FREE VIDEO

Essential Test Tips Video from Trivium Test Prep!

Thank you for purchasing from Trivium Test Prep!
We're honored to help you prepare for your exam.
To show our appreciation, we're offering a

FREE *Essential Test Tips* Video

Our video includes 35 test preparation strategies that will make you successful on your big exam. All we ask is that you email us your feedback and describe your experience with our product. Amazing, awful, or just so-so: we want to hear what you have to say!

> To receive your FREE *Essential Test Tips* Video, please email us at
> **5star@triviumtestprep.com.**

Include "Free 5 Star" in the subject line and the following information in your email:

1. The title of the product you purchased.
2. Your rating from 1 – 5 (with 5 being the best).
3. Your feedback about the product, including how our materials helped you meet your goals and ways in which we can improve our products.
4. Your full name and shipping address so we can send your FREE *Essential Test Tips* Video.

If you have any questions or concerns please feel free to contact us directly at:
5star@triviumtestprep.com.

Thank you!

– Trivium Test Prep Team

CCRN Study Guide 2024-2025:

2 Practice Tests and Review Book for the Adult Critical Care Registered Nurse Exam

2nd Edition

E.M. Falgout

Copyright © 2023 by Ascencia Test Prep

ISBN-13: 9781637985526

ALL RIGHTS RESERVED. By purchase of this book, you have been licensed one copy for personal use only. No part of this work may be reproduced, redistributed, or used in any form or by any means without prior written permission of the publisher and copyright owner. Ascencia Test Prep, Trivium Test Prep, Accepted, and Cirrus Test Prep are all imprints of Trivium Test Prep, LLC.

The American Association of Critical-Care Nurses (AACN) was not involved in the creation or production of this product, is not in any way affiliated with Ascencia Test Prep, and does not sponsor or endorse this product.

Image(s) used under license from Shutterstock.com

TABLE OF CONTENTS

INTRODUCTION xi
    The CCRN Certification Process xi
    The CCRN Exam xi
    CCRN Exam Scoring xii
    Using This Book xii
    Ascencia Test Prep xiii

ONE: Cardiovascular Review 1
    Cardiovascular Physiology
    and Assessment 2
    Electrocardiogram 6
    Cardiovascular Pharmacology 7
    Cardiac Interventions 10
    Acute Coronary Syndrome 13
    Acute Peripheral Vascular
    Insufficiency 17
    Acute Pulmonary Edema 19
    Aortic Aneurysm 21
    Cardiac Tamponade 22
    Cardiac Trauma 23
    Cardiogenic Shock 24
    Cardiomyopathies 25
    Dysrhythmias 26
    Heart Failure 33
    Hypertensive Crisis 35
    Myocardial Conduction System
    Defects 36

    Structural Heart Defects 41
    Respiratory Physiology 45

TWO: Respiratory Review 45
    Respiratory Physiology 45
    Respiratory Assessment Tools 48
    Respiratory Gases 52
    Respiratory Procedures 53
    Mechanical Ventilation 56
    Acute Pulmonary Embolus 61
    Acute Respiratory Distress
    Syndrome 63
    Acute Respiratory Failure 65
    Acute Respiratory Infection 67
    Aspiration 68
    Chronic Conditions 69
    Pleural Space Abnormalities 71
    Status Asthmaticus 75
    Thoracic Trauma 77

THREE: Endocrine Review 83
    Adrenal Insufficiency 83
    Antidiuretic Hormone Imbalances . 85
    Diabetes Insipidus 85
    Diabetes Mellitus 88
    Hyperglycemia 89
    Hypoglycemia 92

    Thyroid Disorders 93

FOUR: Hematology and Immunology Review 97
    Overview of the Hematologic System 97
    Anemia 101
    Coagulopathies 102
    Immune Deficiencies and Leukopenia 104
    Oncologic Complications 105
    Transfusion Reactions 106

FIVE: Gastrointestinal Review 111
    Gastrointestinal Assessment 111
    Nutrition 114
    Abdominal Compartment Syndrome 115
    Acute Abdominal Trauma 117
    Acute GI Hemorrhage 119
    Bowel Infarction 121
    Bowel Obstruction and Perforation 122
    Gastric Surgeries 124
    Hepatic Failure 125
    Malabsorption 126
    Pancreatitis 128

SIX: Renal and Genitourinary Review 131
    Renal Physiology and Assessment 131
    Renal Therapeutic Interventions 134
    Acute Genitourinary Trauma 135
    Acute Kidney Injury 136
    Chronic Kidney Disease 140
    Electrolyte Imbalances 141
    Infections 145

SEVEN: Integumentary Review 149
    Integumentary Interventions 149
    Cellulitis 150
    IV Infiltration/Extravasation 151
    Necrotizing Fasciitis 152
    Pressure Injury 153

EIGHT: Musculoskeletal Review 157
    Compartment Syndrome 157
    Functional Issues 160
    Rhabdomyolysis 163

NINE: Neurology Review 165
    Neurological Anatomy, Physiology, and Assessment 165
    Acute Spinal Cord Injuries 170
    Brain Death 173
    Delirium 174
    Dementia 176
    Encephalopathy 176
    Increased Intracranial Pressure 178
    Stroke (Hemorrhagic) 180
    Stroke (Ischemic) 184
    Neurological Infectious Disease .. 186
    Neuromuscular Disorders 188
    Neurosurgery 189
    Seizure Disorders 190
    Space-Occupying Lesions (Brain Tumors) 191
    Traumatic Brain Injury 192

TEN: Behavioral and Psychosocial Review ... 199
- ABUSE AND NEGLECT ... 199
- AGITATION, AGGRESSION, AND VIOLENT BEHAVIOR ... 200
- ANXIETY ... 202
- MOOD DISORDERS AND SUICIDAL IDEATION ... 203
- POST-TRAUMATIC STRESS DISORDER (PTSD) ... 204
- SUBSTANCE DEPENDENCE AND ABUSE ... 205
- MEDICAL NONADHERENCE ... 209

ELEVEN: Multisystem Review ... 213
- END-OF-LIFE CARE ... 215
- INFECTIOUS DISEASES ... 217
- LIFE-THREATENING MATERNAL/FETAL COMPLICATIONS ... 218
- PAIN ... 221
- SHOCK STATES ... 222
- SEPSIS AND SEPTIC SHOCK ... 224
- TOXIC INGESTION AND EXPOSURE ... 228

TWELVE: Professional Caring and Ethical Practice Review ... 235
- THE AACN SYNERGY MODEL ... 235
- ETHICAL PRACTICE PARAMETERS ... 240
- ETHICAL DECISION-MAKING ... 243
- COMMUNICATION AND TEACHING ... 248

THIRTEEN: Practice Test One ... 255
- PRACTICE TEST ONE ANSWER KEY ... 277

FOURTEEN: Appendix A: Abbreviations ... 293

FIFTEEN: Appendix B: Signs and Symptoms Glossary ... 305

SIXTEEN: Appendix C: Medical Signs ... 307

ONLINE RESOURCES

Ascencia Test Prep includes online resources with the purchase of this study guide to help you fully prepare for your CCRN exam.

Practice Test
In addition to the practice test included in this book, we also offer an online exam. Since many exams today are computer based, practicing your test-taking skills on the computer is a great way to prepare.

Review Questions
Need more practice? Our review questions use a variety of formats to help you memorize key terms and concepts.

Flash Cards
Ascencia Test Prep's flash cards allow you to review important terms easily on your computer or smartphone.

Cheat Sheets
Review the core skills you need to master the exam with easy-to-read Cheat Sheets.

From Stress to Success
Watch "From Stress to Success," a brief but insightful YouTube video that offers the tips, tricks, and secrets experts use to score higher on the exam.

Reviews
Leave a review, send us helpful feedback, or sign up for Ascencia promotions—including free books!

Access these materials at: https://www.ascenciatestprep.com/ccrn-online-resources

INTRODUCTION

Congratulations on choosing to take the CCRN Exam! Passing this exam is an important step forward in your nursing career, and we're here to help you feel prepared on exam day.

The CCRN Certification Process

The **CCRN Exam** is developed by the **American Association of Critical-Care Nurses (AACN)** as part of its certification program for critical care nurses. The CCRN measures the nursing skills necessary to excel as a nurse in critical care settings, including intensive care units, cardiac care units, trauma units, and critical care transport.

To qualify for the exam, you must have a current Registered Nurse license in the United States or its territories. You must also have completed a certain number of clinical hours. There are two paths for meeting these clinical requirements:

1. 1,750 hours in direct care of critically ill patients during the previous two years (875 of those hours accrued in the year before applying for certification)
2. at least five years of clinical experience with a minimum of 2,000 hours in direct care of critically ill patients (144 of those hours accrued in the year before applying for certification)

You can apply for the CCRN exam through the AACN website (www.aacn.org/certification/get-certified/ccrn-adult). You will need to provide proof of clinical hours when applying for the exam. Once you are approved, you will receive an email with directions for scheduling your exam.

The CCRN Exam

When taking the CCRN exam, you will have **three hours** to complete **150 multiple-choice questions**. Only 125 questions will be scored. The other twenty-five questions are pretest items included by the test makers to gauge their appropriateness for future exams. However, these pretest items will not be specified, so you must answer all questions on the exam.

There is no penalty for incorrect answers, so you should answer every question on the exam (even if you aren't sure of the answer).

The CCRN Adult test plan is broken into two sections: clinical judgement (80 percent) and professional caring and ethical practice (20 percent). The clinical judgement section is further broken down into five categories.

A summary of the test outline is given in the table below. The conditions included in each category are listed at the beginning of each chapter in this guide; you can also see the full test plan on the AACN website.

CCRN Exam Outline	
Category	**Percent of Test**
Cardiovascular	17%
Respiratory	15%
Endocrine, Hematology, Gastrointestinal, Renal, and Integumentary	20%
Musculoskeletal, Neurological, and Psychosocial	14%
Multisystem	14%
Professional Caring and Ethical Practice	20%

The questions on the exam will focus on patient care for the conditions listed in each category. You should be able to recognize the most common diagnostic criteria for each condition and understand how each condition is managed in the critical care setting.

CCRN Exam Scoring

If you are taking a computer-based exam, you will receive your score when the exam is over. If you take the pen-and-paper version of the test, you must wait six to eight weeks to receive your results.

To pass the CCRN Adult exam, you must answer **eighty-three questions correctly** out of the 125 scored questions. If you pass the exam, you will receive your certification in the mail. If you do not pass the exam, you may apply through AACN to retake the test.

You can retake the test four times within a year of your original application.

Using This Book

This book is divided into two sections. In the content review, you will find the pathophysiology, risk factors, signs and symptoms, diagnostic findings, and treatment protocols for the conditions included in the CCRN test plan. Throughout the chapters, you'll also see Quick Review Questions that will help reinforce important concepts and skills.

The book also includes two full-length practice tests with answer rationales. You can use these tests to gauge your readiness for the test and determine which content areas you may need to review more thoroughly.

Ascencia Test Prep

With health care fields such as nursing, pharmacy, emergency care, and physical therapy becoming the fastest-growing industries in the United States, individuals looking to enter the health care industry or rise in their field need high-quality, reliable resources. Ascencia Test Prep's study guides and test preparation materials are developed by credentialed industry professionals with years of experience in their respective fields. Ascencia recognizes that health care professionals nurture bodies and spirits, and save lives. Ascencia Test Prep's mission is to help health care workers grow.

1 CARDIOVASCULAR REVIEW

CCRN TEST PLAN: CARDIOVASCULAR

- Acute coronary syndrome (ACS)
- Acute peripheral vascular insufficiency
- Acute pulmonary edema
- Aortic aneurysm
- Aortic dissection
- Aortic rupture
- Cardiac surgery
- Cardiac tamponade
- Cardiac trauma
- Cardiac/vascular catheterization
- Cardiogenic shock
- Cardiomyopathies
- Dysrhythmias
- Heart failure
- Hypertensive crisis
- Myocardial conduction system abnormalities
- Papillary muscle rupture
- Structural heart defects (acquired and congenital, including valvular disease)
- Transcatheter aortic valve repair (TAVR)

Cardiovascular Physiology and Assessment

- During the **cardiac cycle**, the heart alternates between **diastole** (relaxation) and **systole** (contraction) to move blood.
  - When both chambers are in diastole, the atria passively fill the ventricles.
  - During atrial systole, the atria force blood into the ventricles.
  - During ventricular systole, the ventricles force blood into the arteries.

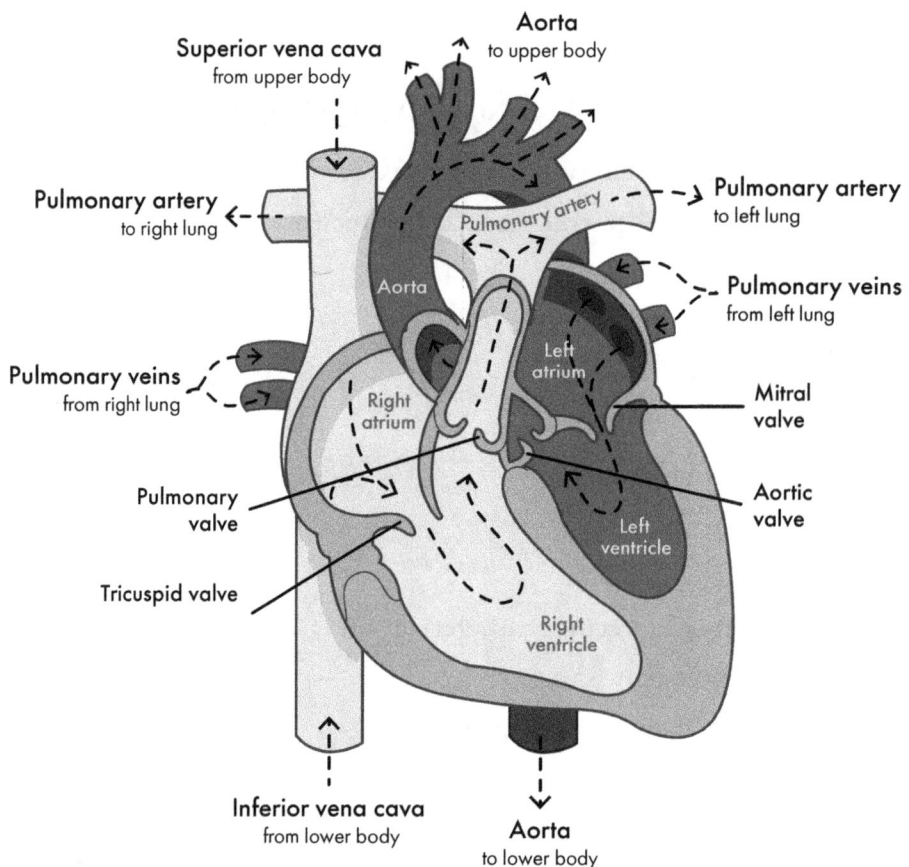

Figure 1.1. Anatomy of the Heart

- **Stroke volume (SV)** is the volume of blood pumped from the left ventricle during one contraction. Stroke volume is determined by:
  - **preload:** how much the ventricles stretch at the end of diastole (a measure of ventricular end-diastolic volume)
  - **afterload:** resistance the heart must overcome during systole to pump blood into circulation (a measure of aortic pressure and systemic vascular resistance [SVR])

☐ **contractility:** the force of the heart independent of preload and afterload

Component of stroke volume	Preload	Afterload	Contractility
	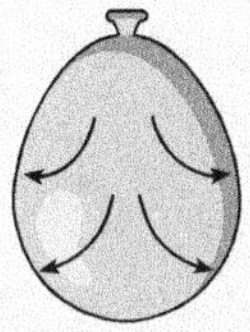	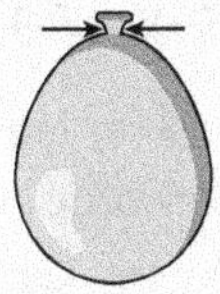	
	How much the balloon stretches.	The resistance to air leaving the balloon.	The force of the air leaving the balloon.
Increase with	vasopressors IV fluids	vasopressors	positive inotropes (e.g., digoxin, dobutamine)
Decrease with	diuretics nitrates	antihypertensives nitrates	negative inotropes (e.g., beta blockers, non-dihydropyridine calcium channel blockers)

Figure 1.2. Management of Stroke Volume

TABLE 1.1. Hemodynamic Parameters

Parameter	Description	Normal Range
Blood pressure (BP)	vascular BP given as systolic blood pressure (SBP, top number) and diastolic blood pressure (DBP, bottom number)	90/60 – 120/80 mm Hg
Central venous pressure (CVP) or right atrial pressure (RAP)	pressure in the vena cava; used to estimate preload	2 – 6 mm Hg
Pulmonary artery pressure (PAP)	pressure in the pulmonary artery	8 – 20 mm Hg
Stroke volume (SV)	volume of blood forced from the left ventricle with each contraction	60 – 100 mL/beat
Cardiac output (CO)	volume of blood pumped in a unit of time (usually per minute) CO = SV × HR	4 – 8 L/min
Cardiac index (CI)	CO relative to patient size CI = CO/BSA	2.5 – 4 L/min/m^2
Mean arterial pressure (MAP)	average BP during a complete cardiac cycle MAP = SBP + (2 × DBP)/3	70 – 100 mm Hg

continued on next page

TABLE 1.1. Hemodynamic Parameters (continued)

Parameter	Description	Normal Range
Systemic vascular resistance (SVR)	total peripheral vascular system resistance to blood flow SVR = 80 × (MAP − CVP)/CO	700 – 1200 dyne · sec/cm^5
Pulmonary artery occlusion pressure (PAOP) or pulmonary capillary wedge pressure (PCWP)	indirect measurement of left atrial pressure; uses Swan-Ganz catheter to "wedge" inflated balloon into a branch of the pulmonary artery	6 – 12 mm Hg
Pulmonary vascular resistance (PVR)	vascular resistance to blood flow in the lungs PVR = 80 × (MPAP − PAOP)/CI	255 – 285 dyne · sec/cm^5
Left ventricular end-diastolic pressure (LVEDP)	pressure in the left ventricle before systole	5 – 12 mm Hg
Arterial oxygen saturation (SaO$_2$)	fraction of oxygen-saturated hemoglobin in arteries	95% – 100%
Mixed venous saturation (SvO$_2$)	fraction of oxygen-saturated hemoglobin in veins (taken from pulmonary artery catheter [PAC])	60% – 80%
Central venous oxygen saturation (ScvO$_2$)	fraction of oxygen-saturated hemoglobin in veins; surrogate for SvO$_2$ (taken from central venous catheter)	>70%
Arterial oxygen content (CaO$_2$)	volume of oxygen delivered to tissue per unit of blood	16 – 22 mL/dL
Oxygen delivery (DO$_2$)	volume of blood oxygen being transported to tissues per unit of time	arterial = 1000 mL/min venous = 775 mL/min
Oxygen consumption (VO$_2$)	volume of oxygen used by the body per unit of time	200 – 250 mL/min

- **Heart sounds** are produced as blood moves through the heart.
    - **S1:** caused by the closure of the AV valves; indicates the end of diastole and the beginning of systole
    - **S2:** caused by the closure of the semilunar valves; indicates the end of systole and the beginning of diastole

- □ **S3 (ventricular gallop):** an extra heart sound heard after S2, caused by a rush of blood into a ventricle; a normal finding in children and young adults
- □ **S4 (atrial gallop):** an extra heart sound heard before S1, caused by the atrial contraction of blood into a noncompliant ventricle; can be a normal finding in older adults

S4 heart sound is associated with decreased ventricular compliance (e.g., hypertrophic cardiomyopathy, hypertension, or aortic stenosis).

- **Cardiac biomarkers** measure damage to heart tissue.

HELPFUL HINT:
S3 heart sound is associated with ventricular dysfunction or volume overload in the ventricles (e.g., MI, systolic heart failure [HF], dilated cardiomyopathy, or mitral valve regurgitation).

TABLE 1.2. Cardiac Biomarkers

Test	Description	Normal Range
Troponin I (cTnI) and troponin T (cTnT)	proteins released when the heart muscle is damaged; high levels can indicate an MI but may also be due to other conditions that stress the heart (e.g., renal failure, HF, pulmonary embolism [PE]); levels peak 24 hours post-MI and can remain elevated for up to 2 weeks	cTnI: <0.04 ng/mL cTnT: <0.01 ng/mL
Creatine kinase (CK)	responsible for muscle cell function; an increase indicates cardiac or skeletal muscle damage	22 – 198 U/L
Creatine kinase–muscle/brain (CK-MB)	cardiac marker for damaged heart muscle; often used to diagnose a second MI or ongoing cardiovascular conditions; a high ratio of CK-MB to CK (high CK-MB/CK) indicates damage to heart muscle (as opposed to skeletal muscle)	normal CK-MB: 5 – 25 IU/L CK-MB/CK suggesting possible MI: 2.5 – 3 IU/L

QUICK REVIEW QUESTION

1. The nurse is reassessing a patient with severe sepsis after a fluid bolus and administration of vasopressors. What hemodynamic value would indicate an improvement?

Electrocardiogram

- A 12-lead **electrocardiogram (ECG)** includes 3 bipolar leads (I, II, and III), 3 unipolar leads (aVR, aVL, and aVF), and 6 precordial leads (V1 – V6).
- **Posterior leads** (V7, V8, and V9) are placed on the patient's back when a posterior infarction is suspected.
- **Right-side leads** (V3R, V4R, V5R, and V6R) are placed on the patient's right side in a mirror image of V3 – V6 when a right ventricular infarction is suspected.

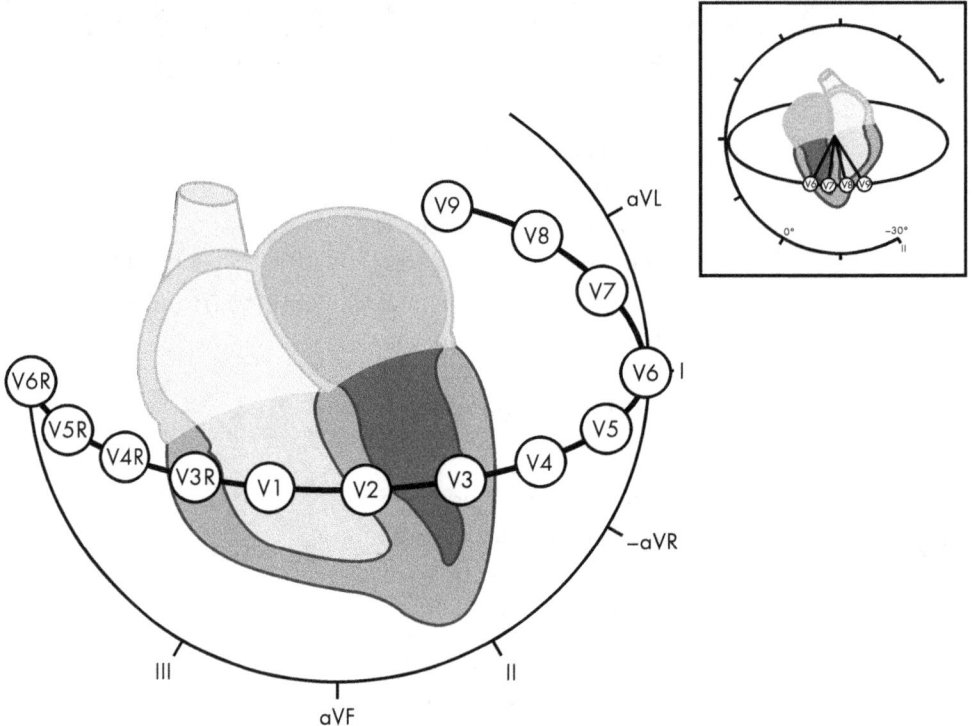

Figure 1.3. ECG Leads

- The waveforms and intervals on the ECG strip correspond to the cardiac cycle.
  - **P wave:** represents atrial depolarization and should measure 0.06 – 0.11 seconds
  - **PR interval:** represents the AV conduction time and should measure 0.12 – 0.20 seconds

- **QRS complex:** represents ventricular depolarization and should measure 0.08 – 0.10 seconds
- **T wave:** represents the repolarization of the ventricles
- **U wave:** theorized to represent late repolarization of the His-Purkinje system
- **QT interval:** represents the total time of ventricular activity (depolarization and repolarization) and should measure 0.36 – 0.44 seconds
- **ST segment:** shows the early part of ventricular repolarization

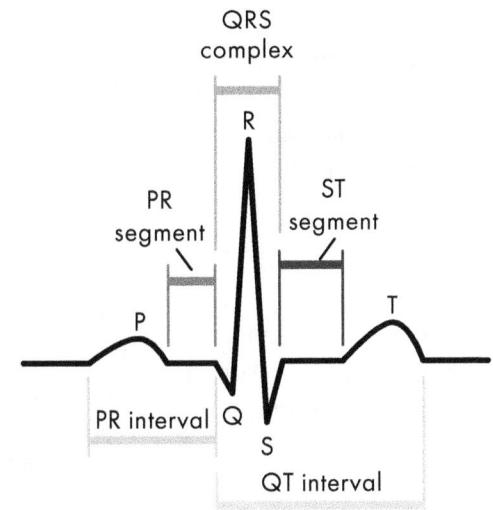

Figure 1.4. Waveforms and Intervals on an ECG

QUICK REVIEW QUESTION

2. A patient with chest pain and ST elevation undergoes a cardiac catheterization with PCI for a right ventricular infarction. The RCA was stented. After 3 hours, the patient starts having chest pain. Which leads of an ECG should the nurse focus on to identify early restenosis?

Cardiovascular Pharmacology

TABLE 1.3. Cardiovascular Medications

Category	Action	Therapeutic Uses
ACE inhibitors (ACE-Is): lisinopril, ramipril, enalapril, benazepril	lower SVR, resulting in decreased BP	- hypertension (first line) - CHF - medical management post-MI
Alpha1-adrenergic agonists: methoxamine, midodrine, phenylephrine	increase SVR, resulting in increased BP	- hypotension - shock

continued on next page

TABLE 1.3. Cardiovascular Medications (continued)

Category	Action	Therapeutic Uses
Beta-adrenergic antagonists (beta blockers): metoprolol, carvedilol, atenolol, propranolol, labetalol	lower BP and heart rate, decrease CO, and slow AV node conduction	• medical management post-MI (first line) • chronic angina • hypertension (second line) • cardiac dysrhythmias (A-fib, SVT)
Angiotensin II receptor blockers (ARBs): valsartan, losartan, irbesartan	use a mechanism of action similar to that of ACE inhibitors but cause fewer adverse effects	• hypertension (second line if intolerant to ACE inhibitors) • HF • medical management post-MI (second line if intolerant to ACE inhibitors)
Anticoagulants: warfarin, apixaban, rivaroxaban, enoxaparin, heparin	increase clotting time via various mechanisms that disrupt production of clotting factors	• known thrombosis (e.g., PE or DVT) • prophylaxis of thrombosis (e.g., after A-fib, cardiac post-op procedures) • adjunct therapy in mechanical valve replacements, MI, and stroke
Antidysrhythmics: amiodarone, flecainide, procainamide	suppress cardiac dysrhythmias and restore normal cardiac conduction	• dysrhythmias (hemodynamically stable)
Antiplatelets: clopidogrel, ticagrelor, prasugrel, aspirin	decrease platelet aggregation and inhibit thrombus production	• unstable angina • PCI/stent placement for ACS • treatment and prophylaxis for ischemic stroke
Calcium channel blockers: amlodipine, nicardipine, diltiazem, verapamil	cause coronary vasodilation, which slows cardiac conduction, decreases heart rate, and decreases myocardial contraction	• hypertension • variant (Prinzmetal) angina • artery vasospasm

Category	Action	Therapeutic Uses
Cardiac glycosides: digoxin	increase myocardial contraction, decrease heart rate, slow cardiac conduction, and increase CO	• atrial dysrhythmias (e.g., A-fib) • paroxysmal SVT conversion • HF
Diuretics: furosemide, bumetanide, mannitol	increase excretion of water and electrolytes	• hypertension • HF • edema • osmotic diuretics: ICP
Nitrates: nitroprusside, nitroglycerin	cause vasodilation, which decreases preload, afterload, and CO; reduces work effort of LV	• ACS • hypertension
Inotropic/vasodilator agents: milrinone	vasodilator; increase SV and CO	• emergent HF
Sympathomimetics: epinephrine, norepinephrine, dobutamine, dopamine	alpha- and beta-adrenergic agonists that cause vasoconstriction, increased force of cardiac contraction, or increased rate of cardiac conduction (depending on the affected receptors)	• hypotension • HF • cardiogenic shock • cardiac arrest, asystole, PEA • acute bronchospasm • anaphylaxis
Thrombolytics (fibrinolytics): tPA or alteplase, tenecteplase	promote destruction of fibrin clots	• MI when coronary angiography is unavailable • acute CVA • massive PE

QUICK REVIEW QUESTION

3. Why are beta blockers contraindicated for patients with second-degree AV blocks?

Cardiac Interventions
Cardioversion, Defibrillation, and Pacing

- **Synchronized electrical cardioversion** uses electrical current supplied by external electrode pads placed on the anterior chest to reset the heart to a normal sinus rhythm.
  - Current is supplied during the R wave of the QRS complex.
  - Cardioversion is indicated for narrow-complex tachycardias, V-tach with a pulse, A-fib, and atrial flutter.
- During **defibrillation**, also known as **unsynchronized cardioversion**, electrical current is used to reset the heart to a normal sinus rhythm.
  - The electrical current is supplied randomly during the cardiac cycle, disrupting the heart's electrical rhythm and allowing the SA node's normal sinus rhythm to restart.
  - Defibrillation is an emergent treatment for patients with V-fib and unstable V-tach.
- An **implantable cardioverter-defibrillator (ICD)** can be programmed to provide cardioversion or defibrillation to prevent sudden cardiac death in patients at high risk for V-tach or V-fib.
- A **pacemaker** is a device that uses electrical stimulation to regulate the heart's electrical conduction system and maintain a normal heart rhythm.
  - **Temporary pacemakers** can include transvenous leads or transcutaneous adhesive pads attached to the chest (**transcutaneous pacing [TCP]**). Temporary pacemakers are controlled by an external pulse generator.
  - **Permanent pacemakers** are implanted subcutaneously, and the leads are then run through the subclavian vein into the heart. The device is battery operated and allows the physician to continuously monitor the patient's cardiac rhythm.

Cardiac Catheterization

- In **cardiac catheter procedures**, a catheter is inserted into a large blood vessel to diagnose and treat damage in the arteries, heart muscles, and valves.
- The most common sites for catheter procedures are the femoral, brachial, or radial arteries.
- Post-procedure complications include:
  - retroperitoneal bleeding
  - cardiac ischemic pain

- excessive bleeding
- dysrhythmia
- hematoma
- neurovascular insufficiency

Angioplasty

- During an **angioplasty**, a balloon is placed in the stenotic artery via a catheter and is inflated to open the artery. A **stent** may be placed to hold the artery open.
- **Percutaneous coronary intervention (PCI)** (also called coronary angioplasty) is used to revascularize the coronary arteries in patients with ACS.
- **Percutaneous transluminal angioplasty (PTA)** is used to widen the arteries in patients with peripheral artery disease or stenosis in the carotid, renal, or coronary arteries.

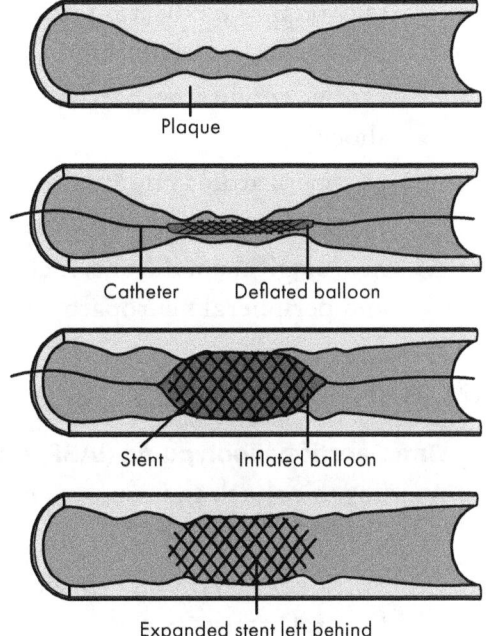

Figure 1.5. Angioplasty with Stent

HELPFUL HINT:

Reperfusion pain—angina without the presence of restenosis—occurs in approximately 20% of patients after PCI. With reperfusion pain, the ECG should not show any significant changes, and the patient will respond to pharmacological treatment.

Coronary Artery Bypass Graft (CABG)

- A **coronary artery bypass graft (CABG)** revascularizes ischemic heart tissue by diverting blood through the left internal thoracic artery or by grafting a section of the great saphenous vein to the aorta.

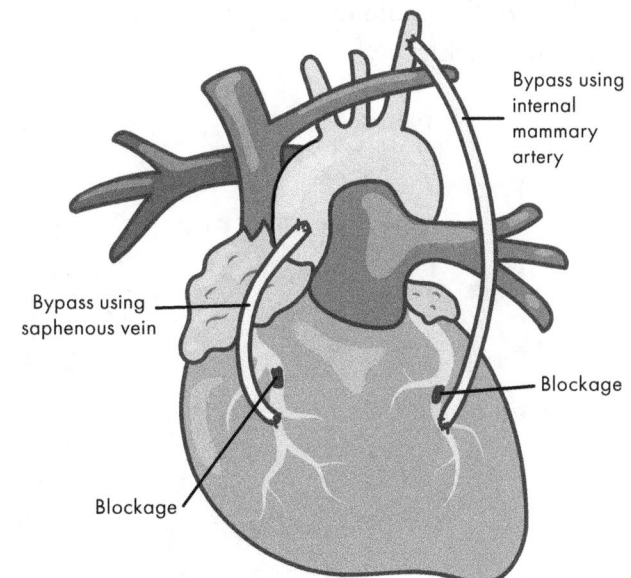

Figure 1.6. Coronary Artery Bypass Graft (CABG)

- CABG is performed in patients with cardiac ischemia who cannot be treated with PCI.
- Post-procedure complications include:
  - excessive bleeding or anemia (around 30% of patients will require a blood transfusion after CABG)
  - dysrhythmias (particularly A-fib): common postoperatively and may require medication or cardioversion; patient may be given prophylactic amiodarone
  - cardiac conditions, particularly perioperative MI and vasodilatory shock
  - post-pericardiotomy syndrome, due to pericardial injury; may cause pericarditis, pericardial effusion, or tamponade
  - neurological conditions, including stroke, post-cardiotomy delirium, and peripheral neuropathy

Intra-aortic Balloon Pump (IABP)

- **Intra-aortic balloon pump (IABP) therapy** is used in patients with cardiogenic shock to increase coronary artery perfusion and raise blood pressure.
- The intra-aortic balloon is inserted into the ascending aortic arch via the femoral artery.
  - The balloon inflates during diastole and forces blood flow back into the coronary arteries.
  - During systole, the balloon deflates, which decreases afterload and increases cardiac output.
- The IABP should only be paused briefly, as thrombus formation can occur quickly.

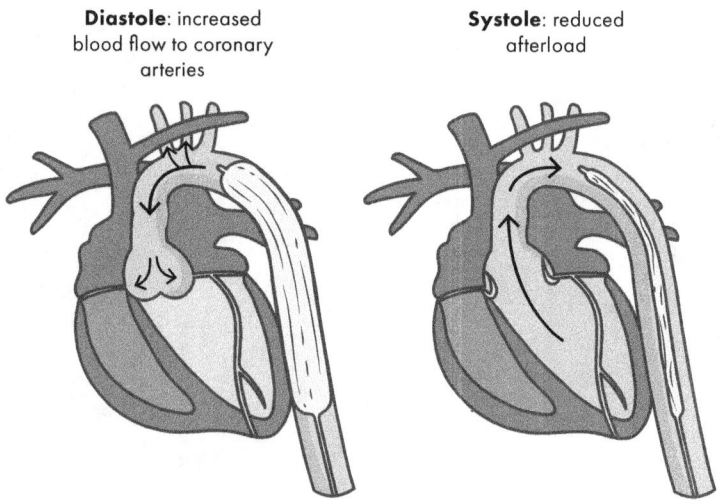

Figure 1.7. Intra-Aortic Balloon Pump (IABP) Therapy

- Contraindications for IABP include coagulopathies, aortic regurgitation, and dissecting/ruptured aortic aneurysm.

QUICK REVIEW QUESTION

4. A patient presents to the ED with chest pain and the ECG shown below. What priority intervention should the nurse expect?

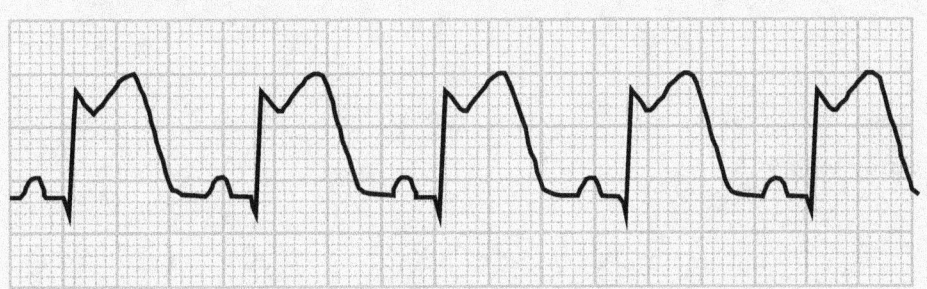

Acute Coronary Syndrome

Pathophysiology

Acute coronary syndrome (ACS) is an umbrella term for cardiac conditions in which thrombosis impairs blood flow in coronary arteries. **Angina pectoris** (commonly called just angina) is chest pain caused by narrowed coronary arteries and presents with negative troponin, an ST depression, and T wave changes.

- **Stable angina** usually resolves in about 5 minutes. It is resolved with medications or rest, and can be triggered by exertion, large meals, and extremely hot or cold temperatures.
- **Unstable angina** can occur at any time and typically lasts longer (>20 minutes). The pain is usually rated as more severe than stable angina and is not easily relieved with nitrates.
- **Variant angina** (also called Prinzmetal angina or vasospastic angina) is episodes of angina and temporary ST elevation caused by spasms in the coronary artery. Chest pain is easily relieved with nitrates.

A **myocardial infarction (MI)**, or ischemia of the heart muscle, occurs when the coronary arteries are partly or completely occluded. MI is diagnosed via positive troponin and ECG changes; it is classified by the behavior of the ST wave. A **non-ST-elevation myocardial infarction (NSTEMI)** includes an ST depression and a T wave inversion. An **ST-elevation myocardial infarction (STEMI)** includes an elevated ST (>1 mm), indicating a complete occlusion of a coronary artery.

HELPFUL HINT:

The starred topics are the ones most likely to appear on the exam.

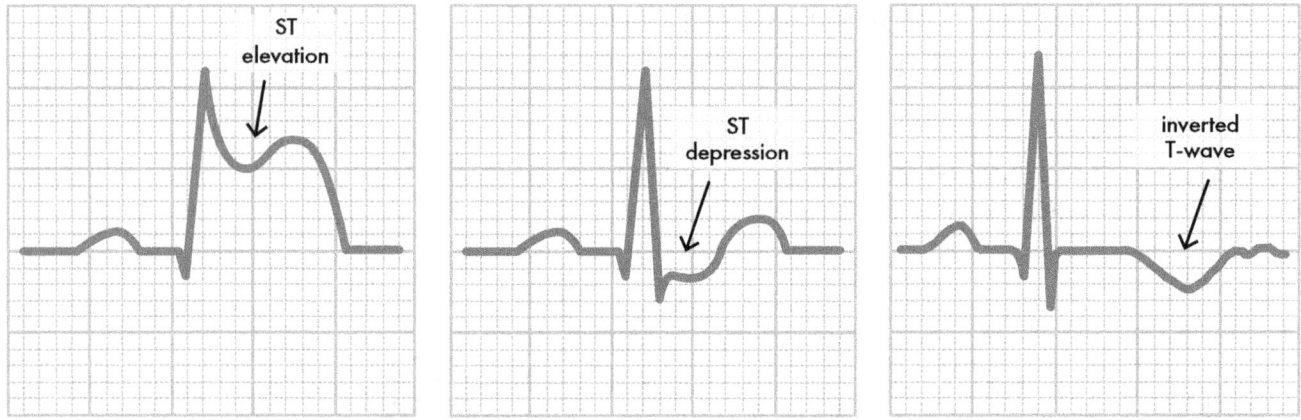

Figure 1.8. ECG Changes Associated with ACS

Signs, symptoms, and diagnostic findings for MI vary according to which coronary artery is occluded. The heart's blood supply comes from the aorta, which branches into the **left coronary artery (LCA)** and **right coronary artery (RCA)**. The LCA further divides into the **left anterior descending (LAD) artery** and **left circumflex artery**.

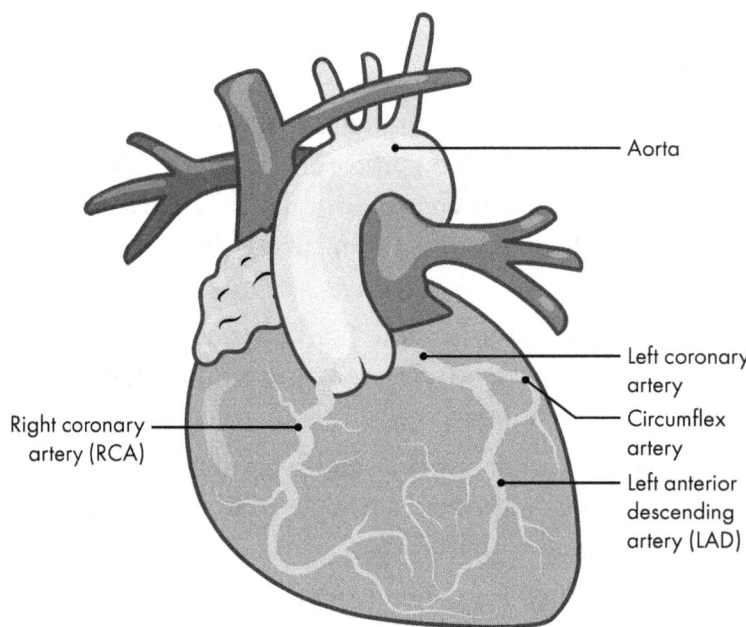

Figure 1.9. Coronary Arteries

- **Anterior-wall MI** is occlusion of the LAD artery, which supplies blood to the anterior of the left atrium and ventricle. **Septal MI** may occur alongside anterior-wall MI (but is rarely diagnosed in isolation).
    - ST changes in V1 – V4
    - increased risk of left ventricular failure (and subsequent cardiogenic shock)

- increased risk of second-degree, type II heart block and BBB
- increased risk of ventricular septal rupture (usually 2 – 7 days post-MI)

- **Inferior-wall MI** is occlusion of the RCA, which supplies blood to the right atrium and ventricle, the SA node, and the AV node.
    - ST changes in II, III, aVF
    - presents with bradycardia and hypotension
    - increased risk of AV heart blocks (e.g., first-degree AV block)
    - increased risk for papillary muscle rupture
    - use beta blockers and nitrates cautiously to avoid reducing preload

HELPFUL HINT:

Papillary muscle rupture is a rare but serious complication that occurs 2 – 8 days post-MI. Patients will present with hemodynamic compromise; pulmonary edema; new, loud systolic murmur; and a large V wave in PAOP. Papillary muscle rupture usually requires immediate surgical repair.

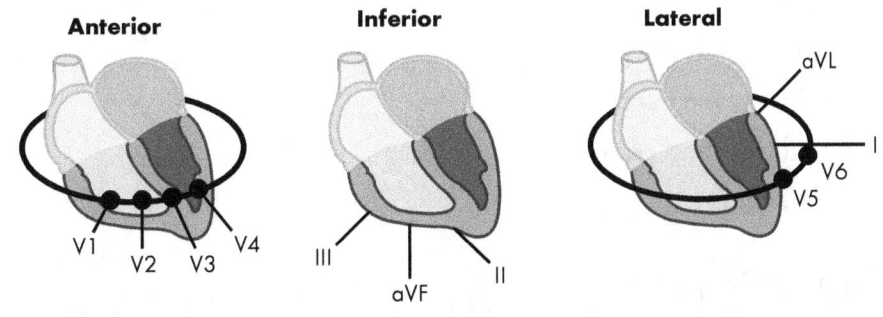

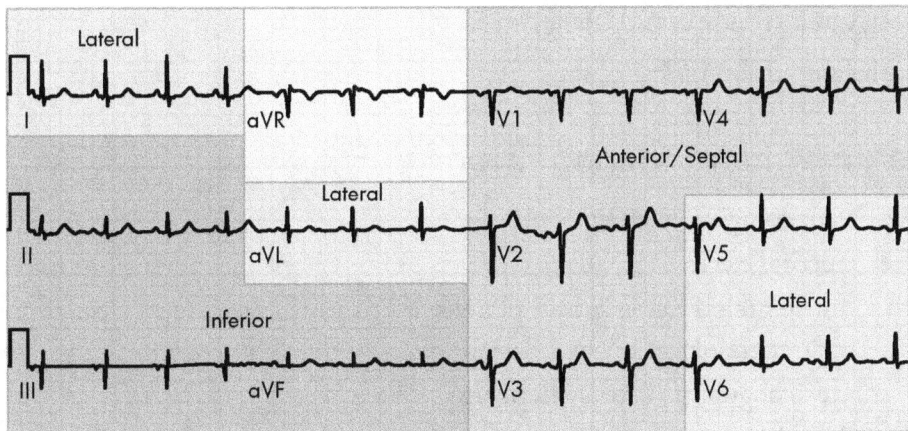

Figure 1.10. ECG Leads and Corresponding MI Location

- **Right ventricular infarction** may occur with inferior-wall MI.
    - ST changes in V4R – V6R
    - presents with tachycardia, hypotension, and JVD
    - treat with positive inotropes
    - avoid preload-reducing medications (beta blockers, diuretics, morphine, nitrates)
- **Lateral-wall MI** is occlusion of the left circumflex artery, which supplies blood to the left atrium and the posterior/lateral walls of the left ventricle. ST changes may be seen in I, aVL, V5, or V6.

> **HELPFUL HINT:**
> Contraindications for beta blocker use during STEMI include bradycardia, hypotension, cardiogenic shock, and heart block.

- **Posterior-wall MI** is occlusion of the RCA or left circumflex artery, with ST elevation in V7 – V9 and ST depression in V1 – V4. Posterior-wall MI is rare but may be missed or read as an NSTEMI on a 12-lead ECG.

Signs and Symptoms

- continuous chest pain that may radiate to the back, arm, or jaw (possible Levine's sign)
- upper abdominal pain (more common in adults >65, people with diabetes, and women)
- dyspnea
- nausea or vomiting
- dizziness or syncope
- diaphoresis and pallor
- palpitations

Diagnostic Tests

- elevated troponin (>0.01 ng/mL)
- elevated CK-MB (>2.5%)

Treatment and Management

- pharmacological management
    - nitroglycerin
    - antiplatelets: aspirin and platelet P2Y12 inhibitors (e.g., clopidogrel or ticagrelor)
    - anticoagulant (usually heparin)
    - beta blocker
    - morphine (only for severe pain not relieved by nitroglycerin)
- isolated right ventricular infarction
    - IV fluids
    - antiplatelets and anticoagulants
    - cautious use of nitrates, beta blockers, and morphine
- NSTEMI: initially treated with medication (may require PCI)
- STEMI: immediate fibrinolytics or PCI
    - goal for door to balloon time: 90 minutes
    - goal for door to fibrinolytics: 30 minutes
    - post-procedure antithrombotic therapy (may include aspirin, clopidogrel, abciximab, eptifibatide, and/or heparin)

> **HELPFUL HINT:**
> Contraindications for beta blocker use during STEMI include bradycardia, hypotension, cardiogenic shock, and heart block.

> **QUICK REVIEW QUESTION**
>
> 5. A 12-lead ECG on a patient with chest pain shows ST elevations in leads II, III, and aVF. Which medications are contraindicated for this patient?

Acute Peripheral Vascular Insufficiency

Arterial Occlusion

Pathophysiology

Atherosclerosis, also called atherosclerotic cardiovascular disease (ASCVD), is a progressive condition in which **plaque** builds up in the tunica intima of arteries. Atherosclerosis that occurs in peripheral arteries leads to **peripheral vascular insufficiency** (also called **peripheral arterial disease [PAD]**).

Acute peripheral vascular insufficiency (also **acute arterial occlusion**) occurs when a thrombus or an embolus occludes a peripheral artery and causes ischemia and possibly the loss of a limb. This condition is a medical emergency requiring prompt treatment to prevent tissue necrosis.

Carotid artery occlusive disease (CAOD), or **stenosis**, is a narrowing or hardening of the carotid arteries, usually caused by atherosclerosis. The artery may be occluded, or plaque may break off and travel to the brain, causing a TIA, or an ischemic stroke. Carotid artery stenosis may be asymptomatic and is usually diagnosed after a CVA. It is the cause of most ischemic strokes.

Signs and Symptoms

- the 6 Ps (hallmark signs) of an arterial occlusion
  - pain (intermittent claudication)
  - pallor
  - pulselessness
  - paresthesia
  - paralysis
  - poikilothermia
- petechiae (visible with microemboli)
- ABPI <0.30 (indicating poor outcome of limb survivability)

→ CONTINUE

Diagnostic Tests

- duplex ultrasonography, CT angiography, or catheter-based arteriography
- elevated D-dimer

Treatment and Management

- medications: IV anticoagulants (usually heparin), thrombolytics, and/or antiplatelet agents
- surgical/catheter intervention: catheter-directed thrombolysis, bypass surgery, or embolectomy
    - ultrasound-enhanced thrombolysis: catheter-directed delivery of thrombolytic with ultrasound pressure
    - **carotid endarterectomy** indicated for patients with severe carotid artery stenosis
- nursing considerations
    - frequent pulse and neurovascular checks
    - do not elevate extremity
    - monitor for signs and symptoms of bleeding following use of anticoagulants or thrombolytics

> **QUICK REVIEW QUESTION**
>
> 6. Catheter-directed thrombolysis is performed on a patient with an acute arterial occlusion in the lower right leg. What nursing interventions are the most important?

VENOUS OCCLUSION
Pathophysiology

A **deep vein thrombosis (DVT)** is the most common form of acute venous occlusion and occurs when a thrombus forms within a deep vein. DVT is most common in the lower extremities. Risk factors for acute venous occlusion include:

- Virchow's triad
    - hypercoagulability (e.g., due to estrogen, contraceptive use, or malignancy)
    - venous stasis (bed rest or any other activity that results in decreased physical movement)
    - endothelial damage (damage to the vessel wall from trauma, drug use, inflammatory processes, or other causes)

- pregnancy, hormone replacement therapy, or oral contraceptives
- recent surgery

Signs and Symptoms

- pain localized to a specific area (usually the foot, ankle, calf, or behind the knee)
- unilateral edema, erythema, and warmth
- positive Homans' sign

Diagnostic Tests

- elevated D-dimer
- venous duplex ultrasonography

Treatment and Management

- pharmacological management: anticoagulants (first line), thrombolytics (second line)
- surgical or endovascular thrombectomy (if medication is ineffective or contraindicated)
- inferior vena cava (IVC) filter may be placed to avoid a PE in patients who cannot tolerate anticoagulants

> **QUICK REVIEW QUESTION**
>
> 7. A patient diagnosed with a DVT complains of dyspnea. What is the priority invention for this patient?

Acute Pulmonary Edema

Pathophysiology

Pulmonary edema (PE) is characterized by fluid accumulation in the lungs and is caused by extravasation of fluid from pulmonary vasculature into the interstitium and alveoli of the lungs. The fluid impairs respiration and may lead to acute respiratory failure.

Cardiogenic pulmonary edema develops secondary to a decrease in left ventricular function. The decrease in left-side function increases pulmonary venous pressure and capillary pressure in the lungs, forcing fluid from the vasculature into interstitial spaces. Common causes of **acute cardiogenic pulmonary edema (ACPE)** include acute decompensated HF, MI, severe dysrhythmias, hypertensive crises, valvular disease, or complications of cardiopulmonary bypass.

Signs and Symptoms

- severe, sudden onset of dyspnea
- blood-tinged sputum
- orthopnea (requiring high Fowler's positioning)
- anxiety, irritability, or restlessness
- tachycardia
- inspiratory fine crackles, rales, or wheezing
- other signs and symptoms of right-sided HF

Diagnostic Tests

- CXR shows intestinal edema
- PAOP >25 mm Hg

Treatment and Management

- immediate objective: to improve oxygenation and reduce pulmonary congestion
- noninvasive O_2 therapy (e.g., BiPAP) preferred; intubation may be required
- medications
    - morphine to reduce anxiety and afterload
    - diuretic to reduce fluid overload
    - vasodilator to reduce preload and afterload
    - medication to improve contractility
    - aminophylline to prevent bronchospasm (may increase risk of tachycardic dysrhythmias)

> **QUICK REVIEW QUESTION**
>
> **8.** A patient being treated for refractory V-tach develops severe orthopnea and dyspnea, and the lung sounds are coarse, with rales throughout. What is the probable cause of these signs and symptoms, and what testing is likely to be ordered to confirm the diagnosis?

Aortic Aneurysm

Pathophysiology

An **aortic rupture**, a complete tear in the wall of the aorta, rapidly leads to hemorrhagic shock and death. An **aortic dissection** is a tear in the aortic intima; the tear allows blood to enter the aortic media. Both aortic rupture and dissection will lead to hemorrhagic shock and death without immediate intervention.

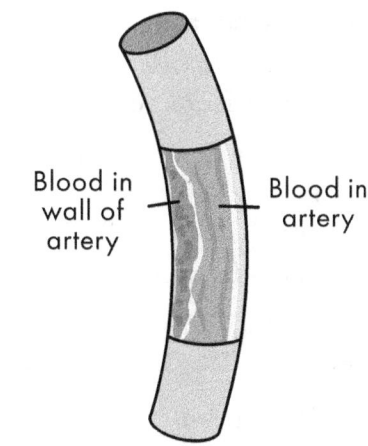

Figure 1.11. Aortic Dissection

Signs and Symptoms

- sharp, severe pain in the chest, back, abdomen, or flank; often described as "tearing"
- rapid, weak, or absent pulse
- a blood pressure difference of ≥20 mm Hg between the left and right arms
- new-onset murmur
- diaphoresis
- nausea and vomiting
- pallor
- hypotension
- orthopnea

Diagnostic Tests

- CT scan, TEE, angiogram, or chest MRI

Treatment and Management

- pain management (usually morphine)
- beta blockers; nitroprusside may also be given
- hemodynamically unstable patients: immediate surgical repair usually required

QUICK REVIEW QUESTION

9. A patient reports new-onset, sharp pain and describes it as tearing. The BP in the right arm is 85/62 mm Hg. What should the nurse do next?

HELPFUL HINT:

Positive inotropes are contraindicated in patients with aortic dissection because the medications increase stress on the aortic wall.

Cardiac Tamponade

Cardiac tamponade is compression of the heart by excess fluid in the pericardium. The increased pressure reduces chamber compliance and filling. With enough pressure, venous return is reduced and cardiac output drops.

The onset of cardiac tamponade may be acute (usually due to trauma) or subacute. The most common etiology of subacute cardiac tamponade is idiopathic (likely viral). Other causes include malignancy, kidney dysfunction, MI, and infection (pericarditis).

> **HELPFUL HINT:**
>
> Constrictive pericarditis is fibrosis of the pericardial sac. It is usually chronic and is often caused by radiation therapy. Definitive treatment is pericardiectomy.

Symptoms and Physical Findings

- Beck's triad
    - low arterial BP
    - dilated neck veins
    - muffled heart sounds
- sudden and severe chest pain
    - increases with movement, lying flat, and inspiration
    - decreases by sitting up or leaning forward
- tachycardia (usually the earliest sign)
- hypotension
- pulsus paradoxus
- pericardial rub
- dyspnea

Diagnostic Tests

- ECG
    - ST elevation possible, usually in all leads except aVR and V1
    - tall, peaked T waves
- CXR showing "water bottle" silhouette in pericardial effusion
- echocardiogram may show pericardial effusion, thickening, or calcifications

> **HELPFUL HINT:**
>
> Positive pressure ventilation should be avoided in patients with cardiac tamponade because the pressure furthers limits venous return.

Management

- definitive treatment: pericardiocentesis or surgical drainage
- hemodynamically stable patients may be monitored while underlying condition is treated
    - maintain fluid volume
    - manage pain (positioning, analgesics)

> **QUICK REVIEW QUESTION**
>
> 10. A patient who is 4 hours post-PCI presents with tachycardia, hypotension, dilated neck veins, and muffled heart sounds. What intervention should the nurse prepare for?

Cardiac Trauma

- **Cardiac trauma** occurs when an outside force causes injury to the heart. Cardiac trauma can cause rupture of heart chambers, dysrhythmias, damage to the heart valves, or cardiac arrest.
- **Blunt cardiac injury (BCI)** occurs when an object forcefully strikes the chest. Damage due to BCI may be caused by compression of the heart between the sternum and spine, pressure fluctuations in the thoracic cavity, or shearing forces. Because the right side of the heart is anteriorly positioned, it is typically the most affected.
    - **Cardiac contusion** is a general term used to describe damage to the heart from blunt trauma.
    - Common consequences of BCI include dysrhythmias; damage to chamber walls, septa, or valves; and decreased contractility and stroke volume.
    - Management of BCI may include antidysrhythmic drugs, temporary pacemakers, medications to manage heart failure, and surgery to repair damaged heart tissues.
    - Fluid and electrolytes should be monitored closely to preserve myocardial conduction and cardiac output.
    - **Blunt aortic injury (BAI)** is a tear in the aorta resulting from compression of the aorta between the vertebrae and anterior chest wall. Patients with BAI are administered antihypertensives (sodium nitroprusside IV infusion) to maintain SBP <90 mm HG and usually require surgery.
- **Penetrating cardiac trauma** involves the puncture of the heart by a sharp object or a broken rib. The penetration causes blood to leak into the pericardial space or mediastinum.
    - The most frequently affected area is the right ventricle (due to its anterior position).
    - Blood leakage can result in cardiac tamponade, and blood loss from penetrating injuries can also result in shock.
    - Penetrating objects should be stabilized and the patient prepped for surgery.

HELPFUL HINT:

The most common cause of blunt cardiac trauma is MVC. Any patient who experiences rapid deceleration forces during an MVC should be assessed for BCI.

HELPFUL HINT:

When assessing patients with suspected BCI, measure blood pressure in both arms; a tear in the aortic arch may create a pressure gradient between the upper extremities. An aortic disruption may also cause upper extremity hypertension and lower extremity relative hypotension.

> **QUICK REVIEW QUESTION**
>
> 11. A patient arrives at the ED with a knife impaled in the chest. The patient is awake and alert but anxious and appears pale. What priority interventions should the nurse perform?

Cardiogenic Shock

Pathophysiology

Cardiogenic shock, a cyclical decline in cardiac function, results in decreased cardiac output in the presence of adequate fluid volume. A lack of coronary perfusion causes or escalates ischemia/infarction by decreasing the ability of the heart to pump effectively. The heart rate increases in an attempt to meet myocardial oxygen demands. However, the reduced pumping ability of the heart reduces cardiac output and the CI, and demands for coronary or tissue perfusion are not met. LVEDP increases, which leads to stress in the left ventricle and an increase in afterload. This distress results in lactic acidosis. Cardiogenic shock is most commonly seen after an MI but can be associated with trauma, infection, or metabolic disease.

HELPFUL HINT:

Left ventricular dysfunction caused by an anterior MI is the most common cause of cardiogenic shock.

Signs and Symptoms

- tachycardia and sustained hypotension (SBP <90 mm Hg)
- oliguria (<30 mL/hr or <0.5 mL/kg/hr output)
- crackles
- tachypnea and dyspnea
- pallor
- JVD
- altered LOC
- cool, clammy skin
- S3 heart sound possible

Diagnostic Tests

- CI <2.2 L/min/m^2
- PAOP >15 mm Hg

- elevated SVR, CVP
- decreased SvO_2, MAP
- elevated lactate
- ABG shows metabolic acidosis and hypoxia

Treatment and Management

- immediate goal: reduce cardiac workload and improve myocardial contractility
- immediate IV fluids
- medications given based on hemodynamic status
    - vasopressor (usually norepinephrine) for hypotensive patients
    - inotrope (usually dobutamine) and vasodilator for normotensive patients
- other interventions
    - IABP to reduce afterload and increase coronary perfusion
    - cardiac catheterization to improve myocardial perfusion and increase contractility
    - LVAD
- monitor patient for cardiac dysrhythmias

> **QUICK REVIEW QUESTION**
>
> 12. A patient presents with tachycardia, pallor, JVD, and crackles after emergent PCI for anterior MI. What hemodynamic findings for this patient would indicate cardiogenic shock?

Cardiomyopathies

Pathophysiology

Cardiomyopathy is abnormal functioning of the heart muscles. Signs and symptoms of cardiomyopathy are similar to those of HF and vary with the location and degree of dysfunction. Types of cardiomyopathies include dilated, hypertrophic, and restrictive.

TABLE 1.4. Pathophysiology and Management of Cardiomyopathy

Type of Cardiomyopathy	Management
Dilated congestive cardiomyopathy (DCCM) occurs when damage to the myofibrils causes dilation in the ventricles, causing enlargement and systolic impairment (<40% ejection fraction).	• beta blockers, ACE inhibitors (ARBs if patient is ACE intolerant), and diuretics • implantable defibrillator or cardiac resynchronization therapy
Hypertrophic cardiomyopathy (HCM) is an inherited disorder characterized by left ventricular hypertrophy and diastolic dysfunction. In **obstructive HCM**, cardiac output is decreased. The stiffening of the ventricle septum obstructs the left ventricle outflow tract and disrupts mitral valve function, resulting in a decreased preload and an increased afterload.	• beta blockers, calcium channel blockers, and antidysrhythmic agents • implantable defibrillator • alcohol septal ablation or surgical septal myectomy for severe symptoms • contraindicated: ACE inhibitors, digoxin, vasodilators, and diuretics
Restrictive cardiomyopathy (RCM) occurs when fibrous tissue builds up within the ventricles, resulting in diastolic dysfunction and decreased cardiac output. Systolic function is usually normal. Unlike other cardiomyopathies, in RCM the ventricles will not be enlarged or hypertrophic.	• diuretics; beta blockers and calcium channel blockers used cautiously • contraindicated: digoxin, nitrates
Ischemic cardiomyopathy is impaired left ventricular functioning caused by CAD and the resulting ischemia and ventricular remodeling.	• ACE inhibitors and beta blockers

QUICK REVIEW QUESTION

13. The nurse is completing a medication reconciliation on a patient admitted with HF symptoms and a history of HCM. Home medications include metoprolol, diltiazem, and digoxin. Which medication should the nurse be concerned about?

Dysrhythmias

A cardiac **dysrhythmia** is an abnormal heartbeat or rhythm. Dysrhythmias are typically caused by a malfunction in the heart's cardiac conduction system. Most dysrhythmias of clinical importance are caused by **reentry**: the re-excitation of the heart by an electrical impulse that did not die out. Reentry dysrhythmias include A-fib, atrial flutter, V-tach, and V-fib.

HELPFUL HINT:

When treating dysrhythmias, medical staff should always consider a hypotensive patient unstable.

TABLE 1.5. The Cardiac Conduction System	
Component	Description
SA node	sets the heart's pace by sending out electrical signals that cause the atria to contract
AV node	relays the electrical impulse of the SA node to the ventricles; the impulse is delayed to allow the atria to fully contract and fill the ventricles
bundle of His	carries the electrical signal from the AV node to the right and left bundle branches
right and left bundle branches	carry the electrical signal from the bundle of His to Purkinje fibers
Purkinje fibers	endpoint of the conduction system; located in the endocardial layer; depolarize muscle cells, causing contraction of the ventricles

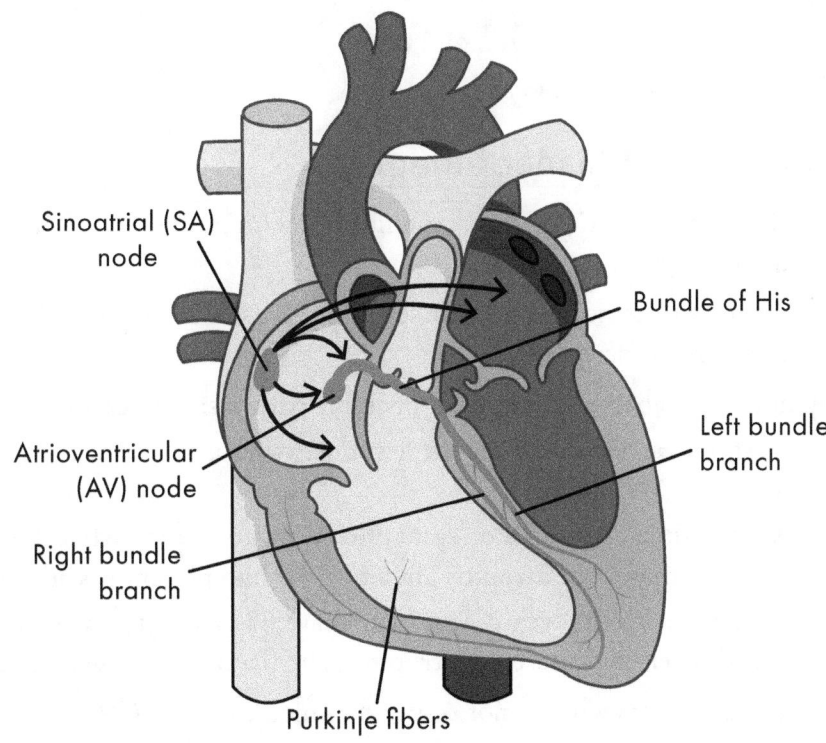

Figure 1.12. The Cardiac Conduction System

Treatment is based on whether the patient is deemed hemodynamically stable or unstable.

- Stable patients can receive noninvasive interventions or drugs as a priority intervention to correct an abnormal rhythm.

- Unstable patients should receive the appropriate electrical therapy.

Bradycardia

Pathophysiology

Bradycardia is a heart rate of <60 bpm. It results from a decrease in the sinus node impulse formation (automaticity). Bradycardia is normal in certain individuals and does not require an intervention if the patient is stable. Symptomatic patients, however, need immediate treatment to address the cause of bradycardia and to correct the dysrhythmia. Symptoms of bradycardia may include hypotension, syncope, confusion, or dyspnea.

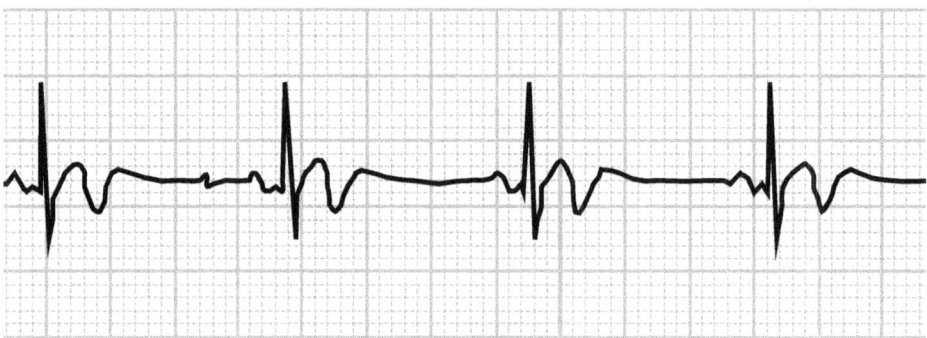

Figure 1.13. ECG: Bradycardia

Treatment and Management

- stable, asymptomatic patients: monitoring with no intervention required
- symptomatic, hemodynamically stable patients: monitor while determining underlying cause
- symptomatic, hemodynamically unstable patients: medication
  - first line: atropine 0.5 mg for first dose, with a maximum of 3 mg total
  - second line: dopamine or epinephrine if atropine is ineffective or if maximum dose of atropine already given and patient is still stable
  - patients with bradycardia and who have had a heart transplant: administer isoproterenol (atropine is ineffective in these patients)
- unstable patients who do not respond to medication: TCP

QUICK REVIEW QUESTION

14. A patient presents with complaints of confusion, dizziness, and dyspnea. The patient's blood pressure is 72/40 mm Hg, with a heart rate of 32 bpm and O_2 saturation of 92% on room air. What priority intervention should the nurse prepare for?

Narrow-Complex Tachycardias
Pathophysiology

Narrow-complex tachycardias (also called **supraventricular tachycardia [SVT]**) are dysrhythmias with >100 bpm and a narrow QRS complex (<0.12 seconds). The dysrhythmia originates at or above the bundle of His (supraventricular), resulting in rapid ventricular activation. Specific SBT rhythms include AV nodal reentrant tachycardia (AVNRT), AV reentrant tachycardia (AVRT), and atrial tachycardia (AT).

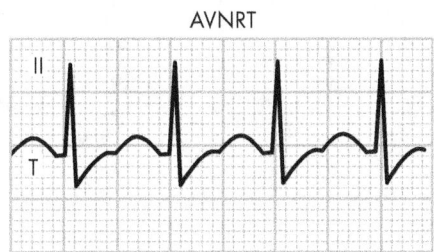

Figure 1.14. ECG: AV Nodal Reentrant Tachycardia (AVNRT)

Narrow-complex tachycardias are often asymptomatic. Symptomatic patients may have palpitations, chest pain, hypotension, and dyspnea.

Treatment and Management

- first line: vagal maneuvers
- second line: medication
    - rapid bolus dose of adenosine (6 mg)
    - second dose (this time 12 mg) if chemical cardioversion does not occur within 1 – 2 minutes
- refractory SVT
    - stable patients: calcium channel blockers, beta blockers, or digoxin
    - unstable patients and patients for whom medications are ineffective: synchronized cardioversion

> **QUICK REVIEW QUESTION**
>
> 15. A patient in SVT is unresponsive to vagal maneuvers. What intervention is likely to be ordered next?

Atrial Fibrillation and Flutter
Pathophysiology

Atrial fibrillation (A-fib) is an irregular narrow-complex tachycardia. During A-fib, the heart cannot adequately empty, causing blood to pool and clots to form, increasing stroke risk. The irregular atrial contractions also decrease cardiac output. The ECG in A-fib will show an irregular rhythm with no P waves and an undeterminable atrial rate.

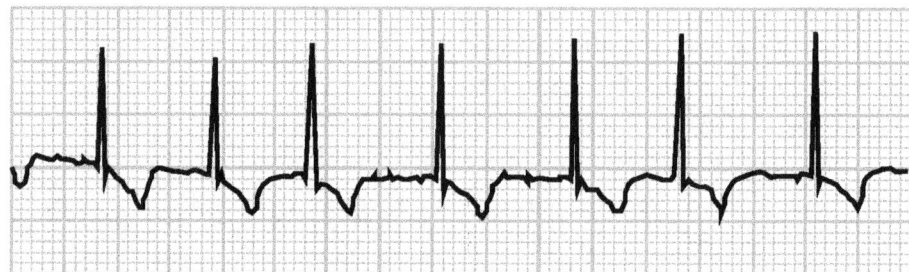

Figure 1.15. ECG: Atrial Fibrillation

During **atrial flutter**, the atria beat regularly but too fast (240 – 400 bpm), causing multiple atrial beats in between the ventricular beat. Atrial flutter can be regular or irregular. The ECG in atrial flutter will show a saw-toothed flutter and multiple P waves for each QRS complex.

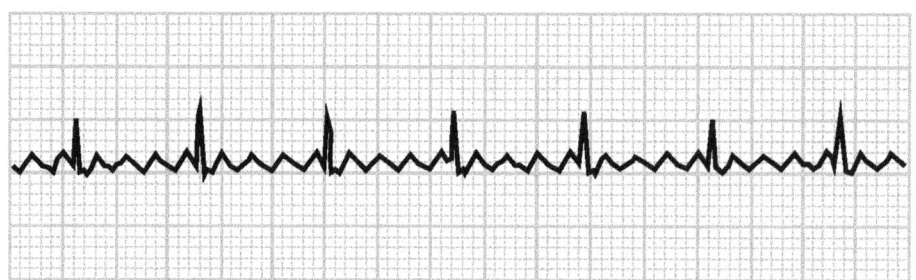

Figure 1.16. ECG: Atrial Flutter

Treatment and Management

- adenosine: slows the rhythm so that it may be identified, but will not convert dysrhythmia to a sinus rhythm
- hemodynamically stable patients: medication
    - calcium channel blockers, beta blockers, or cardiac glycoside to slow the rhythm
    - antidysrhythmics to convert to sinus rhythm
- hemodynamically unstable patients: cardioversion
- anticoagulants to lower risk of stroke
- cardiac ablation may be used to correct A-fib and atrial flutter

QUICK REVIEW QUESTION

16. A patient presents with A-fib. Vital signs are:

BP	125/80
HR	150
RR	23

What intervention should the nurse anticipate?

Ventricular Tachycardia and Fibrillation
Pathophysiology

Ventricular tachycardia (V-tach) is tachycardia originating below the bundle of His, resulting in slowed ventricular activation. During V-tach, ≥3 consecutive ventricular beats occur at a rate >100 bpm. V-tach is often referred to as a **wide-complex tachycardia** because of the width of the QRS complex.

Because the ventricles cannot refill before contracting, patients in this rhythm may have reduced cardiac output, resulting in hypotension. V-tach may be short and asymptomatic, or it may precede V-fib and cardiac arrest.

HELPFUL HINT:

Torsades de pointes, a type of V-tach with irregular QRS complexes, occurs with a prolonged QT interval. It can be congenital or caused by antidysrhythmics, antipsychotics, hypokalemia, or hypomagnesemia.

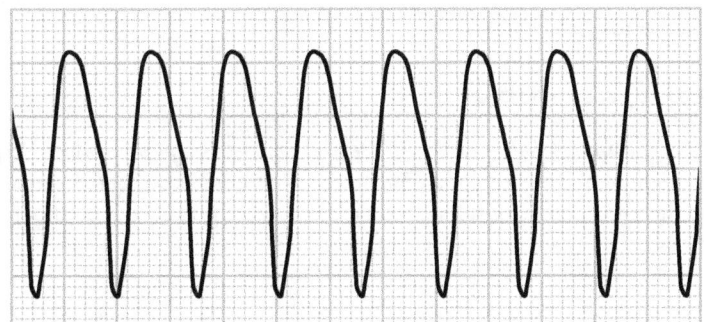

Figure 1.17. ECG: Ventricular Tachycardia

During **ventricular fibrillation (V-fib)** the ventricles contract rapidly (300 – 400 bpm) with no organized rhythm. There is no cardiac output. The ECG will initially show **coarse V-fib** with an amplitude >3 mm. As V-fib continues, the amplitude of the waveform decreases, progressing through **fine V-fib** (<3 mm) and eventually reaching asystole.

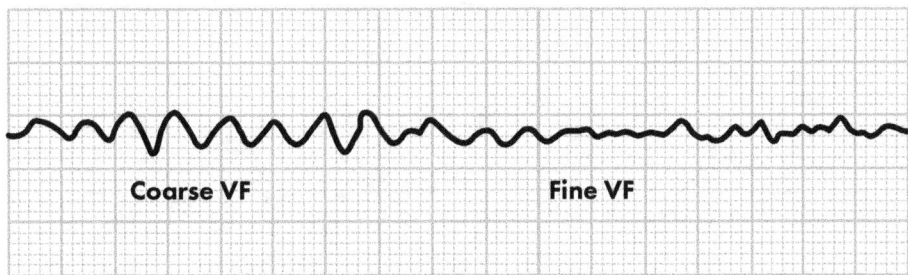

Figure 1.18. ECG: Ventricular Fibrillation

Cardiovascular Review 31

Treatment and Management

- V-fib: follow **advanced cardiac life support (ACLS)** protocols
  - immediately initiate high-quality CPR at 100 – 120 compressions per minute
  - defibrillation ASAP, before administration of any drugs
  - defibrillation doses: 200 J → 300 J → 360 J (biphasic)
  - ≥2 defibrillation attempts should be made for patients in V-fib before giving any medications
  - first line: epinephrine 1 mg every 3 – 5 minutes
  - shock-refractory V-fib: amiodarone (300 mg as first dose and 150 mg for second dose)
- priority intervention for V-tach: check for pulse
  - pulseless V-tach: follow ACLS protocols
  - V-tach with a pulse, patient stable: administer amiodarone
  - V-tach with a pulse, patient unstable: synchronized cardioversion
  - patients with recurrent V-tach: implantable defibrillator or radiofrequency ablation

QUICK REVIEW QUESTION

17. The nurse is participating in a cardiac resuscitation attempt of a patient found in V-fib. A total of 2 defibrillation attempts have been made, and 1 dose of epinephrine has been given 2 minutes earlier. What priority action should the nurse take next?

Pulseless Electrical Activity/Asystole
Pathophysiology

Pulseless electrical activity (PEA) is an organized rhythm in which the heart does not contract with enough force to create a pulse. **Asystole**, also called a "flat line," occurs when there is no electrical or mechanical activity within the heart. Both PEA and asystole are nonshockable rhythms with a poor survival rate.

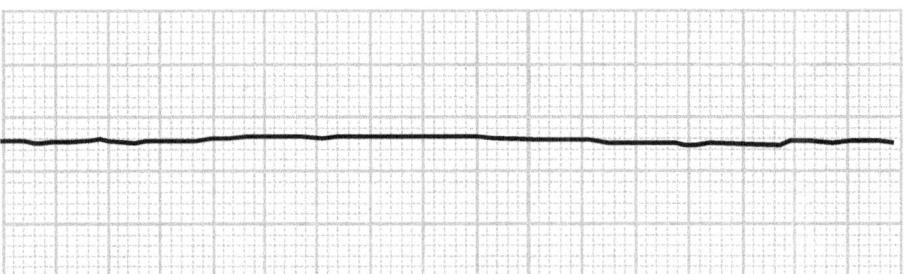

Figure 1.19. ECG: Asystole

Treatment and Management

- immediate CPR
- epinephrine 1 mg every 3 – 5 minutes until circulation returns or a shockable rhythm emerges
- immediate attempts to determine and treat underlying cause, particularly **Hs and Ts** (common causes of PEA and asystole)
    - hypovolemia
    - hypoxia
    - hydrogen ion (acidosis)
    - hyperkalemia/hypokalemia
    - hypothermia
    - toxins
    - tamponade
    - tension pneumothorax
    - thrombosis (coronary or pulmonary)

> **QUICK REVIEW QUESTION**
>
> 18. A patient is found in bed unresponsive to commands. The patient appears cyanotic, and the nurse determines there is no pulse and no breathing present. What should the nurse do first?

Heart Failure

Pathophysiology

Heart failure (HF) occurs when either one or both of the ventricles in the heart cannot efficiently pump blood, resulting in decreased cardiac output. The condition is typically due to another disease or illness, most commonly CAD. **Acute decompensated heart failure** is the sudden onset or worsening of HF symptoms.

HF is classified according to the left ventricular ejection fraction. Impairment of systolic function results in **heart failure with reduced ejection fraction (HFrEF, or systolic HF)**, classified as an ejection fraction of <50%. **Heart failure with preserved ejection fraction (HFpEF, or diastolic HF)** is characterized by an ejection fraction of >50% and diastolic dysfunction.

CONTINUE →

TABLE 1.6. Systolic Versus Diastolic Heart Failure (HF)

Systolic HF	Diastolic HF
• reduced ejection fraction (<50%)	• normal ejection fraction
• dilated left ventricle	• no enlargement of heart
• S3 heart sound	• S4 heart sound
• hypotension	• hypertension

HELPFUL HINT:

Cor pulmonale, or impaired functioning of the right ventricle, is caused by pulmonary disease or pulmonary hypertension.

HF can also be categorized as left-sided or right-sided, depending on which ventricle is affected. **Left-sided HF** is usually caused by cardiac disorders (e.g., MI, cardiomyopathy) and produces symptoms related to pulmonary function. **Right-sided HF** is caused by right ventricle infarction or pulmonary conditions (e.g., PE, COPD) and produces symptoms related to systemic circulation. Unmanaged left-sided HF can lead to right-sided HF.

Diagnostic Tests

- BNP >100 pg/mL
- echocardiogram to assess ejection fraction, ventricular hypertrophy, valve dysfunction
- CXR to show cardiomegaly or pulmonary congestion

Signs and Symptoms

TABLE 1.7. Signs and Symptoms of Right- and Left-Sided Heart Failure (HF)

Left-Sided HF	Right-Sided HF
increased LVEDP and left atrial pressures	increased right ventricular end-diastolic pressure (RVEDP) and right atrial pressures
increased PAP	increased CVP
dyspnea or orthopnea	increased PAP
pulmonary edema	dependent edema (usually in lower legs); ascites
tachycardia	JVD
bibasilar crackles	hepatomegaly
cough, frothy sputum, hemoptysis	right-sided S3 sound
left-sided S3 sound	weight gain
diaphoresis	nausea, vomiting, abdominal pain
pulsus alternans	nocturia
oliguria	

Treatment and Management

- goal of treatment: improve cardiac output and CI
- medications
  - first-line: loop diuretic, ACE inhibitor or ARB, and beta blocker
  - hydralazine and nitrate for patients who cannot tolerate ACE inhibitors or ARBs
  - calcium channel blockers used with caution (amlodipine or felodipine may be used to treat hypertension if first-line mediations are ineffective)
- other interventions: ICD, permanent pacemaker, IABP, VAD, or transplant

HELPFUL HINT:

Management of HF is complex. Patients will have varying needs for pharmacological and surgical interventions, depending on the type and degree of HF.

QUICK REVIEW QUESTION

19. A patient presents with sudden onset dyspnea, JVD, and peripheral edema. What laboratory test would confirm a diagnosis of acute decompensated heart failure?

Hypertensive Crisis

Pathophysiology

Hypertensive crises include hypertensive urgency and hypertensive emergencies. **Hypertensive urgency** occurs when blood pressure is >180/110 mm Hg without evidence of organ dysfunction. A **hypertensive emergency** occurs when systolic blood pressure is >180 mm Hg or when diastolic blood pressure is >120 mm Hg and when either of these is accompanied by evidence of impending or progressive organ dysfunction. Hypertensive crises increase the risk of cerebral infarction, and prolonged hypertension can lead to heart or renal failure.

Signs and Symptoms

- usually asymptomatic
- headache
- blurred vision
- dizziness
- dyspnea
- retinal hemorrhages
- epistaxis
- chest pain

Treatment and Management

- blood pressure reduction: limited to a decrease of ≤25% within the first 2 hours to maintain cerebral perfusion
- first-line medications: labetalol, hydralazine, clonidine, or metoprolol
- quiet, nonstimulating environment
- O_2 administration

QUICK REVIEW QUESTION

20. A patient is found to be alert and oriented with a blood pressure of 200/100 mm Hg and is asymptomatic. What priority intervention should the nurse take?

Myocardial Conduction System Defects

Atrioventricular Blocks

Pathophysiology

An **atrioventricular (AV) block** is the disruption of electrical signals between the atria and ventricles. The electrical impulse may be delayed (first-degree block), intermittent (second-degree block), or completely blocked (third-degree block).

A **first-degree AV block** occurs when the conduction between the SA and the AV nodes is slowed, creating a prolonged PR interval. A first-degree AV block is a benign finding that is usually asymptomatic, but it can progress to a second-degree or third-degree block.

The ECG in a first-degree AV block will show a prolonged PR interval of >0.20 seconds.

> **HELPFUL HINT:**
>
> If the R is far from P, then you have a *first degree*.
>
> Longer, longer, longer, drop, this is how you know it's a *Wenckebach*.
>
> If some Ps just don't go *through*, then you know it's a *type 2*.
>
> If Ps and Qs don't agree, then you have a *third degree*.

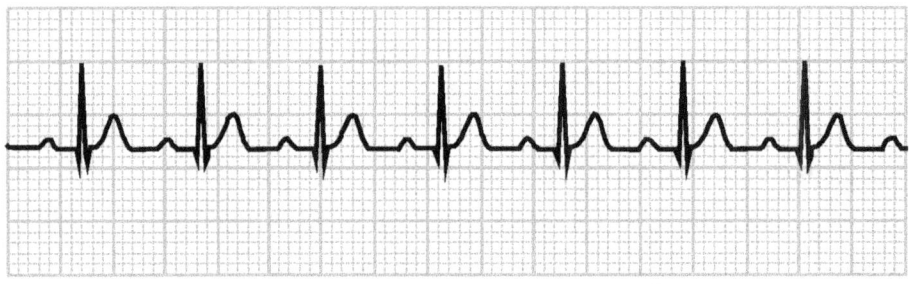

Figure 1.20. ECG: First-Degree Atrioventricular (AV) Block

A **second-degree AV block, type 1** (Wenckebach or Mobitz type 1), occurs when the PR interval progressively lengthens until the atrial impulse is completely blocked and does not produce a QRS impulse. This dysrhythmia occurs when the atrial conduction in the AV node or bundle of His is either being slowed or blocked. This type of block is cyclic; after the dropped QRS complex, the pattern will repeat itself.

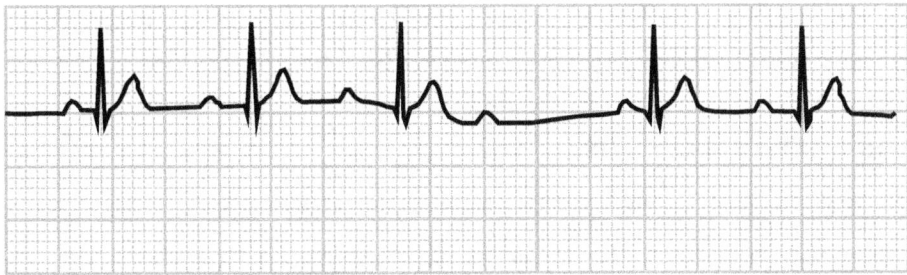

Figure 1.21. ECG: Second-Degree AV Block, Type 1

The ECG in second-degree AV block, type 1, will show progressively longer PR intervals until a QRS complex completely drops.

A **second-degree AV block, type 2** (Mobitz type 2), occurs when the PR interval is constant in length but not every P wave is followed by a QRS complex. This abnormal rhythm is the result of significant conduction dysfunction within the His-Purkinje system.

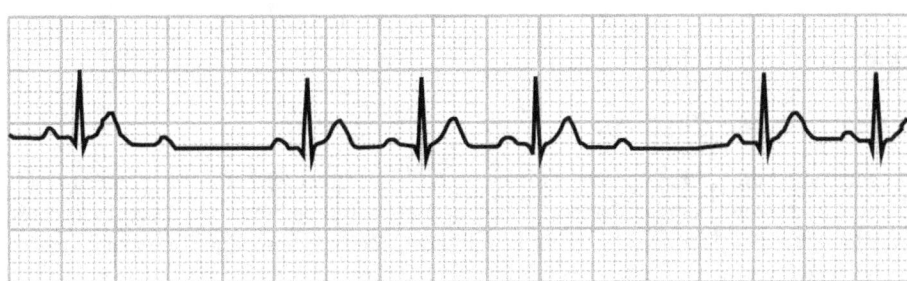

Figure 1.22. ECG: Second-Degree AV Block, Type 2

The ECG in second-degree AV block, type 2, will show constant PR intervals and extra P waves, with dropped QRS complexes.

A **third-degree AV block**, sometimes referred to as a complete heart block, is characterized by a complete dissociation between the atria and the ventricles. There are effectively 2 pacemakers within the heart, so there is no

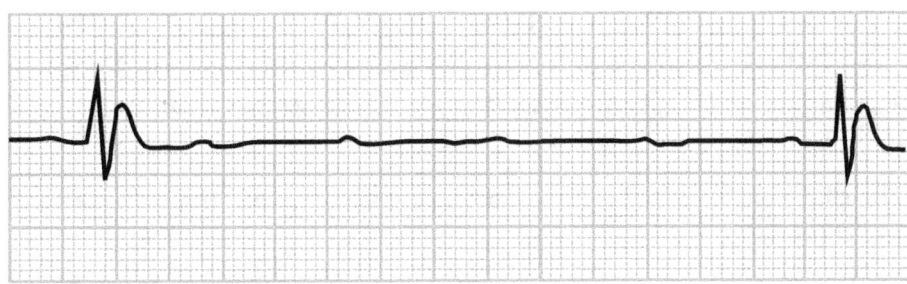

Figure 1.23. ECG: Third-Degree AV Block

correlation between the P waves and the QRS complexes. The most common origin of the block is below the bundle of His, but the block can also occur at the level of the bundle branches of the AV node.

The ECG for third-degree AV block will show regular P waves and QRS complexes that occur at different rates. There will be more P waves than QRS complexes, with P waves possibly buried within the QRS complex.

Signs and Symptoms

- first- and second-degree AV blocks usually asymptomatic
- may show symptoms of reduced cardiac output (e.g., hypotension, dyspnea, chest pain)
- bradycardia

Treatment and Management

- symptomatic patients: TCP possibly needed to manage symptoms
- implantable pacemaker if underlying cause cannot be resolved
- hypotensive patients: dopamine or epinephrine may be needed
- discontinue medications that slow electrical conduction in the heart (e.g., antidysrhythmics)

HELPFUL HINT:

Atropine is ineffective for Mobitz type 2 and third-degree AV blocks. It only increases the firing of the SA node, and the block prevents the SA node from influencing ventricular contraction.

QUICK REVIEW QUESTION

21. A patient begins to complain of dizziness and weakness and appears diaphoretic. The nurse notes from the telemetry monitor that the patient has a third-degree AV block. BP is 71/55 mm Hg, and HR is 30 bpm. What interventions does the nurse expect?

SINUS NODE DYSFUNCTION
Pathophysiology

Sinus node dysfunction (SND), also known as sick sinus syndrome (SSS), refers to dysrhythmias caused by a dysfunction in the SA node. An individual with SND can have bouts of bradycardia or tachycardia or can alternate between the two. SND can also arise from an SA block or sinus arrest. Because of these irregular and usually unpredictable signals, most people with SND will need a permanent pacemaker.

- The ECG for SND will show alternating bradycardia and tachycardia and sinus arrest.

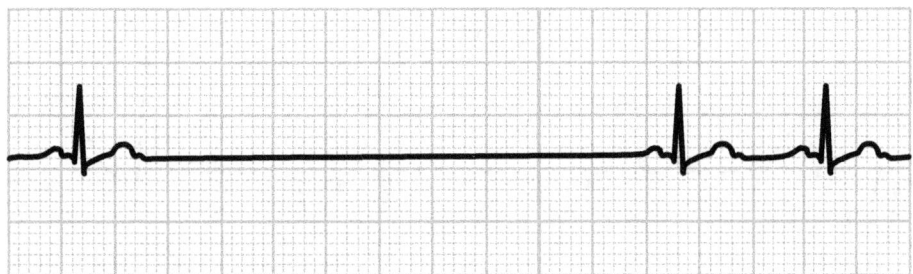

Figure 1.24. ECG: Sinus Arrest

Signs and Symptoms

- syncope
- fatigue
- dyspnea
- palpitations
- confusion

Treatment and Management

- stable, asymptomatic patients: monitoring only
- hemodynamically unstable patients: atropine and temporary pacing to correct bradycardia
- symptomatic patients with recurrent episodes of bradycardia: implantable pacemaker required

> **QUICK REVIEW QUESTION**
>
> **22.** A patient with recurring episodes of bradycardia due to SND tells the nurse that they do not want to have surgery for a pacemaker, since they currently have no symptoms. What is the nurse's best response?

BUNDLE BRANCH BLOCK
Pathophysiology

Right bundle branch block (RBBB) and **left bundle branch block (LBBB)** are interruptions in conduction through a bundle branch. Bundle branch blocks (BBB) usually occur secondary to underlying cardiac conditions, including MI, hypertension, and cardiomyopathies. LBBB in particular is associated with progressive underlying structural heart disease and is associated with poor outcomes post-MI. However, both RBBB and LBBB may occur in the absence of heart disease.

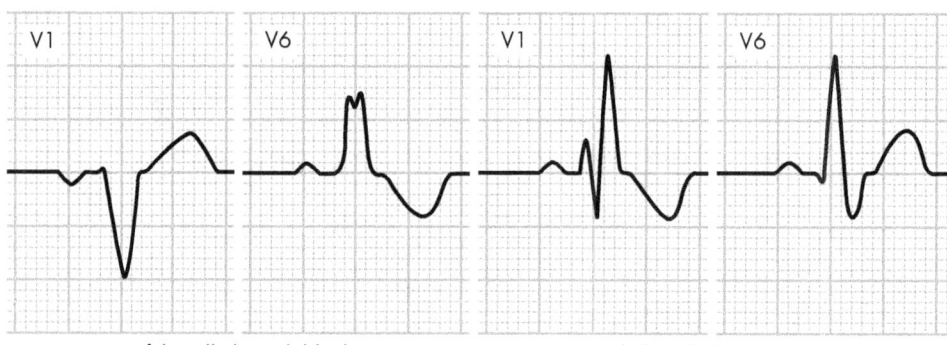

Figure 1.25. ECG: Bundle Branch Blocks

Ischemic heart disease is the most common cause of both RBBB and LBBB. LBBB can also arise from other heart diseases, hyperkalemia, or digoxin toxicity. Other causes of RBBB include cor pulmonale, pulmonary edema, and myocarditis.

If the patient with a BBB is asymptomatic, no treatment is necessary. Patients with syncopal episodes may need to have a pacemaker inserted.

HELPFUL HINT:

LBBB may mask the characteristic signs of MI on an ECG.

QUICK REVIEW QUESTION

23. A patient with HF develops a new-onset LBBB. What medication would be important to consider as a possible cause of the LBBB?

Congenital Conduction Defects

- **Wolff-Parkinson-White syndrome**, caused by an early excitation of an extranodal accessory pathway, results in tachycardia.
    - May be asymptomatic or present as sudden A-fib or paroxysmal tachycardia with HR >150.
    - ECG shows short PR interval (<0.12 seconds) with a slurred QRS upstroke and a wide QRS (>0.12 seconds).
    - Treatment is synchronized cardioversion. Unstable patients may require catheter ablation.
    - Contraindicated medications include adenosine, digoxin, amiodarone, beta blockers, and calcium channel blockers.
- **Long QT syndrome** is a cardiac electrical disturbance that causes a prolonged ventricular repolarization (seen as a QT interval >0.44 seconds on ECG).
    - may be asymptomatic or present with dysrhythmias (especially torsades de pointes), syncope, seizure, or sudden cardiac death
    - management: beta blockers and placement of an ICD

- medications likely to prolong the QT interval contraindicated
- **Brugada syndrome** is a genetically inherited cardiac electrical pathway syndrome that is linked to 4% – 12% of all sudden cardiac deaths.
  - Diagnosed by characteristic ECG findings with sudden cardiac arrest, ventricular tachydysrhythmias, or syncopal episodes.
  - ECG shows pseudo-RBBB and persistent ST-segment elevation.
  - ECG abnormalities may be unmasked by sodium channel blockers.
  - Treated with medication (quinidine or flecainide) or ICD placement.
  - Medications likely to prolong the QT interval are contraindicated.

HELPFUL HINT:

Caution should be exercised when administering antipsychotics, antidepressants, and anticonvulsants if the QT is >0.45 seconds.

QUICK REVIEW QUESTION

24. A combative patient with schizophrenia develops torsades de pointes in the ICU. What medications may have caused this dysrhythmia?

Structural Heart Defects

- In **aortic stenosis (AS)**, blood flow from the left ventricle to the aorta is impeded.
  - The pressure load on the left ventricle is increased, eventually leading to left ventricular hypertrophy, decreased cardiac output, and HF.
- **Aortic regurgitation (AR)** occurs when blood flows backward from the aorta to the left ventricle.
  - Volume overload in the left ventricle leads to left ventricular hypertrophy and systolic dysfunction with a lowered ejection fraction.
- In **mitral stenosis (MS)**, blood flow from the left atrium to the left ventricle is impeded, resulting in an enlarged atrium.
  - Almost all cases of mitral stenosis are caused by rheumatic heart disease, with most patients showing symptoms ≥15 years after the initial infection.
- **Mitral regurgitation (MR)** occurs when the blood flows backward from the left ventricle to the left atrium.
  - This backward flow increases the preload and decreases the afterload.
- Aortic and mitral valve disease presents with signs and symptoms similar to HF; they include dyspnea, exercise intolerance, angina, and dizziness or syncope.

- Symptomatic patients will require surgical valve repair or replacement.
- **Transcatheter aortic valve repair (TAVR)** is the replacement of the aortic valve via catheter. Common postoperative complications include bleeding, thrombosis, and endocarditis.

QUICK REVIEW QUESTION

25. What heart sound is associated with aortic stenosis?

ANSWER KEY

1. The nurse should focus on CVP as CVP is an indirect measure of right ventricular pressure and is highly influenced by fluid status. In sepsis, CVP is <2 mmHg, because of profound systemic vasodilation. Both treatments would be expected to increase preload, thereby increasing CVP.

2. As the initial MI involved the right ventricle, ST elevation changes will be enhanced with placement of leads V3 through V6 on the right side. Restenosis of the stent will present as an acute MI, whereas reperfusion pain will have little to no ECG changes and will respond to medical treatment.

3. Beta blockers depress conduction through the AV node; the reduced conduction may exacerbate an underlying AV block, resulting in severe bradycardia.

4. The patient is experiencing a STEMI and needs immediate transport to the catheterization lab for PCI for reperfusion.

5. The symptoms indicate inferior-wall MI, which puts the patient at risk for right ventricular infarctions. For patients with right ventricular infarction, medications that reduce preload (e.g., nitrates, diuretics, morphine) should be avoided.

6. The nurse should ensure strict bedrest and make sure that the affected extremity is kept straight. The nurse should also assess the site frequently and notify the physician for bleeding, coldness, increased pain, or decreased pulse. NPO status should be initiated 8 hours before reevaluation.

7. Patients with DVT and dyspnea should immediately have a CT scan ordered to rule out a PE. A PE is an emergent condition that needs immediate treatment.

8. Because of the patient's dysrhythmia and the presented symptoms, pulmonary edema should be suspected. Confirmation through a chest X-ray will reveal anomalies, especially pleural effusions and basal congestion due to accumulation of fluid within the alveolar space.

9. Since the patient describes the pain as tearing, the nurse should take the blood pressure in the other arm. A difference of ≥20 mm Hg can be a strong indicator that the patient is experiencing an aortic rupture or dissection.

10. The patient has signs and symptoms of cardiac tamponade, which is a possible complication following percutaneous cardiac interventions. The nurse should prepare for pericardiocentesis to drain the fluid.

11. The object should be stabilized and bleeding controlled. Two large-bore IVs should be placed for the administration of IV fluids and blood if needed. The patient should be prepped for surgery to have the object removed and to be assessed for underlying damage to organs and surrounding areas.

12. Cardiogenic shock is characterized by signs and symptoms of hypoperfusion combined with a systolic BP of <90 mm Hg, a CI of <2.2 L/min/m^2, and a normal or elevated PAOP (>15 mm Hg).

13. Digoxin is contradicted with this type of cardiomyopathy, as the medication is a positive inotropic and can reduce LV filling and increase obstruction of the left ventricular outflow tract. The medication should be verified with the patient, and the admitting physician should be notified immediately.

14. This patient is hemodynamically unstable because of bradycardia. The nurse should prepare to push IV atropine.

15. If the patient in SVT does not respond to vagal maneuvers, the patient will likely be administered 6 mg of adenosine to terminate the dysrhythmia.

16. The nurse should expect a hemodynamically stable patient with A-fib to receive calcium channel blockers, beta blockers, or cardiac glycosides to decrease the heart rate.
17. After 2 defibrillation attempts and the first dose of epinephrine has been given, the nurse should prepare the first dose of amiodarone (300 mg) to be given next.
18. The nurse should activate the code team and begin high-quality compressions immediately. CPR should not be delayed to administer epinephrine.
19. A BNP lab value of >100 pg/mL indicates HF.
20. After confirming that the BP reflects a hypertensive crisis, the nurse should administer an antihypertensive medication but should aim for a reduction of no more than 25% within the first 2 hours.
21. The nurse should prepare the patient for TCP. Dopamine and epinephrine may be appropriate medications to administer for a third-degree block as they will increase the overall heart rate.
22. The nurse should explain that the absence of symptoms does not mean that underlying conditions are gone. Without the pacemaker, the patient risks developing additional dysrhythmias or could go into sudden cardiac arrest without warning.
23. Digoxin, often administered for treatment of HF, has a narrow therapeutic index. Digoxin toxicity may manifest itself as an LBBB. Labs would need to be drawn to assess for digoxin toxicity.
24. There is a strong association between antipsychotic medication use and torsades de pointes in patients with prolonged QT. The patient may have been administered haloperidol, which is one of the most commonly used medications in the ICU associated with torsades de pointes.
25. In aortic stenosis, an S4 heart sound may be heard. This extra heart sound, heard before S1, is caused by the atrial contraction of blood into a noncompliant ventricle.

2 RESPIRATORY REVIEW

> ### CCRN TEST PLAN: RESPIRATORY
> - Acute pulmonary embolus
> - Acute respiratory distress syndrome (ARDS)
> - Acute respiratory failure
> - Acute respiratory infection (e.g., pneumonia)
> - Aspiration
> - Chronic conditions (e.g., COPD, asthma, bronchitis, emphysema)
> - Failure to wean from mechanical ventilation
> - Pleural space abnormalities (e.g., pneumothorax, hemothorax, empyema, pleural effusions)
> - Pulmonary fibrosis
> - Pulmonary hypertension
> - Status asthmaticus
> - Thoracic surgery
> - Thoracic trauma (e.g., fractured rib, lung contusion, tracheal perforation)
> - Transfusion-related acute lung injury (TRALI)*
>
> *Covered in chapter 4, Hematology and Immunology Review

Respiratory Physiology

- The primary functions of the respiratory system are ventilation and respiration. The CCRN exam will focus on trauma- or disease-induced changes in these physiological functions.

- **Ventilation** is the inhalation and exhalation of air by the lungs.
- **Respiration** is the exchange of gas within the lungs.

- **Lung compliance** is a measure of how easily the lungs inflate (distensibility or elasticity).
  - **Static compliance** is measured under no-flow conditions so that only lung compliance (not airway resistance) is being measured. Normal range is 57 – 85 mL/cm H_2O.
  - **Dynamic compliance** is measured during the patient's breathing cycle to measure both lung and airway elasticity. Normal range is 46 – 66 mL/cm H_2O.

- **Lung volumes and capacities** are measured by spirometry at bedside in a critical care unit for clinical application in pulmonary management.
  - **Tidal volume (V_T)** is the volume of air exhaled after a normal resting inhalation. Normal value is 7 mL/kg.
  - **Vital capacity (VC)** is the maximal volume of air that can be exhaled after a maximal inhalation. It increases with height and decreases with age; the normal value is 60 – 70 mL/kg.
  - **Inspiratory capacity (IC)** is the maximal volume of gas that can be inspired from the resting expiratory level.
  - **Functional residual capacity (FRC)** is the volume of gas retained in the lungs when the patient is at rest and at the end of expiration.
  - **Total lung capacity (TLC)** is the volume of gas contained in the lungs at the end of a maximal inspiration.
  - **Normal resting minute ventilation** is the volume of air inhaled or exhaled per minute. Normal is 5 – 8 L/min.

- **Ventilation/perfusion (V/Q) ratio** is the amount of air that reaches the alveoli (ventilation, V) divided by the amount of blood flow in lung capillaries (perfusion, Q).
  - Normal V/Q ratio is 0.8.
  - A **V/Q mismatch** occurs when either perfusion or ventilation is inadequate.
  - A low V/Q ratio (perfusion with low ventilation) causes intrapulmonary shunting (e.g., ARDS).
  - A high V/Q ratio (ventilation with low perfusion) causes increased dead space (e.g., PE).

- **Intrapulmonary shunting (right-to-left shunting)** occurs under normal perfusion but with decreased ventilation, causing blood to enter the arterial system without being oxygenated.
  - PaO_2 decreases as shunting increases; $PaCO_2$ is essentially unchanged.

HELPFUL HINT:

A VC of 10 – 15 mL/kg (accompanied by a spontaneous RR of <24 breaths/min) is the minimal accepted value for weaning from mechanical ventilation.

- If left untreated, tissue demand for oxygen is unmet, leading to cellular hypoxia, lactic acidosis, and multiple organ dysfunction syndrome (MODS).
- Intrapulmonary shunting may occur because of fluid in alveoli (e.g., pulmonary edema), constriction of airways (e.g., asthma), or collapse of alveoli (e.g., atelectasis).

■ **Dead space** in the lungs is the volume of air that does not participate in gas exchange and is expired unchanged.
- **Anatomical dead space** is the volume of inspired air that never reaches the alveoli. It includes the volume of air in the upper and lower respiratory tracts down to the terminal bronchioles.
- **Alveolar dead space** is the volume of inspired air that reaches the alveoli but never participates in gas exchange. It is negligible in healthy lungs and increases because of alveoli hypoperfusion (e.g., PE).
- **Physiologic dead space** is the sum of anatomical and alveolar dead space.

HELPFUL HINT:

Administering O_2 to patients with severe intrapulmonary shunting (very low V/Q) will have little effect on PaO_2 because air is not reaching the area where perfusion occurs.

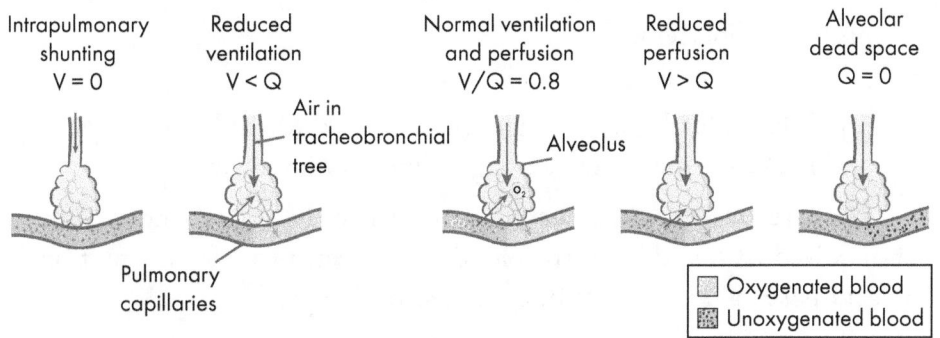

Figure 2.1. Ventilation/Perfusion (V/Q) Ratio

■ **Hypoxemia** is a decreased level of oxygen (O_2) in the blood (as measured by SaO_2, PaO_2, or A-a gradient). It can be caused by several different underlying pathophysiological processes.
- V/Q mismatch (e.g., PE)
- shunting (e.g., pneumonia, ARDS)
- hypoventilation (e.g., sedation, brain injury)
- impaired diffusion (e.g., pulmonary fibrosis)

■ **Hypoxia** is a deficiency in oxygenation at the tissue or cellular level. It may be caused by hypoxemia or other processes, including hypoperfusion (e.g., MI) or the inability of tissues to metabolize O_2 (e.g., cyanide poisoning).

QUICK REVIEW QUESTION

1. A SICU patient is now 5 hours post-extubation after a successful open-abdominal complete hysterectomy. When the nurse auscultates the patient's lungs, there are bronchial breath sounds over the lung fields, indicating consolidation, and the patient's SaO$_2$ is low. The surgical resident orders a mixed venous blood gas analysis after the patient is placed on an initial CPAP mask at 35% FiO$_2$. The nurse knows that a specific lung disease process has initiated. What physiological pulmonary process will the venous blood gas results indicate?

Respiratory Assessment Tools

- **Pulse oximetry** (peripheral capillary oxygen saturation, or **SpO$_2$**) is the noninvasive, continuous monitoring of patient's oxygen saturation.

- **Capnography** (patient end-tidal CO$_2$ measurement, or **PETCO$_2$**) is the noninvasive, continuous monitoring of patient's exhaled carbon dioxide (CO$_2$) gas. PETCO$_2$ is used to assess:
  - ventilation status during procedural sedation
  - proper ET placement
  - effectiveness of CPR
  - physiologic dead space changes (increased gradient between PaCO$_2$ and PETCO$_2$ means worsening pulmonary impairment)

- An **arterial blood gas (ABG) test** measures the pH (acidity) and amount of dissolved CO$_2$ and O$_2$ in the blood. ABG tests provide information on acid-base balance and pulmonary gas exchange.

TABLE 2.1. Normal Values for ABG

Elements of an ABG	Normal Value
pH	7.35 – 7.45
Partial pressure of oxygen (PaO$_2$)	75 – 100 mm Hg
Partial pressure of carbon dioxide (PaCO$_2$)	35 – 45 mm Hg
Bicarbonate (HCO$_3$–)	22 – 26 mEq/L
Oxygen saturation (SaO$_2$)	94% – 100%

  - The following tic-tac-toe method is one of many tools available for understanding the pathophysiology behind the ABG result in critically ill patients.

1. Identify the normal, acidic, and basic values.

Lower	Normal	Higher
	pH	
Acidic ←	7.35–7.45	→ Basic
	$PaCO_2$	
Basic ←	35–45 mm Hg	→ Acidic
	HCO_3^-	
Acidic ←	22–26 mEq/L	→ Basic

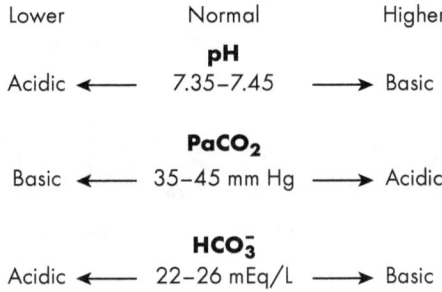

Figure 2.2. Normal ABG Values

2. Draw tic-tac-toe grid.

Acid	Normal	Base

Figure 2.3 ABG Tic-Tac-Toe Grid

3. Plug in the given values in the appropriate column.

Acid	Normal	Base
HCO_3^- 19		pH 7.5
		$PaCO_2$ 26

Figure 2.4 Example of a Completed ABG Tic-Tac-Toe Grid

4. Name the acid-base result by finding the "tic-tac-toe/3-in-a-row."

Tic-tac-toe: respiratory alkalosis

Abnormal: compensated

Acid	Normal	Base
HCO_3^- 19		pH 7.5
		$PaCO_2$ 26

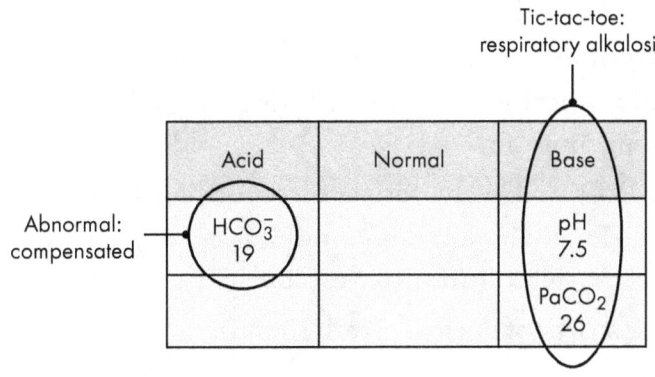

Figure 2.5 Analysis of an ABG Tic-Tac-Toe Grid

5. Determine if uncompensated, partially compensated, or fully compensated.
6. Consider possible causes of acid-base imbalance to implement plan of care.

TABLE 2.2. Common Causes of Changes in ABG Values

Abnormality	pH	ABG	Etiology
Respiratory acidosis	decreased	$PaCO_2$ increased	• asthma (late stage) • cardiac arrest • COPD • Guillain-Barre syndrome, ALS, myasthenia gravis • respiratory depressant drugs
Respiratory alkalosis	increased	$PaCO_2$ decreased	• asthma (early stage) • cirrhosis • CNS disorders • hypoxemia • salicylate overdose • sepsis
Metabolic alkalosis	increased	HCO_3^- increased	• blood transfusions • GI: vomiting • hypokalemia
Metabolic acidosis	decreased	HCO_3^- decreased	• DKA • GI: diarrhea • lactic acidosis • renal failure • rhabdomyolysis

- The **alveolar-arterial (A-a) gradient** is the difference between oxygen concentration in the alveoli and the arterial oxygen concentration (A-a gradient = $PAO_2 - PaO_2$).
    - assesses shunting and level of V/Q mismatch
    - normal gradient is 5 – 10 mm Hg (in young adult, nonsmoker, breathing room air)
- **P/F ratio** is PaO_2 divided by patient's fraction of inspired oxygen (FiO_2).
    - A low P/F ratio indicates poor respiration; oxygen is entering the lungs but is not diffusing to the capillaries.
- There are a variety of normal breath sounds.

- **bronchial:** high pitch, loud, auscultated over trachea
- **bronchovesicular:** moderate pitch, moderate intensity, upper sternum/between scapulae
- **vesicular:** low pitch, soft, peripheral, and basilar lung fields

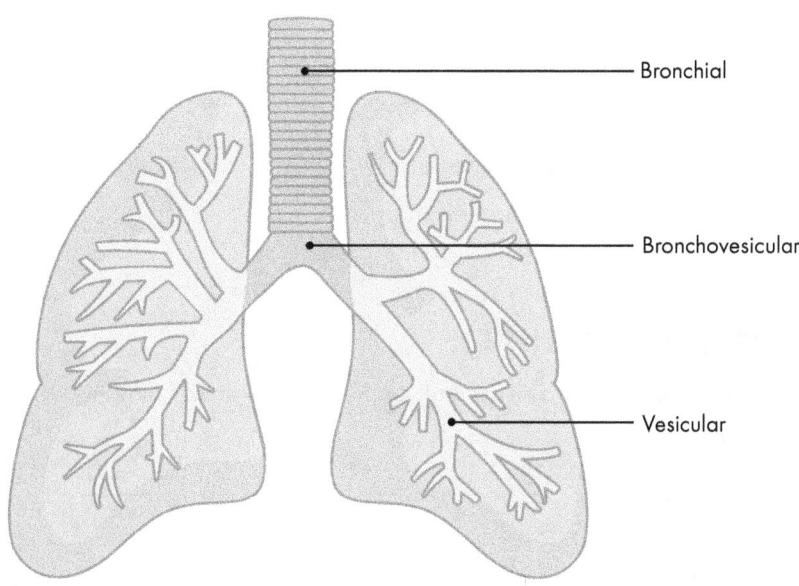

Figure 2.6. Three Types of Breath Sounds

TABLE 2.3. Abnormal and Adventitious Breath Sounds	
Sound	**Etiology**
Abnormal Breath Sounds	
Absent	• complete airway obstruction • pleural effusion • pneumothorax
Diminished	• atelectasis • pleural effusion
Bronchial sounds heard in lung fields	• pleural effusion • pneumonia • pulmonary edema
Adventitious breath sounds	
Crackles (rales)	• atelectasis • pulmonary edema • pneumonia

continued on next page

TABLE 2.3. Abnormal and Adventitious Breath Sounds (continued)	
Sound	Etiology
Abnormal Breath Sounds	
Rhonchi	• asthma • bronchospasm • pneumonia
Wheeze	• asthma • bronchospasm
Friction rub	• pleural effusion • pleurisy

QUICK REVIEW QUESTION

2. A patient is in the critical care unit post-cardiac arrest with the following ABG values:

   pH: 7.30

   PaO_2: 95

   $PaCO_2$: 48

   HCO_3-: 28

   How should the nurse interpret these results?

Respiratory Gases

- **Oxygen (O_2)** is a vasodilator in lungs and a vasoconstrictor in all other vascular beds.
    - Room air = 21% oxygen
    - over-oxygenation can result in **oxygen toxicity**
        - may occur in any patient breathing >50% FiO_2 over 24 hours
        - a risk factor for ARDS
        - reduces hypoxic drive (especially with COPD)
        - clinical signs include substernal chest pain exacerbated by deep breathing, dry cough, tracheal irritation, dyspnea, absorption atelectasis, negative inotropic effects on the heart, and ocular toxicity
- **Nitric oxide (NO)** is a pulmonary selective vasodilator.
    - used with mechanically ventilated patients
    - may be an effective therapy in some respiratory diseases of critically ill adults (e.g., PH, COPD)

- adverse effects include pulmonary edema, bronchospasm, and acidosis
- **Heliox** is a mixture of room air (21% FiO_2) and helium (He).
  - has same viscosity as room air but is less dense, allowing it to move more easily to distal areas of lung
  - generates less airway resistance than room air
  - reduces work of breathing and assists in liberation from mechanical ventilation

> **QUICK REVIEW QUESTION**
>
> 3. A critical care patient has been on >60% FiO_2 via a partial rebreathing mask for 36 hours. The patient tells the nurse about a sharp substernal pain on inhalation that worsens with deep breaths. The nurse notes the patient's RR is 22 – 24, with a frequent dry cough. The bedside monitor shows bradycardia in the 50 – 60 bpm range. What disease process does the nurse suspect has been initiated, and what serious respiratory disease process is a potential sequela?

Respiratory Procedures

Fiber-Optic Bronchoscopy

- **Fiber-optic bronchoscopy** is a common diagnostic and therapeutic bedside procedure in critical care units.
- Pre- and intra-procedure medications include:
  - IV sedation
  - IV analgesia
  - pre-procedure atropine (decreases secretions, reduces vasovagal response)
  - pre-procedure IM codeine (decreases cough reflex)
- Complications include laryngospasm and bronchospasm, vomiting, infection, anaphylaxis, and respiratory or cardiac impairment.

Thoracentesis

- In **thoracentesis**, a needle is inserted with local anesthetic as a diagnostic or therapeutic procedure to remove air or fluid from the pleural space.
- Removal of greater than 1000 mL effusion fluid will increase negative intrapleural pressure and lead to **re-expansion pulmonary edema** if lung does not re-expand to fill the now-available pleural space.

- Signs and symptoms of re-expansion pulmonary edema include severe cough and dyspnea.
- If re-expansion pulmonary edema is suspected:
  - Stop procedure immediately.
  - Administer supplemental oxygen.
  - Consider positive pressure mechanical ventilation.
  - If pneumothorax develops, immediate chest tube insertion is needed.

Chest Tube

- **Chest tubes** (also tube thoracotomy) use suction to reestablish negative pleural pressure and re-expand the lung field; they may also be used to remove fluids from compromised thoracic spaces.
- Serial CXR is used to monitor lung improvement.
- Position patient with "good side" down so that air travels up and is evacuated by chest tube system.
- If chest tube is dislodged, immediately cover surgical insertion site with occlusive dressing and manual pressure.
- The water-seal system has a water-seal chamber, suction-control chamber, and collection chamber.
  - The **water-seal chamber** acts like a one-way valve: air escapes but can't reenter the pleural space.
  - Suction-control chamber is set to 10 – 20 cm H_2O suction on regulator.
  - Collect and measure fluid from collection chamber, per facility policy.
  - Heimlich valve is a one-way valve: air escapes but can't reenter the pleural space.

HELPFUL HINT:

Bubbling in water-seal column is normal only when used for pneumothorax. New bubbling may indicate an air leak in the system or a new pneumothorax.

Extracorporeal Membrane Oxygenation (ECMO)

- During **extracorporeal CO_2** removal, a venous catheter circuit pumps through a modified extracorporeal membrane oxygenation (ECMO) device to extract CO_2 from blood.
- ECMO is used for ARDS and COPD exacerbation.
- Contraindicated for cardiac failure.

Surgical Procedures

Medical and postoperative nursing management of common complications of thoracic surgery may be a brief focus of the CCRN exam.

TABLE 2.4. Respiratory Surgical Procedures

Procedure	Description	Indications
Pneumonectomy	removal of entire lung, with or without resection of mediastinal lymph nodes	• one-sided tuberculosis • unilateral bronchiectasis • malignant tumors • overwhelming hemoptysis • bronchopleural fistula
Lobectomy	resection of one or multiple lung lobes	• tuberculosis in single lobe • tumor in single lobe • cysts or abscesses in single lobe • bronchiectasis • traumatic injury
Segmental resection	resection of bronchovascular section of lung lobe	• bronchiectasis • cysts or blebs • small localized peripheral lesions
Wedge resection	removal of wedge-shaped section(s) of lung	• peripheral granulomas • blebs • small localized peripheral lesions without lymph involvement • empyema drainage • infection
Partial rib resection	removal of one or more ribs	• healing of chronic empyema
Video-assisted thoracoscopic surgery (VATS)	minimally invasive chest wall incisions with small videoscope insertion	• biopsy of lung lesions • recurrent spontaneous pneumothorax incidents • sympathectomy • adhesion lysis

- Common complications of thoracic surgeries
    - acute respiratory failure
    - hemorrhage

HELPFUL HINT:

Lobectomy: position patient with good side down

Pneumonectomy: position patient supine with operative side down.

- bronchopleural fistula (opening into pleural space from suture line failure)
- pulmonary edema
- dysrhythmias
- atelectasis (prevent through deep breathing/incentive spirometry and stabilization of V/Q mismatch)

QUICK REVIEW QUESTION

4. A bedside thoracentesis is ordered for drainage of a pleural effusion for a critical care patient. The ICU resident has determined the needle insertion site by reviewing the previously obtained chest CT scan and has appropriately administered local anesthetic prior to needle insertion. After 1400 mL of effusion fluid has been slowly removed, the patient suddenly demonstrates severe dyspnea and severe coughing. What has occurred, and what is the nursing response to this complication?

Mechanical Ventilation
Overview of Mechanical Ventilation

- **Invasive mechanical ventilation** uses an advanced invasive airway.
- **Endotracheal tube (ETT)** placement (oral or nasal) should be checked after intubation.
  - CXR remains gold standard for placement verification; tip of ETT should be 2 – 3 cm above carina.
  - Waveform capnography is an excellent tool to confirm ETT placement at bedside.
  - Chest auscultation simply identifies that bilateral breath sounds are present and equal, and not in stomach or right main-stem bronchus.
  - Cuff pressure should be 20 – 30 cm H_2O.
- **Tracheostomy tubes** are placed emergently for obstruction and used for long-term ventilator support.
  - Deflate cuff and place one-way valve for patient to talk.
  - Always keep an extra trach tube at bedside (document every shift).
- **Volume-limited ventilation** delivers a set volume.
  - **Assist-control (AC) ventilation** always delivers a set V_T and set respiratory rate (RR).
    - Spontaneous patient breath receives full-delivery V_T.
    - RR maintained even with spontaneous breaths.
    - Requires neuromuscular blockade to not "fight vent."

- □ **Synchronized intermittent mandatory ventilation (SIMV)** always delivers a set V_T and a set RR.
  - □ Spontaneous patient breath receives only patient's own V_T.
  - □ Each ventilator breath is synchronized with patient's own RR.
  - □ Use sedation or neuromuscular blockade, per patient's needs.
- During **pressure-support ventilation (PSV)**, patient-initiated breaths receive positive pressure support on inspiration.
  - □ decreases work of breathing
  - □ very effective during weaning from ventilator
  - □ need backup apnea mode
- Ventilator settings
  - □ RR: 8 – 20 breaths/min
  - □ V_T: customized to the patient's predicted body weight (as part of lung-protective ventilation [LPV] bundles) to prevent volutrauma (6 – 8 mL/kg of patient's body weight)
  - □ The lowest tolerated FiO_2 should be used to maintain SaO_2 without oxygen toxicity.
  - □ **Positive end-expiratory pressure (PEEP)** is positive pressure applied at the end of exhalation to prevent the passive emptying of the lung, which causes end-expiratory alveolar collapse.
    - □ PEEP increases alveolar recruitment and allows for more gas exchange.
    - □ Complications of PEEP include barotrauma, decreased blood pressure and cardiac output, and air-leak disorders.
    - □ For most patients, extrinsic PEEP is set at 5 cm H_2O.
  - □ The normal **inspiratory-expiratory (I:E) ratio** is 1:2.
  - □ The **inspiratory flow rate** is usually set with a peak rate of 60 L/min.
- **Noninvasive ventilation (NIV)** uses a noninvasive interface such as a face mask or mouthpiece.
  - □ **Continuous positive airway pressure (CPAP)** delivers a single level of pressure for both inspiration and expiration. It is primarily used for obstructive sleep apnea and cardiogenic pulmonary edema.
  - □ **Bilevel positive airway pressure (BiPAP or BPAP)** delivers two levels of positive airway pressure, IPAP and EPAP.
    - □ **Inspiratory positive airway pressure (IPAP)** enhances airflow and augments patient's V_T; corresponds to pressure support.
    - □ **Expiratory positive airway pressure (EPAP)** reduces amount of pressure to ease expiratory effort; corresponds to PEEP.

HELPFUL HINT:

Asynchrony occurs when ventilator gas-flow delivery is not efficiently matched to the patient's needs. Machine-delivered breaths may be early or late, or the flow rate may not meet the patient's needs.with operative side down.

HELPFUL HINT:

Volutrauma is injury due to mechanical settings that deliver excessive volume to the alveoli. Ventilated patients with ARDS are at high risk for volutrauma and should receive a lower V_T.

- NIV may be used as an alternative to mechanical ventilation, with fewer risks; it reduces airway injuries, ventilator-associated pneumonia (VAP), and length of stay.
- Contraindications for NIV include:
  - life-threatening conditions, including hypoxemia and dysrhythmias
  - high risk of airway obstruction

QUICK REVIEW QUESTION

5. What is PEEP, and what are the complications of this therapy?

LIBERATION FROM MECHANICAL VENTILATION

- Critical care facilities have specific parameters for liberating patients from mechanical ventilation. Some general parameters are:
  - The patient must be awake and be able to follow commands, perform chin-to-chest movement, lift their head from the pillow, and protect their airway by coughing and deep breathing.
  - ABGs must reflect stabilization of underlying respiratory disease pathology.
  - The Richmond Agitation-Sedation Scale (RASS) must provide evidence of patient tolerance to lightened sedation and analgesia and daily "sedation holidays" that are part of facility-specific protocols.
  - Most patients are off vasopressors.
  - Nutrition status, especially phosphate and albumin levels, has been optimized.
- If all the above criteria are satisfactory, the following are generally accepted parameters for successful liberation from mechanical ventilation:
  - positive expiratory pressure >30 cm H_2O
  - vital capacity >10 mL/kg
  - spontaneous V_T >5 mL/kg
  - FiO_2 <50%
  - minute volume <10 L/min
  - rapid shallow breathing index (RSBI) <105 breaths/min/L
  - negative inspiratory force (NIF) <−20 cm H_2O
- The US Agency for Healthcare Research and Quality (AHRQ) has recommended specific protocols that coordinate the use of **spontaneous**

awakening trials (SAT) and spontaneous breathing trials (SBT) to evaluate patients' tolerance for removal from mechanical ventilation.

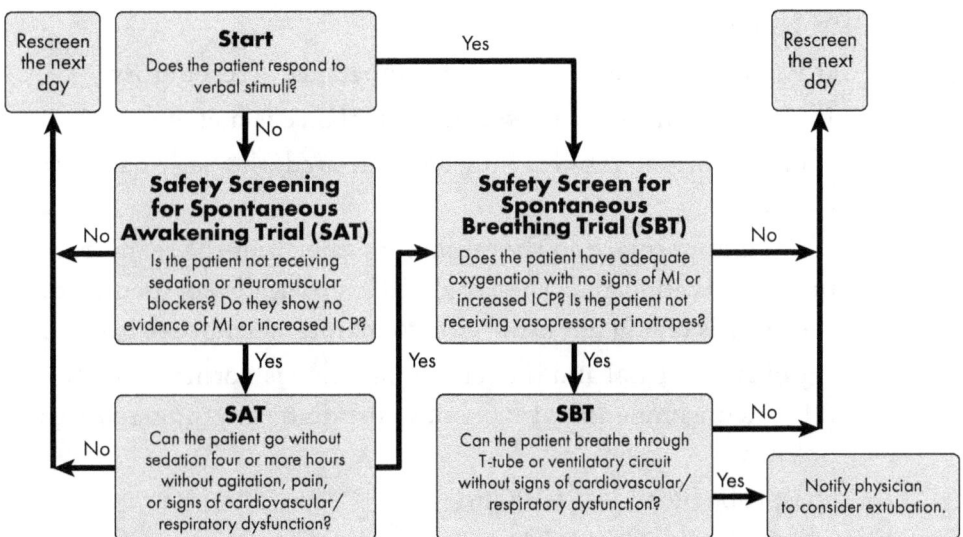

Figure 2.7. Summary of AHRQ Protocols for SAT and SBT

- Post-extubation adverse events include:
  - **stridor:** treated with heliox and steroids to reduce subglottal inflammation
  - **post-extubation laryngeal edema:** airway obstruction from ETT-generated mucosal damage that may require emergent re-intubation

> **QUICK REVIEW QUESTION**
>
> 6. A patient has been successfully liberated from mechanical ventilation after 6 days of intubation, where the oral ETT soft cuff pressure was monitored at every shift and maintained at 20 – 25 cm H_2O, and ETT was repositioned in the mouth, per facility protocol. Then, 5 hours post-extubation, the patient's voice is raspy and they say their throat "feels tight." What does the nurse suspect is occurring?

Ventilator-Associated Events

- Patients on mechanical ventilation are at high risk for ventilator-associated events (VAE).
  - **ventilator-associated conditions (VAC),** which include atelectasis, fluid overload, and ARDS
  - **infection-related ventilator-associated conditions (IVAC),** which include VAP

- The Society of Critical Care Medicine (SCCM) recommends the implementation of an LPV bundle and the ABCDEF bundle to reduce VAP.
  - LPV bundle
    - If $PaCO_2$ is in the tic-tac-toe, the imbalance is respiratory.
    - If HCO_3 is in the tic-tac-toe, the imbalance is metabolic.
    - If pH is normal, ABG is fully compensated; the body has done its job.
    - If pH is abnormal and the remaining value (not the tic-tac-toe/3-in-a-row) is abnormal, then the ABG is partially compensated: the body is trying but is not able to maintain acid-base balance.
    - If pH is abnormal and the remaining value is normal, then the ABG is uncompensated: the body isn't doing anything to fix the problem.
    - chest tube blood loss >100 mL
    - sudden increase in blood loss
    - place patient operative side down
    - emergent return to OR necessary for repair
    - emergent chest tube placement may be done at bedside to drain fluid
    - head of bed raised 30 – 45 degrees (to prevent aspiration)
    - oral care (chlorhexidine every 2 hours)
    - subglottic suction protocol
    - low VT settings
    - Choice of analgesia and sedation: treat pain before sedation, and routinely assess for agitation and depth of sedation
    - Delirium assessment and management
    - Early mobility and exercise
    - Family engagement and empowerment
  - ABCDEF bundle
    - Assess, prevent, and manage pain
    - Both SAT and SBT (see "Liberation from Mechanical Ventilation" section on page 58)
- Additional interventions to prevent VAE include:
  - GI prophylaxis
  - DVT prophylaxis
  - IV fluid administration (prevent fluid overload or dehydration)
  - vigilant monitoring for sepsis, per facility protocol (with targeted antibiotic therapy as needed)

> **QUICK REVIEW QUESTION**
>
> **7.** What components of the LPV bundle help prevent VAP in the critical care setting?

Acute Pulmonary Embolus

Pathophysiology

A **pulmonary embolus (PE)** is a thromboembolus that occludes a pulmonary artery. The most common embolus is a blood clot caused by deep vein thrombosis (DVT), but fat emboli, tumor emboli, and amniotic fluid emboli can also reach the lungs.

Damage to the lungs during PE follows several pathways. The occlusion increases pulmonary dead space and causes V/Q mismatch, resulting in pulmonary shunting and hypoxemia. PE may also trigger bronchoconstriction and disrupt surfactant functioning, resulting in atelectasis and worsening hypoxemia.

Pulmonary hypertension develops from both the mechanical obstruction (clot) and the release of an injury-site mediator that causes pulmonary vasoconstriction. These processes elevate pulmonary vascular resistance (PVR), which in turn increases right ventricular workload and eventually results in right ventricular failure. Left ventricular preload decreases, cardiac output drops, hypotension follows, and shock occurs.

Etiology

- trauma (high risk with fracture)
- surgery
- A-fib
- immobility
- hypercoagulability states

Signs and Symptoms

- pleuritic chest pain
- tachycardia
- tachypnea and dyspnea
- hemoptysis

- increased pulmonary S2
- sudden onset
  - increased PA pressures
  - right-sided HF

Diagnostic Findings

- ABG showing low PaO_2
- increased A-a gradient
- V/Q scan (25% – 30% accuracy)
- spiral CT scan: a 30-second study with >90% sensitivity/specificity
- pulmonary angiogram: definitive diagnosis but with long study time
- ultrasound for DVT in lower extremities
- 12-lead ECG
  - tall, peaked T waves in II, III, aVF
  - transient RBBB
  - right-axis deviation
- D-dimer positive
- $ETCO_2$ value ≥36 rules out PE with high reliability

Treatment and Management

- IV fluid resuscitation
- IV anticoagulants once diagnosis is confirmed
- thrombolytics for unstable patients with no contraindications
- supportive treatment for symptoms
  - O_2 therapy
  - analgesics
  - vasopressors to manage blood pressure

> **QUICK REVIEW QUESTION**
>
> 8. A 52-year-old patient is admitted to the critical care unit with tachycardia, tachypnea, hemoptysis, and chest pain. The patient is currently hemodynamically stable, and a diagnosis of a PE is suspected. What diagnostic study should the nurse expect to be ordered to confirm the diagnosis?

Acute Respiratory Distress Syndrome

Pathophysiology

Acute respiratory distress syndrome (ARDS) is a sudden and progressive form of **noncardiogenic pulmonary edema (NPE)** in which the alveoli fill with fluid following damage to the pulmonary endothelium. ARDS is the systemic response to lung injury and is initiated by the inflammatory-immune system, which releases inflammatory mediators from the site of injury within 24 – 48 hours.

There are three phases of ARDS, but the CCRN exam focuses on phase 1, the exudative phase. When inflammatory mediators injure pulmonary capillaries, the resultant permeability allows blood, proteins, fibrin, and other mediators to leak into the pulmonary interstitium, causing interstitial edema. This fluid is then forced back into the alveoli, causing alveolar edema. The combination of edema and protein in the alveolar fluid disrupts surfactant production, causing the alveoli to stiffen and collapse.

NPE with refractory hypoxemia ensues because of intrapulmonary shunting and V/Q mismatch. Compression also increases the work of breathing, decreases lung compliance, and reduces the functional residual capacity of the lungs. Hypoxic vasoconstriction, microthrombi, and patient fatigue all lead to increased alveolar dead space and pulmonary hypertension, which increases the right ventricular afterload. As increased right ventricular dysfunction continues, cardiac output is reduced.

Etiology

- gastric aspiration, pneumonia
- chemotherapy, transthoracic radiation
- toxic inhalation
- pulmonary contusion
- sepsis
- DIC
- pancreatitis
- TRALI

Signs and Symptoms

- restlessness, anxiety
- tachypnea with increased accessory-muscle usage for work of breathing

HELPFUL HINT:

Historically, respiratory distress with a P/F ratio between 200 and 300 was referred to as acute lung injury (ALI). That term is generally no longer used; instead, ARDS has been divided into mild, moderate, and severe, based on the P/F ratio.

HELPFUL HINT:

Hypermetabolism is an increase in resting energy expenditure often seen in critically ill patients. It is a complex stress response that impairs glucose metabolism, increases risk of infection, and impairs tissue healing. Adequate and early parenteral nutrition is vital to manage hypermetabolism in trauma, SIRS, and ARDS patients.

- elevated PAP
- PAOP normal or low
- progressive hypoxemia
- lungs clear initially; fine crackles as ARDS progresses
- decreased urine output
- tachycardia and hypotension

Diagnostic Findings

- CXR showing pulmonary infiltrates, ground-glass opacity, and an elevated diaphragm
- ABG findings
  - decreasing P/F ratio
    - <300 = mild ARDS
    - <200 = moderate ARDS
    - <100 = severe ARDS
  - refractory hypoxemia
  - increasing hypercapnia
- bronchoscopy showing increase in neutrophils and protein in aspirate
- lab results
  - lactic acidosis
  - elevated SGOT, ALP, bilirubin
  - increased PT/aPTT
  - decreased albumin

Treatment and Management

- use LPV methods
  - goal for reversing hypoxemia and preventing oxygen toxicity: PaO_2 = 55 – 65 mm Hg
  - PEEP: set at lowest possible amount (10 – 15 cm H_2O) to decrease intrapulmonary shunting while improving P/F ratio
  - low V_T (4 – 6 mL/kg) to reduce barotrauma and volutrauma
  - increased mechanical respiratory rate (20 – 30 breaths/min) for sufficient CO_2 elimination in low V_T settings
  - end-inspiratory plateau pressure goal: <30 cm H_2O
  - permissive hypercapnia with arterial pH ≥7.20 to avoid cardiopulmonary effects of acidosis
    - administer IV $NaHCO_3$

HELPFUL HINT:

Low PEEP can cause decreased cardiac output and hypotension.

- increase RR ventilator settings
- increase V_T ventilator settings
- neuromuscular blockade agent; peripheral nerve stimulator (train of four) to titrate paralytic doses, with goal of 1 – 2 twitches
- prone positioning to reduce damage to dependent areas of lungs
  - initiated early in treatment
  - maintained >16 hr/day
- improve tissue perfusion
  - low PAOP (intravascular volume) at 5 – 8 mm Hg through fluid restriction and diuretics
  - positive inotropic therapy and other vasoactive medications to maintain cardiac output

HELPFUL HINT:

Contraindications for permissive hypercapnia include pulmonary hypertension, increased ICP, heart failure, and seizures.

QUICK REVIEW QUESTION

9. A 68-year-old patient was admitted from the ED to the critical care unit for aspiration pneumonitis after being found in bed, lethargic, weak, and confused, with dried vomit on their clothing and gurgling respirations. CXR shows bilateral lung infiltrates. Vital signs: temperature 38.4°C (101.2°F) oral, HR 118 bpm, RR labored at 26 breaths/min, BP 86/50 mm Hg. Fine bibasilar crackles are auscultated, and pulse oximetry reads 83%. ABG on 3 L nasal cannula shows a pH = 7.29, $PaCO_2$ = 62 mm Hg, PaO_2 = 55 mm Hg, and HCO_3^- = 24 mEq/L. The patient is intubated to correct uncompensated respiratory acidosis with hypoxemia secondary to aspiration pneumonitis and ARDS. What components of LPV would be included for this patient?

Acute Respiratory Failure

Pathophysiology

Acute respiratory failure is a critical condition of the respiratory system marked by insufficient gas exchange and pulmonary inflammation caused by direct or indirect injury to the lungs. Acute respiratory failure may be characterized by hypoxemia (acute hypoxemic respiratory failure), hypercapnia (acute hypercapnic respiratory failure), or both. Hypoxemia symptoms are related to impaired oxygen exchange in lung fields; hypercapnia symptoms are related to the retention and inability to clear carbon dioxide, even in the presence of increased FiO_2 delivery.

HELPFUL HINT:

Refractory hypoxemia—low oxygen levels that do not respond to increased FiO_2—is a hallmark of respiratory failure.

TABLE 2.5. Types of Acute Respiratory Failure

Type	Description	Etiology
Type 1	hypoxemic: failure of O_2 exchange, with PaO_2 <60 mm Hg	• ARDS • atelectasis • PE • pneumonia
Type 2	hypercapnic: failure of CO_2 exchange, with $PaCO_2$ >45 mm Hg	• airway obstruction • blunt or penetrating trauma • COPD • drug overdose (e.g., opioids) • postoperative state • neuromuscular disease • spinal injury
Type 3	combined: failure of O_2 and CO_2 exchange, with PaO_2 <60 mm Hg and $PaCO_2$ >45 mm Hg	• ARDS • asthma • COPD

Signs and Symptoms

- hypoxemic
    - increased work of breathing
    - increased minute ventilation
    - tachypnea
    - dysrhythmias
- hypercapnic
    - reduced RR
    - altered mental status (including delirium and paranoia)
    - decreased LOC

Diagnostic Findings

- hypoxemia
    - PaO_2 <60 mm Hg
- hypercapnia
    - $PaCO_2$ >45 mm Hg
    - increased A-a gradient (>20 mm Hg)
    - pH <7.35 (in patients with acute hypercapnia)

Treatment and Management

- primary goals: improve ventilation and treat underlying etiology
- airway support (e.g., suctioning) as needed
- high FiO_2 likely needed, but should be reduced as quickly as possible
- noninvasive or invasive mechanical ventilation as needed
    - BiPAP for hypercapnic failure
    - CPAP for hypoxic failure
- ECMO for hypercapnia
- monitor and manage cardiac complications

> **QUICK REVIEW QUESTION**
>
> 10. A patient with COPD develops acute-on-chronic hypercapnia ($PaCO_2$ 55 mm Hg and pH 7.30) that is unresponsive to bronchodilators and administration of oxygen via nasal cannula. The patient is hemodynamically stable. What intervention should the nurse anticipate?

Acute Respiratory Infection

Pathophysiology

Pneumonia is a lower respiratory tract infection that causes inflammation and consolidation in the alveoli. It is classified according to how it was acquired. **Community-acquired pneumonia (CAP)** is contracted in the community. **Hospital-acquired pneumonia (HAP)**, also called **nosocomial pneumonia**, is contracted in a medical care setting. Patients with gastric feeding tubes are at a higher risk of **aspiration pneumonia** caused by inhalation of oropharyngeal secretions. Patients who have been intubated are at risk for VAP. Signs, symptoms, and treatment of CAP, HAP, aspiration pneumonia, and VAP are similar.

Signs and Symptoms

- productive cough
- pleuritic chest pain
- fever
- dyspnea
- hemoptysis
- abnormalities in affected lung/lobe
    - decreased lung sounds
    - inspiratory crackles
    - dull percussion

Diagnostic Tests and Findings

- elevated WBC count
- CXR showing infiltrates
- positive blood cultures or sputum cultures

Treatment and Management

- oxygen adjuncts or mechanical ventilation where necessary
- broad-spectrum antibiotics until cultures determine sensitivity
- adequate hydration
- good pulmonary hygiene and chest physiotherapy

HELPFUL HINT:

In patients with unilateral lung disease (e.g., right lung pneumonia), the patient should be positioned with the "good" lung down to promote blood flow and perfusion in the healthy lung.

QUICK REVIEW QUESTION

11. A 70-year-old patient is transported from a nursing home with complaints of dyspnea, fever, chills, and a productive cough with thick brown sputum. The patient's pulse oximetry reading is 86% on room air. What are the first actions the nurse should take?

Aspiration

Pathophysiology

Pulmonary aspiration is the entry of foreign bodies or material from the mouth or GI tract into the upper and/or lower respiratory tract. The acidity of the ingested material damages alveoli and capillaries, resulting in inflammation, decreased lung compliance, and possible pulmonary edema.

Etiology

- mechanical ventilation
- NG tube, tracheostomy, or bronchoscopy
- sedation or other altered LOC
- dysphagia
- stroke
- seizures

Signs and Symptoms

- coughing
- dyspnea

- choking
- diminished breath sounds in affected lobe
- crackles
- reduced SaO_2 or SpO_2

Diagnostic Tests and Findings

- CXR, spiral CT scan showing pulmonary infiltrates
- elevated WBC, increasing lactic acid, and positive blood cultures

Treatment and Management

- preventative measures to decrease risk
  - HOB elevated ≥30°, if not contraindicated
  - minimal amount of sedation for patient comfort
  - airway clearing and suctioning, where appropriate
  - maintain endotracheal cuff pressure <30 cm H_2O
  - assess placement of gastric tubes per sepsis protocols
  - continuous feedings instead of bolus; feeding tolerance assessed by monitoring residual formula
  - swallow assessment on extubated patients before PO delivery
- sepsis protocol

> **QUICK REVIEW QUESTION**
>
> 12. An 84-year-old nursing home patient with dementia, a right-side CVA 10 years ago, residual lower extremity weakness, bilateral knee contractures, mild dysphagia, and a history of GERD is transferred to the MICU after 2 – 3 days of increasing lethargy. On arrival, the nurse notes a temperature of 38.5°C (101.3°F) oral, tachycardia, dyspnea, and SpO_2 of 88% on 4 L nasal cannula. Lung sounds are diminished in the RLL, with fine, scattered crackles. CXR on admission shows right-sided pulmonary infiltrates. Which diagnosis would the nurse expect, and which actions should be prioritized?

Chronic Conditions

- The conditions in this section are included in the CCRN text framework but are usually not covered in depth on the exam. Test takers should be familiar with the basic pathophysiology of the conditions and management of acute exacerbations in critical care settings.

- **Chronic obstructive pulmonary disease (COPD)** is characterized by a breakdown in alveolar tissue (emphysema), chronic productive cough (chronic bronchitis), and long-term obstruction of the airways; the condition worsens over time.
    - The most common cause of COPD is smoking, although the disease can be caused by other inhaled irritants (e.g., smoke, industrial chemicals, other air pollution).
    - COPD is characterized by low expiratory flow rates.
    - Acute exacerbations of COPD are characterized by increased sputum production and hypoxia or hypercapnia, which may require emergent treatment.
    - Dysrhythmias are a common complication of acute exacerbations.
    - First-line management of COPD is bronchodilators (not inhaled corticosteroids) such as short-acting beta agonists and anticholinergics with cautious use of oxygen (titrated to SaO_2 88% – 92% or PaO_2 of 60 mm Hg).
    - When administering oxygen, vigilantly monitor for hypercapnia.
    - Intubation is required if respiratory distress is accompanied by progressive deterioration of hemodynamic stability.
- **Pulmonary fibrosis** is a chronic, progressive lung disease in which the tissue surrounding the alveoli is damaged, leading to thickening, scarring, and impaired lung function.
    - Most cases of pulmonary fibrosis are idiopathic, but the condition has been linked to smoking and exposure to some environmental pollutants.
    - Secondary complications include pulmonary hypertension and right-sided HF.
    - Acute exacerbations of pulmonary fibrosis may present with signs and symptoms similar to respiratory infection, PE, or pneumothorax.
    - Management of acute exacerbations of pulmonary fibrosis is supportive and includes O_2 (with possible mechanical ventilation) and corticosteroids.
- **Pulmonary hypertension (PH)** is clinically defined as a mean PAP ≥25 mm Hg measured via right heart catheterization.
    - PH can be hereditary, idiopathic, or secondary to other conditions, including connective tissue disease, left heart disease, respiratory disease, and PE.
    - Compensated PH is characterized by normal cardiac output and RAP with right ventricular hypertrophy.

HELPFUL HINT:

In COPD, inflammation is mainly caused by neutrophils. In asthma, inflammation is caused by eosinophils and activated T cells. Corticosteroids are highly effective against eosinophilic inflammation but mostly ineffective against neutrophilic inflammation.

- ☐ Decompensating PH is characterized by increased RAP and increased right ventricular hypertrophy.
- ☐ Decompensated PH is characterized by decreased PAP and right-sided HF.
- ☐ Treatment of PH focuses on treating the underlying etiology. Long-term management of PH includes selexipag, endothelin receptor antagonists, and calcium channel blockers.

QUICK REVIEW QUESTION

13. A 58-year-old patient is admitted to the critical care unit with a history of COPD. The patient is noncompliant with medical treatment (has continued smoking) and is being treated for bacterial pneumonia that has been worsening over the past 5 days despite antibiotic outpatient management. The patient presents with a diagnosis of acute exacerbation of COPD and is on BiPAP for hypercapnic failure after bronchodilators, IV methylprednisolone, and protocol-specific antibiotics. What signs and symptoms will indicate a worsening condition, and what therapies will the nurse anticipate next?

Pleural Space Abnormalities

AIR-LEAK SYNDROMES

Pathophysiology

Air-leak syndromes occur when air or gas enters the pleural space, resulting in extra-alveolar air accumulation and compression of the lung(s). There are two major categories of air-leak disorders: pneumothorax and pulmonary barotrauma. They have distinctly different pathophysiologies.

Pneumothorax occurs when air accumulates in the pleural space, collapsing the lung. Alveoli are underventilated, resulting in V/Q mismatch and intrapulmonary shunting. Hypoxia and respiratory failure may occur. The increased intrathoracic pressure may cause mediastinal shift, compressing the great vessels and decreasing cardiac output. Pneumothorax may be spontaneous or traumatic.

- **Primary spontaneous pneumothorax (PSP)** occurs spontaneously in the absence of lung disease and often presents with only minor symptoms.
- **Secondary spontaneous pneumothorax (SSP)** occurs in patients with an underlying lung disease and presents with more severe symptoms.
- **Traumatic pneumothorax** is caused by penetration of a blunt or sharp object. Common iatrogenic causes of pneumothorax include central line insertion, needle aspiration, or thoracentesis.

- **Tension pneumothorax**, a late progression of a pneumothorax, occurs when air enters the pleural space on inspiration and is unable to exit, causing increased pressure.

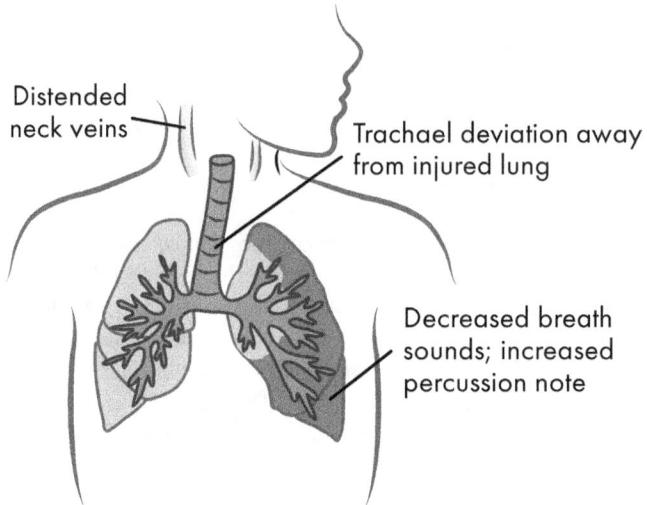

Figure 2.8. Signs and Symptoms of Tension Pneumothorax

Pulmonary barotrauma occurs when the positive pressure from mechanical ventilation causes alveoli to rupture, leaking air into the interstitial space (pulmonary interstitial emphysema). Air may then travel into the mediastinum (pneumomediastinum), where it obstructs the airway and decreases venous return. Air may also travel to the pleural space (pneumothorax, as described above) or the pericardium (pneumopericardium), causing cardiac tamponade.

Signs and Symptoms

TABLE 2.6. Signs and Symptoms of Air-Leak Syndromes	
Disorder	**Signs and Symptoms**
Pneumothorax	dyspnea
	pleuritic chest pain
	tracheal deviation toward affected side
	hyper-resonance over affected area
	absent or diminished breath sounds over affected area
Tension pneumothorax	dyspnea
	agitation
	tracheal deviation away from unaffected side
	JVD
	hypotension
	tachycardia

Disorder	Signs and Symptoms
Pneumomediastinum	subcutaneous emphysema (palpable crepitus from face to upper chest)
	crunching/rasping sound over pericardium on auscultation (Hamman's sign)
	substernal stabbing pain with position changes
Pneumopericardium	friction rub
Tension pneumopericardium	signs and symptoms of cardiac tamponade

Diagnostic Findings

- CXR showing increased translucency on affected side
- in tension pneumothorax, CXR showing mediastinum and heart shift to unaffected side

Treatment and Management

- pneumothorax <15%: supplemental oxygen and monitoring
- pneumothorax >15%: percutaneous needle aspiration of air from pleural space and insertion of chest tube
    - small-bore chest tube (nonventilator patients); large-bore chest tube (ventilator patients)
    - insertion at fourth or fifth intercostal space mid-axillary line on affected side
    - water-seal drainage system or Heimlich valve
    - CXR to confirm lung re-expansion
- emergent treatment of tension pneumothorax: immediate percutaneous placement of large-bore needle (insertion at second intercostal space mid-axillary line on affected side) and chest-tube insertion
- tension pneumopericardium: immediate pericardiocentesis required

QUICK REVIEW QUESTION

14. A 68-year-old patient was intubated and placed on positive pressure mechanical ventilation. CXR post-intubation revealed a right main-stem placement of the ETT, which was pulled back appropriately. Later in the shift, the patient suddenly becomes highly agitated and hypotensive. The cardiac monitor shows tachycardia. The nurse observes JVD with tracheal and mediastinum deviation to the left. What interventions should the nurse anticipate?

Pleural Effusion

Pathophysiology

Pleural **effusion** is the buildup of fluid around the lungs in the pleural space. The fluid can displace lung tissue and inhibit adequate ventilation and lung expansion. There are two types of pleural effusions.

- **Transudative pleural effusions** are fluid leakages caused by increased systemic pressure in the vessels or low serum protein levels. The most common causes of transudative pleural effusions are heart failure (due to increased pulmonary capillary pressure) or cirrhosis (currently believed to be the result of fluid movement from the peritoneal cavity to the thorax).

- **Exudative pleural effusions** are the result of changes in capillary permeability resulting in exudate. They have widely varying etiologies, including malignancy (especially lung cancer), pulmonary embolism, and infections.

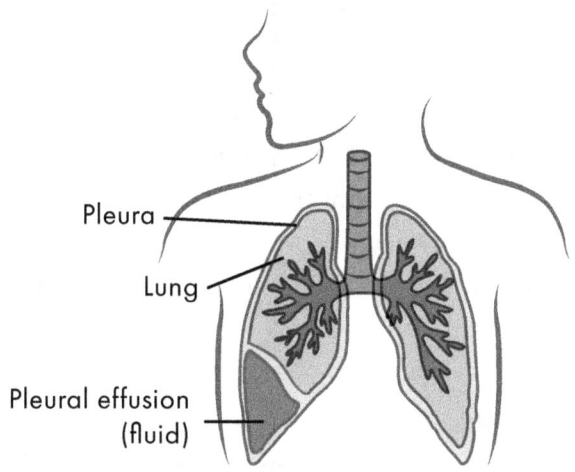

Figure 2.9. Pleural Effusion

Diagnosis

- dyspnea
- dullness upon percussion of the lung area
- asymmetrical chest expansion
- decreased breath sounds on affected side
- cough (dry or productive)
- pleuritic chest pain
- CXR showing white areas at the base of the lungs (unilaterally or bilaterally)

- CT scan to further diagnose the severity of the condition
- thoracentesis to determine the mechanism of effusion

Treatment and Management

- drainage of excess pleural fluid
- multiple thoracenteses necessary for reaccumulated fluid
- pleurodesis or indwelling pleural catheter for recurrent effusions
- medications based on underlying condition (e.g., diuretics, antibiotics)

> **QUICK REVIEW QUESTION**
>
> 15. A nursing student requests assistance with understanding the difference between pulmonary effusion and ARDS. What is the response?

Status Asthmaticus

Pathophysiology

Asthma is a chronic obstructive pulmonary disease characterized by airway inflammation and bronchoconstriction. Asthma exacerbations may be triggered by allergens, infections, exercise, aspirin, and GERD. **Status asthmaticus** is a severe, progressively worsening asthma event that does not respond to bronchodilator therapy; the condition may develop into acute respiratory failure.

When the triggered response occurs, the airway becomes obstructed by a combination of bronchospasm, thick mucus, mucosal edema, and airway inflammation. The increased airway resistance increases the work of breathing. The lungs are hyperinflated, with the increased residual volume creating a V/Q mismatch and hypoxemia. Alveolar dead space increases, worsening hypoxia and leading to "air trapping" with hypercapnia and auto-PEEP (raised pressure in the distal airways).

Increased venous return causes blood to pool in the right ventricle. This distended right ventricle causes a shift of the intraventricular septum, compromising the left ventricle. Cardiac output and SBP drop.

Signs and Symptoms

- tachypnea and severe dyspnea
- bronchoconstriction
    - expiratory wheeze (early stage)

HELPFUL HINT:

Aspirin-exacerbated respiratory disease (aspirin-sensitive asthma) is asthma that develops after taking aspirin or other NSAIDs. It is a pseudoallergic reaction, meaning it is not antibody-mediated, seen in around 14% of people with severe asthma.

HELPFUL HINT:

During severe asthma exacerbations, lactate overproduction occurs in respiratory muscles, resulting in respiratory and metabolic acidosis.

- inspiratory and expiratory wheeze (late stage)
- wheezes may disappear with fatigue or if obstruction prevents wheezing
- increased use of accessory respiratory muscles
  - intercostal and subcostal retractions
  - use of abdominal muscles to overcome airway resistance
- decreased breath sounds in all lung fields (ominous sign, as patient is not moving enough air)
- hypoxia (early); hypercapnia (late)
- tachycardia and hypertension
- pulsus paradoxus >20 mm Hg
- with progression of disease
  - decreased cardiac output
  - hypotension and bradycardia
  - seizure
  - coma

Diagnostic Tests and Findings

- peak expiratory flow rate (PEFR) showing 20% drop from expected response to treatment or baseline best effort
- ABG
  - initial: respiratory alkalosis with hypoxemia
  - worsening: respiratory acidosis with hypercapnia
- ECG may show peaked P wave and right-axis deviation
- CXR to rule out other underlying diseases (e.g., pneumonia, pneumothorax)

Treatment and Management

- medications
  - inhaled bronchodilators (beta 2 agonists)
  - anticholinergics (synergistic effect with beta 2 agonists)
  - corticosteroids
- high-flow O_2 to keep SpO_2 >92%, or heliox to decrease airway resistance
- mechanical ventilation
  - larger ETT if possible (to decrease airway resistance and facilitate suctioning)
  - decrease ventilation rate to extend exhalation phase

- prolonged expiratory pause to reduce auto-PEEP from hyperinflated lungs
- lower V_T to reduce barotrauma
- sedation to reduce patient-ventilator dyssynchrony

QUICK REVIEW QUESTION

16. A critical care patient is admitted with a diagnosis of status asthmaticus. HR is 118 bpm, with diaphoresis, tachypnea, pulsus paradoxus >25 mm Hg, and an inspiratory and expiratory wheeze. Initial ABG shows hypoxia with respiratory alkalosis. One hour later, a repeat PEFR shows a 30% drop from the expected outcome of an initial albuterol treatment, and physical exam shows increased use of accessory muscles with abdominal and intercostal retractions. Although auscultation shows an absence of wheezes after nebulizer treatment, breath sounds are now diminished throughout all lung fields. How would the nurse interpret this change in breath sounds?

Thoracic Trauma

PATHOPHYSIOLOGY

Chest trauma, whether from blunt injury, sharp, invasive penetration, or thoracic surgical procedures, creates a wide range of respiratory complications. To prepare for the CCRN exam, focus on pulmonary contusion, rib fractures, and hemothorax. (Pneumothorax is reviewed above in "Air-Leak Syndromes.")

TABLE 2.7. Thoracic Injuries

Injury	Pathophysiology	Clinical Presentation
Pulmonary contusion	Bruising of the parenchyma of the lung. Capillary rupture causes blood and other fluid to leak into lung tissue, causes localized edema, and may result in hypoxia from diminished gas exchange. Fluid accumulation in alveoli and decreased pulmonary secretion clearance put patients at risk for ARDS and pneumonia.	<ul><li>signs and symptoms may be delayed 24 – 72 hours until edema develops</li><li>hemoptysis (pink, frothy sputum)</li><li>crackles</li><li>tachypnea and tachycardia</li><li>hypoxia</li><li>chest wall bruising</li><li>pain</li><li>decreased $PaCO_2$</li><li>decreased P/F ratio</li></ul>

continued on next page

TABLE 2.7. Thoracic Injuries (continued)

Injury	Pathophysiology	Clinical Presentation
Rib fractures	Commonly caused by traumatic crushing injury to chest or cancer; leads to altered ventilation and perfusion status. Most common fractures are ribs 4 – 8. Ribs 9 – 12 may cause splenic rupture and tears to the diaphragm and liver.	• pain with breathing • shallow breaths • splinting
Hemothorax	Blood in the pleural space, usually resulting from blunt or penetrating trauma to the chest wall. Damage to the lung parenchyma and great vessels causes alveoli collapse. May also present with pneumothorax (pneumohemothorax).	• symptomatic with blood volume >400 mL • absence of breath sounds on affected side • tracheal deviation toward unaffected side • dullness to percussion • tachypnea • hypovolemia • shock
Tracheal rupture (or perforation)	Occurs when there is injury to the structure of the trachea. The perforation can be caused by forceful or poor intubation efforts or by traumatic injury to the trachea such as in crush injuries or hanging injuries.	• hemoptysis • dyspnea • diffuse subcutaneous emphysema
Ruptured diaphragm	Injury to the diaphragm creates a negative pressure gradient, allowing abdominal viscera to enter the thoracic cavity. The shift compresses the lungs and mediastinum, causing decreased venous return and cardiac output.	• respiratory distress • bowel sounds in chest on auscultation • tracheal deviation
Flail chest	Multiple anterior and posterior fractures to 3 or more ribs.	• paradoxical movement of the chest wall (flail segment moves inward during inspiration and outward during exhalation)

Treatment and Management

- pain management as needed (intercostal nerve blocks, thoracic epidural analgesia, opioids, or NSAIDs)
- small contusions: heal in 3 – 5 days, often without treatment
- severe contusions
    - aggressive pulmonary care (e.g., ambulation, turning, incentive spirometry)
    - mechanical ventilation with PEEP
    - fluid management (to avoid overload)
    - infection prevention
- hemothorax: chest-tube insertion or thoracotomy (if bleeding cannot be managed)
- tracheal perforation: maintain airway and prepare for surgical repair
- ruptured diaphragm: prep patient for immediate surgical intervention
- flail chest: aggressive management with analgesics, pulmonary hygiene, and noninvasive positive pressure ventilation

HELPFUL HINT:

A sudden crush injury to the chest wall produces **traumatic asphyxia**. This specific crush injury results in an "ecchymotic mask" characterized by subconjunctival hemorrhage, facial edema, and petechiae and cyanosis of the head, neck, and upper extremities.

QUICK REVIEW QUESTION

17. A 46-year-old patient with A-fib who is on anticoagulant medication suffered a fall from a small step stool in the kitchen, with no head injury or loss of consciousness. Twenty-four hours later, the patient is admitted to the critical care unit with the following symptoms: pink frothy sputum, crackles in the lung fields, tachypnea, tachycardia, and pain. Ecchymosis is evident over ribs 4 – 8. ABG shows hypoxia. CXR has ruled out rib fractures but is not remarkable. The patient is sent for a chest CT scan. What diagnosis would the nurse expect, and why was a chest CT scan ordered?

ANSWER KEY

1. Bronchial breath sounds over the lung fields indicate consolidation and reflect pneumonia. The mixed venous blood gas analysis will show intrapulmonary shunting because of underventilated alveoli. The poor ventilation generates a V/Q mismatch. The results, which show how much venous blood participates in gas exchange, will help the nurse direct appropriate oxygen and possible mechanical therapy.

2. The patient has respiratory acidosis that is partially compensated, meaning the body is attempting unsuccessfully to restore acid-base balance.

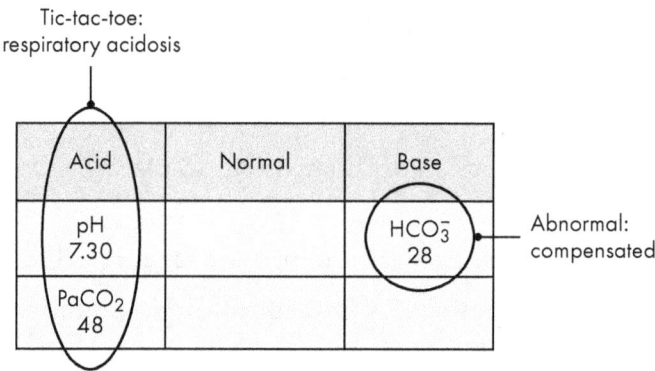

3. Oxygen toxicity has been initiated, as evidenced by the patient's history of >24 hours on >60% FiO_2, clinical signs of substernal chest pain with deep breaths, dyspnea, cough, and bradycardia. Oxygen toxicity places the patient at high risk for ARDS.

4. The patient has developed pulmonary edema because >1000 mL fluid has been removed. This large amount of fluid removal has increased the negative intrapleural pressure, and the lung has not re-expanded to fill the space. The nurse should encourage immediate discontinuation of the procedure, administer oxygen, and evaluate for progression to mechanical ventilation. If the patient deteriorates because of an open pneumothorax, the nurse will prepare for chest tube insertion by the practitioner.

5. PEEP, or positive end-expiratory pressure, allows for more effective gas exchange by keeping the alveoli open especially at end expiration. Complications include barotrauma to the lungs, decreased blood pressure and cardiac output, and air-leak syndromes.

6. The nurse suspects post-extubation laryngeal edema.

7. (1) Elevate HOB 35 – 45 degrees; (2) oral care with chlorhexidine every 2 hours; (3) subglottic suctioning; and (4) low V_T settings.

8. Definitive diagnosis of a PE is by pulmonary angiogram. Because the patient is stable, a faster but less definitive test is unlikely to be ordered.

9. LPV includes low tidal volumes (V_T), higher RR settings, permissive hypercapnia, and PEEP settings at the lowest possible amount to decrease intrapulmonary shunting while improving P/F ratio. Research has shown that a reasonable goal for reversing hypoxemia and preventing oxygen toxicity is a PaO_2 of 55 – 65 mm Hg.

10. The patient will likely receive noninvasive mechanical ventilation via BiPAP. NIV is the standard of care for acute hypercapnia due to COPD because it effectively manages hypercapnia while preventing risks associated with invasive ventilation.

11. The nurse should administer oxygen to the patient, establish IV access, and anticipate drawing blood cultures, collecting a sputum culture from the patient, and administering antibiotics after collection of blood cultures, per facility protocols.

12. Pulmonary aspiration (or aspiration pneumonitis) is the likely diagnosis, and sepsis protocol should be immediately instituted. Priorities should be obtaining blood cultures before the initiation of antibiotic therapy, and anticipating possible mechanical intubation to prevent respiratory collapse.

13. The nurse will monitor for increasing respiratory distress, signs of hemodynamic compromise, worsening acidosis on ABGs, and mental status changes and will plan for emergent intubation.

14. The patient has a tension pneumothorax with evidence of decreased cardiac output. Cardiac deterioration requires immediate percutaneous placement of a large-bore needle at the second intercostal space mid-axillary line on the affected side to relieve pressure from air trapped within the chest. The nurse knows the needle will need stabilization in place until a large-bore chest tube is inserted at the fourth or fifth intercostal space mid-axillary line and connected to either a water-seal drainage system or a Heimlich valve.

15. Pulmonary effusion and ARDS differ in which lung structures are affected. In pulmonary effusion, fluid collects in the pleural space that surrounds the lung and limits the ability of the lungs to expand. In ARDS, pulmonary capillary permeability is compromised, and fluid fills the alveolar sacs within the lungs. The fluid limits the ability of the lungs to exchange oxygen and carbon dioxide.

16. The decrease in breath sounds in all lung fields is an ominous sign, as the increased work of breathing requires more physical effort (recruitment of accessory muscles and abdominal and intercostal retractions) to overcome increasing airway obstruction. The patient is too obstructed or fatigued to overcome the narrowed airways, and wheezing disappears, while diminished breath sounds may indicate impending respiratory failure or arrest.

17. The more sensitive chest CT scan will confirm a diagnosis of pulmonary contusion.

3 ENDOCRINE REVIEW

CCRN TEST PLAN: ENDOCRINE
- Adrenal insufficiency
- Diabetes insipidus (DI)
- Diabetes mellitus (DM), types 1 and 2
- Diabetic ketoacidosis (DKA)
- Hyperglycemia
- Hyperosmolar hyperglycemic state (HHS)
- Hyperthyroidism
- Hypoglycemia (acute)
- Hypothyroidism
- SIADH

Adrenal Insufficiency

Pathophysiology

Adrenal insufficiency is an endocrine disorder characterized by a decrease in circulating corticosteroids (both glucocorticoids and mineralocorticoids). **Primary adrenal insufficiency** (Addison's disease) is caused by the inability of the adrenal glands to produce corticosteroids. **Secondary adrenal insufficiency** is caused by low production of **adrenocorticotropic hormone (ACTH)** in the pituitary gland. (ACTH stimulates corticosteroid production.)

The condition can be chronic or acute. The most common cause of **chronic adrenal insufficiency** is autoimmune conditions that damage the adrenal cortex.

Acute adrenal insufficiency (**adrenal crisis**) causes distributive shock and is a medical emergency that requires immediate care. It usually occurs when infection or trauma exacerbate chronic adrenal insufficiency, but may occur following damage to the adrenal or pituitary glands. Rarely, it may be caused by withdrawal from long-term glucocorticoid use.

During an adrenal crisis, low levels of aldosterone cause vasodilation, increased excretion of sodium, and retention of potassium, resulting in volume depletion and hypotension. Low levels of glucocorticoids lead to hypoglycemia and further depress blood pressure.

The information below describes the diagnosis and management of adrenal crisis.

HELPFUL HINT:

Fever caused by infection may precipitate an adrenal crisis, or the fever itself may be caused by low corticosteroid levels.

Signs and Symptoms

- shock (e.g., hypotension, tachycardia, oliguria)
- abdominal pain/tenderness
- nausea, vomiting, or diarrhea
- fever
- hyperpigmentation (from chronic adrenal insufficiency)

Diagnostic Findings

- low cortisol or aldosterone levels
- ACTH stimulation test shows low cortisol level
- elevated renin
- low serum Na^+
- high serum K^+
- low blood glucose

Treatment and Management

- IV fluid resuscitation
- empiric administration of IV glucocorticoids (usually hydrocortisone or dexamethasone)
- replacement of mineralocorticoids may be required (e.g., fludrocortisone)
- management of hypoglycemia and electrolyte imbalances as needed

QUICK REVIEW QUESTION

1. A patient with refractory hypotension and a fever of unknown origin has the following laboratory results:

    sodium 130 mmol/L

potassium 4.2 mmol/L

plasma cortisol 25 mmol/L

What diagnostic test should the nurse anticipate will be ordered for this patient?

Antidiuretic Hormone Imbalances
Diabetes Insipidus

Pathophysiology

Antidiuretic hormone (**ADH**, also called **vasopressin**) is produced by the hypothalamus and stored in the posterior pituitary gland. When released, ADH constricts blood vessels and signals the kidneys to hold on to water. **Diabetes insipidus (DI)** occurs when an imbalance of ADH prevents the body from regulating blood volume and maintaining a normal serum osmolality. **Central diabetes insipidus** occurs when the body is unable to secrete an adequate amount of ADH; **nephrogenic diabetes insipidus** occurs when the kidneys cannot respond appropriately to ADH.

Excessive excreted free water causes a decrease in urine osmolality and specific gravity, while serum osmolality and serum sodium rise. Because the kidney tubules cannot concentrate urine or hold on to water, extracellular dehydration occurs, leading to hypotension and hypovolemic shock. Continued severe polyuria may lead to decreased cerebral perfusion, seizures, coma, and death.

Etiology

- central DI
  - TBI
  - infection (e.g., meningitis, encephalitis)
  - pituitary or hypothalamic dysfunction
  - increased ICP (can be life-threatening)
- nephrogenic DI
  - medications (e.g., lithium, phenytoin, demeclocycline)
  - hypercalcemia
  - hereditary

Signs and Symptoms

- marked polydipsia
- marked polyuria
- highly dilute urine

Diagnostic Findings

- high urine output (6 – 24 L/day)
- low urine osmolality (<300 mOsm/kg)
- low urine specific gravity (1.001 – 1.005)
- high serum Na^+ (>145 mEq/L)
- high serum osmolality (>295 mOsm/kg)
- low ADH (generally not measured in ICU settings)

Treatment and Management

- primary goals: rapid fluid resuscitation, ADH replacement, and identification and treatment of the underlying condition
- IV or subcutaneous ADH
- IV fluids to increase intravascular volume
  - Initiate with hypotonic IV fluids.
  - Correct fluid volume status slowly over 2 – 3 days.
- monitoring
  - ADH administration increases risk of vasospasm of cardiac, cerebral, and mesenteric arteries
  - cardiac monitoring for ischemia and hypertension
  - overhydration possible after administration of ADH or analogue
  - daily weights and strict I&O
  - urine specific gravity and electrolytes balance (especially Na^+ and K^+).

HELPFUL HINT:

Patients with high calcium levels are unresponsive to ADH administration.

QUICK REVIEW QUESTION

2. A 72-year-old patient is post-op neurosurgery for head trauma from an MVC. The patient's LOC has been variable. Urine output has been 6 L/24 hr, with specific gravity of 1.005. Serum Na+ is 145 mEq/L, with serum osmolality 295 mOsm/kg. The patient is given a diagnosis of CDI. Why should the nurse plan to monitor for angina?

Syndrome of Inappropriate Secretion of Antidiuretic Hormone (SIADH)

Pathophysiology

In **syndrome of inappropriate secretion of antidiuretic hormone (SIADH)**, excess secretion of ADH causes water retention and dilutional hyponatremia (low serum sodium is the result of excess water, not a sodium deficiency). The hallmark signs of SIADH are hyponatremia with decreased serum osmolality (dilute blood) and increased urine osmolality (concentrated urine). Neurological symptoms may occur as a result of cerebral edema caused by hyponatremia.

Etiology

- trauma to head (hypothalamus or posterior pituitary gland)
- oat cell carcinoma (lung cancer)
- infection (pneumonia, meningitis, Guillain-Barré syndrome)
- medications (e.g., chlorpropamide)
- surgery (particularly to pituitary gland)

Signs and Symptoms

- patients may be euvolemic or have signs and symptoms of fluid overload
- signs and symptoms of hyponatremia (see chapter 6, Renal and Genitourinary Review)

Diagnostic Findings

- low serum Na^+ (<120 mEq/L)
- low urine output
- decreased serum osmolality (<275 mOsm/kg)
- high urine osmolality (>100 mOsm/kg)
- high urine specific gravity (>1.030)

Treatment and Management

- primary goals: restore fluid/sodium balance and treat the underlying cause
- manage fluid overload
    - fluid restriction
    - loop diuretics (watch for hypokalemia)
    - daily weights and strict I&O

HELPFUL HINT:

DI is the result of **too little ADH**, causing polyuria. It results in dilute urine, concentrated serum, and high serum Na^+.

SIADH is the result of **too much ADH**, causing water retention. It results in concentrated urine, dilute serum, and low serum Na^+.

- slow correction of Na⁺
    - Rapid correction can cause permanent neurological damage.
    - Limit Na⁺ replacement to 8 – 12 mEq/L in 24 hours.
    - Stop Na⁺ replacement when serum sodium is 130 mEq/L.
- hypertonic IV solutions (3% normal saline) for severe or refractory hyponatremia
    - reduces cerebral edema
    - monitor respiratory status for crackles, increased effort of breathing, and decreases in O₂ saturation
- declomycin inhibits ADH and promotes diuresis (off-label use)

> **QUICK REVIEW QUESTION**
>
> 3. An authorized prescriber has ordered a vasopressin continuous IV infusion per ICU protocol for a neurological ICU patient with a secondary diagnosis of SIADH. Why should the nurse question this order?

Diabetes Mellitus

- **Diabetes mellitus (DM)** is a metabolic disorder affecting insulin production and insulin resistance. It is classified as type 1 or type 2.
    - **type 1:** an acute-onset autoimmune disease most prominent in children, teens, and adults <30. Beta cells in the pancreas are destroyed and are unable to produce sufficient amounts of insulin, causing blood sugar to rise.
    - **type 2:** a gradual-onset disease most prominent in adults 30. Individuals develop insulin resistance, which prevents the cellular uptake of glucose and causes blood sugar to rise.
- Diagnosis includes polyuria, polyphagia, and polydipsia; fasting blood glucose ≥126 mg/dL; 2-hour plasma glucose ≥200 mg/dL (75 g OGTT); and A1C ≥6.5%.
- DM is correlated to poor outcomes in critical care settings, particularly for patients with comorbid cardiovascular conditions. Patients with diabetes are more likely to develop complications (e.g., sepsis) while in the ICU, and are also more likely to be hyper- or hypoglycemic.
- Regular blood glucose monitoring is required for critical care patients, with closer monitoring for patients with DM.
    - Protocols will vary, but current guidelines suggest moderate glycemic controls (140 – 180 mg/dL) that may be tightened for individual patients (e.g., acute MI, neurosurgery post-op).

- Tight glycemic controls (e.g., 80 – 110 mg/dL) place patients at higher risk of hypoglycemia and sequelae such as seizure and dysrhythmias.
- Patients with type 2 diabetes require insulin management in critical care settings, even if their blood glucose is well managed at home. Insulin type and dosage depend on individual patient characteristics.
  - Patients may receive a combination of long-acting (basal) insulin, short-acting insulin following meals, and rapid-acting insulin to manage acute hyperglycemia.
  - Insulin may be given subcutaneously or via IV infusion.
  - Patients with DM who are being fed via TPN or enteral feedings require insulin. It may be delivered IV, subcutaneously, or as part of the nutritional solution (depending on the needs of the patient).
- Patients with type 1 diabetes require regular insulin administration, even if feedings are discontinued. These patients usually receive continuous IV insulin and IV dextrose (to prevent hypoglycemia).
- Oral anti-diabetic agents are usually discontinued in critical care settings because they are contraindicated or only indicated for postprandial use.

HELPFUL HINT:

Use of metformin is contraindicated in patients with renal or hemodynamic dysfunction; sulfonylureas may cause severe hypoglycemia.

QUICK REVIEW QUESTION

4. A patient with a history of type 2 diabetes is being fed via TPN during treatment for necrotizing pancreatitis and is on a continuous IV insulin infusion. The nurse is currently preparing the patient for surgery. Why is it important for the TPN to be discontinued gradually?

Hyperglycemia

Pathophysiology

Diabetic ketoacidosis (DKA) occurs when the body does not produce insulin. The elevated glucose levels increase the serum osmolality, resulting in osmotic diuresis that causes polyuria, with significant water loss. Simultaneously, the body also begins to break down fat cells for fuel, producing a buildup of serum ketones, resulting in acidosis. As acidosis worsens, potassium is shifted out of cells, resulting in an initial presentation with hyperkalemia. However, continued osmotic diuresis eventually leads to hypokalemia in most patients.

Hyperosmolar hyperglycemic state (HHS), also called **hyperglycemic hyperosmolar nonketotic syndrome (HHNK)**, is a slow-onset, high-mortality

HELPFUL HINT:

Stress-induced hyperglycemia is often seen in critical care settings, even in patients with no previous DM diagnosis. It should be managed with insulin to maintain normoglycemic levels.

complication of type 2 DM. It occurs when the pancreas produces insufficient insulin. As with DKA, blood glucose levels become high, resulting in osmotic diuresis and hypovolemia. With decreased kidney perfusion and oliguria from dehydration, less glucose is removed and serum hyperosmolality increases. Serum potassium may be elevated, but total body potassium will be depleted due to osmotic diuresis. In HHS, insulin production is sufficient to prevent ketoacidosis, differentiating it from DKA.

HHS is often mistaken for a neurological event as intracerebral dehydration may cause profound CNS symptoms, including coma. Hemoconcentration also increases the risk of thromboemboli and possible cardiac, cerebral, and pleural infarctions.

HELPFUL HINT:

Look out for questions about HHS that involve an uncharacteristic patient (e.g., a teenager with Crohn's disease on home TPN infusion).

TABLE 3.1. DKA and HHS

DKA	HHS
Etiology	
- undiagnosed/ineffectively managed type 1 DM - destabilized type 2 DM (less common) - acute illness (e.g., MI, pancreatitis) - medications (e.g., steroids, epinephrine, thiazide diuretics, atypical antipsychotics) - stress of critical illness - endocrine disorders (e.g., hyperthyroidism, Cushing's syndrome)	- most common in older adult patients with obesity, type 2 DM, and underlying cardiovascular disease - patients who control diabetes through diet only - TPN - use of steroids or thiazides - pancreatitis - serious illness or infection (e.g., MI, pneumonia)
Signs and Symptoms	
- rapid onset - polyuria (early); oliguria (late) - signs and symptoms of hypovolemia - Kussmaul respirations and fruity breath odor - polyphagia and polydipsia - nausea, vomiting - abdominal pain - malaise and weakness - decreased LOC	- slow onset - polyuria - signs and symptoms of hypovolemia - rapid, extremely shallow breaths - polydipsia - mild nausea or vomiting - weight loss - diplopia - malaise and weakness - stupor or coma

DKA	HHS
Diagnostic Findings	
- elevated blood glucose (250 mg/dL) - metabolic acidosis - pH <7.3 - HCO_3^- <18 mEq/L - anion gap 10 - increased serum ketones - low serum Na^+ and Ca^{++} - increased serum K^+ - elevated BUN and creatinine - fluid deficit (negative 50 – 100 mL/kg common)	- elevated blood glucose (>600 mg/dL) - high serum osmolality (>350 mOsm/kg) - no diagnostic findings of acidosis (i.e., normal pH and serum HCO_3) - serum K^+ normal or high - elevated BUN and creatinine - fluid deficit may be as high as 150 mL/kg total body weight

Treatment and Management

- IV fluid protocols
    - first hour: 1 – 3 L of isotonic fluids (lactated Ringer's or 0.9% normal saline)
    - second hour: 1 L of hypotonic fluids (0.45% normal saline)
    - when blood glucose reaches 250 mg/dL: 1 L of hypertonic fluids with dextrose (D5 in half-normal saline).
- IV K^+ replacement if K^+ <5.3 mEq/L
- continuous IV insulin (0.1 units/kg/hr)
    - initiate only when K^+ 3.3 mEq/L
    - slow blood glucose reduction (decrease by 50 – 75 mg/dL/hr)
- monitoring
    - risk of ventricular dysrhythmias due to hypo- or hyperkalemia (especially in patients with renal insufficiency)
    - blood glucose every hour
- HHS may require management of type 2 DM insulin resistance (due to high levels of stress hormones)
    - High-dose insulin may be used.
    - After IV insulin is discontinued, administer oral agents specific to reducing insulin resistance.

HELPFUL HINT:

For fluid resuscitation in DKA, think "Oh, oh, ease off": isOtonic, hypOtonic, hypErtonic.

> **QUICK REVIEW QUESTION**
> 5. What diagnostic findings differentiate HHS from DKA?

Hypoglycemia

Pathophysiology

Hypoglycemia is the sudden fall of blood glucose below normal levels. The decreased glucose levels result in neurological dysfunction. In addition, the adrenal medulla is triggered to release adrenaline (also called epinephrine) to restore normal glucose levels, leading to increased sympathetic nervous system activity.

Etiology

- use of insulin (IV or subcutaneous)
- interruption of oral, enteral, or parenteral feedings
- adrenal insufficiency
- infection
- pancreatitis
- vomiting
- drinking excess alcohol, or liver disease

Signs and Symptoms

- cardiovascular
    - tachycardia
    - diaphoresis
    - irritability, restlessness
    - cool skin
- neurological
    - lethargy
    - weakness
    - slurred speech or blurred vision
    - anxiety or confusion
    - seizure (at blood glucose 20 – 40 mg/dL)
    - coma (at blood glucose <20 mg/dL)

HELPFUL HINT:

Beta blockers may hide cardiovascular symptoms in patients with hypoglycemia.

Diagnostic Findings

- serum glucose <70 mg/dL

Treatment and Management

- overall treatment goal: maintain blood glucose level 70 mg/dL
    - blood glucose 60 – 70 mg/dL: 4 oz of juice if oral intake is not contraindicated
    - blood glucose 40 – 60 mg/dL: D50 via IV push (12.5 g = 0.5 ampule)
    - blood glucose <40 mg/dL: D50 via IV push (25 g = 1.0 ampule)
- refractory hypoglycemia
    - continuous infusion of D10 (dextrose 10% solution) via peripheral IV
    - continuous infusion of D20 (dextrose 20% solution) via central line
- longer-acting carbohydrates (oral intake, tube feeding, or TPN) after patient is stabilized
- seizure prophylaxis
- identify and treat underlying cause

> **QUICK REVIEW QUESTION**
>
> 6. What hormone is released from the adrenal gland to restore glucose levels in hypoglycemia?

Thyroid Disorders

Hyperthyroidism

Pathophysiology

Hyperthyroidism (thyrotoxicosis) occurs when the thyroid produces an excess of the thyroid hormones triiodothyronine (T3) and/or thyroxine (T4). Chronic hyperthyroidism presents with a characteristic set of symptoms, including anxiety, weakness, palpitations, tremor, and weight loss.

Thyroid storm is a severe form of thyrotoxicosis usually seen in patients with hyperthyroidism after a precipitating event (e.g., trauma, infection). Thyroid storm has a high mortality rate and requires immediate treatment.

The information below describes the diagnosis and management of thyroid storm.

Signs and Symptoms

- tachycardia (140 bmp)
- hypotension
- hyperpyrexia
- altered mental status (agitation, confusion)
- decreased LOC (progressing to coma)

Diagnostic Findings

- elevated T4 and/or T3
- low TSH

Treatment and Management

- pharmacological suppression of thyroid hormones (e.g., thionamides, iodine, and glucocorticoids)
- beta blockers (for cardiac symptoms)
- respiratory support as needed
- aggressive cooling measures (e.g., ice packs)

> **QUICK REVIEW QUESTION**
> 7. A patient is admitted to the ICU with new onset of thyroid storm. Which physiological system should be a main focus of symptom management?

Hypothyroidism

Pathophysiology

HELPFUL HINT:

Myxedema coma caused by hypothalamic-pituitary disease may present with secondary adrenal insufficiency (caused by reduced secretion of ACTH).

Hypothyroidism is characterized by low levels of the hormones T3 and T4. **Primary hypothyroid** disease results from damage to the thyroid. **Secondary hypothyroidism** is the result of a hypothalamic-pituitary disease. Symptoms of chronic hypothyroidism are related to slowing of metabolic process and include fatigue, bradycardia, cold intolerance, weight gain, and localized non-pitting edema (myxedema).

Myxedema coma is severe hypothyroidism usually seen in patients with chronic hypothyroidism after a precipitating event (e.g., MI, infection). It is a medical emergency that requires immediate treatment.

The information below describes the diagnosis and management of myxedema coma.

Signs and Symptoms

- decreased LOC (confusion and lethargy progressing to coma)
- hypothermia
- bradycardia
- hypotension

Diagnostic Findings

- low serum T4
- low serum Na^+
- ABGs show respiratory acidosis

Treatment and Management

- empiric administration of IV levothyroxine (T4) and liothyronine (T3)
- glucocorticoids (usually hydrocortisone)
- fluids and vasopressors
- passive rewarming

QUICK REVIEW QUESTION

8. Why would a patient with suspected myxedema coma be administered glucocorticoids?

ANSWER KEY

1. The patient has symptoms of adrenal insufficiency. The provider will likely order an ACTH stimulation test to diagnose primary or secondary adrenal insufficiency.

2. DI is treated with vasopressin, which can cause vasospasm of cardiac, cerebral, and mesenteric arteries. Coronary artery spasm may precipitate an angina episode, resulting in a myocardial ischemic event.

3. SIADH is a condition of too much ADH in the patient's system. Vasopressin is an ADH. The nurse would know that giving additional ADH would exacerbate this condition.

4. Abruptly discontinuing TPN may lead to hypoglycemia, particularly in patients with DM. The TPN should be tapered and the patient's insulin dose recalculated to match the patient's changing carbohydrate intake.

5. The preferred diagnostic indicator is serum osmolality: patients with HHS will have a higher serum osmolality (350 mOsm/kg) than with DKA. HHS also presents with higher blood glucose (600 mg/dL) than DKA, and patients may have a higher fluid deficit (as high as 150 mL/kg of body weight). Because no ketoacidosis is present with HHS, there will be no significant serum ketones or findings associated with acidosis.

6. Adrenaline (epinephrine) increases blood glucose levels and increases cardiac output.

7. Patients with thyroid storm typically have severe cardiac disturbances and need supportive care to maintain hemodynamic stability. The patient should be placed on cardiac telemetry and the nurse should be prepared for emergent cardioversion and treatment with beta blockers.

8. Myxedema coma is often concomitant with secondary adrenal insufficiency. Because adrenal crisis requires immediate treatment with glucocorticoids, they are often administered to patients with myxedema coma until adrenal insufficiency has been ruled out.

4 HEMATOLOGY AND IMMUNOLOGY REVIEW

CCRN TEST PLAN: HEMATOLOGY AND IMMUNOLOGY
- Anemia
- Coagulopathies (e.g., ITP, DIC, HIT)
- Immune deficiencies
- Leukopenia
- Oncologic complications (e.g., tumor lysis syndrome, pericardial effusion)
- Thrombocytopenia
- Transfusion reactions

Overview of the Hematologic System

- **Plasma**, the liquid part of blood, includes albumin (which maintains osmotic pressure), serum globulins, and clotting factors.
- **Red blood cells (RBCs or erythrocytes)** transport oxygen (and, to a lesser extent, CO_2).
  - High RBC counts may indicate chronic hypoxia, dehydration, bone marrow overproduction, or kidney disease.
  - Low RBC counts indicate anemia caused by disease processes that result in underproduction or destruction of RBCs.
  - **Erythropoiesis**—the production of RBCs—is triggered by the release of erythropoietin from the kidneys. RBCs grow to maturity within the bone marrow.

- RBCs are broken down in the liver and spleen through **phagocytosis**; waste products are excreted as bilirubin and biliverdin in bile.
- **White blood cells (WBCs or leukocytes)** fight infection.
  - High WBC counts occur during infections, physiological distress, and steroid use.
  - Low WBC counts occur during bone marrow suppression and chemotherapy.
- A **WBC differential** includes the percentage or absolute number of different types of WBCs.
  - **Left shift** refers to an increased presence of band neutrophils in the peripheral blood. This shift may be due to inflammation, infection, steroids, or stress.
  - Viral infections show a decreased overall WBC count and high lymphocytes.
  - Malignancies show a high count of one type of WBC or high counts of numerous immature WBCs.

TABLE 4.1. CBC With Differential

Test	Description	Normal Range
Complete Blood Count (CBC)		
White blood cells (WBCs)	cells that fight infection; a high WBC count can indicate inflammation or infection	4,500 – 10,000 cells/µL
Red blood cells (RBCs)	cells that carry oxygen throughout the body and filter carbon dioxide	men: 5 – 6 million cells/µL women: 4 – 5 million cells/µL
Hemoglobin (HgB)	protein that binds oxygen in the blood	men: 13.8 – 17.2 g/dL women: 12.1 – 15.1 g/dL
Hematocrit (Hct)	percentage of the blood composed of red blood cells	men: 41% – 50% women: 36% – 44%
Mean corpuscular volume (MCV)	average size of RBCs	80 – 95 fL
Mean corpuscular hemoglobin (MCH)	average amount of HgB in RBCs	27.5 – 33.2 pg

Test	Description	Normal Range
Complete Blood Count (CBC)		
Mean corpuscular hemoglobin concentration (MCHC)	average concentration of HgB in RBCs	334 – 355 g/L
Platelets	blood components that play a role in clotting	150,000 – 450,000 platelets/μL
WBC Differential		
Neutrophils	first responders that quickly migrate to the site of infection to destroy bacterial invaders	2,000 – 7,000/μL (40% – 60%)
Band neutrophils	immature neutrophils (also called bands)	<700/μL (<5%)
Lymphocytes	B cells, T cells, and natural killer cells; all 3 types develop from common lymphoid progenitors	1,000 – 3,000/μL (20% – 40%)
Monocytes	cells that engulf and destroy microbes and cancer cells	200 – 1,000/μL (2% – 8%)
Eosinophils	cells that attack parasites and regulate inflammation	20 – 500/μL (1% – 4%)
Basophils	cells responsible for inflammatory reactions, including allergies	20 – 100/μL (0% – 2%)

- **Hemostasis**, the process that stops bleeding, occurs through vasoconstriction and coagulation.
    - During **coagulation**, a semisolid **clot** forms from platelets and red blood cells held together by the protein **fibrin**.
    - **Fibrinolysis** is the disintegration of blood clots.
- Coagulation is a cascade of reactions involving proteins called **clotting factors**.
    - Platelet aggregation is initiated by exposure to **von Willebrand factor (vW)** and **tissue factor (TF)**.
    - During coagulation, the protein **fibrinogen** (clotting factor I) is converted to fibrin by the enzyme **thrombin** (clotting factor IIa).

HELPFUL HINT:

The liver is highly involved in the synthesis and removal of clotting components. Chronic liver disease often leads to coagulation disorders caused by decreased synthesis of clotting factors and poor clearance of activated factors.

HEMATOLOGY AND IMMUNOLOGY REVIEW

- **Prothrombin** (clotting factor II) is a precursor to thrombin.

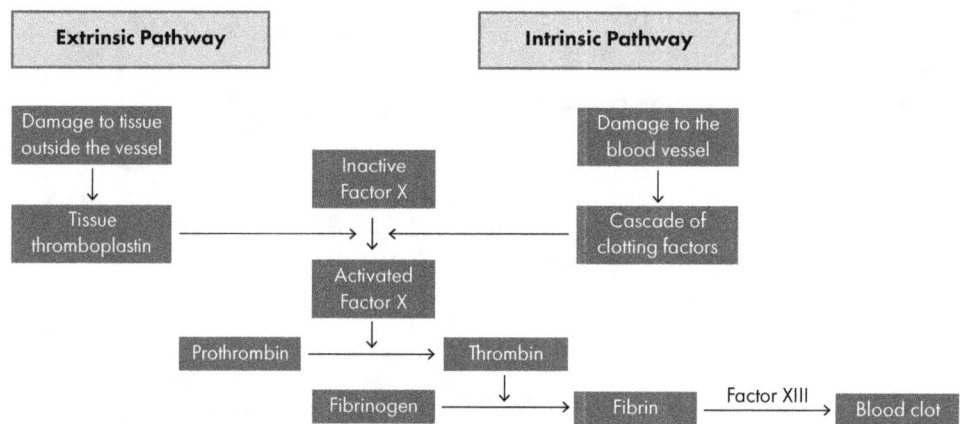

Figure 4.1. The Coagulation Cascade

- Coagulation can follow two possible pathways:
  - The intrinsic pathway is activated via damage within a blood vessel.
    - This pathway is monitored by measuring the aPTT.
    - Heparin disrupts the intrinsic pathway.
  - The extrinsic pathway is activated by damage outside the vasculature.
    - This pathway is monitored by measuring the PT.
    - Warfarin disrupts the extrinsic pathway.
  - Both pathways activate clotting factor X and produce a fibrin clot.

TABLE 4.2. Coagulation Studies and Clotting Factors

Test	Description	Normal Range
Prothrombin time (PT)	how long it takes blood to clot	10 – 13 seconds
International normalized ratio (INR)	ratio of a patient's PT and a standardized PT for patients taking anticoagulants	healthy adults: <1.1 patients taking anticoagulants: 2.0 – 3.0
Partial thromboplastin time (PTT)	the body's ability to form blood clots	60 – 70 seconds
Activated partial thromboplastin time (aPTT)	the body's ability to form blood clots using an activator to speed up the clotting process	20 – 35 seconds
D-dimer	protein fragment produced during fibrinolysis	negative

Test	Description	Normal Range
Fibrin split products (FSP) or fibrin degradation products (FDP)	components produced during fibrinolysis	<10 mg/L
Fibrinogen	amount of fibrinogen (clotting factor I)	200 – 400 mg/dL
Plasminogen	substrate involved in fibrinolysis	10 – 16 mg/dL

QUICK REVIEW QUESTION

1. Congenital hypofibrinogenemia is an inherited condition characterized by low circulating levels of fibrinogen (<150 mg/dL). What signs and symptoms should a nurse expect to see in a patient with severe hypofibrinogenemia?

Anemia

Pathophysiology

Anemia is a reduction in RBCs, usually diagnosed via low levels of HgB and Hct. Anemia can result from destruction or underproduction of RBCs.

- **Hemolytic anemia** is caused by premature destruction of RBCs. Underlying causes of hemolytic anemia may include autoimmune conditions, trauma, infection, and drugs or toxins.
- **Decreased erythropoiesis** can result from dietary deficiencies (e.g., iron deficiency, vitamin deficiency secondary to alcohol abuse) and bone marrow disorders.

Signs and Symptoms

- tachycardia and tachypnea
- weak pulse
- lethargy
- pallor

Diagnostic Tests and Findings

- decreased RBC, HgB, and Hct
- men
    - HgB <13.5 g/dL
    - Hct <41.0%

- women
    - HgB <12.0 g/
    - Hct <36.0%

Treatment and Management

- treat underlying cause
- blood products (PRBCs)
- erythropoiesis-stimulating agents

> **QUICK REVIEW QUESTION**
>
> 2. An ICU patient recently diagnosed with chronic lymphocytic leukemia has lab values flagged with a critical HgB of 6.5. What intervention will the physician most likely order?

Coagulopathies
Disseminated Intravascular Coagulopathy
Pathophysiology

Disseminated intravascular coagulopathy (DIC) is a coagulation disorder with simultaneous intervals of clotting and bleeding. DIC occurs when injury exposes blood to TF, causing a rapid increase in circulating thrombin and fibrin. Microclots cascade throughout the vascular system, causing hypoxia and ischemia in multiple organs. The use of platelets in clot formation results in thrombocytopenia, decreased fibrinogen, and overall increased clotting time. Subsequent fibrinolysis of the clots leads to elevated D-dimer and FSP.

Acute (or decompensated) DIC occurs when the presence of large amounts of TF cause rapid depletion of platelets and clotting factors, resulting in severe bleeding. **Chronic (or compensated) DIC** is the result of long-term exposure to TF. The body is able to compensate for lost platelets and clotting factors, but the risk of thromboembolic complications is high.

Etiology

- sepsis
- trauma
- cancers (especially leukemia and brain tumors)
- blood transfusion reaction
- recent procedure or surgery with anesthesia

- obstetrical complications (e.g., preeclampsia)
- cardiac arrest

Signs and Symptoms

- bleeding (e.g., spontaneous hemorrhage, petechiae)
- thromboembolic event (e.g., PE, DVT)

Diagnostic Tests and Findings

- acute DIC
    - decreased platelets (moderate to severe)
    - prolonged PT and PTT
    - decreased fibrinogen
    - severely elevated D-dimer and FSP
- chronic DIC
    - decreased platelets (mild)
    - normal or slightly prolonged PT and PTT
    - normal or slightly decreased fibrinogen
    - elevated D-dimer and FSP

Treatment and Management

- identify and treat underlying cause
- IV fluid resuscitation
- vasopressors
- transfusion of blood products (FFP, PRBCs, platelets, or cryoprecipitate)
- heparin for chronic DIC

> **QUICK REVIEW QUESTION**
>
> 3. What findings would confirm a diagnosis of acute DIC in a patient recovering from postpartum hemorrhage?

THROMBOCYTOPENIA

- **Thrombocytopenia** is an abnormally low platelet level that can lead to severe bleeding or thrombosis. It can generally be classified by the number of platelets:
    - mild: 100,000 – 150,000/μL
    - moderate: 50,000 – 100,000/μL
    - severe: <50,000/μL

- Thrombocytopenia has a diverse etiology. In the ICU, it is commonly seen in patients with cancer, bone marrow disorders, sepsis, chronic liver disease, and autoimmune diseases.
- **Heparin-induced thrombocytopenia (HIT)** is acute-onset thrombocytopenia in patients receiving heparin therapy.
    - causes platelet activation, significantly increasing risk of thrombosis
    - thrombocytopenia and thrombosis occur 5 – 10 days after exposure to heparin
    - more common after exposure to unfractionated heparin
    - if HIT is suspected, immediately discontinue heparin and administer anticoagulants
- **Idiopathic thrombocytopenic purpura (ITP**, also called **immune thrombocytopenia)** is an autoimmune disorder that causes the destruction of platelets.
    - Signs and symptoms include mild bleeding (e.g., petechiae, purpura); severe GI bleeding and hematuria are rarer.
    - Treatment includes corticosteroids and IV immunoglobulin.
    - Because platelet destruction occurs in the spleen, refractory ITP is treated with splenectomy.

HELPFUL HINT:

Heparin is neutralized with protamine sulfate. Warfarin is neutralized with vitamin K.

QUICK REVIEW QUESTION

4. A patient with sepsis after a complicated PE has been in the ICU for 2 weeks. The nurse calls the physician because the patient has frank blood in the stool and is oozing from around the PICC lines. Why should the nurse consider thrombocytopenia as the cause?

Immune Deficiencies and Leukopenia

Pathophysiology

Immune deficiencies can be primary disorders (i.e., inherited) or secondary to disease, medications, or malnutrition. Immune deficiencies commonly seen in critical care are discussed below.

- **Leukopenia** is the general term for a WBC <4000/μL. It can occur as the result of impaired production or rapid use of WBCs.
- **Acquired immunodeficiency syndrome (AIDS)** is the end-stage progression of HIV. Patients with AIDS have a depletion of

T lymphocytes and are susceptible to opportunistic and sometimes emergent infections.

- **Leukemia**, cancer of the WBCs, occurs in the bone marrow and disrupts the production and function of WBCs. In the absence of functioning WBCs, the patient becomes immunocompromised. The types of leukemia are differentiated by which WBCs are affected (lymphocytes or myeloid cells).
- Patient who have received **organ transplants** are started on a high-intensity regimen of immunosuppressants perioperatively and are at high risk of infection during recovery.
- **Chemotherapy** is conducted with a class of cytotoxic medications that destroy cancer cells by disrupting cell mitosis and DNA replication. A side effect of chemotherapy is severe **neutropenia** (a decrease in circulating neutrophils).
- Poorly managed **diabetes mellitus** and associated hyperglycemia increases the risk of infection. In the critical care setting, patients with diabetes are more prone to postoperative infections and skin infections.

Treatment and Management

- Patients with immune deficiencies require specialized care to prevent opportunistic infections.
- Maintain skin integrity.
- Ensure adequate nutrition and hydration.
- Ensure that patient, providers, and visitors use adequate hand hygiene.
- Place patients in isolation rooms, per hospital policy.
- High-risk patients may receive prophylactic antibiotics.

> **QUICK REVIEW QUESTION**
>
> 5. A patient receiving chemotherapy presents with onset of cough and fever. A CBC reveals a WBC count of 20,000/μL and a left shift. Blood cultures are drawn, with results pending, and the patient's lactic acid level is 2.9 mmol/L. CXR shows bilateral pulmonary infiltrates. What diagnosis does the nurse anticipate?

Oncologic Complications

- Patients with cancer may be admitted to the ICU for conditions directly related to the malignancy or for complications of treatment.

- Common oncologic complications include pericardial effusion/cardiac tamponade (see chapter 1, Cardiovascular Review), PE or respiratory failure (see chapter 2, Respiratory Review), hypercalcemia (see chapter 6, Renal and Genitourinary Review), and sepsis (see chapter 11, Multisystem Review).
- **Tumor lysis syndrome** occurs when tumor lysis releases large amounts of potassium, phosphate, and nucleic acids into circulation. The resulting hyperuricemia and hyperphosphatemia lead to acute kidney injury and high risk for dysrhythmias.
    - The condition is most common in patients with hematological cancers, particularly non-Hodgkin lymphoma and acute lymphoblastic leukemia.
    - Patients present with signs and symptoms of hyperkalemia, hyperphosphatemia, and hypocalcemia.
    - Management calls for allopurinol, febuxostat, or rasburicase (to reduce uric acid levels), pharmacological management of electrolyte imbalances (see chapter 6, Renal and Genitourinary Review), and 108cardiac monitoring.
- **Superior vena cava syndrome** occurs when a malignancy obstructs the superior vena cava either by invading or compressing the vein.
    - The condition is most common in patients with lung cancer and non-Hodgkin lymphoma.
    - Patients present with facial edema, dyspnea, and chest pain. Severe symptoms may include cerebral edema, hemodynamic instability, and airway obstruction.
    - Management involves stabilization (ABCs) and stent placement.

> **QUICK REVIEW QUESTION**
>
> 6. Why would a patient with tumor lysis syndrome be administered allopurinol?

Transfusion Reactions

- Whole blood and blood products are **transfused** to replace lost volume or to replace specific components such as RBCs, platelets, or clotting factors.

TABLE 4.3. Uses of Blood Products

Blood Product	Uses	Notes
Packed red blood cells (PRBCs)	to treat hypovolemia due to hemorrhage to treat anemia for low HgB (<7 – 8 g/dL)	One unit of PRBCs raises hematocrit by 3% and HgB by 1 g/dL.
Platelets	to stop or prevent bleeding in patients with thrombocytopenia	Blood type match is not required but is preferred. One unit increases platelet count by 5,000 – 10,000 platelets/μL.
Fresh frozen plasma (FFP)	to replace clotting factors to reduce bleeding to prevent bleeding in patients with abnormal coagulation tests (e.g., low INR) for massive transfusion of PRBCs	Crossmatching is not required.
Cryoprecipitate	to replace fibrinogen and clotting factors VIII and XIII	Cryoprecipitate has a higher concentration of clotting factors than does FFP.
Whole blood	for massive hemorrhage	Whole blood is used rarely and only as an emergent treatment.
Albumin	for hypovolemic shock to treat hypotension during hemodialysis	Diuretics are often given with albumin.

- In an **exchange transfusion**, the patient's blood is slowly removed in cycles and simultaneously replaced with donor whole blood or plasma. Exchange transfusion is used to treat sickle cell disease, polycythemia vera, and malaria.
- **Plasmapheresis** is similar to dialysis and filters antibodies from blood. It is used for autoimmune disorders such as lupus, myasthenia gravis, and thrombotic thrombocytopenic purpura.
- A blood **type and screen (T&S)** or **type and crossmatch (T&C)** is necessary for the transfusion of some blood products to avoid immunological reactions.
- For suspected transfusion reactions, the nurse should:
    □ Immediately stop transfusion.

HELPFUL HINT:

Leukocyte-reduced RBCs should be used for patients at high risk for transfusion reactions, including patients with a history of transfusion complications.

- ☐ Infuse with normal saline.
- ☐ Notify physician and blood bank.
- ☐ Continue to monitor vital signs.
- ☐ Return blood products to blood bank for investigation.

HELPFUL HINT:

Febrile reactions are the most common complication of blood transfusions. They occur more often in children and in patients receiving RBCs or platelets. Transfusion-associated circulatory overload is the most common cause of transfusion-related death in the United States.

TABLE 4.4. Complications of Blood Transfusions

Complication	Signs and Symptoms	Intervention
Immunological Reactions		
Acute hemolytic reaction (onset <15 minutes)	fever, chills, back pain, hypotension, tachycardia, elevated JVP, pink or dark-brown urine, DIC	normal saline and diuretic to maintain urine output at 100 mL/hr for 24 hours
Delayed hemolytic reaction (onset >24 hours)	dark urine, jaundice, decreased HgB	usually mild symptoms that do not require intervention; monitor renal function
Febrile nonhemolytic reaction (onset 1 – 6 hours)	slight fever, chills, rigor, dyspnea	rule out hemolytic reaction and sepsis; antipyretics
Allergic reaction	mild: urticaria, itching; severe: anaphylaxis	mild: antihistamines; severe: ACLS protocols
Other Complications		
Transfusion-associated circulatory overload (TACO)	signs and symptoms of CHF or pulmonary edema	diuretics; slow the transfusion rate
Transfusion-related acute lung injury (TRALI)	signs and symptoms of ARDS or acute lung injury	discontinue transfusion; O_2 and hemodynamic support per ARDS protocols

QUICK REVIEW QUESTION

7. The nurse began an infusion of PRBCs 30 minutes ago and reassesses the patient. The patient is experiencing lower back pain, diaphoresis, and tachycardia. What is the first thing the nurse should do?

ANSWER KEY

1. Fibrinogen (clotting factor I) is a substrate necessary for coagulation. Patients with very low fibrinogen levels are at risk for severe bleeding and will have prolonged PTs, INRs, PTTs, and aPTTs.

2. The nurse should expect the physician to order an immediate infusion of PRBCs.

3. Obstetrical complications are a common cause of DIC. Diagnostic findings that would confirm this diagnosis include thrombocytopenia, prolonged clotting times (PT and PTT), decreased fibrinogen, and increased levels of fibrinolysis products (D-dimer and FSP).

4. The patient would have been administered heparin to treat the PE, so heparin-induced thrombocytopenia should be considered as a cause of the bleeding.

5. The nurse should suspect septic pneumonia. Chemotherapy immunocompromises patients, making them more susceptible to infection.

6. Tumor lysis syndrome is characterized by the release of large amounts of nucleic acids, which metabolize to form uric acid, leading to hyperuricemia. Allopurinol is a hypouricemic agent that prevents the formation of uric acid.

7. The nurse should immediately stop the blood transfusion, run normal saline wide open through the line, and then notify the physician.

5 GASTROINTESTINAL REVIEW

CCRN TEST PLAN: GASTROINTESTINAL

- Abdominal compartment syndrome
- Acute abdominal trauma
- Acute GI hemorrhage
- Bowel infarction, obstruction, perforation (e.g., mesenteric ischemia, adhesions)
- GI surgeries (e.g., Whipple, esophagectomy, resections)
- Hepatic failure/coma (e.g., portal hypertension, cirrhosis, esophageal varices, fulminant hepatitis, biliary atresia, drug-induced)
- Malnutrition and malabsorption
- Pancreatitis

Gastrointestinal Assessment

1. Inspection: Look for distention, bulges, color, hernias, ascites, and/or pulsations.
2. Auscultation: High-pitched gurgling sounds are normal. Normal bowel sounds can be documented as normal, hypoactive, or hyperactive. Other types of bowel sounds include:
   - **Borborygmi** are loud, rumbling sounds caused by the shifting of fluids or gas within the intestines; these sounds are a normal finding.
   - **High-pitched bowel sounds** are often described as tinkling or rushing sounds and may indicate an early bowel obstruction.

- **Absent bowel sounds** are an indication of an **ileus**, where no peristalsis is occurring. Bowel sounds may be temporarily absent in certain cases (e.g., after surgery), but their absence, combined with abdominal pain, indicates a serious condition.

3. Percussion: **Tympany** (air) sounds are normal, and **dull sounds** are heard over solid organs (liver and spleen).
4. Palpation: Check for guarding, rigidity, masses, and/or hernias.

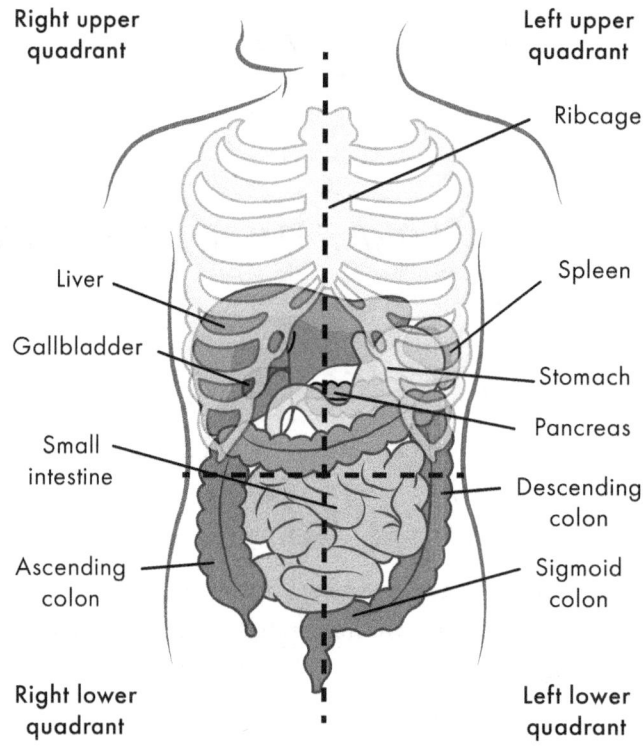

Figure 5.1. Abdominopelvic Anatomy and Quadrants

TABLE 5.1. GI Signs		
Name	**Description**	**Indication**
Kehr sign	referred left shoulder pain caused when the diaphragm irritates the phrenic nerve	splenic rupture diaphragm irritation
Rovsing sign	pain in the RLQ with palpation of LLQ (indicates peritoneal irritation)	appendicitis
Cullen sign	a bluish discoloration to the umbilical area	retroperitoneal hemorrhage

Name	Description	Indication
Grey Turner sign	ecchymosis in the flank area	retroperitoneal hemorrhage
Psoas sign	abdominal pain when right hip is hyperextended	appendicitis, Crohn's disease
McBurney's point	RLQ pain at point halfway between umbilicus and iliac spine	appendicitis
Murphy sign	pain and cessation of inspiration when RUQ is palpated	acute cholecystitis
Markle test (heel drop)	pain caused when patient stands on tiptoes and drops heels down quickly or when patient hops on one leg	appendicitis, peritonitis

- Diagnostic studies for GI assessment
    - A **focused assessment sonography for trauma (FAST)** exam is a quick bedside exam that uses ultrasound to assess for bleeding after trauma.
    - **Esophagogastroduodenoscopy (EGD** or **upper endoscopy)** is an endoscopic procedure that uses a scope to visualize the linings of the upper GI tract.
    - **Colonoscopy** is an endoscopic procedure that uses a scope to visualize the linings of the lower GI tract.
    - **Flexible sigmoidoscopy** is endoscopy of the rectum and sigmoid colon.
    - **Balloon-assisted enteroscopy** is used to assess areas of the GI tract that are hard to access, particularly the small intestine.
    - **Ultrasound** is frequently used to visualize the gallbladder, liver, pancreas, spleen, and abdominal aorta.
    - A **CT scan** is frequently used to diagnose or rule out a cause of abdominal pain.
    - **X-rays** are taken to visualize free air, gas, obstructions, foreign bodies, and dilatation.
- Common laboratory tests for GI conditions
    - liver function panels
    - tests for pancreatic enzymes

CONTINUE

TABLE 5.2. GI Laboratory Tests

Test	Description	Normal Range
Liver Function Tests		
Albumin	protein made in the liver; low levels may indicate liver damage	3.5 – 5.0 g/dL
Alkaline phosphatase (ALP)	enzyme found in the liver and bones; increased levels indicate liver damage	45 – 147 U/L
Alanine transaminase (ALT)	enzyme in the liver; helps metabolize protein; increased levels indicate liver damage	7 – 55 U/L
Aspartate transaminase (AST)	enzyme in the liver; helps metabolize alanine; increased levels indicate liver or muscle damage	8 – 48 U/L
Total protein	low levels may indicate liver damage	6.3 – 7.9 g/dL
Total bilirubin	produced during the breakdown of heme; increased levels indicate liver damage or anemia	0.1 – 1.2 mg/dL
Gamma-glutamyl-transferase (GGT)	enzyme that plays a role in antioxidant metabolism; increased levels indicate liver damage	9 – 48 U/L
L-lactate dehydrogenase (LD or LDH)	enzyme found in most cells in the body; increased levels may indicate liver damage, cancer, or tissue breakdown	adults: 122 – 222 U/L
Pancreatic Enzymes		
Amylase	enzyme that breaks down carbohydrates	23 – 140 U/L
Lipase	enzyme that breaks down fats	<160 U/L

QUICK REVIEW QUESTION

1. A patient presents with severe upper GI bleeding. What diagnostic study will likely be ordered to locate the source of the bleeding?

Nutrition

- **Enteral nutrition (EN)** delivers formula through a tube and is indicated for patients with a functioning GI tract but who cannot maintain oral intake.

- **Total enteral nutrition (TEN)** delivers all required components of nutrition.
- Feedings should start within 48 hours of admission for hemodynamically stable patients who require EN.
- **Prepyloric tubes** (tip ending in stomach) can be nasogastric (NG tube), orogastric (OG tube), or gastrostomy (G-tube).
- **Postpyloric tubes** feed into the duodenum or jejunum.
- Gastric residuals should be monitored per protocols.
- Keep HOB raised at least 30° during administration and for 30 minutes afterward to prevent aspiration.
- Administer metoclopramide to improve motility, as ordered.

- **Parenteral feedings** deliver nutrition via IV catheter and are indicated for patients with GI disorders that prevent the absorption of nutrients (e.g., malabsorption, bowel obstruction, ileus).
  - **Total parenteral nutrition (TPN)** delivers all the required components of nutrition via a central venous catheter. TPN must be delivered via central line to prevent phlebitis or thrombosis.
  - **Peripheral parenteral nutrition (PPN)** delivers more-dilute nutrition through peripheral veins.
  - Monitor strict input/output when starting, with assessment of cardiac and respiratory to assess for fluid overload.
  - Monitor the patient for signs of hypoglycemia or hyperglycemia.
  - Feedings must not be stopped abruptly; give dextrose 5% if TPN is interrupted.

HELPFUL HINT:

Gastric residual volume (GRV or gastric residuals) is the amount of fluid aspirated from the stomach after enteral feedings. High GRV (250 mL) may put the patient at risk for aspiration.

QUICK REVIEW QUESTION

2. A patient receiving TPN has become diaphoretic and shaky and complains of blurred vision. What should the nurse consider?

Abdominal Compartment Syndrome

Pathophysiology

Abdominal compartment syndrome is organ dysfunction caused by increased **intra-abdominal pressure (IAP)**. For most patients, normal IAP will be 5 to 7 mm Hg. Intravesical (bladder) pressure is most commonly used to monitor IAP. Saline is inserted into the bladder via a Foley catheter, and expiration pressure is measured.

HELPFUL HINT:

Chronic obesity increases IAP, and bariatric patients may have elevated IAP with no symptoms.

Intra-abdominal hypertension is IAP >12 mm Hg (although this will vary by patient). Compartment syndrome is usually monitored using **abdominal perfusion pressure (APP)** where APP = MAP – IAP. The goal for adequate abdominal perfusion is APP 60 mm Hg.

Sequalae to intra-abdominal hypertension and abdominal compartment syndrome can be seen in most organ systems.

- Increased IAP displaces the diaphragm, reducing ventricular compliance, venous return, and cardiac output.
- Diaphragm displacement also compresses the lungs.
- Hypoperfusion of the intestines may lead to infarction or infection.
- Increased IAP may lead to increased ICP.

Etiology

- intraperitoneal or retroperitoneal bleeding
- extensive fluid resuscitation
- abdominal packing
- ascites
- burns

Signs and Symptoms

- distended abdomen
- increased peak inspiratory pressure
- oliguria
- JVD
- peripheral edema
- signs and symptoms of hemodynamic instability

HELPFUL HINT:

Applying excess PEEP will further reduce cardiac output in patients with IAP.

Diagnostic Tests and Findings

- IAP >20 mm Hg
- APP <60 mm Hg

Treatment and Management

- definitive treatment: surgical decompression of abdomen (laparotomy) or percutaneous catheter decompression
- noninvasive management
  - fluid restriction
  - supine position (raising head of bed increases IAP)

- nasogastric or rectal decompression
- analgesics, sedation, and/or pharmacological paralysis to improve abdominal wall compliance
- mechanical ventilation: reduced tidal volume, permissive hypercapnia to lower airway pressures

> **QUICK REVIEW QUESTION**
>
> 3. A patient is sedated and on mechanical ventilation after surgical repair of a pelvic fracture that required aggressive resuscitation with fluids and blood products. Monitoring shows increasing IAP, with IAP of 15 mm Hg and APP of 60 mm Hg. If the patient is currently hemodynamically stable, what interventions should the nurse anticipate?

Acute Abdominal Trauma

Pathophysiology

Acute abdominal trauma can be caused by a penetrating injury such as a gunshot or knife wound or by blunt force trauma from a motor vehicle injury or a fall. Abdominal trauma usually involves injury to multiple organs.

- Trauma to the liver and spleen can cause massive hemorrhage because of the high volume of blood that circulates through them.
- Blunt or penetrating trauma can cause rupture of the diaphragm, leading to dyspnea and possible herniation of abdominal organs into the thoracic cavity.
- Hollow viscus perforation may cause leakage of gastric acids or biliary secretions, leading to peritonitis, SIRS, infection, or sepsis.

Signs and Symptoms

- The following physical assessments indicate visceral injuries.
    - Grey Turner sign (ecchymosis in the flank area): retroperitoneal bleeding or pancreatic injury
    - Cullen sign (purple discoloration at umbilicus or flank): blood in the abdominal wall
    - Kehr sign (referred pain to left shoulder): ruptured spleen or irritated diaphragm from bile in peritoneum
    - hematoma in the flank: kidney trauma
    - abdominal distension: accumulated fluid, gas, or blood from ruptured blood vessels or perforated organs

HELPFUL HINT:

All undifferentiated trauma patients should be treated as having hemorrhagic shock until proven otherwise. Fluid resuscitation is the recommended initial treatment following rapid primary and (when possible) secondary survey.

- auscultation of friction rub over spleen or liver: may indicate rupture
- rebound tenderness and rigidity during abdominal palpation: peritoneal inflammation
- subcutaneous emphysema: free air from ruptured bowel
- Signs and symptoms of retroperitoneal bleeding (or hematoma) include hypotension; bradycardia; Grey Turner sign; and abdominal, back, or flank pain.

HELPFUL HINT:

A hemodynamically unstable trauma patient with a positive FAST will likely require emergency surgery.

Diagnostic Findings

- FAST: assess for abdominal fluid, blood, and hemoperitoneum
- abdominal CT: gold standard specific for retroperitoneal hemorrhage
- Foley catheter: assess for frank blood
- NG tube: assess for frank or occult blood (also used for effective gastric decompression)
- diagnostic peritoneal lavage (DPL): invasive insertion of catheter through abdominal wall after bladder emptied
  - frank blood: immediate surgery
  - no blood: if lab analysis positive for occult blood, immediate surgery is necessary; 1L 0.9% NaCl or LR infused through abdominal catheter and fluid drained back into dependent-position IV bag
- hemoconcentration distorts HgB/Hct results (use serial labs to monitor status)

Treatment and Management

HELPFUL HINT:

Removal of the spleen compromises the immune system and places patients at high risk of infection and **postsplenectomy sepsis**. Patients who have undergone full or partial splenectomy should receive vaccinations per hospital policies (usually pneumococcal, meningococcal, and influenza).

- Common conditions requiring management following abdominal trauma include:
  - pre- and post-op hemorrhage (especially with liver injury) and hypovolemic shock
  - coagulopathy (deterioration in serial values may warrant rapid surgical exploration)
  - hypothermia (caused by large cavity wounds, DPL, fluid resuscitation with non-warmed fluids, or massive transfusion protocol)
  - infection and sepsis
- Multiple visceral organ injury generally requires a 3-phase "damage control" surgical plan.

> **QUICK REVIEW QUESTION**
>
> 4. A patient is admitted to the ICU after a motor vehicle accident that included blunt force trauma to the abdomen. What signs and symptoms would the nurse look for to assess for retroperitoneal hemorrhage?

Acute GI Hemorrhage

Upper GI Bleeding

Pathophysiology

An **upper GI bleed** is bleeding that occurs between the esophagus and duodenum. Bleeding may be severe and require immediate hemodynamic management.

Etiology

- **Peptic ulcers** and **esophagitis** (secondary to GERD) are the most common causes of upper GI bleeding.
- **Esophageal varices** occur when veins in the esophagus rupture because of portal hypertension (usually caused by hepatic cirrhosis). Bleeding may be severe and is likely to recur.
- **Esophageal perforation** or **rupture** may be iatrogenic, secondary to trauma, or caused by the severe effort of vomiting (**Boerhaave syndrome**).
- **Mallory-Weiss tears** occur at the gastroesophageal junction and result from forceful vomiting.
- NSAIDs and chronic gastritis can cause or worsen upper GI bleeding.

HELPFUL HINT:

Acid suppressive therapy in the critical care setting is aimed at reducing stress-related peptic ulcer formation and subsequent bleeding. Acid suppression includes a PPI or an H_2 receptor blocker.

Signs and Symptoms

- upper abdominal pain
- hematemesis (may be in nasogastric aspirate)
- melena
- coffee-ground emesis
- hematochezia (if hemorrhaging)
- signs and symptoms of hypovolemia (after significant blood loss)

Diagnostic Tests and Findings

- decreased HgB, Hct, and platelets

- longer PT and aPTT
- electrolyte imbalances (due to hypovolemia)
- elevated BUN and BUN-creatinine ratio
- positive hemoccult
- diagnosed via appropriate endoscopy or angiogram (EGD to locate source of bleeding)

Treatment and Management

- O₂ therapy
- manage hemodynamic status: IV fluids, blood products, and management of coagulopathies
- medications to constrict vasculature: vasopressin, octreotides, and beta blockers
- endoscopic or surgical repair if bleeding persists
    - esophageal varices: endoscopic variceal band ligation (EVL) or esophageal balloon tamponade (e.g., Sengstaken-Blakemore tube)
    - PPI to prevent post-procedure ulcers

> **HELPFUL HINT:**
>
> Elevated BUN-creatinine ratio is associated with decreased kidney function and increased breakdown of protein. It is often seen with upper GI bleeds (due to digestion of blood) but not with lower GI bleeds.

> **QUICK REVIEW QUESTION**
>
> 5. The physician has ordered an octreotide drip for a patient diagnosed with esophageal varices. The critical care nurse knows that this medication is appropriate for this diagnosis because it has what type of action?

Lower GI Bleeding

Pathophysiology

A **lower GI bleed** is any bleeding that occurs below the duodenum. Lower GI bleeds occur less frequently than do upper GI bleeds, are typically less emergent, and may stop on their own.

Etiology

- disease of the colon (e.g., diverticulitis, IBD, colitis)
- colon polyps, cancer, or tumors
- abscess or inflammation of rectum
- hemorrhoids
- anal fissures

Signs and Symptoms

- abdominal or chest pain
- hematochezia
- melena
- bleeding from rectum
- signs and symptoms of hypovolemia (after significant blood loss)

Diagnostic Tests and Findings

- positive hemoccult
- decreased HgB and Hct
- PT and aPTT may be longer
- diagnosed via appropriate endoscopy, CT scan, or angiogram

Treatment and Management

- manage hemodynamic status: IV fluids, blood products, and management of coagulopathies
- endoscopic or surgical repair if bleeding persists

> **QUICK REVIEW QUESTION**
>
> 6. What signs and symptoms would the nurse expect to see in a patient with a lower GI bleed?

Bowel Infarction

Pathophysiology

Bowel infarction, necrosis of part of the intestinal wall, occurs when decreased blood flow causes ischemia in the small bowel (**mesenteric ischemia**) or large bowel (**colonic ischemia**). The most common cause of mesenteric ischemia is embolus or thrombus in the mesenteric artery. Colonic ischemia is usually nonocclusive and is associated with low flow states (e.g., MI, CHF).

Signs and Symptoms

- abdominal pain, cramping, and distension
- nausea and vomiting

- diarrhea
- hematochezia
- altered mental status (in patients 65 years old)

Diagnostic Tests and Findings

- elevated WBC count
- ABG may show metabolic acidosis
- elevated L-lactate or serum amylase
- diagnosed via CT scan of abdomen

Treatment and Management

- fluid resuscitation
- gastric decompression
- anticoagulant therapy and possible angioplasty for arterial occlusion
- broad-spectrum antibiotics
- surgery required to resect necrotic bowel

HELPFUL HINT:

Vasopressors and digitalis should be used cautiously in patients with bowel infarction, as these medications may worsen the ischemia.

QUICK REVIEW QUESTION

7. A patient with infective endocarditis complains of severe abdominal pain, diarrhea, and vomiting. Why should the nurse suspect a bowel infarction?

Bowel Obstruction and Perforation

Pathophysiology

A **bowel obstruction** occurs when normal flow through the bowel is disrupted. **Mechanical obstructions** are physical barriers in the bowel. The most common mechanical obstructions in the small bowel are **adhesions**, **hernias**, and **volvuli** (twisting of the bowels). The most common obstruction in the large bowel are tumors.

Paralytic ileus is the impairment of peristalsis in the absence of mechanical obstruction. It is most common in postoperative patients and can also be caused by endocrine disorders or medications (e.g., opioids).

Increased pressure proximal to the obstruction can lead to **perforation** of the bowel wall. Other common causes of bowel perforation include surgery, abdominal trauma, and neoplasm (in large bowel).

Signs and Symptoms

- nausea and vomiting
- diarrhea
- distended and firm abdomen
- abdominal pain (cramping and colicky)
- unable to pass flatus
- high-pitched bowel sounds (early); absent bowel sounds (late)
- tympanic percussion
- pain, often sudden onset (perforation)

Diagnostic Tests and Findings

- increased WBCs
- elevated BUN and decreased electrolytes from dehydration/vomiting
- abdominal X-ray may show dilated bowel loops
- CT scan to diagnose

Treatment and Management

- bowel rest (NPO) or nutritional support distal to obstruction
- fluid resuscitation
- bowel decompression via tube (NG or Miller-Abbott) with low, intermittent suction
- antibiotics as needed
- medications for GI signs and symptoms: antiemetics, simethicone, and/or magnesium hydroxide
- surgical intervention for obstructions that do not resolve within 48 hours
- surgical closure of perforation

> **QUICK REVIEW QUESTION**
>
> 8. A patient presents with abdominal pain, nausea, and vomiting. A bowel obstruction is suspected and then confirmed by CT scan. What priority interventions should the nurse anticipate for this patient?

Gastric Surgeries

- Resection of portions of the GI tract may be required in patients with Crohn's disease, ulcers, tumors, polyps, or cancers affecting the bowels.
  - **Colectomy** is the surgical partial or full resection or removal of a portion of the large intestine.
  - **Ileal pouch anal anastomosis** occurs after a total colectomy and creates a pocket from the distal end of the ileus by surgically attaching it to the anus to preserve bowel function.
  - **Abdominoperineal** (or rectal) **resection** is the removal of the sigmoid colon, rectum, and anus.
  - **Small bowel resection** is the removal of a diseased portion of the small intestine and reattachment of healthy tissue.
  - **Gastrectomy** is the resection of part or all of the stomach, usually because of cancer.
- **Ostomies** divert fecal matter from its normal path through the GI tract by connecting the intestines to an opening in the anterior abdominal wall.
  - Ostomies are commonly performed with resections.
  - An **ileostomy** bypasses the large intestine.
  - A **colostomy** bypasses the distal colon, anus, and rectum.
  - Waste is collected in an **ostomy pouch**.
- **Bariatric surgeries** are performed to resect, bypass, or band the stomach to promote weight loss. Common complications of bariatric bypass surgery include malabsorption, bowel obstruction, anastomotic leaks, and GI bleeding. (See Ch. 11 Multisystem Review for more detailed information on management of bariatric surgery patients.)
- An **abdominal wall hernia** is an area of weakness within the abdominal cavity; organs or tissue can protrude through this weak area.
  - Large hernias can become incarcerated or trapped, which will lead to **strangulation** and ischemia.
  - Hernias with a large diameter or strangulation need surgical repair.

> **HELPFUL HINT:**
>
> Anastomotic leaks should be considered when patients recovering from GI surgery develop s/s of infection.

QUICK REVIEW QUESTION

9. A patient recovering from a partial colectomy is having loose stools several times a day. What intervention should the nurse expect to provide?

Hepatic Failure

Hepatic (liver) failure can be acute (onset <26 weeks) or chronic. Common causes of acute liver failure (also called **fulminate hepatitis**) include acetaminophen overdose and viral hepatitis; the most common cause of chronic liver failure is alcohol abuse.

Liver failure leads to dysfunction in multiple organ systems.

- **Hepatic encephalopathy** is impaired cognitive function caused by increased serum ammonia (NH_3) levels. NH_3 is produced by bacteria in the bowels and is normally broken down by healthy liver tissue before it enters circulation. Increased NH_3 levels may also cause neuromuscular symptoms, including asterixis and bradykinesia.
- Coagulopathies are caused by impaired synthesis of clotting factors in liver tissue.
- **Jaundice** is caused by hyperbilirubinemia.
- Acute kidney injury occurs in approximately 50% of patients with liver failure. (The mechanism is unknown.)
- Infections and sepsis develop secondary to decreased and defective WBCs.
- Metabolic imbalances may include hypokalemia, hyponatremia, and hypoglycemia.
- Lowered peripheral vascular resistance decreases BP and increases HR.

Chronic liver failure leads to **cirrhosis**—the development of fibrotic tissue in the liver. Cirrhosis in the liver increases resistance in the portal vein, causing **portal hypertension**. Common conditions that occur secondary to portal hypertension include esophageal varices, **ascites**, and **splenomegaly**.

Biliary atresia, a rare condition that affects the hepatic and biliary ducts, presents between 2 and 8 weeks of age. Most individuals require a liver transplant in early childhood. However, approximately 35% of people affected reach adulthood before needing liver transplants.

Signs and Symptoms

- cognitive changes or motor dysfunction
- jaundice
- petechiae or purpura
- spider angiomas
- ascites
- RUQ pain

HELPFUL HINT:

Sedatives should be used cautiously in patients with liver failure because of the liver's inability to clear them. Low doses of short-acting benzodiazepines should be used when sedation is necessary.

- palmar erythema
- nausea and vomiting

Diagnostic Tests and Findings

- elevated AST, ALT, and/or bilirubin
- elevated NH_3 levels
- decreased protein, albumin, and fibrinogen
- decreased WBCs, HgB, Hct, and platelets
- longer PT and PTT, and increased INR
- CT scan or MRI may show fibrosis of liver

Treatment and Management

- IV fluid resuscitation
- lactulose and neomycin to reduce ammonia levels
- diuretics for ascites
- prophylactic treatment for stress ulcers
- monitor ICP
- tight glucose control for nonalcoholic fatty liver disease
- shunt to reduce portal hypertension
    - transjugular intrahepatic portosystemic shunt (TIPS): portal vein to a hepatic vein
    - distal splenorenal shunt (DSRS): splenic vein to the left kidney vein

HELPFUL HINT:

Alcoholic cirrhosis requires special considerations and the implementation of an alcohol withdrawal protocol. (See chapter 10, Behavioral and Psychosocial Review, for more information on alcohol withdrawal.)

QUICK REVIEW QUESTION

10. A nurse is providing care to a patient with acute liver failure. What should the nurse expect to see in the patient's CBC and coagulation tests?

Malabsorption
Pathophysiology

Malabsorption is a dysfunction of the small intestine resulting in the inability to effectively absorb the micro- and/or macronutrients that are needed for health. Malabsorption may be global (inability to absorb any nutrients) or specific to certain nutrients.

Etiology

- impairment of digestive enzyme production (e.g., cirrhosis, resection of pancreas)
- bacterial overgrowth
- small intestine dysmotility
- chronic bowel disease (e.g., Crohn's disease)
- bowel resection
- rapid gastric emptying
- medications that affect the lining of the small intestine
- fluid overload

Signs and Symptoms

- steatorrhea
- diarrhea
- abdominal distention
- signs and symptoms related to malabsorption of specific nutrients (e.g., anemia, edema, peripheral neuropathy)

Diagnostic Tests and Findings

- blood tests for low levels of micro- and macronutrients (e.g., iron, calcium)
- CT scan to look for changes in the wall of small intestine

Treatment and Management

- treat primary illness
- antimotility medications
- investigate possible causes of diarrhea
    - enteral feeding (e.g., osmolality, fiber content, contamination)
    - *Clostridium difficile* (C. diff)
    - medications (e.g., PPIs, NSAIDs, diabetes medications, antibiotics)

> **QUICK REVIEW QUESTION**
>
> 11. A patient has been treated for severe sepsis with antibiotics and fluid resuscitation. The patient remains on mechanical ventilation, and enteral feeding has been started. The nurse notes that the patient has increased diarrhea. What should the nurse consider to prevent malabsorption?

★ Pancreatitis

Pathophysiology

Pancreatitis is caused by the release of digestive enzymes into the tissues of the pancreas. The condition causes autodigestion, inflammation, tissue destruction, and injury to adjacent structures and organs. Pancreatitis can be acute or chronic, but its onset is usually sudden. The most common causes of pancreatitis are gallstones and alcohol abuse.

The tissue damage caused by pancreatitis increases capillary permeability, resulting in fluid shifts into interstitial spaces that cause edema and systemic inflammatory responses (e.g., ARDS). Inflammation may also limit diaphragm movement and cause atelectasis. Severe damage to the pancreas may cause retroperitoneal bleeding.

Signs and Symptoms

- steady, severe pain abdominal pain; usually in the LUQ and may radiate to the back or shoulder
- guarding
- nausea and vomiting
- decreased bowel sounds
- steatorrhea
- fever
- tachycardia and hypotension
- dyspnea
- Cullen sign
- Grey Turner sign

Diagnostic Tests and Findings

- elevated amylase and lipase
- hypocalcemia
- decreased total protein
- hypoglycemia
- elevated Hct, BUN, and CRP
- increased WBCs
- imaging (MRI or CT scan with contrast) to diagnose

Treatment and Management

- fluid resuscitation, including electrolyte replacement
- pain management (usually opioids)
- enteral nutritional support (postpyloric)
- endoscopic retrograde cholangiopancreatography (ERCP) for gallstones and bile duct inflammation
- monitor for respiratory complications, including ARDS and atelectasis

> **QUICK REVIEW QUESTION**
>
> 12. The nurse is caring for a patient who is complaining of sudden, severe abdominal pain in the mid-epigastric area that spreads to the left shoulder. What complications should the nurse assess for?

ANSWER KEY

1. EGD is the diagnostic study most commonly used to visualize sources of upper GI bleeding.

2. The patient may be hyperglycemic or hypoglycemic. The nurse should perform a capillary or serum blood glucose check immediately. If the blood glucose is outside the normal range, protocol to treat for hyperglycemia or hypoglycemia should be followed, and the physician and pharmacy should be notified to adjust the composition of additives.

3. The patient has intra-abdominal hypertension but does not currently have symptoms of abdominal compartment syndrome. The nurse should expect to implement noninvasive interventions to manage IAP, including fluid restriction and supine positioning, and to continue monitoring IAP.

4. Retroperitoneal hemorrhage can lead to ecchymosis (Grey Turner sign, Cullen sign); abdominal, back, or flank pain; and signs or symptoms of hypovolemia (e.g., hypotension).

5. Because octreotide is a vasoconstrictor, it constricts the dilated vessels present in esophageal varices and reduces bleeding.

6. Early signs of a lower GI bleed include hematochezia, abdominal pain, and fatigue. Decreased HgB, decreased Hct, tachycardia, and hypotension may occur after a significant amount of blood loss and would be seen as late signs of a lower GI bleed.

7. Arterial embolus is a common complication of infective endocarditis. When the embolus occludes the mesenteric artery, the resulting hypoperfusion in the bowels may cause ischemia and infarction.

8. Patients with bowel obstructions need IV fluids. During a bowel obstruction, severe vomiting and fluid sequestration in the bowel lumen lead to hypovolemia and electrolyte imbalances.

9. Diarrhea is a common complication of a partial colectomy and is usually temporary. The large intestine is the organ primarily responsible for water absorption, so resection of the colon often results in loose stools. The patient's diet should be adjusted, and the patient may be given an antimotility agent.

10. Patients with liver failure will be pancytopenic with low levels of RBCs, platelets, and WBCs. They will also have prolonged PT and aPTT/PTT, an increased INR, and low fibrinogen.

11. The nurse should collaborate with dietary staff to determine if the correct formula is being used for the patient's needs. Loperamide may help slow the diarrhea. The nurse should also keep in mind that fluid overload may be affecting absorption rates. Finally, because the patient received high-dose antibiotics for sepsis, a diagnosis of *C. diff* should be ruled out with a stool sample.

12. The patient has symptoms of acute pancreatitis. Atelectasis and other respiratory problems are common in patients with acute pancreatitis. The nurse should thoroughly assess lung sounds and note any adventitious or diminished breath sounds, look for signs of orthopnea or other dyspnea, and monitor oxygen saturation levels.

RENAL AND GENITOURINARY REVIEW

CCRN TEST PLAN: RENAL AND GENITOURINARY
- Acute genitourinary trauma
- Acute kidney injury (AKI)
- Chronic kidney disease (CKD)
- Infections (e.g., kidney, urosepsis)
- Life-threatening electrolyte imbalances

Renal Physiology and Assessment

- The renal system consists of the kidneys, ureters, bladder (KUB), and urethra. Functions include:
  - fluid balance
  - blood pressure monitoring and homeostasis
  - electrolyte regulation
  - metabolic waste excretion
  - acid-base balance
  - secretion of erythropoietin
- **Nephrons** are the functioning portion of the kidney within the renal cortex. The **glomerulus**, the network of small capillaries within the nephron, is where filtration occurs. This filtration is a result of hydrostatic and oncotic pressure differences across the capillary bed.

> **HELPFUL HINT:**
>
> ACE inhibitors have a greater vasodilatory effect on efferent arterioles than on afferent arterioles in the glomerulus. This imbalance reduces the intraglomerular pressure that drives filtration and reduces the GFR.

- The **basement membrane** prevents large particles (e.g., proteins) from entering the filtrate.
- Filtrate from the glomerulus travels through the **proximal tubule, loop of Henle,** and **distal convoluted tubule**, where water, electrolytes, and bicarbonate are reabsorbed to maintain fluid, electrolyte, and acid-base balance.

■ Kidney function is assessed by measuring the rate of filtration and buildup of metabolic waste in the blood.

- The **glomerular filtration rate (GFR)** is the approximate volume of fluid filtered from the glomeruli per minute.
- **Creatinine clearance (CrCl)** is the volume of plasma cleared of creatinine per minute. (Normal rate is 90 – 140 mL/min for men and 80 – 125 mL/min for women.)
- **Blood urea nitrogen (BUN)** and **serum creatinine** tests assess the levels of metabolic waste products that are normally cleared by the kidneys.
- During renal hypoperfusion, urea may be reabsorbed in the proximal tubules because of compensating increases in the reabsorption of sodium and water. Creatinine is not reabsorbed, so an increased **BUN-to-creatinine ratio** indicates hypoperfusion.

> **HELPFUL HINT:**
>
> Acidosis increases bicarbonate reabsorption from the tubular fluid and increases hydrogen ion secretion from the collecting ducts.
>
> Alkalosis increases bicarbonate excretion and decreases hydrogen ion secretion.

TABLE 6.1. Kidney Function Tests

Test	Description	Normal Range
Serum Tests		
BUN	byproduct of ammonia metabolism; filtered by the kidneys; high levels can indicate insufficient kidney function	7 – 20 mg/dL
Creatinine	product of muscle metabolism; filtered by the kidneys; high levels can indicate insufficient kidney function	0.6 – 1.2 mg/dL
BUN-to-creatinine ratio	increased ratio indicates dehydration, AKI, or GI bleeding; decreased ratio indicates renal damage	10:1 – 20:1
GFR	volume of fluid filtered by the renal glomerular capillaries per unit of time; decreased GFR indicates decreased renal function	men: 100 – 130 mL/min/1.73 m^2 women: 90 – 120 mL/min/1.73 m^2 GFR <60 mL/min/1.73 m^2 is common in adults 70 years

Test	Description	Normal Range
Serum Tests		
Potassium (K^+)	helps with muscle contraction and regulates water and acid-base balance	3.5 – 5.2 mEq/L
Sodium (Na^+)	maintains fluid balance and plays a major role in muscle and nerve function	135 – 145 mEq/L
Calcium (Ca^{2+})	plays an important role in skeletal function and structure, nerve function, muscle contraction, and cell communication	8.5 – 10.3 mg/dL
Chloride (Cl^-)	plays a major role in muscle and nerve function	98 – 107 mEq/L
Magnesium (Mg^{2+})	regulates muscle, nerve, and cardiac function	1.8 – 2.5 mg/dL
Urinalysis		
Leukocytes	presence of WBCs in urine indicates infection	negative
Nitrate	presence in urine indicates infection by gram-negative bacteria	negative
Protein	presence in urine may indicate diabetic neuropathy, nephritis, or eclampsia	negative
pH	decreased (acidic) pH may indicate systemic acidosis or diabetes mellitus; increased (alkali) pH may indicate systemic alkalosis or UTI	4.5 – 8
Blood	presence in urine may indicate infection, renal calculi, a neoplasm, or coagulation disorders	negative
Specific gravity	concentration of urine; decreased concentration may indicate diabetes insipidus or pyelonephritis; increased concentration may indicate dehydration or syndrome of inappropriate antidiuretic hormone secretion (SIADH)	1.010 – 1.025
Urine osmolality	concentration of urine; more accurate than specific gravity	300 – 900 mOsm/kg
Ketones	produced during fat metabolism; presence in urine may indicate diabetes, hyperglycemia, starvation, alcoholism, or eclampsia	negative

> **QUICK REVIEW QUESTION**
> 1. Why do patients with upper GI bleeding often have a high BUN-to-creatinine ratio?

Renal Therapeutic Interventions

- **Renal replacement therapies** are considered when the GFR is <30 mL/min; options include dialysis and kidney transplantation.
- Filtration may occur via diffusion or convection.
  - Diffusion occurs when blood is exposed to a **dialysate fluid** with water, electrolytes, and osmotic agents. The composition of the dialysate fluid creates an osmotic gradient that moves water and metabolic waste out of the blood.
  - During convection, hydrostatic pressure forces water and permeable molecules out of the blood.
- During **intermittent hemodialysis**, blood is pumped through an external dialyzer.
  - standard method of dialysis for hemodynamically stable patients
  - access through a temporary or permanent dialysis catheter or a surgically created fistula
  - treatments take 3–5 hours
  - heparin administered to prevent microemboli formation
  - complications usually related to shifts in fluid volume; include hypotension, angina, dyspnea, and dysrhythmias
- **Continuous renal replacement therapy (CRRT)** uses an extracorporeal blood pump to continuously move blood through a hemofilter.
  - used in patients who cannot tolerate changes in water and electrolyte levels during intermittent hemodialysis
  - can be used to remove larger particles than those removed by intermittent hemodialysis
  - requires large-bore double-lumen central catheter
- During **peritoneal dialysis**, the dialysate fluid is infused into the peritoneal cavity and allowed to remain there for several hours.
  - preferred method for hemodynamically unstable patients who cannot tolerate hemodialysis
  - requires percutaneous or laparoscopic insertion of catheter into abdominal cavity

HELPFUL HINT:

Continuous venovenous hemofiltration (CVVH) is a type of CRRT that uses convection to remove excess water from the blood.

- patients with diabetes require careful monitoring to ensure stability of blood-glucose level
- most common complication: peritonitis
- signs and symptoms: abdominal pain, cloudy peritoneal effluent, and fever
- **Dialysis disequilibrium syndrome (DDS)** is a set of neurological symptoms that occur during dialysis, due to cerebral edema. Signs and symptoms include headache, blurred vision, and altered LOC or mental status.

> **QUICK REVIEW QUESTION**
> 2. Why is intermittent hemodialysis contraindicated for patients with TBI or increased ICP?

Acute Genitourinary Trauma

Pathophysiology

Genitourinary (GU) trauma can cause injury to the kidneys, bladder, urethra, or external genitalia. GU trauma symptoms can be nonspecific and can be masked by or related to other injuries. Trauma may occur from blunt or penetrating injury.

- Renal: The majority of renal trauma occurs from blunt trauma such as direct impact into the seatbelt or steering wheel in frontal MVCs or from body panel intrusion in side-impact crashes. Renal injuries are ranked graded from 1 to 5 based on severity. Grade 5 renal injuries are referred to as **shattered kidney** and include severe renal vascular laceration.
- Bladder: The majority of bladder trauma occurs from blunt trauma, usually occurring with a pelvic fracture. Bladder rupture can also result from lap belt restraint. Leakage from ruptures may lead to peritonitis or sepsis.
- Urethral: Urethral injuries are more common in males and may result from trauma and pelvic fracture or from iatrogenic injuries resulting from catheterization.

Signs and Symptoms

- pain (suprapubic, abdominal, groin/genital, or flank)
- urinary symptoms (e.g., hematuria, dysuria)
- bleeding at meatus

- ecchymosis
- distended bladder
- abdominal distention
- foul-smelling vaginal discharge

Diagnostic Tests and Findings

- urinalysis (for hematuria)
- decreased hemoglobin and hematocrit
- monitor for
  - elevated BUN and creatinine
  - fluid and electrolyte status
- diagnostic imaging (CT scan, KUB X-ray)

Treatment and Management

- low-grade renal trauma may be admitted for monitoring (Hct, hemodynamic)
- use angioembolization for persistent bleeding
- keep bladder decompressed via Foley catheter (if no urethral injury present)
- manage sequalae (e.g., acute kidney injury, hemorrhage)

> **QUICK REVIEW QUESTION**
>
> 3. A patient with grade 4 blunt renal injury is admitted to the ICU for monitoring. What symptoms and diagnostic findings should the nurse expect to monitor?

Acute Kidney Injury

Acute kidney injury (AKI), previously called acute renal failure, is an acute decrease in kidney function characterized by increased serum creatinine (**azotemia**) with or without decreased urine output. Changes in kidney function may result in multiple systemic conditions that require intervention. These conditions include:

- fluid imbalance (hypo- or hypervolemia)
- electrolyte imbalance
- acid-base imbalance
- hematological abnormalities (e.g., anemia, low platelet count)

AKI has a diverse etiology and is characterized as prerenal, intrarenal, or postrenal, based on the cause of injury. Questions on the CCRN will focus on intrarenal disease.

PRERENAL DISEASE

Pathophysiology

Prerenal disease is renal hypoperfusion caused by hemodynamic compromise (e.g., hypovolemia, systemic vasodilation) or renal ischemia. Prerenal disease presents with no damage to renal tubules and can usually be reversed by treating the underlying condition.

> **HELPFUL HINT:**
>
> NSAIDs, ARBs, and ACE inhibitors can cause or worsen prerenal disease and ATN.

Diagnostic Findings

- increased creatinine and BUN
- elevated BUN-to-creatinine ratio (20:1)
- low urine Na^+ (<20 mEq/L)
- increased urine osmolality and specific gravity
- normal finding on urine microscopy (no casts)
- serum creatinine returns to normal value after fluid repletion

Treatment and Management

- treat underlying cause to maintain MAP 65 mm Hg
  - fluids to rehydrate
  - vasopressors as needed to manage vasodilation

> **QUICK REVIEW QUESTION**
>
> 4. A patient with sepsis has received 3 L of normal saline over the past 24 hours and currently has maintenance fluids at 125 mL/hr. The nurse notes that urine output is at 250 mL for the past 4 hours. The last serum creatinine is 1.8 mg/dL, and BUN is 38 mg/dL. What interventions should the nurse anticipate?

INTRARENAL DISEASE

Pathophysiology

Intrarenal (or intrinsic) disease is caused by damage to the kidneys. The most common intrarenal condition in critical care settings is **acute tubular necrosis (ATN)**, the destruction of the renal tubular epithelium. ATN may be ischemic (usually caused by severe prerenal disease) or nephrotoxic. Common nephrotoxic substances include contrast dyes, NSAIDs, ARBs, ACE inhibitors, and aminoglycosides. ATN may also occur secondary to rhabdomyolysis or after cardiovascular surgery.

Intrarenal disease and recovery occurs in 4 phases.

1. The **onset phase** occurs immediately after the triggering event but before cell injury. Patients may have reduced urine output but few other symptoms.
2. During the **oliguric phase** (1 – 2 weeks), urine output is reduced to <400 mL/day, and creatinine and BUN serum levels will increase. In rare cases, patients may become **anuric** (urine output <100 mL/day). The inability of the kidneys to excrete urine may cause fluid overload, electrolyte imbalances (particularly hyperkalemia), and metabolic acidosis.
3. The **diuretic phase** (1 – 2 weeks) begins when the underlying cause of AKI has been corrected and GFR begins to increase. This phase is characterized by increased urine output (3 L/day). Patients should be monitored for hypovolemia and electrolyte depletion.
4. The **recovery phase** may last up to a year as kidney function slowly returns.

HELPFUL HINT:

Infection is the most common cause of death for patients with AKI.

Diagnostic Findings

- increased creatinine and BUN
- BUN-to-creatinine ratio <20:1
- oliguric phase
    - increased urine osmolality and specific gravity
    - urine Na^+ <10 mEq/L
- diuretic phase
    - decreased urine osmolality and specific gravity
    - urine Na^+ <40 mEq/L
- casts seen through urine microscopy
- serum creatinine does not respond to fluid repletion

Treatment and Management

- treat underlying cause
- discontinue or minimize use of nephrotoxic medications
- fluid volume management
    - IV fluids for hypovolemia
    - loop diuretics for hypervolemia (if not anuric)
    - daily weights and strict monitoring of fluid I/O

- correct electrolyte imbalances and monitor for related complications (including cardiac monitoring)
- sodium bicarbonate for metabolic acidosis
- indications for urgent dialysis in patients with AKI
  - ☐ severe or symptomatic hyperkalemia
  - ☐ severe metabolic acidosis
  - ☐ volume overload
  - ☐ pulmonary edema
  - ☐ uremia

QUICK REVIEW QUESTION

5. Several days after a cardiac catheterization, a patient is suspected of having intrarenal disease related to the imaging contrast dye used. The patient's I/O are being monitored closely, with outputs of approximately 500 mL per shift charted. The patient's assessment is as follows: BP 165/92, HR 85 bpm, 3+ pitting edema, auscultation of crackles in the bases of lungs, and SpO_2 92%. What condition should the nurse suspect, and what intervention will be required?

POSTRENAL DISEASE

Pathophysiology

Postrenal conditions are characterized by the blocked drainage of urine, usually because of prostatic hypertrophy or renal calculi. Treatment addresses the underlying cause of obstruction.

Diagnostic Findings

- oliguria
- increased serum creatinine and BUN
- normal BUN-to-creatinine ratio
- possible pain or hematuria

QUICK REVIEW QUESTION

6. What lab values can be used to differentiate between pre- and postrenal failure?

Chronic Kidney Disease

Pathophysiology

Chronic kidney disease (CKD) is long-term (3 months) kidney damage or dysfunction caused by destruction of nephrons. Like AKI, the etiology of CKD can be categorized as pre-, intra-, or postrenal. Common causes of CKD include:

- decreased perfusion due to heart failure or cirrhosis
- hypertensive nephrosclerosis
- diabetic nephropathy
- renal artery stenosis (usually due to atherosclerosis)
- glomular or tubulointerstitial disease
- chronic urinary obstruction

The kidneys initially compensate by hyperfiltration in individual nephrons, so patients are initially asymptomatic and present only with abnormal creatinine or BUN values. As the kidneys' ability to remove excess fluid and metabolic waste is further impaired, patients show signs and symptoms related to hypervolemia and decreased GFR. Related conditions that may require acute care include pulmonary edema and electrolyte imbalances. Other sequalae include anemia, hypertension, nausea/vomiting, pericarditis, peripheral neuropathy, weakness/lethargy, and altered mental status.

HELPFUL HINT: Patients with CKD have an elevated risk of CAD and worse outcomes after MI, CABG, and PCI.

Diagnostic Findings

- decreased GFR
  - Stage 1: 90 mL/min
  - Stage 2: 60 – 89 mL/min
  - Stage 3: 30 – 59 mL/min
  - Stage 4: 15 – 29 mL/min
  - Stage 5: <15 mL/min (**end-stage renal disease [ESRD]**)
- increased serum creatinine and BUN
- increased K^+ and decreased Ca^{2+}
- decreased HgB
- increased serum bicarbonate

Treatment and Management

- reverse initial cause of kidney injury
- sodium restriction and diuretics for hypervolemia

- sodium bicarbonate for acidosis
- ACE inhibitors or ARBs for hypertension
- erythropoietin for anemia
- renal replacement therapy (hemodialysis, peritoneal dialysis, or transplant)

QUICK REVIEW QUESTION

7. Why would diuretics be prescribed for a patient with CKD?

Electrolyte Imbalances

Imbalance	Clinical Manifestation	Treatment and Management	Etiology
Sodium (normal: 135 – 145 mEq/L)			
Hyponatremia	tachycardia, hypotension, weakness, dizziness, headache, abdominal cramping, cerebral edema, increased ICP	sodium replacement, ≤12 mEq/L/24 hr in a 24-hour period; PO sodium replacement as tolerated; isotonic IV solutions (lactated Ringers or 0.9% normal saline); restrict fluid intake and monitor fluid I/O	dilutional depletion of Na⁺; CHF; diarrhea; diaphoresis; use of thiazides
Hypernatremia	hypotension, tachycardia, polydipsia, lethargy or irritability, edema, warm, flushed skin, hyperreflexia, seizures	restrict dietary sodium; increase PO fluid or free-water intake; diuretics; D5W or other hypotonic IV solutions	sodium overload; volume depletion; impaired thirst; renal or GI loss; inability to replace fluid losses

continued on next page

TABLE 6.2. Electrolyte Imbalances (continued)

Imbalance	Clinical Manifestation	Treatment and Management	Etiology
Potassium (normal: 3.5 – 5 mEq/L)			
Hypokalemia	dysrhythmias • flat or inverted T waves • prominent U waves • ST depression • prolonged PR interval hypotension altered mental status leg cramps or muscle cramps hypoactive reflexes flaccid muscles	potassium replacement PO or IV • IV administration ≤20 mEq/hr • not to exceed 40 – 80 mEq/24 hr in a 24-hour period • stop infusion if urine output <30 mL/hr cardiac monitoring necessary presents with hypercalcemia	acid-base shifts alkalosis true depletion or deficits IV dextrose use diarrhea alcoholism Cushing's syndrome medications • steroids • diuretics • amphotericin • insulin
Hyperkalemia	dysrhythmias or cardiac arrest • tall, peaked T waves • prolonged PR interval • wide QRS complex • absent P waves • ST depression abdominal cramping and diarrhea anxiety	medication or IV solution, depending on severity of symptoms • calcium gluconate • IV insulin and D50 • loop diuretics • sodium polystyrene sulfonate • sodium bicarbonate • beta 2 agonists • hypertonic IV solution (3% normal saline) ECG and continued cardiac monitoring restrict PO intake of potassium-containing foods may require dialysis	increased intake of salt substitutes or potassium-sparing medications hemolysis, burns, crushing injury, or rhabdomyolysis decreased urine output

Imbalance	Clinical Manifestation	Treatment and Management	Etiology
Magnesium (normal: 1.3 – 2.1 mEq/L)			
Hypomagnesemia	dysrhythmias • torsades de pointes • flat or inverted T waves • ST depression • prolonged PR interval • widened QRS complex hypertension Chvostek sign Trousseau sign seizures hyperreflexia	magnesium sulfate IV, 1 – 2 g over 60 minutes monitor for seizures, dysrhythmias, and magnesium toxicity	excessive excretion (from GI tract or kidneys) diuretic use alcoholism
Hypermagnesemia	dysrhythmias or cardiac arrest • prolonged PR interval • wide QRS complex • peaked T waves bradycardia (more common) or tachycardia bradypnea respiratory paralysis altered mental status, lethargy, or coma	calcium gluconate loop diuretics isotonic IV solutions (lactated Ringers or 0.9% normal saline) may require dialysis	increased magnesium intake renal dysfunction hepatitis Addison's disease

TABLE 6.2. Electrolyte Imbalances (continued)

Imbalance	Clinical Manifestation	Treatment and Management	Etiology
Calcium (normal: 4.5 – 5.5 mEq/L)			
Hypocalcemia	dysrhythmias or cardiac arrest; prolonged QT interval; flattened ST segment; hypotension; third-space fluid shift; decreased clotting time; laryngeal spasm or bronchospasm; seizures; Chvostek sign; Trousseau sign; hyperactive deep-tendon reflexes	PO or IV calcium replacement; calcium gluconate, 10 – 20 mL, over 5 – 10 minutes; dilute IV solution with D5W only, never with normal saline; vitamin D supplements (to enhance absorption); seizure precautions	low serum proteins; decreased calcium intake; renal failure; hypoparathyroidism; vitamin D deficiency; pancreatitis; medications; calcitonin; steroids; loop diuretics
Hypercalcemia	anxiety; cognitive dysfunction; constipation; nausea/vomiting; shortened QT interval; muscle weakness	loop diuretics; isotonic IV solutions (0.9% normal saline); glucocorticoids and calcitonin	malignancies; hyperthyroidism and hyperparathyroidism; Paget's disease; medications; lithium; androgens; tamoxifen; excessive vitamin D; excessive thyroid replacement therapy

Imbalance	Clinical Manifestation	Treatment and Management	Etiology
Phosphate (normal: 1.8 – 2.3 mEq/L)			
Hypophosphatemia	respiratory distress or failure, tissue hypoxia, chest pain, seizures, decreased LOC, increased susceptibility to infection, nystagmus	PO or IV phosphate replacement, replace slowly if on TPN, seizure precautions	increased renal excretion
Hyperphosphatemia	tachycardia, Chvostek sign, Trousseau sign, hyperreflexia, soft-tissue calcifications	saline and loop diuretics, phosphate binders (e.g., aluminum hydroxide), limit dietary intake of phosphates, dialysis may be appropriate	decreased renal excretion

QUICK REVIEW QUESTION

8. A patient receiving enteral feedings has had severe diarrhea. The patient becomes irritable and is twitching. The nurse's assessment reveals the following vital signs: BP 92/53 mm Hg, HR 108 bpm, RR 20 breaths/min, and oral temperature 38.3°C (100.9°F). What condition should the nurse suspect?

Infections

- Urinary tract infections (UTIs) include **pyelonephritis** (infection of the kidney or upper urinary tract) and **cystitis** (infection of the bladder or lower urinary tract).
- Most UTIs in critical care settings are associated with urinary catheters (**catheter-associated urinary tract infection [CAUTI]**).
- Signs and symptoms of UTI include costovertebral pain, fever, and dysuria. Patients 65 years old may present with delirium.

- Signs and symptoms are often absent or nonspecific in ICU patients. Patients with catheters or an altered LOC may not be able to communicate signs or symptoms.
- UTIs are diagnosed via urinalysis and culture.
- Symptomatic UTIs (with fever or obstruction) should be treated with antibiotics.

QUICK REVIEW QUESTION

9. A patient in the ICU for a subdural hematoma has ICP monitoring in progress and is receiving mannitol. I/O of fluid is being strictly monitored with an indwelling Foley catheter for output collection. The patient's urine is cloudy and has a foul odor. What is the best action for the nurse to take?

_____

ANSWER KEY

1. The BUN-to-creatinine ratio increases because of hypovolemia. Urea is reabsorbed in the proximal tubules when reabsorption rates of water and sodium (to which urea is passively linked) are increased. Creatinine is not reabsorbed at the same rate. BUN levels are also increased by the breakdown of blood proteins in the GI tract.

2. The rapid removal of urea from the blood can lower plasma osmolality, which results in fluid shift to the intracellular space. For patients at risk for ICP, the resulting cerebral edema can cause neurological deterioration. While cerebral edema may occur with any type of dialysis, it is more common with intermittent dialysis.

3. Patients with kidney injury are at high risk for hemorrhage. The nurse should monitor for signs of bleeding (e.g., serial hematocrit) and shock (e.g., hypotension).

4. The patient is likely experiencing sepsis-induced prerenal disease. The nurse should ensure optimal perfusion through continued fluid replacement and titrating vasopressors to keep MAP 65 mm Hg. The physician should be notified if the patient does not respond with improving urine output.

5. These symptoms may indicate pulmonary edema. The nurse should immediately inform the physician and prepare the patient for hemodialysis.

6. In prerenal disease, the BUN-to-creatinine ratio will be 20:1. In postrenal disease, the ratio will be normal (10:1 – 20:1).

7. Diuretics are prescribed to manage conditions related to hypervolemia in patients with CKD; these conditions include PE and hypertension. Diuretics may also be used to lower K^+ levels (loop diuretics).

8. The patient's history and symptoms suggest hypernatremia, likely due to the dehydration associated with diarrhea and possibly insufficient free water administered with the enteral feedings.

9. The nurse should remove the Foley catheter, obtain a clean-catch urine sample, and monitor for fever and elevated WBCs. The physician should be notified for alternative output monitoring, such as weighing linens or an external female catheter.

INTEGUMENTARY REVIEW

CCRN TEST PLAN: INTEGUMENTARY
- Cellulitis
- IV infiltration
- Necrotizing fasciitis
- Pressure injury
- Wounds

Integumentary Interventions

- **Negative-pressure wound therapy (NPWT)** devices, also known as **vacuum-assisted wound closure (VACs)**, apply a controlled suction to the wound bed to promote healing.
    - Wound VACs promote healing by improving circulation to the wound bed, decreasing fluid in the wound bed, and promoting formation of granulation tissue.
    - Wound VACs are commonly used for wounds with high-volume drainage or that are high risk for infection, surgical wounds, burns, and chronic wounds (e.g., pressure ulcers).
    - Wound VACs should not be used on wounds with necrotic or cancerous tissue, exposed nerves or organs, or underlying coagulopathies.
- A **fecal management device** is a closed system that collects and contains liquid or semiliquid stools.
    - The goals of using a fecal management device are to prevent cross-contamination by virulent stool pathogens and to reduce the threat to skin integrity posed by diarrhea.

HELPFUL HINT:

Suction pressure that is too strong (less than −175 mm Hg) may reduce perfusion in the tissue under the wound and slow healing.

- Contraindications to use of fecal management devices include rectal/anal injury, bleeding, tumor, or stenosis; fecal impaction; recent large bowel surgery; and antithrombic therapy (requires caution).
- Potential adverse outcomes of fecal management include pressure necrosis, leakage of fecal material, and abdominal distension.

QUICK REVIEW QUESTION

1. A patient is 2 days post-op. The patient's left trochanter surgical site has high-volume drainage requiring application of NPWT to promote wound healing. While changing the dressing, the nurse notes purulent discharge and erythema at the wound site. What should the nurse do next?

Cellulitis

Pathophysiology

Cellulitis is a bacterial infection that has compromised the skin through to the hypodermis. The infection is caused by bacterial entry wounds in the skin. While it can develop anywhere on the body, the lower extremities are most commonly affected in adults.

The infection is usually localized at first but may quickly progress to sepsis if not treated promptly. Patient populations with chronic comorbidities such as diabetes, heart failure, and autoimmune diseases are more susceptible to serious complications.

Signs and Symptoms

- erythema, warmth, and tenderness at site
- lymphadenopathy of affected side
- fever

Diagnostic Findings

- elevated WBCs
- culture and sensitivity (most commonly group A *Streptococcus*)

Treatment and Management

- antibiotics
- debridement and drainage
- pain management

> **QUICK REVIEW QUESTION**
>
> 2. The nurse is conducting a skin assessment on a patient admitted with DKA. She notes a localized area of erythema on the left lower extremity that is warm and tender. The patient states that it started as a bug bite. How should the nurse manage this patient's risk for cellulitis?

IV Infiltration/Extravasation

Pathophysiology

IV infiltration is the infusion of fluids into the tissue around a venipuncture site. **Extravasation** is infiltration of a chemotherapeutic drug or vesicant fluid into the tissue around the venipuncture site. **Vesicants** can cause pain, tissue sloughing, loss of mobility in the surrounding areas, blisters, erythema, and infection. Mild symptoms of extravasation may appear immediately, but more serious symptoms may take days or weeks to develop.

Drugs classified as vesicants include:

- electrolyte solutions
- vasopressors
- antineoplastics
- most antibiotics (e.g., doxycycline, nafcillin, and vancomycin)
- radiocontrast infusions
- D10
- phenytoin

Signs and Symptoms

- immediate (at insertion site)
  - tingling, burning, or pruritus
  - swelling
- later (at insertion site)
  - erythema
  - pain
  - discoloration
  - blistering, ulceration, or necrosis

Treatment and Management

- Immediately stop infusion.
- Assess patency of IV ports to determine need for alternative IV access sites.
- Aspirate the infusing medication from the catheter until blood return and waste amount is achieved (hospital-specific policy).
- Flush catheter (hospital-specific protocol).

HELPFUL HINT:

Use of hyaluronidase for extravasations of parenteral nutrition and calcium chloride can be beneficial. Hyaluronidase should not be used for extravasation of vasoconstrictive agents.

QUICK REVIEW QUESTION

3. An intubated patient is hemodynamically stabilizing on a titrated infusion of norepinephrine, with propofol and fentanyl, via a triple-lumen internal jugular venous catheter. The nurse assesses an area of erythema and slight puffiness around the catheter insertion site and sees a scant amount of clear liquid pooling under the transparent dressing during palpation. What should the nurse do first?

Necrotizing Fasciitis

Pathophysiology

Necrotizing soft-tissue infections (NSTIs) are fast-spreading infections that cause soft tissue death. **Necrotizing fasciitis** is an NSTI that affects the muscle fascia and hypodermis. It may spread quickly without noticeable skin symptoms, making it difficult to diagnose. Patients with diabetes or compromised immune systems are at higher risk of NSTIs. Prompt treatment of necrotizing fasciitis is necessary to prevent tissue necrosis, amputation, or death.

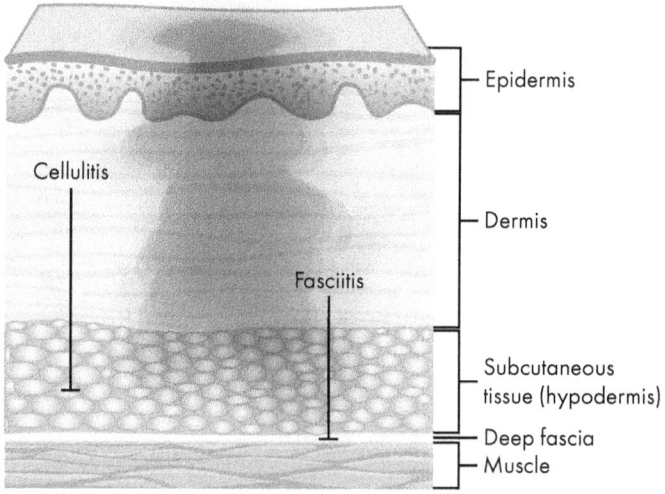

Figure 7.1. Cellulitis and Fasciitis

Signs and Symptoms

- erythema, warmth, and tenderness at site
- progression of necrosis on skin (red to blue to black)
- tingling or lack of sensation in affected area
- significant pain
- crepitus
- hematic or gas bullae
- fever
- sepsis

HELPFUL HINT:

Fournier gangrene is a necrotizing infection of the perineum. It is most common in patients with DM, and is a rare side effect of SGLT2 inhibitors.

Diagnostic Findings

- elevated WBCs

Treatment and Management

- prompt surgical exploration and debridement (should not be delayed for diagnostic labs)
- empiric administration of broad spectrum antibiotics
- IV fluids and vasopressors as needed to maintain hemodynamic stability
- pain management
- hyperbaric oxygen therapy

HELPFUL HINT:

During hyperbaric O_2 treatment, patients with history or increased risk of seizures are at a higher risk for repeat seizure.

> **QUICK REVIEW QUESTION**
>
> 4. An immunocompromised patient is recovering from a hemicolectomy in the ICU. Three days post-op, the nurse notes new areas of erythema and edema on both flanks. The patient is started on IV antibiotics, but the erythema continued to spread and the patient reports significant pain. Four days post-op, the patient presents with fever and decreased LOC, and wound crepitus is observed. What intervention should the nurse anticipate for this patient?

Pressure Injury

Pressure injuries (also known as pressure ulcers, decubitus ulcers, or bedsores) are wounds occurring secondary to tissue ischemia. Unrelieved pressure is the most common cause, with most wounds occurring over a bony prominence. Unrelieved pressure compromises the blood flow to the skin and underlying tissue, which deprives the tissue of oxygen and nutrients and limits waste removal. Pressure ulcers are described as stage 1 through stage 4. They can also be labeled as a deep-tissue injury or unstageable. (Staging of pressure ulcers is not tested on the CCRN.)

Treatment and Management

- Measures to prevent pressure ulcers include systematic position changes and use of positioning devices.
- Stage 1: Begin preventive measures, including repositioning and transparent film.
- Stage 2: Dress wound to maintain moist environment.
- Stages 3 and 4: Debride necrotic tissues (surgical or hydrogel dressing).
- Other interventions include NPWT and topical antibiotics.

> **QUICK REVIEW QUESTION**
>
> 5. An ICU patient is intubated 24 hours post-insertion of an IABP. During a skin assessment, the nurse notices a non-blanchable area of redness on the left heel of the patient. What should the nurse do next?

ANSWER KEY

1. The wound shows signs of infection, so the nurse should discontinue use of NPWT. The wound will need to be cleaned and a wound culture taken so that the patient can receive the appropriate antibiotics.

2. The nurse should note the patient's risk for cellulitis and document the wound size, shape, and location. The circumference of the area should be marked with a skin-safe pen to assess for progression. The physician should be notified, and the nurse should expect a culture and sensitivity and empiric antibiotics to be ordered while awaiting results.

3. The nurse should stop the IV infusions through the central IJ line and begin a quick assessment of each individual port for patency. A quick evaluation, per hospital policy, will indicate whether it is safe to restart vesicant infusions or whether the nurse needs to obtain other IV access. The results of these assessments and interventions can then be communicated to the physician.

4. The patient has symptoms of necrotizing fasciitis. The nurse should anticipate that the patient will undergo immediate surgical exploration and debridement.

5. A non-blanchable red area on the heel is likely a stage 1 pressure ulcer. Because the patient has an IABP and is intubated, they cannot be repositioned laterally. The nurse should use a positioning device, such as a pillow or heel lift device, to reduce pressure on the heel.

MUSCULOSKELETAL REVIEW

CCRN TEST PLAN: MUSCULOSKELETAL
- Compartment syndrome
- Fractures (e.g., femur, pelvic)
- Functional issues (e.g., immobility, falls, gait disorders)
- Osteomyelitis
- Rhabdomyolysis

Compartment Syndrome

Pathophysiology

Compartment syndrome is the result of increased intracompartmental pressure, usually due to a fracture or crush injury. When the increased pressure in the closed compartment exceeds the pressure of perfusion, blood circulation is impaired, resulting in ischemia of the nerves and muscle tissue. Oxygen deficiency and the buildup of waste irritate the nerves, resulting in pain and a decrease in sensation. As ischemia progresses, muscles become necrotic, which can lead to rhabdomyolysis, hyperkalemia, and infection if left untreated.

HELPFUL HINT:

The most common cause of compartment syndrome is extremity fractures.

Signs and Symptoms

- the 6 Ps
    - pain (not proportional to injury and does not respond to opioid medications)
    - paresthesia
    - pallor

- paralysis
- pulselessness
- poikilothermia
- decreased urine output
- hypotension
- tissue tight on palpation
- edema with tight, shiny skin
- intracompartmental pressure 30 mm Hg or within 20 to 30 mm Hg of MAP

Treatment and Management

- Remove casts or dressings to relieve pressure.
- Push IV fluids to maintain urine output >30 cc/hr.
- If intracompartmental pressure >30 mm Hg, prepare patient for fasciotomy.
- If intracompartmental pressure is 10 – 30 mm Hg, monitor pressure and hemodynamic status.

> **QUICK REVIEW QUESTION**
>
> 1. A patient admitted to the ICU following an MVC has a cast on their right wrist for a Salter-Harris fracture. The patient reports acute onset of paresthesia and pain in the distal fingers. The nurse observes pallor in the extremities and is unable to obtain a radial pulse. What should the nurse do first?

Fractures

- While most fractures are uncomplicated and may be treated in an acute care setting, traumatic fractures of the pelvis or femur are often managed in the ICU. These fractures require complex stabilization and place patients at high risk of complications, including internal hemorrhage, organ perforation, hematoma formation, and lipid embolisms.
- Acute care for both pelvic and femur fractures focuses on hemodynamic stabilization and surgical stabilization of the fracture.
- **Pelvic fractures** are caused by high-energy trauma (e.g., MVC) and usually occur alongside injuries to the chest, abdomen, or vertebral column.
    - Pelvic fractures are classified by the location of the fracture. Patients with unstable pelvic ring fractures (fractures that disrupt

the integrity of the pelvic ring) are at the highest risk for complications.

- Patients with pelvic fractures (particularly open fractures) are at high risk of hemorrhage from venous or arterial bleeding, which is the most common cause of mortality related to pelvic fractures.

HELPFUL HINT:

Patients with pelvic fractures should be closely monitored for signs and symptoms of retroperitoneal bleeding.

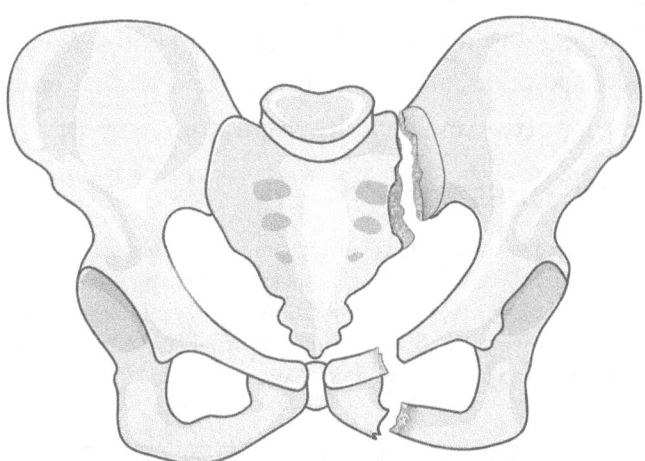

Figure 8.1. Example of an Unstable Pelvic Ring Fracture (Vertical Shear Injury)

- Soft tissue injuries that may accompany pelvic fractures include ruptured bladder, perforation of abdominal organs, and lacerations of the reproductive organs.
- Diagnostic imaging may include pelvic X-rays, pelvic CT scan, pelvic angiogram (when patient has an unstable pelvic ring with ongoing hemorrhage), cystogram (for suspected urinary bladder injury), or retrograde urethrogram (for suspected urethral tears).
- Perforation of the GI tract places the patient at high risk for infection and sepsis, the second most common cause of mortality related to pelvic fractures. Patients may require a temporary colostomy or ileostomy to prevent wound contamination.
- Immobility and hemodynamic disruption in the lower extremities create a high risk of DVT.
- Postoperative care includes hemodynamic monitoring, aggressive DVT prophylaxis, pain management, and care for related injuries.

- **Femur fractures** may be caused by high-energy trauma (e.g., MVC) in young patients, or by low-energy trauma (e.g., falls) in patients 65 years old. Life-threatening complications of femur fractures include hemorrhage, compartment syndrome, fat embolism syndrome, and respiratory distress (ARDS caused by fat embolism or PE).
- **Fat embolism syndrome (FES)** is caused by fat in the pulmonary circulatory system.

- A cardinal cutaneous sign of fat emboli is reddish-brown non-palpable petechiae that appear over the upper body (particularly in the axilla region) 24 – 36 hours after the trauma event.
- Other symptoms include hypoxemia, dyspnea, altered mental status/decreased LOC, and fever.
- The development of progressive altered mental status, restlessness, confusion, seizures, and coma indicate cerebral fat emboli.
- Care is supportive and includes respiratory support and IV fluids.

QUICK REVIEW QUESTION

2. A 28-year-old patient has been receiving supportive care for a closed femur fracture caused by an MVC. After being hemodynamically stable with a GCS of 15 for two days post-injury, the patient is now unable to follow commands. His vital signs are: HR 122 bpm, RR 30, temperature 101°F (38.5°C). What condition should the nurse suspect, and how will it be diagnosed?

Functional Issues

Falls and Gait Disorders

Falls are less common in critical care environments than in acute care settings, but the critical care nurse should be active in fall prevention. Patients should be assessed for fall risk and appropriate precautions put in place. Common risk factors in critical care settings include:

- altered LOC
- agitation or delirium
- medications (particularly analgesics, sedatives, and antipsychotics)

Gait disorders affect patients' ability to walk; they may be neurological or non-neurological. Common causes of gait disorders in critical care settings include stroke, dementia, encephalopathy, injury or infection in limbs, and chronic neurological disorders (e.g., Parkinson's disease).

Treatment and Management

- Assess patients' fall risk each shift with a screening tool (e.g., Morse Fall Scale, Johns Hopkins Fall Risk Assessment Tool).
- Universal fall precautions are designed to provide a safe environment for all patients.

- ☐ Always place nonslip footwear or socks on patients before ambulating or transferring.
- ☐ Keep environment free from fall hazards (e.g., cords or other items that could trip the patient).
- ☐ Ensure patient's call light and personal possessions are within reach.
- ☐ Lower bed to lowest setting and leave bed rails up.
- Moderate and high fall risk precautions should be tailored to individual patients.
    - ☐ Consult physical therapy to collaborate on early mobilization plans.
    - ☐ Encourage use of mobility aids like gait belts, walkers, etc.
    - ☐ Use chair and bed alarms.
    - ☐ Consider using a patient safety companion for confused patients.
    - ☐ Consider restraints only as the last option.

QUICK REVIEW QUESTION

3. A patient who is normally independent at home has gait issues and is deemed a moderate fall risk. What fall precautions should the nurse put in place?

HELPFUL HINT:

Neuromuscular weakness in ICU patients is sometimes referred to as **ICU-acquired weakness**, particularly when there is no obvious underlying cause for the weakness.

IMMOBILITY

Immobility is common in critical care settings and can have negative short- and long-term effects on patient health. Possible side effects of prolonged immobilization include pressure ulcers, muscle atrophy, bone demineralization, and reduced respiratory and cardiac function. Mitigating these side effects during critical care can prevent future complications and shorten recovery time.

Nursing Interventions

- Regularly assess ROM and strength.
- Assess nutritional needs.
- Implement DVT prevention measures.
- Maintain skin integrity.
- Mobilize patient as early as possible.
    - ☐ Use the minimum sedation necessary.
    - ☐ Limit use of neuromuscular blockers.
    - ☐ Collaborate with PT for passive and active ROM exercises.
    - ☐ Encourage patient to participate in their own care as much as they can.

> **QUICK REVIEW QUESTION**
>
> 4. How can a nurse alleviate the effects of immobility on a patient who is vented and sedated?

OSTEOMYELITIS

Pathophysiology

Osteomyelitis is an infection in bone, most commonly caused by *Staphylococcus aureus*. Non-hematogenous osteomyelitis is the result of infection from adjacent tissues or penetrating injuries; hematogenous osteomyelitis is a result of bacteremia. In adults it is most common in the spine, but may affect other areas such as the clavicle, pelvis, or long bones.

Signs and Symptoms

- signs and symptoms of local infection
- musculoskeletal pain
- fever

Diagnostic Findings

- MRI or CT scan
- positive blood culture or culture of bone biopsy

Treatment and Management

- surgical debridement
- IV antibiotics

> **QUICK REVIEW QUESTION**
>
> 5. A patient is admitted to the ICU with bacteremia and sepsis with an unknown cause of infection. The health history reveals that the patient suffers from chronic back pain and has recently received an epidural steroid injection. What diagnostic tests should the nurse anticipate?

Rhabdomyolysis

Pathophysiology

Rhabdomyolysis is muscle necrosis that leads to the release of intracellular components into circulation, including CK, electrolytes, and myoglobin. The resulting serum abnormalities result in organ dysfunction, particularly AKI.

Etiology

- trauma (crush or compartment syndrome)
- sepsis
- cardiac or vascular surgery
- alcohol or drug use

Signs and Symptoms

- myoglobinuria (red-brown urine)
- myalgia
- muscle weakness

Diagnostic Findings

- elevated CK (>5x normal levels)
- urinary myoglobin >250 mcg/mL
- hyperuricemia
- electrolyte abnormalities (hyperkalemia, hypo- or hypercalcemia, hyperphosphatemia)

Treatment and Management

- IV fluids
- correct electrolyte imbalances
- treat underlying condition

> **QUICK REVIEW QUESTION**
>
> 6. The nurse is reviewing labs from a patient who is 2 days post-op of mitral valve repair. The chemistry panel returns with CK 1200 IU/L, myoglobulin 390 mcg/mL, and K+ 6.8. What treatment would be expected for this patient?

ANSWER KEY

1. Remove the cast as soon as possible and reassess circulation, sensation, movement, and neurovascular status. If compartment syndrome is suspected, prepare for emergent fasciotomy or surgery.

2. The patient has signs and symptoms of FES. FES is a clinical diagnosis, so the nurse should assess for other symptoms (e.g., petechial rash) and anticipate a CXR to rule out a PE.

3. The nurse should assess the patient to determine if a mobility device should be used, provide the patient with nonslip footwear and encourage their use whenever the patient is out of bed, ensure the environment is free from fall hazards, and provide stand-by assistance as needed. The nurse should ensure the call light is within reach and encourage the patient to use it rather than getting out of bed.

4. The nurse should determine the patient's prior status and assess their current strength and flexibility. A care plan should incorporate measures to maintain skin integrity and maintain or improve flexibility through passive and active ROM exercises. It should also include collaboration with nutritional services to ensure an optimal diet. The nurse should discuss DVT risk with the interdisciplinary team and use anticoagulation devices and administer medications as ordered.

5. The nurse should suspect osteomyelitis caused by introduction of bacteria to the spine via epidural spinal injections. An MRI or CT scan will be ordered. If imaging shows osteomyelitis, a bone biopsy may be performed to identify the pathogen.

6. The patient is experiencing rhabdomyolysis, which is affecting the efficacy of the kidneys. The nurse can expect to provide supportive care through IV fluid administration and hemodialysis to correct the critical value of potassium.

NEUROLOGY REVIEW

CCRN TEST PLAN: NEUROLOGY

- Acute spinal cord injury
- Brain death
- Delirium (e.g., hyperactive, hypoactive, mixed)
- Dementia
- Encephalopathy
- Hemorrhage
- Increased intracranial pressure (ICP) (e.g., hydrocephalus)
- Neurological infectious disease (e.g., viral, bacterial, fungal)
- Neuromuscular disorders (e.g., muscular dystrophy, cerebral palsy [CP], Guillain-Barré syndrome, myasthenia)
- Neurosurgery (e.g., craniotomy, Burr holes)
- Seizure disorders
- Space-occupying lesions (e.g., brain tumors)
- Stroke
- Traumatic brain injury (TBI): epidural, subdural, concussion

Neurological Anatomy, Physiology, and Assessment

Brain Anatomy and Physiology

- Blood supply to the brain comes by two arterial sources: the internal carotid artery and the vertebral arteries.

> **HELPFUL HINT:**
>
> "Time is brain" is a guiding principle in critical care neurology. The sooner care is initiated, the more brain function can be preserved.

- The **internal carotid artery** branches off from the subclavian artery and divides into the middle cerebral artery (MCA), the anterior cerebral artery (ACA), and the posterior cerebral artery (PCA). Together, these arteries provide 80% of blood to the brain.
- The **vertebral arteries** come up through the brainstem area and fuse together to form the basilar artery just below the pons. In the midbrain area, the basilar artery merges into the posterior cerebral arteries. The vertebral arteries supply blood to the spinal cord, cerebellum, and brainstem.

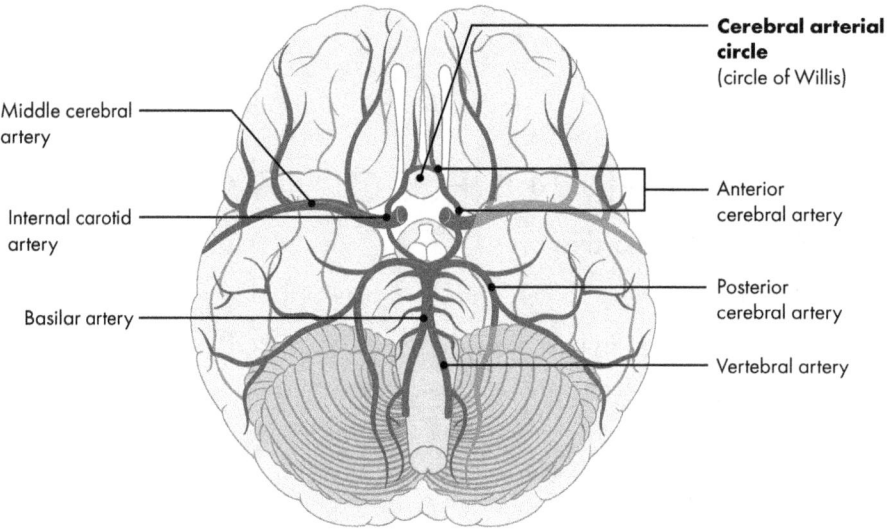

Figure 9.1. Vasculature in the Brain

- Blockage in any of these arteries causes intense temporary or permanent damage to each area of the brain they supply.
- Each area of the brain has specific functions that are affected by localized tissue damage.
  - frontal lobe: thinking, speaking, movement, memory
  - parietal lobe: touch, language
  - temporal lobe: emotions, hearing, learning
  - occipital lobe: vision, color perception
  - cerebellum: balance, coordination
  - brainstem: breathing, heart rate, temperature regulation
  - thalamus: sleep, alertness, sensory processing
- The cerebrum and thalamus have 2 hemispheres, the right and left. Each hemisphere controls movement and sensory processing on the contralateral side of the body.
- **Cerebral spinal fluid (CSF)** is a clear, colorless fluid that circulates around the brain and spinal cord.

- CSF cushions the brain and transports nutrients and waste.
- The normal volume of CSF is 125 – 150 mL.
- CSF is produced and circulated by 4 **ventricles** in the brain. The 2 lateral ventricles are found in the 2 cerebral hemispheres; the third ventricle is located midline between the thalami; and the fourth ventricle is surrounded by the pons and medulla oblongata.
- Fluid drains from the fourth ventricle into the subarachnoid space and the spinal cord.

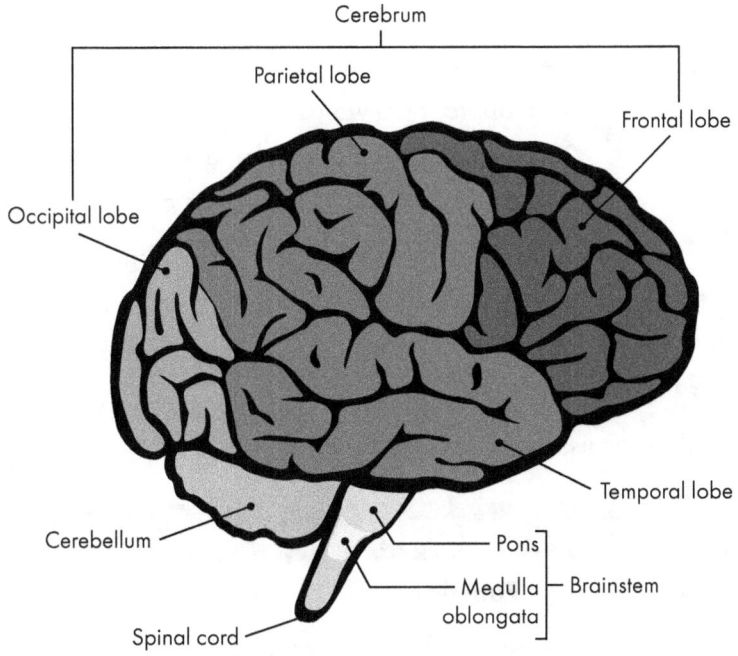

Figure 9.2. Areas of the Brain

QUICK REVIEW QUESTION

1. What type of focal neurological deficits would indicate likely damage to the occipital lobe?

Nursing Neurological Assessment

- Neurological assessment should be done continuously to obtain baseline data and to assess for neurological deterioration or improvements related to treatment.
    - level of consciousness (LOC): earliest indication of neurological deterioration
    - pupillary response: late indication of neurological deterioration
    - mental status

- motor function
- sensation/touch perception
- vision changes
- speech changes
- Glasgow Coma Scale (GCS) (Table 9.1)

TABLE 9.1. Scoring on the Glasgow Coma Scale

Eye Opening (E)	Verbal Response (V)	Motor Response (M)
4 = spontaneous 3 = to sound 2 = to pressure 1 = none	5 = oriented 4 = confused 3 = inappropriate words 2 = incomprehensible sounds 1 = no response	6 = obeys command 5 = localizes 4 = normal flexion 3 = abnormal flexion 2 = extension 1 = none

15: fully awake
<8: severe brain injury
3: coma or death

- cranial nerve assessment (Table 9.2)

TABLE 9.2. Cranial Nerve Function and Assessment

Cranial Nerve	Function
I. Olfactory	sense of smell
II. Optic	central and peripheral vision
III. Oculomotor	constriction of pupils
IV. Trochlear	downward eye movement
V. Trigeminal	facial sensation and motor control of mouth
VI. Abducens	sideways eye movement
VII. Facial	movement and expression
VIII. Vestibulocochlear	hearing and balance
IX. Glossopharyngeal	tongue and throat
X. Vagus	sensory and motor
XI. Accessory	head and shoulder movement
XII. Hypoglossal	tongue position

Other Cranial Nerve Assessments

Doll's eyes reflex	assessment of oculocephalic function (cranial nerves III, IV, VI) in an unconscious patient: **normal** (both eyes roll/move to opposite side of head position) **abnormal** (eyes roll/move in opposite directions of each other): indicates a brainstem injury **absent** (eyes remain midline/move with head position): indicates significant brainstem injury
Consensual response	assessment of CN II and III: constriction of pupil when light shined into opposite eye

- postural indicators of brain damage
    - **decorticate** (patient brings arms to the CORE of the body): damage to cerebral hemispheres (CORtex)
    - **decerebrate** (extended position): ominous sign of brainstem damage and possible brain herniation

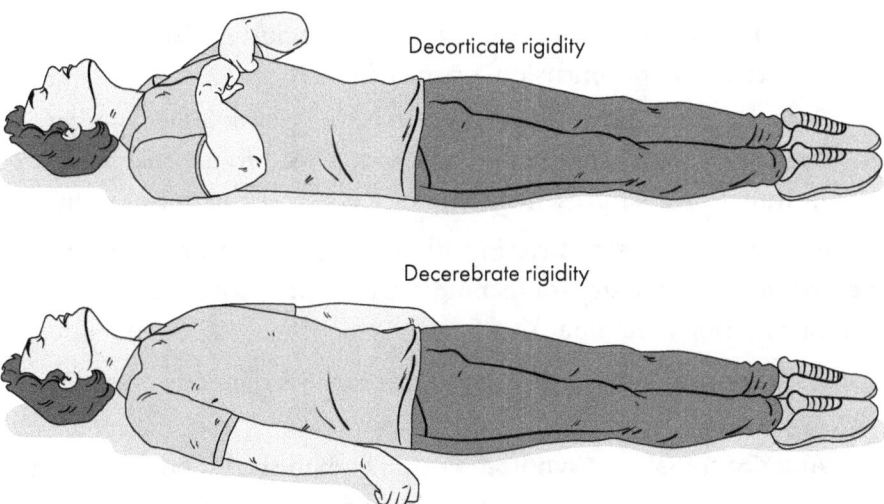

Figure 9.3. Decorticate and Decerebrate Postures

- medical signs of possible brain damage
    - **Kernig's sign** (indicator of meningitis): patient in supine position with the hips and knees flexed, unable to straighten leg due to hamstring pain
    - **Brudzinski's sign** (indicator of meningitis): passive flexion of the neck elicits automatic flexion at the hips and knees
    - **nuchal rigidity** (indicator of meningitis): inability to place the chin on the chest (neck flexion) due to muscle stiffness

- □ **Babinski sign** (indicator of damage to corticospinal tract): a single, firm stroking of the sole of the foot from the heel to toes causes big toe to point up and toes to fan out
- **Cushing's triad** is a late, ominous sign of increased ICP and possible brain herniation.
  - □ widening pulse pressure (elevated SBP and decreased DBP)
  - □ bradycardia
  - □ decreased/abnormal RR (Cheyne-Stokes respiration)

> **QUICK REVIEW QUESTION**
>
> 2. A patient is being assessed with the GCS. There is a slight reaction to pressure, incoherent verbal responses, and decorticate positioning. What would the GCS result be, and what does it indicate?

Acute Spinal Cord Injuries

- **Spinal cord injuries (SCIs)** are injuries to the vertebral column.
  - □ The **primary injury** is caused by trauma, including compression, hyperextension, contusion, or shearing.
  - □ **Secondary injuries** are caused by resulting physiological processes such as hypoxia and ischemia; they may lead to neurological dysfunction that presents hours or days after the initial trauma.
- SCIs may be **complete** (meaning all sensory and motor function is lost below the level of injury) or **incomplete** (meaning some sensory and motor function is retained).
- The location and severity of sensory/motor loss depends on the type of injury.
  - □ **Anterior spinal cord syndrome** occurs when the blood flow to the anterior spinal artery is disrupted, resulting in ischemia in the spinal cord and complete loss of motor and sensory function below the lesion.
  - □ **Brown-Séquard syndrome** is an SCI caused by complete cord hemitransection, typically at the cervical level. Symptoms include ipsilateral motor loss below the lesion and contralateral loss of sensation of pain and temperature.
  - □ **Cauda equina syndrome** is an SCI typically caused by compression of, or damage to, the cauda equina, the nerve bundle that innervates the lower limbs and pelvic organs, most notably the bladder. Symptoms include sensory loss in the lower extremities, bowel and

bladder dysfunction, numbness in saddle area, and loss of reflexes in upper extremities.
- **Central cord syndrome** is caused by spinal cord compression and edema, both of which cause the lateral corticospinal tract white matter to deteriorate. Symptoms include greater motor function loss in the upper extremities than in the lower extremities and paresthesia in the upper extremities.
- Assessment of SCIs: anteroposterior and lateral spinal cord X-rays (to assess lesions), CT of cervical spine and top of T1 (to rule out cervicothoracic junction injury), initial/ongoing spinal cord assessment (American Spinal Injury Association [ASIA] exam)
- Respiratory compromise due to SCI is determined by lesion level.

TABLE 9.3. Respiratory Compromise in SCIs

Level of Lesion	Description
C1 or C2 (high cervical lesions)	vital capacity 5% – 10% of normal cough absent ventilator dependent
C3 – C6	vital capacity 20% of normal ineffective cough variable ventilator support/weaning ability
T2 – T4 (high thoracic lesions)	vital capacity 30% – 50% of normal cough weak compromised respiratory function
Below T4 – T10	vital capacity 50% of normal respiratory function improved
T11	vital capacity normal cough strong minimal respiratory dysfunction

- Management of SCIs
    - goals of management: prevent life-threatening complications, maximize organ system functions, prevent secondary spinal cord damage, and address neurological deficits
    - immediate spinal cord stabilization (tongs, halo traction braces, kinetic therapy beds, body casts)
    - methylprednisolone IV (bolus followed by 24 – 48 hour infusion)
    - monitor for, and treat, cardiac and respiratory complications (both common in SCIs)

> **HELPFUL HINT:**
>
> The use of methylprednisolone following SCI remains controversial because of the high risk of infection in already compromised, sepsis-prone trauma patients.

> **HELPFUL HINT:**
>
> **Spinal shock** refers to depressed or absent reflexes that result from SCIs. It is not related to the circulatory system.

- temperature stabilization
- urinary catheterization (to avoid bladder distension)

- **Neurogenic shock** is a form of distributive shock caused by an injury or trauma to the spinal cord, typically above T6. The injury causes a decrease in sympathetic tone, leading to vasodilation and rapid onset of hypotension. The resulting decrease in SVR causes blood to pool in the lower extremities, and cardiac output is greatly reduced. Bradycardia occurs because of unopposed vagal tone exacerbated by hypoxia and suctioning (common in spinal injury patients). Unless rapidly recognized and treated, multisystem organ failure occurs with a very high mortality. This shock state may persist for more than a month from injury event.
    - Symptoms: rapid onset of hypotension, bradycardia, hypothermia; wide pulse pressure; skin warm, flushed, and dry; priapism
    - Management: IV fluids (first line); vasopressors/inotropes (second line); atropine or isoproterenol (for bradycardia)

- **Autonomic dysreflexia** is the overstimulation of the autonomic nervous system after SCIs above the T6 level. A sympathetic stimulation to the lower portion of the body leads to vasoconstriction below the area of injury and vasodilation above the injury, resulting in bradycardia and hypertension. If left untreated, cardiac status quickly deteriorates, and MI or stroke may occur.
    - Symptoms: flushing and sweating above the level of injury; cold, clammy skin below the level of injury; bradycardia; sudden, severe headache; hypertension
    - Management: anti-hypertensives; elevate HOB to 90°; have patient empty bladder and bowel; remove tight, restrictive clothing

QUICK REVIEW QUESTION

3. A 25-year-old patient was brought into the ED after a 20-foot fall at a construction site. Spinal immobilization was performed in the field. The patient was intubated in the ED, and a primary assessment showed HR 59 bpm, BP 84/50 mm Hg, SaO_2 95%, GCS 6, and no other abnormalities. Secondary assessment showed diffuse abrasions over the back, torso, and extremities, but no abdominal ecchymosis or distension, pelvic instability, or extremity deformities. The patient arrives in the spinal cord ICU post-CT with a suspected partial lesion of the spinal cord at T2. What initial treatment plan would the CCRN expect to implement?

Brain Death

- **Brain death** is the irreversible cessation of all brain functions, including brainstem function. It is determined based on the American Academy of Neurology's clinical diagnosis guidelines, although US state and hospital policies vary.
- To declare brain death, the cause and irreversibility of the coma must be confirmed after all factors that might influence the results have been removed.
- Confirmation of management or absence of confounding conditions includes the following:
  - absence of hypotension: SBP >90 mm Hg; patient may be on vasopressors
  - absence of severe hypothermia (i.e., core temperature >32°C)
  - sedation, opioids, analgesics, intoxicants, and poisons cleared from system
  - absence of recent/current neuromuscular blockade (NMB): 4 twitches with maximal ulnar nerve stimulation by train-of-four peripheral nerve stimulator
  - absence of acid-base, endocrine, or electrolyte dysfunction
- The bedside exam includes the following components:
  - absence of cerebral motor reflexes (note that motor responses seen during apnea testing are considered spinal cord reflexes)
  - absence of brainstem reflexes (oculocephalic reflex, oculovestibular reflex, gag reflex, cough reflex, pupillary response, corneal reflex)
  - absence of respiratory drive (positive apnea test)
- Apnea test conducted to assess respiratory drive:
  - pulse oximeter on with 100% O_2 and 10-minute preoxygenation
  - reduce PEEP to 5 cm H_2O, and reduce vent rate to 10 breaths/minute
  - if O_2 saturation >90%, obtain ABG for baseline
  - disconnect ventilator, and insert insufflation catheter via ETT at level of carina
  - deliver 100% O_2 at 6 L/min flow
  - observe for spontaneous respiratory efforts over 8 – 10 minutes; monitor for abdominal or chest movements that produce adequate tidal volumes
  - abort test if SBP drops <90 mm Hg and if drop continues despite increasing vasopressor dose
  - abort test if O_2 saturation is <80% for >30 seconds

HELPFUL HINT:

Additional tests for confirming brain death include an EEG, somatosensory evoked potential (SSEP), and a cerebral perfusion evaluation (MRI, CT scan, or transcranial Doppler).

- if no respiratory drive seen, obtain ABG after 8 minutes
- if respiratory movements are absent and arterial pCO_2 is ≥ 60 mm Hg or if there is a 20 mm Hg increase in arterial pCO_2 over baseline, the apnea test result is positive (supports the clinical diagnosis of brain death)
- if patient breathes or gasps during test, return to pretest ventilator status and repeat apnea test in a few hours

QUICK REVIEW QUESTION

4. During an apnea test to determine brain death, the patient's BP decreases to 87/55 mm Hg. Norepinephrine is increased to maintain SBP >90. The BP continues to decrease, with the next reading at 78/52. What action should the nurse expect to take next?

Delirium

Delirium, an acute cognitive change from baseline, affects up to 80% of patients hospitalized in ICUs. The patient exhibits confusion and disorientation, with a decreased ability to focus and converse coherently. The delirium may be categorized as hypoactive, hyperactive, or mixed (with characteristics of both). Delirium is a common complication of underlying disease processes (e.g., pneumonia), particularly in the elderly. It may also be trigged by physiological conditions such as pain, fever, intoxication, sleep deprivation, severe burns or trauma, and idiosyncratic response to medications.

HELPFUL HINT:

Pain management is the first-line consideration in preventing delirium, especially in elderly at-risk patients.

Signs and Symptoms

- hypoactive
  - listless and lethargic
  - decreased response or nonresponsive
  - flat affect and slowed speech
- hyperactive
  - combative, agitated, or restless
  - unable to follow commands
  - repeatedly attempts to leave the bed, room, or hospital
  - labile moods

Treatment and Management

- assess for delirium every shift and whenever cognitive changes are observed, using cognitive assessment tools
    - Confusion Assessment Method for the ICU (CAM-ICU)
    - Intensive Care Delirium Screening Checklist (ICDSC)
    - Richmond Agitation-Sedation Scale (RASS)
- identify and treat underlying cause (THINK)
    - toxins
    - hypoxemia
    - infection
    - non-pharmacologic intervention (e.g., remove any unnecessary lines or tubes, reduce use or remove restraints)
    - K^+ (electrolyte imbalances)
- reduce number of medications
    - decrease sedative use and limit benzodiazepines
    - dexmedetomidine (Precedex) has a lower delirium risk than benzodiazepines
- nonpharmacological methods for preventing delirium
    - treating pain
    - maintaining routines and sleep schedule
    - introducing nutrition as soon as tolerated
    - refraining from use of restraints, if possible
    - discouraging the use of unnecessary equipment, tubing, and catheters
    - securing and concealing necessary lines
    - avoiding excessive environmental noise and clutter
    - providing cognitive stimulation (e.g., talking to patient during care)
    - increasing patient's mobility (passive range of motion progressing to baseline ability)

QUICK REVIEW QUESTION

5. An 88-year-old patient was admitted to the ICU with pneumonia and respiratory failure, requiring noninvasive positive-pressure ventilation. Over the past 2 days, the patient has become increasingly withdrawn and confused and is currently responding listlessly and incoherently to the nurse's questions. What interventions are appropriate to include in the care plan?

Dementia

Dementia is a broad term for progressive, cognitively debilitating symptoms that interfere with independent functioning. Patients may show decline in one or more cognitive domains, including language, memory, executive function, motor skills, and social cognition.

Etiology

- Alzheimer's disease (most common form of dementia in older adults)
- vascular dementia (from stroke)
- Lewy body dementia
- frontal temporal dementia
- other dementias (e.g., Huntington's disease, Parkinson's disease)
- mixed (multiple causes)

Treatment and Management

- Assess for dementia using the **mini-mental state exam (MMSE)**. A score less than 24 indicates dementia.
- Unless dementia is caused by a treatable disease process, its progression can be slowed but not cured.
  - antidementia medications: cholinesterase inhibitors (e.g., donepezil) and memantine
  - other medication, including antidepressants and analgesics, to help manage symptoms

> **QUICK REVIEW QUESTION**
>
> 6. A patient in the ICU was recently diagnosed with Alzheimer's disease and began taking donepezil. The patient's spouse asks why the patient has not improved since starting the medication. How should the nurse respond?

Encephalopathy

Anoxic encephalopathy (hypoxic-ischemic brain injury) is a process that begins when **cerebral blood flow (CBF)** stops, resulting in global brain ischemia. In a hypoxic brain injury, restricted oxygen supply to the brain tissue causes the gradual death of brain cells; anoxic brain injuries lead to death of brain cells after 4 minutes without oxygen.

"Watershed" areas of injury (the destruction of cerebral white matter) affect significant parts of the brain and cause motor and sensory disturbances of varying severity. Major brain injury also occurs during reperfusion.

Etiology

- vascular injury
- poisoning (e.g., drug overdose, carbon monoxide)
- drowning
- cardiac or respiratory arrest
- shock
- severe asthma event
- suffocation/strangulation
- electric shock

Signs and Symptoms

- confusion or delirium
- altered LOC (diminished arousal/awareness, coma, or vegetative state)
- sensory impairment
    - eye movement deficit (CN III, IV, and VI)
    - changes in pupil size, shape, or reaction to light
    - impaired consensual response (CN II and III)
    - impaired equilibrium and hearing (CN VIII)
- motor impairment (muscle weakness, paraplegia, or quadriplegia)
- tremor, myoclonus, or asterixis
- recurrent partial or myoclonic seizures

Treatment and Management

- primary treatment goal: prevention of further neurological damage and management of symptoms
- monitor ICP and fluid balance
- manage risk for falls, aspiration, infection, and gastric ulcers
- provide nutritional support

HELPFUL HINT:

Targeted temperature management (therapeutic hypothermia) is used for post-cardiac-arrest patients to prevent neurological damage. Patients should have their core temperature kept at 32 – 36°C for at least 24 hours after resuscitation.

QUICK REVIEW QUESTION

7. A patient is brought into the ED unresponsive after a suicide attempt via hanging. The patient is intubated, vented, and stabilized. What nursing interventions are important for this patient when they are admitted to the ICU?

Increased Intracranial Pressure

Intracranial pressure (ICP) is the pressure within the intracranial compartment (the area enclosed by the cranium). A normal adult cranium encloses a fixed volume of around 1500 mL divided between brain tissue (80% of volume), CSF (10%), and blood (10%). Since the cranium does not expand or otherwise move, insults to brain tissue that increase intracranial volume will increase ICP. **Intracranial compliance** is the change in volume over the change in pressure. When the brain's compensation mechanisms fail, intracranial compliance is reduced, and even small changes in volume can produce large changes in ICP.

When ICP increases, immediate interventions must be implemented to maintain **cerebral perfusion pressure (CPP)**, the net pressure gradient that drives oxygen delivery to brain tissue. Increased ICP may also cause brain tissue to herniate downward through the tentorial notch and foramen magnum into the brainstem; herniation is rapidly fatal.

Normal ICP is 5 – 15 mm Hg. An ICP >20 mm Hg is a neurological emergency that requires immediate treatment. CPP is defined as the difference between MAP and ICP (i.e., MAP – ICP), and should be maintained at 50 – 70 mm Hg. ICP monitoring is always recommended for:

- large-territory acute ischemic stroke
- head injuries with a GCS score <8
- cerebral edema
- hydrocephalus
- when early recognition of ICP changes is needed

Several options are available for ICP monitoring:

- An **external ventricular drain (EVD)** or **intraventricular catheter** is the gold standard for continuous direct measurement of dynamic ICP.
    - the most invasive technique, with the catheter placed into ventricle of nondominant hemisphere
    - device both monitors ICP and drains CSF
    - transducer is placed at level of foramen of Monro
    - high risk for infection and CSF leakage at insertion site
- A subarachnoid "bolt" with intraparenchymal catheter provides subarachnoid access and fixation without penetration of brain tissue.
- Noninvasive monitoring may be done with a transcranial Doppler study (TCD), transcranial color-coded duplex sonography (TCCS), or a handheld infrared pupillometer, which provides a neurological pupil index (NPi).

HELPFUL HINT:

The **Monro-Kellie Doctrine**: The total volume of brain tissue, CSF, and blood in the cranium is constant. An increase in the volume of one of the three elements should cause a decrease in one or both of the others. If not, ICP will increase.

HELPFUL HINT:

An elevated tidal wave (P2) in an ICP waveform indicates reduced intracranial compliance.

- Under normal physiologic conditions, the ICP waveform has three peaks: P1 (percussion wave), P2 (tidal wave), and P3 (dicrotic wave or notch) with descending heights.
  - An elevated tidal wave (P2) indicates reduced intracranial compliance and increased ICP.
  - A single wave with a lack of distinct peaks indicates a critical increase in ICP that requires immediate intervention.

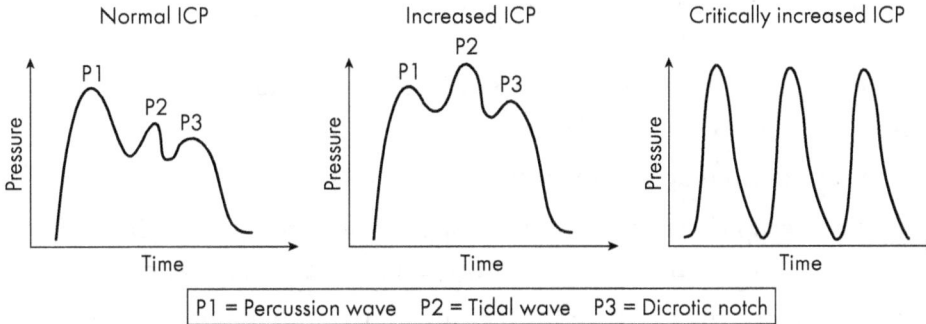

Figure 9.4. ICP Waveform

Etiology

- trauma (TBI, brain contusion)
- mass displacement of brain tissue by tumor, hematoma, or abscess
- hypoxic-ischemic brain injury
- intracranial hemorrhage
- increased CSF production (meningitis)
- blockages to CSF flow/reabsorption (hydrocephalus, meningeal disease)
- seizures
- hyperthermia (core temperature >37.5°C)

Signs and Symptoms

- change in LOC
- headache
- vomiting
- Cushing's triad
- irritability
- photophobia
- lethargy and impaired/slowed decision-making

HELPFUL HINT:

Hypoxia in brain tissue leads to edema and arterial vasodilation, both of which increase ICP. Hypercapnia may also increase ICP by increasing blood flow to the brain and reducing venous return.

Diagnostic Findings

ICP >20 mm Hg

Treatment and Management

- hyperosmolar/hypertonic fluid therapy
  - mannitol 20% (0.25 – 1 g/kg IV bolus)
  - loop diuretics (assess for hypokalemia)
  - hypertonic saline (2%, 3%, 5% NaCl)
- patient positioning: elevate HOB 30 – 35° with midline head alignment, and avoid hip flexion
- maintain normal body temperature
- limit activities that may raise ICP, including coughing, sneezing, vomiting, suctioning, PEEP, restraint use, and the Valsalva maneuver
- stabilize blood glucose: insulin therapy to maintain blood glucose ≤140 mg/dL
- decrease environmental stimuli, and minimize nursing care
- higher-level interventions for refractory ICP
  - mechanical ventilation with hyperventilation (keep PaO_2 at 35 – 40 mm Hg)
  - IV fentanyl (paradoxical ICP increase may occur) or IV morphine
  - sedation (avoid "sedation holidays"), possibly with neuromuscular blockade
  - barbiturate coma
  - decompressive craniotomy

> **HELPFUL HINT:**
>
> Hypotonic solutions (D5W, 0.45% NaCl) should be avoided in patients with ICP. They decrease plasma osmolality and move water from extracellular to intracellular spaces in the brain, increasing ICP.

> **HELPFUL HINT:**
>
> Each 1°C increases cerebral O_2 demand by 7 – 10%, which in turn increases CBF and ICP.

QUICK REVIEW QUESTION

8. A patient is in the ICU after sustaining a head injury during a motorcycle accident. The patient's ICP has risen to 21 mm Hg, and the nurse alerts the physician. The following orders are received: mannitol 20% 0.5 g/kg IV bolus, furosemide 20 mg IV push, and 0.45% sodium chloride 125 mL/hr IV continuous infusion. Which order should the nurse question?

Stroke (Hemorrhagic)

A **hemorrhagic stroke**, the disruption of CBF, is caused by bleeding. The resulting hypoxia rapidly leads to brain cell death, and the excess blood in the cranium also increases ICP, increasing the risk of brain herniation. Bleeding may be caused by the spontaneous rupture of a blood vessel, head trauma, a brain mass, or uncontrolled anticoagulation conditions. The hemorrhage is classified by location as intracerebral or subarachnoid. **Intraventricular hemorrhage (IVH)** is bleeding in the ventricles; it rarely occurs alone and is usually seen with intracerebral and subarachnoid hemorrhages.

Intracerebral Hemorrhage

An **intracerebral hemorrhage (ICH)** is arterial bleeding directly into cerebral tissue. An ICH is most commonly caused by hypertensive rupture of a cerebral artery that has become damaged over time by atherosclerosis. The burst of blood from such a break in the artery causes a hematoma in the brain tissue around the rupture site. Patients with an ICH often present to EMS as unconscious and require immediate intubation for ventilatory support.

> **HELPFUL HINT:**
>
> Hypertension is the most important risk factor for all types of stroke. Other risk factors include hyperlipidemia, smoking, diabetes, and A-fib.

Signs and Symptoms

- acute onset of symptoms that gradually worsen over minutes or hours
- sudden loss of consciousness (hallmark differentiation from ischemic stroke)
- sudden focal deficit (determined by site of bleed)
- severe headache
- nausea and vomiting
- severe hypertension (200/100 – 250/150 mm Hg)
- seizures

Diagnostic Findings

- priority (interpreted in < 45 minutes): noncontrast CT scan of head to differentiate ischemic from hemorrhagic stroke

> **HELPFUL HINT:**
>
> Hematoma expansion is evident on repeat CT scans in nearly 40% of cases within the first 3 hours after onset of symptoms.

Treatment and Management

- priority goal: management of ABCs and reduction of BP
- intubation and mechanical ventilation usually necessary
- moderate BP reduction to reduce bleeding
    - MAP = 110 – 130 mm Hg
    - CPP >70 mm Hg
    - vasopressor therapy after fluid replacement if SBP <90 mm Hg
- treat increased ICP (per above)
- reverse or stabilize anticoagulation state
- management of seizures (prophylactic medication likely)

- DVT prophylaxis
- surgical removal of clot may be considered, depending on ICP and neurological condition

> **QUICK REVIEW QUESTION**
>
> 9. A CT scan has determined a patient with stroke symptoms has had an intracerebral hemorrhage. The patient has a history of hypertension and A-fib and is currently taking hydrochlorothiazide, lisinopril, and warfarin. The patient's SBP was initially 200 mm Hg but has been stabilized to 170/86 mm Hg on a nicardipine IV infusion at 10 mg/hr. Results of coagulation labs find that the INR is 4.5. What medication should the nurse expect to administer?

SUBARACHNOID HEMORRHAGE

A **subarachnoid hemorrhage (SAH)** is bleeding into the subarachnoid space. About 85% of spontaneous SAHs are due to the rupture of a saccular **cerebral aneurysm**, most commonly located at the circle of Willis. When age-related or long-term hypertension places stress on the weakened arterial blood vessel, the dome of the outpouching aneurysm thins and ruptures. The mortality rate is 25 – 50% in the first 24 hours of the event.

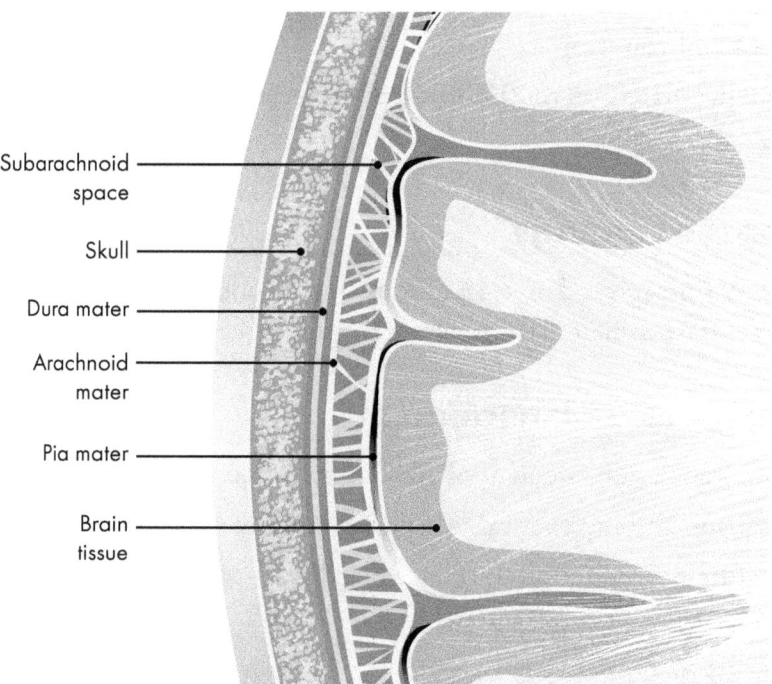

Figure 9.5. Anatomy of the Subarachnoid Space

Around 6% of SAHs are caused by the rupture of an **arteriovenous malformation (AVM)**, a mass of arterial and venous blood vessels that shunt arterial blood directly into the venous system (bypassing the capillary system). Cerebral "feeder" arteries to the AVM become enlarged over time and increase the mass size of the AVM. The high pressure of arterial blood flow engorges the veins, which eventually rupture.

Signs and Symptoms

- abrupt onset of pain, often described as "the worst headache of my life"
- brief loss of consciousness that may progress to coma
- nausea and vomiting
- focal neurological deficits, especially CN III palsy
- nuchal rigidity
- meningeal irritation: positive Kernig's and Brudzinski's signs

Diagnostic Findings

- noncontrast CT scan: blood visualized in subarachnoid space if scan obtained within 48 hours of hemorrhage
- lumbar puncture (if initial CT scan is negative): CSF bloody with RBC >1000 cells/μL
- CT angiogram to locate cause of hemorrhage (for surgical intervention)
- Hunt and Hess Grading Scale

TABLE 9.4. Hunt and Hess Grading System for SAH	
Asymptomatic, mild headache, slight nuchal rigidity	1
Moderate to severe headache, nuchal rigidity, no neurological deficit other than cranial nerve palsy	2
Drowsiness, confusion, mild focal neurological deficit	3
Stupor, moderate to severe hemiparesis	4
Coma, decerebrate posturing	5

Treatment and Management

- priority goal: management of ABCs and reduction of BP
- manage BP (SBP < 160 mm Hg)
- treat increased ICP (per above)
- reverse or stabilize anticoagulation state
- manage seizures (prophylactic medication likely)
- DVT prophylaxis

HELPFUL HINT:

Infectious vegetation from bacterial endocarditis can migrate to cerebral arteries, causing aneurysms that may rupture.

HELPFUL HINT:

Patients with SAH may describe sudden onset of headaches with vomiting in preceding weeks. These symptoms are the result of small amounts of blood leaking from aneurysms ("warning leaks" from preruptured aneurysms).

HELPFUL HINT:

Vasodilators (such as nitroprusside) should be avoided in patients with SAH because they raise ICP.

- surgical intervention (clipping, embolization, or endovascular coiling of aneurysm) within 48 hours
  - monitor post-op for reperfusion bleeding and embolic stroke
- prevention and treatment of secondary conditions
  - rebleeding: monitor for onset of neurological, respiratory, or hemodynamic changes
  - cerebral vasospasm: hypertensive, hypervolemic, hemodilution (HHH) therapy
  - hydrocephalus (due to slowed absorption of CSF) requires ventriculostomy; may require permanent ventriculoperitoneal shunt placement

HELPFUL HINT:

Cerebral vasospasm is a common cause of death after cerebral aneurysm rupture but is rare in SAH due to AVM rupture.

QUICK REVIEW QUESTION

10. A patient returns from CT guided intervention for SAH. What nursing interventions are required?

HELPFUL HINT:

Hemiplegic migraine headaches and severe hypoglycemia can mimic stroke.

Stroke (Ischemic)

During an **ischemic stroke**, blood flow to the brain is interrupted because of either a thrombotic or an embolic clot. Regardless of etiology, loss of CBF leads to hypoperfusion of brain cells, ischemic injury to a focal area, and brain death if anoxia is sustained.

Cerebral edema is expected with large-territory cerebral infarcts and is the leading cause of death in the week after an ischemic stroke. Around 10 – 20% of ischemic stroke patients develop cerebral edema sufficient to increase ICP, which reaches maximal levels at 4 days postevent. Other poststroke pathological sequelae include new-onset seizure disorder and hemorrhagic conversions at the stroke lesion site.

A **transient ischemic attack (TIA)**, a sudden, brief neurological deficit resulting from brain ischemia, does not cause permanent damage or infarction. Symptoms depend on the area of the brain affected. Most TIAs last less than 5 minutes and are resolved within 1 hour. A majority are caused by emboli in the carotid or vertebral arteries.

Signs and Symptoms

- focal neurological signs determined by location and size of the area of ischemia (lesion)

- dominant left hemisphere
  - aphasia or dysarthria
  - emotional lability and/or memory loss
  - vision changes (right hemianopia and conjugate gaze difficulties)
  - right hemiparesis
  - right-sided sensory loss
- nondominant right hemisphere
  - rambling speech or dysarthria
  - vision changes (left visual neglect or hemianopia)
  - left-sided sensory loss and stimuli extinction
  - spatial disorientation
  - difficulty in problem-solving
- posterior hemisphere, cerebellum, or brainstem
  - dysarthria
  - vision changes (nystagmus, disconjugate gaze, bilateral vision-field deficit)
  - sensory loss in all 4 limbs
  - ataxia or loss of fine motor movement control
- subcortical/brainstem (pure motor stroke): face/limb weakness on one side of body; no deficit in sensation, vision, or brain function
- subcortical/brainstem (pure sensory stroke): face/limb decreased sensation on one side of body; no deficit in motor function, vision, or brain function

Diagnostic Testing

- priority (interpreted in < 45 minutes): noncontrast CT scan of head to differentiate ischemic from hemorrhagic stroke
- National Institute of Health Stroke Scale (NIHSS)
  - LOC
  - eye deviation (CN III, IV, VI)
  - visual field loss (tests hemianopia and extinction)
  - facial palsy
  - motor arm (drift)
  - motor leg (drift)
  - limb ataxia (tests for unilateral cerebellar lesion)
  - sensory
  - best language (tests for comprehension/aphasia)

- ☐ dysarthria (tests for speech ability)
- ☐ extinction and inattention (tests for visual/spatial "neglect")

Treatment and Management

- IV or intra-arterial fibrinolytic therapy (alteplase)
  - ☐ dosage: 0.9 mg/kg to a maximum of 90 mg; first 10% as IV bolus dose over 1 minute, with remaining 90% given as IV infusion over 1 hour
  - ☐ must be initiated within 3 hours from "last seen normal"
  - ☐ time window expanded to 4.5 hours for eligible patients (<80 years old, no history of diabetes/stroke, NIHSS score <25)
  - ☐ hypertensive patients: BP should be lowered to <185/110 with antihypertensive medication before administration
  - ☐ aspirin administered 24 hours after alteplase administration
  - ☐ monitor for side effects, including bleeding, angioedema, ICH, pulmonary edema, DVT, seizure, and sepsis
- mechanical thrombectomy for fibrinolytic-ineligible patients or fibrinolytic-eligible patients with high likelihood of stroke due to LVO; may be done in conjunction with tenecteplase administration
- cardiac monitoring for post-reperfusion dysrhythmias
- regular neurological checks, and monitor ICP
- maintain normal body temperature
- maintain blood glucose of 140 – 180 mL/dL (do not administer D5W)
- supplemental O_2 for saturation below 94%
- DVT prophylaxis

QUICK REVIEW QUESTION

11. A patient recovering from TAVR presents with aphasia and right-sided hemiparesis. What is the priority diagnostic test for this patient?

Neurological Infectious Disease

- **Meningitis,** an acute inflammation of the meninges, is caused by bacterial, viral, or fungal pathogens that invade the subarachnoid space.

The infection triggers WBC accumulation and tissue damage, leading to swelling and purulent exudate within the cranium.

- Viral infection is the most common cause of meningitis; bacterial meningitis is a medical emergency because of the rapidity of deterioration and the high mortality rate.
- Diagnosis: headache, nuchal rigidity, fever, altered mental status, rash, positive Brudzinski's and Kernig's signs, photophobia, lumbar puncture to confirm
- CSF finding for viral meningitis: elevated protein and lymphocytes; clear fluid
- CSF finding for bacterial meningitis: very elevated protein, elevated WBCs and neutrophils, low glucose, cloudy fluid
- Management: empirical IV antibiotic therapy; corticosteroids; antivirals (as appropriate); monitor for sepsis, increased ICP, and SIADH/DI

- **Encephalitis**, an infection of the brain parenchyma, may be caused by bacteria, viruses, fungi, or parasites. It may present alone or alongside meningitis.
  - Diagnosis: altered mental status, seizures, focal neurological deficits; lumbar puncture shows elevated protein and WBC
  - Management: antibiotic, antiviral, or antifungal therapy (as indicated); manage seizures, including prophylaxis; monitor for increased ICP

- **Brain abscesses** are localized infections in the brain parenchyma. The infection can be caused by bacteremia or by direct spread from nearby tissues (e.g., otitis media, dental conditions).
  - Diagnosis: headache (on side of abscess), fever, focal neurological deficits, seizures; CT scan or MRI to confirm
  - Management: antibiotics, glucocorticoids; needle aspiration (via trephination) or surgical excision may be required

HELPFUL HINT:

Lumbar punctures are contraindicated for some patients with increased ICP because decompression of the CSF may lead to brain herniation.

QUICK REVIEW QUESTION

12. A 22-year-old college student arrives at the ED with complaints of headache, neck pain, fever, and sensitivity to light. On examination, the patient is positive for Brudzinski's and Kernig's signs. What test would be expected to help with diagnosis?

⟶
CONTINUE

Neuromuscular Disorders

- **Amyotrophic lateral sclerosis (ALS)** (Lou Gehrig's disease) is a neurodegenerative disorder that affects the neurons in the brainstem and spinal cord. Symptoms progressively worsen until respiratory failure occurs.
  - Symptoms: progressive asymmetrical weakness (can affect both upper and lower extremities); difficulty swallowing, walking, or speaking; muscle cramps
  - Management: supportive care for symptoms; respiratory support (high risk of aspiration)
- **Cerebral palsy (CP)** is a group of disorders characterized by permanent, nonprogressive muscle weakness. CP may present with a wide range of comorbidities, including intellectual disability, GI disorders, chronic lung disease, epilepsy, vision/hearing impairment, and chronic pain. Common reasons for ICU admission in patients with CP include infection, refractory seizures, and postoperative care.
- **Guillain-Barré syndrome** is an acquired demyelinating neuropathy believed to result from an immune reaction to recent infection. It is characterized by progressive symmetric muscle weakness, which may lead to respiratory dysfunction.
  - Symptoms: neuropathy and weakness ascending from lower extremities and advancing symmetrically upward; paresthesia in extremities; unsteady gait; absent or diminished deep tendon reflexes; autonomic dysfunction (hypertension, bradycardia, temperature instability)
  - Management: plasmapheresis, IV immunoglobulins; manage signs and symptoms of autonomic dysfunction
- **Multiple sclerosis (MS)** is a neurodegenerative disorder caused by patches of demyelination in the brain and the spinal cord. It has periods of both remission and exacerbation of symptoms, with gradually growing disability.
  - Symptoms: paresthesia; weakness of at least one extremity; visual, motor, or urinary disturbance; vertigo; fatigue; mild cognitive impairment; increased deep tendon reflexes; clonus
  - Management: corticosteroids for inflammation, baclofen or tizanidine for spasticity, gabapentin or tricyclic antidepressants for pain
- **Muscular dystrophy (MD)** is a genetic disorder in which a mutation in the recessive dystrophin gene on the X chromosome causes muscle fiber degeneration. It is usually first noted at 2 – 3 years of age and results in steady, progressive proximal-muscle weakness.

- Symptoms: steady progression of weakness; limb flexion and contraction; scoliosis; dilated cardiomyopathy, conduction abnormalities, or dysrhythmias; respiratory insufficiency
- Management: prednisone or deflazacort; monitor CO_2 levels; noninvasive ventilator support may be needed; supportive treatment of symptoms related to falls and cardiovascular disorders

- **Myasthenia gravis (MG)** is an autoimmune disorder that causes cell-mediated destruction of acetylcholine receptors, resulting in episodic muscle weakness and fatigue. **Myasthenic crisis** is an emergent condition in which MG symptoms rapidly worsen; weakening of the bulbar and respiratory muscles can cause respiratory dysfunction. (The information below is for myasthenic crisis.)
  - Symptoms: dyspnea, respiratory failure, tachycardia, hypertension, no cough or gag reflex, urinary and bowel incontinence
  - Management: IV fluids; IV immunoglobulin; anticholinesterase; respiratory support; long-term medications include pyridostigmine, steroids, muscle relaxants

HELPFUL HINT:

Patients with myasthenia gravis are at risk for a cholinergic crisis if they are given high doses of anticholinesterase medications. Antidotes for anticholinesterase overdoes include atropine and pralidoxime.

QUICK REVIEW QUESTION

13. What type of weakness should a nurse expect to observe in a patient with ALS?

Neurosurgery

- A **craniotomy** is the surgical opening of the skull to gain access to tissues inside the cranium.
- Common reasons for craniotomy include evacuation of hematoma or abscess, clipping or removal of an aneurysm or an AVM, brain tumor resection or removal, cerebral decompression, ICP monitoring, and placement of deep brain stimulators.
- Surgical access may be transcranial (through the skull) or transsphenoidal (through the nose).
- Patients should be closely monitored for the following post-op complications:
  - increased ICP
  - surgical hemorrhage: monitor for increased ICP (transcranial) or postnasal drip/external drainage (transsphenoidal)
  - CSF rhinorrhea: may require continuous lumbar drainage or surgical repair
  - SIADH or DI: monitor fluid balance

HELPFUL HINT:

A transsphenoidal craniotomy is used to remove a pituitary tumor. Patient teaching pre-op must include preparing the patient for nasal packing pressure; mouth breathing required; and the importance of avoiding sneezing, blowing nose, or coughing.

- infection: meningitis, surgical site infection, subdural empyema, or cerebral abscess
- injury to brain tissue: altered mental status, seizures

- **Burr hole trephination** is the drilling of small holes (trepanations) in the skull to drain fluid; the process usually includes the placement of a catheter in the hole.
  - Burr holes are used to drain hydrocephalus, hemorrhages, empyema/abscess, and subdural hematomas. They may also be used for some diagnostic procedures.
  - Postoperative complications of burr holes include infection, hemorrhage, embolism, and brain injury.

QUICK REVIEW QUESTION

14. After a transsphenoidal craniotomy to remove the pituitary gland, a patient experiences increased nasal discharge. What may this indicate, and what action should the nurse take?

HELPFUL HINT:

Patients with a history of seizures are especially at high risk in the critical care setting because of a combination of sleep deprivation, poor nutrition, high levels of stimulation, medications that can lower seizure thresholds, and changes in the therapeutic level of antiepileptic drugs.

Seizure Disorders

Seizure disorders are caused by abnormal electrical discharges in the brain. During a seizure, brain neurons abnormally or excessively fire because the membrane potential is altered in a way that makes those neurons hypersensitive to stimuli. Seizures may be **focal** (limited to one part of the brain) or **generalized**.

Status epilepticus is a medical emergency in which seizure activity continues or recurs for more than 5 minutes. It has a high mortality rate (20 – 30%) and requires immediate intervention.

Etiology

- genetic/congenital
- trauma
- drug toxicity or withdrawal
- fluid or electrolyte imbalances
- hypoglycemia
- hypoxic-ischemic events
- cerebral edema
- sepsis
- tumors

Signs and Symptoms

- convulsive: tonic-clonic (grand mal) seizure pattern of extremities
  - tonic phase: loss of consciousness, rigidity of extremities, dilated pupils
  - clonic phase: rhythmic shaking, violent alternating contraction/relaxation, tachycardia, mouth frothing
  - postictal: impaired mental status and focal neurological deficits (Todd paralysis common)
  - nonconvulsive: EEG tracing of seizure activity with/without clinical signs

Treatment and Management

- manage ABCs
- finger-stick blood glucose: administer 50 mL D50W IV push if blood glucose <60 mg/dL
- prompt pharmacological treatment
  - first-line drugs: IV lorazepam, IV diazepam, or IM midazolam
  - second-line drugs (after 20 minutes of nonresponse to treatment): IV fosphenytoin, IV valproate, or IV levetiracetam
- After status epilepticus is aborted, determine etiology of seizure and begin antiepileptic drug therapy

> **QUICK REVIEW QUESTION**
>
> **15.** A patient with liver cirrhosis is being treated in the ICU for hepatic encephalopathy with refractory increased ICP. Lorazepam IV continuous infusion has been titrated up to 0.1 mg/kg/hr to manage agitation. The patient has a history of seizure, and current EEG monitoring shows a pattern consistent with status epilepticus. What medication should the nurse anticipate will be ordered for the patient?

Space-Occupying Lesions (Brain Tumors)

- **Brain tumors** are space-occupying lesions that, depending on their location, size, and rate of growth, create a range of symptoms.
- **Primary tumors** originate from brain tissue or immediately surrounding brain tissue; they are rare, and can be either benign or malignant.
  - The most common type of primary tumor is a **glioma**, which originates in the glia cells that surround the neurons in the brain.

- Common benign primary brain tumors include meningiomas, schwannomas, and pituitary adenomas.
- **Secondary**, or **metastatic**, **brain tumors** are malignant cancers that have originated elsewhere and migrated to the brain. Metastatic cancer may spread from the primary cancer in any part of the body, including the lungs, breasts, colon, skin, or kidneys.
- Symptoms of brain tumors will vary and may include headaches, seizures, unilateral weakness, and neurological deficits (related to tumor location).
- Disorders that occur secondary to brain tumors and that require critical care include encephalopathy, hemorrhage, and increased ICP (managed as discussed above).
- Patients with brain tumors may also be admitted to manage side effects of treatment, such as sepsis (due to chemotherapy's effects on the immune system) or cardiac disorders (a side effect of radiation therapy).

QUICK REVIEW QUESTION

16. A patient has metastatic pancreatic cancer and is admitted to the ICU because of a secondary brain tumor causing seizures. What lab value requires close monitoring for this patient?

★ Traumatic Brain Injury

Pathophysiology and General Management Guidelines

- **Traumatic brain injury (TBI)** results from a blunt or penetrating blow to the head or from a blast injury.
    - **Primary injuries** are caused by mechanical forces and can cause skull fractures, brain contusions and concussions, lacerations, hemorrhages, hematomas, or damage to white brain matter.
    - **Secondary injuries** occur days or weeks after the TBI event as a result of neurochemical cascades leading to chronic inflammation and vascular changes in the brain.
- In patients with TBI, decreased cerebral perfusion may lead to tissue ischemia and edema. Cerebral vasodilation occurs to compensate for decreased perfusion and to increase O_2 to cerebral tissue. This increased cerebral blood volume leads to increased intracranial volume and ICP.

- Severe cerebral edema causes loss of autoregulation, meaning CPP will vary with changes in MAP. Tight control of MAP is required to main adequate CPP.
- Hypotension is closely associated with poor outcomes in patients with TBI. Hypotension may be a direct result of brain tissue injury but often has other causes (e.g., hemorrhage). Hypotension requires immediate stabilization to maintain CPP.
- The goal of critical care management of TBI is to maintain CPP and decrease secondary injury to the brain.
    - ICP monitoring and management (discussed in detail above)
    - target CPP: minimum 60 mm Hg (70 mm Hg is optimal)
    - maintain MAP 60 mm Hg (fluid management)
    - fluids and vasopressors for hypotension
    - brain tissue oxygen monitoring may be implemented
    - capnography to identify hypo- or hypercapnia
    - serial ABGs to ensure adequate oxygenation
    - manage hyperthermia to reduce CV demand (target 36°C – 37°C)

> **HELPFUL HINT:**
>
> ETT Suctioning for TBI Patients
>
> 2 passes of suction catheter
>
> each pass <10 seconds
>
> hyperventilate patient before and after each pass
>
> minimize stimulation of airway with suction

QUICK REVIEW QUESTION

17. A 36-year-old construction worker is admitted to ICU with TBI after falling from a ladder. The intubated, sedated patient has a subarachnoid screw for ICP and CPP monitoring. Arterial line shows MAP <60, ICP 30 mm Hg, and CPP 40 mm Hg. What interventions should the nurse anticipate?

Specific Traumatic Brain Injuries

- The level of care for **skull fractures** depends on the type and severity of fracture.
    - Nondisplaced fractures generally do well with conservative treatment.
    - No treatment is usually required for a linear fracture, especially as the dura mater usually remains intact in adults.
    - Surgical decompression for a depressed fracture is necessary only when the depression is greater than the thickness of the skull (if the depression is ≥6 mm).
    - Basilar skull fractures require critical care monitoring and intervention.
- **Basilar skull fractures** affect the floor of the skull.
    - may cause rupture of meninges, resulting in pneumocephalus
    - likely injury to CN I, III, VII, and VIII

- associated spinal cord injury common
- signs and symptoms: Battle sign, raccoon eyes, otorrhea, and rhinorrhea

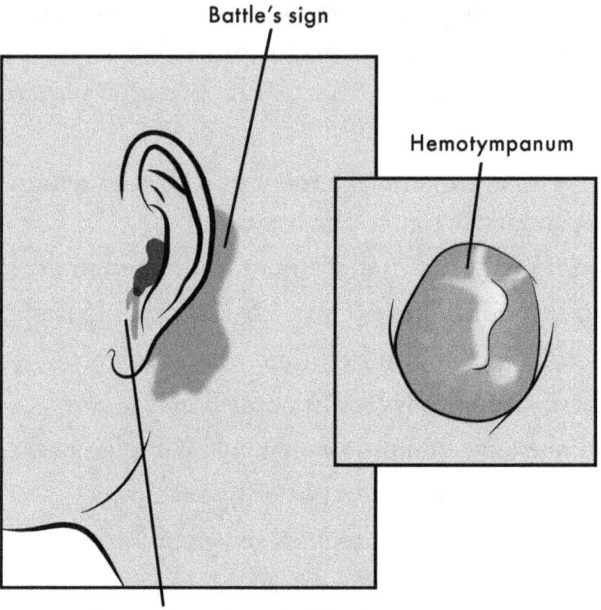

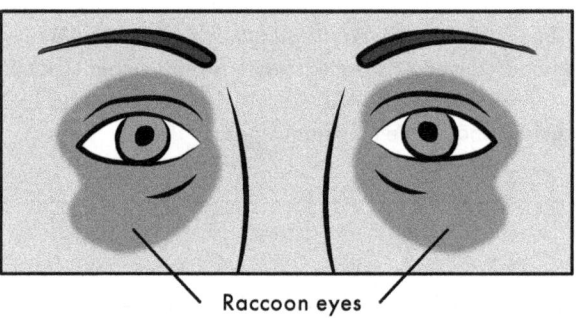

Figure 9.6. Signs and Symptoms of Basilar Skull Fracture

- management: manage ABCs; manage ICP, hemorrhage, and meningeal injury (as described above); avoid NT and oral tube, oral suctioning, and positive-pressure support

■ **Diffuse axonal injury (DAI)** is a shearing injury that occurs during rapid acceleration–deceleration or rotational acceleration. These forces can shear axons in the brain and cause the death of the brain cells to which they were connected. Sufficient force will disconnect the cerebral hemisphere from the reticular activating system.
- signs and symptoms: coma (GCS <8), decorticate or decerebrate posturing, cerebral edema, increased ICP, temperature elevation
- management: manage ABCs; supportive treatment for symptoms; reduce secondary injury

- An **epidural hematoma (EDH)** is a traumatic collection of blood between the dura mater and the skull, usually because of a temporal- or parietal-region skull fracture that causes a laceration of the middle meningeal artery.

    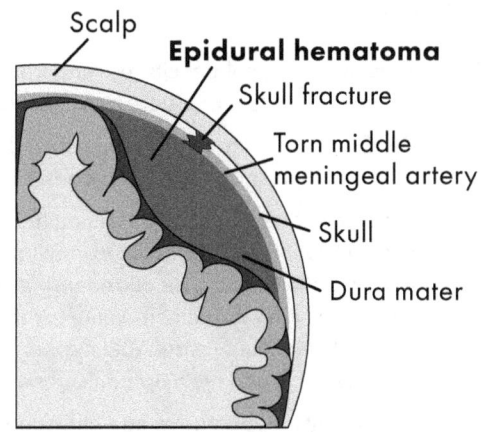

    Figure 9.7. Epidural Hematoma

    □ EDH is a neurosurgical emergency: a rapidly expanding hematoma will increase ICP and quickly progress to uncal herniation of brain tissue.
    □ Diagnosis: CT scan or MRI; lucid interval followed by coma; agitation and confusion; nausea and vomiting; headache; ipsilateral pupil dilation; Cushing's triad
    □ Management: manage ABCs; craniotomy or trephination for hematoma evacuation

- A **subdural hematoma (SDH)** is low-pressure venous bleeding between the dura mater and the arachnoid space. SDH is generally caused either by trauma or by anticoagulation therapy. SDH is categorized into 3 main types, based on the rate of bleed, symptom appearance, and rebleeding subsequent to the initial trauma/event.
    □ Diagnosis: CT scan or MRI; decreasing LOC, headache, confusion, contralateral hemiparesis, increased ICP, ipsilateral pupil dilation
    □ **Acute SDH:** symptoms appear immediately or <4 days from trauma/event
    □ **Subacute SDH:** symptoms appear 4 – 21 days after trauma/event
    □ **Chronic SDH:** symptoms appear 21 days after trauma/event
    □ Management: manage ABCs; craniotomy or trephination for hematoma evacuation

HELPFUL HINT:

Older adults, individuals on antiplatelet therapy, and chronic dialysis patients are at greatest risk for both a spontaneous SDH and a fall-related bleed.

HELPFUL HINT:

Because symptoms of chronic SDH evolve slowly, the condition may be mistaken for dementia, strokes, or brain tumors.

QUICK REVIEW QUESTION

18. A 72-year-old patient is admitted to the ICU after emergent surgical repair of a hip fracture sustained during a fall. The patient remains sedated and vented post-surgery. Before the surgery, the neurology assessment noted that the patient was alert and oriented to person, place, and time (A&O×3) and within normal limits, except for a headache rated at 3/10. The postsurgical assessment shows that the patient is not responding to stimuli and exhibits ipsilateral pupil dilation. What would be appropriate action for this patient?

ANSWER KEY

1. Focal neurological deficits resulting from damage to the occipital lobe, which controls vision, include loss of vision, hallucinations, and cortical blindness.

2. The GCS score would be 7, indicating that the patient has severe brain injury (likely in the cerebral hemispheres, as suggested by decorticate positioning).

3. The immediate treatment for an undifferentiated trauma patient with spinal immobilization and a stabilized ventilatory status is fluid resuscitation. This unstable trauma patient should be considered to be in hypovolemic shock until proven otherwise. If the spinal cord injury is radiologically confirmed and neurogenic shock differentiated, the nurse should expect to administer vasopressors, atropine or isoproterenol, and methylprednisolone.

4. The patient is hypotensive and unresponsive to vasopressors. The apnea test should be aborted, and the ventilator delivery returned to pretest settings.

5. The nurse should review the patient's medications, especially any current or prior benzodiazepine use. The nurse should request an order for a chemistry panel to assess for electrolyte imbalances, replacing deficiencies per protocol. Because the patient has a known infection, a sepsis screen should be completed once per shift and when any changes are observed. A sleep protocol and grouping of care will prevent overstimulation and provide adequate rest. Family should be encouraged to visit and talk with the patient. Dietary staff must be consulted for appropriate nutritional intake.

6. The nurse should answer honestly and explain that the medication does not cure the disease and will not improve the patient's cognitive symptoms. However, the medication will slow the progression of the disease. The nurse should tell the spouse that the patient should continue the medication as directed by the physician, even if they see no obvious improvement.

7. The hanging action has caused a hypoxic-ischemic brain injury. The nurse should expect to obtain baseline readings (vital signs, GCS score, cranial nerves responses, and LOC) and to closely monitor the patient for changes in neurological status. The nurse will also need to closely monitor ICP and tightly manage the patient's fluid balance.

8. The nurse should question the hypotonic solution of 0.45% sodium chloride because it can further increase ICP. A hypertonic solution would be expected in a patient with increased ICP.

9. Phytonadione (vitamin K) 1 mg IV would be administered to reverse the anticoagulation effects of warfarin and prevent further bleeding in the brain. The provider may also order 4-factor PCC or FFP to encourage clotting.

10. Nursing interventions would include monitoring and treating hypertension and ICP per ordered parameters; completing neurological assessments, including NIHSS every 4 hours; and monitoring for signs and symptoms of rebleeding, including hemodynamic or respiratory changes.

11. The priority intervention for a patient with a suspected ischemic stroke is to immediately obtain a noncontrast CT scan of the head.

12. A lumbar puncture with fluid analysis would be completed to determine viral or bacterial meningitis.

13. A patient with ALS presents with a progressive, asymmetrical pattern of weakness that affects both upper and lower extremities.

14. The patient may have a CSF leak, which is a common complication of pituitary surgery done via transsphenoidal craniotomy. The nurse should confirm that the discharge is CSF and alert the physician.

15. The patient will be treated with a second-line antiepileptic medication, most likely IV fosphenytoin or phenytoin. (Note that valproate is hepatotoxic and would not be administered to a patient with liver cirrhosis.)

16. Because the primary cancer is pancreatic, this patient is at greater risk of hypoglycemia which may increase the likelihood of seizures. The patient should be monitored closely for signs and symptoms of hypoglycemia and treated according to facility policy.

17. Hypotension is not usual in TBI and needs to be corrected quickly. The nurse should notify the provider while rapidly assessing for additional trauma sources such as internal crush injuries or hemorrhage. The nurse should anticipate administration of fluids and vasopressors to increase MAP and CPP.

18. Given the history of the fall, the age of the patient, and the noted headache, this patient may be experiencing an SDH. A stat CT scan should be completed. The patient should be prepared for, and family notified of, possible surgery for hematoma evacuation.

10 BEHAVIORAL AND PSYCHOSOCIAL REVIEW

CCRN TEST PLAN: BEHAVIORAL AND PSYCHOSOCIAL
- Abuse/neglect
- Aggression
- Agitation
- Anxiety
- Depression
- Medical non-adherence
- PTSD
- Risk-taking behavior
- Suicidal ideation and/or behaviors
- Substance use disorders (e.g., withdrawal, chronic alcohol or drug dependence)

Abuse and Neglect

Characteristics

Patients presenting with concern for **abuse** and **neglect** generally fall into one of three categories: domestic abuse, child abuse/neglect, and geriatric abuse/neglect. Nursing assessment for each of these concerns begins at admittance, and patients should be screened for signs or indications of neglect. Abuse can include both physical and emotional abuse; neglect may be on the part of caregivers or self.

Diagnosis

- physical signs and symptoms: unexplained injuries, fractures, or bruising at different stages of healing, poor hygiene, weight loss or gain

- emotional signs and symptoms: severe mood swings or changes, agitation, depression, suicidal ideation

Treatment and Management

- Protected populations (including pediatric and geriatric patients) require obligatory reporting of suspected abuse and neglect.
- Priority treatment of the abused or neglected patient should focus on physical injuries.
- Consideration should be made for emotional needs that result from abuse and neglect.
    - Provide same-gender caregivers or a same-gender chaperone for exams.
    - Use organizational resources to provide support for the patient.
    - Ask permission to touch the patient or narrate the physical exam.
    - Warn the patient when and where they will be touched during the exam.

QUICK REVIEW QUESTION

1. A pediatric patient is admitted for acute asthma exacerbation. Upon assessment, the nurse discovers bruising to the abdomen, back, and arms that appears to be in different stages of healing. The patient's parent is at the bedside. What is the nurse's next action?

Agitation, Aggression, and Violent Behavior

Characteristics

HELPFUL HINT:

Urosepsis is a common cause of agitation and aggression in patients over 65 years old.

Agitation is a state of anxiety and restlessness. This is a common challenge in the ICU and must be monitored in patients who are mechanically ventilated, restrained, or otherwise impeded from normal freedom of movement or who are experiencing delirium or a crisis.

Aggression or **violent behavior** in patients may occur for many reasons. These include:

- crisis or psychosis
- influence of drugs or alcohol
- underlying organic processes (e.g., TBI)

Treatment and Management

- recognize early signs and attempt to control situation
- alert security and follow facility protocol
- de-escalation techniques
    - verbal redirection
    - allowing the patient to express needs
    - allowing the patient to exercise
    - decreased environmental stimulation (quiet room time)
    - PRN medication administration (as requested by patient)
- restraint protocols
    - should be used conservatively and only for patients whose behavior cannot be controlled through less restrictive measures
    - require a physician order and initial assessment
    - require frequent assessment
        - every 5 – 15 minutes, depending on organizational policy
        - check vitals; assess pain, circulation, and skin integrity of all restrained extremities; address restroom needs
    - should be removed as soon as they are deemed unnecessary for patient and staff safety
- opioids and benzodiazepines for sedation

The **Richmond Agitation-Sedation Scale (RASS)** is a widely accepted method to assess a patient's level of sedation within a critical care unit. The goal is to maintain an RASS score between −2 and 0.

TABLE 10.1. Richmond Agitation-Sedation Scale (RASS)

Description	Score
Combative	+4
Very agitated	+3
Agitated	+2
Restless	+1
Alert and calm	0
Drowsy	−1
Light sedation	−2
Moderate sedation	−3
Deep sedation	−4
Unarousable sedation	−5

> **QUICK REVIEW QUESTION**
>
> 2. A patient was placed in mechanical restraints after demonstrating violent and aggressive behavior toward nursing staff. It has been 15 minutes since the restraints were applied, and the nurse is preparing to assess the patient. What will the nurse include in the assessment?

Anxiety

Characteristics

Anxiety is feelings of fear, apprehension, and worry that can be characterized as mild, moderate, or severe (panic). Anxiety can affect the respiratory, cardiac, and gastrointestinal systems. A key nursing consideration is to assess for organic causes for reported symptoms, as other illnesses, some life-threatening, may present with similar symptoms (e.g., palpitations, dizziness, dyspnea).

Treatment and Management

- target the level of anxiety the patient presents with (mild to panic)
- non-pharmacological interventions
    - placing patient in a calm environment
    - encouraging rhythmic breathing and the Valsalva technique
    - offering emotional support
    - promoting an open policy for family visitation
    - allowing the patient time to overcome the episode
- pharmacological interventions
    - antihistamines
    - benzodiazepines

> **QUICK REVIEW QUESTION**
>
> 3. A patient presents to the ED reporting a sudden onset of feeling fearful, apprehensive, and on edge. The patient is feeling mild chest pain and shortness of breath. What should the nurse ask in the assessment of this patient?

Mood Disorders and Suicidal Ideation

Characteristics

Mood disorders can include mania and/or depression. **Depression** is a mood disorder characterized by feelings of sadness and hopelessness. Patients may also report feelings of suicidality. Depression can manifest as an exacerbation of bipolar disorder or as its own disease process.

Bipolar disorder (previously called manic-depressive illness) is characterized by shifts in mood accompanied by manic behaviors or depressive behaviors. Severe episodes of either mania or depression can also result in **psychosis**, characterized by hallucinations or delusions.

Suicidal ideation is characterized by considering suicide, thoughts of attempting suicide, or planning suicide. Patients exhibiting suicidal ideation may have vague thoughts without a distinct plan, or they may have a specific plan and the means to carry it out.

Signs and Symptoms

- manic behaviors
    - feelings of elation
    - high levels of energy and increased activity
    - difficulty sleeping; may not sleep for several days
    - increased rate of speech
    - engaging in high-risk activities (e.g., excessive spending, risky sexual activity)
- depressive behaviors
    - deep or intense feelings of sadness, worry, or anxiety
    - decreased energy levels with associated decreased activity
    - sleep and appetite disturbances
    - suicidal ideation or focus on death

Treatment and Management

- screen for depression and suicidal ideation
    - Ask directly if the patient is considering suicide or has recently or in the past attempted suicide.
    - If the patient is having thoughts of suicide, do they have a concrete plan to carry it out?

- □ Determine the presence of risk factors such as a history of substance abuse or chronic pain.
- □ Assess the presence of social supports for the patient.
- interventions for patients with suicidal ideation
    - □ securing a contract of safety that states they will remain safe while in the hospital and in the future
    - □ creating a safe environment (e.g., removing dangerous items from the room)
    - □ establishing a 1:1 watch or line-of-sight supervision for the patient
    - □ having the patient evaluated by a psychiatrist before discharge
- rule out possible medical causes for depression or mania (e.g., metabolic disorders)
- medications used to treat exacerbations of bipolar disorder
    - □ mood stabilizers
    - □ atypical antipsychotics
    - □ antipsychotics and antidepressants (usually used long term)

QUICK REVIEW QUESTION

4. How can the nurse address patient and staff safety when a patient reports thoughts of self-harm?

Post-Traumatic Stress Disorder (PTSD)

Characteristics

Post-traumatic stress disorder (PTSD) is a psychosomatic condition triggered by a traumatic event that involved the real or potential threat of serious injury, violence, or death. The condition can take an unspecified time to present, from a month to several years. It is marked by symptoms including pain, flashbacks, debilitating anxiety, nightmares, and uncontrollable fixation on the initial event.

Patients with **post-intensive care syndrome (PICS)** experience PTSD-like symptoms after critical care, particularly if they required ventilatory support. PICS correlates with delirium and typically presents 1 – 6 months posthospitalization.

HELPFUL HINT:

Never ask family members to monitor or care for patients who are agitated, delirious, violent, or suicidal. This places an undue burden on the family. They may choose to provide support, but the nurse should ensure that appropriate monitoring or restraints are in place.

Treatment and Management

- nursing considerations for patients with PTSD
  - providing a supportive environment
  - initiating safety precautions for patient and others
  - reviewing medications and assessing for unwanted side effects
  - providing facts and reorientation if patient is experiencing flashbacks or delirium
  - announcing self when entering the room
  - explaining care before providing to prevent startling the patient
  - maintaining routines
- measures to prevent PICS
  - limiting use of sedation
  - extubating as soon as safe
  - assessing and treating for delirium
  - encouraging family to talk with patient while the patient is under sedation
  - having patient keep a journal
  - educating patient and family on signs of PICS to monitor for

QUICK REVIEW QUESTION

5. The nurse is transferring a patient from ICU to progressive care. The patient had been in ICU for two weeks to treat sepsis and was intubated and sedated for several days. What should the nurse explain to the family members regarding PICS?

Substance Dependence and Abuse

ALCOHOL WITHDRAWAL

Pathophysiology

Alcohol is a CNS depressant that directly binds to gamma-aminobutyric acid (GABA) receptors and inhibits glutamate-induced excitation. Chronic alcohol use alters the sensitivity of these receptors; when alcohol use is stopped, the result is hyperactivity in the CNS. Alcohol withdrawal can be fatal.

Chronic alcohol use inhibits the absorption of nutrients, including thiamine and folic acid. Consequently, patients admitted with symptoms of alcohol withdrawal are also at risk for disorders related to vitamin deficiency, including Wernicke's encephalopathy and megaloblastic anemia.

Refractory alcohol withdrawal syndrome (RAWS) occurs when the maximum dosage of benzodiazepines is insufficient for treatment, leading to excessive sedation, respiratory depression, hyperosmolar metabolic acidosis, and an increase of morbidity and mortality.

Signs and Symptoms

- mild (6 – 24 hours after last drink)
    - tachycardia and hypertension
    - agitation and restlessness
    - tremor
    - insomnia
    - hyperactive reflexes
    - diaphoresis
    - headache
    - nausea and emesis
- severe
    - hallucinations (12 – 48 hours after last drink)
    - tonic-clonic seizures (6 – 48 hours after last drink)
    - delirium tremens (DTs) (72 – 96 hours after last drink)
        - anxiety
        - tachycardia and hypertension
        - ataxia
        - diaphoresis

Assessment

- Assess withdrawal symptoms using the Clinical Institute Withdrawal Assessment (CIWA-Ar).
    - Scores range from 0 to 67.
    - A score >20 indicates severe withdrawal symptoms.

Treatment and Management

- IV fluids
- monitor for electrolyte imbalances
- treat vitamin deficiencies and malnutrition
- benzodiazepines for agitation
- lorazepam for seizures

- treatment for RAWS: phenobarbital, propofol, and dexmedetomidine
- mechanical ventilation for patients with severe DTs or RAWS

> **QUICK REVIEW QUESTION**
>
> 6. An ICU patient was conscious and alert 48 hours following endovascular aortic repair to an abdominal aortic aneurysm. The patient's wife expresses concern that the patient has become sweaty and confused and has been asking when he can have a drink to relax. What interventions should the nurse anticipate?

OPIOID WITHDRAWAL

Pathophysiology

Opioids are synthetically and naturally occurring substances that bind to opioid receptors in the brain, depressing the CNS. (The term "opiate" is sometimes used to refer only to naturally occurring opioids.) Chronic use of opioids increases excitability of noradrenergic neurons, and withdrawal leads to hypersensitivity of the CNS. Opioid withdrawal is rarely fatal, but death can occur, usually as a result of hemodynamic instability or electrolyte imbalances.

Signs and Symptoms

- drug craving
- nausea, vomiting, diarrhea, and abdominal cramping
- dysphoria and anxiety
- yawning
- rhinorrhea and lacrimation
- mydriasis
- piloerection
- sweating
- muscle pain and twitching
- tachycardia, tachypnea, and hypertension

Assessment

- The **Clinical Opiate Withdrawal Scale (COWS)** is an 11-item scale to help objectively assess withdrawal symptoms and ensure that patients are given the correct amount of medication.
    - ☐ 5 – 12: mild withdrawal
    - ☐ 13 – 24: moderate withdrawal

- 25 – 36: moderate to severe withdrawal
- \>36: severe withdrawal

Treatment and Management

- supportive care for symptoms
    - benzodiazepines for anxiety, tachycardia, and hypertension
    - clonidine for tachycardia and hypertension
    - antiemetics
    - antidiarrheals
- possible treatments for opioid withdrawal
    - Immediately cease taking opioids.
    - Opioid replacement therapy—methadone or buprenorphine relieve symptoms without producing intoxication.
    - Opioid antagonists—naltrexone and naloxone block the effects of opioids.

> **QUICK REVIEW QUESTION**
>
> 7. An opioid-naive patient in the ICU for therapeutic hypothermia treatment was mechanically ventilated for five days and received a fentanyl 0.1 mcg/kg/hr IV continuous infusion as part of the analgesia protocol. After discontinuation of the drip, the patient was treated for discomfort with hydromorphone. The patient has been extubated and opioid treatment withdrawn. What should the nurse do to monitor and prepare for opioid withdrawal in the patient?

Drug-Seeking Behavior
Characteristics

Drug-seeking behavior is a loose term used to describe repeated attempts by a patient to obtain a certain substance or drug. In the critical care setting, opioids and benzodiazepines are the most commonly sought-after substances, although psychotropics are also abused. Patients exhibiting drug-seeking behaviors may display the following:

- reported pain levels that do not match patient symptoms or behavior
- polypharmacy and using several different pharmacies
- requesting drugs by specific name/brand name
- requesting increases to dosing
- escalating requests for a certain drug or displaying aggression
- irritability/anger when requests for medication are denied
- refusal to consider other treatment methods

Treatment and Management

- Be empathetic with patient; avoid judgment or blame, and be cautious of labeling patient as drug-seeking.
- Perform comprehensive pain assessment using a pain assessment tool that describes the pain scale.
- Establish a functional pain goal with patient that is reasonable and realistic.
- Observe and document patterns in behavior.
- If patient requires ongoing IV analgesics and is cognitively capable, patient-controlled administration can offer improved outcomes.
- Discuss alternative or adjuvant treatments available.

> **QUICK REVIEW QUESTION**
>
> 8. One day after a PCI for a STEMI, a patient is sitting up in bed, laughing and talking with family in the room. When the nurse enters the room to complete morning assessments, the patient's demeanor abruptly changes. Cringing, the patient complains of chronic severe lower back pain and specifically requests "Dilaudid." The nurse notes that the home medication list reports oxycodone for back pain. What should the nurse do?

Medical Nonadherence

Characteristics

There are a number of factors that can contribute to **medical nonadherence** to care plans.

- social factors
  - inability to afford medications or lack of insurance
  - lack of transportation or time
  - cultural norms against receiving care
- emotional or spiritual factors
  - depression or fear
  - recourse to prayer or alternative healing methods
- physical factors
  - immobility
  - inability to properly access or use medications
  - medication side effects
- educational factors (i.e., lack of health literacy)

Treatment and Management

- Provide supportive care that individually addresses the patient's barriers, needs, and circumstances.
- Assess for potential barriers to medical adherence when developing a care plan.
- Consult social worker for financial and supportive resources.
- Consult physician to explore alternative medications or treatments that may better meet the patient's needs.
- Maintain open communication with the patient and family over concerns.

QUICK REVIEW QUESTION

9. A patient is readmitted to the ICU with acute-on-chronic COPD exacerbation. Upon questioning, the nurse finds that the patient was not taking the medications prescribed after the last admit. The patient's spouse states there are too many pills to keep track of and they are not able to afford several of the medications. What key interventions can the nurse initiate to mitigate this nonadherence?

ANSWER KEY

1. The nurse should complete the physical assessment and discuss these findings with the physician. She should then complete the screening for child abuse and follow local policy on mandatory reporting of suspected child abuse.

2. The nurse should assess the status of the patient, including orientation, vital signs, neurovascular status of the extremities restrained, and skin integrity at the restraint points.

3. The nurse should obtain prior medical history, including cardiac and respiratory concerns, and find out if the patient has a history of anxiety reactions in the past. Medications the patient is currently taking should be reviewed. The nurse should be prepared to address any life-threatening illnesses before addressing anxiety.

4. The nurse should get a detailed accounting of the patient's plan for self-harm and determine if the patient is in possession of any objects or weapons that could cause harm to the patient or to staff. The patient's surroundings should be assessed for safety, with removal of any objects that could be used for harm. Suicide precautions should be initiated with procurement of a 1:1 safety companion assignment.

5. The nurse should educate the family on the possibility that the patient could develop symptoms of depression, labile moods, excessive fatigue, weakness, or cognitive decline in the upcoming months. The family should be encouraged to talk with the patient about their experiences in the ICU and to validate their feelings about the experience.

6. The nurse should assess the patient and take a thorough history to confirm the patient is experiencing alcohol withdrawal. The nurse should be prepared to administer benzodiazepines and assess for fluid and nutrient imbalances related to chronic alcohol use.

7. A patient who does not have prior opioid use is at risk for opioid withdrawal after more than 96 hours of opioid treatment. Screen patient for withdrawal symptoms using COWS. Anticipate orders for benzodiazepine or clonidine if patient exhibits symptoms of tachycardia, tachypnea, and hypertension.

8. After completing a thorough pain assessment, as well as setting reasonable and realistic pain goals with the patient, the nurse should review the medications and other treatments the patient used at home prior to hospitalization. A discussion with the managing physician regarding restarting the patient's home regimen rather than treating with patient's request for hydromorphone (Dilaudid) is reasonable.

9. The nurse can try to alleviate the cost of medications by working with a social worker to find assistance programs and working with the physician to find less expensive alternative medications. An interview with the patient and family may help identify other specific barriers that can be addressed. Possible interventions may include pill organizers, further education, and increased social support from family or friends.

11 MULTISYSTEM REVIEW

CCRN TEST PLAN: MULTISYSTEM

- Acid-base imbalance*
- Bariatric complications
- Comorbidity in patients with transplant history
- End-of-life care
- Healthcare-associated conditions (e.g., VAE, CAUTI, CLABSI)*
- Hypotension*
- Infectious diseases
- Life-threatening maternal/fetal complications (e.g., eclampsia, HELLP syndrome, postpartum hemorrhage, amniotic embolism)
- Multiple organ dysfunction syndrome (MODS)
- Multisystem trauma*
- Pain: acute, chronic
- Post-intensive care syndrome (PICS)*
- Sepsis
- Septic shock
- Shock states
- a. Distributive (e.g., anaphylactic, neurogenic)
- b. Hypovolemic
- Sleep disruption (including sensory overload)
- Thermoregulation
- Toxic ingestion/inhalations (e.g., drug/alcohol overdose)
- Toxin/drug exposure (including allergies)

*Topic is covered in relevant systems chapter. Bariatric Complications

- The CCRN should be prepared for acute post-op management of bariatric surgery and for delivery of pertinent dietary and lifestyle education to the patient.
- There are three types of bariatric surgical procedures intended to produce weight loss: restrictive, malabsorptive, and combination procedures.
- **Restrictive procedures** reduce the capacity of the stomach.
    - The **vertical band gastroplasty (VBG)** creates a small pouch (15 – 30 mL capacity) and is generally considered a permanent alteration.
    - The **adjustable gastric banding procedure** also creates a small pouch, which can be externally inflated and deflated to allow for flexibility in the amount of food intake.
    - The **vertical sleeve gastrectomy (SG)** surgically removes approximately 80% of the stomach, changes the organ to a sleeve shape, and permanently reduces capacity.
- **Malabsorptive procedures** limit digestion and absorption of food by altering the GI tract itself. The amount of food volume consumed is minimally affected, but the absorption of nutrients is markedly reduced. Nutritional deficits require monitoring over time.
    - The **biliopancreatic diversion with a duodenal switch (BPD)** creates an anastomosis between the stomach and the intestine.
- **Combination procedures** limit capacity and profoundly alter the absorption of nutrients.
    - The **Roux-en-Y gastric bypass (RYGB)** constructs a small gastric pouch (20 – 30 mL capacity) that has a stoma outlet to a Y-shaped section of the jejunum that has been anastomosed to the pouch.
    - This surgery allows food to bypass the lower stomach and the duodenum, decreasing digestive absorption.
- Common complications of bariatric surgery:
    - Post-op GI bleeding markedly increases morbidity and mortality and requires surgical correction.
    - Anastomotic leaks present with pain and fever. They require treatment with broad-spectrum antibiotics and possible drainage or surgical repair.
    - Stenosis is prevalent in the RYGB procedure and often requires endoscopic balloon dilation within 1 week postsurgery.
    - Kinks in the surgical sleeve (after SG) present with recurrent vomiting and inability to tolerate oral intake. This complication generally requires surgical intervention.
    - Gastroenteric or gastrobronchial fistulas are managed according to severity; they may close without intervention or require surgery.

HELPFUL HINT:

VBG is often accompanied by a cholecystectomy to reduce risk of gallstones.

- Common abdominal postsurgical emergent events such as atelectasis, pneumonia, PE, DVT, postoperative pain, and trauma from nasogastric suction are also bariatric sequelae.
- **Dumping syndrome** is a collection of symptoms that result from rapid gastric emptying; it can occur after surgery that removes or bypasses the pyloric sphincter.
  - Early dumping syndrome occurs when fluid shifts into the small bowel because of hyperosmolar stomach contents. Signs and symptoms include abdominal pain, diarrhea, tachycardia, and hypotension.
  - Late dumping syndrome (postprandial hyperinsulinemic hypoglycemia [PHH]) occurs when there is an overproduction of insulin after a high concentration of carbohydrates is delivered quickly into the intestines.
  - Dumping syndrome is managed with dietary changes. Some patients may require medication (self-administered subcutaneous Sandostatin [octreotide injection]).
  - Dumping syndrome may not occur in the critical care setting, as postoperative dietary progression may not include sufficient solids to trigger the syndrome.

QUICK REVIEW QUESTION

1. What are the anatomical changes in an RYGB and the potential adverse emergent situations in the first 3 postoperative days?

End-of-Life Care

- The implementation of high-quality **end-of-life care (EOLC)** is an important part of ICU work. The CCRN should be aware of the aspects, options, and caring responses to this event described by the 2020 AACN recommendations.
- Decision-making process:
  - The decision to withhold or withdraw life-sustaining therapy is made by the individual, with family involvement.
  - Decisions should reflect the patient's values and wishes (if possible) and are documented with input from the entire interdisciplinary team, without excluding other therapies in progress.
- Place-to-die determination:
  - The best location for an actively dying individual is usually the same single-occupancy ICU room.

- If transfer is necessary, complete information is given to the patient early, with staff support, to ease the transition.
    - Discharge to home is also an option.
- Palliative care, patient comfort, and dignity:
    - Assess frequently to manage palliation of pain.
    - Both medical and nonmedical techniques should be used to maintain patient comfort.
    - Respect individual dignity and the patient's wishes for visits, spiritual support, and a nursing surrogate role (if no family is present).
- Family presence in ICU (including children's visiting practices):
    - If congruent with patient's wishes, family should be able to visit at all times.
    - Avoid unnecessary waiting outside room.
    - Provide clear, age-appropriate, and truthful explanation of dying to children before their first ICU visit.
    - When possible, provide an ICU area that children can play in.
- Preparing family and identifying their diverse needs at end-of-life event:
    - Be sensitive to cultural and personal family reactions to the active dying of a loved one.
    - Assess family needs for information and spiritual support systems.
    - Respect family dynamics during the grieving process.
    - Reassure family that the patient's pain is being managed, and frequently assess and treat emergent symptoms while giving family simple explanations.
- Determining staff presence during the active dying of individual:
    - Identify the individual's wishes.
    - If the family prefers to be alone, continue appropriate care in room without intruding on family processes.
- Family participation at end-of-life event, and after:
    - Family-centered bereavement care provides time for grieving, allows the family to participate in care of the expired patient, and continues to support families after they leave the ICU.
    - Most facilities have established policies to allow for personal mementos (e.g., locks of hair, handprints), follow-up notes, visitations, or calls, and bereavement counseling groups to reduce family suffering and PTSD responses to loss.
- Staff grieving: Debriefing honors staff grief and reduces burnout.

> **QUICK REVIEW QUESTION**
>
> 2. What is family-centered bereavement care?

Infectious Diseases

- The CCRN exam will likely not cover signs and symptoms or management of specific infectious diseases. Instead, candidates should expect to see bacterial or viral infections appear as part of background scenarios (e.g., management of sepsis secondary to pneumonia).
- The exam may include questions about standard isolation protocols. Some general guidelines are given below.

Standard Precautions

- Assume that all patients are carrying an infectious microorganism.
- Practice hand hygiene.
    - Use soap and water when hands are visibly soiled.
    - Use antimicrobial foam or gel if hands are not visibly soiled.
- Wear gloves.
    - Gloves must be discarded between each patient visit.
    - Gloves may need to be discarded when soiled and a new pair donned.
    - Practice hand hygiene after removing gloves.
- Prevent needle sticks.
    - Immediately place used needles in puncture-resistant containers.
    - Recap using mechanical device or one-handed technique.
- Avoid splash and spray: wear appropriate PPE if there is a possibility of body fluids splashing or spraying.

HELPFUL HINT:

Antimicrobial foams and gels are not effective against some infectious agents, such as *C. difficile*.

Airborne Precautions

- Patient should be placed in a private room with a negative-pressure air system and the door kept closed.
- Wear N-95 respirator mask: put it on before entering the room, and keep it on until after leaving the room.
- Place N-95 or surgical mask on patient during transport.
- Examples of diseases requiring airborne precautions include chicken pox, measles, and tuberculosis. The precautions are also used for COVID-19 patients undergoing aerosol-generating procedures (e.g., intubation).

Droplet Precautions

- Place patient in a private room; the door may remain open.
- Wear appropriate PPE within 3 feet of patient.
- Wash hands with antimicrobial soap after removing gloves and mask, before leaving the patient's room.
- Place surgical mask on patient during transport.
- Examples of diseases requiring droplet precautions include influenza, pertussis, and COVID-19.

Contact Precautions

- Place the patient in a private room; the door may remain open.
- Wear gloves.
  - Change gloves after touching infected materials.
  - Remove gloves before leaving patient's room.
- Wear gown; remove before leaving patient's room.
- Use patient-dedicated equipment if possible; community equipment is to be used clean and disinfected between patients.
- During transport, keep precautions in place and notify different areas as needed.
- Examples of diseases requiring contact precautions include C. *difficile*, MRSA, and noroviruses.

> **QUICK REVIEW QUESTION**
> 3. A patient is admitted to the ICU with a suspected C. *difficile* infection. What PPE should the nurse use?

Life-Threatening Maternal/Fetal Complications

- **Preeclampsia** is a syndrome that occurs when abnormalities in the placental vasculature cause widespread arterial vasospasms. The multiple, repetitive vasospasms decrease perfusion to organs, eventually leading to tissue ischemia, microangiopathy, and end-organ dysfunction in the mother.

- Symptoms can appear after the twentieth week of pregnancy and most commonly appear after 34 weeks. Maternal **postpartum preeclampsia** generally occurs within 6 days after childbirth but can be delayed up to 6 weeks after delivery. It can occur even if there was no evidence of preeclampsia prior to delivery.
- Signs and symptoms: malignant hypertension, edema (despite strict bed rest), excruciating headache, vision disturbance, dyspnea, changes in LOC.
- Diagnostic findings: proteinuria, hyperuricemia, thrombocytopenia, elevated homocysteine.
- The reduced blood flow seen in severe preeclampsia can cause injury to multiple organs, including the liver (causing elevated liver enzymes), kidneys, (causing elevated creatinine), or myocardium (causing elevated troponin). Labs may also show hemolysis of RBCs (decreased hemoglobin, hyperbilirubinemia).
- Sequalae: pulmonary edema (due to increased capillary permeability), abruptio placentae, intracerebral hemorrhage
- During pregnancy, the only definitive treatment is delivery of the fetus and removal of placental tissue.
- Postpartum preeclampsia requires anti-hypertensives, seizure prophylaxis, and anticoagulants.
- **Eclampsia** is the onset of tonic-clonic seizures in women with preeclampsia. All patients with preeclampsia require seizure prophylaxis (magnesium sulfate [$MgSO_4$] IV pump infusion) to prevent progression to eclampsia. Recurrent seizure may be treated with amobarbital, phenytoin, or benzodiazepines.
- Refractory hypertension is treated with labetalol or hydralazine hydrochloride.

■ **HELLP syndrome** is currently believed to be a form of preeclampsia, although the relationship between the 2 disorders is controversial and not well understood.
- Around 85% of women diagnosed with HELLP also present with symptoms of preeclampsia.
- HELLP is characterized by hemolysis (H), elevated liver enzymes (EL), and low platelet count (LP).
- Signs and symptoms: hypertension, tachycardia, dyspnea, jaundice, fatigue, RUQ pain with epigastric tenderness, dehydration.
- HELLP severity is evaluated using the Mississippi Classification System (based on platelet count, AST/ALT levels, and LDH levels).
- Management is focused on preventing and managing emergent complications, including DIC, pulmonary edema, PE, ARDS, MI, AKI, hepatic rupture, and infection.

HELPFUL HINT:

Be aware of how an exam question on preeclampsia is worded. Do not confuse *prepartum* preeclampsia (which requires delivery of the fetus) with *postpartum* preeclampsia (which requires ICU monitoring and management).

HELPFUL HINT:

HELLP syndrome is often mistaken for acute hepatitis, gastritis, gallbladder disease, or influenza.

- **Postpartum hemorrhage** is bleeding that occurs any time after delivery up to 12 weeks postpartum and exceeds 1,000 mL or that causes symptoms of hypovolemia.
    - Management: IV fluid resuscitation and blood products as needed; identify and treat underlying cause of hemorrhage.
    - Uterine atony: uterine massage; oxytocin 20 – 40 IU/L 0.9% NaCl IV; ergot derivatives (contraindicated for preeclampsia and hypertension); vasopressors.
    - Trauma: surgery to repair cause of bleed.
    - Retained tissue: manual removal of placental tissue.
    - Coagulopathy (thrombin): replace clotting factors (platelets and/or FFP).

HELPFUL HINT:

The causes of postpartum hemorrhage are known as the Four T's: tone, trauma, tissue, and thrombin.

- **Amniotic fluid embolism (AFE)** is an acute, life-threatening allergic reaction that occurs when amniotic fluid enters the maternal circulation during childbirth.
    - Phase 1 exhibits rapid-onset respiratory failure leading to cardiac arrest, ARDS, and multisystem organ failure.
    - Phase 2 (hemorrhagic phase) develops profuse bleeding (usually at the site of placental attachment, cesarean incision, and IV site) and DIC.
    - Treatment focuses on management of symptoms and may include massive blood transfusion protocol, hysterectomy, and management of cardiac arrest, ARDS, and multisystem organ failure.
    - Maternal survivors demonstrate severe neurological injury; infant survivors show cerebral palsy or limited brain function. AFE survivors and their families are at high risk for PTSD.
- **Abruptio placentae** (placental abruption) occurs when the placenta separates from the uterus after the twentieth week of gestation but before delivery. Abruption can lead to life-threatening conditions, including hemorrhage and DIC.
- In **placenta accreta**, the placenta attaches abnormally deeply into the myometrium. Because the placenta cannot detach from the uterus after delivery, placenta accreta can lead to hemorrhage and requires a hysterectomy.

QUICK REVIEW QUESTION

4. A 33-year-old prima gravida previously diagnosed with mild preeclampsia develops headache, double-vision intervals, with BP 180/101 mm Hg at 36 weeks. After a noncomplicated vaginal delivery, BP stabilizes at 145/80. Six days later, the mother presents at the ED with severe headache, overwhelming fatigue, abdominal pain, nausea, vomiting, and generalized edema. With BP of 190/110, she is transferred to ICU for management. What is the admission diagnosis, and what should the nurse anticipate for treatment?

Pain

- **Pain management** is uniquely individualized in the critical care setting, so the CCRN exam will not focus on management of individual patients. Instead, the exam will present questions that target the nurse's understanding of pain assessment and documentation.
- The goal of pain management should be timely and consistent patient responses to interventions.
- The critical care nurse should understand that pain assessment requires asking the right questions and using an appropriate and consistent pain scale (as defined by hospital policy). Pain assessment may include:
  - patient's self-reported pain (on a consistent scale)
  - a detailed interview to determine location, quality, severity, timing, and alleviating/exacerbating factors of pain
  - review of effects of previous interventions
  - use of tools such as the Behavioral Pain Scale (BPS) or Critical Care Pain Observation Tool for patients who cannot verbally communicate
- Planning for pain management is an important component of a care plan.
  - Review with patient and/or family the potential or actual discomfort levels related to the specific clinical situation.
  - Prepare patients for upcoming treatments or bedside procedures (e.g., dressing changes, line insertions or removals, treatments, transfers to testing areas) with appropriate premedication, and ensure sufficient time for premedication to take effect before initiating procedures.
  - Engage patients/family in mobility planning and implementation.
- Pain management interventions should always be properly documented.
- The pain management plan should address the side effects of analgesics (e.g., constipation, nausea, or respiratory depression related to opioid use).

HELPFUL HINT:

Sedation is NOT the correct way to treat pain and should never replace the use of appropriate analgesics.

QUICK REVIEW QUESTION

5. A 28-year-old multi-trauma patient will require, after chest wound surgical repair, intermittent prone positioning to decrease ARDS complications of prolonged ventilator therapy. The patient's wife, upset because she believes her husband is in pain during positioning, demands the nurse "give him something to stop him from hurting." What is the most appropriate pain management plan for the nurse to initiate?

Shock States

Shock is a state of circulatory failure that results in insufficient oxygenation of tissue. Shock is categorized according to the underlying cause of circulatory failure.

- **Hypovolemic shock** is the result of reduced intravascular volume.
- **Distributive shock** is the result of massive vasodilation. Types of distributive shock include anaphylactic, septic, and neurogenic shock. (Neurogenic shock is discussed in chapter 9.)
- **Cardiogenic shock** is the result of cardiac tissue damage that reduces cardiac output. (Cardiogenic shock is discussed in chapter 1.)
- **Obstructive shock** is reduced cardiac output not caused by cardiac tissue damage. Causes of obstructive shock include PE, pulmonary hypertension, cardiac tamponade, and tension pneumothorax.

Understanding the pathophysiology underlying the **three phases of shock**—no matter what the specific type/cause of shock—is the key to answering exam questions on every type of shock state.

HELPFUL HINT:

Specialty knowledge of shock trauma is not part of the CCRN exam, but CCRN candidates should know that the triad of hypothermia, acidosis, and coagulopathy in trauma patients must be stabilized to prevent irreversible damage or death.

TABLE 11.1. Phases of Shock

Phase	Pathophysiology	General Symptoms
Compensatory (early)	Activation of the sympathetic nervous system to increase/maintain blood pressure causes vasoconstriction, increased contractility of heart, and increased HR.	• restlessness, anxiety • tachycardia • tachypnea (impending respiratory alkalosis) • normal PaO_2 on ABG • pallor • oliguria • increased thirst
Progressive	Compensatory system begins to fail, and sympathetic withdrawal syndrome occurs.	• hypotension • change in LOC • increased tachycardia • decreased PaO_2 • metabolic acidosis on ABG • cool, clammy, mottled skin • nausea

Phase	Pathophysiology	General Symptoms
Refractory (late)	Severe systemic hypoperfusion leads to MODS.	- neurological: stroke, encephalopathy - cardiac: ischemia, failure - pulmonary: ARDS - renal: anuria, acute tubular necrosis - hepatic: liver failure - hematologic: DIC

Hypovolemic Shock

Pathophysiology

Hypovolemic shock is characterized by a profound reduction in circulating volume, leading to impaired tissue perfusion. It is the most common type of shock.

External causes of hypovolemic shock include hemorrhage, burns, GI/renal losses, or excessive diaphoresis. Hypovolemic shock can also be caused by fluid pooling in the intravascular compartment (third-spacing). Shock caused by bleeding is categorized as **hemorrhagic shock**; all other causes of hypovolemic shock are **nonhemorrhagic**.

Hemodynamic Changes

- narrowing pulse pressure (decrease in SBP, increase in DBP): cardinal sign of hypovolemic shock
- increased SVR
- decreased cardiac output
- decreased pulse pressure/low BP
- decreased CVP
- decreased PAOP

Treatment and Management

- Determine and treat cause (assessment performed concurrently with fluid resuscitation).
- Secure airway and obtain 2 large-bore IV access sites.
- Rapidly replace volume.
  - 0.9% NaCl or lactated Ringer's (crystalloid fluids)
  - Use fluid warmer if giving more than 2 L/hr

HELPFUL HINT:

During early shock, vasoconstriction occurs with activation of the **renin-angiotensin-aldosterone system (RAAS)**. **Renin** activates angiotensin I, which in turn activates **angiotensin II**, which increases systemic vascular resistance. Angiotensin II also stimulates release of **aldosterone**, which promotes Na^+ and water retention.

HELPFUL HINT:

SVR remains high during hypovolemic state: do NOT give vasopressors.

HELPFUL HINT:

Replacing lost volume helps sustain aerobic metabolism to reduce acidosis, improves oxygen delivery/tissue uptake, decreases tachycardia, and increases renal perfusion to improve urinary output.

HELPFUL HINT:

Cold blood increases hemoglobin's affinity for oxygen and decreases tissue uptake, creates platelet dysfunction, and deforms RBCs.

- Initiate maintenance treatment when HR returns to baseline to meet target parameters:
  - MAP ≥ 65
  - CVP 6 – 10 mm Hg
  - Urine output ≥ 0.5 mL/kg/hr
- Management of hemorrhagic shock:
  - manage bleeding
  - hemorrhagic shock Class I and II (blood loss <1500 mL, BP normal): crystalloid fluids
  - hemorrhagic shock Class III and IV (blood loss >1500 mL, decreased BP): crystalloids and PRBC units
  - because PRBCs do not contain plasma or platelets, actively bleeding patients will also need FFP, cryoprecipitate, and/or platelets
  - indications for massive transfusion resuscitation: traumatic injuries; liver transplants; OB emergencies; ruptured aortic or thoracic aneurisms; Hgb <7.0 (generally transfused at higher level for MI, lactic acidosis, severe hypoxemia, or continued active bleeding)
  - ensure Hgb >7.0 and coagulation profile/platelets normalized before moving to maintenance treatment
- Blood administration risks:
  - hypothermia: use blood warmer if possible
  - hemolytic and nonhemolytic transfusion reactions (see chapter 4 for more detailed information on transfusion reactions)
  - hypocalcemia and hypomagnesemia
  - coagulopathy: requires platelets and plasma therapy
  - viral infections: transmitted from blood products

QUICK REVIEW QUESTION

6. What are the classic signs and hemodynamic changes found in hypovolemic shock?

Sepsis and Septic Shock

Pathophysiology

Sepsis, a dysregulated inflammatory response to infection, leads to organ system dysfunction. What starts as a localized response to infection leads to generalized inflammation, which in turn causes cellular damage across systems. Common organ-specific conditions seen during sepsis include:

- hypotension (due to massive vasodilation)
- pulmonary edema and ARDS
- AKI
- encephalopathy

Sepsis is a progressive process, and the guidelines for classifying its stages continue to evolve. Current Society of Critical Care Medicine guidelines define 3 stages of sepsis:

- **early sepsis:** infection + early indicators of organ dysfunction (e.g., increased RR or decreased SBP)
- **sepsis:** infection + signs of organ dysfunction
  - lung: decreased PaO_2/FiO_2 ratio
  - coagulation: decreased platelets
  - liver: increased bilirubin
  - cardiovascular: hypotension
  - brain: low GCS score
  - kidney: increased creatine
- **septic shock:** sepsis + inability to maintain adequate MAP (MAP ≥65 mm Hg and lactate 2 mmol/L)

MODS is the most severe end of the sepsis spectrum. (Note that MODS is simply a description of organ dysfunction and can have noninfectious causes.) Commonly used indicators of organ dysfunction are given below.

- **neurologic:** confusion, lethargy, disorientation, delirium, coma, seizure
- **cardiovascular:** tachycardia, dysrhythmias, elevated troponin level, hypotension requiring fluid resuscitation and vasopressor support, decreased SVR, abnormal CVP (low or high)
- **pulmonary:** tachypnea, dyspnea, hypoxemia, ARDS
- **renal:** oliguria, decreased GRF, elevated creatinine, critical-level electrolyte imbalances
- **endocrine:** hypoglycemia or hyperglycemia, adrenal insufficiency
- **hepatic:** decreased albumin, jaundice, elevated liver function tests
- **hematologic:** thrombocytopenia, coagulopathy, increased D-dimer levels
- **metabolic:** metabolic acidosis, elevated lactate levels

Older sepsis guidelines also include **systemic inflammatory response syndrome (SIRS)** as part of the sepsis continuum. SIRS is defined as 2 or more of the following:

- HR >90 bpm
- temperature 100.5°F (38.0°C) OR <96.8°F (36.0°C)

- RR >20 or PaCO$_2$ <32 (respiratory alkalosis)
- WBC >12,000 or WBC <4,000 OR a shift of bands to the left 10%

Patients with SIRS and a suspected or confirmed infection are considered to have sepsis. Noninfectious causes of SIRS include pancreatitis, burns, thromboembolism, and trauma.

Regardless of which guidelines are used, the critical care nurse should understand how sepsis may progress from infection to inflammation to organ dysfunction.

Treatment and Management

- Stat lab work:
    - 2 sets of blood cultures: 2 separate sites; obtain before initiating antibiotic therapy
    - CBC with differential, lactate levels
- Implement sepsis bundle (per facility guidelines): broad-spectrum antibiotics, IV fluids, and vasopressors as indicated.
- Identify causative agent: antibiotic/antiviral/antifungal therapy ASAP.
- IV fluid challenges:
    - initiated when lactate level 4 mmol/L
    - 30 mL/kg to start to support BP
    - IV crystalloid concentrations based on other comorbidities present
- Maintain MAP ≥65:
    - first-line vasopressor: norepinephrine infusion
    - second-line vasopressor: epinephrine infusion
    - ionotropic therapy if cardiac dysfunction: dobutamine infusion (not to exceed 20 mcg/kg/min)
    - PRBCs if Hgb <7.0
- Focused reassessment exam after initial fluid resuscitation:
    - assess tissue perfusion and volume status
    - lactate level should decrease by 10% with each fluid bolus
- SvO$_2$/ScvO$_2$ stabilized
    - SvO$_2$ 60 – 75% (target): measured with pulmonary artery catheter; mixed venous sample
    - ScvO$_2$ 70% (target): continuous monitoring (identify/use specific CVP port/line) or intermittent monitoring (CVP multiuse port/line or PICC line)
    - ScvO$_2$ = 5 – 8% higher than SvO$_2$

HELPFUL HINT:

Lactate may be considered a marker of tissue perfusion. Elevated lactate levels sustained 6 hours lead to increased mortality. Lactate 4.0 mmol/L is associated with a 28% mortality rate.

> **QUICK REVIEW QUESTION**
>
> 7. A 69-year-old female patient with oral-medication-controlled type 2 diabetes mellitus has just completed her course of chemotherapy postmastectomy. The patient is admitted from the ED to the ICU with a temperature of 102.6°F (39.2°C), lethargy, and confusion. HR 105 bpm, BP 92/68 mm Hg, RR 22. Admission fingerstick glucose was 122 mg/dL, electrolytes and coagulation panel appeared within normal limits, lactate level was 2.4, and WBC = 14,000. What interventions should the nurse prepare for?

Anaphylactic Shock

Pathophysiology

Anaphylaxis is triggered when a hypersensitive reaction to an allergen (e.g., foods, medications, insect sting, latex, radiocontrast dye, blood/blood products) causes an overwhelming inflammatory response. Symptoms appear minutes to a few hours after exposure to the allergen. If untreated or ineffectively treated, anaphylaxis will progress to anaphylactic shock, refractory hypotension, and possible death.

Anaphylactic shock is characterized by massive vasodilation, resulting in fluid loss into the extravascular space, hemoconcentration, and hypovolemia. Increased pulmonary vascular resistance may lead to pulmonary edema and respiratory arrest. Dysrhythmias (especially tachycardia) are common, and patients are at risk for MI.

Signs and Symptoms

- urticaria, itching, and erythema
- pale skin
- nausea, vomiting, or diarrhea
- angioedema or tongue swelling
- laryngeal edema and difficulty swallowing
- bronchospasm and wheezing
- hypotension
- tachycardia
- alteration in LOC

Treatment and Management

- first-line treatment
  - maintain airway

HELPFUL HINT:

Epinephrine may be administered in nebulized form for laryngeal edema.

- 0.3 mg epinephrine 1:1,000 IM (blocks release of inflammatory mediators)
- glucagon 5 – 15 mcg/min infusion if patient is on beta blocker
- second-line treatment
    - H1 blocker: diphenhydramine (25 – 50 mg IV/IM/PO)
    - H2 blocker: ranitidine (50 mg IV or 150 mg PO)
    - steroids: prednisone (50 mg PO) OR methylprednisolone (125 mg IV)
- shock management
    - airway management: oxygen therapy and bronchodilators (albuterol inhaler)
    - volume resuscitation: IV or IO colloid infusion with volume dependent on response (1 – 3 L rapid administration not uncommon)
    - circulatory management (decrease afterload and preload): epinephrine infusion (2 – 8 mcg/min), dopamine infusion (5 – 20 mcg/kg/min), or norepinephrine infusion (2 – 8 mcg/min)
- Monitor for spontaneous or rebound/reemergence of anaphylaxis.

QUICK REVIEW QUESTION

8. A 33-year-old male patient is undergoing an emergent laparotomy for removal of an inflamed appendix. The circulating nurse hangs a 50 mL antibiotic IV mini bag as the incision is closed and sutured. As the still-intubated patient is being prepared for transfer to the PACU, the cardiac monitor shows SVT of 128, and the patient is markedly hypotensive. IV fluids and a dopamine drip at 8 mcg/kg/min are infusing as the patient is brought to the SICU. The receiving nurse discusses with the surgical resident a possible anaphylactic reaction. What series of initial medication orders should the critical care nurse expect for this patient?

Toxic Ingestion and Exposure

- During **acetaminophen (Tylenol)** overdose, toxic metabolites accumulate in the liver causing hepatotoxicity from mitochondrial dysfunction and cellular destruction.
    - Time and amount of drug are important considerations in acetaminophen overdose treatment. Plasma acetaminophen levels can be measured 4 – 24 hours after ingestion to predict risk of hepatotoxicity using the Rumack-Matthew nomogram.

- Gastritis symptoms usually appear within hours; symptoms of hepatotoxicity may not appear for 48 hours.
- Hepatoxicity rapidly advances to acute liver failure often complicated by encephalopathy, pulmonary edema, pancreatitis, and AKI. (See chapter 5 for detailed information on liver failure.)
- The antidote for acetaminophen overdoes is **N-acetylcysteine (Mucomyst)**; the best response occurs when it is administered within 24 hours of ingestion.
- N-acetylcysteine dosing (IV): IV 150 mg/kg over 1 hour; 50 mg/kg over next 4 hours; 100 mg/kg over next 16 hours
- N-acetylcysteine dosing (PO): 140 mg/kg loading dose; 70 mg/kg every 4 hours
- Activated charcoal may be administered within 4 hours of ingestion but is usually not well tolerated.

- **Beta blockers** block beta-adrenergic receptors in the heart (beta$_1$) and blood vessels (beta$_2$), resulting in lowered BP and HR and decreased cardiac output. They are used to treat a wide range of conditions, and most overdoses are unintentional.
  - Symptoms will vary with the beta blocker ingested, as each medication has different actions, absorption times, half-lifes, and interactions with other medications.
  - Symptoms will be seen 1 – 2 hours after ingestion and usually are most pronounced around 20 hours post-ingestion.
  - General signs and symptoms: bradycardia, hypotension, hypoglycemia, altered mental state.
  - Beta blockers with lipophilic affinity (e.g., propranolol) cross the blood-brain barrier easily and may cause seizures.
  - Beta blockers that block sodium or potassium channels (e.g., propranolol, acebutolol) can cause prolonged QRS/QTc intervals.
  - Glucagon bypasses the beta-adrenergic receptor sites affected by the beta-blocking agent and reverses the beta$_1$ blockade; it increases myocardial contractility and HR with improved AV conduction.
  - Management of symptoms may include vasopressors, MgSO$_4$ IV for prolonged QTc, sodium bicarbonate (NaHCO3) IV for widened QRS, intubation, bronchodilators for bronchospasm, gastric lavage, seizure management, insulin drip (glucose control target 100 mg/dL – 200 mg/dL)

- **Salicylate** (aspirin) overdose affects the brain's respiratory center, resulting in hyperventilation and respiratory alkalosis. The kidneys respond by producing more bicarbonate and excreting more potassium, causing metabolic acidosis.

> **HELPFUL HINT:**
>
> Enteric-coated pills may form a gastric **bezoar** (hard mass or concretion in the stomach) delaying absorption and excretion.

- Peak serum salicylate levels occur at 6 hours after ingestion (for non-enteric-coated pills).
- Diagnostic findings: nausea/vomiting, tinnitus, hyperventilation, hyperthermia, hypoglycemia, hypernatremia, hypokalemia
- Sequelae: seizure, dysrhythmias, noncardiogenic pulmonary edema, coma
- Management: urinary alkalinization (IV $NaHCO_3$ bolus or infusion until urine pH $\geq$ 7.5); fluid resuscitation and electrolyte replacement; hemodialysis
- Intubation is contraindicated unless there is respiratory failure with hypoxemia and uncontrollable acidosis. Even a temporary increase in pCO_2 rapidly increases the flow of salicylates into brain tissue, precipitating cardiovascular collapse and death.

- **Benzodiazepine** overdose causes a depression of spinal reflexes and the reticular activating system by enhancing the neurotransmitter GABA.
  - Generally, respiratory arrest occurs with ingestion of benzodiazepines. Cardiopulmonary arrest is seen in rapid diazepam injections or when benzodiazepines are used with other depressant drugs.
  - Onset of symptoms are seen in 30 – 120 minutes (specific to the benzodiazepine used).
  - Signs and symptoms: lethargy, slurred speech, ataxia, hyporeflexia, hyporeflexia, pinpoint pupils (midline fixated and unresponsive to light), hypothermia, coma.
  - **Flumazenil (Romazicon)** is an antidote that competitively inhibits benzodiazepines receptors. Administer 0.2 mg IVP every 1 – 6 minutes or IV infusion 0.3 – 0.4 mg/hr.
  - Monitor for re-sedation after flumazenil administration: its effects often do not last as long as the drug's toxic effects.
  - Benzodiazepines have a very high therapeutic index, and the majority of benzodiazepine overdose cases do not require the use of an antagonist.

> **HELPFUL HINT:**
>
> The sleep aids zolpidem and zaleplon also bond to GABA/benzodiazepine receptors and are responsive to flumazenil after an overdose.

- **Calcium channel blockers (CCBs)** restrict the flow of calcium into cells in vascular and cardiac tissues and result in vasodilation, decreased contractility, and decreased conduction velocity in the cardiac nodes. They are used to treat hypertension, vasospasms, SVT, and migraine headaches.
  - Dihydropyridines (nifedipine, amlodipine, felodipine, isradipine, nicardipine, nimodipine) act on vascular smooth muscle and are used to treat hypertension.
  - Non-dihydropyridines (diltiazem, verapamil) act on the myocardium and are used for angina and SVT.

- CCBs also reduce insulin secretion from the pancreas, causing insulin resistance and hyperglycemia, and alter glucose catabolism, ultimately increasing lactate levels.
- CCB overdose causes severe hemodynamic instability with hypotension and dysrhythmias, including sinus bradycardia, AV block, junctional rhythms, BBBs, prolonged QT, or sinus tachycardia (nifedipine only).
- Results of tissue hypoperfusion and end-organ ischemia include seizures, MI, bowel infarction, stroke, and ARDS.

TABLE 11.2. Management of CCB Overdose

Symptom Management	Reversal of Toxicity
Emergent intubation with pre-administration of atropine	Activated charcoal (within 2 hours of ingestion); whole bowel irrigation for timed-release medication
Continuous cardiac monitoring; pacing for refractory bradycardia	
IV colloids	10% calcium chloride 10 – 20 mL IV bolus; **not rapid** IVP: will cause hypotension, V-fib, AV dissociation
IV glucagon for refractory hypotension: 5 mg IV bolus, repeat bolus reconstituted in D5W (to avoid propylene glycol toxicity)	Lipid emulsion therapy (LET): high-dose IV lipid administration reverses CCB toxicity
vasopressor and/or positive inotrope to increase MAP	Hyperinsulinemic euglycemia therapy (HIET): ensure serum glucose 200 mg/dL and serum potassium ≥2.5 mEq/L
ECMO, IV catecholamine, and/or IABP for cardiogenic shock	

HELPFUL HINT:

Urinary alkalinization, hemofiltration, and hemodialysis are ineffective decontamination measures because there is large volume distribution and lipophilic affinity with CCB toxicity.

- **Opioids** depress the CNS and lower the perception of pain by stimulating dopamine release.
  - Opioid overdose can be a complication of substance abuse, unintentional or intentional overdose, or therapeutic drug error.
  - Opioid overdose causes an excessive depressive effect on the portion of the brain that regulates RR and can be fatal.
  - Signs and symptoms: opioid overdose triad (pinpoint pupils, respiratory depression, decreased LOC), hypotension, wheezing, dyspnea, nausea, vomiting, gastric aperistalsis, seizure, coma.
  - Priority is airway management and supplemental oxygen.
  - **Naloxone** is an opioid antagonist administered IV or IM; a standard dose is 0.4 mg titrated until adequate ventilation is achieved.
  - In patients who are opioid dependent, a slow dose of naloxone (0.1 – 0.4 mg every 1 – 3 minutes) is administered to prevent withdrawal symptoms.

- Activated charcoal or whole bowel irrigation may be used if indicated.
- **Alcohol** is a CNS depressant that directly binds to GABA receptors and inhibits glutamate-induced excitation. Chronic alcohol use alters the sensitivity of these receptors; when alcohol use is stopped, the result is hyperactivity in the CNS.
    - Alcohol withdrawal can be fatal.
    - Chronic alcohol use inhibits the absorption of nutrients, including thiamine and folic acid. Consequently, patients admitted with symptoms of alcohol withdrawal are also at risk for disorders related to vitamin deficiency, including Wernicke's encephalopathy and megaloblastic anemia.
    - Signs and symptoms: tachycardia, anxiety, irritation, tachypnea, diaphoresis, seizures.
    - Delirium tremens (DTs) may occur 72 – 96 hours after the last drink and is characterized by anxiety, hallucinations, tachycardia, hypertension, ataxia, and diaphoresis.
    - The Clinical Institute Withdrawal Assessment (CIWA) is a 10-item scale used to objectively assess withdrawal symptoms and to ensure that withdrawing patients are given the correct amount of medication.

TABLE 11.3. The CIWA of Alcohol

Patients are given a score of 0 – 7 for each symptom, based on its severity, except orientation, which is scored as 0 – 4.

- nausea and vomiting
- paroxysmal sweats
- level of anxiety
- level of agitation
- tremors
- headache symptoms
- auditory disturbances
- visual disturbances
- tactile disturbances
- orientation

< 8	No medication needed
9 – 14	Medication administration is optional
15 – 19	Administer medications ordered
>20	High risk for complications

- Pharmacological interventions for alcohol withdrawal and DTs include benzodiazepines, chlordiazepoxide (Librium), dexmedetomidine, antipsychotics (e.g., haloperidol, quetiapine), and nonbenzodiazepine anticonvulsants (e.g., phenytoin, carbamazepine, gabapentin).
- Patient will require IV fluids and electrolyte/vitamin replacement (particularly thiamine).

- **Carbon monoxide (CO)** binds to serum hemoglobin with 240 times oxygen's affinity, producing carboxyhemoglobin (CHOB) and resulting in impaired oxygen uptake by tissue. Additionally, CO can initiate an inflammatory cascade that causes delayed neurologic conditions.
  - Sources of CO include malfunctioning heaters and generators, smoke from fires, and motor vehicle exhaust. CO poisoning and cyanide poisoning often occur together.
  - Diagnostic findings: headache, malaise, dizziness, nausea, altered mental status, syncope, seizure, lactic acidosis.
  - SpO_2 pulse oximetry CANNOT screen for CO exposure, because the sensor does not differentiate between oxyhemoglobin and carboxyhemoglobin.
  - Complications: pulmonary edema, ventricular dysrhythmias, MI.
  - Management: 100% oxygen via nonrebreathing mask (high-flow oxygen) or intubation.
  - Hyperbaric oxygen therapy (HBO) initiated within 6 hours of exposure when patient has one of the following indicators: CHOB level 25% (20% in pregnant patients), loss of consciousness, severe metabolic acidosis (pH <7.1), or symptoms of end-organ ischemia (e.g., chest pain).

> **HELPFUL HINT:**
> The "cherry red" skin and lips often cited as indicative of CO poisoning are not reliable diagnostic criteria but may be included in a test scenario.

QUICK REVIEW QUESTION

9. A 58-year-old is brought to the ED after ingesting 25 enteric-coated diltiazem pills 3 hours earlier. He is administered 0.5 mg atropine and intubated. Fluid resuscitation is started with 3 L 0.9% NaCl and he receives IV calcium gluconate 60 mL bolus/10 min. After transfer to the MICU, the patient's hemodynamics are MAP 45 mm Hg, cardiac output 3.0 L/min, CI 2.0 L/min/m2, SVR 90 dynes/sec/cm5, and stroke volume variability 8%. A second 12-lead ECG shows sinus bradycardia of 53 bpm and a slightly prolonged QRS interval. What medications should the nurse anticipate administering?

ANSWER KEY

1. RYGB combines restrictive and malabsorption bariatric surgical procedures to effectively reduce the size of the stomach and to allow ingested food to bypass the lower part of the stomach and duodenum to reduce nutritional absorption. Post-op considerations include monitoring for internal bleeding at the anastomosis site; signs and symptoms of hypovolemic shock, atelectasis, pneumonia, and wound infection; pain management; and DVT prophylaxis with early ambulation.

2. Family-centered bereavement care prepares the family with information and education before the death of their loved one. It continues through the end-of-life event, with all staff demonstrating empathy and respect for the family's social, cultural, and specific grieving processes.

3. *C. difficile* requires contact protections, so the nurse should use gloves and an isolation gown.

4. The diagnosis is postpartum preeclampsia. Targeted treatment would include IV antihypertensive medications, aggressive IV seizure management, and initiation of anticoagulants, with a plan for long-term monitoring and therapy tapering after discharge.

5. The nurse should build a preemptive plan for pain management. The nurse should review the rationale for prone positioning and design a care plan that minimizes maneuvers that appear to cause the patient pain. The nurse should also determine the length of time necessary for position changes and ensure that appropriate premedications are administered. During care, the nurse needs to evaluate and document pain per hospital policies and share this information with the health care team so that consistent feedback can be given to the wife.

6. A narrowing pulse pressure (dropping SBP with increasing or maintaining DBP); decreasing BP; increased SVR; decreased cardiac output; decreased CVP (RAP); and decreased PAOP.

7. The nurse should be prepared to initiate a sepsis bundle per the hospital's protocols. This will likely include administration of broad-spectrum antibiotics and a crystalloid IV bolus fluid challenge. Vasopressors may be administered as part of the bundle if hypotension persists.

8. To stabilize the profound vasodilation response in anaphylaxis, the nurse should expect to initiate an epinephrine drip to titrate for a MAP ≥65. To counteract the histamine release in response to the antibiotic administered, the nurse would expect to give diphenhydramine 50 mg IV. Finally, methylprednisolone 125 mg IV will likely be given to reduce inflammation and potential rebound anaphylaxis.

9. The CCRN should anticipate administering a continuous calcium chloride IV infusion and should determine whether the medical team wants to repeat the 60 mL IV calcium gluconate bolus. The patient may also be administered glucagon (5 mg IV bolus followed by glucagon drip). To improve cardiac output, the nurse would anticipate starting an inotropic infusion rather than a vasopressor, because stroke volume and SVR are within normal limits. The patient may also receive IV regular insulin (1 unit/kg) as part of HIET protocols.

12 PROFESSIONAL CARING AND ETHICAL PRACTICE REVIEW

CCRN TEST PLAN: PROFESSIONAL CARING AND ETHICAL PRACTICE

- Advocacy/moral agency
- Caring practices
- Response to diversity
- Facilitation of learning
- Collaboration
- Systems thinking
- Clinical inquiry

The AACN Synergy Model

The **AACN Synergy Model** for patient care was developed in 1996 as a framework for the certification program of the American Association of Critical-Care Nurses (AACN). This patient-focused model is centered on an understanding that the characteristics of the patient/family unit inform the competencies of the nurse who delivers care.

Eight Core Patient Characteristics

- **Core patient characteristics** reflect the patient's biological, psychosocial, and spiritual developmental characteristics.
- Assessing patients' core characteristics enables the critical care nurse to develop an integrated, individualized plan of care with the patient/family unit.
- Core characteristics are rated from level 1 to level 5.

TABLE 12.1. Core Patient Characteristics

Characteristic	Description	Levels
Resiliency	The ability of an individual to use coping skills and survive in the face of adversity. The relationship between resiliency and a positive patient outcome has been extensively documented.	level 1: minimally resilient level 5: highly resilient
Vulnerability	The susceptibility of patients to harm. This may include physical, psychosocial, or social vulnerability.	level 1: highly vulnerable level 5: minimally vulnerable
Stability	The ability of a patient to maintain a steady state of equilibrium. This generally refers to hemodynamic stability.	level 1: minimally stable level 5: highly stable
Complexity	The entanglement of two or more systems. Complexity requires a multifaceted assessment by the nurse.	level 1: highly complex level 5: minimally complex
Resource Availability	The number and type of resources (e.g., financial, psychological) the patient and family bring to the immediate health care situation. The nurse should be aware that a lack of resources can negatively impact a patient's recovery.	level 1: few resources level 5: many resources
Participation in Care	The extent to which the patient and family take part in care. The nurse plays a critical role in encouraging patient/family to actively participate in care.	level 1: no participation level 5: full participation
Participation in Decision-Making	The extent to which a patient/family is able to understand and make decisions regarding care. The CCRN candidate should expect exam questions that reference barriers to decision-making.	level 1: no participation level 5: full participation
Predictability	A summary of multiple factors present in the patient's condition that allow a health care provider to expect a certain trajectory. Critical pathways are tools-based scoring systems (e.g., APACHE, SOFA) used to guide care of the patient to survival of the critical illness.	level 1: not predictable level 5: highly predictable

HELPFUL HINT:

When hemodynamic measurements reflect hypoperfusion to vital organs, early recognition and rapid intervention by the nurse will prevent further destabilization, avoid multisystem organ dysfunction, and reduce morbidity/mortality.

QUICK REVIEW QUESTION

1. A 30-year-old primigravida (37 weeks) patient is admitted preoperatively to the CVICU after a diagnosis of large dissecting thoracic aneurysm. A plan for an emergent C-section, followed by aneurysm repair, was outlined by the care team and presented to the patient and partner. The couple agreed to this plan, although this deviated significantly from their expectation of a natural childbirth. An advance directive is already on file, and the family verbalizes an understanding that the patient's partner will make medical decisions. Extended family members appear supportive and caring, and clergy related to the couple's spiritual view are present. The patient and partner both have insurance accepted by the hospital, and extended family members verbalize plans to help with the post-op care of patient and infant. The patient is being transferred to the OR as vital signs are labile.

   What level would each of the core patient characteristics be?

HELPFUL HINT:

The Synergy Model requires that the nurse become an advocate for the patient to ensure equitable care.

EIGHT CORE NURSE COMPETENCY CHARACTERISTICS

- The eight **Core Nurse Competency Characteristics** reflect a continuum of knowledge, experience, skills, and attitudes.
- Each competency is rated from level 1 (competent) to level 5 (expert).

TABLE 12.2. Core Nurse Competencies

Competency	Level 1 Nursing Actions	Level 5 Nursing Actions
Clinical judgment: clinical reasoning that incorporates clinical decision-making, critical thinking, a global grasp of the situation, and integration of nursing skills based on formal/informal experiential knowledge and evidence-based practice guidelines	• collects basic data • uses algorithms and protocols (but is uncomfortable deviating from these guidelines) • matches formal knowledge with clinical events • delegates decision-making to others; includes extraneous detail	• synthesizes/interprets complex and often conflicting patient data • makes clinical judgment based on immediate grasp of situation • uses past experience to anticipate problems • recognizes limitations

continued on next page

TABLE 12.2. Core Nurse Competencies (continued)

Competency	Level 1 Nursing Actions	Level 5 Nursing Actions
Advocacy/moral agency: representing the concerns of the patient/family and nursing staff, and acting as a moral agent to identify and help resolve ethical/clinical concerns	• works on behalf of patient • is aware of ethical issues that may occur in clinical settings • makes ethical/moral decisions based on rules	• works on behalf of patient, family, and community • advocates for patient/family regardless of personal values • suspends rules to allow the patient/family to direct moral decision-making • empowers patient/family to represent themselves
Caring practices: the application of nursing concepts like vigilance, responsiveness, engagement, and compassion to promote healing, prevent unnecessary suffering, and create a therapeutic environment	• identifies needs of patient care based on policy, procedure, and standards • manages a safe environment for patient and family • does not anticipate future needs • acknowledges end of life as a potential outcome	• insightfully recognizes/anticipates changing patient/family needs • engages fully with patient/family/community • anticipates obstacles and hazards and takes action to avoid them • promotes safety while allowing expression of grief as death/dying issues present • compassionately stands alongside patient/family transitioning through the end of life continuum
Collaboration: working with patients, families, health care colleagues, and community members to promote individual contributions to optimal and realistic patient/family goals	• is willing to be mentored, coached, or taught • is open to team members' contributions • participates in health care meetings to discuss practice issues/care activities	• reaches out to mentor others and continues self-learning by willingness to be taught • facilitates health care meetings/care delivery discussions and practice decisions • optimizes diverse resources and promotes patient/family outcomes through inclusivity

Competency	Level 1 Nursing Actions	Level 5 Nursing Actions
Systems thinking: the understanding of a body of knowledge and the tools used by nurses to manage system and environmental resources available for the patient/family and staff	<ul><li>has limited strategies and outlook</li><li>sees patient/family within the specific health care unit environment</li><li>sees self as a resource</li><li>is unable to recognize negotiation as a caring tool</li></ul>	<ul><li>develops and applies multiple strategies driven by the needs and strengths of patient/family</li><li>has a global outlook; anticipates and guides patient/family through the health care system</li><li>uses alternative resources when necessary</li><li>knows when and how to negotiate within the health care system on behalf of patient/family</li></ul>
Response to diversity: the ability to recognize, appreciate, and incorporate diversity into care delivery (including differences in culture, gender, lifestyle, spiritual beliefs, race, values, socioeconomics, ethnicity, and age)	<ul><li>assesses aspects of cultural diversity</li><li>is guided by own belief system in provision of care</li><li>is aware of the culture of the health care environment</li></ul>	<ul><li>anticipates and integrates cultural differences into patient/family care delivery</li><li>incorporates diverse and alternative therapies into care as presented</li><li>facilitates merging of health care culture with patient/family strengths to meet patient goals as possible</li></ul>
Facilitation of learning: facilitating formal and informal learning for patients, families, health care colleagues, and the community	<ul><li>has limited knowledge</li><li>follows planned educational program</li><li>sees patient/family education as separate nursing care delivery task</li><li>sees patient as passive</li><li>focuses on nurse's perspective</li></ul>	<ul><li>develops patient education programs</li><li>individualizes and incorporates health care team's educational input</li><li>evaluates patient understanding by recognizing behavioral change related to education</li><li>recognizes patient/family goals and choices</li><li>negotiates in relation to patient/family education needs</li></ul>

continued on next page

TABLE 12.2. Core Nurse Competencies (continued)

Competency	Level 1 Nursing Actions	Level 5 Nursing Actions
Clinical inquiry: the ongoing process of evaluating practice and creating practice change through research, experiential learning, and sharing new evidence-based practice guidelines	• follows standards and guidelines • uses evidence-based clinical changes developed by others • recognizes critical patient status changes • seeks assistance to identify needs and emergent problems	• individualizes standards, guidelines, and policies for individual or patient populations • reviews literature to acquire new knowledge • attends education/learning opportunities to address questions of practice/care delivery improvement • merges clinical judgment and clinical inquiry on the expert level

QUICK REVIEW QUESTION

2. A recently retired 68-year-old prediabetic Muslim neuro-ICU patient received tPa treatment for a left hemispheric stroke in the last 18 hours. The patient has right-sided hemiplegia and has passed a dysphagia screening. The patient is widowed, appears sad, and speaks mostly Farsi. The patient's son was out of state at a business meeting, and will not arrive until much later in the evening. The patient has refused the bacon, egg, and pancake breakfast tray. What should the nurse understand and do for this patient?

HELPFUL HINT:

Although participation in care encourages more positive outcomes, diminishes errors, and increases satisfaction with care, there are patient/family preferences or beliefs that may limit their ability or willingness to participate in care practices.

Ethical Practice Parameters
CODE OF ETHICS

- The **American Nurses Association (ANA)** has defined a clear framework for ethical decision-making that reflects the nurse's professional responsibility to the general public, the nursing profession, and health care colleagues.

- AACN considers the **ANA Code of Ethics for Nurses** the foundation for nursing practice. Questions on clinical competency throughout the CCRN exam will reflect this ethical practice knowledge base.

- The CCRN candidate is expected to read and understand the Code of Ethics. The code can be viewed at the ANA's website: https://www.nursingworld.org/practice-policy/nursing-excellence/ethics/code-of-ethics-for-nurses/.

- The CCRN candidate should expect questions on the CCRN exam that address assisting patients and families through a meaningful end-of-life clinical event.
  - The ANA Code of Ethics 2015 Provision 1.4 specifically defines **The Right to Self-Determination**, which describes the patient's right to make decisions (with family) to accept, refuse, or terminate treatment.
  - The nurse should understand the moral rights of the patient and give support during the process, which includes providing information without duress, coercion, deceit, prejudice, or undue influence.

> **QUICK REVIEW QUESTION**
>
> 3. A 58-year-old female patient who has obesity, hypertension, and DM is confirmed positive for COVID-19. She was transferred to the ICU for emergent intubation. The patient developed ARDS with an unstable hemodynamic status and acute kidney injury requiring dialysis. The nurse has been facilitating virtual visits for the patient with her daughter during the patient's stay. The daughter, who has medical power of attorney, has also been in discussion with the hospital's ICU intensivist about end-of-care decisions. During the most recent discussion, the daughter stated that she wants "everything done to save her mother." During dialysis, the patient becomes hypotensive, resulting in heart block and ACLS measures. The patient is unable to be resuscitated.
>
> What actions should the nurse take to help the family after the patient's death?

Legal and Ethical Principles

- Ethical and legal dilemmas occur daily in the critical care environment. Critical care practitioners must make decisions with speed and synthesize rapidly changing technological data, making resolving dilemmas even more challenging.
- The nurse should combine an ethical decision-making process with a systematic approach of moral examination to support the best interests of the patient.
- The nurse should be able to advocate for identifying ethical/legal issues and use the processes available to address these concerns.
- Candidates should be familiar with the following ethical principles:
  - **Autonomy** is the basic human right of freedom to self-determine a course of action that is respected and supported, without coercion, undue influence, or withholding of information by others.
  - **Beneficence** is the promotion of well-being for patients, based in the compassionate actions of doing good for others or preventing or removing harm, or actively improving another's situation.

HELPFUL HINT:

Some patient empowerment strategies may conflict with religious or cultural views that must be respected by the health care team. Expect relevant exam questions to address the referral of these situations to a facility's ethics committee.

- **Nonmaleficence** is an ethical principle that obliges a nurse to "do no harm" and/or to correct a harmful situation.
- **Veracity**, also known as "truth-telling," requires the nurse to provide information accurately and without bias to patients/family units and colleagues and within the employer-employee relationship.
- **Fidelity** is the idea that faithfulness builds a trusting relationship. It requires loyalty, fairness, truthfulness, patient advocacy, and a commitment by the nurse to keep promises.
- **Confidentiality** is a key element of the ANA Revised 2015 Position Statement on Privacy and Confidentiality,[1] which states that protection of privacy and confidentiality, including individually identifiable health information such as genetic data, is essential in the nurse-patient trust relationship.
- **Paternalism** is when health care providers make decisions they believe to be in the patient's best interests without the knowledge or consent of the patient. Nurses must work to balance patient autonomy with their adherence to other ethical values, like beneficence and nonmaleficence.
- **Justice** pertains to the fair and equitable distribution of scarce goods and resources, based on the assumption that all have equal rights. Everyone has the right to **access** to health care in the US, but health care itself is not a constitutionally mandated right. Quality of life, application of technology, and patient treatment preferences related to their personal value system must be considered in allocating resources.
- **Utilitarianism** is an ethical theory that, in the context of health care, seeks to promote the greatest achievable good based on a health care professional's actions; actions are analyzed based on positive or negative consequences, not fundamental moral principles.

QUICK REVIEW QUESTION

4. A 67-year-old woman is admitted to the ICU for multiple fractures and a closed head injury. She and her husband were hit by a car while walking across a street and the husband subsequently died from his injuries at the scene. The family and admitting physician have directed nursing staff not to tell the patient that her husband has died; however, she keeps asking the nurse if he is okay. Which ethical principles are being violated and what should the nurse do?

---

1   American Nurses Association, "Position Statement on Privacy and Confidentiality," revised June 2015, https://www.nursingworld.org/~4ad4a8/globalassets/docs/ana/position-statement-privacy-and-confidentiality.pdf.

Moral Distress

- **Moral distress** occurs when:
  - the nurse knows the appropriate ethical action but is unable to act on it
  - the nurse is required to act in a manner that violates professional and/or personal values and undermines the nurse's integrity and authenticity
- The AACN provides a framework to help nurses manage moral distress. It involves four key steps.
  1. **Identify what you are experiencing**: distinguish between moral distress, burnout, and compassion fatigue.
  2. **Assess your level of moral distress**: learn to recognize the emotional, physical, and psychological symptoms of moral distress.
  3. **Identify the causes and constraints**: determine the personal or organization constraints causing distress.
  4. **Take action**: find resources and make a plan to move forward.
- To manage the moral distress that is part of the critical care environment, nurses must feel empowered to advocate for themselves, patient/family units, and their colleagues, and to do so in a safe work environment.
- It takes **moral courage** to act in an ethical manner that reflects one's personal and professional integrity when moral principles are being compromised or undermined.
- The CCRN candidate should be prepared to see this issue of moral distress/moral courage reflected in at least one question or scenario on the exam.

> **HELPFUL HINT:**
>
> In March 2020, the AACN released their position statement "Moral Distress in Times of Crisis" to address moral distress during crises like the COVID-19 pandemic. It can be viewed here: https://www.aacn.org/policy-and-advocacy/aacn-position-statement-moral-distress-in-times-of-crisis

QUICK REVIEW QUESTION

5. A CCRN is asked to perform a painful procedure that the nurse feels may cause unnecessary harm to a patient with a poor prognosis. The physician determines that the particular treatment is required and is not interested in the nurse's viewpoint. What makes this situation an example of moral distress?

Ethical Decision-Making

Decisional Capacity

- **Decisional capacity** is the ability of the patient to make informed medical decisions based on knowledge of their illness and treatment options.

- Decisional capacity is assessed using four criteria.
  - the patient's demonstrated **understanding** of the situation
  - the patient's ability to **express a choice**
  - the patient's **appreciation** of how illness or treatment options will affect them
  - the patient's ability to **reason** and understand consequences
- **Diminished decisional capacity** is common in critical care settings. Common situations that may lead to diminished decisional capacity include sedation, underlying medical conditions (e.g., hypoglycemia), and neurological injury or disease.
- If decisional capacity is determined to be diminished, a surrogate or power of attorney may be used.
- **Durable power of attorney (DPOA)** (also called medical power of attorney or health care proxy) may be appointed to make health care decisions for a patient when they do not have the capacity to do so.
  - It may be general or very specific regarding the range of decisions the surrogate can make.
  - It must be present and valid in order to be used for decisions in care.
  - If a patient is alert and competent, their medical decisions cannot be overridden by their health care proxy.

HELPFUL HINT:

Decisional capacity is fluid and can change based on the patient's presentation and status in the critical care setting. For example, a patient with hypoxia may regain decisional capacity after the underlying medical condition is corrected.

QUICK REVIEW QUESTION

6. A patient admitted to the ICU following cardiac arrest and resuscitation tells the nurse that he does not want to be resuscitated again. He also states that he is worried that his spouse, who has DPOA, will reverse this decision if he is not able to communicate. What should the nurse do?

Patient Consent

- Patient **consent** is required for treatment. In general, there are four types of consent: informed, implied, express, and involuntary.
  - **Informed consent** is used in situations where moderately invasive or high-risk procedures are going to be performed. The provider must cover key elements for informed consent to be valid (e.g., description of procedures, risks/benefits, alternatives).
  - **Implied consent** is given in situations where patients are at risk to lose life or limb, and they are unable to provide informed consent. This type of consent is only applicable during resuscitation and is no longer implied if the patient is able to give and/or express informed consent.

- ☐ **Express consent** is the assumption of consent to perform noninvasive to minimally invasive procedures. Some departments require a signature for express consent; others take verbal consent based on words or actions of patients.
- ☐ **Involuntary consent** is given when a patient is deemed not to have decisional capacity. Physicians, law enforcement officers, and psychiatrists typically enact this type of consent.

■ If a pediatric patient presents for care without a legally responsible adult, the nurse must get consent for care from the legal custodian of the patient. There are some exceptions to this rule.
- ☐ Treatment can be provided if there is immediate danger to life or limb.
- ☐ Some states allow pediatric patients to come to the ED for care for STIs or similar issues in the absence of the legal custodian.
- ☐ Treatment can be provided when there is high suspicion of non-accidental trauma or domestic abuse. Consent for treatment is implied until the local child services system can determine temporary legal guardianship terms.

■ Patients who have intact decisional capacity have the **right to refuse any and all care.**
- ☐ The responsibility of the nurse is to provide the patient with as much information as they can to allow the patient to make an informed decision to refuse care.
- ☐ This also applies to surrogates or family members responsible for making care decisions.

■ **Leaving against medical advice (AMA)** is when a patient requests to leave care against the advice of health care providers. If the patient chooses to do so, the physician will counsel the patient on the risks of such a departure, and then ask the patient to provide a signature acknowledging these risks.

QUICK REVIEW QUESTION

7. A diabetic patient being treated for cellulitis and wet gangrenous ulcers of the left lower extremity has been told by the multidisciplinary team that the leg below the knee must be amputated. The patient vehemently disagrees and refuses to undergo an amputation. The patient has been educated about the risks and benefits and is advised of the immediate risk of sepsis, losing her leg above the knee, and possibly death. How should the nurse proceed?

Advance Directives

- **Advance directives** are written statements of individuals' wishes with regard to medical treatment decisions such as resuscitation, intubation, and other interventions. They are made to ensure that the wishes of the individual are carried out in the event the person is unable to express those wishes at the time of care.
- Advance directives must be documented, valid, and up to date before they can be honored in the clinical setting. In order to honor an advance directive, the physician must see the paperwork, validate the paperwork, and place an order that indicates the advance directive status of the patient.
- Advance directives generally dictate the level of lifesaving measures to be taken in certain circumstances.
  - **Do not resuscitate (DNR)** typically indicates that no resuscitation measures (e.g., CPR, defibrillation) should be taken.
  - **Do not intubate (DNI)** indicates that the patient does not wish to be intubated if the need presents.
  - **Allow natural death (AND)** indicates the patient does not want any intervention that may sustain life or prevent a natural progression to death.
- Any combination of DNR, DNI, and AND may be requested, as can other directives present in the documentation if applicable to the patient's circumstance.
- DNR, DNI, and AND all allow for palliative care and comfort measures.
- **Living wills** allow an individual to state which treatments they would like in the event they are unable to express such at the time of illness. They are used in situations such as a patient having a terminal illness or being in a vegetative state.
- In the absence of legal documentation to guide decision-making, a multidisciplinary approach should be taken to inform patients and families of treatment options.

HELPFUL HINT:

Advance directives may also address organ donation and specify which organs a patient is choosing to donate and/or specific recipients

QUICK REVIEW QUESTION

8. An 85-year-old patient arrives at the ED for nausea and dizziness. Soon after arrival, the patient becomes unresponsive and requires CPR. The patient's daughter states the patient does not wish to be resuscitated. What should the nurse do next?

Family Presence

- Family presence in critical care settings, particularly during procedures or resuscitation, is a complex and controversial topic.
- Generally, family presence, even during invasive procedure and resuscitation, is recommended.
- Evidence shows that family members assert that it is their preference and right to be present for these efforts, especially in the case of pediatric care.
- Family members should be invited to be present if appropriate and their presence should be governed by local policy and guidelines for consistency and provision of boundaries.
- If a family member is behaving inappropriately or interfering with care, they should not be present.
  - Aggressive or interfering family members may be taken to a separate, private area to deescalate.
  - Security may be needed if family members are violent or pose a danger to patients or staff.
- The critical care nurse should make every effort available (within hospital policies) to ensure that patients and their families have the time they need together.

HELPFUL HINT:

Family members may find their experience in the critical care unit difficult, and a staff member should be assigned to be available to discuss what is occurring. A chaplain or other community support staff may also be requested.

QUICK REVIEW QUESTION

9. A nurse is caring for a 68-year-old patient in a COVID-19 unit that does not allow visitation. Security has detained the patient's son at the entrance to the unit. The man is calm, but he tells the nurse that he knows his mother is dying and will not leave without seeing her. What actions should the nurse take?

Pain Management

- **Pain management** in critical care is a complex and controversial issue in the context of the current opioid crisis facing the United States.
- Both non-pharmacological and pharmacological approaches to pain should be considered.
  - Non-pharmacological interventions include repositioning the patient, keeping the patient relaxed or distracted, and applying ice, heat, or massage.
  - Pharmacological interventions include acetaminophen, NSAIDs, opioids, muscle relaxants, and local anesthetics.
- Nurses manage expectations for pain relief with patients.

HELPFUL HINT:

It is a common myth that some patients feel less pain. Medication should never be withheld from a patient based on the patient's race, age, religion, gender identity, or cognitive ability.

- Pain assessment is a numerical score as well as a subjective description of the nature of pain from a patient's perspective.
- Measurement of pain should occur as frequently as every measurement of vital signs, or more frequently if indicated.
- Patients may have unrealistic expectations of pain management and will need education on the subject. Establishing a goal for pain with the patient may help mitigate this issue.

QUICK REVIEW QUESTION

10. The nurse is taking care of a 63-year-old patient admitted with septic pneumonia. The patient is refusing any pain medication aside from PO acetaminophen. The nurse observes that the patient is guarding and cringing when coughing and suggests that the patient may get more relief from a different type of pain medication. The patient states that their sibling died of an opioid overdose and that they will never take any opioids. What should the nurse do?

Communication and Teaching
Components of Communication

- **Therapeutic communication** is a set of communication techniques that address the physical, mental, and emotional well-being of patients.

TABLE 12.3. Dos and Don'ts of Patient Communication

Do...	Don't...
• make eye contact with the patient • introduce yourself and use the patient's name • speak directly to the patient when possible • ask open-ended questions • speak slowly and clearly • show empathy for the patient • be silent when appropriate to allow the patient time to think and process emotions	• use medical jargon • threaten or intimidate the patient • lie or provide false hope • interrupt the patient • show frustration or anger • make judgmental statements

- A variety of techniques are used for therapeutic communication.
    - **Active listening** includes facing the client, being attentive to what they are saying, and maintaining eye contact if culturally appropriate.

- ☐ **Sharing observations** may open the conversation up to how the patient is feeling.
- ☐ **Empathy**, or trying to understand and accurately perceive the patient's feelings and experiences, can make the patient more comfortable.
- ☐ **Using touch**, such as a gentle hand on the shoulder or arm, when appropriate or welcome, can offer comfort.
- ☐ **Silence** allows the patient a moment to absorb or process information given.
- ☐ **Summarizing and paraphrasing** information back to a patient helps ensure or confirm understanding.
- ☐ **Asking relevant questions** that pertain to the situation helps the nurse gather information for decision-making.
- Communication includes both verbal and nonverbal components.
  - ☐ **Verbal communication** is the use of language to convey information. Characteristics of verbal communication include tone, volume, and word choice.
  - ☐ **Nonverbal communication** includes behavior, gestures, posture, and other non-language elements of communication that transmit information or meaning.

QUICK REVIEW QUESTION

11. A patient admitted for monitoring post-MI has just been emergently intubated. The spouse enters the room and begins to cry and aggressively accuse the nurse of providing poor care. The nurse tells the spouse, "Your behavior is disrupting the patient's recovery. I need you to calm down and come with me to the conference room."

    Why is the nurse's response inappropriate, and what would a better response be?

Barriers to Communication

- Certain **barriers** can prevent effective communication between the nurse and patient. Such barriers include language differences, sensory impairments, cognitive impairments, time constraints, and personality conflicts.
- **Language barriers** can occur when a nurse does not speak the patient's primary language or speaks it as a second language.
  - ☐ The organization should provide professional interpretation services for the patient when necessary.
  - ☐ It is not appropriate for staff to act as interpreters.

HELPFUL HINT:

When treating patients who are blind or have low vision, describe what actions are being taken throughout assessment and treatment so that the patient understands what is occurring.

- □ If waiting for translation services would prevent the patient from receiving needed care, the nurse should use nonverbal communication (such as gestures) with the patient.
- **Sensory impairments** include hearing or vision loss as a result of heredity, disease, or injury.
  - □ Patients with sensory impairments should be offered interpretation services when needed.
  - □ Whenever possible, the nurse should ask the patient what their preferred method of communication is.
- **Cognitive impairments** can often result from trauma or injury, particularly stroke. In these cases patients may not be able to speak due to motor impairments, or they many have neurological impairments that prevent them from processing communication.
  - □ The nurse should determine the method of communication that works best for the patient.
  - □ The nurse should be aware of changes in a patient's cognitive status.
- **Time constraints** are common in all care settings and can be the result of understaffing, high-acuity patient loads, or unanticipated emergencies. When the nurse is speaking with patients and their families under time constraints, the nurse should share this issue with the patient.

QUICK REVIEW QUESTION

12. A patient is admitted to the critical care unit following an ischemic stroke. The patient's first language is Spanish, but they understand some English. The nurse assigned to perform the admission assessment does not speak any Spanish. What should the nurse do?

EDUCATION PLANS

- The critical care nurse should understand how to develop and implement a **patient education plan** tailored to the learning needs of each patient.
- **Procedural education** should be included if a patient is going to or already has undergone a procedure that they will have to recover from. Such education should include details about the procedure, what the patient can expect after the procedure, and the responsibilities of the patient in their own care after the procedure.
- **Risk factor modification** should be included when a patient needs to make lifestyle changes to promote healthy outcomes, such as quitting smoking or following a restricted diet.

- **Disease management** education should focus on the patient's role in managing a chronic condition. Topics may include the disease process, monitoring and management of disease symptoms, medication administration, and management of medication side effects.
- **Health promotion** education includes ways that patients can prevent deterioration in their health, including diet, exercise, and managing stress.

> **QUICK REVIEW QUESTION**
>
> 13. The nurse is providing patient education after a patient returns from a PTA procedure. The patient appears anxious. What should the nurse include in the teaching plan?

CONDITIONS FOR LEARNING

- Adult learners have several distinct traits that critical care nurses should consider while developing patient education plans.
    - Adult learners are **independent** and **self-directed**. Nurses should actively engage them in the learning process and encourage them to help develop their health plans.
    - Adult learners are **results-oriented** and **practical**. Nurses should give them information that they can apply immediately.
    - Adult learners may be **resistant to change** and will require justification for new behaviors.
    - Adult learners may **learn more slowly** than younger learners. However, they may be more skilled at integrating new knowledge with previous experience.
- Psychologist Benjamin Bloom described three domains of learning.
    - The **cognitive domain** includes collecting, synthesizing, and applying knowledge.
    - The **affective domain** involves emotions and attitudes, including the ability to be aware of emotions and to respond to them.
    - The **psychomotor** domain relates to motor skills, including the ability to perform complex skills and create new movement patterns.
- Patient education plans should address all three learning domains. For example, a patient who is learning about smoking cessation may need to be taught about the negative health impacts of smoking (cognitive domain), how to manage negative emotions related to quitting (affective domain), and how to correctly apply a nicotine patch (psychomotor domain).

HELPFUL HINT:

The "knowledge, skills, and attitude" discussed in nursing education align with the three learning domains: **knowledge** is cognitive learning, **skills** are psychomotor learning, and **attitude** is affective learning.

- The critical care nurse should assess patients' source of **motivation** in the context of managing their health in order to better educate, encourage, and advocate for them.
    - **Intrinsic motivation** is the desire to achieve a goal, seek challenges, or complete a task that is driven by enjoyment and personal satisfaction (e.g., exercising because it is enjoyable).
    - **Extrinsic motivation** is the desire to accomplish a goal that is driven by external rewards or punishment (e.g., exercising to prevent cardiac-vascular disease).
- Patients' **readiness to learn** can be shaped by many factors, including openness to new information, emotional response to illness (e.g., denial, anxiety), religious and cultural beliefs, and social support systems.
- The nurse must assess the **functional status** of a patient before developing an education plan for that patient. Doing so ensures that the plan aligns with the patient's abilities and capacity to learn.
- **Health literacy** is the degree to which an individual has the ability to obtain, process, and understand basic health information needed to make personal health decisions. Interventions for patients with low health literacy include:
    - asking patients questions to assess their current knowledge
    - using plain language and short sentences
    - limiting important points to three or fewer
    - using teach-backs to confirm the patient's understanding
    - using visual materials such as videos or models
    - discussing issues in terms of short time spans (<10 years)
    - being consistent when discussing numeric values (e.g., units, risk, dosage)
    - simplifying procedures and regimens as much as possible

HELPFUL HINT:

Patient health literacy improves as patients become more involved in their own care.

QUICK REVIEW QUESTION

14. A nurse is teaching a patient how to take their own blood pressure. While the patient is trying to apply the cuff, the nurse asks the patient to state their target BP range. The patient becomes visibly frustrated and claims to not know. How can the nurse's teaching style meet this patient's needs?

ANSWER KEY

1. The patient shows level 1 in Vulnerability, Stability, Complexity, and Predictability, and level 5 in Resiliency, Resource Availability, Participation in Care, and Participation in Decision-making.

2. If the patient follows a halal diet, then he would not be able to eat from his breakfast tray (which includes bacon). The patient is also experiencing barriers to communication, including a limited English-speaking ability, and is likely overwhelmed navigating his condition without any family or spiritual support. The nurse can address this patient's needs by using dietary, chaplain, and translator services to promote nutritional intake, address the patient's significant spiritual distress, and help the patient communicate with health care providers.

3. The nurse should be fully engaged with the daughter and create a compassionate, supportive, therapeutic environment. The nurse should provide comfort and an opportunity for the daughter to share her emotions/concerns surrounding her parent's death. During the process, the nurse should respect the daughter's grieving practices. The nurse should describe the postmortem care procedures to the family in a sensitive manner and give the daughter an opportunity to see the patient again. Offering CISM or grief support services to the family is also appropriate.

4. The ethical principle of veracity is being violated. The patient is requesting the truth and it is being withheld. The physician is also practicing paternalism by making decisions without involving the patient. The nurse should consult the ethics committee of the facility to review the situation.

5. When the nurse is required to act in a manner that violates their professional and/or personal values, it undermines their integrity and authenticity, creating an internal locus of moral distress. The recognition that challenging the institutional hierarchy also creates risk to the nurse is an external source of moral distress.

6. The patient is correct that the DPOA may override his decision should he become incapacitated. To prevent this from happening, the patient should be encouraged to have a conversation with his spouse and physician to clarify his wishes. He should also be encouraged to complete the necessary legal forms (e.g., DNR) to ensure that he is not resuscitated again.

7. The nurse can explore the reasons the patient does not want to amputate, further educate on the risks of noncompliance, and assist with answering any questions that the patient may have. If there is a reason to doubt that the patient is competent, a psychiatric consult may be ordered to verify intact decisional capacity. Otherwise, the patient is within her rights to refuse care and the nurse should adopt a supportive role.

8. Continue to resuscitate the patient, and ask the daughter to procure the DNR paperwork, if it is available. Explain that the ED team cannot act on the request until it has been verified as a valid, legal document.

9. The nurse should express empathy for the patient's grief but explain that the hospital visitation policies currently do not allow any visitors to enter the COVID-19 unit. The nurse should offer alternatives to the son that meet the hospital's policies, such as virtual visits. Depending on local policies, the nurse may go through the proper channels to inquire about a compassionate exception to allow for visitation.

10. The nurse should explain to the patient that proper use of opioids in the acute care setting does not increase the chance of addiction. If the patient continues to refuse opioids, the nurse may try other modalities of nonmedicinal pain relief such as repositioning, heat, ice, and distraction. The nurse should discuss the patient's refusal of ordered meds with physician and, if there are no contraindications, request an NSAID.

11. The nurse is not creating a supportive and therapeutic environment aligned with caring practices. The nurse's words place blame for the patient's condition on the spouse. Telling the spouse to calm down invalidates their emotions. The nurse should empathize with the patient's family member and attempt to deescalate the conflict. For example, the nurse could say, "I understand that you are upset. Would you like to come to the conference room with me to discuss the situation?"

12. The nurse should arrange for an interpreter to be present during the admission assessment to communicate information between the patient and the care team. The nurse should not try to communicate with the patient in a language other than Spanish.

13. To reduce the patient's anxiety, the nurse should explain that the health care team is monitoring the patient after the procedure. The nurse could say something like, "We will be checking your vital signs and heart rhythm frequently to assess for any changes." The nurse should not give the patient false reassurance or provide results of the procedure.

14. Psychomotor skills require concentration. When the nurse asked the patient about a BP target while the patient was trying to apply the cuff, the nurse disturbed the patient's focus on this skill. The nurse should help the patient learn to apply the cuff, and once that skill has been mastered, the nurse can ask questions from the cognitive domain.

13 PRACTICE TEST ONE

1. A labetalol IV infusion is started on a patient who was admitted with BP 230/108 and is being continuously monitored. After 1 hour, the patient reports dizziness and a headache. The nurse rechecks the BP and finds it is 120/62. What is the priority intervention for this patient?

    A) Continue to monitor.
    B) Notify physician that therapy is effective.
    C) Decrease rate of drip per titration orders.
    D) Complete an NIH stroke scale assessment.

2. The priority nursing intervention for a patient in pulseless electrical activity is to

    A) administer 1 mg epinephrine IV.
    B) begin high-quality CPR.
    C) prepare to defibrillate the patient.
    D) open the patient's airway.

3. A patient with a GI bleed has a critical HgB value of 4.5 g/dL, and a massive transfusion protocol is initiated. During the blood transfusion, the patient develops crackles in their lung bases and dyspnea. What transfusion reaction is likely occurring?

    A) allergic reaction
    B) febrile nonhemolytic reaction
    C) transfusion-associated circulatory overload
    D) acute hemolytic reaction

4. What classification of medication should be used cautiously in the presence of decreased glomerular filtration rate?

    A) NSAIDs
    B) ACE inhibitors
    C) statins
    D) loop diuretics

5. A 55-year-old female injured in a car accident is in the ICU being treated for a pelvic ring fracture. An hour after bathing and repositioning, the patient's vital signs are as follows: BP 96/54, HR 127, O_2 sat 96%, and RR 24. The patient is diaphoretic and reports pain in the lower back. What is the priority intervention for the nurse?

    A) Administer analgesics.
    B) Reposition patient.
    C) Increase IV fluids because patient is having a vagal response.
    D) Call physician for a pelvic CT order.

6. A patient admitted for difficulty with breathing is found to have unilateral infiltrates in the bases of the right mid and lower lobes. How should this patient be positioned?

   A) on their left side
   B) on their right side
   C) prone
   D) semi-Fowler's

7. After a cardiac catheterization, the cardiologist's report reveals that the patient's pulmonary artery pressure is 35 mm Hg, with right ventricular hypertrophy. What other findings would indicate that this condition is decompensating?

   A) left ventricular hypertrophy
   B) normal cardiac output
   C) increased right atrial pressure
   D) decreased pulmonary artery pressure

8. A 19-year-old male diagnosed with viral meningitis is being treated in the ICU for elevated ICP. The nurse notes an increase in urine output, from 30 mL/hr to 550 mL/hr. What lab values would support a diagnosis of SIADH versus diabetes insipidus?

   A) serum Na+ of 115
   B) urine osmolality 280 mOsm/kg
   C) urine specific gravity 1.003
   D) elevated HgB and Hct

9. A patient is comatose and has been intubated and sedated to reduce encephalopathy after a drug overdose 3 days ago. What factor would prevent confirmation of brain death?

   A) all sedation, opioids, analgesics, intoxicants, and poisons cleared from system
   B) absence of acid-base, endocrine, or electrolyte dysfunction
   C) core temperature 31.9°C
   D) BP sustained at 110/80 with norepinephrine bitartrate titratable IV infusion

10. A family member requests to speak to the charge nurse about the care of her 98-year-old mother. She states that her mother had been in several abusive relationships when younger and is apprehensive about having male nurses and caregivers. How can the charge nurse alleviate patient safety concerns?

    A) Explain that resources and staffing is short; there is no way to assign certain caregivers.
    B) Rearrange patient assignments so that only females are providing care, if possible.
    C) Purposefully assign male caregivers so that the patient can get used to it.
    D) Accompany male caregivers in, and provide an introduction at the beginning of the shift.

11. A 39-year-old morbidly obese patient is recovering from bariatric surgery. The patient was slightly hypertensive at 150/99 in the hour after returning to the unit from PACU. The nurse checks the patient again in 30 minutes and finds that the patient is diaphoretic and difficult to arouse. The vital signs are as follows:
    BP 92/65
    HR 120
    RR 15
    O_2 sat 98% on 2 L
    What action should the nurse immediately take?

    A) Position the patient Trendelenburg and notify physician.
    B) Increase IV fluid rate.
    C) Recheck vitals in 15 minutes since the MAP is within normal limits.
    D) Place a cold cloth on the patient's head since they appear overheated.

12. An 18-year-old female, postpartum 1 day, is being monitored for preeclampsia in the ICU. What clinical sign would indicate the patient is progressing to HELLP syndrome?

A) icteric sclera
B) urine output of 200 mL/hr
C) troponins < 0.012
D) PLT 320,000/mL

13. A 32-year-old patient is admitted after a heroin overdose. The patient has been administered naloxone and is regaining consciousness. The patient becomes extremely agitated and is making indirect threats. What deescalation technique should be attempted first?

    A) Allow patient to freely move around room and halls.
    B) Place patient in seclusion.
    C) With assistance from security, place patient in restraints.
    D) Use firm, but calm verbal redirection.

14. A 43-year-old female with multiple sclerosis is admitted to the ICU after surgical complications for a scheduled hip surgery. The patient was unable to be postsurgically extubated. While repositioning the patient, the nurse notes that the patient's arms are stiff and contracted. What medication would the nurse request from the physician?

    A) gabapentin
    B) amitriptyline
    C) baclofen
    D) fentanyl

15. A patient is being monitored in the CCU with a Swan-Ganz catheter. Assessment reveals the patient is short of breath, and fine crackles are auscultated. The patient tells the nurse that they are coughing up pink-tinged sputum. The nurse inflates the balloon and receives a pulmonary capillary wedge pressure result of 28 mm Hg. What condition should the nurse suspect?

    A) mitral valve regurgitation
    B) cardiogenic shock
    C) acute respiratory edema
    D) hypotension

16. A nurse is admitting a patient for left lower extremity cellulitis with antibiotic treatment. While auscultating the lungs, the nurse notes crackles in the bases. The patient's family member states that the patient's "smoker's cough" has been worse than usual. What should the nurse do after completing the assessment?

    A) Document findings.
    B) Initiate antibiotic as ordered.
    C) Encourage cough and deep breathing.
    D) Obtain sputum sample.

17. A patient with an acute deep vein thromboembolism in the left lower extremity has been treated with catheter-directed thrombolytics for 24 hours. The patient has a history of recurrent GI bleeds with aspirin and clopidogrel. What intervention will likely be ordered to prevent pulmonary embolism?

    A) angiogram
    B) low-molecular-weight heparin
    C) thrombectomy
    D) IVC filter

18. A systolic heart murmur is noted in a patient exhibiting dyspnea and angina. The patient says that they have had a syncopal episode before being brought to the ED. The nurse identifies +3 pitting edema in the lower extremities. What should the patient be asked regarding their health history?

    A) recent viral infection
    B) childhood rheumatic fever
    C) suicide risk
    D) fall risk

19. A patient with severe abdominal cramping has no bowel sounds. What signs and symptoms would support a diagnosis of bowel infarction?

    A) abdominal distension, jaundice, and altered mental status
    B) pH 7.44, serum amylase 200 U/L, and WBC 18,000/mL

C) hematochezia, diarrhea, and LDH 300

D) McBurney's point, intractable abdominal pain, and WBC 12,000/mL

20. A patient with myasthenia gravis is admitted to the ICU with increasing muscular weakness, cramping, and diarrhea. The patients states that she mixed up her medication and took six 180 mg tablets of pyridostigmine that morning. What medication should the nurse expect to administer?

A) atropine

B) labetalol

C) IV immunoglobulin

D) insulin

21. A patient is scheduled to have a bone marrow biopsy at the bedside. The patient requests pain medication to be given for the procedure. How should the nurse address this request?

A) Notify the patient that this is not a painful procedure and medication is not required.

B) Administer the medication 15 minutes before the procedure starts.

C) When the physician is administering lidocaine to the area, administer the medication.

D) Wait to see if the patient needs the medication, and administer it if the patient appears to be in pain.

22. After stabilizing a patient brought in emergently with dyspnea that quickly escalated to respiratory failure requiring intubation and mechanical ventilation, the nurse asks the family if anyone knows what the patient's wishes are and if the patient had a durable power of attorney assigned. The family members are in shock and say that they don't know. What action would protect patient autonomy?

A) Assure family that it does not matter at this point.

B) Review hospital records to check if patient has submitted a living will.

C) Assign the responsibility to the most competent-seeming family member.

D) Enter order for patient to be full code.

23. A facility is going through the Magnet process and is offering a program that will pay for the study guide and exam fees for certification for nurses in the ICU and Med/Surg. What developmental reason should a nurse attempt to seek certification in their area of specialty?

A) to prove that the nurse is smarter than colleagues

B) to certify clinical skills competence

C) to be a part of the hospital's quota of certified nurses

D) to promote personal growth and increase knowledge base in one's specialty

24. A nurse is reviewing a patient's medications on admission. Which medication is NOT of concern when considering fall risk?

A) valproic acid

B) diazepam

C) terazosin

D) cholecalciferol

25. During dialysis, a patient suddenly reports a headache and blurred vision and cannot remember the day. What are they likely experiencing?

A) hypotension

B) cerebral edema

C) onset of migraine

D) dementia

26. Which of the following complications should be monitored in a patient with hyperosmolar hyperglycemic state?

A) metabolic acidosis and hypotension

B) pulmonary embolism, hypokalemia, and fluid deficit

- C) coma, pleural effusion, and tachycardia
- D) fluid overload, increased ICP, and infection

27. A 72-year-old male patient is confirmed with ischemic stroke by a CT scan. The symptoms began approximately 4 hours ago. There is no history of diabetes or stroke. Which of the following would be a contraindication for alteplase therapy?

- A) time window
- B) NIH stroke scale score of 30
- C) patient took aspirin this morning
- D) BP 175/95

28. A patient is admitted to the ED with chest pain. A 12-lead ECG is performed, with ST elevations noted in leads II, III, and aVF. The nurse should prepare to administer

- A) nitrates.
- B) diuretics.
- C) morphine.
- D) IV fluids.

29. A nurse reviews the 12-lead ECG on a patient 2 days after right ventricular infarction. The patient's ECG reads normal sinus rhythm with a first-degree heart block. Which result would the nurse expect to see on the ECG?

- A) a PR interval > 0.20 and consistent throughout the ECG
- B) a PR interval that will lengthen, lengthen, and drop a QRS
- C) 2 P waves for every QRS
- D) no correlation between the P waves and QRSs

30. A patient arrives at the ICU from the ED with a non-rebreathing mask delivering 15 L/min with an O_2 sat of 94%. The patient is resting comfortably and reports no current discomfort. ABG values are as follows:
pH 7.56
pO_2 89 mm Hg
pCO_2 65 mm Hg
HCO_3 24 mEq/L

Which condition noted in the patient's history would require immediate intervention by the nurse?

- A) asthma
- B) COPD
- C) respiratory fibrosis
- D) respiratory hypertension

31. A patient is being treated for an acute occlusion of the superficial femoral artery. Which of the following indicates that the patient is at an optimal level of anticoagulation therapy?

- A) aPTT 94 seconds
- B) fibrinogen ≤ 150 mg/dL
- C) PLT 45,000/mL
- D) elevated D-dimer

32. A patient admitted for treatment of a DVT of the calf complains of dyspnea and chest pain. The nurse should first

- A) administer oxygen at 2 L/min PRN.
- B) place patient in a semi-Fowler's position.
- C) prepare patient for diagnostic tests.
- D) obtain vital signs.

33. A 34-year-old patient is recovering from bilateral PEs after a pelvic fracture during a ski accident. During this stay, the patient was intubated for 3 days. The patient is being readied for discharge after a total of 10 days in the facility. What potential post-ICU complication should the patient be educated about?

- A) need for supplemental O_2 because of being vented
- B) ICU-related PTSD
- C) dysphagia
- D) paying hospital bills without insurance

34. A sentinel event is identified and reported to the charge nurse. After entering the physician's verbal order into the MAR, the dayshift nurse failed to communicate to the oncoming shift that an amiodarone drip was ordered to be discontinued. The medication ran through the night, and at 0300, the patient experienced a hypotensive event that required administration of a vasopressor. What action would be beneficial in a systems-thinking solution?

A) Require all IV drips to be reviewed by the house supervisor.

B) Require all IV drips to be cosigned when initiated.

C) Reassign both nurses to medical/surgical units where they will not encounter vasoactive drips.

D) Require bedside reporting to verify IV infusions with MAR orders.

35. A patient in the ED with chronic pain is requesting more IV pain medication for reported 10/10 pain. The physician will not give any more medication. How should the nurse approach this patient?

A) Inform the patient that it is the physician's decision.

B) Discuss chronic pain relief and realistic expectations with the patient.

C) Ignore the patient's pain complaint.

D) Discuss drug-seeking concerns with the patient.

36. A patient is sedated with fentanyl and midazolam for a lumbar puncture at the beside. The nurse is evaluating the patient 2 hours after the procedure and finds that the patient is lethargic and has pinpoint pupils. What action should be taken?

A) administration of naloxone

B) administration of flumazenil

C) sternal rub to stimulate patient

D) raising head of bed and letting patient wake up on their own

37. A 43-year-old knife wound victim with significant blood loss is transferred to the ICU. The ED nurse notes that a CT has verified that the knife did not puncture any organs. An IV was started in the ED, and the patient received about 300 mL of NS. The patient is now lethargic and having a difficult time answering questions. What intervention should the nurse immediately initiate after checking vitals?

A) Start a vasopressor to treat the patient's hypotension.

B) Initiate fluid protocol for hemorrhagic shock.

C) Continue to monitor.

D) Call security to ensure the patient has no weapons in their belongings.

38. A patient is arriving via EMS with possible ST elevation, and a STEMI code is activated. A subsequent ECG shows elevation in all leads except for aVR and V1. Which of the following medications should be used cautiously?

A) NS bolus

B) nitroglycerin

C) atropine

D) epinephrine

39. Which laboratory finding indicates that a 62-year-old male patient is at risk for ventricular dysrhythmia?

A) magnesium 0.8 mEq/L

B) potassium 4.2 mmol/L

C) creatinine 1.3 mg/dL

D) total calcium 2.8 mmol/L

40. A patient with AIDS has been admitted to the ICU for complications related to pneumonia. What would the nurse expect the ordering provider to initiate immediately?

A) sulfamethoxazole/trimethoprim

B) fluid bolus

C) supplementary nutrition

D) inhaled steroid nebulizer treatment

41. Along with an infection, which of the following conditions would indicate that the patient has sepsis?
    A) PLT 220,000/mL
    B) GCS 10
    C) creatinine 1.6 mg/dL
    D) bilirubin 4.0 mg/dL

42. The nurse is reviewing the history of a patient with heart failure. Which of the following coexisting health problems will cause an increase in the patient's afterload?
    A) diabetes
    B) endocrine disorders
    C) hypertension
    D) Marfan syndrome

43. During assessment, a patient has new-onset confusion, blurred vision, and slurred speech. Their vital signs are within normal limits. What initial assessment would be best for this patient?
    A) NIH stroke scale assessment
    B) ECG
    C) CT scan of head
    D) blood glucose levels

44. Several hours after an emergent percutaneous cholecystectomy, a patient's family reports that the patient is having new, severe pain. An assessment of the patient reveals a firm, distended abdomen and high-pitched bowel sounds, with patient rating the pain as 8/10. What is the nurse's first priority?
    A) Insert nasogastric tube and start low, intermittent suction.
    B) Administer simethicone and continue to monitor.
    C) Administer morphine PRN and reassess in 20 minutes.
    D) Send patient for CT scan.

45. A patient presents to the ED with chest pain, dyspnea, and diaphoresis. The nurse finds a narrow-complex tachycardia with these vital signs: HR 210, BP 70/42, and RR 18. Which priority intervention should the nurse anticipate?
    A) Administer adenosine 6 mg IV.
    B) Defibrillate at 200 J.
    C) Administer amiodarone 300 mg IV.
    D) Prepare for synchronized cardioversion.

46. What comorbidity requires cautious monitoring of the patient when they are being administered desmopressin?
    A) heart failure
    B) psoriasis
    C) rheumatoid arthritis
    D) hypothyroidism

47. A new mother is 3 days postpartum and is being treated in the ICU for postpartum hemorrhage. The nurse notes that the patient is very tearful and despondent during conversation. The patient confides that she is feeling incredibly sad and is having disturbing thoughts about her child. What is the best intervention by the nurse?
    A) Call a rapid response.
    B) Immediately leave to inform the attending physician.
    C) Ask the client if she has thoughts of harming herself or her child.
    D) Assure the patient that these feelings are normal and will pass in time.

48. A Hispanic patient recovering from PE is weaning off BiPAP. She is concerned that she has not been taking the herbs prescribed by her curandero. How can the nurse incorporate the patient's preferences into her current health regimen?
    A) Tell the patient that she should not take medications not prescribed by a medical doctor.

B) Find out what herbs the patient was using, and discuss continuation with the physician.

C) Call the curandero, and tell them to stop giving the patient any herbal preparations.

D) Tell the patient that those herbs are already in the medications she is receiving in the hospital.

49. A patient with suspected occlusion of the left anterior descending artery develops cardiogenic shock. The patient has received a 1000 mL fluid bolus and is on a dobutamine drip. Hemodynamics are measured via a Swan-Ganz catheter, and the cardiac output results are 2 mL/min. The patient's BP has decreased to 89/42. What would be the expected next action?

A) Titrate dobutamine up, to increase cardiac output.

B) Administer another fluid bolus.

C) Start a norepinephrine drip.

D) Begin an esmolol drip.

50. Which type of MI causes ST elevation in leads V1 – V6?

A) lateral

B) right ventricular

C) anterior

D) inferior

51. The nurse is preparing to suction a patient with a tracheostomy tube. The patient has had thick secretions that are hard to suction out. What action is NOT appropriate for this patient?

A) Oxygenate with 100% O_2 for 30 seconds before suctioning.

B) Use a sterile suction catheter.

C) Apply continuous suction for ≤ 15 seconds with each pass.

D) Increase suction to 250 mm Hg.

52. A patient who has tested positive for COVID-19 is being transferred from a step-down unit to the ICU for increasing lethargy, dyspnea, and hypoxemia. A V/Q test returns indicating right-to-left shunting. The blood gas levels return at PaO_2 of 61 mm Hg and $PaCO_2$ of 45 mm Hg. The patient is on a 3 L high-flow nasal cannula. What immediate action is required by the nurse?

A) Administer an albuterol breathing treatment.

B) Increase the high-flow nasal cannula to 4 L.

C) Call respiratory, and prepare patient for intubation.

D) Notify the physician that the patient's condition is responding to treatment.

53. Which diagnosis does the ECG in the exhibit support?

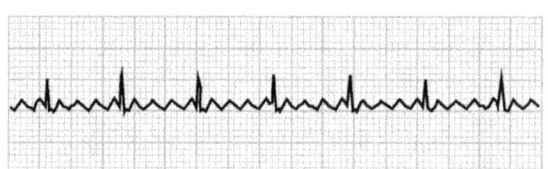

A) atrial flutter

B) atrial fibrillation

C) torsades de pointes

D) ventricular fibrillation

54. The nurse is reviewing the labs of a newly admitted patient. Which of the following findings would be the most critical?

A) ALT 33 units/L

B) BNP 760 pg/mL

C) WBC 10,450/mL

D) direct bilirubin 0.2 mg/dL

55. A patient has started receiving bolus enteral feedings through an NG tube. The patient begins coughing, and rhonchi are heard on auscultation. The feeding is immediately stopped, and a chest X-ray obtained. The feeding tube is positioned correctly, and the cause is attributed to reflux. What interventions would prevent this from happening in the future?

- **A)** bolus feeding at a faster rate
- **B)** keeping the head of bed at > 15 degrees
- **C)** requesting change from bolus feed to continuous
- **D)** keeping patient NPO

56. What diagnostic finding is indicative of DKA?

- **A)** blood glucose level 175 mg/dL
- **B)** metabolic alkalosis
- **C)** presence of serum ketones
- **D)** decrease in serum potassium

57. Before providing patient care, the nurse sees two care assistants whispering outside the patient's room. One of the aides admits to telling the other to make sure to double glove because the patient has AIDS. What is the best response by the nurse?

- **A)** Agree that this would offer more protection.
- **B)** Reproach the aides for discussing a patient in the hallway.
- **C)** Educate both care assistants on the importance of using standard precautions, and explain that no other precautions are needed to keep both staff and patient safe.
- **D)** Notify the manager that the care assistants were breaking HIPAA rules.

58. A patient and the patient's spouse are feeling overwhelmed while the nurse is teaching them how to take care of and flush a new cholecystectomy drain. What is the best method to ensure they will be able to complete the tasks once the patient is discharged?

- **A)** Use the teach-back method.
- **B)** Give instructional pamphlet to take home.
- **C)** Evaluate their learning preferences and needs.
- **D)** Tell them not to worry and that home care will do it.

59. A patient is diagnosed with idiopathic thrombocytopenic purpura and has undergone treatment with IV immunoglobulin and corticosteroids. After being sent home several weeks ago, the patient is now readmitted with epistaxis, generalized purpura, and PLT 26,000/μL. What should the nurse prepare the patient for?

- **A)** platelet transfusion
- **B)** emergent splenectomy
- **C)** antibiotics
- **D)** arterial line for monitoring

60. The treatment that a patient is undergoing for HIV includes the antidepressant imipramine. The patient is admitted to the MICU with anorexia, abdominal pain, weight loss, hypotension, fatigue, confusion without hypoglycemia, electrolyte abnormalities, and hyperpigmentation of the skin. Which of the following is the most likely diagnosis?

- **A)** adrenal insufficiency
- **B)** myxedema
- **C)** SIADH
- **D)** Crohn's disease

61. A patient arrives at the ED extremely agitated and anxious. The patient has a history of anxiety disorder and visits the ED several times a year. Which medication should the nurse expect to administer to the patient?

- **A)** haloperidol
- **B)** phenytoin
- **C)** lorazepam
- **D)** chlordiazepoxide

62. A patient is recovering after a Roux-en-Y gastric bypass, and the nurse is preparing the discharge instructions to review with the patient and family. What post-op complication related to this type of bypass surgery may require a further procedure after discharge?

- **A)** stenosis
- **B)** gallstones
- **C)** post-op GI bleeding
- **D)** anastomotic leak

63. A patient has esophageal varices secondary to portal hypertension and has been medically treated for an upper GI bleed. Vital signs are as follows:
BP 115/82
HR 48
RR 16
temp 38.7°C
The patient is alert and oriented. The nurse is about to administer the patient's morning medications. What order should the nurse question?

- **A)** octreotide 50 mg 4 times per day
- **B)** nadolol 40 mg 2 times per day
- **C)** lansoprazole 40 mg 1 time per day
- **D)** loratadine 10 mg 1 time per day

64. Which of the following medications would be contraindicated for a patient with mesenteric ischemia?

- **A)** heparin
- **B)** digitalis
- **C)** metoprolol
- **D)** cephalexin

65. A patient is admitted to the ICU for peritonitis secondary to an infection around the peritoneal dialysis catheter. The patient's vital signs are as follows:
BP 83/52
HR 120
RR 18
temp 39.3°C
What is the most likely method of dialyzing to be ordered for this patient?

- **A)** peritoneal dialysis with new catheter at different site
- **B)** intermittent hemodialysis
- **C)** delay dialysis until peritonitis is treated
- **D)** continuous renal replacement therapy

66. After a craniotomy to repair an arteriovenous malformation, a patient experiences rhinorrhea. What test may be performed to definitively determine if the fluid is CSF?

- **A)** halo test
- **B)** glucose oxidase
- **C)** beta-2-transferrin
- **D)** CT scan

67. An 84-year-old female patient with a Foley catheter was admitted from an adult care facility. Antibiotics were initiated for a probable UTI. The patient was very agitated and restless for the first 2 days. On the third day, the patient's assessment reveals a flat affect and listlessness. What is the most likely cause for the change in the patient's behavior?

- **A)** The patient has adjusted to the new settings.
- **B)** The patient is experiencing hypoactive delirium.
- **C)** The patient is not getting enough sleep.
- **D)** The delirium has subsided.

68. A patient has an HR of 112 and is diaphoretic. A finger-stick blood glucose result is 43 mg/dL. What is the most appropriate intervention?

- **A)** Check the serum blood glucose level.
- **B)** Have patient drink 4 oz of orange juice.
- **C)** Administer 15 g of glucose gel sublingually.
- **D)** Administer 0.5 ampule of D50 via IV push.

69. A 50-year-old patient is scheduled for a percutaneous alcohol ablation of the intraventricular septum to decrease the size of the septal wall. Which type of cardiomyopathy does this patient most likely have?

- **A)** idiopathic dilated cardiomyopathy
- **B)** restrictive cardiomyopathy
- **C)** ischemic dilated cardiomyopathy
- **D)** hypertrophic cardiomyopathy

70. Which of the following clinical signs is NOT seen in an inferior wall MI?

- **A)** ST elevation in leads II, III, and aVF
- **B)** ST depression in leads I and aVL
- **C)** AV heart blocks requiring temporary pacing
- **D)** tachycardia

71. Which of the following medications is contraindicated in the treatment of heart failure with reduced ejection fraction?

- **A)** hydralazine and isosorbide dinitrate
- **B)** lisinopril
- **C)** carvedilol
- **D)** nifedipine

72. A 36-year-old male in a motorcycle accident is admitted to the ICU after being intubated in the field. During assessment, the nurse notes pink secretions suctioned from the orotracheal tube and crepitus around the neck and upper torso. BP is 101/63 with titratable norepinephrine bitartrate at 4 mcg/min IV infusion. HR is 105, and temperature is 36.2°C. The patient appears to be resting comfortably with a dexmedetomidine infusion. Which of these findings should be immediately reported to the physician?

- **A)** BP
- **B)** HR
- **C)** temperature
- **D)** crepitus

73. Which of the following ABG results should the nurse expect for a patient with acute respiratory distress syndrome in respiratory acidosis?

	pH	PCO_2	HCO_3
A)	7.47	32	24
B)	7.33	46	24
C)	7.30	40	20
D)	7.36	38	26

74. A patient with a history of cirrhosis has arrived at the ED with a new onset of confusion. The patient's skin is jaundiced. Labs are as follows:
ammonia 130 mcg/dL
ALT 98 units/L
blood glucose 128 mg/dL
The nurse should prepare to administer

- **A)** lactulose.
- **B)** bisacodyl.
- **C)** mesalamine.
- **D)** insulin 2 units.

75. A hemodialysis patient is admitted with a potassium level of 7. What would the nurse expect to see on this patient's ECG?

- **A)** shortened PR interval
- **B)** ST elevation
- **C)** tall, peaked T waves
- **D)** extra P waves

76. A patient is being closely monitored after a fall. The nurse notices a slight increase in ICP. The nurse should intervene by

- **A)** increasing oxygen flow.
- **B)** elevating the head of the bed to 90 degrees.
- **C)** turning and repositioning the patient on their side.
- **D)** suctioning the patient at least hourly.

77. The nurse learns that the patient is a member of the local Native American tribe. The nurse recently attended an event celebrating Native American culture and learned about smudging. What is the best way to incorporate the patient's beliefs into care?

   A) Call the local tribe to request a visit from the spiritual leader.
   B) Notify the patient that they can smudge in the room if the door is closed.
   C) Bring aromatherapy supplies into the room as a substitute for smudging.
   D) Ask the patient if they have any cultural preferences for their care.

78. What signs would indicate that a patient with a subarachnoid hematoma is responding to treatment and that ICP is reducing?

   A) The P2 waveform is taller than the P1.
   B) The patient's temperature has increased by 2°C.
   C) Hunt and Hess assessment has been reduced to 2.
   D) Patient has increased rhinorrhea.

79. A patient becomes nauseated after receiving chemotherapy. The nurse has already administered 2 doses of ondansetron, and the patient is allergic to prochlorperazine. The patient requests aromatherapy to help with nausea. The patient is sharing a room with another patient who has severe allergies. What can the nurse do to incorporate the patient's request into care?

   A) Have a discussion with the patient about medications being more effective than home remedies.
   B) Tell the patient it is against hospital policy, even though there is no policy prohibiting alternative therapy.
   C) Allow patient to use oils and scents, and hope that the other patient is not affected.
   D) Try to obtain a private room for the patient so that they may use their aromatherapies.

80. A patient's ECG shows torsades de pointes, and $MgSO_4$ is ordered stat. The nursing priority is to

   A) monitor the patient for bradycardia and respiratory depression.
   B) prepare the patient for synchronized cardioversion.
   C) monitor the patient for tachycardia and hyperventilation.
   D) prepare the patient for Swan-Ganz catheter.

81. A patient has undergone surgery to remove a supratentorial intradural tumor. The patient's urine osmolality decreases to 265 mOsm/kg. What medication is likely to be the cause?

   A) beta blockers
   B) intraoperative NS 0.9% bolus
   C) phenytoin
   D) albuterol

82. A patient is being assessed for adequate abdominal perfusion pressure. The patient's MAP is 65 mm Hg, and IAP measured via intravesical pressure is 14 mm Hg. What should the nurse's next step be?

   A) Increase IV fluids.
   B) Raise the head of the bed to 90 degrees.
   C) Continue to monitor.
   D) Notify the physician.

83. A patient is brought to the ED in supraventricular tachycardia (SVT) with an HR of 220. EMS has administered 6 mg of adenosine, but the patient remains in SVT. What medication should the nurse anticipate administering to the patient next?

   A) 12 mg adenosine IV
   B) 1 mg epinephrine IV
   C) 300 mg amiodarone IV
   D) 0.5 atropine IV

84. Which of the following chest X-ray readings is consistent with acute respiratory distress syndrome?

- **A)** bilateral, diffuse white infiltrates without cardiomegaly
- **B)** bilateral, diffuse infiltrates with cardiomegaly
- **C)** tapering vascular shadows with hyperlucency and right ventricular enlargement
- **D)** prominent hilar vascular shadows with left ventricular enlargement

85. Which of the following increases a patient's risk of Fournier gangrene?

- **A)** well-controlled diabetes
- **B)** dapagliflozin 10 mg 1 time per day
- **C)** nystatin powder
- **D)** straight catheter use at home

86. A nurse is assessing a patient in traction for a complicated fracture of the scapula after a water-skiing collision. The nurse notes maroon petechiae on the upper chest extending to the axilla. What should the nurse suspect?

- **A)** side effect from enoxaparin injections
- **B)** contusions from the accident
- **C)** fat emboli
- **D)** compartment syndrome

87. A 64-year-old female is brought into the ED by her family for new-onset slurring of words, confusion, and unilateral weakness. The triage nurse activates the facility's stroke protocols. Which of the following assessments should the nurse expect to perform before the patient is taken for a CT scan?

- **A)** stat ECG
- **B)** lumbar puncture
- **C)** blood glucose test
- **D)** urinalysis

88. The nurse notices that a food tray being removed from a patient's room is mostly untouched. The nurse goes in to ask the patient if they are experiencing nausea. The patient answers that they are avoiding gluten and cannot eat what is being served. Reviewing the patient's chart, the nurse does not find a diagnosis of celiac disease. What should the nurse do to make sure that the patient is getting enough to eat?

- **A)** Tell the patient to have family bring in food that is gluten-free.
- **B)** While serving the next meal, assure patient that all items are gluten-free even if they contain wheat products.
- **C)** Notify the physician that the diet needs to be modified to be gluten-free.
- **D)** Call dietary for guidance, and provide the patient with a menu that identifies food choices that are gluten-free.

89. A nurse is concerned with the increasing rate of pressure ulcers seen on the unit in the past six months. What action would demonstrate that the nurse is performing at the highest level of competency in clinical judgment?

- **A)** asking a charge nurse for help when encountering a difficult patient situation
- **B)** identifying and defining the issue, then designing an evidence-based practice project for improvement
- **C)** continuing to practice because that is the way it has always been done on this unit
- **D)** notifying the manager about the issue, and hoping that it is fixed

90. Three hours ago, a patient underwent a left heart catheterization with intervention to the right coronary artery. The access site was via the right radial artery, and the radial band was removed 1 hour ago. What sign should the nurse be concerned with?

- **A)** BP 105/62
- **B)** HR 52
- **C)** right digit capillary refill > 3 sec
- **D)** lower back pain

91. The nurse is caring for a patient who presents to the ED with the following ABG results:
pH 7.32
$PaCO_2$ 47 mm Hg
HCO_3 24 mEq/L
PaO_2 91 mm Hg
The nurse should expect the patient to present with

   A) chest pain.
   B) nausea and vomiting.
   C) deep, rapid respirations.
   D) hypoventilation with hypoxia.

92. A patient with a traumatic brain injury has the following labs:
Na^+ 110
serum osmolality 235 mOsm/kg
urinary specific gravity 1.045
What treatment may be ordered for this patient?

   A) hypertonic fluid bolus
   B) torsemide
   C) insulin
   D) beclomethasone

93. A patient with crackles in bases, dyspnea, and fluid overload is admitted to the ICU for treatment of acute pulmonary edema. The physician orders aminophylline. What additional order should the nurse ensure is completed for this patient?

   A) acetaminophen 500 – 1000 mg PRN TID
   B) D5 fluid bolus 500 mL
   C) furosemide 40 mg IV push
   D) telemetry monitoring

94. Five days after percutaneous coronary intervention for MI, a patient develops a new, high-pitched, holosystolic, harsh murmur found at the cardiac apex and widely radiating. A nurse should suspect

   A) papillary muscle rupture.
   B) post-MI aortic stenosis.
   C) ventricular septal defect.
   D) pulmonary embolism.

95. A patient is admitted for an acute asthmatic attack leading to respiratory failure. The patient was stabilized with breathing treatments and O_2 delivery through a high-flow nasal cannula at 30 L/min. After 2 hours, the nurse responds to the call light. The patient has become dyspneic, tachycardic, and extremely anxious. Blood gases are drawn, with these results: PaO_2 46 mm Hg and $PaCO_2$ 62 mm Hg. What intervention would the nurse anticipate from the physician?

   A) increase O_2 of high-flow nasal cannula to 35 L/min
   B) BiPAP
   C) albuterol nebulizer treatment
   D) 0.5 – 2 mg morphine IV push for air hunger

96. A patient arrives in the ICU with family at the bedside. The patient speaks only Vietnamese, but the family speaks English and Vietnamese fluently. Although the nurse sets up the video translator service, it is not functioning, and the images and sound are unclear. What can the nurse do to ensure that the patient understands and participates in their care?

   A) Have the family act as translators, and notify the charge nurse.
   B) Draw pictures for the patient, demonstrating care.
   C) Continue to use a facility-approved video translation service.
   D) Attempt to troubleshoot with IT over the phone.

97. A nurse new to a facility is unsure about the facility's NPO sedation rules. How can the nurse ensure that the appropriate guidelines are being met while caring for a patient who will be having a lung biopsy tomorrow?

   A) Search online for evidence-based practice on NPO before sedation.

B) Refer to the facility's policies and procedures.

C) Call the surgeon to ask their preference.

D) Hold all intake after midnight.

98. A 79-year-old patient is admitted to the neuro-ICU after an ischemic stroke. The patient received TNKase 2 days ago and is still in bleeding precautions. The patient has made significant improvements and is sitting up in bed, eating a soft diet with the assistance of family. The nurse walks by the room and notices that a family member is passing several pills to the patient. What action should the nurse take?

A) Call security to seize the medications and escort the family out.

B) Stop the patient from taking the pills, and seek more information about what they are.

C) Stop the patient from taking the pills, and berate the family for doing such a dangerous act.

D) Assume they are vitamins, and go to the next patient.

99. A patient is admitted to the ICU after an abdominal aortic aneurysm repair that resulted in blood loss of 2000 mL. After surgery, HgB is 6.2 g/dL. The patient's history includes congestive heart failure and the placement of a cardiac stent within the past year. Crystalloid fluids have been administered, and the patient's BP is 80/52. The physician orders 4 units of PRBCs to be transfused immediately. What other orders would the nurse expect?

A) stat HgB

B) transfusion of FFP and PLT

C) furosemide

D) norepinephrine

100. A patient has died after 33 days in the neuro-trauma ICU. What is the best way for the staff to cope with this loss?

A) Increase workload so there is no time to dwell on the experience.

B) Apologize to the family.

C) Refer to a counselor a week after the patient's death.

D) Take time to debrief and share feelings regarding the loss.

101. When caring for a patient with esophageal varices, the nurse should first prepare to administer

A) phenytoin.

B) octreotide.

C) levofloxacin.

D) pantoprazole.

102. A patient is admitted with severe gastroenteritis and fluid loss due to excessive vomiting and diarrhea. CBC results are as follows: WBC 14,000 /mL, HgB 15 g/dL, Hct 53%, and sodium 152 mmol/L. What symptom would be expected?

A) bradycardia

B) hyporeflexia

C) hyperreflexia

D) ICP 20 mm Hg

103. The nurse is reviewing the labs of a patient with renal failure and notes a serum potassium level of 7.2 mEq/L. The nurse should prepare to administer which of the following medications to protect cardiac status?

A) aspirin

B) insulin

C) calcium gluconate

D) digoxin

104. An 18-year-old patient with a crush injury to the right lower extremity develops increased pain at the site. The nurse assesses the pressure bandage and finds that the patient can no longer move the toes and that capillary refill is 6 seconds. What is the priority intervention?

A) Remove dressing.
B) Elevate extremity.
C) Increase IV fluids.
D) Notify the physician, and ask for an increased range for analgesic therapy.

105. The nurse is caring for a patient after transsphenoidal craniotomy. What potential complication would be indicated by fluid balance overload?
A) cardiac dysrhythmias
B) CSF rhinorrhea
C) diabetes insipidus
D) SIADH

106. Which of the following should NOT be done when suctioning the endotracheal tube of a patient with TBI?
A) keeping each pass < 10 seconds
B) 100% oxygenation before and after each suction
C) deeper suction to remove more secretions with fewer passes
D) limit suction passes to 2 times

107. A patient's IV site has infiltrated with dopamine. The nurse stopped the infusion, aspirated the infusing medication until blood was returned, and flushed the catheter per hospital protocol. What intervention would be best to preserve skin integrity?
A) Request an order for a PICC line to infuse dopamine through.
B) Administer NSAIDs.
C) Apply a cold compress to site.
D) Contact physician for hyaluronidase injection.

108. A nurse is freshly off orientation and is caring for a vented patient. The patient suddenly desaturates in oxygen levels to 85%. What action shows that the nurse is progressing in the competency of clinical judgment?

A) immediately calls respiratory for assistance
B) texts the preceptors for advice
C) suctions the patient, repositions them, and then evaluates O_2 sats for improvement
D) calls a rapid response

109. A patient displaying distended neck veins, hypotension, and muffled heart sounds after receiving a penetrating chest trauma from a gunshot injury is most likely experiencing the development of
A) aortic injury.
B) tension pneumothorax.
C) cardiac tamponade.
D) hemothorax.

110. Which definition best describes a hospital facility's ethics committee function?
A) an end-of-life guidance and support group composed of community clergy and hospital health care teams
B) a group of physicians and administrators who develop policies to address legal issues related to advance directive statements
C) a multidisciplinary consulting group that addresses conflicts between doctors, patients, and their families
D) a multidisciplinary team of resource persons for patients, families, health care clinicians, and other members of the facility

111. To clinically evaluate for salicylate consumption, when should the nurse draw salicylate levels?
A) immediately
B) 3 hours after symptoms of overdose first occur
C) 6 hours after ingestion
D) within 24 hours

112. A patient on the ventilator in the ED begins to decompensate. The O_2 sat is decreasing, and the patient is becoming more anxious. There is a noted shift in the location of the patient's trachea. What does the nurse suspect?
    A) ventilator equipment failure
    B) endotracheal tube obstruction
    C) tension pneumothorax
    D) too much positive end-expiratory pressure

113. A 52-year-old patient undergoes emergency surgery for a ruptured appendix with possible peritonitis. During surgery, the patient received 3 L NaCl IV and 2 units PRBCs, and broad-spectrum IV antibiotics were initiated. The patient was stable before extubation and transfer to the SICU. Five hours later, the patient developed respiratory distress and bilateral rales on auscultation. A stat ABG shows the following:
    pH 7.48
    PaO_2 56 mm Hg
    $PaCO_2$ 38 mm Hg
    HCO_3 21 mEq/L
    The patient is placed on high-flow 100% oxygen, without improvement, and a chest X-ray shows bilateral pulmonary opacities. The nurse should suspect
    A) acute post-extubation laryngeal edema.
    B) acute exacerbation of bronchial asthma.
    C) pulmonary edema.
    D) pneumonia.

114. A patient who had a stroke 3 days ago has failed a swallow study. An NG tube has been inserted and verified via auscultating an air bolus. What action would next be appropriate?
    A) Flush the tube with 30 – 60 mL of water.
    B) Infuse fiber-fortified tube feeding formula per order.
    C) Verify placement with an X-ray.
    D) Crush and administer scheduled medication per orders.

115. Which of the following is the recommended intervention for a stage 2 pressure ulcer?
    A) lessening pressure to area and monitoring
    B) skin grafting
    C) moist dressings
    D) debridement

116. The nurse is caring for a patient who says he wants to take his own life. The patient has a detailed, concrete plan. The nurse places the patient on suicide precautions, which include a 24-hour sitter. The patient becomes angry and refuses the sitter. Which action is the most appropriate?
    A) Place the patient in soft wrist restraints.
    B) Have security sit outside the patient's door.
    C) Assign a sitter despite the patient's refusal.
    D) Allow the patient to leave AMA.

117. The rhythm shown in the figure is exhibited by a patient complaining of "heart pounding" and dyspnea.

    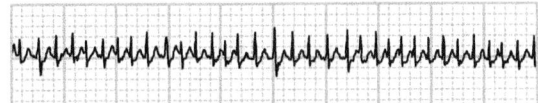

    The telemetry monitoring tech notified the bedside nurse of the rhythm change and the rapidly increasing ventricular response rate. Which of the following drugs should the nurse anticipate administering?
    A) lidocaine
    B) amiodarone
    C) epinephrine
    D) digoxin

118. Which of the following drugs would be contraindicated for a patient with low systemic vascular resistance?
    A) vasopressin
    B) dopamine

C) nitroprusside

D) norepinephrine

119. A mechanically ventilated patient with bilateral pneumonia has sudden-onset anxiety and begins to cough up thick tracheal secretions. Cardiac monitor show sinus tachycardia 118, BP 148/82, RR 32, and a drop in O_2 sat to 88%. Which of the following is an appropriate initial intervention?

A) Administer 100% O_2 manual ventilation via ambu-bag to endotracheal tube.

B) Suction the endotracheal tube using an in-line closed suction system.

C) Discuss FiO_2 adjustment with the respiratory therapist and pulmonologist.

D) Increase IV sedation infusion to manage patient's anxiety.

120. A patient with new-onset diabetes after long-term steroid therapy is concerned about adhering to a new diet and insulin therapy. What referral would best meet the patient's health education needs?

A) follow-up appointment with primary care provider

B) psychiatric consult

C) diabetes educator

D) no referral (patient does not meet criteria for a consult)

121. A physician orders a stat medication for a patient, but in light of the patient's condition, the nurse does not understand why it is being administered. The nurse has looked up the medication in the drug book and still is puzzled. What action should the nurse take before administering the medication?

A) Call the physician to clarify the order.

B) Administer the medication as this is a trusted physician.

C) Do not give it, and mark "Patient not available" in the medication administration record.

D) Tell the charge nurse that the patient is refusing to take it.

122. A 23-year-old female with a history of status asthmaticus is a direct admit to the ICU with severe shortness of breath despite use of her rescue inhaler. Auscultation of her lung fields reveals minimal air movement. She is immediately intubated, and mechanical ventilation is initiated with the following settings:
FiO_2 = 60%
tidal volume = 400ml
positive end-expiratory pressure = 12
respiratory rate = 18
Repeat ABGs after 60 minutes show the following:
PaO_2 = 76
$PaCO_2$ = 60
SpO_2 = 93%
pH = 7.10
Which of the following interventions should the nurse anticipate to improve the patient's respiratory acidosis and hypercapnia?

A) Decrease the tidal volume.

B) Decrease the FiO_2.

C) Increase the RR.

D) Increase the inspiratory time.

123. A patient is admitted to the ICU for management of pancreatitis. During the admission assessment, which complication should the nurse should carefully assess for?

A) atelectasis

B) high blood glucose

C) light sensitivity

D) low urine output

124. Which post-MI complication is characterized by chest pain, ST elevation in all the upright leads, and an auscultated friction rub?

A) ruptured papillary muscle

B) pericarditis

C) re-infarction

D) extension of the original MI

125. What is the most important determinant of adequate coronary artery blood flow to ensure myocardial tissue perfusion?

   A) supraventricular tachycardia
   B) HR
   C) preload
   D) afterload

126. When blood glucose levels fall below normal levels, what organ is triggered to release a hormone to restore normal glucose levels?

   A) liver
   B) pancreas
   C) adrenal medulla
   D) medulla oblongata

127. A nurse responds to the call light of a patient who had a fall from a ladder. The chart notes an injury at T5. The patient is diaphoretic and has marked erythema in the upper half of the body. The tele monitor alarm signals that the patient's HR is 45. What other symptoms would support autonomic dysreflexia?

   A) profound erythema across patient's body
   B) tachycardia and severe headache
   C) severe headache and cold, clammy lower extremities
   D) hypotension > 20 mm Hg drop from baseline BP

128. A 70-year-old patient with a history of Marfan syndrome required an open-reduction internal-fixation of the left femur from a high-velocity motor vehicle crash. Six hours post-op, the patient has become hypertensive and has an acute onset of severe, tearing pain in the abdomen and back; the pain radiates downward. A nurse should suspect

   A) pulmonary embolism.
   B) cardiac tamponade.
   C) aortic dissection.
   D) acute coronary syndrome.

129. A patient with a history of COPD is admitted to the ED with dyspnea. ABGs are drawn with the following results:
   pH 7.30
   PO_2 87 mm Hg
   PCO_2 52 mm Hg
   HCO_3 28 mEq/L
   Which of the following orders should the nurse verify?

   A) Administer high-flow oxygen at 15 L.
   B) Administer nebulized albuterol treatment.
   C) Administer IV fluids.
   D) Administer prednisone dose pack.

130. After receiving treatment for sepsis, what is the most likely reason the patient would develop acute kidney injury?

   A) septic-induced hypovolemia
   B) fluid overload from NS bolus
   C) nephrotoxic antibiotics
   D) underlying kidney disease that was not previously detected

131. A patient admits to having "3 – 4 servings of hard liquor" each night. What symptoms should be monitored in the first 6 hours?

   A) delirium tremens
   B) Wernicke encephalopathy
   C) agitation and restlessness
   D) hyperosmolar metabolic acidosis

132. A 36-year-old female with right upper quadrant pain, jaundice, and fatigue is being worked up for possible acute hepatitis. The patient is 30 days postpartum. What other condition should be ruled out, and what tool would be used to evaluate the patient?

   A) HELLP syndrome; Mississippi Classification System
   B) pre-eclampsia; NIH stroke scale
   C) postpartum hemorrhage; Glasgow Coma Scale
   D) abruptio placentae; Edinburgh Depression Scale

133. A peripheral nerve stimulator is being used to titrate an IV neuromuscular blocking agent dose to maintain an 80% blockade on a patient with no evidence of anasarca. Which of the following sites and corresponding responses should the nurse use to monitor muscle response?

A) ulnar nerve, 2 twitches of the thumb
B) facial nerve, 6 twitches of the eyebrow
C) posterior tibial nerve, 4 twitches of the great toe
D) facial nerve, 0 twitches

134. A nurse has read a new article in a nursing journal that would be of benefit to the neurosurgical unit. What is the best way to share this evidence-based practice with colleagues?

A) Email the article to the manager.
B) Tell a few close coworkers about the article.
C) Wait until the next staff meeting next month to bring it up.
D) Bring in the article and post it in the break room.

135. The nurse is reviewing the discharge instructions with a patient and family. The patient will be continuing to take 2 new medications at home that were started during this hospitalization. The patient asks how much the new medications cost. Which of the following responses advocates for the patient?

A) Tell the patient to contact their insurance company once they get home.
B) Call pharmacy for a free sample.
C) Remind the patient that the medication is needed to prevent rehospitalization.
D) Call pharmacy on patient's behalf for cost, and find out if there are less expensive generic options.

136. A transgender patient is comatose and vented in the ICU with a primary diagnosis of DKA. The patient's family wants the care team to call the patient by the birth name of "Angela," but the patient's chart indicates that the patient uses he/him pronouns and prefers to be called "John." What is the appropriate response by the nurse to recognize the patient's gender identity?

A) Educate the family that the patient has previously stated the preference of being called "John."
B) Call the patient "Angela" while the family is in the room.
C) Use the patient's legal name, which is still Angela, since it would be against policy to use another name.
D) Tell the patient's family that they should be more sensitive and supportive of the patient's choices.

137. A 78-year-old patient with increasing dementia is admitted to the ICU after a family member found her unconscious with an empty bottle of metoprolol. The nurse prints out a telemetry strip and measures the QT to be 500 ms. What medication would be expected to be ordered based on this clinical finding, and why?

A) atropine for bradycardia
B) $MgSO_4$ to prevent torsades de pointes
C) insulin drip for glucose control
D) glucagon to improve atrioventricular conduction

138. A brain death evaluation is being completed on a patient 4 days after discontinuation of therapeutic hypothermia. What action does NOT occur during this test?

A) preoxygenation for 10 minutes with O_2 sat readings of 100%
B) vent settings reduced to 10 breaths per minute and a positive end-expiratory pressure of 5 cm H_2O

C) test aborted if systolic BP decreases to < 100 without vasopressors

D) delivery of 100% O₂ at 6 L/min flow

139. A patient is admitted to the ICU after being struck by a vehicle while crossing a road. The patient has bruising around the eyes and at the base of the skull. When transferring the patient from the cart to a bed, what important action must be taken?

A) log roll

B) seizure precautions

C) monitoring for dysrhythmias

D) hyperventilate before and after movement

Use the following case to answer questions 140 and 141.

A 42-year-old female patient is admitted to the ICU for a malignant pleural effusion related to metastatic breast cancer. A total of 2.9 L of fluid is rapidly evacuated through the left thoracostomy. The patient describes pleuritic chest pain and begins to cough vigorously and uncontrollably. The chest X-ray shows fluffy infiltrates and unilateral haziness.

140. The nurse should suspect

A) hemothorax.

B) re-expansion pulmonary edema.

C) tension pneumothorax.

D) heart failure.

141. Which of the following is the most appropriate immediate intervention for this scenario?

A) Administer IV fluid resuscitation.

B) Intubate, and mechanically ventilate with low VT and high respiratory rate settings.

C) Perform needle decompression of chest.

D) Stop pleural fluid evacuation, and administer supplemental oxygen.

142. Grey Turner's sign in a patient with blunt abdominal trauma most likely indicates which one of the following?

A) retroperitoneal bleed

B) cholelithiasis

C) liver failure

D) hypoxemia

143. A patient 4 weeks after a small bowel resection is admitted to the ICU with a high-output enterocutaneous fistula. The nursing priority is to

A) administer antibiotics.

B) preserve and protect the skin.

C) apply a wound VAC to the area.

D) provide quiet time for relaxation.

144. A patient comes to the ED with complaints of nausea and vomiting for 3 days. The ECG reading is shown in the exhibit.

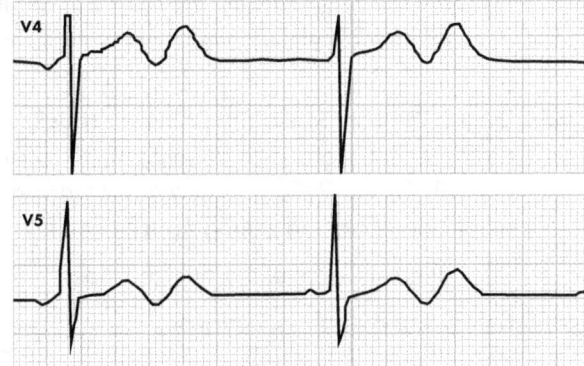

The nurse should suspect

A) hyperkalemia.

B) hypokalemia.

C) hypercalcemia.

D) hypocalcemia.

145. A college student is admitted to the ICU with new-onset confusion, severe headache, pyrexia, and nuchal rigidity. The physician is performing a lumbar puncture at the bedside, and the nurse is preparing to collect the fluid in tubes to send to the lab. The CSF appears clear. What diagnosis is the physician attempting to rule out?

   A) bacterial meningitis
   B) influenza B
   C) viral meningitis
   D) bacterial brain abscess

146. The nurse is caring for a patient who has dementia and who has pulled out 3 peripheral IVs. Which intervention should the nurse use to manage this patient?

   A) Place the patient in restraints or mitts.
   B) Tell the family that they need to stay with the patient.
   C) Replace the IV, and wrap it in gauze to hide it from view.
   D) Tell the patient that if they pull out another IV, the nurse will have to use a PICC line.

147. During the compensatory phase of shock, a patient's vital signs is as follows: BP 105/64, HR 113, O_2 sat 92%, RR 16. What other signs would be expected during this phase?

   A) decreased level of consciousness
   B) urine output < 30 mL/hr
   C) cool, mottled skin
   D) nausea

148. A 67-year-old cancer patient is in the ICU after developing pneumonia secondary to neutropenia after chemotherapy. The patient has discussed her wishes with her physician and has decided that she does not want to pursue any more treatment. She has signed documentation to change her status from Full Code to Do Not Resuscitate. Her daughter speaks privately to the primary nurse, saying she wants the status changed back and that her mother is just giving up. What intervention is most appropriate to maintain the daughter's trust?

   A) Allow time for the daughter to express her feelings.
   B) Tell the daughter that it is her mother's choice.
   C) Call the physician to speak with the daughter.
   D) Say nothing, and continue with another patient's care.

149. The nurse is taking care of a 32-year-old who has been admitted for renal failure due to extensive heroin use. The nurse is angry that this patient continues to be readmitted to the hospital and is exhibiting drug-seeking behavior. What should the first action of the nurse be?

   A) Provide analgesia PRN as requested by the patient.
   B) Notify physician of drug-seeking behavior.
   C) Tell the charge nurse that she needs to switch assignments.
   D) Assess own values to remove personal bias from care provided.

150. A patient with a history of atrial fibrillation is admitted to the ICU for a persistent HR of > 140. The patient is not in distress, and other vital signs are stable. The physician orders adenosine. What is the expected result of this medication?

   A) slow rate to verify underlying rhythm
   B) chemical cardioversion
   C) antidysrhythmic effect
   D) anticoagulation

PRACTICE TEST ONE ANSWER KEY

1. **C)** Treatment for hypertensive crisis should aim to decrease the BP by less than 25% within the first 2 hours. Decreasing more within this time frame can lead to poor cerebral perfusion, as evidenced by the dizziness and headache in this patient. The IV infusion should be reduced per titratable parameters, and the physician notified. It would not be appropriate to continue therapy at the current rate as severe hypotension may result. An NIH stroke scale assessment is appropriate for patients during hypertensive crisis, but this is not the priority intervention at this time.

   Objective: Cardiovascular

   Subobjective: Hypertensive crisis

2. **B)** The priority intervention for a patient in pulseless electrical activity (PEA) is to immediately begin high-quality CPR. Epinephrine is appropriate for PEA but is not the priority intervention. A patient in PEA should not be defibrillated, as it is a nonshockable rhythm. Opening the patient's airway is not a priority.

   Objective: Cardiovascular

   Subobjective: Dysrhythmias

3. **C)** The patient is exhibiting signs of transfusion-associated circulatory overload, with symptoms of congestive heart failure or pulmonary edema.

   Objective: Hematology and immunology

   Subobjective: Transfusion reactions

4. **B)** ACE inhibitors may worsen acute tubular necrosis, which is the most common intrarenal damage seen in the ICU.

   Objective: Renal and genitourinary

   Subobjective: Acute kidney injury

5. **D)** This patient is at elevated risk for hemorrhage. A vessel may have been perforated when the patient was repositioned, and this should be ruled out via CT exam. As the patient had been repositioned a while ago, a vagal response to the repositioning is unlikely. The patient should be moved as little as possible to prevent destabilizing the fracture.

   Objective: Musculoskeletal

   Subobjective: Fractures

6. **A)** Since this patient has disease on the right side, they should be positioned with the "good" lung down (on their left side).

   Objective: Respiratory

   Subobjective: Acute respiratory infection

7. **C)** The elevated pulmonary artery pressure indicates that the patient has been diagnosed with pulmonary arterial hypertension (PAH). If the patient is experiencing right-sided heart failure, the condition has transitioned to decompensated. Increased right atrial pressure also indicates decompensated PAH. Left ventricular hypertrophy is not an indication of worsening PAH. Normal cardiac output indicates that the condition is compensated. Decreased pulmonary artery pressure would indicate that treatment is improving the patient's condition.

   Objective: Respiratory

   Subobjective: Pulmonary hypertension

8. **A)** Both diabetes insipidus and syndrome of inappropriate antidiuretic hormone secretion (SIADH) are the result of inappropriate excretion of ADH, resulting in a sodium/fluid imbalance. In SIADH, ADH is elevated, causing water retention. This would be reflected in a decrease in serum sodium (< 120 mEq/L), because the sodium would be diluted. All the other values indicate a fluid deficit.

   Objective: Endocrine

   Subobjective: SIADH

9. **C)** The patient must have a core temperature above 32°C if they are to be evaluated and declared brain dead. All the other responses meet the conditions required for a brain-death evaluation that is not distorted by potentially influencing factors.

   Objective: Neurological

   Subobjective: Brain death

10. **B)** If at all possible, the charge nurse should attempt to assign per patient preference. Patients and family members should never be told that staffing is short. Purposefully assigning male caregivers will promote distrust of nursing staff and the facility. If it is not possible to assign a female caregiver, response D would be the next-best solution.

    Objective: Professional caring and ethical practice

    Subobjective: Advocacy/moral agency

11. A) Postoperative hemorrhage is a risk after bariatric surgery. The decrease in BP by > 30 systolically is clinically significant even though the MAP is > 60, as is the decrease in cognitive status. The Trendelenburg position will promote perfusion to the brain while the nurse then contacts the physician. Fluids should not be increased without a physician's order. The patient's diaphoresis is unlikely to be caused by overheating, and a cold cloth will not treat this potential medical emergency.

Objective: Multisystem

Subobjective: Bariatric complications

12. A) HELLP is characterized by hemolysis, elevated liver enzymes, and a low platelet count. Hepatic failure and hemolysis lead to elevated bilirubin levels. This presents as jaundice, which would cause the yellowing of the sclera noted in this scenario. The other options are all within normal limits and would not indicate organ failure.

Objective: Multisystem

Subobjective: Life-threatening maternal/fetal complications

13. D) Firm, calm verbal redirection with limit setting should be attempted before placing a patient in seclusion or restraints. For the safety of other patients, the patient should not be allowed to roam hallways.

Objective: Behavioral and psychological

Subobjective: Aggression

14. C) The patient is likely experiencing muscle spasticity secondary to multiple sclerosis. Baclofen is a muscle relaxer that is common for treatment of this condition. The nurse would expect baclofen to be ordered in conjunction with an IV pain medication, such as morphine. Gabapentin and amitriptyline are commonly used to treat pain but are not utilized for acute pain. Fentanyl is a strong opioid and would not be a first-choice medication for treating spasticity or pain.

Objective: Neurological

Subobjective: Neuromuscular disorders

15. C) Pulmonary capillary wedge pressure (PCWP) is an indirect measure of the left atrial pressures. Along with the other symptoms presented, acute pulmonary edema should be suspected with severely elevated PCWP or pulmonary artery occlusion pressure (PAOP). In cardiogenic shock, the PAOP may be normal to > 15 mm Hg. Hypotension will often show a normal or lower PAOP because the heart is inefficiently pumping blood to the pulmonary system. The PAOP will be elevated with mitral valve stenosis, not regurgitation.

Objective: Cardiovascular

Subobjective: Acute pulmonary edema

16. D) The respiratory findings are suspect for community-acquired pneumonia (CAP). The physician should be notified, an order for a culture and screen obtained, and the sputum sample collected and sent to lab before starting antibiotic treatment. It is important to screen for and identify CAP on incoming patients to prevent delays in patient treatment. The other answers are all appropriate once the sample is sent to the lab.

Objective: Respiratory

Subobjective: Acute respiratory infection

17. D) An IVC filter—a small, umbrella-shaped device with metal spines—is deployed within the inferior vena cava and catches emboli before they reach the lungs; the device prevents pulmonary embolism. The patient's history of recurrent GI bleeds is a relative contraindication for anticoagulant use. An angiogram and a thrombectomy are interventions to identify and treat thromboembolism.

Objective: Cardiovascular

Subobjective: Acute peripheral vascular insufficiency

18. B) The patient's symptoms along with the heart murmur are associated with mitral valve disease. This condition would be supported by a history of rheumatic fever, which can damage the heart valves. The damage can lead to heart failure, but the condition usually appears 15 years or more after the initial infection. A viral infection could precipitate pericarditis. All patients should be screened for suicide and fall risks.

Objective: Cardiovascular

Subobjective: Structural heart defects

19. C) Jaundice is a sign of liver failure. Metabolic acidosis, not alkalosis, is usually seen with bowel infarctions. McBurney's point is a sign of appendicitis. Hematochezia, diarrhea, and an elevated LDH (low-density lipoprotein) are all signs or symptoms of bowel infarctions.

Objective: Gastrointestinal

Subobjective: Bowel infarction, obstruction, perforation

20. A) The patient is in cholinergic crisis due to acetylcholinesterase inhibitor overdose. Atropine is effective in addressing the muscarinic effects of excessive acetylcholine by occupying the receptor sites and reducing the nicotinic effects such as muscle flaccidity and respiratory failure. IV immunoglobulin is used as supportive care for myasthenia gravis but is not usually administered for cholinergic crisis. Labetalol and insulin are not used to directly treat cholinergic crisis or myasthenia gravis.

Objective: Neurological

Subobjective: Neuromuscular disorders

21. **B)** A bone marrow biopsy can be extremely painful, and the patient's request should be honored. Providing the pain medication before the procedure allows sufficient time for the medication to take effect. The pain medication will likely not have relieving effects if given only at the start of the procedure. It would not be appropriate to withhold pain medication and administer it only if the nurse deems it necessary.

Objective: Multisystem

Subobjective: Pain

22. **B)** To protect patient's rights, the nurse should verify that the patient has not already filed a durable power of attorney or living will with medical records during a previous visit. If there are no records on file, it would be appropriate for the nurse to request that the physician discuss the options with family. The physician should enter an order for the patient to be full code after this discussion. Answers A and C are not clinically sound and do not promote autonomy.

Objective: Professional caring and ethical practice

Subobjective: Advocacy/moral agency

23. **D)** Certification is an excellent way for a nurse to promote personal growth, advocate for the nursing profession, and increase knowledge in the nurse's specialty. Passing the exam does not prove that the nurse is any smarter. The exam does not evaluate clinical skills; it is knowledge based. Fulfilling a quota for the facility does not provide the nurse development or enrichment.

Objective: Professional caring and ethical practice

Subobjective: Clinical inquiry

24. **D)** Valproic acid is used to treat seizures, diazepam is a benzodiazepine, and terazosin is a vasodilator. These all have associated risks related to falls. Cholecalciferol is a vitamin D_3 supplement.

Objective: Musculoskeletal

Subobjective: Functional issues

25. **B)** Cerebral edema may occur during dialysis. This may also be referred to as dialysis equilibrium syndrome.

Objective: Renal and genitourinary

Subobjective: Manage patients requiring renal therapeutic interventions

26. **B)** Patients with hyperosmolar hyperglycemic state (HHS) are at higher risk for microemboli leading to PE, shifts in serum potassium, and fluid deficits. Metabolic acidosis is associated with DKA. Pleural effusion is not a complication of HHS. Fluid deficit is a primary symptom; fluid overload is not typical.

Objective: Endocrine

Subobjective: Hyperosmolar hyperglycemic state (HHS)

27. **B)** A contraindication for alteplase therapy in this scenario is the NIH stroke scale score of > 25. For eligible patients, the time frame may be increased to 4.5 hours. Although the BP is elevated and should be managed, it is less than the threshold of 185/110. Aspirin is not a contraindication and would be administered again > 24 hours after alteplase is given.

Objective: Neurological

Subobjective: Stroke (ischemic)

28. **D)** The symptoms indicate right-sided MI, so IV fluids are the priority treatment for this patient. When treating patients with right ventricular infarction, nitrates, diuretics, and morphine are to be avoided because of their pre-load-reducing effects.

Objective: Cardiovascular

Subobjective: Acute coronary syndrome

29. **A)** First-degree heart block is associated with an elongated PR interval that is consistent and uniform throughout the reading. An inconsistent lengthening that drops a QRS is associated with a second-degree type I heart block. Two P waves for every QRS may indicate atrial malfunction. No correlation between the P and QRS waves is indicative of a third-degree heart block.

Objective: Cardiovascular

Subobjective: Myocardial conduction system abnormalities

30. **B)** The pO_2 level is elevated for a patient who has COPD. This can decrease their hypoxic drive and lead to an increased retention of CO_2. The nurse should collaborate with respiratory therapy to decrease the O_2 and continue to monitor the ABGs. For this patient population, the pO_2 should be kept around 60 mm Hg, and the O_2 sat at 88 – 94% to reduce the risk of hypercapnia. The other conditions are typically not associated with chronic hypercapnia that would lead to this concern.

Objective: Respiratory

Subobjective: Chronic conditions

31. **A)** An aPTT of 94 seconds indicates that heparin therapy is within the optimal range for preventing blood clot formation. Fibrinogen levels that are ≤ 150 mg/dL and PLT levels < 60,000/μL indicate that the patient is at a higher risk for bleeding issues. D-dimer is a test used to evaluate risk for thrombus or embolus; an elevated result indicates a higher probability of developing an occlusion.

    Objective: Cardiovascular

    Subobjective: Acute peripheral vascular insufficiency

32. **B)** The patient is experiencing symptoms of a PE and should first be placed in a semi-Fowler's position to clear the airway. Vital signs should then be obtained to compare with established baseline data, followed by administration of oxygen as ordered. Finally, the patient should be prepared for diagnostic tests such as blood gases, ventilation-perfusion lung scan, and pulmonary angiography.

    Objective: Respiratory

    Subobjective: Acute pulmonary embolus

33. **B)** Approximately 10% of patients develop post-ICU PTSD, including night sweats, flashbacks, and anxiety issues. The patient should be educated about, and provided resources to address, PTSD.

    Objective: Professional caring and ethical practice

    Subobjective: Caring practices

34. **D)** Systems thinking employs strategies such as root-cause analysis. Analysis would reveal that this situation could happen to any nurse and that it occurred because the nurses did not review the drips of this patient together. Requiring a bedside report that reviews the IV infusions with the MAR (medication administration record) would help prevent this breakdown. Having a house supervisor review all IV drips would be time-consuming and infringe on that role's responsibilities. Requiring all IV drip orders to be cosigned by a nurse might also be time-consuming and could be helpful in initiating a drip but would not have prevented the drip from continuing to run.

    Objective: Professional caring and ethical practice

    Subobjective: Systems thinking

35. **B)** Having a frank, professional conversation about chronic pain relief is the nurse's priority. The nurse should not immediately assume the patient is drug-seeking; nor should the nurse ignore the patient's pain complaint.

Objective: Professional issues

Subobjective: Patient (pain management and procedural sedation)

36. **B)** The administration of sedation has put this patient at risk for oversedation. The cause is most likely the midazolam, a benzodiazepine, because the onset of symptoms is 30 – 120 minutes after administration. Because the symptoms indicate a medical emergency, the reversal drug flumazenil must be administered. Sternal rub is also appropriate, but not the priority.

    Objective: Multisystem

    Subobjective: Toxic ingestion/exposure

37. **B)** Undifferentiated trauma patients should initially be treated for hemorrhagic shock until proven otherwise. As the patient only received a small bolus in the ED, fluid resuscitation per protocol should be started immediately. Once the patient has received sufficient fluids, the BP should be evaluated, and, if necessary, vasopressors started. The patient requires an intervention, so simply continuing to monitor would not be appropriate in this case. Security should be notified of the patient, and the belongings searched, but this action does not take precedence over treating the patient.

    Objective: Multisystem

    Subobjective: Multisystem trauma

38. **B)** ST elevation in all leads except aVR and V1 is indicative of cardiac tamponade. This causes pressure that prevents venous return and decreases BP, which may cause ischemia. Nitroglycerin should be avoided or used under physician direction and close monitoring. Both an NS bolus and epinephrine are appropriate to improve volume status and to stabilize hemodynamics, as needed. Atropine is not contraindicated and would be appropriate if needed to treat bradycardia; however, cardiac tamponade is usually associated with tachycardia.

    Objective: Cardiovascular

    Subobjective: Cardiac tamponade

39. **A)** Abnormalities in magnesium levels may put the patient at risk for ventricular dysrhythmia. A hypomagnesemia level of 0.8 mEq/L would be of concern (normal range is 1.5 – 2.5 mEq/L). The other values are within normal ranges.

    Objective: Cardiovascular

    Subobjective: Dysrhythmias

40. **A)** The first line of treatment for a patient with AIDS and an opportunistic infection is antibiotics. The other

treatments may be a part of the plan of care, but antibiotics would be initiated first.

Objective: Hematology and immunology

Subobjective: Immune deficiencies

41. **D)** A normal bilirubin is between 0.3 and 1.2 mg/dL. A level of 4.0 mg/dL indicates liver damage and could be used alongside an infection to diagnose sepsis. The other lab levels listed are all within normal limits.

    Objective: Multisystem

    Subobjective: Septic shock

42. **C)** A history of hypertension will cause an increase in afterload. Diabetes will cause complications with microvascular disease, leading to poor cardiac function. Endocrine disorders will cause an increase in cardiac workload. Marfan syndrome causes the cardiac muscle to stretch and weaken.

    Objective: Cardiovascular

    Subobjective: Heart failure

43. **D)** The nurse should begin with assessing the patient's blood glucose levels and treat accordingly. While confusion, blurred vision, and slurred speech are symptoms of a stroke, an ECG and NIH stroke scale assessment would be reasonable tests to order if the blood glucose levels were within normal range. A CT scan may be ordered, depending on further assessment.

    Objective: Endocrine

    Subobjective: Hypoglycemia (acute)

44. **D)** Because of the sudden nature and intensity of the pain, a stat CT scan would rule out possible perforation or volvulus. The other interventions would be reasonable after perforation or volvulus is ruled out.

    Objective: Gastrointestinal

    Subobjective: Bowel infarction, obstruction, perforation

45. **D)** With a BP of 70/42, the patient is experiencing unstable supraventricular tachycardia (SVT) and therefore requires immediate synchronized cardioversion. Defibrillation is not indicated, because the patient is awake and has an organized heart rhythm. Adenosine can be used in patients with stable SVT, but this patient is not stable. Amiodarone is not indicated for patients in unstable SVT.

    Objective: Cardiovascular emergencies

    Subobjective: Dysrhythmias

46. **A)** Vasopressin and desmopressin may cause cardiac, cerebral, and mesenteric artery vasospasm. In a patient with heart failure, vasospasm may affect cardiac perfusion and inhibit the pumping function; therefore, cardiac monitoring is indicated.

    Objective: Endocrine

    Subobjective: Diabetes insipidus

47. **C)** Before assuming that the patient is thinking of harming herself or her child, the nurse must collaborate with the patient to address these signs of postpartum depression. The patient is not in immediate danger, and the patient should not be stigmatized for confiding in the nurse. The patient should not be left alone without the nurse's determining any suicidal tendencies. The physician may be contacted later. The patient's feelings should not be dismissed, and the nurse has the opportunity to educate the patient on the symptoms of postpartum depression and provide resources for help.

    Objective: Professional caring and ethical practice

    Subobjective: Collaboration

48. **B)** The safety and efficacy of the herbs should be explored, and the herbs incorporated into the patient's care, if possible. Curanderos are an important part of some Hispanic and Indigenous cultures. Telling the patient to stop the use of these herbs or warning the curandero to stop treatment may cause distrust of Western medicine. Directly lying to the patient should never be a considered an appropriate response.

    Objective: Professional caring and ethical practice

    Subobjective: Response to diversity

49. **C)** If the cardiac output is not improving, a second vasopressor (such as norepinephrine) is typically initiated. Dobutamine is an inotropic but may also cause systemic vasodilation. The patient has already received a fluid bolus, and the pressure remains low. The dobutamine drip would not be increased, given the increasing hypotension, and may be ordered to discontinue. Esmolol is a beta blocker and is contraindicated with cardiogenic shock.

    Objective: Cardiovascular

    Subobjective: Cardiogenic shock

50. **C)** ST elevation in leads V1 – V4 indicates a primarily anterior infarction. Accompanying elevation in leads V5 – V6 suggests some lateral involvement as well. Lateral STEMI will have elevation in leads I, aVL, V5, or V6. Right ventricular (inferior) infarction elicits elevation in leads II, III, and aVF.

    Objective: Cardiovascular

Subobjective: Acute coronary syndrome

51. D) Suction should be kept at the lowest possible pressure, usually between 800 and 120 mm Hg, and < 200 mm Hg if necessary. Catheters should not be reused, and a sterile suction catheter should be used with each suction session. Oxygenating the patient before and after suctioning prevents hypoxia. Continuous, not intermittent suction, is best practice, and passes should be limited to ≤ 15 seconds to prevent a vagal response.

Objective: Respiratory

Subobjective: Tracheostomy

52. C) COVID-19 can cause fluid to build up in the alveoli, resulting in shunting. PaO_2 will continue to decrease as shunting increases, while $PaCO_2$ remains stable. The patient's PaO_2 levels indicate hypoxemia. This emergent condition requires positive airway pressure and intubation and ventilatory support. Increasing O_2 delivery will not improve PaO_2, because the issue is a deficit of gas exchange related to the pulmonary edema.

Objective: Respiratory

Subobjective: ARDS

53. A) In atrial flutter, there are no discernible P waves, and a distinct sawtooth wave pattern is present. The atrial rate is regular, and the PR interval is not measurable. In atrial fibrillation, the rhythm would be very irregular with coarse, asynchronous waves. Torsades de pointes, or "twisting of the points," is characterized by QRS complexes that twist around the baseline and is a form of polymorphic ventricular tachycardia. It may resolve spontaneously or progress to ventricular fibrillation, which is emergent: the ventricles are unable to pump any blood, because of disorganized electrical activity. Untreated, ventricular fibrillation quickly leads to cardiac arrest.

Objective: Cardiovascular

Subobjective: Dysrhythmias

54. B) BNP, or B-type natriuretic peptide, is a hormone released by the heart in response to pressure changes within the heart. This measurement is used to gauge the severity of congestive heart failure. A normal range in a patient with heart failure is 0 – 100 pg/mL. A BNP of 760 pg/mL indicates severe heart failure. ALT (alanine aminotransferase) tests liver enzymes. The normal range of ALT is 7 – 56 units per liter, so a value of 33 units/L is within normal limits. WBC count normally ranges from 4,500 to 11,000/μL, so a value of 10,450 is within normal limits. Direct bilirubin is a by-product of RBC breakdown. Normal lab values for direct bilirubin range from 0 to 0.3 mg/dL, so a value of 0.2 mg/dL falls within normal limits.

Objective: Cardiovascular

Subobjective: Heart failure

55. C) The bolus increases the probability of aspiration due to the noted reflux; delivering the bolus faster would worsen the reflux. The head of the bed should be kept at > 30 degrees during feedings unless otherwise contraindicated. Delivering the enteral nutrition at a slower rate would help prevent reflux and is an appropriate intervention. Because the patient requires nutrition, a restriction of caloric intake could worsen outcomes.

Objective: Respiratory

Subobjective: Aspiration

56. C) The presence of ketones is a highly reliable indicator of DKA. The patient would have a blood glucose level > 250 mg/dL, metabolic acidosis, and an increase in serum potassium.

Objective: Endocrine

Subobjective: Diabetic ketoacidosis

57. C) The best action for the nurse would be to treat this as a teaching moment and provide the care assistants with the information needed to keep themselves safe and to decrease the stigma surrounding this diagnosis. Double gloving offers no more protection during standard patient care than does single gloving. Reproaching the staff may cause a lack of trust and a breakdown of relationships. Since both aides were participating in the care of the patient and were not speaking loud enough to be heard by others, HIPAA laws were not violated.

Objective: Professional caring and ethical practice

Subobjective: Caring practices

58. C) Effective teaching must start with evaluating the learner's preferences and needs. Choices A and B are both appropriate if they align with the information gathered from the evaluation of the patient's and spouse's learning styles. The patient and spouse may not always have home care available and should know and feel comfortable with the basic care and management of the drain.

Objective: Professional caring and ethical practice

Subobjective: Facilitation of learning

59. A) Although the patient may need a splenectomy in the future, the nurse must now stabilize the patient by correcting platelet levels. Antibiotics are not indicated to treat idiopathic thrombocytopenic purpura, and an arterial line is contraindicated because of the bleed risk.

Objective: Hematology and immunology

Subobjective: Coagulopathies

60. **A)** Adrenal insufficiency, a serious pathologic condition found in critically ill patients, is caused by the decreased production of cortisol, aldosterone, and androgen. Imipramine is an inhibitor of glucocorticoid production and may lead to adrenal insufficiency. Myxedema is a deficiency of thyroxine and is also known as advanced hypothyroidism. SIADH, caused by an inappropriate and excessive release of ADH from the posterior pituitary gland, alters the equilibrium of water in the body. Crohn's disease is a regional, chronic, nonspecific inflammatory disease of the bowel.

Objective: Endocrine

Subobjective: Adrenal insufficiency

61. **C)** Lorazepam is a short-acting antianxiety medication used to treat patients with a high level of anxiety. Haloperidol is an antipsychotic used to treat schizophrenia, and phenytoin is an antiseizure medication; neither would be ordered for anxiety. Chlordiazepoxide is a medium- to long-acting benzodiazepine that would take several hours to have a full effect.

Objective: Behavioral

Subobjective: Anxiety

62. **A)** Stenosis is seen specifically with Roux-en-Y gastric bypass (RYGB) and requires endoscopic balloon dilation. Stenosis is usually seen within the first week post-op. Because gallstones are a common complication with vertical band gastroplasty, the gallbladder is often prophylactically removed during the bypass procedure. The risk for post-op bleeding is highest in the immediate post-op period, not after discharge, and would require emergent surgical correction. Anastomotic leaks are a risk with all bypass procedures and are not specific to RYGB.

Objective: Multisystem

Subobjective: Bariatric complications

63. **B)** Nadolol is a beta blocker, and this patient is already bradycardic. Consultation with the physician is required before administration. While loratadine is not utilized to treat esophageal varices, there is no contraindication to administering this medication. The other medications and dosages are all appropriate.

Objective: Gastrointestinal

Subobjective: Hepatic failure/coma

64. **B)** Vasoconstrictors like digitalis are contraindicated with mesenteric and colonic ischemia because they may further decrease blood flow to the bowel. The other options are all part of the medical management of bowel infarctions.

Objective: Gastrointestinal

Subobjective: Bowel infarction, obstruction, perforation

65. **D)** The patient will still require dialysis, but dialysis via the peritoneal route is contraindicated with the presence of infection. The patient's vital signs are not stable enough to handle the fluid shifts of intermittent hemodialysis. Continuous renal replacement therapy is appropriate for hemodynamically unstable patients in the ICU setting.

Objective: Renal and genitourinary

Subobjective: Manage patients requiring renal therapeutic interventions

66. **C)** The gold standard for identifying a fluid as CSF is either the beta-2-transferrin or the beta-trace-protein lab test. The halo test is subjective; it requires interpretation of the presence of a halo appearance on a piece of gauze. The glucose oxidase test may give false positives for patients with diabetes. A CT scan will show where a leak is occurring and would be appropriate if the fluid is determined to be CSF.

Objective: Neurological

Subobjective: Neurosurgery

67. **B)** There are 2 types of delirium: hypoactive and hyperactive. Patients experiencing delirium may have one set of symptoms or the other set, or they may have a mix of both. The patient may need more rest, but lack of rest is not the most likely cause of the flat affect. Moreover, this complacency should not be confused with adjusting.

Objective: Neurological

Subobjective: Delirium

68. **D)** This is a critical blood glucose level. There is no time to wait for a serum blood glucose result. The patient is at high risk for seizures at this low of a glucose level, and oral intake would therefore not be safe. The patient should be administered an 0.5 ampule of D50 (dextrose 50% solution) via IV.

Objective: Endocrine

Subobjective: Hypoglycemia (acute)

69. **D)** Alcohol septal ablations are used to treat left ventricle outflow obstruction caused by hypertrophic

cardiomyopathy. This treatment is not indicated for other cardiomyopathies.

Objective: Cardiovascular

Subobjective: Cardiomyopathies

70. **D)** The AV (atrioventricular) node's arterial supply is from the conus off the right coronary artery. Occlusion interrupts the normal conduction pattern, resulting in the bradycardia and AV heart blocks that are most commonly seen in a right-sided (inferior wall) infarction. The ECG changes listed are also associated with inferior wall MIs.

Objective: Cardiovascular

Subobjective: Acute coronary syndrome

71. **D)** First-generation calcium channel blockers such as nifedipine are contraindicated in the treatment of heart failure with reduced ejection fraction (HFrEF) because they reduce contractility. ACE inhibitors such as lisinopril are the first-line treatment of HFrEF. Hydralazine, a selective arteriole dilator, and isosorbide dinitrate, a nitrate that is a selective venous dilator, are used together to create an effect similar to ACE inhibitors when patients are unable to tolerate an ACE inhibitor. Beta blockers, such as carvedilol, are prescribed to patients with HFrEF to prevent progression of the disease.

Objective: Cardiovascular

Subobjective: Heart failure

72. **D)** Crepitus is an abnormal finding caused by an air leak into the subcutaneous tissue and must be reported to the physician immediately. Because the patient was intubated in the field and has signs of crepitus and hemoptysis, the patient should be evaluated for tracheal perforation. Although the BP is on the lower side, the titratable norepinephrine bitartrate drip is not at max level and may be increased. The HR is high but would most likely decrease if the BP were raised. The patient's temperature is within normal limits.

Objective: Respiratory

Subobjective: Thoracic trauma

73. **B)** A pH of 7.33 with an increased PCO_2 and normal HCO_3 indicates respiratory acidosis. Option A indicates respiratory alkalosis. Option C indicates metabolic acidosis. Option D indicates a normal ABG.

Objective: Respiratory emergencies

Subobjective: Interpret blood gas results

74. **A)** The patient's ammonia level and ALT are elevated, which is expected with cirrhosis. Lactulose is given to lower ammonia levels in patients with cirrhosis. Bisacodyl is a laxative and is not indicated for this patient. Mesalamine is an anti-inflammatory given for ulcerative colitis. The patient's blood glucose is not elevated enough to require 2 units of insulin.

Objective: Gastrointestinal

Subobjective: Hepatic failure/coma

75. **C)** Tall, peaked T waves are a classic sign of hyperkalemia. Other indicators of hyperkalemia include ST depression, prolonged PR intervals, and absent P waves.

Objective: Renal and genitourinary

Subobjective: Life-threatening electrolyte imbalances

76. **A)** Increasing ICP requires nursing intervention; the nurse should increase the rate of oxygen because hypoxia can worsen ICP. Elevating the head of the bed, repositioning the patient, and suctioning the patient are not recommended interventions for patients experiencing (or at risk for) ICP because these interventions can actually increase the pressure.

Objective: Neurological

Subobjective: Increased intracranial pressure

77. **D)** Calling the local spiritual leader without the patient's request or permission may be violating HIPAA laws. Answers B and C indicate that the nurse is making cultural assumptions about the patient. Before assuming that the patient may wish to participate in certain cultural practices, the nurse should ask the patient if there are any cultural preferences that would affect their care.

Objective: Professional caring and ethical practice

Subobjective: Response to diversity

78. **C)** The Hunt and Hess grading scale evaluates severity of symptoms caused by a subarachnoid hemorrhage. The lower the value, the less symptomatic the patient is, indicating that ICP would be reducing and the patient improving. When measuring ICP waveforms, the P1 wave would normally be highest. For every 1°C a patient's temperature increases, there is an increase in ICP. Rhinorrhea is a sign of elevated ICP, which causes CSF drainage.

Objective: Neurological

Subobjective: Increased intracranial pressure

79. **D)** Even though it may not be possible, the nurse should attempt to find a private room so that the patient could use aromatherapy. If the nurse dismisses the purposefulness of a patient's alternative therapies, the nurse is imposing their own belief system onto

the patient. The other patient's health should never be jeopardized. Most health care facilities allow alternative therapies in conjunction with conventional medicine. The patient should never be told something that is not true.

Objective: Professional caring and ethical practice

Subobjective: Response to diversity

80. **A)** Magnesium sulfate (MgSO$_4$) is a CNS depressant and can cause marked bradycardia and respiratory depression. The nursing priority is to monitor the patient's vital signs for CNS depression after this drug is administered. Tachycardia and hyperventilation are not side effects of MgSO$_4$. A Swan-Ganz catheter and synchronized cardioversion are not indicated.

Objective: Cardiovascular

Subobjective: Dysrhythmias

81. **C)** The low urine osmolality is indicative of diabetes insipidus. Phenytoin, used postoperatively to prevent surgically induced seizures, may cause drug-induced diabetes insipidus by making the kidneys unresponsive to the action of ADH.

Objective: Endocrine

Subobjective: Diabetes insipidus

82. **D)** The equation for abdominal perfusion pressure (APP) is MAP – IAP (intra-abdominal pressure). An adequate APP is 60 mm Hg or greater. This patient's APP is 51 mm Hg, which is insufficient for adequate perfusion. The physician should be notified for orders such as increasing IV fluids. Raising the head of the bed and continuing to monitor do not address this specific issue.

Objective: Gastrointestinal

Subobjective: Abdominal compartment syndrome

83. **A)** The drug of choice for supraventricular tachycardia (SVT) is adenosine. The first dose of 6 mg has already been given, so the next appropriate dose would be 12 mg. The other options are not the next appropriate intervention for a patient in SVT.

Objective: Cardiovascular

Subobjective: Dysrhythmias

84. **A)** The typical chest radiography for a patient with acute respiratory distress syndrome (ARDS) is bilateral, diffuse white infiltrates without cardiomegaly. Options C and D show results for abnormal heart tissue but not for lung tissue and give no information about infiltrates.

Objective: Respiratory emergencies

Subobjective: ARDS

85. **B)** Dapagliflozin, an SGLT2 inhibitor used to manage diabetes, does have the rare risk of causing Fournier gangrene. Poorly controlled diabetes is a risk factor for infection and possible gangrene. Nystatin powder, used to treat integumentary yeast infections, does not increase the risk of Fournier gangrene. Long-term indwelling catheters, not straight catheters, may also contribute to the development of necrotizing fasciitis conditions such as Fournier gangrene.

Objective: Integumentary

Subobjective: Necrotizing fasciitis

86. **C)** Petechiae in this region are a cardinal sign of a fat embolism, which is a risk after a fracture of the scapula and long bones. Petechiae related to subcutaneous enoxaparin would appear on the lower abdomen at the injection site. Contusions would appear as mottled blue and purple bruising. Petechiae are not a sign of compartment syndrome.

Objective: Musculoskeletal

Subobjective: Fractures

87. **C)** Severe hypoglycemia can mimic stroke signs; a finger-stick blood glucose test would quickly rule out hypoglycemia without delaying the CT scan. A lumbar puncture may be done if the CT scan is inconclusive and if a hemorrhagic stroke is suspected. The patient is not exhibiting chest pain or signs of MI, an ECG is not necessary. A urine specimen may be difficult to collect at this time because of the patient's condition and may be postponed until after the CT scan.

Objective: Neurological

Subobjective: Stroke (ischemic)

88. **D)** Giving the patient a menu of choices available for various dietary preferences allows the patient to order a meal without waiting for the physician to put in a new dietary order. The physician should be notified of the dietary preference during rounds that day and should clarify if the patient has celiac disease or is gluten intolerant so that this condition may be added to the chart.

If the patient is still unsatisfied by the food selection, suggesting that the family bring in some food choices may be appropriate. It is never appropriate to lie to a patient, and misleading statements about gluten content may cause serious health issues if the patient does indeed have celiac disease.

Objective: Professional caring and ethical practice

Subobjective: Response to diversity

89. B) Level 5 in clinical judgment involves synthesizing and interpreting complex patient data. Taking the initiative to design a project embraces autonomy and contributes to the practice of nursing. The other responses are at the lowest level of clinical practice and involve gathering basic data to identify an issue, but they do not act on that information autonomously.

Objective: Professional caring and ethical practice

Subobjective: Clinical judgment

90. C) The HR and BP are within normal limits, and the scenario does not indicate that the patient is having any distress related to cardiac output. With interventions on the right coronary arteries, the patient may have refractory bradycardia. Because the access site was through the right radial artery, the back pain is highly unlikely to be due to a retroperitoneal bleed; nor is the patient having any signs of hemorrhage. With the radial band now off, the capillary refill to the right hand should have returned to normal. In this situation, neurovascular insufficiency is of concern, and the physician should be notified of this finding.

Objective: Cardiovascular

Subobjective: Acute peripheral vascular insufficiency

91. D) These ABGs indicate acute respiratory acidosis. Common signs of respiratory acidosis include hypoventilation with hypoxia, disorientation, and dizziness. Untreated respiratory acidosis can progress to ventricular fibrillation, hypotension, seizures, and coma. Deep, rapid respirations and nausea and vomiting are signs of metabolic acidosis. Chest pain is not a symptom of respiratory acidosis.

Objective: Respiratory

Subobjective: Interpret blood gas results

92. B) The patient's labs history and labs suggest syndrome of inappropriate antidiuretic hormone secretion (SIADH). Torsemide is used off label to decrease ADH secretion and promote diuresis. Hypertonic fluids may be an appropriate treatment but should be used to slowly correct Na^+ imbalances to decrease the risk of permanent neurological damage. Insulin and beclomethasone are not used primarily to treat SIADH.

Objective: Endocrine

Subobjective: SIADH

93. D) Because aminophylline may cause tachydysrhythmias, the patient's hemodynamic and cardiac rhythms should be monitored closely for sudden changes. Acetaminophen may be indicated to promote patient comfort but is not a priority. A fluid bolus is contraindicated in the case of fluid overload. The patient may require furosemide, but this is related to the disease process and not associated with the aminophylline order.

Objective: Cardiovascular

Subobjective: Acute pulmonary edema

94. A) This heart sound at the cardiac apex is specific to mitral or tricuspid regurg, which would be caused by a papillary muscle rupture. Aortic stenosis would be heard as a harsh systolic murmur over the right second intercostal space, with radiation to the right neck. A pleuritic rub may be auscultated in the presence of pulmonary embolism.

Objective: Cardiovascular

Subobjective: Cardiac/vascular catheterization

95. B) BiPAP is the appropriate choice to improve gas exchange and decrease the patient's respiratory work. The patient is in type 3 respiratory failure, a mix of hypoxemia and hypercapnia. Merely increasing the O_2 concentration will not help with hypercapnia. And because the PaO_2 labs show that the patient is already severely hypoxemic, and 35 L/min is at the maximum delivery rate for the high-flow nasal cannula, increasing the O_2 would be insufficient for type 3 respiratory failure. A breathing treatment has been provided already within the past 2 hours, so albuterol nebulizer treatment is unlikely to provide any improvement at this point. Morphine may help alleviate air hunger, but the sedation may also decrease respiratory depth and worsen hypercapnia.

Objective: Respiratory

Subobjective: Acute respiratory failure

96. A) The patient's care should not be delayed because of translational or technology issues. The charge nurse should be notified that the system is not working so that IT can work on the problem. Drawing pictures and continuing to use the malfunctioning system may increase the risk of misunderstanding. Attempting to troubleshoot over the phone delays patient care. The nurse should continue the care that the patient needs at this time with the family's assistance in explaining what is occurring. The family should not be used to translate information needed for informed consent if the patient is still capable of making their own decisions.

Objective: Professional caring and ethical practice

Subobjective: Response to diversity

97. B) NPO guidelines vary slightly depending on the resource. To ensure best practice within the facility, the nurse should refer to the facility's policy and procedures for guidance. Searching online for evidence-based practice may bring up resources that are not valid or that contradict the facility's standards. It would not be appropriate to call the surgeon for this matter. Deciding to simply hold all intake after midnight would also not be appropriate if the surgery was scheduled later in the afternoon or if the patient has diabetes.

Objective: Professional caring and ethical practice

Subobjective: Clinical inquiry

98. B) The immediate action should be to prevent the patient from taking the pills and to find out what they are and if the patient has already taken any. The patient's family should then be educated about the importance of not giving any medications or supplements to the patient while the person is in the hospital. Calling security or berating the family will not help ensure patient safety or educate the family on why this is a safety risk. Even vitamins may be contraindicated with certain medications, and several herbal supplements may increase bleed risk.

Objective: Professional caring and ethical practice

Subobjective: Clinical judgment

99. B) As the patient may still be actively bleeding from the continued hypotension despite fluid resuscitation, clotting factors such as FFP and platelets should be administered with the PRBCs. HgB should be redrawn after blood has been transfused. After the patient has stabilized, furosemide should be considered, to prevent fluid overload and pulmonary edema due to congestive heart failure. Norepinephrine is a vasopressor and should not be administered until the patient's hypovolemic state has been stabilized.

Objective: Multisystem

Subobjective: Shock states

100. D) Debriefing should occur shortly after the causative event. Doing so has been shown to prevent staff burnout. Apologizing to the family assigns blame to the staff. Increasing workload after a traumatic event will further increase the risk for burnout.

Objective: Multisystem

Subobjective: End-of-life care

101. B) Esophageal varices can lead to death via hemorrhage. Octreotide is a vasoconstrictor used to control bleeding before an endoscopy. Phenytoin is an anticonvulsant, levofloxacin is an antibiotic, and pantoprazole is a proton pump inhibitor; none of these are indicated at this time.

Objective: Gastrointestinal

Subobjective: Acute GI hemorrhage

102. C) The patient is hypernatremic. Hyperreflexia is seen with hypernatremia and may be elicited. Tachycardia is seen with both hyper- and hyponatremia. Hyporeflexia and increased ICP are typical of hyponatremia.

Objective: Renal and genitourinary

Subobjective: Life-threatening electrolyte imbalances

103. C) Calcium gluconate is administered to the patient with hyperkalemia for cardiac and neuromuscular protection. Aspirin is used for acute coronary syndrome but would not be a first-line drug for this condition. Insulin may be given to lower potassium levels but does not protect cardiac status. Digoxin is an antidysrhythmic and is not indicated for hyperkalemia.

Objective: Renal and genitourinary

Subobjective: Life-threatening electrolyte imbalances

104. A) The priority is to prevent tissue ischemia. The pressure dressing may be too tight, or the patient could be developing compartment syndrome. Once the dressing is removed, the nurse must reassess circulatory status. Elevating the extremity is contradicted with compartment syndrome. It would be appropriate to increase IV fluids if the urine output decreased to < 30 mL/hr. The nurse should first assess the patient for the cause of increased pain before administering higher doses of analgesics.

Objective: Musculoskeletal

Subobjective: Compartment syndrome

105. D) Syndrome of inappropriate antidiuretic hormone (SIADH) is a condition where the body makes too much ADH, causing the kidneys to retain too much fluid. Cardiac dysrhythmias are not typical with craniotomies. They may occur as a side effect of anesthesia but typically are not accompanied by fluid retention. CSF rhinorrhea is caused by a CSF leak. Diabetes insipidus would cause polyuria and fluid balance deficit.

Objective: Neurological

Subobjective: Neurosurgery

106. C) Suctioning deeply can induce coughing and overstimulate the patient. The other options are all appropriate for this patient.

Objective: Neurological

Subobjective: Traumatic brain injury

107. A) A PICC line should be placed to continue the dopamine infusion at a different site and to prevent a reoccurrence of infiltration. NSAIDs may be given for pain, but they will not preserve skin integrity. A cold compress may cause further damage by keeping the vesicant in a localized area. Hyaluronidase may be used for parenteral nutrition or calcium chloride infiltrations but is contraindicated with vasoconstrictive medications such as dopamine.

Objective: Integumentary

Subobjective: IV infiltration

108. C) In option C, the nurse is demonstrating clinical competence in using nursing judgment to intervene before delegating a decision. The other options delegate decision making to others. Texting a preceptor for advice without intervening on the patient's behalf would put the patient at risk for serious complications.

Objective: Professional caring and ethical practice

Subobjective: Clinical judgment

109. C) Cardiac tamponade occurs from accumulation of blood in the pericardial sac, decreasing cardiac output. Tension pneumothorax presents with absent or diminished breath sounds, dyspnea, and tachypnea. Aortic injury presents with profound hypotension and a loud systolic murmur. Hemothorax occurs when blood collects in the pleural cavity, causing tachypnea, dyspnea, and dullness upon percussion.

Objective: Cardiovascular

Subobjective: Cardiac trauma

110. D) An ethics committee addresses and provides guidance to any member with an ethics inquiry within the committee's jurisdiction. The committee may be represented by numerous individuals who have a vested interest in providing solutions and support in the facility. The committee is not limited to personal or legal conflicts.

Objective: Professional caring and ethical practice

Subobjective: Advocacy/moral agency

111. C) Labs should be drawn at 6 hours after ingestion, because peak serum levels will occur at this time. The nurse can then base treatment on the severity of the overdose.

Objective: Multisystem

Subobjective: Toxic ingestion/exposure

112. C) Tracheal deviation and decompensation are key characteristics of tension pneumothorax. The nurse should check the ventilator for malfunction and the endotracheal tube for obstruction, but the tracheal shift must be immediately addressed. Too much positive end-expiratory pressure will not cause tracheal shift.

Objective: Respiratory

Subobjective: Pleural space abnormalities

113. C) In this scenario, fluid overload in surgery forced fluid into the alveoli from circulatory burden. This noncardiogenic-based pulmonary edema was evident by both bilateral rales and the lack of PaO_2 improvement on high-flow oxygen. There is no mention of stridor, a classic indication of laryngeal edema post-extubation, and deterioration to respiratory distress in asthma would be distinguished by a silent chest, rather than rales. Diminished air flow/air movement is indicated by the marked reduction of breath sounds over all fields in asthma, whereas rales indicate a collection of fluid in lung tissues or pleural spaces. While pneumonia and pulmonary edema have similar diagnostic qualities, the sudden onset after fluid resuscitation points toward a noninfectious process.

Objective: Respiratory

Subobjective: Noncardiogenic pulmonary edema

114. C) Best practice is to always verify NG tube placement with an X-ray before first use. The other actions are appropriate once placement is verified.

Objective: Gastrointestinal

Subobjective: Intervene to address barriers to nutritional/fluid adequacy

115. C) Stage 2 pressure ulcers are treated with moist dressings such as petroleum-impregnated gauze.

Objective: Integumentary

Subobjective: Pressure injury

116. C) The nurse should assign a sitter because the patient's safety is more important than his right to refuse care. Placing the patient in restraints does not guarantee his safety and may escalate the situation. If the patient manages to get out of the restraints, he might hang himself with the restraints. Having security sit outside the door does not provide direct observation of the patient and uses up a limited resource of the facility. Allowing the patient to leave against medical advice (AMA) leaves the nurse and the facility vulnerable to legal action if the patient hurts himself or dies by suicide after leaving.

Objective: Behavioral and psychosocial

Subobjective: Suicidal ideation and/or behaviors

117. B) Amiodarone has been shown to control the ventricular rate in atrial fibrillation with rapid ventricular response and may assist in a spontaneous conversion to sinus rhythm. Lidocaine, epinephrine, and digoxin are not used to correct atrial fibrillation.

Objective: Cardiovascular

Subobjective: Dysrhythmias

118. C) Nitroprusside is a vasodilator that lowers systemic vascular resistance; it is not appropriate for patients with low systemic vascular resistance. Vasopressin, dopamine, and norepinephrine are vasoconstrictors that increase systemic vascular resistance.

Objective: Cardiovascular

Subobjective: Hemodynamic monitoring

119. B) Removal of the copious secretions causing mechanical obstruction of the patient's endotracheal tube airway is the first priority in this scenario. An in-line closed suction system is an effective and sterile intervention that is immediately available. Manual ventilation will not clear the clogged endotracheal tube or improve oxygenation but will waste time and increase distress for the patient. There is no need to increase IV sedation, because in this example, anxiety is a reasonable response to airway obstruction and a drop in O_2 sat. Increasing sedation is counterproductive to weaning protocols, which are designed to prevent weakening of a patient's breathing musculature while they are intubated. The health care team will continuously discuss management of FiO_2 (fraction of inspired oxygen), but this acute event requires simple, immediate nursing intervention.

Objective: Respiratory

Subobjective: Therapeutic interventions related to mechanical ventilation

120. C) The patient should have a consultation with a diabetes educator before being discharged. Because a follow-up appointment with the primary care provider might not be scheduled immediately, the patient should feel well educated before discharge. A psychiatric consult is not indicated, as the patient's concern is not a mental health disorder related to food, and the new-onset diabetes is a medical condition that requires education. The statement that the patient does not meet criteria is false.

Objective: Professional caring and ethical practice

Subobjective: Facilitation of learning

121. A) Many medications are ordered for off-label use; however, the nurse should verify that this is the correct medication and dosage. Administering a medication without knowing what it is for is reckless and could jeopardize the patient's condition. Options C and D suggest that the nurse make a false statement; the nurse should not attempt to lie to bypass responsibilities. These actions could jeopardize the nurse's career and license.

Objective: Professional caring and ethical practice

Subobjective: Clinical inquiry

122. C) Increasing the minute ventilation (MV = tidal volume [V_T] x RR) would improve both hypercapnia and respiratory acidosis. Increasing either V_T or RR would increase MV, decrease PCO_2 (treating hypercapnia), and help return the pH to normal range (as the acidosis resolves). An increase in V_T is limited by lung size (respiratory mechanics) and would potentially cause lung injury if plateau pressures were raised aggressively; decreasing the V_T will NOT help this patient. Decreasing the FiO_2 is unwarranted, and manipulating it only affects oxygenation, not ventilation. Increasing the ventilator RR will achieve the desired CO_2 reduction and improve acidosis. Increasing the RR is limited by the expiratory time (increasing the RR will reduce expiratory time), and if expiratory time is set too "short," the patient will show evidence of auto-positive end-expiratory pressure.

Objective: Respiratory

Subobjective: Manage patients requiring mechanical ventilation

123. A) Atelectasis and other respiratory problems are common in patients with acute pancreatitis. The nurse should thoroughly assess lung sounds and note any adventitious or diminished breath sounds, look for signs of orthopnea or dyspnea, and monitor O_2 sat levels. High blood glucose, light sensitivity, and low urine output are not complications of pancreatitis.

Objective: Gastrointestinal emergencies

Subobjective: Pancreatitis

124. B) Pericarditis will cause global elevation in upright ECG leads. A ruptured papillary muscle causing valve prolapse or regurg does not produce specific ECG changes and may be heard as a murmur. Re-infarction or extension of initial MI will show specific ECG changes, depending on the location of the infarction, and may be accompanied by a crushing-chest feeling, jaw or back pain, and diaphoresis.

Objective: Cardiovascular

Subobjective: Acute coronary syndrome

125. B) Coronary artery perfusion occurs during diastole, and the length of time the heart is in diastole directly affects coronary artery perfusion. HR is the determinant of blood flow to the coronary arteries: elevated HR reduces the amount of time in diastole, thus reducing the amount of coronary artery perfusion by decreasing both the volume of blood flow and the time for perfusion to occur.

Objective: Cardiovascular

Subobjective: Hemodynamic monitoring

126. C) The adrenal medulla releases epinephrine to stimulate the sympathetic nervous system to achieve homeostasis of blood glucose levels.

Objective: Endocrine

Subobjective: Hypoglycemia (acute)

127. C) Autonomic dysreflexia is the result of overstimulation of the autonomic nervous system for spinal cord injuries above the T6 level. The condition causes flushing and diaphoresis above the injury and cold, clammy skin below the level of injury. Answer C supports this diagnosis. Hypertension and bradycardia are also classic signs.

Objective: Neurological

Subobjective: Acute spinal cord injuries

128. C) The patient has 2 predisposing conditions for the diagnosis of aortic dissection: Marfan syndrome and blunt chest trauma (from the car crash). Patients with aortic dissection typically present with sudden onset of severe, tearing chest pain. Pulmonary embolism would elicit symptoms such as dyspnea, a feeling of impending doom, and chest pain. Cardiac tamponade presents with muffled heart tones, jugular venous distention (JVD), and hypotension. Acute coronary syndrome exhibits crushing chest pain radiating to the left arm and jaw, as well as ST elevation on an ECG.

Objective: Cardiovascular

Subobjective: Aortic dissection

129. A) The patient with COPD should start out with low-flow oxygen delivery. Too much oxygen can decrease the hypoxic drive and cause respiratory arrest. The other interventions are appropriate in the treatment of a patient with COPD exacerbation.

Objective: Respiratory emergencies

Subobjective: Chronic conditions

130. A) The hypovolemic shock experienced during sepsis has a high potential to cause acute kidney injury.

Objective: Renal and genitourinary

Subobjective: Acute kidney injury

131. C) Agitation and restlessness are most common during the first 6 hours after the last drink, and symptoms are generally mild. Delirium tremens and metabolic changes are more likely to occur 72 – 96 hours after the last drink. With Wernicke encephalopathy, the changes in the brain occur slowly over a long period of alcoholism.

Objective: Behavioral and psychosocial

Subobjective: Substance use disorders

132. A) Right upper quadrant pain is often attributed to acute hepatitis, gastritis, or gallbladder disease. But because the patient has recently delivered, this sign, along with signs of hepatic failure, should prompt screening for HELLP syndrome via the Mississippi Classification System. NIH stroke scale assessment is used to evaluate for stroke symptoms. The Glasgow Coma Scale assesses for level of consciousness, and the Edinburgh Depression Scale assesses for postpartum depression.

Objective: Multisystem

Subobjective: Life-threatening maternal/fetal complications

133. A) The testing location of choice is the ulnar nerve, and 2 twitches at any site indicate an 80% blockade. If anasarca is grossly present, the secondary choice of stimulation is the facial nerve. However, 0 twitches indicates a need to troubleshoot electrode placement, retest, and if the response is the same, the nurse must immediately reduce the neuromuscular blocking agent dose (perhaps by as much as 50%). Testing should be repeated every 15 – 30 minutes per hospital protocol/policy until at least 2 twitches are obtained.

Objective: Respiratory

Subobjective: Manage patients requiring mechanical ventilation

134. D) Posting the article in a high-traffic area would be the most effective way to share new knowledge with colleagues. Mailing the article to the manager does not ensure that it will be distributed to the intended audience. As the nurse believes the information will benefit the entire unit, the article should be shared with the unit, rather than just a few select colleagues. Sharing the article now would give colleagues an opportunity to review the article before bringing it up at the next staff meeting so that everyone will be aware of the information.

Objective: Professional caring and ethical practice

Subobjective: Collaboration; clinical inquiry

135. D) When advocating for the patient, the nurse should act to provide a solution. Finding out the cost and less expensive alternatives before the patient's discharge enables the patient to ask the physician for a generic or alternative medication that is more affordable before the patient learns that they cannot pay for it. Telling the patient to call after they are home does not answer their question about the cost and does not give the patient alternatives before discharge. Free samples offer only a short-term solution.

Objective: Professional caring and ethical practice

Subobjective: Advocacy/moral agency

136. A) The patient's declared preference for being called "John" should be respected, and the family should be made aware of the patient's wishes. Calling the patient a different name to appease family is disrespectful to his wishes. Studies have shown that vented, sedated patients often remember conversations and events. While the legal name should still be used as the patient identifier for safety purposes, nicknames or preferred names are acceptable while providing care. The nurse should not pass judgment on the patient's family, but to prevent confusion, the family should be made aware of previous conversations or statements by the patient.

Objective: Professional caring and ethical practice

Subobjective: Response to diversity

137. B) A QT > 470 ms in females is considered prolonged. This places that patient at an increased risk for torsades de pointes. Magnesium sulfate (MgSO4) is utilized in patients with prolonged QT to decrease this risk. The patient may have a prolonged QT without being bradycardic. Insulin and glucagon are both used in the treatment of beta-blocker overdose but are not given specifically for QT prolongation.

Objective: Multisystem

Subobjective: Toxic ingestion/exposure

138. C) Options A, B, and D are all appropriate actions defined by standard brain death evaluations. The evaluation should not be aborted unless the systolic BP decreases to < 90 despite increasing vasopressor dosage.

Objective: Neurological

Subobjective: Brain death

139. D) Battle sign and raccoon eyes indicate that this is a basilar skull fracture, and spinal cord injuries are frequently concurrent. The patient should be log-rolled during transfer to prevent cord injury. The patient should be placed in seizure precautions after being moved to bed. Critical care monitoring is essential for this patient but is not directly related to the patient transfer. Hyperventilation should take place before and after suctioning a patient with a TBI, not with movement.

Objective: Neurological

Subobjective: Traumatic brain injury

140. B) A pleural effusion is excess fluid that has collected in the pleural space. The CCRN candidate is aware that a pleural effusion should be evacuated slowly, with intermittent clamping and that no greater than 1000 – 1500 mL should be removed, to prevent re-expansion pulmonary edema. Removal of a large amount of fluid increases the negative intrapleural pressure and leads to lung collapse when the lung is unable to re-expand sufficiently to fill the thoracic space.

Objective: Respiratory

Subobjective: Pleural effusions

141. D) Immediate stoppage of further evacuation of pleural fluid and giving supplemental oxygen is the most appropriate intervention for this emergent re-expansion pulmonary edema crisis. If patient's condition continues to deteriorate, noninvasive positive-pressure ventilation or intubation with positive-pressure mechanical ventilation may be required. Unless the patient is hypotensive, fluids should not be administered, as the excess fluid would return to the thoracic space. Since the issue is not ventilatory, intubation is unnecessary. Needle decompression is also unnecessary and may worsen this condition.

Objective: Respiratory

Subobjective: Pleural effusions

142. A) Signs and symptoms of retroperitoneal bleed include hypotension, bradycardia, Grey Turner's sign (ecchymosis along flanks), and abdominal or flank pain.

Objective: Gastrointestinal

Subobjective: Acute abdominal trauma

143. B) The nursing priority for patients with fistulas is preserving and protecting the skin. Antibiotics may be given but are not the first priority. Wound VACs (vacuum-assisted closures) should not be used simply to manage drainage or in patients with increased bleeding risk. Providing a quiet environment is important, but skin integrity is the first priority with this patient.

Objective: Gastrointestinal

Subobjective: GI surgeries

144. B) The patient has had nausea and vomiting; the vomiting can cause hypokalemia. A U wave can be noted on an ECG or a cardiac monitor. Hyperkalemia would show peaked T waves. Hypercalcemia may produce a shortened QT interval, and hypocalcemia may show QT prolongation.

Objective: Renal and genitourinary

Subobjective: Life-threatening electrolyte imbalances

145. C) As the patient is a college student and has the symptoms of meningitis, the viral type would be more likely. The clear appearance of the fluid also supports this diagnosis. Bacterial meningitis is less common, and the CSF would appear cloudy. Influenza B is not tested via CFS. While a brain abscess does exhibit similar symptoms, a CT scan or an MRI would be used to rule out.

Objective: Neurological

Subobjective: Neurological infectious disease

146. C) Many patients with dementia pull out an IV because they see it as something unusual attached to their body. Placing the IV in an inconspicuous place, such as where it can be covered by the gown or wrapped up in gauze, prevents the patient from pulling it out, because the patient cannot see it. Restraints should not be the first-line intervention for this patient; this intervention may increase confusion and agitation. Family members can help watch the patient and prevent them from removing the IV, but many patients have no family close by who can stay with them around the clock. Threatening the patient with a more invasive procedure should never be used as a means of obtaining cooperation.

Objective: Neurological

Subobjective: Dementia

147. B) Oliguria (decrease in urine output) is a compensatory mechanism to prevent volume loss associated with this phase of shock. The patient would be more likely to be anxious, not lethargic. The patient would also be extremely thirsty. Nausea and cool, mottled skin are signs of progressive phases.

Objective: Multisystem

Subobjective: Shock states

148. A) The daughter should be allowed time to express her feelings and vent. The nurse has an opportunity to answer questions that the daughter may have and to provide a bridge to encourage further discussion with the patient. Although the daughter may have further questions for the physician, the nurse should not automatically pass along that responsibility.

Objective: Professional caring and ethical practice

Subobjective: Advocacy/moral agency

149. D) The nurse should first recognize any personal bias that may be a barrier in providing care to this patient. The nurse should assess the patient's pain and symptoms before notifying the physician about drug-seeking behavior. Anger at a patient's choices is not an appropriate cause for having a different nurse assigned to the patient.

Objective: Professional caring and ethical practice

Subobjective: Advocacy/moral agency

150. A) Because the patient has a history of atrial fibrillation, the fast rhythm is probably due to this condition, but it may not be easily distinguishable from supraventricular tachycardia, because of the rate. Adenosine would be administered to slow the rate and identify the underlying rhythm before further treatment. The patient is stable, and immediate cardioversion is not indicated. Moreover, adenosine will not cardiovert an atrial fibrillation or atrial flutter. Calcium channel blockers, cardiac glycoside, or beta blockers—not adenosine—would be ordered to treat dysrhythmias. Adenosine has no blood-thinning attributes.

Objective: Cardiovascular

Subobjective: Dysrhythmias

APPENDIX A: ABBREVIATIONS

A

A&O×3: awake and oriented to person, place, and time

A-a gradient: alveolar-arterial gradient

AAA: abdominal aortic aneurysm

ABC: A1c (hemoglobin), blood pressure, and cholesterol

ABCs: airway, breathing, circulation (emergency treatment)

ABG: arterial blood gas

ABPI: ankle-brachial pressure index

AC ventilation: assist-control ventilation

ACA: anterior cerebral artery

ACE inhibitors: angiotensin-converting enzyme inhibitors

ACLS: advanced cardiovascular life support

ACPE: acute cardiogenic pulmonary edema

ACS: acute coronary syndrome *or* abdominal compartment syndrome

ACTH: adrenocorticotropic hormone stimulation test

ADH: antidiuretic hormone

AFE: amniotic fluid embolism

A-fib: atrial fibrillation

AHRQ: US Agency for Healthcare Research and Quality

AIDS: acquired immunodeficiency syndrome

AIS: acute ischemic stroke

AKI: acute kidney injury (formerly called acute renal failure, ARF)

ALI: acute lung injury (no longer used; instead use mild, moderate, or severe ARDS)

ALL: acute lymphocytic leukemia

ALP: alkaline phosphatase

ALS: amyotrophic lateral sclerosis

ALT: alanine aminotransferase *or* alanine transaminase

AMA: against medical advice *or* American Medical Association

AML: acute myeloid leukemia

AND: allow natural death

AOM: acute otitis media

APP: abdominal perfusion pressure

aPTT: activated partial thromboplastin time

AR: aortic regurgitation

ARBs: angiotensin II receptor blockers

ARDS: acute respiratory distress syndrome

ARF: acute respiratory failure (sometimes acute renal failure, which is now called acute kidney injury [AKI])

AS: aortic stenosis

ASCVD: atherosclerotic cardiovascular disease

ASIA: American Spinal Injury Association

AST: aspartate aminotransferase *or* aspartate transaminase

ATN: acute tubular necrosis

AUB: abnormal uterine bleeding

aVF: augmented vector foot (ECG lead)

aVL: augmented vector left (ECG lead)

AVM: arteriovenous malformation

aVR: augmented vector right (ECG lead)

B

BAI: blunt aortic injury

BBB: bundle branch block

BCI: blunt cardiac injury

BiPAP or BPAP: bilevel positive airway pressure

BNP: B-type natriuretic peptide

BP: blood pressure

BPH: benign prostatic hyperplasia

bpm: beats per minute (in all caps [BPM], breaths per minute)

BPS: Behavioral Pain Scale

BRAT: banana, rice, applesauce, toast (e.g., BRAT diet)

BSA: body surface area

BUN: blood urea nitrogen

BZK: benzalkonium chloride (e.g., BZK wipes)

C

CA-MRSA: community-acquired methicillin-resistant *Staphylococcus aureus*

CABG: coronary artery bypass graft

CAD: coronary artery disease

CAM-ICU: Confusion Assessment Method for the ICU

CaO$_2$: arterial oxygen content

CAOD: carotid artery occlusive disease (stenosis)

CAP: community-acquired pneumonia

CAUTI: catheter-associated urinary tract infection

CBC: complete blood count

CBF: cerebral blood flow

CCB: calcium channel blocker

CDC: Centers for Disease Control and Prevention

CHF: congestive heart failure

CI: cardiac index

CISD: critical incident stress debriefing

CISM: critical incident stress management

CIWA-Ar: Clinical Institute Withdrawal Assessment for Alcohol

CK: creatine kinase

CK-MB: creatine kinase–muscle/brain

CKD: chronic kidney disease

CLABSI: central line associated bloodstream infection

CLL: chronic lymphocytic leukemia

CML: chronic myelogenous leukemia

CMP: comprehensive metabolic panel

CN: cranial nerve

CNS: central nervous system

CO: cardiac output

COBRA: Consolidated Omnibus Budget Reconciliation Act

COCA: color, odor, clarity, amount (urinary assessment)

COPD: chronic obstructive pulmonary disease

COWS: Clinical Opiate Withdrawal Scale

CP: cerebral palsy

CPAP: continuous positive airway pressure

CPG: clinical practice guideline

CPP: cerebral perfusion pressure

CPR: cardiopulmonary resuscitation

CrCl: creatinine clearance

CRF: chronic renal failure

CRI: cutaneous radiation injury

CRP: C-reactive protein

CRRT: continuous renal replacement therapy

CRT: capillary refill time

CS: culture and sensitivity

CSF: cerebrospinal fluid

CSM: circulation, sensation, and movement

CT scan: computed tomography scan

cTnI: troponin I

cTnT: troponin T

CTPA: computed tomography pulmonary angiography

CVA: cerebrovascular accident

CVP: central venous pressure

CVVH: continuous venovenous hemofiltration

CXR: chest X-ray

D

D&C: dilation and curettage

D50: dextrose 50% solution

D5W: dextrose 5% in water

DAI: diffuse axonal injury

DBP: diastolic blood pressure

DCCM: dilated congestive cardiomyopathy

DDS: dialysis disequilibrium syndrome

DI: diabetes insipidus

DIC: disseminated intravascular coagulation (or coagulopathy)

DKA: diabetic ketoacidosis

DM: diabetes mellitus

DMARDs: disease-modifying antirheumatic drugs

DNA: deoxyribonucleic acid

DNI: do not intubate

DNR: do not resuscitate

DO$_2$: oxygen delivery

DPL: diagnostic peritoneal lavage

DPOA: durable power of attorney

DSRS: distal splenorenal shunt

DT: diphtheria and tetanus (vaccine)

DTs: delirium tremens

DTaP: diphtheria, tetanus, and pertussis (vaccine)

DTI: deep tissue injury

DTPA: diethylenetriamine pentaacetate

DTs: delirium tremens

DUBB: dangerous underwater breath-holding behaviors

DVT: deep vein thrombosis

E

EAPs: Employee Assistance Programs

EBP: evidence-based practice

ECF: extracellular fluid

ECG: electrocardiogram

ECMO: extracorporeal membrane oxygenation

ECR: extracorporeal core rewarming

ED: emergency department

EDH: epidural hematoma

EEG: electroencephalogram

EF: ejection fraction

EGD: esophagogastroduodenoscopy

EIA: enzyme immunoassay

ELISA: enzyme-linked immunosorbent assay

EMB: ethambutol

EMTALA: Emergency Medical Treatment and Active Labor Act

EN: enteral nutrition

EPAP: expiratory positive airway pressure

ERCP: endoscopic retrograde cholangiopancreatography

ESI: Emergency Severity Index

ESR: erythrocyte sedimentation rate

ESRD: end-stage renal disease

ESWL: extracorporeal shock wave lithotripsy

ETCO$_2$: end-tidal CO$_2$ measurement (capnography)

ETT or **ET tube:** endotracheal tube

EVD: external ventricular drain

EVL: endoscopic variceal band ligation

F

FAST ultrasound (or exam): focused assessment with sonography for trauma

FDP: fibrin degradation products

FES: fat embolism syndrome

FFP: fresh frozen plasma

FiO$_2$: fraction of inspired oxygen

FLT3: fms-related tyrosine kinase 3

FRC: functional residual capacity

FSH: follicle-stimulating hormone

FSP: fibrin split products

G

G-tube: gastrostomy tube

GABA: gamma-aminobutyric acid

GCS: Glasgow Coma Scale

GER: gastroesophageal reflux

GERD: gastroesophageal reflux disease

GFR: glomerular filtration rate

GGT: gamma-glutamyl transferase

GI: gastrointestinal

GRV: gastric residual volume

GSW: gunshot wound

GU: genitourinary

H

H/H: hemoglobin and hematocrit

HA-MRSA: hospital-acquired methicillin-resistant *Staphylococcus aureus*

HAP: hospital-acquired pneumonia

HBO: hyperbaric oxygen therapy

HBSS: Hanks' Balanced Salt Solution

HCAHPS: Hospital Consumer Assessment of Healthcare Providers and Systems

hCG: human chorionic gonadotropin

HCM: hypertrophic cardiomyopathy

HCS: Hazard Communication Standard

Hct: hematocrit

HELLP syndrome: hemolysis, elevated liver enzymes, low platelet count

HF: heart failure

HFpEF: heart failure with preserved ejection fraction (diastolic heart failure)

HFrEF: heart failure with reduced ejection fraction (systolic heart failure)

HgB: hemoglobin

HHH: hypertensive, hypervolemic, hemodilution therapy

HHNK: hyperglycemic hyperosmolar nonketotic syndrome

HHS: hyperosmolar hyperglycemic state

HIET: hyperinsulinemia euglycemia therapy

HIPAA: Health Insurance Portability and Accountability Act

HIT: heparin-induced thrombocytopenia

HIV: human immunodeficiency virus

HOB: head of bed

HR: heart rate

HSV: herpes simplex virus

I

I:E ratio: inspiratory-expiratory ratio

I/O or **I&O**: intake and output

IABP: intra-aortic balloon pump

IAP: intra-abdominal pressure

IBD: inflammatory bowel disease

IBS: irritable bowel syndrome

IC: inspiratory capacity

ICD: implantable cardioverter defibrillator

ICDSC: Intensive Care Delirium Screening Checklist

ICF: intracellular fluid

ICH: intracerebral hemorrhage

ICP: intracranial pressure

ICS: incident command system

ICU: intensive care unit

IgM: immunoglobulin M

IM: intramuscular

INH: isoniazid

INR: international normalized ratio

IO: intraosseous (infusion)

IPAP: inspiratory positive airway pressure

ITP: idiopathic thrombocytopenic purpura

IUD: intrauterine device

IV: intravenous

IVAC: infection-related ventilator-associated conditions

IVH: intraventricular hemorrhage

IVIG: intravenous immunoglobulin

IVP: intravenous pyelography

J

JVD: jugular vein distention

K

KUB: kidney, ureter, bladder

L

LAD: left anterior descending

LBBB: left bundle branch block

LD or **LDH**: L-lactate dehydrogenase

LET: liquid emulsion therapy

LFT: liver function test

LLQ: left lower quadrant

LMA: laryngeal mask airway

LOC: level of consciousness

LPN: licensed practical nurse

LPV: lung-protective ventilation

LUQ: left upper quadrant

LV: left ventricle

LVAD: left ventricular assist device

LVEDP: left ventricular end-diastolic pressure

LVN: licensed vocational nurse

LVO: large-vessel occlusion

M

MAP: mean arterial pressure

MAR: medication administration record

MCA: middle cerebral artery

MCH: mean corpuscular hemoglobin

MCHC: mean corpuscular hemoglobin concentration

MCI: mass casualty incident

MCV: mean corpuscular volume

MD: muscular dystrophy

mEq: milliequivalent

MG: myasthenia gravis

MI: myocardial infarction

MICU: mobile ICU

MMI: methimazole

MMSE: mini-mental state exam

MODS: multiple organ dysfunction syndrome

MPAP: mean pulmonary artery pressure

MR: mitral regurgitation

MRI: magnetic resonance imaging

MRSA: methicillin-resistant *Staphylococcus aureus*

MS: multiple sclerosis *or* mitral stenosis

MSDS: material safety data sheets

MVC: motor vehicle crash/motorized vehicle crash

N

NAAT: nucleic acid amplification test

NG tube: nasogastric tube

NIF: negative inspiratory force

NIH: National Institutes of Health

NIHSS: National Institutes of Health Stroke Scale

NIV: noninvasive ventilation

NMB: neuromuscular blockade

NO: nitric oxide

NPE: noncardiogenic pulmonary edema

NPi: neurological pupil index

NPO: *nil per os* (Latin for "nothing by mouth"; patient should consume no food or fluids)

NPWT: negative pressure wound therapy

NSAID: nonsteroidal anti-inflammatory drug

NSTEMI: non-ST-elevation myocardial infarction

NSTIs: necrotizing soft-tissue infections

O

OG tube: orogastric tube

OME: otitis media with effusion

P

PA: pulmonary arterial

PAC: pulmonary artery catheter

PaCO₂: partial pressure of carbon dioxide

PACU: post-anesthesia care unit

PAD: peripheral arterial disease

PALM-COEIN: polyp, adenomyosis, leiomyoma, malignancy, coagulopathy, ovulatory disorder, endometrial, iatrogenic, not otherwise classified (risk factors for abdominal uterine bleeding)

PAP: pulmonary artery pressure

PaO₂: partial pressure of oxygen

PAOP: pulmonary artery occlusion pressure

PCA: posterior cerebral artery

PCC: prothrombin complex concentrate

PCI: percutaneous coronary intervention

PCR: polymerase chain reaction

PCWP: pulmonary capillary wedge pressure

PE: pulmonary embolism *or* pulmonary embolus

PEA: pulseless electrical activity

PEEP: positive end-expiratory pressure

PEFR: peak expiratory flow rate

PETCO₂: patient end-tidal CO₂ measurement (capnography, also called ETCO₂)

P/F ratio: PaO₂ divided by patient's FiO₂

PH: pulmonary hypertension

PHH: postprandial hyperinsulinemic hypoglycemia

PHI: protected health information

PICC: peripherally inserted central catheter

PICS: post-intensive-care syndrome

PID: pelvic inflammatory disease

PLT: platelet count

PO: *per os* (by mouth)

PPE: personal protective equipment

PPI: proton pump inhibitor

PPN: peripheral parenteral nutrition

PRBCs: packed red blood cells

PRN: *pro re nata* (as needed)

PSP: primary spontaneous pneumothorax

PSV: pressure support ventilation

PT: prothrombin time

PTA: percutaneous transluminal angioplasty

PTH: post-traumatic headaches

PTSD: post-traumatic stress disorder

PTT: partial thromboplastin time

PTU: propylthiouracil

PVC: premature ventricular contraction

PVD: peripheral vascular disease

PVR: pulmonary vascular resistance

PZA: pyrazinamide

R

RAAS: renin-angiotensin-aldosterone system

RAP: right atrial pressure

RASS: Richmond Agitation-Sedation Scale

RAWS: refractory alcohol withdrawal syndrome

RBBB: right bundle branch block

RBC: red blood cell

RCA: right coronary artery

RCM: restrictive cardiomyopathy

RhoGAM: Rho(D) immune globulin

RIF: rifampin

RIG: rabies immune globulin

RLL: right lower lobe (e.g., lung)

RLQ: right lower quadrant

ROM: range of motion

ROSC: return of spontaneous circulation

RPR: rapid plasma reagin

RR: respiratory rate

RSBI: rapid shallow breathing index

RSI: rapid sequence intubation

RSV: respiratory syncytial virus

RT-PCR: real-time polymerase chain reaction

RUQ: right upper quadrant

RVEDP: right ventricular end-diastolic pressure

RYGB: Roux-en-Y gastric bypass

S

SA: sinoatrial

SAH: subarachnoid hemorrhage

SANE: sexual assault nurse examiner

SaO$_2$: arterial oxygen saturation

SARS: severe acute respiratory syndrome

SAT: spontaneous awakening trials

SBP: systolic blood pressure

SBT: spontaneous breathing trials

SCCM: Society of Critical Care Medicine

SCI: spinal cord injury

ScvO$_2$: central venous oxygen saturation

SDH: subdural hematoma

SDS: safety data sheets

SG: vertical sleeve gastrectomy

SGOT: serum glutamic-oxaloacetic transaminase

SIADH: syndrome of inappropriate antidiuretic hormone secretion

SICU: surgical intensive care unit

SIMV: synchronized intermittent mandatory ventilation

SIRS: systemic inflammatory response syndrome

SND: sinus node dysfunction

SpO$_2$: peripheral capillary oxygen saturation or pulse oximetry

SSEP: somatosensory evoked potential

SSP: secondary spontaneous pneumothorax

SSS: sick sinus syndrome

START: simple triage and rapid treatment

STEMI: ST-segment elevation myocardial infarction

STI: sexually transmitted infection

SV: stroke volume

SvO$_2$: mixed venous saturation

SVR: systemic vascular resistance

SVT: supraventricular tachycardia

T

T&C: blood type and crossmatch

T&S: blood type and screen

TACO: transfusion-associated circulatory overload

TAVR: transcatheter aortic valve repair

TBI: traumatic brain injury

TBSA: total body surface area

TCCS: transcranial color-coded duplex sonography

TCD: transcranial Doppler study

TCP: transcutaneous pacing

Td: tetanus and diphtheria (vaccine)

Tdap: tetanus, diphtheria, and pertussis (booster DTaP vaccine)

TEE: transesophageal echocardiogram

TEN: total enteral nutrition

TF: tissue factor

TIA: transient ischemic attack

TIPS: transjugular intrahepatic portosystemic shunt

TLC: total lung capacity

TMJ: temporomandibular joint

tPA: tissue plasminogen activator

TPN: total parenteral nutrition

TRALI: transfusion-related acute lung injury

TSH: thyroid stimulating hormone

TTM: targeted temperature management

U

U/L: units per liter

ULQ: upper left quadrant

URQ: upper right quadrant

UTI: urinary tract infection

V

VAC: ventilator-associated conditions *or* vacuum-assisted wound closure

VAD: ventricular assist device

VAE: ventilator-associated events

VAP: ventilator-associated pneumonia

VATS: video-assisted thoracoscopic surgery

VBG: vertical band gastroplasty

VC: vital capacity

VDLR: venereal disease research laboratories

V-fib: ventricular fibrillation

VO$_2$: oxygen consumption

V/Q ratio: ventilation/perfusion ratio

VRE: vancomycin-resistant enterococci

V$_T$: tidal volume

V-tach: ventricular tachycardia

vW: von Willebrand factor

W

WBC: white blood cell

WHO: World Health Organization

APPENDIX B: SIGNS AND SYMPTOMS GLOSSARY

asterixis: bilateral tremor or "flapping" of the wrist or fingers

ataxia: abnormal, uncoordinated movements

bradycardia: slow heart rate

bradypnea: slow respiration rate

crepitus: abnormal cracking sounds heard in fractures, joints, or the lungs or in subcutaneous emphysema

diaphoresis: excessive sweating

dyspnea: difficulty breathing

ecchymosis: bruising

epistaxis: bleeding from the nose

erythema: redness of the skin

guarding: voluntary contraction of abdominal muscles to avoid pain

hematemesis: blood in vomit

hematochezia: bright red blood in stool

hemoptysis: blood in expectorate from respiratory tract

hepatomegaly: enlargement of liver

hyperpigmentation: darkening of the skin

hyperpyrexia: body temperature > 106.7°F (41.5°C)

hyperreflexia: overreactive reflexes

jaundice: yellowing of the skin or sclera

jugular vein distention: bulging of the superior vena cava due to increased pressure

lacrimation: excessive secretion of tears

lymphadenopathy: swollen lymph nodes

melena: dark, sticky digested blood in the stool

myalgia: muscle pain

mydriasis: pupil dilation

myoclonus: twitches or jerks of muscles

myoglobinuria: urine that is brown due to presence of myoglobin

nocturia: excessive urination at night

nuchal rigidity: inability to place the chin on the chest (neck flexion) due to muscle stiffness (indicator of meningitis)

nystagmus: repetitive, uncontrolled movement of the eyes

oliguria: low urine output

orthopnea: dyspnea that occurs while lying flat

otorrhea: drainage from the ear

pallor: pale appearance

paresthesia: abnormal dermal sensation such as burning or "pins and needles"

pericardial rub: characteristic heart sound caused by inflammation of the pericardium

petechiae: tiny red or brown spots on the skin caused by subcutaneous bleeding

photophobia: sensitivity to light

piloerection: erection of the hair

poikilothermia: inability to regulate body temperature

polydipsia: excessive thirst

polyphagia: excessive hunger

polyuria: abnormally high urine output

pruritus: severely itchy skin

pulsus alternans: alternating strong and weak pulse

pulsus paradoxus: abnormally large drop in blood pressure during inspiration

purpura: purple coloring on the skin caused by blood pooling around damaged blood vessels

rhinorrhea: drainage from the nose

S3 (ventricular gallop): an extra heart sound heard after S2, caused by a rush of blood into a ventricle; a normal finding in children and young adults

S4 (atrial gallop): an extra heart sound heard before S1, caused by the atrial contraction of blood into a noncompliant ventricle; can be a normal finding in older adults

spider angiomas: red skin lesions caused by dilated blood vessels

splinting: voluntary shallow breathing done to avoid pain caused by inspiration

steatorrhea: excretion of excess fat in the stool

syncope: temporary loss of consciousness

tachycardia: fast heart rate

tachypnea: fast respiratory rate

APPENDIX C: MEDICAL SIGNS

Battle sign: bruising behind the ears caused by a basilar skull fracture

Brudzinski's sign (indicator of meningitis): passive flexion of the neck elicits automatic flexion at the hips and knees

Chvostek sign: contraction of facial muscles in response to tapping over the facial nerve (CNVII)

Cullen sign: a bluish discoloration to the umbilical area

Grey Turner sign: ecchymosis in the flank area

Homans' sign: pain in the calf following dorsiflexion of the foot

Kehr sign: referred left shoulder pain caused when the diaphragm irritates the phrenic nerve

Kernig's sign (indicator of meningitis): patient in supine position with the hips and knees flexed, unable to straighten leg due to hamstring pain

Levine's sign: a clenched fist held over the chest in response to ischemic chest pain

Markle test (heel drop): pain caused when patient stands on tiptoes and drops heels down quickly or when patient hops on one leg

McBurney's point: RLQ pain at point halfway between umbilicus and iliac spine

Murphy sign: pain and cessation of inspiration when RUQ is palpated

Psoas sign: abdominal pain when right hip is hyperextended

Rovsing sign: pain in the RLQ with palpation of LLQ (indicates peritoneal irritation)

Trousseau sign: contraction of the hand and wrist following compression of the upper arm

www.ingramcontent.com/pod-product-compliance
Lightning Source LLC
Chambersburg PA
CBHW080935300426
44115CB00017B/2821

HISTORY
OF
WESTERN MARYLAND.

BEING A HISTORY OF

FREDERICK, MONTGOMERY, CARROLL, WASHINGTON, ALLEGANY, AND GARRETT

COUNTIES

FROM THE EARLIEST PERIOD TO THE PRESENT DAY;

INCLUDING

BIOGRAPHICAL SKETCHES

OF THEIR

REPRESENTATIVE MEN.

BY

J. THOMAS SCHARF, A.M.,

AUTHOR OF "CHRONICLES OF BALTIMORE," "HISTORY OF BALTIMORE CITY AND COUNTY," "HISTORY OF MARYLAND;" MEMBER OF THE MARYLAND HISTORICAL SOCIETY AND ACADEMY OF SCIENCES; MEMBER OF THE HISTORICAL SOCIETY OF PENNSYLVANIA; HONORARY MEMBER OF THE GEORGIA HISTORICAL SOCIETY; CORRESPONDING MEMBER OF THE HISTORICAL SOCIETIES OF NEW YORK, WISCONSIN, MINNESOTA, SOUTH CAROLINA, AND VIRGINIA; OF THE HISTORICAL AND PHILOSOPHICAL SOCIETY OF OHIO; OF THE NEW ENGLAND HISTORIC-GENEALOGICAL SOCIETY, ETC., ETC.

IN TWO VOLUMES, ILLUSTRATED.

VOL. I.

Baltimore
REGIONAL PUBLISHING COMPANY
1968

Originally Published
Philadelphia, 1882

Reprinted
Regional Publishing Company
Baltimore, 1968

Library of Congress Catalog Card Number 68-26127

TO

ARUNAH S. ABELL, Esq.,

FOUNDER, EDITOR, AND PROPRIETOR OF THE BALTIMORE SUN,

THIS VOLUME IS DEDICATED;

PARTLY IN TESTIMONY OF THE AUTHOR'S ESTEEM AND HIS ENDURING GRATITUDE FOR MANY
KINDNESSES, ANCIENT AND RECENT; PARTLY, ALSO, AS A TRIBUTE OF THE
AUTHOR'S GENUINE ADMIRATION FOR, AND APPRECIATION OF,

"THE SUN,"

the model newspaper of the United States. This great Structure, as it was Mr. Abell's creation, will also become his monument. It is a Perfect Piece of Work, "not built by envious show," yet symmetrical in all its Parts, and the Pride of the Generous Architect swells chiefly at the Fact that, as it was reared with no man's ruin and to no man's hurt, so there are none who witness its Prosperity with Envy or wish its solid columns less stately in their vista. It is so built that there is always not only encouragement, but necessity, for its expansion; its influence in the community, always large and strong, and always increasing, must ever be on the side of virtue, honor, justice, and enlightenment, since the public will never believe it capable of utterance or suggestion on any other side.

The Founder's Sons may be expected to maintain in its pristine integrity, develop, enlarge, and beautify the original work; but neither They nor the Public will ever fail to uphold him for its creating and perfecting should he depart now, or should his life be spared to us for multiplied years, which all trust and pray, none more fervently than

J. THOMAS SCHARF.

PREFACE.

THE preparation of such a work as the "History of Western Maryland" imposes a vast responsibility and an immense amount of labor. Years of study devoted to the subjects embraced in it, the encouragement of friends, and the enterprise of the liberal publisher induced the author to undertake the work.

In the compilation of this history no authority of importance has been overlooked. The author has carefully examined every source of information open to him, and has availed himself of every fact that could throw new light upon, or impart additional interest to, the subject under consideration. Besides consulting the most reliable records and authorities, over fifteen thousand communications were addressed to persons supposed to be in possession of facts or information calculated to add value to the work. Recourse has not only been had to the valuable libraries of Baltimore, Annapolis, Frederick, and Hagerstown, but the author and his agents have visited personally the entire territory embraced in the six counties of Western Maryland, spending much time in each district, examining ancient newspapers, musty manuscripts, family, church, and society records, conversing with the aged inhabitants, and collecting from them orally many interesting facts never before published, and which otherwise, in all probability, would soon have been lost altogether. In addition to the material partly used in the preparation of his "Chronicles" and "History of Baltimore City and County" and "History of Maryland," the author has consulted an immense number of pamphlets, consisting of county and town documents, reports of societies, associations, corporations, and historical discourses, and, in short, everything of a fugitive character that might in any way illustrate the history of Western Maryland. From these and a large collection of newspapers (more particularly a nearly complete file of the Hagerstown *Torchlight, Mail, Spy,* and *Herald,* which were kindly loaned by Messrs. Mittag, Bell & Williams, and E. W. Mealey) great assistance has been derived.

With the aid of Prof. Philip R. Uhler, the topography and geology, as well as the geography, of Western Maryland have received the attention which their importance demands. Sketches of the rise, progress, and present condition of the various religious denominations, professions, political parties, and charitable and benevolent institutions, societies, and orders form a conspicuous feature of the work. Manufacturing, commercial, and agricultural interests have also a prominent place. An account of the county school system is also given, and a history of the various institutions of learning of which Western Maryland has every reason to be proud. Many of the facts recorded, both statistical and historical, may seem trivial or tediously minute to the general reader, and yet such facts have a local interest and sometimes a real importance.

An honest effort has been made to do justice to both sections in the relation of such events of the civil war as come within the proper scope of a purely local history. The author has made no attempt to obtrude his own political views upon the reader, and has constantly kept in mind the purpose that has guided his labors,—to present a work free from sectional or partisan bias which shall be acceptable to the general public.

Considerable space has been given to biographies of leading and representative men, living and dead, who have borne an active part in the various enterprises of life, and who have become closely identified with the history of Frederick, Washington, Montgomery, Allegany, Carroll, and Garrett Counties. The achievements of the living must not be forgotten, nor must the memories of those who have passed away be allowed to perish. It is the imperative duty of the historian to chronicle their public and private efforts to advance the great interests of society. Their deeds are to be recorded for the benefit of those who follow them; they, in fact, form part of the history of their communities, and their successful lives add to the glory of the Commonwealth.

A distinguishing feature of the work is its statistics of the various districts into which the six counties of Western Maryland are divided. In them the reader is brought into close relation with every part of Western Maryland. The advantage of this method of treatment is obvious, embracing, as it does, narratives of early settlements, descriptions of interesting localities, and personal reminiscences. The maps, views, and portraits are a prominent accompaniment, and add interest and attractiveness to the subjects which they are designed to illustrate and explain. Our acknowledgments are due to many friends, not only for a kindly interest shown in our labors, but for much valuable information, furnished in many cases without solicitation.

In presenting the "History of Western Maryland" to the public the author feels conscious that he sends it forth with many imperfections. In the preparation of a work of this character many minor inaccuracies and errors are almost unavoidable, the existence of which it is impossible to discover until the book has been exposed to the light of general criticism. It may not be considered presumptuous, however, to express the hope that its general conception and execution will be satisfactory to the community for which it has been written, and that it will prove useful and interesting to all classes of readers.

J. THOMAS SCHARF.

BALTIMORE, Feb. 10, 1882.

CONTENTS OF VOLUME I.

CHAPTER I.
Topography and Geology.. 13

CHAPTER II.
The Aborigines... 46

CHAPTER III.
The Early Settlers... 58

CHAPTER IV.
The French and Indian War.. 74

CHAPTER V.
Logan and Cresap.. 101

CHAPTER VI.
Boundary Lines.. 111

CHAPTER VII.
The War for Independence.. 121

CHAPTER VIII.
The Constitution and Union.. 161

CHAPTER IX.
The War of 1812... 174

CHAPTER X.
The Civil War... 194

CHAPTER XI.
First Year of the Civil War... 211

CHAPTER XII.
Maryland Campaign of 1862... 227

CHAPTER XIII.
The Gettysburg Campaign... 262

CHAPTER XIV.
Close of the Civil War.. 283

CHAPTER XV.
Record of Maryland Volunteers in the Union Army in the War of 1861-65... 298

CHAPTER XVI.
Record of Maryland Commands in the Confederate Army during the Civil War of 1861-65... 329

CHAPTER XVII.
Political Progress.. 340

CHAPTER XVIII.
Frederick County.. 358

CHAPTER XIX.
Land Grants and Resurveys... 371

CHAPTER XX.
The Bench and Bar... 380

CHAPTER XXI.
Early Court Proceedings... 416

CHAPTER XXII.
Public Schools, Internal Improvements, and Agricultural Societies....... 432

CHAPTER XXIII.
Distinguished Men of Frederick County................................... 449

CHAPTER XXIV.
County Officers... 476

CHAPTER XXV.
Frederick City.. 483

CHAPTER XXVI.
Religious Denominations and Cemeteries of Frederick City................ 501

CHAPTER XXVII.
Press of Frederick.. 527

CHAPTER XXVIII.
Banks and other Financial Institutions.................................. 538

CHAPTER XXIX.
Secret Orders, Benevolent Societies, etc................................ 545

CHAPTER XXX.
Prominent Institutions and Events....................................... 552

CHAPTER XXXI.
Frederick County Districts and Villages................................. 565

CHAPTER XXXII.
Montgomery County... 640

CHAPTER XXXIII.
Courts and County Officials... 657

CHAPTER XXXIV.
Educational and Miscellaneous Matters................................... 669

CHAPTER XXXV.
The District of Columbia.. 686

CHAPTER XXXVI.
Internal Improvements in Montgomery County.............................. 696

CHAPTER XXXVII.
Montgomery County Districts... 717

ILLUSTRATIONS IN VOLUME I.

	PAGE
Arms of William Penn and Lord Baltimore	116
Baker, Daniel	facing 568
Baltimore City in 1800	166
Barney, Commodore Joshua	188
Barnsley, Wm. B	780
Battle of South Mountain	234
Baughman, John W	532
Biggs, Joshua	facing 580
Bowie, Richard J	" 754
Braddock, Gen.	81
Brooke, Roger	facing 774
Brown, H. C., Residence of	" 573
Burnside's Bridge	246
Cashell, Hazel B	facing 719
Calvert, Charles, Fifth Lord Baltimore	" 113
Carroll, Charles, of Carrollton	" 125
Carroll, Charles, of Carrollton	" 439
Chase, Samuel	" 384
Clagett, Thomas, with Residence	" 544
Clemson, John	603
Clemson, John, Residence of	facing 603
Congress Hall	62
Cooke, Nathan	facing 785
Culler, John	580
Davis, Allen B., Residence of	facing 771
Davis, Eli	" 606
Davis, Henry W	387
Deaver, Capt. H. T., Residence of	facing 622
Downey, William	" 609
Dulany, Daniel	" 382
Dunker Church	239
Feaga, Wm. M	559
Frederick, Sixth Lord Baltimore	facing 360
Gaither, Henry C	" 600
Gorman, Arthur P	" 713
Gott, B. C	" 730
Griffith, H	" 737
Griffith, Lebbeus, Sr	604
Hanson, Alex. C	142
Hanson, John	450
Hobbs, Edward	facing 601
Hopkins, Johns	681
Houck, Ezra	facing 539
Houck, Geo., Residence of	" 571
Howard, Gen. John E	176
Hughes, Hon. C., Jr	192

	PAGE
Hutchinson, H. M., Residence of	facing 644
Johnson, Reverdy	386
Johnson, Governor Thomas	facing 389
Kenly, John R	" 304
Key, Francis S	" 399
Kunkel, Jacob M	" 554
Lakin, D. T	" 435
Lee, Gen. Henry	165
Lewis, C. M., Residence of	facing 623
Lewis, Jacob, with Residence	" 572
Lynch, John A	" 404
Map of Battle of Antietam	" 240
Map of Western Maryland	between 12, 13
Martin, Luther	383
McElfresh, John H	facing 415
McMahon, John V. L	386
McMurray, Louis	facing 492½
McSherry, James	413
O'Donnell, John C., Residence of	facing 620
Palmer, William P	" 778
Peter Cooper's First Locomotive	440
Peter, Maj. George	facing 732
Phillips, Lycurgus	" 615
Pinkney, William	384
Ray, Alfred	facing 763
Riley, P. C	" 783
Rouzer, John	630
Schaeffer, William A	" 735
Scharf, J. Thomas	Frontispiece.
Schley, Fairfax	facing 448
Shriner, E. A., with Residence	" 624
Smallwood, Gen. William	" 138
Smith, Gen. Samuel	167
Staley, Cornelius	facing 557
Steiner, L. H	" 488
Stocks and Pillory	420
Stricker, Col. John	168
Taney, Roger B	394
Thomas, C. K., Residence of	facing 574
Thomas, John H	341
Trail, Charles E	facing 540
Urner, Milton G	" 409
Williams, John T	" 607
Winder, Gen. William H	187
Wirt, William	385
Young, Isaac	facing 727

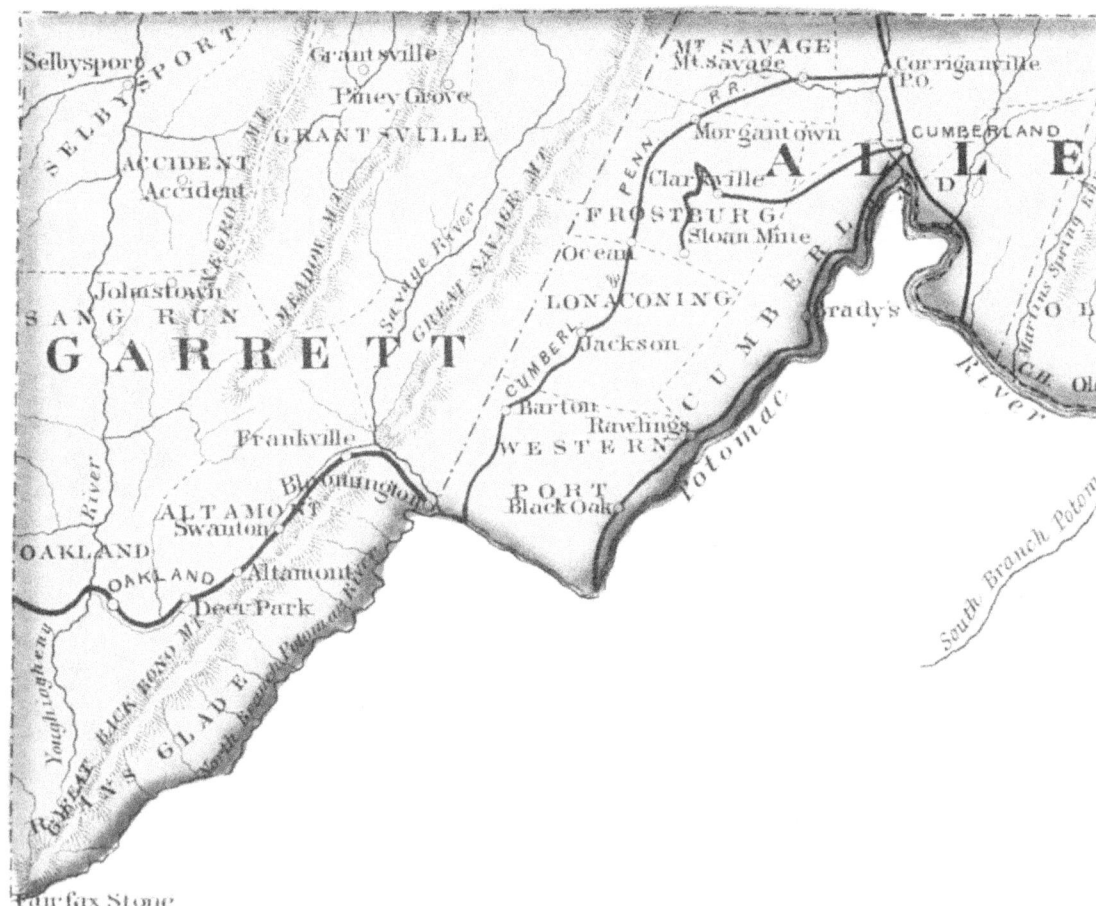

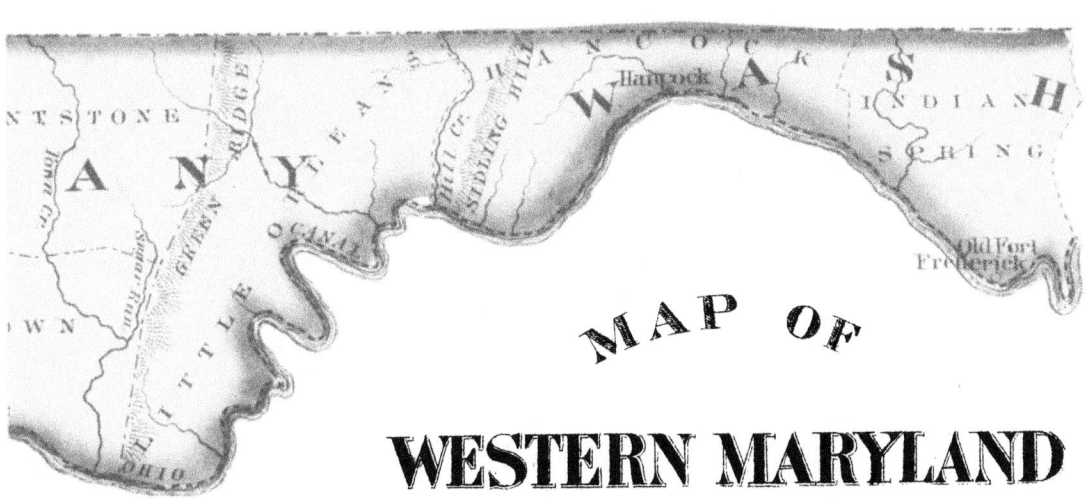

MAP OF WESTERN MARYLAND

Engraved expressly for Scharf's History

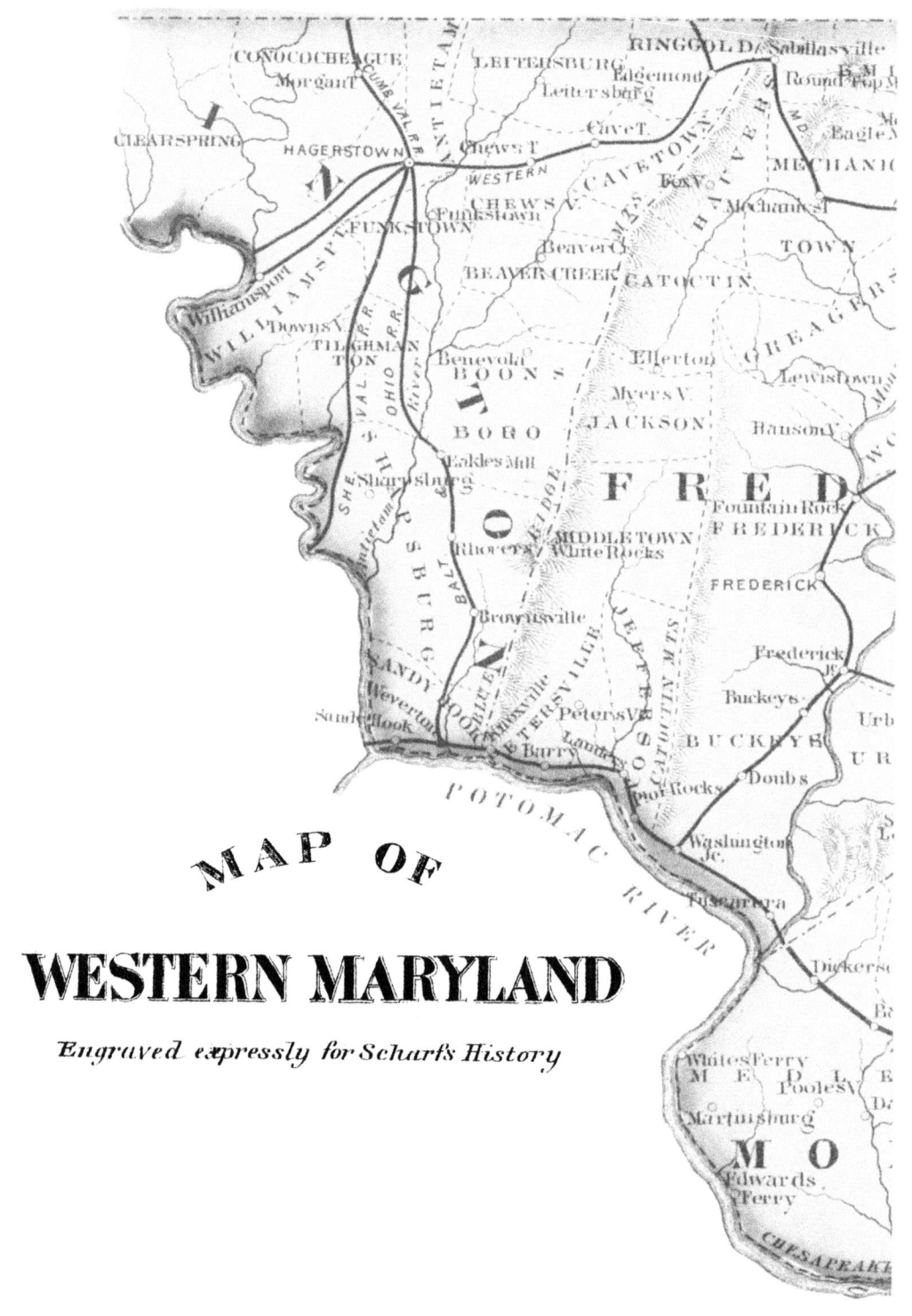

HISTORY OF WESTERN MARYLAND.

CHAPTER I.

TOPOGRAPHY AND GEOLOGY.[1]

THE section of country embraced in the following descriptive outline is a long strip, running from east to west, widened on the ends, and extending from the western boundary of Baltimore County to the extreme limits of Maryland next to West Virginia. It consists of six large counties, among the most fertile, varied, and populous in the State. These are Frederick, Montgomery, Washington, Allegany, Carroll, and Garrett Counties. This region is bounded on the north by Mason and Dixon's line, which separates it from Pennsylvania, and on the south by the Potomac River, whose bending channel breaks the outline into a series of long and short curves, and cuts it off from West Virginia and Virginia. It might be regarded as of the form of a low bridge or arch, the keystone of which would be placed at Hancock (where the county is narrowed to a breadth of only one and a quarter miles); the wider end would rest on the District of Columbia, and the narrower end would stand on the source of the north branch of the Potomac River. The length of this strip is about one hundred and forty miles, and the width is about fifty miles, from north to south, across the east, and nearly thirty-six miles, in the same direction, across the west end.

It embraces almost every variety of surface within the State, the lowlands at tide-water and the ocean shores only being excepted. For convenience, the region may be divided into four great sections, marked by well-distinguished features of the surface, and coinciding sufficiently with the groups of rocks upon which it rests.

As no part of the TIDE-WATER BELT strictly occurs within this territory, the *first* to be noticed is the MIDLAND BELT. It begins about five miles back of the inner limits of the tides in the rivers, such as the Potomac and Patuxent, and extends westward to an oblique line running from the mouth of the Monocacy River to the sources of Piney Creek, in Carroll County.

The *second* is the BLUE RIDGE BELT, which runs from the basin of the Monocacy and the head-waters of Piney Creek to the west side of the summit of the Blue Ridge, or South Mountain range.

The *third* is the GREAT VALLEY, extending from the western side of the summit of South Mountain to the corresponding part of the summit of North Mountain. It is occupied chiefly by the extension of the Cumberland Valley of Pennsylvania, which is widely known as the Hagerstown Valley, and which, southwest of the Potomac River, becomes the great Valley of Virginia.

The *fourth* is the extensive APPALACHIAN BELT. This is pre-eminently the mountain region, and extends from the summit of North Mountain to the western boundary of the State.

Each of these divisions includes smaller belts and tracts of country, which may be recognized by a difference in the quality or color of the soil, and by the kinds of native rocks which rest near the surface.

Midland Belt.—This embraces the greater part of the two most eastward counties, Montgomery and Carroll. The lowest lands occurring within its limits belong to the southern extremity of Montgomery County, where the primitive rocks dip beneath the soil to stretch off under the deep basin of the Chesapeake Bay. These are tracts of clay, gravel, and sand, the former resting directly upon the eroded surfaces of granite, gneiss, and hornblende, and the

---

[1] Contributed by Prof. Philip R. Uhler, president of the Maryland Academy of Sciences.

latter spread over the surface of the low hills of clay and rock by floods and by the retreating tides of a former ocean. Several of these areas reach back into the country for a distance of nearly seven miles, while the more gravelly portions are confined to a belt varying in width from two to five miles. The clay area extends through the District of Columbia and Prince George's County into this region, chiefly along the ancient valleys of the streams, spreading more broadly from thence, and covering parts of the adjacent hills. On the northwest of the former the surface rises gradually by a series of rounded plateaus, until it culminates about twenty miles back in the folds and crest of Parr's Ridge. An altitude of about nine hundred feet is now attained, and the backbone of this range is seen to stretch away from near the Potomac River on the southwest in a wavy line, through the eastern part of Carroll County in a north-northeast direction, then with a backward bend as Westminster is reached, and across the boundary into Pennsylvania. It forms a high fold in the talcose slates, which, decomposing, serve to furnish a fairly light and kind soil, capable of being made very productive of all the cereals and fruits of temperate climates. A fine agricultural tract is also seen to spread away on both sides, presenting large farms of real fertility, and attesting the thrift of the inhabitants, whose ample barns and well-kept houses greet the eye on every hand. The soils belonging to this system of rocks extend as far as to the base of the Sugar-Loaf Mountain on the west, interrupted in the west corner by the red sandstone soils, and on the east extend as far as to the boundary of the archæan lands on Rock Creek. They also send off two tongues of the same kind of soil, the one reaching to near the northern angle of the District of Columbia, and the other running parallel with the Patuxent River as far as to the source of Paint Branch. The ridge forms the dividing line between the creeks and rivers which flow towards the east and south and those which course southwest and west. In most parts the scenery offers a pleasing variety, but the wildest and most romantic spots are to be met with in the thinly-settled section on the head-waters of the various tributaries of the Patuxent River. There the hills are abrupt, high, and broken, flanked along the sides by lower and more rounded knobs, which have lost their former angular summits by reason of the softer and less resisting materials of which they are composed. Deep, sudden ravines, set with angular and piled-up rocks, are seen at frequent intervals, and through these the limpid waters of the rivulets and branches leap with never-ceasing activity over moss-covered bowlders, amid the tangled branches of flowering bushes and creeping vines. On these ridgy hills, too, the principal forests still remain. Second-growth trees of various kinds—oaks, hickory, walnut, beech, maples, sour-gum, dogwood, tulip-poplars, elm, hazel, a few pines, and numerous chestnut-trees—still serve to cover the wilder places and store the moisture to feed springs and rivulets.

As usual, the dark-gray and silvery minerals composing the rocks of this region are attacked by the atmosphere, frost, and heat; they crack into slaty joints, change to a rusty color, and then disintegrate into a pale-yellowish micaceous and aluminous soil. Moisture, supplied by the morning and evening vapors, creeps into these, in common with many other kinds of cleaving, cracking rocks, carries carbonic acid and other solvents into the interstices between the grains, and sets up chemical activities which rapidly reduce them to powder.

Commencing in Montgomery, on the southeast, the country rises by series of water-worn plateaus, or hills, with shallow, narrow depressions intervening, giving the effect of interrupted table-lands. The roads intersect ledges and masses of granite, gneisses, hornblende schists, and, at the lowest levels, the black hornblende rocks. As in Baltimore and Howard, so here, this latter seems to be the bed-rock which underlies, holds, or gives rise to all the later ones of the formation. It crops out in the beds of the streams, such as Rock Creek, Paint Branch, and the tributaries of the Potomac south of the Great Falls, and is also indicated in places adjacent to the Patuxent. It underlies the mica schists where in most places their lower exposures are visible, and it forms bowlders on the sides of the hills and partly in the drift of the lower and central parts of this county.

Crossing the rolling slope which descends immediately west of Parr's Ridge, the valley of the Monocacy River is reached, and the talcose slates become more aluminous. Here and there chains of high domes stretch from the northeast towards the southwest, and the higher swellings are seen to be composed of the tougher beds of the rock, while the lower undulations appear more shattered, broken next the surface into small fragments, and exhibit marked evidences of decay. Near the mouth of the river erosion and frequent washings have opened out a wide basin, which is now covered by the alluvium of this stream. It has thus brought some of the best fertilizing ingredients of the distant rocks within the reach of the agriculturist, who has thus been enabled to profit by the opportunity to secure most abundant crops of Indian corn, clover, hay, etc. On the northwestern side of this county a broad belt of red sandstone hills runs down to the bed of the Potomac River. They begin a little east of Seneca Creek, and extend to within a few rods of the mouth of the Monocacy River. These rise in their more central parts in majestic piles, like huge ranges of masonry, swelling to a height of more than one hundred and fifty feet above the basin of the Potomac. Colossal chimney-rocks stand up like tall sentinels on the dark-brown walls of precipitous sandstone, and craggy peaks jut out at various angles over the vast piles of overthrown blocks, which join to attest the power of the forces that have snapped them apart and pitched their shattered fragments upon the buttresses below. This is a section full of delightful scenery, and beset with a multitude of surprises for the attentive eye. It abounds in objects of the weird and grotesque, and is quite unlike any other part of the great triassic framework to which it belongs. The great river itself spreads away in a silvery sheet through solitudes broken only at distant intervals by the lonely bird or the more fearless hunter or fisherman.

Montgomery County has an area of five hundred and eight square miles; it is the most southern of the counties included in the present notice, and possesses in an eminent degree those peculiarities of surface, soil, and climate which contribute to the health and prosperity of the inhabitants. It is about twenty-eight miles long from northwest to southeast, by about twenty-three miles wide on its northern boundary, and seventeen miles across its southern extremity. No mountain ranges actually exist within its limits, but, instead, the system of high hills known as Parr's Ridge crosses it diagonally a few miles from its northern border. The hills and plateaus already described occupy the chief parts of its surface, and serve to separate the numerous rivulets, branches, and creeks which so abundantly water almost all sections of its territory. Although large tracts of uncleared lands appear on the uplands and undulations next these water-courses, yet large farms have been cleared in most parts of the county, and others of even greater size form the larger part of the area in the more northern and central divisions. The upper part of the great plateau around Sandy Springs, which was originally but little better than a sandy waste, has been almost turned into a garden by the energy and intelligence of the inhabitants. An almost endless variety of soils appears as the different parts of the country are examined, and in nearly all the natural quality is well adapted to the purposes of agriculture. The northern and western portions are especially the home of the grasses and cereals; the warm hillsides promote the growth of the grape and fruit-trees; the small fruits succeed well on the more loamy and sandy depressions of the midlands and more southern sections, and in the bottoms the native bushes, flowering shrubs and plants form a varied and comprehensive collection.

In the expanded portions of the old beds of the creeks the decaying leaves and other vegetable matter, drifted down from the higher levels, joined to the washings brought down by freshets and overflows, has placed vast beds of humus and rich soil within easy reach of the florist and horticulturist. The more rocky streams are decorated by the kalmia, or common laurel, which grows in thickets between the gray rocks, in the loose, rich soil. In the spring the golden blossoms of the leatherwood, the sassafras, the clear lilac of the *Houstonia*, and the delicate pink of the *Claytonia* add a cheerful brightness to the tender verdure of the open woods, while the advancing summer is made rich by the fragrant flowers of the magnolia and azaleas, the showy sepals of the dogwood, the clustering bloom of the snowy viburnum, the odor of the wild grape, and the splendor of the native lily. The waters, too, are studded with the huge, fragrant rosettes of the pond-lilies, and teem with the numerous varieties of pickerel plants, water plantains, arrow-heads, and a host of others too numerous to mention. Alders group themselves on the damp spots of the basins, the swamp-maples spread their broad limbs over the pools, and the greenbrier binds the crown of the bushes in a maze of perpetual green.

Between the mouth of the Monocacy River and Seneca Creek the brown sandstone hills were formerly covered with a luxuriant growth of the sugar-maple. An abundant supply of sugar was obtained from the trees, and this industry was one of great importance to the inhabitants. But now these forests are replaced by other kinds of trees, forming a later growth of uncommon variety. Chestnut, red, black, and other oaks, ash, hickory, elm, walnut, and, most of all, false locust grow in thick woods, set with a dense undergrowth of bushes, creepers, and grape-vines. At intervals, where the hills are eroded to near the water-level, wide lowlands stretch back into the country, the margins of which are occupied by large specimens of the sycamore, sour-gum, and occasionally the tulip-poplar. The vistas across these broad plains are broken here and there by low spurs of hills, which stand out like islands. These are usually wooded, fade out imperceptibly into the lowlands, and form a rich relief of dark color to the paler and yellower greens of the grasses and cereals of the wide-spreading fields. Usually the remote background, two or more miles away, is formed by higher hills of similar dark green, rendered more soft and blue by the distance, while in the interval are large farms of high culture, with excellent houses, immense barns, and numerous haystacks. Herds of cattle, groups of horses, and flocks of sheep have their appropriate places on the open undulations and in the meadows, giving a pleasant air of animation to the scene, and adding to the enjoyments of rural life. Milk is abundant, and the water is soft, pure, and plentiful. Little rills pursue their way in unbroken steadiness through these meadows, or burst with impetuosity from the rocky hillsides to plunge into the creeks beyond.

Much of the successful farming of this county has been due to the free use of lime. The soils being naturally sour, require the addition of this substance or plaster of Paris. Some of the farmers along the high-roads leading into the Frederick Valley, or near the line of the Chesapeake and Ohio Canal, transport the limestone to their farms, where they burn it in kilns, and then offer the surplus for sale to their neighbors. The stone is brought either from the western section of the red sandstone or from the valley of the Monocacy, in Frederick, and is partly of the variety known as calico-rock, or Potomac breccia.

The region around Brookville and the valley of Hawling's River have likewise been enriched by the intelligent use of lime. Although naturally thin, and being composed in part of the magnesian minerals derived from serpentine and talcose slates, they have been transformed into some of the richest and most productive lands in the county. The region west of this gradually changes into the ophiolite, or serpentine formation. It consists of a series of rounded hills, running from the ridge on which Damascus, Cracklintown, etc., are situated, and continued in sloping spurs towards the basin of the Patuxent River. This belt of country, which widens as it enters the county, proceeds southwestward, and maintains a breadth of about three miles, until it fades out before reaching the Potomac River. A wide strip of pine woods stretches along the greater part of its length, occupying a chain of low hills, on which the soil is the poorest and thinnest in the county.

The whole country is abundantly supplied with streams of water, which rise in the uplands, and stretch away towards the creeks and rivers by passing through the bottoms and around the hills. Five principal systems of drainage are found within its limits,—the Patuxent on the east, the northwest branch of the Potomac and Rock Creek on the south, Seneca Creek on the west, and the Monocacy on the northwest.

The Patuxent River rises in the corner of Parr's Ridge next to Howard County, in a region of high hills, very picturesque, and full of rugged rocks, disposed in almost endless variety. More than a dozen of its little tributary branches start from springs in the dark rocks, push their way in tortuous threads, as twisted as the arms of an octopus, leap over sharp bowlders, and whirl along as rapids in the wider gaps, until they have settled to a level low enough to unite with the waters in the deeper trough of the river. At first the river proper is a comparatively narrow creek, forcing its way into deep ravines between the hills, rushing violently through cracks in the rocks, and forming cascades by plunging from the bowlders which stand in its path. But after leaving the barriers west of Triadelphia it rapidly widens, and becomes a strong, full stream, running with great rapidity in a more steeply-cut channel. At occasional intervals it spreads (where the softer rocks have given way) into shallow basins, in the midst of a fine overgrowth of white and other oaks, and through almost impenetrable thickets of bushes, shrubs, and vines of various kinds. East of Sandy Spring the river has piled up for hundreds of feet back beyond its present channel vast areas of clay and reddish micaceous soil, which stand like cliffs and barriers on either side. From a remote period it has been the great sewer for the drainage of a large part of this and the adjoining (Howard) county.

During the great ice ages the amount of solid rock, in the form of bowlders, gravel, mineral paste, grit, and mud that it has contributed to the estuaries of the former Atlantic Ocean is only to be estimated by the enormous beds and deep deposits of these substances to be seen in crossing the counties of Prince George and Anne Arundel. Along the border of Montgomery County it can only be estimated as a broad, rapid creek; but at a distance of twenty-five miles south of this limit it becomes a large river, navigable for schooners and vessels of moderate size.

The Potomac River bounds the whole length of the western side of this county, and receives numerous tributaries from the adjoining hills, but its description properly belongs to the general belt of counties, in and where it will be found.

The northwest branch of the Potomac River is but a small creek in this county. It rises in two principal branches, fed by several small brooks in the region southwest and south of Sandy Spring. It runs in a somewhat zigzag southeast course between the sandy and clay hills, through a rather depleted country in which the red clay and heavy soil abounds. After having pursued a course of about twelve miles amidst the tangled bushes and low woods, it passes beyond the boundary, two miles south of Burnt Mills.

Rock Creek.—The next system of drainage to be noticed is that of Rock Creek. This is an important stream, carrying a large body of water, fed by several tributaries along both banks, and supplying water-power to numerous grist and saw-mills. It rises in the region northwest of Brookville, in the midst of craggy masses of talcose schists, which are traversed by innumerable veins of white quartz. The rills which form its source leap down from the silvery rocks in frequent cascades, cool and limpid, shaded by bushes, tangled vines, and canopies of ferns; then breaking into rapids as they strike the bowlders in their path, they finally spread out in a broad, active stream as the vicinity of Rockville is reached. The creek passes through a pleasantly diversified country, uncovering here and there along its margins the ledges of hornblende, gneiss, steatite, and sienite which underlie the soil. Along its banks the decomposing rocks yield red and yellow lands of decided fertility; a large part of these have been cleared, and while some parts have been worn out by crops of tobacco, others now comprehend some of the best-tilled farms in the county. The copious supply of water afforded by this stream and its tributaries has fed the trees and contributed towards the growth of a luxuriant vegetation. The original forests which here covered the land were formed of the grand old white oaks, with a numerous company of other oaks, of several kinds of hickory, of walnuts, tulip-trees, maples, gums, sycamore, and dogwood, with a varied retinue of bushes, flowering shrubs, and creepers. Now their successors, of less impressive size, still luxuriate in the rich alluvial soils of the bottoms, or spread along the misty summits of the hills. Everywhere the horizon is bounded by a stately belt of verdure, which gives variety and freshness to the dull uniformity of the plowed fields and denuded hillsides. After running in a southwestern course for about fifteen miles, the creek crosses into the District of Columbia, and finally buries itself in the Potomac River within the limits of Georgetown. A great part of its bed is clogged by the bowlders of hornblende and gneiss which have been torn from the sides of the uplands by the furious floods which have penetrated the region.

Seneca Creek next claims attention as forming another separate outlet for the waters of the county. It rises by numerous tributaries in the high country bordering the fork of Parr's Ridge, and is separated from the head-waters of the Patuxent River by only the outlying barrier of talcose slates which curves from the vicinity of Damascus to Cracklintown, and continues thence to Mechanicsville and beyond. Some of its sources start in the dark mounds of serpentine rocks which contain the chrome-iron ore. The tributaries at its head bend in almost countless curves to evade the frequent hills and swells of surface studding that section. On the eastern side it receives three large branches,—the Whetstone, Long Draught, and Dawes' Branch, and on the western side the Little Seneca and the Dry Seneca, all of which are fed by copious and constant springs. Taken altogether, it is a long and wide-reaching stream, extending nearly across the entire width of the county, bending into sudden loops towards the west until Dawsonville is reached; next with equal abruptness it stretches south with fewer bends, and then straightening out, it empties into the Potomac River. It passes in most parts through a country abounding in round-top single hills and short knobs, although the whole system of swells belongs to a broad fold of the surface which runs almost to the Potomac River, and includes two minor folds, known as Oak Ridge and The Pines. This higher district is peculiar to the eastern side of the creek, and is chiefly built into the magnesian rocks, with thin and lean soils. On the western side, north of the Little Seneca, the rocks are chiefly talcose slates of green and red tints, largely invaded by veins of white quartz, and extensively shattered into joints inclosing angular fragments. "Between the Little Seneca and Buck-lodge branch the quartz is more porous, the pores lined with black oxide of manganese, and occasionally inclosing specular oxide of iron. In this direction the talcose slate varies in color from red to grayish and blue, assuming a more decidedly slaty character, and finally passing into the true clay-slate. About the region of the Dry Seneca, and stretching to the mouth of the Seneca proper, the rocks are red and gray sandstones and shales, whilst near the mouth of the Monocacy River, and between it and the Little Monocacy, the sandstone varies in color from gray to red." This rock also assumes a difference in texture and composition, ranging from a fine-grained, uniform sandstone to a gritty and uneven conglomerate. The creek, including its numerous windings, has a total length of about twenty-six miles, and, together with its tributaries, drains an area of more than one hundred and thirty-six square miles. At its head-waters the country is wilder, much diversified, and well pervaded with ledges and beds of broken rocks, but as the creek widens and takes on its well-settled form the region is more extensively cleared, farms appear on every hand, and the woodlands are more restricted to the tops of the hills and to the rocky alluvial basins of the stream. After crossing the Rockville turnpike it becomes a creek fully thirty feet wide, running through a well-defined trough, extensively bounded by alluvial banks, and continuing in a slowly widening channel until, near the splendid aqueduct which crosses it and carries the water of the canal, it becomes a full stream at least sixty feet wide, and almost equaling the Monocacy in its volume of water. The brown soil through which it passes in its lower division imparts some of its color to the creek, so that the stream is usually seen to have a rusty brown tint.

Besides the larger streams already described, a multitude of small branches pour into the Potomac River from the ravines opening out on that side of the county, and thus an abundant supply of water is seen to be secured. But here as elsewhere the injudicious clearing away of the forests has laid the surface open to the sun, and the springs which formerly supplied the rivulets that fed the creeks and rivers have become dry, and a great volume of water has accordingly disappeared from the larger streams.

The Monocacy River has several small tributaries which rise in the slate-lands within the western part of this county. But the only considerable one of these is Bennet's Creek. It starts from many sources among the broad, round, clay-slate hills southwest of Damascus, and bending westwardly, passes behind the Sugar-Loaf Mountain to empty into the river. Like most of the other branches which have their sources in the slates, it bursts forth from cavities in the midst of the shattered rocks, and pursues its course in deep channels along narrow ravines, expanding but little in its course, and finally passing out into the wider stream through alluvial beds of its own construction.

The resources of Montgomery County are adequate to the wants of a large and varied population. Industries of nearly all kinds possible to an inland country can be successfully conducted within its limits. As already noticed, ample water-powers for driving mills and machinery are present in nearly all the larger streams. The Great Falls of the Potomac pours the heaviest volume of water to be found in the State. Broad belts of alluvial soil suitable for meadows and fitted for the grazing of stock are present in the northern and western sections, and the mild climate, pure water, and fresh air of the higher districts supply the first requisites for a healthy and thriving population. Gold, copper, and chrome occur in the metalliferous range of formations bordering the central belt of magnesian rocks; brown sandstones, granites, etc., for building purposes, abound within easy access of the canal, and fruit culture can be conducted to an immense extent.

The native animals of the region have been the black bear, gray wolf, panther, wild-cat, gray and red fox, raccoon, opossum, mink, marten, weasel, field hare, ground-hog, skunk, fox-squirrel, gray squirrel, flying squirrel, chipmunk or ground squirrel, common mole, star-nosed mole, shrew, white-footed mouse, jumping mouse, and several others of this group, the hoary and two other kinds of bats, the otter and muskrat in the waters, and the common rat and mouse in the barns and houses. The wild beasts have been exterminated, and so have the elk and caribou, but the red deer is said to be still a casual visitor of the wilder sections near the Potomac River.

The birds still form a numerous assemblage, rich in species, attractive in habits and song, and finely varied in plumage. The famous mocking-bird, with the brown thrush and meadow-lark, are at home here, with more than twenty varieties of warblers; several kinds of wading birds, and the belted kingfisher, the blue heron, the white egret, the bittern, lesser heron, night heron, fly-up-the-creek, and several other kinds find congenial hunting-grounds along the shores of the streams. The birds of prey, such as the golden and bald eagle, the fish-hawk, and a score of hawks and owls, add to the list, while the various swallows, martins, swifts, pigeons, doves, and woodpeckers serve to furnish a catalogue of forms of great diversity and eminent beauty.

The reptiles and fish likewise comprise numerous species of curious appearance or of value for food. Among the former, the great snapping-turtle, the slider, two kinds of mud-terrapins, the musk-turtle, the land-tortoise, the gray swift, and six-lined skink may be mentioned as conspicuous and well-known creatures. Of the worm-shaped reptiles, the dreaded rattlesnake and the copperhead still occur among the low rocks in the wilder parts of the back country, besides which three kinds of water-snakes, four varieties of garter-snakes, the blowing viper, the chain and milk-snakes, the great horse-runner and common black snake, the delicate green snake, and a dozen other species affect most parts of the region where vegetation grows thickly. Of frogs, most of the kinds common to the Atlantic region occur in moderate numbers. Thus two forms of toad, two tree-toads, the bull-frog, leopard frog, woods frog, savannah cricket, and spring frog are numerous in most of the low grounds and wet meadows. The crustacea are represented by four kinds of crayfish, the fresh-water shrimp, and a host of sow-bugs, besides the minute forms peculiar to the streams and ponds.

The insects form an almost countless assemblage of both noxious and useful forms. Beautiful butterflies of large size and brilliant colors abound in the fields of clover, fly swiftly along the edges of the open woods or settle upon conspicuous flowers standing by the river's brink. Gay sphinxes protrude their long beaks into the throats of the tubular flowers, and four kinds of large silk-worm moths find a home in the forest or field. Attractive but noxious wood-boring beetles destroy the hickory, walnut, and oak trunks or limbs; and the fruit-trees are sometimes attacked by the Ægeria, plumb weevil, apple-moth, or web-weavers, and measuring caterpillars of many varieties. Of horse-flies more than a dozen kinds are more or less known; mosquitoes affect the country along the Potomac River and larger creeks, and the other flies, many of them studded with golden and silvery markings, make a host too great to enumerate. The broad-winged dragon-flies dash with unapproachable swiftness over the surface of every pond and creek, and the crimson-winged Hetærina balances itself over the waters of Rock Creek and the canal.

The next part of this belt which claims attention lies in Carroll County. It forms a triangular tract in the southeastern corner of the county of about ten miles from northeast to southwest, and of about six miles from northwest to southeast. On the east it is bounded by the north branch of the Patapsco River, and on the south by the west branch of the same river. It forms a part of the great archæan belt of rocks which, crossing from Baltimore County, passes through Howard into Montgomery. Here, however, it is built into higher uplands, and is characterized by the prevalence of granitic rocks. These rise in high, broad domes, reaching to an altitude of more than four hundred feet above the level of the sea. The granites and gneiss are exposed in fine sections along the line of the Baltimore and Ohio Railroad near Sykesville, standing at high angles in great dark, forbidding masses. These form but a few hills between the serpentine formation on the northeast and the metalliferous belt on the west. Taken altogether, it constitutes a wedge of country embracing types of most of the mineral aggregations belonging to the oldest formations of the State. Within this small area may be found copper, soapstone, limestone, white quartz, and the minerals of the magnesian and chloritic series, in great abundance. Soapstone has been excavated in considerable quantities from a large quarry, and copper has been worked in the Springfield and adjoining mines. The limestone valley which runs in a line continuous with Marriottsville is a valuable addition to the resources of the neighborhood in supplying the lime as a fertilizer where it is much needed. Crossing the ore-bearing belt, the talcose and slaty rocks are reached, which characterize the region in general.

Carroll County, of which the preceding tract forms but a small corner, is one of the medium-sized but very productive sections of the State. It possesses an area of about four hundred and fifty square miles, and has a form somewhat like that of an anvil with the point broken off. On the north it is bounded by Pennsylvania, on the east by Baltimore County, on the west by Frederick, and on the south by Howard County. The surface of the country is broken by hills in ridges and domes, becoming higher towards Parr's Ridge, and then decreasing in height after the ridge is crossed. The hills are often very wide and rather blunt on top, grouped more or less in chains having a general southwest direction. Broad valleys lie between these, usually running from the direction of Pennsylvania, and intersecting smaller valleys and ravines at frequent intervals. A very large proportion of the county consists of cleared lands, on which are located extensive and highly productive farms. Large barns are to be seen in almost every section, surrounded by numerous outhouses, and with comparatively small dwelling-houses placed a few rods away, usually on some hillside or slight swell of the ground. In the near vicinity of these large hayricks or numerous stacks are conspicuous, and in the adjacent fields or meadows groups of well-kept cattle show the industry and care of the inhabitants. Grazing farms are especially numerous near the public roads which intersect the country in every direction, and along the railroads; and a vast supply of milk, cream, and butter is continually being transported to Baltimore and other cities and towns. Ice cream is also one of the manufactures of the country near the Western Maryland Railroad, and promises to become a great source of income in the near future.

Meadow-lands, derived from the decomposition of slate rocks, and, to a smaller extent, from limestone, spread away in broad tracts near the brooks and rivulets which intersect most parts of the county. The entire region is watered by long streams of medium width, but whose tributaries are so numerous that large sections are charged with a network of constantly running pure water. Almost every extensive farm between Parr's Ridge and the new red sandstone has one or more springs, sending forth a steady stream from a depression in the hillside or from the head of a ravine. As many of these descend from altitudes far above the general level of the surface, they acquire a force which drives them over the rocks in torrents and small cascades, and affords ample power for the numerous mills, factories, and tan-yards. Parr's

Ridge divides the county into two sections, the larger and more irregular one of which lies on its west side, stretching away to Sam's Creek and the Monocacy River. Several very wild tracts still remain to point out the original condition of the country. These are chiefly on the head-waters of the branches of the Patapsco River, on the east side of the county, among the outlying spurs of the ridge, but also in a few places at the source of Bear Creek and Big Pipe Creek. Approaching the ridge from that side, a high backbone of hills appears, which bends into broad curves and incloses wide, open basins of alluvial soil, inclosed like amphitheatres. Through these the various rivulets and brooks pass swiftly over bottoms but little interrupted by the broken rocks. But nearer their sources they pass through the gaps, reach the ledges of dark and hard hydro-mica schists, and at once begin to contend with the rugged barriers that would arrest their farther advance. Here a scene of great attractiveness presents itself. Huge masses of angular rocks rest against the sides and ends of the broken ridges, while above them project the remnants of former ledges, sharp and craggy, disposed at every angle. In the old bed of the stream stand the great broken pieces which have fallen from the crest above, and a scattered heap of fragments of all sizes lies along the depression below. Trees of numerous varieties, chief of which are the oaks, maples, birches, and hickories, range in unbroken lines along the upward slopes, casting deep shadows over the sunny nooks, and giving shelter to a host of shrubs, plants, and vines that intertwine and mix in deep confusion among their piercing branches. On every sheltered rock the green, gray, and purple lichens have painted frescoes of marvelous elegance and beauty, and, crowning all, a dozen forms of ferns have woven their graceful chaplets of exquisite green over the crown of each dripping bowlder. Sparkling little springs sprinkle drops of limpid water upon the slender grasses and delicate creepers, keeping all moist, and adding their quota to the brook which aids to swell the vigorous river. All the streams of water in this region rise high up the slopes, rush down rocky channels choked with loose fragments of stone, form rapids, torrents, and cascades at frequent intervals, and display unceasing activity in wearing their channels ever deeper as they descend. During times of heavy rain they carry down immense quantities of sediments, in conjunction with the washings from the hills, and spread them in layers over the flat lowlands. Thus the bottoms of these basins are rising year by year, and the best ingredients of the forest humus and the mineral soil are carried into these natural meadows, to feed the grasses and wild plants. The open spaces are covered deeply with the soft soil which has been poured upon them through untold ages, and in the dim, far-back past they formed a great chain of fresh-water lakes, which stretched from beyond the Pennsylvania boundary away down into Baltimore County. While these were pent up within their rigid bounds of earth and stone, broad marshes spread along the edges of the barrier of archæan mountains on the southeast that kept back the oceanic waters a few miles north of Baltimore. Later, the melting of the great ice mass, reaching through the broad, deep valleys farther north, sent such vast floods of water into the midst of these lakes that an opening was made at their southern end, through which the waters found an outlet into the lower levels farther south. Thus the surface features of this region have been toned down near to the proportions that appear to-day, the tops of the ridges have been broken away, and the summits of the softer spurs washed into the form of rounded domes.

The region in which Carrollton Post-Office is situated discloses a scene of uncommon wildness. There the branches of the Patapsco River pursue their course in bewildering complexity, bending and turning back at unexpected intervals, and seeming to be ever in the way of the traveler. They drain the country across a width of more than ten miles, and carry a large volume of water into the north branch of the river. The ridges here are narrow and abrupt, everywhere set with broken rocks, some of the ledges of which stand like huge piles of ruined masonry on the edges of precipitous heights. Viewed from a distant hill, these broken ridges and spurs produce an effect of grandeur and variety. They stand in broken series, which seem to fade into others at lower levels, while those at the end terminate in spurs, which taper off and become lost in the general surface of the flat valleys. Crowned with trees of every variety of green, they roll away into the distance like the broken caps of huge waves in a sea of boundless verdure. Proceeding northward and westward, valleys of larger size appear in view. These are usually long depressions between the higher hills, underlaid by limestone, with deep soil of the highest fertility, and well supplied with springs and rivulets in which the water is clear, pure, moderately hard, and delightfully refreshing to the taste. Baughman's Valley is one well known for the fine farms and well-kept homes of an industrious and thrifty people. All the cereals and crops of the most favored portions of the adjoining States grow here in excellence and abundance. Fruit-trees of various kinds grow with ease, and yield fine crops of the best quality, and the smaller fruits are grown with equal facility. Grazing is practiced to a large extent, and large quantities of produce, added to the butter and milk, are transported from thence to the Baltimore market. The soil on the hills is derived from the mica-slates and talcose rocks, which, being decomposed, yield a light and deep stratum, which readily admits of high cultivation.

Between Westminster and Union Bridge is the garden part of the county. Talcose schists form the higher hills, the country rolls away in broad, flattened domes, and the bottoms and ravines are always traversed by streams of spring-water. The hills are to a great extent cleared of woodland, and large farms spread over uplands which are as carefully tilled as the meadows below. Limestone ledges project from the sides of the hills, and yield inexhaustible supplies of the richest fertilizing lime.

The country between Little and Big Pipe Creeks, and northwest of the latter, in which Middleburg and Taneytown are situated, forms a strong contrast to all the preceding districts. It rests upon and is derived from the new red sandstone rocks. The latter jut out in picturesque variety along the banks of the streams just mentioned, and lie scattered in indescribable confusion down the ravines through which they flow. Heavy rains and freshets grind these rocks into fine mud, which marks a trail wherever the floods carry the waters, and which stains the streams for many hours after they have subsided.

These sandstones, being soft and easily acted upon by the atmosphere, have been extensively denuded by moving water, consequently much rather flat country occurs where formerly the high domes uplifted their summits. The hills now generally appear low, wide, and separated by shallow bottoms. But along the Little Bear branch and on the upper sections of the Big Pipe Creek the hills are mixed with talcose slates, remain much more elevated, and furnish valuable water-powers from their more abrupt flanks. Taneytown occupies the centre of a tract about six miles square, based upon a red sandstone, somewhat mixed with slate. The resulting soil is thin, sandy, and sour, but little valued, and which has commanded relatively but a low price in the market. Careful limeing has, however, worked wonders with some of these depauperated lands, and brought them back to their original flourishing condition.

Limestone and Marbles.—These are so valuable, occur in such vast quantities and in so many places west of Parr's Ridge that they demand more than a passing notice in this place. Beginning with the section a little northwest of Manchester, they continue southwest towards the Frederick County line, and across it to a short distance below New Market. At first they seem to occupy but a narrow belt of country, but gradually widen, until, near the line of the Western Maryland Railroad, they stretch over more than one-half the width of the county. Within this range an extraordinary number of varieties may be found. Every color between plain white and black veined with white occurs. Most of them are stratified, while a very few are so much contorted as to hide all trace of their type of deposition. In general they are very fine-grained, of close texture, strong, durable, and susceptible of a very high polish. Samples taken from the exposed surfaces of beds in about fifty localities have shown what a great treasure Carroll County possesses in these remarkable deposits. The weathered superficial parts of the beds form good stones for burning, and when these are cleared away to a depth of a few feet, varying according to the situation, new, clean surfaces of the massive marble are reached, suitable for dressing, trimming, and decorating buildings. On the western outskirts of Westminster large and deep quarries of limestone have been opened and worked to great advantage. Here they form the flanks of prominent hills, and are accessible for twenty-five or more feet above the level of the ground. These are much cracked and jointed, and probably do not yield large slabs or long monoliths, but they are very prettily veined and variegated with black or red through the white body, and take a polish sufficiently good for out-of-door work. Some of these have been used for doorsteps in the city of Baltimore, and they have proved both acceptable and durable. But it is chiefly as a fertilizer that these are most highly prized. Vast quantities have been broken into small blocks and transported in that form to great distances, or have been calcined in the kilns near at hand and shipped in the condition of lime. It is, however, a few miles farther west that the marbles are found in their finest and richest development. In the region around Avondale and in the vicinity of New Windsor the beds of marble seem to vie with each other in putting on their most splendid dress. Several quarries of wine-red rock, exceedingly close and fine-grained, capable of a very high polish, marked with veins or wavy lines of either black or white, resting on massive layers of great extent, invite the builder to employ that which in point of beauty and fineness is one of the most admired of building stones. About three-quarters of a mile north of Avondale, and in the same beautiful valley, a quarry of the deep rich red marble has been opened and excavated below the surface of the ground. It forms a large and very compact bed, of remarkably uniform texture. Blasting the surface has shattered and cleft much of the exposed upper part, but from the general appearance and disposition of the mass it seems capable of yielding very large monoliths, and might also be worked into slabs of almost any desired size. This bed seems to be more uniform in color than most of the others. Its ground tint is of the richest wine-red, toning in a few points to almost madder purple. It takes an exceedingly fine polish, and is admirably adapted for pedestals, altar bases, mosaic pavements, and for the most elegant decorations of churches and palatial residences. Another quarry, belonging to this same belt of rock, and only a few rods distant from the former, yields a bluish-purple or mauve-purple marble of similar character and quality. It takes a surface as fine as glass, and is varied by veins and wavy lines of brown, gray, or black. Large blocks can be easily secured, and it deserves to be held in high esteem for the richness and purity of its combinations of color.

From this point to New Windsor many other beds of marble occur, chiefly of white, streaked, veined, or spotted with some tint of gray, pink, red, or purple. But a particularly marked quarry is a large one, extensively worked for lime, on the property of Mr. Chew, in the first range of hills south of New Windsor. There the strata dip at a moderately high angle, spread from three to five feet in thickness, are quite long, and run deep into the earth. The upper layers are more or less stained with red, in many devices and patterns, while the more deeply-colored blocks are largely invaded by purple, somewhat mixed with green, in zigzag and wavy combinations. These fade out into greenish tints, becoming more blackish as they descend, until the extreme reached is dark gray, variegated, waved, and dappled with black, accompanied by some white. The next very prominent quarry occurs on the farm of Mr. Myers, situated about one mile south of the former. The stone there is of the same excellent quality, takes an equally good polish, and while varying somewhat as to the proportions of red, purple, and pink, presents some wonderfully beautiful patterns of color-figures on either a light or tinted ground. These latter are somewhat noted for the red pipe-clay which passes through them in belts between the layers of marble. This is of the kind that was formerly so much prized by the Indians, and tradition points to their having resorted to these places for their supply of the unwrought material.

From New Windsor to Big Pipe Creek the beds of marble are both numerous and varied. Some of them are small, and set into the earth rather than protruded from the hillsides. But they are none the less rich in stone of fine quality, and of peculiar and curious patterns of deep colors. So little has been the demand for these in the arts of construction and decoration that they have shared the fate of the coarser limestones in being broken and burnt for fertilizers. The farms next to the boundary of Frederick County, along Big Pipe Creek, are well provided with the finer marbles of the Tennessee variety. These have commonly a mixture of reddish brown, with purple, red, and white. Two patterns closely resemble the colored Castile soap, the one having the smaller diagonal spots arranged in loops and bends, while the other has purplish waves of different shades disposed in belts and irregular streaks. Some extremely fine, pure white marbles also occur in this neighborhood, and this region shares with the adjoining parts of Frederick in these treasures which nature has deposited so bountifully for the use of its inhabitants.

The limestones are properly the coarser and softer rocks of the marble group, and often invade the ledges of the more valuable and harder beds, but in general they occupy the outward limits of the belt, more particularly on the east, and yield lime of great strength and permanence as a fertilizer. They are also much used for plaster and building, giving a good surface in plastering of rooms, and forming a tough and durable cement in the construction of brick walls.

Iron Ores.—Every natural division of the State has its peculiar types of iron ore, which are in general not to be met with in places outside. Thus the ores of the mica-slate and talcose belt of Parr's Ridge occur in quartz veins in the hard rocks. The brown hæmatites of the midland belt belong to the earthy series, and are confined, rather narrowly, to depressions in the body of the limestone valleys. The carbonates of iron of the hone series are peculiar to the clays of the tide-water belt, while the carbonates of the coal-fields are of the black band and ball type. Dozens of other kinds occur within the limits of Western Maryland, but these have not yet proved to be in sufficient quantities nor of the proper quality for commercial purposes. The midland belt possesses immense deposits of brown hæmatites and smaller aggregations of specular oxide, and of magnetic oxide. Brown hæmatites abound in Baughman's Valley, and on the west side of Parr's Ridge from the Pennsylvania line to a point five or more miles south of Westminster. This form of ore accompanies the limestone formations, and generally occurs along the margins of the valleys, near the point of contact of the former with the talcose slates. It lies bedded in the brownish or reddish clay soil overlying the limestone. It has attracted a new attention within the last few years, and in consequence the old localities have been revisited, profitable deposits have been reopened, high prices have been realized for neglected ore-banks, and a wide-spread remunerative industry has become established in this region. This widely-known and highly-prized hæmatite is of the limonite series, dark brown or blackish where oxydized, often ochreous when freshly broken, and with a chalky or earthy aspect when dried. It occurs in nodules, chunks, and masses, varying from the size of a large egg to that of a bushel measure. Pieces, and especially nodules, or shell-like lumps of about the size of a quarter-of-a-peck measure, are quite common and of great interest. These are apt to be mixed with the least portion of earthy or foreign matters, and to yield about sixty-one per cent. of pure iron. They are composed of an outer shell of brown iron ore, simple and clean, more or less rounded, and set all around inside with sharp-edged loops, with bunches of knobs, with slender, tapering, tubular stems, or with blackberry-like lumps arranged in groups. Some of these are of great beauty from the fine gloss and splendid iridescence of their rich, deep purples, blues, greens, and bronze. Frequently they are filled with a series of chambers of a cavernous pattern, coated with a film of glossy deep black. This ore is apt to be arranged in more or less spherical shells, which exhibit a circle or circles of denser minerals wherever the surface is broken across. The lumpy masses partake also more or less of this shelly character, and most of this class of ores show that their development has proceeded in somewhat concentric lines. Most of the diggings thus far pursued have been superficial, very few of them having penetrated below a depth of from thirty to forty feet. The ore is extracted from beds, seams, or pockets in the limestone, or from spaces in the talcose slates where the limestone formerly existed. These ores seem to be inseparably connected with the limestones. They were originally derived in part from them, and in some places fade into them by almost insensible degrees. Persistent search is constantly revealing new localities in which these ores occur, and wider experience is determining with increased certainty the probability of their presence in large deposits. Similar localities in Pennsylvania have displayed practically inexhaustible stores of this same class of ores, and doubtless some of the beds recently opened in the central parts of Carroll County will prove equally extensive.

A variety of this iron ore has been raised for several years past from a deep shaft opposite Avondale, on the line of the railroad. It has now penetrated to a depth of over one hundred feet, and seems to be incalculably productive. It is placed on the side of a limestone basin, directly next to a high hill of shattered talcose slate. A stream of water runs through the alluvial basin which overlies the white and variegated limestone. The ore is rather less nodular than that from the northern part of Baughman's Valley, and is somewhat lumpy and less coherent than the former. It is, however, a rich ore, and is shipped from the railroad station in large quantities. The same kind of ore has likewise been taken in large quantities from the section lying about two and a half miles west of Westminster, and also near the suburbs of that city. It contains a certain proportion of manganese, and has been worked from almost the first settlement of the region. A brown hæmatite belonging to the same group has also been found near Brighton, in Montgomery County. The samples thus far exhibited are rather extensively mixed with a gangue rock which holds pockets and seams of the ore in close embrace. It occurs in the metamorphic rocks, and has narrow wedges and layers of limestone spread through the mass. The deposits need deeper excavation in order to prove the value and extent of the metal there present.

The specular oxide (or red oxide of iron) also is found within the limits of Carroll County. The metalliferous range which courses along the east side of Parr's Ridge is the natural resting-place of this form of the metal. The heavy talcose schists near their line of contact with the older archæan rocks are charged with great seams and beds of quartz. In these the pockets and veins of this somewhat silvery-looking oxide occur in great variety and beauty. The highly-polished surface of the metal, as it branches and spreads out through the milk-white quartz, presents a very attractive appearance. Exposure to the atmosphere renders it more black and destroys the lustre of its surface. No very extensive deposits of it have thus far been reported, although it is quite widely distributed. It accompanies the copper-bearing veins at Mineral Hill, it has been broken from quartz near Sykesville, and is not infrequent in the rocks near Carrollton Post-Office and southeast of Manchester. It is a difficult and expensive ore to work, because of the hard matrix in which it is imbedded, and has yet to be found in larger masses in order to prove a profitable metal here.

The magnetic oxide of iron is a black or black-gray mineral, often quite massive, and turning to a black powder when crushed in the mill. It is one of the richest of our iron ores, and sometimes yields as much as seventy per cent. of the metal. Much of it is mixed with the oxides of titanium and of manganese, which lessen its purity and lower its value. Some varieties are highly magnetic, and hence the name magnetic is given to such as possess that property. It belongs to the copper-bearing series of rocks, is most extensively mined in the vicinity of Sykesville, and is smelted at the furnace near that place. The talcose rocks along the eastern side of Parr's Ridge form its chief resting-place, but it has been neglected or overlooked in most of the other localities in this region. It is found in masses or pockets in the metamorphic rocks, and occurs there also in the form of grains or octahedral crystals.

Copper has been mined at the Springfield, Florence, and Mineral Hill veins, and near Finksburg. It has been at various times actively carried on at all of these places, as well as at a few others in the neighborhood of Sykesville, but since the rediscovery and opening of the vast deposits at Lake Superior operations have ceased at all of these mines. Other metals, such as gold, silver, zinc, and lead, have been found in small quantities in the metalliferous belt of both Carroll and Montgomery Counties, but not as yet in profitable quantities. Gold ore has been found near Brighton, in the latter county, and a gold-mine is now being worked west of Brookville, about two miles from the Chesapeake and Ohio Canal.

Frederick County.—The Blue Ridge Belt consists of Frederick County alone. It forms a tract of country extending from the Monocacy River and Little Pipe Creek on the east to the summit line of the South Mountain range on the west. The total area is about seven hundred square miles. It is about thirty-two miles in length from north to south, by twenty-five miles from east to west. In form it is somewhat of an irregular trapezoid, with an uneven triangle taken from its eastern side next the north. The South Mountain ridge separates it from Washington County, while the Potomac River forms its southern boundary, Montgomery County touches it along the southeast, Carroll County stands next to it on the east, and Pennsylvania on the north. The Catoctin range of mountains runs through its whole length from north to south, and forms the dividing line between two great valleys of great beauty, diversity, and fertility. That on the west is the Middletown Valley, while the other on the east is the Frederick, or Monocacy Valley. The former is not a deep trough scooped down to the base of the mountains, but it is a series of intervening foot-hills, which originally constituted the minor elevations of the great group of ranges connecting the Blue Ridge with the Catoctin. At the northern extremity these swellings rise to equal altitudes with the primary ranges, and fade into them by imperceptible degrees. The effect is to build there one great mountain mass, with three principal ridges rising only a few hundreds of feet above the inner depressions, but inclosing minor valleys of enchanting beauty, and throwing off spurs at intervals of from one to three or more miles.

The valley slopes from the central part of Hauver's District, widening as it runs towards the south, and gradually expanding and lowering as it gets nearer to the swellings of the Catoctin range. It is traversed throughout two-thirds of its length by Catoctin Creek, and is plentifully watered in all parts by rapid brooks and branches originating in springs. An unlimited supply of the purest mountain water, poured from the sandstones and slates, is ever present, as well for running mills and factories as for the direct uses of man and animals. Farmers are thus enabled to place their dairies upon streams of perpetual cool water, and every home is accordingly supplied with an abundance of well-kept milk, cream, butter, and cheese. The valley is one of great loveliness, and ranges over a large tract. It is about thirty miles in length by nine miles in its greatest breadth. Beginning at the northern end, it seems to be contracted out of existence by the spurs of abrupt high ridges which press into it from the right and left. But as it is followed towards the south the hills gradually open, become round-top broad swellings, falling lower at every grade, until near the Potomac River they rise to scarcely more than one hundred feet above the alluvial lowlands.

The soils are derived from the decomposition of sandstones next the mountains, or of slates, talcose schists, quartz, and trap rocks upon the more central lines. On the north, and in a few places along the flanks of the South Mountain, decomposing epidote adds another ingredient to the soil, and contributes to its fertility. The Catoctin Creek has built for itself a path of surprising variety, with a tortuous channel cut out of the hard sandstone and slate rocks. It rises by half a dozen brooks of great activity, high up the eastern flank of the South Mountain, in Catoctin and Hauver's Districts. In the midst of untamed grand scenery, where high peaks rise to an altitude of more than two thousand feet above the level of the sea, where the great white sandstone rock-masses have been split and riven asunder with titanic violence, and the dark heavy slates have been pitched into craggy piles of threatening aspect, there the little streams come creeping out of the clefts in the rocks, and leaping, as freed spirits just escaped from prison, to the terrace below, dash against the fragments and bowlders which stand in their way, and force a deep and rugged channel, ever widening as they run. Their advance is strangely attractive. Not by one even and continuous line of water do they quietly press along, but basin by basin, as every new stage is reached, dashing with impetuous force against broken ledges, leaping over huge bowlders which have pitched from the frightful chasm above, creeping between the tangled branches of broken, fallen trees, then roaring beneath the overlapping jaws of the precipice farther down, and then bounding along still lower until the distant valley is reached. Tributary rills add their quota to these at every stage, running out of the mossy and vine-clad banks, from the midst of dense thickets of graceful shrubs and flowering bushes. Here the beech grows, with its fresh lichen-painted gray and white bark, its neighbor being the fringe-fingered spruce, clad in scaly bark of deep brown, with its companions, the birch, peeled by the tearing winds, the chestnut, oak, the maple, and the tulip-tree.

Other branches come rolling into the widening creek from between the sharp mountain spurs, bending around their rocky flanks to find a more peaceful path, and distributing nourishment to the rank undergrowth in the little valleys which they have helped to cut. The Catoctin runs over a course of more than twenty miles from its farthest source, becomes a moderately wide, rapid creek after reaching the base of Middletown Hill, and thence continues widening and baying out in the bottoms until finally it enters the Potomac River through an alluvial basin. Besides the tributaries of the Catoctin, there are two long branches, which rise, likewise, in the South Mountain ridge, flow southeast, and empty into the Potomac. The longest of these is the Little Catoctin. It is a narrow but vigorous creek, with a full body of water running swiftly between the rolling hills, and furnishing power for several flour and saw-mills. That nearer the mountain is an active little brook which runs over the bowlders in the ravines of the farms next the ridge, and comes out bright and clear along the road running through Knoxville. All of these were originally the native places of the speckled trout, that found a congenial home in the little gravelly basins and deeper trenches in the dark sandstone or slate rocks. At present the valley is mostly cleared, and belts of trees rest here and there in rocky places, where the surface is more abruptly broken, or where the soil is too full of large surface bowlders to be made readily available for tillage. The greatest proportion of the Middletown Valley is covered by large farms in a high state of cultivation. Wheat, rye, oats, Indian corn, and forage plants are raised in vast quantities, and large stores of hay, placed in stacks near immense barns, indicate the extensive provision made for the numerous horses and cattle kept by the industrious inhabitants. Large distilleries have also been settled in various parts of the valley, and the production of whisky from the abundant cereals of the region furnishes immense quantities of liquor for exportation. Grazing is also carried on to a fairly large extent, and extensive droves of beef-cattle may at all times be seen in the fields fattening for home consumption, but chiefly for transportation to Baltimore, Washington, and other markets. The greater part of the region is based upon the talcose slates. These are largely invaded by veins of quartz, some of which are of enormous thickness, and the surface of the fields in many places is so full of the fragments of this white rock as to be a great hindrance to the rapid cultivation of the soil. Decomposition of the talcose rocks and the less ready disintegration of the quartz yields a soil more or less chocolate colored, but light, porous, easy to till, and well supplied with the natural nourishment of the cereals.

Wells cut into this rock to a depth of thirty feet or more generally furnish a permanent and abundant supply of water. This is often rendered a little hard by the presence of magnesia; but the taste is sweet, and no unhealthful influences have been attributed to its permanent use for drinking.

This is not one of the limestone valleys, such as those on the other side of the ridge. It belongs to an older system of rocks, and the only limestone yet discovered within its limits is a small bed situated at the western base of the Catoctin range, on the canal, near the mouth of Catoctin Creek. Viewed from one of the more central spurs at the entrance to some of the gaps leading over the South Mountain, the valley presents a picturesque and highly-attractive scene. Instead of a monotonous trough with nearly level bed, curving at the sides directly from the mountains, a series of bold reliefs appear, varying in proportion and arrangement as one or other side of the Catoctin Creek is observed. At the upper end it forms an acute triangle, and becomes lost in the high spurs which stand in wavy lines to unite the Blue Ridge with the Catoctin. Here the forests cover the principal part of the higher ridges; wave after wave of varying green leads off the perspective, until the distant horizon blends into the universal blue of earth and sky. On the south the beautiful groups of houses composing Middletown, with its white spires standing up in the midst, rise out of the hollow and from behind the hills, like a bird ready to take its flight. Bolivar, Burkittsville, and a dozen other villages and little towns nestle between the rolls of surface, almost buried in the sea of waving grain, or only half disclosed among the belts of tall oaks and other woods which decorate the fields, while still more southward the broad opening valley spreads its wide mouth to receive the Potomac, and becomes lost to view in the spreading channel of the mighty river. North of this valley, but placed at a much higher level, the truly mountain-valleys, but of small size, find a place. The larger and nearer one of these is Harbaugh's. It is situated to the east of the extremity of the former, and is separated from it by a scalloped ridge, or series of knobs, terminating in spurs. These taper acutely on their inner ends, and thereby open a passageway for the streams and roads. It is a diagonal eroded basin, having a northeast by a southwest direction. Its base is only a few hundred feet below the summit of the general high levels of the Catoctin range. It has a length of about seven miles by a width of one mile. In crossing its lower end abrupt spurs appear on both sides. These rise in terrible majesty, loaded with heavy projecting ledges of gray, greenish, and blackish rocks, threatening to fall at any moment from the startling precipices into the road below. The mountains are heavily wooded with numerous varieties of trees, of which the chestnut and oaks predominate. Chestnut-oak is here a fine, abundant, and conspicuous tree. In the gap of Owen's Creek, leading up to this beautiful valley, some of the most romantic scenery in the county is to be found. The Catoctin Mountain is cleft in a sinuous line, broken at intervals by the downfall and erosion of sandstones and slates; huge masses of cracked and pointed rocks slant off at every angle, or form beetling cliffs of enormous size far overhead; wide, open spaces, strewn with fragments of rock and bowlders, appear at frequent intervals, in the midst of which the busy little creek comes tumbling down from the terraces above, broken into foam by striking against the ledges in its way, or pouring in cascades over the sandstones blocking its path. The limpid water of the stream shines like molten silver where the sunlight strikes it in the openings between the trees, and many a moss-covered bank projects from the terraced slopes, where the beech-trees lend their graceful branches to shade the pools in the quiet bayed-out nooks. In the wider openings a few pines lend variety to the woods, groups of hemlock offer a still stronger contrast of fringy foliage in the midst of broad-leaved trees, and the cucumber-magnolia decorates the rich spots on which vines, creepers, and ferns form luxuriant masses of fresh green.

The purity and coolness of the atmosphere in this region, combined with the moist exhalations from the tangled growths along its basins, offer most refreshing retreats from the heat and dryness of the summer temperature. A considerable part of the valley and adjoining slopes is already occupied by farms of promising fertility, and the deep alluvium of the lower levels is well watered and rich in elements most important to the growth of cereals and grasses. On the very rocky ridges the trees grow far apart in the soil which has accumulated in the cracks and cavities, and from these places the lumbermen and tanners derive ample supplies of wood and bark. Leaving this region and passing towards the east, four other small valleys, running in the same general direction, occupy the deep depressions between the spurs of the Catoctin. These are Eyler's, Hampton, and two smaller ones which stretch off for a mile or more in the direction of Pennsylvania. The two former are the larger, and are two miles or more in length by about a half-mile in width. All of them are highly picturesque, and placed in the midst of startling and romantic scenery. They occupy the old cracks in the mountain summits, where the floods and streams of past ages have widened the gaps and ground the slate, sandstone, and epidote rocks into rich alluvial soil. Accordingly, pockets of rich earth along the sides of the ridges, kept in place by ledges and fragments of rock, support copious forests of many kinds of trees, while the trough below receives the richest supply of plant food in the transported sands, clays, and humus, and responds in a vigorous outgrowth of ash, oaks, hickory, maple, tulip-trees, etc., and an endless accompaniment of bushes, plants, vines, ferns, mosses, and lichens. Leaving the valleys of the Catoctin side of the mountain mass, proceeding towards the west, and crossing the upper end of the Middletown Valley, the roads traverse the eastern flank of the Blue Ridge. Rising by steep grades the summit is reached, in the midst of farms growing abundant crops of Indian corn and well supplied with orchards of apples and other fruits. A few straggling peach-trees have attempted to develop in the corners of the fences, but at best have only been able to struggle for existence, and to yield small, unpalatable peaches of uninviting aspect. A high, broad plateau stretches out before the eye at this point, and the view is limited by the forest-covered high knobs, connected with ridges, which form the horizon. After ascending to the top and going beyond the flat cultivated lands, the side of the mountain slopes rather steeply into a lovely, well-tilled basin, known as Mount Zion Valley. The common milk-weed grows in astonishing abundance over the cleared slopes, and showers its silky, plume-like seeds all over the region reached by the drift of the winds.

A descent of about one hundred and forty feet reaches the bed of the valley, in the midst of clover-fields and fertile meadows. This depression, placed so high in the great chain of the South Mountain, is about two and a quarter miles long by three-quarters of a mile wide. The boundary line separating Frederick from Washington County passes along the eastern flank of this valley from north to south, consequently the depression is all in the latter county, although still within the limits of the Blue Ridge Belt. Several fine brooks rise in the bed of the valley, and lend a delightful moisture to the air while contributing to the fertility of the soil and stimulating a most varied growth of valuable timber-trees, such as hickory, oaks, walnuts, and maples. A deep dark soil fills the moist woods, where, in the midst of lichen-covered and fern-set bowlders, a thousand bright flowers, rustic vines and creepers adorn the varied scenery. Wild grapevines grow luxuriantly here in the rich depressions, and yield ample supplies of the native grapes. A great gorge leads out between two high abrupt spurs, traversed by an active stream of limpid water. Crossing this stream a few rods farther on, in a southern direction, the mouth of the gorge is passed and another valley, of character very similar to the last, is reached. Its bed is, however, rather more flat, and the bounding ridges are very steep.

On the eastern side of this trough, known as the Bull-Tail Valley, away up near the summit, stands the celebrated Raven Rock. It is not black in color, but derives its name from the ravens which made their homes upon it when the country was first occupied. These birds have long since changed their habitations, and have fled away from the face of man by degrees farther west, until not one seems left to represent the species among the ranges of our eastern mountains. The rock is an immense swelling of jointed white Potsdam sandstone, projecting from the flank of the abrupt mountain spur, in the midst of the thin chestnut forest. It has been rounded off by the heavy storms and rains which have driven against its faces and broken off the sharp cliffs of its upper corners. Time has softened the glaring whiteness of the rock, and gray tints have been added by the fringes of ferns and the patches of lichens which have settled in every inequality of its surface. This little valley is scarcely more than three miles long, by a half-mile wide, but it is full of romantic scenery, shady dells, immense craggy rocks of white, gray, green, and black, disposed in the wildest confusion, in the greatly varied forests or woodless gaps. Dogwood and pawpaw are common growths in the lower parts of the basin, and laurel abounds in thickets along the watered hillocks.

Coal has been dug from a bed of blackish slate in a hillside near the northern end of this valley. It served well for blacksmith's uses, and was reported to resemble anthracite in its hardness and general appearance. Unfortunately, only a single deposit has been discovered, but nowhere else than in the shaly slate, and this was only excavated in a quite small bed.

Mountains.—The mountain ranges of the Blue Ridge Belt deserve especial mention because of the important influence which they exert upon the adjacent country. Standing up as barriers to the clouds, they aid in giving direction to the masses of moisture which form areas of precipitation of rain and snow. On the western faces they rise in general quite precipitously, while on the eastern they mount by a series of gradual slopes of fairly easy ascent. Only in the most northern divisions are the roads excessively steep, and there the gaps or chasms between the spurs and knobs generally open out in a series of terraces, forming resting-places at occasional intervals. Frequently an avenue rises gently along the projecting flank of a ridge, leading up to a chasm nearer the summit, through which it passes to the next stage above. The highest summits of the South Mountain range, as it appears in this State, are met with on the western side, overlooking the Hagerstown Valley. There at the most northern extremity the well-known High Rock rises beyond Pen Mar Park to an altitude of two thousand feet above the level of the sea. The view from this peak is very extensive, and takes in a vast range of country, reaching out into the three States of Maryland, Pennsylvania, and Virginia. A charming country lies spread out before the eye from this point, including the richest regions in the great valley which crosses the three States before mentioned, and takes in to the southward the most varied and romantic parts of the Shenandoah basin. The mountain-side is here strewn with huge bowlders and fragments, the shattered remnants of colossal rocks of the Alp that once rose far above any point now reached by the loftiest pinnacle of this region. On this side of the range, also, two or three high knobs, only a few miles farther south, rise to altitudes of two thousand two hundred to two thousand three hundred feet above the level of the sea. Some of these are almost flat on top, the shattered rocks which formerly rested there having been carried away by the torrents and tempests, and the summits thereby worn off and leveled. On the outer limits of the chain short spurs and ridges have been split off from the ancient mass, and these form the outliers from which the foot-hills swell away into the broad valleys. The South Mountain range, when viewed alone, appears to form an undulating line of nearly horizontal ridges, sloping gradually for a few miles, to be successively more rounded, and then by more abrupt summits, until the whole series of swells is lost in the misty blue of the distance. It is a series of high and very narrow parallel folds, which become a single ridge on the south, and having a general width of less than a mile in that part of its course. This view is, however, somewhat deceptive, since it presents only that part of the system which rises above the beds of the high adjoining valleys. It forms what appears to be only the larger western division of a great fan-shaped synclinorium, or series of depressions, of which the Elk Ridge is the extreme western member and the Sugar-Loaf group the eastern. Both of these outer divisions are superficially detached from the great central body of upfolds, but formed of the same rocks, having continuity throughout along lines below the surface, and produced by the same set of continental forces as those which let down the valleys. The same tremendous agencies have likewise squeezed together the two great chains on the north, breaking enormous cracks and chasms along and across their course, throwing them into curving spurs running nearly east and west, forcing the underlying older rocks, such as the epidotes, porphyries, and amygdaloids, to the surface in huge ranges, and twisting the whole series of strata far out of place. At the southern end of the South Mountain the ridges rise generally to a height from eleven to thirteen hundred feet above the level of the adjoining valley, while farther north several of the more single knobs reach an altitude of nearly five hundred feet higher.

The Catoctin forms a less elevated but wider, alternately contracted and expanded ridge, sloping in general rather gently along its eastern side, and, as usual, more abrupt on the western. It is well buttressed by swelling hills along its whole length, and rises very slowly from the domes, which roll away and become lost in the valley of the Monocacy. It forms a highly picturesque body of mountains as the upper part of its course is pursued; but the lower end, near the Potomac, is rather monotonously blunt and flat, except where relieved at the Point of Rocks by the ragged black slate masses which have been torn asunder by the terrific forces that opened a way through them for the great river. The high billows of the range are succeeded at occasional intervals by sharp ridges and knobs. These rise with some irregularity from a height of about nine hundred feet above the level of the sea, until nearly half-way up the chain, at High Knob, an altitude of fifteen hundred and thirty feet is reached, while two or three outstanding knobs towards the north are reported to rise to a height of sixteen hundred to seventeen hundred feet. Probably the highest of these is Round-Top, which towers in magnificent altitude at a distance of about three and a half miles southwest of Emmittsburg. Eagle Mountain is another single spur, standing out from the great body of the range, on the right of the grand gap of Owen's Creek. On the side of the gap through which the turnpike runs from Frederick to Middletown the Catoctin becomes lowered to a level of about eight hundred and seventy feet above tide. At least seven openings between the spurs make easy entrances for the roads which cross into the Middletown Valley. These rise through comparatively easy grades, are remarkably even and well kept, and open out broadly wherever the swelling terraces of the mountain permit. Only in the most northern division, where the two ranges unite, are the roads steep and difficult, and even there they are so wide and excellent as to greatly facilitate the crossing of such sudden heights. The most conspicuous rock on the higher surfaces, and which lies broken and scattered in endless confusion, is the Potsdam, with its related sandstones. It forms enormous beds above and in the gaps, and crops out at frequent intervals in scattering crags and beetling summits. Hard, compact talcose slates, grading into aluminous sandy rocks, constitute the body of the mountain, while its central core and inner base is found to be filled up with the metamorphosed slaty porphyries, epidote, amygdaloids, and quartz. These hard, almost volcanic rocks have been so distorted and torn by the expansive power of heat that their broken and disjointed fragments are spread around in all directions, and in part may be found in masses lying all along the flank of the higher levels. At intervals of every few miles, and occasionally near the gaps, spurs and knobs stand off, as if monster sentinels to guard the approaches to the peaceful valleys below. These afford a wide view of the lowlands beyond, each having its own peculiar panorama, and no two presenting precisely similar features. At the southern extremity the Potomac basin and Sugar-Loaf Mountain bound the distance; viewed from nearer the middle of the range, the broad valley and its many villages and towns, besides the picturesque city of Frederick, form the central group, while the Linganore hills, the winding Monocacy, and Parr's Ridge fill out the picture; likewise towards the north an almost interminable collection of short ridges, hills, belts of forest, villages, and hamlets, half concealing the network of slender streams, creeps away into the red sandstone and gray slates on the horizon. The lovely valley of the Monocacy lies in full view from several of the high central prominences. In the spring and early summer it is a country full of beauty and bloom. Rich soils, more varied than can be found in any other equal area within the State, yielding abundant crops of all the cereals, fruits, and products of the farm, luxuriant meadows, and extensive dairies characterize the whole of this favored region.

In addition to these, a healthful climate, an exhilarating atmosphere, and a permanent supply of pure water in springs and streams renders the region best calculated to support a large, healthy, and thriving population. The valley is not a simple depression between two ranges of heights, but is a broad, waterworn basin, flat and rolling by turns, less elevated than its counterpart on the other side of the mountains. Swells of highlands and a few ridges push into it from the Catoctin, and high billows range along the eastern side of the Monocacy until they meet the higher uplift of the Sugar-Loaf. It constitutes an area having a width of ten to fifteen miles, and a length of about thirty miles, the lowest level being in the bed of the river, at an altitude of about two hundred and eighty feet above tide. The general average of the surface may be computed to be about four hundred feet above the sea, with a gentle downward slope from the north towards the south, and with a more decided pitch from the sides towards the middle line. This causes the drainage of the whole country to descend into the river, which in its turn empties into the Potomac. The Monocacy is the principal stream in the region. It is a small but long river, not more than a creek in the upper part of the county, but which becomes more than one hundred feet wide in the part near its mouth. It is a moderately sluggish stream in its lower divisions, but rapid and full near its sources. In the great springs near Gettysburg, Pa., are its principal heads, and from thence it bends among the rocks and hills in perpetual windings, until it finally has cut a more decided channel out of the red sandstones of Frederick County. After entering fully into that system of rocks, it spreads out in frequent alluvial basins, into which it has poured the sediments appropriated throughout its upper course. After receiving the waters of Double Pipe Creek it becomes much wider, and passes through a wide channel, bordered by thick bushes, scattered trees, and thickets of greenbrier. It receives a greater number of tributaries than any of the smaller rivers of Maryland, and thus contributes an endless supply of moisture to the whole valley through which it runs. Some of these creeks are of large size and drain wide areas of country.

The principal ones on the east are Piney, Little and Big Pipe, Israel's, Linganore, and Bennet's; and on the west Tom's, Owen's, Hunting, Fishing, Big and Little Tuscarora, Carroll's, and Ballenger's Creeks. Those of the latter division are chiefly rapid mountain streams of great beauty and clearness. Most of the northeasterly tributaries pass through the new red sandstone soils, and carry down large quantities of red sediment, which discolors their waters and stains the country through which they flow. In the northern part of the valley the red sandstone stretches across its whole width, and on the east passes over into Carroll County. But after reaching the vicinity of Frederick City it lies to the westward, becomes narrowed to a width of about two miles, and finally thins out as the Point of Rocks is approached. One of the principal factors in producing the fertility and capabilities of this charming valley is the boundless store of limestone which rests beneath so much of its surface. On the west side of the Monocacy a strip of blue, with some white limestone begins near the Potomac River (having a general breadth of two miles), and runs north by a little east several miles, crossing the Monocacy at the mouth of Israel's Creek, and tapering to a point in the vicinity of Woodsboro'. Besides this, the beautiful breccia, or calico-marble, starts at Mechanicstown, in the midst of the red sandstone, runs south for more than three miles, disappears, then reappears in a new guise southwest of Frederick City, and spreads out in a broad area reaching to the banks of the Potomac River. In this southern end of the valley it has become more silicious, includes larger fragments of coarser rocks, and is not so homogeneous in texture, and not always having the pebbles so firmly cemented together as in that from the upper end. East of the river Frederick County shares with Carroll in the beds of fine marble which pass southwest across Sam's Creek to the vicinity of Union Bridge. These form quarries of all possible dimensions, are abundantly supplied with marbles which take a fine polish, and which can be taken out in monoliths of large dimensions. Only a few of them have been opened deep and far enough to show their capabilities, but such as have had enough of the surface mass removed show bodies of generally solid, broad, and long blocks in even strata. These are often of marvelously beautiful colors and combinations of patterns. Bright reds occur almost plain, and often veined or variegated with black, brown, and white.

Salmon-colored or orange-yellow marbles also occur of similar patterns, likewise the varieties commonly known as Tennessee and Vermont marbles, and others, such as the clear black veined with white, lead color or mauve traced with black, and mottled, spotted, and waved with brown, purple, liver-color, etc. Besides these, there is a pure white statuary marble of fine grain, massive and free from grit. Near Emmittsburg a green variety, resembling verd-antique, occurs in large quantities; while in and below Mechanicstown a bewildering range of varieties of breccia, composed of deep and clear-colored fragments of purple, yellow, drab, brown, white, etc., and of all sizes, are easily obtainable. These can be selected in pieces of almost any useful size, and the supply seems to be practically inexhaustible.

For many years these choice marbles have been broken to fragments for burning in the lime-kilns. Fashion has not yet called them into her celestial train amidst the favored beauties of the decorative arts. Builders send abroad for the blocks and slabs which are to adorn palatial mansions, while these elegant objects, so cheap and easily obtained, are made to do the service of coarse limestones in supplying nourishment to the soil.

Iron, Copper, and Other Metals.—Iron ore is found in large quantities in many parts of the valley. It is chiefly some form of brown hæmatite or limonite which overlies the limestone and is imbedded in the clay or in the ochreous soil. About three miles south of Mechanicstown, near the foot of the Catoctin Mountain, the fibrous and chambered variety occurs in beds and deposits of vast extent. This has been dug and smelted for a period of more than eighty years, and still sustains a good reputation for quality and for tractability in the furnace. The crude much resembles that found in the limestone regions of Washington County. It has the same flaky layers, twisted and rolled back in every direction, and a purplish tinge to the fracture of the more solid parts. A rusty powder rests between the layers or fills the cavities of the cellular portion. It is also accompanied in the beds by nodules of phosphate of iron associated with brown ochre. In this region particularly the ore is characterized by being mixed with an appreciable amount of the carbonate of zinc, which melts when the metal is being fused, and forms a coating on the inside of the furnace. This makes an available form of the oxide of zinc, but it becomes a serious obstacle in the manufacture of the iron unless removed from the walls of the stack. The close proximity of limestone for the flux, and of large bodies of wood for the charcoal, make this deposit of ore immediately available for smelting. A similar deposit of brown hæmatite is found under almost equally propitious circumstances near the base of the same ridge of mountains, not far from the Point of Rocks. The primitive forests no longer remain, but ample supplies of the ore might still be obtained from the same set of beds. Much of this latter is of the variety known as "pipe ore," the cavities of which are more or less occupied by the earthy phosphate of iron. A very compact and rich brown hæmatite is found in quantities near the Monocacy, about four miles northeast of Frederick City. It has a more metallic aspect than those previously mentioned, is very heavy and dense, and often incloses small crystals of opaque white quartz.

Specular oxide of iron also occurs east of the Monocacy River, in the metalliferous belt passing through the country from Middleburg, in Carroll County, to New Market. Very rich specimens of this beautiful ore have been extracted from pockets in the talcose slates in the neighborhood of Liberty and New London. These have not yet, however, been fully opened, nor sufficiently laid bare to determine the amount of ore possibly present. The absence of large tracts of woodland from this section seems to prevent iron manufacturers from erecting furnaces on the spot, and a lack of active local interest hinders the developing of the mines, and so no attempt is made to transport the ore to localities favorable for smelting. A similar specular oxide has likewise been found along the summit of the Catoctin ridge. These ores are rich in iron, and would form important additions to the resources of the county if they were shown to be present in large quantities. The magnetic oxides of iron have also been found in the copper-bearing belt which passes to the south of New Market. These also occur in pockets or masses in the talcose and slaty rocks, and in the joints of the limestone. Some of the varieties are very rich in metal, and might prove very profitable if discovered in large quantities. Copper is very widely distributed through the quartz and next the limestone beds in the talcose slates and new red sandstone formations east of the Monocacy and south of Little Pipe Creek. It sometimes accompanies the magnetic oxide of iron which enters with steatite into the masses of mica-slate. The silicates and carbonates of copper are found near Middleburg, New London, Liberty, etc., and between the two branches of Pipe Creek. But the most promising region for this metal is that drained by the Linganore Creek. The principal rock there is the talcose slate, embracing numerous detached beds and ledges of limestone set into the strata. The latter are always associated with the ore, and wherever they are found stains of copper appear on their surface or in the cracks. Good ore generally has a position between these two kinds of rocks, but is commonly most abundant near the outer limits of the limestone. Rich ores have been extracted from the Dolohyde mine, near Liberty, and at other points in this vicinity, also near New London, in the same formation. The oldest of these workings was begun as early as the time of the Revolution, and has been continued at intervals ever since. A lack of minute information with regard to the relations and form of the masses or pockets has proved an obstacle in the successful development of these mines. New and particular experiences with this class of deposits will alone determine how far these formations will prove profitable, and to what extent the metal can be worked. Copper exists also in the older rocks of the Catoctin summit. Pieces of the native ore have been picked up in Harbaugh's Valley, one of which weighed fourteen pounds. It is not to the native metal, however, that attention need be called, since it is quite improbable that deposits of it can be found in the class of rocks prevailing in this part of the country. More reliance may be placed upon the indications of sulphurets and carbonates of copper, which here may prove to be stored away in the central division of the mountain chain.

Sulphuret of lead, or galena, has been detected in the limestone region near Unionville; but only small pieces have thus far been secured. It occurs, also, in the Dolohyde copper-mine in small quantities. Oxide of zinc is found associated with the brown hæmatites of the Catoctin region, and it is obtained in large quantities as a furnace product from the Catoctin Iron-Works.

Gold and silver have been detected as minute particles in some of the older slates and metamorphic rocks, both of the metalliferous belt and mountain range. The structure of these regions, however, renders it very unlikely that either of these metals will be found there in profitable amounts.

Roofing slates of good quality are present in several localities within the talcose schist region on the eastern side of the county. Among the Linganore hills several quarries of chiefly local interest have been opened, but near Ijamsville, directly on the line of the Baltimore and Ohio Railroad, large beds of even texture and dark-blue color have been worked for many years. These produce excellent thin plates of good quality, which improve in size and firmness as the beds are worked to greater depths. Slates of an entirely different character occur both in the Catoctin and Blue Ridge Mountains, next the roads leading towards Hagerstown. These are tough and very strong, easily and naturally split into slabs of four inches or more in thickness, may be obtained in pieces of the largest size, and are of a nature particularly well fitted for pavements, caps of walls, sills, and for the outside of buildings generally.

A remarkable feature of the county, and one of its most curious monuments, appears in its southeastern corner, near the Monocacy River. At that point representative rocks of three great geological periods centre, and a great fold of the surface has built an isolated group of mountains. These are merely the lateral outliers of the great upthrust produced by the contracting force which raised the Catoctin and Blue Ridge. But here it has assumed a mere local elevation, and constitutes a triple-crested mountain, with a short ridge flanking it on the west. The summit called distinctively Sugar-Loaf is the most southwesterly, the intermediate one is called Round Top, and that at the other end, or northeasterly, is Mount Airy. About three-quarters of a mile to the west stands the nearly straight hog-back called Green Ridge, while beyond its northern end may be seen three minor single knobs of much less altitude. This section forms the place of junction of the primordial series with the new red sandstone and rocks of the Azoic formation, the former being represented by the Potsdam sandstone, constituting the uppermost layers of rocks and overlapping the talcose slates, while the brown sandstone fills the intervening valley, and conceals the ends of the great layers of white sandstone. The grand Sugar-Loaf rises in magnificent prominence to a height of thirteen hundred and seventy feet above the level of the sea, and gives a commanding view of all the country lying east and south to nearly as far as Washington. It is most appropriately named Sugar-Loaf, since it is built from base to summit of the plain white sandstone, which glistens with crystalline brightness in the sunshine.

The white rock is set together in vast walls of immense thickness, forming a curved front bristling with crags and rugged buttresses, like the torn flank of a huge fortress. On top great piles of the rock stand detached from the main mass, and project in frightful crags over the abyss beneath. In spite of the solid masonry which forms the whole body of the peak, it is covered everywhere, even upon the summit, with a growth of trees, which in the distance lends a rich contrast to the white rocks and spots of brown soil. Green Ridge is likewise well named, for it is a verdant billow, standing with refreshing brightness in bold relief beside the dark soils and light stream of the Monocacy. On the southwest side of the group colored sandstones and silicious conglomerates form large beds, and offer beautiful building-stones, which would make superb substitutes for the much-used Scotch granites.

Fauna and Flora.—Great diversity obtains in the natural productions of the Blue Ridge Belt. Everywhere it has at some time supported a varied population of great beasts, of the smaller animals and birds, and of the unnumbered host of creeping things, while a rich and abundant representation of the floral tribes has added grace and beauty to the picturesque landscape. The great American elephant at one time roamed over the fertile valleys, while the elk, caribou, and red deer grazed in the open areas of the forests. Besides those, the bear, panther, wild-cat, gray wolf, two kinds of foxes, raccoon, opossum, ground-hog, and most of the small animals now common to the eastern side of the United States found a home in one or the other parts of this varied region. The beaver especially was formerly abundant here, and built dams across the creeks and river. Unhappily, with the increase of population new demands for cleared lands drove away many of the interesting animals, such as the beaver and elk, and the cupidity of thoughtless men caused the extermination of all the animals most valued in the chase. Of the birds, a vast assemblage once tenanted the lands where now only a few scores can be met with in the longest trip. The wild pigeon still returns in diminished numbers to the vicinity of its former "roosts," but the great birds have chiefly been destroyed, together with the raven, the Carolina parrot, the large white heron, the fish-hawk, and a large company of the sweet warblers and bright-feathered songsters of smaller size, but of inestimable value and gratification. Butterflies and brilliant insects abound, the injurious as well as the useful. But the removal of the forests has opened the way for a thousand crawling enemies to agriculture, while the thoughtless impulses of the population have destroyed numerous species useful and ornamental.

Flora has been lavish in the beauty and variety of her gifts, but the loose rich humus resting in the shadows of the heavy old forest has been swept away, and with it the primitive fairies which charmed the senses on the mountain-side and in the open valley. In their stead, however, still remain a remnant of the azaleas, magnolias, kalmias, orchids, asters, and sunflowers, in company with the blossoming thorns, viburnums, spiræas, dogwoods, and other showy bushes. Judicious planting of trees year by year will bring back some of these lost beauties, but will do even more in retaining and supporting the moisture so much needed to keep the little streams, and through them the creeks, in their former more active condition as sewers of the country.

Coal.—Indications of the presence of coal have been met with in various parts of the new red sandstone formation in the valley of the Monocacy. But the chief localities which have given promise of deposits of this important fuel have been in the ridge of hills at the foot of the Catoctin Mountain, sometimes described as the red hills. This is at the head-waters of the Tuscarora Creek, runs off in a southeast direction, and constitutes the Chapel Ridge. It is formed chiefly of the breccia, or calico-marble, associated with shale of the reddish-brown sandstone, penetrated more or less by broken blocks of the blackish hornblendic trap. The region extends to near the Point of Rocks, where it blends with the talcose slates and becomes lost. Specimens of anthracite coal have been exhibited which were reported to have been taken from some outcrops of blackish shale in these hills. Great doubt has, however, been thrown upon the authenticity of these deposits by the attempts of unscrupulous persons to pass off unquestionable specimens of foreign coal as the products of this section. Carbonaceous shales do undoubtedly occur at the Yellow Springs, six miles northwest of Frederick City, between the branches of Big and Little Tuscarora Creek, but these do not belong to the true coal-bearing series of rocks. The breccia and blue limestone, associated with micaceous sandstone, inclose a bituminous shale, which is charged with impressions and remains of carbonized plants, including thin seams of apparently real anthracite coal. This shale sometimes outcrops at the surface of the ground, and elsewhere seems to be enveloped by the limestone and micaceous sandstone. The ledges of breccia form extensive outcrops on the more elevated places, and inclose a band of blue bituminous limestone. The general direction of this formation concurs with that of the adjoining mountain, and the strata dip in a northerly direction at an inclination of about forty-five degrees. It has been traced throughout a length of three miles, and proved to have a width of about one mile. Excavations have been made in it to a depth of twenty feet, and the adjoining gray sandstone has been penetrated about forty feet. Horizontal drifts have been run through various distances to the belts of coal, but the thickest reached has not exceeded two inches. Fuel of such a nature being so very valuable in the vicinity of a large city might naturally attract the attention of capitalists, but a very thorough examination has shown that these beds do not belong to the carboniferous, or true coal formation, and that accordingly no large important deposits of this mineral need be expected in this region. The specimens examined from other parts of the new red sandstone belt have been fragments of calamites or other plants, having the black color and somewhat the appearance of coal, but possessing none of its most valuable properties.

Washington County, and the Great Valley.—This county is proportionally the longest and narrowest in the State. It extends from the summit line of the South Mountain chain to the western base of Sideling Hill; the creek of that name separating it from Allegany County. It stretches from east to west over a distance of forty-four miles, and its greatest length from north to south is about twenty-eight miles. Pennsylvania bounds it on the north, and the Potomac River separates it from Virginia on the south. Its general outline suggests the shape of a boot, the heel being at the bend of the South Mountain near its northern extremity, the toe at the Potomac River next to Elk Ridge, and the top of the leg at Sideling Hill. The entire area of the county is about four hundred and sixty-three square miles, of which more than three-fourths are included in the Hagerstown Valley. At Hancock the county is contracted to a width of about one mile and a quarter by the great bend in the Potomac River.

The county may be properly divided into two natural sections, of which the smaller and most western belongs to the Appalachian Belt, while the eastern and larger, forming one of the grand divisions closely connected with the Blue Ridge Belt, is the Great Valley.

The Great Valley.—This great feature of the central mountain system forms the most important part of the territory of Washington County. It is a broad depression lying between the South Mountain range on the east and the North Mountain on the west. Its breadth between these two ridges is from twenty to twenty-three miles, while its length from north to south is about twenty-eight miles. That part of it within these limits is known as the Hagerstown, or Antietam Valley. No natural boundary separates this from its northern extension, called the Cumberland Valley, in Pennsylvania, but on the south it is detached from the Shenandoah Valley by the basin of the Potomac River. No depression of the surface of equal magnitude, beauty, and fertility exists on the eastern side of the United States. It forms also the principal valley within the State of Maryland, and yields to none in productiveness of the soil and in the grandeur and variety of its scenery. It is not a simple trough circumscribed by two great elevations of surface, but minor waves of uplift traverse it in various parts, running mainly from north to south. Nor is it a single hydrographic basin, for the Antietam River runs through its principal depression on the east, and the Conococheague River drains the section on the west. On the northern end the eastern division is set with high swells of surface, some of which rise into spurs running parallel to the main body of the South Mountain. The general level of the valley is probably somewhat more than five hundred feet above the level of the sea, and in the more northern parts rises to about seven hundred feet, while its southern extremity, near the Potomac River, slopes down to about two hundred and seventy-five feet.

On the west the Conococheague River winds in great loops through a somewhat less elevated basin, but where the country rises into an abrupt ridge along the belts of slate rocks. Almost the whole valley is spread with large farms of unsurpassed fertility. Being so generally underlaid by limestone, the soil is particularly well adapted to raising cereals and grasses, and accordingly it produces the largest crops of wheat and other grain to be met with in the State.

The limestone is chiefly of the strong, compact, dark-blue variety, invaded by seams and veins of white; but in certain sections, as between Sharpsburg and Boonsborough, drab, yellowish-red, pale blue, and white occur in large beds. Many of the varieties from this section are very fine and massive, they take a fine polish, and can be taken out in monoliths of almost any required dimension. Between Keedysville and Boonsboro' a very hard, dense, bluish, wavy limestone forms a belt about five hundred feet wide, running from northwest towards the southeast, which may be removed in large slabs, and is highly esteemed for pavements and for buildings. It is called knuttle, is easily wrought, and proves to be an attractive and most enduring building-rock. In the neighborhood of Keedysville many varieties of stone suitable for industrial purposes are quarried. About one-half mile south of this place a species of fine-grained calcareous rock, white or yellowish in color, marked with wavy lines and zigzag streaks of brown or black, is extensively quarried, sawed into blocks, and dressed. It is a most novel variety, is easily worked, takes a good surface, and may be taken out in thick slabs of immense size. The ledges, angular hills, and masses of limestone rock, particularly in this part of the valley, are so striking as to arrest the attention, and give a highly picturesque effect to the landscape. A white, coarse-grained, distinctly crystalline limestone also occurs in this vicinity. It is really a hard marble, and is said to take a good polish. South of Boonsboro' a fine variety of this white marble abounds, which is remarkably free from impurities and foreign elements. It equals the Tuscan statuary marble in purity of color and evenness of texture, while it takes a fine polish, and readily admits the chisel of the sculptor. As these latter rocks have not yet been sufficiently developed, it will be necessary to penetrate deeper into their mass to reach the large blocks best adapted for fine monuments and sculpture. The auroral blue limestone, which forms the underlying bed of nearly the whole valley, the chief exceptions being the slates of the Conococheague belt and of the base of the Elk Ridge and South Mountain, belongs to the most extensive formation of this rock in North America.

Caves and Caverns.—A great variety of curious cavities occurs in this limestone, which lines the basin of the Great Valley. This is of the same kind of rock as that in which the Mammoth Cave, the Luray caverns, and all the celebrated caves of the Eastern United States occur. No correct idea can yet be formed of the number and extent of the cavernous spaces which lie concealed in the almost fathomless rock which underlies this valley. Sink-holes and openings in the surface of many farms, and particularly in the neighborhood of Williamsport and Hagerstown, attest the presence of a former deep underground drainage; and even now small streams of water are said to disappear beneath the surface and become lost to further observation. In the vicinity of Keedysville the yellowish calcareous rocks are cavernous, and cavities of a few feet in diameter are frequently discovered. These have usually been excavated by currents of spring and rain-water, carrying a certain amount of carbonic or other acids in solution, and softening and transporting the materials of the rock into which they find an entrance.

The most considerable and well-known caves at present accessible in this valley are those at Cavetown, on the Western Maryland Railroad, about seven miles east of Hagerstown. They are situated in a ridge, along the flank of which the railroad runs, the summit of which rises more than eighty feet above the track. The limestone composing the hill is of two kinds. The upper, or sandy strata, called "rocklime" by the quarrymen, mixed with silicious and other impurities, is from five to fifteen feet in thickness; the lower and bed-rock of the country is the well-known blackish-blue compact limestone, so rich in lime, which is the most highly-prized fertilizer to be found in Washington County.

The entrance to the larger, or Bishop's, cave is a hole formed by the falling in of the wall of rock, leaving an aperture ninety-two feet wide and eight feet high. It is entered at a point about twenty-five feet above the level of the railroad, and is nearly one hundred feet west of Cavetown Station. A great deal of débris has fallen into the mouth of the cave, occupying an area of at least one hundred feet wide by thirty feet long and thirty deep. The first cavern entered forms a large hall, fairly well illuminated by daylight, sloping inward about twenty feet to a nearly level floor. It is almost circular, has a diameter from north to south of two hundred feet, a length of two hundred feet from east to west, and a height varying from thirty-five to forty-five feet. Formerly the walls, ceiling, and floor were studded with an endless variety of stalactites and stalagmites of almost every pattern and peculiarity. Unfortunately, the easy access to this cave made it ever open to the vandalism of curiosity-seekers, and accordingly it has been rifled of all the smaller-sized specimens which once belonged to it. Possibly by the planting of trees upon the hill, and by the consequent return of dripping moisture, it may be once more restored to its pristine beauty and splendor. Fortunately, two objects of interest still remain. The principal one of these is in the southwest corner of this first hall. It consists of a series of Venus' baths, arranged in terraces, rising to a height of about twenty-five feet next the wall, and covering an area of more than nine hundred square feet. The larger basins composing the group are placed above and behind; they are in the form of oval rosettes, with a raised rim about one foot high forming the borders, and the cavities in them about six to nine inches deep, filled with limpid water. The smaller ones gradually extend forward from these at lower levels, and become shallower as they advance stage by stage.

They are also scalloped, and taken together form a piece of fountain-work only excelled by the great basins of similar shape which adorn the valley of the Yellowstone, in the United States National Park. In this cave, however, these baths have been made by the deposit of layers and rims of calcareous matter, while in the latter the material deposited is partly silicious. This group of basins is now badly disfigured by dirt and mud-stains, which hide its chief beauties, but it is capable of being made as clear and pure as it was originally. The other object is a large stalagmite, cylindrical, somewhat tapering, standing erect, and being about six feet in diameter and ten feet in height. It stands on the right, beyond the middle of the hall, a solitary column, the sad and silent witness of the ravages of the past. Going to the end of this first chamber, a hole is reached, about four by seven feet in diameter, leading into an uneven cavern, varying in width from ten to forty feet, with a rising floor, the summit of which contracts the cavity at a point two hundred feet from its entrance, and forms a narrow passage with a downward slope into the next room beyond. The floor of this third cavern is somewhat scooped out, but has a general downward slope towards the rear or western end. The roof at this point descends, slopes nearly concurrently with the floor, and thus produces a narrower passage, which leads down to a cavern with a low ceiling. This latter is situated about three hundred and twenty-one feet from the mouth of the cave, and is mostly occupied by a pond of clear and motionless water.

Apparently this water occupies the whole basin of this inner chamber; it has no visible outlet, and the rocks of the ceiling descend to within a very few feet of its surface. Its bed slopes downward very rapidly at an angle of scarcely less than 45°, so that it appears to be very deep at only a few feet from its first accessible margin. The temperature of the water was 55°, while that of the air in the first hall was 59°, and that outside of the cave 84°. In the second chamber, and on its north side, is a hole leading to a cavern a few feet distant, which runs parallel to the large cave. This is a long, narrow chamber, which descends and terminates at each end, like the bag of a purse. It is one hundred and fifty feet long, about thirty feet high, and from ten to fifteen feet wide. Here, as in the larger one, the walls and floor have been denuded of all their objects of interest, and now only the stumps and vestiges of stalactites and stalagmites remain to indicate their former presence.

Close by this scene of wreck and ruin one almost unmolested cavern still remains to attest the beauties of these wonders of nature. It is entered from above at a point above three hundred and fifty feet south of Bishop's Cave, and is entirely disconnected from the latter. The opening into it has been artificially enlarged, and a series of steps broken into the limestone to render the descent into it less difficult. Upon entering, it is seen to be an enlarged horizontal crack in the rock, about two hundred and forty feet in length, but contracting so rapidly at intervals that a person can hardly squeeze through into the open spaces beyond.

Although small, it is a perfect gallery of splendid objects. In every direction the eye rests on beautiful and bright forms of crystalline groups, which only require adequate illumination to bring them out in indescribable brilliance. This gem-studded chamber might well be styled the Crystal Grotto, for it is literally a cabinet of crystals of almost endless variety and great expressiveness.

The fauna and flora of the caves are very limited. In the first chamber of Bishop's Cave the common striped squirrel, *Tamias striatus*, runs about in the area reached by the light, and here, too, may be found a few of the insects which belong to the limestone region outside. But in the dark chambers the hoary bat, *Lasiurus cinereas*, is the only animal occupant; while in the damp humus a few insects of the *Thysanuran*, or springtail group are found in the vicinity of a meagre growth of minute lichens. No living objects have yet been found in the waters of these caverns, and they appear to be destitute of the wingless crickets and various blind insects which occur in the Mammoth and other caves.

Water-courses.—The valley is well supplied with brooks and rivulets running from springs or bursting from fountains in the rocky hillsides. The latter are remarkable for the large and strong volume of water formed so near their sources. To this circumstance the inhabitants are indebted for the superior water-powers which drive their mills so near the heads of the streams. As the porous nature of parts of the limestone rocks forming the hills allows the formation of large cavities, the underground drainage is caught and stored in places above the general level of the region, and these pour a perpetual outflow through the avenues worn along the old cracks, until an outlet is reached in some ravine or depression at the point of least resistance.

The Antietam River, which rises in Pennsylvania, near Gettysburg, has its source in one of these vigorous outbursts from the side of a hill. At all seasons of the year, and in times of drought as well as during the periods of rain, this class of streams supplies the same abundance of limpid water, while similar sources which simply swell up from the ground are sensitive to prolonged changes of weather, and either fail or flush, in conformity with prevailing physical conditions. The former are evidently supplied in large measure from the nearer mountains, and form a portion of the surplus of the permanent underground water-system. This supply is not derived chiefly from the rainfall, although it may be increased beyond the average measure by additions from such sources. But, as the water comes from distant localities, and from considerable heights, it is found to rise high above its external source, and to be steady in its supply. "The Cold Spring, in the immediate vicinity of Hagerstown, possesses in these respects sufficient interest to deserve the attention of tourists. It pours forth a large steady volume of cold, clear water, sufficient to supply the needs of a large bathing resort, and it is noted for its purity and mineral strength. When exposed to the influence of the sun, the excess of carbonic acid which it contains, and which renders it a solvent of the limestone rocks, escapes, and an efflorescence of neutral carbonate of lime is precipitated along its course. It is probable that formerly these streams were still more abundant than at present, for on both sides of their actual course there are broad and deep deposits of this calcareous sediment. Moreover, in consequence of the copiousness and temperature of the streams of this kind, they never freeze; and the Antietam, which is supplied in this way at every stage of its progress through the country, furnishes a very large amount of never-failing water-power."[1] The tributaries of this river which belong to Washington County rise chiefly between the outlying spurs of South Mountain, the few branches that rise on the west side being only two or three of quite small size, and of little importance. On the northeast, however, a large tributary, proceeding from the mountain chain by several branches, passes through the Fourteenth and Ninth Districts, and makes a fork with the main branch of the river below Leitersburg. Next, and most important of them all, the rapid, romantic Beaver Creek rushes from the mountains through more than a dozen channels, drains a tract of country thirteen miles long, and carries a large stream of water into the river at a point three miles north of Keedysville. The only other tributary of much importance is the interesting, but short, Little Antietam. It rises in several sources from the limestone hills northeast of Rohrersville, bends around to the northwest, and passing Keedysville through a wide, stony channel, glides into the greater Antietam. Probably the most romantic stream in the valley is Israel's Creek. It rises in the ridges adjacent to Rohrersville, pursues its way south between high ledges of broken rocks, over rapids and miniature cascades, and finally rushes down the embankment beneath the canal to enter the Potomac River. The next large water-system has its outlet through the Conococheague River. It is not so broad and extensive as the Antietam; much of its course lies in Franklin County, Pa., and it rises in that region. That part of it in Washington County is broad, rapid, intensely winding, and full of sediment in its lower course. It follows in part the division between the limestone and the slate; but in its upper division it is not confined to either, and is deflected out of a direct course by the hard layers in the limestones with which it comes in contact on its way towards the south. Abundantly supplied by short branches from both sides, at intervals of every two or three miles it is reinforced by new volumes of water, and after passing through the town of Williamsport it empties into the Potomac River. The Little Conococheague is a small, long creek, which rises in a gap of the North Mountain, receives another branch from the region of Clear Spring, flows south, and also empties into the Potomac. It runs through a picturesque region, in a basin of its own construction, at an average distance of about three miles from the base of the mountain ridge, and receives several small tributaries at its headwaters near the Pennsylvania line.

Williamsport is situated in the vicinity of a rich agricultural region, where the limestone soils spread out widely, where also the fertile bottom-lands of the old bed of the Potomac stretch along the canal; but also next the slate ridge, where the surface soils are thin and of less agricultural value. Timber of large size and superior quality formerly covered the greater part of the ridges and bottoms in this section; but it has been greatly thinned out within a quite recent period, and is now replaced in part only by second-growth trees of less value than their predecessors. An important production of this region is the massive black slate, which abounds at a distance of about five miles below the town. It is compact, strong, of fine texture, breaks into even slabs, and takes a high polish. The choice limestone rocks of this vicinity share the characteristics of some of those found on the eastern side of the valley. They are white, or of some tone of drab or yellow, appear fine-grained, take a good polish, and are accessible in fairly large slabs. The principal rock, however, is the blue limestone, which rests in immense beds of unmeasured depth, and shows evidences of being extensively cavernous. No large caves have yet been actually discovered there, but the numerous sink-holes which exist in the farms extend to unknown depths, and indicate a connection with an extensive system of underground cavities, at present apparently too dangerous for exploration. One of these larger sink-holes, at the base of South Mountain, near Cavetown, is remarkable for not being connected with any visible outlet beneath, and accordingly for being always nearly full of water. It consists of a circular, funnel-shaped cavity in the limestone, about one hundred feet in diameter, of unknown depth, filled with clear water, which keeps an almost uniform level regardless of the variations in the seasons.

The central parts of the valley are rolling, and the folds of surface rise higher on both sides until the mountain regions are reached. At the southeastern extremity Elk Ridge rises in majesty, and forms the western boundary of the narrow but charming little basin known as Pleasant Valley. It is an old crack between the two mountain uplifts, which has been eroded and scooped out until it slopes down into a depression somewhat lower than the Great Valley, of

---

[1] J. Ducatel, Geol. Report, 1840.

which it is but a minor outlet. On the east the South Mountain builds its boundary wall of the flinty sandstone, chert, and slate, while on the west Elk Ridge piles its huge walls of white sandstone in a ridge seven miles long, and then bends in a few rods to contract the upper end of this romantic little inclosure. Along these high walls of jointed rock beetling cliffs stand out in threatening attitudes, while the mountain base is buttressed by masses of heavy masonry. In the valley great bodies of dark slates and cherty limestones raise their heads in startling attitudes; the surface is strewn with fragments of rock which once fitted into the cliffs beyond; the stream threads its way with audible murmur among the sharp-cornered slates and sandstones, and the bowlders are overhung by the branches of graceful shrubs and trailing creepers. It is a fruitful corner, set in the peaceful solitude of the mountain embrace. Daily the mist curtain of early morn rests over it; the dark shadows of growing daylight deepen as the mountain walls are brought into sharp relief; and later every rock, spur, and cliff is lighted into glorious splendor by the glowing flashes of the midday sun. Lovely vistas delight the eye, both in the valley and on the mountain-top. Towards the north the frowning brows of the precipitous ridge project in severe contrast to the open expanse of the widening valley, which stretches off in endless variety of reliefs until lost in the dim blue of the distant horizon. While away off southwards the opening gap guides the eye out to the basin of the broad Potomac, then up the winding gorge of the opposite mountains, until the scene glides into the swelling waves of the hills beyond and is lost in the dark borders of the far-reaching forests. On the west the imposing summit is crowned by Maryland Heights; here in the midst of crags and rugged sandstone masses the eye takes in long miles of charming perspective on the channel of the shining river, and over roll after roll of mountain and hill, resting in peaceful sublimity and beauty, until distance levels all into one universal tender gray.

The minerals of the valley are of but few kinds. No copper, gold, or silver need be expected in profitable amounts, but iron ore of the brown hæmatite variety abounds near the Potomac River, about two miles west of Sandy Hook. It is of the species called pipe ore, or sometimes limestone ore, and yields metal of excellent quality, well adapted to the manufacture of bar-iron.

The animals of the county are essentially those of the Blue Ridge Belt. The elephant, elk, caribou, and beaver were formerly residents of the valleys and uplands, but they have long since disappeared. Among the vegetable productions, the cucumber magnolia and rhododendron are conspicuous, while the golden lilies, asters, sunflowers, and the generally known flowers and flowering shrubs of the eastern slope of the continent are well represented. The usual trees of the same region belong here, while on the higher and more exposed mountain summits the spruces and pines of a more northern climate begin to appear.

Appalachian Region.—This great belt of country extends from the summit of the North Mountain chain to the western extremity of the State. It includes the western end of Washington County and the whole of Allegany and Garrett Counties. It stretches from east to west in a direct line over a distance of eighty-five miles, and its greatest breadth from north to south is on its western boundary, and is about thirty-six miles; while on the east it is about eight miles in Allegany, and narrows to one and a quarter miles in the western part of Washington County. No less than fifteen mountain ranges cross this long strip of country, and those in the western division form the highest lands in Maryland. The lowest levels appear next the basin of the Potomac River at Cumberland, where they grade down to a point scarcely five hundred feet above the sea. The highest altitude attained is on the summit of the Great Savage Mountain at Altamont, which rises to an elevation of more than two thousand seven hundred feet above high tide. West of Sideling Hill until the city of Cumberland is passed the mountain ridges are all broken into spurs or backbones of variable length. They have been generally compressed with great force, and are consequently high, narrow, and abruptly elevated. The surface between them forms elevated valleys of moderate simplicity, broken only by slight swells, and traversed by water-courses which have cut their way through winding ravines in deep channels, often encumbered by broken masses of slate and sandstone. Every valley is supplied with its stream of water, usually rapid and pure, running from the north over a rocky bed, increased by several small tributaries near its source, and emptying into the Potomac River. Some of these have cut their way through gorges in the spurs, in the midst of great rocky ledges, overhung by heavy cliffs, overgrown with bushes, ferns, and trailing vines. Near their sources they tumble in wild confusion over the remnants of shattered rocks, in torrents and cascades, and run through wild spots of indescribable attractiveness.

The beginning of the Appalachian region forms the small western division of Washington County.

After crossing the Hagerstown Valley and proceeding towards the west, up the side of the North Mountain, a point is reached on the summit near Fair View, at an altitude of sixteen hundred feet above the level of the sea. Here the eye may roam almost unobstructed from the region of sunrise to where the sun sinks below the western horizon. Viewed during the early morn, the mist is seen hovering over valleys and hiding in the water-courses; a few purple and orange clouds streak the sky beyond the mountains, and the green foliage of the nearer forests seems moistened by a bath of dew; but as the sun lifts his golden face above the edge of the higher uplands, the smoky fleece rises from the streaks of water, the mountains unveil, and the foliage glistens as if studded with countless gems. On the west, in the nearer valley, the narrow chasm of Licking Creek lies beneath the eye; across the broad, high valley, raised into swells and low ridges, the town of Hancock now crops out on the rounded hillsides and then settles down into the adjacent ravine; as the view is lifted a stage higher the heavy back of Tonoloway Mountain, flanked by Round Top beside the canal, arises; and then still higher, behind them all, the great lofty backbone of Sideling Hill ridge sets up a forest-fringed barrier, beyond which the vision cannot penetrate. A few miles to the left the placid bosom of the Potomac River gleams like molten silver in the clear light, while along its margins the tall, spreading sycamores and branching maples join with the dark oaks and glossy-leaved gum-trees in tracing their images down into the limpid water. In the neighborhood of Hancock broken rocks, and occasionally bowlders of white sandstone, lie scattered over the flanks of the hills or rest in piles along the beds of the ravines. Ridges of brown, gray, and olive sandstones and slates project with massive front from places where the torrents of by-gone periods have torn their channels, while on the precipitous sides of the ridges, and from the walls of the frequent gaps, pale cliffs stand out with forbidding sharpness, or threaten to fall from the overhanging heights.

On the Virginia side of the Potomac the country is very rugged, and broken by frequent low ridges of the shattered sandstones and slates; but it is wonderfully picturesque, and the hills are covered by forests and verdure as far as the eye can reach. Frequent shallows in the river open good fords, which form the principal avenues of travel across the country. The absence of bridges, which appears a serious obstacle to the progress of the stranger, is apparently but little felt by the inhabitants of the region. At most times the stream seems to be only moderately rapid, and not at all too swift to be crossed by horses and cattle; but when heavy rains fall on the mountains beyond, it becomes a roaring flood which carries everything before it. Three miles west of Hancock the remarkable knob called Round Top stands at the southeastern angle of Tonoloway Ridge. It rises on that side somewhat in the form of a rounded cone, but from heights in the rear it is seen to be a short backbone extending back in a gradual slope for more than a mile. This detached dome is notable for the singular manner in which its rocky mass has been folded, and for the superior cement limestone that it contains. Here the heavy limestone and sandstone layers forming the rocky skeleton of this huge dome have been bent back and up three times in the lower half of the mass. The result has been to force the cement layers into closely compressed loops, doubling and increasing its thickness accordingly. At the same time the eastern side of the beds has received a diagonal twist, which has thrust them off in a projecting keel at nearly right angles to the rest, and opened a seam along that line.

These cement limestones are mainly of a bluish or drab color, interstratified with other limestones, and with drab and olive sandstones and slates. The cement rock is now excavated from nearly horizontal drifts or tunnels, ranging from eight to twelve feet in height, and fully as much in width, one of which has been pursued quite through the end of the mountain. A part of the great thickness of these layers is owing to a double fold of the thickest portion of the rock being brought in close contact with a second and shorter one. The rock is closely bent together, and fully exposed in at least six outcrops within a distance of scarcely more than six hundred feet along the canal. It appears to be present in practically inexhaustible quantities. The hydraulic cement is calcined, ground, and prepared in a large mill, situated on the spot, and is sent from thence by canal and railroad to all parts of the country. It has a high reputation with United States engineers and master-builders in various part of the country, who have used it extensively in the construction of large buildings for the government, and for various public works, besides those of the aqueducts, locks, and walls of the Chesapeake and Ohio Canal. Nearly half-way up the steep front of this mountain there is a thick layer of calcareous spar of great purity. It is chiefly ribbed with parallel series of narrow, columnar crystals, remarkable for their length. Above this stratum of spar, a nearly square hole leads into a cavern hollowed out of the upfolded limestone by the tremendous forces which have crushed the mountain and split wide open the beds of stone. This cave has never been adequately explored. It is reported to have been the abode of a family of black bears, which were traced into it and finally destroyed. It is supposed to be of enormous length, and to be formed in part of vast fissures extending to fearful depths.

This region varies greatly as to its capacities for agriculture. On the sides of the slate hills the soil is thin, and not supplied with the moisture necessary for the production of large crops. This is also the case in a less marked degree of the blunt ridges capped by the white conglomerate. But on the limestone bottoms and throughout the alluvial basins a deep fertile soil prevails, which yields abundant crops of clover, cereals, and Indian corn. The streams here are of small size, although springs are numerous, and send forth little brooks in many directions. Three creeks wind in tortuous channels across this narrow belt of country, and contribute their quota of fertilizing elements to the narrow valleys through which they run. They are the Big and Little Tonoloway and Deep Creek. Like all the other streams of this region, they run in deep channels through the winding gullies and ravines between the hills, are moderately rapid, and flow for the most part over broken rocks and scattered bowlders.

The majestic Sideling Hill ridge, which forms the most westward summit of Washington County, is a grand, high backbone of red and brown sandstone, capped and flanked by the Oneida white sandstone, and is picturesque, precipitous, and in places almost inaccessible. Its summit near the turnpike rises above an altitude of sixteen hundred feet, and affords some of the finest views of scenery to be had in this country. Looking east the eye takes in the whole range of the Potomac Valley as far as North Mountain, and rests successively upon three or more prominent and beautiful mountain groups set in the intervening landscape. The minerals of this section are of few species, and have not yet been discovered in large quantities. Most important of them all is the specular oxide of iron, which occurs near Sideling Hill, in the calcareous shales. It has not yet been properly developed, but future investigations may determine its presence in profitable amounts. The general color of this ore is red, while bright scales of the dark metal project from the surface of the lumps.

Coal has always been an object of special interest to the people of this part of Washington County. It has been frequently reported as occurring in various places where the black shale crops out at the surface of the ground. Notwithstanding the adverse reports of several competent geologists, extensive drifts were pierced into the precipitous flank of Sideling Hill, next to where the grand, picturesque gorge of the creek opens into the basin of the Potomac River. Several of these have been excavated at a great height above the bed of the creek, and at a heavy expenditure of money and time. The result has been an accumulation of large piles of black, bituminous, decomposed slate and shale, which has proved but a poor substitute for the much-coveted anthracite coal. No true coal-measures exist in this county; the position of the geological series would place them above all the formations found within its limits, and hence they would occur upon the surface and not below.

Sulphuret of iron is met with in small pieces, or in crystals bedded in the slate and limestone rocks, but it has not been found in masses or quantities large enough for commercial purposes.

Gold, silver, zinc, copper, and lead have not thus far been discovered in useful amounts, and the formations peculiar to the country are not in favor of their being so found.

Limestones suitable for agricultural purposes, besides the cement rock, appear in immeasurable deposits, but no true marbles belong to this region. Purple, brown, olive, and white sandstones of compact texture and fine grain abound, and can be obtained of any workable size. Glass-sand of pure white color is found, both in the rock and disintegrated, in vast beds along the western flanks of Tonoloway and of Sideling Hill.

Allegany County has an area of about five hundred square miles, and extends from Sideling Hill Creek on the east to the ridge of the Great Savage Mountain on the west. Its general outline is somewhat that of a bent gourd, with the bowl on the east and the handle running diagonally on the west. It is bounded on the north by Pennsylvania, and separated on the south from West Virginia by the Potomac River. Its length from east to west is about thirty-two miles, and its greatest width from north to south is twenty miles. The surface of the country on the east is frequently broken by abrupt, moderately elevated mountain ridges, with intervening narrow valleys; but on the west it rises to nearly the highest elevation reached in the State.

The first stream reached after crossing Sideling Hill is the romantic Sideling Hill Creek. It rises in Somerset County, Pa., runs along the base of the mountain, and has pierced through numberless obstructions of rock, bluff, and bowlder until it has conquered a deep wide channel all the way to the Potomac. At intervals along its path masses of the heavy-jointed brown sandstone stand in solid masonry as majestic bluffs, while next beyond a broad bayed-out basin rests as it has been worn from the strata by the power of the rushing floods. Occasionally the great mountain swells push into its channels, throwing out huge buttresses of rock, and forming tremendous precipices of the jointed white Oneida sandstone, where the struggling creek labors to force its way through the labyrinths of stone. For wild, undisturbed solitude the basin of this stream has scarcely a counterpart in the State of Maryland. In the midst of half-concealed hollows, from which there seems no outlet, Nature has lavished unnumbered gifts. On the one side a glen appears, overgrown with the lithe forms of varied shrubs, penetrated by alleys bordered with richly-colored flowers. Beyond this, the green banks, which bend over the ledges of rocks, overflow with the fringy ends of trailing vines, while water, trickling down through the tangled moss, feeds the roots of broad tufts of graceful ferns. In the open avenues whole beds of the rich rhododendron grow, next to where the groves of maple and birch luxuriate in the moisture-laden breezes. There, too, on the slopes of rich humus, along the ravines, the kalmias and azaleas grow in company, and interlace their branches in endless confusion.

A broad, gradually rising valley stretches from this creek to Town Hill, a distance of about five miles. The bed of the whole section is brown sandstone, yielding a soil productive of ample crops of Indian corn and oats. The ridge is a repetition of Sideling Hill, but rather less elevated. Beds of black decomposing shale, similar to those previously mentioned, are also met with in this ridge, and have likewise tempted adventurers to dig for coal. But these do not belong to the coal-bearing series, and will not be found to yield that mineral.

Beyond this several ranges of lower mountains, of similar character, enter the county from Pennsylvania, and cross this entire width of region. Of these, Green Ridge, Polish Mountain, and Warrior Mountain stand in close proximity to each other beyond Town Hill, and between these narrow, high, uneven valleys rest, through which small creeks run and transport the drainage of the country into the Potomac. The ridges are composed of closely-pressed strata of the same blue and drab limestones, red sandstones, and variously colored slates as those previously noticed, and on their summits occurs the white sandstone or gray conglomerate. Most of the valleys are two miles or less in width, while that between Warrior and Martin's Mountains is expanded to a breadth of about four miles.

In the latter the red slaty sandstones prevail, and they are also found in the succeeding valleys until the city of Cumberland is reached.

Warrior Mountain is largely built of the massive cavernous limestone, and contains numerous species of fossils peculiar to this formation.

The caverns are known to form subterranean reservoirs of large size, storing the water which finds an outlet at the base of some ridge or hill. In such cases vigorous and permanent springs burst forth, and produce streams which afford the only reliable water-power of the region. Usually the temperature of these springs during the cold season is higher than that of the surrounding atmosphere, and accordingly they are rarely found to freeze, even in the severest weather. This important condition permits the running of the mills throughout the whole winter, at times when it is found impossible to do so in many other localities. Murley's Branch is one of the streams which rises under similar conditions at the western base of Warrior Mountain. After supplying power for several mills, and flowing through a flourishing region, it bends around to the east to pass through the gap in that mountain, then winds south and unites with Town Creek in the pleasant valley below Gilpintown. The upper parts of this and the next two adjoining valleys are distinguished by the presence of mineral springs, both sulphur and chalybeate. Adjoining Flintstone, at the base of the gap in Warrior Mountain, a white sulphur spring of ample volume and of great clearness and mineral strength appears. Several others of the same type are also present between Green Ridge and Polish Mountain, particularly on the Carroll estate. Four of these issue from a fossiliferous slate rock which forms the bed of the valley, and although appearing limpid and free from sediment, nevertheless precipitate all along their margins the deposit known as "white sulphur." The temperature of these springs is 47° or 48° F., and a chemical analysis by experts establishes the presence of carbonic acid gas in large proportion, of sulphuretted hydrogen, and of useful proportions of magnesia, muriate of soda, sulphate of lime, carbonate of lime, and of chlorides in small quantities.

Situated as these springs are in the fertile and beautiful valley of Fifteen-Mile Creek, at a distance of about sixteen miles east of Cumberland, in the midst of a region of invigorating and pure air, together with the facilities offered by the proprietor of the establishment there, should make the locality one of the chief resorts for invalids and tourists who seek for health and pleasure in more distant and far less accessible places. Most of the valleys are seated at an elevation of seven hundred to seven hundred and fifty feet above the sea. These and the cleared parts of the ridges are covered with farms, on which good crops of wheat, rye, Indian corn, oats, and potatoes are commonly raised. Apples, pears, and the common kinds of small fruits succeed well, and the alluvial bottoms are adapted for the grazing and raising of cattle and farm-stock. Springs are numerous along the flanks of the ridges, where they usually give rise to active little brooks which transport their waters to the larger creeks. The mountains are still overgrown with ample forests on their summits and sides, and these are composed of the yellow and spruce pines, with some groves of white pine and large areas of chestnut. On the deeper and moister soils the white, chestnut, and other oaks, together with the magnolia or cucumber-tree, the sycamore, sour-gum, tulip-tree, linden, walnut, hickory, maples, and especially the false locust, grow luxuriantly.

The sugar-maple still grows abundantly in some localities, from which the farmers obtain their annual supply of the maple-sugar. Various flowering trees and small shrubs abound in the sheltered parts of the mountain gaps and in the ravines, among which the dogwood, fringe-tree, hawthorn, haw, Judas-tree, and calico-bush are very conspicuous. But the most magnificent of all, the great rhododendron, forms extensive thickets in the avenues among the trees, and adds its massive bloom to the sweet scent of the delightful azaleas. Along the alluvial levels of the Potomac the region is made gay by groups of bright heads of the native yellow lily, and by numerous varieties of pink, purple, and golden crowns of the ever-present asters and sunflowers. The Virginia creeper, clematis, greenbrier, and other climbing and trailing vines overspread the rocky nooks with waves of refreshing verdure.

Beyond Evitt's Mountain the city of Cumberland rests in an open amphitheatre, set around with high hills and prominent blunt mountain-domes. The Potomac River in making its long bend to pass around Knobby Mountain touches this city and receives the waters of Will's Creek. The latter occupies the bed of the great and startling gap in Will's Mountain, on the western side of Cumberland. This tremendous chasm has a width of five hundred feet at its base, and the abrupt mountain flank on its east side rises to a height of eight hundred feet above the creek. On this side the red sandstone lies at the base and stands up like a great wall, while on the opposite shore the white sandstone is seen in long, heavy walls of immense thickness, which are continuous with the side of the mountain and curve over its summit. The blue limestone forms the end of this ridge next the city, and crops out at various points on the hill beyond the creek. At this point, also, a large bed of the black magnesian limestone stands out prominently, and is quarried for the purpose of making hydraulic cement. This is calcined in kilns near the spot, and is then packed in barrels for exportation. Some of the limestones are slightly bituminous, and are often crossed by wide seams of quartz, which more strongly resist the atmosphere and elements, and are thus left standing in prominent belts, while the adjoining rock is worn away. Such features often constitute great buttresses of fantastic shapes, extending down from great elevations, and always form attractions to the observant and curious. One of these, of more than usual interest, is situated on the northwest slope of Will's Mountain, only a few miles beyond Cumberland. It has been a standing object of awe to the ignorant and superstitious, who dread to be near it during the evening or night, and who have given it the significant name of Devil's Sliding-place.

Crossing Will's Mountain through the valley of Braddock's Run, the higher ridge of Davis Mountain is reached, and then a descent is made into the great Potomac and Allegany coal-basin. It is an oval valley, sloping from the north towards the south, with the rocky sides curving upwards to form the crests of the mountains. On the western boundary the great Savage Mountain forms the highest ridge, while on the eastern side Dan's Mountain rises to a somewhat less elevation. Between these the present general surface of the valley drops down to a depth of five hundred feet below the summits of the ridges. In this county, between the Pennsylvania line and the Potomac River, it has a length of about twenty miles and a width of five to six miles. This is the centre of Allegany's greatest activity, and along its slopes and swells the miners' houses crop out at frequent intervals, where the rugged surface has been denuded of the forests which once gave shade and moisture to the earth. In the midst of the rocks, on the hard, thin soil, the miner's family lives and manages to raise a few potatoes and some vegetables to eke out the scanty fare which the region supplies. All summer long, and until the icy cold of winter has stopped the canal, he works beneath the ground, cutting out the black mineral for transportation to other and distant places. Square holes in the sides of the mountains and in the ravines, kept open by supports of timber, lead to the beds from which the coal is taken. About twenty-seven square miles of area were originally occupied by the seams of this fuel, of which the main stratum, or great bed, fourteen feet in thickness, is the eighth in the descending order, and rests at a distance of about two hundred and seventy-seven feet below the surface.

Enormous quantities of this important mineral are being removed every year, and the rate of excavation is so rapid as to make it appear likely that this principal bed will be exhausted within the next half-century. The coal is of the semi-bituminous kind, containing from seventy-two to eighty-three per cent. of carbon, is jet-black and glossy, and is taken out in blocks often as large as a man can handle.

The valley is traversed by a number of streams, the principal of which is a fine large one, the George's Creek, that winds and bends in a deep channel from north to south, and empties into the Potomac River. The other streams are chiefly its tributaries, and generally rise on the mountain flanks, both east and west, wearing their way though deep channels in the hard sandstones and shales, until they finally become merged with the creek. Towards the northern end of the valley Jennings' Creek and Braddock's Run have cut their way in deep channels through gaps in Dan's and Will's Mountains, and dashing over broken rocks in the midst of startling scenery, they unite with Will's Creek in the great chasm a few miles from Cumberland. The mountains of this region are all quite massive, have been folded into chains of high, broad domes by the enormous pressure which raised them into the air chiefly after the coal period; but before that time marshes bordering the ancient ocean permitted the growth of a dense and rank vegetation, which supplied the material for the beds of carbonaceous mineral, since proved to be such useful fuel. This part of the country is of little interest as to its agricultural capacities, but it is full of remarkable scenery, and contains an ample store of carbonate of iron in connection with its coal-measures.

Garrett County.—Upon crossing the summit of the great Backbone Mountain, Garrett County is reached. It is the most elevated and compact mountain region in the State; the surface is all greatly elevated, and its outline is that of a broad triangle, whose hypothenuse is on the southeast, and is bounded there by the Potomac River. Its western boundary is a straight line, about forty miles long next to West Virginia; on the north it is equally straight, stands next to Pennsylvania, and is about thirty-two miles long. It has an area of about six hundred and seventy square miles, and is traversed from northeast to southwest by six long chains of mountains and two or three spurs running off from their sides. The country is supplied with great numbers of small brooks, most of which are torrents; and its principal river is the Youghiogheny, a rapid stream that rises at the fork of the Little Savage Mountain, and winding northwest through Pennsylvania, empties into the Monongahela River. At least two important coal-basins occur in this region, both of which are now being developed. The most easterly lies between Meadow Mountain and Negro Mountain, forming a long triangular trough, whose widest part is on the north, next Pennsylvania, and the narrow end is on the south, intersected by the valley of Deep Creek. It is about seventeen miles long by from two to five wide; and, like the coal-bearing valley of Allegany, is a downward curve of broad and narrow strata of shale, sandstone, coal, limestone, conglomerate, and iron, resting one above the other in a regular series. The same is the case with the deeper and wider coal-basin which occupies the northwestern section of the country between Keyser's Ridge and Briery Mountain. It is an extremely uneven basin, broken into many small divisions by Winding Ridge and various spurs and knobs, and is traversed from south to north by the Youghiogheny River. This valley extends across the boundary lines of both Pennsylvania and West Virginia; but within the limits of Garrett County it varies in width from five to eight miles, while its length is co-extensive with the width of the western boundary of the State.

The former of these valleys is known as the Meadow Mountain coal-field, and the latter derives its name from the Youghiogheny River, which runs through its lowest level. Neither of these basins contains strata of coal at all comparable to the great fourteen-feet bed of the Allegany Valley, and in some parts of each of the former the eroding waters have carried away vast sections of the coal-rocks; but at least four strata of coal have been detected in both, three of which beds average four or more feet in thickness. Besides the coal strata so important to this section, argillaceous iron ore occurs in large quantities. On Bear Creek a good quality of the oxide of manganese is present, apparently in large quantities, and on the western flank of Winding Ridge an extensive deposit of clay contains nodules of the carbonate of iron in connection with a layer of calcareous earth. At the same place may also be found a mineral composed of lime, clay, and the oxide of iron, well adapted for the production of a strong hydraulic cement.

The country is one of great attractiveness, from the fine resorts for health and pleasure which abound everywhere in the midst of fine scenery and pure air and water. Beautiful meadows of fresh green called glades are present almost everywhere along the mountain-tops, and the speckled trout still lives in the limpid streams which course through these uplands. During the warm seasons these glades are decked with a numerous collection of showy and bright flowering plants, which delight the eye and continually attract the attention. Among these the yellow lily, cardinal flower, phlox, asters, and smaller sunflowers may be cited, together with the fine flowering shrubs and trees, such as the cucumber magnolia, collinsonia, ænothera, monarda, and rudbeckia. The sugar-maple also flourishes upon the mountain-sides, and yields its annual supply of syrup to the farmers who collect it. Wild beasts were formerly numerous in the rugged, rocky ravines and forests of the mountain-sides, but these have been mostly exterminated; and now in their stead may be occasionally found the red deer, raccoon, opossum, rabbits, and several varieties of squirrels. The wild turkey and pheasant are still tenants of the more secluded woods, and small game is yet to be found in the wilder spots. The glades produce rich grasses in great abundance, upon which the sheep and cattle are fed, and consequently the country is noted for the superiority of its mutton, as it is, also, for the fine quality of its well-named "Glades butter." Rattlesnakes are still to be found in the wild rocky parts of the ravines, and a general list of the reptiles of the region would include most of those common to the Allegany belt at large. But the tops of the highest ridges are tenanted by creatures, although becoming more uncommon, such as the Canada porcupine, the white rabbit, and some mice, which belong properly to the Canadian fauna. The flora also, as represented by its trees, has much the same character, and may be distinguished by the northern spruces, hemlocks, and pines which grow in the exposed woods. Fish formerly abounded, among which the native trout was the most beautiful and desired, but over-fishing and neglect of the rivulets have depleted the streams, so that only small numbers can now be found where formerly the waters were almost overstocked with them. Rye, buckwheat, and oats are leading productions of the farms, and tobacco is raised to some extent on newly-cleared lands. Cattle are raised in large numbers for export, and may be seen grazing in herds on the wide-spreading meadows, while long trains of cars are continually being sent off loaded with well-fattened stock from this county. Thus, with all its peculiarities of surface and soil, built upon and out of the massive rocks which lie but a few feet beneath; with bracing breezes, pure air, good water, and extensive ranges of grandly picturesque scenery along the valleys and across the mountains, joined to its immense mineral resources, Garrett County possesses first-class advantages for attracting and sustaining a large and healthy population, while capable of receiving and providing for the ever-increasing number of summer residents and tourists who crowd thither for health and pleasure.

Potomac River.—Connecting all the counties which form the principal body of this great western tract, the historic and celebrated Potomac is at once the grandest and most remarkable surface feature of Maryland. It is in most respects both a river and a bay. Two great divisions, marked by peculiar individualities, distinguish it into the Upper and Lower Potomac. The former lies outside of the territory included within the foregoing description; but it may be briefly noticed as the estuary or bay-portion of the river, or that subject to the rise and flow of the tides of the ocean. It extends from the city of Georgetown to Chesapeake Bay, a distance of one hundred and twenty-five miles.

Below Alexandria it expands to a width of nearly two miles, and all along its winding course receives the waters of wide creeks, which increase its breadth, and spread out into broad, picturesque estuaries upon the lower levels. Some of these bodies of water are from three to five miles wide in conjunction with the river, while the outlet of the Potomac at its mouth forms a bay nearly eight miles wide, which stretches from Point Lookout to the opposite shore in Virginia. In the first part of its course below Washington the banks are composed of clay and sand bluffs, which rise to a height of fifty or sixty feet; but as it proceeds the high border lands gradually slope and wave lower, and finally fade out in points and bars. Before entering this bay-like division the river has left the region of primitive rocks, and from that point to its mouth passes only through alluvial and earthy beds of the upper secondary and tertiary periods.

But that part of it which belongs to the region included in the western counties is the river proper, usually called the "Upper Potomac." It remains at present all beyond the reach of the tides, and probably it has never been affected by them.

Swift and powerful, it rushes in imperturbable grandeur through a channel of its own construction, cut out of the largest mountains in the State. In forming almost the entire western boundary of Maryland, it constitutes also the water border of the western counties. Away up among the high mountain summits where West Virginia touches the great Backbone range, marked by the Fairfax stone, this youngest of our great rivers bursts forth from the sandstones and shales of the carboniferous strata. The region is one of marked interest from the variety of striking objects which it presents. Hill-tops of mountain height, and loftier than the Blue Ridge, shaped by the tremendous floods of past periods, stand between the crests of the summit ridges. Broad belts of hemlock, spruce, and the northern pines bound the highest horizon, and form a dark background for the oak, chestnut, maples, birches, and poplars of the less elevated positions. A most picturesque scene stretches out before the eye as it takes in the winding valley with its silvery thread of water, here and there arrested by a ledge of dark rocks, then flashing the sunlight from the torrent or rapid, or leaping in foam-stirring cascade to the basin scooped in the rocks below. In the deep solitude of the wilderness, where broken masses of rock lie spread around in endless confusion, where the forests are choked with the trunks and branches of the fallen trees, and the moistened slopes are covered with the matted foliage of the vines and creepers; there, too, where the flowering shrubs and sweet-scented ferns weave chaplets and plumes of the tenderest green over the crowns of the weather-worn bowlders, this bright streak of water pursues its onward course, ever forward and downward, with a ceaseless impulse towards the sea. It is the great outlet for the waters which reach the surface in a territory nearly two hundred miles in length, while its tributaries on the north side cross nearly or quite the entire width of the State, its great South Branch in Virginia, with the Shenandoah and a dozen smaller rivers and creeks, draining an area fully twice as great. Indeed, the South Branch is the principal member of the upper river, and to it is largely due the wide expanse of water which it discloses before passing beyond the high mountains. Soon after leaving the head-waters it has worn a deep trough into the firm rocks, torn away huge pieces from the hard ledges, and resistlessly rasped and dug its way downward along the flank of the huge Backbone Mountain until the foot of the great coal-basin has been reached. Its course has hitherto been northeast, it has spread out into a broad creek with shallow but limpid water, running over a strong and pebbly bed, now it makes a broad curve around to the west, then resuming the former course and bending north it receives the waters of a fine branch, the Savage River; another bend is made and the George's Creek adds its narrow stream to the quickened flood which rushes on with new energy. It is now a vigorous and strong creek, able to contend with the obstructions that press in its way. Two miles above the former it had taken a new direction, going in a general southeast course; this is pursued for a distance of about eight miles, during which tearing its way across the end of Dan's Mountain, and then flows on to New Creek. The slope of the country now favors another change of direction, and accordingly the river rushes away northeast through its shallower trough, interrupted by frequent rapids between the ridges of Dan's and Knobby Mountains, a distance of twenty miles, when it bends abruptly around the spur of the latter mountain and touches the city of Cumberland. Will's Creek now adds its quota of water, and the river passes down on the east side of Knobby Mountain. Here it is charged with islands near the Virginia shore, and soon bends into the form of the letter S, to pass through the gorge in Evitt's Mountain. It is now in the very heart of high, abrupt ridges, where barriers must be crossed at right angles. Running in a straighter line towards the southeast, it rushes through the gorges of Martin's, Warrior, and Town Hill Mountains, surrounded by most romantic scenery, decorated in all directions by a boundless stretch of verdure-clad hill and dale. In the interval it has been joined by the great South Branch, and the two have united their waters to dash on with renewed energy in rending the hills and distributing nourishment into the valleys farther away. Having passed Town Hill, it flows in long uneven loops towards the northeast, cutting its way through the dense body of Sideling Hill, and gliding in perfect silence over the wreck of mighty ledges of rock, now lying as scattered bowlders over its bed, it bends once more and runs down the valley of the Tonoloway to where the little town of Hancock stands out upon the hills.

The beautiful dam which feeds the Chesapeake and Ohio Canal has been passed, the arched rocks and the cement-beds of the Round Top have been left behind, and the beautiful, clear river, as smooth and placid as a lake, glistens in the sunshine, and reflects the images of the grand old sycamore-trees that line its banks. Still broad and shallow, pursuing its course over the planed edges of the sandstones, slates, and limestones that lie across its path, it makes a long sweep towards the east, by a little south, until the spurs of the North Mountain are reached. At this point it has broken through a deep gorge, in the midst of a wild, rugged, and most romantic country, to become involved in difficulties which it could only surmount by passing suddenly around the unyielding rocks and forming a long narrow loop. After bending twice more, it strikes the heavy slates at Williamsport, admits the copious current of the Conococheague River, is unable to penetrate farther in the same direction, and is obliged to turn west and retrace nearly three miles of the distance previously gained. A great struggle for mastery now goes on between the river and the limestone-beds, with their layers of chert and strata of dense slate. Thus the river is compelled to run diagonally in a general southeast direction, and to bend back upon itself six times before its conflict with these hard rocks is over. Through an expanse of country more than twenty-five miles in length it has gained and lost, and at best has been obliged to follow the course of the Great Valley, and to submit to its conditions. But now, after Harper's Ferry is reached, the great rapid stream is favored by the tremendous down-slide which split the South Mountain from summit to base, and an avenue is open into the region on the east. Objects of fresh interest now appear on every hand. On the north side the majestic pile of castellated rocks, chimney peaks, the profile of the giant face, and the great arching strata of Maryland Heights rise in overpowering grandeur overhead. On the opposite shore the town of Harper's Ferry is seen straggling up, as if to reach the summit of the mountain bluffs, on the side of which the celebrated Jefferson's Rock is perched. Across the Shenandoah, more than a quarter of a mile distant, the spur called Short Ridge slants precipitously to the brink of the rapids, covered to the very top with close-set trees, between which huge piles of the mountain sandstone lie in indescribable disorder. As far as the eye can reach in this direction spurs, ridges, and peaks stand thrust together in close proximity, hiding all but the two lovely valleys through which the waters of the two great rivers find their outlet. An enormous but unimproved water-power now appears in view, the Potomac becomes fully one-third of a mile wide, and a heavy flood passes over a sloping but nearly flat channel.

The prospect down the river is now indescribably beautiful. The South Mountain, rock and tree clad, stands in silent majesty in the foreground; the Point of Rocks rises as a rocky bluff upon which to rest the eyes; the opposite shore waves away in vast, rounded swells of upland; the mighty river rolls in silvery brightness, losing itself in the mist-softened verdure of the far-off landscape, while all the features of hill, valley, woodland, and plain blend into the tender blue of the scarce bounded distance. Still gradually widening as it runs, and preserving a southeast direction, the river receives the Monocacy at the outlet of the delightful Frederick Valley. A wide, open tract enlarges the view of a luxuriant and picturesque region. The splendid viaduct for the canal over the Monocacy, the highly-cultivated hills on the borders of Montgomery County, and the triple crown of white sandstone of the Sugar-Loaf Mountain stand out as if sculptured monumental objects in the midst of the soft-toned landscape. The river now makes a wide bend in passing the hard slate rocks, and then enters the brown hills of the new red sandstone formation. From this point the slopes gradually increase in steepness, and for a distance of eighteen miles rise and fall in long serpentine waves. About four miles from the beginning of this sandstone its extreme altitude is reached in rocks which rise abruptly to an altitude of more than one hundred fee above the river. A new surprise now bursts upon the senses. The summits of the ridge are made of uplifted crags and chimney-rocks, reaching far above the tops of the tallest trees, resting upon long lines of natural brownstone masonry, and decorated at every turn by tufts, plumes, and festoons of lovely plants, ferns, and creepers. Long wall-like ridges of this picturesque rock, set in a background of far-reaching foliage, appear at frequent intervals along both shores of the river, and here its waters are interrupted at three or four stages by islands which have settled in its path. After passing the new red sandstone a region in strong contrast with the former is reached. The uniform wall-like structure of the hills gives place to the bent, twisted, and upturned ridges of silvery gray or blackish rock. Tremendous forces have been at work here on a grand scale. For a distance of two miles the whole bed and surface of the country has been pressed together with such violent force that the former body of a huge mountain has been shattered into jointed fragments, in part carried away, and only its broken base left in the trough of the river. Throughout this distance rapids succeed each other in such quick succession that the bed of the stream is gradually lowered to a depth of eighty feet.

The Great Falls of the Potomac now appear at the lower end of this scene of ruin. A fall, thirty-five feet in height, now precipitates an enormous volume of water; this is divided into three principal cascades of uncommon grandeur, which, after boiling and chafing amidst the terrible rocks of the deep basin beneath, dash with uncontrollable violence through cañons of their own digging, and sweep out in a broad torrent through the channel below.

On either shore of this great scene of desolation piles of shining rock thrown on end project high into the sky, and send off craggy ledges from the base of every towering peak. The jointed rock fills the whole region as far as the eye can reach, and the prospect is rendered still more wild and impressive by the thinly spread-out forests which straggle over the broken ledges. Nowhere else in the State, if indeed anywhere on the eastern side of the continent, can a more sublime and awe-inspiring spectacle be seen. It is of such an unusual type in this part of the United States, and so remarkable, that the mind is directed first to the region of the Rocky Mountains to find its counterpart in structure and sublimity. The remainder of this division of the river keeps on for fourteen miles, which take it to Georgetown. In this part of its course it has steadily forced its way through the granitic rocks, spread out into a deep channel nearly three-quarters of a mile wide, until, after gathering into a series of cascades at its lower falls, and gliding along over bowlders and broken stones, it finally becomes lost in the waters of the alluvial basin at the head of tide-water.

The most characteristic expressions of this river are in the freshness, vigor, and variety which it everywhere displays. It crosses the Appalachian region in a direction which brings it in direct contact with every geological formation that belongs to the eastern slope of the continent. It winds its way through them all, or only yields where harmony is indispensable, in conformity with unalterable physical conditions. As a continental force its career seems but of yesterday. The ages had been steadily preparing for its advent. Cool morn of a long geological day, succeeded by the glowing heat of an equally protracted noontide, had been followed by the long evening twilight of the carboniferous era. Heavy mists and long periods of rainfall had saturated the low hills and set rivulets to running in the ravines and bottoms. But now the mighty mountains are upfolded, an axis separating the basins of the east from those of the west is built high into the air, and cracks have opened in its flanks to let loose the imprisoned waters of the subterranean cavities. From the end of one of these the young giant arose and burst forth with all the energy of a new life. Pushing aside the deep soil which rested around, and forcing apart the bits of rock that stood in the way, it soon worked a deep path out and along the dark mountain-side. Plunging, butting, and leaping against the ridges standing in its path, a narrow trough was cut away up in the midst of the highest uplands, and then gradually working, forced its way down to the lower levels, until the sea was reached beyond the lower hills. As the ages have rolled on it has pursued its onward course in nearly the same direction, ever deepening its channel and spreading so wide that it has been at one time a roaring flood of more than two miles in breadth.

From the time of Washington to the present it has been recognized as the great avenue leading to the West, and its great usefulness in the future will depend upon the skill and judgment with which it is employed to facilitate commercial relations between the two sides of a continent.

CHAPTER II.

THE ABORIGINES.

The Algonquin Stock—The Iroquois—Warlike Susquehannoughs—Capt. Fleet's Expedition—The Jesuit Missionaries—Treachery of Trueman and Washington—Murder of Susquehannough Chiefs and Bacon's Rebellion—The Senecas and Shawnees of Western Maryland—Indian Manners and Customs.

THE Indians anciently occupying the vast expanse of country lying between the Atlantic and the Mississippi, and reaching from the St. Lawrence to the Gulf, have been classified by ethnologists, according to the affinities of language, into three great stocks. The first was the Algonquin stock, the most numerous and wide-spread of all, whose territories extended north as far as Hudson's Bay, and south to Pimlico Sound, and from the coast to the Mississippi, and in the northwest as far as Lake Winnipeg. The tribes of this stock were numerous. Among the most important were the great nation of Lenni Lenape, or Delawares, the Chippewas, Ottawas, Pottawatomies, Mohegans, and Shawnees. To them also belonged all the New England tribes, and most of those of Maryland and Virginia. South of the Algonquins, occupying part of North Carolina, South Carolina, Georgia, and the Gulf region, was the Muscogee stock, comprising the Natchez, Uchees, and Creeks, forming the Muscogee Confederacy, and the Yamassees, Cherokees, Choctaws, Chickasaws, and Seminoles. In the midst of the Algonquin territories, thrust in like a wedge, its base resting on the St. Lawrence and Lake Huron, and its apex reaching North Carolina, was the powerful Iroquois stock, comprising the famous confederacy of the Five Nations, the Mohawks, Oneidas, Onondagoes, Cayugas, and Senecas. To the same stock, though not confederate with them, belonged the Hurons, the Susquehannoughs, and the Tuscaroras, which last tribe in 1712 joined the confederacy, which was thenceforth known as the Six Nations.[1]

The Iroquois, though less numerous, were the bravest, the fiercest, and the most intelligent of all, and were the terror of the surrounding tribes. It is these who have furnished the typical Indian of romance; grave, taciturn, patient in suffering, untiring in action, defiant in death; faithful to friends, remorseless to foes; adroit in all the arts of the chase; cunning in strategy, surprises, and ambuscades; fierce and vindictively cruel in war. They possessed a higher degree of political and military genius than the rest; and their famous league

---

[1] See the writer's "History of Maryland," vol. i. p. 83, *et seq.*

or confederacy of the Five Nations was far more firmly organized than the loose Algonquin federations, and carried dismay as far west as Lake Superior, and as far south as North Carolina. The Iroquois were of a nobler and more martial appearance than their neighbors, and all early travelers were struck with the tall, sinewy forms, stern but commanding features, and majestic demeanor of their warriors. Those whose personal knowledge of the Indian is confined to the degraded remnants still lingering in the North, or the wretched savages of the far West, can form no idea of a Mohawk or Cayuga chief as he was seen two hundred years ago. Native tradition assigns the origin of this people to the far Northwest, whence they removed to the upper waters of the St. Lawrence and the mountainous region about the Saranac Lakes. As they increased in numbers they spread over the high forest country in Northern and Middle New York, where game was abundant, and a fertile soil and a milder climate yielded them an ample supply of maize. Skillful boatmen, their war-fleets descended the Hudson, the Delaware, the Susquehanna, and carried fire and slaughter among the coast tribes, many of whom they subjugated, and among the rest the once powerful Delawares, whom—probably in mockery of their proud name of Lenni Lenape, or " Manly Men"—they reduced to the condition of " women,"—that is, forbidding them to undertake wars, meddle with military matters, or alienate the soil. Some confusion has arisen from the various names they bore; they were called Mingoes in some regions, and in others Nadoues, Nattoways, or Nadowassies, a name said to signify "cruel." Smith mentions one of their nations, probably the Mohawks, under the name of Massawomekes.

"Beyond the mountains, from whence is the head of the river Patawomeke (Potomac), the Salvages report inhabit their most mortall enemies, the Massawomekes, upon a great salt water, which by all likelihood is either some part of Cannada, some great lake, or some inlet of some sea that falleth into the South Sea. These Massawomekes are a great nation and very populous. For the heads of all those rivers, especially the Pattowamekes, the Pautuxuntes, the Susquesahanocks, the Tockwoughes, are continually tormented by them; of whose cruelties they generally complained, and very importunate they were with me and my company to free them from these tormentors. To this purpose they offered good conduct, assistence, and continuall subjection."

The importance of the Iroquois was so great that they were included in all the early treaties made by the white colonists. During the English and French wars they were almost constantly allied with the English, who sought their friendship to use them against the Chippewas, Ottawas, Shawnees, and other tribes of Algonquin stock who were the firm allies of the French. Although the Susquehannoughs, the most powerful tribe in Maryland, belonged to this stock, they were not members of the Iroquois confederacy, but, on the contrary, were their fiercest enemies.

It is probable that the Susquehannoughs separated from the Iroquois about the time when the latter migrated eastward from the far northwest, and coming south, established themselves on the fertile and well-wooded shores of the great river that still bears their name. The Susquehannoughs being hunting Indians changed their abodes as game grew scarce, and so scattered themselves over a large extent of country. When Capt. John Smith in the summer of 1608 penetrated the territory of Baltimore County, he found it inhabited by the Susquehannough Indians, whose chief settlement was about twenty-one miles northward from the mouth of the Susquehannough River. At this time the tribe numbered about fifteen hundred fighting men, and exercised dominion over a considerable part of the eastern and western shores of the Chesapeake Bay, being the lords of some and the allies of other tribes and confederacies. The Susquehannoughs were one of the fiercest and most warlike nations on the Atlantic coast, and kept all the tribes within their reach in a state of almost continual alarm. Their warlike appearance, grave and haughty carriage, and sonorous speech seem to have strongly impressed the early voyagers, for Smith describes them as very noble specimens of humanity. He speaks of them as a race of giants. "Such greate and well-proportioned men are seldome seene, for they seemed like giants to the English, yea, and unto their neighbours." He speaks of them as in other respects the "strangest people of all those countries." They were of a simple and confiding temper, and could scarcely be restrained from prostrating themselves in adoration of the white strangers. Their language seemed to correspond with their proportions, "sounding from them as a voyce in a vault." They were clad in bear and wolf-skins, wearing the skin as the Mexican his poncho, passing the head through a slit in the centre, and letting the garment drape naturally around from the shoulders.

"Some have cassocks made of beares' heads and skinnes that a man's head goes through the skinne's neck, and the eares of the beare fastened to his shoulders, the nose and teeth hanging down his breast, another beare's face split behind him, and at the end of the nose hung a pawe; the halfe sleeves comming to the elbowes were the necks of the beares, and the armes through the mouth with pawes hanging at their noses. One had the head of a wolfe hanging in a chaine for a jewell, his tobacco pipe three-quarters of a yard long, prettily carved with a bird, a deere, or some such devise at the great end, sufficient to beat out one's braines."

Smith has given us a spirited sketch of one of these gigantic warriors, "the greatest of them," thus attired:

"The calfe of whose leg was three-quarters of a yard about, and all the rest of his limbes so answerable to that proportion, that he seemed the goodliest man we ever beheld. His hayre, the one side was long the other shave close, with a ridge over his crowne like a cock's combe. His arrows were five quarters long, headed with the splinters of a white chrystall-like stone, in forme of a hearte an inche broad, and an inche and a halfe or more long. These he wore in a wolve's skinne at his backe for his quiver, his bow in the one hand and his club in the other, as is described."

All the territory now comprised in Cecil, Harford, Baltimore, Howard, Carroll, Frederick, and Montgomery Counties was the favorite hunting-ground of this formidable tribe, which scoured all the country between the Delaware and the Potomac, and spread terror and dismay through the distant and less warlike tribes of Southern and Western Maryland and parts of Virginia.

About the year 1621 the pinnace "Tiger," with twenty-six men, was sent from Jamestown, under the direction of an experienced trader named Spilman, to trade for corn with the Indians near the head of navigation on the Potomac. Arriving opposite the present site of Washington City, Spilman left five men on board of his vessel, and with the remainder landed among the Nacostines, or Anascostan Indians, who lived in that vicinity.[1] Soon after, he was attacked by the Indians, and all of his party were either killed or taken prisoners, and among the latter was Capt. Henry Fleet. Remaining in captivity for several years, Fleet returned to England, where a contemporaneous writer thus mentions him:

"Here is one, whose name is Fleet, newly come from Virginia, who being lately ransomed from the Indians, with whom he hath long lived, till he hath left his own language, reporteth that he hath oftentimes been within sight of the South Seas; that he hath seen Indians besprinkle their paintings with powder of gold; that he had likewise seen rare precious stones among them, and plenty of black fox, which of all others is the richest fur."

By his flattering representations he induced, in September, 1627, William Cloberry, a prominent merchant of London, to place the pinnace "Paramour," of one hundred tons burden, under his charge.[2] He returned to the Indian town of Yowaccomoco (afterwards St. Mary's City), where he had lived with the Indians, and traded largely with them for furs. He made a number of voyages across the Atlantic with cargoes of fur, and, with Gov. Leonard Calvert, before landing his company, made a reconnoissance of the Potomac as far as Piscataway. From his "Journal of a voyage made in the bark 'Virginia' to Virginia and other parts of the continent of America," it is evident that his trading operations brought him into communication with many of the most powerful Indian tribes of Southern and Western Maryland.[3] Arriving at Yowaccomoco, he learned that one Charles Harman had been trading with the Indians of that region for furs during his absence, and had succeeded in securing three hundredweight of beaver-skins by representing that Fleet was dead.

"This relation," he says, "did much trouble me, fearing (having contrary winds) that the Indians might be persuaded to dispose of all their beaver before they could have notice of my being in safety, they themselves having no use at all for it, being not accustomed to take pains to dress it and make coats of it. Monday, the 21st of May (1632), we came to an anchor at the mouth of the river, where hastening ashore I sent two Indians in company with my brother Edward to the Emperor, being three days' journey towards the Falls."

By the 26th of May he "came to the town of Patomack" (Potomac Town, supposed to be, at the mouth of Potomac Creek, in Virginia), and on the 1st of June, "with a northwest wind, we set sail, and the 3d we arrived at the Emperor's." There was but little friendship, Fleet relates, between the Emperor and the Nacostines, "he being fearful to punish them, because they are protected by the Massomacks, or Cannyda Indians." The 13th of June Fleet

"had some conference with an interpreter of Massomack, and of divers others Indians that had been lately with them, whose relation was very strange in regard to the abundance of people there, compared to all the other poor number of natives which are in Patomack and places adjacent, where are not above five thousand persons, and also of the infinite store of beaver they use in coats. Divers were the imaginations that I did conceive about this discovery, and understanding that the river was not for shipping, where the people were, not [nor] yet for boats to pass, but for canoes only."

The neighboring Indians endeavored to dissuade Fleet from his design of penetrating into this new country, but he declined to listen to their representations, and sent his brother and two trusty Indians with presents to the chiefs of this region.

"I find the Indians of that prosperous place," he says, "are governed by four kings, whose towns are of several names,—Tonhoga, Mosticum, Shaunetowa, and Moserahak,—reported above thirty thousand persons, and that they have palisades about the towns, made with great trees, and with scaffolds upon the walls. On Monday, the 25th of June, we set sail for the town of Tohoga, where we came to an anchor two leagues short of the Falls,[4] being in the latitude of 41°, on the 26th of

---

[1] The suburb opposite the navy-yard is now called Anacostia, and Mason's Island is often called Analostan, both designations derived from the name of this tribe.

[2] Bruce's "British State Papers."

[3] This voyage was commenced on the 4th of July, 1631.

[4] Nine miles above Washington.

June. This place, without all question, is the most pleasant and healthful place in all this country, and most convenient for habitation, the air temperate in summer and not violent in winter. It aboundeth with all manner of fish. The Indians, in one night commonly, will catch thirty sturgeons in a place where the river is not above twelve fathoms broad. And as for deer, buffaloes, bears, turkeys, the woods do swarm with them, and the soil is exceedingly fertile, but above this place the country is rocky and mountainous like Cannida. The 27th of June I manned my shallop and went up with the flood, the tide rising about four feet in height at this place.

"We had not moved above three miles, but we might hear the Falls to roar about six miles, by which it appears that the river is separated with rocks, but only in that one place, for beyond is a fair river. The 3d of July my brother with the two Indians came thither, in which journey they were seven days going and five days coming back to this place. They all did affirm that in one palisado, and that being the last of thirty, there were three hundred houses, and in every house forty skins at least, in bundles and piles."

On the 11th of July he received a visit from "seven lusty men, with strange attire," of haughty language and demeanor, who called themselves Mostikums, but who, as Fleet afterwards learned,

"were of a people three days' journey from there, and were called Herecheenes (Iroquois?), who with their own beaver, and what they get of those that do adjoin upon them, do drive a trade in Cannida at the plantation, which is fifteen days journey from this place."

The Susquehannoughs, or Minquas, or Andastes, or Conestogues, or Gaudastogues, as they were sometimes called, were engaged in active hostilities against the colonists and friendly tribes from the first settlement of the colony on March 27, 1634. The policy of the early settlers of Maryland was to treat the Indians with justice, moderation, and kindness, and to buy the land from them. The settlement of St. Mary's was purchased by Leonard Calvert for a quantity of axes, hoes, and broadcloth, articles of real value to the Indians, who, indeed, were the more ready to part with the territory from the fact that they were suffering from the continued inroads of the fierce Susquehannoughs, who had harassed them so cruelly that they had already determined to abandon their lands and seek safer homes elsewhere.[1] Some were allowed to remain on part of the purchased territory, and their wives and children were employed as servants in the settlers' families; others were allotted reservations, with full rights of hunting and fishing in the woods and streams. They very cheerfully submitted to the dominion of the whites for the sake of the protection against the Susquehannoughs, which their ancestors tried to purchase from Smith with the offer of perpetual subjection. The friendly Indians were protected against their enemies and secured in the enjoyment of their rights, and many of them, such as the Yaocomicos, Potopacos, Piscataways,[2] Patuxents,[3] and others, rarely wavered from their amicable relations. The two strong and warlike tribes of Maryland—the Nanticokes and Susquehannoughs—preserved an independent existence, and at the time of the first settlement of the province there was a feud between them, and the former, as well as the latter, were often invaded by the Iroquois. As if this were not enough, the Nanticokes were frequently embroiled with the whites, and war was several times declared against them. Under this double pressure they yielded at last, and requested to be put on the same footing as the Piscataways. The Iroquois, however, continued to harass them, and finally brought them under subjection. About the middle of the eighteenth century, by advice or command of the Six Nations (who stipulated in a treaty with the province that the Nanticokes should be permitted to leave Maryland and settle where the Six Nations should appoint), a portion of the tribe left the province, carrying with them the bones of their ancestors, and removed to Otsiningo (now Binghamton, N. Y.), where they joined some fragments of the Shawnees and Mohickanders, and made a league under the name of the Three Nations. Others seem to have settled in Wyoming, Pa., and others again, if the theory be correct which identifies the Conoys, or Kanawhas, with the Nanticokes, to have removed to the vicinity of the rivers which now bear their name. As late as 1852 a remnant of the tribe (about one hundred) was living on Grand River, north of Lake Erie, in Canada West.

The interposition of the colonists in behalf of the peaceable and friendly tribes of Piscataways, Patuxents, and Yoamacos had from the first secured the hostility of the Susquehannoughs, who took occasion as they followed the war-path against their savage enemies of the south, or the back settlers of Virginia, to strike a blow at the unprotected Marylanders; and at times they organized expeditions with the express purpose of surprising the frontier plantations, mur-

---

[1] Father White's Narrative, pp. 36, 37.

[2] Mr. Davis, in his "Day-Star," says "the territory of the Piscataways, whose prominent chief bore the title of emperor, was bounded in one direction by the country of the Susquehannoughs, in another by the region of the Patuxents. It also embraced a part of the country bordering upon the Patapsco and upon the Potomac, including Piscataway Creek, and probably the sites both of Washington and of Baltimore." The confederates of the Piscataways were the Doags, Mattawomans, Chapticos, and the Mattawas. The latter tribe inhabited the lands near Baltimore.

[3] The Patuxents, whose principal seat was upon the river of that name, included a large number of smaller tribes, remarkable for their friendliness towards the whites.

dering their occupants and plundering their dwellings. Even the devoted and fearless Jesuit missionaries who were engaged in converting the Indians to Christianity began seriously to think of abandoning their station on the Patuxent River and establishing themselves at Potupaco (Port Tobacco), which was less exposed to the ravages of this cruel and warlike tribe.

Friendly relations having been re-established in the beginning of 1639 with the Patuxent Indians, the Jesuit missionaries immediately improved the favorable circumstance by dispersing themselves among the Indians in such places as seemed to be most favorable for the general diffusion of Christianity. The annual letter of 1639 says,—

"Father Andrew White is distant" from St. Mary's City "one hundred and twenty miles, to wit: at Kittamaquindi, the metropolis of Pascatoe, having lived in the palace of the king himself of the place, whom they call Tayac, from the month of June, 1639. . . . The salvation of Maquacomen being despaired of, Father Andrew White betook himself to him [the Tayac], and being treated by him very kindly at the first interview, so attached the man to him that he was afterwards held by him in the greatest love and veneration; of which thing this is the strongest proof that he was unwilling that the father should use any other hospitality than of his palace. Nor was the queen inferior to her husband in benevolence to their guest, for with her own hands (which thing the wife of our treasurer also does willingly) she is accustomed to prepare meat for him and bake bread, with no less care than labor.

"So not long after the coming of Father White to his palace, the Tayac was in danger from a severe disease; and when forty conjurers had in vain tried every remedy, the father, by permission of the sick man, administered medicine, to wit: a certain powder of known efficacy mixed with holy water, and took care, the day after, by the assistance of the boy whom he had with him, to open up one of his veins for blood-letting. After this the sick man began daily to grow better; not long after became altogether well. Restored from the disease entirely, of himself he resolved, as soon as possible, to be initiated in the Christian rites; not himself only, but his wife also and two daughters; for as yet he has no male offspring. Father White is now diligently engaged in their instruction; nor do they slothfully receive the heavenly doctrine, for, by the light of heaven poured upon them, they have long since found out the errors of their former life. The king has exchanged the skins, with which he was heretofore clothed, for a garment made in our fashion; he makes also a little endeavor to learn our language.

"Having put away his concubines from him, he lives content with one wife, that he may the more freely (as he says) have leisure to pray to God. He abstains from meat on the days in which it is forbidden by the Christian laws; and men that are heretics who do otherwise, or are of that name, he thinks ought to be called bad Christians. . . . But the greatest hope is, that when the family of the king is purified by baptism, the conversion of the whole empire will speedily take place."

The writer then proceeds to describe the execution of an Indian convicted of the murder of an Englishman. The culprit was converted to Christianity before his death, which he met with fortitude, and his remains were buried with the solemn rites of the Catholic Church. The writer adds,—

"No one, however, was more vehemently moved at the sight of the dying neophyte than the Tayac, who afterwards earnestly insisted that he too should receive the gift of baptism. The thing being considered in council, it appeared that it would be for the greater glory of God if it be deferred a little until it could be performed with splendid display, in the greatest solemnity, and in the sight of his countrymen; his wife also, and his children, coming to a participation of his joy and gladness. The king, at length, won over by the attentions of the Catholics, and greatly delighted with their prolonged hospitality, returned home, the same Father White being his attendant, whither as soon as he came he gave command to his people to prepare the church by next Pentecost, the time appointed for the next baptism. On that day, at Kittamaquindi, the Governor and other distinguished men of the colony contemplated honoring by their presence, and by whatever other means they can, the Christian sacraments and the second better birth of the Tayac, a merciful God causing this thing to turn out to the good of all,—to his glory, to our reward, and to the salvation of the whole tribe."

The Tayac mentioned in the last letter as king or emperor of Piscataway was also called Chitomacon, or Chitomachen. The latter appears to have been his proper name, and Tayac an appellation expressing his rank or dignity. He had been represented as a chief of great power, exercising authority over several of the neighboring tribes. His capital, called Kittamaquindi, was at or near the present village of Piscataway, about fifteen miles from Washington City.

The annual letter of 1640 gives an account of the baptism and marriage of this barbaric prince. So important was the event considered, that we find Governor Calvert and others of the principal men in the colony making a journey into the wilderness to be present at it. As an incident in history it may be placed beside the baptism of Pocahontas, which has so often inspired the artist's pencil. As that ceremony secured for Virginia the friendship of the great chief Powhatan, so the baptism of the Tayac gained for the infant colony of Maryland the good will and alliance of the most powerful of the neighboring chieftains, without whose friendship its existence would probably have been seriously imperiled. The letter runs,—

"In this mission this year have been four priests and one coadjutor. We stated last year what hope we had conceived of converting the Tayac, or the emperor of what they call Pascatoe. From that time, such is the kindness of God, the event has not disappointed the expectation, for he has joined our faith, some others also being brought over with him, and on the 5th of July, 1640, when he was sufficiently instructed in the mysteries of the faith, in a solemn manner he received the sacramental waters in a little chapel, which, for that purpose and for divine worship, he had erected out of bark, after the manner of the Indians. At the same time the queen, with an infant at the breast, and others of the principal men, whom he especially admitted to his councils, together with his little son, were regenerated in the baptismal font. To the emperor, who was called Chitomachen before, was given the name of Charles; to his wife, that of Mary. The others, in receiving the Christian faith, had Christian names allotted to them. The Governor was present at the ceremony, together with his secretary and many others; nor was anything wanting in display which our means could supply.

"In the afternoon the king and queen were united in matrimony in the Christian manner; then the great holy cross was erected, in carrying which to its destined place the king, Governor, secretary, and others lent their shoulders and hands; two of us in the mean time chanting before them the litany in honor of the Blessed Virgin."

In the mean time the Susquehannough Indians continued their depredations, for the records exhibit for many years lamentable accounts of the murders, house-burnings, and robberies committed by them upon the inhabitants of the territory now embraced in Montgomery, Ann Arundel, Prince George's, Baltimore, Harford, Cecil, and Kent Counties. In 1662 the colonists were at peace with the Susquehannoughs, but both of these were at war with the Senecas, who were devastating the few scattered settlements of the English along the western tributaries of the Chesapeake Bay.

In the spring of 1662 they penetrated as far south as the head of South River, which seems to have alarmed the Council, for they ordered all the powder and shot to be seized for the use of the colony, and that scouts should be sent to the head-waters of all rivers emptying into the head of the bay, with orders to arrest or kill all Indians found there. The troubles with the Senecas grew worse, and on July 4, 1663, the Council was informed by the inhabitants of Baltimore County at the head of the bay that the Indians had recently murdered two of the settlers, and another near Patapsco River, with two youths whom it was believed they had either killed or carried off. For nearly twelve years a fierce war was kept up between the Susquehannoughs and Senecas, success being mostly on the side of the former tribe; but a more formidable enemy than even the Senecas had by this time invaded them,—the smallpox, which first appeared among them in 1661, and whose ravages became terrible. In 1673 they only numbered about three hundred warriors, while ten years before they had been able to muster seven hundred; and probably the mortality was even greater among the women and children.

When the Hurons, who were of Iroquois stock, were finally overthrown, the survivors fled for refuge to the Andastes, or Susquehannoughs, from whom they had before received promises of assistance. The protection thus afforded seems to have been resented by the Iroquois Confederacy, or Five Nations, and war being declared between them and the Susquehannoughs in 1662, the warriors of the latter tribe carried such devastation into the land of the Senecas (one of the Five Nations) that these were forced to seek the aid of the French. The Dutch writers, under date of 1661-62, relate that the Susquehannoughs, or Minquas, though they had suffered severely from the smallpox, had engaged in a war with the Senecas, and that "in May, 1663, an army of sixteen hundred Senecas marched against the Minquas and laid siege to a little fort defended by a hundred men, who, armed with firearms and even cannon, relying, too, on speedy aid from their countrymen, and from the Marylanders, with whom they had really made peace, defended themselves vigorously, and at last compelled the Senecas to raise the siege." The war between the Andastes and Iroquois continued for many years, with almost constant victory for the former. But disease accomplished what the Five Nations could not, and the reduced tribe was finally defeated, the Relation of 1676-77 speaking of the Andastes as utterly exterminated after a resistance of twenty years. That Maryland took part in the final defeat of this heroic nation is evident from the language of the Iroquois deputies at the treaty of Lancaster in 1744. "We do not remember," they say, "that we have ever been employed by the Great King to conquer others; if it is so, it is beyond our memory. We do remember we were employed by Maryland to conquer the Conestogues (Susquehannoughs), and that the second time we were at war with them we carried them off."

The Susquehannoughs having been reduced by disease and warfare to about three hundred warriors, in 1674 were terribly defeated by the Senecas, and driven from their homes at the head of the Chesapeake to the territory formerly occupied by the Piscataways, near the Maryland and Virginia boundary, the latter tribe having been removed by the Assembly to lands on the Potomac River, near the present site of Georgetown, afterwards in Frederick County. Here they established themselves in an old Indian fortification. Here the Senecas pursued them, and did some damage to the plantations on both sides of the river.

In the summer of 1675 a white man was found lying covered with wounds at the door of his house near Stafford, Va., and the corpse of a friendly Indian by his side. Before dying he declared that Indians had been the murderers. Col. Mason and Capt. Brent at once collected a party of militia, and followed the trail up the Potomac and across that river into Maryland.

Here the party divided; the detachment under Brent found a wigwam belonging to some of the Doage tribe, surrounded it, and summoned the inmates to come forth. A chief obeyed, and was at once shot dead by Brent. The others within rushed forth, and all, ten in number, were shot down, only a boy being spared. In the mean time Mason's party had also found and surrounded a wigwam, and as the Indians came out at his summons they were fired on and fourteen killed, the firing only ceasing when a chief running up to Mason called out that they were Susquehannoughs and friends. The survivors denied all knowledge of the murder, which they said had been done by a marauding band of Senecas. Shortly after this several other murders were committed on both sides of the river, and terror and excitement prevailed. Disbelieving the innocence of the Susquehannoughs, or desirous of ridding themselves of their neighborhood, the Marylanders and Virginians organized a joint attack upon their fortress, the Virginia troops being led by Col. John Washington (great-grandfather of Gen. George Washington), Col. Mason, and Maj. Alderton, and the Marylanders by Maj. Thomas Trueman, one of the Governor's Council. The Maryland force were assisted by Piscataway, Chaptico, Matawoman, Pamunky, and Nansemy Indians. On Sunday morning, Sept. 25, 1675, the Maryland troops appeared before the fort, summoned the chiefs to a parley, and charged them with the recent murders, which they solemnly denied, laying the blame on the Senecas. These, they said, were now near the head of the Patapsco, and they offered guides for their pursuit. During the conference the Virginians had joined the Marylanders, and their commanders reiterated the charges, which the Indians persisted in denying, insisting that they were friends, and as proof of their assertions showing a silver medal with a black and yellow ribbon—the Baltimore colors—and certain papers which had been given them by Governor Calvert as a safe-conduct and pledge of amity. Trueman, it is said, professed himself satisfied of their innocence, and promised that no harm should befall them. On the following morning, however, Capt. Allen, who had been sent to one of the scenes of recent murder, returned, bringing with him the bodies of the victims, and arrived at the camp while the conference was being held with the chiefs. The passions of the militiamen were roused to fury by the sight of the mangled bodies, and the Virginia officers demanded the instant execution of the chiefs, Col. Washington, according to the testimony of a witness, being particularly furious, shouting, "What! should we keep them any longer? Let us knock them on the head."

Despite the reluctance of Trueman, five of the chiefs were bound, led away, and tomahawked, one only being spared. The remainder in the fort bravely defended themselves for six weeks, after which time, their provisions giving out, they made their escape by night.

For this breach of faith Maj. Trueman was cited before the bar of the Lower House, and Robert Carville, attorney-general, Messrs. Burgess, Cheseldyn, Stephens, and others brought in articles of impeachment against him, addressed to the proprietary, and supported by affidavits. These charge, first, that he caused the chiefs to be seized and executed after they had come out under assurance of safety, and had shown the paper and medal as evidence of their being friends to Maryland. Secondly, that he caused the execution without previously obtaining the proprietary's authority. Thirdly, that he failed to procure a signed declaration of the Virginia officers that the execution was by their advice and consent. They therefore conclude that Trueman had broken his commission and instructions, and pray his lordship and the Upper House " to take such order with the said Maj. Thomas Trueman as may be just and reasonable."

These articles and depositions being laid before the Upper House, Trueman was brought to trial on May 27, 1676, before the Lord Proprietary, Col. Samuel Chew, chancellor and secretary, and Cols. Wharton and Tailler, sitting as a court of impeachment, and it was voted, *nemine contradicente*, that the accused was guilty of the first article of impeachment, and the Upper House was requested to send a message to the Lower House, desiring them to draw a bill of attainder against him. The bill was at once drawn and sent to the Upper House, which on the 1st of June responded by a message saying that the penalties therein prescribed were far too light for "so horrid a crime" and breach of the public faith. That if Trueman escaped so lightly the justice and dignity of the province would be brought into contempt, and the Indians set an example of bad faith likely to have disastrous consequences. That, moreover, the Assembly will be looked upon as countenancing rather than abhorring the acts of Trueman.

To this the Lower House replied that circumstances were shown at the trial that extenuated the conduct of the accused; for instance, " the eager impetuosity of the whole field, as well Marylanders as Virginians, at the sight of the Christians murdered at Mr. Hinson's," the identification of several of the chiefs as the murderers, and the necessity of the act to prevent a meeting. They therefore refused to recede from their former position.

The Upper House on the 12th answered that the bill was an attainder only in name; that they never would consent "to inflict a pecuniary punishment upon a person accused of murder by one house and condemned by the other; and that it was against their privileges for the bill to be pressed on them any further." The Lower House unanimously decided that Trueman, though guilty of the charge, was not deserving of death, and the Upper House remaining firm, he escaped his deserved punishment. He was, however, dismissed from the Council.

It has been said that the Indians left in the fort after the massacre of the chiefs defended themselves until their provisions gave out and then escaped by night. They went with the fires of rage and revenge burning in their hearts, and marked their southward march by a track of devastation and slaughter. At least sixty settlers paid the penalty of that deed of treachery and cruelty. One of them was a servant of Nathaniel Bacon, of Virginia; and this aroused Bacon, a man of bold and adventurous spirit, to apply for a commission to raise and command a force against the Susquehannoughs, the consequences of which were the utter crushing of the tribe and the revolt which bears Bacon's name in Virginian history.

A remnant of the Susquehannoughs that had been carried off by the Iroquois in a war with that nation must have maintained a separate existence, for we find that Penn, in 1701, entered into a regular treaty with Conoodagtok, king of the Susquehannoughs, Minquays, or Conestoga Indians; but it would seem that on this occasion a representative from the Onondago tribe was present. As a subject tribe we meet with the Susquehannoughs for many years in the negotiations of the league, and though some of them appear to have been removed to Onoghguage, a little band remained at Conestoga, where, joined by some Nanticokes, they formed a small village. In 1763, we are told, "they were still at their old castle, numbering only twenty, inhabiting a cluster of squalid cabins, living by beggary and the sale of baskets, brooms, and wooden ladles. An Indian war (Pontiac's) then desolated the frontier, and the Paxton boys, suspecting these poor wretches, and finding in the Bible sufficient commission to destroy the heathen, attacked the village, and killed six of them, the only occupants at the time. The fourteen survivors were taken to Lancaster by the sheriff, and shut up in the jail-yard for protection, but they could not escape the Paxton boys, who, while the townspeople were at church, burst into the jail and massacred the helpless objects of their fury." Thus perished at the hands of a cowardly mob the last remnant of that once powerful and noble tribe which had lorded it over the whole of Maryland, and which had often vanquished the fiercest and most formidable of the Indian confederacies.

The Indians that roamed over the upper counties of Western Maryland belonged to the Shawanese tribe, a subdivision of the Algonquin group. According to a tradition of recent origin, the Shawnees, or Shawanese, were primarily identical with the Kickapoo nation; but they moved eastward, and a part are said to have remained in 1648 along the Fox River, while the main body, met south of Lake Erie by the Iroquois, were driven to the banks of the Cumberland River.

The basin of the Cumberland River is marked by the earliest geographers as the locality of the Shawnese, who connected the southeastern Algonquins with the western,[1] and there is authority for the statement that they were inhabitants of this territory before the settlement of the Europeans on the continent. In 1682, when Penn made his celebrated treaty with the Indians, in the neighborhood of the present city of Philadelphia, the Shawnees were a party to the treaty in common with other tribes who composed the great nation of Algonquins, and they must have been considered a very prominent band from the fact of their having preserved the treaty in their own possession, as we are informed that at a subsequent conference held with them and the Mingoes many years afterwards, probably in 1701, by the Governor of Pennsylvania, the Shawnees produced this treaty written on parchment.

It would seem that after the treaty of 1682 a part of the Shawnees lived near Winchester, Va., but that the principal band removed from their hunting-ground in Kentucky, on the Cumberland River, to the headwaters of one of the great rivers of South Carolina, perhaps the Congaree; and at a later day four hundred of them who had wandered in the woods for four years were found a little north of the head-waters of the Mobile River, on their way to the country of the Muscogees, or Creeks.

In the year 1684, La Salle, a Frenchman, set out on a second expedition for the discovery of the mouth of the Mississippi, but before he had effected his object he was murdered by the Indians. In 1694, M. Iberville set out on a voyage of the same character, and on the 14th of August a basket was found in the possession of some Indians containing a paper upon which the names of many individuals belonging to La Salle's expedition were written, and a letter addressed to M. D. Zanti, from which it was learned that he had

---

[1] Harvey's "History of the Shawnee Indians."

descended to the sea with twenty Canadians and thirty Shawnee Indians from the river Wabash. This appears to have been on the first expedition of La Salle, which was of course prior to the one above mentioned, which was in the year 1684, but how long before is unknown. Thus it seems that previous to the year 1684 some of the Shawnees lived on the Wabash, but what became of the thirty Shawnees who accompanied La Salle we are not informed; it is thought, however, that they made their way into Florida or Texas, and never returned to the Wabash country. About 1678 seventy families of the Shawnees removed from South Carolina and settled on the Susquehanna River, in Pennsylvania. Others of the same tribe soon followed, so that the number of fighting men of this tribe in Pennsylvania in 1732 amounted to seven hundred, half of whom were from the South. This number, it is presumed, only included the band that had gone to South Carolina; but as it is evident that these seven hundred warriors did not include all the Shawnees, the remainder can be accounted for by another band, referred to by Cadwallader Colden, who, after remarking, in 1745, that the Shawnees were the most restless of all the Indian tribes, says that one tribe of them had gone to New Spain (now Florida). This band of four hundred and fifty, who were found north of the head-waters of the Mobile River, probably never returned to Pennsylvania, while the band which had lived near Winchester probably removed to the Alleghany, near Fort Duquesne, and afterwards to Cape Girardeau, between the Whitewater and Mississippi Rivers.

The Iroquois claimed sovereignty over the Shawnees, and drove them to the West, where they took active part in the various Indian wars that from time to time broke forth in vain attempts to stay the progress of white civilization. In 1731, rejecting the English missionaries, they negotiated with the French, and gave early aid to them in the final struggle; but in 1758 they were won over by the appearance of Gen. Forbes. After the fall of Canada they joined Pontiac, and were active in hostilities till subdued by Bouquet. In 1774 they participated in the battle of Point Pleasant, and in 1779 twice repulsed the attacks of Col. Bowman. They joined in the peace of 1786, but under English influence took part in the Miami war, in the campaigns against Gens. Harmar and St. Clair, till they were finally reduced by Gen. Wayne, and submitted under the treaty of Greenville in 1795. The main party were at this time on the Scioto, but some had crossed into Missouri, where the Spaniards gave them land. Another band moved South. In the war of 1812 some of the bands were won by the English. Urged by Tecumseh and his brother, the Prophet, they endeavored to unite all the Indians of the West against the Americans, but those in Ohio remained faithful. The Missouri band ceded their lands to the government in 1825, and the Ohio band in 1831. In 1854 the band of Shawnees proper in that part of the Indian Territory now included in Kansas numbered nine hundred, on a reservation of one million six hundred thousand acres; but by treaty the tribal relation was ended, and the lands were divided in severalty. Besides these, there were in 1872 ninety in the Quapaw agency, and six hundred and sixty-three in the Sac and Fox agency.

Of the region bordering on the Upper Potomac, however,

"there is no history," says a distinguished writer, "either written or oral, to enlighten us as to the events of an epoch earlier than about 1728.

"At that date there was located in the province of Maryland, at the junction of two streams known as the Cohongaronta and the Caiuctucuc, an Indian town, which also bore the latter name. The town of Caiuctucuc was built on the ground lying between these streams, from their confluence to a point some distance up the river Cohongaronta, the greater portion of the town being located upon the site of the west side of the present city of Cumberland. Other towns were dotted along the river's bank for a distance of more than forty miles, the most easterly being the present site of Oldtown, Allegany Co., Md. A century ago the settlement at that point was called 'Shawanese Oldtown,' but of late years the explanatory prefix has been entirely dropped, and the place is now simply known as Oldtown. Other villages were scattered about between the Virginia and Pennsylvania lines, two of which were not far distant from Caiuctucuc. One of these was located in the narrow valley, three miles westward, on the banks of Braddock's Run, on what is now known as the Eckles' place, and within a few yards of the line of the present National road, just where it is crossed by the Eckhart Railroad. Within the memory of men now living there were many relics of this village in existence.

"The ground was heavily timbered throughout that valley, and a clearing of several acres had been made there, in which were still to be seen the remnants of the small huts used by the natives. Just across the ridge, in Cash Valley, was another village of the same character, and still another of greater dimensions was situated near the spot on which Cresaptown stands, probably a little nearer the river. The date of the decline and fall of the town of Caiuctucuc is left to conjecture, but it was abandoned prior to 1751, as is shown by the earliest map of this region, made in that year, which simply marks the territory in question as 'Abandoned Shawanese Lands,' and at that time 'many bands of Indians of other tribes, with scattered lodges, were found here by the hardy pioneers, whose venturesome spirits led them so far beyond the limits of civilization, while the Shawanese thickly peopled the banks of the Ohio and the Monongahela west of the Alleghanies.'"[1]

In its day and generation, however, Caiuctucuc was a town of respectable dimensions, built after the fashion of Indian villages in general. It was simply an

---

[1] Lowdermilk's "History of Cumberland."

aggregation of cabins or wigwams, constructed by fixing saplings in the ground in a circle and tying the flexible ends together at the top, so as to form a conical cage or frame-work, which was covered with skins or sheets of bark. A better style of house, such as the chiefs used, was constructed by inclosing an oblong space in the same manner. Holes were cut in the sides for windows, and an opening left at the top to allow the smoke to escape, the fireplace occupying the centre part of the floor. Mats of grass or rushes were sometimes used to partition off an apartment. The mode of fortification was by inclosing the whole town, or a part of it, including the chief's house, with a strong and close stockade. Within this stockade was the council-fire, around which they gathered to discuss public matters or for religious ceremonies.

The land about the village was held in common, but to each family a portion was allotted for cultivation, the agricultural tasks devolving upon the women. Each family delivered a part of the crop to the chief, and it was placed in a general store-house to be used for the chief's subsistence, for the entertainment of guests, and as a reserve in case of scarcity or siege. They cultivated maize, beans, tobacco, and several varieties of the melon and gourd. The confederate tribes exercised common rights of forestry over the surrounding wilderness; but certain natural boundaries, such as rivers and streams, distinguished the territory of each from its neighbors.

The tribe was subject to its chief, who had absolute power over his people, and whose authority descended in the female line. When the chief died he was succeeded by his brother of the same mother, or failing a brother, by his sister's son; the alleged reason being that descent derived through the mother is certain, while that through the father was uncertain. This custom would seem to point to a time when conjugal fidelity was rarer among the women than the early writers represent it. Next to the chief, or "king," of the tribe was the *werowance*, or general, who had command of all expeditions, whether peaceful or hostile. Such warriors as had distinguished themselves in council or battle were honored with a title which the early travelers and historians give as *cockarouse*, and these, with the chief, the werowance, and a "medicine-man," or conjuror, formed the ordinary council of the tribe.

This medicine-man was a person of great importance, combining in himself the functions of physician and magician, as is generally the case among savage tribes, who look upon disease as the result of a hostile incantation or the anger of a malignant or offended spirit. They were usually initiated into their profession by a long period of preparation, including protracted fasting, solitude, severe penances, and frequently the administration of narcotic drugs. This regimen produced hallucinations, in which medicines or charms were revealed to them by spirits, and a hysterical or epileptic tendency superinduced, which, under nervous excitement, readily gave rise to paroxysms.

Their modes of *powwowing* were various, but usually began with drum-beating, shaking of rattles, and chanting by the assistants, and furious dancing and gesticulation on the part of the conjuror, until he was seized with convulsions, real or simulated, and rolled upon the ground with face distorted and mouth foaming. Sometimes he howled forth his oracle in this condition, and then it was understood to be a spirit that possessed him speaking with his voice; at other times he fell prostrate and apparently lifeless, and did not deliver his oracle until he recovered his senses, when he announced that his soul had quitted his body and journeyed to the world of spirits, whence it brought the desired answer. In their medical practice they combined these conjurations with treatment of a more orthodox sort, administering drugs, using scarification, cauterization, and other remedies; and in both capacities they were regarded with great veneration. These medicine-men also took a prominent part in the religious ceremonies, solemn fasts, and other rites. These had mostly reference to the change of seasons and other events, the chief feast being at the maize-harvest, while others signalized the return of certain sorts of migratory game, the ripening of certain fruits, etc. Their festivals were celebrated with various ceremonies of a symbolical character, with singing, dancing, and a grand banquet.

Neither at these festivals nor in their ordinary life did these Indians use any beverage but water, sometimes sweetened with the sap of the sugar-maple, until after they had learned the use of spirituous liquors from the whites; and to these, Father White tells us, the Maryland Indians had at first a great repugnance, though afterwards drunkenness became a prevalent vice with them. The custom of smoking tobacco was universal among the tribes at the time of the first arrival of the whites. It was regarded, however, in a far different light from the same practice among ourselves. Tobacco was a sacred herb, a precious gift of the Great Spirit to his children, and the act of smoking had always something of a ceremonial or even religious character. In some tribes the chief, standing at the entrance of his cabin at sunrise, saluted the first appearance of the solar disk with solemn wafts of smoke from his pipe. In councils and other ceremonies the *calumet* played an important part. It was solemnly lighted by the chief, who gave a few whiffs, sometimes directing these to the four cardinal points, and then opened the matter for consideration; the pipe was next handed to the second in rank, who in turn took two or three whiffs, and then delivered his opinion, and thus the pipe made the circuit of the assembly. A large and ornamental pipe was kept in each village for the ceremonious reception of strangers, whose peaceful or hostile intentions were known by their reception of it. The chief of the village filled and lighted the peace-pipe in the presence of the visitors, and after smoking a little handed it to their principal men. If he refused to smoke, it meant that their intentions were hostile, but if he received and smoked it, it was a sign of peace, and it was passed alternately according to rank between hosts and guests. These pipes were adorned with feathers and wings of birds, and whatever other ornament their fancy could devise, and served also as credentials to traveling ambassadors, and, like the herald's tabard of feudal times, was a safe-conduct even among foes.

At the time of the arrival of the first colonists the Maryland Indians clothed themselves in skin, mostly of the deer, which the women had the art of dressing extremely soft and pliant. Some, according to Smith, used ingeniously-woven mantles of turkey-feathers. Their weapons were bows and arrows, pointed with pieces of deer-horn, the spurs of the wild turkey, or flints skillfully chipped to the requisite shape and keenness; hatchets of hard grit-stone ground to an edge and grooved for the attachment of a handle, and war-clubs of hard wood, sometimes edged with flints. As defensive armor they had shields of bark, and Smith mentions a kind of light target used by the Massawomekes, made of small sticks woven between strings of hemp and silk grass, and proof against arrow-shots. The introduction of firearms, however, rendering these simple contrivances useless, they were gradually abandoned. They soon learned to buy improved arms, implements, and clothing from the Europeans, giving in exchange furs and peltries, and getting coarse, heavy cloths, hatchets and knives of steel, guns and ammunition, and pieces of iron out of which they cut lighter and better heads for their arrows. Though iron ore was abundant, none of the Indians had the art of melting it, their skill in metallurgy being limited to the manufacture of rude articles out of native copper, and occasionally gold. Penn's description of Indian manners and customs is as graphic as it is accurate.

"Of their manners and customs," he says, "there is much to be said. I will begin with children. So soon as they are born they wash them in water, and while very young, and in cold weather to choose, they plunge them in the river to harden and embolden them. Having wrapped them in a cloth, they lay them on a straight thin board, a little more than the length and breadth of the child, and swaddle it first upon the board to make it straight,—wherefore all Indians have flat heads,—and thus they carry them at their backs.

"The children will go very young, at nine months old commonly. They use only a small cloth round their waist till they are large. If boys, they go a-fishing till ripe for the woods, which is about fifteen; then they hunt, and after giving some proofs of their manhood, by a good return of skins, they may marry, else it is a shame to think of a wife. The girls stay with their mothers and help to hoe the ground, plant corn, and carry burthens; and they do well to use them young, which they must do when they are old, for the wives are the true servants of their husbands. Otherwise the men are very affectionate to them.

"When the young women are fit for marriage they wear something on their heads for an advertisement, but so as their faces are hardly to be seen but when they please. The age they marry at, if women, is about thirteen or fourteen; if boys, seventeen or eighteen; they are seldom older.

"They are great concealers of their own resentments, brought to it, I believe, by the revenge that hath been practiced among them; in either of these they are not exceeded by the Italians. In sickness they are impatient to be cured, and for it give everything, especially for their children, to whom they are extremely natural. They drink at those times a teran, or concoction of roots in spring water; and if they eat any flesh, it must be the female of any creature. If they die, they bury them with their apparel, be they men or women, and the nearest of kin fling in something precious with them as a token of true love; their mourning is blacking of their faces, which they continue for a year. They are choice of the graves of their dead, lest they should be lost by time and fall to common use. They pick off the grass that grows upon them, and heap up the fallen earth with great care and exactness. These poor people are under a dark night in things relating to religion; to be sure the traditions of it they have only, yet they believe in a God and immortality without the help of metaphysics; for, say they, there is a great king that made them, who dwells in a glorious country to the southward of them, and that the souls of the good shall go thither, where they shall live again. Their worship consists of two parts, sacrifice and cantico; their sacrifice is their first fruits, the first and fattest buck they kill goeth to the fire, where he is all burnt, with a mournful ditty of him that performeth the ceremony, but with such marvelous fervency and labor of the body that they will even sweat to a foam. The other part is their cantico, performed by round dances, sometimes words, sometimes songs, then shouts; two being in the middle tent begin, and by singing and drumming on a board direct the chorus.

"Their postures in the dance are very antique and differing, but all keep measure. This is done with equal earnestness and labor, but great appearances of joy. In the fall, when the corn cometh in, they begin to feast one another. There have been two great festivals already, to which all come that would. I was at one myself. Their entertainment was a great seat by a a spring, under some shady trees, and twenty fat bucks with hot cakes of new corn, both wheat and beans, which they make up in square form, in the leaves of the stem, and bake them in the ashes, and after that they fall to dancing. But they that go must carry a small present in their money; it may be sixpence, which is made of the bone of a fish; the black is with them as gold, the white, silver. They call it all wampum. The justice they have is pecuniary; in case of any wrong or evil fact, be it murder itself, they atone by feasts and presents of their wampum, which is proportioned to the offense or person injured, or of the sex they are of; for in case they kill a woman, they pay double, and the reason they render is that she can raise children, which men cannot do. It is rare that they fall out if sober, and if drunk forgive it, saying it was the drink and not the man that abused them."

Their mode of warfare was altogether of the guerrilla sort, consisting chiefly of surprises and ambuscades, in which they displayed great skill and cunning. Such a thing as a pitched battle between two armies in the open field was contrary to all their notions of good strategy. When a hostile expedition had been determined on by the chief and leading warriors in council, it was made known to the tribe, who celebrated the occasion by a solemn dance, in which the warriors, bedizened in paint and feathers, stated their past or projective exploits, and imitated in expressive pantomime the shooting, tomahawking, and scalping of their foes. On the appointed day they set out in one or more parties, moving, as they approached their destination, with extreme wariness to prevent discovery, marching often by night in single file, slipping from shadow to shadow, or gliding through the forest so stealthily that hardly a twig snapped or leaf rustled under the tread of a moccasined foot, until at a given signal they burst upon the village with terrific war-whoops. Those of their foes who survived after the rage of slaughter was glutted they made prisoners, and reserved for death by the most cruel tortures their ingenuity could devise; in inventing and enduring which the Iroquois—who, indeed, have the credit of introducing the custom—seem to have surpassed all others. Instances are recorded of the tortures of distinguished warriors lasting for days, a sort of contest arising between the power of cruelty to inflict and that of fortitude to endure. In the intervals of torment the victim would sometimes smoke his pipe and talk on indifferent matters with his tormentors; while amid his suffering he sang his own exploits, or derided the unskillfulness of his torturers, and taught them devices for inflicting more exquisite pain. Women were sometimes tortured, but usually they were tomahawked or shot, unless the captors wanted women, in which case they were adopted into the tribe.

One of the most noted species of ornament, which answered all the purposes of a circulating medium among the Eastern Indians, was wampum. This consisted of small circular bits of sea-shell, smoothly ground and polished, with a hole drilled through the centre of each, by which it might be strung or attached ornamentally to the belt or other parts of the dress. The "quahog," or round clam, furnished the principal material for this coin, the variegated purple portions of the shell being much the most valuable. The great labor in preparing it was the boring, which was effected by a sharp flint.[1]

"The wompompeague," says Gookin, "is made principally by the Block Islanders and Long Island Indians. Upon the sandy flats and shores of those coasts the wilk shells are found. With this wompompeague they pay tribute, redeem captives, satisfy for murders and other wrongs, purchase peace with their potent neighbors, as occasion requires; in a word, it answers all occasions with them, as gold and silver doth with us."

To effect a clearing and secure a crop with such rude implements of stone as they possessed appears to us almost an impracticable undertaking; but we are assured by early writers that they obtained as large a yield from a given quantity of ground as can be produced by the assistance of all modern conveniences and contrivances.[2]

Two dishes greatly in vogue among the Indians, says Brownell, have maintained their popularity among their European successors. Green corn, the ripening of which was celebrated by a national dance, is sought as eagerly as when it supplied a grateful refreshment to the red men, emaciated, as Smith describes them, by their spring diet of fish and roots. A preparation denominated "succotash," consisting of maize boiled with beans and flavored with fat bear's meat or fish, still remains a favorite dish.

It is a singular fact that the use of milk should have been entirely unknown before the advent of the whites, although there were various animals in the country from which it might have been procured. This fact has been adduced as a strong argument against the hypothesis that immigrants from the nomadic tribes of Tartary have mingled with the red race in comparatively modern times.

A favorite article of diet was a cake made of maize, beaten as fine as the means at command would permit, mixed with water, and baked upon a flat stone, previously heated in the fire. These cakes, it is said, were called "Shawnee cakes," the name, in the course of a few years, being corrupted into the "Johnny-cake" so well known in the South and other sections of the country at the present day.[3]

---

[1] Brownell's "Indian Races of North and South America."
[2] Ibid.
[3] Lowdermilk. It must be confessed, however, that this derivation is more plausible than probable, and will scarcely stand the test of criticism. "Johnny-cake" is more probably a corruption of "Journey-cake," an article cooked hastily for travelers, or upon the spur of a hurried and unexpected journey.

"The lands in the vicinity of Cumberland," says Lowdermilk, "are rich in Indian relics, and an interesting collection of stone pipes, tomahawks, rings, tablets, quoits, etc., has been made by F. M. Offutt. These were taken from graves which were opened by various persons. Along the banks of the Potomac the curious may still find these graves, and the writer has himself assisted in the exploration of a number of them. The custom of the Indians was to lay their dead upon the surface of the earth, and to deposit beside them their bows, arrows, tomahawks, and food in jars or crocks of pottery made of clay mixed with finely-crushed flint, and burned. The friends then deposited such articles as they chose, and the bodies were afterwards covered with stones, which were laid on to the height of about two feet. Usually the stones used were bowlders from the bed of the river. It is probable that the graves thus constructed were those of parties who were on the war-path, or traveling from one place to another, as usually not more than two or three graves are found together. This is rendered more probable from the fact that few such graves are found in the vicinity of their towns. At Brady's Mills a number of skeletons were unearthed some years ago by workmen who were excavating the ground for the production of a distillery built there by Samuel Brady. These were, beyond doubt, the remains of Indians, and were buried in a sitting posture some depth below the surface. This was doubtless the burial-ground of the Indian village which lay between that place and Cresaptown. On the farm of Mr. Christopher Kelly, fourteen miles below Cumberland, one of these stone-piles was opened recently, and a beautiful serpentine pipe of green tinted stone, besides rings, etc., taken therefrom. In that neighborhood, and on the opposite side of the river, are several other graves of a similar character, while in the valley of the South Branch they have been discovered in great numbers, and hundreds of relics taken from them have found their way to the Smithsonian Institute. The articles thus recovered were all of stone or bone, the latter being used freely as ornaments."

CHAPTER III.

THE EARLY SETTLERS.

The First Pioneers—German Immigration—Herman and the Labadists—Germans in the Revolution—Palatine Refugees—Their Religious Character—The English and Scotch—Irish Settlements—Primitive Manners and Customs of the Early Settlers.

IT was many years after the first settlement of Maryland before the advance of white civilization reached the western section of the province. The population of that region was so sparse that it was not until 1748 that it was considered sufficient to justify the formation of another county, and even then the new county of Frederick was so thinly settled that it was made to embrace the whole territory now included in Montgomery, Washington, Allegany, Garrett, and part of Carroll Counties, besides that comprised at present within its own limits, forming about three-fourths of the land area of Maryland. Although traders and hunters had penetrated the wilds of Western Maryland as early as 1715, and perhaps fifteen years earlier, few attempts at white settlements were made in the remoter portions of this region for many years afterwards. In 1732, Joist Hite, with his family and his sons-in-law, George Bowman, Jacob Chrisman, and Paul Froman, with their families, accompanied also by Robert McKay, Robert Green, William Duff, Peter Stephens, and several others, numbering in all sixteen families, removed from Pennsylvania, cutting their road from York, and crossing the Cohongoronton about two miles above Harper's Ferry. Hite settled on Opequon, about five miles south of Winchester, on the great highway from Winchester to Staunton. Peter Stephens and several others settled at Stephensburg and founded the town; Jacob Chrisman, at what was afterwards called Chrisman's Spring, about two miles south of Stephensburg; Bowman, on Cedar Creek, about six miles farther south; and Froman, on the same creek, eight or nine miles northwest of Bowman. Robert McKay settled on Crooked Run, eight or nine miles southeast of Stephensburg. Hite and his party were probably the first immigrants who settled west of the Blue Ridge, but it was not long before they were followed by others.[1]

Benjamin Allen, Riley Moore, and William White had settled upon the Monocacy, in Maryland, prior to 1734, and in the same year Richard Morgan obtained a grant for a tract of land in the immediate neighborhood of Shepherdstown, on or near the Cohongoronton. Among the first settlers on this watercourse and its vicinity were Robert Harper (from whom Harper's Ferry derives its name), William Stroop, Thomas and William Forester, Israel Friend, Thomas Shephard, Thomas Swearengen, Van Swearengen, James Forman, Edward Lucas, Jacob Hite, John Lemon, Richard Mercer, Edward Mercer, Jacob Vanmeter and brothers, Robert Stockton, Robert Buckles, John Taylor, Samuel Taylor, Richard Morgan, and John Wright. The first settlers on the Wappatomaka (South Branch) were Coburn, Howard, Walker, and Rutledge.

The more southern part of Western Pennsylvania (Greene, Washington, Fayette, and part of Somerset, which were supposed to be within the boundaries of Virginia) was visited by adventurous settlers from Maryland prior to 1754. Among them were Wendel Brown and his two sons, and Frederick Waltzer, who settled four miles west of Uniontown, Pa. David Tygart had settled in the valley which bears his name in Northwestern Virginia, and several other families

---

[1] Kercheval's "History of the Valley of Virginia."

joined him a few years afterwards. These, with those of Gist, Cresap, and several others, of whom more will be said hereafter, were probably the only settlements (west of the Blue Ridge Mountains) attempted prior to Braddock's defeat, and those made immediately afterwards or before 1760 were repeatedly molested by the Indians, and alternately abandoned and reoccupied.

William Jacob settled at the mouth of Redstone Creek in 1761, but was obliged to remove on account of the Indians in 1763, and in 1769 applied for a location. James Gondin erected a house at Eleven-Mile Run in 1762, and in the same year William Shearer and Harry Shrihack made improvements in this region by order of Col. Bouquet. From the application of James Burd, in 1769, we learn that a house had been erected at a place called Somerset, five or six miles from Fort Pitt, as early as 1760, and in 1762, Casper Toup, by permission of Col. Bouquet, improved land four miles from the present site of Pittsburgh. Among the early settlers of this territory, then claimed by Virginia, was Col. Crawford, who was the intimate friend of Washington. He settled in the valley of the Youghiogheny, on the river, precisely at the place where Braddock's army had crossed. Whether Col. Crawford fixed upon this location by design or accident is not known; but it was undoubtedly an excellent selection. It was then on the only road leading to this remote section of the country, and he was thus enabled to see all travelers visiting the Indian country; and being an intelligent and hospitable man, his house was made the stopping-place of the weary pioneer. Gen. Washington was frequently an inmate of his humble dwelling during his frequent visits to the western country, and more than once refers to him in his journal. A considerable number of emigrants from Maryland, about 1768, settled on the Youghiogeny, Monongahela, and its several tributaries, and the settlements in Western Pennsylvania, Western Maryland, and Western Virginia began to attract attention. "The forts at Redstone, now Brownsville, and at Wheeling were among the first and most conspicuous; the route the settlers pursued was the scarce practicable path called 'Braddock's trail,' which they traveled with no better means of conveyance for their furniture and provisions than that offered by pack-horses.[1] The great object of most of these persons was to obtain possession of the lands, the title to which cost little more than the payment of office fees. The Indian title was not then considered by individuals as presenting any obstacle, and Virginia (whose charter, it was then supposed, embraced this region of country) confirmed the titles of settlers with no other restrictions than such as were necessary to prevent the confusion of interfering claims. At an early period that colony appointed three commissioners to give certificates of settlement rights, which were sent with the surveyor's plot to the land-office, where they remained six months to await the interposition of caveats by other claimants to the same land. If none were offered within that period the patents were issued. There was an inferior kind of title invented by those rude borderers called a 'tomahawk-right,' which was made by deadening a few trees near a spring, and marking others by cutting in the bark, by the person who thus took possession. This ceremony conferred no legal property, but was respected by the settlers as establishing a priority of claim with which it was thought discreditable to interfere. These rights were, therefore, often bought and sold, because those who wished to secure favorite tracts of land chose to buy the tomahawk improvements rather than quarrel with those who had made them."

To the German immigrants from Pennsylvania and the Palatinate, however, must be ascribed the largest share of honor in that wonderful development of the fertile plains and valleys of Western Maryland which has added so much to the general growth and prosperity of the State. As in other portions of the country so in Western Maryland, the German element has played an important part from the earliest period of colonial history, and at the present day, woven in by time with the general prosperity and progress, forms one of the chief constituents of the industrial, agricultural, moral, and intellectual well-being of Western Maryland, as well as of other portions of the State. Even before Penn and his followers made their settlement upon the Delaware, certain German Protestants, in quest of a refuge from religious oppression, had come into the province and had been hospitably received.

Among the earliest German emigrants was Augustine Herman (Harman, Heermans, as the name is variously spelled), a Bohemian surveyor, a man of culture and influence, a native of Prague, and very probably a sectary of the school of Huss or Jerome. In early youth he had left his native country and settled in Holland. From Holland, in 1647, he emigrated to New York as clerk to John and Charles Gabry, of Amsterdam. He acquitted himself so well that he soon got to be a member of the Dutch Council, and in that capacity was sent to St. Mary's to confer with the provincial Governor in regard to the claims of Maryland to the territory on the Delaware Bay.

---

[1] Hall's "Sketches of the West," p. 193.

After this mission had been completed he removed to Maryland, and in 1663 took up land on Elk River, now Cecil, but then Baltimore County, where "Bohemia Manor" and "Port Herman" still preserve his memory. Various reasons have been assigned for his removal from New York, but the true cause seems to have been some disagreement with Governor Stuyvesant. At all events, it is certain that about 1661 he proposed to Lord Baltimore to make an exact map of the country, if his lordship would be pleased to grant him "a certain tract of land as an inheritance to his posterity, and the privileges of a manor." This offer was accepted, and the land patented to him Oct. 12, 1663, under the name of Bohemia, or Bohemia Manor. By subsequent additions it was increased to nearly twenty thousand acres, lying in both Maryland and Delaware and just east of Elk River. In 1666 he and his family were naturalized by an act of Assembly, the first act of the kind passed in the colonies. In 1670 his map was published, and copies of it are still extant. It is adorned with his portrait, representing a gentleman of about fifty years of age, of rather saturnine but not unpleasing features, set off by the full-bottomed periwig of Charles the Second's time, the whole surrounded by the legend, "Augustine Hermann, Bohemensis."

Herman seems to have taken up his residence on what is now known as the Ferry farm, near the present Bayard mansion, but no trace of his house now remains, nor can even its site be definitely located. It cannot have been far from the stream, however, for Dankers and Sluyter tell us in their journal that the screeching of the geese and other wild fowl in the Bohemia River, before the door, greatly disturbed their rest at night. Herman probably resided on the manor for more than twenty years, during which time, it is said, he once rode to New York on the back of his favorite horse to reclaim his long-neglected possessions there. He found his land occupied by "squatters," who not only declined to vacate it, but imprisoned him in their round-house, which was built with high steps for better protection against the Indians. He was sentenced to death, but " a short time before he was to be executed he feigned himself to be deranged in mind, and requested that his horse should be brought to him in prison." The horse ascended the steps without difficulty, much to the astonishment of Herman's captors, and was mounted by his master, who, while pretending to be performing military exercises, suddenly " bolted through one of the large windows that was some fifteen feet above ground, leaped down, swam the North River, ran his horse through Jersey, and alighted on the bank of the Delaware opposite New Castle, and thus made his escape from death and the Dutch." This daring feat, tradition says, he had transferred to canvas, himself represented as standing by the side of his charger, from whose nostrils the blood was flowing. It is said a copy of this painting still exists. Herman never suffered this horse to be used afterwards, and when he died had him buried, and honored his grave with a tombstone.

Herman's death is said to have occurred in 1686; but two years before, on Aug. 11, 1684, he conveyed by deed to Peter Sluyter *alias* Vorsman, Jasper Dauckeats *alias* Schilders, of Friesland, Petrus Bayard, of New York, and John Moll and Arnoldus de la Grange, of Delaware, jointly, three thousand seven hundred and fifty acres of land, bounded on the west by Long Creek, north by the great cart-road leading to Reedy Island, in the Delaware, east by the Appoquinimink path leading from the great cart-road to the head of Bohemia River, and south by Bohemia River, known afterwards as the Labadie tract. The whole of this tract, with the exception of a few acres, lay in Cecil County, the line between Delaware and Maryland crossing its eastern extremity just before reaching the Bohemia River. The grantees in the deed from Herman were members of a religious community at the small village of Wieward, in Friesland. The sect was founded by and named after Jean de Labadie, a French enthusiast, who had left the order of the Jesuits and founded this new " Evangelical Church" in Amsterdam about 1669. Owing to the opposition met with in Amsterdam, De Labadie and his adherents removed to Erfurt, from whence they removed in 1672 to Altona, where De Labadie died. From this point they were compelled to remove to Wieward, in Friesland, and at length, in the hope of securing a safe and permanent retreat, they turned their eyes towards America. Jasper Dankers and Peter Sluyter, two of the leading members of the community, were sent in advance on a tour of observation, and to select a proper location for a colony, and being attracted by the situation and advantages of Bohemia Manor, they resolved to settle there, and accordingly obtained from Herman the tract of land which has been mentioned. A company of men and women, including several families, shortly afterwards arrived from Wieward, and were joined " by a few persons from New York. Sluyter declared himself bishop, and sent to Friesland for his wife, whom he installed as a kind of abbess over the female portion of the establishment. The members belonging to this community did not at any time greatly exceed one hundred men, women, and children. They had all their possessions in common, so that none could claim any more right than another

THE EARLY SETTLERS.

to any part of the property. They worked at different employments in the house or on the land, such as the manufacture of linen, the cultivation of corn, tobacco, flax, and hemp. Their meals were eaten in silence, the men by themselves and the women by themselves, the former with their heads covered, except during a short season spent in inaudible thanksgiving. They slept in the same or adjoining buildings, but in different rooms, which were not accessible to each other. Their dress was plain and simple. Gold and silver ornaments, jewelry, carpets, lace, and other fancy work were prohibited. But the seeds of dissolution were developing themselves, and as early as 1698, Peter Sluyter, who had become sole proprietor of the lands of the colony, resolved to divide the property. He conveyed three of the four necks of land embraced in the tract to Herman van Berkels, Nicholas de la Montaigne, Peter de Koning, Derrick Kolckman, John Moll, Jr., Hendrick Sluyter, and Samuel Bayard, and retaining one of the necks himself, became a wealthy man in his own right." In the year 1722 Sluyter died, and the Labadist colony expired about the same time.

It was, however, in the western portion of the State that the first considerable settlement of German refugees was made. In common with the neighboring province of Pennsylvania, Maryland was the favorite goal of the Protestants, who were forced to flee from the relentless persecution which devastated some of the fairest portions of France and Germany in the seventeenth and eighteenth centuries. During the reign of Queen Anne many of these exiles were attracted to Pennsylvania, not only by the promise of religious toleration, but probably through the kindly intervention of the queen herself, who displayed so keen solicitude for them, and contributed so liberally to their relief, as to provoke the criticism that she was encouraging pauperism. The reproach was most unjust, for these exiles were skillful artisans, who afterwards contributed immensely to the development of British manufactures in the colonies. At first the German immigrants settled in the vicinity of Philadelphia, but gradually advancing westward, soon spread over the southern counties of Pennsylvania, and crossed the border into Maryland. The enviable reputation which the latter province had enjoyed, by reason of its toleration of different religious creeds, had been seriously marred by the proscription of the Catholics, which followed the Puritan revolution, and which was revived under William and Mary, Anne, and the first two Georges. In the reign of William, on the other hand, the Dissenters had enjoyed especial favor and immunity, and under George II. we find Methodism making rapid headway in Maryland, though here and there antagonized and threatened by occasional outbursts of fanaticism on the part of individual members of the Established Church. To this, however, must be opposed the fact that Methodist ministers were permitted, and even invited, to preach in the Anglican (Episcopalian) churches in various portions of the province. To the special toleration thus accorded Protestants, together with their remoteness from the centres of clerical and legislative authority, the German settlers in Western Maryland doubtless owed the immunity from persecution which they enjoyed from the first. Doubtless, too, the authorities of the province were wise enough to see that it would be impolitic in the highest degree to molest the brave pioneers, whose axes were constantly ringing in the western forests, clearing through the hitherto untrodden wilderness a path to the virgin plains of the Ohio and Mississippi Valleys. Whatever the reason, the German settlements were permitted to worship God in their own fashion without let or hindrance, and new sects sprang up among them on every side. The Germans who had settled chiefly in the vicinity of Lancaster and York drifted westward and southward, dotting the fertile country with smiling and thrifty settlements, and as early as 1748 had taken possession of many valuable tracts along the Monocacy River and the Catoctin Creek. They were also very numerous in the northern part of Frederick County, and in a few years had established settlements in various portions of what are now the election districts of Hauver's, Mechanicstown, Catoctin, Creagerstown, and Emmittsburg. In 1735 the Schleys, with about one hundred families from Germany, Switzerland, and France, established themselves on the Monocacy, the first house in Frederick Town being erected by Thomas Schley. The younger members and descendants of these families were the pioneer Germans in Baltimore, and contributed more largely towards building up that city than any other nationality.

In the words of one of Baltimore's representative German citizens, it may be said that "Germans were among the founders of this city, Germans sat at her cradle, German merchants helped to develop her commerce, German industry contributed to establish her renown abroad, and the thrift and enterprise of our German mechanics have done much to secure for Baltimore the prosperity she enjoys. I can assert with pride to-day that German blood flows in the veins of every second resident of our city, that every third name in our city directory is of German origin, that every fourth Baltimorean is descended in one way or the other from Germans, that every fifth one understands German, and every sixth can read and speak that language."[1]

Among the Germans who removed to Baltimore from Frederick County were the Schleys, Steiners, Shrivers, Slingluffs, Warners, Pipers, Raborgs, Rineharts, Lurmans, Miltenbergers, Yeisers, Littigs, Mayers, Ramsburgs, Hoffmans, Mantzes, Baltzells, Gists, Baers, Harbaughs, Strickers, and Amelungs. Peter Hoffman, founder of the well-known Hoffman family of Baltimore, came from Frankfort-on-the-Main and settled in Frederick, whence he removed to Baltimore in 1778 and established a flourishing dry-goods trade. Peter Hoffman was a commissioner of Baltimore Town along with Engelhardt Yeiser and George Lindenberger, and was one of the founders of Calvert Street Spring, at one time a fashionable resort. About the time of Hoffman's arrival there was an important accession of young and enterprising immigrants, who came direct from different portions of Germany, and from the towns of Hamburg, Bremen, Frankfort, etc. They were attracted by the fact that the Germans of Frederick imported largely of German goods by way of London. Baltimore was the port for the arrival and shipment of goods to and from the rich and flourishing settlements of Western Maryland, Southern Pennsylvania, and the Cumberland Valley, and many of the immigrants accordingly located there, while others decided to push their fortunes in the interior towns of the province.

This was in 1774, on the eve of the Revolution, and we find the well-known names of Frick, Diffenderfer, Raborg, Leypoldt, Schultze, Heide, and Schaeffer as among Germans who came to us from Europe just as the war broke out. The part which our German fellow-citizens took in that great struggle was manly, patriotic, distinguished. They furnished a great many soldiers, and the Baltimore, Frederick, and Lancaster Germans fought face to face with the Hessians on many a bloody field. The majority of the battalions of sharpshooters which Daniel Morgan and Michael Cresap took to Cambridge as soon as Bunker Hill was fought was recruited from among the Germans in Frederick, Conococheague, and the Valley of Virginia. Maryland had nearly a full German regiment in service during the whole war, and Western Maryland always had one company and sometimes two in this regiment. These brave fellows were among the steadiest and sternest fighters under the banners of Smallwood and Gist. Among the officers of the Second Brigade we find the names of Lieut.-Col. George Stricker, Maj. Ludwig Weltner, Captains George Hubley, William Keiser, Henry Fisher, Philip Graybill, Peter Boyer, Charles Baltzell, William Keeports, Bernard Hubley, Michael Boyer, and Martin Schugardt, and Lieuts. Christian Meyers, Adam Hoops, Jacob Reybold, Jacob Gomath, George Lora, Jacob Kotz, Samuel Gerock, Adam Smith, William Ritter.

But the Germans who did not draw the sword did the civil state quite as valuable and indispensable service. In Baltimore, John Deaver, Barnet Eichelberger, Isaac Griest, and George Lindenberger were on the first Committee of Safety and Correspondence; Isaac Griest and Isaac Van Bibber were on the committee to watch vessels in port, and both these gentlemen were particularly active in keeping up the patriot spirit and in making it "hot" for the Tories. Griest and Loudenslager were appointed to build the water-battery on Whetstone Point, now Fort McHenry, and Peter Hoffman, Anthony Houck, and George Warner, new-come Germans, were full of zeal. Jacob Fite lent his new building, southwest corner of Sharpe and Baltimore Streets, thence called

CONGRESS HALL.

Congress Hall, to the Continental Congress in 1776, and some of his descendants still own the property. In the militia home guards of Baltimore we find George Lindenberger, Isaac Griest, and Henry Schaefer among the commissioned officers.

In 1782 Baltimore had a sort of municipal government set up, the first she had ever enjoyed, and of the seven commissioners composing the board, three—Engelhart Yeiser, George Lindenberger, and Peter Hoffman—were Germans. In this year another German, Gabriel Vanhorn, established a stage-line to Philadelphia.

After the war everybody went to work with intense energy, immigration flowed in in a full tide, and the State advanced on wheels. There was a most valuable influx of young merchants from the towns in the Hanseatic Bund and the other commercial cities of Germany and Holland. We had flour and tobacco to export in immense quantities, and Maryland tobacco was just what the Germans wanted. We had

---

[1] Sesqui-Centennial Oration of Col. Frederick Raine.

potash also, roasted bark, raw-hides, hemp, flax, lumber, hard-wood, etc., to export. It was at this time that our intimacy with Bremen and Bremen merchants, so long and so honorably sustained, was first established. A great number of merchants came in from other parts of the country, among whom we find the names of Van Wyck, Stouffer, Slubey, Kimmell, Starck, Solomon, etc.; while among those who came from Bremen and Hamburg, etc., occur the honored names of Brune, Brantz, Schroeder, Von Kapff, Seekamp, Zollicoffer, Leib, and Konig. Among the justices of the peace of the day are named the leading Germans who took part during the Revolution.

It is a significant fact that nearly all the German immigrants who came into Maryland soon established themselves in permanent homes, and in almost every instance took rank at once as thrifty and enterprising citizens. The greater number were skilled in agriculture, but there was a large percentage of first-rate mechanics, harness-makers and saddlers, weavers, tailors, tanners, shoemakers, paper-makers, butchers, watchmakers, bakers, smiths, iron-workers, etc. It is a generally recognized fact that the Protestant population of France and Germany supplied the best class of workmen in the various branches of manufacture. Thus we are told by the historian Lecky that "twenty thousand Frenchmen, attracted to Brandenburg by the liberal encouragement of the elector at the time of the revocation of the Edict of Nantes, laid the foundation of the prosperity of Berlin and of most of the manufactures of Prussia." The same is true in a greater or less degree of all the Protestant refugees, and it would be difficult to overestimate the industrial value to our own country of the successive immigrations of whole communities from the different German states.

At first the immigration of Germans into Pennsylvania was confined to the sectaries, the Quietists, and the other religious denominations who, on account of their extreme views, found it difficult to get along with their more conservative Protestant brethren. The Labadists, for instance, were followed by the Mennonites, who took up much land and formed many communities in York, Lancaster, and Adams Counties; by the Seventh-day Baptists, who established their monastery at Ephrata; by the Voetists and the Cocceians, and by the hundred other sects of the day. But after these sectaries came the deluge. The Germans had found out that there was a land of peace on the other side of the Atlantic, and they knew by sad experience that their own country was a land of war. The peace of Westphalia had turned out to be only a hollow truce after all, as far as Protestant Germany was concerned. A man was not only deprived, practically, of the enjoyment of his own religion, he was robbed also incessantly of the fruits of his labor. No matter how forehanded, how industrious he might be, he could not certainly lay aside anything against a rainy day. This was a state of things which he naturally rebelled against, and emigration afforded him a relief.

The religious fanaticism of Louis XIV., which so long desolated the Low Countries, and which deprived that monarch (when he revoked the Edict of Nantes) of half a million of his best and most thrifty subjects, broke in upon the Palatinate in the shape of the most desolating war of which we have any authentic record in history. What is told of Tamerlane was practiced by the "enlightened" monarch and his able but savage lieutenants. Turenne, Saxe, Vendôme, Villars, Villeroy, Taillard, Marsin, Berwick, Noailles, Luxembourg, each in his turn helped to desolate the Palatinate and to contribute immigrants to the colonies. The homeless and ravished peoples of Germany sought and found homes in the new land of peace and plenty. At one time the immigration of German Palatines into Pennsylvania and Maryland was in excess of all other immigration.

In "A Memorial of the Case of the German Emigrants settled in the British Colonies of Pennsylvania and the Back Parts of Maryland, Virginia, etc.," published in London in 1754, it is stated that

"by the most authentic accounts, for many years last past very large numbers of Germans have transported themselves into these British provinces of North America; the greatest part of them from Switzerland and the Palatinate, many from Würtemberg, Swabia, Julien, and Berg, and other places along the Rhine, and some few lately from the lower Saxony; above thirty thousand of them within the last ten years, and in one single year, 1750, more than ten thousand.

"The causes of their removal from their native countries were various. Some of them fled from the severe persecutions they were exposed to at home on account of their being Protestants; others from the oppressions of civil tyranny and attracted by the pleasing hopes of liberty under the milder influence of the British government; others were drawn by the solicitations of their countrymen, who had settled there before them; but for the greatest part by the prospect they had of relieving themselves under their deep poverty, and providing better for themselves and their families, in the provinces to which they respectively retired. In the single colony of Pennsylvania the inhabitants, exclusive of the Indian natives, are reckoned to be about one hundred and ninety thousand; amongst these are above one hundred thousand Germans, or High Dutch, of whom about thirty thousand are of the Protestant Reformed religion, near as many of them Lutherans, above twelve thousand papists, and the rest of them Baptists, Herenhutters, and of various other sects and denominations."

As a rule, the Germans brought their own means with them, but sooner than not immigrate they were glad to indenture themselves as redemptioners. Many hundreds thus came into Maryland, many thousands into Pennsylvania. They came chiefly from the harried Palatinate, but also from Alsace, Suabia, Saxony, and Switzerland. There were Wittenbergers, and people from Darmstadt, Nassau, Hesse, Eisenberg, Franconia, Hamburg, Mannheim,—all classed as "Palatines." They brought the Heidelberg Catechism with them, even if they brought nothing else, and many of them were so plundered *in transitu* that they were not able to bring anything else.

The number of these immigrants was prodigious. In 1731 there were fifteen thousand members of the German Reformed Church in Pennsylvania from the Palatinate. Rupp and Kapp note, in order to show the rapid rate of the depopulation of these provinces on the Rhine, that in 1709, from the middle of April to the middle of July, there arrived in London eleven thousand two hundred and ninety-four German Protestants, males and females, who were vine-dressers and husbandmen, bakers, masons, carpenters, shoemakers, tailors, butchers, millers, tanners, weavers, locksmiths, barbers, coopers, saddlers, lime-burners, glass-blowers, hatters, brick-makers, smiths, potters, turners, etc. More than one-half of these came to this country. In 1790 there were one hundred and forty-five thousand Germans in Pennsylvania, the total population not exceeding four hundred and thirty-five thousand. These included the sectaries above referred to, the Palatines, the Dunkers, and the Hessian soldiers who preferred not to be exchanged after the Revolution. These German *huelfs truppen*, or subsidiary troops, were bought in Brunswick, Hanau, Anspach, Waldeck, Anhalt, Hesse-Cassel, Hesse-Darmstadt, Brandenburg, etc., in large numbers. They cost George III. eight million one hundred thousand dollars, and eleven thousand of them died or perished in battle. A great many of these people settled in Pennsylvania, Maryland, and the Valley of Virginia after the war. The other immigrants were German Calvinists, Moravians, Schwenkenfelders, Omishites, Dunkers, Mennonites, and Separatists (or Seventh-day Baptists).

Up to about 1760 the Germans in Maryland were supplied from these plentiful sources. A good many Palatines came in by direct consignment to Chesapeake Bay, but the great majority of the Germans drifted down from York and Lancaster. They came into Baltimore County in small parties, but they settled in Frederick County and the Valley of Virginia by the wholesale. It was the custom in Germany for all young mechanics to make a "peregrination" of one or more years in order to perfect themselves in their trades, and this and other regulations of the trade-guilds produced a class of workmen of a very superior character. But this must be apparent at once when we reflect that the German immigrants in many cases reached our shores with little or nothing, and often so destitute that, as previously stated, they were forced to bind themselves and their children to masters for a term of years in order to obtain the money to pay for the passage over. "Many who at home," says Rupp, the Pennsylvania historian, "had owned property and converted it into money, were robbed *in transitu* by ship-owners, importers, sea-captains, and Neulaender. The emigrants' chests, with their clothes and sometimes their money, were put on other vessels or ships and left behind. These chests were rifled of their contents. The German immigrants thus treated, on their arrival at Philadelphia, were obliged to submit to being sold as *Loskaeuflinge Redemptioners*, they and their children, to pay the passage-money. In not a few cases persons who still had means were held responsible to pay the passage for the poorer. This was the practice for more than fifty years. In this way persons of substance were necessitated, and did become very frequently common beggars." According to Dr. Benjamin Rush, in his "Manners of the Germans of Pennsylvania," "a few pieces of silver coin or gold, a chest with clothes, a Bible and Prayer or Hymn Book, constituted the whole stock of most of them. . . . A clergyman always accompanied them when they came in large bodies." Dr. Rush also gives a vivid description of the customs and characteristics of the early Germans of Pennsylvania, which answers for the Germans of Western Maryland. "The Germans," he says, "taken as a body, especially as farmers, are not only industrious and frugal, but skillful cultivators of the earth." "The German's farm," says Rupp, "was easily distinguished from those of others by good fences, the extent of orchard, the fertility of soil, the productiveness of the fields, the luxuriance of the meadows." They always provided the best accommodations for their horses and cattle, and paid special attention to the cultivation of grass. They were great economists in the use of wood, and almost invariably lived frugally with respect to diet, furniture, and apparel. They seldom permitted themselves to get in debt, and saved considerable sums by the cultivation of a variety of vegetables, which enabled them to be sparing consumers of meat. The work on the farm was done almost exclusively by the family, the women often assisting the men.

The German mechanic possessed the same characteristics of frugality and industry, and his first object was to save up sufficient money to purchase a home of his own. As merchants the early Germans of Pennsylvania and Maryland were also very successful. In fact, whatever they essayed to do was done thoroughly and well. It was one of their distinguishing traits to settle as near one another as possible, not only from a kindly fellow-feeling, but in order that they might enjoy the advantages of proximity to a common place of worship and to a school-house. "Their churches," says Dr. Rush, "are . . . large, and furnished in many places with organs. The clergy belonging to these churches have moderate salaries, but they are punctually and justly paid. . . The Lutherans and Presbyterians (German Reformed) live in great harmony with each other, insomuch that they preach in each other's churches, and in some instances unite in building a church, in which they both worship at different times." Dr. Rush sums up the general character of the German population in the following pregnant sentence: "If it were possible to determine the amount of all the property brought into Pennsylvania by the present German inhabitants of theState and their ancestors, and then compare it with the present amount of their property, the contrast would form such a monument of human industry and economy as has seldom been contemplated in any age or country." Among the German sects the Mennonites, Moravians, German Brethren, German Seventh-day Baptists, and Schwenkfelders held war to be unchristian and unreasonable, and it is worthy of note that the German Friends of Germantown, as early as 1688 (ten years before the passage of the act by the British Parliament for the encouragement of the slave-trade, by throwing it open to all British subjects and exempting cargoes of negroes from the African military tax), addressed the Philadelphia Yearly Meeting, protesting against buying, selling, and holding men in slavery, and declaring it in their opinion an act irreconcilable with the precepts of the Christian religion.

Of these denominations, the first to emigrate to America appears to have been the Mennonites. This sect had been persecuted in Switzerland, and forced to leave that country. Some had fled to Alsace, above Strasburg, and others to Holland. A number of those about Strasburg, with other Germans, attracted by the toleration extended to all religions by William Penn, set out for Pennsylvania in 1683, and on reaching the colony on the Delaware located themselves at what is now the suburb of Germantown. The greater part were naturalized in 1709. A few years previous the people of Heidelberg and vicinity had just been delivered from the persecutions of the French army, which had twice destroyed the town, only to be made the victims of still more cruel oppression by the Catholic Elector Palatine, their prince. To the number of six thousand they fled to England, drawn thither by a proclamation of Queen Anne offering them protection and aid. Many more had determined to seek a refuge in America. Christopher de Graffenried and Louis Michelle were sent out by the canton of Berne, with instructions to inspect the unoccupied districts of Pennsylvania, Virginia, and Carolina. Michelle had previously visited America, and is believed to have built a fort not far from Connejahera, "many miles above Conestoga," in Pennsylvania. In 1709 the refugees from Berne sailed for America. They landed in New York, Pennsylvania, and North Carolina. In the same year a company of Mennonites left Strasburg and sailed for America. Those who emigrated to Pennsylvania came from the cantons of Zurich, Berne, and Schaffhausen, in Switzerland. In their new homes they not only enjoyed toleration, but practiced it towards other denominations, resembling in this respect the early colonists of Maryland and the followers of Roger Williams and of Penn. Before leaving Europe they had made an agreement with William Penn for lands to be taken up. Several families from the Palatinate emigrated to America and settled in Lancaster County in 1709. In the same year a Swiss company procured a grant of ten thousand acres on the north side of Pequa Creek, in Lancaster County, and settled there. Among the settlers at Pequa we find the familiar Maryland names of Fouts, or Foutz, Zimmerman, Funk, Hoover, Stouffer, Boyer, Hostater, Darby, Miller, Mayer, Witmer, Kauffman, Faber, Boehm, Kaufmann, Baughman, Steiner, and Beatty. So well pleased were the settlers with the country around them that they decided to send one of their number back to Europe to induce others of their denomination to share their fortunes. Martin Kendig was selected, and embarked at Philadelphia. Returning from Europe, he brought with him a number of immigrants, who joined the colony at Pequa. The settlers were surrounded by Indians, but were not molested, and "mingled with them in fishing and hunting." So successful was the little colony (numbering some thirty families in all) that German and French refugees were attracted to it. Among these were the Ferrees, Isaac Lefevre, and the Slaymakers, who had been driven by religious persecution from the Palatinate. The mother of Hon. Abraham Schriver, of Frederick County, was a Ferree. Her name was Rebecca, and she was the wife of David Schriver. The name is variously spelled, in the early colonial records, Ferree, Ferrie, Ferie, Fiere, Fierre, and Firre. In the wake of these two companies came numerous bands of German, Swiss, Dutch, and Huguenot immigrants, who scattered themselves over Southern Pennsylvania and crossed the border into Maryland. During 1727 twelve hundred and forty Palatines arrived in Pennsylvania. In the two years that followed, however, the number of German immigrants was greatly diminished.

Among those who came over about this time was Michael Dieffenderfer, father of David Dieffenderfer, and one of the earlier settlers of Lancaster. David Dieffenderfer served in the Revolutionary army under Col. George Stricker, father of Gen. Stricker, who was prominent in the defense of Baltimore in the war of 1812. In 1725 or 1726 was commenced the Dunker or Tunker settlement of Ephrata, in Lancaster County. The Dunkers were seceders from the German Baptists, and one of their distinctive tenets was the practice of baptism by immersion. In 1725 a number of them, under the leadership of Conrad Beissel, separated from the others owing to their conviction that there was an error among the Dunkers in the observance of the Sabbath, and that the seventh day was the true Sabbath. In 1732 a monastic society was established by Beissel and his followers, and the habit of the Capuchins, or White Friars, was adopted by both brethren and sisters. In 1740 there were thirty-six single brethren and thirty-five sisters in the cloister, and the community, including members living in the vicinity, numbered nearly three hundred. A school was established, which attracted general attention, and which numbered among its pupils young men from Philadelphia and Baltimore. The sect was known to the outside world as the Seventh-day Baptists. George Thomas, an Antigua planter, who was appointed Governor of Pennsylvania in 1737, visited Ephrata in 1741. He was accompanied by "a retinue of twenty horses and a large number of distinguished gentlemen from Maryland and Virginia; they were all honorably received by the brethren." Among the descendants of members of the society are the Urners, the Negleys, the Funks, the Hoehns, the Weisers, and the Gorgases.

Among the Germans and other foreigners who settled in Lancaster County prior to 1735 were the Hoffmans, Bezores, Byerlys, Owens, Emmets, Snevelys, Newcomers, Longneckers, Stakes, Zieglers, Snyders, Koenigs, Graafs, Herseys, Templemans, Fultons, Meixells, Baughmans, Haineses, Lightners, McKimms, Boyds, Alexanders, Lloyds, Buchanans, McClures, and Hugheses. All these names have long been familiar in different portions of Maryland.

About 1732 and subsequently the people living along the border in Pennsylvania and Maryland became involved in a serious quarrel, arising out of the boundary difficulties. The first difficulty was occasioned by the arrest of Daniel and William Lowe, two Marylanders who had settled in Pennsylvania, by a Pennsylvania constable for killing a horse which had strayed to their farm. Capt. Thomas Cresap, the famous Indian-fighter and scout of Frederick, pursued the constable and attempted to rescue the prisoners. His party wounded John Hart, one of the constable's assistants, but were forced to desist, and the Lowes were carried safely to Lancaster. This affair was followed by more "unhappy frays," which finally culminated in a formidable raid of the Lancaster people against Cresap and other Marylanders. According to Rupp, Cresap's party were beaten and driven out of Pennsylvania. At this time Lancaster County embraced the present boundaries of York, Adams, Franklin, Cumberland, and Perry Counties, or, in other words, the whole of Pennsylvania bordering on Western Maryland. The boundary between Maryland and Pennsylvania had not been accurately defined as yet, and the absence of such definition gave rise to serious disputes, which are treated more at length in this work in the chapter on "Boundaries." A large number of Germans had settled in what is now York County, Pa., under Pennsylvania titles, but in order to avoid paying taxes imposed by that province they accepted titles from Lord Baltimore, but subsequently becoming satisfied "that adhesion to him might ultimately prejudice their interests, they formally renounced their allegiance and sought protection from Pennsylvania." The Maryland settlers across the border were greatly incensed at this and determined to eject the "miscreants" from their holdings. "The German settlers," says Rupp, "were harassed perpetually, in many instances driven from their farms, and in others deterred from any attempt to plant or improve."

In 1738 a number of Swiss and Germans in Lancaster County were naturalized upon their own application. Among them were Michael and William Albert, Jacob Bare, or Baer, Casper Stump, George Klein, or Kline, and Frederick Eighelberger, or Eichelberger.

The immunity of the German settlers both in Pennsylvania and Maryland from Indian attacks was sensibly increased by the treaty with the Six Nations, which was signed by representatives of Pennsylvania, Maryland, and Virginia at Lancaster in 1745. The Six Nations, or Iroquois, engaged to prevent the French and Indians from marching through their country to attack the English settlements, and to give the earliest information of the enemy's design. They also surrendered their titles to the lands settled by the

THE EARLY SETTLERS.

English in Pennsylvania, Maryland, and Virginia. Six hundred pounds were paid by the three colonies in consideration of the concessions made by the Indians. This treaty did not, however, secure the settlers from the attacks of Indians who had been wronged or defrauded by traders and unprincipled men; and while free from organized incursions up to the period of the French and Indian war, they were compelled to be continually on the alert, especially in the more exposed and isolated frontier settlements. They found ample time, however, to thoroughly cultivate the rich virgin soil on which they had settled, and to develop the manufacturing industries which are mentioned elsewhere as those most successfully undertaken by the German colonists in Maryland. The same distinguishing characteristics of the Germans in Pennsylvania, as noted by Dr. Rush and Mr. Rupp, were conspicuous among the Maryland Palatines. Like their neighbors and brethren over the border, they preferred to build the most modest dwellings in order that they might erect commodious and comfortable quarters for their stock. Usually the settler in the Monocacy region was content to live in a log cabin, the spaces between the logs being closed up with mortar or clay, and the chimney built outside the structure and of the rudest materials. "The favorite style of building of the stout Germans and Palatines of Frederick County and Western Maryland contemplated a house that was seldom more than one story high, but had large garret-rooms and a deep cellar well filled. The chimney, an immense stack, was in the middle of the building to accommodate the kitchen, which was also the living-room, and had a great fireplace, furnished with pot-hooks and cranes of massive construction. . . . The bedrooms in these houses were not very elaborately furnished, . . . but the housekeeping was always neat and clean, and the larder liberally supplied." The German farmers were prudent, far-seeing men. They never spent more than they could afford, and while they lived in comfort, were careful not to indulge in excess of any kind. The result was that their lands and cattle soon waxed fat, and they were enabled to transmit to their children the heritage not only of material prosperity, but of an unblemished reputation for honest dealing and patient industry and thrift. Their descendants at the present day are scattered all over Western Maryland, and the old methods, except where they have had to be discarded in obedience to the necessities of modern improvement, are still adhered to with the best results. To the German housewife and maiden of these early times is due a large portion of the credit attaching to the immigrants as a class, for the women of the family did not hesitate to lend a hand in the field, and were always busy within-doors, either at the spinning-wheel or in the dairy, or at the kitchen fire. The productive capacity of the Germans was therefore immense, and as they were economical and cautious, though seldom niggardly where liberal expenditure was advisable or when their benevolent impulses were appealed to, it was inevitable that they should outstrip the rest of the province in prosperity.

Of the religious denominations among the Germans, the Lutherans and German Reformed were the most numerous and influential, and, as in Pennsylvania, these two bodies fraternized cordially, and while maintaining their distinctive principles and tenets, worshiped in meeting-houses erected by the joint efforts of both congregations. Besides these there were the Moravians and the other sects already enumerated. As a rule, the members of all these denominations were strict in the observance of their religious duties, and to this fact doubtless is to be ascribed in great part the preservation of the virtues of morality, temperance, and industry which have always distinguished the population of Western Maryland, and which have contributed so much to its prosperity.

"Frederick," says one of its distinguished citizens, "was laid out by an English gentleman, but its lots and the rich farms immediately surrounding it were soon taken up by a host of honest, thrifty, laborious German emigrants, who had fled from the oppressive restrictions of their own fatherland to seek a refuge here for themselves and their families, and whose names underwent many a distortion and mutilation at the hands of the English representatives of the Lord Proprietor, as they labored to write them down from sound upon the pages of our early records. The German was spoken one hundred years ago more freely and frequently upon the streets of Frederick than the English, two of their congregations had their service entirely in that language, the children were instructed in both languages in the schools, the style of houses and barns introduced was that of German rather than of English origin, and, in various degrees of modification, had so held its place here that strangers who have had the opportunity of European travel invariably notice how much Frederick resembles a continental town. But these emigrants brought with them more than their mother-tongue and familiar forms of worship and architecture. They brought also German thrift, industry, and honesty, with ardent love of home—wherever it might be, whether native or adopted,—they brought laborious habits, virtuous lives, truthful tongues, unflinching courage, and an intense longing to do their duty to their families, the community, and the State. And of such ancestry a large number of this assembly may proudly boast,—a nobility of origin worth more than that which is based upon deeds of violence and unrestrained lawlessness. Says a German traveler who visited this place, May 6, 1747, of one of its congregations, 'It appears to me to be one of the purest in the whole country, and one in which I have found the most traces of the true fear of God.'"[1]

---
[1] Address by Dr. Lewis H. Steiner at the Frederick Centennial Celebration, June 28, 1876.

In the immense and constant stream of emigration which the Old World is pouring into America, no element forms a larger or more important part than that which is contributed by the German race. In all the splendid empire of territory which stretches from the Atlantic to the Pacific, and from the Canadian border to the remotest southern limits, there is not a city, a town, or hamlet of the United States which has not been vitalized by the energizing and quickening influences of German enterprise and industry. The brief and imperfect recital that has been given of the part which the German population of Western Maryland have borne in the development of this rich and important section of the State, is but a poor tribute to the all-pervading influence which they have exercised in every period of its history and at every stage of its progress. In the limited space of a notice like the present it is impossible to do justice to a theme so rich in facts as well as suggestions, and the writer must dismiss this portion of the subject with the hope that the time may not be far distant when some more efficient chronicler will record at the length and with the careful detail they deserve the history and achievements of the German population of Western Maryland. But until that task has been accomplished they can at least draw some measure of satisfaction from the reflection that their history has already been written in enduring characters in the progress and prosperity of the section in which they live.

While the large majority of the early settlers in Western Maryland were of German origin, other nationalities were not unrepresented. Settlers of English birth or descent had made their way towards the western boundary of the province in small numbers at a comparatively early period, and, like Cresap and other pioneers of the same nationality, soon made themselves prominent in the new section by their bold and adventurous dispositions, and the courage and determination with which they addressed themselves to the difficult and dangerous duties of border life. From Pennsylvania also flowed in a considerable stream of Scotch-Irish emigrants, many of whom passed into the Valley of Virginia, settling along Back Creek, the North Mountain, and Opequon, while many others remained to try their fortunes in Western Maryland.

The ancestors of the Glasses, Allens, Vances, Kerfoots, etc., were among the earliest settlers on the upper waters of the Opequon. The ancestors of the Whites, Russells, etc., settled near the North Mountain. There was a mixture of Irish and Germans on Cedar Creek and its vicinity, the Frys, Newells, Blackburns, and Wilsons being among the number. The proximity of these early Scotch-Irish settlements in the Valley of Virginia to settlers of the same nationality and religious creed in Western Maryland naturally caused more or less communication between them, and by frequent intermarriages families which originally settled on one side of the border have since been transferred to the other, and have now their representatives both in Maryland and Virginia.

By the treaty of Paris, in 1763, a large territory was ceded to England, within which it became necessary to organize colonial governments. For this and other purposes the king, on the 7th of October, 1763, issued a proclamation, by which the colonial governments generally were prohibited from granting any lands lying west of the sources or heads of any of the rivers flowing into the Atlantic from the west and northwest. On the 16th of April, 1764, instructions were issued to the judges of the land-office, setting forth that the proprietary was desirous of having reserved for him ten thousand acres of land in the western part of Frederick County, to be held as a manor; and that he had therefore directed the surveyor of that county not to execute any warrant on any lands lying beyond Fort Cumberland until this reserve had been selected. In the mean time Governor Sharpe thought proper to survey five different tracts of land, aggregating one hundred and twenty-seven thousand six hundred and eighty acres, from which his lordship might make his selection. This general interdict of the crown, and the reserve to the proprietary, each had a tendency to check the progress of settlements in the direction of the debatable territory. In March, 1774, the subject of the reserve on the lands lying westward of Fort Cumberland being brought before the proprietary's board of revenues, it determined that the object of the reserve had been accomplished in the surveys actually made for the proprietary, and therefore took off the reserve. Large grants of land on the reserve were immediately made, and continued to be made until October, 1774, when instructions were received from the proprietary directing the judges of the land-office to suspend all further grants of the reserved lands. Two years later the proprietary's rights and reservations were swept away by the Revolution, and Washington and Montgomery Counties were created. When the barriers erected by the crown and the proprietary had been removed, new settlements at once began to be made in the territory thus thrown open. Among those who flocked into what had been the forbidden land were a number of the representatives of some of the oldest families of Maryland. Among them were Samuel Ringgold, who patented a tract of twenty thousand acres in Washington County; William Fitzhugh, who also purchased a large estate; Nathaniel Rochester, after whom Rochester, N. Y., was called; Charles Carroll, of Duddington; Otho H. Williams, who owned all the land in the neighborhood of the present town of Williamsport; Frisby Tilghman, of the noted Eastern Shore family of that name; and many others whose descendants are now among the most prominent citizens of Western Maryland.

Manners and Customs of the Early Settlers.—Most of the early settlers were an industrious, frugal, and temperate people, and especially well qualified for the dangerous and difficult task of subduing the splendid but wild territory upon which they had entered, and of driving out before them the savage tribes which they encountered.

As has been truly said, the task of making new establishments in a remote wilderness in time of profound peace is sufficiently difficult, but when the farmer must be at the same time both a warrior and a hunter, must earn his bread not only with sweat but with blood, and must constantly defend by force what his energy and enterprise have won, his position is one which demands the highest degree of human courage and fortitude. Such was the condition of the first settlers of Western Maryland; making their way into the very heart of a hostile country and in the face of a savage foe, far from friendly succor and exposed to constant danger of Indian attacks, they reared their humble structures in the wild wastes with the pride and confidence of monarchs, and with the rifle in one hand and plowshare in the other,—the weapons of war side by side with the implements of peace,—went forth into forest and field to make good the sovereignty which they claimed.

Their buildings were generally of the rudest character, but were substantially constructed, and were not without a sort of solid comfort. When after a painful and dangerous journey of weeks, and perhaps months, the emigrant had reached his destination, he selected a spot for his new residence, and calling together his neighbors, if he had any, proceeded at once with its erection. If he were the first settler in the neighborhood, he had to rely upon his own skill and resources, and upon the aid of the male members of his family. But the early emigrants generally traveled in parties, so as to render each other mutual assistance in the tasks and difficulties of their new life, and if there was no one to help them in their forest homes, they were men who could help themselves. The first step in the erection of their dwelling was the felling of trees of proper size and character for the purpose, and while this was being done, and the logs were being hauled or carried to the place selected, the carpenter of the party would be in search of a straight-grained tree for making clapboards for the roof. The boards were split four feet long with a large frow, and as wide as the timber would allow, and were used without planing. While this work was in progress others were employed in getting puncheons for the floor of the cabin; this was done by splitting trees eighteen inches in diameter, and hewing the faces of them with a broad-axe. They were half the length of the floor they were intended to make. These were the usual preparations for the first day. The second day the neighbors collected, raised and finished the house. The third day's work generally consisted of "furnituring" the house,—supplying it with a clapboard table, made of a split slab, and supported by four raised legs set in auger-holes. Some three-legged stools were made in the same manner. Some pins stuck in the logs at the back of the house supported some clapboards, which served for shelves for the family furniture, consisting of a few pewter dishes, plates, and spoons, but mostly of wooden bowls, trenchers, and noggins. If these last were scarce, gourds and hard-shelled squashes made up the deficiency. The iron pots, knives, and forks were brought from the east side of the mountains, along with salt and iron on pack-horses.[1]

A single fork, placed with its lower end in a hole in the floor, and the upper end fastened to a joist, served for a bedstead, by placing a pole in the fork, with one end through a crack between the logs of the wall. This front pole was crossed by a shorter one within the fork, with its outer end through another crack. From the first pole, through a crack between the logs of the end of the house, the boards were put on which formed the bottom of the bed. Sometimes other poles were pinned to the fork a little distance above these, for the purpose of supporting the front and foot of the bed, while the walls were the support of its back and its head. A few pegs around the walls for the display of the coats of the women and hunting-shirts of the men, and two small forks, or buck's horns, to a joist, for the rifle and shot-pouch, completed the carpenter-work. The cabin being finished, the next ceremony was "the house-warming," which consisted of a dance of a whole night's duration, prior to the occupation of the new abode. Hog and hominy, johnny-cake and pone, milk and mush, with such wild meats as the forests offered and the trusty rifle supplied, was the diet upon which the early settlers mainly lived, and which made strong men and buxom women.

---

[1] Doddridge, chap. v. p. 134.

Their dress partook both of the Indian and the European styles, and, like their lives, was a combination of the savage and the civilized. The hunting-shirt was in universal use, and was a sort of loose frock, coming half-way down the thighs, with large sleeves, open before, and so wide as to lap over a foot or more when belted. The cape, which was large, and sometimes handsomely fringed with a raveled piece of cloth, added to the comfort of the wearer as well as to the appearance of the garment. The bosom of this convenient dress furnished a receptacle where the hunter might deposit a small stock of provisions, his tow for cleaning the barrel of his rifle, and any other article necessary in a short march or journey. To the belt, which held the shirt closely to the body of the wearer, were suspended the tomahawk and scalping-knife, the former on the right side and the latter on the left, while the bullet-bag sometimes hung from the front. The hunting-shirt was made of various materials, generally of linsey, sometimes of coarse linen, and occasionally of dressed deerskin, which latter, however, were cold and uncomfortable in wet weather. The shirt and jacket were made after the common fashion, while the drawers or breeches and leggings, with the moccasins, of dressed deerskin, with cap or hat of various form and material, completed the attire.

The moccasins were generally made of a single piece, with a gathered seam along the top of the foot, and another from the bottom of the heel without gathers, reaching as high as the ankle-joint, or a little higher. The moccasin was lined with deer's hair, or dry leaves in cold weather, and flaps on each side reaching some distance up the legs, and tied with deer-thongs, gave warmth to the extremities, and protected the feet from the entrance of dust, gravel, and snow.

In the latter part of the French and Indian war many of the young whites adopted the Indian costume in its entirety, with the exception of the match-coat. "The drawers," Dr. Doddridge tells us, "were laid aside, and the leggings made larger, so as to reach the upper part of the thigh. The Indian breech-clout was adopted. This was a piece of linen or cloth, nearly a yard long and eight or nine inches broad. This passed under the belt before and behind, leaving the ends for flaps hanging before and behind over the belt. These flaps were sometimes ornamented with some coarse kinds of embroidery work. To the same belt which secured the breech-clout, strings, which supported the long leggings, were attached. When this belt, as was often the case, passed over the hunting-shirt, the upper part of the thighs and part of the hip were naked. The young man, instead of being abashed by his nudity, was proud of his Indian-like dress. In some instances I have seen them go into places of public worship in this dress. Their appearance, however, did not add much to the devotion of the young ladies."

The women wore linsey petticoats and bed-gowns, going barefooted in warm weather, and in cold covering their feet with moccasins, overshoes, or shoe-packs.

The wardrobes of the family were hung in full view upon the walls of the cabin, and while often serving to stop a crack and keep the wind away, also proclaimed the wealth or poverty of the occupants.

"Many of the early sports were imitations of the exercises and stratagems of hunting and war. Boys were taught the use of the bow and arrow at an early age; but, although they acquired considerable adroitness in the use of them, so as to kill a bird or squirrel sometimes, yet it appears to me that, in the hands of the white people, the bow and arrow could never be depended upon for warfare or hunting, unless made and managed in a different manner from any specimens of them which I ever saw. One important pastime of our boys was that of imitating the noise of every bird and beast in the woods. This faculty was not merely a pastime, but a very necessary part of education, on account of its utility in certain circumstances. The imitations of the gobbling and other sounds of wild turkeys often brought those keen-eyed and ever-watchful tenants of the forest within reach of the rifle. The bleating of the fawn brought its dam to her death in the same way. The hunter often collected a company of mopish owls on the trees about his camp, and amused himself with their hoarse screaming. His howl would raise and obtain responses from a pack of wolves, so as to inform him of their neighborhood, as well as guard him against their depredations. This imitative faculty was sometimes requisite as a measure of precaution in war. The Indians, when scattered about in a neighborhood, often collected together by imitating turkeys by day and wolves or owls by night. In similar situations our people did the same. I have often witnessed the consternation of a whole neighborhood in consequence of a few screeches of owls. An early and correct use of this imitative faculty was considered as an indication that its possessor would become in due time a good hunter and a valiant warrior.

"Throwing the tomahawk was another boyish sport in which many acquired considerable skill. The tomahawk, with its handle of a certain length, will make a given number of turns in a given distance. Say in five steps it will strike with the edge, the handle downwards; at the distance of seven and a half, it will strike with the edge, the handle upwards, and so on. A little experience enabled the boy to measure the distance with his eye when walking through the woods, and strike a tree with his tomahawk in any way he chose. The athletic sports of running, jumping, and wrestling were the pastimes of boys in common with the men. A well-grown boy at the age of twelve or thirteen years was furnished with a small rifle and shot-pouch. He then became a fort soldier, and had his port-hole assigned him. Hunting squirrels, turkeys, and raccoons soon made him expert in the use of his gun. Dancing was the principal amusement of our young people of both sexes. Their dances, to be sure, were of the simplest forms,—three or four-handed reels and jigs. Country-dances, cotillons, and minuets were unknown. I remember to have seen once or twice a dance which was called 'The Irish Trot,' but I have long since forgotten its figure. Shooting at a mark was a common diversion among the men when their stock of ammunition would allow it. This, however, was far from being always the case. The present mode of shooting off-hand was not then in practice. This mode was not considered as any trial of the value of a gun, nor indeed as much of a test of the skill of a marksman. Their shooting was from a rest, and at as great a distance as the length and weight of the barrel of the gun would throw a ball on a horizontal level. Such was their regard to accuracy in those sportive trials of their rifles, and of their own skill in the use of them, that they often put moss or some other soft substance on the log or stump from which they shot, for fear of having the bullet thrown from the mark by the spring of the barrel. When the rifle was held to the side of a tree for a rest, it was pressed against it as tightly as possible for the same reason. Rifles of former times were different from those of modern date; few of them carried more than forty-five bullets to the pound. Bullets of a less size were not thought sufficiently heavy for hunting or war.

"Dramatic narrations, chiefly concerning Jack and the Giant, furnished our young people with another source of amusement during their leisure hours. Many of these tales were lengthy, and embraced a considerable range of incident. Jack, always the hero of the story, often encountering many difficulties and performing many great achievements, came off conqueror of the Giant. Many of these stories were tales of knight-errantry, in which some captive virgin was restored to her lover. These dramatic narrations concerning Jack and the Giant bore a strong resemblance to the poems of Ossian, the story of the Cyclops and Ulysses in the 'Odyssey' of Homer, and the tale of the Giant and Greatheart in 'Pilgrim's Progress.' They were so arranged as to the different incidents of the narration that they were easily committed to memory."

Singing was another but not very common amusement among our first settlers. Their tunes were rude enough, to be sure. Robin Hood furnished a number of our songs, the balance were mostly tragical. These last were denominated "love-songs about murder;" as to cards, dice, backgammon, and other games of chance, we knew nothing about them. As a general rule, the early settlers married young. There was no distinction of rank, says Dr. Doddridge, and very little of fortune. On these accounts the first impression of love resulted in marriage, and a family establishment cost but a little labor and nothing else. In the first years of the settlement of the country a wedding engaged the attention of a whole neighborhood, and the frolic was anticipated by old and young with eager expectation. This is not to be wondered at when it is told that a wedding was almost the only gathering which was not accompanied with the labor of reaping, log-rolling, building a cabin, or planning some scout or campaign. On the morning of the wedding-day the groom and his attendants assembled at the house of his father for the purpose of reaching the home of his bride by noon, which was the usual time for celebrating the nuptials, and which for certain reasons must take place before dinner. Let the reader imagine an assemblage of people without a store, tailor, or mantua-maker within a hundred miles, and an assemblage of horses without a blacksmith or saddler within an equal distance. The gentlemen dressed in shoe-packs (tanned leather), moccasins, leather breeches, leggings, linsey hunting-shirts, and all home-made. The ladies dressed in linsey petticoats, and linsey of linen bed-gowns, coarse shoes, stockings, handkerchiefs, and buckskin gloves, if any. If there were any buckles, rings, buttons, or ruffles, they were the relics of olden times, family pieces from parents or grandparents. The horses were caparisoned with old saddles, old bridles or halters, and pack-saddles, with a bag or blanket thrown over them; a rope or string as often constituted the girth as a piece of leather.

The march, in double file, was often interrupted by the narrowness and obstructions of our horse-paths, as they were called, for we had no roads, and these difficulties were often increased, sometimes by the good and sometimes by the ill will of neighbors, by fallen trees, and tying grapevines across the way. Sometimes an ambuscade was formed by the wayside, and an unexpected discharge of several guns took place, so as to cover the wedding-party with smoke. Let the reader imagine the scene which followed this discharge: the sudden spring of the horses, the shrieks of the girls, and the chivalrous bustle of their partners to save them from falling. Sometimes, in spite of all that could be done to prevent it, some were thrown to the ground. If a wrist, elbow, or ankle happened to be sprained, it was tied with a handkerchief, and little more was said or thought about it. The ceremony of the marriage preceded the dinner, which was a substantial backwoods feast of beef, pork, fowls, and sometimes venison and bear-meat, roasted and boiled, with plenty of potatoes, cabbage, and other vegetables. During the dinner the greatest hilarity always prevailed, although the table might be a large slab of timber hewed out with a broad-axe, supported by four sticks set in auger-holes, and the furniture some old pewter dishes and plates, the rest wooden bowls and trenchers; a few pewter spoons, much battered about the edges, were to be seen at some tables. The rest were made of horns. If knives were scarce, the deficiency was made up by the scalping-knives, which were carried in sheaths suspended to the belt of the hunting-shirt. Every man carried one of them. After dinner the dancing commenced, and generally lasted till the next morning. The figures of the dances were three and four-handed reels, or square sets and jigs. The commencement was always a square four, which was followed by what was called "jigging it off;" that is, two of the four would single out for a jig, and were followed by the remaining couple. The jigs were often accompanied with what was called "cutting out;" that is, when either of the parties became tired of the dance, on intimation the place was supplied by some other person without interruption to the dance. In this way a dance was often continued until a musician was heartily tired of his situation. Towards the latter part of the night, if any of the company, through weariness, attempted to conceal themselves for the purpose of sleeping, they were hunted up, paraded on the floor, and the fiddler ordered to play "Hang Out Till To-Morrow Morning." About nine or ten o'clock a deputation of the young ladies stole off the bride and put her to bed. In doing this it frequently happened that they had to ascend a ladder instead of a pair of stairs, leading from the dining and ball-room to the loft, the floor of which was made of clapboards lying loose. This ascent, one might think, would put the bride and her attendants to the blush; but as the foot of the ladder was commonly behind the door, which was purposely opened for the occasion, and its rounds at the inner ends were well hung with hunting-shirts, dresses, and other articles of clothing, the candles being on the opposite side of the house, the exit of the bride was noticed by but few. This done, a deputation of young men in like manner stole off the groom, and placed him snugly by the side of his bride. The dance still continued; and if seats happened to be scarce, which was often the case, every young man, when not engaged in the dance, was obliged to offer his lap as a seat for one of the girls, and the offer was sure to be accepted. In the midst of this hilarity the bride and groom were not forgotten. Pretty late in the night some one would remind the company that the new couple must stand in need of some refreshment; *black Betty*, which was the name of the bottle, was called for, and sent up the ladder; but sometimes black Betty did not go alone, but was accompanied by as much bread, beef, pork, and cabbage as would afford a good meal for half a dozen hungry men. The young couple were compelled to eat and drink more or less of whatever was offered. It often happened that some neighbors or relations not being asked to the wedding took offense, and the mode of revenge adopted by them on such occasions was that of cutting off the manes, foretops, and tails of the horses of the wedding company.

On returning to the infare, the order of procession and the race for black Betty was the same as before. The feasting and dancing often lasted several days, at the end of which the whole company was so exhausted with loss of sleep that a long rest was necessary to fit them to return to their ordinary labors.[1]

The custom of stealing the bride's shoe while at dinner, though perhaps of later date, was one which long prevailed, and which afforded great amusement to the wedding guests. She was protected from the attacks by the waiters (or, as we call them nowadays, groomsmen and bridesmaids), and to succeed in accomplishing the theft the greatest dexterity was required; and if they failed to defend her successfully, they were in honor bound to pay a penalty for the redemption of the shoe. This penalty was a bottle of wine or one dollar, which was commonly the price of a bottle of wine; and as a punishment to the bride, she was not permitted to dance until the shoe was restored. The successful thief on getting the shoe held it up in triumph to the view of the whole assemblage, which was generally pretty numerous. This was almost exclusively a German custom, but that of throwing the stocking was also known to the Irish, and is celebrated by an Irish poet in his "Irish Wedding."

---

[1] Dr. Doddridge.

After the bride and groom had been put to bed, the young people were admitted to their room, and a stocking rolled into a ball would be given to the young women, who one after the other would go to the foot of the bed, stand with their backs towards it, and throw the stocking over their shoulders at the bride's head; and the first that succeeded in touching her cap on her head was the next to be married. The young men then took up the stocking and threw it at the groom's head, the greatest earnestness and eagerness being shown by both sexes to prove successful.[1]

The race for the bottle, already alluded to, was one of the most interesting and exciting incidents of the wedding. A bottle of the best spirits that could be obtained was prepared at the bride's residence and ornamented with a white ribbon, and when several miles distant the competitors in the race would start, on even terms, and with their horses at full speed, disdaining rocks, stumps, and ravines, and disregarding all impediments, would dash madly forward for the tempting prize. The father, or next friend of the bride, expecting the racers, stood, bottle in hand, ready to deliver it to the successful contestant. On receiving it, he immediately returned to meet the bridal party, and presented the bottle first to the bride, next to the groom, and then to the rest of the company, all of whom, both men and women, were required to give it a hearty salute.

In the earlier days of the settlements, and upon the frontiers, and in positions especially exposed to attack, self-preservation required the erection of places of defense, to which the harried inhabitants might retire upon the approach of hostile Indians. The forts of these early days were, however, not simply fortified points of refuge, but often the residence of a small number of families of the same neighborhood. As the Indian mode of warfare was an indiscriminate slaughter of all ages and of both sexes, it was as requisite to provide for the safety of the women and children as for that of the men.[2] The fort consisted of cabins, block-houses, and stockades, a range of cabins commonly forming at least one of its sides, divisions or partitions of logs separating the cabins from each other. The walls on the outside were ten or twelve feet high, the slope of the roof being wholly inward. The block-houses were built at the angles of the stockade inclosure, and projected about two feet beyond the outer walls of the cabins and stockades. Their upper stories were about eighteen inches larger in every way than the lower, leaving an opening at the beginning of the second story, so that the inmates could shoot from above upon an enemy attempting to climb the walls. But one door opened into these rude structures, and that was always very strong, so as to defy entrance by any ordinary means of assault. In some cases the angles of the stockades were furnished with bastions instead of with block-houses. A large folding-gate, made of thick slabs, nearest the spring, closed the fort. The stockades, bastions, cabins, and block-house walls were provided with port-holes at proper heights and distances, and the whole of the outside was made completely bullet-proof. The whole of this work was accomplished without the aid of a single nail or spike of iron, and for the very good and sufficient reason that there were none to be had.[3]

In some places less exposed a single block-house, with a cabin or two, constituted the whole fort. Such defenses, though wholly insufficient for protection against artillery, answered all the purposes of the times, and were seldom attacked and scarcely ever taken by the Indians.

Although, according to a distinguished writer, " there was, for many years after the settlement of the country, neither law nor gospel" among the frontier communities, there was an unwritten code, both of morals and property, to which general obedience was cheerfully accorded. The want of legal government in the extreme western frontier was due to the dispute as to sovereignty between Virginia and Pennsylvania, and for a long period the people of that section knew nothing of courts, lawyers, magistrates, sheriffs, or constables. Public opinion was the sole and the supreme tribunal, but it was one which was universally respected, and whose decrees were always enforced. "The punishment," says Dr. Doddridge, " for idleness, lying, dishonesty, and ill-fame generally was that of 'hating the offender out,' as they expressed it. This mode of chastisement was like the *atimia* of the Greeks. It was a public expression in various ways of a general sentiment of indignation against such as transgressed the moral maxims of the community to which they belonged. This commonly resulted either in the reformation or banishment of the person against whom it was directed. At house-raisings, log-rollings, and harvest-parties, every one was expected to do his duty faithfully. A person who did not perform his share of labor on these occasions was designated by the epithet of 'Lawrence,' or some other title still more opprobrious; and when it came to his turn to require the like aid from his neighbors, the idler soon felt his punishment in their refusal to attend to his call. Although there was no legal

---

[1] Kercheval's "History of the Valley of Virginia."
[2] Dr. Doddridge.

[3] Dr. Doddridge.

compulsion to the performance of military duty, yet every man of full age and size was required to do his full share of public service. If he did not do so he was 'hated out as a coward.' Even the want of any article of war-equipments, such as ammunition, a sharp flint, a priming-wire, a scalping-knife or tomahawk, was thought highly disgraceful.

"Debts, which make such an uproar in civilized life, were but little known among our forefathers at the early settlement of the country. After the depreciation of the Continental paper they had no money of any kind; everything purchased was paid for in produce or labor. A good cow and calf was often the price of a bushel of alum salt. If a contract was not punctually fulfilled, the delinquent's credit was at an end. Any petty theft was punished with all the infamy that could be heaped on the offender. The first settlers had a kind of innate or hereditary detestation of the crime of theft, in any shape or degree, and their maxim was, 'a thief must be whipped.' If the theft was of something of some value, a kind of jury of the neighborhood, after hearing the testimony, would condemn the culprit to Moses' law, that is, to forty stripes save one. If the theft was of some small article, the offender was doomed to carry on his back the flag of the United States, which then consisted of thirteen stripes. In either case some able hands were selected to execute the sentence, so that the stripes were sure to be well laid on. This punishment was followed by a sentence of exile, the offender being told that he must decamp in so many days on penalty of having the number of his stripes doubled.

"If a woman was given to tattling and slandering her neighbors, she was punished by common consent with a kind of patent right to say whatever she pleased without being believed. Her tongue was then said to be harmless, or to be no scandal.

"With all their rudeness, these people were given to hospitality, and freely divided their rough fare with a neighbor or stranger, and would have been offended at the offer of pay. In their settlements and forts they lived, they worked, they fought and feasted or suffered together in cordial harmony.

"They were warm and constant in their friendships. On the other hand, they were revengeful in their resentments. And the point of honor sometimes led to personal combats. If one man called another a liar, he was considered as having given a challenge, which the person who received it must accept or be deemed a coward, and the charge was generally answered on the spot with a blow. If the injured person was decidedly unable to fight the aggressor, he might get a friend to do it for him. The same thing took place on a charge of cowardice or any other dishonorable action. A battle must follow, and the person who made the charge must fight either the person against whom he had made the charge or any champion who chose to espouse his cause. The mode of single combat in those days was dangerous in the extreme. Although no weapons were used, fists, teeth, and feet were employed at will; but, above all, the detestable practice of gouging, by which eyes were sometimes put out, rendered this mode of fighting frightful indeed. Instances of seduction and bastardy did not frequently happen in our early times."

CHAPTER IV.

THE FRENCH AND INDIAN WAR.

The Ohio Company—The Cresaps—Frontier Forts—Braddock's Defeat—Indian Outrages—Capture of Fort Du Quesne—Pontiac's War.

DIFFICULTIES between England and France had arisen at intervals since the peace of Utrecht (1713), though not assuming the character of war. In the North and East, France was sparing no effort to extend her power and crush that of England. This vexatious contest was continued with feeble efforts and various success almost down to 1756. It came at last to be distinctly understood, or fully believed, that a preponderating ascendency in America must decide the long and arduous contest between those rival powers. It was a singular phenomenon, that a great question of national aggrandizement between the courts of London and Paris should be decided in the interior of America. Such, however, was the fact; and the banks of the St. Lawrence, and the shores of the American lakes, and the borders of Maryland and Virginia were destined to be the theatre on which the great prize was to be contended for. The vigor of the contest was proportionate to the magnitude of the stake. The efforts of England were cheerfully and promptly seconded by those of her colonies through four successive years, until at length the Plains of Abraham witnessed the triumph of their united valor, and the gallant and lamented Wolfe planted the cross of St. George upon the ramparts of Quebec. The peace of Fontainebleau, which soon followed, secured the conquest which valor and perseverance had won. France relinquished her pretensions, and left Great Britain without a rival upon this great field of glory and enterprise. The first signal of alarm to the French was the grant of five hundred thousand acres of territory on the south side of the Ohio, between the Monongahela and Kanawha Rivers, and west of the Alleghanies, made by the English government in 1749 to a small number of Marylanders and Virginians of wealth and influence, styling themselves the "Ohio Company."

By its charter the company was required to select a large portion of its lands immediately, to settle upon them one hundred families within seven years, to erect a fort, and maintain a garrison against the Indians. They at once set about the exploration of the country, and employed for the purpose Christopher Gist, of Maryland, an energetic, fearless pioneer, and a man of considerable intelligence. Gist was instructed to examine the quality of the lands, keep a journal, draw plans of the country, and report in full. He arrived at Will's Creek in October, 1749, and on the 31st started on his mission, following an Indian trail, his only guide through the wilderness. His explorations occupied several months, and took him almost to the falls of the Ohio, near the present site of Louisville, Ky., and included the region bordering on the Miami River. Gist also succeeded in obtaining from the Indian tribes friendly assurances, which, by his influence and that of George Croghan, a popular trader, were reiterated at the Council held at Logstown in 1752.[1]

In 1750 the Ohio Company built a small store-house at Will's Creek, and stocked it with goods for the purpose of trading with the Indians, and in the following year, 1751, Col. Thomas Cresap, who still lived at Oldtown, laid out and marked a road from Will's Creek to the mouth of the Monongahela, the present site of Pittsburgh. He was assisted by a friendly Indian named Nemacolin, and the work was so well done that Gen. Braddock with his army afterwards pursued the same route, which thenceforward took the name of Braddock's road. Col. Cresap was one of the earliest settlers of Western Maryland, and it may be said without exaggeration was one of the most remarkable men of his day. He emigrated to America from Yorkshire, England, when only fifteen years of age, and about fifteen years afterwards married a Miss Johnson, and settled on the Susquehanna River, either at or near Havre de Grace, in Harford County. He subsequently removed higher up the river, to Wright's Ferry, opposite the town of Columbia, where he proceeded to take possession of a tract of five hundred acres of land obtained under a Maryland patent. The land, however, was part of the debatable ground claimed by both Penn and Lord Baltimore, and Cresap soon found that it was necessary to make good his title by force of arms. He appears to have been nothing loath to engage in the border troubles that ensued, and took so active a part in defense of Lord Baltimore's claim that he soon came to be regarded as an especially dangerous enemy by the Pennsylvanians, who resorted to the basest means to compass his destruction. "An Indian was hired to assassinate him in his own house; yet, won by his kindness and hospitality, the savage disclosed the plot and was pardoned for his meditated crime." At length, however, a regular battle took place between the factionists, and Cresap's party having wounded several of Penn's partisans, gained the day and kept the field.

The Pennsylvanians, however, soon returned to the attack, and coming upon Cresap by night laid siege to his house, which he defended with his customary boldness and vigor.

---

[1] "Christopher Gist was of English descent. His grandfather of the same name was one of the earliest settlers of Baltimore County, where he died in 1691. His grandmother was Edith Cromwell, whose death occurred in 1694. Their only child, Richard, was surveyor of the Western Shore, one of the commissioners appointed to lay off Baltimore Town, and presiding magistrate in 1736. In 1705 he married Zipporah Murray, and Christopher, the able agent of the Ohio Company, was one of three sons. He married Sarah Howard; his brother Nathaniel married Mary Howard; and Thomas, the third brother, married Violetta Howard, aunts of Gen. John Eager Howard. From either Nathaniel or Thomas descended Gen. Gist, who was killed at the battle of Franklin, Tenn., near the close of the late civil war. Christopher had three sons—Nathaniel, Richard, and Thomas—and one daughter,—Nancy,—none of whom, except Nathaniel, were married. Because of his knowledge of the country on the Ohio, and his skill in dealing with the Indians, Christopher Gist was chosen to accompany Washington on his mission in 1753, and it was from his journal that Sparks and Irving derived their account of that expedition. With his sons Nathaniel and Thomas he was with Braddock on the fatal field of Monongahela, and for his services received a grant of 12,000 acres of land from the king of England. Richard was killed in the battle of King's Mountain. Thomas lived on the plantation, and was a man of note in his day, presiding in the courts till his death, about 1786. Nancy lived with him until his death, when she joined her brother Nathaniel, and removed with him to the grant in Kentucky about the beginning of the present century. Nathaniel, the grandfather of the Hon. Montgomery Blair, of Maryland, married Judith Carey Bell, of Buckingham County, Va., a grandniece of Archibald Carey, the mover of the Bill of Rights in the House of Burgesses. Nathaniel was a colonel in the Virginia line during the Revolutionary war, and died early in the present century at an advanced age. He left two sons, Henry Carey and Thomas Cecil. His eldest daughter, Sarah Howard, married the Hon. Jesse Bledsoe, United States senator from Kentucky, and a distinguished jurist; his grandson, B. Gratz Brown, was the Democratic candidate for Vice-President in 1872. The second daughter of Col. Gist, Anne (Nancy), married Col. Nathaniel Hart, a brother of Mrs. Henry Clay. The third daughter married Dr. Boswell, of Lexington, Ky. The fourth daughter married Francis P. Blair, and they were the parents of Hon. Montgomery Blair and Francis P. Blair, Jr. The fifth daughter married Benjamin Gratz, of Lexington, Ky."—*Lowdermilk*, p. 28.

Finding they were unable to carry the position by assault they set fire to the house, and Cresap being forced to leave the burning building, was taken prisoner after a desperate struggle, in which one of his assailants was wounded.

His captors carried him in triumph to Philadelphia, where, as he was marched through the streets before the assembled citizens, he taunted the crowd by exclaiming, half in derision, half in earnest, "Why, this is the finest city in the province of Maryland!" After more than a year's confinement he was released by the king's order, and returning to Maryland removed to Antietam, to a valuable farm called the Long Meadows, afterwards owned by the Sprigg family, in Washington County. Here he built over a spring a house of stone, which was designed not only for a residence, but as a fort, as the locality was then on the frontier, in advance of white population and exposed to the danger of Indian attack. Obtaining a loan of five hundred pounds from Mr. Dulany, he commenced to trade in skins and furs, and shipped a large quantity to England, which, however, were captured by a French vessel on the way over, to the financial ruin of the unfortunate trader. But he was not the sort of man to be frowned down by fortune, and so settling his indebtedness to Mr. Dulany by transferring to him his farm of fourteen hundred acres, he removed to what is now known as Oldtown, in Allegany County, but which he called Skipton, after the place of his nativity, where he took up his permanent residence, and where he acquired an immense landed estate, lying in both Maryland and Virginia. Col. Cresap having thus made his way to the extreme outposts of civilization, soon became one the most distinguished pioneers of the West, and his name was a household word not only among the whites, but the Indians as well.

"In early times," says Jacob, "when there were but few taverns, and these few were very indifferent, his house at Old Town was open and his table spread for all decent travelers, and they were welcome. His delight was to give and receive useful information; nor was this friendly disposition limited to the white people only. The Indians generally called on him in pretty large parties as they passed and repassed from north to south in their war expeditions, and for which special purpose he kept a very large kettle for their use; and he also generally gave them a beef to kill for themselves every time they called, and his liberality gained for him among them the honorable title of the 'Big-spoon.'"

In person Col. Cresap was not large, but firmly set, and of very great muscular strength; he had a sound constitution, and lived to the age of one hundred and five or six. When seventy years old he made a voyage to England, where he was commissioned by Lord Baltimore to run the western line of Maryland, in order to ascertain which of the two branches of the Potomac was the larger, and which was actually the fountain-head of that river. On his return home he employed surveyors to run the line, and the map of this work, prepared by Col. Cresap, was the first ever made to show the course and fountains of the north and south branches of the Potomac River. When more than eighty years of age he married his second wife, and at the age of one hundred performed a journey, partly by sea and partly by land, from his residence at Oldtown to an island near the British province of Nova Scotia, and returned in safety. When ninety years of age he "conceived and digested a plan to explore as far west as the Pacific, and nothing but his advanced years prevented the accomplishment of an enterprise which he described with the enthusiasm of an early borderer."[1] From this his enthusiastic biographer is justified in declaring,—

"that had Providence placed Col. Cresap at the head of our army, or state, or kingdom, he would have been a more conspicuous character. He was not inferior to Charles XII., of Sweden, in personal bravery, nor to Peter the Great, of Russia,—whom in many things he much resembled,—in coolness or fortitude, or that peculiar talent of learning experience from misfortune, and levying a tax upon damage and loss to raise him to future prosperity and success."

Col. Thomas Cresap had five children, three sons—Daniel, Thomas, and Michael—and two daughters,—Sarah and Elizabeth.[2]

Michael, the youngest son of Col. Thomas Cresap, was no less distinguished than his father in the early history of Western Maryland. He was born in that part of Frederick which is at present Allegany County, on the 29th of June, 1742, and was sent to the celebrated school of Rev. Thomas Craddock, in Baltimore County. Not fancying the restraints of school-life,

---

[1] Jacob's "Life of Cresap."
[2] On the 14th of September, 1751, Christopher Gist, Michael Aldridge, and James Martin made affidavit "that four captains of Indian warriors, with their men, consisting of fifty or thereabouts, camped in said Col. Thomas Cresap's pasture. They killed several of his hogs, took his corn, his flour, and bread, which made the said Cresap fall into a passion and threaten to load his guns and shoot among them at night." They persuaded him not to do so, but to complain to the Governor.

Several Indians made affidavit about the same time that "Brother Cresap" of late seemed angry, and "did not give us victuals so cheerful as usual. Our young men went out and killed sundry of his hogs, at which he flew into a passion.

"'As the white people has killed up the deer, buffaloes, elks, and bears, there is nothing for us to live on but what we get from the white people; and having no white people on the road from Onondaga to our brother Cresap's house, we are often very hungry, and stays three or four days to rest ourselves, and our young men very unruly goes into the woods and kills our brother Cresap's hoggs and sometimes cattle.'"

young Cresap left his preceptor and made his way back to his father's house, traveling alone one hundred and forty miles through a dangerous wilderness to reach his destination, where, however, he received only a flogging for his pains, and was returned to his teacher, with whom he remained until the completion of his studies.

Soon after leaving school he married Miss Whitehead, of Philadelphia, and set up as a trader. His operations were not successful, however, and "urged by necessity as well as a laudable ambition," early in 1774 he engaged six or seven active young men, and "repairing to the wilderness of the Ohio commenced the business of building houses and clearing lands, and being among the first adventurers into this exposed and dangerous region, he was enabled to select some of the best and richest of the Ohio levels."[1]

Here, on or near the present site of Brownsville, Ky., he built himself a house of hewed logs, with a shingled roof nailed on, which is believed to have been the first shingled house west of the Alleghany Mountains. He retained the title to this land for years, and at last disposed of it to Thomas and Basil Brown, two brothers from Maryland, from whom the present town of Brownsville takes its name. This point became an attractive place to the whites as it had evidently been to the savages, as we may judge from the ingenious works with which they fortified it. This post, known in border history as Red-Stone Old Fort, became the rallying-point of the pioneers, and was familiar to many an early settler as his place of embarkation for the "dark and bloody ground." In the legends of the West, Michael Cresap is connected with this Indian stronghold. In those mountains Cresap is spoken of as remarkable for his brave, adventurous disposition, and awarded credit for often rescuing the whites by a timely notice of the savages' approach, a knowledge of which he obtained by unceasing vigilance over their movements. This fort was frequently Cresap's rendezvous as a trader, and thither he resorted with his people, either to interchange views and adopt plans for future action, or for repose in quieter times when the red men were lulled into inaction, and the tomahawk was temporarily buried.[2]

Michael Cresap was prominently engaged in all the border conflicts with the Indians, and has been portrayed in a celebrated piece of Indian rhetoric as the instigator if not one of the chief actors in the massacre of Logan's family,—a charge which has been sufficiently refuted by Jacob in his "Life of Cresap," and by Brantz Mayer in his "Taj-Gah-Jute, or Logan and Cresap." Nevertheless the war of 1774 has often been called "Cresap's War," and although Cresap was entirely guiltless of all connection with the butchery which brought it on, he rendered good service while it was in progress, under a captain's commission from the Governor of Virginia. After its conclusion, Cresap returned to Maryland, spending the autumn of 1774 and the following winter with his family, and early in the spring of 1775 proceeded again to the Ohio to complete the work begun the preceding year. Ill health, however, compelled him to retrace his steps to Maryland, and while on his way he was met by a messenger, who informed him that he had been appointed by the Committee of Safety at Frederick to take command of one of the two rifle companies required to be raised in Maryland by a resolution of the Continental Congress. In spite of bad health Cresap accepted the commission, and joined Washington at Boston in August with the first company of riflemen raised in Maryland. His illness increased, and after about three months' service he was compelled to leave the army, with the intention of returning to his home; but he was unable to proceed farther than New York, where he died of fever on the 18th of October, 1775, at the early age of thirty-three. His remains, attended by a vast concourse of people, were interred with military honors in Trinity churchyard, New York. His tombstone bears the following inscription, beneath the rude sculpture of a winged head:

"IN MEMORY OF MICHAEL CRESAP FIRST CAP^t OF THE RIFLE BATALIONS, AND SON OF CO^l THOMAS CRESAP, WHO DEPARTED THIS LIFE OCTOBER THE 18th, 1775."

In June, 1752, Mr. Gist, as agent of the Ohio Company, with Col. Fry and two other gentlemen, went to Logs-town, about seventeen miles below the Forks,[3] and made the treaty with the Indians to which allusion has been made. By this treaty the Indians bound themselves not to disturb any settlement on the southeast side of the Ohio. After the treaty at Logstown Gist was appointed surveyor for the company, and was directed to lay off a town at Shutee's Creek, a little below the present site of Pittsburgh, on the east side of the Ohio, and four hundred pounds were appropriated to pay for the construction of a fort. Gist, with several other families, then settled in the valley of the Monongahela, not far from the creek above named. During the same year the company erected another post on the Virginia side of the river, which was known as the "New Store-house," and was

---

[1] Jacob's "Life of Cresap."
[2] Mayer's "Logan and Cresap."
[3] Pittsburgh.

located "at the foot of the bluff on which now stands the beautiful residence of Capt. Roger Perry, very near the point occupied by the abutment of the Potomac bridge at Cumberland." The first store-house was located on the west side of Will's Creek, north of the river, and the ground on both sides of the creek was surveyed and laid off into a town, with streets, lines, etc., and called Charlottesburg in honor of Princess Charlotte Sophia, afterwards wife of George III.[1]

The territory granted to the Ohio Company, however, was claimed by the French, and the establishment of the trading-posts described was followed by prompt and decisive measures of reprisal on the part of the French military commanders. Some of the English traders among the Indians were seized and imprisoned, and several of the trading-posts of the company were reduced and pillaged. Indignant at these outrages, Governor Dinwiddie introduced upon the theatre of affairs a youth—George Washington—to perform an important and hazardous mission for his native colony, and to prepare himself to serve the whole country. Col. Washington was dispatched to the French commandant to protest against his proceedings and to demand the evacuation of the territory.

On the 30th of October, 1753, Washington set off from Williamsburg on his dangerous mission through a hostile Indian region with that courage, zeal, and perseverance which afterwards, in a higher station, made him the savior of his country. He reached Will's Creek on the 14th of November, where he engaged Col. Nathaniel Gist, the intrepid pioneer, to accompany him on the expedition. The demands of Virginia were rejected, and nothing was left but a recourse to hostilities. In the war which ensued Maryland became involved simply in self-defense and for the assistance of the sister colonies, while Virginia and Pennsylvania were contending for the acquisition of a large and fertile territory.

The intentions and movements of the French being understood, the Governor of Virginia prepared for immediate war. He summoned the House of Burgesses to meet at an early day, and also wrote letters to the Governors of the other provinces calling on them for aid, drawing a vivid picture of the common danger, and making moving appeals to their patriotism and sense of duty to their sovereign. The English government recognized the dangerous consequences likely to result to her possessions from these encroachments unless they were instantly repelled, and responded fully to the spirit of Virginia. Upon representations made by Governor Dinwiddie to the Earl of Holderness (then Secretary of State) circulars were addressed to the English colonies to repel by force all attempts by the French to intrude upon the settlements within the colonies. That addressed to the province of Maryland was submitted to its Assembly, October session, 1753, but its requisitions, although sustained and urged by its Executive, were without effect. The Lower House assured the Governor "that they were resolutely determined to repel any hostile invasion of the province by any foreign power, and that they would cheerfully contribute to the defense of the neighboring colonies when their circumstances required it, but they did not deem this a pressing occasion." At the next session of the Assembly, held in February, 1754, the Upper House expressed its willingness to concur in proper measures of defense.

In the mean time the French had not been idle. In the spring of 1753 they had built at Presque Isle, on Lake Erie, a strong fort, and, leaving a large garrison there, they marched to the Rivière aux Bœufs, where they erected another fort, cutting a wagon-road twenty-one feet in width between the two. Here garrisons were maintained during the winter of 1753–54, and here a strong force gathered in 1754, fully prepared to march to and occupy the head of the Ohio. On the 17th of April, 1754, M. de Contrecœur, the French commander, at the head of from five hundred to a thousand men, with eighteen pieces of artillery, captured the defenseless works afterwards known as Fort Du Quesne, which occupied the spot where now stands the city of Pittsburgh. Washington was at Will's Creek (now Cumberland, Md.) when the news reached him of the surrender of the fort. He resolved to proceed to the mouth of Red Stone Creek (Brownsville, Pa.), and there to erect a fort, and await the advancing foe. He arrived at the Great Meadows on the 28th of May, and encountered a detachment of thirty-five men, under M. de Jumonville, sent out from Fort Du Quesne as ambassadors, as was alleged by M. de Contrecœur, to warn him to withdraw. Washington, however, mistook their character, and a sharp skirmish ensued, in which M. de Jumonville and several of his men were killed, and the rest surrendered, and were sent under guard to the Governor of Virginia. Having heard of large reinforcements at Fort Du Quesne, and expecting an attack, Washington retreated to the Great Meadows, where he commenced the erection of a fort, to which was given the suggestive title of Fort Necessity. While thus engaged, they were surprised by the approach of a superior French force, and, after a conflict of some hours, obliged to surrender on honorable terms. On the 4th

---

[1] Lowdermilk.

of July, 1754, the little garrison evacuated its feeble fort and retreated to Will's Creek, and the unprotected frontiers of Pennsylvania, Maryland, and Virginia were exposed to the plundering bands of French and Indians. Leaving his force at Will's Creek under the command of Col. Innes, Washington hastened to Williamsburg, to communicate in person to Governor Dinwiddie the result of his expedition, while messengers were dispatched with letters to the Governors of Maryland and Pennsylvania, explaining his weak and exposed situation, and soliciting aid. Governor Sharpe, however, aware of the situation of affairs, had already convened the Assembly, which met in Annapolis on the 17th of July. The news of the defeat of Col. Washington reached Annapolis the day after the Assembly had met, and created great surprise and alarm, and it had the effect of hastening the action of the Legislature, which, on the 25th of July, appropriated six thousand pounds

"to his excellency Horatio Sharpe, Esq., for his majesty's use, towards the defence of the colony of Virginia, attacked by the French and Indians, and for the relief and the support of the wives and children of the Indian allies that put themselves under the protection of this government."

Immediately upon the passage of this act, Governors Sharpe notified Governor Dinwiddie, who recommended that a company of one hundred soldiers be raised in the province, to act in conjunction with the forces then gathering at Will's Creek, to serve under the command of Col. Innes. Governor Sharpe issued a commission to Capt. Thomas Cresap, who had behaved himself on all occasions as a good servant to the government, "to raise a company of riflemen to serve beyond the Allegany Mountains." In August the Governor gave orders that two additional companies should be raised to join Col. Innes, and on the 15th the *Gazette* announced that we "are now raising recruits to go against the French on the Ohio." The privates were to receive eight pence a day, and clothes, arms, and accoutrements. On the 23d of September a part of a company left Annapolis, under the charge of Capt. Forty, on their way to Frederick, and on the 30th another detachment marched for the same place, under the command of Lieut. John Bacon. John Ross also enlisted a company. All were to serve under the command of Capt. Dagworthy.

Col. Innes, who commanded a few companies of North Carolina troops, was ordered, after the battle of the Great Meadows, to march to Will's Creek, and to construct a fort, which would serve as a rallying-point and a defense to the frontiers.

On his arrival at Will's Creek he commenced the construction of fortifications, and selected for the purpose the hill lying between the Potomac River and the creek, near the mouth of the latter. This work, which was commenced on the 12th of September and completed about the middle of the following month, was built of stoccadoes, and called by Col. Innes "Fort Mount Pleasant." Log houses were then built for the men, which were finished by the 25th of December, and soon after their completion Governor Dinwiddie received instructions from England to erect a fort at Will's Creek "of such dimensions and character of construction as the importance of the position seemed to require." Gov. Dinwiddie transmitted these instructions to Col. Innes without delay, and the fort was erected and garrisoned during the winter of 1754–55. At the request of Gen. Braddock it was named Fort Cumberland, in honor of the captain-general of the British army. The troops engaged in its construction were Rutherford and Clarke's independent companies of foot from New York, Demerie's independent company from South Carolina, and three independent companies under the command of Col. Innes from North Carolina, assisted by a Maryland company, which arrived on the ground in November. Fort Cumberland stood upon the bank of Will's Creek, near its junction with the Potomac, "opposite to the new store,"[1] on the site of the present city of Cumberland, in Allegany County. "The citizens of our city," says Lowdermilk, in his interesting history of Cumberland,

"have for generations past pointed out the spot upon which this fort was located, but they had no information or conception of the size, shape, and character of the work or its surroundings. Fortunately a sketch of the fort was found by the author among the king's manuscripts in the library of the British Museum in London. A photographic copy of this sketch was secured. It was drawn by one of the officers in the fort at the time of Gen. Braddock's arrival. The fortifications were drawn to a scale, but the proportions were not preserved in mapping out the river, creek, and surrounding grounds. This fact made it somewhat difficult to establish the exact lines of the work, and compelled a resort to the memory of our oldest inhabitants. Mr. Jesse Korns has a distinct recollection of climbing over the remaining earth-works when a boy, and he fixes the easterly line of the fort—that portion of it which runs to a point nearest Will's Creek—some forty feet east of Emmanuel Church. The conformation of the ground at that spot is strongly confirmatory of his opinion, as well as other circumstances, which fix the western line near the boundary of Prospect Street. The greater portion of Fort Cumberland was a palisado work,—all of it, in fact, except the small bastioned work on the western end. The palisades were logs cut to a length of eighteen feet, and planted in the earth to a depth of six feet, forming a close wooden wall twelve feet in height. These logs were spiked together with strips and pins on the inner side, and the wall was pierced with openings for musketry along its entire face. Two water gates are shown in the plot, and from each of these a trench was excavated leading to the creek, so that the men might secure

---

[1] Pennsylvania Colonial Records, vi., p. 180.

therefrom a supply of water without being exposed to the fire of the enemy. In 1756, after Braddock's defeat, the Indians became so numerous and so bold as to approach near enough to shoot those who ventured to the water's edge, and in consequence thereof a well was sunk inside of the palisade near the main gate on the south side. This well was in use not many years since, and is still in existence on the property of Hon. Hopewell Hebb. It was about eighty feet in depth, and within the memory of the writer was furnished with an immense wheel and two buckets, by which excellent cold water was drawn from it. About the year 1799 this well was first cleaned out after the abandonment of the fort, and the father of Mr. John B. Widener was present when part of a gun-carriage, a wheel, and a large quantity of cannon-balls, musket-balls, etc., were taken therefrom.

"Inside the stockade were built barracks sufficient to furnish quarters for two hundred men and the company officers. Besides, there was a parade or drill-ground for the companies. At the west end of the stockade was built a fort with bastions, parapets, and ditches, where sixteen guns were mounted, which commanded all the ground north, west, and south, as well as the north and south lines of the stockade. These guns were of different calibre, four of them being twelve-pounders and twelve four-pounders. Besides these there were several swivels. A part of this armament was ships' guns, brought from Admiral Keppel's fleet. On the west face was a sally-port, and inside the fort were the houses used as quarters for the commanding officer, for storing provisions, and for the guard details while on duty. The entire work was four hundred feet in length and one hundred and sixty in width, extending from the point indicated below Emmanuel Church to within a short distance of Prospect Street, the northern line extending along nearly the centre of Washington Street. The fort proper occupied almost the identical spot on which now stands the residence of Mr. James A. Millholland, known as the 'Hoye House.' This fortification was of considerable strength, and commanded the approaches from the north, east, and south. The ground to the northwest was somewhat higher, but a small earth-work of a temporary character was constructed on the crest, on the site of the residence of the late James W. Jones, Esq. The ground on the south side of the river, opposite the fort, was high enough to overlook the work, and somewhat interfered with its efficiency. The company parade and drill-ground was inside the palisades, but the dress parades were held on the ground now occupied by the court-house and academy. Quite a number of log houses for barracks were built near the crest, and as far back as Smallwood Street, but these were made use of only when there was present a greater force than could be accommodated in the fort and the barracks immediately adjoining."

In October, 1754, the Virginia House of Burgesses made an appropriation of twenty thousand pounds for the public service, and with the grant of ten thousand pounds and supply of arms made by the home government, Col. Washington contemplated an extensive expedition against Fort Du Quesne. At the same time, " for settling the ranks of the officers of his majesty's forces when serving with the provincials in North America," the king directed,—

"That all officers commissioned by the king or his general should take rank of all officers commissioned by the Governors of the respective provinces; and further, that the general and field officers of the provincial troops should have no rank when serving with the general and other commissioned officers commissioned by the Crown, but that all captains and other inferior officers of the royal troops should take rank over provincial officers of the same grade having senior commissions."

The effect of these instructions was to reduce Washington from the rank of colonel to that of captain. This humiliation he was not content to submit to, but resigned his commission and retired to private life. The Duke of Newcastle, upon learning of the resignation of Col. Washington, issued a commission to Governor Horatio Sharpe, appointing him commander of the provincial forces at Fort Cumberland. Immediately on the receipt of the information that the vessel bearing it had arrived, Governor Sharpe proceeded to Williamsburg and "received his majesty's commission appointing him commander-in-chief of all the forces that are or may be raised to defend the frontiers of Virginia and the neighboring colonies, and to repel the unjustifiable invasion and encroachments of the French on the river Ohio."

After an interview with Governors Dinwiddie and Dobbs, of North Carolina, who brought out the commission, he returned to Annapolis, November 3d. It was concluded to raise immediately seven hundred men, with whom and the independent companies the French fort should be attacked and reduced before reinforcements could be brought from Canada or Louisiana. This effected, that post and another, which he thought would be necessary to erect on a small island in the river, were to be held for the king. To garrison these and Fort Cumberland would require all his forces, and he concluded it would be useless for them to attempt anything further against the enemy on La Rivière aux Bœufs and Lake Erie "without they be supported with such a body of troops from home as he dare not presume to hope for the direction of."

Governor Sharpe, who was now commander-in-chief of all the forces against the French, with instructions to make his headquarters in Virginia, attended by some officers of the Virginia regiment and a few personal friends, set out from Annapolis on the 12th of November to take command of the army. During the occasions of his absence in visiting the military posts and in attending to his official duties as Governor, Col. Fitzhugh, of Virginia, was to have charge of the forces.

Knowing the value of Col. Washington's experience and reputation, Sharpe at once took steps to induce him to re-enter the army, and before he left Annapolis he requested Col. Fitzhugh to induce him to change his resolution. Washington, however, who was deeply wounded at what he thought an act of deep injustice, was not to be persuaded.

An officer writing from Fort Cumberland on November 21st, thus speaks of the arrival of Governor Sharpe at that place:

"We now have got a fort completed, with barracks for our men at the back of it, well built, comfortable for the winter. We had the pleasure of being joined three days ago by his Excellency Col. Sharpe, with one company from Maryland. Mr. Sharpe appears to be a stirring, active gentleman, and by his method of proceeding I believe a very good soldier; cheerful and full of good conduct, and one who won't be trifled with. In the spring, if we have a good body of men, I make no doubt but we shall be able to do something to the purpose. By the present situation of the French, they are not to be driven out of their forts unless our numbers are greatly increased."

Governor Sharpe now carried on with vigor the preparations for the spring campaign. Military stores, ordnance, etc., were collected in Frederick and Alexandria, and the militia were properly organized and disciplined.

Indeed, an unwonted energy seems at this time to have inspired the people of the province. Finding the militia law defective, the Governor convened the Assembly on December 24th, when they passed an act to levy troops for the following campaign. As an inducement to the enlistments, they enacted "that if any citizen of the province shall be so maimed in the service as to be incapable of maintaining himself, he should be supported at the public expense." In the ensuing session of February, 1775, they regulated the rates of transportation of military stores, and the mode of quartering soldiers in the province, and prohibited by severe penalties any inhabitant from supplying the French or their Indian allies with stores, ammunition, or provisions. Governor Sharpe, however, did not find it difficult to procure volunteer soldiers, for he had more applications than he could provide for. As an instance, the *Maryland Gazette* of Feb. 6, 1755, says, "We are assured that in Chestertown, in Kent County, several men enlisted immediately upon the arrival of the officer in that town, before the drum was beat, and that the officer, who wanted but thirty men, got his complement and marched with them." The *Gazette* adds,—

"Such is the commendable spirit of that place." "They are gone for Will's Creek, and some young Maryland gentlemen (patriots) are gone from thence as volunteers; the mother of one of them at parting took leave of him, saying, 'My dear son, I shall with much greater pleasure hear of your death than your cowardice or ill conduct,' and Governor Sharpe, in a letter to Lord Baltimore, dated Jan. 12, 1755, also says,—

"'As to levying any number of men, I conceive we shall not find it difficult . . . but the difficulty will be to get money from the Assemblies after they are raised for their support; indeed, this I look upon as impracticable, or not to be expected without the Legislature of Great Britain shall make a law to be binding on all these several colonies, and oblige them to raise such a fund as may be thought expedient for the support of their own troops.''

The appointment of Governor Sharpe to the chief command was but a measure of temporary expediency. His friends would have persuaded the king to have retained him, urging in his behalf his exceeding honesty, while compelled to admit he was not possessed of remarkable ability. "A little less honesty," replied the king, "and a little more ability might, upon the present occasion, better serve our turn." The government, although still amusing the French with their professions of peace, had decided to maintain vigorously all its pretensions on this continent, and with this view to send out an adequate force under one of the bravest and most accomplished soldiers of the empire. Such, in the opinion of the Duke of Cumberland, captain-general of the army, was Maj.-Gen. Edward Braddock, whom Horace Walpole describes as "desperate in his fortune, brutal in his behavior, and obstinate in his sentiments," but admits that he was still "intrepid and capable." Gen. Braddock was ordered to proceed to Virginia, as commander-in-chief of all the British troops in North America, on Sept. 24, 1754, but did not sail until the 21st of December. He set sail in the "Norwich,"

GENERAL BRADDOCK.

convoyed by the "Centurion," flag-ship of Commodore Keppel, and arrived in Hampton Roads on the 20th of February. He was soon followed by the rest of the fleet, with two regiments, each of five hundred men, one under Col. Sir Peter Halket, and the other under Col. Thomas Dunbar. Two more regiments, each of one thousand men, were to be raised in the colonies at the king's expense, and commanded by Sir William Pepperell and Governor Shirley, of Massachusetts. These, with the independent companies, the levies expected of the several colonies, and such Indians as enlisted, it was thought would make up an effective force of not less than twelve thousand men. When Governor Sharpe received information of the appointment of Gen. Braddock, he proceeded, on the 13th of January, 1755, on a tour of inspection to the scene of anticipated operations, in the neighborhood of Will's Creek. In one week after his arrival he was joined by Sir John St. Clair, lieutenant-colonel of O'Farrell's Twenty-second Regiment of Foot, and quartermaster-general of all the British forces in America, who was then actively engaged in visiting military posts, making contracts for supplies, and acquainting himself generally with the scene of his future operations.[1] Having procured from every source all the maps and information that were obtainable respecting the country through which the expedition was to pass, he and Governor Sharpe descended the Potomac River two hundred and fifty miles in a canoe, and reached Annapolis on the 2d of February, whence they went to Williamsburg, Va., to await Gen. Braddock's arrival, which was hailed with great joy by the people of Virginia, Maryland, and Pennsylvania, as they looked forward with confidence to the defeat of the French and the early termination of the war, and possibly thought that the cost of the undertaking would mainly fall where it justly belonged, upon the mother-country.

On the 10th of March Gen. Braddock forwarded letters to the Governors of the different colonies, desiring them to meet him at Annapolis on the 1st of April for consultation and to settle a plan of operations. On the 26th, accompanied by Governor Dinwiddie and Commodore Keppel, he arrived at Alexandria, where the troops were encamped, and issued his first general order the next day. Here Governor Sharpe paid him a visit on the 28th. On the 3d of April the general, with a numerous suite, arrived at Annapolis, but, owing to the absence of Governors Shirley, De Lancey, and Morris, the council was postponed till the 14th, the place of meeting being changed to Alexandria. On the 11th and 12th, Governors Shirley, of Massachusetts, De Lancey, of New York, and Morris, of Pennsylvania, arrived at Annapolis, and, in company with Governor Sharpe, proceeded to the general's headquarters at Alexandria, where, on the 14th, he laid before them his instructions and his plans for the summer's operations. He proposed to proceed in person against Fort Du Quesne, while Shirley commanded an expedition against Niagara, and Sir William Johnston one against Crown Point. The plan having been agreed upon, and the details arranged, the council broke up, and Governors Shirley, De Lancey, and Morris returned to Annapolis on the 17th with Governor Sharpe, whose hospitality they enjoyed for several days.

Gen. Braddock had written to the Duke of Newcastle from Williamsburg on the 1st of March, that he should be beyond the Alleghanies by the end of April; and, in compliance with this promise, he now hurried his arrangements for a forward movement.

By Col. St. Clair's advice, it was decided to march from Alexandria in two divisions: one regiment and a portion of stores were to be sent to Winchester, Va., whence a new road was nearly completed to Fort Cumberland, and the other regiment, with the remaining forces, were to move by the way of Frederick, Md. Accordingly, on the 8th and 9th of April the provincials and six companies of the Forty-fourth Regiment, Sir Peter Halket, set out for Winchester, Lieut.-Col. Gage and four companies remaining to escort the artillery. On the 18th of April the Forty-eighth Regiment, under Col. Dunbar, marched for Frederick, detaching a company to the mouth of the Conococheague Creek (a large stream which flows into the Potomac in Washington County) to hasten the forwarding of the stores gathered there. Arriving at Frederick, Col. Dunbar found there was no road through Maryland to Fort Cumberland, and he accordingly, on the 1st of May, crossed the Potomac at the mouth of the Conococheague, and took the Winchester route. For the purpose of expediting the necessary preparations for transporting the supplies, Governor Sharpe, on the 22d of April, went to Frederick, where a portion of the army was then quartered. At this point, on the 24th of April, he met Gen. Braddock, Col. Washington, and Benjamin Franklin, the two latter having met for the first time. Washington had been invited by Gen. Braddock to serve as one of his aides-de-camp in the campaign. Franklin, then the British postmaster-general of the colonies, had met Braddock here for the purpose of concerting a plan for forwarding supplies, and learning the scarcity of wagons, undertook to furnish them from Pennsylvania. By adroit means he succeeded in obtaining from the counties of Lancaster, York, and Cumberland one hundred and fifty wagons with four horses to each, and fifteen hundred pack- or saddle-horses needed for the expedition. Besides this assistance, Governor Sharpe tells us Gen. Braddock did

"not scruple in enlisting and taking away a good many servants from the inhabitants of Frederick, Prince George's, and Baltimore Counties, as well as impressing their wagons, horses, teamsters, carriages, and carriage horses."

To such an extent were the seizures made that the contractors for the new court-house, which was then being erected in Frederick, found it impossible to obtain horses to haul the materials to the site of the building. "He was extremely warm and angry" at this time, "and stormed like a lion rampant."

Braddock, while at Frederick, purchased of Governor Sharpe an English chariot, with six horses, in which he rode, and on the 1st of May, accompanied by his staff and guard of light-horse, he left Frederick for Will's Creek, by the way of Winchester, the

---

[1] Sir John's Station on the Baltimore and Ohio Railroad, and Sir John's Run and Sir John's Road, in Berkeley County, Va., are named after Sir John St. Clair.

road along the north side of the Potomac not being yet made. The discomforts of the rough road were increased for Gen. Braddock by his mode of traveling, which was not suited to the mountainous country through which he was passing. Accompanied by his staff, he overtook Dunbar's division near Will's Creek, his body-guard of light-horse galloping on each side of his chariot, the drums beating the Grenadier's March as he passed. In this style, too, he arrived at Fort Cumberland on May 10th, amid a thundering salute of seventeen guns.

By this time he discovered that he was not in a region fitted for such display, and his traveling chariot was abandoned at Fort Cumberland; otherwise it would soon have become a wreck among the mountains beyond.

On arriving at the fort on the 10th of May, Braddock found Sir Peter Halket already there, with six companies of the Forty-fourth, with which he had marched from Alexandria. The remaining four companies of his regiment, which had been left with Lieut.-Col. Gage to escort the artillery, were still delayed, but by the 22d of the month all the forces were assembled at the appointed rendezvous, with the exception of a North Carolina company, which did not reach there until the 30th. Braddock now mustered two thousand effective men.

The regiments of Dunbar and Halket, originally one thousand strong, were now increased to fourteen hundred by volunteers and conscripts, principally procured in Maryland; and besides these there were the two independent companies from New York; five companies of rangers, and two of carpenters and pioneers, principally from Virginia; one company of rangers from Maryland, two companies of rangers from North and South Carolina, and thirty seamen, under a lieutenant of the navy, furnished by Admiral Keppel, having four pieces of cannon, which they were to assist in dragging over the mountains. Among the officers present who afterwards distinguished themselves in the Revolution were Thomas Cresap, Hugh Mercer, George Washington, Daniel Morgan, Thomas Gage, and Horatio Gates.[1]

Being at last ready to undertake the long and tedious journey that was before him, Gen. Braddock gave orders for the army to advance. On the 30th of May, Sir John St. Clair, with Maj. Chapman and six hundred men of the Forty-fourth Regiment, were sent forward to clear the road to the Little Meadows, on the Youghiogheny, thirty miles distant, where they were to erect a fortified camp. The army followed in three divisions: the first, under Col. Halket, on the 7th of June; the next, under Lieut.-Col. Gage, on the 8th; and the third, under Col. Dunbar, on the 10th, when Braddock also set off, with his aides-de-camp and others of his staff and his body-guard of light-horse. Fort Cumberland, with the hospital filled with invalids, was left under the care of Col. Innes.

Braddock's army consisted of the Forty-fourth Regiment of (English) Infantry, Col. Sir Peter Halket; the Forty-eighth, Col. Thomas Dunbar; sundry independent (colonial) companies; a company of horse, another of artillery, a company of marines, etc.; in all, two thousand one hundred and ninety, besides the usual train of non-militants who always accompany an army. The other field-officers were Lieut.-Cols. Burton and Gage (of Bunker Hill notoriety); Majs. Chapman and Sparks; Maj. Sir John St. Clair, deputy quartermaster-general; Matthew Leslie, his assistant; Francis Halket, brigade-major; William Shirley, secretary; and Robert Orme, Roger Morris, and George Washington, Esqs., aides-de-camp to the general. Among the captains were: Stephen, Lewis, Polson, Hogg, Peyronie, Mercer, and Waggoner. These commanded provincial troops, chiefly from Virginia. The New York independent companies were commanded by Capts. Rutherford and Horatio Gates, the Gen. Gates to whom Burgoyne surrendered at Saratoga. Christopher Gist and his son Nathaniel accompanied the army as guides; George Croghan, the Indian agent of Aughwick, with Montour, interpreter, also accompanied the army, trying to be useful in the Indian department, aided by Monacatootha and Capt. Jack, the "wild hunter of the Juniata."

Among the Virginia surgeons were Drs. James Craik and Hugh Mercer, men of imperishable fame.

---

[1] The route of march of the army after leaving Frederick, on the 28th of April, was as follows: On the 1st of May, Col. Dunbar, after building a bridge over the Antietam, crossed the Potomac at the mouth of the Conococheague, so as to strike the Winchester road. On the 5th he crossed the Little Cacapon, and on the 8th was again ferried over the Potomac to Maryland from a spot near the mouth of Cacapon, which has since that day borne the name of the Ferry Fields. Thence along the riverside, through Old Town, the dwelling place of Col. Thomas Cresap, it passed through the narrows at the foot of Will's Mountain into Cumberland. The house of Cresap, the ruins of which are still standing near the canal, was half dwelling and half fortress. To this strongly fortified castle the settlers in this section of the province repaired whenever there was danger of an Indian attack. Cresap then called the place Skipton, after the place of his nativity in England. It is situated on the north fork of the Potomac, a few miles above the junction of the north and south branches of the Potomac. The residence of his son, Michael Cresap, a large stone building, is still standing in the centre of the town.

They were both Scotchmen, the latter having fled to Virginia from the fatal field of Culloden. Dr. Craik had followed Washington in his campaign of 1754, was his companion in his journey to the West in 1770, and was his physician at his death. Dr. Mercer became a field-officer in the Revolution, and fell at Princeton in January, 1777.

Some idea of the difficulties Braddock's forces encountered may be had when it is stated that they spent the third night only five miles from the first. The place of encampment, which is about one-third of a mile from the toll-gate on the National road, is marked by a copious stream bearing Braddock's name. For reasons not easy to divine, the route across Will's Mountain, first adopted for the National road, was selected, instead of the more favorable one through the narrows of Will's Creek, to which the road was subsequently changed for the purpose of avoiding that formidable ascent. The traces are very distinct on the east and west slopes, the modern road crossing it frequently. From the western foot the route continued up Braddock's Run to the forks of the stream, where Clary's tavern now stands, nine miles from Cumberland, when it turned to the left in order to reach a point on the ridge favorable to an easy descent into the valley of George's Creek. It is surprising that having reached this high ground, the favorable spur by which the National road accomplishes the ascent of the Great Savage Mountain did not strike the attention of the engineers, as the labor requisite to surmount the barrier from the deep valley of George's Creek must have contributed greatly to those bitter complaints which Braddock made against the colonial government for their failure to assist him more effectually in the transportation department.

Passing then a mile to the south of Frostburg, the road approaches the east foot of Savage Mountain, which it crosses about one mile south of the National road; and thence by very favorable ground through the dense forests of white pine peculiar to this region, it got to the north of the National road, near the gloomy tract called the "Shades of Death." This was the 15th of June, when the dense gloom of the summer woods, and the favorable shelter which these enormous pines would give an Indian enemy, must have made a most sensible impression on all minds of the insecurity of their mode of·advance. This doubtless had a share in causing the council of war held at the Little Meadows next day. To this place, distant only about twenty miles from Cumberland, Sir John Sinclair and Maj. Chapman had been dispatched on the 30th of May to build a fort, as we have already seen, and the army having been seven days in reaching it, it follows, as the line of march was upwards of three miles long, the rear was just getting under way when the advance were lighting their evening fires.

Here it may be well enough to clear up an obscurity which enters into many narratives of these early events from confusing the names of "Little Meadows" and "Great Meadows," "Little Crossings" and "Great Crossings," which are all distinct localities.

The "Little Meadows" have been described as at the foot of Meadow Mountain; it is well to note that the "Great Meadows" are about thirty-one miles farther west, and near the east foot of Laurel Hill. By the "Little Crossings" is meant the ford of Cassleman's River, a tributary of the Youghiogheny itself. The Little Crossing is two miles west of the Little Meadows, and the Great Crossing seventeen miles farther west.

The conclusion of the council was to push on with a picked force of twelve hundred men and twelve pieces of cannon, and the line of march, now more compact, was resumed on the 19th.

While these events were occurring in the western part of Maryland, the Governor and the Lower House of Assembly were quarreling over the requisitions made by Gen. Braddock for supplies for his army.

On June 28th the Governor sent to the Lower House the following message:

"GENTLEMEN OF THE LOWER HOUSE OF ASSEMBLY:

"I have just received letters from Col. Innes at Fort Cumberland, and from the back inhabitants of Frederick County, advising me that a party of French Indians last Monday morning (June 23) fell on the inhabitants of this province, and killed two men and one woman (who have been since found dead), eight other persons they have taken prisoners and carried off. The names of the persons who were murdered and left are John Williams, his wife, and grandson, and with their bodies also was found that of a French Indian. The persons carried off are Richard Williams (a son of John who was murdered), with two children, one Dawson's wife and four children. Richard Williams' wife and two brothers of the young man that is killed have made their escape. This accident, I find, has so terrified the distant inhabitants that many of them are retiring and forsaking their plantations. Another letter from Winchester, in Virginia, informs me that a party of Indians have also attacked the back inhabitants of that province, of whom they have killed eleven and carried away many captives. Apprehending the French would proceed in this manner as soon as Gen. Braddock and the troops under his control should have passed the mountains, and being confirmed in my opinion by an intimation in the general's letter, I issued a proclamation near a month since, cautioning the distant and other inhabitants of this province to be on their guard, and unite for their common defence and safety. At the same time I sent peremptory orders and instructions to the officers of the militia of Frederick County frequently to muster and discipline their several troops and companies, once a fortnight at least, and in case of alarm that the enemy was approaching or had fallen on the inhabitants, to march out and act either offensively or defensively, and use all means to protect and defend the inhabitants from the devastations of the French or Indians. However, I find neither the proclamation nor instructions will be effective unless the militia can be assured that they shall receive satisfaction, and be paid for the time they are out on duty. I should consider it highly proper for us to have about one hundred, or at least a company of men, posted or constantly ranging for some time on the frontiers for our protection. In this I desire your advice, and that you will enable me to support such a number.

"Gentlemen:

"At the general's request, and that I might receive early intelligence at this time from the camp and back inhabitants, I have engaged several persons between here and Will's Creek to receive and speedily convey any letters that shall come to them directed for the general or myself. I doubt not that you will be convinced of the necessity of such a measure, and provide for the expense thereof."

The House, on the same day, took into consideration the Governor's message, and immediately passed the following resolutions:

"*Resolved*, That this House will make suitable arrangements for the maintaining of eighty men, including officers, for four months (if occasion) for ranging on the frontiers of this province, to protect the same against the incursions or depredations that may be attempted or made by the French or their Indian allies.

"*Resolved*, further, That this House will defray the reasonable expense of conveying intelligence from Will's Creek to Annapolis and back thither for four months."

With some slight amendments the Upper House agreed to the resolutions, and two thousand pounds were appropriated for the purposes therein mentioned.

On the 5th of July the Governor sent another message to the Lower House informing them that bands of hostile Indians were entering the province, and that fifteen persons in Frederick County on their way to Fort Cumberland for protection had been killed or captured by the savages.

During all this time the possibility of Braddock's defeat had been as little dreamed of by the colonists as by that confident commander himself. The immense superiority of the English over French troops had become, since Marlborough's time, an article of the British creed, and to the regulars at least their Indian allies, who knew nothing of drill or discipline, who never met a foe in the open field, and carried into warfare the tactics and strategy of the forest hunter, seemed beneath contempt, and only formidable to sentinels, stragglers, and "raw militia-men." The colonists, however, knew them better, and the general had been warned of the possibility of a surprise, and had received the caution with the scorn he had bestowed on the militia and all their doings. But even of the provincials, only a few who were with the army thought any disaster possible; elsewhere victory was regarded as settled. Preparations were made in Philadelphia and Annapolis for celebrating the assured triumph, and money was freely subscribed for illuminations and general festivities as soon as the couriers should bring the joyful news.

Resuming the march, and passing over ground to the south of the Little Crossing and of the village of Grantsville, which it skirted, the army spent the night of the 21st of June at the Bear Camp, a locality supposed to be about half-way to the Great Crossings, which it reached on the 23d. The route thence to the Great Meadows, or Fort Necessity, was well chosen, though over a mountainous tract, conforming very nearly to the ground now occupied by the National road, and keeping on the dividing ridge between the waters flowing into the Youghiogheny on the one hand, and the Cheat River on the other. Having crossed the Youghiogheny, the army was now on the classic ground of Washington's early career, where the skirmish with Jumonville and the battle of Fort Necessity had occurred the year before. About one mile west of the Great Meadows, and near the spot now marked as Braddock's Grave, the road struck off more to the northwest, in order to reach a pass through Laurel Hill, that would enable them to strike the Youghiogheny at a point afterwards known as Stewart's Crossing, and about half 'a mile below the present town of Connellsville. This part of the route is marked by the farm known as Mount Braddock.

One month was spent in the march from Fort Cumberland to the fatal field. The route as far as Gist's was that of Washington the year before; and although Washington had marched from Will's Creek to the Meadows in twenty-three days, *making the road as he went*, yet it took Braddock eighteen days to drag his slow length along over the same distance, and Dunbar eight days longer. Truly did Washington say that "instead of pushing on with vigor, without regarding a little rough road, they were halting to level every mole-hill and erect bridges over every brook." This needless delay, like everything else in this campaign, contributed its share to the disastrous result; for while Braddock was halting and bridging the enemy was collecting a force for resistance and attack which three days' prompter movement would have anticipated. At the Little Meadows (Tomlinson's) a division of the army in the march was made: the general and Col. Halket, with select portions of the two regiments and of the other forces, lightly incumbered, going on in advance, being in all about fourteen hundred. Col. Dunbar, with the residue, about eight hundred and fifty, and the heavy baggage, artillery, and stores, were left to move up by "slow and easy marches," an order which he executed so literally as to earn for himself the sobriquet of "Dunbar the tardy." When, on the 28th of June, Braddock was at Stewart's Crossing (Connellsville), Dunbar was only at the Little Crossings. Here Washington, under a violent attack of fever, had been left by Braddock, under the care of his friend Dr. Craik and a guard, two days in advance of Dunbar, to come on with him when able, the gallant aide requiring from the general a "solemn pledge" not to arrive at the French fort until he should rejoin him; and as Washington did not report himself until the day before the battle, this pledge may be some apology for Braddock having consumed eighteen precious days in marching about eighty miles. According to Capt. Orme's journal, the encampments, etc., of Braddock in Fayette County, Pa., were as follows:

On the 24th of June he marched from Squaw's Fort (near Somerfield) six miles to a camp east of the Great Meadows, near the "twelve springs." He crossed the Yough without bridging about half a mile above where the National road now crosses it. In this day's march they passed a recently-abandoned Indian camp, indicating by the number of huts that about one hundred and seventy had been there. "They had stripped and painted some trees, upon which they and the French had written many threats and bravadoes, with all kinds of scurrilous language." This encampment of Braddock was between Mount Augusta and Marlow's road, south of the National road.

June 25th. The army moved about seven miles, and encamped in what is now the Old Orchard, near and northwest of "Braddock's Grave," called then, two miles west of Great Meadows,—the general riding in anticipated triumph over the very spot which in twenty days was to be his last encampment. The army seems to have passed the ruins of Fort Necessity without a halt or a notice. It is singular they did not encamp there, for Orme says they were late in getting to their ground, because that morning, about a quarter of a mile after starting, they had to let their carriages down-hill with tackle. In this day's march three men were shot and scalped by the enemy, and the sentinels fired upon some French and Indians whom they discovered reconnoitering their camp,—an annoyance now become so frequent that on the next day Braddock offered a bounty of five pounds for every scalp that his Indians or soldiers would take.

June 26th. They marched only about four miles by reason of the "extreme badness of the road," arriving at what Orme calls Rock Fort, on Laurel Hill, a place now known as the Great Rock, near Washington Spring and the Half King's old camp, being a little more than two miles southward of Dunbar's camp. "At our halting-place," says Orme, "we found another Indian camp, which they had abandoned at our approach, their fires being yet burning. They had marked in triumph upon trees the scalps they had taken two days before, and many of the French had written on them their names and sundry insolent expressions. We picked up a commission on the march, which mentioned the party being under the command of the Sieur Normanville. This Indian camp was in a strong situation, being upon a high rock, with a very narrow and steep ascent to the top. It had a spring in the middle, and stood at the termination of the Indian path to the Monongahela at Redstone. By this pass the party came which attacked Mr. Washington last year, and also this which attended us. By their tracks they seem to have divided here, the one party being straight forward to Fort Du Quesne and the other returning by Redstone Creek to the Monongahela. A captain's detachment of ninety-four men marched with guides, to fall in the night upon the latter division. They found a small quantity of provisions and a very large batteau, which they destroyed, but saw no men, and the captain joined the general the next day at Gist's."

June 27th. "We marched from the camp at Rock Fort to Gist's Plantation, which was about six miles, the road still mountainous and rocky. Here the advancing party was relieved, and all the wagons and carrying horses with provision belonging to that detachment joined us." This advanced party consisted of about four hundred, under Lieut.-Col. Burton, who, with Sir John St. Clair, had been sent in advance to cut and make the road, taking with them two six-pounders, with ammunition, three wagons of tools, and thirty-five days' provisions, all on pack-horses.

June 28th. The army marched from Gist's, where the encampment was near Washington's of the previous year, to a camp near to and west of Stewart's Crossing of the Yough, a short half-mile below New Haven, on land subsequently belonging to Daniel Rogers, formerly Col. William Crawford. It has been commonly supposed that a division of the army here took place, the English troops, etc., crossing the river and bearing northward, while the Virginia or colonial forces went down the river and crossed at the Broad Ford, thence bearing more to the west, crossing Jacob's Run at Stouffer's mill, the two divisions reuniting at Sewickley, near Painter's Salt-Works. Orme's journal has no notice of any such division. The Broad Ford route may be that which was traversed by the detachments or convoys of provisions, etc., from Dunbar's division, which were from time to time sent up to the main army; one of which, Orme says, came up at Thicketty Run, a branch of Sewickley, on the 5th of July. Another detachment of one hundred men, with pack-horse loads of flour and some beeves, according to Washington's letters, left the camp west of the Great Meadows on the 3d of July, with which *he* went, joining the army on the 8th, the day before the battle, "in a covered wagon." This convoy took up the one hundred beeves which were among the losses in the defeat. It is a noticeable fact that Washington, enfeebled by a consuming fever, was so invigorated by the sight of the scenes of his discomfiture the previous year as to seize the opportunity of celebrating its first anniversary by hastening on to participate in an achievement which, as he fondly hoped, would restore to his king and country all that had been lost by his failure.

June 30th. The army to-day crossed the Yough at Stewart's Crossing or Ford in strict military style, with advanced guard first passed and posted. There is here a little confusion in Capt. Orme's journal. Not only does he make the west to be the east side of the Yough, but he says, "We were obliged to encamp about a mile on to the west (east) side, where we halted a day, to cut a passage over a mountain. This day's march did not exceed two miles!" It would seem the halt was on the 29th, before crossing the river, for the march is resumed on the 1st of July. This "mountain" is the bluff known as the "Narrows," below Davidson's mill. The camp is not certainly known, probably on land late of Robert Long, deceased; perhaps south of the Narrows, on Mr. Davidson's land.

July 1st. Says Orme, "We marched about five miles, but could advance no farther by reason of a great swamp, which required much work to make it passable." The course was northeastward. The swamp can be no other than that fine-looking champaign land above the head-waters of Martin's Creek and Jacob's Creek, north and east of the Old Chain Bridge, embracing lands formerly belonging to Col. Isaac Meason, and afterwards to George E. Hogg and others.

July 2d. The army moved in the same direction (east of north) about six miles, to "Jacob's Cabin."

The localities of this and the last preceding camp cannot be precisely fixed, and the curious reader and topographer is left to his own conclusion from the data given. Jacob's cabin was doubtless the abode of an Indian, who gave his name to the creek on which he trapped and hunted.

July 3d. "The swamp being repaired, we marched about six miles to Salt-lick Creek." This Salt-lick Creek is Jacob's Creek, and the camp at the end of the day's march was near Welshouse's mill, about a mile below Mount Pleasant. From Welshouse's mill the course was northward, passing just to the west of Mount Pleasant; thence crossing Sewickely (Thicketty) Run near Painter's Salt-Works; thence bearing a little westward, it crossed the present tracks of the Pennsylvania Railroad and turnpike, west of Greensburg, to the Bush Fork of Turtle Creek. Here Braddock abandoned his wise design to approach the French fort by the ridge route, or Nemacolin's path, being deterred by the difficulties of crossing the deep and rugged ravines of the streams. Turning, at almost a right angle, westward, he got into the valley of Long Run at or near Stewartsville, and went down it past Samson's mill, encamping on the night of the 8th of July, where Washington joined him, about two miles east of the Monongahela. The army moved from this encampment early next morning, turning into the valley of Crooked Run, which they followed to its mouth, and crossed the river at "Braddock's upper ford," below McKeesport; thence down the river on the west side about three miles to Braddock's lower ford, just below the mouth of Turtle Creek and Dam No. 2, where they recrossed to the fatal encounter of the 9th of July. This double crossing of the river was to avoid the intervening narrows.

Braddock had conducted the march hitherto with most commendable care and with signal success; and now, as he neared the object of his labor and ambition, he took all the precautionary measures to avoid surprise and disaster which his military education suggested. But, unfortunately, he knew nothing of Indian strategy or backwoods tactics. He was sensible that his near approach was known at the French fort, and that all his movements were closely and secretly watched. Hence at the crossings of the river he had his advanced guards well posted, and having caused his soldiers to be well appareled and their arms brightened, he made a display well calculated to strike terror into the enemy. Washington was wont to say that he never saw a more animating sight than the army's second crossing of the Monongahela. Nevertheless, Sir Peter Halket, Mr. Secretary Shirley, and Maj. Washington were not without anxious forebodings. Controcœur, the commandant of the fort, frightened at the exaggerated reports of the numbers of the English, had prepared to surrender or to fly, as his successor did before Gen. Forbes in 1758. Indeed, he reluctantly yielded assent to any resistance. And when, on the 8th, MM. Beaujeau, Dumas, and De Ligneris sought a detachment of regulars and Indian aid, it was merely to dispute the river passes, and to annoy and retard the march of the English. They had caused the ground to be thoroughly examined, and knew well the ravines, or natural trenches, which so well served them for attack and protection in the conflict. To comprehend the nature of the action and the inevitableness of Braddock's defeat one must visit the ground. He will there, even yet, see the two ravines, dry, with almost perpendicular banks, just high enough to conceal, protect, and fire from, capable of containing an army of two thousand men. And if he will imagine the second bank to be densely wooded, and covered with a thick and tangled web of pea-vine and other undergrowth, with a newly-cut road, twelve feet wide, passing about midway between the ravines, and at no place more than eighty yards distant from one or the other, he will have fully before him the scene of the disaster. The French and Indians were about nine hundred strong, the latter being more than two-thirds of the force. They arrived on the ground too late to dispute the passage of the river. The army had crossed, formed its line of march, and was moving —marching into the snare—when the enemy appeared right in front, and near the heads of the ravines.

As if by magic, at a preconcerted silent signal from M. Beaujeau, the chief in command, the Indians at once disappeared right and left into the excavations, leaving only the little French line visible. These were engaged with spirit and success by Lieut.-Col. Gage, and until the Indians began to pour in their invisible deadly shots fortune seemed to incline to the English. It soon changed, and no efforts could restore it. Even tree-fighting could not have saved the doomed English soldiery, who held their ground, fought well, and obeyed their officers as long as they had officers to command them. They were in the jaws of death, and nothing could have delivered them except perhaps a raking fire of grape or round-shot up and down the ravine. The excuse for not essaying this expedient is that the ravines were unknown and invisible. Even yet, when all is clear around them, you do not discern them until you are almost upon them.

In the narrow road, but twelve feet wide, the men were huddled into a confused mass, firing at random into the trees, while the enemy, whom they could not see, but whose numbers seemed multiplied tenfold by their hideous yells and whoopings, mowed them down by a well-directed fire. Frantic with rage and excitement, Braddock endeavored to restore order and extricate his force from this slaughter-pen; and four horses were shot under him as, reckless of his own life, he flew from point to point. His officers dismounted and formed into platoons, to set their men an example, and thus made themselves fair marks for the Indians' rifles, but their self-devotion was fruitless. The provincials, skilled in forest-fighting, at once sheltered themselves behind trees, and the regulars would have followed their example had Braddock allowed it, but he refused to give the order; and such was the force of discipline, or the bewildering effects of panic, that the men were mowed down as they stood, neither flying or taking cover. Many were slain by the fire of their own comrades, who had lost the power of distinguishing friend from foe.

Thus for hours the slaughter went on. The ammunition was giving out; the officers were nearly all killed or wounded, not a single aide but Washington being left; more than half the army had fallen, and the rest could do nothing where they were but die. Braddock gave the order for retreat, and almost at the same moment a ball pierced his right arm and entered his lungs, inflicting a mortal wound. The retreat became a headlong flight, which the dying general in vain attempted to check. A few men gathered around him, bore him from the field, and obeyed his orders; and despite his agonies he employed every remaining moment of his life in endeavoring to provide for the safety of the survivors, repair in what slight measure he could the disaster his rashness had caused, and bring back the shattered remnant of his great army to Great Meadows, where he died.[1]

Of the fourteen hundred and sixty, besides women and other camp-followers who crossed the Monongahela, four hundred and fifty-six were killed, four hundred and twenty-one wounded, many of them mortally. Out of eighty-nine commissioned officers, sixty-three were killed or wounded.

---

[1] It is uncertain whether Braddock was killed by the enemy or by one of his own men. There is a strong probability that he was killed in revenge by Thomas Fossit, a Pennsylvania provincial, whose brother Joseph, it is said, Braddock struck dead with his sword for having taken shelter behind a tree during the battle. Braddock was buried about two miles west of Fort Necessity, near the banks of a small stream, immediately in the road, a short distance from the present National road. About 1824, says Lowdermilk, a party of workmen, engaged in repairing the old road, came upon the remains of a human skeleton, supposed to be that of Braddock. The remains were carried to a point about one hundred and fifty yards eastward, and buried in a field at the foot of a large oak-tree, some twenty-five yards from the National road. By the direction of Hon. Andrew Stewart the spot was marked by a board, upon which was inscribed the fact that this was the last resting-place of Maj.-Gen. Edward Braddock, and this board was nailed to the tree. Some twelve years ago the tree was blown down, leaving nothing but a portion of the trunk to mark the place. In 1871 a party of English visitors had the spot inclosed with a strong board fence.

The *Gentleman's Magazine*, of August, 1755, gives the following list of officers who were present, and of those who were killed and wounded in this disastrous engagement:

STAFF.

Edward Braddock, Esq., General and Commander-in-Chief, mortally wounded.

Robert Orme, Esq., Roger Morris, Esq., George Washington, Esq., Aides-de-Camp; wounded.

William Shirley, Esq., Secretary; killed.

Sir John St. Clair, Deputy Quartermaster-General; wounded.

Matthew Leslie, Gent., General Assistant Quartermaster-General; wounded.

Francis Halket, Esq., Major Brigade.

FORTY-FOURTH REGIMENT.

Officers' Names.	Rank.	Killed or Wounded.
Sir Peter Halket	Colonel	Killed.
Gage, Esq	Lieut.-Colonel	Wounded.
Tatton	Captain	Killed.
Hobson	"	
Beckworth	"	
Githins	"	Killed.
Falconer	Lieutenant.	
Sittler	"	Wounded.
Bailey	"	
Dunbar	"	Wounded.
Pottenger	"	
Halket	"	Killed.
Treby	"	Wounded.
Allen	"	Died of wounds.
Simpson	"	Wounded.
Lock	"	"
Disney	Ensign	"
Kennedy	"	"
Townsend	"	Killed.
Preston	"	
Clarke	"	
Nortlow	"	Killed.
Pennington	"	

FORTY-EIGHTH REGIMENT.

Burton, Esq	Lieut.-Colonel	Slightly wounded.
Sparks, Esq	Major.	
Dobson, Esq	Captain.	
Cholmondeley	"	Killed.
Bowyer, Esq	"	Wounded.
Ross, Esq	"	"
Barbutt, Esq	Lieutenant.	
Walsham, Esq	"	
Crymble, Esq	"	Killed.
Widman, Esq	"	"
Hansard, Esq	"	
Henry Gladwin, Esq	"	Wounded.
Hotham, Esq	"	
Edmund Stone, Esq	"	Wounded.
Cope, Esq	"	
Brereton, Esq	"	Killed.
Stuart, Esq	"	
Montresore	Ensign	Wounded.
Dunbar	"	
Harrison	"	
Colebatt	"	
Macmullen	"	Wounded.
Crowe	"	"
Stirling	"	"

VIRGINIA OFFICERS.

Stevens	Captain	Wounded.
Waggoner	"	
Polson	"	Killed.
Peyronie	"	
Stewart	"	
Hamilton	Lieutenant	Killed.
Woodward	"	
Wright	"	Killed.
Spittdorph	"	
Stewart	"	Wounded.

Officers' Names.	Rank.	Killed or Wounded.
Waggoner	Lieutenant	Killed.
McNeill	"	

INDEPENDENTS.

Gates	Captain	Wounded.
Sumani	Lieutenant	Killed.
Miller	"	
Haworth	"	Wounded.
Grey	"	"

ARTILLERY.

Orde	Captain.	
Smith	Capt.-Lieutenant	Killed.
Buchanan	Lieutenant	Wounded.
McCloud	"	
McCullor	"	Wounded.

ENGINEERS.

McKeller, Esq	Major	Wounded.
Gordon, Esq	Captain	"
Williamson, Esq	Capt.-Lieutenant	"

NAVAL OFFICERS.

Spendelowe	Lieutenant	Killed.
Haynes	Midshipman.	
Talbot	"	Killed.

VOLUNTEERS.

Stone	Captain	Killed.
Hager	"	Wounded.

Capt. Evan Shelby's name was omitted by the *Gentleman's Magazine*, by mistake no doubt. He was a captain of rangers, and participated in the battle. He was a Welshman by birth. He subsequently served in Forbes' expedition with great honor, and was the father of Gen. Isaac Shelby, a distinguished Revolutionary officer. Lieut. Henry Gladwin, of the English Forty-eighth Regiment, afterwards was deputy adjutant-general in America.

All the artillery and ammunition, baggage, provisions, wagons, and many horses were lost. The general lost his military chest, containing, it is said, £25,000 in specie ($125,000) and all his papers.

Washington also lost many valuable papers. In short, the officers and soldiers who escaped the carnage lost nearly everything except the clothes on their backs and the arms in their hands, many abandoning even the latter. Capt. Orme saved his journal, now almost the only authentic continuous record of this most disastrous campaign.

Braddock displayed, in the perplexing circumstances of the action, great activity and courage. He had four horses shot under him, and after having mounted a fifth, while in the act of issuing an order, near the head of one of the ravines, and near the end of the conflict, he received a mortal wound, the ball shattering his right arm and passing into his lungs. He fell to the ground, "surrounded by the dead and almost abandoned by the living;" and had it not been for the devotedness of his aide, Capt. Orme, and the almost obstinate fidelity of Capt. Stewart, of Virginia, who commanded the light-horse, the fallen general would have had his wish gratified,—that the scene of his disaster should also witness his death. He was borne from the ground at great risk, at first in a tumbril, then on a horse. Every officer above the grade of a captain was now either killed or disabled except Washington, who escaped unhurt, though two horses were shot under him and his clothes pierced with balls, so feeble and emaciated that day (from his late sickness with the fever) that he had to ride upon a pillow. The drums had beat a retreat before Braddock fell, and now Washington undertook to give it whatever of order it was susceptible of, for it was a headlong flight.

The retreat was by the same route as the advance, crossing the river at the same fording. The enemy did not pursue, but remained to riot in scalps and plunder. Braddock was carried with the little remnant of his army that could be held together. It is not probable that the panic-stricken fugitives all returned to Gist's by the same path, many, through fear of pursuit, betaking themselves to the woods and by-ways. The Pennsylvania wagoners, it is said, escaped to a man, astride their fleetest horses. Certain it is, by ten o'clock next morning several of them were in Dunbar's camp, on Laurel Hill, nearly forty miles distant, with the tidings, and one or two wounded officers were carried into the camp before noon of that day.

After crossing to the west side of the river in the flight, a rally was effected of about one hundred men, with whom were Braddock, Burton, and Washington. From this point Washington was sent to Dunbar for aid and wagons to convey the wounded. The road was then new, and hard to find in the night. There had been a coldness between the general and Dunbar, hence it was deemed necessary, to insure obedience, that Washington, as aide-de-camp, should go with orders. Weak and exhausted as he was, he shrank not from his duty. He set out with two men, in a night so wet and dark that frequently they had to alight from their horses and grope for the road. Nevertheless, they reached Dunbar's camp about sunrise. Braddock and his followers reached Gist's about ten o'clock that evening.

Nathaniel Gist, son of Christopher, with "Gist's Indian," were dispatched from the battle-field to Fort Cumberland with tidings of the overthrow, but with instructions to avoid passing by or disturbing the repose of Dunbar. They traveled afoot and through unfrequented paths to avoid the Indians. While snatching some repose during the first night of their journey, in a thicket of bushes and grapevine on Cove's Run, a branch of Shoutis Run, within view of the camp-fires of Dunbar, they mistook the noise of the movement of some bird or beast for Indians, and taking to flight, became separated in the darkness. But each wended his way cautiously alone. When nearing their destination, upon emerging from the bushes into the open road, Gist saw ahead a few rods his long-lost Indian, who had also just taken to the highway. Although the sufferings of Braddock in mind and body were intense, he was not unmindful of his wounded soldiers. Upon the arrival, on the morning of the 11th, at Gist's of some wagons and stores from Dunbar, he sent off a convoy of provisions for the relief of those supposed yet to be behind, and ordered up more wagons and troops from the camp, to bring off the wounded.

It is probable these humane provisions were available but to few, except the general officers, and perhaps a few others. All the badly wounded were left on the bloody field to the merciless cruelties of the savages, or perished in its vicinity. In after-years human bones were found plentifully all around, some as far off as three miles. Having made these arrangements, had their wounds dressed, and taken some food, Braddock and the remnant of his command, on Friday, the 11th, moved up to Dunbar's camp.

Dunbar, as will be remembered, was at the Little Crossings on the 20th of June, with about eight hundred and fifty of the army, and the heavy artillery and the stores. On the 2d of July he passed the Great Meadows, and on the 10th is found at his camp on the top of Laurel Hill. How long he had lain there is uncertain, probably several days.

It is, perhaps, ample apology for the slow movements of Dunbar that, besides the rugged and steep passes of the mountains, the troops he had with him were the refuse of the army, very many of whom sickened and died on the way with the flux and for want of fresh provisions.

The Indians and French constantly annoyed his march and beset his camps, and having got in his rear, cut off much of his scanty supplies. But the great cause of delay was the want of horses to move his heavy train. After one day's toil at half the wagons and other vehicles, the poor jaded beasts had to go back the next day and tug up the other half, often moving not more than three miles a day, and consuming two days at each encampment. So exhausted were the horses that an officer of the train estimated it would require twenty-five days for Dunbar to overtake Braddock from the Great Meadows. And in the council of war held by Braddock at Jacob's Creek, on the 3d of July, to consider Sir John St. Clair's suggestion to halt and send back all their horses to bring up Dunbar's division, it was adjudged that with this aid he could not be brought up in less than eleven days, so weak were all the horses. Besides, it was never designed that Dunbar should overtake Braddock until the fort was captured. And this setting apart of him, his officers, and soldiers to an ignoble service—making it a "foregone conclusion" that they were not to share the honors or spoils of victory—soured their tempers and relaxed their exertions.

Dunbar's camp was situated southeast of the summit of Wolf's Hill, one of the highest points of Laurel Hill Mountain, and about three thousand feet above the level of the ocean. The site is in full view of Uniontown, to the eastward about six miles distant, and is visible from nearly all the high points in Fayette County and the adjacent parts of Greene and Washington Counties, Pa. The camp was about three hundred feet below the summit, and about half a mile's distance on the southern slope. It was then cleared of its timber, but has since become much overgrown with bushes and small trees. Near it are two fine sand springs, below which a dam of stones and earth, two or three feet high, was made to afford an abundant supply of water. This dam is still visible, though much overgrown by laurels. Into this spring, pool, or basin, it is said, when Dunbar's encampment was broken up, fifty thousand pounds of powder, with other material of war, were thrown, to render them useless to the enemy. Old Henry Beeson, of Uniontown, used to relate that when he first visited this locality, in 1767, there were some six inches of black nitrous matter visible all over this spring basin.

The Turkey's Foot, or "Smith's road," from Bedford, crossed Braddock's, or Nemacolin's road just at this camp. Both are yet plainly visible, and the remains of an old stone chimney near the cross-roads indicate the site of an ancient tavern, where many a pioneer halted and many an old emigrant and settler took his ease.

When the remains of Braddock's division rejoined Dunbar here, on the 11th of July, the camp was found in great confusion and disorder. Many had fled the day before on the first tidings of the slaughter of the 9th, and as had been the case upon that disaster, the wagoners and pack-horse-drivers were among the first to fly, and were the earliest messengers of the defeat to Governor Morris, of Pennsylvania, then at Carlisle superintending the forwarding of supplies.

Orders still continued to be issued in Braddock's name, though his life was fast ebbing away. Retreat became inevitable. The camp was abandoned on the 12th. All the stores and supplies, artillery, etc., which had been brought hither at such great labor and expense, were destroyed. Nothing was saved beyond the actual necessities of a flying march. These included two six-pounders and some hospital stores, horses and light wagons for the sick and wounded, of whom there were three hundred. The rest of the artillery, cohorns, etc., were broken up, the shells burst, the powder thrown into the spring basin, the provisions and baggage scattered, and one hundred and fifty wagons burned. A few days afterwards some of the enemy came up and completed the work of destruction.

It has been a current tradition, based upon contemporary statements, that some of the field-pieces and other munitions of war, and even money, were buried or concealed near the camp, and much time and labor have been spent in fruitless search for them. This story, it seems, reached the ears of Dunbar while on his retreat from Will's Creek through Pennsylvania, and he and all his officers, in a letter to Governor Shirley, dated Aug. 21, 1755, expressly contradict it in these words: "We must beg leave to undeceive you in what you are pleased to mention of guns being buried at the time Gen. Braddock ordered the stores to be destroyed, for there was not a gun of any kind buried." However, such things as cannon-balls, bullets, brass and iron kettles, crowbars, files, some shells, irons of horse gears and wagons, etc., have been found by the early settlers and other explorers.

The remains of the reunited army encamped on the night of the 13th of July at the old orchard camp, "two miles west" of Fort Necessity. Here Braddock died, having, before he expired, it is said, but rather apocryphally, bequeathed to Washington his favorite charger and his body-servant, Bishop. Mr. Headley has endeavored to give to Braddock's funeral the romantic interest of the burial of Sir John Moore,—"darkly, at dead of night," by the light of a torch, instead of "lanterns dimly burning," and with the addition of Washington reading the funeral service. But he was buried in daylight, on the morning of the 14th, in the road near the run and old orchard, and the march of the troops, horses, and wagons passed over the grave to obliterate its traces, and thus prevent its desecration by the enemy. The tree labeled "Braddock's Grave" indicates the place, near by, where were reinterred, about 1820, some of the bones of a man supposed to be Braddock. The military accompaniments said to have been found with them indicate that they were. They had been dug out of the bank of the run in 1812, in repairing the old road. These may or may not have been the bones of Braddock. Several of the bones were carried off before the reinterment at the tree, many of which, it is said, were afterwards collected by Abraham Stewart (who was the road supervisor when they were dug out) and sent to Peale's Museum at Philadelphia as curiosities. Col. Burd says he found the spot of his interment about "twenty rods from a little hollow," etc., when he came out in 1759. But Washington says that when he buried him "he designed at some future day to erect a monument to his memory, which he had no opportunity of doing till after the Revolutionary war, when he made, in 1784, a diligent search for his grave, but the road had been so much turned, and the clear land so extended, that it could not be found."

On July 11th, Col. Innes, who had been appointed by Braddock governor of Fort Cumberland, received the first unfavorable news of a great reverse to the army, and hurried away expresses to the neighboring provinces. On the 16th the tidings reached Annapolis, and on the next day Governor Sharpe set out for Fort Cumberland, accompanied by his secretary, Mr. Ridout, Lieut. Gold, and Ensign Russel, of His Majesty's forces, and a band of volunteers who had taken up arms to aid in the defense of the frontier. When the Governor reached the fort all was alarm and confusion. Numbers of the terrified inhabitants had hastened to its walls for safety from the now defenseless frontier, and to complete their misery Col. Dunbar had announced his intention of abandoning everything and retreating to Philadelphia, a resolution which he carried into effect in spite of all the remonstrances and pleadings of the Governor.[1]

This pusillanimous retreat excited the greatest indignation and alarm throughout the colonies, for it left the whole frontier uncovered, and the enemy now harried at his pleasure all the western borders of Maryland, Virginia, and Pennsylvania, plundering and murdering everywhere. To add to the alarm, the Shawanese and Delaware Indians, who had hitherto continued faithful, now went over to the French side, and began to ravage and slay the unhappy colonists. The outposts were everywhere driven in, some of the smaller forts taken, and universal panic prevailed. Fort Cumberland was still held by the provincials, under Capt. Dagworthy, but this isolated post could afford no protection against the roving bands of savages, who plundered the country round, and the garrison themselves were subject to frequent annoyance. There are two high knobs of the mountain, one on the southern or Virginia side of the Cohongornton, and the other on the Maryland side, within a short distance of the fort, from which the Indians frequently fired into it. On one occasion a rather large party of savages were posted on the knob on the Maryland side, and had given considerable annoyance, when a captain and seventy men volunteered to dislodge them. On a very dark night they sallied out from the fort, surrounded the knob, and cautiously ascending until they were within musket-shot of the foe, waited for daybreak. As soon as it was light they opened a brisk fire upon the Indians from all quarters, which threw them into utter confusion. Not knowing which way to escape, they were killed almost to a man, and the knob to this day bears the name of "Bloody Hill." Shortly after this "Killbuck," a distinguished chief, attempted to take the fort by stratagem. He approached it at the head of a large force of warriors, and pretending that they came as friends and allies, asked to be admitted. The commander appeared to be deceived by the stratagem and opened the gates, but no sooner had the chief and his principal warriors entered than the gates were closed and the wily savage caught in a trap. The commander charged him with his treachery, and as a punishment dressed his prisoners in women's clothes and drove them from the fort, a humiliation which, to the haughty savage, was more bitter than a torturing death.

The alarm which the disaster on the Monongahela, the flight of the British troops, and the advance of the enemy occasioned spread over the whole province. Many of the inhabitants of the western settlements fled to Baltimore, and preparations were even made by the people of that town to place the women and children on board the vessels in the harbor and send them to Virginia, while some of the Virginians were so alarmed as to think there was no safety short of England itself. But there were others of firmer temper who proposed to meet the coming danger. In September, Lieut. Stoddert, assisted by fifteen pioneers from the surrounding settlements, erected a stockade fort, which served as a rallying-point for the settlers around. All those who lived beyond Tonalloway Creek abandoned their habitations, and the country, as far east as thirty miles east of Col. Cresap's, who lived about five miles west of the mouth of the South Branch of the Potomac, was deserted. Col. Thomas Cresap himself moved down the river to the plantation of his son, Michael Cresap, who lived near the Conococheague. The two Cresaps were distinguished among the hardy frontiersmen for courage, intelligence, and skill in Indian warfare.

---

[1] On the return of the Maryland troops from their expedition against the Indians, under Braddock and Washington, Capt. Evan Shelby, who commanded a company of Frederick County Rangers, was received with every demonstration of joy.

They were always on the alert, and their timely warnings saved many of their neighbors from massacre. Their block-house, which was strong enough to resist the savages, served as a place of refuge in case of an invasion, and as a rendezvous for the settlers in more peaceful times, where they met to hear and tell their news, to try their skill as marksmen, or engage in friendly trials of strength or dexterity, and at night, seated around a huge log fire, they would tell adventures of war or the chase, and if by good luck any of them possessed a jewsharp or fiddle, and had the cunning to awaken its harmony, the evening wound up hilariously with a dance.

So now the frontiersmen gathered at Cresap's and strengthened his block-house for defense; others sought protection at Fort Cumberland and Frederick. Governor Sharpe, as we have already seen, had raised a number of volunteers at this town when on his way to the fort, and to defray their expenses subscriptions were raised throughout the province, Annapolis and the surrounding country alone furnishing in a very few days one thousand pounds. The people of Baltimore raised a large sum, with which they purchased arms and ammunition, and established a public armory in the town. The news from the frontiers, telling of Indian raids and massacres, kept up the alarm. In the *Maryland Gazette* of October 9th we have the following account of affairs in the West:

"By a person who arrived in town last Monday (October 6th) from Col. Cresap's, we are told that last Wednesday (October 1st) morning the Indians had taken a man prisoner who was going from Frazier's to Fort Cumberland, and had also carried off a woman from Frazier's plantation, which is four miles on this side Fort Cumberland. The same morning they fell in with a man and his wife who had left their plantations, and were retiring into the more populous part of the country; they shot the horse on which the man was riding, but as it did not fall immediately he made his escape. The woman, it is supposed, fell into their hands, as neither she or the horse on which she was riding have been seen since or heard of. The same party of Indians also have carried off or killed Benjamin Rogers, his wife, and seven children, and Edmund Marle, one family of twelve persons, besides fifteen others, all in Frederick County. On Patterson's Creek many families have within this month been murdered, carried away, or burnt in their houses by a party of these barbarians, who have entirely broke up that settlement.

"Another person, who left Stoddert's fort last Sunday, acquaints us that the inhabitants in that part of the country were in the greatest consternation. That near eighty persons were fled to the said fort for protection, and many more gone off in the greatest confusion to Pennsylvania. This, it seems, had been occasioned by a dispatch sent to Lieut. Stoddert and the neighborhood by Col. Cresap, advising them that a party of seventeen Indians had passed by his house and had cut off some people who dwelt on the Town Creek, which is a few miles on this side of Cresap's. One Daniel Ashloff, who lived near that creek, is come down towards Conococheague, and gives the same account. He says also that as himself and father, with several others, were retiring from their plantations last Saturday they were attacked by the same Indians, as he supposes, and all but himself were killed or taken prisoners. It is said that Mr. Stoddert, who has command of fifteen men, invited a few of the neighbors to join him and to go in quest of the enemy, but they would not be persuaded, whereupon he applied himself to Maj. Prather for a detachment of the militia, either to go with a party of his men in pursuit of the savages, or garrison his fort while he made an excursion. We hope there will be no backwardness in the militia to comply with such a reasonable request, especially as any party or person that shall take an enemy prisoner will be rewarded with six pounds currency, and the person who will kill an enemy, with four pounds, provided he can produce witnesses, or the enemy's scalp, in testimony of such action."

In consequence of these outrages, Governor Sharpe, on the 18th of October, called out the militia of the province. At the same time Capt. Alexander Beall and Lieut. Samuel Wade Magruder with thirty volunteers from the lower part of Frederick County, and Col. Henry Ridgely with thirty more from Anne Arundel County, hastened to the invaded district. A few days afterwards sixty more volunteers, fully armed and equipped, went from Prince George's County to the West at their own expense. They arrived too late to punish the marauders, who had already made off with their booty and prisoners, but they remained to protect those who were left from further outrage.

Meanwhile, the alarm increased, and the wildest rumors were afloat. It was reported early in November that a large body of French and Indians were advancing upon the interior settlements, and this rumor reaching Frederick Town on Sunday, November 2d, the inhabitants, expecting an immediate attack, rang the bells as an alarm, and dispatched messengers to Baltimore and Annapolis for help. Several companies of volunteers at once mustered in Baltimore and the neighborhood, and marched without delay. The Indians came to within about fifteen miles of Frederick Town.

Governor Sharpe ordered into service the militia of Frederick, Prince George's, Baltimore, Cecil, Anne Arundel, Calvert, Charles, and St. Mary's Counties, to rendezvous at Frederick, Oct. 10, 1755. The troops were to march to Frederick, where James Dickson was to furnish them with provisions for five days; thence they were to march to the mouth of the Conococheague, where George Ross was to furnish provisions to subsist them for eight days, or till they could reach Col. Cresap's, where they were to assist in the protection of the frontier.

In August, 1755, Col. Nathaniel Wickham commanded the militia of Frederick County, and ordered all to be called to the protection of the frontier. Some of the scalping-parties approached within thirty miles of Baltimore, and though many of them were killed, terror spread from the very fact of their approach; but in the West the peril was real and constant; scarce any out-door labor was carried on except under the protection of the troops, or of armed bodies of settlers. It was at the risk of life that any one ventured a few rods away from his door; women visiting their sick neighbors were shot down or carried off; children bringing in the cattle from the field were tomahawked and scalped by the ambushed murderers. The plantations were being deserted, and homes and property abandoned to plunder or the torch, and all the remoter settlements were fast becoming a wilderness. Washington, harassed by want of sufficient support, and deeply pained by the scenes which he witnessed, wrote to Governor Dinwiddie, April 16, 1756,—

"I have done everything in my power to quiet the minds of the inhabitants by detaching all the men I have any command over to the places more exposed. There also have been large detachments from Fort Cumberland in pursuit of the enemy these ten days past, yet nothing, I fear, will prevent the people from abandoning their dwellings and flying with the utmost precipitation."

Six days later he writes,—

"The supplicating tears of the women and moving petitions of the men melt me into such deadly sorrow, that I solemnly declare, if I know my own mind, I could offer myself a willing sacrifice to the butchering enemy, provided that would contribute to the people's ease."

On the 24th he writes,—

"The deplorable situation of this people is no more to be described than my anxiety and uneasiness for their relief. You may expect by the time this comes to hand that, without a considerable reinforcement, Frederick County will not be mistress of fifteen families. They are now retiring to the securest parts in droves of fifties."

In consequence of this state of things, Governor Sharpe authorized Prather to organize all the forces on the frontiers, except those at Fort Cumberland, and operate between the Potomac and the Pennsylvania line. By the 11th of March, Prather had under his command one hundred and fifty efficient and hardy backwoodsmen skilled in Indian fighting. Capt. Alexander Beall, who commanded a company of volunteers, was also authorized to raise a force of one hundred men and join Maj. Prather. Extracts from the papers of the times will show the state of affairs and the public excitement. The *Maryland Gazette* of the 4th of March says,—

"Our accounts from the westward are truly alarming. All the slaughters, scalpings, burnings, and every other barbarity and mischief that the mongrel French, Indians, and their chieftain, the devil, can invent are often perpetrated there, and approach us nigher and nigher.

"By a person come to town this day from Frederick County we are told that last Sunday two boys, near Lawrence Wilson's, in that county, were killed and scalped, and a son of one Mr. Lynn was found dead and scalped, himself and three more of his family missing. At the Little Cove all the houses were burned last week. The house of Ralph Matson, about half a mile from Stoddert's Fort, was burned on Tuesday, last week. Some sheep which were in the pen near the house the Indians flung in the fire alive, others they killed, and some they scalped."

And on March 11th the *Gazette* published this extract from a letter dated Conococheague, February 29th:

"My last was of the 26th instant. On our march to Toonaloways, about five miles this side Stoddert's Fort, we found John Meyers' house in flames, and nine or ten head of large cattle killed. About three miles and a half farther up the road we found a man (one Hynes) killed and scalped, with one arm cut off and several arrows sticking in him; we could not bury him, having no tools with us for that purpose. Half a mile farther (within a mile of Stoddert's Fort) we found Ralph Watson's house burnt down, and several hogs and sheep killed. When we came to Stoddert's Fort we found them all under arms, expecting every minute to be attacked. From thence we went to Combe's Fort, where we found a young man about twenty-two years of age killed and scalped; there were only four men in this fort, two of which were unable to bear arms, but upwards of forty women and children, who were in a very poor situation, being afraid to go out of the fort, even for a drink of water. The house caught fire during the time the Indians were surrounding the fort, and would have been burnt down, but luckily there was some soapsuds in the house, by which they extinguished it. The young man mentioned above was one Lynn's son, and was sitting on the fence of the stockyard with Combe's son, when they discovered the Indians, upon which they ran to get into the fort, and before they reached it Lynn's son was shot down, and an Indian pursued the other man with a tomahawk within thirty yards of the fort, but he luckily got into the fort and shot the Indian. We searched the woods to see if we could discover where the Indian was buried (as they supposed him to be mortally wounded). We found in two places great quantity of blood, but could not find the body. We saw several creatures shot, some dead, and others going around with arrows sticking in them. About half a mile on this side Mr. Kenney's (in Little Toonaloways) we found a load of oats and a load of turnips in the road, which two boys were bringing to Combe's, and it is imagined the boys are carried off by the Indians. When we came to Mr. Kenney's we saw several sheep and cattle killed. From thence we went to one Lowther's, about two miles farther, where we found his grain and two calves burnt, two cows and nine or ten hogs killed, and about fifty yards from the house found Lowther dead and scalped, and otherwise terribly mangled; his brains were beat out, as it is supposed, with his own gun-barrel, which we found sticking in his skull, and his gun broken; there was an axe, two scythes, and several arrows sticking in him. From here we returned to Combe's and buried the young man, and left ten of our men here to assist them to secure their grain, which soon as they have done they purpose to leave that fort and go to Stoddert's, from hence we went to Stoddert's Fort, where we laid on Friday night and yesterday. On our way down here we buried the man we left on the road.

"ISAAC BAKER."

Under date of March 11th the *Gazette* reports that "one Mrs. Inglis, who was taken prisoner by the

Shawanese when Col. Patton was killed, had made a wonderful escape from the Lower Shawnee Town, and that she was fourteen days in the woods on her way home, was naked all the time, and lived on chestnuts." The murders and burnings continued without abatement, and on April 8th the *Gazette* recites the "deposition" of James Tucker, who related that he was

"at Capt. Waggoner's Fort in Virginia, and heard some of Capt. Waggoner's company say that Mr. John Bacon, lieutenant of Capt. Dagworthy's company, was killed and scalped by the Indians about four or five miles from Cumberland Fort, and also that two men with Lieut. Bacon were wounded, but made their escape to the fort. That he had heard that five men under the command of Capt. Ashby were killed by the enemy, and that the Indians had attacked one Cox Fort, but were repulsed. By the same express we have deposition of Aaron Ryley, taken yesterday (April 7, 1756), to the following effect: that he was at Adam Hoop's on the 5th instant, where he saw an express who brought letters to several people there, which he did not hear read, but was told by the man who brought them that on the 1st instant William M. Coard's Fort, within about five miles from Col. Chambers' Fort, which he thinks is about thirty miles from Fort Lyttleton, was taken, and thirty people were there killed and taken. Upon the news of this, Capt. Alexander Culverson marched from among the inhabitants with a party of men in pursuit of the Indians, and were joined by another party from Fort Lyttleton, the whole amounting to about fifty men. That the Indians were about twelve miles from Fort Lyttleton. That they came up with the Indians, fired upon them and killed several, and at length put them to flight; that they were so eager in pursuit that, though Indian Isaac, our friend, advised them to cut loose some of the prisoners which they had tied to trees, yet they omitted it. That the party had not pursued far before the Indians were joined by fifty more, as they supposed, who soon routed the white men, and of the whole fifty only fifteen were returned to Fort Lyttleton Sunday night last (April 4th)."

At the burning of Coard's Fort "one of the young women was very big with child, whom they ripped open, and scalped the infant."

While the Indians were thus laying waste the frontier settlements, a heartless attempt was made by some white adventurers on the border to turn the general alarm to their own advantage by pillaging the distressed inhabitants. In March (1756),

"Thomas Mills, who came from Conococheague the beginning of last week, says that the inhabitants of that part of Frederick County were lately thrown into the greatest consternation by some parties firing guns and hallooing, with a design to terrify the inhabitants and make them desert their habitations. He further says that upon the people's flying, the villains went and robbed their houses, and some of them have been since approached, and confessed what is above mentioned."

In the mean while the people of Frederick, Prince George's, and Baltimore Counties assailed the Lower House of Assembly with petitions. A memorial from Frederick Town urged them to decline unnecessary disputes, and demanded that means should be afforded them to defend their lives and protect their property, as the destructive inroads of the enemy were now compelling them to desert their homes. On the 25th of April, 1756, forty-one persons,—six men, five women, and thirty children,—with a small portion of their cattle, to avoid the fury of the enemy deserted their cabins and clearings near Conococheague and came to Baltimore. Their houses were destroyed and their cattle killed. And on the 23d of April, 1756, Thomas Cresap, Jr., and Daniel Cresap, sons of Col. Thomas Cresap, with sixty riflemen, "dressed and painted like Indians," with "red caps," started on an expedition "to kill the women and children in the Indian towns and scalp them, while the warriors are committing the like destruction on our frontiers." The result of this expedition is given in the *Maryland Gazette* as follows:

"On the 23d of April, as Thomas Cresap, Jr., lay in ambush near the Little Meadow, they saw a party of Indians coming by them, but one of the party firing too soon alarmed them, and they fled as fast as possible into thickets, leaving their horses and baggage, which our people took and brought off with them. Among their baggage one scalp was found. One of the Indians taking a different course from the rest, Mr. Cresap and two others ran after him near a mile; when the Indian found that Mr. Cresap gained on him and would overtake him, he dodged behind a large tree, and Mr. Cresap stopped behind one smaller, and they fired at one another so near together that it could not be distinguished which fired first. Cresap was shot with large shot in the breast, and the others of the party coming up, he told them not to mind him, he was a dead man, but to pursue the enemy, and then dropped down dead. The Indian was shot through the right breast, but was not dead when they came up to him, so they dispatched him with a tomahawk and scalped him. Mr. Cresap's body they buried as privately as they could. He was a young widower, and left two little children, and his death was lamented by all who knew him."

This account was not quite correct. Cresap was shot with a bullet and seven buckshot, the ball going through his breast, and he was not shot behind a tree, but in an open space while he was pursuing his foe.

Col. Cresap's men were dressed in red caps, and in July "four Indians dressed in the same made a foray among the inhabitants near Conococheague, and killed and scalped two persons and then made off. A party of forty-six men started in pursuit, but were unable to overtake them."

Col. Cresap soon got together another band of volunteers, "and with his two surviving sons, Daniel and Michael, and a negro of gigantic stature, marched again, taking the same route on Braddock's road. They advanced this time as far as Negro Mountain, where they met a party of Indians. A running fight took place; Cresap's party killed an Indian, and the Indians killed the negro; and it was this circumstance—the death of the negro on the mountain—that has immortalized his name by fixing it on this ridge forever."[1]

On the 30th of June, 1756, Col. Cresap, with a party of thirteen young men, had a skirmish with the Indians, in which Abraham Johnson, Jacob Ashcroft, and James Lowry were killed, the Indians losing two of their number.

After the defeat of Braddock, the inhabitants of Western Maryland inaugurated for their defense a series of private forts or block-houses, which were occasionally garrisoned by companies of rangers. Each of the forts were generally in charge of a few men, but they only afforded protection to those who fled to them for safety. Separated as they were from each other by so great a distance, the Indians in their incursions readily avoided them, and still found a wide field for their inhuman warfare, where they could strike a deadly blow and retreat to the mountains before the settlers could be gathered together in pursuit. The butchery continued for seven long years, and the Indians boasted that they had killed fifty white people for every Indian killed. While there was great truth in the boast, it scarcely conveys an accurate impression of the prowess of the red men, for they always avoided equal and honorable combat, and butchered men, women, and children in cold blood, for whose scalps they were liberally paid by the French. It is scarcely possible to convey in words a correct idea of the deplorable condition of Western Maryland at this period. Families were surprised in their dwellings at midnight, every member murdered and scalped, their houses and crops burned, and their cattle gathered together in the lurid light of the flames, and driven off to the mountains. Delicate women were carried into captivity worse than death; little children, driving cattle to the fields, were killed and scalped in sight of their homes. The ground was plowed, the seed sown, and the harvest gathered in constant dread of the tomahawk and rifle. Scarcely any out-door work was attempted, unless some of the laborers carried arms in their hands; and the men usually plowed or harvested in companies, that they might defend each other.

In November, 1755, a band of Indians, under Shingas, the Delaware chief, attacked the frontier settlements of Western Maryland and Pennsylvania, burned the houses, and murdered or made prisoners of those of the inhabitants who did not escape. Shingas was the most cruel and blood-thirsty warrior of his tribe. His exploits form a sickening record of the murder and torture of innocent victims, equaled in fiendish malignity by those of no other human being on the North American continent. He is said to have been small in stature, but in point of courage and activity and in savage prowess was equaled by few. A settler speaking of this inroad of Shingas, said, "Last night I had a family of upwards of one hundred women and children, who fled for succor. You can form no just idea of the distress and distracted condition of our inhabitants, unless you saw them and heard their cries." Another says, "The cries of widows and fatherless children were heart-rending, while those who escaped with their lives had neither a mouthful to eat, nor a bed to lie on, nor clothes to cover their nakedness or keep them warm; all they had being consumed in their burning dwellings." Fifty persons at this time were killed or taken prisoners, twenty-seven houses were burned, a great number of cattle were killed or driven off, and out of ninety-three families on the borders of Maryland and Pennsylvania who settled in what was called the two "coves," members of forty-seven families were either killed or captured, and the remainder deserted their homes, so that the settlements were entirely broken up. One woman, over ninety years of age, was found lying dead with her breasts torn off and a stake driven through her body. The infuriated savages caught up little children and dashed their brains out against the door-posts in presence of their shrieking mothers, or cut off their heads and drank their warm blood.

The cold indifference of the Lord Proprietary, who refused to allow his immense estates to bear a share of the tax demanded for the purpose of raising troops and money for the defense of the frontier, awoke the deepest indignation throughout Western Maryland against him and the Assembly. The patience of the western settlers was worn out with the interminable disputes between the Governor and Assembly, and they threatened to adopt the emphatic measures of their friends in Pennsylvania.[2]

The resolute men of Western Maryland, under the leadership of Col. Thomas Cresap, who appears to be at this time the guardian genius of the frontier settlements, assembled in Frederick Town and threatened to march with guns and tomahawks to Annapolis and compel the Assembly to cease their unseasonable

---

[1] Jacob's "Life of Cresap."

[2] The dead bodies of three people that had been murdered and scalped by the Indians were brought down to Philadelphia by the distant inhabitants and hauled about the streets, with placards announcing that these were victims of the Quaker policy of non-resistance. A mob of four thousand people surrounded the House of Assembly, placed the dead bodies in the doorway, and demanded immediate relief for the people on the frontier, which was granted.

wranglings and come to their relief. The Assembly immediately acquiesced in their demands, and notwithstanding the prognostications of the Governor, appropriated £40,000 for purposes of defense. Of this sum £11,000 were to be applied to the erection of a fort and block-houses on the frontier, and for raising, arming, and maintaining a body of two hundred men to garrison them; £3000 were appropriated for engaging the services of the Southern Indians, for which purpose two commissioners, Col. Benjamin Tasker and Charles Carroll the younger, were appointed to take charge of the fund and conduct the negotiations. One thousand pounds were allotted as bounties for Indian scalps or prisoners, at the rate of £10 for each; £25,000 were set apart for the proposed joint expedition against Fort Du Quesne. William Murdock, James Dick, and Daniel Wolstenholme were appointed agents to pay out these sums, with a commission of two and a half per cent.

Though England and France had kept up hostilities in the colonies since 1754, the peace was not openly broken in Europe until the 17th of May, 1756, when a formal declaration of war was made. New exertions were now made to put the frontiers in a state of defense. Under the act passed at the previous session (1755-56) of the Assembly, Governor Sharpe purchased one hundred and fifty acres of land near the present town of Hancock, and began to erect a substantial stone fort, which he named Fort Frederick. It had barracks for the accommodation of two hundred men, and on an emergency could contain twice that number. It had bastions and curtains faced with stone, and on each bastion was mounted a six-pounder. It was built upon an elevated plateau about a quarter of a mile from the Potomac, which was navigable from thence almost to Fort Cumberland. The fort was quadrangular in shape, its walls being strengthened with earth embankments, and each of its exterior lines was three hundred and sixty feet in length. It was expected to cost only about two thousand pounds, but cost three times that sum when completed. By the middle of August, 1756, it was so far completed as to receive a garrison of two hundred men, under command of Capt. Dagworthy. The walls of this fort are still standing, firm and strong, covered with wild vines. It is thirteen miles east of Hancock, and may be seen from the railroad cars in passing over the Baltimore and Ohio road, near Green Spring Run station.

During this time the audacity of the Indians had increased with their success. A party of Indians advanced within a short distance of Frederick, and emboldened by the success of their confederates on the head-waters of the Ohio, the forks of the Monongahela and the Alleghany, made their way even to the neighborhood of Emmittsburg, assailed that then thinly-settled region, and after shooting a man named Alexander McKeasy near his own house, and capturing his son, made good their escape without any loss. At this critical juncture, according to Washington's report to Lord Fairfax, the whole settlement of Conococheague had fled, and there only remained two families between that point and Frederick Town.[1]

"That the Maryland settlements are all abandoned," says Washington, "is certainly a fact, as I have had the accounts transmitted to me by several hands, and confirmed yesterday by Henry Brinker, who left Monocacy the day before, and who also affirms that three hundred and fifty wagons had passed that place, to avoid the enemy, within the space of three days." In consequence of this alarming condition of affairs, the people below Conococheague raised a subscription sufficient to arm and equip a patrol of twenty men, under Lieut. William Teagard, of Capt. Rench's company of militia, for their protection. Their services were soon demanded, for on August 18th the enemy plundered the settlers near Baker's Ridge, and on the 20th attacked a funeral train, killing two persons (George Hicks and Lodovick Claymour). They were followed by a party of thirteen of Teagard's men, under Luke Thompson, until they came within two miles of the mouth of Conococheague, on the Pennsylvania road, when five shots were heard about three hundred yards in advance, which threw the pursuing party into some confusion; but Matthias Nicholls, "a young lad of eighteen, insisted they should run up and come upon the enemy while their pieces were unloaded, and set off immediately." The others, however, ran off, but he continued the pursuit, and rescued William Postlewaite, who had been seriously wounded by the Indians, and conducted him in safety to Col. Cresap's. An effort was made at this time by Washington to secure the consent of Governor Dinwiddie to the abandonment of Fort Cumberland, the former regarding the post as of no value in a military point of view, and as a source of useless expense and anxiety. After

---

[1] A beautiful young lady, well known in those days as a daring heroine, was taken prisoner by the Indian freebooters on the farm where Henry W. Dellinger now lives, and after a desperate struggle broke loose from her captors. After running for some distance, with the Indians in close pursuit, she dodged behind a tree to escape the arrows of her pursuers, when her flowing hair caught in the bark and stopped her flight. At this moment one of the Indians threw his tomahawk at her head, but the weapon, missing its aim, severed her hair and set her free, when she again took to flight and made good her escape.

considerable correspondence on the subject, however, Washington's advice was rejected, and by Dinwiddie's order the garrisons were withdrawn from the smaller frontier posts and sent, with most of the troops from Winchester, to Fort Cumberland, which was made the headquarters of the army. On the 29th of April, 1757, a body of Cherokee Indians arrived at Fort Frederick and offered their services to Governor Sharpe, and the Governor's secretary, John Ridout, and Daniel Walstenholme were sent as commissioners to Fort Frederick to treat with these Indians, carrying with them a wagon-load of presents and two hundred pounds in goods for the scalps of four hostile Indians, whom the Cherokees had killed while waiting for an answer.

The enemy, however, still kept up their forays, almost under the walls of the forts, and the settlements west of the Blue Ridge were well-nigh deserted. In the summer of 1757 there was a general flight from the upper waters of the Potomac, and on the 18th of June the report came that a large force of French and Indians, with artillery, were advancing on Fort Cumberland. Sharpe immediately called out the militia, and gathering a body of volunteers, started to relieve the threatened post, but on reaching Frederick found that it was a false alarm.

William Pitt, appointed Secretary of State the previous June, resolved that the campaign of 1758 should be conducted after a different fashion, and it was determined that another expedition should be sent against Fort Du Quesne, under Gen. Forbes. In June the forces of Maryland, Pennsylvania, and Virginia received orders from Gen. Forbes to begin their march upon Fort Du Quesne. The troops destined for this expedition numbered between six and seven thousand, of whom Maryland furnished a contingent of about five hundred, under Lieut.-Col. Dagworthy. Early in July the Maryland and Virginia troops were assembled at Fort Cumberland, and the Pennsylvanians at Raystown (now Bedford), in their own province, about thirty miles from the fort. An army of seven thousand men had now assembled under the command of Gen. Forbes, who, disregarding the advice of Washington to advance by the road already opened by Braddock, ordered a new road cut from Raystown. The working-party, under the command of Col. Bouquet, to whom this task was assigned, had early in September arrived at Loyal Hanna, ten miles beyond Laurel Hill, and on the 21st of September Maj. Grant, of Montgomery's battalion, with eight hundred Highlanders, a part of Washington's regiment, eighty-one Marylanders, and a number of Pennsylvanians were detailed from this advanced post to reconnoitre the enemy's position at Fort Du Quesne. The French commander of that fort, observing the want of precaution with which Grant executed his orders, took speedy measures to punish him. Having posted Indians in ambuscade on his enemy's flank, he made a sudden sally from the fort, and soon spread dismay and confusion among the ranks of the British soldiers. With gleaming knives and brandished tomahawks the Indians rushed yelling from the thickets, and fell upon the astonished Highlanders with terrible effect. Hand to hand they fought until, overpowered, the whole detachment fled in dismay, pursued by the furious savages. The Highlanders for a time stood their ground well, but the Marylanders and Virginians bore the brunt of the battle, the Pennsylvanians breaking at the first fire. The Marylanders behaved with the greatest gallantry, and gave evidence of the thorough manner in which they had been trained for border warfare. Out of eighty-one men, their loss was twenty-seven privates and one officer—Lieut. Duncan McRae—killed, and nearly one-half of their whole force missing.

"The Marylanders," says the *Maryland Gazette*, "concealing themselves behind trees and the brush, made a good defense, but were overpowered by numbers, and not being supported, were obliged to follow the rest." The total loss was two hundred and seventy killed and forty-two wounded.

The fugitives were rallied by Capt. Bullitt, who checked the enemy until the whole force could retreat out of danger. Capt. Ware, Lieut. Riley, and Ensign Harrison brought off in safety the remaining Marylanders. On the 12th of October the enemy, who had watched the movements of the army, thinking it a favorable time to strike another blow and complete their victory, attacked Col. Bouquet at Loyal Hanna. After a few hours' struggle, during which the English lost sixty-seven officers and men killed and wounded, the enemy were repulsed. In this engagement Lieut. Prather and two privates of the Maryland troops were killed, Ensign Bell and six privates wounded, and eleven missing. In another skirmish, on the 12th of November, near Loyal Hanna, Capt. Evan Shelby, of Frederick County, killed with his own hand one of the greatest chiefs of the enemy. With fifty miles of road to open across the forests, the winter rapidly approaching, and the disheartened troops beginning to desert, it was decided that it was inexpedient to proceed further in the campaign. Fortunately, Capt. Ware, of the Maryland troops, with a scouting-party, brought in three prisoners, from whom information was obtained of the actual condition of Fort Du Quesne. They learned the weakness and distress of the French garrison, and nerved by this intelligence, Gen. Forbes determined to make a vigorous effort to gain possession of the place before it could be reinforced. Leaving their tents and heavy baggage at Loyal Hanna, they advanced within a few hours' march of the fort, when the French garrison set fire to the works and retreated down the Ohio. Gen. Forbes took possession of the abandoned fort, caused the works to be repaired, and gave it the name of Fort Pitt, in honor of the prime minister, assigning a garrison of four hundred and fifty men, taken from the Maryland, Pennsylvania, and Virginia troops, for its defense.

The contest which commenced in America between England and France was ended by a treaty signed at Paris on the 10th of February, 1763, and as there appeared to be safety for settlers west of the mountains, emigration began to move over those hitherto impassable barriers of civilization. These encroachments aroused Pontiac, a sagacious Ottawa chief, who went secretly from tribe to tribe among the Indians, and obtained their solemn pledges to a confederation, whose object was the expulsion of the English from all the forts and settlements on the frontier. So adroitly were their plans matured that the commanders of the Western forts had no suspicion of the conspiracy until it was ripe and the first blow had been struck, in June, 1763. Their plan was that the border settlements were to be invaded during harvest, the men, corn, and cattle to be destroyed, and the outposts to be reduced by famine. Pursuant to these plans, the Indians massacred traders whom they had invited among them, and seized their property; and large scalping-parties advanced to the frontiers of Maryland, Pennsylvania, and Virginia, marking their way with blood and devastation. The most remote outposts were attacked about the same time, and within a fortnight all those west of Oswego, except Niagara, Fort Pitt, and Detroit, fell into their hands. The whole country west of Fort Frederick became the prey of the savages, who burned barns and houses, and surprised and massacred the settlers in the fields or asleep in their dwellings. "Another tempest has arisen upon our frontiers," Washington wrote to a friend, "and the alarm spreads wider than ever. In short, the inhabitants are so apprehensive of danger that no families remain above the Conococheague road, and many are gone below. The harvests are, in a manner, lost, and the distresses of the settlements are evident and manifold."

On the 15th of July, 1763, Col. Thomas Cresap wrote from Old Town to Governor Sharpe, as follows:

"I take this opportunity in the highth of Confusion to acquaint you with our unhappy and most wretched Situation at this time, being in Hourly Expectation of being massacred by our Barberous and Inhumane Enemy the Indians, we having been three days successively attacked by them, viz.: the 13, 14, and this Instant. On the 13th, as 6 men were shocking some wheat in the field, 5 Indians firing on them as they came to do it and others Running to their assistance;—on the 14th 5 Indians crept up to and fired on about 16 men who were sitting and walking under a Tree at the entrance of my Lane, about 100 yards from my House, but on being fired at by the white men, who much wounded some of them, they Immediately Run off, and were followed by the white men about a mile, all which way was a great Quantity of Blood on the Ground. The white men got three of their Bundles, containing sundry Indian Implements & Goods. About 3 Hours after several gunns were fired in the woods, on which a party went in Quest of them and found 3 Braves Killed by them. The Indians wounded one man at their first fire, tho' but Slightly.

"On this Instant, as Mr. Samuel Wilder was going to a house of his about 300 yards D:stant from mine with four men and several women, the Indians rushed on them from a rising Ground, but they perceiving them coming, Run towards my House hollowing, which being heard by those at my house, they run to their assistance, and met them and the Indians at the entrance of my lane, on which the Indians Immediately fired on them to the amount of 18 or Twenty, and Killed Mr. Wilder. The party of white men Returned their fire, and killed one of them dead on the Spot and wounded severall of the others, as appeared by Considerable Quantity of Blood strewed on the Ground as they Run off, which they Immediately did, and by their leaving behind them 3 Gunns, one pistole, and Sundry other Emplements of warr, &c., &c. I have Inclosed a List of the Desolate men, Women, and Children who have fled to my house, which is Inclosed by a small stockade for safety, by which you'll see what a number of poor Souls, destitute of Every necessary of Life, are here penned up and likely to be Butchered without Immediate Relief and assistance, and can expect none, unless from the province to which they Belong. I shall submit to your wiser Judgement the Best and most Effectual method for such Relief, and shall conclude with hoping we shall have it in time."[1]

The inhabitants of Frederick Town did all in their power to relieve the unhappy fugitives, a large part of whom were women and children, who had lost their all, and crowded the streets in a state of destitute misery. Their immediate necessities were relieved by food and shelter, and a considerable sum for their relief was subscribed throughout the province. An interesting contemporary account of the state of things in and about Frederick is given in the following letter published in the *Gazette*, written from Frederick Town, under date of July 19, 1763:

"Every day, for some time past, has offered the melancholy scene of poor distressed families driving downwards through this town with their effects, who have deserted their plantations for fear of falling into the cruel hands of our savage enemies, now daily seen in the woods. And never was panic more general or forcible than that of the back inhabitants, whose terrors at this time exceed what followed on the defeat of Gen.

---

[1] The *Maryland Gazette* of July 21, 1763, informs us that the colonel was not yet cut off by the savages, though it is feared he would be if not quickly relieved. Subsequent accounts show that ten men were sent to Cresap's assistance.

Braddock, when the frontiers lay open to the incursions of both French and Indians. Whilst Conococheague settlement stands firm we shall think ourselves in some sort of security from their insults here. But should the inhabitants there give way, you would soon see your city and the lower counties crowded with objects of compassion, as the flight would in that case become general. Numbers of those who have betaken themselves to the fort, as well as those who have actually fled, have entirely lost their crops, or turned in their own cattle and hogs to devour the produce, in hopes of finding them again in better condition should it hereafter appear safe for them to return. The season has been remarkably fine, and the harvest in general afforded the most promising appearance of plenty and goodness that has been known for many years. But alas! how dismal an alteration of the prospect! Many who expected to have sold and supplied the necessities of others now want for themselves, and see their warmest hopes defeated, the fruits of their honest industry snatched from them by the merciless attack of these blood-thirsty barbarians, whose treatment of such unhappy wretches as fall into their hands is accompanied with circumstances of infernal fury, too horrid and shocking for human nature to dwell upon even in imagination. We were so sensible of the importance of Conococheague settlement, both as a bulwark and supply to this neighborhood, that on repeated notice of their growing distress Capt. Butler, on Wednesday last, called the town company together, who appeared under arms on the court-house green with great unanimity. Just as the drum beat to arms we had the agreeable satisfaction of seeing a wagon sent up by his excellency (whose tender care for the security of the province raised sentiments of the highest gratitude in the breast of every one present) loaded with powder and lead,—articles of the greatest importance at this critical juncture, when the whole country had been drained of those necessary articles by the diligence of our Indian traders, who had bought up the whole for the supply of our enemies, to be returned, as we have dearly experienced, in death and desolation among us. A subscription was then set on foot and cheerfully entered into, in consequence of which twenty stout young men immediately enlisted under Mr. Peter Grosh to march immediately to the assistance of the back inhabitants, and with other volunteers already there raised, to cover the reapers, in hopes of securing the crops. Had not the Governor's supply arrived so seasonably it was doubted whether the whole town could have furnished ammunition sufficient for that small party, half of which marched backwards in high spirits on Thursday, and the remainder on Friday morning. And on Sunday subscriptions were taken in the several congregations in town for sending up further assistance. On Sunday afternoon we had the pleasure of seeing Mr. Michael Cresap arrive in town with mokosins on his legs, taken from an Indian whom he killed and scalped, being one of those who had shot down Mr. Wilder, the circumstances of whose much-lamented murder and the success of Col. Cresap's family you no doubt have received from other hands. Money has been cheerfully contributed in our town towards the support of the men to be added to Col. Cresap's present force, as we look upon the preservation of the Old Town to be of great importance to us, and a proper check to the progress of the savages; but notwithstanding our present efforts to keep the enemy at a distance, and thereby shelter the whole province, our inhabitants are poor, our men dispersed, and without a detachment from below it is to be feared we must give way, and the inundation break upon the lower counties."

In consequence of these outrages, the Governor convened the Assembly on the 4th of October, 1763, and further provision was made for the protection of the frontiers. The commissioners of the loan-office having £2120 still unexpended of the several sums appropriated by the act of 1756, were directed to pay to Daniel and Michael Cresap, John Walker, Nathan Friggs, William Young, Abraham Richardson, and Ezekiel Johnson fifty pounds for the scalp of an Indian taken by them in July, and the same amount to James Davis, of Virginia, who, in August, with a party of frontiersmen, had pursued a party of Indians from Cape Capon, on the south side of the Potomac, to George's Creek, in Maryland, where they overtook the savages, killing one, and rescuing James Coniston and his wife, whom they were carrying off as prisoners.

On July 25, 1764, two women were killed by the Indians near Fort Loudon, and on the following day, at a *school-house* near Capt. Potter's, in Conococheague, Robert Brown and nine children were scalped by four Indians, and four children carried off prisoners. Two of the nine children scalped were left living. The schoolmaster was killed.

Fort Pitt was in the mean time surrounded and cut off from all communication with the interior. In July, Gen. Amherst directed Col. Bouquet to proceed with five hundred men to reinforce it and drive back the savages. At Bushy Run Bouquet's command was attacked by Indians on the 5th of August, and the fight continued all day without decisive result. On the next day the contest was renewed, and the Indians were put to flight. Four days later Bouquet reached Fort Pitt.

In Col. Bouquet's expedition against the Mingoes, Delawares, and Shawnees in 1764 there were two companies of Maryland volunteers, one consisting of "forty-three brave woodsmen, besides officers, all of them well equipped with good rifles, and most of them born and bred on the frontiers of Frederick County," under Capt. William McClellan, and the other under the command of Capt. John Wolgomatt. In his letter to the Governor, dated Forks of Muskingum, Nov. 15, 1764, after giving a detailed account of his expedition, Col. Bouquet says, " As such a public spirit ought to be encouraged in our colonies, I beg leave to recommend them to your notice, that they may obtain pay, if possible, from your Assembly. Their conduct has given me great satisfaction, and it would be very agreeable to me if they could receive some gratification, as they (Capts. McClellan and Wolgomatt) have put themselves to considerable expenses to equip the men."[1]

---

[1] The following are the muster-rolls of the two companies: Wm. McClellan, captain; John Earl, James Dougherty, lieu-

Although the scenes of 1763 were never again repeated within the limits of Maryland, it was many years before the settlements on the western frontiers of the province were entirely relieved from the danger of savage inroads. In 1778 the Indians commenced hostilities on the frontiers, and it was found necessary to call into service the Washington County militia, under Col. Beatty, in conjunction with the militia of Virginia and Pennsylvania. In the following year (1779) we learn by a letter from Washington County, dated April 20th, that the Indians about two weeks previously "struck the settlement of the Yock [York?] Glades, about ten or twelve miles within the State line. It appears that as five men were covering a cabin they were fired on; four were killed on the spot, the other escaped, and says the number of Indians was about thirty-five. A large number of savages were discovered lurking about the Horse-shoe Bottom, no doubt with hostile intentions."[1]

CHAPTER V.

LOGAN AND CRESAP.

Logan's Speech—Murder of his Family—The Cresaps—Massacre at Baker's Fort—Jefferson's Charge Refuted—He Retracts—Vindication of Capt. Michael Cresap.

THE massacre of the family of the great Indian chief, Logan, in the early part of the year 1774, has been so frequently discussed from the time when Mr. Jefferson first sought to place the responsibility upon Col. Michael Cresap, that the evidence and argument have grown too voluminous to be presented in full in such a work as the present.

The narrative of the Indian wars in Western Maryland and on the frontier would be incomplete, however, without at least a brief reference to a subject which has become one of the celebrated questions of Indian history, and which is closely connected with one of the most prominent figures in the early settlement of this portion of the State. The charge as originally made by Mr. Jefferson in his "Notes on Virginia," published in 1787, was as follows:

"Col. Cresap, a man infamous for the many murders he had committed on those much injured people (the Indians), collected a party and proceeded down the Kanhaway in quest of vengeance. Unfortunately, a canoe of women and children, with one man only, was seen coming from the opposite shore unarmed, and unsuspecting an hostile attack from the whites. Cresap and his party concealed themselves on the bank of the river, and the moment the canoe touched the shore singled out their objects, and at one fire killed every person in it. This happened to be the family of Logan, who had long been distinguished as a friend of the whites. This unworthy return provoked his vengeance. He accordingly signalized himself in the war which ensued. In the autumn of the same year a decisive battle was fought at the mouth of the Great Kanhaway, between the collected forces of the Shawnees, Mingoes, and Delawares and a detachment of the Virginia militia. The Indians were defeated and sued for peace. Logan, however, disdained to be seen among the suppliants. But lest the sincerity of a treaty should be distrusted from which so distinguished a chief absented himself, he sent by a messenger the following speech to be delivered to Lord Dunmore:

"'I appeal to any white man to say if ever he entered Logan's cabin hungry and he gave him not meat, if ever he came cold and naked and he clothed him not. During the course of the last long and bloody war Logan remained idle in his cabin, an advocate for peace. Such was my love for the whites that my countrymen pointed as they passed and said, "Logan is the friend of white men." I had even thought to have lived with you but for the injuries of one man. Col. Cresap, the last spring, in cold blood and unprovoked, murdered all the relations of Logan, not sparing even my women and children. There runs not a drop of my blood in the veins of any living creature. This called on me for revenge. I have sought it; I have killed many; I have fully glutted my vengeance. For my country, I rejoice at the beams of peace. But do not harbor a thought that mine is the joy of fear. Logan never felt fear. He will not turn on his heel to save his life. Who is there to mourn for Logan? Not one.'"

The charge thus brought by Mr. Jefferson was not known to the Cresap family until 1797, when Luther

---

tenants; Joseph Hopewell, Henry Graybill, sergeants; David Blair, John Moran, Edmund Moran, ensigns; Privates, David Shelby, George Rout, Wm. Beadles, John Dean, Richard Arsheraft, Nicholas Carpenter, Thomas Vaughan, James Ross, Isaac Flora, Joshua Young, George Mattison, Isaac Wilcocks, Wm. Hanniel, John Dougherty, Wm. Colvin, Wm. Flora, Thomas Edington, James Bradmore, Richard Coomore, Wm. Sparks, Thos. Clemens, John Sealon, John Doughland, Patrick O'Gullen, Robert Ford, Joseph Clemens, James Small, Wm. Lockhead, James Ware, Thos. Williams, John Masters. John Murray, Felix Leer, Bartholomew Pack, Charles Hays, and Wm. Polk.

John Wolgomatt, captain; Matthew Nicholas, lieutenant; John Blair, ensign; Privates, James Booth, James Dulany, Wm. Fife, Wm. Dunwidie, Peter Ford, Thomas Davis, David Johnson, Samuel McCord, Robert Blackburn, Abraham Enocks, James Myres. Wm. Marshall and James Fox.

[1] The *Maryland Journal* of June 26, 1789, contains the following: "Last week a person passed through this town on his way from Kentucky, who informs us that on the 22d of May last he and eleven persons were in company, at the distance of four days' journey from the Crab Orchards, in the wilderness, and were fired upon by a party of Indians. Five of the company were killed; the rest made their escape, but lost all their horses except two. A young man by the name of Funk, from Funk's Town, another of the name of Lewis Myers, from Pike Creek, and a Mr. Blayer, from near Harper's Ferry, were among the unfortunate victims. As this fact is to be depended upon, it induces us to credit the many various reports that have been lately so much circulated respecting the horrid murders and depredations committed by the Indians upon the frontiers, and makes humanity shudder at the idea of the bloody consequences which must ensue from a war with those barbarians."

Martin, who married a daughter of Michael Cresap, published his defense, and since his day many able writers have taken up the pen in answer to Mr. Jefferson, and in vindication of the character of Cresap.[1] Cresap himself could make no answer to the charge, for he had yielded up his life in defense of his country at the very outbreak of the Revolutionary struggle; but fortunately he left behind him many friends and witnesses, who came promptly forward to defend his name from the infamy with which it was sought to be associated. Falsehood and slander, however, run at a swifter pace than truth, and it was long before the latter was enabled to overtake the false charge and nail it to the counter. Thus for many years the war which followed the massacre of Logan's relatives was known as "Cresap's war," and he was represented as guilty not only of butchering in cold blood and unprovoked cruelty an unprotected party of women and children, but as responsible for all the horrors of the Indian hostilities which followed. Of both counts in this historical indictment it has been demonstrated beyond the shadow of a doubt that Michael Cresap was wholly guiltless; but it is clear from the history of that period that even were it possible to fix upon Cresap the guilt of the massacre, it could not be shown that the war which ensued was the result of that deed of blood. In point of fact, hostilities had already commenced before Logan's family was slaughtered, and although that piece of indefensible barbarity may have added fresh fuel to the fires of Indian animosity and vengeance, war had been declared in the fashion of that period by such overt acts as shooting and scalping, and would inevitably have followed whether Logan's relatives had fallen or not. "During the ten years," says Mr. Mayer, "subsequent to the treaty made by Bouquet, the gradual advance of the whites to the West had been a constant source of alarm to the Indians. Collisions and violent disputes were the natural and necessary results. The slow, eager, resistless encroachments of civilization brought the two uncongenial and incongruous races face to face in contact, and the slightest breath was sufficient to fan into conflagration the fire that smouldered in the hearts of each. Besides this, there had been no scrupulous fulfillment of Bouquet's treaty on the part of the Indians; and I am informed by one of our ablest border historians and scholars that in these ten years of nominal peace, but in truth of quasi-war, more lives were sacrificed along the Western frontiers than during the whole outbreak of 1774, including the battle of Point Pleasant." So lightly did the Indians regard this treaty that the Shawanese refused to surrender their white prisoners, Red Hawk, one of that tribe, insulting Col. Bouquet with impunity, and another Indian killing the colonel's servant on the very day after the nominal peace was concluded. In the following year further murders were committed by the Indians on New River, and not long afterwards others were waylaid and killed while on their way to Illinois; and following these outrages, "a number of men employed in slaughtering cattle for Fort Chartres were slain, and

---

[1] Thomas Cresap, the father of Col. Michael Cresap, was named in the treaty between the Six Nations and the province of Maryland, dated the 30th of June, 1744, as having "a hunting or trading cabin, about two miles above the uppermost fork of Congorontan, or Potomac, on the north branch of said fork." This Thomas Cresap, usually called "the English colonel," was a much trusted agent of Charles, Lord Baltimore (the fifth of that title), and was sent to that portion of the province to guard the interest of Lord Baltimore against the claim of Lord Fairfax. The family of Col. Cresap was therefore one of the oldest Maryland families in that section of the State, and from the time of "the English colonel" to the present have occupied a high position among "the first families" of Western Maryland. "The English colonel" built a stone house, since known as Cresap's Fort, where his trading cabin stood, opposite the Green Spring Run, a station of the Baltimore and Ohio Railroad Company, which is still standing and occupied, and can be seen from that station. At an early day settlers built around it, and so near that on any alarm being given all fled to the fort for protection. Col. Thomas Cresap called the place "Skipton," after the place or village of his residence in England. The village is now called "Old Town," situated on the Potomac, about sixteen miles east of Cumberland. Col. Michael Cresap (in Mr. Jefferson's "Notes on Virginia"), said to be "a man *infamous for his many Indian murders*," had three daughters and two sons. At the time of this publication the eldest daughter was the wife of the celebrated Luther Martin, a lawyer of whom Maryland has always been justly proud. He was one of the counsel for Aaron Burr, who was tried for treason, and was denounced by Jefferson as "the Bulldog of the Federal Party." The second daughter married his brother, Lenox Martin, a lawyer of that portion of Maryland, who raised a large and respectable family, still residing in Allegany County. The third daughter married Osborn Sprigg. Their children were the Hon. Michael Cresap Sprigg, a member of Congress from Allegany County, and whose descendants now hold "a first position" in society in this State. Michael C. Sprigg was also at one time president of the Chesapeake and Ohio Canal Company. There was no higher-toned gentleman or man of fairer character in Western Maryland in his day than Michael C. Sprigg. The Hon. James C. Sprigg, his brother, was a member of Congress from Kentucky. His son, James Cresap, was a man of high standing, who married (his second wife) the widow of Capt. Van Bibber, a most accomplished and excellent lady, by whom he had one son, Luther Martin Cresap, a worthy and respectable gentleman, who now resides near Old Town, in the old family residence. A man of unexceptionable character, with a liberal education, and, Cresap-like, of a mild and amiable disposition. The widow of Col. Michael Cresap married John I. Jacobs. Their son, Hon. J. J. Jacobs, ex-Governor of West Virginia, is a man of no ordinary ability, and now holds a high position among the citizens of that State. Such was, has been, and now is the position of the Cresap family in Western Maryland for over a century.—*Thomas J. McKeig, in his MS. notes to the author.*

their rifles, blankets, and accoutrements carried to the Indian villages." And thus, as it has been well pointed out, "the Indian hatchet was never buried. The summer after Bouquet's treaty the savages killed a white man upon the Virginia frontiers; the next year eight Virginians were butchered on the Cumberland, and their peltries brought to the Indian towns, where they were sold to Pennsylvania traders. Some time after, Martin, a Virginia trader, with two companions, was killed by the Shawanese on the Hockhocking, only, as it was alleged by Lord Dunmore, because they were Virginians, at the same time that the savages allowed a certain Ellis to pass simply because he was a Pennsylvanian. In 1771 twenty Virginians and their party of friendly Indians were robbed by savages of thirty-eight horses, as well as of weapons, clothes, and trappings, which they delivered to Callender and Spears, and certain other Pennsylvania traders, in their towns. In the same year, within the jurisdiction of Virginia, the Indians killed two remote settlers, and in the following year Adam Stroud, another Virginian, with his wife and seven children, fell beneath their tomahawks and scalping-knives on the waters of the Elk. In 1773 the savages were still engaged in their work of destruction. Richards fell on the Kanawha, and a few months after, Russell, another Virginian, with five whites and two negroes, perished near the Cumberland Gap, while their horses and property were borne off by the Indians to the towns, where they fell a prey to the Pennsylvania traders. These and many other butcheries and robberies of a similar character were committed in the savage raids and forays anterior to the year 1774, and long before Shawanese blood was wantonly shed in retaliation by the irritated people. A Dutch family was massacred on the Kanawha in June of 1773, and the family of Mr. Hog and three white men on the Great Kanawha early in April, 1774.

"On the 25th of April, 1774, the Earl of Dunmore, at Williamsburg, his seat of government in Virginia, issued his proclamation, which, as dates are of great importance in this narrative, we should regard as unveiling other causes of border difficulty besides the Indian hostilities which were then occurring. In this proclamation of the 25th of April, 1774, before there could have possibly been a communication of any retaliatory murders on the Ohio, committed by the whites upon the Indians, the British earl, then at Williamsburg, declares, that inasmuch as there is trouble within his jurisdiction at Pittsburgh, and the authorities in that place and its dependencies will endeavor to obstruct His Majesty's government thereof by illegal means, and inasmuch as that 'settlement is in danger of annoyance from Indians also,' he has thought proper, with the advice and consent of His Majesty's counsel, to require and authorize the militia officers of that district to embody a sufficient number of men to repel *any assault whatever*. The events that caused the issuing of this proclamation must necessarily have occurred both among the white and the red men a considerable time before, so as to have allowed the messenger to cross the mountains prior to the 25th of April."

Withers, in his "Chronicles of Border Warfare," expresses the decided opinion that the hostilities of 1774 were not the result of the outrages of that year alone, but of injuries repeated and continued through a long period of time, and the following letter from Lord Dunmore to Gen. Haldimand, written from Williamsburg on the 24th of December, 1774, "is good authority at least for the fact that it was no 'Cresap's war,' as it has been called by some writers:"

"You have been very much imposed upon by the account given you, which you have thought fit to transmit to his Majesty's minister. There is no other Col. Cresap than an old man of ninety years of age, who has not removed from his habitation for many years,—for some from my own knowledge, and for the rest from incontestable authority. There is, indeed, one Michael Cresap (not a colonel, but a trader), who with others *is said* to have killed those Indians (not on a scout, but) returning from the back settlements, *where he had been on his private business, and where he found the Indians ravaging the country, and murdering every white man they could lay their hands on, and, therefore, very far from being the cause of a war as you suggest, or even of hostilities.* It was the consequence of repeated hostilities committed by the Indians on the people of our frontiers; and both these Cresaps are not Virginians, or even inhabited Virginia, but belonging to Maryland; with respect, however, to which, or the cause of the war with the Indians, I conceive it not necessary for me to send you proofs."

Early in 1774, Michael Cresap, who had emigrated from Maryland to the new lands of the Ohio with the hope of mending his broken fortunes, was engaged, with the help of laborers brought from his native province, in opening and locating farms in the vicinity of Pittsburgh and Wheeling. His errand was an eminently peaceable one, and his course through all this exciting period shows that he was especially anxious to avoid hostilities with the Indians. While thus engaged he "suddenly received a summons which terminated his agricultural projects in the West. After this region had been explored in 1773, a resolution was formed by a band of hardy pioneers, among whom was George Rogers Clark, who afterwards, as a general officer, became so celebrated in the annals of Kentucky, to make a settlement during the following spring; and the mouth of the Little Kanawha was appointed as the place of general rendezvous, whence the united party should descend the river. Early in 1774 the Indians had done some of their habitual mischief. Reports of further and perhaps meditated dangers were rife along the river, as coming from the Indian towns. Many of the promised settlers, alarmed by the news, remained at their homes, so that at the appointed time not more than eighty or ninety men assembled at the rendezvous. In a few days the anticipated troubles with the savages commenced. A small party of hunters, encamped about ten miles below Clark's emigrants, was fired on by the Indians; but the red men were repulsed, and the hunters returned to camp. This hostile demonstration, coupled with the rumors already spoken of, satisfied the Americans that the savages were bent on war. Accordingly, the whole band was enrolled for protection; yet it was resolved to adhere to the original project of settling in Kentucky, inasmuch as the camp was amply furnished with everything needful for such an enterprise. An Indian town called the Horse-head Bottom, on the Scioto, near its mouth, lay in the pioneers' way, and they forthwith resolved to cross the country and surprise it. But when the question arose who should command so perilous an adventure, it was found that in the whole band no one possessed sufficient experience in Indian warfare to be intrusted confidently with the fortunes of his companions. It was known, however, that Michael Cresap dwelt on the river about fifteen miles above the camp, engaged with certain laborers in settling a plantation, and that he had resolved to follow this band of pioneers to Kentucky as soon as he had established his people. His experience of frontier life was notorious. The eager settlers with one voice resolved to demand his services in the hour of danger, and a messenger was forthwith dispatched to seek him. In half an hour he returned with Michael, who learning of the unwise resolution to attack the Indian town, had already set out to visit the pioneer camp. The emigrants at once thought their army, as they called it, complete, and the destruction of the savages certain. But a council was called, and to the surprise of all, the intended commander-in-chief promptly dissuaded his companions from the meditated enterprise." In his address to the pioneers he especially called their attention to the fact that though outrages had been committed, war had not actually commenced, and that the course they meditated would unquestionably provoke an outbreak of hostilities. Cresap's advice was considered so wise that it was determined to return to Wheeling and await further intelligence. On their way to this point they met Killbuck, a celebrated Indian chief, who had been concerned in many of the previous Indian wars, and had "a long but unsatisfactory" interview with him in regard to the anticipated troubles. During this interview Cresap remained on the opposite side of the river, "declaring that he was afraid to trust himself with the Indians, especially as Killbuck had frequently attempted to waylay and murder his father in Maryland, and that if they met his fortitude might forsake him, and he might put the savage to death." All this shows how anxious Cresap was to avoid everything which might give the Indians a pretext for the inauguration of a regular war. When the party reached Wheeling, they found the inhabitants of that section greatly alarmed by the apprehension of an Indian attack, and Cresap's party was soon greatly augmented by the large numbers of farmers, hunters, and woodsmen who flocked to the camp, both to obtain and afford protection. The general apprehension was soon increased by an express from Connolly, Lord Dunmore's representative at Pittsburgh, to Capt. Cresap, informing him that messengers returned from the Indian country announced war to be inevitable, that the savages would begin operations as soon as the weather permitted, and "begging him to use his influence with the party to cover the country with scouts until the inhabitants could fortify themselves."

This message was received about the 21st of April, and its reception, says Gen. George Rogers Clark, a member of the party,

"was the epoch of open hostilities with the Indians. The War Post was planted, a Council Called and the Letter read and the ceremonies used by the Indians on so important an occasion acted, and War was formally declared. The same evening two scalps were brought into camp. The following Day some Canoes of Indians were discovered descending the River, taking advantage of an Island to cover themselves from our View. They were chased by our men 15 miles down the River, they were forced ashore and a Battle ensued, a few were wounded on both sides and we got one scalp only; On examining their Canoes we found a considerable quantity of ammunition and other Warlike Stores. On our return to Camp a Resolution was passed to march next Day and attack Logan's Camp on the Ohio, about 30 miles above Wheeling. We actually marched about five miles, and halted to take some Refreshment, here the Impropriety of executing the proposed Enterprize was argued, the Conversation was brought forward by Cresap himself; it was generally agreed that those Indians had no hostile Intentions, as it was a hunting Camp composed of Men, Women & Children with all their Stuff with them. This we knew as I myself and others then present had been at their Camp about four weeks before that time on our way down from Pittsburg; In short every Person present particularly Cresap (upon reflection) was opposed to the projected Measure. We returned and on the Same evening Decamped and took the Road to Red-Stone. It was two Days after this that Logan's Family was killed."[1]

---

[1] Some time before these events, William Butler had sent off a canoe loaded with goods for the Shawanese towns, and on the

But while Cresap and his men had thus abandoned the proposed attack, his prudent and friendly advice was not heeded by others, and on the 30th of April, 1774, the murder of Logan's family was committed.[1]

Logan's camp, as has been said, was about thirty miles above Wheeling, near the mouth of Yellow Creek, and on the opposite side of the Ohio, near the river-bank, was the cabin of a certain Baker, "who sold rum to the Indians, and of course received frequent visits from them. This man had been particularly desired by Cresap to remove his liquors, and seems to have prepared to take them away at the time of the murder."

In the latter part of April, 1774, Michael Myers and two companions, who had been called forth to guard the frontier at Baker's Bottom, crossed the Ohio in order to examine the country along the banks of Yellow Creek. While thus engaged they discovered an Indian endeavoring to steal their horse, whereupon Myers fired upon and killed him. A second Indian appeared and shared the same fate, when the whites, fearing to remain longer in this dangerous neighborhood, recrossed the Ohio and took refuge in Baker's cabin. The evening or night before the tragedy a squaw came over to Baker's from the Indian camp on the opposite side of the river, and after some reluctance confessed that the Indians had resolved to kill the white woman and her family the next day.

In consequence of this information, Baker, says Mr. Mayer, "summoned a number of his neighbors, who all reached his house before morning, when it was resolved the strangers should conceal themselves in a back apartment, whence the assailing Indians might be watched. It was also determined that if they demeaned themselves peaceably they should not be molested, but if hostility was manifested they should show themselves and act accordingly. Early in the morning a party of eight Indians, composed of three squaws, a child, and four married men, one of whom was Logan's brother, crossed the river to Baker's cabin, where all but Logan's brother obtained liquor and became excessively drunk. No whites except Baker and two of his companions appeared in the cabin. After some time Logan's relative took down a coat and hat belonging to Baker's brother-in-law, and putting them on, set his arms akimbo, strutted about the apartment, and at length coming up abruptly to one of the men, addressed him with the most offensive epithets and attempted to strike him. The white man, Sappington, who was thus assailed by language and gesture, for some time kept out of his way, but becoming irritated, seized his gun and shot the Indian as he was making to the door, still clad in the coat and hat. The men, who during the whole of this scene had remained hidden, now poured forth and without parley slaughtered the whole Indian party except the child. Before this tragic event occurred, two canoes, one with two and the other with five Indians, all naked, painted, and completely armed for war, were descried stealing from the opposite shore, where Logan's camp was situated. This was considered as confirmation of what the squaw had said the night before, and was afterwards alleged in justification of the murder of the unarmed party which had first arrived. No sooner were the unresisting drunkards dead than the infuriated whites rushed to the river-bank, and ranging themselves among the concealing fringe of underwood, prepared to receive the canoes. The first that arrived was the one containing two warriors, who were fired upon and killed. The other canoe immediately turned and fled, but after this two others, containing eighteen warriors, painted and prepared for conflict as the first had been, started to assail the Americans. Advancing more cautiously than the former party, they endeavored to land below Baker's cabin, but being met by the rapid movements of the rangers before they could effect their purpose, they were put to flight with the loss of one man, although they returned the fire of the pioneers."[2]

16th of April, some ten days before the formal declaration of war by the whites, it was attacked about forty miles below Pittsburgh by three Cherokees, who killed one of the white men composing the party and wounded another, the third making his escape, and the boat falling into the hands of the assailants.

[1] There is some conflict of testimony as to the date of the massacre. Benjamin Tomlinson, in his testimony, in Jacob's "Life of Cresap," places it on "the third or fourth of May;" but John Sappington's statement in the 4th appendix to Jefferson's "Notes on Virginia" fixes it on the 24th of May. Mr. Mayer, to whose "Tah-Gah-Jute" the author is indebted for much of the information contained in this sketch, says, "I am satisfied the massacre occurred on the 30th of April, 1774, and that Sappington's date of the 24th May, given from memory, after a lapse of twenty-six years, is inaccurate. An examination of Washington's MSS. in the archives of the State Department at Washington has disclosed a letter from Valentine Crawford to Col. G. Washington, from Jacob's Creek, on the Monongahela, and dated 'May 7, 1774.'" The following is an extract from it. After describing some of the Indian and pioneer fights before the Yellow Creek massacre, he adds,—

"And on *Saturday* last, about twelve o'clock, there was one Greathouse and about twenty men fell on a party of Indians at the mouth of Yellow Creek, and killed ten of them, and brought away one child a prisoner, which is now at my brother William Crawford's." By reference to the almanac for 1774, it will be seen that the Saturday before the 7th of May of that year, the date of Valentine Crawford's letter, was the 30th of April. Valentine Crawford was Washington's land agent in the West."

[2] All accounts appear to agree in representing the victims of this massacre to have been under the influence of "fire-water"

According to the statement of John Sappington, the only relative of Logan killed at Baker's was his brother; none of the squaws slain was his wife; two of them were old women, while the third, whose infant was spared, was the wife of Gen. Gibson, who was at that time an Indian trader, "and subsequently took care of the child as if it had been his own." It is probable, however, that his mother and sister were also among the slain. Logan's wife was a Shawanese woman, was not present at Baker's on the day of the tragedy, and lived for many years afterwards. She never had any children by Logan. Tod-kah-dohs, or "The Searcher," and probably a son of Logan's sister, did not die until about 1844, at the Cold Spring, on the Allegany Seneca reservation; "so that, in spite of Logan's speech, *some* of his 'blood' *still* 'ran' in human veins ninety years after the Yellow Creek tragedy."

Such, as far as they can now be learned, were the circumstances connected with this famous, or rather infamous, incident in border warfare. It fully merited all the indignation which it aroused at the time and all the denunciation which it has since received, and excited a universal feeling of horror even at a period when deeds of violence and death were of every-day occurrence. But the truth of history as well as the demands of justice require that the responsibility for the deed should be clearly placed where it belongs, and that the character of an innocent man should not be made the victim of posthumous vengeance. In considering the evidence on which Mr. Jefferson based his charge against Michael Cresap, it is impossible to repress surprise at the insufficiency of the testimony on which he made it. In point of fact, the only evidence against Cresap is the unsupported statement of Logan, who at the time of the massacre was on the other side of the Ohio, and who based his belief in Cresap's guilt solely upon the fact that he had recently been at the head of a large war-party of white settlers. Of the fact that Logan considered Cresap the chief actor in the tragedy there cannot be any reasonable doubt. Apart from the statement of Gibson, in whose presence Logan pronounced his celebrated speech, and who declares that Logan insisted in charging Cresap with the murder, the Indian chief himself left unmistakable record of his conviction in another place and another way. During the open war which blazed forth without concealment or disguise after the affair at Yellow Creek, Logan destroyed the family of a settler named John Roberts, and left in the house of the murdered family the following note, written in "gunpowder ink," and attached to a war-club:

"CAPT. CRESAP,—What did you kill my people on Yellow Creek for? The white people killed my kin at Conestoga a great while ago, and I thought nothing of that. But you killed my kin again on Yellow Creek, and took my cousin a prisoner. Then I thought I must kill too, and I have been three times to war since; but the Indians are not angry, only myself.

"CAPTAIN JOHN LOGAN.
"July 21, 1774."

Against this unsupported statement of a man who had no possible opportunity of obtaining the real facts in the case there is a large mass of positive evidence showing the entire innocence of Cresap.

Gen. George Rogers Clark, to whom reference has already been made, and who was one of the party which had sought the advice of Cresap, and under his command returned from their projected expedition against Logan's camp, in response to inquiries on the subject wrote as follows, under date of June 17, 1798:

"I was of the first and last of the active Officers who bore the Weight of that War, and on perusing some old Papers of that Date I find some Memoirs, but independent of them I have a perfect Recollection of every Transaction relative to Logan's Story. The Conduct of Cresap I am perfectly acquainted with; he was not the Author of that Murder, but a family of the Name of Greathouse. But some Transactions that happened under the Conduct of Capt. Cresap a few days previous to the murder of Logan's Family gave him sufficient Ground to suppose it was Cresap who had done him the Injury."

After relating the "incidents which gave rise to Logan's suspicions"—Cresap's command of the party of proposed emigrants to Kentucky, which returned at his suggestion to Wheeling—Gen. Clark continues,—

"The war now raged with all its Savage Fury until the following fall, when a Treaty of Peace was held at Dunmore's Camp within five Miles of Chilicothe, the Indian Capital on the Siotho. Logan did not appear. I was acquainted with him, and wished to be informed of the Reason of his absence by one of the Interpreters. The Answer he gave to my Enquiry was 'that he was like a Mad Dog, that his Bristles had been up and were not yet quite fallen—but that the good Talks now going forward might allay them.' Logan's Speech to Dunmore now came forward, as related by Mr. Jefferson, and was generally believed, and indeed not doubted to have been genuine and dictated by Logan. The Army knew it was wrong so far as it respected Cresap, and afforded an Opportunity of rallying that Gentleman on the subject. I discovered that Cresap was displeased, and told him that he must be a very great Man, that the Indians shouldered him with every Thing that had happened—he smiled, and said he had a great mind to tomahawk

---

at the time of its occurrence; is it not just possible that the whites may have been in the same condition? This would account for and to a certain extent palliate the wanton and barbarous murder of the women. It should be remembered also, in considering the weight of the provocation or excuse for the attack upon the unarmed and helpless party of Indians, that we have only the testimony of *white* witnesses to the occurrence, who would naturally endeavor to put the best face upon the affair possible.

Greathouse about the matter. What is here related is Fact. I was intimate with Cresap, and better acquainted with Logan at that Time than with any other Indian in the Western Country, and had a Knowledge of the Conduct of both Parties. Logan is the Author of the Speech, as related by Mr. Jefferson, and Cresap's Conduct was such as I have related."

The testimony of Jacob Tomlinson, the brother-in-law of Baker, is of the same positive character. "The attacking party at Baker's Bottom," he says, "had no commander. I believe Logan's brother was killed by a man named Sappington; who killed the others I know not, but this I know well, that neither Capt. Michael Cresap nor any other person of that name was there, nor do I believe within many miles of the place." The testimony of Col. Gibson, to whom Logan's speech was delivered, of Gen. John Minor, Dr. Wheeler, and, in short, of every one who has been called upon to give evidence in this celebrated historical cause, completely exonerates Cresap from all connection with the Yellow Creek tragedy.

Col. Thomas J. McKaig, of Allegany County, who was born in 1804, at Steubenville, Ohio, about thirty miles below the place of the murder, in a recent communication to the writer, furnishes some interesting facts bearing upon this subject.

"Baker's Fort, as it was called," says Col. Mc-Kaig,—

"was nothing more than a comfortable, well-built log cabin, in which Mr. Baker and his wife resided at the time of the murder. The house remained standing for many years, and could be seen from steamboat or rail-car in passing up or down the river. When I was but a small boy my father removed from Steubenville and made him a home on the West Fork of Beaver, some fourteen miles from where it empties into the Ohio, below Wellsville. I resided with my father until I was over twenty years of age. I was therefore well acquainted with the 'settlers' both on the Ohio and Virginia sides of the river. I was familiar with the story of the murder of Logan's family from my earliest recollection, and had heard it told and retold by those who at the time of the murder lived in our neighborhood. I have heard all the particulars of the murder when a boy from Adam Poe, who resided at the time of the murder a few miles farther up the river. I spent a night with his elder brother, Andrew Poe, who resided at the old homestead in the Virginia Neck, some few miles above Baker's house, where the murder was committed. In the course of the evening he gave me the particulars of his terrible fight, on the banks of the Ohio, with the Indian 'Big Foot' and his companion. He also, on that evening, told me the story of the murder of Logan's family, the same as I had heard it frequently from his brother Adam, who lived, from my earliest recollection, within a mile of my father's house in Ohio. The fact is unquestionable that all the particulars of the murder of Logan's family, and who was responsible for that murder, and who were present when the murder was committed were perfectly and universally known to all the settlers of that region of country, and there was no dispute about who were the perpetrators for they were all known. Benjamin Sappington and his party, from Buffalo Creek, in Washington County, Pa., about fifteen miles from 'Baker's Fort,' perpetrated the murder. This was the universal understanding, denied by none in that region of country. The veracity of the Poes was unquestionable. They were men of large size and of unusual bodily strength, and he would have been a bold man that dared to question the truth or veracity of either, for they were men of unimpeachable character.

"Adam Poe was the grandfather of the Rev. Adam Poe, who with the eloquent Bascum, opened with prayer the convention at Baltimore in 1840 that ratified the nomination of 'Tippecanoe and Tyler too.'

"But more especially have I heard 'Old Pew' (for I forget his Christian name, everybody called him 'Old Pew') defending himself and the party who was with him. He lived, when I knew him, in the 'Virginia Neck,' not far from Andrew Poe. He was old and poor, but I never heard his veracity questioned. When a boy I had a great admiration for 'Old Pew,' for his Indian stories, for his fights, and his hairbreadth escapes from the rifle-ball and the tomahawk of the Indian. Whilst I listened I could have exclaimed with Horace, 'Oh, that the first earth had borne me amongst those heroes!'

"The old man, Pew, told me he was one of Ben Sappington's party; was present at the murder, and knew every man of the party, and I know he lived in that neighborhood until his death at a very advanced age. He never denied his presence at the murder, nor his participation in it. I well remember his justification of the act. The Sappington party were residents of a portion of the country that lay some fifteen miles distant from the Ohio River, and on that account had but little intercourse with the Indians, for the public highway of the Indian, 'the trail,' as we called it, was by the valley of the Ohio River. Nor did those pioneers of Buffalo Creek understand the absolute necessity that lay upon the sparse settlers of the Virginia side of the Ohio River to cultivate the friendship of the Indian. A quarrel with the Indian was death to the sparse settler on the banks of the Ohio. The settlers were but few, the Indians were numbered by the hundred. The settlers could make no resistance if the Indians, for any offense or outrage by the whites upon one or more of these people, were excited to revenge. This party from Buffalo, not understanding the position of the settlers on the Ohio, thought that the killing of Logan's family was justifiable in anticipation of the reported attack on Baker's Fort.

"Mr. Pew said it was reported that an attack would be made that morning upon the fort; that it was said and believed that it was the custom of the Indians to send the families of their chiefs before the attack was made to the point to be attacked, that they might be the first to share the plunder. That morning the family of Logan, the Mingo chief, came to the fort, and they expected every moment to see the boats of the attacking party push off from the opposite side of the river. There was no time for consultation. They considered the danger imminent, and they killed those that had arrived, knowing that they were the family of their chief. Mr. Pew, therefore, to the day of his death insisted that they were justified in the act under all the circumstances. Unfortunately for the whites, they killed their friends, and brought upon themselves the swift vengeance of all the surrounding savages, the Indian war of the summer of 1774. I never heard Mr. Pew or the Poes speak of Michael Cresap, nor do I believe that Mr. Pew ever knew or saw him. Cresap's settlement was at Grave Creek, more than seventy miles below Baker's Fort, and in the West I never heard Cresap's name connected with the murder of Logan's family.

"In October, 1826, after receiving my baccalaureate from Washington College, Pennsylvania, I came to Cumberland, Md., where I obtained the position of principal of the Allegany County Academy. Being poor but proud, I was fortunate enough to procure board with Mrs. Mary Cresap, the widow of James Cresap, the son, as before stated, of Col. Michael Cresap, one of the most amiable and accomplished ladies I ever met.

"I was admitted into the family, not because her circumstances required her to take boarders, but because she wanted her son, the present Luther Martin Cresap, of Allegany County, to be under my personal control in the academy. At Mrs. Cresap's house I made the acquaintance of all the Cresaps, 'much people,' for the connection was a large one, and in point of rank and character second to none in Western Maryland. Among the many, not the least, was that excellent old man, the Rev. J. J. Jacobs, the father of ex-Governor Jacobs, of West Virginia. 'Father Jacobs,' as everybody called him, had been brought up from boyhood in the family of Capt. Michael Cresap, was his man of business, knew, I might say, all the acts of his life, and after his death married his widow, and had then in the press his defense of Capt. Cresap, a small volume of about one hundred and twenty pages, now on my desk. Here I first saw Jefferson's 'Notes on Virginia,' and heard Capt. Michael Cresap's name in connection with the murder of the Logan family. To charge that 'Col. Michael Cresap,' as my ancestors would have said, 'the chief and hero of the clan,' after he had given his life for his country, and after he had rested over twenty years in an honored grave, 'was a man famous for his many Indian murders' was certainly a cruel and grievous charge, and was so regarded by his friends and by all the community who had known him. It is therefore not 'wondrous strange' that it was resented with so much bitterness. It was utterly repugnant to the well-known character of Col. Cresap, and to every trait of character that belonged to the Cresap family.

"Some short time after I came to Cumberland to reside I paid a visit to Benjamin Tomlinson, an old gentleman, who then resided on his farm some four miles north of Cumberland. Mr. Tomlinson at that time (the close of the year 1826), I would say, from his appearance, must have been over eighty years of age, of fine personal appearance, large stature, and of great dignity of character; his character for truth and veracity 'unimpeached and unimpeachable.' No man in that community stood higher than Benjamin Tomlinson. During the course of our conversation it occurred to me that in passing and repassing from my home in Ohio to Washington College, Pennsylvania, I had frequently crossed a run in the 'Virginia Neck' which old Mr. Pew called 'Tomlinson's Run.' I asked him if he knew anything about it, or how it got its name. He answered, 'Oh, yes; when I was a young man I had my hunting camp on that run, and it was called after me.' I then said to him, as that run is but a few miles from 'Baker's Fort,' you may know something of the murder of the Logan family. His answer was emphatic. 'I know all about it. I know every man who was present at the murder. Mr. Baker was my brother-in-law. He built the house called Baker's Fort, and resided in it with his wife, my sister, at the time of the murder. He had settled at that place and built the house for a permanent home.

"'I made my home with my sister at that time. On the night before the murder, as was my usual mode of sleeping, I lay down before the fire, with my rifle at my side on the floor, wrapped in my blanket. At early dawn I was awakened by a knock at the door. I sprang up, seized my rifle, and called out, "Who is there?" A voice from without answered, "Is that you, Ben?" The voice was familiar, and I proceeded to open the door by removing the cordwood which was placed with the end of the wood against the door. When the door was opened I found at the door Benjamin Sappington and a party, some fifteen in number, who lived at a settlement on Buffalo Creek, in now Washington County, Pa., distant fourteen or fifteen miles. I cannot now recall the names of any of the party except the names of Benjamin Sappington, Daniel Greathouse and his two sons, and Mr. Pew, my old acquaintance, "Old Pew." They were much excited, and said that it was reported in their settlement that "Baker's Fort" would be attacked by the Indians that morning.'

"Mr. Tomlinson said he assured Sappington and his party that he did not think that there was any danger of an attack, that there had been some uneasiness felt amongst them on account of the killing of an Indian in a canoe down the river towards Steubenville, but the Indians knew that the settlers had nothing to do with it. The Indian was shot in his canoe by some strolling hunters out of mere wantonness. For the consequences the passing huntsmen cared nothing. The vengeance of the Indians could not affect them, and that the Indian knew this as well as the settler. They seemed, as Mr. Tomlinson said, to be much relieved, and said they would return to their homes. Mrs. Baker said as they had come so far to defend them, they must not go until she had prepared breakfast. To this all agreed. Mr. Baker, my brother-in-law, said Mr. Tomlinson, was very near-sighted, and could not see an animal at any time in the forest, so he asked me to go with him to bring in the horses while my sister got the breakfast. We were but a short time in the forest, not far distant from the house, when we heard the report of several rifles towards the house. We ran with all our speed for the house. When we got there we found Sappington and his party had shot the Logan family. When I heard their story I drew my rifle on Ben Sappington, and would have killed him had not others interfered. It appeared, said Mr. Tomlinson, that within a few minutes from the time we left, a canoe pushed off from the Ohio side containing Logan's mother, brother, and sister, the wife of a renegade white man, Simon Girty, who had a child in her arms that was not killed. Their object apparently was to visit Baker's house, and they crossed the river directly, went to the house, and sat down, when Sappington's party shot and killed the mother, brother, and sister, believing, as they said, that they were the advance of the attacking party. There was no breakfast that morning. Sappington and his party left, and we knew that it was death to the settler or instant flight. We took with us the child and what we could conveniently carry, and fled for an unexposed settlement that same morning.' That this is a correct statement of the facts and circumstances under which the murder was committed, I have no doubt. It agrees with what was universally believed, and held to be the truth in all that portion of the country where the murder was perpetrated. I asked, 'was Michael Cresap present at the murder?' Mr. Tomlinson said he was not, nor was he at that time in that portion of the country. If on the Ohio at all, he was at his settlement at the flats of Grave Creek, seventy-four miles lower down the river. No settler would have done a deed of that kind, for the settlers on the Ohio at that time were too few to defend themselves against the Indians on the opposite bank of the Ohio."

The evidence in favor of Cresap was so overwhelming that Mr. Jefferson felt it necessary to substantiate or correct his statement, and on the 21st of March, 1800, he addressed a letter to Col. Gibson, in which he says,—

"I was within a day or two of putting into the press the evidence I had collected on this subject. I have been long in collecting it, because of the distance and dispersion of those acquainted with the transaction. However, I have at length that of a dozen or fifteen persons who clear up the mystery which threw doubt on this piece of history. It appears that instead of one, there were four different murders committed on the Indians. The first by Cresap and his party, a little above Wheeling, on two Indians. The second by the same persons, on the same or the next day, on a party of Indians encamped below Wheeling, at the mouth of Grave Creek, among whom were some of Logan's relatives. The Indians here returned the fire, and wounded one of Cresap's party. The third by *Greathouse and Tomlinson*, a few days after. *This was a hunting-party of Indian men and women, encamped at the mouth of Yellow Creek, opposite to Baker's Bottom.* Greathouse went to their camp as a friend, found them too strong, and invited them over to Baker's to drink. They came over, were furnished with as much rum as they would drink, and, when the men were quite drunk, *Greathouse's party* fell on and massacred the whole except a little girl, Logan's cousin, whom they made prisoner. Here his sister was murdered and some of his relations. The Indians over the river, alarmed at the guns, sent over two canoes of men to seek for their friends. Greathouse and his party received them as they approached the shore with a well-directed fire, and killed and wounded several. The popular report at a distance from the scene had blended all these together and made only one transaction of it; and passing from one to another unacquainted with the geography of the transaction, the Kanhawa had been substituted for the Ohio. Hence, too, arose the doubt whether it was not Greathouse instead of Cresap who killed Logan's relations. *The principal murder was by Greathouse, at Yellow Creek, but some of them had been killed a few days before, by Cresap, at Grave Creek.*"

In this letter Mr. Jefferson directly acquits Cresap of all participation in the Yellow Creek massacre, but endeavors to support his previous assertion that Cresap had been concerned in the murder of Logan's relatives by reference to the affair at Grave Creek, where he alleges some of Logan's relatives had been killed a few days before by Cresap's party. As a matter of fact there is no proof that any of Logan's relatives were killed in that encounter. Logan, in the note left at the house of John Roberts during the war, charges that the murder of his people occurred "*on Yellow Creek*," and refers to that alone as the cause of his anger. As regards the two Indians killed "a little above Wheeling," it appears from a contemporaneous account published in Philadelphia, that a man of the name of Stephens with two Indians were descending the Ohio in a canoe, in which one white man had been killed and another wounded a few days previous by three Cherokees, as he (Stephens) alleged; that they saw another canoe with some persons in it, whom he supposed to be Indians; that he tried to avoid them by crossing the river, and was fired upon and the two Indians killed. To this account Stephens added that " he *suspects* the murder was committed (not by Cresap himself), but by persons in confederacy with him." That was the first case of "murder" referred to by Mr. Jefferson, and yet Stephens does not charge Cresap with any participation in it, but " *suspects* it was done by some persons in confederacy with him." Even if this murder was committed by members of Cresap's party, could he be held responsible for the acts of a set of wild borderers, among whom the restraints of military discipline were not recognized?

The second affair mentioned by Mr. Jefferson in his letter of " confession and avoidance" was a fight between Cresap and fifteen men with fourteen Indians, who were concealed at the mouth of a creek " with the expectation of being attacked." Certainly there is no resemblance between a fair battle between men and the treacherous and bloody massacre of unarmed women and children. In the last edition of his "Notes on Virginia," Jefferson substituted the following in place of the original charge made against Cresap: " Capt. Michael Cresap and a certain Daniel Greathouse, leading on these parties, surprised at different times traveling and hunting-parties of the Indians, having their women and children with them, and murdered many. Among these were unfortunately the family of Logan, a chief celebrated in peace and in war, and long distinguished as a friend of the whites." This, as Mr. Mayer observes, " is certainly a *mitigation* of the charge against Capt. Cresap, but it leaves altogether indefinite the fact as to whether Greathouse and Cresap conjointly directed these parties, or which of the two murdered Logan's relatives. It relieves Cresap, however, altogether from the charge of murdering the Logan family in *canoes* on the Kanawha." As already pointed out, Mr. Jefferson, in his letter to Col. Gibson, had previously abandoned the charge that Cresap had committed the murders at Yellow Creek, and had shifted his ground to the assertion that a party under his command had killed a brother of Logan in an open fight at Grave Creek.

The authenticity of Logan's speech has often been called in question, and its genuineness may, perhaps, still admit of doubt. While it is unnecessary in this connection to enter into a full discussion of the probability or improbability of its being the production of the person to whom it is credited, it is not irrelevant to the subject under consideration to call attention briefly to the evidence which tends to establish it as the original production of Logan, and to that which has been collected against its authenticity. The first witness on this point is John Gibson, who on the 4th day of April, 1800, twenty-six years after the event occurred, made affidavit that while the treaty of peace was under consideration by Lord Dunmore and the Indian chiefs, Logan " came to where this deponent was sitting and asked him to walk out with him; that they went into a copse of wood, where they sat down, when Logan, after shedding abundance of tears, delivered to him the speech *nearly* as related by Mr. Jefferson in his 'Notes on the State of Virginia;' that he, the deponent, *told him then that it was not Col. Cresap who had murdered his relatives*, and although *his son*, Capt. Michael Cresap, was *with* the party who had killed a Shawanese chief and *other* Indians, yet he was not present when his relatives were killed at Baker's, near the mouth of Yellow Creek, on the Ohio; that this deponent, *on his return to camp, delivered the speech to Lord Dunmore;* and that the murders perpetrated as above *were considered* as ultimately the cause of the war of 1774, commonly called Cresap's war." The testimony of Gen. George Rogers Clark, on the same side, has already been given, and according to his evidence it appears that Cresap's name was in Logan's speech as read by Lord Dunmore. James Dunlap, of Pittsburgh, in a letter to Mr. Brantz Mayer, declares that he frequently heard Col. Gibson give the same account of the speech as contained in his affidavit, with the addition that Gibson stated "he returned at once to his friends and wrote down the language of Logan immediately, and delivered it to Lord Dunmore in council." "The message or speech," says Mr. Mayer, "was circulated freely at Williamsburgh immediately after Dunmore's return from his campaign in the winter of 1774, and was *published* then in the *Virginia Gazette* on the 4th of February, 1775, and in New York on the 16th of February, 1775." William McKee testifies in the IVth Appendix to Jefferson's "Notes," that being in the camp on the evening of the treaty made by Dunmore, he heard "*repeated conversations* concerning an *extraordinary speech made at the treaty, or sent* there by a chieftain of the Indians named Logan, and *heard several attempts at a rehearsal of it.*"

Against the authenticity of the speech, there is, in the first place, the argument of Luther Martin, son-in-law of Capt. Michael Cresap, dated the 29th of March, 1797, which may be found in the *Olden Time Magazine*, vol. ii. p. 51. Withers, in his "Chronicles of Border Warfare," says, "Two *interpreters* were sent to Logan by Lord Dunmore, requesting his attendance; but Logan replied that 'he was a warrior, not a counselor, and would not come.'" Mr. Withers, commenting on this, says, "Col. Benjamin Wilson, Sr., then an officer in Dunmore's army, says that he had conversed freely with one of the interpreters (Nicholson) in regard to the mission to Logan, and that neither from the interpreter, nor from any other one during the campaign, did he hear of the charge preferred in Logan's speech against Capt. Cresap as being engaged in the affair at Yellow Creek. Capt. Cresap was an officer *in the division under Lord Dunmore;* and it would seem strange, indeed, if Logan's speech had been made public at Camp Charlotte, and neither he (who was so naturally interested in it, and could at once have proven the falsehood of the allegation it contained) nor Col. Wilson (who was present during the whole conference between Lord Dunmore and the Indian chiefs, and at the time when the speeches were delivered sat immediately behind and close to Dunmore) should have heard nothing of it until years after." Mr. Neville B. Craig, in the second volume of the *Olden Time*, says, "We will state that many years ago, Mr. James McKee, the brother of Alexander McKee, the deputy of Sir William Johnson, stated to us distinctly *that he had seen the speech in the handwriting of one of the Johnsons,* whether Sir William or his successor, Guy, we do not recollect, *before it was seen by Logan.*" The following testimony of Benjamin Tomlinson, of Allegany County, Md., and a brother-in-law of Baker, given in Cumberland on the 17th day of April, 1797, twenty-three years after the occurrence to which it relates, is of the same positive character:

"Logan was not at the treaty. Perhaps Cornstalk, the chief of the Shawanese nation, mentioned among other grievances the Indians killed on Yellow Creek; but *I believe* neither Cresap nor any other person were named as the perpetrators; and I perfectly recollect that I was that day officer of the guard, and stood near Dunmore's person, that consequently I saw and heard all that passed; that also, *two or three days before the treaty,* when I was on the outguard, Simon Girty, who was passing by, stopped with me and conversed; he said he was going after Logan, but he did not like the business, for he was a surly fellow; he, however, proceeded on, and I saw him return on the day of the treaty, and Logan was not with him; at this time a circle was formed, and the treaty began. I saw John Gibson, on Girty's arrival, get up and go out of the circle and talk with Girty, after which he (Gibson) went into a tent, and soon after returning into the circle drew out of his pocket a piece of clean new paper, on which was written in his own handwriting a speech for and in the name of Logan. This I heard read three times, once by Gibson, and twice by Dunmore, the purport of which was that he, Logan, was the white man's friend; that on his journey to Pittsburgh to brighten this friendship, or on his return thence, all his friends were killed at Yellow Creek; that now when he died who should bury him, for the blood of Logan was running in no creature's veins; *but neither was the name of Cresap or the name of any other person mentioned in this speech.* But I recollect to see Dunmore put this speech among the other treaty papers."

There are many letters and documents of a highly interesting character throwing further light upon the subject, but more than enough has been adduced to convince the reader of Cresap's entire innocence of all participation in the massacre at Yellow Creek. That some Indians may have been killed by the party under Cresap's command is not denied, but they were killed after the commission of similar outrages by the Indians themselves, after information from the most reliable sources that the Indian tribes had determined upon and were about inaugurating hostilities, after the formal declaration of war by the whites, and in a fair encounter between men, in which there was no surprise or treachery, and for which both sides were prepared.

In regard to Logan's speech, Mr. Mayer, after an impartial consideration of all the testimony, expresses the opinion that "Gen. Clark's letter seems to prove conclusively that Cresap's *name was* in the message when read in the camp, for he jeered him with his asserted importance in originating the war, whereupon Cresap broke forth in bitter invective against Greathouse; and, moreover, it is evident that Logan had previously charged Cresap with the murder, as will be seen by reference to the note addressed to 'Capt. Cresap,' which the Indian left in the house of Roberts, whose family he had murdered in 1774."

Col. Gibson, upon whose testimony the authenticity of the speech mainly rests, "was always regarded," says Mr. Mayer, "as an honest and truthful person. He enjoyed the confidence of Washington, who in 1781 intrusted him with the command of the Western military department. In 1782, when Gen. Irvine had succeeded him, Gibson was intrusted with the command during the general's absence, which continued for several months. Jefferson, Madison, and Harrison respected him. He was a major-general of militia, secretary of Indian territory under the administrations of Jefferson and Madison, member of the Pennsylvania Convention in 1778, and an associate judge of the Court of Common Pleas of Alleghany County, Pa. Chief Justice Gibson and Gen. George Gibson, sons of Col. George Gibson, who was mortally wounded at St. Clair's defeat, are his well-known and esteemed nephews."

In a letter dated "Alleghany, March 8, 1848," addressed to J. W. Biddle, of Pittsburgh, Rev. William Robinson, Jr., says, "I knew Gen. Gibson from my earliest childhood. He was one of the most artless and unsophisticated men in the world, and the last man on earth that would make a false statement in narrating events. He was a pretty good English scholar, with a remarkable memory, yet without any fancy or imagination, though watchful and observant of all around him."

In a letter to Lyman C. Draper, written in November, 1846, John Bannister Gibson, chief justice of Pennsylvania, and a nephew of Col. John Gibson, says,—

"At his return to camp, Mr. Gibson made an accurate translation of it (Logan's speech), which, as it was much admired, was probably preserved by Lord Dunmore among the archives of the government. After the lapse of almost half a century, Gen. Gibson would not assert that the speech published by Mr. Jefferson was a literal copy of his translation; but he was sure it contained the substance of it. Here it is proper to remark that he was as competent as Mr. Jefferson, or any one else, to give it the simple dress in which it appears. But whoever was entitled to the merit of it, Gen. Gibson said it was a poor picture of the original, uttered, as it was, in accents dictated by an abiding sense of his wrongs, and in tones expressive of the hopeless desolation of his heart. It was its last passionate throb. The man was done with impulses, even of revenge. He sunk into apathy from intemperance, and in the course of a year was murdered in a drunken fray."[1]

CHAPTER VI.

BOUNDARY LINES.

Dutch and Swedes on the Delaware—Border Warfare—Pennsylvania Squatters—Capture of Col. Thomas Cresap—Wm. Penn's Duplicity—Mason and Dixon's Boundary Line—Southwestern Virginia Boundary—Mason and Dixon's Line.

THE territory granted by Charles I. on June 20, 1632, to Cecilius Calvert, the second Lord Baltimore, under the name of the province of Maryland, was bounded on the east by the Atlantic Ocean and Delaware Bay and river, on the north by the fortieth parallel of north latitude, on the west by a line drawn from the northern boundary southward to the most western source of the Potomac River, and thence down the southern bank of that river to the Chesapeake Bay, and on the south by a line running from the last point to Watkins' Point, on the Eastern Shore of the bay, and thence east to the ocean. It will at once be perceived that these boundaries of the province are not those which now define the limits of the State. By examination of the original boundary of Maryland, it will be seen that the State has been deprived of the whole State of Delaware, and a strip of territory about twenty miles wide now forming part of the State of Pennsylvania, including in its limits the present city of Philadelphia, and a great part of Chester, Delaware, Lancaster, York, Adams, Franklin, Fulton, Bedford, and Somerset Counties. The whole number of acres of territory lost to Maryland may be summed up thus: to Delaware, one and a quarter millions; to Pennsylvania, two and a half millions; and to Virginia, half a million; making a total loss of four and a quarter millions of acres, besides about one hundred and fifty thousand acres

---

[1] The precise manner of Logan's death seems involved in some obscurity. By one account he is represented as having been killed by his nephew, Tod-kah-dahs.

"left out" between Onancock River and the Scarborough line on the Eastern Shore.

Of the most of this valuable territory Maryland was deprived on the alleged ground that the Swedes and Dutch had established settlements in Delaware before Lord Baltimore's charter was obtained; and this plea was not only urged by the Penns, but has been repeated by historians, without any authentic proof of the assertion on which it is founded.[1] It is certain no settlements of any kind had been made upon the territory granted to Lord Baltimore down to the time he received his charter, either under the authority of the crown or of the charter governments, except the trading-post established by Claiborne on Kent Island and the unauthorized settlements of the Dutch on the Delaware in 1631, which were abandoned in March of the following year. No permanent settlements were made upon the Delaware until the arrival of the Swedes in 1638, when disputes arose between them and the Dutch at Manhattan (now New York), who in 1655 finally succeeded in conquering "New Sweden." A number of the Swedes fled to Maryland, where they were kindly received.

Lord Baltimore, hearing of the proceedings of the Dutch, ordered Col. Nathaniel Utie, of Baltimore County, to notify the settlers on the Delaware within the limits of his grant that they must depart the province or submit to his government. This proceeding led to considerable negotiations between the contending parties for the settlement of their difficulties, without any definite result. On the 19th of October, 1659, the government of Maryland gave an answer to the Dutch ambassadors appointed by Governor Stuyvesant to wait upon the Maryland authorities at Patuxent, insisting on the right of the proprietary to the territory on the Delaware, and refusing to submit the matter in dispute to the governments of England and Holland. This refusal of Maryland to recognize the authority of the Dutch to treat with the province about the disputed territory bordering on the Delaware was followed by constant collisions between the Dutch and Maryland settlers near the disputed land.

In the mean time doubts had arisen in the Council of Maryland whether the Dutch settlement at New Amstel, on the Delaware, was really below the fortieth degree of north latitude, and as the Dutch West India Company appeared determined to maintain their possessions by force, while there was no prospect of any aid from the colonies should a forcible reduction be attempted, all further action was deferred until the will of the proprietary could be ascertained. Lord Baltimore, however, took care to obtain from the king, on July 21, 1661, a confirmation of his patent.

Charles II., provoked by the continued encroachments of the government of New Netherlands, determined to effect the conquest of the whole settlement. To accomplish this, on the 12th of March, 1664 (O. S.), he granted to his brother James, Duke of York and Albany, all that tract of country extending from the west banks of the Connecticut River to the eastern shore of Delaware Bay (including Long Island). The duke took possession in September, not only of the settlement on the Hudson, but of those on the Delaware south of forty degrees of north latitude, which, as we have seen, were within the limits of Lord Baltimore's charter. By the terms of capitulation the Dutch colonists were admitted to all the rights and privileges of English subjects. Under the new government the name of the town of New Amstel was changed to that of New Castle, and Altona to that of Christiana, while the river and the bay into which it flows lost their old names, and received the English name of Delaware. From this period until the grant by Charles II. to William Penn, on the 4th of March, 1681 (O. S.), of the territory of Pennsylvania, the settlements on the Delaware were dependencies of the government of New York, although clearly within the limits of Maryland. The singular definition of the southern boundary in Penn's charter, which left open the question whether the boundary circle was to be a circle of twelve miles in circumference, or to be drawn around a diameter of twelve miles passing through New Castle, or with a radius of twelve miles beginning at New Castle, was the origin of the present boundary line ("Mason and Dixon's") dividing the North and South, and was one of the principal sources of the contention between Baltimore and Penn. The latter soon discovered that if his province extended no farther south than the fortieth degree he would not have a good port for ships; so he managed to have the southeast corner of his province fixed at twelve miles north of New Castle, and thus within Lord Baltimore's land. He then further obtained from the Duke of York the grant of the counties south of New Castle, or what is now the State of Delaware, which the duke had no right to convey, as these also were included in the charter of Maryland. Penn, however, claimed this territory on the ground that Baltimore's charter called for "uncultivated land," whereas a portion of this, he asserted, was cultivated by the Dutch at the time that charter was granted. This, as we have seen, was not the case.

---

[1] See a full review of the boundary troubles in the writer's "History of Maryland," vol. i. pp. 230, 395, etc.

CHARLES CALVERT, FIFTH LORD BALTIMORE.

The Board of Trade, however, decided in favor of Penn.

On the 20th of April, 1681, Penn commissioned his cousin, William Markham, as deputy governor, and in May following he was dispatched to the province. He arrived at Upland, now Chester, Delaware, about July, 1681, and in December, 1682, Penn, who had arrived on the 27th of October, had an interview with Lord Baltimore at the house of Col. Thomas Tailler, in Anne Arundel County, to settle the disputed question of their boundaries. Though both charters fixed the fortieth parallel of north latitude as the line between Maryland and Pennsylvania, Penn tried hard to persuade Lord Baltimore to let the line be run farther south, so as to give him a tract of land about twenty miles wide running along the northern border of Maryland, while Lord Baltimore was to repay himself by taking from Virginia a small strip of the narrow peninsula below what is now Worcester County. Lord Baltimore naturally refused to make such an unfair bargain as this, or to rob Virginia for the benefit of Penn, and so the matter remained unsettled until 1732, when John, Richard, and Thomas Penn by some means succeeded in obtaining from Charles, fifth Lord Baltimore, a written agreement conceding to the Penns all their claims.

A large strip of territory about twenty miles wide, now forming part of the State of Pennsylvania, and running westward along the northern border of Western Maryland, was a portion of this disputed region, and in the troubles which arose from the antagonistic claims of the two provinces many of the principal citizens of this section of the province were involved. As early as December, 1732, Lord Baltimore, who had come to Maryland to settle the disputes, wrote to Governor Patrick Gordan, of Pennsylvania, calling his attention to the fact that "a most outrageous riot had lately been committed in Maryland by a great number of people calling themselves Pennsylvanians." John Lowe, of Baltimore County, his wife and family, were the victims of this border raid, which seems to have been entirely without justification or excuse, as far as Lowe, at least, was concerned. The dwellers on the Maryland side of the border, as may be supposed, were not slow in retaliating, and in May, 1734, John Hendricks and Joshua Minshall from their settlements on the Susquehanna, and two others from the borders of New Castle County, were carried off by the Maryland authorities and confined in the Annapolis jail. These troubles, however, would seem really to have begun with Penn's first settlement in the province, for we learn from the Pennsylvania records that at a council held at Philadelphia in 1684 a letter from one Samuel Lands was read "concerning Col. George Tallbot's goeing with three musqueters to ye houses of Wm. Ogle, Jonas Erskin, and Andreis Tille, and tould them if they would not forthwith yield Obedience to ye Lord Baltimore, and Own him to be their Propor, and pay rent to him, he would Turne them out of their houses and take their Land from them." And from the same source we learn that, in 1686, "ye Marylanders have lately reinforced their fort at Christina, and would not suffer John White to cut hay, but thrittend those he imployed to do it with their gunns presented against them, and that what hay they had cut ye Marylanders sayd they would throw it into river." Moreover, it appears that about this same time one Maj. English "came into ye county of New Castle with about fourty armed horsemen; left them at John Darby's whilst Maj. English and a Marry Land Capt. came to New Castle, where John White meeting him, made complaint to him of the abuses don him by ye Mary Landers at ye fort. Maj. English tould him that if thou wilt say 'you drunken dogg, Ned English, lett me cutt hay,' I will give you leave."

Inroads and exasperations of this character continued on both sides for a long period, and appear not to have ceased even after the king himself had commanded the peace. In 1717 we hear complaints of "certain persons from Maryland who had lately surveyed out lands not far from Conestoga, and near the thickest of our settlements to the great disturbance of the inhabitants there;" and in 1722 "the secret and underhand practices of persons" from Maryland are referred to with virtuous indignation in the minutes of the Pennsylvania Councils,—" these secret and underhand practices" consisting apparently in an attempt to survey and take up lands on the west side of the Susquehanna. In the same year Governor Keith sent a letter to the Governor of Maryland, in which he refers to a report that "two magistrates of Pennsylvania, with some others, had been taken prisoners by a party of men in arms from Cecil County and carried before the justices of Kent County, who detained them in custody two days, and afterwards dismissed them upon a verbal promise to appear there next court."

In 1735, William Rumsey, a surveyor of Maryland, was apprehended by the sheriff of New Castle County and taken before the Governor of Pennsylvania, charged with committing and causing others to commit great abuse and violence against several inhabitants of Chester and Lancaster Counties, for no other reason "than that those persons asserted the jurisdiction of this province [Pennsylvania] in those parts where they live." In 1736, Governor Ogle directed Thomas White, deputy surveyor, to lay out two hundred acres of land in the disputed territory of Baltimore County, and lying on the west side of the Susquehanna, for each of the following persons: Henry Munday, Edward Leet, Charles Higginbotham, James Kaine, John Smith, Hugh Kaine, James Nickleson, Robert Trotter, Robert Rowland, William Miles, William Greenlee, Stephen White, John Cross, John Kaine, Sr., John Kaine, Edward Ryly, Patrick Savage, Arthur Browlee, James Love, Anthony Dixon, Benjamin Dixon, James Morrow, Thomas King, Ralph Higginbotham, John McNabb, James McGee, Barnibe Clarke, Thomas Moore, Richard Ryan, George Bond, Thomas Linass, William Linass, John Linass, John Coats, Robert Jesson, George Moore, Robert Moore, Gibbons Jennings, Thomas Scarlet, William Carpenter, Richard Pope, Thomas Charlton, John Charlton, Sr., Edward Charlton, John Charlton, Thomas Charlton, Jr., Arthur Charlton, Henry Charlton, Jr., Richard Sedgwick, William Betty, William Betty, Jr., William Webb, Thomas Dawson, and John Dawson. Henry Munday and Edward Leet, however, were arrested by the Pennsylvania authorities, and the design to occupy the debatable land fell through. Among those who suffered in these border frays was Elisha Gatchel, a member of the Society of Friends, and a justice of the peace for the county of Chester, who was carried off by a party of Marylanders under Capt. Charlton, taken across the line, and made to give bail to answer the charge of speaking disrespectfully of Lord Baltimore. The most striking incident of these border feuds was the attack upon the house of Thomas Cresap, a citizen of Maryland, which was made by a body of armed men from Pennsylvania, who set fire to the house in which himself and family and several neighbors had taken refuge, and attempted to murder them as they made their escape from the flames. In this sharp contest one of Cresap's men was killed and himself wounded. He was also made prisoner, and conveyed to Philadelphia, where he was lodged in jail.

The Governor of Pennsylvania, in his report to his Council, gives the following account of the arrest of Cresap, who lived at this time at Wright's Ferry, opposite the town of Columbia, now Pennsylvania, where he obtained a Maryland title to five hundred acres of land:

"The sherif of Lancaster, having called to his assistance twenty-four persons, went over Susquehannah on Tuesday night, the twenty-third of November [1736], in order to be at Cresap's early next morning and to have taken him by surprise, but they being discovered, Cresap secured himself in his house, and having six men with him he stood on his defense; that the sherif read the warrant to Cresap and required him to surrender, but he and those with him swore they would defend themselves to death; that the sherif finding all persuasive means ineffectual sent for more assistance, but Cresap had so fortified his house and fired so furiously on the sherif and his company that they could not storm the house without the utmost hazard, there being near a hundred firearms in it; that they had taken an oath to stand by one another, with a resolution to kill any one that offered to capitulate; one, however, found means to desert him by getting out at the chimney; that the sherif and his assistants having waited till near sunset and finding they must either return without executing their warrant or destroy the house to come at him, they set fire to it, but offered to quench it if he would surrender; he nevertheless obstinately persisted in his refusal, neither would he suffer his wife or children to leave the house, but fire at those who proposed; that when the fire prevailed and the floor was ready to fall in, those with him rushed forth loaded with arms, which as they fired at the sherif and his assistants they threw away, and in the confusion one of Cresap's men, Michael Reisner, shot down by mistake another of the gang, named Lauchlan Malone, on whose body the coroner was taking an inquisition; that Cresap was at length apprehended."

Cresap before his capture had formed, with the knowledge of Governor Ogle, an association of about fifty men for the purpose of driving out the German settlers on the west side of the Susquehanna, and in the prosecution of their design they killed one Knowles Dant, who had resisted them. Cresap was then attacked, as related, made prisoner, and carried to Philadelphia, where the streets and doors were thronged with spectators to see the "Maryland Monster," who taunted the crowd by exclaiming, half in earnest, half in derision, "Why, this is the finest city in the province of Maryland!"

Before the formation of Cresap's association the sheriff of Baltimore County, with the sanction of the Maryland authorities, had marched with three hundred men at his back to eject the German settlers from their possessions, but was persuaded to relinquish his design on a pledge from the Germans that they would consult together, and give an answer to Lord Baltimore's requisition to acknowledge his authority. The attack upon Cresap added fresh fuel to the bitter feeling already prevailing, and Governor Ogle, after in vain demanding the release of Cresap, "ordered reprisals, and four German settlers were seized and carried to Baltimore, and a band of the associates, under one Higginbotham, proceeded forcibly to expel the Germans. Again the Council of Pennsylvania ordered out the sheriff of Lancaster and the power of his county, with directions to dispose detachments in proper positions to protect the people; when the sheriff entered the field the invaders retired, but returned as soon as his force was withdrawn. Captures were made on both sides; the German settlers were harassed perpetually, in many instances driven from their farms, and in others deterred from every attempt to plant or improve." In October, 1737, sixteen Marylanders, under the leadership of Richard Lowder, broke into the jail at Lancaster and released Lowder's brother and a number of others who had been apprehended by the sheriff of Lancaster County.

This fierce border warfare at length attained so alarming a character that the Governor and both Houses of Assembly of Maryland found it necessary to make a true representation to the king and the proprietary "of the impious treatment which this Province in general, and more particularly your Majesty's subjects residing on the northern borders thereof, have of late suffered from the Government and inhabitants of the Province of Pennsylvania."

From this address it appears that the German settlers, of whom so much has been said, had in the first place applied to the authorities of Maryland for permission to settle on the land in dispute, that considerable quantities of land had been allotted to them (in what is now York County, Pa.), and that for a time they had paid taxes to the government of Maryland, and in every other way acknowledged its jurisdiction. The address charged, however, that they had been seduced from their allegiance by emissaries from Pennsylvania, who had promised them lighter taxes under that province, and they had accordingly refused to yield any further obedience to Maryland, under the pretense that their lands were within the limits of Pennsylvania. It was to reduce these people to submission and to maintain the proper authority of Maryland that Cresap's association was formed, and it was in the attempt to defend her territory from encroachment that he was subjected to the violence and imprisonment for which the Governor and Assembly now sought redress. This address had the effect of drawing from the King an order in Council, dated Aug. 18, 1737, in which the Governors of Maryland and Pennsylvania were commanded, on pain of His Majesty's highest displeasure, to put a stop to the tumults, riots, and outrageous disorders on the borders of their respective provinces. The dangerous situation of affairs in the two provinces at this time, and the desire to conciliate the crown, produced a ready compliance with this order, and an agreement was made in 1738 providing for the running of a provisional line between the provinces, which was not to interfere with the actual possessions of the settlers, but merely to suspend all grants of the disputed territory as defined by that line until the final adjustment of the boundaries. Col. Levin Gale and Samuel Chamberlaine on the part of Maryland, and Richard Peters and Lawrence Snowden on the part of Pennsylvania, were appointed commissioners to run the line, and began operations in the spring of 1739, when Col. Gale was called away by sickness in his family, and Mr. Chamberlaine declining to proceed in the absence of his colleague, the Pennsylvania commissioners, by the order of Governor Thomas, continued the work alone, and ran the line westward of the Susquehanna "to the most western of the Kittochtinny hills" (now called North Mountain).

Though this provisional line put a stop to the border troubles, the boundary question remained a subject of contention until the 4th of July, 1760, when it was finally determined by an agreement between the Penns and Lord Baltimore. In 1763 the east-and-west line between Maryland and Pennsylvania, known as Mason and Dixon's line, from the names of the surveyors, Charles Mason and Jeremiah Dixon, was established. Mason and Dixon, whose services had been secured by Lord Baltimore and Thomas and Richard Penn in London, arrived in Philadelphia on the 15th of November, 1763, and having settled upon their " tangent point, they proceeded to measure on its meridian fifteen miles from the parallel of the most southern part of Philadelphia, the north wall of a house on Cedar Street, occupied by Thomas Plumstead and Joseph Huddle." They thus determined what was to be the northeastern corner of Maryland, the beginning of the parallel of latitude that had been agreed upon as the boundary between the provinces.

On the 17th of June, 1765, the surveyors had carried the parallel of latitude to the Susquehanna River, and thereupon received instructions to continue it " as far as the province of Maryland and Pennsylvania were settled and inhabited." On the 27th of October they had reached North Mountain, and they record in their journal that they got Capt. Shelby to go with them to its summit, " to show them the course of the Potomac," when they found that they could see the Allegany Mountains for many miles, and judged it " by its appearance to be about fifty miles' distance, in the direction of the line." On the 4th of June, 1766, we find them on the summit of the Little Allegany, and at the end of that summer's work. The Indians were now troublesome, and the surveyors and their assistants began to feel alarmed for their safety. In 1767 the surveyors began their operations late in the season. A negotiation with the Six Nations was necessary, which Sir William Johnson had promised to conduct; but this was not concluded before May, so that it was not until the 8th of June that the surveyors reached their halting-place of the preceding year, on the summit of the Little Allegany Mountain. On the 14th of June they had advanced as far as the summit of the Great Allegany, where they were joined by an escort of fourteen Indians, with an interpreter, deputed by the chiefs of the Six Nations to accompany them. On the 25th of August the surveyors note that "John Green, one of the chiefs of the Mohawk nation, and his nephew, leave them in order to return to their own country." The roving Indians of the wilderness, regardless of the escort, began also to give the white men uneasiness, and on the 29th of September twenty-six of the assistants quit the work for fear of the Shanees and Delawares. Mason and Dixon had now but fifteen axemen left with them; but, nothing disheartened, they sent back to Fort Cumberland for aid, and pushed forward with the line. At length they reached a point two hundred and forty-four miles from the river Delaware, and within thirty-six miles of the whole distance to be run. And here, in the bottom of a valley, on the borders of a stream marked Dunkard Creek on their map, they came to an Indian war-path winding its way through the forest. And here their Indian escort told them that it was the will of the Six Nations that the surveys should be stayed. There was no alternative but obedience, and retracing their steps, they returned to Philadelphia, and reporting all these facts to the commissioners under the deed of 1760, they received an honorable discharge on the 26th of December, 1767. Subsequently, and by other surveyors, the line was carried out to its termination. A cairn of stones some five feet high, in the dense forest not far from the Board Tree Tunnel on the Baltimore and Ohio Railroad, now marks the termination of Mason

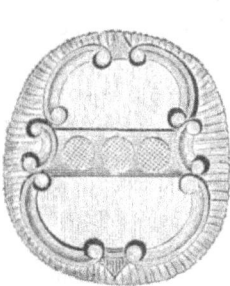

ARMS OF WM. PENN.   ARMS OF LORD BALTIMORE.

and Dixon's line, calling by that name the southern boundary of Pennsylvania.

The boundary line thus run between Maryland and Pennsylvania was directed by the agreements of the parties to be marked in a particular manner, and the surveyors accordingly planted at the end of every fifth mile a stone, graven with the arms of the Penns on the north side, and of Frederick, sixth Lord Baltimore, on the south side. The intermediate miles were marked with smaller stones, having a P on the north side, and an M on the south. The stones with the sculptured arms were all sent from England. These were planted on the parallel of latitude as far as Sideling Hill; but here, all wheel transportation ceasing in 1766, the further marking of the line was the vista of eight yards wide, with piles of stone on the crests of all the mountain ranges, built from six to seven feet high, as far as the summit of the Allegany, beyond which the line was marked with posts, around which stones and earth were thrown, the better to preserve them.

The Southern and Western Boundary.—Having adjusted her eastern and northern boundaries, Maryland next turned her attention to the settlement of her southern and western boundaries. This related to, and grew out of, the description of "the first fountain of the Potomac," as the terminus of the western and southern boundaries of Maryland. This was predicated upon a grant made by Charles II., in the first year of his reign, to Lord Hopton, Lord Jermyn, Lord Culpeper, Sir John Berkeley, Sir William Morton, Sir Dudley Wyatt, and Sir Thomas Culpeper, of "all that tract of land lying and being in America, and bounded within the heads of the rivers Rappahannock and Quiriough, or Potomac (the courses of the said rivers as they are commonly called and known by the inhabitants), and the Chesapeake Bay." The validity of the grant was subsequently drawn in question, when it was surrendered, and a new one given in May, 1669, to the Earl of St. Albans, Lord Berkeley, Sir William Morton, and John H. Trethaway. Subsequently the title of this grant was vested in Thomas, Lord Culpeper, to whom a new patent was granted of the northern neck of Virginia by King James II. in the fourth year of his reign, and from him it descended to his daughter and only child, who was married to Lord Fairfax, and thus passed into the Fairfax family. This grant of the northern neck called for the lands lying on the south side of the Potomac to its *head*, while the charter of Lord Baltimore called for all the land to the *fountain* or *source* of the Potomac, which was of course its *head*. At first there were no disputes about the true location of the common call, but as soon as the settlements began to extend towards the head of the Potomac, jealousies and difficulties broke out between the two proprietaries. Lord Baltimore, who claimed from the head of the South Branch of the

Potomac, its first fountain, remonstrated at a very early period with the Virginians, who had undertaken to define his limits by granting lands to the North Branch. Notwithstanding these protests, from the year 1753, Fairfax continued to adhere to the line as adjusted by him, and the proprietary of Maryland continued to assert his claim to the first fountain as provided by his charter.

For some years after the controversy was opened the attention of the government of the province was wholly engrossed with its internal concerns, and its efforts, in common with the other colonies, in the prosecution of the French and Indian wars; but these being terminated by the definitive treaty of peace, concluded at Paris in February, 1763, it is probable that the settlements of Maryland would soon have been pushed to its extreme limits. Had this occurred, there would soon have ensued a collision between the grants of the proprietary and of Fairfax, and this collision would at once either have brought about an amicable adjustment of the boundaries, or have forced it for determination before the King in Council. At this moment, when the conflict seemed inevitable, two causes for its suspension arose, which held this difference in abeyance until the Revolution came to convert it into a contest between free and independent States.

By the treaty of Paris, in 1763, a large territory was ceded to the English, within which newly-acquired territory it became necessary to organize colonial governments. For this and other purposes a proclamation was issued by the king on Oct. 7, 1763, by which, and to enable the English government to carry into effect its engagements to the Indians, the colonial governments generally were prohibited from granting any lands lying west of the sources or heads of any of the rivers flowing into the Atlantic from the west and northwest. On the 16th of April, 1764, instructions were issued by Governor Sharpe to the judges of the land-office, which set forth that the proprietary was desirous to have reserved for him ten thousand acres of land in the western part of Frederick County, to be held as a manor; and that he had therefore instructed the surveyor of that county not to execute any warrant on any lands lying beyond Fort Cumberland until that reserve was taken off. Until the manor of Lord Baltimore should be ascertained, Governor Sharpe thought proper to survey, in lieu thereof, five different tracts, containing in the whole 127,680 acres. This general interdict of the Crown, and the reserve to the proprietary, each tended to check the progress of the settlements in the direction of the debatable territory, and the proprietary and his officers now waited for the first favorable opportunity of bringing the question before the council which might present itself. In 1771 the first actual examination and survey of the two branches of the Potomac was made by Col. Thomas Cresap, under the direction of the proprietary, and he decided that the South Branch was the most western source, and therefore *the first fountain.*

In March, 1774, the subject of the reserve, on the lands lying westward of Fort Cumberland, being brought before the proprietary's board of revenue, which had been organized in 1766–67, that board determined that the object of the reserve had been accomplished in the surveys actually made for the proprietary, and therefore took off the reserve. This determination led to a correspondence between them and Daniel (of St. Thomas Jenifer), his lordship's agent and receiver-general, which fully establishes the fact that Lord Baltimore always claimed the South Branch of the Potomac as the most western source, and therefore the first fountain, and the point at which the meridian for the western boundary ought to start, and that he was only waiting for a favorable opportunity of bringing it before the King in Council. The board, however, still adhered to their determination, and large grants of land on the reserve were immediately made, and continued to be made, until October, 1774, when instructions were received from the proprietary directing the judges of the land-office to suspend all further grants of the reserved lands, and to prepare and transmit to his guardians an accurate list of all warrants issued under the order of the preceding March, and of all settlements and locations made within the territory thrown open by that order since the year 1763.[1]

From the year 1753 to the Revolution the proprietary and his government continued to assert the Maryland claim, and were restrained from making grants of the disputed territory[2] only through the apprehension of the interference of the Crown, and because of the adjustment between the Crown and Lord Fairfax. And if any doubts could arise from the possession of Fairfax, anterior to the Revolution, they are all removed by the constitution of Virginia adopted in June, 1776, which in its twenty-first ar-

---

[1] "The titles acquired under warrants issued between the 22d of March and the 6th of October, 1774, to affect lands lying westward of Fort Cumberland, were saved by the act of 1784, chap. 75."—*McMahon's History of Maryland.*

[2] At the time of the Revolution the following manors belonging to Lord Baltimore were undisposed of in Western Maryland: Monocay manor and the reserves thereon, as returned by the surveyor of Frederick County, 13,143 acres; My Lord's two manors and reserves, westward of Fort Cumberland, Allegany County, 125,130 acres.

ticle, after making certain reservations as to the navigation and use of the Potomac and Pocomoke, etc., expressly cedes and confirms to the State of Maryland "all the territory contained within its charter, with all the rights of property, jurisdiction, and government, and all other rights whatsoever, which may at any time heretofore have been claimed by Virginia." Thus, then, at the Revolution, by the express concession of the State of Virginia, the claims of Maryland to her charter limits existed in their full force, and are sustained by an express surrender of all counter-claims which Virginia might have. On the 6th of October, 1777, after the recognition by Virginia of the right of Maryland "to all the territory contained within its charter," by a resolution of the Assembly of Maryland Daniel (of St. Thomas) Jenifer, Thomas Stone, and Samuel Chase were appointed commissioners on the part of Maryland for the purpose of adjusting with the commissioners on the part of Virginia (George Mason and Alexander Henderson) "the navigation of, and jurisdiction over, that part of the Chesapeake Bay which lies within the limits of Virginia, and over the rivers Potomac and Pocomoke," subject to the ratification of the General Assembly. The result of the conferences of these commissioners was a compact, formed at Mount Vernon on the 28th of March, 1785, which accomplished all the purposes of their appointment, and which received the ratification of the Legislatures of both States at their next session.[1]

The compact contains a series of commercial regulations, constituting a treaty of commerce predicated upon the basis of free and equal rights in the navigation of these rivers, to be maintained for their common benefit by their common efforts, and at their joint expense, and securing these in a manner eminently calculated to promote and establish an harmonious and beneficial intercourse. These regulations have been superseded by the adoption of the Constitution of the United States, which devolved upon Congress the power of regulating commerce with foreign nations, and among the several States; but they are worthy of all commendation, says McMahon, and deserve to be the most cherished part of our history, when we remember that to these may be traced the germ of the causes which called that Constitution into being.

Thus by this compact, irrevocable, except by the assent of both States, all differences were ended which could arise about the rights reserved by Virginia under her constitution; and Maryland was now, by the concessions of that very constitution itself, as well as by the intrinsic efficacy of her charter, confessedly entitled to all the territory which fell within her chartered limits, subject to the compact. Had she known and pursued her interests, this compact would never have been formed without making the adjustment of the western boundary a part of it; and had the consideration of it been introduced into the negotiation, and its settlement insisted upon by Maryland, it would doubtless have been conceded. Virginia was too much alive to the deep interests which she had staked upon that negotiation, and which might be lost by its failure, to have hazarded all for an interest comparatively so unimportant as her claim to mere jurisdiction over a portion of what was then her remote territory. That it should have been passed by whilst a subject so intimately connected with it was under consideration, and that it should not have been brought up, even as a subject-matter for negotiation, until 1795, is truly surprising. In that year, by a resolution of the General Assembly of Maryland, Messrs. William Pinkney, William Cooke, and Mr. Key were appointed commissioners on the part of Maryland to meet such commissioners as might be appointed on the part of Virginia, with power to adjust, by compact between the two States, the western and southern limits of Maryland, and the dividing lines and boundaries between it and Virginia, and also any claim of either State to territory within the limits of the other; and in the event of agreement, the compact was to be reported to the Legislature for its confirmation. Delay still followed delay, Mr. Pinkney having left the province, and Mr. Cooke having declined acceptance. In 1796, Charles Carroll of Carrollton and J. T. Chase were appointed in their stead. Mr. Key removed from the State, and Messrs. Carroll and Chase declined acceptance, and thus the State was again left without commissioners until 1801, when, by a resolution of that year, the power of appointment was given to the Governor and Council. Messrs. Duvall, McDowell, and Nelson were now appointed commissioners, and a correspondence upon the subject took place between Governors Mercer and Monroe. The result of it was that a resolution was passed by Virginia authorizing the appointment of commissioners to meet those appointed on the part of Maryland, but limiting their powers to the adjustment of the western line. Virginia was unwilling even to enter into a discussion of her right to the territory between the two branches, whilst Maryland went upon the broad principle of referring the whole subject to the commissioners. The power of the Virginia commissioners being thus restricted, Gov-

---

[1] See a full review of this question in the writer's "History of Maryland," ii., p. 529, etc.

ernor Mercer deemed it unnecessary to request a meeting, and the negotiation ended. At December session, 1803, this correspondence and the acts and resolutions of the two States to which it related were referred to the consideration of a committee of the House of Delegates of Maryland, by whom a report was made recommending the running of a provisional boundary line (by agreement with Virginia), to start from the extreme western source of the North Branch, which should be held to be the boundary line of the two States until further and definitive measures could be taken to ascertain the southern boundary. This report was not acted upon, and the subject does not appear to have been revived until 1810, when another resolution was passed similar to that of 1801, under which nothing was done, and the subject again slept until it was revived by Maryland in the act of 1818.

Maryland had now become wearied with her efforts to reclaim the territory south of the North Branch, and hence this act of 1818, in proposing to Virginia the appointment of commissioners, agrees to adopt the most western source of the North Branch as the point from which the western boundary shall start. At December session, 1821, of the Assembly of Virginia, an act was passed which purported to meet and reciprocate this proposition of the State of Maryland, but was, in fact, materially variant from it. The Virginia act did, in fact, beg the whole question, and left nothing open for negotiation. The act itself undertook to determine the point from which the line should start, and left nothing to the commissioners but the power of locating it, in conformity to its instructions. They were specially instructed to commence the western boundary at a stone planted by Lord Fairfax on the head-waters of the Potomac, and thus they were tied down to the old adjustment between Fairfax and the Crown.[1]

The Virginia act was, therefore, entirely different from that of Maryland, which directed the commissioners to begin at the most western source of the North Branch, be that where it might, and being dissimilar, it did not justify the appointment of commissioners on the part of Maryland. The Maryland act of 1818 expressly directed that the appointment, on the part of this State, should be made only after Virginia had embraced its propositions by the passage of a similar act; and no act could be considered similar which did not confide to their commissioners the same powers of adjustment and adopt the same basis of settlement. This was, however, overlooked by the Executive of Maryland, and commissioners were appointed on the part of both States, who assembled on the head-waters of the North Branch in the summer of 1824. The commissioners who acted on this occasion on the part of Maryland were Ezekiel Chambers and James Boyle.

Chancellor John Johnson, who was joined with them in the commission, died at Hancock, Washington Co., when on his journey to the place of assemblage, to the deep regret of his fellow-citizens, among whom he was conspicuous for his abilities as

---

[1] "This adjustment, which was the only one that ever took place, was one growing out of controversies between Fairfax and the government of Virginia, having reference solely to the conflicting territorial claims, and concluding by proceedings to which Lord Baltimore was in nowise a party, and of the existence of which he and his government appear to have had no knowledge before they were terminated. It appears that in 1733 a petition was preferred by Fairfax to the King in Council, praying that a commission might issue for running and marking the dividing line between his grant and the province of Virginia, and that the commission was accordingly issued, and the survey made and reported in August, 1737. In December, 1738, the several reports were referred to the consideration of the Council for plantation affairs, by whom a report was made in 1745, which determined the head-springs of the Rappahannock and Potomac, and directed that a commission should issue to extend the line. The report was confirmed by the King in Council; and the line being adjusted in conformity to it, an act was passed by the General Assembly of Virginia in the year 1748 which adopts the order in Council, and confirms all previous grants made by the Crown of lands lying within the limits of the Fairfax grant. The line thus settled adopted the North Branch of the Potomac as the first head of that river, by which location of it, thus passing over the Fairfax grant to this branch, without even considering, much less respecting, the claims of the proprietary of Maryland, each of these interested parties were to be benefited at his expense. On the one hand the territory subject to the jurisdiction of Virginia was enlarged, and on the other Fairfax gained a more valuable territory lying between the North and South Branch than that which he lost lying east of the head of the South Branch, and between it and a meridian passing over the head of the North Branch. During all this period the situation of the proprietary of Maryland afforded to these parties the most favorable opportunity for practicing the usurpation of his rights. His petition for the confirmation of his grant, so as to exclude the claims of the Penns, was then pending before the King in Council, to await the issue of the proceedings in chancery upon the agreement of 1732, which was all the while progressing. The momentous character of that proceeding was well calculated to engross his attention, and to divert it entirely from these *ex-parte* transactions on the part of Fairfax, which did not upon their face even profess to interfere with his grant, and to the purpose of which he was awakened only by the knowledge of the actual location from the North Branch. His death shortly afterwards prevented the proprietary from adopting any decisive measures for the vindication of his rights, but the instructions of his successors in 1753, immediately after his accession to the proprietaryship, excluded all inference of acquiescence in these unwarrantable acts, and manifested a full determination on his part to exclude all settlements which might be attempted under them upon his territory."—*McMahon's Maryland*, p. 54.

a lawyer and his worth as a man. His body is buried in a marble tomb in the cemetery at Hancock.

Upon the instant of the assemblage of the boundary commissioners, it was discovered that the positive instructions to the Virginia commissioners would operate as a bar to all further proceedings. The Maryland commissioners came instructed to locate the western line from the most western source of that branch, whilst those on the part of Virginia were limited to Fairfax's location, without regard to the inquiry " whether it was or was not so located." Fairfax's stone is not, in fact, planted at the extreme western source; and even had it been so situated, it was scarcely consistent with the rights and dignity of Maryland to have entered into an adjustment with commissioners who were thus restricted without regard to the question of right. Maryland having by her act offered to relinquish all claim to the territory south of the North Branch, it was not to be expected, after this concession, that she should adopt as the source of that branch a point determined as such by her interested adversaries during the progress of the controversy. The spirit of amity and concession which had characterized all her proceedings in her repeated efforts to close this controversy had been met at every step by one of obstinate adherence on the part of Virginia to the full extent of her pretended claims, and it did not become her dignity as a State to submit herself implicitly to any terms which the latter might dictate. Her commissioners, therefore, properly insisted that the whole question as to the true source of the North Branch should be thrown open for investigation, and this being declined the negotiations ended.

So rests the controversy even to this day, and the proffer of Maryland to confine herself to the North Branch, as contained in her act of 1818, being thus rejected by Virginia, she is remitted to her original rights. Hitherto the course of Maryland has never contemplated aught but an amicable adjustment, and she has already made every advance towards this except that of unqualified submission to the demands of Virginia. Every effort has failed, and the inhabitants of our western borders begin to feel more sensibly every day the consequences of the protracted struggle. It is a matter of reproach to the two States that this boundary, so extensive and important, should be unsettled to this day; and to Maryland it especially belongs to redeem herself from this reproach by adopting on the instant some legal or equitable decisive measures to bring about its adjustment. Our citizens would deeply regret the necessity of an adversary proceeding against a sister State which has held so high a place in our affections, yet in reviewing the conduct of our State they will find no cause for censure. As to the *chartered* extent of Maryland there can be little room for doubt. " *The first fountain of the Potomac*" is evidently a descriptive term intended to designate the most westerly source, and applies to the South Branch, the source of which lies considerably west of that of the North Branch. The extent of territory lying between the two branches is estimated at half a million of acres, including some of the most fertile lands in Mineral, Grant, Pendleton, and Hampshire Counties in West Virginia. In the event of adversary proceedings, the claims of Maryland will of course extend to her chartered limits, and the sovereignty over this extensive country will be the high prize for the victor. The citizens of our sister State will, perhaps, smile at pretensions so extensive, yet that they were once well founded can scarcely be doubted, and if so, it will be difficult to show in what way they have been lost. If this be admitted, Virginia can rest her claims only upon prior occupancy and long-continued possession, and these will avail her but little in such a case as the present.[1]

---

[1] The distinguished lawyer and historian, John V. L. McMahon, in summing up this question, says, "The claim of Maryland, as the successor to the proprietary rights, extends both to the right of soil and the jurisdiction, and it seems to be now well settled that where there is a controversy between States involving the right of soil the Supreme Court of the United States has original jurisdiction over it, and one State may in that court enforce such a right against another State of the Union. It has been doubted whether, upon such a right as that of mere sovereignty or jurisdiction, a State could proceed at law, but even in such a case it has been held that there is at least an equitable remedy by bill praying to be quieted as to the disputed boundaries. Besides this direct mode of bringing the question to an issue, there is also an indirect mode of producing a decision of it which would eventually be equally as efficacious. It is but necessary for the State of Maryland to make a grant within the disputed territory, upon which a suit could immediately be instituted against those claiming it under a Virginia grant, and the question of superior right to grant would at once come up. It being then a case of conflicting claims under grants of different States, it might be at once transferred to the proper Circuit Court of the United States, and thence (if of sufficient value) to the Supreme Court for final determination. These are the modes of proceeding open to Maryland, and if she still retains and intends to adhere to her original claim, she should be prompt in the prosecution of it. All further hopes of obtaining it by concession are at an end, and whatever course she may resolve to adopt should be at once determined upon. *What the boundary line may be* is not a matter of such moment to her citizens *as that it should be definite and undisputed*. In any issue of the contest, it would be the duty of Maryland to confirm all the anterior grants from the proprietaries of the neck. No attempt would be made to disturb titles so derived, and the contest would be mainly for the sovereignty of the territory. Thus respecting and protecting private rights, her claim would be stripped of all its harshness, and, if successful, whilst it enlarged and enriched her territory, would be a monument of her justice."

CHAPTER VII.

THE WAR FOR INDEPENDENCE.

The Stamp Act—Declared Unconstitutional in Frederick—The Sons of Liberty—Cresap's Riflemen—The Maryland Line—Connolly's Treason—Hanging of Tories in Frederick—Peace and Independence.

THE treaty of Paris of Feb. 10, 1763, gave to Great Britain all the territory east of the Mississippi, from the Gulf of Mexico to Hudson's Bay, and to the American colonies peace along the western borders with the savage enemies who had for nearly a century made them the scenes of pillage, devastation, and murder.

In their joy and exultation it is not wonderful that the colonists believed that a brighter day was about to dawn, and that a future of happiness and prosperity was opening before them. Patriotic and loyal addresses were sent to the king, and public sentiments of gratitude were offered. Yet in the midst of all their happiness and hope lay the *amarum aliquid*, the drop of bitterness which was in time to turn all the sweetness to gall.

The main objects of the parliamentary measures which followed the peace of 1763, were to relieve the financial embarrassments of Great Britain, and to punish the colonies for the reluctance and insubordination they had shown in meeting her demands. The manner in which the royal requisitions had been canvassed in the provincial Legislatures, and particularly in that of Maryland, had exhibited a growing spirit of freedom in the colonial governments which was by no means pleasing to the mother-country, and which it was now resolved to repress before it should be too late.

It had long been the avowed right as well as the policy of England to keep to herself the colonial trade, and many acts of Parliament had been framed with this view. The Navigation Act of 1651 has been generally supposed to have been the beginning of that system which had for its object the suppression of the colonial carrying trade; but this is an error. Long before this period, in consequence of the heavy duties and impositions levied by the Crown, the Southern planters sent their tobacco to Holland, to the considerable detriment of English revenue and commerce. To counteract this an order was issued by the King in Council "that no tobacco or other productions of the colonies should thenceforth be carried into any foreign ports until they were first landed in England and the duties paid." This was the beginning of a system of commercial monopoly which continued until the American Revolution.

But though the system of monopoly proved as prejudicial to those who bore its restraints as it was profitable for those for whose benefit it was imposed, it was yet professedly for the regulation of trade and not for the acquisition of revenue. The fundamental principle of exemption from the taxation of England was not only established by the express words of the charter of Maryland, but had been the uninterrupted practice of the colony from the first settlement. The war with France in 1754, however, revived the proposition to tax the colonies; and it was accordingly resolved "to raise funds for American affairs by a stamp duty and a duty on products of the West Indies imported into the continental colonies." A tax upon "stamped paper" was also suggested, and these projects were pressed upon Pitt immediately upon his accession to the ministry, but he "scorned to take an unjust and ungenerous advantage" of the colonies. Others with less lofty ideas of national principle and policy were found to carry out these purposes, and on the 22d of March, 1765, the Stamp Act received the royal assent.

It provided that all bills, bonds, leases, notes, ships' papers, insurance policies, and legal documents, to be valid in the courts, must be written on stamped paper, which was to be sold by public officers at prices that constituted a tax. In America the announcement of the passage of the Stamp Act aroused a strong spirit of indignation and determined resistance to its mandates. Public assemblies put forth protestations the most eloquent, resolves the most determined in opposition, while the merchants of the larger cities, whose patriotism preferred the public weal to private emolument, entered into engagements not to import goods from England until the act should be repealed; and from one end of the continent to the other the love of civil liberty strengthened the nerve and animated the hearts of the colonists. The English ministry selected as stamp distributor for Maryland,—Zachariah Hood, a native of the province, and a merchant of Annapolis. In no section of the province was more determined opposition manifested to the obnoxious measure than in Western Maryland, and on Aug. 29, 1765, the new stamp distributor was burnt in effigy by the people of Frederick Town. While public feeling was thus agitated, the Governor called the Assembly together to take such measures as might be deemed advisable, and Frederick County, which at that time constituted the whole of Western Maryland, sent as her representatives in the important deliberations of this body, Thomas Cresap, Joseph Chaplaine, Fielder Gantt, and James Smith.

The Assembly appointed delegates to the Continental Congress proposed by Massachusetts, and adopted resolutions protesting against the Stamp Act; but the bold and aggressive temper of the hardy frontiersmen of the western section of the province did not suffer them to await the uncertain result of petitions, protestations, and deliberations. An opportunity of manifesting their spirit and determination was soon presented. The fall term of the Frederick County Court commenced on the 15th of November, 1765, and among those present were the worshipful justices Thomas Beatty, William Luckett, Charles Jones, Thomas Price, and David Lynn; Sheriff, George Murdoch, and Clerk, John Darnall. On the 18th Justices Joseph Smith, David Lynn, Charles Jones, Samuel Beall, Joseph Beall, Peter Bainbridge, Thomas Price, Andrew Hugh, William Blair, William Luckett, James Dickson, and Thomas Beatty were present, and ordered the following resolution and opinion to be recorded among the minutes of the court:

"Upon application of Michael Ashford Dowden, bail of James Veach, at the suit of a certain Stephen West to surrender said James Veach in discharge of himself, which the court ordered to be done, and an entry of the surrender to be made accordingly, which John Darnall, Clerk of the Court, refused to make, and having also refused to issue any process out of his office, or to make the necessary entries of the Court proceedings, alleging that he conceives there is an Act of Parliament imposing stamp duties on all legal proceedings, and therefore that he cannot safely proceed in exercising his office without proper stamps,

"*It is the unanimous resolution and opinion of this Court* that all the business thereof shall and ought to be transacted in the usual and accustomed manner, without any inconvenience or delay to be occasioned from the want of *Stamped Paper, Parchment, or Vellum, and that all proceedings shall be valid and effectual without the use of Stamps*, and they enjoin and order all Sheriffs, Clerks, Counsellors, Attorneys, and all officers of the Court to proceed in their several avocations as usual, which Resolution and Opinion are grounded on the following and other reasons:

"1st. It is conceived that there has not been a legal publication yet made of any Act of Parliament whatever imposing a Stamp Duty on the Colonies. Therefore this Court are of opinion that until the existence of such an Act is properly notified, it would be culpable in them to permit or suffer a total stagnation of business, which must inevitably be productive of innumerable injuries to individuals, and have a tendency to subvert all principles of civil government.

"2d. As no Stamps are yet arrived in this Province, and the inhabitants have no means of procuring any, this Court are of opinion that it would be an injustice of the most wanton oppression to deprive any person of a legal remedy for the recovery of his property for omitting that which it is impossible to perform."

The clerk of the court, apprehending damage to himself if he made any entry or issued any process without stamped paper, refused to comply with the order of the court, upon which it passed the following order:

"*Ordered*, that John Darnall, clerk of this Court, be committed to the custody of the sheriff of this county for a contempt of the authority of this court, he having refused to comply with the foregoing order of this Court relative to the execution of his office in issuing processes and making the necessary entries of the Court's proceedings; and that he stands committed for the above offense until he comply with the above mentioned order."

The clerk then submitted to the order of the court, and upon paying the costs was discharged.

The decision of the court was celebrated in Frederick Town on the 30th of November in a manner most characteristic of the times.

The following amusing description of it is published in the *Maryland Gazette* of Dec. 16, 1765:

"The Stamp Act having received a mortal wound by the hands of justice on Saturday last gave up the ghost, to the great joy of the inhabitants of Frederick County. The lifeless body lay exposed to public ignominy till yesterday, when it was thought proper, for preventing infection from its stench, to bury it in the following manner: The Sons of Liberty assembled at the house of Mr. Samuel Swearingen in the afternoon, and the coffin was taken up exactly at three o'clock.

"*Form of the Funeral.*

"1. The colors of the Town Company.

"2. Drums.

"3. The banner displayed with this inscription in large characters: 'Constitutional Liberty asserted by the Magistrates of Frederick County, 22d November, 1765.'

"4. The Cap of Liberty mounted on a staff with the several following inscriptions: 'Magna Charta, Charter of Maryland, Trials by Juries Restored, Oppression Removed, Liberty and Loyalty.'

"5. Conductors.

"6. The coffin with this inscription on the lid: 'The Stamp Act expired of a mortal stab received from the genius of liberty in Frederick County Court, 23d November, 1765, Aged 22 days.' On the ends, sides, and ledges of the coffin appeared several inscriptions, which were all together deposited in the ground as appendages to the Stamp Act, viz.: 'Tyranny,'—'Villenage,'—'Military Execution,'—'Soldiers quartered in Private Houses,'—'Court of Vice-Admiralty,'—'Guarda de Costas to Prevent Corruption in North Americans from a Redundancy of Spanish dollars,'—'Britons Employed in Fastening Chains on the Necks of British Subjects,'—'Fines,'—'Imprisonment,'—'Ruin,'—'Desolation,'—'Slavery taking Possession of America in order to Extend Her Dominion over Great Britain.'

"7. Z—— H——, Esq. (Zachariah Hood), as sole mourner, carried in an open chariot. His countenance pale and dejected, his dress disorderly, unsuitable to his rank, and betraying great inward distraction of mind, and his tottering situation (being scarce able to keep his seat) demonstrated the weakness to which he was reduced, and plainly indicated the melancholy catastrophe which shortly ensued.

"8. Sons of Liberty, two and two.

"During the whole procession, which marched through the principal streets till it arrived at the gallows erected on the Court-house Green, the bells continued ringing; and on every huzza by the crowd, or loud laugh of female spectators, Z—— H——, Esq., was observed to nod, or drop his head into his bosom, in token of the utmost sorrow and confusion.

"On their arrival at the gallows, under which the grave was

dug, the drums ceasing, and proclamation made for silence, Z——— H———, Esq., was observed to be struck with such astonishment that tho' he seemed to demand audience by a weak motion of his head, he was not able to utter a word, and his features were fixed as death. Being asked whether he had anything to say, he made no answer, but a paper appearing in his bosom, was taken out; and it being demanded whether that paper contained the substance of what he had to say on the occasion, he continued silent, but was seen to make a faint nod of approbation.

"The paper, which was ordered to be read, contained the following words, and appears to have been composed by him by way of funeral oration or lamentation over the body of that beloved act which had engrossed his whole mind and affections: 'Good people,—for countrymen I dare not call you, having forfeited all claim or title to that appellation,—wonder not at my hesitation of speech, or my sighs and groans on this sad occasion, the powers of utterance being, in a great measure, taken from me by the sight of that mournful object! Cursed be the day, that direful day, in which my eyes beheld the fatal catastrophe of the beloved of my soul! May the 23d November be struck out of the Calendar, and never be reckoned in the future annals of time! And shall a record appear to eternize the downfall of my beloved, naked and unadorned with the beautiful stamp which ought to have been annexed by my influence? Can I possibly survive the dreadful thought? And must all my hopes perish, my schemes for advancing my fortune at the expense of my country be blasted, and public emolument triumph over private gain? Shall Maryland freely export her wheat and corn and find out markets for her flour and provisions without my participation in the fruits of the toil and sweat of her laborious sons? Shall the press continue free, and exist only to publish my disgraces, and instill notions of constitutional rights and liberties into the minds of North Americans? Shall the power of taxing the poor (who are chiefly involved in the duties of the Stamp Act), by imposing an arbitrary price on stamped paper, be wrested from me? and instead of lording it over my countrymen, must I need be reduced to the state of an exile, a fugitive, and a vagabond on the face of the earth? Forbid it, all ye black infernal powers of tyranny, avarice, and oppression! For to you have I devoted myself! But, soft! Your powers are enervated and your dominion blasted by the bold Sons of Liberty, before whom I now stand. Pardon, good people, this last testimony of my affection to the deceased. For her I despised country, humanity, friendship, kindred, and all the ties of honor, nature, gratitude, and honesty. For her was every motive of justice, benevolence, piety, and compassion banished from my breast. For her could I have sacrificed the good of the public, the happiness of individuals, and (encircled in her embraces) have smiled at the curses of the poor, the tears of the orphan, the cries of the widow, the groans of the oppressed, and without one pang of remorse have viewed the land of my birth gnashing her teeth under the load of bondage, whilst I enjoyed the sunshine of ministerial influence, and decked myself in the spoils of the wretched and unfortunate! Dear object of my warmest wishes! thou art now expired under the hand of Justice. The same spirit animated us both, and the cold grasp of fate is now upon me! My faculties sink together with thee, and death freezes my stagnating fluids! Let me be buried together with thee, and one grave receive our breathless remains! I hope, good people, you will not refuse this last request of a dying person. And, Oh! Oh! Oh!'

"No sooner had the person appointed to read it come to the 'Oh! Oh!' &c., than Z——— H———, Esq., was seen to sink suddenly down and tumble out of the chariot, his body becoming instantaneously cold and stiff, so violent an assault had grief made on all his vital faculties, and left him a lifeless figure scarce resembling humanity. As he was falling, a Son of Liberty, with a voice like thunder, cried out, 'Let him die like a dog!' A loud huzza and roll of the drums immediately followed, and, according to his own request, his corpse was deposited in the earth together with that of his beloved.

"The grave being filled up, and acclamations repeated, the company marched in their former order, with colors, banner, &c., to the house of Mr. Samuel Swearingen, where an elegant supper was prepared, and a ball given to the ladies, who made a brilliant appearance on the occasion. Many loyal and patriotic toasts were drank, and the whole concluded with the utmost decorum!"

The opposition against the government was now organized into a compact and enterprising party, strengthening itself throughout the province, and making itself known by its influence over the action of representatives in the Assembly. In Maryland its more aggressive members, under the name of "Sons of Liberty,"—a phrase used by Barré in his celebrated speech in Parliament in February, 1765,—by a series of bold and defiant attacks upon the government of the province, soon increased their power and steadily sapped the reverence for British law and legislative authority. In October (1765) the Sons of Liberty in Frederick County formed an organization under the leadership of Col. Thomas Cresap, and in December about three or four hundred of them, "armed with guns and tomahawks," assembled at Fredericktown, and threatened to "march down in companies to Annapolis, in order to settle the disputes between the two Houses of Assembly."[1]

The bold example of Frederick Court, and the firm

---

[1] Dr. David Ross, in his deposition, submitted to the Assembly, said that about the 27th or 29th of October a "writing addressed to the Lower House of Assembly" was circulated in Frederick County for signatures, which was in substance as follows: "It expressed a satisfaction of the conduct of the Lower House in opposing the Stamp Act, and intimated a reliance that they would endeavor, like the renowned, true, ancient Roman Senate, to suppress any future attempts to deprive them of their liberty; it also expressed that the signers were informed that a very large unjust claim in tobacco was made against the public by particular gentlemen in Annapolis [alluding to the Governor and his Council, who insisted on the collection of the twelve pence per hogshead on tobacco exported under the act of 1704, and which the Lower House, since 1739, had constantly and ineffectually declared that his lordship had no right to collect], preventing the payment of other just claims, and desiring that if the said unjust and dishonorable claim should still be insisted upon the Lower House would give speedy intelligence, in order that the signers might come down and cause justice to take place." These threats produced considerable excitement in Annapolis, as it was rumored at one time that some of the "Sons" were already at Elk Ridge, on their march to the capital. The Governor became alarmed, and immediately summoned his Council together, and laid the whole matter before them. (See House Journal, Dec. 11, 1765.)

and determined spirit of the yeomanry of Western Maryland, inspired the Sons of Liberty in other sections, and on the 31st of March, 1766, the Provincial Court at Annapolis, yielding to the stern demands of these representatives of the people, passed the following order, which was at once obeyed by the public officers, and the detested Stamp Act was in Maryland forever *null* and *void:*

"It is by the court here ordered that the clerk of this court from henceforth issue all manner of process, file all pleadings, give copies, and transact all business whatsoever in his office for which application shall be made to him by any inhabitant of this province, as usual, *without stamped paper.*"

The universal opposition in the colonies provoked by the Stamp Act, and the injury resulting from it to English commerce and manufactures, caused its repeal on the 18th of March, 1766, and the news of its repeal, which was received in Annapolis on the 22d of May, was celebrated with every manifestation of private and public delight in Western Maryland and every other part of the province.

The first exultation that followed the repeal of the Stamp Act was not destined to be of long duration. In May, 1767, Charles Townshend, Chancellor of the Exchequer, introduced in Parliament a series of revenue acts, the principal of which passed and received the royal assent on June 29th, to go into effect on the 20th of November. These acts, in brief, imposed duties on glass, paper, pasteboard, white and red lead, painters' colors, and tea imported into the colonies; established a board of customs at Boston to collect the revenue throughout America, and legalized writs of assistance. This new scheme of taxation at once revived the spirit of resistance in Maryland, and led to the reorganization of the non-importation associations which had sprung into existence during the previous agitation. The Maryland non-importation association was sustained in vigorous operation by special committees, appointed by kindred associations in each of the counties, who were charged with the duty of inquiring into and reporting the facts of every case of actual or suspected violation of the agreement, and was continued up to the breaking out of the Revolutionary war. In October, 1769, a number of wagons of contraband goods, valued at three hundred pounds, were shipped from Pennsylvania to Frederick, and not being accompanied with the proper certificates, they were stored at the risk and cost of the owners. Meetings were held in all parts of the province to give expression to the popular feeling in regard to the despotic course of the government. The first meeting held in Frederick County, as published in the *Maryland Gazette* at Annapolis, was convened at the old school-house, not far from Troxell's mill, on Tom's Creek, on Sunday, the 28th of August, 1770. The meeting was largely attended by the old inhabitants, who were deeply impressed by the situation. There were present on that occasion William Blair, an old resident of Scottish descent, James Shields, Sr., William Shields, Charles Robinson, Patrick Haney, Robert Brown, Henry Hockersmith, William Elder, son of Guy, Samuel Westfall, Moses Kennedy, Alexander Stewart, William Curran, Jr., Charles Carroll, William Koontz, Christian Hoover, John Smith, Daniel McLean, John Faires, John Long, Arthur Row, John Crabs, Moses Ambrose, George Kelly, Walter Dulany, Thomas J. Bowie, James Park, Robert Agnew, John Corrick, Frederick Troxell, Rudolf Nead, Octavius S. Taney, George Ovelman, Dominick Bradley, Thomas Hughes, Philip Weller, Jacob Valentine, William Brawner, Thomas Martin, Daniel Morrison, William Munroe, Henry Brook, and others. It was agreed by a "show of hands" that William Blair should be called to the chair, and John Faires appointed secretary. The meeting was then addressed by Walter Dulany and William Elder, son of Guy, who concluded by offering the following resolution:

"*Resolved,* by the inhabitants of Tom's Creek, Frederick County, in the province of Maryland, loyal to their king and country, that we reaffirm the great Magna Charta of our Civil and Religious Rights, as granted by Charles of England to Lord Baltimore and the inhabitants of this colony, as reaffirmed on the first landing of the Pilgrim Fathers of Maryland, that there shall be a perfect freedom of conscience, and every person be allowed to enjoy his religious and political privileges and immunities unmolested."

The resolution was read and re-read and adopted by a "showing of hands." It was further

"*Resolved,* That the proceedings of this meeting be published in the Annapolis *Gazette* and Bradford's paper at Philadelphia."

In the mean time local causes of complaint served to intensify public feeling and increase the general opposition.

The Assembly having failed to provide for the fees of public officers, or for the assessments for the support of the clergy, Governor Eden undertook to regulate the former by proclamation, leaving the latter to be collected under an old act of 1702, which he claimed had been revived by the failure of the Assembly to legislate on the subject. Governor Eden's action was a virtual assumption of the legislative prerogative of taxation, and involved in a measure the principle at stake in the contest with the mother-country. It immediately gave rise to great public excitement, warm advocates appeared on either side of the question, and the discussion assumed a tone of

CHARLES CARROLL OF CARROLLTON.

much bitterness and animosity. Among the champions of the proclamation appeared a writer who put forth his views in a dialogue between two citizens, one of whom attacked the obnoxious measure, and the other defended it, the victory being given to the "Second Citizen," its defender. The great ability and adroitness of his article marked it as the production of no common mind, and called forth an antagonist of corresponding strength. Charles Carroll of Carrollton stepped forward on February 4th, and assumed the cause and the signature of the "First Citizen," whereupon Daniel Dulany, the provincial secretary, and the ablest lawyer in the province, became Mr. Carroll's antagonist, under the signature of "Antilon." The elections held in May, 1773, during the progress of this discussion, were attended with great excitement, and resulted in the complete triumph of the anti-proclamation party. Immediately after the result had been announced the people of Frederick and other counties celebrated the victory with great rejoicings; and at a public meeting the thanks of the people of Frederick were ordered to be formally presented by their delegates to the "First Citizen" for the patriotic service which he had rendered to the popular cause in his discussion with "Antilon," which was accordingly done in the following communication:

"MAY 25, 1773.

"To the First Citizen:

"*Sir*,—The freemen of Frederick County (to so few of whom you are personally known) are generally acquainted with your merit. The service you have done your country in plainly and clearly stating and evincing the illegality of the late proclamation for officers' fees appears to them justly to claim their thanks, they have therefore directed us, their representatives, to make known their sentiments to you, and we with pleasure take this early opportunity of returning you the thanks of the freemen of Frederick County for your spirited, manly, and able opposition to that illegal, arbitrary, and unconstitutional measure.

"We are, Sir, with the greatest respect, your most obedient servants,

"THOMAS SPRIGG WOOTTON,
"CHARLES BEATTY,
"JONATHAN HAGAR,
"HENRY GRIFFITH."[1]

---

[1] On Saturday, May 22, 1773, the polls closed in Frederick County, and Messrs. Thos. Sprigg Wootton, Charles Beatty, Jonathan Hagar, and Henry Griffith were declared duly elected. On the afternoon of that day a numerous and very respectable body of the freemen of the county assembled at the coffee-house, when the proclamation was read, and unanimously declared illegal, unconstitutional, and oppressive, and sentenced to be carried to the gallows and hanged thereon, and afterwards to be buried face downwards, that by every ineffectual struggle it might descend still deeper into obscurity. The proclamation was then put in a coffin prepared for the purpose and carried to the place of execution, attended by a large concourse of at least one thousand people, who moved in slow and regular order, attended with drums, fifes, bag-pipes, playing slow music suitable

The non-importation policy of the colonists had been so generally adopted and so faithfully observed that very little tea (upon which article alone the duty had been retained) was imported into the country. One of the great markets of the East India Company being thus closed, a heavy stock of tea accumulated in their warehouses. To relieve them of this, while at the same time maintaining the principle of taxation, seemed to the government a master-stroke of policy; and it was proposed to accomplish this by allowing the company on tea exported to America, a drawback of the duties paid in England. As soon as it was announced in America that the Tea Act was to be carried into effect, it was generally denounced as a scheme to establish the right of Parliament to tax the colonies and to give the East India Company the monopoly of their trade. On the 28th of November, 1773, a vessel containing the tea arrived in the harbor of Boston, and in a few days was followed by two others. On December 16th a party disguised as Indians went on board the vessels, and warning their officers and those of the custom-house to keep out of the way, opened the hatches, hoisted the chests of tea on deck, cut them open, and hove the tea overboard. This action provoked the "Boston Port Bill," introduced in the House of Commons on the 14th of March, 1774, which interdicted all commercial intercourse with Boston, and prohibited after the 1st of June following the landing or shipping of any goods, wares, or merchandise whatsoever at that port. On the arrival of the news of the passage of these measures, the people of Maryland made common cause with those of Massachusetts, and in various ways expressed their sympathy for the inhabitants of Boston. Frederick County, which had been foremost in the opposition to the Stamp Act, was not slow at this crisis in giving expression to her sentiments of sympathy for Boston and hostility to the oppressive course of the British government. On the 11th of June a large meeting of the inhabitants of the lower part of Frederick County was held at Charles Hungerford's tavern, at which Henry Griffith was chosen moderator, and the following resolutions adopted:

"*Resolved, unanimously,* That it is the opinion of this meeting that the town of Boston is now suffering in the common cause of America.

"*Resolved, unanimously,* That every legal and constitutional measure ought to be used by all America for procuring a repeal of the act of Parliament for blocking up the harbor of Boston.

"*Resolved, unanimously,* That it is the opinion of this meeting that the most effectual means for the securing American

to the occasion. The sentence was executed, to the universal joy and satisfaction of the spectators, under a general discharge of small-arms.

freedom will be to break off all commerce with Great Britain and the West Indies until the said act be repealed, and the right of taxation given up on permanent principles.

"*Resolved, unanimously*, That Mr. Henry Griffith, Dr. Thomas Sprigg Wootton, Nathan Magruder, Evan Thomas, Richard Brooke, Richard Thomas, Zadok Magruder, Dr. William Baker, Thomas Cramphin, Jr., and Allen Bowie be a committee to attend the general committee at Annapolis, and of correspondence for the lower part of Frederick County, and that any six of them shall have power to receive and communicate intelligence to and from their neighboring committees.

"*Resolved, unanimously*, That a copy of these our sentiments be immediately transmitted to Annapolis, and inserted in the *Maryland Gazette*.

"Signed per order.

"ARCHIBALD ORME, *Clerk*."

On the 20th of June a meeting of the citizens of Frederick County was held at the court-house in Frederick Town, at which the following resolutions were adopted, John Hanson presiding:

"I. *Resolved*, That it is the opinion of this meeting that the town of Boston is now suffering in the common cause of America, and that it is the duty of every colony in America to unite in the most effectual means to obtain a repeal of the late act of Parliament for blocking up the harbor of Boston.

"II. That it is the opinion of a great majority of this meeting that if the colonies come into a joint resolution to stop all imports from, and exports to, Great Britain and the West Indies till the act of Parliament for blocking up the harbor of Boston, as well as every other act oppressive to American liberty, be repealed, the same may be the means of preserving to America her rights, liberties, and privileges.

"III. That, therefore, this meeting will join in an association with the several counties in this province and the principal colonies in America to put a stop to all exports to, and imports from, Great Britain and the West Indies, shipped after the 25th day of July next, or such other day as may be agreed on, until the said acts shall be repealed, and that such association shall be upon oath.

"IV. That we, the inhabitants of Frederick County, will not deal or have any connections with that colony, province, or town which shall decline or refuse to come into similar resolutions with a majority of the colonies.

"V. That no suit shall be commenced after the stop shall be put to imports and exports for the recovery of any debt due to any person whatsoever, unless the debtor be about to abscond, or being appealed to shall refuse to give bond and security.

"VI. That Messrs. John Hanson, Thomas Price, George Scott, Benjamin Dulany, George Murdock, Philip Thomas, Alexander C. Hanson, Baker Johnson, and Andrew Scott be a committee to attend the general congress at Annapolis, and that those gentlemen, together with Messrs. John Cary, Christopher Edelen, Conrad Groth, Thomas Schley, Peter Hoffman, and Archibald Boyd, be a committee of correspondence to receive and answer letters, and in any emergency to call a general meeting, and that any six shall have power to act.

"Ordered, that these resolves be immediately sent to Annapolis, that they may be printed in the *Maryland Gazette*.

"Signed per order.

"ARCHIBALD BOYD, *Cl. Com*."

Another meeting was held at Elizabeth Town on the 2d of July, of which the *Maryland Gazette* gives the following account:

"On Saturday, the 2d of July, 1774, about eight hundred of the principal inhabitants of the upper part of Frederick County, Md., assembled at Elizabeth Town, and being deeply impressed with a sense of the danger to which their natural and constitutional rights and privileges were exposed by the arbitrary measures of the British Parliament, do think it their duty to declare publicly their sentiments on so interesting a subject, and to enter into such Resolutions as may be the means of preferring their freedom. After chosing John Stull, Esq., their Moderator, the following resolves were unanimously entered into:

"I. That the Act of Parliament for blocking up the harbor of the Town of Boston is a dangerous invasion of American liberty, and that the town of Boston is now suffering in the common cause, and ought to be assisted by the other Colonies.

"II. That the stopping all commercial intercourse with Great Britain will be the most effectual means for fixing our Liberties on the footing we desire.

"III. That a general congress of Delegates from the several colonies to effect a uniform plan of conduct for all America is highly necessary, and that we will strictly adhere to any measure that may be adopted by them for the preservation of our Liberties.

"IV. That the surest means for continuing a people free and happy is the disusing all luxuries, and depending only on their own fields and flocks for the comfortable necessaries of Life.

"V. That they will not, after this day, drink any Tea, nor suffer the same to be used in their Families, until the Act for laying duty thereon be repealed.

"VI. That they will not, after this day, kill any sheep under three years old.

"VII. That they will immediately prepare for manufacturing their own clothing.

"VIII. That they will immediately open a subscription for the relief of their suffering Brethren in Boston.

"After choosing John Stull, Samuel Hughes, Jonathan Hager, Conrad Hogmire, Henry Snebley, Richard Davis, John Swan, Charles Swearingen, Thomas Brooke, William McGlury, and Elie Williams as a committee, they proceeded to show their disapprobation of Lord North's Conduct with regard to America by Hanging and burning his Effigy, after which a subscription was opened for the relief of the Poor of Boston. In consequence of the Fifth Resolve, a number of mercantile Gentlemen solemnly declared they would send off all the Tea they had on hand, and that they would not purchase any more until the Act laying a duty thereon be repealed, among which number was a certain John Parks."[1]

---

[1] As indicating how the poor, out of their limited means, contributed to these subscriptions, we append an interesting memorandum:

"LINGANORE, FREDERICK COUNTY,
"April 3, 1775.

"As much for the satisfaction of the subscribers to this paper, as the contradicting malicious reports lately propagated in this county to the detriment of the character of the collector of this place, he has thought proper to give the public a state of his collections, with the receipt of the treasurer (appointed by the committee for said county) for the money, as may appear below. A copy of the subscription paper, with the subscribers' names affixed to it, as followeth: 'We, the subscribers, inhabitants of Frederick County, have paid to David Moore the sums of money affixed to our names, in consequence of an unanimous resolve of the committee for the middle part of said county, to make up, by the first Monday of next January, the sum of one hundred dollars currency, to be sent immediately to Boston, there

The following correspondence, which occurred a few months later, shows how generously these promises of assistance were redeemed:

"FREDERICK TOWN, FREDERICK CO., MD.,
"17th February, 1775.

"TO THE HON. THOMAS CUSHING, ESQ.:

"Sir,—We, the Committee for the middle part of Frederick County, Maryland, have this day forwarded £200 currency to Messrs. William Lux and Samuel Purviance, of Baltimore, who are directed to forward the same to you for the relief of the poor of your place, either specie or bills, as may appear to them most advisable. A line from you acknowledging the receipt of the money will oblige the Committee, as it will serve to convince the people from whom it was collected that it had been applied to its proper use.

"Signed for order and in behalf of the Committee.
"JOHN HANSON, *President*."

"BOSTON, M'ch 15, 1775.

"TO MR. JOHN HANSON, IN FREDERICK TOWN, MD.:

"Sir,—I am to acknowledge your letter of the 17 of February last, directed to Mr. Cushing, who is a member of the committee appointed by the Town to receive and distribute the donations from our friends to the sufferers by Act of Parliament, commonly called the Boston Port Bill, and to acquaint you that agreeable to your directions Mr. Samuel Purviance, Jr., has remitted in a bill of exchange the sum of two hundred pounds, your currency, being a contribution from the gentlemen of the Middle Division of Frederick County, in Maryland, for that charitable purpose. You will be pleased to return the hearty thanks of our committee to those gentlemen for their generous donations, and to assure them that it will be applied to its proper use.

"It will doubtless afford them satisfaction to be informed that their brethren in this place endure the sufferings inflicted upon them by that unrighteous and barbarous edict with patience and fortitude, and that they continue to bear oppression and count it all joy so to do, rather than to stain their reputation by a base compliance with the demands of arbitrary power.

"With very great regard, I am, in behalf of the committee, your obliged and affectionate friend and countryman,
"S. ADAMS, *Chairman*."

On the 22d of June, 1774, deputies from all the counties assembled in general convention at Annapolis and adopted non-importation resolutions of the strongest character. The convention adjourned on the 25th, but it was not long before a serious infringement of the non-importation agreement occupied public attention. In August the brigantine "Mary and Jane," Capt. George Chapman, arrived in St. Mary's River from London with eleven chests of tea, consigned to Robert Findlay, a merchant of Bladensburg, Robert Peter, of Georgetown, and several other merchants at Norfolk, Va. In consequence of this "alarming" intelligence the Committee of Correspondence of Frederick County held a meeting on the 11th of August, and requested these gentlemen to appear before them. After hearing their statements the committee unanimously resolved "that the importation of any commodity from Great Britain liable to the payment of a duty imposed by an Act of Parliament is in a high degree dangerous to our liberties, as it implies a full assent to the claim asserted by the British Parliament of a right to impose taxes for the purpose of raising a revenue in America." And in order "to discourage the pernicious practice" the committee determined that the "detestable plant" should not be landed in America, but that "it should be sent back in the same ship."[1]

On the 5th of September, 1774, the Continental Congress, which was first proposed by Maryland, and to which she elected the first set of delegates, assembled at Carpenters' Hall, Philadelphia, and adopted a plan "for carrying into effect the non-importation, non-consumption, and non-exportation" association.

At a meeting of the inhabitants of Frederick County "qualified to vote for representatives," held at the court-house, on Friday, the 18th of November, the following resolutions were adopted:

"*Resolved*, That Charles Beatty, Henry Griffith, Thos. Sprigg Wooton, Jacob Hunk, Nath. Magruder, Richard Thomas, Evan

"'Nov. 30, 1774.

"'Wm. Winchester, 7s. 6d.; John Chamberlain, 7s. 6d.; John Chrisman, 10s.; William Carey, 1s. 8d.; Christian Efrey, 3s. 9d.; William Kende, 1s. 3d.; John Becrast, 4s.; John Weaver, 5s.; John Umsteat, 5s.; J. McDaniel, Sr., 7s. 6d.; Charles Wood, 7s. 6d.; James Frazer, 9s.; Sol. Longworth, 5s.; Enoch Moore, 3s. 9d.; Francis Mathews, 7s. 6d.; John Lindsey, 2s. 6d.; John Henckle, 2s.; James Hoops, 2s.; Conrad Carkess, 3s.; Peter Kemp, 5s.; Gerrard Davis, 2s. 6d.; Jacob Hosler, 2s.; Green Shurear, 5s.; Anthony Linsey, 5s.; Edward Hodgskiss, 5s.; John Chamberlain, 5s.; W. Winchester, Jr., 5s.; James Winchester, 5s.; Hugh McKniel, 2s.; Thomas Wheeler, 5s.; Joshua Grimes, 2s. 6d.; Aran Richards, 5s.; Geo. Becrast, 5s. 4d.; John Lawrance, £1; Joseph Wood, Sr., 5s. 8d.; J. McDaniel, Jr., 5s. 8d.; Edward Evans, 5s. 8d.; Francis McDaniel, 5s.; William Condon, 3s. 9d.; Amos Wright, 3s. 9d.; David Moore, £1 6s. 5d. Total, £11 10s.'

"Received, Jan. 26, 1775, of Mr. David Moore, the sum of £11 10s., a sum collected by him for the support of the poor in Boston.

---

[1] The women of Western Maryland were by no means behind the men in patriotic support of all the measures looking to the protection of American rights and liberties. Madeline Sheffey, a woman of fine mind and strong character, and the mother of the celebrated Daniel Sheffey, of Staunton, Va., speaking for the women of Frederick County, said, "We have resolved to drink no more tea for years to come,—not until the war is ended; but we will eat mush and milk, drink water, and live frugally until our fathers, sons, husbands, and brothers achieve a brave victory."

Thomas, Richard Brooke, Zadock Magruder, William Baker, Thomas Cramphin, Jr., John Murdock, Thomas Jones, Allen Bowie, Jr., William Deakins, Jr., Bernard O'Neal, Brook Beall, Edward Burgess, Charles G. Griffith, Henry Griffith, Jr., Wm. Bayley, Jr., Samuel W. Magruder, Nath. Offutt, Archibald Orm, Joseph Threlkeld, Walter Smith, Thos. Beall of George, Richard Crab, William Luckett, William Luckett, Jr., Greenbury Griffith, Samuel Griffith, John Hanson, Thomas Price, Thomas Bowles, Conrad Grosh, Thomas Schley, Jonathan Wilson, Francis Deakins, Casper Schaaff, Peter Hoffman, George Scott, Baker Johnson, Philip Thomas, Alexander C. Hanson, Archibald Boyd, Arthur Nelson, Andrew Scott, George Stricker, Adam Fisher, Wm. Ludwick, Weltner Van Swearengen, William J. Beall, Jacob Young, Peter Grosh, Æneas Campbell, Elias Bruner, Frederick Kemp, John Haas, John Romsburg, Thomas Hawkins, Upton Sheredine, John Lawrence, Basil Dorsey, Charles Warfield, Ephraim Howard, Joseph Wells, David Moore, Joseph Wood, Norman Bruce, William Blair, David Schriver, Roger Johnson, Henry Cock, Robert Wood, William Albaugh, Jacob Mathias, Henry Crawle, Jacob Ambrose, David Richards, Wm. Winchester, Philip Fishburn, William Hobbs, Thomas Cresap, Thomas Warren, Thos. Humphreys, Richard Davis, Jr., Charles Clinton, James Prather, George Brent, James Johnson, James Smith, Joseph Chapline, John Stull, Samuel Beall, Jr., William Baird, Joseph Sprigg, Christian Orendorf, Jonathan Hager, Conrad Hogmire, Charles Swearengen, Henry Snavely, Richard Davis, Samuel Hughes, Joseph Perry, John Jugerhorn, Joseph Smith, Thomas Hog, Thomas Prather, William McClary, John Swan, Eli Williams, Stophall Burkett, and Thomas Brooke be a committee to represent this county to carry into execution the association agreed on by the American Continental Congress, and that any five have power to act.

"*Resolved*, That Charles Beatty, Thos. Sprigg Wooton, John Hanson, Thomas Bowles, Caspar Shaaff, Thomas Price, Baker Johnson, Philip Thomas, George Murdock, Alexander C. Hanson, Thomas Cramphin, Jr., William Bayley, Jr., Evan Thomas, Richard Brooke, Thomas Johns, Walter Smith, William Deakins, John Murdock, Bernard O'Neal, John Stull, Samuel Beall, Jr., James Smith, Joseph Chapline, Joseph Sprigg, Charles Swearengen, Rich. Davis, Jonathan Hager, and Joseph Perry be a committee of correspondence for this county, and that any five have power to act.

"*Resolved*, That Charles Beatty, Henry Griffith, Thos. Sprigg Wooton, Jacob Funk, Evan Thomas, Richard Brooke, Upton Sheredine, Baker Johnson, Thomas Price, Joseph Chapline, and James Smith attend the provincial meeting on the 21st inst. according to appointment, and that any five have power to act and represent this county."

This convention, after an adjournment from the 21st of November to the 8th of December, adopted resolutions encouraging the colonies to rely upon the products of their own fields and their own industry, and recommending "such of the inhabitants of this province as are from sixteen to fifty years of age to form themselves into companies of sixty-eight men; to choose a captain, two lieutenants, an ensign, four sergeants, four corporals, and one drummer for each company, and to use their utmost endeavors to make themselves masters of the military exercise. That each man be provided with a good firelock and bayonet fixed thereon, half a pound of powder, two pounds of lead, and a cartouch-box or powder-horn, and a bag for ball, and be in readiness to act in any emergency." It was further recommended that £1333 should be raised in Frederick by subscription to be expended by the committee of the county in the purchase of arms and ammunition.

At a meeting of the inhabitants of Frederick County, held at the court-house, on Tuesday, the 24th of January, 1775, John Hanson, chairman, Archibald Boyd, clerk, the association and resolves of the American Congress and the proceedings of the last Provincial Convention were read and unanimously approved. It was also

"I. *Resolved*, That Messrs. Charles Beatty, Henry Griffith, Thomas Sprigg Wooton, Jacob Funk, and Nathan Magruder, Richard Brooke, Zadock Magruder, William Baker, Thomas Cramphin, Jr., Alexander Bowie, Jr., William Deakins, Jr., John Murdock, Thomas Johns, Bernard O'Neal, Brooke Beall, Edward Burgess, Charles G. Griffith, Henry Griffith, Jr., William Bayley, Jr., Samuel Magruder, Nathaniel Offutt, Archibald Orme, Joseph Threlkeld, Walter Smith, Thomas Beall of George, Richard Crabb, William Luckett, William Luckett, Jr., Greenbury Griffith, Samuel Griffith, John Hanson, Thomas Price, Thomas Bowles, Conrad Grosh, Thomas Archley, Jonathan Wilson, Francis Deakins, Caspar Schaaff, Peter Hoffman, George Scott, Baker Johnson, Philip Thomas, Alexander C. Hanson, Archibald Boyd, Arthur Nelson, Andrew Scott, George Stricker, Adam Fisher, Wm. Ludwick, Weltner Van Swearingen, Wm. M. Beall, Jacob Young, Peter Grosh, Æneas Campbell, Elias Brunner, Frederick Kemp, John Haas, John Remsburg, Thomas Hawkins, Upton Sheredine, Basil Dorsey, John Lawrence, Charles Warfield, Ephraim Howard, Joseph Wells, David Moore, Joseph Wood, Norman Bruce, William Blair, David Schriver, Roger Johnson, Henry Cock, Robert Wood, William Albaugh, Jacob Mathias, Henry Crawle, Jacob Ambrose, David Richards, William Winchester, Philip Fishburn, William Hobbs, Thomas Cresap, Thomas Warren, Thomas Humphreys, Richard Davis, Jr., Charles Clinton, James Prather, George Bent, James Johnson, James Smith, Joseph Chapline, John Stull, Samuel Beall, Jr., William Baird, Joseph Sprigg, Christian Orendorff, Jonathan Hager, Conrad Hogmire, Chas. Swearingen, Henry Snavely, Richard Davis, Samuel Hughes, Joseph Perry, Joseph Smith, Thomas Hog, Thomas Prather, William McClary, John Swan, Eli Williams, Christopher Burkett, Thomas Brooke, Michael Raymer, Nicholas Tice, John Adlum, Samuel Norwood, Bartholomew Booth, Jacob Boyer, Michael Grosh, Jacob Miller, Andrew Bruce, John Darnall, John Remsburg, William Dorran, John Key, John Beall, John McCallister, Charles Beall, Lewis Kemp, John Stoner, Thomas Beatty, Thomas Gilbert, Abraham Hoff, P. Henry Thomas, Jacob Good, Westel Ridgely, Samuel Carrick, Abraham Hosteter, Baltzer Kelcholumer, Samuel Emmet, John Cary, Christopher Edelin, Amos Riggs, John Grimber, Leonard Smith, Nicholas Hower, Richard Northcraft, John Herriot, Richard Smith, Zacharias Ellis, Azel Waters, Martin Cassil, James Johnson, George Bare, Benjamin Johnson, and Abraham Paw be a committee of observation, with full powers to prevent any infraction of the said institution, and to carry the resolves of the American Congress and of the Provincial Convention into execution; that any seventy-five of those gentlemen have power to act for the county, and any five in each of the larger districts be authorized to act in any manner that concerns such Division only.

"II. *Resolved*, That the gentlemen appointed at the last meeting of this County a committee of Correspondence be hereby continued, and that the duration of their authority be limited to the second Tuesday in October next.

"III. *Resolved*, As the most convenient and effectual method of raising the sum of $1333, being this County's proportion of the $10,000 which the provincial convention has appointed to be raised for the purchase of arms and ammunition, that a subscription be immediately opened in every part of the County, and the following gentlemen be appointed to promote such subscriptions in their several Hundreds:

"For Salisbury Hundred, Jonathan Hager, Henry Snavely, and Jacob Sellers.

"For Upper Catoctin, Peter Bainbridge, Benjamin Eastburn, Caspar Smith, and Thomas Johnson.

"For the Lower part of New Foundland, Edward Burgess, Walter Beall, Joseph Perry.

"For Skipton, Thomas Cresap, Moses Rawlings, and Richard Davis, Jr.

"For Georgetown, William Deakins, Thomas Johns, Walter Smith.

"For Sharpsburg, Joseph Chapline and Christian Orendorf.

"For Lower part of Potomack Hundred, William Bayley, Samuel Wade Magruder, Andrew Hugh, and Charles Jones.

"For Tom's Creek Hundred, William Blair, William Sheales, and Benjamin Ogle.

"For Catoctin Hundred, George Stricker, William Luckett, Jr., and Westel Ridgely.

"For Upper Antietam Hundred, Jacob Funk, Conrad Hogmire, Joseph Perry, John Ingram.

"For Linton Hundred, Martin Johnson and Joseph Flint.

"For Cumberland Hundred, Charles Clinton.

"For Middle Monocacy, Thomas Beatty, Mathias Ringer, Christopher Stull, and T. Flemming.

"For Rock Creek Hundred, Thomas Cramphin, Zadock Magruder, W. Baker, and Allen Bowie.

"For Sugar Loaf Hundred, Francis Deakins, R. Smith, L. Plummer, Z. Waters, and Z. Linthicum.

"For Burnt Woods Hundred, Ephraim Howard, Charles Warfield, David Moore, John Lawrence, Henry Crowle, and William Hobbs.

"For Lower Antietam Hundred, Thomas Hog, Henry Butler, and Thomas Cramphin.

"For Linganore Hundred, John Beall, Charles G. Griffith, Nicholas Hobbs, Basil Dorsey, and William Duvall.

"For Conococheague, David Jones, Isaac Baker, and Jacob Friend.

"For Piney Creek Hundred, Jacob Good, John McCallister, Samuel McFarren, Abraham Hiter, and John Key.

"For Lower Monocacy Hundred, Lewis Kemp, John Darnall, Thomas Nowland, and Leonard Smith.

"For Northwest Hundred, Samuel Harwood, Peter Becraft, and Richard Beall, of Samuel.

"For Marsh Hundred, Charles Swearingen, Eli Williams, James Smith, Richard Davis, and George Swimley.

"For Upper Part of Potomac Hundred, Brooke Beall, Samuel West, Nathaniel Offutt, and Alexander Clagett.

"For Seneca, Charles Perry, Richard Crabb, Gerard Briscoe.

"For Pipe Creek Hundred, Andrew Bruce, William Winchester, David Schriver, and Nathaniel Norris.

"For Manor Hundred, William Beatty, Joseph Wood, Jr., Azel Waters, John Remsbury, Abraham Hoff, and Valentine Creager.

"For Upper Part of Monocacy Hundred, Henry Cox, Roger Johnson, Richard Butler.

"For upper part of New Foundland Hundred, Henry Griffith, Richard Brooke, and Henry Gaither, Sr.

"For Elizabeth Hundred, John Stull, Otho Holland Williams, John Swan, and John Rench.

"For Fredericktown Hundred, Phil. Thomas, Thomas Price, Baker Johnson, Peter Hoffman, and Ludwick Weltner.

"For Fort Frederick Hundred, Ezekial Cox.

"For Sugar Land Hundred, Æneas Campbell, John Fletcher, John Luckett, Alexander Whitaker, and Solomon Simpson.

"The said gentlemen are instructed to apply personally, or by Deputy, to every freeman in their respective Districts, and to solicit a generous contribution.

"They are ordered to state accounts of money received, and pay it to the Committee of Correspondence, which is hereby appointed to meet at Fredericktown, the 23d day of March next: and they are further ordered to report to the said Committee the names of persons (if any) who shall refuse to subscribe.

"IV. That Messrs. Thomas Johnson, William Deakins, Charles Beatty, George Murdock, John Stull, and John Swan, or any one of them, be empowered to contract, in behalf of the Committee of Correspondence, for any quantity of powder and Lead, to be paid for on the said 23d day of March.

"V. In order that a committee of observation may be more conveniently chosen, and a more proper representation of the people may be had, the several collectors in each Hundred are desired to give notice to those qualified by their estates to vote for Representatives of some time and place of meeting in the Hundred, to elect members for a Committee, agreeably to the following regulation:

"When the number of taxables exceed two hundred, and amounts to not more than four hundred, the District shall elect three members. The Collectors are ordered to return such Representatives to the Committee of Correspondence on the said 23d day of March; the Committee so chosen shall then meet, and the authority of the present Committee of Observation shall be dissolved.

"VI. *Resolved*, That Messrs. John Hanson, Charles Beatty, Upton Sheredine, Baker Johnson, Philip Thomas, Jacob Funk, Samuel Beall, Joseph Chapline, John Stull, James Smith, Henry Griffith, Thomas Sprigg Wootton, Richard Brooke, William Deakins, and Thomas Cramphin, or any five of them, shall represent this County to any Provincial convention to be held at the city of Annapolis before the second Tuesday of October next. A petition from the People called Dunkers and Mennonists was read. They express a willingness freely to contribute their money in support of the common cause of America, but pray an exemption from the Military Exercise on the score of their Religious Principles.

"*Resolved*, That this petition be referred to the Committee to be chosen agreeably to the fifth Resolve. In the mean time it is strictly enjoined that no violence be offered to the person or property of any one, but that all grounds of complaint be referred to said Committee.

"ARCH. BOYD, *Clerk.*"[1]

On the 15th of June, 1775, Col. George Washington, one of the Virginia delegates in Congress, was nominated by his friend and associate, Thomas John-

---

[1] As arms became necessary, a gun-lock factory was ordered by the convention in December, 1775, to be erected in Frederick, and the land was purchased. (Land Record B. D., No. 2, folio 471.) The site of the factory is now occupied by the coal-yard of Mr. Groshon, Messrs. Tyson & Son's warehouse, and J. E. Gifford's marble-works. By the act of 1778, ch. 4, it was ordered to be sold.

son, of Frederick, to be commander-in-chief of the Continental forces, and he was unanimously chosen. Having accepted his commission from the "United Colonies," Washington left Philadelphia on the 21st of June to take command of the army.

On the 17th of June the battle of Bunker Hill was fought, and from this hour the colonists were fully roused. In Maryland all was vigilance and activity. The manufacture of gunpowder, arms, and ammunition of every kind was encouraged. The two companies, assigned as the quota of the province under the resolution of Congress, were raised with the utmost spirit and dispatch in Frederick County, which then embraced, besides its present territory, all of Washington, Montgomery, Allegany, Garrett, and part of Carroll Counties. At a meeting of the Committee of Observation of Frederick, held in the court-house in Frederick Town on the 21st of June, a letter was read by John Hanson, chairman, from the delegates of Maryland in Congress, accompanied by the resolution passed on the 14th. The latter represented that two companies of expert riflemen were required of the county to join the army at Boston, "to be there employed as light infantry." The committee thereupon

"*Resolved*, That agreeable to the resolution of the Congress, and on the terms by them proposed, two companies of expert riflemen be forthwith raised and officered by the following gentlemen: Of the first company—Michael Cresap, captain; Thomas Warren, Joseph Cresap, Jr., Richard Davis, Jr., lieutenants. Of the second company—Thomas Price, captain; Otho Holland Williams, John Ross Key, lieutenants; another lieutenant to be chosen by Capt. Price and approved by the committee."

By the terms of enlistment the captains were to receive $20 per month; the lieutenants, $13¼; the sergeants, $8; the corporals, $7¼; the drummers, $7¼; and the privates, $6⅔; "that they find their own arms and clothes; that each company consist of a captain, three lieutenants, four sergeants, four corporals, a drummer, and sixty-eight privates; that the form of enlistment be as follows:

"I, A. B., have this —— day of —— voluntarily enlisted myself as a soldier in the *American* Continental Army for one year, unless sooner discharged. I do bind myself to conform in all instances to such rules and regulations as are or shall hereafter be established for the government of the said Army."

The character and appearance of the riflemen, and their skill as marksmen, excited the curiosity of a gentleman in Frederick, who, in a letter to a friend in Philadelphia, dated Aug. 1, 1775, thus describes them before they left Frederick:

"Notwithstanding the urgency of my business, I have been detained in this place by an occurrence truly agreeable. I have had the happiness of seeing Capt. Michael Cresap marching at the head of a formidable company of upwards of 130 men from the mountains and backwoods, painted like Indians, armed with tomahawks and rifles, and dressed in hunting shirts and moccasins; and though some of them had traveled near eight hundred miles from the banks of the Ohio, they seemed to walk light and easy, and not with less spirit than at the first hour of their march. Health and vigor, after what they had undergone, declared them to be intimate with hardships and familiar with danger. Joy and satisfaction were visible in the crowd that met them. Had Lord North been present, and could have been assured that the brave leader could raise thousands of such to defend his country, what think you?—would the hatchet and block have intruded upon his mind? I had an opportunity of attending the captain during his stay in town, and watched the behavior of his men and the manner in which he treated them; for it seems that all who go out to war under him do not only pay the most willing obedience to him as their commander, but in every instance of distress look upon him as their friend or father. A great part of his time was spent in listening to and relieving their wants without any apparent sense of fatigue and trouble. When complaints were before him he determined them with kindness and spirit, and on every occasion condescended to please without losing his dignity.

"Yesterday the company were supplied with a small quantity of powder from the magazine, which wanted airing, and was not good for rifles. In the evening, however, they were drawn out to show the gentlemen of the town their dexterity at shooting. A clapboard, with a mark the size of a dollar, was put up; they began to fire off-hand, and the bystanders were surprised, so few shots being made that were not close to or in the paper.

"When they had shot for a time in this way, some lay on their backs, some on their breast or side, others ran twenty or thirty steps, and, firing, appeared to be equally certain of the mark. With this performance the company were more than satisfied, when a young man took up the board in his hand, not by the end, but by the side, and holding it up, his brother walked to the distance, and very coolly shot into the white; laying down his rifle, he took up the board, and, holding it as it was held before, the second brother shot as the former had done.

"By this exercise I was more astonished than pleased. But will you believe me, when I tell you, that one of the men took the board, and placing it between his legs, stood with his back to the tree, while another drove the centre? What would a regular army of considerable strength, in the forests of America, do with one thousand of these men, who want nothing to preserve their health and courage but water from the spring, with a little parched corn, with what they can easily procure in hunting, and who, wrapped in their blankets, in the damp of night, would choose the shade of a tree for their covering and the earth for their bed?"

At the time Cresap was appointed to command the Western Maryland Rifles, he was returning to his home at Old Town, now Washington County, from his settlement on the Ohio. He was met, it is said, near Cumberland, by a faithful friend with the message that he was chosen to command one of the two rifle companies.

"When I communicated my business," says the messenger, "and announced his appointment, instead of becoming elated, he became pensive and solemn, as if his spirits were really depressed, or as if he had a presentiment that this was his death-warrant. He said he was in bad health and his affairs in a deranged state, but that, nevertheless, as the committee had selected him, and as he understood from me his father had pledged himself that he should accept of this appointment, he would go, let the consequences be what they might. He then directed me to proceed to the west side of the mountains, and publish to his old companions in arms this his intention. This I did, and in a very short time collected and brought to him, at his residence in Old Town, about twenty-two as fine fellows as ever handled a rifle, and most, if not all, of them completely equipped."

The riflemen set out from Frederick Town on the 18th of July, 1775, on their march to Cambridge, Mass., and after traveling five hundred and fifty miles over the rough and difficult roads of that period, they arrived on the 9th of August at their destination, thus making the journey in twenty-two days without the loss of a man.[1]

Cresap's company was the first from the South to reach Cambridge, and although in bad health, he marched on the 13th of August with Capt. Daniel Morgan's company of Virginia riflemen to Roxbury, on the south side of Boston, where they joined the American army under the command of Gen. Washington. Mr. Thatcher in his military journal of August, 1775, in noticing their arrival, says,—

"They are remarkably stout and hardy men, many of them exceeding six feet in height. They are dressed in white frocks, or rifle shirts, and round hats. These men are remarkable for the accuracy of their aim, striking a mark with great certainty at two hundred yards' distance. At a review, a company of them, while on a quick advance, fired their balls into objects of seven inches diameter at the distance of two hundred and fifty yards. They are now stationed on our lines, and their shot have frequently proved fatal to British officers and soldiers, who expose themselves to view, even at more than double the distance of common musket-shot." [2]

McCurtin's journal gives some interesting particulars of the earlier experiences of these representatives of Western Maryland in the theatre of war. On the 15th (of August), he says, "we had a most amazing shout of cannon thunders, which at this time seemed strange and shocking to our young soldiers, during this our first alarm." Three days later he relates that as "he was at breakfast in the former dwelling-house of Dr. Williams they (the British) fired four thirty-two-pounders at the house, one of which rushed through the room and dashed one side out of the chimney, broke two partitions, and filled our dishes with plastering, ceiling, and bricks. George Switcher, Sergt. Torrel, and William Johnson were in the room when this happened. Any man may judge whether or no this did not surprise us four young heroes; however, as I cannot say for the minds of them who were in company with me, but I know, to the best of my thinking, that I went down two pair of stairs of three strides without a fall, and as soon as I was out of doors ran to the breastwork in great haste, which is our place of safety, without the least concern about my breakfast, to James McCancie's amazement." [3]

In 1776 these companies were incorporated in a rifle regiment, of which Stephenson, of Virginia, was appointed colonel, Moses Rawlings, of Old Town, Frederick (now Washington) County, lieutenant-colonel, and Otho Holland Williams, of Frederick (now Williamsport, Washington County), major. Upon Stephenson's death the command devolved upon Rawlings, and the regiment formed part of the garrison of Fort Washington, in the State of New York, at the time it was attacked by Sir William Howe. In this attack the rifle regiment behaved with splendid courage, but were made prisoners of war with the rest of the command on the capture of the fort.

---

[1] Extract from a letter from a gentleman in Frederick Town to his friend in Baltimore Town, dated July 19, 1775:

"On Monday last, July 17th, Capt. Morgan, from Virginia, with his company of riflemen (all chosen), marched through this place on their way to Boston. Their appearance was truly martial, their spirits amazingly elated, breathing nothing but a desire to join the American army and to engage the enemies of American liberties. They were met a mile out of town by three companies, viz.: Capt. Price's company of riflemen, Capt. Grosh's and Capt. Beatty's companies of militia, and escorted a few miles out of town, amidst the acclamation of all the inhabitants who attended them. And yesterday Capt. Price with his company also marched, and surely never were two finer companies raised in any country more determined to conquer or die than those two companies are. Capt. Cresap also with his brave company have marched. I need not say anything of Capt. Cresap's undaunted courage. Not an American but knows him to be an intrepid warrior, and of course he knows his men, and has culled them from the many. We are also in hourly expectation of Capt. Stinson with his company in this town, on his way to Boston. God grant him a speedy and happy arrival there. So many offered to join the above companies, that not one of them but might have had one hundred men at least."

[2] Capt. Cresap, as we have before stated, after about three months' efficient service in the neighborhood of Boston, was forced by continued illness to obtain leave to return home; but, finding himself too sick to proceed, stopped in New York, where he died of fever on the 18th of October, 1775, at the early age of thirty-three. On the following day his remains, attended by a large concourse of people, were buried with military honors in Trinity Churchyard. Mr. Brantz Mayer says that on a visit to the churchyard of Trinity on the 2d of June, 1860, he discovered the long-neglected grave and gravestone of the pioneer immediately opposite the door of the north transept of the church. It was of sandstone, and when last seen, in 1865, was broken off near the ground and propped up.

[3] On the 30th of August William Norris, a member of one of the rifle companies, died "with a long sickness, and was buried in as genteel a manner as we could get it done."

In the mean time the citizens of Frederick were not idle. At a meeting of the freeholders and others of the freemen of the middle district of Frederick County at the court-house in Frederick Town, the 12th of September, 1775, agreeable to the resolve of the last Provincial Convention, the following gentlemen were chosen a Committee of Observation of said district, viz.: George Stricker, Charles Beatty, Christopher Edelin, Upton Sheredine, Baker Johnson, William Blair, Dr. Adam Fisher, Conrad Grosh, John Hanson, George Murdock, John Adlum, Michael Raymer, Dr. Philip Thomas, William Luckett, John Haas, Joseph Wood, Jr., John Stoner, and made choice of Messrs. Charles Beatty and Baker Johnson, by a ballot, to attend the Provincial Convention.

At a meeting of the middle district committee of Frederick County, the 14th of September, 1775, there were present Messrs. George Stricker, Charles Beatty, Christopher Edelin, Upton Sheredine, Baker Johnson, William Blair, Adam Fisher, William Beatty, Conrad Grosh, John Hanson, George Murdock, John Adlum, Michael Raymer, Dr. Philip Thomas, William Luckett, John Haas, Joseph Wood, and John Stoner.

On the 12th of September a meeting of the freemen of the upper district of Frederick County was held for the purpose of choosing a Committee of Observation and delegates to the Provincial Convention, and the following persons were elected: for the Committee of Observation, John Stull, Charles Swearingen, Andrew Rench, Jonathan Hager, John Sellars, Col. Cresap, James Smith, John Rench, Ezekiel Cox, Samuel Hughes, William Baird, Joseph Smith, William Yates, Conrad Hogmire, Christian Orendorff, George Zwingly, Joseph Chaplain, and Col. James Beale. Delegates, William Beard and John Stull.

The committee met for the first time on the 14th of September, 1775, when the following members were present: John Stull, Esq., president; Samuel Hughes, secretary; James Smith, John Rench, Conrad Hogmire, William Rench, Z. Cox, George Zwingly, C. Orendorff, Andrew Rench, John Sellars, W. Baird, Charles Swearingen.

A letter being received from the Committee of Correspondence for the middle district of the county relative to the raising of two companies of minute-men, the committee of the upper part of the county met for that purpose on Monday, the 18th of September, 1775, at Elizabethtown (now called Hagerstown) with the following persons present: John Stull, Esq, president; Samuel Hughes, secretary; Capts. Hogmire, Smith, Hager; Messrs. John Rench, John Sellars, Andrew Rench, George Zwingly, Charles Swearingen. It was

"*Resolved*, That Messrs. Henry Shryock and James Chaplain be appointed to enroll two companies of minute-men, being the number allotted for this district; and they are hereby appointed for that purpose."

The committee then adjourned to the first Monday in October, 1775.

The following persons were also appointed to serve as a committee for licensing suits in Frederick County: James Smith, Samuel Hughes, Conrad Hogmire, Col. Beall, John Rench, John Sellars, and Charles Swearingen. Capt. Jonathan Hager was appointed to receive all sums of money that might be voluntarily given for the public good. It was also

"*Ordered*, That the following persons carry the association to all freemen resident in this district, and require their subscription to the same: Linton Hundred, Thomas Hynes; Fort Frederick, Benj. Johnson; Conococheague, Thomas Swearingen, David Jones, Isaac Baker; Salisbury, Doct. Schnebly, Henry Cellar; Elizabeth Town, Danl. Clapsadle, Ludwick Young, Andrew Link; Upper Antietam, Daniel Perry, Christian Lantz, Geo. Dement; Lower Antietam, Thomas Crampton, Conrad Schnebly; Sharpsburg, Doct. Cruse, John Reynolds, Jr.; Marsh Hundred, Richard Davis, Ignatius Sims, Peter White. Application being made to the committee by the committee of George's Creek, on the Monongahela, for Ammunition, it was

"*Ordered*, That Mr. Stull deliver unto Mr. J. Swearingen, for the use of the said committee, seventy-four pounds of gunpowder, at 3s. 6d. per pound, and eighty pounds of lead, at 6d. per pound, and receive the money for the same, and keep it until further directions from this committee.

"*Resolved*, That each member of this committee shall pay 5s. fine for each day's non-attendance without a lawful excuse; Col. Cresap excepted.

"*Resolved*, That each member pay his club of the expenses attending this committee, present or absent."

The committee then adjourned to the first Monday in October, 1775.

From the proceedings of the Committee of Observation for Elizabethtown (now Hagerstown) district we make the following interesting extracts, which show that the hearts of the colonists of this section of the province were full of sympathy for the patriotic cause, and that their hands were full of aid:

"The committee met according to adjournment. Present, Joseph Smith, Esq., in the chair; Samuel Hughes, secretary; James Smith, C. Orendorff, Z. Cox, C. Swearingen, Capts. Hager and Stull, C. Hogmire, G. Zwingly, J. Sellars, W. Yates, W. Rench, and W. Baird.

"It appears to this committee (from the representation of some of the members who have endeavored to get their neighbors to enroll in companies of militia) that the greatest number refuse in consequence of several religious sects being excepted by the resolves of the convention.

"*Resolved*, That this committee is of opinion that it is highly reasonable that every person who enjoys the benefit of their religion and protection of the laws of this free country ought to contribute, either in money or military service, towards the defence of these invaluable rights.

"*Resolved*, That two shillings and sixpence, currency, per week (for all those who are constrained by religious principles from contributing their proportion in military service) would be equal to mustering, agreeable to the directions of the convention.

"*Resolved*, That a remonstrance be sent to the next convention, setting forth the cause and substance of the above resolve.

"*Ordered*, That the commissioned officers of the militia companies in this district attend at Elizabeth Town on the third Monday of this month, in order to vote for persons to be recommended to the council of safety, as field-officers.

"The committee adjourns till the 16th October.

"The committee met according to adjournment. Present, John Stull, Esq., in the chair; Samuel Hughes, secretary; George Zwingly, James Smith, J. Rench, C. Orendorff, C. Swearingen, and W. Rench, Capt. Hager, W. Baird, John Sellars, Z. Cox.

"On a motion being made and seconded, it was

"*Ordered*, That a letter should be written to the committee of correspondence in the middle district that it is the opinion of this district that the battalion of minute-men for this county would receive great advantage by being kept together and instructed, and that this committee are desirous such a plan should be adopted, and that a meeting of the three districts of this county would be advisable; and, in case such meeting should be appointed, Messrs. James Smith and Samuel Hughes are appointed to attend at said meeting, with full power to act for this committee in the aforesaid business.

"*Ordered*, That all those who have enrolled with Mr. Brook and Mr. Dement, do join and form one company, and immediately proceed to the choice of officers.

"On motion of Mr. Thomas Frinck, Sr., of the Upper District of Frederick County, that he hath been often jostled by the residents of the upper part of Frederick County by refusing to pay their public dues, it is the opinion and advice of this committee that they ought to pay their levies and all their public dues for the support of the civil government.

"A motion being made by a member of the committee that as sundry companies of the militia that are not yet made up and ordered according to the directions of the provincial convention, and as the numbers of the said companies appointed to be raised do not amount to make up two battalions, it is

"*Resolved* by the committee, in order to satisfy the populace, that an election be held for the Hagerstown battalion on the 22d day of October, 1775, and for the lower battalion on the 30th day of October; and that the said lower battalion shall transmit a full and clear copy of their election to the committee of correspondence for the said district, in order that they may transmit the same to the Council of Safety of this province that they may take order therein.

"Committee adjourns to 23d.

"The committee met on the 11th of November, 1775, Col. Joseph Smith in the chair.

"*Agreed*, That Capts. Stull, Hogmire, Baker, Rench, Hughes, Kershner, Shryock, Clapsadle, be the first battalion; Capts. Orendorff, Shelley, Williams, Davis, Smith, Demond, Swearingen, Walling, be the second battalion.

"Whereas it hath been represented to this committee by Mr. John Swan that his character has been much aspersed by a certain John Shryock, as having said that he suspected the said Mr. Swan of having been an enemy to America, the said John Shryock being called to this committee, and making nothing appear against him, the said John Swan is honorably acquitted by this committee of said charge.

"The committee adjourns to Monday the 20th inst.

"At the meeting of the committee on the 20th of November, 1775. Present, Mr. James Smith, president; Messrs. Stull, Baird, Swearingen, A. Rench, Zwingly, John Rench, and S. Hughes. Doct. John C—— [Connolly], of Fort Pitt, and certain persons called Doctor S—— [Smith], and M. C—— [Cameron] were bro't before the committee and accused of being inimical to the liberties of America.

"*Resolved, unanimously*, That the said doct. C—— (from certain papers produced to this committee, and acknowledged to have been written by him) is a dangerous enemy to the colonies, and as such shall be sent to the council of safety or convention for further trial.

"It was also *Resolved*, That the aforesaid Doctor S—— and M. C—— being found guilty of many equivocations, and coming in company with the aforesaid Doct. C—— from the dangerous councils of Lord Dunmore, that it is the opinion of this committee that the said S—— and C—— shall be sent to the council of safety or convention for further enquiry. The committee adjourns till the 1st Monday in December.

"The committee met accordingly. Present, Mr. Jas. Smith in the chair; Christian Orendorff, John Rench, Andrew Rench, C. Swearingen, George Zwingly, S. Hughes. By order the committee appointed Daniel Heaster to arbitrate and award on an affair of controversy now depending betwixt William Sitsster and Christian Shneakenberger, in the room of Capt. Jonathan Hager, dec'd.

"*Ordered*, That Samuel Hughes and Andrew Rench do attend at Mr. Harry's on Thursday next, in order to receive the accounts of necessaries supplied the rifle companies, and transmit the same to the treasurer in Philadelphia for payment.

"The committee adjourn till the fourth Monday in this month.

"December the 18th, 1775, the committee met: Jos. Smith in the chair.

"Christian Orendorff, Andrew W. Rench, George Zwingly, John Rench, John Sellars, Conrad Hogmire.

"*Agreed*, That Capt. Shryock is to have one pound of powder and four pounds of lead, for which he was out in taking C——.

"*Agreed*, That each captain of the two battalions is to have two pounds of powder and six pounds of lead, to be applied only to the use of the public in case of an invasion, and to be returned if demanded.

"*Agreed*, That if Capt. H—— comes home before the first day of January next, and does not come to this committee upon the complaint of Lieut. William Hyser, Adam Smith, and John Oster, he then shall be sent for.

"The committee was called on the 10th of January, 1776, Samuel Hughes in the chair.

"Capts. Hogmire, Smith, Swearingen, and Rench, Messrs. Zwingly, Sellars, John Rench. Dr. S——, who made his escape from Frederick Town, was brought before the committee, and several letters of consequence from Dr. C—— to the enemies of America in the back country were found with him.

"*Resolved*, That the said Dr. S—— be sent under safe guard to the congress.

"The committee adjourns till Monday next.

"The committee met, according to adjournment, January 15. Present, Joseph Smith in chair; John Rench, C. Hogmire, James Smith, A. Rench, John Sellars, C. Orendorff, G. Zwingly, S. Hughes.

"*Ordered*, That Henry Yost be supplied with six pounds of powder to prove his muskets with.

"The committee adjourned until the first Monday in February.

"The committee met, according to adjournment, on Monday, Feb. 5, 1776. Present, John Stull, Esq., in the chair; A.

Rench, John Sellars, C. Hogmire, C. Swearingen, G. Zwingly, Saml. Hughes, John Rench, E. Cox, Wm. Yates, Wm. Baird.

"*Ordered*, That Thomas Brooke be clerk to this committee. The committee proceed to the trial of Capt. S. H——, and after examination of the evidence do honorably acquit him, they not being able to make anything appear against him. Henry Y—— having been charged with making use or selling the powder allowed him by this committee to prove his muskets, is honorably acquitted, as he has fully satisfied the committee he is clear of the charge.

"*Ordered*, That Basil Prather be recommended by this committee as a captain, and Henry Prather as lieutenant, to the Continental Congress.

"The committee adjourns to the third Monday in this month.

"The committee met, according to adjournment, the 19th February. Present, Maj. Joseph Smith, in chair; Col. John Stull, Majs. C. Swearingen and A. Rench, Capts. J. Sellars, C. Orendorff, C. Hogmire, Mr. John Rench.

"Capt. John Sellars and Lieut. M'Laughlin appointed to enquire what number of the country's arms are in the hands of Capt. Baker, and to know what order they are in.

"*Ordered*, That Capt. S. Hughes have nine pounds of powder to prove one of the cannon.

"*Ordered*, That Mr. Moses Chapline be recommended by this committee to the Continental Congress as a fit person to take the command of a company as a captain in the service of his country.

"*Ordered*, That Lieut.-Col. Smith, of the Thirty-sixth Battalion, be recommended to the council of safety or convention of this province as first colonel to said battalion in the place of Col. Beall, who has refused his commission; and Capt. Orendorff as lieutenant-colonel to said battalion, and Jno. Reynolds captain, and George Kefer first lieutenant to Capt. Orendorff's company.

"The committee adjourns to the first Monday in March.

"The committee met, according to adjournment, the 4th March, 1776. Present, Capt. Conrad Hogmire in the chair; Col. John Stull, Capt. J. Sellars, John Rench, Capt. Samuel Hughes, Col. A. Rench, G. Zwingly.

"*Ordered*, That the following persons hand about the associations: Thomas Brooks, George Demont, John Charlton, Joshua Barnes, Jas. Walling, J. Rench, J. Sellars, David Jones, John Barnett, J. Stull, Saml. Hughes, Peter Shelley, Daniel Perry, John Reynolds.

"*Ordered*, That the captains of each hundred take an association paper and present it to the inhabitants of their hundred for signing, and make an exact account of those that sign and those that refuse, with their reasons for refusing, Conocheague hundred excepted, David Jones, J. Barnett, Balsar Mondy, and Matthias Oats being appointed for that purpose.

"*Ordered*, That Col. J. Stull, Capt. S. Hughes, and Col. Joseph Smith be judges of the election for the choice of six members in the place of Capt. Hager (deceased), Col. Samuel Beall, Col. Thomas Cresap, Mr. Joseph Chapline (who refused), Messrs. Cox and William Yates, who are taken into the upper hundred.

"*Ordered*, That Henry R—— be kept under a guard of six men until sent to the Council of Safety for trial; but, in case he shall sign the association, enroll into some company, ask pardon of this committee, and give good security for his good behavior for the future, to be released.

"*Ordered*, That the sheriff of Frederick County obtain a general warrant on his list of public levys and clergy for the last year.

"The committee adjourns to the third Monday in this month.

"The committee met on Monday, the 18th March. Present, William Baird in the chair; John Stull, Conrad Hogmire, A. Rench, Michael Fockler, William Heyser.

"The committee was called the 6th of April. Present, Henry Shryock in the chair; Col. A. Rench, Capts. Michael Fockler, J. Sellars, William Heyser, Messrs. J. Rench, C. Lantz. Was brought before this committee E—— and P—— G——, for speaking unbecoming word against the association, acknowledged their fault, and signed.

"The committee adjourns to the 8th of April, nine o'clock.

"The committee met, according to adjournment, on the 8th of April. Members present, Col. Beall in the chair; Charles Swearingen, M. Fockler, A. Rench, J. Sellars, C. Orendorff, W. Heyser, Henry Shryock, John Rench, G. Zwingly, C. Lantz, John Stull, Joseph Smith, C. Hogmire, J. Chapline, William Baird.

"'IN COUNCIL OF SAFETY, ANNAPOLIS,
"'March 23, 1776.

"'*Gentlemen*,—The great difficulty we find in providing blankets for the regular forces raised for the defence of this province obliges us to apply to the committee of observation for the several counties and districts, earnestly requesting that they would use their endeavors to procure from the housekeepers in their respective counties and districts all the blankets or rugs that they can with any convenience spare, for which the council will pay such prices as the committees shall agree on, as well as any expense that may arise in collecting them together; and when you have procured any quantity, you will send them to Annapolis, to Col. Smallwood, or, in his absence, to the commanding officer on this station, who will receive the same, and give orders on the council for the payment thereof.

"'We hope that the friends to our cause in the county will contribute everything in their power to the comfortable subsistence of the soldiery in this respect; it will be an act of great humanity, and render an essential service to the public.

"'We are, Gentlemen, your most O^{bt} servants. By order.

"'DANIEL, OF ST. THOS., JENNIFER, P.'

"In consequence of the preceding letter from the honorable the council of safety of this province, we have, agreeably to their request, furnished them with what quantity of blankets and rugs the inhabitants of this district can with any convenience spare, and a price estimated on them by this committee as follows:

	£	s.	d.
Wm. Baird, 1 blanket	0	17	6
John Parks, 1 rug	0	12	0
Andrew Rench, 1 blanket	0	12	6
Simon Myer, "	0	15	0
Philip Rymeby, 3 coverlets	2	10	0
Geo. Fry, 1 blanket	0	7	6
Felty Safety, 1 blanket	0	5	0
Jacob Lazear, "	0	12	6
Joseph Birely, 1 coverlet	1	8	0
" " 1 blanket	0	5	0
Richard Davis, "	0	10	0
Thos. Prather, "	0	18	0
Ch'n Rhorer, "	0	10	0
Leonard Shryock, "	0	12	0
Robert Guthrie, 1 coverlet	1	10	0
Christian Miller, "	1	10	0
Jacob Prunk, 1 blanket	0	14	0
Jacob Rohrer, "	0	12	6
Ellen Miller, "	0	9	0
Chas. Swearingen, 1 blanket	0	10	0
Ch'n Eversole, "	0	9	0
" " 1 quilt	0	15	0
" " 1 coverlet	0	17	6
John Ingram, 1 blanket	0	15	0
Adam Grimer, 2 blankets	1	18	0
Wm. Douglass, 1 blanket	0	10	0

		£	s.	d.
Matthias Need, 1 blanket		0	12	0
Michael Ott,	"	0	5	0
John Feagen,	"	0	16	0
" "	"	0	16	0
Jerentiah Wells,	"	0	10	0
Joseph Rench,	"	0	11	0
Zach'h Spires,	"	0	10	0
Matthias Nead,	"	0	10	0
Henry Startzman,	"	0	12	0
George Swingly,	"	0	16	0
George Hoffman,	"	0	7	6
Jacob Brumbaugh,	"	21	3	0
Michael Miller,	"	42	17	0
George Hartte,	"	0	18	0
John Roltrer,	"	20	10	0
Christ'r Burgard,	"	0	12	0
Jacob Good, 1 rug		0	16	0
John Rench, 1 blanket		0	12	0
John Stull,	"	0	14	0

"Received of Conrad Sheitz forty-four blankets for the use of this province, which were delivered him by the committee of Observation of Elizabeth Town district.

"Received by me this 12th day of April, 1776.

"GEO. STRICKER.

"Col. John Stull, Received the remaining seven blankets, for the use of the province. Col. Stull delivered 112 lbs. Powder (belonging to the public) to Capt. Burgess, in order to prove the cannon at D. & S. Hughes' works.

"*Ordered*, That the said quantity remain in the possession of D. & S. Hughes until this committee gives further order thereon.

"The committee adjourns till Saturday next, two o'clock.

"The committee met according to adjournment. Present, Col. Samuel Beall in the chair; Joseph Smith, John Keller, Mich'l Fockler, Wm. Heyser, John Stull, Henry Shryock, A. Rench, Christian Lantz, G. Zwingly, J. Rench, Conrad Hogmire.

"The committee orders that Major Henry Shryock and Capt. Michael Fockler shall receive of Mr. Daniel Heister what money is in his hands, for arms and other necessaries purchased here for Capt. Mich'l Cresap's company, signed and ordered by the committee.

"The committee adjourns to the 29th day of April.

"April the 29, 1776, the committee met according to adjournment. Present, Col. J. Smith, Geo. Swingly, S. Hughes, Wm. Baird, John Rench, Saml. Beall, Jr., C. Swearingen, Ch'n Lantz, Wm. Heyser, Christian Orendorff, John Sellars, John Stull, Conrad Hogmire. Samuel Beall, Jr., chosen chairman, and James Clark appointed clerk. Appeared Maj. Henry Shryock and Joseph Chaplin.

"*Resolved*, That this committee do pay the clerk seven shillings and sixpence for each day that he shall attend, and that he consider himself under the ties of honor not to disclose or reveal the secrets of the said committee.

"The committee adjourns to three o'clock in the afternoon.

"The committee met according to adjournment. On motion, *Resolved*, That the several returns of non-enrollers and non-associators be considered [here follow sundry lists of the names of persons who refused to enroll or associate]. On motion that the committee sit at Sharpsburg once in three times, the committee concurs therewith.

"The committee adjourns until the first Tuesday in May.

"May 7, committee met according to adjournment. Members present, Col. S. Beall in the chair; Andrew Rench, G. Chaplin, Henry Shryock, C. Hogmire, S. Hughes, Wm. Heyser, John Sellars, Chs. Swearingen, George Swingly, John Stull. James Clark continued as clerk. It was resolved that no personal disputes and reflections should pass in committee. No questions to be put and voted to without a motion being made and seconded. The committee adjourn.

"*Resolved*, That consideration be had of the summonses issued at the last committee for the appearance of sundry persons before them this day, to show cause why they do not enroll and associate, and deliver up their arms, in which the committee concurred, and proceeded to examine the returns made thereon, when it appeared that sundry persons had due notice accordingly, and were called in turn.

"And as such as have appeared not, or are not able to give any satisfactory reasons to this committee, why they did not or do not enroll and associate, and deliver up their arms, according to the resolve of the late convention in December last, be fined and proceeded against.

"The committee adjourned for half an hour, met accordingly, and adjourns to the morrow, to meet at 9 o'clk A.M.

"Wednesday, 8 May, 1776. The committee met according to adjournment,—all the members present as on yesterday, except Capts. Hughes, Hogmire, and Sellars. Appeared Mr. John Rench.

"*Ordered*, That the sundry persons do pay the sums annexed to their names in one month from the date hereof, and deliver up their fire arms immediately, if they have any, except pistols, to the several persons appointed to receive the same." [Here follows a long list of names, with the fines annexed.]

"This day Col. J. Stull made known to this committee that he received from the treasurer, Thomas Harwood, by order of the council of safety, £137 9s. 6d. current money, it being the sum due for 51 blankets purchased by the committee for the use of the province, by order of the council of safety.

"*Ordered*, That Captains James Walling, P'r. Reed, Basil Williams, Michael Fockler, Martin Kershner, John Sellars, S. Hughes, and C. Hogmire be empowered by Warrant to receive the sundry sums of money heretofore assessed by this committee against the several persons, as per lists to be made and annexed thereto, who have not enrolled, and the fire arms they may have from those who have not associated, agreeably to the resolution of this convention in December last, within each of their districts, to be made out in manner and form following:

"'You are hereby authorized or empowered to receive from sundry persons the sums of money annexed to each of their several names, as per list hereunto annexed, at the end of one month from the date hereof, and such fire arms immediately, except pistols, that are or may be in their possession, or otherwise may be their or either of their properties, whenever found, and make return thereof; to sit next after the time aforesaid, being the sums levied and assessed on them and each of them for not enrolling and associating, agreeably to the directions of the convention of December last. And this shall be your authority. Given under my hand this 8 of May 1776, by order of the committee.'

"The above warrant, with the separate lists of names and sums annexed to the several gentlemen appointed for that purpose, to be by them collected, agreeably to the order of the committee.

"The committee adjourned to the first Tuesday in June."[1]

---

[1] Great difficulty was experienced at the beginning of the war in obtaining supplies; the arsenal at Annapolis was almost empty. To overcome these difficulties the convention gave encouragement and gratuities for the manufacture of saltpetre, materials for clothing, and munitions of war. Powder-mills were erected, and Col. Hughes, of Washington County, agreed to furnish cannon for the province, and established a foundry on the Potomac River, one mile above Georgetown, where the

While her sons were rendering gallant service to the cause of American liberty in a distant section of the country, Frederick itself was threatened with a formidable danger. As early as July, 1775, John Hanson, Jr., wrote to Peyton Randolph, of Virginia, the first president of the "Continental Congress:" "There is too much reason to believe that an expedition will be set on foot by the British and Indians in Canada against the western frontiers of this State (Maryland), Virginia, and Pennsylvania. Agents and allies of the king and parliament, of Gen. Gage and Lord Dunmore, it is believed in this place, are now operating with the Delaware and Shawnese Indians in Ohio, and bands in Kentucky and Canada, with a view to destroy our frontier towns and desolate our homes and firesides. We are determined to keep a vigilant eye on all such agents and emissaries, but it would be highly prudent to take early measures to supply the arsenal and barracks at Fredericktown with arms and ammunition, to enable the male population to defend all the inhabitants, in case the emergency should arise in which it will become our solemn duty to act." These fears were not without foundation. Governor Dunmore, of Virginia, who had been making ineffectual efforts to maintain the royal authority in that colony, being at length forced to fly from Williamsburg, sought refuge on board an English man-of-war, and inaugurated a predatory warfare upon the coast, extending his operations to Maryland. Instigated by a ferocious spirit of revenge he reduced the town of Norfolk to ashes, and with the double design of cutting off communication between the Northern and Southern colonies, and of compelling a division of the Continental army under Washington, employed Dr. John Connolly, a native of Lancaster, Pa., to incite the Indians to a war upon the frontier and to raise an army at Detroit, which was to seize Pittsburgh, and from this base invade the back settlements of Virginia and Maryland. After establishing a strong post at Cumberland it was proposed to seize Alexandria, where Governor Dunmore was to meet them with a fleet and a body of runaway slaves from the lower part of the Potomac. Alexandria was to be strongly fortified, and communication cut off between the Northern and Southern colonies.

Connolly was born and bred near Wright's Ferry, Pa., and according to Ormsby, led a roving life in the Illinois country "till he could subsist there no longer." He appeared at Pittsburgh a few years before the commencement of the Revolution, where he was introduced to Lord Dunmore, " who traveled through the western country to sound the inclinations of the inhabitants as well as the Indians. Connolly, like a hungry wolf, closed with Dunmore a bargain that he would secure a considerable interest among the white inhabitants and the Indians on the frontier. In consequence of this agreement my lord made him a deed of gift of two thousand acres of land at the Falls of Ohio." Connolly showed himself a serviceable agent in the border troubles between Virginia and Pennsylvania, and when the struggle with the mother-country began, willingly lent himself to the designs of Lord Dunmore. On the 25th of July, 1775, Connolly, who had been stationed at Fort Pitt, joined Lord Dunmore on board the "Fowey" man-of-war, where the plan of attack already described was formed. Lord Dunmore feeling that it was necessary to secure the indorsement and authority of Gen. Gage, sent him to Boston, where Connolly presented the following proposals to the British commander:

"*Proposals for raising an Army to the Westward, and for effectually obstructing a Communication between the Southern and Northern Governments.*

"As I have, by direction from his Excellency Lord Dunmore, prepared the Ohio Indians to act in concert with me against his Majesty's enemies in that quarter, and have also dispatched intelligence to the different officers of the militia on the frontiers of Augusta County, in Virginia, giving them Lord Dunmore's assurances that such of them as shall hereafter evince their loyalty to his Majesty by putting themselves under my command, when I shall appear among them with proper authority for that purpose, of a confirmation of titles to their lands, and the quantity of three hundred acres to all who should take up arms in the support of the constitution, when the present rebellion subsided, I will undertake to penetrate through Virginia, and join his Excellency Lord Dunmore at Alexandria early next spring, on the following conditions and authority:

"1st. That your Excellency will give me a commission to act as Major-commandant of such troops as I may raise and embody on the frontiers, with a power to command to the westward and employ such serviceable French and English partisans as I can employ by pecuniary rewards or otherwise.

"2d. That your Excellency will give orders to Captain Lord on the Illinois to remove himself, with the garrison under his command, from Fort Gage to Detroit, by the Aubache, bringing with him all the artillery, stores, &c., &c., to facilitate which undertaking he is to have authority to hire boats, horses, Frenchmen, Indians, &c., &c., to proceed with all possible expedition on that route, as the weather may occasionally permit, and to put himself under my command on his arrival at Detroit.

"3d. That the commissary at Detroit shall be empowered to furnish such provision as I may judge necessary for the good

---

first cannon were made in this country. A portion of the old stone building still remains, while broken fragments of cannon are at this time to be found in the stream of water that flows at the base of the building. Daniel and James Hughes, of the Antietam Iron-Works, in Washington County, and John Yoast, of Georgetown, also made cannon for the Revolution. Shells and cannon were also manufactured at Catoctin Furnace, in Frederick County, by James and Thomas Johnson during the Revolution, and some were used at the siege of Yorktown.

of the service, and that the commanding officer shall be instructed to give every possible assistance in encouraging the French and Indians of that settlement to join me.

"4th. That an officer of artillery be immediately sent with me to pursue such route as I may find most expedient to gain Detroit, with orders to have such pieces of light ordnance as may be thought requisite for the demolishing of Fort Dunmore and Fort Fincastle, if resistance should be made by the rebels in possession of those garrisons.

"5th. That your Excellency will empower me to make such reasonable presents to the Indian chiefs and others as may urge them to act with vigor in the execution of my orders.

"6th. That your Excellency will send to Lord Dunmore such arms as may be spared, in order to equip such persons as may be willing to serve his Majesty at our junction, in the vicinity of Alexandria, &c., &c. If your Excellency judges it expedient for the good of the service to furnish me with the authority and other requisites I have mentioned, I shall embrace the earliest opportunity of setting off for Canada, and shall immediately dispatch Lord Dunmore's armed schooner, which now awaits my commands, with an account of what your Excellency has done, and that I shall be ready, if practicable, to join your Lordship by the twentieth of April, at Alexandria, where the troops under my command may fortify themselves under the cover of the men of war on that station.

"If, on the contrary, your Excellency should not approve of what I propose, you will be good enough to immediately honor me with your dispatches to the Earl of Dunmore, that I may return as early as possible."

Gen. Gage approved the design, and on the 14th or 15th of September, Connolly left Boston, and in October again joined Dunmore, who, in accordance with the instructions of Gen. Gage, on the 5th of November granted him a commission as lieutenant-colonel commandant of the Queen's Royal Rangers, to be raised "in the back parts and Canada." About the 13th of November he left Lord Dunmore on his way to Detroit, where he expected to meet his commission and instructions. He was accompanied by Allan Cameron and Dr. John Smith. The former, a native of Scotland, had left his country on account of an affair of honor, and had come to Virginia with the intention of purchasing lands in that colony; but finding it difficult to pass through the back country, encouraged by Lord Dunmore and the promise of advancement, he agreed to accept a commission as first lieutenant in the regiment to be raised by Connolly. Dr. Smith, also a native of Scotland, had left Charles County, Md., for political reasons, intending to go to the Mississippi, but finding it impracticable he returned to Norfolk, where he was induced by Lord Dunmore by promises of preferment to accept the appointment of surgeon under Connolly.

The party, consisting of Connolly, Cameron, Smith, and a servant, departed from Norfolk on a flat-bottomed schooner, intending to proceed in this vessel up the Chesapeake into Potomac River, and land if possible near to Dr. Smith's house (about two miles below Cedar Point), on Port Tobacco Creek, and to pass through the country on horseback until they reached Detroit.

Fortunately, the people of Frederick County were on the alert, and to their vigilance was due the discovery and frustration of this well-conceived plot. Patrols and minute-men were constantly scouring the country, ready to apprise the inhabitants of the first signs of danger, and Connolly and his companions happening to fall in with one of these parties near Hagerstown, and not being able to give a satisfactory account of themselves, were arrested on suspicion and taken to Frederick. Connolly had concealed his papers in the mail pillion-sticks, which were hollow, encased in tin plates covered with canvas.

"When we arrived at Frederick," says Smith, "we were stripped and searched again, and examined separately before the committee, where one of the most illiberal, inveterate, and violent Rebels, named Samuel Chase (son of a respectable and very worthy clergyman of this Province), a lawyer and a member of the Congress, presided. At this place we were not a little alarmed lest they should discover our instructions, papers, &c., as they examined everything so strictly as to take our saddles to pieces, and take out the stuffing, and even rip open the soles of our boots, in vain, for the object of their search was not found, although they so frequently handled what contained it. However, by some neglect of Col. Connolly's servant, an old torn piece of paper was found in his portmanteau, which discovered some part of our design; and then Col. Connolly, to prevent our falling immediate sacrifices to a frantick mob, acknowledged our commissions. The servant, however, who was faithful to his trust, being allowed to go at large from the first of our confinement, took care to destroy the mail pillion-sticks containing the papers, commissions, and instructions, which we dreaded so much being discovered, as soon as he could effect it with safety, which put an end to our anxiety and alarms on that account."

On the following day John Hanson, Jr., chairman of the Committee of Observation, transmitted to the president of Congress copies of the examinations of the prisoners, a letter to John Gibson, an early resident of the region, a speech of Lord Dunmore to White-Eyes, an Indian chief, and Connolly's proposals to Gen. Gage.

In the latter part of December, Connolly was sent to Philadelphia under guard of Dr. Adam Fisher and ten privates. Smith made his escape just before this, but was recaptured in January, 1776, at Little Meadows, with a number of letters from Connolly to British officers and others, which he had written while in confinement at Frederick. Connolly was kept imprisoned for more than a year in Philadelphia, and was afterwards removed to Baltimore. He was subsequently released on parole, but remained a prisoner until near the close of the war.

Among the companies raised in Frederick County in 1775 were those of Capts. William Blair, William

Shields, Jacob Ambrose, and Benjamin Ogle. The "game-cock" company of Capt. Blair, which went first to the front, was officered as follows:

William Blair, captain; Jacob Hockersmith, ensign; George Hockersmith, first lieutenant; Henry Williams, second lieutenant; William Curran, Jr., George Kelly, John Smith, Christian Crabbs, sergeants; John Crabbs, George Matthews, Arthur Row, James Park, corporals; Daniel McLean, drummer; and fifty-four privates.

The Second Company, raised in 1775, William Shields, captain; John Faires, first lieutenant; Michael Hockersmith, second lieutenant; John Shields, ensign; Charles Robinson, James Shields, Sr., Patrick Haney, Robert Brown, sergeants; Moses Kennedy, John Hawk, John Long, Thomas Baird, corporals; and fifty-two privates.

The Third Company, raised in 1775, Jacob Ambrose, captain; Peter Shover, first lieutenant; Henry Bitzell, second lieutenant; John Weller, ensign; Martin Bartz, Frederick Schultz, John Gump, Casper Young, sergeants; John Protzman, George Kuhn, Dominick Bradley, Lawrence Creager, corporals; John Shaw, drummer; Philip Weller, fifer; and fifty privates.

The Fourth Company, raised in 1775, Benjamin Ogle, captain; Henry Matthews, first lieutenant; George Nead, second lieutenant; James Ogle, ensign; John Syphers, Lawrence Protzman, Peter Leonard, Conrad Matthews, sergeants; Jacob Valentine, Adam Knauff, Daniel Protzman, William Elder, son of Guy, corporals; John Roche, drummer; Daniel Linebaugh, fifer; and fifty-two privates.

These companies formed portions of the battalions which were raised in Frederick County, and they were conspicuous during the war for their ardent devotion and steady valor.[1]

On the 7th of December, 1775, the Maryland Convention assembled, and immediately set about the formation of a military force for the protection of the province. After appointing Messrs. Charles Beatty, James Johnson, and John Hanson, Jr., a committee to establish a gun-lock manufactory at Frederick, they resolved on the 1st of January, 1776, that fourteen hundred and forty-four men should be raised for the defense of the province, that eight companies of the troops, of sixty-eight privates each, should be formed into a battalion, and that the remainder should be divided into companies of one hundred each. William Smallwood was elected colonel of the first battalion, Francis Ware lieutenant-colonel, Thomas Price (who commanded the second company of Frederick riflemen) first major, and Mordecai Gist (of Baltimore) second major. The province was then divided into districts, and a brigadier-general was assigned to the command in each. Frederick County constituted the Third District, and was placed under the command of Thomas Johnson, Jr., who ranked as the first brigadier-general. The officers of militia for Frederick County were as follows:

First Battalion.—Charles Beatty, colonel; William Beatty, lieutenant-colonel; Ludwick Weltner, first major; Benjamin Johnson, second; Louis Bush, quartermaster. *Second Battalion.*—James Johnson, colonel; Joseph Wood, lieutenant-colonel; Benjamin Ogle, first major; Roger Johnson, second; Azel Waters, quartermaster. *Third Battalion.*—Jacob Good, colonel; William Blair, lieutenant-colonel; Samuel Shaw, first major; William Shields, second; Joseph McKillip, quartermaster. *Fourth Battalion.*—Baker Johnson, colonel; William Luckett, lieutenant-colonel; Jacob Miller, first major; Henry Darnall, second; Nicholas Tice, quartermaster. Lower District—*Lower Battalion.*—John Murdock, colonel; Thomas Johns, lieutenant-colonel; Richard Brooks, first major; William Deakins, second; Richard Thompson, quartermaster. *Upper Battalion.*—Zadock Magruder, colonel; Charles G. Griffith, lieutenant-colonel; Francis Deakins, first major; Richard Crabb, second; Samuel Duvall, quartermaster. Upper District.—*First Battalion.*—John Stull, colonel; Andrew Rench, lieutenant-colonel; Henry Shryock, first major; George Woltz, second; Elie Williams, quartermaster. *Second Battalion.*—Dr. Samuel Beall, colonel; Joseph Smith, lieutenant-colonel; Richard Davis, first major; Charles Swearingen, second; James Chapline, quartermaster.[2]

Independence of Great Britain was not generally desired at the beginning of the troubles. All the conventions of the province had, down to June, 1776, met and adjourned without the expression of a single opinion in its favor. Time was requisite to convince the great mass of the people of the necessity of a complete separation from the parent-country and the establishment of independent governments. The ablest pens were employed throughout the colonies in the winter and spring of 1776 on this momentous subject. In Maryland, under the influence of Chase, Paca, Johnson, and Robert Goldsborough, the strongest opposition was gradually waning.[3]

---

[1] On the 8th of December, 1775, the Convention, by resolution, appropriated two hundred pounds currency for building a strong log jail in Fredericktown, thirty feet long, twenty broad, to be lined with two-inch planks, two stories, with split logs and plank floors, the upper story to be divided into three rooms, with a stove in each. That a small house be built for a keeper and guard, and that the treasurer of the Western Shore pay to James Johnson and Thomas Beatty the said sum. The jail was built as directed on Second Street, a few perches east of the present Mechanics' Bank, and the logs were fastened by iron bolts made by Frank Mantz, a Tory blacksmith, and was used as such during the continuance of the war, after which it was converted into a stable, a part of which remained standing in 1846.

[2] In March, 1776, powder belonging to the province was stored in the market-house at Frederick. The first prisoners confined in Frederick arrived there from North Carolina in May, 1776.

[3] As an illustration of the determined spirit which animated the representative men of Western Maryland at this period the following incident is worthy of preservation. Some time after the commencement of hostilities, but long before the Declaration of Independence, Mr. Eden, the last proprietary

GEN. WILLIAM SMALLWOOD.

On the 7th of June, 1776, Richard Henry Lee, of Virginia, submitted to Congress a resolution declaring "That the United Colonies are and ought to be free and independent States; that they are absolved from all allegiance to the British crown; and that all political connection between them and the State of Great Britain is and ought to be totally dissolved." On the 11th of June, Matthew Tilghman, Thomas Stone, and John Rogers wrote to the Council of Safety for instructions, and asking that the county committees call the people together to express their sentiments on the question of independence. In response the freemen of Frederick County, June 17th, unanimously resolved, "That what may be recommended by a majority of the Congress, equally delegated by the people of the United Colonies, *we will*, at the hazard of our lives and fortunes, support and maintain; and that every resolution of the Convention tending to separate this Province from a majority of the colonies, without the consent of the people, is destructive to our internal safety and big with public ruin." The freemen of the upper district of Frederick County "resolved unanimously" that they would "support the union of the colonies" with their "lives and fortunes."

The same spirit was manifested in all the counties, and urged forward by these expressions of the popular will, the Convention repealed its former resolutions and authorized the Maryland representatives in Congress to concur with the other United Colonies in such measures as should be "adjudged necessary for securing the liberties of America." These instructions were followed on the 4th of July by the adoption by Congress of the Declaration of Independence, and the decisive step having thus been taken, Maryland at once proceeded to strengthen her military force. The Convention determined to raise 3405 men—the proportion authorized by Congress—to form a flying camp to act with the militia of Pennsylvania and Delaware in service in the Middle Department (from New York to Maryland, both included) until the 1st of December following. This force was to be divided into four battalions of nine companies each, of which nine were to be furnished by Frederick County, five by Anne Arundel, four by Baltimore, three by Prince George's, two each by Charles, Harford, Cecil, Kent, Queen Anne's, and Caroline, and one each from St. Mary's, Calvert, and Talbot; the whole to be commanded by Brig.-Gen. Thomas Johnson, Jr.[1]

On the 4th of July, the Convention "being of the opinion that it is of very great importance to the welfare of this province that it should not be deprived of the advice and assistance of the said Thomas Johnson in the public councils of the United Colonies, and that his place can be supplied with less inconvenience in the military than in the civil department, therefore, resolved, that a brigadier-general should be elected by ballot in the room of the said Thomas Johnson, Esq.," and John Dent was elected to fill the vacancy. He resigned shortly afterwards, and Gen. Beall was chosen. Otho H. Williams was elected colonel of the Frederick County battalion, but declined the appointment, because of his previous acceptance of a commission as major in a United States rifle battalion.

The battalion composing Frederick County's contribution to the Flying Camp was largely composed of Germans, and rendered valuable service in the ensuing campaign.[2]

In addition to this battalion, the Convention by another resolve, in obedience to a requisition of Congress, passed on the 27th of June, directed two companies of riflemen to be raised, one in Harford County, and the other in Frederick, and four companies of

---

Governor of Maryland, requested Barrister Carroll to invite Thomas Johnson, afterwards of Frederick, and Samuel Chase, to dine at the Government House. Mr. Chase and Mr. Johnson were among the most distinguished of the Whig leaders of the time, and the invitation occasioned some little embarrassment. The difficulty was finally solved by inviting the Governor, Messrs. Johnson and Chase, and other distinguished gentlemen to Mr. Carroll's. Shortly after the company sat down to dinner the Governor said, "It is understood in England that the Congress are about forming a treaty of alliance with France." A momentary silence prevailed, when Mr. Johnson answered, "Governor, we will answer your question, provided you will answer one for us." The Governor assenting to this proposition, Mr. Johnson said, "Well, sir, we will candidly acknowledge that overtures have been made to France, but that they are not yet accepted. Now, sir, we understand that the king, your master, is about subsidizing a large body of Hessians to join his forces to come over to cut our throats." He answered that he believed the report was true. Mr. Johnson immediately rejoined in the following words, "The first Hessian soldier that puts his foot on the American shore will absolve me from all allegiance to Great Britain." Chase exclaimed, "By G—d, I am for declaring ourselves independent." The Governor immediately dropped his knife and fork, and did not eat another mouthful.

[1] The parade-ground and place of rendezvous of the Frederick County troops was Gantt's Common, near Frederick Town.

[2] Many of the descendants of the brave soldiers composing the battalion are to be found in Frederick, Washington, and Carroll Counties. Jacob Sheets, who built Sheets' mill on Piney Creek, in Carroll County, was a private in Capt. Baltzell's company. His descendants reside in the Tom's Creek Valley, near Emmittsburg. Among the German families prominent in the Revolutionary annals of Western Maryland are the Hockersmiths, the Williamses, the Baltzells, the Creagers, the Steiners, and the Millers.

Germans, two in Baltimore County and two in Frederick.[1]

In the battle of Harlem Heights, on the 16th of September following, Griffith's and Richardson's regiments, of Gen. Beale's brigade of the Maryland Flying Camp, with Maj. Price's three independent companies, greatly distinguished themselves. A letter from headquarters, dated September 17th, says, "Never did troops go to the field with more cheerfulness and alacrity, when there began a heavy fire on both sides. It continued about one hour, when our brave Southern troops dislodged them from their posts; the enemy rallied, and our men beat them the second time. They rallied again; our troops drove them the third time, and were rushing on them, but the enemy got on an eminence, and our troops were ordered to retreat, the general considering there might be a large number of the enemy behind the hill concealed, which was the case."

On the 19th of September, by a general order, the six independent companies under Maj. Price were attached to the battalion. By the army returns of September 21st, Gen. Beale's brigade of militia, consisting of Griffith's, Hall's, Richardson's, and Ewing's regiments, had a total rank and file of 2189 men, of which number only 1717 were present and fit for duty. At this time over half the Maryland troops were sick and unfit for service, but those who were able to take part in the campaign did not fail to render a good account of themselves in every engagement with the enemy. After the battle of White Plains, in which Beale's brigade displayed great nerve and steadiness, Col. Moses Rawlings' rifle regiment was sent to reinforce Fort Washington.

This regiment was composed of four companies of Virginians and four of Marylanders, and were at first commanded by Col. Stephenson, of Virginia, who was succeeded by Lieut.-Col. Rawlings. Two of the companies were those raised in Frederick by Cresap and Price at the beginning of hostilities, and were subsequently commanded by Capt. Philemon Griffith and Capt. Richard Davis. The other two companies were commanded by Capt. Thomas Beale and Capt. Smith, and were raised the former in Frederick, the latter in Harford County. Fort Washington was attacked on the 16th of November (1776) by a large force of the enemy, and captured after a struggle, in which the Frederick County riflemen displayed all the nerve and courage of veterans. About four hundred Marylanders were taken prisoners, among whom were Col. Rawlings, Maj. Otho H. Williams, and Lieut. Peter Contee Hanson, who died a prisoner in New York. Lawrence Everhart, of Frederick, and some of his men escaped in a boat after the surrender. The loss of the enemy was nearly nine hundred killed and wounded, more than half of which was sustained in the attack upon Rawlings' riflemen. Some authorities put the loss even higher. Gordon in his "History of the American Revolution," says, "it cost Knyphausen 'near upon eight hundred men' to force the 'single regiment of Rawlings' back.'"

In Green's "Life of Greene" the author says, "Had Rawlings been supported, Knyphausen could not have gained the north lines. But the men refused to man them, and crowded into the redoubt, where they became a compact mass for the enemy's guns. The defense on the east was still more irresolute, and there are questions connected with that on the south which will, it is probable, never be solved. But had it been like that of Rawlings' riflemen it would have well-nigh crippled the enemy." Gen. Washington, in a letter to his brother, John A. Washington, dated Nov. 19, 1776, in referring to the capture of Fort Washington, only mentions the services rendered by Rawlings' regiment. He remarks, "The enemy have suffered greatly on the north side of Fort Washington. Col. Rawlings' regiment (late Hugh Stephenson's) was posted there, and behaved with great spirit."

While the representatives of Western Maryland were thus winning distinction where the soldiers of some other sections only earned disgrace, many important events had occurred at home. The shadow of the proprietary government having vanished by the departure of Governor Eden, the Convention, in pursuance of instructions from the several counties, resolved upon the establishment of a permanent form of government. For this purpose a new Convention was to be elected, consisting of four representatives from each district of Frederick County, four from each of the other counties, and two each from Annapolis and Baltimore Town. In pursuance of these resolutions, elections were held throughout Maryland on the 1st of August, 1776, for delegates to a Convention, which assembled at Annapolis on the 14th of the same month, for the purpose of framing a State constitution and bill of rights. On the 6th of September the Convention divided Frederick County, and erected out of parts of it the new counties of Washington and Montgomery; the former named after the commander-in-chief of the army, and the latter after

---

[1] The four companies of Germans raised were commanded respectively by Capts. Heiser, Graybill, Fister, and Keeports. Together with four companies raised in Pennsylvania they formed a regiment, and were officered by Col. Hausegger, of Pennsylvania, and Lieut.-Col. Geo. Stricker and Maj. Weltner, of Frederick County.

Gen. Richard Montgomery, who was killed in the attack on Quebec. The declaration of rights and the constitution having been formally adopted, the new government was organized on the 13th of February, 1777, by the election of Thomas Johnson, afterwards of Frederick County, as the first Governor of the State. In the mean time Congress, dismayed by the successive disasters which had overtaken the American arms, had adjourned to Baltimore, and a general feeling of despondency prevailed. Washington's troops were reduced to a mere handful, and it was uncertain whether he would be able to obtain reinforcements. Disappointed in his hopes from New Jersey, where the spirit of disaffection was prevalent, he could not tell what reliance could be placed on Pennsylvania and Maryland. In the latter State he was not disappointed, and so soon as intelligence was received of his retreat through the Jerseys every preparation was made to sustain him. Congress dispatched Col. Ewing, of the Maryland Flying Camp, on the 9th of December, to the Maryland Council of Safety with the news of the disasters that had overtaken the army, and immediately the militia of Cecil, Baltimore, Harford, and Frederick Counties were put in motion for the seat of war.

On the 1st of December (1776), the term of enlistment of Gen. Beall's Maryland Brigade of the Flying Camp expired, and, owing to the unpopularity of their commander, Washington was compelled to discharge the greater portion in the face of the enemy. Some few remained as volunteers, and many re-enlisted after their return to the State. Maj. Gist's regiment, however, the seven independent companies, and the two artillery companies, with the Maryland part of the rifle and German regiments,—four companies in each,—making a total of 2280 men, all re-enlisted for three years on the Continental plan. On the 19th of January, 1777, Washington made another appeal for reinforcement, and on the 25th the militia of Frederick and other counties, under the command of Thomas Johnson, were ordered to join Gen. Washington at once in the Jerseys. The Legislature also immediately took steps to raise recruits, and barracks were ordered to be erected in Frederick and at other points for their accommodation while preparing for the army. In consequence of an apprehended attack, all the powder and military stores were removed in February from Annapolis to Frederick, and the prisoners confined at Baltimore were sent to the same point, and placed in charge of Lieut. William Beatty.[1]

As the spring of 1777 opened the urgent necessity of reinforcing the army became apparent, and in accordance with Washington's request Maryland raised five full regiments of infantry, in addition to the two she already had in the field. These seven regiments, with the German battalion, part of which had been raised in Frederick County, were divided into two brigades; one, composed of three regiments and the German battalion, was placed under the command of Chevalier Deborre, and the other, formed of the four remaining regiments, was assigned to Gen. Smallwood.[2]

These troops all participated in the campaign of 1777, and well sustained the reputation of the Maryland line.

Early in the following year, 1778, in accordance with the earnest request of Congress, the Legislature passed an act to raise 2902 men, including the two artillery companies already in camp and the volunteers already on hand within the State. To insure their speedy enlistment, the Legislature apportioned to each county the number of men required according to the number of militia in each. The proportion assigned to Frederick was 309, to Washington 120, and to Montgomery 156.

About this period hostilities broke out along the Western frontier with the Indians, Tories, refugees, and other border desperadoes. To suppress the outrages committed by them, Washington fitted out three expeditions,—the first from Fort Schuyler, under Col. Van Schaick, the second under Gen. Sullivan, and the third under Col. Brodhead, from Pittsburgh, up the Allegany,—against the Mingo, Muncey, and Seneca tribes. The force under Brodhead consisted of the militia of Washington and Montgomery Counties, in Maryland, under the command of Col. Beatty, and the militia of Virginia and Pennsylvania. To supply this force with provisions Maryland pressed into service fifty wagons, and on the 5th of August

---

[1] In August, Lieut. Beatty was promoted to a captaincy in the First Maryland Regiment, and joined the army under Washington. He was succeeded by Col. Rawlings, and in August the prisoners were removed to Sharpsburg and placed in charge of Lieut. Charles Hughes.

[2] Late in December, 1777, the commander of Frederick, Col. Beatty, received one hundred prisoners, whom he was compelled to confine in jail until Fort Frederick was fitted up for their reception. Late in the afternoon of Christmas-day they set fire to the jail, and upon the alarm being given the colonel ordered every man to arm himself as quick as possible, and upon reaching the jail-yard the gate was opened by the jailer, and about one-third of the prisoners attempted to make their escape, which compelled the small party of militia to charge them and knock them down with their arms, which had the effect of driving them back. They were finally removed to the Tory House and the fire put out, with little damage. A few days after this they threatened to break out, but were told that they would be sacrificed, which put an end to the disturbance.

(1778) loaded them with stores, etc., in Washington County, and sent them to Carlisle, Pa.[1]

Early in December, 1778, Washington distributed his troops in winter-quarters in a line of cantonments from Long Island Sound to the Delaware. The Marylanders, under Lord Stirling, were near Middlebrook, in the Jerseys, and Frederick and Hagerstown were occupied by Baylor's regiment of cavalry. In May, 1779, Col. Moses Rawlings was ordered to march to Fort Pitt, and in consequence of the refusal of Gen. Washington to place the German regiment under his command he resigned, and Capt. Beale was placed in command at Frederick. The German battalion and Rawlings' rifle regiment during the same year were merged into one regiment, known as the Eighth Maryland. The Frederick troops were actively engaged in the campaign of 1779, and were transferred with the rest of the Maryland line in 1780 to the South, where they once more illustrated the quality of Maryland courage.[2]

After the defeat of Gen. Gates and the advance of Lord Cornwallis into the interior of North Carolina, on the 16th of October, 1780, Gen. Leslie sailed from New York with about three thousand troops, with orders to penetrate into Virginia and await the orders of Lord Cornwallis. Leslie entered the Chesapeake, and took possession of Norfolk and Portsmouth. His expedition formed part of a design to invade the Western frontier and to release a large number of British prisoners who were confined at this time in Winchester, Strasburg, Leesburg, Sharpsburg, Fort Frederick, and Frederick. Gen. Johnston, with a large force of the enemy, was to operate in the neighborhood of Pittsburgh, while Col. Connolly, who had been exchanged for Lieut.-Col. Nathaniel Ramsey, with the aid of Gen. Leslie and the Tories and refugees on the frontiers and the Eastern Shore, was to co-operate with him. And to procure the aid and assistance of the loyalists in the campaign of 1781, in pursuance of instructions from the king, Sir Henry Clinton in February issued a commission to William Franklin, Governor of New Jersey, Josiah Martin, Governor of North Carolina, Timothy Ruggles, Daniel Coxe, George Duncan Ludlow, Edward Lutwyche, George Romer, George Leonard, Anthony Stewart, and Robert Alexander, constituting them a board of directors for the control and management of the "Associated Loyalists of America." The board of directors of this association were authorized to employ "such of his majesty's faithful subjects in North America as may be willing to associate under their direction, for the purpose of annoying the sea-coasts of the revolted provinces and distressing their trade, either in co-operation with his majesty's land and sea forces, or by making diversions in their favor when they are carrying on operations in other parts."

Large numbers of the Tories were enrolled on the frontier, on the Eastern Shore, and in the neighboring States to execute the royal commission of robbing and murdering the inhabitants, when the conspiracy was providentially discovered at Frederick. It is stated that a disguised British officer was to meet a messenger of the enemy at a designated place, to put him in possession of all the plans relating to the conspiracy. The watchfulness of the Americans deterred the officer from fulfilling his appointment, and the papers fell into the hands of a patriotic officer, "who, by a singular coincidence, was at that moment standing where the Tory messenger expected his correspondent." The plot and the names of the prominent conspirators were at once disclosed, and secret and efficient measures were instantly taken to put them under arrest.

ALEXANDER CONTEE HANSON

Numbers were accordingly arrested and imprisoned, and on the 25th of July, Peter Sueman, Nicholas Andrews, John George Graves, Yost Plecker, Adam Graves, Henry Shett, and Casper Fritchie were

---

[1] After the Maryland militia returned from New Jersey, a draft was ordered of one company from each regiment in the State. The regiment commanded by Col. James Johnson, in the upper part of the county, was mustered on the appointed day, when a sufficient number of men turned out, and double the required number of officers, among whom were two captains named Smith and Creager. The question now arose who should take command of the company, and it was agreed to be decided by throwing up a dollar. Accordingly it was done, and Creager was the fortunate winner. With a magnanimity worthy of imitation he addressed himself to Smith: "Sir, I have won the command, but, as you are the oldest and most experienced officer, you must take the command, and I will act as your lieutenant." The arrangement was reluctantly agreed to, and the company so officered marched to headquarters.

[2] In March, 1778, Gen. Greene accepted the appointment of quartermaster-general of the army, and soon after established his department in Maryland for the collection of military supplies for the army. On the 10th of September, 1779, he appointed Thomas Richardson assistant commissary of purchases for Montgomery, Prince George's, Charles, and St. Mary's; George Murdock for Frederick; and Moses Rawlings for Washington County. On September 13th, Gen. Greene appointed Charles Beatty deputy quartermaster-general for Frederick County; on the following day, Richard Butler and Nicholas Tice deputy quartermasters for Frederick; on the 17th, John Greer assistant deputy quartermaster-general for the lower part of Frederick and the upper part of Baltimore Counties, and Henry Shryock the same for Washington County.

brought to trial before a special court at Fredericktown, consisting of Alexander Contee Hanson, afterwards Chancellor of the State, Col. James Johnson, and Upton Sheredine. After an impartial trial they were found guilty of high treason, in "enlisting men for the service of the king of Great Britain and administering an oath to them to bear true allegiance to the said king, and to obey his officers when called on."

The following sentence was delivered by Judge Hanson:

"Peter Sueman, Nicholas Andrews, John George Graves, Yost Plecker, Adam Graves, Henry Shett, Casper Fritchie, attend. It has been suggested to the court that notwithstanding your guilt has been ascertained by an impartial jury, you consider the proceedings against you nothing more than solemn mockery, and have adopted a vain idea, propagated by the enemies of this country, that she dare not punish her unnatural subjects for engaging in the service of Great Britain. From the strange nsensibility you have heretofore discovered, I was indeed led to conclude that you were under a delusion, which might prove fatal to your prospects of happiness hereafter. I think it is my duty, therefore, to explain to you your real situation. The crime you have been convicted of, upon the fullest and clearest testimony, is of such a nature that you cannot, ought not, to look for a pardon. Had it pleased heaven to permit the full execution of your unnatural designs, the miseries to be experienced by your devoted country would have been dreadful even in the contemplation. The ends of public justice, the dictates of policy, and the feelings of humanity all require that you should exhibit an awful example to your fellow-subjects, and the dignity of the State, with everything that can interest the heart of man, calls aloud for your punishment. If the consideration of approaching fate can inspire proper sentiments, you will pour forth your thanks to that watchful Providence which has arrested you at an early state of guilt. And you will employ the short time you have to live in endeavoring, by a sincere penitence, to obtain pardon from the Almighty Being, who is to sit in judgment upon you, upon me, and all mankind.

"I must now perform the terrible task of denouncing the terrible punishment ordained for high treason.

"You, Peter Sueman, Nicholas Andrews, Yost Plecker, Adam Graves, Henry Shett, John George Graves, and Casper Fritchie, and each of you, attend to your sentence. You shall be carried to the gaol of Fredericktown, and be hanged therein; you shall be cut down to the earth alive, and your entrails shall be taken out and burnt while you are yet alive, your heads shall be cut off, your body shall be divided into four parts, and your heads and quarters shall be placed where his excellency the Governor shall appoint. So Lord have mercy upon your poor souls."

Three of the number were executed in the court-house yard at Frederick, the remainder having been pardoned.[1]

---

[1] At various times judgment of outlawry for treason was rendered in the General Court at Annapolis against about one hundred leading Tories, among whom were Daniel Dulany, of Daniel, Daniel Dulany, of Walter, Lloyd Dulany, Jonathan Boucher, Henry Addison, William Edmiston, John Montgomery, Bennett Allen, Anthony Stewart, Walter Dulany, Philip Key, of Frederick County, and William Dickson, of Montgomery County.

The Southern campaign of 1781 under Gen. Greene turned the tide of war in favor of the American cause. The brunt of this campaign was borne by the Maryland line, and although it does not come within the scope of the present work to follow in detail the operations which resulted in the virtual recovery of the South from the British armies, it can be said without exaggeration that no troops contributed so largely to the accomplishment of these important ends as those from Maryland. The Maryland line was the "Stonewall" legion of every contest, and came out of every conflict with fresh honors and distinction. In the battle of Eutaw Springs, which was one of the most desperate battles of the war, they displayed a gallantry that drew from Gen. Greene the highest expressions of admiration, and to their charge, "exceeding anything he ever saw," he ascribed the success which attended the Americans in the earlier part of the day. The following letter from a gallant soldier who took part in that engagement will be found interesting in this connection:

"HIGH HILLS, SANTEE, Sept. 25, 1781.

"DEAR BROTHER,—I expect before this reaches you you will hear of the severe action that happened on the 8th instant with a body of British troops at the Eutaw Springs, commanded by Col. Stewart. I also expect you will have the particulars of the action before this reaches you, so shall say nothing concerning it, only inform you of the loss of officers killed and wounded in our Line. I have the misfortune myself to be one of the latter. We had 4 killed, which are as follows: Capts. Dobson and Edgerly, of the 2d Regiment, Lieuts. Duvall and Gould, of the 1st Regiment. Wounded: Lt.-Col. Howard, Lt. Ewing, Lt. Woolford, Lt. Moore, and myself, of the 2d Regiment; of the 1st, Capts. Gibson and Hugon. My wound is in the left leg and has much shattered the big bone. Its between the calf and ankle. I have had no fevers these several days. The Doctor has taken, I believe, at least forty pieces of bone out of it, though the most of them were very small. The wound has a very good appearance, and I have not the least doubt but that I shall be able to go upon crutches in the course of two months. Col. Howard's wound is through one of his shoulders, and is mending fast; Capt. Gibson's through the right arm, and like to do well; Capt. Hugon's in the right groin, and like to do well; Lt. Ewing has two of his ribs broke, was shot through the left thigh, and, I believe, will do well; Lt. Moore has the end of his right thumb shot off, and is doing well. We were brought here upon litters from near the field of action, which is 50 or 60 miles from this place, and are to move again to-morrow to the Warsaw Settlement, about 70 miles from this place,—a very healthy country, where I expect we shall stay till we get well. If you can possibly send me some hard cash do it, for I am in great want of it. I have had no money since last fall. I shall want as much as will purchase me a horse. If I could ride I have no horse; and I have no hat, and had none to wear all the summer but an old borrowed one. If you can procure me one, do send it by the first safe hand, and two or three pairs of stockings. You will please excuse the incorrectness of this letter, for I can write no other way than as I lie upon my side. I can't sit up with any ease. You'll make my love to my Mother and Sisters, and George, to Col. Brooke and Little Nancy, and to all the neighbours. Tell them I expect to be with them in the course of this winter. Adieu.

"Y^r Affect^e Brother,   J. LYNN.

"P. S.—Tell my Mother not to make herself uneasy upon my account. For I would not regret the other leg being broke to give the enemy such another drubbing.

"To CAPT. DAVID LYNN, Montgomery County, Maryland.
"By CAPT. BRUFF."

In compliance with the request of Congress, Washington, on the 20th of February, 1781, directed Lafayette to march southward for the purpose of capturing Arnold and checking the enemy's operations in Virginia, and he accordingly set out on his march two days later. To expedite his progress, Thomas Beatty, of Frederick, George Murdock and Thomas Beall, of Montgomery, and the lieutenants of other counties were instructed to seize all the salt and fresh meats in their districts, and impress all the wagons, carriages, teams, drivers, etc., and send them to the head of the Elk for the purpose of transporting the troops, cannon, stores, and baggage to Virginia.[1]

This assistance was promptly rendered, but after a short campaign in Virginia Lafayette was obliged to abandon Richmond and retreat towards Fredericksburg before the superior forces of Lord Cornwallis. Continuing his retreat, he crossed the Rapidan, where he was joined on the 7th of June by Gen. Wayne, who had passed through Frederick on the 31st of May with about one thousand troops to join him. The retreat of Lafayette towards Maryland excited apprehensions of invasion, and on the 4th of June the lieutenant of Frederick County was ordered immediately to arm and equip five hundred militia, the lieutenant of Montgomery two hundred and fifty, and of Prince George's two hundred and fifty, and march with them to Georgetown. The troops of horse in Frederick, Baltimore, and Kent Counties received similar orders, and such was the alacrity of the people that two new regiments were formed in a few days, the third under Lieut.-Col. Peter Adams, and the fourth under Lieut.-Col. Thomas Woolford. The Frederick troop of horse was commanded by John Ross Key, who, on the 10th of June, 1781, transmitted the following letter to the Governor:

"SIR,—I have the Honor and Satisfaction to inform Your Excellency that the Frederick Co. Troop of Horse under my Command are now on their Rout to George Town, where I expect to arrive this evening. We are tolerably well mounted and Equipped, and with pleasure Assure you I find a Desire and Anxiety prevails among the men that compose the Troop to render every Service in their Power to their Country, and wish to join the acting Army should your Excellency think it necessary.

"I am with every Sentiment of Respect and Esteem your Excellency's Most Ob^t S^t
"J^{no} ROSS KEY.
"Road to GEORGE TOWN, 10^t June, 1781."

In company with the "Baltimore Light Dragoons," under Capt. Nicholas Ruxton Moore, the "Frederick Light Dragoons" crossed the Potomac on the 18th of June, and joined Lafayette on the 6th of July.

About the time Lafayette was encamped near the Rapidan, intelligence was received that Tarleton was on his way to Winchester to liberate the British prisoners who, to the number of several hundred, were then confined in the place. By order of Lafayette they were removed without delay to Fort Frederick, in Maryland, and placed in charge of Col. Moses Rawlings, deputy commissary-general of prisoners.[2]

On the 30th of August, when Washington was on his southward march towards Yorktown, the Governor called upon the commissaries of the several counties, directing them to purchase supplies, and to procure from each county a certain number of cattle, the quota of Frederick being 400, of Montgomery 300, and of Washington 300. At the same time warrants were issued to Thomas Beall, at Georgetown, and other quartermasters throughout the State, directing them to impress all vessels capable of transporting troops or military stores; and James Calhoun was ordered to impress all the wagons and teams in Frederick and Washington Counties to haul flour and

---

[1] On the 29th of June, 1777, the General Assembly appointed Charles Beatty lieutenant of Frederick, Daniel Hughes lieutenant of Washington, and Charles Greenbury Griffith lieutenant of Montgomery.

[2] "A meeting was called in Frederick County, at the courthouse in Frederick Town, on Friday, the 17th of August, 1781, in consequence of public notice for that purpose (Col. Thomas Price in the chair). The resolutions entered into by the meeting on the 7th, respecting the new paper money, were read and approved. It being represented from the chair that Messrs. James Smith, John Neil, and Adam Jacobs were refusing the same paper money, they were sent for, and appeared, and on examination acknowledged they had for some days stopped receiving it, from a persuasion that it did not circulate freely in Baltimore Town, but declared they were not aware that such conduct would be considered a breach of the resolutions of the first meeting, whereupon they were dismissed upon promising respectively to comport themselves in future as good citizens, and to receive the paper money aforesaid at par with silver and gold in all future transactions until, by some future meeting of the *people*, agreeable to the said resolutions of the 7th instant, they shall be authorized to discontinue so doing.

"On motion, *Resolved unanimously*, that we will exert our utmost endeavors in supporting the credit and circulation of the said new paper money at par, and we will punish by Tarring and Feathering, and expulsion from the county, any person who shall hereafter be so hardy as to act contrary to the tenor of the aforesaid mentioned resolutions of the 7th instant, and that these proceedings be published in the newspapers."

military supplies to Georgetown. At this time all was activity in Maryland. The arrival of Washington, and the prospect of capturing Cornwallis, re-awakened the spirit of the people, and measures of co-operation were effectually and promptly carried out. The third regiment of Continentals was speedily completed and dispatched to the scene of action, while the fourth regiment, under Maj. Alexander Roxburgh, mustering upwards of six hundred men, rank and file, and "said to contain the best men who had enlisted from this State since the war," marched from Annapolis on the 4th of September to join Lafayette.

After the surrender of Cornwallis the Maryland Continentals were sent to the support of Gen. Greene in the South, and the British prisoners were marched to Fort Frederick, Md., and Winchester, Va. Those confined at the former point were subsequently removed to Lancaster, Pa. The triumph at Yorktown virtually ended the war and freed the people of Maryland from further serious apprehension. No section of the State contributed more generously to the common defense than Western Maryland, and none were represented in the armies by braver or better soldiers.[1]

The declaration of peace was celebrated with public demonstrations of joy in Frederick Town and in all parts of the western section of the State.

On the 25th of April (1783) it is related that a number of the people living on Israel's Creek

"met at Rocky Hill Chapel, having previously engaged a clergyman, instead of the *Hessian Bond*, thinking it their duty before they gave loose to the effusions of joy, so natural on being relieved from the calamitous circumstances under which they had so long labored, to pay the tribute due to the Supreme Dispenser of all good by offering up their most grateful and hearty thanks for blessed interference in favor of the American cause, and for his having been pleased to conduct us through the war in so miraculous a manner, and at the conclusion of the same to make us free, sovereign, and independent States. To pray for his Divine blessings, etc., after which there was delivered an excellent sermon, much to the purpose. Upon leaving the chapel they were all most kindly invited to Col. Wood's, where there was a most elegant entertainment prepared. After dinner the following toasts were drank:

"1. The United States of America.
"2. Gen. Washington and the Northern army.
"3. Gen. Greene and the Southern army.
"4. The King of France.
"5. The King of Spain.
"6. The United Provinces.
"7. The Marquis de Lafayette.
"8. Count de Grasse and his fleet.
"9. Count Rochambeau and his army.
"10. The American ambassadors in Europe.
"11. The French ambassadors at Congress.
"12. Peace, Liberty, and Independence.
"13. May the peace now concluded be perpetuated.

"During the times the toasts were going around there were fired thirteen platoons, and as many cheers given by nearly two hundred people, in whose countenance you might see joy and gladness. In the evening the colonel's (Wood) house was illuminated and bonfires made. The whole was concluded with propriety and decorum."

The Soldier Lands.—To discharge the engagements of the State towards its officers and soldiers for their services during the Revolution, the General Assembly, at the November session of 1781, appropriated all the vacant lands westward of Fort Cumberland (within the present limits of Allegany and Garrett Counties), reserved or otherwise, except so far as they were fairly covered by warrants, etc., to fulfill these obligations. By this act it was also provided that there should be a land-office for the Western Shore at Annapolis, and another on the Eastern Shore, where the General Court was held. In April, 1787, the Legislature passed a resolution authorizing the Governor to employ a competent person to lay out the vacant lands belonging to the State westward of Fort Cumberland, in lots of fifty acres each. In pursuance of this resolution, Francis Deakins was appointed, and at the November session of the Legislature of 1788, having finished a general plat of the lands, he reported to the General Assembly, whereupon an act was passed "to dispose of the reserved lands westward of Fort Cumberland." To each of the Maryland officers who had served in the Revolution were assigned four lots, and to each private one lot, as follows:

LIST OF OFFICERS AND SOLDIERS ENTITLED TO LOTS WESTWARD OF FORT CUMBERLAND.

OFFICERS.

Rank.	Names.	Numbers.
Captain	George Armstrong	2367, 2368, 2395, 2396
Captain	Richard Anderson	3249, 3252, 3253, 3221
Lieutenant	William Adams	2379, 2380, 2381, 2382
Captain	James Bruff	2711, 2712, 2713, 2714
Colonel	Peter Adams, 1st Regt	2312, 2313, 2314, 2317
Major	Archibald Anderson	2391, 2392, 2393, 2394
Chaplain	James Armstrong	2589, 2590, 2591, 2592
Major	Benjamin Brooks	2383, 2384, 2385, 2386
Captain	William Beatty	2421, 2422, 2423, 2424
Captain	Lloyd Beall	2773, 2774, 2767, 3310

---

[1] In looking over the old records of the clerk's office of Frederick County the following criminal proceedings, among others, were discovered in the prosecutions of Tories, instituted near the close of the Revolutionary war: State against one A. C., presented for saying "he wished all persons who went about warning people on militia duty might be all hanged, not by the necks but by the heels." Fined £25 specie. State against J. H., presented for "damning Gen. Washington and the Congress of the United States of America." Fined £15 specie. State against E. L., presented for "drinking health to King George, and damnation to Gen. Washington." Fined £5 specie. The minutes of the court show numerous orders passed by the court appropriating money for the support of the wives and the children of the soldiers in the Maryland line.

Rank.	Names.	Numbers.
Captain	Jacob Brice	3222, 3224, 3228, 3229
Major	William Brown	1664, 1665, 1680, 1682
Captain	Joseph Burgess	2603, 2604, 2605, 2606
Major	William Dent Beall	2489, 2490, 2583, 2584
Captain	William Bruce	2387, 2388, 2389, 2390
Captain	Perry Benson	1635, 1636, 1637, 1638
Lieutenant	Thomas Boyd	2599, 2600, 2601, 2602
Captain	Michael Boyer	2268, 2269, 2270, 2271
Lieutenant	Henry Baldwin	3200, 3201, 3198, 3199
Captain	John Sprigg Belt	3258, 3259, 3260, 3261
Captain	Richard Bird	1454, 1455, 1456, 1457
Lieutenant	Joshua Burgess	2493, 2494, 2585, 2588
Lieutenant	Samuel B. Beall	2347, 2348, 2349, 2350
Lieutenant	Basil Burgess	3237, 3238, 3059, 3061
Lieutenant	Henry Baker	2777, 2778, 2779, 2780
Lieutenant	Thomas Beatty	1666, 1667, 1668, 1669
Lieutenant	Malachi Bonham	2734, 2672, 2670, 2661
Lieutenant	Jacques Bagues	1660, 1661, 1662, 1663
Captain	Charles Baltzell	2607, 2608, 2609, 2610
Lieutenant	Joseph Britain	2498, 2499, 2573, 2574
Lieutenant	John Brevett	3331, 3340, 3344, 3262
Lieutenant	Joseph Cross	1683, 4128, 4129, 4130
Captain	Horatio Claggett	2954, 2955, 2956, 2957
Lieutenant	Henry Chapman	2258, 2259, 2260, 2261
Lieutenant	John Cary	2709, 2710, 2719, 2720
Surg.-Gen	James Craig	2781, 2782, 2783, 2784
Lieutenant	John Chever	2326, 2327, 2328, 2329
Lieutenant	Jacob Crawford	2355, 2356, 2357, 2358
Lieutenant	Edward Compton	3202, 3205, 3088, 3090
Lieutenant	Henry Clements	2359, 2360, 2361, 2362
Captain	John Carlile	3191, 4140, 4141, 4142
Lieutenant	John Carson	2280, 2282, 2284, 2285
Ensign	Peter Cockey	2272, 2273, 2274, 2275
Captain	Charles Croxall	2363, 2364, 2365, 2366
Major	John Davidson	2875, 2877, 2878, 2880
Captain	Rezin Davis	3345, 3346, 3347, 3348
Major	Richard Dorsey	3600, 3601, 3602, 3349
Lieutenant	Isaac Duvall	2293, 2281, 2283, 2134
Surgeon	Levin Denwood	2322, 2323, 2324, 2325
Lieutenant	Robert Denny	2575, 2576, 2577, 2578
Captain	Henry Dobson	2189, 2190, 2069, 2070
Lieutenant	Thomas A. Dyson	2620, 2622, 2623, 2624
Lieutenant	Edward Duvall	2950, 2951, 3135, 3136
Lieutenant	Walter Dyer	3203, 3204, 3205, 3209
Major	John Deane	3234, 3051, 3053, 4151
Captain	Edward Dyer	3218, 3219, 3220, 3223
Lieutenant	Richard Donovan	3615, 3616, 3617, 3618
Major	John Eccleston	3611, 3612, 3613, 3614
Captain	Edward Edgerly	3607, 3608, 3609, 3610
Captain	James Ewing	3603, 3604, 3605, 3606
Surgeon	John L. Elbert	2621, 3246, 3248, 3251
Captain	Elijah Evans	3063, 3065, 3239, 3240
Lieutenant	Samuel Edmiston	3055, 3057, 3235, 3236
Lieut.-Col	Benjamin Ford, 6th Regt.	3206, 3207, 3211, 3213
Lieut.-Col	Uriah Forrest, 1st Regt	2715, 2716, 2717, 2718
Lieutenant	Samuel Farmer	3266, 3333, 3334, 3337
Captain	Ebenezer Finley	2214, 2215, 2216, 2217
Lieutenant	Benjamin Feckel	2660, 2664, 2668, 2669
Lieutenant	Hezekiah Ford	3274, 3275, 3276, 3265
Brig.-Gen	Mordecai Gist	2209, 2213, 2262, 2263
Captain	Edward Gale	2208, 2210, 2211, 2212
Colonel	John Gunby, 7th Regt	2266, 2267, 2264, 2265
Captain	Jonathan Gibson	3242, 4145, 4146, 1679
Major	Henry Gaither	2136, 2137, 2138, 2139
Captain	John Gassaway	3338, 3341, 3342, 3343
Captain	John Gale	2300, 2301, 2290, 2291
Lieutenant	Henry Gassaway	2876, 2893, 2894, 2895
Lieutenant	Richard Grace	2470, 2471, 2472, 2473
Captain	James Woolford Gray	2765, 2768, 2775, 2776
Lieutenant	Benjamin Garnett	2059, 2115, 2117, 2152
Captain	John Gist	2225, 2226, 2227, 2228
Lieutenant	Jacob Gromith	2736, 2737, 2738, 2739
Lieutenant	James Gould	3137, 2964, 2966, 2968
Lieutenant	William Goldsborough	3099, 4147, 4148, 1677
Lieutenant	Nicholas Gassaway	3241, 4143, 4144, 1681
Lieutenant	John Hardman	3079, 3080, 3081, 3082
Lieutenant	John Hamilton	3214, 3215, 3216, 3217
Captain	George Hamilton	1570, 1571, 1572, 1573
Lieut.-Col	John E. Howard, 5th Regt.	3243, 3244, 4149, 4138
Colonel	Josiah C. Hall, 4th Regt.	3083, 3084, 3085, 3086
Lieutenant	Philip Hill	4136, 3273, 3272, 3271
Lieutenant	Robert Hatkerson	2060, 2061, 2066, 2067
Lieutenant	Samuel Hanson	2294, 2295, 2296, 2297
Lieutenant	Arthur Harris	3305, 3306, 3307, 3313
Captain	John A. Hamilton	2482, 2483, 2484, 2485
Lieutenant	Rignel Hillery	3193, 4134, 4139, 4132
Lieutenant	Isaac Hanson	2611, 2612, 2613, 2614
Lieutenant	Edward Hamilton	2286, 2287, 2288, 2289
Captain	George Handy	3267, 3268, 3369, 3270
Lieutenant	Henry Hawkins	2318, 2319, 2298, 2299
Lieutenant	William Hanson	2252, 2253, 2255, 2257
Surgeon	Ezekiel Haynie	2248, 2249, 2254, 2256
Captain	Thomas B. Hugon	2701, 2703, 2704, 2698
Surg'n's Mate	Elisha Harrison	2343, 2344, 2345, 2346
Major	David Hopkins	2351, 2352, 2353, 2354
Lieutenant	John Hartshorn	2468, 2469, 2449, 2450
Major	Henry Hardman	2997, 2998, 2999, 2883
Captain	Edward Hall	2302, 2303, 2315, 2316
Captain	Adam Hoops	2478, 2479, 2480, 2481
Captain	John Courts Jones	2702, 2705, 2708, 2699
Captain	John Jordan	3303, 3304, 3314, 2871
Lieutenant	Adam Jamison	1565, 1670, 1672, 1673
Surgeon	William Kilty	2454, 2455, 2456, 2457
Captain	John Kilty	2140, 2141, 2142, 2128
Surg'n's Mate	Samuel Y. Keene	2118, 2129, 2130, 2131
Major	Thomas Lansdale	3210, 3212, 3231, 3233
Captain	David Lynn	2375, 2376, 2377, 2378
Major	John Lynch	1578, 1579, 1580, 1632
Captain	James M. Lingan	4124, 4125, 4126, 4127
Lieutenant	John Tolson Lowe	2593, 2594, 2496, 2497
Lieutenant	John LeNashu	2132, 2133, 2321, 2320
Lieutenant	John Lynn	2474, 2475, 2476, 2477
Captain	Thos. H. Luckett	2428, 2430, 2434, 2435
Captain	William Lamar	2444, 2443, 2447, 2427
Captain	David Luckett	2671, 2673, 2674, 2675
Captain	Samuel McPherson	1498, 1671, 1676, 1678
Captain	John Mitchell	3194, 3195, 3196, 3197
Captain	John Morris	2062, 2063, 2064, 2065
Captain	Thomas Mason	2058, 2071, 2072, 2079
Captain	Nicholas Mangers	2124, 2125, 2126, 2078
Captain	Joseph Marberry	2073, 2074, 2076, 2077
Lieutenant	Mark McPherson	2276, 2277, 2278, 2279
Captain	Christian Myres	2075, 2114, 2116, 2119
Captain	James McFadden	2676, 2677, 2680, 2681
Captain	Walker Muse	2461, 2462, 2491, 2480
Lieutenant	John McCoy	2700, 2689, 2688, 2697
Lieutenant	Zedekiah Moore	2690, 2685, 2684, 2682
Ensign	Caleb Mason	2595, 2596, 2597, 2598
Lieutenant	Lawrence Myers	2465, 2466, 2492, 2495
Lieutenant	David Morgan	2304, 2306, 2308, 2309

THE WAR FOR INDEPENDENCE.

Rank.	Names.	Numbers.
Captain	Jacob Norris	2582, 2586, 2587, 2683
Lieutenant	Roger Nelson	2845, 2847, 2849, 2868
Lieutenant	John Nelson	2336, 2337, 2338, 2436
Captain	Edward Oldham	3302, 3279, 3280, 4119
Lieutenant	Thomas Price	2881, 2882, 2888, 2889
Captain	Edward Prall	1574, 1575, 1576, 1577
Captain	Benjamin Price	2110, 2111, 2143, 2145
Lieutenant	William Pendergast	2112, 2113, 2135, 2292
Surgeon	Richard Pindell	4120, 4121, 4122, 4123
Colonel	Nath'l Ramsey, 30th Regt.	2127, 2144, 2146, 2147
Captain	Christopher Richmond	2740, 2741, 2742, 2743
Captain	William Riley	1457, 1458, 1459, 1460
Captain	Philip Reed	2096, 2097, 2098, 2099
Major	Alexander Roxburgh	3230, 3232, 3226, 3227
Lieutenant	Isaac Rawlings	3184, 3185, 3186, 3187
Major	John Rudolph	3225, 3245, 3247, 3250
Lieutenant	Joshua Rutledge	2691, 2692, 2693, 2694
Lieutenant	Jacob Raybolt	2846, 2848, 2850, 2896
Captain	Francis Revely	2728, 2729, 2730, 2731
Lieutenant	Nicholas Ricketts	2870, 2872, 2873, 2874
Lieutenant	Thomas Rouse	2401, 2402, 2403, 2404
Lieutenant	William Raison	2405, 2406, 2407, 2408
Captain	Michael Rudolph	2764, 2766, 2726, 2727
Maj.-Gen'l	William Smallwood	2409, 2410, 2411, 2412
Colonel	John H. Stone, 1st Regt.	2399, 2400, 2334, 2335
Major	Alex. L. Smith	2721, 2722, 2724, 2725
Major	Jonathan Sellman	3894, 3895, 3893, 2525
Captain	Edward Spurrier	2987, 2988, 2989, 2990
Captain	John Smith, 3d Regt	2958, 2959, 2961, 2963
Captain	James Somerville	2962, 2960, 2949, 2945
Captain	Clement Skerrilt	2723, 2732, 2733, 2735
Lieut.-Col	John Stewart	2756, 2757, 2758, 2759
Lieutenant	John Sears	2748, 2749, 2750, 2751
Major	John Swan	2706, 2707, 2695, 2696
Lieutenant	William Smoot	3315, 3316, 2869, 2867
Surgn's Mate	Alex. Smith	2975, 2976, 2977, 2978
Lieutenant	Martin Shugart	2983, 2984, 2985, 2986
Captain	John Smith, 6th Regt	2969, 2071, 2973, 2974
Lieutenant	Edward M. Smith	2441, 2442, 2460, 2463
Captain	James Smith, Artillery	2970, 2972, 3138, 3139
Lieutenant	William T. Stoddart	2413, 2414, 2415, 2416
Captain	Joseph Smith	4131, 4133, 4135, 4137
Ensign	Jacob Shoemaker	3188, 3189, 3190, 3192
Major	Alexander Trueman	2617, 3263, 3264, 3619
Lieut.-Col	Edward Tillard	1566, 1567, 1568, 1569
Captain	Adomson Tannehill	2371, 2372, 2373, 2374
Lieutenant	Josiah Tannehill	2887, 2890, 2891, 2892
Lieutenant	John Trueman	3180, 3181, 3182, 3183
Captain	Lilburn Williams	2615, 2616, 2618, 2619
Brig.-Gen'l	Otho Holland Williams	2687, 2686, 2678, 2679
Colonel	Thomas Woolford	1656, 1657, 1658, 1659
Captain	William Wilmot	2752, 2753, 2754, 2755
Lieutenant	William Woolford	2979, 2980, 2981, 2982
Captain	Richard Waters	2946, 2947, 2944, 2879
Lieut.-Col	Levin Winder	2884, 2885, 2886, 2996
Captain	James Winchester	2760, 2761, 2762, 2763
Lieutenant	Robert Wilmot	2744, 2745, 2746, 2747
Surgn's Mate	Gerrard Wood	2148, 2149, 2150, 2151
Lieutenant	Francis Ware	2952, 2953, 2965, 2967
Surgn's Mate	William Wate	2339, 2340, 2341, 2342
Lieutenant	Gassaway Watkins	2244, 2245, 2246, 2247
Surgeon	Walter Warfield	2837, 2842, 2843, 2844
Lieutenant	Nathan Wright	2092, 2093, 2094, 2095
Lieut.-Col	Lud'ck Weltner, Ger. Rgt.	3254, 3255, 3256, 3257
Lieutenant	George Winchester	2451, 2452, 2453, 2448

Rank.	Names.	Numbers.
Lieutenant	Young Wilkinson	2305, 2307, 2310, 2311
Captain	Nathan Williams	2330, 2331, 2332, 2333
Lieutenant	Basil Waring	2445, 2446, 2464, 2467
Lieutenant	William Towson	2431, 2432, 2433, 2429
Captain	Peregrine Fitzhugh	3335, 3336, 3332, 3339
Lieutenant	William Fitzhugh	2940, 2941, 2942, 2943
Lieutenant	William Murdoch	2417, 2418, 2419, 2420

SOLDIERS.

Names.	Rank.	Regiment.	Number.
Adam Adams	Private.	1	1876
Ignatius Adams	"	1	1163
John Alvey	"	2	2033
John Appleby	"	3	1131
Daniel Anderson	"	4	1318
James Allen	"	5	27
Thomas Ayres	"	5	1168
Emanuel Allen	"	5	1160
John Andrews	"	5	2537
William Ayhern	"	6	3174
John Armstrong (1)	"	2	1956
John Ashmore	"	7	3121
George Abbot	"	2	2544
Cuthbert Able	Sergeant.	7	1146
John Adams	Corporal.	3	1117
Thomas Arthur	Private.	State.	2528
John Auber	"	"	2520
John Ashbury	"	"	2571
John Armstrong (2)	"	6	1901
Harris Austin	"	5	138
Josias Alvey	"	1	2034
Jacob Adams	"	Rawlings'.	4059
John Adams (2)	"	State.	1748
John Anderson (1)	"	3	62
Peregrine Asque	M.	Artillery.	930
William Allen	"	"	1949
Thomas Adams	Private.	3	876
James Ashley	"	German.	950
William Absolum	"	Recruit 81.	......
Travers Alvey	"	3	......
Nathan Aldridge	"	German.	......
John Anderson	"	7	......
Henry Austin	"	2	......
Thomas Aspin	"	2	......
Frederick Ayres	"	6	......
Thomas Allison	"	1	......
Michael Anderson	"	Hazen's.	......
Barnet Alley	"	Lee's Legion.	......
James Arrants	"	"	......
James Addy, or Eddy	"	2	......
Thomas G. Alvey	"	3	......
Daniel Basil	Fifer.	1	1882
John Baker	Private.	1	2545
George Bateman	"	1	1825
John Brookbank	"	1	3118
Levy Burk	"	2	1256
Thomas Buckley	Sergeant.	2	1330
William Brookes	Private.	2	1992
Barruch Butt	"	2	1970
Thomas Butt	"	2	4036
Edward Butt	"	2	1818
Frederick Bennett	Fifer.	2	2040
Solomon Brittenham	Private.	2	131
Levy Button	"	2	1893
Levin Bramble	"	2	3129

Names.	Rank.	Regiment.	Number.	Names.	Rank.	Regiment.	Number.
John Blades	Private.	2	1585	James Bigwood	Private.	State.	......
Thomas Brown	Corporal.	3	951	Peter Bushell	"	4	......
John Brown (1)	Private.	3	1948	Thomas Baker	"	State.	......
Richard Butler	"	3	1169	James Balip	"	"	......
John Barrett	"	3	1142	J. Berriman, or Banneman	"	4	......
Basil Brown	"	3	1780	James Brannan	"	2	1057
George Brown	"	3	2084	John Brian	"	State.	1112
Zachariah Burch	"	3	91	John Biggs	"	"	1859
Leonard Bean	Corporal.	3	1827	Jacob Blake	"	"	1785
Gabriel Brand	Private.	3	471	John Brown (3)	Corporal.	Rawlings'.	75
John Bean	"	3	814	Benjamin Burch	Sergeant.	"	1123
Thomas Bird	"	3	3015	George Bough	Private.	German.	1134
Benjamin Boyd	"	3	2027	Samuel Boswell	"	"	2521
John Blair (2)	"	3	997	William Batten	"	Rawlings'.	1351
Peter Bochard	"	3	873	Zachariah Berry	"	"	2547
Thomas Bailey	"	3	1043	James Bryan	"	1	3166
John Buckley	"	3	872	John Bayley (1)	"	3	1147
Joshua Barret	Sergeant.	4	101	William Burgess	"	3	3001
George Bradley	Corporal.	4	1407	George Belfast	"	Recruit 1781.	1051
Peter Bowler	Private.	4	194	Charles Buckliss	"	State.	3044
Joshua Batchley	"	4	1381	John Brady	Sergeant.	"	1416
Robert Bowen	Fifer.	4	2535	James Barrow	Private.	"	888
Philip Bailey	Private.	4	1037	Thomas Baxter	"	"	936
John Beach	Drummer.	4	1148	James Blewer	"	3	1369
John Buchanan	"	1	2025	John Butcher	"	3	188
Daniel Buckley	Private.	2	1757	Nathan Bateman	"	5	2016
James Biass	"	3	1139	John Bennet	"	State.	63
John Barnett	"	5	1026	Joseph Burch	"	2	1089
Perry Burtham	"	5	1072	Thomas Bishop	"	2	1127
John Brent	Fifer.	5	1411	William Braithwait	"	2	4107
George Blackham	Private.	5	3	Richard Blansford	"	2	1076
James Barron	"	5	159	Thomas Brown	Sergeant.	Artillery.	1904
James Bailey	"	5	2000	Isaac Burton	M.	"	2549
Abram Bowen	"	5	1940	Thomas Brown	"	"	1199
John Bantham	"	5	41	Edward Berry	"	"	4104
Solomon Barrett	"	5	1797	Thomas Bowler	"	"	881
James Burk (1)	"	6	1771	John Brady	"	"	1510
John Brown (2)	Sergeant.	6	1059	Thomas Barber	"	"	1170
Henry Billop	Private.	6	1275	Thomas Barclay, or Bartley.	Private.	3	1905
Thomas Bear	"	6	1849	William Bruff	"	7	1782
George Bumgardner	"	6	2035	David Bramble	"	2	1888
Benjamin Burch (2)	Corporal.	6	1556	John Burnes	"	Recruit 81.	2538
Thomas Brady	Private.	6	1464	Benjamin Bough	"	"	57
Joseph Blaize	"	7	2002	John Boudy	"	"	1561
Joseph Botts	"	7	986	John Boody	"	"	891
Moses Barney	"	7	1360	John Britton	"	"	26
Richard Boone	"	7	3120	John Briley	"	"	103
Joshua Brown	"	7	1881	Benjamin Belcher	"	"	1846
Josiah Burgess	"	7	1603	Thomas Burch (2)	"	"	1149
Humphrey Beckett	Sergeant.	7	1086	Nathaniel Barley	"	"	393
Laurence Brannan	"	7	1581	Andrew Bramble	"	"	1698
George Brown	Private.	7	2541	John Baxter	"	"	3058
George Buck	"	7	182	James Bowen	"	"	1185
Abijah Buxton	"	1	1875	Joel Baker	"	7	1177
Jesse Barnett	Fifer.	7	1489	William Brady	"	Recruit 81.	992
Thomas Bowser	Private.	5	1935	John Blair (1)	"	7	3023
James Baber	"	State.	4111	George Bowers	"	6	3152
Daniel Bulger	"	7	4113	James Bayley	Drummer.	3	993
Jesse Boswell	Corporal.	State.	1831	James Berry	M.	Artillery.	1703
Joseph Barton	Private.	"	3027	Robert Britt	Private.	1	1052
Martin Bowles	"	7	......	Luke Burnes	"	1	4029
John Brewer	"	State.	......	William Bowles	"	2	4066
John Branson	"	"	......	Daniel Boyles	"	2	1963
Jeremiah Brown	"	"	......	Ezekiel Burnes	"	2	989
Richard Biddle	"	"	......	John Burnes	"	2	1465

THE WAR FOR INDEPENDENCE.

Names.	Rank.	Regiment.	Number.
Zachariah Butt	Private.	2	1934
Charles Byrn	"	2	1903
James Banny	"	3	1181
Hugh Burns	"	3	1154
Thomas Buttery	"	3	1536
William Bolton	"	3	1172
James Brown	"	5	1742
John Benny	"	5	4096
Alexander Beck	"	5	887
Michael Burns	"	5	1537
Hugh Batton	"	6	1981
Robert Body	Fifer.	6	3008
John Brown	Private.	6	3064
James Boyle	"	6	1918
Harvey Burnes	"	Hazen's.	1115
John Batton	"	"	29
William Brown	"	"	4103
Nehemiah Barns	"	"	1221
Richard Basset	"	Lee's Legion.	1763
George Bowe	"	"	1267
John Bennet	"	"	434
James Brown	"	"	1207
Thomas Broome	"	"	1840
William Bright	"	4	953
Robert Barnet	"	German.	1740
William Clary	"	1	4153
David Caile	"	1	2397
John Carroll (1)	"	1	2504
James Collard	Fifer.	1	4044
Wm. Clements (2)	Private.	1	1182
Michael Cole	"	1	1178
Thomas Campher	"	2	493
Patrick Cavenaugh	"	State.	1266
William Cato	"	2	1675
Hugh Cain	"	2	1063
David Conner (1)	"	2	1092
Morris Citizen	"	2	1095
William Chatland	"	2	1922
William Cutler	"	2	1910
John Camphen	"	2	2369
Hampton Coursey	"	2	821
William Conner (1)	"	2	193
George Childs	Corporal.	3	79
Daniel Claney	Private.	3	1832
John Craig	"	3	3094
Barton Cecil	"	3	90
Charles Clements	"	3	4165
Luke Carter	"	3	4152
John Claggett	"	3	3161
Thomas Clark (1)	"	3	123
Heze. Carr	Drummer.	3	472
John Courts	Private.	3	1604
Michael Clark	"	4	1931
John Colin	Sergeant.	4	4157
Thomas B. Clements	Private.	Recruited 81.	1911
William Cartro (2)	"	4	1135
Emanuel Carthagone	"	4	1020
Abram Catchsides	"	4	4022
Thomas Clinton	Fifer.	4	1108
Michael Callahan	Private.	4	158
Aseph Colegate	"	4	1919
Andrew Crummy	"	2	1132
John Carr	"	3	911
Robert Cornick	"	5	191
John Carroll (2)	"	5	459
Charles Crouch	Sergeant.	5	1028
Augustine Cann	Private.	5	1833
Thomas Carney	"	5	1067
Michael Claney	Fifer.	5	1066
Thomas Cahoe, Sr	Private.	6	4100
Thomas Cahoe, Jr	Fifer.	6	4109
Benjamin Cleaver	Private.	6	1417
Christopher Cusick	"	6	1006
Robert Callahan, or Clemmahan	"	6	1805
William Cook	"	6	1175
William Craile	"	7	962
Darby Crowley	"	7	474
John Cheshire	Sergeant.	7	475
William Casey	Private.	7	461
Adam Crow	"	Recruited 81.	1704
William Cummins	"	7	1446
Aquilla Chitham	Sergeant.	7	1562
Owen Carey	Corporal.	7	21
Ignatius Compton	Private.	7	1032
James Curren	"	7	168
Stephen Carr	"	7	162
Edward Claney	Fifer.	7	167
John Cochran	Private.	7	166
William Collis	Sergeant.	State.	1208
Jonathan Chubb	Private.	"	3119
William Chapman	"	"	1402
Henry Crook	"	"	3035
William Cox	"	"	909
Henry Craine	"	"	1033
George Clarke	"	"	808
Thomas Cooper	"	"	1487
Bennet H. Clements	"	"	1920
James Casey	"	"	1913
Lewis Cunningham	"	"	1520
Calothile Carmile	"	"	1755
David Crady	Fifer.	"	1802
Michael Casner	Private.	"	1058
Samuel Callahan	"	3	1753
John Cooper (1)	"	State.	1752
George Craigs	"	4	3164
Dominick Coins	"	6	906
Benjamin Cole	"	German.	477
John Connelly (1)	"	Gist's.	3033
Isham Coleman	"	State.	1467
William Carter (1)	"	"	1497
James Crozier	"	"	2570
Peter Carberry	"	"	56
Samuel Chapple	"	"	1982
Michael Curtis	"	"	176
William Clements (1)	"	5	1790
Kindall Cobb	"	Recruited 81.	4155
Thomas Cannady	"	3	1149
Valentine Clapper	"	State.	4052
Charles Cooper	"	2	1167
John Carson	Sergeant.	Recruited 81.	297
Elijah Cockendall	Corporal.	Rawlings'.	1506
John Crosby (1)	Private.	4	278
Dennis Cragan	"	1	340
Joseph Cooley	"	1	1282
Thomas Craig	Sergeant.	Rawlings'.	960
Edward Cosgrove	Private.	1	298
John Clancey (2)	Corporal.	1	458
James Crawford	Private.	3	1214
William Civill	"	5	1294

Names.	Rank.	Regiment.	Number.	Names.	Rank.	Regiment.	Number.
Timothy Cahill	Private.	German.	23	William Collier	Private.	3	52
Jacob Carnant	"	7	921	William Cougleton	"	4	1490
John Carter	"	State.	923	Simon Chappoik	"	4	946
Owen Coffield	"	Grayson's.	924	James Conner	"	5	1813
George Collins	"	3	4144	John Caves	"	5	1907
Bryan Carroll	"	2	3126	Michael Claney, Sr	Sergeant.	5	1789
Michael Coyle	"	6	479	Peter Carwell	"	6	1102
Edward Cain	"	4	1104	Michael Corr	"	6	414
Joseph Crouch	"	3	1035	John Crozier	"	6	412
Thomas Cardiff	"	3	973	Peter Cunningham	Private.	7	82
John Cole	"	Recruited 81.	1150	John Clarke	"	7	25
Jacob Collins	"	2	902	Richard Clarke	"	7	342
James Chambers	"	Recruit 81.	183	Nicholas Campbell	"	7	3171
John Collins	"	"	1130	Hugh Connelly	"	Hazen's.	436
Thomas Clarke	"	"	1155	John Craig	"	"	3172
Thomas Condron	Corporal.	Artillery.	1126	John Coomy, or Kumy	"	"	4031
Arthur Carns	"	"	1068	John Collins	"	"	437
Hugh Chaplin	M.	"	1861	Jessie Crasbie	"	Lee's Legion.	438
Timothy Connelly	Sergeant.	"	1860	Robert Crouch	"	"	1038
William Cornwall	"	"	857	Wm., or Benj. Chesnut	"	"	846
Samuel Carter	"	"	1950	Charles Dawkens	Sergeant.	1	156
John Clark	Gunner.	"	432	Dennis Dunning	Drummer.	1	445
Michael Conner	M.	"	1307	John Dixon (1)	Private.	1	1985
John Compton	"	"	1483	Francis Dunar	"	1	2572
Robert Campbell	"	"	4156	William Dortch	"	1	1244
James Clarke	"	"	858	Henry Dixon	"	1	497
John Curl	Private.	State.	1044	John Denson	"	2	867
John Cleverdence	"	Recruited 81.	42	George Dixon	"	2	84
Arthur Coffin	"	"	105	William Dixon	"	3	1082
Joshua Cox	"	"	47	John Dyer	"	3	1674
Edward Chambers	"	"	979	Aquilla Deaver	"	3	4045
James Chard	"	"	1159	Luke Dempsey	"	3	1354
James Cochran	"	"	925	Thomas Drudge	"	3	1505
John Cannon	"	"	1491	John Donovan	"	4	121
Thomas Compton	"	"	1194	William Downes	"	4	130
James Collins	Sergeant.	7	1607	Thomas Doyle	"	4	1628
William Cork	Private.	Recruit 81.	1631	Peter Degafzoon	"	4	454
George Carney	"	"	1060	James Daffin	Corporal.	4	485
Robert Carnes	"	"	1252	Edmund Dougherty	Sergeant.	4	1714
Matthias Cyphart	"	"	1418	Francis Dunnington	Private.	2	1692
James Clements	"	"	1593	James Doyle	"	5	1543
William Coe	"	"	1595	John Duhague	"	5	1508
James Crasbury	"	"	800	John Downey	"	5	1507
William Cann	"	"	1295	Elijah Deane	"	5	212
Zachariah Clark	Fifer.	3	1983	Robert Davis	"	6	1717
Samuel Clark	Private.	7	1425	Richard Duvall	"	6	1550
Robert Campbell	"	Recruit 81.	1218	Patrick Doran	Sergeant.	6	1481
John Campbell (2)	"	"	1109	John Denson	Drummer.	6	1909
John Connelly (2)	"	Gist's.	1812	James Devereux	Sergeant.	6	1504
William Coursey	"	Recruit 81.	1626	George Devit	Private.	7	480
Patrick Conner	"	2	3078	Robert Dunkin	"	7	1527
Peter Casey	"	7	1118	Samuel Davis (1)	Sergeant.	7	1716
Michael Carr's Adm'r			457	Samuel Denny	Private.	7	1232
Benjamin Carns	"	2	1866	James Dyer (1)	"	3	1602
John Curritt	"	1	4110	John Delanaway	"	7	1525
Thomas Chapman	"	1	1473	Matthias Dyche	"	6	1627
Samuel Chinn	"	1	3004	John Deakins	"	State.	1689
Robert Cooley	"	1	1300	Edward Dominick	"	"	1954
John Cole	"	2	864	Joseph Donahoe	"	"	1858
John Cornish	"	2	1245	James Davidson	"	1	443
Joseph Cullamine	"	3	1298	William Deaver	"	3	1697
Bennet Cheser	"	3	1343	James Due	"	5	1161
Barney Cassaday	"	3	53	William Devine	"	State.	1848
John Cox	"	3	189	James Dyer (2)	"	German.	1800
Justinian Carter	"	3	38	John Donaghan	"	State.	1189

THE WAR FOR INDEPENDENCE.

Names.	Rank.	Regiment.	Number.
Wm. Dunnington, or Derrington	Private.	3	114
Joseph Deford	"	5	1027
Alexander Downey	"	5	1011
Richard Dixon	"	7	1085
Francis Duvist	"	Rawlings'.	466
James Dowden	"	"	1583
Butoc Deveaux	"	1	4038
John Dent	"	3	4039
John Dove	Sergeant.	7	1941
Beryer Dominick	Private.	6	1197
James Denison	"	Rawlings'.	1736
Richard Downs	"	7	1474
Pearce Deakon	"	Rawlings'.	1761
William Day	"	State.	1921
James Davidson	"	1	1727
Thomas Dutton	"		1788
Charles Davis	"	Recruit 81.	397
William Davis	M.	Artillery.	1255
William Dixon	B.	"	3130
Peter Davis	D.	"	427
John Davis (1)	Private.	Recruit 81.	293
William Dawson	"	"	273
Barnaby Dorothy	"	5	314
Jacob Duders	"	Recruit 81.	241
Terrence Duffy	"	6	428
John Deane	"	Recruit 81.	1121
John Dobson	"	"	490
James Drian	"	Recruit 81.	1235
Thomas Duffy	"	"	812
Thomas Davis (1)	"	"	1625
Abram Dugan	"	"	963
Thomas Dickison	"	"	338
Charles Deane	"	"	1957
Richard Dolvin	"	"	324
Richard Dunby	"	"	426
James Dawson	"	"	240
Timothy Donovan	M.	Artillery.	272
Thomas Dutton's Adm'r	Private.	1	292
Thomas Daley	"	2	317
John Davis	"	3	337
John Davis, of Bailey's Co.	"	3	364
James Douglas, " "	"	3	385
James Divine, " "	"	4	406
Michael Duffy	"	4	1953
John Deford	"	5	1210
Patrick Durgan	"	5	407
Peter Dunston	"	6	1421
Thomas Disharoon	"	7	1426
George Dice, or Dias	"	5	467
Francis Duffy	S.	Recruited 81.	1094
Jeremiah Driskill	Private.	4	1524
George Dyer	"	5	1600
John Davis	"	Recruited 81.	1119
Patrick Dennison	"	4	448
William Deakins	"	Hazen's.	1588
Thomas Deavor	"	"	1427
William Douley	"	"	446
William Dowdle	"	Lee's Legion.	1549
Joseph Deale	"	Artillery.	386
Michael Dowlan	"	N. Gist's.	1712
Henry Evans	"	Recruited 81.	1539
Edward Ellicott	"	1	1432
Peregrine Evans	Sergeant.	2	439
Bartholomew Esom	Corporal.	2	949
Michael Ellis	Fifer.	2	1434
Thomas Evans (2)	Private.	3	1705
Thomas Ellicott (2)	"	3	1433
William Ellis	"	4	1589
Edward Evans (1)	"	4	972
William Evans	"	4	1204
Thomas Edwards	Sergeant.	4	1428
Jarvis Eccleston	Private.	5	239
Joseph Ellicott	"	6	1685
George Elms	Fife-Major.	6	1231
John Ellicott (1)	Private.	6	382
Edward Evans (2)	Sergeant.	State.	1271
William Elkins	Private.	"	365
Thomas Ellis (1)	"	"	969
Enork Ennis	"	"	850
Leonard Ennis	"	"	1236
John Ennis	"	"	1249
John Edwards	"	Recruited 81.	465
Peter Equidowney	"	"	494
James Evans	"	"	316
Thomas Elliott (1)	"	"	817
Samuel Evans	Corporal.	"	1738
Thomas Evans (1)	Private.	"	4041
Heathesat Edwards	"	"	1794
Emanuel Ebbs	"	Gist's.	1750
Euel Evans	"	State.	1883
Thomas Ellison	"	1	1863
John Edwards	Sergeant.	3	391
Richard Ellis' Adm'r	"	5	449
Frederick Eyen	"	Artillery.	441
John Evans	M.	"	1553
Benjamin Evans	"	6	1310
John Etheridge	"	6	1691
Richard Ellison	Private.	7	901
James Ervine	"	Recruited 81.	1304
Nicholas Elliott	"	"	932
James Edes	"	Hazen's.	220
Edward Ervine	"	"	255
Jacob Flora	"	1	1083
Francis Fairbrother	"	1	34
John Franeway	"	1	1898
Stephen Fresh	"	1	20
Joseph Fowler	"	1	914
William Fisher	"	1	844
Jonathan Fowler	"	1	328
Geo. Fellason, or Fenlayson	"	2	213
Henry Fisher (2)	"	German.	1423
James Farrel	"	2	341
James Fitzjerald	"	2	16
Francis Freeman	"	2	1424
John Ferguson	"	2	1781
Edward Furriner	"	3	2501
James Forster	"	3	1845
Alexander Francis	"	3	1841
Richard Freeman	"	3	164
Wm. R. Franklin	"	3	1077
John Farrell	"	3	1750
Richard Farraby	"	4	1141
Frederick Flinon	"	4	1042
Stafford Fosdale	"	4	3098
Peter Fountain	"	4	2486
Benjamin Folliott	"	4	153
Rigby Foster	"	5	947
Wm. Foreman	Sergeant.	5	3113
Wm. Farrell	Drummer.	5	148

Names.	Rank.	Regiment.	Number.	Names.	Rank.	Regiment.	Number.
John Fulham	Private.	5	3062	John Green (1)	Private.	1	2018
Edward Flowers	"	5	810	William Griffin	Fifer.	1	1997
Mark Forster	"	5	1284	Thomas Glover	Private.	1	1978
Benjamin Fitzgerald	Sergeant.	7	172	Andrew Garnet	Fifer.	2	3123
Absolom Fardo	Private.	7	22	William Gould	Private.	2	1923
John M. Funner	"	7	3165	Mark Griffin	"	2	1959
Doras Filmont	"	7	1062	Nathan Griffin	"	2	822
Nicholas Fitzgerald	"	7	1871	Rubin Goostry	"	2	1333
Moses Forster	"	7	2024	Henry Green	"	2	1340
Samuel Filson	Sergeant.	7	3131	Thomas Gossage	"	2	1205
Stephen Fluhart	"	1 and 7	3097	Anthony Geohagan	Drummer.	3	1563
Dennis Flanagan	M.	Artillery.	3178	Jesse Grace	"	3	1229
Emanuel Farara	Private.	State.	174	John Gibson	Private.	3	811
Philip Fisher	"	"	1339	Isaac Green	"	3	33
John Folling	"	"	1924	William Glascow	"	3	1258
Robert Farrel	"	"	1211	Charles Goldsborough	"	3	1828
Jeremiah French	"	"	896	John Gordon (1)	"	3	1253
Philip Fitzpatrick	"	"	905	William Gates	Drummer.	3	1610
Charles Fitzgerald	"	"	971	John Goddard	Private.	3	3107
Wm. Fitzgerald	"	"	1932	Hugh Gainer	"	3	210
John Frawney	"	"	1329	James Garth	"	4	415
George Finlay	Sergeant.	Recruited 81.	4159	John Gwynn	Sergeant.	4	1309
Robert Folger	Private.	"	1328	James Gray (1)	Private.	4	1176
Peter French	Corporal.	"	965	John Gorman (1)	"	4	3032
Thomas Foxall	Private.	"	893	Thomas Gillon	"	5	1824
Edward Fincham	"	"	1816	Henry Gilby	"	5	3072
John Fosset	"	"	345	Abraham Gamble	"	5	3010
Walter Farrel	"	"	815	James Greenwood	Drummer.	6	1996
David Foxall	"	"	128	Moses Grahame	Private.	6	3056
Stephen Fennell	"	State.	1049	Isaac Graves	"	6	201
George Ford	"	5	1162	Edward Garrish	"	6	1515
John Fulford	"	State.	1737	Paul Grenard	"	6	100
George Fields	Sergeant.	3	1003	Richard Gee	"	7	1762
Robert Firth	"	Rawlings'.	938	Samuel Gerry	"	7	484
Thomas Flemming	"	"	994	Joseph Gordon	"	7	1928
Joseph Fisher	"	Recruited 81.	2085	Henry Goldsborough	"	3	4049
John Fennel	"	German.	933	John Gordon (2)	"	Rawlings'.	1855
Charles Fulham	Corporal.	"	2088	William Glory	"	State.	1881
John Franklin	Private.	"	4097	William Groves	"	"	1744
Joseph Folliott	"	4	55	John Green (2)	"	"	413
Thomas Frumley	"	5	4105	Benjamin Gilbert	"	"	1884
Henry Fisher (1)	"	Recruited 81.	2001	Thomas Gadd	"	"	1614
William Fairburn	"	3	3167	Philip Graham	"	Recruited 81.	1720
Jeremiah Fitzjerald	"	7	455	Bennet George	"	"	1929
Richard Fenwick	"	4	1729	Lambert Goody	"	"	1721
Andrew Fernan	"	3	1452	John Gee	"	"	1767
Thomas Fanning	M.	Artillery.	1019	Amos Griffith	"	"	3101
John Fitzjerald, Jr.	"	"	907	John Graham	Fifer.	"	2542
Benjamin Freshwater	"	1	3009	Charles Girdler	Private.	State.	883
Robert Ford	Sergeant.	4	1373	Thomas Gilham	"	"	1710
John Fairbank	"	5	1408	Solomon Greene	"	Recruited 81.	1477
William Fountain	"	5	1530	Charles Goff	"	1	884
Edward Fennel	"	7	1730	John Gregory	"	2	1605
Massey Fluart	"	Hazen's.	1995	James Gravey	"	State.	1545
Samuel Frazier	"	"	2029	William Greenage	"	5	1296
James Flood	"	"	1974	Smart Greer	"	Recruited 81.	941
William French	"	Lee's Legion.	1196	Samuel Gray	"	State.	1945
Edmund Flowers	"	5	3160	William George	"	6	456
Robert Freemoutt	"	3	1041	Southey George	"	Recruited 81.	943
James Flack	Sergeant.	6	1074	Joseph Green	"	State.	1518
Peter Farrell	Corporal.	State.	462	William Gudgeon	"	Recruited 81.	1494
Benjamin Gray	Sergeant.	7	1973	John Gather	"	5	1951
Amos Green	Private.	1	3054	Jacob Games	"	Recruited 81.	1739
Abraham Garcena	"	1	899	Benjamin Gater	"	"	1952
Samuel Green	"	1	1972	William Gillespie	"	State.	1599

THE WAR FOR INDEPENDENCE.

Names.	Rank.	Regiment.	Number.	Names.	Rank.	Regiment.	Number.
Marshall Galloway	Private.	3	1760	John Head	Drummer.	2	1378
James Goodwin	"	3	1784	John Hughes (1)	Private.	2	358
William Grant	"	Recruited 81.	2019	Richard Harper	"	2	4032
Vincent, or Willson Gray	"	Grayson's.	1701	James Hill	"	2	2030
Michael Grosh	"	German.	1528	John Howard	"	2	4061
Robert Gelhampton	"	4	1475	John Holmes	"	3	144
Thomas Gray	"	4	78	Edward Hurley	"	3	3066
Jacob Gray	Sergeant.	2	1870	William Harris	"	3	380
Richard Gray	Private.	2	915	Elias Hardy	"	3	95
John Giles	"	2	401	Isaac Hill	Drummer.	4	829
Moses Graves	"	5	1260	Josias Harris	Private.	3	1383
Jonathan Gill	M.	Artillery.	359	John Howell	"	4	267
Mark Goldsborough		"	289	William Howe	"	4	218
Charles Groom	M.	"	416	Jacob Hines	"	4	1451
Thomas Gleeson	"	"	266	Nathaniel Hull	"	4	296
William Grimes	"	"	102$_3$	Henry Hines	"	3	1400
Enoch Ganet	Private.	5	398	Zadock Harvey	"	5	1326
Harvey Gray	"	7	1582	Charles Hill	"	6	310
Sylvester Gatting	"	1	3048	Wm. Harris (1)	"	6	403
John Gordon	"	Lee's Legion.	165	Nicholas Huster	"	7	290
Walter Glasgow	"	3	1873	Thomas Hoye	"	7	311
William Hutton	Corporal.	Artillery.	1021	Walter Hagan	"	7	1800
William Hellen	B.	"	3112	Randolph Hoskins	"	1	1619
Cornelius Harling	M.	"	417	Lazarus Higgs	"	State.	222
Michael Hughes	"	"	1933	James Hagan	Corporal.	"	3087
William Hallen	B.	"	1933	George Haden	"	5	926
John Howard	M.	"	351	Thomas Harrison (2)	Sergeant.	Grayson's.	2086
James Hendrickson	M.	"	1420	George Holton	"	Recruit 81.	1649
Robert Harding	Private.	1	151	George Hagarthy	"	2	1980
Thomas Hart	"	2	1478	John Hood, or Wood	Private.	3	1718
William Harper	"	2	1190	Vachel Hayes	Drummer.	2	4065
John Hall	"	2	217	James Hare	Private.	2	1826
Conrad Hodibuck	"	2	1164	Samuel Hughes	"	2	1320
Joseph Hoole	"	3	1016	Cornelius Howard	Sergeant.	3	1854
John Hackett	"	4	3116	John B. Haslip	Private.	3	31
Jeremiah Hooper	"	4	1686	Isaac Holliday	"	4	1803
John Hulls	"	4	1501	Leonard Hagan	"	7	1338
Isaac Hines	"	4	1166	Wm. Hughes	"	1	496
Josiah Hurley	"	5	413	John Higgens	"	State.	2081
Richard Harper	"	5	319	John Hare	"	"	3002
John Hall	"	5	1209	Peter Howard	"	"	3011
Charles Heath	"	5	470	John Hood (2)	"	"	3029
Richard B. Haslip	"	German.	1488	John Hillary	"	6	3006
Thomas Hutchcraft	"	"	3888	John S. Hunt	"	Recruited 81.	102
Richard Hayes	"	Recruited 81.	4046	Edward Hennisee	"	1	1265
William Hartman	"	"	277	Pompey Hollis	"	Recruited 81.	154
James Humphries	"	"	1749	James Halleron	"	"	1314
Hercules Hutchings	"	"	224	John Haynes	"	"	3075
John Hannan	"	1	322	David Hatton	"	"	1216
Charles Hickey	"	2	244	Wm. Hamston	"	7	1430
John Hutson (2)	"	Recruit 81.	1431	Samuel Harrison	"	Recruit 81.	1342
Calib Haley	"	State.	1925	John Haney	"	2	303
John Holston	"	Recruit 81.	976	Austen Howard	"	3	1136
Samuel Hughes	"	"	389	Joseph Horsfield	"	2	238
William Hamilton	D.	3	321	Joseph Hukell	"	2	383
Henry Harris	Private.	3	245	Barney Haney	"	3	335
Lawrence Hurdle	"	7	225	Richard Hall	"	3	420
Michael Hawke	Corporal.	Artillery.	1151	John Hamilton	"	3	808
Henry Higgs	M.	"	276	Peregrine Howard	"	3	362
Daniel Harvey	"	"	361	Charles Harvey	Sergeant.	4	1743
John Head	"	"	920	John Hyde	Private.	4	1642
James Hutton	Sergeant.	"	150	Robert Harpham	Sergeant.	4	1915
James Hammond	Corporal.	"	4108	Thomas Harris (1)	Private.	Recruited 81.	4
William Herrington	Private.	1	2559	Francis Hopkins	"	3	3176
Raphael Hagan	"	1	93	John Holder	"	5	2557

Name.	Rank.	Regiment.	Number.	Names.	Rank.	Regiment.	Number.
John Harris (1)	Private.	5	1093	Joshua, or Matthew Harvey		Lee's Legion.	1463
Wm. Horney	"	5	3115	Abijah Hickell		"	967
John Hull	Drummer.	5	1775	George Hill		"	181
John Holliday	Private.	6	1609	Joseph Hemphill		"	3095
John Housley	"	6	1906	Samuel Huggins		6	483
John Hall (2)	Corporal.	6	1837	William Haney		Artillery.	1325
Jacob Hunt	Private.	7	1836	William Hickenson	Private.	"	1394
Frederick Harty	"	7	379	Benton Harris	"	State.	58
Wm. Hurley	"	7	1621	Thomas Harrison (1)	"	2	344
John Hulet	"	7	400	Robert Johnston	"	2	1829
John Harrell	"	1	136	Thomas Jones (2)	"	5	1075
Joseph Hall	"	1	36	Zachariah Jacobs	"	3	132
John Haden	"	7	1379	Thomas Jones (3)	"	3	283
Wm. Hillman	"	5	981	John Johnston (3)	"		1872
Walter Howe	"	State.	1395	Isaac Johnston	"	Rawlings'.	486
Edward Holland	Drummer.	"	3127	William Johnston	Sergeant.	1	980
William Hicks	Private.	"	1517	William Johnston	"	German.	824
George Hamilton	"	"	134	Robert Issable	"	2	1587
Philip Huston	"	"	402	David Jones	Corporal.	2	269
Nathan Harper	"	"	1890	John Johnston	Private.	State.	1864
Samuel Hamilton	"	"	481	William Joice (2)	"	4	180
Samuel Harper	"	"	334	William Joice (1)	"	1	291
Lazarus Harman	"	"	11	Archibald Johnston	Sergeant.	1	468
Nehemiah Hadder	"	"	4116	Edward Ervin	Private.	1	255
Ed. Hammond	"	"	209	Joseph Jenkins	"	1	378
John Hancock	"	"	249	Henry Jacobs	"	2	207
Elijah Hutt	"	"	1278	Nealy Jones	"	2	279
Ralph Hope	"	Recruited 81.	190	Joseph Jones (1)	"	2	1179
Wm. Hill (1)	"	5	60	William Jinkins	"	2	1283
James Hewett	"	State.	1419	John Jones (1)	"	2	2090
James Harris (2)	"	2	1521	James Jackson	Sergeant.	2	1765
Thomas Hawson	"	1	1165	Benjamin Johnston	Fifer.	3	1804
Stephen Hancock	"	State.	1243	Thomas Jones (1)	Private.	3	895
John Hickens	"	"	2037	Joseph Johnston	"	4	4056
Daniel Howe	"	Rawlings'.	43	Adam Jameson	"	4	161
Richard Huggens	Sergeant.	"	332	John Johnston (1)	"	4	430
Thomas Hill	Private.	"	374	William Ingles	"	5	1830
William Hope	"	State.	1976	Aaron Jones	"	5	46
John Hurley	"	"	331	Jesse Jacobs	Sergeant.	6	3074
Leonard Holt	"	"	1541	Daniel Jarvis, or Javins	Private.	6	1586
Nicholas Hiner	"	4	1917	Joseph Jeans	Sergeant.	Rawlings'.	827
Richard Harrington	"	Recruited 81.	444	John Jones, Sr. (3)	Private.	State.	2556
Levin Harrington	"	"	163	William Jones (1)	"	"	375
William Harper	"	"	3039	William Jones (2)	"	"	1531
Daniel Holdman	"	"	169	Jacob Jeffers	"	Recruited 81.	1756
John Hudson (1)	"	"	489	Thomas Johns	"	"	889
Samuel Hurst	"	"	1053	Robert Johnston	"	2	3175
James Hudson (1)	"	2	299	John Jones (2)	"	State.	1270
William Hedge	"	4	3887	Ed. Jackson	"	Recruited 81.	86
William Hutcheson	"	1	1806	Frederick Ijams	"	"	1319
William Harrison (1)	"	1	1702	George Jennings	"	State.	1793
Michael Hartman	"	German.	1045	John Jackson	"	State and 1.	1285
John Hopkins	"	7	1927	Joseph Isaacs	"	Recruit 81.	390
William Hammond	"	7	1250	Abram Irvine	"	2	76
Henry Harley	"	3	1323	Thomas Jones (2)	"	Recruit 80.	1111
James Homes	"	1	1317	Charles Jones	"	German.	10
Joseph Harper	"	Recruited 81.	1289	George Jones	"	Recruit 81.	879
John Harris (2)	"	"	1241	Thomas Jones (4)	"	"	206
Thomas Hammond	"	"	1403	John Irons	"	1	863
Daniel Hall	"	7	1315	James Isaacs	"	State.	1371
William Harris (2)	"	6	4035	Francis Johnston	M.	Artillery.	875
John Holliday, Sr	"	6	495	John Ireland	"	"	1203
James Hopkins		Hazen's.	381	Philip Jones	"	"	1099
James Heaton		"	959	Benedict Johnston	"	"	231
David Henderson		Lee's Legion.	318	John Jordan	Q. M. S.	5	3021

THE WAR FOR INDEPENDENCE.

Names.	Rank.	Regiment.	Number.	Names.	Rank.	Regiment.	Number.
William Jones	Private.	7	1156	William Laws	Private.	2	1611
John Jarvis		1	1321	Roger Landers	"	2	913
Samuel Jenkins		Lee's Legion.	4063	John Lucas (1)	"	2	1534
Thomas Johnston		Gist's.	1914	Benjamin Loffman	"	5	1786
Dennis Kelly	Sergeant.	1	1303	Levi Lord	"	2	3005
Edward Killman	Private.	2	4154	Henry Laws	"	3	3117
James Kelly	"	3	98	William Lynch	"	3	1735
John King	"	7	1516	John Love (1)	"	3	1233
Michael Kernon	"	6	1967	John Lee (1)	"	3	1212
William Kindle	"	7	839	Michael Lawler	"	3	1368
Walter Keech	"		2004	John Lynch (2)	"	4	4030
Jacob Kiser	"	German.	107	Alexander Levi	"	4	4024
John Knox (1)	"	4	1733	Robert Legg	"	State.	202
Joseph Kerrick	Corporal.	6	1269	John Linkon	"	6	1984
Francis Kitely	Private.	7	179	Joseph Long	"	6	1410
Peter Kinkade	"	5	1754	Joshua Leister	"	7	4027
Stephen Kemble	"	3	230	William Leakins	"	7	1331
William Kellow	Sergeant.	1	1312	David Love	Sergeant.	7	1994
Thomas King	Private.	1	931	Francis Long	Private.	State.	3038
Adam Kephart	"	2	1694	John Lewin	"	"	1409
Jacob Knight	"	2	4026	Christopher Lambert	"	"	99
John Kidd	"	4	1225	George Linton	"	"	1263
John King	"	4	1229	Paul Lapine	"	State and 1.	433
William King	"	4	1230	Dudley Lee	"	6	301
David Kelly	"	5	1288	Theophilus Lindsay	"	1	1120
George Kelson	"	5	1639	Thomas Larrimore	"	German.	1811
Benjamin H. Kerrick	"	6	1157	Joseph Lewis (2)	"	Recruit 81.	1273
James Kelly	Corporal.	7	1247	John Lynch (3)	"	Rawlings'.	3028
James Keckland	Private.	7	1344	John Lesley	"	Recruit 81.	826
John Kildee	"	State.	112	William Lee (2)	"	"	284
Jacob Kelly	"	Recruited 81.	1248	Thomas Long	"	3	1237
Thomas P. Kittle	"	"	215	Nehemiah Lingard	"	Recruit 81.	3022
Benjamin Karns	"	2	1887	Timothy Langrel	"	"	1226
Edward Kearsey	"	6	77	Jesse Locker	"	"	1493
James Knott	"	State and 1.	868	William Little	"	3	4040
Edward Kirk	"	Rawlings'.	918	Theophilus Lomax	Sergeant.	5	373
Francis Kearns	"	German.	1313	Edward Legg	Private.	State.	1613
David Kettle	"	"	129	Thos. Loveday, or Lovely	D.	Rawlings'.	1447
Abram Kettle	"	"	1620	Dennis Leary	Private.	State.	1374
Matthew Kelly	"	4	4095	Robert Livingston	M.	Artillery.	990
John Knox (2)	"	7	1257	Joshua Lovely	"	"	1791
James Killagan	"	2	418	Richard Lewis	Sergeant.	"	1526
Nathaniel Knott	"	3	1311	Peter Laurence	M.	"	1316
William Kennedy	"	6	1695	Jacob Lion	Sergeant.	"	254
Richard Kisby	"	State.	1191	Daniel Longest	Private.	3	3111
David Kennedy		Hazen's.	353	John Lavender	"	2	1017
John Kennard		Lee's Legion.	110	James Lowry	"	5	916
John Kincade		"	1276	John Laton	"	5	1741
Thomas Kearns		6	2500	John Lindsay	"	4	187
George Laws	"	2	1350	Barney Lemmon	"	4	350
William Lettman	"	2	280	Peter Ledington	"	1	3026
William Lee	"	2	1187	Jeremiah Lee	"	5	171
William Lilly	"	3	410	Thomas, or John Luff	"	3	802
John Loveday	"	7	203	John Majors	"	1	247
William Lucas	"	1	288	Richard Mudd	Sergeant.	1	1687
Kinsey Lanham	"	Recruit 81.	309	Walter Miles	Corporal.	1	1448
John Lonass	"	German.	1015	Gifford Minikee	Private.	1	1234
Zachariah Lyles	"	2	236	William Mann	"	2	3049
Thomas Lewis	"	3	830	James Magraw	"	2	370
John Lowry	"	7	4163	Frederick Miles	Corporal.	2	1853
Darby Lanahan	"	6	3133	John Morris	"	3	1012
Charles Leago	"	German.	1847	Valentine Murray	"	3	404
Jacob Lowe	Sergeant.	"	3067	Jonathan Mayhew	"	3	1346
Jonathan Lewis	Private.	1	825	John Miles (1)	"	3	1048
Michael Lloyd	"	2	3037	James Matthews	"	4	1183

Name.	Rank.	Regiment.	Number.	Names.	Rank.	Regiment.	Number.
William Marshal	Corporal.	5	3151	John Moore (1)	Private.	7	425
Robert Matthews	"	6	256	Charles McNable	Sergeant.	7	1220
Thomas McCernan	"	5	352	Joseph Managa	Private.	7	4060
John Mantle	Sergeant.	6	377	Joseph Murphey	"	7	1724
Joseph Mattingly	Private.	7	1363	Peter Maguire	"	7	1098
Arthur McClain	Sergeant.	7	469	John Macanally	"	7	3013
Samuel McConnell	"	6	208	Enoch McClain	Sergeant.	7	3108
Joseph McNamara	Private.	State.	2039	John Maxwell (1)	Private.	7	3153
Jeremiah Mudd	Sergeant.	"	327	William Moade	"	7	4043
John Matthews (2)	"	"	1000	John Mick	"	7	294
John Moore (3)	"	"	286	Neal Norris	"	7	999
Hezekiah Massey	"	5	1415	John Mills (2)	"	6	1979
John McCay (1)	"	State.	871	Nicholas Milburn	"	6	5
John McDonald	Fifer.	Recruit 81.	1334	William McNeal	Corporal.	6	274
Michael Maguire	Private.	3	1324	James McDonald	Private.	7	4037
Thomas Mahoney	"	German.	242	Thos. Matthews	Corporal.	State.	1629
Stephen Magraw	"	"	339	John McGuinis	Private.	"	1287
Jacob Moses (2)	"	"	1699	Isachea Mason	Corporal.	"	813
Bennet Mudd	Sergeant.	1	1297	William Manly	Private.	"	1962
Humphrey Miniken	Private.	4	4099	Henry Mansfield	"	"	2540
Benjamin McHaffee	"	5	94	John Moore (2)	"	"	966
Benjamin Moran	"	6	3043	John C. Miller	"	"	482
John Martin (2)	"	6	1559	Jesse McKinsey	"	German.	234
Christian Myers	"	7	1050	John McNeill	"	4	419
John M. Laughlin	"	7	320	John Moore (4)	"	4	307
Andrew Moore	"	7	1277	Adam Mushler	"	German.	251
William Martin	Corporal.	6	845	John McGall	"	Recruit 81.	1706
Timothy McLamar	Private.	State.	1010	David Meadows	"	"	1280
Michael McGower	"	"	3179	Roderick McKinsey	"	Rawlings'.	87
Joseph McAtee	"	"	252	Aaron Michell	"	Recruit 81.	1640
Thomas Mahoney	"	6	221	Aleard Melville	"	"	1966
Thomas Maloney	"	7	3050	Robt. Mitchell	"	"	1509
Michael Miller	"	1	59	Daniel Murphy	"	"	211
Darby McNamara	"	1	4102	Francis McCann	"	"	1548
John Martindale	Fife-Major.	1	1286	John Morris (2)	"	"	1393
Peter McNaughton	Sergeant.	1	1722	John Mills (3)	"	7	3170
John Morrison	Fifer.	1	1622	John Murray (1)	"	7	1719
Wm. McLoughlin	Private.	2	1486	John McDonald	Sergeant.		141
Christopher Magraw	Drummer.	2	1125	John McNight	Fifer.		135
James Mason	Private.	2	4106	Edward Mahoney	Private.	State.	330
Wm. Moore (1)	"	2	1778	Benjamin Marsh	"	1	968
Richard Mitchel	"	2	3070	Wm. Marlow	Sergeant.	Rawlings'.	1612
Wm. Moore (2)	"	2	205	Luke Merriman	Private.	Recruited 81.	910
John Martin (1)	"	2	1372	John McCaliff	Drummer.	"	1795
Cornelius McLaughlin	"	3	1056	Wm. Mansfield	Private.	State.	1215
Charles Murphy	Sergeant.	3	3157	John Maglin	"	"	4033
Wm. McGee	Private.	3	1389	Daniel Mann	"	"	1709
John Matthews (1)	"	3	1388	Peter Melvin	"	2	1801
Charles McGee	"	3	355	John McClain	"	3	1367
Matthew Moore (1)	"	3	235	John Moore (5)	"	7	983
Wm. Mitchell	"	3	1390	Thomas Matthews (2)	"	Recruited 81.	2026
John McCann	"	3	1079	Joshua McKinsey	"	German.	882
Patrick Mahorn	"	3	1404	Moses McKinsey	"	"	3020
Matthew Moore (2)	"	4	1843	Francis McGauran	Sergeant.	"	1939
Thomas Murphy	"	4	387	Patrick McKinsey	Private.	Rawlings'.	1088
Christopher McAway	"	4	1965	John McBride	"	"	326
Hugh McMillan	Sergeant.	4	1856	Thos. McKinsey	"	"	323
James Mead	Drum-Major.	2	429	Zachariah Mills	"	Recruit 81.	3114
John McCoy	Private.	5	1364	Abraham Manning	"	"	1238
George Mantle	"	6	939	Thomas Mie	"	2	1396
Michael McCann	"	6	336	John Milstead	"	1	140
James Maxwell	Corporal.	6	285	James Moore	G.	Artillery.	1356
Wm. Moore (3)	Private.	6	106	Peter Maynor	Fifer.	"	108
Boston Medler	Drummer.	7	2012	Charles Muiritt	M.	"	1397
Wm. Mann (1)	Private.	7	384	Robert Myers	M.	"	395

THE WAR FOR INDEPENDENCE.

Names.	Rank.	Regiment.	Number.	Names.	Rank.	Regiment.	Number.
Dennis McCormick	Corporal.	Artillery.	1349	James Neale	M.	Artillery.	186
Philip Masterson	M.	"	860	Daniel Neal	"	"	253
Hugh McDowell	"	"	492	Martin Noble	"	2	1384
Peter Maynor, Sr.	"	"	363	Nathaniel Nott			127
James McGowen	"	"	1535	George Nicholson		4	2543
Cruise Moser	Private.	2	396	Samuel J. Nelme		Artillery.	1869
James Murphy	"	2	4064	Leonard Outerbridge	Private.	2	1358
John McDougle	"	2	3034	Samuel Oram	"	4	1009
John McConnikin	"	2	1261	John O'Brian	"	State.	2038
John McGran	"	2	1547	John Osburn	"	3	3007
John Murray (Bugley's Co.)	"	3	1290	Joseph Overereek	"	3	3025
John Miller	"	2	24	Daniel O'Quinn	"	4	1031
Richard Maxwell	"	4	1711	Stephen Owens	"	6	1723
Archibald Morton	"	4	369	James Owens	"	5	2522
John McIntosh	"	5	3092	Charles Orme	"	7	1040
Thomas Morgan	"	5	1100	Henry Osten, or Austin	"	2	955
Dennis Murley	"	5	1557	John Onion	Fifer.	State.	3155
Wm. McKinley	"	6	1646	Peter Outhouse	Private.	"	1495
Barney McManus	"	7	1944	Samuel Owens	"	1	1202
Jacob Moses	"	3	3104	Michael O'Brian	Bugler.	Artillery.	37
William Matthews	"	6	4062	Philip O'Brian	Corporal.	"	219
Jacob Myers	"	State and 2.	325	Michael O'Farrel	M.	"	869
Timothy McMahon	"	3	1106	Jacob Owens	"	"	4034
Patrick Mollohon	"	Recruit 81.	1930	John Owens	Private.	3	1538
Wm. McPherson	"	"	3077	Richard O'Quynn	"	German.	1968
George Miller	"	"	1779	Elijah Oakley	"	Recruit 81.	1855
Nicholas McManiard	"	"	1029	Joseph Owens	"	Lee's Legion.	985
James McIntire	"	Hazen's.	1989	James Onants	"		842
John McColgan	"	"	50	George Parker	"	Rawlings'.	2426
Charles March, or Marsh	"	"	2532	Nathan Peak	Sergeant	1	834
Alex. Matthewson	"	"	155	Henry Phillips	Private.	2	1889
George McDonald	"	"	977	Cupid Plummer	"	2	1792
Martin Mulloy	"	"	847	George Patrick	"	Rawlings'.	995
Jamer McCrakin	"	Lee's Legion.	49	Gabriel Peters	"	5	1279
John Manley	"	"	1240	John Purdy	"	6	405
Hugh McCoy	"	1	372	Henry Purdy	"	6	1991
Marmaduke McDonald	"	3	1822	George Phillips	"	7	1644
James McCarty	"	4	1113	John Pease	Sergeant.	7	1114
Nicholas Nicholson	Sergeant.	1	1519	Jesse Powers	Private.	State.	1110
John Neary	"	1	1081	Obadiah Plummer	"	2	3042
Asael Nicholls	Private.	3	1129	Thomas Phipps	"	2	809
John Neighbours	"	7	137	Samuel Pleasants	"	4	248
John Newton (2)	"	State.	3160	James Phillips	"	State.	488
Michael Noland	"	6	1896	George Plumley	"	"	3017
Richard Nelson	"	State.	1173	Thomas Pollhouse	"	German.	3110
Patrick Nolan	"	4	1947	Thomas Peacock	"	7	1895
Thomas Neill	"	1	1259	John Pickering	"	2	3000
Henry Nicholson	Corporal.	2	1332	William Poland	"	1	2008
Stephen Nicholson	Sergeant.	2	1348	Simon Perry	"	1	1327
Wm. Newton	Private.	2	1630	William Pherson	"	1	1264
Morris Neagell	"	3	1514	Aquilla Pearce	D.	2	1128
Wm. A. Needhand	Sergeant.	4	1274	William Purchase	Corporal.	2	198
Joseph Nabb	Private.	5	1987	John Peany	D.	2	1137
Wm. Nailor	"	5	450	Stephen Preston	Private.	3	287
James Narvel	Fifer.	6	4028	Richard Proctor	"	3	424
Isaac Nicholls	Private.	Recruit 81.	113	William Peters	"	3	1251
Basil Norman	"	7	1281	William Pursell	"	4	388
Wm. Niblet	"	7	1564	William Prior	"	4	3100
John Newton (1)	"	Recruit 81.	894	William Pecker	"	4	3163
Charles Nabb	"	7	177	Joseph Purdy	D. Major.	5	1047
John Nelson	"	4	6	James Poole	Private.	5	2014
John Nevit (2)	"	2	152	George Pierce	"	5	1598
Joseph Neale	"	Rawlings'.	367	Neal Peacock	"	7	1798
John Nicholson	"	Recruit 81.	3041	Stephen Price	Sergeant.	6	1600
John Nave	"	"	111	Elijah Pepper	Private.	7	1645

Names.	Rank.	Regiment.	Number.	Names.	Rank.	Regiment.	Number.
Thomas Pinder	Private.	State.	2567	William Rogers	Private.	1	831
Thomas Pennyfield	"	"	862	Cristian Ross	"	Recruit 81.	1158
Lambert Phillips	"	"	1990	William Smith	"	1	961
Thomas Patterson	"	Recruit 81.	160	Thomas Sanders	"	1	1787
Nathaniel Price	"	"	1583	William Smith	"	1	1492
Thomas Perry	"	"	1546	John Snelling	"	1	1746
Joshua Pierce	"	1	837	Anthony Smith	D.	1	1772
Michael Pilkerton	"	5	3014	David Smith	Private.	2	870
Joseph Pherson	Corporal.	1	1399	Leonard Swan	"	3	1335
William Prather	Fifer.	Recruit 81.	478	Jesse Simons	Corporal.	3	3030
William Paul	Private.	"	104	Thomas Smith	Private.	4	1648
Thomas Porter	"	"	1476	Andrew Stewart	"	2	1700
Robert Pennington	"	5	836	Thomas Sappington	Sergeant.	5	1769
William Porter	"	Recruit 81.	4047	William Sharp	Corporal.	5	1998
William Pagram	"	2	2546	William Simmons	Private.	Recruit 80.	1684
Thomas Pettit	"	Recruit 81.	1357	John Stackhouse	"	6	3019
Arthur Pritchet	"	"	4054	Michael Sours	"	6	1751
Joseph Pogue	M.	Artillery.	329	Aquilla Smith	"	7	2023
Thomas Potter	Fifer.	"	1097	William Sly	Corporal.	7	3132
John Prout	M.	"	2534	Jeremiah Sullivan	Private.	State.	1385
John Paine	"	"	422	Richard Smith	Sergeant.	"	1345
Francis Popham	"	"	487	Alexander, or Andrew Smith	Private.	5	1018
John Pearson	"	"	2089	Samuel Scott	"	State.	157
Jonas Phillips	"	"	1429	Benjamin Smith	"	Recruit 80.	3016
Benjamin Phelps	Private.	2	81	James Stewart (1)	"	"	1532
Joseph Peters	"	2	72	John Smith	"	3	2022
James Pritchard	"	2	1365	Leonard Smith	"	State.	908
Andrew Preston	"	2	1975	Nathan Speak	"	6	1242
Emanuel Polston	"	4	175	Frederick Stoffee	"	Recruit 81.	196
James Paivel	"	5	1352	Edward Sute	Corporal.	2	453
James Pack	"	6	473	Murphy Shee	Private.	Recruit 81.	1359
Thomas Price	"	6	1201	George Silver	"	German.	1046
Jacob Plaine	"	Lee's Legion.	237	Joseph Smith	"	3	142
John Parkinson	Private.	1	3169	John Smithard	"	German.	2032
John Parsons	"	6	1103	Robert Shipley	"	2	1239
Edward Purdy	"	6	1555	William Sherley	"	State.	117
John Quick	Sergeant.	2	3177	Ignatius Smith	"	Recruit 81.	900
Joseph Quinn	Private.	3	1336	Jonathan Short	Sergeant.	"	214
William Quintin	"	7	948	Josiah Smith	"	State.	897
Patrick Quinn	"	Rawlings'.	1437	Charles Schoudrick	Corporal.	5	1398
John Quinn	M.	Artillery.	1500	Robert Scriviner	Sergeant.	2	3134
James Quay	Private.	1	1246	Thomas Stokes	Private.	2	360
William Rowles	"	4	1441	Noah Sears	"	3	1301
William Roberts (1)	"	1	125	James Stewart (2)	"	4	1337
Andrew Riggs	"	2	1946	Reuben Smith	"	4	184
Edward Richardson	"	3	801	Abraham Schockee	"	Gist's.	1002
John Rock	"	3	1943	Peter Smith	Sergeant.	1	1217
William Rock	"	3	4164	William Sykes	Private.	1	227
Jeremiah Rodes	"	3	1355	Charles Scott	"	1	1143
Adam Raines	"	3	1707	John Smith (2)	"	7	1306
John Robertson	"	3	306	Humphrey Spencer	Sergeant.	2	1293
Robert Richardson	"	3	1443	Jesse Suite	"	2	859
Thomas Redman	"	4	304	John Salmon	Private.	2	2536
Benedict Reynolds	"	3 or 4.	1213	James Shaur	"	2	1512
Bennet Rawlings	"	2	1005	John Shouell	"	2	1977
Robert Rise	"	6	956	Aaron Spalding	Sergeant.	2	1438
Michael Rhytmire	"	German.	823	James Smith (2)	Private.	3	1036
Edward Riely	"	State.	1770	John Smith (4)	Corporal.	2	2003
Alexander Rutherford	"	"	3018	John Scott	Drummer.	3	937
William Richardson	"	"	3040	William Smith (2)	"	4	311
John Radly	Sergeant.	4	88	Conrad Smith	Private.	4	1299
James Ryly	Private.	3	3091	Thomas Slade	"	4	44
Charles Reynolds	Sergeant.	State.	354	Elijah Smith	"	4	2017
Charles Riddle	Private.	Recruit 81.	833	William Sinclair	"	5	1073
Horatio Roberts	"	7	4055	Levy Smith	Sergeant.	5	1391

THE WAR FOR INDEPENDENCE.

Names.	Rank.	Regiment.	Number.
Daniel Smith (1)	Private.	5	1868
William Sullivan	"	5	1807
John Smith (1)	Corporal.	5	1078
Perry Sullivan	Private.	5	2083
Roger Shorter	"	5	832
Solomon Summers	"	5	124
George Sanders	"	5	1401
Robert Sharpless	Corporal.	6	1200
Alexander Stephenson	Drummer.	6	40
John Summers	Private.	6	1206
William Stonestreet	"	6	1347
Joseph Sloop	"	6	1445
James Sewall	"	6	3109
Thomas Smith (1)	"	6	1030
Michael Standly	"	6	3889
George Steem, or Stumm	"	6	1370
James Smith (3)	"	7	1726
Christopher Simpkins	"	7	28
Abraham Stallings	Drummer.	7	178
Peter Stephens	Private.	7	890
Daniel Smith (2)	"	7	2502
Christopher Seymore	"	State.	1902
James Sullivan	"	"	282
John Smith (3)	"	"	1782
John Shanks	"	"	1223
Bennet Sherley (2)	"	"	1025
Job Sylvester	"	"	143
Levi Scott	Drummer.	"	1783
Robert Streets	Private.	"	1484
William Sterling	"	"	39
John Smallwood (2)	"	"	1435
John Smallwood (1)	"	Recruited 81.	1054
John Starkey	"	"	1186
James Shepherd	"	"	2028
John Spire	"	"	1777
Charles Sickle	"	"	1937
Solomon Sullivan	"	"	73
Richard Spires	"	"	1198
John Sheffer	"	"	1862
Solady Stanley	"	"	368
Thomas Smith (2)	"	State.	1544
Luke Sanson	"	7	228
Thomas Summers	"	2	4112
William Silwood	"	German.	1857
Benjamin Steward	"	State.	1124
Laurence Simpson	"	Recruited 81.	61
William Steward	Fifer or Private.	6	1440
John Stoffle, or Stoffe		Recruited 81.	1731
Philip Savoy	Private.	1	1479
Samuel Street	Fifer.	4	173
Joseph Sidney, or Sidmer	Private.	5	2031
Elias Smith	"	6	1308
Michael Smith (2)	"	German.	954
Christopher, or Christian Smith	"	"	3041
Michael Smith (1)	"	"	927
Samuel F. Shoemaker	"	"	1001
John Stanton	"	"	922
Oliver Stephens	"	Recruited 81.	1096
Cato Snowden	"	"	1153
Basil Shaw	Sergeant.	Rawlings'.	2080
Thomas Scoudrick	Private.	5	3149
Joseph Southall	"	3	1091
Thomas Sheridan	"	1—81	1732
Walter B. Smallwood	"	Recruited 81.	1180
William Standley	Private.	State.	934
James Sappington	"	Recruited 81.	1961
James Smith (1)	"	German.	1439
Jacob Standley	"	7	1375
James Scott	Sergeant.	State.	3158
George Scone	Corporal.	5	45
William Sizeland	Private.	7	411
Joseph H. Spencer	Sergeant.	2	1810
Henry Slack	"	Artillery.	491
John Slack	"	"	1926
Charles Sutton	"	"	1145
John Sillman	M.	"	1341
William Stalker	"	"	1055
Robert Smith	"	"	2538
Reuben Scott	"	"	1955
Thomas Smith	"	"	1533
James Simmonds	"	"	442
Andrew Shrink	"	"	3046
John Sandall	"	"	1133
John Standley, Jr.	"	"	2560
John Smith	"	"	892
Thomas Standley	"	"	929
Rawling Spinks	"	"	1219
Valentine Smith	Private.	1	3036
Thomas Salsbury	"	1	1865
Nathaniel Smith	"	1	1745
Richard Sweeny	"	2	1821
John Smith	Sergeant.	2	2013
James Sweeny	Private.	2	451
Thomas Sergeant	"	2	2533
Charles Snow	"	2	3173
Charles Simpson	"	2	1590
John Sanders		3	1008
James Sheridan	"	3	2007
Joseph Spinks	"	3	4053
Jeremiah Scrabbles	"	3	1014
John Spriggs	"	3	423
James Simms	Sergeant.	3	952
Thomas Sylvester	Private.	5	1174
Darby Sullivan	"	5	1376
Robert Sturton	"	5	216
Noble Simmons		6	293
William Spyers		6	409
John Sloop		6	1462
John Shaw		7	1823
Patrick Scott	Private.	7	440
Peter Shoemaker		7	452
John Sankey		7	2398
William Smith			944
William Smith		Hazen's.	1815
Bartholomew Sheridan		"	984
George Summerville		"	3052
John Strahan		Lee's Legion.	1912
Abraham Sutton		"	1654
Tamerlane Spencer		Artillery.	1405
Philip Shoebrick	Invalid.	2	1362
Edward Timms	Private.	1	281
John Tucker	"	1	2530
Dennis Tramwell	"	1	878
William Townsend	"	7	1584
Richard Taylor	"	7	1773
Francis Thompson	"	1	1084
Solomon Turner	"	7	1908
Giles Thompson, or Thomas.	"	State.	1747
Samuel Trigg	"	3	250

Names.	Rank.	Regiment.	Number.	Names.	Rank.	Regiment.	Number.
John Tomlin	Private.	German.	464	John Vincent	Private.	2	917
Peter Tippet	"	3	70	John Vanzant	"	4	1122
John Trusty	"	3	1496	Samuel Vermillion	"	1	1886
Samuel Taylor	"	7	1116	George Vernon	"	State.	1171
Thomas Tanner	"	7	1161	John Vaughan	Sergeant.	Artillery.	1071
James Tite	"	German.	4101	James Veazy		Lee's Legion.	3047
Anthony Tucker	"	5	1759	Thomas Woolford	Private.	German.	1834
Christopher Touchstone	"	6	1069	Daniel Williams	"	"	275
William Taylor	"	1	996	John Williams	"	1	1450
Natley Tippet	"	1	392	George Ward (1)	"	1	431
William Toland	"	2	1305	David Williams	"	2	243
Lambert Tompson	"	2	1377	William Wheatley	"	2	223
John Taylor (1)	"	2	1960	Andrew Wingate	"	2	366
James Thomas, Jr.	"	3	3103	York Waters	"	2	1809
John Turner (3)	"	3	3068	Samuel B. White	"	3	2009
Bartholomew Tompson	"	2	1696	George Windham	"	3	145
Richard Tasco	"	3	1513	William West	"	3	1254
Henry Townley	"	3	333	William Wilkeson	"	3	1623
Thomas Thompson	"	3	118	Charles Williams (1)	"	3	1641
Peter Topping	"	4	1708	George Willson	"	5	3045
John Taylor (2)	"	4	1193	Jonathan Windell	"	6	139
Evin Tumbleson	"	4	4025	Michael Wiser	"	7	4048
Robert Taylor (2)	Sergeant.	5	903	Motley Whitcomb	"	7	1774
Cornelius Tomson	Private.	5	3003	Gabriel Williams	Sergeant.	7	1414
George Taylor	"	5	1690	Richard Wheeler	Corporal.	State.	1413
John Turner	"	7	2036	John Whitcomb	Private.	"	919
James Terry	"	3	3124	Walter Watson	"	"	71
William Taylor (2)	"	Rawlings'.	1969	Benjamin Ward	Sergeant.	"	1601
William Taylor, Jr. (3)	"	7	2529	Joseph White	Private.	5	904
James Thomas, Sr.	Sergeant.	State.	1064	Sylvester Wheatley	"	2	1466
Allen Townsend	Private.	Recruit 81.	1392	Jonathan Weeden	"	Rawlings'.	1007
Levin Thomas	"	"	3012	Alexander West	"	1	1184
James Tigner	"	"	2503	William Willson	"	7	1353
John Thomson (1)	"	"	975	Edward Wright	"	4	1262
Edward Tanner	"	"	1529	William Wedge	"	7	982
Thomas Thomas	"	"	199	John Willing	"	Recruit 81.	2425
John D. Tully	"	"	942	Philip Welsh	"	" 4th Reg.	2548
John Thomas (2)	"	"	232	John Wilkerson	"	"	119
George Twench	Sergeant.	Rawlings'.	394	Samuel Wright	"	German.	1988
Henry Tucker (2)	"	Recruit 81.	820	George Watson	"	State.	1322
John Turner (2)	"	7	1796	Charles Willett	"	Recruit 81.	1552
John Thomas (1)	"	6	74	John Willing	(formerly of Artillery.)		998
Samuel Tindall	"	3	957	John Wade (1)	"	German.	35
Joseph Thompson	"	3	865	Edward Wade (2)	"	3	1101
Thomas Tyack	"	Artillery.	1087	William Whaland	"	Recruit 81.	978
John Turner	M.	"	1195	John Willis	"	"	1900
Rezin Thacknill	Private.	1	1485	Nicholas Welch	"	" 80.	315
James Trego	"	2	126	Benjamin Williams (3)	"	" 81.	1897
William Tutten	"	2	1999	Thomas Wood (3)	"	"	877
John Tuff	"	6	1387	Thomas Windom	Sergeant.	1	3106
John Thomas	"	6	4098	John T. West	Fifer.	1	3069
Aaron Townsend	"	7	807	Jonathan White	Private.	1	886
John Turner (of Morris' Co.)	"	7	109	Jesse Wright	"	2	1412
Francis Taylor	"	Recruit 81.	122	John Welch (1)	"	2	885
Evan Thomas	"	"	1222	Thomas Wood (1)	"	2	1558
Dennis Ternan	"	7	1406	James Willson (1)	"	2	1986
Francis Tycowit	"	Hazen's.	64	Thomas Wimber	"	2	2087
John Towlin	"	Lee's Legion.	1502	Thomas Wate, or Wyatt	"	2	343
John German Thomas	"	"	1386	Robert Walker	"	3	302
Jesse Thompson	Sergeant.	Artillery.	856	Michael Woolford	"	3	1560
Cornelius Vaughan	Private.	German.	1942	Frederick Willmott	"	3	3122
Stephen Varlow	"	2	3071	Thomas Watson	"	3	408
John Varlow	"	5	1523	John Williams (1)	"	3	2558
Edward Vickers	"	State.	1080	Barney Willson	"	3	912
William Vaughan	"	2	1192	Robertson Wood	"	4	1268

Names.	Rank.	Regiment.	Number.
Thomas Wood (2)	Private.	4	1380
Jeremiah Williams	Corporal.	4	1776
James Wood (2)	Private.	4	1606
Daniel Willis	D.	5	1936
David Willson	Private.	5	1842
John Wilkenson	Sergeant.	5	1764
Daniel Warrior	D.	6	1713
Michael Wiery	Fifer.	6	1468
Benjamin Williams (2)	Private.	6	2523
Absalom Wright	"	6	835
William Willson (2)	"	Rawlings'.	2554
Samuel Wedge	"	7	92
James White	"	7	1361
Michael Waltman	"	7	3089
John Wells	"	State.	3150
Richard Wiely	"	"	1453
John Wilson (1)	"	"	51
Rhody Woodland	"	"	1938
John Walker (3)	Sergeant.	State, late 1st.	1470
Banks Webb	Private.	State.	1899
John West (2)	"	"	2020
William Watkins	Drummer.	"	2006
James Willson (2)	Private.	"	1647
Charles Wheeler	"	Recruit 81.	4050
George Williams	Sergeant.	"	1024
Humphrey Wells	Private.	"	1594
Wm. Willson (1)	"	"	958
James West	"	"	3096
James Wood (1)	Sergeant.	"	1034
John Wright	Private.	"	3076
Zadock Whaley	"	7	1766
Anthony Weaver	"	1	2041
Benjamin Williams (1)	"	7	185
Wm. Whitton, or Whittaker.	"	Recruit 81.	1366
John Walker (1)	"	German.	2550
John Welch (2)	"	2	1596
James Williams	"	Recruit 81.	861
Samuel Willson	Sergeant.	State.	3128
Edward Walter	Private.	Recruit 81.	974
Jarvis Williams	"	4	4058
James Welch	B.	Artillery.	2082
James Whaling	G.	"	4067
James Welch	M.	"	1618
Thomas Williams	Drummer.	"	4057
Wm. Withorm, or Whitton	M.	"	83
David White	"	"	1039
David Welch	Sergeant.	"	1817
John Wheeler		"	1734
Thos. Webster		2	880
Wm. Willson		2	1597
James Welch		2	1140
Peter Ward		2	1844
Zachariah Williams		3	1616
James Williams		5	1615
Abraham Waters		5	1892
Solomon Watts		5	1944
David Woods		6	2021
John Waters		6	4023
Thos. Wheeler		7	204
Garret Welch		Recruit 81.	1422
Benjamin Willson		Hazen's.	964
Edward White		"	1655
Edward Wall		"	970
John Wysham		Lee's Legion.	89
John Ward		"	2015
William Wade	M.	Artillery.	1469
Samuel Young	Private.	6	1449
John Young (2)	Corporal.	6	2552
Godfrey Young	Private.	6	1715
Jacob Yeast, or Yost	"	Recruit 81.	1188
Henry Young	"	"	3024
John Young (1)	"	4	1090
David Young	M.	Artillery.	1013
Richard Yates		2	994
William York		7	1819
Jacob Young	Drummer.	Recruit 81.	3073
Thos. Yeates		Artillery.	2091

CHAPTER VIII.

THE CONSTITUTION AND UNION.

The Society of the Cincinnati—Unhappy Political Divisions—Whisky Insurrection—Washington in Cumberland—Militia Organizations.

AFTER the conclusion of the Revolutionary war, the remnants of the Maryland regiments returned to their native State to be disbanded. Many of these veterans bore honorable scars, still more had their health broken down by hardship and disease, and nearly all were penniless and in rags. The Maryland line, now numbering about five hundred men, under the command of Brig.-Gen. Gist, embarked at Charleston, S. C., on transports, and arrived at Annapolis late in July, 1783. They soon after marched to Baltimore, arriving there on the 27th. Before their departure, Gen. Greene, in a letter to Governor Paca, thus referred to the Maryland troops in the Southern army:

"Many of your officers are on their return home. I should be wanting in gratitude not to acknowledge their singular merit and the importance of their services. They have spilt their blood freely in the service of their country, and have faced every danger and difficulty without a murmur or complaint. I beg leave to recommend Col. Williams, who has been at the head of your line, to the particular notice of your State, as an officer of great merit and good conduct. A very considerable number of these (Maryland line) returned are not, nor ever will be, fit for service again. They are incapable of doing active duty, and ought to be turned over to the Invalid Corps."

The British prisoners confined at Frederick and Winchester, numbering about fifteen hundred, were marched to Baltimore in May, 1783, and embarked in vessels sent to transport them to New York. By a proclamation of Congress, dated October 18th, all officers and soldiers absent from the army on furlough were discharged from further service, and all others who had engaged to serve during the war were to be discharged from and after the 3d of November. On the 25th of November the British troops under Sir Guy Carleton evacuated New York, and Washington, accompanied by Governor Clinton, immediately took possession. A few days afterwards Washington took an affectionate leave of Gen. Knox and his companions in arms, and then set out for Annapolis, where he resigned his command on the 23d of December, 1783.

While Congress was sitting in Annapolis, on the 14th of January, 1784, it ratified the definitive treaty which had been concluded and signed at Paris on the 3d of the preceding September; and on the 20th of January, Governor Paca issued his proclamation announcing the same to the people of the State.

The Society of the Cincinnati.—Before the dissolution of the army on the Hudson, Gen. Knox, "ever noted for generous impulses," suggested as a mode of perpetuating the friendships which had been formed, and keeping alive the brotherhood of the camp, the formation of a society composed of the officers of the army. The suggestion met with universal concurrence and the hearty approbation of Washington. On May 10, 1783, a meeting of the general officers and one officer from the line of each regiment was held at the headquarters of Baron Steuben, at the cantonment on Hudson River. Baron Steuben presided, and proposals for establishing "The Society of the Cincinnati" were considered. They were referred to a committee composed of Maj.-Gen. Knox, Brig.-Gen. Hand, Brig.-Gen. Huntington, and Col. Shaw. After three days they made a report which was unanimously adopted, and the plan as revised by them was carried into complete effect with little opposition, and is still in force. The next preliminary meeting was again held at the cantonment on June 19, 1783, when Gen. Washington was elected temporary president-general; Maj.-Gen. McDougall, treasurer-general; and Maj.-Gen. Knox, secretary-general. The first general meeting after the disbanding of the army took place at the City Tavern, at Philadelphia, in May, 1788, when permanent officers were elected. On the 15th, Washington was unanimously chosen president; Maj.-Gen. Gates, vice-president; and Maj.-Gen. Knox, secretary. The *Maryland Gazette*, on the 6th of November, 1783, published the following notice:

"Oct. 30th, 1783.

"The officers of the Maryland Line, upon the present and half-pay establishments, are requested to meet at Annapolis on the 20th of November, where several matters very interesting to the line in general will be communicated and necessarily brought under consideration.

"W. Smallwood, M.-G."

In pursuance of this notice a large number of the officers of the Maryland line assembled at Mann's Tavern, in Annapolis. In consequence of the absence of Maj.-Gen. Smallwood and Brig.-Gen. Gist, the two senior officers of the Maryland line, the meeting was adjourned until the following morning at eleven o'clock. The two officers not appearing, the meeting was again adjourned until the afternoon at three o'clock, when it was organized by selecting Brig.-Gen. Otho H. Williams, of Washington County, as temporary chairman, and Lieut.-Col. Eccleston secretary. The institution of the Order of Cincinnati was read and adopted, and after each officer had signed the constitution they adjourned until the next day. Upon reassembling they proceeded to the election of officers, whereupon Maj.-Gen. Smallwood was elected president; Brig.-Gen. Gist, vice-president; Brig.-Gen. Williams, secretary; Col. Nathaniel Ramsay, treasurer; and Lieut.-Col. Eccleston, assistant treasurer. After the transaction of some minor business, the society then elected Gen. Smallwood, Gen. Williams, Governor Paca, and Col. Ramsay delegates to the general society.[1]

The Indians on the frontier, as has been seen, had given more or less trouble all through the Revolutionary war, and still continuing their hostile demonstrations, Congress on the 29th of September, 1789, authorized the President to call out the militia for the protection of the border settlements, and "to break the power of the savages." On the 6th of October in the same year Gen. St. Clair, then Governor of the Northwest Territory, was directed by Washington to collect fifteen hundred men from the western counties of Virginia, Maryland, and Pennsylvania, and march against the hostile Indian towns on the Maumee. Col. Henry Lee, of Virginia, was to command one regiment of levies to be raised in Maryland, Virginia, and Pennsylvania. These troops assembled in the vicinity of Fort Washington (now Cincinnati) early

---

[1] While The Society of the Cincinnati was in session at Annapolis, on the 24th of November, 1783, Governor Paca sent the following brief message to the General Assembly: "This morning one of the officers of the Maryland Line called upon me and gave information that a number of soldiers had collected in the city and expressed a design of surrounding the General Assembly, and of making use of some violence to obtain satisfaction of their claims on the public." As a matter of precaution, he ordered Col. James Brice to hold in readiness to march at a moment's warning one company of the Annapolis militia, to protect the treasury and suppress any violent proceedings. It is scarcely necessary to add that the rumor was false. Great as was the need of these veterans, and however just their cause of complaint at the delays of Congress in settling their long arrears of pay, they showed no turbulent disposition, but patiently returned to their farms and workshops.

in September, and consisted nominally of two thousand regulars and one thousand militia, including a company of artillery and several squadrons of horse. On the 4th of November, being reduced to fourteen hundred effective men, after penetrating to a tributary of the Wabash, fifteen miles south of the Miami villages, and almost a hundred from Fort Washington, they were fiercely attacked by a large number of Indians. For two hours and a half the Indians, concealed in the woods, slaughtered the troops from every point, when they fled in disorder, leaving their artillery, baggage, etc., in the hands of the enemy.

The entire loss was estimated at six hundred and seventy-seven killed, among whom was Gen. Butler, and two hundred and seventy-one wounded.[1]

Ensign George Chase, of Baltimore, was killed, and Capt. William Buchanan and a number of Marylanders were wounded.

This defeat produced great alarm on the borders, and Congress took prompt and immediate action by authorizing an army of five thousand men to be equipped for frontier service. Various obstacles, however, prevented a speedy organization of this force, and it was not until the spring of 1794 that an army strong enough to strike a decisive blow could be collected. Gen. Anthony Wayne was appointed commander-in-chief, and Col. Otho H. Williams, of Washington County, and Col. Rufus Putnam brigadier-generals under him.

In May, 1791, Henry Gaither, of Western Maryland, was "appointed commandant of levies now raising in this State," vice Col. Rawlings, who declined; and Capts. William Lewis and Benjamin Price were appointed to the command of two companies.

Among the Maryland troops engaged in this expedition were the companies of Capt. Campbell Smith, of Baltimore, and of Capts. Lewis, Carberry, and Benjamin Price, of Frederick. The entire force consisted of two thousand regular troops, fifteen hundred mounted volunteers from Kentucky, and some other volunteer organizations, and assembled at Greenville. On the 20th of August, 1794, Gen. Wayne met the Indians at the foot of the rapids on the Maumee, and, after a short but sanguinary struggle, completely defeated them. In this battle Capts. Smith and Price were severely wounded.

In September, 1790, Thomas Sprigg was authorized to collect all the arms in Washington County belonging to the State, and persons having arms in their possession were directed to deliver them to Capt. Ott, at Hagerstown.

In October, 1790, M. Lacassagne, to encourage twenty families to emigrate and improve a tract of land which he possessed on the northwest side of the Ohio, in sight of Louisville, at the rapids, offered to give, among other inducements, two hundred acres of land in fee-simple to each family. Col. Thomas Sprigg, Col. John Barnes, and Dr. Henry Schnebely, near Hagerstown, Col. Wm. Bentley, near Frederick, and James Chapline, near Sharpsburg, were his agents.

The *Hagerstown Spy* of Oct. 18, 1793, says that on "last Saturday marched from this town, in order to join the main army in the Western country, a detachment of troops, under the command of Lieut. Whistler. The most of this corps was raised in this town, and too much praise cannot well be bestowed on Lieut. Whistler for his indefatigable assiduity in disciplining his men, and rendering them orderly and inoffensive to the inhabitants. We wish them an agreeable march and successful campaign."

While these events were occurring on the border, the country was agitated by apprehensions of war with foreign powers, and by actual insurrection at home. On the 1st of February, 1793, the French National Convention declared war against England and Holland. One of their first acts was to appoint a representative to the United States to solicit the support of the sister republic, and to claim the privileges to which they considered France to be entitled under the two treaties made with Benjamin Franklin on the 6th of February, 1778. Under Articles XVII. and XXII. of the first treaty of friendship and commerce the French assumed that they might claim the exclusive right to arm and commission privateers within American ports, to bring into them their prizes, to cause the prizes thus brought in to be condemned by French consuls and sold, and even to capture vessels of the enemy within the limits of the maritime jurisdiction of the United States. At least such were the pretensions of their envoy, Monsieur, or, as he styled himself, Citizen Genet, a Girondist of the most radical type, whose avowed object was to excite the people of the United States to a war with Great Britain.

On the other hand, Washington, then entering on his second term of office as President, was determined to preserve the neutrality of his country, and immediately on receiving intelligence of the outbreak of war, hastened from Mount Vernon to Philadelphia, summoned his cabinet together, and soon after, on the 22d of April, 1793, issued a proclamation of neutrality. The sympathies of the people of the United States were warmly engaged on the side of France, and Genet was so much encouraged by the popular

---

[1] Included in the killed were thirty women.

sentiment that on his arrival in Charleston, in April, 1793, he at once proceeded to disregard the President's proclamation and to organize a system of privateering. He had not been in the country a week before he had commissioned four vessels to sail as privateers. He also authorized the French consuls in one town to hold prize-courts and condemn and sell vessels captured by his privateers, and he then made a triumphant progress from Charleston to Philadelphia, organizing red republican clubs and preaching hostility to England. In consequence of the depredations committed by the American privateers under the French flag against British commerce in 1794, and the extraordinary pretensions and naval power of the British government, the President recommended serious preparations both for offense and defense, and the fortifications at Baltimore and other exposed points were put in readiness to repel attack. In compliance with the act of Congress and the provisions made by the Legislature, Governor Thomas Sim Lee reorganized the militia of the State, and appointed as major-generals John E. Howard, John Hoskins Stone, and Levin Winder. John Davidson was appointed brigadier-general for Calvert and Anne Arundel Counties; John H. Briscoe for St. Mary's and Charles; Uriah Forrest for Prince George's and part of Montgomery; Jeremiah Crabb for part of Montgomery and Frederick; Mountjoy Bailey for Fredericktown; Moses Rawlings for Washington and Allegany Counties; Samuel Smith for Baltimore Town; Charles C. Ridgely for Baltimore County; Josias C. Hall for Cecil and Harford; James Lloyd for Kent and Queen Anne's; John Eccleston for Dorchester, Caroline, and Talbot; and Alexander Roxburgh for Somerset and Worcester.

For Washington County: Lieut.-Cols. Thomas Sprigg, Rezin Davis, William Van Leer; Majs. Josiah Price, Charles Carroll, William Fitzhugh, Jr., Adam Ott, Hanson Briscoe, Christopher Orondors.

Allegany County: Lieut.-Col. Daniel Cresap; Majs. John Lynn, Gabriel Jacobs.

Frederick County: Lieut.-Cols. George Murdock, Edward Tilyard, William Lucket, John Ross Key, Joshua Gist, William Lamar; Majs. John McPherson, Stephen Shelmerdine, Philemon Griffith, Thomas Darnall, Thomas Hawkins, John Thomas, Michael Bayer, Joseph Sim Smith, Stephen Winchester, Francis Brown Sappington, Nicholas Randall, Robert Cumming.

Montgomery County: Lieut.-Cols. Francis Deakins, Richard Anderson, William Deakins; Majs. Davis Lucket, Benjamin Murdock, Aquila Johns, Thomas Plater, John Mason, Lloyd Beall.

The Whisky Insurrection.—While these military preparations were in progress some of the western counties of Pennsylvania lifted the arm of defiance against the Federal government, and acts were committed to defeat the execution of the laws imposing duties upon spirits distilled within the United States. These treasonable measures called for the prompt interference of the executive authority, and hence arose the episode in our history known as the "Whisky Insurrection." Distillers, who resided in Allegany, Fayette, Washington, and Westmoreland Counties, Pa., who were willing to comply with the excise laws passed by Congress, were abused; mails were robbed, outrages committed on the government revenue officers, and Gen. Neville, the chief inspector of revenue, was twice attacked and his house burned to the ground by these lawless insurgents. The government of Maryland watched with interest the efforts of Pennsylvania to suppress this rebellion, and prepared to furnish help if necessary. On May 19th the Secretary of War directed Governor Lee "to organize, arm, and equip, according to law, and hold in readiness to march at a moment's warning 5418 of the militia of Maryland, officers included." In the mean time the rebels were making preparations to seize Fort Fayette in Pennsylvania, and the insurrectionary spirit seemed to be spreading into the adjoining counties of Maryland and Virginia. One Bradford, a native of Maryland, who had assumed by common consent the position of commander-in-chief of the insurgents, issued a call for the assembling of the militia on Braddock's Field on August 1st, with arms and accoutrements, and provisions for four days. Within three days seven thousand men assembled, the greater part with the determination to follow Bradford in resistance to the Federal and State governments wherever he might lead. Mr. Lossing says, "It was Bradford's design to seize Fort Pitt and its arms and ammunition; but he found most of the militia officers unwilling to co-operate in such an overt act of treason. But they readily consented to the perpetration of outrages against excise officers, and the whole country in that region was governed for the moment by the combined powers of mobocracy and military despotism." Upon the receipt of this intelligence the President immediately called his cabinet together to take the necessary measures for the preservation of peace and the enforcement of the laws. It was agreed in the cabinet council that forbearance must now end, and the effective power of the government be put forth to suppress the rising rebellion. Accordingly, on August 7th Washington issued a proclamation warning the insurgents to disperse, and declaring that if tranquillity should not be restored in the disturbed counties before September 1st an armed force would be employed to compel submission to the laws. At the same time the President made a requisition on the Governors of Maryland, Virginia, Pennsylvania, and New Jersey for militia sufficient to compose an army of twelve thousand men. This number was subsequently increased to fifteen thousand. The troops of New Jersey and Pennsylvania were directed to rendezvous at Bedford, and those of Maryland and Virginia at Cumberland. The command of the expedition was conferred by Washington on Governor Richard Henry Lee, or "Light Horse Harry," as he was generally called, of Virginia. Governor Mifflin, of Pennsylvania, and Governor Howell, of New Jersey, commanded the militia of their respective States. Gen. Daniel Morgan commanded the militia of Virginia, and Gen. Samuel Smith, the hero of Fort Mifflin in 1777, and at this time the able representative of Baltimore in Congress, commanded those of Maryland. The latter took command August 17th, and immediately proceeded to organize his forces. Volunteers flocked to Baltimore from all portions of the State to await marching orders to the seat of war.

GEN. HENRY LEE.

The friends of the government in Western Maryland were in the mean time taking steps for their own protection and for the maintenance of the laws. The following notices published in the newspapers of the period show that in spite of its proximity to the disaffected region the spirit of loyalty was still strong in this section:

"The different Companies of Militia in Hagerstown are requested to assemble at the Court-House, on Saturday next, at two o'clock, at which time the troop will beat.

"DANIEL STULL, *Capt.*
"ROBERT DOUGLASS, *Capt.*
"JOHN GEIGER, *Capt.*
"JOHN LEE, *Capt.*
"CASPER SHAFFNER, *Capt.*

"HAGERSTOWN, Aug. 27, 1794.

"All those Gentlemen who are desirous of joining the volunteer company of Light Horse of Washington County, will please make application to Jacob Schnelby, captain.
"Aug. 27, 1794."

"ELIZABETH TOWN, MARYLAND, September 3.
"The following Citizens are Draughted in Col. Thomas Sprigg's Regiment, viz.: From Capt. Joseph Hurst's Company, George Fuls, Peter Miller, Robert Mills, Clark Linn, and Samuel Henry; Captain Ankeny's Company, Jacob Fiery, Jacob Haynes, Henry Praither, Philip Miller, and Andrew Walker; Captain Bowles' Company, David Butterbough, John Murry, Samuel Bowles, and Christian Mettz; Capt. Thomas Allen's Company, John Kee, Joseph Wolgamott, Robert Chalmbers, Edmond Norris, Basel Berry, and Henry Ensmouser; Captain Lantz's Company, John Schriver, William Thompson, and Frederick Shoop; Captain Downey's Company, Isaac Young, John Raby, Casper Henry, Charles Carroll, of Dudington, and John Howard; Captain Zellers' Company, John Newonnser, Jacob Orendorff, John Schnebely, and John Fisher; Capt. James McClain's Company, James McClain, jun., Henry Moudy, Archibald Talbot, and Robert McClain. The subsequent gentlemen of Capt. John Johnson's Company offered themselves as volunteers on the present important crisis, viz.: Captain John Johnson, Lieutenant David Miskimman, Ensign Samuel Thomas, David Roberts, Gaas Roberts, Henry Proizman, Soloman Taylor, William Johnson, Joseph Johnson, Peter Johnson, Joshua Johnson, William Donnell, James McCallister, John Sowders, John Smith, Benjamin Berry, Robert Boyd, Jeremiah Dugan, William Flint, Owen Dougherty, William Lamey, and William McGaughey."

On the 6th of September a meeting of such of the inhabitants as were exempt by law from military duty was held at the court-house in Frederick, Thomas Johnson in the chair, "to consider of the steps necessary to be taken to quiet the alarm occasioned by the insurgents. Besides the military guards on duty, it was unanimously agreed that a company should be formed of persons thus exempt to serve as guards at this place, whenever it may be necessary to act in support of the constitutional civil authority, or to repel any attempt that may be made to disturb the peace of the town or neighborhood. It was further resolved that as soon as fifty persons should enroll themselves, a meeting should be held to choose the proper officers to command the company, and on the same day they were enrolled; but the evening being then too far advanced to complete the business, they adjourned till Monday, eleven o'clock, when Mr. Johnson was unanimously chosen captain, Col. Price lieutenant, and Maj. Miller ensign."

The forces assembled at Baltimore were joined by various military organizations of the town and its vicinity, among which were Capt. Mackenheimer's "First Baltimore Light Infantry," Capt. Stricker's "Independent Company," Capt. Coulson's "Mechanical Company," Capt. James A. Buchanan's "Baltimore Sans Culottes," Capt. Jessup's rifle company, Maj. Lowry's "First Baltimore Battalion," in which were included Capt. Hugh Thompson's company of grenadiers, and Capt. William Robb's company of light infantry, and two troops of horse under Capt. John Bowen and Capt. Ruxton Moore.

Most of these organizations had been formed previous to this time. Capt. Mackenheimer's company was raised about 1787. Its uniform was light blue faced with white, and its parade-ground was on the present site of the Front Street Theatre, in Baltimore. The Independent Company, the Mechanical Company, the Baltimore Sans Culottes, and Capt. Jessup's rifle company are said to have been organized about 1792. These, when the State militia was organized, constituted the Fifth Regiment. The First Baltimore Battalion was raised about the same time, and comprised Capt. Hugh Thompson's company of grenadiers, two companies of hatmen, as they were called, wearing cocked hats, and Capt. Robb's company of light infantry. The uniform of the organization was blue coat faced with red and edged with white, white vest and breeches, black knee-bands, short-laced boots, and white cotton hose. Capt. J. Bowen's troop of horse was associated with them; uniform, green faced with red.

BALTIMORE CITY IN 1800.

This body on parade made a splendid appearance, and were drilled twice a week in citizens' dress, on the west side of Harford Run, near old Trinity church,—this afterwards became the Twenty-seventh Regiment. The first rifle company adopted the dress of Morgan's riflemen of the Continental army,—hunting-shirt, with a profusion of fringe. The second rifle company was raised by Capt. Reese, father of John Reese, who was for many years president of the Firemen's Insurance Company of Baltimore; uniform, green faced with yellow. The uniform of Capt. Moore's company was blue and buff. In this troop were several gentlemen who had belonged to Pulaski's Legion. The uniform of the Sans Culottes, afterwards called the Independent Blues, was copied from the marine uniform of the frigate "Astrea," then lying at Baltimore. It was worn buttoned close to the body, with the cartouche-belt inside. It was the first company that adopted pantaloons, breeches and stockings being then universally worn.

Messrs. Daniel Cresap, John Lynn, and Gabriel Jacob, in a letter to Governor Lee, dated Cumberland, Sept. 2, 1794, say,—

"We are very sorry to add, but we conceive it to be our indispensable duty to inform your Excellency that the spirit of insurrection is not confined to the western counties of Pennsylvania; those to the eastward of the Allegany mountains are infected with the contagion; and unless speedily prevented, may rise to a formidable height, and, perhaps, end in our destruction. Cumberland hath been threatened, an attempt hath been made there to raise a liberty-pole (which is the insignia or badge by which the insurgents are now discriminated), but by the exertions of the most respectable citizens it was prevented. In other parts of the country they have succeeded. The papers of the excise officers have been demanded. We are threatened with the Pennsylvanians, whom, the disaffected here say, they will call to their assistance. Should it take place, God only knows what will be the event; however, let the event be what it may, our exertions, friended, we trust, by the most respectable of the country, will not be wanting. In our situation, we think it our duty to request of you to forward to us arms and accoutrements, these we will distribute amongst the men in whom we may confide. Those who are willing to support the measures of the government have it not in their power. Should you be able to obtain the approbation of council, you will please forward us two hundred stand of arms, and order to our protection a small detachment of militia, consisting of cavalry and infantry, to be selected from those counties which are well disposed to the laws of the Union, and particularly the Excise law. We hope the example of Baltimore Town will sanction the transmitting of public arms, and that your conduct will, on this occasion, as it then did, meet with the approbation of the Legislature."

On September 6th, Secretary Hamilton wrote to Governor Lee,—

"WAR DEPARTMENT, Sept. 6, 1794.

"SIR,—I am directed by the President to notice to your Excellency that information has been received that some riotous proceedings have taken place in the upper part of Baltimore County and in the neighborhod of Hagerstown, connected with the insurrection in the western counties of Pennsylvania. He instructs me to observe that it appears to him of the highest importance that efficient measures should be pursued to suppress the first beginning of this spirit in your State, and thereby to check the progress of an evil which radically threatens the order, peace, and tranquillity of the country. Much depends, in such a crisis as the present, on an early display of energy under the guidance of the legal precaution. It is understood that the magazine of arms of the State is at Frederick. Adequate means no doubt will be used to prevent the possibility of these falling into bad hands.

"With great respect, I have the honor to be your Excellency's most obedient and humble servant,

"A. HAMILTON.

"His Excellency THOMAS S. LEE, Esq., Governor of Maryland."

Again on September 15th, Hamilton wrote to Governor Lee that

"it is the President's desire that no time should be lost in uniting the whole of the militia of Maryland at Fort Cumberland. If the commanding officer has not already taken the field, it is desirable that he should do so without delay, in order to combine, arrange, and accelerate their ulterior movements."

On September 15th the Governor sent by express a requisition for Baltimore troops, in consequence of a report that the insurgents had assembled in considerable numbers near Cumberland, with the intention of marching to Frederick to seize the State arms deposited in the arsenal. The order reached Baltimore on Sunday, while the people were at their several places of worship. General Smith was at the time attending service at the First Presbyterian church, and was immediately sent for. He at once ordered the drums to beat and the troops to assemble on the parade-ground near Harford Run. A correspondent in the *Maryland Gazette* of the 18th gives the following graphic description of this call to arms:

GEN. SAMUEL SMITH.

"A more warlike appearance, perhaps, our town has not exhibited since the year 1776 than it did yesterday, in consequence of an express from the Governor to General Smith. The militia of this town were requested to meet on the parade, near the old theater, at 4 P.M. They met accordingly, when a circle was formed, and Gen. Smith, in a short but energetic address, informed them of the object of their meeting; that it was in consequence of an intended attack by the insurgents beyond the mountains upon the arsenal at Frederick Town, with a view of taking off all the arms, etc., and that three hundred volunteers of infantry, besides artillery and cavalry, were required immediately to march under the command of Col. Stricker and secure it. ' It is not,' said he, ' against an enemy that we have to march, but a set of men more daring than the rest, a lawless banditti, who set themselves up to govern. Shall we permit them to seize our arms and give us laws, or shall we keep them and give laws to ourselves?' (We could not hear the whole of the general's speech.) He concluded his harangue by putting the question, 'Will you go as volunteers or will you be drafted?' Melancholy as the circumstances are, it is with pleasure we have it in our power to inform the public that they turned out voluntarily to nearly treble the requisition, and that the unanimity displayed on the occasion could hardly be surpassed. This is the test of patriotism."

The Fifth Regiment was ordered to parade at the court-house on Monday morning following at nine o'clock, in marching order, and at the time appointed took up the line of march for Frederick under the command of Col. Stricker, being twenty-five cavalry and two hundred and twenty-five infantry. The Twenty-seventh Regiment set out on Tuesday morning, followed by a company of volunteers from Worcester County. On the 18th over three hundred more marched, and later in the week six hundred additional men. On the 15th a part of the volunteer militia of Annapolis marched to Frederick, and on the succeeding day a detachment of light dragoons. In a letter dated from Frederick a few days later, after the arrival of part of the militia, a correspondent writing to a friend in Baltimore says,—

"I know your anxiety to hear from us. Reports have, I fear, pictured our situation dreadful. The march of the troops from both Baltimore and Georgetown has been singularly expeditious. Capt. Moore and his troop, that would do honor to any army, arrived about the middle of yesterday. Col. Stricker and a most beautiful corps of fine young fellows are now refreshing themselves at Monocacy. The troops from Georgetown left that place at five o'clock Sunday evening, and arrived here Monday before night. The grenadiers from the city of Washington, and other troops from the neighborhood, came in yesterday. The militia of the county have behaved truly praiseworthy, and as becomes freemen they are returning to their homes; for, rest assured, we shall never see the face of an insurgent unless he is sought for in the mountains, as you would a wolf. We are not, nor ever have been, in any danger. A number of idle reports have alarmed some of our citizens without cause."

On the 19th twenty men on horseback arrived in Frederick from Hagerstown with an account "that the deluded people of Allegany and Washington Counties were embodying, and might be expected to attack Frederick the next day." There were then, according to contemporaneous accounts, five hundred troops at Frederick, "well armed, in high spirits, and desirous that the insurgents would make the attack; and besides, the Baltimore horse were within a few miles; the first detachment of foot would be at New Market on Tuesday evening; the second detachment were apprised of the alarm."

The following letter from Elizabeth Town, Washington County, under date of the 24th of September, gives an interesting account of the condition of affairs in that locality at this crisis:

"Saturday last his Excellency the Governor of this State arrived here, and returned on Monday morning. The opposition of the excise law grew, by progression, as well to an opposition to all law and authority as to a personal enmity to individuals in this town, inasmuch as the pole, which had been erected in this town by the rabble, was secretly cut down, perhaps by one of themselves, in order to have a colorable pretext again to insult the peaceable citizens, and wreak vengeance on those to whom they had at any time hitherto taken umbrage. As a prelude to another affray, some dark assassin put a handbill at the market-house, ordering, by name, some of the principal citizens of the town to erect another pole or they should be put to death. This order and threat was valiantly despised by those worthy citizens. In the mean time a party were assembling along the verge of the South Mountain, in order, as was said, to attack the magazine and town of Frederick. That expedition, however, failed. At this stage of the business, and finding the turbulence of faction still increase, some volunteers of our cavalry and infantry mounted guard, patrolled the streets, sent detachments into the country, apprehended some of the principals, and brought them to justice. The vigilance and alacrity of our citizens on this occasion to support government was too conspicuous to be passed over in silence, and, without detracting any merit from the many distinguished patriots of this town, the names of Capts. Lee and Schnebly are honorably mentioned. At this juncture, on last Friday, a detachment of volunteers and drafts arrived in town, under the command of Gen. Bailey, consisting of seventy cavalry and two hundred and fifty infantry, from Baltimore, Georgetown, and Fredericktown. Their presence had a good effect; . . . they assisted in the work which had been begun of bringing the culprits to justice; . . . a tribute of gratitude is due to those troops for their kind and prompt assistance, . . . but finding there remained little occasion for them here they returned home on last Monday morning, . . . about which time arrived two hundred volunteers and drafts, under the command of Maj. Lynn, who are destined for the Western country, but are to remain here till further orders, and are now under the command of that old veteran soldier, Maj. Ott. Those fascinated oppositionists, who defied the arm of government, have at length tamely submitted to the law, . . . even sixteen of them surrendered to five of the cavalry. They in general plead ignorance as their shield, notwithstanding that incomparably eloquent and persuasive oration delivered by Mr. Mason two days before the riots began, and notwithstanding the expostulation and exertions of Col. Spring, Col. Shryock, Maj. Price, and others, at the risk of their lives, when they were about erecting the pole in the town.

"The Hon. Judge Craik, and some of the magistrates of the county, have been busily employed in the examination of the culprits, and have, we understand, admitted sundry to bail. Upon the whole, we doubt not that justice will be done, and that every species of unnecessary severity will be avoided on the occasion, . . . well knowing that affection as well as submission is requisite to the security of a Republican government, . . . and that affection arises from a sense and experience of the blessings of liberty and order."

On the morning of the 23d September the volunteers who had marched from different parts of the State to Fredericktown to act against the insurgents, met on the grand parade in Baltimore, and having performed the manual, were drawn up in a large circle, when Col. Stricker, accompanied by the Governor himself, read the following address from his Excellency:

"The commander-in-chief feels it incumbent on him, on this occasion, to present on the part of the State, whose character, peace, and security were so largely endangered, and for himself, his warmest acknowledgments to all the officers and soldiers who had given their services under this requisition, and who by so doing have not only effected the restoration of order and safety in their own State, but have given a material check to the views of the insurgents in Pennsylvania, who will despair hereafter of aiding their wretched designs by the seduction of their neighbors. Thus, conceiving that an important service has been rendered by the militia serving under his orders, the commander-in-chief, with congratulations and thanks, discharges them from the present service.

"THOMAS S. LEE."

COL. JOHN STRICKER.

At a meeting of a number of the people of Washington County held at the court-house in Elizabeth Town, on Friday, the 26th of September, 1794, Col. Henry Shryock, chairman, and John Thomson Mason, secretary,

"it was proposed and agreed to, that Messrs. Nathaniel Rochester, Henry Schnebely, Samuel Ringgold, William Clark, and John Thomson Mason be requested to prepare an address from the meeting to Col. Thomas Sprigg, who prepared the following, which was read, approved, and ordered to be printed in Washington, Frederick, and Baltimore newspapers:

"'TO COL. THOMAS SPRIGG:

"'Sir,—By the unanimous voice of the persons present at this meeting you are solicited once more to permit us to cast our suffrages upon you as the person, in our opinion, most proper to represent this district in Congress. We beg leave to return you our thanks for your past services in that station, and to manifest our approbation of your conduct as our representative. We beg leave, more particularly at this time, to thank you for your late constant, unremitted, prudent, and spirited exertions in endeavoring to suppress those unhappy tumults that have disturbed the peace and threatened the safety of the well-disposed citizens amongst us. The manner in which certain reports have been secretly and industriously circulated, and the inexcusable misrepresentations that have been made, excite our highest indignation, and we feel ourselves injured in the attempts made to calumniate you. But whilst we assure you of our determination to support you at the ensuing election, we hope, and confidently trust, that every honorable and manly exertion will be made on your part to gratify the wishes and effectuate the endeavours of your friends.

"'Signed, by order of the meeting.

"'H. SHRYOCK, Chairman.
"'JOHN T. MASON, Secretary.'

"We do certify that, in company with Mr. George Price and others at Col. Sprigg's, it was mentioned that the Frederick light-horse intended to march to Hagerstown to cut down the liberty-pole which a mob had some days before erected. In answer to which Col. Sprigg observed, he was very sorry to hear it; that, if it was necessary, he could cut the pole down himself, and that, if he knew when they intended to come up, he would oppose their cutting it down; that he had seen a very disagreeable day in Hagerstown, and that if the pole was cut down, and no force remained in that place to prevent its being set up again, the mob would return more enraged than before, set up the liberty-pole, and insult the inhabitants, who were not in a situation to protect themselves. That it would reflect, too, upon Washington County, and that it would be better to suspend cutting the pole down for a short time, until a force sufficient to prevent its being set up again should arrive in Hagerstown to protect the inhabitants, and bring those to justice who had thus offended against the laws of their country.

"WILLIAM FITZHUGH, JR.,
"WILLIAM FITZHUGH, SR.

"Sept. 28, 1794."

"N.B.—Capt. Hunter, from Baltimore, Capt. William Campbell, and Maj. Taylor, and some others, were present when this conversation took place. I am satisfied that the above statement represents the substance of Col. Sprigg's conversation therein alluded to, and, although it is not probably in his words, it fully conveys the ideas received from his expressions.
"GEORGE PRICE.

"Sept. 28, 1794."

"We certify that we were present in Hagerstown on the 1st day of September, 1794, when the mob so much talked of happened. We also certify that Col. Thomas Sprigg was then present, and that he exerted himself in a most singular and spirited manner to prevent the erection of the liberty-pole, that was then raised, and to disperse the mob. We were witness to many insults that he received from the mob in consequence of his exertions, and we often supposed his person in danger. We have also been witness to the active and decided part which Col. Sprigg has since taken to bring those insurgents to justice, and do think this county under particular obligations to that Gentleman for the part he has acted.

"ADAM OTT,
"H. SHRYOCK,
"REZIN DAVIS,
"WM. LEE,
"BENJ. CLAGETT,
"N. ROCHESTER,
"JOSIAH PRICE."

At the time Washington issued his first proclamation he appointed Senator Ross, Mr. Bradford, the Attorney-General, and Mr. Yates, a judge of the Supreme Court of Pennsylvania, commissioners on the part of the Federal government to visit the insurgent counties with discretionary powers to offer lenient terms to the offenders, and, if possible, induce them to submit to the laws, and disband before the 14th of September. They were joined by Chief Justice McKean and Gen. Irvine, commissioners appointed on the part of Pennsylvania. These commissioners visited the insurgents, who refused all compliance, and they returned to Philadelphia and reported the failure of their mission. The President then issued his proclamation of the 25th of September, in which he vividly described the defiant spirit with which the lenient propositions of the government had been met, and declared his determination to reduce them to submission by coercive measures. As if anticipating the result of the commissioners' mission, Alexander Hamilton had previously addressed the following letter to Governor Lee:

"WAR DEPARTMENT, Sept. 17, 1794.
"SIR,—The intelligence received from the western counties of Pennsylvania, which comes down to the 13th instant, and announces, as far as it was then known, the result of the meetings of the people in the several townships and districts to express their sense on the question of submission or resistance to the laws,—while it shows a great proportion of the inhabitants of these counties disposed to pursue the path of duty, shows, also, that there is a large and violent party which can only be controlled by the application of force. This being the result, it is become the more indispensable and urgent to press forward the forces destined to act against the insurgents with all possible activity and energy. The advanced season leaves no time to spare,—and it is extremely important to afford speedy protection to the well disposed, and to prevent the preparation and accumulation of greater means of resistance and the extension of combinations to abet the insurrection. The President counts upon every exertion upon your part which so serious and eventful an emergency demands.

"With perfect respect, I have the honor to be, sir, your obedient servant,
"ALEXANDER HAMILTON.
"His Excellency THOS. S. LEE, Governor of Maryland."

In October Washington left Philadelphia, determined to lead the army in person, and, accompanied by the Secretary of War, he proceeded to Fort Cumberland, the place of rendezvous for the Maryland and Virginia troops, where he arrived on the 16th.[1]

---

[1] The following notices throw light upon some of the local military movements at this time in progress in Western Maryland:

"A TROOP OF HORSE.

"Those persons who are desirous of joining a troop of Horse will apply to Samuel Ringgold, he being authorized by the Field-officers to raise a troop.
"HAGERSTOWN, Oct. 1, 1794."

"BATTALION ORDERS.

"The Captains of companies composing my Battalion, in the Twenty-fourth Regiment of militia of this State, will meet on the parade at the court-house, on Thursday, the 30th, to march to Cannon Hill for exercise.
"ADAM OTT,
"Major Twenty-fourth Regiment M. M.
"WASHINGTON COUNTY, October 28th."

"ELIZABETHTOWN, October 28th.
"Capt. John Lee's company of infantry is desired to parade on Thursday next at one o'clock. A full attendance is expected."

"A meeting of Capt. Schnebly's troop of Horse is requested at Mr. Ragan's tavern, on Friday evening next, at six o'clock, in order to consult upon the most eligible method of having the said troop equipped."

"ELIZABETH TOWN, MARYLAND, October 7th.
"Accounts from all quarters mention the marching of the militia against the Western insurgents . . . the troops which were stationed here, as well as the quota of this place, marched yesterday, in order to join the other troops of the State at Williamsport, under the command of Gen. Smith."

The Pennsylvania and New Jersey troops had moved from Carlisle on the 10th of October. A large number of the Maryland and Virginia troops were assembled at Cumberland. Upon Washington's arrival he received such information as convinced him that the spirits of the insurgents were broken, and hastened on to Bedford, thirty miles distant, and there this intelligence was confirmed. " The assembling of the militia from Maryland and Virginia at Cumberland created great excitement in the village. How long they remained here is not exactly known, but on the 18th of October Washington arrived, and spent several days inspecting the condition of the men and their supplies. On the 19th he appeared in full uniform, and held a review on the old parade-ground of Fort Cumberland, at which the entire population of the town was present. This was the last occasion upon which he wore his uniform. The troops had been encamped along Will's Creek, on what was known as the 'Island,' where they had good water from a spring near by. On the 19th the command was marched up to the parade-ground, where the court-house now stands, and drawn up for inspection.

" Gen. Washington rode along the line, from the right to the left, and was loudly cheered by the men. Afterwards the command marched in review, and Washington raised his hat as a salute while they passed. Gens. Lee and Morgan were both present and participated. Hon. Alexander R. Boteler has in his possession an oil-painting representing this review. It was the work of an amateur artist, and upon its completion passed into the hands of Gen. Daniel Morgan."[1]

Satisfied that his presence would be no longer needed with the army, Gen. Washington returned to Philadelphia, leaving Governor Lee, of Virginia, in command. The troops crossed the Allegany Mountains in a heavy rain, marching sometimes in mud up to their knees, and the two wings formed a junction at Union Town. As they advanced into the insurgent country all signs of rebellion disappeared, and the leaders fled. After the adoption of a few precautionary measures, most of the troops were sent to their homes, and thus, without the shedding of a drop of blood, ended a rebellion which at one time threatened the very existence of the Union.

The following letter was addressed by Alexander Hamilton to Governor Lee shortly after the suppression of the insurrection :

"WAR DEPARTMENT, Nov. 24, 1794.

" SIR,—I have the honor to acknowledge the receipt of a letter of the 18th instant from the Executive Council of Maryland, and to congratulate you and them on the disappearance of the insurrection in Maryland.

" The President has seen with great satisfaction the laudable vigor with which it was met by the Government, the excellent disposition manifested by the citizens, and the speedy termination of the disturbance. Such an example cannot but have the best effect.

" Though severity towards offenders is to be avoided as much as can consist with the safety of society, yet impunity in such cases is apt to produce too much promptitude in setting the laws at defiance. Repeated instances of such impunity in Pennsylvania are perhaps the principal cause of the misfortune which now afflicts itself, and through it the United States. The disturbers of the peace familiarly appeal to the past experience of unpunished offences as an encouragement to the perpetration of new ones. This general reflection will no doubt be duly adverted to by the judiciary and other authorities of Maryland.

" With great respect and esteem, I have the honor to be, Sir, your most obedient servant,

" ALEXANDER HAMILTON.

" His Excellency THOMAS SIM LEE, Governor of Maryland."

Upon the return of the Maryland troops, Gen. Lee acknowledged their services in the following letter to the Governor :

"HEADQUARTERS, Nov. 26, 1794.

" SIR,—The period having arrived when the army entrusted to my direction by the President of the United States, having accomplished the object of their advance into this country, are about to return home, I should commit violence on my own feelings were I not to express to your Excellency my very high ideas of their merit. Suddenly brought into the field, they were unprepared for the hardships which they encountered. Nevertheless, disregarding the distress to which they were consequently in a greater degree exposed, they continued to evidence, with firmness and zeal, the purity of the principles by which they were moved, and terminated their campaign in perfect correspondence with the patriotism which impelled them to exchange domestic enjoyments for the toils and privations inseparable from military life. To all is due the tribute of applause which ever attends the faithful and animated discharge of duty, but to one class something more is due. Those inestimable and friendless citizens who fill the ranks seem to have been scarcely noticed in the legal provisions for compensation.

" If the example exhibited by my companions in arms is deemed worthy of attention, I derive great consolation from my hopes that the State Legislature will take into consideration the inequality which at present exists in the pay allowed to the officers and to the soldiers, and, so far as respects the faithful army under my orders, will be pleased to manifest their sense of the conduct of the troops by rendering the pecuniary compensation of the soldiers proportionate to that given to the officers. The justice and policy of such interposition are alike evident, and will be peculiarly acceptable.

" Another point, in which both officers and soldiers are interested, claims, in my humble opinion, legislative notice. Although the wise and temperate system adopted by the President of the United States averted the heaviest of all human calamities, and saved the effusion of blood, yet the sufferings which the army experienced from the extreme severity of the weather have deprived many families of their dearest friend and chief support. To alleviate their miseries, by extending to them, with equity and liberality, the public aid, is the only possible retribution which can be made by the community, and I flatter myself it is only necessary to make known the existence of such cases to secure to the sufferers the requisite legal provision.

---

[1] Lowdermilk.

"I forbear to gratify my affectionate attachment to my fellow-citizens in arms with me, by yielding to my solicitude for their welfare, and subjoining the many observations which my knowledge of their virtue and sufferings crowds upon my mind, in the confidence that their conduct best bespeaks their worth, and that the General Assembly will take pleasure in manifesting their respect to real merit.

"I have the honor to be, with great respect, your most obedient servant,   "RCH. HY. LEE."

And as a further recognition of their services, the General Assembly, on the 24th of December, 1794,

"*Resolved, unanimously*, That the thanks of this Legislature be given to the officers and privates of the militia of this State, who on the late call of the President rallied round the standard of the laws, and in the prompt and severe services which they encountered bore the most illustrious testimony to the value of the Constitution and the blessings of internal peace and order; and that the Governor be requested to communicate the above vote of thanks in such manner as he may judge most acceptable to the patriotic citizens who are its subjects."[1]

---

[1] The military revival caused by the Whisky Insurrection and the anticipated trouble with France did not die out with the suppression of the outbreak in Western Pennsylvania, but continued with increasing force until after the conclusion of the war with England in 1812. Such Washington County notices as the following show that the militia laws were strictly enforced, and the military organizations carefully maintained and kept in a state of preparation and discipline:

"The different companies forming Maj. Ott's battalion are desired to attend parade on Saturday, the 25th instant. It is expected every member will be punctual.

"DANIEL STULL, *Captain*.
"JOHN GEYER, *Captain*.
"ROBERT DOUGLASS, *Captain*.
"CASPER SHAFFNER, *Captain*.
"JOHN LEE, *Captain*.

"ELIZABETHTOWN, April 14, 1795."

"The companies commanded by Capt. Bowles, Ankeny, McClain, Hurst, and Johnston are desired to meet at the lower Quarter of John Barnes, Esq., on the third Saturday in August next, at one o'clock, in order to exercise in battalion, agreeable to law.   JOSIAH PRICE,

"*1st Major Eighth Regt., Washington County Militia, Maryland.*
"July 28, '95."

"The companies commanded by Capt. Wellar, Lantz, Rench, and Allen are desired to meet at Gen. Sprigg's quarter, on Saturday, the 29th instant, to exercise in battalion, agreeably to law.   CHARLES CARROLL, *Major*.
"ELIZABETHTOWN, Aug. 18, 1795."

BATTALION ORDERS.

"The different companies forming my Battalion are desired to meet in Mr. Ringgold's Lane, on the third Tuesday in this month, to exercise in Battalion, agreeably to law.
"Aug. 11, 1795."

"The different companies forming Maj. Ott's Battalion, are desired to attend parade on Saturday, the 30th instant. It is expected every member will be punctual.

"DANIEL STULL, *Captain*.
"CASPER SHAFFNER, *Captain*.
"JOHN GEYER, *Captain*.
"ROBERT DOUGLASS, *Captain*.
"JOHN LEE, *Captain*.

"ELIZABETHTOWN, April 14, 1796."

REGIMENTAL MUSTER.

"The officers with their companies composing the Eighth Regiment are requested to attend regimental muster on the last Saturday in this month, precisely at twelve o'clock, at Mr. Rowland Chambers's tavern, near Mr. Jacques's Furnace.

"JOSIAH PRICE,
"*Colonel Eighth Regiment, Maryland Militia.*
"Oct. 6, 1796."

April 9, 1797, M. Bartgis was captain of the Fredericktown riflemen, and August 9th, same year, Valentine Brother was captain-commandant of the Fredericktown battalion.

"HAGERSTOWN, Aug. 2, 1798.

"The Companies commanded by Capts. Klinger, Rutledge, Davis, Langley, Able, and Brookbank, and Maj. David Funk, will meet at the cross-roads at Capt. John Langley's, on Saturday, the 11th inst., precisely at twelve o'clock."

"GEORGETOWN, Jan. 13, 1799.

"The following army officers from Maryland have just been appointed: Capts. William Spencer, John C. Beatty, Thomas Beatty, Jr., Lloyd Beall, Gerard Briscoe, Rezin Davidge, Bradley Beans, Isaac Spencer, William Nicholson, Jacob Norris, Lieuts. Richard Tilghman, William Elliott, Edward A. Howard, Richard W. West, John B. Barnes, Ninian Pinkney, Levi Alexander, Matthew Tilghman, Henry C. Neale, Aquilla Beall; Ensigns, Alexander Cooper, John Brengle, Enos Noland, Thomas Dent, Levi Hillary, John Warren, William Swan, Levi G. Ford, Daniel Hughes; Cornet, Richard Cook; Lieut.-Col., Josias C. Hall."

"HAGERSTOWN, April 18, 1799.

"The Volunteer Troop of Washington Blues are requested to attend at their usual place of parade on Saturday, the 27th inst., precisely at one o'clock in the afternoon. Every member is requested to be punctual and in full uniform.

"By order of the Captain,
"GEORGE PRICE, *Secretary*."

"HAGERSTOWN, Apr. 25, 1799.

"In consequence of the resignation of Lieut.-Col. Rezin Davis, the Governor and Council have been pleased to appoint me to command of the 24th Regt. of the Maryland Militia. The officers commanding companies in the 24th Regt. are therefore requested, on or before the first day of May next, to make returns thereof, as directed by the 14th section of the supplement to the Militia act, passed at November session, 1798.

"WILLIAM FITZHUGH,
"*Lieut.-Col. 24th Regt. Militia.*"

"HAGERSTOWN, Aug. 1, 1799.

"All persons between the ages of twenty-one and thirty years, belonging to the 8th Regiment, are requested to meet at Kersner's Tavern, at the Cross roads (where said Regiment annually meets), on the third Saturday in August next, at 12 o'clock, for the purpose of completing the Select Company of said Regiment agreeably to Law. It is expected that those Captains who have not yet returned their lists to me, will bring them to the above place, in proper time for business.

"JOSEPH PRICE,
"*Lieut.-Col. 8th Regt., Washington County, Maryland.*"

"HAGERSTOWN, Sept. 19, 1799.

"Ordered, that the 8th Regiment of the 2nd brigade of Militia, be paraded on Saturday, the 19th day of October next,

---

The Encroachments of England and France.—The war between France and England transferred a large portion of the laboring population of the former from their usual avocations to the armies, and this, with other causes, produced a scarcity of provisions in France. Induced by this state of things, France opened her ports to neutral commerce, while Great Britain, in the hope of reducing her enemy by famine, determined to cut off all external supplies. Instructions were accordingly issued on the 8th of June, 1793, and renewed on the 6th of November, 1794, by the British Privy Council to the commanders of British ships-of-war and privateers, directing them " to stop and detain all ships laden with goods, the produce of any colony belonging to France, or carrying provisions or other supplies for the use of such colonies, and to bring the same, with their cargoes, to legal adjudication in our Courts of Admiralty."

This Order in Council, which was a most lawless invasion of neutral rights, in a few weeks swept the seas of our commerce. Hundreds of our vessels engaged in the French West India trade were without previous notice captured, and many of our merchants were reduced to bankruptcy. The intelligence of this procedure excited universal indignation throughout the United States. There was a general clamor for war among all parties. Several violent measures were moved and debated in Congress,—among the rest, the sequestration of all British property in the United States for the purpose of indemnifying our merchants. While Congress was engaged in debating on various modes of procuring redress for the outrages committed on American commerce by the English and French nations, President Washington arrested its career by the appointment of Chief Justice John Jay, of New York, as minister extraordinary to the British government. He embarked from New York on the 12th of May, 1794, and on the 19th of May, 1795, he concluded a treaty with Lord Grenville in London, which was submitted to their respective governments for ratification.

This celebrated treaty, which bears Minister Jay's name, was defective in many parts and very objectionable in others; but owing to the troubled state of Europe, it was the best that he could obtain. The ratification of it disturbed the political atmosphere to such an extent that it shook the Union to its foundation, and produced intense excitement throughout the country. On the 1st of June, 1796, at the close of the exciting session of Congress in which Jay's treaty had been the chief topic of debate, Washington retired for partial repose to his home at Mount Vernon. While there he determined to leave public life at the close of his term of office in March following; and, with this object in view, he prepared his " Farewell Address to the People of the United States," to be published in time to enable them to choose his successor at the appointed season. As this hour was drawing near, the President's enemies did everything in their power to prejudice him in the public mind. His most intimate friends knew that he would not consent to a re-election; but his reserve on the subject and the long delay of making public announcement of his determination puzzled the politicians. However, while political and partisan abuse of the grossest kind was being heaped upon the head of the President, his " Farewell Address" appeared. It was made public about the middle of September, 1796, and produced a great sensation throughout the country. For a time the ribald voice of party spirit was subdued in tone, and to detraction and attack succeeded expressions of veneration and love for the author of the Address.

At the Presidential election which succeeded, John Rousby Plater, Francis Deakins, George Murdock, John Lynn, Gabriel Duvall, John Archer, John Gilpin, John Roberts, John Eccleston, and John Done were chosen electors for Maryland. The votes of the Electoral College for President of the United States were opened and counted in the United States Senate on the 8th of February, 1797, and resulted in the election of John Adams as President, and Thomas Jefferson as Vice-President.

The difficulties with France still continued, and created no little public excitement and agitation. Meetings were held in all sections of the country demanding a vigorous policy against France, and approving the firmness with which the new administration seemed about to deal with the important questions involved. Many meetings of this character were held in Western Maryland.

---

the 10th Regiment on the 22nd, and the 24th Regiment on the 26th day of the same month, each at nine o'clock in the morning.

"T. Sprigg, *Brig.-Gen. 2nd Brigade.*
"Sept. 19, 1799.

" The Lieutenant-Colonels are requested to let me know where they intend to parade their respective Regiments.

"J. Buchanan, *Brigade Major 2nd Brigade.*
"Hagerstown, Sept. 19, 1799."

"Hagerstown, Oct. 31, 1799.

" The members composing the Troop of Washington Blues are requested to meet at their usual place of parade, on Saturday the 9th of November next, at one o'clock precisely, in complete uniform, and six rounds of blank cartridges. It is expected that the troopers will be punctual in their attendance, as there is some business to be laid before them.

"By order,   O. H. Williams, *Sec.*"

"Hagerstown, Aug. 21, 1800.

" Captain Schnebly's Troop of Horse are requested to parade on Saturday next, the 23rd instant, at 9 o'clock in the morning with the Batallion."

"At a numerous meeting of the citizens of Fredericktown and county, held at the court-house in Fredericktown on Saturday, the 28th of April, 1798, after public notice being given, Thomas Johnson in the chair, Valentine Brother was appointed secretary, and the following resolutions were adopted and ordered to be published:

"1st. *Resolved unanimously*, That the President of the United States is entitled to the thanks of his fellow-citizens for his wise, firm, and patriotic conduct in endeavoring to bring our differences with France to a speedy, amicable, and honorable adjustment; that his instructions to our ministers and their powers of negotiations were ample, candid, and liberal; and that our envoys ought to have experienced a reception very different from the one they have met with.

"2d. *Resolved unanimously*, That our envoys have discharged their duty in a manner calculated to impress their fellow-citizens with the greatest respect for their ability and patriotism, and with gratitude for their services.

"3d. *Resolved unanimously*, That it is our fixed determination to support the Constitution of the United States as now established, and the liberty and independence of America against all foreign nations whatsoever; and we view with the utmost detestation the attempts made by foreigners to divide the citizens of this country, and to set them at variance with a government of their own choice.

"4th. *Resolved*, That the chairman be requested to inclose the foregoing resolutions to the representative of this district, to be by him laid before the President and the Congress of the United States."

The following reply was received from the President:

"TO THE CITIZENS OF FREDERICKTOWN AND COUNTY, IN THE STATE OF MARYLAND:

"*Gentlemen*,—A copy of your resolutions of the 23d of April has been presented to me by your Representative in Congress, Mr. Baer.

"The honorable testimony of your thanks to me, of your applause of our envoys, of your determination to support the Constitution and independence of America against all foreign nations, your detestation of the attempts made by foreigners to divide the citizens of this country, and to set them at variance with the government of their choice, would be highly pleasing under all circumstances, and are increased in value to me by having been passed and certified under the auspices of one of the few who remain of my ancient and most respected colleagues in the first councils of the nation.

"JOHN ADAMS.

"PHILADELPHIA, May 8, 1798."

Washington did not remain long in retirement, for on the 2d of July, 1798, owing to the attempts of the French to degrade the United States into a tributary of France, the indignities offered to the representatives of our government, and the injuries inflicted upon our commerce, President Adams nominated and the Senate confirmed him as "lieutenant-general and commander-in-chief of all the armies raised and to be raised in the United States." At the same time Congress ordered the army to be increased by twelve regiments, four of which were to be raised in Maryland. The difficulties with France were, however, arranged in a manner satisfactory to both governments, and there was no immediate necessity for the services of the troops which had been called for by Congress.[1]

The unsettled state of our foreign relations, however, served to keep alive the military spirit of the country, and each new difficulty with England or France added fresh fuel to the military ardor of the times. The hardy inhabitants of Western Maryland, always ready for combat, and by reason of their exposed position rather more accustomed to war than peace, needed no urging to prepare themselves for hostilities, and the large number of military organizations in existence at this period in that section of the State shows the eagerness with which they had responded to the calls of patriotism. Prominent among these organizations during the years immediately succeeding 1800 were the companies of horse known as the "American Blues," at Hagerstown, Capt. Otho H. Williams[2] commanding, and the "Washington Hussars," at Williamsport, commanded by Capt. Frisby Tilghman. Hagerstown at the same time also boasted of two infantry companies, viz., the "Select Volunteers" and another commanded by Capt. Timothy Monahan, the battalion being commanded by Maj. John Reynolds. Besides the frequent militia parades, the people were often gratified by visits from detachments of the United States army as they marched westward *via* Hagerstown, Cumberland, and Wheeling. Among the frequent references to the passage of troops through Western Maryland at this period we find the following paragraph in the columns of the *Herald*, under date of April 26, 1805: "On Wednesday morning last a small detachment of soldiers, under the command of Capt. McClellan, marched through this town on their way to St. Louis, in Upper Louisiana." In December of the year, "Passed

---

[1] "FREDERICKTOWN, May 28, 1800.

"On Saturday evening last arrived in this town, on his way to the city of Washington, the President of the United States. He was met near Monocacy by the troop of horse belonging to Frederick County, headed by our Republican Elector, Dr. Tyler, and by Capt. Brother's company of infantry belonging to the Provincial army. Every respect due the office of Chief Magistrate was paid him by our citizens.

"On Sunday the President attended divine worship, performed by the Rev. Mr. Samuel Knox, in the Lutheran Church (it being more spacious than his own), and the subject was happily adapted to the occasion, while a negotiation is pending with France. The happiness and advantages of peace were fully portrayed, and contrasted with the misery and destruction of war, the curse of any nation. The text was Matthew 5th and 9th, 'Blessed are the peace-makers, for they shall be called the children of God.'"

[2] The other original officers of this troop were First Lieut. Isaac S. White, Second Lieut. John I. Stull, and George Beltzhoover, cornet.

through this town on their way to Washington a detachment of troops and a deputation of twenty-two Indian chiefs, who attended the treaty lately held at St. Louis by Gen. Wilkinson and Governor Harrison. They consist of five of the Little Osage nation, two Missouris, seven Sacs and Foxes, one Canzas, two Ayowas, one Poutowatamis, one Sioux, two Panis, and one Altooes."

During the winter of 1806–7 a company of the Second United States Infantry, Lieut. John Miller commanding, was stationed at Hagerstown.

CHAPTER IX.

THE WAR OF 1812.

The Aggressions of Great Britain—Orders in Council—Attack upon the Chesapeake—Declaration of War—Campaign in Canada—Battle of Bladensburg—Muster-Rolls—War Songs.

PRESIDENT JEFFERSON was inaugurated the second time as President of the United States on the 4th of March, 1805, and on the 2d of December of the same year the Ninth Congress opened its first session. The message of the President was chiefly devoted to our foreign relations, which it represented as being in an unfavorable condition, owing to the proceedings of France and England, which were then at war. He said,—

"Our coasts have been infested and our harbors watched by private armed vessels, some of them without commissions, some with illegal commissions, others with those of legal form, but committing piratical acts beyond the authority of their commissions. They have captured in the very entrance of our harbors, as well as in the high seas, not only the vessels of our friends coming to trade with us, but our own also. They have carried them off under pretence of legal adjudication, but not daring to approach a court of justice, they have plundered and sunk them by the way, or in obscure places where no evidence could arise against them, maltreated the crews, and abandoned them in boats in the open seas or on desert shores without food or covering." [1]

In the new European war, France, Holland, and Spain were allied against Great Britain, and the exposure to capture of the merchant vessels belonging to these nations had caused their withdrawal from the ocean. The United States and other neutral nations from this cause were enjoying an immensely profitable carrying trade, not only with the colonies of the belligerents, but with the mother-countries, and on principles recognized by Great Britain and the established rule of international law, "that the goods of a neutral, consisting of articles not contraband of war, in neutral vessels, employed in a direct trade between a neutral and belligerent country, are protected, except in ports invested or blockaded." In conformity to this principle a direct trade was carried on with the enemies of Great Britain and their colonies, and chiefly by American vessels; and not well pleased to see American merchants so rapidly amassing fortunes, and her enemies receiving by American ships the productions of their own colonies without the hazard which would attend transportation in vessels of their own, Great Britain ordered the capture of our vessels, alleging that the trade was unlawful, on the principle that "a trade from a colony to its parent country, not being permitted to other nations in time of peace, cannot be made lawful in a time of war."

The Attack on the Chesapeake.—While the depredations on our commerce were yet under discussion, three of the crew of the British frigate "Melampus," engaged with the British squadron in watching some French frigates blockaded at Annapolis, deserted, and enlisted on the United States frigate "Chesapeake," lately built in Baltimore, and destined to compose part of an American squadron against the Barbary powers. Four separate demands were made for these men, but without success,—one on Lieut. Sinclair, of the "Chesapeake," one by the British consul on the mayor of Norfolk, one on Capt. Decatur, and one by Lord Erskine, the British minister, on the Secretary of State. The government, willing to be just and anxious for honorable peace, instituted inquiries concerning the deserters, and Commodore Barron, in a letter to the Secretary of the Navy, dated April 7, 1807, thus gives an account of the men:

"William Ware, pressed from on board the brig 'Neptune,' Capt. Crafts, by the British frigate 'Melampus,' in the Bay of Biscay, has served on board the said frigate fifteen months.

"William Ware is a native American, born on Pipe Creek, Frederick County, State of Maryland, at Bruce's Mills, and served his time at said mills. He also lived at Ellicott's Mills, near Baltimore, and drove a wagon several years between Hagerstown and Baltimore. He also served eighteen months on board the United States frigate 'Chesapeake,' under the com-

---

[1] The following is a correct statement of the returns from the different districts of Frederick County, at an election held on Monday, the 12th November, 1804, for Electors of President and Vice-President of the United States:

District.	John Tyler.	Frisby Tilghman.
No. 1	33	33
" 2	278	276
" 3	410	410
" 4	127	127
" 5	117	117
" 6	130	130
" 7	208	208
" 8	101	100
" 9	119	120
	1523	1521

mand of Commodore Morris and Capt. James Barron. He is an Indian-looking man.

"John Strachan, born on the Eastern Shore of Maryland, Queen Anne's County, between Centreville and Queenstown. Strachan sailed in the brig 'Martha Bland,' Captain Wyvill, from New York to Dublin, and from thence to Liverpool. He then left the brig and shipped on board an English Guineaman. He was pressed off Cape Finisterre."

The other, a colored man named Martin, was a native of Massachusetts, and was pressed at the same time and place with William Ware. Ware and Strachan had protections, but Martin had lost his. The "Chesapeake" sailed with these men on board, and on the 21st of June, 1807, when at sea, not far from the Capes of Virginia, was overtaken by the British frigate "Leopard," of fifty-six guns, commanded by Capt. Humphreys. The "Chesapeake" carried forty-four guns. Capt. Humphreys sent his boat with a note to Commodore Barron informing him that his commanding officer, Vice-Admiral Berkeley, by instructions dated June 1st, had directed him to take any British deserters on board the "Chesapeake," by force if necessary, and to allow on his part a search for American deserters. Barron, astonished at the insolence of Humphreys and the assumptions of Berkeley, refused permission to search, and stated that he had no deserters on board the "Chesapeake," and that his crew should not be mustered except by their own officers. On the receipt of this answer the "Leopard" opened fire upon the "Chesapeake," and the latter being taken by surprise, and unprepared for action, did not return the fire, and immediately struck her flag. Three men were killed and eighteen wounded upon the unresisting ship. When the American ensign was lowered, several of the British officers went on board, mustered the crew, arrested the three deserters from the "Melampus," and took a fourth named John Wilson, who had deserted from the "Halifax."[1]

Capt. Humphreys refusing to receive the "Chesapeake" as a prize, she returned to Norfolk. John Hayden, of Baltimore, was wounded in the attack upon the "Chesapeake."

This outrage excited the utmost indignation throughout the United States, and for a time united all parties in the common clamor for reparation of the insult and injury, or for war. Public meetings were held in all the principal cities from Boston to Norfolk, in which the feelings of the people were vehemently expressed.

The citizens of Western Maryland were in nowise behind their fellow-countrymen, and at a meeting held at the court-house in Hagerstown, July 14, 1807, for the purpose of expressing their sentiments "upon the dastardly outrages committed by the British squadron stationed on our coast on the flag and citizens of the United States," Dr. Richard Pindell was called to the chair, and Upton Lawrence was appointed secretary.

After the proclamation of President Jefferson had been read, it was resolved, "That Col. Nathaniel Rochester, Gen. Thomas Sprigg, Samuel Hughes, Jr., Esq., Dr. Richard Pindell, Col. William Fitzhugh, Maj. Charles Carroll, Dr. Frisby Tilghman, Col. George Nigh, Dr. Christian Boerstler, Upton Lawrence, Esq., Dr. Jacob Schnebly, Col. Daniel Hughes, Col. Adam Ott, Mr. William Keyser, and Mr. Alexander Neill be appointed a committee to report resolutions expressive of the abhorrence in which this meeting holds the recent conduct of the British squadron near Norfolk, and our determination to support the constituted authorities of our country, in all such measures as they may think proper to adopt for obtaining satisfaction for the insult and murders committed."

The committee having retired for a short time, returned and reported several vigorous resolutions, which were unanimously adopted; and it was ordered that the chairman and secretary of the meeting transmit copies of the resolutions to the President of the United States and the Governor of Maryland, and that they be published in the newspapers of Hagerstown.

The critical situation of our foreign relations induced the President to convene the Tenth Congress on the 25th of October, 1807, and in a special message on the 18th of December he recommended to that body the passage of an act laying an embargo on all vessels of the United States. The subject was immediately discussed in Congress in secret session, and an embargo bill passed on the 22d of December, 1807. At this session of Congress measures of defense were adopted, and on the 6th of July the President made a requisition on the States for one hundred thousand men to take the field at a moment's warning. Of this number the Governor of Maryland was authorized to furnish a quota of five thousand eight hundred and sixty-three men, and such was the enthusiasm of the people that double that number volunteered their services to the government.[2]

---

[1] "The unfortunate deserters were taken to Halifax and sentenced to be hung. The three Americans were reprieved on condition that they should re-enter the British service, but Wilson, the English subject, was hanged. One of the Americans died in captivity in the English navy, and the others, after five years' hard service, were restored to the deck of the 'Chesapeake.'"—Lossing, "War of 1812."

[2] Among the volunteers was the Third Regiment, commanded by Levy Philips, Montgomery County.

On the 17th of July, in response to the call of the President, the following notice was published in the newspapers of Hagerstown:

"THE SPIRIT OF '76!!!

"*When our country demands our aid it is a species of treason to be deaf to her call.*

"A meeting of the young men of Washington County is requested at Mr. Smith's tavern on Saturday evening next at four o'clock, for the purpose of forming a volunteer corps, whose services are to be at the command of the President as exigencies may demand, or as the public good may require."

As a result of this meeting, a company known as the "Hagerstown Volunteer Rifle Company" was formed, and the officers chosen were as follows:[1] John Ragan, Jr., captain; Thomas Post, first lieutenant; and William B. Rochester, second lieutenant. This company was soon after mustered into the United States service for a period of six months, but was not called upon to perform any active duty.

Besides the companies already mentioned, there were in existence at that time those of the Eighth Maryland Militia, commanded respectively by Capts. Daniel Hughes, Jr., Henry Lewis, John Abel, Joseph Chapline, George Binkley, John Harry, and others; and this regiment was placed in as efficient condition as possible, as is shown by the following order from its veteran commander, Col. John Carr:

"The officers commanding companies in the Eighth Regiment are requested to make out rolls of their respective commands and attend with them at Hagerstown on Saturday, the 15th inst., which will enable me to make out a regimental return to forward to the brigadier-general.[2] I hope the officers will be accurate in their returns and punctual in their attendance at this interesting crisis, as their injured country calls aloud for the exertions of its citizens.

"JOHN CARR,
"*Lieut.-Col. Eighth Regiment.*

"Aug. 5, 1807."[3]

In May, 1808, Gen. Thomas Sprigg's brigade,—composed of Col. John Carr's Eighth, Col. Samuel Ringgold's Tenth, and Lieut.-Col. Jacob Schnebly's Twenty-fourth Regiments of Maryland Militia,—together with Capt. Otho H. Williams' company of American Blues, Capt. Frisby Tilghman's company of Washington Hussars, and Capt. John Ragan's company of volunteer riflemen, was reviewed at Hagerstown by Gen. John E. Howard, of Baltimore.

GEN. JOHN E. HOWARD.

Great exertions were then being made to raise, by volunteering, Maryland's quota of the one hundred thousand militia required for national defense, but it was not until December, 1808, that the requisite number of volunteers was obtained in Washington County. At that time, however, from among the organizations just mentioned, many more than were

---

[1] These officers all became prominent in subsequent years. Col. John Ragan, Jr., was appointed a captain in the United States army in 1808, and served in that capacity at New Orleans and Camp Terre au Bœuf about eighteen months. In 1810 he returned to his native place (Hagerstown), and upon his marriage resigned his commission in the regular service. He was afterwards appointed by the Executive of Maryland lieutenant-colonel of the Twenty-fourth Regiment of militia, and during the war of 1812 was in command of a regiment of militia at the battle of Bladensburg, where, although his command early in the engagement broke and fled in the utmost disorder, he particularly distinguished himself in his brave efforts to rally his raw and panic-stricken troops, but in the fruitless attempt was thrown from his horse, severely injured, and finally taken prisoner by the enemy. In private life Col. Ragan was generous and upright, a valuable neighbor, and a most worthy member of society. He died at his residence in Hagerstown, May 4, 1816, in the thirty-fourth year of his age.

Capt. Thomas Post, besides serving as sheriff of Washington County for a number of years, commanded a company of Washington County militia during the war of 1812, and filled most creditably many other public positions.

William B. Rochester was the eldest son of Col. Nathaniel Rochester, and was born in Washington County. He removed to the Genesee country with his father in 1810, and afterwards became one of the most prominent citizens in Western New York. During the war of 1812–14 he served as captain of a company of New York State Volunteers, and with his command was present at Buffalo and its vicinity during the series of warlike operations carried on there. He held many important civil positions in the State of his adoption, and was a man of fine legal acquirements, and much respected for his ability. He was a representative in Congress from New York from 1821 to 1823, and subsequently held the office of circuit judge in New York, but resigned to compete with De Witt Clinton for the office of Governor. He was lost, with many others, off the coast of North Carolina, by the explosion of the steamer "Pulaski," June 15, 1838.

[2] Thomas Sprigg, who died in December, 1809, and was succeeded by Col. Samuel Ringgold, who assumed command in July, 1810.

[3] Aug. 12, 1807, the volunteer company in Frederick was officered by Capt. Henry Steiner, Lieut. John Ritchie, and Ensign Lawrence Brengle.

Aug. 17, 1809, Henry Kemp was elected captain of the first Frederick troop of cavalry. April 19, 1810, Stephen Steiner chosen lieutenant-colonel of Sixteenth Regiment Militia. June 13, 1811, the Governor appointed John Cook captain, Otho Sprigg first lieutenant, Nicholas Hall, Jr., second lieutenant, and Joshua Johnson cornet of a troop of horse attached to the Seventh Brigade, Frederick County; Oct. 26, 1811, John Cook chosen captain of New Market Light Dragoons; May 9, 1812, Ezra Mantz was appointed major First Battalion Maryland Militia, and John Ritchie lieutenant-colonel of the Sixteenth Regiment Militia.

wanted signified their readiness to march at a moment's notice. The members of the Washington Hussars met at Rockland, and listened to a spirited address from their commander, Capt. Frisby Tilghman, in which he ably proved the necessity of rallying around the country's standard. He then drew his sword, as a token that he was ready to obey her call. His patriotic example was instantly followed by the rest of the officers, and almost[1] unanimously by the whole of the troopers present. The following resolutions were also adopted by the troop:

"*Resolved*, That though fully sensible of the blessings of peace where they can be enjoyed without the sacrifice of national honor, yet we consider WAR a lesser evil than submission to any foreign power under any form or pretence whatever.

"*Resolved*, That we are ready and willing to offer up our all in defense of the rights or of avenging the wrongs of our much injured country, and therefore make a VOLUNTARY tender of our services as a part of the quota called for from Maryland by the President of the United States."

Capt. Tilghman's company enlisted on the 9th of December, and on the 17th of the same month Col. Schnebly's regiment, also Capt. Williams' company of horse, tendered their services to the general government. The editor of the *Herald* speaks of the event as follows in his issue of the 23d:

"On Saturday, the 17th inst., the Twenty-fourth Regiment of Maryland Militia, under the command of Col. Jacob Schnebly, assisted by Majs. Beard and Reynolds, paraded on their customary ground in the neighborhood of this town. The call by Brig.-Gen. Sprigg was for *volunteers*, to the end that a draft might not be made on the citizens whose *will* might urge them to the field, but whose *peculiar circumstances* (for the present) admonished them to remain at home. It was with *heartfelt gratification* we witnessed the patriotic spirit of our regiment in volunteering the whole, and more than the whole, of their proportionate numbers. We will not make invidious distinctions, but we were pleased in noticing some of the companies turning out with Spartan mind a number uncalled for from among them.

"Capt. O. H. Williams' troop, called 'American Blues,' behaved as we had expected,—all his men on parade (thirty-seven in number) tendered their services. It is said that Capt. Williams is not an admirer of the present administration; but we know that he is friendly to American Independence and honor.

"The times *were* which tried men's souls,—the times may shortly come which *will* try men's souls; but, be it as it may, happy and safe are we in our defense."

Capt. George Binkley, of the Twenty-fourth Regiment, in addressing his company previously to their volunteering, spoke as follows:

"Citizens! soldiers! You have appeared on this ground to-day in obedience to the commands of your general, but more especially in obedience to the call of patriotism.

"Fellow-soldiers! we have a triple call,—our general, our country, but most of all a lively sense of honor and independence sounds the alarm. Shall we be heedless to these calls? No; as a band of brother patriots we will erect a proud crest against every foe, foreign or domestic.

"Soldiers! your captain and other officers of this company now tender their services to their country. Will you follow them? I know many of you will; then those who are so disposed advance *forty* paces in front. The God of battles is on our side."

Thereupon twenty-two men of the forty-one present volunteered.

Before the date last mentioned, however, Capt. Ragan's company of riflemen was mustered into the service of the United States as part of its regular force, and in October, 1808, marched from Hagerstown to the barracks at Carlisle, Pa. From thence the company was soon after sent forward to New Orleans, La.

Thus did the people of Western Maryland attest their devotion to their country during the years 1807, 1808, and 1809; but, although British naval officers still continued to impress our seamen, and to offer indignities to the American flag wherever encountered on the high seas, the crisis, as regarded an open rupture with Great Britain, was, in the summer of 1809, considered passed, and the volunteers under pay of the general government were mustered out of service.

There was another feature connected with the history of the period mentioned deserving of notice, perhaps, in this connection,—the original poetic effusions which appeared in the " Poet's Corner" of the newspaper prints of that time. The following were published in the *Maryland Herald*. Some were written by the Hon. Thomas Kennedy, of Williamsport (afterwards of Hagerstown), who was (if we may use the term) the poet-laureate of Washington County in his day, as well as one of the ablest and best-known writers in the State of Maryland. He also represented Washington County many years in the State Legislature, where he distinguished himself in debate, but more particularly as the originator and champion of the bill abolishing the " religious test," an old law which denied to the Hebrews political rights in common with all other citizens.[2]

---

[1] Thirty-one out of thirty-four members who were present.

[2] In 1810 he published a volume entitled
"POEMS.
"Composed on several occasions,
"*In sundry places and in divers manners.*
"BY THOMAS KENNEDY,
"WASHINGTON COUNTY, MD."

"Ye generous sons of lov'd Columbia's soil,
'Tis yours to recompense the poet's toil,
'Tis yours to give or to withhold applause,
To weigh his merits and to judge his cause."
Prologue to the Poems.

The prospectus likewise stated that "the Poems will be printed on good paper, and decently bound and lettered. They

"A NEW SONG.

"TUNE.—'*John Anderson my Jo.*'

"The Volunteers of Hagers-town,
    Great praise to them is due,
They've tender'd down their services
    To face old Britain's crew,
And every other warlike tribe
    That dares to be our foe;
With courage great, fair steps we'll take
    Their schemes to overthrow.

"When Britain's host, some years ago,
    Did try us to enslave,
The sons of freedom forward came,
    With courage stout and brave;
Though undisciplin'd as they were,
    Undauntingly did go
Into the field where none would yield,
    Resentment for to show.

"Old Georgy's crew they try'd their best,
    Their plans were made to nought,
The Hessian crew, and Dunmore too,
    They all against us brought;
The savages and all their aids
    Were soon reduced so low,
That home they flew, with part their crew,
    To let old Georgy know.

"Now they've begun the second time
    Our courage for to try,
So, Volunteers, we'll all rouse up,
    And fight them till we die;
And every tender-hearted soul
    That with us cannot go,
May keep behind, some kind of blind,
    While we do face the foe.

"America has oft received
    Insults of every kind,
But Jefferson, that worthy man,
    For peace was still inclined;
So their abuse did still increase,
    For which we'll let them know
That we're prepar'd, and on our guard,
    To give them blow for blow.

"So here's a health to all the Greens,
    And every Volunteer
Who is intent, and fully bent
    With honor for to steer;
We'll to a man join hand in hand
    To meet our treacherous foe,
With fire and ball we will them maul,
    And drink before we go.

"HAGERSTOWN, Dec. 21, 1808."

---

are now preparing for the press, and will form a volume of a handsome size. The price to subscribers two dollars each copy, payable on delivery. Those who procure ten subscribers and become responsible for the payment shall have one copy gratis." In conclusion he said,—

"When an author makes his first appearance before the public he is apt to think it necessary to state some reasons by way of excuse for his presumption; in the present instance this must be dispensed with. Nor is it now necessary to enter into any commendation of the intended work, its merits are yet to be examined and its worth decided by an impartial tribunal. Suffice it therefore to say that, in the humble opinion of the author, the publication will be found deserving all the encouragement it may receive, and hope promises as favorable a reception as it deserves. If in this he is disappointed, if the present generation treats the labors of his Muse with neglect, like other authors, he must enter an appeal on his behalf to the supreme court of posterity.

"The charms of beauty and the love of liberty first awakened his Muse, and with honest pride he can say that there are none among the numerous pieces in the volume that owe their origin to mean or mercenary motives, and may he cease to be ere he becomes a flatterer, ere he prefers fortune to fame, or the private to the public good.

"Those who intend to become subscribers are requested to do so immediately. And let them all remember that the author does not pretend to the sublime in poetry, his verse is unpolished and clad in homely attire. But if—

"—— And flattering hope does this presage—
If in some future time, some distant age,
These strains shall some sweet pleasing thrills impart,
E'er sorrow soothe, or cheer a drooping heart,
E'er stop a struggling sigh, or check a tear,
He will be blest; such fame is truly dear,
And such the laurels that he longs to wear."

"MR. PRINTER:

"*Be so good as to let the following epigram have a place in your Poet's Corner :*

"God in his wrath may often change
    A Whig into a Tory;
The circumstance is nowise strange,
    'Tis on record in story.
But no such instance can we show,
    Thro' all the Tory race,
A Tory once, will still be so,
    In spite of God and Grace.

"WASHINGTON COUNTY, August, 1809."

"THE SOLDIER'S CALL.

"A SONG.

"TUNE.—'*The Soldier's Return.*'

"Rouse, rouse, ye brave, ye gallant souls,
    Who cherish Independence,
That country you so dearly love
    Demands your quick attendance.
Injured, insulted, she has been
    By Britain—haughty nation;
Then haste to arms, for honor calls
    Aloud for reparation.

"Remember your forefathers bold,
    For freedom who contended,
Who nobly dear Columbia's cause
    With their best blood defended.
O! do not sully their fair fame;
    O! tarnish not their glories;
Discard the deeds, despise the name
    And actions of old Tories.

"In infant days Columbia bore
    The storms of war unmoved,
For tyrant's wrath and deep designs
    More than a match she proved;

O! who can think upon those times
  Nor feel his bosom glowing,
Nor feel sensations, sweet, sublime,
  His patriot soul o'erflowing.

"And if in infancy she foiled
  The plans of wild ambition,
To her united youthful might
  Vain will be opposition.
In Him who rules the hosts of Heaven
  Her hope, her stay, and trust is,
He will with victory crown the cause
  Of liberty and justice.

"Too long has our lov'd country sought,
  By mild negotiation,
To have her rights restored in peace,
  For wrongs, some compensation.
But patience hitherto has made
  Her claims be more neglected,
The last resort then must be tried,
  She then may be respected.

"Though war we never do desire,
  We do not dread its terrors.
Columbia's thunder shall once more
  Show kingcraft all its errors.
Her *Volunteers* will rally round
  The starry flag of freedom.
Nor shall Quebec arrest their march,
  If heroes only lead 'em.

"Then beat the drum, the trumpet sound,
  And let the cannons rattle;
Gird on your swords, your muskets seize,
  Be all prepared for battle.
Go forth to conquer or to die,
  The cause is good, is glorious,
And sacred Union will ensure
  The final end victorious.
"Washington County, Jan. 16, 1810."

"THE BIRTHDAY OF WASHINGTON.

"As the blush of the rose in the dew of the morn,
  As the beautiful blossoms of Spring,
When snow-drops and hyacinths sweetly adorn
The fields and the forests, and from every thorn
  Wild warblers their sonnets do sing,

"So sweet's the remembrance of virtue most dear,
  Of valor with wisdom combin'd,
Of the patriot sage, whose great name we revere,
Whose praises with pride and with pleasure we hear,
  Whose worth is impressed on each mind.

*   *   *   *   *   *   *

"O! Washington, when recollection recalls
  Thy noble, illustrious deeds,
The tear of warm gratitude glistens and falls,
Sublime admiration each bosom enthralls,
  And in pleasing captivity leads.

"Thy courage, thy prudence, thy patriot zeal,
  Thy constancy in truth's great cause,
Thy attention alive to America's weal,
Will furnish forever, while freemen can feel,
  Fit themes for their love and applause.

"And O! may foul factions thy hallowed name
  To cloak their designs ne'er assume;
Ye assassins pollute not the shrine of his fame,
Lest the blaze of his glory burst forth in a flame
  And you with just vengeance consume.

"For who are his friends? Not all they who pretend,
  But those who his precepts obey,
Who cherish firm Union, who nobly contend
For the rights of Columbia, and them to defend
  Are ready to act in his way.

"Immortal his actions, his name shall descend
  To ages unknown, distant climes;
Far and wide as the earth or the sea does extend,
The friend of his country—the friend of mankind,
  Shall be honored in all future times,

"Applauding historians his worth shall recite,
  The muses his praise in sweet strains,
His example will fire future warriors to fight,
And patriot statesmen shall read with delight
  The instruction his maxims contain.

"But chiefly Columbians his deeds shall inspire,
  And their bosoms with ardor inflame,
His story shall pass from the son to the sire,
Even innocent infants will learn to admire,
  And prattling lisp his dear name.

"For he was the friend of their forefathers brave,
  And for them, O! what toils he endured,
His greatest ambition his country to save,
Or find in her wreck and her ruin a grave—
  How blest when his aim was secured!

"And sooner shall sink in the midst of the main
  Columbia, earth's favorite spot,
Of old Allegany no vestige remain,
And time to eternity yield up the rein,
  Ere Washington can be forgot.

"Yea, even when time and when space are no more,
  When the sun and the stars cease to shine,
His fame, like the sovereign eagle, shall soar
Bright worlds unknown, and immortal explore,
  And rank high in the regions divine."

"THE WASHINGTON HUSSARS.[1]

"A song.

"Tune—'*Hail Columbia.*'

"Ye brave Hussars who nobly stand,
  Prepar'd to guard with sword in hand
The laws and rights you hold so dear,
The laws and rights you hold so dear,
Who bear the high, immortal name
Of Washington, the great in fame,
Like him, undaunted, meet the foe,
Like his, may all your bosoms glow
With liberty's celestial fire,
The goddess freemen most admire.
  "*Chorus.*—When the trumpet sounds attend,
    Your lov'd country to defend;
    Fear not danger, death, nor scars,
    Act like Washington Hussars.

---

[1] An organization that was composed of residents of Williamsport and its vicinity.

"With Honor, Friendship full in view,
 The path of glory still pursue.
  O! cherish union's sacred ties,
  O! cherish union's sacred ties,
 For freedom ev'ry danger dare,
 Your country's weal your constant care,
 For her no perils ever shun,
 For her no duty leave undone,
 For her no sacrifice refuse,
 Nor life itself regret to lose.
   "*Chorus.*—When the trumpet, etc.

"Your fathers bold, they knew not fear,
 Their names, their deeds will long be dear.
  Hark! from the tomb their spirits cry,
  Hark! from the tomb their spirits cry,
 'Shall coward sons our glory stain,
 And have we bled and died in vain?'
 No. Rest in peace, ye truly brave,
 And let green laurels round you wave,
 The flame of freedom still inspires,
 The sons are worthy of their sires.
   "*Chorus.*—When the trumpet, etc.

"Hussars, in arms you're not alone,
 The *Blues* are, too, of Washington,
  And they, like you, are volunteers,
  And they, like you, are volunteers.
 With you as friends they will unite
 At the feast or in the fight;
 With you, the foe they will engage,
 And in the battle's hottest rage
 Hussars and Blues shall firmly join
 And force the enemy's strongest line.
   "*Chorus.*—To the charge when trumpets call,
     On each side, when thousands fall,
     Laugh at danger, death, and scars,
     Act like Blues, and like Hussars.

"And O! how blest, the battle o'er,
 When war's alarms are heard no more,
  When beauty bids you welcome home,
  When beauty bids you welcome home,
 And with approving, sweetest smiles,
 Repays your troubles and your toils.
 From your lov'd country then you'll hear
 Such praise as this to charm your ear:
 'None were distinguished in the wars
 More than the Washington Hussars.'
   "*Chorus.*—When the trumpet sounds attend,
     Your dear country to defend;
     And in love, in peace, or wars
     Act like Washington Hussars."

"THE AMERICAN BLUES.[1]

"A SONG.

"TUNE.—'*To Anacreon in Heaven.*'

"Ye American Blues, who have gallantly drawn
 Your swords in defense of the rights of the Union,
 Whose glory is bright as the sun at the dawn,
  Whose souls are all joined in sweet, sacred communion,
   Let honor still guide,
   With truth at her side!
 May valor and wisdom with pleasure preside,
 And furnish for ages a theme for the Muse,
 Be worthy the name of American Blues!

[1] Capt. O. H. Williams' company of Hagerstown.

"The rich vale you inhabit receiv'd its dear name
  From Washington, he who in arms was victorious,
 Whose actions immortal, whose talents and fame
  Shine brightly and pure, with a lustre most glorious,
   That loved name when you hear
   Will banish all fear.
 Like him, . . . may yours be a noble career,
 And furnish for ages a theme for the Muse
 Deserving the name of American Blues!

"Remember the heroes in liberty's cause,
  Who fought and who bled with a brave resolution,
 Their patriot names with deserved applause
  Will be gratefully honor'd till Time's dissolution.
   Like them, O! be brave,
   Independence to save,
 And swear that no despot this soil shall enslave,
 And furnish for ages a theme for the Muse
 Deserving the name of American Blues!

"The tyrants of Europe, e'en should they combine,
  Can ne'er conquer freemen whose bosoms are glowing
 With liberty's flame, and whose hands ever join
  In supporting the cause . . . with a zeal overflowing.
   Then let Britain or France,
   Or both, e'er advance,
 They will fall 'neath the stroke of America's lance,
 And furnish for ages a theme for the Muse
 And prove that Americans all are True Blues!

"And troopers, see where a brave squadron appears,
  The Hussars who bear Washington's name, too, assemble;
 Should war e'er approach, you are all volunteers,
  And united will make every enemy tremble.
   When the trumpets do sound,
   And your foes bite the ground,
 The Blues and the Hussars shall together be found,
 And furnish for ages a theme for the Muse
 Deserving the name of Hussars and of Blues!

"Returning with glory, received with regard,
  As troopers who faithfully have done their duty;
 How blest when enjoying the noble reward
  That you'll meet from the eye, from the sweet smile of beauty!
   The fav'rites of Mars,
   All covered with scars,
 The American Blues will return from the wars,
 And furnish for ages a theme for the Muse
 Deserving the name of American Blues!

"Columbia, our country, oh, pure be thy peace!
  Thy freedom be lasting as old Allegany!
 The bonds of thy Union in strength still increase,
  Thy foes few and feeble, thy friends firm and many.
   While foremost among
   The patriot throng
 May the Blues be seen rushing undaunted along,
 And furnish for ages a theme for the Muse
 Deserving the name of American Blues!"

"A SONG.

"Come, all ye hearts of temper'd steel,
 Come, leave your flocks and farms,
 Your sports, your plays, and holy-days,
 And haste away to arms.

A soldier is a gentleman,
  His honor is his life,
And he that won't stand by his post
  Will ne'er stand by his wife!
    And he that won't, etc.

"Sure, love and honor are the same,
  Or are so near allied
That neither can exist alone,
  But flourish side by side.
Then farewell, sweethearts, for awhile,—
  Our sweet, dear girls, adieu,—
But when we've drove those foes away,
  We'll come and stay with you!
    But when, etc.

"We'll chase our foes from post to post,
  Attack their camp and lines,
And by some well-concocted schemes
  We'll baffle their designs.
No foreign power shall make us slaves,
  No British tyrant reign,
'Twas our fathers' prowess made us free,
  And freedom we'll maintain.
    'Twas our fathers' prowess, etc.

"In shady tents, by curling streams,
  With hearts both firm and free,
We'll drive the cares of life away
  With songs of liberty;
And when the wars are over, boys,
  We'll sit us down at ease,
We'll plow, we'll sow, we'll reap and mow,
  And do just as we please,
    We'll plow, we'll sow, etc.

"This rising world shall sing of us
  Ten thousand years to come,
And children to their children tell
  The wonders we have done;
Brave, honest fellows, here's my hand,
  My heart, my very soul,
With all the joys of liberty,
  Our sweethearts and our bowls,
With all the joys of liberty,
  Our good wives and our bowls!
"WASHINGTON COUNTY, 1810."

During the days of Federalism Washington County was one of the Republican strongholds of Maryland, and upon the inauguration of President Madison, March 4, 1809, a large number of her citizens convened at the court-house (which then occupied the present public square in Hagerstown) for the purpose of rejoicing and celebrating the event.

The day was ushered in by the ringing of bells, martial music, and the firing of cannon. At twelve o'clock William L. Brent delivered an address to the meeting, and recommended the propriety of adopting resolutions expressive of their sentiments upon the political situation of the country. Col. Nathaniel Rochester was appointed chairman, and William L. Brent secretary of the meeting, when, upon motion, it was

"*Resolved*, That Col. David Schnebly, Dr. Christian Boerstler, Mr. H. Gaither, Mr. M. Collins, Col. Samuel Ringgold, Col. Adam Ott, Col. Jacob Schnebly, Col. N. Rochester, and Dr. Wm. Downey be a committee to prepare and report resolutions for the consideration of this meeting. All of which having been done, and a resolution passed that the full proceedings of the meeting be transmitted to Mr. Madison, President of the United States, it was further resolved,

"That William L. Brent, Esq., Maj. Martin Kirshner, Col. Jacob Schnebly, Capt. Henry Lewis, and Col. Nathaniel Rochester be a committee to prepare and report a suitable address to the late President of the United States, Thomas Jefferson, upon his retiring from office."

Having expressed their sentiments as to the situation of their country, the vast concourse present then partook of a feast prepared for the occasion. The table was furnished with the best viands and vegetables that the season would afford; and among many excellent meats which were dressed, a large bullock was spitted and roasted whole. After dinner the following toasts were drank amidst the loud acclamations of the people and the roaring of cannon, fired at intervals between the toasts:

"1. The day we celebrate, which placed the destinies of this country, eight years ago, in the hands of our worthy and beloved fellow-citizen, Thomas Jefferson, late President of the United States, and a Republican majority in Congress, and this day in the hands of James Madison, his successor, and a greater Republican majority in Congress.

"2. James Madison, President of the United States, the patriot, statesman, and uniform friend of the people, may he show to the world, and particularly to disorganizers and traitors, that a republic is not only the best but the strongest government in existence.

"3. The patriotic members of the late Congress who would not barter their country's rights for a tributary commerce, nor be driven from their duty by a weak and unprincipled faction.

"4. The heads of departments, superior in wisdom and integrity to the ministers and councils of European potentates.

"5. The militia of the United States, the grand bulwark of American liberty and independence.

"6. The army and navy of the United States, composed of patriots and not mercenaries.

"7. The memory of Gen. George Washington, the father of his country, may his valedictory address be ever remembered, and the advice therein given to his countrymen be better observed than it recently has been by the Essex Junta and other British advocates in the United States.

"8. Thomas Jefferson,—'well done, thou good and faithful servant,'—may your patriotic and useful labors for our common country be a guide to present and future statesmen in conducting the political affairs of this happy land of freedom, and may your remaining days, in the retirement you have chosen, be peaceful and happy, until you partake of the joys above with other benefactors of mankind.

"9. The patriotic Governor of Massachusetts (Levi Lincoln) and other friends to their country in that State, who have declared their determination to support the laws and reduce to order a daring faction that has reared its head in favor of anarchy and confusion, with a view to dissolve the union of these United States.

"10. John Quincy Adams, William Gray, and William L. Smith, who have proved themselves friends to their country by seceding from their party and supporting the measures of their government when they discovered the machinations of the Essex Junta, in conjunction with a foreign power, were exciting opposition to the laws, with a view to destroy the best government in the world.

"11. The agriculture of the United States, may it never pay tribute to a foreign power to gratify the avarice or ambition of the dishonest part of our merchants.

"12. The manufactories of the United States, may they soon be capable of furnishing substitutes for those of foreign powers.

"13. Commerce, unshackled by foreign orders or decrees, but no foreign commerce subject to tribute.

"14. Peace with all the world, if to be had on honorable terms, but no alliance with any power while they disregard the law of nations, and war, with all its privations and other evils, rather than disgraceful submission to French decrees or British Orders of Council.

"15. The friends of the government throughout the United States, their numbers and firmness, will support the laws and appall the spirit of faction.

"16. A speedy passage to Europe of Tories and apostate Whigs, where they may enjoy their favorite government of master and vassals.

"17. The fair daughters of America, may they smile on the defenders of their country's liberty and laws, and leave in the forlorn state of celibacy cowards and the enemies of their own country."

In the evening a more brilliant illumination took place than had ever been witnessed in Hagerstown upon a like occasion. A band of music paraded the streets with a large lantern, exhibiting on the four sides a portrait of President Madison and figures emblematic of agriculture, commerce, and manufactures, which was carried by some of the most prominent men of the county. However, among the many individual illuminations and displays of transparent paintings, the one which attracted universal attention and applause was an elegant full-length portrait of James Madison, which was displayed in a large door in the second story of Capt. Henry Lewis' residence.

During the years of Madison's administration, from March, 1809, to June, 1812, the English continued their insults, aggressions, and depredations. Our harbors were insulted and outraged, our commerce swept from the ocean, our seamen impressed into British fleets, scourged and slaughtered, fighting the battles of those who held them in bondage, and studied indignities were offered to our national flag wherever displayed. All efforts for redress from the British government had failed, and at length (acting in accord with a majority[1] of the Senate and House of Representatives of the United States) the President issued his proclamation declaring war against Great Britain on the 18th day of June, 1812.

Anticipating this event, however, and determined to place the militia of the State in as effective condition as possible, the Legislature, by an act approved Jan. 18, 1812, provided that the State be divided into eleven regimental (cavalry) districts and one extra squadron. In the formation of these districts, Washington and Frederick Counties were to constitute the first, while Allegany County was to furnish the extra squadron, which (for the time being, or until a regiment could be formed in that county) was attached to the first regimental district.

In February following, Capt. Frisby Tilghman was appointed lieutenant-colonel in command of this regiment, while Capt. O. H. Williams was appointed major of the same. Thereupon, to fill the vacancy in the "Blues" occasioned by the promotion of Capt. Williams, a meeting was held at Strauss' tavern, in Hagerstown, Feb. 25, 1812, when Moses Tabbs was elected captain, Jacob Barr first lieutenant, David Clagett second lieutenant, and David Newcomer cornet. At about the same time Edward Greene Williams (brother of Maj. O. H., and both sons of Gen. Otho H. Williams, of Revolutionary fame) was appointed to the command of the Hussars, *vice* Capt. Frisby Tilghman promoted.

To add to the military excitement, Lieut. John Miller, of the United States army, established a recruiting station at Hagerstown during the same month. The inducements held out by him to encourage enlistments were as follows:

"Every able-bodied man from the age of eighteen to thirty-five years who shall be recruited for the army of the United States for the term of five years will be paid a bounty of sixteen dollars; and whenever he shall have served the term for which he enlisted, and obtained an honorable discharge, he will be allowed, in addition to the aforesaid bounty, three months' pay and one hundred and sixty acres of land; and in case he should be killed in action or die in the service his heirs and representatives will be entitled to the said three months' pay and one hundred and sixty acres of land.

"JOHN MILLER, *Lieut.*

"HAGERSTOWN, Feb. 18, 1812.

"N.B.—Pay, FIVE DOLLARS per month."

Col. J. P. Boyd,[2] one of the heroes of the battle of

---

[1] The final vote was carried in the Senate by nineteen to thirteen, and in the House of Representatives by seventy-nine to forty-nine. In the House of Representatives the Maryland delegates voted as follows: In the affirmative—Stevenson Archer, Joseph Kent, Peter Little, Alexander McKim, Samuel Ringgold, and Robert Wright. In the negative—Charles Goldsborough, Philip Barton Key, and Philip Stuart. In the Senate, Gen. Saml. Smith voted aye, and Philip Reed voted no. Those voting in the negative were Federalists; and Philip Barton Key, of their number, though an American, was a British officer under half-pay during and for many years succeeding the war of the Revolution.

[2] Col. Boyd, then about forty years of age, was born at Boston, Mass. Having qualified himself for a military life at the place of his nativity, he emigrated to the East Indies with but little more than his sword and his personal bravery. He soon

Tippecanoe, visited Hagerstown, Friday, Feb. 28, 1812, and as a mark of respect due to him for his undaunted conduct in that battle a dinner was given by the citizens. After drinking to seventeen regular toasts, the following "volunteers" were added:

By Col. Boyd:

"The Militia of Maryland—Energetic Men and Measures."

After Col. Boyd had retired, Maj. O. H. Williams gave the following:

"Col. John P. Boyd—a hero of Tippecanoe. His services are recorded in our hearts, and may his example stimulate the bosom of every soldier."

By Col. John Ragan:

"The New Army—
"Be the sword of our vengeance erected on high,
And forever be it waved for Columbia's woes;
May its bright, dazzling beam when flash'd to the sky
Be quenched in the blood of her foes."

In leaving the town on his way to the seat of government Col. Boyd was escorted a short distance by the American Blues and the command of Capt. Tabbs.

As a rule the county gave a warm support to the war, although a majority was evidently against its declaration; but when once begun the great body of the people rallied in its favor. Still there were some who steadily opposed it as unwise and unnecessary. At a district-meeting of the friends of peace, at New Windsor, now Carroll County, on July 28, 1812, it was recommended that each district in the county appoint a committee to meet in general committee at the "Washington Hotel," August 12th. Col. Joshua Gist, Curtis Williams, and John Mittens were appointed for Westminster. At a similar meeting in Liberty (Frederick County) District, of which F. B. Sappington was chairman and Samuel Thomas was secretary, the following were appointed a committee, to meet in general committee: Gen. R. Cumming, Col. Henry Barrick, D. D. Howard, John Duddem, Joshua Delaplane, Sebastian Groff, Dennis Poole. Until the third week of August, 1812, the people of Frederick Town witnessed but little of the war movements. On August 17th a troop of cavalry, enlisted in Virginia and commanded by Capt. White,

passed through *en route* to Trenton, N. J.; and on the 20th, Capt. Worthington's company of drafted militia from the town and neighborhood marched for Annapolis. These men were to supply the place of a part of the Fifth United States Regiment ordered to the North. Capt. Worthington was escorted out of town by the companies commanded by Capts. Henry and Stephen Steiner. On August 25th there arrived in Frederick the Hagerstown Volunteers, under Capt. Thomas Quantrill, who two days later left for the front. They were a part of the State's quota ordered in compliance with the Secretary of War's request for three hundred and fifty men for the defense of Annapolis.

Meantime the most strenuous exertions were being put forth by the executive (Governor Winder) to place upon a war footing the infantry commands of the State militia; also to furnish the State's quota of six thousand men, and to organize, arm, and equip the latter ready for service at a moment's warning. Gen. Samuel Ringgold's Second Brigade of the Third Division (Maj. Thomas B. Pottinger, Brigade Inspector) was at this time composed of Lieut.-Col. David Schnebly's Eighth Regiment (Majs. John McClain and Christian Hager), Lieut.-Col. Daniel Malott's Tenth Regiment, Lieut.-Col. John Ragan's Twenty-fourth Regiment, and Maj. O. H. Williams' squadron of horse,—*i.e.*, the "Blues" and "Hussars." Among the company commanders of militia infantry were Capts. Thomas B. Hall (of the "Washington Rangers"), David Cushwa, Joseph Hunter, Wherritt, Stonebraker, Miller, Stevens, Chapline, Lewis, and Blackford.

Volunteering progressed favorably during the spring and summer months of 1812, and the quota of Washington County was filled without resorting to a draft. On Monday, Aug. 24, 1812, the "Homespun Volunteers" of Hagerstown, under command of Capt. Thomas Quantrill, marched *en route* to Fort Madison, Annapolis, escorted for several miles by Capt. Tabbs' troop (the "Blues") and many enthusiastic citizens; and on the 31st of the same month Capt. Parker's detachment of United States troops passed through Williamsport and Hagerstown on their march to Albany, N. Y. They were *fêted* at Williamsport, Gen. Samuel Ringgold, Col. Frisby Tilghman, and Capt. E. G. Williams forming the reception committee, and the "Hussars" doing escort duty. The general government was then concentrating all of its available regular force on the Canadian frontier, and in April, 1813, a detachment of three hundred and twelve regulars from Virginia, under command of Lieut.-Col. James Preston, passed through Hagerstown on their

---

obtained a position in the military service there, and rapidly rose to the rank of general. In 1802 he returned to America with fame, honor, and fortune; and though rich, sought and obtained military employment in the service of the United States. How well he deserved the confidence of his country was amply attested by his conduct during Harrison's campaign against Tecumseh and the Prophet in the fall of 1811, and the war with Great Britain in 1812–14.

march to Black Rock, in the vicinity of Buffalo, N. Y.

In March, 1813, Maj. Williams' squadron, the "Blues" and the "Hussars," were ordered to Annapolis, where they performed duty for a brief period; and in May of the same year companies of volunteers, under the command of Capt. Wherritt, of Funkstown, Capt. Miller, of Sharpsburg, Capt. Stevens, of Hancock, and Capt. Bell, of Allegany County, proceeded to Baltimore.

On May 8, 1813, Capt. Steiner's artillery and Capt. Dawson's infantry companies left Frederick for Baltimore to aid in the defense of that city, then threatened by the British. Two days previous Capt. Flant's rifle and Capt. Samuel Ogle's infantry companies had gone to the same rendezvous. On the 9th two other companies from Washington and Allegany Counties passed through Frederick for Baltimore. On the 7th thirteen wagons loaded with specie arrived at Frederick from Baltimore. On the 16th of May thirty-seven regulars left Frederick under Ensign W. G. Shade, who had all been recruited in the county. On May 19th about a hundred militia from various parts of Frederick County went to Annapolis. On the 3d of July a general discharge took place of the troops called for the defense of Baltimore, who were highly extolled in a general order, particularly Capt. Henry Steiner's company of artillery, which arrived home on the 5th. On the 6th the companies of Capt. Samuel Dawson and of Capt. Miller, of Sharpsburg, and also most of the troops of Washington and Allegany Counties, returned. On the 16th of September, Capt. Marker's fine company of "Mountain Rangers," which had been summoned to Annapolis, passed through Frederick *en route* home. On October 21st there was a grand illumination in Frederick in honor of the victory of the American arms in Canada. In 1814 the entire militia of the county went again to the defense of Baltimore, and many participated in the bloody engagement at North Point. Large numbers of the citizens of Frederick County entered the regular service of the United States, and served with honor on the Western frontiers and the Canada line.[1]

While these events were transpiring in the State the sons of Western Maryland were winning fame on the Canadian frontier. The projected invasion of Canada in 1812 resulted in the battle of Queenstown, in which the Maryland troops under Col. Winder bore a conspicuous part. The expedition resulted in a failure, however, which Gen. Smythe attempted to atone for by organizing another for the same object. He gave orders on the 25th of November, 1812, for "the whole army to be ready to march at a moment's warning." Everything being in readiness, an advance was embarked near Buffalo, in two divisions, at three o'clock on the morning of the 29th.

The first division, under the command of Lieut.-Col. Charles G. Boerstler,[2] with about two hundred men of Col. Winder's regiment, in eleven boats, was to cross the river at a point about five miles below Fort Erie, capture the guard stationed there, kill or take the artillery horses, and with the prisoners, if any, return to the American shore. The second division was under the command of Capt. King, who with one hundred and fifty regular soldiers, and seventy sailors under Lieut. Angus, in ten boats, was to cross higher up the river at the "Red House," and storm the British batteries. Col. Winder was to remain on the American side to give directions.

At the appointed hour the boats started for their respective destinations. King's division, when within about a quarter of a mile from the shore, was discovered by the enemy, who opened upon him with such good effect as to compel six of his boats to return. The other four made good their landing, and forthwith carried the British batteries by storm. But the enemy came upon them from distant stations, and with no more help from Gen. Smythe, these gallant men were soon overpowered, Sailing-master Watts killed, and their commander taken prisoner, the rest getting back to the American side of the river in great confusion.

Col. Boerstler and his party mean time had been placed in great danger. The firing upon King had aroused the enemy all along the river-bank, and they were moving rapidly to the attack. Mr. Lossing, the historian, in his account of this movement, says,—

"Boerstler's boats became separated in the darkness. Seven of them landed above the bridge to be destroyed, while four others that approached the designated landing-place were driven off by a party of the enemy. Boerstler landed boldly alone, under fire from a foe of unknown numbers, and drove them to the bridge at the point of the bayonet. Orders were then given for the destruction of that structure, but owing to the confusion at the time of landing, the axes had been left in the boats. The bridge was only partially destroyed, and one great object of this advance party of the invading army was not accomplished.

"Boerstler was about to return to his boats and recross the river, because of the evident concentration of troops to that point in overwhelming numbers, when he was compelled to form his lines for immediate battle. Intelligence came from the commander of the boat-guard that they had captured two

---

[1] Middletown contributed a fine company of volunteers under Capt. Jacob Alexander.

[2] He was a son of Dr. Christian Boerstler, of Funkstown, and died while stationed at New Orleans, La., Nov. 21, 1817.

British soldiers, who informed them that the whole garrison at Fort Erie was approaching, and that the advance guard was not five minutes distant. This intelligence was correct. Darkness covered everything, and Boerstler resorted to stratagem when he heard the tramp of the approaching foe. He gave commanding orders in a loud voice, addressing his subordinates as field-officers. The British were deceived. They believed the Americans to be in much greater force than they really were. A collision immediately ensued in the gloom. Boerstler ordered the discharge of a single volley, and then a bayonet charge. The enemy broke and fled in confusion, and Boerstler recrossed the river without annoyance."

Disaster awaited the gallant Boerstler, however, for in June, 1813, he encountered an overwhelming force of the enemy at Beaver Dam, Canada, and after an engagement of three hours' duration was forced to surrender, or sacrifice the lives of the survivors of his brave command. The following letter, written the day after the fight, and addressed to his father, will prove interesting:

"Head of Lake Ontario,
"Upper Canada, June 25, 1813.

"Dear Father,—It becomes my unfortunate lot to inform you that yesterday I was taken prisoner with a detachment under my command amounting to near five hundred men, after an engagement of about three hours. I lost not many killed, about forty wounded, and five or six officers,—myself a flesh-wound of no consequence. I am on my way to Kingston, and shall write to you every opportunity. The officers under my command must say whether your son did his duty. I need only state to you that I was seventeen miles from Fort George, and surrounded on all sides by more than my numbers, and the enemy's force increasing, while mine was constantly diminishing; ammunition nearly exhausted, men wearied with a march of ten miles without a mouthful of refreshment; then the engagement, and then to fight our way back the whole distance surrounded by woods filled with Indians. On the score of humanity I determined to capitulate, as it was extremely doubtful whether a man of us would reach Fort George. What I say above will be sufficient for you; my country must apply to those under my command.

"Your son,
"Charles.

"Col. Scott will please seal and forward the above."

"Dear Sir,—I pray you to believe that your son is not condemned for being unfortunate.

"Respectfully, sir,
"Your most obed't serv't,
"W. Scott.

"Dr. C. Boerstler."

On the 20th of July, 1813, the *Buffalo Gazette* published the following account of Col. Boerstler's fight at Beaver Dam:

"On Wednesday night last, Maj. C. Chapin arrived in this village, having, together with his company, escaped from the enemy on Monday preceding. The major has given us the following narration of the action at Beaver Dam, which we now lay before the public.

"On the 23d of June last a party of the regular troops, consisting of five hundred infantry and twenty light dragoons, under the command of Lieut.-Col. C. G. Boerstler, together with forty-four mounted riflemen, composed of militia from the country, under Maj. Chapin, were detached from the American encampment at Fort George, for the purpose of cutting off the supplies of the enemy, and breaking up the small encampments they were forming through the country. On the 24th, about nine miles west of Queenstown, they were attacked by a body of above five hundred Indians and nearly one hundred British regulars, who lay concealed in the woods near the road they were passing. The attack commenced on the dragoons, who were placed in the rear. The infantry was soon brought into a position to return the enemy's fire to advantage, and succeeded in driving them some distance into the woods.

"In a short time the Indians, having taken a circuitous route, appeared in front, and opened a fire upon the mounted riflemen who were stationed there. Here they met with so warm a reception that they were compelled a second time to retreat in much haste. After this every exertion was made to draw the Indians from the woods to the open ground, but without much effect. The few who were bold enough to venture were handled so roughly that they soon returned to their lurking-places. Meanwhile the enemy were receiving considerable reinforcements, which at length gave them a great superiority. A retreat for a short distance was ordered, and effected with very little loss. The Indians soon made their appearance upon our right and left, the British regulars and some Canadian militia in front. Our troops were formed into close columns for the purpose of opening themselves a way through the enemy's lines with their bayonets.

"At this juncture a British officer rode up and demanded the surrender of the American party. The demand was made, he said, to prevent the further effusion of blood. He asserted upon his honor, and declared in the most solemn manner, that the British regular force was double that of the American, and that the Indians were seven hundred in number. Lieut.-Col. Boerstler, under a belief of these facts, and thinking it impracticable to get off the wounded, whom he was unwilling to abandon to the mercy of the savages, and deeming it extremely uncertain whether a retreat could be effected, thought proper to agree to terms of capitulation, which were at length signed by himself on the one part, and Lieut. Bishop on the other. By these it was stipulated that the wounded should be taken good care of, the officers permitted to retain their side-arms, private property to be respected, and the militia permitted to return home immediately.

"The articles of capitulation were no sooner signed than they were violated. The Indians immediately commenced their depredations, and plundered the officers of their side-arms. The soldiers, too, were stripped of every article of clothing to which the savages took a fancy, such as hats, coats, shoes, etc. It is impossible to give any correct account of the killed and wounded, as the enemy did not furnish a list. The loss of the enemy is supposed to be much greater than ours. Between thirty and forty Indians were counted that lay dead on the field, and from their known practice of carrying off their killed and wounded, it is believed they have suffered severely.

"The regular troops were in a few days sent to Kingston, from whence it is probable they have proceeded to Quebec.

"Maj. Chapin and his corps were detained under guard at the head of Lake Ontario, and no attention paid to that article of capitulation which provided for their being paroled. On the 12th instant they were ordered down the lake to Kingston, for which place they were embarked in two boats, accompanied by a guard of fifteen men under a lieutenant. Thirteen of the guard, with the lieutenant, were stationed in the forward boat with Maj. Chapin and the other officers, while the remaining two (a sergeant and one private) took the direction of the other boat which contained the soldiers. An agreement had been entered into by the prisoners—previous to their departure—of seizing the first opportunity that offered to regain their liberty, which they determined to effect or die in the attempt.

"When they were within twelve miles of York (now known as Toronto), the boat which was filled with the prisoners was rowed by them alongside the other, under pretence of taking something to drink. The signal being given they sprang upon the guard, who little expected such a manœuvre, and in a moment disarmed them and gained possession of the boats. They immediately changed their course from Kingston to Fort Niagara, and after rowing hard for most of the night, and with difficulty escaping from one of the enemy's schooners which gave them chase, arrived in safety with their prisoners at the American garrison.

"When the major and his company arrived in this village they were welcomed with many demonstrations of the public feeling."

Notwithstanding the friendly assurances of Col. Scott, there were those who basely misrepresented Col. Boerstler's conduct on the occasion alluded to, and his character as an officer and soldier was most shamefully traduced. That these aspersions upon the name and fame of a brave and generous spirit were without foundation, were the emanations of such creatures as fight best on dress-parade, or of insignificant newspaper scribblers who *never* fight, was shown by his complete exoneration by a court of inquiry, as also by the following extract from a letter written by an officer of rank and distinction in the army (and who was with Col. Boerstler at the time of his surrender) to his friend and brother-officer in Virginia:

"You have seen, no doubt, in the newspapers an account of Boerstler's unfortunate affair, and on my return to Fort George I found to my great mortification that the public prints had handled him very roughly. Never was there a man more unjustly censured. The blame ought to rest with Gen. Dearborn, who ordered him to go on so foolish an expedition from the information he received from lying deserters.

"However, we fought them three hours and twelve minutes at close action, against almost double our force. Boerstler was struck with four bullets, one of which wounded him in the thigh. I was twice in the heat of the action, and my horse received two wounds while I was on him, but Providence protected me. I could not but admire Boerstler's coolness, when, enveloped in smoke, he rode from right to left encouraging the men (who, by the by, fought like devils) to charge them; and as often as we charged did the British and Indians retreat. At length, overcome by numbers, having seventy-three killed and wounded, and knowing we could receive no reinforcements in time, and being surrounded, the British sent in a flag demanding us to surrender, which Boerstler peremptorily refused.

"The British officer then offered to let any officer go and see his force, and pledged his honor that he had double that of ours. Col. Boerstler sent Karney, who returned, and gave it as his opinion they had nearly double our force; it was impossible for us to retreat, and if we attempted it our wounded would be massacred by the Indians. It was then determined, in a council of war, to surrender. You can guess what was the mortification of your friend Boerstler and mine at such a time. Boerstler wished ten thousand bullets through him, and I wished I was in hell."

Returning to the seat of war in the State of Maryland, we find that nothing of importance occurred wherein Western Maryland men were represented during the remainder of the year 1813. But in July, 1814, when the British, under Admiral Cockburn and Gen. Ross, threatened all points along the Chesapeake Bay and its adjoining waters, Lieut.-Col. John Ragan, Jr., with more than one hundred volunteers obtained from the ranks of his regiment (the Twenty-fourth Militia), marched from Hagerstown to Baltimore, where he was joined a few days later by one hundred and twenty more from the same command. Among the company commanders were Capt. George Shryock, of Hagerstown, Capt. Gerard Stonebreaker, of Funkstown, and Capt. Henry Lowry.

Allegany's quota towards filling the State's requisition was readily supplied, there being a considerable degree of enthusiasm manifested. Two companies of infantry were formed in the county, one under Capt. William McLaughlin, and the other under Capt. Thomas Blair. The first was made up in the lower part of the county, while Capt. Blair's company was composed largely of citizens of Cumberland. Capt. McLaughlin's company marched to Baltimore in August, 1814, and joined the First Regiment of Maryland Militia, under Col. John Ragan, on the 11th of August, serving until October 13th, when it was mustered out, returned to the county and disbanded.

The company formed in Cumberland was made up of excellent material. By frequent drills it attained a state of enviable discipline and proficiency. It marched to Baltimore in the latter part of August, and was in the service of the government as part of the national army from Sept. 2 to Nov. 6, 1814, which time was spent at Camp Diehl near Baltimore.[1]

Battle of Bladensburg.—Early in August, 1814, Maj. O. H. Williams' squadron of cavalry (of Col. Frisby Tilghman's regiment), composed of the American Blues, Capt. Jacob Barr, and the Washington Hussars, Capt. Edward G. Williams, well mounted, armed, and equipped, marched from Hagerstown for the lower counties. They proceeded first to Georgetown, and thence to Washington, D. C., where they encamped at "Camp Stuart," until a short time before the battle of Bladensburg. On the 16th of August two hundred and seventy militia from Allegany County passed through Hagerstown *en route* to Baltimore, where they joined Col. Ragan's regiment. Thus were included, in the commands already men-

---

[1] Lowdermilk, pp. 296–97.

tioned, all or nearly all of the volunteers and militia from Washington County who participated in the disastrous "battle of Bladensburg," which was fought in the afternoon of Aug. 24, 1814.

Before proceeding to give an account of this battle, to obviate the necessity of tedious interruptions or repetitions, we will give a brief description of the troops which Gen. Winder had collected for the defense of Washington. The first in order were the troops of the District of Columbia, composed of militia and volunteer companies of Washington and Georgetown, formed into two regiments, the first commanded by Col. Magruder, the second by Col. William Brent. These, with two companies of light artillery, having each six six-pound guns, and commanded respectively by Maj. George Peter, an officer of distinguished ability, and Capt. Benjamin Burch, a soldier of the Revolution, and two companies of riflemen, armed with muskets, under Capts. Doughty and Stull, were organized into a brigade, which was commanded by Gen. Walter Smith, of Georgetown. These troops, well disciplined and officered, and comprising some of the most respectable inhabitants of the District, marched from Washington on the 20th of August for the scene of action, and numbered about one thousand and seventy men.

GEN. WM. H. WINDER.

Gen. Robert Young organized another brigade of District militia, consisting of volunteer companies from Alexandria and its vicinity, a company of cavalry, under Capt. Thornton, and a company of light artillery, with two brass six-pounders and one brass four-pounder, commanded by Capt. Marsteller. This brigade numbered about five hundred men, and reported to Gen. Winder on the 18th of August. They were not engaged at the battle of Bladensburg, having been employed to defend the approach to Fort Washington.

As soon as the enemy appeared in the Chesapeake, the President called the Third Brigade of Maryland militia into active service, and on the 19th of August, Gen. Samuel Smith, who commanded the defenses in Baltimore, ordered them to hold themselves in readiness, "completely armed and equipped," to march at a moment's notice. On the following day, Gen. Tobias Stansbury's brigade, composed of two regiments of militia, one of about five hundred and fifty men, under Lieut.-Col. John Ragan, Jr. (late captain of United States Rifles), and another of eight hundred and three men, under Lieut.-Col. Schutz, marched out of Baltimore. This force halted at the Stag Tavern on the evening of the 21st, and on the 22d advanced towards Bladensburg, near which place they encamped, and on the 23d began moving towards Marlborough, the orders of Gen. Winder being to take a position on the road not far from that place. On the evening of the 23d, Lieut.-Col. Sterrett's command, consisting of the Fifth Baltimore Regiment of Volunteers, comprising some of the most substantial merchants and business men of the city and some distinguished professional men, with the rifle battalion of Maj. William Pinkney (previously Attorney-General of the United States), and two companies of volunteer artillery from the same city, under Capts. Myers and Magruder, with six six-pounders, in all about eight hundred men, reached Bladensburg and joined Gen. Stansbury. On the next morning arrived, after a march of sixteen miles, several detachments of Maryland militia, comprising a part of two regiments, and numbering seven hundred and fifty men, under the command of Col. William D. Beall, an efficient officer of the Revolution, and Col. Hood. Another small detachment of two hundred and forty men was under the command of Col. Kramer, and two battalions, amounting to one hundred and fifty men, were under Majs. Waring and Maynard.

The Virginia militia were under the command of Col. George Minor, and consisted of one regiment of about six hundred men and a cavalry company of about one hundred. The regular United States infantry were under the charge of Lieut.-Col. William Scott, and amounted to about three hundred men, and a company of about eighty men from the Twelfth Regiment. Barney's command, numbering about four hundred sailors and about one hundred and fifty marines, with two eighteen-pounders, joined the army on the morning of the 22d of August.

The Maryland cavalry, about three hundred men, were commanded by Lieut.-Col. Frisby Tilghman, Majs. Otho H. Williams and Charles Sterett. Capt. J. C. Herbert commanded the "Bladensburg Troop of Horse." The United States cavalry, numbering about one hundred and twenty-five, were commanded by Lieut.-Col. Lavel. The whole American force, therefore, amounted to about seven thousand men in or near Bladensburg at the time of the battle, and the British not more than four thousand five hundred.

Bladensburg, at which this unlucky engagement was fought, is at the head of small craft navigation on the Eastern Branch of the Potomac, about six miles northeast of Washington, on the old post-road from that city to Baltimore. North of this road is another joining the Washington road, running from Georgetown, and these roads form an acute angle a few yards from the bridge in the town. In the triangular space thus formed, and near the old mill, Gen. Stansbury's command was posted on the morning of the 24th of August. About four hundred yards from the Bladensburg bridge, on a slight eminence in that triangular field, between a large barn and the Washington road, the Baltimore Artillery, under Capts. Magruder and Myers, occupied a temporary breastwork of earth, commanding the bridge and road. Part of the battalion of riflemen, under Maj. William Pinkney, and one other company took position on the right of the artillery, near the junction of the roads, and partially protected by a fence and brush on the low ground near the river.

On the left of the battery, leading to the rear of the barn and near the Georgetown road, two companies of militia from Col. Shutz's regiment, under the command of Capts. Gorsuch and Ducker, and the other portion of Maj. Pinkney's riflemen were stationed. Col. Ragan was posted in the rear of Maj. Pinkney, his right resting on the Georgetown road, Col. Schutz continuing the line on the left, with a small vacancy between the two regiments; and Col. Sterrett formed the extreme left flank of the infantry. In the midst of these confused preparations for battle Cols. Beall and Hood entered Bladensburg with other Maryland militia, after a forced march of sixteen miles that sultry morning from Annapolis, crossed the bridge, and took a position on the most commanding height on the right of the Washington turnpike, about three hundred yards from the road, to secure the right flank. In the mean time (about eleven o'clock) intelligence was received at headquarters that the enemy was in full march to Bladensburg, on which Gen. Winder put in motion his whole force, except a few men and a piece of artillery left at the Eastern Branch bridge to destroy it.

The march to Bladensburg was rapid, though the day was excessively hot and the road deep in dust. On the arrival of the cavalry and mounted men, they were placed on the left flank a little in the rear. Gen. Winder now arrived on the field, and informed Gen. Stansbury and Col. Monroe that his whole force was on the march to the scene of action, and approved the dispositions which had been made. At this time, however, it had become impracticable, in the opinion of the officers present, to make any essential change, as the enemy had already appeared on the opposite heights of Bladensburg, about a mile distant, where he halted fifteen or twenty minutes. This was about twelve o'clock.

The troops from Washington were disposed of as they came up. Capt. Burch, with three pieces of artillery, was stationed on the extreme left of the infantry of the first line, and a rifle company, armed with muskets, near the battery to support it. About this time the Secretary of War arrived, and a few moments after the President and the Attorney-General, and proceeded to examine the disposition of the troops. In the mean time the enemy, who had been standing in the blazing sun on the opposite hill, advanced into Bladensburg, while the officers were rapidly forming the second line. At this time Gen. Winder became greatly annoyed by "numerous self-constituted contributors of advice, suggesters of position, and intermeddlers with command, gentlemen of respectability and good will; committees, whole democracy of commanders, industriously helped to mar all singleness of purpose and unity of action. Arriving at the bridge while Col. Monroe was displacing the corner-stones of the combat, Gen. Winder met several gentlemen, among the rest Mr. Francis S. Key, not only recommending, but showing where they thought the troops ought to be posted, riding to the spots designated and confounding the outset. Other bystanders were present at the spectacle as such, among them Alexander McKim, the Baltimore member of Congress, on one of his fast trotting horses,—a rich merchant, who said that having voted for war, he could not find it in his conscience if not to fight for it, at least to stand by those who did."[1]

In the midst of this confused preparation for battle Commodore Barney, with two eighteen-pounders and his flotilla-men, came up at a trot, and formed his men on the right of the main road in a line with the commands of Cols. Beall and Hood, but with considerable space between them, owing to the formatoin of the ground. Commodore Barney planted his heavy guns in the road, a portion of the semen acting as artillerists. Capt. Miller, who commanded the flotilla-men and marines as infantry to support the artillery, stationed three twelve-pounders to the right

COM. JOSHUA BARNEY.

---

[1] Ingersoll, ii., p. 174.

of Barney. Lieut.-Col. Kramer, with a battalion of Maryland militia, was posted in a wood a short distance in advance of the marines and Cols. Beall and Hood's command. The regiment under Col. Magruder was stationed on the left of Barney, and the regiment of Col. Brent and Maj. Waring's battalion and some other detachments formed the left flank of the second line, and in the rear of Maj. Peter's battery. Lieut.-Col. Scott, with the regulars, was stationed in advance of Col. Magruder, and to the left, forming a line towards Maj. Peter's battery, other small detachments in various directions.

Such was the disposition of the American army when, about half-past twelve o'clock on Aug. 24, 1814, the enemy descended the hills beyond Bladensburg, and the battle commenced which ended so disastrously to the American arms.

The British entered Bladensburg without opposition, and then began crossing by the bridge. When their advance was crowded upon it, the Baltimore battery and Maj. Pinkney's battalion opened upon them with deadly effect, nearly a whole company being swept away at the first discharge. They pressed across, however, threw the first American line into some confusion, and captured one of their guns.

The second line stood firm, and received the enemy with so heavy a fire of musketry and artillery that they were driven back in disorder to the river's bank. The second British brigade had now crossed, and came to the support of the first. Both brigades now pressed forward, Ross extending his line so as to turn the American left flank, and sending at the same time a flight of rockets into their ranks. Two regiments of militia broke and fled, in spite of Winder's efforts; but Sterett's Baltimore volunteers stood firm until Winder ordered a retreat.

The British now attacked the position held by Barney with his guns, Miller's marines, and Beall's militia. The militia (who had arrived on the field that morning, after a trying march of sixteen miles) soon fled, leaving Barney's and Miller's corps uncovered, still fighting like heroes. A party of the British now climbed a hill which commanded the artillery and opened a fire upon them, killing a number, and desperately wounding Barney himself, while the main body charged them with the bayonet. The brave sailors, however, stood to their guns, loading and firing, until some of them were bayonetted at their pieces, and their wounded commander ordered them to retire and leave him a prisoner. As it was evident that they were about to be outflanked, and further resistance was useless, Gen. Winder ordered a general retreat, which soon became a flight, and the day was lost.

Col. Minor was ordered to cover the retreat of the army until all had marched for the capital. The most of the troops, however, instead of moving towards Washington, had scattered in every direction, and, as it afterwards appeared, the greater part had fled towards Montgomery Court-House. Gen. Winder, after consultation with the Secretary of War, decided that it would be useless to think of defending Washington, and therefore proposed to rally the troops on the heights of Georgetown. But the general soon found that but few of the militia could be collected, the greater part having strayed off in search of food or refreshments, and on the 25th orders were given for all the troops to assemble at Montgomery Court-House. Gen. Winder seems to have taken this position with a view to collect his forces and to interpose for the anticipated attack upon Baltimore. On the 26th the army again took up its line of march for the latter city, where it arrived in due time.

Meanwhile, the British forces marched into Washington without further molestation, and destroyed the Capitol, including the Senate chamber and House of Representatives, the President's house, arsenal, navy-yard, Treasury buildings, and the bridge across the Potomac. Besides pillaging many private dwellings and stores, the public property alone destroyed at Washington was worth more than two millions of dollars.

To describe more fully the operations of the cavalry forces during and subsequent to the battle of Bladensburg, we append the following extract from a letter written by an officer in Col. Frisby Tilghman's cavalry regiment to his friend in Hagerstown:

"MONTGOMERY COURT-HOUSE,
"Aug. 27, 1814.

"I have this moment returned from Bladensburg, to which place I was sent yesterday morning by Gen. Winder, for the purpose of ascertaining the situation of several officers who were said to have been wounded and made prisoners in the battle at Bladensburg on Wednesday last. You have no doubt by this time heard the issue of that battle, perhaps in a thousand different ways, and have had much anxiety about the fate of several of your friends. I have with my cavalry escaped unhurt, although the enemy directed his first fire with the rockets at the cavalry, which must have appeared to them very formidable, posted upon the left of the army. The cavalry did not participate much in the fight, being ordered not to charge until the enemy showed a disposition to retire, which, unfortunately, did not take place. The left wing of our army first gave way, and we were obliged to retire with them, there being no troops left in that quarter to support us in case of a charge.

"I felt very anxious about Col. Ragan, who was said to have been badly wounded and in the possession of the enemy. I found, however, upon my arrival in Bladensburg, that he had been thrown from his horse in the action, taken prisoner, and paroled. He left there yesterday morning for Baltimore, and

I presume will return home in a few days, as he cannot serve until exchanged Commodore Barney and several other officers are wounded and now in Bladensburg.

"The British left their men[1] and horses unburied on the field of action. I saw many of them lying in and near the main road, and had them buried before I left.

"A party of the cavalry last night took about one hundred prisoners at Bladensburg, among them were several officers. Reinforcements are coming in daily to our aid; part of them have been ordered to Baltimore, and a part to Washington.

"The enemy have returned to their shipping, and it is thought they will next attack Baltimore. They left the city without destroying the paper-mill, foundry, or Parrott's ropewalk. They did not burn Stull & Williams' powder-works at Bladensburg. They became alarmed, and retreated with a great deal of caution. A British captain informed me they were fearful that Gen. Winder was making arrangements to cut off their retreat to their shipping.

"We have had very arduous service, having been hovering about the enemy ever since we have been in service. We have been for twenty-four hours without provisions or sleep. Our horses and men are literally broken down with fatigue, yet the men bear it like soldiers; and I can truly say they are an honor to any corps.

"You have no doubt heard of the destruction of the Capitol, President's house, navy-yard, and very much other property in and about the city. The scene which Washington this day exhibits cannot be described."

Political Controversy in Washington County. —During this exciting period in the history of the State, Gen. Samuel Ringgold, commanding the Second Brigade of Maryland militia in Washington County, was not inactive. The moment he heard of the disastrous results of the battle at Bladensburg and the capture of the national capital he ordered the whole of his brigade into service, Boonsboro' being named as the place of rendezvous. The orders were promptly obeyed by the citizens, and on the 27th of August six hundred men were assembled, and armed with muskets hastily procured from Harper's Ferry. However, as it was concluded by those in command that the State's militia already in the field were sufficient to defend Annapolis, Baltimore, and other points threatened on the Western Shore, the members of Gen. Ringgold's brigade were permitted to return to their homes on the 28th.

Strange to relate, in consequence of the zeal and patriotism displayed by Gen. Ringgold on this occasion he was as a candidate for re-election to Congress beaten by a Federalist, a "peace candidate" (Mr. Baer, of Frederick County), in October, 1814, upon the strength of assertions that he had unlawfully ordered his brigade into service; also that he had proposed to the brigade that the *single men should march*, while the married men remained at home for the defense of the county.

However, in the three counties of Allegany, Frederick, and Washington, which then composed the Fourth Congressional District, Mr. Baer received a majority of but one hundred and seventy-five votes in Frederick County, and one hundred and forty-four in Allegany, while Gen. Ringgold had one hundred and fifty majority in Washington. The latter county then had in the field at Baltimore and Annapolis more than five hundred men. A large majority of these men were Republicans, and had they been at home, notwithstanding the delusive cry of peace and its influence over the weak, the ignorant, and the cowardly, Gen. Ringgold would have been returned.

In 1816, Gen. Ringgold was again a candidate for Congressional honors (and was elected), and in September of that year a citizen through the press queried him as follows : " By what power or authority did you call out your brigade in the month of August, 1814? and why did you not march them after they had assembled and were armed?" To this and other questions Gen. Ringgold replied one week later in the following manner :

" To the Voters of the Fourth Congressional District of Maryland.

" Fellow-Citizens,—In reply to certain questions put to me by one of you in the last *Maryland Herald*, I beg leave to state that I ordered out the brigade in August, 1814, by virtue of the power and authority vested in me by the 6th section of the Militia Law of this State, in the following words : . . .

" And also in pursuance of the order of Gen. Winder of the 20th day of August, 1814, which is as follows :

" ' Adjutant-General's Office,
" ' Headquarters Military District No. 10,
" ' Washington City, 20th August, 1814.

" ' *General Orders.*

" ' The commander of the Tenth Military District has made requisitions on the proper officers for such militia aid as the present threatened pressure on his district demands, and he relies with confidence that this demand will be obeyed with the utmost promptitude and alacrity.

" ' But since the formal proceedings of regular demand may be too slow for the urgency of the occasion, and will certainly be too tardy for the zeal and patriotism of the freemen of America, who see their Capitol threatened by an insolent foe, who insists upon dictating terms to them there, after having desolated their shores and sacked their cities, the spontaneous efforts of the people are demanded. In this momentous period, therefore, the commander of the district appeals with confidence to the people within and contiguous to his command, and calls upon all not included in the requisition already made who wish to avert the calamities which threaten us voluntarily to rally round the standard of their country without waiting for the slower progress of legal calls.

" ' Organized companies or individuals who will hasten to the scene of action and will perform the services which may be required, armed in the best manner possible, will be received,

---

[1] According to their own statement, the loss on the part of the British was five hundred men killed and wounded, a large majority of whom fell in front of Barney's and Miller's batteries. The American loss was comparatively nothing.

and may finally enjoy the satisfaction of reflecting that they have contributed to save their country from devastation and plunder.

"'By order of the commanding general.
"'R. G. Hite,
"' Asst. Adjt.-Gen. Tenth Mil. Dist.'

"So much has heretofore been said in relation to the call of the brigade at that time that I think it my duty, as an opportunity is offered me, to give you a minute detail of that transaction. On Wednesday, the 24th of August, I received the above order of Gen. Winder, and on the next morning by express the account of the capture of Washington; also that the main body of the enemy, after burning and pillaging the city, were in full march towards Baltimore, and a strong detachment towards Fredericktown, with a view of seizing the treasure of the banks deposited there; and from thence to Harper's Ferry, to destroy the public works and gain the arms and public stores at that place.

"On receiving this information I sent a messenger to Maj. Pottenger and Capt. Thomas Kellar, my two aides, to repair to my house. On their arrival a consultation was held, at which were present those gentlemen, with Maj.-Gen. James Wilkinson and Maj. Upton Lawrence. They unanimously coincided in opinion with me that I not only had the power, but that the danger with which the State was threatened fully justified the measure and rendered the call of the brigade absolutely necessary.

"The order was immediately issued for the brigade to assemble at Boonsboro', and arms were procured from Harper's Ferry ready for distribution on their arrival. Late in the evening of the assemblage of the troops at Boonsboro' I received from a respectable citizen information that the enemy had precipitately left Washington, and were retreating to their shipping at the mouth of the Patuxent. Not wishing to march the troops without there was an absolute necessity, well knowing how very inconvenient it would have been to most of them at that season of the year to leave their homes, I sent the following letter by express to Gen. Armstrong, the then Secretary of War, then at Fredericktown. On the next morning I received from the chief clerk of the War Department the letter which also follows, in consequence of which I disbanded the brigade.

"I feel confident this candid statement of facts will satisfy every unprejudiced mind I did on that occasion what other generals did in adjoining States, and for which they have received the applause and thanks of their country. I did what it was my duty to do, and what I should do again did the same necessity exist.

"With regard to the Compensation Law, I take occasion to say that I am opposed to it, and should I be honored by a majority of the suffrages of the district, I will use my best endeavors to procure its repeal.

"Once more I am nominated by my Republican fellow-citizens as a candidate for Congress. After serving in public life for a period of twenty years it cannot be necessary that I should make a new profession of my political creed; it is sufficient to say that the principles which have dictated and governed my conduct heretofore afford a sure indication of the course I shall in future pursue.

"I am, most respectfully,
"Your fellow-citizen,
"Samuel Ringgold.

"Fountain Rock, Sept. 16, 1816."

"Headquarters, Boonsboro',
"Aug. 27, 1814.

"The moment I heard of the capture of the metropolis of the nation I ordered the whole of my brigade into service, to rendezvous at this place. The orders have been promptly obeyed by the citizens, and this day I had under arms six hundred men, independent of the last requisition of Gen. Winder.

"This morning a fine volunteer company marched from Hagerstown through this place, and another company of the last requisition.

"I have dispatched this express for the purpose of consulting you as to the marching of the men to-morrow. If the enemy have returned to their shipping, it will be unnecessary until further orders; if not, they will march at eight o'clock, and can reach Baltimore the next day or the day after.

"I am, sir, respectfully yours,
"Samuel Ringgold.

"P.S.—Two companies of the requisition made by Gen. Winder will march to-morrow morning at all events.
"Gen. John Armstrong, *Secretary of War,*
"*Frederick-Town, Md.*"

"Frederick-Town, Aug. 27, 1814.
"11 o'clock in the evening.

"Dear Sir,—Your letter of this date to the Secretary of War has just arrived by express. I carried it to Gen. Armstrong in his bed. He directs me to offer you his respects, and inform you that so many militia troops are already in motion to meet or overtake the enemy that it is deemed unnecessary for you to march your brigade. The two companies ordered out on Gen. Winder's requisition should march according to orders.

"The President has this evening sent notice to the Secretaries of War and Treasury at this place that he will meet them in Washington as soon as they can make it convenient. They set out to-morrow morning, when all the public papers, etc., will follow, to resume the proper routine of office as usual in Washington.

"I hope you will do me the honor to accept the assurances of my great respect and esteem.
"Daniel Parker, *C. C. War Dep't.*
"Gen. Ringgold."

In September, 1814, nearly all of the Western Maryland troops who were present at Bladensburg participated in the operations around Baltimore, caused by the efforts made by the British to capture that city. The "Homespun Volunteers," of Hagerstown, under Capt. Thomas Quantrill, were attached to Lieut.-Col. Joseph Sterett's Fifth Baltimore Regiment. They behaved most gallantly throughout their entire term of service, and were especially complimented for the bravery displayed by them at the battle of North Point. Col. Frisby Tilghman's cavalry also came in for a word of commendation, Gen. Samuel Smith stating in his congratulatory "general orders" that their duties "were performed with an alacrity and promptness highly honorable to the officers and men."

The emergency having passed which rendered it necessary for the volunteers and militia of the county to take the field, they were, in November following, mustered out of service. The peace commissioners representing England and the United States completed their labors at Ghent, Dec. 24, 1814, and the tidings of peace were brought to the United States by Hon. Christopher Hughes, Jr., of Baltimore, who was then our *charge d'affaires* at Stockholm, and secretary to the commissioners. He arrived in Annapolis on the 13th of February, in the schooner "Transit," and immediately set out for Washington.

HON. C. HUGHES, JR.

The Prince Regent ratified the treaty on December 30th, and on the 18th of February, 1815, the President's signature was attached to it, thus perfecting that instrument, and concluding the second war between Great Britain and the United States.[1]

---

[1] Pursuant to public notice, a meeting of the surviving officers and soldiers of the war of 1812, residing in Washington County, met at the court-house in Hagerstown, on Tuesday, the 26th day of December, 1854, and on motion Col. John Miller was called to the chair, and Daniel Hauer was appointed secretary, and Capt. James Biays assistant secretary. The object of the meeting having been stated by the chair, on motion of William H. Handey a committee of five was appointed by the chair to draft resolutions for the adoption of the meeting. The following gentlemen were appointed as the committee: William H. Handey, Capt. George Shryock, Capt. James Biays, William McCardel, and Charles G. Downs. On motion, also, a committee of five was appointed to name twelve delegates to attend the general convention to assemble at Washington City on the 8th of January ensuing, when the following persons were appointed: David Newcomer, Henry Blessing, William Grove, Andrew Duble, Jacob Powles. The meeting then adjourned, to meet again at two o'clock P.M. At two o'clock the meeting reassembled, pursuant to adjournment, when the committee to appoint delegates reported the following: Col. John Miller, Capt. James Biays, David Newcomer, Henry Blessing, Charles G. Downs, Capt. George Shryock, Frederick Humrichouse, Frederick Betts, Daniel Hauer, Capt. John Byer, William Freaner, and William McCardel. It was also

Resolved, That the thanks of this meeting be tendered to A. K. Syester, Esq., for the very appropriate address delivered on this occasion, and also to the officers of the meeting and the members of Heyser's Band.

Resolved, That the proceedings of this meeting be published in all the papers in the county.

JOHN MILLER, *President*.
DANIEL HAUER,
JAMES BIAYS, *Secretaries*.

Names of the officers and soldiers taking part at the meeting: Col. John Miller, Capt. James Biays, Daniel Hauer, Capt. George Shryock, David Newcomer, William Grove, Charles G. Downs, Richard Davis, Rezin James, John Dovenberger, Nathan Davis, William McCardel, Jesse Long, Daniel Oster, Jacob Powles, Frederick Humrichouse, William Johnston, John Brown, James Swales, John Plummer, Matthias Wegley, Samuel Feigley, James Dillehunt, Spencer Lushbaugh, David Long, Jacob Kayler, William Biershing, David Tschudy, John Neff, Ezekiel Cheney, John Murry, William Cline, George Hauer, Capt. Gerard Stonebraker, Anthony Campbell, George Spangler, Andrew Burns, Benjamin Simpson, Solomon Stine-

Military Organizations of Western Maryland Participating in the War of 1812.

Washington County.—Capt. George Shryock's company of volunteer infantry raised in Washington County marched from Hagerstown, July 23, 1814, for the defense of Baltimore, and remained in service to the close of the war. It contained the following members, and was disbanded at Annapolis on the 10th of January, 1815:

Capt. George Shryock, 1st Lieut. Nathaniel Posey, 2d Lieut. David Artz,[2] 3d Lieut. Christian Fechtig, 1st Sergt. Nat. Bateman, 2d Sergt. Henry Beigler, 3d Sergt. Samuel Baar, 4th Sergt. Henry Protzman, 1st Corp. Thomas Sturr, 2d Corp. William Miles, 3d Corp. William Smith, 4th Corp. Jacob Hess, Drummer, Henry Creager, Fifer, Frederick Kinsell. Privates, Jacob Apprecht, James Adams, William Armstrong, Samuel Abbott, Jas. Aldnage, John Buterbaugh, Henry Buterbaugh, Andrew Burns, Jacob Baker, Joseph Bradshaw, Thomas Bond, Joseph Bowman, John Blackburn, Conrod Blentlinger, Moses Bower, Frederick Bets, William Baily, Jacob Baar, Samuel Abbott, John Creager, William Creager, John Cook, James Curry, George Craul, Rezin Derumple, Jacob Emrich, Samuel Feigley, Michael Fague, George Fockler, Jacob Geiger, John Gray, George Grubb, Peter Geiser, Jacob Gower, Samuel Hawkey, Henry Huntzberry, George Harrison, Henry House, William Heath, John Henry, V. P. G. Irving, Arthur Johnston, William Jackson, Jacob Kline, Henry Kinkle, Zebulon Lover, Samuel Lutz, Jeremiah Leonard, Jacob Lizer, Jonas Lizer, William Lizer, John Locher, John Lora, George Morgentall, William McMon, Wm. M. Moore, John Murray, Thomas Moore, James Matere, Michael Monahan, John Matsabaugh, Lambert Mackerson, Jesse Right, Michael Ridenour, John Ropp, Peter Riner, Joseph Palmer, Henry Patdurf, Daniel Rench, George Rinoll, Daniel Smith, George Smith, Gerrard Smith, William Stephen, Samuel Saylor, William Soaper, John Sowers Matthias Saylor, John Stokes, William Shaw, Jacob Shaw, John Sager, Thomas Parkes, James M. Thomson, Rudolph Tarlton, Josiah Tally, John Troxell, John Traver, David Thomas, John Tice, David Tschudy, James Wilkinson, George Washington, Mathias Wallick, Jonas Wolleslager, John Yeider, John Yost, William Yostler, Peter Zimmer, Philip Wingert.

Hagerstown Volunteers.[3]—Capt. Thomas Quantrill, 1st Lieut. Daniel Sprigg, 2d Lieut. George Harry, Ensign William Hall, 1st Sergt. Thomas Keen, 2d Sergt. William McCardel, 3d Sergt. George Kreps, 4th Sergt. John Harry, 1st Corp. John Hunter, 2d Corp. Daniel Oster, 3d Corp. Benjamin Smith, 4th Corp. John Cellers, Musician, Chas. Dumetz, Peter Snyder, John Anderson, Jacob Middlekauff, Christian Coy, John Rockwell, John Harrigan, Jacob Hose, Thomas Combs, Jacob Burkart, Frederick Kinsel, Henry Creager, John Hull, Jacob King, Philip Mouse, Henry Blessing, Andrew Duble, Frederick Betts, Joseph Barkdoll, Capt. David Artz, John Cramer, Robert Campbell, Abraham Crum, John Marteney, Maj. Elias Baker, Valentine Wachtal, David Shinn, Henry Sweitzer, William Freaner, Daniel Creager, John Kealhoffer, Jacob Borvard, Samuel Creager

[2] Promoted to first lieutenant.

[3] Attached to the Thirty-ninth Regiment Maryland Militia at the battle of North Point, Baltimore.

wasser. Privates, John Anderson, William Allison, William Armour, Samuel Bayley, Jacob Beehart, John Billenger, Samuel Bennet, Samuel W. Barnes, John Conley, John Cramer, Andrew Collins, Alexander Cake, John T. Cook, John Deitz, Daniel Daup, Peter Glassbrener, John McDonough, Solomon Mann, John N. Miller, Jacob Morter, John Martiney, Robert McClanhan, Anthony B. Martin, Joseph Neal, James Noble, John O'Ferrall, Columbus Patton, Andrew Poffenbarger, John Schnebly, Thomas Soper, Joseph Stroud, Samuel Shank, Jacob Gayer, William Harry, Joseph Hemphill, Philip Helser, Frederick Humrickhouse, Samuel Harry, Daniel Hawkin, John Johnston, Jacob Keally, Jesse Keallyer, Jacob Kinkerly, Frederick Knease. George Lynes, Jacob Loney, Jacob Locker, William McPherrin, Daniel Smith, John Shipley, William Schleigh, James Sterett, David Shryock, Peter Smith, John Snecdor, John Smith, John Strit, John Nagman, Lazarus Wilson, Samuel Wilson. Joseph Wareham, Levin West, George Winters, George Wise.

Hagerstown Cavalry.—Capt. Jacob Barr, 1st Lieut. David Newcomer, 2d Lieut. Samuel Rohrer, Cornet, Henry Kealhofer, Sergts. Jacob Huyett, Benjamin Kershner, Otto Adams, Jacob Kershner, Corps. Samuel Alter, Levy Rench, Frederick Rohrer, John Walgamot, Q.M.-Sergt. Philip Burkley, Saddler, John Kealhofer, Blacksmith, Jacob Leider, Trumpeter, Joseph Eakle. Privates, Jacob Adams, William Adams, William Anderson, John Winders, Jacob Binkley, John Miller, Henry Miller, James Dillihunt, Jacob Knode, John Witmore, Jacob Eakle, John Repp, Edward H. Wilson, Joseph Kindell, John Allers, Moses Fabbs, George Krider, Daniel Kline, Henry Gurlaugh, James Berry, Abraham Degraft, Henry Waller, Frederick Kitz, Daniel Miller, George Thomas, David Clagett, John Gall, John Howard, George Kershner, Perry Wayman.

Muster-roll of Capt. John Brengle's company of volunteers, raised in four hours by marching through the streets of Frederick, Aug. 25, 1814. This was the day after the battle of Bladensburg, when the news of that battle was received. Rev. David F. Schaeffer rode by the side of Capt. Brengle through Fredericktown, encouraging men to volunteer:

Capt. John Brengle, 1st Lieut. Matthias E. Bartgis, 2d Lieut. William Kolb, Ensign Ormond F. Butler, 1st Sergt. Alexander Robertson, 2d Sergt. Joseph Adlum, 4th Sergt. John Brunner, of Jacob, 1st Corp. John Dinsmore Smith, 2d Corp. John Wilson, 3d Corp. Henry Bante, 4th Corp. John Sloan. Privates, Hezekiah Applebee, John Balderston, Christian Bartel, John Bante, David Baer, Lawrence Brengle, of Clinton, Alexander Bevins, Jacob Bougher, Tobias Butler, Abraham Kalkloescher, Henry Kauffman, David B. Devitt, Joshua Dean, Peter Doll, James Doury, Michael Doll, William Ely, Eli Ebert, Jacob Firestone, Jacob Geyer, Jonas Geyer, John Gouso, Jacob Gouso, Reuben Grove, John Houck, John Hirsley, Miles Hilton, Daniel Hane, Andrew Hoffman, Zephaniah Harrison, David Hane, Philip Haller, Jacob Heffner, George Kelly, Greenbury Knauff, John Keller, Charles Keller, Jacob Kessler, George Loche, Peter Lipsley, David Markey, Gabriel J. Mattingly, Basil Mobley, Jacob Mixsell, Sr., David McVicker, John Ortner, John A. Porter, Charles Peters, Frederick Poole, John Pobst, Jacob Riehl, John Richter, William Rattler, William Rowe, Henry Scholl, David Springer, John Schoto, John Schivaller, George Solmon, George B. Shope, George Zeiso, Jacob Strickstrock, Henry Stahl, George Schuantiegel, Henry Snyder, George Wissinger, Samuel Webster, Peter Wissinger, David Young, Thomas Young, Andrew Young, David Webster.

The whole town was in commotion at the time of their volunteering. The court-house yard was full of wagons, filled with government archives sent from Washington, and the Central Bank was stocked with specie sent from the Baltimore banks to Frederick for safe-keeping.

Steiner's Frederick Artillery.—Capt. Henry Steiner, 1st Lieut. R. G. McPherson, 2d Lieut. Lewis Green, 1st Sergt. John Buckey, 2d Sergt. William Houser, 3d Sergt. George Dertzback, 4th Sergt. David Mantz, 1st Corp. Jacob Kieffer, 2d Corp. William Steiner, 3d Corp. Henry Hauer, 4th Corp. Marcus Y. Graff, Musicians, Jacob Fowble, John Stouffer. Privates, Peter Ambrose, Michael Baer, of John, Samuel Barns, Thomas Blackford, Lloyd Belt, Samuel Brent, David Boyd, Robert Boone, Daniel Burhart, William Cassell, Thomas Dean, James Dixon, George Evett, Peter Freburger, Jacob Feagler, Nich. Goldsborough, Thomas Grahame, Henry Hanshew, George Hauer, John L. Harding, Michael Heffner, Henry Holler, Daniel Holter, John Jamieson, William Jenkins, William Johnson, Thomas M. Jolly, John Kontz, George McClain, Peter McFarland, William McPherson, Richard B. Murdoch, John Miller, Abraham Neaff, Henry Nixdorff, Adam Nichols, Philip Pyfer, Philip Potts, Henry Rye, Jacob Schaffner, Charles Salmon, John Thomas Steiner, Jacob Shellman, Thomas Scott, James Somerville, John Schissler, Jacob Schriver.

Allegany County.—*McLaughlin's Company.*

Capt. Wm. McLaughlin, 1st Lieut. James Hook, 2d Lieut. Geo. Shuck, Ensign Frederick Rice, Sergts. Robert Little, Frederick Deems, John Porter, James M. White, Jacob Waggoner, Corps. Rezin Hook, Daniel Poland, John Walts, William Street, Joseph S. Stafford, John North. Privates, John Busey, Benjamin Brown, James Bryan, David Barr, Nathaniel Barnes, Michael Bevins, Samuel Banks, Thomas Breeman, Nathaniel Bryan, Wm. Broadwater, James Boyer, Charles Busey, Elias Burrows, Martin Clabaugh, Bernard Connelly, Lewis Clemmer, David Cox, Samuel Chapman, John Creamer, Jacob Clark, Edward Connelly, Samuel Crawford, Isaiah Davis, Benjamin Deverbaugh, Michael Entler, Joseph Erb, Frederick Garey, Nicholas Gowar, Samuel Hoblitzell, George Hager, Jacob Isenhart, Thomas Jodwin, Benjamin Jolley. William Johnson, John Johnson, William Jolley, Robert R. Kennedy, James Kempton, David Kinsey, John Loatz, Benj. H. Lacy, Daniel Letters, George Loar, James Lee, Jacob Lee, John Lee, Archibald Love, John Laughridge, Frederick Lee, James Morrow, John Martin, John McIntire, John Markee, Peter Myers, James Moore, George Miller, Abraham Michaels, Francis Madore, John Neff, Jr., M. Northcraft, Joseph Perrin, Joseph Paxton, William Paxton, Henry Porter, George Rice, Arjalon Resonor, Daniel Rhodes, John Russell, Frederick Rice, Elizophr Robinette, Thomas Riley, Jacob Sterner, Henry Shellhorn, Moses Spencer, James Sherry, Peter Spillman, Jacob Saylor, Jacob Schoffer, John Shuck, Absalom Stoyer, Jacob Tumbuster, Jonathan Willson, Isaac Willson, Joshua Willson, Samuel White, Levi Whalley Amos Willson, Jacob Zumbuly. Total in company, 104.

Blair's Company.—Capt. Thomas Blair, 1st Lieut. Walter McAtee, 2d Lieut. Samuel Lowdermilk, 1st Sergt. William Shaw, 2d Sergt. Alpheus Hinkle, 3d Sergt. Jacob Shuck, 4th

Sergt. George M. Houx, 1st Corp. John Delouhrey, 2d Corp. Robt. Stahan, 3d Corp. James Keath, 4th Corp. James Taney, Drummer, Moses McKinsey, Fifer, Thomas Clinton. Privates, John Allen, James Bernard, Jacob Bowlie, John Bucker, James Burns, Nathaniel Britton, Francis Bruce, Alpheus B. Beall, Alfred Burgess, William B. Bumbsy, Charles Broadwater, Robert Britt, John Cox, Robert Coddington, John Case, Zodock Clark, Michael Conrade, John Dart, Aaron Devore, John Deaking, Thomas Drain, James Drain, Reuben Elbin, John Fisher, John Fling, John Foley, Joseph Forsyth, George Fryer, Elisha Frazce, Adam Gross, John Griffey, William Golding, William Gordon, Jacob Hoffman, Frederick Hoff, John Humphrey, John Harding, John J. Hoffman, Solomon Hall, Thos. Hendrixon, James Irons, Thomas Irons, William Knott, Cornelius Kight, James Kennedy, William Kelly, Joseph Kelly, Charles Korns, Moses Kelly, Samuel Kelly, John Lafoot, John Lowery, George Long, Stephen Millholland, John Moor, Gabriel M. Moore, Joseph Martin, John Massor, Henry Martz, James Murphy (1), James Murphy (2), Arthur Morrison, Godfrey Miller, Jesse McKinsey, David Muman, James McCartney, William Majors, George W. Morrison, Elisha Morris, William Neptune, John C. Newman, George A. Newman, Edward Northcraft, Athanias Newton, John Potter, Joseph Porter, John Polard, David Potter, Thomas Plummer, Wm. Parkeson, George Peters, John Peterman, Thomas Riland, James Ravenscraft, Elisha Riley, Jacob Roads, John Rizer, William Stephen, David Siford, Samuel Savage, Adam Sapp, John Shepherd, Adam Spiker, Jacob Shriver, Henry Smith, Lewis Shircliff, Joshua Stanton, John Shockey, John Shelhouse, Elisha Tasker, Peter Thrasher, Jesse Tomlinson, Abner A. Trull, Mal Taylor, Zachariah Vansickle, Jacob Wolfe, James T. White, William Wilson, Samuel Woodrough, William Winzett. Total in company, 123.

In the organization of the Maryland militia the Fiftieth Regiment was ordered by the Council to be organized in Allegany County, and the following officers were appointed: Thomas Greenwell, lieutenant-colonel; John Folck, major; captains, John McElfish, Dennis Beall, Conrad Corbus, Joseph France, and Thomas Porter; adjutant, Levi Hilleary.[1]

CHAPTER X.

THE CIVIL WAR.

Public Feeling—Town-Meetings and Resolutions—Opposition to Secession—Western Maryland Home-Guards—The Public Safety Bill—Arrest of Maryland Legislature—Secret Correspondence.

On the 6th of November, 1860, the long political struggle between the North and the South on the slavery question, which began in 1803 with the purchase of Louisiana, ended with the election to the Presidency of Abraham Lincoln, and the triumph of the Republican party. The accession of the anti-slavery party to power filled the South with dismay, and created the greatest excitement throughout the country. Hardly had the result been ascertained before some of the extreme Southern States began military preparations, and set on foot measures to carry into effect their oft-repeated threats of secession and combination in resistance to alleged Northern encroachments.

Public feeling was, perhaps, even more intense in Maryland than in other States, from the obvious danger to which she was exposed by her geographical position in event of conflict between the North and South, and from the very strong counter-currents which existed in popular sentiment. This conflict of opinions and sympathies was nowhere more marked than in Western Maryland, and while the majority of the people of that section were pronounced and decided in their support of the Union after hostilities had actually commenced, there was a very large and respectable element which sympathized with the South, and which deprecated the coercion of the Southern States. Meetings were soon called to give expression to public sentiment, and the tone and character of the resolutions adopted forcibly illustrated the condition of the popular mind in Western Maryland at that period. In accordance with the recommendation of "the National Union Democratic Central Committee of the State of Maryland," a large meeting of citizens of the Fifth Election District of Washington County, without respect to former party associations, was held at the house of Lloyd H. Barton, in the town of Hancock, on Tuesday evening, November 27th, "for the purpose of taking into consideration the present crisis in our public affairs, and to appoint ten delegates to represent the district in the State Convention to meet in Baltimore on the 6th of December." After the selection of Joseph Graves as chairman and R. E. Taney as secretary, a committee of three, consisting of David E. Price, Joseph Harrison, and Devalt Stottlemyer, reported a series of resolutions, which were unanimously adopted, and which accurately portrayed the feeling of a large proportion of the people of Western Maryland upon the questions then agitating the country. After the expression of regret at the formation of sectional parties and at the triumph of "Northern sentiment," the resolutions proceeded to declare "that notwithstanding some of our fellow-citizens of the South profess to look upon the result of our recent election as a justification for a withdrawal from the National Union, and consequently a disruption of our government, we, standing as we do between the two extremes, and after the most mature consideration, cannot look upon the said result in so

---

[1] Lowdermilk.

disastrous a light, but view it only as another evidence of the great truth of the sentiment, that 'The price of liberty is eternal vigilance.' *Resolved*, That we believe that under the provisions of our Constitution the legislative and executive departments of our national government possess ample powers to cause the people of the North to do justice to the people of the South in the rendering up of fugitive slaves, and that by a judicious exercise of these powers, and proper appeals to the justice, the sense of right, and the patriotism of the people of the North, all causes of complaint may be easily and speedily removed."[1]

On the 17th of December, in pursuance of a call signed by Richard Potts and other prominent citizens without regard to party, a convention of the people of Frederick County assembled in Frederick City "to consider all constitutional means of vindicating and securing our constitutional rights within the Union, and to petition the Governor, if deemed expedient, to convene the Legislature for the sole purpose of passing a law for a State Convention to take into consideration the present perilous condition of public affairs, to devise such measures as the exigencies of the crisis may call for, and to appoint delegates to represent the State in such general convention of the slaveholding States as may be convoked to guard and protect Southern interests and Southern rights."

The Hon. Richard Potts presided, assisted by a number of vice-presidents and secretaries. After prayer by Rev. J. McK. Riley, the following committee on resolutions was appointed: Grayson Eichelberger, William P. Maulsby, L. J. Brengle, S. D. Walker, B. A. Cunningham, Governor E. L. Lowe, and Outerbridge Horsey. This committee reported a series of resolutions, a portion of which had been previously adopted by a meeting of the workingmen of Frederick. The resolutions protested against disunion and secession; called for conciliatory measures on the part of the North; rebuked many of the public men for want of patriotism; urged the Maryland congressmen to vote for such measures as would be likely to restore harmony to the country; declared that while the mere fact of President Lincoln's election did not justify secession, the conduct of the "anti-slavery fanatics of the North" in the passage of personal liberty bills, their persistent agitation of the slavery question in the pulpit, the press, and in political assemblages, and their active and determined opposition to the return to their owners of fugitive slaves, evidenced unfriendly feeling towards their Southern brethren, was in direct violation of the letter as well as the spirit of the Constitution, was subversive of all good government, deserved the severest reprobation of every good citizen, and warranted the Southern States in asking for further constitutional guarantees from their Northern brethren. The resolutions also requested the Governor of Maryland, when in his judgment it should become necessary, or so soon as a convention of the Southern States should be determined upon, to convene the Legislature, for the sole purpose of providing for the calling of a State Convention and of the election of delegates thereto, "to take into consideration the dangers by which we are environed, to take all necessary constitutional steps for our relief, and, if necessary, to appoint delegates to a convention of slaveholding States to take counsel with our Southern brethren."

Ex-Governor Lowe made a minority report to the following effect: "that each State is sovereign, the Federal Constitution being equally binding upon all as a compact, which compact as (Daniel Webster declared) if broken on one side the other contracting parties are at liberty to consider annulled. Therefore the nullification of the fugitive slave law by several free States is sufficient to justify the Southern States in considering the compact broken, while the election of Lincoln upon an avowed policy of irrepressible conflict with the institution of the South, guaranteed by the Federal Constitution, demonstrated the determination of the controlling political party at the North to convert the Union into an engine of oppression." The resolution further declared "that the Union, as our fathers made it, ought to be preserved, but can only be by the North fully recognizing all the constitutional rights of the South, the latter never having been the aggressor, while the former has caused all the perils which now endanger the Union; that while deprecating the precipitate action of South Carolina and other adjoining States, before consultation with sister Southern States, the provocation is acknowledged to be excessive, and comes exclusively from the North; that Maryland and Virginia can never go to the North, but must ever remain at the great column of Southern States; that a convention should be held as early as possible to determine the measures of preserving the Union upon the basis of the Constitution, and failing in that, then to devise some way to avert the calamities of a civil war." In conclusion, the resolutions repudiated the idea of coercion by the Federal

---

[1] A committee, consisting of John S. Hedding, Joseph P. Bishop, and Charles Barton, was appointed at this meeting to select ten persons to represent the district in the State Convention at Baltimore, and reported the names of Jacob Snively, David E. Price, Robert Bridges, Benjamin B. Bootman, John J. Bowles, A. B. Taney, Jacob Reel, James D. Hook, John J. Brosius, and D. Stottlemyer.

government, and demanded an early session of the Maryland Legislature. The minority report of Governor Lowe was seconded by John A. Lynch, and supported at length by William J. Ross, J. M. Killgour, and Governor Lowe himself. The majority report was advocated by Col. William P. Maulsby, Grayson Eichelberger, and W. Hobbs. Col. E. Shriver then called the previous question, which was sustained, when Governor Lowe's report was rejected, and that of the majority (substituted by Mr. Eichelberger) was adopted. The former received two hundred and one, and the latter three hundred and fourteen, votes.

On the 1st of January, 1861, a large mass-meeting of the people of Montgomery County was held at Rockville. John Brewer was chosen president; Thomas Griffith, Sr., E. J. Hall, Z. Waters, Robert Sellman, W. B. Howard, John H. Gassaway, S. C. Viers, S. T. Stonestreet, P. Palmer, B. Brush Roberts, vice-presidents; and John T. Varrison, G. W. Dawson, R. W. Carter, John T. Benson, G. R. Braddock, secretaries. A committee on resolutions was appointed, which, through its chairman, Hon. Richard J. Bowie, reported resolutions sympathizing with the South, but declaring that "every sacrifice should be made before Maryland consents to separate herself from the Union."

The resolutions suggested a convention of the slave States to devise measures to secure their constitutional rights within the Union, and that the Governor of this State "be requested, when in his judgment it shall become necessary, or as soon as such convention in the slave States shall be determined on, to convene the Legislature for the sole purpose of providing for the call of a State Convention and of the election of delegates thereto, to take all necessary constitutional steps to avert the dangers by which they were environed." The resolutions also demanded the repeal of the obnoxious laws of the free States, opposed the abolition of slavery in the District of Columbia, and concluded as follows:

"*Resolved*, That if, unfortunately, the slavery question cannot now be settled permanently upon terms acceptable to the South and the North, and the Union should be dissolved, then Maryland ought to go with the South or Central Southern Confederacy, and we pledge ourselves to use our influence to that object, which will clearly protect our rights and institutions."

The committee was equally divided on the latter resolution, and the meeting finally laid it upon the table. Upon the resolution relative to an extra session the committee was also equally divided. W. Viers Bowie offered a substitute " that the Governor be requested to convene the Legislature without delay, to consult with him and determine upon the course the State ought to take to protect herself and the Union in the present alarming condition of the country." This led to an earnest and animated discussion, in which the substitute was advocated with much ability by W. Viers Bowie and George Peter, Jr., and the original resolution by A. Bowie Davis, Richard J. Bowie, and E. J. Hall. The substitute was rejected,—ayes 131, nays 133. Thereupon the resolution was adopted by the same vote. The other resolutions, which had been unanimously reported by the committee, were also unanimously adopted by the meeting.

The committee which reported the original resolutions consisted of Richard J. Bowie, William V. Bowie, Samuel Biggs, of R., Zachariah Waters, Robert Sellman, Howard Griffith, and Benjamin C. Gott.

On the 3d of January a lofty pole was raised at Williamsport and decorated with a Union flag bearing the motto, "Constitution and the Union." "Strong and eloquent" Union speeches were made by Hon. Judge Weisel, J. V. L. Findlay, and A. K. Stake, member of the Legislature.

On the 15th, pursuant to a previous call, an immense meeting of the citizens of Washington County assembled at the court-house in Hagerstown "to give expression to their views in relation to the alarming crisis in the country." The call was addressed to the people without distinction of party, and was responded to by large numbers from nearly every portion of the county.

Dr. Charles Macgill and John McKee were made temporary chairmen, with Joseph A. Skinner and Richard Sheckles as vice-presidents, and Charles J. Nesbitt and Lewis P. Fiery, secretaries. On motion of R. H. Alvey, a committee of seven, consisting of R. H. Alvey, L. T. Brien, Dr. William A. Riddlemoser, Elias Davis, David Brumbaugh, David Troup, and William Reynolds, was appointed to report permanent officers, and in accordance with their recommendation the temporary officers were made permanent. Hon. William T. Hamilton, seconded by Dr. William A. Riddlemoser, moved the appointment of a committee of twenty to report resolutions, and the following gentlemen were appointed: R. H. Alvey, L. T. Brien, Dr. Wm. A. Riddlemoser, Elias Davis, David Brumbaugh, David Troup, Williams Reynolds, Hon. William T. Hamilton, Hon. Daniel Weisel, George Freaner, Col. George Schley, William Motler, George Harmon, John W. Breathed, Peter B. Small, Emanuel Tice, Alexander Neill, Joseph Beeler, James Wason, and Isaac Nesbitt.

The committee retired, and upon full consultation

reported unanimously a series of resolutions, declaring "that in our opinion and judgment the present evils of the country have been produced and precipitated upon us by a persistent and dogmatical course of fanaticism in the Northern States of this Union, and that by the legislation and conduct of the people, as well official as unofficial, in said section of the Union, the letter and spirit of the Constitution of the United States, as also the comity of the States, have been violated, and the constitutional obligations and rights set at defiance; that the Northern States should repeal the laws violative of the Constitution and arrest all further aggression of their people upon the rights of the South; that while the Southern and slaveholding States of this Union have suffered much at the hands of the people of the Northern States, and are now menaced by their hostile position, and therefore have just cause of complaint, yet we think and hope that by mutual forbearance and wise counsels the difficulties may be adjusted under the Constitution, by proper amendments thereto; and that we earnestly appeal to those in authority to exert themselves to the utmost to accomplish such a result; and that an amendment of said Constitution such as that proposed by Mr. Crittenden would be acceptable as a measure of peace; that, in view of the prospect of a total dissolution of the Union, the true policy of all who are attached to the same and desire to see a reconstruction thereof is to desist from all provocations of hostility between the several States, or between the Federal government and the seceding States; and that a resort to force would be but the certain means of engendering lasting hostility and of alienating the people of the States, and thus render the reconstruction of the Union impossible; that the action of the people of Maryland in this important crisis ought, if possible, to comport with the forms of law and order, and therefore to be more effective in results, as the Governor of Maryland has recently announced that he has no power by proclamation to call upon the people to take their sense upon the propriety of holding a State Convention, nevertheless, as an expression of the views of this meeting, we most respectfully request that he recommend to the people of Maryland to assemble upon a day designated by him at their several places of voting, that their sense may be had upon calling such convention, and that as good citizens we will cheerfully observe and abide by the same."

A minority of the committee reported as supplemental and additional to the foregoing a series of resolutions declaring "that at the time of the adoption of the present Constitution of the United States the several States adopting the same were free and independent republics; and that the Constitution being adopted and the Union of the States formed by the separate assent of the States respectively, as expressed through and by the several Legislatures or Conventions held in the several States for that purpose, such States, whenever they think themselves aggrieved and oppressed, and that the ends and purposes of their Federal association have been defeated, and their rights and liberties endangered, and therefore withdraw from the Union, cannot, consistently with freedom and the nature of the republican institutions guaranteed to each, be forced to remain in and maintain the Union; and that the employment of force by the general goverment against any seceding State from said Union would be in violation of the true principles of the Union, and of the rights of the States; that it would be a radical and despotical perversion of the principles and objects of the Union, as well as of the rights of the States, that any such resort to force by the general government should be made; that it is right and expedient that the people of the State should consult and determine in regard to the crisis impending over them, and as to the position and welfare of the State, and to that end a convention of the people should be called by the sanction of law." After the committee had made their reports, the meeting adjourned until the 26th of January, when it reassembled in the "County Hall" at Hagerstown. The proceedings, however, were inharmonious, and the Union men withdrew from the hall and proceeded to the public square, where they organized by the appointment of Daniel Startzman, Sr., as chairman, Peter B. Small, of Hagerstown, Lewis P. Fiery, of Clear Spring, and Joseph F. Davis, of Funkstown, as vice-presidents, and J. D. Bennett and B. F. Lushbaugh, of Hagerstown, as secretaries. The resolutions reported to the former meeting, on motion of Joseph A. Skinner, were unanimously laid on the table, and a new committee on resolutions appointed, consisting of Daniel Weisel, chairman, Elias Davis, Frederick Bell, Martin Startzman, B. F. Kendall, David Spigler, Henry Newcomer, Isaac Wilson, John Lesher, Jonathan Toby, John Sprecker, David Smith, and Dr. N. B. Scott. The committee reported resolutions, which were unanimously adopted, declaring "that as much as we deeply regret the election of men to the highest offices of the republic nominated and sustained by a section, yet we do not regard their election as a cause for revolution; that we agree with the President of the United States in his recent annual message that secession is no constitutional mode of redress, but revolution; and that we regard all the States that have by acts of secession declared themselves out of the Union and independent of the general government as in a state of revolt against the authority of the United States; that all good citizens should sustain the government in maintaining its rights and the public property of the nation, and enforcing its authority and laws wherever it can be done without endangering the Union; that all laws passed by any of the States in contravention of the Constitution and laws of the general government, called 'personal liberty bills,' and such like, should be at once repealed, as alike due to the patriotism and justice of those States and the harmony of the Union; that we are ready to adopt all amendments of the Constitution which will secure now and forever the constitutional rights of the South, and every other section of the Union, and that such amendments should, without delay, be proposed and ratified in the mode pointed out by the Constitution; that the people of Maryland should vigorously oppose all attempts at secession and revolution; that her true position *is in the Union*, and that for all her grievances the Constitution provides adequate remedies; that the course of Governor Hicks meets with the hearty approval of this meeting; that in any future contingency that may arise out of our present national difficulties Maryland should not consent to be the border State, but her true policy is to look to such a position in any new confederacy as will best comport with her safety, peace, and prosperity; and that in the opinion of this meeting a central confederacy presents the best guarantees for her future destiny, if unhappily the present Union should be dissolved; that among the proposed amendments of the Constitution we earnestly recommend the election of the Electors of President and Vice-President of the United States to be by the district system, instead of by general ticket, as a measure eminently calculated to prevent the election of sectional candidates, as more conformable to our system of representation, and as affording to minorities their just weight in the government." Addresses in favor of the Union were made by Judge Weisel, Joseph A. Skinner, Lewis P. Fiery, of Clear Spring, Capt. Elias Davis, of Boonsboro', S. M. Fiery, of Hagerstown, Capt. Isaac Nesbitt, and others, and a letter from Governor Hicks was read.[1]

[1] Among other meetings held at this period in Western Maryland to give expression to the popular views upon the issues of the day were the following: A meeting of the workingmen of Hagerstown on Jan. 19, 1861, indorsing the policy of Governor Hicks. William Miller was called to the chair, A. J. McGruder, William Biershing, and William Ratcliff were elected vice-

On the 16th of January, in pursuance of a previous call from prominent citizens of the county, a convention was held in Frederick City " of those who

presidents, and William Updegraff, secretary. William Colklesser, P. B. Small, John Knodle, B. A. Garlinger, and Martin Braley reported resolutions condemning secession and approving the compromise measures of Mr. Crittenden. On the 12th of January a Union meeting of the citizens of District No. 7, in Washington County, was held in Mr. Pearson's school-house in the town of Smithsburg, which assembled again at the same place on the 19th, having first appointed Messrs. William B. McAtee and J. D. Price to report the proceedings of the County Convention to the adjourned meeting. George Winters was called to the chair, and Philip Oswald appointed secretary, when Messrs. McAtee and Price reported the resolutions prepared by the committee of twenty at Hagerstown, and unanimously adopted the first four. A Union meeting was held at Rohrersville by the citizens of District No. 8 of Washington County on the 18th of January, 1861, at which Elias E. Rohrer presided, and Josiah E. Mullendore acted as secretary. On the 23d of January a Union meeting of the citizens of Clear Spring District No. 4, Washington County, was held at the academy in Hagerstown. Denton Jacques was called to the chair, George Ernst chosen vice-president, and Dr. H. F. Perry, secretary. On January 22d a Union meeting of the citizens of the Covetown, Leitersburg, and part of Hagerstown District, Washington County, was held at Pleasant Hill school-house. James M. Leiter was made president, Jacob Eckstine, vice-president, and D. M. Good, secretary. Resolutions were prepared by George W. Lantz, A. J. Hartman, and John Slick. On the 12th of January a Union meeting was held at Boonsboro', at which George C. Rohrer presided. Jacob Rudy and Anselm Walters were vice-presidents, and Drs. William Beal and H. B. Wilson, secretaries.

On the 5th of January a very large and influential meeting of the citizens of Mount Pleasant District, of Frederick County, irrespective of party, was held at Mount Pleasant. Resolutions presented by John Houck, Samuel D. Walker, John W. Ogborn, Simon W. Stauffer, and Esau D. Creager were adopted, protesting against any and every attempt from any and every source to commit the State to any sectional issue, asserting a determination not to go, nor to be driven out of the Union, and fully sustaining the course of Governor Hicks.

On the 11th of January a mass-meeting of the people of Districts No. 1, 10, and 15 assembled at Oakland, now Garrett County, at which William Tyler Duval presided, with Messrs. Wright, Thayer, John Stoyer, and Jonathan Hinebaugh, vice-presidents, and M. Fallon and Dr. J. Lee McComas, secretaries. Addresses were delivered by C. W. White and John Matthews, and strong Union resolutions adopted. On the 10th of January a large Union meeting was held at Lonaconing, at which John Douglas was chosen chairman, and John Love, secretary. Addresses were delivered by Dr. G. E. Porter, A. Chamberlin, and others, and resolutions adopted protesting against secession and favoring the Crittenden Compromise.

On the 12th of the same month a meeting was held by the citizens of Westernport District, Allegany Co., at the Barton Hotel, in the town of Barton. James S. Inskeep was called to the chair, and A. W. Tennant appointed secretary. A committee, consisting of J. W. Parker, William Armstrong, G. K. Berkybile, B. B. Dawson, and John Barnes, reported resolutions, which were adopted, condemning the course of South Carolina, and expressing a desire for the adoption of compromise measures.

advocated the Union upon the basis of the Constitution and a full recognition of the rights of the South."

On the same day a Union meeting was held at Grantsville, Allegany Co., at which Jacob Arendt presided, and Michael Durst acted as secretary. Resolutions condemning secession, and approving efforts for compromise, were reported by Capt. Henry Brown, Maj. William Dehaven, Elijah Fuller, Perry Shultz, and Elisha Durst, and were unanimously adopted.

On the same day a Union meeting was held by the citizens of Woodsboro' District, Frederick Co., at Christian Barrick's hotel, at which John D. Crumbaugh presided, with John M. Smith, of M., and Nicholas Fogle as vice-presidents, and J. Q. Stitely and John Fulton as secretaries; and another at Myersville, in the same county, with George Leatherman as president, Jacob Smith, of M., Jacob Young, of D., and John W. Bussard as vice-presidents, and Charles F. Hornevick as secretary.

On the 15th of January a meeting was held at Hancock, at which John J. Thomas presided, James D. Hork was appointed vice-president, and Robert Bridges, secretary, and conservative resolutions adopted.

On the 7th of February a Union meeting was held at Johnstown, in the Fourteenth Election District of Allegany County, at which nearly four hundred persons were present. John L. Hook was elected president, E. Hoye, J. M. Armstrong, and John McCleary, vice-presidents, and David Zosker, S. Switzer, and A. W. Cook, secretaries. Resolutions reported by James Dewitt, of J., Denton D. Brown, D. H. Friend, and John Brady were adopted, and addresses were made by C. W. White, of Oakland, John Matthews, and others.

On the 9th of February a Union meeting was held at Clear Spring, Washington Co., at which the Union flag was thrown to the breeze, and addresses delivered by Lewis P. and Samuel M. Fiery.

Another Union flag-raising occurred at Middletown on February 23d, at which ex-Governor Francis Thomas delivered an eloquent and impressive address of two hours' duration. Pursuant to a call, signed by more than five hundred persons, the citizens of Carroll County, without distinction of party, assembled in the court-house at Westminster on the 13th of April. Capt. William Ecker was called to the chair, Nimrod Gardner and Jacob Zacharias were chosen vice-presidents, and J. H. Christ and J. D. Hoppe were appointed secretaries. Addresses were delivered by Col. William P. Maulsby, of Frederick, and John E. Smith, of Westminster, and resolutions, reported by Joseph M. Parke, John E. Smith, Robert T. Shipley, Thomas S. Brown, and Jacob Campbell were adopted, condemning secession, opposing coercion, approving the course of Governor Hicks, and directing the appointment by the chairman of five delegates from each district to represent Carroll in the State Convention called by the friends of the Union in Frederick County, to meet in Baltimore on the 2d of May.

On January 30 (1861), the citizens of Blair's Valley, District No. 4, Washington County, held a Union meeting at John Feidt's school-house, at which John Bartel presided, and Samuel Bartel acted as secretary. An address was delivered by Dr. William Fiery.

On the 2d of February a Union meeting was held at Keedysville, Washington Co. Jacob H. Cost was called to the chair, Samuel Pry and Washington Kitzmiller were appointed vice-presidents, and Dr. H. G. Chritzman, secretary. Resolutions were reported by a committee, consisting of George C. Rohrer, chairman, Samuel Keedy, Frederick Wyand, Washington Snively, Jacob Lantz, Alfred N. Cost, and Martin Line, and an address was delivered by Capt. Elias Davis, of Boonsboro'.

The delegates to this convention were chosen at district meetings held at the usual polling-places on the 12th.

Dr. William Waters presided, assisted by a large number of vice-presidents and secretaries. A committee on business having been appointed, the chairman, Bradley T. Johnson, reported an address to the people of Maryland, declaring "that the rejection of the Crittenden Compromise by the Republicans of the United States Senate has destroyed all hope from that quarter of a settlement of the existing national troubles, and that in view of the fact that the Northern States are threatening on the incoming of Lincoln's administration to use coercion against Southern seceding States, it becomes the duty of Maryland, attached as she ever has been to the Union under the Constitution as adopted by our fathers, to speak and act as promptly and decidedly as her circumstances will permit for the preservation of peace between the sections and ultimate reconstruction and continuance of the Union."

The committee also reported the following resolutions:

"*Resolved*, By the people of Frederick County in convention assembled:

" That we are now as ever faithful to the Federal Union under the constitution as adopted by our fathers, and are willing and ready to make every effort and proper sacrifice to restore and perpetuate it.

"*Resolved*, That any attempt to preserve it by force will be vain and criminal; that coercion means war; that war means disunion, certain, inevitable, irreversible; and that we will stand by our Southern brethren in resisting it.

"*Resolved*, That we believe we pronounce the nearly unanimous feeling and intention of the people of Maryland that they will hold on to the Union while a hope of restoring it remains, but that when we shall be obliged to make a choice between the Southern Confederacy and the Northern States, we are then determined to go with the South, and stand by the South at all hazards and to the last extremity.

"*Resolved*, That there ought to be co-operation and consultation among the border slave States for the purpose of averting war, preserving peace, restoring the Union, if possible, by procuring a recognition of Southern rights, and failing in this, to take necessary steps to protect themselves.

"*Resolved*, That there ought to be a convention of the people of Maryland to be selected and meet at an early day for the purpose of conference among the people of the State as to what action might be necessary to protect their rights and honor.

"*Resolved*, That the president of this convention do appoint fourteen delegates to said convention to represent this county, and that the delegation have full power to fill vacancies.

" *Resolved*, That the president appoint a committee of twelve on correspondence and organization, who shall have full power to do whatever may be necessary to carry out the object of the address and resolutions adopted by said convention."

The address and resolutions were ably advocated by Mr. Johnson and ex-Governor Lowe, and, on motion of John A. Lynch, were unanimously adopted; whereupon Capt. Ritchie presented a series of resolutions, accompanied by an address in their favor, for the consideration of the convention. The resolutions were seconded by William Tyler, Jr., and unanimously adopted. They

"disclaimed any wish to foster sectionalism, expressed warm attachment to the Union as established by our fathers on the basis of the Constitution, but that in view of abolition aggressions and the mighty pecuniary interests of Maryland involved in the present controversy, we should be impoverished if appended to a Northern Confederacy; therefore our interests and sympathies are Southern in contradistinction to Northern, if the North, by refusing to acknowledge our rights and redress our wrongs, shall destroy the spirit of nationality and drive us to make such a discrimination. . . ."

The convention was subsequently addressed by ex-Governor Lowe, Bradley T. Johnson, J. M. Kilgour, J. A. Lynch, and Capt. John Ritchie. The president of the convention appointed the following gentlemen delegates to represent the county in the State Convention: William S. Bantz, Lewis M. Thomas, Henry Boteler, George Smith, Bradley T. Johnson, E. Louis Lowe, Daniel S. Biser, J. Mortimer Kilgour, H. W. Dorsey Waters, John Ritchie, Thomas G. Maynard, Jacob Summers, of J., Joseph P. McDevitt, and Dr. James T. Johnson. The following gentlemen were appointed a committee on organization and correspondence: John A. Lynch, chairman; George K. Shellman, Dr. William T. Tyler, Jr., O. Horsey, M. F. Sefton, George H. Haason, Thomas E. Pope, Thomas H. O'Neal, Charles E. Worthington, George Saylor, Richard Thomas, and Lingan Boteler.[1]

In pursuance of previous notice the people of Allegany County assembled in mass-meeting at Cumberland on the 17th of January. D. W. McCleary was appointed temporary chairman, and Thomas Devecmon, Alexander King, and John M. Buchanan were appointed to nominate permanent officers of the meeting. George A. Pearre was elected president, H. P. Tasker, Richard Fairall, John McLaughlin, H. B. Elbin, Hanson Willison, John Douglas, A. Chamberlain, Robert Bruce, George M. Blocher, Jesse Korns, Francis Mattingly, Thomas Whalen, John Cullen, and Moses Rawlings, vice-presidents, and J. J. McHenry and C. Slack, secretaries.

A committee, consisting of J. P. Roman, William Shaw, C. M. Thruston, J. M. Buchanan, William Walsh, John G. Lynn, Joseph Shriver, Nelson Beall, Samuel M. Semmes, and C. Slack, reported resolutions declaring "that while we feel that the Southern States of the Union have just right to complain of the growing hostility of the Northern people to their institutions, and of the enactment by various States of what is known as 'personal liberty laws,' which we believe to be in violation of the Constitution and of the sacred obligations which those States owe to our common country, and although Maryland, bordering on, and separated only by an imaginary line from, one of these States which have thus violated one of her obligations, has more cause than any of her sister States to complain of this unfriendly legislation, yet we believe that the proper remedies for these evils and aggressions is within the Union, and not outside of it." Patriotic addresses were delivered by ex-Governor Francis Thomas, Mr. Roman, and others.

The Legislature of South Carolina, which had been convened for the purpose of choosing Presidential electors, was still in session when the election returns made it certain that Mr. Lincoln had been elected President; and Governor Pickens sent them a message recommending that they should remain in permanent session, and take action to prepare the State for the threatened crisis. In response to this suggestion the Legislature passed an act calling a convention of delegates to assemble at Columbia on the 17th of December, 1860. The convention met at the time appointed, but adjourned on the following day to Charleston, where, on the 20th of December, it passed the ordinance of secession. Although the action of South Carolina created the most intense excitement in all parts of the country, efforts were still made in various quarters to prevent the impending conflict.

On the 10th of January, in accordance with an invitation from prominent citizens of Baltimore, a number of gentlemen of all shades and classes of opinion, representing all parts of the State, met in the Law Buildings in that city "for the purpose of conferring relative to the threatening condition of public affairs." This "Conference Convention" adopted resolutions expressing devotion to the Union, approving the Crittenden Compromise, and appointing Hon. R. B. Carmichael, Hon. William T. Goldsborough, and Messrs. Allen Bowie Davis, of Montgomery, John Contee, A. B. Hagner, and Ross Winans, to request the Governor to issue his proclamation calling on the people to vote on the last Monday in January for or against the calling of a convention.[2]

---

[1] On Jan. 21, 1861, the Union men of Frederick raised a splendid pole at the west end of Fourth Street, surmounted with a national flag, the streamer bearing the name of Governor Hicks. Col. Maulsby, F. J. Nelson, and J. S. Cooper made stirring speeches to an enthusiastic crowd.

[2] Among those invited to attend this conference from Washington County were James Wason, Andrew K. Syester, Joseph O'Neal, James Dixon Roman, Elias Davis, Jacob H. Grove,

The delegates present at this convention from Frederick County were Outerbridge Horsey and Benedict Boone; from Montgomery County, A. Bowie Davis and Col. Benjamin Shreeves; from Washington County, James Wason; from Allegany, John M. Buchanan and Horace Resley; from Carroll, George W. Manro, Micajah Rogers, and Somerset R. Waters.

On the 18th of February another State Conference Convention assembled in Baltimore, at which all the counties in Maryland were represented by gentlemen reflecting all shades of political opinion. This convention was held in pursuance of the recommendation of the Frederick County Convention of the 16th of January. The delegates were selected at informal meetings throughout the State on the 12th of February.

The delegates from Allegany County were J. H. Gordon, W. W. McKaig, J. P. Lyles, Samuel Smith, Richard Farrell, Patrick Murray, T. A. Hopkins, Thomas J. McKaig, Jr., Charles McBlair, Col. James M. Schley; from Carroll County, Dr. Jacob Showers, Thomas Tipton, and Henry Falkenstien; from Frederick County, William S. Bantz, Lewis M. Thomas, Henry Boteler, George Smith, Bradley T. Johnson, E. Louis Lowe, Daniel S. Biser, J. Mortimer Kilgour, H. W. Dorsey Waters, John Ritchie, George A. Hanson, Jacob Summers, of J., Joseph P. McDevitt, and Dr. James T. Johnson; from Montgomery County, E. B. Hutton, Warner Welsh, Samuel C. Vies, Lemuel Clements, Col. Robert T. Dade, and Francis Valchar; from Washington County, George Freaner, A. Rench, R. H. Alvey, A. K. Syester, L. T. Brien, Dr. Macgill, W. T. Hamilton, John Murdock, T. H. Crampton, J. Thompson Mason, G. E. Stonebreaker, and J. Beeler.

Col. James M. Schley, of Allegany County, was made secretary *pro tem.* of the convention, and Andrew Rench, of Washington County, elected one of the vice-presidents. After a session of two days the convention unanimously adopted an address "To the people of Maryland" and a set of resolutions, and adjourned to meet in Baltimore on the 12th of March following. On the day appointed the convention reassembled in Baltimore, and appointed Messrs. Walter Mitchell, E. F. Chambers, William Henry Norris, E. L. Lowe, of Frederick, Isaac D. Jones, and J. Hanson Thomas to wait upon the Virginia Convention and urge that body to recommend a conference of the Border States.

The suspense in which the country had been kept was finally dissipated by the terrible certainty that the crisis had at last come. The attack upon Fort Sumter on the 12th of April indicated the determined resolution of the people of the seceded States to maintain the position they had assumed, and the departure southward of the armament which sailed from New York proved the purpose of the administration to coerce the Gulf States into obedience. Thus began the war between the government of the United States and the people of the Confederate States.

The proclamation of President Lincoln on the 15th of April, calling for an army of seventy-five thousand men, created the most intense excitement in Maryland, as it showed that it was determined to make instant and desperate war upon the South, and the announcement of the Northern press that Maryland was to be held by the North only served to increase it. This excitement was greatly heightened by the riot in Baltimore on the 19th of April, and serious apprehensions were felt in all parts of the State that Baltimore would be attacked in revenge by the Federal troops that were gathering on the borders of Pennsylvania. The authorities of the city made hasty preparations for defense, and sent dispatches to various sections of Maryland asking for assistance. The aid of Southern sympathizers in Western Maryland was invoked, and on the 20th of April, the day after the riot, the following hand-bill was widely circulated throughout Frederick and other counties:

"LATEST NEWS!

"MARYLANDERS AROUSE!

"FREDERICK, Saturday, seven o'clock A.M., 1861.

"At twelve o'clock last night I received the following dispatch from Marshal Kane, of Baltimore, by telegraph to the Junction and express to Frederick:

"'Thank you for your offer. Bring your men by the first train, and we will arrange with the railroad afterwards. Streets red with Maryland blood! Send expresses over the mountains and valleys of Maryland and Virginia for their riflemen to come without delay. Fresh hordes will be down upon us tomorrow (the 20th). We will fight them, or whip them, or die.

"'GEO. P. KANE.'

William Dodge, James Nesbitt, Sr., Jacob Snively, James P. Mayherd, Otho Williams, and Dr. E. L. Boteler.

Among those invited from Frederick County were Hon. R. H. Marshall, Hon. Richard Potts, Wm. J. Ross, Col. John McPherson, L. J. Brengle, George R. Dennis, of Frederick City; Col. Thomas Hammond, Liberty; Benedict Boone, Petersville; Outerbridge Horsey, Burkettsville; D. W. Naill, Sam's Creek; Dr. N. O. Shipley and Jesse Wright, New Market; B. A. Cunningham, Buckeystown; and S. G. Cockey, Urbana. The conference was called by an informal meeting of citizens held at Barnum's Hotel on the 27th of December, 1860. The following gentlemen composed the committee appointed to invite citizens of influence from all the counties of the State to attend the convention: Wm. H. Norris, chairman; Ross Winans, Hon. John C. Legrand, L. P. Bayne, S. G. Wyman, James H. Stone, Austin Doll, Hon. Henry May, and Wm. T. Walters.

"All men who go with me will report themselves as soon as possible, providing themselves with such accoutrements and equipments as they can; double-barreled shot-guns and buckshot are efficient. They will assemble, after reporting themselves, at ten and a half o'clock, so as to go down in the eleven and a half train.

"BRADLEY T. JOHNSON."[1]

On the 22d of April, Governor Hicks, in compliance with the will of a majority of the people of the State, convened the Legislature, to meet in special session at Annapolis on the 26th, "to deliberate and consider of the condition of the State, and take such measures as in their wisdom they may deem fit to maintain peace, order, and security within our limits." The capital of the State being occupied by Federal troops, the Governor, on the 24th, selected Frederick City for the deliberations of the Assembly, which accordingly met at that place on the day appointed. Upon the opening of this session intense interest was felt as to the course which would be pursued in relation to secession. On the 27th, the second day of the session, the Senate settled this question in an "Address to the people of Maryland," in which it said, "We cannot but know that a large proportion of the citizens of Maryland have been induced to believe that there is a probability that our deliberations may result in the passage of some measure committing this State to secession. It is, therefore, our duty to declare that all such fears are without just foundation. *We know that we have no constitutional authority to take such action. You need not fear that there is a possibility that we will do so.*" This address was unanimously adopted. The House of Delegates two days afterwards, on the 29th, by a ballot of fifty-three to twelve, declared that they did not possess the power to pass an ordinance of secession. On the 10th of May the Committee on Federal Relations in the House of Delegates, consisting of Messrs. S. Teackle Wallis, chairman; J. H. Gordon, S. W. Goldsborough, James T. Briscoe, and Barnes Compton, presented a report and set of resolutions " in regard to the calling of a sovereign convention," which met the hearty approval of an overwhelming majority of the members of that body. In the House the vote stood, ayes 43, nays 12; and in the Senate, ayes 11, nays 3. On the 13th both Houses adopted a resolution providing for a committee of eight members (four from each House) to visit the President of the United States and the President of the Southern Confederacy. The committee to visit Jefferson Davis were instructed to convey the assurance that Maryland sympathized with the Confederate States, and that the people of Maryland were enlisted with their whole hearts on the side of reconciliation and peace.[2]

On the 2d of May, at the evening session of the Senate, Coleman Yellott, of Baltimore, reported the following bill to provide for the safety and peace of the people of Maryland:

"*Whereas*, The present extraordinary state of the country and the disturbed condition of the people demand that prompt and efficient measures should be adopted by the General Assembly of Maryland to secure the safety and peace of the people, and to avoid the evils and horrors of civil war; therefore

" *Be it enacted by the General Assembly of Maryland*, That Ezekiel F. Chambers, of Kent County; John V. L. McMahon and Thomas Winans, of Baltimore City; Thomas G. Pratt, of Anne Arundel County; Enoch Louis Lowe, of Frederick County; and Walter Mitchell, of Charles County, together with the Governor of the State of Maryland for the time being, or whoever

---

[1] On Dec. 29, 1860, a new military company was organized in Frederick, under the title of Frederick Mounted Dragoons. It numbered over fifty-five, and was officered as follows: Captain, Bradley T. Johnson; First Lieutenant, J. Oliver Meyers; Second Lieutenant, William Smith, Jr.; Third Lieutenant, Alfred Heming; Cornet, Daniel McGramvine; First Orderly Sergeant, B. Henry Schley; Second Orderly Sergeant, William T. Preston; Third Orderly Sergeant, George Gallion; Fourth Orderly Sergeant, John C. Fleming; First Corporal, F. Marion Getzendanner; Second Corporal, John H. Sin; Third Corporal, Robert Q. Lewis; Fourth Corporal, Charles Miller.

Jan. 10, 1861, the United Guards of Frederick elected the following officers: Captain, Gabriel Beckley; First Lieutenant, Frederick Keefer (promoted); Second Lieutenant, Philip Buddey; Third Lieutenant, Henry J. Norris; Ensign, William Bradshaw; First Sergeant, Michael Blumenaner (promoted); Second Sergeant, N. J. Wilson; Third Sergeant, J. Milton McDaniel (promoted); Fourth Sergeant, Joshua T. Dayhoff (promoted); Fifth Color Sergeant, Hezekiah Bailey; First Corporal, Charles E. Albaugh (promoted); Second Corporal, Charles H. Abbot (promoted); Third Corporal, Thomas A. McDaniel (promoted); Fourth Corporal, Charles Bishop (promoted); Fifth Corporal, John E. Haller; Secretary, Edward Y. Goldsborough; Treasurer, Henry J. Norris.

[2] On the 4th of May an election was held in Washington County for a member of the House of Delegates. There was but one candidate in the field, Mr. Fiery, the nominee of the Union party. The vote in the several election districts was as follows:

	Fiery.	Whole Number Votes in 1860.
Sharpsburg	374	438
Williamsport	235	436
Hagerstown	685	1027
Clear Spring	346	444
Hancock	216	302
Boonsboro'	435	573
Cavetown	313	415
Pleasant Valley	181	212
Leitersburg	224	273
Funkstown	154	336
Sandy Hook	125	158
Tilghmanton	200	244
Conococheague	202	197
Ringgold	66	144
Indian Spring	196	228
	3952	5427

The total vote polled was 4084, there having been 136 scattered votes cast in the several districts, most of which were for the Union without Mr. Fiery's name.

may be lawfully acting in the capacity, be and they are hereby appointed a Board of Public Safety, in and for the State of Maryland, a majority of whom may act in any case wherein said Board may be authorized to act under the provisions of this or any supplemental act; and

"*Be it enacted*, That the Board of Public Safety so constituted and appointed shall have full power and authority to provide for the better organization, arming, and regulation of the militia of this State, and may remove and appoint any officer of the militia above the rank of captain, and may commission any such appointee in the name and under the Great Seal of the State of Maryland; and the said Board of Public Safety shall have full power to provide for the protection, safety, peace, and defense of the State; and

"*Be it enacted*, That if any vacancy shall occur in the said Board, it may be filled by a majority of the remaining members of said Board, and the person or persons so appointed shall hold office until one month after the commencement of the next regular session of the General Assembly of Maryland; provided, nevertheless, in the event of a sovereign convention being elected by the voters of Maryland, in pursuance of a call of the present or of any succeeding General Assembly, said Board of Public Safety shall be subject to such sovereign convention, which convention shall have power to remove any or all of the members of said Board of Public Safety; and

"*Be it enacted*, That the said Board of Public Safety shall report any or all of their acts and proceedings to the General Assembly of Maryland, whenever required so to do by order or resolution adopted by a majority of all the members of each branch thereof, and the members of said Board of Public Safety, before entering upon the duties of their office, shall take and subscribe the following oath or affirmation:

"That in any and every appointment or removal to be made by the Board of Public Safety, under the authority given to them by law, I will in no case and under no pretext appoint or remove any officer of the militia or other person for or on account of his political opinions, or for any other cause or reason than the fitness or unfitness of such person in my best judgment for the place to which he shall be appointed, or from which he shall be removed; and

"*Be it enacted*, That the members of said Board, except the Governor of this State, shall be entitled to compensation at the rate of —— dollars per month, payable monthly; and

"*Be it enacted*, That the sum of —— dollars, as a contingent fund, be and the same is hereby appropriated to carry out the provisions of this law; and that all orders drawn by the Board of Public Safety on the Treasurer of Maryland shall be paid out of said appropriation, such orders so drawn to be attested by the signatures of at least two members of said Board; and

"*Be it enacted*, That this law shall take effect from and after the date of its passage; and

"*Be it enacted*, That Sections 1, 2, 12, and 13 of Article 42, relating to the Governor, of the Code of Public General Laws, and Sections 14, 32, 33, 34, 35, 36, 37, 38, 39, 40, 43, 55, 61, 71, 96, 97, 99, 103, 107, 111, and 112 of Article 63, relating to the militia, of the Code of Public General Laws, in so far as the same are in any manner inconsistent with the provisions of this act, be and the same are hereby repealed."

The bill was strenuously opposed by Messrs. Smith and Kimmell, but was ordered to a second reading by a vote of ayes 14, nays 8, as follows: Ayes, Messrs. Brooke, Blackiston, Duvall, Franklin, Dashiell, Graham, Gardner, Hackart, Lynch, McKaig, Townsend, Watkins, Whittaker, Yellott; nays, Messrs. Bradley, Goldsborough, of Talbot, Goldsborough, of Dorchester, Miles, Nuttle, Smith, Stone, Kimmell. On the 4th, on motion of Senator Yellott, the bill was referred back to the Committee on Federal Relations. In the mean time many public meetings were held in Western Maryland and in other sections of the State protesting against the adoption of a measure which was regarded as simply a substitute for an ordinance of secession. On the 3d of May the citizens of District No. 7, of Washington County, assembled at Smithsburg, and adopted a memorial to the Legislature protesting against Senator Yellott's bill as unnecessary and unconstitutional. William Adams presided, J. W. Barkdoll was appointed secretary, and the resolutions of remonstrance were drafted by Dr. E. Bishop, William B. McAtee, A. C. Hildebrand, Dr. T. E. Bishop, and J. L. Vogle. A committee of ten, consisting of George Pearson, Philip Oswald, Adam Vogle, John Fessler, W. H. Eackle, Samuel Houser, Jeremiah Besore, John W. Barkdoll, John N. Shank, and Samuel Welty, were appointed to obtain signatures to the memorial. On the same evening a meeting of similar character was held at Clear Spring, at which Jonathan Nesbitt presided, with Dr. H. F. Berry as vice-president, and Dr. J. Rufus Smith as secretary, and resolutions were adopted declaring "that the Legislature of Maryland has been convened contrary to law; that we ignore the present assembly at Frederick as the Legislature of Maryland; that we regard it as illegally convened, illegally constituted, and engaged in revolutionary and despotic measures without a parallel in the annals of American legislation; that as true and loyal citizens of the State of Maryland we are not bound to obey the decisions of a body who have no legal constitutional existence, but that we are subserving the best interests of the State and constitution in resisting their pretensions; that the Committee of Public Safety about to be established by the *so-called* Legislature is an arbitrary and despotic power, not warranted by the condition of the country, but a usurpation of authority extremely dangerous to our liberties, if not to our lives and fortunes, bidding us beware of these despotic officials as the Robespierres, Marats, and Dantons of another kindred revolution." On the 6th an immense meeting was held at Cumberland to protest against the creation of the "Board of Public Safety," and Col. Charles M. Thruston was chosen president, with John Gephart, Benjamin Kegg, A. M. L. Bush, John B. Widener, Joseph Shriver, John Everett, Alpheus Beall, William Armbuster, S. M. Semmes, James J. McHenry, Lewis Smith, Samuel Luman, John Kolb, Jonathan W. Magruder, Andrew Gouder, John B. H. Campbell, William

Evans, Robert Bruce, J. H. Young, John B. Hays, Alexander King, Richard D. Johnson, and Joseph Hughes as vice-presidents, and John H. Shaw, George White, Samuel Shipley, and George Deetz as secretaries. Resolutions were adopted "solemnly protesting against the lawless and desperate attempt now making in the Legislature of this State to inaugurate a military despotism by the enactment of the bill to create a committee of public safety." The Conditional Union men also held a public meeting in Cumberland, and resolved that if the general government failed to grant the Southern States certain guarantees it would become the bounden duty of Maryland to quit the Federal Union. A resolution offered by Daniel Blocher to postpone such proceedings until the conclusion of the Peace Congress then in session was followed by lengthy and violent speeches, and the meeting adjourned in the wildest disorder and confusion. All manner of opinions were entertained by the people, and nearly every shade of thought found a representative in the city, but from the very first a majority of its citizens were for the preservation of the Union under any circumstances and at all hazards.

On the 4th of May a meeting was held by the citizens of Lonaconing, and resolutions adopted condemning the action of the Legislature "in attempting to create a (so-called) committee of safety in defiance of all constitutional law." John Douglass presided, and the committee on resolutions consisted of John S. Coombs, G. E. Porter, A. Chamberlin, Alexander Shaw, Henry Hennekauf, John Bell, Andrew Speir, and Robert Cowen. A petition circulated at the meeting protesting against the passage of the bill received three hundred and fifty signatures. Great excitement was created in Frederick City by the proposed measure, and some of its opponents went so far as to threaten personal violence to Senator Yellott, and to call upon the "freemen" to "arouse and strike for their liberties." Awed perhaps by these popular demonstrations, the friends of the bill deemed it best not to press it further.[1]

On the 14th of May the Legislature adjourned until the 4th of June. When it reassembled the two committees appointed to visit the President of the United States and the President of the Confederate States made their reports. Messrs. John B. Brooke, G. W. Goldsborough, George H. Morgan, and Barnes Compton, the committee appointed to visit President Lincoln, and "secure, if possible, through the instrumentality of Maryland, peace to our distracted country, and, if failing in that, then a cessation of hostilities on the part of the armies of the Federal and Confederate troops until Congress should express its opinion on the subject which now agitates the people," submitted a report, in which they said, "These purposes being defeated in the movement of the Federal troops on Virginia, and an active commencement of hostilities, we have considered our mission as ended, and therefore have not felt authorized, on the part of the sovereign State of Maryland, to present a request which has in advance been repudiated." At the same time Messrs. Thomas J. McKaig, Coleman Yellott, and Charles A. Harding, the commissioners appointed to visit Jefferson Davis at Montgomery, Ala., presented their report, accompanied by a letter from Mr. Davis, dated May 25th, expressing his gratification at hearing that the State of Maryland was enlisted on the side of peace and reconciliation, and avowing that the Confederate government would readily entertain any proposition from the government of the United States looking to a peaceful settlement of the existing difficulties. On the 25th of June the Legislature adjourned until the 30th of July.

Previous to its adjournment, however, on the 22d of June, the Legislature passed a resolution requesting the Governor "to return to the armories of the State the arms which have been removed by his order from said armories and deposited in Fort McHenry, or placed in the hands of ununiformed companies or associations of individuals, and that he return to all regularly organized and uniformed volunteer companies of the State the arms reclaimed from them, or either of them, by his order." This resolution was immediately denounced by the friends of the Union as an attempt to disarm legal citizens and strengthen the enemies of the government, and many of the military organizations at which it was supposed to be aimed promptly expressed their determination to resist its enforcement.

On the 24th of June, two days after the passage of the resolution, the "Home Guards" of Frederick assembled at their armory and adopted the following resolutions:

"WHEREAS, The Legislature of Maryland, now in session in this city, have passed a resolution requesting the Governor to return to the armories of the State the arms which have been 'placed in the hands of ununiformed companies,' and

"WHEREAS, The Home Guards of Frederick City, an ununiformed company, having been regularly organized and mustered into the Sixteenth Regiment Maryland Militia, in accordance with law, would naturally come under the purview of that resolution, having probably excited the ire of this body by their

---

[1] On the 7th of May the Home Guard of Frederick City were presented with a national flag by the ladies of that place. Hon. Reverdy Johnson delivered a patriotic address, to which earnest responses were made by Col. William P. Maulsby, on behalf of the Brengle Guards, and ex-Senator Cooper.

honest zeal and careful efforts in protecting the town from the villanous designs of incendiaries and unprincipled scoundrels who have been found prowling our streets at night; and

"WHEREAS, The present Legislature, by its high-handed legislation, unparalleled in the history of any civilized nation, have legalized riot, robbery, and bloodshed in the city of Baltimore by passing a certain law, presented by a citizen of Baltimore, one T. Parkin Scott, now unjustly and shamefully holding a seat in the Legislature of this State, and thereby taught us a lesson which must be looked upon with indignation and horror by all good citizens; and

"WHEREAS, We, the members of the Home Guard of Frederick, have organized the company for the purpose of protecting life and property from mobs and rioters, and have obtained our arms legally from the proper military authorities of the State;

"*Therefore, be it unanimously Resolved*, by the Home Guard of Frederick, That we will resist the enforcement of said order or requisition, if made on us, *at all hazards and to the death.*

"*Resolved*, That all the companies of Home Guards in this county be requested to concur in the above determination.

"*Resolved*, That the foregoing preamble and resolutions be signed by the officers of this meeting, and published in all the newspapers of the county favorable to the UNION AND TRIUMPH OF THE STARS AND STRIPES.

"LIEUT. WM. D. REESE, *Chairman.*
"J. A. STEINER, *Secretary.*"

The Home Guards of Middletown, through their commanding officers, expressed their determination not to submit in the following emphatic language:

"WHEREAS, The secession majority of the Maryland Legislature, in their attempts to usurp the military power of the State and divest the Governor of his constitutional authority, have passed an act to disarm the Home Guards, organized and enrolled under the militia laws of the State,

"Therefore, the undersigned, captains of the Middletown Home Guards, in the name and on the behalf of the companies under their respective commands, solemnly protest against this legislative usurpation and invasion of their rights as citizens, and pledge themselves, by all that freemen hold dear, to oppose to the death any and every attempt to take away their arms, under the pretended authority of the act referred to.

"And if any person or persons, under the pretended authority of the legislative usurpers, feel disposed to carry their illegal act into effect, we invite them to commence operations on the Middletown Home Guards.

"JACOB RUDY, *Captain of Company A.*
"STEPHEN R. BOWLUS, *Captain of Company B.*
"HORATIO ZITTLE, *Captain of Company C.*
"HANSON T. RUDY, *Captain of Company D.*"

On the 28th of June the Home Guards of Williamsport adopted a resolution declaring that "they stood ready to co-operate with the Home Guards of Frederick and Middletown, and all other loyal citizens of our good State of Maryland, in resisting to the death any and all attempts which may be made to enforce the illegal and despotic act of the late traitorous Legislature, organized and sitting unconstitutionally at Frederick City, designed to disarm the loyal citizens of the State, and hand them over, helpless and unprotected, like our suffering neigh... of Virginia, to a ferocious military despotism, under the treasonable plea of the execrably false doctrine of State's Rights, justifying secession and rebellion." The resolution was signed by William B. Kennedy, captain; S. Holenberger, first lieutenant; J. B. Masters, second lieutenant; and D. Anderson, third lieutenant. In response to these resolutions, Col. Ward H. Lamon addressed a letter to Capt. Kennedy and the officers of the Home Guards, "pledging his influence to sustain the loyal citizens of Maryland in their resolution to support the Federal government against all treasonable attempts to deprive them of their rights," and "assuring the loyal citizens of Maryland that the whole power of the Federal government will be exerted to sustain them in their rights."

On the 30th of July the Legislature reassembled and continued in session until the 7th of August, when it adjourned until the 17th of September. In the mean time the State had passed into the control of the Federal government, and orders had been issued for the arrest of the secession members of the General Assembly. When the 17th of September arrived it found but few members of the Lower House in Frederick, and at one o'clock, the hour for assembling, there were but three senators in the city, Messrs. Bradley, Nuttle, and Kimmel, all of whom were Union men. Determined to prevent a session of the Legislature, they refused to enter the Senate chamber, and met for consultation at the reading-room opposite to the hall in which the General Assembly was to assemble. They had previously notified the clerk of the Senate that they proposed to consult as to their course, and would communicate their joint determination in half an hour. At the expiration of that time notice was conveyed to the clerk that there would be no meeting of the Senate, when they were informed that he had called the roll in the empty chamber, and gone through the formality of announcing that, "there being no quorum present, the Senate stands adjourned until one o'clock on Wednesday."

The Union members of the House of Delegates had also come to a similar determination to do all in their power to prevent the meeting of that body, but the opposition members who were in the city moving towards the hall, they went also, and at ten o'clock Thomas H. Moore, the reading clerk, went through the formality of calling the House to order, and proceeded to call the roll. The members present were Messrs. Salmon, Kessler, Gordon, Maccubbin, Jones, of Talbot, S...aughn, Durant, McIntire, Long, Keene, and Mills, being seven of the Opposition to four Union members. Messrs. Naill and Fiery were in the city, but declined to go to the hall. There were but four responses, and Mr. Long immediately moved that the House adjourn until noon on Wednesday.

The refusal of the Senate to convene, it was argued, had virtually annulled any legal assemblage of the Legislature, though the clerks declared their intention to continue to call the roll daily until a quorum should appear, denying the right of less than a quorum to adjourn the body.

A few minutes after the formality of opening the Legislature had thus been gone through with by the clerks, and they had dispersed, small squads of the Wisconsin regiment, each under charge of an officer, were observed moving through the city, all taking different directions towards the outskirts. Thus in about a half-hour a cordon of armed pickets circled the entire town, with instructions to allow no one to pass out without a written permit from a member of Gen. Banks' staff, who had been appointed provost-marshal. This had scarcely been accomplished before a squad of police-officers from Baltimore, consisting of Lieut. Carmichael, Sergt. Wallis, Sergt. Watt, and Officer West, accompanied by a military escort of the Third Wisconsin Regiment, Col. T. H. Ruger, which had been encamped for some days near the railroad depot, commenced to search the city for parties they were ordered to arrest. In the course of the 17th and 18th the following arrests were made:

Milton Y. Kidd, clerk of the House.

Thomas H. Moore, reading clerk of House.

William Kilgour, clerk of Senate.

S. P. Cormack, assistant clerk of Senate.

John N. Brewer, reading clerk of Senate.

William E. Salmon, of Frederick, House of Delegates.

Thomas J. Claggett, of Frederick, House of Delegates.

Andrew Kessler, of Frederick, House of Delegates.

Josiah H. Gordon, of Allegany, House of Delegates.

Richard C. Maccubbin, of Anne Arundel, House of Delegates.

D. Bernard Mills, of Carroll County, House of Delegates.

William R. Miller, of Cecil, House of Delegates.

Clark J. Durant, St. Mary's, House of Delegates.

J. Lawrence Jones, Talbot, House of Delegates.

The following citizens were also arrested: John W. Elkins and John Hagan, with E. A. Hanson, William Mason, William Hanson, and his two sons.

E. Riley, editor of the *Annapolis Republican* and printer of the House, was also arrested.

The sudden embargo on egress from the city, without previous notice, soon occasioned considerable excitement. The pickets were stationed on every road and across every field, and no one could leave without a pass. One gentleman who lived about ten steps beyond the picket-guard was compelled to return to town, and all manner of vehicles soon commenced to move towards the headquarters of Col. Ruger. Among others, Col. Maulsby's carriage was turned back for a pass. The passes were given freely to those who could prove their loyalty, and in order to facilitate operations Gen. Shriver attended at headquarters, at the request of citizens, to identify the applicants.

The prisoners were all taken to the barracks as fast as arrested, and when Dr. Jones, of Talbot, was arrested on Wednesday morning, the guards around the town were withdrawn, and the ancient city of Frederick again fell back into the control of the civil authorities.

There were various rumors in circulation as to the purposes of the majority of the Legislature, had that body been permitted to assemble. "It is, however, known," says a contemporary account, "that letters have been intercepted by the First Maryland Regiment, Col. Kenly, looking to a collusion between the Legislature and Gen. Johnston, as to his crossing the Potomac with a Confederate army and occupying Frederick, and the simultaneous passage of a secession ordinance under the protection of Confederate bayonets. It is also asserted that when one of the Frederick delegates was arrested a similar letter from Virginia was found in his possession." On Tuesday evening (the 17th), immediately after the arrest of the officers of the Legislature, nearly thirty thousand copies of the report of Mr. Wallis on Federal Relations were seized by order of the provost-marshal and taken to the camp of the Wisconsin regiment, where they furnished the materials for a grand conflagration. At the preceding session of the Legislature fifty thousand copies of this document were ordered to be printed, and when seized were in readiness for mailing.

At noon (Wednesday, the 18th) the train brought up Messrs. Miller, of Cecil, McCoy, of Harford, Bayless, of Harford, and Lawson, of Somerset, and immediately on its arrival Mr. Miller was arrested and conveyed to the guard-house. The others being loyal men, were welcomed by their Union friends, and returned in the afternoon with their colleagues to Baltimore on their way home. Mr. Steake, of Washington County, also arrived Wednesday morning, and approved of the action of his Union colleagues.

The afternoon train, which usually left Frederick at one o'clock, was detained until three to bring down the prisoners, the delay being permitted for the purpose of giving the officers of the Legislature an opportunity to obtain their discharge by taking the oath of allegiance, which was administered to E. Riley, Milton Y. Kidd, Thomas H. Moore, William Kilgour, and S. P. Cormack, who were then released. John N. Brewer, reading clerk of the Senate, refused to take the oath, and was sent off on the train with the members of the House, who were not allowed to take it. Mr. Marshall, postmaster of the House, was arrested just as the cars were about to start, and marched back to headquarters to take the oath. At three o'clock on Wednesday, the 18th, the prisoners were brought from the barracks and marched under guard of a company of Wisconsin military to the cars, and an armed guard seated with each of them, the remainder of the car being filled with soldiers. The arrested parties were at first confined in Fort McHenry, and were finally sent to Fort Lafayette with those arrested in Baltimore.

The following correspondence, with the indorsements, captured in Frederick in 1862 by Gen. "Stonewall" Jackson from Gen. N. P. Banks, contains the secret history of this memorable transaction:

"WAR DEPARTMENT, Sept. 11, 1861.

"GENERAL,—The passage of an act of secession by the Legislature of Maryland must be prevented. If necessary, all or any part of the members must be arrested. Exercise your own judgment as to the time and manner, but do the work effectively.

"Very respectfully your obedient servant,
"SIMON CAMERON, *Secretary of War.*
"MAJ.-GEN. N. P. BANKS,
"Commanding near Darnestown, Md."

Legislative matters.

"HEADQUARTERS ARMY OF THE POTOMAC,
"WASHINGTON, Sept. 12, 1861.

"*Confidential*—MAJ.-GEN. N. P. BANKS, U.S.A.:

"GENERAL,—After full consultation with the President, Secretaries of State, War, etc., it has been decided to effect the operation proposed for the 17th. Arrangements have been made to have a government steamer at Annapolis to receive the prisoners and carry them to their destination. Some four or five of the chief men in the affair are to be arrested to-day. When they meet on the 17th, you will please have everything prepared to arrest the whole party, and be sure that none escape. It is understood that you arranged with Gen. Dix and Governor Seward the *modus operandi*. It has been intimated to me that the meeting might take place on the 14th; please be prepared. I would be glad to have you advise me frequently of your arrangements in regard to this very important matter. If it is successfully carried out it will go far towards breaking the backbone of the Rebellion. It would probably be well to have a special train quietly prepared to take the prisoners to Annapolis. I leave this exceedingly important affair to your tact and discretion, and have but one thing to impress upon you—the absolute necessity of secrecy and success.

"With the highest regard, I am, my dear general, your sincere friend,
"GEO. B. MCCLELLAN, *Maj.-Gen. U.S.A.*"

Copeland's report, Legislature, September 16th.

"FREDERICK, Sept. 16, 1861.
"MAJ.-GEN. BANKS:

"DEAR SIR,—I find that there is some probability of no quorum,—this is particularly Gen. S.'s opinion. He thinks the whole thing is crushed by the arrest. But there is reason to believe he is mistaken. Noakes is here, and says there are at least twenty-five in town; that they have spread the rumor that there will be no quorum in order to lull attention, but that there will be enough to meet and adjourn to a place outside of the town. He saw to-night four carriages and a party of men come in one of the back roads and go to a drinking-saloon, where they were loud and deep in threats and imprecations; they left the tavern and came into the town and separated, where he could not tell, as he was on foot. He has got no evidence of any messenger from Virginia,—thinks no one is here. But there is one bad thing: Gen. Dix has sent his son here, and a major, and the provost-marshal of B——, and party of police to make arrests. I have tried to get them sent back early in the first train to-morrow, accompanied at least as far as Monocacy by Mr. Dix. He does not like to get up and go at that time. It is a mistake. Gen. S. has no particular information and wants to shield some personal friends,—would like, *for the future,* to make it easy for some men. I think that I shall get a plan arranged to take a number at any rate. The arrests in B. have terrified them very much, and all profess obedience there. None of the members from the Eastern Shore have come up yet, which inclines me to wait for day after to-morrow. I regret your letters to Col. R. did not put the matter more under my especial control, as he is rather disinclined to be as careful and patient as is desirable, and I do not feel authorized to direct. If anything occurs to you send by messenger to me, care of Col. R. I am at the U. S. Hotel.

"In haste, very respectfully,
"R. M. COPELAND.

"Young Dix tells me his errand was to meet you, and give you a list of names of men to be arrested,—nothing more. He will give me the paper to-morrow and await orders. You will get this at six,—a messenger can return in three hours."

Copy of letter of instructions concerning Legislature.
"Important and confidential.
"HEADQUARTERS, CAMP NEAR DARNESTOWN,
"16th September.
"LT.-COL. RUGER, Commanding Third Wisconsin Reg't.
"On special service at Frederick:

"SIR,—The Legislature of Maryland is appointed to meet in special session to-morrow, Tuesday, September 17th. It is not impossible that the members or a portion of them may be deterred from meeting there, on account of certain arrests recently made in Baltimore. It is also quite possible that on the first day of meeting the attendance of members may be small. Of the facts as to this matter, I shall see that you are well informed as they transpire. It becomes necessary that any meeting of this Legislature, at any place or time, shall be prevented. You will hold yourself and your command in readiness to arrest the members of both Houses. A list of such as you are to detain will be inclosed to you herewith; among them are to be especially included the presiding officers of the two Houses, secretaries, clerks, and all subordinate officers. *Let the arrests be certain, and allow no chance of failure.* The arrests should be made while they are in session, I think. You will, upon receipt of this, quietly examine the premises. I am informed that escape will be impossible if the entrance to the building be held by you; of that you will judge upon examination. If no session is held, you will arrest such members as can be found in Frederick. The process of arrest should be to enter both Houses at the same time, announcing that they were arrested by orders of the Government; command them to remain, as they are subject to your orders. Any resistance will be forcibly suppressed, whatever the consequences. Upon the arrests being effected, the members that are to be detained will be placed on board a special train for Annapolis, where a steamer will await them. Everything in the execution of these orders is confided to your secrecy, discretion, and promptness."

Copeland's report, Maryland Legislature, September 17th.

"FREDERICK, MD., Sept. 17, 1861.

"DEAR SIR,—The arrests in Baltimore have entirely broken down and disorganized the secession element in the Legislature, and much less than a quorum have assembled. Of the members present the larger number are Union men, who, encouraged by our presence, are here to face the enemy. I have had pickets set since noon in all the roads leading to this place, with orders to let no one go out unless down to Frederick Junction, with a trusty man to see who should come up and make arrangements for them,—only seven came. We find that there are only about six bad specimens here, but that there is a chance that more may arrive. We have spotted the house where these men board, and shall arrest them to-night. I have let the train go to B—— with a sergeant, who will come up on the train, and will spot and, if needs be, arrest any man who tries to leave the train at Monocacy. To-day some persons left at the station below M—— to drive here in a carriage. As yet the Legislature has not convened; when it does I shall have the trap sprung on them. Your letter has just arrived. I will attend to it as you wish. You have by this time learned of the arrests in Baltimore yesterday, which has alarmed all. I sent Mr. Dix and the policemen away on the train and went myself, as we were surrounded by a crowd in which were ten of the worst men. They now think we are all gone. I and two of the policemen returned afoot. Noakes is on the watch to find out where every man lives, and I do not think we can fail to get some; but the worst men are too wary to come here. I shall send this to you just as soon as I can find a messenger, and shall telegraph when the arrest is completed. Gen. S. and all his friends believe that nothing can be effected, as those whom we shall take are the least conspicuous. I shall arrest the clerks of the two Houses, who are mentioned as particularly venomous. Nothing more occurs to me now. I will add whatever happens later.

"Truly, your obedient servant,

"R. MORRIS COPELAND."

"To MAJ.-GEN. N. P. BANKS:

"It is now 5 P.M. We have arrested twelve of the worst men, and are progressing very well. We shall get the whole eighteen I think, and if any come in on the train to-night we will bag them too. Gen. S. is invaluable. We have been besieged for passes,—every avenue being blocked. It has taken three men all the time to write and inquire into the merits of the case. No news from Virginia; all seems quiet as far as we can learn. The House met to-day; was called to order by the clerk; four members present, and adjourned until to-morrow at noon.

"Respectfully,

"R. M. C."

Copeland's report of arrest of members of the Maryland Legislature, September 18th:

"FREDERICK, MD., Sept. 18, 1861.

"To MAJ.-GEN. BANKS, Darnestown:

"SIR,—I have just telegraphed to Gen. Dix that we have seized seven members of the House of a very bitter character, and four officers, clerks, etc., who are intensely bitter, and are said to have been very forward, and to have kept some of the weaker men up to the work. Several arrests made of violent or resisting persons, whom I shall let go after the others are gone. I shall send four men at least to Gen. Dix, at Baltimore, who are very bad men. I have advised Col. Ruger to send to Sharpsburg landing to seize five hundred sacks salt which are waiting for the Southerners to come and take them; they have tried twice to do it. We have also heard of some arms, which the colonel will look up. There is a very bitter man here, a Mr. Sinn, who is currently reported by Gen. Shriver and others to be the medium of communication with the Southern Confederacy. The names of the members are B. S. Salmon, R. C. Maccubin, J. H. Gordon, C. J. Durant, Thomas Claggett, Andrew Kessler, and Bernard Mills. We shall get T. Lawrence Jones. The officers of the Legislature, J. N. Brewer, chief clerk, Senate; Thos. Moore, reading do.; Samuel Penrose, Jr., assistant; N. Kilgore, reading do.; Milton Kidd, chief of the House. Mr. Jones is taken; Edward Houser, citizen; Riley (very bad), printer to the House; John Hogan (very bad), citizen; Joseph Elkins, do.; Mr. Mason, folder to the House. We shall leave here for headquarters this afternoon. The arrests were nearly all seized by the policemen.

"I am yours respectfully,

"R. MORRIS COPELAND, *Aide-de-Camp.*

"Mr. Macubbin is a person whom I should recommend you to set at large if he takes the oath, which I have no doubt he will. He is brother-in-law to Gen. Hammond, and a man much respected; also a man of rather timid nature, and greatly troubled by his arrest. Gen. Shriver has been very active for us, and is very earnest that we should let him go on these terms. If you can do it, it will be well to telegraph to Annapolis to have the oath tendered and reelase him. I should do it under my instructions, only that Col. Ruger thinks he has no authority to allow any man on the list any liberty.

"R. M. C."

United States Military Telegraph.

"To MAJ.-GEN. N. P. BANKS:

"*The rations have gone.*

"R. M. COPELAND."

"FREDERICK, MD., September, 1861.

"To MAJ.-GEN. DIX, Commanding Fort McHenry, Md.:

"SIR,—The member from Annapolis City, Mr. McCubbin, has many qualifications which recommend him to you as a person to be released on his taking the oath. I have communicated the facts to Maj.-Gen. Banks, and have urged him to telegraph to Annapolis that he may be released on taking the oath. I will communicate further in my report. Will you attend to this matter?

"I am yours respectfully,

"R. MORRIS COPELAND,

"*A. A. to Maj.-Gen. Banks.*

"The bearer of this communication, Gen. Hammond, is well known as true to the Government.

"R. M. C."

U. S. Military Telegraph, received from Washington Sept. 20, 1861.

"To MAJ.-GEN. BANKS:

"Have you any more of our friends to send from Frederick to Annapolis? Please answer at once. I wish to know on account of ordering off boat.

"MAJ.-GEN. MCCLELLAN."

"HEADQUARTERS, CAMP NEAR DARNESTOWN,
"Sept. 20, 1861.
"MAJ.-GEN. MCCLELLAN, Commanding Army of Potomac:
"HON. W. H. SEWARD, Secretary of State:

"SIR,—I have the honor to report, in obedience to the orders of the Secretary of War and the general commanding the Army of the Potomac, transmitted to me by letter of the 12th instant, that all the members of the Maryland Legislature assembled at Frederick City on the 17th instant known or suspected to be disloyal in their relations to the government have been arrested. The opening of the session was attended chiefly by Union men, and after rigid examination but nine secession members were found in the city. These were arrested, with the clerk of the Senate, and sent to Annapolis, according to my orders, on the 18th instant, under guard, and safely lodged on board a government steamer in waiting for them. Of their destination thence I had no direction. The names of the parties thus arrested and disposed of were as follows, viz.: B. F. Salmon, Frederick; William R. Miller, Cecil County; J. H. Gordon, Allegany County; Lawrence Jones, Talbot County; Bernard Mills, Carroll County; R. C. McCubbin, Annapolis; Thomas Claggett, Frederick; Clark J. Durant, St. Mary's County; Andrew Kessler, Jr., Frederick; J. N. Brewer, chief clerk of the Senate. No meeting of the Senate occurred. But three senators were in town, and these were Union men. Three subordinate officers of the Senate, the chief clerk and printer of the House, and one or two citizens were also arrested, but released after the departure of the members for Annapolis upon taking the oath of allegiance. Milton Kidd, clerk of the House, is in the last stages of consumption, beyond the power of doing harm, and was released upon taking the oath and making a solemn declaration to act no further with the Legislature under any circumstances whatever. This course was adopted upon the urgent solicitation of the Union members of the Legislature present. The same parties desired the release of R. C. McCubbin, of Annapolis, upon the same conditions. I telegraphed to the commander of the steamer that he might be left at Annapolis under sufficient guard until the orders of the government could be ascertained. Col. Ruger, Third Wisconsin Regiment, my aide-de-camp, and a detachment of police rendered efficient aid. Sufficient information was obtained as to preparation for board, etc., to lead to the belief that the attendance of members would have been large had not the arrests of some of the leaders been made at Baltimore on Saturday and Monday before the day of meeting. I regret the attempt at Frederick was not more successful.

"*Classification of the Members of the Legislature.*—A classification of the members of the Legislature is given, in which the numbers from one to four attached to their names indicates the intensity of secession principles. Among them we find the following bad cases: R. M. Denison, 4; J. W. Dennis, 4; John B. Brown, 4; G. W. Goldsborough, 4; Barnes Compton, 3; H. M. Warfield, 3; T. Parkin Scott, 3; S. Teackle Wallis, 3; W. H. Legg, 3; G. Kilborn, 3. In the Senate: Franklin Whittaker, 4; Coleman Yellott, 4; Thomas J. McKaig, 3; Teagle Townshend, 3.

"*Suggestions of Arrest—Altered Complexion of the Legislature.*—I suggest the arrest of the following members, J. A. D.: Senate: Anne Arundel, Thomas Franklin; Cecil, John J. Heckart; Charles, John F. Gardiner; Dorchester, Charles F. Goldsborough; Harford, Franklin Whittaker; Howard, John S. Watkins; Kent, David C. Blackston; Prince George's, John B. Brooke; St. Mary's, Oscar Miles. McKaig, of Allegany, and Lynch, of Baltimore City, is in Richmond. Teagle Townshend, of Worcester, should not be arrested—great rascal. House: Allegany, Josiah H. Gordon and William B. Bernard; Anne Arundel, B. Allen Welch, McCubbin E. G. Kilbourn; Calvert, James T. Briscoe and Benjamin Parran; Caroline, G. W. Goldsborough; Carroll, Bernard Mills; Cecil, James M. Maxwell and W. Miller; Charles, Barnes Compton; Frederick, Andrew Kessler, Jr., Thomas J. Claggett, N. E. Salmon, and John A. Johnson; Howard, John R. Brown; Kent, Philip F. Raisin; Prince George's, E. Pliny Bryan, Richard Wooten, Ethan A. Jones; Montgomery, Howard Griffith; Queen Anne, William H. Legg, William L. Sharkey; St. Mary's, Clark J. Durant, George H. Morgan; Somerset, James W. Dennis; Talbot, Alexander Chaplain, J. Lawrence Jones; Washington, Martin Eakle, John C. Brining; Worcester, George W. Landing. Wallis, Pitt, Scott, Sangston, Morfit, Winans, Thomas, Harrison, and Warfield, of Baltimore City, and Dennison and Quinlan, of Baltimore County, are in custody.

"The list I marked with you has been carefully revised and corrected by the Legislative journals, so that the propriety of the foregoing selection is unquestionable.

"If these arrests are made the Senate will stand thus:

Secessionists arrested 11
" absent from the State 1
" at large 3
Union men at large 6
Doubtful men at large 1
—
Total 22

"The House will stand thus:
Secessionists arrested 40
" at large 10
Union men at large 15
Doubtful men at large 8
—
Total .... 73"

The following correspondence relating to the State election of November, 1861, also captured from Gen. N. P. Banks by Gen. T. J. Jackson at the same time, will be found of interest in this connection:

"CUSTOM-HOUSE, COLLECTOR'S OFFICE,
"BALTIMORE, Oct. 17, 1861.

"DEAR GENL.—Your note in reply to my request was received this morning.

"I owe you many thanks for the prompt order given to Major Gould and the trouble you have taken to furnish me with so speedy an acknowledgment.

"So far as we are able to perceive there will be no regular or serious opposition to the Union State ticket.

"The peace men will struggle to maintain their supremacy in one branch of the Legislature (Senate), and to prevent which it will be necessary for us to carry the doubtful and hardly-contested counties of Queen Anne's, Calvert, and Prince George. To this end we shall devote all our energies until the day of election.

"The bold and vigorous policy inaugurated by yourself whilst in command here has been productive of the most salutary results. We no longer hear the mutterings of secession upon the corners of the streets. As one decided step has followed another, the mutterings have grown fainter each day, until secession, if it has not become extinct, has at least been subdued and thoroughly humiliated.

"I have no fears that the result of the election in November will not be a complete vindication of the loyalty and patriotic devotion of Maryland to the Union and Constitution as made by our Fathers.

"Once again accept my thanks for your kindness, and sincerely your friend,
"HENRY W. HOFFMAN.
"MAJ.-GEN. N. P. BANKS, U.S.A."

Gov. Hicks in relation to election. Received November 1st, answered at once by telegraph.

"STATE { State arms. } MARYLAND.

"EXECUTIVE CHAMBER,
"ANNAPOLIS, Oct. 26, 1861.

"MAJ.-GEN. N. P. BANKS, U.S.A.:

"MY DEAR SIR,—I should have written at an earlier day, but delayed for return of Geo. W. Howard, who had been sent down the Potomac by Maj.-Gen. McClellan, and soon after his (H.'s) return the papers represented you to have gone with your forces into Virginia. Indeed I dislike to occupy a moment of your closely occupied time, and write now only because I feel it due from me in view of your uniform courtesy and kindness to me, of which I shall always entertain most grateful recollections. You will excuse me, I am sure, for suggesting the importance of looking closely to Maryland until our election is over, 6th November.

"The Confederates will endeavor to effect something by which to operate on our elections. You may suppose, my dear sir, that I am anxious to have a killing majority rolled up against secessionism. Not only am I and is Maryland deeply interested, but the Government is greatly concerned. Will it be possible to have Col. Kenly's regiment placed near Baltimore temporarily so as to save their vote? I hope so. I have the honor to be with very great respect,

"Your ob't servt.,
"THO. H. HICKS."

Order from Secretary of War and Gen. McClellan relative to the voting of Maryland troops.

"HEADQUARTERS ARMY OF THE POTOMAC,
"WASHINGTON, Oct. 29, 1861.

"MAJ.-GEN. N. P. BANKS, Commanding, etc.:

"GENERAL,—Pursuant to directions from the Secretary of War of the 28th instant, of which I inclose a copy, the major-general commanding directs that such soldiers of the First, Second, and Third Regiments of Maryland Volunteers as may be within the limits of your command receive furloughs for such a length of time as will enable them to reach the place wherein they may be entitled to vote by the 6th of November. Wherever it may be necessary, in order to facilitate the presence of these men at their place of voting, to furnish them transportation, it may be furnished. It is desired that the most liberal and prompt circulation may be given to these instructions in order to secure with certainty the carrying into effect the design proposed. Sufficient time is to be allowed the soldiers thus furloughed to enable them to return after voting, without exceeding the term fixed for their furlough; but a prompt return is desired.

"Whenever it may be necessary, the absent soldiers should be replaced for the time by other troops.

"The general commanding desires that the receipt of this communication be acknowledged at once.

"I have the honor to be, general,
"Very respectfully,
"Your obedient servant,
"J. WILLIAMS,
"Asst. Adjt.-Genl."

"WAR DEPARTMENT,
"WASHINGTON, Oct. 28, 1861.

"MAJ.-GEN. MCCLELLAN, Commanding:

"SIR,—In order to have a full vote in Maryland at the coming election, Wednesday, November 6th, so that the legal voters may decide by their ballots all public questions, you are hereby directed to grant three days' furlough to the soldiers of the First, Second, and Third Regiments of Maryland Volunteers, all to return to duty on Thursday, November 7th.

"Very respec'y,
(Signed) "SIMON CAMERON,
"Sec'y of War."

"HEADQUARTERS ARMY OF THE POTOMAC,
"WASHINGTON, Oct. 29, 1861.
"Official. J. WILLIAMS,
"A. A. G."

Instructions from R. B. Marcy, chief of staff, concerning Maryland elections.

"HEADQUARTERS ARMY OF THE POTOMAC,
"WASHINGTON, Oct. 29, 1861.

"GENERAL,—There is an apprehension among Union citizens in many parts of Maryland of an attempt at interference with their rights of suffrage by disunion citizens on the occasion of the election to take place on the 6th of November next. In order to prevent this, the major-general commanding directs that you send detachments of a sufficient number of men to the different points in your vicinity where the elections are to be held to protect the Union voters, and to see that no disunionists are allowed to intimidate them, or in any way to interfere with their rights.

"He also desires you to arrest and hold in confinement till after the election all disunionists who are known to have returned from Virginia recently and who show themselves at the polls, and to guard effectually against any invasion of the peace and order of the elections. For the purpose of carrying out these instructions you are authorized to suspend the 'habeas corpus.' Gen. Stone has received similar instructions to these. You will please confer with him as to the particular points that each shall take the control of.

"I am, sir, very respectfully,
"Your ob't serv't,
"R. B. MARCY, *Chief of Staff.*

"To MAJ.-GEN. N. P. BANKS,
"Commanding division, Muddy Branch, Md."

Gen. Shriver, Frederick, on election districts in Frederick County. No answer.

"FREDERICK, Nov. 1, 1861.

"GEN. N. P. BANKS:

"MY DEAR SIR,—On my return home to-night your favor of the 30th ult. was handed me by Capt. Stone.

"In one county there are two or three districts in which our friends apprehend interference by disloyal men on election-day. I have consulted with some of our most reliable friends, and we all concur in the opinion that a body of men thrown into Frederick on Monday and Tuesday next, and then divided into squads and placed in the different districts of the county on the day of election, will not only prevent disloyal men from interfering with and overawing our friends, but will have the additional effect of keeping such men from the polls. Cavalry would answer better than infantry, as our county is divided into seventeen districts, and some of them twenty and twenty-five miles off in a mountainous country. I would also suggest that whatever force is sent here be placed under command of Capt. Stone, who seems fully to understand the duty to be performed. In the First Maryland Regiment, commanded by Col. Kenly, there are at least fifty men entitled to their votes in our county,—they are principally to be found in the company commanded by Capt. B. H. Schley,—we should be gratified to have these men sent home to the election.

"With great respect, I am very truly yours,
"EDWD. SHRIVER."

Maj. Stone, provost-marshal. Election at Frederick. Received 7th November.

"United States Military Telegraph. Received Nov. 7, 1861.
"From Frederick, Md.

"To MAJ.-GEN. N. P. BANKS:

"The election passed off quietly. Had all the rum-shops closed. Union majority in the city seven hundred (700), Union majority in the county twenty-seven hundred (2700), much exceeding the most sanguine expectations. Every district in the county gone Union.

"H. B. STONE, *Provost-Marshal.*
"39, 78. Paid."

Report from Col. J. W. Geary concerning elections, etc.

"ENCAMPMENT TWENTY-EIGHTH REGIMENT P. V.
"POINT OF ROCKS, Nov. 8, 1861.

"CAPT. R. MORRIS COPELAND,
"Acting Assistant Adjutant-General:

"SIR,—Previous to the election a number of enemies to the Union in this State preliminated schemes for disturbing the peace of the various precincts. I had several of the most prominent actors in this, among whom was a candidate for senator, arrested before election, and held until to-day. I had detailments from various companies of my regiment, with proper officers, stationed in Sandy Hook, Petersville, Jefferson, Urbana, New Market, Buckeystown, Frederick City, and other places where the polls were held. Owing to the presence of the troops everything progressed quietly, and I am happy to report a Union victory in every place within my jurisdiction. Some of the Maryland troops visited the polls with their muskets, which I directed to be given up, to be returned at the expiration of their furloughs, mostly dating until to-day. A few days previous to election, bodies of cavalry, equipped, varying in numbers from fifty to several hundred, were visible in and about Harper's Ferry, and several encampments were seen in the direction of Charlestown. They gave every evidence of the intention of a combined attack upon our force in that neighborhood. During Monday their action was openly insolent, and their preparations and activity indicated that an attack was imminent. Dragoons rode about the town, and women were seen leaving with bundles for the direction of Bolivar and Charlestown.

"A cannon was also brought into the town.

"A few shots were fired across the river at a group of my officers standing near the canal bridge, and my upper pickets, nearly opposite the Virginia Ore-Banks, were fired upon by about twenty-five cavalry, but fortunately without effect.

"I had issued orders not to engage them until their movements would assume a shape by which we could find them in a force guaranteeing a battle, meanwhile deluding them into an idea of our incapacity to defend ourselves.

"Upon receipt of the news of the gathering of their forces, on Monday evening, with a detachment of picked men and a gun of the battery, I went to Harper's Ferry, and before daylight had the gun placed in a position on Maryland Heights to command both Harper's Ferry and Bolivar, and then posted my detachment at intervals, concealed, opposite the Virginia Ore-Banks, where numbers of rebel cavalry were seen for days previous. A most vigilant watch was kept from all these points, but the town was perfectly deserted and quiet, and only a small body of men appeared opposite the infantry post, who were put to flight by a few shots.

"The presence of my men encouraged a great number of Union men to vote, who otherwise would not have done so through fear of molestation.

"Harper's Ferry is now avoided by the rebels, either from change of intention or fear of demonstrations being made against them. On the evening of my departure a number of the enemy were seen half-way up the mountain opposite Point of Rocks. I had one of the guns taken down, and fired several shells among them, which put them to flight without an answering shot.

"I have reliable authority from Leesburg that many of the troops at that point have been called off in the direction of Lewinsville, at or near which place it is the intention of the rebels to give battle to our troops. The same authority informs me that a large number of troops have been withdrawn from Manassas and sent to Charleston, under the personal command of Beauregard. I have information that there is but one regiment at Leesburg. If it is desirable to take the place, this would be a favorable opportunity to do so.

"Very respectfully, your obedient servant,

"JNO. W. GEARY,
"*Col. Twenty-eighth Regiment Pennsylvania Volunteers, commanding post.*"

CHAPTER XI.

THE FIRST YEAR OF THE CIVIL WAR.

Organizing Maryland Troops in Defense of the Union—Picket Firing on the Potomac—Evacuation of Harper's Ferry—Invasion of Virginia—Battle of Leesburg—The Federal Defeat at Manassas—Jackson's Brilliant Campaign in the Valley—Marylanders in the Union Army—Devotion of the People to the Union—Enrolling Officers.

WHILE these events in the civil and political history of the State were in progress, war between the sections had been recognized as inevitable, and military preparations actively commenced on both sides. Owing to the unsettled condition of affairs in Maryland, Governor Hicks did not comply with President Lincoln's first call for troops until the 14th of May, when he issued a proclamation "calling for four regiments of volunteers for three months, to serve within the limits of Maryland or for the defense of the capital of the United States, and not to serve beyond the limits aforesaid." In consequence of the delay and the short time they were to serve, the government did not accept any of the three months' men offered by the State, but on the 3d of May the President called for forty-two thousand and thirty-four volunteers, to serve for three years, and a large number who had enlisted under the first call immediately joined companies that were enlisting under the second.[1]

---

[1] Immediately after the President's call was issued, John R. Kenly, then a prominent member of the Baltimore bar, and a number of other citizens of the State, proceeded to organize military companies for the support of the Federal government. By the 14th of May two full regiments were organized and placed under the command of Brig.-Gen. Kenly (Maryland Militia). In consequence of the short term for which they were called upon to serve they were declined by the government, and on the 16th of May, 1861, they were disbanded by Gen. Kenly, with his thanks for "taking up arms for the maintenance of the Union."

Under this call Hon. James Cooper, of Frederick City, was appointed by the War Department a brigadier-general, and assigned to the duty of raising and organizing the volunteers of the State. Recruiting offices were immediately opened in Baltimore and elsewhere, and vigorous measures instituted for the enlistment of men. In a short time the First Maryland Regiment was organized, and Col. John R. Kenly, a gallant soldier of the Mexican war, was appointed its commander, and at once proceeded to put it into condition for active service. Company H of this regiment, commanded by Capt. Benjamin H. Schley, was formed by the consolidation of two detachments of about equal strength,—one raised by Capt. Schley at Frederick, and the other by Capt. William H. Taylor at Baltimore. On Sunday evening, July 7th, the First took its departure from Baltimore, under command of Lieut.-Col. Dushane, accompanied by Gen. Cooper, and proceeded by rail to Frederick City. A march of eight miles over the Western turnpike on the afternoon of the 8th brought the regiment to its first bivouac, near Middletown. The next night, after a march of sixteen miles, it bivouacked on Antietam Creek, beyond Boonsboro', and on the 10th marched to Downsville, Washington Co., where it encamped. Col. Kenly resumed command of the regiment at this place on the 16th of July, and on the 23d the First moved its camp to Williamsport, three miles distant. About this time several of the companies were detached and stationed at different points along the Potomac, from Williamsport to the mouth of the Antietam, to guard the fords and ferries of the river; and although some of these posts were several times attacked, especially that opposite Shepherdstown, Va., they were maintained, and no successful crossing by the Confederates was effected while the First Maryland remained at these points.

In the mean time other regiments and "home guards" were organized in various sections of the State, and were soon in active service.

The Southern sympathizers were not idle; finding that they could not succeed in securing the secession of the State, they determined that Maryland should not be wholly unrepresented in the Confederate armies. Large numbers of volunteers flocked to the Southern colors, and were enrolled in the Confederate service, among whom were Capt. Bradley T. Johnson, of Frederick, who, on the 8th of May, 1861, joined the Confederate forces at Harper's Ferry with a company which he had raised in his native county.[1]

On the 23d of May a sharp skirmish occurred at McCoy's Ferry, on the Potomac, about a mile and a half above the Four Locks. The Virginia side of the river was guarded by the Virginians from Camp Allen, opposite Williamsport, under Col. Allen, and the Maryland side by the home guard of Clear Spring. The Virginians were anxious to capture the ferry-boat, carry it to the opposite side of the river, and thus secure possession of the ferry. On the 22d of May, Col. Allen commanded some of his men to take the ferry-boat that night at any risk, and the attempt was made about two o'clock Thursday morning. The Clear Spring Guards had retired to a house in the vicinity, but had been there only a few minutes when one of them thought he heard the sound of oars or of setting-poles. He ran out, and saw a half-dozen men in the ferry-boat making for the Virginia shore. He gave the alarm, and the guards sprang to their arms and rushed out to the bank. They hailed the Confederates three times but received no answer, when the command was given to fire. The Confederate troops in the boat returned the fire. Again the guards fired, and again it was returned, when the Confederates, thinking it was getting a little too hot, jumped into a skiff which they had with them and made for Virginia, leaving the ferry-boat to float down the river.

The morning fog was rising on the river, and the guards could not see how much damage was done; but it is supposed that one of the Confederate soldiers was killed and another wounded, as one of their number seemed to be missing, and when they left the skiff one was heard to say to a comrade, "Jim, can you get out without help?" Not one of the guards was injured. The boat was recaptured and taken to a place of safety on the Maryland side of the Potomac. Another skirmish occurred at Lemon's Ferry on the 1st of June. Camp Allen was broken up on the last day of May, but two companies of Confederates were left to guard the ferry. These retired on the same night, and on Saturday morning a company of Confederate cavalry and a company of riflemen were sent with orders to sink the ferry-boat.

The cavalry left about nine o'clock, and the rifle company (Capt. Patrick's) proceeded to sink the boat. They had accomplished their design before it was discovered on the opposite shore. As soon as it

---

[1] On the following day a body of thirty-seven men under Capt. Henry Wellmore, another of nineteen under Capt. Price, and another of about eighty under Capt. C. C. Edelin, passed through Frederick on their way to join the Southern forces at Harper's Ferry. On the 13th, about one o'clock at night, a train of two or three cars, filled with Federal troops from the Relay House, arrived in Frederick. The officer in charge, in company with several citizens of Frederick, visited the barracks and reconnoitred the position, but returned soon after to the Relay House with his command, which did not leave the cars.

was discovered that they had sunk the boat, an officer of the Williamsport Guards stepped to the shore and commanded the Virginians to leave the boat in twenty minutes, or he would fire upon them. The twenty minutes passed; the fire was opened and returned. Capt. Patrick sent a dispatch for aid. A brisk fire was kept up, the balls whistling over the men's heads, till some seventy shots were exchanged. A few splinters were knocked from the bridge and trees, but no one was injured. The Union men saw that they were wasting ammunition, of which they had but little, and the firing ceased. Soon the Virginia cavalry were seen coming back down the turnpike at full speed. It was known that the Confederates had artillery and thousands of soldiers at no great distance. Soon after dinner the Virginia soldiers were seen to enter the ferry-boat and lighten her; soon she floated again. Some soldiers were put on board, and also three of the ferryman's sons, and they began to make their way down the river. It was evident that they intended to take her around to Falling Waters. The presence of the ferryman's three boys in the boat, who had been pressed into the service, prevented the Federals from firing into her; they were unwilling to kill them, so the boat passed on. She had proceeded about a quarter of a mile, when a squad of the guards started in pursuit. The Virginia soldiers ran the boat against the Virginia bank and fled to the woods near by. Under a flag of truce (in the form of a man stripped to the skin and swimming the river), a message was sent to them that they could take the boat no farther except at their peril. Reinforcements were then sent down to the Virginia soldiers with axes to cut the boat in pieces, when they were again informed that the first man who entered the boat with an axe in his hand would be shot dead on the spot. Under these circumstances the Confederate captain deemed it advisable to take the boat back to the ferry and sink her there.[1]

On the 24th of May the first forward movement of the Federal forces from Washington took place under the command of Gen. J. K. F. Mansfield. The entire force, consisting of thirteen thousand men, proceeded to cross the Potomac, and took possession of Alexandria and all the heights which commanded Washington on the Virginia side of the river. The Confederates having occupied Harper's Ferry in large force, under command of Gen. Joseph E. Johnston, the Federals commenced operations to recapture it. With this view a large force was collected at Chambersburg, Pa., under Maj.-Gen. W. H. Keim. On the 2d of June, Maj.-Gen. Robert Patterson took command of this force, and soon after, with an army of ten or twelve thousand men, made a forward movement by way of Hagerstown towards Harper's Ferry, while another force moved up the north bank of the Potomac from the District of Columbia. Gen. Patterson's command reached Hagerstown on Saturday, the 15th of June, the First Pennsylvania Regiment, under Col. Yohe, forming the advance, and being followed by the Second Pennsylvania, under Col. Stambaugh, the Seventh Regiment, Col. Irwin, the Eighth Regiment, Col. Emley, accompanied by Gen. Williams and staff, the Tenth Regiment, Col. Meredith, and the Scott Legion, Col. Gray. At the same time a large force, under Gen. Cadwallader, passed down the Greencastle turnpike to Williamsport. Col. Yohe's, with the Third and Twenty-fourth Pennsylvania Regiments, encamped on the lands of Mr. Hunter, a short distance below Funkstown; the Fourteenth and Fifteenth Pennsylvania Regiments, Col. Starkweather's Wisconsin Regiment, the Eleventh Pennsylvania, and the Fourth Connecticut encamped in a field on the Baltimore turnpike belonging to Jonathan Hager, about a mile and a half from Hagerstown; while another portion of the army encamped near the College of St. James, where it remained only one night, moving the next day to Williamsport for the purpose of crossing the Potomac. Near the Franklin Railroad, just beyond the suburbs of Hagerstown, Capt. Doubleday and his men of Fort Sumter renown encamped, and attracted quite a large share of public attention. Maj.-Gen. Patterson and staff occupied the Hagerstown Female Seminary as the headquarters of the army. The court hall at Hagerstown was occupied as a guard-house, and the market-house and town hall were used for the storage of munitions and provisions. The Hagerstown Academy and the county hall were subsequently converted into hospitals. The large field belonging to the estate of Michael Hammond, on the southwestern suburbs of Hagerstown, was used as a sort of wagon-yard by the government. Speaking of these first stirring scenes of the war, a contemporaneous account says, "Our town and surrounding neighborhood resemble a vast military camp. Soldiers are seen in every street, and guards on almost every corner. Companies are constantly parading, and strains of music are wafted to the ear on every breeze. On the Sabbath long lines of bristling bayonets glittered in our streets, and the peals of church-bells blended with the stirring notes of the drum and fife, presenting a striking

---

[1] On the 5th of June, —— Rench, a young man about twenty-three years of age, visited Williamsport on business, and becoming involved in an altercation with some members of the Home Guard, fired upon them, when they returned his fire, killing him instantly.

contrast with the order and quietude which usually mark the holy day in our midst." The troops were hospitably entertained by the citizens of Hagerstown, and many substantial attentions were shown both officers and privates.[1]

As Gen. Patterson's forces approached Harper's Ferry the Confederates evacuated the Maryland Heights, which they had for some time occupied, and where they had some artillery mounted, and fell back to their main body on the Virginia side of the river. On the 15th of June, Gen. Johnston, after deciding that Harper's Ferry was untenable, evacuated it and retreated towards Winchester. Before leaving the place he destroyed the fine bridge over the Potomac, the government buildings, and forty-six locomotives and over three hundred cars, valued at five hundred thousand dollars, belonging to the Baltimore and Ohio Railroad. The railroad bridge at Martinsburg was also destroyed.[2]

Col. Wallace with the Eleventh Indiana Regiment was stationed at Cumberland, and on the 18th of June intelligence was received that a force of from three to five thousand Confederate troops were in Romney, and were about to march upon Cumberland. Intense excitement was created by the news, the Continentals and Union Home Guards were called to arms, dispatches were sent to the various military organizations of the county for aid, and every preparation was made for defense. A military company from Frostburg, under Maj. F. A. Mason, another under Col. Petrie, from Wellersburg, Pa., and others from Grantsville, Centreville, and Bedford, responded promptly to the call, but the report proved to be false, and there was no necessity for their services.[3]

During the latter part of June the first division of Gen. Patterson's army, with the exception of Col. Burnside's Rhode Island regiment and battery, and the Second and Third United States Infantry, which had been sent to Washington, was quartered on the banks of the Potomac, at Williamsport and its vicinity. Of the second division, which had encamped near Funkstown and Hagerstown, Col. Yohe's regiment was at Frederick, and Col. Owens', Col. Johnson's, and Col. Oakford's regiments, commanded by Brig.-Gen. Negley, were at Sharpsburg, where they had been sent to occupy the Maryland Heights opposite the Ferry. Company F, Fourth United States Artillery, with six batteries, commanded by Capt. Perkins, was encamped on the Agricultural Fairgrounds, near Hagerstown. On the 20th of June, Maj. Doubleday, who had also been encamped near Hagerstown, marched to Williamsport, where he placed his batteries in position to command the opposite side of the river.[4]

On the 21st of June the following special order, No. 42, was issued by Col. Burnside from Camp Sprague, the headquarters of the First Regiment of Rhode Island Volunteers:

"The colonel commanding the First Regiment Rhode Island Volunteers would hereby acknowledge the kindness and generosity of the citizens of Greencastle, Pa., Williamsport, Hagerstown, Boonsboro, and Middletown, Md., as shown by the very cordial reception given to the command. Particular thanks are due to the citizens of Frederick City, Md., for the hearty welcome which they extended, and the lavish hospitality which they dispensed, to the regiment. Their good will is fully reciprocated, and their kindness will long be gratefully remembered."

---

[1] A. H. Hager, of Hagerstown, equipped his colored servant, Dan Fox, eighteen years of age, and made a present of his services to Col. W. H. Irwin, of the Seventh Pennsylvania Regiment, for an indefinite period, or as long as the war should last.

[2] On the arrival of the Rhode Island regiment in Frederick City, in June, 1861, an attempt was made to mob the office of the *Herald*, which was supposed to sympathize with the South. The prompt intervention of Col. Burnside and other officers saved the office from destruction.

[3] Cumberland was very much exposed to the dashes of the enterprising Confederate commands that operated in the counties south of it. Many were the panics produced by movements of Imboden, Jenkins, Neil, and others, to say nothing of those of "Stonewall" Jackson still farther south. For some reason or other the military authorities never considered the city of sufficient importance to be held at much hazard, but to be evacuated whenever anything like danger impended.

On the 26th of August, 1861, the bells of the city commenced ringing in lively metre. Soon the old cry of "The Confederates are coming!" was heard. At the intersection of Baltimore and George Street, in the northern part of the city, Capt. H. Clay Hagen, of the Third West Virginia Regiment (Federal), formed his company of some seventy-five men in line of battle, and awaited the approach of the enemy.

A reconnoitring party was sent out to carefully feel the enemy, and ascertain his force and whereabouts. The supposed Confederates were to be seen on the hill beyond Col. J. G. Lynn's residence manœuvring; still they came no closer. The reconnoitring party came back and reported that the supposed Confederates were about fifty German Catholic priests (who were then located at Sts. Peter and Paul's Churches) *taking their daily exercise!* The harmless priests thereafter selected quite another direction for their recreation and innocent manœuvring.—*Lowdermilk.*

[4] On the 19th of June, Hon. Richard H. Alvey, of Hagerstown, and now one of the associate judges of the Maryland Court of Appeals, was arrested by order of Gen. Patterson; on the 12th of July, John W. Baughman, of Frederick, was arrested by the Federal authorities; on the 26th of August, Senator Thomas J. McKaig, of Allegany, and other prominent citizens of the county, were arrested.

On the 2d of July, Silas Hines, a citizen of Rohrersville, Washington Co., was shot and killed by a Federal picket near Keedysville. Mr. Hines was challenged by the sentinel, but either did not hear the summons or did not understand it, and, failing to halt, was fired upon and killed.

On the 2d of July, Maj.-Gen. Patterson's division was put in motion with a view of proceeding to Martinsburg. Early in the morning the advance column, consisting of Capt. McMullen's Rangers, the Philadelphia City Troop, Col. Thomas' United States Cavalry, Maj. Perkins' battery, and the First Wisconsin and Eleventh Pennsylvania Regiments, commanded by Cols. Starkweather and Jarrett, the whole accompanied by Maj.-Gen. Patterson and staff, crossed the Potomac at Williamsport, and moved in the direction of Martinsburg, leaving the main body to follow by easy stages. About four and a half miles from the river an engagement occurred between the Federal advance and a body of Confederates, which continued for about half an hour, the latter finally abandoning the field.

On the following day the Federal forces entered and occupied Martinsburg.

In the mean time the army in front of Washington was organized, and preparations were made for an advance against the Confederate forces collected at Manassas. Accordingly, on the 16th of July a forward movement was begun, and the "Grand Army" in four divisions, under the command of Maj.-Gen. Irwin McDowell, took up its line of march for Fairfax and Manassas. McDowell's force consisted of about sixty thousand men. On the 21st of July the opposing forces met, and fought the celebrated battle of Bull Run, or Manassas. The result of this engagement naturally produced the greatest consternation among the friends of the Union in Western Maryland, and as soon as the first feeling of alarm had subsided active measures were taken to provide for the general defense. Immediately after the battle Maj.-Gen. George B. McClellan, who had been operating in Western Virginia, was assigned to the command of the Federal forces in and around Washington and Northeastern Virginia. Upon taking command of the army Gen. McClellan at once proceeded to strengthen the defenses of Washington, and the small remnant of Patterson's army was removed to the Maryland side of the Potomac, and reinforced from time to time by new troops. Maj.-Gen. N. P. Banks was assigned to this division of the army, which was posted in the vicinity of Poolesville, with picket-lines extending along the banks of the Potomac from Harper's Ferry to Georgetown. The Federal forces also occupied the Maryland shore of the Potomac below Washington, the lines being gradually extended towards the mouth of the river. In front of this line the Confederates were posted in strong force, constantly threatening an attack, and making movements which required vigilant watching and counter-movements on the part of the Federal forces. Frequent skirmishes occurred between the pickets and reconnoitring and foraging parties of the two armies, with various success and more or less loss.

On the 19th of July, Hon. Francis Thomas was authorized to provide for the organization of four regiments of the loyal citizens, resident on both sides of the Potomac River from the Monocacy to the western boundary of Maryland, for the protection of the canal, and of the property and persons of loyal citizens of the neighborhood, "to be stationed in the vicinity whilst in the service." A few days later, on the 26th of July, the government accepted Mr. Thomas' offer of four companies of cavalry, one to be attached to each of the four regiments of infantry. This force was designated as the Potomac Home Brigade, and was rapidly organized after the battle of Manassas.

In August the President appointed Wm. P. Maulsbury colonel, Chas. E. Trail lieutenant-colonel, and Lewis P. Fiery, of Washington County, major of the First Regiment of the Potomac Home Brigade, seven companies of which were mustered into service and encamped in August near the turnpike, about a mile and a half north of Frederick.

The organization of the brigade proceeded with equal spirit and energy in other parts of Western Maryland, and by the 17th of August eight companies had been raised in Allegany, and others were being rapidly formed.[1]

Although the Home Brigade was not intended to be employed outside of the State, it did not insist upon its exemption from foreign duty, and frequently rendered good service outside of the sphere assigned it. An opportunity of proving their mettle was soon presented, and the result showed that the Home Brigade was composed of no mere holiday soldiers. On the 23d of August, Capt. James D. Roberts, with forty men of Company B of the Second Infantry, marched from Oldtown, Md., to Springfield, Va., where a sharp skirmish took place with some fifty or sixty of the enemy, in which the company behaved with great gallantry and steadiness, three of the command being slightly wounded. These were the first Marylanders to shed their blood for the Union. Three

---

[1] On the 23d of August, Mr. Thomas arrived in Cumberland, and addressed a meeting of the citizens on the subject of the formation of a regiment for the Potomac Home Brigade. In the course of his address he was interrupted by a Southern sympathizer, who was attacked and beaten by the crowd, which then proceeded to wreck the office of the *Alleganian*, the editor of which had interposed in behalf of the person assaulted. The crowd also visited the residence of Senator McKaig, breaking the windows, etc. On the following morning an attempt was made about seven miles west of Cumberland to wreck the train on which Mr. Thomas was traveling, and shots were fired into it, but fortunately without effect.

days later another detachment of the same company was sent over the river to prevent the destruction of the property of a loyal citizen named Croagan, and attacked and pursued the enemy to Blue's House, where they made their escape.

On the 20th of September a skirmish occurred between the Confederates at Shepherdstown and the Federal forces on the Maryland side of the river, under Capt. David Souders. Capt. Souders planted two pieces of artillery opposite Shepherdstown and fired several shots into the place. His fire was answered on the following morning by the Confederates, but the citizens fearing the Federal forces would be reinforced and the town destroyed, requested a cessation of the firing. Capt. Wilson, of the First Maryland, crossed the river and had an interview with the mayor of the town, when it was agreed that no more firing should take place at that point by either party.[1]

No engagement of any magnitude took place in the fall of 1861 until the battle of Ball's Bluff, or Leesburg, which occurred on the 21st of October. In this affair one-half of the Federal force which crossed the Potomac under the command of Col. Baker to attack the Confederates never returned. Many were shot while in the water, many were drowned, many surrendered, and others succeeded in swimming to Harrison's Island. In this battle no Maryland troops were engaged; but on the 22d of October the First Maryland Regiment, which was then stationed at Darnestown, Montgomery Co., received orders to reinforce the command of Brig.-Gen. C. P. Stone at Edward's Ferry. Upon their arrival they were directed to man the boats and rescue the brigade of Gen. Gorman, which had been sent over the Potomac to act in conjunction with Col. Baker's command, and which was in momentary danger of being cut to pieces or captured. Notwithstanding the river was very high, the current strong, and the wind blowing a gale, these brave men almost alone, with coal-boats worked with poles, brought out of the jaws of danger and death a whole brigade. All night long they worked diligently to bring off those whom folly had sent to the Virginia side of the river, and this too when troops from other States refused to perform so dangerous a service. Col. Kenly in his official report of the affair concludes with the remark: "I feel it to be a duty to say that the soldiers of the First Maryland Regiment of Infantry saved numbers of our army from destruction or capture. I am very proud of that night's work." The First Maryland Regiment remained in the vicinity of Edward's Ferry until the 26th of October, when it returned to Darnestown.

During the night of October 25th the Second Maryland Infantry, under Col. Thomas Johns, with Capt. Fiery's company of cavalry, were concentrated at North Branch bridge on the Baltimore and Ohio Railroad, and early the following morning marched in the direction of Romney, Va., to co-operate with a force from New Creek (now Keyser) under Gen. Kelley in an attack on the Confederates at Romney. Passing through Frankfort, the column arrived at a point one and a half miles from Springfield, where it had a slight skirmish with the enemy, losing two men severely wounded. After a short delay the march was continued through Springfield, distant twenty miles from Cumberland, to the Chain bridge over the South Branch of the Potomac, seven miles below Romney. Here the enemy was discovered strongly intrenched on a wooded eminence immediately fronting the bridge on the opposite side of the river. A brisk fire at once commenced. After skirmishing across the river about half an hour, Col. Johns determined to force the passage of the bridge. Capt. Alexander Shaw, of Company A, who had the advance, was, with his company, directed to lead the way at a double-quick step, supported by the remainder of the regiment. The company moved promptly, and when about half-way across the bridge discovered the flooring torn up and its further progress stopped. The enemy on seeing the movement opened fire by volley, killing one man (Private Andrew Hewes) and wounding six, and causing the company to seek shelter be-

---

[1] On the 23d of September, Capt. Waltemyer, with about forty members of Company B, First Maryland Regiment, proceeded to Boonsboro' and seized the arms belonging to the Boonsboro' Guards, which had disbanded some time before. About the 20th of September, John Marrow, of Sharpsburg, a member of Capt. Cronise's company of the Home Brigade, was accidentally killed at Frederick by one of his comrades.

On the 21st of September the Union Washington County Convention assembled in Hagerstown. Hon. Daniel Weisel was elected president, Michael Newcomer and Henry W. Dellinger, vice-presidents, and Isaac Nesbitt and Joseph O'Neal, secretaries. Addresses were delivered by John V. L. Findley and others, and strong war resolutions adopted. On the 24th of September, Messrs. Bradford and Maffitt, Unconditional Union candidates for Governor and Comptroller, delivered political addresses at Hagerstown to a large meeting, at which Capt. Elias Davis, of Boonsboro', presided, with Capt. George Shryock, of Hagerstown, and Alexander Shafer, of Williamsport, as vice-presidents, and Col. Henry W. Dellinger, of Clear Spring, as secretary. On the 30th of September Dr. Charles Macgill, of Hagerstown, was arrested by Capt. Waltemyer, of the First Maryland Regiment, and after being taken to the headquarters of Col. Kenly, at Williamsport, was sent North on the following day. On the 23th of September, Messrs. Bradford and Maffitt addressed a large Union meeting at Cumberland.

Nov. 19, 1861, Charles J. Brown, second lieutenant in Capt. Faithful's company of the First Maryland Regiment, Home Brigade, stationed at Frederick, was promoted to the captaincy of Company K.

hind the pillars and abutments of the bridge. After some further skirmishing, and not hearing the firing of Gen. Kelley's column for an hour, Col. Johns concluded Romney had been taken and the object of his movement—to create a diversion in Gen. Kelley's favor—accomplished. He therefore withdrew his command to Old Town, twenty-five miles distant. The next day it returned to Cumberland.

In this affair Company B, Potomac Home Brigade Cavalry, commanded by Capt. Fiery, rendered very efficient service by drawing the fire of the enemy from the infantry at the bridge.

On the 11th of November the regiment marched from Cumberland to Old Town, whence the several companies were distributed along the line of the Baltimore and Ohio Railroad at Green Spring, Little Cacapon, Great Cacapon, Springfield, and Paw Paw. Headquarters were established at Green Spring. Capt. Fiery's company was placed at Green Spring and Springfield.

The Third Brigade of Gen. Banks' army, Gen. Williams commanding, arrived in Frederick Dec. 9, 1861, and encamped near the hamlet of Fairview, three miles out on the Hagerstown turnpike. The brigade, regimental supply, and baggage-trains followed immediately in the rear of the regiments. The First and Second Brigades, commanded by Gens. Abercrombie and Hamilton, arrived respectively on Tuesday (December 3d) and Wednesday (December 4th). The former encamped on the Monocacy and Baltimore turnpike, and the latter on the Monocacy, near Ijamsville, both from four to five miles from Frederick. Two cavalry companies and the artillery battalion under Capt. Best, of the Fourth United States, arrived about the same time.

Gen. Banks' headquarters were in the spacious mansion of Bradley T. Johnson, then absent in the Confederate army. It had been unoccupied, except by his servants, since his departure. The only troops that were located in the city were Gen. Banks' bodyguard, composed of the Zouaves d'Afrique and Company A, Capt. Fitzsimmons, and Company K of the Allen Cavalry.

The First Maryland Regiment, under Col. Kenly, went into winter quarters about four miles west of Frederick City, but on the night of December 18th, Col. Kenly was directed to proceed with his command towards Sharpsburg or Williamsport, as he might deem advisable, to repel a threatened advance of the Confederates into Maryland. The regiment started from its camp at midnight, and after a very rapid march reached Williamsport at ten A.M. Believing the enemy were moving farther up the river, the colonel pushed on with his regiment, and established his headquarters at the Four Locks, a point midway between Williamsport and Hancock.

The several companies were now again distributed along the Potomac for the protection of the Chesapeake and Ohio Canal, and to guard the fords and ferries of the river. They were posted as follows: Companies B, C, D, E, and G, at the Four Locks; Company F, at Dam No. 5; Company A, at Cherry Run; Company H, at old Fort Frederick; and Companies I and K, near Fogel's Ferry, opposite Little George Town, Va. This assignment (with the exception of Company F, transferred from Dam No. 5 to No. 4) remained unchanged until the night of Jan. 7, 1862, when, in obedience to orders from Gen. Lander, commanding the United States forces at Hancock, Col. Kenly started with Companies A, B, C, E, G, and I, and marched to Hancock, where he arrived in time to render valuable assistance to the besieged garrison, and, with the other reinforcements that had been sent, prevented the surrender of the town, which had been demanded by Gen. "Stonewall" Jackson. This march over the North Mountain was made on one of the coldest nights of midwinter, through a severe storm of sleet and snow, and Col. Kenly received the commendation and warm thanks of Gen. Lander for the succor afforded his command by the timely arrival of the battalion of the First Maryland.

After the retreat of the Confederates from before Hancock, the headquarters of the regiment were established at Millstone Point, five miles east of the former town, and the following distribution of the companies was made, viz.: A, B, E, and G, at Millstone Point; D, at old Fort Frederick; F, at Four Locks; H, at Cherry Run; I, at Bevan's Hill; K, at Licking Creek bridge; and C, at Baer's schoolhouse. During the whole of the winter of 1861 and 1862 frequent attempts were made by the Confederates to drive the companies and detachments of the regiment from their posts on the river, and several spirited engagements took place between them, especially at old Fort Frederick, Cherry Run, and Dam No. 5, but in every instance the Confederates failed to accomplish their purpose.[1]

Companies A, C, and D, Potomac Home Brigade, spent the fall in camp at Frederick, perfecting themselves in cavalry tactics. In December they moved to Williamsport, and were employed in doing picket duty along the Maryland side of the Potomac, and watching the Confederate pickets under Ashby on the opposite bank.

---

[1] Kirkley's "Historical Record of the First Regiment."

During the same month the Confederates, under Gen. T. J. (Stonewall) Jackson, moved from Winchester into Jefferson and Berkeley Counties, Va., tore up and removed the rails of the Baltimore and Ohio Railroad between Harper's Ferry and North Mountain, and made several attempts to render the Chesapeake and Ohio Canal useless by breaking the dams from which it is fed. These attempts brought on some heavy skirmishing along the river.

On the 6th of December, Capt. G. P. Robinson's company of Lamon's regiment, which afterwards became Company C of the Third Maryland, exchanged compliments with small parties of the Confederates at Dam No. 5 and Back Creek.

Next day a larger Confederate force, infantry and artillery, made its appearance at the dam, and commenced throwing shell and shot at the work as well as the houses on the Maryland shore.

Capt. Robinson's company answered with musketry, and the firing continued until dusk. A small detachment of this company, under Lieut. Day, was on picket at Faulkwell's Ferry, where an incessant firing was kept up all day and throughout the night.

At the dam musketry firing recommenced about 9 P.M. on the part of the Confederates, the object of which was to cover a party endeavoring to destroy the cribs of the structure. Capt. Robinson's men responded, and the firing was continued until past midnight.

At dawn of the 8th the Confederates resumed the throwing of shot and shell across the dam, and also opened artillery at Faulkwell's Ferry. At the dam the Confederates succeeded in setting fire to and destroying a barn owned by John Sterling. Mr. Stanhope's dwelling-house, near by, had been burned to the ground the previous day.

Firing at both places was kept up all day, with but little intermission on either side. The force at the dam had been strengthened during the night of the 7th by a company of the Thirteenth Massachusetts from Williamsport.

Before daylight of the 9th the Confederates withdrew without accomplishing their designs on the canal.

Later in the month, Jackson made a stronger demonstration against Dam No. 5, which he covered by a feint movement of a portion of his troops towards Williamsport and Falling Waters. Sharp skirmishing with considerable cannonading occurred at the dam on the 17th, 18th, and 19th of December, in which Capt. Robinson's and Capt. Kennedy's companies of Maryland Volunteers participated.

It was these operations of the Confederates that caused the movement of the First Maryland from Frederick, as already mentioned.

On this occasion no serious impression was made upon the dam. It was so slightly injured that the damages were repaired within two days.

At night of the 19th a volunteer party from Capt. W. B. Kennedy's company (afterwards Company A of the Third Maryland) crossed the river in a skiff and burnt Colston's mill, which had afforded a good shelter to the Confederate riflemen.

At the close of the year the various commands, whether organized or in process of organization, were stationed as follows:

First Cavalry, at Camp Carroll, Baltimore (organizing).

Company A, Potomac Home Brigade Cavalry, near Williamsport.

Company B, Potomac Home Brigade Cavalry, at Springfield, W. Va.

Company C, Potomac Home Brigade Cavalry, at Williamsport.

Company D, Potomac Home Brigade Cavalry, at Hagerstown.

Battery A, Light Artillery, at Camp Blair, near Eastville, Va.

Battery B, Light Artillery, near Drummondtown, Va.

First Infantry, on the Upper Potomac.

Second Infantry, at Camp Carroll, Baltimore.

Third Infantry, at Camp Belger, Baltimore (organizing).

Fourth Infantry (German Rifles), at Camp Carroll, Baltimore (organizing).

Fifth Infantry, at Camp Hoffman, Baltimore.

First Infantry, Potomac Home Brigade, at Frederick.

Second Infantry, Potomac Home Brigade, on line of Baltimore and Ohio Railroad, in Western Virginia.

First Infantry (Eastern Shore), at Salisbury, etc., Eastern Shore, Md.

Second Infantry (Eastern Shore), at Camp Vickers, Chestertown (organizing).

Purnell Legion, Infantry, at Eastville, Hengas Creek, Cape Charles, Franktown, and near Chuystown.

Company A, Purnell Cavalry, at Pikesville Arsenal.

Company B, Purnell Cavalry, at Pikesville Arsenal.

Patapsco Guards, at Ellicott's Mills.

The position of the Federal troops in Maryland at the beginning of the year 1862 was as follows: Gen. Dix commanded in Baltimore; Gen. Hooker, in Charles County and south of Washington; Gen. McClellan, southwest of Washington; Gens. Keys and Casey, in and around Washington; Gen. Stone, at and near Poolesville, and Banks near Darnestown, with detachments on the Potomac to Williamsport. Cumberland was the headquarters of Gen. Kelley.

The Federal government had determined to respond to the call of the people of the North for the vigorous prosecution of the war, and the accession of Mr. Stanton to the War Department was followed by a more active and energetic conduct of military affairs. A general plan of operations was adopted, and on Jan. 22, 1862, all the land and naval forces of the United States were ordered to move on the 22d of February following "against the insurgent forces."

New Year's day of 1862 found Gen. Banks' division, consisting of Abercrombie's, Hamilton's, and Williams' brigades, Maulsby's First Potomac Home Brigade Infantry, First Michigan Cavalry, and two batteries of artillery, in winter quarters near Frederick City, where Gen. Banks had established his headquarters. Four regiments of his command, the Twenty-eighth Pennsylvania, Col. Geary, the Twelfth Indiana, Col. Link, the Thirteenth Massachusetts, Col. Leonard, the First Maryland, Col. Kenly, and Cole's and Horner's companies of Maryland cavalry, held positions on the Maryland side of the Potomac, guarding the river-line from the mouth of the Monocacy to near Hancock. Geary's headquarters were at Point of Rocks, Link's at Sharpsburg, Leonard's at Williamsport, and Kenly's at Four Locks.

The companies of the First Maryland were stationed as follows: A, at Cherry Run; B, C, D, E, and G, at Four Locks; F, at Dam No. 5; H, at old Fort Frederick; and I and K, at Faulkwell's Ferry, opposite Little Georgetown.

Gen. Kelley, commanding the district of Romney, had troops at Romney, Bath, and Springfield, with detachments along the Baltimore and Ohio Railroad, from a point opposite Hancock to Cumberland. In this district the Second Maryland Potomac Home Brigade Infantry and Firey's, Sahl's, and Russell's companies of Maryland cavalry were serving.

On January 1st, the Confederate Gen. Jackson started from Winchester, with a considerable force of volunteers and militia, and moved towards Bath. The place was held by eight companies of the Thirty-ninth Illinois, Col. Osborn, and a section of Best's regular battery, under Lieut. Muhlenberg.

Gen. Jackson's plan, it would seem, was to capture the small force at Bath, push across the Potomac at Hancock, six miles distant, then move by the National turnpike to Cumberland, and cut off the Federal forces occupying Romney and adjacent country.

Reaching the neighborhood of Bath on the afternoon of January 3d, Jackson's advance encountered three companies of the Thirty-ninth Illinois, sent out on the Winchester road to feel and reconnoitre his column. After a spirited skirmish the scouting party retired in good order and unmolested to Bath.

During the night the garrison was reinforced from Hancock by the Eighty-fourth Pennsylvania and Patterson's company of Maryland cavalry. Col. Murray, of the Eighty-fourth, assumed command of the entire force, and at four o'clock the next morning advanced to an eminence beyond the town and deployed in line of battle. Muhlenberg's guns, already in position, commanding the numerous roads centring in Bath, opened a lively fire as soon as the enemy came in view, advancing by the Winchester and Martinsburg roads. The Federal commander, however, soon learned that a well-appointed force of cavalry, artillery, and infantry, greatly superior to his own, was in his front. At eight o'clock Gen. Jackson began to press upon him, driving in his skirmishers. But by skillful manœuvring, presenting a bold front, the enemy was kept at bay until near nightfall, when the command fell back by the Sir John's road towards Hancock. On the way thither it was joined by the Thirteenth Indiana and Russell's cavalry company from Green Spring Run. At Alpine Depot, just opposite Hancock, a brisk fight took place, but the Federal troops finally succeeded in crossing to the Maryland shore.

Two companies of the Twenty-ninth Illinois, and Company F, Second Potomac Home Brigade Infantry, Capt. L. F. Dyche, stationed at Great Cacapon bridge, were also attacked, and for several hours maintained their position. A heavy force was approaching, and these companies not being able to ford the Potomac, retreated up the railroad to Green Spring Run.

Capt. Sahl's cavalry company, while reconnoitring from Springfield, fell into an ambuscade near Stone's Cross-Roads. The captain and one man (Peter Martin) were mortally wounded. The troops at Bath sustained no serious loss except in the matter of camp and garrison equipage. At Alpine Depot some army supplies also fell into the hands of the Confederates.

That night Gen. F. W. Lander arrived at Hancock, *en route* to Cumberland, to relieve Gen. Kelley, who was disabled by the wound he had received at Philippi. He immediately assumed command of the post, and Gen. Jackson, who had taken position on the bluffs opposite Hancock, and was vigorously shelling the town, sent Col. Turner Ashby, on the morning of the 5th, with a flag of truce to demand its immediate surrender. Gen. Lander defiantly refused, and, having been reinforced by Hampton's Pennsylvania battery and a section of Matthews' Pennsylvania battery, under Lieut. Ricketts, a spirited cannonade ensued, which was kept up during the entire day following. The Confederate bombardment was vigorously conducted, and several houses in the town were struck by shells, while the inhabitants, men, women, and children, ran wildly through the streets, seeking an escape from the fire. Lander's guns, however, returned the fire with such fatal accuracy as to drive the Confederate batteries from the bluff. Foiled in his efforts perhaps to force a passage of the river and capture Hancock, Jackson withdrew on the morning of the 7th, and put his army in motion towards Romney. As soon as this was discovered, Gen. Lander resumed his journey to Cumberland, being followed on the 10th by the Eighty-fourth and One Hundred and Tenth Pennsylvania, Thirty-ninth Illinois, and two guns of Best's Battery.

The force in Hancock during the bombardment consisted of the Thirty-ninth Illinois, Eighty-fourth and One Hundred and Tenth Pennsylvania, four companies Thirteenth Massachusetts, Cole's, Patterson's, and Horner's companies Maryland cavalry, and eight Parrott guns from Best's, Hampton's, and Matthews' batteries.

Williams' brigade arrived from Frederick on the 8th, after the enemy had withdrawn. Gen. Lander having already left for Cumberland, Gen. A. S. Williams assumed command of the post.

Col. Kenly, with Companies A, B, C, E, G, and I of the First Maryland, marched from Four Locks to Hancock on the night of the 7th. The regiment was soon after distributed as follows: Companies A, B, E, and G, with headquarters at Millstone Point, five miles east of Hancock; D, at old Fort Frederick; F, at Four Locks; H, at Cherry Run; I, at Bevan's Hill; K, at Licking Creek Bridge; and C, at Baer's schoolhouse.

The day before Jackson retired from Hancock, Gen. Kelley ordered Col. Dunning, Fifth Ohio, commanding at Romney, to attack a force of the Confederates that had been left to hold Blue's Gap, a strong position, twelve miles from Romney, on the road to Winchester.

On the night of January 6th, Col. Dunning moved from Romney with a column of two thousand men, and on the morning of the 7th surprised the Confederates completely, driving them from their intrenchments, capturing stores, equipage, prisoners, two pieces of artillery, and entirely dispersing the whole force.

Gen. Jackson, who at this time had begun his retirement from Hancock, moved on Romney. Gen. Lander in person reached that place on the night of the 8th, and on the 10th he withdrew the command, *via* Springfield and Frankford, to the mouth of Patterson's Creek, leaving to the Confederate general the barren occupancy of Romney, which, in addition to his losses of men and material in battle, cost him many men disabled from cold and exposure. Besides, he was soon obliged to abandon the place, retiring into winter quarters at Winchester.

After passing Springfield, the rear of Lander's column was covered by Companies D, G, I, and K, Second Maryland Potomac Home Brigade, under Col. Robert Bruce, and Fiery's and Sahl's companies of cavalry, with other troops.

For several days after Jackson's departure the garrison of Hancock was kept in constant readiness to go to the support of Gen. Lander should he be attacked. Alarms were frequent, and reconnoitring parties were thrown forward almost daily in the direction of Bath. In this duty the Maryland cavalry rendered efficient service.

On one of these scouting expeditions Cole's cavalry penetrated to within a few miles of Winchester, and ascertained that Jackson had gone into winter quarters there. Russell's, Fiery's, and Redpath's (formerly Sahl's) companies also performed similar service with Gen. Lander's command in Virginia.

At the end of January the companies of the Second Potomac Home Brigade were posted as follows: A, at Little Orleans; B, at Little Cacapon; C, D, E, H, I, and K, with headquarters at Old Town; F, at South Branch; and G, at Cumberland.

On the 14th of February Russell's and Fiery's cavalry companies participated in a brisk fight at Bloomery Gap, in which the Confederate commander, with his staff and part of his command, were captured.

The time was now approaching when an active spring and summer campaign in the Shenandoah Valley was to be inaugurated. As a part of the grand plan for the advance of McClellan's army, the commands of Banks and Lander were to enter the valley, cover the reconstruction of the section of the Baltimore and Ohio Railroad lying between Harper's Ferry and Hancock, and at the same time draw the attention of the Confederates to their left flank, held by Jackson, which was threatened by the movement.

Gen. Lander having cleared his district of the forces of the enemy, movement was then commenced lower down the river by a portion of Gen. Banks' division. On the 25th of February the Twenty-eighth Pennsylvania, Col. Geary, crossed the Potomac from Sandy Hook, took possession of Harper's Ferry, and drove the enemy's scouts from Bolivar Heights. This was the first step towards seizing and holding the valley.

On the 27th, Abercrombie's and Hamilton's brigades, with Col. Maulsby's regiment, moved from Frederick to Harper's Ferry, and thence on March 1st to Charlestown, meeting with no opposition from the enemy. In this advance Col. Maulsby's regiment led the van. Col. Geary, with his own regiment, Knap's battery, and a battalion of the First Michigan Cavalry, crossed the Shenandoah on February 28th, drove the enemy from Loudon Heights, advanced through Lovettsville and Waterford, and on the 8th of March occupied Leesburg.

The operations of crossing the Potomac and the occupation of Charlestown were superintended by Gen. McClellan in person.

To strengthen the advance into the valley two brigades of Sedgwick's division, under Gens. Gorman and Burns, were brought from Poolesville, reaching Harper's Ferry on the 2d of March, and proceeding thence to Charlestown on the 7th.

These brigades remained with Gen. Banks until Jackson had evacuated Winchester, but did not advance beyond Berryville. They then rejoined their corps, and embarked with McClellan's main army for the Peninsula. Upon the retirement of these troops Charlestown was garrisoned by Col. Maulsby's regiment.

Meantime Gen. Williams' brigade, which included Gen. Kenly's First Maryland and Cole's cavalry battalion, marched from Hancock on the 28th of February, occupying Martinsburg on the 2d of March. In this movement Cole's battalion led the van, and were the first to enter the town, after a slight skirmish.

Advancing cautiously, Hamilton's and Williams' brigades were united at Bunker Hill on the 10th, and marched to Stephenson's Depot on the 11th. At the last named place the advance-guard encountered and repulsed Ashby's cavalry. On the 12th the two brigades marched upon and occupied Winchester, Jackson's force having retired the previous night. Cole's cavalry was the first to enter the town, dashing through and capturing a few prisoners. At this time Abercrombie's brigade and a portion of Sedgwick's division were at Berryville.

Moving with Gen. Williams' column on the direct road from Martinsburg, Cole's battalion had several spirited encounters with Ashby's cavalry. In one of these affairs three men of Company A were wounded, one mortally.[1] Capt. Cole had his horse killed under him, but sustained no injury himself. The gallantry of the command on this occasion was acknowledged by the brigade commander as follows:

---

[1] Private Dennis E. Stull.

"HEADQUARTERS THIRD BRIGADE, GEN. BANKS' DIVISION,
"BUNKER HILL, VA., March 8, 1862.
"CAPT. H. A. COLE, Commanding Cavalry:

"CAPTAIN,—I take great pleasure in offering you and your command my thanks and congratulations on the good conduct and gallantry displayed in the affair of yesterday in advance of this town. My staff-officers, who were with you, speak in high terms of the cool and steady conduct of yourself and Lieut. Vernon, and of all your non-commissioned officers and men. Be pleased to make known to your command my appreciation of their good services, and my regret that three of your brave fellows suffered wounds.

"I am, captain, with much respect,
"Your obedient servant,
"A. S. WILLIAMS,
"Brig.-Gen. Comdg."

Towards the close of February, Gen. Lander removed his troops from Patterson's Creek to Paw Paw. At this place, on the 2d of March, the gallant commander died, and was succeeded temporarily by Col. Nathan Kimball, of the Fourteenth Indiana. On the 7th of March the division moved towards Martinsburg, and thence to Winchester. At Martinsburg Gen. James Shields assumed command.

Two days after the occupation of Winchester Gen. Banks' command, consisting of his own and Shields' division, was designated the Fifth Army Corps. By this reorganization Gen. Williams was assigned to the command of Banks' old division, Col. Dudley Donnelly, Twenty-eighth New York, to the First Brigade, Gen. J. J. Abercrombie to the Second Brigade, and Col. George H. Gordon, Second Massachusetts, to the Third Brigade. The First Maryland, Twenty-eighth New York, Fifth Connecticut, and Forty-sixth Pennsylvania constituted the First Brigade.

The initial movement in Gen. McClellan's plans having been accomplished by the advance on Winchester, and the Confederate forces at Manassas under Gen. Johnston having fallen back behind the Rappahannock, preparations were made to transfer the Army of the Potomac to a new base of operations on the Peninsula.

To Gen. Banks was assigned the duty of covering the line of the Potomac and the capital after the withdrawal of McClellan's army, and he was ordered to place the bulk of his force in the vicinity of Manassas, and to repair the Manassas Gap Railway, so as to have a rapid and direct communication with the Shenandoah Valley. On March 1st he moved to Charlestown, meeting with no opposition from the enemy, Col. Maulsby's regiment leading the advance. On the night of March 6th an unfortunate affair occurred at Kabletown, by which one man of the First Michigan Cavalry was wounded and two horses killed. In anticipation of an attack from a superior force of the enemy, known to be in the vicinity, Col. Maulsby, who held the outpost at that place, had sent to Gen. Banks for reinforcements of cavalry. The general replied that he had none available, but subsequently, without notifying Col. Maulsby, sent a detachment of the First Michigan Cavalry to his support. By mistake the cavalry took a circuitous route and approached the village from the direction whence the enemy was expected. Col. Maulsby immediately formed his men in line and fired a volley on the supposed enemy, with the result above mentioned. The sad mistake was soon discovered, and the firing stopped before further harm was done.

The line of the Baltimore and Ohio Railroad being now clear of the Confederates, its employés repaired the great bridge at Harper's Ferry, and others which had been burnt or broken down, and relaid the rails where they had been torn up, and on the 30th of March, all the repairs being completed, a resumption of business took place between Baltimore and Wheeling. The first through passenger-train for Wheeling which had gone over the road since May, 1861, left Baltimore on April 1, 1862.

After the battle of Kernstown, Fiery's company of cavalry was ordered back to the Romney district. Under command of Col. Downey, of the Third Potomac Home Brigade Infantry, it was actively employed in scouting after guerrillas. On the 23d of April it had a severe skirmish at Grass Lick, near Romney, in which the opposing force was defeated, with the loss of their leader (John Umbaugh) and others killed, besides a number wounded and twenty captured. The company lost two men killed, Robert Elms and John H. Rockwell. At the beginning of Gen. Banks' movement from Strasburg, ten companies of Cole's cavalry battalion were posted in Jefferson County, Va., Company A (Cole's) was at Charlestown, C (Horner's) at Kearneysville, and D (Curll's) at Wadesville. As the Confederates under Jackson advanced in pursuit of Banks, after the battle of Front Royal and Winchester, these companies were actively employed in scouting, skirmishing, and picket duty.

Gen. Jackson had halted his infantry a short distance from Winchester, but his cavalry had followed Banks' retreating column to Martinsburg, where the pursuit ended.

On the 28th of May the Confederate advance moved upon Harper's Ferry by way of Summit Point and Charlestown, followed the next day by the whole army, which encamped in the vicinity of Halltown. At this time Harper's Ferry was held by troops hastily gathered together, and consisting of two brigades of infantry, commanded by Gens. James Cooper and John P. Slough, with some light artillery and cavalry, the whole under Gen. Rufus Saxton. On Maryland Heights there was a battery of heavy guns, called the "naval battery," which commanded the town and all its approaches.

The most of these troops were new levies and militia regiments turned out for the emergency. The following-named Maryland organizations constituted a part of the garrison: Cole's cavalry; Companies D, F, H, K, and L of the First Cavalry, under Maj. Deems; the First Potomac Home Brigade Infantry, Col. Maulsby; the Third Infantry, Col. De Witt; and the Purnell Legion, Col. Leonard.

The two latter and the battalion of the First Cavalry had been hurriedly forwarded from Baltimore to assist in checking Jackson's threatened invasion of Maryland.

Col. Maulsby's regiment had been posted along the Baltimore and Ohio Railroad from Harper's Ferry as far east as Marriottsville, with headquarters at Monocacy Junction, but upon the first intimation of the enemy's approach it was concentrated at Harper's Ferry. On the night of the 27th, Gen. Saxton sent Companies I (Capt. Saunders) and F (Capt. Whittier) of this regiment, under Maj. John A. Steiner, to make a reconnoissance of Loudon Heights, where the enemy was reported in position. While cautiously ascending the mountain about eleven o'clock, and when near a spring not far from the top, the detachment was suddenly fired upon by dismounted Confederate cavalry concealed in the bushes on the east side of the narrow road. Sergt. Conradt Mehrling, of Company I, was killed and several others wounded. After returning the fire with considerable effect, as was afterwards learned, the command fell back to Harper's Ferry. Next morning Loudon Heights were briskly shelled from the naval battery on Maryland Heights, and in the afternoon Maj. Steiner was again ordered up the mountain with two companies (A, Cook, and D, Baugher) to observe the effects of the firing and engage the enemy should he still be there. The detachment proceeded to a point near the summit of the mountain, as far as Nicewauer's house, but found no enemy. It then returned to camp. In the forenoon a reconnoissance in force was also made towards Charlestown by the One Hundred and Eleventh Pennsylvania, the Second Battalion First Maryland (Maj. Deems), and Cole's cavalry, with one section of artillery. When within two miles of the town the enemy's skirmishers were met and driven through and beyond it. Having developed the fact that the enemy was in force in front and advancing, the command returned to Harper's Ferry. The First Maryland Cavalry had three men wounded, and one officer (Capt. Vincent Von Koerber) and eight men captured. Upon the return of this reconnoitring column, Gen. Saxton formed his troops in line of battle, extending along the crest of Bolivar Heights, or "Smallwood's Hill," across the peninsula from the Potomac to the Shenandoah. Small bodies of the enemy appeared in the neighborhood during that and the forepart of the ensuing day, as if with the object of alluring the Federal forces from their strong defensive position to one where they would be more easily attacked and overpowered. By the afternoon of the 29th the whole of Jackson's army was before Harper's Ferry, and Gen. Saxton's pickets being driven in, his forces were again formed in order of battle on Bolivar Heights, Gen. Cooper's brigade to the right and Gen. Slough's brigade to the left of the road leading to Charlestown.

Learning in the course of the evening that the enemy had sent a force across the Shenandoah at Key's Ferry to occupy Loudon Heights, and that another strong detachment had moved towards Shepherdstown, with a view of crossing the Potomac and thus turning his position, Gen. Saxton determined to withdraw his troops from Bolivar Heights and take up a second line of defense on the height known as Camp Hill, immediately above the town of Harper's Ferry. With the force rendered by this contraction of his front available for other purposes, he deemed it prudent to occupy the crest of Maryland Heights above the naval battery, to frustrate any attempt of the enemy to take that position in the rear and turn his batteries against him. Accordingly, about midnight, Gen. Cooper's brigade, including the Third Maryland, was set in motion, and by daylight had succeeded in crossing the river and occupying the heights on the Maryland side. Gen. Slough's brigade at the same time fell back to the new position on Camp Hill. To this brigade the Purnell Legion was attached.

About dark on the 30th the enemy advanced beyond Bolivar Heights to storm the works on Camp Hill. The light batteries on Camp Hill and the heavy guns on Maryland Heights opened upon him. The scene at this time was very impressive. The night was intensely dark; the hills around were alive with the signal-lights of the enemy; the rain descended in torrents; vivid flashes of lightning illumined at intervals the grand and magnificent scenery, while the crash of thunder echoing among the mountains drowned into comparative insignificance the roar of the artillery. After an action of about an hour's duration the enemy retired. He made another unsuccessful attack at midnight, and after a short engagement disappeared. During the operations of the 29th and 30th the Purnell Legion had three men wounded. A reconnoissance next day ascertained that the rear of the Confederate army had passed through Charlestown in the direction of Winchester about an hour before the arrival of the reconnoitring force. Gen. Jackson was now moving rapidly to the rear. Gen. Fremont from the west and Gen. McDowell from the east were on the march to intercept him.

The narration of the pursuit by Shields and Fremont, and the battles of Cross Keys and Port Republic, does not come within the province of this work, as no Federal troops from Western Maryland or any other section of the State participated therein. Suffice it to say that early in June the First Cavalry, Third Infantry, and Purnell Legion advanced with Gen. Banks' command, now known as the Second Corps, Army of Virginia, to Winchester and Cedar Creek, whence they subsequently moved into Eastern Virginia.

Col. Maulsby's regiment was again distributed along the line of the Baltimore and Ohio Railroad, and Cole's cavalry operated in the lower valley, while the remnant of the First Infantry proceeded to Baltimore to reorganize and recruit. The enlisted portion of the regiment captured at Front Royal was held in confinement at Lynchburg and Belle Isle, Va., and the captive officers at Salisbury, N. C., until September, 1862. On account of the severity of his wounds, Col. Kenly was paroled at Winchester, and returned to Baltimore City.

Great excitement was created in Hagerstown by the defeat of Banks and the approach of the Confederates. "The town," says a correspondent, under date of May 28, 1862, "is filled with refugees and escaped soldiers, who give a most horrible account of the sufferings of the Union men. A regular Union force destroyed the rebel newspaper office in which the Hagerstown *Mail* was published. The presses, type, and other material were demolished, together with the building. The building being the property of a Union man, that party at once raised funds and compensated the owner fully for his loss. The proprietor fled for his life." A large crowd assembled in front of the residence of Col. McKaig, at Cumberland, when it is said a pistol was fired from a window of the house. The crowd then commenced throwing stones at the windows, which they completely demolished, and Mr. McKaig's stable was set on fire and destroyed.[1]

---

[1] The Union Military Hospital in Frederick was situated on the outskirts of the town, and had an area of about four acres, inclosed by a board fence. The hospital consisted of one stone

On the 17th of June, 1862, "another outbreak," according to the Hagerstown *Herald and Torch*, "occurred in this town, during which Rhodes' restaurant was attacked and demolished, and the proprietor and his son driven off. On the same night the silversmith-shop of George Gruber was also destroyed. Comment upon these scenes at the present time is neither advisable nor necessary. Those who sympathize with this hellish rebellion, inaugurated for the overthrow of government, law, and order, are beginning to see and feel its consequences."

On the 5th of August a large and enthusiastic meeting of the friends of the Union was held at Hagerstown "to take into consideration the means best calculated to promote the object of the call of the President of the United States for more troops." On motion of Judge Weisel, Col. John Miller was called upon to preside. Messrs. Jonathan Toby and John J. Thomas were appointed vice-presidents, and Edward G. W. Stake and Isaac Nesbitt were selected as secretaries. A committee of thirteen, consisting of Lewis P. Fiery, Samuel Rohrer, Raphael E. Taney, Joseph F. Davis, James D. Bennett, Peter Negley, Levin Benton, E. G. W. Stake, James M. Leiter, Lewis B. Nyman, Henry W. Dellinger, William Rulett, and Thomas Hassett, reported resolutions, which were adopted, declaring "that our allegiance and patriotic duty to our whole country exactingly demand of us to suppress this causeless and gigantic rebellion by every available means in our power; that one of the most efficient means of doing so is to remove all secession incumbents from office, and to express everywhere and at all times our abhorrence of the crime of resistance to our national government; that we conceive that the speedy, effectual suppression of this rebellion can be accomplished only by the most rigorous punishment of all acts of disloyalty, and expressions of disaffection to our government; that the clemency hitherto extended to civic traitors, though we commend the motive that prompted it, has emboldened and encouraged them in our midst to the embarrassment of the government and great injury to its loyal citizens; that it is the duty of all loyal citizens to contribute to the necessary support of the families of such soldiers as may enter the service of the government, and that we recommend the appointment of committees in the various districts of the county for that purpose." In accordance with these resolutions the following committees were appointed for the patriotic service suggested: Sharpsburg, Levin Benton, Dr. A. A. Biggs, Benjamin F. Cronise; Williamsport, John A. Ensminger, Ed. G. W. Stake, Lewis Ripple; Hagerstown, F. Dorsey Herbert, Peter B. Small, Isaac Nesbitt; Clear Spring, H. W. Dellinger, Samuel M. Reitzell, George Cook; Hancock, Richmond Gregory, Raphael E. Taney, Dewalt Stottlemeyer; Boonsboro', Elias Davis, Lewis B. Nyman, Lewis Watson; Cavetown, A. C. Hildebrand, John P. Shank, Jeremiah S. Besore; Pleasant Valley, Jonathan Toby, Samuel Rohrer, David G. Potter; Leitersburg, George W. Lantz, Fred. K. Zeigler, James M. Leiter; Funkstown, Joseph F. Davis, Samuel Baker, Henry Landis; Sandy Hook, Jacob A. Miller, Michael Barthelow, Joseph Lewis; Tilghmanton, John Miller, A. J. P. Tabler, John Reichard; Cunningham's Cross-Roads, Daniel Cearfoss, Joseph O. Fiery, John Tice; Ringgold, Isaac H. Durborow, Isaac Garver, George Fulton; Indian Spring, Denton Jacques, J. Thomas Mason, Hugh McKenna.[1]

On the 9th of August a war-meeting was held at Westminster, Carroll Co., which was largely attended. Augustus Shriver acted as president; Thos. S. Brown and Joseph Schaeffer, as vice-presidents; R. Bernie and J. W. Boring, as secretaries.

A committee on business, consisting of one person from each district, was appointed by the chair, as follows: Joseph M. Parke, Henry Shriner, Granville S. Haines, William Tagg, J. F. Gardner, R. F. Jenkins, James Kelly, A. F. Myers, Col. J. C. Gist, S. W. Angel, S. S. Ecker.

Resolutions were adopted declaring "that we heartily approve of the measures taken by the government for the prompt increase of the Federal army, believing that the only means to preserve the lawful authority of the government and the unity of our great country against the wanton assaults of unprincipled traitors is to meet force with still greater force, and to prosecute the war in the most vigorous manner; that Carroll County will do her whole duty in raising her portion of the four regiments of volun-

---

and seven frame buildings. The stone structure was an old-fashioned two-story house. It was built by Gen. Braddock, and used by him as a hospital, and it is stated that Gen. Washington, then a colonel in Braddock's army, had his headquarters in one of the rooms. The other seven buildings were frame, one-story, and were built in the most substantial manner. The rooms were filled with small bedsteads, which had good and neat bed-clothing. It was probably at this time the best and largest hospital in the United States, and in June, 1862, contained six hundred and ninety patients. It held seven hundred (including attendants), and buildings were erected for two hundred more. The hospital was under the charge of Dr. R. F. Weir, Assistant Surgeon U.S.A., assisted by Dr. Goldsborough and several other efficient and capable surgeons.

[1] About the 20th of June, Benjamin Garver, of Ringgold District, was shot by a drunken soldier on the road between Ringgold and Leitersburg. Fortunately, the wound was only a slight one.

teers and other troops called for from Maryland, and for this purpose we will do all that we can to urge the brave and gallant men of our county to join, as volunteers, the standard of our country, raised in our midst by patriotic sons of Carroll. That we respectfully recommend that the commissioners for Carroll County advance, on the faith of the county, to each person who volunteers in the county the sum of fifty dollars, to be applied to the use of said volunteers, in common with the funds raised in Baltimore and elsewhere, so as to secure to each volunteer of the four regiments the sum of one hundred dollars, in addition to the bounty offered by the government; that a committee of three persons be appointed by the president to wait on the county commissioners, and lay before them the proposition of this meeting in regard to the pecuniary aid expected from them."

Under the last resolution, Messrs. John Smith, Grove, Shipley, and Andrew K. Shriver were appointed the committee. Addresses were delivered by Hon. John E. Smith, Lieut. William A. McKellip, John Smith, J. H. Christ, and R. Birnie.

On the 19th of August a large public meeting was held at Hagerstown, at which resolutions were adopted directing the Board of County Commissioners to borrow sixty thousand dollars, "to be expended and paid in bounties to volunteers already enlisted, and who may hereafter enlist from this county in the military service of the United States, under the recent calls of the President for more troops, one hundred dollars to each volunteer." The county commissioners being present at the meeting, at once convened and passed a formal order calling for a loan of sixty thousand dollars for the purpose indicated. The first loan of ten thousand dollars was obtained from the Hagerstown Bank to pay the bounty to Capt. Mobley's company, the commissioners themselves, as individuals, with some other patriotic gentlemen, leading off on the indorsement of the bond upon which the money was raised.

A contemporary writer, speaking of the patriotism and devotion of the people of Washington County at this time, says, under date of Sept. 3, 1862,—

"Washington County has led the State in furnishing troops. Indeed, there are few counties in the free States that have proportionately furnished more troops than she has. Out of a voting population of fifty-five hundred, she has already furnished fourteen companies of one hundred men each, and will, doubtless, have another, if not two, in the field by the 15th, making over one-fourth of her voting population. She has four companies that hold the right in as many regiments; she has five companies in the First Regiment Potomac Home Brigade; she has one father and seven sons in one company, and yesterday one of our old citizens, D. L. Smith, who has four sons all in the service, left with Lieut. Ratcliff to offer his services as a drummer to the Seventh Maryland Regiment. She was the first county in the State to pay her volunteers a cash bounty of one hundred dollars; she was the first to organize Union Relief Associations, and to-day that association is at work gathering lint, material for bandages, etc. Notwithstanding her undying attachment and determined energy, she has never had but one officer in the service above a captain (Maj. Kennedy, who was wounded and captured at Cedar Mountain)."

Another correspondent from Clear Spring, under date of Aug. 19, 1862, says,—

"In your issue of to-day I noticed a puff from Chestertown, Md., giving the amount of sixty-two soldiers volunteered for the war out of less than two hundred voters, and they think it hard to beat. In justice to our patriotic sons who have volunteered from our village of Clear Spring, Washington Co., Md., they should be heard from. You will please give this a notice in your valuable paper. I have taken pains by actual count to know positively our full vote of the village proper, and, all told, is but one hundred and twenty-four votes, and we have sent seventy-three volunteers to the war out of the village. We can further boast of sending seven out of one family,—the father and six sons. George W. Chace has that honor of six sons in the service, and a few more boys left home with the mother. We have also another family which has sent four sons, and still another three. Can Chestertown beat that, or any other town or city in the Union? If so, we will knock under."

On the 13th of August a large "war mass-meeting" was held at Cumberland, for the purpose of adopting measures for raising troops in response to the recent call of the President. Gen. C. M. Thruston was called to the chair, Lloyd Lowndes and F. A. Mason made vice-presidents, and William R. McCully and William Hoblitzell secretaries. Messrs. Charles H. Ohr, S. P. Smith, M. Sherry, G. E. Porter, and Hopewell Hebb submitted resolutions, which were adopted, declaring it to be the duty of the people to maintain the government, and requesting the county commissioners to appropriate fifty thousand dollars, to be applied to the payment of bounties to volunteers.

Apprehending a raid from the Confederate forces in West Virginia, the city authorities of Cumberland organized a city guard, consisting of three volunteer companies, which were officered as follows:

First District: Captain, Caspar Kassen; First Lieutenant, Joshua Steiner; Second Lieutenant, James A. Buckey; Orderly Sergeant, D. B. Myers. Second District: Captain, Jacob Wickard; First Lieutenant, William R. McCulley; Second Lieutenant, J. M. Koerner; Orderly Sergeant, Charles A. Seay. Third District: Captain, Horace Resley; First Lieutenant, J. J. McHenry; Second Lieutenant, J. F. Troxell; Orderly Sergeant, George M. Read. Horace Resley was subsequently elected lieutenant-colonel, to command the city guard. Allegany's quota was 874, but by October, 1862, she had furnished 1463 volunteers, and there was no necessity for the enforcement of the draft within the county limits.

All the militia in the State having been ordered to be enrolled, Charles Gilpin was appointed commissioner of enrollment for Allegany County, and completed his work early in September, the whole number enrolled being 4714.[1]

The Bradford Guards, of Hagerstown, Capt. Ed. M. Mobley, were raised in about ten days, and departed for Baltimore on the 18th of August, 1862. The following is a list of the members of the company, with the exception of a few who joined the organization after it left Hagerstown: George Adams, Jacob Armstrong, Thomas Baltz, John Baltz, H. H. Barnhart, J. Bingaman, J. A. Buxton, D. S. Bolmer, William W. Bovey, Andrew Bower, Valentine G. Brewer, John C. Bowman, A. Bragonier, W. Buck, W. H. Buck, George C. Burkitt, Charles C. Byers, John Carver, —— Lewis, William Colklesser, James Coon, J. T. A. Crager, George F. Crissinger, James R. Lorrance, Otho W. Dunner, William Earhart, Henry Everhart, Samuel Eyster, George Feigley, W. H. File, George Fisher, G. W. Fravel, Daniel Garver, Luther Gelwicks, H. A. Guyer, William Gumbert, Elias Hammond, William B. Harris, Pard Hartman, Robert Hatfield, Thomas Haney, Luther Helferstay, S. Herbert, J. M. Hicks, J. P. Himes, William H. Horine, A. H. Houck, Jonas Huffer, Isaac N. James, Walter Johnston, Jacob F. Johnson, George Kiose, J. H. Laney, Jacob Latt, Daniel Linebaugh, Henry Linebaugh, William H. Little, Charles F. Little, Daniel Long, Charles Lowman, Martin Mangin, Henry May, George McKain, William McKain, Thomas McKain, Jacob Moatz, William E. Moatz, Carver E. Mobley, Walter A. Mobley, J. Monroe, James Myers, H. C. Nesbitt, Thomas J. Nesbitt, Aug. Nickols, S. T. Nigh, James Peitz, Charles Poffenberger, J. T. Reichard, Moses S. Rinehart, J. T. Rinehart, John Sager, William L. Schuff, Amos Smith, David L. Smith, Frisby Spielman, David Stephey, John Swope, L. P. Thompson, J. N. Titlow, Washington Tracy, D. M. Tritle, George C. Updegraff, George Wantz, James A. Weise, Charles H. Wolford, J. H. Zeigler, and George H. Zeigler.

On the 21st of August a committee, consisting of Messrs. William Updegraff, Joseph P. Mong, Thomas A. Boullt, Henry Gantz, Benjamin Harris, F. A. Heard, D. C. Aughinbaugh, and Charles F. Gelwicks, in behalf of the citizens of Washington County, proceeded to Baltimore, paid the members the one hundred dollars bounty which Washington County had appropriated for the benefit of its volunteers, and presented to the officers of the company three elegantly finished swords, which had been purchased from a fund raised in Hagerstown for the purpose.

The following were the officers of enrollment appointed under the President's call for troops in 1862:

Washington County.—First District, John Rowlett, Sharpsburg; Second, Arthur F. Welch, Williamsport; Third, Robert C. Thornburg and Richard Wise, Hagerstown; Fourth, J. Rufus Smith, Clear Spring; Fifth, Samuel Oliver, Hancock; Sixth, Famose H. Irwin, Boonsboro'; Seventh, John P. Shank, Smithsburg; Eighth, Capt. W. McCoy, Rohrersville; Ninth, James H. Leggett, Leitersburg; Tenth, Henry Fritch, Funkstown; Eleventh, John W. Drenner, Sandy Hook; Twelfth, John Miller, Tilghmanton; Thirteenth, Joseph O. Fiery, Hagerstown; Fourteenth, Benton Schull, Ringgold; Fifteenth, Lewis G. Stanhope, Indian Spring.

Carroll County.—First District, William Fisher, Taneytown; Second, Jacob H. Christ, Uniontown; Third, Henry Wirt Shriver, Union Mills; Fourth, Thomas S. Brown, Carrollton; Fifth, Rezin S. Jenkins, Winfield; Sixth, Jonas Winters, Manchester; Seventh, Henry W. Wampler, Westminster; Eighth, Joseph Armcost, Hampstead; Ninth, Somerset R. Waters, Watersville; Tenth, Samuel Shuch, Union Bridge; Eleventh, Mordecai C. McKinstry, McKinstry's Mills.

Allegany County.—First District, Ephraim G. Blackburn, Summitville; Second, Ralph Thayer, Selbyport; Third, Jacob Arendt, Grantsville; Fourth, Thomas E. Jones, Westernport; Fifth, Nathan Frost, Frostburg; Sixth, Jacob Wickard, Cumberland; Seventh, John H. Stalling, Old Town; Eighth, George Price, Orleans; Ninth, Daniel Duncan, Flintstone; Tenth, Isaac J. Thompson, Oakland; Eleventh, Jacob W. Boyer, Occident; Twelfth, James Thomas, Mount Savage; Thirteenth, Henry D. Wineon, Cumberland; Fourteenth, John Brady, Johnstown; Fifteenth, Charles W. White, Oakland; Sixteenth, Herman Hahnecamp, Lonaconing.

Montgomery County.—First District, Henry N. Harris, Olney P. O.; Second, James G. House,

---

[2] On the 13th of August, John V. L. Findley "addressed his fellow-citizens of Hagerstown in a speech of great power and thrilling effect. Mr. Findley is engaged in raising a company for the war, and made a strong and eloquent appeal to the loyal citizens of the county to buckle on their armor in response to the President's call, and nobly battle for their imperiled liberties, homes, and firesides, whilst he denounced the secret traitors in our midst with a scorching, withering, but well-merited severity, which elicited frequent outbursts of applause from the numerous audience which had assembled upon a brief notice to hear him."

Clarksburg; Third, George W. Davidson, Poolesville; Fourth, Joseph G. White, Rockville; Fifth, John W. Baker, Olney.

Frederick County.—First District, Arthur Delasthmut, Buckeystown; Second, Joseph M. Ebberts, Frederick City; Third, Lewis H. Hill, Frederick City; Fourth, Peter G. Schlosser, Middletown; Fifth, John W. Staub, Creagerstown; Sixth, David Agnew, Emmittsburg; Seventh, Hiram H. Muller, Wolfsville; Eighth, Thomas A. Smith, Urbana; Ninth, John Baker, Liberty; Tenth, Robert W. Phelps, New Market; Eleventh, Jacob F. Miller, Sabillsville; Twelfth, Benjamin Smith, Woodsboro'; Thirteenth, Jeremiah G. Morrison, Weverton; Fourteenth, Robert Lease, Mount Pleasant; Fifteenth, Charles J. Little, Jefferson; Sixteenth, John S. Pennel, Mechanicstown; Seventeenth, Daniel V. Harp, Myersville; Eighteenth, John S. Repp, Johnsville.

On the 28th of August a company of Confederate cavalry made a dash into Smithfield, Jefferson Co., Va., where a picket-guard of Capt. Curll's cavalry of the Potomac Home Brigade were stationed, and captured Andrew J. Boyd, Christian Newcomer, Duncan McConnell, John Seifert, Thomas Eltonhead, James C. Orr, Sergt. Stephen Bryan, Corp. J. J. Goff, Corp. Wm. H. Bowman, R. C. Welsh, John H. Edy, Samuel B. Sigler, Jeremiah Leutzer, Charles E. Ball, George E. Steele, James Grubs, and Wm. H. Gregg.

CHAPTER XII.

THE MARYLAND CAMPAIGN OF 1862.

How the Confederates were Received—Lee's Invasion of Maryland—Occupation of Frederick—Battles of Crampton's Gap and South Mountain—Battle of Sharpsburg, or Antietam—Capture of Harper's Ferry—Movements of Maryland Troops—Stuart's Cavalry Raid into Maryland and Pennsylvania.

On the 26th of June, 1862, Gen. John Pope was assigned to the command of the Army of Virginia, and speedily commenced his memorable campaign "in the saddle."

While Gen. Pope's main army was operating in Northeastern Virginia, Cole's cavalry was ordered out from Harper's Ferry to operate on the left flank of the Confederate army. In the performance of this duty the battalion struck Col. Mumford's cavalry regiment near Leesburg on the 2d of September. The enemy was promptly attacked and driven back, but the battalion soon found itself surrounded by two of Stuart's regiments. For a while it seemed that this gallant little band would be overwhelmed by the largely superior force brought against it. But by one last desperate effort, in which both officers and men showed the best of mettle, it succeeded in charging through the enemy's lines, and escaped back to Harper's Ferry, losing in killed,[1] wounded, and missing over seventy men. Sergt. Hall and Corp. Apple, of Company A, were cut off and surrounded by the enemy, and, refusing to surrender, perished, fighting gallantly to the last, fairly riddled with bullets and hacked with sabre-cuts. Many of the command who escaped also bore the marks of the fray in the shape of sabre-strokes and pistol-wounds. After the second battle of Manassas the Confederate army, on the 31st of August, 1862, was moved towards Little River turnpike for the purpose of turning Gen. Pope's right. Anticipating this movement of the Confederates, Pope prepared to resist it, and on the evening of the following day a battle occurred at Chantilly, in which Gen. Kearney and Gen. Stevens, of the Federal forces, were killed. The immediate design of the Confederates was frustrated, but Pope's army was compelled to seek shelter in the fortifications around Washington. Pope now resigned his command, and was succeeded by Gen. McClellan.

As soon as the Union forces had reached the fortifications of Washington from the hard-fought fields of Manassas, Gen. Lee put his army in motion towards Leesburg, and on the 4th of September his advance division, under Gen. D. H. Hill, crossed the Potomac near the mouth of the Monocacy. The passage of the river was stoutly resisted for several hours by a detachment of Company E, First Potomac Home Brigade Infantry, consisting of only thirty-one men, under Lieut. Jerome B. Burk, stationed at the Monocacy aqueduct. After dark the lieutenant conducted his command along the east bank of the Monocacy to Monocacy Junction, and thence to Frederick City. Here it joined Capt. Faithful's company of the same regiment, and the two proceeded, as hereafter described, to Sandy Hook, where the remainder of the regiment was posted. In the skirmish at the aqueduct Lieut. Burk had one man wounded. After crossing, the enemy made an unsuccessful attempt to blow up the aqueduct.

Another detachment of Company E, under Lieut. Alonzo Carroll, on duty at Edward's Ferry, fell back to the vicinity of Poolesville, where, on the 5th, it had a skirmish with the enemy's advance, losing one man wounded. Being cut off from the regiment it

---

[1] The killed were First Sergt. Joseph J. Hall and Corps. Julius C. Apple and John C. Beeler, Company A; Private George Cease, Company C; Saddler Charles F. Davis and Privates John Kernan and John W. Sullivan, Company D.

repaired, *via* Washington, to Baltimore, and reporting to Gen. Wool, was sent thence to Frederick City.

"Lee's object in invading Maryland," says John Esten Cooke in his life of the Confederate commander, "has been the subject of much discussion, one party holding the view that his sole aim was to surround and capture a force of nine or ten thousand Federal troops stationed at Harper's Ferry, and another party maintaining that he proposed an invasion of Pennsylvania as far as the Susquehanna, intending to fight a decisive battle there, and advance thereafter upon Philadelphia, Baltimore, or Washington. The course pursued by an army commander is largely shaped by the progress of events. It can only be said that Gen. Lee doubtless left the future to decide his ultimate movements; meanwhile, he had a distinct and clearly-defined aim, which he states in plain words. His object was to draw the Federal forces out of Virginia first. The movement culminating in the victory over the enemy at Manassas had produced the effect of paralyzing them in every quarter.

"On the coast of North Carolina, in Western Virginia, and in the Shenandoah Valley had been heard the echo of the great events in Middle and Northern Virginia. Gen. Burnside's force had been brought up from the South, leaving affairs at a standstill in that direction; and, contemporaneously with the retreat of Gen. Pope, the Federal forces at Washington and beyond had fallen back to the Potomac. This left the way open, and Lee's further advance, it was obvious, would now completely clear Virginia of her invaders. The situation of affairs and the expected results are clearly stated by Gen. Lee. 'The war was thus transferred,' he says, 'from the interior to the frontier, and the supplies of rich and productive districts made accessible to our army. To prolong a state of affairs in every way desirable, and not to permit the season for active operations to pass without endeavoring to inflict other injury upon the enemy, the best course appeared to be the transfer of the army into Maryland.' . . . Such were the first designs of Lee; his ultimate aim seems as clear. By advancing into Maryland and threatening Baltimore and Washington, he knew he would force the enemy to withdraw all their troops from the south bank of the Potomac, where they menaced the Confederate communications with Richmond; when this was accomplished, as it clearly would be, his design was to cross the Maryland extension of the Blue Ridge, called there the South Mountain, advance by way of Hagerstown into the Cumberland Valley, and, by thus forcing the enemy to follow him, draw them to a distance from their base of supplies, while his own communications would remain open by way of the Shenandoah Valley. This was essentially the same plan pursued in the campaign of 1863, which terminated in the battle of Gettysburg. Gen. Lee's movements now indicated similar intentions. He doubtless wished, in the first place, to compel the enemy to pursue him, then to lead them as far as was prudent, and, if circumstances were favorable, bring them to decisive battle, success in which promised to open for him the gates of Washington or Baltimore, and end the war. It will now be seen how the delay caused by the movement of Jackson against Harper's Ferry, and the discovery by Gen. McClellan of the entire arrangement devised by Lee for that purpose, caused the failure of this whole ulterior design."

Gen. Lee, after the retreat of Pope, moved the main body of his army to Leesburg. Thence he moved to the Potomac, near Point of Rocks, and on the same day, the 5th of September, that Gen. Bragg, on a similar duty, entered Kentucky, Lee crossed at White's Ford, five miles below, and at a ford three miles above. His force consisted of the divisions of Gens. Jackson, Ewell, A. P. Hill, D. H. Hill, and Longstreet. When it became known that the army was destined for Maryland enthusiasm ran wild. Old and young along the route of march thronged the roadsides with banners and waving handkerchiefs. Upon entering Leesburg the bands played, colors waved, men shouted, women wept, and all was a scene of dust, confusion, and noise. "Maryland, my Maryland," "Dixie," the "Bonnie Blue Flag," and the "Marseillaise" of the various regimental bands were drowned in the tumult of voices, rumble of wagons, jingling of artillery, and the heavy tramp of infantry.

Jackson's division crossed near the Point of Rocks, tore up the Baltimore and Ohio Railroad tracks, and cut off all telegraphic and other connection from Harper's Ferry to Washington. The crossing of the Potomac was a holiday for the Marylanders in the Confederate army. All of them were filled with joy and many wept with gladness when they touched the "sacred soil of old Maryland." Old and young tossed their hats in the air with delight, others kissed the sod, and the bands constantly played "Maryland, my Maryland," until the sound was oppressive. The troops were wretchedly clothed and shod, and greatly in want of all necessaries. "Thousands of the troops," says Lee, "were destitute of shoes." "Never," says Gen. Jones, who commanded Jackson's old brigade, "had the army been so dirty, ragged, and ill-provided for as on this march." The wagons were empty, except extra ammunition; and as soon as the troops had crossed, their first meal on Maryland soil was green corn cut from the stalk growing in the cornfields. Soon, however, the quartermasters and commissaries brought in from the surrounding country supplies of provisions, which had been unknown to Lee's army for many months. No violence, no incivility was shown by the Confederate agents, and all transactions were satisfactorily arranged. Of the citizens of Western Maryland, a large majority favored the Union cause, many were indifferent, and a few warm secessionists. A Confederate newspaper correspondent traveling with the army says, "The few inhabitants we met betrayed evident pleasure at our arrival, but were extremely cautious and circumspect in showing it. They would look on and smile as we passed, but seemed much constrained in manner, as if feeling certain that Union men were in their midst quietly taking note of all actions or expressions, and ready to divulge names at fitting opportunities. Some few young men openly avowed their Southern feeling and joined us,[1] but the greater number stood as if thinking, 'I should much like to assist you if I dare, but how long will they remain? I am between two fires; I must sacrifice principle and secure my home.'"

The advance of the Confederate forces reached a point but three or four miles from Frederick on the night of the 5th. Their approach was already announced, and created great commotion, which spread rapidly through the surrounding country, and to other towns and cities in Maryland, and on the borders of Pennsylvania. On the 6th the army entered Frederick City, and was placed under the strictest orders to respect personal rights and private property. A brigade took possession of the hospital buildings for the sick and wounded Confederates, while a large portion of the army marched through Frederick and camped on the other side of the city at Norman's mill. The main body encamped about Monocacy Junction, near the Baltimore and Ohio Railroad bridge, on the side towards Baltimore.

The reception of the Confederate troops by the inhabitants of Frederick was decidedly cool. Not the slightest manifestation of joy or enthusiasm was exhibited. With all places of business closed, and the streets deserted by the people, the old town wore a gloomy appearance, in striking contrast to the resplendency it displayed upon the entry of the Union army one week later. On the approach of the Confederate army many of the citizens fled towards Pennsylvania and Baltimore. The military force in the city consisted of but one company,—C, First Potomac Home Brigade Infantry,—commanded by Capt. William T. Faithful, which could make no opposition. Capt. Faithful, who was provost-marshal of the town, removed all the military stores possible, and, leaving a sufficient supply for the hospitals, containing about six hundred patients, burned the remainder. Lieut. George T. Castle, of the First Potomac Home Brigade Infantry, had charge of the commissary depot.

The following report made by Capt. Faithful contains an interesting description of the scenes and occurrences in Frederick and the vicinity on the approach of the Confederates:

"Having been made aware that the rebel army was crossing the Potomac River at, and in vicinity of, Point of Rocks and the mouth of Monocacy, I immediately mounted my horse and reconnoitred the different roads leading from Frederick in the direction of the Potomac; returning to Frederick, I immediately detailed a sufficient number of my company to establish a line of telegraph pickets extending five miles from Frederick, in the road leading to the Point of Rocks. Having done this, I at once repaired to the telegraph-office, accompanied by Assistant Surgeon Weir, in charge of general hospital at Frederick, and Lieut. G. Castle, acting assistant quartermaster, when I desired that they should remain with me during the night and notice how things were going on. At eleven o'clock P.M. I was made aware our small force had been driven from Point of Rocks, and that the rebels were in possession; but in a short time, reinforcements arriving, I received the intelligence that our forces had regained possession of Point of Rocks, and held it at daylight. By this time people had begun to leave their homes and rush to Frederick, circulating rumors of all kinds. This created great excitement among the citizens of Frederick, which I endeavored to allay as much as possible. On the morning of the 5th some twenty canal boatmen, with their mules, arrived in Frederick at seven o'clock, stating that the rebel army was within six miles of Frederick. Just at this moment a gentleman from Buckeystown (about six miles out on the Point of Rocks road) arrived en route for Pennsylvania, informing me that the rebel Gen. Jackson and staff were eating supper at his house. I at once telegraphed to Col. D. S. Miles, commanding at Harper's Ferry, informing him of the news I had received, and the excitement of the place, when I received the following dispatch, to wit: that I should run off all horses that I had to a place of safety in Pennsylvania; to destroy all quartermaster and commissary stores, and start with my company, and all others that belonged to the regiment, for Knoxville, and report to Col. W. P. Maulsby. I immediately called the attention of Assistant Surgeon Weir, in charge of general hospital, and Post Quartermaster Castle, to my orders, and advised the saving of all property possible, instead of destroying it; and ordered all the horses in pasture to Pennsylvania. I then called upon Mr. Quinn, the Baltimore and Ohio Railroad agent at Frederick, and secured every car possible. With a small engine, the only one which could be had, I had all the quartermaster and commissary stores loaded into the cars, to their utmost capacity, under direction of Lieut. Castle; and with the energy displayed by Assistant Surgeon Weir, we succeeded in getting off all the most valuable hospital stores in wagons and ambulances, together with about three hundred convalescents from the hospital, to a place of safety in Pennsylvania. After having sent off all the most valuable stores by all availing means at hand, we set about destroying by fire the remains of some old and worthless stores,

---

[1] It is thought that not over two hundred Marylanders joined the Confederates during their invasion of Maryland in 1862.

which were of no great value to the government, but might have been made useful to the rebels. Everything of value having been sent off, and the flames consuming the balance, by the aid of Assistant Surgeon Weir and Lieut. Castle, I then ordered Mr. Kelly, the telegraph operator, to detach his instrument and secure a conveyance and start for Pennsylvania, that he might get to Baltimore and report to the general superintendent of the line.

"This having been accomplished, I ordered in my pickets, formed my company, and started for my regiment at Knoxville by the Sharpsburg road, expecting to come in contact with some of the rebel pickets (cavalry) as I passed in the neighborhood of Petersville and Jefferson, but by a rapid march I succeeded in passing this point but a short time before they became occupied by their pickets.

"The time consumed in the saving of the government property in Frederick, which amounted to several hundred thousands, was about five hours."

In Frederick martial law was proclaimed by the Confederates, and Col. Bradley T. Johnson, a native of the place, was appointed provost-marshal, with a strong guard of soldiers to patrol the streets and preserve order. Immediately on assuming command he issued the following proclamation:

"TO THE PEOPLE OF MARYLAND:

"After sixteen months of oppression more galling than the Austrian tyranny, the victorious army of the South brings freedom to your doors. Its standard now waves from the Potomac to Mason and Dixon's line. The men of Maryland, who during the last long months have been crushed under the heel of this terrible despotism, now have the opportunity for working out their own redemption, for which they have so long waited and suffered and hoped.

"The government of the Confederate States is pledged by the unanimous vote of its Congress, by the distinct declaration of its President, the soldier and statesman, Davis, never to cease this war until Maryland has the opportunity to decide for herself her own fate, untrammeled and free from Federal bayonets.

"The people of the South, with unanimity unparalleled, have given their hearts to our native State, and hundreds of thousands of her sons have sworn with arms in their hands that you shall be free.

"You must now do your part. We have the arms here for you. I am authorized immediately to muster in for the war companies and regiments; the companies of one hundred men each, the regiments of ten companies. Come all who wish to strike for their liberties and homes. Let each man provide himself with a stout pair of shoes, a good blanket, and a tin cup. Jackson's men have no baggage.

"Officers are in Frederick to receive recruits, and all companies formed will be armed as soon as mustered in. Rise at once!

"Remember the cells of Fort McHenry! remember the dungeons of Fort Lafayette and Fort Warren! the insults to your wives and daughters, the arrests, the midnight searches of your houses!

"Remember these, your wrongs, and rise at once in arms and strike for liberty and right!

"BRADLEY T. JOHNSON, *Col. C. S. A.*

"Sept. 8, 1862."

"Personne," the correspondent of the Charleston *Mercury*, who was an eye-witness to all the stirring scenes of Lee's campaign in Maryland, in a letter dated at Frederick, September 7th, the day after the Confederates arrived, says,—

"Thus far we have everywhere met with cordial hospitality. Along the road the farmers have welcomed the presence of our men with a sincerity that cannot be misunderstood, opened their houses, and spread their boards with the fat of the land. One Marylander whom I met has fed, in twenty-four hours, six hundred hungry men, free of charge. Others have been proportionately liberal. Our reception, up to this point, has been all that we could desire. With a few the enthusiasm has been highly demonstrative, but the majority content themselves with quiet manifestations of the warm sympathy they feel. Nearly all the houses along the route of march were open, and invitations were freely extended to the officers to spend the day and night. A slight indication of the grateful outbursts of the people was in the presentation of a magnificent horse to Gen. Jackson, by the farmers, within an hour after he touched Maryland soil. In the sentiment of the people we are not much disappointed. It is apparently about equally divided, and there is yet little expressed enthusiasm. As Jackson's army marched through their houses were mostly closed, and from between the window-blinds the citizens could be seen anxiously peering, as if they expected to see a crowd of bugaboos, intent upon nothing but rapine and slaughter. A few of the residences were open, however, and in those ladies and gentlemen were waving their handkerchiefs and displaying the Confederate flag."

On Sunday the churches were opened as usual, and were filled with Confederate officers and soldiers. Gen. Jackson attended the Presbyterian and German Reformed churches. On Monday, September 8th, "Personne" writes,—

"Frederick to-day presents a busy scene, more like that of a Fourth of July festival than a gathering of armed invaders; a majority of the stores are closed to general admission, because of the crowds eager to press and buy, but a little diplomacy secures an entrance at the back door, or past the sentinel wisely stationed to protect the proprietor from the rush of anxious customers. Prices are going up rapidly. Everything is so cheap that our men frequently lay down a five-dollar bill to pay for a three-dollar article, and rush out without waiting for the change. The good people here don't understand it. Bitter complaints are uttered against those who refuse Confederate money, and it is understood that the authorities will insist upon its general circulation.

"The people are beginning to recover from their surprise at our sudden appearance, and to realize the magnitude of our preparations to advance through and relieve Maryland from her thraldom. Some are still moody, and evidently hate us heartily, but we are more than compensated by the warm welcome of others, who now begin to greet us from every quarter. Only a few moments ago I met a lady who confessed that although she had Confederate flags ready to expose in her windows as we passed, she was afraid to wave them lest, being discovered by her Union neighbors, she should be reported to the Federals in case of our retreat, and be therefore subject to insult, if not imprisonment, at their hands. To assure me how true were her sentiments, she introduced me to a large room in her house, where there were fourteen ladies, young and old, busy as bees making shirts, drawers, and other clothing for the soldiers. She also distributed money and tobacco to the soldiers.

"Though thousands of soldiers are now roaming through the town, there has not been a solitary instance of misdemeanor. I have heard no shouting, no clamor of any kind, and seen but a single case of intoxication,—a one-legged Yankee prisoner.

"All who visit the city are required to have passes, and the only persons arrested are those who are here without leave. This quiet behavior of our men contrasts so strongly with that of the Federals when here as to excite the favorable comment of the Unionists.

"None of the latter have to my knowledge been interfered with, and, as far as I can learn, it is not the policy of our commander to retaliate. We shall, on the contrary, pursue a conciliatory course, and by kindness endeavor to show those misguided people that our home should be their home, and our God their God.

"One of these men frankly confessed to me that he feared his own neighbors more than he did our troops, and he should regret to see us depart. We pay for everything as we go, the farmers being compensated for all damage by the burning of rails, use of forage, or destruction of crops before we break up camp.

"Recruiting here goes on rapidly. Within two days ago five companies have been formed, and it is stated that from the surrounding country over seven hundred entered our ranks while *en route*. Pennsylvania, the border line of which is only some twenty-five or twenty-eight miles distant, has sent us nearly a hundred recruits, who prefer service in the Confederate army to being drafted into that of the North.

"Altogether, our movements have been thus far marked by the most gratifying success. Every detail has been successively carried out, the troops are in good health and full of enthusiasm, the commissariat is improving, and we wait for nothing more anxiously than the order to resume our march onward."

On the same day Gen. Lee issued the following address to the people of Maryland, setting forth the object of his invasion:

"HEADQUARTERS ARMY N. VA.,
"NEAR FREDERICK TOWN, Sept. 8, 1862.

"TO THE PEOPLE OF MARYLAND:

"It is right that you should know the purpose that has brought the army under my command within the limits of your State, so far as that purpose concerns yourselves.

"The people of the Confederate States have long watched with the deepest sympathy the wrongs and outrages that have been inflicted upon the citizens of a Commonwealth allied to the States of the South by the strongest social, political, and commercial ties.

"They have seen with profound indignation their sister State deprived of every right, and reduced to the condition of a conquered province.

"Under the pretence of supporting the Constitution, but in violation of its most valuable provisions, your citizens have been arrested and imprisoned upon no charge, and contrary to all forms of law; the faithful and manly protest against this outrage, made by the venerable and illustrious Marylander to whom in better days no citizen appealed for right in vain, was treated with scorn and contempt. The government of your city has been usurped by armed strangers; your Legislature has been dissolved by the unlawful arrest of its members; freedom of the press and speech has been suppressed; words have been declared offenses by an arbitrary decree of the Federal Executive, and citizens ordered to be tried by a military commission for what they may dare to speak. Believing that the people of Maryland possessed a spirit too lofty to submit to such a government, the people of the South have long wished to aid you in throwing off this foreign yoke, to enable you to again enjoy the inalienable rights of freemen, and restore independency and sovereignty to your State.

"In obedience to this wish our army has come among you, and is prepared to assist you with the power of its arms in regaining the rights of which you have been despoiled.

"This, citizens of Maryland, is our mission, so far as yourselves are concerned.

"No restraint upon your free will is intended; no intimidation will be allowed.

"Within the limits of this army at least Marylanders shall once more enjoy their ancient freedom of thought and speech.

"We know no enemies among you, and will protect all of every opinion.

"It is for you to decide your destiny, freely and without constraint.

"This army will respect your choice whatever it will be, and while the Southern people will rejoice to welcome you to your natural position among them, they will only welcome you when you come of your own free will.

"R. E. LEE, *General Commanding.*"

It was hoped by the South that Johnson's proclamation and Lee's stirring appeal would arouse the people of the State, but few responded to the call. The section occupied by the Confederate army was inhabited by people who had, for the most part, very different views and feelings from those of the more southern counties. In the latter and in Baltimore thousands would have flocked to the standard of Lee had they not been restrained by the Federal occupation. Moreover, the wretched appearance of the Confederate troops had a discouraging effect, and damped the martial ardor of many who visited the camp with intent to enter the service. The cavalry and artillery were nearly all barefooted, and many of the infantry in the same condition, some having their feet tied up with rags, pieces of carpet, or covered with raw-hides, while the more fortunate had some battered remnants of shoes, through which the toes protruded. It was no unusual sight to see tracks of blood on the turnpike left by a marching regiment. While the Confederates occupied Frederick, their cavalry scouted the entire country for forage, provisions, recruits, etc. They established pickets on the Baltimore turnpike, at New Market, Liberty, Middletown, Union Bridge, Pikesville, Poplar Springs, and other places. Col. Piper, with about three hundred and fifty of Stuart's cavalry and one piece of artillery, occupied Westminster, where they arrested Dr. Billingslea, the provost-marshal, but afterwards released him on parole. All the books and papers relating to the enrollment were seized and destroyed. They also seized the post-office and carried off the postage-stamps. In their intercourse with the citizens they professed the greatest friendship for the peace of the State, and desired to be received as friends. No one was interfered with, or questioned with regard to their sentiments. They had plenty of money (such as it was), and spent it freely, purchasing what they wanted from the stores.

Recruiting-offices were opened in Frederick, and citizens invited to enlist. Very few volunteers, however, were obtained, not enough to compensate for the loss the army sustained by desertion.

Scouting parties were thrown out in various directions for considerable distances. Middletown was occupied by a small force on the 9th. In anticipation of such an event, many of the residents had already left their homes and sought refuge elsewhere. A body of cavalry moved as far east as Uniontown, while another party penetrated to within four miles of Ellicott's Mills.

The excitement in Pennsylvania was quite as great as in Maryland. An invasion of the North had been loudly proclaimed by the Confederates, and threats of devastation and retaliation were freely uttered. The advance to Frederick was directly towards Pennsylvania, and the invasion of that State seemed imminent. While the infantry were at Frederick the Confederate cavalry had entered Pennsylvania, and their numbers had been greatly exaggerated by rumor. In the excited state of the people it was believed the whole army was advancing towards Harrisburg, with the purpose of moving thence upon Philadelphia. Gov. Curtin summoned the people, and they hastened in great numbers to Harrisburg, while from other States new levies and volunteers were hurried forward to the defense of the capital. Jackson's division was encamped on Norman's, near the suburbs, to the north of Frederick, except the brigade of Gen. J. R. Jones (Col. Bradley T. Johnson commanding), which was encamped in the barracks inclosure in the city as provost-guard. Ewell's and Hill's divisions occupied positions near the railroad bridge over the Monocacy, guarding the approaches to Washington. On the occupation of Frederick, Gen. Lee supposed the Federals would evacuate Harper's Ferry, and thus open his line of communication through the Valley of Virginia to Richmond. As this did not occur, it became necessary, if possible, to dislodge the Federals from this position before concentrating the army west of the mountains. With this object in view, Gen. Lee directed Jackson to proceed with his command to Martinsburg, and after driving the Federals under Gen. White from that place, to move down the south side of the Potomac on Harper's Ferry. Gen. McLaws, with his own and R. H. Anderson's divisions, was ordered to seize Maryland Heights, on the north side of the Potomac, opposite Harper's Ferry, and Brig.-Gen. Walker to take possession of Loudon Heights, on the east side of the Shenandoah at its junction with the Potomac. These several commands, after reducing Harper's Ferry and clearing the valley, were ordered to join the rest of the army at Boonsboro' or Hagerstown. These troops, in pursuance of their orders, on the morning of the 10th of September broke up camp at Monocacy Junction, and passing rapidly through Middletown, Boonsboro', and Williamsport, recrossed the Potomac at Light's Ford on the 11th. Gen. A. P. Hill moved with his division on the turnpike direct from Williamsport to Martinsburg. The divisions of Jackson and Ewell proceeded towards the North Mountain depot, on the Baltimore and Ohio Railroad, about seven miles northwest of Martinsburg, to prevent the escape of Gen. White's troops. Maj. Myers, commanding the cavalry, sent part of his force as far south as the Berkeley and Hampshire turnpike. Gen. White, learning of these movements, evacuated Martinsburg on the 11th, and retreated to Harper's Ferry. On the following day Jackson's command took possession of Martinsburg, and on the morning of the 13th they arrived before the Federals drawn up in force upon Bolivar Heights. Before beginning the attack, Gen. Jackson proceeded to put himself in communication with the co-operating forces of McLaws and Walker. The latter took possession of Loudon Heights on the 13th, and on next day was in readiness to open fire upon Harper's Ferry.

The former entered Pleasant Valley on the 11th, and on the following day Gen. Kershaw, with his own and Barksdale's brigade, proceeded to ascend the ridge whose southern extremity is known as Maryland Heights and attack Col. Thomas H. Ford, who occupied that position with infantry and artillery, protected by intrenchments. He disposed of the rest of his force to hold the roads leading from Harper's Ferry eastward through Weaverton, and northward from Sandy Hook, guarding the pass in his rear, through which he had entered Pleasant Valley, with the brigades of Semmes and Mahone.

In the meanwhile events occurred in Maryland which threatened to interfere with the reduction of Harper's Ferry. On the 10th of September Gen. Longstreet moved from Frederick for Hagerstown, and reached there with part of his command on the 11th. Gen. D. H. Hill with his division constituted the rear-guard, and had charge of the immense wagon-train moving in the direction of Hagerstown. On the 13th he was ordered by Gen. Lee to dispose of his troops so as to prevent the escape of the Federal garrison from Harper's Ferry, then besieged, and also to guard the pass in the Blue Ridge near Boonsboro'.

When Gen. McClellan arrived in Washington, about the middle of August, he was in the department of Gen. Pope, which included the District of Columbia. On the 2d of September, Maj.-Gen. Halleck relieved Gen. Pope, and placed Maj.-Gen. McClellan in "command of the fortifications of Washington, and of all the troops for the defense of the capital." On the 4th he assumed command of the forces under Gen. Pope, together with some new levies which had arrived at Washington under the call of the President. On the invasion of Maryland he received orders to pursue Gen. Lee with all the troops which were not required for the defense of Washington, and on the next day most of his army was in motion and rapidly advanced into Maryland. Gen. Banks was placed in command of the defenses at Washington, and Gen. Heintzelman in charge of the forces on the Virginia side. The command of Fitz John Porter's corps was given to Gen. Hooker, and that of Gen. McDowell was assigned to Gen. Reno, late of the North Carolina Department.

"Having assumed command of the army, I pushed forward," says Gen. McClellan, "the First and Ninth Corps under Gens. Reno and Hooker, forming the right wing. under Gen. Burnside, to Leesburg on the 5th inst.; thence the First Corps, by Brooksville, Cooksville, and Ridgeville, to Frederick; and the Ninth Corps, by Damascus, on New Market and Frederick. The Second and Eleventh Corps, under Gens. Sumner and Williams, on the 6th were moved from Tenallytown to Rockville; thence, by Middlebury and Urbana, on Frederick, the Eleventh Corps moving by a lateral road between Urbana and New Market, thus maintaining the communication between the centre and right wing, as well as covering the direct route from Frederick to Washington. The Sixth Corps, under Gen. Franklin, was moved to Darnestown on the 6th inst.; thence, by Dawsonville and Barnville, on Buckeystown, covering the road from the mouth of the Monocacy to Rockville, and being in a position to connect with and support the centre, should it have been necessary (as was supposed) to force the line of the Monocacy. Couch's division (composed of the brigades of Gens. Howe, Devens, and Cochrane) was thrown forward to Offut's Cross-Roads and Poolesville by the river road, thus covering that approach, watching the fords of the Potomac, and ultimately following and supporting the Sixth Corps. The object of these movements was to feel the enemy, to compel him to develop his intentions, at the same time that the troops were in position readily to cover Baltimore or Washington, to attack him should he hold the line of the Monocacy, or to follow him into Pennsylvania, if necessary."

Attached to the Army of the Potomac at this time were the following Maryland organizations: The Second Infantry with the Ninth Corps, the Third and Purnell Legion with the Twelfth Corps, and Batteries A and B, Light Artillery, with the Sixth Corps. The Fifth Infantry was brought from Fort Monroe *via* Washington, and joined the Second Corps *en route* to Antietam.

Gen. McClellan started in pursuit of the enemy with his right and centre spread out towards the north to guard against any attempt of Lee to sweep around and capture Baltimore. Franklin's command was kept on the left along the river line to prevent a *coup de main* in the direction of Washington.

Burnside's column, moving *via* Leesboro', Brookville, Damascus, and New Market, arrived at the bridge over the Monocacy on the Baltimore pike during the afternoon of the 12th. The bridge, held by a small force of the enemy, was carried after a slight resistance. An hour or two later a charge was made by Cox's division of the Ninth Corps upon Frederick, the enemy's rear-guard driven out and the city occupied. Pleasonton's cavalry entered the town by the road from Georgetown simultaneously with Reno's corps. The entrance of the latter into Frederick was a most brilliant scene. It was greeted with a cordial and enthusiastic welcome. An eye-witness says,—

"The entire corps advanced in a long, splendid line, Harland's brigade emerging through the hospital barracks just in time to see the last of the rebel cavalry dash out of the streets pursued by our own. Women blessed God and the soldiers, and rushed out to kiss the old flag; gray-haired men hobbled forth with radiant faces, and the young shouted their welcome, while children capered in holiday glee. If Dame Barbara Fritchie alone had dared,

"'When Lee marched over the mountain wall,'

to set the starry flag defiantly in her attic window, thousands had kept the loved emblem, and the line had not been five minutes in the street before national banners, large and little, were flung from the windows, and draped with inspiring grace almost every threshold."[1]

Another wrote,—

"Gen. Burnside's reception was especially enthusiastic. The people crowded around him, covered his horse and himself with flowers, saluted him with cheers and shouts of welcome, and manifested their joy in every method of demonstration. Gen. McClellan's reception, at a later hour, was equally cordial and demonstrative. The citizens of Frederick felt as though they had been delivered from a great affliction, and the Army of the Potomac had the opportunity of enjoying a new sensation."[2]

Of Gen. McClellan's reception, another says,—

"When Burnside rode through the acclamations were universal, but nothing to the reception given McClellan when he entered some time after. Bouquets were thrown; men, women, and children rushed to him, he bowing and speaking to all; girls embracing his horse's neck and kissing the animal, only because they could not reach the general."[3]

A participant thus describes the passage of the Second and Twelfth Corps through the city:

---

[1] "Military History of Connecticut during the War," page 261.
[2] "Burnside and the Ninth Army Corps," page 121.
[3] "Moore's Rebellion Record," vol. v. page 608.

"On the 14th Sumner's column passed through Frederick, and was greeted by the loyal citizens of the place with a reception as handsome as it was unexpected. Flags that had been concealed while the enemy held possession now decorated the dwellings, and were waving along with the emblem that made Barbara Fritchie historical; and on the streets by which the army entered the people pressed forward to greet the soldiers with expressions of warmest sympathy.

"These patriotic manifestations were not confined to the town of Frederick, but frequently along the line of march through this portion of Maryland the inhabitants gave the strongest evidence of attachment to the Union cause. Ladies of all ages and stations in life stood by the roadside, in front of their dwellings, with pails of milk, or, if the supply had been exhausted, a cup of cold water and a word of cheer."[1]

To these extracts from contemporary histories we may add that the Union element in the section of Maryland traversed by the two armies was very strong. The secession element was chiefly limited to Baltimore City and the tier of counties lying between the Chesapeake Bay and the Potomac River, and on the Eastern Shore. By the 13th of September the whole of McClellan's army had crossed the Monocacy, the larger portion being concentrated around Frederick.

During the Confederate occupation of Frederick, Capt. Russell, with Companies H and I, First Maryland Cavalry, made a raid on their picket-lines near that city, and captured over two hundred prisoners, whom he carried back to Harper's Ferry. On the afternoon of the 12th the Federal advance drove the Confederates out of Middletown, and Sunday morning, the 14th, found them posted on the east side of the Blue Ridge Mountains, and stretching on a line from north to south from points immediately opposite Middletown and Jefferson, both of which villages are about eight miles from Frederick. Middletown is on the road to Hagerstown, and Jefferson on the direct road to Harper's Ferry. The right of the Federal army, at this time under Gen. Burnside, rested on Middletown, and the left, under Gen. Franklin, on Jefferson.

At Frederick, McClellan found a copy of Lee's order to Gen. D. H. Hill, disclosing to him the movements of the Confederate forces. From this it appeared that Lee intended to capture the garrison of Harper's Ferry. McClellan immediately gave orders for a rapid and vigorous forward movement. The Confederate cavalry under Gen. Stuart fell back before him, materially impeding his progress towards Boonsboro'. The Confederate line of battle was formed with the left resting upon Turner's Gap and the turnpike road towards Hagerstown, which passes through the gap, and the right covering Crampton's

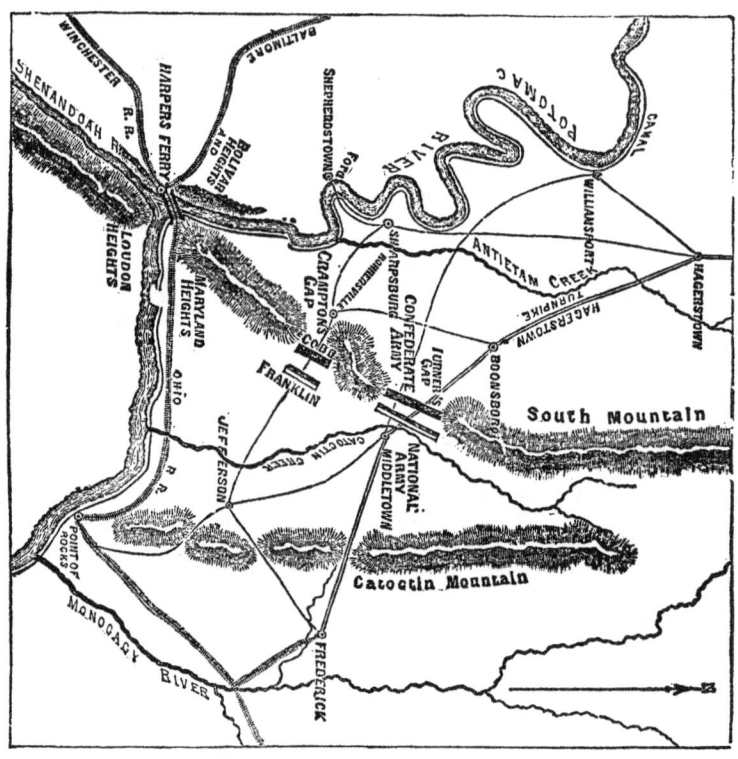

BATTLE OF SOUTH MOUNTAIN.

---

[1] Banes' "History of the Philadelphia Brigade," page 107.

Gap and the road leading to Harper's Ferry. To check the advance of the enemy, and to prevent the relief of Harper's Ferry, Hill was directed to guard Crampton's Gap, and Longstreet was ordered from Hagerstown to his support.[1]

On the morning of September 14th, the Federal column under Gen. Franklin, then near Jefferson, was put in motion towards Harper's Ferry, with orders to secure and hold Crampton's Gap, "cut off, destroy, or capture McLaws' command, and relieve Col. Miles."

Gen. Franklin pushed his corps rapidly forward to the vicinity of Burkettsville, immediately in the rear of which he found the Confederate infantry posted in force on both sides of the road leading through the pass, with artillery in strong positions to defend the approaches thereto. Slocum's division was formed upon the right of the road, and Smith's upon the left. As the line advanced the Confederates were forced back into the gap, where they made a most determined stand, but after a spirited action of three hours the crest was gained by Gen. Franklin's troops, the Confederates hastily retreating down the western slope of the mountain.

During the engagement Battery A of the Federal Maryland Light Artillery was stationed on the left and to the rear of Burkettsville, and maintained a steady fire on the positions of the Confederates until they were assailed and carried by the infantry.

The close of the action found Gen. Franklin's advance in Pleasant Valley, within three and a half miles of the point on Maryland Heights where he might, on the same night or the following morning, have formed a junction with the garrison at Harper's Ferry had not the force on the heights been previously withdrawn.

But Col. Miles surrendered at an early hour on the morning of the 15th, and it was now too late to accomplish the principal object of Gen. Franklin's movement. He was therefore directed to watch the enemy in his front and protect the left and rear of the main body of the army. This he did until the night of the 16th, when he was ordered to unite with the other corps confronting the enemy on the Antietam.

---

[1] Longstreet's corps was to remain at Hagerstown until the fall of Harper's Ferry. D. H. Hill's division, with Stuart's cavalry, constituted the rear-guard of this corps. Longstreet's advance entered Hagerstown on the morning of the 11th. The sheriff and other officials left the place as soon as the enemy entered, carrying with them the public records and other valuables in their different offices. Numbers of private citizens also left the town. On the 6th and 7th the banks, anticipating the enemy's approach, had removed their deposits to Harrisburg and other places east for safety. The government stores there were also removed.

While the events just described were transpiring at Harper's Ferry and Crampton's Gap, the right of the Federal army was engaged in a contest for the possession of Turner's Gap, through which runs the main road from Frederick to Hagerstown.

On the morning of the 13th, Gen. Pleasonton moved with a portion of his cavalry in the direction of Middletown. After some sharp skirmishing he reached the town, out of which he drove the Confederate rear, and held it during the night. The enemy was found occupying Turner's Gap in strong force, and apparently determined to dispute the passage of the mountain. Cox's division of Reno's corps was advanced in the afternoon as a support to the cavalry, followed before night by the other divisions of the corps.

On the morning of the 14th the several corps constituting the right wing and centre, which had been united at Frederick, were posted as follows:

The First (Hooker's) on the Monocacy, the Second (Sumner's), the Fifth (Sykes' division), and the Twelfth (Williams') at or near Frederick.

The advance division (Cox's) of the Ninth Corps (Reno's) was at Middletown, with the other three divisions (Willcox's, Rodman's, and Sturgis') within easy supporting distance.

At an early hour Hooker began the march towards Middletown, followed at intervals by the other corps.

Gen. Burnside, commanding the right wing, had orders to carry Turner's Gap.

The combat of the day really commenced about 6 A.M. at the bridge over Catoctin Creek, half a mile west of Middletown, where the enemy had concentrated his artillery to resist the passage. D. H. Hill's division of Longstreet's corps held the crest of the mountain from three miles north of the gap to two miles south. This included Fox's Gap, at the point where a country road leading to Sharpsburg crosses the mountain, south of the main pike, and the "old Hagerstown road" on the northerly side.

About 9 A.M., the passage over the Catoctin having been forced, Cox's division moved up the acclivity towards Fox's Gap, and after a severe contest carried the crest. Cox's division was supported in the course of the day by the divisions of Willcox, Rodman, and Sturgis.

While moving forward with the latter division, the Second Maryland was detached and placed in position near the turnpike, where it was held in reserve and lay under a galling artillery fire, but did not become actively engaged.

After very hard fighting the Ninth Corps repulsed several attacks of the enemy, and held full possession of the summit at Fox's Gap. Gen. Reno, its gallant commander, was killed just before sunset, and Gen. Cox assumed the command. About the middle of the afternoon Gen. Hooker, with Meade's and Hatch's divisions, attacked the heights on the right of Turner's Gap, and after a desperate resistance carried the crest about dark and held it. Just before dark Gibbon's brigade of Hatch's division advanced up the main road against the enemy in the gap, and after an obstinate conflict gained the entrance to the pass. At night the entire army except Franklin's column was massed in the vicinity of the field of battle.

The battle had raged during the day with fearful effect against Hill's small force until the afternoon, when Longstreet, who had made a forced march from Hagerstown, arrived to his assistance about half-past three o'clock. Longstreet hurried his troops to Hill's assistance as rapidly as their exhausted condition would admit of, and they succeeded for some time in repulsing the repeated and powerful attacks of the Federal army, and prevented the passage of the Federal forces till night put an end to the conflict. The superiority of numbers enabled McClellan to extend his army beyond both flanks of the Confederate line. By this means he succeeded in reaching the summit of the mountain beyond the Confederate left, and pressing heavily upon them from that direction, gradually forced Gen. Rhodes back, till darkness prevented a further advance of the Federals.

Having accomplished all that was required,—the delay of the Federal army until Harper's Ferry could not be relieved,—the Confederates during the night retreated to Sharpsburg, covered by the cavalry brigade of Gen. Fitzhugh Lee. Gen. Hill, in summing up the results of this battle, says, "Should the truth ever be known, the battle of South Mountain, as far as my division was concerned, will be regarded as one of the most remarkable and creditable of the war. The division had marched all the way from Richmond, and the straggling had been enormous, in consequence of heavy marches, deficient commissariat, want of shoes, and inefficient officers. Owing to these combined causes, the division numbered less than five thousand men on the morning of the 14th of September, and had five roads to guard, extending over a space of as many miles. This small force successfully resisted without support for eight hours the whole Federal army, and when its supports were beaten still held the roads, so that our retreat was effected without the loss of a gun, a wagon, or an ambulance."

In the battle of South Mountain the Confederates lost in killed the following prominent officers: Gen. Garland, Col. B. B. Gayle, of the Twelfth Alabama; Col. J. B. Strange, of the Nineteenth Virginia. The Federals lost Gen. Reno and several minor officers.[1]

While these events were in progress, Gen. Jackson had been vigorously engaged in the attack upon Harper's Ferry.

The Federal Maryland troops at Harper's Ferry and immediate neighborhood were Companies H and I, First Cavalry, A, C, and D, Cole's cavalry battalion, and the First and Third Potomac Home Brigade Infantry.

Gen. Jackson, as has been said, left Frederick on

---

[1] Gen. Reno was born in the State of Virginia, and was appointed as a West Point cadet from Pennsylvania in 1842. He graduated in 1846, in the same class with Maj.-Gen. McClellan; was breveted second lieutenant of ordnance; went to Mexico, and participated in every engagement from Vera Cruz to the city of Mexico. He was breveted first lieutenant on the 18th of April, 1847, for gallantry at Cerro Gordo. In this battle, as at Chapultepec, he commanded a battery, and in the latter action he was wounded. For gallantry at Chapultepec he was breveted captain, Sept. 13, 1847.

After the close of the war he was for six months Assistant Professor of Mathematics at West Point, and for eighteen months afterwards secretary to the Artillery Board, during which he was engaged in testing heavy ordnance and compiling tactics for heavy artillery. Various employments succeeded, in all of which he brought to bear judgment, good scientific attainments, and industry. He was for a time on the coast survey, then on topographical duty in the West; for a year engaged in building a military road from Big Sioux River to St. Paul, Minn. From 1854 to 1857 he was stationed at Frankford Arsenal, near Philadelphia. He was afterwards chief ordnance officer to Gen. Johnston in the Utah expedition, and remained there till 1859, when he was detached and sent to the Mount Vernon Arsenal, Alabama. He was afterwards stationed at Leavenworth, Kansas, where he was when the Rebellion broke out.

He was one of the officers selected by Gen. Burnside himself to accompany him in his expedition, and approved by his unvarying gallantry and conduct the choice of his superior general. He was appointed brigadier-general of volunteers Nov. 12, 1861, distinguished himself at Roanoke and Newbern, and was considered one of the bravest and most promising officers in the service. When Burnside's army was brought up from North Carolina, Reno was put in command of a division, and in the battles before Washington so distinguished himself that his name is among the foremost of those honorably mentioned in reports. Gen. Reno's remains were conveyed to Baltimore, where they were embalmed by John H. Weaver. On the 16th they were placed in a patent air-tight coffin and removed to the President Street depot, to be conveyed by the one o'clock train of the Philadelphia Railroad to Boston, Mass., where his family resided. During the morning a large number of persons, including ladies, visited the establishment of Mr. Weaver to view the body, which was exposed to view. He was dressed in his full uniform, and had quite a natural appearance. The following members of his staff accompanied the remains from Frederick to Baltimore, and thence to Boston: Capt. E. M. Neale, assistant adjutant-general, Capt. B. F. Reno, aide-de-camp to the general (his brother), and Lieuts. John A. Morris, Thos. A. Marsh, and Charles Hutton, aides-de-camp.

the 10th, and marching rapidly *via* Williamsport, occupied Martinsburg on the 12th, the Federal garrison having fallen back east of Sandy Hook, and was now approaching Loudon Heights; and McLaws having gained the summit of Maryland Heights by way of Solomon's Gap, confronted Col. Ford's command, posted there for the defense of Harper's Ferry on the north. During the afternoon portions of the Thirty-second Ohio and One Hundred and Twenty-sixth New York were deployed along the mountain near to the Gap. Skirmishing commenced at about half-past three, continuing until sundown. Owing to the thick underbrush, the skirmish was of a bushwhacking character, as, indeed was all the fighting on the heights. After dark a strong picket-line was established from one side to the other of the mountain, and a renewal of the conflict awaited with sleepless anxiety.

At daybreak on the 13th a line of battle was formed some three hundred yards in front of a barricade constructed four hundred yards in advance of what was known as the "lookout." Companies K and B, First Potomac Home Brigade Infantry, held the extreme right, the One Hundred and Twenty-sixth New York next in order, Thirty-second Ohio front and centre, and the Thirty-ninth New York the extreme left. Companies H and I of the First Maryland Cavalry, under Capt. Charles H. Russell, advanced on foot about three hundred yards in front of the line of battle. But the enemy appearing in superior force, firing heavily, these companies fell back after discharging two volleys. The enemy then, about seven o'clock, opened with musketry on the front and right, and made two partial charges, in which he was handsomely repulsed. Fighting now became general along the whole line, continuing one hour. At the end of this time, the Confederates, receiving reinforcements, advanced with great vigor and determination. Under this pressure the whole line fell back to the barricade, fighting as it retired.

On reaching the barricade a stand was made and the position maintained for several hours, Company K, First Potomac Home Brigade Infantry, with its handful of men, preventing a flank movement on the right. But the enemy having succeeded in turning the left compelled the command to again fall back some distance. At this juncture the Third Potomac Home Brigade Infantry, under Lieut.-Col. S. W. Downey, arrived from below, and the line advanced, reoccupying the "lookout."

Again, however, the Confederates succeeded in flanking the defenders of the heights, and they were obliged to fall back, first to the naval battery overlooking Harper's Ferry, and ultimately, about four P.M., down the mountain and across the river into the town. Capt. Russell, of the First Maryland Cavalry, displayed much gallantry. Capt. Charles J. Brown, of Company K, First Potomac Home Brigade Infantry, also exhibited much heroism. Lieut.-Col. Downey, of the Third Potomac Home Brigade Infantry, was complimented by Col. Miles for his courage and skill in handling his troops. Col. Downey, while in command of a small reconnoitring force of cavalry, nineteen men of First Maryland Cavalry, under Capt. Shamburg, from Kearneysville, had been slightly wounded in a skirmish with the enemy's column passing through Boonsboro' on the 10th. Lieut. D. C. Hiteshew, of Company H, First Maryland Cavalry, showed conspicuous bravery, and was mortally wounded while encouraging his men to stand firm under a deadly fire. Sergt. P. L. Hiteshew, of Company I, a brother of the lieutenant, was severely wounded, and it is a singular circumstance that these brothers were the only ones injured in the two companies.

At the close of the day Gens. Jackson and Walker closely invested Harper's Ferry on the west and south, and McLaws held Maryland Heights, which was the key of the position.

Next morning the remainder of the First Potomac Home Brigade Infantry, under Col. William P. Maulsby, took position near the Virginia end of the pontoon-bridge spanning the Potomac, with orders to destroy it should the enemy attempt to make a crossing. The Third Potomac Home Brigade Infantry occupied a position behind the earthworks on Bolivar Heights. In the forenoon Col. Miles' batteries opened on Loudon and Maryland Heights, and continued shelling them for several hours.

About two P.M. the Confederates began a furious artillery fire simultaneously from Loudon and Maryland Heights and from Sandy Hook. The Federal artillery replied with much spirit, and for a time silenced the Loudon batteries. The enemy also opened other guns from the Sheperdstown and Charlestown roads. Heavy cannonading was thus brought to bear on the doomed garrison from five different points. Notwithstanding this the Union forces held their ground manfully until the firing ceased, towards sunset.

About dusk the Confederates in front opened a musketry fire on the left flank, posted near the Shenandoah, which was promptly returned by Companies A and I (Cook and Samuels), First Potomac Home Brigade Infantry, and five companies of the Eighty-seventh Ohio Regiment. But the Union line was finally forced to contract itself, the enemy having succeeded in turning the flank. After nightfall all became quiet, and the exhausted soldiers slept on their arms.

Under cover of the night the enemy planted additional batteries in every direction, and at five A.M. began pouring a concentric fire on Bolivar Heights from seven different points, and so arranged as to completely enfilade the Union line.

This bombardment was answered vigorously for some time. But between seven and eight o'clock the white flag was raised by order of Col. Miles, and arrangements made for the surrender of his entire command. The terms of capitulation were agreed upon within one hour. The Confederate artillerists, not perceiving the signal of surrender, continued to fire some time after it had been displayed. By one of these shots Col. Miles was mortally wounded, being struck by a fragment of shell.

On the evening previous the cavalry was ordered to cut its way through the enemy's encircling lines. Cole's battalion was given the post of honor (and of danger) at the head of the column, in accordance with the following order:

"HEADQUARTERS, HARPER'S FERRY, VA.,
"14 September, 1862.

"*Special Orders* }
No. 120. }

"1st. The cavalry forces at this post, except detached orderlies, will make immediate preparations to leave here at eight o'clock to-night, without baggage, wagons, ambulances, or led horses, crossing the pontoon and taking the Sharpsburg road.

"2d. The senior officer, Col. Voss, will assume command of the whole, which will form in the following order, the right at the quartermaster's office, the left up Shenandoah Street, without noise or loud command, viz.: Cole's cavalry, Twelfth Illinois, Eighth New York, First Rhode Island, and First Maryland Cavalry.

"No other instructions can be given the commander for his guidance than to force his way through the enemy's lines to our army.

"By order of Col. Miles,
"H. C. REYNOLDS,
"*Lieut. and A. A. Genl.*"

This movement of cavalry was so unexpected that before the Confederates properly comprehended its nature the command had penetrated through their lines immediately investing Harper's Ferry from the Maryland side. Moving cautiously on through the numerous Confederate camps that lined the Sharpsburg road, and passing right through the town (Gen. Lee's headquarters being near by), the column struck the Hagerstown and Williamsport turnpike at daylight on the 15th. Here an ammunition train belonging to Gen. Longstreet was captured.

A large force of the enemy coming up immediately after, a portion of the train was burned, and the remainder conveyed safely into Chambersburg. In all these transactions Cole's cavalry and Companies H and I, First Maryland Cavalry, bore their full share.

Two noteworthy incidents in which Marylanders figured prominently occurred during the investment.

On the night of the 13th, after the evacuation of Maryland Heights, Col. Miles directed Capt. Charles H. Russell, of the First Cavalry, to take a few men, pass through the enemy's lines, and report to Gen. McClellan the condition of the beleaguered garrison.

Shortly after dark Capt. Russell, accompanied by five men, started from the Ferry, and moving up the Potomac, on the Virginia side, until he reached the mouth of the Antietam, crossed into Maryland, and surprised and captured some Confederate pickets, whom he bucked and gagged to prevent their giving the alarm. He then pushed his way through the mountains, often in sight of the enemy's camps. Reaching Gen. McClellan's headquarters at Frederick early the next morning, he reported as directed by Col. Miles.

Maj. H. A. Cole, another energetic and daring officer, with one man, also made his way on foot through the investing lines, and carried dispatches to Gen. McClellan representing the desperate situation of Harper's Ferry. The major received orders to return and advise Col. Miles to hold out, as succor was approaching, but before he could get back Col. Miles had been killed and the humiliating surrender consummated.

After the capitulation the Maryland troops were sent to Camp Parole, at Annapolis. Their losses in killed and wounded were as follows:

Companies H and I, First Cavalry, had one officer (Lieut. Hiteshew) mortally, and one enlisted man severely, wounded in the fight on Maryland Heights.

Companies B and K, First Potomac Home Brigade Infantry, lost in the action on Maryland Heights six enlisted men killed[1] and six wounded.

The Third Potomac Home Brigade Infantry had one officer (Capt. Jacob Sarbaugh) killed and one officer (Maj. C. L. Graffton) and seven enlisted men wounded in the combat on Bolivar Heights, and one man (William H. Harrison) killed and one man wounded on Maryland Heights.

The number of troops surrendered at Harper's Ferry was eleven thousand five hundred and eighty-three, half of them being from New York, and the remainder from Ohio and Maryland. Among the latter was Col. Maulsby's First Maryland Regiment, Potomac Home Brigade, nine hundred men; Col. Downey's Third Maryland Regiment, of the same brigade, six hundred men.

---

[1] Charles W. Oursler, George Frank, Robert N. Gill, James E. Huggins, William T. Martin, and Charles Mann.

Seventy-three pieces of artillery, thirteen thousand small-arms, two hundred wagons, and a large quantity of tents and camp equipage fell into the hands of the Confederates.

Leaving Gen. A. P. Hill to receive the surrender of the Federal troops and secure the captured property, Gen. Jackson, with Ewell's division (Gen. Lawton commanding) and Jackson's (Gen. Jones commanding), set out at once to join Gen. Lee at Sharpsburg, ordering Gens. McLaws and Walker to follow without delay. By a forced march he arrived at Sharpsburg on the morning of the 16th, where he was joined on the 17th by the remainder of his command. McLaws crossed the Potomac at Harper's Ferry, and destroying the bridge behind him, moved through Martinsburg and Shepherdstown to Sharpsburg.

On the morning of the 15th the whole right wing and centre of the Federal army was pushed forward in pursuit of the commands of Gens. D. H. Hill and Longstreet, who had retreated from South Mountain during the night. The Confederates reached Sharpsburg about daylight on the morning of the 15th of September. Pleasonton's cavalry, followed by the corps of Sumner, Hooker, and Mansfield (the latter having assumed command of the Twelfth), moved by way of the National pike.

The Ninth Corps, under Cox, and Sykes' division of the Fifth, the whole commanded by Gen. Burnside, marched by the old Sharpsburg road. The cavalry advance, supported by Richardson's division of Sumner's corps, had a severe skirmish with the Confederate rear-guard at Boonsboro', and followed the retreating foe to a new position he had taken on the heights behind Antietam Creek, in front of Sharpsburg. Late in the afternoon Gen. McClellan put his army in position on the eastern side of the creek, opposite the enemy's lines.

In the course of the day Gen. Lee, having learned of the capture of Harper's Ferry, ordered Jackson, Walker, and McLaws to join him at Sharpsburg without delay.

At daylight on the 16th the Confederate batteries opened on McClellan's army, and a heavy cannonading on both sides was kept up throughout the day. At two P.M. the advance of Hooker's corps crossed Antietam Creek at the upper bridge and a ford close by, engaged the enemy near the house of Daniel Miller, and drove him from his position.

The firing lasted until after dark, when Hooker's troops rested on the ground won from the enemy. During the night Mansfield's corps (the Twelfth) also crossed the creek, and bivouacked about a mile in the rear of Hooker's position.

Gen. Lee had drawn up his army in front of the town of Sharpsburg, on the high ground west of the Antietam, a narrow and winding stream which flows through fields dotted with homesteads and clumps of fruit and forest-trees to the Potomac. "The Confederate commander," says Swinton, "formed his troops on a line stretched across the angle formed by the Potomac and Antietam; and as the Potomac here makes a sharp curve, Lee was able to rest both flanks on that stream, while his front was covered by the Antietam." Longstreet's corps was posted on the right of the road from Sharpsburg to Boonsboro', his right flank guarded by the waters of the stream, which here bends westward. On the left of the Boonsboro' road D. H. Hill's command was stationed; two brigades under Gen. Hood were drawn up on Hill's left, and when Jackson arrived Lee directed him to post his command on the left of Hood, his right resting on the Hagerstown road, and his left extending backward obliquely towards the Potomac, here making a large bend, where Stuart with his cavalry and horse artillery occupied the ground to the river's bank.[1]

About half a mile in the rear of the Confederate left, and on the west of the Hagerstown road, was a small meeting-house known as the Dunker church.

DUNKER CHURCH.

It was surrounded by a skirt of woods, which extended in a circular form northward to the Hagerstown road. In this woods and near the church were limestone ledges, behind which, at times, the Confederates took shelter. Four stone bridges crossed the Antietam,—one in front of Longstreet, on the Con-

---

[1] "Life of Gen. Robert E. Lee," by John Esten Cooke.

federate right, a second in front of Hill, in the centre, a third opposite Jackson, by the Dunker church, near which was also a ford, and a fourth beyond the Confederate left flank. The upper bridge was on the Keedysville and Williamsport road, the second on the Keedysville and Sharpsburg pike, and the third on the Rohrersville and Sharpsburg road. Between the first and second bridges the distance is about two and a half miles, and from the second to the third about one mile. By the morning of the 16th the whole Confederate force had concentrated at Sharpsburg, with the exception of McLaws' and A. P. Hill's divisions, which had not yet returned from Harper's Ferry.

Confronting the Confederate lines on the left were the corps of Hooker and Mansfield, supported by Sumner's and Franklin's; Burnside was on the extreme right, and Porter in the centre. Porter's corps was posted on the left of the turnpike, opposite bridge No. 2; Burnside's Ninth Corps, on the Rohrersville and Sharpsburg turnpike, directly in front of bridge No. 3. McClellan determined to throw his right across the creek by the upper and unguarded bridge, beyond the Confederate left flank, and when this manœuvre should have shaken the enemy, the centre and left were to carry the bridges in their front.[1]

"The turning movement," says Swinton, "was intrusted to Hooker's corps, to be followed by Sumner's two corps. Towards the middle of the afternoon of the 16th Hooker's corps was put in motion, and crossed the stream at the upper bridge and ford, out of range of the hostile fire. Advancing through the woods, Hooker soon struck the left flank of the Confederate line, held by Hood's two brigades," on the extreme left of Longstreet's line, between Antietam Creek and the village of Sharpsburg. "Lee," continues Swinton, "had anticipated a menace on that flank, and had made his dispositions accordingly, Hood's brigade forming a crotchet on the Confederate left."[2]

It was towards dusk when the troops of Hooker and Hood met, and after a smart skirmish between the Confederates and the division of Pennsylvania Reserves under Gen. Meade, the opposing forces rested on their arms for the night, both occupying a skirt of woods which form the eastern and northern inclosure of a considerable clearing on both sides of the Hagerstown road. This movement across the Antietam on the 16th was of no advantage; it was made too late in the day to accomplish anything, and it served to disclose to Lee his antagonist's purpose. The Confederate commander made no change in his dispositions, save to order Jackson, who lay in reserve in the rear of the left, to substitute a couple of his brigades in the rear of Hood's worn-out command. Gen. McClellan strengthened the turning column by directing Sumner to throw over during the night the Twelfth Corps, under Gen. Mansfield, to the support of Hooker; and he ordered Sumner to hold his own corps (the Second) ready to cross early in the morning.

The strength of the two armies was by no means equal. "Our forces at the battle of Antietam," said Gen. McClellan, in his testimony before the committee of investigation, "were, total in action, eighty-seven thousand one hundred and sixty-four." Gen. Lee says in his report, "This great battle was fought by less than forty thousand men on our side."[3]

---

[1] Swinton.

[2] "In anticipation of a movement to turn the line of Antietam, Hood's two brigades had been transferred from the right to the left, and posted between D. H. Hill and the Hagerstown road."
—LEE: *Reports of the Army of Northern Virginia,* vol. i. p. 32.

[3] Col. Walter H. Taylor, adjutant-general of the Army of Northern Virginia, and a member of Gen. Lee's staff, says,—

"The command of Gen. Jackson embraced the division under Gen. J. R. Jones and that under Gen. Lawton. After Gen. Lawton was wounded, the command of the latter division devolved upon Gen. Early. Gen. J. R. Jones reports the effective strength of his division to have been sixteen hundred when the battle began. Gen. Early reports the effective strength of his division as follows; Lawton's brigade, eleven hundred and fifty; Hayes' brigade, five hundred and fifty; Walker's brigade, seven hundred; and his own brigade, one thousand; total effective of the division, three thousand four hundred, and the total effective of Jackson's command was therefore five thousand men.

"The command of Gen. Longstreet at that time embraced the six brigades under Gen. D. R. Jones, the two brigades under Gen. Hood, and an unattached brigade under Gen. N. G. Evans. His other three brigades were temporarily detached under Gen. R. H. Anderson.

"Gen. Jones reports his strength to have been two thousand four hundred and thirty effective, the strength of Hood's division at the commencement of the campaign was three thousand eight hundred and fifty-two. Gen. Hood puts the losses of his division in its encounters with the enemy previous to the battle of Sharpsburg at fifteen hundred and twenty; this, making no deduction for straggling, would make his effective in that engagement but two thousand three hundred and thirty-two. Gen. Evans states that his brigade numbered two thousand two hundred effective at the opening of the campaign, and reports his loss in the battles about Manassas at six hundred and thirty-one; his brigade was also engaged at South Mountain, and could not have exceeded fifteen hundred effective at Sharpsburg. Gen. Longstreet's command therefore numbered six thousand two hundred and sixty-two effective. Gen. D. H. Hill in his report puts his effective at three thousand on the morning of the 17th.

"Gen. R. H. Anderson's division, embracing on this occasion the brigades of Mahone, Wright, Armistead, Wilcox, Pryor, and Featherston, and temporarily assigned to Gen. D. H. Hill, is stated by the latter to have been three or four thousand strong,—call it three thousand five hundred.

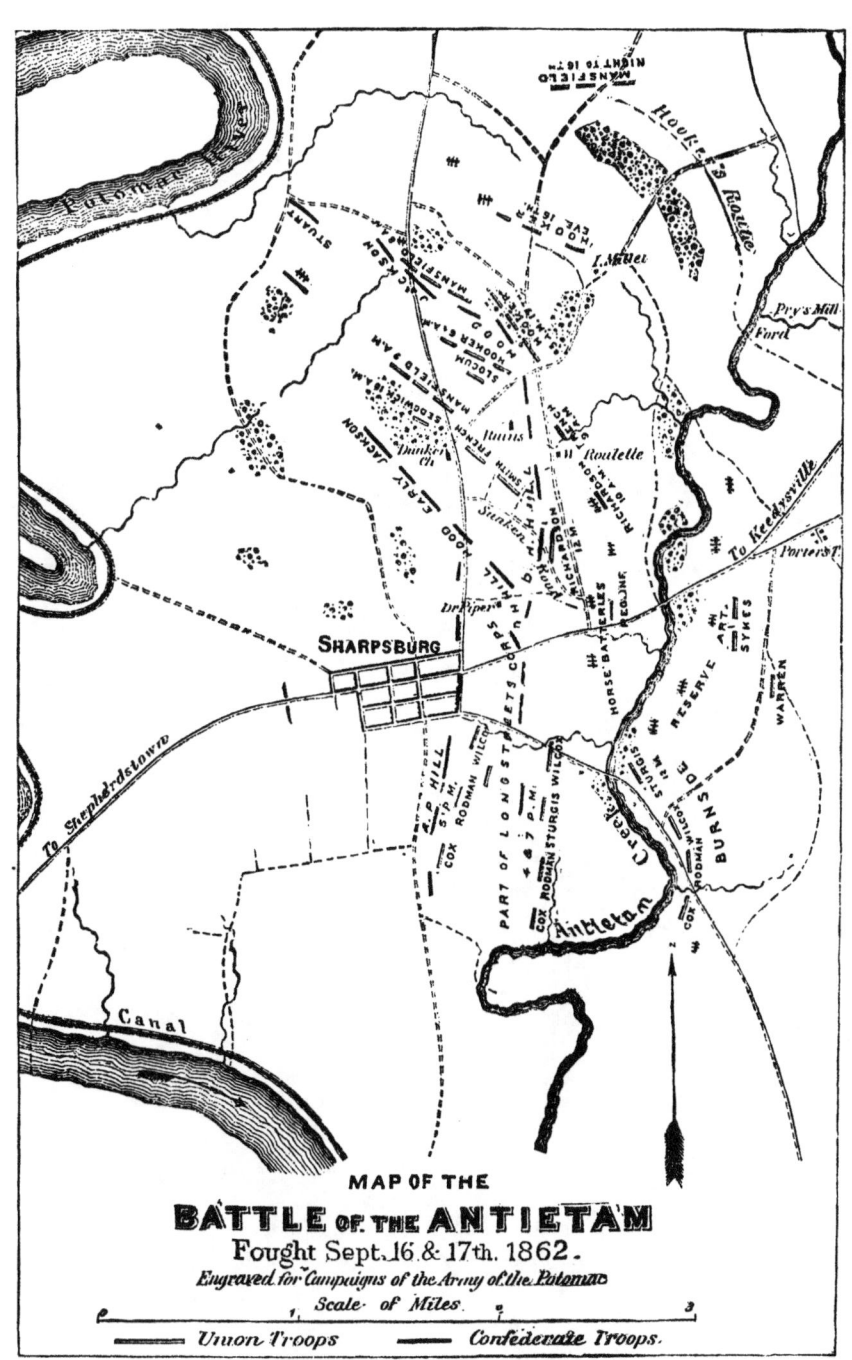

At daylight on the 17th the combat was opened by Hooker, who assailed the Confederate left, now held by Jackson's force. "The ground on which the battle opened," says Swinton, "was the same field on which the action continued to be waged during the day, and it has already been indicated in that opening extending to the east and west of the Hagerstown road, bounded on each side by woods. In the fringe of forest on the eastern side of the road Hooker had the previous evening effected a lodgment, though morning found the Confederate riflemen still clinging to its margin, while the main force of Jackson lay in the low timbered ground on the west side of the road, where the Confederate troops were pretty well protected by the out-cropping ledges of rock. But though it had this tactical advantage for the defense, the position was really untenable, for it was completely commanded and seen in reverse by high ground a little to the right to where Hooker formed his line of battle. This height was the key-point of all that part of the field, and had it been occupied by Union batteries, as it should have been, the low timbered ground around the Dunker church, where Jackson's line lay, could not have been held fifteen minutes. It is a noteworthy fact that neither Gen. Hooker nor Gen. Sumner, who followed him in command upon this part of the field, at all appreciated the supreme importance of this point. The former, beginning the combat, opened a direct attack with the view of carrying the Hagerstown road and the woods on the west side of it; and this continued to be the aim of all the subsequent attacks, which were made very much in detail, and thus lost the effective character they might have had with more comprehensive dispositions."

The attack was ushered in by a heavy fire from the Federal batteries on the ridge on the east side of the Antietam, and by those which had accompanied Hooker and Mansfield across the stream the night before, and was promptly replied to by the Confederate batteries under Poague, Carpenter, Brockenbrough, Raines, Caskie, and Wooding. Hooker, under a terrific storm of shell, canister, and musketry, advanced his corps of eighteen thousand men, with Doubleday's division on the right, Meade's in the centre, and Ricketts' on the left. Jackson met him with two divisions, Ewell's and Jackson's, commanded respectively by Lawton and Jones, and numbering only four thousand men.[1]

"Just as the light broadened in the east above the crest of mountains rising in rear of the Federal lines, Gen. Hooker made his assault. His aim was plainly to drive the force in his front across the Hagerstown road and back on the Potomac, and in this he seemed about to succeed. Jackson had placed in front Ewell's division of twenty-four hundred men. This force received Gen. Hooker's charge, and a furious struggle followed, in which the division was nearly destroyed. A glance at the casualties will show this. They were remarkable. Gen. Lawton, division commander, was wounded and carried from the field; Col. Douglas, brigade commander, was killed; Col. Walker, also

---

"Gen. A. P. Hill's command consisted of the brigades of Branch, Gregg, Archer, Pender, and Brockenbrough. He stated the strength of the first three at two thousand, and allowing the average of seven hundred each for the other two, we have for his division a total effective of three thousand four hundred. The other brigade of this division (Thomas') was left at Harper's Ferry.

"The division of Gen. McLaws consisted of the brigades of Kershaw, Barksdale, Semmes, and Cobb. He reports the effective strength of the four brigades to have been two thousand eight hundred and ninety-three.

"There remains but the small division of two brigades under Gen. J. G. Walker. Gen. Ransom states his effective strength at sixteen hundred. Gen. Walker does not give the strength of his brigade, but I have put it at sixteen hundred, on the authority of Gen. Ransom, who says, 'So far as my memory serves me, my brigade was stronger all the time than the other of Walker's division.' With the exception of the single brigade last mentioned, the following recapitulation is established upon indisputable and contemporaneous authority, being nothing less than the testimony of the commanding officers, as shown by their official reports, made at the time:

"Longstreet... 6,262
Jackson's command............................... 5,000
D. H. Hill's division................................ 3,000
R. H. Anderson's division...................... 3,500
A. P. Hill's division................................. 3,400
McLaws' division.................................... 2,893
J. G. Walker's division........................... 3,200
                                                              ———
Total effective infantry........................... 27,255

"I cannot verify the estimate made for the cavalry and artillery, viz., eight thousand, but I am sure it is rather excessive than the reverse."

Swinton, a Northern historian, says, "So greatly had the Confederate army become reduced by its previous losses and by straggling that Lee was unable to count above forty thousand bayonets."

[2] "Incredible though this return of Jackson's two divisions may appear," says Swinton, "it is vouched for by official evidence. So reduced had his numbers become by the heavy losses of the campaign, and by the great straggling that attended the march through Maryland, that Jackson's old ('Stonewall') division numbered but one thousand six hundred men. Gen. J. R. Jones, who commanded this division at Antietam, says of it, 'The division was reduced to the numbers of a small brigade, and at the beginning of the fight numbered not over one thousand six hundred men.' Of the number of the three brigades of Ewell's division, holding the advanced line, Gen. Early, who at a subsequent part of the day came into command of it, reports as follows: Lawton's brigade, one thousand one hundred and fifty; Hayes' brigade, five hundred and fifty; Walker's brigade, seven hundred. This would make a total for the two divisions of four thousand men,—the number above given."

commanding brigade, was disabled. Lawton's brigade lost five hundred and fifty-four killed and wounded out of eleven hundred and fifty, and five out of six regimental commanders. Hayes' brigade lost three hundred and twenty-three out of five hundred and fifty, and all the regimental commanders. Walker's brigade lost two hundred and twenty-eight out of less than seven hundred, and three out of four regimental commanders; and of the staff-officers of the division scarcely one remained."[1]

This heavy slaughter had been effected in Ewell's division within an hour after dawn, but in spite of their stubborn resistance they were unable to hold their ground and fell back in disorder from the "hither woods" across the open fields. The Union batteries on the opposite bank of the Antietam had secured an enfilade fire on Jackson's advance and reserved line, and, together with the batteries in front, had contributed largely to the loss sustained by the Confederates. Hooker, perceiving his advantage, at once advanced his centre under Meade to seize the Hagerstown road and the woods beyond, with the design of crushing the whole Confederate left, but was met by Jackson's old division of sixteen hundred men, who had been held in reserve, and by Hood's two small brigades, one numbering about eight hundred and sixty-four men, which Gen. Lee had hastened to the threatened point. With this force Jackson now met Gen. Hooker's advancing column, "delivering a heavy fire from the woods upon the Federal forces. In the face of this fire they hesitated, and Hood made a vigorous charge, Gen. Stuart opening at the same time a cross-fire on the enemy with his horse artillery. The combined fire increased their disorganization, and it now turned into disorder. Jackson seized the moment, as always, throwing forward the whole line, and the enemy were first checked and then driven back in confusion, the Confederates pursuing and cheering."[2]

"At the same time," says Swinton, "Ricketts' division on the left became hotly engaged with three brigades of Hill's division, which were at this time closed up on the right of Jackson in support; and Hooker's right division, under Doubleday, was held in check by the fire of several batteries of Stuart's horse artillery, posted on commanding ground on his right and front. Hooker had suffered severely by the enemy's fire; but, worse still, had lost nearly half his effective force by straggling. In this state of facts his offensive power was completely gone, and at seven o'clock Mansfield's corps, which had crossed the Antietam during the night and lay in reserve a mile to the rear, was ordered up to support and relieve Hooker's troops. Of this corps the First Division, under Gen. Williams, took position on the right, and the Second, under Gen. Greene, on the left. During the deployment that veteran soldier, Gen. Mansfield, fell mortally wounded. The command of the corps fell to Gen. Williams, and the division of the latter to Gen. Crawford, who, with his own and Jordan's brigade, made an advance across the open field, and succeeded in seizing a point of woods on the west side of the Hagerstown road. At the same time Greene's division on the left was able to clear its front, and crossed into the left of the Dunker church. Yet the tenure of these positions was attended with heavy loss; the troops, reduced to the attempt to hold their own, began to waver and break, and Gen. Hooker was being carried from the field severely wounded, when opportunely, towards nine o'clock, Gen. Sumner, with his own corps, reached the field.

"Of the extraordinary statement respecting this part of the battle made by Gen. Hooker, in his evidence before the Committee on the Conduct of the War, it must be said, at least," continues Mr. Swinton, "that it is not justified by facts. 'At that time' (nine o'clock), said Gen. Hooker, 'my troops were in the finest spirits; they had whipped Jackson and compelled the enemy to fly, throwing away their arms, their banners, and saving themselves as best they could.' Now not only is this contradicted by the facts above recited, and which are derived from the reports of both sides, but Gen. Sumner, who at the time spoken of reached the field, says, 'On going upon the field I found that Gen. Hooker's corps had been dispersed and routed. I passed him some distance in the rear, where he had been carried wounded, but I saw nothing of his corps at all as I was advancing with my command on the field. I sent one of my staff-officers to find where they were, and Gen. Ricketts, the only officer we could find, stated that he could not raise three hundred men of the corps.'"

The combat up to this time, though attended with murderous loss to both sides, had not resulted in decisive triumph for either. The tide of battle had raged with varying fortune, victory now inclining to the Confederate and now to the Federal forces. "Hooker, after driving one of Jackson's divisions, was in turn forced back by the other; and Mansfield's corps having caused this to retreat, found itself overmastered by the fresh battalions of Hood."

---

[1] "Life of Gen. Robert E. Lee," by John Esten Cooke. Report of Gen. Early, Army of Northern Virginia, ii., pp. 190, 191. Gen. Jackson said, "The carnage on both sides was terrific."

[2] Cooke's Life of Lee.

The arrival of Gen. Sumner, however, entirely changed the aspect of affairs, and as his fresh troops advanced, Mansfield's and Hooker's corps had an opportunity to reform. This was rapidly effected, and throwing Sedgwick's divisions on his right across the open field into the woods in which Crawford had been fighting, "he easily drove the shattered Confederate troops before him, and held definitive possession of the woods around the Dunker church." While this movement was in progress Sumner advanced French's divisions on what had hitherto been the left, and Richardson's division still further to the left, to oppose the Confederate centre under D. H. Hill, and they were both soon actively engaged. Gen. Lee had sent to the left the brigades of Colquitt, Ripley, and McRae, and with these, the troops of Hood, and his own shattered division Jackson presented a stubborn front, but his loss was heavy. Gen. Starke, of the old division, was killed; the brigade, regimental, and company officers fell almost without an exception, and the brigades dwindled to mere handfuls.[1]

For a time Sumner's division flanked the Confederates, who retired slowly, fighting every inch. It was a trying time; Sumner saw his advantage and pressed it with vigor. Eight batteries were in full play upon the retreating Confederates, and the din of heavy guns, whistling and bursting of shells, and the roar of musketry were almost deafening.

"This," says John Esten Cooke, "was undoubtedly the turning-point of the battle of Sharpsburg, and Gen. Lee had witnessed the conflict upon his left with great anxiety. It was impossible, however, to send thither more troops than he had already sent. As will be seen in a moment, both his centre and right were extremely weak. A. P. Hill and Gen. McLaws had not arrived from Harper's Ferry. Thus the left had been reinforced to the full extent of Lee's ability, and now that portion of his line seemed about to be crushed."

Just at this critical moment, when Sedgwick "appeared to grasp victory, and the troops of Jackson and Hood were retiring in disorder,"[2] the divisions of McLaws and Walker, which had just come up from Harper's Ferry, were hurried to the left, and at once changed the fortunes of the day. The Confederates had fought until their ammunition as well as their strength were almost exhausted. "It was then ten o'clock, and in that one hour the fighting of an entire day seemed to have been concentrated." Encouraged by the opportune reinforcements, the whole Confederate line rallied, and the fight was resumed with redoubled energy. Splendidly manœuvred, the divisions of McLaws and Walker swept on like a wave upon Sumner's columns that had so stubbornly forced their way to the original position held by the Confederates in the morning. A considerable interval had been left between Sumner's right division under Sedgwick and his centre division under French. Through this the Confederates penetrated, enveloping Sedgwick's left flank, and pressing heavily at the same time on his front, forced him out of the woods on the west side of the Hagerstown road, and back across the open field and into the woods on the east side of the road, the original position held in the morning. The Confederates did not follow up their advantage on this end of the line, but retired to the original position held by them at the beginning of the battle.[3]

From the ground thus occupied the Federal forces were unable to dislodge the Confederates, "and the great struggle 'of the left at Sharpsburg' was over. It had begun at dawn, and was decided by ten or eleven o'clock, and the troops on both sides had fought as resolutely as in any other action of the war."

In the mean time the divisions of French and Richardson, composing Sumner's centre and left, had not been idle. "When the pressure on Sedgwick became the hardest, Sumner sent orders to French to attack, as a diversion in favor of the former. French obeyed with the brigades of Kimball and Weber, and succeeded in forcing back the enemy to a sunken road which runs almost at right angles with the Hagerstown road. This position was held by the division of D. H. Hill, three of whose brigades had been advanced to assist Jackson in his morning attacks, and it was these that were assailed by French and driven back in disorder to the sunken road. These brigades were respectively those of Colquitt, Ripley, and McRae, and Gen. Hill mentions the following curious circumstance as the cause of the repulse that befell them: 'The men advanced with alacrity, secured a good position, and were fighting bravely, when Capt. Thompson, Fifth North Carolina, cried out, "They are flanking us!" This cry spread like an electric shock along the ranks, bringing up vivid recollections of the flank fire at South Mountain. In a moment they broke and fell to the rear. Efforts were made to rally them in the bed of an old road, nearly at right angles to the Hagerstown pike,

---

[1] Cooke's "Life of General Lee." [2] Swinton.

[3] Swinton. Of this attack McLaws says, "The troops were immediately engaged, driving the enemy before them in magnificent style at all points, sweeping the woods with perfect ease. They were driven not only through the woods, but over a field in front of the woods and over two high fences beyond, and into another body of woods about half a mile distant from the commencement of the fight."

and which had been their position previous to the advance.'" Uniting here with the other brigades of Hill, they received the attacks of French and of Richardson's division to his left. The latter division was composed of the brigades of Meagher, Caldwell, and Brooke. Meagher first attacked, and fought his way to the possession of a crest overlooking the sunken road in which Hill's line was posted. After sustaining a severe musketry fire, by which it lost severely, this brigade, its ammunition being expended, was relieved by the brigade of Caldwell, the former breaking by companies to the rear, and the latter by companies to the front. Caldwell immediately became engaged in a very determined combat, and was supported by part of Brooke's brigade, the rest of the latter being posted on the right to thwart an effort on the part of the enemy to flank in that direction. The action here was of a very animated nature, for Hill, being reinforced by the division of Anderson, assumed a vigorous offensive, and endeavored to seize a piece of high ground on the Union left, with the view of turning that flank. This manœuvre was, however, frustrated by the skill and promptitude of Col. Cross, of the Fifth New Hampshire (Caldwell's brigade), who, detecting the danger, moved his regiment towards the menaced point. Between his command and the Confederate force there then ensued a spirited contest, each endeavoring to reach the high ground, and both delivering their fire as they marched in parallel lines by the flank. The race was won by Cross. The effort to flank on the right was handsomely checked by Brooke, French, and Barlow, the latter of whom, changing front with his two regiments obliquely to the right, poured in a rapid fire, compelling the surrender of three hundred prisoners with two standards. A vigorous direct attack was then made, and the troops succeeded in carrying the sunken road and the position in advance, around what is known as Piper's House, which, being a defensible building, formed, with its surroundings, the citadel of the enemy's strength at this part of the line. The enemy was so much disorganized in this repulse that only a few hundred men were rallied on a crest near the Hagerstown road. This slight array formed the whole Confederate centre, and there is little doubt that a more energetic following up of the success gained would have carried this position and fatally divided Lee's wings. The few Confederates showed a very bold front, however, and deceived by this, Richardson contented himself with taking up a position to hold what was already won."[1]

Of this incident in the attack upon the centre, John Esten Cooke, in his "Life of Gen. Lee," gives essentially the same account. "In the centre," he says, "a great disaster was at one time imminent. Owing to a mistake of orders, the brave Gen. Rhodes had drawn back his brigade posted there; this was seen by the enemy, and a sudden rush was made by them with the view of piercing Lee's centre. The promptness and courage of a few officers and a small body of troops defeated this attempt. Gen. D. H. Hill rallied a few hundred men, and opened fire with a single gun, and Col. Cooke faced the enemy with his regiment, 'standing boldly in line,' says Gen. Lee, 'without a cartridge.' The stand made by this small force saved the army from serious disaster."

"Three of the six corps of the Army of the Potomac, and they the strongest," says Swinton, "had thus been drawn into the seething vortex of action on the right, and each in succession, while exacting heavy damage of the enemy, had been so punished as to lose all offensive energy, so that noon found them simply holding their own. Porter with his small reserve corps, numbering some fifteen thousand men, held the centre, while Burnside remained inactive on the left, not having yet passed the Antietam. Between twelve and one o'clock, Franklin, with two divisions of his corps, under Slocum and W. F. Smith (Couch remaining behind to occupy Maryland Heights), reached the field of battle from where the action at Crampton's Pass had left him. Gen. McClellan had designed retaining Franklin on the east side of the Antietam, to operate on either flank or on the centre as circumstances might require. But by the time he neared the field the strong opposition developed by the attacks of Hooker and Sumner rendered it necessary for him to be immediately pushed over the creek to the assistance of the right. The arrival of Franklin was opportune, for Lee had now accumulated so heavily on his left, and the repulse of Sumner's right under

---

[1] Swinton. Gen. D. H. Hill says, "There were no troops near to hold the centre except a few hundred rallied from various brigades. The Yankees crossed the old road which we had occupied in the morning, and occupied an orchard and corn-field in advance of it. *Affairs looked very critical.* They had now got within a few hundred yards of the hill which commanded Sharpsburg and our rear. I was satisfied, however, that the Yankees were so demoralized that a single regiment of fresh men could drive the whole of them in our front across the Antietam. I got up about two hundred men, who said they were willing to advance to the attack if I would lead them. We met, however, with a warm reception, and the little command was broken and dispersed. Col. Iverson had gathered up about two hundred men, and I sent them to the right to attack the Yankees in flank. They drove them back a short distance, but in turn were repulsed. These two attacks, however, had a most happy effect. The Yankees were completely deceived by their boldness, and induced to believe there was a large force in our centre."

Sedgwick had been so easily effected, that the enemy began to show a disposition to resume the offensive, directing his efforts against that still loose-jointed portion of Sumner's harness between his right and centre. Gen. Smith, with quick perception of the needs of the case, of his own accord filled up this interval with part of his division; and his third brigade, under Col. Irwin, charged forward with much impetuosity, and drove back the advance until abreast the Dunker church. Though Irwin could not hold what he had wrested from the Confederates, his boldness, seconded by another charge made soon after by the Seventh Maine Regiment alone, served to quell the enemy's aggressive ardor. Franklin then formed the rest of his available force in a column of assault, with the intention of making another effort to gain the enemy's stronghold in the rocky woodland west of the Hagerstown turnpike,— the woods Hooker had striven for and Sumner had snatched and lost. But Sumner, having command on the right, now intervened to postpone further operations on that flank, as he judged the repulse of the only remaining corps available for attack would peril the safety of the whole army."

Referring to the attack on the Confederate left, Col. Walter H. Taylor, adjutant-general of the Confederate Army of Northern Virginia, says, "It is established upon indisputable Federal evidence that the three corps of Hooker, Mansfield, and Sumner were completely shattered in the repeated but fruitless efforts to turn this flank, and two of these corps were rendered useless for further aggressive movements. The aggregate strength of the attacking columns at this point reached forty thousand men,[1] not counting the two divisions of Franklin's corps, sent at a late hour in the day to rescue the Federal right from the impending danger of being itself destroyed; while the Confederates, from first to last, had less than fourteen thousand men on this flank—consisting of Jackson's two divisions, McLaws' division, and the two small divisions of two brigades each under Hood and Walker—with which to resist their fierce and oft-repeated assaults."

The attack upon the Confederate right had been intrusted to the Ninth Corps, under Gen. Burnside. This force lay massed behind the heights on the east side of the Antietam, and early in the morning Gen. Burnside was ordered to hold his troops in readiness to force a passage over the Antietam by the lower stone bridge, with the view of assailing the Confederate right, carrying the Sharpsburg crest, and forcing Gen. Lee from his line of retreat by way of Shepherdstown. At eight o'clock, " on learning how much opposition had been developed by Hooker, Gen. McClellan ordered Burnside to carry the bridge, gain possession of the heights, and advance along their crest upon Sharpsburg, as a diversion in favor of the right. Burnside's tentatives were frivolous in their character, and hour after hour went by, during which the need of his assistance became more and more imperative, and McClellan's commands more and more urgent. Five hours, in fact, passed, and the action on the right (the Confederate left) had been *concluded*, in such manner as has been seen, before the work that should have been done in the morning was accomplished. Encouraged by the ease with which the left of the Union force was held in check, Lee was free to remove two-thirds of the right wing under Longstreet,—namely, the divisions of McLaws and Walker; and this force he applied at the actual point of conflict on his left, where the arrival of these divisions served to check Sumner in his career of victory and hurl back Sedgwick. This step the Confederate commander never would have ventured on had there been any vigor displayed on the part of the confronting force; yet this heavy detachment, having been made from the hostile right, should have rendered the task assigned to Gen. Burnside one of comparative ease, for it left in that entire wing but a single hostile division of two thousand five hundred men under Gen. Jones, and the force actually present to dispute the passage of the bridge did not exceed four hundred.[2] Nevertheless it was one o'clock, and after the action on the right (the Confederate left) had been determined, before a passage was effected; and this being done, two hours passed before the attack of the crest was made. This was successfully executed at three o'clock, the Sharpsburg ridge being carried, and a Confederate battery that had been delivering an annoying fire captured. It was one of the many unfortunate results of the long delay in this operation on the Federal left that just as this success was gained the division of A. P. Hill, which Jackson had left behind to receive the surrender of Harper's Ferry, reached the field from that place by way of Shepherdstown, and uniting his own reinforcement of two thousand men with the troops of Jones that had been broken through in the attack, he assumed the offensive, recaptured the battery, and drove back Burnside over all the ground gained and to the shelter

---

[1] Gen. Sumner's testimony, " Report on the Conduct of the War," Part I., p. 368.

[2] The force covering the bridge-head consisted of two regiments under Gen. Toombs, numbering four hundred and three men.

of the bluff bordering the Antietam. This closed the action on the (Federal) left, and as that on the (Federal) right had been suspended, the battle closed for the day."[1]

To Swinton's account of Gen. Burnside's attack upon the Confederate right may be added the following from another source: "While the attack upon the Confederate left and centre was in progress, Gen. Burnside made repeated efforts to force the bridge over the creek opposite Longstreet's right wing, defended by Gen. Toombs with two regiments of his own brigade and the batteries of Gen. Jones. This small force repulsed five different assaults made by greatly superior numbers. In the afternoon Gen. Burnside made a feint, as if intending to pass by the bridge below, and then threw a heavy force upon Toombs, and drove the Confederates from their position. But the timely arrival of Gen. A. P. Hill with his command from Harper's Ferry entirely changed the position of affairs. He was ordered to reinforce Gen. Jones, commanding Longstreet's right wing, and moved to his support with the brigades of Archer, Branch, Gregg, and Pender, who attacked the Federals, and with the assistance of several batteries of artillery arrested their progress. After an obstinate resistance the Federals began to waver. At this moment Gen. Jones ordered Toombs to charge the flank, while Archer, supported by Branch and Gregg, charged them in the front." Gen. A. P. Hill, in his official report, says that "the enemy had already advanced in three lines, had broken through Jones' division, captured McIntosh's battery, and were in the full tide of success. With a yell of defiance, Archer (of Maryland) charged them, retook McIntosh's guns, and drove them back pell-mell. Branch and Gregg, with their veterans, sternly held their ground, and pouring in destructive volleys, the tide of the enemy surged back, and breaking in confusion passed out of sight." Burnside made a brief resistance, then broke and retreated in confusion towards the Antietam, pursued by the Confederates, until he reached the protection of his batteries on the other side. In this attack the Confederates lost Gen. L. O'B. Branch, killed. The troops of Gen. Hill were now recalled, and they occupied the position originally held by Gen. Jones in the morning.

Referring to the arrival of the reinforcements under Gen. A. P. Hill, John Esten Cooke says, "These attacked the enemy, drove him from the hill across the Antietam again; and so threatening did the situation at that moment appear to Gen. McClellan that he is said to have sent Gen. Burnside the message, 'Hold your ground! If you cannot, then the bridge, to the last man! Always the bridge! If the bridge is lost, all is lost!' The urgency of this order sufficiently indicates that the Federal commander was not without solicitude for the safety of his own left wing. Ignorant, doubtless, of the extremely small force which had thus repulsed Gen. Burnside,—in all four thousand five hundred men,—he feared that Gen. Lee would cross the bridge, assail his left, and that the hard-fought day might end in disaster to his own army. That Gen. Lee contemplated this movement, in spite of the disproportion of numbers, is intimated in his official report. 'It was nearly dark,' he says, 'and the Federal artillery was massed to defend the bridge, with Gen. Porter's corps, consisting of fresh troops, behind it. Under these circumstances,' he adds, 'it was deemed injudicious to push our advantage further in the face of fresh troops of the enemy much exceeding our own.' The idea of an advance against the Federal left was accordingly abandoned, and a movement of Jackson's command, which Lee directed, with the view of turning the Federal right, was discontinued from the same considerations."

BURNSIDE'S BRIDGE.

Burnside has been severely criticised for his delay in forcing the bridge and carrying the Sharpsburg heights, but the task, to say the least, was one of no inconsiderable difficulty,—a high-banked stream, bordered by willows, a narrow bridge, a steep hill,

---

[1] Swinton.

cleared lands, with no shelter from the batteries in front and on both his flanks after he should have succeeded in crossing the stream. The road crossing the Antietam farthest south, instead of being at right angles, runs diagonally to Sharpsburg up the hill. The ground is undulating, lying in ridges or swells," with dry ravines between, all cleared land, and at the time of the battle beautiful fields of corn and clover, or newly plowed for the fall wheat sowing. The Confederate batteries were so posted that any force crossing either bridge or advancing directly upon the town would be exposed to a severe cross-fire.[1]

The losses on both sides had been terrible. Swinton places that of the Federal army at twelve thou-

---

[1] The following description of the battle-field and of the positions of the armies is taken from a contemporaneous account:

"Antietam River, which rises near Gettysburg, Pa., runs nearly south along the western slope of Elk Ridge. The Keedysville and Williamsport road crosses it a mile west from Keedysville by a stone bridge.

"A mile farther down is a second stone bridge, on the Sharpsburg and Shepherdstown turnpike, and two miles below that a third, which must be kept in special remembrance, for there gallant deeds were done.

"The enemy selected the ground, choosing a line where the two armies would be face to face, with but little opportunity for flank movements, a line about four miles long,—a gateway four miles wide, where he put up his batteries. Harper's Ferry was in his possession, also Shepherdstown, Williamsport in ours, so that the enemy could not flank us in that direction, neither escape them if defeated. McClellan could not flank Lee or get in his rear. Neither could Lee outflank McClellan. Neither was there an opportunity for the cutting round policy pursued against Pope.

"It is a mile from the turnpike to the Potomac, measuring from Joel Paffenburgh's house, which stands east of the turnpike. Right behind Paffenburgh's house is a ridge of land, a cleared field running nearly parallel with the turnpike. Standing on this ridge and looking west we see first a mown field of ten or twelve acres, then a corn-field on the eastern slope of a parallel ridge, which is crowned with an oak grove. The distance between the two ridges is about one-half mile. Just below Paffenburgh's is an old toll-house and gate. Walking southeast we find that we are gradually crossing the ridge; that there is a slope east towards the Antietam, and a gentle slope, with hills, knolls, and ravines, west towards the Potomac; that the turnpike is on the high ground between the two streams. A short distance, through a beautiful oak grove, and we come to a large plowed field. The grove extends along the turnpike a half-mile. East of the plowed field is another grove —the distance between the two groves half a mile. Continuing our walk we find the slope more abrupt as we gradually near the lower stone bridge. The eastern slope is bare of trees, but mottled with corn-fields, the stalks beginning to wear the russet hues of autumn. There are a few farm-houses with white-washed outbuildings. Conspicuous in the panorama is the house of William Roulet, in a ravine, three-fourths of a mile northeast of Sharpsburg. Numerous fences, smooth fields, a few apple-orchards, and a burial-ground, with the white head-stones standing in pleasant contrast against the greensward.

"Looking east we have the valley of the Antietam,—a winding stream, sparkling in the sunlight, fringed with willows, the village of Keedysville, undulating lands, farm roads, with the Elk Ridge green to its summit, and the South Mountain lying beyond.

"Crossing the upper stone bridge into the village, and along the base of Elk Ridge opposite the lower bridge, then turning towards the west, we have a view of two-thirds the entire line, —from the ridge near Paffenburgh's to a mile below Sharpsburg. Right before us, a mile and a half distant from the river, is the town, pleasantly situated, two church steeples piercing the sky above the horizon. North of the town is a considerable elevation, also south of it. If we should go up there and look towards Keedysville we should behold the valley like an elongated basin below us, in a great measure commanded by the two elevations. There is a ford between the lower and turnpike bridge. It was not used, however, as a crossing for our troops till after our line of battle was formed. With this view of the ground we are prepared to see how Gen. McClellan disposed his army corps.

"It is not easy to give the line of battle with distinctness,— that is, the disposition of the different corps. Let it be kept in mind that the nature of the ground was such that there was necessarily wide gaps between some of the corps. Gen. Hooker was assigned the extreme right, near Paffenburgh's house; next Gen. Mansfield, commanding Banks' army corps; next Sumner, next Franklin, next Richardson. All of these were west of the river, extending from the Sharpsburg and Boonsboro' turnpike bridge to the Potomac. East of the Antietam was Porter and Burnside, the latter at the lower stone bridge. Franklin did not arrive on the ground till Wednesday forenoon. He came up Pleasant Valley, crossed the upper bridge, turned in column to the left, moved over the fields and took his position partly between Richardson and Sumner, his right overlapping Sumner's left.

"Of course this is but approximately accurate, as nearly accurate as can be made at present. I have shown Franklin at right angles with Sumner, and the rebels also at right angles, but an angle of forty-five degrees would more nearly represent it. You are to imagine an elevation in front of Sumner's left, crowned by the grove before mentioned. Between Franklin and Richardson, and between the rebels in front of Richardson, three-fourths of a mile, is an unobstructed sweep of ground. The distance between Sumner and the rebels in front of him is not more than a third of a mile. Sumner is in a western border of a grove, the rebels in an eastern, the rebels on ground fifty to seventy-five feet highest. In front of Mansfield is a grove; in front of Hooker the mown land, the corn-field, and the wood-crowned ridge beyond, already mentioned, occupied by the rebels. The batteries in front of Richardson are fifty feet above him, on the highest land in the vicinity, and were turned at times upon Sumner, Franklin, Richardson, Porter, and Burnside. The rebel batteries at Sharpsburg played upon Richardson, Porter, and Burnside. Burnside also had a heavy rebel battery in front and on his flank.

"It will be seen that the lines were near together in the centre, opposite Sumner, but more widely separated on the flanks. The centre was the rebel stronghold. Hooker took the extreme right, having Doubleday's, Ricketts', and Meade's divisions. He did not know that the enemy were in full force. Jackson, when last heard from, was at Harper's Ferry, with only Longstreet's, A. P. Hill's, and Ewell's corps in the vicinity of Sharpsburg. I do not think our generals comprehended that Lee had chosen the locality for a great battle till the batteries began to play on Tuesday afternoon."

sand five hundred men, and that of the Confederates at above eight thousand. This latter estimate, he admits, is only approximate. "Gen. Lee," he says, "gives his aggregate loss in killed and wounded in the Maryland campaign as ten thousand two hundred and ninety-one. As the killed and wounded in all the other actions save Antietam were not above two thousand two hundred and ninety-one, it leaves about eight thousand for the casualties of that battle. Gen. McClellan states that about two thousand seven hundred of the Confederate dead were buried; and taking this as a basis and uniting the usual proportion of five wounded to one killed, the aggregate would be very much in excess of Gen. Lee's statement." Speaking of the losses suffered in the battle, Gen. McClellan, in his testimony before the Committee on the Conduct of the War,[1] said,—

"The next morning (the 18th) I found that our loss had been so great, and there was so much disorganization in some of the commands, that I did not consider it proper to renew the attack that day, especially as I was sure of the arrival that day of two fresh divisions amounting to about fifteen thousand men. As an instance of the condition of some of the troops that morning, I happen to recollect the returns of the First Corps,—Gen. Hooker's,—made the morning of the 18th, by which there were about three thousand five hundred men reported present for duty. Four days after that the returns of the same corps showed thirteen thousand five hundred."[2]

---

[1] "Report," Part I., p. 441.

[2] The Second Maryland Infantry, operating with the Ninth Corps under Burnside, and attached to the First Brigade, Nagle's, of the Second Division, under Sturgis, was posted in the immediate vicinity of the third bridge, better known in history as "Burnside's bridge."

Gen. J. D. Cox, in his official report, said, "The bridge is a stone structure of three arches, with stone parapet above, this parapet to some extent flanking the approach to the bridge at either end. The valley in which the stream runs is quite narrow, the steep slope on the right bank approaching quite to the water's edge. On this slope the roadway is scarped, running both ways from the bridge end, and passing to the higher land above by ascending through ravines above and below, the upper ravine being some six hundred yards above the bridge, the turn about half that distance below. On the hillside immediately above the bridge was a strong stone fence running parallel to the stream. The turns of the roadway were covered by rifle-pits and breastworks made of rails and stone, all of which defenses, as well as the woods which covered the slope, were filled with the enemy's infantry and sharpshooters. Besides the infantry defenses, batteries were placed to enfilade the bridge and all its approaches." An attempt to carry the bridge by other troops of the corps having failed, Gen. Sturgis was ordered about ten A.M. to take it at all hazards and seize the heights beyond. The force selected to make this desperate attempt was composed of two regiments, the Sixth New Hampshire and the Second Maryland, commanded respectively by Col. S. G. Griffin and Lieut.-Col. J. Eugene Duryea. At this point the Antietam was not fordable, and the road by which the attacking column was to move struck the creek about two hundred yards below the bridge, then turned at right angles and ran along the bank of the stream, with only the narrow creek between it and the enemy, then turned again at right angles to cross the bridge. The side held by the enemy was a steep, high bluff, heavily wooded. Behind the trees and behind a stone wall and a barricade of logs he held a very strong position, his fire covering the whole ground over which the assailants must pass to reach the objective.

The two regiments were formed in the field below where the road strikes the creek, directly under the fire of the concealed foe. The residue of the brigade lay still farther down the stream under cover of fences and corn-fields. The assaulting regiments formed by the flank, the Second Maryland leading, fixed bayonets, and moving forward at the double-quick, passed through a narrow opening in a post-and-rail fence which there was no time to remove, and charged in the most gallant manner directly up the road towards the bridge. Batteries from the heights opposite plunged their shot into them, sharpshooters singled them out, musketry thinned their lines, but on they kept, and had nearly gained the bridge, when a murderous charge of grape and canister dealt death and destruction in their ranks. Many went down never to rise again, and of the first hundred men who passed through the opening in the fence a large number were either killed or wounded. So near was the enemy and so completely did his fire command the road that almost every shot took effect. Neither physical nor moral courage could withstand such a withering fire of shell, canister, and musketry, and the shattered regiments halted near the hither end of the bridge, and the men sheltered themselves behind the abutments, fences, trees, logs, and whatever cover they could find.

The regiment was highly complimented by Gen. Burnside for its gallant behavior. Its losses amounted to two officers (Capts. Malcolm Wilson and James A. Martin) and nineteen men killed or fatally wounded, three officers and forty men wounded, and three men missing. Company A, commanded by Lieut. T. L. Matthews, which led the charge, suffered most, losing eighteen out of thirty-four men. Capt. John M. Santenyer and Lieuts. T. L. Matthews and R. C. Wills received wounds. Those killed were, Company A, Wm. Burman, George Connelly, James Kirby, Christian Lukebart, George Waltjen, Harry H. Stewart, James S. Clark, Charles Hauptman; Company C, Wm. Kuhl, John Q. Adams, John Huber; Company F, John M. Frazer; Company G, John A. Osborn; Company H, Joseph Clark, Wm. Kelly, John Ward; Company I, Peter Daily; Company K, Jacob Mueller, Martin Becker.

The Third Maryland Infantry, Lieut.-Col. Joseph M. Sudsbury commanding, entered the conflict on the right with the Second Brigade, Second Division (Greene's), Twelfth Corps (Mansfield's). The Third went into action with one hundred and forty-eight officers and men, of which it lost two men (Henry Ashler and Francis Bruner) killed, two officers (Lieuts. Wm. E. Hacker and Charles Stevens) and twenty-two men wounded, and four missing.

The Purnell Legion, under Maj. Wm. T. Fulton, was ordered into action with the Third Brigade, Second Division, Twelfth Corps, but was detached and sent to the support of the Sixtieth New York and One Hundred and Twenty-fourth Pennsylvania.

Such was the battle of Sharpsburg, or Antietam, one of the most sanguinary and protracted engagements of the war. The results of the battle may be briefly summed up. Every effort of Gen. McClellan to dislodge Gen. Lee from his position had been defeated with great loss. Nowhere did McClellan gain any permanent advantage over the Confederates. Varying as were the fortunes of the day, Lee was left intact, unbroken, and an equal master of the field with his antagonist. Both armies fought well, and were handled in a masterly manner. McClellan had the advantage, not only in numbers, but of a position from which he could assume an offensive or defensive attitude at will, besides which his signal-stations on the Blue Ridge commanded a view of every movement of Lee's army. Lee could not make a manœuvre in front or rear that was not instantly revealed to the Federal lookouts; and as soon as the intelligence could be communicated to the Federal batteries below, shot and shell were poured upon the moving columns.

The following distinguished Confederate officers were killed in this battle : Longstreet's division,—Col. Liddell, Eleventh Mississippi; Lieut.-Cols. Coppens and Holmes, of the Second Georgia Volunteers. Jackson's division,—Gen. Starke, Col. Douglas, and thirty-six other officers. D. H. Hill's division,—Brig.-Gen. G. B. Anderson ; Col. C. C. Tew, Second North Carolina Regiment; Col. W. P. Barclay, Twenty-third Georgia; Col. Levi B. Smith, Twenty-seventh Georgia; Lieut.-Col. J. M. Newton, Sixth Georgia; Maj. Tracy, Sixth Georgia; Maj. Robert S. Smith, Fourth Georgia. In the Twenty-seventh Georgia Regiment every commissioned officer was killed; in the Fourth North Carolina all the officers were killed or wounded. Gen. A. P. Hill's division lost Gen. L. O'B. Branch, of North Carolina, and Col. Barnes; Gen. McLaws lost his adjutant-general, Maj. T. S. McIntosh. Among the Federal killed were Maj.-Gen. Mansfield, Maj.-Gen. Israel B. Richardson, Brig.-Gen. Isaac P. Rodman, Col. Kingsbury, of Connecticut; Cols. Crossdale, Childs, and McNull, of Pennsylvania; Col. Hinks, of Massachusetts; Col. Coleman, of Ohio; and Lieut.-Col. Dwight, of Boston.[1]

Capt. Noyes, who visited the field soon after the battle, gives the following graphic description of what he saw:

"My route carried me over the battle-field, and I spent much of the afternoon, part of the time in company with a friend, in visiting some of the most severely contested points, to be awe-struck, sickened, almost benumbed with its sights of horror.

Afterwards it was marched to and fro as the exigencies of the battle seemed to require. The Legion had three men (A. C. Spicer, James English, and John Means) killed, Capt. Wm. Mitchell, Lieuts. G. W. Brown, S. H. Bogardus, and twenty men wounded.

The Fifth Maryland Infantry, under Maj. Leopold Blumenberg, was attached to Weber's (Third) Brigade, French's (Third) division of Sumner's (Second) Corps. The regiment went into action with nearly six hundred officers and men, of whom thirty-nine were killed and one hundred and nine wounded.

Lieut. Magnus Moltke was killed. Maj. Leopold Blumenberg, Capts. Wm. W. Bamberger and Charles A. Holton, and Lieuts. Evan W. Thomas and Joseph M. Rothrock were among the wounded. The enlisted men killed or mortally wounded were as follows: Company A, George L. Flintham, Oliver McCullough, John A. Leonard, John S. West, John Alexander, Wm. T. Brown, George W. McClure, Asa R. Mattox, Benjamin K. Streeper; Company B, George W. McComas; Company C, Albert Warmboldt, Christopher Preiss; Company D, Joseph Daley, Martin Kenny, Edward Smith, Benjamin N. Tracey; Company E, Edward Waltham, Gersham Edwards, Marshall Ensey, Wm. Parker, Andrew Stahl; Company F, August Harochkamp, Francis J. Bruder, Bernhard Kohler, Geo. J. Merling; Company H, Charles Kohlman, Luder Bremerman; Company I, Robert Ottley, Wm. McSoiley; Company K, John C. Braun.

Battery A, Maryland Light Artillery, under Lieut. J. H. Rigby, serving with Capt. Emory Upton's artillery brigade of Slocum's division, lost one man (Sergt. Charles Marsden) killed and six wounded.

Battery B, Lieut. T. J. Vanneman commanding, was attached to Capt. R. B. Ayres' artillery brigade of Smith's division, but suffered no loss.

[1] "The Confederate reports are replete," says Swinton, "with evidence of the enormous straggling that attended the Maryland campaign. Says Lee, in his official report, 'The arduous service in which our troops had been engaged, their great privations of rest and food, and the long marches without shoes over mountain roads had greatly reduced our ranks before the action began. These causes had compelled thousands of brave men to absent themselves, and many more had done so from unworthy motives. This great battle was fought by less than forty thousand men on our side, all of whom had undergone the greatest labors and hardships in the field and on the march. Nothing could surpass the determined valor with which they met the large army of the enemy, fully supplied and equipped, and the result reflects the highest credit on the officers and men engaged.' Says Hill, 'Had all our stragglers been up McClellan's army would have been completely crushed or annihilated. Thousands of thievish poltroons had kept away from sheer cowardice.' As an illustration of the privations endured it is stated that Walker's command, which marched from Harper's Ferry the night before the battle, had nothing to eat except green corn from the time they left Harper's Ferry until after the conclusion of the battle. Speaking of the heroism displayed by the Southern troops, a Northern journal said in its description of the battle, 'It is beyond all wonder how men such as the rebel troops are can fight as they do. That those ragged and filthy wretches, sick, hungry, and in all ways miserable, should prove such heroes in fight is past all explanation. Men never fought better. There was one regiment that stood up before the fire of two or three of our long-range batteries and of two regiments of infantry, and though the air around them was vocal with the whistle of bullets and the screech of shells, there they stood and delivered their fire in perfect order, and there they continued to stand until a battery of six light twelves was brought to bear on them, and before that they broke. Nothing mortal can stand a battery of six light Napoleon guns, if there is plenty of grape and canister in the ammunition chests.'"

Within this space of little more than a mile square, this spot, once beautiful with handsome residences and well-cultivated farms, isolated, hedged in with verdure, sacred to quiet, calm content, the hottest fury of man's hottest wrath had expended itself, burning residences and well-filled barns, plowing fields of ripened grain with artillery, scattering everywhere through corn-fields, wood, and valley the most awful illustrations of war. Not a building about us which was not deserted by its occupants and rent and torn by shot and shell; not a field which has not witnessed the fierce and bloody encounter of armed and desperate men.

"Let us first turn off to the left of the Hagerstown turnpike; but we must ride very slowly and carefully, for lying all through this corn-field are the victims of the hardest contest of our division. Can it be that these are the bodies of our late antagonists? Their faces are so absolutely black that I said to myself at first, 'This must have been a negro regiment.' Their eyes are protruding from their sockets; their heads, hands, and limbs are swollen to twice the natural size.

"Passing through this corn-field, with the dead lying through its aisles, out into an uncultivated field beyond, I saw bodies, attired mainly in rebel gray, lying in ranks so regular that Death, the reaper, must have mowed them down in swaths. Our burying-parties were already busily engaged, and had put away to rest many of our own men. Still here, as everywhere, I saw them scattered over the fields. The ground was strewn with muskets, knapsacks, cartridge-boxes, and articles of clothing, the carcasses of horses, and thousands of shot and shell. And so it was on the other side of the turnpike, nay, in the turnpike itself. Ride where we may, through corn-field, wood, or ravine, and our ride will be among the dead, until the heart grows sick and faint with horror. Here, close to the road, were the haystacks near which our general and staff paused for a while when the division was farthest advanced, and here, at the corner of the barn, lay one of our men killed by a shell, which had well-nigh proved fatal to them also.

"Just in front of these haystacks was the only pleasing picture on this battle-field,—a fine horse, struck with death at the instant when, cut down by his wound, he was attempting to rise from the ground. His head was half lifted, his neck proudly arched, every muscle seemed replete with animal life. The wound which killed him was wholly concealed from view, so that I had to ride close up before I could believe him dead. Hundreds of his kind lay upon the field, but all were repulsive save himself, and he was the admired of every passer-by. Two weeks afterwards I found myself pausing to gaze upon him, and always with the wish that some sculptor would immortalize in stone this magnificent animal in the exact pose of his death-hour.

"One would like to see something from a battle-field not wholly terrible.

"Over this graveyard of the unburied dead we reached a wood, every tree pierced with shot or cut with bullets, and came to the little brick Dunker church on the turnpike. This must have been a focal point in the battle, for a hundred round-shot have pierced its walls, while bullets by thousands have scarred and battered it. A little crowd of soldiers was standing about it, and within a few severely wounded rebels were stretched on the benches, one of whom was raving in his agony. Surgical aid and proper attendance had already been furnished, and we did not join the curious visitors within. Out in the grove behind the little church the dead has been collected in groups waiting for burial, some of them wearing our uniform, but the large majority dressed in gray. No matter in what direction we turned, it was all the same shocking picture, awakening awe rather than pity, benumbing the senses rather than touching the heart, glazing the eye with horror rather than filling it with tears.

"I had, however, seen many a poor fellow during my ride, something in whose position or appearance had caused me to pause; and here, lying side by side with three others, I saw a young rebel officer, his face less discolored than the rest, whose features and expression called forth my earnest sympathy, not so much for him as for those who, in his Southern home, shall see him no more forever. No one among the burying-party knew his name, and before night he was laid in a trench with the rest,—no headstone to mark his resting-place,—one of the three thousand rebel dead who fill nameless graves upon this battle-field.

"Very slowly, as men move through the burial-places of the dead, we rode through the woods at the back of the church, and reached the rocky citadel, behind which crouched the enemy to receive our charging battalions, sweeping their ranks with destruction and compelling their retreat. I was astonished to see how cunningly nature had laid up this long series of rocky ledges, breast-high, for the protection of the rebel lines. In front of this breastwork we found a majority of the dead dressed in blue. At this point also commenced a long barricade of fence-rails, piled closely, to protect the rebel lines, and stretching off towards the north. Here is one more evidence of the use to which the rebel generals put ever spare moment of time, and of their admirable choice of position.

"One more scene in this battle picture must be seen, and with a visit to it our ride may end. It is a narrow country lane, hollowed out somewhat between the fields, partially shaded, and now literally crowded with rebel corpses. Here they stood in line of battle, and here, in the length of five hundred feet, I counted more than two hundred of their dead. In every attitude conceivable,—some piled in groups of four or six, some grasping their muskets, as if in the act of discharging them, some evidently officers, killed while encouraging their men, some lying in the position of calm repose,—all black and swollen, and ghastly with wounds. This battalion of the dead filled the lane with horror. As we rode beside it—we could not ride in it—I saw the field all about me black with corpses, and they told me that the corn-field beyond was equally crowded. It was a place to see once, to glance at, and then to ride hurriedly away, for, strong-hearted as was then my mood, I had gazed upon as much horror as I was able to bear."

"All around," says a Northern correspondent, "were evidences of the terrible strife, of the long-continued contest, such as I do not like to dwell upon. The enemy had buried many dead. There were many long trenches, where they had laid their fallen, thrown a few inches of earth upon them, and covered them with fence-rails. The slaughter on their side must have been terrific. Horses were thickly strewn where our artillery had plowed the ground, cut down the tall forest-trees, and hurled destruction in their ranks. The enemy had strengthened the ridge by constructing rifle-pits of rocks, logs, and loose stones, gathered from the ledges. Passing down to the spot where through the day they had held the ground, it was easy to see why they clung to it with such tenacity: if they had been driven from the spot they would have been forced out into a large open field, and the place would have been equally strong to Gen. McClellan. So long as they held it they could hope to keep McClellan at bay, but if once lost there could be for them but little hope of success.

"Continuing on, I reached the line where French and Richardson had moved up the road leading to the farm-house of Mr. Roulet. The enemy had held it as a rifle-pit, and there across the fences fifteen thousand muskets had blazed, there the shells had fallen like thunder-bolts from heaven. Some had fallen upon their faces towards our advancing columns; some in the act of leaping the fence behind them; some while loading their guns; one while tearing a cartridge with his teeth had received a bullet through his heart, and had fallen with all his features fixed to that end. There was an officer, with his face towards heaven, bald-headed, yet not far advanced in years, his insignia of rank cut from his gray frock-coat. He fell while cheering his men, with all his muscles set, his system under tension, nerved up to the great exigencies of the moment.

"It was a fearful sight along the roadway, in the corn-fields. Thousands of dead were there.

"The army was moving on through Sharpsburg. There our shells had fallen in a continuous shower, tearing houses to pieces, killing one young child, and driving from the place all but a few persons, who took refuge in the cellar of a strong stone house.

"Gen. McClellan was there, with a careworn, troubled countenance. The people greeted him loyally. Nearly every house had its Union banner out, and there was a general rejoicing that the enemy was gone."

Another contemporaneous account says,—

"Upon walking over the field so hotly contested the evidences abound, especially near the centre and the right of the centre of our lines, of the terrible carnage that occurred. Among our forces, where the brigades mentioned charged over the crest of the hills and were repulsed from the woods, the slaughter was most fearful, the ground, as far as bodies could be distinguished, being thickly strewn with them. To the left of where Capt. Frank's battery of French's division was stationed—one of the most effective volunteer batteries in the service—a large group of dead horses attracted attention. Wounded and turned loose at different points where the fight was the hottest in this part of the field, they had herded together in their affright and pain, to perish in every attitude that makes the picturesque in a field of battle. One especially looked as if in the act of rising up once more to take part in the strife. On all sides was abundant evidence of the obstinacy of the struggle in the impromptu breastworks which abounded. Wherever a few panels of fence afforded opportunity to do so, these were thrown down and then piled thickly together, perhaps two feet high, and from behind them, and to the last moment possible, the rebels poured forth a deadly fire upon their assailants. Small ledges of rocks also, along the hillside which descended to the woods so fatal to our advance, served for shelter at every few steps, and while the shot and shell from our batteries, as they gained the crest of the hill, tore the trees to fragments over their heads, it was very hard to dislodge them except by an actual charge through, which ended in strewing the whole neighborhood with their killed. A brick school-house on a slight knoll in front of the woods was riddled with shot and shell. To the rear of this piece of woods a splendid steel gun was left by the rebels, a shot having slightly injured one of the axles.

"Passing back again through the woods, two rebel colonels and one brigadier were found on the ground, and interspersed with the multitudes of their fallen were so many of those in the National uniform that at a glance one might see how fearful was the cost of the victory. Upon one dead body was found a large black dog, dead also from some chance shot which had struck him whilst stretched upon his master's corpse caressingly, his forepaws across the man's breast. Ride where one might for a space of perhaps a mile and a half in width in places, and four or five miles in length, the dead were on every side, interspersed with the arms that had fallen from their hands. Shattered cannon-wheels and caissons and enormous quantities of round-shot and conical shell gave more evidence of the deadly storm that had come with destruction in its track.

"Sharpsburg was sadly cut up, almost every house in it giving proof of the terrible force of the missiles which were rained upon it so abundantly. Dead horses, too, were scattered around, to make the scene afforded more revolting, if possible, whilst the excitement of the occasion was painfully apparent in the faces of its inhabitants, such of them as had ventured to stay. . . .

"Returning to the field again, and looking into the houses and barns of the neighborhood, sights were seen calculated to harrow the hearts of the most hardened in such scenes. We came to the great barn and stack of wheat straw of the Roulett farm, and here might have been seen lying in the straw a large number of wounded rebels, hardly yet assured of the kindness of their captors, although their wounds had been dressed, and all had been done for them which the circumstances of the case permitted. The great cry was for water, and it was a sad reflection as one filled their canteens and put them to white feverish lips that another day would place them beyond the want of it. Returning to the unfortunate group the next morning, we found that several of them were dead, those capable of being removed having been taken to more comfortable quarters. Go where one might, in every place that afforded the slightest chance of shelter, the wounded of the battle-field were found. Every farm-house became a hospital, whilst whole regiments were detailed to bury the dead."

"In one part of the battle-field, a large corn-field," says another account, "just at the edge of a wood, where the rebels appear to have suffered most, their dead lay so thick that their dark forms could be plainly distinguished a long distance. A rifle-pit which was charged upon by a Pennsylvania regiment contained heaps of dead, lying just as they had fallen, one upon the other. In a ravine three rebels had met their death apparently while eating their breakfast. A plate lay before them with food upon it, containing a spoon, and around them lay the scattered fragments of a shell which had doubtless exploded in their midst, taking off the top of the head of one, and giving death wounds also to the others.

"But if to look upon the mangled bodies of the dead was horrible, still more terrible was the spectacle which the wounded on this vast blood-stained battle-field presented on Wednesday night, Thursday, and Friday. Many of the wounded remained on the field for twenty-four hours or more before their wounds received any attention. The surgeons were taxed beyond their ability by the multitude of sufferers, and I regret to say there was a lamentable deficiency in the supply of the various appliances needed at such a time. But for the many volunteer helpers on the field, there must have been a fearful aggravation of the sufferings of many of the heroic men who were stricken down in their country's service. Every church and school-house and nearly every private dwelling in Boonsboro' was a hospital.

"The fence-posts and panels and the trees of the woods were shivered and scattered around in every direction, covering the dead and the wounded, who lay piled up and scattered over miles of the country. They were mostly shot through with minié bullets, torn with grape and shell, and mangled with cannon-balls. Here lay a Wisconsin man with his hand and leg shot away with a round-shot; here lay two Mississippi brothers, one, with his head propped against a tree, mortally wounded, and the other by his side locked in the embrace of death. I saw a Thirteenth Massachusetts man propping the head of a wounded South Carolinian, and filling his canteen with water by draining his own; I saw our Union wounded sharing water and food with the wounded rebels, and I saw, during Wednesday and Thursday, hundreds of rebel wounded succored by the hands of our own soldiers as they lay on the field.

"After the rebel left had been driven back across the pike, they retreated in order from their front directly across the country, over well-made roads, striking the Sharpsburg and Shepherdstown road about one and a half miles from the latter place. Near this point, on the farm of Capt. D. Smith, we found one of the rebel hospitals, in which were about an equal number of rebel and Federal wounded, and here we learned from our own wounded that our left under Burnside had been unsuccessful in driving in the rebel right, and that they had been repulsed and lost the ground they had taken early in the morning. Had they been as successful on the left as on the right, we would have captured a large portion of the rebel left before they could have reached Shepherdstown; but the rebel right then resting on the Potomac, and their centre about the town of Sharpsburg, the nature of the country covered them with such strong fortifications that they successfully resisted every attack of our left, and from Monday till Wednesday evening our artillery poured a continuous stream of shell and shot into the loyal and patriotic town of Sharpsburg and along their entire right, but with no effect in driving them out of this line.

"In Sharpsburg the houses of the Widow Homes and the Widow Shackleford and the barn of Jacob H. Grove were burnt to the ground; but few houses of the town escaped the shot and shell. The women and children of the town suffered terribly from fright and hunger. For three days and nights they were gathered together in the cellars of the stone houses of the town, while the rebel soldiers despoiled their homes. They carried off everything in the stores, robbed the women of their clothing, flour, meat, preserves, fruits, vegetables, and everything they could use. We stopped at the house of Judge Smith, a Union refugee. He invited us in to take a drink of water, the only thing left to supply the wants of his family. His wife and family had remained at home, but the rebels crowded his house and ate every particle of food they had. A cannon-ball passed through his front door and out the rear door into his pantry, and demolished his dishes and crockery-ware.

"At the rebel hospital, on Capt. D. Smith's farm, about two miles from Shepherdstown, I noticed the rebel graves of W. T. Mulligan, colonel of the Fifteenth Georgia Regiment; Maj. Smith, Fourth Georgia; Lieut.-Col. N. Lutter, South Carolina Volunteers, and some fifteen dead rebels in a pile. On the farm adjoining I noticed some twelve graves of rebel officers, and about thirty of their dead unburied.

"Gen. McClellan stopped at the house of Col. Miller, a good Union man. We had seen Gen. McClellan in the front, at the right, on Wednesday and Thursday, but here we had the extreme pleasure of shaking hands with him and conversing with him. Just at that time Mr. Knowles, of Martinsburg, came in and introduced himself as Col. White's scout, who had piloted all our cavalry out of Harper's Ferry and through the rebel lines to Williamsport, where they captured Longstreet's ammunition train. The general shook his hand cordially and warmly, thanked him for his successful effort in saving our cavalry, and asked him several questions concerning the fight at Harper's Ferry, and then remarked, 'Had Col. Miles held Harper's Ferry twenty-four hours longer it would have insured the destruction of the Confederate army.'"

A correspondent of the New York *Tribune*, describing the field of battle, says, under date of September 18th,—

"I have just returned from the sickening spectacle. Soldiers who went through all the battles of the Peninsula say Fair Oaks and Malvern Hill were as nothing compared with it. The dead lie in heaps, the wounded are coming in by thousands. Around and in a large barn, about half a mile from the spot where Gen. Hooker engaged the enemy's left, I counted eleven hundred and twenty wounded. Along the same road, and within the distance of two miles, are three more hospitals, each having from six hundred to seven hundred in them, and long trains of ambulances standing in the road waiting to discharge their bloody loads. Surgeons, with hands, arms, and garments covered with blood, are busy amputating limbs, extracting balls, and bandaging wounds of every nature in every part of the body. Rebel soldiers in great numbers lie among our own and receive the same attention. I saw a rebel officer of the Twenty-seventh Alabama Regiment endure the amputation of his leg without the use of chloroform. Every muscle in his face was contracted, his jaws looked as if in a death-spasm, but no sound of pain issued from him. The saw and the knife did their work, but they could not wring from him an expression of physical agony.

"Keedysville, Boonsboro', Middletown, and Frederick are rapidly being filled with the wounded from the battles of Sunday and yesterday. The inhabitants in all these villages are laboring night and day to relieve the dying and the suffering. A more Christian people, in the practical significance of that word, I never saw. Every private dwelling is filled with the wounded. Carpets are torn up, costly furniture removed, and comfortable mattresses spread upon the floor, awaiting the arrival of the ambulances. And much of this preparation for the wounded is without one word from the medical directors in regard to it. In the pleasant village of Middletown especially I have seen nothing in the hospitals in Washington that indicated so much thoughtfulness and devotion. All the ladies in the village are spending night and day with the wounded."

Another correspondent, writing from Frederick under date of September 22d, says,—

"The number of sick and wounded at present in this city exceeds four thousand. To accommodate this large number every exertion has been made by the medical director and his staff, who have been nobly assisted by the ladies of Frederick. Last Friday two thousand one hundred and eighty rations for the sick and wounded were served out; Saturday, four thousand two hundred; and to-day, about four thousand one hundred. As the badly wounded who can be removed are being brought in, the convalescing are being sent away, and now that the railroad communication is complete, they are being sent North at the rate of about seven hundred a day; but no sooner are they gone than others take their place, as those that lie at Middletown and Boonsboro' are brought in here, where they can be made more comfortable.

"It takes an immense staff of surgeons, doctors, and nurses to attend to four thousand patients. I have visited all the hospitals in the city, and I have not met one man to complain that he was not well attended to at all times. We have twenty hospitals in Frederick City. The largest is the one known by the name of the United States General Hospital. This building is situated on a hill just as you enter the city. It was used as a barrack by Gen. Banks when he was quartered in this city last winter. It is capable of accommodating nearly one thousand patients. There are nineteen other buildings which have been converted into asylums for the sick and wounded, namely, the City Hotel, the United States Hotel, the Lutheran, Methodist, New and Old Episcopal, Presbyterian, and African churches, the three upper or high schools of the city, Nos. 70, 71, and 72, also two German Reformed churches, the Frederick Female Seminary, Bronson's Academy, a portion of the large building called the Jesuits' Noviciate, the left wing of the convent occupied by the Sisters of the Visitation Convent, and a private house used as the hospital for Confederates.

"Dr. H. S. Henertt presides over the Noviciate and Convent Hospitals. Dr. R. F. Wier, of New York, has charge of the general hospital; he has also been acting as assistant medical director. Mr. M. J. Fitzgerald is the general steward for all the hospitals in town. At all hours of the day, and even at night, you can find the good ladies of Frederick at the bedsides of our poor sick and wounded soldiers. The men get well rapidly under their kind treatment. No words of mine could describe their kindness and attention. A train full of mattresses, beds, pillows, and hospital furniture generally arrived here today. They were much wanted and will soon be in use. There are two hundred and fifty very bad cases, Confederates, in hospital. There has been more deaths among the few Confederates than among our large numbers in hospital."

"From Hagerstown to the southern limits of the county," said the Hagerstown *Herald and Torch* of September 24th, "wounded and dying soldiers are to be found in every neighborhood and in nearly every house. The whole region of country between Boonsboro' and Sharpsburg is one vast hospital. Houses and barns are filled with them, and nearly the whole population is engaged in waiting on and ministering to their wants. In this town the Washington House, County Hall, and Lyceum Hall have been appropriated to the use of the wounded, and our citizens, especially the ladies, are untiring in their efforts to relieve them."

A correspondent writing from Hagerstown says,—

"Our Ladies' Union Relief Association, at the head of which stands Mrs. Harry, has been at work night and day. At night they assembled at different houses, sewed bandages, scraped lint, and made up such things as would relieve the sufferers, and from sunup to sundown you could find them in the hospitals, in every nook of the town and through the country, searching for, begging, and buying such articles as the sufferers might ask for or want. At morning, noon, and evening, on every street of the town, you could see these ladies, accompanied by their husbands, children, and servants, with baskets, buckets, pitchers, and plates in their hands, wending their way to the hospitals, where each one vied with the other in serving out delicate morsels and relieving the wounded, and many an unfortunate fellow wept tears of joy as gentle and kind words invited him to partake of the refreshing food served with fair hands and the gifts of loyal hearts. This was a kindness that many of them had almost become strangers to, yet it served to refresh and brighten the fond recollections of sweet home. Would that I could pay a just tribute to the energy, industry, and constant devotion of Mrs. Harry and the ladies of the Union Relief Association. They have now been organized and extending relief to our sick and wounded for more than sixteen months, and still they do more, and contribute more, than on any former occasion."

In October the hospitals at Clarysville were transferred to Cumberland, under the direction of Dr. George H. Oliver, medical director. The Belvidere Hall, the old Presbyterian church, and the "Old Mill" on South Mechanic Street were among the buildings taken for the purpose.

The destruction of property in the section of country through which the two armies passed, and in which the battles of the Maryland campaign were fought, was necessarily very great. The Chesapeake and Ohio Canal for the distance of twelve miles "presented a scene of desolation;" the canal was tapped in five places, several flood-gates were torn to pieces, large bowlders were dislodged and rolled into the basin, and an attempt was made to blow up the aqueduct at Monocacy. The bridge about one mile west of Middletown, in Frederick County, was destroyed by the Confederate forces. A barn and shop belonging to Mr. Koogle, near the bridge, were burned, and the Baltimore and Ohio Railroad bridge at Monocacy Junction, near Frederick, was destroyed, while more or less damage was done to the railroad and telegraph lines. During the battle of Antietam a number of houses and barns were destroyed, among them the house and barn of Samuel Mumma, which were between the two armies and were ignited by shells. Mr. Mumma lost all his household furniture, including the wardrobe of his family, and all his grain, hay, and farming implements. His neighbor, William Rulett, one of the county commissioners, lost his horses and cattle and other property. He was in his house while the battle raged around it, and was obliged to seek refuge in his cellar. There he remained until the Federal troops drove back the Confederates temporarily and afforded him an opportunity to escape. The barns of Samuel and Henry Reel were also destroyed by fire, and nearly all the houses along the whole line of battle from Sharpsburg to Keedysville exhibited marks of having been under fire. Some were penetrated in three or four different places by shot and shell, and in many instances their inmates made narrow escapes from destruction.

When the Confederates approached Hagerstown many Union men sought refuge in Pennsylvania, and the *Herald and Torch* was suspended for two weeks. In its issue of September 24th it gave the following account of the Confederate occupation of the town:

"The advent of a Federal force under Gen. Reynolds, on Monday of last week, relieved our community from the suspense caused by the presence of the rebel army under Gen. R. E. Lee. Five days had been passed amid the greatest excitement, during which the rebels occupied Frederick County. Day brought partial relief, but night was passed amid perfect terror, until Thursday, the 11th instant, when the advance-guard, a squad of the First Virginia Cavalry, came dashing into our midst. These were followed by the whole regiment under L.

T. Brien, of our county, which numbered about three hundred and fifty. During the afternoon Toombs' brigade of Georgians passed through, and encamped on the railroad. The advance-guard captured Lieut. A. Nesbitt and four of his men, all of Russell's cavalry. During the day a few others were made prisoners, all of whom were paroled. In the meanwhile the stores of the town were quickly thronged, and Confederate scrip passed upon our merchants. Many of our citizens having fled with their goods and chattels, the amount of worthless paper forced upon the community was much lessened. As it was, but a few hours elapsed ere the quartermaster-general impressed stores of various kinds, boots, shoes, hats, caps, clothing, medical stores, and produce of every description, paying a few in United States Treasury notes, but by far the greater part and the larger amounts in scrip, or its equivalent, certificates of indebtedness. On Friday morning, about eleven o'clock, Longstreet's division, headed by Gen. R. E. Lee, made its appearance, and for three hours continued in one uninterrupted stream. But about 2 P.M. it became evident from the movements that there was some change of programme, the march having ceased, and the ammunition trains were started for the rear, with artillery following.

"Thus, having camped in two localities on the southwest and southeast of town, they remained until early on Sunday morning, when the line of march was again formed, but with a retrograde movement. Jackson, Taliaferro, and Hill's forces had crossed from Boonsboro' to Williamsport, over the Manor road, thence to Virginia. By noon of Sunday all had passed, and seeming quiet again prevailed until midnight, when Toombs' brigade moved down the Sharpsburg pike to Jones' Cross-Roads, thence on the Manor road to Williamsport, and about two o'clock Brien's cavalry left for the same place. Thus we were left in a state of doubtful uncertainty until about 2 P.M. of Monday, when a company of United States regular cavalry, under Lieut. Tarleton, came charging into town, and were received with wild and enthusiastic applause.

"The condition and *morale* of the Confederate army is beyond description. They came among us not only badly clothed and unclean in person, but in a half-starving condition. For days, indeed, since the fights at Centreville they had subsisted on rations of bread, irregularly issued, and green corn and fruits. Hundreds are weakened by diarrhœa and worn out by their long marches, but they fight desperately because forced by hunger and want."

The following interesting description of the Confederate occupation of Frederick is from the report of Dr. Lewis H. Steiner, inspector of the United States Sanitary Commission:

"FRIDAY, September 5th.—Left Washington at six o'clock, under the impression that the Confederate army had crossed the Potomac the preceding evening and were then in Frederick. Anxiety as to the fate of my friends, as well as to the general treatment my native place would receive at rebel hands, made the trip by no means a pleasant one. Along the road at different stopping-places reports reached us as to the number of Confederates that had crossed into Maryland. The passengers began to entertain fears that the train would not be able to reach Frederick. These were, however, quieted by a telegram received at a station near Monrovia, which announced the road open. Arriving at twelve o'clock, I found the town full of surmises and rumors. Such information had been received by the post quartermaster and the surgeon in charge of hospital that they were busy all the afternoon making arrangements to move off their valuable stores. The citizens were in the greatest trepidation. Invasion by the Southern army was considered equivalent to destruction. Impressment into the ranks as common soldiers or immurement in a Southern prison, these were not attractive prospects for quiet, Union-loving citizens!

"Towards nightfall it became pretty certain that a force had crossed about the mouth of the Monocacy. Telegrams were crowding rapidly upon the army officers located here, directing that what stores could not be removed should be burnt, and that the sick, as far as possible, should be sent on to Pennsylvania. Here began a scene of terror seldom witnessed in this region. Lieut. Castle, assistant quartermaster, burned a large quantity of his stores at the depot. Asst.-Surg. Weir fired his storehouse on the hospital grounds, and burned the most valuable of his surplus bedding, contained in Kemp Hall, on Church Street near Market. Many of our prominent citizens, fearing impressment, left their families and started for Pennsylvania in carriages, on horseback, and on foot. All the convalescents at the hospital that could bear the fatigue were started also for Pennsylvania, in charge of Hospital Steward Cox. The citizens removed their trunks, containing private papers and other valuables, from the bank vaults, under the firm belief that an attack would be made on those buildings for the sake of the specie contained in them. About $1\frac{1}{2}$ o'clock A.M. it was ascertained that Jackson's force, the advance-guard of the Southern army, was encamped on Moffat's farm, near Buckeyestown, and that this force would enter Frederick after daylight, for what purpose no one knew. Having possession of this amount of information, I retired about two o'clock, being willing to wait the sequel whatever it might be.

"SATURDAY, September 6th.—Found, on visiting the market in the morning, that a very large number of our citizens had left the town last night. Every mouth was full of rumors as to the numbers, whereabouts, and whatabouts of the Confederate force. One old gentleman, whose attachment to McClellan has become proverbial, declared that it was an impossibility for the rebels to cross the Potomac; and another, who looks upon Banks as the greatest of generals, declared that Banks' force had been taken for Confederates, and that the supposed enemies were friends.

"At length uncertainty was changed into certainty. About nine o'clock two seedy-looking individuals rode up Market Street as fast as their jaded animals could carry them. Their dress was a dirty, faded gray, their arms rusty and seemingly uncared for, their general appearance raffish or vagabondish. They shouted for Jeff Davis at the intersection of Patrick Street, and then riding to the intersection of Church and Market Streets, repeated the strange jubilant shout. No one expressing an opinion as to the propriety or impropriety of this proceeding, they countermarched and trotted down the street. Then followed some fifty or a hundred horsemen, having among them Bradley T. Johnson. These were received with feeble shouts from some secession sympathizers. They said 'the time of your deliverance has come.' A force of cavalry entered the hospital grounds and took possession of hospital and contents. All the sick were carefully paroled, not excepting one poor fellow then in a moribund condition. After some hours the medical officers and hospital stewards were allowed to go about town on horses.

"At ten o'clock Jackson's advance force, consisting of some five thousand men, marched up Market Street, and encamped north of the town.

"During the afternoon a provost-marshal was appointed for the town, and he occupied the same office which had been the headquarters of the United States provost-marshal. Guards were posted along our streets, and pickets along the roads leading from Frederick. Our stores were soon thronged with crowds. The shoe-stores were most patronized, as many of their men were shoeless and stockingless. The only money that many of them had was Confederate scrip, or shinplasters issued by banks, corporations, individuals, etc., all of equal value. To use the expression of an old citizen, 'the notes depreciated the paper on which they were printed.' The crowded condition of the stores enabled some of the chivalry to take what they wanted ('confiscate' is the technical expression) without going through the formality of handing over Confederate rags in change. But guards were placed at the stores whenever requested, and only a few men allowed to enter at a time. Even this arrangement proved inadequate, and the stores were soon necessarily closed.

"An attack on the *Examiner* printing-office being anticipated, a small guard was placed at the door. About nine o'clock P.M. a rush was made on the guard by some of the Southern soldiers, the door was driven in, and the contents of the office thrown in the street. W. G. Ross, Esq., a prominent lawyer of Frederick, called on the provost-marshal, who soon arrived with a strong force, suppressed the riot, and having obliged the rioters to return everything belonging to the office, put them in the guard-house. During the continuance of this struggle the oaths and imprecations were terrible. Every one in the neighborhood expected that a general attack would be made on the Union houses. Fortunately a quiet night ensued.

"SUNDAY, September 7th.—The rebels obliged most of our shoe-stores to be kept open during the day, so that their men could obtain shoes. The reign of terror continued, although no personal violence was done to any citizen. Pickets are posted miles out of town. The main body of the rebel troops is said to be encamped about Urbana. Gen. Robert E. Lee is in command, and there are three divisions, or it may be four, commanded by Jackson, Longstreet, D. H. Hill, and some one else. At the Evangelical Reformed church the pastor, Rev. Dr. Daniel Zacharias, offered up prayers for the President of the United States, notwithstanding the presence of a number of Confederate officers. In the evening Gen. Jackson attended the same church.

"The commissioner for the enrollment of the State militia was seized to-day and made to hand over the enrollment-books. No further requirement was made of him, except that he should report himself daily at the office of the provost-marshal.

"Mr. Heard (formerly editor of the *Frederick Herald*, a secession paper) issues a card calling for recruits to a company he is forming.

"JOHN W. HEARD'S PROCLAMATION.

"'Men of old Frederick, arouse! Defend your homes! Under the authority of the Confederate government, I am now engaged in raising a company of infantry. The great army of the South, unconquered and unconquerable, is now in your midst, and has determined that Maryland shall be free. What say you, Marylanders? Are you willing to fight for the liberties for which you have so long been clamorous, or are you so abject as to accept them as a boon at the hands of another? No! no! sons of Maryland, inheritors of her Revolutionary glory, by your own right arm achieve the independence of your own State. Falter not, hesitate not, now that the opportunity is offered you, but rally at once and vindicate your history.

"'☞ Recruiting-office next door to the provost-marshal's, where there will always be found an officer in attendance.

"'JOHN W. HEARD.

"'SEPTEMBER 9, 1862.'

"The following was also issued by Capt. White:

"CAPTAIN E. V. WHITE'S PROCLAMATION.

"'*Marylanders to the Rescue!*

"'I am a Marylander! I have been in the service eighteen months, opposing the tyranny which would have made of the South a subjugated and ruined country. I come to Maryland with the Southern army to do what I can to carry her where she belongs, to the Southern Confederacy. I want Marylanders to join me. I am authorized to raise a regiment of Maryland cavalry. I have no recruiting-office. I can be found at Gen. Lawton's headquarters, where I will be happy to receive recruits. Come at once, or make up your minds to be slaves to the Northern despotism forever.

"'E. V. WHITE,

"'*Captain Commanding Gen. Lawton's Body-Guard.*

"'SEPT'R 8, 1862.'

"CAVALRY NOTICE.

"'I have been detailed to recruit for Capt. White's cavalry regiment. All persons desiring to join this far-famed corps will apply to me at the provost-marshal's.

"'J. M. KILGOUR.

"'SEPTEMBER 10, 1862.'

"WEDNESDAY, September 10th.—At four o'clock this morning the rebel army began to move from town, Jackson's force taking the lead. The movement continued until eight o'clock P.M., occupying sixteen hours. The most liberal calculations could not give them more than sixty-four thousand men. Over three thousand negroes must be included in this number. These were clad in all kinds of uniform, not only in cast-off or captured United States uniforms, but in coats with Southern buttons, State buttons, etc. These were shabby, but not shabbier or seedier than those worn by white men in the rebel ranks. Most of the negroes had arms,—rifles, muskets, sabres, bowie-knives, dirks, etc. They were supplied in many instances with knapsacks, haversacks, canteens, etc. They were seen riding on horses and mules, driving wagons, riding on caissons, in ambulances, with the staff of generals, and promiscuously mixed up with all the rebel army.

"Some of the rebel regiments have been reduced to one hundred and fifty men; none number over five hundred.

"This force had about one hundred and fifty guns with the letters U. S. This rebel army seemed to have been largely supplied with transportation by some United States quartermaster. Uncle Sam's initials were on many of its wagons, ambulances, and horses. One neat spring-wagon was lettered '*General Casey's Headquarters.*' Each regiment was supplied with but one or two wagons. The men were mostly without knapsacks, some few carried blankets, and a *toothbrush* was occasionally to be seen at the buttonhole of a private soldier, whose reminiscences of home-life were not entirely eradicated.

"THURSDAY, September 11th.—Gen. Hill's division, numbering about eight thousand men, marched through the streets on their route westward this morning. This division moves more rapidly than either of the others. This was held to indicate the approach of the National army. Three of the buildings on the hospital grounds were taken possession of by the Confederates for the accommodation of the sick.

"FRIDAY, September 12th.—Stuart's cavalry passed through town to-day on their way to Hagerstown. It is said to be composed of Ashby's cavalry and the Hampton Legion. The men are more neat and cleanly than the infantry that preceded them, and their horses, of good stock, are well groomed and fed.

"The advance cavalry of the Federals charged into our streets, driving the rebels before them. They were met by a counter charge of Stuart's men, made in grand style. Saddles were emptied on both sides. Stuart's men fell back, carrying with them seven of our men as prisoners, and leaving many of their own men wounded on the ground. The accidental discharge of a cannon caused the death of seven horses and the wounding of a few men. Martial music is heard in the distance; a regiment of Ohio volunteers makes its appearance, and is hailed with the most enthusiastic demonstrations of joy.

"SATURDAY, September 13th.—The town was effervescent with joy at the arrival of the Union troops; no business was done. Every one felt jubilant, and congratulated himself and neighbor that the United States troops were once more in possession. Gen. McClellan and his staff rode through about nine o'clock, and was received on all sides with unlimited expressions of delight.

"In the afternoon I found McClellan, with a large portion of his army, encamped on my farm, west of Frederick. The nature of the camp and its arrangements prevented one forming any other conclusion than it was a bivouac, and only intended for temporary occupation. Some onward movement of the army was evidently already in contemplation, but what it might be was kept concealed in the breast of the general commanding.

"One thing may be said with perfect truth of the rebel army, and that is, but few stragglers are left behind as they march through the country. Depredations on private property in this neighborhood have been comparatively rare. This is understood to be the result of some very stringent rules adopted by Gen. Lee with special reference to the invasion of Maryland.

"The experience of one week with the rebel army satisfies me that the men are in a high state of discipline, and have learned implicit obedience.

"SUNDAY, September 14th.—Maj.-Gen. Banks' corps d'armee, commanded by Brig.-Gen. A. S. Williams, passed through town this morning on its way to the front. The men were in the best possible spirits, all eager for the fray.

"During the afternoon of the day the memorable engagement at the South Mountain Pass took place, in which our new levies vied with the veterans in pressing the Confederates up the side of the mountain, and then over into the valley beyond. Our military commanders will bear testimony, in proper form, to the heroic courage shown by our army in this well-fought action. The rebels had tried to make a stand at several points on the road prior to this engagement, but were gallantly driven forwards by our troops.

"On Wednesday the great battle of Antietam was fought, with such a display of strategy and power on the part of our general, and of heroism and daring from our men, that the enemy was glad to resign all hopes of entering Pennsylvania and withdraw his forces across the Potomac. A great victory had been gained; the enemy had been driven from loyal soil, and McClellan had shown himself worthy of the love (amounting almost to adoration) which his troops expressed on all sides.

"The battles fought at South Mountain and Antietam," continues Dr. Steiner, "opened up an extensive field of operations for the Sanitary Commission. This had been anticipated at the central office, and Inspectors Andrew, Chamberlain, and Smith had accompanied the army on its march from Washington, with wagons furnished with such articles as were most essential in the emergency. After a few days of duty in the front, Inspector Smith returned to Washington, and Inspector Andrew was assigned to duty in the hospitals at Frederick."

The force then representing the United States Sanitary Commission in Western Maryland was as follows:

Frederick: Lewis H. Steiner, M.D., Sanitary Inspector and Superintendent; George L. Andrew, M.D., Sanitary Inspector; Horace Howard Furness, Esq., Mr. Atherton Blight, Mr. Edwin R. Cornwall, assistants.

Sharpsburg: E. A. Crane, M.D., Sanitary Inspector; Mr. Clampitt, Mr. Watson, Mr. Parsons, assistants.

On the night of the 18th, having previously sent over all his trains, artillery, and stores at the ford near Shepherdstown, Lee moved his army to the south bank of the Potomac, entirely unmolested, the last body crossing about ten o'clock on the following morning. Anticipating pursuit, he made no display of force to intimidate the Federals, who followed on the night of the 19th. The passage of the river was undisputed, except by a few shots from a four-gun battery, whose gunners fled when the Federal advance reached the Virginia side. Supposing that the Confederates were in full retreat, they pressed on with loud cheers. Jackson, who was bringing up the Confederate rear, at once ordered A. P. Hill's division to drive them back. Arriving about half a mile from Boteler's Ford, Hill drew his men up in two lines, the first composed of the brigades of Pender, Gregg, and Thomas, under command of Gen. Gregg, and the second of Lane's (Branch's brigade), Archer's, and Brockenbrough's, under the command of Gen. Archer, of Harford County, Md.

"The enemy had lined the opposite hills," says Gen. Hill, "with some seventy pieces of artillery, and the infantry, who had crossed, lined the crest of the high banks on the Virginia shore. My lines advanced simultaneously, and soon encountered the enemy. This advance was made in the face of the most tremendous fire of artillery I ever saw, and too much praise cannot be awarded my regiments for their steady, unwavering step. It was as if each man felt that the fate of the army was centred in himself. The infantry opposition in front of Gregg's centre and right was but trifling, and soon brushed away. The enemy, however, massed in front of Pender, and extending, endeavored to turn his left. Gen. Pender became hotly engaged, and informing Archer of his danger, he (Archer) moved by the left flank, and forming on Pender's left, a simultaneous, daring charge was made, and the enemy driven pell-mell into the river. Then commenced the most terrible slaughter that this war has yet witnessed. The broad surface of the Potomac was blue with the floating bodies of our foes. But few escaped to tell the tale. By their own account they lost three thousand men killed and drowned from one brigade alone. Some two hundred prisoners were taken. My own loss was thirty killed and two hundred and thirty-one wounded. Total, two hundred and sixty-one. This was a wholesome lesson to the enemy, and taught them to know it may be dangerous sometimes to press a retreating army. In this battle (Shepherdstown) I did not use a piece of artillery." [1]

Leaving the dead behind, and unheeding the constant cannonade maintained from the north bank of the Potomac, the Confederates withdrew towards the Opequan, and drew up in line of battle on the west side of that stream, with their left extending to Williamsport and the Potomac. They maintained this position for several days, but McClellan declining to advance, they retired leisurely to the Opequan near Martinsburg, where they remained a few days, and then removed to the vicinity of Bunker Hill and Winchester, carefully removing all army stores as they went.

On the 2d of October, Gen. Lee issued the following order, giving a summary account of his campaign:

"HEADQUARTERS ARMY NORTHERN VIRGINIA,
"Oct. 2, 1862.

"General Orders No. 116.

"In reviewing the achievements of the army during the present campaign, the commanding general cannot withhold the expression of his admiration of the indomitable courage it has displayed in battle, and its cheerful endurance of privation and hardship on the march.

"Since your great victories around Richmond you have defeated the enemy at Cedar Mountain, expelled him from the Rappahannock, and after a conflict of three days utterly repulsed him on the plains of Manassas, and forced him to take shelter within the fortifications around the capital.

"Without halting for repose, you crossed the Potomac, storming the heights of Harper's Ferry, made prisoners of more than eleven thousand men, and capturing upwards of seventy pieces of artillery, all their small-arms, and other munitions of war.

"While one corps of the army was thus engaged, the other insured its success by arresting at Boonsboro' the combined armies of the enemy, advancing under their favorite general to the relief of their beleaguered comrades.

"On the field of Sharpsburg, with less than one-third of his number, you resisted from daylight until dark the whole army of the enemy, and repulsed every attack along its entire front of more than four miles in extent.

"The whole of the following day you stood prepared to renew the conflict on the same ground, and retired next morning without molestation across the Potomac.

"Two attempts subsequently made by the enemy to follow you across the river have resulted in his complete discomfiture and being driven back with loss.

"Achievements such as these demanded much valor and patriotism. History records few examples of greater fortitude and endurance than this army has exhibited; and I am commissioned by the President to thank you, in the name of the Confederate States, for the undying fame you have won for their arms.

"Much as you have done, much more remains to be accomplished. The enemy again threatens us with invasion, and to your tried valor and patriotism the country looks with confidence for deliverance and safety. Your past exploits give assurance that this confidence is not misplaced.

"R. E. LEE, *General Commanding.*" [2]

The official returns of the Army of Northern Virginia of the 22d of September, 1862, after the return of the Confederate army to Virginia, and when the stragglers left behind in the extraordinary marches in Maryland had rejoined their commands, show present for duty thirty-six thousand one hundred and eighty-seven infantry and artillery; the cavalry, of which there is no report, would perhaps increase these figures to forty thousand of all arms.

The returns of the Army of the Potomac of the 20th of September, 1862, show present for duty at that date of the commands that participated in the battle of Sharpsburg eighty-five thousand nine hundred and thirty of all arms, as follows:

Gen. McClellan, staff, and engineer brigade, etc.	1,393
First Army Corps, Gen. Meade	12,237
Second " Gen. Sumner	13,604
Fifth " Gen. Porter	19,477
Sixth " Gen. Franklin	11,862
Ninth " Gen. Burnside	10,734
Twelfth " Gen. Williams	8,383
Cavalry Corps, Gen. Pleasonton	4,543
Detached commands at Frederick, Williamsport, and Boonsboro'	3,697
	85,930

This is exclusive of Couch's division of the Fourth Corps (seven thousand two hundred and nineteen), which reached Gen. McClellan after the battle.[3]

In the battle of Sharpsburg and other engagements fought in Maryland quite a number of the Maryland commands in the Federal and Confederate armies suffered severely. The Third Maryland Federal Regiment, as has been seen, occupied a prominent position on the right of the line at the battle of Sharpsburg, and was reduced to about two hundred effective men. They fought with the greatest gallantry, driving the Confederates before them, and only retired when the remainder of the army fell back. This gallant command also suffered in the various engagements in Virginia. At the battle of Slaughter Mountain, under Col. De Witt, they lost in killed Maj. Kennedy, and in killed and wounded seventy-two. At Beverly Ford, on the 21st of August, they were

---

[1] The Federal loss was undoubtedly severe; but John Esten Cooke, while expressing the opinion that this bloody repulse deterred McClellan from further pursuit, says that Gen. Hill's estimate of his enemy's loss "appears to be exaggerated."

[2] Gen. Longstreet says, "In one month these troops had marched over two hundred miles, upon little more than half rations, and fought nine battles and skirmishes, killed, wounded, and captured nearly as many men as we had in our ranks, besides taking arms and other munitions of war in large quantities."

[3] Taylor's "Four Years with Gen. Lee," p. 75.

again called into action, and had in killed and wounded seventeen, and forty-three taken prisoners. Col. De Witt being sick, Lieut.-Col. Sudsburg took command at Georgetown, on their march to Frederick, and fought the regiment at the battle of Sharpsburg. The Fifth and Second Regiments also evinced distinguished bravery in the battle of the 17th of September. The former regiment, as has already been said, was under the command of Major Blumenburg, who was severely wounded, and it lost forty-two killed and one hundred and forty-two wounded. The latter, under Lieut.-Col. Duryea, fought on the left of the Federal line, under Burnside, near the stone bridge. This regiment had also performed hard service in Newbern, N. C. At that time it numbered seven hundred and seventy-nine men, and after the campaign in Maryland it only numbered two hundred and fifty men and officers. It lost in battle by death and wounds one hundred and forty-four men. At the battle of Sharpsburg the Purnell Maryland Legion fought in the third brigade of Brig.-Gen. George S. Greene's second division of the Eleventh Army Corps. They were complimented by Gen. Greene for their gallant conduct on the field, having lost three killed and twenty-four wounded out of one hundred and ninety-three men with which they went into the engagement. The First Maryland (Federal) Artillery, or the Gist Artillery, as it was sometimes called, also won great distinction in this memorable battle. It occupied an advanced position.

Gen. Kenly with his brigade left Baltimore for the army on the 18th, and arrived at Williamsport on the 20th, to reinforce the Pennsylvania militia drawn up in line of battle near the town. The Pennsylvanians were very much alarmed at the presence of the Confederates, and had made preparations to destroy the stores, etc., in case of an attack. But the presence of Gen. Kenly's command, notwithstanding their long and forced march and the great need of rest and subsistence, "encouraged us," says Governor Curtin, "and proved a material influence in compelling the enemy to withdraw to the right bank of the Potomac, and in checking the demonstration he was making on Hagerstown." Governor Curtin, in a very complimentary letter, acknowledged the valuable services of the Maryland Brigade at that time, and expressed his thanks to Gen. Kenly personally " for the cheerful alacrity with which you obeyed the orders of Gen. Reynolds, and for the faithful discharge of all the duties which devolved upon you."

In the Confederate army, besides Gen. Trimble, Gen. Archer, Col. Bradley T. Johnson, Col. Charles Marshall, Maj. Henry Kyd Douglass, and other prominent Marylanders, who held distinguished positions and took a prominent part in the battles in Maryland, the State was represented in the ranks by the First Maryland Artillery, Chesapeake Artillery, Baltimore Light Artillery, and several companies of cavalry, besides scouts, etc.

After the campaign in Western Maryland, the entire country around, as has already been seen, was turned into a vast hospital for the sick and wounded soldiers of the two armies. Federal and Confederate sufferers were lying side by side in the hospitals, and received equal attention and relief, no distinction being made between them. The ladies of opposite sentiments united as relief associations and accomplished their humane and benevolent objects. The Christian Commission of Baltimore visited the battle-fields and hospitals, and distributed food, clothing, and bandages to the sick and wounded, and rendered all possible aid to the needy soldiers. Among those who rendered valuable assistance to the sufferers was Dr. Lewis H. Steiner, of Frederick City.

Subscription lists were opened in all sections of the State by the association for the relief of the sick and wounded, and soon large sums of money, clothing, and necessaries were contributed. Many who had slight wounds made their way to Baltimore, stopping at the railroad stations, etc., to have their wounds dressed.

Governor Bradford and his staff, with eighteen volunteer surgeons, visited the hospitals around the battle-fields of Sharpsburg, and the latter remained to assist the army surgeons in their duties. After the Governor's return he issued an address thanking the Marylanders under McClellan—the Second, Third, and Fifth Regiments, the Purnell Legion, the First Regiment of the Potomac Home Brigade, and First Maryland Artillery—for their courage and conduct, and expressing acknowledgments on behalf of the State to Gen. McClellan and Governor Curtin, of Pennsylvania. On the 1st of October, President Lincoln, accompanied by John W. Garrett, president of the Baltimore and Ohio Railroad; Mr. Kennedy, superintendent of the United States census; Marshal Lamon, of the District of Columbia, and several other distinguished personages, visited Gen. McClellan, and remained several days. He visited the battle-fields of South Mountain and Sharpsburg, and spent some time viewing the important points of historical interest.

Upon arriving at the scene of the recent battle of South Mountain the whole party took horses and rode over the battle-field, spending some time in visiting the localities rendered historical by the severe struggles of September 14th and 15th. After this was done, Gen. McClellan and his staff took leave of the

President and returned to headquarters. The President and his party occupied two large ambulances, in which they returned to Frederick.

At fifteen minutes before five the Presidential salute, which was fired by Battery K of the First New York Artillery, announced their approach. Patrick Street was lined with people anxious to see and welcome the President of the United States. Just at this time a smart shower commenced falling, accompanied by a heavy wind, which raised suffocating clouds of dust. But this could not drive in the crowds, who had been long and anxiously waiting his approach. The procession was led by Col. Allen, the military governor of Frederick, followed by the ambulances containing the Presidential party, accompanied by a detachment of the First Maine Cavalry, under the command of Capt. Smith, the provost-marshal, as a guard of honor. The President was enthusiastically received by the multitude as he rode up Patrick to Court Street, where the procession turned off and proceeded to the residence of Mrs. Ramsey, on Record Street, where Gen. Hartsuff was stopping and being attended upon since he was wounded at the battle of Antietam. The President had expressed a desire to pay his respects to this gallant soldier on his way through the city.

Here he remained for a few moments, and upon making his appearance he was again enthusiastically cheered and called upon for a speech. He briefly addressed the assemblage as follows:

"In my present position it is hardly proper for me to make speeches. Every word is so closely noted that it will not do to make foolish ones, and I cannot be expected to be prepared to make a sensible one. If I were as I have been most of my life, I might perhaps talk nonsense to you for half an hour, and it wouldn't hurt anybody. As it is, I can only return thanks for the compliment paid our cause. Please accept my sincere thanks for the compliment to our common country."

Here repeated cheers were given for the President and Gen. McClellan. Mr. Lincoln then re-entered the ambulance, and was driven to the railroad station, closely followed by the rapidly increasing crowd. The party immediately entered the handsomely fitted up cars, which had been in readiness to receive them for nearly forty-eight hours. The President was again loudly called for by the throng of citizens and soldiers, and upon making his appearance another speech was demanded. He good-naturedly responded as follows:

"I am surrounded by soldiers, and a little further off by the citizens of this good city of Frederick. Nevertheless I can only say, as I did five minutes ago, it is not proper for me to make speeches in my present position. I return thanks to our good soldiers for the services they have rendered, the energy they have shown, the hardships they have endured, and the blood they have shed for this Union of ours; and I also return thanks, not only to the soldiers, but to the good citizens of Frederick, and to the good men, women, and children in this land of ours, for their devotion in the glorious cause, and I say this with no malice in my heart towards those who have done otherwise. May our children and children's children for a thousand generations continue to enjoy these benefits conferred upon us by a united country, and have cause yet to rejoice under these glorious institutions, bequeathed to us by Washington and his compeers. Now, my friends, soldiers and citizens, I can only say once more, farewell."

Cheers for the President and Gen. McClellan were alternately given. Just as the cars moved off Gen. McClellan was loudly called for, and he stepped out on the platform and bowed a farewell to the multitude. At twenty minutes past five the train started for Washington, and the crowd dispersed. Frederick Schley, editor of the *Examiner*, telegraphed an invitation to the President to accept the hospitalities of his mansion, but Marshal Lamon, on behalf of Mr. Lincoln, declined it on account of the necessarily brief time that he would remain in the city. The President's car was ornamented by a very large and beautiful bouquet, presented to him by Mrs. Schley, with which he appeared to be much pleased.[1]

Not long after the battle of Sharpsburg the State was again thrown into excitement by an adventurous inroad of the Confederate cavalry under Gen. J. E. B.

---

[1] A Washington correspondent who accompanied President Lincoln in this visit to the battle-fields of Sharpsburg and South Mountain relates the following incident:

"After leaving Gen. Richardson the party passed a house in which was a large number of Confederate wounded. By request of the President, the party alighted and entered the building. Mr. Lincoln, after looking, remarked to the wounded Confederates that if they had no objection he would be pleased to take them by the hand. He said the solemn obligations which we owe to our country and posterity compel the prosecution of this war, and it followed that many were our enemies through uncontrollable circumstances, and he bore them no malice, and could take them by the hand with sympathy and good feeling. After a short silence the Confederates came forward, and each silently but fervently shook the hand of the President. Mr. Lincoln and Gen. McClellan then walked forward by the side of those who were wounded too severely to be able to arise, and bid them to be of good cheer, assuring them that every possible care should be bestowed upon them to ameliorate their condition. It was a moving scene, and there was not a dry eye in the building, either among the Nationals or Confederates. Both the President and Gen. McClellan were kind in their remarks and treatment of the rebel sufferers during this remarkable interview."

Stuart. The following official reports contain the history of this daring expedition:

"HEADQ'RS ARMY NORTHERN VIRGINIA,
"CAMP NEAR WINCHESTER, VA., 8th Oct., 1862.
"MAJ.-GEN. J. E. B. STUART,
"Commanding Cavalry, etc.

"GENERAL,—An expedition into Maryland with a detachment of cavalry, if it can be successfully executed, is at this time desirable. You will therefore form a detachment of from twelve to fifteen hundred well-mounted men, suitable for such an expedition, and should the information from your scouts lead you to suppose that your movement can be concealed from bodies of the enemy that would be able to resist it, you are desired to cross the Potomac above Williamsport, leave Hagerstown and Greencastle on your right, and proceed to the rear of Chambersburg, and endeavor to destroy the railroad bridge over the branch of the Conococheague.

"Any other damage that you can inflict upon the enemy or his means of transportation you will also execute. You are desired to gain all information of the position, force, and probable intention of the enemy which you can, and in your progress into Pennsylvania you will take measures to inform yourself of the various routes that you may take on your return to Virginia.

"To keep your movement secret, it will be necessary for you to arrest all citizens that may give information to the enemy, and should you meet with citizens of Pennsylvania holding State or government offices, it will be desirable, if convenient, to bring them with you, that they may be used as hostages, or the means of exchange for our own citizens that have been carried off by the enemy. Such persons will, of course, be treated with all the respect and consideration that circumstances will admit.

"Should it be in your power to supply yourself with horses, or other necessary articles on the list of legal captures, you are authorized to do so.

"Having accomplished your errand, you will rejoin the army as soon as practicable. Reliance is placed upon your skill and judgment in the successful execution of this plan, and it is not intended or desired that you should jeopardize the safety of your command, or go farther than your good judgment or prudence may dictate.

"Col. Imboden has been desired to attract the attention of the enemy towards Cumberland, so that the river between that point and where you may recross may be less guarded. You will, of course, keep out your scouts to give you information, and take every other precaution to secure the success and safety of the expedition.

"Should you be led so far east as to make it better, in your opinion, to continue around to the Potomac, you will have to cross the river in the vicinity of Leesburg.

"I am, with great respect,
"Your obedient servant,
(Signed) "R. E. LEE, General.
"Official—R. H. CHILTON, A. A. General."

"HEADQUARTERS CAVALRY DIVISION,
"October 9, 1862.

"SOLDIERS.—You are about to engage in an enterprise which, to insure success, imperatively demands at your hands coolness, decision, and bravery, implicit obedience to orders, without question or cavil, and the strictest order and sobriety on the march and in bivouac.

"The destination and extent of this expedition had better be kept to myself than known to you. Suffice it to say that, with the hearty co-operation of officers and men, I have not a doubt of its success,—a success which will reflect credit in the highest degree upon your arms.

"The orders which are herewith published for your government are absolutely necessary, and must be rigidly enforced.
(Signed) "J. E. B. STUART,
"Major-General Commanding."

"HEADQUARTERS CAVALRY DIVISION,
"October 9, 1862.

"Orders No. 13.—During the expedition into the enemy's country on which this command is about to engage, brigade commanders will make arrangements for seizing horses, the property of citizens of the United States, and all other property subject to legal capture, provided that in no case will any species of property be taken except by authority, given in person or in writing, of the commander of brigade, regiment, or captain of a company in the absence of his superior officers. In all cases a simple receipt will be given to the effect that the article is seized for the use of the Confederate States, giving place, date, and name of owners, in order to enable the individual to have recourse upon his government for damages.

"Individual plunder for private use is positively forbidden, and every instance must be punished in the severest manner, for an army of plunderers consummates its own destruction. The capture of anything will not give the captor any individual claim, and all horses and equipments will be kept, to be apportioned, upon the return of the expedition, through the entire division. Brigade commanders will arrange to have one-third of their respective commands engaged in leading horses, provided enough can be procured, each man linking so as to lead three horses, the led horses being habitually in the centre of the brigade, and the remaining two-thirds will keep at all times prepared for action.

"The attack, when made, must be vigorous and overwhelming, giving the enemy no time to reconnoitre or consider anything except his best means of flight. All persons found in transit must be detained, subject to the orders of division provost-marshal, to prevent information reaching the enemy. As a measure of justice to our many good citizens who, without crime, have been taken from their homes and kept by the enemy in prison, all public functionaries, such as magistrates, postmasters, sheriffs, etc., will be seized as prisoners. They will be kindly treated, and kept as hostages for our own. No straggling from the route of march or bivouac for the purpose of obtaining provisions, etc., will be permitted in any case, the commissaries and quartermasters being required to obtain and furnish all such supplies in bulk as may be necessary.

"So much of this order as authorizes seizures of persons and property will not take effect until the command crosses the Pennsylvania line.

"The utmost activity is enjoined upon the detachments procuring horses, and unceasing vigilance upon the entire command.

"Maj. J. P. W. Hairston is hereby appointed division provost-marshal.

"By command of Maj.-Gen. J. E. B. STUART.
"R. CHANNING PRICE, 1st Lieut. and A. D. C."

"HEADQUARTERS CAVALRY DIVISION,
"Oct. 14, 1862.
"COL. R. H. CHILTON,
"A. A. General Army Northern Virginia:

"COLONEL,—I have the honor to report that on the 9th instant, in compliance with instructions from the commanding general Army Northern Virginia, I proceeded on an expedition into Pennsylvania with a cavalry force of eighteen hundred men and four pieces of horse artillery, under command of Brig.-

Gen. Hampton and Cols. W. H. F. Lee and Jones. This force rendezvoused at Darksville at 12 M., and marched thence to the vicinity of Hedgesville, where it camped for the night. At daylight next morning (October 10th) I crossed the Potomac at McCoy's (between Williamsport and Hancock) with some little opposition, capturing some two or three horses of the enemy's pickets. We were told here by citizens that a large force had been camped the night before at Clear Spring, and were supposed to be *en route* to Cumberland. We proceeded northward until we had reached the turnpike leading from Hagerstown to Hancock (known as the National road). Here a signal-station on the mountain and most of the party, with their flags and apparatus, were surprised and captured, and also eight or ten prisoners of war, from whom, as well as from citizens, I found that the large force, alluded to, had crossed but an hour ahead of me towards Cumberland, and consisted of six regiments of Ohio troops and two batteries under Gen. Cox, and were *en route*, *via* Cumberland, for the Kanawha. I sent back this intelligence at once to the commanding general. Striking directly across the National road, I proceeded in the direction of Mercersburg, Pa., which point was reached about 12 M. I was extremely anxious to reach Hagerstown, where large supplies were stored, but was satisfied from reliable information that the notice the enemy had of my approach and the proximity of his forces would enable him to prevent my capturing it. I therefore turned towards Chambersburg. I did not reach this point till after dark in a rain. I did not deem it safe to defer the attack till morning, nor was it proper to attack a place full of women and children without summoning it first to surrender.

"I accordingly sent in a flag of truce, and found no military or civil authority in the place; but some prominent citizens who met the officer were notified that the place would be occupied, and if any resistance were made the place would be shelled in three minutes. Brig.-Gen. Wade Hampton's command being in advance took possession of the place, and I appointed him military governor of the city. No incidents occurred during the night, during which it rained continuously The officials all fled the town on our approach, and no one could be found who would admit that he held office in the place. About two hundred and seventy-five sick and wounded in hospital were paroled. During the day a large number of horses of citizens were seized and brought along. The wires were cut, and railroads were obstructed. Next morning it was ascertained that a large number of small-arms and munitions of war were stored about the railroad buildings, all of which that could not be easily brought away were destroyed, consisting of about five thousand new muskets, pistols, sabres, ammunition, also a large assortment of army clothing. The extensive machine-shops and depot buildings of the railroad and several trains of loaded cars were entirely destroyed.

"From Chambersburg I decided, after mature consideration, to strike for the vicinity of Leesburg as the best route of return, particularly as Cox's command would have rendered the direction of Cumberland, full of mountain gorges, particularly hazardous. The route selected was through an open country. Of course I left nothing undone to prevent the inhabitants from detecting my real route and object. I started directly towards Gettysburg, but, having passed the Blue Ridge, turned back towards Hagerstown for six or eight miles, and then crossed to Maryland by Emmittsburg, where, as we passed, we were hailed by the inhabitants with the most enthusiastic demonstrations of joy. A scouting party of one hundred and fifty Lancers had just passed towards Gettysburg, and I regret exceedingly that my march did not admit of the delay necessary to catch them. Taking the road towards Frederick, we intercepted dispatches from Col. Rush (Lancers) to the commander of the scout, which satisfied me that our whereabouts was still a problem to the enemy.

"Before reaching Frederick I crossed the Monocacy, continued the march through the night, *via* Liberty, New Market, Monrovia, on the Baltimore and Ohio Railroad, where we cut the telegraph wires and obstructed the railroad. We reached at daylight Hyattstown, on McClellan's line of wagon communication with Washington, but we found only a few wagons to capture, and we pushed on to Barnsville, which we found just vacated by a company of the enemy's cavalry. We had here corroborated what we had heard before, that Stoneman had between four and five thousand troops about Poolesville and guarding the river fords. I started directly for Poolesville, but instead of marching upon that point avoided it by a march through the woods, leaving it two or three miles to my left, and getting into the road from Poolesville to the mouth of the Monocacy. Guarding well my flanks and rear, I pushed boldly forward, meeting the head of the enemy's column going towards Poolesville.

"I ordered the charge, which was responded to in handsome style by the advance squadron (Irving's) of Lee's brigade, which drove back the enemy's cavalry upon the column of infantry advancing to occupy the crest from which the cavalry were driven. Quick as thought Lee's sharpshooters sprang to the ground, and engaging the infantry skirmishers, held them in check till the artillery in advance came up, which, under the gallant Pelham, drove back the enemy's force to his batteries beyond the Monocacy, between which and our solitary gun quite a spirited fire continued for some time. This answered, in connection with the high crest occupied by our piece, to screen entirely my real movement quickly to the left, making a bold and rapid strike for White's Ford, to make my way across before the enemy at Poolesville and Monocacy could be aware of my design. Although delayed somewhat by about two hundred infantry, strongly posted in the cliffs over the ford, yet they yielded to the moral effect of a few shells before engaging our sharpshooters, and the crossing of the canal (now dry) and river was effected with all the precision of passing a defile on drill.

"A section of artillery being sent with the advance and placed in position on the Loudon side, another piece on the Maryland height, while Pelham continued to occupy the attention of the enemy with the other, withdrawing from position to position until his piece was ordered to cross. The enemy was marching from Poolesville in the mean time, but came up in line of battle on the Maryland bank, only to receive a thundering salutation, with evident effect, from our guns on this side. I lost not a man killed on the expedition, and only a few slight wounds. The enemy's loss is not known, but Pelham's one gun compelled the enemy's battery to change its position three times. The remainder of the march was destitute of interest. The conduct of the command and their behavior towards the inhabitants is worthy of the highest praise; a few individual cases only were exceptions in this particular.

"Brig.-Gen. Hampton and Cols. Lee, Jones, Wickham, and Butler, and the officers and men under their command, are entitled to my lasting gratitude for their coolness in danger and cheerful obedience to orders. Unoffending persons were treated with civility, and the inhabitants were generous in proffers of provisions on the march. We seized and brought over a large number of horses, the property of citizens of the United States.

"The valuable information obtained in this reconnoissance as to the distribution of the enemy's force was communicated orally to the commanding general, and need not here be repeated. A number of public functionaries and prominent citizens were taken captives and brought over as hostages for our own unoffending citizens whom the enemy has torn from their homes and confined in dungeons in the North. One or two of my men lost their way, and are probably in the hands of the enemy.

"The results of this expedition in a moral and political point of view can hardly be estimated, and the consternation among property-holders in Pennsylvania beggars description.

"I am especially indebted to Capt. B. S. White, South Carolina Cavalry, and to Mr. ——, and Mr. ——, whose skillful guidance was of immense service to me. My staff are entitled to my thanks for untiring energy in the discharge of their duties.

"I inclose a map of the expedition, drawn by Capt. W. W. Blackford to accompany this report, also a copy of orders enforced during the march.

"Believing that the hand of God was clearly manifested in the signal deliverance of my command from danger, and the crowning success attending it, I ascribe to Him the praise, the honor, and the glory.

"I have the honor to be, most respectfully, your obedient servant,

(Signed) "J. E. B. STUART,
"*Maj.-Gen. Commanding Cavalry.*"

"HEADQUARTERS DEPARTMENT OF NORTHERN
"VIRGINIA, Oct. 18, 1862.

"GEN. S. COOPER, Adjutant and Inspector-General:

"GENERAL,—In forwarding the report of Maj.-Gen. Stuart of his expedition into Pennsylvania, I take occasion to express to the Department my sense of the boldness, judgment, and prudence he displayed in its execution, and cordially join with him in his commendations of the conduct and endurance of the brave men he commanded. To his skill and their fortitude, under the guidance of an overruling Providence, is their success due.

"I have the honor to be, most respectfully, your obedient servant,

(Signed) "R. E. LEE, *General.*"

In the mean time the Confederates had destroyed about thirty-five miles of the Baltimore and Ohio Railroad, beginning at Harper's Ferry and running to a point about ten miles west of Martinsburg. This portion of the road had the rails torn up, and either carried off or twisted and rendered useless. All the bridges throughout this extent were destroyed, and at Martinsburg one of the great store-houses of the company, and an immense amount of damage was done. Switches and sidings were torn up, the various repair-shops, water-tanks, coal-dumps, offices, machine-shops, engines, cars, and, in short, everything pertaining to the railroad was destroyed as far as possible.

CHAPTER XIII.

THE GETTYSBURG CAMPAIGN.

Movements of Maryland Troops—Formation of the Maryland Brigade—Confederate Occupation of Cumberland—Battle of Chancellorsville—Battle of Winchester—Confederate Invasion of Maryland—Occupation of Hagerstown—Battle of Gettysburg—Confederate Occupation of Westminster—The Pursuit of Lee through Maryland—Capture of the Ninth Maryland Federal Regiment.

AFTER the termination of the Maryland campaign, the Army of the Potomac remained on the north bank of the river, in the vicinity of Sandy Hook, Sharpsburg, and Williamsport, with a large detachment thrown across at Harper's Ferry, occupying Loudon and Bolivar Heights.

Reconnoissances were made on the 16th and 17th of October from Sharpsburg in the direction of Reameysville, Leetown, and Smithfield, Va., and from Harper's Ferry to Charlestown. In the latter the Fifth Maryland participated. On the 21st of October a reconnoissance was also made from Loudon Heights to Lovettsville, in which the Third Maryland bore a part. On the 26th of October, Gen. McClellan began his second advance into Virginia from the line of the Potomac. Early on that day a cavalry force under Gen. Pleasonton crossed the Potomac at Berlin, and moved in the direction of Purcellville. Soon after the Ninth Corps began to cross in light marching order, and took position near Lovettsville. The First, Sixth, and Ninth Corps, the cavalry and the reserve artillery crossed at Berlin between the 26th of October and the 2d of November. The Second and Fifth Corps crossed at Harper's Ferry between the 29th of October and the 1st of November. The Twelfth Corps was left in the vicinity of Harper's Ferry, to guard against another invasion of Maryland. Attached to it at this time were the Third and Fifth Maryland Infantry Regiments, Purnell's Legion, and Cole's cavalry.

On the 7th of November an order was received from Washington relieving Gen. McClellan of command and appointing Gen. Burnside as his successor. On the 13th of December, Burnside made an assault upon the Confederate heights in the rear of Fredericksburg, when "a slaughter the most bloody and most useless of the war" took place. Gen. Jackson commanded on the right of the Confederate line, and Gen. Longstreet on the left. On the Federal side Franklin was on the left, Hooker occupied the centre, and Sumner the right. The Federal attack was repulsed with a loss on the Union side of about fifteen thousand killed and wounded, and on the Confederate side of about five thousand. After the battle of Fredericksburg, Gen. Burnside was relieved of the command, and Gen. Hooker appointed in his stead. The Twelfth Corps, which had been left at Harper's Ferry when McClellan advanced towards the Rappahannock, again joined the main army in the latter part of December. During its stay on the upper Potomac several reconnoissances were made to ascertain the location and strength of the Confederate forces in the Shenandoah Valley. In one of these expeditions, made by the Second Division, under Gen. Geary, on the 9th of November, the Third Maryland and Purnell's Legion participated. The division moved from Bolivar Heights to Rippon, within six miles of Berryville, driving back the enemy, and capturing prisoners, arms, horses, and cattle.

From the 2d to the 6th of December, Cole's cavalry and the Third Infantry formed part of a column under Gen. Geary, which marched to Winchester. *En route* Cole's cavalry skirmished with the enemy's cavalry at Charlestown, Berryville, and Ash Hollow. On the withdrawal of the Twelfth Corps from Harper's Ferry, Cole's cavalry and the Fifth Infantry were left in that vicinity, while the Purnell Legion was sent to Frederick City.

The First Maryland Cavalry did not accompany the Army of the Potomac in the Maryland campaign of 1862. It was given a more arduous duty in the defenses of Washington south of the Potomac. During the fall and winter months it made numerous reconnoissances through the section of country lying between the Bull Run Mountains and the Potomac and Rappahannock Rivers. The regiment was kept almost incessantly in motion, picking up guerrillas, watching dangerous defiles, scouting across the country, always on the *qui vive* against attack or surprise.

On the 25th of October, 1862, while making one of these reconnoissances, a detachment of the regiment was attacked near Manassas Junction by a superior force of the enemy, and had one man (Robert Starkey) killed, two officers (Lieuts. A. S. Dorsey and N. P. Patterson) wounded, and seven men captured. Again, on the 27th of December, a portion of the regiment, under Capt. Joseph H. Cook, aided in repulsing Stuart's attack upon the town of Dumfries. After a sharp and determined fight, lasting several hours, the enemy was driven off with considerable loss. Capt. Cook was highly commended by Col. Candy, commanding the post, for his efficient services on this occasion. In the morning a detachment of the First, commanded by Capt. J. K. Buckley, had been sent from Dumfries on a scout in the direction of Stafford Store and Springs. Next day, while *en route* from Fairfax Station to the relief of the garrison of Dumfries, the Third Maryland Infantry took part in a skirmish with the enemy at a point between Occoquan Creek and the town of Dumfries. Finally, on the 31st of January, 1863, the First Cavalry left Hall's Farm, four miles from Washington, and marched to Stafford Court-House, where it arrived on the 4th of February, and was attached to the cavalry brigade of the Eleventh Army Corps, Col. Kielmansegge, of the First, commanding. On the 12th of February it changed camp to Aquia Creek. Upon being assigned to the Second Brigade, Third Division, Cavalry Corps, Feb. 21, 1863, the First moved to near Belle Plain Landing. While here it performed picket duty on the Rappahannock.

In the mean time steps had been taken to reorganize the First Maryland Infantry, which had so greatly distinguished itself at Front Royal. On the 8th of June, 1862, the Secretary of War ordered the remnants of the regiment, then at Williamsport, to proceed without delay to Baltimore for reorganization, recruiting, and equipment. In accordance with this order the depleted regiment, under Capt. Thomas S. J. Johnson, proceeded to Baltimore, where Col. Kenly resumed command on the 15th of August. On the 22d of the same month Col. Kenly was promoted brigadier-general of United States Volunteers for "gallant conduct at the battle of Front Royal," and on the 6th of September he was directed to organize and command a brigade of new troops. Two days after, on the 8th of September, 1862, Gen. Kenly assumed command of the "Maryland Brigade," which was composed of the First, Fourth, Sixth, Seventh, and Eighth Regiments of Maryland Volunteers, then in process of formation in or near Baltimore, and Capt. Alexander's battery of Baltimore Light Artillery. On the morning after the battle of Antietam the Maryland Brigade, except the Sixth Infantry and Alexander's battery, left Baltimore for Hagerstown, which it reached at 2.30 A.M. on the 20th. It immediately marched towards Williamsport to reinforce the Pennsylvania militia, whom they found formed in line of battle about two and a half miles from the town, and engaged in a brisk skirmish with the advance cavalry of the enemy, who were approaching in the direction of Hagerstown. The brigade remained in line and under arms until the next day, when it marched in and occupied Williamsport, the enemy meantime having withdrawn to the Virginia side of the river.[1]

---

[1] "Historical Record of the First Regiment Maryland Infantry."

The significance of this movement of the brigade is explained in the following extract from a letter of Governor Curtin, of Pennsylvania, addressed to Gen. Kenly:

"The enemy crossed at Williamsport in force, with cavalry, artillery, and infantry, on the afternoon of the 19th of September, 1862, and attacked the pickets of Gen. Reynolds between that place and Hagerstown. After night they approached his lines, then about three miles from the latter place. In the mean time large commissary and quartermaster stores and ammunition for the Army of the Potomac had arrived at Hagerstown. Gen. Reynolds had his men in line of battle, and kept me informed as to the movements of the enemy. Between twelve and one o'clock the general came to Hagerstown, and a council was held in my room, composed of Gens. Andrew Porter and Herman Haupt, Maj. Vogdes, Capt. Gentry of Gen. Porter's staff, and Col. John A. Wright of my staff. It seemed to be the united judgment of the military gentlemen that the enemy would attack in the morning, if not before, and serious apprehensions were entertained as to the result.

"Our troops were raw and undisciplined, and we were without efficient artillery. Preparations were ordered to be made for the destruction of military stores and the removal of the troops, to be carried out if the enemy should attack in force, and if it should become apparent that we could not resist him. At two o'clock on the morning of the 20th you arrived with your command, the Maryland Brigade, *en route* to report to Gen. McClellan. I deemed the danger so imminent at that point that at my instance Gen. Reynolds was notified of your arrival and took command of yourself and troops. Your arrival relieved us all, and your troops marched directly to the front (notwithstanding the long and rapid march they had made and their need of rest and subsistence), where you remained until the enemy recrossed the Potomac, and Gen. Reynolds, by my direction, ordered the militia under his command to return to Pennsylvania. Although no battle was fought, your presence and the strength of your command encouraged us, and proved a material influence in compelling the enemy to withdraw to the right bank of the Potomac, and in checking the demonstration he was making on Hagerstown."

The brigade went into camp just outside of Williamsport, on the road leading to Hagerstown and Clear Spring. Company A of the Seventh Regiment, Capt. E. M. Mobley, was detailed as the provost-guard of the town.

The command now formed part of Gen. Franklin's Sixth Army Corps. The pickets of either army faced each other across the river, easily fordable and within comparatively short range. This led to an occasional interchange of compliments more spicy than courteous, but the practice was soon suppressed. Shortly after reaching Williamsport the brigade was again united by the arrival of the Sixth Infantry and Alexander's battery, which had been left behind when the other regiments moved from Baltimore. During the night of September 23d the Eighth Infantry, under Col. Denison, marched to Clear Spring, reaching there about daybreak. When the inhabitants of the village awoke their profuse hospitality demonstrated that the regiment was among friends. In a short time the whole command was breakfasted, and often in after and more dangerous times the generous reception at Clear Spring was pleasantly recalled by the soldiers of the Eighth.

On the afternoon of the 24th the regiment fell back some three miles towards the river, and took position on Cowton's farm in support of a battery posted at Dam No. 5. It was relieved of this duty on the 10th of October, and returned to Williamsport. That day information was received by Gen. Kenly that Stuart's cavalry was crossing the river at McCoy's Ferry and moving towards Williamsport. The whole brigade was turned out under arms, the streets of the town barricaded, and every disposition made to hold the post. Capt. Russell's company of the First Maryland Cavalry was dispatched in the direction of Clear Spring to watch the movements of the enemy. It was soon discovered that he was heading for Pennsylvania. After remaining under arms for three rainy days and nights the brigade was ordered back to camp. During this period of excitement there were the usual flying rumors and false alarms, with frequent "falling in," as if the enemy was actually at hand, and reported demonstrations upon the advanced pickets, concluding with the intelligence that Stuart had finally succeeded in effecting his escape across the river near the mouth of the Monocacy. In the pursuit of Stuart, Fiery's cavalry company marched from New Creek, Va., to Mercersburg, Pa., whence it returned to Clear Spring, where for some time it was employed in guard and picket duty along the river front from Dam No. 5 to Cherry Run. The other companies of Cole's battalion pursued the enemy vigorously on his return march, harassing him upon every occasion, and capturing seven men with horses and equipments of Wade Hampton's Legion, about the only loss that Stuart suffered in this raid around the Army of the Potomac. Towards the end of October everything about Williamsport in the military line quieted down for the time. On the 29th of October the Seventh Infantry marched to Four Locks, where its headquarters were established. The several companies (except Company A, which remained at Williamsport) were distributed along a front of some five miles, guarding the fords of the Potomac and the culverts and draw-bridges of the canal from a point above McCoy's Ferry to below Dam No. 5. On the 2d of November, 1862, the Fourth Infantry, at the request of Governor Bradford, took its departure from Williamsport for Baltimore for service as guards at Camp Bradford, the general rendezvous of drafted men. On the 11th of December, Gen. Kenly marched with the First and Sixth Infantry for Maryland Heights, under orders to take post there. Next day the Seventh Infantry, under Lieut.-Col. Charles E. Phelps, marched back to Williamsport, leaving only Company I, Capt. Anderson, at Four Locks. Company G, Capt. Bragonier, continued its march to Dam No. 4. On the 13th of December four companies of the Seventh were ordered on provost duty at Hagerstown, and Capt. Bennett, of Company E, was appointed provost-marshal. On the 21st the Seventh Regiment (except Company B, left on provost duty in Hagerstown) was assembled at Williamsport, and in company with the Eighth and Alexander's battery, and a squadron of the First Cavalry under Capt. Russell, proceeded, *via* Sharpsburg, to Maryland Heights.[1]

Here the entire Maryland Brigade (the Fourth Regiment having rejoined it from detached service at Camp Bradford on the 17th of December) went into winter quarters, and the regular routine of drill and discipline was re-established.

The sojourn of the brigade in Western Maryland was a bright page in its history. The feeling of the people towards the soldiers was, with very few exceptions, cordial and thoroughly sympathetic. When the brigade first entered Williamsport, upon the heels of the enemy's cavalry, they were welcomed as deliverers, and, so far as opportunity for intercourse was permitted, with hospitality. The Union sentiment seemed to increase in volume and intensity as you approached the border. It was in some measure doubtless owing to the spirit inspired by the Virginia Union refugees that the loyalty of this southern border of Maryland was of a flavor that the word bitter would but feebly characterize.

As the Confederates had lost all hopes of making these people their friends, there was no special motive for forbearance, and hence repeated raids and invasions had stamped desolation upon the face of the country, and upon the minds of the inhabitants many recollections of personal wrongs and losses.

After the withdrawal of McClellan's army from the vicinity of Harper's Ferry, Cole's cavalry remained in that neighborhood, scouting, picketing, and meeting the enemy in several minor conflicts. On the 20th of December, 1862, a detachment of sixty men from Companies A and C, under command of Capt. Vernon, left the Ferry on a reconnoissance. After proceeding about three miles up the left bank of the Shenandoah, it was learned that Capt. Baylor's guerrillas, one hundred and twenty strong, were at Charlestown, but it was subsequently understood they had gone to Halltown. Moving rapidly to that point, Capt. Vernon succeeded in capturing the guerrilla chief, who was visiting a farm-house near by. On its return the detachment encountered a Confederate force drawn up in line on the crest of a hill. Receiving the enemy's fire, Vernon's command immediately charged upon him, breaking his ranks and putting him to flight. A running fight ensued, in which Lieut. W. W. Wilson, of the Twelfth Virginia Cavalry, a private, and five riderless horses were captured. One of Vernon's men received a slight wound.

Shortly after the arrival of the Maryland Brigade at Maryland Heights, Companies A and E of the First Regiment were posted at Duffield Station, on the Baltimore and Ohio Railroad, while Company K, with Companies F and H of the Seventh, were sent to garrison the "Stone Fort" and signal-station on the crest of the mountain. This fort was located on the ground upon which had occurred the fight preceding the surrender of Col. Miles. It was still in an unfinished condition. Heretofore the brigade had enjoyed little opportunity for target practice, from the fact that its operations had been mainly confined to picketing in the immediate presence of the enemy. At Maryland Heights this essential part of a soldier's practical education was systematically attended to, not only in the brigade, but throughout the entire command of all arms of the service. On some days there was noise enough for a regular battle.

The "naval battery" of Dahlgren guns threw "flour-barrel" shell with a noise like that of a locomotive and a long train of cars going through mid-air at the rate of several hundred miles an hour. Alexander's field battery and others in the vicinity were also busily engaged in practice, and musketry firing from all the regiments at the post added to the general din.[2]

---

[1] On the 29th of October, 1862, Gen. Wade Hampton, commanding the Confederate forces opposite Williamsport, sent a communication by flag of truce to Gen. Kenly; "but before the truce party had made its appearance, or anything was known of its mission on the Federal side, an expedition, consisting of Lieut. McMahon and fifteen men of the First Maryland Cavalry, was sent across the river by order of Gen. Kenly to surprise and capture a picket guard of the enemy stationed on the neck opposite Williamsport. On crossing the Potomac near Sharpless' warehouse, Lieut. McMahon kept the woods until he struck the Williamsport and Martinsburg turnpike beyond the picket station, when he took to the road, and with a dash came so suddenly upon the guard as to completely surprise them, all of whom, six in number, were captured. Gen. Hampton claimed the unconditional release of the prisoners, on the ground of a violation of military law and usage governing flags of truce," but Gen. Kenly refused to surrender the prisoners, and his action was sustained by superior authority.—*Historical Record of the First Regiment Maryland Infantry.*

[2] On the 28th of February, 1863, a beautiful national flag, sent by a number of Marylanders residing in San Francisco,

With the opening of spring some changes were made in the location of the regiments of the Maryland Brigade. On the 14th of March the camp of the Eighth on Maryland Heights was broken up, and the regiment crossed the river and pitched tents on Bolivar Heights, a fine plateau on the Virginia side above Harper's Ferry, stretching away from a steep bluff overlooking the Potomac. The Seventh followed on the 4th of April, and the First on the 9th of the same month.

On the 27th of March, 1863, the Maryland Brigade was officially designated the First Brigade, forming part of the First Division, Eighth Army Corps. The same order transferred the Sixth Regiment and Alexander's battery to Gen. Milroy's command, and they left for Berryville on the 28th of March. On the 27th of April the Fourth and Seventh Regiments, Cols. Bowerman and Webster commanding, were transferred by rail to Oakland, under orders which indicated a campaign in West Virginia, then alarmed by a dashing raid of Confederate cavalry under Imboden and Jones. Upon arriving at Altamont, it was found that the railroad track had been torn up the day before and hastily relaid. Several bridges had been burned and the telegraph wires cut. The fidelity of the engineer was questioned, and Col. Webster, who by reason of seniority commanded the force, took his position upon the leading locomotive, and at all doubtful places an advanced guard marched ahead of the train. Oakland was found in a state of intense excitement, created by the recent presence of the raiders, who had carried off with them a large number of valuable horses belonging to the citizens. The town and its approaches were at once picketed by the Seventh, supported by the Fourth, which came up during the day. The men were under arms all night, during almost the whole of which there was constant telegraphing of reports, rumors, and inquiries in all directions. The result of all this was that early on the morning of the 29th the Seventh left knapsacks behind at Oakland, in charge of the Fourth, and marched westward along the line of the railroad, or parallel with it. The bridge over the Youghiogheny, some two or three miles out, having been destroyed by the raiders a few hours before, some delay occurred before a crossing could be effected, the creek being high and the banks steep and miry. A march of ten miles brought the regiment to Cranberry Summit. This little town had made a spirited defense, but the Confederates were much too strong for the citizens and the few soldiers who were there, and the stores had been plundered and all the horses seized. The regiment left Cranberry about 7 P.M. in a thunder-storm, and made a forced march of thirteen miles farther to "No. 72," a water-station near Rowlesburg. The distance by the railroad between these points, passing through tunnels, was less, but the line of march was over rough country roads, climbing and descending the mountains. Nothing could be worse than the condition of these roads, or more trying than this march. The steep slippery roads were crossed and recrossed by Salt Lick and other creeks, through which the men waded a dozen times, sometimes almost waist-deep, and wound along the brink of precipices, up and down rough mountain-sides, and through the dense darkness of gloomy gorges. After marching all day and nearly all night, twenty-three miles in the rain over the Alleghanies, at two o'clock on the morning of the 30th of April a picket-guard was posted, and while these watched, their weary comrades slept. The memory of this forced march became the standard of comparison for the Seventh Regiment in all its future campaigns. At an early hour of the 30th the regiment resumed its march, following the railroad four miles to Rowlesburg. This place had been defended not only with spirit but success, and after a hot skirmish the enemy's cavalry had been repulsed with loss by a detachment of the Sixth Virginia Volunteers under Maj. Showalter. Singularly enough, these troops evacuated the town soon after the enemy's departure, leaving the important railroad structures unguarded.

Up to this point the orders were to watch and follow, intercept, and, if possible, capture the enemy. The Seventh had followed close upon their heels, but naturally without gaining on them. The companies were now so disposed as best to guard the railroad bridge over Cheat River and the elaborate trestles in the vicinity, and Capt. Bennett with his company (E) was sent on a scout to St. George, twenty miles distant.

On the 1st of May, Gen. Kenly, who had left Harper's Ferry the day before, passed up the road with the First and Eighth Regiments *en route* for Clarksburg, whither he had been ordered to the support of Gen. Roberts' command, which was hard pressed by the enemy. Large quantities of government stores were collected at Clarksburg, it being the supply depot for all the Federal forces operating in

---

was presented to the First Regiment as a token of admiration for its gallant conduct at Front Royal. The presentation speech was made by Hon. F. F. Lowe, member of Congress from California, and was responded to on behalf of the regiment by Archibald Sterling, of the Baltimore bar. Brief and appropriate addresses were also made by Gen. John R. Kenly and John G. Wilmot.

that section of country. Gen. Kenly reached Grafton at 1 P.M., May 1st, and upon receiving information that the bridge near Bridgeport, on the Parkersburg Railroad, had been burned, and that a large force of the enemy was near that town preparing to attack Gen. Roberts, he at once pushed on to the relief of that officer and his command. On arriving at Bridgeport, at 7 P.M., it was ascertained that the Confederates had retired, having doubtless been informed by telegraph from Grafton of the approach of the Federal troops with exaggerated numbers. Gen. Kenly, however, continued his march to Clarksburg, where he arrived at midnight, much to the relief of Gen. Roberts, who no doubt would have been attacked that night but for the opportune arrival of these reinforcements. The command remained at Clarksburg, watching the movements of the enemy, who threatened the Parkersburg Railroad and Wheeling, until the 11th of May, when it marched five miles on the road to Weston, bivouacking for the night near Janelen. On the 13th it proceeded through Weston, and camped near the bridge over Stone Coal Creek, where it remained until the 23d, guarding the approaches to West Union, on the line of the Parkersburg road. On the last-mentioned date it resumed the march, and passing through Buchanan and Philippi, arrived at Webster on the 26th of May. Here the command took cars and returned to Harper's Ferry, reoccupying the old position on Bolivar Heights. The Seventh Regiment had already returned from Rowlesburg, and on the 2d of June the Fourth Regiment came back from Oakland. Respecting the services of the Maryland Brigade in this campaign, Gen. Kelley, the division commander, in a letter to Gen. Kenly, says,—

"When the rebel Gens. Jones and Imboden, in April last, threatened to overrun the entire State of West Virginia, your prompt movement under orders to the support of Gen. Roberts at Clarksburg alone saved from destruction much valuable public property, as well as that of the Baltimore and Ohio Railroad. Your services afterwards in aiding to drive the enemy from the State were not less valuable, and deserve great praise."

Upon returning to Harper's Ferry the daily routine of camp was re-established, and preparations were made for the summer campaign. About this time the Eighth Regiment was the recipient of a national ensign and a set of guidons, the gift of Marcus Denison, of Baltimore. Col. A. W. Denison presented the colors in the name of his father, and they were received on behalf of the regiment by Lieut.-Col. J. G. Johannes.

On the 30th of May the First Regiment recrossed the river and again occupied the site of the old camp on Maryland Heights. It was followed on the 9th of June by the Seventh. Company B of this regiment was still at Hagerstown, where it had been stationed since December.[1]

Gen. Hooker took command of the Army of the Potomac on the 26th of January, 1863, and at once proceeded to reorganize it. In his testimony before the Committee on the Conduct of the War, Gen. Hooker thus describes the condition of the army when he assumed command:

"It had recently returned from two unsuccessful efforts to cross the river and drive the enemy from his position, the first resulting so disastrously as to render a second effort soon after, even with propitious weather, almost futile. Before the second effort ended the winter rains set in, and all operations for a while were suspended, the army literally finding itself buried in mud, from which there was no hope of extrication before spring. With this prospect before it, taken in connection with the gloom and despondency that followed the disaster of Fredericksburg, the army was in a forlorn, deplorable condition. At the time the army was turned over to me desertions were at the rate of about two hundred a day. So anxious were parents, wives, brothers, and sisters to relieve their kindred that they filled the express-trains to the army with packages of citizen clothing to assist them in escaping from service. At that time perhaps a majority of the officers, especially those in high rank, were hostile to the policy of the government in the conduct of the war. The Emancipation Proclamation had been published a short time before, and a large element of the army had taken sides antagonistic to it, declaring that they never would have embarked in the war had they anticipated this action of the government. I may also state that the moment I was placed in command I caused a return to be made of the absentees of the army, and found the number to be 2922 commissioned officers and 81,964 non-commissioned officers and privates. These were scattered all over the country, and the majority were absent from causes unknown. When it was announced to me that I had been placed in command of the Army of the Potomac I doubted, and so expressed myself, if it could be saved to the country."

Having thoroughly reorganized his army and matured his plans for a campaign against Richmond, Gen. Hooker on the 27th of April, 1863, commenced his advance, and on the 2d and 3d of May fought the

---

[1] The Hagerstown *Herald and Torch* of March 25, 1863, says, "Some ten or twelve rebel guerrillas crossed the Potomac in the vicinity of Sharpsburg on Monday night, the 10th instant, and after stealing some eight or ten horses (five of which were taken from Mr. Adam Hutzell, living near the Smoketown Hospital) they returned to the river at the ferry opposite Shepherdstown. The ferry is kept by two brothers named Entler, formerly citizens of Shepherdstown, and these the rebels called up and asked them to take them over the river, asserting they were Federal soldiers with important dispatches. The Entlers refused to cross them, and they then thereupon fired upon the brothers, killing one of them, a young man of excellent character, while the other made his escape into the house before they had time to assassinate him. They then seized the ferry-boat and made their way over the river with a portion of their booty, several of the horses having broken away from them, and were found in the road the next morning."

battle of Chancellorsville, in which he was defeated with dreadful loss. The Confederates under Lee gained a great victory, but this was more than counterbalanced by the death of Gen. "Stonewall" Jackson, who was mortally wounded by the fire of his own men in his attack on Howard's corps, and died on the 10th of May. His loss was irreparable, and was deeply felt throughout the South.

"After the battle of Chancellorsville, the position occupied by the enemy," says Gen. Lee, "opposite Fredericksburg being one in which he could not be attacked to advantage, it was determined to draw him from it. The execution of this purpose embraced the relief of the Shenandoah Valley from the troops that had occupied the lower part of it during the winter and spring, and, if practicable, the transfer of the scene of hostilities north of the Potomac. It was thought that the corresponding movement on the part of the enemy, to which those contemplated by us could probably give rise, might offer a fair opportunity to strike a blow at the army then commanded by Gen. Hooker, and that in any event that army would be compelled to leave Virginia, and possibly to draw to its support troops designed to operate against other parts of the country. In this way it was supposed that the enemy's plan of campaign for the summer would be broken up, and part of the season of active operations be consumed in the formation of new combinations and the preparations that they would require. In addition to these advantages, it was hoped that other valuable results might be attained by military success."

Having arranged his plan of campaign, Gen. Lee proceeded with great energy to put it into execution. The infantry were organized into three corps, under Longstreet, Ewell, and A. P. Hill, each of these corps containing three divisions, the cavalry under J. E. B. Stuart, consisting of the brigades of Fitzhugh Lee, Hampton, and W. H. F. Lee, which were concentrated at Culpeper Court-House. All his preparations having been made, on June 3, 1863, McLaws' division of Longstreet's corps left Fredericksburg for Culpeper Court-House, and Hood's division of the same corps was ordered to the same place. On the next day Ewell marched in the same direction, leaving A. P. Hill to occupy the lines at Fredericksburg. On the 11th and 12th, Hooker broke up his encampments on the line of the Rappahannock and moved cautiously northward, followed by Hill. Meanwhile Gen. Lee had continued his march to the north.

On the 14th of June, Milroy was attacked near Winchester by the Confederates under Ewell, and on the next day was defeated with the loss of nearly his whole command. After their return to Harper's Ferry, the Sixth Maryland (Federal) Regiment and Alexander's battery were permanently attached to Gen. Milroy's command in the valley, and in the defense of Berryville and Winchester bore the brunt of the heavy fighting, and suffered severely, the latter losing their guns at the battle of Winchester. The remnant of Milroy's force after this disastrous engagement retreated to Maryland Heights, where with the Maryland Brigade they strengthened the fortifications, and observed the movements of the Confederate forces.

During these operations Cole's cavalry had come in for its usual share of hard service. On the 12th of June, when Rodes' Confederate division was approaching Berryville, Company A, under Capt. Vernon, made a scout into Loudon County to ascertain the enemy's movements. Next day it boldly attacked a superior force of Confederate infantry at Berryville, which proved to be a part of Rodes' division. The company was compelled to retreat with the loss of several men, but the object of the reconnoissance was accomplished. Having ascertained that the enemy was pushing in the direction of the Winchester and Martinsburg pike, in rear of the Union forces at Winchester, Capt. Vernon dispatched a scout through the Confederate lines to apprise Gen. Milroy of his danger. On the 14th the company skirmished all day with the enemy on the roads leading from the Potomac to Winchester.

Capt. Summers' company ran into a large body of the enemy's cavalry near Berryville. After losing one man wounded and two men captured, the company fell back to Charlestown and then to Halltown, contesting every inch of the ground, and inflicting some punishment on its pursuers.[1]

On the 15th of June, Vernon's company was at Charlestown and on the roads beyond, covering the retreat of remnants of Milroy's command, then endeavoring to effect their escape to Harper's Ferry. On the 16th it skirmished with the enemy's advance, then moving on the roads from Winchester to the Poto-

---

[1] On the night of the 15th of May, 1863, this company, numbering seventy-seven men, had been completely surprised by the enemy at Charlestown. The Confederate cavalry dismounted outside the town, and passing unobserved in squads through the company's pickets and patrols, attacked the men in their quarters. The company made a spirited resistance, but was finally overpowered, and one officer (Lieut. McKinsley) and fifty-five men were forced to surrender. The lieutenant and two men were wounded. A force of Federal cavalry sent out from Winchester by Gen. Milroy to intercept and attack the enemy overtook him at Piedmont Station, in Fauquier County, on the afternoon of the 16th, and recaptured all of Capt. Summers' men except one, who was seriously wounded and left in the enemy's hands.

mac. At Charlestown, Capt. Vernon's squadron, consisting of his own and Capt. Summers' company, was summoned to surrender. To this demand Capt. Vernon responded, "I did not come to Charlestown to surrender, but to fight to the best of my ability, and I propose to do it." By skillful manœuvring he succeeded in extricating his command, and at night fell back within easy striking distance of the Federal lines at Harper's Ferry. On the 14th and 15th, Company C scouted the country from Kearneysville to Shepherdstown, Hallstown, and Harper's Ferry.

On Sunday, the 14th of June, about 4 P.M., Gen. Rodes, who had been instructed, after dislodging the force at Berryville, to cut off the communication between Winchester and the Potomac, appeared before Martinsburg, held by two regiments of infantry, Fiery's company of Maryland cavalry, and one battery of artillery, the whole commanded by Col. B. F. Smith, One Hundred and Twenty-sixth Ohio Volunteers. Gen. Jenkins, commanding the Confederate advance, demanded the surrender of the town, which was refused, and an attack was then made, which Col. Smith resisted until dark, when he began to evacuate the position. The cavalry and artillery moved towards Williamsport, and the infantry towards Shepherdstown. The enemy followed on the Williamsport road, and succeeded in capturing the battery and about seven hundred prisoners. After crossing the river at Shepherdstown, Col. Smith marched his infantry to Maryland Heights.

In this affair Capt. Fiery's company acquitted itself with its accustomed gallantry. Having skirmished nearly all day with the enemy's cavalry, it was confronted in the evening by a heavy force massed on the Winchester road to turn the right of the Federal line. With great impetuosity the enemy charged up the pike, and despite a stubborn resistance by the company and some infantry (not over one hundred in all) he pushed forward, and a running fight was kept up through the town, Capt. Fiery bravely contesting every inch of the ground. Taking the Williamsport road, the company hurried in retreat towards the river, which was crossed before midnight. Next morning learning that the enemy would cross at Dam No. 5, Capt. Fiery started for that point with twenty-five men to harass him. On the road he met a small squad of Confederate cavalry and dashed after them. He soon ran into a large force concealed behind a hill and the fences close by. In this encounter Lieut. Jacob A. Metz, of Washington County, was killed, and Capt. Fiery was taken prisoner, but soon after escaped. The rest of the detachment escaped unharmed. From this point the company kept constant watch on the enemy as far as Harrisburg, and on his return followed him back to the river, capturing nearly two hundred prisoners in the course of the campaign.

Upon receipt of the first news of the attack on Winchester every preparation was made by the garrison of Maryland Heights and Harper's Ferry to give the enemy a warm reception should he again try the stronghold which he had once assailed with success.

The fortifications were greatly strengthened, heavy and light artillery advantageously posted, and strong picket-lines established. The troops remained on the alert, performing heavy fatigue and guard duty for two weeks, with rainy days and nights disagreeably frequent.

But the attack, which was so confidently expected by the military authorities, did not occur.

On the 13th of June, when Rodes' division appeared in front of Berryville, the First and Seventh Maryland were on Maryland Heights, and the Fourth and Eighth Maryland, with Miner's Indiana Battery, under the personal direction of Gen. Kenly, occupied Bolivar Heights. With these troops Gen. Kenly strengthened the line of works on Camp Hill, between the Potomac and the Shenandoah, picketed Loudon Heights, and reconnoitered almost daily into Loudon County and towards and beyond Charlestown. Holding this outpost until the night of June 17th, Gen. Kenly was then ordered by Gen. Tyler (who had just arrived and assumed command, relieving Gen. Kelley) to abandon Harper's Ferry and remove his troops to Maryland Heights. At nine P.M. the command withdrew from the Virginia side (all the army stores having been previously removed from Harper's Ferry), the Eighth Maryland being the last regiment to cross.

Before daybreak of the 15th the Seventh was marched about a mile west of its camp on the heights and thrown into line with the First Maryland and the Sixth New York Artillery, its left resting on the Sharpsburg road.

The report was that the enemy had appeared on the river opposite Sharpsburg. This was the beginning of a long and exciting day. About sunrise the line was heavily reinforced, and during the day the tongue of rumor was busy with a thousand startling reports, all of which centred around the one established fact that Milroy's command at Winchester had been crushed before an overwhelming force of the enemy on their march to transfer the seat of war to the Northern States. It was with especial regret that the soldiers of the Maryland Brigade heard that their old comrades of the Sixth Maryland and Alexander's battery had shared in the general disaster.

A very gratifying incident, and one which aroused the enthusiasm of the Seventh Maryland, was the arrival this day of Company B from Hagerstown. Capt. Makechney had been charged with the collection of government property, and had a train of fifteen loaded wagons and about two hundred horses. By strenuous exertions he succeeded in getting all this property away in safety before the enemy crossed over from opposite Williamsport and occupied Hagerstown.

On the 16th the First and Seventh were relieved from their position of the day before and moved up to the crest of the heights. Here they were joined by the Fourth and Eighth Regiments from Bolivar Heights, and the entire brigade threw up timber breastworks and abatis.

A private letter, written by an officer of the Seventh Maryland, thus describes the condition of affairs on the heights at this time:

"Our position here is impregnable and supplies abundant. We are nearly on the summit of the heights, overlook the surrounding country for miles, cannot be taken by surprise, and cannot be whipped. Our men were never in better trim for service, confident and impatient. Although not actually engaged as yet, we have been by no means idle. It would not be proper to state what has been done towards strengthening the natural defenses of this position. Suffice it to say that we have done enough in that way to make it very desirable that we should be attacked here. All we fear is that Lee is too old and too cunning a rat to nibble at our cheese."

On the 25th of June the same correspondent wrote as follows:

"The evidences of a heavy force in front of us and around us continue to be visible. For several days past we have seen trains of wagons of almost endless length creeping along our front from left to right, and crossing the Potomac at Shepherdstown and perhaps Williamsport. Lee's headquarters are reported at Berryville, and in that direction, along the base of the Blue Ridge, we see heavy columns of dust and the smoke of camp-fires. Yesterday a train of cars arrived from Baltimore, an event which caused an agreeable excitement."

On the 27th of June, Gen. Hooker came and directed the heights to be abandoned, and orders were issued for the troops to be ready to move in light marching order at 6 A.M. of the 28th. It was intended by Gen. Hooker that the force on the heights, in conjunction with the Twelfth Corps, then in the vicinity, should march upon the enemy's line of communication at Williamsport, destroy his pontoon-bridge at that point, and stop the enormous quantities of provisions, horses, and cattle which were steadily flowing from Pennsylvania and Maryland into Virginia. But Gen. Halleck would not consent to the abandonment of the heights, and this order to march was soon countermanded.

Gen. W. H. French, a regular army officer and a Marylander, was now in command of the heights, having relieved Gen. Tyler on the 26th. His command at this time consisted of four brigades, commanded by Gens. Elliott, Morris, and Kenly and Col. Smith.

On the last day of June, after some previous preparations, Maryland Heights was evacuated. All unmovable property was rendered useless, the heavy ordnance was dismounted, and the ammunition, commissary stores, camp equipage, etc., destroyed. Some property—artillery, forage, stores, etc.—was loaded upon canal-boats for shipment to Washington *via* the Chesapeake and Ohio Canal, under escort of Gen. Elliott's and Col. Smith's brigades, which had been specially assigned to that duty. The Sixth Maryland accompanied this force as a part of Gen. Elliott's brigade. The remainder of Gen. French's command, comprising the brigades of Gens. Kenly and Morris, marched to Frederick City.

During the evacuation of the heights rain was pouring in sheets, and the mountain roads were becoming the beds of torrents. As the Maryland Brigade moved down the mountain, it found the road blockaded with wagons, and the march was interrupted at intervals of about five minutes by halts of fifteen.

An accidental explosion in the magazine of the thirty-pounder battery filled the air with fragments of shell, rock, and timber, and human bodies also. Limbs without bodies and bodies without limbs flew in all directions, and the wounded and the dead, horribly mutilated, were borne away on stretchers. There were nine killed and twelve wounded by the accident. Among the number were some members of the Sixth and Eighth Regiments.

On Monday, June 15th, Jenkins' brigade of Confederate cavalry crossed the Potomac at Williamsport without opposition, and immediately moved through Hagerstown to Greencastle, and thence to Chambersburg, Pa., arriving there on Tuesday night. No Federal troops were at either of these places to oppose this force, and its only hostile acts were the seizure of horses, cattle, and forage. Goods were purchased at the stores, and paid for in Confederate scrip.

On Tuesday afternoon, June 16th, a small force of Confederate infantry crossed the Potomac at Williamsport for the purpose of guarding the passage until the return of the cavalry expedition.

On the 17th, Jenkins, having already gathered a large number of horses and cattle from the Pennsylvania farmers, evacuated Chambersburg and retired to the vicinity of Hagerstown, there to await the arrival of the main army.[1]

---

[1] On the 15th of June, the day of the dispersion of Milroy's force at Winchester, Rodes moved to Williamsport, and sent

In his official report Gen. Rodes says,—

"As soon as possible after arriving at Williamsport a strong guard was placed over it, and the necessary instructions were given to Gen. Jenkins about obtaining supplies of cattle and horses. In obedience to orders the command remained at Williamsport during the 16th, 17th, and 18th (of June), in which time, with the aid of Gen. Jenkins' cavalry, the commissaries and quartermasters obtained in a proper manner large supplies in their respective departments. The pioneers, under Capt. Chichester, were busy during our rest here trying to destroy the aqueduct over the Conococheague. Some five thousand pounds of leather were bought by Maj. Paxton at Williamsport and sent to the rear. At Hagerstown and Williamsport thirty-five kegs of powder were purchased and sent back. I may as well mention here that at Williamsport, Hagerstown, Chambersburg, etc., large quantities of such articles as were suitable for government use were obtained by purchase or certificate and sent back by Quartermasters Paxton, Rogers, and Harman. During the march into Pennsylvania some two or three thousand head of cattle were taken, and either appropriated for the command or sent to the rear for the other divisions. Some twelve or fifteen hundred were thus sent back. The horses were almost all seized by the cavalry of Gen. Jenkins, and were rarely accounted for. My best efforts were made to suppress all irregularities, and being very generally and cheerfully seconded by officers and men, they succeeded satisfactorily. Some few cases of fraud and some (at Greencastle) of violence to property—the latter traceable to the cavalry—were heard of. A few instances of forced purchases were reported, but never established. I believe that one quartermaster seized such articles as velvet, etc., but I could not find him out. In all cases of purchase that came before me the parties were fully paid and satisfied."

Upon the invasion of the State the citizens of Western Maryland were thrown into the greatest excitement. In Frederick hundreds of the citizens left the city, while many more made preparations to do so. The free negroes were thrown into the greatest perturbation, fearing that they would be carried South and sold as slaves by the Confederates. They crowded the freight-trains to Baltimore, and in a short time there was a general flight of them towards the Pennsylvania line and other directions. The government on the 15th of June removed its surplus commissary and quartermaster stores from Frederick, and cleared the hospitals of all patients who could be moved.

Jenkins' brigade of cavalry, which had been placed under his orders, to Hagerstown. Jenkins went on to Chambersburg, and returned on the 20th, while Rodes waited for the remainder of Ewell's corps. This was being moved up, Johnson, with the Maryland infantry and artillery, crossing and camping at Sharpsburg on the 18th, and Early crossing and going on to Boonsboro' on the 22d. After remaining in camp at Sharpsburg three or four days, the Second Maryland (Confederate) Infantry moved on towards Hagerstown, which place they passed through, and encamped a short distance beyond. On the 26th they left Hagerstown, and crossing the Pennsylvania line, and passing through Greencastle, Mercersburg, McConnellsburg, etc., arrived at Chambersburg on the same day. On the 27th they passed through Chambersburg, and on the 28th went into camp about three miles beyond Carlisle.—*The writer's History of Maryland.*

On the 16th of June it was reported that the Confederates were rapidly approaching Cumberland in force, whereupon a number of citizens retired hastily towards Pennsylvania. Early the next morning a small squad of men on the brow of the hill east of the city, on the Williams road, were discovered; several of Milroy's escaped cavalry advanced to ascertain who they were, and were saluted by the discharge of two small field-pieces, the shells dropping in the vicinity of McKaig's foundry, and putting the Federal scouts to flight. In a short time two Confederate soldiers rode into the town with a flag of truce, and after consultation with acting Mayor V. A. Buckey and a deputation of citizens, obtained the formal surrender of the place. About three hundred and fifty of Imboden's cavalry with two pieces of artillery soon appeared, and after securing such horses as they could find, induced some of the merchants to open their stores, paying for their purchases with Confederate money. No damage was done to either public or private property, beyond the partial destruction of the telegraph-lines. The invading force soon departed, doing no violence to any one except in the case of Griffin Twigg, Sr., living near Murley's Branch. The particulars are involved in some doubt, but the old man was killed, after having killed two of his assailants and wounded another. Gen. Kelley and staff had arrived in Cumberland from Pennsylvania on Tuesday night, and left for New Creek about the time of the arrival of Imboden's men next morning. Discovering a portion of the Baltimore and Ohio Railroad torn up a short distance from the city the train returned, and proceeded over the Cumberland and Pennsylvania Railroad to Piedmont, and thence to New Creek. On the following day a force of Federal cavalry from New Creek arrived in Cumberland and captured several of Imboden's command who had remained with friends in town.

On the 24th, Gen. Ewell, with Rodes' and Johnson's divisions, had reached Chambersburg, and Early was at Greenwood. On this day Hill and Longstreet crossed the Potomac at Shepherdstown and Williamsport, and moved towards Hagerstown. The Confederate scouts penetrated as far as the line of the Susquehanna, which was defended by militia hastily summoned from Pennsylvania, New York, and New Jersey. Strong foraging parties were sent out, and Ewell's corps occupied Carlisle, York, and the intervening country. A force under Gen. Gordon, sent by Gen. Early from York, captured Wrightsville, on the Susquehanna, where a sharp skirmish for the possession of the bridge at that point occurred. Some Pennsylvania militia, with Capt. McGovern's company of Maryland infantry, were driven across the river, but succeeded in burning the bridge. On the 22d of June the Union army lay stretched from Leesburg, through Centreville and Gainesville, to Thoroughfare Gap and Bristoe Station.

Lee's movements had been conducted with so much skill that Gen. Hooker was kept for some time in doubt as to his real designs. Having at length learned that Lee's whole force had crossed into Maryland, on the morning of June 25th he sent over Stahl's cavalry, followed by Gen. Reynolds with the First, Third, and Eleventh Corps, at Edwards' Ferry. On the next day he crossed over with the Twelfth, Fifth, Second, and Sixth Corps, the cavalry bringing up the rear. The main army was concentrated near Frederick, while the Twelfth Corps was advanced towards the passes in the South Mountain leading to Hagerstown, and Stahl's cavalry thrown forward to scour the country in the neighborhood of Gettysburg. On the 28th, Gen. Hooker, at his request, was relieved of the command of the Army of the Potomac at Frederick, and Gen. George H. Meade was appointed in his stead. On the same day Lee, with the corps of Longstreet and Hill, reached Chambersburg.

In the mean time, on the Baltimore and Ohio Railroad all trains ceased to be run farther than Harper's Ferry. A vast quantity of freight and locomotives were sent to Baltimore, the bridges over Patterson's Creek, Evett's Creek, North Branch, South Potomac country road, Great and Little Cacapon, and Opequan were all destroyed, and the railroad between Harper's Ferry and Cumberland was very much damaged. On June 29th telegraphic communication with the Baltimore and Ohio Railroad ceased beyond Marriottsville at an early hour, the Confederate cavalry doing much damage along the line in that vicinity. At this point, which is only thirty-one miles from Baltimore, the telegraph wires were cut, the rails torn up, bridges burned, and other damage done. The Confederates also spread themselves over Montgomery County, but for the most part abstained from plunder, except seizing all the horses they could find. A large body of cavalry also carried on their operations undisturbed at Rockville, and a small body also appeared at Colesville, a few miles from Beltsville, on the Washington Branch of the Baltimore and Ohio Railroad. At Westminster, Carroll Co., a body of about one hundred of the First Delaware Regiment of Federal cavalry, being surrounded by the Confederates under Maj. Harry Gilmor, were nearly all captured, and others were chased by the Confederates beyond Pikesville, eight miles from Baltimore. A newspaper correspondent, speaking of the occupation of Westminster, says,—

"During ten days previous to July 9, 1863, this usually quiet town was the scene of the wildest excitement and unanticipated events, the people having had the opportunity of witnessing warlike measures in a manner quite new to them, experiencing some of its horrors in their own streets that before they had only read of elsewhere.

"On Sunday morning, June 28th, the citizens and the congregations at the different churches were considerably startled by a squad of cavalry suddenly dashing into town, and as a Confederate raid had for some time been anticipated, many readily supposed it to be their advance. They, however, proved to be a portion of the First Delaware Cavalry, about one hundred and fifteen strong, under command of Maj. N. B. Knight, who had been detailed for special duty at this place. Late on Sunday evening some of the pickets who had been stationed on the different roads leading into town came hurrying in, reporting the advance of a heavy Confederate force from the direction of Littlestown, and soon all were in the saddle, and repaired to a position a short distance below town, and within reach of reinforcements, to await events. The alarm, however, proved causeless, and within a few hours they returned and quiet was again restored.

"About four o'clock on Monday afternoon, however, affairs assumed a more serious aspect. A number of rebel cavalry dashed suddenly into the east end of town, and succeeded in capturing three of the Delaware boys, who were having their horses shod at a blacksmith-shop. Information being at once taken to their camp, they immediately started in pursuit, supposing the Confederate force to be merely a small raid; in this they were mistaken, as it proved to be the brigades of Fitzhugh Lee and Stuart. They met the advance at the junction of the Washington road, and actually held them in check for a few moments, fighting most desperately, being armed as they were with only revolvers and sabres; but observing the overpowering numbers which menaced them, they retired. Their loss was two privates killed and some five or six wounded, and, as far as we can learn, some thirty captured. The rebel loss was two lieutenants killed and some eight wounded. Too much praise cannot be bestowed upon this mere handful of men for their bravery in this attack. Lieutenant Bowman, the provost-marshal, with twelve of his men were soon after captured, only two making their escape.

"The Confederates immediately afterwards occupied the town. In some cases Confederate scrip was offered in payment, and in others no equivalent whatever was made. Several citizens were arrested, some of whom were paroled, while others were taken with them. A large number of horses were taken off with them, and the merchants suffered heavily. Some few private residences were searched by them, but with these exceptions private property was not molested.

"Their force was variously estimated at from five to eight thousand, the greater portion of which made no halt, but pushed steadily forward. By seven o'clock on Tuesday morning the rear-guard passed out of the west end of town, and simultaneously Gen. Gregg with a brigade of Federal cavalry entered at the east end. Advance-guards were thrown out by the Federals, and some twenty stragglers of the Confederates captured, among whom was the clerk of Gen. Lee. The cavalry followed close upon the heels of the Confederates in the direction of Littlestown, and had hardly cleared the town when the advance of Gen. Sedgwick's Sixth Army Corps entered the town, and continued passing through until a late hour in the evening. The number composing the corps was quite large and appeared very formidable. The Confederates mostly were jaded and fatigued, while the Federal troops exhibited the very best of spirits. The citizens without exception tendered to them the kindest hospitalities, for which all appeared greatly thankful, many of them offering payment for the most trifling articles.

"On Wednesday the citizens enjoyed a rather quiet day, but few incidents transpiring to remind them of the close proximity to the two contending armies, until the afternoon, when heavy cannonading was heard in the direction of Gettysburg, where a most sanguinary contest was raging. On Thursday the wagon-trains from the different army corps began to arrive under heavy escorts, and to encamp in the fields in and around town, and it was soon ascertained that this place was to be a grand centre for supplies, as the government had taken possession of the railroad for the emergency, and trains were running day and night. During the balance of the week the streets presented a continual mass of moving wagons, horses, and train-guards, with all the paraphernalia requisite for a large army passing and re-passing. Headquarters of the different departments were established, and for the time all business was suspended. Little of moment was heard during this time from the contending armies in front, save by the large numbers of rebel prisoners arriving, and a considerable number of sick and wounded which arrived during Friday. Hospitals were hastily and temporarily established at the Union church, and the large school-house near it, and also on the Catholic chapel grounds, where the patients received all the time and care the citizens could bestow. Quite a number were sent to Baltimore on Sunday evening, where they received more prompt and necessary attention.

"Orders were received from headquarters on Saturday evening, July 4th, for a removal from here to Gettysburg, and a movement was at once commenced, the trains leaving in an almost unbroken line. Subsequently orders for a portion of the troops and trains to remove to Middletown and Frederick were received, and during Sunday night and Monday morning many moved in that direction, rather indicating an attempt of the rebels to retreat towards the Potomac. On Tuesday afternoon Lieut.-Col. Butler, provost-marshal, with his guard left for the front, and with the exception of a small number of sick and wounded and a few stragglers, the town, after a week's occupation, once more assumed its usual quiet serenity. The streets were rendered almost impassable by the recent rains and extraordinary travel."

All the operations of the Confederate cavalry were under the direction of Stuart, who had crossed the Potomac from Loudon County, Va., into Montgomery County, Md., pushed through Rockville, crossing the Baltimore and Ohio Railroad at Marriottsville, and passed up through Carroll by Westminster to Carlisle, in Pennsylvania. His flanking and scouting parties extended over a wide stretch of country on each side of his line of march, and spread terror and confusion by the impression this produced of the presence of overpowering forces.

Gens. Hill and Longstreet on the 29th moved towards Gettysburg from Chambersburg, and Ewell was directed to march from Carlisle to the same place. These marches were conducted slowly, the position of Gen. Meade being unknown, and Gen. Lee, in the absence of any information from Stuart, his cavalry leader, did not know that the Federal army was so near him. The concentration of Lee's army was so admirably ordered that Ewell from Carlisle, Early from York, and Hill from Chambersburg all reached Gettysburg within a few hours of each other on July 1st.

Although the change of command in the Army of the Potomac was made on the march, and almost in the very face of the enemy, it caused no hindrance to the onward movement, no loss of confidence on the part of the army. The appointment of Gen. Meade was received with unusual satisfaction, and under his leadership the veteran troops hurried forward to meet the Confederate forces. The Federal army was put in motion on the 29th of June, and on the night of the 30th, after two days' marching, Gen. Meade arrived at Taneytown; the First Corps was at Marsh Run, near Gettysburg, the Second at Uniontown, the Third at Bridgeport, the Fifth at Union Mills, the Sixth at Manchester, the Eleventh at Emmittsburg, supporting the First at Marsh Run, and the Twelfth at Littlestown. The cavalry was kept well to the front and on both flanks, and the night of the 30th found Gamble's and Devin's brigades of Buford's division at Gettysburg, Gregg's division at Manchester, and Kilpatrick's division at Hanover.

Gettysburg, the capital of Adams County, Pa., at which the two armies were soon to meet in the most desperate and best-fought battle of the war, lies on the northern slope of a gentle eminence known as Cemetery Hill. On the west of the town, one mile distant, is another eminence called Oak, or Seminary Ridge. This ridge slopes to the west into a little open valley of plowed fields and meadows, interspersed with clumps of timber. Beyond this valley is another ridge, thickly wooded, along the western base of which flows Willoughby Run. The distance between these two ridges is one-half mile. Southeast from Cemetery Hill, between the Baltimore turnpike and Rock Creek, is Culp's Hill, and beyond the creek in that direction is Wolf's Hill, a rugged wooded eminence. Between these two hills, extending from the Baltimore pike to Rock Creek, is Spangler's meadow, partially wooded. Spangler's spring lies near the eastern debouch of this swale. Two miles southwest of Cemetery Hill is a knob of considerable elevation, called Round Top, and adjoining it on the north, with only a narrow valley intervening, is a rocky hill of less altitude called Little Round Top. This extends in diminished altitude to Zeigler's grove, on Cemetery Ridge, the general name for the entire eminence lying between Little Round Top and Cemetery Hill proper. North of the town the country is a rolling plain. Beginning on the right at Culp's Hill, as one faces the north, and bending around Cemetery Hill and following the ridge south to Round Top is a distance of four miles. The whole ridge is shaped somewhat like a fish-hook, the barb being Culp's Hill, and the shank ending in the rocky peak of Round Top. In the town a number of roads converge, making it easy of access from every direction. Here on the 1st, 2d, and 3d of July was fought the great battle of Gettysburg, in which the Confederacy virtually received its death-blow.

In this, as in all the great contests of the war, the sons of Maryland, under either flag, bore a distinguished part. The Second Maryland Confederate Infantry, under Lieut.-Col. James R. Herbert, which was the pride and the boast of the Confederate army, made an assault on the Federal breastworks on Culp's Hill. On the first day it captured the first line of works, but on the next, in attempting to storm the hill in the face of heavy masses of infantry and artillery, they were compelled to fall back with heavy loss. Nearly all the commissioned officers were killed or wounded, and of the five hundred of the command who went into the fight only two hundred escaped unhurt. In this terrible conflict the commander of the Chesapeake Maryland Artillery, Capt. William H. Brown, was killed. Capt. Dement's battery of First Maryland Artillery also suffered greatly. On the Federal side, Col. Maulsby's First Potomac Home Brigade displayed conspicuous gallantry, and suffered severely in killed and wounded. When the invasion commenced this command was stationed on the lower Potomac, and on the 17th of June, the very day that Jenkins' cavalry entered Chambersburg, Pa., Gen. Lockwood received orders to move all his forces to Baltimore, and in obedience to these orders they were immediately concentrated at Point Lookout. The First Potomac Home Brigade, under Col. Maulsby, was put on board the steamer "John A. Warner" early on the morning of June 21st, and landing at Baltimore about noon, immediately marched to Druid Hill Park, where it bivouacked for the night. The regiment remained in Baltimore until the 25th, when Gen. Lockwood received orders to march his command, consisting of the First Potomac Home Brigade, First Eastern Shore and One Hundred and Fiftieth New York Volunteers, to Monocacy Junction, for assignment to the Army of the Potomac. Col. Maulsby's regiment, in company with the One Hundred and Fiftieth New York, left Baltimore during the afternoon, and on the 27th reached Monocacy Junction, where it passed the 28th, moving thence on the 29th to Boyd's Lot, north of Frederick. Leaving the latter place on the morning of the 30th, in the midst of a rain-storm, the First took up the line of march towards Pennsylvania, reaching Bruceville late in the evening. The next morning the men were astir at early light, and soon the regiment was again upon the march, hurrying on through Taneytown towards Gettysburg. That night it bivouacked near Two Taverns, on the Baltimore pike, about four miles from Gettysburg. While on the march this day sounds of the battle between the Union advance and that of the Confederates could be distinctly heard, and late in the afternoon the wounded, on foot and in ambulances, carriages, and every kind of vehicle that could be used, were met coming from that desperate encounter.

At 2.30 A.M. of July 2d the regiment was moved to the front, and at 8 A.M. was placed in position, with Ruger's first division of the Twelfth Corps, along the west bank of Rock Creek, near McAllister's mill. Here the regiment threw up breastworks of rails and earth, behind which it remained until six in the evening, when the brigade, consisting of the First Potomac Home Brigade and One Hundred and Fiftieth New York (the First Eastern Shore not having yet arrived), was ordered to the left of the Union line, then the scene of a heavy action. Lockwood's brigade led the advance of the reinforcements sent from the Twelfth Corps, and upon reaching the summit of Cemetery Ridge was immediately formed in two lines, the First Potomac Home Brigade in front. With a shout of defiance the brigade rushed down the declivity, and sweeping obliquely to the left across the plain, amid a most terrific fire of artillery and musketry, continued its rapid advance without pause until it reached the vicinity of Sherfy's peach-orchard, where the severest contest of the day had occurred. Before this impetuous charge the enemy fell back, leaving his dead and wounded within the Federal lines. Reaching the line originally held by the Third Corps, the men of the First Potomac Home Brigade raised a shout of triumph which rang through the valley and over the hills, and it was with the utmost difficulty they could be restrained from following the enemy farther. While advancing the First Regiment recovered from the enemy three guns of Bigelow's Massachusetts battery that had been lost during the fearful onset of the Confederates. After dark the regiment returned by a circuitous route to the Baltimore pike, near the cemetery, where the men stretched their weary limbs to rest, and slept regardless of the skirmishing of the pickets, which was kept up, with brief intermissions, all night. Before daybreak of the 3d, Col. Maulsby was ordered to post his regiment in position to support Knapp's Pennsylvania battery, posted on a slight ridge west of the Baltimore pike and opposite Spangler's house.

At daylight the artillery opened a rapid fire,

which was continued for more than an hour. But, although severe, it failed to dislodge the enemy, who still held the captured breastworks. At about six o'clock orders were given Col. Maulsby's regiment to advance across Spangler's meadow and carry the position held by the enemy at the base of Culp's Hill, near Spangler's spring. It seemed certain destruction, but such were the orders, and Col. Maulsby gave the command, "Forward, double quick!" With deafening cheers the line sprang forward and advanced as rapidly as the nature of the ground would allow. Maj. Steiner, with the left wing of the regiment, moved directly through a tongue of woods jutting out from Culp's Hill, and extending half-way across the meadow, while the right wing, under Col. Maulsby, advanced across the open swale, and then into the woods. From behind every tree and rock the enemy's fire was poured in, but the regiment with undaunted courage pushed forward towards the stone wall, from which the adversary sent death-dealing missiles. The fire of his sharpshooters, posted in trees on the other side of the creek, was also very close and annoying. Already many had fallen and the regiment seemed devoted to destruction, but onward it went, its officers leading and cheering the men. Gaining a position within twenty yards of the stone wall, and while preparing for a final charge, orders were given for the regiment to return to the turnpike, as a movement of another regiment on the enemy's flank would expose it to an enfilading fire from its friends. Collecting its dead and wounded, the regiment retired to an orchard near the pike, where it was held in reserve for a short time. During the charge at Spangler's spring, Company I, under Capt. Walter Saunders, had a lively skirmish with the enemy at Culp's Hill. After resting in the orchard until about nine o'clock the regiment was advanced to the front on Culp's Hill, where it occupied rifle-pits and engaged the enemy. Here, too, it fought earnestly and bravely, and not a man faltered or displayed the least sign of fear. Its loss in this last engagement was severe, but the heaviest loss was sustained at Spangler's spring. Among the killed were Lieut. James T. Smith, Company C, and Lieut. John S. Willman, Company D. In the action at Culp's Hill, Lieut. Charles E. Eader, Company I, was killed. These officers were all citizens of Frederick County. Lieut. Smith was a young lawyer of Frederick City, and one of the editors of the *Maryland Union*. Lieut. Eader, also of Frederick City, was an educated mechanic of brave and generous impulses. Lieut. Willman, who was from Mechanicsburg, was a young officer of great gallantry, accomplishments, and promise.

The total loss of the regiment at Gettysburg was three officers and twenty-two enlisted men killed or mortally wounded, three officers and sixty-nine men wounded, and one man missing. Capt. Joseph Groff, Company B, Lieut. George H. Wain, Company C, and Lieut. Frank H. Hardesty, Company G, were among the wounded.[1]

During the night of the 3d the regiment lay in the works near its original position at McAllister's mill, on Rock Creek.

On the 4th of July, Lee took a position to receive an attack, but as Meade showed no disposition to disturb him, he began to retreat on the night of the 4th, and reached Hagerstown on the 6th and 7th. Finding the river too full to cross, he took up a position covering the Potomac from Williamsport to Falling Waters. While at Hagerstown he issued the following address to his army:

"HEADQUARTERS ARMY OF NORTHERN VIRGINIA,
"July 11, 1863.

"*General Orders No.* 16:

"After long and trying marches, endured with the fortitude that has ever characterized the soldiers of the Army of Northern Virginia, you have penetrated to the country of our enemies, and recalled to the defense of their own soil those who were engaged in the invasion of ours. You have fought a fierce and sanguinary battle, which, if not attended with the success that has hitherto crowned your efforts, was marked by the same heroic spirit that has commanded the respect of your enemies, the gratitude of your country, and the admiration of mankind.

"Once more you are called upon to meet the enemy from whom you won, on so many fields, names that will never die. Once more the eyes of your countrymen are turned upon you. Again do wives and sisters, fathers and mothers, helpless children lean for defense on your strong arms and brave hearts. Let every soldier remember that on his courage and fidelity depend all that makes life worth having,—the freedom of his country, the honor of his people, and the security of his home. Let each heart grow strong in the remembrance of our glorious past, and in the thought of the inestimable blessings for which we contend; and, invoking the assistance of that benign power which has so signally blessed our former efforts, let us go forth in confidence to secure the peace and safety of our country. Soldiers, your old enemy is before you. Win from him honor worthy of your right cause, worthy of your comrades dead on so many illustrious fields.

"R. E. LEE,
"*General Commanding.*"

The pursuit by the Union army is thus stated by Gen. Meade in his report:

---

[1] Those killed or mortally wounded in the First Potomac Home Brigade at Gettysburg were, Company A, John J. Farling; B. Alpheus Hesson, John W. Stockman; C, Thomas Vance, Henry Miller; D, Stephen Ford; E, Teater French; F, Philip Warner, John Conner, H. H. Hartman, George Must; G, David Krebs, Silas Frizell, Peter L. Miller, Uriah Flagle; H, George H. Barger, Andrew Caswell; I, Joseph Ballis, Daniel Karnes K, John H. R. Broose, George G. Lowrey, and Daniel Sherburt.

"The 5th and 6th of July were employed in succoring the wounded and burying the dead. Maj.-Gen. Sedgwick, commanding the Sixth Corps, having pushed the pursuit of the enemy as far as the Fairfield Pass, in the mountains, and reporting that the pass was a very strong one, in which a small force of the enemy could hold in check and delay for a considerable time any pursuing force, I determined to follow the enemy by a flank movement, and accordingly, leaving McIntosh's brigade of cavalry and Neill's brigade of infantry to continue harassing the enemy, put the army in motion for Middletown, Md. Orders were immediately sent to Maj.-Gen. French at Frederick to reoccupy Harper's Ferry, and send a force to occupy Turner Pass, in South Mountain. I subsequently ascertained Maj.-Gen. French had not only anticipated these orders in part, but had pushed a cavalry force to Williamsport and Falling Waters, where they destroyed the enemy's pontoon-bridge and captured its guard. Buford was at the same time sent to Williamsport and Hagerstown. The duty above assigned to the cavalry was most successfully accomplished, the enemy being greatly harassed, his trains destroyed, and many captures of guns and prisoners made. After halting a day at Middletown to procure necessary supplies and bring up the trains, the army moved through the South Mountain, and by July 12th was in front of the enemy, who occupied a strong position on the heights of Marsh Run, in advance of Williamsport. In taking this position several skirmishes and affairs had been had with the enemy, principally by the cavalry and the Eleventh and Sixth Corps. The 13th was occupied in reconnoissances of the enemy's position and preparations for attack, but on advancing on the morning of the 14th it was ascertained he had retired the night previous by a bridge at Falling Waters and the ford at Williamsport. The cavalry in pursuit overtook the rear-guard at Falling Waters, capturing two guns and numerous prisoners."

Speaking of the recrossing of the Potomac by the Confederate army, John Esten Cooke, in his "Life of Gen. Lee," says, "Towards dawn on the 14th the army commenced moving, in the midst of a violent rain-storm, across the river at both points, and Lee, sitting his horse upon the river's bank, superintended the operation, as was his habit on occasions of emergency. Loss of rest and fatigue, with that feeling of suspense unavoidable under the circumstances, had impaired the energies of even his superb physical constitution. As the bulk of the rear-guard of the army safely passed over the shaky bridge, which Lee had looked at with some anxiety as it swayed to and fro, lashed by the current, he uttered a sigh of relief, and a great weight seemed taken from his shoulders. Seeing his fatigue and exhaustion, Gen. Stuart gave him some coffee. He drank it with avidity, and declared, as he handed back the cup, that nothing had ever refreshed him so much." The last of the Confederate troops did not cross the river at the bridge until 1 P.M. on the 14th, and in the skirmish of the rear-guard with the Federal cavalry the gallant Pettigrew fell, who had supported Pickett in the great charge at Gettysburg, where in spite of a painful wound he had done all in his power to rally his troops.

"The pursuit," says Gen. Meade, "was renewed by a flank movement, the army crossing the Potomac at Berlin and moving down the Loudon Valley. The cavalry were immediately pushed into the several passes of the Blue Ridge, and having learned from scouts the withdrawal of the Confederate army from the lower valley of the Shenandoah, the army, the Third Corps, Maj.-Gen. French, in advance, was moved into the Manassas Gap, in the hope of being able to intercept a portion of the enemy. The possession of the gap was disputed so successfully as to enable the rear-guard to withdraw by way of Strasburg, the Confederate army retiring to the Rapidan. A position was taken up with this army on the line of the Rappahannock, and the campaign terminated about the close of July."

The organizations from Maryland actually engaged on the Federal side in the battle of Gettysburg were the First Cavalry, Company A, Purnell's Legion, Cole's battalion of cavalry (in detached bodies, as guides, orderlies, etc.), Rigby's battery, First Potomac Home Brigade Infantry, First Eastern Shore Infantry, and the Third Infantry.

The First Cavalry, under Lieut.-Col. Deems, with McIntosh's first brigade of Gregg's (second) cavalry division, broke camp at Aldie on the 26th of June, and marched to Leesburg, covering the rear of the army advancing into Maryland. Thus was commenced that series of rapid, continuous, and exhausting marches which brought it upon the field of Gettysburg, and continued with scarcely an intermission until the opposing armies were once again confronting each other on the line of the Rappahannock. In the pursuit of the Confederates after the battle of Gettysburg, the First Maryland Cavalry did valuable service, capturing many stragglers, participating in a skirmish near Emmittsburg, in which one man was wounded, and encountering the enemy in a spirited engagement on the 10th of July at Old Antietam Forge.

On the 5th of July the First Potomac Home Brigade, whose gallant conduct at the battle of Gettysburg has already been described, started with the army in pursuit of the enemy, marching, *via* Littletown, Frederick City, and Crampton's Gap, to the neighborhood of Bakersville, where it arrived on the 10th, threw up breastworks, and remained four days. Advancing on the 14th, the enemy's works were found deserted. On the 16th the regiment reached Sandy Hook, where its connection with the Army of the Potomac ceased.

In this campaign the officers and men of the First Potomac Home Brigade were subjected to the severest hardships, besides trials and dangers of every description, yet throughout the trying ordeal all behaved with a nobility of spirit well worthy of record. Each and every one seemed aware of the great issues involved and the importance of the struggle in which they were engaged. From the time the regiment left Baltimore, on the 25th of June, until it reached Sandy Hook, on the 16th of July, it marched more than one hundred and fifty miles, engaged the enemy on three occasions at Gettysburg, built breastworks and other fortifications, suffered great hardships of every character, and under all circumstances exhibited the greatest fortitude and courage.

On the 19th of June the Second Potomac Home Brigade was ordered, with the First Virginia Volunteers and a section of artillery, to Cumberland. On the 6th of July, Gen. Kelley, who was in command, moved these forces from Cumberland to co-operate with the Army of the Potomac, then in pursuit of the Confederates. The Second Potomac Home Brigade was attached to Col. Mulligan's brigade, Department of West Virginia. Leaving Cumberland at 9.30 A.M., July 6th, Col. Bruce marched his regiment, the Second Potomac Home Brigade, eastward over the National pike. One mile from Cumberland, Company B, Capt. Morrow, was detailed to return to town and proceed down the Baltimore and Ohio Railroad, for the purpose of repairing the telegraph-line along that route. At 6 P.M. the regiment halted for the night at Gilpintown. Marching all day of the 7th, and until 2.30 A.M. of the 8th, it reached a point one mile east of Hancock. After daylight the regiment returned one mile west of Hancock, where it encamped through the night, and where it was joined by Company B. Continuing the movement eastward, the Second bivouacked the night of the 10th at Indian Spring, and the night following at Clear Spring, where it remained until the 14th, when the march was renewed to Williamsport, at which place a junction was effected with Gen. Meade's army.

The Confederate army having retired into Virginia, Gen. Kelley's command on the 15th of July moved to Cherry Run, where it crossed the Potomac and advanced to Hedgesville, where skirmishing with the enemy was maintained until the 20th. During the night Gen. Kelley learned through a loyal citizen of Martinsburg that the enemy in force was moving on his rear, and immediately retreated into Maryland. The enemy approached and threw a few shells across the river, but soon withdrew. At North Mountain, during the advance into Virginia, the Second Potomac Home Brigade supported a heavy skirmish line. On the 24th of July the regiment again crossed the river with Gen. Kelley's command, and marched to Hedgesville. Leaving this place on the 1st of August, it arrived at New Creek on the 7th, having marched *via* Shanghai, Pughton, Great Cacapon Bridge, Blue's Gap, Romney, Mechanicsburg Gap, and Burlington. At New Creek the Second remained some time, performing heavy guard and picket duty, also furnishing escorts to government supply trains to Romney and Petersburg. The frequent details for this service allowed little or no respite from duty.

The Third Potomac Home Brigade Infantry, commanded by Col. W. Gilpin, embarked on transports at Annapolis, June 27th, and moved to Baltimore, whence it proceeded next day by rail to Elysville, on the Baltimore and Ohio Railroad. Two important iron bridges, crossing the Patapsco at this point, were threatened with destruction by Stuart's cavalry, then advancing on the right flank of the Army of the Potomac towards Pennsylvania. The preservation of these bridges was of great importance to the government, the Baltimore and Ohio Railroad being the principal route of supply and communication between Washington, Baltimore, and Gen. Meade's army. The service, therefore, rendered by the Third at Elysville and vicinity, although not of a nature involving much personal danger or hardship, like that in the field, was of vast importance, and the most valuable of all the railroad arteries upon which the Union army depended for supplies was successfully guarded at this vital point. The regiment, with detachments posted at different stations from Ellicott's Mills to the Monocacy Junction, remained on railroad guard duty during the ensuing fall and winter and the following spring.

As has already been stated, Vernon and Summer's companies of Cole's cavalry crossed the Potomac from Virginia into Maryland at Harper's Ferry on the 16th of June. Next day White's battalion of Confederate cavalry (mostly Marylanders) made the passage of the river at Point of Rocks and captured a small squad of Mean's Virginia (Union) cavalry. It afterwards intercepted a train of freight-cars, and captured a number of men belonging to Alexander's battery *en route* from Harper's Ferry to Baltimore. They were all sent South as prisoners of war. Vernon's and Summer's companies, while marching from Harper's Ferry to Point of Rocks, for the purpose of guarding the fords of the Potomac, encountered White's command at Catoctin Creek. Mistaking the enemy for friends, both companies were at first surprised and thrown into confusion by his attack, but after the loss of a few men they rallied and drove back the foe, capturing one prisoner. In Capt. Summer's company one man (Joseph L. Michael) was killed, three wounded, and four captured. Capt. Vernon also lost several men taken prisoners. On the 18th of June three of Summer's men, sent with some of Vernon's company on a scout to Frederick, were captured in the town after a lively resistance. Summer's company then went to Berlin, where it remained until the 30th of June, on which date it moved by way of Maryland Heights to Frederick City. At this place it was employed in scouting through the surrounding country and doing patrol duty in the city. Two of its members (couriers) were captured near Emmittsburg on the 5th of July by Stuart's cavalry. Meantime, from the 18th to the 21st of June, Companies A, C, and D of Cole's battalion were kept constantly in motion watching the movements of the Confederate army. The former operated east of the mountains, and the two latter on the west. As a central point from which to direct the movements of his command, Maj. Cole established his headquarters at Burkettsville. On the 22d, Company A, Capt. Vernon, numbering but thirty men, entered Frederick by the Manor road, and dashing along Market and Patrick Streets, drove out the First Maryland (Confederate) Cavalry Battalion, commanded by Maj. Harry Gilmor. Boldly charging through the streets, Company A, with Lieut. Link leading the advance, pushed the enemy beyond the city limits on the Hagerstown road. Discovering a larger force outside the city preparing to re-enter, Capt. Vernon prudently withdrew his company towards Point of Rocks. One of the Confederates was badly wounded and taken prisoner. He was paroled and left in the hospital. This brilliant dash was executed amid the plaudits of the parents, wives, and friends of many of the men. While the bullets whistled, these patriotic friends waved their handkerchiefs and cheered the men on to victory. Next day the entire battalion, under Maj. Cole, moved on a reconnoissance over South Mountain to Boonsboro'. On the 24th it skirmished with the enemy's column advancing into Pennsylvania, and captured quite a number of prisoners. From this point Company C, Lieut. W. A. Homer, pushed forward on the right flank of the Confederate army, through Wolfsville and Sabillasville, into Pennsylvania, making some effective dashes at the enemy and capturing a number of prisoners, among them a bearer of dispatches from Gen. Lee to Gen. Ewell. At Fountaindale, on the 28th of June, it had a lively skirmish with a small body of the enemy's cavalry, capturing the lieutenant in command, three sergeants, and eight privates, with their arms and equipments and twenty horses. Companies A and D had returned from Boonsboro' to Knoxville, where they were rejoined on the 30th of June by Company C. On the 1st of July these companies established camp at Frederick, where they performed provost duty and operated in different directions as occasion required through the month of July. On the 4th of July a squad of the enemy's cavalry, which dashed into Frederick on the Harper's Ferry road, was driven back and pursued to Knoxville by the battalion. Next day it drove a party of Confederates from Sandy Hook across the bridge at Harper's Ferry and burnt the bridge.

From the time the enemy entered until he withdrew from the State, many of Maj. Cole's command, both officers and men, were detailed as guides, couriers, etc., to the various corps commanders of the Army of the Potomac. In this capacity they rendered most valuable service, their familiarity with the country being thus turned to good account.

After the evacuation of Maryland Heights by the Maryland Brigade, as described at the beginning of the Maryland and Pennsylvania campaign, it proceeded to Frederick City, where it arrived on the afternoon of July 1st. The command bivouacked just outside the city in a clover-field, with the exception of the Seventh Regiment, which, having had the advance on the march, was detailed for picket duty. Next day, July 2d, the great battle of the war raged at Gettysburg, within hearing of the troops at Frederick, and Gen. French, commanding the Federal forces, fully appreciated the responsibility of his position. On the morning of that day he issued a ringing order, concluding with the announcement that "any officer, no matter how high his rank, or soldier who fails to do his duty at this moment will be made to *suffer death under immediate trial before a Drum-Head Court.*" Gen. French followed this up in a way that showed he meant business. He visited the outposts and camps, found fault with everything, reprimanded everybody, and put under arrest men and officers of all grades. Upon the whole, it had a capital effect.

At night the Seventh was relieved on picket by the Eighth, and the next morning the entire force was paraded through town in column of platoons (equalized), field-music playing, on the march to Monocacy Junction. The brigade never appeared to better advantage.

At the corner of Market and Patrick Streets the column passed Gen. French in review, and at all points was loudly cheered. When Gen. Meade ordered the evacuation of Maryland Heights, he directed Gen. French to march his column rapidly northward and unite with the main army. He was, however, subsequently directed to hold Frederick, camping his troops in the immediate vicinity, to guard the rail and turnpike bridges over the Monocacy. He was further directed to guard the Baltimore and Ohio Railroad from Frederick to a junction with Gen. Schenck, and in the event of the Federal army being compelled to retire before the enemy, to fall back into the defenses of Washington. At Monocacy Junction the brigade guarded the bridges over the Monocacy and the approaches from Nolan's and other ferries of the Potomac, and kept open the line of communication between Washington and Meade's army.

Soon the news of a victory at Gettysburg flew like wildfire. There was, however, no time for a Fourth of July celebration. All was activity and vigilance, constant marching and countermarching, posting of pickets and calling them in again, and hourly expectation of something important to happen. During the afternoon of the 4th the brigade was countermarched back to its old bivouac on Rizer's farm, west of Frederick, on the Harper's Ferry road.

At reveille on the morning of the 6th, when the men paraded for roll-call, they descried an object swinging from the limb of a tree in an adjoining field. It was soon learned that it was the body of an alleged Confederate spy, caught with the evidences in his boots, and hung by order of Gen. John Buford, who commanded a brigade of Union cavalry, which had arrived during the night from Gettysburg. The deceased was recognized as a visitor to the camps of the Maryland Brigade on Maryland and Bolivar Heights, offering various small articles for sale, and getting up ornamented company rolls.

On the afternoon of the 6th of July, Gen. Kenly was ordered to march with the First, Fourth, and Eighth Regiments and Miner's Indiana battery to retake and occupy Maryland Heights. Starting immediately, and making a forced march, Gen. Kenly reached Knoxville early next morning. It was here learned that the enemy was in full possession of Harper's Ferry, and engaged in repairing the railroad bridge, which had been partially destoyed by Cole's cavalry the day previous, and that they had been and were still employed in collecting the ammunition and stores which were left on the evacuation of the heights.

Upon receiving this information Gen. Kenly pushed forward, and when the column reached the mouth of Pleasant Valley, he detached Lieut.-Col. Wilson, with the First Maryland, instructing him to ascend the heights by way of the eastern slope, and to carry and hold them.

Gen. Kenly then moved with two companies of the Fourth Maryland, followed by the remainder of the Fourth and Eighth Regiments, by the road leading along the canal.

As the advance-guard neared the bridge they found the road obstructed, and the enemy at the same time opened upon them a sharp fire. The advance immediately dashed forward in gallant style, turned the point of the precipice which abuts on the road, and, taking cover, by their rapid firing soon materially lessened that of their opponents.

The balance of the command was then brought up the road and placed in position on the western slopes of the mountain. A section of Miner's battery was also placed in position on the points of the heights overlooking Harper's Ferry, and a few well-directed shots soon dispersed a body of Confederate cavalry which made its appearance on Bolivar Heights.

About this time a detachment of troops, with several pieces of light artillery, mounted on an iron-plated car, under command of Lieut. John R. Meigs, U.S.A., which had been sent up from Baltimore by Maj.-Gen. Schenck, arrived, and assisted in silencing the Confederate sharpshooters, who were annoying the Federal column from the Virginia side of the river.

The heights gained, a picket-line was at once established, extending from the river to Solomon's Gap, and before dark several squads of the enemy's cavalry came down the road from Sharpsburg and the Shepherdstown ferry; but after remaining a short time, and being apparently surprised at finding the position occupied by Federal troops, they withdrew.

The great importance of this movement may be more fully appreciated on reading the following acknowledgment from Gen. French:

"HEADQUARTERS THIRD ARMY CORPS,
"Jan. 22, 1864.
"BRIG.-GEN. JOHN R. KENLY,
"Commanding Third Division First Army Corps:
"GENERAL,—My sudden and unexpected transfer to the command of the Third Army Corps prevented me from making the recognition of the important services of yourself and the Maryland Brigade, under your command, to which you and it are eminently entitled.

"The fact that Maryland Heights had been reoccupied after a forced march, surprising the enemy and compelling him to abandon the bridge-head and the heights, is a part of the history of the Gettysburg campaign of which you and your troops may be justly proud.

"I am, general,
"Very truly yours,
"WM. H. FRENCH, Maj.-Gen. Vols."

When Gen. Kenly started from Frederick the Seventh Regiment was on picket, and did not accompany the brigade. As soon as the Seventh was relieved by its namesake, the Seventh New York Militia, it marched back and rejoined the brigade on Maryland

Heights. At an early hour on the 10th of July the brigade left the heights in the care of the Ninth and Tenth Maryland Regiments, which had arrived from Baltimore, and moved out through Pleasant Valley, passing Locust Grove and Rohrersville, to a point near Boonsboro', where it arrived at nine P.M. The march was directly towards the sound of cannon, which was heard early in the day. It was necessarily a forced march, and the day becoming excessively hot, there was much straggling from sheer exhaustion. Men dragged themselves along until they dropped down in their tracks.

Next day the brigade was assigned to the First Corps, and became the Third Brigade of its Third Division. Gen. John Newton commanded the corps, Gen. Kenly the division, and Col. Dushane, of the First Regiment, the brigade.

On the following day (July 12th), about noon, the corps moved from Beaver Creek, through Funkstown, which Lee's army had evacuated in the morning, and took position fronting the enemy's line, formed on the south of the town, and extending from Falling Waters, on the Potomac, along the Salisbury Ridge to the Conococheague, six miles west of Hagerstown.

All this day the rain poured, and the fields were heavy with the tenacious clay of this limestone country, so that the order, "Close up, men; close up your files," was constantly in the mouth of every officer from colonel to file-closers.

Suddenly the sharp crack of rifles and whistle of bullets indicated the immediate presence of the foe. The men of the Maryland Brigade closed up with a spring and formed in line. Skirmishers were advanced across the fields towards the Sharpsburg and Hagerstown pike, held by the enemy, and a lively fire was kept up until after dark. Just about dark the brigade skirmish line went forward with a rush and cleared the enemy out of Stover's barn, from which their fire had been somewhat annoying.

Skirmishing was renewed with daylight of the 13th, and for some time became quite brisk. About five o'clock Private Scoffin, of Company I, Seventh Maryland, was sent to the rear in a blanket, shot through the thigh. The skirmish-line was gradually pushed forward until within easy point-blank range of the enemy's main works. The firing of musketry was scattering but incessant until mid-day, when the enemy opened with artillery and fired several rounds of spherical case-shot. They put four shot into Stover's barn, but hit nobody. All day there was skirmishing and some cannonading along the whole line, but no severe fighting, although the two armies were in close proximity to each other.

During the night it was evident to the pickets on certain portions of the line that Lee was withdrawing his army. One of the first to discover this movement was a member of the First Maryland, who, about midnight, stealthily approached the enemy's rifle-pits and found them deserted. He at once reported the fact to the officer in charge of the brigade picket-line, Maj. Faehtz, of the Eighth Regiment, who promptly communicated the intelligence to the division commander, and by him was directed to push forward his line as far as he could go. This was done forthwith, and the line advanced without opposition to within one mile of Williamsport, capturing twenty-nine Confederate stragglers on the way.

The main body of the Confederate army was already over the Potomac, having effected a successful escape under cover of the night; but their rear-guard was overtaken by Kilpatrick's cavalry at Falling Waters and severely punished. Meade's entire army was then put in motion towards the river. The First Corps, following the Sixth, marched through the two strong lines of earthworks just abandoned by the enemy, the men of the Maryland Brigade noticing the fresh graves of a number of the Confederates who fell in their front during the two days' skirmish. They also soon found themselves traveling over the same ground that was familiar as the scene of their operations in September, 1862, and at night bivouacked near Williamsport. For the First Regiment this was the fifth time it had encamped in that vicinity.

The next morning the march was resumed, and, passing through Smoketown, Keedysville, and Rohrersville, the First Corps bivouacked for the night at the foot of South Mountain, near Crampton's Gap. From Crampton's Gap another day's march brought the corps to a resting-place between Petersville and Knoxville, the Maryland Brigade bivouacking on Hilleary's farm. Here it remained, refitting and reclothing generally, until the 18th, when the corps crossed the Potomac at Berlin, and marched through Lovettsville and bivouacked just outside of Waterford, a neat and loyal little Quaker village. From Waterford the next march was to Hamilton, where the Maryland Brigade slept in Janney's woods. Marching thence on the 20th, *via* Middleburg, White Plains, Warrenton, Warrenton Junction, and Bealton Station, the brigade finally reached Rappahannock Station on the 1st of August, and crossing the river threw up intrenchments. Here the Gettysburg campaign ended.

While these military operations were in progress intense excitement prevailed in Maryland. Upon the invasion of the State, the people of the western counties were greatly alarmed. In Frederick, Hagerstown, Boonsboro', Williamsport, Cumberland, and other towns hundreds of the citizens left their homes, while many more made preparations to do so. The panic also spread wildly through the country. Valuable stock of all descriptions was put *en route* northward, and did not halt in its flight until some haven of safety was reached. Horses, wagons, and cattle crowded every avenue leading to the mountains and other safe hiding-places.

During the Confederate retreat a brisk skirmish occurred at Hagerstown on the 6th of July between Stuart and Kilpatrick.

The Hagerstown *Herald and Torch* of the 22d of July, 1863, says,—

"Before our people had completely settled down after the entry of Stuart, leading the advance of the rebel retreat on Monday, the 6th, they were again aroused by the cry, 'The Yankees are coming!' About half-past one o'clock the advance of Kilpatrick's division appeared, and formed in line of battle on the crest of the hill near Funkstown. Stuart seemed thunderstruck, and wild hurry and bustle characterized all his movements. Approaching gradually line after line was formed, until the advance line of the Federal forces rested near Mr. A. Hager's mill. From here, led by Capt. Snyder, of the First Michigan Cavalry, a charge of not more than fifty men was made about half-past two o'clock. Hastily advancing, they met and received the fire of the enemy, about one hundred and fifty strong, posted on Potomac Street, just where the road to Frederick breaks off to the left, and rushing on them, sabre in hand, they drove the rebels pell-mell up Potomac Street to beyond the Reform church, where the main body of the force rested. Here they fell back in an orderly manner to meet the skirmishers, deployed and led forward by Capt. Dahlgren (son of Rear-Admiral Dahlgren), of Gen. Kilpatrick's staff, who advanced beyond the town hall. Capt. Dahlgren was wounded in the right ankle by a pistol-ball from the market-house as he led his skirmishers up. The main column was soon deployed, part of them dismounted and put in ambuscade, and a general charge prepared for. In the meanwhile the rebel battery opened with shell, which proved inefficient to move or check the gradual advance of the Federals. Elder's battery was quickly put in position on the north of the seminary and replied, while Gen. Custer, with his brigade, was sent to the right, to work to the enemy's flank and rear. An ambuscade of the rebels on Grove's farm, a mile north of town, being discovered, Kilpatrick made dispositions to attack it in the rear, while he led a charge of two regiments in person into the front of the main body of the rebels. All his arrangements were made; Gen. Custer had reached a position where he could attack the left flank of the enemy, and Kilpatrick himself actually moving off to lead the charge, when Custer, whose skirmishers had reached the Leitersburg road, in the rear of the rebel column, discovered the advance of a brigade of rebel infantry, the beginning of the retreat of the shattered columns which Lee had so triumphantly led through an unarmed valley but two weeks before, and with which he was to conquer and bring back a treaty of peace. Thereupon Gen. Kilpatrick ordered his men to draw off gradually, to go to the assistance of Buford at Williamsport, who was attacking the enemy's trains. His loss was not over five killed and twenty wounded during this spirited skirmish. On his route to Williamsport he was pursued by cavalry and mounted infantry, about six thousand strong, and there met and cut up at least five hundred of their men with but slight loss, notwithstanding he was hemmed in between two columns, one of infantry, the other of cavalry and infantry mounted."

When Gen. Lee reached Hagerstown on his retreat from Gettysburg, and discovered that the Potomac was too high to effect a crossing, he took a position west of the town and proceeded to protect it by fortifications. His line of intrenchments extended about twelve miles, his extreme left resting on the farm of Frederick Bryan, a mile northwest of Hagerstown, and a few miles from the Pennsylvania line, and his right reaching the Potomac River in the vicinity of Falling Waters. These works were thrown up in about two days, and, together with the great natural strength of the positions chosen for them, were formidable in the extreme. A contemporaneous writer, speaking of the spectacle presented after the passage of the two armies, says,—

"The rebel line of intrenchments, as well as our own, which were hastily thrown up opposite to them, extend for a distance of twelve miles through one of the most fertile portions of Washington County. Along these lines farms have been terribly devastated. Fences have been destroyed, timber cut down, embankments thrown up, ditches dug, wheat, corn, and cloverfields destroyed, the whole presenting a scene of desolation and destruction painful to behold. Some farmers estimate their losses at six, eight, and ten thousand dollars, and renters and others say that they are entirely ruined."[1]

---

[1] During the skirmish at Hagerstown on the 6th of July John F. Stemple, a citizen of the place, was instantly killed. He had ascended to the roof of Marshall & Cranwell's business house to witness the fight, and was killed by a ball from the neighborhood of the market-house. On the 1st of July, when the Confederate forces occupied Hagerstown, some one reported to them that Andrew Boward, Sr., a respectable citizen living in the suburbs of the town, had on the previous day displayed the national flag while Kilpatrick's forces occupied the place; whereupon a squad of Confederates at once repaired to his residence and demanded its surrender. Mr. Boward, being slightly deaf, did not understand the nature of the demand and did not comply with it, upon which, it is said, one of the Confederates leveled his carbine and fired at him, the ball entering his left arm below the elbow. On Monday, the 13th of July, during a skirmish between Gen. Kilpatrick's cavalry and the Confederates, Andrew Hagerman, a well-known citizen of Hagerstown, seized his gun, rushed into the streets, and commenced firing upon the Confederates. He was mortally wounded in the skirmish, and died a few days afterwards. After the retreat of the Confederate army large bodies of Pennsylvania militia were encamped for some time in the vicinity of Hagerstown. The Washington House and Lyceum Hall of Hagerstown were used after the battle of Gettysburg as hospitals for Union soldiers, and the seminary as a hospital for Confederate soldiers.

On the 25th of August an affray occurred at Clear Spring, in which Capt. Isaac T. Prather, a highly respectable citizen of that district, lost his life. The affair, it is said, grew out of an assault by a paroled soldier, named Samuel Masters, upon some colored men whom Capt. Prather had recruited for the United States service, and who had assembled preparatory to being sent to join the colored regiment then being formed in Baltimore. During the *melée* Capt. Prather was shot in the abdo-

On the 20th of August, by order of Brig.-Gen. Lockwood, Col. Benjamin L. Simpson was directed by his brigade commander, Col. George D. Wells, to proceed with the forces under him from Loudon Heights and encamp in the woods on the east side of the village of Charlestown, W. Va. Col. Simpson's command consisted of portions of seven companies of the Ninth Maryland Volunteers, amounting to about three hundred and fifty men, and a cavalry force of about eighty men. His instructions from his brigade commander were that the holding of Charlestown itself was of no importance, but to watch the movements of the Confederate forces, scout the country thoroughly, and if attacked to resist or retire as the force opposed to him should suggest. At half-past five o'clock on the morning of the 18th of October a Confederate force under Imboden attacked and drove in the pickets on the different roads about Charlestown, planted a battery north and south of the town, and sent in a flag of truce demanding the surrender of the place. This was refused, and the attack was soon after begun by the Confederates.

When the presence of the enemy in the vicinity was first discovered by the attack on the Federal pickets, Col. Simpson posted his men in the court-house, the jail, and another building, making loop-holes for muskets. The Confederate batteries were so planted behind buildings at a distance of two or three hundred yards that their fire was very effective, while the cannoneers were completely protected from the musketry of Col. Simpson's force. The first shot fired struck the court-house, and several others followed, killing and wounding several men and an officer. Col. Simpson then ordered the men to evacuate the building, and form column by company in the street, and ordered the cavalry force, consisting of about eighty men, under Lieut. Moore, to reconnoitre the roads and find the weak points of the enemy. Lieut. Moore led his men out on the road leading to Harper's Ferry, and finding the enemy ordered a charge, which resulted in the killing or capture of all but the lieutenant and seventeen men. Col. Simpson had in the mean time learned the force of the enemy and the number of pieces of artillery, and his men, who had been organized but two months, and had never been in action before, became panic-stricken, could not be kept in line, broke in confusion, destroyed their arms, and were very soon all made prisoners.

Col. Simpson was remarkably cool, and at the head of his column, assisted by his officers, endeavored to rally his men, that an orderly retreat might be effected; but all efforts to do so failing, and the command having scattered in every direction, he struck off through the fields in company with his mounted officers and succeeded in escaping capture. In consequence of this disaster a court of inquiry was convened to investigate the case, and acquitted Col. Simpson of all blame, the court expressing the opinion "that the surprise and capture of the greater part of the forces under command of Col. Benjamin L. Simpson, Ninth Maryland Infantry, at Charlestown, on the morning of the 18th of October ult., were inevitable, because of the peculiar location of the place, which, surrounded by an open country for several miles on all sides, and approached by a large number of roads from all directions, was easy to be flanked and surrounded, and because of the superior force by which it was attacked, and of the inferior force for its defense. The rebel attacking force was two thousand men, with six pieces of artillery. The defending force, under command of Col. Simpson, consisted of three hundred and seventy-five infantry and seventy-five cavalry."

Gen. Kelley forwarded the record of the case, with the statement that he did not concur in the findings of the court, but believed that Col. Simpson was derelict in allowing himself to be surprised, and that he should have maintained himself in his position until the reinforcements reached him, which started from Harper's Ferry as soon as the cannonading was heard. He therefore recommended that Col. Simpson should be dismissed the service. The War Department, however, approved the finding of the court, and the judge-advocate-general, in declining to concur in Gen. Kelley's recommendation, said, "After a disaster of this kind has occurred it is much less difficult for a military commander to review the details, and remark what should or should not have been done, than for a subordinate to anticipate the strength, position, and design of the enemy, and to successfully have met or withstood their attack."

Among the officers who escaped capture were Lieut.-Col. Thomas Clandeley, Maj. George Church, Surgeon Morgan, Asst. Surgeon Kemp, Chaplain G. T. Gray.[1]

---

men, and died in about forty-eight hours afterwards. On the 27th of August the First Maryland Cavalry was paid off, and on the 29th its members forwarded by express to their families at home over seven thousand dollars. Company I, of Washington County, alone forwarded over two thousand. Altogether the regiment sent home over ten thousand dollars of the money received on the last pay-day.

[1] Company F, Second Maryland Potomac Home Brigade, Capt. George D. Summers, formed part of the cavalry force at Charlestown. While stationed here the company was engaged in continual skirmishes, in which the command was very much reduced and Capt. Summers killed.

CHAPTER XIV.

CLOSE OF THE CIVIL WAR.

Grant in Command of the Union Army—Battle of the Wilderness—Gallantry of Cole's Cavalry—Early's Invasion of Maryland—Contributions Levied on Hagerstown and Frederick—The Distressed Citizens—Battle of Monocacy—Defeat of the Federals—Great Excitement in Baltimore and Washington—Operations of Confederate Cavalry—Assessing Farmers for Confederate Damages—Captures of Gens. Crook and Kelly in Cumberland—Peace.

WHILE the Army of the Potomac lay on the north of the Rapidan, Maj.-Gen. U. S. Grant, who had been made lieutenant-general, was assigned by President Lincoln, on the 10th of March, 1864, to the command of all the "armies of the United States." Gen. Meade was selected as his second in command of the Army of the Potomac, and to him was intrusted the execution of his plans. This portion of the army was consolidated into three corps, the Second, Fifth, and Sixth, commanded respectively by Gens. Hancock, Warren, and Sedgwick, and numbering, with Burnside's independent corps, about one hundred and forty thousand men. The Confederates under Lee numbered about sixty thousand men. By the consolidation of the Army of the Potomac on the 23d of March, 1864, into three corps, the Maryland Brigade, under Col. N. B. Dushane, of the First Maryland Regiment, became the Third Brigade in the Second Division of the Fifth Army Corps. Brig.-Gen. John C. Robinson commanded the division, and Maj.-Gen. G. K. Warren the corps. Gen. Kenly, much to the regret of his command, was assigned a district in the Middle Department. During the temporary absence of Col. Dushane (afterwards killed at the battle of Weldon Railroad) the command of the brigade devolved upon Col. Andrew W. Denison, of the Eighth Maryland Regiment.

On the 3d of May, 1864, Gen. Meade issued an address to his army, and on the following day it left Culpeper for the Rapidan. In the evening Meade reached that tangled forest where was fought, from the 5th to the 9th, the battle of the Wilderness, the most terrible and bloody of the war. In this series of bloody engagements, fought in a mass of tangled underwood, the Maryland Brigade took a conspicuous part in Warren's corps and met with severe loss. On Sunday, the 8th of May, with its division, they charged Longstreet's command, posted in a skirt of wood at Laurel Hill, near Spottsylvania Court-House, in the face of a galling fire of musketry and a storm of both canister and shell from both front and flank. The First, Seventh, and Eighth Maryland Regiments pushed on to within fifty yards of Longstreet's intrenchments, but the terrible fire poured into their depleted ranks forced them to retire, leaving the field covered with their dead and wounded. Gen. Robinson, their division commander, was wounded in the leg, and Col. Denison, who commanded the brigade, lost his arm. The command of the brigade then devolved upon Col. Charles E. Phelps, who had succeeded Col. E. H. Webster, elected to Congress. While gallantly leading his men into action, Col. Phelps was struck down within the Confederate line and was taken prisoner, but was afterwards recaptured by Custer's cavalry. Col. Richard M. Bowerman, of the Fourth Regiment, was then assigned command of the brigade. In consequence of the disabling wound of Gen. Robinson, his division was broken up, and the various regiments, with the exception of the Maryland Brigade, were assigned to other commands. The Maryland Brigade, as a light corps, was placed under the immediate command of Gen. Warren. It was employed in various duties until the 29th of May, when the old Second Division was reorganized, and the Maryland Brigade again became the Third Brigade, Second Division, Fifth Army Corps, which it retained until the 6th of June, when it was designated the Second Brigade of the same division and corps. Brig.-Gen. R. B. Ayres was assigned to the command of the division, and the Purnell Legion, Maryland Infantry, under Col. Samuel A. Graham, was joined to the brigade. In all the various battles in which their division was engaged, from Spottsylvania Court-House to the Chickahominy, which they crossed on the 14th of June, the Maryland Brigade bore a distinguished and active part, and suffered severe loss in killed and wounded. On the 16th, moving by way of Charles City Court-House, it crossed the James at Wilcox's Landing with the Second and Fifth Corps, and proceeded towards the lines near Petersburg, where it arrived early on the morning of the 17th.

While the Maryland Brigade was thus operating with Grant in his movements against Richmond, other Maryland commands were performing active service in other sections of the country. The Sixth Maryland Regiment of Infantry, under Col. Horn, was in the Sixth Corps, under the distinguished and lamented Gen. Sedgwick; and the Second and Third Regiments, in the Ninth Corps, under Gen. Burnside, on more than one occasion proved their patriotism by their valor. At the battle of Cold Harbor the Second and Third Regiments were in all the severe engagements in which the Ninth Corps participated, and was part of the rear-guard when Grant and his army crossed the James. On the 17th of June this brigade was ordered to charge the Confederate breastworks in front of Petersburg, and the command was successfully executed. They held the breastworks until late at night, when for want of support their whole line fell back to their former position.

At early dawn on the morning of the 10th of January, 1864, Mosby's Confederate battalion of cavalry made an attack upon the camp of Maj. Cole's Maryland cavalry, on Loudon Heights, Va. They avoided the pickets, dashed into the camp with a yell, and poured a volley of bullets into the tents where the officers and men were sleeping. The following is Maj. Cole's official report of this spirited affair:

"H'DQ'RS BATT'N P. H. B. CAV., MD. VOLS.,
"LOUDON HEIGHTS, VA., Jan. 10, 1864.
"WM. M. BOONE,
"Asst. Adjt.-Gen. First Division, Dept. West Virginia:

"SIR,—I have the honor of addressing you for the purpose of reporting the facts of an attempt by Maj. Mosby's battalion of guerrilla cavalry to surprise and capture my camp between the hours of three and four A.M. of this day. They studiously avoided my pickets, divided themselves into small bodies, which were speedily consolidated in sight of my camp; they then made an impetuous charge with a yell on the right of the same. In consequence of the suddenness of the same this company could offer but a feeble resistance. In the mean time Company A, the second in the line, was speedily rallied by its commanding officer, Capt. Vernon, who contested their further advance in such a sanguinary manner that formed a rallying-point for the balance of the command, who were now thoroughly aroused of the danger that threatened them, and one and all, from the officer to the private, entered into the contest with such a determined zest as led to the utter rout and discomfiture of the enemy and the signal failure of their base attempt. They experienced a loss of one captain, two lieutenants, and two privates killed, and two privates mortally wounded, and one prisoner; it was also very evident that they removed a large portion of their wounded with them in their precipitate flight, as a detachment of the command subsequently sent in pursuit found evidence of blood all along their line of retreat. I experienced a loss of four enlisted men killed and sixteen wounded. Capt. Vernon experienced a serious wound in the head, but it is the opinion of the battalion surgeon, W. R. Way, that it will not prove fatal. I am deeply indebted to the officers and men of my command for the daring displayed by them on this occasion, and earnestly commend them to the division commander for his favorable consideration.

"I have the honor to remain,
"Very respty yr. obt. servt.,
"HENRY A. COLE, *Major Commanding.*"

The following is a list of the killed and wounded of Maj. Cole's command, as shown by the report of the medical director:

"MEDICAL DIRECTOR'S OFFICE,
"HARPER'S FERRY, VA., Jan. 10, 1864.
"Brig.-Gen. J. C. SULLIVAN,
"Comdg. 1st Division, Dept. of West Virginia:

"SIR,—I have the honor to report the following list of killed and wounded in the Independent Battalion, Maryland Cavalry, Maj. Cole commanding, during an attack made on the camp on Loudon Heights, Va., by Mosby's and White's forces, at 3 A.M. of the 10th January, 1864:

"*Killed.*—Company B, Sergt. J. J. Kerns; Company D, Private George Burford.

"*Wounded.*—Company A, Capt. G. W. F. Vernon, wound of head and left eye; Ord.-Sergt. Zimmerman, flesh wound of the left leg; Private D. W. Carnes, gunshot compound fracture of right leg; Private H. F. Null, wound of abdomen; Private I. Craighton, flesh wound of left leg; Private E. Godwin, gunshot compound fracture of left leg; Private Samuel Stone, wound of abdomen.

"*Company B.*—Lieut. Samuel Rivers, flesh wound of left foot; Ord.-Sergt. J. C. Stouffer, flesh wound of left hip; Sergt. C. W. Ham, flesh wound of left arm; Private Samuel Rivers, gunshot compound fracture of left thigh; Private Gotlieb Foos, wound of shoulder and left lung; Private B. F. Filler, wound of right shoulder; Private A. Sosy, wound of abdomen.

"*Company C.*—Private Weaver, flesh wound of left thigh.

"*Company D.*—Private R. Cross, wound of right hip; Henry Howard, flesh wound of right thigh.

"The above I believe to be a correct list of the casualties.
"Very respectfully,
"Your obedient servant,
"WILLIAM HAYES, Surgeon U.S.V.
"*Medical Director.*"

For the gallantry displayed by Maj. Cole and his command upon this occasion the following complimentary orders were issued:

"HEADQUARTERS OF THE ARMY,
"WASHINGTON, D. C., Jan. 20, 1864.
"BRIG.-GEN. B. F. KELLEY, Cumberland, Md.

"GENERAL,—I have just received through your headquarters Maj. Henry A. Cole's report of the repulse of Mosby's attack upon his camp on Loudon Heights on the 10th instant. Maj. Cole and his command, the battalion of P. H. B. Cavalry, Maryland Volunteers, deserve high praise for their gallantry in repelling this rebel assault.

"Very respectfully,
"Your obedient servant,
"H. W. HALLECK, *General-in-Chief.*"

"HEADQUARTERS DEPARTMENT WEST VIRGINIA,
"CUMBERLAND, MD., Jan. 25, 1864.
"Respectfully transmitted to Brig.-Gen. Sullivan, commanding post:

"I take great pleasure in thus conveying to the officers and men of Maj. Cole's command this evidence of appreciation on the part of the general-in-chief of the gallantry displayed by them. B. F. KELLEY, *Brigadier-General.*"

"HEADQUARTERS FIRST DIVISION, DEPARTMENT WEST
"VIRGINIA, HARPER'S FERRY, VA., Jan. 26, 1864.

"Respectfully transmitted to Maj. Henry H. Cole, who will cause this communication to be read to his command. I take great pleasure in transmitting the thanks of the general-in-chief, which the command so richly deserve.

"JOHN C. SULLIVAN, *Brigadier-General Volunteers.*"

While Lee was defending his lines at Cold Harbor, Hunter was ravaging the Valley of Virginia and moving on Lynchburg, for the purpose of destroying the stores, manufactories, and railroad bridges at that place. Gen. Early, who had received orders on the 12th of June at Cold Harbor to move with two battalions of artillery and the infantry of Ewell's corps, numbering about nine thousand men, to destroy or disperse Hunter's force, arrived with his advance at Lynchburg on the 18th. In the mean time Gen. Breckenridge, who had been sent from Cold Harbor to Waynesboro' with a small force, by a forced march had arrived at the same place. Hunter with his command arrived before Lynchburg on the 18th of June, and made a slight attack on Early's lines, which was repulsed. Fearing that he would be cut off from his base, Hunter rapidly retreated during the night, closely pursued in the morning by Early and Breckenridge. He continued retreating across the mountains towards Charlestown, Kanawha, leaving Washington exposed. Lee, seeing the opportunity to make an attempt on the capital, and believing that such a demonstration might lead to the raising of the siege of Petersburg, telegraphed to Early whether, in his judgment, the condition of his troops would permit such a movement across the Potomac. Gen. Early determined to make the attempt, and immediately set about to carry out his plans. With a force of about twelve thousand men in rags, and many shoeless, he moved down the valley on the 28th of June from Staunton, and in spite of the intense heat and almost intolerable dust, advanced by forced march about twenty-five miles a day. He reached Winchester on the 2d of July, and on the 3d, dividing his force into two columns, he sent one under Breckenridge to drive Sigel out of Martinsburg, and with the other marched to drive Mulligan out of Leestown. Both columns were successful. Sigel retreated across the Potomac at Shepherdstown. Col. Bradley T. Johnson, who had been promoted to brigadier-general of cavalry, and assigned to the cavalry brigade of W. E. Jones, who was killed at New Hope, led the advance of Early's command, encountered Mulligan's advance, and after a severe fight drove them out of Leestown with loss. Gen. Weber, in command at Harper's Ferry, evacuated the town, and after destroying the bridges over the Potomac, retired to Maryland Heights. Early destroyed the Baltimore and Ohio Railroad, the Chesapeake and Ohio Canal, and boats along his line from Shepherdstown to Harper's Ferry.

On the 5th of July, Gen. Johnson with his cavalry crossed the Potomac at Sharpsburg, part going to Hagerstown and part to Boonsboro'. Breckenridge with his command crossed the Potomac the same afternoon, followed on the next day by the rest of Early's command. After receiving some stores, which he was greatly in need of, Early on the 8th of July marched twenty miles to Jefferson and Middletown, where he was joined by the cavalry, which had been scouting in the vicinity of Frederick.

The sudden and unexpected invasion of Maryland by the Confederate forces under Early created intense excitement in the State, especially in Frederick and in the Cumberland Valley.

The movements of the Confederates on the upper Potomac were not sufficiently developed to afford a clear estimate either of their force or intentions until the 6th of July, when a skirmish between the pickets took place about half-way between Frederick and Point of Rocks. The Confederates retired, leaving several of their men in the hands of the Federals, who gave the intelligence that the Confederates were advancing, and that it was not simply a raid, but an invasion in force with the purpose of capturing Washington or Baltimore.

On receipt of intelligence that the Confederates were crossing the Potomac, the inhabitants of the border towns of Pennsylvania were greatly alarmed. Hundreds of men, women, and children passed through York and Harrisburg on their way to the interior, and the roads were lined with horses, cattle, and wagons, loaded with goods and provisions, being driven in the same direction. Many hid their property and cattle in the mountains. The merchants in Chambersburg, Shippensburg, and Carlisle packed up their goods and valuables and shipped them to points of safety. The machinery in the shops of the Chambersburg Railroad Company was removed, and every precaution taken to prevent anything valuable falling into Confederate hands. The live-stock of the farmers in Adams, Fulton, and Cumberland Counties was all removed, and every train from Cumberland Valley moving eastward was crowded with refugees.

The Confederate cavalry, under Brig.-Gen. John McCausland, entered Hagerstown on the 6th of July, and took possession of the place. The United States quartermaster had in the mean time abandoned the town, with a large quantity of his stores and several hundred horses, and arrived safely at Carlisle. A large majority of the stores were closed and their contents removed.

As soon as McCausland found that he was in undisturbed possession of Hagerstown he requested an interview with the town council. As soon as this was had he presented them with the following order, and told them that if the demand was not complied with within a limited time the town would be laid in ashes:

"HEADQUARTERS CAVALRY BRIGADE,
"HAGERSTOWN, MD., July 6, 1864.
"*General Order No. ——.*

"1st. In accordance with the instructions of Lieut.-Gen. Early, a levy of 20,000 dollars is made upon the inhabitants of this city. The space of three hours is allowed for the payment of the sum in United States funds.

"2d. A requisition is also made for all government stores.

"3d. The following articles will also be furnished from the merchandise now in the hands of the citizens or merchants, viz.: 1500 suits of clothes, 1500 hats, 1500 pairs shoes or boots, 1500 shirts, 1900 pairs drawers, and 1500 pairs socks. Four hours allowed for their collection.

"The mayor and council are held responsible for the execution of this order, and in case of non-compliance the usual penalty will be enforced upon the city.

"JOHN MCCAUSLAND, *Brigadier-General C.S.A.*"

Upon receipt of this order a town-meeting was immediately called to assemble in the court-house, where the demand of Gen. McCausland was discussed; and it was decided that under the circumstances the town council should raise the money and as much of the clothing as it was possible for them to obtain within the time allowed. The money was soon raised, but it was found that it would be impossible to furnish the clothing. Additional time was asked in which to raise it, but McCausland was deaf to every appeal, and repeated his threat that if his demand was not complied with within the time specified he would lay the town in ashes. At last, however, when he found that there was a disposition on the part of the council and the people to furnish the required amount, he extended the time two hours, telling them that if his requisition was not filled by that time they knew what they had to expect. He then marched a regiment of his cavalry into the town, and stationed them in front of the court-house, as it was supposed, for the purpose of intimidating the citizens, or with a view of carrying out his threat, provided the money and goods were not promptly handed over at the hour stipulated. Every effort was put forth by the distressed citizens, and clothing of every hue and material was taken to the court-house, where it was placed in the hands of a committee, whose duty it was to hold it and transfer it to McCausland. The supply in town, however, was found to be sadly deficient, and the fact was soon announced to the Confederate leader, who swore to them that if it was not "forthcoming by the time specified he would carry out his threat, should it cost him his own life and that of his whole command." He told them that before doing so he would give them half an hour to remove the women and children from the town, and that they might expect no lenity at his hands. At last, through the influence of several members of his staff, to whom the citizens had appealed, he was induced to accept the twenty thousand dollars and the amount of clothing that they had raised. Upon receiving the following assurance, written on the bottom of the original demand, that the money and clothing was satisfactory, the ransom was handed over to McCausland:

"The town of Hagerstown having complied with the foregoing requisition by paying in cash twenty thousand dollars ($20,000), and having also furnished the specified articles therein mentioned to the utmost of their ability, I hereby certify to the facts, and place the town under the protection of the Confederate forces, releasing the citizens and their property from further contribution, and agreeing to shield both from further requirements.

[Signed]   "JOHN MCCAUSLAND, *Brig.-Gen. C.S.A.*

"Coats	243	Shoes	123
Pants	203	Hats	830
Drawers	132	Shirts	225
Hose	737	Piece Goods, 1370½ yards.	
Boots	99	Clothing, 70 pieces ass'd.	

"J. C. VAN FOSSEN, *Quartermaster.*"

Among the sufferers in Hagerstown whose stores were rifled were Messrs. Knodle and Small, shoe-dealers, and Messrs. Rourkulp and Updegraff, dealers in hats.

While the citizens of Hagerstown were occupied in complying with McCausland's demands, a number of prowling cavalrymen entered and plundered the drug-stores. At the same time other bodies were scattered over the country plundering stores, seizing horses and cattle, and destroying property in retaliation for Gen. Hunter's devastations in Virginia. In Williamsport, Sharpsburg, Boonsboro', and Middletown they entered the stores, and in some instances private dwellings, and carried off whatever suited their purpose. At Boonsboro' they also destroyed the printing materials of the *Odd-Fellow* newspaper, and in their march through the country they took wagons, horses, cattle, and sheep. A large steam distillery, about a mile and a half from Williamsport, belonging to Mr. Dahl, was fired and consumed.

After the money and clothing had been handed over to McCausland by the citizens of Hagerstown he left the place, marching in the direction of Middletown and Boonsboro'. On the next day (Thursday, July 7th) several squads of Confederates passed through the town, but no damage was done to any property, and no one was molested. On Friday morning, however, a band of guerrillas, numbering about one hundred and eighty men, under command of Maj. Davis, entered the town, and broke into a number of shoe- and hat-stores, helping themselves freely to their contents. They also set fire to the hay belonging to the United States government and to the Franklin Railroad depot, which were consumed. They were about to destroy a large quantity of oats and corn belonging to the government, stored in several private warehouses, when the citizens remonstrated with them, and called their attention to the fact that they had already paid the amount of indemnity demanded by McCausland and were ransomed.

This Davis' party was not satisfied with, but they consented to spare the warehouses, and perhaps the town, provided they were paid the sum of five hundred dollars, and that one of the citizens would give bond in one hundred thousand dollars that the grain would be burned, his life, besides, to be forfeited in case of default. Isaac Nesbitt, clerk of the court, agreed to the conditions and gave the requisite bond; and the people proceeded to carry out the grain and set it on fire in accordance with the terms. They then demanded ten pair of boots, with the understanding that on receipt of them they would vacate the place. This was agreed to; the boots were furnished, and the marauders left the place. On Saturday evening the town was occupied by Federal cavalry, and thus ended the raid on Hagerstown.

After Gen. Johnson with his brigade of cavalry had crossed the Potomac on July 5th at Shepherdstown, he moved through Sharpsburg, sending a scouting party in the direction of Hagerstown, and camped at Keedysville that night. The next day (the 6th) he moved through Boonsboro' by the turnpike and camped on the top of the mountain, between Boonsboro' and Middletown, in the gap which was the scene of Reno's attack, where ex-President (then Col. R. B.) Hayes was wounded, just before the battle of Sharpsburg, in September, 1862. On the 7th, being still held back by the orders of Maj.-Gen. Ransom, commanding Early's cavalry, who insisted upon his keeping within reach of the infantry, he made another slow movement towards Frederick. Early had passed part of his force over the Potomac on the evening of the 5th, and was manœuvring to oust the Federal force from Maryland Heights, being unwilling to expose his flank to it while moving on Washington, as well as to leave it in his rear.

In Middletown Johnson's advance came in contact with the Eighth Illinois Cavalry, Col. Clendenin, which had moved from Frederick on a reconnoissance. Col. Clendenin's force consisted of about three hundred of the Eighth Illinois, Cole's Maryland cavalry battalion, and two pieces of Alexander's Baltimore artillery. After a sharp skirmish the Federals were driven back, and made a stand on the top of the mountain between Frederick and Middletown. Gen. Johnson deployed the two Maryland battalions under Col. Harry Gilmor and pressed them on the Federal position, when Col. Clendenin, finding he was about to be flanked, withdrew into Frederick, the Confederates pressing hotly on his retreat, moving to within a mile of Frederick on the Hagerstown turnpike. Johnson's brigade consisted of about eight hundred effectives and the Baltimore Light Artillery with four guns.

As he passed the hamlet of Fairview, at the toll-gate he detached Lieut.-Col. Dunn with a Virginia regiment by the road that passes from the right of the road behind the estate of Prospect Hill to the Harper's Ferry road. Dunn passed rapidly down the road in a sweeping gallop, and turning into the Harper's Ferry road, moved sharply towards the city, pushing his dismounted skirmishers as far as Rizer's barn, and across through Mount Olivet Cemetery towards the Georgetown turnpike. These operations created the utmost excitement in the city. From early dawn on the 7th it was rumored in Frederick that the Confederates were only a short distance from the city, and that they would soon enter and occupy it. The arrival of couriers and wounded from the skirmish beyond Middletown, bringing the news that the force sent out to hold the Confederates in check until reinforcements arrived was unable to cope with them, and was slowly falling back towards Frederick, raised higher the alarm, and by noon business was suspended, stores closed, and many fled from the city. All the sick and stores were hastily removed. About half-past three o'clock the Federal forces came down the Hagerstown turnpike, and immediately took position on the edge of the city. It was an exciting time for the citizens of Frederick, as it was impossible to resist a direct assault upon the city with the light force at the command of Col. Clendenin. At this time, however, Gen. Wallace, the commander of the department, sent up from Monocacy Junction the Third Maryland Regiment, which was promptly marched to the front under Col. Gilpin, the senior officer present, who assumed command and disposed of his forces for battle. The whole force under his command at this time in defense of the city was the Third Maryland, seven hundred men; Eighth Illinois Cavalry, three hundred men; three pieces of Alexander's battery (Baltimore), about fifty men; and two companies of Col. Maulsby's Potomac Home Brigade, and Maj. Cole's Maryland cavalry.

About four o'clock the Confederates were to be seen from the roofs of the houses in Frederick coming down the Hagerstown road, and also the Harper's Ferry or Jefferson road, apparently in strong force. Capt. Alexander opened his battery upon the advancing foe, when they closed up and formed their line of battle on the west front of the city, covering the Harper's Ferry and Hagerstown roads, planting their guns on "Hogan's Hills" and the "Red Hills," and posting their cavalry in the valley formed between the two hills named and the Catoctin Mountains. The engagement opened about half-past four o'clock with an artillery duel between Alexander's guns in Zimmerman's fields and the Confederate guns on Hogan's Hill. The skirmishers soon advanced, and the sharp crack of musketry was heard for about two hours with no result on either side, when the Third Maryland Regiment was advanced and drove the Confederates out of Rizer's field, lying on the Harper's Ferry road, on the west side of the city, which they held for the remainder of the day. The two companies of Col. Maulsby's regiment supported the guns at the head of Patrick Street, and the Eighth Illinois Cavalry were dismounted and rendered effective service on the skirmish-line. During the artillery duel several shots from the Confederate batteries entered the heart of the city and did some damage. All the houses on the west side of the city were deserted, as they were in range of the Confederate guns.

The Confederate line of battle held its position, pushing its skirmishers along the front of the Federal line to conceal the movement Johnson was preparing to make by the reservoir road at the northwestern end, and by the Georgetown road at the southern end of the city. He was perfectly informed by his friends of the forces and condition of things within the Federal line, and he proposed sending in one regiment by the reservoir road, while Lieut.-Col. Dunn charged with his regiment down through Market Street, by the Georgetown road, and the main body moved directly on in front. This attack on both flanks and in front, he believed, would result in the capture of the entire force engaging him. Gen. Ransom, who was with Johnson's column, prohibited him from attempting to execute this plan, and ordered him to withdraw his troops to the top of the mountain as soon as night covered the movement.

Chagrined and mortified, Johnson saw a brilliant victory eluding his grasp and a substantial success thus escaping him, and sullenly withdrew about nine o'clock the night of the 7th. His headquarters during the engagement that afternoon had been on the range of hills not far from the house of George Wm. Smith.

All day of the 8th the Confederates lay inactive, leaving the garrison of Frederick in the greatest anxiety, which feeling was intensely shared by the administration at Washington.

Col. Clendenin and the Eighth Illinois Cavalry made another reconnoissance from Frederick by way of the Mountain or Shookstown road on the 8th, but were driven back with loss by Gilmor and the First and Second Maryland Cavalry. The head of Early's column of infantry reached Middletown the evening of the 8th, and the same evening Gen. Wallace, having assumed command at Frederick, ordered the evacuation of that place.

Hastily gathering the stores and ammunition, he forwarded them by rail to Monocacy Junction, and withdrew his forces by the turnpike road to the same place. The whole movement was executed quietly, and by midnight there was scarcely a Federal soldier in the city, except a few scouts who had been stationed to watch the movements of the Confederates.

The feelings of the Union people of Frederick when it became known that the Federal troops were about to evacuate the city, cannot be described. Hundreds left with the troops in every manner of conveyance, and many on foot. On the withdrawal of the Federal forces many of the Southern sympathizers made their way out the Hagerstown road and communicated the intelligence to the Confederates, who immediately entered the city with cavalry and hoisted their flag over the court-house. The capture was a barren victory, so far as military supplies were concerned, as everything in the way of stores, horses, ammunition, wagons, etc., belonging to the Federal government had been removed long previous to its evacuation. Nearly all the horses of citizens were sent away, and many people had sent their valuables to a point of safety. The banks had made ample arrangements to secure their property. The collector of internal revenue sent over seventy thousand dollars in his possession to Washington, and the Baltimore and Ohio Railroad Company secured all their rolling-stock and motive-power on the road.

On taking possession of Frederick the Confederates appointed a provost-marshal, etc., and on the morning of the 9th addressed the following communications to the authorities of the city:

"FREDERICK CITY, MD., July 9, 1864.

"HON. MAYOR,—I am directed by Lieut.-Gen. Early, commanding, to require of you for the use of his troops—

"(500) Five Hundred Barrels of Flour.
"(6000) Six Thousand Pounds of Sugar.
"(3000) Three " " " Coffee.
"(3000) " " " " Salt.
"(20,000) Twenty " " " Bacon.

"I am respectfully, Your Obt. Sert.,
"W. J. HAWKS, *Chief C. S. Army of Va.*"

"HD. QRS. V. D.
"FREDERICK TOWN, MD., July 9, 1864.

"By order of the Lieut.-Gen. Comdg.

"We require of the Mayor and Town authorities two hundred thousand dollars ($200,000) in current money for the use of this army. This contribution may be supplied by furnishing the Medical Depart. with fifty thousand dollars ($50,000) in stores at current prices, the Commissary Depart. with the stores to the same amount, the Ordnance Depart. with the same, and the Quarter Master Depart. with a like amount.

"WM. ALLEN, *Lieut.-Col. and Chief Ord. V. D.*
"W. J. HAWKS, *Chief Com. C.S.A., V. D.*
"HUNTER MCGUIRE, *Surg. and Med. Director.*
"JOHN A. HARMAN, *Maj. and Chief Q. M., V. D.*"

Mayor Cole called the members of the corporation remaining in the city together, and to save the city from threatened destruction it was decided to ransom it by paying the sum demanded. The amount was accordingly paid in "greenbacks" of various denominations, which were placed in baskets and removed to one of the wagons. When the ransom had been paid the following receipt was given:

"FREDERICK, July 9, 1864.

"Received of the Mayor, Aldermen, and Common Council of Frederick the sum of two hundred thousand dollars in full payment of said sum, which this day was levied and demanded to be paid to the Confederate States Army by said corporation of Frederick.

"J. R. BRAITHWAITE,
"*Major and Q. M.*"

The stores were visited by a number of the cavalrymen, who took what they wanted, in some instances offering Confederate currency in payment, but generally helping themselves without compensation. On Sunday Cole's cavalry had quite a skirmish on Patrick Street, opposite the City Hotel, with a portion of the rear-guard of the Confederates, who were moving out towards the Washington turnpike.

On the 5th of July, Governor Andrew G. Curtin, of Pennsylvania, made an urgent call for twelve thousand troops to repel the Confederate invaders, and volunteers not coming forward with the desired promptitude, he on the next day issued another proclamation, calling for twelve thousand men, in accordance with President Lincoln's proclamation, which required to meet the exigency twelve thousand men each from New York and Pennsylvania, and five thousand from Massachusetts, all to serve one hundred days. Gen. Grant, on learning that Early had crossed the Potomac, also detached the Sixth Corps from the Army of the Potomac and forwarded it by transports to Washington. It happened, too, at this juncture that the Nineteenth Corps under Gen. Emory, which had been ordered from New Orleans after the failure of the Red River expedition, had just arrived in Hampton Roads. Without debarking it was sent to follow the Sixth. The advance division of the Sixth Corps, under Gen. Ricketts, having arrived at Baltimore, Gen. Wallace, with that added to his own force, determined to cover the turnpike road leading to Baltimore and Washington, and to preserve communication with his forces at Harper's Ferry. With this view, after withdrawing his force from Frederick on the evening of the 8th, he took up a strong position on the east side of the Monocacy River, along the crest of a ridge running obliquely to the left from the river. The troops forming Ricketts' division of the Sixth Corps, which had arrived on the ground from the Army of the Potomac, were posted to the left of the railroad crossing the Baltimore turnpike, with their front resting on the Buckeystown road, while the remaining portion of Gen. Wallace's forces were posted to the right of the railroad. Gen. E. B. Tyler, with a small force, defended the turnpike bridge across the Monocacy. In Gen. Wallace's front lay an open field, which he commanded with his artillery, while in the rear ran a valley nearly parallel with the general direction of his lines of battle. About nine o'clock on the morning of the 9th, Gen. McCausland's cavalry brigade (dismounted) advanced and felt Wallace's line, but after considerable skirmishing they were driven back by superior numbers. McCausland occupied the attention of the Federal force until about noon, when the advance of Early's force, which had marched fourteen miles that morning from Middletown and Jefferson, arrived at the scene of action. Early determined, if possible, to disperse Wallace's command before he moved in the direction of Washington, and as soon as Breckenridge's corps arrived on the field the action began.

About 2.30 o'clock Maj.-Gen. John B. Gordon received orders to move his division, consisting of about two thousand five hundred men, to the right and cross the Monocacy about one mile below the bridge and ford (on the Georgetown pike), which was then held by the Federals. While he was carrying out this movement, Breckenridge was to occupy Wallace from the front on the opposite side of the river, with a portion of McCausland's cavalry, numbering about five hundred men. Gordon's division rapidly crossed the river, and then filed to the left to the point where McCausland's cavalry had been skirmishing. Gen. Gordon reconnoitred the Federal position, and as soon as he obtained the range of their lines he ordered his skirmishers, under Capt. Keller, of Evans' brigade, to deploy, and directed Evans' brigade, under the protection of a dense woodland about seven hundred yards in front of the Federals' left, to move by the right flank and form so as to overlap them. Gen. York, with the brigades of Hays and Stafford, was ordered to form on the left of Gen. Evans, and Terry's brigade to move in support of the left of Gordon's line. These dispositions having been made, Gordon advanced *en echelon* by brigades from the right. The troops emerged from the woods in front of the Federal left under a heavy fire of artillery and infantry. This force advanced but a short distance when Gen. Evans was struck down and several of his regimental commanders were killed, which threw his brigade into slight confusion. This, however, did not check their advance, for they forced Wallace to change his front under fire.

"At this point," says Gen. Gordon, "the Louisiana brigades, under the command of Brig.-Gen. York, became engaged, and the two brigades (Evans' and York's) moved forward with much spirit, driving back the enemy's first line in confusion upon his second. After a brief halt at the fence from which this first line had been driven, I ordered a charge on the second line, which was equally successful. At this point I discovered a third line, which overlapped both my flanks, and which was posted still more strongly in the deep cuts along the Georgetown road, and behind the crest of the hill near the Monocacy bridge, and at once ordered Brig.-Gen. Terry, who as yet had not been engaged, to attack vigorously that portion of the enemy's line nearest the river, and from which my troops were receiving a severe flank fire. This brigade advanced with great spirit and in excellent order, driving the enemy from his position on a portion of the line. He still held most stubbornly his strong position in front of the other two brigades and upon my right. He also advanced at the same time two fresh lines of troops to retake the position from which he had been driven by Terry's brigade. These were repulsed with heavy loss and in great confusion. Having suffered severe loss in driving back two lines, either of which I believed equal in length to my command, and having discovered the third line longer than either of the others, and protected by the cuts in the road, in order to avoid the great loss it would require to drive the enemy from his position by a front attack, I despatched two staff-officers in succession to ask for a brigade to use on the enemy's flank. Ascertaining, however, that a considerable length of time must elapse before these could reach me, I at once ordered Brig.-Gen. Terry to change front, with his brigade to the right, and to attack the enemy's right. This movement, promptly executed, with a simultaneous attack from the front, resulted in the dislodging of this line and the complete rout of the enemy's forces.

"The battle though short was severe. I desire in this connection to state a fact of which I was an eye-witness, and which, for its rare occurrence and the evidence it affords of the sanguinary character of the struggle, I consider worthy of official mention. One portion of the enemy's second line extended along a branch, from which he was driven, leaving many dead and wounded in the water and upon its banks. This position was in turn occupied by a portion of Evans' brigade in the attack on the enemy's third line. So profuse was the flow of blood from the killed and wounded of both these forces, that it reddened the stream for more than a hundred yards below."

Gen. Gordon's loss was heavy in both officers and men, amounting in the aggregate, as shown by reports of brigade commanders, to six hundred and ninety-eight. Among the killed were Col. J. H. Lamar, and Lieut.-Col. Von Valkenburg, both of the Sixty-first Georgia Regiment, of Evans' brigade. Lieut.-Col. Hodges, of the Ninth Louisiana Regiment, Hays' brigade, and several other regimental commanders were severely wounded. The Federal loss was about sixteen hundred killed, wounded, and missing. The retreat soon became a perfect rout, and the Confederate cavalry, pursuing closely, secured a large number of prisoners. All the Federal wounded and killed in the latter part of the action were abandoned where they fell. A great number of men, principally slightly wounded, managed to reach the train stationed at New Market, and were immediately sent to Ellicott's Mills, the Confederate cavalry following the retreating column to nearly the same point, at which Wallace made a stand with the remnant of his force the next morning. The following official reports of the battle show the part taken in this engagement by several of the Federal commands:

REPORT OF CAPT. F. W. ALEXANDER.

"CAMP NO. 24, BALTO. BATTY. LT. ARTY,
"NEAR BALTIMORE, July 13, 1864.

"SAMUEL B. LAWRENCE,

"A. A. G., 8th Army Corps:

"SIR,—In pursuance of orders, I have the honor to make the following statement regarding the fight at Frederick and the battle of Monocacy.

"At 1 A.M. Thursday, 7th, I received an order to send a section to Frederick to report to Lieut.-Col. Clendenin, Eighth Illinois Cavalry. Lieut. Leary, of the battery, reported at 4.30 A.M. with his section at Frederick to Lieut.-Col. Clendenin, and advanced at 6 A.M. along the road leading westward to Middletown. The enemy were encountered two miles this side of Middletown, and the section gradually retired towards Frederick. At 11 A.M. of the same day I received orders to go to Lieut. Leary's assistance with another gun and ammunition. I met them at 12.30 P.M., and with Col. Clendenin formed a line of defense on the edge of the town. The enemy opened on us with three guns about 4 P.M. About 6 P.M. we dismounted one gun, and began to silence their artillery fire. Shortly before dark Col. Gilpin, who on his arrival had assumed command, charged and forced back the rebels, and they appeared no more that night.

"On Friday, 8th, the battery was filled by the arrival of the remaining three pieces at 9 A.M. No engagement took place, except slight skirmishing on the Middletown road, but the battery was constantly on the move until 4 A.M. Saturday, 9th, when it returned to the Monocacy, somewhat short of ammunition, as the fire on Thursday had been continuous all day. On Saturday, 9th, at 9 A.M., I was ordered to place three guns on the hill beyond Monocacy towards Frederick, and commenced firing on the enemy as they advanced on both sides of the pike from Frederick. They soon returned with artillery, but with little effect. Finding this they proceeded around towards the left of our position, where the ground gradually rose in the distance, while on our side it sloped away. The other three guns were then placed on the hill on this side of the Monocacy, so as to meet their movement to our left. The enemy brought, as nearly as I can judge, about sixteen guns to bear on us, but, owing to the advantage of the ground, and the infantry preventing them from gaining ground to our left, where they could have commanded the battery, did but little damage, though some of their guns were of heavier calibre. (The guns of the battery are three-inch rifle.) When more guns of the enemy began to appear on our left with infantry, I moved two more guns from the hill on the right to the hill on our left. Finally, about 3 P.M., our troops made a charge, and drove them back, and they then uncovered their forces, and came on in about three lines, and forced our troops to retreat. Our ammunition almost gave out about 4 P.M., but the guns were kept in position until the order was given from Gen. Ricketts to retire by the Baltimore road. We moved out along the road at a walk, which led to the Baltimore pike, and I was ordered by Gen. Wallace at New Market to proceed along the road to Baltimore. Two of the guns were left in the rear to assist in guarding the column, though with little ammunition left, and joined the battery at Ellicott's Mills at 11 A.M., Sunday, July 10th, when I moved to Baltimore, as ordered, for ammunition and supplies. I cannot speak too highly of the conduct of the officers and men of the battery, viz.: Lieut. Evans, Lieut. Leary, and Lieut. Hall. Lieut. Alexander was absent as A. A. I. General on Gen. Kenly's staff. My loss was four men wounded and five horses killed, one caisson-body (empty), and the body of the battery-wagon left behind in order to attach a twenty-four-pounder howitzer, which did not belong to the battery, to the limber. I succeeded in bringing it safely to Baltimore, as also a mountain howitzer which had been used to defend the Monocacy bridge.

"I am, sir, very respectfully,
"Your obedient servant,
"F. W. ALEXANDER,
"Comdg. Balto. Battery of Light Artillery."

REPORT OF BRIG.-GEN. E. B. TYLER.

"HEADQUARTERS FIRST SEP. BRIG., EIGHTH A. C.,
"RELAY HOUSE, MD., July 14, 1864.
"LIEUT.-COL. SAMUEL B. LAWRENCE,
"Asst. Adjt.-General:

"COLONEL,—I have the honor, sir, to submit the following report of the part taken by my command in the late engagements at Frederick City and Monocacy Junction.

"On Thursday the 7th inst., Lieut.-Col. Clendenin, of the Eighth Illinois Cavalry, under the immediate orders of the major-general commanding, drew the enemy from the mountains west of Frederick City, and I reinforced him with three guns of Alexander's Maryland battery and the Third Regiment, Potomac Home Brigade, Maryland Volunteers, under Col. Charles Gilpin, then at Monocacy Junction. The promptness of these troops soon brought them in front of the enemy, who were occupying a commanding position a short distance west of the city. The action soon became warm and spirited, continuing some five hours, the enemy being handsomely repulsed just as darkness came upon us. The conduct of both officers and men was brave, gallant, and creditable. Col. Gilpin and Lieut.-Col. Clendenin conducted themselves in the most gallant manner, deserving great credit for their skill and efficiency from first to last. These officers speak in very high terms of the officers and men under them, and they deserve it all. The three guns of Alexander's battery were served splendidly under the command of Capt. Alexander, and I do but simple justice when I say that the officers and men are entitled to high esteem and admiration for their skill and bravery exhibited in this action.

"Receiving information that the enemy were being heavily reinforced, I went forward with the regiment, composed of companies of the One Hundred and Forty-fourth and One Hundred and Forty-ninth Ohio National Guard, commanded by Col. Brown, who took possession of the enemy's deserted lines soon after daylight Friday morning. The most of Friday was spent in cavalry skirmishing with the enemy, under the personal directions of Lieut.-Col. Clendenin, and was very efficiently done. I continued to receive reports during the day of the increasing strength of the enemy, which was communicated to the commanding general, who directed me to fall back on Monocacy Junction, which was successfully done during the night, leaving the One Hundred and Forty-ninth Ohio National Guards to hold the stone bridge across the Monocacy on the National or Baltimore pike.

"Saturday morning found us in line of battle, my command forming the right of the line, my left resting on the Baltimore and Ohio Railroad and connecting with Gen. Ricketts; the One Hundred and Forty-ninth Ohio National Guards and three companies of the One Hundred and Forty-fourth Ohio National Guards holding the extreme right, Col. Gilpin's Third Regiment, Potomac Home Brigade, Maryland Volunteers, and three companies of the First Maryland, Potomac Home Brigade, under Capt. Barnford, extending along the base of the hill, holding the ford between the stone bridge and junction, and the Eleventh Maryland, Col. Landstreet, completing my line. The enemy appeared directly in my front about 9 A.M., and opened on us with artillery, and attacked in considerable force our skirmish-line formed on the west bank of the Monocacy, and composed of the troops of the First Maryland, Potomac Home Brigade, under command of Capt. Brown. Three guns of Capt. Alexander's battery (three having been sent to Gen. Ricketts) and a twenty-four-pounder howitzer soon checked their advancing lines, and the action in my front, with the exception of sharpshooters and skirmish firing, was an artillery fight. This at times was quite spirited, continuing until near the close of the action. We maintained our position without serious loss.

"The conduct of Capt. Brown, of First Maryland, Potomac Home Brigade, and his command merits special notice; they successfully maintained their skirmish-line against a superior force to the close, and resisted several charges of the enemy.

"Capt. Alexander, with his officers and men, behaved in the most gallant manner, serving their guns with great coolness and effect. I desire particularly to call the commanding general's attention to their conduct during the three days we were in front of the enemy.

"The One Hundred and Forty-ninth Ohio and three companies of the One Hundred and Forty-fourth Ohio National Guards, under Col. Brown, considering their inexperience, behaved well, successfully resisting several charges of the enemy.

"Col. Gilpin's regiment, with the three companies of the First Maryland, Potomac Home Brigade, that were assigned him, although serving in detachments along an extended line, fully sustained the enviable reputation they had won on Thursday.

"The Eleventh Maryland was not brought into action, but was exposed for a time to the artillery fire of the enemy.

"The cavalry was placed under the direction of Lieut.-Col. Clendenin, who will furnish a separate report; and I would very respectfully call the attention of the major-general to this gallant and valuable officer and the officers and men serving under him. They certainly acquitted themselves with great credit.

"A force of the enemy's cavalry came down upon me while on the right of the line near the stone bridge, and forced me, Capt. Webb and Lieut. Goldsborough, of my staff, into the woods surrounding us, and, with their persistent watchfulness, prevented our following the column for nearly three days.

"To the officers of my staff—Capt. W. H. Wiegel, Capt. F. J. D. Webb, and Lieuts. Goldsborough, George W. Startzman, and R. E. Smith—I am greatly indebted for their untiring efforts and energy during the whole movement. Capt. Wiegel in the heat of the engagement took command of the twenty-four-pounder howitzer on the bank of the river, serving it with marked courage and ability, and with telling effect upon the enemy. His conduct must have been observed by the commanding general.

"I send you herewith a list of the casualties, as far as we are able to obtain them at this time.

"Very respectfully submitted,
"E. B. TYLER, *Brig.-Gen. Comdg.*"

REPORT OF CAPT. CHARLES J. BROWN, FIRST MARYLAND, POTOMAC HOME BRIGADE.

"HEADQUARTERS, FORT WORTHINGTON,
"July 20, 1864.

"CAPT. R. H. OFFLEY, A.A.G. Defenses of Baltimore.

"CAPTAIN,—I have the honor to submit the following report of my command at the battle of the Monocacy. My two companies, C and K, First Maryland Regiment, Potomac Home Brigade, were occupying at the commencement of the fight the block-house on the west side of the Monocacy, which I, in obedience to orders from the general commanding, evacuated and burned. I was then ordered to hold the bridge over the railroad on the Georgetown pike, one company of the Tenth Vermont Infantry and one company of the Ninth New York Heavy Artillery being added to my command. This position I held until the left of our army fell back, when, having received a discretionary order to fall back while I could do so with safety, I left my position, fell back across the railroad bridge, and occupied the rifle-pits on the east side of the Monocacy, covering the retreat of our army for a short time, and then following the line of march until my command was increased by Companies B, G, and H, First Maryland, Potomac Home Brigade, by being added to it at Ellicott's Mills, where I was furnished transportation to Baltimore, Sunday, July 10th, and ordered to report to Col. Gilpin, commanding First Separate Brigade, Col. Gilpin being in command of Fort Worthington. On Wednesday, July 13th, Col. Gilpin being ordered elsewhere, I was placed in command of the fort, which I now occupy with Companies B, C, G, H, and K of the First Maryland Regiment, Potomac Home Brigade.

"I have the honor to be
"Very respectfully,
"Your obt. servt.,
"CHARLES J. BROWN,
"*Capt. Comdg. 1st Md., P. H. B., Detcht. Inftry.*"

The loss of the Third Regiment, Potomac Home Brigade, at the battle of Monocacy was two killed, seven wounded, four missing, and ten captured.

After the defeat of Wallace the Confederates had everything their own way. Small parties traversed the country in every direction without opposition, collecting forage, grain, horses, and army supplies of all sorts. Gen. Early, after burying his dead and caring for his wounded at the Monocacy, on the morning of the 10th took up his line of march towards Washington, and made twenty miles that day, camping within four miles of Rockville.

On Sunday afternoon, July 10th, at about three o'clock, the Federal forces, numbering about twelve hundred, passed through Rockville, closely pursued by the Confederate advance, consisting of a brigade of cavalry, numbering some sixteen hundred, under the command of Gen. McCausland. Of this latter force several hundred constituted "pressmen," who scoured the adjacent farms in search of horses, which they appropriated "without money and without price." They made no distinction between citizens on the ground of sympathy.[1]

On Monday, the 11th, Early resumed his march, and appeared before the defenses of Washington on the Seventh Street pike. His force at this time had been reduced to eight thousand infantry, one thousand cavalry, and forty pieces of artillery, manned by about seven hundred men. The rest of his cavalry force had been detached at Frederick on the 9th, under Gen. Bradley T. Johnson, with special orders from Gen. Lee to destroy the communication between Baltimore and the north, threaten Baltimore, break the railroad and cut the telegraph wires between Baltimore and Washington, and thence move on Point Lookout, so as to attack on the morning of the 12th, when an attack was also to be made on the bay side, After releasing the prisoners, some fifteen thousand, Gen. Johnson was to take command of them and rejoin Early at Bladensburg, while that general was in the mean time to attack Washington and carry it by assault. As soon as Early's movements in the neighborhood of Washington were disclosed, however, Gen. Kenly, Gen. Rawlings, and most of the regular troops engaged in the defenses of Baltimore hastened to Washington and manned the fortifications.

Johnson moved his whole force to Cockeysville, and after destroying the bridges there he detached the First and Second Maryland Cavalry under Gilmor, and directed that officer to burn the railroad bridges over the Bush and Gunpowder Rivers. At Texas, Baltimore Co., on the line of the Northern Central Railway, the telegraph wires were cut and poles pulled down; the bridge above Cockeysville was destroyed and a portion of the track torn up; the Hanover bridge was destroyed, and two others south of the junction; the bridge at Ashland was burnt and the telegraph wires cut. After operating with the greatest boldness on the north of Baltimore, the Confederates pushed across the country, cutting the telegraph wires

---

[1] The damage done in the Medley district of Montgomery was greater than in any other part of the county. About fifteen hundred head of cattle were seized, which in some instances were paid for in Confederate money at the rate of twenty cents a pound. A few farmers saved some of their cattle by driving them into the woods. The merchants in Poolesville suffered heavily.

on the Harford and Philadelphia turnpikes. A small detachment came down Charles Street Avenue and burned the country house of Governor Bradford, five miles from Baltimore, with all his household furniture, valuable library, paintings, etc. This was done in retaliation for Gen. Hunter's destruction of Governor Letcher's residence at Lexington, Va., in his movement upon Lynchburg. The main body of the Confederate cavalry passed on by the Joppa road, and struck the Philadelphia Railroad at Magnolia Station, eighteen miles from Baltimore. Here they captured the morning express-train from Baltimore, turned the passengers out, and setting fire to the cars ran the train back upon the bridge over the Gunpowder River. The burning train set fire to the bridge, which was much damaged. In one of the cars Maj.-Gen. William B. Franklin, who was going North from Baltimore, was recognized and taken prisoner; but he afterwards escaped. The Confederates captured a way train, which they also destroyed. In their movements in the neighborhood of Baltimore, they visited Towsontown, Reisterstown, Relay House, Mount Washington, Texas, Randallstown, Union Bridge, and other points, helping themselves to whatever they fancied, especially horses.

In a recent narrative of the Maryland campaign of 1864, Gen. Johnson gives the following account of his subsequent operations:

"While these events were taking place I was pressing in hot haste through Howard and Montgomery Counties. I reached Triadelphia about nine o'clock that night, and unsaddled and fed my horses and let the men get a little sleep. By twelve o'clock I received information that a large force of Federal cavalry had gone into camp since my arrival at Brookeville, only a few miles out. I at once got ready and started to attack them, but on reaching the point found that they, too, had information of their unwelcome neighbors and had left. Thence I moved to Beltsville, on the railroad between Baltimore and Washington. There I found about one thousand cavalry of Wilson's division, which had been dismounted in a recent raid in lower Virginia and sent North to recuperate. They were mounted on green horses, and we drove them, after a short affair, down the road towards Bladensburg. It was now the morning of Tuesday, the 12th. I was due that night at Point Lookout, the extreme southeast point of Maryland, in St. Mary's County. It was physically impossible for men to make the ride in the time designated. I determined, however, to come as near it as possible. I sent an officer with a detachment to ride at speed through the country, impressing fresh horses all the way, and inform the people along the route that I was coming. They were unanimously my friends, and I requested them to have their horses on the roadside, so I could exchange my broken-down animals for their fresh ones, and thus borrow them for the occasion. During the preceding day I had been taking horses by flankers on each side of my column, and kept a supply of fresh ones at the rear of each regiment. As soon as a man's horse broke down he fell out of the ranks, walked until the rear of his regiment came up, got a fresh horse, left his old one, and resumed his place. By this means I was enabled to march at a trot, which with a cavalry column is impossible for any length of time without breaking down horses, and broken-down horses speedily break down men. With fresh horses, however, I hoped to make a rapid march and get to Point Lookout early on the morning of the 13th.

"After returning from the pursuit of Wilson's cavalry, I turned the head of the column towards Upper Marlboro', and had proceeded only a short time when I was overtaken by a courier from Gen. Early. He brought me orders to report at once to headquarters at Silver Spring, on the Seventh Street road. I moved down the Washington road to the Agricultural College, and thence along the line of the Federal pickets, marching all night, occasionally driving in a picket, and expecting at any moment to be fired upon from the works, within range of which I was moving. I reported to Gen. Early after midnight, and found the whole army in retreat. I was directed to close up the rear, with Jackson's cavalry brigade behind me. We reached Rockville during the day, where Jackson was pushed by the Second Massachusetts Cavalry, who hung on his rear and rendered things very uncomfortable generally. Finding matters getting disagreeable, I put in a squadron of the First Maryland, under Capt. Wilson G. Nicholas and Lieut. Thomas Grew, and charged into the town, scattering our pursuers, who got out of the way with expedition. Their dismounted men, however, stuck to the houses and fences and poured in a galling fire. The dust was so thick that the men in their charge could not see the houses in front of them. The horses of Nicholas and Grew were killed, and their riders wounded and taken prisoners. As soon as this loss was discovered, I put in another charge and recaptured Grew, but was unable to retake Nicholas, whom they had mounted on a spare horse and run off the field.

"During the rest of the 13th our pursuers treated us with more respect. All night long we marched and stopped, and stopped and marched, with that terrible tedious delay and iteration so wearing to men and horses, and it was not until Thursday, the 14th, we reached Poolesville. Here we were obliged to stand and keep back the pursuit while the infantry and artillery were passing over the Potomac. I got my artillery in position and deployed a strong skirmish-line in front of Poolesville, and checked the enemy for several hours. At last, in the afternoon, a wide line of skirmishers could be seen stretching far beyond each end of those we had been engaged with, and which moved steadily forward with a steady alignment very unusual for dismounted cavalry. I sent for Gen. Ransom to come up to my position, that the infantry had arrived, and that it was about time for the cavalry to leave. He soon joined me, and while we were looking at the advancing line through our glasses, which showed their cartridge-boxes and canteens plainly, puff! puff! puff! went their fire all along the line. There was no mistaking the sound. The swish of the minié-ball was so clear and so evident that it could not possibly come from carbines. We held on nevertheless, making a great show with the artillery and repeated attempts to charge them with cavalry, so that we delayed them until supports could deploy.

"By this time, however, the enemy had become far advanced, and having been notified that everything, including my own ordnance and baggage-train, had crossed, I withdrew comfortably and got into Virginia about sundown. We had been marching, working, and fighting from daylight, July 9th, until sundown, July 14th, four days and a half, or about one hundred and eight hours. We had unsaddled only twice during that time, with a halt of from four to five hours each time, making nearly one hundred hours of marching. We had isolated Baltimore from the North and cut off Washington from the United States, having made a circuit from Frederick to Cockeysville to the east, to Beltsville on the south, and through Rockville and Poolesville towards the west. We had failed in the main object of the expedition, which was to relieve the prisoners at Point Lookout, convert them into a new army, capture Washington, establish our communications across the Potomac by Manassas Junction with Gordonsville and Richmond, and by making this a new base of operations force Grant to let go his hold and come to the rescue of Pennsylvania. I have always considered the movement one the audacity of which was its safety, and that no higher military skill was displayed on either side than that shown by Gen. Early in this daring attempt to surprise the capital of his enemy with so small a force."

Early had arranged all his plans for an assault upon the defenses of Washington at daylight on the 12th, but during the night received a dispatch from Gen. Johnson informing him that the Sixth and Nineteenth Federal Corps had reached Baltimore some time before and were moving to the defense of Washington. This caused Gen. Early to defer his contemplated assault, and as soon as it was light he rode to the front and found the fortifications lined with troops in every direction. He therefore abandoned his design, and, as has already been stated, immediately sent an order to Gen. Johnson to join him without delay, which he did early the next morning at the house of Francis P. Blair, Sr., Silver Springs, Montgomery Co.

During Gen. Early's absence from Virginia, Gen. Hunter had been plundering, burning, and laying waste, in his usual style of warfare, without check. The Federal troops had also burned and devastated towns and villages in other parts of the South, and, as far as could be seen, public sentiment at the North approved this mode of conducting the war. Gen. Early therefore determined to follow these examples by way of retaliation. Chambersburg, in Pennsylvania, was selected for the sacrifice, and thither Gen. McCausland was ordered to proceed with his cavalry brigade and that of Gen. Bradley T. Johnson and a battery of four guns, and demand of the municipal authorities the sum of one hundred thousand dollars in gold, or five hundred thousand dollars in United States currency, as a compensation for the wanton outrages of Gen. Hunter in the Valley of Virginia, and in default of payment to lay the town in ashes. On the 29th of July, McCausland crossed the Potomac near Clear Spring, above Williamsport, while Vaughan drove a cavalry force from Williamsport and entered Hagerstown, where he captured and destroyed a train of cars loaded with supplies. Several infantry divisions also crossed the Potomac at Shepherdstown, and took positions at Sharpsburg, to be within supporting distance. On the 30th of July, McCausland reached Chambersburg, and made the demand as directed. It was not complied with, and the greater part of the town was burned.

McCausland then moved in the direction of Cumberland, but finding it defended by a force under Gen. Kelley, after a slight skirmish at Folck's Mill, about two miles from the town, withdrew towards Hampshire County, Va., and crossed the Potomac near the mouth of the South Branch. He then moved to Moorefield, in Hardy County, where he was overtaken by Gen. Averill, who had been in pursuit since he left Chambersburg, and his entire command was routed and his four pieces of artillery captured. The remnants of the command finally made their way to Mount Jackson in great disorder.[1]

On Saturday, August 6th, business was still suspended in Cumberland, and a feverish uncertainty pervaded the public mind as to the whereabouts and intentions of the Confederates. Official information told, however, that the force which attacked New Creek was retreating towards Moorefield, pursued by the Federals.

The railroad west was intact, trains running regularly, and in a day or two trains were expected to run east to Hancock, the road having sustained no damage this side of Sleepy Creek. The residents in the neighborhood of Flintstone had had another scare, caused by a report that the Confederates had again made their appearance at Green Spring, but the newcomers proved to be Federals.

On Sunday, the 7th, the city wore its usual Sabbath sedateness. The war rumors were numerous. One placed Gen. Breckenridge in strong force at Romney, while a contradictory report said Averill was there; another said Breckenridge was making for Beverly, W. Va.; another asserted that Early had crossed the Potomac and established his headquarters at Hagerstown. On Sunday night a detachment of Averill's and DeFoe's cavalry reached Cumberland from Hancock, bringing fifteen Confederate prisoners. On Monday, the 8th, a new excitement seemed to have possessed a portion of the citizens, who packed up and sent off their goods, under the stimulus of a report that the Confederates had again entered Maryland.

Monday afternoon the One Hundred and Fifty-second Ohio Regiment, Col. Putnam, paraded the

---

[1] When it was known that McCausland was approaching Cumberland the citizens made determined preparations for defense. Gen. Kelley's force was a small one, composed of a few regulars and some hundred-day men from Ohio. A meeting of the citizens was held at the market-house, and three companies were organized on the spot, under Gen. C. M. Thruston, and were united with the command of Gen. Kelley.

streets, and in the evening a meeting of the citizens was held to make preparations for a demonstration of gratitude to the military for their noble and successful defense of the city on Monday, the 1st, Gen. Kelley having, in compliance with the request of the mass-meeting, designated Thursday as a convenient time for a street parade.

On Tuesday, August 9th, the city was unusually quiet, but some of the merchants continued to ship their goods, feeling that Cumberland was even then a very unsafe place. A train that day went east, loaded with lumber, workmen, and a guard, with a view to repair bridges, etc., along the line. The citizens were greatly elated at the confirmation of the rout of McCausland's and Bradley T. Johnson's forces by Gen. Averill, and the recapture of horses and a large amount of plunder, and were likewise pleased that Gen. Sheridan had been placed in command of the division of the country embracing the departments of West Virginia and Susquehanna and the Middle Department.

Thursday, August 11th, was a day of jubilee in Cumberland. Assurances the day before by telegraph that the Confederates had all left Maryland allayed considerably the fears of the business men, some of whom began to bring back their goods. Flags floated in all directions, and preparations were going on for the grand demonstration of thanks to the military, Gen. Kelley having appointed a parade for the afternoon, at the request of the citizens through their town-meeting held on the 5th.

According to the programme, the troops stationed at the post, and who participated in the late defense of the city, were drawn up in line on the old race-ground. Gen. Kelley having arrived on the ground, the review took place, in which the citizen-soldiers were assigned their position. After passing in review they resumed their position in line; the column was then brought into close column, and the thanks of the people of Cumberland tendered to the brave defenders.[1]

In consequence of the sympathy displayed by certain persons in Frederick County towards the command of Gen. Early and his troops, Gen. Hunter issued the following characteristic order:

"HEADQUARTERS DEPARTMENT WESTERN VIRGINIA,
"HARPER'S FERRY, July 18, 1864.

"MAJ. JOHN I. YELLOTT, First Maryland P. H. B. Infantry, Commanding officer, Frederick, Md.:

"MAJOR,—Your communication of this date relating to persons in Frederick City, Md., having 'pointed out to the rebels during their late raid the property of Union citizens, and otherwise manifested their sympathy with the enemy,' has been submitted to the major-general commanding the department.

"In reply he directs that you arrest at once all persons who are known by Union citizens to have given such information, and to send them, with their families, to this place under suitable guard, that the males may be sent to the military prison at Wheeling, W. Va., and their families beyond our lines South. You will seize their houses, to be used for hospitals, government offices, and store-houses, and for government purposes generally. Their furniture you will have sold at public auction for the benefit of Union citizens of the town who are known to have suffered loss of property from information given by these persons.

"The major-general commanding further directs that all male secessionists in Frederick, with their families, must be sent here at once. You will make the same disposition of their houses and furniture as has been directed already in this letter for the houses and furniture of those who gave information as to the property of Union men.

"I am, major, very respectfully,
"Your obedient servant,
"P. G. BIER,
"Assistant Adjutant-General."

"To prevent infliction of such punishment as is specified in the above order, it is ordered that every male citizen of this town, and that portion of Frederick County lying within the limits of the department of West Virginia, shall appear at this office between the hours of eight o'clock A.M. and five o'clock P.M, beginning on the 25th day of July, 1864, and ending on the 30th day of July, 1864, and subscribe to an oath of allegiance to the government of the United States. In default of thus appearing and swearing allegiance to the national government, all persons thus failing will be regarded as secessionists and treated as directed in the above order.

"JOHN I. YELLOTT,
"Major Commanding Post and Provost-Marshal."

In pursuance of this order many of the most respectable citizens of Frederick County, male and female, were seized and imprisoned or driven from their homes and sent within the Confederate lines.

It having been alleged that the Confederates during their invasion of the State had destroyed the barn of one Thomas Harris, Gen. Wallace assessed the following persons residing in the Liberty District, Frederick County, for the amounts set opposite their respective names to indemnify him for his loss:

James Pearre	$1296.30
William Hobbs	1037.04
Anthony Kimmel	518.52
Luther Welch	388.89
Thornton Pool	388.89
Dr. G. R. Sappington	194.45
Jesse Devilbiss	194.45
Henry Clary	259.26
George Gaither	259.26
John D. Gaither	194.45
C. A. Lawrence	259.26
C. W. Dorsey	259.26
Thomas G. Maynard	194.45
William G. Wilson	129.63
John P. Devilbiss	324.08
Milton Carter	129.63
Dr. Thomas W. Simpson	64.82
Joseph Smith	64.82
Henry A. Peddicord	64.82
Hamilton Lindsay	64.82

---

[1] Lowdermilk's "History of Cumberland."

John G. Norris	$129.63
Thomas H. Hammond	194.45
D. V. Hammond	129.63
R. Emory Simmons	64.82
James H. Steele	194.45

With McCausland's raid hostile operations in Western Maryland virtually ceased, and with the exception of a brilliant dash by the Confederates into Cumberland in the winter of 1865, little more of military importance occurred in that section during the remainder of the war.

After the death of Capt. John Hanson McNeill, mortally wounded near Mount Jackson bridge, in the Valley of Virginia, Oct. 4, 1864, in a charge on a company of the Twelfth Pennsylvania Cavalry, his son Jesse, first lieutenant of the company, determined to capture Maj.-Gens. Crook and Kelley, then in command of the Federal forces at Cumberland.

S. S. Lynn, a native of the place, having previously penetrated into the very heart of the city on four different occasions, obtained thorough information as to the number of troops in Cumberland, the location of the various headquarters, pickets, etc., and reported to Maj. Harry Gilmor, stationed at Moorefield, W. Va. John B. Fay and C. Ritchie Hallar, a young Missourian, were sent by McNeill to procure similar information, which they obtained through George Stanton, in the employ of the Baltimore and Ohio Railroad Company. With this fund of knowledge they returned and reported the facts to Lieut. McNeill. The command, then in camp ten miles north of Moorefield, was ordered about noon on the 21st of February, 1865, to march rapidly towards Cumberland, a distance of fifty miles. Crossing the South Branch of the Potomac near Romney, and feeding their horses at the house of Boss Herrod, a farmer, the command crossed Middle Ridge and struck the Nobley Mountain road at its base, and crossed the mountain to the North Branch of the Potomac at a point five miles from Cumberland. Here the command was halted almost within pistol-range of a cavalry picket. A portion of the command, composed of Lieut. McNeill, Fay, Lynn, Vandiver, Kuykendall, Dailey, and Nichols, went to the house of S. D. Brady, where a consultation was held. Here it is alleged McNeill's courage failed him, and he proposed to capture the pickets and return, and gave as a reason that he was afraid it was too late to do more than this before daylight.

Fay and Lynn vehemently opposed this, and the command was speedily pushed forward again. Lynn here took the advance alone, with the advance-guard in hailing distance in his rear. Just below the three-mile water-station on the Baltimore and Ohio Railroad the first cavalry picket post, composed of three men, was encountered. "Halt! Who comes there?" "Friend, without the countersign, bearing important dispatches to Gen. Kelley," was Lynn's response. "Dismount, advance, and give the countersign." The words hardly escaped the sentinel's lips before Lynn dashed by the astonished picket and reined up where the two in reserve were quietly sleeping, who were ordered to surrender, which they promptly did. Putting a pistol in each boot, the prisoners were halted in the road until the command came up. A pistol-shot fired by McNeill at the first sentinel passed had but one meaning, which was to retrace their steps; and again the proposition was made, and as promptly repelled by Fay and Lynn. With one voice the whole sixty-five men, composed of Marylanders and Virginians, whispered, "Go ahead; we will follow." At this juncture the command virtually devolved on Fay and Lynn, and the command was ordered forward. Lynn again placed himself in the advance, and at the junction of the river road and the old pike the second picket post was encountered. Again rang out on the frosty air, "Halt! Who comes there?" "Friend, with the countersign." "Dismount, advance, and give the countersign," demanded the sentinel on duty. The countersign having been obtained from the three first pickets, Lynn dismounted, and leading his horse walked to the sentinel and whispered "Bull's Gap" in his ear. "All right," replied the sentinel. Lynn then ordered the advance forward, and quickly the astonished infantry pickets, six in number, were ordered to surrender, which summons they promptly obeyed, and trying the ramrod in each barrel of the guns, it was discovered that every gun was empty, and that the hammer of the pistol of the first sentinel could not be raised. The guns were placed on the comfortable log fire burning in front of their quarters and destroyed, and the command again ordered forward.

Lynn here overheard a conversation between McNeill, Kuykendall, and Vandiver, placing the former in command of a party of ten men to secure Gen. Kelley, and the latter, with ten men, to secure Gen. Crook, the previous arrangement being that Lynn was to capture Kelley, and Fay, Crook, a compensation for services rendered as scouts. Lynn communicated these facts to Fay, who was so incensed at the duplicity practiced that he simply remarked, "I can stand it if he can."

Passing down Green Street, a company of regulars were passed who were encamped in an old brick house on the Potomac, near the present water-works. As the command moved forward an interchange of words passed as to the state of the weather, their destination, etc. Reaching the iron bridge across Will's Creek,

Lynn selected John Dailey, Charles Nichols, and Charlyle to accompany him on foot up Baltimore Street. Their horses were led by friends in the command, and hurrying ahead of the command, Lynn and his followers hastened to the St. Nicholas Hotel.

Leaving the men at the steps of Alpheus Beall's, he went alone to the hotel. Here he saw an orderly sergeant leaning against the railing at the entrance of the house. Across George's Street he also discovered the sentinel pacing his beat in front of Gen. Kelley's headquarters at the old Barnum House. How to capture the sergeant without being observed by the sentinel was the question to solve. The thought then flashed into his mind that the advance of the column would naturally attract the sergeant's attention, and he would advance to the curbstone to ask questions, etc. So Lynn walked to the curb and awaited results. Soon the tramp of horses was heard, and the sergeant took up his position alongside of Lynn, who, placing his left hand on his shoulder, covered him with his pistol and ordered him to surrender, which he did by saying, "I have no arms." Lynn told him to lead him to Kelley's room, and being joined by his companions, they proceeded across the street, walked up to the sentinel, disarmed him, and entered the hall leading to the general's room. Ascending the stairway and reaching the top, the sergeant said, "Through this door you will enter Adjutant Thayer Melvin's room, and through a door in his room you will enter the general's." Lynn opened the door, and to the left lay the sleeping form of the adjutant. Stepping to his bedside, Lynn caught him by the shoulder, raised him up, and ordered him to speedily dress, that he was a prisoner in the hands of the Confederates. A guard was left with him, and Lynn then entered the general's room, and found him sound asleep. Rousing him in like manner, the general indignantly demanded what he wanted. Lynn then introduced himself, and taking in the situation the general made a hasty toilet, and the two were guarded to the pavement below, where both were mounted up behind some of the men.

Meantime a similar scene was being enacted at the Revere House, where General Crook was sleeping in fancied security. James Dailey sent word that he had secured Gen. Crook, soon joined the command, drawn up in line in front of the old Barnum Hotel, and the command was ordered to retrace their steps down Baltimore Street. Lynn mounted his horse and rode rapidly down the street to the stables near the bridge, where the staff horses were quartered. Riding into the yard he secured the sentinel guarding the stables, and calling to the men, they secured eight of the finest horses, among them Gen. Kelley's horse "Philippi." Taking the tow-path, they encountered about twenty pickets stationed at the dam, whom they captured, throwing their arms into the river. Reaching Wiley's Ford, three miles below town, they were halted by another picket, who was stationed behind a stone wall leading to the bridge across the canal. The fourth time the sentinel called upon the retreating Confederates to halt he called to the sergeant of the guard, and said, "Sergeant, I have halted four times; they won't stop; I am going to shoot." The sergeant then stepped forward and said, "Who are you?" "Gen. Crook's body-guard on a scout; in a hurry; 'rebs' near town." The sergeant replied, "All right; go ahead and give them hell." Passing quickly under the bridge and across the river, orders were given to keep well closed up, and a guard placed in the rear to prevent straggling. Shortly after the departure the alarm was given and a company of mounted men went in pursuit. The fugitives were overtaken near Romney, and a skirmish followed, but the prisoners were beyond recapture. Taking the old Trough Hollow road, the command soon came in sight of Moorefield, where they had hoped to exhibit the prisoners to the people of that hospitable town and procure supplies. Their attention being attracted across the river, it was soon discovered that a force had been sent from New Creek to intercept them and, if possible, recapture the generals. Lynn was ordered to the ford at the river to hold them in check until the command, by a flank movement to the left, gained the mountain and left Moorefield far to the right. The Federals drove Lynn and his men, who kept the road, before them to Moorefield, and thus the recapture of the generals was frustrated. This event caused much excitement throughout the country, and was commented upon largely in every direction. The captured officers were sent to Richmond, and shortly afterwards exchanged.[1]

The capture of Gens. Crook and Kelley was one of the last exploits of the war. On the 3d of April, 1865, Gen. Lee's lines at Petersburg were broken, and on the 9th the remnant of the Confederate army was surrendered to Gen. Grant at Appomattox Court-House. Five days after the surrender of Lee the country was shocked by the intelligence of the assassination of President Lincoln and the attempted murder of members of his cabinet. The news was received in Western Maryland, as it was throughout the land, with a universal feeling of regret and indignation, and men of all parties joined heartily in deploring the untimely end of the Chief Magistrate of

---

[1] Lowdermilk.

the nation, and in denouncing the crime of which he was the victim.

The excited state of feeling growing out of the assassination of the President and the return of Confederate paroled prisoners led in Baltimore and elsewhere to intemperate measures, and it was therefore considered desirable to define the legal status and rights of those who had recently been serving in the armies of the Confederacy. At the request of the War Department, Attorney-General Speed, on the 24th of April, 1865, gave an opinion in regard to certain paroled Confederate prisoners whose homes before the war had been in the States north of the Potomac. By the terms of the agreement entered into by Gens. Grant and Lee, all the officers and men of Lee's army were to be allowed to return to their homes, and were not to be disturbed by the United State authorities so long as they observed their parole and the laws in force at the place of their residence.

Attorney-General Speed, however, held that this agreement did not apply to Confederate soldiers from Maryland and other States north of the Potomac, and in accordance with this opinion Maj.-Gen. Wallace issued an order directing the commanding officers and provost-marshals in the Middle Department to arrest and hold in confinement all Confederate officers, soldiers, and citizens who had returned to their former homes to await exchange, and to report each case to headquarters for such disposition as might be directed by the government at Washington. In accordance with this order a large number of ex-Confederates were arrested "for coming into this department without authority," and upon taking the oath of allegiance were sent North, where they were tolerated. On the 18th of July, 1865, Gen. Winfield S. Hancock assumed command of the Middle Department, embracing the States of West Virginia, Pennsylvania, Delaware, and Maryland, excepting the counties of Anne Arundel, Prince George, Calvert, Charles, and St. Mary's. On the 2d of August, Gen. Hancock issued an order requiring "paroled prisoners of the late rebel armies who have not been pardoned by the President of the United States," upon arriving within the limits of the department, to report their presence and residence immediately to the nearest provost-marshal and register their names, and announcing that paroled prisoners non-residents of the department would not be allowed to remain in it without the sanction of the department commander or higher authority.

On the 12th of January, 1866, another military order was issued, in which it was announced that,—

"The provost-marshal's office will cease to exist in this command on the 31st of January. Brevet Brig.- Gen. John Woolley, United States Volunteers, provost-marshal, will take measures to close the books and records pertaining to his office upon that date, and turn them over to the adjutant-general of the department." In accordance with this order all the books, papers, and records of the office of the provost-marshal-general of the Middle Department of the Eighth Army Corps were turned over on the 31st of January, 1866, to Adam E. King, brevet colonel, adjutant-general of the Middle Military Department. The closing of the provost-marshal's department in Baltimore closed the reign of the military commanders in Maryland. President Johnson had, on June 23, 1865, rescinded the blockade proclamations issued April 15 and 17, 1861; on Aug. 29, 1865, he had removed further restrictions, and on the 1st of December following he annulled the suspension of the writ of *habeas corpus*, and finally, on the 2d of April, 1866, formally announced by proclamation that the Rebellion had ended.

CHAPTER XV.

RECORD OF MARYLAND VOLUNTEERS IN THE UNION ARMY IN THE WAR OF 1861-65.

General Statistics.—From the beginning to the close of the late civil strife the number of organizations put into the service of the United States by the State of Maryland was three regiments, two battalions, and one independent company of cavalry, six batteries of light artillery, and nineteen regiments and one independent company of infantry. There were also three incomplete regiments,—viz.: the Baltimore (or Dix) Light Infantry, Fourth Potomac Home Brigade, and the original Fourth Infantry, or German Riflemen,—which having failed to perfect an organization were consolidated with other commands.

This entire force, with the respective original commanders and the term of service for which mustered, is thus enumerated:

Three Years.

First Cavalry, Col. Andrew G. Miller.
First Cavalry (Potomac Home Brigade), Col. Henry A. Cole.
Third Cavalry (Bradford Dragoons), Col. C. Carroll Tevis.
Purnell Legion Cavalry (three companies), Capts. Robert E. Duvall, Thomas H. Watkins, and Theodore Clayton.
Independent Company Cavalry, Capt. G. W. P. Smith.
Battery A, Light Artillery, Capt. John W. Wolcott.
Battery B, Light Artillery, Capt. Alonzo Snow.
Battery D, Light Artillery, Capt. John M. Bruce.
Baltimore Battery Light Artillery, Capt. F. W. Alexander.
First Infantry, Col. John R. Kenly.

[1] First Infantry (Potomac Home Brigade), Col. William P. Maulsby.
First Infantry (Eastern Shore), Col. James Wallace.
Second Infantry, Col. John Sommer.
Second Infantry (Potomac Home Brigade), Col. Thos. Johns.
Second Infantry (Eastern Shore), Col. Edward Wilkins.
Third Infantry, Col. John C. McConnell.
Third Infantry (Potomac Home Brigade), Col. S. W. Downey.
[2] Fourth Infantry (German Rifles), Capt. Joseph M. Sudsburg.
Fourth Infantry, Col. W. J. L. Nicodemus.
[2] Fourth Infantry (Potomac Home Brigade) Lieut.-Col. Geo. R. Kennis.
Fifth Infantry (Public Guard Regiment), Col. W. Louis Schley.
Sixth Infantry, Col. George R. Howard.
Seventh Infantry, Col. Edwin H. Webster.
Eighth Infantry, Col. Andrew W. Denison.
Purnell Legion Infantry, Col. William H. Purnell.
[2] Dix Light Infantry, Lieut.-Col. Thomas B. Allard.
Independent Company Infantry (Patapsco Guards), Capt. T. S. McGowan.

One Year.

Eleventh Infantry, Col. John G. Johannes.

Six Months.

Second Cavalry (battalion), Capt. W. F. Bragg.
Battery A, Light Artillery (Junior Artillery), Capt. John M. Bruce.
Battery B, Light Artillery (Eagle Artillery), Capt. Joseph H. Audoun.
Ninth Infantry, Col. Benjamin L. Simpson.
Tenth Infantry, Col. William H. Revere, Jr.

One Hundred Days.

Eleventh Infantry, Col. William T. Landstreet.
Twelfth Infantry, Lieut.-Col. John L. Bishop.

In the foregoing commands, as original members or as recruits, there was, according to the records of the provost-marshal-general's office, an aggregate of thirty-seven thousand nine hundred and twenty men. In addition to these there were eight thousand seven hundred and eighteen colored soldiers recruited in the State, making a total of forty-six thousand six hundred and thirty-eight. These figures of course do not include the men who enlisted in the navy and marine troops, nor those who paid commutation money and were thereby exempted from service. Of the former class there were two thousand two hundred and seventeen, and of the latter three thousand six hundred and seventy-eight. The enlistments in the naval service and marine corps, added to the military force, gives a grand aggregate of forty-eight thousand eight hundred and fifty-five men furnished by the State.

The number of veterans who re-enlisted at the expiration of their first term of service was two thousand five hundred and eighty-one.

---

[1] Designation changed to Thirteenth Infantry, April 8, 1865.
[2] Failed to complete its organization.

The Fourth, Seventh, Ninth, Nineteenth, Thirtieth, and Thirty-ninth United States Colored Infantry Regiments and Battery B of the Second Light Artillery were wholly recruited in Maryland. Besides these, many men enlisted in the State were assigned to regiments raised elsewhere. The regiments thus receiving recruits from Maryland were the First and Second Cavalry, First, Second, Sixth, Eighth, Tenth, Twenty-third, Twenty-eighth, Twenty-ninth, Thirty-first, Thirty-sixth, Thirty-eighth, Forty-first, Forty-fourth, Forty-fifth, One Hundred and Second, One Hundred and Ninth, One Hundred and Fourteenth, One Hundred and Fifteenth, and One Hundred and Sixteenth Infantry. In the Twenty-eighth, Twenty-ninth, and Thirty-eighth Regiments Maryland was largely represented.

These organizations were mustered directly into the service of the United States, and were commanded by officers acting under the authority of the general government, and not of any particular State. But few Marylanders held commissions in this branch of the service.

The credits allowed for men furnished under the different calls were as follows:

Under the call of—
May 3, 1861, and calls under acts approved July 22 and 25, 1861, for three years' service	9,355
July 2, 1862, for three years	3,586
June 15, 1863, for six months	1,615
Oct. 17, 1863, for three years	6,244
March 14, 1864, for three years	9,365
April 22, 1864, for one hundred days	1,297
July 18, 1864, for one, two, or three years	10,235
Dec. 19, 1864, for one, two, or three years	4,941
Sailors and marines not credited to specific calls	2,217
Aggregate	48,855

Of this number, forty-four thousand nine hundred and seventy-three were volunteers, one thousand four hundred and twenty-six drafted men, and two thousand four hundred and fifty-six substitutes.

Reduced to a three years' standard, this force aggregated forty-one thousand two hundred and seventy-five.

The casualties by death and discharges for disability on account of wounds or disease contracted in service among the white soldiers were as follows:

	Officers.	Men.
Killed or died of wounds received in action	45	685
Died of disease or other causes	32	1147
Discharged for disability	165	1224

Among the enlisted men of colored troops, composing the six regiments of infantry and one battery of artillery, organized exclusively in Maryland, the casualties in battle were 193 killed or died of wounds and 868 wounded.

Battle List.[1]

Aldie, Va., June 19, 1863, First Cavalry.
Alpine Depot, Va., Jan. 4, 1862, First Cavalry.
Amissville, Va., Oct. 12, 1863, First Cavalry.
Antietam, Md., Sept. 17, 1862, Batteries A and B, Light Artillery; Second, Third, Fifth, and Purnell Legion Infantry.
Antietam, Md., Aug. 5, 1864, First Potomac Home Brigade Cavalry.
Antietam Iron-Works, Md., Aug. 27, 1861, First and Third Infantry.
Appomattox, Va., April 9, 1865, First Cavalry; First, Second, Fourth, Sixth, Seventh, and Eighth Infantry.
Ashby's Gap, Va., 1863, Cole's Cavalry.
Ashby's Gap, Va., July 19, 1864, First Potomac Home Brigade Cavalry.
Auburn Mills, Va., Oct. 14, 1863, First Cavalry.
Back Creek, Va., Dec. 6, 1861, Third Infantry.
Ball's Bluff, Md., Oct. 21, 1861, First Cavalry.
Bath, Va., Jan. 4, 1862, First Cavalry.
Benevola, Md., July 10, 1863, First Cavalry.
Bermuda Hundred, Va., June 17, 1864, First Cavalry.
Berryville, Va., Dec. 3, 1862, Cole's Cavalry.
Berryville, Va., June 13, 1863, Baltimore Battery Light Artillery; Sixth Infantry.
Berryville, Va., Aug. 13, 1864, First Potomac Home Brigade Infantry and Third Potomac Home Brigade Infantry.
Berryville, Va., Sept. 3, 1864, Second Eastern Shore Infantry.
Bethesda Church, Va., May 31 and June 1, 1864, First, Fourth, Seventh, Eighth, and Purnell Legion Infantry.
Beverly Ford, Va., Aug. 20 and 21, 1862, Third Infantry.
Beverly Ford, Va., June 9, 1863, First Cavalry.
Blain's Cross-Roads, Tenn., Dec. 17, 1863, Second Infantry.
Bloomery Gap, Va., Feb. 14, 1862, First Cavalry and Fiery's company of cavalry.
Bloomfield, Va., ———, 1863, Cole's Cavalry.
Blue's House, Va., Aug. 26, 1861, Second Potomac Home Brigade Infantry.
Blue Springs, Tenn., Oct. 10, 1863, Second Infantry.
Boissieux House, Va., Oct. 5, 1864, Second Infantry.
Bolivar Heights, Va., Sept. 14, 1862, Third Potomac Home Brigade Infantry.
Bolivar Heights, Va., Aug. 6, 1864, Third Potomac Home Brigade Infantry.
Boonsboro', Md., Sept. 7, 1862, First Cavalry.
Brandy Station, Va., June 9, 1863, First Cavalry.
Brandy Station, Va., Nov. 8, 1863, Sixth Infantry.
Bristoe Station, Va., Oct. 14, 1863, First Cavalry.
Brownsville, Md., ———, 1864, First Potomac Home Brigade Cavalry.
Buchanan, Va., June 14, 1864, First Potomac Home Brigade Cavalry.
Bull Run, Va., Aug. 30, 1862, First Cavalry; Second Infantry.
Bunker Hill, Va., March 5, 1862, Cole's Cavalry.
Burgess' Mills, Va., April 3, 1865, First Cavalry.
Burlington, Va., Nov. 16, 1863, Second Potomac Home Brigade Infantry.
Campbell's Station, Tenn., Nov. 16, 1863, Second Infantry.

Cape Charles, Va., ———, 1863, A, Purnell Cavalry.
Catlett's Station, Va., Aug. 22, 1862, Purnell Legion Infantry.
Catoctin Creek, Md., June 17, 1863, Cole's Cavalry.
Catoctin Mountain, Va., Sept. 14, 1863, Cole's Cavalry.
Cedar Creek, Va., Oct. 19, 1864, Sixth Infantry.
Cedar Mountain, Va., Aug. 9, 1862, First Cavalry; Third Infantry.
Centreville, Va., Aug. 28, 1862, First Cavalry.
Chaffin's Farm, or New Market Road, Va., Sept. 29, 1864, First Cavalry.
Chambersburg, Pa., July 30, 1864, Patapsco Guards.
Chancellorsville, Va., May 1–5, 1863, Third Infantry.
Chantilly, Va., Sept. 1, 1862, First Cavalry; Second Infantry.
Chapel House, Va., Oct. 1–3, 1864, B and C, Purnell Cavalry; First, Fourth, Seventh, Eighth, and Purnell Legion Infantry.
Charles City Road, or Fair Oaks, Va., Oct. 27, 1864, First Cavalry; Fifth Infantry.
Charlestown, Va., May 28, 1862, First Cavalry and Cole's Cavalry.
Charlestown, Va., Nov. 14, 1862, Cole's Cavalry.
Charlestown, Va., Dec. 2, 1862, Cole's Cavalry.
Charlestown, Va., Dec. 5, 1862, Cole's Cavalry.
Charlestown, Va., Oct. 18, 1863, Cole's Cavalry; First Potomac Home Brigade, Second Potomac Home Brigade, and Ninth Infantry.
Charlestown, Va., Aug. 9, 1864, Third Potomac Home Brigade Infantry.
Charlestown, Va., Aug. 22, 1864, First Potomac Home Brigade Cavalry.
Charlestown, Va., Aug. 26, 1864, Sixth Infantry.
Cherry Run. Md., Dec. 25, 1861, First Infantry.
Clark's Mountain, Va., Aug. 18, 1862, Second Infantry.
Cold Harbor, Va., June 2–5, 1864, First, Second, Third, Fourth, Sixth, Seventh, Eighth, and Purnell Legion Infantry.
Corbin's Cross-Roads, Va., Nov. 10, 1862, Second Infantry.
Crampton's Pass, Md., Sept. 14, 1862, Battery A, Light Artillery.
Crampton's Pass, Md., 1864, First Potomac Home Brigade Cavalry.
Culpeper Court-House, Va., Sept. 14, 1863, First Cavalry.
Dabney's Mill, Va., Feb. 6, 1865, First, Fourth, Seventh, and Eighth Infantry.
Dam No. 5, Md., Dec. 6–8, 1861, Third Infantry.
Danville Railroad, Va., April 5, 1865, First Cavalry.
Darbytown Road, Va., Oct. 13, 1864, First Cavalry.
Deep Bottom, Va., July 27, 1864, First Cavalry.
Deep Creek, or Danville Railroad, Va., April 5, 1865, First Cavalry.
Deep Run, Va., Aug. 16 and 18, 1864, First Cavalry.
Duffield's Station, Va., June 29, 1864, First Potomac Home Brigade Infantry.
Dumfries, Va., Dec. 27, 1862, First Cavalry.
Dumfries, Va. (near), Dec. 28, 1862, Third Infantry.
Edinburg, Va., March 24, 1862, Cole's Cavalry.
Edinburg, Va., Dec. 17, 1863, Cole's Cavalry.
Emmittsburg, Md., July 5, 1863, First and Cole's Cavalry.
Fair Play, Md., July 10, 1863, First Eastern Shore Infantry.
Fair Oaks, or Charles City Road, Va., Oct. 27, 1864, First Cavalry; Fifth Infantry.
Falling Waters, Md., July 14, 1863, Second Eastern Shore Infantry.
Falling Waters, Va., July 26, 1864, First Potomac Home Brigade Cavalry.
Farmville, Va., April 6, 1865, First Cavalry.
Faulkwell's Ferry, Md., Dec. 7 and 8, 1861, Third Infantry.

---

[1] In the compilation of this summary of battles, etc., it was found impracticable in many instances to designate with exactitude the particular companies or detachments where such only were engaged, therefore the whole command has uniformly been given credit for the action. Wherever practicable the preceding chapters on the civil war have particularized the portions actually brought into collision with the Confederates.

Fisher's Hill, Va., Sept. 22, 1864, Sixth Infantry.
Five Forks, Dinwiddie Co., Va., April 1, 1865, First Cavalry; First, Fourth, Seventh, and Eighth Infantry.
Five Forks, Amelia Co., Va., April 4, 1865, First Cavalry.
Flemming's Ford, La., Feb. 11, 1864, Third Cavalry.
Flusser's Mill, Va., Aug. 14, 1864, First Cavalry.
Fort Blakely, Ala., April 9, 1865, Third Cavalry.
Fort Frederick, Md., Dec. 25, 1861, First Infantry.
Fort Gaines, Ala., Aug. 8, 1864, Third Cavalry.
Fort Morgan, Ala., Aug. 23, 1864, Third Cavalry.
Fort Stedman, Va., March 25, 1865, Third Infantry.
Fountaindale, Pa., 1863, Cole's Cavalry.
Franklin, Va., May 12, 1862, Third Potomac Home Brigade Infantry.
Frederick, Md., June 22, 1863, Cole's battalion cavalry.
Frederick, Md., July 8, 1864, Baltimore Battery Light Artillery; Third Potomac Home Brigade Infantry.
Frederick, Md., July 11 and 12, 1864, First Potomac Home Brigade Cavalry.
Fredericksburg, Va., Dec. 11–15, 1862, First Cavalry; Batteries A and B, Light Artillery; Second Infantry.
Freeman's Ford, Va., Aug. 22, 1862, First Cavalry.
Front Royal, Va., May 23, 1862, First Infantry.
Front Royal, Va., Dec. 11, 1863, Cole's Cavalry.
Funkstown, Md., July 12, 1863, First, Fourth, Seventh, and Eighth Infantry.
Gainesville, Va., Aug. 28, 1862, First Cavalry.
Gettysburg, Pa., July 1–3, 1863, First Cavalry, A, Purnell Cavalry; Battery A, Light Artillery; First Eastern Shore, First Potomac Home Brigade, and Third Infantry.
Grass Lick, Va., April 23, 1862, Fiery's company Potomac Home Brigade Cavalry.
Great Cacapon Bridge, Va., Jan. 4, 1862, Second Potomac Home Brigade Infantry.
Groveton, Va., Aug. 29, 1862, First Cavalry; Second Infantry.
Hagerstown, Md., July 10, 1863, First Cavalry.
Hagerstown, Md., July 29 and 30, 1864, First Potomac Home Brigade Cavalry.
Halltown, Va., Dec. 20, 1862, Cole's Cavalry.
Halltown, Va., Aug. 8, 1864, Third Potomac Home Brigade Infantry.
Hancock, Md., Jan. 5–6, 1862, First and Cole's Cavalry.
Harper's Ferry, Va., May 28–30, 1862, First Cavalry; Third and Purnell Legion Infantry.
Harper's Ferry, Va., June 9, 1862, First Cavalry.
Harper's Ferry, Va., Sept. 14 and 15, 1862, First and Cole's Cavalry; First Potomac Home Brigade, and Third Potomac Home Brigade Infantry.
Harper's Ferry, Va., July 6, 1863, Cole's Cavalry.
Harper's Ferry, Va., July 27, 1863, Purnell Legion Infantry.
Harris' Farm, Va., May 18, 1864, First, Fourth, Seventh, and Eighth Infantry.
Harrisonburg, Va., Dec. 21, 1863, Cole's Cavalry.
Harrisonburg, Va., June 3, 1864, First Potomac Home Brigade Cavalry.
Hatcher's Run, Va., Oct. 27, 1864, First, Second, Fourth, Seventh, and Eighth Infantry.
Hatcher's Run, Va., April 2, 1865, First Cavalry.
Haymarket, Va., Oct. 19, 1863, First and Seventh Infantry.
Herndon, Va., 1864, First Potomac Home Brigade Cavalry.
Hyattstown, Md., Oct. 12, 1862, Cole's Cavalry.
Keedysville, Md., Aug. 5, 1864, First Potomac Home Brigade Cavalry.
Kelly's Ford, Va., Aug. 21, 1862, Second Infantry.
Kernstown, Va., March 22, 1862, Cole's Cavalry.

Kernstown, Va., March 23, 1862, Cole's Cavalry and First Infantry.
Kernstown, Va., July 23 and 24, 1864, First Potomac Home Brigade Cavalry.
Knoxville, Tenn., Nov. 18–Dec. 6, 1863, Second Infantry.
Laurel Hill, Va., May 8, 1864, First, Fourth, Seventh, and Eighth Infantry.
Leesburg, Va., Sept. 2, 1862, Cole's Cavalry.
Leesburg, Va., 1863, Cole's Cavalry.
Leetown, Va., July 3, 1864, First Potomac Home Brigade Cavalry.
Lexington, Va., June 13, 1864, First Potomac Home Brigade Cavalry.
Loudon, Tenn., Nov. 15, 1863, Second Infantry.
Loudon Heights, Va., May 27, 1862, First Potomac Home Brigade Infantry.
Loudon Heights, Va., Jan. 10, 1864, Cole's Cavalry.
Lynchburg, Va., June 18, 1864, First Potomac Home Brigade Cavalry; Battery B, Light Artillery; Second Eastern Shore and Second Potomac Home Brigade Infantry.
Madison Court-House, Va., Aug. 8, 1862, First Cavalry.
Malvern Hill, Va., July 1, 1862, Batteries A and B, Light Artillery.
Manassas Junction, Va., Oct. 25, 1862, First Cavalry.
Mansura, La., May 14 and 16, 1864, Third Cavalry.
Marksville, La., May 17, 1864, Third Cavalry.
Martinsburg, Va., March 3, 1862, Cole's Cavalry.
Martinsburg, Va., June 14, 1863, Cole's Cavalry.
Marye's Heights, Va., May 3, 1863, Battery A, Light Artillery.
Maryland Heights, Md., Sept. 12 and 13, 1862, First Cavalry; First Potomac Home Brigade and Third Potomac Home Brigade Infantry.
Maryland Heights, Md., July 7, 1863, First, Fourth, and Eighth Infantry.
Maryland Heights, Md., 1864, First Potomac Home Brigade Cavalry.
Mechanicsville Gap, Va., January, 1864, Cole's Cavalry.
Meddley, Va., Jan. 30, 1864, Second Potomac Home Brigade Infantry.
Middleburg, Va., June 23, 1863, First Cavalry.
Middletown, Va., May 24, 1862, First Cavalry.
Middletown, Md., July 7, 1864, Baltimore Battery Light Artillery; Third Potomac Home Brigade Infantry.
Millerstown, Md., July 5, 1863, First Cavalry.
Mine Run, Va., Nov. 26–Dec. 2, 1863, First Cavalry; Sixth Infantry.
Monocacy, Md., July 9, 1864, Baltimore Battery Light Artillery; First Potomac Home Brigade, Third Potomac Home Brigade, and Eleventh Infantry.
Monocacy Aqueduct, Md., Sept. 4, 1862, First Potomac Home Brigade Infantry.
Moorefield, Va., June 29, 1862, Third Potomac Home Brigade Infantry.
Moorefield, Va., Jan. 1864, Cole's Cavalry.
Moorefield Junction, Va., Jan. 8, 1864, Second Potomac Home Brigade Infantry.
Morgan's Ferry Road, La., June 9, 1864, Third Cavalry.
Mount Jackson, Va., Nov. 17, 1863, Cole's Cavalry.
New Bridge, Va., June 5, 1862, Battery B, Light Artillery.
New Market, Va., Dec. 18, 1863, Cole's Cavalry.
New Market, Va., May 13, 1864, First Potomac Home Brigade Cavalry.
New Market, Va., May 15, 1864, First Potomac Home Brigade Cavalry and Battery B, Light Artillery.
Nollichucky Bend, Tenn., March 12, 1864, Second Infantry.

North Anna, Va., May 23–27, 1864, First, Third, Fourth, Seventh, and Eighth Infantry.
Opequan, Va., June 13, 1863, Baltimore Battery Light Artillery; Sixth Infantry.
Peeble's Farm, Va., Oct. 7 and 8, 1864, B and C, Purnell Cavalry; First, Fourth, Seventh, Eighth, and Purnell Legion Infantry.
Petersburg, Va., 1864–65, First and B and C, Purnell Cavalry; First, Second, Third, Fourth, Fifth, Sixth, Seventh, Eighth, and Purnell Legion Infantry.
Piedmont, Va., June 5, 1864, First Potomac Home Brigade Cavalry; Battery B, Light Artillery, and Second Eastern Shore Infantry.
Pollocksville, N. C., May 16, 1862, Second Infantry.
Poolesville, Md., Sept. 5, 1862, First Potomac Home Brigade Infantry.
Poplar Spring Church, Va., Sept. 30, 1864, B and C, Purnell Cavalry; First, Second, Third, Fourth, Seventh, Eighth, and Purnell Legion Infantry.
Purcellville, Va., July 16, 1864, First Potomac Home Brigade Cavalry.
Rapidan Station, Va., July 13, 1862, First Cavalry.
Rapidan Station, Va., Sept. 16, 1863, First Cavalry.
Rappahannock Station, Va., Aug. 22, 1862, First Cavalry.
Rector's Cross-Roads, Va., 1863, Cole's Cavalry.
Rectortown, Va., Jan. 1, 1864, Cole's Cavalry.
Richmond, Va., April 3, 1865, Fifth Infantry.
Richmond and Petersburg Railroad, Va., June 19, 1864, First Cavalry.
Ridgeville, Va., Jan. 4, 1864, Second Potomac Home Brigade Infantry.
Romney, Va., Jan. 1864, Cole's Cavalry.
Sailor's Creek, Va., April 6, 1865, First Cavalry; Sixth Infantry.
Salem, Va., June 21, 1864, First Potomac Home Brigade Cavalry; Battery B, Light Artillery.
Salem Heights, Va., May 3 and 4, 1863, Battery A, Light Artillery.
Shady Grove, Va., May 30, 1864, First, Fourth, Seventh, Eighth, and Purnell Legion Infantry.
Sharpsburg, Md., Sept. 15, 1862, First and Cole's Cavalry.
Sharpsburg, Md., 1863, Cole's Cavalry.
Shepherdstown, Va., Sept. 9, 1861, First Infantry.
Shepherdstown, Va., July 14, 1863, First Cavalry.
Shepherdstown, Va., July 3, 1864, First Potomac Home Brigade Cavalry.
Slane's Cross-Roads, Va., Jan. 4, 1862, First Cavalry.
Smithfield, Va., Dec. 7, 1864, First Cavalry.
Snicker's Ford, Va., July 18, 1864, First Potomac Home Brigade Cavalry; Second Eastern Shore, Second Potomac Home Brigade, and Third Potomac Home Brigade Infantry.
Snicker's Gap, Va., July 25, 1864, First Potomac Home Brigade Cavalry.
Snickersville, Va., 1863, Cole's Cavalry.
South Branch Bridge, Va., Oct. 26, 1861, Fiery's company cavalry; Second Potomac Home Brigade Infantry.
South Mountain, or Turner's Gap, Md., Sept. 14, 1862, Second Infantry.
Southside Railroad, Va., April 2, 1865, First Cavalry.
Spanish Fort, Ala., April 9, 1865, Third Cavalry.
Spottsylvania, Va., May 9–20, 1864, First, Second, Third, Fourth, Sixth, Seventh, and Eighth Infantry.
Springfield, Va., Aug. 23, 1861, Second Potomac Home Brigade Infantry.
Springfield, Va., Oct. 26, 1861, Second Potomac Home Brigade Infantry.
Staunton, Va., Dec. 21, 1863, Cole's Cavalry.
Stephenson's Depot, Va., March 7 and 11, 1862, Cole's Cavalry.
Stoneman's Raid, Va., April–May, 1863, First Cavalry.
Strawberry Plains, Tenn., Jan. 22, 1864, Second Infantry.
Summit Point, Va., Oct. 7, 1863, Second Potomac Home Brigade Infantry.
Summit Point, Va., Aug. 30, 1864, First Potomac Home Brigade Cavalry.
Sutherland's Depot, Southside Railroad, Va., April 5, 1865, First Cavalry.
"The Crater," Va., July 30, 1864, Second, Third, and Fifth Infantry.
Tolopotomy, Va., May 31, 1864, Second Infantry.
Tye River Gap, Va., June 12, 1864, First Potomac Home Brigade Cavalry.
Upperville, Va., June 23, 1863, First Cavalry.
Upperville, Va., Sept. 25, 1863, Cole's Cavalry.
Upperville, Va., Dec. 10, 1863, Cole's Cavalry.
Wardensville, Va., May 7, 1862, Fiery's company, Potomac Home Brigade Cavalry.
Wardensville, Va., May 29, 1862, Third Potomac Home Brigade Infantry.
Weldon Railroad, Va., Aug. 18–21, 1864, B and C, Purnell Cavalry; First, Second, Fourth, Seventh, Eighth, and Purnell Legion Infantry.
White Oak Road, Va., March 31, 1865, First, Fourth, Seventh, and Eighth Infantry.
White Post, Va., Sept. 3, 1864, First Potomac Home Brigade Cavalry.
White Sulphur Springs, Va., Aug. 23, 1862, First Cavalry.
White Sulphur Springs, Va., Aug. 24, 1862, Second Infantry.
White Sulphur Springs, Va., Nov. 15, 1862, Second Infantry.
White Sulphur Springs, Va., Oct. 13, 1863, First Cavalry.
Wilderness, Va., May 5–7, 1864, First, Third, Fourth, Sixth, Seventh, and Eighth Infantry.
Williamsport, Md., June 15, 1863, Cole's Cavalry.
Winchester, Va., March 12, 1862, Cole's Cavalry.
Winchester, Va., May 24, 1862, First Cavalry.
Winchester, Va., Dec. 5, 1862, Cole's Cavalry.
Winchester, Va., June 13–15, 1863, Baltimore Battery Light Artillery, Fifth and Sixth Infantry.
Winchester, Va., July 19, 1864, First Potomac Home Brigade Cavalry.
Winchester, Va., July 24, 1864, Second Eastern Shore Infantry.
Winchester, Va., Sept. 19, 1864, First Potomac Home Brigade Cavalry, Sixth Infantry.
Woodstock, Va., 1863, Cole's Cavalry.
Wrightsville, Pa., June 28, 1863, Patapsco Guards.
Yellow Bayou, La., May 18, 19, 1864, Third Cavalry.

Classification of Engagements by States.

Pennsylvania	4
Maryland	39
Virginia	190
Tennessee	7
North Carolina	1
Alabama	4
Louisiana	5
Total engagements	250

Military Department.[1]—April 9, 1861, to April 27, 1861.—The entire State was in the Department of Washington.

[1] For the purpose of military administration the whole area of the United States is divided into geographical divisions and departments. During the war the departments within whose limits the State of Maryland was embraced are here set forth.

April 27, 1861, to July 25, 1861.—Fort Washington and the adjacent country as far as Bladensburg, inclusive, in the Department of Washington; the country for twenty miles on each side of the railroad from Annapolis to the city of Washington, as far as Bladensburg, in the Department of Annapolis (changed to the Department of Maryland, July 19, 1861); the remainder in the Department of Pennsylvania.

July 25, 1861, to Aug. 17, 1861.—The counties of Washington and Allegany in the Department of the Shenandoah; all of Prince George's County, including the section of country lying east of the District of Columbia, and south of a line twenty miles from the south side of the railroad from Annapolis to the city of Washington, as far as Bladensburg, and the counties of Montgomery and Frederick, in the Department of Washington; the remainder in the Department of Pennsylvania.

Aug. 17, 1861, to March 3, 1862.—The entire State in the Department of the Potomac.

March 3, 1862, to March 11, 1862.—That part lying west of Flintstone Creek, in Allegany County, in the Department of Western Virginia; the remainder in the Department of the Potomac.

March 11, 1862, to March 22, 1862.—That part lying west of Flintstone Creek, in Allegany County, in the Mountain Department; the remainder in the Department of the Potomac.

March 22, 1862, to April 4, 1862.—The Eastern Shore and counties of Cecil, Harford, Baltimore, and Ann Arundel in the Middle Department; that portion west of Flintstone Creek, in Allegany County, in the Mountain Department; and the remainder in the Department of the Potomac.

April 4, 1862, to June 26, 1862.—That part west of the Blue Ridge and east of Flintstone Creek in the Department of the Shenandoah; that part west of Flintstone Creek in the Mountain Department; the country between the Potomac and the Patuxent in the Department of the Rappahannock; and the residue in the Middle Department.

June 26, 1862, to Sept. 2, 1862.—The sections embraced within the limits of the Departments of the Shenandoah, Rappahannock, and the Mountain Department (as described in the preceding paragraph) were under the jurisdiction of the commanding general of the Army of Virginia, the remainder continued in the Middle Department.

Sept. 2, 1862, to Feb. 2, 1863.—The district of country lying within a line beginning at Fort Washington, on the Potomac, and running thence to Annapolis Junction, and thence to the mouth of Seneca Creek, in the defenses of Washington; the rest in the Middle Department.[1]

Feb. 2, 1863, to June 24, 1863.—The district of country north of the Potomac River, from Piscataway Creek to Annapolis Junction, and thence to the mouth of the Monocacy, in the Department of Washington; the residue in the Middle Department.

June 24, 1863, to July 23, 1863.—That part lying west of Hancock, Washington Co., in the Department of West Virginia; that north of the Potomac River, from Piscataway Creek to Annapolis Junction, and thence to the mouth of the Monocacy, in the Department of Washington; the remainder in the Middle Department.[2]

July 23, 1863, to Aug. 3, 1863.—The county of St. Mary's in the St. Mary's District; that part west of Hancock, Washington Co., in the Department of West Virginia; that north of the Potomac River, from Piscataway Creek to Annapolis Junction, and thence to the mouth of the Monocacy, in the Department of Washington; the remainder in the Middle Department.

Aug. 3, 1863, to Dec. 21, 1863.—The county of St. Mary's in the District of St. Mary's; that part west of the Monocacy River in the Department of West Virginia; that north of the Potomac River, from Piscataway Creek to Annapolis Junction, and thence to the mouth of the Monocacy, in the Department of Washington; the residue in the Middle Department.

Dec. 21, 1863, to June 21, 1864.—The county of St. Mary's in the Department of Virginia and North Carolina; that part west of the Monocacy River in the Department of West Virginia; that north of the Potomac River, from Piscataway Creek to Annapolis Junction, and thence to the mouth of the Monocacy, in the Department of Washington; the rest in the Middle Department.

June 21, 1864, to close of war.—That portion between the Patuxent, the Chesapeake Bay, and the Potomac River, including the prisoners' camp at Point Lookout, and south of a line from Annapolis Junction to the mouth of the Monocacy, in the Department of Washington; that west of the Monocacy in the Department of West Virginia; the residue in the Middle Department.[3]

---

[1] During the Maryland campaign, from Sept. 3 to Nov. 2, 1862, the Army of the Potomac also operated in the counties of Montgomery, Frederick, and Washington.

[2] The Gettysburg campaign belongs to this period, during which the Army of the Potomac operated in the counties of Montgomery, Frederick, Carroll, and Washington.

[3] At the time of the Confederate invasion of Maryland and threatened attack on the city of Washington, in July, 1864,

Department Commanders whose Headquarters were at Baltimore City.

Brevet Maj.-Gen. George Cadwalader, May 15 to June 11, 1861.
Maj.-Gen. Nathaniel P. Banks, June 11 to July 23, 1861.
Maj.-Gen. John A. Dix, July 23, 1861, to June 9, 1862.
Maj.-Gen. John E. Wool, June 9, 1862, to Dec. 22, 1862.
Maj.-Gen. Robert C. Schenck, Dec. 22, 1862, to Aug. 10, 1863.
Brevet Brig.-Gen. Wm. W. Morris, Aug. 10 to 31, 1863.
Maj.-Gen. Robert C. Schenck, Aug. 31 to Sept. 28, 1863.
Brig.-Gen. Erastus B. Tyler, Sept. 28 to Oct. 10, 1863.
Maj.-Gen. Robert C. Schenck, Oct. 10 to Dec. 5, 1863.
Brig.-Gen. Henry H. Lockwood, Dec. 5, 1863, to March 22, 1864.
Maj.-Gen. Lew Wallace, March 22, 1864, to Feb. 1, 1865.
Brevet Brig.-Gen. Wm. W. Morris, Feb. 1 to April 19, 1865.
Maj.-Gen. Lew Wallace, April 19 to July 18, 1865.

HISTORICAL OUTLINES.

INFANTRY.

First Regiment of Infantry.—Under the President's call of May 3, 1861, the Hon. James Cooper, of Frederick City, was appointed a brigadier-general, and assigned by the Secretary of War to the duty of raising and organizing the volunteers from Maryland. Recruiting-offices were immediately opened in Baltimore City and elsewhere, and vigorous measures instituted for the enlistment of men.

The first company (A) was enrolled by Capt. John C. McConnell at Baltimore. This officer is unquestionably entitled to the credit of having opened the first recruiting-office for three years' volunteers in the State of Maryland.

Company B was recruited by Capt. F. G. F. Waltemeyer at Baltimore; C, by Capt. George Smith at Baltimore; D, by Capt. Charles W. Wright at Baltimore; E, by Capt. Thomas R. Evans at Baltimore; F, by Capt. Robert W. Reynolds at Ellicott's Mills; G, by Capt. John W. Wilson, chiefly at Cockeysville.

Company H, commanded by Capt. Benjamin H. Schley, was formed by the consolidation of two detachments of about equal strength, one raised by Capt. Schley at Frederick, and the other by Capt. William H. Taylor at Baltimore.

Company I was organized by Capt. Lemuel Z. Lyon at Baltimore, and K, commanded by Capt. T. S. J. Johnson, was composed principally of Germans, recruited in Baltimore and Washington.

By the 28th of May a sufficient number of men for one regiment had been enrolled, and on that date the organization of the First Infantry was completed at Elkridge Landing (the place of general rendezvous, whither all the companies had been previously ordered) by its acceptance into the service of the United States for three years unless sooner discharged.

The muster in of the several companies dated as follows: A, May 10th; B and C, May 11th; D, May 16; E, May 20th; F, G, H, and I, May 27th; and K, May 28th.

On the 11th of June the field-officers of the regiment were appointed by the President.

The colonelcy was bestowed on John R. Kenly, a lawyer of Baltimore, who had seen active field service in Mexico, and at this time held a commission as brigadier-general of Maryland militia. Nathan T. Dushane, of Baltimore, was commissioned as lieutenant-colonel, and George Chorpenning, of Pennsylvania, as major. Dr. Thomas E. Mitchell, of Ellicott's Mills, was appointed surgeon, and Dr. Edward R. Baer, of Baltimore, assistant surgeon.

The company officers as originally mustered in were as follows:

Company A.—Capt. John C. McConnell, Lieuts. George W. Kugler and David C. Huxford.
Company B.—Capt. F. G. F. Waltemeyer, Lieuts. Thomas Saville and Henry R. Gillingham.
Company C.—Capt. George Smith, Lieuts. J. Baily Orem and Charles R. Colgate.
Company D.—Capt. Charles W. Wright, Lieuts. Fredk. C. Tarr (regimental adjutant) and Christopher C. Gillingham.
Company E.—Capt. Thos. R. Evans, Lieuts. Robert A. Morris (regimental quartermaster) and Wm. T. Hilleary.
Company F.—Capt. Robert W. Reynolds, Lieuts. Frank M. Collier and Virgil T. Mercer.
Company G.—Capt. John W. Wilson, Lieuts. Robert S. Smith and Isaac Wilson.
Company H.—Capt. Benj. H. Schley, Lieuts. John McF. Lyeth and Maurice Albaugh.
Company I.—Capt. Lemuel Z. Lyon, Lieuts. Josiah B. Coloney and Henry C. Hack.
Company K. Capt. Thos. S. J. Johnson, Lieuts. N. G. Starkweather and Julius Veidt.

Col. Kenly was promoted to brigadier-general Aug. 22, 1862, for gallant conduct at Front Royal. His successors were Nathan T. Dushane, who was killed at the battle of the Weldon Railroad, Aug. 21, 1864; John W. Wilson, killed in action at Dabney's Mill, Va., Feb. 6, 1865, and David L. Stanton, mustered out with the regiment. The latter rose from the ranks, having entered the service in May, 1861, as first sergeant of Company A.

During the winter of 1863 and 1864 a large majority of the original members re-enlisted as veterans, by which act the organization of the regiment was preserved till the end of the war.

The following is a list of the actions in which the regiment, as a whole or in part, was engaged:

Skirmish at Antietam Iron-Works, Md., Aug. 27, 1861.
Skirmish at Shepherdstown, Va., Sept. 9, 1861.

---

troops of the Sixth and Nineteenth Army Corps and the Department of West Virginia also operated in the counties of Montgomery and Frederick.

John R Kenly

Skirmish at Cherry Run, Md., Dec. 25, 1861.
Skirmish at Fort Frederick, Md., Dec. 25, 1861.
Skirmish at Kernstown, Va., March 23, 1862.
Battle of Front Royal, Va., May 23, 1862.
Skirmish at Maryland Heights, Md., July 7, 1863.
Skirmish at Funkstown, Md., July 12, 1863.
Skirmish at Haymarket, Va., Oct. 19, 1863.
Reconnoissance from Culpeper to Raccoon Ford, Va., Feb. 6 and 7, 1864.
Battle of the Wilderness, Va., May 5 to 7, 1864.
Battle of Laurel Hill, Va., May 8, 1864.
Battle of Spottsylvania Court-House, Va., May 9 to 20, 1864.
Battle of Harris' Farm, Va., May 19, 1864.
Battle of North Anna, Va., May 23 to May 27, 1864.
Battle of Shady Grove, Va., May 30, 1864.
Battle of Bethesda Church, Va., May 31 and June 1, 1864.
Battle of Cold Harbor, Va., June 2 to 5, 1864.
Assault on Petersburg, Va., June 17 and 18, 1864.
Siege of Petersburg, Va., 1864-65.
Battle of Weldon Railroad, Va., Aug. 18 to 21, 1864.
Battle of Poplar Spring Church, Va., Sept. 30, 1864.
Battle of Chapel House, Va., Oct. 1 to 3, 1864.
Battle of Peeble's Farm, Va., Oct. 7 and 8, 1864.
Battle of Hatcher's Run, Va., Oct. 27, 1864.
Raid to Hicksford, Va., Dec. 7 to 12, 1864.
Battle of Dabney's Mill, Va., Feb. 6, 1865.
Battle of White Oak Road, Va., March 31, 1865.
Battle of Five Forks, Va., April 1, 1865.
Surrender at Appomattox, Va., April 9, 1865.

The regiment served in the Department of Annapolis and Department of the Shenandoah from its muster in to Aug. 17, 1861; Banks' division, Army of the Potomac, to Feb. 18, 1862; Third Brigade, Banks' division, Army of the Potomac, to March, 1862; First Brigade, First Division, Fifth Army Corps, to June 8, 1862; Middle Department, Eighth Army Corps, to July 11, 1863; Third Brigade, Third Division, First Army Corps, to January, 1864; Second Brigade, Third Division, First Army Corps, to March 23, 1864; Third Brigade, Second Division, Fifth Army Corps, to June 6, 1864; Second Brigade, Second Division, Fifth Army Corps, to June, 1865; and First Brigade, Second Division, Fifth Army Corps, to July 2, 1865.

After four years of arduous campaigning in Western Maryland and Western Virginia, in the Shenandoah Valley, and with the Army of the Potomac in Virginia, up to the surrender at Appomattox, the regiment finally took up its line of march homeward, leaving the scenes and employments of war for those of peace.

On the 2d day of July, 1865, it was mustered out of service at its camp on Arlington Heights, near Alexandria, Va. The next day it proceeded to Camp Bradford, near Baltimore, where final payments were received, and with an earnest "Well done, good and faithful servants," from the hearts of a grateful people, the officers and men repaired to their homes, once more to join their fellow-citizens in cultivating the arts of peace.

From first to last the regiment had within its ranks 2317 officers and men. Of this number 86 were killed or mortally wounded, 118 died of disease, and 255 received wounds which did not prove fatal.

No regiment from the State won a prouder name or made a more honorable record than the old veteran First. Along the banks of the Upper Potomac, in the Valley of the Shenandoah, and wherever the old Army of the Potomac met the Confederates subsequent to their bloody repulse on the rocky heights of Gettysburg, there lie its dead.

Second Regiment of Infantry.—This regiment, like the First, was raised under the President's call of May 3, 1861. A few of the companies were mustered into the United States service in June, but the recruiting of several other regiments at the same time somewhat delayed the completion of the organization, and it was not until the month of September that the tenth company was mustered in. The dates of the muster in of the several companies were as follows: A, June 13th; B, June 18th; C, July 9th; D, July 10th; E, July 23d; F, August 8th; G, August 9th; H, I, and K, September 18th; all at Camp Carroll, Baltimore. Both officers and men were mainly from Baltimore City.

On the 8th of October, 1861, the field-officers were appointed by the President. John Sommer, of Towsontown, a soldier of the Mexican war, was commissioned as colonel; J. Eugene Duryee, of New York, lieutenant-colonel; and David P. De Witt, of New York, as major. Lieut.-Col. Duryee had already seen some service as a company officer in the Fifth New York Zouave Regiment, and Maj. De Witt was a graduate of the West Point Military Academy.

The company officers, as originally constituted, were as follows:

Company A.—Capt. Henry Howard, Jr., Lieuts. W. O. Bigelow (regimental adjutant) and James D. Spangler.
Company B.—Capt. Andrew B. Brunner, Lieuts. George A. Zimmerman and J. Emory Gault.
Company C.—Capt. William G. Hunt, Lieuts. George F. Armor (regimental quartermaster) and Milton C. Dove.
Company D.—Capt. William F. Bragg, Lieuts. Charles H. Bowen and John W. Davis.
Company E.—Capt. J. D. Stinchcomb, Lieuts. James A. Martin and James Cooper, Jr.
Company F.—Capt. Malcolm Wilson, Lieuts. Benjamin F. Matthews and Benjamin F. Dougherty.
Company G.—Capt. William E. Conoway, Lieuts. Charles Z. O'Neill and William H. Prince.
Company H.—Capt. John M. Santmyer, Lieuts. William H. Taylor and Richard C. Wills.
Company I.—Capt. Robert Karns, Lieuts. John A. Thompson and David E. Whitson.

Company K.—Capt. Joseph M. Sudsburg, Lieuts. F. W. Heck and Louis Fleckenstein.

Edwin P. Morony was the surgeon, Joseph E. Beatty assistant surgeon, and Robert S. Hitchcock the chaplain.

Col. Sommer held his position until April 21, 1862, when he resigned, and was succeeded by Thomas B. Allard, of Baltimore, formerly lieutenant-colonel of the Dix Light Infantry, who also resigned Jan. 19, 1864. Subsequent to this the regiment had no colonel, its numerical strength, greatly reduced by hard service, not being sufficient, under the rules of the War Department, to entitle it to an officer of that grade. Lieut.-Col. Henry Howard was therefore the ranking officer of the regiment until July 30, 1864, when he was mortally wounded at the battle of "The Crater." He was succeeded by Benjamin F. Taylor, originally an enlisted man of Company B, who had risen step by step to the rank of lieutenant-colonel. This officer was promoted colonel, but not mustered as such.

In the spring of 1862 the Second joined the command of Gen. Burnside in North Carolina, and from that time forward it shared in all the operations of the Ninth Corps.

Its list of battles, skirmishes, etc., comprises the following:

Skirmish at Pollockville, N. C., May 16, 1862.
Skirmish at Clark's Mountain, Va., Aug. 18, 1862.
Skirmish at Kelly's Ford, Va., Aug. 21, 1862.
Skirmish at White Sulphur Springs, Va., Aug. 24, 1862.
Battle of Groveton, Va., Aug. 29, 1862.
Battle of Bull Run, Va., Aug. 30, 1862.
Battle of Chantilly, Va., Sept. 1, 1862.
Battle of South Mountain (Turner's Gap), Md., Sept. 14, '62.
Battle of Antietam, Md., Sept. 17, 1862.
Skirmish at Corbin's Cross-Roads, near Amissville, Va., Nov. 10, 1862.
Skirmish at White Sulphur Springs, Va., Nov. 15, 1862.
Battle of Fredericksburg, Va., Dec. 12 to 15, 1862.
Engagement at Blue Springs, Tenn., Oct. 10, 1863.
Skirmish at Loudon, Tenn., Nov. 15, 1863.
Engagement at Campbell's Station, Tenn., Nov. 16, 1863.
Siege of Knoxville, Tenn., Nov. 18 to Dec. 6, 1863.
Skirmish at Blain's Cross-Roads, Tenn., Dec. 17, 1863.
Skirmish at Strawberry Plains, Tenn., Jan. 22, 1864.
Skirmish at Nollichucky Bend, Tenn., March 12, 1864.
Battle of Spottsylvania, Va., May 12 to 20, 1864.
Battle of Tolopotomy, Va., May 31, 1864.
Battle of Cold Harbor, Va., June 3 and 4, 1864.
Assault on Petersburg, Va., June 16 and 17, 1864.
Siege of Petersburg, Va., 1864-65.
Battle of "The Crater," Va., July 30, 1864.
Battle of Weldon Railroad, Va., Aug. 18 to 21, 1864.
Battle of Poplar Spring Church, Va., Sept. 30, 1864.
Skirmish at Boissieux House, Va., Oct. 5, 1864.
Battle of Hatcher's Run, Va., Oct. 27, 1864.
Raid to Nottoway River, Va., Dec. 10 to 12, 1864.
Storming of Petersburg, Va., April 2, 1865.
Surrender at Appomattox, Va., April 9, 1865.

The regiment served in Dix's division, Army of the Potomac, from muster in to March 26, 1862; First Brigade, Second Division, Department of North Carolina, July 22, 1862; First Brigade, Second Division, Ninth Army Corps, to April, 1863; First Division, Twenty-third Army Corps, to August, 1863; First Brigade, Second Division, Ninth Army Corps, to January, 1864; Second Brigade, Second Division, Ninth Army Corps, to May, 1864; and Second Brigade, Third Division, Ninth Army Corps, to July 17, 1865.

By the re-enlistment of three hundred and ten of the original members in the winter of 1863-64, the regiment secured its continuance in service as a veteran organization until the termination of hostilities.

After the surrender at Appomattox the Second turned its steps homeward, and was mustered out of service July 17, 1865, near Alexandria, Va. Thence it was transported to Baltimore, and there paid off and disbanded on the 25th of July, 1865.

Nothing can be found in the history of the Second Maryland which need cause any of its members to feel ashamed of the regiment in which they served. On the contrary, it has an imperishable record of gallant deeds and heroic sacrifices equal to any and second to none of its sister regiments, and of which every true soldier may well be proud.

Third Regiment of Infantry.—The organization of this regiment was commenced at Baltimore in August, 1861, by Col. John C. McConnell, under special authority from the Secretary of War. Five companies were raised and officered as follows:

Company A (mustered in Sept. 1, 1861).—Capt. Wm. P. Ferguson, Lieuts. Joseph H. Allen and Alfred Fairall.

Company B (mustered in Sept. 12, 1861).—Capt. Benjamin Berkley, Lieuts. Washington A. Danskin and Samuel B. Clements.

Company C (mustered in Oct. 1, 1861).—Capt. Ellison J. Lockwood, Lieuts. James A. Williams and John W. Jordan.

Company D (mustered in Nov. 21, 1861).—Capt. George Arnold, Lieuts. George W. Reay and William W. Waite.

Company H (mustered in Sept. 1, 1861).—Capt. John Krein, Lieuts. James Binau and James H. Sherwood.

On the 16th of February, 1862, four companies organized at Williamsport, Md., in the summer and autumn of 1861 for the First Virginia Union Volunteers, Col. Ward H. Lamon commanding, and containing many refugees from Jefferson and Berkeley Counties, Va., were assigned to the Third Regiment and designated as Companies A, B, C, and I. In consequence of this consolidation the original Companies A, B, C, and D became Companies D, E, F, and G respectively. The companies thus added to the regiment were originally officered as follows:

Company A.—Capt. Wm. B. Kennedy, Lieuts. James Farrow and Samuel Woolford.

Company B.—Capt. Joseph Kerns, Lieuts. James D. Fayman and John Lowman.

Company C.—Capt. Gilbert P. Robinson, Lieuts. Caleb T. Day and Harry Littlejohn.

Company I (incomplete).—Second Lieut. Theodore P. Butler.

On the 11th of May, 1862, the companies bearing the designation of E, F, H, and I were broken up and the men distributed among Companies A, B, C, D, and G. These discontinued companies were replaced by four companies, comprising the members of the Fourth Maryland Infantry (German Rifles) and the Baltimore (or Dix) Light Infantry, both of which had failed to perfect their organization. The companies transferred from the Fourth Infantry were styled E and H, and those from the Dix Light Infantry, I and K.

As now constituted the regiment numbered nine companies, viz.: A, B, C, D, E, G, H, I, and K. A tenth company (F), composed of nine-months' drafted men, organized Oct. 15, 1862, at Easton, Talbot Co., was assigned in February, 1863. This company was mustered out of service Sept. 2, 1863.

Capt. John C. McConnell, of the First Maryland, was promoted colonel of the Third, Aug. 5, 1861, and served therewith until Feb. 18, 1862, when he was discharged.

Up to this time no other field-officers had been appointed. On the 29th of March, 1862, David P. De Witt, who had served as major of the Second Maryland, was commissioned colonel, and on the 7th of May, 1862, Joseph M. Sudsburg, the senior captain of the Fourth Maryland, was made lieutenant-colonel, and Capt. William B. Kennedy, of Company A, was promoted major.

At the date of Col. De Witt's appointment the staff-officers of the regiment stood as follows: Quartermaster, Richard F. Gardner; Adjutant, George H. Dobson; Surgeon, Alphonso A. White; Assistant Surgeon, James H. Currey; Chaplain, Samuel Kramer.

Col. De Witt was discharged Oct. 8, 1862, to accept the colonelcy of the One Hundred and Forty-third New York Volunteers, whereupon Lieut.-Col. Sudsburg was advanced to the colonelcy of the Third. He was mustered out June 24, 1864, in consequence of his command becoming reduced below the minimum standard of strength. Subsequently the ranking officer of the command was Lieut.-Col. Gilbert P. Robinson.

On the 24th of May, 1862, the Third abandoned Camp Belger and its associations for active field service, and proceeded to Harper's Ferry, Va., then endangered by the advance of "Stonewall" Jackson's army down the Shenandoah Valley. Here it became a part of Gen. Banks' command, subsequently better known as the Twelfth Army Corps, with which it performed most gallant and meritorious service in Maryland, Virginia, Tennessee, and Alabama, until the termination of its veteran furlough in April, 1864, when it joined the Ninth Army Corps, in the Army of the Potomac, and continued therewith to the close of the war. Two-thirds of the original members having re-enlisted as veterans after two years' service, its organization was maintained throughout the war and until the government had no further use for its services.

On the 24th of June, 1864, by reason of its greatly-reduced strength, the Third was consolidated into a battalion of four companies,—A, B, C, and D.

The command participated in the following engagements, etc.:

Skirmish at Antietam Iron-Works, Md., Aug. 27, 1861.
Skirmishes at Dam No. 5, Md., and Back Creek, Va., Dec. 6, 1861.
Skirmishes at Dam No. 5, Md., and Faulkwell's Ferry, Md., Dec. 7 and 8, 1861.
Defense of Harper's Ferry, Va., May 29 and 30, 1862.
Battle of Cedar Mountain, Va., Aug. 9, 1862.
Skirmish at Beverly Ford, Va., Aug. 20 and 21, 1862.
Battle of Antietam, Md., Sept. 17, 1862.
Reconnoissance from Loudoun Heights to Lovettsville, Va., Oct. 21 and 22, 1862.
Reconnoissance from Bolivar Heights to Rippon, Va., Nov. 9, 1862
Reconnoissance from Bolivar Heights to Charlestown, Va., Nov. 26, 1862.
Reconnoissance from Bolivar Heights to Winchester, Va., Dec. 2–6, 1862.
Reconnoissance from Fairfax Station to Dumfries, Va., Dec. 27–30, 1862.
Skirmish between Occoquan Creek and Dumfries, Va., Dec. 28, 1862.
Battle of Chancellorsville, Va., May 1–3, 1863.
Battle of Gettysburg, Pa., July 1–3, 1863.
Battle of the Wilderness, Va., May 5–7, 1864.
Battle of Spottsylvania, Va., May 10–20, 1864.
Battle of North Anna, Va., May 23–27, 1864.
Battle of Cold Harbor, Va., June 1–3, 1864.
Assault on Petersburg, Va., June 17, 1864.
Siege of Petersburg, Va., 1864–65.
Battle of "The Crater," Va., July 30, 1864.
Battle of Poplar Spring Church, Va., Sept. 30, 1864.
Raid to Hicksford, Va., Dec. 8–12, 1864.
Engagement at Fort Stedman, Va., March 25, 1865.
Capture of Petersburg, Va., April 3, 1865.

The regiment served in Dix's division, Army of the Potomac, from muster in to March, 1862; Middle Department, Eighth Army Corps, to May 24, 1862; First Brigade, Sigel's division, Department of the Shenandoah, to July, 1862; First Brigade, Second Division, Second Corps, Army of Virginia, to August, 1862; Second Brigade, Second Division, Second Corps, Army of Virginia, to September, 1862; Second Brigade, Second Division, Twelfth Army Corps, to March, 1863; Second Brigade, First Division, Twelfth Army Corps, to May, 1863; First Brigade, First Division, Twelfth Army Corps, to April 25, 1864; Second Brigade, First Division, Ninth Army Corps, to Sept. 1, 1864; and Third Brigade, First Division, Ninth Army Corps, to July 31, 1865.

The final muster out of the veteran battalion took place July 31, 1865, on Arlington Heights, Va., and it immediately proceeded to Baltimore, where it was paid off and disbanded. The Third Maryland earned for itself an honorable name in the struggle for the Union, and is justly entitled to the gratitude of the State and nation.

Fourth Regiment of Infantry (German Rifles).—The organization of this regiment was begun at Camp Carroll, Baltimore, during the winter of 1861-62, in accordance with the authority embodied in the following communication:

"WAR DEPARTMENT,
"WASHINGTON, Nov. 5, 1861.
"BRIG.-GEN. JAMES COOPER, Washington, D. C.:

"SIR,—You are hereby authorized to raise and organize in the State of Maryland a regiment of infantry, as the fourth regiment from that State, to serve for three years or during the war. This authority is with the distinct understanding that this Department will revoke the commissions of all officers who may be found incompetent for the proper discharge of their duties.

"Your men will be mustered into the service of the United States in accordance with General Orders No. 58, 61, and 70, herewith inclosed.

"Very respectfully,
"THOMAS A. SCOTT,
"*Assistant Secretary of War.*"

Failing to secure the requisite complement of men for a regimental organization, those who had been enlisted were transferred to the Third Infantry, May 7, 1862, and became Companies E and H of that regiment. Some of the officers were provided with positions in the Third, and the remainder were mustered out of service.

The officers engaged in organizing the regiment are embraced in the following list. Those who went into the Third Regiment are indicated by an asterisk:

Captains.—*Joseph M. Sudsburg, George Hoffman, Albert Lonyi, *Charles M. Schad, and *Louis Beyer.

First Lieutenants.—*James Gillette, adjutant; *Cyrus D. Culbertson, quartermaster; *Charles Durand, *Louis Scherzer, *Michael Schmidt, John B. Cantel, Adolph Kogelshatz, and Charles L. de Charlier.

Second Lieutenants.—Lewis Binder, George Ruths, Charles M. Stacks, Julius Pellicott, and Henry Kirzingsky.

Assistant Surgeon.—John M. P. Pannetti.

Under the President's call of July 2, 1862, another regiment, known as the Fourth Infantry, was organized, a description of which appears hereafter.

On the 2d of July, 1862, the President issued a call for three hundred thousand volunteers for three years. The adjutant-general of the State immediately published the following order:

"STATE OF MARYLAND,
"ADJUTANT-GENERAL'S OFFICE,
"ANNAPOLIS, July 19, 1862.

"Four regiments of infantry being required of this State by the War Department, and to be raised as soon as practicable, as a part of Maryland's quota of the three hundred thousand men lately called for by the President, the Governor is authorized by a recent order of the Department to commission immediately a second lieutenant to each company of said regiments, who will act as the recruiting and mustering-in officer of his company.

"These officers are now being appointed, and will be assigned to duty, as they are appointed, in the city of Baltimore and all the principal towns in the State.

"Other persons desiring to fill company offices can also receive authority to recruit, and will be selected from those forwarding their testimonials to the Governor.

"When the half of a company is recruited and mustered in the first lieutenant will be commissioned, and the captain when the whole company is mustered in; and in issuing these commissions regard will be had to the wishes of the company and the efficiency and promptness exhibited by those thus employed in recruiting. Camps of rendezvous for these several regiments, which will be respectively designated the Fourth, Sixth, Seventh, and Eighth Regiments, will be established at Baltimore, and the cost of transportation from the place of muster to the place of rendezvous will be paid by the quartermaster at the latter place.

"By a recent order of the War Department recruits for the new regiments are entitled to a premium of $2, to be paid when they are inspected by the surgeon and mustered into service, and which payment may be made either to the person bringing the recruit or to the recruit in person, in case he presents himself.

"A further advance of $25 will be paid to every recruit (on account of the $100 bounty to which he is entitled at the end of his service), which advance will be paid when his company is organized and mustered in.

"In addition to these advances of premium and bounty, a month's pay in advance will be made to each recruit, under such regulations as the paymaster-general may establish. Any further information may be obtained by application to this office, or to Col. Schley, superintendent of recruiting, Baltimore.

"By order of the Governor,
"N. BREWER, of John,
"*Adjt.-General of Maryland.*"

Fourth Regiment of Infantry.—By authority from Governor Bradford the organization of a regiment of infantry, to be styled the Fourth, was begun at Baltimore about the time the original Fourth (German Rifles) was merged into the Third, by Maj. Joseph P. Warner, of the Baltimore City Guard Battalion. Maj. Warner, who was to have been the colonel of the new regiment, commenced recruiting in the latter part of May, 1862, but died before much progress had been made, and the organization of the regiment was then carried forward under the President's call of

July 2d and the Governor's order of July 19th, already cited. With the exception of Company E, raised in Carroll County, the entire regiment was almost wholly from the city of Baltimore.

The several companies were mustered into the United States service as follows:

A, June 28; B, July 17; C and D, July 31; E, Aug. 14; F, Aug. 15; G, Aug. 20; H, Aug. 29; and I, Oct. 4, 1862. Throughout its term of service the regiment consisted of but nine companies.

The original field and staff-officers were: Colonel, W. J. L. Nicodemus, a graduate of the West Point Military Academy, and captain of the Twelfth United States Infantry; Lieutenant-Colonel, Richard N. Bowerman, formerly a captain in the Eleventh New York Volunteers, or First Fire Zouaves, and the Seventy-third New York, or Fourth Excelsior, and who had also previously served in the ranks of the celebrated Seventh New York State National Guards; Major, Henry P. Brooks, a lawyer of Baltimore; Adjutant, John A. Thompson, Jr., who had recently resigned from the Second Maryland; Quartermaster, William T. Adreon; Surgeon, Wm. W. Valk; Assistant Surgeons, Henry W. Owings and John C. Carter; Chaplain, Edwin R. Hera.

As originally composed the following were the company officers:

Company A.—Capt. Isaac L. Boyd, Lieuts. Harrison Adreon and Robert Watson.
Company B.—Capt. Edward Hyde, Lieuts. John W. Brown and George Ruths.
Company C.—Capt. J. Bailey Orem, Lieuts. Wm. H. Allen and Oscar A. Mace.
Company D.—Capt. Anthony C. Williams, Lieuts. Wm. H. Davis and Robert B. Meads.
Company E.—Capt. John L. Bishop, Lieuts. John Deveney and John G. Barber.
Company F.—Capt. Gregory Barrett, Jr., Lieuts. John Schley and David Crouch.
Company G.—Capt. Martin Suter, Lieuts. John H. Millender and Thomas A. Mills.
Company H.—Capt. Charles Z. O'Neill, Lieuts. Albert S. Husband and John W. Isaacs.
Company I.—Capt. Louis A. Carl, Lieuts. Josiah Bankerd and Robert M. Gorsuch.

Col. Nicodemus resigned Nov. 17, 1862, and was succeeded by Col. Bowerman. The latter was mustered out with the regiment.

The Fourth was hurried to the field Sept. 18, 1862, before its organization was fully completed, and served with distinction in the Army of the Potomac, bearing an honorable part in the following engagements, etc.:

Skirmish at Maryland Heights, Md., July 7, 1863.
Skirmish at Funkstown, Md., July 12, 1863.
Reconnoissance from Culpeper to Raccoon Ford, Va., Feb. 6-7, 1864.
Battle of the Wilderness, Va., May 5 to 7, 1865.
Battle of Laurel Hill, Va., May 8, 1864.
Battle of Spottsylvania, Va., May 9 to 20, 1864.
Battle of Harris' Farm, Va., May 19, 1864.
Battle of North Anna, Va., May 23 to 27, 1864.
Battle of Shady Grove, Va., May 30, 1864.
Battle of Bethesda Church, Va., May 31 and June 1, 1864.
Battle of Cold Harbor, Va., June 2 to 5, 1864.
Assault on Petersburg, Va., June 17 and 18, 1864.
Siege of Petersburg, Va., 1864-65.
Battle of Weldon Railroad, Va., Aug. 18 to 21, 1864.
Battle of Poplar Spring Church, Va., Sept. 30, 1864.
Battle of Chapel House, Va., Oct. 1 to 3, 1864.
Battle of Peeble's Farm, Va., Oct. 7 and 8, 1864.
Battle of Hatcher's Run, Va., Oct. 27, 1864.
Raid to Hicksford, Va., Dec. 7 to 12, 1864.
Battle of Dabney's Mill, Va., Feb. 6, 1865.
Battle of White Oak Road, Va., March 31, 1865.
Battle of Five Forks, Va., April 1, 1865.
Surrender at Appomattox, Va., April 9, 1865.

The Fourth served in the Middle Department, Eighth Army Corps, from muster in to July 11, 1863; Third Brigade, Third Division, First Army Corps, to January, 1864; Second Brigade, Third Division, First Army Corps, to March 23, 1864; Third Brigade, Second Division, Fifth Army Corps, to June 6, 1864; and Second Brigade, Second Division, Fifth Army Corps, to May 31, 1865.

The war having ended and their services being no longer required by the government, the members of the regiment whose terms of service expired prior to Oct. 1, 1865, were mustered out at Arlington Heights, Va., May 31, 1865, and the residue (thirty-one enlisted men) were transferred to the First Maryland.

The Fourth experienced much hard service, made long and fatiguing marches, and fought bravely on many hotly-contested battle-fields. Its record is as imperishable as it is splendid. In its various encounters with the enemy the regiment suffered a loss of three officers and twenty-six enlisted men killed, ten officers and eighty-eight men wounded, and two officers and thirty-nine men captured.

Fifth Regiment of Infantry.—In the latter part of August, 1861, William Louis Schley, a lawyer of Baltimore, who had served with credit in the war with Mexico, received verbal authority directly from the War Department at Washington to raise a regiment of infantry, to be known as the "Public Guard Regiment," whose specific duties were to be the guarding of railroad lines and the protection of government property. On the 4th of September, 1861, the regiment was conditionally accepted into the service of the United States, as will be seen by the following communications:

"State of Maryland,
"Executive Chamber,
"Annapolis, Sept. 9, 1861.
"Hon. H. W. Hoffman:
"Dear Sir,—Please find inclosed authority from War Department to Col. William Louis Schley to form and report his regiment.
"Your obedient servant,
"Thos. H. Hicks."

[Inclosure.]
"War Department, Sept. 4, 1861.
"Col. William Louis Schley,
"Care of Henry W. Hoffman, Esq., Baltimore, Md.:
"Sir,—The regiment of infantry which you offer is accepted for three years or during the war, provided you have it ready for marching orders in thirty days. This acceptance is with the distinct understanding that the Department will revoke the commissions of all officers who may be found incompetent for the proper discharge of their duties.
"You will be mustered into the service of the United States in accordance with General Orders Nos. 58 and 61, herewith inclosed.
"Very respectfully
"Your obedient servant,
"Thomas A. Scott,
"Asst. Secretary of War."

The rendezvous of the regiment was established at Lafayette Square, situated in the northwestern section of the city of Baltimore. Commodious barracks were erected and known as Camp Hoffman, having been so named in compliment to the Hon. Henry W. Hoffman, of Allegany County, then collector of the port of Baltimore.

John C. Holland, of Catonsville, was selected as lieutenant-colonel, and Leopold Blumenberg, of Baltimore, as major.

The original staff-officers were Judson Gilman, surgeon; William H. Norris, assistant surgeon; James M. Stephens, adjutant; James H. Cook, quartermaster; and John W. Bull, chaplain.

The organization was speedily completed, and the regiment mustered into the United States service for three years from the 19th of September, 1861, with one thousand officers and men.

Company A (Maffit Guards) was organized at North East, Cecil Co., with the following officers: Captain, C. Davis Irelan; Lieutenants, Samuel Ford and George W. Benjamin.

Company B (Bradford Guards) was raised in Baltimore City, and officered as follows: Captain, Wm. W. Bamberger; Lieutenants, Salome Marsh and Wm. H. Irving.

Company C (Montgomery Blair Guards) was enrolled in Baltimore City. Its officers were: Captain, Nicholas Ganster; Lieutenants, Edward M. Koch and Magnus Moltke. This company was raised by Capt. Blumenberg, who upon being appointed major was succeeded in the captaincy by the first lieutenant, Ganster.

Company D (Hoffman Guards) was enlisted in Baltimore City, and had for its officers: Captain, Charles A. Holton; Lieutenants, Bruff W. Tall and Edwin C. Kirkwood.

Company E (McClellan Guards), recruited in Frederick County and Baltimore City, was officered by Capt. Alfred Schley, Lieuts. John P. Gleeson and Wm. H. Walters.

Company F (Schley Guards) was enrolled in Baltimore City. Its officers were Capt. John W. Horn, Lieuts. William A. Noel and Joseph M. Rothrock.

Company G (Steuben Guards) was raised in Baltimore City, and had for its officers Capt. John C. Sehrt, Lieuts. Uriah Garber and William L. Adkisson.

Company H (Ellsworth Guards) was enlisted in Baltimore City, and officered by Capt. Frederick Memmert, Lieuts. William H. Chaney and Nicholas B. Talbott.

Company I (Elkton Guards) hailed from Elkton, Cecil Co., and had in its ranks a number of men from Wilmington, Del., with some from Baltimore City. Its officers were Capt. E. F. M. Fachtz, Lieuts. Evan W. Thomas and John Carroll.

Company K (John A. Dix Guards) was organized in Baltimore City, and had for its officers Capt. Christian Bitter, Lieuts. Edward Stein and Joseph Sachs.

On the 28th of October, 1861, the several companies voted unanimously to offer their services to the government for duty anywhere, and to be called and known from that date as the Fifth Regiment Maryland Volunteers. This proposition was submitted to and approved by the War Department.

The Fifth left Camp Hoffman March 11, 1862, for the seat of war in Virginia, and during its subsequent history was identified with Gen. Dix's command in the vicinity of Fort Monroe, the Army of the Potomac under McClellan, the Eighth Army Corps under Schenck, and the Army of the James under Butler and Ord. A large number of its original members re-enlisted as veteran volunteers.

The battle list of the regiment is as follows:

Battle of Antietam, Md., Sept. 17, 1862.
Reconnoissance from Harper's Ferry to Charlestown, Va., Oct. 16 and 17, 1862.
Battle of Winchester, Va., June 13 and 15, 1863.
Siege of Petersburg, Va., June to September, 1864.
Battle of "The Crater," Va., July 30, 1864.
Siege of Richmond, Va., October, 1864, to April, 1865.
Battle of Fair Oaks, Va., Oct. 27, 1864.
Occupation of Richmond, Va., April 3, 1865.

The regiment was mustered out of service at Fredericksburg, Va., Sept. 1, 1865, and at once repaired to Baltimore City, where it was paid off and disbanded. As an organization the Fifth Maryland thus ceased to exist, but its record still remains. Some other regiments from the State may have participated in more engagements and lost a greater number of men, but none ever fought more gallantly, endured hardships with greater fortitude, or performed every duty imposed upon them more faithfully.

Sixth Regiment of Infantry.—This regiment was raised under the President's call of July 2, 1862. Its rendezvous was established at Baltimore City. The companies were organized at the following-named places, and mustered into the United States service on the dates affixed thereto.

A, Carroll County, Aug. 12, 1862; B, Cecil County, Aug. 20, 1862; C, Carroll County, Aug. 23, 1862; D, Frederick County, Aug. 23, 1862; E, Cecil County, Aug. 27, 1862; F, Baltimore City, Sept. 8, 1862; G, Cecil County, Aug. 28, 1862; H, Washington County, Sept. 5, 1862; I, Baltimore City, Aug. 25, 1862; and K, Queen Anne's County, Sept. 2, 1862.

The original field, staff, and company officers were as follows:

George R. Howard, of Elkton, colonel; John W. Horn, of Baltimore City, formerly captain in the Fifth Maryland, lieutenant-colonel; William A. McKellip, of Westminster, major; Jacob B. Ash, adjutant; James Touchstone, quartermaster; Charles F. M. Nelson, surgeon; Charles T. Simpers and Edwin K. Foreman, assistant surgeons; and Joseph T. Brown, chaplain.

Company A.—Capt. Albert Billingslea, Lieuts. Charles N. Kuhn and William H. Burns.

Company B.—Capt. Joseph C. Hill, Lieuts. Isaac N. Benjamin and Erastus S. Narvel.

Company C.—Capt. George Webster, Lieuts. J. L. Beaver and Ira Tyler.

Company D.—Capt. Martin Rouzer, Lieuts. John R. Rouzer and Charles A. Damuth.

Company E.—Capt. Francis A. Crouch, Lieuts. John Pryor and William T. Cain.

Company F.—Capt. Clifton K. Prentiss, Lieuts. Norris G. Starkweather and Harry Coggins.

Company G.—Capt. John S. Christie, Lieuts. Wm. J. Grant and Samuel H. Jack.

Company H.—Capt. Adam B. Martin, Lieuts. Melville R. Small and James H. C. Brewer.

Company I.—Capt. John J. Bradshaw, Lieuts. Henry J. Hawkins and Demarest J. Smith.

Company K.—Capt. Jacob L. Goldsborough, Lieuts. John A. Schwartz and William E. Thompson.

Col. Howard resigned May 5, 1863, and was succeeded by Lieut.-Col. Horn, promoted in his stead. Col. Horn resigned Feb. 4, 1865, when the command devolved upon Lieut.-Col. Joseph C. Hill. This officer was commissioned as colonel, but owing to the reduced numbers of the regiment was not mustered into that grade.

The Sixth left Baltimore Sept. 20, 1862, for the front, and proceeded *via* Frederick City to Williamsport, Md., where it united with the other regiments of the Maryland Brigade, which had gone to that place by way of Harrisburg, Pa.

It was attached to the Maryland Brigade, Eighth Army Corps, from muster in to March 28, 1863; Third Brigade, Second Division, Eighth Army Corps, to June 16, 1863; First Brigade, Second Division, Eighth Army Corps, to July 9, 1863; Second Brigade, Third Division, Third Army Corps, to March 23, 1864; and Second Brigade, Third Division, Sixth Army Corps, to June 20, 1865.

The Sixth took part in the following engagements, etc.:

Skirmish at Berryville, Va., June 13, 1863.
Skirmish at the Opequan, Va., June 13, 1863.
Battle of Winchester, Va., June 14 and 15, 1863.
Skirmish at Brandy Station, Va., Nov. 8, 1863.
Battle of Mine Run (Locust Grove), Va., Nov. 29, 1863.
Reconnoissance to Mitchell's Station, Va., Feb. 6 and 7, 1864.
Battle of the Wilderness, Va., May 5–7, 1864.
Battle of Spottsylvania, Va., May 9–20, 1864.
Battle of Cold Harbor, Va., June 1–3, 1864.
Siege of Petersburg, Va., June 19 to July 6, 1864, and Dec. 7, 1864, to April 2, 1865.
Skirmish at Charlestown, Va., Aug. 26, 1864.
Battle of Winchester, Va., Sept. 19, 1864.
Battle of Fisher's Hill, Va, Sept. 22, 1864.
Battle of Cedar Creek, Va., Oct. 19, 1864.
Reconnoissance to Vaughan Road, Va., Dec. 7–10, 1864.
Assault on Petersburg, Va., April 2, 1865.
Battle of Sailor's Creek, Va., April 6, 1865.
Surrender at Appomattox Court-House, Va., April 9, 1865.

The loss among the enlisted men of the regiment in these actions was seventy-eight killed and two hundred and thirty-three wounded. Of the latter, thirty-six died from the effects of their wounds, making a total of one hundred and fourteen slain.

On the 20th of June, 1865, the regiment, as an organization, was mustered out of service near Washington, D. C. (the recruits, forty in number, whose terms expired subsequent to Oct. 1, 1865, being transferred to the First Maryland), and returned to Baltimore, where the officers and men received their pay, spoke their final adieus, and dispersed to their homes.

By its undaunted courage, remarkable coolness, unwavering persistence, and sturdy reliability on trying occasions the Sixth Maryland won a reputation that was always recognized and appreciated by its commanding generals. Associate regiments from other States also acknowledged its worth, and the services herein recorded fully sustain the reputation it gained.

Seventh Regiment of Infantry.—This regiment was organized and mustered into the United States service at Baltimore City in August and September,

1862, under the President's call of July 2, 1862. Its rendezvous, styled Camp Harford, was located upon a spot now included within the limits of Druid Hill Park.

The regiment originally consisted of nine companies, enrolled as follows: A, Hagerstown, Washington Co.; B, Frederick City; C, Belair, Harford Co.; D, Towsontown, Baltimore Co.; E, Frederick City; F, Carroll County; G, Middletown, Frederick Co.; H, Havre de Grace, Harford Co.; and I, Boonsboro', Washington Co.

Pressing exigencies of the service hurried it into the field before it had received its tenth company, the men recruited for which being mustered into other regiments. Company K was added in April, 1864, and was composed of the re-enlisted men of the Tenth Maryland, a six-months' organization.

The following were the original field, staff, and company officers:

Colonel, Edwin H. Webster; Lieutenant-Colonel, Charles E. Phelps; Major, William H. Dallam; Adjutant, Richard R. Brouner; Quartermaster, Thomas S. Nesbitt; Surgeon, James H. Jarrett; Assistant Surgeon, Robert K. Robinson; and Chaplain, William H. Keith.

Company A (Bradford Guards).—Capt. Edward M. Mobley, Lieuts. William Colklesser and A. James Weise.

Company B.—Capt. John Makechney, Lieuts. Thomas W. Harn and Joshua T. Dayhoff.

Company C.—Capt. Richard E. Bouldin, Lieuts. Joseph P. Webster and F. Stanley Beacham.

Company D.—Capt. William D. Morrison, Lieuts. Charles A. Connor and Richard G. Dunphy.

Company E.—Capt. David T. Bennett, Lieuts. Isaiah Devilbiss and John Howard.

Company F.—Capt. Daniel Rinehart, Lieuts. Charles T. Reifsnider and George L. Tyler.

Company G.—Capt. A. C. Bragonier, First Lieut. John K. Smith.

Company H.—Capt. James B. Cochran, Lieuts. S. C. Gorrell and Joseph Robinson.

Company I.—Capt. Ephraim T. Anderson, Lieuts. William D. Ratcliff and Charles S. Knodle.

Company K.—Capt. Henry W. Wheeler, Lieuts. Henry C. Smith and W. H. Burnham.

Col. Webster was a resident of Harford County who had served as a member of the State Senate from 1855 to 1859, as Presidential elector on the Fillmore and Donelson ticket in 1856, and at the time of entering the service was a representative in Congress.

Lieut.-Col. Phelps, a prominent lawyer of Baltimore, had been a member of the City Council in 1860, and at the outset of the war held the position of major in the "Maryland Guard," a thoroughly drilled volunteer militia organization, but resigned this commission April 19, 1861, rather than obey an order that he deemed inconsistent with his oath to support the constitution of the United States.

Maj. Dallam had been for many years the State's attorney of Harford County.

The captains of companies were all well-known and highly respected citizens of their several counties. Capt. Rinehart, of Carroll County, was a brother of the sculptor.

Col. Webster resigned his commission Nov. 6, 1863, consequent upon his re-election to Congress. He was succeeded by Col. Phelps, who also resigned Sept. 9, 1864, on account of disability from wounds received at the battle of Spottsylvania. The command then devolved upon Maj. Edward M. Mobley, who in turn was succeeded by Lieut.-Col. David T. Bennett.

The Seventh left Baltimore Sept. 18, 1862, and formed a part of the Maryland Brigade, Eighth Army Corps, to July 11, 1863; Third Brigade, Third Division, First Army Corps, to January, 1864; Second Brigade, Third Division, First Army Corps, to March 23, 1864; Third Brigade, Second Division, Fifth Army Corps, to June 6, 1864; Second Brigade, Second Division, Fifth Army Corps, to May 31, 1865.

It bore an active and honorable share in the following engagements, etc.:

Skirmish at Funkstown, Md., July 12, 1863.
Skirmish at Haymarket, Va., Oct. 19, 1863.
Reconnoissance from Culpeper to Raccoon Ford, Va., Feb. 6 and 7, 1864.
Battle of the Wilderness, Va., May 5–7, 1864.
Battle of Laurel Hill, Va., May 8, 1864.
Battle of Spottsylvania, Va., May 9–20, 1864.
Battle of Harris' Farm, Va., May 19, 1864.
Battle of North Anna, Va., May 23–27, 1864.
Battle of Shady Grove, Va., May 30, 1864.
Battle of Bethesda Church, Va., May 31 to June 1, 1864.
Battle of Cold Harbor, Va., June 2–5, 1864.
Assault on Petersburg, Va., June 17 and 18, 1864.
Siege of Petersburg, Va., 1864–65.
Battle of Weldon Railroad, Va., Aug. 18–21, 1864.
Battle of Poplar Spring Church, Va., Sept. 30, 1864.
Battle of Chapel House, Va., Oct. 1–3, 1864.
Battle of Peeble's Farm, Va., Oct. 7 and 8, 1864.
Battle of Hatcher's Run, Va., Oct. 27, 1864.
Raid to Hicksford, Va., Dec. 7–12, 1864.
Battle of Dabney's Mill, Va., Feb. 6, 1865.
Battle of White Oak Road, Va., March 31, 1865.
Battle of Five Forks, Va., April 1, 1865.
Surrender at Appomattox, Va., April 9, 1865.

With the exception of Company K, and the recruits of other companies whose terms of service expired subsequent to Oct. 1, 1865, and who were transferred to the First Maryland, the regiment was mustered out of service May 31, 1865, at Arlington Heights, Va.

Thus, after nearly three years of arduous and honorable service, the Seventh Maryland ceased to exist as a body, and its war-worn members returned to their peaceful avocations. To say that throughout the whole of this time the Seventh sustained its reputation for bravery and heroic endurance would be but faint praise for the gallant deeds performed. May a grateful country do them justice, written history never can.

Eighth Regiment of Infantry.—This regiment was organized at Baltimore City under the call of July 2, 1862. It originally consisted of seven companies, raised as follows: A in Cecil County, B, C, D, F, and G at Baltimore, and E in Frederick County. These companies were mustered into the United States service at different dates between Aug. 13 and Oct. 28, 1862, to serve for three years. Companies H, I, and K, composed of nine-months' drafted men and substitutes, were mustered in from December, 1862, to April, 1863. These companies were mustered out as their terms of service expired. The veterans and recruits of Companies B and C, Purnell Cavalry (dismounted), were transferred to the regiment Nov. 17, 1864, and designated as Companies H and I.

Andrew W. Denison, who had been prominently identified with the volunteer militia organizations of Baltimore City, was commissioned as colonel, and held the position until the final muster out of the regiment. John G. Johannes, of Baltimore, was promoted to the lieutenant-colonelcy from the captaincy of Company D, and Ernest F. M. Fachtz, who had served as captain in the Fifth Infantry, was appointed major. The latter became lieutenant-colonel upon the promotion of Lieut.-Col. Johannes to the colonelcy of the Eleventh Infantry, Feb. 25, 1865.

The original company officers were as follows:

Company A.—Capt. C. Davis Irelan, Lieuts. Louis R. Cassard and John W. Simpers.

Company B.—Capt. Frederick W. Simon, Lieuts. David F. Hullett and James Fay.

Company C.—Capt. William F. Larrabee, Lieuts. Alexander Murray and Richard L. Gross.

Company D.—Capt. Eugene J. Rizer, Lieuts. James Bride and James R. Hosmer.

Company E.—Capt. Charles T. Dixon, Lieuts. Edward Y. Goldsborough and William W. Roderick.

Company F.—Capt. Beal D. Riddle, Lieuts. William E. Andrews and Bowie F. Johnson.

Company G.—Capt. Richard F. Gardner, Lieuts. Louis Chaney and F. C. Garmhausen.

Company H.—Capt. David F. Hullett (promoted from first lieutenant of Company B), Lieuts. B. E. Greaser and Wallace A. Bowie.

Company I.—Capt. Stephen P. Heath, Lieuts. William P. Cole and William J. Biays.

Company K.—Capt. George W. Shriver, Lieuts. Thomas Latchford and McKendree C. Furlong.

Alphonso A. White was appointed surgeon; William B. Wheeler, assistant surgeon; William B. Norman, adjutant; Christopher C. Adreon, quartermaster; and John J. Suman, chaplain.

The regiment took the field Sept. 18, 1862, and was attached to the Maryland Brigade, Eighth Army Corps, until July 11, 1863; Third Brigade, Third Division, First Army Corps, to January, 1864; Second Brigade, Third Division, First Army Corps, to March 23, 1864; Third Brigade, Second Division, Fifth Army Corps, to June 6, 1864; Second Brigade, Second Division, Fifth Army Corps, to May 31, 1865.

It participated with credit in the following engagements, etc.:

Skirmish at Maryland Heights, Md., July 7, 1863.
Skirmish at Funkstown, Md., July 12, 1863.
Reconnoissance from Culpeper to Raccoon Ford, Va., Feb. 6-7, 1864.
Battle of the Wilderness, Va., May 5-7, 1864.
Battle of Laurel Hill, Va., May 8, 1864.
Battle of Spottsylvania, Va., May 9-20, 1864.
Battle of Harris' Farm, Va., May 19, 1864.
Battle of North Anna, Va., May 23-27, 1864.
Battle of Shady Grove, Va., May 30, 1864.
Battle of Bethesda Church, Va., May 31 to June 1, 1864.
Battle of Cold Harbor, Va., June 2-5, 1864.
Assault on Petersburg, Va., June 17-18, 1864.
Siege of Petersburg, Va., 1864-65.
Battle of Weldon Railroad, Va., Aug. 18-21, 1864.
Battle of Poplar Spring Church, Va., Sept. 30, 1864.
Battle of Chapel House, Va., Oct. 1-3, 1864.
Battle of Peeble's Farm, Va., Oct. 7, 1864.
Battle of Hatcher's Run, Va., Oct. 27, 1864.
Raid to Hicksford, Va., Dec. 7-12, 1864.
Battle of Dabney's Mill, Va., Feb. 6, 1865.
Battle of White Oak Road, Va., March 31, 1865.
Battle of Five Forks, Va., April 1, 1865.
Surrender at Appomattox, Va., April 9, 1865.

In these actions the regiment sustained a loss of three officers and thirty-seven enlisted men killed, ten officers and two hundred and one enlisted men wounded, and forty-five enlisted men missing. Of the missing only eight returned, whilst of the wounded five officers and eighty-eight enlisted men never recovered sufficiently to resume duty.

The regiment was mustered out of service at Arlington Heights, Va., May 31, 1865. The members whose terms of service expired subsequent to Oct. 1, 1865, were transferred to the First Infantry.

The services of the Eighth cannot be reviewed by its surviving members without the proud consciousness that the command upon every occasion did its whole duty, and as an organization reflected honor upon the State and the cause for which it fought.

Ninth Regiment of Infantry.—This regiment was organized at Baltimore City in June and July, 1863, to serve for a period of six months, in accordance with the President's proclamation of June 15, 1863, calling for an additional military force to repel the invasion of Maryland and Pennsylvania by the enemy under Lee. It had its nucleus in the "Independent Grays," a well-known and thoroughly-drilled volunteer militia organization, which became Company

A. All the companies (excepting I from Baltimore County) were raised in Baltimore City.

Benjamin L. Simpson, of Baltimore City, who had already seen service as lieutenant-colonel of the Purnell Legion, was appointed colonel; Thomas Clowdsley, a former captain in the Tenth New York Volunteers, was commissioned lieutenant-colonel; and Royal W. Church, of Baltimore City, major. Charles H. Richardson received the appointment of adjutant; John Turner, quartermaster; Wilbur P. Morgan, surgeon; Henry C. Kemp, assistant surgeon; and G. Farring Gray, chaplain.

As originally constituted the company officers were as follows:

Company A.—Capt. Stephen W. Jones, Lieuts. Martin Callahan and Lloyd J. Haslup.
Company B.—Capt. James W. Brady, Lieuts. William Fensley and Edward Wilson.
Company C.—Capt. Thomas Clowdsley (promoted lieutenant-colonel), Lieuts. George L. Sollers and Harman F. Meyer.
Company D.—Capt. William E. Conoway, Lieuts. William H. Prince and Joseph F. Carter.
Company E.—Capt. John B. Herold, Lieuts. Nicholas Undutch and William L. Snyder.
Company F.—Capt. Martin Callahan (promoted from first lieutenant of Company A), Lieuts. Horace Noble and George W. Moore.
Company G.—Capt. Perley R. Lovejoy, Lieuts. Nathaniel D. Porter and William S. Stewart.
Company H.—Capt. Jonathan P. Cummins, Lieuts. Charles A. Lutz and William T. Wheeler.
Company I.—Capt. J. Marche McComas, Lieuts. Alfred S. Cooper and Hanson P. Jordan.

On the 6th of July, before its organization was completed, the command left Baltimore and proceeded by rail to Sandy Hook, Md., where it joined the troops under Gen. French and took part in the reoccupation of Maryland Heights. It subsequently crossed the Potomac at Harper's Ferry and encamped on Loudon Heights. Company B was stationed at Duffield's Station, and C at Brown's Crossing, on the Baltimore and Ohio Railroad. Afterwards Company B was relieved at Duffield's by Company A, the former being detailed as provost-guard in Harper's Ferry. About the middle of August Companies D, E, F, G, H, and I were moved forward to Charlestown, Va., where they had an engagement with the enemy on the 18th of October, but being surrounded by overpowering numbers and unsupported were forced to surrender. Only about one-half of those that were captured lived to return to their homes. Some of them were held as prisoners of war until hostilities ceased.

Companies A, B, and C continued on duty in the vicinity of Harper's Ferry until February, 1864.

Its term of service having expired, the regiment was mustered out at Baltimore Feb. 23, 1864. A number of the officers and men immediately re-entered the service for three years, and were assigned to the Third Infantry.

The Ninth was composed of excellent material, and had a better opportunity been afforded, none can doubt but that it would have won for itself a brilliant record on the field of battle.

Tenth Regiment of Infantry.—This regiment, like the Ninth, was organized at Baltimore City in June and July, 1863, under the President's proclamation of June 15, 1863. It had its nucleus in the Baltimore City Guard Battalion, an independent militia organization, which had its origin in 1830.

The original officers of the regiment were as follows:

William H. Revere, Jr., colonel; William E. W. Ross, lieutenant-colonel; J. Townsend Daniel, major; Edmund Simon, adjutant; Abram G. Smith, quartermaster; D. W. Onderdonk, surgeon; and William T. Urie and Edward Borck, Jr., assistant surgeons.

Company A.—Capt. John D. Ehlers, Lieuts. Charles Jones and George C. Cassard.
Company B.—Capt. William F. Rogers, Lieuts. George W. James and John A. Brownell.
Company C.—Capt. David Keener, Lieuts. John G. Harryman and W. Edward Paul.
Company D.—Capt. Thomas W. Webster, Lieuts. John B. Richardson and John H. Torney.
Company E.—Capt. John B. Airey, Lieuts. John Sullivan and Henry W. Wheeler.
Company F.—Capt. John W. Hamilton, Lieuts. Alexander Rutherford and Henry C. Smith.
Company G.—Capt. George N. Holloway, Lieuts. L. P. Stone and John M. Palmer.
Company H.—Capt. Charles M. Schad, Lieuts. Julius Pellicot and John Mohr.
Company I.—Capt. Ernest Osswald, Lieuts. George L. Ott and Andreas Moser.
Company K.—Capt. Charles Reddehase, Lieuts. Edward Wollman and William R. C. Jenks.

Companies H and I were raised as Companies A and B of the Eleventh Maryland, another six-months' regiment, which was to have been commanded by Col. Herman Ryter, but failing to complete the regimental organization, these companies were, by order of Governor Bradford, assigned to the Tenth.

The regiment was mustered out of service at Baltimore, Jan. 29, 1864. A portion of the regiment, consisting of one company of eighty-seven men and three officers and a squad of fifty-seven men with one officer, having re-enlisted for three years, was assigned to the Seventh Infantry, April 11, 1864.

The *esprit de corps* of the Tenth was second to none in the service, and every duty devolving upon it was most cheerfully and faithfully discharged.

Eleventh Regiment of Infantry (One Hundred Days).—On the 13th of May, 1864, the Secretary of War telegraphed Governor Bradford as follows:

"In the present juncture it might be of great service if you would call out two thousand of your State militia, to take charge of the works in Baltimore and relieve the same number of other troops, for the period of one hundred days, and upon the same terms as were agreed upon by the President and the Governors of Ohio, Indiana, Illinois, Iowa, and Wisconsin. Our army now appears to be victorious, and a helping hand at the present moment from you might contribute greatly to the speedy restoration of peace. Will you do this? Please answer immediately."

The Governor promptly replied,—

"I have no doubt that a volunteer militia force of two or three regiments could be at once organized in Baltimore if they could be furnished immediately with eligible arms. Gen. Wallace promised me several days ago to communicate with you on that subject. I will go to Baltimore this afternoon and confer with him again. Please communicate to the general or myself at that city whether you can supply the arms and equipments as soon as organized."

Satisfactory arrangements for the necessary supply of arms having been made, recruiting was begun in the city of Baltimore, and on the 15th and 16th of June, 1864, the Eleventh Regiment was mustered into the United States service at Camp Bradford.

William T. Landstreet, Thomas Sewell, Jr., and William E. George, all of Baltimore City, were commissioned respectively as colonel, lieutenant-colonel, and major. The latter had been previously connected with the First Infantry. Jacob Norris was appointed adjutant; Richard C. Cushing, quartermaster; and Harvey Buhrman, assistant surgeon.

The company officers were as follows:

Company A.—Capt. William E. Conoway, Lieuts. Joseph R. Keene and Charles A. Wilson.
Company B.—Capt. James H. B. Otto, Lieuts. Edward W. Phillips and John L. Cost.
Company C.—Capt. W. Edward Paul, Lieuts. Charles E. Lowe and James H. Tucker.
Company D.—Capt. Archibald D. Ferguson, Lieuts. James A. Dicus and Emanuel Myers.
Company E.—Capt. Samuel J. Syford, Lieuts. Jacob Fox and Joshua N. Richardson.
Company F.—Capt. Edward Jones, Lieuts. John T. Ford and Thomas M. Sumption.
Company G.—Capt. James A. Courtney, Lieuts. Alexander Rutherford and Benjamin B. Owens.
Company H.—Capt. William P. Vaughan, Lieuts. Jesse A. Reynolds and Charles L. Lilly.
Company I.—Capt. Max Killmeyer, Lieuts. Charles L. Kaupp and William P. Cole.
Company K.—Capt. William Diver, Lieuts. Thaddeus S. Smith and William H. Pierce.

Leaving Baltimore July 1, 1864, the regiment moved by way of the Baltimore and Ohio Railroad to Monocacy Junction, where it participated in the engagement with the enemy on the 9th of July. Falling back to Baltimore, it subsequently performed guard duty at Monrovia and Mount Airy, on the Baltimore and Ohio Railroad.

Before the expiration of its term of service a large number of the men re-enlisted for one year, forming the nucleus of another regiment bearing the same numerical designation.

Returning to Baltimore, the remaining members of the several companies were mustered out as follows: E and G, September 28th; B, C, and D, September 29th; F, September 30th; and A, H, I, and K, with the field and staff, Oct. 1, 1864.

Although but once engaged with the enemy, the duties performed by the regiment were valuable, from the fact that it took the place of veteran soldiers, who were thus permitted to reinforce the army operating against Richmond.

Eleventh Regiment of Infantry (One Year).—Companies A, B, and C of this regiment were composed principally of the re-enlisted men of the Eleventh (100 days) Regiment. In January, 1865, seven companies from the First Eastern Shore were added, thus making the regimental organization complete.

John G. Johannes, James C. Mulliken, and Martin Suter were commissioned severally colonel, lieutenant-colonel, and major. The first named had already seen service in the Purnell Legion and Eighth Infantry, and the two latter with the First Eastern Shore.

Company C did duty at the Relay House, on the Baltimore and Ohio Railroad; I in Baltimore City, and the residue at Fort Delaware.

The regiment was mustered out of service at Baltimore, June 15, 1865. All members whose term of service expired subsequent to Oct. 1, 1865, were transferred to the Second Infantry.

Twelfth Regiment of Infantry.—This regiment, consisting of five companies, was organized at Camp Bradford, Baltimore, in the summer of 1864, pursuant to orders from the War Department, dated May 13, 1864, for one hundred days. All the companies were mustered into the United States service July 30, 1864.

John L. Bishop, of Baltimore City, a former captain in the Fourth Infantry, was commissioned as lieutenant-colonel. No other field-officers were assigned to the regiment, its numerical strength being insufficient to warrant such appointments.

The company officers were as follows:

Company A.—Capt. Theodore M. Bartholomew, Lieuts. Thos. J. Evans (acting adjutant) and Benj. F. Moore.
Company B.—Capt. Benjamin F. Reichard, Lieuts. Charles M. Betts and Daniel Le Fever.

Company C.—Capt. Levi M. Haverstick, Lieuts. Edward Marshall and John W. Henderson (acting quartermaster).

Company D.—Capt. Caleb P. Spicer, Lieuts. Ogden M. Clow and Robert E. Duvall.

Company E.—Capt. George W. Shriver, Lieuts. Israel G. Powell and John Stinemetz.

During its term of service the regiment performed guard duty at various points along the Baltimore and Ohio Railroad between Baltimore and Kearneysville, Va. It was mustered out at Baltimore, Nov. 6, 1864. A number of the men who, prior to the muster out of the regiment, had re-enlisted for one year were assigned to the First Eastern Shore Regiment.

Potomac Home Brigade.—Hon. Francis Thomas, of Frederick County, a member of the United States House of Representatives, and ex-Governor of the State of Maryland, was the father of the Potomac Home Brigade. He obtained from the Secretary of War the following letters authorizing its formation:

"WAR DEPARTMENT,
"WASHINGTON, July 19, 1861.

"HON. FRANCIS THOMAS:

"You are hereby authorized to provide for the organization of four regiments of the loyal citizens resident on both sides of the Potomac River from the Monocacy to the western boundary of Maryland, for the protection of the canal and of the property and persons of loyal citizens of the neighborhood, and to be stationed in the vicinity whilst in the service.

"The men will be permitted to elect their own company officers, the field-officers to be appointed by the President. Arms will be forwarded as soon as practicable.

"Respectfully,
"Your obedient servant,
"SIMON CAMERON, *Sec'y of War.*"

"The Secretary of War has my approbation to sign this letter.
"A. LINCOLN."

"WAR DEPARTMENT,
"WASHINGTON, July 26, 1861.

"HON. FRANCIS THOMAS, Frederick, Md.:

"SIR,—The four companies of cavalry offered by you, one to be attached to each of the four regiments of infantry heretofore accepted, are accepted for three years or the war.

"This acceptance is with the distinct understanding that the Department will revoke the commissions of all officers who may be found incompetent for the proper discharge of their duties.

"You will advise Adjt.-Gen. Thomas, at Washington, the date at which the men will be ready for mustering, and he will detail an officer for that purpose.

"By order of the Secretary of War.
"JAMES LESLEY, JR., *Chief Clerk.*"

By the terms of the Secretary's letter of July 19, 1861, it will be observed these troops were to be organized for a specific duty and a restricted field of operations, but it is perhaps proper to remark that whenever called upon to perform duty outside the prescribed limits they promptly and cheerfully responded, and rendered good service, both in Pennsylvania and Virginia.

From the very beginning the war was waged on their immediate border, at times in their very midst, and they stood a trusty bulwark of defense between the foe and the homes of soldiers from sister States frequently in danger of invasion and harm.

First Regiment of Infantry, Potomac Home Brigade.[1]—Companies A, B, D, and I of this regiment were recruited in Frederick County; C, in Baltimore City; E, F, and H, in Washington County; G, in Baltimore, Carroll, and Frederick Counties; and K, in Baltimore City and Frederick County. All were mustered into the United States service at Frederick City during the summer and fall of 1861.

The original field-officers were William P. Maulsby, Sr., colonel; George R. Dennis, lieutenant-colonel; and John A. Steiner, major, all of whom were residents of Frederick City.

Jerningham Boone was appointed surgeon; Jacob Baer, acting surgeon; George T. Castle, adjutant (succeeded, Nov. 30, 1861, by William P. Maulsby, Jr.); Thomas M. Wolfe, quartermaster; and William G. Ferguson, chaplain.

The company officers were:

Company A.—Capt. Roger E. Cook, Lieuts. Jacob Hewett and James Wilson.

Company B.—Capt. William Glessner, Lieuts. Joseph Graff and George T. Castle.

Company C.—Capt. William T. Faithful, Lieuts. Theodorick B. Hall and Charles J. Brown (promoted captain of Company K on its organization).

Company D.—Capt. Charles H. Baugher, Lieuts. John L. Willman and Gideon Staley.

Company E.—Capt. William H. H. Youtz, Lieuts. Jerome B. Burk and John M. Martin.

Company F.—Capt. Samuel G. Prather, Lieuts. Tacitus N. Halley and John Beard.

Company G.—Capt. John I. Yellott, Lieuts. Frank H. Hardesty and Peter Wolfe.

Company H.—Capt. William M. Cronise, Lieuts. Robert C. Bamford and Martin L. Fry.

Company I.—Capt. Walter Saunders, Lieuts. Charles E. Eader and David H. Kolb.

Company K.—Capt. Charles J. Brown, Lieuts. Daniel L. Hoover and Stephen L. Bridge.

The battle list of the regiment embraces the following:

Skirmish at Loudon Heights, Va., May 27, 1862.
Skirmish at Monocacy Aqueduct, Md., Sept. 4, 1862.
Skirmish at Poolesville, Md., Sept. 5, 1862.
Action at Maryland Heights, Md., Sept. 13, 1862.
Defense of Harper's Ferry, Va., September 14 and 15, 1862.
Battle of Gettysburg, Pa., July 2 and 3, 1863.
Skirmish at Duffield's Station, Va., June 29, 1864.
Battle of Monocacy, Md., July 9, 1864.

The commands to which the regiment was attached are as follows: Banks' division, from muster in to

---

[1] Designation changed to the Thirteenth Maryland Infantry, April 8, 1865.

April 4, 1862; Middle Department, to July 2, 1863; Twelfth Army Corps, to July 17, 1863; Department of the Susquehanna, to Aug. 3, 1863; and Department of West Virginia, to May 29, 1865.

On the expiration of its term of service the original members (except veterans) were mustered out, and the organization, composed of veterans and recruits, retained in service until May 29, 1865, when the entire command was discharged, leaving behind them a record for valor of which this State and the United States may well be proud.

Second Regiment of Infantry, Potomac Home Brigade.—This regiment was organized at Cumberland, from August to October, 1861.

The companies were mainly recruited as follows: A, at Lonaconing; B, at Old Town; C, at Frostburg; D, at Piedmont, Va.; E, H, and K, at Cumberland; F, near Hancock; G, at Mount Savage; and I, in Allegany County at large.

The original field-officers were: Colonel, Thomas Johns; Lieutenant-Colonel, Robert Bruce; and Major, J. Ellis Porter. The two former were citizens of Cumberland, the latter of Lonaconing.

Orlando D. Robbins was appointed adjutant; Kennedy H. Butler, quartermaster; Samuel P. Smith, surgeon; Patrick A. Healey, assistant surgeon; and John H. Symmes, chaplain.

The officers of the line were:

Company A.—Capt. Alexander Shaw, Lieuts. John Douglas and Andrew Spier.

Company B.—Capt. James D. Roberts, Lieuts. John Irvine and James A. Morrow.

Company C.—Capt. John H. Huntley, Lieuts. John Weir and George W. McCulloch.

Company D.—Capt. Benjamin B. Shaw, Lieuts. Robert Powell and Mark Powell.

Company E.—Capt. James C. Lynn, Lieuts. Theodore Luman and George Conter.

Company F.—Capt. Lewis Dyche, Lieuts. George D. Summers and Norval McKinley.

Company G.—Capt. Charles G. McClelland, Lieuts. Robert Cowan and Lloyd Mahaney.

Company H.—Capt. George H. Bragonier, Lieuts. Samuel T. Little and David C. Edwards.

Company I.—Capt. J. Floyd McCulloch, Lieuts. James M. Shober and John F. Troxell.

Company K.—Capt. Peter B. Petrie, Lieuts. Jason G. Sawyer and Moses Bickford.

The regiment entered upon active duty in Western Maryland and Virginia as soon as organized, and stands credited with the following engagements, etc.:

Skirmish at Springfield, Va., Aug. 23, 1861.
Skirmish at Blue's House, Va., Aug. 26, 1861.
Skirmish near Springfield, Va., Oct. 26, 1861.
Skirmish at South Branch Bridge, Va., Oct. 26, 1861.
Skirmish at Great Cacapon Bridge, Va., Jan. 4, 1862.
Skirmish at Summit Point, Va., Oct. 7, 1863.
Skirmish at Charlestown, Va., Oct. 8, 1863.
Skirmish near Burlington, Va., Nov. 16, 1863.
Affair at Ridgeville, Va., Jan. 4, 1864.
Affair at Moorefield Junction, Va., Jan. 8, 1864.
Affair at Medley, Va., Jan. 30, 1864.
Engagement at Lynchburg, Va., June 18, 1864.
Engagement at Snicker's Gap, Va., July 18, 1864.

It served with the following commands: Kelley's division, to January, 1862; Landers' division, to March 11, 1862; Mountain Department, to June 26, 1862; Middle Department, to Sept. 19, 1862; Department of the Ohio, to December, 1862; Middle Department, to June, 1863; and Department of West Virginia, to May 29, 1865.

On the expiration of its term of service the original members (except veterans) were mustered out, and the veterans and recruits consolidated into a battalion of three companies,—A, B, and C. A new company, raised in March, 1865, to serve one year, was assigned to the battalion as Company D.

The organization was mustered out of service May 29, 1865.

That the Second Potomac Home Brigade fully sustained the reputation of Maryland soldiers for bravery and fidelity will never be questioned.

Third Regiment of Infantry, Potomac Home Brigade. — The organization of this regiment was begun at Cumberland in the fall of 1861, and before midwinter three full and two partially-filled companies had been mustered into the service of the United States. These companies (except B) were raised principally at Cumberland and other localities in Allegany County. Company B hailed from Warfordsburg, Pa.

The officers of these companies at muster in were as follows:

Company A.—Capt. Crawford W. Shearer, Lieuts. James S. Inskeep and John Coles.

Company B.—Capt. Wm. F. Cardiff, Lieuts. Wm. H. Hipsley and Moses Whitford.

Company C.—Capt. Henry C. Rizer, Lieuts. C. S. Jones and Wm. R. Jarboe.

Company D.—First Lieut. Theodore A. Ogle.

Company E.—First Lieut. Wm. A. Falkenstine.

On the 11th of August, 1862, three companies raised for the Fourth Regiment, Potomac Home Brigade, were transferred to the Third, as Companies E, F, and G, the designation of the original Company E being thereby changed to H. About the same time a company organized at Oakland by Capt. Michael Fallon, with John M. Armstrong and Joseph L. Forsyth as lieutenants, joined the regiment and took the place of Company D, whose designation was changed to I. This company was broken up Jan. 23, 1863, and the men transferred to Company C. In the spring of 1864 two new companies (I and K) were organized with the following officers:

Company I.—Capt. N. M. Ambrose, Lieuts. Gustave Valvis and Augustine Robinett.

Company K.—Capt. John W. Dodson, Lieuts. Wm. J. Donoghue and Wm. H. Foreman.

The first colonel of the regiment, Stephen W. Downey, of Cumberland, resigned Nov. 6, 1862, and was succeeded by Charles Gilpin, of the same city. Col. Gilpin was mustered out on expiration of term of service, Jan. 2, 1865. Thereafter the command devolved on Lieut.-Col. Henry C. Rizer.

The original staff-officers consisted of N. M. Ambrose, adjutant; John Matthews, quartermaster; Henry C. Stewart, assistant surgeon.

In detachments or as a whole the regiment participated in the following actions:

Skirmish at Franklin, Va., May 12, 1862.
Skirmish at Wardensville, Va., May 29, 1862.
Skirmish at Mooresfield, Va., June 29, 1862.
Skirmish at Maryland Heights, Md., Sept. 13, 1862.
Engagement at Bolivar Heights, or defense of Harper's Ferry, Va., Sept. 14-15, 1862.
Engagement at Frederick, Md., July 7 and 8, 1864.
Battle of Monocacy, Md., July 9, 1864.
Engagement at Snicker's Gap, Va., July 18, 1864.
Skirmish at Bolivar Heights, Va., Aug. 6, 1864.
Skirmish at Halltown, Va., Aug. 8, 1864.
Skirmish at Charlestown, Va., Aug. 9, 1864.
Skirmish at Berryville, Va., Aug. 13, 1864.

It served with the following commands: Lander's division, to March 11, 1862; Mountain Department, to June 26, 1862; Middle Department, to August, 1864; and Department of West Virginia, to May 29, 1865.

The original members (except veterans) being mustered out as their terms of service expired, the organization, composed of veterans and recruits, was retained in service until May 29, 1865.

That the services of this regiment were fully appreciated its favorable mention by superior commanders will attest.

Fourth Regiment of Infantry, Potomac Home Brigade.—During the winter of 1861–62, Lieut.-Col. George R. Dennis, of the First Potomac Home Brigade Infantry, undertook the organization of a fourth regiment of the brigade, but the effort did not succeed. Three companies were raised, one (A) at Hagerstown, one (B) at Baltimore, and one (C) in Frederick County.

These companies were officered as follows:

Company A.—Capt. Charles A. Welsh, Lieuts. Peter J. Mayberry and Robert Maxwell.

Company B.—Capt. Jacob Sarbaugh, Lieuts. Henry B. McCoy and John W. Dodson.

Company C.—Capt. Eli D. Grinder, Lieuts. Daniel C. Shriver and Charles Pratt.

James Resley was appointed quartermaster.

The battalion performed guard duty in Western Maryland, and on the Baltimore and Ohio Railroad between Harper's Ferry and Martinsburg, until Aug. 11, 1862, when it was consolidated with the Third Infantry, Potomac Home Brigade.

First Regiment of Eastern Shore Infantry.—Upon the recommendation of Governor Hicks, approved by President Lincoln, the Secretary of War authorized the organization of this regiment for special service on the Eastern Shore of Maryland. This authority was contained in the following communication:

"WAR DEPARTMENT, Aug. 16, 1861.
"COL. JAMES WALLACE, Cambridge, Md.:

"SIR,—The regiment of infantry you offer is accepted for three years, or during the war, provided you have it ready for marching orders in sixty days. In accordance with the letter of Governor Hicks of the 15th inst., you will be mustered into the service of the United States to act as a home guard, to be stationed on the Eastern Shore of Maryland.

"By order of the Secretary of War,
"JAMES LESLEY, JR., *Chief Clerk.*"

The formation of the companies which made up the regiment began at once, under the personal supervision of Col. Wallace, and within the time specified the regimental organization was completed and the command mustered into the service of the United States.

Companies A, B, and C were organized, respectively, at Cambridge, Strait's District, and Church Creek, in Dorchester County; D, E, F, and G, respectively, at Greensboro', Preston, Denton, and Federalsburg, in Caroline County; H, at Trappe, in Talbot County; I, at Baltimore City; and K, at Annamessex, in Somerset County.

Upon organization the roster of officers was as follows:

James Wallace, of Cambridge, colonel; William H. Comegys, of Greensboro', lieutenant-colonel; William Kirby, of Cambridge, major; John E. Rastall, adjutant; William H. Gootee, quartermaster; Francis P. Phelps, Jr., surgeon; Granville B. Lecompte, assistant surgeon; and Thomas L. Poulson, chaplain.

Company A.—Capt. John C. Henry, Lieuts. Thomas H. Coburn and Clement T. Mobray.

Company B.—Capt. John E. Graham, Lieuts. George B. Hart and William J. Robinson.

Company C.—Capt. John R. Keene, Lieuts. William R. Tall and William A. Bailey.

Company D.—Capt. William H. Comegys (promoted lieutenant-colonel), Lieuts. James L. Clendening and Richard H. Comegys.

Company E.—Capt. Andrew Stafford, Lieuts. James R. Hooper and Jesse W. Blades.

Company F.—Capt. Thomas Numbers, Lieuts. James B. Austin and Robert J. W. Garey.

Company G.—Capt. William H. Watkins, Lieuts. L. Shanley Davis and John E. Mobray.

Company H.—Capt. Charles R. Mullikin, Lieuts. Argalus G. Hennisee and James C. Mullikin.
Company I.—Capt. George W. Evans, Lieuts. William H. Pearson and John H. Shane.
Company K.—Capt. Littleton Long, Lieuts. Hance Lawson and William J. Porter.

The regiment served in Dix's division from muster in to April 4, 1862; Middle Department, to July 2, 1863; Twelfth Army Corps, to July 17, 1863; Department of the Susquehanna, to Aug. 3, 1863; and Middle Department, to Feb. 23, 1865.

Company A was mustered out of service Aug. 16, 1862. On the expiration of their terms of service the original members (except veterans) of the other companies were mustered out at Baltimore City, and the organization, composed of veterans and recruits, together with the veterans and recruits of the Second Eastern Shore Regiment (consolidated with the First, Jan. 23, 1865), was retained in service until Feb. 23, 1865, when it was consolidated with the Eleventh Infantry.

The First Eastern Shore was not brought face to face with the enemy, except on the field of Gettysburg, where it bore an honorable and gallant part, and again in a skirmish near Fairplay, Md., during Lee's retreat towards Virginia. But it performed valuable, onerous, and oftentimes most disagreeable duties. A detachment of the regiment accompanied Gen. Lockwood's expedition to Accomac and Northampton Counties, Va., in November, 1861. Much of its time was spent on the Eastern Shore of Maryland and Virginia, where it assisted materially in the efforts of the government to suppress the illegitimate trade carried on between the Eastern Shore counties and the insurgent district west of the Chesapeake Bay.

Second Regiment of Eastern Shore Infantry.—Authority to organize this regiment was given by the Secretary of War in the following communication:

"WAR DEPARTMENT, Sept. 14, 1861.
"COL. EDWARD WILKINS, Chestertown, Md.:
"SIR,—You are authorized to raise and organize a regiment of infantry to serve for three years, or during the war, with the understanding that it is for service in the State of Maryland, unless special necessity shall require their presence elsewhere, of which the Department will determine.
"Very respectfully
"Your obedient servant,
"THOMAS A. SCOTT,
"*Asst. Secretary of War.*"

The rendezvous for organization was established at Charlestown, whither the companies repaired and were mustered into the service of the United States during the fall and winter of 1861.

The men of Companies A, B, C, D, and E came chiefly from Kent County; F, from Baltimore City; and G and H, from Harford County. A small detachment, recruited for Company I, was transferred to Company H, March 19, 1862.

But eight companies were raised for the regiment. Edward Wilkins, of Chestertown, was commissioned colonel; Elijah E. Massey, of Queen Anne's County, lieutenant-colonel; Robert S. Rogers, of Havre de Grace, major; Alfred C. Wortley, adjutant; John N. McDaniel, quartermaster; William W. Valk, surgeon; Robert K. Robinson, assistant surgeon; and William B. Watson, chaplain.

The line-officers at this time were:

Company A.—Capt. Jesse K. Hines, Lieuts. William H. Hamilton and Thomas F. Hamilton.
Company B.—Capt. Simon Wickes, Lieuts. John H. Redue and Charles A. A. Stanley.
Company C.—Capt. Robert M. Smith, Lieuts. Justus B. Sheppard and John K. Evans.
Company D.—Capt. Wilson W. Walker, Lieuts. William T. Chance and William D. Burchinal.
Company E.—Capt. Charles H. Wickes, Lieuts. James M. Vickers and Benjamin H. Gardner.
Company F.—Capt. William H. Jones, Lieuts. George T. Mitchell and Socrates A. Smith.
Company G.—Capt. Seth W. Herrick, Lieuts. George W. Wilson and George Toy.
Company H.—Capt. Harrison Hopper, Lieuts. Oliver T. Lyon and William J. Vannort.

The actions in which the regiment participated are as follows:

Falling Waters, Md., July 14, 1863.
Piedmont, Va., June 5, 1864.
Lynchburg, Va., June 18, 1864.
Snicker's Ford, Va., July 18, 1864.
Winchester, Va., July 24, 1864.
Berryville, Va., Sept. 3, 1864.

The regiment served in Dix's division from organization to April 4, 1862; Middle Department, to July 8, 1863; Twelfth Army Corps, to July 17, 1863; Department of the Susquehanna, to Aug. 3, 1863; Middle Department, to November, 1863; and Department of West Virginia, to January, 1865.

Like its companion regiment, the Second Eastern Shore was mostly employed in the performance of arduous guard and garrison duty. Though it is true that it was not called to the more illustrious fields of strife, yet it is nevertheless the fact that its history is a record of faithful and meritorious service.

On the expiration of its term the original members (except veterans) were mustered out, and the organization, composed of veterans and recruits, retained in service until Jan. 23, 1865, when it was consolidated with the First Eastern Shore Infantry.

Purnell Legion.—On the 19th of August, 1861, Hon. William H. Purnell, postmaster of Baltimore, obtained permission from the Secretary of War to raise a regiment of infantry, two batteries of artillery, and two companies of cavalry, to serve for three years.

Pikesville Arsenal, near Baltimore, was selected as the place of rendezvous, and during the fall and early winter of 1861 nine companies of infantry, two batteries of artillery, and two companies of cavalry were mustered into the United States service. Companies A, B, C, H, and K of the infantry were recruited at Baltimore City; D, in Somerset County and Baltimore City; E, in Cecil Co., Md., and Chester Co., Pa.; F, in Baltimore County; and G, in Somerset and Worcester Counties.

Battery A of the artillery came from Baltimore City, and B from Cecil County. Company A of the cavalry was raised in Harford County, and B in Anne Arundel and Cecil Counties.

The field and staff-officers were Wm. H. Purnell, of Worcester County, colonel; John G. Johannes, of Baltimore City, lieutenant-colonel; Wm. J. Taylor, of Somerset County, major of infantry, and Edward R. Petherbridge, of Baltimore City, major of artillery; Josiah S. Hubbell, adjutant of infantry, and John Bigelow, adjutant of artillery; John T. Graham, quartermaster; John T. Hall, surgeon; Charles W. Cadden, assistant surgeon of infantry, James H. Jarrett of cavalry, and James S. O'Donnell of artillery; Vaughan Smith, chaplain.

The line-officers of infantry were:

Company A.—Capt. Benj. L. Simpson, Lieuts. Wm. Gibson and John F. Reinecker.
Company B.—Capt. Wm. Mitchell, Lieuts. Wm. H. Hogarth and Albert J. Brooks.
Company C.—Capt. Robert G. King, Lieuts. Alexander S. Williamson and Z. W. Christopher.
Company D.—Capt. Samuel A. Graham, Lieuts. Francis I. D. Webb and Wm. W. Thorington.
Company E.—Capt. Wm. T. Fulton, Lieuts. Samuel Burns, Jr., and Howard M. Newton.
Company F.—Capt. H. C. McAllister, Lieuts. Washington Stonebraker and Martin Callahan.
Company G.—Capt. George S. Merrill, Lieuts. Thomas A. Kennard and George W. Brown.
Company H.—Capt. Wm. H. Boyle, Lieuts. John W. Cooper and Stephen H. Bogardus.
Company K.—Capt. Wm. R. Patterson, Lieuts. Wm. H. Watkins and Thomas P. Hammitt.

Of the artillery—

Battery A.—Capt. John W. Wolcott, First Lieuts. James H. Rigby and Thomas Binyon, Second Lieuts. Edgar G. Taylor and Lowell A. Chamberlain.
Battery B.—Capt. Alonzo Snow, First Lieut. Lucius A. C. Gerry and T. J. Vanneman, Second Lieuts. James H. Kidd and John M. Bullock.

Of the cavalry—

Company A.—Capt. Robert E. Duvall, Lieuts. John Smiley and Joseph W. Strong.
Company B.—Capt. Thomas H. Watkins, Lieuts. Henry L. Clayton and Charles W. Palmer.

Upon the resignation of Col. Purnell, in February, 1862, the "Legion" organization of mixed arms was discontinued, and the infantry, cavalry, and artillery were made independent of each other.

The two batteries of artillery continued to serve as a battalion under Maj. Petherbridge until he resigned, in July, 1862, after which they were regarded as separate organizations.

The infantry participated in the following engagements:

Defense of Harper's Ferry, Va., May 29–30, 1862.
Action at Catlett's Station, Va., Aug. 22, 1862.
Battle of Antietam, Md., Sept. 17, 1862.
Skirmish at Harper's Ferry, Va., July 27, 1863.
Battle of Shady Grove, Va., May 30, 1864.
Battle of Bethesda Church, Va., May 31 and June 1, 1864.
Battle of Cold Harbor, Va., June 2–5, 1864.
Assault on Petersburg, Va., June 18, 1864.
Siege of Petersburg, Va., June 19–Oct. 24, 1864.
Battle of Weldon Railroad, Va., Aug. 18–21, 1864.
Battle of Poplar Spring Church, Va., Sept. 30, 1864.
Battle of Chapel House, Oct. 1–3, 1864.
Battle of Peeble's Farm, Va., Oct. 7–8, 1864.

The regiment served in Dix's division, Army of the Potomac, to March, 1862; Middle Department, Eighth Army Corps, to May 25, 1862; Second Brigade, Second Division, Second Corps, Army of Virginia, to September, 1862; Third Brigade, Second Division, Twelfth Corps, Army of the Potomac, to October, 1862; Second Brigade, Second Division, Twelfth Corps, to December, 1862; Middle Department, Eighth Army Corps, to May 26, 1864; Second Brigade, Second Division, Fifth Corps, Army of the Potomac, to October, 1864.

The original members (except veterans) were mustered out Oct. 24, 1864, and the veterans and recruits transferred to the First Infantry.

By bravery displayed on the field of battle the Purnell Legion earned for itself a high and lasting reputation.

Baltimore, or Dix Light Infantry.—In the summer of 1861, Gen. John A. Dix, who commanded the Department of Maryland, with headquarters at Baltimore, proposed to the Secretary of War to raise and arm a regiment of eight hundred and fifty picked men in Baltimore.

This proposal was accepted by the authorities at Washington, and Gen. Dix was authorized, on the 27th of July, "to organize and equip a regiment as suggested." Recruiting was soon commenced under the personal supervision of Dr. George W. Wayson, a prominent physician of Baltimore. Failing, however, to effect a regimental organization, five companies only being raised, the men were consolidated into two companies and transferred to the Third Infantry,

May 7, 1862, forming Companies I and K of that regiment.

The following is a list of its officers: Lieutenant-Colonel, Thomas B. Allard, of Baltimore City; Assistant Surgeon, Henry P. P. Yeates; Captains, Joshua Lynch, James Roff, Thomas H. Evans, Charles W. Crocker, and James H. Foy; First Lieutenants, Jesse W. Lee, Jr. (adjutant), Edward T. Sweeting (quartermaster), William J. McNelly, Carlton A. Uber, William H. Allen, Isaac L. Boyd, and Augustus M. Leary; Second Lieutenants, Robert B. Meads, Charles W. Edgar, Charles G. Downs, and Robert Watson.

All of these officers were discharged the service by reason of the consolidation except Capts. Roff and Crocker, First Lieuts. Lee, McNelly, and Leary, and Second Lieut. Downs, who were transferred to the Third Infantry.

Patapsco Guards.—On the 3d of September, 1861, Capt. Thomas S. McGowan, of Ellicott's Mills, was authorized by the War Department to raise an independent company of infantry, to be styled the Patapsco Guards.

The organization of the company was completed by Oct. 11, 1861, with the following officers: Captain, Thomas S. McGowan; First Lieutenant, Jacob Timanus; and Second Lieutenant, Lemuel Bewley.

Much of the company's time was passed in the performance of ordinary guard and provost duty at Ellicott's Mills, Md., and York, Harrisburg, and Chambersburg, Pa. During the Gettysburg campaign it took part in a skirmish with the enemy at Wrightsville, Pa., June 28, 1863, and again during McCausland's raid, near Chambersburg, Pa., July 30, 1864.

The original members were mustered out Oct. 17, 1864, and the company, composed of veterans and recruits, retained in service until Aug. 17, 1865, when it was mustered out.

Company C, Second Delaware Infantry.—Besides the troops regularly enrolled within the State of Maryland and credited to its quota was a company of infantry organized at Elkton, Cecil Co., and mustered into the service of the United States at Wilmington, Del., June 19, 1861, as Company C, Second Delaware Volunteers.

Benj. Ricketts was captain, with William F. A. Torbert and John G. Simpers lieutenants.

The company served with its regiment in the Army of the Potomac, and participated in all the memorable campaigns of that army.

The battle list comprises White Oak Swamp, Malvern Hill, Antietam, Fredericksburg, Chancellorsville, Gettysburg, Auburn, Mine Run, Spottsylvania, Cold Harbor, and Petersburg.

The company was mustered out of service June 23, 1864, John G. Simpers, the original second lieutenant, being then the captain. He re-entered the service Sept. 2, 1864, as captain of Company K, Sixth Maryland, to which he brought forty-eight recruits, thirty of whom had served three years in his old company.

CAVALRY.

First Regiment of Cavalry.—The formation of this regiment was commenced in the summer of 1861, under the first call of the President for three-years' men.

Companies A, B, C, D, and E were recruited in Baltimore City; F, at Baltimore and Cockeysville; G and K, at Pittsburgh, Pa.; H and I, in Allegany and Washington Counties; and L and M, at Washington, D. C. Companies G, H, I, and K were organized for the First Virginia Cavalry, attached to Ward H. Lamon's brigade, but by order of Gen. McClellan, dated Jan. 28, 1862, they were assigned to this regiment. Companies L and M, organized as independent companies District of Columbia Cavalry, were attached to the regiment in April, 1862, and December, 1863, respectively.

On the 20th of December, 1861, Andrew G. Miller, of Wisconsin, was appointed lieutenant-colonel, and James M. Deems, of Baltimore, major.

On the 1st of May, 1862, Miller was commissioned colonel, and Capt. Charles Wetschky, of Company B, lieutenant-colonel. The original staff-officers consisted of Burr H. Grover, adjutant; David C. Steiner, quartermaster; J. Edward Warner, surgeon; Charles C. Lee, assistant surgeon; and Arthur O. Brickman, chaplain.

The line-officers at original organization of the several companies were as follows:

Company A.—Capt. Joseph B. Merritt, Lieuts. David C. Steiner and Francis Shamburg.

Company B.—Capt. Charles Wetschky, Lieuts. Otto Von Borries and Henry Appel.

Company C.—Capt. Thomas Galloway, Lieuts. Burr H. Grover and John M. Tibbs.

Company D.—Capt. Charles F. Hillebrand, Lieuts. Jacob Seibert and Herman Von Marsdorf.

Company E.—Capt. John Axer, Lieuts. George Stuart and Randolph Norwood.

Company F.—Capt. Robert A. Wilson, Lieuts. Milton C. Dove and Henry C. Hack.

Company G.—Capt. Robert H. Patterson, Lieuts. John H. Stewart and John Hancock.

Company H.—Capt. Joseph R. Zeller, Lieuts. William H. Grafflin and Daniel C. Hiteshew.

Company I.—Capt. Charles H. Russell, Lieuts. Alexander H. Nesbitt and Christian E. Stonesifer.

Company K.—Capt. Leopold Sahl, Jr., Lieuts. Irvin Redpath and John Seiferth.

Company L.—Capt. George Thistleton, Lieuts. Joseph G. White and Joseph H. Cook.

Company M.—Capt. Louis F. Whitney, Lieuts. William H. Orton and F. A. Whitney.

The following list exhibits the engagements, etc., in which the First Cavalry participated, either as a whole or in detachments:

Ball's Bluff, Va., Oct. 21, 1861.
Slanes' Cross-Roads, Va., Jan. 4, 1862.
Bath, Va., Jan. 4, 1862.
Alpine Depot, Va., Jan. 4, 1862.
Hancock, Md., Jan. 5-6, 1862.
Bloomery Gap, Va., Feb. 14, 1862.
Middletown, Va., May 24, 1862.
Winchester, Va., May 24, 1862.
Charlestown, Va., May 28, 1862.
Harper's Ferry, Va., June 9, 1862.
Rapidan Station, Va., July 13, 1862.
Madison Court-House, Va., Aug. 8, 1862.
Cedar Mountain, Va., Aug. 9, 1862.
Rappahannock Station, Va., Aug. 22, 1862.
Freeman's Ford, Va., Aug. 22, 1862.
White Sulphur Springs, Va., Aug. 23, 1862.
Centreville, Va., Aug. 28, 1862.
Gainesville, Va., Aug. 28, 1862.
Groveton, Va., Aug. 29, 1862.
Bull Run, Va., Aug. 30, 1862.
Chantilly, Va., Sept. 1, 1862.
Boonsboro', Md., Sept. 7, 1862.
Maryland Heights, Md., Sept. 13, 1862.
Harper's Ferry, Va., Sept. 13-14, 1862.
Sharpsburg, Md., Sept. 15, 1862.
Manassas Junction, Va., Oct. 25, 1862.
Fredericksburg, Va., Dec. 13, 1862.
Dumfries, Va., Dec. 27, 1862.
Stoneman's Raid, Va., April and May, 1863.
Brandy Station, Va., June 9, 1863.
Beverly Ford, Va., June 9, 1863.
Aldie, Va., June 19, 1863.
Middleburg, Va., June 23, 1863.
Upperville, Va., June 23, 1863.
Gettysburg, Pa., July 1-3, 1863.
Millerstown, Md., July 5, 1863.
Benevola, Md., July 10, 1863.
Shepherdstown, Va., July 14, 1863.
Culpeper, Va., Sept. 14, 1863.
Rapidan Station, Va., Sept. 16, 1863.
Amissville, Va., Oct. 12, 1863.
White Sulphur Springs, Va., Oct. 13, 1863.
Auburn Mills, Va., Oct. 14, 1863.
Bristoe Station, Va., Oct. 14, 1863.
Mine Run, Va., Nov. 26th to Dec. 2, 1863.
Bermuda Hundred, Va., June 17, 1864.
Richmond and Petersburg Railroad, June 19, 1864.
Deep Bottom, Va., July 27, 1864.
Flusser's Mill, Va., Aug. 14, 1864.
Deep Run, Va., Aug. 16 and 18, 1864.
Siege of Petersburg, Va., Aug. 25–Sept. 27, 1864.
Chaffin's Farm, Va., Sept. 29, 1864.
Darbytown Road, Va., Oct. 13, 1864.
Fair Oaks, Va., Oct. 27, 1864.
Smithfield, Va., Dec. 7, 1864.
Five Forks (Dinwiddie Co.), Va., April 1, 1865.
Hatcher's Run, Va., April 2, 1865.
Southside Railroad, Va., April 2, 1865.
Burgess Mill, Va., April 3, 1865.
Five Forks (Amelia Co.), Va., April 4, 1865.
Sutherland's Depot, Va., April 5, 1865.
Richmond and Danville Railroad, Va., April 5, 1865.
Farmville, Va., April 6, 1865.
Appomattox Court-House (Clover Hill), Va., April 9, 1865.

The original members were mustered out as their terms of service expired, and the organization, composed of veterans and recruits, was retained in service until Aug. 8, 1865, when it was mustered out.

History alone can do full justice to the brave men who composed this regiment. Suffice it here to say that the First Maryland Cavalry maintained a reputation for fidelity and bravery second to no other cavalry regiment.

First Regiment, Potomac Home Brigade Cavalry.—This regiment had its nucleus in a battalion recruited chiefly in Frederick and Washington Counties during the summer of 1861, in accordance with the authority granted Hon. Francis Thomas to organize the Potomac Home Brigade, and was familiarly known as Cole's cavalry.

The four companies constituting the battalion were raised as independent organizations, and served as such until June, 1862, when they were consolidated under the command of the senior captain, Henry A. Cole, who was promoted major Aug. 1, 1862.

Company B did not formally unite with the battalion until March 21, 1863, when the four companies were first brought together at Kearneysville, Va.

The original officers of these companies were:

Company A.—Capt. Henry A. Cole, Lieuts. Richard W. Coomes and George W. F. Vernon.

Company B.—Capt. William Fiery, Lieuts. Alexander M. Flory and Jacob A. Metz.

Company C.—Capt. John Horner, Lieuts. John M. Annan and Washington Morrison.

Company D.—Capt. Pearce K. Curll, Lieuts. Robert H. Milling and Francis Gallagher.

In the spring of 1864 the battalion was increased to a full regiment of twelve companies.

While in process of augmentation Maj. Cole was advanced to the rank of lieutenant-colonel, and Capt. Vernon, of Company A, to that of major.

Upon the completion of the regimental organization its roster of officers stood as follows:

Henry A. Cole, colonel; George W. F. Vernon, lieutenant-colonel; J. Townsend Daniel, Alexander M. Flory, and Robert S. Mooney, majors; Oliver A. Horner, adjutant; H. F. Winchester, quartermaster; H. H. Vernon, commissary; Walter R. Way, surgeon; D. W. Onderdonk, assistant surgeon; and Charles Cole, chaplain.

Company A.—Capt. Daniel Link, Lieuts. Franklin Hitchcock and Lewis M. Zimmerman.

Company B.—Capt. William Fiery, Second Lieut. Jonathan L. Rivers.

Company C.—Capt. A. M. Hunter, Lieuts. W. A. Horner and H. Buckingham.

Company D.—Capt. Francis Gallagher, Lieuts. Samuel T. Mills and Samuel B. Sigler.

Company E.—Capt. George J. P. Wood, Lieuts. Charles V. Duncan and John T. Hickman.

Company F.—Capt. William F. Bragg, Lieuts. Hiram B. Younger and Uriah Garber.

Company G.—Capt. George M. Kersner, Lieuts. Frank D. Kerr and Thomas J. McAtee.

Company H.—Capt. Benjamin F. Houck, Lieuts. Elijah H. Johnson and Joseph A. Swaney.

Company I.—Capt. William L. Atkinson, Lieuts. Robert S. Mooney and Alexander M. Briscoe.

Company K.—Capt. Lewis M. Zimmerman, Lieuts. George E. Owens and Benjamin F. McAtee.

Company L.—Capt. John H. McCoy, Lieuts. Alexander A. Troxell and Charles J. Gehring.

Company M.—First Lieut. George W. Lease, Second Lieut. Leonard H. Greenewald.

Of the additional companies, E, F, and I were organized mainly at Baltimore City; G, H, and L, at Frederick City; and K and M, at large.

Company D having become reduced below the minimum standard, an independent company, organized at Cumberland in the summer of 1864 by Capt. Tappan W. Kelly, with Henry A. Bier and Columbus F. Benchoff as lieutenants, was assigned in its stead Jan. 30, 1865.

In the capacity of independent companies, or as a battalion and regiment, the services of this command were of the most active and efficient character. It took over one thousand prisoners, and captured or destroyed an immense amount of the enemy's property. Its engagements were numerous, and its marches continuous and severe. The following are some of the places where, as a whole or in part, it fought the enemy:

South Branch Bridge, Va., Oct. 26, 1861.
Hancock, Md., Jan. 5-6, 1862.
Bloomery Gap, Va., Feb. 14, 1862.
Martinsburg, Va., March 3, 1862.
Bunker Hill, Va., March 5, 1862.
Stephenson's Depot, Va., March 7 and 11, 1862.
Winchester, Va., March 12, 1862.
Kernstown, Va., March 22-23, 1862.
Edinburg, Va., April 1, 1862.
Grass Lick, Va., April 23, 1862.
Wardensville, Va., May 7, 1862.
Charlestown, Va., May 28, 1862.
Leesburg, Va., Sept. 2, 1862.
Harper's Ferry, Va., Sept. 13-14, 1862.
Sharpsburg, Md., Sept. 15, 1862.
Hyattstown, Md., Oct. 12, 1862.
Charlestown, Va., Nov. 14, 1862.
Charlestown, Va., Dec. 2, 1862.
Berryville, Va., Dec. 3, 1862.
Winchester and Charlestown, Va., Dec. 5, 1862.
Halltown, Va., Dec. 20, 1862.
Berryville, Va., June 13, 1863.
Martinsburg, Va., June 14, 1863.
Williamsport, Md., June 15, 1863.
Catoctin Creek, Md., June 17, 1863.
Sharpsburg, Md., 1863.
Fountaindale, Pa., June 28, 1863.
Frederick, Md., June 22, 1863.
Gettysburg, July 1-3, 1863.
Emmittsburg, Md., July 5, 1863.
Falling Waters, Va., July 6, 1863.
Harper's Ferry, Va., July 6, 1863.
Catoctin Mountain, Va., Sept. 14, 1863.
Snickersville, Va., 1863.
Leesburg, Va., 1863.
Rector's Cross-Roads, Va., 1863.
Bloomfield, Va., 1863.
Upperville, Va., Sept. 25, 1863.
Charlestown, Va., Oct. 18, 1863.
Mount Jackson, Va., Nov. 17, 1863.
Woodstock, Va., 1863.
Ashby's Gap, Va., 1863.
Upperville, Va., Dec. 10, 1863.
Front Royal, Va., Dec. 11, 1863.
Edinburg, Va., Dec. 17, 1863.
New Market, Va., Dec. 18, 1863.
Harrisonburg and Staunton, Va., Dec. 21, 1863.
Rectortown, Va., Jan. 1, 1864.
Loudon Heights, Va., Jan. 10, 1864.
Romney, Va., Jan. —, 1864.
Moorefield, Va., Jan. —, 1864.
Mechanicsville Gap, Va., Jan. —, 1864.
New Market, Va., May 13 and 15, 1864.
Harrisonburg, Va., June 3, 1864.
Piedmont, Va., June 5, 1864.
Tye River Gap, Va., June 12, 1864.
Lexington, Va., June 13, 1864.
Buchanan, Va., June 14, 1864.
Lynchburg, Va., June 18, 1864.
Salem, Va., June 21, 1864.
Leetown and Shepherdstown, Va., July 3, 1864.
Frederick, Md., July 11 and 12, 1864.
Maryland Heights, Md., 1864.
Brownsville, Md., 1864.
Crampton's Gap, Md., 1864.
Herndon, Va., 1864.
Purcellville, Va., July 16, 1864.
Snicker's Ferry, Va., July 18, 1864.
Ashby's Gap, Va., July 19, 1864.
Winchester, Va., July 19, 1864.
Kernstown, Va., July 23 and 24, 1864.
Snicker's Gap, Va., July 25, 1864.
Falling Waters, Va., July 26, 1864.
Hagerstown, Md., July 29 and 30, 1864.
Reedysville and Antietam, Md., Aug. 5, 1864.
Berryville, Va., Aug. 13, 1864.
Charlestown, Va., Aug. 22, 1864.
Summit Point, Va., Aug. 30, 1864.
White Post, Va., Sept. 3, 1864.
Winchester, Va., Sept. 19, 1864.

From 1861, when it first entered upon the arduous labors peculiar to the cavalry branch of the service, until peace dawned upon the land, Cole's cavalry was always ready for any duty, and in its performance gained for itself a well-merited reputation, and did honor to the State that sent it into the field. Although generally employed only upon the border of their own State, the service performed by these troops was none the less honorable than that performed by others on more glorious and renowned fields. Their duties in some instances were more perilous and arduous, and if fewer laurels were gained, the consciousness of important services performed is their best reward.

The regiment was mustered out of service June 28, 1865.

Second Regiment of Cavalry.—Under the President's proclamation of June 15, 1863, calling for six-months' volunteers, an effort was made to organize a regiment of cavalry, to be styled the Second. Five companies only were raised,—A, B, and E, at Baltimore; C, in Howard County and at Baltimore; and D, at Washington, D. C., and at Baltimore.

The original officers consisted of: Captains, George W. Hack, William F. Bragg, Thomas McCrea, William J. Hoffman, and John Sommer; First Lieutenants, B. F. T. Dulaney, Charles E. Dudrow, Peter Rush, Joseph F. Lewis, and Hiram B. Younger; Second Lieutenants, Francis A. Poisal, Elijah H. Johnson, George Munn, William W. Hoffman, and Daniel Shealy.

Soon after its organization the battalion, under command of Capt. Bragg, moved from Baltimore to Annapolis, and was employed at various points in Anne Arundel and Calvert Counties, with part of one company on provost duty in the city of Annapolis.

Companies A and B were mustered out of service Jan. 26, 1864; C and D, Feb. 6, 1864; and E, Jan. 31, 1864.

Before the expiration of their terms about seventy men re-enlisted for three years, and, with Lieut. J. F. Lewis, went into Company K of the Third Maryland Cavalry. Some of the other officers and men also re-entered the service in the First Potomac Home Brigade Cavalry.

Third Regiment of Cavalry.[1]—This regiment, consisting of ten companies, was organized at Baltimore City in the summer and fall of 1863. Companies A, B, C, H, I, and K were recruited at Baltimore. Companies D, E, F, and G were composed of men enrolled at Fort Delaware from among Confederate prisoners of war who had taken the oath of allegiance. In Company I were some men from Frederick County, and a portion of Company K consisted of men re-enlisted from the Second Cavalry.

---
[1] Also called "Bradford Dragoons."

C. Carroll Tevis, a graduate of the West Point Military Academy, was appointed colonel; Byron Kirby, lieutenant-colonel; William Kesley and Henry E. Clark, majors; William M. Crossland, adjutant; Stillman Williams, quartermaster; John M. Stevenson, surgeon; Edward Borck, Jr., and Joseph S. Claridge, assistant surgeons.

The line-officers were:

Company A.—Capt. Charles C. Moore, Lieuts. William H. Brown and J. Woodfin Minifie.
Company B.—Capt. Joseph C. Hodges, Lieuts. John S. Parker and Thomas W. Caulfield.
Company C.—Capt. Adolph Bery, Lieuts. H. P. Anderson and DeeLaroo Wilson.
Company D.—Capt. Joseph S. Gregory, Lieuts. Harry P. Eakin and Charles Seager.
Company E.—Capt. A. J. Pemberton, Lieuts. Thomas W. Caulfield and Kentuck B. Piatt.
Company F.—Capt. Henry E. Clark, Lieuts. William F. De-Vere and William H. Coulston.
Company G.—Capt. Samuel P. Walsh, Lieuts. Francis R. Haight and William Q. Moore.
Company H.—Capt. Douglas E. Jerrold (son of the celebrated London journalist), Lieuts. John Brownley and George W. Barnett.
Company I.—Capt. Eli D. Grinder, Lieuts. Hiram S. McNair and John W. Snively.
Company K.—Capt. Henry R. Crosby, First Lieut. Joseph F. Lewis.

The battle list of the Third Cavalry comprises the following affairs:

Skirmish at Fleming's Ford, La., Feb. 11, 1864.
Skirmishes at Mansuria, La., May 14 and 16, 1864.
Engagement at Marksville, La., May 17, 1864.
Engagement at Yellow Bayou, La., May 18 and 19, 1864.
Skirmish at Morgan's Ferry Road, La., June 9, 1864.
Capture of Fort Gaines, Ala., Aug. 8, 1864.
Capture of Fort Morgan, Ala., Aug. 23, 1864.
Capture of Spanish Fort, Ala., April 9, 1865.
Capture of Fort Blakely, Ala., April 9, 1865.

The regiment was consolidated into six companies Dec. 14, 1864, by the transfer of A to B, C to I, D to E, and G to F, H, and K.

Much reduced in numbers, the battalion was mustered out at Vicksburg, Miss., Sept. 7, 1865. Its service in Louisiana, Alabama, Florida, and Mississippi had sadly thinned its ranks.

Purnell Cavalry.—Two companies of cavalry (A and B) were organized in the fall of 1861, as a part of the Purnell Legion, from which they were permanently detached in the spring of 1862.

The roster of officers of these companies, as it stood at the date of organization, is given in the outline sketch of the Purnell Legion.

Company A left Pikesville Arsenal Jan. 6, 1862, and proceeded to the fair-grounds near Baltimore, afterwards known as Camp Bradford. It was subsequently stationed at Eastville, Franktown, Drummondtown, and Pungoteague, on the Eastern Shore of Virginia, and in St. Mary's County, Md. It also took part in the Gettysburg campaign, being present at the battle fought on the 2d and 3d of July, 1863, and was in frequent skirmishes during the retreat of the enemy towards Virginia. In the fall of 1863 it had a spirited skirmish with some pirates or guerrillas at Cape Charles, Va. It was mustered out of service July 28, 1865.

Company B moved from Pikesville Arsenal to the fair-grounds, near Baltimore, on the 6th of January, 1862, and subsequently did duty at Camp Carroll, Camp Parole, Baltimore City, Smyrna, Del., Bryantown, Monocacy Junction, and with the Army of the Potomac in front of Petersburg.

From Oct. 14, 1862, to Jan. 27, 1863, it was on duty at the State capital, under the orders of Governor Bradford. It was dismounted and equipped as infantry May 28, 1864, and joined the Army of the Potomac June 7, 1864, when it was temporarily attached to the Purnell Legion Infantry.

With this regiment it participated in the following engagements:

Assault on Petersburg, Va., June 18, 1864.
Siege of Petersburg, Va., June–October, 1864.
Battle of Weldon Railroad, Va., Aug. 18–21, 1864.
Battle of Poplar Spring Church, Va., Sept. 30, 1864.
Battle of Chapel House, Va., Oct. 1–3, 1864.
Battle of Peeble's Farm, Va., Oct. 7–8, 1864.

The original members (except veterans) were mustered out Oct. 26, 1864, and the veterans and recruits transferred to Company C, which was subsequently transferred to the Eighth Maryland.

Company C was organized at Baltimore City in September, 1862, with Theodore Clayton as captain, and Charles W. Palmer (promoted from second lieutenant of Company B) and Washington I. Purnell as lieutenants. It was stationed at Camp Bradford to Feb. 5, 1863, when it moved to Harper's Ferry, Va., thence to Drummondtown, Va., thence to Wilmington, Del., and finally, in June, 1864, to the Army of the Potomac in front of Petersburg, where it was assigned temporarily to the Purnell Legion Infantry. With this regiment it bore a part in the same engagements, etc., enumerated in the list of Company B.

The veterans and recruits of Company B were transferred to this company Oct. 26, 1864, and the consolidated force was transferred to the Eighth Maryland, Nov. 17, 1864.

In point of intelligence, courage, and endurance, these companies were not excelled by any in the service, and eminently deserve honorable mention.

Smith's Independent Company of Cavalry.—This company was organized at Snow Hill, Md., in September, 1862, in accordance with authority granted Col. George W. P. Smith by the Secretary of War "to raise a company of cavalry for special duty in Worcester County, unless the exigency of the service should require it to be attached to some regiment for general service."

The company was originally officered by George W. P. Smith, captain; Arthur J. Wallis, first lieutenant; and Charles F. Foster, second lieutenant.

During its term of service the company was stationed at Snow Hill, Newtown, Point Lookout, Eastville, Drummondtown, Salisbury, Relay House, Barnesville, etc.

It was mustered out of service June 30, 1865.

ARTILLERY.

Maryland furnished six batteries to the artillery arm of the service. Two of them were formed in the early part of the war, and performed distinguished services in many of the most important campaigns of the Army of the Potomac.

Battery A, originally attached to the Purnell Legion, was enrolled at Baltimore City in the fall of 1861. Its first complement of officers consisted of Capt. John W. Wolcott, who had served as a lieutenant in Nim's Massachusetts battery; First Lieuts. James H. Rigby and Thomas Binyon, Second Lieuts. Edgar G. Taylor and Lowell A. Chamberlain. It was engaged with the enemy at

Malvern Hill, Va., July 1, 1862.
Crampton's Pass, Md., Sept. 14, 1862.
Antietam, Md., Sept. 17, 1862.
Fredericksburg, Va., Dec. 13, 1862.
Marye's Heights, Va., May 3, 1863.
Salem Heights, Va., May 3–4, 1863.
Gettysburg, Pa., July 2–3, 1863.

In all its campaigns the battery won the commendation of its superior officers and the admiration of the commands with which it served. On the expiration of its term of service the original members (except veterans) were mustered out, and the organization, composed of veterans and recruits, retained in service until March 11, 1865, when it was consolidated with Battery B.

Battery B was recruited in Cecil County in the fall of 1861, and was at first attached to the Purnell Legion. The officers at date of organization were Capt. Alonzo Snow, First Lieuts. Lucius A. C. Gerry and T. J. Vanneman, Second Lieuts. James H. Kidd and John M. Bullock.

Its battle list comprises the following:

New Bridge, Va., June 5, 1862.
Malvern Hill, Va., July 1, 1862.
Antietam, Md., Sept. 17, 1862.
Fredericksburg, Va., Dec. 13, 1862.
New Market, Va., May 15, 1864.
Piedmont, Va., June 5, 1864.
Lynchburg, Va., June 18, 1864.
Near Salem, Va., June 21, 1864.

Like Battery A, this one was distinguished for efficiency, and won high praise from its commanding generals.

On the expiration of its term of service the original members (except veterans) were mustered out, and the organization, composed of veterans and recruits, together with the men of Battery A, consolidated with it March 11, 1865, was retained in service until July 3, 1865, when it was mustered out.

The Baltimore Battery, more generally known as "Alexander's Battery," was organized in the summer of 1862, at Baltimore, by Capt. F. W. Alexander, under special authority from the Secretary of War, dated July 28, 1862.

In eight days three hundred and twelve men were enlisted, from which Capt. Alexander selected one hundred and fifty-six of the best for his battery.

As originally constituted the officers were Capt. F. W. Alexander, First Lieuts. H. E. Alexander and Charles H. Evans, Second Lieuts. Peter Leary, Jr., and J. Thomas Hall.

The battery was engaged with the enemy at

Berryville, Va., June 13, 1863.
Opequan, Va., June 13, 1863.
Winchester, Va., June 14-15, 1863.
Middletown, Md., July 7, 1864.
Frederick, Md., July 8, 1864.
Monocacy, Md., July 9, 1864.

Its muster out June 17, 1865, ended the honorable service of a battery the superior of which, in intelligence, *morale*, and courage, was not found in the army.

Battery D was organized at Baltimore in the month of February, 1864, to serve three years, under the President's call of Feb. 1, 1864.

Its original officers were Capt. John M. Bruce, First Lieuts. Richard M. Ray and Charles A. Talbott, Second Lieuts. George Smith and Sidney S. Allen.

Unlike the batteries above mentioned, this one did not have the good fortune to particularly distinguish itself on the field of battle or in active campaigning. Its theatre of operations for the most part was in the defenses of Washington, where it did garrison duty at Forts Tillinghast, Lyon, Willard, Richardson, Ward, Barnard, C. F. Smith, and Whipple.

It was mustered out of service June 24, 1865.

Battery A (Second), otherwise known as the Junior Artillery, was organized at Baltimore in July, 1863, under the President's proclamation of June 15, 1863, calling for six-months' men.

Its original officers consisted of Capt. John M. Bruce, First Lieuts. Jacob W. Miller and Richard W. Pryor, Second Lieuts. David Duncan and Richard M. Ray.

The duties this battery performed were strictly of a local character.

It was mustered out of service Jan. 19, 1864.

Battery B (Second), better known as the Eagle Artillery, was organized at Baltimore in July, 1863, under the President's proclamation of June 15, 1863.

Upon organization its officers were Capt. Joseph H. Audoun, First Lieuts. Thomas W. Binyon and Edgar G. Taylor, Second Lieuts. Charles H. Dexter and John H. Jenkins.

It was mustered out of service Jan. 16, 1864.

COMMISSIONED OFFICERS FROM THE COUNTIES OF FREDERICK, WASHINGTON, MONTGOMERY, ALLEGANY, AND CARROLL IN THE VOLUNTEER FORCE OF THE UNITED STATES ARMY DURING THE WAR OF 1861-65.[1]

Appointed from Frederick County.

Albaugh, Maurice, captain First Infantry.
*Annan, John M., first lieutenant First (P. H. B.) Cavalry.
Baer, Jacob, acting surgeon First (P. H. B.) Infantry.
Baugher, Charles H., captain First (P. H. B.) Infantry.
Baugher, Eugene C., major First (P. H. B.) Infantry.
Beatty, Charles W., first lieutenant First (P. H. B.) Cavalry.
Beatty, Joseph E., surgeon Second Infantry.
Bennett, David T., lieutenant-colonel Seventh Infantry.
Boone, Jerningham, surgeon First (P. H. B.) Infantry.
Bragonier, A. C., captain Seventh Infantry.
Bromett, Michael, captain and acting quartermaster U. S. Vols.
Buhrman, Harvey, assistant surgeon Eleventh Infantry, and assistant surgeon Seventh Infantry.
Burr, Frank, first lieutenant First (P. H. B.) Cavalry.
Butler, Robert, second lieutenant First (P. H. B.) Cavalry.
Byrne, John, captain Third Infantry.
Carlin, David J., second lieutenant First (P. H. B.) Infantry.
Castle, George T., first lieutenant First (P. H. B.) Infantry, and captain and commissary subsistence U. S. Vols.
Cole, Charles, chaplain First (P. H. B.) Cavalry.
Cole, Henry A., colonel First (P. H. B.) Cavalry.
Coomes, Richard W., first lieutenant First (P. H. B.) Cavalry.
*Cooper, James, brigadier-general U. S. Vols.
Cooper, James, Jr., captain Second Infantry.
Creager, Noble H., first lieutenant Seventh Infantry.
Crever, Benj. H., hospital chaplain U. S. Vols.
Cromwell, Wm. H., second lieutenant Seventh Infantry.
Cronise, Wm. M., captain First (P. H. B.) Infantry.

---

[1] Only the highest rank attained in any particular regiment or corps is given. Those who died in the service are indicated by an asterisk. See the writer's History of Baltimore City and County for other officers who served in the Union army.

Crum, Isaac B., second lieutenant First (P. H. B.) Infantry.
Damuth, Charles A., captain Sixth Infantry.[1]
Dayhoff, Joshua T., second lieutenant Seventh Infantry.
Dennis, George R., lieutenant-colonel First (P. H. B.) Infantry.
*Devilbiss, Isaiah, first lieutenant Seventh Infantry.
Dixon, Charles T., captain Eighth Infantry.
*Eader, Charles E., first lieutenant First (P. H. B.) Infantry.
Eck, Samuel T., captain Third (P. H. B.) Infantry.
Eichelberger, G. M., captain Sixth Infantry.[2]
*Ely, Wm. J., second lieutenant Third Cavalry.
Foreman, Edwd. K., surgeon Sixth Infantry.
Fox, Henry J., captain First (P. H. B.) Infantry.
Gannon, Edward V., first lieutenant First (P. H. B.) Cavalry.
Glessner, Geo. W., second lieutenant First (P. H. B.) Infantry.
Glessner, William, captain First (P. H. B.) Infantry.
Goldsborough, Edward Y., first lieutenant Eighth Infantry.
Green, Hanson T. C., second lieutenant First (P. H. B.) Cavalry.
Grinder, Eli D., captain Fourth (P. H. B.) Infantry, and captain Third Cavalry.
Groff, Joseph, captain First (P. H. B.) Infantry.
Hagan, Peter A., second lieutenant Seventh Infantry.
Hammett, David C., second lieutenant Sixth Infantry.
Harn, Thomas W., first lieutenant Seventh Infantry.
Hergesheimer, Robert H., second lieutenant Seventh Infantry.[3]
Hitchcock, Franklin, captain First (P. H. B.) Cavalry.
Horner, Oliver A., major First (P. H. B.) Cavalry.
Howard, John, captain Seventh Infantry.
Kerr, Frank D., first lieutenant First (P. H. B.) Cavalry.
Kolb, David H., second lieutenant First (P. H. B.) Infantry.
Koogle, Jacob, first lieutenant Seventh Infantry.
Kuhn, Leander H., captain First (P. H. B.) Infantry.
Lease, George W., first lieutenant First (P. H. B.) Cavalry.
Link, Daniel, captain First (P. H. B.) Cavalry.
Long, Charles H., first lieutenant First (P. H. B.) Infantry.
Lugenbeel, Henry G., second lieutenant Seventh Infantry.
Lyeth, John McF., captain First Infantry.
Makechney, John, captain Seventh Infantry.
Maulsby, William P., Sr., colonel First (P. H. B.) Infantry.
Maulsby, William P., Jr., first lieutenant and adjutant First (P. H. B.) Infantry.
Maxell, Samuel J., first lieutenant and commissary First (P. H. B.) Cavalry.
McLane, Rufus A., captain First (P. H. B.) Infantry.
McMillan, Oscar D., first lieutenant First (P. H. B.) Cavalry.
Morrison, Washington, first lieutenant First (P. H. B.) Cavalry.
Orrison, David E., second lieutenant First (P. H. B.) Cavalry.
Ostrelli, Charles, first lieutenant and adjutant First (P. H. B.) Cavalry.
Otto, James H. B., captain Eleventh Infantry.
Ramsburg, John E., captain First (P. H. B.) Infantry.
Reay, George W., first lieutenant Third Infantry.
Roderick, William W., second lieutenant Eighth Infantry.
Rouzer, John R., captain Sixth Infantry.[4]
Rouzer, Martin, captain Sixth Infantry.

Ryan, Joseph P., first lieutenant First (P. H. B.) Infantry.
Saunders, Walter, captain First (P. H. B.) Infantry.
Schley, Alfred, captain Fifth Infantry.
Schley, Benjamin H., major First Infantry.
Smith, Francis M., first lieutenant and adjutant First Infantry.[5]
*Smith, James T., first lieutenant First (P. H. B.) Infantry.
Staley, Gideon, first lieutenant First (P. H. B.) Infantry.
Steiner, John A., lieutenant-colonel First (P. H. B.) Infantry.[6]
Suman, John J., chaplain Eighth Infantry.
Sweadner, John, second lieutenant Fifth Infantry.
Tabler, Franklin C., second lieutenant First (P. H. B.) Infantry.
Thrasher, Joseph E., first lieutenant First (P. H. B.) Infantry.
Troxell, Alfred A., first lieutenant First (P. H. B.) Cavalry.
Tyler, George L., first lieutenant and adjutant Seventh Infantry.[7]
Tyler, Henry, first lieutenant Sixth Infantry.
Vernon, Geo. W. F., lieutenant-colonel First (P. H. B.) Cavalry.
*Vernon, Henry H., first lieutenant and commissary First (P. H. B.) Cavalry.
Willard, James, assistant surgeon First (P. H. B.) Infantry.
Willman, J. T. C., second lieutenant Third (P. H. B.) Infantry.
*Willman, John L., first lieutenant First (P. H. B.) Infantry.
Winchester, B. F., captain and commissary subsistence United States Volunteers.
Winchester, Hiram F., first lieutenant and quartermaster First (P. H. B.) Cavalry.
Wolfe, Thomas M., first lieutenant and quartermaster First (P. H. B.) Infantry.
Woodrow, William E., second lieutenant Third Infantry.
Zimmerman, Lewis M., captain First (P. H. B.) Cavalry.

Appointed from Washington County.

Anderson, Ephraim F., captain Seventh Infantry.[8]
Barnford, Robert C., captain First (P. H. B.) Infantry.
Barnett, George W., second lieutenant Third Cavalry.
Barnett, James, first lieutenant Third Infantry.
Beard, John, first lieutenant First (P. H. B.) Infantry.
Beard, Samuel M., first lieutenant First (P. H. B.) Infantry.
Brewer, James H. C., first lieutenant and quartermaster Sixth Infantry.
Brewer, Valentine G., first lieutenant Seventh Infantry.
Bromley, John, first lieutenant Third Cavalry, and captain First (P. H. B.) Infantry.
Burk, Jerome B., first lieutenant First (P. H. B.) Infantry.
Colklesser, William H., captain Seventh Infantry.
Cook, Roger E., colonel First (P. H. B.) Infantry.
Drenner, John W., second lieutenant First (P. H. B.) Infantry.
Edwards, Henry, hospital chaplain United States Volunteers.
Embrey, Charles W., second lieutenant First Cavalry.
Ferguson, William P., chaplain First (P. H. B.) Infantry.
Fiery, William, captain First (P. H. B.) Cavalry.
Flory, Alex. M., major First (P. H. B.) Cavalry.
Foreman, Wm. H., first lieutenant Third (P. H. B.) Infantry.
Forsyth, Joseph L., second lieutenant Third (P. H. B.) Infantry.
Fry, Martin L., second lieutenant First (P. H. B.) Infantry.
Halley, Tacitus N., captain First (P. H. B.) Infantry.

---

[1] Breveted major for gallant and meritorious services at the battle of Sailor's Creek, Va.

[2] Breveted captain for gallant and meritorious services before Petersburg, Va.

[3] Awarded a medal of honor for capturing a battle-flag from the enemy at Five Forks, Va., April 1, 1865.

[4] Breveted major for gallant conduct at the battle of Winchester, Va., and lieutenant-colonel for gallant and meritorious services during the war.

[5] Breveted captain for gallant and meritorious services at the battle of Five Forks, Va.

[6] Breveted colonel and brigadier-general for faithful and meritorious services.

[7] Breveted captain for gallant and meritorious conduct at the battle of the Wilderness, Va.

[8] Breveted major for gallantry at the battle of the Wilderness, and lieutenant-colonel for conspicuous gallantry at the battle of Spottsylvania Court-House, Va.

Herbert, F. D., additional paymaster United States Volunteers.
Hewitt, Jacob, captain First (P. H. B.) Infantry.
*Hiteshew, Daniel C., first lieutenant First Cavalry.
Hiteshew, Philip L., captain First Cavalry.
Horine, Wm. H. H., second lieutenant Seventh Infantry.
*Houck, Benj. F., captain First (P. H. B.) Cavalry.
*Irvin, Wm. H., first lieutenant First Cavalry.
*Kennedy, Wm. B., major Third Infantry.
Kershener, George M., captain First (P. H. B.) Cavalry.
Kimble, Robert J., second lieutenant First Cavalry.
King, Harrison E., first lieutenant First (P. H. B.) Infantry.
Knodle, Charles S., second lieutenant Seventh Infantry.
Mann, Charles W., second lieutenant First (P. H. B.) Cavalry.
*Martin, Adam B., captain Sixth Infantry.
Martin, John M., second lieutenant First (P. H. B.) Infantry.
Mason, Daniel, second lieutenant First (P. H. B.) Infantry.
Maxwell, Robert, second lieutenant Fourth (P. H. B.) Infantry, and captain Third (P. H. B.) Infantry.
Mayberry, Peter J., first lieutenant Fourth (P. H. B.) Infantry, and first lieutenant Third (P. H. B.) Infantry.
McAtee, Benj. F., second lieutenant First (P. H. B.) Cavalry.
McAtee, Thomas J., second lieutenant First (P. H. B.) Cavalry.
McBride, Edward, second lieutenant Third Infantry.
McCoy, John H., captain First (P. H. B.) Cavalry.
McKee, Charles E. S., surgeon Third (P. H. B.) Infantry.[1]
McKinley, Norval, captain Second (P. H. B.) Infantry.
McMachan, Henry M., captain First Cavalry.
*Metz, Jacob, second lieutenant First (P. H. B.) Cavalry.
Mobley, Edward M., major Seventh Infantry.[2]
Morrison, George W. B., first lieutenant Third Infantry.
Mullendore, Josiah E., second lieutenant First (P. H. B.) Infantry.
*Nape, John, second lieutenant Third Infantry.
Nesbitt, Alexander A., captain First Cavalry.
Nesbitt, Thomas S., first lieutenant and quartermaster Seventh Infantry.
Noile, John T., second lieutenant First (P. H. B.) Cavalry.
Pennell, David, second lieutenant First (P. H. B.) Infantry.
Pennell, Hezekiah C., first lieutenant First (P. H. B.) Infantry.
*Prather, Samuel G., captain First (P. H. B.) Infantry.
Ratcliff, William D., captain Seventh Infantry.
Resley, James, first lieutenant and quartermaster Fourth (P. H. B.) Infantry.
Rivers, Jonathan L., captain First (P. H. B.) Cavalry.
Robinson, James A., second lieutenant Sixth Infantry.
Russell, Charles H., major First Cavalry.
Seidenstricker, William H., captain First (P. H. B.) Infantry.
Sigler, Samuel B., second lieutenant First (P. H. B.) Cavalry.
*Small, Melville R., first lieutenant and adjutant Sixth Infantry.
Smith, John K., first lieutenant Seventh Infantry.
Snively, George W., first lieutenant Third Cavalry.
Speaker, Frederick, second lieutenant First Cavalry.
Startzman, George W., second lieutenant Third (P. H. B.) Infantry.
Stinemetz, John, second lieutenant Twelfth Infantry, and second lieutenant First (P. H. B.) Infantry.
Stonesifer, Christian E., second lieutenant First Cavalry.
*Summers, George D., captain Second (P. H. B.) Infantry.
Suter, Charles M., first lieutenant Seventh Infantry.

[1] Breveted lieutenant-colonel for faithful and efficient services.

[2] Breveted lieutenant-colonel for gallant and meritorious services during the campaign terminating with the surrender of Lee's army, and colonel for faithful and gallant services.

Troupe, Joseph C., first lieutenant First (P. H. B.) Infantry.
Van Lear, John, captain and commissary subsistence United States Volunteers.
Weaver, David J., captain Third Infantry.
Weise, Arthur J., first lieutenant Seventh Infantry.
Wilson, James, first lieutenant First (P. H. B.) Infantry.
Yountz, William H. H., captain First (P. H. B.) Infantry.
Zeller, Joseph R., captain First Cavalry.

Appointed from Montgomery County.

Brooke, E. H., additional paymaster United States Volunteers.
*Engle, M. P., captain and assistant quartermaster United States Volunteers.
Lewis, Joseph S., first lieutenant Second Cavalry, and first lieutenant Third Cavalry.

Appointed from Allegany County.

Ambrose, Nathaniel M., captain Third (P. H. B.) Infantry.
Armstrong, John M., first lieutenant Third (P. H. B.) Infantry.
Benchoff, Columbus F., second lieutenant First (P. H. B.) Cavalry.
Bier, Henry A., first lieutenant First (P. H. B.) Cavalry.
Blocher, Daniel, first lieutenant and quartermaster First (P. H. B.) Infantry.
Bragonier, George H., captain Second (P. H. B.) Infantry.
Brinkman, Harman, second lieutenant Second (P. H. B.) Infantry.
Browning, Richard T., second lieutenant Second (P. H. B.) Infantry.
Bruce, Robert, colonel Second (P. H. B.) Infantry.
Buckey, Jacob H., second lieutenant First (P. H. B.) Infantry.
Butler, Kennedy H., first lieutenant and quartermaster Second (P. H. B.) Infantry.
Coles, John, first lieutenant Third (P. H. B.) Infantry.
Couter, George, first lieutenant Second (P. H. B.) Infantry.
Cowan, Robert, captain Second (P. H. B.) Infantry.
Cross, Wm. A., second lieutenant Third (P. H. B.) Infantry.
Douglass, John, captain Second (P. H. B.) Infantry.
Downey, Stephen W., colonel Third (P. H. B.) Infantry.
Edwards, David C., second lieutenant Second (P. H. B.) Infantry.
Falkinstine, Wm. A., captain Third (P. H. B.) Infantry.
Fallon, Michael, major Third (P. H. B.) Infantry.
Friend, Hanson B., second lieutenant Third (P. H. B.) Infantry.
Friend, Wm. H. H., first lieutenant Third (P. H. B.) Infantry.
Garrahan, James E., captain Third (P. H. B.) Infantry.
Gilpin, Charles, colonel Third (P. H. B.) Infantry.
Gross, Richard L., second lieutenant Eighth Infantry.
Hartsock, Henry H., captain Second (P. H. B.) Infantry.
Healy, Patrick A., assistant surgeon Second (P. H. B.) Infantry.
Huntly, John H., major Second (P. H. B.) Infantry.
Irvine, John, first lieutenant Second (P. H. B.) Infantry.
Irvine, Thomas, second lieutenant Second (P. H. B.) Infantry.
Jarboe, Wm. R., captain Third (P. H. B.) Infantry.
Jenkins, Wm. H., second lieutenant Third (P. H. B.) Infantry.
Johns, Thomas, colonel Second (P. H. B.) Infantry.
Kelley, Tappan W., captain First (P. H. B.) Cavalry.
Little, Samuel T., first lieutenant Second (P. H. B.) Infantry.
Luman, Theodore, first lieutenant and adjutant Second (P. H. B.) Infantry.
Lynn, A. Browne, first lieutenant Second (P. H. B.) Infantry.
Lynn, James C., lieutenant-colonel Second (P. H. B.) Infantry.
Mahaney, Lloyd, first lieutenant Second (P. H. B.) Infantry.

Matthews, John, first lieutenant Third (P. H B.) Infantry.
McAleer, Charles F., first lieutenant Third (P. H. B.) Infantry.
McCulloh, George W., second lieutenant Second (P. H. B.) Infantry, and second lieutenant Eighth Infantry.
McCulloh, J. Floyd, captain Second (P. H. B.) Infantry.
McKee, James A., second lieutenant Second (P. H. B.) Infantry.
Morrow, James A., captain Second (P. H. B.) Infantry.
Ogle, Theodore A., first lieutenant Third (P. H. B.) Infantry.
Owens, George E., first lieutenant First (P. H. B.) Cavalry.
Pelton, Emory W., second lieutenant Second (P. H. B.) Infantry.
Petrie, Peter B., captain Second (P. H. B.) Infantry.
Porter, G. Ellis, lieutenant-colonel Second (P. H. B.) Infantry.
Powell, Mark, second lieutenant Second (P. H. B.) Infantry.
Powell, Robert, first lieutenant Second (P. H. B.) Infantry.
Rizer, Henry C., colonel Third (P. H. B.) Infantry.
Robbins, Orlando D., first lieutenant and adjutant Second (P. H. B.) Infantry.
Roberts, James D., captain Second (P. H. B.) Infantry.
Robinett, Augustine, first lieutenant Third (P. H. B.) Infantry.
Sansom, Richard C., first lieutenant Second (P. H. B.) Infantry.
Schilling, Joseph G., chaplain First Infantry.
Shaw, Alexander, major Second (P. H. B.) Infantry.
Shaw, Benjamin B., captain Second (P. H. B.) Infantry.
Shaw, Levi, second lieutenant Second (P. H. B.) Infantry.
Shearer, Crawford W., lieutenant-colonel Third (P. H. B.) Infantry.
Shearer, James, first lieutenant and adjutant Third (P. H. B.) Infantry.
Shober, James M., first lieutenant Second (P. H. B.) Infantry.
Smith, Samuel P., surgeon Second (P. H. B.) Infantry.
Spier, Andrew, first lieutenant Second (P. H. B.) Infantry.
Swaney, Joseph A., first lieutenant First (P. H. B.) Cavalry.
Symmes, John H., chaplain Second (P. H. B.) Infantry.
Tennant, Alexander, first lieutenant Second (P. H. B.) Infantry.
Thayer, Charles H., first lieutenant Second (P. H. B.) Infantry.
Thompson, James, second lieutenant Second (P. H. B.) Infantry.
Thruston, C. M., brigadier-general U. S. Vols.
*Troxell, Jacob L., second lieutenant Eighth Infantry.
Troxell, John F., second lieutenant Second (P. H. B.) Infantry.
Wardwell, Ernest H., captain and assistant quartermaster U. S. Vols.
Weir, John, captain Second (P. H. B.) Infantry.
White, James W., first lieutenant Third (P. H. B.) Infantry.
Wigley, George, second lieutenant Second (P. H. B.) Infantry.

Appointed from Carroll County.

*Angel, Samuel W., first lieutenant Sixth Infantry.
Beaver, J. L., captain Sixth Infantry.
Billingslea, Albert, captain Sixth Infantry.
*Burns, William H., second lieutenant Sixth Infantry.
Byers, Lewis F., captain Sixth Infantry.
Easton, William T., first lieutenant Fourth Infantry.
Hoover, Daniel L., first lieutenant First (P. H. B.) Infantry.
Jordan, John W., second lieutenant Third Infantry, and second lieutenant Second (P. H. B.) Infantry.
Kuhn, Charles N., first lieutenant Sixth Infantry.
Lightner, Isaiah, captain Seventh Infantry.
Mathias, O. H. P., first lieutenant Sixth Infantry.[1]

McKellip, William A., lieutenant-colonel Sixth Infantry.
*Myers, Alexander F., second lieutenant Sixth Infantry.
*Ocker, Thomas J., captain Sixth Infantry.[2]
Reckard, John W., second lieutenant Fourth Infantry.
Reifsnider, Charles T., first lieutenant Seventh Infantry.
Rinehart, Daniel, captain Seventh Infantry.
Webster, George, captain Sixth Infantry.
Wheeler, William B., assistant surgeon Eighth Infantry.[3]

CHAPTER XVI.

RECORD OF MARYLAND COMMANDS IN THE CONFEDERATE ARMY DURING THE CIVIL WAR OF 1861-65.

The First Maryland Infantry.—During the session of the General Assembly at Frederick, in April and May, 1861, it was waited upon by Hon. James M. Mason, formerly United States senator from Virginia, as commissioner from that State, authorized to negotiate a treaty of alliance offensive and defensive with Maryland on her behalf. While in Frederick upon this business, Capt. Bradley T. Johnson, a native of that place, procured from Mr. Mason authority to raise troops for the Confederate service, on the pledge of Mr. Mason that all such troops would be welcomed there. Armed with this indorsement, Capt. Johnson visited Col. Jackson, then in command of the Virginia troops at Harper's Ferry, and obtained from him permission to rendezvous his troops at the Point of Rocks. Accordingly, on May 8, 1861, Capt. Johnson marched his company out of Frederick to the Point of Rocks and crossed to the Virginia side. On the 9th of May he was joined by Capt. C. C. Edelin with a company from Baltimore. Other skeleton companies were rapidly formed at Harper's Ferry under Capts. James R. Herbert, Wilson G. Nicholas, Harry McCoy, Holbrook, Price, and Wellmore. By the 15th of May eight companies had been organized, and Capt. George H. Steuart, of the regular cavalry of the Confederate army, was placed in command of them as lieutenant-colonel by Col. Jackson. Lieut.-Col. Steuart had been a captain in the First Regiment United States Cavalry, and being a Marylander, was placed in command of the First

---

[1] Breveted first lieutenant for gallant and meritorious services at the battle of Sailor's Creek, Va.

[2] Breveted major for gallant and meritorious services before Petersburg, Va.

[3] We are indebted for the historical sketches of the various military organizations from Maryland in the Federal service, as well as for the names of the officers from Western Maryland, and for much of the material in the chapters upon the civil war, to Joseph W. Kirkley, one of the most gallant representatives of the famous First Maryland (Federal) Regiment, who is preparing a history of the Maryland commands in the Union armies during the war.

Maryland Battalion, which when first formed numbered about four hundred and fifty men enlisted for the war. At this time the organization of the battalion was as follows: Lieutenant-Colonel, George H. Steuart; Company A, Captain, Bradley T. Johnson; Lieutenants, George R. Shellman, Charles Blair, G. M. E. Shearer; Company B, Captain, C. Columbus Edelin; Lieutenants, James Mullen, Thomas Costello, James Griffin; Company C, Captain, Frank S. Price; Company D, Captain, James R. Herbert; Lieutenants, George Booth, Nicholas Snowden, William Key Howard; Company E, Captain, Harry McCoy; Lieutenants, John Lutts, Joseph Marriott. Afterwards Capt. McCoy resigned, and Edmund O'Brien succeeded him in the captaincy. Company F, Captain, Thomas Holbrook; Company G, Captain, Wilson Carr Nicholas; Lieutenants, Alexander Cross, J. Louis Smith, John Deppish; Company H, Captain Wellmore. For several weeks after its organization the battalion remained at Harper's Ferry. Through the exertions of Mrs. Bradley T. Johnson, five hundred Mississippi rifles were obtained from North Carolina for the command, and uniforms, underclothes, and tents from Richmond, Va. On the 21st and 22d of May the battalion was regularly mustered into the Confederate service by Lieut.-Col. George Deas, assistant inspector-general Confederate States army. In the mean time other Maryland commands were being organized at Richmond, among them four companies commanded by Capts. J. Lyle Clark, E. R. Dorsey, William H. Murray, and M. S. Robertson. Capt. Clark elected to unite his company with the Twenty-first Virginia. The other three companies were united with the battalion at Harper's Ferry, the companies of which were reorganized, and the First Maryland Regiment formed, with Arnold Elzey, late captain of artillery, United States army, colonel; George H. Steuart, late captain of cavalry, United States army, lieutenant-colonel; and Bradley T. Johnson, major; Acting Adjutant, Frank X. Ward; Quartermaster, G. D. Spurrier; Surgeon, Dr. Galliard; Company A, Captain, W. W. Goldsborough; Lieutenants, G. R. Shellman, Charles Blair, G. M. E. Shearer; Company B, Captain, C. C. Edelin; Lieutenants, James Mullin, T. Casteltor, Joseph Griffin; Company C, Captain, E. R. Dorsey; Lieutenants, S. H. Stewart, R. C. Smith, William Thomas; Company D, Captain, T. R. Herbert; Lieutenants, George Booth, Nicholas Snowden, W. Key Howard; Company E, Captain, H. McCoy; Lieutenants, J. Lutts, Joseph Marriott, J. Cushing; Company F, Captain, J. Louis Smith; Lieutenants, Joseph Stewart, William Broadfoot, Thomas Holbrook; Company G, Captain, Willie C. Nicholas; Lieutenants, Alexander Cross, John Deppish; Company H, Captain, William H. Murray; Lieutenants, George Thomas, F. X. Ward, Richard Gilmor; Company I, Captain, M. S. Robertson; Lieutenants, Hugh Mitchell, H. H. Bean, Eugene Diggs. The regiment numbered over seven hundred men at the time of its organization. Company A was brought by Capt. Johnson from Frederick; Companies B, C, E, and F were composed of Baltimoreans; Company D, of men from Prince George's, Anne Arundel, Baltimore, and other counties; Company G, of men from Baltimore City and County, Pikesville and its vicinity; Company I, of men from Charles and St. Mary's; and Company H, of men drawn from all parts of the State. The regiment performed gallant service at the battle of Manassas, where Col. Elzey was made brigadier-general on the field. The casualties in the First Maryland at the battle of Manassas were Corp. John Berryman and Private W. H. Codd, of Company C, badly wounded, and John Swisher, of Company A, mortally wounded, the latter being the first Marylander killed in battle. Capt. E. R. Dorsey, of Company C, was promoted major, 21st of July, 1861, and subsequently made lieutenant-colonel. First Lieut. S. Hunter Stewart, of the same company, was appointed assistant quartermaster, with rank of captain, and Second Lieut. R. Carter Smith was elected captain of Company C in 1861. About the same time Lieut.-Col. Steuart was promoted to the colonelcy, and Maj. Bradley T. Johnson was made lieutenant-colonel. After the battle of Manassas the regiment was ordered to Fairfax Court-House, where it remained about two weeks, when it rejoined the brigade at their camp near Fairfax Station. Here it stayed until the 19th of October, when it withdrew to Centreville, and late in November removed to a pine forest near Manassas, where it went into winter quarters. On the first day of 1862 the "furlough and bounty law" went into effect, and in accordance with its terms, two companies of the First Maryland, A and B, being twelve-months' men, re-enlisted, and received furloughs of from thirty to sixty days. Companies C, H, and I, which had also enlisted for twelve months, did not re-enlist for the war, preferring to enter some other branch of the service. The other four companies had originally enlisted for the war. In the early part of 1862, Lieut.-Col. Bradley T. Johnson was made colonel, and Maj. Edward R. Dorsey lieutenant-colonel of the regiment, which had been detached from Elzey's brigade to form, with the Baltimore Light Artillery, the nucleus of a Maryland brigade under the command of Gen. George H. Steuart, who was promoted to a brigadier-generalcy on the 6th of March. On the 19th of May, 1862, the term of enlistment of Company C expired, and the men were discharged. All, with but two or three exceptions, re-enlisted in the cavalry or artillery. Company C was composed mainly of former members of two crack Baltimore military organizations,—the Baltimore City Guards and the Maryland Guards. At its organization at Harper's Ferry it had four commissioned and eight non-commissioned officers and sixty-five privates. The discharge of these men naturally revived the question of discharge in reference to Companies H and I, which were also enlisted for twelve months. Some of the companies "in for the war" also contained twelve-months' men, who had been assigned to them from Companies C and H when the latter, in the reorganization at Winchester in June, 1861, were broken up. All these men claimed their right to a discharge at the expiration of their term of service, or at least an admission on the part of the military authorities of their right to enter other branches of the service. The dispute grew so warm that it was found necessary to put many of the men under arrest. Jackson's Valley campaign was then in progress, and the discontent was at its height when, on the 20th of May, 1862, Ewell, to whose division the First Maryland was then attached, joined his forces with those of Jackson at New Market. The difficulties were still unsettled when, on the morning of the 23d, Col. Johnson received an order from Gen. Jackson directing him to move the First Maryland to the front and attack the Federals at Front Royal. The order was obeyed with alacrity, the regiment acquitting itself with great gallantry in the action which followed. Through the efforts of Adjt. Frank X. Ward and others, the men agreed to submit their grievances to the Secretary of War. The regiment distinguished itself in all the battles of Jackson's famous Valley campaign, and after their defeat of the Pennsylvania "Bucktails," near Harrisonburg, were complimented with the following order:

"HEADQUARTERS THIRD DIVISION.
"*General Orders No.* 30.

"In commemoration of the gallant conduct of the First Maryland Regiment on the 6th of June, when, led by Col. Bradley T. Johnson, they drove back with loss the 'Pennsylvania Bucktail Rifles' in the engagement near Harrisonburg, Rockingham Co., Va., authority is given to have one of the captured 'bucktails' (the insignia of the Federal regiment) appended to the color-staff of the First Maryland Regiment.
"By order of MAJ.-GEN. EWELL."

The First Regiment fully sustained its enviable reputation in the terrible battles around Richmond which followed Jackson's junction with Gen. Lee, and after the campaign was over returned to Richmond and encamped on the Central Railroad, about three miles from the city. Shortly afterwards it removed to Charlottesville to recruit, arriving there on the 15th of July. The severe service of the last few months had so diminished its numbers that it scarcely mustered two hundred men, and but little progress was made in filling up its ranks. On the 4th of August, 1862, the regiment was ordered to Gordonsville, and here an order to disband was received from the Secretary of War. This was considered the readiest and best means of settling all disputes as to the length of time for which the men had enlisted. It was about the 16th of August that Col. Johnson drew the regiment up in line for the last time, and after a few remarks read the Secretary's order, and it was with no little sorrow that the men parted from each other and from the flag presented them by the ladies of Baltimore on the day of the first battle of Manassas.

The Second Maryland Battalion.—In anticipation of the disbandment of the First Maryland Battalion, Capt. William H. Murray, of Company H, early in the summer of 1862 secured from the War Department authority to raise a new company. With such of his old company as had re-enlisted "for the war" and desired to remain with him, he opened a recruiting rendezvous at the fair-grounds, near Richmond, and soon filled up his company from among the Marylanders who were then coming South in large numbers.

About the same time Capt. J. Parran Crane, of St. Mary's County, undertook the organization of a company, to be composed mainly of recruits from Southern Maryland. His company and Murray's were filled up about the same time, and were mustered in the service at Richmond on Aug. 27, 1862, as Companies A and B, with the following officers:

Company A.—Captain, William H. Murray, of Baltimore; First Lieutenant, George Thomas, of St. Mary's; Second Lieutenant, Clapham Murray, of Baltimore; Junior Second Lieutenant, William P. Zollinger, of Baltimore.

Company B.—Captain, J. Parran Crane, of St. Mary's; First Lieutenant, John H. Stone, of Charles County; Second Lieutenant, Charles B. Wise, of St. Mary's County; Junior Second Lieutenant, James H. Wilson, of St. Mary's County.

Company A was composed of men drawn from Baltimore City, Anne Arundel, the Eastern Shore, and the southern part of the State. Company B was made up of St. Mary's and Charles County men.

Capt. Murray having been chosen commander of the battalion, Lieut. George Thomas, of Company A, was designated as acting adjutant, and J. Winder

Laird, of Company A, as sergeant-major. On the 12th of September the battalion left Camp Maryland, beyond Winder Hospital, for Charlottesville, Va., where Gen. George H. Steuart was endeavoring to organize a force of Marylanders of all arms, to be known as the Maryland Line. At Winchester the command was joined on the 28th of September by Companies C, D, and E, commanded respectively by Capts. Herbert, McAleer, and Torsch. These companies had been rapidly organized, and contained a strong infusion of the old battalion, though in the main composed of new recruits.

Company C was mustered in on the 11th of September, 1862, with the following officers: Captain, James R. Herbert; First Lieutenant, Ferdinand Duvall; Second Lieutenant, Charles W. Hodges; Junior Second Lieutenant, Joseph W. Barber.

Company E was mainly raised by John W. Torsch, who had served during the first year of the war as lieutenant in Zarvona's Zouaves. His new company was mustered into service about the 14th of September, and was composed of men from Baltimore and the Eastern Shore, some having been members of the old First Maryland Battalion, some members of his former command, and some of them new recruits. The men of Capt. McAleer's company, which was mustered in shortly after Capt. Torsch's command, were largely from Western Maryland, with a few from Baltimore and Anne Arundel County.

The officers of Companies D and E were as follows: *Company D.*—Captain, Joseph L. McAleer, from Frederick; First Lieutenant, James S. Franklin, Annapolis; Second Lieutenant, J. T. Bussey, Baltimore; Junior Second Lieutenant, S. T. McCullough, Annapolis.

Company E.—Captain, John W. Torsch, Baltimore; First Lieutenant, William Broadfoot, Baltimore; Second Lieutenant, W. R. Byus, Talbot; Junior Second Lieutenant, Joseph P. Quinn, Baltimore.

While at Winchester Company F was organized, from material drawn mostly from Southern Maryland, and was officered as follows: Captain, Andrew J. Gwinn, Prince George's; First Lieutenant, John W. Polk, Eastern Shore; Second Lieutenant, John G. Hyland, of the same section; Junior Second Lieutenant, Joseph Forrest, of Prince George's County.

Company G was added to the battalion on the 2d of January, 1863, it having been mustered into the service at Richmond on the 20th of December previous. The men were principally from Southern Maryland and the Eastern Shore, and were officered as follows: Captain, W. W. Goldsborough, Baltimore; First Lieutenant, Thomas R. Stewart, of Talbot County; Second Lieutenant, James Davis, of the same county; Junior Second Lieutenant, W. W. Wrightson, of the Eastern Shore.

Near the close of September, 1862, an election was held for field and staff-officers, which resulted in the choice of Capt. Herbert as major; and upon the addition of Company F the battalion had the number of companies requisite to entitle it to two field-officers; whereupon Maj. Herbert, on the 26th of January, 1863, was elected to the lieutenant-colonelcy, and not long afterwards Capt. Goldsborough was promoted to the majority. The battalion organization now became what it continued to be to the close of the war:

Field and Staff.—Lieutenant-Colonel, James R. Herbert, of Baltimore; Major, W. W. Goldsborough, of the same place; Acting Adjutant, Lieut. George Thomas, of St. Mary's; Quartermaster and Commissary, Capt. John Eager Howard, Baltimore; Surgeon, De Wilton Snowden, Prince George's.

Non-Commissioned Staff.—Sergeant-Major, J. Winder Laird, Cambridge, Md.; Color-Sergeant, Cole Moore, Talbot County; Quartermaster-Sergeant, Edward S. Judge, Baltimore; Commissary-Sergeant, Edwin James, Washington County; Hospital Steward, John W. McDaniel, Baltimore. Drum Corps: Drum-Major, Michael Quinn; Drummers, William Gannon, Joseph E. Smith, Tobias Aubrey, Charles Drewry.

To fill the vacancies occasioned in Companies C and G, caused by the promotion of their commanding officers, Lieut. Ferdinand Duvall was elected to the command of Company C, and Lieut. Thomas R. Stewart to the command of Company G. "At this time," Maj. Goldsborough says, "I think, without any exception, that the Second Maryland was the most perfect command, in matters of drill and discipline, that was or had ever been in the Confederate army."

On June 16, 1863, the battalion was formally attached to Gen. George H. Steuart's brigade, which was then composed of the First and Third North Carolina, the Tenth, Twenty-third, and Thirty-seventh Virginia. Steuart's brigade was then the Third Brigade of the Third (Johnson's) Division of the Second (Ewell's) Army Corps. At the battle of Gettysburg the Second Maryland Battalion lost on Culp's Hill over two-thirds of the command, the estimate being about two hundred and forty-five killed and wounded. It was here that the brave and chivalrous Capt. Murray fell, pierced through the neck, as he was waving his sword as a signal to his men to retire from their assault on the second line of the enemy's works. Among the seriously wounded were

Col. Herbert, Maj. Goldsborough, and Adjt. George Thomas.

On the 1st of November, 1863, the battalion was transferred from Steuart's brigade to the Maryland Line. This name was given to a command consisting of the First Maryland Cavalry, Second Maryland Infantry, and the Baltimore Light Artillery, to be commanded by Gen. George H. Steuart, of Baltimore. The intention was to make it, if possible, the nucleus of a much larger force,—a division perhaps,—which should consist wholly of Marylanders. There were, it is supposed, at this time more than twenty thousand men from Maryland in the Confederate service, and it was thought desirable, for the name and fame of their native State, that they should be collected under one command. Hitherto the credit of their services had fallen to other States, in whose regiments they had been enrolled. Gathered into one body sufficiently large to play a separate part in action and gain an individual character, they would develop the *esprit de corps* for which Maryland troops have always been so distinguished, and accomplish all that could be expected of men of their superior intelligence and gallantry.

But the effort to organize such a body never wholly succeeded. The men preferred the associations they had already formed, and were loath to leave them. According to the new arrangement, the infantry, cavalry, and artillery were to rendezvous at Hanover Junction, where they would be under the command of Col. Bradley T. Johnson.

The movement began on the 2d of November, 1863, and by the end of April, 1864, Col. Johnson found himself in command of the First Maryland, Chesapeake, and Baltimore Light Artillery, in addition to the Second Maryland Infantry and the First Maryland Cavalry. About the 1st of April, Gen. Arnold Elzey, of Maryland, by a general order was placed in command, and fixing his headquarters at Staunton, proceeded to take such steps as were thought to be most likely to lead to the desired result. Permission was accorded to every Marylander throughout the Confederacy to receive a transfer from the command in which he was enrolled, and Capt. Torsch was sent on a recruiting expedition to Charleston, S. C., where there was a considerable body of Marylanders, who went South about the time of the first bombardment of Fort Sumter. While some additions were made to the Line from various sources, the same result attended all the efforts to recruit the Maryland Line to the dimensions of a division, or a brigade at least. The attempt to augment the Line and give it a permanent organization was therefore abandoned. Col. B. T. Johnson was promoted to brigadier-general for saving Richmond from the attacks of Gens. Kilpatrick and Dahlgren, and placed in command of a brigade of cavalry, under Early, in the Valley, and took the First Maryland Cavalry with him. The Second Maryland Infantry was attached to Breckenridge's division till after Cold Harbor, when it was transferred to Walker's (subsequently McComb's) brigade. Finally the artillery also, early in June, was sent to the Valley; and so the Line was broken up, never again to be reunited.

On the 20th of May, 1864, the Second Maryland Battalion joined Breckenridge at Hanover Junction, and on the last of the month fought under him at the second battle of Cold Harbor. In this engagement the battalion won from Gen. Breckenridge the expression, "What could not be done with a hundred thousand such men!" In a letter to the author Gen. Breckenridge thus speaks of the Marylanders who served under him:

"LEXINGTON, KY., Jan. 6, 1874.

"MY DEAR SIR,—Since September last I have, until very recently, been hindered by sickness from attending to my correspondence, and I offer this as an apology for the delay in not answering your letter of Nov. 30, 1873. You desire me to tell you something of a Maryland regiment that was in my command toward the close of the war, with a view to use the information in your proposed 'History of Baltimore.' When I crossed over from the Shenandoah Valley in May, 1864, and joined Gen. Lee on the North Anna, near Hanover Junction, a battalion of Maryland infantry was sent to me, and it remained under my command until I returned to the Valley in the following month. It had seen rough service, and I think all the field-officers were absent from disabling wounds. While with me it was commanded by Capt. Crane. I had occasion to observe this battalion along the North Anna, on the Tolopotomy, and in a series of other engagements of greater or less importance, ending with the battle of Cold Harbor early in June, and I take pleasure in saying that its conduct throughout was not merely creditable, but distinguished. Not being incorporated into any brigade, it came more frequently under my eye, and I presently fell into the habit of holding it in hand for occasions of special need. For an instance, at Cold Harbor, where a point in my line was very weak, and was actually broken for a time by Gen. Hancock's troops, the Maryland battalion and Finnegan's Florida brigade (the latter borrowed from Gen. Hoke for the occasion) aided decisively to restore the situation, and behaved with the greatest intrepidity. During their brief service with me I was every way favorably impressed by those Marylanders. Not in courage only, but also in discipline, tone, and all soldierly qualities they were quite equal to any troops I saw during the war. After my return to the Valley I did not see them any more, yet I never think of them but with admiration and affection. Some Maryland cavalry and artillery under the command of Col. (afterwards Brig.-Gen.) Bradley Johnson reported to me for a few days after my arrival at Hanover Junction. They seemed to be fine troops and well instructed, but I cannot speak of them more particularly.

"With good wishes, I am yours truly,
"JOHN C. BRECKENRIDGE.

"COL. J. THOMAS SCHARF, Baltimore, Md."

The following is what "a Virginian" says, in the Richmond *Sentinel*, of the part taken by the Marylanders in the second battle of Cold Harbor:

"NEAR RICHMOND, June 6, 1864.

"MR. EDITOR,—The public have already been informed, through the columns of the public journals, of the great results of the late engagements between the forces of Gen. Lee and Gen. Grant. But they have not yet learned the particulars, which are always most interesting, and in some instances, owing to the confusion which generally attends large battles, they have been misinformed on some points. It is now known by the public that the enemy were momentarily successful in one of their assaults on the lines held by Maj.-Gen. Breckenridge's division, which might have resulted in disaster to our cause. It will be interesting to all to know what turned disaster into victory, and converted a triumphant column into a flying rabble. The successful assault of the enemy was made under cover of darkness, before the morning star had been hid by the light of the sun. They came gallantly forward in spite of a severe fire from Gen. Echols' brigade, and in spite of the loss of many of their men, who fell like autumn leaves, until the ground was almost blue and red with their uniforms and their blood. They rushed in heavy mass over our breastworks. Our men, confused by the suddenness of the charge, and borne down by the rush of the enemy, retreated, and all now seemed to be lost. At this juncture the Second Maryland Infantry, of Col. Bradley T. Johnson's command, now in charge of Capt. J. P. Crane, were roused from their sleep. Springing to their arms they formed in a moment, and rushing gallantly forward, poured a deadly fire into the enemy and then charged bayonets. The enemy were in turn surprised at the suddenness and vim of this assault. They gave back, they became confused, and Gen. Finnegan's forces coming up, they took to flight, but not until nearly a hundred men were stretched on the plain from the fire of the Second Maryland Infantry, and many others captured. Lieut. Charles B. Wise, of Company B, now took possession of the guns which had been abandoned by our forces, and with the assistance of some of his own men and some of Gen. Finnegan's command, poured a deadly fire into the retreating column of the enemy. Thus was the tide of battle turned, and this disaster converted into a success. I am informed that the whole force of the enemy which came within our lines would have been captured had it not been for the mistake of an officer who took the enemy for our own men, and thus checked for a few moments the charge of the Second Maryland Infantry. I take pleasure in narrating these deeds of our Maryland brethren, and doubt not you will join in the feeling.   A VIRGINIAN."

At the battle of Reams' Station, on the Weldon Railroad, on the 19th of August, the Second Maryland Battalion again proved of what material it was made. A contemporaneous writer said,—

"Disdaining to retreat without the command, when all others were seeking safety in flight, they stood to their post to the last. Again and again were they assaulted, but again and again they drove their assailants back with heavy loss. At length in overwhelming numbers the enemy came upon them and reached the breastworks. But there that little band remained for a time as firm as the rock of Gibraltar. But the enemy crossed the breastworks, and the struggle was hand to hand. Desperately the bayonet was thrust, and the butts of muskets crashed through human skulls. But this unequal struggle could not be of long duration, and surrounded and overwhelmed, the survivors sought to fight their way out. Many succeeded, but one-third of that gallant band lay dead and wounded or were prisoners in the hands of the foe."

On the 30th of September, at the battle of Peeble's Farm, the Second Maryland Confederate Infantry took a conspicuous part in that desperate engagement, losing fearfully in killed and wounded. Out of one hundred and forty-nine men that went into the fight, forty-three were killed and wounded. On the next day, October 1st, they again encountered the enemy on the Squirrel Level road, and repulsed them after a sharp engagement with severe loss. For a long while after the battle of Squirrel Level road the Second Maryland remained in the trenches or were engaged in picketing along their front. It had been reduced to about one hundred men, and still these men were compelled to do the duty of a battalion. So numerous were the desertions in the brigade to which they belonged that it at last became necessary to keep the Marylanders almost constantly on picket, for as sure as this duty was intrusted to other troops just so sure were they to find deserted posts in the morning. And still these brave men never complained of what was imposed upon them. Throughout that dreary fall and the long cold winter, nearly naked and hardly half fed, they silently did their duty, whilst thousands were proving recreant to the cause. Elegant and refined gentlemen, who at home never knew what it was to want for a single comfort, were in rags and tatters, sleeping in mud and filth; and when the bleak winds of December pierced many a rent in their wretched garments, they only drew their sorry blankets the closer around their gaunt and shivering limbs, and cheerfully responded to the call for any duty.

The remnant of this gallant band, under Capt. John W. Torsch, continued steadfast to the last, and bore uncomplainingly the many privations that were imposed upon them. The crisis, however, was approaching when they would cease to exist as a military organization. On the 9th of April, 1865, Capt. Torsch surrendered with the Army of Northern Virginia, sixty-three officers and men, the survivors of a battalion conspicuously marked by unsurpassed courage and fortitude.

At the time of the surrender the Second Maryland Battalion was in McComb's brigade, and that officer upon taking leave of his favorite battalion gave Capt. Torsch, its commander, the following very complimentary letter:

"RICHMOND, VA., April 26, 1865.

"CAPTAIN,—I leave the city this morning. I hope we may meet again under more favorable circumstances. If not, I will commend you to any country to which you may elect to go as a true and gallant officer.

"Words cannot express the high esteem I have for the brave and gallant officers and enlisted men in your command. They have proven themselves in every battle in which they have participated BRAVE AS THE BRAVEST IN THE ARMY OF NORTHERN VIRGINIA.

"I am, with much respect,
"Your Obd't Ser't,
"WM. M. MCCOMB,
"*Brig.-Gen. C.S.A.*
"To CAPT. JOHN W. TORSCH, Second Maryland Infantry.
"McComb's Brigade,
"Heth's Division,
"Third Corps, A. N. V."

In the same connection, after the war, Jefferson Davis sent the author the following letter:

"MEMPHIS, August 28, 1873.
"COL. J. THOMAS SCHARF, Baltimore, Md.:
"DEAR SIR,—Yours of the 22d inst. received, and I am glad to know that you are about to make a durable record of the services of the Baltimoreans in the great struggle for the assertion of State rights and the preservation of constitutional government. The world will accord to them peculiar credit, as it has always done to those who leave their hearthstones to fight for principle in the land of others. I am glad that your old commander, so distinguished for skill and gallantry, survives to bear testimony to the individual merit of the members of his company. Wishing you long life, prosperity, and happiness,
"I remain very respectfully and truly yours,
"JEFFERSON DAVIS."

Zarvona's Zouaves.—About the 15th of June, 1861, Richard Thomas, of St. Mary's County, whose name was afterwards changed by the Legislature of Virginia to Zarvona, and who had served under Garibaldi in his Sicilian campaign, with George W. Alexander, who had recently resigned from the United States navy, went to Baltimore and enlisted sixty-two men for the Confederate service. They were taken on the steamers of the Weems' Patuxent Line to Millstone Landing, St. Mary's County, but soon after crossed the Potomac into Virginia, where it organized as a Zouave company with the following officers: Captain, Richard Thomas; First Lieutenant, George W. Alexander; Second Lieutenant, J. W. Torsch; Third Lieutenant, Frank Parsons.

In June, 1861, Capt. Thomas conceived the idea of capturing the steamer "St. Nicholas," running between Baltimore and Washington, in which he was successful. About ten days after this bold exploit Capt. Thomas, or the "French Lady," as he was called, from the disguise he assumed in his first enterprise, was captured on his return to Baltimore and incarcerated in Forts McHenry and Lafayette. About the same time Lieut. Alexander was captured on the Eastern Shore, and was also confined in Fort McHenry, from which, by the aid of his devoted wife, he managed to escape. From close confinement the mind of Capt. Thomas became impaired, and after his release he went to France to live, but returned to this country shortly after the war, where he died. Lieut. Alexander after his release was made provost-marshal of the Eastern District of Virginia. After Capt. Thomas was permanently detached from his command, William Waters was elected captain. The company remained for some weeks on the Rappahannock, and was then assigned as Company H to the Forty-seventh Virginia Regiment. It remained with the Forty-seventh till October, when it was detached to the batteries at Evansport, to aid in blockading the Potomac during the winter of 1861–62. Upon the evacuation of Evansport, Lieut. John W. Torsch with eight men was left to finish blowing up the magazines. The company joined its command at Fredericksburg, and participated in the campaign on the Peninsula. At the reorganization of the army the company was transferred to the Second Arkansas Battalion, under the command of Maj. Brenan, consisting of three companies, and remained with it until about the 10th of June, 1862, when, its term of service having expired, the company was disbanded.

The Maryland Guard, or Company B, Twenty-first Virginia Regiment, was mustered into the Confederate service at Richmond, Va., for one year on the 24th of May, 1861, numbering one hundred and nine commissioned and non-commissioned officers and privates. The larger portion of its members formerly belonged to the Maryland Guards, a volunteer militia organization, formed in Baltimore in 1860, and nearly all were Baltimoreans. The commissioned officers were as follows:

Captain, J. Lyle Clarke; First Lieutenant, R. Curzon Hoffman; Second Lieutenant, W. Stewart Symington; Third Lieutenant, Joseph Selby.

On the 29th of May, 1861, the company was ordered to the south side of the James River at Petersburg. After a brief campaign in this locality the company was attached to Col. Gillam's Twenty-first Virginia Regiment, becoming Company B. About the 15th of July, 1861, Col. Gillam's regiment left Richmond to join Gen. Lee in his operations in Northwestern Virginia, and participated in that severe campaign. The last battle at which the Maryland Guard were present was that at Front Royal, on May 23, 1862. Its term of service having expired on the 24th, it was put in charge of the prisoners captured in that battle and sent to Richmond, where it was mustered out of service. The command almost unanimously joined other Maryland organizations which were then in service or forming in Richmond. J. Lyle Clarke, the first commander of the Maryland Guard, was commissioned captain in the Confederate

States army, May 24, 1861; promoted to major in February; and commissioned May 1, 1862, to serve as assistant adjutant-general to Maj.-Gen. W. W. Loring; promoted to lieutenant-colonel Oct. 5, 1862, to command the Thirtieth Virginia Battalion of Sharpshooters. He was disabled near Staunton, on Early's march to Maryland, in 1864. R. Curzon Hoffman was commissioned first lieutenant May 24, 1861; promoted to captain April 3, 1862; appointed captain of Company E, Thirtieth Virginia Battalion of Sharpshooters, Oct. 5, 1862. W. Stewart Symington was commissioned second lieutenant May 24, 1861; promoted to first lieutenant April 3, 1862; afterwards promoted to captain and major on Gen. George E. Pickett's staff. Joseph Selby was commissioned third lieutenant May 24, 1861; promoted to second lieutenant April 3, 1862; appointed first lieutenant Company E, Thirtieth Virginia Battalion of Sharpshooters, Oct. 5, 1862. James Adams was second lieutenant of this company, and Wm. T. Iglehart was third lieutenant.

First Maryland Artillery.—In April, 1861, R. Snowden Andrews, of Baltimore, received authority of Governor Letcher, of Virginia, to organize a company of light artillery, to be known as the First Maryland Artillery. With the aid of the Virginia Ordnance Department, then under the charge of Col. Dimock, Mr. Andrews proceeded with that industry and energy for which he has always been remarkable to instruct and equip with guns, caissons, horses and harness, as well as enroll, organize, and drill the men for his company. From designs of his own, the first three brass twelve-pound Napoleon guns made in the Confederate States and three twelve-pound brass howitzers were cast by Col. Dimock. These were the models for all other Napoleons cast in the Confederacy. While constructing the battery and equipments, Mr. Andrews enlisted and organized one hundred and forty-seven Marylanders, by whom he was elected captain, with William T. Dement, of Charles County, first lieutenant; Charles Snowden Contee, of Prince George's, junior first lieutenant; Frederick Dabney, of Mississippi, second lieutenant; and Dr. DeWilton Snowden, orderly sergeant. The company was mustered into the Virginia service in June, 1861, and the next day transferred with the other Virginia forces to the Confederate army. The company was mustered into the Virginia service by the request of Governor Letcher, in order that he might supply the Marylanders with their celebrated battery. These guns were cast at the Tredegar Works in June and July, 1861, and used in all the battles of the Army of Northern Virginia, and by their great success induced the Confederate authorities to recast all of their six- and twelve-pound howitzers into Napoleon guns of Andrews' pattern. The first service of this celebrated battery was in the blockade of the Potomac at Evansport, Va. From Evansport it was transferred to Magruder's line at Yorktown, and took part in all the engagements from Yorktown to the relief of Richmond from the army of McClellan. At the battle of Mechanicsville the First Maryland Artillery, under Capt. Andrews, had the honor of firing the "first gun," and during the engagement he was wounded in the leg. For the gallantry displayed by Capt. Andrews during the Seven Days' fights around Richmond, at the recommendation of Gen. Lee, he was promoted to major, and subsequently rose to the high rank of lieutenant-colonel of artillery.

Upon the promotion of Capt. Andrews to major, Lieut. Dement became captain of the company. Lieut. Dabney having received a higher appointment in the Engineer Corps, he was transferred to the Southwestern army, where he subsequently acquired great distinction. To fill the vacancies in the company, Charles Contee was promoted to first lieutenant; John Gale, of Somerset County, to junior first lieutenant; William J. Hill, of Prince George's, second lieutenant; J. Harris Stonestreet, of Charles, junior second lieutenant. The company participated in all the engagements in which the Army of Northern Virginia was engaged up to the battle of Winchester, where it was particularly distinguished. In the report of Gen. Ewell of his summer campaign of 1863 he says,—

"Lieut.-Col. Andrews, of the artillery, not fully recovered from his serious wound at Cedar Run, was again wounded at Winchester, and while suffering from his wounds appeared on the field at Hagerstown and reported for duty. At Winchester, Lieut. Charles S. Contee's section of Dement's (First Maryland) battery was placed in short musket-range of the enemy on the 15th of June, and maintained its position till thirteen of the sixteen men in the two detachments were killed or wounded, when Lieut. John A. Morgan, of the First North Carolina Regiment, and Lieut. R. H. McKim, A. D. C. to Brig.-Gen. George H. Steuart, volunteered and helped to work the guns till the surrender of the enemy. The following are the names of the gallant men belonging to the section: Lieut. C. S. Contee, A. J. Albert, Jr., John Kester, William Hill, B. W. Owens, John Glascock, John Harris, William Wooden, C. C. Pease, Frederick Frayer, —— Duvall, William Compton, John Yates, William Brown, William H. Gorman, Thomas Moore, Robert B. Chew. Col. Brown, chief of artillery, recommends Lieut. Contee for promotion to the captaincy of the Chesapeake (Maryland) Artillery, vice Capt. W. D. Brown, a most gallant and valuable officer, killed at Gettysburg."

During Mahone's attack along the line of the Weldon Railroad, on June 22, 1864, the First Maryland Artillery silenced a battery that was annoying the Confederate infantry. The men left their guns, and with the horses rushed forward to the Federal battery, hastily by hand worked the four pieces (three-inch steel Dahlgren rifles) over the breastworks, and brought them into the Confederate lines. The absolute capture of a battery by another was so rare in the annals of warfare that it created a great furore in the army, and the Marylanders received great praise the following day from Gen. Mahone in his congratulatory address. From this time to the springing of the Crater mine the First Maryland had no part in any general engagement. After this event the company was sent to Drury's Bluff, and occupied quarters there until its evacuation, April 2d. The men of the First Maryland, who had stood by their guns during the whole of the war and had never lost one, were now ordered to spike their guns and leave them in the pits, as there were no horses to remove them, and take muskets and follow the retreating army.

On Sunday following, April 9th, the surrender took place, and thus ended the career of a company that won a proud name in an army distinguished for every soldierly virtue.

The Baltimore Light Artillery, or Second Battery, was organized early in the war by Capt. J. B. Brockenborough. Its officers at various times during the war were as follows: Capt. Brockenborough, promoted to major; First Lieut. W. H. Griffin, promoted to captain; Second Lieut. W. B. Bean, promoted to first lieutenant; Junior Second Lieut. J. W. Goodman; Third Lieut. John McNulty, promoted to captain and major. Non-commissioned officers: Orderly Sergeant, W. Wirt Robinson; Quartermaster-Sergeant, James Smith; Commissary-Sergeant, Louis Claus; Ordnance Sergeant, William Quinn; First Sergeant, G. W. Poindexter; Second, Joseph Bean; Third, Harry Marston; Fourth, James Morrison; First Corporal, John A. Watter; Second, Christopher Pohlman; Third, George Pilleto; Fourth, James F. Owens. This company served with distinguished gallantry during the entire war in the Army of Northern Virginia.

The Third Maryland Artillery was recruited at Richmond, Va., in October, 1861, by Henry B. Latrobe, eldest son of John H. B. Latrobe, of Baltimore, John B. Rowan, William L. Ritter, and other Marylanders. The first rendezvous was at Ashland; from thence on the 4th of November it was ordered to Camp Dimock for instruction. On the 4th of December it was ordered into winter quarters at Camp Lee, on the fair-grounds, two miles from Richmond, and on Jan. 14, 1862, the battery was mustered into the Confederate service as "Third Maryland Artillery," with the following officers:

Captain, Henry B. Latrobe, of Baltimore; Senior First Lieutenant, Ferdinand O. Claiborne, of New Orleans; Junior First Lieutenant, John B. Rowan, of Elkton, Md.; Second Lieutenant, William Thompson Patten, of Port Deposit, Md.; Orderly Sergeant, William L. Ritter, of Carroll County, Md.; Quartermaster's Sergeant, Albert T. Emory, of Queen Anne's County, Md.; First Battery Sergeant, James M. Buchanan, Jr., Baltimore County; Second Battery Sergeant, John P. Hooper, of Cambridge, Md.; Third Battery Sergeant, Edward H. Langley, of Georgia; Fourth Battery Sergeant, Thomas D. Giles, of Delaware; Battery Surgeon, Dr. J. W. Franklin, of Virginia.

The company was composed of ninety-two men, exclusive of commissioned officers. Of the former about twenty were from Maryland, and ten from Washington City or its vicinity. The battery consisted of two six-pounders, smooth-bores, two twelve-pounder howitzers, and received afterwards two three-inch iron rifled pieces.

On the 4th of February, 1862, the company was ordered to report at Knoxville, Tenn., and arrived there on the 11th. During the remainder of the war the battery played an important part in the Southwestern Department of the Confederate army, and performed gallant service in the Confederate operations at Vicksburg and on the Mississippi River, in the mountains of East Tennessee and the open fields of Kentucky.

On May 1, 1862, it was made a six-gun battery, and Holmes Erwin, of Nashville, Tenn., was appointed junior second lieutenant. On March 1, 1863, Capt. Henry B. Latrobe left the service and Lieut. Holmes Erwin resigned; at the same time Lieut. F. O. Claiborne was promoted to captain to fill the vacancy. On the 17th of March, 1863, Orderly Sergt. William L. Ritter was elected junior second lieutenant, and on the 21st of the same month was promoted to senior second lieutenant, and Sergt. Thomas D. Giles elected to fill the vacancy. April 14, 1863, Lieut. William T. Patten was killed aboard the "Queen of the West," on Grand Lake, and on the 22d of June following Capt. Ferdinand O. Claiborne was killed at Vicksburg, Miss. On the 30th of June, 1863, Lieut. John B. Rowan was promoted to captain, and J. W. Doncaster elected junior second lieutenant. Dec. 16, 1864, Capt. John B. Rowan was killed before Nashville, Tenn., and Lieut. William L. Ritter was promoted captain to fill the vacancy. The battery, after displaying conspicuous gallantry on many hard-fought fields, surrendered at Meridian, Miss., May 4, 1865, and on the 12th the men were paroled.

The Fourth Maryland, or Chesapeake Artillery, was organized at Camp Lee, Richmond, Va. The following were the officers: Captain, Wm. Brown, of Baltimore; Senior First Lieutenant, John Plater, of Baltimore; Junior First Lieutenant, Walter Chew, of Washington, D. C.; Senior Second Lieutenant, John Grayson, of Queen Anne's County. The office of junior second lieutenant was left vacant and afterwards filled by Lieut. Roberts, of St. Mary's County. Orderly Sergeant, Martin L. Harvey; First Sergeant, Thomas Le Compt; Second, Robert Crowley; Third, Philip Brown; Fourth, James Wall; Corporals, Thomas Coubray, Bey Hopkins, Henry C. Buckmaster, Daniel Dougherty; Commissary-Sergeant, John P. Hickey; Quartermaster, George McCubbin; Bugler, Henry Wilkinson; Blacksmith, Thomas Brady.

The Fourth Maryland Artillery participated in nearly all the engagements in which the Army of Northern Virginia was engaged. At the battle of Chancellorsville, Lieut. Grayson, Corp. Hopkins, and Private Graham were killed, and a large number of others severely wounded. At Gettysburg the battery lost heavily. Capt. Brown, Lieut. Roberts, Sergt. Brown, Corp. Dougherty, and several others were killed, besides a large number wounded. The command took a prominent part in the gallant defense of Fort Gregg, near Petersburg, and surrendered with the rest of the Army of Northern Virginia.

The First Maryland Cavalry.—The nucleus of this gallant command was a body of eighteen men, who at Richmond on the 15th of May, 1862, organized Company A. They had belonged to Capt. Gaither's company, then connected with the First Virginia Cavalry. The new organization was officered as follows: Captain, Ridgely Brown, of Montgomery County; First Lieutenant, Frank A. Bond, of Anne Arundel County; Second Lieutenant, Thomas Griffith, of Montgomery County; Third Lieutenant, James A. V. Pue, of Frederick County.

The command being recruited to a full company, it was speedily mustered into service, and joined Jackson in the Valley, and participated in all the engagements in which that distinguished officer was engaged. After the return of Lee's army from the Maryland campaign of 1862, Company A was joined in Virginia by three companies of Marylanders, organized by Capts. Emack, R. C. Smith, and Warner Welsh. On the 25th of November, 1862, the battalion was organized with the following field and staff-officers:

Major, Ridgely Brown; Adjutant, Lieut. George W. Booth; Quartermaster, Ignatius Dorsey; Surgeon, Wilner McKnew.

Company A.—Captain, Frank A. Bond; Lieutenants, Thomas Griffith, J. A. V. Pue, Edward Beatty.

Company B.—Captain, George W. Emack; Lieutenants, M. E. McKnew, Adolphus Cook, Henry Blackiston.

Company C.—Captain, Robert C. Smith; Lieutenants, George Howard, T. Jefferson Smith, W. S. Turnbull.

Company D.—Captain, Warner E. Welsh; Lieutenants, W. H. Dorsey, Stephen D. Lawrence, Milton Welsh.

The battalion, as thus organized, was afterwards augmented by the addition of other companies.

Company E.—Captain, W. I. Raisin; Lieutenants, John B. Burroughs, Nathaniel Chapman, Joseph K. Roberts.

Company F.—Captain, Augustus F. Schwartz; Lieutenants, C. Irving Ditty, Fielder C. Slingluff, Samuel T. G. Brown.

In July, 1864, the company of Capt. Dorsey, which had up to that time served with distinction in the First Virginia Cavalry, joined the battalion. Its third lieutenant, Randolphus Cecil, was killed during the company's connection with the Virginia regiment. At the time it joined the Maryland battalion Company H was officered by Capt. Gustavus W. Dorsey and Lieuts. N. C. Hobbs and Edward Pugh. Maj. Brown was then elected lieutenant-colonel of the battalion, and Capt. R. C. Smith was promoted to major to fill the vacancy.

In the campaign of 1864 the First Maryland Cavalry saved the city of Richmond from being destroyed by Gen. Dahlgren's raiders, and on June 1, 1864, the brave Lieut.-Col. Ridgely Brown lost his life in battle near Dabney's Ferry on the South Anna. Maj. R. C. Smith received a disabling wound at Greenland Gap, in Western Virginia, and was retired, no one being appointed to fill the vacancy. After the death of Lieut.-Col. Brown, however, Capt. Dorsey was promoted to a lieutenant-colonelcy and put in command of the battalion. On the last day of the existence of the Army of Northern Virginia, while the articles of capitulation were being prepared, the First Maryland Cavalry broke through the Federal lines and escaped to Lynchburg, where the command remained about ten days, and then took up the line of march for Gen. Johnston's army. At Cloverdale, Botetourt Co., Va., on April 28, 1865, the command learned from Gen. Munford that Gen. Johnston had surrendered. The general being sick, he sent his favorite battalion the following complimentary letter:

"CLOVERDALE, BOTETOURT COUNTY, VA.,
"April 28, 1865.
"LIEUT.-COL. DORSEY, commanding First Maryland Cavalry:

"I have just learned from Capt. Emack that your gallant band was moving up the Valley in response to my call. I am deeply pained to say that our army cannot be reached, as I have learned that it has capitulated. It is sad, indeed, to think that our country is all shrouded in gloom. But for you and your command there is the consolation of having faithfully done your duty. Three years ago the chivalric Brown joined my old regiment with twenty-three Maryland volunteers, with light hearts and full of fight. I soon learned to admire, respect, and love them for all those qualities which endear soldiers to their officers. They recruited rapidly, and as they increased in numbers so did their reputation and friends increase, and they were soon able to form a command and take a position of their own. Need I say, when I see that position so high and almost alone among soldiers, that my heart swells with pride to think that a record so bright and glorious is in some part linked with mine? Would that I could see the mothers and sisters of every member of your battalion, that I might tell them how nobly you have represented your State and maintained our cause. But you will not be forgotten. The fame you have won will be guarded by Virginia with all the pride she feels in her own true sons, and the ties which have linked us together memory will preserve. You who struck the first blow in Baltimore, and *the last in Virginia*, have done all that could be asked of you; and had the rest of our officers and men adhered to our cause with the same devotion, to-day we would have been free from Yankee thraldom. I have ordered the brigade to return to their homes, and it behooves us now to separate. With my warmest wishes for your welfare, and a hearty God bless you, I bid you farewell.
"THOMAS T. MUNFORD,
"*Brigadier-General Commanding Division.*"

Company B of White's (Thirty-fifth Virginia Battalion of Partisan) Rangers was composed almost exclusively of Marylanders, drawn from Poolesville and its vicinity. It began to be organized under George W. Chiswell, at Charlottesville, Va., towards the close of June, 1862, though it appears an organization was effected some time before in Maryland. On the 12th of September, 1862, the company was completely organized and serving under Capt. White, who at that time had but two companies under his command, being engaged in scouting in the neighborhood of Harper's Ferry, on the Maryland and Virginia side of the Potomac. The command soon grew to six companies, and a battalion was organized and mustered into the Confederate service on the 28th of October, 1862. Capt. White, of Company A, was made major, and selected Lieut. Crown, of Company B, as his adjutant. At this time the Maryland company (B) was officered as follows: Captain, George W. Chiswell; First Lieutenant, Joshua R. Crown; Second Lieutenant, Nicholas W. Dorsey; Third Lieutenant, Edward J. Chiswell. About the middle of December, 1862, the battalion made a raid to Poolesville, Md., and captured a large amount of property, including sixty horses. In June, 1863, the command took part in the engagement at Brandy Station, where Capt. Chiswell was so badly wounded in a charge upon a Federal battery that he was disabled the service. By an effective charge made at Parker's Store, Nov. 29, 1863, the battalion won the name given to it by Gen. Rosser,—the "Comanches." After this time the "Comanches" shared in the fortunes of the cavalry of the Army of Northern Virginia, and at Appomattox Court-House did not surrender, but broke through the lines to Lynchburg. Here subsequently they went by twos and threes to the Federal officers and were paroled.

Company G of the Seventh Virginia Cavalry Regiment was formed in Romney, Hampshire Co., W. Va., June 17, 1861. A few months later an election of officers was held at Morgan Springs, near Shepherdstown, Jefferson Co., W. Va., which resulted as follows: Captain, Frank Mason, of Virginia; First Lieutenant, T. Sturgis Davis, of Towson, Baltimore Co., Md.; Second Lieutenant, Thadeus Thrasher, of Frederick County, Md. (killed at Kernstown, March 22, 1862). At the close of the first year T. S. Davis was elected captain; Benjamin P. Crampton, of Frederick County, Md., first lieutenant; Rodney Howell, of the same county, second lieutenant; and Blanchard Philpot, of the same county, third lieutenant. Harry Gilmor, who afterwards became distinguished as a cavalry leader, was at the first election a private in this company, which was a favorite with Col. Turner Ashby. Company G never lost its identity as a Maryland command, and did as effective service as any other cavalry company in the Confederate army.

Besides the foregoing exhibit, Maryland had in various other commands a large number of men in the Confederate army. There was a company of infantry in the Thirteenth Virginia Infantry, under the command of Capt. Clayton Hill; a battalion of six companies of cavalry, under Maj. Harry Gilmor, of Baltimore, who has published a very thrilling narrative of its adventures on the border; the Howard County Dragoons, commanded by Capt. G. R. Gaither, and attached till July, 1864, to the First Virginia Cavalry, after which date it became the seventh company in the First Maryland; Company D of Mosby's battalion of partisan rangers, commanded by Capt. R. P. Mountjoy (of Mississippi) and Lieuts. C. E. Grogan, W. Trunnel, and D. Briscoe, the latter all Marylanders. There were many other Marylanders in the cavalry commands of Mosby, White, and McNeal; a large number served as staff-officers, and in various positions requiring special intelligence and skill. Two-thirds of "Stuart's horse artillery" (Breathed's battery) were Marylanders, and much the larger part of Purcell's battery was of the same material. In general officers Maryland made an excellent showing: Arnold Elzey, appointed Aug. 28, 1861, promoted major-general Dec. 4, 1862; Gen. Isaac Trimble, appointed Aug. 9, 1861, promoted major-general Jan. 17, 1863; Mansfield Lovell, promoted major-general Oct. 7, 1861; Bradley T. Johnson, appointed June 28, 1864; W. W. Mackall, appointed March 6, 1862; George H. Steuart, appointed March 8, 1862; Charles S. Winder, appointed March 7, 1862; John H. Winder, appointed March 7, 1861. Marylanders held important commands in the Confederate navy. Among those who attained special prominence were Admiral Raphael Semmes, Admiral Franklin Buchanan, Capt. George N. Hollins, Capt. Isaac S. Sterett, Commander C. H. McBlair, Commander R. F. Pinkney, Commander J. E. Barney, and Commander Frederick Chatard.

CHAPTER XVII.

POLITICAL PROGRESS.

Sources of Government—The First Assemblies—The Right of Franchise—Property Qualifications—Reform and Revolution—The Van Buren Electors—State Repudiation—John Brown Insurrection—Anti-Slavery Agitation—Abolition of Slavery—Anti-Registry Law—State Politics.

UNDER the charter of Maryland the legislative power was lodged in the hands of the proprietary, with the proviso that it should be exercised " by and with the advice, assent, and approbation of the freemen, or of the delegates or deputies," the right being reserved to him of selecting the mode in which they should be assembled. The warrants for convening the Assemblies issued by the Governors at the foundation of the province determined whether they should be convened in person or by deputies; or if by deputies, the number of deputies to which each county should be entitled and the manner in which they should be elected. From the first Assembly of the province until the government passed into the hands of Cromwell's commissioners there was no settled or uniform mode of convening Assemblies. At that time the elective franchise was not highly appreciated, and there are several instances showing that the inconvenience of personal attendance and the obligation to defray the expense of delegates occasionally caused it to be considered a grievance. " Until 1650 the delegates were elected for hundreds or settlements, and the warrant for each Assembly specified the number to be elected for each hundred. There was no regular delegate system before this period, and perhaps this arose from the existence of the right then generally conceded to the freemen of appearing in the Assembly in person or by proxy. It was not until 1659, when the Lower House was made to consist only of delegates, that its organization became regular. At the session of 1659 four delegates were called from each county, and from this period until 1681, with one exception, the summons permitted the election of two, three, or four delegates in each, at the option of the people. In the latter year the number was reduced to two by the proprietary's ordinance; but in 1692, after the establishment of the royal government, the constitution of the Lower House was regulated by law, and four delegates were again allotted to each county. The right of representation thus established upon the basis of equality among the counties existed without alteration until the American Revolution." Thus it appears that from the colonization until 1650 the right of representation had no regular character. Sometimes the Assemblies had the nature of the " Ecclesia"[1] of the Athenians. They were assemblies of the freemen generally rather than of representatives. Every freeman had a right to be personally present, and this right being a personal privilege, like that of a member of the English House of Peers, he might either appear in person or by proxy. When the Assemblies were so constituted the government was a pure democracy, being administered by the people in person. At other times the freemen were permitted to appear only by delegates or deputies, elected in the manner prescribed by the warrants of election. The three sessions of 1640, and those of July, 1641, and 1642, were of the latter character; the other sessions were of the former, which was the prevailing character. After the commotions of the civil war in England had ceased, and the government was restored to the proprietary by Cromwell's commissioners, viz., from 1659, the Assembly consisted only of delegates, and from that period the right of appointing proxies or appearing personally wholly ceased. Yet it was not until 1681 that any restrictions appear to have been imposed upon the people in the choice of delegates. It was the disposition of both the proprietary and the people to extend rather than to abridge the right, and it was not until it was esteemed a privilege that restrictions were imposed. By the proprietary's ordinance of the 6th of September, 1681, the same qualifications were required for delegates as for voters, and these qualifications were continued as to both until the Revolution. This ordinance confined the privilege of being delegates to

---

[1] McMahon.

all freemen having a freehold of fifty acres, or residents having a visible personal estate of £40 within the county. The qualifications were re-established by law in 1692, and continued by the successive acts of 1704, 1708, 1715, and 1716[1] until the beginning of the Revolution, and they were then preserved by the provisional government. When Maryland joined in the Declaration of Independence, in 1776, a new constitution was adopted, by which it was provided that the House of Delegates should be chosen in the following manner: "All freemen above twenty-one years of age, having a freehold of fifty acres of land in the county in which they offer to vote and residing therein, and all freemen having property in this State above the value of £30 current money, and having resided in the county in which they offer to vote one whole year next preceding the election, shall have a right of suffrage in the election of delegates for such county." These provisions were continued without alteration until 1802, when the property qualification for voters was entirely abolished, and the elective franchise was placed under new regulations applicable as well to elections in Western Maryland as in other parts of the State. These regulations excluded persons of color, previously enjoying the right of franchise when free and possessing the necessary property qualifications, and conferred the right to vote *exclusively* upon "free *white* persons, citizens of the State, above the age of twenty-one, and having a residence of twelve months next preceding the election in the city or county in which they offered to vote." Elections by *viva voce* vote and the property qualifications were still required "in persons to be appointed or holding offices of profit or trust;" but in November, 1809, John Hanson Thomas, of Frederick County, introduced a bill in the Assembly by which all such clauses of the constitution were repealed, and in the following year the act was confirmed. Under the constitution of 1776 the qualifications of a member of the House of Delegates included, besides the other requisites of a voter, the possession of an estate of £500. The time of election was the first Monday of October in each year; the mode was *viva voce*; the judges of elections in the counties were the sheriffs; in Annapolis the municipal authorities; and in Baltimore, at first its commissioners, but after its erection into a city the mayor and Second Branch of the City Council, with whom it remained until 1799. Until that year "there had been but one place for holding the elections in Baltimore as well as in the counties, but a new system was then adopted for both."[2]

JOHN HANSON THOMAS.

Before 1776 Baltimore had enjoyed no separate representation in the Assemblies; but under the constitution of that year it was allowed two representatives in the House of Delegates. The Senate consisted of fifteen members, taken indiscriminately from any part of the State, with the sole restriction that nine of them were to be residents of the west and six of the east side of Chesapeake Bay. Their term of office was five years, and they were chosen by an electoral college, composed of two electors from each of the counties, and one each from Annapolis and Baltimore. The electors were required to possess the qualifications necessary for delegates, and met at Annapolis on the third Monday in September after their election, to proceed to the election of a Senate. The qualifications of a senator were that he should be above the age of twenty-five, should have resided in the State for the three years next preceding his election, and should have real or personal property above the value of £1000.

After the conclusion of the Revolution political sentiment in the State was divided between those who favored the enlargement of the powers delegated to the Federal Congress and those who, fearing that such an enlargement would imperil the independence and sovereignty of the States, insisted that these powers should be strictly confined within the original limits. After the adoption of the Federal Constitution in 1787, and its subsequent ratification by the States, a struggle for supremacy at once began between these two parties, which was nowhere more earnestly conducted than in Western Maryland. The depth and intensity of public feeling was manifested in the State and Federal elections of the day, and a degree of bitterness developed scarcely exceeded in the political agitations of any subsequent period.

In compliance with a resolution of Congress, the General Assembly of Maryland, on the 22d of December, 1788, passed "an act directing the time, places, and manner of holding elections of representatives of this State in the Congress of the United States, and for appointing electors on the part of the State for choosing a President and Vice-President of the

---

[1] There was one change, however: Catholics were not permitted to hold office or to vote, and were, moreover, required to pay a double tax on their lands.

[2] McMahon, p. 462.

United States, and for the regulation of the said elections." By this law the State was divided into six districts, which were numbered from one to six. The first district was composed of St. Mary's, Charles, and Calvert Counties; the second of Kent, Talbot, Cecil, and Queen Anne's Counties; the third of Anne Arundel (including Annapolis) and Prince George's Counties; the fourth of Baltimore (including Baltimore Town) and Harford Counties;[1] the fifth of Somerset, Dorchester, Worcester, and Caroline Counties; the sixth of Frederick, Washington, and Montgomery Counties.

It was provided that the first election should be held on the first Wednesday in January, but after this on the first Monday of October in every second year thereafter. The electors were to consist of eight persons, five to be residents of the Western Shore and three of the Eastern Shore. There were to be six representatives, who were to be residents of the district they were to represent, but every person coming to vote for such representative "shall have a right to vote for six persons," thereby giving each voter the right to vote for the general ticket. The elections to be free and made *viva voce*. The mode of electing senators to represent Maryland in the United States Senate at this time engaged the attention of the public, and after considerable discussion the State Senate proposed to the House of Delegates, and it agreed, "that the two Senators to represent this State should be elected by a *joint ballot* of both houses; and that no person should be elected a senator from this State *unless* by a majority of the attending members of both houses."

Tuesday, Dec. 9, 1788, being the day appointed for the election, thirteen members of the Senate and seventy of the House of Delegates attended in joint convention, when a resolution was adopted declaring "that one senator should be a resident of the Western and the other of the Eastern Shore." Hon. Charles Carroll of Carrollton and Uriah Forrest, of Montgomery County, were put in nomination for the Western Shore, and Hon. John Henry and George Gale for the Eastern Shore, and upon counting the ballots Henry received 41, Gale 41, Forrest 41, and Carroll 40. There being 83 ballots cast and neither of the candidates receiving a majority, a second ballot was taken with the following result: Henry 42, Gale 40, Carroll 41, and Forrest 41. Mr. Henry receiving a majority, was declared elected United States senator, after which the Legislature adjourned until the next day, when Mr. Carroll was elected by 42 to 39. The first constitutional election for representatives in Congress and electors for President and Vice-President took place in January, 1789, and resulted in the triumph of the Federal ticket. The successful Presidential electors in Maryland were Chancellor John Rogers, Col. George Plater, Col. Wm. Tilghman, Wm. Richardson, Alexander C. Hanson, Robert Smith, Dr. Philip Thomas, and Dr. Wm. Matthews. The highest vote cast in Frederick County was 790, the highest in Washington 1164, and in Montgomery 320. Political excitement ran high at this election, and in Baltimore and other sections of the State the anti-Federalists made a strong fight. Western Maryland, however, was almost solid for the Federal electors, the highest number of votes for the opposition ticket in Montgomery County being 44, in Frederick County being 3, while in Washington County every vote was cast for the Federal candidates. A German farmer in Washington County, writing to a gentleman in Baltimore, Jan. 11, 1789, says, "We had pain when we heard of the people in your district that they were wrong, and we thought it right to call the friends of the new government to give in their votes at the court-house, so we made out so many as 1164 for the Federal ticket, and no man said against it. The last day you would wonder to see so much people together, two or three thousand, may be, and not one 'anti.' An ox roasted whole, hoof and horn, was divided into morsels, and every one would taste a bit. How foolish people are when so many are together and all good-natured! They were so happy to get a piece of Federal ox as ever superstitious Christians or anti-Christians were to get relics from Jerusalem."

When the Constitution of the United States went into operation, Maryland, as has been said, was divided into six districts for the election of representatives to Congress, and one member assigned to each, but all the members were voted for by general ticket throughout the State. At this election in 1789, when there was nothing particularly or locally interesting to Baltimore, she cast a comparatively small vote, which was divided almost equally between the two sets of candidates. From some unknown cause Baltimore afterwards became dissatisfied with five of the members then elected, and at the next election it was determined to leave them out. Accordingly a short time before the election of 1790 a caucus was held, and Philip Key, Joseph Seney, William Pinkney, Samuel Sterett, William Vans Murray, and Upton Sheredine were nominated as candidates. Upon the announcement of this ticket the counties became alarmed at the supposed assumption of power and

---

[1] After the census of 1800, Maryland was entitled to nine representatives in Congress, and the electoral districts were again altered by act of Assembly.

influence on the part of Baltimore, and immediately called a convention of deputies in Baltimore, on the 23d of September, 1790, who were authorized to nominate candidates. On the day appointed the counties' deputies nominated as their candidates Michael Jenifer Stone, Benjamin Contee, George Gale, and Daniel Carroll, four of the old members, and James Tilghman, of James, and Samuel Sterett.[1]

When the election came off Baltimore cast upwards of three thousand votes for her own ticket, while six votes was the highest number which any one of the county candidates received. In the counties the vote was very much divided between the two tickets, and as a consequence Baltimore elected her ticket by a large majority, and thereby took control of the politics of the State.[2]

The counties now regarded the plan of electing members of Congress by general ticket as "destructive of their influence and interests," and at the next session of the Legislature, on the 19th of December, 1790, the law was changed, so that the elector only voted for a candidate in his own district, it being enacted "that every person entitled and offering to vote for representatives for this State in the Congress of the United States shall have a right to vote for one person being a resident of his district at the time of his election." This change of the law confined the direct influence of Baltimore to the election of its own ticket, as at present, and the counties were restored to their "proper station, dignity, and independence." The electors of President and Vice-President were still to be chosen by general ticket, but five of them were to be residents of the Western Shore and three of the Eastern Shore.

In 1815 considerable discussion arose in the larger counties and in the city of Baltimore over the fact that the minority of the people of the State were governing the majority. Under the constitution, as it then existed, the delegates were the representatives of the counties of the State and not of the people, thereby giving one man as much political weight in some of these counties as ten men in others. Annapolis had at this period from two hundred and thirty to two hundred and sixty voters, while Baltimore had from five to six thousand; but each under the existing constitution were equal.

At the election of 1815 seven counties and two cities, notwithstanding they had a majority of nearly nine thousand votes cast in the State, were only entitled under this system to thirty-two members, while twelve counties which were in the minority sent forty-eight members. This question was discussed with great animation during subsequent campaigns; and in 1816 the political writers declared the attack of the "Baltimore Jacobins" the "most daring upon the rights of the people that ever was conceived in a country professing to be free to increase representatives." The election in September of that year is described "as the most bitter that ever transpired in Maryland. Not only had the Federal party to encounter the arts and zealous operations of the Democrats of the State, but the general government lent the aid of its influence in the election. The contest was opened early in the winter by transporting voters from places where they could be spared, where the Federal majority was usually not very large. This the Federalists soon discovered and counteracted. A number of United States soldiers were ordered from Baltimore to man the condemned works at Annapolis, but with the greater object in view to endeavor to vote through the expected acquiescence of the corporation officers. This scheme failed on account of the tardiness of their motions, as they did not reach the city more than six months before the election. Great quantities of money, and false and licentious papers, almost outraging shame itself, were poured forth everywhere by both parties. Truth and probability were set at defiance; the most virtuous private characters were aspersed and acriminated; nothing was left unessayed, however nefarious, which might conduce to gain success for either party."[3]

Such was the force of prejudice in Maryland that until 1826 no Israelite could hold any office, civic or military, in the State government. The subject was brought before the Legislature in 1818 and at each succeeding session until 1822, when a bill removing these disabilities was passed, mainly through the efforts of Thomas Kennedy, of Washington County, and R. B. Taney, of Frederick, but, in accordance with the constitution of the State, before it could become a law it was necessary that it should be confirmed by the Legislature of 1823. The measure was very unpopular with the people, and its passage created an extraordinary influence on their minds, so much so that in the election of members for the Legislature of 1823, out of forty members that voted in favor of the

---

[1] Gen. Wm. Smallwood was president of this convention.

[2] Samuel Sterett received the highest number of votes cast in the State, 16,420.

[3] At the State election held in October, 1818, the soldiers stationed at Fort McHenry and the sailors and marines on board the United States vessel "Nonesuch" were mustered, furnished with ballots, marched to the polls and voted. The soldiers themselves said that their ballots were dealt out to them by a sergeant on parade, that they were then marched to the polls and ordered to vote the tickets with which they had been furnished.

bill only sixteen were returned to the next Assembly. As there were about one hundred and fifty Hebrews in the State, representing a capital of about half a million dollars, the prejudice of the people soon subsided. The measure gained strength, and finally, after a struggle of six or seven years, on the last day of the session of 1824 (Saturday, Feb. 26, 1825) the "Jew Bill," as it was then called, or the bill to alter the constitution so as to relieve persons from political disqualifications on account of their religious opinions, again passed the Assembly,—in the House of Delegates by a vote of 26 to 25, only fifty-one out of eighty members being present. It was ratified by the Assembly of 1825 in the House of Delegates by a vote of 45 to 32.

Before the Presidential election of 1836 the manifest injustice of a minority of the people of the State governing the majority, which had been the subject of complaint for years, again violently agitated the people, who made it the engrossing topic of discussion and the great object in State politics. As has before been stated, the constitution of the State, as framed in 1776, apportioned the representatives in the House of Delegates and in the Senate electoral college among the several counties and cities, without regard to population. There were conflicting interests in the State, springing from its geographical position, which had little or no existence in other States. The lower or Eastern Shore counties in 1776 were densely and the upper or western counties sparsely populated; the former contained a large proportion of slave population, while the settlers of the latter were almost exclusively white. The city of Annapolis and the town of Baltimore required peculiar and special attention. And, above all, the division of the territory of Maryland into the Eastern and Western Shores required such recognition and protection of the rights and interests of each as infused into the constitution somewhat of the appearance, if not of the spirit, of a compact between the counties of the opposite shores of the Chesapeake Bay. By the constitution the State was a confederation of counties, each with the same voice in the Legislature, without regard to population or wealth.

The House of Delegates was composed of four members from each county and two each from Annapolis and Baltimore. The Senate, composed of fifteen members, was chosen by a body of electors of two from each county. The Governor and Council were elected by the two houses on joint ballot. By this system, it will be seen, the smaller and less populous counties had as much political weight in the Legislature as the larger, so that by the organization of the legislative powers the counties of Kent and Calvert, with a population of nineteen thousand four hundred and one, were at this time allowed as many representatives in the senatorial electoral college and the House of Delegates as the counties of Frederick and Washington, with a population of seventy-one thousand and fifty-six, and Kent and Calvert each had double the number of delegates allowed to the city of Baltimore, with a population of eighty thousand six hundred and twenty-five. The executive department was the creature of the Legislature, being elected thereby, and most of the civil officers received their appointment from the executive, so that a minority of one-fourth of the people, having a right to elect a majority of the members of the Legislature, controlled all the departments of the government.

Since the adoption of the State constitution in 1776 the resources of the western counties had greatly developed, and their population had largely increased, so that the operation of the system as originally established was no longer just and equal. The lower counties, however, refused to recognize the changed conditions or to grant the reasonable and just rights of the people of the western section of the State. Arranging themselves behind the strict letter of the constitution, they disregarded the great principles upon which it was originally based, and its inadequacy to the wants of the people at this time. They forgot the great change the State had undergone in point of population, commerce, and trade in the course of sixty years, and that a constitution which was republican at an earlier date in our history in consequence of that change had grown anti-republican. The mode of electing the Senate was particularly objected to, and the small number of representatives allowed Baltimore City. As early as 1807 a strong effort had been made to change the system by electing one senator from each county by the people; and in the bill which passed the House for that purpose an attempt was made to engraft a provision regulating the number of delegates for each county in proportion to its population. The bill, however, was defeated in the Senate, and a similar one met with a like fate in the ensuing year.

Year after year repeated and earnest petitions were presented to the Legislature, asking, praying for redress of these gross grievances of which the majority of the people had long complained. These petitions and memorials were again and again rejected. The smaller counties, which had ruled for nearly half a century the majority of the people, declined to surrender the undue share of power they possessed. At length the representatives of both political parties in the larger counties and the city of Baltimore united and proposed that a convention of reformers, without distinction of party, should be held in Baltimore to agree upon such measures as would insure success.

On the 6th of June, 1836, the Reform Convention, composed of delegates from Cecil, Harford, Baltimore, Frederick, Montgomery, and Washington Counties and Baltimore City, assembled and adopted resolutions recommending the people of the State to elect at the next October election delegates pledged to introduce and support a bill providing for taking the sense of the people on the question of reforming the constitution of the State on the first Monday in May, 1837; and in the event of a majority of the people declaring themselves in favor of such reform, providing in the same bill for the calling of a convention for that object. It was further resolved that the members of the convention should be distributed equally among the several congressional districts with the exception of the Fourth, which being a double congressional district was to have twice the number of representatives of any other district. It was also agreed that if the Legislature should refuse to pass the desired bill the president of the convention should reconvene it for the adoption of such ulterior measures as might then be deemed expedient.

The people seemed disposed to fully sustain the recommendations of the convention, for the Assembly of 1835 had passed laws which tended to enlarge the representation of the more populous districts, and which only needed the confirmation of the ensuing Legislature to become a law. By this act two additional delegates were given to Baltimore City, and Carroll County was erected out of portions of Frederick and Baltimore Counties, thus giving four more representatives to this section of the State, and making the Reformers more urgent in their demands.

But these movements suddenly took a most unexpected turn. The Presidential election was approaching, and the opposition or Whig party, although they were unable to concentrate their forces upon a single candidate, had strong hopes of defeating the election of Mr. Van Buren by throwing the final choice into the House of Representatives. Party spirit was at its height in Maryland; a new State Senate was to be elected, and the combination of parties in the interest of reform was scarcely to be expected. The Senate of Maryland was composed of fifteen members, who were elected every five years, not immediately by the people, but by a college of electors, forty in number, who were elected by the people. Two of these electors were chosen from each of the nineteen counties, and one each from Baltimore and Annapolis.

On the 5th of September, 1836, the election came off, and resulted in the choice of twenty-one Whig and nineteen Van Buren electors.

On the third Monday of September, in accordance with the constitution of the State, they assembled at Annapolis to go into an election of senators. By the constitution of Maryland no Senate could be elected unless twenty-four electors were present in the college. On the day appointed the twenty-one Whig electors qualified by taking their official oath, but the nineteen Van Buren electors, availing themselves of this provision, which seems to have been designed for the protection of the counties on the Eastern Shore, acted in accordance with the following instructions, given by the Democrats of Frederick County to their electors:

"*Whereas*, The fifteenth section of the constitution declares that no Senate can be formed unless twenty-four electors agree to meet for the appointment of the members of which it is to consist:

"*Therefore resolved*, That the senatorial electors of this county be instructed to require of the twenty-one Whig electors a pledge that no member of the former Senate and no member of the House of Delegates who opposed the bill calling a convention of the people shall be elected to the next Senate of the State; that at least eight of the members of the Senate to be chosen by the electoral college shall be selected from among persons known to entertain opinions and sentiments coinciding with the principles and opinions held by and governing a majority of the people (two hundred and five thousand nine hundred and twenty-two), who have elected nineteen Van Buren electors; and that in the formation of the Senate there shall be a majority of members known to be favorable to such a thorough and radical reform of the constitution of the State as will insure to all citizens living under it equal political rights and privileges.

"*Resolved*, That unless the pledges required by the preceding resolution are solemnly given in true faith, the two electors from this county be requested to refuse to enter into an election of senator, provided that the electors from other counties and cities having a majority of the white population of the State therein will co-operate with them to defeat the election of a Senate hostile to a reform in the constitution to the extent required in the first resolution.

"*Resolved*, That our friends in the counties and cities that have elected Van Buren Reform electors are earnestly invited and recommended to join us in these measures, as the only means by which we can avoid the fate of being compelled to submit for five years at least to the tyranny of a government wielded and controlled by a small and aristocratic minority of the people of the State."

The nineteen Van Buren electors met in caucus in Annapolis on the 19th of September, and determined, in accordance with the instructions they had received, that as they represented a majority of the voters in the State, it was right that they, although a minority in the electoral college, should have the nomination of eight members.

Contrary to the hopes and expectations of the Van Buren electors, the Whig electors declined to receive or reply to the propositions submitted to them. Finding that the Whig electors refused to hold any communication with them until they had qualified, according to the requirements of the constitution, the nineteen Van Buren electors, on the 21st of September, abandoned Annapolis and retired to their homes. Before doing so, however, they issued an address "to the people of Maryland," in which they announced their determination not to take part in the election of the Senate, setting forth the reasons for their course, to which the Whig electors immediately published a reply. This sudden and hostile demonstration excited serious alarm throughout the State, and it was feared that a most painful and perilous crisis was at hand; public meetings were held in many places; at Baltimore an immense meeting of citizens expressed their indignation in forcible language at the "Reform or Revolution" in Maryland. Similar meetings were held in Washington, Frederick, and Allegany Counties, at which all party distinctions were ignored, and all pledged themselves to sustain the supremacy of the law; and on the 18th of October (1836) the grand jury of Allegany presented the nineteen recusant electors "as unfaithful public agents and disturbers of the public peace."

In the meanwhile the Whig electors continued at Annapolis, patiently waiting until a sufficient number of the recusants should qualify to enable them to proceed to business. The Presidential election took place on the 7th of November, and on the following day Governor Thomas W. Veazey issued his proclamation, denouncing in severe terms the conduct of the "recusant electors and their abettors," calling on the people, civil and military, to hold themselves in readiness to maintain the law, and convening the old Senate and House of Delegates to assemble on the 21st of November. On the 12th of November, Wesley Linthicum, a Van Buren elector from Anne Arundel County, addressed a note to his associates, informing them that, in accordance with "the will of the people," he had determined to repair to Annapolis, and on the 19th qualify as an elector of the Senate. John S. Sellman, the colleague of Mr. Linthicum, had entered the college and qualified early in October.

In the mean time the people of Maryland, in the election for delegates and for the President, had expressed at the ballot-box their opinion of the conduct of the Van Buren electors. The contest was conducted with much spirit, and the result may be considered as a fair criterion of the strength of parties in those counties where they were arrayed in opposition. In Worcester and Frederick the Van Burenites had no ticket in the field. In the latter county the Van Buren delegate ticket was withdrawn, on the ground that, as it had been determined to hold a convention in Annapolis on the third Monday of November, 1836, to make provisional arrangements for the "continuance of the government until the old constitution is amended or a new government instituted, it was not necessary to elect delegates to the Assembly." The election resulted in the choice of sixty Whig and nineteen Van Buren members of the House of Delegates.

The result of this election changed the aspect of affairs very considerably. The recusant electors found that their action had not been sustained by the approval of the people, and a number of them determined to obey the popular will, and the electoral college, reinforced by the electors from Anne Arundel, Queen Anne's, and Caroline, proceeded on the 19th of November to the election of fifteen senators.

The Reform convention held another session in Baltimore on the 16th of November, and adjourned to meet in Annapolis on the first Monday of January, 1837. This meeting never took place, for the Assembly convened a few days afterwards and immediately entered upon the work of reform. They first confirmed the law, passed at the last session of the Assembly, to increase the delegation from Baltimore from two to four members; and in March, 1837, coerced by the state of public feeling produced and manifested by the course of the nineteen electors, the Legislature passed a law making many of the desired changes in the constitution. The people were given the power of electing the Governor; the Senate was entirely reorganized, one member being assigned to each county and the city of Baltimore, to be elected immediately by the people. The constitution of the House of Delegates was materially altered, five members being assigned to Baltimore City, Frederick, and Baltimore Counties each, four to Montgomery, Carroll, and Washington each, and three to Allegany; and it was provided that after 1840 every county having a population of over thirty-five thousand souls should have six delegates, and Baltimore City as many delegates as the most populous county. The first Democratic State Convention under the reformed constitution was held in Baltimore on the 31st of May, 1838, and resulted in the nomination of William Grason, whose opponent was John L. Steele. At the ensuing election Mr. Grason was elected Governor.

At an early period in the history of the country the dangerous policy of unlimited internal improvement by the Federal government—"to set apart and pledge certain funds for constructing roads and canals and improving the navigation of water-courses, in order to facilitate, promote, and give security to internal commerce among the several States, and to render more easy and less expensive the means and provisions of the common defense"—had attracted public attention, and had received its temporary quietus at the hands of President Jackson in 1832 by his veto of the Maysville road bill. Unfortunately for Maryland, this opinion, which had been confirmed by the general approval of the country, was not shared by the State government. It refused to abandon altogether an extravagant system of roads and canals that could not be perfected at that period, when the population of the country was comparatively so small and scattered over such an immense area of territory. Measures were taken to place Maryland in the van of those States ambitious of rivaling Great Britain, Holland, and other countries, where the population was crowded and dense, and where vast numbers justified large expenditures to facilitate intercourse. In the short space of seven years succeeding the veto of President Jackson the debt of Maryland was augmented more than twelve millions of dollars. Within the same period other roads and canals were projected, until the little State of Maryland, having ten thousand square miles of territory and 318,194 white inhabitants, was staggering under a load of debt under which any less determined people would have sunk in financial ruin.

We were at one and the same time projecting or constructing a railroad from Baltimore to Washington, another from Baltimore to New York, another on the Eastern Shore, another from Baltimore to the Ohio, and a magnificent canal from tide-water on the Potomac to the Ohio River. If the people of the State had foreseen the distresses which these works were destined to bring upon them, or had then understood, as they did afterwards, the financial measures devised to insure the punctual payment of interest, few persons would have been hardy enough to invest their capital in these securities. Our citizens had not the remotest idea that taxes were ever to be the result of these debts, nor was any allusion to that contingency ever permitted. On the contrary, the vast revenues to be derived from these works to enrich the State was the sole theme of newspaper discussion, stump oratory, and the plausible estimates of contractors and jobbers,—a vast army eager to obtain the money that the people were urged to vote.

Such was the indignation of many, when first awakened to a true conception of the whole subject, that a strong disposition existed to deny all obligations to pay the debt on account of the alleged absence of constitutional power in the Legislature to contract it. To overcome the pecuniary embarrassments which threatened to overwhelm her creditors, Maryland, in 1837, when there was a general bank suspension and no currency but depreciated bank-paper, stepped forward and displayed to her sister States a noble example by passing a law ordering that the State creditors should be paid in gold or silver, or its equivalent, and this law was made retrospective. Unfortunately, this could not be long maintained, for the embarrassments into which the State was drawn by her system of internal improvements, exaggerated by the deceptive manner in which the affairs of the Chesapeake and Ohio Canal were managed, resulted in such a deficit in revenue that when the foreign markets were no longer open to the sale of stock the payment of interest on the State debts became impossible, and as no system of taxation had previously existed in Maryland, difficulties in levying and collecting a tax were encountered, and in January, 1842, the State failed to pay its interest. The revenue of the State would meet only its current expenditure, and it became necessary to raise the whole interest, of over $600,000 per annum, by taxation. Although it had thus become evident, at the close of 1840, that taxes were inevitable, the Legislature, at the session of 1841, was disposed to dodge the question by false estimates and chimerical paper speculations, but was finally compelled to take effective measures, and on the 23d of March, 1841, passed a law which, with a supplement enacted in the following December, imposed a tax for the first year of twenty cents, and for the next three years of twenty-five cents on the one hundred dollars of assessed value of real and personal property. This was expected to yield $456,000 per annum, and, together with other laws passed, it was hoped the State would realize $200,000 more. All these estimates proved fallacious, mostly from causes incident upon the commencement of a system of taxation. It was contested by the ship-owners, banks, and others, who required time. When it is recollected that before the act of March, 1841, the largest amount of direct taxation ever levied upon the people of Maryland in any one year was $60,818, and that even that imposition was continued but for a few years, it is not surprising that grave doubts of the ability of the State to raise in this way more than $600,000 were entertained, and this apprehension operated very injuriously by leading people to resist what they supposed would ultimately not be enforced. Under the impression that no serious attempt would be made to pay the State interest, the several companies also that had received aid from the State held back in their payments, showing an evident disposition to cast off the obligation to the public creditors by throwing the odium of repudiation upon the commonwealth at large. When the direct tax was levied the value of the assessed property in Maryland was estimated at $300,000,000. If this estimate had been correct, the rate of tax then imposed would have been sufficient. When, however, the actual value of the property was ascertained to be $190,723,788, subsequently reduced to $177,139,645 by the action of the appeal tax courts, there was no alternative for those who intended to pay the interest on the public debt by taxation except to increase the rate of the levy from twenty to thirty cents on the one hundred dollars, but instead of doing this the Legislature undertook to rely upon other doubtful sources of revenue. Another fatal error was in the failure to enforce the laws against the first delinquents, the result of which was that in seven counties the tax laws were not enforced, and as a consequence, in January, 1842, the State suspended the payment of interest on its debts.

Various expedients were tried by the people to meet the progressive increase of interest, which had grown from $859,656 on the 1st of December, 1842, to $1,171,872 on the 1st of December, 1843, and to $1,450,961 on the 1st of December, 1844.

Among the many laws enacted for raising a revenue the act of 1844, ch. 280, imposing the "stamp tax," was the most objectionable. This law, which was popularly known as the "British Stamp Act," required stamps to be used "for every skin or piece of vellum, or parchment, or sheet, or piece of paper, or other material upon which shall be printed or written any or either of the instruments of writing following, to wit: On any bond, obligation, single bill, or promissory note or notes, made or executed in this State, above one hundred dollars, and not made or issued by any incorporated bank of this State, and on any foreign or inland bill of exchange, or other evidence of debt, above one hundred dollars, whether indorsed or otherwise, and whether made or issued by any incorporated institution, individual, or firm." This act went into operation on the 10th of May, 1845, and from its passage it was denounced in all sections of the State in unmeasured terms, through the public press, from the hustings, and in every other shape which the ingenuity of its opponents could devise. In several sections of the State resistance to the law was strenuously urged, and insisted upon as a rightful measure. In Carroll, Washington, Harford, and other counties many of the citizens formed anti-tax associations, and declared their inability to meet the demands made upon them by the State.

Finally a number of the prominent citizens of Somerset County, irrespective of party, signed a notice calling "a united convention of tax-payers, farmers, mechanics, and workingmen" at the court-house in Princess Anne on the second Tuesday in June, 1845. The object of the convention was stated to be "to confer and consult upon measures of policy and practice deeply interesting in the present depressed condition of the country;" and all were invited to attend who were "disposed to unite in endeavoring to devise means to avoid ruinous taxation and provide for the reduction of the public debt,—in fine, to arrest the downward course of the great interests of the people, and to save the State from desolation and disgrace."

On the 9th of June the convention met and adopted a memorial asking the Legislature to pass an act providing for the election of delegates to a State Convention to form a new constitution. They also appointed delegates to an informal State Convention which had been proposed, at a meeting of the citizens of Harford County, to be held in Baltimore on the first Wednesday of August following. In response to the call of these counties, the other counties of the State appointed delegates to the "Reform Convention," which assembled in Baltimore on the 27th of August, 1845. It was composed of some of the ablest men of the State of both political parties, and organized by the selection of Col. Anthony Kimmell, of Frederick County, president, and various vice-presidents, among whom was Dr. E. L. Boteler, of Washington County. The convention adopted resolutions recommending the organization of reform associations throughout the State, and calling upon the people to vote for no candidate for either branch of the Legislature who would not pledge himself to vote for the call of a convention, the abolition of all useless offices, and the retrenchment of all unnecessary expenses. These efforts produced a good moral effect, and, with the improvement in business generally, as the country emerged from the disastrous effects of the great collapse of the credit system which attended the final explosion of the corrupt United States Bank, the taxes were more readily paid, and the machinery for collecting them worked more smoothly. The actual produce of the taxes gradually approximated to the estimates, and the reduction in the State expenses by the curtailment of many outlays enabled a large amount to be appropriated to the payment of interest. At length it became evident that the finances had by able management been worked up to a position which would permit of resumption, and at the session of 1847 the Legislature, in compliance with the earnest recommendations of Governor Thomas G. Pratt, passed a law directing the State treasurer to resume payment of the current interest on the public debt on the 1st of January, 1848. This law also authorized and directed the commissioner of loans, after Oct. 1, 1847, to issue six per cent. bonds, the interest payable annually, to the holders of coupons or certificates of interest. The interest on the main debt to be first paid; and if then, after defraying the ordinary expenses of the State, there should not remain in the treasury funds adequate to pay the full amount of six per cent. interest on the bonds, then what was remaining should be appropriated *pro rata* among said bonds, and certificates given for the balance due. All taxes and State dues were to be paid in current money. The law was carried into effect, and resumption took place January, 1848. The amount of arrears funded under its provisions was $854,003.43 in six per cent. stock, redeemable at the pleasure of the State.[1]

Upon the assembling of the Legislature the committee appointed by the "Reform Convention" held in the city of Baltimore in August, 1845, laid before that body the memorial suggesting "alterations in the existing, or the call of a convention for the adoption of a new, constitution." The Legislature declined to accede to this recommendation, but passed a law submitting to the people the question of biennial sessions of the General Assembly, and it was ratified by the popular vote on the 7th of October, 1846. Upon the assembling of the Legislature, on the 3d of January, 1848, Governor Philip Francis Thomas laid before that body a message of great force and power, principally upon the question of constitutional reform and retrenchment, and in a lengthy argument favored the call of a convention for the purpose of revising the constitution. This act of justice was again, however, denied the people. For more than thirty years a large majority of the people of Maryland had been ineffectually importuning the Legislature to give them the opportunity to revise the constitution. Bills directing the call of a convention for that purpose had been repeatedly passed by the Lower House, and as often rejected by the Senate. Within the last four years a "Reform party" had been organized, the members of which bound themselves not to vote for any candidate for the Legislature who would not pledge himself to support the call for a convention. This party, notwithstanding the opposition of the smaller counties on the Eastern Shore, had now acquired power and influence, and assembled in convention in Baltimore on July 25, 1849, to make public declaration of their objects, which was done in a set of strong resolutions. At the fall election of 1849 in a number of the counties the Whigs and Democrats united in running "Reform" tickets for members of the Legislature, without reference to political distinctions, and in others and in Baltimore City the candidates of both parties were pledged to constitutional reform. The efforts for reform were successful, and a new constitution was framed and went into effect on the 4th of July, 1851. By the new constitution the State was divided into three gubernatorial districts, from each of which, in regular rotation, the Governor was to be selected. St. Mary's, Charles, Calvert, Prince George's, Anne Arundel, Montgomery, and Howard Counties, with the city of Baltimore, were to form the first; the eight counties of the Eastern Shore the second; and Baltimore, Harford, Frederick, Washington, Allegany, and Carroll to form the third.

Every county in the State and the city of Baltimore to be entitled to elect one senator. In the House of Delegates Allegany was assigned four representatives; Carroll, three; Frederick, six; Montgomery, two; Washington, five. The greatest change was in Baltimore City, which gained five delegates, while the counties collectively lost seventeen. The State was to be divided into four judicial districts,—Allegany, Washington, Frederick, Carroll, Baltimore, and Harford Counties to compose the first; Montgomery, Howard, Anne Arundel, Calvert, St. Mary's, Charles, and Prince George's, the second; Baltimore City, the third; and Cecil, Kent, Queen Anne's, Talbot, Caroline, Dorchester, Somerset, and Worcester, the fourth. The State was further divided into eight judicial circuits, of which Montgomery belonged to the second, Frederick and Carroll formed the third, and Washington and Allegany the fourth. In the election for members of the House of Delegates, held in the fall of 1851, under the provisions of the new constitution, the Democrats succeeded in electing forty-three members, and the Whigs thirty. The Senate stood eleven Democrats and ten Whigs, with one vacancy, caused by a tie vote in Washington County, which gave the Democrats political control of the State. In the Presidential election of 1852 the Democrats again carried the State. In Baltimore the Whigs were defeated by a majority of 4474 out of 23,616 votes polled, and in the State the Democratic electors, R. M. McLane, C. Humphries, J. Parren, R. H. Alvey, Carroll Spencer, C. J. M. Gwynn, J. A. Wickes, and E. K. Wilson, were elected by a majority of 5077.

After the defeat of the Whig Presidential candidates in Maryland that party reorganized, and with

---

[1] In the fall election of 1845 a repudiation ticket for the Legislature was run in Carroll County, which received 866 votes, but was defeated by the Whigs, who polled 1574.

the help of the "American party," which was now assuming shape, placed in the field Richard J. Bowie, of Montgomery, as their candidate for Governor, to whom the Democrats opposed T. Watkins Ligon, of Howard County. The result was the election of Mr. Ligon, but with a Whig majority in both branches of the Legislature, the Lower House standing thirty-nine Whigs to thirty-five Democrats, and the Senate fourteen to eight. The American or Know-Nothing party, in the fall of 1854, determined to place in nomination in Baltimore City a straight-out mayoralty ticket, and selected Samuel Hinks as their candidate, who was opposed by William G. Thomas, the Democratic nominee. The election resulted in the triumph of the American party, and in the State election of 1855 the American ticket was successful by a majority of 2699. The American party elected four out of the six congressmen, and eight of the eleven State senators chosen. The House of Delegates, which contained seventy-four members, was divided politically as follows: Americans, fifty-four; Union, ten; Democrats, nine; Whig, one. Strengthened by their majority in the Legislature, the American party soon obtained full and supreme control in Baltimore, where they inaugurated a reign of terror and lawlessness which all the efforts of its respectable citizens were for several years unable to overthrow. The Legislature, with its Know-Nothing majority, was deaf to all the appeals of the citizens of Baltimore for protection from the organized ruffianism which had taken possession of the city government, and treated the suggestions and recommendations of the Democratic executive with indifference and contempt. In the November election of 1857, by the help of the "Plug-Uglies," "Blood-Tubs," and other Know-Nothing organizations in Baltimore, they elected their candidate, Thomas Holliday Hicks, Governor by a majority of 8400 over John C. Groome, the Democratic candidate. They also secured forty-three members in the House of Delegates to thirty-one elected by the Democrats, and fifteen members of the Senate to seven Democrats. They, moreover, elected all the other State officers, thus obtaining complete political control of the State. The supremacy of the American party continued until 1860, when the General Assembly at length gave ear to the appeals of the people of Baltimore, and by the passage of the reform bills enabled them to restore their city to the position of a law-abiding, self-governed community.

Early in July, 1859, Capt. John Brown, or "Ossawatomie Brown," of Kansas notoriety, appeared in the neighborhood of Harper's Ferry, under the assumed name of Isaac Smith, attended by two of his sons and a son-in-law. He pretended to be a farmer from New York who desired to rent or purchase land in that vicinity with a view to farming and mining. Soon afterwards he rented a small farm from Dr. Kennedy on the Maryland side of the Potomac, about four or five miles from Harper's Ferry, in Washington County, and began farming operations in a small way. He lived in an obscure manner and attracted but little attention. Two or three of his friends were posted at Chambersburg, Pa., who received and forwarded to him arms of different kinds.

A man named Cook, whom Brown had sent to Harper's Ferry about a year previous to await his orders, now joined him, and on Sunday night, the 16th of October, 1859, between eleven and twelve o'clock, Brown and his party, some eighteen in number, crossed the bridge connecting the village of Harper's Ferry with the Maryland shore, and on reaching the Virginia side proceeded to take possession of the armory and arsenal of the United States. Each member of the party was armed with a Sharp's rifle carbine and with revolvers. The inhabitants of the village being asleep, the presence of Brown's party was not known until they demanded admittance at the arsenal gate, which was locked. The watchman refusing to admit them, they burst open the gate, made him prisoner, and established themselves in a strong brick building used as an engine-house. They brought with them a wagon containing arms and prepared torches. During the course of the night and the following morning they arrested many of the citizens of Harper's Ferry and the vicinity, and detained them in the engine-house as hostages.

The intelligence of the invasion of Harper's Ferry at first seemed so improbable that little credit was given it, but the news was soon confirmed, and created the most intense excitement. The Frederick military telegraphed to the President, proffering their services, which were immediately accepted. Other military organizations from Baltimore also started promptly for Harper's Ferry, and were joined on the way by a detachment of marines and Col. Robert E. Lee. In the mean time a number of Virginia volunteer companies, and three from Frederick under Col. Shriver, had arrived at Harper's Ferry and forced the insurgents to withdraw within the armory inclosure. The next morning Brown was summoned to surrender, and refusing to do so, the doors of the engine-house were battered down by the marines and the party captured or killed. After the citizens arrested and held prisoners by Brown were liberated, Lieut.-Col. S. S. Mills, of the Fifty-third Maryland Regiment, with the Baltimore Independent Grays, Lieut. B. F. Simpson commanding, were sent on the Maryland side of the river to search for Cook, and to bring in the arms of the insurgent party, which were said to be deposited in a school-house two and a half miles distant. Subsequently Lieut. J. E. B. Stuart with a party of marines was dispatched to the Kennedy farm, which had been used by Brown as a depôt for his arms and a rendezvous for the members of his party. Col. Mills found boxes containing Sharp's carbines and belt revolvers, and Lieut. Stuart found also at the Kennedy farm a number of sword-pikes, blankets, shoes, tents, and all the necessaries for a campaign. The prisoners were escorted to Charlestown, Va., by a detachment of marines under Lieut. Green, and were shortly afterwards tried, convicted, and hanged by the authorities of that State.[1]

[1] The list of insurgents was as follows: John Brown, Aaron C. Stevens, Edwin Coppic, Oliver Brown, Watson Brown, Albert Hazlett, William Leeman, Stuart Taylor, Charles P. Tidd, William Thompson, Adolph Thompson, John Kagi, Jeremiah Anderson, and John E. Cook, white; and Dangerfield, Louis Leary, Green Shields, Copeland, and O. P. Anderson, colored. Of the insurgents, Oliver Brown, Watson Brown, Hazlett, Leeman, Taylor, Tidd, William Thompson, Adolph Thompson, Kagi, Jeremiah Anderson, Dangerfield, and Leary were killed; and John Brown, Stevens, Coppic, Shields, Green, and Copeland were executed, as were also John E. Cook and Hazlett, who at first escaped, but were captured in Pennsylvania and delivered to the Virginia authorities. Those killed or wounded by the insurgents were Fontaine Beckman, mayor of Harper's Ferry, killed; G. W. Turner, of Virginia, killed; Thomas Boerly, of Virginia, killed; Heywood Shepherd (colored), killed; Private Quinn (marine corps), killed; and Messrs. Murphy, Young, Richardson, Hammond, McCabe, Dorsey, Hooper, Woollet, and Private Rupert (marine), wounded. The John Brown raid was the climax of a long series of aggravations inflicted upon the slaveholding States by extremists and fanatics at the North. The Gorsuch case, in which a citizen of Baltimore County was murdered while endeavoring to reclaim some fugitive slaves in Pennsylvania, is familiar to all readers of State history; but the murder of James H. Kennedy, of Hagerstown, in June, 1847, while endeavoring to reclaim his fugitive slaves in Carlisle, Pa., though in every way as infamous and unjustifiable as that of Gorsuch, does not seem to have attracted as much attention from historical writers. Mr. Kennedy, a young gentleman under thirty years of age, of liberal education and easy fortune, and a resident of Hagerstown, pursued his slaves, who made their escape into Pennsylvania, and on the 2d of June, 1847, arrested them in Carlisle. Under legal advice he appeared with them before the court, claiming their restitution under the Constitution and the act of Congress of 1793. The facts were not disputed. The judge declared his undoubted right to return them to Maryland, but decided that by a recent act of Pennsylvania, passed in 1847, commonly known as the "personal liberty bill" of that State, "the court was forbidden to hold jurisdiction, and the sheriff forbidden to render assistance or to use the jail for safe-keeping." Being thus deprived of official aid, while passing from the court-house door to his carriage at the curbstone he was attacked by an infuriated mob, and although a few citizens, personal friends, who were with him, aided by some others, fought manfully in defense, they were overpowered, the slaves rescued, and Mr. Kennedy left prostrate on the street, with severe bruises in the region of the chest and his knee-cap broken. Mr. Kennedy remained confined in his bed until the 25th, when he died from his injuries. When his body was brought home to Hagerstown his funeral was attended by a vast concourse of citizens, and the circumstances of his death called forth the most intense feeling of indignation against the hostile legislation of Pennsylvania.

The execution of Brown and his associates increased the political feeling in the North of which it was one of the manifestations, and the utterances and actions of the popular leaders on both sides only served to increase sectional hate and bitterness. The history of the political events immediately preceding the great civil conflict, as well as the narrative of Western Maryland's share in that tremendous struggle, are recited elsewhere, and it is not necessary to rehearse them in this connection. As a matter of interest in the military history of Western Maryland, it is not inappropriate to refer once more in passing to the readiness and enthusiasm with which the great majority of her people responded to the appeals for the support of the Union. On the 4th of August, 1862, the President ordered a draft of three hundred thousand militia for nine months, unless sooner discharged, and directed that if any State should not by the 15th furnish its quota of the additional three hundred thousand authorized by the act of Congress of July 17, 1862, the deficiency of volunteers in that State would be made up by special draft from the militia. On the 13th of August the enrolling officers of the State began to enroll the militia, under the direction of Hon. John A. J. Creswell, assistant adjutant-general of Maryland. In Baltimore City the work of enrolling was completed by Messrs. John B. Seidenstricker, Frederick Fickey, Jr., and Henry Stockbridge, the commissioners, on the 22d of August. The aggregate quota assigned to Allegany County was 872 men, but when this enrollment commenced, under the call of President Lincoln, it was found that this patriotic little county, with a population of only 27,895, had already furnished 1463 volunteers, or 591 in excess of its quota. The quota of Washington County was 943, but no draft was needed within its borders, for it had already given 1048 soldiers to the Union armies. Thirteen hundred and fifty-four men was Frederick's proportion, of which 1019 had been raised and sent to the field in volunteer organizations before the call of August, 1862, was made; while Carroll, out of a total quota of 742, had voluntarily and eagerly contributed 499 without the necessity of any other spur or stimulus than that of earnest patriotism.

Montgomery was the only county of Western Maryland in which enthusiasm for the Union cause was lacking at the beginning of the contest, and here the absence of this sentiment was so marked that out of a quota of 486 only seven volunteers had been furnished up to the date of this enrollment.

As the war proceeded and the power of the Republican party increased, it was more and more emboldened to adopt many anti-slavery measures on the plea of military necessity. On the 6th of August, 1861, a bill was approved declaring free all slaves used by the Confederates in aid of military purposes. On the 13th of March, 1862, the President also approved a bill dismissing from the service officers guilty of surrendering fugitive slaves. On the 16th of April, 1862, he approved a bill abolishing slavery in the District of Columbia. On the 10th of June, 1862, slavery was prohibited in the Territories, and on the 17th of July, 1862, Congress authorized the enlistment of negro soldiers. Upon the first Confederate invasion, in September, 1862, "I made a solemn vow before God," said Lincoln, "that if Gen. Lee was driven back from Maryland, I would crown the result by a declaration of freedom to the slaves." Accordingly, three days after the retreat of Lee across the Potomac, on the 22d of September, 1862, he issued his emancipation proclamation, declaring that on the 1st day of January, 1863, "all persons held as slaves within any State, or designated part of a State, the people whereof shall then be in rebellion against the United States, shall be then, thenceforward, and forever free," and on the 1st of January, 1863, issued another proclamation in which he designated the States and parts of States in which emancipation was to take effect.

In the mean time anti-slavery sentiments were making rapid strides in Maryland, and entered largely into the politics of the times. As early as May 28, 1862, the Union Convention of Baltimore unanimously adopted a series of strong resolutions recommending a new Constitutional Convention and approving a system of gradual emancipation. The subject continued to be discussed from time to time by the press and people until the year 1863, when the ultra Union party, aided by the administration, determined to make emancipation the paramount and leading issue in the fall canvass. They demanded peremptory emancipation, without regard to constitutional rights and laws of the State, or even the reasonable convenience of those who were slaveholders, and who had been from the beginning of the war as strong in support of the government as the emancipationists. As the campaign opened the deepest interest was felt by the country in the result of Maryland's choice. The election was for comptroller of the treasury, commissioner of the land-office, members of Congress, members of the General Assembly, judges of the courts, clerks of courts, sheriffs, and minor officers. In Baltimore there were four tickets in the field: the Independent Union, Regular Union, Conditional Union, and Unconditional Union. The Independent Union, Regular Union, and Unconditional Union had the same State officers, with some differences in the candidates for local offices. The candidates for Congress on the Unconditional tickets were: First District, John A. J. Creswell; Second District, Edwin H. Webster; Third District, Henry Winter Davis; Fourth District, ex-Governor Frank Thomas; and Fifth District, John C. Holland. The candidates on the Conditional Union were: First District, John W. Crisfield; Fifth District, Charles B. Calvert and Benjamin G. Harris. The five Unconditional Union candidates were all pledged to vote for the administration candidate for Speaker. In the election for State officers the question of emancipation or slavery was to be tested. Those who were for the speedy abolition of slavery in the State voted for Henry H. Goldsborough for comptroller of the treasury; and those who wished to retain slavery in the State, and who were opposed to the calling of a convention for its abolition, voted for Samuel S. Maffit for that office. In Baltimore the entire regular Unconditional Union ticket was elected, and in the State the same State ticket was elected, with the nominees of the same ticket from the First, Second, Third, and Fourth Districts for Congress. In the Fifth District, where there were two Union candidates running, Benjamin G. Harris, the Constitutional Union candidate, was elected. In Baltimore City Goldsborough received 10,942 votes, and Maffit 368. In the State the former received 33,901, and the latter 12,951, making a total vote of 46,852, and a majority of 20,950 votes for Goldsborough. The Legislature was largely in favor of the abolition of slavery and the calling of a convention to alter the constitution of the State.

Under the anti-slavery agitation slave property became almost valueless. This was strikingly illustrated in July, 1863, when Col. William Birney, of the bureau for the organization of colored troops, liberated all the slaves in Campbell's slave-prison, on Pratt near Howard Street, Baltimore. The course pursued by Col. Birney in enlisting negroes excited universal comment, and considerable correspondence grew out of it. Among those who participated in the discussion were Governor Bradford and ex-Governor

Francis Thomas. Judge Hugh L. Bond, who became one of the most strenuous advocates of unconditional emancipation in the State, addressed a long and urgent letter to the Secretary of War, Mr. Stanton, which attracted a great deal of attention at the North, and was widely copied by the journals of that section of the country. He pointed out that in Maryland the free negroes were nearly equal in numbers to the slave population, their aggregates being in 1860 eighty thousand of the former to eighty-seven thousand of the latter. If enlistments were to be confined to the former class, he observed, Baltimore and the adjoining free counties of the northern and western section of the State would suffer materially in being deprived of the laboring force necessary for their welfare. The enlistment of free negroes only, he argued, tended to appreciate the value of slave property and to put money in the pockets of the planters of the lower counties, a majority of whose inhabitants, he declared, were at heart disloyal. He therefore recommended that a proclamation should be issued stating explicitly that the acts of Congress before referred to authorized the enlistment of all classes of persons of African descent, and inviting free negroes and slaves alike to join the army.

In the meanwhile, however, the abduction and recruiting of slaves was kept up in Maryland by the various colored companies in the State. It was practiced to a very large extent on the Eastern Shore, and in the southern counties of the Western. In the fall of 1863 a circular was issued from the War Department for the organization of colored troops, and the establishment of recruiting stations for negro troops in Maryland, among which were Monocacy and Hagerstown. All claims for enlisted slaves were laid before a board appointed by President Lincoln, consisting of Hugh L. Bond, Thomas Timmons, and L. E. Straugh. No claim was entertained from any person who was or had been in arms against the government, or who in any way had given aid or comfort to the Confederates, and all claimants were to file with their claims an oath of allegiance to the government of the United States.

The General Assembly convened at Annapolis on Jan. 6, 1864, and one of its first acts was the introduction of a bill calling a State Convention with a view to the abolition of slavery. This bill passed both houses on the 28th of January, and became a law on the 3d of February. The vote in the Senate was, ayes 13, nays 2; and in the House, ayes 45, nays 17. By this act the people of Maryland were called upon to vote on the first Wednesday in April "for" or "against" holding a State Convention to frame a new constitution, and on the same day they were to vote for delegates to the convention. The election took place on the 6th of April, and resulted in the calling of a State Constitutional Convention. The Governor stated that the whole vote cast was 51,117, of which 31,593 were for, and 19,524 against a convention. He thereupon called the convention by proclamation to meet at Annapolis on Wednesday, the 27th of April. The vote in Washington County was 3298 for the convention and 651 against; in Montgomery it was 516 for and 746 against; in Frederick it was 3231 for and 1957 against; in Allegany it was 2307 for and 1135 against; and in Carroll it was 1898 for and 1635 against. The Constitutional Convention assembled at Annapolis on the 27th of April, 1864, and after a session of over four months it adopted a new constitution and form of government, and adjourned on the 6th of September. The most important changes made by the new constitution in the organic law of the State were the articles abolishing slavery and declaring "paramount allegiance" to be due to the Constitution and government of the United States. The new constitution was submitted to the people for their ratification in Baltimore City on the 12th of October, and in the several counties of the State on the 12th and 13th. The total vote in Baltimore on the adoption of the constitution was 11,832, of which 9779 was for and 2053 against. In Allegany County the vote was 1839 for and 964 against; in Carroll, 1587 for and 1690 against; in Frederick, 2308 for and 1916 against; in Montgomery, 422 for and 1367 against; and in Washington, 2441 for and 985 against. The result was a majority in the State of 1995 against the new constitution. To counteract this result provision had been made for taking the soldiers' vote at their camps outside of the State. The soldiers voted as the Prussian army prays, at the word of command, and the final result was: citizens' vote for, 27,541, against, 29,536; soldiers' vote out of the State 2633 for and 263 against; total, 30,174 for, 29,799 against; declared majority in favor of the constitution, 375. As soon as it was known that the constitution was defeated in the State, Thomas S. Alexander, of the Baltimore bar, on the 24th of October, on behalf of Samuel G. Miles, a slave-owner, applied to the Superior Court of that city for a writ of *mandamus* to compel Governor Bradford to reject the soldiers' vote on the ground of illegality. The application was refused *pro forma* by Judge Martin, and an appeal was taken the same day to the Court of Appeals, which affirmed the decision on the 29th, Judge Bartol dissenting. Governor Bradford on the same day issued a proclamation declaring that the constitution and form of government had "been adopted by a majority of the voters of the State, and that in pursuance of the provisions therein contained the same will go into effect as the proper constitution and form of government of this State, superseding the one now existing, on the 1st day of November next."[1]

The constitution of 1864 virtually disfranchised nearly two-thirds of the citizens of the State. When the military *regime* came to an end and civil authority was once more fully established, a bitter struggle for political supremacy at once commenced.

The Legislature, which was largely Republican, passed "an act relating to the registration of the voters of the State," which was the first general and permanent registration law in Maryland. By this act the Governor was to appoint from the citizens "most known for loyalty, firmness, and uprightness three persons for each ward in the city of Baltimore, and for each election district in the several counties of the State," who were to be styled officers of registration. They were to "register all free white male persons claiming and entitled to the elective franchise resident in or temporarily absent from the several wards of the city of Baltimore, and the several election districts of the counties." Three persons were also appointed to register the soldiers and sailors of the State in the service of the United States, stationed at convenient and accessible points, who were absent from their regular places of voting on account of the nature of their service, and qualified voters at the various camps, hospitals, etc.

To all persons registered they were to administer the oath of allegiance prescribed by the constitution of 1864, and also a further oath that they would answer truly all questions propounded touching their right to vote. They were empowered to exclude from the lists the name of any person who had done any of the acts enumerated in the third, fourth, and fifth sections of the constitution, notwithstanding the applicant had taken the oath of allegiance prescribed in section four of the first article. In pursuance of this law, the Governor appointed registers, who held a convention in Baltimore on the 2d of August, 1865, and adopted regulations for the guidance and government of registers throughout the State. A series of questions were formulated, to be propounded to the applicant for registration, which effectually excluded from the privileges of the elective franchise not only those who had shown but even those who had felt the slightest sympathy for the Southern cause. The registration, when completed, showed that in Baltimore, out of a voting population of forty thousand, only ten thousand persons were considered qualified to take part in the political government of the city. The total number of persons registered throughout the State was only about thirty-five thousand in a voting population of ninety-five thousand.

The first election under the registration law took place on the 7th of November, 1865, when the people of Baltimore were called upon to vote for a member of Congress, State senator, two members of the House of Delegates, sheriff, clerk of the Circuit Court, and city surveyor. In the counties elections were also held for county officers and judges of the Circuit Courts.

Early in January, 1866, at the instance of a number of gentlemen from the counties, a meeting was formally called and held in Baltimore for the purpose of ascertaining whether the people of the city were willing to co-operate in calling a State Convention of those who were opposed to the registration law. At this meeting resolutions were adopted calling upon the people of the different counties of the State and of Baltimore who were opposed to the registration law to hold primary meetings, and through them to appoint delegates to meet in convention in Baltimore on the 24th of January, 1866.

The convention met at Temperance Temple, Baltimore, on the day appointed. Allegany County was represented by Richard D. Johnson, James M. Schley, Dr. Robert T. McKaig, John S. Daily, J. Philip Roman, and Peter Baker; Carroll by Dr. Henry Betz, J. M. Parke, Jacob Ponder, Sterling Galt, T. W. Manro, L. P. Slingluff, John Frizzle, Henry Motter, Michael Murdock, Dr. Butler, James Blizzard, John B. Boyle, and E. M. Shipley; Frederick by Col. J. M. Kunkel, John Barthalow, Hon. Anthony Kimmell, Frederick J. Nelson, Harry W. Dorsey, Valentine Ebbarts, Upton Worthington, Hugh McAleer,

---

[1] According to the census of 1850 there were then in Maryland 16,040 slaveholders, of whom 4825 were owners of only one slave, 5331 were owners of over one and under five, 3327 of over five and under ten, 1822 of over ten and under twenty, 655 of over twenty and under fifty, 72 of over fifty and under one hundred, 7 of over one hundred and under two hundred, and 1 of over three hundred and under five hundred. From 1850 to 1860 the population of the State increased 148,631,—that is, from 583,034 in 1850 to 731,665 in 1860; and during the same time the number of slaves decreased 4986,—that is, from 90,368 in 1850 to 85,382 in 1860. The entire population of Allegany County in 1860 was 29,524, and the whole number of slaves 824, the percentage of slaves to the whole population being 2.8; in Carroll the whole population in 1860 was 24,361, and the number of slaves 802, a percentage of slave population of 3.2; in Frederick the entire population was 46,879, the number of slaves 3248, a slave percentage of 6.9; in Montgomery the whole population was 18,398, the slaves 5363, a percentage of 29.1; in Washington County the aggregate population was 24,248, the number of slaves 1126, a percentage of 4.6.

John Ritchie, J. D. Zeiller, James McSherry, Jr., Joseph Brown, N. B. Hendry, Robert Pattengall, John E. Sifford, John Lapatsall, N. J. Wilson, and Joseph Bowlus; Montgomery County by Hon. Montgomery Blair, Wm. Thompson, of R., and Joseph A. Taney; Washington County by R. H. Alvey, James Wason, Z. S. Claggett, David Cushwa, William Dodge, and Hon. George Schley.

Hon. Montgomery Blair, of Montgomery County, was chosen president, with Col. James Wallace, of Dorchester County, Hon. John Wethered, of Baltimore County, George M. Gill, of Baltimore City, J. Oden Bowie, of Prince George's, and George Schley, of Washington County, as vice-presidents; and Milton Y. Kidd, of Cecil County, William H. Neilson, of Baltimore City, and Thomas E. Williams, of Prince George's County, as secretaries. The convention adopted an address "to the people of Maryland," in which were set forth the grievances which had called the body together, and appealed to the Legislature to correct the evils complained of. After a two days' session, before adjourning, committees were appointed to proceed to Annapolis and present the resolutions of the Convention to the General Assembly then in session, and to procure signatures throughout the State to a memorial praying a repeal or modification of the constitution. The committee appointed to appear before the Legislature were accorded a respectful hearing, and in due time petitions signed by over twenty thousand citizens were presented to the General Assembly, but that body, on the 8th of February, 1866, resolved "that neither the temper or conduct of the people of this State who have been hostile to the government, nor the condition of our national affairs, nor the provisions of the constitution of the State warrant any interference with the registry law, and that it ought to be vigorously enforced."

On the 6th of June the ultra wing of the Unconditional Union party in Maryland assembled in convention in Baltimore, and adopted a platform declaring that "the registered loyal voters of Maryland will listen to no proposition to repeal or modify the registry law," and cordially indorsing the reconstruction policy of Congress. This convention again met in Baltimore on the 15th of August, and after adopting similar resolutions, and appointing delegates to the Southern Loyalists' Convention, to be held at Independence Hall, Philadelphia, on the 3d of September, nominated Col. Robert Bruce, of Allegany County, as their candidate for State comptroller.

The Conservative wing of the Unconditional Union party in Maryland assembled in convention in Baltimore on the 25th of July, 1866, and nominated for comptroller Col. William J. Leonard, of Worcester County. After the adoption of a long series of resolutions and the appointment of delegates to the Philadelphia National Convention, it adjourned. In the meanwhile a new set of officers of registration were appointed, who gave a more liberal construction to the law than their predecessors.

On the 10th of October following the municipal election was held, and resulted in the success of John L. Chapman, the ultra Republican candidate. The total number of votes cast was 7993, of which 5392 were given to Chapman, and 2601 to Daniel Harvey, the Conservative candidate. As the act of 1862, ch. 131, provided that for official misconduct any of the police commissioners might be removed by a concurrent vote of the two houses of the General Assembly, or by the Governor during the recess thereof, those who felt aggrieved at the result of the recent election determined to make an effort to have the police commissioners removed for their alleged partisan conduct. A meeting of citizens was accordingly held on the 16th of October, when committees were appointed "to gather information touching the official misconduct of the police commissioners and appointees," and to prepare memorial lists to the Governor asking for their removal, and that the election should be set aside.

In a few days a memorial signed by over four thousand citizens was presented to Governor Swann, accompanied by numerous affidavits, praying for the removal of the commissioners. In their petition the memorialists represented that the commissioners, "disregarding alike the appeals of their fellow-citizens and their own explicit oaths, appointed the two hundred and forty judges almost without exception from the political party of which they themselves are members."

They moreover charged that "the Board of Police, in violation of law and the liberty of the citizens, gave orders to the police justices not to hear any case, or take bail, or in manner release any person arrested or committed on the day of election, but in all cases to keep them confined until after six o'clock in the evening of that day." On the 18th of October, Governor Swann notified Messrs. Nicholas L. Wood and Samuel Hindes, the police commissioners, that he would take up their case on the 22d, at the executive chamber at Annapolis, and inclosed copies of the memorial and affidavits for their inspection. The police commissioners denied the power of the Governor to try them for "official misconduct," or to find them guilty thereof. Governor Swann, however, proceeded to try their case, and on the 1st of November announced his intention to remove Messrs. Hindes and

Wood on several grounds which he distinctly specified. Pending the decision of Governor Swann, the State was threatened with invasion by armed partisans from other States, and military organizations were formed in Baltimore for the open and avowed purpose of resisting the authority of the laws. On the 24th of October, Gen. Grant wrote to President Johnson, declaring that there was no occasion to send troops to Baltimore, and on the 25th President Johnson asked for the number of troops at convenient stations near Baltimore, to which Gen. Grant replied on the 27th, giving the desired information. On the 1st of November, President Johnson announced to Secretary Stanton that, "in view of the prevalence in various portions of the country of a revolutionary and turbulent disposition which might at any moment assume insurrectionary proportions and lead to serious disorders, and of the duty of the government to be at all times prepared to act with decision and effect, this force is not deemed adequate to the protection and security of the seat of government. I therefore request that you will at once take such measures as will insure its safety, and thus discourage any attempt for its possession by insurgent or other illegal combination."

When Governor Swann made his decision removing the police commissioners, President Johnson, on the 2d of November, gave Secretary Stanton the following order:

"EXECUTIVE MANSION, WASHINGTON, D. C., Nov. 2, 1866.

"SIR,—There is ground to apprehend danger of an insurrection in Baltimore against the constituted authorities of the State of Maryland, on or about the day of the election soon to be held in that city, and that in such contingency the aid of the United States might be invoked under the acts of Congress which pertain to that subject. While I am averse to any military demonstration that would have a tendency to interfere with the free exercise of the elective franchise in Baltimore, or be construed into any interference in local questions, I feel great solicitude that should an insurrection take place the government should be prepared to meet and promptly put it down. I accordingly desire you to call Gen. Grant's attention to the subject, leaving to his own discretion and judgment the measures of preparation and precaution that should be adopted.

"Very respectfully yours,
"ANDREW JOHNSON.
"HON. EDWIN M. STANTON, Secretary of War."

On the same day Gen. Grant sent an order to Gen. Canby, inclosing the orders from the President, and directing him to hold troops in readiness for the anticipated difficulties in Baltimore. Gen. Canby came immediately to Baltimore, and was followed in a few days by Gen. Grant, who reported on the 5th that "collision this morning looked almost inevitable. Wiser counsels now seem to prevail, and I think there is strong hope that no riot will occur. Propositions looking to the harmonizing of parties are now pending." Messrs. Wood and Hindes, the police commissioners, having been removed by Governor Swann, Messrs. William Thomas Valiant and James Young were appointed on the same day to fill the vacant offices. The superseded board, however, procured the arrest of the new appointees and the sheriff, William Thomson, who was assisting Messrs. Valiant and Young, and had them all lodged in jail. They were arrested on a warrant issued by Judge Bond, of the Criminal Court, and were charged with inciting a riot. Judge Bond required them not only to give bail to keep the peace, but to bind themselves not to attempt to execute the duties of their office, and to this demand they refused to submit, and were therefore committed to jail. This proceeding caused the most intense excitement in the city, but there was no serious disturbance of the peace. Several regiments of troops organized and were quartered at Fort McHenry, and Gens. Grant and Canby were besieged by the several factions at their headquarters in the city. Messrs. Hindes and Wood mustered in about three thousand five hundred regular and special police, and guarded the station-houses, their office, and prominent places in the city. As soon as the new police commissioners and sheriff were committed to jail, their counsel waited upon Hon. James L. Bartol, one of the judges of the Court of Appeals, who was at his home in the city, and procured a writ of *habeas corpus*, which was made returnable on Monday, November 5th, at 9 A.M., before the judge of the Superior Court. The writ was directed to the warden of the Baltimore City jail, commanding him to produce the bodies of William Thomas Valiant, James Young, and William Thomson, and have them before the judge at the time named. At the time appointed it was stated to the judges that the writs had been served, but it was understood that they would not be obeyed. The court adjourned until November 8th, and in the mean time the police commissioners were kept confined. During their confinement, on the 6th of November, the election took place, and resulted in a triumph of the Conservative party. In the city a total vote of 16,006 was polled for State comptroller, of which the Conservatives cast 8513, and the stalwart Republicans 7493.

Messrs. Valiant and Young, the new police commissioners, were brought before Judge Bartol on the writ of *habeas corpus* on November 8th, and on the 13th the judge rendered his decision releasing the commissioners, who immediately took possession of the office and entered upon the discharge of their duties. The marshal of police during the day surrendered the force under his charge to their orders, and on the 15th Messrs. Hindes and Wood surrendered their books, and turned over the station-houses and other property to the new commissioners, thus settling one of the most exciting difficulties that ever occurred in Baltimore.

The success of the Conservatives was followed by appeals to Congress on the part of their opponents, and by charges that the State had been revolutionized, and that the safety of loyal men, and especially of the colored population, was endangered. These charges first took definite and official form in a notice of contest by Joseph J. Stewart, Republican candidate for the Fortieth Congress from Baltimore, defeated by Charles E. Phelps, Conservative, and then a member of the Thirty-ninth Congress. Mr. Stewart charged "that Thomas Swann, Governor of the State of Maryland, conspiring with officers of his own appointment to defeat the law and revolutionize the State, did resort to measures revolutionary in their character, as against the loyal body politic of Maryland." After considerable testimony had been taken on both sides, Mr. Stewart abandoned the contest in a published letter to Mr. Phelps, dated April 12, 1867, admitting that the evidence had failed to present matter of serious controversy, and offering to indemnify his opponent for the costs.

The Republican State Convention which assembled in Baltimore on the 28th of March, adopted resolutions which were presented to Congress, calling upon that body "to protect the loyal majority of the people of Maryland, both white and colored, in defeating the scheme of the revolutionists in the Legislature," and declaring that " we will oppose any new constitution set up in subversion of the existing constitution under the convention bill which does not express the will of the majority of the people without regard to color ; and we will, with the aid of the loyal representatives of the nation, and by all means in our power, resist and destroy any such constitution as revolutionary usurpation." The Baltimore City Council also asked Congress to "assist the people of Maryland to form a State government, republican in form, and in unison with the spirit of the age." A petition for an injunction to prevent the election authorized by the Legislature on the 20th of March, 1867, to decide whether or not a Constitutional Convention should be called, was filed in the Superior Court of Baltimore on the 30th of March. After an extensive argument on both sides, Judge Martin, on the 2d of April, rejected the application.

The election was held on the 13th of April, and the whole number of votes cast in the State was 58,718, of which 34,534 were for a convention, and 24,136 against it. After a session of over three months the convention completed its work, and adjourned on the 17th of August, 1867. The election for the adoption or rejection of the new constitution was held on the 18th of September. The whole number of votes cast in the State in favor of its adoption was 47,152, and the whole number cast in opposition to it was 23,036, a majority of 24,116 in its favor. The first election under the new constitution was held in Baltimore on Oct. 23, 1867, for judge of the Court of Appeals, chief and four associate judges of the Supreme Bench of Baltimore, and mayor and City Council. The vote for mayor was: R. T. Banks, Democratic-Conservative, 18,420 ; A. W. Denison, Republican, 4896. At the State election on November 5th the candidates for Governor were Oden Bowie, Democratic-Conservative, and Judge H. Lennox Bond, Republican. The total vote of the State was 85,744, of which Bowie received 63,694, and Bond 22,050.

In the Presidential election of Nov. 3, 1868, Allegany County cast 2721 votes for Seymour, and 2428 for Grant; Carroll, 2607 for Seymour, and 2300 for Grant; Frederick, 3813 for Seymour, and 3869 for Grant; Montgomery, 1745 for Seymour, and 399 for Grant; Washington, 3114 for Seymour, and 3056 for Grant.

In March, 1870, the Legislature passed a law incorporating Towsontown, the county-seat of Baltimore County, and on April 4th an election was held for five commissioners to serve one year. This was the first election in the State under the Fifteenth Amendment to the Federal Constitution, and was the first occasion on which colored men had been allowed to vote in Maryland since 1802. They were duly impressed with the importance of the new privilege, and cast a full vote for the Republican ticket, which was elected by a large majority. The election of Nov. 2, 1870, passed off quietly considering the excitement of the campaign and the introduction of a new political element. All the colored voters appeared at the polling-places at an early hour, and the day seemed to be almost a holiday with them. United States deputy marshals were present at the polls in Baltimore, in accordance with the provisions of the Enforcement Act, but there was no necessity for their services. The total vote in the State was 134,525, of which 76,796 were cast for the Democratic and 57,729 for the Republican candidate, leaving a Democratic majority of 19,067.

In Allegany County the vote was 2843 for the Democratic candidates, and 1980 for the Republican ;

Carroll, 2966 for the Democrats, and 2558 for the Republicans; Frederick, 4739 for the Democrats, and 4664 for the Republicans; Montgomery, 2436 for the Democrats, and 1791 for the Republicans; Washington, 3756 for the Democrats, and 3284 for the Republicans.

In the State election for Governor, comptroller, attorney-general, and members of the Legislature, held on the 7th of November, 1871, the Democrats were again successful. On the State ticket the Democratic candidates were William Pinkney Whyte, of Baltimore City, for Governor; A. K. Syester, of Washington County, for attorney-general; Levin R. Woolford, of Somerset County, for comptroller. The Republican candidates were Jacob Tome, of Cecil County, for Governor; Alexander Randall, of Anne Arundel County, for attorney-general; and Lawrence J. Brendle, of Frederick, for comptroller. The total vote of the State was 132,728, against 134,525 at the congressional election in 1870. The total number of votes cast for the Democratic candidate for Governor was 73,908, and for the Republican candidate 58,820; Democratic majority, 15,088.

At the Presidential election of 1872, Greeley or the "new departure" candidate received in the State 67,687 votes, and Grant 66,760. Majority for Greeley, 927. Allegany County cast 2695 votes for Greeley, and 3301 for Grant; Carroll, 2505 for Greeley, and 2587 for Grant; Frederick, 4065 for Greeley, and 5186 for Grant; Montgomery, 2121 for Greeley, and 1949 for Grant; Washington, 3204 for Greeley, and 3664 for Grant.

The State election of Nov. 2, 1875, for Governor, attorney-general, comptroller of the treasury, and members of the Legislature, was one of the most animated political contests ever known in Maryland. The Democratic candidates were John Lee Carroll for Governor, Charles J. M. Gwinn for attorney-general, and Levin Woolford for comptroller. The opposition Reform candidates were J. Morrison Harris, of Baltimore County, for Governor; S. Teackle Wallis, of Baltimore City, for attorney-general; and Col. Edward Wilkins for comptroller. The total vote cast in the State was 157,984, of which Carroll received 85,454, and Harris 72,530. In the counties Harris was successful, but his majority in the State was overcome by the vote in Baltimore City, which stood 36,958 for Carroll and 21,863 for Harris, the total vote of the city being 58,821. Great frauds were alleged, and the election was contested before the Legislature of 1876, which decided in favor of the Democratic candidates. At the Presidential election of Nov. 7, 1876, the Democratic electors were elected by 19,799 majority, the vote for Samuel J. Tilden, of New York, and Thomas A. Hendricks, of Indiana, being 91,780, against 71,981 for R. B. Hayes, of Ohio, and William A. Wheeler, of New York.

In the political campaign of 1879 the contest was narrowed down to a struggle between Democrats and Republicans. The issues of the campaign were, however, above the level of personal altercations or attacks upon individual character, as there was no personal objection that could be alleged against either of the gubernatorial candidates.

Hon. William T. Hamilton, of Washington County, was the Democratic nominee for Governor, and Mr. James A. Garey the Republican nominee. The election was held on the 4th of November, 1879, and resulted in the success of the entire Democratic State ticket by heavy majorities, the vote being 90,820 for Hamilton and 68,612 for Garey, the Democrats carrying, among other counties, Carroll, Montgomery, and Washington.

FREDERICK COUNTY.

CHAPTER XVIII.

INTRODUCTORY.

The First Settlers—Boundaries of the County—Character of Inhabitants—Frederick, Lord Baltimore—Trade and Manufactures—Religious Habits of the People—Population—Industrial Statistics — Education — Post-Offices — County Finances.

FREDERICK, the parent-county of Western Maryland and the fourteenth in the order of formation in this State, was created by an act of the General Assembly passed June 11, 1748. This act, however, did not take effect until the 10th of December of the same year. The territory of Frederick County originally belonged to Charles County, created in 1658, the bounds of which, as defined by the commission appointing officers for it, were "the river Wicomico to its head, and from the mouth of that river up the Potomac as high as the settlements extend, and thence to the head of Wicomico." Charles County had then on the east St. Mary's and Calvert Counties, and in its general and vague boundary it included all the territory in the western part of the province, or what are now Prince George's, Montgomery, Frederick, Washington, Allegany, and Garrett Counties and the District of Columbia, and so continued for thirty-six years.

The early settlers of Maryland and Virginia kept

to the navigable streams, and it was many years afterwards before the fertile lands in the valleys in the neighborhood of the Blue Ridge and Allegany Mountains began to be dotted with the log cabins of an advancing frontier. No pioneer had ventured into these solitudes, whose sleeping echoes were only waked by the scream of the eagle or the whoop of the painted warrior. Neither Gist nor Cresap had yet seen the wilds of Western Maryland. The Potomac then flowed in solitary grandeur for more than three hundred miles through an unbroken wilderness, its gentle surface only disturbed by the wing of the wildfowl or the dip of the savage paddle. It now washes shores studded on either side with the habitations of civilized and Christianized men, reflecting in its mirror-waves the jocund harvests and golden fruits of regulated and active tillage, is adorned with smiling villages and cities, and for one hundred and twenty-five miles from its mouth it bears upon its bosom the diversified commerce of mighty commonwealths.

As we have seen in another place, the Potomac had been explored as far as the Little Falls, above Georgetown, by Henry Fleet, thirty-four years before the erection of Charles County. Fleet, however, was not the first white man who ever looked upon the site of Washington, for this locality was explored by Capt. John Smith, of Virginia, as early as 1608. When Leonart Calvert arrived in the "Potomac" in 1634, he went up to confer with Fleet, the adventurous fur-trader, who had been many years in the country. "The place," said Fleet, alluding to the Potomac just above Georgetown, and afterwards in Frederick County, "is, without all question, the most healthful and pleasant place in all this country, and most convenient for habitation, the air temperate in summer and not violent in winter. It aboundeth with all manner of fish. The Indians in one night commonly will catch thirty sturgeons in a place where the river is not over twelve fathoms broad. And for deer, buffaloes, bears, turkeys the woods do swarm with them, and the soil is exceedingly fertile; but above this place the country is rocky and mountainous, like Canada. . . . We had not rowed above three miles but we might hear the falls to roar."

The progress of settlements up the Potomac was slow, and we have learned little respecting them. "Blue Plains," a tract of ten hundred acres east of the Anacostia,—*i.e.*, the Eastern Branch of the Potomac,—was surveyed for George Thompson, June 4, 1662. "St. Elizabeth," of fourteen hundred and thirty acres, was on a survey Sept. 30, 1695, made "Oxon Hill Manor." "Glennings," of three hundred and forty-nine acres, and "Giesborough," of eight hundred and fifty, surveyed May 5, 1663, on a resurvey Feb. 3, 1695, by Col. John Addison, were made "Barnaby Manor." These settlements continued to grow rapidly until 1695, when Prince George's County was formed out of the territory lying north of the Mattawoman and Swanson's Creek, and a straight line connecting their heads, and between the rivers Patuxent and Potomac. In 1748, Prince George's received its first definite western limits by the creation of Frederick County, from which it was separated by a straight line, beginning at the lower side of the mouth of Rock Creek, and running thence with Hyatt's plantation to the Patuxent River. Since that period no change has been made in its bounds, except by the interposition of the District of Columbia (ceded to the United States by Maryland in 1789), which has given to it as its present southern and western boundaries the Potomac River until it meets the lines of the District, then with those lines lying in Maryland until they intersect the former line from Rock Creek, and with that line to the Patuxent.

Frederick County, at the time of its formation, embraced all that portion of the province lying north and west of Prince George's, Anne Arundel, and Baltimore Counties which is now contained in the counties of Carroll (partly), Montgomery, Frederick, Washington, Allegany, and Garrett and the District of Columbia. In other words, Frederick County originally embraced the whole of that section of the State now known as "Western Maryland."

The act of 1748 was passed in response to repeated petitions sent annually for the preceding nine years by many of the inhabitants of the western part of Prince George's County, the first of which was delivered by Benjamin Tasker from the Upper House to the Speaker of the Lower House on the 10th of May, 1739. These petitions asked leave to have a separate county formed from that in which the petitioners resided, to have separate magistrates, and to build a court-house. The bill of 1748 enacted "That from and after Dec. 10, 1748, a new county is erected out of Prince George's County, the bounds whereof to be as followeth, viz.: Beginning at the lower side of the mouth of Rock Creek, and thence by a straight line joining to the east side of Seth Hyatt's plantation to Patuxent River, the said line to be run by the surveyor of Prince George's County, and trees marked, etc.; then with Patuxent River to the lines of Baltimore County, and with the said county to the extent of the province; and all the lands lying to the westward and northward of the said lines to be included within the new county aforesaid, which shall be called Frederick County, and the inhabitants thereof to have and enjoy equal privileges with the other counties of this province in sending delegates to the Assembly, having county courts, sheriffs, justices, etc., and the court-house and prison to be built in or adjoining to Frederick Town." Provision was made for holding the county courts on the third Tuesday of March, June, August, and November, and the assize on the Monday next after that in Prince George's County. Exactly what were the western lines of Baltimore County had not been determined, and accordingly in 1750 an act was passed establishing a definite line, beginning at Parr's Spring, and running thence with artificial metes to the Pennsylvania line.

"By this act it was provided that that part of Frederick County which was formerly included in Prince George's County is hereby divided from Baltimore County in manner following, viz.: Beginning at a spring called Parr's Spring, and running thence north 35° east to a bounded white oak standing on the west side of a wagon-road called John Digg's road, about a mile above a place called the Burnt House Woods, and running thence up the said road to a bounded white oak standing on the east side thereof, at the head of a draught of Sam's Creek, thence north 55° east to a Spanish oak standing on a ridge near William Roberts', and opposite to the head of a branch called the Beaver Dam, and running thence north 20° east to the temporary line between the provinces of Maryland and Pennsylvania, being near the head of a draught of Conewago, at a rocky hill called Rattlesnake Hill, which said lines are hereby established as the boundaries between the said counties, and all the lands on the southeast side of the said lines to be deemed to be in Baltimore County, etc., and all the lands on the west-northwest sides to be part of Frederick County," etc.

It is probable that the first settlements in what was afterwards known as Frederick County were made in the neighborhood of Georgetown, D. C., which was for a long time the chief mart and the only seaport of the county. It is also evident that the glowing descriptions given by the early voyagers to this locality fired the imaginations of many of the colonists of Virginia and the Old World, and led many to take up their homes at the head of navigation on the Potomac. The attractions and advantages of this section of the province had become familiar in the other colonies some years before Cæcilius Calvert received his charter. Whatever, indeed, may have been the date at which the first settlements in Frederick County were made, it is certain that it was indebted at an early period for much of its population to Virginia and Pennsylvania. The religious persecutions in Virginia and political troubles in that colony, and the uprisings in Scotland in 1715 and 1745 led many persons to come to Maryland and settle near the headwaters of the Potomac, and the dispute with the Dutch over the title to the Delaware drove a few of the Swiss to this locality. Our border troubles with Pennsylvania led many of the inhabitants of the adjacent counties of that province to remove to Maryland, who in the early days settled mostly in the neighborhood of Frederick Town. The lower part of the county, at Georgetown and Rockville (now in Montgomery County), was at first the most thickly settled, and there is conclusive evidence in the old Episcopal Parish records to show that it long maintained this numerical superiority. Settlements in the beginning, as we have stated, clung to the shores of the bay or the banks of the large rivers, and nearly every plantation of consequence was placed within easy distance of some water highway, the only sort of road which the early colonists found already prepared for them. Thus from the first the "backwoods" was the wilderness, and the backwoods was simply the unsettled region removed from navigable water; and thus it happened that both shores of the bay and its large estuaries were settled before the interior of even St. Mary's, Charles, Talbot, and Kent Counties had ceased to be called the "backwoods." The tide of immigration from the South, as far as the original Frederick County was concerned, was met by a downward current from the North, and accordingly we find among the early settlers of Western Maryland emigrants from Virginia, Southern Maryland, Delaware, and England on the one hand, and from Pennsylvania, New York, and Germany on the other. The settlements on the Potomac continued to be the most populous until about the time of the formation of the county, when the Governor and Council stated to the Board of Trade in England that "the population of Maryland had been much increased by the influx of Germans, who had been assigned lands in Frederick County." These settled principally in the neighborhood of Frederick Town, and when the county was created Frederick Town was made by law the county-seat, and the court-house was ordered to be erected there. The town of Frederick had been laid out in 1745, three years before the creation of the county, and there had been a settlement of pioneers from Southern Maryland in what is now the Urbana district as early as 1730. In 1733 a company of German immigrants came down from Pennsylvania and established themselves in the valley of the Monocacy, and from this time onward we can date the rise and progress of this interesting section of our State.

The county was named after Frederick, the Sixth and the last of the Barons of Baltimore. He was the only son of Charles, the Fifth Lord Baltimore, who died on the 24th of April, 1751, aged fifty-two years. Before the death of Charles he made and published his will, which was afterwards proved in

FREDERICK, SIXTH LORD BALTIMORE.

the Prerogative Court of the Archbishop of Canterbury, England, bearing date Nov. 17, 1750, whereby he devised to trustees therein mentioned the province of Maryland and all his estates, " of what nature or kind soever the same were (except the manor of Anne Arundel, in the county of Anne Arundel, in the said province), to the use of his only son, Frederick Calvert, afterwards Lord Baltimore, in strict settlement, with the reversion in fee to his the testator's eldest daughter, Louisa Calvert."

Frederick, the last of the Barons of Baltimore, married Lady Diana Egerton, youngest daughter of the Duke of Bridgewater, in 1753. She died Sept. 4, 1771, without issue. Frederick was a fast young man, and did not live to be an old one. His memory is not precious, and his deeds were anything but meritorious. In 1768 he was indicted and tried for committing rape, but notwithstanding he was acquitted by the court, he was most severely censured by the press and people for this atrocious act, and the conviction of his guilt was universal. He had an insurmountable propensity to flourish as an author, but he never gained any literary reputation, although he published several works. He died in Naples, Sept. 14, 1771, leaving two illegitimate children by Hester Wheland,—Henry Harford and Frances Mary Harford. Hester Wheland, *alias* Harford, afterwards married Peter Prevost, and her daughter, Frances Mary Wheland, *alias* Harford, married Robert Morris, of England. Frederick Calvert upon his death bequeathed the province of Maryland in tail mail to his illegitimate son, Henry Harford, a child nine years of age, then under the care of Rev. Dr. Loxton, at Richmond School, remainder in fee to his younger sister, the Hon. Mrs. Norton, and several minor bequests.

Henry Harford, instead of repairing to Maryland to take possession of the province under Frederick's will, remained in England during the Revolutionary struggle, and as a consequence all their property, revenues, etc., valued at two millions of dollars, were confiscated. As Frederick left no legitimate issue, the title of Lord Baltimore became extinct, and by the results of the war for independence Henry Harford was the first and last proprietary of Maryland.

At the time of the formation of Frederick County some thirty persons from New York joined the German and English colonists near Frederick Town in clearing the surrounding country and in building up the town. In addition to these there were important accessions from the Scotch-Irish of the Cumberland Valley and from Swiss refugees. These pioneers found themselves in a wild country, in close proximity to the Indians, and confronted by all the difficulties and dangers of the frontier life. They were, however, a hardy, adventurous people, and soon succeeded in permanently establishing themselves in their new home. So compact, indeed, and well ordered was the little colony that it not only kept the Indians at a respectful distance, but developed rapidly in the peaceful arts. Undoubtedly the great natural advantages of the region in which the immigrants had settled contributed largely to their success. To a kind and fertile soil, abundantly watered by numerous streams, were joined a bracing climate and delightful scenery of a character peculiarly fitted to stimulate all the energies of the thrifty and industrious pioneers who had chosen it as their abiding-place. The abundance of mineral deposits and the utilization of the valuable water-power provided by the various rivers and creeks were important factors of industrial development, and it was not long before iron and copper-works and two glass manufactories were in active operation. Thus in an early writer (1807) we find: " Frederick County contains abundance of iron ore, slate, and limestone, a copper-mine near Liberty Town, and flintstone for making glass. There are two furnaces and two forges in operation, which manufacture pig, hollow-ware, and bar-iron to a considerable amount. Within a few miles of Frederick Town are two glass-houses which carry on the manufacture of glass with much spirit." The two glass-houses mentioned were probably those of John Frederick Amelung & Co., who issued a prospectus Feb. 9, 1785, announcing that " a company of German manufacturers being lately arrived in the State of Maryland, and having made a plan of establishing a complete glass manufactory in the United States," were prepared to make " all kinds of glassware, viz.: window-glass from the lowest to the finest sorts, white and green bottles, wine and other drinking-glasses, as also optical glasses and looking-glasses finished complete." The firm purchased a tract of land on the Monocacy, near Frederick, erected factories, and soon began the regular manufacture of glass. They established agencies in New York, Philadelphia, Baltimore, and Frederick. In Baltimore their representative was Melchior Keener, and in the town of Frederick, Abraham Faw. This was undoubtedly the first glass manufactory established in America. In common with the rest of the country, however, Frederick County was hampered in the development of manufactures by the restrictive and almost prohibitory legislation of the British Parliament against all American manufactures which competed with English goods, and under the circumstances their progress prior to the Revolution was remarkable.

So rapid was the growth of the settlements in Western Maryland that within the comparatively brief period of twenty-five years it was found necessary to erect two new counties in addition to Frederick. That county had been established on the 11th of June, 1748. On the 6th of September, 1776, the Colonial Convention divided Frederick County, and formed the new county of Washington on the west and Montgomery on the south. Carroll, which now bounds Frederick on the east, was not established until 1835, and previous to that year was comprised in Frederick and Baltimore Counties. The ordinance for the establishment of the new counties provided "that after the 1st day of October next such part of the said county of Frederick as is contained within the bounds and limits following, to wit: beginning at the place where the temporary line crosses the South Mountain, and running thence by a line on the ridge of the said mountain to the river Potowmac, and thence with the lines of the said county, so as to include all the lands to the westward of the line running on the ridge of the South Mountain, as aforesaid, to the beginning, shall be and is hereby erected into a new county by the name of Washington County," and "that after the first day of October next such part of the said county of Frederick as is contained within the bounds and limits following, to wit: beginning at the east side of the mouth of Rock Creek, on Potowmac River, and running with the said river to the mouth of Monocacy, then with a straight line to Parr's Spring, from thence with the lines of the county to the beginning, shall be and is hereby erected into a new county by the name of Montgomery County." For Washington County, Messrs. Joseph Sprigg, Joseph Smith, John Barnes, Andrew Rench, Daniel Hughes, William Yates, and Conrad Hogmire, and for Montgomery County, Messrs. Nathan Magruder, John Murdock, Henry Griffith, Thomas Crampton, Jr., Zadock Magruder, Allen Bowie, and John Wilson were named as commissioners. These lines still constitute the boundaries of Frederick County on the south and west, but by the formation of Carroll County in 1835, which cut off a large part of Frederick, the eastern boundary of the county was changed, so that it now runs as defined by the act (1835, ch. 256) creating Carroll County: "Beginning at the Pennsylvania line where Rock Creek crosses said line, thence with the course of said creek until it merges in the Monocacy River, thence with the Monocacy to the point where Double Pipe Creek empties into Monocacy, thence with the course of Pipe Creek to the point of juncture of Little Pipe Creek with Big Pipe Creek, thence with the course of Little Pipe Creek to the point where Sam's Creek empties into Little Pipe Creek, thence with Sam's Creek to Warfield's Mill, thence with the road called the Buffalo road and to a point called Parr's Spring." In 1789, Allegany County was formed out of Washington County, and embraced all of that part of the State lying west of Sideling Hill Creek until 1872, when it was divided to make the new county of Garrett.

Frederick is one of the most picturesque, diversified, and interesting counties in the State. Along its western boundary extends the Blue Ridge, or South Mountain, and its surface is divided by the Catoctin Mountains into two beautiful valleys, the Valley of the Monocacy River and the Middletown Valley, drained by the Catoctin River or Creek. The scenery on both sides of the Catoctin range and along the base of the Blue Ridge is of the most charming character, presenting a diversity of effects, a boldness of outline, and a warmth of color (at certain seasons of the year) which fully justify the local pride which is felt in them. The soil, especially of the two valleys, is famous for its fertility. Frederick, in fact, is, agriculturally, the most productive county in the State. The pasturage is so superior that stock-raising has long been one of the distinctive features of Frederick County farming, and in certain districts tobacco and potatoes are important crops. The surface of the country is undulating, with gently-swelling hills, rising in the western portion to a beautiful spur of the Blue Ridge, geographically known as the Catoctin Mountains; not rugged, barren, and forbidding in their aspect, but covered to the summit with well-cultivated farms or dense forests of valuable timber. The South Mountain, or Blue Ridge Range, which divides Frederick from Washington County, is noted for the grandeur and beauty of its scenery and the purity of its atmosphere. Frederick County embraces many varieties of soil, most of which have been improved to the highest degree and are in the best state of cultivation. The soil is mostly limestone, with some slate and flint lands and considerable red soil. The extensive tracts of comparatively level land in the basins of the valleys are sufficiently rolling to drain well, and there are no marshes or swamps of any extent in the country, so that it is exempt from all malaria. In quality the soils comprise the best varieties of the clay limestone, mica slate, roofing-slate, and red lands. Each of these soils has its peculiar excellence and adaptation to particular crops, but all of them produce large yields of wheat, rye, oats, corn, and the cultivated grasses, and, as a consequence, the best cattle, sheep, horses, and other domestic animals. The climate is salubrious, and the county renowned for its healthfulness. The inhabitants are intelligent and industrious, and mainly devoted to agriculture. The farms are finely improved with large barns and substantial dwellings that bespeak the prosperity of the owners. Orchards abound, and the apple and peach are extensively grown. The eastern slope of the Catoctin Mountains and the Linganore hill country are especially adapted to the culture of the grape. Here is the native home of the Catawba, while other varieties are also largely cultivated with success. There are also several large and flourishing vineyards in the vicinity of the Monocacy River. The Concord grape thrives best on limestone lands, but in the hill country the Catawba, Iona, Isabella, Delaware, and Clinton are singularly exempt from the ravages of the phylloxera.

The mountains are covered with oak, hickory, and chestnut timber, the latter affording an inexhaustible supply of fencing material, while in the valleys, at frequent intervals, there are strips of woodland, which give variety to the landscape and furnish fuel and fencing. The county is watered by innumerable streams. The Monocacy River and Cactoctin, Linganore, Owen's, Hunting, Fishing, Carroll, Tom's, Bennett's, Bush, Israel's, Tuscarora, Middle, Sam's, Pike's, Broad, and Beaver Dam Creeks traverse the county and provide an abundance of water-power, besides that existing on the Potomac.

Large tracts of land in Frederick County were taken up or purchased by the Dulanys, the Carrolls, and other leading families of the province, who early appreciated its great value for agricultural purposes. Patrick Dulany owned the land on which Frederick City now stands, and a considerable tract besides. Charles Carroll of Carrollton's manor on the Monocacy, in what is now Buckeystown District, was much more productive than the family-seat in Howard County. Land was taken up in what is now Linganore District by James Carroll as early as 1727. The abundance of water-power and the discovery of valuable deposits of copper, iron, and other minerals naturally gave a great impetus to manufactures and to industrial occupations of various kinds. Paper-mills were erected, and during the Revolution a gun-lock factory was established at Frederick, and Daniel and Samuel Hughes, of Antietam, were given a contract for casting cannon. Long ere this the manufacture of linen had been established by the German settlers. Large quantities of flax were grown, the soil being especially suited to its cultivation. The men prepared it for spinning, and the women wove it into coarse linen, which found a ready sale. Thread of different colors was also made and sold at a profit, and the seed of the flax was sent to Baltimore and Philadelphia, where it was easily disposed of. Thus in every German household an important industry was added to the ordinary avocations of the farm, and it is not to be wondered that the Frederick County Germans should have so soon outstripped their Southern neighbors in the race for material prosperity. Nor did they stop at a single branch of manufactures, but occupied themselves with a great variety of profitable employments. Thus they knitted long yarn stockings, very useful to the frontiersman and farmer; they tanned leather and worked it up into harness; and they prepared butter in firkins, honey, apple-butter, dried apples, etc., which they exchanged in Frederick and in Baltimore for salt, lead, gunpowder, and other necessary supplies. These, in turn, were often exchanged with the frontiersmen for furs and peltries, hides, game, etc. The natural consequence was that Frederick expanded rapidly, and soon became the second town in Maryland in population and importance. As early as 1760, and probably even earlier, a public road was established between Frederick and Baltimore, and another about the same time between Frederick and Annapolis. In addition to the trade with Baltimore, Frederick carried on an extensive traffic with the people of Georgia. That colony was established about the same time (1733) that the first settlement was made at Frederick, and under the direction of the eccentric but able Oglethorpe had developed rapidly. There was a bond of sympathy between the Germans of Frederick and the people of Georgia, from the fact that Moravians and Protestant refugees from Salzburg had settled in the Southern colony. The goods sent from Frederick were boots and shoes, saddles and harness, woolen goods, linen and woolen and flaxseed threads. They were carried on pack-horses, and were exchanged for cotton, indigo, and money. Frederick also had a lucrative trade with the posts of the Ohio Company, the first of these being situated on the Potomac, on the present site of the city of Cumberland. Annapolis, during this period, was an important post, and the road to that point was chiefly used for the transportation of tobacco and flax intended to be shipped abroad.

A turnpike road between Frederick and Baltimore was commenced in 1805. Writing of Frederick in 1807, Joseph Scott, the geographer, says, "It (Frederick) is a flourishing place, and carries on a brisk trade with the Western country, and when the great Western turnpike which is to pass through it into Pennsylvania and the State of Ohio is completed it will add greatly to the trade, wealth, and prosperity of the place. Frederick Town will then become the great thoroughfare between Baltimore and Philadelphia to the Western country." In another portion of his book he says, "The great Western turnpike . . . has been begun, and twenty miles of it completed from the city of Baltimore. It is expected that during the ensuing summer it will be finished as far as Frederick Town." This fact alone serves to prove the industrial importance and prosperity which Frederick County had already attained. It was the more marked from the fact that in the other counties of Maryland the people devoted themselves almost exclusively to the cultivation of tobacco with slave labor, and led, on the whole, a very easy, indolent life. Naturally, the prosperity of the German families of the rich Monocacy and Middletown Valleys excited the cupidity of adventurers, and we read in "Eddis' Letters" that large sums of money were made by those who had influence with Governor Ogle by the lease and sale of fertile lands in Frederick County of which they had secured possession. These lands speedily found their way into the hands of comparatively small holders, who cultivated them closely, and improved them so that now they form one of the most productive agricultural regions in the country. The Monocacy and the Catoctin, both of which flow southward into the Potomac, have numerous branches, so that the county is abundantly supplied with water-power, which was utilized at a very early date in the erection of mills, tanneries, etc. As early as 1796 there were thirty-seven grist-mills on the Monocacy and its branches. Copper-mines were worked as far back as 1760. On the 20th of November, 1765, a copartnership was entered into between Stephen Richards and John Stevenson to raise copper ore from a tract known as Spring Garden. James Smith was appointed manager, and work was commenced. Comparatively little success was met with until 1767, when some of the ore was shipped to London. The Fountain Copper-Works were in operation in 1760. These veins of ore are situated in the Linganore Section, near Liberty, and are still worked with profit. The rich marble quarries of the Catoctin Mountain and of the Monocacy Valley were also developed at a very early day. From the Monocacy region came the marble which was used in the columns of the old hall of the House of Representatives in the capitol at Washington. Very handsome limestone marble of various tints of blue and gray is found in quantities between Woodsboro' and the Potomac River, and another variety of light and dark red is seen west of Frederick City. To Frederick County is due the credit of having first manufactured that useful article, the friction-match, which was discovered and first made in the village of Mechanicstown, by Joseph Weller and two others, in 1831. Large quantities were manufactured and sent to Baltimore, Cincinnati, Philadelphia, Wheeling, and Nashville, Tenn. Mr. Whittaker, druggist, at the corner of Howard and Baltimore Streets, was the agent for Baltimore. Owing to a defect in the preparation, the "heads" of the matches became soft in hot weather, and this of course had the effect of greatly diminishing their popularity for a while. The manufactory was twice blown up, and one of the proprietors with it. Mr. Weller narrates that he sent an agent into the Middletown Valley, and that the prudent and wary farmers ran him and his matches off, saying, "You rascal, you want to sell articles to set our barns and houses on fire!" At first the matches sold for twenty-five cents per box, and afterwards for ten cents. Every box had a piece of sand-paper in it on which to strike the match.

The geographical position of the town of Frederick has made it the scene of many stirring events. Situated on the great highway to the South and West, it became during the Revolution one of the most conspicuous of the colonial towns. During the French and Indian war it was the nearest English settlement of importance to the theatre of military operations, and was the rallying-point for the British and colonial troops. Here Gen. Braddock swore and foamed over the vexatious delays which preceded his fatal advance upon Fort Du Quesne, and here George Washington, then a colonel in the colonial service, and Benjamin Franklin, postmaster-general for the colonies, met for the first time. No community contributed more liberally to the Revolutionary cause than did Frederick County, whose companies of the "Flying Camp," under the gallant Johnson and Rezin Beall, and of the German Battalion, commanded by Col. George Stricker, did gallant service throughout the war. The people appear to have been practically a unit in their devotion to the principles for which the colonies contended, and under the leadership of Thomas Johnson, John Hanson, Thomas Sim Lee, Alexander Contee Hanson, and other patriotic men, were untiring in their exertions in behalf of the cause. A hardy, independent race, they were naturally impatient under the oppressive legislation of the British government, and though peaceable by nature and slow to violence, were tenacious of their rights and determined to assert them at all hazards. It was not to be expected that the men who had braved the perils of the wilderness for freedom's sake would sit down tamely under the iniquitous burdens which the British ministry was seeking to impose, and consequently we find many of the bravest soldiers of the Revolution in the ranks of the German companies which were recruited in Frederick County. Among the earliest manifestations of the Revolutionary spirit were the demonstrations of the Sons of Liberty, who not only denounced the Stamp Act in 1765, but threatened to march to Annapolis, in order to compel the Governor and Council to abolish a certain tax on tobacco which they continued to levy in opposition to the Lower House of the General Assembly. This was not the first time the men of Frederick had asserted themselves in a similarly bold and independent manner. In 1756, Capt. Thomas Cresap publicly announced his intention to lead a band of riflemen to Annapolis to compel the provincial government to give them necessary aid in repelling Indian attacks, but as the aid was granted he did not execute his threat.

The settlements of Frederick and in the vicinity extended rapidly westward, and the more adventurous spirits did not hesitate to establish themselves in isolated situations, exposed to sudden assaults from the neighboring Indian tribes. Among these pioneers the Cresaps, the Shelbys, the Poes, the Gists, and the Wetsels stand forth conspicuous in local history for daring and success. Previous to and during the French and Indian war the savages made frequent incursions into thinly-settled portions of the county, and their depredations caused the inhabitants to organize a band of riflemen for the protection of the frontier. The constant presence of danger and the necessity for unflagging vigilance inured the people to military service, and produced a warlike race of frontiersmen. In fact, the settlements outside of Frederick Town were all established in the midst of no ordinary perils, and were subjected to many severe trials before their permanent safety was secured. Frederick itself does not appear to have been seriously threatened at any time, except during the French war and once during the Revolution by the famous Dunmore,—White Eyes' conspiracy, which was frustrated by the energetic measures of the patriotic John Hanson. The Swiss settlement, in what is now known as Hauver's District, was one of the most advanced of the frontier villages. The country around it was wild and desolate, but the Swiss preferred it on account of its mountainous character, and their industry soon caused it to blossom like the rose. The Indians were dangerously near, but as the French war had practically terminated, the settlers were not often molested except in individual cases. For some years the population of the county was composed mainly of the emigrants from Germany and Switzerland, but as this portion of Maryland began to assume importance as a region of uncommon productiveness, it attracted persons from other portions of the province and from Pennsylvania, and became a favorite point with emigrants newly arrived from Great Britain. Among those who repaired thither from other counties of Maryland were the well-known families of Howard, Dorsey, Claggett, Carroll, Fitzhugh, Johnson, Grahame, Gaither, Wood, Cockey, Worthington, Duvall, Hanson, Thomas, and Tilghman. Daniel Dulany owned more than eight thousand acres of land in Frederick County, and previous to the Revolution his son, Walter Dulany, was one of its representative men. Charles Carroll of Carrollton had a vast estate on the Monocacy River. James and Baker Johnson, brothers of Governor Thomas Johnson, and William Elder, the first settler in the Emmittsburg District, were attracted to the flourishing new country from Southern Maryland and soon acquired valuable property there. Frederick, the last Lord Baltimore, had a manor of thirteen thousand one hundred and forty-eight acres on the Monocacy, and two manors and reserves, aggregating one hundred and twenty-five thousand one hundred and thirty acres, west of Fort Cumberland. By his order these, with his other manor lands, were nearly all sold in 1766 by his agents, Governor Sharpe, Daniel Dulany, and Mr. Jordan, at prices ranging from twenty to thirty shillings per acre. The influx of English settlers was followed by the establishment of churches of the Anglican communion. At this period, however, the Episcopal Church in Maryland had the misfortune of being largely in the hands of dissolute and unprincipled ministers. Their lives were a daily scandal and reproach; but, as the church was established by law, and their livings were held independently of the will or wishes of their parishioners, they continued to perpetrate the worst excesses with impunity. The inevitable consequence was that many of their parishioners and the people generally turned to other denominations, and we find that even the oppressed and persecuted Catholics made considerable headway in the western portion of the State. The Lutherans, Presbyterians, Reformers, Mennonites, Friends, and various German sects made rapid progress in Western Maryland, and the numerous churches of these denominations which are scattered over the country are enduring memorials of the early religious activity of that region.

From an Episcopalian stand point, however, the condition of the people was simply deplorable. The Rev. Thomas Bacon, compiler of the early laws of Maryland, who had a parish in Frederick County, writes to the Society for the Propagation of the Gospel, in England, that "infidelity has indeed arrived to an amazing and shocking growth in these parts." By "infidels," however, he probably meant all who did not subscribe to the doctrines of the Established Church. A curious picture of the profligacy of the clergy is found in the adventures in Maryland of the Rev. Bennett Allen, who succeeded Rev. Thomas Bacon as rector of All Saints' parish, in Frederick County, in 1768. All Saints' was the richest parish in Maryland, yielding about one thousand pounds per annum. Mr. Allen had come over to Maryland with letters from Lord Baltimore commending him to the consideration of Governor Sharpe. He sought to have himself made rector of St. Ann's, at Annapolis, and for a time succeeded. Not satisfied with this living, however, he undertook to get possession of St. James' parish, near Annapolis, but his conduct was so tricky and unprincipled that the vestry of St. James' would not consent to the union. Enraged at his failure he quarreled with one of the vestrymen, Samuel Chew, who thereupon ejected him from his house. Mr. Allen returned to Annapolis and challenged Mr. Chew to fight a duel. After several letters had been exchanged, Mr. Chew consented to fight, and named the time and place, adding that he was determined that one of them should never leave the field alive. It was agreed that they should fight with pistols, and that there should be no witnesses. Fearing treachery on Allen's part, however, Chew took with him a servant armed with a blunderbuss. Allen did not appear, and afterwards alleged that he had received "timely information" that Chew had brought a third party to the field with the intention of murdering him. This duel, therefore, never came off, but Mr. Allen afterwards fought Lloyd Dulany, son of Daniel Dulany, in England, and killed him. On being told that the income from St. James' parish was about three hundred pounds sterling, Mr. Allen replied, "It will hardly supply me with liquors." He carried pistols and "a cane with a spear in it," and seems to have led a turbulent, dissolute life. He made his appearance at Frederick on Tuesday, May 3, 1768, and having had the keys to the church stolen from the sexton by "a tippling, itinerant barrister," proceeded to the church and read prayers in the presence of witnesses. The people were very much opposed to him, having doubtless heard of his scandalous behavior in Annapolis. On the following day (Sunday) he attempted again to enter the church, when he was met by the vestry, who remonstrated with him. He persisted, however, and entering the chancel took his place at the desk and began to read the prayers. The vestry retired, but the congregation were much incensed, and one of them approached the desk and asked Mr. Allen to desist from a performance which seemed little short of sacrilege. For reply the clergyman drew a pistol and declared with an oath that if the person offered to touch him he would shoot him through. But the people persisted, and at length Allen, becoming frightened, descended from the desk and left the church. Outside he was assailed with stones and compelled to yield the church keys, which he dropped to the ground as he ran. The parishioners then shut up the church. Mr. Allen appears to have returned to Annapolis, as he published a card in the *Maryland Gazette*, Sept. 29, 1768, in which he gave his version of the affair. He was severely criticised for his conduct, as would appear from the fact that he threatened to "knock up" Mrs. Green's press if she published "any more pieces against him." The only effect of his threats, however, was to cause Mrs. Green to be elected provincial printer by the General Assembly. He seems to have had a special grudge against the Dulany family, for his animus appears not only in the fatal duel with Lloyd, but also in the fact that he sought to bribe a man named David Atchison to shoot Walter Dulany, Lloyd's brother.

It would be unfair to select Mr. Allen as a representative of his class, but we have the strongest contemporary testimony for the assertion that many of his fellow-ministers were ignorant, neglectful, and too often dissolute. The Revolution did away with the arbitrary appointment of rectors, and produced a marked improvement in the character of the Episcopalian clergy. In the mean time Methodism had been making rapid growth. The first regular Methodist congregation established in the colonies was that at Sam's, or Pipe Creek, Frederick Co., which was organized by Robert Strawbridge, a Wesleyan lay preacher, who had come to America from Ireland in 1760 and had settled there. He formed in his own dwelling a class-meeting of twelve or fifteen persons, which Bishop Asbury says was "the first society in Maryland and America." He preached regularly at his house and at various places in the neighborhood, and gradually extended his work to Baltimore and Harford Counties, the Eastern Shore, Fairfax County, Va., and Lancaster County, Pa. The first society of Methodists in Baltimore County was formed under his direction at the house of Daniel Evans. For this society a chapel, one of the first in the country, was afterwards built. Mr. Strawbridge licensed preachers, the first of them being Richard Owen, of Baltimore County, who was the first native American to preach the Methodist doctrines. Mr. Strawbridge resided at Sam's Creek for sixteen years, when he removed to Long Green, Baltimore Co., to a farm given him for life by Capt. Charles Ridgely, of Hampden. He died about 1781. In 1764 the congregation at Sam's Creek built a log meeting-house. It remained standing until 1844, when it was demolished. It is believed to have been the first chapel erected in this country, preceding the next in order about three years. A stone chapel was built near it in 1783, and rebuilt in 1800. In 1772 the congregation were visited by Francis Asbury, afterwards bishop. John and Charles Wesley had preached in Georgia as early as 1736, and John Wesley and George Whitefield in various portions of the country afterwards, but there seems to be no reason to doubt that the first regular meeting or society was organized at Sam's, or Pipe Creek. Mr. Strawbridge was not regularly licensed to exhort until 1772, when authority was given him by Francis Asbury. Methodism was introduced into Frederick Town by Mr. Strawbridge on an invitation from Edward Drumgole, who, on coming from Ireland in 1770 with a letter to Mr. Strawbridge, went to Pipe Creek. He heard him preach, and was so well pleased that he gave him an invitation, which Mr. Strawbridge accepted, to preach in Frederick. Mr. Drumgole afterwards became a Methodist minister himself. The celebrated Methodist minister, Freeborn Garretson, began his career in the Frederick District in 1776. Frederick County may in fact be termed the cradle of Methodism in America, and from the humble efforts of Srawbridge, Drumgole, Owen, and others rose the mighty structure of the present Methodist denomination. In its earlier stages Methodism exerted a powerful influence in correcting the abuses of the Established Church, and for that reason it is not at all surprising that it should have met with harsh treatment and misrepresentation in various portions of the province, until at length it grew to be strong enough to command both toleration and respect.

It is impossible to state with certainty the date of the establishment of the first Presbyterian congregation in Frederick County. But as the Scotch-Irish settlers of the Cumberland Valley and vicinity were mostly Presbyterians, and as they crossed the line into Maryland at an early period, it seems highly probable that Presbyterianism was among the earliest denominations on the field. Thus, for instance, we find that Samuel Cavin, a licentiate from Ireland, was sent by the Presbytery of Donegal on the 16th of November, 1737, to Conococheague (now Chambersburg). This settlement was first mentioned in September, 1736, when the Presbytery refused to sanction the employment of Mr. Williams, from England, who was then preaching there. The settlement embraced Falling Spring (or Chambersburg), Greencastle, Mercersburg, and Welsh Run. The congregation was soon divided into two portions, the dividing line being Conococheague Creek, and they were denominated respectively East and West Conococheague. Mr. Caven accepted the call of the East Side, April 4, 1739. In the following winter he visited the settlements on the South Branch of the Potomac. In 1741 he severed his relations with Conococheague, and spent some time in ministering to settlers on the present site of Hagerstown, Marsh Creek, Opequon, and the South Branch of the Potomac. The settlement at Conococheague remained without a regular minister for some years. In September, 1760, the Rev. Robert McMordie was appointed by the Presbytery of Donegal to "supply" the settlers on the Monocacy. One year later provision was made for ministerial service for congregations on Tom's and Pipe Creek.

The earliest organized religious bodies in Frederick County were the Protestant denominations represented among the German and Swiss emigrants. There was quite a number of these sects, and all of them appear to have maintained the lines of demarcation between them with scrupulous care. The immigrants from Germany were indiscriminately denominated "Palatines," from the fact that many of them came from the Palatinate, along the Rhine (afterwards incorporated in Prussia, Bavaria, Baden, Hesse-Darmstadt, and Nassau). After the revocation of the Edict of Nantes, which had secured toleration for the Protestants of France, the latter were relentlessly persecuted by the government of Louis XIV. and his successors, the Regent and Louis XV. It is estimated that more than five hundred thousand persons fled from France during this reign of terror to Holland, England, and America; and when the victorious French army invaded Germany a similar expatriation of the Protestant population took place. Many thousands fled to America, and being attracted to Pennsylvania by the mild and tolerant rule of Penn and his representatives, the greater portion settled in that province. Thus, for instance, Governor George Thomas, of the province of Pennsylvania, writing to the Bishop of Exeter in 1747, says, "The Germans of Pennsylvania are, I believe, three-fifths of the whole population (whole population two hundred thousand). They have by their industry been the principal instruments of raising the State to its present flourishing condition beyond any of His Majesty's colonies in North America." The religious sects into which they were divided were the Lutherans, the German Reformed, the Moravians, the Mennonites, the Calvinists, the Amish Brethren (rigid Mennonites), and the German Seventh-Day Baptists. There were also the Labadists, the Society of the Woman in the Wilderness, the Separatists, the Quietists, and others. Of these none were more devout, frugal, and industrious than the Mennonites, who took their name from the Protestant reformer, Menno Simon, a native of Friesland, who founded many communities in Germany and Switzerland. His teaching extended even to Russia, where in our own day the Mennonites are a large and prosperous community. Many of the immigrants were robbed before leaving home, and were compelled to sell their services and those of their children for a term of years in order to pay the passage-money. And yet in a comparatively short time these Redemptionists, as they were termed, had become well-to-do farmers or mechanics, so universal among them was the practice of the closest economy and thrift. They seem to have had keen eyes for fertile soil, and many of them were speedily attracted from Pennsylvania to the blooming plains and valleys of Western Maryland. They soon spread over the entire region east of the South Mountain, and even penetrated as far west as the Conococheague Creek. Owing to the danger from predatory Indians, the settlements advanced no farther for some time. With the exception of the trading-post of the Ohio Company at Fort Cumberland, they were the most western of the European settlements in the eastern section of America. Nearly all the leading sects established in Pennsylvania soon came to be represented in Maryland, and some of them grew rapidly there.

We find, therefore, that three distinct and widely divergent elements entered into the composition of the early population of Frederick County, viz.: (1) the English and colonial settlers from other portions of Maryland; (2) the Scotch-Irish from just across the Pennsylvania border; and (3) the German and Swiss immigrants, some newly arrived from Europe, and the rest previously settled in Pennsylvania, chiefly in the counties of Lancaster, York, and Adams. It was to have been expected that the interests, the habits, and the prejudices of these communities would have kept them apart, but in the presence of common dangers and difficulties they speedily joined hands and worked together harmoniously, forming in course of time a practically homogeneous population, distinguished equally for judicious liberality and thrift, and second to none in the country in the general distribution of intelligence and wealth.

It will be seen that Frederick was deprived of a very large slice of its original territory, more than one-half in fact. However, it was still quite large enough, and could even afford to spare the portion annexed to that taken from Baltimore County in 1835 to form the new county of Carroll. It was peopled by a superior class of immigrants, who found ample room for development in its fertile valleys and high, breezy table-lands, and it has held from the beginning the front rank among the counties of Maryland for the beauty of its scenery, the fertility and productiveness of its soil, and the industry, energy, and thrift of its inhabitants. As constituted at present, Frederick County is bounded on the north by Adams County, Pa., on the east by Carroll County, on the southeast by Howard and Montgomery, on the south by Montgomery and the Potomac River, which divides it from Virginia, and on the west by Washington County, from which it is separated by the Blue Ridge, or South Mountains. Its area is 652 square miles, and its population is 50,122.

Census Returns of Population.—According to the census of 1880, the population by districts is as follows:

District No. 1.—Buckeystown. Town, 415; Adamstown, 66; Point of Rocks, 290; District, 2547.

No. 2.—Frederick. City, 8659; District, 12,231.

No. 3.—Middletown. Town, 705; District, 2821.

No. 4.—Creagerstown. Town, 140; District, 1054.

No. 5.—Emmittsburg. Village, 847; District, 3560.

No. 6.—Catoctin, 1502.

No. 7.—Urbana. Village, 180; Park Mills, 44; Centreville, 80; District, 2576.

No. 8.—Liberty. Liberty Town, 542; District, 1650.

No. 9.—New Market. Village, 402; New London, 97; Kemptown, 62; Ijamsville, 71; Bartonville, 98; District, 3097.

No. 10.—Hauver's. Sabillasville, 151; District, 1505.

No. 11.—Woodsboro'. Village, 336; District, 2305.

No. 12.—Petersville. Village, 192; Berlin, 217; Burkittsville, 280; Knoxsville, 265; Weverton, 100; District, 2603.

No. 13.—Mount Pleasant. Village, 139; Walkersville, 160; District, 1598.

No. 14.—Jefferson. Village, 274; District, 1578.

No. 15.—Mechanicstown. Town, 730; Graceham, 151; District, 2738.

No. 16.—Jackson. Beallsville, 108; Myersville, 138; District, 1499.

No. 17.—Johnsville. Village, 171; District, 1727.

No. 18.—Woodville. Village, 39; District, 1126.

No. 19.—Linganore. District, 1439.

No. 20.—Lewistown. Town, 210; Utica Mills, 45; District, 1326.

Total population, 50,122.

There are eight incorporated towns in the county,—viz., Emmittsburg, Mechanicstown, Middletown, Woodsboro', Jefferson, New Market, and Point of Rocks.

In 1790, Frederick County contained 27,150 free persons and 3641 slaves; and in 1800, 26,941 free persons and 4572 slaves. On the other hand, Montgomery, with a much smaller population in 1790,—viz., 11,973 free persons,—had 6030 slaves; and in 1800, with only 8770 free persons, 6228 slaves; clearly demonstrating the difference in the habits and

FREDERICK COUNTY.

pursuits of the people of the two counties. In Frederick the population was chiefly engaged in small farming, manufacturing, and mining, while in Montgomery it was mainly occupied with planting, for which slave labor was in great demand, although flourishing manufactories had also been established there.

Following are the census returns of population for Frederick County since and including the first census of 1790 up to 1870, inclusive:

Aggregate.

1870	47,572
1860	46,591
1850	40,987
1840	36,405
1830	45,789
1820	40,459
1810	34,437
1800	31,523
1790	30,791

Free Colored.

1870	7,572
1860	4,957
1850	3,760
1840	2,985
1830	2,716
1820	1,777
1810	783
1800	473
1790	213

White.

1870	39,999
1860	38,391
1850	33,314
1840	28,975
1830	36,703
1820	31,997
1810	27,983
1800	26,478
1790	26,957

Slave.

1860	3,243
1850	3,913
1840	4,445
1830	6,370
1820	6,685
1810	5,671
1800	4,572
1790	3,641

Chinese.

1870	1

AGRICULTURAL STATISTICS OF FREDERICK COUNTY IN 1870.

Improved land, acres	287,750
Woodland, acres	73,228
Other land, not improved, acres	1,553
Present cash value of farms	$19,463,749
" " " farming implements and machinery	656,150
Wages paid annually, including board	832,389
Value farm productions, including betterments and additions to stock	4,094,567
Orchard products	83,050
Market-garden products	9,367
Forest products	71,594
Value of home manufactures	2,763
Value of animals slaughtered or sold for slaughter	693,266

NUMBER AND SIZES OF FARMS IN FREDERICK COUNTY IN 1870.

Number of farms of all sizes	716
" " under 3 acres	5
" " over 3 and under 10 acres	90
" " 10 and under 20 acres	72
" " 20 and under 50 acres	109
" " 50 and under 100 acres	106
" " 100 and under 500 acres	330
" " 500 and under 1000 acres	4

MINING STATISTICS OF FREDERICK COUNTY IN 1870.

	Establishments.	Steam-Engines. Horse-power.	Steam-Engines. Number.	Hands Employed. All.	Hands Employed. Men above Ground.	Hands Employed. Men under Ground.	Hands Employed. Boys above Ground.	Capital Invested.	Wages.	Materials.	Products.
Copper	1	75	2	65	17	28	20	$150,000	$30,000	$7810	$65,000
Iron ore[1]	1	10	1	60	60			56,000	18,000	1375	42,800
Slate	2			9	9			2,700	950	56	5,000
Stone	1			4	4			800	500	22	3,200

[1] The product of iron ore in tons was 12,000.

In 1791 the county had over eighty grist-mills busily employed in the manufacture of flour, two glass-works, two iron-furnaces, two forges, two paper-mills, and four hundred stills. Twelve towns and villages enlivened its surface.

In 1811 its two furnaces annually turned out 380 tons of pig-metal and 400 tons of pots, stoves, etc., valued at $42,920. The other articles manufactured annually were:

230 tons bar-iron	$27,600
400 boxes glass and 7000 bottles	7,600
730 barrels beer	4,380
5,175 gallons oil	4,140
5,247 pounds powder	3,670
4,150 reams paper	8,945
145,000 gallons whisky	70,500
34,168 hides and skins, tanned	140,109
15,000 pounds nails	1,800
84,080 pounds flour	756,109
10,740 fur and 14,510 wool hats	56,842
45,380 pairs shoes and 1509 pairs boots	27,609
2,264 saddles and 4969 bridles	89,142
208,194 yards of linen, cotton, and woolens	152,583
34 carriages	10,200
Total	$1,404,760

Eleven fulling-mills fulled 44,000 yards of cloth, nine carding-machines carded 35,600 pounds of wool, and five spinning-machines had in operation 362 spindles.

The industrial statistics of the county, as returned in the census of 1870, are the following:

Number of establishments, 550; steam-engines, 24, aggregating 367 horse-power; water-wheels, 140, aggregating 2638 horse-power; hands employed, 1703, of whom 1614 were males above sixteen years of age, 72 females above fifteen years of age, and 17 youths; capital invested, $1,694,712; wages paid, $313,758; value of materials used, $2,262,012; products, $3,252,634.

In 1870 the chief productions were 1,133,623 bushels wheat, 54,995 rye, 1,360,420 corn, 250,069 oats, 138,484 potatoes, 32,893 tons hay, 877,784 pounds butter, 34,533 pounds wool, 274,369 pounds tobacco. There were 11,860 horses, 11,907 milch cows, 10,188 other cattle, 9,817 sheep, 29,939 swine, 16 manufactories of carriages and wagons, 1 of charcoal, 15 of clothing, 25 of barrels and casks, 2 of fertilizers, 15 of furniture, 6 of lime, 16 of saddlery and harness, 3 of sashes, doors, and blinds, 11 of tin, copper, and sheet-iron ware, 10 of cigars, 8 of woolen goods, 4 of bricks, 47 flour-mills, 4 iron-works, 21 tanneries, 10 currying establishments, and 2 distilleries.

The following is a detailed statement for 1870 of the number of establishments, with statistics of production, etc.:[2]

[2] The industrial statistics for the census of 1880 had not been compiled up to the date of going to press.

	Number of Establishments.	Hands Employed.	Capital.	Wages.	Materials.	Products.
Agricultural implements..	4	20	$44,250	$6,900	$5,250	$17,135
Boots and shoes...............	3	26	4,700	8,300	7,521	16,550
Bread and other bakery products..................	6	17	10,300	1,450	6,556	16,600
Brick............................	4	70	18,150	10,165	6,174	22,970
Carriages and wagons......	16	72	37,325	19,086	22,102	64,740
Charcoal	1	60	49,000	21,000	17,000	60,480
Clothing, men's...............	15	72	16,580	12,180	34,432	63,050
Confectionery	4	9	4,700	1,734	6,911	13,407
Cooperage	25	105	21,267	25,027	43,365	89,001
Fertilizers.....................	2	12	26,000	2,100	47,700	62,875
Flouring-mill products.....	47	128	467,600	16,974	1,069,364	1,209,009
Furniture........................	15	38	22,350	5,780	8,384	24,600
Gas...............................	1	5	50,000	2,100	4,000	13,700
Iron, forged and rolled.....	1	5	8,000	1,872	4,920	10,000
Iron pigs.......................	1	62	150,000	12,000	105,580	142,800
Iron castings..................	2	14	35,400	4,400	4,600	13,000
Leather tanned...............	21	81	226,400	21,295	239,440	314,704
Leather curried...............	10	17	57,200	4,947	95,706	115,008
Lime.............................	6	36	33,450	7,485	17,939	31,300
Liquors distilled..............	2	8	16,000	3,050	21,927	54,300
Lumber sawed	3	4	4,600	225	2,700	13,500
Machinery	1	17	16,000	9,000	3,200	15,000
Masonry, brick, and stone.	11	25	7,200	4,400	29,260	43,910
Printing and publishing...	5	19	20,000	3,530	5,869	30,760
Saddlery and harness	16	39	26,775	5,214	18,750	36,268
Sash, doors, and blinds...	3	43	55,724	18,325	41,380	68,633
Soap and candles............	2	4	4,300	750	9,526	12,270
Tin, copper, and sheet-iron ware..........................	11	35	24,550	8,909	13,687	31,150
Tobacco, cigars...............	10	32	9,000	6,275	8,400	23,250
Woolen goods.................	8	38	25,000	6,194	16,596	29,853

According to the United States census returns, the agricultural statistics of Frederick County for 1880 are the following:

	Acres.	Bushels.
Barley	51	1,723
Buckwheat.............	206	2,328
Indian corn............	52,002	1,774,256
Oats.....................	5,051	94,267
Rye......................	4,013	42,592
Wheat...................	83,767	1,418,542
		Pounds.
Tobacco	429	370,840

Statistics of Public Schools and Illiteracy in 1880.—Whole number of elementary schools, 153; schools for colored children, 24; whole number of school buildings, 158; number of buildings having more than one study-room, 20; number of school buildings having two or more recitation-rooms, 2; whole number of seats now provided, 8303; total seating capacity, 9396; number reported in good condition, 98; number improperly heated and ventilated, 16; number having insufficient ground, 1; number simply reported in bad condition, 27; teachers in high schools (white), male 103, female 67, total 170; colored, male 16, female 10, total 26; whole number of teachers, white and colored, 196; number of teachers educated at high schools or academies, 62; number educated at normal schools, 28; number educated at colleges or universities, 16; number holding certificates other than preceding, 90; average of teachers' salaries per month, $33.25; average number of months employed, 7.10.

Total population over ten years of age who cannot read... 4779
White population over ten years of age who cannot write... 2878
Native white population "   "   "   "   ... 2768
Foreign white   "   "   "   "   ... 110
Total colored   "   "   "   "   ... 3450
Grand total of colored and white population over ten years of age who cannot write... 6328

White population from ten to fourteen years who cannot write:
Male.. 237
Female... 170
Total... 407

White population from fifteen to twenty years who cannot write:
Male.. 140
Female... 117
Total... 257

White population from twenty-one years and over who cannot write:
Male.. 864
Female... 1350
Total... 2214

Colored population from ten to fourteen years who cannot write:
Male.. 213
Female... 204
Total... 417

Colored population from fifteen to twenty years who cannot write:
Male.. 163
Female... 212
Total... 375

Colored population from twenty-one years and over who cannot write:
Male.. 1277
Female... 1381
Total... 2658

Post-Offices.—The post-offices in Frederick County are the following:

Adamstown.	Licksville.
Araby.	Limekiln.
Barry.	Linganore.
Bolivar.	Mechanicstown.
Bridgeport.	Middletown.
Broad Run.	Monrovia.
Buckeystown.	Motter's.
Burkittsville.	Mount Pleasant.
Catoctin Furnace.	Myersville.
Creagerstown.	New London.
Cromwell.	New Market.
Ellerton.	New Midway.
Emmittsburg.	Oak Orchard.
Fountain Mills.	Owen's Creek.
Frederick.	Park Mills.
Graceham.	Petersville.
Greenfield Mills.	Plane Number Four.
Hansomville.	Point of Rocks.
Harmony.	Rocky Ridge.
Harmony Grove.	Sabillasville.
Ijamsville.	Sam's Creek.
Jefferson.	Unionville.
Johnsville.	Urbana.
Kemptown.	Utica Mills.
Knoxville.	Walkersville.
Ladersburg.	West Falls.
Lander.	Wolfsville.
Lantz.	Woodsboro'.
Lewistown.	Woodsville.
Liberty Town.	

County Finances.—The last published financial exhibit of the county is as follows:

Total value of real property—assessed value, $17,421,745; estimated full value, $23,228,993. Total value of personal property—assessed value, $7,966,105; estimated full value, $7,966,105. Aggregate value of real and personal property—assessed value, $25,387,850; estimated full value, $31,195,098. Total receipts from taxation for all purposes except schools, $129,714.75. Total receipts from taxation for school purposes—teachers' salaries, etc., $25,310.20; new school-houses and furniture, $9,491.34. Total receipts from State tax for all purposes, $44,822.11. Expenditures for schools, $25,310.20 and $9,491.34—total, $34,801.54; roads, special appropriation, $19,615.40; roads and bridges, contingent, $7200; poor in Montevue Hospital, $10,000; poor on pension list, $7795; all other purposes, $85,104.35—total expenditures, $164,516.29. Bonded indebtedness—1865, bounty to volunteers, bonds running from one to seven years before maturity, date of maturity from Jan. 1, 1880, amount paid, $10,000, amount outstanding, $35,000, 6 per cent. interest; 1875, new jail, five to twenty years, amount outstanding, $18,200, 6 per cent. interest; 1876, new jail, five to twenty years, $25,000, 6 per cent. interest; 1880, new jail, five to twenty years, $25,000, 5 per cent. interest; 1876, for schools, sixteen to twenty years, $2000 yearly, $5000, 6 per cent. interest; 1879, refunding almshouse bonds, five to twenty years, $80,000, 5 per cent. interest; 1880, floating debt, twelve months or pleasure, $37,150, 5 per cent. interest—total indebtedness, $225,350. The floating debt enumerated in bonded debt exhibit was occasioned by building new iron bridges and subscriptions to turnpike companies from 1872 to 1876, and since funded in county 5 per cent. notes, payable in twelve months from April, 1880, but may not be paid for years unless demanded. There is no sinking fund. A levy is made in June of each year for so much as will be required to pay off bonds falling due on the 1st of January or July of the following year. The county's assets are: Farm and Montevue Hospital, about $120,000; court-house lot and furniture, about $48,000; county jail and sheriff's house, erected at a cost of about $72,000—total, $240,000.

The early assessment valuations of property were, 1789, £963,675 9s. 0d.; 1793, £1,021,520 19s. 2½d.; 1797, £1,045,850 15s. 5½d.

The rate of taxation for 1881, levied by the county commissioners, was sixty-two cents on the one hundred dollars.

CHAPTER XIX.

LAND GRANTS AND RESURVEYS.

The Landlord of Maryland—Quit-Rents—Caution Money—Alienation Fines—The Payment of Ground-Rent—"Conditions of Plantation"—Creation of Land Office—Confiscated British Lands—Soldiers' Lots—Original Resurveys.

UNDER the charter of Maryland, the proprietary was both the ruler of the province and the owner of its soil, and hence the exclusive landlord of Maryland. The revenues arising from his land grants consisted in quit-rents, caution money paid at the time of the grant, and alienation fines, including fines upon devises. The *quit-rents*, or ground-rents, as we now call them, were the annual rents, renewed by the proprietary in his grants, and to be perpetually paid from year to year by the owner of the land granted, in acknowledgment of the tenantcy. They were rent charges, charged upon the land when it was first granted out by the proprietary, and they constituted the only revenue from land grants which was looked to in the first settlement of the province. The quantum of the rent to be reserved was always regulated by the proprietary's proclamations or instructions, and it varied continually throughout the government with the varying value of the lands to be granted and the views of the proprietary. In the earliest grants, under the first conditions of plantations, the rent was made payable in wheat, but in general, with regard to the rights acquired after the year 1635, the rent was payable either in money alone or in the commodities of the country, at the option of the proprietary and his officers. This right of the proprietary to require payment of his rents in money was attended with great inconvenience and oppression to the people, and hence, as early as 1671, it was commuted for payment in tobacco. The act of 1671, which originated this commutation, imposed a duty of two shillings sterling on all exported tobacco, of which one-half was given to the then proprietary for his own use, and the residue for the defense of the province, in consideration of his agreeing to receive tobacco for his quit-rents and alienation fines at the rate of twopence per pound. This mode of payment was continued until 1717 by a variety of acts, when the Assembly resorted to the expedient of buying out the rents and alienation fines as the only effectual mode of relief from the harassing petty officers scattered over the whole province. The act of 1717 gave to the proprietary for his own benefit a duty on all exported tobacco of two shillings sterling on every hogshead, and fourpence sterling per hundred on all tobacco exported in box or case, etc., and so *pro rata*, " in full discharge of his quit-rents and alienation fines." This temporary law was continued by several acts until 1733, when it was suffered to expire; and from that period until 1780, there being no commutation, the quit-rents were payable according to the requisition of the patents. During this interval it appears that all the evils of the old system of collection returned in full force. Scarcely a session of Assembly elapsed without some complaint of outrage or oppression on the part of the collectors of these rents, and every effort was made by the Assembly to induce the proprietary to accept an equivalent for them. Of the value of the quit-rents throughout the proprietary government it is difficult for us at the present day to speak with accuracy, but from the best estimate which can be collected from the debt-books it appears that in the year 1770 their gross amount was about £8400 sterling, and the net revenue of the proprietary from them, after deducting the expenses of collection, upwards of £7500 sterling.

The sagacity of the wise and benevolent Cæcilius, the first proprietary of Maryland, is conspicuous in the policy pursued by him in granting the lands of the province. The first wish of his heart was to see its population increase and its commerce prosper. Looking to the future, beyond the petty ambitions and interests of the moment, he saw that his reputation and permanent interests were identified with the prosperity of the colony; and with the sagacity to perceive, and the heart to feel this, he made his rights of property in the province minister to its advancement. His lands were offered as *premiums for emigration*. Adventurers were encouraged to come into the province, and to bring their servants and dependants with them. Every person transporting himself into it was entitled to a certain quantity of land, without paying any caution or purchase money, and the land granted was charged only with a moderate quit-rent. If he brought others with him he was allowed for their transportation a further quantity, which was proportioned to the numbers, age, and sex of the persons transported, the highest premiums being given, in some of the earliest conditions of plantation, for the transportation of males between fifteen and sixty, and of females between fourteen and forty-three. These land rights were prescribed by various proclamations, issued from time to time by the proprietary, which were familiarly called "The Conditions of Plantation." They were frequently varied, according to the necessity for inducements to emigration, or to promote the establishment of settlements in particular portions of the province.

These plantation rights were the only modes of acquiring lands recognized in the "Conditions of Plantation," but besides these there were land rights acquired under warrants for land granted by the proprietary to particular individuals. The inducements granted to the first settlers were abolished by the new proprietary in 1683, and a new system was then adopted, under which all persons were permitted to sue out warrants for lands upon payment of a definitive amount of purchase money, which was called "caution money," because no warrant could issue until it was paid or secured. Thus was fully introduced the system of granting lands which has prevailed in Maryland until to-day. Fines for alienation were the incidents of the feudal tenures generally, as they originally existed in England. They appear to have belonged as well to the *socage* tenure as to that *in chivalry*, and the same feudal reasons existed for their connection with both. They were transplanted to the province of Maryland, with the socage tenure, and notwithstanding their abolition in the mother-country in 1660, they continued to exist until the American Revolution.

The sale and lease of the proprietaries' lands in Maryland formed the principal part of their revenue, and consequently the Land Office became from the first the chief office of the province.

In the year 1680, from the natural increase of business, it was found necessary to create a Land Office, distinct and not blended with other offices, as it had been up to that period. From the year 1680 the Lord Proprietary managed the land affairs of his province by a Land Council, the clerk of which was called the register. In 1684 certain formal instructions were given by the Lord Proprietary to his Land Council, the principal and most important of which are here subjoined:

"The Land Council is first authorized to give, grant, lease, or otherwise dispose of all land escheatable for want of heirs. Any error made by surveyor or clerk in certificate or patent to be corrected, rectified, and amended, as the case shall require.

"Any person owning two or three or more tracts of land contiguous or adjoining, upon application the Land Council may grant special warrant to resurvey or to lay out the same into one entire tract and grant patent for the same.

"May grant land of an alien, not naturalized, that may escheat to the proprietary.

"Where it hath been discovered or made known to the Land Council that any grant hath been illegally or surreptitiously obtained, the Land Council are required to order *scire facias* to issue forth out of the Chancery Court of Records to the patentee, or other present owner and possessor, to show cause why the same should not be vacated.

"Should the land be adjudged and condemned to the proprietary for the reasons aforesaid, then the Land Council may, by letters patent or otherwise, give, grant, or dispose of the same to the discoverer thereof.

"The Land Council may, upon the death of the surveyor-general, extend or continue any special warrant or warrants of resurvey.

"They cannot grant any patent for any tract of land that is part or parcel of a greater tract formerly granted.

"Authority is given to the Land Council to sign all patents legally obtained and affix the great seal."

When the war with Great Britain culminated in the independence of the colonies, the first act of the State to assume the control of the Land Office was contained in the act of Assembly of April session, 1777, ch. 15, entitled "An act to open the courts of justice, etc.," by the eighth section of which act it was ordained, among other things, in order, as the act stated, that individuals might not suffer by the change of government, that all the land warrants granted and issued out of the Land Office before the appointment and qualification of the new register should continue to be in force for the same time, and should be executed by the new officers in the same manner as if the former government had continued; and that all officers who might have in their possession any such land warrants, or any record-books or papers, should deliver them to the proper officers immediately after their qualification, or as soon as they should be thereunto required.

The next act of the Legislature is that of October session, 1777, ch. 8, by which the State appeared to have in view its succession to the bodies of land still remaining vacant, by promising certain bounties of land to recruits for the army and to recruiting-officers, with a declaration, however, that if no other method should be provided within the time specified in the act for laying out the quantity of land required to make good that engagement, it should be procured within the limits of the State at the public expense.

The acts of October session, 1780, chs. 45, 49, and 51, by which, for reasons therein set forth, all property, debts only excepted, belonging to British subjects was declared, under certain exceptions, to be confiscated to the use of the State, are presumed to have ended the struggle and decided the question as to what was to be the future destination and employment of the Land Office.

The act of November session, 1781, ch. 20, "to appropriate certain lands to the use of the officers and soldiers of this State and for the sale of vacant lands," and which, by subsequent acts, as well as by general acceptance, is termed the law opening the Land Office, is the first that makes arrangements for disposing of the State's right to vacant land.

Under this law provision was made for the appointment of two registers of the Land Office, one on the Eastern and one on the Western Shore. By the act of 1841 the former office was abolished, and all the papers, etc., were transferred to the Western Shore Land Office, at Annapolis.

The original "patents" or "surveys" for lands in Frederick County varied in extent from one up to tens of thousands of acres, were irregular in shape, and had bestowed upon them names as quaint and odd as human ingenuity could suggest. The commissioners empowered by Lord Baltimore to sell his reserved lands and manors, on Nov. 9, 1767, offered for sale at the house of Col. Thomas Prather, in Frederick County, his lordship's manor of "Conococheague," with the reserve, containing over eleven thousand acres. The original patents of lands in Frederick County are not now found in the county clerk's office, but the following are the resurveys made since their issuing down to 1800, which in some cases are exact duplicates of the originals, and in other instances are subdivisions of the first patents:[1]

Names of Resurveys.	Acres.	Party.	Date.
Addition to Brimour's Misfortune....	62⅓	Thomas Beatty	1791
Addition	9	George Weaver	1791
Addition to Summer Hill	72	Jacob Harbaugh	1791
Antigua	5¾	Samuel Owings	1788
All that is left	188	Henry Griffith	1788
Addition to school-lot	13	Jacob Ridgely	1788
Addition to May Fall	245	Wm. Duvall	1787
Adam's Hill	64	Adam Roughsong	1786
Appeal	106	Daniel Root	1786
Addition to Hunting-Ground	32	James Morrison	1785
Ask and ye shall receive	20	Wm. Ballinger	1786
All disputes settled	234	John Mathews	1785
Almost lost	20	Conrad Mangin	1784
Addition to Quakers' Mistake	3	Adam Roughsong	1784
" Molly's Fancy	11½	Daniel McKinsey	1784
" Smith's Chance	3½	Philip Smith	1789
All that is left	12	Michael Troutman	1784
Addition to Acorn Hill	4	Christian Bowers	1784
Adam's Content	383	John and Chris. Getzendanner	1791
Amended	481¼	Ulrick Miller	1788
Acquisition	16	Jacob Snider	1795
Part of addition to Hazel Thicket	115	Fielder Gantt, etc.	1791
Anvil	180½	John Creager	1792
"	203	Christiana Smith	1791
Addition to Narrow Bottom	9⅜	Stephen Winchester	1795
Acorn Hill	85	Greenbury Majors	1791
Apple Brandy	14	Jacob Fulwiler	1791
Addition to Miller's Purchase	52¾	Peter Miller	1791
All is safe now	382	Jacob Knouff	1798

[1] The first deed recorded conveying in fee simple land in the county was that of George Matthews, dated Jan. 21, 1749, and recorded the same day. This instrument conveyed to Charles Davis, for the consideration of thirty pounds, one hundred acres of land, one *moiter* or part of a tract called "Good Luck," on Ballenger's Creek. The next deed is that of William Bigerstaff to Thomas Harris, dated Feb. 24, 1749. It conveyed, for fifty pounds, a plantation called "The Pleasant Level," "situated on the south side of a branch of Tom's Creek, between the mountains, being a draught of Minocacy." The third conveyance was that of Joseph Chapline to Samuel Kelsy, dated March 8, 1749, conveying, for twenty-five pounds, part of a tract of land called "Hunting the Hare," being fifty acres. The first deed recorded in the new volume of records opened after the adoption of the first State constitution in 1776 was that of Peter Hoffman to His Excellency Thomas Johnson, Governor of Maryland. It is dated Aug. 24, 1778, and conveyed, in consideration of four thousand pounds current money of Maryland, all that tract called "Rose Garden," being part of the survey called "Tasker's Chance." The piece thus conveyed "contained two hundred and twenty-five acres, except the graveyard now paled in on the said land."

Names of Resurveys.	Acres.	Party.	Date.
All in the right	4½	Peter Mantz	1798
Addition to Rich Barrens	91½	Lawrence Brengle, Jr.	1798
All I can get	4½	Thomas Beatty	1787
Addition to Daniel Small's tract	8	Wm. Ballinger	1787
Arnold's Inheritance	216	Anthony Arnold	1792
Addison's Choice	40⅜	Joseph Sim	1792
Addition to Deer-Park	3¼	Solomon Shepherd	1792
" Little Worth	82¾	Christopher Kogle	1796
" Narrow Hollow	4¾	Henry Koontz	1796
Almost night	31	Jacob Delaughter	1796
A stopper for the full bottle	9	Jacob Burton	1796
Addition to Deer-Park	104½	Joshua Wright	1796
" Turkey Plight	4	Samuel Plummer	1793
" Mill Right's Design	6¼	Normand Bruce	1789
Addison's Choice	51	James Beatty	1787
" "	31½	" "	1787
Addition to Chance	16	Mary Biers	1787
Attraction	42	Thomas Beatty	1787
All night	23	Charles Cheny	1789
Acre lot	1	Dani l Levister	1799
Addition to John's Fancy	93	Wm. Lamsby	1799
" Red Rock	2¾	Michael Wachtee	1799
All wood	2	Michael Smith	1799
All's my own	4¼	Malachi Flannagan	1799
Adam's Expense	357	Adam Roughsong	1792
Addition to the Garden	5½	Godfrey Leather	1792
" the Triangle	1⅞	Jacob Apler	1800
" Clark's Discovery	283		1785
" Deep Hole	70½	Adam Neif	1785
" Elbert's Inheritance	109	Philip Elbert	1790
" Enlarged	66	Frederick Weaver	1794
" Rich Barrens	83		
" Small Venture	2¼	Wm. Dickenshutz	1790
" Middle Land	8	Godfrey Leatherman	1792
" Daily's Labor	39	John Clarke	1792
" Mount Misery	10	John Hoover	1795
" Friendship	202	Frederick Fox	1797
" Sugar Tree Valley	100	Stephen Winchester	1797
" Expensive	3	Thomas Beatty	1797
" What's Left	25½	Joseph Swearingen	1797
Appeal	101¾	Daniel Root	1790
Asp Hill	160	Henry Feror	1794
Adam's Fall	268	Peter Luckinbill (Lugenbeel)	1790
Adam's Isle	4¼	Wm. Jenkins	1794
Albaugh's Chance	27¼	David Albaugh and Joseph Baker	1788
Arnold's Integrity	269½	Arnold Hardy	1795
Arnold's Remnant	110½	Archibald Arnold	1792
All neighbors confused	176½	Jacob Haynes	1792
All talk and no cider	39½	Peter Mantz	1792
As you see fit	8¾	Aaron Lurman	1795
All in haste	70	Valentine Summer	1795
Anticipated	2¼	Norman Bruce	1795
All the remainder	138	John Trammel	1774
A mile long	182	Peter Leatherman	1795
Acorn Bottom	92	Peter Crist	1795
Acorn Hill	43½	Christian Bowers	1784
Apple Brandy	242½	Barbara Flooke	1795
Abraham's Fancy	20	Thomas, James and John Conrad Beatty	1795
All's fast now	1⅝	Joseph Swearingen	1797
Altogether	230	Melchor Staley	1785
"	138	Nicholas Crall	1787
Abraham's Intrigue	7	Norman Bruce	1795
All bottles full }	172		
and Rocky Ridge. }	50		
Albin's Choice	300	John Radford	1726
Benjamin's Choice	13½	Benjamin Ridge	1760
" Advice	233	George Devilbess	1785
Blacksmith Hall	248	John Lock	1800
Bachelors' Refuge	191	John Clary	1786
" "	54½	Robert Israel, Jr.	1791
Beard's Delight	191	Peter Beard	1791
Brothers' Lot	283	Abm. Lakins	1786
Berkeley	8	Joseph Plummer	1791
Boyers' Neglect	5¼	Peter Haubert	1791
Black-Oak Neck	349	Jacob Weller	1789
Browning's Inheritance	296¼	Jeremiah Browning	1788
Big Spring	23½	Abraham Faw	1789
Beatty's Loss	4¼	Jacob Ridgely	1788
Baltzell's Content	406	Jacob Baltzell	1790
Bale's Industry	340	Peter Bale	1791
Bite me softly	33	Charles Hammond	1791
Bear's Den.	156	John Cookerly	1786
Bare Hill	180	John Stevenson	1791
Beiser's First Chance	10½	Daniel Bieser	1784
Bowles' Compass	8	Peter Mantz	1785
Beard's Luck	42	Peter Beard	1789
Bowers' Struggle	30½	Christian Bowers	1784
Breeches Pocket	194	Yellos Stouffer	1791
Bite him softly	371	Benjamin Hall	1791
Bloomsbury	1788		1791
Barbadoes	28	Samuel Owings	1787
Bell View	670	Richard Potts	1791
Brothers' Agreement	139¾	Philip Delacourse	1800
Boat Harbor	32	Samuel Hook	1790
Benedict's Rest	118	Benedict Holtz	1789
Black-Oak Ridge	25½	John Harbaugh	1793
Bannester's Home	3½	William Billinger	1789
Bone him, secure him	141	Charles Beatty	1787

Names of Resurveys.	Acres.	Party.	Date.
Baker's Lot	15	Godfry Leatherman	1789
Beauty-Spot	2¾	Alexander Ogle	1787
Beggar-Head	32	Jacob Harbaugh	1795
Boyle's Retreat	195	Daniel Boyle	1800
Boar Swamp Forest	701		1795
Brandy Bitters	13½	Norman Bruce	1800
Brown's Adventure	36	Robert Brown	1800
Benders' Retreat	242	John Painter	1800
Behind the bush	4¾	Jacob Wissman	1799
Bowers' good right	112		1784
Bald Eagle Knob	13	Philip Yearst	1797
Brown's Neglect	7⅛	Stephen Winchester	1797
Bigg's Lot	32½	Adam Gamant	1795
Basket Ridge	14½	James Warren	1795
Baker's Conclusion	277	Henry Baker	1800
Buckingham House	334	Carlton Tannyhill	1760
Bone him, secure him	2¾	Lawrence Everhart	1795
Biegley's Displeasure	222	Chris. Hearshman	1792
Better for worse	139	John Poltz	1785
Boyer's Fancy	25	John Boyer	1790
Bitts Added	544		
Brass Buckle	50	Bigger Head	1785
Better than none	35	Joseph Wood	1787
Brothers' Content	419	Jacob Warnfelt	1787
Better than none	74	Conrad Crick	1790
Brotherly Kindness	227½	Henry Staley	1794
Bravleton's Neighbor	2	George Winter	1790
Better than none	174¾	Joseph McDaniel	1790
Biggis' Delight	12	William Biggis	1790
Bull-Pasture	16¼	Peter Kerny and Geo. Shoup	1792
Clifford's Lookout	12	Michael Clifford	1766
Chance it	17½	Thomas Beatty	1786
Conclusion	380	Charles Warfield	1785
Conrad's Purchase	157	Conrad Shaver	1791
" Paradise	420½	Conrad Matthews	1791
Carmack's Advice	165½	Lazarus Funderburgh	1791
Second on Cat-Tail Branch	558	Geo. Smith	1785
Carmack's Chance	30⅝	John Brown	1794
Chance	153½	Alex. Brandon	1792
Chargeable	1100	Orlando Griffith	1787
Chew Farm	5191½	Samuel Chew, etc	1786
Church-lot	65 poles.	On second choice	1786
Confusion	5⅞	Adam Markell	1791
Caty's Garden	5¾	Daniel Arnold	1791
Chestnut Hill	51	Samuel Cock	1788
Chance Medley	358	Christian Keefer	1787
Chase About	187	Michael Bumgardner	1787
Conclusion	104½	Thos. Beatty	1787
Chestnut Level	25	Michael Neip	1784
Catch it if you can	124	Valentine Lingenfelter	1784
Convenient	18	Wm. Ballinger	1784
Carter's Discovery	23½	John Carter	1791
Cobblers' Hall	109½	Lawrence Brengle, Jr.	1798
Circumbendibus	145	" " "	1798
Chisholm's Chance	4½	John Chisholm	1787
Chisholm's Addition	3½	" "	1787
Casper's Loss	602½	Casper Devilbess	1787
Carmack's Trouble	25	Joseph Wood	1787
Civility	21	Thomas Beatty	1787
Crook About	134½	John Hawn	1792
Cherry-Tree Grove	86	Geo. Cook	1792
Crawford's Delight	35	Norman Bruce	1793
Crown Point	50	Geo. Dulinger	1766
Connected	112½	Matthias Fickle	1796
Confusion Amended	127	Philip Fink	1796
Conclusion	155	Joseph Wilson	1796
Confirmation	8¾	Ignatius Davis	1796
Crumbaugh's Chance	60	John Lock	1789
Caldwell's Intentions	6¼	Samuel Caldwell	1793
" Design	8¾	" "	1793
Campbell's Camp	561	Wm. Campbell	1789
Crowl's Good Will	132¼	Leonard Young	1789
Cost's Content	369	George Cost	1789
Chance All	13¼	Henry Shrader	1787
Carver's Lot	153¼	Samuel Garber	1789
Carrick's Farewell	71½	Samuel Carrick	1799
Content	2 15/160	Ignatius Davis	1800
Children's Inheritance	499	James Wells	1792
Crum's Safeguard	21	Wm. Crum	1795
Crawford's Delight	35	Norman Bruce	1793
Charles and Elizabeth	376½	Charles Howard	1797
Clark's Disappointment	152¼	Christian Lance	1795
Cow-Pasture	2½	Wm. Ballinger	1795
"	20¼	Peter Kerny and Geo. Shoup	1792
Carolina	2902	Norman Bruce	1795
Creager's Scheme	390	John Creager	1795
Casper's Reserve	17	Joshua Howard	1792
Caty's Memorandum	393	Geo. Custard	1792
Content	393	Peter Troxell	1794
Christmas Good Will	335	Valentine Summers	1764
Contention Agreed	124½	Joseph Gordon	1785
Creager's Farm	20	Lawrence Creager	1785
Cherry-Tree Point	76	Peter Mantz	1786
Carolina	252	Mashack Hyatt	1787
"	3012	Benedict Calvert	1763
Conrad's travels by night	318½	Conrad Mangin	1793
Chestnut-Oak	95	John Troxell	1787
Close by	10½	Peter Kemp	1794

Names of Resurveys.	Acres.	Party.	Date.
Cock's Orchard	201	Samuel Cock	1790
Caleb's Content	11½	Caleb House	1790
Calf-Pasture	39	Geo. Sharp	1792
Dear bought neglected	17	Edward Stevenson	1791
Daniel's Diligence	394	James Hook	1780
David's addition to part of Disappointment	94	David Martin	1786
Dry Hill	14	Geo. Custard	1784
Drunkard's not mistaken	304	S. Deaver	1771
Don't lose your beginning	9¼	Andrew Stewart	1791
Deer-Park	15	Thos. Castle	1787
Double Trouble	270	Geo. Cook	1792
Deficiency Regained	11¾	Samuel Owing	1789
Delanter's Luck	110	Jacob Delanter	1789
Dear Enough	1⅛	Henry Landis	1793
Discontentment	244	Jacob Geger	1793
Dissolution	33	Lodwick Kissilling	1793
Doubts Removed	334½	John Hockman	1799
Daniel's Delay	47	Anthony Poultney	1799
Derr's Purchase	3½	Lawrence Brengle	1797
Discovery	25¾	Andrew Hull, Jr	1786
Daniel's race-ground	25	Henry Ulricht and Godfrey Tagoot	1792
Part of Drunkard's not mistaken	1	John Van Swearingen.	1791
David's Delight and the Blue-Bird's Nest	138	Jacob Fister	1791
Drummine	742	Basil Dorsey	1798
Part of Dyer Mill Forest	68	Henry Koontz	1792
Part of Duvall's Forest	223	Wm. Duvall	1786
Daniel's Conquest	198	Daniel McCormack	1790
Duble's Luck	73	Isaac Duble	1780
Durbin's Mistake	776	Thomas Durbin	1785
Dodson's Tent	259	Philemon Barnes	1785
" "	5½	Ignatius Davis	1794
Diffidence	176	Geo. Ramsberg	1790
Dry Weather	18	John Beard	1796
Erb's Pursuit	26¾	Christopher Erb	1786
Etzlir's Contentment	9¼	Wm. Roberts	1786
Even Measure	111	Wm. Reynolds	1786
Establishment	217½	Christian Harden.	1786
Erb's Pleasure	773	Christopher Erb	1798
Edinburgh's lot	6½	Henry Mottler	1798
Expensive	2½	Thos. Beatty	1787
Ebenezer	120	Christian Hamman	1796
Even Measure	217	Wm. M. Beall	1796
Eiler's Request	7	Benj. Farquhar	1796
Enough and to spare	224	Thos. Thrasher	1796
Every little helps	3¼	Jeremiah Gilbert	1799
Edmund's Lot	8½	Edmund Dwyer	1792
Evans' Lot	7¼	Ezekiel Evans	1792
Eiler's Correction	137¼	Conrad Eiler	1794
Elisha's Profit	124	Elisha Beall	1785
Enlargement	880	Christian Smith	1797
Errors Corrected	592¾	Valentine Baist	1794
Exchange	27	Daniel Ballinger	1791
Escape	115	Daniel Deleser	1784
Empty Cupboard	120	Ulrick Shiller	1784
Fox's Last Shift	72	Robert Smith	1764
First come first served	3	Jacob Ringer	1791
Fallen Timbers	54	Thos. Beatty	1791
Fair Warning	9	" "	1791
Far in Swamp	58	Geo. Zimmerman	1786
Family Study	452	Conrad Hochersmith	1788
" "	145	" "	1788
Fishery	2¾	Jacob Valentine	1788
Federal	317	Thos. Beatty	1788
Fox Chase	80	Albert Flora	1788
Fry's Good Will	50	Enoch Fry	1791
Fast bind fast find	8	George Murdock	1786
Fox's Hall	60	John Crouise	1784
Frog's Bottom	17	Peter Mantz	1785
Flemming's Loss	13½	Thos. Castle	1785
Fielderea Manor lots	8150	Dr. Thomas Gantt	1791
Felty's Neglect	20	Henry Kerny	1791
Falconer's Adventure	25	Gilbert Falconer	1787
Fredericksburg	75	Frederick Fox	1792
Fowler's Chance	122	Walter Fowler	1793
Fielder's Neglect	8	Valentine Brother	1796
Frederick's Contentment	106	Frederick Shutenhelm	1796
Father's Farewell	137	Leonard Fearon	1796
Fiction	2⅞	James Hughes	1796
Fruitful Valley	92¾	James Plummer	1789
Fairly Fixed	100¾	Henry Finprock	1793
Flag Band	4	Barnett Renn	1787
First come first served	5	John Rees	1793
Fine Wood	13	John Grousneiker	1765
Five Brothers	57½	Philip Milhoff	1799
Fox Parlor	233	Jacob Bigges	1799
Final	264¾	Thos. Beatty	1788
Fox-Tai	15	Geo. Shoup	1798
Fox Town	37	Charles Robertson	1795
Friendship	231½	Frederick Fox	1795
Frankendale	356	Christopher Brown	1798
Father's Gift	539	Adam and Gabriel Marckel	1797
Frosty Morning	9	Joseph Swearingen	1797
Fair Dealing	223	Henry Matthews	1797
Fox's Chase	286	Albright Flora	1792
Fogle's Conclusion	214	Philip Fogle	1794
Fink's Purchase	5½	Thomas Van	1790
Farewell Owl	23	Frederick Leatherman	1762

Names of Resurveys.	Acres.	Party.	Date.
Forrest's Purchase	250	John Flora	1792
Foul Play	2130	Thomas Johnson, Jr.	1790
First come first served	8½	John Weller	1790
Part of Fountain Low	330	John Snowden	1797
Father's Gift	1071½	Richard Owings	1790
Fancy	112¼	Peter Bale	1790
Four tracts	401	Joab Waters	1788
Greenbury's First Attempt	236	Elias Majors	1784
Get Honestly	80	Charles Beatty	1765
Gilbert's Inheritance Enlarged	392	Thomas Gilbert	1786
Good Pasture	2½	Adam Markley	1785
Greenbury's Second Attempt	21⅞	John Bower	1791
Gumbar's Range	126	Peter Mantz	1788
Gassaway's Garden	17	Adam Gassaway	1788
Guadaloupe	56¼	Samuel Owings	1788
Gombare's First Trial	3	Jacob Gombare	1786
Groff's Forests	525	John Groff	1786
Groff's Content	149	Henry Groff	1788
Good Luck	21	Elizabeth Shartzen	1785
Good Spring	29	Simon Hay	1785
Gibraltar	364	Peter Mantz	1786
Good Intent	12	Charles Warfield	1786
Garber's Disappointment	2½	Norman Bruce	1791
Good Water	119	John Keller	1791
Gist's Forests	1131	Joshua Gist	1798
George's Good Will	1⅞	George Zimmerman	1787
George's Inheritance	115½	George Widrick	1792
Ground-Oak Thicket	39½	Charles Angel	1783
Green Bottom	178	Jacob Holtz	1789
Gaver's Recovery	197	Peter Gaver	1789
Got by chance	8¾	Valentine Brother	1796
Good Wife	44	Peter Troxell	1787
Good Fair	152	Frank Kyler	1780
Griffith's Folly	4	Philemon Griffith	1787
Good Fortune	91	John Biggs	1787
Good Economy	15		1797
Ground-Oak Remnant	197	Charles Angel	1792
Good Hope	260	Christian Gilbert	1798
Greenbriar Maple Spring United	94	John Kulp	1795
Groff's Forest	500	(By order of court)	1794
Good Hope	308½	Christian Gilbert	1797
Germanicus	106	Gen. Heister	1795
Good-Friday	34	William Duvall	1786
Green Meadow	231	John Cove	1786
Give and take	320	William Duvall	1791
Good Spring	153	John Delplan	1786
Gunder's Delight	200	——— Staley	1786
Good Neighborhood	164	Joseph Wood	1787
Grammer's Deer-Park	260	Frederick Grammer	1794
Gerhart's Forest	16½	Peter Mantz	1790
Green Castle	55	Peter Shever	1790
Hog-Pasture	20	Charles Beatty	1761
Hobson's Choice	615	John Nelson	1742
Hap-Hazard	5¾	Norman Bruce	1791
Hammer and Tongs	186	George Lusa	1790
Hard Bargain	13	George Free	1788
Hills and Valleys.	256⅝	Abraham Hockman	1788
Hook's Conclusion	1002	James Hook	1788
Holmes' Chance	8	William Stansbury	1786
Hodges' Silence	15	Michael Troutman	1785
Hog Range	240	John Cronise	1799
Hard Bargain	362	William Goo 'win	1798
Haines' Inheritance	416	Samuel Haines	1790
Part of Hammond's Slip	306	Henry Gaither (pat.)	1765
" " "	96	Jacob Ake	1787
High Germany	1558	Charles Carroll (pat.)	1753
Houge's New Design	400	William House	1787
Hard to find	38	Henry Griffith	1784
Haste makes waste	259	Thomas Beatty	1789
Handsome Wife	10½	Michael Troutman	1784
Howard's Discovery	551½	Solomon Whiller	1786
Homing's P rchase	138	Peter Homing	1786
Haines' Security	184¾	Jacob Haines	1798
Hard Climbing	177½	John Whiteneck	1798
Hard Fortune	176	John Maynard	1787
Hope for the best	47	Abraham Plummer	1793
High Up	57½	George Cost	1792
Hull's Neglect	3	Yost Greenwo d	1789
Huckleberry Hills	364	Iloburtus Boyer	1787
Hap-Hazard	28	William Ballinger	1787
Harbaugh's Delight	67	John Harbaugh	1793
Hope for the best	520	William M. Beall	1799
Hope Well	202	Jacob Troxell	1799
Haines' Retirement	128	Dr. Samuel Haines	1800
Henry and Elizabeth	204	Henry Osherman	1790
Hard Dealing	183	Henry Darst	1791
Harbaugh's Chance	32	Christian Harbaugh	1792
High Germany and part of Ohio	220	Jacob Feaser	1792
Hampton Court	1710		
Henry's Loss	170	Henry Myers	1792
Hit or miss	5½	James Hughes	1797
Heart's Delight	16	John Fitzpatrick	1780
House's New Design.	74	William House	1751
Hide and Seek	1000	William Hobbs	1797
" "	1616	" "	1795
Howard's Paradise	576	Ephraim Howard	1789
High-Top Spring	30⅝	Henry Smouse	1786
Henry's Delight	34	Jeremiah Browning	1794
Howard Discovery	5¼	Joshua Howard	1794
Hog Range.	43	Elizabeth Luckett	1790

Names of Resurveys.	Acres.	Party.	Date.
Huckleberry Hills	270	Jacob Doupe	1790
Holtz's Lot	50	Nicholas Holtz	1790
Hedge's Range	282	Joseph Hedge	1786
Hitchbaugh	207	Philip Burrier	1785
Johnson's Neglect	30	John Johnson	1754
I am looser still	496	Murdock Beall	1785
John's Contrivance	216	John Clay	1785
It's worth taking	168	Daniel Ballinger	1791
If I don't keep all I'll keep some	159	Jacob Burgesser	1791
Joseph's Tricks	21	Peter Copeland	1791
Just by chance	316	Christian Harbaugh	1791
Jacob's Chance	88	Jacob Ridgeley	1788
Industry is fortune's right hand pocket	77¾	Benjamin Norris	1788
I am first	28	Jacob Dusing	1788
Israel's Lot	438	Thomas Riley	1791
Iron intention	2774	Norman Bruce	1786
" "	2713	" "	1786
Inclosure	224	Upton Sheredine	1788
John's Safeguard	32¾	John Whitmore	1799
Joshua's lot rectified	539¼	Joshua Wright	1796
Jacob's Loss	969	Jacob Harbaugh	1792
Jedburg Forest	1055	John Chisholm	1789
John's Fancy	118	John Huckwell	1798
Intended mill-seat	25	Thomas Beatty	1786
John and Catherine	104	John Houke	1786
Jacob's Neglect	11	Hugh Reynolds	1784
I'll get a little if I can and think I am as good a man	11½	Peter Mantz	1785
Jacob's Study	10	Thomas Beatty	1785
I have come at last	131½	John Snyder	1790
I have lost most	195	John Smith	1790
I believe it will do	9	Thomas Johnson	1790
Industry and frugality	270	Leonard Burrier	1790
If I don't keep all I'll keep some	123½	Jacob Burgesser	1792
I got home in time	10	Jacob Crist	1796
John's Discovery	12½	William Morsell	1796
I wish there was more	136	George Shoup	1796
In war a Tory, in peace a Rebel	122	Ludwig Michael	1793
James' Isle	2	James S. Hook	1796
It's bad enough	14¼	Henry Peagley	1796
John's Home	43½	Benedict Holtz	1789
Ijams' Resolution	156	Plummer Ijams	1787
Ielers' Content	572	Frederick Ieler	1793
Ijams' Lot	19	John James	1787
Jones' Conclusion	86	Thomas Jones	1787
Jacob's Lot	26	Jacob Yingland	1787
John's Lookout	19	John Evans	1789
Ins and Outs	34	Richard Potts	1793
John Toms' Luck	209	John Toms	1799
Just as you like	121	Charles Cheney	1789
John's Beginning	52	John Mackissick	1789
Jacob's Contrivance	184½	Jacob Staley	1789
I have waited long enough	32	Peter Mantz	1799
James' Mistake	157¼	Christian Bower	1800
I don't know what	5	Lawrence Brengle	1797
If you won't I will	15	Wm. Ballinger	1797
John's Friend	4	Abraham Goshong	1797
Job's Hole	7⅜	Jeremiah Gilbert	1797
Foxes' "	3⅜	" "	1797
Peep "	3⅝	" "	1797
I want the spring	142	John Neff	1797
Jones' Conclusion	86	Thos. Jones	1787
I offered them fair	10½	Peter Mantz	1795
I'll see who's the land will be	406	Andrew Hearnsman	1792
Ivy Plains	60	Nicholas Holtz	1790
I'll take it all	153	Yost Blickenstaff	1797
Ifert's Risque	34	Devault Willard	1790
Jacob's Last Chance	510	Jacob Harbaugh, Sr.	1794
Jacob's lot well bounded	145	Jacob Barrack	1790
Jeremiah's Vision	109	Jeremiah Steward	1790
Jacob's Plains	59	Jacob Burton	1786
John's Friendship	41	John Harbaugh	1794
John's Fancy	25	John Hockwoll	1793
Karr's Habitation	161	Thos. Karr	1785
Kemp's Lookout	10½	Henry Kemp	1786
Kline's Good Will	21	Geo. A. Kline	1788
Knave's Neglect	5¾	Joseph Swearingen	1788
Kline's Old Field	10	Geo. A. Kline	1788
Kittoctin Bottom	595	Wm. Luckett	1755
Kemp's Content	16	Christian Kemp	1784
Kookerly's Purchase	28	John Kookerly	1787
Kemp's Request	14	Wm. Stansbury	1792
Kiddeman's Purchase	145	Wilfred Neale and Bernard O'Neale	1792
Kemp's Good Luck	184½	Peter Kemp	1790
Keefer's Range	527¼	Frederick Keefer	1790
Long Trusted	7	Philip Thomas	1791
Lambert's Purchase	5½	Joseph Stevenson	1791
Long Timber	146	Anthony Miller	1791
Long Spring	56	Samuel Cock	1788
Little Bottle	7¾	Philip Keller	1788
Little Valley	3⅝	David Mirley	1788
Lynchburg	125	Adam Zolman	1788
Locust Spring	6	Godfrey Leather	1787
Land Gate	122	John Israel	1786
Long Bottom	53	Michael Troutman	1785
Long Strip	15	Bigger Head	1785
Lost Kitty	2½	Henry Kemp	1786
Little did I think it	15	Thos. Beatty	1785
Lydia's Home	15	John Farrell	1785

Name of Resurveys.	Acres.	Party.	Date.
Luckett's merry midnight	652	John Farrell	1780
Part of Locust Neck	129	John Reagle	1784
Long Tail	127¾	J. G. Kedderman	1790
Locust Level		James Ryan.	
Long Field	311	Lucas Fleck	1785
Locust Level	457	James Marshall	1794
Lock's Chance	43	John Lock	1789
Locust Thicket	6	Bigger Head	1785
Look Well	15	John Grosenickel	1785
Lawrence's Neglect	36½	Henry Kemp	1792
Little Piece	3	Chas. Warfield	1786
Lost and found	432	James Ogle	1780
Land Gate	109½	Robert Israel	1791
Long's Lost Chance	131	John Long	1791
Laurel Bank	10	Chas. Angel	1786
Loss and gain	1	Edward Waters	1787
Locust Valley	368	Lawrence O'Neal	1792
Ludwig's Content	562	Ludwig Harbaugh	1792
Long Chance	6¾	Christian Benner	1796
Langton's Rainy Day	6	Thos. Langton	1796
Low's Addition	2½	Joshua Wright	1796
Lemmon's Resurvey	222¼	Jacob Lemmon	1793
Luck	10½	Thos. Johnson	1793
Little Lot	11	Fogle Heirs	1789
Long Measure	565	Philemon Griffith	1793
Loss and gain	205¾	Jacob Englar	1789
Lock's Lookout	71	John Lock	1789
Level Farm	248½	Andrew Worman	1789
Little Scrap	2⅜	Daniel House	1793
Lovely Prospect	202	Geo. Shoup	1793
Low Berney	2¾	Michael Aikart	1795
Little Worth	10½	Christian Kogle	1795
Longfield	287	Lucas Fleck	1787
Lemmon's Range	162	John Lemmon	1787
Look to it in time	10	Adam Rawsawn	1792
Luck's all	207	William Murdock	1769
Long looked for come at last	454	Sam'l & Ignatius Lilley	1797
Leatherman's Chance	206	Henry Leatherman	1795
Last choice	222	David Delaughter	1796
Linked together	483¾	Henry Reed	1774
Lambeth	509	Jno and Pat. McGill	1791
Locust Valley	384	T. Van Swarrington	1790
Little did I think it	23½	Thomas Price	1775
Long Bottom	72	William House	1752
Link's Content	100	Adam Link	1785
Little Pound	7¾	Lawrence O'Neal	1776
Landstool	151	Thomas Price	1782
Long Bottom enlarged	239	Henry Nelson	1793
Little Worth	28½	Adam Bowman	1794
Last Scrap	5⅝	John Campbell	1794
Long trusted	7	Philip Thomas	1791
Lambson	216	Peter Shaver	1790
Laurel Hill	56	George Duttero	1790
Loss recovered	30¼	Joseph Haines	1790
Ludwig's Content	562		
Leave it so	182	Jacob Ridgeley	1799
Last Choice	3½	Samuel S. Thomas	1800
Meadow Land	9	George A. Kline	1788
Myers' Profit	4	Sebastian Myers	1788
Mountain Lock	36	Jno. & Jacob Heffner	1812
Moore's Policy	7¼	Tobias Moore	1797
" Contentment	7¾	" "	1797
Miller's Delight	45	Jacob Miller	1761
Mill Place	50	Adam Miller	1762
Madman's Defeat	321	Devault Willyard	1791
Mount Pleasant	23	Thos. Van Swearingen	1791
Markley's Discovery	14¼	Adam Markley	1791
Moore's Delight	5½	" "	1791
Markley's Discovery	50	" "	1788
Mount Hope	566	Ignatius Davis	1790
Mesner's Content	269	Peter Mesner	1785
Mother's Care	185	Catharine Ruff	1780
Make Haste	257	Thomas Beatty	1785
Mason's Folly	177	P. Mantz	1788
" "	260½	"	1788
Matthew's Inclosure	12½	Joseph Matthews	1785
Make the meadow bigger	22½	Joseph Ogle	1785
Mad George	17	Peter Mantz	1785
Major's Inclosure	10½	Elias Major	1784
Mount Pleasant	1281	John Dorsey	1764
Martin's Delay	6½	Martin Hinds	1798
Miller's Retreat	252	Jacob Miller	1798
Mantz's Management	255½	Catharine Thomas	1787
Maple Spring	23	John Kolb	1787
Mount Misery	11½	William Welsh	1792
Mad Wife	54½	Samuel S. Thomas	1792
Michael's Tricks	65	Michael Ulrick	1793
Montpelier	90	Joseph Swearingen	1796
Menfelt	713	Jacob Doupe	1796
Mason's Folly	76	Henry Gollman	1789
Mount Pleasant	39½	Adam Helm & Co.	1796
Mantzsylvania	433	Peter Mantz	1785
Mountain Fields	298	Joseph Hill	1796
Michael's Neglect	7	George Scott	1796
More than was expected	14½	Norman Bruce	1793
More bad than good	265	William House	1793
Mount Pleasant	174	Richard Richardson	1787
Martin's Neighbors	9	John Orr	1787
Mistake Discovered	132	Casper Young	1787
Miller's Purchase	121	Peter Miller	1789
Melingah	101	Adam Reass	1789

Names of Resurveys.	Acres.	Party.	Date.
Mikesell's Discovery	1⅜	Andrew Shriver	1800
Miller Lot	5¼	Jacob Miller	1800
Mount Lofty	165	John Waggoner	1792
Miller's Timberland	16	John Miller	1797
Mount Vernon	5⅛	L. Brengle	1797
Mother and Son	150	Henry Protsman	1797
Murdock's Inheritance	142½	William Murdock	1795
Main's Last Chance	5	George Main	1795
Marker's Delight	296	George Marker	1795
More plague than profit	3½	Martin Grimes	1795
Monocacy Bank	17½	John C. Beatty	1795
More loss than gain	188	Michael Sadler	1796
Mend in time	20	Jacob Myers	1792
Mount Philip	209	Philip Thomas	1784
Mountain Vacancy	75	George A. Kline	1792
Mantz's Fatigue	368	George Burkhart	1784
Mount Vesuvius corrected	84	John Graham	1790
McGorgan's Fancy	44½	Thomas McGorgan	1800
Meadow's something	391¼	Michael Font	1789
Middle Dam	200	James Ryan	1788
Mill lot	223¾	Jacob Castle	1791
Mason's Lot No. 4	176	George Scott	1793
Many tracts	551	Upton Sheredine	1786
Mason's Folly, part of	436½	Daniel Dulany	1793
Mountain lot	125	John Molton	1789
Mill-seats (5)	620	Allen Farquhar	1796
March weather	211	Daniel Delosier	1795
Mount Felicity	266	Basil Dorsey	1793
Mischief prevented	1¾	John Diffindal	1794
Margaret and Jonalis' partnership	760	Margaret McKissick	1794
Michael's Farewell	88	Michael Hibner	1791
Maiden Island	9¼	Thomas Johnson	1794
Magnetic variation	55¾	David Shriver	1790
Monocacy Manor resurveyed in 1787 to 85 different parties.			
Near the spot	128	G. P. Cooperixder	1762
Newfoundland	77	Thomas Dorsey	1785
"	3½	Nehemiah Hall	1803
New Purchase	61	Wm. Ballinger	1786
Neighbors' Agreement	360	Peter Stittey	1791
" Contention	216	John Ingleman	1791
Nantucket	9½	Jacob Christ	1788
Neighbors accommodated	100	Valentine Linanfelter	1795
Nothing loss	207	John Smith	1791
New Haven	294	Peter Musser	1791
Nicodemus' Inheritance	722	Henry Nicodemus	1791
Neif's Folly	121	John Neif	1784
Neck or nothing	33	Wm. Head	1791
Neighbors' Alarm	303	Wm. Rice	1787
Nail's Profit	68	P. D. Nail	1784
Nicholas' Content	188	Nicholas Bowlass	1787
No matter what	210	Henry Flooke	1792
Now or never	188½	John Ross Key	1793
Nothing hardly	13½	Adam Neff	1793
Newey's Retreat	27½	Joshua Wright	1790
Nicholas' Oversight	4½	Wm. Ballinger	1796
New Harbor	83	Charles Beatty	1796
Now for it	2	Wm. Ballinger	1796
Norris Lot	186½	John Norris	1789
Needful	423½	Charles Hammond	1789
Neglected	5	Norman Bruce	1793
Nazareth	143	D. Leatherman	1786
Now or never	16	Wm. Ballinger	1797
Neck or nothing	40	Charles Beatty	1797
Now look about	118	Peter Hubbert	1795
No more left	10	Michael Smith	1795
No more to be had	7¾	Andrew Hime	1795
No help for my loss	480	Philip Crist	1795
Nehamah's Lot	1	Nicholas Price	1795
Nicholas' Last Chance	10	Nicholas Holtz	1795
Neiff's Ill Will	52	Peter Swinehart	1784
No whisky	14	Joseph Wood	1787
Noah's Lot	5	Wm. Ballinger	1797
Notley's Leaving	97½	James Marshall	1792
Needs must	4¼	John Miller	1792
New Purchase	38	Wm. Ballinger	1786
Nathan's grief and joy	299	Nathan Grief	1786
Neighbors Agreed	280	Samuel Cock	1788
Nathan's Undertaking	1208	Thomas Maynard	1785
New Bremen	1788	John F. Amelung	1786
Nigh Nicking	497	Samuel Carrick	1794
Neighbors' Mistrust	44	Jacob Merch	1794
Neighbors' Agreement	528	Jacob Sheets	1794
New Market Plains	1515	Nicholas Hall	1794
Naught's never in danger	160	Wm. Tams	1794
Nightingale	233	Stephen Howell	1786
Necessity enlarged	251½	Wm. Murphy	1794
Nothing venture nothing gain	44	Samuel Templing	1790
Neighbors' Content	180	Andrew Smith	1790
Neighborly Kindness	107¾	Daniel Zachariah	1770
Olive Branch	48	Thomas Beatty	1780
Ogle's Ferry	5¼	Alex. Ogle	1785
Outlot	47	George Mindack	1791
Ogle's Ferry	1	Alex. Ogle	1787
Oversight enlarged	165	James Sergeant	1796
One Brother	293	Benjamin Biggs	1796
Ogle's Necessary Compact	440	Alex. Ogle	1787
O'Hara's Inheritance	231¼	Henry O'Hara	1793
Owen's Choice and Angels' Rest	50½	Charles Angel	1773
Owing's Venture	40½	John Owens	1744
Oppa	35	Christopher Brown	1795

Names of Resurveys.	Acres.	Party.	Date.
Owl Hollow	27		
Philip's Luck	16¼	Charles Beatty	1772
Pleasant Orchard	119½	Wm. Turner	1791
Piney Hills	31½	Jacob Valentine	1788
Preparatory	562	Wm. Hobbs	1797
Puzzlesome corrected	839	John Beatty	1785
Peace all round	159	Peter Shiver	1785
Pleasant Level	55	John Stevenson	1786
Prelate	507	Richard Lawrence	1786
Philip's want supplied	7½	Philip Crist	1785
Providence	26	Thomas Beatty	1785
Perseverance	10	Peter Mantz	1784
Mount Pisgah	2832	Francis Deakins	1786
Partnership	53	Jacob Holtz	1789
Porter's Second Addition	137	Henry Williams	1788
Part of Sixth Dividend	172	Geo. Brown	1788
Peach Blossom	103¼	William Currents	1791
Pay Cost	8	J. Wood	1784
Plain's Second Attempt	5	David Plain	1785
Profit and loss	106	John Weller	1786
Part of addition to Clark's Discovery	142	Dudley and Ann Deggs	1780
" " " "	115	Wm. Deggs	1780
Pearre's Retreat	241¼	James Pearre	1798
Pleasant Stream	106½	Joseph Ramsey	1798
Pleasant Level	287	Aloysius Elder	1798
Prospect Hill	38¾	Geo. Ellicott, etc	1798
Poplar Grove	599	L. Brengle, Jr	1797
Potato Ridge	96½	Redmond McDaniel	1787
Pipe Creek Hill	188	John Flower	1787
Pittinger's Lot	4	Wm. Ballinger	1787
Plummer's Addition	3¼	Edward Waters	1787
Pleasant Meadow	222	Jacob Young	1787
Poplar Spring	12	John Matthews	1793
Piny Batter	21¼	" "	1796
Peter's Neglect	37	Adam Rawsawn	1796
Peace and plenty	374	Frederick Kemp	1796
Partnership	456	Elizabeth Ellicott, etc.	1796
Pebo	48	Joshua Howard	1789
Polly's Inheritance	185½	Vachel Hammond	1789
Pretty improvement	163	Jacob Snider, Sr	1793
Peace and good will	11¼	" " Jr	1793
Philemon's Surrounded	211	Stephen Bassford	1793
Plummer's Lick	154	Adam Clay	1794
Pleasant Hill	25	Benj. Hall	1793
Part of resurvey of Mason's Folly	65¾	Geo. Markel	1789
" " " "	76	Henry Gollman	1782
Paris	24	John Ijams	1787
Part of resurvey on Cold Friday	447	John Lawrence's heirs	1787
Plumb Garden	18	Jacob Keplinger	1787
Preventative	2¼	Norman Bruce	1799
Precaution	3	" "	1799
Perplexity	203	Samuel Boggess	1792
Poulson's Reserve	274¾	Andrew Poulson	1791
Philip's wish granted	17¼	Philip Hufford	1792
Peace and plenty	76	James Ogle	1784
Porter's Second Addition	121½	Patent dated Sept. 29,	1764
Pool's Policy	7	Henry Pool, Jr	1795
Payplat's Purchase	5⅝	Stephen Winchester	1792
Part of Hammond's Portion	2115	Vachel Dorsey *et al.*	1797
Partnership by many	191½	John Clark	1795
Peter's cow-pasture	2	Peter Suman	1795
Pumpkin Hall	100	Wm. Murdock	1795
Partnership	909	Solomon Turner	1765
Pool's Industry	1022½		
Pleasant Grove	404	Amos Davis	1787
Pleasant Level	67	John Stevenson	1792
Partnership	809	Wm. Cumming	1793
Poor Pay	2½	Jno. Diffendal	1794
Paraphrase	499	Henry Bitesell	1768
Partnership by many	521	Philip Steel	1794
Philip's Bargain	34	Devault Willard	1790
Plumb Orchard	35¾	Benj. Biggs	1790
Peace established	128	Conrad Krickbaum	1790
Poplar Spring	82	David Gearinger	1790
Pleasant Hill	366	Joseph Miller	1797
Perfection disputed	143	Abraham Hoff	1787
Polipotamia	½	Saml. Farquhar	1794
Pardner's Alley	22½	John Whiteneck	1786
Peace and quietness	101	Wm. Runkel	1797
Philip's Care	17	Philip Hufford	1787
Piney Meadows	101	Christian Gilbert	1796
Peter's Hurry	250	Peter Zollinger	1792
Quakers' Good Will	4½	Joseph Wood	1784
Quick work	14¾	Jacob Myers	1792
Quakers' Folly	32	Ludwig Kemp	1790
Rocky Hill	150	John Howard	1749
Rusher's Purchase	148	John Rusher	1798
Rectitude	213	Allen Farquhar	1785
Rock Oak Spring	40	David Shryock	1792
Richard's Hunting-Ground		John Diggs	1742
Raspberry Plains	640	Geo. Cook	1791
Rabbit Harbor	21½	James Armstrong	1791
Range and timber	567	Wm. Ballinger	1788
Raccoon Walk	20	Albert Flora	1788
Rocks and stones	255	John Witherow	1788
Rocky Hill Resurvey, and called Troublesome Job	398¾	John Sturrum	1791
Rocky Hill	321	Chris'r Hull	1786
Rocky Ridge	23½	Andrew Fogle	1789
Rich meadow unexpected	20	Michael Troutman	1784
Reynard	4¼	William Roberts, Jr	1786

Names of Resurveys.	Acres.	Party.	Date
Rattle Weed Forest	483	Joseph Talbot	1786
Root s Disappointment	7	Daniel Root	1791
Road in the middle	4¾	John Whiteneck	1798
Ridgley Rest	251	(By order of court)	1787
Rip Shin	179	Charles Beatty	1787
Rail Trap	6	Wm. Beatty	1787
Rich meadow land	14⅛	Peter Mantz	1796
Richard and Elizabeth	393	Richard Anchrum	1792
Roe Buck	27½	John Creager	1793
Resolution	127½	George Pusey	1789
Rowser's Addition	237	Peter Shiver	1796
Richard's Delight	91	Daniel Richards	17{8}7
Rum Spring	40	Michael Fair	1787
Rocks and Timber	70	Leonard Hoyl	1794
Rocky Hills	150	John Howard	1749
Resist and be free	4¾	Jacob Gomber	1797
Right is right	251	Jacob Cost	1797
Rocky Comfort	54	John Biggs	1795
Ridgeley's Good Will	302½	John Hobbs	1773
Rattle Weed Forest	470	Joseph Talbot	1786
Rough and Smooth	107	Jacob Keplinger	1794
Runnymede enlarged	3820½	Dr. Upton Scott	1794
Ripley's Safeguard	78	Jacob Ripley	1794
Raccoon Walk	20	Frederick Weaver	1794
Rabbit Range	13¼	Benjamin Biggs	1790
Rose Garden	225	Thomas Johnson.	
The Remainder	3½	Norman W. Bruce	1789
Ridgeley's Loss	44	Charles Beatty	'791
Rest and explanation	330	Westall Ridgeley (pat.)	1753
Rodenpeller's Ramble by Quakers' Tricks and Lost Bottle	244½	Philip Rodenpeller	1786
Rich Level	218	Casper Rice	1790
Resurvey of Dear Bought	213	Adam Devilbiss	1785
Rocky Hill	96	Frederick Heffner.	
Stilley's Chance	42	Peter Stilley	1764
Small Glade	55	Thomas Price	1774
Stowder's Lookout	192	Christian Stowder	1771
Shaver's Rest	189½	Henry Shaver	1786
Stony Hill	11¼	Ulrich Stuller	1791
Sherman's Retreat	146¼	Jacob Sherman	1791
Stony Land	503¾	Peter Kowell	1788
Strausburg	646	Philip Rodenpeller	1788
Stony Garden	8	Joseph Blick	1788
Switzerland	10	Samuel Owings	1788
Stony Ridge	37	" "	1788
Stony Batter	2¾	Peter Mantz	1788
Salt Trough	16	John Weller	1791
Stevenson's Garden	1605	Edward Stevenson	1791
Stony Cabin	11½	Wm. Beckwith	1787
Single Delight	254	Matthias Zacharias	1786
Seek and ye shall find	36	Mary Becraft, etc	1786
Stone Quarry	9	Thomas Beatty	1780
Snider's Content	13	Jacob Snider	1786
Second Chance	36	Michael Smith	1786
Shrader's Beginning	15½	Henry Shrader	1786
Small Ridge	9½	Jacob Fulwiler	1785
Staley Desire	14½	Thomas Beatty	1785
Sink Hole	3½	P. Kemp	1785
Small Venture	4½	Adam Markley	1785
Steel's Good Luck	12	George Steel	1785
Seed Tick Bottom	6½	Levy Philips	1800
Snowy Ridge	88	Andrew Hull	1786
Staley's New Addition	127½	Jacob Staley	1798
Samuel's Advice	126	Lazarus Ferderbergh	1798
Second Addition to Sugar-Tree Valley	127	Stephen Winchester	1798
Soon Done	58	Henry Collman	1787
Stophel's Neglect	14	John Fitzpatrick	1787
Sure bind sure find	254	Valentine Creager	1787
Shrader's Luck	63	Henry Griffith	1787
Shryor's Blessing	326	(By order of court)	1787
Stony land	12	George Custard	1792
Small Exchange	2¾	Joshua Stevenson	1792
Stony Batter enlarged	167	James Ogle, etc	1792
Surveyor's Industry	243	Daniel Biser	1792
Samuel's Kindness	5	Samuel S. Thomas	1792
Sugar-Tree Valley	354	Benjamin Farquahar	1796
Second Thought	196	" "	1796
Shryor's Blessing	330	Christian Koones	1786
Short Measure	145	Wm. Morsell	1793
Saum's Purchase	177¼	George Koontz	1789
Sweepstakes	90	William Dorsey	1793
Standing Stone	70	Absalom Hedges (pat).	1771
Spring Lot	1 65/160	S. S. Thomas	1792
St. Patrick's day in the morning	2¾	L. Brengle	1797
Six acres gained	202	Philip Price	1795
Simon's Delight	150	Peter Shover	1795
Saw-mill assistance	63	John Weller	1795
Smithton	14¼	Christian Smith	1795
Smithfield	14¾	" "	1795
Seven bits united	196½	John Karn	1795
Shiverdeforge	289	Christian Harbaugh	1795
So much saved	2	J. F. Heffner	1800
Sure bind sure find	430⅜	Henry Herring	1799
Sweepstakes	37½	Peter Mautz	1793
Safe bind safe find	154	Henry Creager	1789
Shepherds' Delight	447	Benjamin Ogle	1787
Springfield	108	Col. Thomas Price	1785
Strawberry Plains	293½	Henry Maynard	1787
Self-defence	305	Gen. O. H. Williams	1789
Sevenfold	240	Peter Ricker	1800

Names of Resurveys.	Acres.	Party.	Date
Sweet Apple	139	Henry Leatherman	1796
Saw-mill Place	7	Yost Blickenstaff	1789
Sappington's Retreat	195½	F. B. Sappington	1790
Square Bottle	48	Jacob Brown	1798
Stevenson's Conclusion	357½	Charles Stevenson	1792
Settled in peace	150	Adam Hoffman	1800
Shoemakers' Tricks	25¾	Adam Roughsong	1787
St. Mary's Valley	154	John Troxell	1784
" "	55	" "	1787
Small expense	318	Andrew Arnold	1793
Shingle Timber	23½	William Madden	1793
Second Best.	60	Peter Kemp	1793
Sour Apple	60		
" "	5	Henry Leatherman	1797
Shover's Disappointment	3¼	Peter Shover	1795
Stover's Good Luck	32	Peter Mantz	1799
Strong Spring	15	Jacob Klitz	1790
Speculation	4½	Christian Shoup	1790
Short Commons	4½	Elias Delashmeet	1792
Shaver's bad luck	184¾	Henry Shaver	1774
Stouder's Desire	10	Thomas Beatty	1787
Speelman's Canoe	3½	Andrew Shriver	1800
Second Purchase	3½	Joseph Wood	1787
Stony Point	16	John Whiteneck	1785
Second Purchase	52	Peter Slyder	1784
Summer Hill	25	Philip Smith	1790
Second Attempt	11	John Thomson	1795
Stony Meadow	20	Jacob Foosinger	1792
Small Addition	1¾	Joshua Wright	1797
Southgate's Chance	99 138/160	Washington Southgate	1866
Sandy Spring	14	William Deakins	1785
Snow in May	63	Jacob Warnfelt	1797
So much saved	2½	Peter Mantz	1790
Shriner's Content	80½	Philip Shriner	1786
Shoup's Conclusion	218	Christian Shoup	1790
Smith's Good Will	281¾	Philip Smith	1789
Spring Garden		Joel Rite	1792
Smith's Lot	273	Jacob Smith	1792
Sheridan's Range	227½	Thomas Franklin	1790
Stony Corner	705	L. Creager *et al.*	1791
Stricker's timber land enlarged	284	Andrew Arnold	1793
Stony Point	50	Zeph. Wakland	1784
" better part	40½	Joseph Wells	1793
Snipe's Head	226½	Moses Farquhar	1796
Addition to Lemmon's vineyard	127	Stephen Winchester	1796
Stony Hill	131½	Samuel Singer	1798
Stripe's Purchase	865	Joshua Waddington	1790
Six Originals	277¾	George Winter	1790
Seven Originals	289	Walter Funderberg	1789
Stephen's Purchase	356	Stephen Winchester	1792
Shady Grove part	305	Daniel Snygart	1797
Sheridan's Range	329	Thomas Franklin	1792
Several lots	152¾	Henry Landes	1787
St. Elizabeth part	98½	John Weller	1797
Stony Spring	72	John Slutts	1787
Shot Proof	157	James Wistman	1787
Spittlefield	10	Michael Smith	1788
Tailors' Bodkin	129½	Jacob Weller	1791
This or none	62¼	William Goodwin	1791
The Gap	219½	Henry Peakly	1798
The 10 tracts	598¼	Peter and John Erb	1800
The Transylvania	104	John Connell	1794
Timber Hills	192	John Norris	1791
" Land	103	Joseph Gambay	1785
Tom's Gift	150	Henry Beakley	1771
Turnstile	108	Richard Butler	1787
The Forest of Needwood	945	Bartholomew Booth	1775
The mistake is rectified	513	Frederick Eichelberger	1799
The Corn Harrow	67	Daniel Root	1795
Three Partners	390	Charles Beatty	1770
The addition to Cumberland	20	Joseph Cumberlidge	1764
The Two Sisters	169	Susanna and Esther Kemp	1792
The Resy Mt. Pleasant	189	Messrs. Creagers	1765
" Right and good reason	12	L. Brengle, Jr	1798
" Mason's Folly	384	(For the State)	1781
" Albaugh's Delight	125	Wm. Albaugh	1765
This is the way	265	Elisha Beall	1786
Take all	108	Chas. Martin	1783
The resy on wett work	1404	James Marshall	1786
The end of strife	155	Philip McCatthews	1795
The second choice	256	Allen Farquhar	1795
The five mill-seats	34	" "	1795
The rocky mantle-piece	60	Tobias Butler	1795
The little field saved	4	Peter Shaver	1795
The rights of man	496	Wm. Duvall, Sr	1795
The third chance	20½	Thos. James, etc	1795
The land of perplexity	152	Ludwig Leaman	1784
The three Jacobs	168	Jacob Bowlus	1798
The Snipe	5¾	Daniel Arnold	1791
The hardest send off	413	Jacob Crist	1787
The Discovery	136½	Jacob Sherman	1793
The birthday of American independence	1¼	John Brunner	1799
The Addition	1⅞	Stephen Winchester	1797
The bone of contention	99	Wm. Dickensheets	1788
The quilting frolic	606	Chas. Warfield	1786
The Heater	7½	Greenbury Hoffs	1789
The barn secured	6¼	Adam Rowsown	1793

Names of Resurveys.	Acres.	Party.	Date.
The end of trouble	114	Matthias Smith	1795
The Vacancy	1060		
The forked stump	14½	Norman Bruce.	1792
The grape field	54	Baltis Foutz	1784
The apple orchard	23½	Conrad Tutterer	1784
The country seat	225	Peter Kemp	1793
The Discovery	140	Jacob Sherman	1793
The nail factory	7½	Peter Mantz	1793
The second trapezium	3½	Andrew Hull	1792
The generous offer	1⅝	S. S. Thomas	1792
The spring	1¼	Jacob Bergesser	1792
The long farm	468	Joshua Gist	1791
The spider's leg	1¼	Joseph Roop	1793
The sickly season	101	Wm. Stevens	1793
The third addition to New London	15	Upton Scott	1793
The Narrows	18	Samuel Emmett	1787
The Separation	169½	John Biggs	1792
The hog range	130	John Cronise	1792
The crooked billet	139	Joseph Wood	1787
The new location	18½	Jacob Snider, Jr.	1793
The least of the two	31	John Mackissick	1789
The best policy	264	Jacob Toosing	1794
The pleasant ridge	149¼	Joseph Swearingen	1797
The trapezia	3	Norman Bruce	1789
The Quakers' bite	83	Charles Beatty	1769
The Fishery	13	Thos. Beatty	1797
The 1st day of June	387	Philip Baer	1797
The end of dispute	214	Samuel Toms	1788
The mill-stone pick	24½	Joseph Boyler	1788
The Remnant	82	Peter Erb	1791
The second thought	108	Thos. Beatty	1791
The last of all	47	“	1791
The young beginner	112	Philip Keller	1788
The Agreement	24½	Ulrick Mesler	1788
The three springs	92	Thomas Price	1788
The crooked slipe	31	Peter Mantz	1788
The hidden treasure	6½	Jacob Crist	1788
The addition to Ramsburg struggle.	5½	Michael Temple	1792
The sand in stone quarry	6	Henry Kemp	1792
The eldest son	207	John Cronise	1790
The wood-trap	2¼	Samuel Hook	1796
The peach orchard	2½	Jonathan Fry	1800
The small triangle	⅜	Jacob Apler	1800
The winter month	7	Henry Motter	1799
The meadow is safe	14	Frederick Kemp	1799
The safest way	182	“ “	1799
The distillery	25	John Geyer *et al.*	1797
The obtuse triangle	1½	L. Brengle	1797
The six brothers	887	Wm. Biggs.	1786
The case is altered	152	Samuel Shoup	1797
The second surprise	35½	Richard Lawrence	1793
The drooping robin	233	Lodwick Kellsellring.	1793
The worst of all	78	Joseph Wood	1787
The small meadow	5000	Edward Lloyd and Wm. Paca	1774
The bad wife	92	John Everly	1775
The adventure	8	Jonathan Howard	1789
The lower slipe	26¼	Norman Bruce	1789
The summer side of the hill	36	Daniel Smith	1793
The stag	18	John Willyard	1793
The paper factory	170	Geo. Zimmerman	1792
The two sisters	66½	Samuel Waters	1792
The blooming month of May	214	John Flooke	1792
The sheep-bell	8¼	Peter Mantz	1799
The widow's lot	7	“ “	1799
The plug	16½	Zachariah Barnes	1795
The cold Friday in April	28	Baker Johnson, April.	1795
The new-born	319	Wm. Crum	1796
The bullet moulds	5	Jacob Burton	1792
The compass square	5	“ “	1792
“ “ “	10	Daniel Arnold	1792
The rifle-gun	20½	Jacob Burton	1792
The small triangle	1⅜	Stephen Winchester	1792
The first trapezium	4⅛	Andrew Hull	1792
The last scrap	4¼	Peter Mantz	1793
The standing stone	375	Anthony Bostani	1790
The mill-seat secured	45	Valentine Evert	1790
The old story over again	7	Adam Everty	1794
The least said the soonest mended	287	Jacob Champer	1794
The bayberry tree	6¼	Thos. Johnson *et al.*	1794
The third purchase	22	Adam Gernant	1794
The last spot	4	Peter Kemp	1794
The title is good	141	Bernard Hersberger	1798
The four springs	16½	John Sours	1792
The last gap stopped	4½	Geo. Grice	1794
The trapezia	10	Jacob Ripley	1794
The crooked billet	139	Azel Waters	1700
The bootjack	137	Thos. Beatty	1790
The land of promise	904	Daniel Gaver	1797
The apple orchard	13	Conrad Tutterer	1784
The orchard	25	Michael Trautman	1784
The surprise	35	Wm. Hall	1784
The famous mill-seat	12	Henry Kemp	1791
The western mill-seat	112	Moses Farquahar	1800
The triangle	5¼	Solo. Miller	1789
The boat	13	Felter Fleegal	1789
The upper slipe	7½	Norman Bruce	1789
The leavings	42	John Stevenson	1796
The snipe's head	13½	Joshua Wright	1796
The hawk's nest	69½	Daniel Shryock	1796
The chestnut-oak ridge	138	Samuel Shoup	1796

Names of Resurveys.	Acres.	Party.	Date.
The salt trough's long enough	246	John Weller	1796
The secret revealed	28½	L. Brengle	1796
The supply	597	Christian Smith	1796
The saving plan	116½	Wm. Burgess	1796
The third time of asking	640	Chas. Kline	1796
The four friends	115	Adam Link	1796
The near neighbor	48	Jacob Crist	1788
The three Jacobs	168	Jacob Bowlus	1790
The four partners	16	Joseph Staley	1798
The last of the two made bigger	223	John Mackissick	1798
The top of the Blue Ridge	45	Joseph Myers	1791
The treat	535⅛	Wm. Potts	1790
The amicable swap	186	Samuel Shoup	1794
The mountaineer's disappointment	1307	Thomas Beatty	1790
The hammer	11	James Beatty	1790
The tailor's mistake	4¾	George Winter	1790
The trouble's approaching	229	John Thompson	1794
The world's wonder	594	Joshua Gist *et al.*	1794
The finishing stroke	532	Thomas Beatty	1785
The long race	332	Michael Knife	1794
The range about the three miserable knobs	1278	Yost Blinkenstaffer	1787
The case of necessity	794	John Devilbess	1797
The good spring	12	Daniel Gaver	1791
The first and second addition to first.	3½	Jacob Burton	1796
The Koontz's purchase	2	“ “	1796
The nest egg	136	Valentine Brother	1796
Three brothers' lot	470	Basil Wood *et al.*	1790
Taylor's lot	15¼	George Winter	1790
Trouble enough	148	Henry Baker	1784
Timber plenty	309	Christian Koon.	1788
Taken in time	12½	Thomas Beatty	1784
Timber lot	6¼	Jacob Sherman	1791
Troublesome job	398¾	John S urrum	1791
This or none	7½	Thomas Beatty	1786
Timber Ridge	54	Joshua Howard	1789
Thomas' Profit	673	S. S. Thomas	1792
Toms' Safeguard	21	John Toms.	1794
Toms' Farewell	243	“ “	1794
Timber Valley	20	Conrad Mangin	1784
Take what's left	82	John Harbaugh	1795
That or none	173	James McDaniel	1786
Three-acre lot	3	Daniel L ster	1799
Triangle	½	S. S. Thomas	1800
Turkey Hill	11½	Jacob Linepaugh	1787
Trail's Jaunt	52	Michael Menser	1799
Touch and go	7¼	Nathan Trail	1800
Turkey Ramble	39½	Jacob Fulwiler	1785
Turkey Foot	6	Henry Callman	1788
Timberland	60	S. C. Shoup	1797
Tradesmen's Garden	7¼	Upton Sheredine	1793
Three tracts all together	259	Andrew Hearsman	1786
That is the last	8	William Ballinger	1797
Timber Plenty	103	Christian Smith	1793
“ “	493½	Chr stiana Smith	1791
Trouble enough indeed	2492	Thomas Whitton	1763
Thereabouts	22	John Creager	1793
Try it again	25	Thomas Johnson *et al.*	1787
Town Tract	603	Thomas Beatty	1786
Tanner's Purchase	100½	Henry Raep	1789
Unexpected	15	E. McKinsey	1785
Union	406	James Johnson	1787
Umstead's Inheritance	260½	Nicholas Umstead	1789
Under heaven	5½	L. Brengle	1797
Usher's Freehold	119	Thomas Usher	1785
Unity	74¼	Philip Engler	1790
Venture	217	Paul Wolf's exrs	1786
Violet Bank	10½	George Cock	1791
Value in time	5½	Jacob Burton.	1786
Valentine's Day	5¼	L. Brengle	1798
“ “	13	Hugh Jones	1799
“ Retirement	389	Valentine Matter	1789
“ Good Will	120	Jacob Valentine	1787
Value in time	20	William Murdoch	1795
Venture	244	Paul Wolf's ex'rs	1786
Van's Discovery	128	Van Swearingen	1775
Venture and luck	230	Garnit Lingenfelter	1775
Virgin's Delight Part	163	Thomas Piper	1791
Value in time	83	William Murdock	1796
War's proclaimed	3	Law. O'Neal	1776
Wood's Gain	182½	Richard Wood	1786
Wood's Town Land	100	Joseph Wood.	1785
Why not	3¾	Thomas Beatty	1791
Warfield's good luck	485	Davidge Warfield	1788
William's beginning	645	William Dorsey, Jr.	1793
What you please	73	George Steel	1786
Well enough	209	Melchior Tabler	1786
What you please, I am easy	139	Henry Wolf	1786
Woodcock head	38	Peter Mantz	1786
Wood's gain	188	Richard Wood	1786
Wet to the skin	8½	Peter Mantz	1785
Water's Gain	2½	Samuel Waters	1784
West Indies	8½	Peter Harmer	1785
We have got the bird in the cage	268	V. Lingenfelter	1791
Wet to the skin	4½	Norman Bruce	1791
Whiteneck's Alley	14½	John Whiteneck	1798
Wood's mill-land	229	Joseph Wood	1787
Windy Friday	3½	Adam Fisher	1787
White Hall	8	Thomas Beatty	1787
Water Lot	4½	William Ballenger	1787
Ward's Palace	7½	Francis Ward	1787

Names of Resurveys.	Acres.	Party.	Date.
Warman's Content	158	Jacob Warman	1787
White Oak Hills	55	John Cockey	1787
War Spring	17½	Yost Blickenstaffer	1787
William's Wish	18	William Renner	1787
Who could have thought it	13½	Legh Master	1792
William and Amelia	15½	Peter Mantz	1792
Wilson's Inheritance	415	Samuel Wilson	1793
Worth the taking	1167¾	Thomas Beatty	1796
Worth something	30½	Richard Winchester	1796
Wolf Range	32	John Harbaugh	1793
Woodrow's Discovery	5	Joseph Roop	1793
Wide Brake	77	George Markell	1789
Wayman's Retreat	126	Philemon Griffith	1787
Well secured	107	John Shriner	1793
William is never at home	32	Peter Mantz	1799
We could not agree	119½	Henry Lydert	1800
Worth the taking	1010	James Williams	1799
Wet work resurveyed	1278	James Marshall	1797
Westphalia	646¾	Daniel Heister	1797
Wood enough	48	Michael Knife	1795
Well paid for	165	Jacob Harbaugh	1795
Wolf's Mistake	7¼	Wm. Ballinger	1795
Weaver's last renewal	281	Geo. Weaver	1795
Wood's mill-land	223¼	(By court)	1790
Who could have thought it	3½	Legh Master	1792
William's Home	25	Wm. Shilkney	1792
White Oak Ridge	98½	John Clarke	1792
William's Intention	145	Chris'r Kiddeman	1791
White Oak Hill	50		
Warfield's lot	308¾	Alex. Warfield	1788
Woodland	330	Baker Johnson	1796
Wayman's Retreat	116	W. C. Marsh	1794
Wolf's Den enlarged	30	Norman Bruce	1784
White Castle	62	Guy Elder	1790
Weinpinny Till	101	Philip Hungleberry (pat.)	1761
Wallisell escheated	25	Philip Price	1784
Wet Work	1340	James Marshall	1793
Wells' Invention	126	Francis Hoffman	1789
Whisky-Bottle	122	Henry Whitmore	1786
Yost's Narrow Chance	20	Y. Blickinstaff	1796
" Claim	50	Albert Flourey	1786
" " enlarged	175	Joseph Blickinstaff	1787
Young's Purchase	202	Peter Young	1791
Zachariah	632	Elizabeth Boardley	1791

CHAPTER XX.

THE BENCH AND BAR.

Its Professional Standing—The Early Leading Lawyers—The Courts — Martin, Pinkney, and McMahon — Biographical Sketches.

THE bar of Maryland has long been distinguished for its learning, its probity, and the lofty professional standard it has maintained. It has been equally renowned for the prominence of its leaders, who have conjoined in a marked degree knowledge of the law, familiarity with the statutes, and acquaintance with the rules of practice and pleading to signal powers and graces of oratory, no less than it dominates the jury, and makes the court wish, like Ulysses, to be tied to the mast. Colony and State, the Maryland bar can point to an unbroken succession of these conspicuous leaders from the earliest periods down to our own very day. Each gem in that galaxy is a bright particular star, yet so closely do they succeed one another that there seems no interval between. The Bordleys, Dulanys, Jenningses, Tilghmans, and Carrolls of the earlier periods are followed in unbroken order by the Chases and Johnsons of the Revolutionary age, to whom Martin and Pinkney are rather younger brothers than children. When Wirt, Harper, Winder, and others of that "old school" fell into the "sere and yellow leaf" the mantle was not dropped before it was caught by the brilliant circle in the centre of which McMahon, Nelson, and Schley, of Western Maryland, shone brightest, nor can these be said to have left a vacuum so long as we have Wallis, Steele, Alvey, Ritchie, Walsh, Darby, Douglas, Syester, Urner, Roberts, the Schleys, and their associates.

The bar of Maryland has not lost any of its old-time brilliancy. It is still distinguished for its eloquence, its integrity, and for its solid learning as of yore. But these qualities are not so conspicuous now as their singularity made them in the period from 1750 to 1820, when, for two generations, the lawyers of Maryland were almost without peers in their profession upon this continent. Massachusetts and Virginia were rivals, but not superiors, if even equals. In that period Annapolis, and afterwards Baltimore and Frederick, were centres of legal rivalry such as are seldom seen. A style of oratory, ornate and elegant, yet precise, correct, and elaborated upon the best models of pure English, furnished the fitting capstone to a solidly-built column of carefully-studied principle and precedent; the judges were worthy of the barristers who pleaded before them, and neither judges nor barristers were content unless they seemed at least to measure themselves with the most conspicuous lights of Westminster Hall and the great English circuits. During this period, indeed, our bar prided itself upon closely following English models. It claimed to have its Erskines and its Mansfields, its Scarlets and its Broughams; it followed most rigidly the precedents of old English law and the practices of the English courts, and certainly refreshed itself more frequently with English methods and English studies than the bars of either Massachusetts or Virginia. The courts of these States were provincial, the one from necessity, the other from a certain lordly and aristocratic indifference which regarded Williamsburg as good enough for the men who followed legal pursuits in Virginia, as the cream of the tobacco noblesse did not. But estates were not so large in Maryland, while, on the other hand, the rewards of the law as a profession were much more tempting in our State than in Virginia. It paid for the younger sons of a family to pursue the law in Maryland, and the competition was so keen that it paid the fathers of those younger sons to give them a good legal education in the London Inns of Court. Hence a surprisingly large number of our young lawyers, during the colonial period, studied their profession in the Temple and Lincoln's and Gray's Inns. The Bordleys, the

Dulanys, the Taskers, the Carrolls, the Tilghmans, the Jenningses, the Pacas, and Bennetts, and Helmsleys were all represented, at one time or another, in those classic walks. After the Revolutionary war these fashions were not resumed; yet Pinkney went twice to London to defend and secure American interests, and it was proudly believed by those who knew him best that he had found no rival there with whom he feared to cope.

There must have been sufficient causes for this exceptional brilliancy of the early Maryland bar, nor are these causes far to seek. They are the same as those which subsequently gave their great eminence to the bars of Kentucky and some other Western States,—the certainty of handsome emoluments and the existence of much litigation. It was the confusion of titles and the multiplicity of claims to the rich lands of Kentucky which involved that whole State in lawsuits and feuds after its first settlement, and afforded, in both the criminal and the equity sides of the courts, such an opportunity as is rarely offered for the profitable exercise of legal talents and legal skill. The same causes are now at work to give peculiar brilliancy to the bar of Texas. In Maryland, when the colony was settling, while the lands were being cleared, the Indians pushed back, and all society was seething with the hand-to-hand struggle between Protestant and Catholic, Puritan and Cavalier, there were practically no lawyers, the courts were mere justices' courts and, later, vestry courts, and the bench—outside, at least, of St. Mary's, if we may trust the author of the "Sot-Weed Factor"—was boorish and ignorant if not venal. But there came a swift change with the settlement of the provincial government at Annapolis, the clearing of the "backwoods," the large importation of labor, both white and colored, and the general growth of the colony in wealth and importance. Three or four elements are noticeable right here as concerting together for the rapid development of an able and brilliant bar. The rapidly-increasing forces of labor could only be profitably employed by a correspondingly rapid opening up of new lands, and of these there was great variety of choice. The old planters rested contented upon their inherited estates, but their overseers and factors, busy, pushing, ignorant men, took negroes and convicts to the newer settlements, worked them for all they were worth, grew rapidly rich, and were correspondingly arrogant and litigious. When they came to Annapolis they had money to spend and lawsuits to adjust, in respect to both of which they found plenty of young lawyers to accommodate them. Every lease or sale of land made by the provincial government implied an addition to the income of the Lord Proprietary, and quick sales and hasty surveys necessarily involved the validity of many a title. Besides this, the proprietary government, claiming and exercising extraordinary powers, felt constrained to maintain its pretensions by extraordinary means. It was the fountain of patronage for both State and Church, and it made this patronage profitable. There were many offices, and all these were in the gift of the Lord Proprietary, or his deputy at Annapolis. Surveyorships, advowsons, parishes, clerkships, tobacco-inspectorships, collectorships of rents and taxes, sheriffalties, coronerships,—all were appointed from Annapolis. A sheriffalty in that time was a plum indeed, and the prothonotary of a county might grow rich on the fees of office in ten years.[1]

Besides these there were militia commands, commands in the wood rangers, and a very great variety of other patronage, paid for from the fees of office. Any young scion of a good family who studied law, came to Annapolis, and showed his loyalty to the existing government, winking at its abuses and courting its leading spirits, might be sure of securing an office such as would yield him a good support. If it were necessary he could be made a pluralist. John Coode, miserable rebel agitator and atheist as he was, held commissions militant, civil, and apostolic at once, —he was in holy orders, he was collector of customs, and he was colonel of county militia. Rev. Bennett Allen, controversialist, brawler, duelist, murderer, and sot, was incumbent of St. Ann's parish, in Anne Arundel, and the best parish in Frederick County. In 1770, among other fees and salaries, Governor Sharpe was paid, besides his salary of £1000 as Governor, £226 as surveyor-general, and an unstated amount as chancellor. Benjamin Tasker was president of Council, member of Upper House, and joint commissary, his pay in the latter position amounting to £483. Benjamin Tasker, Jr., was councilor, member of Upper House, and naval officer, the fees of the latter office being £318. Edmund Jennings was councilor, member of Upper House, and secretary for county clerks, register in chancery, clerk of provincial court, and notary public, his six offices yielding him £1307. George Steuart was judge of the land office and commissioner of the land office, receiving £517 salary. Daniel Dulany, to the practice at Annapolis courts, added the place of joint commissary, with £483 salary.

---

[1] As early as 1689 one of the alleged grounds for Coode's rebellion was excessive fees of office and extortionate tolls, against which no remedy can be found, "the officers themselves that are partyes and culpable, being Judges."

These various causes soon built up a strong legal circle at Annapolis. In 1710, when Daniel Dulany the elder came to the bar, then fresh from England, there were but few lawyers, and these chiefly provincial born and educated at the provincial court. Among these, Dulany, Stephen Bordley, and the father of Edmund Jennings were the chief. In 1771 the bar of Annapolis was illustrious for its great lawyers and the great number of lesser lights revolving about them. They made a society of their own, witty, ingenious, dissipated. They fought, gambled, dissipated, had their clubs, wrote for the newspapers, patronized the theatres, the cock-pit, and the race-course, and all the province paid toll to them. They rode the circuits to some extent, going to Marlboro', Joppa, Frederick, Chestertown, and Easton; but Annapolis was their home and the fountain of their business. Here was Daniel Dulany the younger, of whom Pinkney, who only saw him in the evening twilight of his greatness, said that "even among such men as Fox, Pitt, and Sheridan he had not found his superiors," and of whom McMahon said, "For many years before the downfall of the proprietary government he stood confessedly without a rival in this country as a lawyer, a scholar, and an orator." He was regarded as "an *oracle* of the law." Here was John Beale Bordley, just retiring from the Governor's Council and the emoluments of office in Baltimore County to become the Cincinnatus of the Eastern Shore. Here was Samuel Chase, first and one of the greatest of our patriots, whose energies "quickened all that he touched, and whose abilities illustrated all that he examined."[1]

"What he felt he expressed," says the lawyer historian of Maryland, "and what he expressed came stamped with all the vigor of his mind and the uncompromising energy of his character; if his manner was a fault it leaned to virtue's side. It is not for my feeble pen to portray his virtues and abilities, they are registered in the nation's history, and there is no true American to whom his name, recorded on the imperishable roll of American independence, does not bring back the grateful recollection of his services. He was a son of Maryland, and when will she have his like again?" Here was Charles Carroll of Carrollton, fresh from his law studies in the Temple, eager and able to challenge Daniel Dulany's masterly pen in a pamphlet controversy about American rights and American liberty,—the wealthiest citizen in the province, and the most keen to stake his fortune for independence and sacred honor, and "to win or lose it all." Here was "Barrister" Carroll, another law student of the Temple, another leader of public opinion, another patriot, whose able pen may be traced in many of our tersest and most effective State papers of the Revolutionary period.

The courts at that time were but little altered from the provincial, or, in other words, the old English model. They were much more formal and precise than now, more stern in rule, more rigid as to precedent, more complicated in practice. They were, in fact, overloaded with formalisms, and the official documentary language was but little removed from an utterly barbarous jargon. The business of the courts was apportioned into more numerous, minuter, and sharper divisions, and the predominant rule, which is now simplicity, tended in those days constantly towards over-refinement. Chancery was then by no means a name, but the labyrinthine way by which alone most men could reach after long wanderings the adytum of equity as to property and goods, estates, and hereditaments. The chancellor was the most important judge in the State, and was paid the highest salary. There was the Court of Appeals, which had then but minor jurisdiction, the Admiralty Court, superseded by the United States District Court after the adoption of the Federal Constitution, and the chief judge and his associates of the General Court. These, after their appellate business at Annapolis was concluded, used to separate and preside over the Oyer and Terminer terms of the County Courts. In 1777 the chancellor's salary was £650 (in Maryland currency), the chief judge of the General Court got £600, and his two associates £500 each; the five judges of the Court of Appeals received £200 each, and the judge of the Admiralty Court was paid £250. This pay does not seem large, but it sufficed to secure for the bench some of the best lawyers in the State. They were appointed by the Governor for life, they did not have to court the popular favor, they were as good, if not better, lawyers than the barristers who pleaded and the attorneys who practiced before them, and they kept up a dignified presence and attitude which would appear astonishingly severe at the present day. The wig was not part of the judge's costume, but the gown was until quite a late period, and there was a certain *state* about the courts which must have admirably upheld what it was meant to enforce, the dignity and elevation of the judiciary. This was well conceived for a bench which had such unlimited power over the persons as well as estates of the citizens, which could retain property in chancery for unlimited intervals, could imprison for debt while life lasted, which could pillory, or brand, or whip,

---

[1] McMahon.

DANIEL DULANY.

or hang in chains and gibbet for offenses which to-day scarcely cause a year or two's imprisonment. It must not be inferred from this, however, that these severe punishments were very often imposed in Western Maryland during the later colonial days and the early State history of Maryland.

The bench held to its dignity as severely as it held to its ancient forms and complicated and involved terminology. The lawyers were kept in order by a rigid construction of the contempt rules, and the judges also sought to apply these rules as rigidly to the press. In fact, for many years the courts, in Frederick, Baltimore, and Annapolis, attempted to control the relations between the press and the public, so far as their sessions were concerned, much more according to the precepts of Lord Thurlow than in obedience to the suggestions of common sense in a free and enlightened country, and collisions between the two powers were consequently quite frequent, the courts seeking to maintain themselves upon a very high plane of constructive dignity, the papers resolute to give the people the news as promptly and fully as possible, with such editorial comments as they thought necessary to make.

The courts had not so many officers as they now have, but the officers were worthy of much more consideration, and were consequently supplied from a better class of materials. The prothonotary, afterwards clerk, held office for life, as did also the register of wills, and both were paid in fees. These officers were appointed. The sheriff, who had great power, was appointed under the provincial government, but elected under the State government. He also received his pay in fees, and the position was as lucrative as it was influential and responsible. Under the colonial government the sheriff was tax and tithe collector, and his influence upon and intercourse with the people must have been extensive to a very unusual degree. Down to quite a recent period the sheriffs of the counties were selected from among persons of the first consequence, and their criminal functions were looked upon as the least part of their charge.

Among the members of the Constitutional Convention of 1777 was Luther Martin, representing Harford County. The constitution then matured provided for an attorney-general of the State, and after Thomas Jennings, James Tilghman, and Benjamin Galloway had one after another declined the appointment, thought to be particularly perilous in a time of war, in which the party which might chance to lose would be treated as rebels, Governor Johnson tendered the post to Mr. Martin, who accepted it Feb. 11, 1778, and performed the duties of the office until December, 1805, when he resigned, and was succeeded by William Pinkney. From 1778 until the reorganization of the Court of Appeals in 1805 the judges of the court were Benjamin Rumsey, chief judge; Benjamin Mackall, Thomas Jones, Solomon Wright, and James Murray. Judge Wright dying in 1801, Littleton Dennis succeeded him, and Richard Potts was the same year appointed to fill the vacancy caused by Judge Murray's death.

The world never produced a better lawyer than the great legal genius, Luther Martin, whose knowledge was as broad as his judgment was unerring, who had so many of the solid parts of the law at his command that he could afford to neglect the graces in his pleadings. Unlike Patrick Henry, who trusted to eloquence and genius to carry him through, Martin was all his life a student. They lower themselves who think of this man as a simple case lawyer, earning fees in order that he might besot himself with brandy. He was a profound student, and a student of principles. At Princeton College, in addition to the studies necessary to give him the highest honors in a class of thirty-five, Martin took a course of French and Hebrew. His parents were poor, but he said that in giving him a liberal education they had endowed him with "a patrimony for which my heart beats towards them with a more grateful remembrance than had they bestowed upon me the gold of Peru or the gems of Golconda." Luther Martin was born in New Brunswick, N. J., in 1744; he was graduated in 1762, and immediately set out to this State in search of a school, securing one at Queenstown, Queen Anne's Co., under the patronage of Edward Tilghman. While teaching school he studied law, borrowing books from Judge Solomon Wright, and laboring indefatigably. He was often arrested for debt, even at that early day, but his studies were never arrested. "I am not even yet," he said long after this period, "I was not then, nor have I ever been, an economist of anything but time." Even while walking on the street he would be seen reading some volume or document lest a moment should be wasted.

LUTHER MARTIN.

Martin was admitted to the Virginia bar in 1771, began to practice in 1772, removed to Accomac, and thence to Somerset, in Maryland, where his practice was soon worth one thousand pounds per annum.

In his first term in a criminal court, of thirty cases he had, twenty-nine resulted in acquittal. He took an active and ardent part in the struggle for American independence, was member of the Maryland Constitutional Convention, and the only leading lawyer who dared accept the office of attorney-general. Tories were abundant in Somerset County at that time, and Martin prosecuted them and confiscated their goods with an unsparing vigor, and with such an intimate knowledge of the law that none escaped. Martin, like Chase, was an ardent Federalist politician. He defended Chase when impeached, and his defense of Burr in his trial for treason is not only one of the *causes célèbre* of the United States, but secured for Martin the active, life-long gratitude of the most heartless man the country ever produced. This great man died paralytic, imbecile, in penury, a pensioner. Yet the Maryland bar had such a sense of his greatness and of his broad contributions to legal science, and their obligations to him on that account, that they willingly consented to pay an annual license tax for his maintenance, and procured an act of the Legislature legalizing the assessment and collection of the tax, a case probably without precedent in professional history. Martin stands out among lawyers for presenting the sound sense of the law without trick or ornament, in beauty unadorned. His knowledge was always broader than his case; his mind seemed to grasp, co-ordinate, and classify the principles of the law as if it were one of the exact sciences, and his professional accuracy was so generally acknowledged that his mere opinion was considered law, and is still deemed sound authority before any of our tribunals.

It is commonly said that when William Pinkney returned from Europe (where he had been serving as commissioner under the Jay treaty), in the full flush of his extraordinary powers, and with his eloquence pruned and chastened down to the tone of English models, Martin's great position at the bar fell away. But when Pinkney came back Martin, who was twenty years his senior, had already seen his best days, and these two were never rivals, nor can they well be compared together. Their methods were entirely different. Martin's cases and his arguments on them grew out of his knowledge of the law, as the tree springs from the soil; but Pinkney built up his cases as the architect, with magic design and exact eye and selection of faultless material, builds a Strasburg cathedral or an Alhambra. The art is wonderful, supernatural if you will, but it is art nevertheless.

William Pinkney, this magic mechanician, was born at Annapolis, March 17, 1764, had a private tutor in classics, began to study medicine, finally studied law with Samuel Chase, and came to the bar in 1786. He held some legislative offices, and practiced his profession successfully until 1796, when he went to England on the Jay treaty claims commission, and also to reclaim Maryland's Bank of England stock from chancery. Mr. Pinkney removed to Baltimore in 1806. He was attorney-general of Maryland and of the United States, State senator, member of Congress, minister to Russia, and United States senator, dying in 1822, in the height of his fame. He was the most brilliant lawyer the State ever produced, but not so sound nor so solid as Martin. Vain, chary of his reputation, he never went into a case without the most careful and elaborate preparation. He did not wish to appear so, but was the most laborious of men, studying each theme like an actor preparing his part. He knew the law deeply, but only regarded it as his instrument. He was philosophical and poetical in the same way, so that he might fill out and round up his nosegay; yet so consummate was this great actor's art—on the country's broadest stage, moreover—that his hearers thought him the most perfect of orators, and said that he conjoined to Burke's turbid thought and tropical rhetoric the chaste sentiment of Canning, the sonorous declamation of Pitt, the vivid fancy of Sheridan, Fox's ardor and passion, and Erskine's rapid but eloquent flow. Why not? William Pinkney was the aptest pupil that ever lived, and during his nine years in England he was at school to all these masters. The traditions of his triumphs, however, are something wonderful, and show him to have been a man of extraordinary force and versatility. These triumphs, however, were always the personal victories of Mr. Pinkney, and only legend tells of them, while the victories of Martin were the victories of the law, and its applications such that the courts even to this day respond to their influence. The distinction is as great as that between the appearance and manner of the two men,—Martin, awkward, matter-of-fact, slovenly in speech and dress, a great snuff-taker, and often using his sleeve in lieu of a handkerchief, sometimes hardly sober enough to appear in court, yet never losing or tangling the thread of his argument;[1] Pinkney, with

WILLIAM PINKNEY.

---

[1] In his latter days Martin could not plead unless under the influence of stimulants, and the story is familiar of the case

SAMUEL CHASE.

the airs of a *petit maitre*, coming into court gloved and dressed in the height of fashion, or hurrying in, booted and spurred, as if he had only remembered the case at the last moment, making good play with his handkerchief and his pinch of snuff *à la marquise*, always the actor, affected even to himself and his own thoughts, yet always fortified at every point in regard to his own case, terribly in earnest to win it, and terribly determined to let no rival eclipse him in the argument.

If to these names we add those of Roger Brooke Taney, the late chief justice of the United States, and William Wirt, whose lives, public property, do not need to be recited here, it will be admitted that the early bar of Maryland deserves all and more than the encomiums that have been bestowed upon it. Taney, though he lived down to our own times, was the contemporary of Harper and Winder, of Pinkney and Martin. He was attorney-general of Maryland, and at the head of the profession in the city and State, when Andrew Jackson took him and in rapid succession made him Attorney-General of the United States, Secretary of the Treasury, and chief justice of the Supreme Court.

WILLIAM WIRT.

A man of the purest character, the loftiest principles, the calmest judgment, the most unblenching courage, his spotless life and record were proof against the foulest breath of calumny and the most frantic convulsions of cant. He served his State and his country well, and rests peacefully in his honored grave.

Around these giants in law gathered many men who but for comparison with them would have shown themselves to be far above the ordinary stature. Of these it is only possible to mention the names of Thomas Beale Dorsey, William Frick, John Purviance, Nicholas Brice, Elias Glenn, and Alexander Nesbet, all of whom ascended the bench; Joseph Hopper Nicholson, of the old Eastern Shore family of that name, who was chief judge of the Baltimore County circuit, and afterwards (in 1805) was appointed to the Court of Appeals; William Ward, Theodorick Bland, who became chancellor; Zebulon Hollingsworth, Stevenson Archer, also chief judge of Baltimore County circuit; John Kilty, David Hoffman, the author; William Gwynn, editor of the *Federal Gazette*, and prince of the Delphian Club, etc. Jonathan Meredith, a contemporary of all these, lived right down into our own times, and deserves the title which was accorded him of "the Nestor of the bar."

And meantime the students of all these elders were coming forward to restore for a second time the golden age, the *Saturnia regna*, of the Baltimore and Western Maryland bar. A good focal point from which to glance at these would be the date of the amended constitution of 1838, when the Governors of the State were first elected by the people. By that time there had been a general reaction against the State's policy of internal improvements, which had involved the community in overwhelming debt. The protest of the "glorious nineteen" had succeeded in arousing the people to a consciousness that the State government was degenerating into a mere rotten borough system, and the general sentiment was being effectually "democratized," so to speak. This had its decided influence upon the temper and character of the bar, and though the incoming leaders were still Whigs, they were Whigs of a very different stamp from the semi-Federalists of the Harper school. Fogyism was departing, like silk stockings and hair powder, and the railroad spirit had already made its distinct and recognizable impress upon society.

Easily first and foremost of the new school, legitimate and worthy successor of Martin and Pinkney, Winder and Harper, stands the towering form of John Van Lear McMahon. Born at Cumberland in 1800, taking first honors at Princeton when only seventeen years old, and coming to the bar at nineteen, Mr. McMahon was as distinctly a nineteenth century man as Messrs. Harper and Carroll were of the eighteenth. His immediate success at the bar did not prevent him from plunging at once into politics, and in his second term in the House of Delegates he became the recognized leader of that body, taking a memorable stand in favor of granting equality of civil rights to the Hebrews. In 1826 he removed to Baltimore to live, was twice again elected to the Legislature as a Jackson Democrat, and declined a nomination to Congress. It was rather a personal issue with the Jackson party than a change of principles which made McMahon turn Whig; his Cumberland birth, education, and associates inclined him to favor internal improvements from the first, and this he did in a masterful way, not only by his eloquent voice, but by his equally effective pen, in pamphlets, memorials, reports, and in bills and charters which embodied and vivified

---

where his client made his fee contingent upon Martin's keeping his promise not to drink. He stammered, stumbled, broke down, and at last, sending for a pint of brandy and a loaf of bread, *ate* the requisite stimulant with his bread soaked in it, and won his case.

the spirit of the institutions he aided in creating. He drew the charter of the Baltimore and Ohio Railroad, the first incorporating act of the kind ever prepared in this country, and the model for all that have succeeded it. This fragment of Maryland history, which is one of the monuments to Mr. McMahon's memory, has caused the best judgments to regret that he did not devote himself entirely to literary pursuits, for it is in this field that his broad and philosophical mind seemed to exercise itself most freely. He was a man of towering genius, the equal of any political speakers, a lawyer profound, astute, full of resources, and knowing at once the authority, the precedent, the principle, and the "right reason" of every point he made. He was an insatiate reader, and a teacher of such winning powers that those who listened to him were never conscious of the lapse of time. His oddities and eccentricities were harmless, and he was the most charming and fascinating of companions.

JOHN V. L. McMAHON.

John Nelson, one of McMahon's rivals at the bar, though not thought to be a larger and broader man, was by many esteemed to be a better lawyer than even that eloquent pleader, who boasted that he never lost a case. Mr. Nelson was a most accomplished and able barrister; he was a skillful and astute diplomatist, and a man all of whose varied parts were rounded up into perfection by close and exhaustive study, by acute analysis and a power of conjoined comprehension and apprehension such as is vouchsafed to but few men. He was a genial, kindly, warm-hearted, thoroughly well-balanced man. His natural endowments were great, his intellect was luminous and vigorous, and he regarded law as a science, the most intricate problems of which it was his province, his privilege, and his delight to master and unravel. In the didactic parts of his profession, before the court and before a jury, his reasoning was close and exhaustive, his logic masterly, but this did not preclude him from the exercise of a genuine eloquence that was pleasing without being florid, and persuasive without vehemence. The late Reverdy Johnson, in speaking of Mr. Nelson's powers, said, "I have heard more eloquence, more brilliant imagery, more power of amplification, and more affluence of learning, but I do not think that in force of analysis, clearness of arrangement, perspicuity of statement, simplicity of language, closeness of logic, and concentration of thought I have ever seen Mr. Nelson much, if at all, excelled." John Nelson was born in Frederick, Md., in 1790; he was elected to Congress when only twenty-five years old; appointed minister to Naples by Andrew Jackson, and made Attorney-General by John Tyler. In the latter position he succeeded the brilliant Hugh Swinton Legare, of South Carolina, but did not suffer in the least by the comparison. He died in Baltimore in 1860, after a severe fit of the gout.

It is natural when we speak of McMahon and Nelson for the thought to revert to Reverdy Johnson. This sturdy oak of the law was the senior of the great triumvirate, in some respects likewise the greatest of the three. A man of wonderful power, both physical and mental, combative, yet subtle, acute, yet never wasting time on hair-splitting, Mr. Johnson's scope and range were remarkable.

REVERDY JOHNSON.

He could talk to a jury of plain farmers in a simple diction of which they understood every word (or thought they did), and so make them have perfect faith in a new medical theory of "moral insanity," invented by him for the nonce and enforced by precept and example. He knew—none better than he—how to address the venerable judges of the Supreme Court so as to win their approbation while securing their attention, and giving them the pleasing sense of relief from the deluge of verbiage perpetually rising around and threatening to overwhelm them. He was the readiest of debaters in the Senate, where his profound grasp of constitutional subjects kept him ready armed in any emergency. He was skillful, astute, and *au fait* in all the language and terms of diplomacy, never losing sight of the main issue of his case, while affecting, with the *politesse* of Talleyrand, the indifferent attachment of a Walpole to the middle way of compromise, and as an after-dinner speaker he was as clear, as genial, as sparkling, and as delightful as a draught of old southside Madeira, sunny and golden as the rays in which it had ripened. His capacity for work and business was almost miraculous. It despised the weight of years and the loss of sight, and when his last fatal accident befell him, on Feb. 9, 1876, at Annapolis, his mind and his powers seemed to be in their full vigor. Mr. Johnson was bred in the law. The son of Chancellor Johnson the first, the brother of Chancellor Johnson the second, he was born in Annapolis, May 21, 1796, educated at St. John's College, and taught law in his father's office. In 1817 he came to Baltimore to challenge the stalwart elders whose history we have already sketched. He never hesitated to throw down the gauntlet to any one. His success was immediate and continuous, nor did his loss of popularity in consequence of the Bank of Maryland troubles affect his standing at the bar. He was Attorney-General of the United States in 1849, United States senator in 1863, minister to England in 1868, and besides these received many other important appointments at the hands of his State and the Federal government.

The last of the lawyers whom we shall attempt to mention in connection with this period as fertile in legal ability of the first order will be William Schley.

Mr. Schley, of Frederick, was one of the most competent and successful barristers and pleaders of his time. He knew the law well, both the common law, the statutes, and the rulings; he was an excellent judge of human nature, full of sound practical common sense, and no man could be plainer or more logical than he in statement and argument. In many respects he resembled Luther Martin, and he had the faculty in a remarkable degree, both before judge and before jury, of following up, pursuing, and hunting down with pertinacity and the unerring instinct of a sleuth-hound the point of all others which was the material, vital, and hinging-point of the case upon which he was engaged.

In 1851 the issue raised by the "glorious nineteen" was finally settled. Governor Philip Francis Thomas, in his message to the General Assembly when it met in January, 1850, speaking of the long-deferred question of constitutional reform, very plainly told them that "unless the wishes of the people in this behalf are gratified, the sanction of the Legislature will not much longer be invoked." A "Reform Bill" calling a Constitutional Convention was accordingly adopted; the Convention met in November, and adopted the new constitution of May, 1851.

This instrument did away with the Court of Chancery, made judges and court officers elective by the people, abolished imprisonment for debt, and radically changed the whole court apparatus of the State, simplifying practice and processes, deeds, and instruments, and paving the way for codifying the statutes. The State was divided into eight judicial districts for county courts; there was a Court of Appeals with four judges, and for Baltimore City there were established a Court of Common Pleas, a Superior Court, and a Criminal Court, to which was afterwards added a City Circuit Court. The office of attorney-general was abolished. Under this new system John C. Legrand was elected chief judge of the Court of Appeals, with John Bowie Eccleston, William Hallam Tuck, and John Thompson Mason, associates.

One of the most accomplished and most beloved members of the Frederick and Baltimore bar was Charles H. Pitts, who died in 1864. Mr. Pitts was endowed with those qualities which give usefulness and honor to his calling, thoroughly grounded in the principles of his profession, and quick and able in their perception and application. He was distinguished for his taste and judgment as an advocate, was eloquent, witty, and forcible, full of manliness, honor, and loyalty to duty and to friendship. Mr. Pitts was a native of Frederick, but made Baltimore his home from the time that he came to the bar. The profession had no greater favorite than Mr. Pitts.

Henry Winter Davis, despite the political estrangements to which his radical opinions and his boldness in expressing them gave rise, is acknowledged on all hands to have been one of the brightest and most conspicuous ornaments of the bar of Maryland. He was but forty-nine years old when his death occurred, in December, 1865, yet he had reached a prominent and commanding position in national affairs. Born in Annapolis in 1817, he was educated at Kenyon College, Ohio, and the University of Virginia, with the idea of becoming a minister of the Protestant Episcopal Church. He, however, passed the bar in Alexandria, Va., and after practicing there a while came to Baltimore in 1850. He was always fond of polemics, however, and shone in ecclesiastical controversy. He was in every way a ripe scholar, full of various attainments carefully elaborated, and must have attained success as a writer if his oratorical powers had not swept him away. As an orator he scarcely had his equal, and he was as impressive on the stump as he was in legislative halls. As elector on the Scott ticket in 1852, he canvassed the State as it had never been canvassed before. Then he

HENRY WINTER DAVIS.

joined the Know-Nothing movement, and represented Baltimore in the Thirty-fourth, Thirty-fifth, and Thirty-sixth Congresses, and again in the Thirty-eighth, having been defeated for the Thirty-seventh by Hon. Henry May. Mr. Davis was a master of elocution. His mind was a store-house of immense reading, which his memory kept ready parceled for his service; he was highly imaginative, had great power of invective, and his wit and sarcasm were mordant to the last degree. He was one of the ablest debaters who ever went to Congress, and a man of superb genius, imposing presence, and possessing the faculty of command in a distinguished degree.

The bar of Western Maryland to-day, as reflected in its living and active members, both those upon the shady side of the hill and those younger men who are gallantly climbing towards the summit, is not unworthy in any respect of the distinguished ancestry whose faint outline has been painted in the preceding pages. The profession holds out the same high rewards to honorable industry, cultivated talents, probity, and integrity, and our contemporaries toil with an inherited zeal and compete with an ardor transmitted through unbroken generations for the same sort of distinction as that which compensated Chase and Martin, Pinkney and McMahon. Those who lightly pretend to believe the bar has degenerated are not familiar with its past or have neglected to measure the stature of its present.

In making comparisons between the lawyers of the past and present, it must not be forgotten that much more is demanded of advocates nowadays than was the case a hundred or even fifty years ago. The rules and forms of practice have been greatly simplified, statutes codified, reports made more complete and comprehensive, and the profession wears much more the aspect of a science than formerly. But at the same time the sphere of the advocate has both widened and deepened enormously. Precedents and rulings have multiplied on all sides, and the *juris-consultus* must nowadays be ready at a moment's warning to thread the intricate labyrinths of a dozen branches of science which had no existence in the times of Martin and Pinkney. Then expert testimony was almost unknown, now it is called in the majority of important issues. Patent law, railroad law, telegraph law, all open new and most arduous fields to the profession, and compel it to specialize itself more and more every day. Business law is assuming a thousand new shapes, each more complicated than the other, nor can the vast body of decisions, rapidly as it accumulates, keep pace with the ever-swelling volume of new issues daily coming up for adjudication. A lawyer who would embrace the whole scope of his profession nowadays must travel very far beyond Coke and Blackstone, Chitty and Greenleaf, Kent and the code. He must be an accountant, a civil engineer, an architect, a mechanician, a chemist, a physician, he must know the vocabulary and technology of all the arts and professions, he must be a theologian and a metaphysician, with the experience of a custom-house appraiser and the skill in affairs of an editor. And after all, with all these stores in his possession, so great is the competition that he may scarcely be able to hew out a living in his profession.

At an early period in the history of Maryland jurisprudence, the bar of Frederick County, then embracing the whole of Western Maryland, numbered among its members some of the most distinguished lawyers in the State. It furnished the fifth Chief Justice of the United States, Roger Brooke Taney; the first Governor of Maryland, Thomas Johnson; the second United States senator from the Western Shore, Richard Potts, who was also one of the early judges of the Court of Appeals; and two Attorney-Generals of the United States, Roger B. Taney and John Nelson. Among the other prominent members may be mentioned Alexander Contee Hanson, John Hanson Thomas, Francis Scott Key, author of the "Star-Spangled Banner," Francis Thomas, Governor of Maryland, John Thomson Mason, William Schley, Charles H. Pitts, Robert J. Brent, Madison Nelson, Wm. P. Maulsby, John Ritchie, Enoch Louis Lowe, Governor of Maryland, John A. Lynch, James McSherry, a historian of Maryland, Bradley T. Johnson, and Milton G. Urner. Alexander Contee Hanson, the younger, who figured during the anti-Federalist riots in Baltimore upon the declaration of war with Great Britain in 1812, was a son of Alexander Contee Hanson, Chancellor of Maryland. His grandfather, John Hanson, who removed to Frederick County from Charles County in 1773, was one of the most conspicuous Revolutionary leaders of Maryland, and was elected President of the Continental Congress. William Cost Johnson, the famous lawyer, politician, and duelist, was also a member of the Frederick bar.

In the olden days there were visiting lawyers, men distinguished for ability and eloquence, and regarded as patriarchs in the legal profession of Maryland, who met at various courts to measure weapons with each other. There were giants in those days in the country court-houses, and many of them who attended the first and later courts at Frederick became the country's pride in legal lore and political reputation. The first mention of the appearance of any attorney at the Frederick courts is that of William Cumming, in 1749, and the next name found in the court minutes is that of Daniel Dulany, in the same year. Of the latter it has been well said, "For many years before the downfall of the proprietary government he stood confessedly without a rival in this colony as a lawyer,

GOV. THOMAS JOHNSON.

a scholar, and an orator." Thomas Johnson, the first Governor of the State, who settled at Frederick after his first gubernatorial term expired, was in the front rank of Maryland lawyers, but retired from practice about 1795. John Thomson Mason, another eminent barrister, quit practicing about 1800, at which date the brilliant Arthur Shaaf removed to Annapolis, though often appearing afterwards in the Frederick courts. Roger Brooke Taney came to the Frederick bar in March, 1801, shortly after which his brother-in-law, the gifted poet and attorney, Francis Scott Key, left Frederick and settled in Georgetown, D. C. William Ross came from Lancaster, Pa., in 1805, married in Frederick, and began practicing at its bar. John Nelson, afterwards Attorney-General of the United States, and one of the ablest of American lawyers, was a contemporary of Mr. Taney and John Hanson Thomas, the latter the deep lawyer and politician, who died universally regretted in May, 1815. Joseph M. Palmer, whose name appears so often in the reports of cases in the Court of Appeals of Maryland, came in 1817 from the Connecticut to the Frederick bar. James Dixon came from Pennsylvania. He was of humble birth, little education, and had no friendly influences to help him forward in his profession. He studied law under Mr. Taney, who, when made attorney-general of the State in 1827, appointed Mr. Dixon as his deputy for Frederick. Mr. Dixon was one of the ablest criminal lawyers in the land, and in the height of his fame often ascribed his success to the kindness of Mr. Taney. The oldest living member of the bar from the date of admission is the venerable Judge Richard H. Marshall, admitted in 1822, and who for long years adorned the bench as associate judge.

We append biographical sketches of the more prominent members of the Frederick bar.

Thomas Johnson, first Governor of Maryland, was the grandson of Thomas Johnson, who came to this country about 1660 from Poole, near Yarmouth, England. The Johnsons were descended from Sir Thomas Johnson, of Great Yarmouth, who was of an old and distinguished family. The Johnsons had been members of Parliament and bailiffs or mayors of Yarmouth since 1585. Thomas Johnson, the immigrant, was a lawyer, and falling in love with Mary Baker, a chancery ward, eloped with her to America, thus committing a penal offense against the crown. They came over in a vessel commanded by Capt. Roger Baker, and settled at the mouth of Leonard's Creek, Calvert Co., Md. A keen desire to see his native land once more prompted him to brave the dangers of apprehension by the British authorities, and accordingly he embarked in a vessel for England. The ship was captured by the Spaniards, but after being detained some time, Johnson succeeded in making his escape to Canada in a destitute condition. From Canada he traveled on foot to his home in Calvert County, only to find on arriving there that his house had been burned by the Indians. Exhaustion caused by anxiety, fatigue, and privations had injured him so seriously that he did not long survive. His wife died soon afterwards, and they were buried side by side on the farm. They left an only son, Thomas Johnson, who married Dorcas Sedgwick, daughter of Joshua and Elizabeth Sedgwick, and had a number of children, of whom Thomas, James, Baker, and Joshua (whose daughter married John Quincy Adams) became distinguished men and ardent Revolutionary patriots. Thomas Johnson was born in Calvert County, Nov. 4, 1732, married Ann Jennings, of Annapolis, and died Oct. 26, 1819, aged eighty-seven, at the residence of his son-in-law, John Graham, in Frederick Town. Governor Johnson had eight children, viz:

1. Thomas Johnson, who was first married to Mary Hesselius, who died *sine prole*. His second wife was Elizabeth Russell, of Baltimore, by whom he had children, viz.: Mary Ann (who married Hugh W. Evans, of Baltimore), Elvira (never married), and Fanny (married to Col. John McPherson).

2. Ann Jennings, married to Maj. John Graham.

3. Rebecca, who died in infancy.

4. Elizabeth, who died young.

5. Rebecca, married to Thomas, son of James Johnson.

6. James, who died young.

7. Joshua, who married Miss Harriet Beall.

8. Dorcas, never married.

Thomas Johnson was to a certain extent a self-made man, as the only advantages of education obtained by him were of a plain and unpretentious character. He spent some time at a common school, after which he was sent to Annapolis to study law under the talented John Beale Bordley. At the commencement of the controversy with Great Britain he was still a young man, but had already risen to eminence in his profession. He was among the first to antagonize the British government, and soon became the trusted associate of Charles Carroll of Carrollton, Paca, Chase, Matthew Tilghman, and the other leading patriots of Maryland.

Mr. Johnson was sent as one of the delegates from Maryland to the first Continental Congress of 1774, and nominated George Washington as commander-in-chief of the army. The fact having been denied in a publication in the Baltimore *Clipper*, James Johnson, of Baltimore, made the following statement in substantiation of the claim:

"The credit of nominating Gen. Washington for commander-in-chief of the American armies has at various times been attributed to Mr. Jefferson and John Adams, but till recently I have never heard it claimed for Samuel Adams. The plain history of the nomination, which I have heard repeatedly from my uncle, Governor Johnson, is this: The eyes of all America were turned to Col. Washington, then a delegate from Virginia to Congress. The delegates from Virginia thought as a matter of delicacy that the nomination should be made by a delegate from another State. Richard Henry Lee, who introduced the resolution to declare the United States free and independent, came to Mr. Johnson, of Maryland, and told him the delegates from Virginia felt a delicacy in nominating their colleague for commander-in-chief, and wished the nomination to be made by a member from another State. Mr. Johnson agreed with him, and on the morning on which the nomination was made and unanimously confirmed, he met Mr. John Adams on the State House steps in Philadelphia, and told him that the Virginia delegation felt a delicacy in nominating Mr. Washington, and he wished him (Mr. Adams), the representative of a large State, the cradle of liberty, to nominate him. Mr. Adams made no reply, turned on his heel, and left him. As soon as the House was called to order, Mr. Johnson arose in his place and nominated Col. Washington commander-in-chief, which, as before stated, was confirmed. Mr. Johnson in all his conversation with me never claimed any peculiar merit in making the nomination, but one merit he always claimed, in preventing Charles Lee from being second in command. When he was nominated Mr. Johnson, in a speech of some length, portrayed his character as a disappointed foreigner, and not to be trusted. When he sat down the whole delegation from New York arose in a body, and said that every word the gentleman from Maryland had said was true. Gen. Ward, of Massachusetts, was appointed first major-general, and Charles Lee the second."[1]

---

[1] In this connection the following letters are appended:

[Extract of a letter from John Adams to Timothy Pickering, dated Aug. 6, 1822.]

"This was plain dealing, Mr. Pickering, and I must confess there appeared so much wisdom and good sense in it that it made a deep impression on my mind, and had an equal effect on all my colleagues. The conversation, and the facts and instances suggested in it, have given a color, character, and complexion to the United States from that day to this. Without it Mr. Washington would never have commanded our armies, nor would Mr. Johnson have ever been the nominator of Mr. Washington for general. Nor Mr. Jefferson the author of the Declaration of Independence, nor Richard Henry Lee the mover of it, nor Richard Chase the mover of dissolving forces in connection.

"If ever I had cause to repent of any of this policy, that repentance ever has been and will be unavailing."

[Letter from Judge Cranch to George Johnson, in answer to one written to him March 14, 1833.]

"DEAR SIR,—I received your letter of March last while the court was sitting, and in consequence of my absence from home since the court adjourned, I have not had time to look over my notes of the memoirs of Mr. Adams to send my authority for the statement that the nomination of Gen. Washington as commander-in-chief of the armies of the United Colonies in 1775 was made by the late Governor Johnson, of Maryland. I have looked over my notes, but find no reference to any authority for the fact.

Thus is the fact clearly established both by Mr. Johnson's repeated declarations to his nephew, James Johnson, and the testimony of Mr. Adams' biographer, that Governor Johnson did nominate Gen. Washington, with only this difference, that he did it of his own choice after Mr. Adams had silently declined his proposition, and not at his instigation. That Mr. Adams deserved great credit for his foresight in differing with his colleagues no one will deny, but if any merit is attached to the mere nomination, it belongs to Governor Johnson.

In a letter from "Civi Debutur" to the *National Intelligencer*, dated Sept. 17, 1833, we find the following:

"The deservedly high estimation in which Governor Johnson was held by Gen. Washington is well known by the writer, and it is well assured that no prominent public man of those 'heart-stirring times' enjoyed more of the confidence, esteem, and affection of the 'pater patriæ' than did Thomas Johnson, first Governor of Maryland.

"On public occasions, and after periods of separation from him, Gen. Washington has been often seen to single out this individual from the crowd, and, approaching him with open arms, press him to his bosom. This fact certainly shows the intimate relation that existed between them."

The same correspondent having the honor of Mr. Johnson's acquaintance, and being much in his company during the last three years of his life, received the following communication written with his own hand, though he was quite blind at the time:

. . . . "I inclose you one of Gen. Washington's letters to me, of which I have several others, in the like style of confidence and friendship. You are welcome to keep this, its length being convenient for your designed purpose, and the possession of the others fully answering any purpose with me.

"But you must consider this favor as laying you under the obligation of calling on me now and then and improving our acquaintance, which I consider and esteem happily commenced.

"With true regard,
"Your obedient servant,
"TH. JOHNSON.
"Oct. 5, 1805."

"I believe, however, that I took it from some publication published in Boston, made by authority of Mr. Adams himself. I was well satisfied of the truth of the statement when I made it.

"With great respect, I am, dear sir,
"Your obedient servant,
"WILLIAM CRANCH."

We add the following corroborative statement from the biography of Mr. Adams: "The eyes of all the New England States were turned upon Gen. Ward, then at the head of the army of Massachusetts. At a meeting of them, when that officer was proposed, Mr. Adams alone objected, and urged the appointment of George Washington, of Virginia. He was resisted, and left the meeting with the declaration that on the next day Washington should be nominated. He was accordingly nominated, at the instigation of Mr. Adams, by Governor Johnson, of Maryland, and chosen without an opposing vote."—*Encyclopædia Americana*, vol. i. p. 48.

Copy of the letter inclosed in the above communication, written in Gen. Washington's own hand:

"PHILADELPHIA, July 14, 1791.

"DEAR SIR,—Without preface or apology for propounding the following question to you at this time, permit me to ask you with frankness, and in the fulness of my friendship, whether you will accept an appointment in the Supreme Judiciary of the United States?

"Mr. Rutledge's resignation has occasioned a vacancy therein, which I should be glad to see filled by you.

"Your answer to this question by the post (which is the most certain mode of conveying letters), as soon as you can make it convenient, will very much oblige, dear sir,

"Your most obedient
"And affectionate h'b'le serv't,
"GEO. WASHINGTON.
"The Hon. THOS. JOHNSON."

While some doubts existed about the ratification of the Federal Constitution, Washington, who was instrumental in its formation and very anxious for its success, wrote the following letter:

"MOUNT VERNON, April 20, 1788.

"DEAR SIR,—As well from report as from the ideas expressed in your letter to me in December last, I am led to conclude that you are disposed (circumstanced as our public affairs are at present) to ratify the Constitution which has been submitted by the General Convention to the people, and under this impression I take the liberty of expressing a *single* sentiment on the occasion. It is, that an adjournment (if attempted) of your convention to a later period than the decision of the question in this State will be tantamount to the rejection of the Constitution. I have good grounds for this opinion, and am told it is the blow which the leading characters of the opposition in the two States have aimed against it, if it shall be found that a direct attack is not likely to succeed in yours. If this be true, it cannot be too much deprecated and guarded against. The postponement in New Hampshire, although made without any reference to the convention of this State, and altogether free from the local circumstances of its own, is ascribed by the opposition here to complaisance towards Virginia, and great use is made of it. An event similar to this in Maryland would have the worst tendency imaginable, for indecision there would have considerable influence upon South Carolina, the only other State which is to precede Virginia, and submits the question almost wholly to the determination of the latter. The pride of the State is already touched upon this string, and it will be strained much higher if there is an opening for it. The sentiments of Kentucky are not yet known here. Independent of these, the parties with us, from the known or presumed opinion of the members, are pretty equally balanced. The one in favor of the Constitution preponderates at present, but a small matter cast into the opposite scale may make it heaviest.

"If in suggesting this matter I have exceeded the proper limit, my motive must excuse me. I have but one public wish remaining. It is that in peace and retirement I may see this country rescued from the danger which is pending, and arise to respectability, maugre the intrigues of its public and private enemies.

"With very great esteem and regard,
"I am, dear sir,
"Your most obedient humble servant,
"GO. WASHINGTON.
"To THOMAS JOHNSON, ESQ."

Mr. Johnson was re-elected to Congress at every successive election until Feb. 13, 1777, when he was chosen first Governor of Maryland. Besides representing his constituency in Congress, he filled other important public trusts. In December, 1774, he was appointed by the Convention of Deputies from the different counties one of the Committee of Correspondence for the province, and was chosen by the Convention of 1775 as one of the Council of Safety for Maryland. In December of that year he was appointed with others as a committee to "devise the best ways and means to promote the manufacture of saltpetre." On the 6th of January following he was elected by the convention a brigadier-general, and took command of the famous "Flying Camp." He did not serve very long, however, for on the 4th of July, 1776, the convention passed a resolution withdrawing his commission, on the ground that his services in Congress could not be spared, and that his place could be supplied "with less inconvenience in the military than in the civil department." His presence was also desired in the State Convention, and was deemed of so much importance that Col. Richardson, a delegate from Caroline, resigned his seat, conveyed to him a farm in Caroline County, and had Gen. Johnson elected in his place. With William Paca, George Plater, and James Holliday, he was of that committee which invited Governor Eden to vacate his seat and leave the province. In June, 1776, he was at Annapolis urging the convention to authorize the Maryland delegates to Congress to unite with the other members in declaring the United Colonies free and independent States. He voted in Congress for the Declaration of Independence, but did not sign that instrument owing to his absence at the bedside of a sick member of his family. On the 13th of February, 1777, he was elected by the Legislature of Maryland first Governor of the State, receiving forty out of fifty-two votes. He was inaugurated on the 21st of March at the State-House in Annapolis. There was a procession from the "Assembly House" in the following order: The high-sheriff, president of the Senate, senators, Governor, Council, sergeant-at-arms, bearing the mace, Speaker of the House of Delegates, delegates, mayor of the city, and recorder, aldermen, Common Council, military officers, visiting strangers, citizens. "Silence being commanded, the high-sheriff then proclaimed that Thomas Johnson, Jr., was the elected Governor of the State of Maryland. Three volleys were then fired by the soldiery, who were paraded in front of the State-House, followed by a salute of thirteen cannon,—one for each of the United States,—after which the procession returned, the

Governor and his Council taking positions immediately after the high-sheriff, the rest of the cortege being in the same order as before. All then repaired to the Coffee-House, where an entertainment was provided" and toasts were drunk. The whole concluded with a brilliant ball and illumination in the evening. Governor Johnson fulfilled the duties of his office during a trying period with remarkable fidelity and success, and retired with the love and esteem of the people. He removed from Annapolis to Frederick Town (he had several brothers living in the county), and was elected to represent Frederick County in the House of Delegates. When Mr. Johnson was eligible, once more he was re-elected Governor, but declined the office. In the State Convention which adopted the Constitution of the United States, he was pitted against Martin, the Chases, Mercer, and other opponents of the Constitution, and with his associates succeeded in procuring its indorsement. On the death of Mr. Harrison, chief judge of the General Court of Maryland, Mr. Johnson was chosen to succeed him, and was appointed one of the associate justices of the United States Supreme Court by Washington in 1791, in place of John Rutledge. He retained this position until 1793, when ill health compelled him to resign. Subsequently Gen. Washington asked him to accept the Secretaryship of State, but he declined. He consented, however, to serve with Dr. Stuart and Daniel Carroll as one of the commissioners for laying off the city of Washington, and for selecting the sites of the Capitol, President's house, and other public buildings.

Mr. Johnson's was a singularly vigorous and well-balanced mind, and his character exhibited the rare combination of ardent impulses with strong good sense and remarkable power of self-control. His honesty inspired universal respect and confidence, and his counsel was always sought by the people and by his associates as being the wisest and safest that could be obtained. Upon his retirement from public life he returned to Frederick, and resided until his death with his daughter, the wife of the accomplished and wealthy John Graham. In 1800 he performed the last public act of his life, in pronouncing a eulogium upon his beloved friend and chieftain, Washington, on the occasion of a large funeral procession in his honor in the old German Reformed church of Frederick. Mr. Johnson was about the middle stature, slender in person, with keen, penetrating eyes, and a highly intellectual countenance. He was irascible in temper, and rather unpopular in manners, but had a warm, generous heart, and was a sincere friend and a kind husband and father. He was very temperate in his habits, and thus preserved a constitution naturally weak to extreme old age. Mr. Johnson was a lawyer of great learning and ability, and had a large and very lucrative practice. "It is said," says Col. George A. Hanson, in a biographical sketch of Mr. Johnson, "that when John Adams was asked why so many Southern men occupied leading positions and possessed great influence during the struggle for independence, he replied that 'if it had not been for such men as Richard Henry Lee, Thomas Jefferson, Samuel Chase, and Thomas Johnson there never would have been any revolution.'" Although Governor Johnson was a native of Calvert County, he was a resident of Frederick County for more than forty years, and was actively engaged with his brothers, James, Baker, and Roger Johnson, in the operation of iron-furnaces on the Bush and Catoctin Creeks. Mr. Johnson's remains, attended by his family, his numerous relatives, the court and bar of the county, the orphans' court, the mayor, aldermen, and common councilmen of the city, the clergy, physicians, and a very numerous assemblage of citizens from all parts of the country, were interred in the family vault in the Episcopal burial-ground at Frederick.

Richard Potts was born in July, 1753, in Upper Marlborough, Prince George's Co., Md. He was the seventh child of William Potts (born 1718, died 1761), who emigrated from Barbadoes to the colony of Maryland about the year 1740, and after his settlement married Sarah, daughter of Philip Lee. The father returned with his family in 1757 to Barbadoes, where he died in 1761. Richard Potts, not long after his father's death, returned to Maryland and resided in Annapolis for some years. He must have received in that city the education required in those days prior to entrance upon the study of a learned profession. He read law, probably with Judge Samuel Chase, in Annapolis, and then removed to Frederick, which place he made his home during the remainder of his life. The exact date of his removal cannot now be ascertained, but the oldest letter directed to him at that place in the possession of his family is dated Dec. 27, 1775.

At an early age he was made, March 5, 1776, clerk to the Committee of Observation for Frederick County. A contemporary authority says, "When the Maryland militia, in the gloomy and ill-boding winter of '77, marched for the purpose of reinforcing Gen. Washington, Mr. Potts, who never held back in times of danger, served in the expedition as aide to the illustrious patriot, Thomas Johnson, who commanded the Virginia detachment in the Flying Camp."

After his return he was appointed, May 20, 1777, clerk of the Frederick County Court. This office he held until the end of 1778, when he resigned and commenced the practice of law in Frederick, Montgomery, and Washington Counties, whereby he acquired considerable reputation and a handsome property. During the sessions of the Legislature in 1779 and 1780 he served as a member of the Maryland House of Delegates, and afterwards during the sessions of 1787 and 1788.

He served in 1781 as a delegate from the State of Maryland in the Continental Congress, taking his seat on the 12th of June.

On the 1st of November, 1784, he was appointed by Hon. Luther Martin attorney-general of the State, to act as State's attorney for the counties of Frederick, Montgomery, and Washington. On the 3d of December, 1787, he was chosen as a State senator in place of Thomas Stone, but, declining the position, Thomas Johnson, of Frederick County, was selected in his stead, May 24, 1788. In 1788 he was elected a member of the State Convention, which met on April 21, 1788, in Annapolis, to consider the proposed Federal Constitution, to which it gave its assent, April 28, 1788. He was commissioned attorney of the United States in and for the Maryland District by President Washington, in a commission still in the family, dated New York, Sept. 26, 1789; and on the 8th of January, 1791, he was appointed chief judge of the Fifth Judicial District, composed of the counties of Frederick, Montgomery, and Washington, although not commissioned until Jan. 17, 1791.[1] On his resignation of this office afterwards, William Craik was appointed in his place, Jan. 16, 1793.

On the 6th of December, 1792, he was elected United States senator to take the place of Charles Carroll of Carrollton, but did not take his seat in the Senate until Jan. 10, 1793. This office he held until October, 1796, when he resigned, and John Eager Howard was chosen as his successor, and qualified Nov. 30, 1796. Judge Potts was chosen November, 1792, one of the electors for the State of Maryland at the election of Gen. Washington for the second term to the Presidency of the United States.

A letter is still extant from Edward Randolph, dated July 24, 1794, to Mr. Potts, stating that the President had resolved to appoint him as one of the commissioners for the Federal City, with a salary of sixteen hundred dollars per year. This appointment he declined.

On the resignation of Hon. William Craik as chief judge of the Fifth Judicial District, he was appointed, Oct. 15, 1796, the second time to that office, and was named a justice of the Court of Appeals of the State, Oct. 10, 1801, when William Craik was reappointed to fill his position as chief judge. This position in the Court of Appeals he held until the revision of the judiciary in 1804. In testimony of its appreciation of his legal attainments and acknowledged professional abilities, he received from Princeton College the honorary degree of LL.D. in 1805.

Mr. Potts married, on April 15, 1779, Elizabeth Hughes, of Hagerstown, Md., sister of Capt. James Hughes, who bandaged André's eyes. They had nine children. His second wife was Eleanor Murdoch, of Frederick (married Dec. 19, 1799), by whom he had four children.

He died Nov. 26, 1808, in the fifty-sixth year of his age, and was interred in the old graveyard belonging to All-Saints' Parish. Subsequently his remains were removed to Mount Olivet Cemetery, Frederick, where they now rest along with those of his two wives and many of his kindred.

One of his sons, Richard Potts (born 1786, died 1865), was a prominent member of the Frederick County bar, and was one of the leading residents of his native city. He served as Senator from Frederick County in the State Senate from 1838 to 1844. There are now only two children of Judge Potts living, a son and a daughter, both being citizens of Frederick.

A contemporary obituary notice, printed in the Frederick Town *Herald*, Dec. 3, 1808, said to have been written by the distinguished John Hanson Thomas, thus speaks of Judge Richard Potts:

---

[1] A copy of this commission is herewith given. The seal employed is the same as that furnished to the colony in 1648, and which has been ordered by a recent resolution of the General Assembly to be hereafter employed as the Great Seal of the State.

"*The State of Maryland to Richard Potts, of Frederick County, Esq., Greeting:*

"Be it known that, reposing great trust and confidence in your integrity and sound Judgment in the Law, you are appointed and assigned Chief Justice of the County Courts of the Fifth District, as described by the Act entitled 'An act for the better administration of Justice in the several counties of this State,' to do equal Right and Justice, according to Law, in every case in which you shall act as Chief Justice of the said District, freely without sale, fully without denial, and speedily without delay; to execute the same office of Chief Justice justly, honestly, and faithfully, according to Law; and you are to hold and exercise the said office of Chief Justice during your good behavior in said office.

"Given under the seal of the State of Maryland this seventh day of January, in the year of our Lord one thousand seven hundred and ninety-one.

"J. E. HOWARD.

"Witness the Honorable ALEXANDER CONTEE HANSON, Esquire, Chancellor.

"A. C. HANSON, *Chanr.*"

"It is not necessary to speak of the many proofs of his genius given at the bar by Mr. Potts. The high and unlimited confidence reposed in him, the attention and respect with which his opinions on legal subjects were listened to, to the latest hour of his life, gave the strongest assurance of his integrity and knowledge. . . . He was a member of the State Convention that ratified the present Constitution of the United States, and in supporting that measure gave proofs of talents and eloquence that have not often been excelled. . . . In his speeches at the bar and in the council, he disdained the trammels of form, and never courted the graces of oratory. His was the eloquence of reason urged home to the hearers by the warmth and animation of an honest heart. Whatever was necessary to place the subject in the clearest point of view he was very sure to say, and he never attempted or wished to say more. Had Mr. Potts been ambitious, his career of life would unquestionably have been still more splendid. But he accepted his many appointments in the councils of the nation in trying times from a sense of duty, and eagerly returned to the blessings of quiet and domestic life, and no man in the various relations of private life discharged his duties more tenderly and affectionately than Mr. Potts. It was in the bosom of an affectionate family, in the freedom of intimate social intercourse, when the business and cares of the world were thrown aside, that Mr. Potts exhibited those excellent qualities that most particularly endeared him to his family and friends. Long, very long, will his loss be felt. The many helpless and indigent whom he has watched over and aided with his labor and his purse will look in vain for a heart equally benevolent, and a hand equally capable and ready. He died as he had lived, a firm and faithful believer in the Christian religion. He was for some days perfectly sensible that his dissolution was near, but he met its approach with characteristic firmness. He had so lived that he feared not to die. And in the fifty-sixth year of his age, without a struggle, without a groan, in full possession of his manly understanding, he left this vain and troublesome world, to repose, we trust, forever in the bosom of his Saviour and his God."

Roger Brooke Taney. This distinguished jurist and statesman was born March 17, 1777, in Calvert County, Md. His father, Michael Taney, owned a good landed estate and a number of slaves. His plantation was situated on the banks of the Patuxent River, about twenty miles from its mouth, where the river is more than two miles wide and navigable for vessels of the largest size.

ROGER BROOKE TANEY.

The British fleet anchored opposite the house during the war of 1812, in the expedition against Washington City. Michael Taney's paternal forefathers were among the early emigrants to Maryland, and had owned and lived upon this beautiful estate for many generations before he was born. There are no records showing the precise time of their arrival or the country from which they came. They were devoted and zealous Roman Catholics. Michael Taney was sent to the English Jesuits' College at St. Omer's, and removed with it to Bruges, when it was expelled from France. He finished his education and returned home some years before the commencement of the American Revolution, and his father being dead, he took possession of his estate and married Monica Brooke about 1770. She was the daughter of Roger Brooke, who owned a large landed estate on Battle Creek, directly opposite the Taney plantation. Roger Brooke was descended from Robert Brooke, born at London, England, 3d June, 1602. Robert Brooke left England and arrived in Maryland the 29th day of June, 1650, in the forty-eighth year of his age, with his wife and ten children. He was the first settler on the Patuxent, and located himself about twenty miles up the river, at Delabrooke, and had one son, born there in 1651, called Basil, who died the same day. In 1652 he removed to Brooke Place, "being right against Delabrooke," and on the 28th of November, 1655, two children, Eliza and Henry, twins, were born. Robert Brooke died on the 20th day of July following, and was buried at Brooke Place Manor. His wife, Mary Brooke, died on the 29th of November, 1663.

Soon after his arrival Robert Brooke was appointed by Lord Baltimore commander of Charles County, and was chosen by the commissioners appointed by Cromwell for the reducing of the plantations Governor of Maryland.

Roger Brooke Taney was the third child and second son of a family of four sons and three daughters. When eight years old he went with his elder brother and sister three miles to a school kept in a log cabin by an ignorant old man. Afterwards with his elder brother he attended the grammar-school of the county, ten miles distant, kept by a Scotchman named Hunter, but in the course of three months this teacher's mind became disordered and he was found drowned in the Patuxent River. His father then employed a family tutor, an educated Irishman, who died before his year was out with consumption. The second tutor was an American, who remained a year, when happily David English, a graduate of Princeton and a thorough teacher, was secured, under whom young Taney was fitted for college. He entered Dickinson College, Carlisle, Pa., when little more than fifteen years of age. He graduated in the fall of 1795, and received the highest honors of that institution, being chosen to deliver the valedictory. In the spring of 1796 he went to Annapolis, to read law in the office of Jeremiah Townley Chase, then one of the judges of the General Court of Maryland.

At that time Annapolis was considered as the place

of all others in the State where a man should study law if he expected to attain eminence in his profession. While reading law young Taney had for a brother student William Carmichael, of Queen Anne County, with whom he roomed for a year. At Annapolis he saw and heard those great legal lights, Luther Martin, Philip Barton Key, John Thomson Mason, John Johnson, Arthur Shaaf, and James Winchester,—Pinkney being abroad, a commissioner under the British treaty. In the spring of 1799, Mr. Taney was admitted to the bar. His first case was in the Mayor's Court of Annapolis, presided over by Gabriel Duvall, then a judge of the General Court, in defending a man indicted for an assault and battery. In this case he secured a verdict of acquittal for his client. He then returned to his home in Calvert County and began the practice of his profession, and in the fall of 1799 was elected by the Federalist party, to which he and his family were attached, a delegate to the General Assembly. He took part in the legislative discussions, and the experience gained proved of great advantage to him in his future life. In 1800 he was a candidate for re-election, but the State and his county going largely against the Federalists, he suffered defeat with the others on his ticket. He then determined to make Frederick his home, from the fact that its bar was a young one, most of its members being but a few years older than himself. Besides, he had at Annapolis formed friendships with some young men near his own age who resided in Frederick, and he felt that he should not be lonely there or destitute of friends. Another inducement in selecting Frederick as his permanent location was, that next to Annapolis and Baltimore, it was with a view to profit the best point of practice in the State. The two lawyers who had been for years at the head of the profession in Frederick were John Thomson Mason and Arthur Shaaf, and the former had recently retired from practice, and the latter had removed to Annapolis. In March, 1801, Mr. Taney took up his residence in Frederick. Soon afterwards he appeared in court and made his first speech, a volunteer effort of great ability, Mr. Shaaf, who still practiced there, having invited him to take part in one of his cases in order to give him an opportunity of appearing before the public. From his first appearance at Frederick Mr. Taney was a diligent student. Law was his chief study, but he devoted much time to history and general literature. In 1803 he became a candidate on the Federal ticket for the House of Delegates. He canvassed the county and made a deep impression by his speeches, but at this early period in Mr. Jefferson's administration the county was very decidedly Republican, and he was defeated. Though it was only in the fifth year of his residence in Frederick, Mr. Taney had already acquired such a position at the bar, and his practice was so lucrative, that he was about to be married. Francis Scott Key, afterwards the author of the "Star-Spangled Banner," had been a fellow-student and friend at Annapolis. Mr. Key and a sister were the only children of their parents. Mr. Taney had met Miss Key in Annapolis, and her beauty and bright mind, united with womanly graces of the most attractive character, had won his heart. Mr. Key was practicing law in Frederick when Mr. Taney went there, but afterwards moved to Georgetown, D. C. John Ross Key, the father of Miss Key, was a lieutenant in the First Artillery, which went to Boston from Maryland at the outbreak of the Revolutionary war, and owned a large estate in Frederick County, where Miss Key was born and was now living with her parents. The mansion was of brick, and consisted of a spacious structure with wings and long porches. It was situated in the midst of a large lawn, shaded by trees, with an extensive terraced garden adorned with shrubbery and flowers. Near by flowed Pipe Creek through a dense woods. A copious spring, where young people loved to retire and sit under the sheltering oaks in summer, was at the foot of the hill, and a meadow of waving grass spread out towards the Catoctin Mountain, which could be seen at sunset curtained in clouds of crimson and gold. It was at this happy home that Mr. Taney was married, on the 7th of January, 1806, to Anne Phebe Charlton Key. For years afterwards Mr. Taney and Mr. Key and their families met annually at this parental home to enjoy the pleasures of a family reunion. At evening, when the labors of the farm were over, the negroes were summoned to prayers with the family, which were usually conducted by Francis Scott Key when he was there, and by his mother when he was away. After prayers, almost every night, as was common on plantations in Maryland, music and dancing might be heard at the quarters of the negroes. No man was ever more happily married than Mr. Taney, and his home-life shed a benign influence over his studious and contemplative pursuits, and nurtured that bland suavity of manner which so distinguished him.

Mr. Taney was for years a director in the Frederick County Bank, and hardly ever missed a meeting of the board of directors. He was also for twenty years a visitor of the Frederick Academy, a State institution of great note, and for a long time was president of the Board of Visitors (trustees). Although, during his life in Frederick, Mr. Taney was strict in his religious observances, he was nevertheless fond of social relaxations. It was common for gentlemen to dine together on the Fourth of July under the shade of the beech-trees on the banks of the Monocacy River, which flowed between wooded banks two miles from Frederick. As Mr. Taney was, like all Southern Marylanders, a good horseman, he took much pleasure in horseback excursions when professional duties required him to go into the country to try cases before juries upon view. In these excursions, the picturesque aspects of the Catoctin Mountain had become so familiar to him that when in after-years he would speak of them, his descriptions were so accurate that they seemed as if frescoed on his memory. In the summer he would sometimes retire, with his family, a few miles from Frederick to Arcadia, the country-seat of the eminent lawyer, Arthur Shaaf, a bachelor, and a cousin of Mrs. Taney, to recruit his exhausted energies and refresh his overtasked mind. In his love of nature Mrs. Taney participated with the romantic ardor of a woman, who, like her brother, was inspired by its beauties with "thoughts that voluntary move harmonious members." In 1811, Gen. Wilkinson, then commander-in-chief of the United States army, was tried on a series of charges before a military court convened at Frederick. He was a Marylander by birth, and knew the professional reputation of Mr. Taney, whom he selected, with John Hanson Thomas, as his counsel. Gen. Wilkinson labored under much public odium. He was suspected of having been an accomplice of Aaron Burr in his supposed treasonable enterprise, and in order to cover his supposed guilt to have turned State's evidence against Burr upon his trial at Richmond. So bitter was the feeling against him that his counsel shared in his unpopularity. Mr. Taney, however, did not shrink from the task, but labored for several months with singular zeal and ability against Walter Jones, of Washington City, the judge-advocate, the subtlest and most casuistic of lawyers, and Gen. Wilkinson was acquitted and his sword returned to him. Both Mr. Taney and Mr. Thomas had shared the general suspicion of Wilkinson's treachery to Burr, and, because of their conviction of the injustice done him in entertaining this opinion, refused to receive a fee for their professional services, communicating the fact to him, and begging him to acquiesce in their course, as it would gratify their feelings.

Mr. Taney was of the Federal party, and shared in the opposition to a declaration of war in 1812, but as soon as war was declared he gave his support to the government, and so did most of the Federalists in Maryland. Mr. Taney, and the Federalists in Frederick County who followed his lead in supporting the government, were nicknamed by the other wing of his party "Coodies," and he, because of his great influence, was called King Coody. John Hanson Thomas, an able lawyer of the Frederick bar, was the leader of the other wing of the Federal party. Such was the bitterness of feeling between the two wings, and such the estrangement between Mr. Thomas and Mr. Taney, that it was not until Mr. Thomas was on his death-bed, some three years subsequently, that he forgave him for his course. He then sent for Mr. Taney, who hastened to his bedside, and gave him a greeting so generous and so tender that their reconciliation was consecrated by mutual tears. Mr. Thomas died in May, 1815, and few followed him to the grave in deeper sorrow, or with more sincere admiration for his high qualities, than Mr. Taney. While the division in the Federal party produced by the war was at its height Mr. Taney was nominated for Congress, and, notwithstanding the great strength of the Republican party in the congressional district, he was defeated by only three hundred majority. In 1816 he was elected to the State Senate. That period was marked by some of the most important legislation in regard to the courts of law, of equity, and of the Orphans' Courts. Many of the statutes were drawn by him, and all the others received his close attention. His defense of Rev. Jacob Gruber in the Frederick court in 1819, indicted for inciting slaves to insurrection, attracted national attention, and is elsewhere detailed at length. Such was Mr. Taney's reputation at this period that he argued appeals from every county on the Western Shore of Maryland, as may be seen in the reports of cases. As Mr. Martin and Mr. Pinkney—by the retirement of the former and death of the latter—had left a favorable opening at the Baltimore bar, the high reputation of Mr. Taney at once suggested that he might now place himself at the head of the leading bar in the State. With all his love of Frederick, therefore, he could not resist the demands of duty and professional ambition, and he decided to remove to Baltimore. His mother, whom he loved with singular devotion, had left her home in Calvert County during the war of 1812, and had taken refuge from the British under her son's roof, and continued to live with him until her death in 1814. Before his departure from Frederick Mr. Taney made an arrangement with a particular friend, William Murdoch Beall, a much younger man than himself, for his own burial by the side of his mother, no matter when and where his death should occur.

In the little Catholic chapel Mr. Taney for many years could be seen every morning, in sunshine and in rain, during his residence in Frederick, at his religious devotions. He moved to Baltimore in 1823, and at once became the leading and most distinguished lawyer at its bar. Mr. William Wirt, who was several years older than Mr. Taney, did not take up his residence in Baltimore until 1829. Although Mr. Taney had been born and educated a Federalist, he warmly supported the war of 1812, and considered the conduct of the Federal party generally,—especially that of the Eastern Federalists,—in opposing that war by factious methods, as greatly reprehensible. He further considered that the war disrupted that party, and that its dissolution was brought about by its own unpatriotic course. Therefore, in the Presidential campaign of 1824, he appeared as a stanch supporter of the election of Gen. Jackson. He was now employed in most of the important cases in the Court of Appeals of Maryland, embracing every variety of legal controversy. In 1827, upon the unanimous recommendation of the Baltimore bar, Mr. Taney was appointed attorney-general of the State. As attorney-general he had the selection of deputy attorneys in the several judicial districts, and in the one embracing Frederick he appointed James Dixon, who years before had read law in his office at Frederick.

On June 21, 1831, President Jackson appointed Mr. Taney to be Attorney-General of the United States, in place of Mr. Berrien, who had resigned. Mr. Taney accepted this position in the cabinet, and became Gen. Jackson's most intimate and confidential friend.

On Sept. 23, 1833, Gen. Jackson peremptorily removed from office his Secretary of the Treasury, William J. Duane, for refusing to remove the deposits of the government from the United States Bank, and on the same day appointed to this great financial position Mr. Taney, who assumed the position on September 24th, and on the 26th gave the order for the removal of the deposits, to take effect October 1st. Under the pretense that the loss of the deposits compelled it, the bank called in its loans and discounts to such an extent as to make the whole country groan under the pressure of the most fearful financial embarrassment, —producing hard times and ruin everywhere. History records the fact that this action of Gen. Jackson and Mr. Taney was sustained by the people. Mr. Taney had been appointed to the Treasury during the recess of Congress, and when it assembled, the President, near the close of its session, on June 23, 1834, sent to the Senate Mr. Taney's nomination as Secretary of the Treasury for confirmation. Next day he was rejected, and it was the first time in the history of our government that a cabinet minister had been rejected by the Senate. That body, however, with its Whig majority and its personal animosity towards the President, refused to confirm Mr. Taney, who the next day resigned his commission and returned to the Baltimore bar. He was the recipient in Baltimore and many other cities of public dinners and large demonstrations of the people, who sustained the course taken by him and President Jackson. But the grandest demonstration indorsing his official action took place at Frederick on August 6th, where he was received by Hon. Francis Thomas, in behalf of the thousands assembled, and tendered a public dinner by his old neighbors and friends, among whom for twenty-two years he had been daily associated in the business affairs of life. After Mr. Taney closed his speech in reply to the reception address of Mr. Thomas, he repaired with the committee to the court-house yard, where under the trees seventeen tables were spread with a sumptuous feast, of which many hundreds of citizens and guests partook. Here, after the toasts were over, Mr. Taney made an elaborate speech, reviewing with the most masterly exposition all the topics involved in the politics of that trying time. He is said to have considered this compliment, tendered before the old court-house, whose bar he had so long adorned, as one of the most gratifying events of his life. Personal friendship entered largely into the compliment, giving to its political signification the higher tribute to his character as a man. In January, 1835, Gabriel Duvall, of Maryland, one of the Associate Justices of the Supreme Court of the United States, and a special friend of Mr. Taney, resigned the commission given him as judge by President Madison in 1811.

Judge Duvall, though strongly opposed to Gen. Jackson and his policy, resigned when he saw there was a likelihood of Mr. Taney being appointed his successor, because, although the latter differed with him politically, he fully appreciated his great legal attainments and purity of character, and held them in the highest esteem. On his resignation on account of his advanced age, Gen. Jackson immediately nominated Mr. Taney to supply the vacancy. The great Chief Justice Marshall was still presiding over the Supreme Court. He had a peculiar dislike to Gen. Jackson and his policy. But so high was his estimate of Mr. Taney, that he privately endeavored to secure the confirmation of his appointment. With that view he wrote the following letter to Benjamin Watkins Leigh, a senator from Virginia, who was opposed to Gen. Jackson's administration:

"MY DEAR SIR,—If you have not made up your mind on the nomination of Mr. Taney, I have received some information in his favor which I would wish to communicate.
"Yours, J. MARSHALL.
"MR. LEIGH."

At the last moment of the session the nomination of Mr. Taney was brought up in the Whig Senate so violently opposed to Gen. Jackson and his policy, and was indefinitely postponed, which was equivalent to a rejection. Chief Justice Marshall died in the summer of 1835. On the succeeding 28th of December President Jackson nominated Mr. Taney to fill his place in the Supreme Court. Since his nomination as associate judge the political complexion of the Senate had changed, but yet his nomination was strongly antagonized by the Whigs, few of whom were aware that Chief Justice Marshall had endeavored to help Mr. Taney to a seat by his side as an associate justice. On March 15, 1836, his nomination was confirmed by a majority of fourteen votes. His opinions from April term, 1836, to April term, 1861, as a judge at the Circuit Courts, were reported by his son-in-law, the late James Mason Campbell, of the Baltimore bar. At the beginning of a Circuit term in Maryland, when the list of jurors was called, he attended to every name, and if a juror from Frederick County, where he had lived so long, was called, he always asked the marshal to tell the juror to come to him after adjournment. He generally found him to be the son or relative of some one of his old professional acquaintances and friends, and made the kindest inquiries concerning his family. Chief Justice Taney had the great blessing of a wife of rare loveliness of person and heart, who was to him "the gust of joy and the balm of woe." On the forty-sixth anniversary of their marriage he wrote her from Washington City a letter of pathetic tenderness, pledging to her again a love as true and sincere as that offered on their wedding-day. A great affliction soon followed which made Judge Taney peculiarly a man of sorrows. He had repaired, as was his custom, to Old Point Comfort with his family in the summer of 1855. The yellow fever suddenly made its appearance, and on September 29th carried off Mrs. Taney, and the next day took away the youngest child, Alice, a lovely girl.

On the 6th of March, 1857, the famous Dred Scott decision was made by the Supreme Court, wherein Judge Taney delivered the opinion, indorsed by himself and five of the associate judges, with dissenting opinions by Justices McLean and Curtis. That decision was that it was not competent for the Congress of the United States, directly or indirectly, to exclude slavery from the Territories of the Union. The opinion of Judge Taney, and a supplement which he afterwards prepared, because of the clamor against him, to justify his opinion before the publicists of the world, and before the judgment of future ages, constitute one of the most comprehensive and best-reasoned politico-judicial opinions ever pronounced by any tribunal. No such question could have arisen before any other judicature in the world, and it sprung out of our peculiar polity and form of government. Just previous to the death of Judge Taney a new epoch began in the political history of the land. Civil war ensued, and darkness spread over the country, torn by strife and discord. In the John Merryman and other habeas corpus cases Judge Taney nobly illustrated and maintained the peculiar functions of his court, and the principles and letter of the Constitution, amidst the clang of arms and the tread of soldiery. His body-servant, Madison, was drafted, and, although he was subject to heart disease and might have been excused, Judge Taney bought for him a substitute for one hundred dollars, while the government, in violation of law, was withholding three per cent. of his judicial salary. In his professional life Judge Taney was compelled to walk over the hottest plowshares that could be put beneath the feet of a public man by his countrymen, but he passed through the ordeal unscathed, though doubtless wounded to the quick. He was a man of iron will, determined purpose, undaunted courage, and of heroic type of character, yet he possessed the most delicate qualities of kindness and courtesy, as his private and public life bore witness, in his intercourse with all. His letters to his wife, running through a period of nearly fifty years, show the inner life of a man possessed of Spartan courage united with extraordinary mildness and simplicity of temperament. He was a devout Catholic, his wife a devout Protestant, but so sure was each that the other was a Christian that no doubt ever suggested itself to either that they would meet in heaven. He died Oct. 12, 1864, in the full possession of his intellectual faculties, and to the last retained the keenest interest in public affairs. In the summer of 1870, Judge Richard H. Marshall, of Frederick City, and Gen. James H. Coale, of Liberty, both distinguished members of the Frederick bar, caused a marble slab to be erected over the grave of Judge Taney, which occupies a secluded spot in the old Catholic graveyard immediately in the rear of the Novitiate, between East Second and Third Streets, of Frederick City. The slab is of Italian marble, highly polished, about three and a half feet in width and six in length, set in brownstone. It is neat and unpretentious, and bears the following inscription:

"I. H. S.
"ROGER BROOKE TANEY,
"Fifth Chief Justice of the United States of America, born in Calvert County, MD., March 17th 1777, died in the city of Washington, October 12th 1864, aged 87 years, 6 months and 25

FRANCIS S. KEY.

days. He was a profound and able lawyer, an upright and fearless Judge, a pious and exemplary Christian. At his own request he was buried in this secluded spot near the grave of his mother.

"May he rest in peace."

Philip Barton Key. This distinguished statesman, the brother of John Ross Key, of Frederick County, was born in Cecil County, Md., in 1761. He was liberally educated, and entered the English army, in which he held a commission as captain. When the Revolutionary war broke out he refused to bear arms against the colonies, and was given a small command at Pensacola, Fla. He afterwards studied law, and on the conclusion of peace with Great Britain returned to Maryland, and settled in Annapolis, where he soon took high rank as a lawyer. He represented Annapolis in the State Legislature, and was a representative in Congress from Maryland from 1807 to 1813. He died at Georgetown, D. C., July 28, 1815. The following obituary of Mr. Key appeared in the *Federal Gazette* at the time of his death :

"Seldom has a more general and unaffected sorrow pervaded a community than has shown itself on the occasion of this mournful bereavement. The kind affability, active humanity, and warm friendship, so conspicuous in his deportment, had bound the hearts of all to him, and his memory will be consecrated no less by those amiable traits than by the splendor of his uncommon intellectual acquirements and capacity.

"The fame of his character as an advocate and senator is spread everywhere, but the affection of his neighbors constitute the only honorable and unerring monument of the value of the man and the Christian. Mr. Key was a native of Cecil County, Md. He was grounded in the knowledge of the law under the direction of Judge Duvall, now of the Supreme Court of the United States, who entertained for him the highest regard through life. Such were the fruits of those studies and the efficacy of his own genius that he rose to the summit of his profession, through the labors of which he secured a fortune to his family. In eloquence his high powers were attested by the general applause of his hearers and the success of his forensic contentions. His legal attainments were profound and comprehensive. Like Sir William Blackstone, in his younger years he cultivated a talent for poetry, which was displaced by the austere occupation to which his profession afterwards devoted him. We have seen a handsome specimen of his proficiency in that elegant art. He served many years as a member of the Legislature of Maryland, and lately a member of Congress. In these capacities he acted with distinction to the good of his country, and with the approbation of his constituents. In the trying period which preceded and followed the declaration of the late war he was a member of the latter body, where his masterly exertions were never wanting to avoid the needless provocations to hostility, to preserve our commerce and peace, and for the re-establishment of that blessing as soon as it could be regained.

"We believe his pen adorns a portion of that able and elegant paper which in the commencement of the war was issued by the minority explanatory of its motives and their conduct. A more candid, dignified, and convincing piece of eloquence, a like evidence of the intelligent patriotism and unchangeable principles of its signers, is nowhere to be found. To the many marks of the confidence reposed in him by his country may be added the appointment of chief justice of one of the circuits of the United States, which he received from the nomination of President Adams. But the system having been prematurely doomed to its destruction by its enemies, he was allowed but a short time for the display of the rare qualities which in a high degree fitted and accomplished him for the most arduous and venerable exercise of the human faculties, the impartial administration of justice."

Francis Scott Key, author of the "Star-Spangled Banner," and a distinguished lawyer, was born at the residence of his father, John Ross Key, near Pipe Creek, in Frederick County, a short distance from Emmittsburg, on the 1st of August, 1779, and died in Baltimore while on a visit to his son-in-law, Charles Howard, on Wednesday, the 11th of January, 1843. His father was a Revolutionary officer, who died in Frederick County, Oct. 12, 1821. Francis S. Key was educated at St. John's College, Annapolis, and studied law in that city in the office of his uncle, Philip Barton Key. In 1801 he commenced the practice of law at Frederick, but in a few years removed to Washington City, D. C., where he was chosen United States District Attorney. Mr. Key was a gentleman of the highest order of talent, of ardent feelings, and benevolent mind; the intimate friend and counselor of the Hon. John Randolph of Roanoke in his last days, and of Gen. Andrew Jackson during his Presidential term. He was also an early and zealous supporter of the African Colonization Society. His chief title to fame, however, rests on his patriotic and soul-stirring poem, "The Star-Spangled Banner," written to commemorate a Maryland triumph, but so thoroughly impregnated with the true spirit of patriotism that it has become a national lyric. The circumstances under which it was composed are as follows:

"On the retreat of the British army from Washington through Marlborough," says Mr. Gleig, who was with them, "though there appeared to be no disposition on the part of the American general to follow our steps and to harass the retreat, the inhabitants of that village, at the instigation of a medical practitioner called Beanes, had risen in arms as soon as we were defeated, and falling upon such individuals as strayed from the column, put some of them to death and made others prisoners. A soldier whom they had taken, and who had escaped, gave this information to the troopers just as they were about to return to headquarters; upon which they immediately wheeled about, and galloping into the village, pulled the doctor out of his bed (for it was early in the morning), and compelled him, by threat of instant death, to liberate his prisoners, and mounting him before one of the party, rode into the camp in triumph."

Dr. Beanes was the leading physician in Upper Marlborough, and an accomplished scholar and a popular gentleman. It is said his house, which was one of the best in Upper Marlborough, was selected by Admiral Cockburn and some of the principal officers of the army as their headquarters when the British troops encamped there on their march to Washington. As the British officers had shown him much courtesy and protected his property, they were greatly incensed at his actions. Mr. Taney says the British "entered Dr. Beanes' house about midnight, compelled him to rise from his bed, and hurried him off to their camp, hardly allowing him time to put his clothes on; he was treated with great harshness and closely guarded; and as soon as his friends were apprised of his situation they hastened to the headquarters of the English army to solicit his release, but it was peremptorily refused, and they were not even permitted to see him, and he had been carried as a prisoner on board the fleet." Alarmed for the safety of Dr. Beanes, a number of his friends hastened to Georgetown to procure the assistance of Francis S. Key, who was then serving as a volunteer in Maj. Peter's artillery. Mr. Key promptly undertook to obtain the release of his friend, and immediately obtained the President's permission to visit the British fleet, Mr. John S. Skinner, the government's agent for the exchange of prisoners in Baltimore, who was well known as such to the officers of the fleet, being directed to accompany him. As soon as the necessary arrangements were made they embarked at Baltimore and sailed for the British fleet, which was then at the mouth of the Potomac, preparing for the expedition against Baltimore. Mr. Taney says that Mr. Key "was courteously received by Admiral Cochrane and the officers of the army as well as of the navy. But when he made known his business his application was received so coldly that he feared it would fail.

"Gen. Ross and Admiral Cockburn, who accompanied the expedition to Washington, particularly the latter, spoke of Dr. Beanes in very harsh terms, and seemed at first not disposed to release him. It, however, happened, fortunately, that Mr. Skinner carried letters from the wounded British officers left at Bladensburg, and in these letters to their friends on board the fleet they all spoke of the humanity and kindness with which they had been treated after they had fallen into our hands. After a good deal of conversation and strong representations from Mr. Key as to the character and standing of Dr. Beanes, and of the deep interest which the community in which he lived took in his fate, Gen. Ross said that Dr. Beanes deserved much harsher punishment than he had received; but that he felt himself bound to make a return for the kindness which had been shown to his wounded officers whom he had been compelled to leave at Bladensburg, and upon that ground, and that only, he would release him. But Mr. Key was at the same time informed that neither he nor any one else would be permitted to leave the fleet for some days, and must be detained until the attack on Baltimore, which was then about to be made, was over. On the other hand, he was assured they would make him and Mr. Skinner as comfortable as possible during their detention. Admiral Cochrane, with whom they dined on the day of their arrival, apologized for not accommodating them in his own ship, saying that it was crowded already with the officers of the army, but that they would be well taken care of on the frigate 'Surprise,' commanded by his son, Sir Thomas Cochrane. To this frigate they were accordingly transferred.

"Mr. Key," says Mr. Taney, "had an interview with Dr. Beanes before Gen. Ross consented to release him. I do not recollect whether he was on board the admiral's ship or the 'Surprise,' but believe it was the former. He found him in the forward part of the ship, among the sailors. He had not had a change of clothes from the time he was seized; was constantly treated with indignity by those around him, and no officer would speak to him. He was treated as a culprit, and not as a prisoner of war. This harsh and humiliating treatment continued until he was placed on board of the cartel. . . .

"Mr. Key and Mr. Skinner continued on board the 'Surprise,' where they were very kindly treated by Sir Thomas Cochrane, until the fleet reached the Patapsco and preparations were made for landing the troops. Admiral Cochrane then shifted his flag to the frigate, in order that he might be able to move farther up the river and superintend in person the attack by water on the fort; and Mr. Key and Mr. Skinner were then sent on board their own vessel, with a guard of sailors and marines, to prevent them from landing. They were permitted to take Dr. Beanes with them, and they thought themselves fortunate in being anchored in a position which enabled them to see distinctly the flag of Fort McHenry from the deck of the vessel. He (Mr. Key) proceeded then, with much animation, to describe the scene on the night of the bombardment. He and Mr. Skinner remained on deck during the night, watching every shell from the moment it was fired until it fell, listening with breathless interest to hear if an explosion followed. While the bombardment continued it was sufficient proof that the fort had not surrendered. But it suddenly ceased some time before day, and as they had no communication with any of the enemy's ships, they did not know whether the fort had surrendered or the attack had been abandoned. They paced the deck for the residue of the night in painful suspense, watching with intense anxiety for the return of day, and looking every few minutes at their watches to see how long they would have to wait for it; and as soon as it dawned, and before it was light enough to see objects at a distance, their glasses were turned to the fort, uncertain whether they should see the Stars and Stripes or the flag of the enemy. At length light came, and they saw that 'our flag was still there,' and as the day advanced they discovered, from the movements of the boats between the shore and the fleet, that the troops had been roughly handled, and that many wounded men were carried to the ships. At last he was informed that the attack on Baltimore had failed, and that the British army was re-embarking, and that he and Mr. Skinner and Dr. Beanes would be permitted to leave them and go where they pleased as soon as the troops were on board and the fleet ready to sail.

"He then told me that, under the excitement of the time, he had written the song, and handed me a printed copy of 'The Star-Spangled Banner.' When I read it and expressed my astonishment, I asked him how he found time, in the scenes he had been passing through, to compose such a song. He said he commenced it on the deck of their vessel, in the fervor of the moment, when he saw the enemy hastily retreating to their ships, and looked at the flag he had watched for so anxiously as the morning opened; that he had written some lines of brief notes, that would aid him in calling them to mind, upon the back of a letter which he happened to have in his pocket, and for some of the lines, as he proceeded, he was obliged to rely altogether upon his memory, and that he finished it in the boat on his way to the shore, and wrote it out as it now stands at the hotel on the night he reached Baltimore, and immediately after he arrived. He said that on the next morning he took it to Capt. Joshua N. Nicholson, commander of the Baltimore Fencibles and chief justice of the Baltimore Court, and one of the judges of the Court of Appeals of Maryland, to ask him what he thought of it; that he was so much pleased with it that he immediately sent it to a printer and directed copies to be struck off in hand-bill form; and that he, Mr. Key, believed it to have been favorably received by the Baltimore public."

The song was first set in type by Mr. Samuel Sands, who was then an apprentice-boy at the office of the Baltimore *American*, on the east side of Harrison Street near Baltimore, and who afterwards became the proprietor and editor of the *American Farmer*. It was set to the tune of "Anacreon in Heaven." It is said it was first sung in camp, afterwards nightly in the Holliday Street Theatre. Mr. Key was the father of eleven children. One of his sons, Philip Barton Key, was killed in Washington by Gen. Sickles, and another, Daniel S. Key, was slain in a duel near Bladensburg by Mr. Sherburne, a New Hampshire man. Both were midshipmen in the United States navy. On the ground Sherburne said, "Mr. Key, I have no desire to kill you." "No matter," said Key; "I came to kill you." "Very well," replied Sherburne; "then I will kill you," which he did at the first fire.

While studying law at Annapolis Mr. Key became the intimate friend of Roger Brooke Taney, afterwards chief justice, who, as previously stated, married Mr. Key's only sister. Besides the "Star-Spangled Banner," Mr. Key wrote a number of other verses, but it is doubtful whether he ever intended them for publication, as they appear to have been hastily composed on the impulse of some passing fancy. Mr. Key was a contemporary of Edward Coote Pinkney, and contributed to the same periodicals for which Edgar Allen Poe wrote. He was a thorough gentleman, and a man of cultivated tastes, but literature was not the serious business of his life, his time being mainly occupied with the practice of his profession. In her "Biographical Sketches of Distinguished Marylanders," Esmeralda Boyle relates the following characteristic anecdote of Mr. Key: "Mr. Key was on intimate terms of friendship with Mr. Randolph (John Randolph of Roanoke), who, being confined to his room by illness upon one occasion, was engaged in conversation with Mr. Key, who had called upon him at the hotel. Not long after Mr. Key entered the room, an officer of high rank in the British navy, deeming himself on intimate terms with Mr. Randolph, merely knocked at the door, then opening it, entered unannounced. Turning hastily around, Randolph cried out in a rude manner, 'Busy, my lord, busy! Always apply to my servant before you enter my lodgings.' 'Beg pardon,' said the officer, who immediately withdrew. Mr. Key said, 'Mr. Randolph, how can you treat a gentleman in this way? He meant nothing wrong.' 'Neither do hogs mean wrong when they enter my cornfields, but I always turn them out,' was the answer of John Randolph." An old friend of Mr. Key said of him,

"Everybody who knew Frank Key loved him, and there was not a more agreeable companion to be found." Mr. Key was a member of the Episcopal Church, and for many years taught a Sunday-school class at Rock Creek Church. His wife was Mary Taylor Lloyd, daughter of Col. Edward Lloyd, of Talbot County, Md., a charming lady, who contributed greatly to the attractiveness of their hospitable home. During the Nullification troubles in South Carolina he was sent in an unofficial capacity to that State, and it is said contributed not a little by his personal efforts to the peaceful settlement which was finally obtained. Mr. Key conducted the prosecution of the would-be assassin of Gen. Jackson in 1835, and acted with great circumspection and a due regard for the rights of the prisoner. The man was adjudged insane and sent to an asylum. Of Mr. Key's appearance in an important case in the United States Supreme Court, ex-Governor Foote, of Mississippi, in his "Reminiscences," says, "I was very much entertained with the whole argument, but I was particularly with the speech of Mr. Key and that of Mr. Berrien. Mr. Key was tall, erect, and of admirable physical proportions. There dwelt usually upon his handsome and winning features a soft and touching pensiveness of expression, almost bordering on sadness, but which in moments of special excitement, or when anything occurred to waken the dormant heroism of his nature or to call into action the higher power of vigorous and well-cultivated intellect, gave place to a bright ethereality of aspect and noble audacity of tone which pleased while it dazzled the beholder. His voice was capable of being in the highest degree touching and persuasive. His whole gesticulation was natural, graceful, and impressive, and was completely free from everything like affectation or rhetorical grimace as any public speaker I have known. . . . On this occasion he greatly surpassed the expectations of his most admiring friends. The subject was particularly suited to his thoughts, and was one which had long enlisted in a special manner the generous sensibilities of his soul. It seemed to me that he said all that the case demanded, and yet no more than was needful to be said, and he closed with a thrilling and even an electrifying picture of the horrors connected with the African slave-trade which would have done honor to either a Pitt or a Wilberforce in their palmiest days." One of the most convincing proofs of Mr. Key's great benevolence and kindness of heart is found in the fact that he manumitted all his slaves and was one of the founders of the African Colonization Society. While visiting his daughter, Mrs. Charles Howard, in Baltimore, Mr. Key was seized with pneumonia, and died suddenly in January, 1843. The United States Supreme Court adjourned in his honor on being acquainted with his death, and next day the Attorney-General of the United States, Mr. Legaré, of South Carolina, presented resolutions of condolence passed by the bar, and made an address testifying to Mr. Key's great intellectual attainments, and to his admirable qualities of heart and mind. Similar action was taken by the bar of Frederick and of Baltimore City and County, and his remains were borne to the grave universally regretted and beloved. Mr. Key was buried at Greenmount Cemetery, Baltimore, but subsequently the remains were removed to Frederick, where they lie beside those of his wife in the cemetery of Mount Olivet. His grave is marked by a simple slab. A bill appropriating five thousand dollars for a monument was introduced into the State Legislature, but failed for want of funds. A handsome monument has, however, been erected in San Francisco through the munificence of the late James Lick.

Alexander Contee Hanson. This distinguished jurist was the son of John Hanson (elected President of the Continental Congress Nov. 6, 1781) and Jane Contee, and was born in Frederick County, Oct. 22, 1749. In early life he was assistant private secretary to Gen. Washington, and was one of the first judges of the General Court of Maryland. Upon the formation of the General Court in 1777, Charles Carroll, barrister, was appointed chief justice, and Benjamin Rumsey and Solomon Wright judges. They declined to accept, and William Paca, chief judge, and Henry Hooper and Alexander Contee Hanson, associate judges, were appointed, Feb. 12, 1778, to fill the vacancies. Upon the death of John Rogers, chancellor of the State, Robert Hanson Harrison was appointed, Oct. 1, 1789, to fill the vacancy, but declined, and Alexander Contee Hanson was appointed, Oct. 3, 1789, to the office, which he held until his death, at Annapolis, Jan. 16, 1806. He was elector for President in 1789, and again in 1792. Under the direction of Mr. Hanson and Samuel Chase the laws of Maryland passed from Nov. 26, 1763, to the close of the session of the Assembly of 1784 were published. In 1789 he was appointed to digest the testamentary laws of the State. He was also the author of a number of celebrated political pamphlets. He married Rebecca Howard, of Annapolis, and had three children,—Charles Wallace Hanson, who was appointed associate judge of the Sixth Judicial District, composed of Baltimore and Harford Counties, in the place of Zebulon Hollingsworth, removed; Alexander Contee Hanson; and a daughter, who married Thomas Peabody Grosvenor, of New York.

Judge Hanson sat at the trial of the seven Tories convicted in Frederick Court during the Revolution, and sentenced them to death. Mr. Hanson's son, Alexander Contee Hanson, Jr., was one of the prominent leaders of the anti-war section of the Federalist party during the war of 1812. He was born in Maryland, and died at Belmont, Frederick Co., April 23, 1819. In 1813-16 he was a member of Congress, and in 1816-19 United States senator from Maryland. At the beginning of the war Mr. Hanson was associated with Jacob Wagner in the publication in Baltimore of a stanch Federalist paper, the *Federal Republican*, which bitterly antagonized the war with Great Britain. Its course infuriated the war-party in Baltimore, and the office of the paper was mobbed, and the types, presses, paper, etc., destroyed. The house itself, a frame building, was demolished. Soon afterwards the paper, which in the mean time had been published in Georgetown, reappeared in Baltimore from a house on South Charles Street which Mr. Hanson occupied with his friends, among whom were Gen. James M. Lingan, Otho Sprigg, Richard J. Crabb, Henry C. Gaither, Charles J. Kilgour, Dr. P. Warfield, J. E. Hall, Gen. Henry Lee, Ephraim Gaither, and John Howard Payne, the actor. An attack was made by the mob, and the occupants of the house fired upon it from the windows, killing a Dr. Gale. The mob brought a field-piece to bear, but by this time a military force had arrived, and Hanson and his friends surrendered to the officer in command. They were taken to the jail, which that night was broken into by the mob. Gen. Lingan was killed, and eleven others dreadfully beaten. Gen. Lee and Mr. Hanson were treated with peculiar brutality, and were seriously hurt. The violence of the mob caused a reaction in Mr. Hanson's favor, and largely contributed to his subsequent political success. Mr. Hanson was a man of exceptional ability and rare personal courage. While in Congress he fought a duel with Capt. Gordon, of the United States navy, and badly wounded him, hitting him exactly where he said he would.

John Hanson Thomas. This eminent lawyer, the son of Dr. Philip Thomas and Jane Contee Hanson, was born in Frederick Town. He was married Oct. 5, 1809, to Mary Isham Colston, a niece of Chief Justice Marshall. In 1808 he was elected to the House of Delegates by the Federalists. By his eloquence and brilliant talents he rose to great distinction in the politics of the State. He was elected a member of Congress, and had been selected by his party for a seat in the United States Senate, but dying on May 2, 1815, before the election, the Federalists honored his cousin, Alexander Contee Hanson, with a seat in that body. His father, Dr. Philip Thomas, the son of James Thomas and Elizabeth Bellicum, of Kent County, was born near Chestertown, June 11, 1747, and commenced the practice of medicine in Frederick Town, Aug. 1, 1769. He was a sterling patriot, and did much to aid the cause of the Revolution. The doctor died April 25, 1815.

John Hanson Thomas was regarded as the most brilliant man of his day in the State, at the bar and on the stump. The late Dr. John Hanson Thomas, of Baltimore, was his son.

Francis Thomas was born in Frederick County, Md., Feb. 3, 1799, and was nearly seventy-seven years old when accidentally killed. He was educated at St. John's College, Annapolis, was admitted to the bar about the year 1820, and acquired a large practice in the counties of Western Maryland. He was at one time the possessor of a comfortable fortune, the most of which he had acquired by the practice of his profession. He was member of the House of Delegates of Maryland in 1822, 1827, 1829, serving the last term as Speaker. He was president of the Chesapeake and Ohio Canal in 1839 and 1840. Ex-Governor Thomas was the second Governor of Maryland elected by the people. He succeeded William Grason in 1841, held the office three years, and was succeeded by Thomas G. Pratt. He was a representative in the 22d, 23d, 24th, 25th, 26th, 37th, 38th, 39th, and 40th Congresses. While in Congress he applied to the Legislature of Maryland for a divorce from his wife, who was a Miss Sallie McDowell, a daughter of Governor McDowell, of Virginia, and a lady of rare accomplishments. He failed to obtain a divorce in Maryland, but Mrs. Thomas was subsequently divorced from her husband by the Legislature of Virginia. She afterwards married Rev. Mr. Miller, a Presbyterian clergyman of Philadelphia. Governor Thomas was a Democrat prior to 1861, and frequently stumped the State, either as a candidate or in behalf of the State and national ticket. He possessed extraordinary popularity as a political orator, and took a prominent part in the reform movement of 1849 and 1850. He was elected to the Constitutional Convention of 1850, and was a leading member of that body. He was re-elected to Congress in 1861, and remained in that body four terms, acting with the Republican party. After the election of President Grant in 1870, he was appointed collector of internal revenue for the Cumberland District, and held that office until 1872, when he was appointed minister to Peru, which position he resigned in 1875, when he retired from public life, and engaged in the practice of law at Cumberland and in wool-growing upon his farm in Garrett County.

Governor Thomas' life was in many respects an eventful one, and his talent and vigor in political life were recognized in all parts of the State. Among the incidents in the stormy portion of his career was his duel fought with the late William Price, a distinguished lawyer of Maryland, growing out of a heated public discussion at Hagerstown. Neither of the combatants were wounded, Governor Thomas' ball glancing from the toe of Mr. Price's boot. The duel was fought at Bath, Berkeley Co., Va., and created a great deal of excitement at the time. He also had a personal encounter with Governor McDowell, of Virginia, in 1843, but owing to the interposition of friends no duel was fought. Governor Thomas was accidentally killed Saturday afternoon (January 23d), 1876, on the railway track, about one mile east of Frankville Station, Baltimore and Ohio Railroad, while engaged in superintending improvements for breeding fine sheep procured by him in Peru, and brought to this country on his return. While standing on the track he saw a freight-train approaching from the east, and stepped to the south track to avoid it. At the same moment a "helper" engine came upon him from the west, "tender" foremost, the approach of which he had not noticed and did not hear. There is a short curve at this point, and the engineer said that as his engine rounded the curve he saw Governor Thomas walking on the track with his arms folded behind him and his head bent in a meditative mood. It was too late to give an alarm or check the speed of the engine, and in a moment it struck him in the back, knocking him twenty feet to a pile of railroad bars beside the road. The locomotive was stopped as soon as possible and assistance summoned, but life was extinct. The body was not mutilated, a severe contusion on the back of his head and several bruises near the spinal column being the only apparent injuries. The remains were taken to Frankville on a hand-car and thence to his house.

A telegram was received from John Sifford, of Frederick City, stating that he had been an intimate friend of the deceased, and had been by him requested to have his body interred in the family burying-ground, Petersville, Frederick Co. This request was made before the Governor had started on his mission to Peru, and Mr. Sifford was also authorized to procure a monument to be erected at the grave. Accordingly, his remains were taken to Petersville and there interred.

In the Legislature, in Congress, and in the gubernatorial chair, Mr. Thomas made a deep and lasting impression. As a political orator he had few equals, and his elocution was so ringing and clear as to obtain for him the title of "Silver-tongued." After having been Governor of the State he retired in 1844, and, brooding over his domestic calamity, led the life of a recluse for many years, until the outbreak of the late civil war, when he emerged from his retirement, and, taking an active part in behalf of the Union cause, was sent to Congress, where he had years before distinguished himself as a Democratic member of the House.

Ex-Governor Thomas was in many respects one of the most extraordinary men ever sent by his State to the Federal Congress. He was a leading supporter of Jackson throughout the stormy congressional contest concerning the United States Bank, and by his commanding gifts of eloquence and fascinating personal address acquired, in a service of ten years in Congress, a national reputation as a debater of uncommon force. From his retirement on leaving the Governor's chair he emerged in 1851, as a member of the Constitutional Convention, and at the commencement of hostilities in 1861 he threw himself with ardor into the work of encouraging enlistments and organizing regiments for the Union cause. Leaving to younger men, like Col. Maulsby, the duty of leading these regiments into the field, he accepted in 1861 the "Union" nomination to Congress, and after an interval of twenty years again found himself a member of the House of Representatives. His course throughout the war was that of an earnest, though not extreme, supporter of the government. Indeed, he inclined more to the views of Border State Union men like Crisfield and Webster than to the more advanced opinions of Henry Winter Davis and his followers. With the shrewd instinct of an experienced political leader, he never allowed himself to get too far in advance of his constituency, and was very formidable on the stump, from the fact that he could always appeal to his own record for moderation and conservatism as an effective argument in favor of the reasonableness of his views.

Judge John Alexander Lynch was born on the 3d day of October, A.D. 1825, near the village of Jefferson, in Frederick County, Md., and now resides in Frederick City, in Frederick County. His father, William Lynch, was born on the 15th of February, A.D. 1788, near the village of Jefferson, and died near the place of his birth on the 7th of August, 1857. He three times represented Frederick County in the Legislature of Maryland. John A. Lynch's mother was Eliza Boteler, who was born in Washington County, Md., near the village of Weverton, on the 10th of Febru-

ary, A.D. 1797, and died near the village of Jefferson on the 14th of January, 1832. His grandfathers on both sides were soldiers in the Revolutionary war.

John A. Lynch married Isabella C. Beckenbaugh, in Frederick City, on the 17th of November, 1856. They have had no children. He was educated at a country school near the place of his birth, and at Pennsylvania College, Gettysburg. He did not graduate, but the degree of A.M. was subsequently conferred upon him by that institution. He was obliged to leave college in March, 1847, on account of failing health, and went to the State of Alabama, where he remained (teaching school a part of the time) until the month of August, 1849, when he returned to Frederick County with restored health, and commenced the study of the law in Frederick City, in the office of Mountjoy B. Luckett, Esq. He was admitted to the bar in November, 1851, and commenced the practice of law in Frederick City, where he has since continued to reside. He was elected State's attorney for Frederick County in November, 1855, and was re-elected in November, 1859, having performed the duties of that office for two terms. He was elected without opposition associate judge of the Sixth Judicial Circuit of the State in November, 1867, which office he now holds. He and his wife are members of the Episcopal Church.

He is a member of the Masonic fraternity, having joined that institution in August, 1849, and is a member of the Grand Lodge of Maryland. He is a Royal Arch Mason, a Knight Templar, and is now Eminent Commander of the commandery in Frederick City. He has never engaged in any business but such as was connected with the profession of the law. He is a Democrat, and previous to his election as judge took an active part in politics in his native county, but never was an aspirant or candidate for any political office. He has always been fond of his profession, and has given to it his almost entire attention. He has written no work for publication, only an occasional address, and numerous legal opinions in the performance of his duties as judge. Devoting himself thus exclusively to the law, it is not strange that he should have won so distinguished a position at the bar and such high honors upon the bench. As both lawyer and judge he has gained an enviable reputation among the people of Western Maryland and of the whole State, and without courting popular favor has secured, by his high character and talents, the esteem and admiration of his fellow-citizens of all parties. Though elected as a Democrat, he knows no party upon the bench, and recognizes in his decisions only the principles of the law. Just, firm, able, and conscientious, it is to be hoped that it may be long before the bench of Maryland shall be deprived of his valuable and able services.

John Nelson was born in Frederick in 1794, and died at his residence in Mount Vernon Place, Baltimore, on Wednesday evening, Jan. 18, 1860, in the sixty-seventh year of his age. Mr. Nelson studied law and was admitted to the bar of Frederick, and when twenty-five years of age, as soon as he was eligible, was elected congressman from his native district. In Congress he was regarded as an exceptionally brilliant and promising young man. On resuming the active practice of his profession he decided to remove to Baltimore, where he continued to reside, with the exception of a comparatively brief residence in Washington, until his death. He rose steadily in the estimation of the bar and the general public as a lawyer of uncommon ability, and in 1843, when Vice-President Tyler succeeded Gen. Harrison as President, he made Mr. Nelson attorney-general. In announcing the nomination the Richmond *Whig* said, "We never heard of Mr. Nelson before," whereupon the Baltimore *Sun* rejoined, "We were very near saying this confession argues yourself unknown. Mr. Nelson is one of the most distinguished members of the Maryland bar. His name has never been bandied about by pot-house politicians, and hence it is not so well known as many others who might be named. The only public position Mr. Nelson has ever held, we believe, was the post of minister to Naples, to which he was appointed by President Jackson. There he performed the duties of his mission with satisfaction to himself and to his government. Mr. Nelson is in this city highly esteemed, both as a citizen and a lawyer, and his friends have full faith that the attorney-generalship will never be disgraced by his person."

Mr. Nelson retired from the cabinet in March, 1845, and returned to Baltimore, where he was a leading member of the bar until his death. On the announcement of his death a special meeting of the bar of Baltimore was held in the Superior Court room. The Baltimore *Clipper* of Jan. 21, 1860, gives the following account of the meeting:

"The specially called meeting of the Baltimore bar to do honor to the memory of the late Hon. John Nelson met yesterday (January 20th) at one o'clock, pursuant to the announcement, in the Superior Court room, which was densely crowded with members of the legal profession in Baltimore, including many of its brightest ornaments.

"Shortly after the hour named Judge R. N. Martin was, upon motion of Jonathan Meredith, Esq., called to preside, and Reverdy Johnson, Jr., elected secretary.

"Upon motion of Mr. Meade Addison, United States district attorney, the president appointed Messrs. Reverdy Johnson,

Jonathan Meredith, J. V. L. McMahon, Nathaniel Williams, and Grafton Dulaney, Esqs., a committee of five to draw up suitable resolutions. The committee retired to the Law Library, and after a few minutes' absence returned, when Jonathan Meredith arose, and spoke as follows:

"'The Baltimore bar, Mr. Chairman, has seldom sustained a heavier loss than we are now assembled to deplore in the death of a distinguished brother.

"'With great natural endowments, a luminous and vigorous intellect, a mastery of law as a science, the fruits of early and patient labor, a power of analysis to disentangle the most complicated problems, the closest reasoning, and an eloquence natural and persuasive, with all these great gifts Mr. Nelson has long stood in the foremost rank of the Baltimore bar.

"'But his legal reputation had a much wider range than his native State; before the most august tribunal of our country, in the Supreme Court of the United States, elevated to the high office of attorney-general, he stood side by side with the distinguished leaders of that bar, and won by his forensic efforts and the faithful discharge of his official duties the respect and confidence of the court.

"'This, sir, is but a tribute to his memory as a lawyer. His worth as a man, his courteous and gentlemanlike bearing to all who met him, his freedom from arrogant pretensions, his equability of temper, his natural cheerfulness in society,—charms which attracted so many to his companionship and made them friends,—remembrance of these will long be cherished, no less than his professional eminence.

"'To record our sorrow for his death and our heartfelt sympathies for those whom it has bereft, I move you, sir, that the resolutions of your committee, which will be read by the secretary, be entered on the minutes of the several courts of this city.'

"The usual resolutions of respect and condolence were then read and adopted.

"Hon. Reverdy Johnson then delivered the following eulogium:

"'Mr. Chairman, the affecting event which has brought us together has filled us with a sorrow that makes it almost impossible for me to participate, except as a silent auditor, in the business of our meeting.

"'It has come upon me with such comparative suddenness that I am unable to meet it even with a becoming fortitude. And although every hour is telling us that it is wanting his presence to make us complete, yet days and weeks and months shall pass before I shall be able to realize the death of John Nelson. It seems to me as if but yesterday that he met us in this chamber, and, as was ever his wont, with a genial smile and friendly grasp, gave us assurance that with us he was ever happy. And then he must have seen (and that in some measure should console us), from the manner in which his salutations were returned, that with him our hours too always passed pleasantly, and that we valued him not less for his social qualities than for his professional eminence.

"'But he is gone, never in this world to be seen by us more. His friendly grasp, as warm as his heart was kind, is now cold as the winter's ice. His tongue and brain are now mere inanimate matter. They will soon be but the dust from which they sprang. The spirit, which was alone immortal, and which gave them the power to persuade and convince, as we so well knew they had, has gone by the summons of its God to the native sky, there to account for its conduct on earth. Nor, at the moment of its departure, did our brother evidence the slightest fear of the result. With a sincere faith in our revealed religion, from a conviction of its truth, the happy result of careful reading and deep meditation, as I have every reason to know he entertained, he met his inevitable hour with the fullest confidence in heaven. In this thought there is much, very much to reconcile us to our bereavement, and yet that is so severe that time can alone enable us to sustain it unmoved.

"'Of Mr. Nelson's professional character it would be difficult to speak in terms of exaggeration. His mind was admirably fitted for the bar. It was naturally acute, discriminating, methodical, and logical, and these capacities were improved almost to perfection by the most careful cultivation, by study and practice. Some of his brethren who knew him less intimately may have supposed that his great efforts at the bar—and when the occasion required they were ever great—were rather the result of peculiar and extraordinary natural endowment than of much general professional reading or careful preparation. If this be so, they are, as I know, in error. From the first he was a diligent student, and for his cases he exhausted all the necessary learning within his reach, and stretched his power of thought to the utmost capacity. He knew—as who does not who has observed much of our profession?—that excellence at all, much more the highest excellence, is not to be obtained without giving days and nights to study.

"'I would not be understood by this that all is accomplished by reading; that much of it is absolutely necessary, but to be valuable it must be accompanied by close, concentrated thought, and of this our brother was eminently competent. A career now of forty-four years' duration, and the opportunity of seeing the great men of the American bar and a few of the bar of England, enabled me to compare, as I have often done when hearing him, Mr. Nelson with others, and with this result: I have heard more eloquence, more brilliant imagery, more power of amplification, and more affluence of learning, but I do not think that in force of analysis, clearness of arrangement, perspicuity of statement, simplicity of language, closeness of logic, and concentration of thought I have ever seen him much, if at all, excelled. When his case demanded an effort, as when the facts were numerous and complicated and the legal questions many and abstruse, I have ever felt, when his arguments were concluded, that the entire argument was exhausted.

"'As a colleague he was invaluable, and whoever measured conclusions with him without feeling that as an adversary he was ever formidable? Whilst guarding with skill his own defenses, he knew with equal skill how to assail those of his opponent, and kept him, whoever he may have been, to the utmost of his capacity. But his talents were not alone suited for the bar.

"'At the early age of twenty-five, the first moment of his being eligible in the district of his nativity and earlier residence, he was elected a member of the House of Representatives of the United States. The body at that time contained men of great ability, and, as I have heard from several of them, young as he was, Mr. Nelson was at once appreciated as a young man of great promise, an estimate which was the more confirmed at the termination of his services. In the Senate of our State, at a subsequent period, his power was yet more evident: he stood first among the first. His superior was not known.

"'In the service of his country abroad afterwards, during the administration of Gen. Jackson, he proved himself the equal of the ablest of our diplomatists, and received on his return, as he well merited, the honor due to a successful treaty, accomplished by the overwhelming power with which he maintained the rights of our people.

"'His mission ended, he made this city his home and the theatre of his subsequent professional life. He was for a short period called from us by President Tyler to assume the duties of Attorney-General of the United States, and although immediately succeeding the accomplished and elegant Legaré, he was at once recognized by the Supreme Court of the United States and by his brethren of that bar as the equal of any of his predecessors. The archives of the office contain enduring evidence of his learning and unsurpassed comprehension. I do not know that in the many opinions given by him a single error was discovered. They constitute now a resource which can be resorted to with confidence to ascertain the law on all the questions he was called upon to consider. How he discharged his duties afterwards in our courts this auditory need not be reminded. His voice, even now, seems to me to fill the hall with its energy, and his mind to explain with the clearness of light the abstrusest inquiries.

"'What a void in our ranks must be caused by the death of such a brother! Can we ever find one every way fitted to supply it? On reflection I do not at all despond. There are young brethren around me full of talent, industry, and noble ambition. Let them study as Nelson studied; let them have their knowledge as accurate as his; let them attain a perfect comprehension of the principles of our science, and rely mainly on those in their examination of adjudged cases, and although the keenness of our bereavement may be long felt, we shall in a few years see the vacant place filled, and the fame of our bar restored to its recent brightness.

"'But, Mr. Chairman, there is a higher lesson taught us by our loss than his example teaches to the aspirant of professional honor.

"'During the pendency of the case now on trial we have had to mourn the deaths of four of our members. The judge who presided in this court and three of our brethren within that period have died. What a lesson does this teach! The frequency of the event would almost tell us that the only business of life is to look about us and die. But such is not the voice that really speaks from the tomb. That voice tells us that the true business of life is so to live that we may be prepared to die; that there are brighter rewards in store for us in a world where happiness pure and immortal awaits us if we are true to our duty to man and to heaven. Let these recent warnings, therefore, excite us to a holy ambition, which will secure us more, inconceivably more, than all the honors that this world are worth.

"'I forbear, Mr. Chairman, to intrude within the sacred circle of the bereaved home, where men can offer now no words of consolation. The blow that has crushed its inmates to the earth can only be borne by communion with God.'

"Several times during the course of his remarks Mr. Johnson was so deeply moved as to be scarcely able to proceed, and at their conclusion he quickly seated himself and covered his face with his hands to conceal the tears which were trickling down his cheeks.

"Judge Martin responded as follows:

"'Before submitting for the adoption of the bar the resolutions that have just been read, expressive of affection and respect for the memory of our lamented friend and brother, the late John Nelson, I have only to remark that I cordially concur in all that has been said by my brothers who have addressed you in commendation of his character, his public services, and professional ability.

"'He was a most accomplished and able lawyer, profoundly versed with the principles of jurisprudence in all its branches, and in discharging the arduous duties of the bench I have been often aided and enlightened by his accurate learning, his lucid reasoning, and his strong argumentative powers.

"'I unite with you all, gentlemen, in deploring an event which has deprived each of us of an attached personal friend, and the profession of one of its brightest ornaments; and, as an enduring memorial of affection and respect for our lamented brother, I shall at the proper time direct these proceedings of the bench and bar to be entered upon the records of the Superior Court.'

"Upon motion of Mr. Meredith, the meeting adjourned upon the conclusion of his honor the judge's remarks."

That Mr. Nelson's reputation was not merely local is shown by the proceedings of the judges and the bar of the United States Supreme Court in relation to his death. The meeting was held in Washington on the 19th of January, 1860, Hon. J. J. Crittenden presiding. Hon. James A. Bayard submitted a series of resolutions, which were adopted, in honor of Mr. Nelson. On the following day they were laid before the United States Supreme Court by Attorney-General Black, who embraced the occasion to deliver a brief but eloquent eulogy of the deceased, in the course of which he remarked:

"It was here that he won what he valued more than anything else, the character of a great lawyer. You can testify to the industry with which he prepared his cases, to his large intellectual resources, to his extensive learning, to his uniform politeness with the court, and to his never-failing frankness in his intercourse with the bar. From July, 1843, until March, 1845, he was in the public service of the United States as their attorney-general. I know whereof I affirm when I say that he left behind him on the records of that department enduring evidence that he was not only a man of great ability, but a most upright, honest, and virtuous officer."

Mr. Justice McLean also testified in warm terms to the high estimation in which Mr. Nelson's attainments and personal qualities were held by the court.

Mr. Nelson was buried at Greenmount Cemetery, Baltimore, and was followed to the grave by the judges of the Baltimore courts and by the leading members of the bar and many prominent citizens.

Hon. Madison Nelson, judge of the Court of Appeals of Maryland, and a half-brother of Hon. John Nelson, was also born in Frederick, and died there Jan. 1, 1870, aged about seventy years.

Judge Nelson and the Hon. John Nelson were both sons of Gen. Roger Nelson, an officer of the Revolutionary army, who achieved distinction at the battles of Camden and Eutaw Springs.

Madison Nelson studied law, was admitted in Frederick, and soon became one of the leading lawyers of Western Maryland. He was elected judge of the Circuit Court for Frederick County in opposition to the Democratic party, but when the new constitution went into effect he was nominated by the Democrats and Conservatives as chief judge of the judicial district composed of Frederick and Montgomery Counties. He was elected, and became, by virtue of his office as chief judge, a member of the Court of Appeals. After his election, however, his health grew feeble, and for some time before his death he was unable to attend the sessions of the court. He was a man of decided talents, and had a quick, sagacious, and penetrating mind.

Hon. Frederick J. Nelson, born in 1833, a distinguished member of the Frederick bar and a member of the Constitutional Convention of 1867, is a son of the late Judge Nelson.

William Schley, one of the shining lights of the Baltimore bar, was born in Frederick City, Oct. 31, 1799, and died March 20, 1872, in his seventy-third year. The Schleys were among the earliest settlers of Frederick, having arrived there in 1735. The builder of the first house in Frederick, John Thomas Schley, was the grandfather of William.

William Schley graduated at Princeton College in 1821, with first honors in every department of study. He was admitted to the bar in 1824, and practiced with success in Frederick till 1837, when he removed to Baltimore and rapidly rose to distinction. In 1824, Mr. Schley married a daughter of Gen. Samuel Ringgold, of "Fountain Rock" Manor, Washington County, and sister of Maj. Samuel Ringgold, who was killed in the Mexican war, at Palo Alto. This lady died in 1870.

In 1836, Mr. Schley was elected to the Senate of Maryland, and as chairman of the Committee on the Constitution took a leading part in the debates of the interesting reform agitation of that time, which involved him in a personal dispute with William Cost Johnson, to whom Mr. Schley sent a challenge. The parties met at Alexandria, Va., Feb. 13, 1837, and exchanged one shot, in which each was wounded. Mr. Schley was accompanied to the field by Daniel, of St. Thomas, Jenifer, of Maryland, and Governor Pickens, of South Carolina. Mr. Johnson's seconds were Governor Henry A. Wise, of Virginia, and Governor Campbell, of South Carolina. The parties were reconciled on the ground and remained firm friends ever after. The affair received the name at the time of the "Pattern Duel," from the extreme punctilio which was observed.

Mr. Schley was in politics a Whig. He was defeated by one vote in the caucus nomination for the United States Senate in 1838. He took an active part in the political campaign of 1850, when Mr. Fillmore was a candidate, and in 1864, when Gen. McClellan was a candidate. Mr. Schley was on terms of friendly and confidential intercourse with Clay, Webster, Crittenden, Gen. Scott, Chief Justice Taney, and many others of the more distinguished men of the last half-century. His life and energies were given with earnestness to the profession of the law, in which he continued actively engaged up to his last sickness. His professional reputation, which was of the very highest character within his State, extended beyond those limits, and no man was more frequently consulted by clients from abroad or from other States. In personal or social intercourse he was distinguished by that peculiar courtesy and gracefulness of manner which is recognized by the appellation of "the old school."

Mr. Schley's death resulted from confluent smallpox, which he is supposed to have contracted while traveling to Baltimore in a railroad train. He had never been vaccinated, and when the nature of his disease was ascertained he was with his own acquiescence removed to the Marine Hospital, where he died. He was attended by Dr. E. Lloyd Howard, and by his affectionate and devoted daughter, Mrs. Wm. Woodville, who nursed him with assiduous tenderness and care throughout his illness. On the night of his death, when Dr. Howard, exhausted, lay down to rest in an adjoining room, Mrs. Woodville remained at his bedside, and was alone with him when he died. A meeting of the bar of Baltimore was held, at which resolutions in honor of Mr. Schley's memory were adopted, and addresses highly eulogistic of his character delivered. Personally, Mr. Schley was a generous, warm-hearted man, and his legal attainments and mental abilities were of the highest order. Unfortunately, in early life, from a mistaken sense of duty, he assumed the indebtedness of his father-in-law, Gen. Samuel Ringgold, and was forced to struggle through life beneath a crushing burden.

The peculiar qualities of Mr. Schley's character were accurately described in the remarks of Judge Giles at the meeting of the bar:

"Before taking a vote upon the resolutions submitted," said the judge, "I would express the deep sorrow I felt on learning this morning (March 20th) of Mr. Schley's death. Thirty-seven years since, at Annapolis, I made his acquaintance. He was then a senator of Maryland from the county of Frederick. During the winter of 1837 he resigned and moved to this city. During the many years since that time he has been in full practice as a leading member of our bar, and no more patient, hard-working, and willing member could be found in the profession. He was an accomplished scholar, an able advocate, and a learned jurist. In very long service on the bench in the District and Circuit Courts of the United States, he has tried very many causes before me, and I always felt I was a learner at his feet. He was courteous and kind to all, and I shall long miss him as a friend whom I shall see here no more. The last few years of his life has been of much sorrow. Death had broken up his family circle, and taken from him those who once adorned it, but he bore blow after blow with an uncomplaining spirit, and toiled on. His passage from the strife and active scenes of this life to the solitude and quiet of the grave has been under circumstances the most painful; but through the dark cloud there breaks a ray of glory from a daughter's love. But a few days since I stood with him at this bar to pay our last tribute to the

patriarch of our profession. Little did I dream that his name would be called from the master of death. But he has bowed to that decree, from which there is no appeal, and has gone on that journey from which there is no return."

William Cost Johnson. This famous lawyer and politician was born in Jefferson District, Frederick Co., in 1806. He received an academic education, studied law, and was admitted to practice in the United States Supreme Court in 1831. He was a member of Congress from 1833 to 1835, and again from 1837 to 1843. He also served in the State Legislature before entering and after leaving Congress, and was a member of the Maryland Constitutional Convention of 1851. He was elected president of the Young Men's Convention which met in Washington to nominate Henry Clay for President. Whilst in Congress he was chairman of the Committee on Public Lands, and was also a member of the Judiciary Committee. Mr. Johnson was an ardent Whig, and a political debater of uncommon ability. He was a man of great energy of character, and of indomitable will and courage. He fought several duels, among them one with William Schley, which has already been described. An anecdote is related of Mr. Johnson which serves to forcibly illustrate his firmness of character, while also throwing a strong light on the customs of his time. On one occasion the House of Representatives was sitting in committee of the whole. Hon. R. M. T. Hunter was Speaker, but the chair was temporarily occupied during his absence by Joseph L. Tillinghast, of Rhode Island.

"Tillinghast," we are told, "was a good sort of a fellow, but nowhere as a chairman. And in about half an hour the House, which had not much to do, and was bent upon 'larks,' got into such a state of uproar that poor Tillinghast, being at his wits' end, sent for the Speaker. When the Speaker came he was for a moment at loss what to do; but casting his eyes around the turbulent benches he observed a young member named Johnson, a Representative from Maryland, whose determination, tact, and knowledge of the forms of the House had been proven on several occasions. Johnson accepting the instructions, took the chair, rapping smartly with the gavel. . . . There was silence for a moment, the House being curious to see what the new-comer would do or say. What he said was, 'The House will please be in order.' An invitation which was received with a roar of laughter."

Among his other claims to distinction Mr. Johnson was well known as a quick, sharp hand with the pistol, and not unaccustomed to the duello. For a moment he stood glaring at the disorderly mob. Then he rapped loudly with the gavel, and, silence being temporarily restored, he spoke to the following effect:

"Gentlemen of the House of Representatives, in compliance with the request of your regular presiding officer, I have taken the chair to preside over your deliberations. It is my sworn duty to preserve order with a view to the speedy dispatch of the business of the country. I devoutly trust you will appreciate the responsibility devolved upon me as well as yourselves, and that we shall proceed with decorum and regularity. You will find me neither tyrannical nor unreasonable, and if you respond to advances in a spirit of amity and conciliation, we shall get along pleasantly and to the benefit of our constituents. On the other hand, if you are inclined to insist in the course of unbridled license that has prevailed here for some time past, I give you fair intimation I will not endure it for one moment. When I call a member to order, he must take his seat quietly until the committee has formally determined upon the propriety of his conduct, and I will make it a personal thing with any member who is unruly or makes unseemly disturbance hereafter. I will show neither favor nor partiality, and if the dearest friend I have on this floor, be he Whig or anti-Whig, violates the rules of this House and refuses to respect the decision of the presiding officer, I will send him a hostile message the moment the committee arises."

This belligerent announcement is said to have had the desired effect, and the House came to order without more ado. Mr. Johnson was an earnest opponent of slavery, and made an eloquent speech in the House proposing its abolition by a system of graduations.

Milton George Urner. Early in the history of this country the Urner family emigrated to America from the canton of Uri, in Switzerland, and made a settlement in Chester County, Pa., where many of the name still reside. Samuel of that name, who was born in Chester County, Dec. 25, 1797, came to Frederick County when a lad, in company with his father, Jonas, who located upon a farm near Sam's Creek, then in Frederick but now in Carroll County. Jonas was, like his ancestors, a farmer, and died on the Sam's Creek farm. Of his ten children two are living,—Mrs. Hannah Cunningham, in Tiffin, Ohio, and Sarah Price, in Pennsylvania. His son Samuel, already spoken of, following in the footsteps of his forefathers, devoted himself to agricultural pursuits, and upon a farm in Liberty District, where he spent the greater portion of his life, died in August, 1872, in his seventy-fifth year. He was twice married,—first, to Elizabeth, daughter of Jacob Snader, of Frederick County, and, second, to Susannah, daughter of Amos Norris, likewise of Frederick County. By his first marriage he had two sons, both of whom are living, and by his second five children, of whom but two are living. His second wife, the mother of the subject of this sketch, died in March, 1853. Samuel Urner was a man of sound judgment and of more than ordinary intelligence and mental vigor. He lived a simple, unpretentious life, and enforced a wholesome parental discipline with religious care. Being a very industrious man himself, he enjoined habits of industry upon his children. Susannah Urner was a woman of intelligence and earnest piety. She was widely known for her zealous activity in matters of benevolence and religion. She was a lady of rare domestic virtues, great force of character, and untiring devotion to the interests of her family and friends. One of the children of his second marriage was Milton G., who was born in Liberty District, Frederick Co., July 29, 1839. His early life was passed upon his father's farm, and his early education acquired first in the district school, later at Freeland Seminary, Montgomery Co., Pa., and still later at Dickinson Seminary, Williamsport, Pa. He spent the years 1856 and 1857 at the latter institution, but by reason of ill health was compelled to relinquish his studies there while his course was yet uncompleted. In 1861 he began the study of the law in the office of Hon. Grayson Eichelberger, of Frederick City, and in October, 1863, was admitted to the Frederick County bar,—meanwhile having taught school during the winters of 1859, '60, '61, and 1862. In 1863 he entered upon the career of law practitioner, and in December, 1878, associated with him as law-partner Edward S. Eichelberger, the son of his old preceptor. In 1871, Mr. Urner was elected State's attorney for Frederick County on the Republican ticket by a majority of about five hundred. After a four years' service in that office he returned to the cares of his extensive law practice. In 1876 he was candidate for Presidential elector at large on the Republican ticket, and in 1878 he was elected to Congress from the Sixth District of Maryland as the Republican candidate, over George Peter, Democrat, and Horace Resley, Greenbacker, and still occupies his seat as a member of that body. During the last session he served on the Committee on the Revision of the Laws and on the Committee on Mines and Mining. With public enterprises Mr. Urner has been prominently associated. He originated and projected in 1880 the Frederick Mechanical and Mercantile Library, is now a director of the Farmers' and Mechanics' National Bank, a trustee of the Frederick Female Seminary, a trustee of the Frederick public schools, and for a long time has been actively and prominently engaged in the promotion of the interests of four of Frederick's building associations. He is a leading member of the Frederick Methodist Episcopal Church, one of its stewards, a member of its board of trustees, and superintendent of its Sunday-school. In May, 1880, he was a delegate to the Methodist Episcopal General Conference that assembled at Cincinnati.

Jan. 10, 1866, Mr. Urner married Laura A., daughter of Dr. Richard T. Hammond, of Frederick County, still living at Woodsboro', and a descendant of the Hammonds of England who settled first in this country at Annapolis, and later became among the early settlers in Frederick County. Mrs. Urner has won considerable local fame as a poetess, and is a lady of refined accomplishments. Of Mr. and Mrs. Urner's eight children four are living.

Gen. Bradley T. Johnson is the son of Charles Worthington Johnson and Eleanor Murdock Tyler, and grandson of Col. Baker Johnson. He married Jane Claudia Saunders, daughter of Hon. R. M. Saunders, of North Carolina, and Anna Hayes, his wife, daughter of Hon. William Johnson, of South Carolina, justice of the Supreme Court of the United States. Hon. R. M. Saunders was member of Congress, judge of North Carolina, and United States minister to Spain in the administration of President Polk. Gen. Johnson graduated at Princeton in the class of '49, finished his law course at Harvard in 1851; the same year was married, and elected State's attorney for Frederick County. In 1857 he was Democratic candidate for comptroller of the treasury, and a delegate to the Democratic National Convention at Charleston and Baltimore in 1860. In 1859, '60, and '61 he was chairman of the Democratic State Central Committee.

On the 8th of May, 1861, he left Frederick in command of the first organized company that entered the Confederate service from Maryland,—all Frederick men, sixty in number, who marched around to the Point of Rocks. He was mustered into the Confederate army May 21, 1861, as captain Company A, First Maryland Regiment; major June 16, 1861; lieutenant-colonel July 21, 1861; and colonel of the regiment March 18, 1862. His regiment was thanked in general orders by Gen. Joseph E. Johnston, June 22, 1861, for soldierly conduct, exemplary discipline, and faithful and exact obedience to orders.

He commanded the Second Brigade, Jackson's division, at the second battle of Manassas, Aug. 26, 29, 1862, and the affairs at Chantilly and Germantown, and during the first Maryland campaign. On Sept. 6, 1862, he entered his native town at the head of his brigade, and was assigned to command the city by Gen. Jackson during the stay of the Confederate army there. He detailed Lieut. Lewis Randolph, First Battalion Regulars, to duty as provost-marshal, which duty he performed with exactness and order.

In that campaign Col. Johnson served and commanded without a commission, his regiment, the First Maryland, having been disbanded for the purpose of reorganization Aug. 18, 1862. This is probably the only case on either side during the war in which a commander actually directed troops in the field and in action without a commission as officer. But Gen. Jackson had such an opinion of Col. Johnson that he assigned him to the command of his Second Brigade with the consent and approbation of every officer in it, although at the time he was not legally in the military service.

On Dec. 16, 1862, he was commissioned colonel of cavalry, and June 22, 1862, colonel First Regiment Maryland line. On joining the army, then before Gettysburg, he was assigned on the last day of the battle to command his old brigade, the Second, of Jackson's division. He continued in command during the retreat from Gettysburg, and at the affair at Martinsburg, until December, when he was transferred to the Maryland line, then first concentrated into one command. It consisted of the Second Maryland Infantry, First Maryland Cavalry, Second Maryland Artillery, and subsequently of the First and Fourth Maryland Artillery also. He was stationed with his command at Hanover Junction to protect Gen. Lee's communications and guard his flank in the winter of 1863–64.

On Feb. 4, 1864, while absent on duty, he was unanimously elected colonel and commander of the Maryland line. On June 28, 1864, he was promoted brigadier-general of cavalry, in recognition of his extraordinary service in defeating with a detachment of sixty of his cavalry the junction of Kilpatrick and Dahlgren before Richmond, and thus frustrating their attack and effort to burn that city. Gen. Johnson was in active and arduous service in the field all through the war. In 1861 he was in the battle of Manassas and the affairs at Mason's Hill, Munson's Hill, and Upton's Hill.

In 1862 he commanded his regiment in the engagements at Rappahannock Station, Front Royal, Winchester, Harper's Ferry, Harrisonburg, Cross Keys, and Port Republic, in Jackson's celebrated Valley campaign, and at Cold Harbor, Malvern Hills, and Westover. He commanded the Second Brigade in the second battle of Manassas and the engagements at Groveton, Chantilly, and Warrenton Springs.

In 1863 he commanded the same brigade at Gettysburg, Martinsburg, Hainesville, Chester Gap, Culpeper, Brandy Station, and Centreville.

In 1864 he commanded the Maryland line at Pollan's Farm and Trevillian's Station, and Johnson's cavalry brigade in the affairs at Leetown, Frederick, Beltsville, Winchester, and Middletown. He was in command of his brigade with McCausland at the burning of Chambersburg; at the battles of Winchester, Sept. 19, 1864; at Fisher's Hill, Sept. 21; at Cedar Creek, Oct. 8; and at Woodstock, Oct. 19, 1864.

In Early's raid into Maryland and around Washington in 1864 he commanded the advance in the invasion and the rear-guard in the retreat.

From the 3d of July to the 1st of November, 1864, he fought every day, with a few exceptions of occasional rest, and continued in active service until May 1, 1865, when he surrendered, while in command of the post at Salisbury, N. C.

Maj.-Gen. Ewell, in his official report of the Valley campaign, said,—

"The history of the Maryland regiment, gallantly commanded by Col. Bradley T. Johnson, during the campaign of the Valley would be the history of every action from Front Royal to Cross Keys. On the 6th, near Harrisonburg, the Fifty-eighth Virginia Regiment was engaged with the Pennsylvania 'Bucktails,' the fighting being close and bloody. Col. Johnson came up with his regiment in the hottest period, and by a dashing charge in flank drove the enemy off with heavy loss, and capturing Lieut.-Col. Kane, commanding. In commemoration of this gallant conduct I ordered one of the captured bucktails to be appended as a trophy to their flag.

"The action is worthy of acknowledgment from a higher source, more particularly as they avenged the death of the gallant Ashby, who fell at the same time. Four color-bearers were shot down in succession, but each time the colors were caught before reaching the ground, and were finally borne by Corp. Daniel Shanks to the close of the action. At Cross Keys they were opposed to three of the enemy's regiments in succession."

At the close of the war Gen. Johnson engaged in the practice of the law in Richmond, Va., where he achieved success. He served as member and president of the City Council, and senator from the city of Richmond in the Virginia Legislature. During his term in the Senate he introduced and procured to be passed a law establishing a railroad commission for the State of Virginia, another law organizing a non-partisan police for the city of Richmond, and one providing for a new, complete, and just registration of voters.

He was the author of the report to the Senate on the public debt of the State, and the report of the joint Committee on Federal Relations on the Rives case, and the relations of the States to the Federal Government under the amended Constitution of the United States. This report received the sanction of a unanimous vote of both committees and of both Houses. In 1879 he returned to his native State, and is now settled in the practice of the law in Baltimore.

Joseph M. Palmer was a native of Connecticut, but came to Frederick in 1819, and was kindly received, especially by Hon. John Buchanan and Roger B. Taney. He soon acquired a lucrative practice, and was sent to the Legislature from Frederick County. In course of time he gained a wide-spread reputation as a lawyer of eminent abilities, and at the time of his death, which occurred Feb. 22, 1870, at Frederick, was the oldest lawyer at the bar of Frederick County, and the senior member of the profession in Western Maryland.

Hon. Richard H. Marshall was born in Charles County, Md., in 1800, and after his educational training had been completed was sent by his father to Frederick to study law, under the supervision of Roger B. Taney. He entered Mr. Taney's office in February, 1820, and continued under his instruction for nearly three years. At the fall term of the Frederick County Court in 1822 he was admitted as a member of the bar. He then returned to Charles County and opened an office in Port Tobacco. In the spring of 1823, Mr. Taney determined to remove to Baltimore, but before leaving Frederick he advised Mr. Marshall to locate himself in Frederick, which then offered a fine opening for a young lawyer. Mr. Marshall decided to take Mr. Taney's advice, and accordingly settled in Frederick in the latter part of 1823. He gradually progressed in public confidence until his practice became a lucrative one. In 1842 he was appointed associate judge by the Governor, and had for his colleagues Chief Judge John Buchanan and his brother, Judge Thomas Buchanan, both accomplished gentlemen and able jurists. After their death Judge Marshall was associated with Judge Robert N. Martin and Judge Daniel Weisel, of Washington County. When the election of judges was substituted for their appointment by the Governor, Judge Marshall retired to private life, and resumed the practice of the law. When the war broke out he found himself unable to accede to the principles asserted by the Republican party, or to continue the practice of his profession in a manner satisfactory to himself, he therefore decided to retire from the bar. Since then he has not resumed his practice, but has led the life of a private gentleman, ever taking, however, a keen interest in public affairs, and especially in the interest of the community among whom he resides. Judge Marshall is eighty-one years of age, and in his peaceful retirement enjoys the confidence and respect of all classes of his fellow-citizens.

Charles H. Pitts was born in Frederick Co., Md., and educated as a lawyer. He passed the bar in Frederick City, and at the suggestion of a prominent lawyer removed to Baltimore, where he soon acquired a large practice.

In the exciting times which prevailed prior to the breaking out of the late civil war the people insisted upon his becoming their representative, and he, along with a number of prominent citizens, was sent to the Legislature which assembled in Frederick City in 1861. As a consequence he was arrested by the military authorities and cast into prison at Fort Warren. Mr. Pitts died Aug. 14, 1864, after an exceptionally brilliant legal career. At a meeting of the bar held in his honor, S. Teackle Wallis paid the following beautiful tribute to his memory:

"I have no intention, even if it were appropriate, and I could command myself, to analyze the admirable gifts which gave to our lamented brother his rare success. All around me knew him well and witnessed the triumphs of forensic eloquence and talent with which his cases were crowded. I need not say then in this presence that they were triumphs fairly won,—the achievements of professional ability and knowledge, directed by courage, sagacity, and skill. Prominent among his endowments was a downright sturdy common sense which could not easily be cheated or misled, and which found for him the straightest path to the solution of all questions, and taught him the directest method of leading to conviction the minds of other men. Thus he was always practical and forcible,—never beguiled for a moment from the duty and the end before him, even by the seductions of his playful fancy and abounding wit and humor. In the moral qualities, which are so large an element in all enlarged professional distinction, he had no superior, for he was brave and true, with a high manly sense of right, and that deep scorn which true men feel for wrong. The traits of his professional intercourse were so attractive to us all that they will linger with us as the memory of a fascination, and those who shared his confidence and knew him in his private and domestic hours will feel that a light has been extinguished with his life, which was among the brightest and gladdest that ever cheered them."

James McSherry, the author of the well-known "History of Maryland," was born in the village of Liberty Town, Frederick Co., on the 29th July, 1819, and died in Frederick City, July 13, 1869. His father, James McSherry, was a native of Adams County, Pa., and was born on the 28th July, 1776. His mother's maiden name was Ann Ridgely Sappington, who was the daughter of Dr. Francis Brown Sappington, a very prominent physician of Frederick County.

The paternal ancestors of James McSherry were from Ireland, from whence Patrick McSherry, born 1725, emigrated to this country with his wife, who was Catharine Gartland, of Armagh. They had twelve children, of whom James McSherry, the father of the subject of this sketch, was the eleventh. Patrick McSherry died in 1795. His son James was a very prominent man in Pennsylvania. In 1807 he was elected a member of the House of Delegates from Adams County, and was re-elected for five years, until

1813, in which year he was elected to the Senate by the people of York and Adams Counties, and served until 1817. While a senator, and exempted from military service, when Baltimore was menaced by a

foreign foe, he enlisted as a private in Capt. McClevis' company of horse at Gettysburg, and remained in service until the company was disbanded. In 1821 he was elected to Congress, and in 1824 was again elected to the Legislature, and served for six successive years, and again during the sessions of 1834, 1835, and 1836. In 1837 he was elected to the Constitutional Convention. He died February, 1849.

James McSherry, the subject of this sketch, married, Sept. 30, 1841, Eliza Spurrier. By this marriage there were five children. The eldest, James McSherry, is a leading attorney of Frederick City, and receiver of Mount St. Mary's College; the second, Dr. William S. McSherry, died in 1876; the third, Dr. Ed Coale McSherry, is a dentist, and the two daughters are married. He was educated at Mount St. Mary's College, where he was graduated in June, 1838. He then read law with Gen. James M. Coale in Frederick, and was admitted to the bar in 1840, and practiced in Gettysburg with the late Hon. Thaddeus Stevens, but at the close of 1841 returned to Frederick, and continued there until his death.

His tastes were much inclined to literary pursuits, and he became a contributor to the *United States Catholic Magazine*. In 1846 he published "Père Jean, or the Jesuit Missionary," which in 1860 was republished under the name of "Father Laval." He was also a contributor to the *Metropolitan Magazine*, published in Baltimore.

But he is better known by his "History of Maryland," published in 1848, in which the principal events of Maryland history are compressed into a popular form, such as would interest and instruct the general reader. The settlement of the colony, its rise and progress, troubles and revolutions, and its periods of peace and prosperity are all told in simple narrative, at once attractive and instructive. Only those battles of the Revolution in which the sons of Maryland were engaged are dwelt upon by the historian. He avoided the strife of politics; and the contentions of parties in that period of the country's history embracing the adoption of the Constitution of the United States, when the foundations of political parties were laid, have no place in this history. Yet, being the second history of Maryland, and treating its subjects with fullness and fairness, it will always retain a prominent place in the libraries of her sons.

In 1851 he published "Willitoft, or the Days of James the First," which was republished in 1858 in Frankfort-on-the-Main. In 1850–51 he lectured frequently in New York and Philadelphia for the benefit of Catholic churches, and in 1858 he delivered the address at the semi-centennial celebration of Mount St. Mary's College. There is a strong Catholic sentiment pervading all his writings, as both himself and ancestors were devotedly attached to that church. He was a strictly religious man, an excellent citizen, discharging every duty with fidelity and zeal.

His son, James McSherry, is the receiver of Mount St. Mary's College, and a lawyer of high standing at the Frederick bar. Like his father, his tastes are literary, and he has been a frequent contributor to the daily and monthly press of the State.

For a number of years Hon. John Ritchie has been one of the leading lawyers of Western Maryland. He was born in Frederick in 1832. His great-grandfather was a Scotch immigrant (probably from the Cumberland Valley), who settled in Frederick County at an early period. His great-uncle was clerk of the Frederick County Court for thirty years, and other members of the family held the responsible positions of sheriff, register, etc. His father was Dr. John Ritchie, a well-known and talented physician of Frederick. Dr. Ritchie married twice, the children by the first marriage being John and Albert

Ritchie, and a son, William, and a daughter by the second. John Ritchie, after receiving an academic education, completed his law education at Harvard University. He then returned to Frederick and began the practice of law with William P. Maulsby, then residing in Frederick, and who afterwards was a member of the Court of Appeals. He soon gained a lucrative practice, and was acknowledged as one of the best speakers in the forum as well as on the stump. His first appearance on the field of public activity was as captain of a militia company in Frederick, and which was the first militia organization that offered its services to President Buchanan for the suppression of the John Brown raid at Harper's Ferry. The services of the company, "The Junior Invincibles," were accepted by the President, and the company marched to Harper's Ferry. In 1860, Mr. Ritchie was an elector on the Breckenridge Presidential ticket. Some years afterwards he was elected State's attorney for Frederick County, and at the end of his four years' term was re-elected. In 1870 he was elected to Congress from the Sixth District by a majority of over eighteen hundred. Mr. Ritchie was the Democratic candidate, and the district was generally expected to give a Republican majority. He was renominated in 1872, but was defeated. Mr. Ritchie has held no political position since then, but has been a prominent figure in Democratic State politics. In the Democratic State Convention of July, 1875, he was the leader of the section of the party which favored the nomination of Hon. William T. Hamilton for Governor, and in 1879 nominated Mr. Hamilton for the same position in an eloquent speech. Mr. Hamilton was elected Governor, and on the 16th of March, 1881, he appointed Mr. Richie chief judge of the Sixth Judicial District of Maryland, comprising the counties of Frederick and Montgomery. Judge Ritchie is by virtue of his office a member of the Court of Appeals. Mr. Ritchie has been prominently mentioned as a candidate for the United States Senate and president of the Chesapeake and Ohio Canal. He is a lawyer of great ability and an eloquent orator. His brother, Albert Ritchie, is a well-known lawyer of Baltimore. Judge Ritchie's wife is a daughter of ex-Judge W. P. Maulsby.

Enoch Louis Lowe was born Aug. 10, 1820, in Frederick County, and entered St. John's College in 1829. He went to Europe and entered Clongore's College, Ireland, and afterwards Stonyhurst, England, where he received medals for proficiency. He left Stonyhurst in 1839, and after a continental tour returned to Maryland. He studied law, and was admitted to the bar of Frederick County in 1842. In 1845 he was elected a member of the Maryland House of Delegates, and in May, 1850, was nominated for Governor before he was thirty years of age. He was elected Oct. 2, 1850, and served as Governor until 1854. He was a member of the Democratic National Convention in 1856, and was appointed minister to China in 1857, but declined the mission. He voted for Breckenridge and Lane in 1860, and in 1861, at the breaking out of the war, went South, and remained there until 1865, when he returned to Maryland. He removed to Brooklyn in 1866 and resumed the practice of the law. Governor Lowe is a finished orator and a lawyer of uncommon talents. He married Esther Winder Polk, daughter of Col. James Polk, of Somerset, a cousin of ex-President Polk.

Robert J. Brent, a prominent member of the Baltimore bar, was born in Louisiana in 1811, his father, a Marylander, having adopted that State as his home. The elder Brent was a member of Congress from Louisiana at the time of his son's birth, and subsequently removed to Washington, where he engaged in the practice of the law, having for his associates such men as Clay, Webster, and Calhoun. His son Robert studied law in his office, as also in the office of the late Gen. Walter Jones, of that city. In 1834, Mr. Brent was admitted to the bar, and practiced for a short space in the courts of the District, but subsequently moved to Frederick, and later to Hagerstown, where he married Miss Lawrence, a member of the well-known Hager family. Mr. Brent afterwards removed to Baltimore City, where he at once established himself as a lawyer of great attainments and wonderful energy. Mr. Brent interested himself to some extent in politics, and though a Whig at the beginning of his career, subsequently espoused the principles of the Democracy. He was elected a member of the State Constitutional Convention of 1851, and while serving as a member was appointed by Governor E. Louis Lowe State's attorney for Baltimore City, to succeed George R. Richardson. Mr. Brent took no active part in politics afterwards save to represent his congressional district in the famous Charleston Convention of 1860, where he figured as a sturdy supporter of Stephen A. Douglas. He devoted himself to his profession with an ardor which has characterized few lawyers, and his practice rapidly extended to all the courts of the State, and at his death, which occurred Feb. 4, 1872, he was regarded as one of the leaders of the Maryland bar. At a meeting of the Baltimore bar, held shortly after his death, Hon. Reverdy Johnson offered a series of resolutions, from which the following is extracted: "In the decease of Mr. Brent the bar has lost a sound

JOHN H. McELFRESH.

and thoroughly educated lawyer, whose intimate acquaintance with his profession was only equaled by the extraordinary energy and activity of his practice, and the intelligence, earnestness, and force with which he pursued it." Mr. Brent was eminently social in disposition, and it was a marvel to his friends how he accomplished so much work and at the same time devoted so many hours to their pleasure. He was passionately fond of yachting, and was as well known to the pilots and mariners of the Chesapeake Bay as to his associates at the bar.

John Hammond McElfresh, son of Henry McElfresh and Ariana Hammond, was born May 27, 1796, near New Market, Frederick Co. The first of his paternal ancestors in America was David McElfresh, a house-carpenter, who came over from Scotland early in the eighteenth century and settled on the river Severn, Anne Arundel County, Md. His son, John H. (likewise a carpenter), removed early in life to Frederick County, near New Market, and turning his attention to farming became wealthy. He married Rachel Hammond. The fourth of their eight children was Henry, father to John Hammond McElfresh. Henry McElfresh was conspicuous for his mental accomplishments, and especially for his acquaintance with Biblical history, concerning which it was of common remark that few ministers of his day were more conversant with the Bible than he. His son, John Hammond, was the fourth of thirteen children, and in his youth even possessed a mind that made him a subject of more than ordinary notice. Under such village pedagogues as Griffith, Whittaker, and Comerford, he bravely fought his way through trigonometry and surveying at the age of thirteen, and at fourteen conquered Greek and Latin. He finished his school education in the classical department of Frederick College, under John V. Weylie, and in 1813 began the study of medicine with Dr. L. T. Hammond, of Anne Arundel County. In the winter of 1816–17 he attended a course of lectures at the University of Maryland, and Feb. 28, 1817, graduated from that institution as a doctor of medicine. He practiced in Frederick until 1822, when he elected to abandon medicine for the profession of the law, having previously (1820) been chosen register of the town and a trustee of Frederick Academy.

After studying law three years with John Nelson, of Frederick, he was admitted to the bar in 1825. He took immediate rank as an eloquent pleader, and as an ardent advocate of the cause of the poor exhibited much sympathetic energy. In 1830 he was elected to the House of Delegates, and exerted himself with persistent effort during his term on behalf of the passage of a law providing for the abolishing of imprisonment for debt. The final success of the measure was largely due to his labors in the cause. In 1831, Governor Martin appointed him on his staff with the rank of colonel. In November, 1836, he was elected a member of the State Reform Convention, while as an incident in his strictly home career it may be mentioned that he was one of the members of Frederick's first fire company. As an orator Col. McElfresh was an acknowledged model, and as a scholar won high approval. His law practice was extensive and greatly successful, and called him into the courts not only of Frederick, but of Washington and Montgomery Counties, and the Court of Appeals of the State. His memory was so remarkably retentive that upon one occasion he repeated Milton's Paradise Lost entire, an affidavit from one of his auditors to that effect being now in the possession of one of his descendants. He was a lover of the poets, and frequently entertained his friends with glowing recitations from his favorite authors.

March 27, 1820, he married Teresa, daughter of Francis Mantz and Anna Mary Burkhardt. Francis Mantz was one of Frederick County's wealthiest citizens, and stood high in public esteem. The bulk of his great fortune descended eventually to his daughter Teresa. While yet in the full flush of manhood and the height of a useful career, Col. McElfresh died, Aug. 4, 1841, aged forty-five. One of his sons (Henry) died at Annapolis while serving as a member of the Legislature. One of his daughters married Hon. Jacob M. Kunkel. The only surviving daughter of Col. McElfresh is Ariana, wife of Col. Charles E. Trail, of Frederick.

Samuel Tyler. This distinguished author and philosopher was born in Prince George's County, Oct. 22, 1809. He was admitted to the Maryland bar in 1831, and established himself at Frederick. In 1836 he became a contributor to the *Princeton Review*, in which he published some of his most valuable productions. In 1844 he published a "Discourse on the Baconian Philosophy," which gained him the friendship of Sir William Hamilton, the eminent Scottish philosopher. His other works are "Burns as a Poet and as a Man," "The Progress of Philosophy in the Past and in the Future," and the "Life of Judge Taney,"—the latter a work of standard authority and high literary and legal excellence. He is also the author of a report on the subject of law reform in the State of Maryland.

George W. Sands. This gentleman has published a volume of poems called "Mazelli and other Poems," which were dedicated to Samuel Tyler. Born in

Frederick, he removed to Howard County, where he became a leading lawyer. He was elected State's attorney of that county, and subsequently was appointed collector of internal revenue.

Charles C. Smeltzer, son of Col. Henry R. Smeltzer, late of Middletown District, and grandson of Sergt. Lawrence Everhart of Revolutionary fame, read law with ex-Governor Lowe. He subsequently removed to Iowa, and in 1858 was elected judge of the court in Clay County.

J. H. C. Jones. This eminent lawyer was born in Frederick City, and was the son of Rev. Joseph H. Jones, the eloquent Baptist preacher, and a brother of Hon. Spencer C. Jones, clerk of the Maryland Court of Appeals. He was in 1870 appointed circuit judge of the district composed of King and Queen and Middlesex Counties, Va.

The following is a list of members of the Frederick bar, with the dates of their admission or of licenses granted them to practice:

Name	Year	Name	Year
William Cumming	1749	Franklin Anderson	1818
Daniel Dulany, Jr.	1749	Robert N. Martin	1819
Henry Darnall	1752	F. A. Schley	1819
Edward Dorsey	1752	Roger Perry	1819
Stephen Bordley	1755	C. Birnie, Jr.	1821
Richard Chase	1755	J. T. Brooke	1821
Lloyd Buchanan	1755	Richard H. Marshall	1822
Eastburn Bullit	1760	Benjamin Price	1822
Thomas Johnson	1760	Wm. M. Blackfoot	1823
James Keith	1761	William Schley	—
James Tilghman	1765	James M. Cole	1828
Townly Rigby	1768	William J. Ross	1828
Thomas Johnson	1778	Alex. Manning	1828
Robert Smith	1783	Samuel Tyler	1831
David Ross	1783	Edward Schley	1833
John McDowell	1784	James Dixon Roman	1834
Henry Ridgely	1785	John R. Key	1834
Edward Nicholls	1785	James Raymond	1835
Joshua Dorsey	1785	James Williams	1835
Roger Nelson	1786	Charles H. Pitts	1835
Richard Potts	—	A. M. Sterett	1835
John Gardner Hamilton	1789	James W. Pryor	1835
Basil Howard	1790	Frederick Coppersmith	1836
Abraham Shriver	—	Eugene H. Lynch	1837
George Price	1791	George A. Pearre	1838
Arthur Shaaf	1791	John Miller	1838
John Thomson Mason	1791	Charles B. McKierna	1838
William Claggett	1792	Thomas M. Markell	1839
James Cookery	1792	James McSherry	1840
James Johnson	1795	Robert Ford	1840
Richard Brooke	1797	Francis B. Sappington	1840
John Hanson Thomas	—	Worthington Ross	1841
William Cranch	1798	Robert J. Taylor	1841
Francis Scott Key	—	M. B. Luckett	—
John Buchanan	1800	Jervis Spencer	1842
Roger Brooke Taney	1801	Enoch L. Lowe	1842
Upton Lawrence	1802	William McSherry	1842
William Ross	1805	John W. Baughman	1843
R. S. Pigman	1806	John H. O'Neill	1843
Wm. T. T. Mason	1806	Grayson Eichelberger	1843
Upton Scott Reid	1808	William M. Merrick	1844
Otho Lawrence	1812	Joseph P. Jenks	1844
John S. Shriver	1812	L. P. W. Balch	1845
John Nelson	—	Charles Schley	1845
James Dixon	—	Jacob M. Kunkel	1845
Dennis Hagan	1815	Corydon Beckwith	1845
James Somerville	1815	Henry D. Motter	1846
John Kilgore	1816	Wm. C. Sappington	1846
John Andrews	1816	Henry McElfresh	1847
Thomas C. Worthington	1817	Robert Wilson	1847
Joseph M. Palmer	1817	Francis D. Young	1847
Benjamin Jones	—	B. F. Wright	1847
Perry A. Rice	1848	Milton G. Urner	1863
Wm. D. Philips	1848	Lloyd Luckett	1864
M. P. Gallagher	1849	D. S. Wright	1865
John F. Tchan	1849	Francis Brengle	1865
Luther M. Reynolds	1850	Charles V. S. Levy	1866
Ross Johnson	1850	Adolphus Fearake, Jr.	1866
John A. Lynch	1851	Joseph Trapnell	1866
Hunter Brooke	1851	Charles Webster	1867
Frederick J. Nelson	1851	John E. R. Wood	1867
John J. Harding	1851	John L. Carlisle	1867
John E. Smith	1852	B. F. M. Hurly	1867
William L. Schley	1852	I. F. McCreery	1867
Ephraim Carmack	1852	George A. Pearre	1868
Z. S. Claggett	1852	Cyrus W. Poole	1868
George K. Shellman	—	John C. Motter	1868
J. W. Price	1853	Isaac E. Pearson, Jr.	1868
George A. Hanson	1853	Valerius Chriswell	1869
John F. Baughman	1853	Robert Stokes	1870
John Johns	1853	John B. Tyler	1870
Charles Lee Ammon	1853	H. G. Sleeper	1870
William P. Maulsby	1854	Charles H. Maulsby	1870
John Ritchie	1854	Carlton Shafer	1870
Charles H. Hoffman	1854	Joseph P. Ryan	1871
George W. Sands	—	George E. Price	1872
Isaac E. Pearson	1854	William H. Hinks	1872
B. J. Semmes	1855	Charles W. Derr	1872
W. H. Wills	1855	W. Otis Tyler	1873
A. K. Syester	1856	Noah Bowles	1873
Thomas M. Monroe	1856	Charles H. Wood	1874
John H. Falconer	1856	William Ritchie	1876
A. K. Venimel	1857	William Wilcoxon	1876
George Schley	1858	Robert H. MacGill	1877
Charles W. Ross	1858	Benjamin H. Richmond	1877
Andrew H. Dill	1858	Charles M. Gilpin	1878
Edward O'Brien	1859	P. Frank Pampel	1878
John P. Poe	1860	Edward S. Eichelberger	1878
Spencer C. Jones	1860	Clayton O. Keedy	1878
John W. Hedges	1860	Silas M. Morgan	1879
Calvin C. Raymond	1861	Charles Light Wilson	1879
William T. Hamilton	1861	Frank C. Norwood	1879
James H. Grove	1862	Zachary T. Brown	1879
James W. Pearre	1862	James B. Trail	1880
James Murdock	1863	Charles F. Markell	1881

Present members of the bar not in the foregoing list:

Edward Shriver, William B. Nelson, Edward Y. Goldsborough, C. H. Eckstein, John H. Handy, Belva A. Lockwood, Roger W. Cull, Michael A. Mullen.[1]

CHAPTER XXI.

EARLY COURT PROCEEDINGS.

First Court—Refreshments for Juries—Judges and Constables—Notable Trials and Executions—Court-houses and Jails—Early Marriages and Wills.

THE laws in force in this State consist of the emanations from three distinct systems: the usages and laws of England,—the mother-country, the usages and laws of the provincial or ante-Revolutionary government of Maryland, and the laws of the present State government. And these, too, are subject to certain modifications and restrictions, flowing from the

---

[1] Some of the above were admitted in other counties and obtained leave to practice in the Frederick courts, while others were admitted in Frederick but resided elsewhere.

FREDERICK COUNTY.

eminent dominion of the Constitution of the United States.

The first court in Frederick County was the "County Seat," consisting of justices of the peace appointed and commissioned by the Governor and his Council. These justices, in addition to their judicial functions proper, performed all the duties now imposed upon the present county commissioners. They were allowed eighty pounds of tobacco per day during their attendance at court. The act creating the county provided that the County Court should begin and be held on the third Tuesday of the months of March, June, August, and November yearly, and assizes therein to begin and be held upon the Mondays following after the assizes in Prince George's County.

The following is a copy of the order of the Lord Proprietary creating the first court in the county:

"Anno Dom 1748.
"FREDERICK COUNTY, ss.

"This day to wit the Thirteenth day of December, Anno Dom 1748, Nathaniel Wickham, Junior, produced the following Commission of the peace and Dedimus Potestatem which was publicly read in these words To wit, Maryland ss—Charles Absolute Lord and Proprietary of Maryland and Avalon, Lord Baron of Baltimore &c. To Benjamin Tasker, George Plater, Edmund Jennings, Charles Hammond, Samuel Chamberlain, Philip Thomas, Daniel Dulany, Edward Lloyd, Benjamin Young, Benjamin Tasker Junior, Richard Lee, and Benedict Calvert, Esquires, Nathaniel Wickham, Junior, Thomas Owen, Thomas Cresap, Thomas Beatty, Joseph Chaplain, Henry Munday, Thomas Prather, George Gordon, Joseph Ogle, William Griffith, John Rawlings, of Frederick County Gentlemen, Greeting, know ye that we have assigned you and every one of you jointly and severally our justices to keep our peace within our County of Frederick and to do equal law and right to all the king's subjects rich and poor according to the Laws, customs and Directions of the Acts of Assembly of this Province so far forth as they Provide and where they are silent according to the Laws Statutes and reasonable Customs of England as used and practiced within this Province for the conservation of the Peace and quiet Rule and Government of the King's Subjects within our said County and to Chastise and punish all or any Person or persons offending against the said Acts, Laws, Statutes and Customs or any of them according to the Directions thereof and to call before you or any of you all those who in our County aforesaid shall threaten to do any bodily Harm to any of the King's subjects, or to Burn their Houses or otherwise break our peace and misbehave themselves to find sufficient Security of the Peace and good Behavior to us and the said Subjects and if they shall refuse to find such security that then you cause them to be committed into safe Custody until they shall be delivered by due course of Law from thence: Also we have assigned you and every three or more of you of whom we will you the said Benjamin Tasker, George Plater, Edmund Jennings, Charles Hammond, Samuel Chamberlain, Philip Thomas, Daniel Dulany, Edward Lloyd, Benjamin Young, Benjamin Tasker Junior, Richard Lee, and Benedict Calvert Esquires, Nathaniel Wickham Junior, Thomas Owen, Thomas Cresap, Thomas Beatty, Joseph Chaplain, Henry Munday, or one of you always to be one our Justices to Enquire by the oaths of good and Lawful men of our county aforesaid by whom the truth of the Premises may be the better known of all and all manner of Felonies Petty Treasons Murders Rapes upon White Women willful burning of any dwelling house or any other outhouse contiguous to and used with any dwelling house or any other outhouse wherein there shall be any Person or any Goods or Merchandizes Tobacco Indian Corn or Fodder and all other Capital Offences done or perpetrated by any Negro or other Slave and likewise all Consulting Advising and Conspiring of Negroes and other Slaves to Rebel or raise any Insurrection or to Murder or poison any person or to Ravish any White Woman or to attempt to Burn any Dwelling house or outhouses Contiguous to or used therewith and of all Trespasses Engrossings Regratings Forestallings and Extortions whatsoever and of all other Misfeasances and Offences whatsoever of which Justices of our peace lawfully may or ought to Enquire by whomsoever or howsoever in our County aforesaid done or committed or which may hereafter happen to be done or committed and also of all those who in our County aforesaid in Riotous manner have gone or rode or shall hereafter presume to go or ride with armed force against our peace to the Disturbance of the King's Subjects, and of all such who in our County aforesaid have lain or shall hereafter presume to lye in Wait or Kill any of the King's Subjects, And also of all ordinary Keepers and other persons who have Offended or hereafter shall presume to Offend in the abuse of Weights or Measures against the Acts of Assembly for the common good and profit now in this Province made and used, and also of the Sheriffs Bailiffs Constables and other Officers who have or shall hereafter misbehave themselves in the Execution of their offices or have been Remiss or Negligent in the Execution thereof or shall hereafter happen so to be within our County aforesaid and of all and every the Articles Matters and Things whatsoever howsoever or by whomsoever in our County aforesaid done or committed or that shall hereafter happen to be done or Committed concerning the Premises or any of them and to Inspect all indictments before you or any of you taken or to be taken or before our late Justices of the peace within our said County had and taken and not yet determined and Process thereon against all or any person or persons so indicted or which shall hereafter happen to be indicted within our County aforesaid to make and Continue until they shall be taken or surrender themselves or be Outlawed and to hear and determine all and every the Felonies Petty Treasons Murders Rapes upon White Women willful Burning of any Dwelling house or outhouse contiguous to and used with any Dwelling house or any other Outhouse wherein there shall be any Person or any Goods or Merchandizes Tobacco Indian Corn or Fodder and all other Capital Offences done or perpetrated by any Negro or other Slave to Rebel or raise any Insurrection or to Murder or Poison any Person or to Ravish any white Woman or attempt to burn any Dwelling house or Outhouses contiguous to or used therewith Trespasses Forestallings Regratings Riots and Indictments and all the other matters aforesaid according to the Laws Customs and Direction of the Acts of the Assembly aforesaid so far forth as they provide and where they are silent according to the Laws Statutes and reasonable Customs of England as used and practiced within this Province and the said Delinquents and every of them to Chastise and Punish by Fines Ransoms Amercements Forfeitures and otherwise according to the Laws Customs and Directions of the Acts of Assembly aforesaid so far forth as they provide and where they are silent according to the Laws Statutes and reasonable Customs of England as used and practiced within this Province. But we will not that you proceed in any of the Cases aforesaid to take Life or Member except of Negroes and other Slaves but that in every such case you send the Prisoners with their Indictments and the whole Matters depending before you to our own Justices of Assize, Nisi prius and Gaol Delivery at the next Court of Oyer & Terminer to be held for our said County be it wheresoever and whensoever to be holden there to be Tried. And we Command you and every one of you Diligently to Intend the Keeping of the Penal Acts of Assembly Laws Customs and Statutes aforesaid and all and every of you the Premises and that at your County Courts you make Inquisition and hear and determine as aforesaid doing therein what to Justice appertains according to the Laws Customs and Directions of the Acts of the Assembly aforesaid so far as they provide and where they are Silent according to the Laws Statutes and reasonable customs of England as used and practiced within this Province. And further we do constitute Ordain and appoint you the said Benjamin Tasker, George Plater, Edmund Jennings, Charles Hammond, Samuel Chamberlain, Philip Thomas, Daniel Dulany, Edward Lloyd, Benjamin Young, Benjamin Tasker Junior, Richard Lee and Benedict Calvert, Esquires, Nathaniel Wickham Junior, Thomas Owens, Thomas Cresap, Thomas Beatty, Joseph Chaplain, Henry Munday, Thomas Prather, George Gordon, Joseph Ogle, William Griffiths, John Rawlings or any three or more of you as aforesaid to issue out Writs Precepts Process and Attachments and hold plea of all Actions Popular and of all Actions personal of what sort soever wherein the demand doth not exceed the sum of one hundred Pounds Sterling or Thirty thousand pounds of tobacco and all Actions Personal now depending before you and after Judgment Execution to Award in all such Cases and Actions aforesaid according to the Laws, Customs and Directions of the Acts of Assembly aforesaid so far forth as they provide and where they are Silent according to the Laws Statutes and reasonable Customs of England as used and practiced within this Province in which said Actions so to be tried we do Constitute ordain and appoint the said Benjamin Tasker, George Plater, Edmund Jennings, Charles Hammond, Samuel Chamberlain, Philip Thomas, Daniel Dulany, Edward Lloyd, Benjamin Young, Benjamin Tasker Junior, Richard Lee, and Benedict Calvert, Esquires, Nathaniel Wickham Junior, Thomas Owen, Thomas Cresap, Thomas Beatty, Joseph Chaplain, Henry Munday, Thomas Prather, George Gordon, Joseph Ogle, William Griffith, John Rawlings and none others to be Judges. Also by these presents we do command the Sheriff of our said County of Frederick to give his Attendance and cause to come before you or any three of you as aforesaid such and so many Good and Lawful men of this Bailiwick out of each and every hundred thereof by whom the Truth of the Matter in the Premises may be the better Known and Enquired of. Lastly you shall cause to be brought before you at your said Court all Writs Precepts Process and Indictments to your Courts and Jurisdiction belonging that the same may be Inspected and by due Course of Law Detirmined.

"Witness our trusty and well Beloved Samuel Ogle, Esquire, Lieutenant General and Chief Governor of our said Province of Maryland this Twelfth day of December in the Thirty fourth year of our Dominion, &c. Anno Dom. 1748."

Whereupon Nathaniel Wickham, Jr., Thomas Beatty, Henry Munday, Thomas Prather, and William Griffiths, gentlemen, qualified themselves as justices for the county by taking the several oaths appointed by the act of Assembly to be taken to the government, together with the oath of judge, signing the oath of abjuration, and repeating and signing the test. The court as thus formed was then called, with the above justices present and sitting. John Darnall, clerk of the county; John Thomas, sheriff; and James Dickson, under-sheriff, exhibited their commissions, and, having qualified, took their respective official seats. The court then adjourned to March 21, 1749.

In accordance with the act of Assembly entitled "An act for amending the staple of tobacco, for preventing frauds in His Majesty's customs," a court was held March 10, 1749. Justices present Daniel Dulany, chief justice, Nathaniel Wickham, Jr., Henry Munday, Thomas Owen, and George Gordon. John Rawlings and George Gordon, both justices, were then appointed to inspect the weights and scales belonging to the warehouse at Rock Creek. The first regular session of the County Court convened March 21, 1749, with Daniel Dulany, chief justice, and the following justices of the peace: Henry Munday, John Rawlings, Thomas Beatty, Joseph Chaplain, Nathaniel Wickham, Jr., William Griffith, Thomas Prather, Thomas Cresap, and George Gordon. The following grand jury appeared and were charged as to their presentments:

David Linn (foreman), Edward Owen, Benjamin Perry, James Perry, William Murdock, Joseph Wood, Elias Delashmutt, John Perrin, Moses Chapline, Samuel Magruder, Mirian Magruder, Jr., Aaron Prather, John Swearingen, John Lemar, Charles Higginbotham, William Beatty, Abraham Alexander.

The following bills of indictments were returned: Staffel Barnard, assault and battery on the wife of George William Lawrence; James Kendal, for remarking two sows and putting a wrong mark on "ten shotes," the property of Van Swearingen; Peter Williams, perjury; John House, Sr., assault and battery on Mary Devilbess; Thomas Appleton, for altering the mark of two hogs, the property of William Garthing; John Nichols and Stephen Richards, felony. The court appointed Alexander Jones as "court-cryer." George Thompson, for *swearing* in court, was committed to the sheriff's custody until he paid his fine. A summons was issued for Peter Hoggins to testify before the grand jury. George Grouse appearing to be a very "antient and infirm person" was set levy free for the future; also Nathan Gregg, Robert Owen, and Baltazer Miller. Basil Beall was sworn in as bailiff to the grand jury. The first petition for a road was presented by Joseph Wood and others, who prayed that a road be "layed out" from Frederick Town by Abraham Miller's mill, and from thence by Ambrose's mill to ye temporary line, and Joseph Ogle and Nathaniel Wickham, Jr., were appointed to lay out said road. The first petition filed was by Stephen Julian and Darby Ryan, who had been bound to Widow Parr, administratrix of John Parr, deceased, and averred that she being dead, and the effects of said Parr being likely to be made way with, petitioned that some method be taken for their safety, and an attachment was issued for Arthur Parr, returnable the third Tuesday in June following.

The petition of Richard Snowden and other inhabitants on Patuxent River was received, asking for the building of two bridges, one at Richard Greene's ford, and the other at Peter Murphy's ford, and forty-five pounds was appropriated for the building of the same, one-half to be levied the ensuing year, and the other half the year after. Cleburn Simms was granted a license for "ordinary keeping,"—*i.e.*, for keeping a tavern or inn.

The grand jury on being discharged were allowed four hundred pounds of tobacco for their services in the next county levy. Van Swearingen was required to appear at the next court as a witness against Peter Williams in the full and just sum of ten pounds. Simon Harden, an orphan child aged eight or nine years, was bound to Charles Higginbotham until his majority. A contract was entered into with William Luckett to keep a ferry over the mouth of Monocacy, for which he was to be allowed in the next levy twenty-two pounds. Said Luckett obligated himself, when his boat or scow could not pass by reason of low water, to provide a cart to transport tobacco and other things, and it was ordered that he should not take more than four pence for carrying a man and horse over, and three shillings for wagons belonging to non-residents. Thomas Reynolds contracted with the court to keep ferry over the Monocacy opposite the plantation where John Hussey formerly dwelt, and Edward Wyatt was appointed to keep one at the mouth of Conococheague. The court purchased of Daniel Dulany six volumes of the statutes and "Nelson's Justice," in two volumes, for £40 15s., to be paid out of next county levy. George Gordon was ordered to purchase blocks and ropes for the prizes and cranes in the Rock Creek tobacco warehouse. William Griffith was approved and recommended to the Governor as a proper person to be appointed " Ranger." Reverdy Ghiselin took the oath as "under" clerk of court. George Gordon was ordered to buy a standard weight for the county.

The court settled the rates of liquors and other "hot-water" accommodations in the county as follows:

	£	s.	d.
Hot Dyet for a Gentleman with a pint of small beer, in the country	0	1	0
Hot Dyet for a Gentleman with a pint of small beer, in towns	0	1	3
Rum Pr Sealed Quart and so pro rata	0	4	0
Hot Dyett for a Gentleman with a pint of beer	0	0	9
Lodging in a bed Pr night	0	0	2
Cider Pr Gallon	0	2	0
Maryland good strong beer Pr Gallon Sealed	0	3	0
A Bowl of punch made with a Sealed Quart of Rum & loaf sugar & so pro rata	0	6	0
Stabling and good fodder for one horse Pr night	0	1	0
Corn and Oats Pr Bushell and so pro rata	0	4	0
A Sealed Quart of Madeira Wine	0	4	0
Good Small beer Pr Quart Sealed	0	0	4
A Cold Dyct	0	0	8
Maryland Spirits distilled from Grain Pr Gallon	0	9	8
Peach Brandy Pr Gallon	0	13	4
All other European Wines	0	5	0

Kennedy Farrell was granted license to keep Ordinary (tavern).

The justices established the "hundreds" and appointed the following constables:

Potomack Hundred, lower part	Charles Jones.
Upper Potomack Hundred	James Offutt, Jr.
Newfoundland Hundred	William Waters.
Middle part Rock Creek Hundred	John Bean.
Sugarland Hundred	Thomas Fletchall.
Sugar loaf "	John Norris.
Linganore "	Thomas Manyard.
Manor "	John Martin.
Pipe Creek "	Joseph Wood.
Kittocton "	John Johnson.
Antietam "	Moses Chapline.
Marsh "	Nathan Tombleson.
Salisbury "	Robert Downey.
Conococheague "	William Ervin.
Linton "	Edmund Martin.
Monocacy " upper part	Joseph Faress.
" " middle part	Stephen Julian.
" " lower part	Joseph Wilson.

The first condemnation suit, on attachment, was that of Robert Lemar against Jacob Eades, and the latter's cow and calf, valued at five pounds, and six hundred pounds of inspected tobacco were condemned for plaintiff's benefit. The first case in the court was that of Capt. Robert De Butts *versus* John Dauphilmire, in which the writ is returned, " Cepi, then agreed." The first trespass suit was that of Henry Lancaster *versus* John Harper. In the suit of Charles Carroll *versus* Robert De Butts, administrator of Isaac Bloomfield, was the first judgment rendered (and by confession), for sixty-six pounds debt and two hundred and seventy-one pounds tobacco, charges and costs.

At the June term of Court 1749, the following were the grand jury: Thomas Stoddert, William Wilburn, Charles Wood, Charles Cheney, John Adamson, John Johnson, Isaac Baker, William Boyd, William Shepherd, Samuel Ellis, Nathaniel Magruder, Hugh Conn, William Pritchett, William Gray, Thos. Boystone, Walter Evans, and William Nichols.

Indictments were found against Van Swearingen, Samuel Swearingen, and Robert Wells, Jr., for refusing to assist a constable (Nathaniel Tomlinson) to carry before a magistrate the body of George Parker, taken with a warrant for debt. The style of all criminal cases were Lord Proprietary *versus* (prisoner's name). The following were the constables appointed by the County Court for the years 1750 and 1751:

Hundreds.	1750.	1751.
Lower part Potomac..	Charles Jones.	Hugh Rielly.
Upper " " ..	William Offutt.	Clement Davis.
Newfoundland..........	William Waters.	Lewis Duvall.
Middle pt. Rock Creek	John Bean.	John Bean.
Lower " " "	Hugh Conn.	Hugh Conn.
Sugarland	Thos. Fletchall.	George Jewell.
Sugar loaf.................	Nathan Veach.	Alex. Perry.
Linganore.................	Henry Beall.	Joseph Beall.
		Ninian Long.
Manor.......................	Jacob Barton.	John Barrick.
Pipe Creek............	James Whitacre.	Michael Hodgkiser.
Kittocton..................	Jos. McDonald.	Wm. Johnson.
Antietam	James Wallen.	Wm. Bonell.
Marsh.......................	John Perins.	Joseph Smith.
Salisbury	David Jones.	James Downing.
Conococheague..........	James Davis.	Owen Davis.
Linton	John Nicholls.	John Nicholls.
Monocacy, upper part.	Thos. Wilson.	Wm. Emmitt.
" middle " ..	Jos. Mayhew.	Peter Stilly.
" lower " ..	John Nelson, Jr.	Notley Thomas.

For the years 1750 and 1751, Joseph Wood, of Israel Creek, and John West were "press-masters." The courts were held in the "Dutch meeting-house" for the first two years, as the court records show that allowances were ordered to be made in the levies for holding it in that building.

By the act of 1748 creating Frederick County, the commissioners therein appointed were authorized to purchase three acres of land in or adjoining Frederick Town, whereon to build a court-house and prison for Frederick County. The land to be surveyed and "laid out in an exact square, and staked, and well bounded: the court-house to be built in the centre of the square, and the county prison on the south side of the same square, within ten feet of the southernmost outline of the three acres aforesaid." In accordance with these provisions the lot was purchased, and on March 21, 1749, the court ordered that the clerk make out advertisements notifying that the magistrates of the county, or the major part thereof, would meet on the 8th of May following to contract with any person or persons to build a court-house, which advertisements the sheriff was ordered to set up in the most convenient places of the county. On Nov. 21, 1749, Joseph Hardman, bricklayer, and John Shellman, carpenter, in court engaged themselves to build the "hull" of a court-house in Frederick Town, and offered Thomas Beatty, Abraham Miller, and Patrick Matthews as their securities, whom the court approved of; and the same court appointed Nathaniel Wickham, Jr., William Griffith, and Henry Munday, or any two of them, to agree with the said Joseph Hardman and John Shellman for the same, and the said gentlemen were desired to lay before the next County Court the bond and articles of agreement for building the "hull" of the court-house aforesaid.

On Nov. 24, 1750, the justices of the county having viewed the court-house lately built in Frederick Town, approved the same, and Joseph Hardman obligated himself "to point the gavel end" and fill up the scaffold-holes. This edifice remained until the building of the second one in 1785.

At March term, 1749, Conrad Cross was fined forty shillings on his confession for selling liquors without a license; the first conviction for this offense. At June term following, Stoaffel Bernard was fined one shilling for breach of the peace. Mary Ryan, for bastardy, was taken to the whipping-post and there received on her bare body five lashes, well laid on by the sheriff, and her time of servitude with her master, Benjamin Harris, was extended nine months, as payment of costs.

At November court, 1749, "Negro Peter," the slave of James Wardrop, for stealing a hat and axe from Richard Smith, was sentenced to receive thirty lashes at the whipping-post.

The first petit jury impaneled was in the case of Lord Proprietary vs. William Roberts, on trial for felony, and were as follows: Robert De Butts, Joseph Doddridge, Moses Chapline, Herbert Wallace, Peter Stull, John Johnson, of Kittocton, Shadrach Hyatt, Patrick Matthews, Elias Delashmutt, John Purdom, James Spurgeon, and John Jones, who acquitted the prisoner. "Negro George," the slave of Maj. Joseph Ogle and Morris Manyan, for stealing a bushel and a half of rye of the value of fifty pounds of tobacco, the property of said Ogle, received seventy-five lashes. Jacob Beney, for keeping a tippling-house, was fined forty shillings, as were also eight others at the same term.

At June term, 1750, John Claggett and George Gordon were ordered to have erected a pair of stocks at the mouth of Rock Creek. Mary Macknane, for purloining a snuff-box of the value of ten pounds, the property of Nicholas Brundrick, was ordered to be set up in the pillory during

STOCKS. PILLORY.

the space of five minutes, and that afterwards she be set to the whipping-post and there receive on her bare body five lashes, restore to the said Brundrick the snuff-box, and pay him twenty-eight pounds, the fourfold value thereof. Andrew Ringle, for the theft of an axe of Henry Six, was fined and whipped with twenty lashes. At this court it was ordered that a pillory be erected on the court-house lot in Frederick Town, and Nathaniel Wickham, Jr., and Thomas Beatty were appointed to attend to the building of the same.

The August court, 1758, established the rates of liquor and other ordinary accommodations, to wit:

	£	s.	d.
Hot dyett for a Gent with a pint of beer or cider.....	0	1	3
Same for a Gent's servant with do.........................	0	0	9
A cold dyett with do			
Corn and Oats Pr bushel & so pro rata...................	0	4	0
Stabling & Good Fodder or hay for a horse Pr night..	0	0	3
Do for 24 hours..	0	1	0
Pasturage for horse 24 hours...............................	0	0	6
Lodging in a bed Pr night...................................	0	0	6
Good small beer Pr gallon sealed & so pro rata.........	0	2	0
Peach Brandy Pr gallon sealed & so pro rata...........	0	10	8
Cider Pr Gall sealed & so pro rata........................	0	1	8
Maryland spirits distilled from grain Pr gallon sealed &c &c...	0	8	0
Rum Pr sealed Quart & so pro rata.......................	0	4	0
Bowl of punch, sealed Quart of rum & loaf sugar & so pro rata..	0	5	0
Ditto with brown sugar......................................	0	4	0
A quart of Madeira wine sealed & so pro rata.........	0	4	0
Vidonia wine sealed Pr quart & " " "	0	3	0
Port wine " " " " " "	0	3	0
All European wines not here mentioned Pr Sealed Quart & so pro rata...	0	5	0
English strong beer Pr sealed quart......................	0	1	8
French brandy Pr Quart made into punch with loaf sugar & so pro rata...	0	8	0
Arrach Pr Quart sealed made into punch with loaf sugar & so pro rata...	0	15	0

At the August court, 1759, the following justices were present: the worshipful Joseph Wood, Wm. Luckett, Thomas Norris, Peter Bainbridge, Major Chaplaine, Thomas Prather, and D. Lynn. The grand jury sworn were Arthur Nelson, Peter Stilly, John Fletshall, Jeremiah Virgin, Joseph Ramsburg, Van Swearingen, Jr., Jon. Hagar, Martin Casner, John Cartwright, Geo. French, Geo. Loy, Garat Davis, Serratt Dickerson, John Shelman, Michael Miller, Walter S. Greenfield.

John Jacobs was sworn as their bailiff.

At the August court the following constables were appointed:

Hundreds.	Names.
Lower part Potomac	Ninian Beall Magruder.
Upper " "	Samuel West.
Newfoundland	John Riggs, Junr.
Lower part Newfoundland	Samuel I. Goodman.
Middle part Rock Creek	Thomas Dowden.
Sugarland	Arthur Hickman.
Sugar loaf	Wm. Patrick.
Linganore	Philip Turner.
Manor	Stephen Richards.
Pipe Creek	Biggar Head.
Piney Creek	Thomas Glann.
Burnt-House Woods	John Segar.
Upper part Monocacy	Richard Branner.
Middle " "	Charles Hedge.
Lower " "	Arthur Nelson.
Frederick town	John Kimball.
Lower part Kattocton	Samuel Magruder, Jr.
Upper " "	Thomas Johnson.
Lower " Antietam	Henry Boteler.
Upper " "	James Walling, Jr.
Marsh	Van Swearingen, Jr.
Salisbury	Daniel Jones, Jr.
Conococheague	Neal McFaul.
Linton	Ralph Matson.
Old Town	John Nicholls.

The court records show that the justices often adjourned for a half-hour or an hour, and most generally to some tavern, where it is supposed the inner man was refreshed, to enable them to better dispatch business.

At the August term of 1768, Mrs. William Beard produced to the court the best piece of white linen, for which she was allowed 1000 pounds tobacco, as per act of Assembly; for second best, Mrs. Sarah Watson was allowed 1000 pounds; and for third best, Charles Swearingen received 900 pounds; for the fourth best piece, David Carlisle got 800 pounds, and also 700 pounds for best sixth piece. For the best piece of brown linen, Catherine Kimball was allowed 900 pounds tobacco; Eleanor McKain for second best, 800 pounds; George Gillespie for third best, 600 pounds; John Swearingen for fourth best, 600 pounds; and Thomas South for fifth best, 500 pounds.

The first instance of the reception of a colored man's testimony in Frederick County occurred as late as July 9, 1866, before Justice Mahoney.

Notable Trials and Executions.—The most momentous case which has ever come before a Frederick County court was the trial of the seven Tory leaders, Peter Sueman, Nicholas Andrews, John George Graves, Yost Plecker, Adam Graves, Henry Shell, and Casper Fritchie, for high treason. These men belonged to an association of loyalists, who had banded themselves together for the purpose of co-operating with a strong force of British and Indians in an expedition against Virginia and Maryland. Their place of meeting was discovered, and a descent was made, which resulted in the capture of the persons whose names are given above. A special court was empowered to try them, of which Alexander Contee Hanson was the principal judge. The trial had a most important significance, from the fact that the opinion prevailed among the Tories that the Revolutionary government would not venture to proceed to extreme measures. It was therefore necessary to make a terrible example, and the prisoners on being convicted were sentenced to death, as stated in the Revolutionary chapter of this work.

The Gruber Trial.—Another case before a Frederick County court which attracted national attention was the famous Gruber trial. On August 16, 1818, a camp-meeting was held in Washington County, Md., under the auspices of the clergy and laity of the Methodist Episcopal Church. The Rev. Jacob Gruber, who was presiding elder of the district, preached the sermon. It was shown afterwards that the sermon was unpremeditated, and that he preached only after his failure to induce another minister to do so. No substitute could be procured, and, as presiding elder, it was his duty to preach. "Righteousness exalteth a nation, but sin is a reproach to any people," was the text of his discourse. By sin, he said, the text meant not individual sin alone, but also national sin, and among the national sins which he proceeded to elaborate was that of slavery. His congregation consisted of from three to five thousand whites and several hundred colored people. Towards the close of the sermon he directed himself to his colored hearers, urging them to bear their lot with resignation, to obey their masters, and to seek consolation in religion. The grand jury of the county subsequently indicted Mr. Gruber for wickedly and maliciously inciting slaves to rebellion. At the trial, Mr. Gruber availed himself of his legal privilege, and procured the removal of his case to Frederick County, where he was acquitted.

The following is the bill of indictment found by the grand jury of Washington County upon which the defendant was tried in the Frederick County court, March term, 1819, and acquitted:

"*Charge* 1.—State of Maryland, Washington County, to wit. The jurors for the State of Maryland, for the body of Washington County, upon their oath present: That Jacob Gruber, late of the said county, clerk, being a person of an evil, seditious, and turbulent disposition, and maliciously intending and endeavoring to disturb the tranquillity, good order, and government of the State of Maryland, and to endanger the persons and property of a great number of the peaceable and quiet citizens of the said State, on the 6th day of August, in the year of our Lord 1818, at the county aforesaid, unlawfully, maliciously, and wickedly intended to instigate and incite divers negro slaves, the property of divers citizens of said State, to mutiny and rebellion, for the disturbance of the peace of the said State, and to the great terror and peril of the peaceable citizens thereof; and the said Jacob Gruber, in prosecution of his said wicked intention and purpose, and for the effecting and the accomplishment thereof, on the said 16th day of August, with force and arms, at the county aforesaid, unlawfully, wickedly, maliciously, and advisedly did endeavor to stir up, provoke, instigate, and incite divers negro slaves, whose names to the jurors aforesaid are yet unknown, the property of divers citizens of said State, and inhabiting in the county aforesaid, with force and arms, unlawfully, seditiously, and wickedly, to commit acts of mutiny and rebellion in the said State, in contempt, and in open violation of the laws, good order, and government of this State, to the evil and pernicious example of all others in like case offending, and against the peace, government, and dignity of the State."

(There were two other charges of a similar character which we omit.)

"FRANKLIN ANDERSON,
"*Dist. Atty. 5th Judicial Dist.*
"OTHO H. WILLIAMS, *Clerk.*"

Mr. Anderson, in opening the case, observed that it was well known that slaves were property according to our laws, and that masters were entitled to protection, and any attempt to incite slaves to insubordination and resistance to the lawful commands of their masters ought to be punished. But in the prosecution of the inquiry on this occasion it must not be forgotten that liberty of opinion and speech is the privilege of every citizen, and if Mr. Gruber had no criminal intent in his sermon he committed no offense. It was, he added, the duty and the province of the jury to judge of the intent from the facts disclosed.

Roger Brooke Taney, afterwards chief justice of the United States, opened the case on the part of the Rev. Mr. Gruber.

"The statement," he said, "made by the district attorney had informed the jury of the interesting principles involved in the trial then pending before them. It was, indeed, a prominent and important case, in which the entire community as well as the accused were interested. The prosecution," said Mr. Taney, "is without precedent in the judicial proceedings of Maryland, and as the jury are the judges of the law as well as the fact, it becomes my duty not only to state the evidence we are about to offer, but to show you the grounds upon which we mean to rest the defense. I need not," he continued, "tell you that by the happy and liberal institutions of this State the rights of conscience and the freedom of speech are fully protected. No man can be prosecuted for preaching the articles of his religious creed, unless, indeed, his doctrine is immoral and calculated to disturb the peace and order of society. And all subjects of national policy may at all times be freely and fully discussed in the pulpit or elsewhere without restraint or limitation. Therefore the reverend gentleman, whose cause I am now advocating, cannot be liable to prosecution in any form or proceeding for the sermon mentioned by the district attorney, unless his doctrines were immoral and calculated to disturb the peace and order of society. The sermon, in itself, could in no other way be an offense against the laws. If his doctrines were not immoral, if the principles he maintained were not contrary to the peace and good order of society, he had an undoubted right to preach them and to clothe them in such language, and to enforce them by such facts and arguments, as to him seemed proper. It would be nothing to the purpose to say that he offended, or that he alarmed some or all of his hearers. Their feelings, or their fears, would not alter the character of his doctrine, or take from him a right secured to him by the constitution and laws of the State. . . . But the accused merits a defense on very different grounds. The counsel to whom he has confided his cause cannot content themselves with a cold and reluctant acquittal, and abandon Mr. Gruber without defense to all the obloquy and reproach which his enemies have industriously, and most unjustly, heaped upon him. We cannot consent to buy his safety by yielding to passion, prejudice, and avarice the control of future discussion on this great and important question. He must not surrender the civil and religious rights secured to him in common with others by the Constitution of this most favored nation. Mr. Gruber feels that it is due to his own character, to the station he fills, to the respectable society of Christians in which he is a minister of the gospel, not only to defend himself from this prosecution, but also to avow and to vindicate here the principles he maintained in his sermon. There is no law that forbids us to speak of slavery as we think of it. Any man has a right to publish his opinions on that subject whenever he pleases. It is a subject of national concern, and may at all times be freely discussed. Mr. Gruber quoted the language of our great act of national independence, and insisted upon the principles contained in that venerated instrument. He rebuked those masters who, in the exercise of power, are deaf to the calls of humanity, and he warned them of the evils they might bring upon themselves. He spoke with abhorrence of those reptiles who live by trading in human flesh, and who enrich themselves by tearing the husband from the wife, the infant from the bosom of its mother, and this I am instructed was the 'head and front of his offending.' Shall I content myself with saying that he had a right to say this? that there is no law to punish him? So far is he from being the object of punishment in any form of proceedings that we are prepared to maintain the same principles, and to use, if necessary, the same language here in the temple of justice, and in the presence of those who are the ministers of the law. A hard necessity, indeed, compels us to endure the evils of slavery for a time. It was imposed upon us by another nation, while we were yet in a state of colonial vassalage. It cannot be easily or suddenly removed. Yet while it continues it is a blot on our national character, and every real lover of freedom confidently hopes that it may be effectually, though it must be gradually, wiped away, and earnestly looks for the means by which this necessary object may be attained. And until it shall be accomplished, until the time shall come when we can point without a blush to the language held in the Declaration of Independence, every friend of humanity will seek to lighten the galling chain of slavery, and to better, to the utmost of his power, the wretched condition of the slave. Such was Mr. Gruber's object in that part of his sermon of which I am now speaking. Those who have complained of him and reproached him will not find it easy to answer him, unless complaints, reproaches, and persecution shall be considered an answer."

The counsel associated with Mr. Taney for the defense were Messrs. Martin and Pegman.

The Black-McKaig Trial.—On April 11, 1871, the Circuit Court of Frederick County convened in special session for the trial of Harry Crawford Black, indicted for murder in shooting Col. W. W. McKaig, Jr. Mr. Black was indicted by the grand jury of Allegany County for killing Col. McKaig on Oct. 17, 1870, in Cumberland, for the alleged seduction of his sister, Miss Myra Black. The defendant procured a change of venue to Frederick County. William Pinkney Maulsby, chief justice of the Sixth Judicial District, presided. The two associate justices at this trial were John A. Lynch and William Veirs Bouic. The counsel for the prosecution were Francis Brengle, State's attorney of Frederick County, Isaac D. Jones, attorney-general of Maryland, and Milton Whitney, of Baltimore. The counsel for the defense were Hon. Daniel W. Voorhees, of Indiana, A. K. Syester, of Hagerstown, Frederick J. Nelson, Lloyd Lowndes, of Cumberland, and William M. Price, of the same city. The jury were William M. Feaga, Joseph W. Etzler, Ephraim Stoner, George W. Foreman, Henry T. Deaver, Robert Lease, Pottinger Dorsey, Benjamin P. Crampton, Jonathan Biser, George H. Fox, Michael Zimmerman, and Daniel T. Whip.

The defendant, Black, was born in Cumberland, May, 1846, and was a relative of the late Hon. J. Dixon Roman and Hon. J. Philip Roman, who when living were recognized as leading men in the political and financial affairs of the State. Col. William W. McKaig, Jr., who fell by Mr. Black's hands, was descended from a long line of wealthy and respectable ancestors. He was the second son of Hon. W. W. McKaig, and nephew of Gen. Thomas J. McKaig. He was born April 5, 1842, was a cavalry captain in the Confederate army, and when killed was largely engaged in manufacturing in Cumberland. He was killed on Baltimore Street, the principal thoroughfare of Cumberland, on the morning of Oct. 17, 1870.

On the tenth day of the trial Mr. Voorhees rose to close the argument for Mr. Black, and paused as though oppressed by a sense of the great responsibility resting on him. All eyes were riveted on him. In a clear, firm voice Mr. Voorhees proceeded to address the jury, dwelling at first upon the remarkable character of the boy at the bar, as developed even in the testimony of adverse witnesses. With great skill he then pointed out the difference in position and circumstances of the families of McKaig and Black, the influence and wealth of the one, the simple integrity and respectability of the other. The speech lasted three and a half hours, and when he closed there was a murmur of applause, which was promptly checked by the court. Chief Judge Maulsby ordered a recess for a few minutes, after which the closing address of Mr. Whitney for the prosecution was delivered, and the case was given to the jury. In an hour the jury reappeared and rendered the verdict of "Not guilty." The pent-up emotions of the assemblage could no longer be controlled, and a deafening cheer shook the building from dome to foundation, and the entire assembly rushed forward as if to seize Black in their arms and bear him out of the court-room. Releasing himself as soon as possible from the throng, Black joined his mother, who stood weeping within the bar.

The Thomas Murder Trial.—John Thomas murdered Sophia Preston, April 24, 1849, was indicted for murder in the first degree, and tried during the latter part of the year. The jury were E. S. Annan, A. Anderson, Daniel House, H. Boteler, B. S. Lamar, John Tehan, John Myers, Edward Howard, Charles Cole, Jonathan Buranner, Theodore Delaplane, Daniel S. Biser. The attorney for the State was William M. Merrick, and for the prisoner, Governor Francis Thomas, Jacob M. Kunkel, E. L. Lowe, and M. Gallagher. The judges who sat in the case were Messrs. Martin, Marshall, and Weisel. After a hotly-contested trial of nearly a week, the jury found the defendant guilty as charged in the indictment. He was sentenced to be hanged, but his sentence was commuted to imprisonment for life.

Executions and Capital Crimes.—On Dec. 13, 1749, a "dead warrant" was issued for the execution of John Murphy, condemned at a special court for felony and burglary. He was the first person hanged within the limits of Frederick County.

On Thursday, April 22, 1762, just after sunset, as Uriah Wirt, an elderly man of sixty-five years of age, and his son were traveling from Virginia to Frederick Town, in Frederick County, and when they were about seven miles from town, they were attacked by a man on horseback, who demanded their money, and almost at the same instant fired his pistol at the old man. The bullet went in at his shoulder and thence into his breast, inflicting a wound of which he died in about two hours. The murderer, who was named Richard Crosby, made off, but was subsequently taken and confined in Frederick County jail.

On April 29 a special commission was granted for holding a court of Oyer and Terminer at Frederick for the trial of said Richard Crosby *alias* Den, and on May 6th he was tried and convicted and sentenced to death. He was executed June 10th.

Oct. 8, 1762, Michael Peck was executed for the murder of George Jacob Poe in July preceding.

Oct. 22, 1773, four convicts who some time previously had murdered their master, Archibald Moffman, were, pursuant to their sentence, duly hanged.

Feb. 2, 1792, a man named Curran was committed to jail on a strong suspicion of being the person who had robbed Joseph H. Nicholson and Richard Chew on the highway.

In 1803, negro "Sam" was executed for killing a black woman.

Nov. 3, 1815, Edward C. Owings was murdered by his own slaves, Jonathan, Harry, Nimrod, and Solomon, who were hanged Jan. 26, 1816. An immense concourse of people were present from adjoining counties and States.

May 20, 1820, Judge Shriver sentenced the negro Kitty to death for setting fire to the barn and dwelling-house of Mr. Troxell, near Emmittsburg.

March 2, 1821, the negroes Peter and Kitty (brother and sister) were executed for murdering their mistress, Mrs. William Baker, in August, 1819. They were sentenced by Judge Buchanan, Nov. 14, 1820.

Nov. 3, 1827, at a husking at Walter Kemp's, a man named Davis stabbed a negro, Sam, who died instantly. Davis was indicted on the 4th, and on the 9th was found guilty of manslaughter and sentenced to ten years in the penitentiary.

June 24, 1831, John Markley was hanged for the murder, on Dec. 29 or 30, 1830, of six persons, viz.: Mr. Newey, his wife, father-in-law, Mr. Tressler, two children, and an apprentice. This barbarous murder occurred in Harbaugh's Valley, and the prisoner was defended by William Ross and Joseph M. Palmer. The execution took place at the barracks, and was witnessed by over four thousand people.

June 25, 1831, John Livure was killed in an affray by Thomas Fowler.

Dec. 19, 1834, Joseph O'Conor, for killing Mary Gower, was sentenced to eighteen years in the penitentiary on the jury's verdict of manslaughter.

Nov. 23, 1849, John Thomas was sentenced to be hanged for the murder of Mrs. Sophia Preston on April 24, 1849, but the Governor commuted the sentence to imprisonment for life in the penitentiary.

Jan. 7, 1858.—Philip Hawkins (free colored) was hanged for the murder of James Diggs (free colored), committed in Urbana District, Feb. 17, 1857.

May 28, 1869, Geo. Truman (colored) was hanged for murder of an unknown white man, Jan. 30, 1869.

June 21, 1878, Edward H. Costley (colored) *alias* Edward H. Dorsey, who murdered his cousin, Solomon Costley, April 7, 1877, was executed in a drenching rain-storm. The murder took place in Liberty District. He was executed in the jail-yard in the presence of three thousand people, who stood in the rain to witness the hanging.

Felix Munshour was hanged at Frederick on the 11th of November, 1881, for the murder of his cousin, James L. Wetsel, near Emmittsburg, on the 5th of August, 1879. He protested his innocence on the scaffold.

Court-House and Jail.—The first courts for a year or so were held in the "Dutch Meeting-House," and subsequently for a while in the upper story of Mrs. Charlton's tavern, on the southwest corner of Market and Patrick Streets, Frederick Town, where now stands Messrs. Stewart & Price's hardware-store.

On the 10th of May, 1750, Daniel Dulany made a deed for lots 73, 74, 75, 76, 77, 78, containing by estimation three acres, to Nathaniel Wickham, Jr., Thomas Beatty, Joseph Ogle, Wm. Griffith, Edward Sprigg, Jr., and John Kimbal, the commissioners appointed by act of Assembly to purchase three acres of ground for building a court-house thereon. The consideration was eighteen pounds. The erection of the building was pushed forward vigorously, and was completed all save the inside, on Nov. 24, 1750. The General Assembly, by an act of Nov. 17, 1753, authorized the County Court to levy two hundred and ten pounds to finish the interior, etc., but it was not completed until about 1756, as Braddock's expedition through the county the previous year retarded the progress of the work, owing to the general's having taken the workmen away to labor for him. The Legislature in 1784 authorized the justices at the March and August courts of 1785 to levy two thousand pounds to build a new court-house,—the second one erected. Its architect was Andrew McCleery, who copied the model of the old court-house of assizes in Dublin, Ireland. The court on April 8, 1785, appointed Jacob Young, Wm. M. Beall, and George Murdock to contract for building it, and drew orders on the collector for payment of expenses. It was ordered to be erected in the centre of the court-house ground, fifty feet back from the old court-house, and in its erection part of the material of the old one was used. The first court-house was a wooden structure of a story and a half, having a kind of gallery or steps to go up, and two jury-boxes. The next, or second, one burned down May 8, 1861. It had been the theatre of many hotly-contested legal battles, and its old walls had resounded with many able and eloquent speeches. On June 17, 1861, the county commissioners resolved to construct a new court-house, in pursuance of an act of the General Assembly authorizing them to assess forty thousand dollars for that purpose, or rather borrow that amount for its erection. Thomas Dixon, of Baltimore, was the supervising architect. J. Edward Sifford & Co. contracted on August 8th to do the granite-work, cut-stone work, marble steps, sills, plinths, and floor-tiling for four thousand and fifty dollars, to be completed by Sept. 1, 1862. S. H. & J. F. Adams, of Baltimore, on the same date contracted to build the remainder of the edifice in the same period of time for thirty-three thousand one hundred and ninety dollars. The court-house was finished in the fall of 1862, and is one of the best and most commodious in the State. Its court-room in the matter of acoustics is hardly surpassed by any in the country. The first jail, a rude and not very safe structure, was built about the time the first court-house was erected, and prior to 1753. It stood on a lot just opposite the court-house, and where Judge Richard H. Marshall's residence is now situated. The whipping-post was on the corner of the court-house lot, immediately opposite to the lot where the Central National Bank is located, and remained there until after the war of 1812. In May, 1804, the jail was broken open and several prisoners escaped. The General Assembly, by act of 1766, authorized the county justices to levy thirty thousand pounds of tobacco to build a stone wall around the jail and a house for the jailer. The next jail was erected on the site of the present county prison, and was rebuilt in 1862, after the fire of September 13th, by James Hopwood. The present jail, with sheriff's house, was erected in 1875 and 1876, at a cost of seventy-two thousand dollars. Frank E. Davis, of Baltimore, was the architect; David Frazier, general superintendent; David H. Kolb, carpenter; and Haller & Hergasheimer did the masonry and bricklaying. Routzhan & Bowers furnished the lumber, Flinn & Emmick the steam-heating apparatus, Calvin Page the iron-work, and Ebbert & Son did the plumbing. It is a solid and substantial structure, well ventilated, and a safe receptacle for the most hardened criminals. It is three stories high, and has separate cells for the prisoners.

Early Marriages.—The first law directing the issuing of marriage licenses in Maryland was passed in 1777, the second year of the State constitution. The following is an official list of the licenses issued for the first three years after the passage of the law:

1778.
March 19. William Logan to Margaret Shelar.
" 24. Archibald Morrow to Margaret Hitton.
" 25. Benjamin Padgett to Ann Green.
" 28. Samuel Archibald to Catherine Cock.
April 6. Richard Boseman to Susanna Holtz.
" 7. John Silver to Ann Springer.
" 17. Joseph McDonald to Anna Shell.
" 18. George Scutehall to Catherine Cline.
" 21. Richard Wells to Edith Coe.
" 23. David Miller to Catherine Heffner.
" 23. Maj. Peter Mantz to Catherine Howard.
" 23. Peter Humbert to Rebecca Bunn.
" 24. John Kemp to Barbara Huff.
" 25. John Keller to Mary Yost.
May 4. John McElfresh, Jr., to Rachel Dorsey.
" 5. Benjamin Beale to Ann Bardle.
" 5. Samuel Norris to Catherine Miller.
" 5. Thomas Hazlewood to Sarah Coffin.
" 8. Moses Farsten to Mary Cavenor.
" 9. Matthias Campbell to Teney Voagh.
" 11. Lawrence Still to Rebecca Gassaway.
" 11. Thomas Brown to Lydia Ann Chambers.
" 11. James Eddie to Mary Hammond.
" 12. Thomas Farroll to Hannah Dalton.
" 20. Zachariah Linton to Mary Maynard.
" 21. James Stipe to Mary Down.
" 22. Richard Barrick to Catharine Heartsock.
" 23. Jacob Smedley to Elizabeth Cline.
" 25. Conrad Gatuldig to Catharine Snider.
" 27. Adam Devilbiss to Catharine Barrick.
" 28. Joseph Johnson to Catharine Miller.
" 30. Jacob Shallman to Catharine Bentz.
June 2. Peter Mottis to Philopœna Heckathen.
" 2. Archibald Thomas to Sarah Farnsell.
" 3. Rudolph Hindes to Sarah Huff.
" 4. William Beaver to Susannah Temple.
" 6. William Bowden to Elizabeth Ryley.
" 8. Philip Aller to Jane Grimes.
" 13. William R. Howe to Ann Strider.
" 15. Peter Pebble to Mary Cepherton.
" 21. Michael Stoker to Mary Adams.
" 25. Abraham Deaver to Ann Laken.
" 27. John Parkinson to Ann Lisle.
" 27. John Smith to Elizabeth Kiser.
" 29. John Compston to Sarah Knotts.
July 4. William Heartsock to Catherine Fogle.
" 9. George Gander to Rosanna Dillon.
" 10. Joseph Taylor to Eleanor Riley.
" 12. James Poole to Rachel Shipley.
" 19. Henry Cline to Mary Jumper.

July 19. Bedwell Parnell to Ruth Easton.
" 19. Andrew Lowe to Mary Peckenpaugh.
" 23. Thomas Simmons to Mary Adams.
" 25. Peter Alvy to Elizabeth Heffner.
" 25. Michael Little to Mary Quinner.
" 27. George Woods to Mary Lloyd.
Aug. 1. Joseph Butler to Mary Ogle.
" 8. Samuel Leatherwood to Hannah Buckingham.
" 8. Gudlip Sidle to Eve Shiveley.
" 10. John Maginnis to Hetty Moran.
" 12. John Snowden Hook to Elizabeth Ward.
" 19. Job Jenkins to Sarah Ann Tucker.
" 21. Richard Creale to Eve Livingstone.
" 22. Chrisholm Griffith to Mary Ann Scott.
" 24. Thomas Porter to Susanna McDonald.
" 25. James Cumming to Keziah Coale.
" 27. William Edward Head to Mary Walker.
" 31. Henry Curtis to Hannah Fulston.
Sept. 1. John Whitmore to Mary Cox.
" 3. Basel Johnson to Sarah Tracey.
" 5. Benjamin Hill to Sarah Scaggs.
" 8. David Gillespie to Christie Berry.
" 9. Michael Hawn to Christianna Eichelberger.
" 12. Jonathan Hollard to Drusilla Ridgeley.
" 14. Jacob Buzzard to Mary Sheffer.
" 16. Joseph Will, Jr., to Margaret Row.
" 18. George Shoup to Charlotte Loy.
" 18. Henry Shrader to Susanna Horine.
" 22. Patrick Ryley to Hannah Price.
" 22. William Dobson to Mary Ray.
" 23. Peter Kemp to Mary Leaman.
" 25. James Conner to Elizabeth Sipes.
" 25. Matthew Myler to Elizabeth Fowler.
" 26. William Anderson to Cavey Brashears.
" 26. Henry Bucey to Ann Trueman.
Oct. 3. Joseph Kenneday to Christianna King.
" 9. Jacob Miller to Margaret Dentlinger.
" 9. Adam Sollman to Susanna Isenbergh.
" 9. Richard Wood to Elizabeth Head.
" 12. Daniel Ale to Madeline Keller.
" 12. Richard Gassaway to Ann Arnold.
" 17. Charles Schweirt to Elizabeth Castle.
" 17. Joseph Brayn to Martha Matthews.
" 19. Christopher Hart to Elizabeth Richards.
" 29. John Richardson to Mary Noble.
" 26. Charles Fleagle to Catherine Fisher.
Nov. 4. Thomas White to Sarah Gavin.
" 4. Josiah Hedges to Ann Barnett.
" 4. William Harrison to Mary Davis.
" 7. Robert Deane to Elizabeth Reynolds.
" 14. George Read to Margaret Mugg.
" 16. John Howard to Mary Crale.
" 16. William Jacobs to Dorcas Stokes.
" 25. Hugh Biggon to Eleanor Fenton.
" 26. Wm. Messer to Eleanor Smith.
" 27. John Bonsam to Elizabeth Wedin.
Dec. 3. John McGalvain to Elizabeth McKinley.
" 4. George Rodgers to Jane Patten.
" 12. Simon Colbert to Eleanor Reed.
" 16. Jacob Harris to Jane Grimes.
" 19. George Hagarty to Elizabeth Kennedy.
" 27. David McCollom to Mary Crips.
" 29. James Calhoun to Catherine McAtee.
1779.
Jan. 1. Henry Lilley to Hannah Harland.
" 2. Henry Cook to Sarah Whitehead.

Jan. 2. William Farwaid to Mary Lambert.
" 4. Martin Everheart to Christina Fulsin.
" 11. William Powell to Mary Edwards.
" 18. Allen Garrett to Mary Barton Phillpott.
" 25. Samuel Flower to Janey Bowlany.
" 29. George Street to Elizabeth Cotton.
" 29. Wm. Carrill to Elizabeth Fee.
Feb. 1. Benjamin Ricketts to Ruth Wells.
" 5. Francis Winpigler to Sarah Ridgeley.
" 8. Michael Ryne to Eleanor Smith.
" 9. Wm. Richardson to Nancy Davis.
" 10. John Bricker to Nancy Boyer.
" 11. Wm. Blackburn to Ann Carr.
" 12. Jacob Neatch to Frances Masten Willson.
" 13. John Lynch to Mary Ridgeley.
" 13. Bigger Head to —— Livers.
" 15. James Polson to Rachel Durbin.
" 15. Henry Barkshire to Gressilla Burton.
" 16. Jacob Smith to Soloney Koontz.
" 16. John Louis to Mary Keplinger.
" 16. Robert Bysert to Mary Falconer.
" 18. Frederick Moyas to Mary Fine.
" 20. Jacob Cueable to Matty Campbell.
" 20. James Ball to Rachel Hinton.
" 22. Lindsay Delashmutt to Sarah Trammell.
" 26. Charles Johnson to Mary Ann Jamison.
" 28. John Greengrass to Catherine Cain.
March 1. Zepheniah Spires to Catherine Walker.
" 2. John Jacobie to Catherine Weane.
" 5. Mathias Ringer to Elizabeth Plank.
" 6. John Peter Schoolmyer to Mary Eve Rineheart.
" 8. John Hendshaw to Elizabeth Knowse.
" 11. Gabriel Thomas to Mary Rainsbergh.
" 13. Edward Richards to Jane Roote.
" 17. Wm. Mathews to Catherine Burchell.
" 17. Isaac Jones Naylor to Barbara Goodman.
" 18. Richard Hinton to Ruth Cash.
" 18. George Boyrley to Elizabeth Inch.
" 19. Henry Shreiver to Barbara Welfley.
" 20. Jacob Amrum to Elizabeth Clark.
" 20. Wm. Moore to Catherine Grimes.
" 20. George Shibeler to Elizabeth Everley.
" 22. Peter Snowdagle to Christina Eckman.
" 26. Wm. Cash to Cassie Nicholls.
" 26. John Faris to Sarah McDonnah.
" 27. Charles King to Elizabeth Risener.
" 31. Daniel Ball to Catherine Boyer.
April 1. Joseph Thompson to Ann Elizabeth Brooke.
" 2. Christian Yesterday to Elizabeth Huff.
" 3. Abram Hill to Judey Clabaugh.
" 3. William Hill to Mary Perkinson.
" 3. Charles King to Mary Middagh.
" 5. Thomas Flowers to Mary Murphey.
" 7. Melchor Tabler to Philopœna Berger.
" 10. Nicholas Vanderlin to Mary Null.
" 10. John Scott to Mary Strane.
" 10. John Cook to Susannah Willson.
" 12. George Cutler to Mary Asbill.
" 13. Charles Smith to Mary Ringer.
" 17. John Flucke to Eve Young.
" 17. Leonard Young to Barbara Crowl.
" 17. Benjamin Hark to Elizabeth Danniwolf.
" 19. Philip Ebert to Mary Swadner.
" 23. Christopher Yoatvell to Elizabeth Dickoutt.
" 24. George Willson to Jeremiah Bonham.
May 1. Henry Burton to Catherine Hill.

May 3.	Jesse Pritchard to Elizabeth Stoner.	Oct. 19.	John Howard to Keziah Veatch.
" 4.	Charles Roads to Abigail Pursley.	" 22.	William Wyer to Catherine Stull.
" 8.	Wm. Winson to Elizabeth Blackamore.	" 23.	Jacob Roar to Catherine King.
" 10.	Jacob Heanmyer to Catherine Steiner.	" 26.	Philip Iser to Anna Albaugh.
" 11.	Michael Fullam to Mary Ropp.	" 29.	Hugh Cochran to Elizabeth Hobstone.
" 11.	Jacob Prauff to Ann Mary Buckey.	Nov. 1.	Joseph Boyer to Mary Hall.
" 18.	Valentine Gaver to Elizabeth Switter.	" 1.	James Campbell to Clara Seharu.
" 21.	Robert Crane to Nancey Hagan.	" 6.	George Stottlemire to Catherine Calon.
" 21.	Adam Tabler to Philopœna Yesterday.	" 6.	Henry Baer to Elizabeth Shellman.
" 26.	Thomas Beatty to Jane Waters.	" 8.	Archibald Cope to Mary Ramsey.
" 28.	Peter Barkman to Ullianna Crandler.	" 11.	Samuel Bayley to Mary Campbell.
" 31.	Alex. Shultz to Eleanor Freeman.	" 13.	Jacob Miller to Aliena Long.
" 31.	Roger Craigg to Mary Ford.	" 15.	Thomas Bayman to Mary Smith.
June 1.	Abraham Hargate to Mary Pentrin.	" 16.	Christian Luther to Allie Sewell.
" 2.	Jacob Valentine to Mary Fred.	" 16.	John Lewis to Verlinda Gatton.
" 3.	Peter Berkman to Catherine Litchard.	" 17.	Joseph Chadbourne to Ann Gates.
" 3.	Thomas Knox to Mary Duffle.	" 18.	Wm. Bradley to Jane Fulliston.
" 3.	Simon Groseman to Elizabeth Fogle.	" 19.	Charles Robinson to Elizabeth Robinson.
" 12.	William Stevens to Lydia Ovria.	" 23.	Uriah Laton to Rachel Hinton.
" 12.	John Anderson to Catherine Loney.	" 27.	Wm. Plummer to Margaret Jones.
" 12.	James Elder to Elizabeth Burn.	Dec. 3.	John Yantsey to Catherine Iseminger.
" 14.	Lackey Flannigan to Jane Barnett.	" 4.	Henry Gay to Judy Silverin.
" 15.	Wm. Wallace to Elizabeth Hopkins.	" 9.	Samuel Kauff to Mary Colebank.
" 15.	Philip Yost to Mary Hayes.	" 12.	John Gurnbard, Jr., to Esther Mantz.
" 15.	Samuel McGowan to Agnes Griffey.	" 13.	David McElfreth to Lucy Nellson.
" 21.	Adam Flarver to Elizabeth Keplar.	" 14.	Charles Swayne to Catherine Gire.
July 4.	Adam Boyer to Charlotte Mantz.	" 16.	Adam Emery to Sarah Hipps.
" 13.	Thomas Gilbert to Hannah Burton.	" 17.	Zachariah Barlow to Eleanor Hickman.
" 17.	John Harrison to Betty Clann.	" 17.	Wm. Cooper to Mary Harrison.
" 19.	Henry Kemp to Madeline Ritter.	" 20.	Jesse Bennett to Priscilla Knight.
" 20.	James Carey to Mary Hodge.	" 24.	Henry Wilson to Sophia Poole.
" 24.	Hugh Burn to Sarah Temple.	" 27.	Christian Gummert to Margaret Read.
" 25.	Jacob Boyer to Catherine Link.	" 30.	Alex. Marshall to Susanna Pearl.
Aug. 3.	Josias Harrison to Elizabeth Davis.	" 31.	Henry Shover to Rosanna Baker.
" 4.	John Pickett to Ann Gannan.	1780.	
" 4.	Samuel Hulse to Margaret Knight.	Jan. 12.	Thomas Hande to Catherine Whitner.
" 6.	Joseph Davis to Ann Howe.	" 16.	John Bryan to Elizabeth Carrill.
" 10.	James Root to Mary Umstatt.	" 16.	James Froud to Mary Sage.
" 10.	Anthony Bastian to Catherine Fogle.	" 27.	Ormond Hammond to Elizabeth Duckett.
" 11.	Valentine Fleagle to Christina Censor.	" 29.	Henry Haring to Catherine Peckenpaugh.
" 14.	Robert Addison to Remela Darlon.	" 29.	Daniel Thomas to Peggy Donnolly.
" 19.	Charles Clabaugh to Elizabeth Hill.	" 29.	William Holland to Catherine Holland.
" 19.	Jacob Inch to Elizabeth Boyrley.	" 29.	Gordon Roland to Elizabeth Dawson.
" 21.	Simon Byrley to Ann Boyle.	" 31.	George Rizeing to Dorothy Whitehair.
" 21.	John Dutterar to Catherine Summer.	Feb. 3.	Thomas Larymore to Sarah Grear.
" 23.	Daniel Huffard to Elizabeth Cassell.	" 4.	Caleb Philips to Sarah Darbey.
" 23.	Jacob Laman to Hannah Peterson.	" 5.	Patrick Collins to Elizabeth Pepper.
" 26.	Frederick Heater to Mary Ann Shroiner.	" 8.	Nicholas Klien to Margaret Smith.
" 27.	Edward Robinson to Catherine Methard.	" 14.	Charles Thomas Phillpott to Elizabeth MacLaboy.
" 28.	John Warner to Beddey Henson.	" 15.	Jacob Iseaberger to Margaret Hosplehaun.
" 31.	Matthias Furrow to Christina Beaghell.	" 20.	George Garnett to Elizabeth Messerley.
Sept. 11.	Matthias Oberfete to Anna Maria Hardman.	" 23.	Christian Runner to Elizabeth Thomas.
" 13.	Michael Cramer to Mary Winpigler.	" 28.	Henry Marker to Clary Shotts.
" 14.	Henry Taylor Francks to Margaret Buskerk.	" 28.	Jacob Frizzle to Margaret McKinley.
" 16.	Gassaway Sellmon to Catherine Davis.	March 1.	George Rineheart to Priscilla Weaver.
" 18.	John W. Bourmaster to Mary Eve Dowlan.	" 1.	Thomas Cartey to Margaret Nicholls.
" 18.	Adam Markel to Mary Dickensheets.	" 3.	Basil Lakin to Hannah Smith.
" 21.	Henry Valentine to Elizabeth Frey.	" 4.	Michael Paine to Peggy Cartey.
" 23.	Henry Ridenhour to Mary Smith.	" 6.	James Candle to Ann Richards.
Oct. 4.	John Asquire to Sarah Woolverton.	" 6.	Richard Lawrence to Ann Warfield.
" 6.	John Rodgers to Mary Tannehill.	" 6.	Thomas Carter to Mary Roach.
" 8.	Michael Heffner to Margaret Reed.	" 7.	Levin Spurrer to Eleanor Clarey.
" 9.	Peter Beall to Margaret Weddle.	" 7.	Ninian Beall to Ann Maria Stricker.
" 9.	John Brooner to Susanna Delanter.	" 8.	Elias Cooperider to Susannah Iseminger.
" 12.	Benj. Johnson (free negro) to Lucy Todd (free negro).	" 9.	Kensey Harrison to Sarah Saffle.
		" 9.	Charles Jemison to Mary Molley.

March 9. Wm. Hatton to Mary Cartey.
" 17. John McElfresh to Jane Cumming.
" 21. Jacob Ringer to Anna Beamer.
" 22. John Lock to Sarah Bastian.
" 28. Samuel Coffin to Catherine Creable.
" 30. Peter Sneike to Julianna Mottis.
April 1. Wm. Guthrie to Eleanor Elder.
" 6. John Snyder to Dorothy Waltz.
" 7. Michael Crowl to Mary Hosplehawn.
" 8. Jacob Roads to Nancy Cash.
" 8. John Maddon to Dolly Steward.
" 20. Archibald Hutchinson to Barbara Bruber.
" 22. George Hitradanner to Elizabeth Darr.
" 22. Nathan Bookey to Christina Grush.
" 25. George Poole to Catherine Baberdoe.
May 8. Samuel Brandenberger to Madeleine Hargishymer.
" 9. George McDonald to Catherine Sutherland.
" 13. Elias Brooner to Mary Ann Zimmerman.
" 13. Jacob Depos to Charlotte Nicholls.
" 16. Thomas Carrens to Ruth Baldwin.
" 20. John Crouse to Catherine Umstatt.
" 22. Richard Simpson, Jr., to Catherine Cumming.
" 27. Henry Lyder to Catherine Staley.
" 30. Andrew Robinson to Margaret Knave.
June 2. Denton Jacques to Elizabeth Powell.
" 5. John Able to Magdalen Derloe.
" 10. Jacob Staley to Ann Castle.
" 16. William Tabler to Margaret Yesterday.
" 17. Henry Hagan to Susannah Hyatt.
" 17. Martin Bower to Barbara Handshew.
" 19. John Waughtstell to Elizabeth Summers.
" 21. John Snyder to Charity Barrick.
" 23. Peter Woolf to Catherine Bruner.
" 26. Basil Israel to Eleanor Mansfield.
" 29. William King to Elizabeth Wright.
July 1. Philip Piper to Elizabeth Huffman.
" 7. Richard Warfield to Anne Delashmutt.
" 11. John Welsh, Sr., to Susannah Mansfield.
" 18. Andrew Miller to Rachel Foutz.
" 22. George Burrell to Elizabeth Lince.
Aug. 1. William Dryden to Philopœna Kissinger.
" 5. John Coome to Catherine Roar.
" 5. Jacob Meassell to Eleanor Bougher.
" 9. Richard Richards to Elizabeth Nevin.
" 9. Jacob Frout to Elizabeth Reed.
" 19. John Alfort to Margaret Ashman.
" 26. Samuel Shower to Catherine Hargishymer.
" 26. Jacob Weast to Eve Saline.
" 30. Edward Hosselton to Magdalen Welton.
" 31. Frederick Kemp to Susanna Ritter.
Sept. 9. Henry Barrick to Margaret Keller.
" 18. Peter Cile to Elizabeth King.
" 18. Benjamin Unkles to Margaret Plaister.
" 19. Jacob Koontz to Mary Clay.
" 22. Jeremiah Cullister to Margaret Chisholm.
" 25. William McCain to Mary McDonnaugh.
" 29. William Harnflower to Ann Aves.
" 30. Henry Wells to Jemimah Coe.
Oct. 12. Caleb Barnes to Margaret Walker.
" 13. Hugh Reynolds to Allie Fleming.
" 16. Jacob Wandle to Mary Goldie.
" 17. William Drake to Elizabeth Hinckle.
" 20. Peter Shoup to Rebecca Goodman.
" 21. Ephraim Ridge to Catherine Creager.
" 21. Christopher Burkitt to Elizabeth Hobbs.
" 27. Truman Hilton to Christina Patrick.

Oct. 27. Christopher Wolfley to Philopœna Hildebrand.
" 30. Samuel Markin to Rachel Lakin.
" 31. Alexander Wright to Susanna Gilbert.
Nov. 17. Jonathan Mason Grover to Sarah Musgrove.
" 21. Jacob Durff to Juliana Grindler.
" 21. Andrew Bash to Barbara Hanes.
" 21. Philip Bower to Sarah Perry.
" 23. Lewis Mobley to Trescilla Dorsey.
" 23. William Barnett to Sarah Piggman.
" 24. Benjamin Bennett to Rebecca James.
" 25. James McDaid to Mary Barnett.
" 28. William Ridge to Barbara Flemming.
" 30. James Groom to Rebecca Ricketts.
Dec. 1. Jehosophat Gartrill to Elizabeth Bissell.
" 5. John Ream to Esther Plunk.
" 9. Thomas Bowden to Eleanor Mahony.
" 10. Peter Cunningham to Elizabeth Bird.
" 12. Nicholas Isenbergh to Mary Smouse.
" 14. William Smith to Phœbe Bodington.
" 16. Henry Jefferson to Mary Howard.
" 17. Jacob Sewalt to Barbara Kurtz.
" 21. John Ninwonger to Ann Noffsinger.
" 21. Henry Allbright to Anna Margaret Swavin.

1781.
Jan. 8. William Goodard to Catherine Donavan.
" 24. Daniel Lear to Mary Pancartson.
" 30. Michael Carney to Margaret English.
" 31. John Lockett to Hittey Monro.
" 31. George Plumb to Mary Magdalen Eater.
Feb. 1. Roger Johnson to Elizabeth Thomas.
" 5. Adam Surprower to Susanna Cronise.
" 12. William Holland to Ann Wayman.
" 14. Joseph Madden to Elizabeth Hillary.
" 17. William Dorchester to Mary Kenear.
" 20. William Taylor to Pugvear Waleare.
" 21. Abraham Deerdarff to Catherine Bowersmith.
" 22. Philip McElfresh to Lydia Griffith.
" 24. William Markell to Mary Boyer.
" 27. Henry Lambergh to Mary Everhart.
March 10. Henry Kemp to Margaret Matthews.
" 15. Solomon Bentley to Rebecca Wood.

The rate or duty on marriage licenses issued by the clerk of the court was twenty-five shillings, and the act passed at the June session of the Assembly, 1780, made the tax payable in hard money. The moneys arising from these licenses were paid into the State treasury by the clerk.

The more important licenses issued subsequently, and up to 1830 inclusive, were the following:

January, 1788. John Graham, of Calvert County, to Miss Johnson, daughter of Hon. Thos. Johnson.

January, 1788. David Harris to Mrs. Frances Moale.

Dec. 9, 1792. Capt. Henry Carberry, of the U. S. Army, to Sybela Schnertzell.

Feb. 2, 1793. William Carey to Barbara Fritchie.

Aug. 10, 1797. By Rev. Joseph Bend, Capt. Wm. Thompson to Mrs. Anderson.

May 4, 1797. Frederick M. Amelung to Sophia Furnival, eldest daughter of Alexander Furnival, Esq.

Feb. 2, 1797. By Rev. Bower, Roger Nelson to Betsy Harrison.

April 5, 1801. John Ritchie to Nancy Darnall.

April 6, 1801. John Weast to Lydia Shuck.

Sept. 5, 1802. Elijah Beatty to Sarah Wigle.

Feb. 11, 1802. By Rev. Mr. Knox, Thomas Johnson to Rebecca Johnson.

April 22, 1802. By Rev. Mr. Snyder, Isaac Shriver, merchant, to Polly Leatherman.

Feb. 15, 1803. By Rev. Mr. Waggoner, Mr. Cromwell to Peggy Kephart.

March 29, 1803. John Brengle to Elizabeth Zeiller, daughter of Henry Zeiller.

April 19, 1803. By the Rev. Mr. Higgins, John Cummings to Annie Louisa Spurrier.

May 1, 1803. Peter Brengle to Kitty Mautz.

May 1, 1803. Mr. Dickson to Elizabeth Raser.

May 1, 1803. By Rev. Mr. Knox, Samuel Aunin, of Harper's Ferry, Va., to Martha Cross, of New Jersey.

Oct. 20, 1803. By Rev. Mr. Wagner, Abraham Shriver, merchant, to Peggy Leatherman.

Nov. 6, 1803. Dr. Henry Carroll to Margaret Candle.

Feb. 13, 1804. By Rev. Dr. Dubois, Conrad Shaffer to Mrs. Hagen.

April 24, 1804. By Rev. Mr. Josinosky, Henry Ruth, merchant, to Peggy Meddart.

May 15, 1804. By Rev. Mr. Wagner, John Smith to Miss Brunner, daughter of Elias Brunner.

May 31, 1804. By Rev. Mr. Bower, John L. Harding to Eleanor Marshall, daughter of James Marshall, deceased.

June 3, 1804. By Rev. Wm. Dankin, Samuel Poulsory to Polly Julia Gist, daughter of Col. Joshua Gist.

June 24, 1805. By Rev. Mr. Higginbottom, Alexander C. Hanson to Priscilla Dorsey.

April 30, 1805. By Rev. Dr. Rattoone, Wm. L. Schmidt to Miss Mariah Furnival.

Nov. 19, 1805. By Rev. George Bower, Alexander C. Magruder, of Annapolis, to Rebecca Thomas, daughter of Dr. P. Thomas, of Baltimore.

Jan. 7, 1806. By Rev. Mr. Dubois, Roger B. Taney to Annie Key, daughter of Gen. Key.

Feb. 4, 1806. By Rev. Mr. Wagner, Jacob Houck to Margaret Getzendanner.

March 4, 1806. By Rev. Mr. Bower, Wm. Ross to Kitty Johnson, daughter of Col. Baker Johnson.

April 15, 1806. By Rev. Mr. Wagner, Wm. Thomas to Catharine Houser, daughter of Capt. Houser.

May 20, 1806. By Rev. Mr. Wagner, Henry Steiner to Rachel Murray.

Oct. 26, 1806. By Rev. Mr. Wagner, Augustus Graham, merchant, to Patty Cock, daughter of Capt. Cock.

Oct. 27, 1806. By Rev. Mr. Wagner, Dr. John Ott to Annie Ritchie, daughter of Abner Ritchie, of Georgetown.

Nov. 11, 1806. By Rev. Mr. Wagner, John Cromwell to Catherine Gephart.

Jan. 11, 1807. By Rev. Mr. Wagner, J. Batesman, of Baltimore, to Elizabeth Bierly.

Jan. 13, 1807. Dr. John Harrison, U.S.N., to Eliza Hoffman.

March 17, 1807. By Rev. Mr. Bower, Wm. Potts to Susannah Campbell, daughter of Capt. William Campbell.

April 7, 1807. George Creager, Sr., late sheriff of Frederick County, to Mary Apler.

May 3, 1807. Jacob Boyer to Miss Mary Knoof.

May 14, 1807. William R. Sanderson, of Winchester, to Elizabeth Leatherman.

Dec. 8, 1808. By Rev. L. Browning, John Wireman, merchant, to Elizabeth Campbell.

Nov. 21, 1809. By Rev. Mr. Rawhauser, Rev. Frederick Rawhauser, of Emmittsburg, to Elizabeth Wagner.

Jan. 16, 1810. By Rev. Mr. Shaeffer, Septimus Stevens to Emelia Shryock.

April 12, 1810. By Rev. Mr. Ryland, Dr. George Colgate to Mary M. Cannon.

April 19, 1810. By Rev. Mr. Shaeffer, Frederick Reel to Catherine Zimmerman.

Oct. 2, 1810. By Rev. Mr. Beastly, Baker Johnson, Jr., to Sophia Grundy.

Nov. 27, 1810. By Rev. David Shaeffer, Lewis Smith to Elizabeth Eichelberger.

Dec. 6, 1810. By Rev. Mr. Shaeffer, John M. Beatty to Charlotte Hughes.

Dec. 6, 1810. John P. Thompson, editor of the Frederick Town *Herald*, to Mary Barnhold.

Jan. 17, 1811. By Rev. Bower, Mr. Hilery to Ann Johnson, daughter of John Johnson.

March 19, 1811. By Rev. Mr. Davison, David M. Quickery to Elizabeth Hoffman.

April 2, 1811. By Rev. Mr. Shaeffer, John Titlow to Mary Folger.

April 9, 1811. By Rev. Mr. Bower, Richard Potts to Ann L. Murdock.

April 25, 1811. By Rev. Mr. Davidson, John McPherson to Miss Catherine Lienhart.

May 2, 1811. By Rev. Mr. Geistwit, Jacob Buckey to Maria Spangler.

May 30, 1811. By Rev. Mr. Martin, David Boyd to Mary Mixell.

June 9, 1811. By Rev. Mr. Martin, Henry Berger to Mrs. Nellie Davis.

June 26, 1811. By Rev. Mr. Bower, George Graff to Mary Charlton.

June 23, 1811. By Rev. Mr. Shaeffer, Gideon Bantz, merchant, to Ann Maria Sower.

July 2, 1811. By Rev. Mr. Dashiells, Samuel Raborg to Henrietta Winemiller.

Aug. 4, 1811. By Rev. Mr. Malevie, George Littlejohn to Elizabeth Geisinger.

Sept. 10, 1811. By Rev. Mr. Martin, John Stallinger to Sophia Haller.

Sept. 17, 1811. Rev. Mr. Browning, Lewis Baltzell, merchant, to Anna Maria James.

Feb. 11, 1812. By Rev. Mr. Schaeffer, John Johnson to Ann Harding.

Feb. 17, 1812. By Rev. Mr. Schaeffer, Henry Jarboe to Eleanor Crampton.

March 16, 1812. The Hon. Outerbridge Horsey, U. S. senator from Delaware, to Eliza Lee, daughter of Thomas Sim Lee.

March 29, 1812. By Rev. Mr. Halfenstein, John Hamilton to Catharine Evitt.

April 23, 1812. By Rev. Mr. Schaeffer, George Geltz to Rebecca Reese.

June 11, 1812. By Rev. Mr. Davidson, Samuel Fleming, of Arthur, to Harriet Hughes.

Aug. 2, 1812. By Rev. Mr. Browning, Philip Keyholtz to Susanna Fuz.

Aug. 16, 1812. By Rev. Mr. Helfenstein, Philip Pyser, Jr., to Rachel Brengle.

Oct. 15, 1812. By Rev. Mr. Kurtz, Frederick L. Amelung to Sophia Seekamp.

April 13, 1813. By Rev. Mr. Schaeffer, Morris Jones to Elizabeth Medtart.

April 15, 1813. By Rev. Mr. Schaeffer, Solomon Boon to Martha Merryman.

Nov. 9, 1813. By Rev. Mr. Higgins, Peter Hines, merchant, to Margaret Campbell.

Nov. 30, 1813. By Rev. Mr. Davidson, David Ott to Mary Ritchie, daughter of Col. J. Ritchie.

Dec. 14, 1813. By Rev. Jonathan Helfenstein, John Brengle to Margaret Leas.

Dec. 14, 1813. By Rev. Mr. Hubbs, Peter Meyers to Hannah Engle.

Jan. 4, 1814. By Rev. Mr. Schaeffer, John Mossberg to Catherine Kurtz.

June 6, 1814. By Rev. Mr. Schaeffer, Henry Alexander to Catherine Robb.

Feb. 24, 1814. By Rev. C. Williams, Samuel Taggart to Susanna Miller.

April 28, 1818. By Rev. Mr. Schaeffer, Henry Hoffman to Margaret Kemp, daughter of Col. H. Kemp.

April 13, 1819. By Rev. Mr. Blake, Jacob Harbaugh to Mary A. Harbaugh.

March 17, 1821. By Rev. Mr. Helfenstein, Col. Stephen Steiner to Elizabeth Bausman.

April 13, 1822. By Rev. Mr. McCain, Wm. Tew to Susan Ritchie.

May 14, 1822. By Rev. Mr. Johns, Worthington Johnson to Mary J. T. Potts, daughter of Hon. Richard Potts.

Sept. 10, 1822. By Rev. Mr. Johns, Thomas Grahame to Caroline Johnson.

April 8, 1823. By Rev. Mr. Shaeffer, Henry Getzendanner to Catharine Kemp; John Berry to Mary Getzendanner; and John Snyder to Mary Whip.

June 12, 1823. By Rev. Mr. Johns, Richard H. Marshall to Harriet Potts, daughter of Hon. Richard Potts.

Nov. 25, 1823. By Rev. Mr. Nevins, Wm. T. Johnson to Dorothea, second daughter of Alex. Mactier, of Baltimore.

Nov. 17, 1825. By Rev. Mr. Martin, John Keedy to Elizabeth Kenege.

Nov. 18, 1825. By the Most Reverend Archbishop Marechal, Robert Coleman Brien to Ann Elizabeth Tierman.

Dec. 2, 1831. By Rev. Mr. Jackson, Neilson Poe, editor of the Frederick *Examiner*, to Josephine E. Clemm.

March 15, 1832. By Rev. Mr. Johns, Wm. G. Harrison to Anne E. Ross, daughter of Wm. Ross.

June 5, 1832. By Rev. Mr. Hughes, John Lee to Harriet Carroll, of Baltimore.

Jan. 26, 1836. By Rev. Mr. Phillips, Chas. A. Gambrill, merchant, to Ann Elizabeth, oldest daughter of Col. George M. Eichelberger.

March 13, 1838. By Rev. John Johns, John Nelson to Matilda Tennant.

July 17, 1838. By Rev. Mr. Slaughter, Rev. John Johns, D.D., to Margaret Jane Shaaf.

Feb. 15, 1844. By Rev. Mr. Zacharias, C. Slack to L. E. Leas.

Wills.—The following is the first will recorded in Frederick County:

"In the Name of God, Amen. This seventeenth day of January in the year of our Lord one thousand seven hundred & fifty, I, Theodores Malot in Frederick County and province of Maryland, plantive, being very sicks & weak of body but of perfect Mind & memory thanks to God there for, calling to mind the mortality of my Body & Knowing that it is appointed for all men to dye, Do make & ordain this my last will & testament, that is to say, principally, first of all I give & Recommend my Soul into the hands of God that gave it & my body I recommend to the Earth to be buried in a Decent Christian burial at the Discretion of my Executors, nothing doubting but at the general Resurrection I shall receive the same again by the mighty power of God, and as touching such worldly Estate wherewith it hath pleased God to bless me in this World's Life, I give devise & dispose of the same in the following manner & Form:

"First I order all my funeral Charges & Debts to be paid. I likewise Constitute make & ordain John Perren & Joseph Pridmore my sole Executors of this my Last will & testament. Item—I give to my Son Peter Malot two Mares & a yearling Colt & a rifle Gun by him freely to be possessed. I give to my Son John Malot one shilling & to Theodores Malot one shilling. I give to my well beloved Daughter Mary a two year old heifer. Item—I give to my beloved daughter Elizabeth Malot a three year old heifer, and to my Son Benjamin a two year old Mare, and a smooth Bore Gun. Item—I give to my well beloved wife all my stock of horses & Mares, Cattle, Sheep & Hogs during her Widowhood, and afterwards to be equally divided amongst all my Children. And I do hereby utterly disallow revoke & disannull all and every of former Wills & Testaments, Wills, Legacies & Requests & Executors by me in any ways before named willed & Bequeathed, Ratifying & confirming this and no other to be my Last Will & Testament. In Witness whereof I have hereunto set my hand & Seal the Day & year above written.

"THEODORUS MALOT. [SEAL.]
  mark
"JOSEPH X LAZUR, SENIOR.
  his
"DAVID ENOCHS, JOSEPH LAZUR."

The following was the entry of its proof:

"March 19th 1751 Joseph Lazur Sen' & David Enochs two of the subscribing Witnesses to the Within Will being duly sworn on the holy Evangells of Almighty God, depose & say that they saw the Testator Theodorus Malot sign the within Will, and heard him publish and declare the same to be his last Will & Testament, that at the Time of his doing so he was to the best of their apprehensions of sound & disposing mind & memory, and at the same Time, they saw Joseph Lazur Junr subscribe the within will as an Evidence & which they subscribed in the presence & at the Request of the Testator.

"JOHN DARNALL, *Depty Comy*."

The next will recorded was that of John Thompson, dated Sept. 25, 1748, and proven March 19, 1751. The testator devised to his son William the tract of land known as "Thompson's Pasture," also sixty-one acres at the lower end of "Thompson's Hop-yard," and one hundred and forty-eight acres at the head of a tract called the "John & Yacomintye," on the Potomac; to his son John one hundred and thirty-five acres, called "The Conjuror Outdone," also one hundred and forty-eight acres out of "John & Yacomintye," and seventy-three acres on the lower end of Derby Island; to his son Cornelius the tract called Cool Springs, also forty-nine acres of "Thompson's Hop-yard," with a small island of twelve acres lying against it, and one hundred and forty-eight acres of the "John & Yacomintye" tract; and to his daughter Ann the tract of land lying on the Potomac of one hundred and five acres and called the "Duck Folly," also an island in the Potomac of twenty acres. The third will recorded was that of Charles Friend, dated Feb. 27, 1750–51, and proven March 20, 1756. The

FREDERICK COUNTY.

fourth recorded will was that of Henry Munday, dated June 28, 1750, and proven March 21, 1756. In it occurs this bequest: "I give and Bequeath unto Mr. William Nughbourg one of the Moravian ministers my Saddle and my hair to make him a Wigg." As showing who then lived, died, and left property, we give a full list of all persons who made wills from the organization of the county up to 1777, including some proved before the erection of the county, with the dates of their being proven:

Jacob Neff	1751
Margaret Markland	1751
Baltish Fought	1751
Alex. Magruder, Sr.	1751
Susanna Beatty	1745
Wm. Norris	1748
John Thomas	1749
Charles Scraggs	1749
Thomas Ball	1749
John Jones	1749
Thomas Gittings	1749
Wm. Coliar	1744
Elizabeth Blair	1749
John Stull	1749
Edward Offut	1749
Cornelius Carmack	1749
Daniel Stull	1749
Wm. Forster	1749
John Davis	1749
Benjamin Ridley	1750
George Winters	1750
Adam Mirra	1750
James Osfut	1749
John Mitchell	1750
Godfried Mong	1750
Wm. Barrack	1750
John Nelson	1750
John Haymond	1750
Wm. West	1750
Daniel Matthews	1755
Wm. Tracey	1755
Susannah Beatty	1755
Absalom Wilson	1755
David Pierpont	1755
Grove Temlison	1755
Robert Downing	1755
Edward Beatty	1755
John Willcoxan	1754
Abraham Millar	1754
Wm. Norris	1754
Martin Adam	1754
Thomas Harges	1754
George Pack	1754
James Jack	1754
Joseph Dickerson	1754
Cornelius Eltinge	1754
Basil Beall	1753
John Kenedy	1753
John Pierpont	1753
Charles Polke	1753
Jacob Julien	1759
John Pigman	1751
John Harding	1752
John House	1752
Wm. Turner	1752
Samuel Durbin	1752
Samuel Deval	1752
Robert Debutts	1752
George Krouse	1753
Thomas Davis	1753
Joseph Hedges	1753
James Holland	1753
Rebecca Eltinge	1756
Edmund E. Rutter	1755
Wm. Beall	1756
Joseph Ogle	1756
John Tinney	1756
John Williams	1756
John Rawlings	1756
Isaac Eltinge	1756
Frederick Unseld	1755
Francis Foy	1756
Wm. Bruce	1756
Jacob Sterm	1757
Wm. Cooper	1757
Raychall Harris	1757
Patrick Doran	1757
Wm. Griffith	1757
Joshua Hickman	1757
Wm. Beatty	1757
Joseph Arnold	1757
Isabel Ryan	1758
Samuel Selty	1758
Ninian Magruder	1759
Wm. Wallace	1759
John White	1759
Daniel Jenkins	1759
Michael Denden	1759
Alex. Beall	1759
Daniel Linn	1759
Wm. Williams	1759
Sarah Hickman	1759
Wm. O. Nail	1759
Thomas Conn	1760
Thomas Culver	1760
Gabriel Friend	1760
Wm. Ray, Sr.	1760
Edward Branner	1760
Francis Alexander	1760
John Vandiver	1760
Valentine Grave	1760
John Jones	1760
Ignatius Perry	1761
Samuel Pruitt	1760
Jacob Steyley	1761
John Biggs	1761
Joseph Wood	1761
Alice Charlton	1761
Margaretha Staley	1761
Peter Shaver	1761
John Gartrill	1761
Josiah Jenkins	1761
Richard Richardson	1761
Samuel Offut	1761
Lawrence Arven	1761
Elizabeth Graw	1761
David Marchand	1761
John Hook	1761
Jacob Barton	1762
Stephen Baldwin	1762
Samuel Richardson	1762
William Ellerburton	1762
Francis Cook	1762
Edward Johnson	1762
George Sultner	1762
Gilbert Crum	1762
Moses Chapline	1762
John Sterm	1762
Ann Perry	1762
Caleb Letton	1763
Henry Ervy	1763
Charles Trail	1763
Joseph Mayhew	1763
John Gilberth	1763
James Lee	1764
Henry Hickman	1764
John Beard	1764
Jacob Syder	1764
Thomas Glenn	1764
Bartholomew Jessurang	1764
William Simmeus	1764
James Goudy	1764
Thomas Wilson	1764
Nicholas Baker	1764
Samuel Richardson	1764
Ham Deal Bone	1764
Garrah Davis	1764
John Williams	1764
Abraham Furry	1764
Peter Troxell	1766
Jacob Syderman	1764
Peter Butler	1764
Isabella McCheaver	1764
James Pilly	1764
Jacob Staley	1764
Jacob Duckett	1764
John Kemp	1764
Jemima Beall	1764
John Ripeley	1764
William Dutcher	1764
Michael Beighler	1764
John Shepherd	1765
Jacob Crous	1765
Robert Owings	1765
Meredith Davis	1765
Jacob Hoffman	1765
Adam Millar	1765
Francis Edwards	1765
Jacob Lockman	1765
John Ludwig Peck	1765
Catherine Jennings	1765
Benjamin Adams	1765
Benjamin Beall	1765
Ludwig Hann	1765
Alex. McKeen	1765
William Andrew	1765
Ezekiel Gosling	1765
Peter Stilly	1765
John Baptist Lovelace	1765
John Cregett	1765
John Hildebrand	1765
John George Syb	1765
Burgess Nelson	1765
Joseph Richardson	1765
Philip Fuss	1765
Casper Kreeger	1765
Kayll Payn	1764
Robert Pearl	1765
Thomas Payn	1765
Hugh Tomlinson	1765
John Eylenier	1766
John Wilds	1766
John West, Sr.	1766
Josias Holland	1766
William Ritchett	1766
Edward Northcross	1766
John Charkton	1766
Daniel Veirs	1766
Stephen Gartrell	1766
William Jones	1766
Spicer Owens	1766
William Hickman	1766
Zephaniah Plumer	1767
Christian Getzendanner	1766
Leonhard Shuebely	1767
John Hoyle	1767
David Delader	1767
Anna Mary Deter	1767
Miriam Richardson	1767
Elizabeth Talbot	1767
Jacob Shingleacker	1767
John Swann	1767
William Wheat	1767
Benjamin Marshall	1767
Thomas Clark	1767
Thomas Windom	1767
Drusilla Plumer	1767
John McKinley	1767
Christian Smith	1767
Thomas Johnson	1767
John Veath	1767
Miriam Tannehill	1767
Nicholas Bugar	1767
Nicholas Hayman	1767
James Brook, Jr.	1767
Absalom Warfield	1767
William Dyell	1766
William Sanders	1768
John Buxtone	1768
John M. Hoffner	1768
John Dannall	1768
Richard Gatten	1768
George Owler	1768
John Hobbs	1768
Daniel Walker	1768
John Hupman	1768
Jacob Werts	1768
Josiah Harper	1768
Eberhard Eply	1768
Dines Ensey	1768
Christian Creager	1768
Teter Danner	1768
John Gillespie	1768
William Richardson	1769
David Watson	1769
Peter Light	1769
George Zewell	1769
Francis West	1769
William Williams	1769
Joseph Chapline	1769
Thomas Beatty	1768
Elizabeth Shiles	1768
Rudolph Keller	1769
James Magenty	1769
George Lawrence	1769
Benjamin Whitmore	1769
John Matthews	1769
John Rutter	1769
Elizabeth Harding	1769
Christian Shot	1769
Ezekiel Cheney	1769
Martin Kirshner	1769
James Riggs	1770
John Perins	1770
Erhart Bomgardner	1770
John Kimbol	1770
George Brown	1770
James Carrick	1770
Daniel Cover	1770
Daniel Haines	1770
Jacob Smith	1770
Peter Sterp	1770
Cornelius Davis	1770
Samuel Matthews	1770
Benjamin J. Perry	1770
R. R. Stallinges	1770
Jacob Pervlis	1770
Henry Sinn	1770
John Philips	1770
Rachel Eplar	1769
John Allison, Sr.	1769
Catherine Toms	1770
Frederick Jollagh	1770
Daniel Zacharias	1770
Ann Durbin	1770
Andrew Smith	1770
George Snagler	1770
Thomas Ambler	1770
Michael Fickel	1771
Thomas Walker	1771
Jacob Auld	1771
Catherine Malot	1771
James Perry	1771
Godfrey Kephart	1771
Richard Percival	1771
David Cox	1771
Robert Wells	1771
Jacob Doub	1771
John Trundle, Sr.	1771
Richard Merry	1771
Joachim Joan	1771
Baker Erbach	1771
John Ritter	1771
Arthur Charleton	1771

432   HISTORY OF WESTERN MARYLAND.

Benjamin Perry	1771	Samuel Busey	1774
Jacob Mullendore	1771	Matthew Logan	1774
James McLane	1771	Orlando Griffith	1774
William Cochran	1772	Maria Barbara Wolheiser	1774
Catherine Cardman	1772	John Yingling	1770
Peter Rentch	1772	Conrad Hearse	1774
William Denney	1772	Rebecca Wilson	1774
George Gue	1772	Jacob Hoy	1774
John Adamson	1772	Thomas Norris	1774
Edward Willitt	1772	Peter Toughman	1774
John Orme	1772	Joseph Bunneston	1774
Benjamin Hall	1772	John Welds	1774
Rebeccah Perry	1772	Daniel Pearl	1774
John Boyd	1772	Philip Hocker	1774
Smith Carnall	1772	James Wallace	1774
John Denden	1772	Wm. Willson	1774
Henry Tom	1772	John Wye	1774
Westall Ridgeley	1772	Balser Hilfliperver	1775
Rudolph Aspey	1772	Elinor Shedley	1775
Nathan Garrett	1772	Joseph Wolgamot	1775
Sarah Needham	1772	Samuel Enghand	1775
George Reid	1772	Andrew Beall, Jr.	1775
Adam Stull	1772	Jacob Lambert	1775
Ann Arr	1772	Peter Buckey	1775
Samuel Wishham	1772	John Head	1775
Matthew Clark	1772	Frederick Iseminger	1775
Wm. Stevenson	1772	Peter Apple	1775
Lorando Tracey	1772	James McDaniel, Sr.	1775
Edward Shaw	1773	Matthias Gray	1775
Wm. Howard	1773	John Lingenfelder	1775
Matthew Lanny	1773	Paul Wolf	1775
Samuel Blackmore	1773	Magdalena Snouffer	1775
Henry Hill	1773	Matthias Ebart	1775
Melcher Leuthert	1773	James Howard	1775
Henry Miller	1773	John Marker	1775
John Nichol	1773	James Rimmer	1775
Peter Little	1773	Michael Cresap	1775
Elizabeth Osfut	1773	Middleton Garrett	1775
Samuel Hardy	1773	Jacob Fout	1775
Wm. Michael	1773	Geo. Buckley	1776
Jacob Clunt	1773	Henry Brunner	1776
Vachel Davis	1773	Ann Self	1776
Uncle Unkles	1773	Stephen Hickman	1776
Robert Ferguson	1773	Thomas Dyson	1776
Lucy Watson	1773	Thos. Powell, Sr.	1776
James Gast	1773	John Brunner	1776
Joseph Wright	1773	Nicholas Kemp	1776
Tobias Harien	1773	Catherine Neff	1776
John C. Smith	1773	John Young	1776
Matthias Zacharias	1773	Devalt Shafer	1776
Philip Knewel	1773	John Garrett, Sr	1776
Wm. Halsey	1773	William Elder	1776
John Hargereder	1774	William Carmack	1776
Richard Watts	1774	Alex. White	1776
Thomas Plummer	1774	Peter Fout	1776
Adrian Hageman	1774	John Banks	1776
Edward Owen	1774	John Bishop	1776
Peter Erb	1774	Wm. Pennebaker	1776
Richard Self	1774	Jacob Howard	1776
Ezra Beatty	1774	James Hagan	1776
Simon Shover	1774	Mary Whitehead	1776
John Miller	1774	Geo. Hartley	1776
John Patterson	1774	Robert Barnes	1776
Wm. Campbell	1774	John Justice	1776
Balser Filler	1774	George Nools	1776
Thos. Addison	1774	Nicholas Jones	1776
Nicholas Grable	1774	Alex. Beall	1776
John Stoner	1774	Juliana Lutz	1776
John Wotgamote	1774	Michael Tanner [1]	1777
Balser Hison	1774		
John Whiteneck	1774		

[1] The wills proven before 1748 in above lists were in Prince George's County and there recorded, but on the erection of Frederick copied into the will book (A) of the latter. The first will proved was that of Thomas Ball, on April 4, 1749.

CHAPTER XXII.

PUBLIC SCHOOLS, INTERNAL IMPROVEMENTS, AND AGRICULTURAL SOCIETIES.

NEITHER the charter granted by Charles I. to Lord Baltimore in 1632, nor the State constitution of 1776, nor its amendments adopted in 1812 or 1815, made any provisions for *free* schools. By the act of 1694 provision for free schools was made, and a school fund was derived from a tobacco tax, and from a tax of twenty shillings per poll laid upon each Irish Catholic servant and each negro slave imported into the colony. There was also a three pence per hogshead tax on exported tobacco, of which one-half went to schools. The earliest school fund, however, was provided by the act of 1695, entitled an act for the "encouragement of learning," by which all persons residing in the province were forbidden to export any furs or skins therein mentioned except on the payment of certain specified duties, to be appropriated to the maintenance of free schools. As the fur trade was a large and profitable one at this period, the revenue derived from it constituted the school fund for nearly thirty years. By this act every exported bear-skin paid 9*d.* sterling; beaver, 4*d.*; otter, 3*d.*; wild-cats, foxes, minks, fishers, wolves' skins, 1½*d.*; musk-rat, 4*d.* per dozen; raccoons, 3 farthings per skin; elk-skins, 12*d.* per skin; deer-skins, 4*d.* per skin; young bear-skins, 2*d.* per skin. All non-resident exporters of these furs were to pay double.

Gratuitous teaching was provided in 1728 for poor children, it being ordered that masters receiving twenty pounds a year from the State should teach as many poor children as the visitors should see fit to admit. In 1754 the following persons were keeping schools in Frederick County, viz.: John Wilkinson, who "took the oaths to government by information of Mr. David Linn;" Martin Moran, upon information by Thomas Prather; John Chamberlain, upon information by J. Smith Prather; Henry Levatt, upon information by John Rawlins; Thomas Flint, upon information of John Rawlins. It was enacted by the act of 1763 that the Rev. Mr. Thomas Bacon, rector of All Saints' parish, Col. Thomas Cresap, Nathan Magruder, John Darnall, Thomas Beatty, Col. Joseph Chapline, and Col. Samuel Beall should be the trustees of Frederick County Free School, and that a school-house should be built on an acre of land to be purchased in Frederick Town, and the school was to have an equal dividend with the other schools from the taxes, etc., collected in the province and appropriated to this purpose. In 1768 the visitors or trustees to the Frederick County school were changed by act of the Assembly, and Jonathan Wilson, Thomas Bowles, George Murdock, Maj. Joseph Wood, Thomas Price, Caspar Shooff, and Charles Beatty were appointed visitors, and they were directed to purchase half an acre of ground in Frederick Town and build the school-house thereon. In 1779, in reply to the "prayer of sundry inhabitants of the State, the Rev. Bartholomew Booth was, by act of the Assembly, permitted to teach and preach the gospel, and also to teach and educate youth in any public or private school, upon taking the oath of fidelity. He had removed from Georgetown to Frederick County, and the children of Benedict Arnold were educated by him. The Rev. Mr. Booth died in 1785, having spent a long life in teaching. He came from Virginia to Maryland. Agreeably to the acts of 1763 and 1769, the half-acre had been purchased and the seminary of learning erected thereon, and by act of 1796 it was declared to be the Frederick County school, and George Murdock, Richard Potts, Philip Thomas, Francis Mantz, John McPherson, and George Baer were appointed visitors with corporate powers, but no person should act as visitor or teacher before he had taken the oath of fidelity. Chapter II. of the acts of 1801 is an additional supplement to the act of 1763 for erecting a public school in Frederick County; the first four sections relate to a lottery for the benefit of the school, and appoint William Luckett, William Hobbs, of Sam., Roger Nelson, Peter Mantz, John Schley, Joshua Dorsey, Daniel Clarke, Jr., and Robert Cummings visitors. In 1802 it was provided by law that any three of these visitors might be a quorum to transact business. In 1808 a lottery was authorized for the erection of a suitable building for a school-house for the accommodation of the youth of Emmittsburg and its vicinity in Frederick County by raising thereby not exceeding twelve hundred dollars. In 1809 a seminary in Middletown, Frederick Co., was provided for by an act authorizing a lottery, and it was provided that no vacancies were to be filled till the number was reduced to nine.

In 1815 an act was passed authorizing a lottery for building a school-house near Taneytown, in Frederick County. In 1816 it was enacted that nine persons were to be appointed in each county as commissioners of public schools, and the treasurer of the Western Shore was directed to pay to the said commissioners each county's legal proportion upon application. The commissioners were to report annually to the General Assembly, but not to accept any compensation. The treasurer was to pay to the order of the Levy Courts of Frederick, Washington, and Allegany Counties their proportion respectively of the school fund, to be invested by said court in such manner as should be most likely to secure the means of education as contemplated in the act, providing the fund until the principal and interest should be sufficient to provide a central free school in each election district. The Franklin School Association of Monocacy and Tom's Creek, in Frederick County, was incorporated in 1824 in the same act the Frederick Town Free School Society was incorporated, with Richard Potts, William Ross, Dr. W. B. Tyler, George Baltzell, Lewis Medtart, John Schley, John McPherson, John Nelson, and W. R. Sanderson as a body politic. In 1824 an act was passed to appropriate a part of the school fund belonging to Frederick County to Frederick Town Free School and the pastor of St. John's Church.[1]

The General Assembly, in February, 1823, passed an act for the public instruction of youth in primary schools throughout the State. It provided for a State superintendent, whose duty was to digest and prepare plans for the organization, improvement, and management of such a school system as might be adopted, and of such revenues as might from time to time be assigned and appropriated to the general objects of the institution. Provision was made that the justices of the Levy Courts in each county should annually appoint nine of the inhabitants to be commissioners of the primary schools; also a suitable number of discreet persons, not exceeding eighteen, who, together with the aforesaid commissioners, constituted the inspectors of the primary schools. The commissioners were authorized to divide their respective counties into a convenient number of school districts. Each district held annually a meeting to select a clerk and three trustees and a district collector. These annual meetings designated sites for school-houses, and voted a tax on the resident inhabitants, and made proper arrangements for fuel, books, stationery, and appendages, and

---

[1] In 1827 an act was passed to promote education in Frederick County, and in 1828 an act authorizing visitors to sell a school-house in Frederick. Mount Nebo School, Frederick County, and the Valley School were incorporated in 1831. Resolutions in favor of St. John's Literary Institute of Frederick were adopted by the Legislature in 1832, and the old county school became Frederick College in 1833; in the same year Luzerne school-house was incorporated. In 1836, St. John's Female Benevolent School and St. John's Literary Institute were incorporated. The Central School, Frederick County, was incorporated in 1836, and the Female Benevolent School of All Saints' parish received the school fund of Frederick Free School. The Orphan House and Episcopal Free School was incorporated in 1837. The Female Seminary of Frederick City was established by law in 1839. The Frederick Academy of Visitation was incorporated in 1846.

had power to repeal, alter, regulate, and modify all such proceedings or any part thereof, from time to time, as occasion required. Whenever a district meeting voted a tax, it was the duty of the trustees to make a tax-list and annex to the same a warrant and deliver it to the tax collector. These trustees employed teachers and paid the salaries, and semi-annually made a report to the school commissioners, specifying the length of time a school had been kept, the amount of moneys received by them and how expended, the number of white children taught, and the number residing in the district between the ages of five and fifteen years, inclusive. No teacher could be employed unless he had been duly examined by the inspectors and received a certificate. The inspectors were compelled at least quarterly to visit and examine all the schools within their respective counties, and the school commissioners to make an annual report to the county clerks.

The law authorized them to hold property as a body politic. All the State funds assigned and appropriated for the support and maintenance of the public schools were distributed according to the ratio of white inhabitants. This act was left to the voters of the several counties to be voted for or against, accepted or rejected, and in the county voting against its adoption it was void and of no effect. Although a good law, it was far in advance of the times, and was only partially accepted, and never substantially adopted and put into practice.

A supplementary act of March 20, 1837, provided that the Levy Court of Frederick County should appoint a board of inspectors of the primary schools in this county, of one person from each election district, to be charged with the same duties and powers as before invested in the inspectors and commissioners. This law ordered the payment by the Levy Court to the school inspectors of the interest arising from the school fund invested by said court, and authorized said court to levy upon the assessable property of the county such amount as would discharge the principal and interest due by the county to the school fund. These inspectors on July 1st of each year distributed the aforesaid interest, the annual school fund of the county, and other school funds among the several districts. The Levy Court annually levied a sum not less than five or more than eight thousand dollars for the primary schools. The district clerk and collector were abolished, and the county collector thereafter collected the school taxes, and paid the same over to the school inspectors. This act was not to be in force until adopted by the majority of the voters of the county. A later act provided that all white children between five and eighteen years of age, inclusive, in Frederick County were entitled to public school instruction. An act of March 21, 1838, provided for the establishment of a separate female school in each school district if desired by a majority of the inhabitants thereof. An act especially relating to Frederick County, passed Feb. 21, 1840, provided that the trustees have power to apply the school funds for the various school purposes as their judgment dictated. Each county received from the State treasury eight hundred dollars for an academy, but in Frederick County four hundred dollars more was allowed for the Rev. John McElroy's school.

The free-school fund was a different one, being derived from a bonus paid by the banks, and partly from the surplus revenue paid to the State by the general government, and appropriated to this purpose.

This fund was afterwards appropriated to the use of the Baltimore and Washington Railroad, and an annuity of thirty-four thousand dollars paid by it to the State therefor, which was annually divided among the counties. The amount of this fund due to Frederick County in 1846 was thus invested:

In the Mechanics' Bank....................	$2805.00
" Commercial and Farmers'........	5160.00
" Baltimore	1500.00
" hands of farmers....................	9600.00
Cash	178.50

The interest of this sum, together with the portion of the thirty-four thousand dollars annuity received by the county, was appropriated to the benefit of the free schools. In addition to which the county yearly levied about eight thousand dollars (as per act of 1836). Also, at the discretion of the trustees, the sum of twenty-five cents per month was assessed each pupil who was able to pay.

The following were the amounts received by the county from the State in the years mentioned:

1840	$2181.46	1843	$6905.34
1842	2314.95	1845	4449.25

In 1846 the county was divided into eighty-two school districts, having about ten thousand pupils in attendance, making one hundred and twenty-two to each district. The county levy of eight thousand dollars gave eighty cents to each pupil, and the State donation gave about forty-five cents, making altogether one dollar and twenty-five cents paid for the tuition of each scholar per year, besides the sum paid by the pupils.

The constitution of 1864 authorized the State superintendent of public instruction to adopt a uniform system of public instruction in Maryland, which that officer, L. Van Bokkelen, prepared and reported to the Legislature in February, 1865. This was the

D. T. LAKIN.

first regular free-school system in the State, and is the basis of the present free schools.

We give below the report for fall term ending Nov. 15, 1865, of the schools in the county, as made by Dr. Lewis H. Steiner, the efficient president of the board of school commissioners:

District.	Boys.	Girls.	Salaries.	Incidentals.	Repairs.
1st	477	309	$1372.12	$315.64	$51.70
2d	191	197	684.42	101.86	83.87
3d	349	365	1185.34	235.68	......
4th	262	291	744.38	32.85	116.49
5th	456	500	1532.45	127.97	......
6th	281	288	844.52	27.88	74.92
7th	222	228	644.25	107.50	......
Total	2238	2178	$7007.48	$949.41	$326.78

This was the last year of the old school system, and the report shows the inefficiency of the system.

We now give the report (likewise made by Dr. Lewis H. Steiner) for the year ending June 30, 1866, the first year of the free schools. This report shows 7888 pupils in attendance, an increase of nearly fifty per cent. over the previous year. The number of school districts 108, in 94 of which schools were opened for ten months. The cost of educating each scholar was $4.83½, computing the entire expenditure, which amounted to $36,356.78, over five hundred per cent. larger than that of the previous year under the old régime. This new system went into operation July, 1865, and at first, as was natural to be expected, the opposition made to it was very great. It involved the introduction of order and system into the educational operations of the county, and the supervision of the entire field of labor by men selected for that purpose by the State board of education. The friction, however, manifested in the first introduction of the system gradually diminished during the first year, and at the end of the second the new method was universally accepted and approved.

The present school law in force (with some amendments made since) was passed April 1, 1872, in pursuance of the constitution of 1867, making it obligatory upon the General Assembly to provide a uniform free-school system by taxation. This act created a State board of education, five school commissioners in Frederick County, and three trustees for each district. All white youths between the ages of six and twenty-one years are admitted into the free schools. Ample provision is made for the education of the colored youth in separate schools of one or more in each election district, where the average attendance is not less than fifteen scholars.

The following are the school statistics of the county for the year ending Jan. 31, 1881:

Number male pupils (white)	4517
" female " "	3459
" male " (colored)	642
" females " "	487
Total	9105
Expenditures for incidental expenses	$972.79
" " blackboards, stoves, etc.	27.48
" " teachers' salaries	15,522.00

COUNTY SCHOOL COMMISSIONERS.

1865.—Dr. Lewis H. Steiner, president, Charles McElfresh, John W. Charlton, George Koogle, Joshua Biggs, John S. Repp, James Russell, and Leonard Picking and Grafton Duvall to fill two vacancies.

1868.—Richard Thomas, Alexis O. Baugher, Tilghman F. Gaver, William H. Todd, John Walter, A. W. Warenfels, C. Keefer Thomas, president, James H. Steele, Dr. Harry W. Dorsey, George P. Fox, J. M. Newman, Michael William Font, E. A. Shriver, Andrew Kessler, John Landers, William Metzgar, John Clemson, being one from each election district.

1870.—Henry S. Michael, C. W. Haller, Peter W. Shafer, Peter T. Waltman, John Walter, A. N. Warenfels, John T. Williams, A. W. Devilbiss, Dr. H. W. Dorsey, George H. Crawford, Randolph G. Barrick, J. M. Miller, Ephraim Zimmerman, Daniel T. Lakin, president, John Landers, Joseph Brown, John S. Repp.

1872.—Daniel T. Lakin, president, John W. White, Lewis M. Nixdarf, Ephraim Stover, James A. Divan. Mr. Lakin having resigned, was succeeded by Andrew Kessler, and thereupon John W. White was elected president of the board.

1876.—James W. Pearre, president, Joseph Brown, Dr. J. W. Hilleary, James Troxell, Harry Boyle, present incumbents in 1881. From 1865 to 1868, Dr. Lewis H. Steiner was school examiner, and from 1868 to 1876, John W. Page secretary, treasurer, and examiner, with H. G. Sleeper as assistant. From 1876 to present time Daniel T. Lakin has been secretary, treasurer, and examiner, with Charlton Shafer as assistant.

The report of the public school board of this county for the year ending Sept. 30, 1881, shows the receipts to have been $66,929.78, and disbursements $64,341.41. The amount paid in salaries to teachers was, to white $11,904.58, to colored $3898.56. The enrollment of scholars was, white 8835, colored 1275, making a total of 10,110. The number of teachers employed was, white 167, colored 122. During the year ten new school-houses were built by the county commissioners for public school purposes.

Daniel Thomas Lakin, now secretary, treasurer, and examiner of the board of county school commissioners of Frederick County, was born near Jefferson, in Frederick County, March 8, 1842, upon a tract of land that was taken up as a "hatchet claim" by Mr. Lakin's great-grandfather, one of the earliest among the early settlers of Frederick County. The land in question has since that time, about two hundred years ago, been in continuous possession of a bearer of the Lakin family name, the owners and occupants at present being the heirs of Capt. William Lakin.[1] The original deed for the land is still in their possession.

Daniel T. Lakin's father, Abraham, was born upon the old Lakin place March 10, 1792, where, too, Mr. Lakin's grandfather first saw the light. Mr. Lakin's mother was Elizabeth, daughter of Charles Gross, of Frederick County. She was born Oct. 24, 1812. Her grandfather, Charles Gross, came to Maryland from Pennsylvania at a very early day. Her mother was Betsey Cost, of Loudon County, Va.

Daniel T. Lakin taught school about ten years previous to 1869, in which year he was chosen to be a member from Jefferson District of the board of county school commissioners. Although the youngest member he was elected president of the board, and in 1871, when the power to appoint school board members was vested by legislative act in the judge of the Circuit Court, Mr. Lakin was, of the seventeen members of the old board, the only one called to be one of the five members fixed upon to constitute the new board. He was again chosen the board's president, and in 1871 tendered his resignation, so that he could take an appointment as superintendent of the Monocacy Division of the Chesapeake and Ohio Canal. In that place he remained for eighteen months, and in the fall of 1875 was a Democratic nominee for the Legislature. Although defeated he handsomely led his ticket. In January, 1876, the newly-appointed board of school commissioners elected Mr. Lakin secretary, treasurer, and examiner, and as such he has served continuously to the present time. He has, therefore, as has been seen, held offices of public trust uninterruptedly since 1869, save for a period of six months,—from June, 1875, to January, 1876.

During the campaign of 1880, being himself a "total abstinence" advocate, he warmly espoused the local option cause by vigorous efforts upon the stump, and enjoyed the subsequent satisfaction of knowing that seven districts in his native county voted for the measure and now enjoy its fruitful blessings. From his youth Mr. Lakin has attended the Reformed Church, and in his political convictions has always been a stanch member of the Democratic party.

Internal Improvements.—The construction of roads connecting the settlements with one another and with Baltimore, Georgetown, Annapolis, and the Pennsylvania towns, was actively begun at a very early period.

On May 14, 1739, the inhabitants about Monocacy and to the northward of the Blue Ridge petitioned that a road might be cleared up through the country to Annapolis, to enable them to bring their grain and other commodities to market. It was referred to the next session, and granted.

Upon the petition of Joseph Wood and other inhabitants between Monocacy and the mountains towards Pennsylvania, a road was by the County Court ordered at March court, 1749, to be laid out from Frederick Town by Abraham Miller's mill, and from thence by Ambrose's mill to ye temporary line. Nathaniel Wickham, Jr., and Joseph Ogle appointed to lay it out. This was the first road laid out in Frederick County after its erection.

A road was ordered to be laid out from Capt. Joseph Ogle's to John Biggs' ford on Monocacy, and from thence to Frederick Town.

Col. Thomas Cresap, Thomas Prather, and James Dickson were appointed to lay out one from the mouth of Conococheague to Pennsylvania line, and another one from the mouth of the creek into the road near Moses Chapline's, also another from said creek to Hugh Gilliland's into the former road.

William Wilburn was ordered to lay a road from Frederick Town to the top of Kittocton Mountain.

A new road (the old one being very crooked and stopped up by falling trees) was ordered to be laid out from Monocacy ford leading to Lancaster, crossing his Lordship's Manor, Little Pipe Creek, and Great Pipe Creek to the temporal line of ye province.

Lewis Duvall, Henry Gaither, and Edward Gaither petitioned for a road from the head of Hawling's River to a convenient place on Snowden's River, near Richard Green's; also from this road near the "Chappill," in the said fork, down to a main road near John Thomas', which were ordered to be laid out.

At March court, 1779, the justices ascertained the following roads to be main roads of Frederick County, and appointed the several persons following overseers of the same:

From the Inspection House at Rock Creek down to the Common Landing on Potomac, and from the Inspection House to Nathan Peddycoat's, and from thence down to Rock Creek bridge upon Potomac.—George Gordon.

From Nathan Peddycoat's to Capt. John's bridge, the road that leads to William Wallace's, and then up the main road to Capt. John's bridge by Lee's quarter, and then from Nathan Peddycoat's to Grove Tomlinson's ford on Rock Creek.—John Claggett.

From Capt. John's bridge to Lawrence Owen's, and from thence down to Rock Creek bridge beyond Caleb Linton's, and from thence down to Rock Creek bridge near James Smith's, and from Lawrence Owen's to a bridge over Rock Creek by Peter Butler's.—John Linton.

From Lawrence Owen's to Muddy Branch, and from the cross-roads by Lawrence Owen's to Thomas Leman's, Lawrence Gates', and then up to Luke Barnett's road.—John West.

All the roads in the forks of Rock Creek which have been formerly cleared by overseers.—John Beckwith.

From Capt. John's to Isaac Ettinge's mill.—John Thompson.

From Muddy Branch to Seneca bridge by Henry Cramphin's, and from the fork road to John Ettinge's mill.—Ninian Hamilton.

From Isaac Ettinge's mill to the "Horse-pen" in the Sugarlands.—Gowen Hamilton.

From the "Horse-pen" to the upper part of that road.—John Wilcoxon.

From Seneca bridge to mouth of Monocacy.—James Veatch.

From Charles Trail's ford to Lower Bennett's Creek and to the ford on Seneca above Richard Watt's.—John Buckston.

---

[1] Capt. William Lakin was a soldier in the Federal service during the war of 1812, and when Lafayette visited Frederick City in 1825, en route through America, Capt. Lakin was the officer in charge of the military, and enjoyed the distinction of assisting Lafayette to alight from his carriage.

FREDERICK COUNTY. 437

From Thomas Lemar's gates to the ford to Charles Trail's, and from his own plantation to John Rawlings'.—Robert Lemar.

From Lower Bennett's Creek to Monocacy.—Joseph Beall, son of Ninian.

From the mouth of Rock Creek up to Slego bridge.—Edward Busey.

From the county bridge on Rock Creek to Slego, to the lower end of the county, and from Thomas Williams' mill to the Watry Branch near John Bean's.—William Murdock.

From Rock Creek bridge till it intersects with the old road, and from Nathan Magruder's to Thomas Owen's, and from thence to Rock Creek bridge.—John Sweringen.

From Rock Creek to Seneca.—John Kennedy.

From Seneca to James Brook's.—Matthew Pigman.

From James Brook's to Charles Williams'.—Higginson Belt.

From Charles Williams' to the lower end of the county.—Thomas Case.

From Richard Snowden's manor to the lower end of the county.—Samuel Rogers.

The main road leading through the forks of Haling's River.—James Williams.

From Monocacy ferry to Henry Ballinger's Branch.—Robert Pearle.

From the main road by William Griffith's to the top of Kittocton Mountain.—Alexander Duvall.

From Henry Ballinger's to Hussey's ford, the new road to the Middle ford, and from Frederick Town to John Bigg's ford on Monocacy, and from Frederick Town to the top of Kittoctin Mountain.—John Cramphin.

From Linganore ford to the extent of this county.—William Turner.

From Monocacy to Linganore, and from Linganore to the extent of the county near Parr's.—William Cumming, Jr.

The river road and Richard Touchstone's road.—Richard Touchstone.

From the top of Kittocton Mountain to the top of Shanandore, the road that leads from the top of Kittocton to Shanandore by Richard Touchston. From the top of Kittocton Mountain to the top of Shanandore that leads by John George's. From the road that leads out of John George's road that leads by Robert Evan's to the top of Shanandore.—William Johnston.

All the main roads in Antietam Hundred.—Robert Turner.

From the Great Marsh to Antietam; from the river to Stull's.—Charles Higginbotham.

Between the Great Marsh to Potomack, and from thence to Conecochegue, up Conechochegue to Vulgamot's mill, and from that to the head of the Great Marsh.—George Moore (son of George).

All the main roads in Salisbury; road to the southwest side that leads from Baker's to Stull's mill.—Martin Casner.

From Baker's to Stull's mill, between that road and the temporary line in Salisbury Hundred.—John William Smith.

All the main roads in Conochochegue Hundred.—Hans Wagoner.

From Nicholl's Neck to Fifteen-Mile Creek.—Thomas Cresap.

From Fifteen-Mile Creek to Great Towoloways.—Charles Polk.

From the road from Monocacy ford, where John Hussey lived, that leads to Lancaster and from Monocacy, crossing my Lord's Manor, crossing Little Pipe Creek to Great Pipe Creek, and from Great Pipe Creek to the temporary line of the province. Lower part to Henry Smith's branch; from thence to John Carnack's; thence with a straight line to Linganore.—Joseph Wood.

Middleport, from Smith's Branch to Great Pipe Creek, and from John Diggs' Forks to Baltimore County.—Dudley Diggs.

Upper part from Great Pipe Creek to the temporary line.—Joseph Sparks.

From Capt. Ogle's ford to John Bigg's ford on Monocacy, and from thence to Frederick Town.—Joseph Dodderidge.

From the temporary line to William Ambrose's.—William Elder.

From Ambrose's mill to Abraham Miller's mill.—Martin Whetser.

From Abraham Miller's mill till it intersects the nearest main road that leads to Frederick Town.—Jacob Nafe.

Col. Thomas Cresap was ordered to lay out a road from Nicholl's Neck to Fifteen-Mile Creek.

At the June term, 1749, a road was ordered to be laid out from the main road leading to John Tenney's, on Sligoe Branch, down Rock Creek, through Carroll's quarters, to intersect the main road to Rock Creek.

The following road was adjudged a main road of the county: From Sligoe bridge to Charles Perry's old field, and from the Northwest Branch to Sligoe by the school-house (the first mentioned).

A road was ordered to be laid out from Frederick Town to Dulany's mill.

The first bridges built were across Patuxent River,—one at a ford called Richard Green's ford, and the other at Peter Murphy's ford. On the petition of Richard Snowden, the March court of 1749 ordered their construction, and appropriated forty-five pounds for the same, to be put half on the next levy and the balance on the succeeding one.

Thomas Prather, Hugh Parker, and James Dickson were appointed to view Sideland Hill Creek and build a bridge across the same.

At the June term a bridge was allowed for Rock Creek, which was built by Edward Bewsie for fourteen pounds ten shillings,—and it being longer than he expected, he wanted five pounds ten shillings more, which extra pay was rejected instanter.

On May 20, 1809, a bridge over the Potomac was opened. The one over the Monocacy, on the Baltimore pike, was opened in 1808.

At the March court of 1749 Thomas Reynolds contracted with the court to keep a ferry over the Monocacy, opposite to the plantation where John Hussy formerly dwelt, until the last day of November court, for which he was to receive fifteen pounds. The rates for ferriage were put at four pence for carrying a man and horse, and three shillings for wagons of non-residents. William Luckett in like manner agreed to keep one over the mouth of the Monocacy, and at same rates,—agreeing in low water to provide a cart to take over tobacco and other things. Edward Wyatt, for ten pounds, agreed to keep the ferry at the mouth of Conecochegue. Daniel Ballinger contracted to keep one over the Middle ford on Monocacy for ten pounds.

In 1750, Wm. Luckett kept the ferry at the mouth of the Monocacy, and Wm. Osborne kept it in 1751.

Other public improvements soon followed, and in 1783 the General Assembly passed a resolution appointing Thomas Beatty, Joseph Sprigg, Andrew Bruce, David Poe, George Keeport, and Robert Long commissioners to lay out a common road from Baltimore Town to Elizabeth Town (now Hagerstown), in Washington County, and from thence to the western limits of the State. In 1805 a turnpike from Baltimore to Frederick was commenced, and carriages were substituted for horseback-riding, which, owing to the inferiority of the public roads, had previously been the most popular mode of conveyance for both sexes. This turnpike was finished in 1808. It passed by Ellicott's lower mill, and through Frederick Town, Hagerstown, and Cumberland; thence crossing the Allegany Mountains to Uniontown, Pa., Brownsville, and Washington, to Wheeling, on the Ohio. At Ellicott's, "on the Great Falls of Patapsco," arched bridges and extensive walls were built. Years before the Messrs. Ellicott had constructed a road from their mills to Baltimore, and had laid out a continuation of it to Frederick, which was built by them in conjunction with the property-owners along the route. At Frederick a road branched off from the turnpike, and, passing through Winchester and Staunton, extended into Tennessee. For many years the people of Tennessee transported large quantities of cotton on this road to Baltimore. At Ellicott's Mills another road branched off through Montgomery County to Leesburg, Va. The public roads, previous to the establishment of the penitentiary system, were kept in order by gangs of convicts, known as wheelbarrow men. Each "gang" had an overseer, who carried a musket and side-arms. Houses built of logs were erected at intervals along the road, in which the convicts were confined at night. "One of these depots," says Martha E. Tyson, in her account of the settlement of Ellicott's Mills, "five miles from Baltimore, on the Frederick road, was standing until 1831, and continued to be pointed out as the spot where on two occasions an overseer had been murdered with bludgeons by the men under his charge. The murderers were tried, condemned, and executed." In the same memoir we find that "before the year 1783 the supply of wheat from the counties of Anne Arundel and Frederick having so much increased, the proprietors of Ellicott's mills, in anticipation of a peace with Great Britain, and the conclusion of the Revolutionary war, determined to make preparations for exporting their flour." The following is a list of the officers of turnpike companies in Frederick County:

Baltimore and Frederick Turnpike Company.—At an election held May 13, 1805, the following officers were elected:

President, Jonathan Ellicott; Treasurer, William Cook; Managers, John McPherson, John Eager Howard, Samuel Smith, Thomas Sprigg, John Ellicott of John, Solomon Etting, John Donnell, George Baer.

Frederick and Catoctin Mountain Turnpike Company.—Officers for 1881:

President, W. M. Feaga; Secretary, Theodore Schultz; Treasurer, D. C. Kemp; Additional Directors, A. W. Burkhart, McClinton Young, George T. Dill, John M. Whitmore, Albert F. Ramsburg.

Frederick and Emmittsburg Turnpike Company.—Directors for 1881:

G. W. Miller, Val. S. Bruner, Joseph Cronise, Dr. Charles Smith, Joseph Hays, Col. John R. Rouver, John Roelky, Daniel J. Snook, Jeremiah C. Cramer.

Besides the above three there are ten (thirteen in all) turnpike roads, well graded and macadamized, in the county,—the National, Woodsboro', Liberty, Buckeystown, Liberty and New Windsor, Liberty, Johnsville and Pipe Creek, Sprunt Spring, Monocacy and Linganore, Union Bridge and Monocacy, and Urbana roads.

The Monocacy is a fine stream, passing from York County, in Pennsylvania, through Frederick County, Md., and discharging itself into the Potomac about forty miles above Georgetown. In 1804 the rich farmers on that river advanced to the Potomac Company a sum of money on condition that it should be applied to improving the navigation from the junction of the Monocacy with the Potomac into the heart of Frederick County, and the work was completed in a manner to insure an uninterrupted communication by water between Washington and Frederick for at least nine or ten months in the year. It appears that the improvement was very beneficial to Georgetown, which was then one of the flourishing trading towns. In 1808 a bridge was built over the Monocacy on the line of the Baltimore turnpike.

On the 28th of June, 1823, a cave was discovered on the land of Mrs. Catharine Thomas, near the Monocacy, but was not then explored.

On Friday, March 17, 1854, the bridge, built in 1832–33, over the Monocacy, on the line of the Baltimore and Ohio Railroad, fifty-nine miles from Baltimore, at the junction of the Branch road to Frederick City, was destroyed by fire.

Baltimore and Ohio Railroad.—It can readily be conceded that nothing has tended more advantageously to the benefit of a country than the establishment of a railroad, and therefore, in considering the growth and progress of Western Maryland, this factor must be largely taken into consideration. "Cabined, cribbed, and confined" as this portion of Maryland naturally is; hemmed in by apparently unaccessible mountains, and yet having within herself the means to branch out and advance the interests of not only one but many States, the question which presented

CHARLES CARROLL OF CARROLLTON.

itself was, how to overcome physical obstacles and bring her advantages before the general community? The inception, the struggles, and the ultimate triumph of the Baltimore and Ohio Railroad are known not only to the people of this State, but to those of others which are rivals in commercial and industrial progress. The scheme, visionary as at first it may have been supposed to have been, which contemplated joining by iron bands the waters of the Patapsco with those of the Ohio, was not intended simply for the benefit of Baltimore City, but aimed at giving to each part of Western Maryland, whether rich in cereals or in minerals, an opportunity for development and a chance to show to the rest of the continent the value of its products. In this the acumen and forethought of the first projectors of the Baltimore and Ohio Railroad were plainly visible, and, in fact, it may be said of them that they builded better than they knew. They remembered that away back in the old days the National turnpike over the Alleganies was the great high-road to the West; they saw that the disciples of old Brundley, the English engineer, who believed that God made the rivers to feed the canals, were clamoring for a hearing for their schemes, and so availed themselves of the new invention, feeling confident that soon every part of Western Maryland would have a share in the benefit and the glory. The result of to-day shows how far-seeing they were, how aptly all of their schemes have adapted themselves to the general good of the State, and how other parts of the country have learned a lesson from the perseverance and faith of such wise and patriotic men.

It might almost be considered unnecessary here to go into the history of the Baltimore and Ohio Railroad, nor would it be, further than to show its connection with Western Maryland, and as it is an axiom that the greater includes the lesser, therefore that railroad of to-day comprises within it elements the strength of which has been gained simply by their connection with a productive section and clear-headed natives of Maryland. And yet the story is one which has in it so much of the practical, and yet withal so much of the romantic, that it deserves to be recorded.

There were two citizens of Baltimore, Philip E. Thomas and George Brown, who felt that not all the canals on the continent could ever surmount the Alleganies, and who, after careful consideration, came to the conclusion that only railroads could be made practicable for such a purpose. A meeting was held by leading citizens of Baltimore for an interchange of views, and a plan for organization of the Baltimore and Ohio Railroad drawn up, a committee of citizens of Baltimore being appointed to present it to the General Assembly, then in session in Annapolis, February, 1827. A few days only had elapsed when the act of incorporation was passed. All the preliminary conditions prescribed by the act of incorporation having been complied with, the construction of the railroad began.

On the 23d of April, 1827, the company was organized, and books of subscription to the capital stock were opened. Mr. Thomas was chosen president, and Mr. George Brown, treasurer. The directors elected were Charles Carroll of Carrollton, William Paterson, Robert Oliver, Alexander Brown, Isaac McKeen, William Lorman, George Hoffman, P. E. Thomas, John B. Morris, Thomas Ellicott, Talbot Jones, and William Stewart.

The Legislature of Maryland in 1828 passed a bill subscribing five hundred thousand dollars to the stock of the company, and this, with the subscriptions of the city of Baltimore and those of individuals, rendered the capital stock of the company four millions of dollars. On the 4th of July, 1828, a day memorable in the history of Baltimore, the first stone of the railroad was laid by Charles Carroll of Carrollton with imposing Masonic ceremonies. On the 28th of July of the same year work on the road-bed was begun, and on May 22, 1830, the road was formally opened to Ellicott's Mills. From that time it was rapidly pushed westward, and on November 12, 1831, was formally opened to Frederick. Up to this time horses had been the motive-power used on the road, but the period soon came when the locomotive outdistanced all competitors, and at the close of 1831 the practicability of using locomotives had been fully demonstrated.

In the location of the road the directors had determined to pass around the Point of Rocks and get through the Blue Ridge by way of Harper's Ferry Gap, but in 1828 an injunction was sued out in Washington County Court by the canal company, restraining the railroad company from acquiring title to the land until its own works had been located through the pass. Another injunction stopped the railroad from proceeding with the construction of the road beyond Point of Rocks. Litigation lasted until 1832, when the Court of Appeals decided that the Chesapeake and Ohio Canal Company, as assignee of the Potomac Company, had the right of choice of route along the banks of the Potomac, and that the railroad company could not occupy any place along the river to restrict the canal company in the location of its works. This stopped the further progress of the road until the canal company had decided how much of the narrow strip of ground between the river and the precipitous walls of the mountain it desired to appropriate, and after it had exercised its right of election in this regard there was no room left for the railroad. Nothing remained for the railroad company but a "compromise" which would permit the joint occupation of the narrow passes between the Point of Rocks and Harper's Ferry, and to this end application was made to the Legislature for an act proposing a plan of agreement between the two companies. A committee of the House of Delegates, after inspecting the disputed passes, reported that there was room enough for both the canal and the railroad, and severely reprobated the canal company for stopping the westward extension of the road. No remedy could be applied, however, except to give the sanction of the Legislature to a compromise, the terms of which were set forth in the act of December, 1832. The railroad company was authorized to subscribe for 2500 shares of the canal stock, and the canal company was to be permitted to grade the road through the disputed passes, and to receive $100,000 for the work. The appointment of two commissioners was provided for in the act, who were empowered to carry its provisions into effect, both companies consenting thereto. After some negotiation, a settlement was effected, which closed the whole controversy. The railroad company paid the canal company in lieu of the stock subscription, and in satisfaction of all the conditions of the compromise act, the sum of $226,000; and further agreed that the railroad should not be pushed beyond Harper's Ferry until the canal reached Cumberland, provided that it got there at the time fixed in its charter, the year 1840. On the 9th of May, 1833, the construction of the railroad from Point of Rocks to Harper's Ferry was resumed, the work having been stopped five years by the controversy with the canal company.

The five years' blockade at the Point of Rocks, however, was not entirely without compensation. During that period the art of transporting passengers and freight by rail was thoroughly studied and mastered. The completed division of the main stem between Point of Rocks and Baltimore and the Washington branch were put into successful operation, and the speed and strength of the "iron horse" had been developed to a degree not dreamed of when the controversy with the canal company began. At the trial of locomotives in the summer of 1831 the "York" was regarded as a magnificent motor because it could draw a load of fifteen tons at the rate of fifteen miles an hour; but in 1834 the "Arabian," built by Phineas Davis, was making daily trips of eighty miles, oftentimes drawing a load of two hundred and twelve tons. Five other locomotives of equal power were doing the same service on the Washington branch, and when the road was opened between the two cities they made the trip in two hours and ten minutes. At the close of the year 1835 the company had seven locomotives, forty-four passenger-cars, and one thousand and seventy-eight freight-cars in daily use.

From 1835 to 1838 nothing was done towards the extension of the road beyond Harper's Ferry except the surveying of routes by the engineer corps. On April 2, 1838, the Virginia Legislature passed the act which required the company to locate the next ninety-two miles of its road in that State, and also to make Wheeling the western terminus. Work was resumed in the latter part of the year 1838, and during the next four years the company devoted its energies and resources mainly to the construction of the road from Harper's Ferry to Cumberland, a distance of ninety-seven miles. The approach to the Harper's Ferry bridge on the Virginia side was covered by the reservation on which the United States armory was located, but the Secretary of War gave the company permission to lay its track through these grounds. By taking the southern bank of the Potomac the railroad company left the canal company to the full enjoyment of its "paramount right" to the

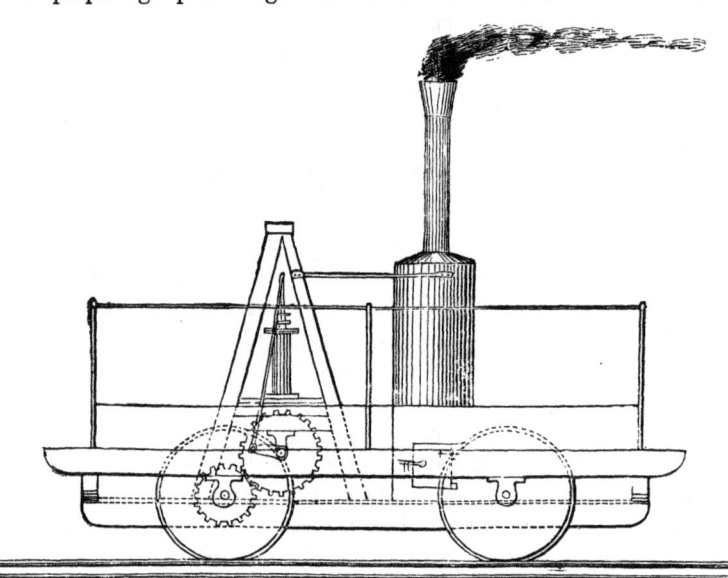

PETER COOPER'S FIRST LOCOMOTIVE.

northern bank, while the act of June 4, 1836, so far modified the compromise of 1833 as to allow the two works to proceed in the direction of Cumberland *pari passu*. The first division of one hundred miles of the main stem of the Baltimore and Ohio road ended at Martinsburg, and here extensive repair-shops were subsequently erected.

The road was opened to Cumberland, Nov. 5, 1842, and that city remained its western terminus during the next seven years. Singular as it may appear, but little importance was attached to the transportation of coal at the time the railroad company established its western depot there. The only mode of bringing coal to Cumberland in those days was by hauling it in wagons over mountain roads. The great mines which have since yielded many millions of tons had not then been opened, and it was in reality the wonderful impulse given to manufactures and to steam navigation on the ocean by the building of the great railways between the East and the West that created a demand for Cumberland coal.

During the year 1843 the president and directors of the Baltimore and Ohio Company scarcely thought it necessary to make any special preparations for the carrying of coal, and only four thousand nine hundred and sixty-four tons were brought to Baltimore during that year. Ross Winans had constructed an engine as early as 1842 which was capable of drawing eleven hundred tons on a level road and one hundred and seventy tons up a grade of eighty-two feet to the mile, so that the motive-power of the company was supposed to be equal to all the demands likely to be made upon it for the transportation of coal until railway communications had been established with the mines. The development of the Cumberland coal-mines, however, followed close upon the completion of the railroad to that point. In the year 1843 the Maryland and New York Iron and Coal Company began operations, and a railway connecting its extensive mines with the Baltimore and Ohio Railroad was projected. It was represented to the railroad company that the success of the mining company would depend largely upon the rate at which coal could be transported by rail from Cumberland to Baltimore, and that this would have to be determined in advance. At first the railroad company refused to enter into a permanent contract, because it would involve the expense of building a large number of cars especially designed for carrying coal; and in the event of a failure in the demand for coal, these cars could not be advantageously used in the transportation of ordinary freight. Subsequently, however, upon a guarantee being given that one hundred and seventy-five tons of coal per day would be furnished for three hundred days in the year, the company entered into a contract by which it agreed to transport coal from Cumberland to Baltimore for one and one-third cents per ton per mile, with ten cents per ton added for hauling the cars through the streets of Baltimore to the point of delivery, the cost of loading and unloading to be borne by the mining company. This contract was made early in January, 1844, but it was not to take effect until the projected railway to the mines had been completed.

In the mean time the canal had "stretched its slow length" along the tortuous banks of the Potomac as far as dam No. 6, forty-five miles east of Cumberland, and in the summer of 1843 was ready to begin the transportation of coal from that point. An arrangement was made between the canal company and the railroad company by which the latter agreed to carry coal from Cumberland to dam No. 6 and deliver it to the boatmen for two cents per ton per mile. At the ensuing session of the Legislature the subject of coal transportation was taken up by the House of Delegates, and an order was passed Jan. 25, 1844, calling upon the president of the Baltimore and Ohio Railroad Company to answer certain interrogatories as to the cost of transporting coal by rail, and as to the facilities of the company for supplying the canal with coal at dam No. 6. The canal company had exhausted all its means, and was unable to prosecute its work any further without additional aid from the State, and the object of this inquiry seemed to be to determine whether it would be better to make dam No. 6 the terminus of the canal and depend upon the railroad for a supply of coal, or to postpone the liens of the State so as to permit the company to pledge its revenues for additional loans to complete the canal to Cumberland. In response to these inquiries, Mr. McLane submitted a statement to show that according to the established rates coal could be delivered at Georgetown at about the same cost for transportation whether the boats should be loaded from the railroad-trains at Cumberland or at dam No. 6. Mr. McLane further expressed the opinion that the demand for Cumberland coal would not exceed 100,000 tons a year for many years to come.

In this prediction Mr. McLane was mistaken, although the experience of the Baltimore and Ohio Company during the first four years after the opening of the coal trade was far from encouraging. Only 5433 tons were carried in 1844; the next year the amount rose to 16,020 tons. The whole transportation of coal for four years was 44,840 tons. From this time forward the coal trade grew so rapidly that the company often found it difficult to provide transportation. Six new freight-engines built by Ross Winans were placed on the road in 1846, and nine more were added during the two succeeding years. In 1849 the coal carried eastward from Cumberland by rail aggregated 142,449 tons, and in 1850 the amount increased to 192,806 tons. The canal having been completed to Cumberland in 1850, began carrying coal from that point, and the immediate effect of the competition was largely increased shipments by rail. In 1860 the Baltimore and Ohio brought 493,031 tons of coal to Baltimore, 1,112,938 tons in 1870, and 2,255,146 tons in 1880.

The construction of the road westward from Cumberland did not begin until the year 1849. During the seven years' delay there public confidence had become weakened in the project; the increased demand for transportation imposed a large additional expense on the company for new rolling-stock; the credit of the State of Maryland having suffered through her temporary failure to pay interest on her bonds, it was impossible to dispose of the securities in which she had paid her last subscription, except at a ruinous sacrifice, and therefore the net revenue derived from working the road was yearly absorbed in expenditures, and no dividend could be declared. In the beginning of 1848, and at a critical period in the history of the road, Mr. Thomas Swann was elected one of the directors of the company, and very soon his energy and intelligence were seen. On Oct. 10, 1848, he was elected president of the company, and under his administration the road was built from Cumberland to Wheeling. He found the road resting at Cumberland in a state of semi-paralysis. Although a portion of the capital contributed by the State for its completion still remained, it was not available because the credit of both company and State was seriously impaired. Mr. Swann re-established this credit, and then succeeded in inducing the directors to proceed with the works and to let contracts for the construction of the whole western division. Heretofore the company had built its road mainly with the capital furnished by the State and the city of Baltimore, but the bounty of both the State and the city had been exhausted, and the company had nothing to rely on now save its own credit and its own resources. The remainder of the sterling bonds were sold, and when the money derived from this source had been expended, the president and directors of the road courageously faced the situation and advised the sale of the company's coupon bonds, authorized to be issued at the discretion of the president and directors by the act of 1845. Prior to this none of these bonds had been put on the market because the president and directors feared that they would fall below par, and the effect would be to still further impair the credit of the company. But when the alternative was presented of submitting to a discount or stopping work on the western division of the road, the company had no hesitation in deciding what ought to be done. The first lot of bonds offered were taken by a banking-house at eighty cents on the dollar, and then the price rose to eighty-seven cents. The effect upon the credit of the company was precisely the reverse of what had been predicted by those who opposed the selling of the bonds below par.

As already stated, the extension of the road westward from Cumberland was commenced in 1849. The engineers had not proceeded far before they again came in collision with the old claim of the Chesapeake and Ohio Canal Company to the "paramount right" to occupy the narrow passes of the Potomac, but the difficulty was settled without litigation, and the company was permitted to build its road across and *through* the mountains without any further interruption from the "assignee of the Potomac Company, chartered in 1784," and soon got out of the region supposed to be covered by this ancient grant. On the 22d of July, 1851, the road was opened for travel to Piedmont, twenty-eight miles west of Cumberland, and on the 22d of June, 1852, the first train reached the Monongahela River. The conditional subscription of $500,000 to the capital stock of the company made by the city of Wheeling became available when the road crossed the Monongahela, and that sum was now added to the construction fund. In the fulfillment of a promise or a prophecy made by Mr. Swann two years before, the road was completed to Wheeling Jan. 1, 1853, and was formally opened from the Chesapeake to the Ohio by an excursion from Baltimore to Wheeling, Jan. 10, 1853. The municipal authorities of Wheeling gave a grand complimentary banquet to the visitors on January 12th, at which George Brown, the first treasurer of the company, and who, in connection with Philip E. Thomas, had first suggested the building of a railway from tide-water to the Ohio River, gave a most interesting historical sketch of the early history of the road.

No railroad two hundred miles in length was ever before constructed through a region presenting so many natural obstacles in so short a time as the western division of the Baltimore and Ohio. The contracts were given out in the summer of 1849, and the road was opened for travel throughout its entire length Jan. 10, 1853. Notwithstanding the vastly improved appliances that have been invented since

1853 for boring tunnels and building bridges, no such rapidity of construction has been witnessed on this side of the Rocky Mountains up to the present time. There are twelve tunnels between Cumberland and Wheeling, the aggregate length of which is ten thousand five hundred feet (two miles); the longest is the great tunnel at Kingwood, four thousand one hundred feet, which cost $460,000. There are also one hundred and fourteen bridges on this division of the road, some of which are splendid structures. The construction of a railroad two hundred miles in length across a series of parallel mountain ranges, tunneling such as could not be outflanked or graded, in the space of three years was a marvelous achievement. This division of the road cost, in round numbers, $8,000,000. Up to the time of its completion the whole line between Baltimore and Wheeling had cost $17,500,000, in round numbers, and the laying of a second track, the purchase of real estate, and the stocking of the road with locomotives and cars had brought the whole expenditure up to $22,000,000, this sum being more than three times the amount of the original estimate. The common stock of the company had been issued to the amount of $9,091,500, of which 6855 shares ($685,500) were held by the State of Maryland, 42,582 shares ($4,258,200) by the city of Baltimore, 5000 shares ($500,000) by the city of Wheeling, and 46,478 shares ($4,647,800) by individuals. To this must be added the 30,000 shares of preferred six per cent. stock issued under the provisions of the act of June 4, 1836, and held by the State of Maryland ($3,000,000), making the entire stock debt of the company $13,091,500. Up to this time coupon bonds secured by mortgage had been issued to the amount of $5,677,012.

Since that time the history of the road has been one of progress. As soon as the line had been laid to the Ohio River, Mr. Swann resigned the presidency, and Chauncey Brooks was elected to the position. On Nov. 17, 1858, he in turn resigned, and John W. Garrett was elected to fill the place. Eminently fitted by a severe course of business training for the work, he applied all his energies to the development of the road and to the pushing of it forward into the West, where formerly other lines had a monopoly of traffic. The wisdom of this aggressive policy was soon felt, and in spite of difficulties and opposition the road grew in importance, until now the whole State feels the benefit of its presence, and agricultural and mechanical industries have grown fourfold.

The act of the Legislature of Maryland of June 4, 1836, imposed certain restrictions and limitations upon the railroad company relating to its construction from Harper's Ferry westward, most of which were avoided by crossing to the south side of the Potomac River; but the railroad company, by locating this division of the road in Virginia, violated one of the provisions of the act, which gave great dissatisfaction in Western Maryland, and led to further controversy in the Legislature and in the courts. It was enacted that the road should run through Boonsboro' and Hagerstown, and thence to Cumberland, and it was provided that in the event of any other route being chosen the company should forfeit one million of dollars to the State of Maryland, for the use of Washington County. The company having selected the Virginia route, the commissioners of Washington County brought suit in Frederick County Circuit Court for the amount forfeited. The Legislature repealed the act of June 4, 1836, and upon appeal the Court of Appeals decided that the forfeiture was in the nature of a *penalty*, which the Legislature could remit, and which was in fact remitted by the repeal of the act.

At the close of the year 1843 the railroad company found itself without authority to enter either Virginia or Pennsylvania, through one or the other of which it was necessary to pass to reach the Ohio River. The five years' limitation of the Virginia act had expired, as well as the fifteen years' limitation of the Pennsylvania act.

Other railroads from the East to the Ohio River were contemplated, and new interests had arisen to antagonize the company. The Pennsylvania act of 1828, authorizing the company to locate its road through that State, contemplated Pittsburgh as its western terminus, or in the event of any other route being selected, that a branch road to Pittsburgh should be constructed. The Pennsylvania act of 1836 provided for a railroad connection with the Baltimore and Ohio at Hagerstown or Williamsport. The people of Western Pennsylvania had been and as late as 1846 were anxious that the road should go to Pittsburgh. After a protracted contest in the Legislature of Pennsylvania in 1846, an act was passed authorizing the construction of the "Connellsville Road," and at that early day a large number of the merchants of Baltimore, as well as the stockholders of the railroad, favored Pittsburgh as the western terminus. The Virginia Legislature refused the right of way through that State as long as there was any probability that Pittsburgh would become the western terminus. It was not until 1847 that an act unencumbered with restrictions conferred the authority to enter the State of Virginia, and this grant was coupled with the imperative condition that Wheeling should be the western terminus of the main stem. This act the company accepted. The idea of a connection with Pittsburgh was not abandoned because the road had been driven by Virginia to Wheeling. The extension of the Connellsville road to Cumberland was regarded as a matter of vital importance to Baltimore, and hence that city authorized, in 1856, a loan of $1,000,000 in city stock to the Connellsville company, upon which the city paid the interest for nineteen years, without receiving any return. In 1875 the Baltimore and Ohio Railroad Company assumed the payment of the principal and arrears of interest, amounting together to $2,235,000. The route from Cumberland to Pittsburgh is comparatively direct, and one hundred and forty-nine miles in distance, and passes through a highly productive country. Benjamin H. Latrobe, in 1856, became president of the Connellsville company, and devoted his energies to the completion of the road to Cumberland, and during his administration the road was extended from Turtle Creek to Pittsburgh, which was accomplished in 1861. The breaking out of the war put an end for the time to the construction of the road, and left an unfinished gap of ninety-one miles, upon which about $200,000 had been expended. Upon the return of peace work was resumed, and prosecuted as well as the means at hand would permit until April 11, 1871, when the cities of Baltimore and Cumberland and Pittsburgh were united by rail. The Connellsville road is located for a very great distance along the route surveyed in 1754 by Gen. Washington for an available wagon road to transport army supplies from Fort Cumberland to Fort Duquesne.

The Washington County Branch, which connects the Baltimore and Ohio Railroad with Hagerstown, was completed in September, 1867; the railroad company furnishing $400,000, Washington County $150,000, and private subscriptions $200,000 of the capital.

The progress of the road is marked by the periods of opening to the principal points along its route, as follows:

Opened to Ellicott's Mills by horse-power, 24th May, 1830.
" " Ellicott's Mills by steam, 30th August, 1830.
" " Frederick " 1st Dec., 1831.
" " Point of Rocks " 1st April, 1832.
" " Harper's Ferry " 1st Dec., 1834.
" " Bladensburg " 20th July, 1834.
" " Washington " 1st June, 1842.
" " Opposite Hancock " 25th August, 1834.
" " Cumberland " 5th Nov., 1842.
" " Piedmont " 21st July, 1851.
" " Fairmount " 22d June, 1852.
" " Wheeling " 1st Jan., 1853.
" " Hagerstown " Sept., 1867.
" " Pittsburgh " 11th April, 1871.
" " Metropolitan Branch " 25th May, 1873.

The Metropolitan Branch from Washington, D. C., to the main stem at the Point of Rocks was constructed under the act of 1870, reviving the power and provisions of the expired act of 1856. It is forty-three miles in length, and cost $3,583,497. The junction at the Point of Rocks is sixty-nine miles west of Baltimore.

The Packersburg Branch of the Baltimore and Ohio Railroad—formerly the Northwestern Virginia Railroad—was chartered in 1851 and completed in 1857. It extends from Grafton on the main stem to Packersburg on the Ohio River, a distance of one hundred and four miles, and is the middle division of the "short" line between Baltimore and Cincinnati. The road was built principally with funds furnished by the Baltimore and Ohio Railroad Company by indorsement of the bonds for $1,500,000, and cash advanced at various times amounting to $2,000,000. The city of Baltimore also indorsed the bonds of the company for $1,500,000, the payment of which the Baltimore and Ohio afterwards assumed. The road is leased to the Baltimore and Ohio Railroad Company.

The Frederick City Branch of the Baltimore and Ohio Railroad enters Frederick County at a point near Parr's Spring, and extends across the southern portion of it to Weverton, a distance of thirty-six miles, with a branch from Monocacy Junction to Frederick City of three miles.

The stations, entering the county from the east, are Plane Number Four, Monrovia, Ijamsville, Frederick Junction, Lime-Kiln, Adamstown, Washington Junction (Point of Rocks), Lander (Catoctin Switch), Berlin, Knoxville, and Weverton.

The road was opened to Frederick, Dec. 1, 1831, a distance of sixty-one miles from Baltimore. The event was celebrated with appropriate ceremonies, the president, Philip E. Thomas, and directors participating, accompanied by a large number of guests, among whom were Hon. George Howard, Governor of Maryland, Judge Baldwin of the Supreme Court of the United States, the mayor and the corporation of Baltimore (specially invited by the Board of Aldermen and Common Council of Frederick), Gen. Steuart, William Gwynn, Gen. Marriott, J. S. Skinner, and a large number of others. Five cars came from Baltimore, in which were passengers the president (Hon. Philip E. Thomas) and directors of the road, the mayor and both branches of the City Council, the Governor of the State (Hon. George Howard), and a number of the officers of the company, about seventy persons in all. The citizens of Frederick gave the entire party a grand reception and dinner at Talbott's (now the City Hotel). The arrival of the cars was announced by the firing of cannon, the ringing of bells, and other jubilating demonstrations. The car "Frederick" was placed first in the train. The Baltimore and Ohio Railroad, at that time sixty miles in length, was the longest railroad in the world. The fare from Frederick to Baltimore was one dollar and eighty cents, or three cents per mile,—just five cents more than the present competing rate of one dollar and seventy-five cents. One train left there daily at nine A.M. From the commencement of its running passengers from the West by stage over the National turnpike, the great thoroughfare of that era, were brought only as far as this point.

The Railroad Accident of 1877.—On June 12, 1877, an excursion-party of over six hundred persons left Frederick City at 6.45 A.M. for Washington and Mount Vernon. In this party was represented nearly every family of Frederick and many from the county. The train was composed of thirteen coaches, and was in charge of Capt. R. Cooper, with Frank Bond, an old employé, in charge of the passengers. The train sped smoothly along, until suddenly, at about 7.45 A.M., within half a mile of the junction of the main stem with the Metropolitan Branch Road, and without a word of warning or the sound of a whistle, there was a sudden jar followed by a crash, and the train was a wreck. It had collided with an east-bound train. The passengers in the rear cars, which fortunately were not involved in the wreck, were seized with consternation. Some jumped out of the rear windows and from the platforms, but so sudden was the accident, and so soon the cessation of the jar, that comparatively few of them became panic-stricken. But the scene presented by the cars which had suffered was appalling in the extreme. The coaches attached to the locomotive of the eastward-bound train were unoccupied. When the engines collided the concussion drove them back about a hundred yards from the wreck. The engines were both complete wrecks, and the two adjoining cars of the train. Coaches Nos. 56 and 67, containing about one hundred excursionists, were completely telescoped. Some were crushed to death, and many maimed and injured. Five were killed outright. Of these, one was Charles H. Keefer, the head of the firm of Keefer & Knauff, of the Frederick *Examiner*. He was the son of the late Hiram Keefer, and was born in 1835. As an apprentice he entered the *Examiner* printing-office in 1849, and became a member of the firm of Schley, Haller & Co. in 1858. By a subsequent change in 1863 he became second member of the firm, then known as Schley, Keefer & Co. Again, in 1865, another business change made Mr. Keefer senior partner, under the name of Keefer, Smith & Co., while in 1875 the present firm of Keefer & Knauff was established. Mr. Keefer, at the time of his death, was a member of the Republican State Central Committee, president of the board of trustees of Montevue Hospital, corresponding secretary of the County Agricultural Society, one of the managers of the Poor Association, a director in the Franklin and Citizens' Building Association, a member of the Standing Committee of the Junior Fire Company, and a member of the O. U. A. M. and I. O. O. F. In 1859 he married a niece of the late Abram Kemp. He was a member of the Reformed Church, in which he had been deacon, and treasurer of its Sunday-school. He was one of Frederick's most popular and influential citizens. Another of the killed was Richard P. T. Dutrow, a prominent farmer, and formerly a member of the Legislature. He had not been on the train over five minutes, having joined the excursionists at Adamstown. He was born in Buckeystown District in 1828, and in 1868 was elected a delegate to the Legislature, and in 1875 chosen as a county commissioner. He married a daughter of Capt. William Lakin, of Jefferson District. The third was Howard Eugene Dixon, about twenty years of age, who lived in West All-Saints' Street with his widowed mother. He was employed at McMurray's packing establishment, and was highly esteemed. The fourth, J. Dorsey Walker, lived in New Market District, and was not quite twenty-one years old. He was a young man of industrious habits and greatly respected. The fifth was Louis H. Schley, a son of Dr. Fairfax Schley, a most popular and promising young man, who had his legs broken, crushed, and fearfully lacerated, and also received internal injuries, which resulted the same day in his death. On the same train with him were his father, mother, and his two sisters. He was born December, 1854, and in 1875 graduated with high honors at Franklin and Marshall College. On his graduation he delivered the "Franklin and Marshall" oration, the highest honor of the institution. On his return from college his father retired from business, and transferred his drug-store to his two sons, Steiner and Lewis H. At the annual election for elders and deacons in the Reformed Church, on Easter Monday, 1877, young Mr. Schley was chosen to the diaconate by the congregation, an honor seldom conferred upon one so young in years. His remains were interred in Mount Olivet Cemetery June 13th, Rev. E. R. Esbach officiating. Among the injured were Col. Charles E. Trail, Leonard C. Mullinix, leg broken; William Bartgis and Henry Brashears, each with a leg broken; Enoch Green, leg broken and serious internal injuries; engineer George Buckley, arm badly hurt; the fireman of engine No. 410, head badly cut; a son of Col. George R. Dennis, arm broken; Luther Knoodle and Isaac Ely, internal injuries; John B. Thomas, John Dadishman, Peter Lugenbeel, L. Clinton Moberly, William Nash Young, William Harrison, Adam Notnagle, H. N. Etchison, G. Fenton Snouffer, and his son William Snouffer, all badly cut or bruised. The extent of the calamity being unknown when the first news reached the city, the entire population of Frederick were overwhelmed with grief. The telegraph-office was besieged by the anxious friends of the excursionists, and as the news began to arrive of the deaths of some and the injuries that had befallen others, it was at first feared that the entire train had been destroyed and the whole party more or less injured. The day will long be remembered in Frederick as one of the darkest in its history.

Agricultural Societies.—About 1821 there was a marked awakening among the agricultural population of Frederick County as to the necessity of adopting improved methods of husbandry and of infusing new life and energy into their work, if they would maintain their standard as the most prosperous and enterprising community in the State. One of the first steps in this direction was recognized at once to be the combination of their individual energies, in order that they might advance in order and harmony and reap the benefit of the experience and advice of all. Accordingly, on the 7th of November, 1821, the Frederick County Agricultural Society was organized. The officers elected were:

President, William E. Williams; Vice-Presidents, District 1, Col. Henry Kemp; 2, Col. John McPherson; 3, John Thomas; 4, James Johnson; 5, Col. G. M. Eichelberger; 6, William P. Farquhar; 7, Jesse Slingluff; 8, Joshua Delaplaine; 9, William Marsel; Secretary, Henry Willis; Treasurer, Thomas Shaw.

Its first exhibition, then called "cattle-show and fair," was held on May 23 and 24, 1822, at George Creager's tavern, Monocacy Bridge, two miles east of Frederick City, and was the first ever held in the county, and the second in the State. At this fair liberal premiums in money were paid to the successful competitors of fine stock.

The next venture was the "Farmers' Club," organized Nov. 22, 1849. Its officers were:

President, Gideon Bantz; Treasurer, Ezra Houck; Recording Secretary, S. H. O'Neal; Corresponding Secretary, E. B. Baltzell; Vice-Presidents, one from each election district, as follows: Frederick, Richard Potts; Middletown, Peter Schlosser; New Market, Harry Dorsey; Liberty, S. D. Warfield; Woodsborough, Chester Coleman; Creagerstown, William Todd; Emmittsburg, Peter Grable; Petersville, Henry Dunlap; Buckeystown, J. L. Davis; Jefferson, William Lynch; Urbana, John Montgomery; Catoctin, George Blessing; Hauver's, J. Harbaugh; Managers, Edward Buckey, Christian Steiner, T. H. O'Neal, Valentine Adams, J. Browers.

On March 5, 1850, William Baer delivered an address before the club on "The different combinations of the soil, effects, mode of treatment, etc." No exhibition seems to have been held by it, though it held many meetings for discussion, at one of which a committee was appointed on manure and inspection, consisting of Wm. Baer, Samuel O. Tyler, and Chester Coleman, who made thereon a very interesting and exhaustive report.

On Jan. 12, 1853, in obedience to a call of many farmers, there was organized "The Agricultural Club of Frederick County," which was to hold annual exhibitions, and monthly meetings for instruction, discussion, etc. It adopted the constitution and by-laws of its predecessor, the "Farmers' Club." Its officers were:

President, Lewis Kemp; Vice-Presidents, William Richardson, Gideon Bantz, H. W. Dorsey, D. W. Naill, R. Y. Stokes, David Thomas, John C. Lane, Noah Phillips, Joseph Eichelberger, George P. Fox, Michael Sluss, Henry Dunlap, William Lynch, George Blessing, David Schindler; Secretary, S. H. O'Neal; Corresponding Secretary, Charles E. Trail; Treasurer, Christian Steiner; Managers, Valentine Adams, R. J. Lamar, B. A. Cunningham, William A. Albaugh, Cornelius Staley.

Its first exhibition was held Oct. 12, 13, and 14, 1853, on the "Barracks" grounds, the east wing of the Barracks being fitted up for domestic fabrications, machinery, etc. The officers in different years were as follows:

1854.—President, Lewis Kemp; Vice-Presidents, William Richardson, Gideon Bantz, H. W. Dorsey, Gen. Anthony Kimmel, R. Y. Stokes, Griffin Taylor, John S. Motter, John Norris, Dr. William S. McPherson, George P. Fox, John Grable, William Lynch, David Schindler, George Blessing, William C. Landers; Secretary, S. H. O'Neil; Managers, Frederick District, Cornelius Staley, W. F. Johnson, Ross Johnson, John F. Clingan, Lewis G. Kemp, John McPherson, of Wm., John Bender, Valentine Albaugh, John H. Bruner, Abraham Kemp, Worthington Johnson; Mount Pleasant District, R. J. Lamar, Joseph Rontzahn, William S. Miller; Buckeystown, Michael Keefer, Dr. G. Gibson, J. M. Buckey, A. J. Snouffer; Woodsborough, William A. Albaugh; Petersville, Outerbridge Horsey; Urbana, R. G. McPherson; Jefferson, J. Q. A. Kemp, J. W. Charlton, G. P. Ramsburg; Middletown, Samuel Bowles; New Market, Dr. N. V. Shipley; Liberty, John Phillips, G. W. Dutrow; Creagerstown, Michael Zimmerman; Emmittsburg, Matthew Moran; Hauver's, David Wolf; Catoctin, Samuel Wolf; Jackson, David Kailor, John C. Lane. On June 3, 1854, "The Agricultural Club" was incorporated into "The Agricultural Society of Frederick County," which name it has borne under that act of incorporation to the present day.

1855.—President, Outerbridge Horsey; Secretary, S. H. O'Neal; Managers, J. M. Buckey, R. G. McPherson, William Richardson, H. Duvall, J. Q. A. Kemp, Samuel Ahalt, E. L. Delashmutt, L. G. Cockey, John McPherson, L. G. Kemp, J. B. Thomas, Roderick Dorsey, W. T. Preston, R. J. Snouffer, Charles Gross, James Finney, Cornelius Staley.

1856.—President, O. Dorsey; Secretary and Treasurer, S. H. O'Neal.

1857 and 1858.—President, Valentine Adams; Secretary and Treasurer, Christian Thomas.

1859.—President, Cornelius Staley; Secretary and Treasurer, Christian Thomas.

1860.—President, Cornelius Staley; Secretary and Treasurer, Edward Shriver.

1861.—President, Edward Buckey; Vice-President, Lewis M. Thomas; Secretary, William Mahony; Treasurer, Edward Shriver. The war stopped all exhibitions, and from the fair held in 1860, the last one on the Barracks grounds, no exhibitions were again held until 1868. The officers elected for the year 1861 held over for six years, during which period no election took place.

1867.—President, C. Keefer Thomas; Vice-President, John Loats; Recording Secretary, William Mahony; Corresponding Secretary, James McSheery, Jr.; Treasurer, Edward Shriver. In September of this year the society purchased for $4500 about thirty acres of land of Gen. Edward Shriver, and subsequently a small addition of Mr. Falconer, making its total area some thirty-three acres, on which it erected commodious and substantial buildings.

1868.—President, C. Keefer Thomas; Secretary, H. C. Koehler; Treasurer, Calvin Page. This year the first fair held since 1860 was held on the new grounds.

1869.—President, C. Keefer Thomas; Vice-President, John Loats; Secretary, H. C. Koehler; Treasurer, Calvin Page.

1870.—President, Dr. Fairfax Schley; Secretary, H. C. Koehler; Corresponding Secretary, Charles H. Keefer; Treasurer, Calvin Page.

1871.—President, John Loats; Vice-President, Dr. F. Schley; Secretary, H. C. Koehler; Corresponding Secretary, Charles H. Keefer; Treasurer, Calvin Page.

1872 and 1873.—President, Dr. Fairfax Schley; Vice-President, B. J. Snouffer; Secretary, H. C. Koehler; Corresponding Secretary, Charles H. Keefer; Treasurer, Calvin Page.

1874.—President, B. J. Snouffer; Vice-President, William H. Falconer; Secretary, H. C. Koehler; Corresponding Secretary, Charles H. Keefer; Treasurer, Calvin Page.

1875.—Same officers except Otis Johnson, secretary.

1876 and 1877.—President, William H. Falconer; Vice-President, James H. Gambrill; Secretary, George Morgan; Corresponding Secretary, Charles H. Keefer; Treasurer, Calvin Page.

1878 and 1879.—President, James H. Gambrill; Vice-President, Dr. Fairfax Schley; Secretary, W. Nash Young; Corresponding Secretary, J. William Baughman; Treasurer, Calvin Page.

1880.—President, Dr. Fairfax Schley; Vice-President, Eugene L. Derr; Treasurer, Calvin Page; Secretary, Frederick A. Markey; Corresponding Secretary, J. William Baughman; Board of Managers, Dr. Fairfax Schley, Eugene L. Derr, Calvin Page, James A. Gambrill, Cornelius Staley, C. Keefer Thomas, Daniel J. Snook, John T. Sinn, George William Smith, A. T. Snouffer, William H. Falconer; Chief Marshal, John T. Best; Assistant Vice-Presidents, 1st District, Christian Thomas; 2d, Theodore Schultz; 3d, J. D. Koogle; 4th, John W. Staup; 5th, Rev. John McCloskey; 6th, D. W. Blickenstaff; 7th, John T. Worthington; 8th, George C. Gaither; 9th, Charles L. Anders; 10th, Lewis Crawford; 11th, George F. B. Crumbaugh; 12th, Henry T. Deaver; 13th, Edward A. Shriner; 14th, Ezra M. Thomas; 15th, John B. Kunkel; 16th, Daniel V. Harp; 17th, Maurice T. Starr; 18th, William R. Dorsey; 19th, Thornton W. Poole; 20th, George W. Miller; Committee on Reception of Invited Guests, Dr. Fairfax Schley, Hon. John A. Lynch, John H. Williams, Charles E. Trail, J. Alfred Ritter, Hon. John Ritchie, George Markell, Outerbridge Horsey, Philip B. Kunkel, A. J. Delashmutt, Z. J. Gittinger, Hon. Lewis H. Steiner, James McSherry, Frederick J. Nelson, D. C. Winebrener, T. T. Hershperger, Gen. E. Shriver, Capt. B. F. Brown, Col. John B. Thomas, Col. George R. Dennis; Committee on Ground, Calvin Page, James H. Gambrill, E. L. Derr, John T. Sinn, William H. Falconer.

For many years the Frederick County fair, acknowledged to be the best in Maryland, and probably not surpassed by any in the country, has been visited by the Presidents of the United States, accompanied by other distinguished dignitaries, civil and military. The exhibition of 1880 was universally fine. Among those present were President Hayes and part of his cabinet. The unsightly booths which formerly disfigured the grounds and incommoded progress, gave way in that year to a more convenient and systematic arrangement. Additional stalls were erected for the accommodation of stock, and an experienced veterinary surgeon was in attendance, who inspected the entries and prevented the introduction of infectious diseases. The half-mile race-track is one of the finest in the Union, and the grand stand is a large, commodious structure. The exhibition of 1880 surpassed in attraction and interest any of its predecessors, and proved a fruitful source of pride and pleasure to the citizens of the county. The society is entirely exempt from debt, and has a surplus sufficient for all emergencies and to meet the requirements and improvements which the experience of the past has suggested. The annual address was delivered by Hon. Daniel W. Voorhees, United States senator from Indiana, and on the same day occurred the grand bicycle tournament. A military parade and review followed on the next day (Thursday). The fair was held on October 12, 13, 14, and 15th. The various committees were as follows:

In the *Cattle department*—For short-horns, the assistant marshal was Daniel Padgett; Judges, Jacob Walker, Ezra M. Thomas, Dr. Charles Goldsborough. For Devons, Marshal, C. T. F. Howard; Judges, John L. Nicodemus, Samuel H. Brown, George C. Gaither. For Alderneys, Marshal, George Bruner; Judges, D. C. Kemp, Christian Thomas, George W. Padgett. For Herefords, Marshal, Charles Hargate; Judges, Wm. S. Miller, Francis T. Lakin, L. C. Cookerley. For Holsteins, Marshal, Worthington Glaze; Judges, Reuben G. G. Rice, John Diller, Samuel Miller. Fat Cattle, Marshal, R. Claude Dutrow; Judges, Wm. Kolb, Frederick Heniline, Geo.

H. River. In the *Hog department*—For Chesters, the assistant marshal was Granville Thomas; Judges, W. H. Blintlinger, Charles T. Brosius, Richard W. Simpson. For Berkshires, Marshal, John Cronise; Judges, Simon Cronise, Geo. W. Roderick, Christian Eyler. For Poland Chinas, Marshal, Wm. A. Kolb; Judges, J. Alf. Fleming, John Diffendal, B. J. Lamar. For mixed grades, Marshal, Rodger Neighbours; Judges, Burgess Hammond, Wm. W. Walker, Thomas C. Resler. *Sheep department*—For Cotswolds, the marshal was Shafer Hargett; Judges, Wm. Downey, John Fulton, Samuel Ahalt. For Lincolnshire, Marshal, George Hoke; Judges, David Derr, John O. Holtz, Robert E. Delander. For Southdowns, Marshal, Glen Worthington; Judges, J. L. Rontzahn, O. P. Harding, Thos. Ogle. For fine wool, Marshal, George M. Warman; Judges, Wm. Feaga, W. Harry Best, Lewis H. Staley. For mixed wool, Marshal, James Cutsail; Judges, James O. Steiner, A. Cromwell, John B. Brenneman. *Horse department*—For blooded horses, Marshal, G. A. Snouffer, Jr.; Judges, J. N. Chiswell, Dr. Wm. S. McPherson, Dr. Wm. E. McKinney. For quick-draught, saddle, and carriage-horses, Marshal, Wm. Roderick; Judges, Thos. R. Jarboe, S. G. Cockey, H. W. D. Waters. For quick-draught colts, Marshal, Wellington Hammond; Judges, G. W. Miller, D. C. Winebrenner, W. O. Denegre. Heavy-draught horses, Marshal, G. Fenton Snouffer, Clarence Hilliery, Daniel Mainhart. For heavy-draught colts, Marshal, N. J. Worthington; Judges, G. F. B. Crumbaugh, Ed. Nichols, John T. Worthington. *Poultry department*—Marshal, D. Frank Clingan; Judges, G. B. Hammond, Dr. John Goldsborough, Henry E. Smith. *Farm and garden productions*—Marshal, Isaac Reich; Judges, Joseph Cronise, Elias Zimmerman, Lewis Bruner; Class 22 of same, Marshal, Wm. S. Bantz; Judges, A. H. Hargate, Jesse Bailer, George W. Buckey. *Pomological department*—Marshal, Wm. S. Bantz; Judges, Chas. W. Ross, J. G. Miller, J. P. Rodgers, H. C. Henshaw, Geo. Markell, Arthur Potts. *Flower department*—Marshal, W. S. Bantz; Judges, Mrs. D. J. Snook, Mrs. A. L. Edder, Mrs. D. C. Winebrenner, Mrs. Lewis Bantz, Mrs. F. B. Carlin, Mrs. Dr. Maynard, Mrs. Dennis Scholl, Mrs. Dr. R. B. Tyler, Mrs. B. F. Brown, Miss M. C. Kunkel, Miss Ella Houck, Miss Rosa Fearhake, Miss Lizzie Mainhart, Miss A. Dennis, Miss Catherine Markell, Mrs. Ella Rohrback. *Machinery and agricultural implement department*—Marshal, Cyrus Fout; Judges, McC. Young, Samuel Hoke, James Forney; Class 26 of same, Marshal, Nelson Diehl; Judges, Lewis M. Thomas, Joseph Glaze, Frank Snook. *Carriage department*—Marshal, Wm. McGill; Judges, Edward Linn, J. O. Myers, Charles E. Mealey. *Harness and leather department*—Marshal, Charles Cronise; Judges, J. H. Hood, Jonathan Biser, Pottinger Dorsey. *Department of bacon, hams, wines, dairy, etc.*—Marshal, Charles H. Baughman; Judges, the Executive Committee. *Household department*—Assistant Marshal, Maj. B. H. Schley; Judges, Mrs. Dr. F. Schley, Mrs. W. H. Falconer, Mrs. J. H. Gambrill, Mrs. Geo. Wm. Smith, Mrs. Cornelius Staley, Mrs. Jno. T. Worthington, Mrs. C. K. Thomas, Mrs. L. S. Clingan, Mrs. Ellen Williams, Mrs. Joseph Cronise, Mrs. Samuel H. Brown, Mrs. George R. Dennis, Mrs. F. A. Markey, Mrs. Ellen Snouffer, Mrs. D. J. Snook, Mrs. Dr. Bowlus, Miss Lizzie Houck, Miss C. Baughman, Miss Kate Thomas, Miss Ella Shriver, Miss S. Gaither. *Needle-work*—Marshal, Gen. John A. Steiner; Judges, Mrs. E. L. Derr, Miss A. T. Snouffer, Mrs. John T. Sinn, Mrs. W. O. Denegre, Mrs. J. F. McMullen, Mrs. John A. Lynch, Mrs. W. H. Miller, Mrs. T. T. Horsperger, Mrs. W. N. Young, Mrs. P. B. Kunkel, Mrs. Arthur Potts, Mrs. Henry Williams, Mrs. P. B. McClurg, Mrs. Geo. T. Kohlenberg, Mrs. Dr. J. W. Downey, Mrs. P. H. Griffith, Mrs. Thos. Harwood, Mrs. A. Y. Anderson, Mrs. Dr. J. N. Wood, Miss F. Maynard. *Oil-paintings*—Marshal, Gen. John A. Steiner; Judges, Col. Charles E. Trail, A. L. Eader, C. C. Smith, Dr. L. H. Steiner, Col. L. V. Baughman, Gen. Edward Shriver. *Musical instruments*—Marshal, Lewis Rice; Judges, Prof. Geo. E. Smith, Prof. John Englebrecht, Miss Annie Campbell. The judges for the trials of speed were, first day, for $150 and $100 purses, Thomas M. Wolfe, H. T. Deaver, Geo. W. Cramer; second day, for $100 and $300 purses, Lewis S. Clingan, Capt. B. F. Brown, Raymond C. Reich; third day, for $200 and $500 purses, Louis McMurray, E. Y. Goldsborough, G. J. Doll; fourth day, for $100 and $150 purses, James A. Doll, Dr. H. H. Hopkins, Lawrence Bantz.

The financial exhibit of the society for the year ending Dec. 31, 1880, showed the following:

Receipts.

Balance on hand Dec. 31, 1879	$453.31
Net proceeds bonds and loans	3942.33
Membership fees annual meeting	78.00
" " and other resources by secretary	1448.85
Financial Committee during fair	1922.78
Railroad coupons	610.00
County appropriation	100.00
Hon. George Merryman's refunded premiums	44.00
Water-rents up to Oct. 1, 1880	224.00
W. T. Preston's note in Probate Court	542.52
Collections to be made	250.00
Interest on water bonds to July 1, 1880	87.50
Total	$9403.30

Disbursements.

Premiums for 1879 and 1880	$2888.00
Employés during fair	553.13
Printing, telegrams, and postage	714.11
New buildings and repairs	4079.41
Discount on $2500 note (renewal)	38.75
Music and incidental expenses	533.08
W. T. Preston's note	242.53
Collections yet to be made	250.00
Cash balance on hand	156.29
Total	$9403.30

The fair-grounds are eligibly and beautifully located some three-eighths of a mile east of Frederick City, and comprise in utility and beauty everything necessary to promote the accommodation and pleasure of visitors.

To the active agency and energetic labors of Dr. Fairfax Schley, more than to any other person, is due the great success of the Frederick County Agricultural Society in the last few years. With his administration began a new era in the history of the society. In the midst of all his business engagements he has devoted much time and given great attention to its affairs, until now it is one of the most successful agricultural societies in the country.

Although retired from active medical practice since the year 1855, Fairfax Schley, of Frederick City, is still best known as Dr. Schley. His great-great-grandfather, Thomas Schley, came from the Palatinate, in Germany, about 1740, and in 1745 erected the first house upon the site of what is now Frederick City. One of his sons, Jacob Schley, was a captain in the Revolution. One of Thomas Schley's grandsons was William Schley, member of Congress and Governor

of Georgia, in which Schley County was named for him. John, his brother, occupied the Supreme Bench in Georgia, while another brother rose likewise to eminent judicial honor. Henry Schley, father to Fairfax Schley, was born in Frederick City in 1793, and died there in 1871. In early life he was engaged in business in Baltimore with his uncles, Henry Schroeder and Jacob Schley. In 1814 he entered the Federal service as adjutant of a Maryland regiment (of which Col. Cramer was commander), and participated in the battles of Bladensburg and North Point. Upon the termination of the campaign he made his home in Frederick City, and during many subsequent years occupied various places of important public trust, notably as clerk of Frederick County and cashier of the Frederick County Bank. He married Sarah Maria, daughter of Dr. Edward Worrell, of Kent County, Md., where the Worrells have ranked for full a century among the most prominent of families. Mrs. Schley died in 1869. Three sons survive,—Col. John Edward Schley, of West Virginia, Charles Schley, of Milwaukee (who married one of Bradley T. Johnson's sisters), and Dr. Schley, of Frederick. Dr. Schley was born in Frederick City, Oct. 11, 1825, and in Frederick has always had his home. He attended school at Frederick College, and completed a full classical course. Upon the foundation thus obtained he so improved and expanded his knowledge, that for years, and to this time, he has stood as a recognized authority in the field of classics.

He studied medicine under Dr. William Tyler, of Frederick, afterwards attended the University of Pennsylvania, and in 1847 graduated at the University of Maryland. Frederick City was the field of his first practice, and, indeed, his last, for after pursuing his professional labors until 1855 his health gave way and he was reluctantly compelled to desist. His active temperament was not, however, disposed to let him rest, and concluding that, as business he must have, he would follow that most in sympathy with his profession; he therefore embarked in the drug trade, and for twenty years, or until 1876, gave it his close attention, and gained therefrom bountiful results. In 1876 he retired from the business in favor of his two sons, Steiner and Lewis H. The latter, a youth of brilliant promise, a graduate of Franklin and Marshall College, and a finished scholar, lost his life in a railway collision at Point of Rocks in July, 1877. Dr. Schley was married in 1847 to Ann R., daughter of Christian Steiner, of Frederick. Of their four children two daughters and one son survive. Although of decided political opinions and keenly alive to the movement of public affairs, he is, and ever has been, opposed to participation in the pursuit of office or the active direction of party politics, despite the fact that he has often been urged to stand in nomination. The satisfaction he finds in life is largely made up of the results that flow from the exercise of his philanthropy and charity. He is connected in many ways with public charities, stands among the foremost as a practical worker in that field, and beyond that devotes much of his time and substance in a private way to the noble work of assisting the worthy poor. Besides being president of the Frederick County Agricultural Society, he is a director in the Central National Bank, a trustee of Frederick College, and chairman of the executive committee of the Deaf and Dumb Institution, in which last named he has always felt a deep and abiding interest,—an interest that has been manifested by earnest and zealous labors in behalf of the progress and prosperity of the institution, and the placing thereof upon a model which should stand as an object of approval and admiration abroad as well as at home.

CHAPTER XXIII.

DISTINGUISHED MEN OF FREDERICK COUNTY.

FREDERICK COUNTY has furnished much more than its quota of men of exceptional capacity in various walks of life. In addition to the great lawyers whose careers have already been described, some of the most distinguished statesmen and soldiers of the Revolution and of later periods have either been born in Frederick or have made that county their home. Of these none has been more conspicuous than John Hanson, president of the Continental Congress in the fall of 1781. John Hanson was the son of Samuel and Elizabeth Hanson, and was a member of one of the oldest and most influential families in Maryland. He was born in Charles County, Md., in 1715, and represented his native county in the House of Delegates at every session, with few exceptions, from 1757 to 1773, when he removed to Frederick County, which he likewise represented in the same body until his election to the Continental Congress in 1781. He took an active and leading part in the preliminary agitation against the arbitrary legislation of the British Parliament, and in June, 1769, he signed, with others, the non-importation agreement of Maryland. In June, 1774, he was elected chairman of a meeting in Frederick County which adopted resolutions to stop all exports to and imports from Great

Britain and the West Indies until the blockade of the port of Boston should be raised by the British government. Upon the formation of the Committee of Observation for Frederick County, in September, 1775, he was elected chairman, and retained that position until the Constitution of 1776 was carried into effect. He also filled positions on various important committees, among them the Provincial Committee for Licensing Suits, the Provincial Committee of Correspondence, and the Committee for the building of a military jail, or barracks, at Frederick, where a large number of prisoners of war were confined. During his chairmanship of the Committee of Observation the formidable Tory conspiracy of Lord Dunmore and White Eyes, an Indian chief, was discovered and frustrated. In 1775 he was commissioned treasurer of the county, and was appointed by the Convention of Maryland to establish a gun-lock factory at Frederick. With James Lloyd Chamberlaine, Benjamin Ramsey, and Thomas Contee, he was appointed member of a commission by the Convention of Maryland, Oct. 9, 1776, to appoint officers and to encourage the re-enlistment of Maryland militia and regular troops whose terms of service in the Continental army were about expiring. Mr. Hanson was elected to the Continental Congress, and presented his credentials Feb. 22, 1781. He was elected president on the 5th of November following, which position he filled for one year, with such fidelity as to receive the formal thanks of Congress. Under instructions from the Legislature of Maryland, John Hanson and Daniel Carroll signed the Articles of Confederation on the part of their State, March 1, 1781. Mr. Hanson was not only a man of conspicuous ability, but possessed great firmness and energy of character, and probably contributed more than any other individual to vivify and strengthen the Revolutionary cause in Western Maryland. He married Miss Jane Contee, and had a number of children, among them Alexander Contee Hanson, afterwards chancellor; another son, Samuel Hanson, was surgeon of Washington's Life-Guards; and still another, Peter Contee Hanson, was a lieutenant in the First Battalion Maryland Infantry, and was mortally wounded at Fort Washington in 1776. John Hanson died Nov. 22, 1783, at Oxen Hill, Prince George's Co., while visiting his nephew, Thomas Hanson.

JOHN HANSON.

Isaac Shelby. The life and character of Isaac Shelby is well worthy of the attention of every American, and Maryland may enjoy great pride in having given birth to a man so remarkable. The record of his father, Gen. Evan Shelby, is that of a man distinguished for indomitable courage, iron constitution, and clear intellect. A Welshman by birth, Gen. Evan Shelby came to this country a mere lad, who settled near Hagerstown, then in Frederick, but now Washington County, Md. In 1758 he distinguished himself as a captain of rangers under Gen. Forbes, leading the advance upon Fort Du Quesne. In 1772 he removed to the West, and in 1774 commanded a company, under Lewis and Dunmore, in an expedition against the Indians on the Scioto River. In 1779 he led a strong force against the Chicamauga Indians on the Tennessee River, and for his services and gallantry was appointed a brigadier-general by the State of Virginia, the first officer of that grade appointed in the West.

Such was the father of Isaac Shelby. He was born near Hagerstown, now Washington County, but then in Frederick County, Md., Dec. 11, 1750, and blessed with a firm and herculean frame, inured to the use of arms, capable of sustaining great fatigue, he was peculiarly fitted for the scenes in which he was destined to become so prominent an actor. In the great battle of Kanawha, Oct. 10, 1774, on the Ohio River, he had his first experience of fighting as a lieutenant in a company commanded by his father. The action, one of the most severe and sanguinary conflicts of the Indian wars, was fought with varying success from sunrise to sunset; night closed the conflict; in the darkness Cornstalk, who commanded the Indians, abandoned the ground. He was employed as a surveyor under Judge Henderson's company in Kentucky, amid the dangers, privations, and difficulties that beset the "dark and bloody ground," under which his health gave way, and he returned home.

In 1777, Governor Patrick Henry, of Virginia, appointed him commissary of supplies for a large body of troops guarding the frontier, and the commissioners who were appointed to treat with the Cherokees, at Long Island, on the Holston River. In 1778 he represented Washington County in the Virginia House of Delegates, and was appointed by Governor Thomas Jefferson a major in the escort of guards to the commissioners for extending the boundary line between Virginia and North Carolina; by this line as established his residence was found to be in North Carolina, and he was appointed by Governor Richard Caswell, of North Carolina, colonel of Sullivan County. The fall of Charleston in 1780 recalled him from his surveying and locating of lands in Kentucky, and he enlisted for the war, determining never to leave the service till the liberty and independence of the country were established. On his arrival in Sullivan County, N. C., he found a requisition from Gen. Charles McDowell to furnish all the aid in his power to check the enemy, who, having overrun Georgia and South Carolina, had entered North Carolina. In a few days he enlisted three hundred mounted men from the militia, and crossed the Allegany Mountains, and reported to Gen. McDowell, near Cherokee Ford, on Broad River, and was detached with Cols. Sevier and Clarke to surprise and capture a fort held by Capt. Patrick Moore, a Tory, on the waters of Pacolet, which was accomplished without loss of time or men. The enemy surrendered as prisoners of war. Maj. Ferguson, of the British army, had been detached by Gen. Cornwallis with a strong force to overcome the western part of North Carolina and win them to the support of the crown. The vigilance and activity of Shelby frustrated every attempted surprise, and on the 1st of August, 1780, at Cedar Spring, the advance of the British force came up and attacked Shelby on ground selected by that adventurous spirit. A sharp conflict ensued, which lasted half an hour, when the whole force of Ferguson advanced. Shelby fell back, carrying with him fifty prisoners, including two British officers, who were secured notwithstanding the vigorous pursuit of Ferguson. At Musgrove's Mills, and at the Cowpens and Ninety-Six, Shelby rendered such valuable services that the Legislature of North Carolina voted him their thanks, accompanied with a splendid sword. In 1781, Shelby served under Marion, and captured a British force of one hundred and fifty men at Fairlawn, near Monk's Corner. He obtained leave of absence to attend the Legislature, of which he was a member, and in 1782, while a member, was appointed a commissioner to settle the pre-emption claims upon the Cumberland, and lay off the lands allotted to the officers and soldiers south of where Nashville stands. Having performed this service, he returned to Boonsboro', Ky., and married Susanna Hart. After peace was established he settled upon his farm, which was the first pre-emption and settlement granted in Kentucky. He was a member of the Convention in Kentucky to obtain a separation of that State from Virginia, and was a member of the Convention, in April, 1792, that formed the constitution of that State, and was elected the first Governor of Kentucky. He was again elected Governor in 1812-16, and with spirit not calmed by the frost of age, at the request of the Legislature, though sixty-three years of age, he headed in person four thousand troops, and marched under Gen. Harrison in 1813 to Canada, and for his gallantry at the battle of the Thames Congress honored him with a gold medal. In 1817 he was called to the War Department by President Monroe, but he declined the honor on account of advanced age. In 1818, with Gen. Jackson, he was appointed to treat with the Chickasaw Indians for the cession of their lands west of the Tennessee River. This was his last public act. In February, 1820, he was attacked by a paralytic affection, and expired in Lincoln County, Ky., on the 18th of July, 1826, from a stroke of apoplexy, in the seventy-sixth year of his age. In honor of him nine counties in the States of Alabama, Texas, Tennessee, Kentucky, Ohio, Indiana, Illinois, Iowa, Missouri, as well as several towns and one college now perpetuate his name. His son, Gen. James, was born in 1784, and died September, 1848. He was a major in the campaign of 1813.

Thomas Sim Lee, second Governor of Maryland, was born in 1743, and lived in what is now the Petersville District of Frederick County for a number of years. He was a descendant of Philip Lee, who came to the province from Virginia in the latter part of the seventeenth century and became a member of the Council of the Lord Proprietary. Thomas Sim Lee was an ardent supporter of the Revolutionary cause, and soon became conspicuous for his zeal and energy in its behalf. In 1779, Governor Thomas Johnson was no longer eligible, having served three successive years, and the Legislature proceeded to elect his successor. Two candidates were named, Col. Edward Lloyd, of Talbot, and Thomas Sim Lee, of Frederick. On the 8th of November, 1779, the election took place, and Mr. Lee was chosen Governor. In December the Governor issued a proclamation urging the local authorities of the different counties to press forward as speedily as possible the collection of supplies for Washington's suffering troops. His wife, Mrs. Mary Lee, was also untiring in her efforts in behalf of the cause. In a letter addressed to her, bearing the date of Oct. 11, 1780, Washington acknowledges in grateful terms "the patriotic exertions of the ladies of Maryland in behalf of the army." In the fall of 1780, Gen. Greene visited Annapolis and conferred with Governor Lee as to the practicability of raising additional troops in Maryland, and the Governor went vigorously to work, assisted by Gen. Gist, and succeeded in recruiting valuable reinforcements for the Southern army. In the same year the British army under Gen. Leslie devastated the shores of the Chesapeake, and Governor Lee addressed an urgent petition to Congress for assistance. Congress was so straitened at this time, however, that it was unable to give any aid, and the people of Maryland were thrown upon their own resources. Under the intrepid lead of the Governor and kindred spirits, the Legislature passed an act appropriating money for the equipment of a fleet of barges, etc., for the defense of the bay. A troop of horse to defend the coast of Worcester and Somerset was also organized. The depredations of the British in the Chesapeake were part of a general scheme for a Tory rising in the disaffected districts, the invasion of Virginia and Maryland, and the release of the British prisoners at Frederick, Sharpsburg, Fort Frederick, Leesburg, Strasburg, and Winchester. The plot was discovered, however, and three of the Tory ringleaders in Western Maryland were apprehended. Leslie was replaced by the traitor Arnold, who again ravaged the shores of the Chesapeake, plundering in particular the plantations of Hon. Edward Lloyd and John Beale Bordley on the Eastern Shore. Washington ordered Lafayette, with twelve hundred men, to proceed to Maryland, and Governor Lee at once took vigorous measures to provide the command with the means of transportation and subsistence. The merchants of Baltimore co-operated with him and furnished valuable aid. A squadron was got together and placed under the command of Commodore James Nicholson. Lafayette's army embarked on the transports, and under the protection of the squadron set sail for Annapolis, where it arrived in safety on the 13th of March. About this time a formidable British expedition was fitted out for transferring the seat of war to the Chesapeake, and active preparations for defense were made by the people of Maryland. This movement culminated in the siege of Yorktown and the final overthrow of the British arms. During all this trying and critical period Governor Lee was unremitting in his patriotic exertions, and by his bold demeanor and exhibition of unwavering confidence infused new hope and courage into many a wavering heart. On the 17th of June, 1782, Governor Lee issued a proclamation inviting the citizens of the State to celebrate the birth of a son and heir to the king of France, as an evidence of the gratitude of the colonies for the assistance rendered by that nation. The day was celebrated in Baltimore with an elegant dinner. On the 4th of August the French forces then stationed in Baltimore, to the number of about five thousand, were reviewed by the Governor, who subsequently entertained Count Rochambeau and the other French officers at Annapolis. When Governor Lee had served three years as Governor he was no longer eligible, and was succeeded by William Paca, who was elected over Daniel, of St. Thomas Jenifer. The distinguished services of the late Governor were recognized by the Legislature by the presentation of a formal address on the 22d of November, 1782. In 1792, Mr. Lee again became eligible, and was elected Governor a second time. He served in that office from 1792 to 1794. He had also served as a delegate to the Continental Congress in 1783 and 1784. On the 23d of April, 1787, he was elected by the Legislature, with Charles Carroll of Carrollton, Robert Hanson Harrison, Thomas Stone, and James McHenry, as deputies to represent Maryland in the convention which prepared the Federal Constitution, but he declined the honor. He was a member of the State Convention which ratified the Constitution, and in 1792 was one of the Presidential electors, and voted for Washington's second election. His second term as Governor embraced the period of the "Whisky Insurrection" of 1794, during which he reorganized the State militia. He very ably seconded the endeavors of President Washington to suppress this rebellion and put the whole State on a war footing, and sent with dispatch and promptness Maryland's quota to the scene of the insurrection.

It was also during Governor Lee's second administration, in 1793, that the famous case arose of the San Domingo privateer "Industry," which, it was alleged, took on part of her armament in Baltimore, and sallying forth captured the British ship "Rockhampton." The principles maintained then by Secretary Jefferson are those which were contended for by the United States throughout the "Alabama" controversy, and are now in a fair way of being universally accepted as part of the law of nations.

Charles Carroll, a grandson of the signer of the Declaration of Independence, married Mary Digges Lee, granddaughter of Governor Lee. From this union was born John Lee Carroll, Governor of Maryland from 1875 to 1879. Governor Thomas Sim Lee died at Medwood, Frederick Co., Md., Nov. 8, 1819, in the seventy-fifth year of his age.

Moses Rawlings was commissioned on the 1st of July, 1776, lieutenant-colonel of the rifle regiment of which Col. Stevenson was commander, and Otho H. Williams, major. In the absence of the colonel he commanded the regiment at Fort Washington, but during the assault by the Hessians was badly wounded, and when the fort capitulated he fell into the hands of the enemy with the rest of the command. At this time Washington said of him, "I entertain a very high opinion of Col. Rawlings and his officers, and have interested myself much in their behalf." His four companies of riflemen were joined to the German Battalion, and the command was afterwards known as the Eighth Maryland Regiment. In 1779 he was ordered by Washington to Fort Pitt (on the present site of the city of Pittsburgh), and on the refusal of Washington to permit the German troops to accompany him he resigned, in April, 1779. Capt. Beale took charge of his command at Fort Frederick, and in May, 1779, marched with it to Fort Pitt. On Sept. 27, 1779, Col. Rawlings was placed in charge of the prisoners at Frederick Town, where he remained until the close of the war. In 1794, there being danger of a war with Great Britain, the militia of Maryland was reorganized, and Col. Rawlings was appointed brigadier-general for Washington and Allegany Counties. He died in Hampshire Co., Va., in May, 1809.

The Johnson Family. Among the promoters of resistance to the usurpation of Parliament there were in each county certain families which from their force, education, and social position naturally assumed, or were by circumstances forced into the position of leaders of public opinion and organizers of popular movements.

The Lloyds had been for more than a century leaders on the Eastern Shore counties, and with them the Tilghmans, the Hollidays, the Hemsleys, the Bordleys, the Wrights, and such families had shaped and directed society.

From St. Mary's, as the settlements extended westward, the cadets of the proprietaries who had established themselves on the Potomac and the Patuxent gradually controlled and dominated the fertile valleys of the Alleganies. The Dents, the Calverts, the Barrons, the Briscoes, of the lower counties, the Howards, the Carrolls, the Goldsboroughs, the Worthingtons, of the Severn, the South and West Rivers, and the Patapsco, controlled all that section. The great county of Frederick was largely dominated from 1765 to 1790 by the Johnson family.

Among the hardy population of Frederick the Johnsons settled themselves just after the French war. They were a bold, aggressive, self-reliant family, who assumed importance and arrogated to themselves consideration, which they maintained by sturdy effort and by leading in all works of usefulness and public concern.

They were descended from a well-known family of their name in the county of Norfolk, in England. They had been long settled at Great Yarmouth, and had commanded ships in the great fleet that Yarmouth sent out to fight the Grand Armada. They had been members of Parliament and bailiffs of Yarmouth since 1585. One of the family sat in the Parliament of 1625, which resisted the usurpations of the king. Another, Capt. Thomas Johnson, was commander-in-chief of the militia of Great Yarmouth in the great rebellion, first against the king and for the Parliament, and then, when the Commonwealth proposed to overthrow the monarchy, for the king and against the Puritan.

Capt. Thomas Johnson was granted an alteration of the family arms in consideration of his great loyalty and suffering, so that after the Restoration they were emblazoned: "Three lions' heads erased gules, ducally crowned or, on a field argent. Between a fess battled counter-embattled gules. Crest—a leopard's head on a ducal coronet. Motto—'Trust and Strive.'"

His son James was knighted by Charles II., and the grandson of Sir James emigrated to Maryland in 1700 and settled in Calvert County, on St. Leonard's Creek.

He ran off with a chancery ward, Mary Baker, and had one son, Thomas, born in Calvert at the family place on St. Leonard's, Feb. 19, 1702.

Thomas Johnson married Dorcas Sedwick and had eleven children. Among them were Thomas Johnson, born Nov. 4, 1732, who married Ann Jennings, daughter of Thomas Jennings, the register of the land office at Annapolis. Although born in Calvert, and spending a large part of his life in Anne Arundel, Thomas Johnson must be considered a Frederick County man. His last years were passed and he is buried there. A sketch of Governor Johnson has already been given.

James Johnson, son of Thomas and Dorcas, and brother of Governor Thomas Johnson, was born on the 30th of September, 1736, died Dec. 3, 1809. He emigrated from his father's residence to Frederick County, now Washington County, where he built for the firm, Jacques & Johnson, Green Spring Furnace, a mile from old Fort Frederick, where his son James was born on the 28th of May, 1774, and also Licking Creek Forge at the mouth of said creek. In November, 1774, he established himself permanently in Frederick County, where, in partnership with his brothers Thomas, Baker, and Roger Johnson, he built Catoctin Furnace and Bush Creek Forge, Johnson Furnace near the mouth of the Monocacy, and Potomac Furnace in Loudon County, Va., opposite to the Point of Rocks. During the Revolutionary war, besides casting a large number of cannon, he furnished the Continental army with one hundred tons of bombshells, which assisted in bringing about the surrender of Cornwallis at Yorktown.

He was for many years justice of the peace in Frederick County, a member of the court, and in 1779, in conjunction with Alexander C. Hanson and Upton Sheredine, composed a special court for the trial of the Tories who were executed on the Court-house Creek in Frederick Town. He commanded a battalion of infantry in the Flying Camp under his brother, Brig.-Gen. Thomas Johnson, in the Jerseys in the winter of 1776 and 1777, the most gloomy period of the Revolution. He married Miss Peggie Skinner, of Calvert County, by whom he had three children.

Joshua Johnson, son of Thomas and Dorcas, was born June 25, 1742, being harvest-day, died April 17, 1802. He went to London early in life, and entered into a counting-house before the Revolutionary war. He married in England, and had a son and seven daughters. One of them, Louisa C., married John Quincy Adams, afterwards President of the United States, and became the mother of Charles Francis Adams. At the commencement of the Revolutionary war Mr. Johnson removed to Nantes, France, where he remained until the treaty of peace in 1783, when he returned to London, and was appointed by Gen. Washington first American consul for that port, in which capacity and that of merchant he continued until 1797, when he returned to his native country, taking up his residence in Georgetown, D. C. He was appointed by John Adams stamp-master, which office he held until his death.

John Johnson, son of Thomas and Dorcas, was born on Aug. 9, 1745, died April, 1811. He was a physician by profession, and a surgeon in the Maryland Line during the Revolution.

Baker Johnson, son of Thomas and Dorcas, was born on the 30th of September, 1749, died June, 1811. He was a lawyer, and commenced his practice in the Frederick County Court about the year 1776, and continued until November, 1794. Before that year he had been attorney for the proprietary. By industry and economy he acquired a handsome independence. He commanded a battalion of infantry in his brother's, Gen. Johnson's, brigade in the summer and fall of 1776, and was at the battle of Paoli, near Philadelphia, famous for the slaughter of Wayne's men. He married Kitty Worthington, eldest daughter of Col. Nicholas Worthington, of "Summer Hill," near Annapolis, by whom he had six sons and five daughters. After the Revolution he was a leading member of the bar of Frederick and of the General Court.

Roger Johnson, son of Thomas and Dorcas Johnson, was born March 18, 1749, and died March 3, 1831. He was an iron-master, and built Bloomsburg Forge on Bennett's Creek, Frederick County. He was also major of his brother James' battalion in the Revolutionary war. He married Betsy Thomas, daughter of Richard Thomas, of Montgomery County, by whom he had seven sons and four daughters.

Gen. Bradley T. Johnson, of whom a sketch is given in the chapter on the Bar of Frederick, is a grandson of Col. Baker Johnson.

While Thomas was serving the State as Deputy Governor and judge, the Johnson brothers were leading the patriot cause in Frederick County. They established iron-works at Catoctin Furnace, glass-works at the mouth of Monocacy, and paper-mills. They acquired great possessions of land and left large patrimonies to their descendants.

The family is now represented in Frederick by Worthington Ross Johnson and Dr. George Johnson, grandsons of Col. Baker Johnson, and by William Johnson Ross and Charles Worthington Ross, grandson and great-grandson of Col. Baker Johnson.

Governor Thomas Johnson's descendants are his granddaughter, Mrs. Fanny Johnson McPherson, her daughter, Mrs. Anne Graham Ross, and her daughter, Fanny McPherson Ross, and the Dennises' granddaughter, Mrs. McPherson. Maj. Roger Johnson's representatives are Dr. James T. Johnson and his family.

Lawrence Everheart. This heroic soldier of the Revolution was born in Middletown, Frederick County, on the 6th of May, 1755, and enrolled himself on the 1st of August, 1776, as a member of the first battalion, "Flying Camp." His company was commanded by Capt. Jacob Goode. Everheart was then in his twenty-second year, and was a tall, stalwart youth, of great physical endurance and indomitable pluck. With his regiment he joined the brigade commanded by Gen. Rezin Beall, which was then stationed at New York. He was, with the other Maryland troops, at the battle of White Plains, and also at Fort Washington. When the latter was surrendered, however, he managed to escape. In 1778, after the expiration of his term of service, he enlisted at Frederick, with a number of others, in Col. Washington's regiment of cavalry. At the battle of Cowpens he was wounded and captured by the enemy. Everheart, with seventeen men, were selected by Col. Washington to reconnoitre Col. Tarleton's command. As the enemy's horses, impressed from the South Carolina plantations, were much fleeter than those of Everheart and his companions, the scouting-party was overtaken. A bloody contest ensued, and Everheart was captured after his horse had been shot under him. He was taken before Tarleton, when the following conversation occurred: "Do you expect Mr. Washington and Mr. Morgan will fight me to-day?" asked

Tarleton. "Yes," replied Everheart, "if they can keep together two hundred men." "Then," said the former, "it will be another Gates' defeat." "I hope to God it will be another Tarleton's defeat," replied Everheart. "*I* am Col. Tarleton, sir!" cried the British commander. "And I," replied the sturdy patriot, "am Sergt. Everheart, sir!" His wounds, which were numerous and severe, were carefully dressed by the British surgeons, and he was treated with great kindness and consideration. He was, however, taken to the field of action, and during the battle which ensued the enemy, finding that they could no longer keep Everheart in their possession, "shot him in the head, over one of his eyes." The wound was not serious, and Washington's cavalry being then intermingled with the British, Everheart pointed out to Col. James Simons the man who had shot him. The British soldier was at once shot down, and his horse was handed over to Everheart. In the eagerness of his pursuit, Col. Washington advanced some thirty yards in front of his command. Observing this, three British officers wheeled about and charged on him. The officer on the right was in the act of cutting him down when Sergt. Everheart sprang forward and saved Col. Washington by disabling the officer's sword arm. The officer on the left was also about to make a stroke at him when a waiter fired his pistol and wounded Col. Washington's assailant. At the same moment the officer in front (believed to have been Col. Tarleton) made a thrust at him, which Washington parried, whereupon the officer fired his pistol, wounding Col. Washington in the knee. On returning from the pursuit, Washington embraced Sergt. Everheart and sent him to the rear, where his wounds were dressed. Everheart was disabled for active service for some time, but was present at the surrender of Yorktown, where he made the acquaintance of Lafayette. In 1782 he was honorably discharged. He returned to Middletown Valley and settled on a farm. He then married, and was the father of several children. He afterwards became a Methodist minister. Col. Washington paid him a visit in 1799, and on meeting the veterans "rushed into each other's arms, kissed, and gave vent to their feelings in tears of joy." Sergt. Everheart died in 1839.

George and John Stricker. Col. George Stricker, of the Revolutionary army, was the descendant of Swiss immigrants who settled in North Carolina at an early period of our colonial history. His mother was a native of one of the French districts of Switzerland. His first wife was named Springer, the mother of all his children; his second wife, it is said, was the mother of John V. L. McMahon, of Baltimore.

Col. Stricker removed to Frederick some time prior to the Revolution, and when the war broke out he raised a company in the neighborhood and repaired to the scene of military operations. He commanded under Gen. Smallwood, and in 1776 was stationed at Annapolis. At Long Island so great was the havoc in his company that scarcely a single member escaped being wounded or killed. In the mean time, Capt. Stricker had been promoted to the lieutenant-colonelcy of the German Battalion, and continued in that position until the death of the colonel, when, considering himself ill treated in the promotion of Baron Hanseigger to the chief command, he resigned his commission and left the army. Subsequently he was elected a member of the Maryland Legislature. He removed to an estate in the vicinity of Wheeling, W. Va., where he died in 1810, aged seventy-eight, and was buried. In person Col. Stricker was dignified and imposing, and his military talents were of a high order.

His son, John Stricker, was born in Frederick on the 15th of February, 1759, and served as a cadet in Capt. George P. Keeport's company in the German Battalion, of which his father was lieutenant-colonel, until commissioned as officer in Boctar's artillery, in which he rose to the rank of captain. He was at the battles of Trenton, Princeton, Brandywine, Germantown, Monmouth, and others, and accompanied Gen. Sullivan on his expedition against the Indians. He was sent from New Jersey with the Hessians captured at Trenton under his charge to Frederick, Md. He was present at the execution of Maj. André, within a few paces of the gallows.

At the close of the war Capt. Stricker married the daughter of Gunning Bedford at Philadelphia. About the same time Commodore Barney married Ann, another daughter of Gunning Bedford. In 1783, Capt. Stricker removed to Baltimore and associated himself in business with Commodore Barney. He took a keen interest in the organization of the militia, and himself formed and trained one of the earliest commands in Baltimore. He was soon made brigadier-general, and accompanied Gen. Sam. Smith as second in command of the Baltimore troops on the expedition for the suppression of the Whisky Insurrection in 1794. In 1801 he was made naval agent of Baltimore, and held the position for a number of years.

Gen. Stricker was a Republican, or Anti-Federalist, and was bitterly censured by the friends of Hanson and others for his course as commander of the State militia during the terrible riots which culminated in the death of Gen. Lingan at the Baltimore City jail. During the attack on Baltimore in 1814 by the British troops under the command of Gen. Ross, Gen. Stricker commanded the brigade which was sent forward to check the enemy's advance, and performed this difficult task with rare discretion and success.

In November, 1814, Gen. Stricker resigned, owing to the appointment of Robert Goodloe Harper, an inferior in rank, to the major-generalship vacated by the resignation of Gen. Smith. He was elected to the State Senate in 1820, but declined, and Reverdy Johnson was chosen in his place. In 1824 he was a member of the committee to receive Gen. Lafayette, and in 1825, on the death of Gen. Harper, the major-generalship was tendered him, but was declined on the score of ill health. He died on the 23d of June, 1825.

Among the most distinguished and prominent men of Frederick County was Upton Sheredine. His father, Maj. Thomas Sheredine, emigrated from the north of Ireland early in the eighteenth century, and took up land in Baltimore County as early as 1721. In 1729 he was sheriff of Baltimore County, and from 1732 to 1749 represented it in the Legislature. In 1742 he was one of the presiding justices, and in 1752 was again elected sheriff. By the act creating "Jones Town," now called "Old Town," in Baltimore City, he was appointed one of the four commissioners, and was one of the first to take up lots in Baltimore. He was a consistent member of the Episcopal Church, and in January, 1728, was appointed by St. Paul's Parish with Richard Gist to purchase a site for the erection of a new church. In 1749, in connection with Thomas Sleigh, he purchased about eighteen acres of ground on the east side of Jones' Falls, in Baltimore, which was added to the town and is now a most valuable section of that city. In 1751 he was among the largest contributors in Baltimore for the erection of a market-house and town hall. He filled many other important trusts, and died about 1754.

His son Upton was born in Baltimore County in 1740, and after a long and useful life died greatly lamented in December, 1800. He is buried on his farm near Liberty, in Frederick County, where is also the grave of his mother, Mrs. Ellenore Sheredine. Upton Sheredine took a most active part in the struggle for independence, was a member of the first State Constitutional Convention from Frederick County, was elected to the First Congress, was a justice of the County and Orphans' Court, and held many other prominent positions. Being possessed of large means, he resided in Frederick Town during the winter, in the house now owned by Mrs. Ezra Houck, which he had built, and during the summer he lived on his farm near Liberty, where he died. He was a highly-cultivated gentleman of pure and lofty principles, and the peer of any man in Maryland. He was also greatly admired for his many fine qualities, and together with Basil Dorsey, Sr., John Lawrence, and others, he did much to mould public sentiment in Western Maryland. He married Sophia, daughter of Basil Dorsey, Jr., and left no children. His property, after providing for his widow, was willed to his nephews, Daniel Sheredine and William Hammond.

Capt. Henry Williams, of Revolutionary fame, was the son of John and Mary Williams, who emigrated from Chester County, Pa., to Frederick County about the year 1753, and settled in the valley of Flat Run below Emmittsburg. His parents were contemporaries of the Reids, Marshalls, Hugheses, Cochrans, Shieldses, Annans, Cawicks, Bayards, Pattersons, Nobles, Porters, Coopers, McKessons, and McNairs, etc., who were among the early immigrants from Pennsylvania. They were of Scotch-Irish descent Capt. Williams' first wife was a Miss McDonald, and his second wife was a Mrs. Cooper (whose maiden name was Witherow). By his second wife he had several children, one of whom still survives, and is now president of the Frederick County National Bank. Mr. William Patterson, one of Capt. Williams' earliest and warmest friends, used to relate that Mrs. Williams (his first wife) often repaired to an old graveyard in Pennsylvania to visit the graves of her parents and strew flowers over them. It was the oldest graveyard in the settlement of Adams County, or in that section of country, except that of the Elders of Frederick County. Upon the breaking out of the Revolutionary war, Capt. Williams, then quite a young man, was elected second lieutenant of Capt. William Blair's company, belonging to the regiment commanded by Col. John Eager Howard. When Capt. Blair fell mortally wounded at Brooklyn Heights, L. I., Capt. Williams took charge of the "Game Cock" company, First Lieut. Hockersmith yielding the palm to Lieut. Williams on account of his great popularity with the non-commissioned officers and privates of the company. The company participated in many hard-fought battles, and Capt. Williams was always in the thickest of the fray. Capt. Williams was a member of the Masonic order, and at an early period of the Revolutionary era enjoyed the friendship of Washington and Lafayette. When Gen. Lafayette was in this country in 1824–25, The Society of the Cincinnati in Baltimore gave him a dinner, and it was agreed that each one would in turn relate something of a personal nature. When it came to the turn of Gen. Lafayette, he related a story highly characteristic of the American troops, as showing their eagerness to rush into battle.

At the siege of Yorktown, he said, there were two columns, one of French the other of Americans, drawn out to assault two bastions, and both were to move at the same moment. Of course there was much excitement as to who should make the capture first. In compliment to Gen. Lafayette he was assigned to the command of the American column as an American officer. Both columns started simultaneously, each one watching the other. On the march an American sergeant (William Curran, Jr., of Capt. Williams' company) stepped up to the general and, tapping him on the shoulder, said, "Hurry, general; those d———d Frenchmen will get in before us yet."

Capt. Williams had often related the same story, but did not live to hear Gen. Lafayette repeat it.

An old resident of Frederick supplies the following concerning Capt. Williams: "My first acquaintance with Capt. Williams was in 1811. He was then a hale and hearty old country gentleman of sixty summers. He had quit the sword, and, like Cincinnatus, had taken to the plow. I often saw him riding in his plain country wagon driven by his trusty yellow servant, Gabriel Briscoe, and his other colored servant, Sam Diggs, accompanying him. I was told by my father that Capt. Williams was a prominent man in the Emmittsburg District, and had served with distinction in the stormy periods of the nation's birth."

In the language of a writer in the *Maryland Chronicle* of May, 1786, Capt. Williams and his company (recruited chiefly in the Emmittsburg District) "covered themselves with glory and received the special commendation of Washington and Lafayette." Capt. Williams was also very useful and active as the commander of one of the scouting-parties which were engaged in unearthing the Dunmore-White Eyes conspiracy.

When the war was over he returned home to his estate near Emmittsburg, where, until his death, he followed the quiet pursuits of a farmer. He also took an active part in the politics of the county, the State, and nation from 1786 to 1816, but seldom appeared as a candidate for office, although frequently solicited to stand for the House of Delegates, which he invariably declined. He sided with the Democratic party and generally supported its nominees. In 1812, however, believing with the Democrats of New York and many other States of the Union that De Witt Clinton was a more energetic statesman, and would carry on the war then waging against Great Britain with more spirit and success than President Madison, and holding to the one-term principle for the Presidency, he yielded to the earnest solicitations of his friends in this county, and announced himself (without any nomination) as a candidate for Presidential elector in the district composed of Frederick, Washington, and Allegany Counties. He was chosen in conjunction with Daniel Rentch, of Washington County, by 450 or 500 majority in Frederick County, and about 150 in the district, over Frisby Tilghman and Joshua Cockey, two very popular men, who were the Madison candidates for electors. It was no doubt owing to Capt. Williams' Revolutionary record and great personal popularity that the district was carried for Clinton. Capt. Williams frequently filled the position of a member of the Levy Court and county magistrate, and at the time of his death, in 1821, was a justice of the peace. He was a firm and consistent member of the Presbyterian Church, but was universally respected by the members of other creeds.

That Capt. Williams bestowed special attention to the science of farming appears from the fact that the first essay on that subject ever published in a Frederick paper was written by him, and appeared in the *Maryland Chronicle* of May 3, 1786.

Capt. Williams named one of his sons (since deceased) Washington, after the Father of his Country. His other son, John H. Williams, formerly editor of the Frederick *Examiner*, is now president of the Frederick County National Bank.

Capt. Henry Williams and Gen. John Ross Key, who resided only about twelve miles apart in Frederick, were bosom friends. Both entered the Revolutionary war about the same period, and both died about the same time. Gen. Key died at his residence near Middleburg, Frederick Co., May 21, 1821. The people of Emmittsburg and Taneytown District, then in Frederick County, passed resolutions at the time of their decease eulogizing their memories and extolling their public and private virtues.

Charles Beatty. This patriot acted a conspicuous part in the Revolutionary war. At the darkest period of those troubled times, when Washington was retreating through New Jersey, and every man's heart sunk within him, the call to arms was heard to resound through the generally quiet and peaceable town of Frederick, and the people sprang to the rescue of their country. The troops were marshaled on the beautiful green inclosures now occupied by the Catholic institutions. There was a whole battalion present, consisting of eight companies. Col. Charles Beatty addressed them, and invited those who were willing to aid "to step forward," whereupon the whole battalion advanced except three men, who afterwards, amid the jeers of their comrades, also volunteered. The soldiers marched under Col. Beatty, and saw some service at the battle of Brunswick, where three men were killed out of one company. Among them was Lieut. Grosch. The colonel was a wealthy, public-spirited man, and built the house occupied by Mr. Ross in 1841.[1]

William Beatty was born in Frederick County, in the State of Maryland, on the 19th of June, 1758. He was the eldest of twelve sons. In stature he was erect and stately, and in person vigorous and athletic, capable of enduring the greatest fatigue and of suffering the utmost privation; his attachments were warm and permanent, his feelings glowing and enthusiastic, and his patriotism ardent and almost romantic.

In 1776, when but eighteen years of age, he obtained the appointment of ensign in Col. Griffith's regiment, in what was termed the "Flying Camp" of Maryland. This regiment, which was hastily raised in the early part of the summer, and was to serve until the 1st of December following, received orders to march in July to the city of New York, which it reached without accident, and thence proceeded immediately to headquarters on York Island. The regiment to which young Beatty was attached continued, during the campaign, under the command of Gen. Washington, and at the expiration of his period of service he returned to his native State. He did not, however, remain long in this state of inglorious inaction, for in a short time he was appointed a lieutenant in the Maryland Line of Continental troops, and spent the winter in raising recruits for the regiment to which he belonged. In the discharge of this unpleasant and difficult duty he acquitted himself with much credit, and in the following spring joined the army at Middlebrook, in New Jersey.

His merit as an officer was soon discovered by the commander-in-chief, and he was promoted to a captaincy in the First Maryland Regiment, which had the honor of being for some time under Gen. Washington's immediate command.

The First Regiment, however, under the command of Col. Gunby, to which Capt. Beatty was transferred, and of which he was now the senior captain, was finally ordered to join the Southern division of the American army in the Carolinas. The distinguished feats of this division are familiar to every American. The First Regiment, according to Marshall, "gained the battle of Cowpens, and was pre-eminently distinguished in the retreat through North Carolina, and at the battle of Guilford." In this last battle, which was fought on the 15th of March, 1781, young Beatty signalized himself in a particular manner by engaging in single combat a gallant British soldier, whom he pierced to the heart with his espontoon. This brave regiment, to whose valor the glory of the day must be partly attributed, sustained its high character for courage and discipline, and acquired a reputation that never will be lost. Young Beatty rose high in the estimation of his superior officers and of the army. His conduct had been such as to merit and receive no ordinary praise, and his patriotism and personal courage promised, at no great length of time, to elevate him to high rank in the army of his country. But his brilliant career was destined soon to be brought to a close. At the battle of Hobkirk's Hill, near Camden, which was fought on the 25th of April, in the same year, Capt. Beatty, while gallantly leading on the right company of the First Maryland Regiment, received a mortal wound. Thus fell, in the twenty-third year of his age, this brave and promising young officer, who has been emphatically termed by Judge Johnson, "the delight of his command." Gen. Lee, in his memoirs of the war in the Southern department, speaking of this battle, says, "The British lost no officer of distinction, which was not the case with us. The wound of Lieut.-Col. Ford proved mortal, and Capt. Beatty, of the First Maryland, was killed, than whom the army did not possess an officer of more promise." Col. John E. Howard does justice to the gallantry of Capt. Beatty in the following extract of a letter to William B. Rochester, member of Congress from New York: "It would give me much pleasure to add my testimony to that of Gen.

---

[1] During the Revolution large numbers of British prisoners were confined at Frederick. The privates were quartered at the barracks, while the officers were paroled and allowed their liberty. The latter, it is said, rode fine chargers, and were great favorites with the Tory ladies in the neighborhood. Some of them at length "became so insolent that they would ride out abreast and make the country people give the road to them. They went further, and rode out early in the morning to meet the country girls coming to market and insulted them. It happened that they met Miss Cassell, a daughter of a prominent farmer, who had an uncle living in town, a most powerful and giant-like young man, about nineteen or twenty years old. She complained to him that a certain British officer whom she pointed out to him had insulted her. It was during the session of the court. Daniel provided himself with a cowhide, and gave him a just and severe cowhiding on the court-house green. The British officer ran into the court-house and complained to the judges of the assault on him by Cassell. Daniel was called into court. He came in blubbering, and when asked what he had done to the officer, answered that he had whipped him, the 'damn beast.' The judge said, 'That's right, Daniel, whip him well; and whenever you hear of any British officers insulting any country women, whip them good.' 'Good God,' said old Jacob Young, who was tainted with Toryism, 'Col. Johnson (the judge), that you should give such advice from the bench!' He repeated it, 'Whip them well, Daniel.' He waited at the court-house door for the officer to come out, and ran his cowhide under his nose; the officer ran back to the judge with his second complaint, but fared no better than at first."

Greene and others of the great merit of Capt. William Beatty. Indeed, the general, in few words, has so strongly portrayed his character that little can be added." " Among the killed," says Gen. Greene, in his report to Congress, " is Capt. Beatty, of the Maryland Line, one of the best of officers, and an ornament to his profession."

The Hoffmans. The founder of the Hoffman (formerly spelled Huffman) family in Maryland it is supposed was Jacob Huffman, who resided in Frederick Town. Jacob, who was of German parentage, had a vegetable farm, from which he supplied the Frederick market. He died on his farm. His son Peter is said to have come to Baltimore in 1771. He was a frugal, industrious man, and after a while had saved enough to begin the dry-goods business at "53 Old Market Street." His business increased until he was compelled to remove to No. 4 Calvert Street. In 1794 he abandoned the retail business, and founded the wholesale house of Hoffman & Co., North Charles Street. Of Peter's sons, Jacob removed to Alexandria, Va., and established there a dry-goods store. Another son, George, married Miss Tilghman, of the Eastern Shore, who died leaving no issue. He then married Henrietta Rogers, by whom he had four sons and one daughter, viz.: Rogers, married the beautiful Miss Key, of Georgetown; George B., married Louisa, the daughter of Gen. Benjamin C. Howard; William Henry, married Miss Travers, of New York. Peter Hoffman, son of Peter, married a daughter of Samuel Owings and had four sons, viz.: William Alfred, died unmarried, Latimer, George, and Samuel Owings Hoffman. His daughter Sarah married Mr. Guest, another daughter married a son of Mr. Birckhead, and a third daughter, Henrietta, remained unmarried. Samuel Owings Hoffman married a daughter of William Gilmor. Samuel, son of Peter, married Miss Curson, by whom he had five children,—four daughters and one son, Curson Hoffman. Jeremiah, son of Peter, married in England. David, youngest son of Peter, married a daughter of Governor McKean, of Pennsylvania, by whom he had one son, who died young. The Hoffmans have long been one of the most distinguished and wealthy families of Baltimore.

The McPhersons. John McPherson, Sr., was born in Pennsylvania in 1760, and removed to Frederick in 1781. Not long before the conclusion of the Revolutionary war he received a lieutenant's commission in the service of his native State, but as a cessation of hostilities soon after ensued, no demand was made upon him for active field duty. He went to Frederick as an agent for the supply of prisoners then quartered there. In 1783 he married there, which confirmed his residence in Frederick, where he lived until his death, in December, 1829. He served with honor in the Legislature, and as an associate judge of the court.

Col. John McPherson, Sr., was the largest manufacturer of iron and owner of real estate in Western Maryland.

Col. John McPherson, Jr., a prominent citizen of Frederick, was born in 1796. He married, Dec. 23, 1823, Fanny, daughter of Thomas Jennings Johnson, and granddaughter of Governor Thomas Johnson. While in Washington City, during the Presidency of John Quincy Adams, the guest of her relative, Mrs. Louisa Catherine Adams, daughter of Joshua Johnson, formerly of Frederick County, Mrs. McPherson was regarded as one of the most beautiful women of the land, and was a great favorite at the White House. Col. McPherson in early life was closely associated with every enterprise projected in the interest of Frederick City and County. For a long time he managed with marked success the Branch Bank, now Central National Bank. He died March 11, 1874. In his early life he was largely connected with the iron interests of the county, and for a number of years was the owner of Catoctin Furnaces. He was one of the prominent projectors of the National turnpike from Washington to Wheeling, and of the Frederick waterworks. When Lafayette visited Frederick in 1825 he was the guest of Col. McPherson, who was then captain of the troop of soldiers known as the Light-Horse Cavalry, in which he took great pride. He left two daughters, Mrs. Worthington Ross and Mrs. Col. George R. Dennis.

The Thomas Family. Dr. Philip Thomas, father of Hon. John Hanson Thomas, was born near Chestertown, June 11, 1747, and removing to Frederick, commenced the practice of medicine in that town, Aug. 1, 1769, after having studied four years under Dr. Vandyke. He had also attended professional lectures in Philadelphia, and the hospital and a "bettering house" in that city, under Professors Bond, Shippen, and Morgan; also a series of lectures by Dr. Smith on Natural and Experimental Philosophy. Dr. Thomas took an active and prominent part in the Revolutionary war. He was chairman of the Frederick County Committee of Safety, and was one of the Presidential electors who voted for Gen. Washington at the first election. He was also the first president of the Medical Society of Maryland. Dr. Thomas died on the 25th of April, 1815.

The career of John Hanson Thomas, son of Dr. Philip Thomas, has already been narrated in the chapter on the bar of Frederick.

Dr. John Hanson Thomas was born in Frederick City, Sept. 23, 1813, was the son of the Hon. John Hanson Thomas, at that time congressman, and his mother was Mary Isham Colston, a niece of Chief Justice John Marshall. Dr. Thomas graduated at the University of Virginia in 1834, and afterwards studied medicine in the office of Dr. Alexander, a well-known and successful practitioner of Baltimore. Dr. Thomas graduated at the Maryland University, and practiced medicine for a short time in Baltimore. He took up his permanent residence there, and in 1837 married Miss Annie Campbell Gordon, a daughter of Mr. Basil Gordon, a wealthy merchant of Fredericksburg, Va., and a sister of Douglas H. Gordon, now a citizen of Baltimore. In 1839 the doctor was made a director of the Farmers' and Mechanics' Bank of Baltimore, and the following year was elected its president. The duties of this position he performed with marked ability and success until January, 1879, when, after re-election, he resigned on account of declining health. During his presidency, on two separate occasions, he employed his private fortune to tide the bank over threatened difficulties and possible disaster. He was for several years chairman of the State Central Whig Committee, and in 1853 made an unsuccessful campaign with Hon. W. Pinkney White for the State comptrollership on the Whig ticket. He was also elected to the State Legislature, and for several years was a member of the Baltimore City Council. While in that body he originated the idea of a system of boulevards around that city, which has been partially carried out in the case of Boundary Avenue.

In 1861, just before the breaking out of the war, Dr. Thomas, Judge Chambers, Governor Lowe, Col. William H. Norris, and other distinguished gentlemen were appointed a peace commission, which went to Richmond and vainly sought to avert impending hostilities. He then became a member of the well-remembered Legislature which met at Frederick the same year, where he was, with ten other members, arrested by the United States authorities and taken to Fort McHenry, and afterwards successively to Forts Monroe, Warren, and Lafayette, being under arrest in all six months. Among other positions of trust and honor held by Dr. Thomas was that of director and first president of the Baltimore Academy of Music Company, and it was largely owing to his active, intelligent efforts that the building was so successfully completed. Two days before the famous 19th of April, 1861, he was one of the committee of citizens which went to Cockeysville to meet the United States troops on their way to Washington, and earnestly sought to persuade those in command to march them around instead of through the city. Dr. Thomas held several private trusts, such as directorships of insurance companies and the presidency of the Baltimore Academy of Music Company. He died July 15, 1881, at Greenbrier, White Sulphur Springs, and left the following children, viz.: Mrs. H. Rieman Duvall, of New York; Mrs. John Carroll, of the "Caves," Baltimore Co.; Basil Gordon, J. Hanson, Raleigh C., Douglas H., and J. Marshall Thomas,—all of whom are grown.

Hon. John Lee, born in 1788, was also a distinguished politician. He was educated at Harvard College, but did not graduate. He was well known and much respected in public and social life in Maryland for more than half a century. He was a representative in Congress from his district in Maryland for the term ending March, 1825, and served as senator and delegate in the Maryland Legislature for a number of years. While in Congress Mr. Lee was chairman of the House Committee appointed to escort the Marquis de Lafayette from Frederick City to Washington. He was then thirty-seven years of age. In 1860 he supported Bell and Everett. In the latter years of his life he espoused the cause of the Conservatives, and never ceased to feel a deep interest in their success. Mr. Lee was one of the pioneers of the Chesapeake and Ohio Canal, and of the Baltimore and Ohio Railroad, and never ceased, even at the advanced age of fourscore, to evince a deep interest in all the internal improvements of his native State. Mr. Lee died at his residence in Frederick County, May 17, 1871, aged eighty-three years.

Maj. Michael Buyer was a lieutenant in the Revolutionary war, and at the battle of Brandywine was ordered by Col. Parker, of Virginia, to station a picket-guard of fourteen men on the top of the hill between the American and British lines, and not to abandon it on point of death. Accordingly, he took the station and threw up a small breastwork. After remaining at his post for some time, he saw the regiment of grenadiers called the Queen's Regiment advancing up the hill to attack him. He thought of his orders and the folly of opposing a whole regiment with fourteen men, but he determined to have one fire. He ordered his men to wait until the British advanced in point-blank shot, to take good aim, and then retreat to the main body at the bottom of the hill. His orders were obeyed, and he drew his men off in safety. Some time afterwards a number of British officers who were in the battle of Brandywine were made prisoners and were quartered at the house of Col. William Beatty, about four miles from Frederick, the native place of Col. Buyer. He met with one of them, and asked him what had become of the regiment which advanced up the hill to a breastwork and received the fire of the picket-guard at the top. The British officer replied he remembered the circumstance well, and that the fire from the picket-guard killed the captain and eleven men, and that when they marched up to the breastwork they found it so slight that they kicked it over with their feet.

William Elder, son of Guy Elder, a native of Calvert County, in this State, during the Revolutionary period was a resident of the Emmittsburg Hundred or District, in Frederick County, near the Pennsylvania line. As early as 1770 he took an active part in the Tom's Creek and Monocacy Valleys in rousing the people of that section to resist the encroachments of the British government against the rights and privileges of the American colonies and to throw off their allegiance to George III.

William Elder, son of Guy, was a quiet, thoughtful, peaceful man, like Goldsmith, schoolmaster, lord of ferule and hickory birch, well read in ancient lore, and withal a natural-born orator. His eloquent voice was heard calling upon the people to rally to the rescue and arm for the defense of American liberty. What Samuel and John Adams and James Otis were to the people of Massachusetts, and Patrick Henry and Richard Henry Lee were to Virginia, William Elder was to the people of the north end of Frederick County. The inhabitants of Tom's Creek Valley heard Mr. Elder's clarion tones, and they listened with eagerness to his vivid and startling denunciations of the king and British Parliament.

Mr. Elder belonged to a Quaker family, and when he espoused the American cause it is said to have "created no little flutter in the royal camp." He helped to organize and equip the Game-cock company of Frederick County, so called from their jaunty cap and waving plume or cockade, the distinguished frontiersmen of Tom's Creek. Of this company William Blair was elected captain, Henry Williams first lieutenant, and George Hockensmith second lieutenant. Mr. Elder was also a member of this organization, and at the sound of the bugle "to arms! to arms!" it early came to the front, and reported to John Hanson, chairman of the Committee of Safety, Frederick Town, that it was ready for duty, equipped for the conflict.

It was in the hottest of the fight at Brooklyn Heights, Long Island, N. Y., where its gallant captain, Blair, fell mortally wounded; participated in all the most important engagements of the war, and assisted at the siege of Yorktown and in the capture of Cornwallis. Capt. Blair was of Scotch-Irish extraction, and was noted for his gallantry and indomitable pluck.[1]

Henry Meyers. The following is from Miner's "History of Wyoming County, Pennsylvania:" "Lieut. Lawrence Meyers was married to Miss Sarah Gore, Jan. 3, 1782. She was of the patriotic family that sent five brothers and two brothers-in-law into battle. That she was very handsome cannot be doubted, for in 1837, then eighty years of age, the round face, regular features, and pleasing expression told of remarkable youthful beauty. Lieut. Meyers was of a German family from Frederick Town, Md. Robust in early manhood, he became corpulent with advancing age, and presented a singular contrast with the spare forms of the Yankees, worn down by exertion and care. But he was ever a favorite. The large round face seemed radiant with benevolence and cheerfulness. Besides having held several offices in the militia, he was for several years a magistrate, and in 1800 commissioner of the county. The plan of the court-house, a cross, was introduced by him, taken from that at Frederick Town, which doubtless owes its origin to the Roman Catholic settlers of Maryland, under their liberal and tolerant founder, though that it was an emblem of Catholicism or had any Christian significance was probably unknown to Mr. Meyers or those in Luzerne who approved thereof. The delight of his life was to talk of Frederick, and anything that existed or came from there was an object of his special regard."

Gen. Anthony Kimmell, popularly known for many years as "the Farmer of Linganore," was the son of a prominent merchant of Baltimore, and was born in that city in 1799. He was educated at St. Mary's College, Baltimore, after leaving which he engaged in mercantile pursuits until attaining the age of twenty-three, when he married a wealthy lady of Frederick County, and removed to that portion of the

---

[1] We are indebted for these particulars to a writer in one of the Frederick journals, whose name is unknown to us. The writer says,—

"A grandson of old Grandmother Hoover, who died near Emmittsburg many years ago, an aged lady who lived over one hundred years, and personally witnessed some Indian forays on Tom's Creek and the upper Monocacy, informed the writer of this sketch that she personally knew nearly all the men in Capt. Blair's company, and was present when they left the Tom's Creek settlement for the Revolutionary campaign. She and the neighbors gave them a good shake of the hand, and, like the mother of the Gracchi, bid them return with their swords or muskets or be transfixed on them."

After the battle of Long Island a meeting was held at the old tavern of Henry Bear, at the sign of John Wilkes, Patrick Street, Frederick Town, and measures taken to fill up the ranks decimated by De Heister's and Knyphausen's Hessians.

State. In 1814, when a mere boy, he entered the army, and from that period identified himself with the State militia, rising to the rank of major-general. He traveled extensively in Europe, and was the vice-president of the American delegation to the Great World's Fair held in London in 1851. In 1840 he was a member of the electoral college which elevated Gen. Harrison to the Presidency, and subsequently was twice defeated as the Whig candidate for Congress, the Democratic party in his district being too strong for even his popularity to overcome. In 1860 he was elected to the State Senate from Frederick County, and although an extreme Southern man, escaped arrest at the time the Maryland Legislature was either dispersed or arrested by the government.

At the age of twenty-two he became a member of the Masonic fraternity, rising to the position of Grand Master of the State, and with the exception of Gen. B. C. Howard, was at one time the oldest Mason in Maryland. He was a member of Baltimore Commandery, No. 2, Knights Templar, and took a great interest in the welfare of the fraternity. He was also a member of the Association of Defenders of Baltimore in 1814, and was always present at the annual meetings of the members on each recurring 12th of September, the anniversary of the battle of North Point. Gen. Kimmell went to Baltimore at the last celebration prior to his death, which occurred April 24, 1871, and attended church on Sunday with the surviving members, and dined with them on the following day, although quite feeble at the time. Gen. Kimmell had been a widower for many years, and left an only son, a Frederick County farmer, to inherit his large estate. The remains were taken to Baltimore by a delegation of Masons from Frederick, and were placed in the Masonic Temple. The funeral took place the same day, and the body was interred in the family burial-ground, corner of Paca and Lombard Streets.

Rev. Thomas Bacon[1] was a native of the Isle of Man, an island in the Irish Sea, about equally distant from the coasts of England, Scotland, and Ireland, and forming part of the diocese of the Bishop of Sodor and Man. He must have been born not far from 1720. As to his family, he was of good descent, his brother being Sir Anthony Bacon.

Of his early education, all that is known is that he was the pupil and *protégé* of the pious and celebrated Bishop Wilson, of Sodor and Man. Having completed his theological studies, he was ordained deacon by Bishop Wilson, Sept. 23, 1744, and in March following priest, with a view to his going to one of the American "plantations." Soon after this he received the appointment of chaplain to Lord Baltimore, the proprietary of Maryland, and came over to that province. He arrived there in the autumn of 1745, and went at once to Oxford, the then port of entry for the Eastern Shore, in Talbot County. There was an intelligent merchant residing there from his own Ireland, to whom he brought letters, and by whom he was very cordially welcomed. Mr. Bacon was accompanied by his wife and a young son. The rector of the parish (Rev. Samuel Maynadier), a good old French Huguenot, who had received orders in the English Church, was very near his end, and he appointed Mr. Bacon his curate. His (Mr. Maynadier's) sermons had gained for him the character of a sober, good, and learned man, and he was found to be most agreeable in the social circle. He was devoted to music, was a good composer, and played well on two or three instruments.

The old rector died late in the year 1745, and Mr. Bacon succeeded to his place. His ministry proved most acceptable, and his congregation so increased that it was found necessary to enlarge his church in the first year of his pastorate. He lived at Oxford some two years, and then removed about twelve miles higher up the country to Dover, near the head of tide-water. About that time he thus wrote to his people:

"Upon being appointed your minister, I began seriously and carefully to examine into the state of religion in the parish, and I found a great many poor negro slaves belonging to Christian masters and mistresses, yet living in as profound ignorance of what Christianity really is as if they had remained in the midst of those barbarous heathen countries from whence they and their parents had been first imported. Being moved, therefore, with compassion at seeing such numbers of poor souls wandering in the mazes of sin and error, as sheep having no shepherd, no kind, tender-hearted Christian to set them right, and considering them as a part of the flock which the Almighty had placed under my care, I began seriously to consider in what manner I could best discharge my duty to them and deliver my own soul from the guilt of their blood, lest they should perish through my own negligence. My first attempt towards it consisted in occasional conversation and advice as often as I happened to meet with any of them at my own house, or at a neighbor's, or upon the road, etc., and, in short, familiar exhortations as opportunity brought a number of them together at any quarter where I visited their sick, or at their funerals or marriages. I then determined to speak to them."

In carrying out this determination he preached two sermons, which he sent to London and had published just as they had been delivered, as containing simply the general points of his instruction. One of his reasons for publishing them was that "possibly it

---

[1] Condensed from Sprague's "Annals of the American Pulpit." The author is Rev. Ethan Allen.

might raise a spirit of emulation among his brethren to attempt something in their parishes towards the bringing home so great a number of wandering souls to Christ." "In setting forth this scheme of instruction," he says, "I consulted nothing but conscience, and had no other view than the discharge of that duty I so solemnly took upon me at my being admitted into Holy Orders." Before the end of the third year of his ministry a chapel was erected for the convenience of those in its neighborhood in a distant part of his parish, in which he ministered at stated intervals. But Mr. Bacon did not stop with what he had already done in behalf of the colored people. In 1749 he preached and published "four sermons upon the great and indispensable duty of all Christian masters and mistresses to bring up their slaves in the knowledge and fear of God." Having mentioned what he felt it his own duty to do, and spoken of the greatness and difficulty of the work, he says, "I found that I must have help, which put me upon considering where laborers might be had; and finding upon the strictest and most impartial inquiry that it is the indispensable duty of all masters and mistresses to bring up their slaves in the knowledge and fear of God, I was determined to call in assistance from where it was due. I therefore, as steward, and in the name of the Lord of the harvest, do press and invite you to work in His vineyard, and do promise, on His part, that whatsoever is right and equal that shall ye receive." Of these four sermons to say that his language is classical yet plain, his thoughts fresh yet well digested, his positions sustained ably yet conclusively, and sometimes eloquently, and that the gospel is distinctly and faithfully presented, and all with the most intrepid, yet affectionate and Christian spirit, is nothing more than every impartial reader must acknowledge to be true. But the colored people in his parish were not the only ones who awakened his interest and enlisted his efforts. About this time he undertook the establishment of a charity and working school. With this view he preached a sermon on the subject, which he also published. He then purchased a tract of land for the purpose, about a mile west of the church, on the road to Oxford. A copy of this sermon, together with a letter explaining his object, was sent by him to Lord Baltimore, who approved of the scheme, and sent him one hundred guineas to assist in erecting the house, and gave direction to the receiver-general in the colony to pay him twenty pounds, equal to ninety-three dollars and twenty cents, annually. Lady Baltimore added to this five pounds, equal to twenty-three dollars and thirty cents, and his nephew, who was his private secretary, the same amount. Bishop Wilson a short time after, learning what the Baltimores had done, sent him a letter of congratulation and encouragement, and told him he had fifty pounds more to aid in the instruction of negroes, and that it might be laid out in purchasing a boy and girl who might be taught and made useful servants for the school. A brick building was erected, and in 1755 a master was employed and the school removed into it. Not long after this Mr. Bacon lost his wife and son, and his own health and spirits seem to have suffered much, owing to his bereavement and the sickly atmosphere of the neighborhood. How long it was after the death of his wife before he married again does not appear, but it must have been in the course of two or three years. He then married one of his own parishioners, Elizabeth, the daughter of Col. Thomas Bozman, of Oxford Neck, a gentleman in easy circumstances. The laws creating parishes, relating to the rights of clergymen, and the duties of vestrymen, were all enactments of the General Assembly. Since 1727 no edition of the laws of Maryland had been published save the annual acts of the Legislature in pamphlet form, and as the Legislature busied themselves at almost every session in making some change in them, it had become difficult for the clergy to understand what their legal rights or restrictions were, or for the vestry to know what their legal duties were or what the penalties for neglecting them. As Lord Baltimore's chaplain in Maryland (a place which he still held), it seemed right that Mr. Bacon should set himself to supply for the church this manifest want. But as he was not accustomed to do anything by halves, he undertook to give the enactments of every General Assembly from the beginning of the colony, retaining, however, those which had been repealed only so far as to give their titles and state the fact of such repeal. In this exhibit the church would have the whole history of the legislation of the province respecting it, and the civil community would derive from it an equal advantage.

He had not been long engaged in this work when All Saints' Parish, in Frederick County, became vacant by the death of its rector, and Mr. Bacon, in 1757, was appointed to it. This was, in point of emolument, decidedly the first parish in the province, being worth, it is said, a thousand pounds, equal to four thousand six hundred and sixty-six dollars per annum, and the bestowal of it upon Mr. Bacon showed the estimation in which he was held. His new parish was on the Western Shore, some seventy miles northwest of Annapolis. Mr. Bacon went there with impaired health, and being obliged to be much in Annapolis, in order to complete the work which he had undertaken he employed a curate to assist him in his parochial charge. It was not till the year 1765 that his work made its appearance. It was a large folio of a thousand pages, printed on thick white paper, making a handsome volume. It was printed in Annapolis, and it may be questioned whether its superior, in point of mechanical execution, was ever issued from the American press.

Whatever the utility of this work may have been to the church and to the civil community, it has now a higher value as a book of reference. It is, in fact, the history of the progress of Maryland from its earliest days, not only as to its legislation, but as to its civil and ecclesiastical legal provisions and changes for one hundred and thirty years. The conclusion of his "Laws of Maryland" found Mr. Bacon's health irrevocably gone. He lingered on for three years, and died on the 24th of May, 1768.

He left behind him a widow and three daughters, who returned to Talbot. The eldest, Elizabeth, at the request of his brother, Sir Anthony Bacon, of Glamorganshire (he having no children), went to England to reside with him, and from him, at his death, she inherited ten thousand pounds sterling. She married George Watkins Price, of Brecon, in Wales, whose public charities were so munificent, but left no children. Mr. Bacon's daughter Rachel married Rigdon Bozman Harwood, of Talbot County, who left two daughters. The other daughter, Mary, married Moses Passapas, of Dorchester County. Mr. Bacon's successor as rector of All Saints' Parish was the notorious Bennett Allen.

Bennett, or Benedict Allen, of whom traditions are still preserved in Frederick County, was one of the most extraordinary figures in the colonial history of Maryland. He was a graduate and Fellow of Wadham College, Oxford, was ordained deacon of the Church of England by the Bishop of Oxford on the 23d of September, 1759, and priest by the same diocesan two years afterwards, on the 20th of September, 1761. He was licensed for Maryland on the 3d of September, 1766, by the Bishop of London, and came over to the province in 1768, with letters to Governor Sharpe from Frederick, last Lord Baltimore, who commended him to the Governor's special consideration as one of his most particular friends, desiring that he might have the first good living or parish of the Established Church that offered itself, or if one good living could not be had, then two indifferent ones. His object evidently was to obtain Mr. Allen a comfortable berth. The character of Frederick Calvert was none of the best, and it is more than probable that Allen had been his boon companion and associate in dissipations which were anything but seemly for a clergyman even in those days. Governor Sharpe seems to have suspected his true character even from the outset, as there is abundant evidence in his correspondence with Lord Baltimore of a deep reluctance to help Mr. Allen forward in his designs, a reluctance which brought down upon him the full weight of the dissipated proprietary's anger and ill will. The Governor finally inducted Mr. Allen into the rectorship of St. Ann's, at Annapolis, and for a time everything went smoothly enough. He was a man of considerable tact, and could be pleasant enough when his interest lay that way; but he could not brook opposition, and as soon as he was crossed gave way to violent outbursts of temper. At first he seems to have been quite intimate with the Dulany family, especially with Walter Dulany, and with Samuel Chew and other leading men of Annapolis and vicinity. It was not long, however, before he got into hot water. Desiring to augment his income, he attempted to secure the living of St. James' Parish, in addition to that of St. Ann's, but his course was characterized by such duplicity that the vestries, some members of which had in the beginning favored the project, refused to give their consent to it. He ascribed his failure largely to the opposition of Walter Dulany and Mr. Chew, and quarreled with both of them. The former he attempted to cane on the street, but seems to have met with a Christian equally muscular; and he insulted Mr. Chew so grossly in the latter's own house that he was compelled to take the irate parson by the collar and put him out of the front door. Mr. Allen's clerical blood was now fully up, and he sent Mr. Chew a challenge, which the recipient, not knowing it to be a hostile message, threw contemptuously, unopened, into the fire. Learning subsequently the nature of the communication, he promptly accepted Mr. Allen's invitation to the field of honor, providing, however, that they should both repair to the appointed place unaccompanied, and that the contest should be to the death. Mr. Chew was on hand at the appointed time, but Mr. Allen failed to make his appearance; but fearing that his reputation for belligerency might suffer, he took care to explain that his failure to keep the appointment was due to the fact that Mr. Chew had violated the terms of the duel by taking with him to the field a servant armed with a blunderbuss. Mr. Chew replied that he had taken this precaution because he was afraid Mr. Allen would attempt to assassinate him, as he had previously done in the case of Mr. Dulany.

St. Ann's not furnishing sufficient revenue for the

support of Mr. Allen, who had complained that even the £300 living of St. James' was not enough to keep him in liquors, Governor Sharpe, apparently worn out by his importunities and the repeated commands of Calvert, determined to give Allen the important post of the Lord Proprietary's agent for the province, and actually appointed him to the place, displacing, in order to do so, Col. Edward Lloyd, a prominent member of the provincial government, and one of the most influential planters in Maryland. Alarmed lest the appointment of Allen should breed discontent and weaken his authority, the Lord Proprietary wrote to the Governor, asserting that he had not intended Mr. Allen to have an office of so much consequence. About this time the rich parish of All Saints', in Frederick County, the best living in the province, became vacant by the death of the venerable rector, Rev. Thomas Bacon, and Mr. Allen was inducted into it by the Governor. As soon as Mr. Allen got the appointment he hastened to seize the rich rectorship. His unsavory reputation, however, seems to have preceded him, and he found it necessary to get possession of the church keys by stealth, and to force his way into the church through opposing vestrymen. Having gotten inside the sacred edifice, he at once leaped into the reading-desk and commenced to rattle off the service. Remonstrances were in vain, and the terrified congregation withdrew for a time to the outside of the church. At last, losing all patience, several of them went in again and approached the chancel to repeat their protests, when Mr. Allen suddenly put a pistol to the head of the foremost, and with a sounding oath told him he would kill him if he came a step nearer. This naturally had the effect of speedily emptying the church, but the repulsed congregation soon made it so unpleasant for the rector, by means of volleys of stones, that he was compelled to evacuate the position and retire from the field. In spite of this little unpleasantness, Mr. Allen managed to hold on to his salary of £1000 per annum until 1777, though he did not perform his duties in person, being represented by his curate, Mr. Goldie.

In that year the Church of England in Maryland was deprived of its livings and Mr. Allen forced to return to England. He carried back to his native country the same violent temper he had exhibited in Maryland, and an intense hatred of the Dulanys, which manifested itself in 1779 in a bitter anonymous attack in the London *Morning Post* upon the character of Daniel Dulany. To this Lloyd Dulany replied in terms of equal bitterness, but no notice was taken of his answer by Allen until 1782, when he avowed himself the author of the attack upon Daniel Dulany, and challenged Lloyd Dulany for his utterances in reply to him. The challenge was accepted, and Mr. Dulany was killed by Mr. Allen at the first fire. What became of Mr. Allen is not known, but according to tradition he died in England a poor abandoned drunkard.

Rev. Dr. Daniel Zacharias was born near Clear Spring, Washington Co., Md., and was early trained in a knowledge of the duties and doctrines of the Christian religion. While still a youth he connected himself with the St. Paul's German Reformed Church, near his father's residence, under the pastorate of the Rev. James R. Reilly. His classical studies were commenced at the Hagerstown Academy, and he afterwards entered Jefferson College, Cannonsburg, Pa., and continued there until the close of the junior year. This institution subsequently, in 1839, conferred upon him the degree of A.M. In 1826 he entered the theological seminary at Carlisle, Pa., which had been opened the previous year, with the Rev. Dr. Lewis Mayer as principal. At the same time he availed himself of the opportunity afforded him to attend some of the lectures at Dickinson College, of which the Rev. Dr. Nesbit was then president.

In 1828 he was licensed and ordained to the Christian ministry of the Reformed Church, along with the Rev. John H. Crawford, Henry Wagner, John G. Fritchey, Jacob F. Dieffenbocker, and J. Caspar Bucher, the first graduates of the theological seminary. The Revs. Dr. T. L. Hoffeditz, Frederick Rahauser, and Dr. S. Helffenstein officiated at the ordination. He had accepted a call from the Creutz Creek and Conondogly Churches, in York County, to which he ministered about two years. In 1830 he received a call from the Harrisburg and Schupp's congregations. In this field he labored until 1835, in the spring of which year he removed to Frederick City, of the church at which place he continued pastor until the time of his death. Dr. Zacharias attained to considerable prominence in the ministry of the Reformed Church, in whose welfare he took a deep and active interest. He was president of the Synod of the Reformed Church in the United States which convened at Chambersburg, Pa., in 1835, and also of the General Synod, at its second triennial session, in Dayton, Ohio, in 1866. He several times filled the same position in his classis. He was also for a number of years a member of the board of visitors of the theological seminary, and likewise of the Boards of Home and Foreign Missions. In these several capacities he was efficient and active. He likewise served on important committees, such as those to prepare an appendix to the English Hymn-Book, to compile what is commonly known as the Chambersburg German Hymn-Book, and to prepare the "Liturgy of the Reformed Church;" also, subsequently, to revise and publish it, as "An Order of Worship for the Reformed Church." He was a member of the committee which prepared the Tercentenary edition of the Heidelberg Catechism in the original German, Latin, Modern German, and English languages. He likewise took a deep interest in the educational enterprises and various charitable interests in the immediate vicinity of Frederick, and lent his efforts sometimes also, in the shape of public addresses, to promote their success. He was taken sick during a visit to the West, made in the autumn of 1872 for the purpose of seeing an aged brother, who has since died. After his return he was so indisposed that he preached but few sermons, the last one of which was delivered Dec. 29, 1872, and was on the text, "But when the fullness of time was come, God sent forth His Son, made of a woman, made under the law." Gal. iv. 4. On the 12th of January he was in his pulpit for the last time, when he made a few touching remarks, after a sermon by Rev. J. T. Glodhill, asking his people to pray that if it was God's will he might be restored to health. On the subsequent Sunday he baptized an infant in the church in the presence of the Sunday-school, which was his last ministerial act in his church. After this, and up to his death, he baptized at the parsonage some of the children of his congregation, and probably performed the marriage service in a few instances. On Thursday, March 20, 1873, he was seized with a complication of symptoms, which caused his physicians to look upon the approach of death as near at hand. He lingered, however, for twelve days before he died. Among his last words were, "At the foot of the cross." It will be long before the community of Frederick will lose the remembrance of this gentle servant of his Master. For thirty-eight years he had the Reformed Church of Frederick under his care, and few men have been so loved by their congregations, or have so grown into the affections of the community in which they lived.

Father John McElroy was born at Enniskillen, Ireland, in May, 1782, and was at the time of his death, which occurred at the Novitiate, Frederick, Sept. 12, 1877, in his ninety-sixth year, being the oldest Jesuit priest in the world. He received an elementary education at home, and came to America in 1803, being then twenty-one years old. Jefferson was at that time President of the United States, and was the object of Father McElroy's high esteem. After a short experience of mercantile life he entered Georgetown College, where he had been appointed treasurer and book-keeper. He remained in this position about eight years, during which time he prosecuted his classical studies. He was ordained priest May 3, 1817, being at that time thirty-five years of age. In 1822 he was sent to Frederick to succeed Father Maleve, pastor of St. John's Church, and remained there for twenty-three years. Father McElroy was appointed chaplain of the United States army under Gen. Taylor, during the Mexican war, at the close of which he went to Boston as pastor of St. Mary's Church, at which place the Immaculate Conception Church and College were reorganized through his instrumentality. About five years before his death he returned to Frederick, to which his heart was indissolubly bound by ties of the tenderest character, and although weighed down by the burden of fourscore years and ten, he was enabled on several occasions to say mass and deliver brief sermons to his former flock. Father McElroy had been on the superannuated list for twelve years, suffering the greatest portion of that time from blindness, and latterly from a dislocated thigh, caused by a fall, which confined him to his bed until his death. His long pastoral career in Frederick was characterized by marked liberality. It was a habitual custom of his to make frequent visits to the parsonages of the Protestant ministers here, Rev. Mr. Schaeffer's, Dr. Zacharias', and others, and his social relations with these gentlemen were frank, open, and whole-souled. From the time of his death to the date of his burial hundreds of people visited the Novitiate to take a last view of his remains. On Saturday morning, September 15th, his remains were taken to St. John's church, and masses were offered continually between 5 and 8.30 A.M., when the offices of the dead were chanted by forty seminarians in the sanctuary, unaccompanied by the organ. Then followed the Benedictus, chanted by a quintet from the Novitiate, assisted by a full chorus of seminarians. Mass was then celebrated by Rev. Father Brady, provincial of Maryland, during which Prof. Dielmon, of Mount St. Mary's, Emmittsburg, rendered in a subdued tone a voluntary on the organ. Rev. Father McGuire delivered the funeral discourse. After sketching Father McElroy's life the speaker coupled his name with that of the late Chief Justice Taney, and held up the two men before the congregation as living epistles to be read and known of all men for their sterling character, vigorous intellect, and spirituality of temperament. Father McGuire pleaded eloquently for the imitation of such models of true greatness, and mentioned the fact that he owed his own soul's salvation to the Christian, humane, considerate treatment of Father

McElroy, who had taken him in his youth from the moral corruption and evil associations of canal life, had given him an education, and had placed him on the road to blessedness. Upon the conclusion of the sermon the funeral procession moved to the grave in the following order, as the quintet chanted the "Miserere": William Judge (a novice), cross-bearer; Durney and Woods, acolytes, censer-bearers; forty seminarians with lighted candles; Father Brady, provincial of Maryland; Fathers Gache, Ward, Stonestreet, Tisdall, Gaffney, Colledevito, Bric, Sumner, Nagle, Holland, Scanlon, Toul, of the Novitiate, Frederick; McCloskey, of Emmittsburg; McGuire, of Boston; McMullen, of Emmittsburg; Healy, of Georgetown College; Jenkins, of Washington; Kelly, of Loyola College, Baltimore; Parron, of Woodstock; Hough, of California; Connolly, of Missouri; Fulmar, of Boston; Fulton, of Boston; and Tilton, of Providence, R. I. Then came the bier, borne by eight brothers, followed by a long train of citizens. After the absolution and litany for the dead the body was committed to the earth in a portion of St. John's graveyard set apart for ecclesiastical burials, and near the grave of James McSherry, the historian.

Rev. Bernard Michael Houseal, the founder of the First Evangelical Lutheran Church of Frederick Town, then known as Monocacy Station, was born at Heilbronn, in Würtemberg, and was the son of Rev. Bernard Houseal, of that place. Just before embarking for America he married, at Rotterdam, in Holland, in 1752, Sybilla Margaretha Mayer, daughter of Christopher Bartholomew Mayer, of Ulm, in Würtemberg. Mrs. Houseal was a cousin of Christian Mayer, of Ulm, who came to Baltimore in 1784 and was the progenitor of the Mayer family of that city, of which the late Charles F. Mayer, the distinguished lawyer, and the late Col. Brantz Mayer, the well-known author, were members. Mr. and Mrs. Houseal, with Christopher Bartholomew Mayer and his two sons and one other daughter, landed at Annapolis in the early part of 1752, and thence they all proceeded to the western part of the province of Maryland, and settled at Monocacy Station. As they disembarked from their voyage at Annapolis, it is probable that Daniel Dulany, then dwelling there, and whose landed possessions in Western Maryland were large, induced the thrifty Germans to look at his lands in and about Frederick Town; nor is this conjecture weakened by the fact that the ground for the church begun at that village subsequently by Houseal was given to him for that purpose by Dulany. Even at that early day, three years before Braddock's defeat, Lutherans were coming in numbers to the converging valleys of the Shenandoah and Potomac Rivers, so that a community from the Fatherland, speaking a common language, and devoted to Lutheranism as a common faith, was already established to welcome the new-comers. Yet the bravery of the enterprise will always be undisputed, for Monocacy Station was then only a frontier settlement, bordering on a wild country thronged with savages. Here the Houseals and the Mayers stopped, and the Rev. Mr. Houseal began his ministrations (he was then a man of twenty-five years of age) as clergyman of the Evangelical Lutheran Church, having been presented by Daniel Dulany with the deed of the property, as before stated, on which the first church was erected, and on which the new church now stands. The completion of the church was stopped by the French war and Indian hostilities. It was afterwards finished, and the Rev. Mr. Houseal continued his pastoral labors in Frederick Town until 1759, when, at the instance of the venerable Dr. Muhlenberg, he was transferred to Reading Town, in Pennsylvania, where he served until about 1768. He was afterwards at Easton, in Pennsylvania, and in Philadelphia. In 1770 he was transferred to New York, and there became "senior minister of the ancient Lutheran Church" of that city. He was one of the governors of the New York College, and one of the corporators of the New York Hospital. When the troubles began which culminated in the war of independence, Houseal took his stand at once as an adherent of the crown. From the historical records of New York we find him to have been loud in his declarations of loyalty to England, as one of the "addressers of Lord Howe and Sir William Howe" after the occupation of New York in 1776. Houseal's church and dwelling were burnt by the Americans when they left the town on its occupation by the British. Houseal remained in New York during the war, and at the peace of 1783 departed with many of his congregation as loyalist refugees to Halifax, Nova Scotia. He afterwards went to England, and having conformed to the Church of England, was ordained to its ministry by the Bishop of London in 1785, and sent back to Nova Scotia, where he resided as rector of St. George's Parish—his church being known as the old "Dutch Chicken-Cock Church" —till his death on the 9th of March, 1799. It may be interesting to mention that his wife's family, with whom he came from Rotterdam, removed to Pennsylvania before Houseal left Frederick Town, and that his wife (née Mayer) survived him, and died at the age of *ninety-one* years, in 1824, at Stonehouse, Devonshire, England, where after her husband's death she lived with her children and grandchildren.

The Rev. Mr. Houseal is described as a man of commanding stature, stately manners, and dignified address, thoroughly educated in ancient and modern languages, as well as theology, and speaking Latin—an accomplishment of his day—with remarkable fluency. He served for thirty-one years as a minister of the Lutheran Church, preaching as the occasion demanded in English, German, Dutch, or French. The sixteen years of his after-life in Nova Scotia were devoted as a clergyman to the Church of England. No reason is assigned for his leaving the church of his fathers, but it was doubtless due to individual convictions.

Jacob Englebrecht. This highly-respected and venerable citizen of Frederick was born in that town Dec. 11, 1797, and died Feb. 22, 1878, in his eighty-first year. Blessed with a strong constitution and a kindly disposition full of genial humor, endowed with earnest admiration for everything that was truthful, honest, and patriotic, and thoroughly interested in the prosperity and success of his native place and country, he was a most valuable citizen, and his death was a serious loss to the whole community. His tastes led him to gather up scraps of local history, so that he became the authority of Frederick in this particular, and every one was ready to acknowledge the accuracy of his reminiscences, fortified as they generally were by a written diary of local events which he had carefully kept since the year 1819. He was frequently called upon to serve the community in an official capacity,—in the council board from 1831 for several years, in the mayoralty for three years (from Feb. 28, 1865), and also as the city tax collector. An ardent lover of vocal music, and possessed of a rich, sonorous voice, Mr. Engelbrecht was for several years before 1825 the leader of the choir in the Reformed Church, and from 1836 to 1842 of that attached to the Lutheran Church. The citizens of Frederick will recollect with what a ringing tone he led the choir on the Decoration Day of 1878 as they sung the "Star Spangled Banner" at the grave of the author of its stirring words in Mount Olivet Cemetery, and how the employment of some favorite old melody by the choirs in the church worship could always inspire him to bring his voice to their aid. On Sunday following his death he was buried in the cemetery, being followed to the grave by a large number of personal friends. The funeral services were conducted by Rev. George Diehl, D.D., and Rev. H. Bilfield.

George Trisler. Among the many men of mark to whom Frederick County has given birth, the subject of this sketch stands forth conspicuous. George Trisler was born in Frederick Town in the year 1768, about the period when the Whigs of Frederick were debating the question of separation from Great Britain, and died in 1845, aged seventy-seven. His parents emigrated from Lancaster County, Pa., to Frederick Town soon after the establishment of Mason and Dixon's line. His father was of German descent, and George received the rudiments of a good German and English education, and spoke both languages with great fluency. He was somewhat familiar with the classics and French and Latin languages. As he grew up to manhood he became acquainted with Mathias Bartgis, who, in 1779, was the first printer in Frederick, and he resolved to learn the art of printing. In connection with Bartgis & Wilcox, he subsequently edited and published a paper at Winchester, Va., before he had attained the age of twenty-one. He subsequently resolved, however, to abandon types and the editorial chair, and sedulously devoted himself to mercantile pursuits. He entered the house of Henry Schroeder, of Baltimore City, then an extensive importer and dealer in German and Irish linens and staple goods. By close application to business he gained the good will and confidence of his employer, and became his principal clerk and salesman. In 1794 he married a young lady in Baltimore. The following notice of the wedding appeared in the Baltimore *Daily Intelligencer*:

"MARCH 28, 1794.—Married, last evening in the city of Baltimore, by the Rev. Mr. Kurtz, Mr. George Trisler, merchant of this place, to the amiable Miss Kittie Breidenbough (daughter of John Breidenbough, of this town), a young lady endowed with every accomplishment to render the marriage state happy.

"[We wish the young and gifted pair long life and all the pleasures which can flow from a happy and agreeable union of wedded life.—EDS. INT.]"

In 1795, Mr. Trisler returned to Frederick Town, and entered the mercantile business there on Market Street upon an extensive scale. Mr. Trisler took a keen interest in politics, and espoused the Republican side of the question in 1796 and 1800, supporting Thomas Jefferson for President against John Adams. He was a warm supporter of Jefferson's administration and the embargo measures of 1808. He was the author of an address to the voters of Frederick, Washington, and Allegany Counties in 1808, and supported the claims of Dr. John Tyler, of Frederick, and Col. Nathaniel Rochester, of Hagerstown, for the electoral college, pledged to the election of James Madison and George Clinton for President and Vice-President. Mr. Trisler was a gentleman of infinite humor, and his "Bulletins from Paris Row," published in the *Political Examiner*, excited the curiosity of the Frederick folks whenever they made their appearance in print. He was the life and soul of the social circle, and always had something to say that was pleasant and laughable.

Mr. Trisler's fugitive poetical productions, written off-hand at his desk behind the counter, if collected would make two large volumes. His effusions were printed in Bartgis' *Maryland Chronicle*, in the *Federal Gazette*, Dr. Carey's *Key*, Winter's *Rights of Man*, *Independent Volunteer*, Colvin's *Republican Advocate and Political Examiner* of Frederick Town, and in the *Virginia Museum* and *Philanthropist* of Winchester, Va., the Baltimore *Daily Intelligencer*, *Telescope*, and *Post*, in Edward Coate Pinkney's *Marylander*, the *Oracle of Dauphin*, the Washington *Monitor*, and a number of other publications. Some of these poems embody deep thought and study, while others are full either of humor or of pathos.

In the social circle of Frederick Town from 1800 to 1840, and among such choice spirits as Henry Kuhn, Joseph M. Cromwell, Jacob Rohr, George Baltzell, Wm. R. Sanderson, Dr. Wm. Tyler, Gen. Joseph Swearingen, Gen. Thomas C. Worthington, Dr. John S. Miller, Mathias E. Bartgis, Frederick Loehr, Benjamin Rutherford, Lewis Medtart, Henry Bantz, William C. Russell, Capt. Jacob Houck, George Webster, Wm. M. Beall, Richard English, John Schissler, Samuel Barnes, Thomas Carlton, Thomas W. Morgan, and many others, Mr. Trisler was the head-centre in wit, humor, and repartee.

He was a generous, open-hearted man, and when Mount St. Mary's College was destroyed by fire in 1824, although he was a Protestant, he contributed a handsome sum towards rebuilding it, and also tendered the president and his associates all the goods they needed from his store on credit at their own terms.

In December, 1824, when Lafayette visited Frederick, Mr. Trisler was among the most zealous and active citizens in honoring him. He wrote an ode and had it painted in large letters on the arch of triumph at the intersection of Market and Patrick Streets.

James Cooper was born in Frederick County, May 8, 1810; he was educated at St. Mary's College, and at Washington College, Pennsylvania. He studied law, and was admitted to the bar in Pennsylvania in 1834. In 1838, and again in 1840, he represented that State in Congress, and 1843, 1844, 1846, 1848 was a member of the State Legislature, serving as Speaker in 1847. He was appointed attorney-general of Pennsylvania in 1848, and was chosen a senator in Congress in 1849 for the term of six years. Feeble health prevented him from active participation in the debates. He subsequently returned to Frederick, Md. He was a brigadier-general in the army, and died in Columbus, Ohio, 1863.

George Baer was born in Frederick, and was a representative in Congress from 1798 to 1801, and again from 1815 to 1817. He died in Frederick at an advanced age.

Francis Brengle, born in Western Maryland, was a representative in Congress from that State from 1843 to 1845. Died Dec. 10, 1846.

Daniel Sheffey was born at Frederick, Md., in 1770. He had but a limited education, and was a shoemaker by trade, but a man of vigorous mind and great intelligence. He removed to Staunton, Augusta Co., Va., and studied law while working at his trade. When admitted to the bar he attained a very lucrative practice, and was frequently a member of the State Legislature. He was a representative in Congress from 1809 to 1817. His speech in favor of renewing the charter of the first Bank of the United States was a masterly production. To John Randolph's sneer, " *Ne sutor ultra crepidam*," he sent back the stinging retort that " Randolph could never have risen from the shoemaker's bench." He died Dec. 3, 1830.

John A. McMahon was born in Frederick, Md., Feb. 19, 1833, and was graduated from St. Xavier's College, in Cincinnati, in 1849; he was admitted to practice in 1854; he was a delegate at large from Ohio to the Baltimore Convention of 1872, and was a representative in the Forty-fourth Congress from Ohio.

Adamson Tannehill was born in Frederick County, Md., in 1752, and served as a captain through the Revolutionary war. He removed to Pennsylvania, and settled near Pittsburgh; he was a justice of the peace at the breaking out of the " Whisky Rebellion," and firmly opposed that outbreak. He served as a brigadier-general in the war of 1812, and was a representative in Congress from 1812 to 1815. He died at Grant's Hill in 1817.

David Ross was a delegate from Maryland to the Continental Congress from 1786 to 1787.

William Schley was born in Frederick City, Md., Dec. 15, 1786. He received an academic education in Georgia, studied law, and was admitted to the bar at Augusta in 1812. He was in 1825 elected judge of the Superior Court of the Middle District of Georgia. In 1830 he was elected to the State Legislature; from 1833 to 1835 he was a representative in Congress, and for the following year was Governor of Georgia. He published a " Digest of the English Statutes," and died at Augusta, Ga., Nov. 20, 1838.

John H. Farquhar was born in Frederick, Md., Dec. 20, 1818, and removed with his father to Indiana in 1833. He was a civil engineer in the service of the State from 1837 to 1840, when he studied law and practiced his profession. In 1842 and 1843 he was secretary to the Indiana Senate, chief clerk, in 1844, of the House of Representatives of the State, Presidential elector in 1860, and was commissioned a captain in the Nineteenth United States Infantry in 1861, and served until 1864, when he resigned and was elected to the Thirty-ninth Congress, and served on the Committees on Post-Offices and Post-Roads and on the Militia.

Roger Nelson was born in Frederick County, and was a general in the Revolutionary army, receiving severe wounds at the battle of Camden. He was a representative in Congress from Maryland from 1804 to 1810, and was for several years a member of the Virginia Legislature, and from 1810 to 1815 he was judge of the Upper District of that State. He was the father of John Nelson, and died at Frederick, Md., June 7, 1815.

Henry S. Geyer was born in Frederick, Md., in 1798, and removed in early life to Missouri. He saw some service in the war of 1812, and was captain of the first militia company formed in the State. He was an eminent practitioner of the law, and took also an active part in politics. He was a member of the convention that framed the first constitution of the State, and an active member for two sessions of the Legislature, of which he was Speaker during his last term. He succeeded Thomas H. Benton in the United States Senate, and served from 1851 to 1857. He was an attorney in the celebrated Dred Scott case. A man of decided ability, he possessed pleasing manners and a high character. He died at St. Louis, March 5, 1859.

Necrology of Frederick County since 1749.— The following is a list of the deaths of leading individuals born in or identified with Frederick County since 1749:

Jan. 1, 1750.—John Thomas, high sheriff.
May 20, 1756.—Richard Burdus, formerly clerk of the Provincial Court.
November, 1756.—Isaac Brooke, surveyor of Frederick County.
July, 1757.—Aleander McKeafy and Samuel Wilson, shot and killed near Frederick Town.
October, 1758.—Rev. Samuel Hunter, rector of All Saints' Parish.
Feb. 19, 1764.—Saul Richards, aged 58.
January, 1764.—Capt. Peter Butler.
1766.—Edmund Key, leaving "Paradise," 335 acres, "Good Hope," 300 acres, and "Friendship," 206 acres. One of these plantations was on the Potomac, and all of them were between Great Conecocheague and Little Conecocheague.
Jan. 29, 1768.—John Darnall, one of the judges of the Provincial Court.
January, 1768.—Capt. Joseph Chapline, for many years a representative of the General Assembly.
September, 1771.—George Scott, farmer of the quit-rents in Frederick County, and deputy commissary of Prince George's County, died in the latter county. William Turner Wootten, of Frederick County, was appointed deputy commissary in his place.
Nov. 26, 1778.—Col. William Blair, aged 48.
May 8, 1786.—John Macgill.
Aug. 27, 1787.—Dr. Adam Fischer, aged 51.
June 2, 1789.—Baron Knyphausen, the Hessian general, who served in America during the greater part of the Revolutionary war.
Nov. 24, 1790.—John Thomas Schley, who built the first house in Frederick in 1746, aged 78.
Oct. 29, 1792.—Mrs. Catherine Ritchie, wife of John Ritchie.
Oct. 28, 1793.—Mrs. Elizabeth Potts, wife of Hon. Richard Potts.
Nov. 27, 1793.—Col. Joseph Sim.
Nov. 22, 1794.—At Rich Hill, four miles from Frederick, Mrs. Ann Johnson, wife of Thomas Johnson.
July 27, 1795.—Rev. Edward Jones, formerly minister of the Protestant Episcopal Church at Moorefield.
Dec. 30, 1797.—Mrs. Eleanor Sheredine, wife of Upton Sheredine, of Midhill.
Feb. 8, 1799.—Melchior Geisser, a native of Germany, said to be 110 years old. He lived to see the fifth generation. Buried February 10th, in Middletown.
1799.—Maj. Henry Hardman, an old soldier.
Jan. 14, 1800.—Upton Sheredine, at Midhill, of yellow fever. He was the first U. S. tax commissioner for the State of Maryland.
Feb. 11, 1801.—John Gambier, aged 78.
March 9, 1802.—Mrs. Patty Brunner, aged 83.
March 13, 1802.—Mrs. Barbara Schnou, aged 65.
March 14, 1802.—Frederick House, schoolmaster, aged 77.
Oct. 23, 1802.—Henry Dorst.
Oct. 25, 1802.—Jacob Baltzell.
Aug. 26, 1803.—At Woodborough, Rev. George Hale, aged 48.
April 6, 1803.—Joseph McCully, coppersmith, aged 32.
April 14, 1803.—William Biggs, aged 78. He left eight children and forty-two grandchildren.
Dec. 18, 1803.—Christain Steiner, aged 67.
May 1, 1803.—At his plantation, Col. William Beatty, aged 64.
April 25, 1803.—John Tobias Reisner, aged 87.
April 15, 1803.—James Marshall, aged 74.
Oct. 13, 1804.—Mrs. Elizabeth Fey, aged 73.
June 21, 1804.—Nicholas Freydenger, a native of Germany.
May 2, 1804.—Mrs. Elizabeth Hoffman, aged 80.
Feb. 24, 1804.—Jacob Kline.
Jan. 3, 1804.—James Smith, merchant, and one of the wealthiest inhabitants of Frederick County, aged 66.
March 23, 1804.—Col. Benedict Jamison, at his farm.
Feb. 23, 1804.—Martin Studor.
Feb. 18, 1804.—Baltzel Hinkle.
March 27, 1804.—William Robertson.
Feb. 26, 1804.—Mrs. Peale, of the Museum.
Feb. 21, 1804.—Miss Rebecca Potts, daughter of Richard Potts.
Jan. 16, 1805.—Andrew Shriver, merchant, aged 27.
Jan. 21, 1805.—Mrs. Mary Lee, wife of Thomas Sim Lee, formerly Governor of Maryland.
April 10, 1805.—George Burkhart, an old merchant.
April 19, 1805.—Archibald Campbell, aged 58.
April 28, 1805.—Mrs. Writh French, aged 72.
April 30, 1805.—Mrs. Beatty, wife of Thomas Beatty.
April 30, 1805.—Louis Kemp.
Jan. 16, 1806.—Alexander Contee Hanson, chancellor of Maryland.

March 3, 1806.—Mrs. Ellis Fleming, aged 86.
March 11, 1806.—Mrs. Mary Hymes, a native of Germany, aged 103.
May 6, 1806.—Mrs. Beall, wife of Upton Beall.
Feb. 10, 1807.—Mr. William Dearn.
Nov. 25, 1808.—Richard Potts.
Dec. 27, 1808.—Henry Winemiller.
Feb. 1, 1809.—Jacob Boyer, Sr.
June 30, 1809.—Edward Salmon.
March 27, 1810.—The Louisiana papers record the death of the wife of Governor Henry Johnson. The deceased was born in Maryland in 1796, and was a cousin of the author of the "Star Spangled Banner." Her father was the Hon. Philip B. Key, formerly a distinguished member of Congress, and one of the most eminent lawyers in the United States. Mrs. Johnson resided for many years in Georgetown, D.C., and her husband was for several years a United States senator.
April 10, 1810.—Mrs. Stickle, wife of Solomon Stickle.
April 26, 1810.—Mrs. Beall, wife of Wm. M. Beall, postmaster.
May 27, 1810.—Thomas McElderry, Esq., one of the senators of the Maryland Legislature.
July 10, 1810.—Capt. Thomas Sprigg.
July 19, 1810.—Hieronimus Size.
Sept. 15, 1810.—Mr. Leaver.
Nov. 22, 1810.—George Schnertzell, Sr.
Nov. 24, 1810.—Erickson H. Stone.
Nov. 24, 1810.—Jacob Wise.
Nov. 25, 1810.—Maj. Jacob Miller.
Nov. 29, 1810.—Col. George Stricker, at his residence in Virginia, aged 78. He was formerly of Frederick County, Md., and took an active and prominent part in the Revolutionary war.
Dec. 17, 1810.—Rev. Daniel Wayman, at York, Pa., aged 61, formerly pastor of the German Reformed Church of Frederick.
Jan. 17, 1811.—Samuel Duvall, surveyor of Frederick County.
Feb. 26, 1811.—Rev. Peter Kemp.
Feb. 27, 1811.—John Baltzer, an inn-keeper.
April 13, 1811.—Thomas Noland.
April 25, 1811.—Col. Normand Bruce.
May 26, 1811.—Roger Edminson.
May 27, 1811.—George Jacob Schley.
June 16, 1811.—Col. Baker Johnson.
Oct. 1, 1811.—Mrs. Margaret Hoff, aged 86.
Feb. 14, 1812.—Samuel Potts.
Feb. 21, 1812.—At Frederick Town, in the 85th year of her age, Mrs. Jane Hanson, relict of Hon. John Hanson, a delegate from Maryland to the old Revolutionary Congress, and president of that body in Philadelphia in the period of 1781–82. Mrs. Hanson, whose maiden name was Jane Contee, was a native of Prince George's County, but had resided a great part of her life in Frederick, of which, at the time of her death, she was one of the oldest inhabitants. She survived her husband thirty years, and had lived to mourn the last of a numerous family of children. One of them, her youngest son, Lieut. Peter Contee Hanson, just entering into manhood, devoted himself to the service of his country in the struggle for independence, and fell at the battle of Fort Washington in 1776. Her eldest son, and the last of her children to die before her, was Alexander Contee Hanson, chancellor of Maryland.
March 7, 1812.—Mrs. Elizabeth Brengle, wife of Christian Brengle.
March 7, 1812.—Daniel Stouffer, Sr., at an advanced age.
May 8, 1812.—Valentine Shriner.

Dec. 24, 1812.—Rebecca Shriver, wife of David Shriver, aged 71.
Sept. 5, 1813.—Mrs. Margaret Johnson, relict of Col. James Johnson, aged 64.
Nov. 12, 1813.—Philemon Barnes, aged 90.
Dec. 31, 1813.—Maj. Charles Baltzell, at his farm near Woodborough, aged 77. He was a native of Germany, and in his youth served several campaigns in the Seven Years' war. He subsequently emigrated to this country and settled in Maryland. He was a soldier in the Revolutionary war from the beginning until the army was disbanded, when he became a member of The Society of the Cincinnati.
June 9, 1814.—Mrs. Catherine Johnson, widow of Col. Baker Johnson.
July 1, 1814.—Rev. Frederick V. Melsheimer, aged 64, for many years pastor of the Lutheran congregation at Hanover. He was master of Arabic, Syriac, Hebrew, Greek, and Latin.
July 28, 1815.—At his home near Georgetown, D. C., Philip Barton Key, member of Congress.
May 2, 1815.—John Hanson Thomas, one of the most eminent and eloquent of the legislators of the State, aged 39.
Jan. 13, 1817.—Wm. Potts, aged 76.
May 15, 1817.—Arthur Shaaf, in the 49th year of his age, a native of Frederick County, but for many years a resident of Annapolis, where he practiced law.
Jan. 3, 1818.—James M. Haffie, formerly postmaster, and president of the Bank of Westminster, aged 39.
April 26, 1818.—John Baer, aged 63.
Feb. 2, 1819.—David Stoner.
Feb. 2, 1819.—Conrad Englebrecht.
Feb. 26, 1819.—John Brunner.
March 30, 1819.—John Hughes.
April 23, 1819.—Alexander C. Hanson, aged 33.
May 7 or 14, 1819.—At Giesborough, John T. Shaaf, aged 56.
May 8, 1819.—Richard Brooks, aged 44. Mr. Brooks was a distinguished member of the bar.
June 22, 1819.—Madame De La Vincendiere, aged 65.
Aug. 26, 1819.—Wm. Baer, Sr.
1819.—John Payan Baneuff, a refugee from San Domingo in 1794; had 800 acres of land at Frederick Junction, and owned many slaves.
Nov. 9, 1819.—Ex-Governor Thomas Sim Lee, in his 75th year.
May 27, 1820.—Francis Bingest, a native of Germany, aged 103 years.
June 27, 1820.—John Thomas Steiner, aged 31.
Nov. 5, 1820.—Peter Hawman.
Nov. 7, 1820.—John Fessler.
Nov. 11, 1815.—Johannes George Meyer.
Dec. 1, 1820.—James Wright, tailor.
Dec. 8, 1820.—Mrs. Jacob Hoffman, aged 52.
April 5, 1821.—William Findlay, a soldier of the Revolution.
April 19, 1821.—Jacob Medtart, aged 67.
July 3, 1821.—Richard White (printer), aged 34.
July 6, 1821.—Sarah, wife of Col. John McPherson, aged 55.
Jan. 10, 1821.—Elizabeth C. Potts.
Jan. 11, 1821.—Peter Hardt, Sr., schoolmaster, and organist of German Reformed Church. He was a Hessian prisoner.
Jan. 17, 1821.—Jacob Steiner, aged 27.
Jan. 21, 1821.—Michael Allix, oldest person in town, aged 94.
March 29, 1821.—Henry Koontz, aged 94; came to Frederick at the age of 22. By trade a blacksmith, he soon made enough money in that business to purchase a small farm on Pipe Creek, where he lived for 57 years. He raised ten children, and left six children, one hundred grandchildren, and one hundred and thirty-five great-grandchildren.

July 23, 1821.—Francis Marcilly, a Frenchman.
July 24, 1821.—Edward Carlton, aged 93.
July 26, 1821.—Barbara Grove, widow of Jacob Grove, lime-burner.
Aug. 21, 1821.—Peter Brumsberger, aged 54.
Aug. 31, 1821.—Harriet, wife of Dr. William Bradley Tyler, and daughter of George Murdock.
Sept. 11, 1821.—Jacob Smith, son of late Jacob Smith, tavern-keeper, "up the pike 3 miles."
Sept. 16, 1821.—Independent Gist, son of Gen. Mordecai Gist, aged 40.
Sept. 11, 1821.—Capt. William Campbell, a wealthy citizen.
Sept. 12, 1821.—Michael Baltzell, Sr.
Sept. 30, 1821.—John Doll, aged 46.
Oct. 2, 1821.—Peter Brumer, aged 97, the oldest inhabitant of the county.
Oct. 4, 1821.—Jacob Malambre, shoemaker, aged 52.
Oct. 10, 1821.—Lewis B. Appollo, a native of San Domingo, and a resident of Frederick since the insurrection of that island in 1793.
Oct. 17, 1821.—Gen. John Ross Key, an officer of the Revolution.
Oct. 18, 1821.—John Woodrow, aged 70, late county surveyor.
Nov. 22, 1821.—Mrs. Rebecca Ogle.
Dec. 14, 1821.—John Bruner, miller.
Dec. 26, 1821.—Dr. Gerard Joseph Schneider, a native of Dusseldorf, Germany, and partner of Dr. Godfrey Wise.
1821.—Michael Allex, butcher, aged 90.
March 1, 1822.—William Housz, aged 90.
March 5, 1822.—Jacob Bruner, aged 63.
March 26, 1822.—Henrietta, widow of the late Rev. John A. Krug, pastor of Lutheran Church, aged 71.
May 26, 1822.—Gen. Henry Carbery, aged 66.
June 4, 1822.—At his residence in Washington, Lawrence Brengle, formerly of Frederick.
Sept. 9, 1822.—Henry Getzendanner, aged 48.
Oct. 3, 1822.—The Rev. Francis Malevie, aged 52 years, and for 13 years pastor of the Catholic congregation of Frederick.
Oct. 19, 1822.—Gen. Thomas H. Cushing, collector of the New London (Conn.) port, aged 67.
Oct. 19, 1822.—Henry Koontz, aged 37.
Oct. 24, 1822.—Robert Patterson.
Oct. 26, 1822.—John Slisor, aged 80.
Nov. 9, 1822.—Lieut. Charles T. Stallings, of the United States navy, a victim to the epidemic in Havana.
Nov. 15, 1822.—Thomas Hoffman, aged 29.
Dec. 18, 1822.—John J. Ott, aged 68.
Dec. 31, 1822.—Rev. James Redmond, aged 47, for several years pastor of the Roman Catholic congregation of Washington and Allegany Counties.
Jan. 28, 1823.—Col. John Bowie, of Bladensburg, while attending service in Dr. Lowrie's church.
Feb. 22, 1823.—Henry Groff, aged 64.
Feb. 7, 1823.—Robert T. Dade, formerly a representative of Montgomery County in the State Legislature, and an officer in the war of 1812, aged 80.
March 10, 1823.—Dr. Wm. Bantz, aged 34.
March 10, 1823.—Richard Mills, keeper of the poor-house.
April 25, 1823.—Wm. Miller, pump-maker.
May 22, 1823.—Francis Mantz, aged 75.
Sept. 6, 1823.—Richard Neakes, tailor.
Sept. 6, 1823.—George Creager, ex-sheriff, aged 46.
Oct. —, 1823.—John G. Harpner and Benj. Winter, both formerly of Frederick, of yellow fever, at Natchez, Miss.
Oct. 21, 1823.—Augustus Taney, aged 36.

Nov. 5, 1823.—Wm. M. Beall, aged 81.
Dec. 13, 1823.—James Lindsey, weaver, a native of county Tyrone, Ireland.
March 1, 1824.—Samuel Mixdorf, aged 79.
April 17, 1724.—William Stewart, a native of Leeds, England, a painter and musician.
July 28, 1824.—Monsieur Joseph B. Charles, dancing-master.
Aug. 20, 1824.—Thos. Bailey, a Revolutionary soldier.
Nov. 24, 1824.—Adam Coons, negro, aged 85, the only colored man ever confirmed in Frederick County as a regular member of the Lutheran Church. He was formerly a slave of Michael Boemer, one of the founders of the church, and was the first colored man buried in the Lutheran graveyard.
Feb. 3, 1825.—Anna Maria Ramsburg, widow of John Ramsburg, Sr., aged 84.
April 6, 1825.—Mathias Bartgis, who established the first newspaper in Frederick.
May 18, 1825.—Capt. Henry Steiner, register of wills.
June 5, 1825.—A colored man belonging to John Hughes stabbed to death by Francis Martin, son of John Martin, a tailor.
July 15, 1825.—Gen. Joseph Swearingen, late of the Ninth Brigade Militia.
Aug. 28, 1825.—Rev. Peter A. Thomson, of St. Mary's County, at Tarbut's inn. His death was occasioned by mortification, resulting from the breaking of his jaw-bone in the drawing of a tooth.
Sept. 10, 1825.—Jacob Faubel, a mason, aged 70. He was one of the Hessian regiment during the Revolution, and was taken prisoner in New Jersey.
Oct. 4, 1825.—Daniel Leab, aged 21. While he was drawing a load from a gun it went off, and the bullet passed through his left eye, causing death in twenty minutes.
Nov. 14, 1825.—Maj.-Gen. Robert Cummings, commander of the Second Division of Maryland militia, aged 72.
Dec. 1, 1825.—Mrs. Lucy Sprigg, widow of Thomas Sprigg, aged 74.
Jan. 6, 1826.—Adolphus Wilhelm, killed by a runaway accident.
Jan. 27, 1826.—Benjamin Harwood, trustee of the State of Maryland, and treasurer of the Western Shore.
Feb. 1, 1826.—Lewis Green, teller in the Branch Bank, and brother of the editor of the *Maryland Gazette*.
Feb. 1, 1826.—Mrs. Ann Maria Meyers, aged 81.
Dec. 4, 1826.—Col. John C. Cockey and John R. Pitt, members-elect of the Legislature.
Nov. 16, 1826.—Col. John Ritchie, aged 70.
Dec. 15, 1826.—Mrs. Anna Ritchie, wife of John Ritchie, aged 55.
Feb. 28, 1827.—Capt. John R. Corberly, aged 45; buried in Catholic cemetery.
April 22, 1827.—Harriet, wife of John Brein, and daughter of Col. John McPherson, at Catoctin Furnace, aged 43.
June 9, 1827.—George Getzendanner, surveyor of Frederick County.
Sept. 1, 1827.—Frederick Markley, aged 31.
Sept. 14, 1827.—Francis Kleinert, aged 76. He was a Hessian soldier in the Revolutionary war, was captured in New Jersey, and was buried in a vault made by himself.
Sept. 28, 1827.—Thomas Bond, aged 60.
Dec. 28, 1827.—Rev. Nicholas Smith (colored), of the Methodist (Asbury) Church.
March 30, 1828.—Joseph Smith, aged 64, and for forty years agent of "Carroll's Manor." He was buried in the Catholic graveyard.

Sept. 4, 1828.—Mrs. Francina Chestor Schley, wife of Frederick A. Schley, and daughter of Capt. David Lynn, of Allegany County.

Sept. 15, 1828.—Christopher Hickman, who came to America with the Hessian regiments during the Revolutionary war, aged 76.

Nov. 2, 1828.—Mrs. Sophia Brunner, aged 80.

April 4, 1829.—Miss Dehouline, aged 80, a native of France, who with a sister, who died the year previous, settled at Frederick immediately after the San Domingo revolution of 1793.

May 28, 1829.—John Brunner, aged 81.

Sept. 8, 1829.—Col. Stephen Steiner, aged 61.

Oct. 16, 1829.—John Jacob Schley, in Louisville, Jefferson Co., Ga., father of Frederick A. Schley, and born in Frederick County, aged 77.

Dec. 2, 1829.—Col. John McPherson.

March 23, 1830.—Christian Froelich, aged 75, a Revolutionary soldier.

June 23, 1830.—Joseph Bell and —— Klaus, killed by falling off a bank of earth on the railroad just where it crosses the Georgetown turnpike.

Aug. 17, 1831.—John Walker (tobacconist), aged 77, a Revolutionary soldier.

Aug. 18, 1831.—Daniel Hauer, who lived in Frederick since 1771, aged 84.

Sept. 10, 1831.—John Leather, aged 76, a Revolutionary soldier, who was wounded at Brandywine. For a number of years he was an elder in the Lutheran Church.

Sept. 13, 1831.—Catharine Tyler, wife of Dr. John Tyler, aged 61.

May 29, 1829.—At Marseilles, France, the Rev. Michael Du Bourg Egan, nephew of the first Catholic Bishop of Philadelphia, and formerly president of Mount St. Mary's Seminary, at Emmittsburg, aged 29.

May 4, 1831.—Rev. Basil D. Higgins, a member of the Baltimore Annual Conference, aged 24.

Aug. 31, 1832.—Rev. Samuel Knox, aged 76.

Sept. 11, 1832.—Judge Jacob Steiner, of the Orphans' Court, aged 70.

Oct. 27, 1832.—John Gebhardt, aged 82.

Dec. 7, 1832.—Prof. John M. Schenck, organist of All Saints' Church; found dead in his bed at Mrs. Murray's tavern.

Jan. 10, 1833.—Maj. Peter Mantz, aged 81.

March 6, 1833.—Peter Brengle, high sheriff.

March 20, 1833.—John Graham, president Frederick County Bank, aged 73.

June 14, 1833.—Mrs. Ann E. Harrison, wife of Wm. G. Harrison, of Baltimore, and daughter of Wm. Ross.

June 10, 1833.—Abraham White, in the 88th year of his age. A native of Pennsylvania, he emigrated to Frederick County, Md., some time prior to the Revolutionary war, and was among the first to enter the Revolutionary army. He was active in recruiting troops, and by his exertions in a short time organized a company, of which he became captain, and which was attached to Capt. Bruce's battalion. He remained in command until 1780, when he was appointed by the commander of the French forces, then at Williamsburg, first conductor of the First Brigade of Artillery, with a major's commission, in which capacity he acted until the general disbandment. In 1802 he removed to Baltimore, where he resided for many years.

Oct. 28, 1833.—Thos. Gordon, inn-keeper.

Dec. 29, 1833.—Adam Sluival, aged 74; came to America in 1777, and was of the "Bayreuth Regiment."

Feb. 12, 1834.—George Mayberry, tavern-keeper.

July 23, 1834.—Mrs. Anna Catharine Hauer, widow of Daniel Hauer, and a native of Germany, aged 92.

Dec. 11, 1834.—Wm. Coleman Brier, aged 22, at Antietam Iron-Works.

Dec. 18, 1834.—Mrs. Ann Key, relict of Philip B. Key, at the residence of her son-in-law, Rev. Mr. Nevins.

July 17, 1835.—John Reich, Sr., aged 71.

Oct. 31, 1835.—John Schley, clerk of the court since 1815.

Nov. 23, 1835.—Ex-Sheriff Thomas Carlton, aged 54.

Jan. 7, 1836.—Capt. J. L. Kuhn, United States army.

Jan. 27, 1836.—Rev. Frederick D. Schaeffer, D.D., aged 76.

March 9, 1837.—Dorothea, sister of Chief Justice Taney.

May 5, 1837.—Rev. David F. Schaeffer, of an apoplectic fit, formerly pastor of the Lutheran Church. He was found dead in his bed, aged 51.

May 26, 1837.—John R. Key, son of F. S. Key.

Oct. 14, 1837.—Hon. L. Harding, chief justice of the Orphans' Court of Frederick County, aged 59.

Aug. 16, 1837.—J. P. W. Amelung, originally from Germany, and a resident of Baltimore, aged 48.

Dec. 16, 1837.—Dr. Henry Baker, one of the elders and class-leaders of the Methodist Episcopal Church at Liberty Town, aged 60.

January, 1838.—Mordecai Vore, keeper of toll-gate at Catoctin Mountain.

April 29, 1838.—Col. Philemon Griffith, an officer of the Revolutionary war, at New Market, aged 82.

May 31, 1838.—John Jacob Baltzell, aged 87.

Sept. 8, 1838.—James Dixon, attorney-at-law.

July 19, 1838.—Christian Getzendanner, proprietor of the *Frederick Times and Democratic Advocate*, aged 47.

July 13, 1838.—Near Tallahassee, Col. Baker Johnson, formerly of Frederick Co., Md., in the 50th year of his age, leaving a wife and five children to mourn their irreparable loss. Col. Johnson was the son of Col. Baker Johnson, of Frederick Town, Md.

Nov. 14, 1838.—At the residence of his son-in-law, Daniel Wetler, near Creagerstown, Frederick Co., Md., Maj. Frederick Willhide, a soldier of the Revolution, in the 85th year of his age. Maj. Willhide on the 2d of November, 1776, enlisted in the German regiment of this State for three years, during which period he was promoted to orderly sergeant in the company to which he was attached, and faithfully served out the term of his enlistment; he afterwards acted as volunteer until the close of the war. During the period of his service he was engaged in some of the hardest-fought battles of the Revolution, having been present at Brandywine, Germantown, Trenton, and Monmouth, and witnessed the closing struggle at Yorktown. Maj. Willhide afterwards commanded a company of volunteers, and was subsequently commissioned a major in the old Maryland line, though he was never in any active service after the war.

Nov. 25, 1838.—Joseph Little, 77 years of age.

Oct. 31, 1839.—Casper Mantz, aged 64.

Dec. 22, 1840.—Wm. Carlton, almost instantly killed while running with the Junior Fire Company.

July 2, 1839.—Sister Genevieve, Superior of St. John's Female Academy and Orphan Asylum. Her family name was Resetha Tyler.

Dec. 17, 1839.—Rev. Wm. McSherry, president of the Georgetown College.

June 29, 1841.—Valentine Brunner, aged 84, a Revolutionary soldier.

Aug. 22, 1841.—Dr. Grafton Duvall, aged 62.

Sept. 16, 1841.—Daniel Hauer, aged 74.

Oct. 15, 1841.—Dr. John Tyler, aged 79.

May 17, 1842.—Capt. Daniel Prengle, of the "Mohawk Invincibles."

Nov. 28, 1843.—Frederick Englebrecht, born in Frederick, Aug. 3, 1786.

Feb. 20, 1845.—Rev. Nathaniel L. Mills, of the Methodist Episcopal Church, and member of the Baltimore Annual Conference, aged 79, and in the 58th year of his ministry.

July 2, 1846.—Rev. Dennis Mouldon, of smallpox.

Dec. 15, 1846.—Hon. Francis Brengle, aged 40. He was formerly a member of the Maryland Legislature, and afterwards a member of Congress.

Feb. 17, 1848.—Henry Bear, aged 91, the last of the Revolutionary survivors of Frederick County. He entered the army in 1776 as a volunteer. He was one of the company that marched from Frederick under the command of Capt. Peter Mantz, and which formed a part of the old Maryland line.

July 29, 1848.—Judge Abraham Shriver.

Jan. 31, 1849.—Thomas Turner, editor of the Frederick *Herald*. Mr. Turner was collector of the port of Georgetown, D. C., about 1837, at which time he was also editor of the *Potomac Advocate*. He was shortly after appointed clerk of the Chesapeake and Ohio Canal Company, and followed the office on its removal from Washington to Frederick City, where he subsequently resided. On the removal of the office from Frederick to Cumberland he resigned his post, and devoted himself entirely to the editorial management of the *Herald*, in which position he continued up to the time of his death. He also represented Frederick City in the Legislature.

Aug. 5, 1849.—M. E. Bartgis, mayor of Frederick. He was by profession a printer, and edited and published a paper in Frederick for many years.

Aug. 10, 1849.—At Petersville, Col. John Thomas, father of ex-Governor Francis Thomas, of Maryland, aged 85.

Nov. 10, 1849.—John Casper Freitchie, aged 70, husband of Barbara Freitchie, of Whittier's poem.

1851.—Dr. Edward Goldsborough.

1851.—Col. Thomas C. Brashear.

April 1, 1851.—John Ebert, aged 79.

May, 1851.—Thomas S. Dulany, merchant.

March 25, 1852.—Henry McElfresh, member of Assembly, elected only a few weeks before his death to fill a vacancy.

Dec. 19, 1852.—William Ross, a prominent member of the Frederick bar, and president of the Frederick Branch of the Farmers' Bank of Maryland, aged 81.

Oct. 14, 1852.—David Schley, for several years editor of the Frederick *Examiner*.

April 30, 1852.—David Shriver, a native of Frederick County, but for many years a resident and prominent citizen of Cumberland, Md., in the 85th year of his age. Mr. Shriver was selected by the Hon. Albert Gallatin, the Secretary of the Treasury, as engineer to lay out and construct the great National road from Cumberland to Wheeling, and on its completion was appointed by the general government commissioner of public works. He surveyed and superintended the construction of the Reisterstown turnpike, and took a prominent part in building the plank-road from Cumberland to West Newton. He also served as a delegate in the Legislature from Frederick County, and for a long time was president of the Cumberland Bank of Allegany.

Oct. 20, 1853.—Wm. Thompson Palmer, in St. Louis.

Feb. 25, 1854.—Rev. Nicholas Dorsey, of the Methodist Protestant Church, at New Market.

March 1, 1855.—John P. Thompson, the founder and for a long time the editor of the Frederick *Herald*, and president of the Frederick County Bank, aged 79.

Nov. 8, 1855.—George Bowlus, formerly a member of the Maryland Legislature.

Feb. 9, 1856.—Samuel Geyer, the father of Dr. J. W. Geyer, editor of the Frederick *Union*.

July 26, 1856.—Dr. Samuel Tyler, aged 36.

April 12, 1857.—Col. Edward Schley.

April 13, 1857.—Mary Ann Evitt.

Nov. 27, 1857.—John Rohr, born in Frederick in 1757.

Nov. 1, 1858.—Ex-Governor Wm. Schley, of Georgia. The deceased was born at Frederick, Md., in 1776, but for many years was a prominent citizen of Georgia, having been a judge of the Superior Court as early as 1825, a member of the Legislature in 1830, and of Congress from 1832 to 1835, when he was elected Governor of the State. For twenty-five years he was the Grand High Priest of the Royal Arch (Masonic) Chapter of the State, and at the time of his death president of the Medical College of Georgia.

June 22, 1858.—Caspar Mantz, ex-sheriff of Frederick County.

Dec. 29, 1858.—Clark Koontz, formerly one of the editors of the Frederick *Union*.

April 14, 1860.—Hon. William Cost Johnson, a native of Frederick County, at Washington City, aged 54.

Feb. 12, 1862.—Mrs. Agnes Houston, widow of James F. Houston.

July 7, 1862.—Dr. William Waters, aged 62.

Dec. 18, 1862.—At 6 P.M., Mrs. Barbara Freitchie, the heroine of Whittier's poem. She was born Dec. 3, 1766, and was the widow of John C. Freitchie. She lived in a house next to the Bentztown bridge, south side, which the corporation bought in 1868 with the lot of George Eissler, and on April 3, 1869, sold the house to James Hopewood for $300, who removed it. The corporation found it necessary to widen Carroll Creek, running through the town, and this house being in the way had to be removed.

Jan. 16, 1863.—Rev. Josiah Varden, aged 57. He joined the Methodist Protestant Church in 1828, soon after its organization, and was at once placed among the active preachers, and continued in the service until about ten years before his death, when failing health compelled him to ask retirement to the superannuated list. While an active member he was for three successive terms chosen president of the Maryland Annual Conference, and was twice stationed in Baltimore, at the East and West Baltimore Churches.

March, 1865.—Rev. Mr. Olemieyer, Professor of Chemistry of St. Mary's College, Emmittsburg.

June 7, 1866.—Professor Wm. Baer, aged 79, a well-known chemist and specialist in agricultural chemistry.

1867.—Dr. John W. Dutrow.

May, 1867.—Benjamin F. Bartgis, aged 73, formerly editor of the Republican *Gazette*, and subsequently of the *Hornet* newspapers, which were published in the interests of the Republican party, under old party divisions and in fierce opposition to the Federal party.

Feb. 21, 1868.—At Frederick, Father Matthaw Sanders, a well-known Catholic priest. He was born in Holland in 1807, and was there ordained in 1831. The next year he came to America, and entered the novitiate of the Society of Jesus in Maryland. He was appointed to take charge of some of the missions in Charles County, later he was transferred to St. Mary's and Prince George's Counties, and in 1858 was removed to the Eastern Shore, where he continued until within a few months of his death.

Feb. 22, 1870.—Joseph M. Palmer, the eminent lawyer.

March 8, 1871.—Mrs. Lucinda Greenwell, aged 101 years 9 months and 23 days.

May 17, 1871.—John Lee, of Medwood, aged 83. He was the son of Thomas Sim Lee, Governor of Maryland.

March 11, 1871.—Louis Elder, of Emmittsburg, aged 73; he left a large number of relatives in Baltimore.

April 1, 1871.—Maj. Henry Schley, an aged and influential citizen, at the residence of his son, Dr. Fairfax Schley. He was adjutant of Col. Chambers' regiment during the war of 1812, and served at Bladensburg and Baltimore. Prior to the constitution of 1851 he was clerk of the Frederick County Court, and afterwards for several years the cashier of the Frederick County Bank. He was a brother of William Schley, the well-known lawyer.

April, 1872.—John E. Naill, brother of Hon. David W. Naill, at his residence in Illinois. He was born at Taneytown, Md., graduated at Pennsylvania College, Gettysburg, Pa., studied law in the office of Hon. James Cooper, formerly a United States senator from Pennsylvania, and went to Illinois when quite a young man. There he accumulated a very considerable estate. He was a Democrat, and in 1860 served on the Breckenridge and Lane electoral ticket. His party repeatedly tendered him the nomination for Congress in his district, and he was also solicited to accept the nomination for Governor of his adopted State, but having no taste for public life declined both nominations.

Sept. 21, 1872.—Col. A. B. Hanson, an old merchant, who served honorably in the war of 1812.

March 11, 1874.—Col. John McPherson, aged 78.

Feb. 27, 1877.—Col. Daniel S. Biser, at Burkittsville, aged 75. Of Mr. Biser it may be said that he was in official harness during nearly the whole course of his life. He was elected to the State Legislature many times (once on the reformed Union ticket with Hon. Francis Thomas and Gen. Edward Shriver). In the winter of 1842-43 he was Speaker of the House of Delegates, and presided over that body with marked ability. He held various other positions also, prominent among which were assistant flour inspector under Governor Lowe, flour inspector-general under Governor Ligon, clerk of the Circuit Court of this county, by appointment from Judge Nelson, to fill the unexpired term of J. W. L. Carty, member of the Chesapeake and Ohio Canal Board for a number of years, etc. Although an active politician and a stanch Democrat, he was highly respected and esteemed by his political opponents as well as friends.

June 18, 1879, the dead body of Rev. John M. Friday, pastor of the Lutheran Church at Harper's Ferry, was found in the Chesapeake and Ohio Canal, just above the lock and below the bridge at Harper's Ferry. The circumstances attending his death were stated by a newspaper account, written at the time, to have been as follows: "On last Thursday evening he was engaged by a young couple from Halltown to marry them with the utmost secrecy on the Maryland side of the river. At the close of the ceremony, some distance above the bridge, he was requested to tarry until the bridal pair could cross the bridge, so that no suspicion of their marriage would be excited by being seen on the bridge in the presence of a minister. On Friday morning the dead body of Mr. Friday was found in the canal above the lock. A silver watch-chain was wound around his left hand, a position habitual to him when standing or leisurely walking. There was a wound along the right temple, extending a little behind the ear. The theory of some is that while waiting for the fifteen minutes to pass, in order that the bridal couple might reach the Virginia shore, and standing on the bank of the canal, a robber stealthily approached and dealt a blow which, striking the temple, produced instantaneous paralysis, and the body fell forward into the water of the canal, without getting the left hand out of the watch-guard. The robber becoming alarmed at the fatal result, not anticipated by him, and the body not rising to the surface, regarded it too perilous to remain long enough to rifle the pockets." Mr. Friday's wife was a daughter of George Whip, of Jefferson, Frederick Co., and the body was interred at that place. The identity of the supposed murderer was never established.

Oct. 14, 1881, at Frederick, Dr. Joseph C. Cockey. Dr. Cockey was a graduate of the University of Maryland, and for many years an intimate friend of the late Prof. Nathan R. Smith. Besides practicing medicine, Dr. Cockey took a great deal of interest at times in local politics. About twenty-five years ago he represented the Fourth Ward of Baltimore in the City Council, and in 1877 was an unsuccessful candidate for the State Senate. He was identified with the Republican party. At one time Dr. Cockey had an exceedingly large practice, but as he was compelled to visit Frederick frequently to attend kinspeople there, his practice gradually fell off. He was comparatively well-to-do, however. In the summer of 1881 a kinsman, Dr. J. Hanson Cockey, of Rye, N. Y., died, and he went there to settle his business affairs. The funeral took place at Frederick, and the remains were interred in Mount Olivet Cemetery.

The General Assembly in 1778 passed an act for the relief of the maimed officers, soldiers, and seamen from Maryland engaged in the Revolutionary cause. Under its provisions those in necessitous circumstances were entitled to half-pay, and the children of those deceased to certain annuities. The records of the Orphans' Court show that the children and wives of the following soldiers from Western Maryland availed themselves of this act:

William Parsons, died in service.
William Bright, died in service.
Charles Williams, died in service.
David Miller, died in service.
Samuel Hanniss, wounded.
Spera Migea, wounded.
John Meek, Seventh Regiment, wounded at Guilford.
John Brown (sergeant), Sixth Regiment, wounded at Camden.
Robert Kerns (sergeant), Second Regiment, wounded.
James Burk, Second Regiment, wounded at Cowpens.
James Garth, Second Regiment, wounded at siege of Ninety-Six.
John Alsop, Second Regiment, wounded at Cowpens.
George Burklup, First Regiment, wounded at Eutaw.
Christopher Lambert, Third Regiment, wounded in Carolinas.
Michael Waltman, First Regiment, wounded at Guilford.
Philip Fisher, First Regiment, wounded at Guilford.
John Ober, wounded.
John Auber (sergeant), Second Regiment, wounded.
Luke Lawson, First Regiment, wounded at Guilford.
James Shehan, Second Regiment, wounded at Monmouth.
Peter Cunningham, Seventh Regiment, wounded in South Carolina.
John Stresner, Seventh Regiment, wounded at Germantown.

Edward Rose, wounded in New Jersey.
John Snider (corporal), lost his leg in Flying Camp.
Paul Haggerty, disabled.
John Shovell, Sixth Regiment, wounded at Camden.

CHAPTER XXIV.

COUNTY OFFICERS.

THE first election ever held in Frederick County took place March 7, 1749, for delegates to the General Assembly. The following were elected: Henry Wright Crabb, Thomas Owen, Joseph Chapline, Daniel Dulany.

The first election held in the county after the practical abolition of the Lord Proprietary's government was that at which were chosen the delegates to the convention of the province which assembled at Annapolis on the 22d of June, 1774. This convention, while affirming the allegiance of the people to King George, took care to make due provision for armed defense by the formation of a militia composed of companies of sixty-eight men each, who were to be provided " with a good fire-lock with bayonet fixed thereon," and the requisite quantity of ammunition. The cost of the equipment was to be defrayed by contributions from the different counties, of which Frederick was expected to furnish thirteen hundred and thirty-three pounds, a sum greater by four hundred pounds than that assessed to any other county in the province. In September, 1775, the freeholders of Frederick County met for the purpose of selecting a Committee of Observation (to consist of fifty-three members) for Frederick County. For "the ease and convenience" of the people of Frederick County it was provided that that county should be divided into three districts. The Upper District was bounded by the South Mountain and the lines of the county westward; the Middle District extended from the South Mountain to the Monocacy; the Southern District was bounded by the Monocacy from its mouth to Bennett's Creek, and with that creek to the headwaters of the Patuxent. The place for holding the elections in the Upper District was Elizabethtown (now Hagerstown); in the Middle District, Frederick Town; and in the Lower District, Hungerford's (now Rockville, Montgomery County). In the articles of association adopted at Annapolis, July 26, 1775, it was provided that forty companies of minute-men should be enrolled, of which Frederick was to furnish eight, or thrice as many as any other county with the exception of Baltimore County, whose quota was five companies. The companies in Frederick County were to compose a battalion of themselves. At the convention which met at Annapolis, Dec. 7, 1775, the delegates elected from Frederick County were: Middle District, Charles Beatty and Baker Johnson; Lower District, Henry Griffith. In the convention of May, 1776, the same delegates served, with the addition of William Baird as the representative from the Upper District (now Washington County). On the 16th of May it is recorded that George Brent, a member "for that district of Frederick County which lies west of Locking Creek," appeared and took his seat. In June, 1776, John Stull was associated with Mr. Baird on the representation from the Upper District. On the 2d of July, 1776, the convention adopted resolutions providing for the election of representatives from the different counties to choose a permanent form of government for the State. The judges of election for Frederick County were: Upper District, Noah Hart, Christian Orndorff, and Eli Williams; Middle District, Christopher Edelen, William Luckett, Jr., and David Shriver; Lower District, Jonathan Wilson, Zadock Magruder, and William Luckett, Sr. The convention met at Annapolis, Aug. 14, 1776, and the delegates from Frederick County were: Upper District, Samuel Beall, Samuel Hughes, John Stull, Henry Schnebely; Middle District, Adam Fischer, Upton Sheredine, Christopher Edelen, and David Shriver; Lower District, Thomas Sprigg Wootton, Jonathan Wilson, William Bayly, Jr., and Elisha Williams. On the 8th of November, 1776, the convention adopted a constitution and form of government for Maryland, and an election for officers under the new constitution was held November 25th of the same year. The judges for Frederick County at this election were William Luckett, John Adhun, and Joseph Wells. The justices of the peace who formed the County Court of Frederick at the organization of the new government in 1777 were Normand Bruce, William Blair, Upton Sheredine, William Beatty, Joseph Wells, Jacob Young, George Scott, Christopher Edelen, James Johnson, William Murdock Beall, Carleton Tannehill, William Luckett, Jr., John Lawrence, Basil Dorsey, David Shriver, Joseph Wood, Jr., Ephraim Howard, John Haas, James Fleming, Charles Warfield.

The justices of the Orphans' Court for Frederick County were Normand Bruce, William Blair, Upton Sheredine, William Beatty, and Joseph Wells, and the surveyor was John Hanson, Jr.; the register of wills George Murdock, and the coroners Benjamin Ogle, Leonard Smith, Van Swearingen, and William

Hobbs. At the election of 1786 the following notice was issued:

"Public Notice to the electors of Frederick County is hereby given, that on Monday, the 4th day of September next, is the day appointed by the Constitution for the election of two persons for this county to be Electors of the Senate; and as our representation under the present form of government is a subject of the first magnitude, 'tis to be hoped every person inspired with real or true patriotism will not fail in giving his personal attendance on that day.

"THOMAS BEATTY, *Sheriff.*
"FREDERICK-TOWN, Aug. 28, 1786."

At that time the State Senate, consisting of fifteen members, was chosen by electors from the different counties, and in pursuance of the above notice the electors of Frederick County met at the court-house (the only election precinct), where a poll was opened, which resulted in the unanimous choice of Thomas Johnson and Thomas Sim Lee as electors for the county to choose the Senate, as directed by the State constitution.

On the 18th of September, 1786, the electors met at Annapolis, and selected the following State senators to serve for five years:

Western Shore.—Charles Carroll of Carrollton, Thomas Stone, Thomas Johnson, Richard Barnes, Daniel Carroll, George Plater, John Hall, Richard Ridgely.
Eastern Shore.—John Henry, George Gale, Edward Lloyd, William Hemsley, William Paca, William Perry.

On Oct. 23, 1828, two barbecues were held at Frederick, that of the Adams party at Bentz' pump, and that of the Jackson men in Nixdorff's meadow.

A public meeting of the Jackson Democrats of Frederick County was held at the court-house on the 24th October, 1832, at which it was unanimously decided to withdraw the Democratic electoral ticket of that district, not on account of any objection to Gen. Jackson, but owing to the manner in which the ticket was gotten up.

At the Presidential elections of 1824 and 1828 Frederick, Washington, and Allegany Counties composed an electoral district, and were entitled to choose two electors of President and Vice-President. At each election the friends of Jackson were successful by a small majority. After which time, owing to the wise policy of Gen. Jackson's administration, his friends had increased, and at the approaching election of the fall of 1832 it was supposed that he would receive in the district a majority of at least five hundred votes.

Of this condition of the public sentiment of the counties the Legislature of the State, which was anti-Jackson, was fully sensible, having learned it from Mr. Adams' defeat in 1824 and 1828, and more recently by the vote for electors of the State Senate in September, 1831, when nearly five hundred votes more were given to the friends than to the enemies of Jackson. With the intention, as was alleged, of preventing the fair expression of this sentiment at the November election, the Legislature at its previous session, by a new arrangement of the electoral districts, united with the above-named counties six other counties and the city of Annapolis, in which Mr. Adams in 1828 obtained a majority of seventeen hundred votes, and in which his party still maintained the supremacy. With regard to this action of the Legislature the people of Western Maryland declared that "a more flagrant, a more disgraceful, a more arrogant violation of popular rights is not to be found in the history of any government professing to be republican." The opposition sought to justify their friends in the Legislature with the pretext that the new apportionment of representation by Congress created the necessity of a new arrangement of electoral districts in Maryland. This subterfuge, however, did not screen from public indignation a measure by which the people of Western Maryland were deprived of their political rights. Under the new apportionment law Maryland was entitled to ten electors of President and Vice-President, instead of eleven as before. Under the new law enacted by the Legislature in their arrangement of the districts, the city of Baltimore, then containing 80,625 inhabitants, was authorized to elect two electors, and the people of Baltimore County, which contained 40,251 inhabitants, were empowered to choose one elector. It was asked, if this distribution of three electors was deemed equitable, why did the Legislature suppose it necessary to alter the electoral district composed of Frederick, Washington, and Allegany Counties, in which there were 81,660 inhabitants? These three counties were, however, united with Charles, St. Mary's, and Calvert, which were remote, and with which they had no interests in common equal to those with the adjoining county and city of Baltimore. The friends of Jackson in the district thought it was a design to deprive them of the aid of a large Jackson majority (not less than 2000) in Baltimore County and City, and overwhelm them with the anti-Jackson majority of 1500 in the three southern counties. The reason for the separation of the city from the county of Baltimore was alleged to be as follows: in the county there was a well-known Jackson majority of more than 1500. If to these figures the Legislature had added the majority of 500 in the city, all hope of giving these electors to Mr. Clay would have been vain and futile. Instead of creating one district with a privilege of choosing three electors, the county was authorized to elect one and the city two others. By this arrangement it was hoped that two electors would be added to the Whig ticket. In the other district similar peculation was discernible. The Jackson majorities of Harford, Cecil, and Queen Anne's Counties were to be counterbalanced by the Clay majorities of the other counties of the Eastern Shore, with which they had been associated.

On the 20th of April, 1840, a Whig County Convention was held. There were five log cabins and several barrels of hard cider. The procession was a mile long. Speeches were made by Richard J. Bowie, John P. Kennedy, Governor John Pope, of Kentucky, Edward Stanley, of North Carolina, George H. Proffit, of Indiana, Daniel Jenifer, Wm. Cost Johnson, and S. Teackle Wallis. On June 8, 1840, a Democratic County Convention was held. There were two thousand three hundred persons in the procession. The speakers were Felix Grundy, of Tennessee, Dr. Duncan, of Ohio, Dr. Risteau, Messrs. Ely, Spencer, Mitchell, and Francis Thomas. On June 10, 1840, John W. Bear, "the Ohio Blacksmith," addressed a Harrison meeting in Frederick. In 1840 the "Junior Tippecanoe Club" was organized, with Alex. Russell, president; Lewis H. Steiner and Joseph Yearkle, vice-presidents; Morgan Smallwood, secretary; and Sydney Bantz, treasurer. On Oct. 28, 1840, a Whig barbecue was held at Slater's Woods. On Oct. 23, 1852, a Democratic barbecue was held on Barracks Hill, and speeches were made by Benjamin C. Presstman, Col. W. W. W. Bowie, and Thos. J. McKaig. On Oct. 30, 1852, a Whig barbecue was held, and speeches were made by J. B. Ricaud, A. R. Boteler, R. T. Merrick, J. T. B. Dorsey, and others.

Civil List.

Citizens of Frederick County who have filled the Office of Governor of the State.

Thomas Johnson, 1777-79; Thomas Sim Lee, 1779-82, 1792-94; Francis Thomas, 1841-44; Enoch Louis Lowe, 1851-54.

Citizens of Frederick County who have represented Maryland in the Senate of the United States.

Richard Potts, 1793.

Congressmen from Frederick County to the Continental Congress.

John Hanson, 1781-83; Thomas Sim Lee, 1783-84; Richard Potts, 1781-82.

Natives of Frederick County who have been members of either House of Congress since the adoption of the Constitution.

Upton Sheredine, the first member-elect; George Baer, formerly cashier of Frederick County Bank; Daniel Sheffey, Representative from Virginia; Henry S. Geyer, Senator from Missouri (married Sheffey's sister); James Cooper, Senator from Pennsylvania; Francis Brengle; Francis Thomas; George Cary, Representative from Georgia, son of Dr. John D. Cary, editor of *The Key*; William Schley, Representative from Georgia, and elected Governor of Georgia (1834) on the Union Jackson ticket; John H. Farquhar, Representative from Indiana; Henry R. Warfield; Henry W. Hoffman; Roger Nelson; John Nelson; William Cost Johnson; Jacob M. Kunkel; John Ritchie: Frederick Green, Representative from Tiffin District, Ohio, son of Capt. Lewis Green; John F. O'Neil, Representative from Zanesville District, Ohio; John A. McMahon, Representative from Ohio; Milton G. Urner.

Judges of the Court of Appeals from Frederick County.

Richard Potts, appointed 10th October, 1801; Madison Nelson, elected 1867; William P. Maulsby, appointed 1870, to fill vacancy caused by death of Madison Nelson, until next general election; John Ritchie, appointed in 1881, and afterwards elected to fill the vacancy caused by the death of Richard J. Bowie.

Judges of the General Court from Frederick County.

Alexander Contee Hanson, appointed 9th March, 1778.

Chancellors of the State from Frederick County.

Alexander Contee Hanson, appointed 3d October, 1789.

Judges from Frederick County in the County Courts for the Fifth Judicial District, comprehending the Counties of Frederick, Washington, Montgomery, and Allegany.

Richard Potts, chief justice, appointed 8th January, 1791, and reappointed chief justice 15th October, 1796; William Claggett, chief justice, appointed 28th January, 1802.

Judges from Frederick County in the County Courts for the Fifth Judicial District, comprehending the Counties of Frederick, Washington, and Allegany.

John R. Key, associate judge, appointed January, 1791; Upton Sheredine, associate judge, appointed January, 1791; William Claggett, associate judge, appointed 28th January, 1806; Abraham Shriver, associate judge, appointed 29th January, 1806; Roger Nelson, associate judge, appointed 7th May, 1810; Richard Marshall, associate judge, appointed 1842.

Judge of the Third Judicial Circuit, comprising Frederick and Carroll Counties.

Madison Nelson, elected 1851.

Judge of the Fourth Judicial Circuit, comprising Frederick County.

Madison Nelson, elected 1864.

Judges from Frederick County in the Sixth Judicial Circuit, comprising Frederick and Montgomery Counties.

Madison Nelson, chief judge, elected 1867, died Jan. 1, 1870; John A. Lynch, associate judge, elected 1867; William P. Maulsby, chief judge, appointed 1870, to fill vacancy caused by death of Madison Nelson, until next general election; John Ritchie, appointed March 16, 1881, chief judge, to fill vacancy caused by death of Richard J. Bowie, elected in 1870, and who died in March, 1881.

Frederick County State Senators.

1776, Upton Sheredine; 1781, Abraham Faw; 1786, Thomas Johnson; 1791, Joshua Dorsey; 1801, Dr. John Tyler; 1804, Roger Nelson; 1806, David Shriver; 1811, Thomas Hawkins; 1816, Roger Brooke Taney; 1821, Joshua Cockey; 1826, John Nelson; 1831, Thomas Sappington; 1836, Wm. Schley; 1837, John Lee; 1838, Richard Potts;

1844, Casper Quynn; 1846, David W. Naill; 1850, Jacob M. Kunkel; 1854, Wm. Bradley Tyler; 1857, Anthony Kimmel; 1861, Grayson Eichelberger; 1865, Charles E. Trail; 1867, Joshua Biggs; 1871, Dr. Lewis H. Steiner. Dr. Steiner is the present senator, having been re-elected in 1875 and in 1879.

Members of the House of Delegates from Frederick County from 1749 to 1882.

1749, Henry Wright Crabb, Thomas Owens, Joseph Chaplaine, Daniel Dulany, Jr.; 1750, Thomas Owens, John Smith Prather; 1751-53, Daniel Dulany, Jr., Nathan Magruder, Capt. Henry Wright Crabb, Joseph Chaplaine; 1754-55, Capt. Henry Wright Crabb, Joseph Chaplaine, Capt. Edward Sprigg, Josiah Beall; 1756, Joseph Chaplaine, Josiah Beall; 1757, Capt. Joseph Chaplaine, Edward Dorsey, Thomas Beatty, Col. Thomas Cresap; 1758, Capt. Henry Wright Crabb, Edward Dorsey, Capt. Joseph Chaplaine, Col. Thomas Cresap; 1759-60, Capt. Joseph Chaplaine, Edward Dorsey; 1761, Col. Thos. Cresap, Thomas Beatty, Nathan Magruder, Joseph Chaplaine; 1762, Capt. Joseph Chaplaine, Nathan Magruder; 1763, Col. Thomas Cresap, Capt. Joseph Chaplaine, Nathan Magruder, Thomas Beatty; 1764-65, Col. Thomas Cresap, Joseph Chaplaine, Fielder Gantt, James Smith; 1766, John Gantt, Joseph Chaplaine, James Smith; 1767, Capt. Wm. Luckett, Col. Thos. Cresap, Capt. Joseph Chaplaine, Thomas Jennings; 1768, Thomas Cresap, Thomas Jennings, Wm. Luckett; 1769, Thomas Jennings, Wm. Luckett; 1770, Wm. Luckett; 1771, Wm. Luckett, Jonathan Hager, Thomas Sprigg Wootton, Charles Beatty; 1773, Thomas Sprigg Wootton, Charles Beatty, Jonathan Hager, Henry Griffith; 1774, Henry Griffith, Jacob Funk; 1775, in Provincial Convention, Middle District, Charles Beatty, Baker Johnson; Lower District, Henry Griffith; Upper District, Wm. Baird. For June, 1776, in addition to the above, John Stull. 1776, Provincial Convention, August 14th, Lower District, Thomas S. Wootton, Jonathan Wilson, Wm. Bayly, Jr., Elisha Williams; Middle District, Adam Fischer, Upton Sheredine, Christopher Edelen, David Shriver; Upper District, Samuel Beall, John Stull, Henry Schnebely, Samuel Hughes; 1777, Christopher Edelen, Philip Thomas, Jacob Young, Upton Sheredine; 1779, George Stricker, John Hanson, John Beatty, Fielder Gantt; 1780, Fielder Gantt, Richard Potts, Normand Bruce, John Hanson; 1781, John Hanson, Thomas Beatty, Samuel Duvall, David Shriver; 1782, David Shriver, Thomas Ogle, Samuel Duvall, Peter Mantz; 1783, Thomas Beatty, David Shriver, Nathan Hammond, Thomas Ogle; 1784, Thomas Beatty, Thomas Gantt, John D. Carey, David Shriver; 1785, Abraham Faw, John Beatty, Mountjoy Bayly, John D. Carey; 1786, Abraham Faw, Peter Mantz, Thomas Johnson, Mountjoy Bayly; 1787, Thomas Sim Lee, Thomas Johnson, Abraham Faw, Richard Potts; 1788, Richard Potts, Abraham Faw, John McPherson, John Gwinn; 1789, Abraham Faw, David Shriver, Mountjoy Bayly, Joshua Dorsey; 1790, Jacob Gomber, Thomas Beatty, Mountjoy Bayly, John McPherson; 1791, John Ross Key, William Beatty, Patrick Sim Smith, George Burkhart; 1792, William Beatty, Joshua Dorsey, Francis Brown Sappington, Roger Nelson; 1793, Wm. Beatty, Mountjoy Bayly, Roger Nelson, Benedict Jameson; 1794, George Baer, Jr., Benedict Jameson, Wm. Beatty, David Shriver; 1795, George Baer, Valentine Brother, William Beatty, David Shriver; 1796, Valentine Brother, Allen Quynn, Jr., Wm. Beatty, David Shriver; 1797, Henry Ridgely Warfield, John Thomas, Upton Bruce, Joshua Gist; 1798, Henry Ridgely Warfield, John Gwinn, John Thomas, Upton Bruce; 1799, Francis B. Sappington, Henry R. Warfield, John Thomas, David Shriver; 1800-2, David Shriver, Thomas Hawkins, Roger Nelson, Henry Kemp; 1803, Thomas Hawkins, David Shriver, Daniel Clark, Henry Kemp; 1804, Daniel Clark, Joab Waters, Joshua Cockey, Thomas Hawkins; 1805, Thomas Hawkins, Joab Waters, Joshua Cockey, Henry Kuhn; 1806, Thomas Hawkins, Joab Waters, Henry Kuhn, Benjamin Biggs; 1807, Benjamin Biggs, Thomas Hawkins, Henry Kuhn, David Shriver, Jr.; 1808, George Baer, John H. Thomas, Francis B. Sappington, John Thomas; 1809, John Thomas, George Baer, John H. Thomas, John Schley; 1810, John Schley, Richard Brooke, Joseph Swearingen, Joshua Cockey; 1811, Joseph Swearingen, Thomas Jones, Isaac Shriver, William Tyler; 1812, John Graham, Ignatius Davis, Richard Potts, Joshua Delaplane; 1813, John Thomas, John Delaplane, John Hanson Thomas, John Grahame; 1814, John Thomas, Joshua Howard, Joseph Taney, Sr., John H. Thomas; 1815, John Thomas, Joseph Taney, Joseph Howard, James Johnson; 1816, Richard Potts, Joseph Taney, Joshua Howard, Ignatius Davis; 1817, Thomas Hawkins, Beane S. Pigman, William Downey, George Buckey; 1818, Joshua Cockey, Thomas C. Worthington, John H. Smith, Thomas Hawkins; 1819, Alexander Warfield, William Ross, Plummer Ijams, Thomas Hawkins; 1820, Alexander Warfield, Robert G. McPherson, Ignatius Davis, Joshua Cockey; 1821, Henry Kemp, Beane S. Pigman, Henry Culler, Upton Bruce; 1822, Henry Kemp, Francis Thomas, William P. Farquhar, John Fisher; 1823, Henry Kemp, John Fisher, Nicholas Turbutt, Joseph M. Cromwell; 1824, Henry Kemp, Joseph M. Cromwell, William P. Farquhar, Samuel Barnes; 1825-26, John C. Cockey, Samuel Barnes, Thomas Sappington, William P. Farquhar; 1827, Francis Thomas, David Kemp, Nicholas Holtz, Isaac Shriver; 1828-29, David Kemp, George Bowlus, William S. M. McPherson, Jacob Shriver; 1830, David Richardson, David Kemp, Evan McKinstry, John H. McElfresh; 1831, William C. Johnson, Davis Richardson, Evan McKinstry, Abraham Jones; 1832, William C. Johnson, Abdiel Unkefer, David Schley, Thomas Hammond; 1833, David Schley, Joseph M. Palmer, Abdiel Unkefer, John Sifford; 1834, William Roberts, Robert Annan, Francis Brengle, Daniel Duvall; 1835, William Willis, Robert Annan, Daniel Duvall, Isaac Shriver; 1836, Francis Brengle, George Bowlus, Joshua Doub, Jacob Matthias; 1837, Daniel S. Biser, John W. Geyer, George W. Ent, Ezra Cramer; 1838, John McPherson, George Schley, Daniel S. Biser, Grafton Hammond; 1839, John McPherson, Daniel S. Biser, Jacob Firor, John H. Simmons, Casper Quynn; 1840, David Richardson, Joshua Motter, William Lynch, Edward A. Lynch, David W. Naill; 1841, Cornelius Staley, John H. Simmons, James M. Schley, Daniel S. Biser, John W. Geyer; 1842, Davis Richardson, Wm. Lynch, James J. McKeehan, Thomas Crampton, Daniel S. Biser; 1843, Edward Buckey, Wm. Lynch, Otho Thomas, David W. Naill, Edward Shriver; 1844, Edward Shriver, Daniel S. Biser, John H. Worthington, Wm. Cost Johnson, Thomas E. D. Poole; 1845, Daniel S. Biser, Enoch Louis Lowe, Henry Boteler, George Zollinger, Francis J. Hoover; 1846, Peter Grabill, Jacob Root, George Doub, Thomas Turner, Jeremiah G. Morrison; 1847, Wm. Lynch, Gideon Bantz, John Need, Peter Graybill, John D. Gaither; 1849, Thomas H. O'Neal, Wm. P. Anderson, Benjamin A. Cunningham, Jacob Root, Daniel S. Biser; 1852, Davis Richardson, James M. Coale, John Lee, William P. Anderson, James M.

Geyer; 1853, Davis Richardson, James M. Coale, John Lee, Wm. P. Andersen, Joseph M. Geyer, George W. Ent; 1854, Lewis M. Motter, W. C. Sappington, J. T. Johnson, W. T. Gittings, William E. Salmon, David Thomas; 1856, Lawrence J. Brengle, James L. Davis, James S. Carper, Daniel Grove, Peter Hauver, Wm. N. Wolfe; 1858, John B. Thomas, Oliver P. Harding, Stephen R. Bowlus, Jacob Root, John Koons, Ulysses Hobbs; 1860, Thomas J. Claggett, David W. Naill, Jonathan Routzahn, John A. Johnson, Wm. E. Salmon, Andrew Kessler; 1861 (December session), Thomas Hammond, James M. Coale, Hiram Buhrman, Joshua Biggs, Thomas Johnson, Henry R. Harris, (April session) Andrew Kessler, Jr., Thomas J. Claggett, Jonathan Routzahn, John A. Johnson, Wm. E. Salmon; 1862, Thomas Hammond, James M. Coale, Henry R. Harris, Hiram Buhrman, Joshua Biggs, Thomas Johnson; 1864, Chas. E. Trail, Upton Buhrman, Joshua Biggs, David Rinehart, Oliver P. Snyder, Thomas Hammond; 1865, David J. Markey, Samuel Keefer, David Agnew, Thomas A. Smith, Upton Buhrman, David Rinehart; 1867, J. R. Rouser, Upton Buhrman, Henry Baker, John L. Linthicum, Thomas Gorsuch, J. A. Steiner; 1868, Ephraim Albaugh, R. P. T. Dutrow, Charles F. Wenner, Noah Bowlus, Thomas G. Maynard, Joseph Byers; 1870, Noah Bowlus, John B. Thomas, Wm. White, John T. McCreery, J. Alfred Ritter, Henry R. Harris; 1872, Lycurgus N. Phillip, Charles W. Miller, Theodore C. Delaplane, Jonathan Routzahn, Charles W. Rowe; 1874, John A. Koons, Job M. Miller, Lewis Lamar, John L. Nicodemus, Andrew Annan; 1876, Christopher M. Riggs, William H. Hinks, Henry Clay Naill, Robert E. Linthicum, John A. Koons; 1878; Christopher M. Riggs, Peter Lugenbeel, Lot Hartsock, William H. Hinks, Wm. J. Leib; 1880, Charles L. Wilson, George W. Remsburg, Christopher M. Riggs, Edward Bernard, Wm. L. Culler; 1882, Charles L. Wilson, T. E. R. Miller, Joseph E. Webster, B. D. Chambers, P. Lugenbeel.

Deputy Commissioners.

1749-54, John Darnall; 1754-57, Reverdy Ghiselin; 1757-59, J. Dickson; 1759-61, John Darnall; 1761-64, Peter Butler; 1764-76, Thomas Bowles.

Registers of Wills.

1776-1805, George Murdock; 1805-15, Richard Butler; 1815-25, Henry Steiner; 1825-45, George M. Eichelberger; 1845-51, Thomas Sappington; 1851-57, George Hoskins; 1857-63, Absalom P. Kessler; 1863-67, Thomas L. McLain; 1867-73, Sebastian G. Cockey; 1873-79, John R. Rouzer; 1879, John P. Perry.

Mr. Perry's deputies are Capt. H. Clay Naill and George Koogle.

Clerks of Circuit Court.

1776-78, Richard Potts; 1775-79, Richard Butler; 1779-1815, William Ritchie; 1815, Tobias Butler; 1815-35, John Schley; 1835-45, Henry Schley; 1845-51, William Bradley Tyler; 1851-57, Edward Shriver; 1857-63, B. G. Fitzhugh; 1867, Daniel S. Biser; 1867-73, Charles Mantz; 1873-79, Thomas Gorsuch; 1879, Adolphus Fearhake, Jr.

Mr. Fearhake's deputies are Judge William Mahony, William Nash Young, Ed. McIntire, Alfred Ritter, William H. Hillary.

Sheriffs.

1748, John Thomas; 1750, George Gordon; 1759, James Dickson; 1760, Samuel Beall; 1763, Thomas Prather; 1765, George Murdock; 1766, George Scott; 1769, Normand Bruce; 1772, James Hackman; 1773, Lawrence O'Neil; 1775, Thomas French; 1776, William Beatty; 1779, Valentine Brother; 1782, Christopher Edelin; 1785, Thomas Beatty; 1788, Peter Mantz; 1791, Tobias Butler; 1794, Richard Butler; 1797, Abner Ritchie; 1800, Lawrence Brengle; 1803, George Creager, Sr.; 1806, George Creager, Jr.; 1809, Ezra Mantz; 1812, Maris Jones (died); 1814-15, Joseph M. Cromwell; 1818, William M. Beall; 1821, Thomas W. Morgan; 1824, Thomas Charlton; 1827, John Rigney; 1830, Peter Brengle (died); 1832, Matthias E. Bartgis; 1833, Mahlon Talbot; 1836, Thomas Gourley; 1839, Henry Houck; 1842, George Rice, of James; 1845, Adam Custard; 1848, Norman B. Harding; 1851, Casper Mantz; 1853, Israel C. O'Neil; 1855, Mahlon Roderick; 1857, Michael H. Haller; 1859, Joseph M. Ebberts; 1861, Michael Zimmerman; 1863, John A. Steiner; 1865, William B. Tabler; 1867, Nathan O. Neighbors; 1869, Hiram Bartgis; 1871, Robert Lease; 1873, Thomas H. Willard; 1875, John Sweadner; 1877, William Richardson; 1879, J. S. B. Hartsock.

The General Assembly, by an act of February, 1777, established the Orphans' Court, to be held by not less than three justices of the peace. This court was empowered to take all probate of wills, grant letters of administration and letters testamentary, also warrants to appraisers in cases where there was no dispute, and in every respect had the same power, jurisdiction, and authority in connection with the register of wills that the deputy commissary had before that time in connection with the County Court. This court was authorized to bind out as apprentices orphan children the profits of whose estates were not sufficient for their maintenance, the children of beggars, illegitimate children, and the children of parents out of the State, where a sufficient support was not afforded. By the act of 1798 the Governor, by and with the advice and consent of the Council, had authority to appoint and commission three men of integrity and judgment to be justices of the Orphans' Court, and to hold their offices until their successors were appointed. Under the constitution of 1838 and legislative enactments in pursuance thereof, the judges held office for four years.

The first court was held Oct. 13 and 14, 1777. The following is a full list of its judges from 1777 to the present time:

Judges of the Orphans' Court.

1777, William Blair, Upton Sheredine, William Beatty, Joseph Wells, Normand Bruce; 1778, William Beatty, Upton Sheredine, Christopher Edelin, William Blair; 1779, Philip Thomas, William Beatty, Christopher Edelin, Upton Sheredine; 1780, Upton Sheredine, William Beatty, Philip Thomas; 1781, William Beatty, William M. Beall, Philip Thomas, Upton Sheredine; 1782, Upton Sheredine, William Beatty, William M. Beall; 1783, George Scott, John Harrison, William Beatty, William M. Beall; 1784, Upton Sheredine, William Beatty, John Harrison, William M. Beall, George Scott; 1785-86, William Beatty, George Scott, Upton Sheredine; 1787-91, Henry Darnall, William Beatty, William M. Beall, George Scott, Upton Sheredine;

1791, William Beatty, Francis B. Sappington, Patrick S. Smith, William M. Beall, Henry Darnall; 1792-95, Upton Sheredine, F. B. Sappington, William M. Beall; 1795-1800, Upton Sheredine, Francis B. Sappington; 1801, John N. Charlton, Henry Darnall, F. B. Sappington; 1802-4, Patrick McGill, John Schley, William Ballinger; 1804-6, John Schley, Henry Kuhn, Patrick McGill; 1806-13, Henry Kuhn, Henry Kemp, John Schley; 1813, John McPherson, Ignatius Davis, George Baer, Robert Cummings; 1814, Henry Steiner, Ignatius Davis, John McPherson; 1815-19, Ignatius Davis, John McPherson, Peter Mantz, John Graham; 1819-27, Henry Kemp, Henry Kuhn, Peter Mantz; 1827-31, Jacob Steiner, Henry Kemp, Henry Kuhn; 1831-35, Davis Richardson, Henry Kemp, John L. Harding; 1835-39, Robert Boone, Nicholas Turbutt, Davis Richardson; 1839-43, M. E. Bartgis, George Smith, John Harritt; 1843-47, George Bowlus, Gideon Bantz, Washington Burgess; 1847-51, William Mahony, Joshua Dill, Isaac Brower; 1851-55, E. L. Delashmutt, William Lowe, Joseph Easterday; 1855-59, William Lowe, John Montgomery, John A. Simmons, A. P. Kessler; 1859-63, B. A. Cunningham, John McPherson, John A. Simmons; 1863-67, Amos Cunningham, George Hoskins, James Brunner, L. J. Brengle, Joseph Routzahn; the last two *vice* Cunningham and Hoskins, resigned; 1867-71, Henry Houck, Jonathan D. English, John A. Simmons; 1871-75, H. G. Maynard, George W. Dudderar, W. J. Black; 1875-79, John Higman, Thomas M. Holbruner, W. J. Black; 1879-83, John T. Lowe, Daniel Castle, of T., Augustus W. Nicodemus.

The auxiliaries to the court are the Register of Wills, J. P. Perry, and his deputies, Henry Clay Naill and George Koogle.

Nov. 18, 1756, John Murdock was appointed surveyor in the room of Isaac Brooke, the only two in the county until after the convention of 1776, as disclosed by the records.

The first surveyor in the county under the first constitution was John Hanson, Jr., and the next one George Dent, appointed in April, 1782, and who served until he resigned, Dec. 20, 1783. His successor was Samuel Duvall, qualified Jan. 3, 1784, and went out in 1811.

Surveyors.

1811, Lawrence Brengle; 1814, John Woodrow; 1823, George Getzandanner; 1825, Corbin West; 1830, Horatio G. O'Neil; 1838, Elihu H. Rockwell; 1839, Thomas H. O'Neil; 1845, A. I. Barney; 1853, Singleton H. O'Neil; 1855, Joel Hall; 1857, Jesse Rupp; 1859, W. H. Hilleary; 1861, John S. Ramsbaugh; 1865, I. Thomas Browning; 1873, John S. Ramsbaugh; 1879, R. A. Rager, and yet in office.

State's Attorneys.[1]

Bradley T. Johnson, John A. Lynch, E. Y. Goldsborough, John Ritchie, Francis Brengle (appointed), Milton G. Urner, John C. Motter.

Collectors and Treasurers.

1803, Lawrence Brengle; 1806, George Creager; 1809, George Baltzell; 1830, Adam Larentz; 1832, Joseph Schell; 1840, John Sifford; 1841, George Beckenbaugh; 1843, Patrick O'Neal; 1844, Elias L. Delashmutt; 1846, Elisha Howard; 1848, Thomas C. Brashear; 1850, Dr. John W. Geyer; 1852, John Bartholow; 1854, John Need; 1856, Arthur Delashmutt; 1858, Zachariah T. Windsor; 1860, Daniel Castle; 1862, Samuel D. Geisinger; 1866, William M. Fenga; 1868, Daniel Michael; 1870, Lloyd H. Herring; 1872, George W. Miller; 1875, William H. Miller; 1878, Peter W. Shafer; 1880, D. H. Routzahn.

Trustees of County Poor.

1786, Basil Beall, Thomas Price, Jacob Steiner, Nicholas Tice.

The Levy Courts originally consisted of the justices of the peace, and by the act of 1798 were seven in number. By later enactments the number was increased, and the county was divided into districts, with one from each district sitting on the board.

Subsequently five commissioners took their places, and performed the duties previously transacted by the Levy Courts.

The Levy Court, or board of commissioners, had general charge of the business of the county in making levies, laying assessments, appointing supervisors, constables, school officers, and other local and county officials. It had jurisdiction over all the county's finances, over all roads, bridges, and highways. Until the creation of Levy Courts the duties performed by them had before that been under the control of the County Courts, but as population increased new boards were found necessary to meet the exigencies of the time.

We give a full list of the justices of the Levy Court and of the commissioners from 1803 to the present time, a period as far back as the public records show them:

Levy Courts and Commissioners.

1803.—Ignatius Davis, Joseph Swearingen, Henry Williams, Alexander Warfield, of Charles, Henry Kuhn, Andrew Shriver, Benjamin Farquhar. This court appointed Adam Frusham to take care of the hay-scales and court-house. The following judges of election in the different districts were chosen: First, Edward Tillard, Francis Hoffman, Christian Kemp; Second, Richard Butler, Jacob Getzendanner, Nicholas Holtz; Third, Edward Boteler, Devalt Williard, Joseph Miller; Fourth, John Briggs, Nathaniel Porter, Peter Shover; Fifth, Normand Bruce, James Mark, Ludwig Kesseling; Sixth, Joseph Wells, Charles Stevenson, Dr. John Baker; Seventh, Joab Waters, Jeremiah Browning, Isaac Wright. The constables appointed for the year were Jacob Boyer, Jr., East Frederick Town Hundred; Adam Frusham, West Frederick Town; John Stults, Israel's Creek; Thomas Knox, Upper Monocacy; Joseph Hedges, Manor; John Westfall, Tom's Creek; Abraham Bankert, Piney Creek; John Gibbony, Taney Town; Wm. Dern, Pipe Creek; Merryman Stevenson, Westminster; Jacob Kiler, Union; Horatio Marlow, Linganore; Francis Hagan, Sugar Loaf; John Kepbart, Lower Monocacy; Jacob Martin, Lower Catoctin; Arthur Boteler, Middle Catoctin; William Brown, Upper Catoctin; John Shepherd, Berlin; Jacob Lawrence, Middletown.

---

[1] This list is exclusively for Frederick County after the office was made elective by the people under the constitution of 1851.

1804-5.—Joseph Swearingen, Henry Williams, Alexander Warfield, of Charles, Andrew Shriver, Benjamin Farquhar, Christian Kemp, John Hoffman.

1806.—John Clempson, John Hoffman, Christian Kemp, Andrew Shriver, Alexander Warfield, Henry Williams, Joseph Swearingen.

1807-11.—Same board save Benjamin Biggs, vice Henry Williams.

1812.—Same board save Mordecai Haines, vice John Clempson.

1813.—Col. John Thomas (Maryland tract), James Johnson, Alexander Warfield, John Hoffman, Benjamin Biggs, Joseph Taney, Stephen Steiner.

1814.—Above board save William Hilloary and Joseph M. Cromwell, vice Thomas and Hoffman.

1815.—Same board save James Morrison and John McKalys, vice Hilloary and Taney.

1816.—Alexander Warfield, Benjamin Biggs, Stephen Steiner, James Morrison, Otho Sprigg, Wm. P. Farquhar, Joshua Gist.

1817-18.—Alexander Warfield, Benjamin Biggs, Stephen Steiner, James Morrison, Wm. P. Farquhar, William Murphy, Jacob Matthias.

1819.—Same board save Wm. B. Head, vice Benjamin Biggs.

1820.—Andrew Shriver, John Hoffman, Christian Kemp, John Mantz, John Kniver, Lewis Birely, William Morsell.

1821.—Same board save Robert Fulton, vice John Mantz.

1822-23.—John Hoffman, Christian Kemp, William Morsell, Robert Fulton, Joseph Swearingen, John Fisher, William Shepherd.

1824.—Same board save Evan McKinstry, vice William Shepherd.

1825.—John Hoffman, Christian Kemp, William Morsell, Robert Fulton, Joseph Swearingen, John Fisher, Evan McKinstry, Zebulon Kuhn, John McGeehan, Henry Baker, John Harbaugh.

1826.—Same board save Nelson Luckett, vice Joseph Swearingen.

1827.—Same board save Adam Lorentz, vice Nelson Luckett.

1828.—John Hoffman, Christian Kemp, William Morsell, Robert Fulton, Evan McKinstry, Zebulon Kuhn, Henry Baker, Adam Lorentz, John Harbaugh, Abraham Wampler, George Troxell.

1829.—Christian Ramsburg, Valentine Shryock, Henry Burkman, George Troxell, Abraham Wampler, Henry Baker, Evan McKinstry, Robert Fulton, William Morsell, Christian Kemp, John Hoffman.

1830.—George Zollinger, John H. Simmons, Christian Getzendanner, Jacob Weller, Jesse Slingle, Frederick Crabbs, William Shaw, Joseph Smith, Henry Smith, Wm. H. McCannon. This board ordered the sale of the old poor-house establishment, but possession of same to be retained until the new building was completed and ready for receiving the poor.

1831.—Grafton Duvall, Moses Warman, James Simmons, Abraham Jones, William Miller, Singleton Wootten, David Foutz, Martin Eichelberger, Frederick Troxell, Solomon Forrest, Abraham Wampler. Moses Warman was appointed to superintend the new poor-house and farm.

1832.—Moses Warman, James Simmons, Abraham Jones, William Miller, Singleton Wootten, David Foutz, Martin Eichelberger, Frederick Troxell, Solomon Forrest, John Cost, Thomas Springer.

1833.—Moses Warman, James Simmons, William Warman, Elisha Nelson, William Miller, David Foutz, Martin Eichelberger, Jacob Matthias, John Cost, Thomas Springer, Henry Culler.

1834.—Moses Warman, James Simmons, William Warman, William Miller, Martin Eichelberger, Frederick Troxell, Solomon Forrest, Jacob Matthias, Thomas Springer, Henry Culler, James L. Higgins, James Smith, Jeremiah G. Morrison.

1835.—Moses Warman, James Simmons, William Warman, Martin Eichelberger, Frederick Troxell, Solomon Forrest, Jacob Matthias, Thomas Springer, James Smith, Jeremiah G. Morrison, William Lynch, James L. Higgins, Evan McKinstry.

1836.—The same board with exception of William Dudderar, vice William Warman.

1837.—James Simmons, Patrick O'Neill, Thomas Springer, M. Eichelberger, Frederick Troxell, William Dudderar, Solomon Forrest, William Miller, William Lynch, J. G. Morrison, Abel Russell, Elias Crutchley.

1838-39.—Same board save Daniel Duvall, vice James Simmons.

1840.—George Zollinger, Daniel Duvall, Abel Russell, Israel Ramsburg, Patrick O'Neill, John R. Curtis, Benedict Boone, William Dudderar, R. Annan, J. J. McKeehan.

1841.—William Lakin, Israel Ramsburg, George Zollinger, Daniel Duvall, Jacob Trayer, Valentine Adams, William Dudderar, Daniel Hoover, Jacob Root, George Kuhn.

1842.—George Harmon, Elias Lilly, John Smith, L. D. Warfield, Valentine Adams, John Lease, Daniel Duvall, William Lakin, Israel Ramsburg, George Zollinger.

1843.—Joseph Easterday, William Grove, J. T. C. Miller, Daniel Duvall, John Lease, Valentine Adams, L. D. Warfield, Michael Sluss, M. Eichelberger, David Devilbiss.

1844.—B. A. Cunningham, J. T. C. Miller, M. Eichelberger, John F. Elder, L. D. Warfield, Washington Burgess, Samuel Wolfe, E. Cramer, Henry Dunlap, Henry Boteler.

1845.—B. A. Cunningham, C. Staley, J. T. C. Miller, M. Eichelberger, J. F. Elder, L. D. Warfield, John Bartholow, S. Walp, E. Cramer, Henry Dunlap, Henry Boteler.

1846.—Thomas H. O'Neil, J. J. McSheehan, J. T. C. Miller, Otho Thomas, Jacob Fox.

1847.—Thomas H. O'Neill, George P. Fox, William Norris, Noah Phillips, John F. Elder.

1848.—Winchester Clingan, Jacob T. C. Miller, William Norris, Noah Phillips, Joseph Willhide.

1849.—W. Clingan, Harry W. Dorsey, L. D. Warfield, Jacob T. C. Miller, George W. Shank.

1850.—William C. Martin, Thomas Crampton, John B. Thomas, John Reifsnider, George W. Shank.

1851-53.—James Pearre, Valentine Adams, John B. Picking, David Schindle, Joel Hall.

1854-55.—J. G. Morrison, George Thomas, of H., Samuel Keefer, Michael Keefer, David Kailor.

1856-57.—Nathan Nelson, Samuel Keefer, Stephen R. Bowlus, John R. Mills, Solomon Krise.

1858-59.—Valentine Adams, Hiram H. Mullen, Thomas Winter, Michael Shank, R. P. T. Dutrow.

1860-61.—Valentine Adams, George T. Whip, David Rinehart, John Witherow, William Metzger. Mr. Adams, president of the board, died in March, 1860, and was succeeded by John Montgomery.

1862-63.—Nicholas Norris, Joseph Routzahn, Horatio Little, Joseph G. Miller, William Watkins.

1864-65.—Joseph Routzahn, Z. G. Harris, M. S. Hensperger, Joseph G. Miller, Lewis Crawford.

1866-67.—Joseph G. Miller, Lewis Crawford, Z. G. Harris, George W. Dudderar, Hanson J. Rudy.

1868-69.—D. C. Johnson, Daniel Leatherman, John W. Buzzard, M. T. Starr, Charles Gross.

1870-71.—D. C. Johnson, Joshua Motter, Lebbeus Griffith, C. Keefer Thomas, Joseph B. Brown.
1872-73.—Joseph Cronise, Lewis Crawford, Joshua Albaugh, Charles Hooper, John W. Staup.
1874-75.—Lewis Crawford, George J. Whip, John W. Staup, Z. G. Harris, A. W. Nicodemus.
1876-77.—Joseph Wood, Ezra Toms, Samuel Hargett, A. R. Simmons, Daniel Biser.
1878-79.—John Witherow, S. R. Bowlus, D. M. Whip, Joseph Cronise, S. D. Devilbiss.
1880.—Thomas A. Smith, of T., George H. Ambrose, Peter Dudderar, Daniel Smith, of J., Thomas R. Jarboe, Samuel M. Buzzard, *vice* Mr. Ambrose, deceased; clerk of board, H. F. Steiner.

Commissioners of the Tax.

Under the act of Assembly of 1797, five commissioners were appointed in each county to ascertain the quantity of land in the respective counties, and to calculate the amount of the average value thereby established. No clergyman, practicing attorney, physician, sheriff, clerk, ordinary keeper, mariner, or inspector could be appointed. To them were returned the lists of able-bodied men liable for militia duty. They were empowered to call the assessors before them and correct their valuations of property, and to alter and correct the accounts on the change of property. The commissioners for the years 1798, 1799, and 1800, while the law was in operation, were Joshua Howard, Peter Mantz, Thomas Beatty, Samuel Skinner, Thomas and John Gwinn.

Frederick County Members of Constitutional Conventions.

First State Convention in 1776, Adam Fischer, Upton Sheredine, Christopher Edelin, David Schriver.

State Convention of 1788 to ratify the Federal Constitution, Thomas Johnson, Thomas Sim Lee, Richard Potts, Abraham Faw.

State Constitutional Convention of 1851, Francis Thomas, Edward Shriver, Wm. Cost Johnson, John D. Gaither, Daniel S. Biser, Robert Annan.

State Constitutional Convention of 1864, Samuel Keefer, Frederick Schley, David J. Markey, Andrew Annan, Henry Baker, B. A. Cunningham, Peter G. Schlosser.

State Constitutional Convention of 1867, William P. Maulsby, Frederick J. Nelson, Harry W. Dorsey, Outerbridge Horsey, William S. McPherson, John B. Thomas, De Witt C. Johnson.

Justices of the County Courts at the first organization of the State Courts in 1777.

Normand Bruce, William Blair, Upton Sheredine, William Beatty, Joseph Wells, Jacob Young, George Scott, Christopher Edelin, James Johnson, Wm. Murdock Beall, Carleton Tannehill, William Luckett, Jr., John Lawrence, Basil Dorsey, David Shriver, Joseph Wood, Jr., Ephraim Howard, George Haas, James Flemming, Charles Warfield.

CHAPTER XXV.

FREDERICK CITY.

Laid Out as a Town—Incorporated—Officers—Taverns and Inns—Early Physicians—Trade Industries—Amusements—Races—Stage-coaches and Mails—Market-houses and City Hall—Fire Companies—Libraries—Societies—Schools.

FREDERICK CITY is charmingly situated on both sides of Carroll Creek, a branch of the Monocacy River, from which it is three miles distant, in a valley remarkable for the fertility of its soil and the beauty of its scenery. Some eight miles to the eastward are the Linganore Hills, extending from north to south, while parallel with them on the west lies the Catoctin Range, a spur of the Blue Ridge, which rises still farther westward. On the north the valley seems shut in by the converging hills, and at its southern extremity the Sugar-Loaf Mountain looms up like some mighty sentinel placed there to bar the way. Beyond it, and some twelve or fifteen miles distant from the city, flows the Potomac River. In every direction the landscape is a feast to the eye, and without the least exaggeration Frederick may be termed the fairest jewel of the State. In the words of Whittier,—

"The clustered spires of Frederick stand
Green-walled by the hills of Maryland;
Round about them orchards sweep,
Apple and peach-trees rooted deep,
Fair as the garden of the Lord."

Frederick is sixty-one miles from Baltimore, seventy-five miles northwest of Annapolis, and forty-three miles from Washington. The city is regularly laid out, with broad streets intersecting at right angles, and is lighted with gas. Its churches are spacious and handsome, and many of its private dwellings are costly and elegant. In the immediate vicinity of Frederick there are many handsome country-seats, and the society both of the city and the neighborhood is hospitable, intelligent, and refined. One of the quaint institutions of the city is the old town-clock, which notifies people of the passing hour with one double stroke for the first quarter, two for the second, and three for the third. One of the pleasantest spots in the town is the ancient square which surrounds the court-house. No healthier or purer water can be found than that which supplies the city from the mountains on its west. The geographical situation of Frederick early made it an important seat of trade, and its historic reminiscences and associations date back to early colonial times, when all the country west of it was a wilderness inhabited only by the red men. Frederick City and its environs were first settled in

1733 by hardy German immigrants, some of whom came direct from the Old World, and the others chiefly from Pennsylvania, where they had previously settled. The Rev. Mr. Muhlenberg, of Pennsylvania, was among the earliest clergymen who held divine service in Frederick County, with the exception of the Catholic missionaries who attempted to convert the Indians of the Linganore and Monocacy Valleys. About this time a colony of thirty-odd persons from the province of New York arrived in the vicinity of Frederick. The advent of the pioneers created a great commotion among the Indians, and was the forerunner of an emigration destined in the next decade to fill up the valley.

The mode of erecting a town at that period was nearly always the same. Commissioners were appointed to agree with the owner of the land for a tract of fifty or a hundred or more acres, which was then staked off and divided into lots of an acre each, intersected by proper streets, lanes, and alleys. The lots being numbered and prices attached to them, the owner of the land was then allowed to select one lot, and the rest, or so many as there were applications for, were divided among the "takers-up," who received the freehold in consideration of a yearly quit-rent, usually of one penny, to the Lord Proprietary. In case the experiment failed, as it often did, the embryo towns were declared to "be annulled and untowned," and the land reverted to its former owner. In September, 1745, Patrick Dulany laid out Frederick Town, on part of the survey called "Tasker's Chance." The commissioners, in laying out its streets, intended that they should run towards the cardinal points; but their surveyor, having but very rude instruments and a defective compass, accomplished this object but imperfectly. The original plat had three hundred and forty lots. All the streets were sixty feet wide save Pence and North, both of which were thirty-three feet. The lots from Patrick to Church Street were three hundred and sixty-three feet in length and sixty-two in width. From Patrick Street to the creek the lots were three hundred and fifty-five feet in length, being a deduction of thirty feet in front for street-way and eight feet for water-way. All the rest were three hundred and ninety-three feet in length and sixty-two in width, except some on the west side, which were irregular from the situation of the land. Lots from numbers seventy-three to seventy-seven, inclusive, were reserved for the court-house, and number seventy-eight for the church. On Aug. 10, 1782, a plat of the town was prepared at the request of Clement Hollyday, one of the commissioners for the preservation and sale of confiscated property held or owned by persons inimical to the Continental Congress and the patriot cause. This resurvey and plat of the town by Samuel Duvall, surveyor, showed that part of lots numbers 217, 218, 261, 262, 263, and 264 lay in lands of Jacob Bentz, and not on "Tasker's Chance." This was occasioned no doubt by the variation of the magnetic needle. Samuel Duvall made an addition of twenty lots, swelling the total number to three hundred and fifty-one. Another survey of the town was made June 15, 1821, by Lawrence Brengle, with commissioners appointed by an ordinance of the corporation, to establish more definitely the metes and boundaries of certain streets and lots. The two main streets are Patrick and Market; the former running east and west, the latter north and south. Parallel to Patrick Street on the north run Church, Second, Third, Fourth, Fifth, Sixth, and Seventh Streets, and parallel to it on the south, All-Saints', Jail, South Streets, etc. Market Street is nearly a mile in length. The great Western turnpike road to Baltimore passes through Patrick Street, and near its eastern extremity stands the forty-second milestone from that city. Through Market Street passes the road leading from Gettysburg, Westminster, etc., towards Georgetown, D. C.

Up to the period of the Revolutionary war German was the language generally heard upon the streets. The immigrants, as stated in another chapter, had fled from religious oppression, and their names underwent many a distortion and mutilation at the hands of the English representatives of the Lord Proprietary as they labored to write them down from sound upon the pages of the early records. The original intention was to locate the town on the banks of the Monocacy; but in consequence of the person to whom the present site of Frederick had been sold regretting the purchase of the land, Mr. Dulany, to whom all the land in the neighborhood belonged, took back this tract, and the town was laid out on Carroll's Creek, instead of being placed on the banks of the Monocacy, at Ceresville, as Mr. Dulany had intended. The greater part of the lots were subject to a quit-rent of a shilling sterling to Mr. Dulany, to which the Revolutionary war put an end. The lots were all laid out north and south with reference to Patrick as the main street; consequently those on Market, now the principal street, have now only the depth of sixty feet. At that time the Pennsylvania and Virginia road passed through the town along the alley of which the residence of Maj. Daniel Hughes, a few years ago, formed the corner. Bentstown, from the bend at Patrick Street, was laid out subsequently, and in consequence of the creek and marshy ground took a southwesterly turn.

It was generally termed in deeds and lease instruments "an addition to Frederick Town." Hallerstown, which is the south end of Frederick, derives its name from a Mr. Haller, the crier, whose numerous descendants gave its name to this part of the city. Among the early immigrants were John Thomas Schley, the Shellmans and Brunners, who came over from Germany in 1745. Then came the Kemps, Raymers, Groshes, etc. Mr. Shellman carried the chain in laying out the town. The building of the town was commenced at what is now the lower part of Patrick Street. The first house was built by John Thomas Schley about 1746, and was on the lot now owned by William Reinhardt on Stein Alley. It was torn down in 1853. Mr. Schley built at the mouth of that alley a "stone well," which had a statue of stone representing a man with a girdle around him looking to the rising sun. A part of this stone Dr. Fairfax Schley, a descendant of John Thomas Schley, now has on his farm near the city. John Thomas Schley carried on a great variety of business, and was a most enterprising citizen. He also superintended the school, and was the organist of the German Reformed Church, of which he was a leading member. The Baltzells came over later, leaving the old country in consequence of religious proscription. In conformity with their fatherland customs, these German settlers introduced the practice of ringing bells on Saturday evening, which was kept up for a century. The first brick house was built by Jacob Steiner, and was occupied as a tavern, and occasionally the County Court sat there. It was located on the corner of Market and Patrick Streets, where Stewart & Price's store now stands. The first child born in Frederick Town was Eve Catherine Schley, daughter of John Thomas Schley, born in 1747. She married Jacob Bier, and died in Baltimore City, May 26, 1843, aged ninety-six years.

On the 7th of March, 1787, in conformity and for the purpose of carrying into execution an act of Assembly passed at the November session, 1786, to improve and repair the streets in Frederick Town, and for other purposes, the following commissioners qualified: Jacob Young, Jacob Miller, Michael Allex, John McPherson, Conrod Doll, and John Hoffman. This board appointed Lawrence Brengle clerk. John Shellman, one of the commissioners nominated in the above act, having declined to serve, the board selected in his place Henry McCleary. In 1788 the board appointed Henry Cronise collector of taxes assessed for street purposes. In 1789 the commissioners were Baker Johnson, Abraham Faw, Henry McCleary, John Hoffman, Jacob Young, Michael Allex, Conrad Doll, and Abner Ritchie, clerk.

1792, Jacob Young, Henry McCleary, Conrod Doll, John Hoffman, Baker Johnson, John Graham, and Henry Kuhn; 1794, George Baer, Jr., Jacob Young, Henry McCleary, George Burkhardt, and Michael Hauser (*vice* McCleary, resigned), Baker Johnson, John Hoffman; 1798, John Hoffman, David Levy, Jr., Michael Hauser, Isaac Mantz, Lawrence Brengle, Charles Glover, clerk; 1802, Baker Johnson, Henry Kuhn, Isaac Mantz, George Creager, Michael Hauser; 1803, John Hoffman, Michael Hauser, Isaac Mantz, David Levy, Jr., John Markell, clerk; 1805, John Gebhart, David Levy, Isaac Mantz, Michael Hauser, John Deale; 1807, new member, Stephen Stoner; 1810, new members, G. Hauer, William Michael; 1814, new member, Frederick Steiner; 1816, new member, George Rice; 1817, John L. Harding, George Rice, —— Doffler, Henry Kuhn, William Michael, Michael Hauser, G. Hauer.

This year the board gave way to the municipal government chosen under the charter and franchises granted in an act passed by the General Assembly at the session of 1816–17, incorporating Frederick Town.

The limits of the city were designated thus: beginning at the forty-fourth mile-stone on the Baltimore and Frederick Town turnpike road, about three-quarters of a mile from the east end of Frederick Town, and running thence with a straight line so as to include John Hughes' brick house; thence with a straight line to include John McPherson's house (formerly Schnertzell's); thence with a straight line to include the late Christopher Mayer's house; thence with a straight line to include John Graham's house; thence with a straight line to the mouth of Carroll Creek; and thence with a straight line to the aforesaid forty-fourth mile-stone. But for taxable purposes the boundaries were made, to wit: all the lots originally laid out as Frederick Town, with all additions thereto, including Bentz Town, and Jacob and Michael Buckey's dwelling-house and tan-yard, and Jacob Buckey's factory, at the east end of the town, and Stephen Steiner's dwelling and tavern-stand on the west end, and George Lease's on the north end of said town; also Ramsburg's mill, also the English Presbyterian church, and the lots fronting on the west side of Bentz Street, from Ramsburg's mill to the aforesaid church, both inclusive. The act of incorporation provided for the election of a mayor and five aldermen for three years, and for dividing the town into seven wards, from which annually one councilman was to be elected. Under its provisions the first election was held on the last Monday in February, 1817. The following is a full list of the mayors, and a partial list of other officers for different periods:

1817.—Mayor, Lawrence Brengle; Register, John J. McCulley; Councilmen, F. A. Schley, Frederick Nurr, John McPherson, Henry McCleary, John Cromwell, Rev. David Martin (president), William Kolb; Aldermen, Stephen Steiner, B. S. Pigman, George W. Ent, George Rice, William Ross (president); Assessor, Henry Koontz; Surveyor, L. Brengle; Flour Inspector, Jacob Meixall, Sr.; Town Commissioner, L. Harding; Town Weigher, John Dice.

1818.—Mayor, Henry Kuhn, *vice* Lawrence Brengle, resigned; Councilmen, George A. Ebbert, Michael Hauser, John Cromwell, John McPherson, Henry Kuhn, William Kolb, Henry Stern; Register, John J. McCulley; Constables, Joseph Walling, Conrad Kaufman, John M. Lowe; Town Commissioner, George Dofler.

1819.—Councilmen, George A. Ebbert, P. Degrange, Frederick Steiner, William Kolb, Michael Hauser, —— Buckey.

1820.—Mayor, George Baer; Register, John J. McCulley.

1823.—Mayor, John L. Harding; Register, Isaac Mantz.

1826.—Mayor, George Kolb; Register, David Steiner.

1829.—Mayor, Thomas Carlton; Register, David Steiner. On March 21st, John M. Lowe sent in a petition to the joint Board of Aldermen and Council for permission to erect a "cock-pit" within the taxable limits of Frederick Town, and on motion leave was given the petitioner to withdraw the same.

1832.—Mayor, Thomas Carlton; Register, David Steiner.

1835.—Mayor, Daniel Kolb; Register, Wm. H. Rigney.

1838.—Mayor, Michael Baltzell; Register, Godfrey Koontz.

1841.—Mayor, George Hoskins; Register, Abner Campbell.

1844.—Mayor, George Hoskins; Register, David Schley.

1847.—Mayor, M. E. Bartgis; Register, David Schley.

1849.—Mayor, James Bartgis, *vice* M. E. Bartgis, deceased; Register, David Schley.

1850.—Mayor, James Bartgis; Register, David Schley.

1853.—Mayor, James Bartgis; Register, D. B. Hunt.

1856.—Mayor, Lewis Brunner; Register, P. L. Storm.

1859.—Mayor, W. G. Cole; Register, William Mahony.

1862.—Mayor, W. G. Cole; Register, William Mahony.

1865.—Mayor, J. Englebrecht; Register, J. W. Birely.

1868.—Mayor, Valentine Ebert; Register, Andrew Henderson.

1871.—Mayor, Thomas M. Holbruner; Register, John M. Ebert.

1874.—Mayor, Lewis H. Moberly; Register, Godfrey Koontz.

1877.—Mayor, Lewis H. Moberly; Register, Godfrey Koontz.

1880.—Mayor, Lewis H. Moberly; Register and Tax Collector, Charles C. Smith.

The Legislature in 1878 abolished the Council, and delegated all the powers previously enjoyed by it and the aldermen to the latter.

The last councilmen in 1878 were W. H. Shipley, S. W. Jarboe, J. H. Bruner, Henry Miller, Adam Eichelberger, L. H. Doll, Benj. Stewart, C. H. Haller, Daniel P. Whip, C. F. W. Roelkey.

The aldermen elected in 1877 were J. N. Wilson, C. C. Smith, Thos. M. Wolf, A. L. Eader, J. H. Abbott.

The aldermen of 1881 (elected in 1880) are David O. Thomas, Lewis H. Doll, B. F. Winchester, B. F. Phoebus,—there being a vacancy occasioned by the death of John H. Brunner, president of the board. Their clerk is Joseph F. Eisenhauer.

1881.—Superintendent of Water-Works, Julius Gray; Collector of Water-Rents, Hiram Bartgis; Market Master, Chief of Police, Hay and Cattle Weigher, Keeper of City Hall, Luther C. Derr; Constables, Geo. F. Miller, Joshua Young, Charles A. Porter, Joseph E. Harper; Clock-Winder, William Simmons; Commissioners of Tax, James Carlin, Lewis Rees, G. J. Lambert.

According to the financial exhibit for the year ending Jan. 31, 1881, the entire indebtedness of the city was as follows:

Frederick and Pennsylvania Railroad bonds	$250,000
Bank bonds (in part payment of money paid Gen. Jubal Early)	123,000
Water-works bonds	70,000
Market-house bonds	55,000
Carroll Creek bonds	50,000
Floating debt	12,500
Total	$560,500

All these bonds drew six per cent. interest until 1880, when they were converted by Charles C. Smith, city register, into five per cent. bonds.

The average annual expenditures proper of the city amount to about eight thousand dollars, of which a fraction over one half is expended in salaries. The city's credit is first-rate, and the municipal government meets its obligations with prompt fidelity.

In 1840, during the hard times prevailing all over the land, it issued its checks in sums of twelve and a half, twenty-five, fifty, and one hundred cents on the various city banks to relieve the existing monetary pressure, which it redeemed and paid when the financial storm had spent its force.

Taverns, or Inns.—The keeping of "ordinaries," or "inns," was commenced very soon after the laying out of the town. After the Revolution, and until the completion of the Baltimore and Ohio Railroad, the town and county were filled with hostelries of all sorts, owing to the fact that Frederick was on the direct route of travel from the East to the West. At these inns the presidents, vice-presidents, senators, congressmen, and other public functionaries from the South and West were wont to stop for rest and refreshment on the journey to and from the national capital. In 1749 the inn-keepers were John Cramplin, Kennedy Farrell, and Jacob Beney, who were granted licenses as "ordinary keepers" by the County Court.

In 1750, Mrs. Charlton kept a tavern on the corner of Patrick and Market Streets, on the lot where Stewart & Price's hardware-store is, and in her upper chambers the County Court held several sessions until the completion of the first court-house. On Dec. 30, 1756, Christopher Lowndes advertised to let by the year, or for a term, and to be entered upon on the beginning of the following March, a very good public-house with all necessary outbuildings, situated in the middle of the town, and then in the occupation of William Beall, and that any person inclined to rent the said house might know the conditions by applying to Christopher Edelin, on the premises, or to him.

In 1786, Capt. Jacob Marres had an inn. On Dec. 22, 1796, A. Josse was landlord of the "Sign of the Sorrel Horse," at the upper end of Market Street. Sept. 18, 1797, Capt. James Neale kept the "Sign of the Spread Eagle," formerly occupied by Maj.

Henry Brother, on Patrick Street, where the Central Hotel is now located.

In September, 1797, the following advertisement appeared:

"George Nelson respectfully informs the public in general and his old customers in particular, that he has opened a House of Entertainment in Frederick Town, in the house formerly occupied by Mrs. Zimmer, nearly opposite Mr. Thomas Johnson's, in Market Street. He flatters himself that he will be able to give general satisfaction to those who please to favor him with their custom. A few Boarders will be taken on reasonable terms.

"N.B.—Weaver's Reeds made and sold by the subscriber.
"G. N.
"Sept. 27, 1797."

In 1799, Henry Brother conducted the tavern formerly kept by his father-in-law, Christian Brengle, on Patrick Street, next door to Maj. Mantz'. In 1801, George Cregar kept public-house, and in 1803, David Levy had a tavern on Patrick Street. Mrs. Kimball had an inn in 1803. On May 1, 1807, William R. King moved from Liberty to Frederick and took the tavern-stand of Mr. Schley, lately occupied by Mr. Miller. In the same year Mrs. Whitecraft kept the "Sign of the Seven Stars," on Market Street. Sept. 17, 1808, Conrad Shaffer kept the "Fountain Inn." In 1810, John Dertzback was landlord of the "Sign of the Eagle and Review," on Market Street. March 13, 1813, Henry Fogler kept the "Washington Inn," at the upper end of Market Street. May 20, 1814, John Huston took the "Globe Inn," corner of Market and Second Streets, lately occupied by George Creager. In 1819, William Kolb opened the "Sign of the Sheaf of Wheat and Plow" in "his new building," North Market Street, on the direct road to Pennsylvania and Liberty road to Baltimore. In January, 1819, Kelvie Hammett kept the "Sign of the Ship," at the upper end of Market Street, on the direct road to Baltimore, Washington, and Pennsylvania. In 1824, W. R. Stuchberry kept a tavern. On May 10, 1825, there were nineteen public-houses in the town, to wit: Robert Roach, David Lambert, Jacob Welty, Eli Mobley, John L. Levy, Nicholas Turbutt, Joseph Talbot, William S. Williamson, George Miller (all on Patrick Street), Mary M. Storm, William Michael, John M. Lowe, Harriet Brish, William Kolb, George Nichols, M. E. Bartgis, Henry Fogler, Sr., George Lease, and John Dill (all on Market and other streets). Matthias E. Bartgis was the proprietor of an inn for thirty-three years. He died in 1849. On the 31st of August, 1830, Isaac Williamson succeeded Robert Roach in the latter's tavern.

Early Physicians.—At an early period the people of Frederick enjoyed the services of skillful and talented physicians, and ever since the standard thus established has been jealously maintained by the members of the profession who have been the leading practitioners there. The first "physician," however, appears to have been an "irregular" doctor named Jacob Fought, who settled in Frederick May 9, 1754. He was from Germany, and announced that he could cure the "country distemper" in four weeks, and would undertake to remove a wen without cutting it off. He advertised several other cures, and, like some modern quacks, desired no money until the cure was completed. He boarded at first with Michael Jeffrey.

On the 1st of August, 1769, Dr. Philip Thomas located at Frederick, and was followed by Dr. John Fischer and Dr. John N. A. Bogen. The latter was a Hessian, and for some time was confined at the "Barracks" as a prisoner of war. After the war he married a daughter of Henry Koontz, and occupied the house on West Patrick Street where the office of B. F. Brown is now located.

On the 17th of January, 1786, Dr. John Tyler, who had just returned from Europe, announced that he was about to practice physic, surgery, etc., and on the 1st of May in the following year Dr. Adam Fischer informed the public that, as smallpox was then in adjacent towns, he would inoculate "as low" as any other physician. Dr. Fischer had been educated at a German university, and was an accomplished physician. His practice soon became very large, and extended over a wide area of territory. He died from a kick received from his horse at Reisterstown, Md., and left two sons and three daughters. One of them was Dr. John Smith Fischer. His son Adam and his daughter Elizabeth left over a hundred descendants.

On Nov. 27, 1792, Dr. Thomas Sim commenced the practice of medicine in Frederick, and in 1803 Dr. Runkel lived on Patrick Street, opposite Benjamin Ogle's store. On April 25, 1806, Dr. Fischer removed from Patrick to Market Street, to the house formerly occupied by Mrs. Colgate, next door to Conrad Shafer's tavern, and opposite to Adam Keller's. For several years preceding 1807 Dr. Edward Anderson had practiced in Frederick, but afterwards removed. In 1820, Drs. John Baltzell, Gerard J. Schneider, William Bradley Tyler, and Godfrey Weise were popular practitioners. Subsequently we find, in 1821, Dr. Jacob Baer; in 1822, Drs. William Bantz and Grafton Duvall; in 1827, Dr. H. Staley; in 1829, Dr. Montandon (dentist); in 1833, Dr. Albert Ritchie; in 1834, Dr. R. E. Dorsey; in 1838,

Dr. W. S. McPherson; in 1839, Dr. William M. Kemp; and in 1852, Drs. Richard Potts and Basil Norris.

Hon. Lewis Henry Steiner, M.D., was born in Frederick City on the 4th of May, 1827. His father, Christian Steiner, born Jan. 14, 1797, and his mother, Rebecca Weltzheimer, born April 20, 1802, were both natives of Frederick. Dr. Steiner is a great-great-grandson of Jacob Steiner, who emigrated from Germany to Frederick County, and a great-grandson of John Steiner, who was born about 1750, in Frederick County, about three miles from the present residence of Dr. Steiner; commanded a company of militia against the Indians in 1775, and was a member of the Committee of Observation for Frederick County during the Revolutionary war. Dr. Steiner was prepared for college at Frederick Academy, and entered the sophomore class of Marshall College, Mercersburg, Pa., in 1843, receiving in 1846 the degree of A.B., and in 1849 that of A.M. He studied medicine with Dr. William Tyler, of Frederick, and graduated from the University of Pennsylvania in 1849 with the degree of M.D., commencing the practice of his profession in his native city in 1850. In 1852 he removed to Baltimore, where he was associated with Dr. J. R. W. Dunbar for several years in the conduct of an institution for medical instruction. In 1853 he was appointed Professor of Chemistry and Natural History at Columbia College, Washington, and Professor of Chemistry and Pharmacy at the National Medical College of the same city; in 1854, Lecturer on Chemistry and Physics at the College of St. James, Maryland; in 1855, Lecturer on Applied Chemistry at the Maryland Institute; and in 1856, Professor of Chemistry at the Maryland College of Pharmacy. In 1852 he was elected a member of the American Medical Association; in 1853, Fellow of Medical and Chirurgical Faculty of Maryland, and in the same year member, and in 1874, Fellow, of the American Association for Advancement of Science; in 1855 he was elected correspondent of the Academy of Natural Sciences, Philadelphia; in 1869, corresponding member of the Maryland Academy of Sciences; in 1872, member, and in 1876, Vice-President, of the American Public Health Association; and in the latter year member of the International Medical Congress (Philadelphia); in 1876, Fellow, in 1876 and 1877, Vice-President, and in 1878, President, of the American Academy of Medicine. In 1861, Dr. Steiner returned to Frederick, where he has since resided.

At the outbreak of the civil war he took an active interest in the Union cause, assisted in raising troops, and when the Sanitary Commission was organized, in 1861, he was appointed inspector, and in 1863 chief inspector, and assigned to the Army of the Potomac. In this service he labored indefatigably until the close of the war, and distinguished himself so greatly by his zeal and skill that in 1868, in recognition of his services, he was elected by the New York Commandery companion (third class) of the Military Order of the Loyal Legion of the United States. After the close of the war he took great interest in adapting the system of public education to the changed condition of affairs, and as president of the school board of Frederick County from 1865 to 1868 reorganized all the schools of the county. Dr. Steiner's contributions to literature and science have been constant since 1851, and have given him a high place both in and out of his profession. Dr. Steiner has also been a frequent contributor to reviews, medical and literary journals, and was for several years assistant editor of the *American Medical Monthly*, published in New York. The honorary degree of A.M. was conferred upon Dr. Steiner by the College of St. James in 1854, and by Yale College in 1869. He is a corresponding member of the Maryland Historical Society and the New Haven Colony Historical Society, trustee of the Hampton Normal and Agricultural Institute at Hampton, Va., and honorary member of the Harrisburg Pathological Society. Before the war Dr. Steiner was a member of the Whig party, but became a Republican when that organization passed away. Since 1871 he has represented Frederick County in the State Senate, having been elected for three successive terms over strong Democratic opponents. In 1876 he was a member of the Cincinnati Republican Convention which nominated Mr. Hayes for the Presidency.

Dr. Steiner's scientific and professional attainments have won for him a national reputation, and given him a high place among the most distinguished names known to medical science in this country. Although he has been frequently honored by the political confidence of the people of Frederick County, he is not a politician in the ordinary acceptation of that term, and stands high above the petty arts and devious methods which too often characterize the politics of the day. In the Senate, Dr. Steiner is the recognized leader of the Republican party; but while loyal to the political principles of that organization, he never forgets the superior fealty due his constituents and the State at large, and his services in the General Assembly have gained him an enviable place in the estimation of the people of all sections of Maryland, and of every political complexion. An elegant scholar,

an able physician, a man of high scientific attainments, of the purest personal character, a refined and genial gentleman, Dr. Steiner is a representative whom Western Maryland may be proud to claim, and whom Maryland at large is happy to count among her sons.

Dr. Steiner was married on the 3d of October, 1866, to Sarah Spencer, daughter of Hon. R. D. Smyth, a distinguished lawyer and genealogist of Guilford, Conn., and has five children, two sons and three daughters.

Business Notes.—The following advertisement appeared April 23, 1761:

"The subscriber having furnished himself with a large quantity of fine fresh Hairs, both curled and uncurled, now carries on the business of Peruke making in Fourth Street, Frederick Town, Frederick County, Maryland, where all gentlemen may furnish themselves with Perukes made after the beautifullest, neatest, and newest fashion. He also makes Tates and Frazetes for ladies in any form required, so that no person can distinguish them from the ladies' own hair. He also sells all sorts of hair for Peruke makers' use, either in the rough or ready prepared after the most approved method. A good preparer, peruke maker, or a barber that can shave well, may have immediate and constant employment by applying to the subscriber. WILLIAM B. WALLS."

"Well's Invention," lying near Fielder Gantt's *iron mine*, in Frederick County, containing five hundred and seventeen acres, was offered for sale in 1763.

On Dec. 29, 1763, Francis Sanderson, coppersmith from Lancaster, removed his business to Frederick, where he made all sorts of copper articles, such as stills, brewing-kettles, fish and wash-kettles, tea-kettles, saucepans, and other copperware, pewter, lead, etc.

In 1764, William Banks was a barber and peruke-maker, and because some enemy of his had inserted in the papers an advertisement that another one was needed by the inhabitants, he became very angry.

On Oct. 10, 1769, a number of wagons arrived containing about three hundred pounds' worth of goods from Philadelphia and Baltimore, not accompanied with the proper certificates, and were stored at the risk and cost of the owners.

In September, 1770, a factory for weaving and the manufacture of weaving-machines was established.

A letter from Frederick in the *Maryland Journal (Gazette?)* of Nov. 6, 1773, says, "Frederick County is amazingly improving, and the condition of the German emigrants is astonishing. We have plenty of stocking and worsted weavers. Our church is the only one in the province that has got a steeple."

In March, 1776, powder belonging to the State was stored in the market-house.

July 5, 1781, Robert Wood, proprietor of the "wire-mill," also added to his business a cotton and wool-card manufactory, and continued the nail business.

May 4, 1786, Peter Engels was appointed armorer of the new arsenal. In the same year Frederick Heisley was a clock and watch-maker opposite the German Reformed church; also kept shop at the "Sign of the Dial," opposite Jacob Steiner's saddlery-shop and store, on Market near Patrick Street.

"Constitution" Smith was a hatter in 1789, so called from his endless talk about the new Federal Constitution.

The first grist-mill was located on West Patrick Street, on the lot now owned by Jacob Schmitt, and where he keeps a hotel.

The merchant and custom flouring-mill, now owned by Lewis Bruner, was built in 1790 by Ramsburg & Beltz. Mr. Bruner purchased it in 1848, and has since operated it successfully.

In 1793 Christian Koontz opened a currying-shop, corner Patrick and Market Streets.

July 17, 1799, William Robertson, weaver, opened shop next door to Henry Gardner's blacksmith-shop, and opposite James Smith's store, on Market Street.

From 1795, and for many years, John Reich carried on a blacksmith-shop on South Market Street, where William Reich now lives, and the same shop is now operated by Alex. Noland (colored).

Michael Allex carried on butchering and slaughtering from 1778 to 1800.

Oct. 25, 1797, William King commenced the cabinet-making and turning business.

April 20, 1797, Peter Smith had a boot and shoe manufactory a few doors below George Burkhart's, on Patrick Street.

In 1799 the making of arms for the service of the United States was largely prosecuted in Frederick.

Dec. 10, 1802, Philip Hauptman opened a boot and shoe manufactory at Gorge Tice's, nearly opposite the "stone well" on Patrick Street.

Feb. 4, 1803, John Geyer carried on saddling and harness-making opposite Mrs. Kimball's tavern, on Patrick Street.

In the same year Peter Storm had his coppersmith-shop two doors below David Levy's tavern, on Patrick Street.

In the spring of 1805, John Bautz was a dyer and weaver.

Jan. 14, 1809, Jacob Kimmerly and Nicholas Hoover carried on the rope-making business on Patrick Street, facing Harman's blacksmith-shop.

Candy-making was begun in 1812 by M. A. Miller (called "Cat-Fish" Miller), in a building located on the lot where part of the City Hotel stands. This candy was made of molasses.

In 1822, Mrs. Getz, from Lancaster, Pa., opened a kind of bakery where B. F. Brown's place of business now stands, on East Patrick Street. She made the first ice-cream known in the town.

Sept. 19, 1833, a meeting was held for the purpose of establishing a carpet-manufactory, with $8000 capital.

The following advertisement appeared in the *Maryland Gazette* of 1749:

"Sept. 1st, 1749.

"The subscriber hath obtained a patent for keeping a fair at Frederick Town, near Monocacy, on the 21st day of October and the tenth day of May next, each fair to continue three days, and for a market to be held there every Saturday after the first of November next.

"All persons who will bring any goods, merchandise, cattle, or any thing else to the said fairs, or markets, to sell, shall be free and exempt from the payment of all toll, stallage, piccage, or any other charge, for the term of five years next ensueing this last day of Aug. 1749. D. DULANY."

December, 1763, Robert Peter kept store as agent for John Glassford & Co., merchants, of Glasgow, Scotland.

Mr. Lowndes advertised, Sept. 20, 1764, as follows:

"WANTED.—To assist in a store in Frederick Town, in Frederick County. A youth about fifteen years old, that writes a good hand, understands arithmetic, and is willing to engage for 5 or 6 years. Any person wanting such employ, on application to the printing-office, may be informed as to the rest."

Feb. 19, 1793, Benjamin Ogle kept store.

Feb. 9, 1796, A. Peticolas, miniature-painter, advertised to paint miniatures at twenty-six dollars apiece at Mrs. Hauser's, opposite Dr. Thomas', on Patrick Street.

May 5, 1796, Lewis Weltzheimer opened "a new medicinal store" next door to Francis Kleinert's, at the "Sign of the Golden Mortar," near the jail.

July 19, 1797, Levi Noyes had a wholesale and retail grocery-store, corner of the market-house.

In the same year Adam Deshler kept a general store in the stone corner house near the German Presbyterian church, and opposite Rev. Mr. Runckel's.

Oct. 14, 1801, A. and J. Shriver kept a general store.

Nov. 5, 1802, James Huey, wishing to remove from town, advertised his entire stock of general goods for sale.

In 1803, Adams & Ruth had a large dry-goods and grocery-store next door to market-house.

Up to 1803, James Smith kept store where the United States Hotel now is, and had a tobacco warehouse. He died that year. From a poor redemptioner he had become a wealthy merchant.

April 9, 1804, the sign of the "Cash and Sugar-Loaves Store" was next to George Baer's, on Patrick Street.

Nov. 11, 1806, Amelia Wolfenden announced her removal to the new store on Patrick Street, between Bailey's and Graham's. She kept ladies' dry-goods.

In 1811, Dr. Jacob Baer kept a drug-store on Patrick Street, opposite the "Indian Queen."

Aug. 31, 1826, W. L. Helfenstein opened a store in a house of Col. John Ritchie's, corner of Market and Patrick Streets.

Amusements.—On May 10, 1786, the Frederick Town Theatre opened at Mr. Graff's room; tickets three shillings and ninepence.

Aug. 17, 1786, a "new theatre" was opened by the old "American Company," under the management of Messrs. Hallam and Henry, with the comedy of "School for Scandal." Also the same night was presented at the market-house the tragedy "Zara." This entertainment concluded with "a little hornpipe by a little man, and a little epilogue by a little lady." Tickets were 3s. 9d., "sold at Capt. Morris' and at Mrs. Owens';" children 1s. 10d. The money was appropriated to the use of Mrs. Tobine.

On June 5, 7, and 9, 1792, at Mrs. Kimball's tavern, a company of French dancers performed.

Sept. 11, 1797, Rickett's equestrian circus exhibited; box, one dollar; "standing room," fifty cents.

Dec. 11, 1802, Mr. Powers, the ventriloquist, exhibited at Baer's "ball-room."

June 20, 1809, Mr. Durang opened a new theatre at Mr. Stalling's "Sign of the Spread Eagle." The curtain was raised at a quarter to eight; box, fifty cents; gallery, twenty-five cents.

April 20, 1821, an African lion, a buffalo, an elk, and a calf with six legs were exhibited at Shimmell's tavern.

June 5, 1822, Williams & Herbert's company of tragedians appeared at the City Hall, and on the 26th added to their number Mrs. Burke and Mrs. Placide.

June 8, 1822, it was advertised that the prices at the theatre over the market-house were, for box, seventy-five cents; pit, fifty; "tickets sold at Talbot's bar, Robinson & Co.'s lottery-office, and W. C. Russell's grocery-store."

July 18, 1822, a menagerie exhibited at Shafer's tavern, and feats of agility were performed by Master Daniel Munich.

Aug. 22, 1822, a company of rope-dancers, comprising three Italians, two Spaniards, and one Chinese, appeared.

July 23, 1824, another troupe of rope-dancers exhibited at Stuchberry's inn.

In 1824, Mr. Sturne kept a museum at the house of Mrs. Mary Gantz.

May 4, 1825, Taylor, the ventriloquist, performed at Williamson's tavern.

Jan. 8, 1826, Magee, the Irish giant, exhibited.

July 26, 1826, a circus of eight men and eighteen horses performed at the Barracks ground.

Oct. 4, 1826, a circus exhibited on East Fourth Street, outside of "St. Domingo."

Sept. 28, 1829, a menagerie appeared, and Dec. 13, 1827, the bones of a mastodon were exhibited at the court-house.

May 27, 1830, Carl Blisse, the Prussian singer, gave a concert.

July 14, 1831, Stickney & Co.'s circus exhibited.

Oct. 15, 1831, a caravan performed at Brush's lot, in Mill Alley.

Jan. 23, 1832, Chang and Eng, the Siamese twins, exhibited. They returned October, 1868.

May 2, 1832, Nicholls, the ventriloquist, and Nov. 13, 1833, Hugh Hagan, another ventriloquist, appeared.

April 23, 1833, a menagerie exhibited, and April 1, 1834, another menagerie appeared at "Cannon Hill."

Frederick Races.—Horse-racing was very popular in Frederick County at an early period, having probably been introduced by the settlers from Southern Maryland. Thus, for instance, under date of April 26, 1749, only four years after the town was laid out, we find the following advertisement:

"To be run for at Frederick Town, in Frederick County, A subscription of Twenty Eight Pounds Two shillings and six-pence, and the Entrance Money of each day. The horses, &c., to carry weight for inches as on the two preceding days, and to pay after the rate of it in the Pound Entrance. The winning horses to be excepted each day. The horses, &c., are to be entered with Kennedy Ferrell by 12 o'clock the day before they run, and if any differences arise, they are to be decided by John Darnall, Esq., and Capt. Nathaniel Wickbawn."

On Aug. 12, 1757, an extremely hot day, a remarkable race was run from Frederick Town to Annapolis by a large horse with a man on his back, and a small mare with a boy, for seventy-five pistoles, fifty to twenty-five being laid on the horse, which won, performing it exactly in eleven hours, four of which the two horses traveled very gently together.

In the *Maryland Gazette* of Sept. 27, 1759, appeared the following:

"On the Twenty-third day of October, 1759, next will be run for, at Frederick Town, in Frederick county, a purse of thirty pounds, by any horse, mare, or gelding. On the twenty-fourth all the entries and what other money may be made up, the winning horse the first day excepted. Each Horse to carry nine stone weight, to run three heats, two miles each heat. If any disputes shall arise, the same to be determined by Messrs. James Dixon and Christopher Edelin. Every horse, etc., to be entered with Mr. Arthur Charlton, in the Town aforesaid, the day before the Race, and the owners to pay thirty shillings entrance-money."

On Monday, the 20th day of October, 1766, was run for, "on the usual race-ground in Frederick Town," a purse of thirty pistoles, offered for any horse, mare, or gelding, each carrying ten stone, saddle and bridle included. The entries were made with George Stricker, and three horses were to start, the winner to obtain two heats out of three one-mile heats. A second day's race for a purse of fifteen pistoles was also run.

Races were also held on the north side of Piscataway Town, about a half-mile from it, Oct. 21, 1766, and at Old Fields, Bladensburg.

In 1772, Moses Rawlings inaugurated a series of races in Frederick County.

Sept. 25, 1797, the Frederick Town races opened, to last three days, under the charge of Henry Brother.

On Sept. 20, 21, and 22, 1809, races were run at Middletown, with John Stottlemire and Jonathan Levy as managers; entrance, "one shilling in the pound."

In 1811, John Adams and George Nichols conducted the Boonsboro' races near Frederick.

On the 5th of September, 1820, races began on Mr. Stubbs' lands; William B. Bourke, manager.

At the August races (1821) at the "Dry Tavern," on the Liberty road, H. Holly won the prize.

Posts, Stages, and Mails.—On the 28th of August, 1773, Absalom Bonham announced that he "rode post from Baltimore to Frederick once a week." From Frederick another post extended to Winchester, Va. Bonham set off from Wm. Adams', at the "Sign of the Race Horses," every Saturday at one o'clock P.M.

On Feb. 22, 1786, Matthias Bartgis informed the public,

"that as he intends to establish the Post from Frederick Town to Baltimore and back to Frederick Town, from thence to Hagers Town and Sharpsburg and back to Frederick Town, &c., &c., every fortnight, until he has a sufficient number of subscribers to pay expenses of the Post; and then to be continued weekly. That those who subscribe will have their letters and papers carried gratis; non-subscribers will have to pay for their letters from Frederick Town to Baltimore One Shilling; from thence to Frederick Town one shilling; to Hagers Town and to Sharpsburg six-pence; from thence to Frederick Town six-pence; and so in proportion for each letter that is sent; paid to me, M. B."

Dec. 29, 1786, the public were informed that the new Frederick and Hagerstown post-rider put up at Mr. Steele's tavern, at the sign of "General Hand," in Market Street, opposite Wm. Stenson's, where letters for and from those places "are received and will be carefully delivered."

Following is a post advertisement of December, 1797:

"Starts from the house of Wm. Fares, Lancaster, every Monday and Thursday morning at five o'clock; arrives in Frederick Town on Tuesday and Friday evenings; and likewise starts from the house of Mrs. Kimball, Frederick Town, every Monday and Thursday at six o'clock, and arrives at Lancaster on Tuesday and Friday evenings; next morning proceeds on to the city of Philadelphia in the Turnpike line of stages, owned by Messrs. David Witmer & George Weed.

"A stage of Mr. Winemiller starts from Mrs. Kimball's, Frederick Town, every Wednesday morning at six o'cock, arrives in George Town on the evening of the same day. Sets out again from Georgetown on every Saturday morning at six o'clock and arrives in Frederick in the evening.

"Likewise a stage of Messrs. McClellan & Spangler starts from the house of Mr. Balster Spangler, Little York, on every Monday at one P.M. for Baltimore; leaves Baltimore every Wednesday at ten o'clock, and arrives in York on Thursday evening.

"Passengers going on to George Town or Baltimore may, by taking the Monday's stage from Lancaster, arrive at either place without being detained on the road. And, in returning from the above place, the line will immediately go on to the city of Philadelphia.

"The fare from Lancaster to Frederick Town is $4.50; from Frederick Town to George Town, $3.00. The usual allowance of fourteen pounds gratis to each passenger; one hundred and fifty pounds the same as a passenger.

"JOHN RILEY."

April 13, 1797, the Frederick Town stage was advertised to start from the house of Wm. Fares, in Lancaster, for York and Frederick Town every Tuesday at nine o'clock A.M., and from the house of Mr. Kimball, in Frederick Town, every Monday for York and Lancaster.

"The Mail Stage from Frederick Town to Susquehannah," says another advertisment, "will commence running three times a week, for spring, summer, and fall seasons, on the last Monday of February, 1803, starting from Mrs. Kimball's, sign of the Golden Lamb, Patrick Street, Frederick Town, every Monday, Wednesday, and Friday at four A.M., and arrive at Susquehannah evening of same days. Returning, will start from house of Mr. John Morrison, Susquehannah, every Tuesday, Thursday, and Saturday at four A.M., and arrive at Frederick Town on the evening of the same days. The line passes through Woodsborough, Taney Town, Petersburg, Hanover, and York, and meets the line of stages from Philadelphia at Susquehannah, and also the mail stage from city of Washington at Frederick, three times a week, which forms a regular line from Philadelphia to Washington.

(Signed) "WM. SCOTT,
"JOSHUA HALLAR,
"JOSEPH HALLAR.

"Feb. 14, 1803."

On the 24th of October, 1806, a new line of stages from Frederick Town to Winchester, Va., was established. It left Mrs. Kimball's, sign of the "Golden Lamb," Sunday morning at six o'clock, arriving at Winchester Monday morning at ten o'clock. It left Winchester Wednesday at one o'clock P.M., and arrived at Mrs. Kimball's Thursday evening. Fare $3.50; way passengers seven cents a mile.

The summer mail schedule of 1819 was as follows: Arrives at Frederick from the East, *via* Baltimore, on Sunday, Tuesday, and Thursdays from twelve to two P.M., other days at four P.M. Closes Monday, Wednesday, and Friday at eight A.M. and five P.M., and Saturday at five P.M.

Statistics of Frederick in 1798.—In 1798 there

were seven religious congregations of different denominations in Frederick, viz.: the Roman Catholic, the Episcopalian, the Lutheran, the Calvinists, the Presbyterian, the Baptists, and the Methodists. Each of these had a place of public worship. The German Presbyterian, or Calvinist, church had a handsome and lofty stone steeple, in which were two good bells and the town-clock. The German Protestant, or Lutheran, church had likewise a steeple and two bells of very sweet tone. The other buildings of a public nature were a spacious poor-house, a court-house, an academy, or county school-house, and two market-houses, all of brick, likewise a stone jail, with a large yard surrounded by a stone wall, four hundred and forty-nine dwelling-houses, besides a number of shops, etc., composed the town, which in 1797 contained the following number of inhabitants, viz.:

White males under ten years	387
" " from ten to sixteen	176
" " from sixteen upwards	682
Total of white males	1245
White females under ten years	325
" " from ten to sixteen	146
" " from sixteen upwards	584
Total white females	1055
Total of white males and females	2300
Colored males under ten years	50
" " from ten to sixteen	24
" " from sixteen upwards	44
Total colored males	118
Colored females under ten years	54
" " from ten to sixteen	25
" " from sixteen upwards	109
Total of colored females	188
Total of colored males and females	306
Total number of inhabitants, white and colored	2606

The industrial occupations were represented as follows: two tobacconists, fifteen blacksmiths, eleven saddlers, sixteen joiners, two comb-makers, twenty-nine shoemakers, twelve weavers, one worker in paste, five wagon-makers, several taverns, eleven hatters, three stocking weavers, five gunsmiths, three nailers, thirteen tailors, thirty-four stores and mercantile shops, three painters, one portrait-painter, thirteen masons, two skinners, six tanners, two curriers, three printers, six butchers, two clock and watch-makers, one silversmith, four coppersmiths, four tinners, three wheelwrights, three chair-makers, one harness-maker, four potters, four leather breeches makers and glovers, two apothecaries, two brewers, one well-digger, five barbers, two cabinet-makers, one pump-maker, two saddle-tree-makers, one brick-maker, one brush-maker, nine bakers, five carpenters, two turners, one cooper, one "white-smith," two reed-makers, two distillers, one miller, two heel-makers, two blue dyers, two plasterers, and several teachers, doctors of divinity, physic, and law.

The greater part of the mechanics employed journeymen and apprentices. From the above statement it will be seen that manufacturing industries must have been carried on with a good deal of enterprise and on a considerable scale.

Market-House and City Hall.—In the early history of the province and State, and, indeed, up to less than half a century ago, lotteries were authorized by the Legislature to raise money for the erection of churches, public buildings, bridges, etc., and were a favorite means of making public improvements without resorting to taxation. On the 21st of December, 1769, a "drawing" was held in Frederick and Prince George's Counties for three thousand one hundred and eighty acres of land, divided into numerous prizes. On May 25, 1811, a lottery was held in Frederick Town for paving Market Street, for which there were 8000 tickets at $5, $40,000, all prizes, 20 per cent. profits, $8000 to be raised. The managers of this municipal scheme were John McPherson, Henry Steiner, Seth Clarke, William Ross, and Raymond Sanderson.

In December, 1768, a scheme for a lottery was devised for raising $600 for finishing the market-house and town hall in Frederick. There were 2000 tickets at $2 each, and 557 prizes. The profits retained were 15 per cent. The managers to conduct the lottery were Christopher Edelin, Casper Shaaf, Thomas Price, George Murdock, Levi Cohen, Jacob Young, Lodowick Weltner, Charles Beatty, Joseph Gaither, George Scott, Adam Fisher, John Horse, William Parker, Jacob Schley, Daniel Hughes, Upton Sheredine, George Stricker, James Cramplin, Jr., William Deakin, Jr., Andrew Steigar. This lottery was drawn with great success in the coming year, 1769, and the work on the building was immediately commenced. It was erected on Patrick Street, on the lot where John H. Ramsburg's carriage-manufactory is now situated. The General Assembly, by an act passed Nov. 2, 1770, fixed an ordinance making Wednesday and Saturday market days, which continued in force until 1788. An act to establish a market in Frederick Town, passed Nov. 17, 1787, provided that a deed made Jan. 20, 1786, by William Murdock Beall, Henry McCleary, John Gebhart, and Henry Zeiler, of a lot of central ground containing sixty feet by one hundred and eighty feet, more or less, and an alley of twelve feet by one hundred and fifty-five feet, and transferred to Baker Johnson, Richard Potts, George Murdock, John Bruner, Jacob Steiner, John Adlum, and Peter Mantz, as trustees, etc., to be set apart for the use of the inhabitants of Frederick Town, together with other ground for the widening of alleys, shall be used for market buildings, etc., to remain free and open for the benefit of the public.

Louis McMurray was born in Baltimore (now Carroll) County, twenty-eight miles northwest of Baltimore City, on the 27th of February, 1823. He was the son of Samuel and Sarah McMurray. His father was a farmer, and continued farming until 1832, when he moved to Baltimore. John McMurray, father of Samuel, came to this country from Ireland with his wife, and went to Virginia in 1788, where a daughter was born,—Anne McMurray. Her mother brought her to Baltimore, where she was baptized at the cathedral in 1789 by the Rev. John Carroll, afterwards Archbishop of Baltimore. Anne McMurray married John Little, brother of Peter Little, who was a representative in Congress for twenty-one years. Shortly before her death she was confirmed by Archbishop Gibbons. She was thus baptized by the first Archbishop of Baltimore and confirmed by the last, who still fills the office.

Samuel McMurray, father of Louis, was born on his father's farm, in Baltimore County, in 1792. This farm was purchased in 1789. Samuel McMurray came to Baltimore in 1813–14, and took an active part in defending the city during the war of 1812. At the termination of the war he returned to his farm. He married, in 1815, Sarah Sellman, daughter of Vachel and Eleanor Sellman. John Sellman, of William, father of Vachel, Jonathan, and Johanzee, came to this country in 1750, and established the furnace or iron-works situated about two miles west of Westminster. These have been worked, with longer or shorter intermissions, to the present time.

Vachel Sellman married, in 1793, Eleanor Gill, of Baltimore County, whose father resided near Black Rock, and was one of the leading farmers in his section.

Louis McMurray has three sisters,—Catharine, Ann, and Caroline McMurray. Catharine married twice, her first husband being Adolphus Dellinger, who was a prominent merchant in Baltimore, and afterwards in Cincinnati, Ohio. He died in 1844. In 1846 she married Ira S. Holden, a merchant of New Orleans. They are both now deceased and buried in Greenmount Cemetery.

Ann S. McMurray married Micajah Young, a native of Baltimore County, but a resident of Montgomery, Ala.

Caroline McMurray married Charles E. Houghton, a merchant of Cincinnati, Ohio, now a resident of Baltimore.

Samuel McMurray and family moved to Baltimore in 1832, where he engaged in the hotel business as proprietor of the Western Hotel, corner of Howard and Saratoga Streets. He retired from the Western Hotel in 1838 to a residence on Pearl Street. In 1840 he commenced keeping a restaurant, and his son Louis engaged in the business with him. He continued in that business until his death in 1850.

In 1851, Louis McMurray was married to Jane Monica McDermott by the Rev. Alexius Elder, at the residence of her uncle, Thomas Smith. She is the daughter of Francis McDermott, of York, Pa., a distinguished classical teacher in his day. Mrs. McMurray, on the mother's side, is a niece of the late Rev. Andrew Smith, of Georgetown College, and Rev. John Smith, for many years pastor of St. James' Church, New York City.

Louis McMurray continued in the restaurant business about one year after his father's death, when, in the fall of 1851, he commenced in a small way packing hermetically sealed goods. After packing the goods they were consigned to Ira S. Holden, of New Orleans, La. The goods were sold at enormous prices. Previous to this time Mr. McMurray had had no knowledge of the packing business, and he had to grope his way in the dark. He was confident that hermetically sealed goods would come to be used in every household, and this caused him to make special efforts to be one of the successful packers. The profits arising from the first shipment dazzled his eyes, and, as Mulberry Sellers says, he thought "there were millions in it." But he was somewhat disappointed, not in the profits, but in the keeping of the packed goods, particularly oysters, of which he packed a considerable quantity. The losses and difficulties were many and great, as the method of packing was not very perfect. At that date very little was known about the use of steam in the preparation of oysters. Many experiments were tried to ascertain the temperature necessary to keep oysters, peas, and the different kinds of vegetables. After various trials it was found that a higher temperature was required than the boiling-point of water, 212°, and after various experiments Mr. McMurray discovered that the proper temperature could be obtained by a solution of calcium potash, or salt. This discovery enabled him to pack oysters and vegetables so that they would keep with but a small percentage of spoilage, and he shipped the goods readily to all parts of the world. Mr. McMurray soon found it necessary to enlarge his business, and commenced building extensive factories on the property purchased of Sellman Shipley and others, the heirs of Johanzee Sellman. The factories were built of such dimensions as to enable Mr. McMurray in the busy season of fruit to employ, as he has frequently done, eight hundred to a thousand hands in preparing peaches and other fruits and vegetables. In the winter season the oysters were packed in the same factory and required about three hundred hands. These extensive accommodations enabled him to pack large quantities of goods to meet the demands both of the home and foreign markets. He also built his dwelling, 268 West Biddle Street, adjoining the factory, where he now resides. In 1868, owing to the failure of the peach crop in Maryland, Mr. McMurray went to Cincinnati that season to pack peaches. There he became familiar with the taste of sugar-corn. Previous to that he had very little knowledge of sugar-corn, as the corn packed in the Baltimore factory was what is termed field-corn, and not of that delicious sweetness which sugar-corn retains after packing. For a few years Mr. McMurray had for partners Messrs. Alexander B. Ellis and Charles E. Houghton. Mr. McMurray consulted them about the packing of sugar-corn, but they did not approve the idea. In the fall of 1868 he visited Frederick, and having satisfied himself that the venture was practicable, bought a lot of four acres from Peter Manse in Frederick, opposite the former residence of Chief Justice Taney. In the spring of 1869, Mr. McMurray commenced the erection of his factories at Frederick.

He contracted with the farmers of the vicinity at high prices to raise several hundred acres of corn, and one hundred acres of tomatoes and peas were planted out. One of the farmers of the region called on Mr. McMurray and said, "Mr. McMurray, don't you think you are doing very wrong? No sane man would plant that much corn and tomatoes; they would not be used in Frederick in all your life." Mr. McMurray replied that it would be all right. Twenty-five practical tinners from Baltimore were sent to Frederick, and commenced making cans; but the farmers who had agreed to raise corn for him by the acre thought it was a wild-goose speculation, and gave very little attention to the corn-fields and cultivation, consequently the crops were poor, and there was very little corn to pack. This was the cause of a very heavy loss the first year. But this did not deter Mr. McMurray, as he knew sugar-corn could be raised successfully in Maryland. He accordingly consulted Thomas H. Smith, his foreman, and they concluded that they must commence farming the lands themselves to make a success. The first year or so Mr. McMurray rented the land, and afterwards commenced purchasing farms as they were offered for sale. The doubts of the Frederick County farmers were shared by Baltimore canners, one of whom, Thomas Kensett, said to him one day, "Mr. McMurray, you had better burn down your factory in Frederick, and you will make money by stopping the corn business." Mr. McMurray smiled and thanked him, but told him he would stick it out to the last. Mr. Kensett said there could be no sugar-corn raised equal to that grown in Maine, but Mr. McMurray has proved to the contrary. In 1870, the second year of Mr. McMurray's Frederick enterprise, the men who did the scaling up of the cans, and who had contracted with him to the end of the packing season, business becoming a little slack for a few days, became restless and wanted to return to Baltimore. Mr. McMurray immediately set to work and invented and obtained a patent for a machine for sealing up the cans by unskilled labor. This enabled a boy of sixteen years of age to seal up twice as many cans as could be formerly done with the old capping-iron and skilled labor. This is the principle used in nearly all the factories in the United States. Mr. McMurray also invented a stove for heating the irons which are used. He also obtained several other patents for soldering devices, which he uses in his factories. With the help of his invention, thirty unskilled boys, who have never capped a can before, can cap up one hundred thousand cans a day. Without this it would require fifty men skilled in the art of tinning to do the same amount of work. Mr. McMurray has purchased one thousand acres of land of Miss Emily Harper, being part of "Carrollton Manor," and now owns two thousand five hundred acres of land in Frederick County, which is regularly cultivated in connection with his canning business. His agricultural operations are conducted with his own teams and under the foremanship of Thomas H. Smith, and it requires three millions of cans to contain the corn thus raised. When in full operation last season from eighty to one hundred thousand cans were packed each day, and eleven hundred and fifty hands employed in the various departments of the Frederick business.

Mr. McMurray's success has been recognized, not only by the increasing demand for his goods, but by the awards of several international expositions. At the Centennial Exposition in 1876 he received the highest medal and diploma for canned sugar-corn, and also the highest diploma and medal for canned oysters. At the Paris Exposition in 1878 he received a gold medal and a diploma, the highest awards of the Exposition, for the superiority of his corn and the excellence of his oysters. It may be added that Mr. McMurray can justly claim to be the first person to raise and pack sugar-corn to any large extent in Maryland. In 1872, Mr. McMurray purchased a lot at the foot of Cross Street, Baltimore, from Charles M. Dougherty, where he had erected extensive factories for the packing of oysters, fruits, etc. Soon after, Mr. Ellis died, and Mr. Charles E. Houghton withdrew from the business. The Baltimore factory fronts seven hundred and fifty feet on Cross Street, employing during the oyster season from four hundred to five hundred hands, canning four thousand bushels per day, and during the fruit season from six hundred to seven hundred hands.

The present market-house and town hall was built in 1872. On June 19th of that year an ordinance was passed appropriating $40,000 for its erection, but the cost of construction with the purchase of some additional ground made the total expenditure $55,000. The city hall, one of the finest rooms in the State, has a comfortable seating capacity for eleven hundred people, and is well arranged and ventilated.

Fire Companies.—The first fire company in Frederick was organized in the year 1760, but its name has not been preserved. In that year a lottery was gotten up for raising five hundred dollars for purchasing a fire-engine, consisting of seventeen hundred and fifty tickets, at two dollars each. The surplus, if any, it was announced, would be applied towards the erection of a market-house in the town. By this scheme there were little more than two and a quarter blanks to a prize, and the profits retained were not quite fifteen per cent. upon the whole. The managers were Thomas Schley, James Dickson, Conrad Grosh, Arthur Charlton, Christopher Edelin, Michael Roman, Casper Shaaf, Thomas Price, Levi Cohen, John Cary, and George Murdock.

On Feb. 14, 1806, another lottery was announced for purchasing a fire-engine with hose. The scheme was—

1500 tickets at $2	$3000
Prizes	2177
Sum to be raised	$823

Its managers were Henry Steiner, Francis Mantz, Henry Bentz, George Creager, Sr., Levi Welteheimer, Charles Shell, Jacob Medtart, C. Adam Ebert, Peter Burckhardt.

In 1807 the "Friendship Fire Company" existed. Its engine was made in London, England, and was the best in America when brought over.

In 1813, at a meeting of the "Union Fire Company," the following distribution of the members was made, and on September 1st was published for the information of the citizens of the town:

Property-men, Daniel Hauer, Sr., Henry McCleary, Conrad Doll, John Gebhart, William House; Engineers, George Baer, Frederick Heisler, Vezey Koontz; Lane-men, Henry Steiner, Jacob Baer, Michael Hauser, John Rigney, William Michael, John McPherson; Bucket-men, Jacob Steiner, Woodward Evitt; Axe-men, William Baer, of Henry, John Haw; Trumpet-men, John Hanson Thomas, George Littlejohn; Councilors to the trumpet-men, Abraham Shriver, Jacob Steiner, and Woodward Evitt; Hook-men, Harry Baer, John Dill, John Fisler, Sr., Michael Kolb, Frederick Reed, George Hauer; Ladder-men, Joshua Dorsey, John Reich, John Baltzell, Philip Hauptman, Solomon Steckle, David Boyd, John Fritchie, James Robertson, Peter Fout, Charles T. Melsheimer, Thomas Shaw, James Archy, Benjamin Williams, Jacob Rohr, William Wirtenburger.

Independent Fire Company.—This veteran company, the oldest existing in Maryland, is sixty-four years of age, having been organized in 1818. Its records prior to 1836 are lost, but its performances in subduing conflagrations live in the grateful recollections of the citizens, the oldest of whom, like the venerable Peter Reich, ran with its engine over three-score years ago. Its officers have been as follows:

1836.—President, G. M. Conradt; Vice-President, Jacob Doll; Secretary, D. J. Markley; Treasurer, Gideon Bantz, Sr.; Principal Engineer, D. B. Devitt; Assistants, George Hoskins, Daniel Haller; Directors, William Small, John Fessler; Pipe Director, G. M. Conradt; Hose Director, Jacob Doll; Engine Director, John Fessler; Lane Director, William Small; Property Guards, William Schley, Joseph Schell; Superintendents fire-plugs, John Schaeffer, Mark Besore; Ladder-men, Jacob Neckle, Henry Kepler; Lane-men, F. A. Schley, Samuel Cormack, Casper Quinn; Axe-men, John Hanshan, Henry Rhodes; Hosemen, George Salmon, Philip Reich, Henry Young, V. J. Brunner, Henry Hansfield, Edward Trail, George J. Fischer, Gideon Bantz, Sr., W. C. Russell.

1837.—President, Casper Quynn; Secretary, D. J. Markley.
1838-39.—President, Casper Quynn; Secretary, George Markell.
1840.—President, Casper Quynn; Secretary, Robert Johnston.
1841.—President, Casper Quynn; Secretary, Edward Shriver.
1842-43.—President, Casper Quynn; Secretary, F. A. Rigney.
1844.—President, Casper Quynn; Secretary, A. G. Quynn.
1845.—President, Edward Shriver; Secretary, W. H. Spangler.
1846-47.—President, Edward Shriver; Secretary, F. A. Rigney.
1848-52.—President, Edward Shriver; Secretary, H. C. Steiner.
1852.—President, Edward Shriver; Secretary, J. Willie Rice.
1853.—President, Edward Shriver; Secretary, H. C. Steiner.
1854.—President, Edward Shriver; Secretary, J. Willie Rice.
1855-67.—President, Edward Shriver; Secretary, P. W. Englebrecht.
1867-79.—President, Edward Shriver; Secretary, John W. Kaufman.
1879-80.—President, James McSherry; Secretary, Joseph F. Eisenhauer.
1881.—President, James McSherry; Vice-Presidents, John W. Baughman, George C. Derr; Treasurer, John C. Hardt; Secretary, Joseph F. Eisenhauer; Assistant Secretary, S. Harry Hauer; Directors, W. E. Getzendanner, C. B. Tyson, Warren Tyson, W. A. Simmons, H. C. Keefer, Dr. F. T. Burck; Foreman, H. B. Tyson; Assistants, J. S. Veit, George Kline, Charles Holm, Charles Mullen; Chief Engineer, D. H. Kolb; Assistants, Casper Brust, Frank Ross, Samuel Jones, Dorsey Tyson; Firemen, Henry Brust, George Salter, James Lowe, Christopher Hiltner; Chief Pipeman, Charles A. Porter; Assistants, Edward Oden, M. Miller, William Angerine, William Hiltner, Edward Mulhorn, Edward Eader, C. B. Shipe, J. C. Woodward, E. L. Green, J. C. Bobst; Surgeon, Dr. Frank T. Burck.

In September, 1876, the company got its first steam-engine, "Romeo," costing four thousand dollars, and in 1881 exchanged it, damaged by a fire, for its second one, "Juliet," costing three thousand two hundred dollars. In 1876 it sold its old hand-engine, previous to getting a steam one, to a fire company in Winchester, Va. Its present membership is four hundred and forty, and it has eight hundred feet of hose. Its engine-house is on West Church Street, near the old Reformed church. Since 1836 it has had but three presidents, to wit: Casper Quynn, serving eight years; Gen. Edward Shriver, serving thirty-four; and Capt. James McSherry, the past three. In forty-five years it has had only eleven secretaries.

Junior Fire Company.—The origin of this company arose from the casual meeting in the last week of November, 1838, of William Carlton, Alex. K. Mantz, and George F. Webster in Mr. Mantz' drugstore. These gentlemen published a notice in the *Herald* for a meeting to be held for the formation of a young men's fire company at the Dill House, at which Mr. Carlton presided, and Mr. Mantz was secretary. On December 15th another meeting was held and committees appointed to solicit subscriptions. These committees reported from time to time the amounts subscribed, until, in January, 1839, the City Council voted to make up the amount necessary to secure to the company an engine, hose-carriage, etc. The full organization took place in that month by the election of William Pitts, president; William Carlton, vice-president; Ezra Dadysman, secretary; William Gittinger, treasurer; James Brunner, William F. Johnson, George F. Webster, Samuel Canby, James Bartgis, and A. K. Mantz, directors. The company contracted with John Rogers, of Baltimore, for an engine for one thousand dollars, and the lot twelve feet front in the rear of the Farmers' and Mechanics' Bank was secured for the purpose of erecting an engine-house upon it. At a meeting held Feb. 16, 1839, the hose and hose-reels were ordered, one from Mr. Rogers, of Baltimore, and the other from H. Boetler, of Frederick. Aug. 24, 1839, the engine was received and placed in the engine-house, which had been erected on the lot above mentioned. On March 23d it was ordered that the engine be painted a vermilion red. The officers have been the following:

1840.—President, Ezra Houck; Vice-President, Samuel Duer; Secretary, Ezra Dadysman; Treasurer, E. P. Eberts; Directors, James Brunner, Peter Goodmanson, Henry Boteler, Samuel Canby, George L. Brengle, A. A. Stambaught; Chief Engineer, John Bender; Assistant Engineers, John W. Birely, John D. Himmell.

1841–42.—President, Ezra Houck; Chief Engineer, John Bender.

1843.—President, Ezra Houck; Chief Engineer, John H. Birely.

1844–45.—President, Ezra Houck; Chief Engineer, John Bender.

1846.—President, Ezra Houck; Chief Engineer, William Bartgis.

1847.—President, Ezra Houck; Chief Engineer, Henry Titlow.

1848.—President, Ezra Houck; Chief Engineer, J. W. Birely.

1849–50.—President, Ezra Houck; Chief Engineer, John Lambright.

1851–53.—President, Ezra Doub; Chief Engineer, William Bartgis.

1854–55.—President, Ezra Doub; Chief Engineer, John Lambright.

1856.—President, Ezra Doub; Chief Engineer, G. James Buckey.

1857–70.—President, John W. Birely; Chief Engineer, Jacob Buckey.

1870.—President, John W. Birely; Chief Engineer, J. J. Shindler.

1871–74.—President, John W. Birely; Chief Engineer, Jacob Buckey.

1874.—President, Edward Koontz; Chief Engineer, G. Jacob Buckey.

1875–77.—President, Edward Koontz; Chief Engineer, William F. Buesing.

1877–81.—President, Edward Koontz; Chief Engineer, Francis T. Rhodes.

1881.—President, Edward Koontz; Vice-Presidents, Albert T. Rice, L. V. Baughman; Secretary, Alexander Brengle; Treasurer, William P. Rice; Investigating Committee, John D. Zeiler, J. Henry Lampe, George S. Rhodock; Foreman, Nicholas Blumenour; Assistant Foremen, C. P. Smith, W. C. Birely; Chief Engineer, Francis T. Rhodes; Assistant Engineers, William Winebrenner, E. C. Ebbert, Lewis Boyer, Clarence C. Rice; Firemen, Joseph Brunchey, W. H. Buesing, Edward Stoner, William Kushmaul; Chief Hose Director, M. A. Woodward; Assistants, Richard Lipps, M. C. Rice, Henry Haller; Chief Pipe-men, C. T. Topper; Assistants, George Groshon, H. W. Falk, George Mulhorn, George Ketler, W. H. Shipley, Edward Nursz, Philip Whisner, Howard Kushmaul; Surgeon, Dr. S. F. Francis.

The present engine-house on Market Street was built in 1846, on the old Hart lot, and in 1872 was enlarged at an expense of six thousand five hundred dollars. The first engine-house, on the lot in the rear of the Farmers' and Mechanics' Bank, was a one-story brick building. The company bought its present steam-engine in the fall of 1876 for four thousand dollars. It is called the Silsby engine, and was made at Seneca Falls, N. Y. It now has five hundred feet of hose attached. This company has two hundred and fifty-three active and eighty-three life members.

United Fire Company.—The United Fire Company was organized in 1845, with Charles Mantz as its first president, and was the successor of the old Washington Hose Company, which had a short time before ceased to exist. Its first engine was one of the old-fashioned hand-engines. In 1848 its present engine-house on Market Street was erected. All its records and books up to July 24, 1868, were lost by the flood of that date, when Quintman S. J. Beckley was its secretary. Since then its officers have been as follows:

1869.—President, John Loats; First Vice-President, John T. Sim; Second Vice-President, Augustus Boteler; Secretary, Q. S. J. Beckley; Treasurer, Charles E. Tabler; Directors, Hiram Bartgis, J. D. Zeiler, Jacob B. Tyson, Jacob Lillich, Milton McDaniel, Edward Sim; Chief Engineer, N. J. Wilson.

1870-75.—President, John T. Sim; Secretary, F. M. Faubel.

1875.—President, John T. Sim; Secretary, L. T. O. Frazier.

1876-78.—President, Gabriel Beckley; Secretary, John H. Bennett.

1878-81.—President, Hiram Bartgis; Secretary, John H. Bennett.

1881.—President, Hiram Bartgis; First Vice-President, Frederick J. Nelson; Second Vice-President, A. L. Butler; Secretary, John H. Bennett; Treasurer, Lewis Rice; Directors, David A. Castle, George Wentz, J. Sahm, N. J. Wilson, David Kolb, George W. Vanforsen, E. N. Hobbs; Chief Engineer, Moses Fisher; Assistant Engineers, Joseph Chew, Charles Chew, Charles B. Clabaugh, William Need; Chief Fireman, Frank Chew; Assistant Firemen, Oscar L. Haller, William Duvall, Lewis Albaugh, George Moberly; Chief Pipe-man, F. T. Kesserling; Foreman, Jacob B. Tyson; Assistant Foremen, E. D. Frazier, Willie Bartgis.

Its present engine, "The Lily of the Swamp," was purchased Feb. 22, 1878, and is one of the best steam fire-engines in the State. Over four hundred and fifty persons are members of this company. It has turned out in the past year on parade over one hundred and twenty-five members dressed in tasteful uniforms.

Schools, Libraries, Societies, Etc.—The General Assembly of the Province of Maryland, Oct. 26, 1723, passed an act for the encouragement of learning and the erection of school-houses in the several counties. It provided for one school in every county, to be under the control of seven visitors. On Nov. 26, 1763, another act was passed for erecting a public school in Frederick County, and authorizing the purchase of an acre of ground in Frederick Town, to be bought by the following persons nominated as school visitors, viz.: Col. Thomas Cresap, Thomas Beatty, Nathan Magruder, Capt. Joseph Chapline, John Darnall, Col. Samuel Beall, and Rev. Thomas Bacon. These visitors were empowered to erect a school-house out of certain funds collected for the use of the county schools. By an act passed June 22, 1768, it was recited that, as it was apprehended that the purchase of one acre for the school would be attended with too much expense, and as the first visitors appointed lived so remote and distant from each other that it was inconvenient for them to attend and execute the duties of their office, therefore it was enacted that the following new visitors be appointed, viz.: Jonathan Wilson, Thomas Bowlus, George Murdock, Maj. Joseph Wood, Thomas Price, Casper Shaaf, and Charles Beatty, who were authorized to purchase half an acre and erect thereon a school-house. By an act passed Dec. 20, 1769, it was recited that the funds appropriated were insufficient to purchase ground and make the necessary buildings thereon. It was therefore enacted that the justices of the County Court cause to be laid out and butted and bounded with stones, or good locust posts, one-half acre of the lots laid off for public uses in Frederick Town, on the northwest corner of the said court-house, and which said half-acre was vested in the said school visitors and their successors in office for the use of said school. The funds appropriated by the Assembly for said school being insufficient to erect the buildings, the inhabitants of the county got up a lottery to raise nine hundred dollars to make up the deficiency. The managers were Jonathan Wilson, Thomas Bowlus, George Murdock, Joseph Wood, Thomas Price, Casper Shaaf, Charles Beatty, Samuel Beall, Jr., Normand Bruce, Andrew Heugh, Eneas Campbell, Christopher Edelin, John Cary, Lodowick Weltner, Peter Gosh, Thomas Neil, Nicholas Tice, Samuel Hughes, Thomas Johns, and James Brand. Three thousand tickets were sold, at two dollars each, and there were eight hundred and fifty-two prizes. The drawing took place Nov. 2, 1769. The history of the school up to 1797 is very meagre, and whether there was any school building erected before that time is uncertain. Hugh Montgomery Brackenridge taught an academy, beginning Aug. 1, 1778. He had fifteen scholars, and charged thirty pounds per pupil, without board, but this was depreciated currency of the Revolution. Rev. George Ralph opened an academy Jan. 16, 1792. James Clark opened a seminary April 11, 1793, in Dr. Philip Thomas' house, near the Baptist church. The General Assembly, at the November session of 1796, passed an act reciting that, under the act of 1763, the specified one acre had been purchased, and that under that of 1769 the designated one-half acre had been appropriated out of lots for public uses, and that commodious buildings thereon had been erected and nearly completed. Therefore it was enacted that there be founded a school or seminary of learning in Frederick Town, to be known as "Frederick County School."

This act appointed George Murdock, Richard Potts, Dr. Philip Thomas, Baker Johnson, Francis Mantz, John McPherson, and George Baer, Jr., as school visitors, who were made a corporation and body politic. This act would seem to establish the fact that prior to 1797 no school building had been erected on these lots. The "Academy" was opened Oct. 2, 1797, under Samuel Knox, principal, at which time William Potts took the place of Francis Mantz, resigned, in the board. October 7th, Hatch Dent became teacher of the English department, at a salary of one hundred and twenty-five pounds per annum and the tuition fees of three pounds per annum, he to collect them from the pupils.

An act passed by the Assembly in 1798 (November session) appropriated eight hundred dollars, payable annually, to this school out of the treasury of the Western Shore.

In 1799, Thomas Barnaby was the junior English teacher, and Mr. Cairon the French. Tuition fees: twenty dollars per annum for Latin and Greek, twelve dollars for English until entering on some branch of mathematics, and from that period to be sixteen dollars.

An act passed at the November session, 1801, provided for a lottery for the benefit of the school, and made the appointment of additional school visitors, to wit: William Luckett, William Hobbs, of Samuel, Roger Nelson, Peter Mantz, John Schley, Joshua Dorsey, Daniel Clark, Jr., and Robert Cummings. But in place of Peter Mantz, resigned, William Campbell was appointed, who after a few weeks declined, and Oct. 30, 1804, Roger Brooke Taney was chosen to fill the vacancy. Francis McHenry was a teacher in the first English school in 1806. On July 19, 1803, Thomas Luckett, a student in the classical department, and Richard Smith, of the advanced English school, were charged with having fought a duel, Smith sending the challenge, and George Mason acting as second to Luckett. Smith was expelled and the other two pupils reprimanded, or rather Mason was only slightly censured. It appears that one shot passed between the combatants, when the second (Mason) seized the pistols and stopped further proceedings. On July 20th the resolutions expelling Smith and reprimanding Luckett were rescinded. This duel and subsequent proceedings relative thereto created great exitement. On Sept. 22, 1803, Samuel Knox, principal of the school, resigned, and was succeeded by Dennis Dunlevy, with John McDonald in the introductory English school, and Lewis St. Martin teacher of French.

July 26, 1805, George Murdock having died and Daniel Clarke removed from the county, their places as visitors were filled by electing Dr. John Baltzell and Maj. John Graham. In 1804, John H. Thomas became a visitor, vice John Schley, resigned, and Mr. Guillou was appointed, in 1806, the French teacher. In 1807, Edward Salmon was the mathematical teacher. In 1809, Dr. Edward Anderson was chosen visitor, vice William Potts, resigned, and S. Markell was made master of the introductory school, and Charles Cresolles the French teacher. August 15th, Rev. Patrick Davidson was made master of the mathematical department. July 8, 1809, William Ross became visitor, vice Richard Potts, deceased. On the 12th of December, 1810, Dr. Philip Thomas was elected president of the board of directors, and Dr. J. Baltzell secretary. To fill the vacancy in the principalship, caused by the resignation of Dennis Dunlevy, Sept. 1, 1809, John V. Weylie was elected March 2, 1811. On March 22, 1813, a rule was promulgated against students dancing, and Charles James Wolfender was expelled for sending to his brother student, Peachy H. Williams, a challenge to fight a duel. Samuel Markell, teacher of the inferior English school, established the Lancasterian system on May 4, 1813.

There is no record of the board from June 3, 1814, to July 24, 1815, between which periods Dr. Philip Thomas (president), John Hanson Thomas, and Roger Nelson died. Francis A. Schley and Richard Potts were chosen to fill two of the vacancies, and John McPherson was made president. In 1819, on the death of Joshua Dorsey, John Brien was made visitor in his place. Feb. 1, 1819, Roger Brooke Taney resigned as visitor, and Dr. William Tyler was chosen in his stead, and on the 14th John Nelson was appointed. At the same date Rev. Samuel Knox was chosen principal of the school. June 13th, John H. McElfresh was chosen visitor, vice George Baer, resigned, and Frederick Ellsworth was selected as teacher in place of Rev. Mr. Davidson, deceased. Sept. 26, 1826, John Graham and John Brien, two of the visitors, having resigned, their places were filled with Abraham Shriver and Dr. Grafton Duvall. On May 4, 1827, after a heated controversy, the Lancasterian system was abolished by a vote of four to three. Ayes: John McPherson, Abraham Shriver, John McElfresh, Frederick A. Schley. Nays: Dr. John Baltzell, William Tyler, John Nelson.

On June 27, 1827, Samuel Markell was appointed teacher in place of Frederick Ellsworth, deceased. August 20th, James G. McNeely was appointed principal of the classical department, and C. J. Haderman teacher of the mathematical department. David F. Schaffer became a visitor this year. On June 17, 1828, a ball-alley was ordered to be built with two sides in the yard of the academy, and trees to be planted in said yard. On July 12th the resolution ordering the erection of a ball-alley was rescinded, and one adopted substituting nine-pins and quoits for the recreation of the pupils. Sept. 23d, Mr. Grillet was elected as French teacher.

The General Assembly passed an act at its December session, 1828, authorizing the visitors to sell the school-lots and buildings, and buy ground elsewhere and erect more commodious buildings. This act also created the school into "Frederick College," with power to grant diplomas and degrees after a regular course of studies pursued under the prescribed curriculum of the board of visitors.

April 4, 1829, Mr. McNeely, the principal, resigned, and on May 4th, Nathaniel Vernon was elected mathematical teacher. May 9th, David F. Shaffer was elected superintendent of the institution and professor of moral philosophy and belles-lettres, and Samuel Hubbell teacher of the languages. July 30th, Rev. Mr. Swan was elected teacher, *vice* Mr. Hubbell, resigned.

Dec. 28, 1831, Dr. William McPherson and George M. Eichelberger were elected visitors, *vice* John Nelson and W. Schley. Mr. Eichelberger refusing to serve, William Ross was appointed. Freeman Converse was appointed teacher of the classics. April 9, 1832, the college's scheme of lottery was ordered to be sold at not less than two thousand five hundred dollars. August 29th, Mr. Converse resigned as teacher. July 20, 1833, the academy and lot were offered for sale. July 31, 1834, G. F. Stein was elected principal. April 22, 1835, Mr. Stein resigned, and Mr. Freeman Converse became principal. In 1837, Thomas W. Morgan, Worthington Johnson, Jacob Markell, and Dr. A. Richie were visitors. June 30, 1838, Mr. Converse resigned the principalship, and August 13th, Rev. Joseph Smith, of Franklin College, was elected in his place. In 1843, on the resignation of William Ross and the death of John H. McElfresh, William J. Ross and Samuel Tyler were elected visitors. In 1843, William Baer was professor of chemistry. June 10, 1844, Rev. Joseph Smith resigned as principal. November 18th, Dr. William Bradley Tyler was elected visitor, *vice* Dr. W. S. McPherson. Feb. 24, 1845, James Thompson, principal for the past year, resigned, and was succeeded by J. S. Bonsall. Thomas Turner succeeded Dr. John Baltzell as visitor. Aug. 16, 1848, Rev. James Barrow was elected to the English department. April 7, 1849, Mountjoy Luckett was elected visitor, *vice* Thomas Turner, deceased, and Jan. 4, 1851, J. M. Kunkell and Samuel Tyler were elected trustees, *vice* Drs. S. B. Tyler and A. Ritchie.

Dec. 12, 1851, Rev. Dr. Zacharias was elected a trustee, *vice* J. Markell, resigned, and Edward Shriver was also elected. Aug. 22, 1854, J. S. Bonsall was re-elected principal, Nathaniel Vernon teacher of mathematics, and Rev. E. W. Reinecke professor of English language, etc. Sept. 4, 1855, the salary of the principal was raised to nine hundred dollars, and the children of the teachers were ordered to be educated free. May 21, 1856, Prof. E. W. Reinecke resigned, and Mr. Harris was elected in his place. In 1856 the board consisted of Samuel Tyler, M. B. Luckett, Edward Shriver, Jacob Kunkel, Dr. Zacharias, Thomas Morgan, F. A. Schley, Jacob Markell, and L. J. Brengle. John D. Wilson was elected a teacher, *vice* Professor Harris, resigned. In 1857, Bradley T. Johnson was elected a visitor, and in 1861, Grayson Eichelberger and Dr. George Johnson, and in 1866, Gideon Bantz. In 1867, Charles Shafer was made professor of mathematics. In 1868, Dr. Fairfax Schley and Dr. W. H. Baltzell came into the board. In 1870, Col. G. R. Dennis and Jacob Reifsnider, and in 1873, Charles W. Ross, were elected members. In the same year G. C. Dearner succeeded J. S. Bonsall as principal, and was succeeded in 1876 by the present incumbent, Henry A. Gatch. Since then visitors have been elected as follows: In 1874, Francis Markell; 1877, Dr. Lewis H. Steiner and C. V. S. Levy; and in 1879, John H. Williams.

The officers for 1881 were as follows:

Board of Visitors.—General Edward Shriver, president; Fairfax Schley, M.D., William H. Baltzell, M.D., Gideon Bantz, C. V. S. Levy (secretary), L. H. Steiner, M.D., John H. Williams, Charles W. Ross, Francis Markell (treasurer). *Corps of Instructors.*—Principal, Thomas A. Gatch, A.M., Professor of Latin and Greek; E. C. Shepherd, Professor of Higher English Mathematics and Sciences; William H. Harry, Professor of Mathematics and Elementary English.

This institution is pleasantly situated at the corner of Counsel and Record Streets, away from the noise and bustle of the business part of the city. Its leading object is to make sound and accurate scholars, and to prepare those who are there educated to do honor to themselves in all the various relations of life. The scholastic year consists of two sessions, and the number of pupils average annually about ninety. It has a large, well-selected library, a valuable cabinet, and costly apparatus for its philosophical and chemical departments. Although in its reorganization of 1828 it was empowered as a college to confer degrees, it has remained a first-class academy.

On Oct. 24, 1806, Mrs. King opened a select school at the house occupied by Mrs. Reilner, nearly opposite the "Stone Well."

At a meeting held in Mr. Shafer's tavern it was agreed to commence a "Public Debate" every Saturday night, the first one to begin Dec. 16, 1809.

Sept. 22, 1810, the Frederick Town "Library Company" was organized and elected its officers.

On Feb. 22, 1811, "The Ugly Club" met at the house of C. G. Mueller to celebrate Washington's birthday.

May 4, 1812, the Lutheran Church Academy was opened under the charge of Rev. David F. Schaeffer, A.M., pastor of the Lutheran congregation, who taught Latin, Greek, "Logick," "Rhetorick," and the various branches of mathematics, English grammar, arithmetic, reading and writing, as well as the English and German languages.

On Dec. 18, 1817, at a town-meeting convened at the academy for the purpose of forming a "Bible Society," Rev. Patrick Davidson was called to the chair, and Rev. Charles Mann appointed secretary. A constitution was adopted, and the society called the "Frederick Bible and Charity Fund Society." It was ordered that all copies of the Scripture distributed by the society should be without notes or comments. The initiation fee was one dollar and annual subscription the same. Life membership was put at twenty dollars. The following were the committee to collect subscriptions: Revs. P. Davidson, D. F. Schaeffer, Chas. Mann, J. Helfenstein, Hatch and D. Martin, and Col. John Ritchie and John Brien.

"The Frederick County Bible Society" met Sept. 15, 1821, at the Lutheran church, and elected the following officers: President, John Graham; Vice-President, Jacob Steiner; Recording Secretary, Dr. Jacob Baer; Treasurer, Col. John Ritchie; Corresponding Secretaries, Revs. Jonathan Helfenstein, John Johns; Board of Managers, John Graham, F. A. Schley, Geo. Baer, John Nelson, Jacob Steiner, Jacob Baer, John Ritchie, Richard Potts, Wm. Ross, John Baltzell.

On Sept. 18, 1821, the first annual meeting of "The Young Men's Bible Society" was held in the German Reformed Presbyterian church, when the following directors were chosen for the ensuing year: Christian Steiner, Valentine J. Brunner, F. A. Gebhart, John Reitzell, Robert McCleary, Thos. H. Flemming, James M. Shellman, Wm. Fischer, John Fessler, Cyrus Mantz, Jas. F. Houston, David Boyd, Geo. Salmon, Thomas Sim, Singleton Duvall, John T. Brooke, W. V. Morgan, Wm. Waters, Geo. Englebrecht, Lewis Medtart. At a subsequent meeting of this board the following officers were elected: President, Cyrus Mantz; Vice-Presidents, John T. Brooke, Singleton Duvall; Treasurer, Geo. Englebrecht; Corresponding Secretary, J. F. Houston; Recording Secretary, L. Medtart.

On Oct. 13, 1821, the Frederick Town "Mechanics' Debating Society" met at Capt. Turbot's at early candle-light.

"The Frederick Benevolent Society" met (agreeably to adjournment) on Jan. 21, 1822, and elected the following officers for the ensuing year: President, John L. Potts; Secretary, Benjamin M. Miller; Treasurer, Lewis Medtart; Directors, John T. Brooke, J. M. Shellman, Wm. Y. Magill, Wm. Blackford, Robert McCleary, D. Shrengle, P. Tormey.

On March 1, 1823, "The Education Society of Frederick" was organized, its object being to educate orphans, or children whose parents were in reduced circumstances, to such knowledge as might be deemed requisite and necessary by the board of directors, who were David E. Shaeffer, F. Nurz, Geo. W. Ent, Geo. W. Conradt, Jacob Keller, Lewis Medtart, Geo. Englebrecht.

On March 12, 1827, a meeting of the citizens was held to establish a "Religious Tract Society." Wm. Ross was in the chair, and Geo. Englebrecht secretary. A constitution was formed, and the society called "The Auxiliary Tract Society of Frederick and Vicinity." Annual subscription, fifty cents; young persons, twenty-five cents. The officers elected for the year were: President, Lewis Medtart; Vice-Presidents, Frederick Ellsworth, David Boyd; Secretary, Geo. Englebrecht; Treasurer, Wm. L. Helfenstein.

On Aug. 22, 1853, Dr. Lewis H. Steiner was appointed professor of chemistry in the National Medical College.

In 1821 it was determined by the Synod of the Reformed Church to found a theological seminary at Frederick City, and on Jan. 12, 1822, the financial committee, through its chairman, John McPherson, announced that at the General Convention of the Reformed Church held at Reading, Pa., this seminary had been permanently located at Frederick, and Rev. Dr. P. Milledoller, of New York, elected its president.

In March, 1827, D. H. Bingham, formerly of Capt. Partridge's military school at Norwich, Vt., opened a military academy. A company of his cadets visited Hagerstown December 5th of that year. Their uniforms were neat, and their marching and manœuvres unusually correct and precise. During the visit they were entertained by Col. Williams and others, of Hagerstown, and by Dr. Boerstler, of Funkstown, by Mr. Fitzhugh, near that place, and Mr. Edwards, of Boonsboro'. The following committee of the cadets returned thanks in a card to the above gentlemen, viz.: H. H. Abbott, Wm. Harding, Joseph Webster, Wm. Foltz, H. Steiner. The institution was in successful operation for some time, and students came from distant States. Many of its pupils afterwards became distinguished in the late civil war, both in the Federal and Confederate ranks.

The Frederick Female Seminary has been in existence for nearly forty years, and during all that period has maintained a high standard of efficiency. It obtained its charter from the State Legislature in 1840, and subsequently received authority from the same source to raise fifty thousand dollars and erect suitable buildings. These buildings were completed in 1843, and are believed to equal those of any similar institution in the country. They consist of two commodious edifices in the Ionic style, each fifty feet front by ninety feet deep, with high basement and three stories. The Collegiate Hall, in which the commencement and other public exercises are held, is a fine apartment, forty by forty-eight feet and seventeen feet high, handsomely frescoed. To Hiram Winchester, the first president of the seminary, the community is principally indebted for the establishment of this institution. Through his instrumentality the charter was obtained and funds were raised for the erection of the buildings. The school was opened under its chartered privileges in 1845, and in 1846 the first catalogue was issued. The trustees that year were Gideon Bantz, David Boyd, and Christian Steiner, and over eighty students were in attendance, many of them from abroad. In process of time, as the school became popular and numbers increased, the buildings were found to be too small. Hence, in 1843, an additional grant was obtained from the Legislature authorizing the raising (before mentioned) of fifty thousand dollars. Of this sum twenty thousand was held as an endowment fund, and a part of the remainder appropriated to the erection of a second building, in design and architecture identical with the first. This is the western building and present school edifice, the eastern one being now used only as a dwelling. The history of the school was for many years one of great prosperity; numbers increased, and the names of many young ladies from the South appeared upon the roll of students. George D. Prentice, in the Louisville, Ky., *Journal* of Dec. 14, 1858, said, "We do not remember to have ever seen in any part of the United States such elegant and handsome edifices devoted to educational purposes as those of the Frederick Female Seminary." Mr. Winchester remained as president from 1846 to 1865. For a short time during the civil war the school was suspended, and the building was used by the United States forces for hospital purposes. This interregnum lasted during the autumn and winter of 1863 and '64 and the spring of 1864. Mr. Winchester resigned Aug. 18, 1865, and was succeeded by Rev. Thomas M. Cann. His administration continued through a term of eight years, until August, 1873, when he resigned. Prof. J. H. Hackelton was then elected to the presidency. In addition to the three first-mentioned trustees, the following names have at different periods appeared on the list: David Schley, G. M. Eichelberger, Lewis Ramsburg, Lewis T. Coppersmith, Dr. Lewis H. Steiner, David J. Markey, Grayson Eichelberger. The first graduating class of 1846 numbered three, and the total number of graduates is over two hundred and seventy-five. Prof. Hackelton died in 1877, since which time the seminary has been under the charge of his widow, Mrs. M. W. Hackelton. Prof. Hackelton was born in Bristol, Me., April 7, 1817, and was the youngest of a family of eight children of James Hackelton, a well-known shipbuilder. He graduated at Bowdoin College in 1844, and then went to Philadelphia, where he was admitted to the bar. About this time, being attacked with a serious bronchial affection, he visited Mississippi, in the hope that change of climate would effect a cure. There he engaged in teaching, first as professor of natural science and languages in the Holly Springs Female Institute, and afterwards as principal of Chalmers' Institute for Boys, in Holly Springs. In 1855 he became connected with the Female College at La Grange, Tenn., first as vice-president, and afterwards as president, on the death of his old friend and classmate, Prof. D. Z. Johnson, with whom he had been associated. Here he met and married Miss Maria W. Nash, of Hadley, Mass., and the next year returned to Holly Springs, to take charge of its Female Institute. The war interrupting for a time all educational effort, he was engaged in mercantile business in Memphis, Tenn., but soon returned to his much-loved profession of teaching, and in 1873 came to Frederick. He was a communicant of the Episcopal Church and a man of the highest character. His labors as an educator extended over a period of about thirty years. As a home for girls during the period allotted to their education, no more healthful or delightful location could well be found than the Frederick Seminary. It is easy of access, being directly upon the line of the Baltimore and Ohio and the Pennsylvania Railroads, and within two and a half hours' ride of Baltimore and Washington. The course of study is extensive, but particular attention is given to the common English branches. The seminary confers upon its post-graduates the degree of A.M., and upon those who complete the course of belles-lettres a gold medal. Pupils enjoy the advantages of a well-selected library, a good chemical and philosophical apparatus, a cabinet of minerals, maps, charts, globes, etc. Mrs. Hackelton, the principal, is assisted by her daughters and by a corps of teachers and professors.

The years 1870–80 were signalized by the erection of a mural tablet in Collegiate Hall in memoriam of Hiram Winchester, the founder of the institution, on which occasion Dr. Lewis H. Steiner delivered an eloquent address. The officers of the seminary are as follows:

Board of Trustees.—Charles E. Trail (president), J. Wm. Birely, Francis Markell, Milton G. Urner, Lewis M. Nixdorff. *Visiting Committee.*—Rev. Geo. Deihl, D.D., Rev. Osborne Ingle, Rev. S. V. Leech, D.D., Rev. Irvin P. McCurdy, Rev. E. R. Eschbach, D.D., Rev. H. Bielfeld, Rev. H. P. Hammill, Hon. Wm. J. Ross, Thomas M. Wolfe (last two appointed by the Governor). *Faculty.*—Mrs. M. W. Hackelton (president), Biblical Literature, Mental and Moral Science, Belles-Lettres, and Elocution; Rev. Irvin P. McCurdy, M.E., A.B., Professor of Greek and Higher Mathematics; Elizabeth J. Watt, A.M., Mathematics and Latin; Alicia S. Bleby, English Literature, Natural Science, and French; Ethel G. Hackelton, Latin and English; Maud V. Hackelton, History, Ancient and Modern; Prof. George Linck, Vocal Culture, Piano, Organ, and Modern Languages; Mrs. M. W. Hackelton, Harp and Guitar; Ethel Hackelton, Piano; Alicia S. Bleby, Piano; Florence W. Doub, Drawing and Painting.

The teachers in the Frederick City schools for the term ending April 15, 1881, were as follows:

School No. 9, Male Department.—George W. McBride, principal; Katie M. Bartgis, V. S. Weagley, Josie Pearre, assistants; 219 pupils. *Female Department.*—Helen J. Rowe, principal; M. S. Yearkle, C. H. Steiner, Susie Steiner, A. E. Shope, assistants; 258 pupils.

School No. 10, Male Department.—A. P. Works, principal; A. C. Hilleary, Lola Frazier, Carrie Haller, assistants; 182 pupils. *Female Department.*—M. A. Trumbull, principal; E. C. Keller, T. W. Delaplane, assistants; 146 pupils.

Colored School No. 1.—J. E. Purdy, principal; Mary E. Gross, assistant; 140 pupils.

Colored School No. 2.—D. B. Washington, principal; Anna McBrown, assistant; 92 pupils.

Maryland Deaf and Dumb Institution.—This institution was incorporated by an act of the General

Assembly passed at the January session of 1867. On October 3d, at the first meeting of the board of visitors, the organization of the board was effected, and at its next meeting, held April 22, 1868, the board decided to open the institution on the first Wednesday in September. The original act set apart the State grounds at Frederick, together with the buildings thereon (the old Barracks and grounds built and fitted in the French and Indian war, and repaired in the Revolutionary struggle), for its use, and gave it an annual endowment of five thousand dollars, and appropriated twenty-five thousand more for furnishing and building purposes. The necessary arrangements having been made and the building constructed, the institution was formally opened on the first Wednesday of September, 1868, with appropriate exercises and the reception of thirty-four pupils. This number was increased during the session to fifty-nine, of whom forty-one were males and eighteen females. Twenty-eight had been in the Columbian Institution, at Washington, D. C., four at the Deaf and Dumb Asylum of Virginia, one at that of Pennsylvania, one at that of Connecticut, and twenty-five had never been in any institution.

The first officers and visitors were: President, A. Fuller Crane; Vice-President, William J. Ross; Treasurer, Lawrence J. Brengle; Secretary, H. Clay Naill; Executive Committee, J. B. Brinkley, George R. Dennis, John Loats, W. H. Falconer, F. S. Jones; Visitors, Grayson Eichelberger, P. F. Thomas, Thomas Sims, M.D., R. B. Carmichael, James H. Cole, Isaac D. Jones, A. C. Green, William Galloway, J. R. P. Gillis, Daniel Wiesel, O. Miller, Jacob Reese, R. J. Bowers, W. J. Albert, James T. Briscoe, Curtis Davis, Barnes Compton, George F. Maddox, Oden Bowie, C. F. Goldsborough, William H. Watkins, Grafton Duvall, J. P. Roman, Joseph Baugher, James Blair, Enoch Pratt, George Vickers, Fairfax Schley, M.D., J. A. J. Creswell; Board of Instructors—Principal, William D. Cooke, A.M.; Teachers, Charles L. Cooke, Charles M. Grow, Lucinda E. Grow; Physician, W. H. Baltzell, M.D.; Steward, W. H. Waddell; Housekeeper, Mrs. Maggie Waddell; Matron, Mrs. L. E. Grow.

Charles W. Ely, A.M., of the Ohio State Institution for the Deaf and Dumb, was unanimously elected principal, to date from Sept. 1, 1870, to supersede Mr. Cooke, who had filled that position since its organization. Having graduated in one of the first universities in the United States, and having been an instructor of the deaf and dumb for seven years in one of the most prominent institutions in the country, Professor Ely combines with a thorough education and large experience that decision of character and forbearance, which qualify him in an eminent degree for that position. He has remained at its head to the present time. The General Assembly, at the January session of 1870, appropriated one hundred thousand dollars to erect a new building, and on August 29th of that year the contract for its erection was awarded to William L. Brown, of Baltimore, at $93,400. Ground was broken on that day for the commencement of the building, and on May 31, 1871, its corner-stone was laid with appropriate ceremonies, conducted by Hon. John H. B. Latrobe, Grand Master, assisted by the Grand Lodge of Free Masons of Maryland. The oration was pronounced by Rev. Richard Fuller, D.D., of Baltimore. The First and Second Branches of the City Council of Baltimore, the Knights Templar of that city, the mayor, aldermen, and Council of Frederick, the various benevolent orders and societies, and the fire department of the city, together with a large concourse of citizens, were present to witness the ceremonies. The architect, William F. Weber, of Baltimore, who had drawn the plans for its construction, was appointed superintendent of the building. Two sections of the new building (the centre and south wing) were completed prior to, and occupied since, Jan. 1, 1873, and these afforded accommodations greatly in contrast with those offered by the Barracks, which were wholly unsuited to the wants of the institution. The Legislature of 1874 appropriated an additional $125,000 for the completion of the building according to the plan originally adopted. The contract to build the north wing was awarded to the former contractor, William L. Brown, and it was completed in the summer of 1875, and occupied at the opening of the term commencing September 1st. The building is imposing in appearance, and is greatly admired for its architectural beauty. The work throughout is massive and substantial. An iron fence has been erected in front on Market Street, and the grounds are beautifully graded and ornamented, making the institution attractive in all its surroundings. There are one hundred and twenty-one pupils, representing every part of the State, who find employment in two shops, a cabinet- and shoe-shop, while several scholars versed in printing publish a very interesting newspaper, called *The Maryland Deaf-Mute Bulletin*. The girls are taught dress-making and light house-work. This institution is supported and controlled by the State. Applicants are received to be educated, and not for medical treatment. All deaf and dumb children in the State, as well as those who though able to speak are so deaf as to be unable to receive instruction in ordinary schools, are admitted. The pupil learns to write rapidly and well, and studies arithmetic, geography, grammar, and history, using the ordinary school-books. In some cases the course of study is further extended. The time of one teacher is given entirely to instruction in speech and lip-reading. The institution is practically free, since those who are unable to pay are admitted free of charge upon presenting the proper certificate. The session begins the second Wednesday of September, and closes on the last Wednesday in June. Visitors are received at the institution on Tuesdays and Thursdays between two and four P.M., and are shown all over the building. The institution is an honor to the State and an ornament to Frederick, whose citizens have always taken the greatest interest in its welfare and success.

The officers and visitors are—

President, Enoch Pratt; Vice-President, William J. Ross; Treasurer, Geo. R. Dennis; Secretary, H. Clay Naill; Executive Committee, Enoch Pratt, *ex officio*, Fairfax Schley, M.D., J. B. Brinkley, W. H. Falconer, W. R. Barry, John H. Williams; Visitors, A. F. Crane, P. F. Thomas, R. B. Carmichael, A. C. Green, Wm. Galloway, J. P. R. Gillis, Daniel Weisel, Oliver Miller, Richard J. Bowie, J. A. J. Creswell, John K. Longwell, Isaac D. Jones, Chas. E. Trail, Geo. Markell, Henry Baker, James T. Briscoe, Curtis Davis, Barnes Compton, Oden Bowie, Daniel M. Henry, Wm. W. Watkins, James Blair, Benj. G. Harris, James McSherry; Principal, Charles W. Ely, A.M.; Teachers, Cornelius H. Hill, Charles M. Grow, Lucinda E. Grow, Mollie M. Ijams, Rose R. Harris, Annie B. Barry; Teacher of Articulation, Florence H. Veitch; Physician, Wm. H. Balzell, M.D.; Matron, A. O. Crumbacker; Assistant Matron, M. E. Vickers; Supervisor of Boys, David A. Stoner; Foreman of Shoe-shop, Robt. F. Thomas; Foreman of Cabinet-shop, Peter Heyduck; Engineer, Samuel Trimmer; Night-watchman, Michael Whisner.

CHAPTER XXVI.

RELIGIOUS DENOMINATIONS AND CEMETERIES OF FREDERICK CITY.

BY an act of the Provincial Assembly, adopted and approved in 1692, the English Church was made the established religion in Maryland. Frederick County with the rest of Western Maryland was included at first in St. John's Parish, Prince George's County, but in 1722 all of St. John's Parish north of the Eastern Branch of the Potomac River was made Prince George's Parish, and the Rev. George Murdock became its rector.

All Saints' Parish.—During the pastorate of Mr. Murdock (in 1742) all of his parish north of the Great Seneca Run was made into All Saints' Parish on the petition of its inhabitants. The act of Assembly read as follows:

" An act for dividing Prince George parish in Prince George County, and for erecting a parish out of the same called by the name of All Saints' parish. By this Act, from and after the 22d of November next, all that part of Prince George parish beginning at Great Seneca run mouth, and running by and with said run to the head thereof, from thence with a due East line to the head of one of the droughts of the Patuxent River, and so bounding all around as the upper part of said County is bounded, shall be separated, constituted, and created into a parish to be called by the name of All Saints' parish, and it is hereby adjudged, deemed, and taken to be a separate and distinct parish, and the free holders of said parish are empowered to elect Vestrymen and church Wardens, and to build and found a church thereon, to have and to hold and enjoy all privileges and advantages that are held and enjoyed by any other parish within this province."

The petition asking the establishment of the parish was signed by nearly two hundred persons. The territory included in the parish comprised a part of what is now Montgomery County, all of Frederick County, part of Carroll County, and Washington, Allegany, and Garrett Counties. The petition for the creation of the parish reads as follows:

"To the Honble the upper and lower houses of Assembly. The humble petition of the inhabitants of Seneca & Monocacy in Prince George County There with,

"That, whereas the parish of Prince George in the County aforesaid is so vastly large, being about 90 miles in length and populous, and the parish at so great a distance from your petitioners that it is not in their power to attend the church or receive the benefit therefrom they would, which is a great trouble to them, & withal the minister of the said parish being growing in years and incapable of taking journeys as formerly,

"Your petitioners therefore humbly pray that your honors, according to your accustomed piety and goodness, would be pleased to provide an act of assembly for the dividing of the aforesaid parish of Prince George at great Seneca Run mouth, & with the said river to the head, from thence to the head of Patuxent river, or where your Honors by inspecting into it shall think most proper, which would tend much to the honor of God and edifying of your petitioners, & they as in duty bound ever pray.

"Thomas Wilson.	John Wilcoxon, Jr.
Thomas Wilson, Jr.	James Deekson.
Robert De Butts.	Francis Toy.
William Ferrill.	William Jones.
Jno. Cramphin.	Wm Wilcoxon.
Henry Cramphin.	Nathaniel Cotman.
Barol Cramphin.	William Cotman.
Jno. Owen.	Jos. Hickman.
Thos Jones.	John Winsor.
Flower Swift.	James Rimmen.
Mark Whiteacre.	Philip Taylor.
Thos Whiteacre.	Nehemiah Lasson.
Benj. Williams.	Michael Dent Cordel.
Jos. Scidmore.	Nicolai Elam.
John Poole.	John Shelton.
Jno. Johnson.	Charles Shelton.
John Veatch.	Richard Lasson.
Samuel Ellis.	Wm Hickman.
Nathan Masters.	Thomas Compton, Jr.
Robert Masters.	John Adams.
John Wilcoxon, Senr.	William Jinnenss.

John Prester.
Peter Prester.
Thomas Prather.
J⁰ Nellson.
James Hook.
Thomas Gitterss.
George Williams.
William Walts.
John Pyburn, Jr.
George Calvin.
Joseph Wells.
Andrew Cottrell.
John Colliar.
Francis Colliar.
Charles Hays.
Wᵐ Hays.
Thos. Charter.
William Wheat.
James Arns.
George Weaver.
Charles Coats.
William Williams.
James Veatch.
Matthew Markland.
Jo. W. Stinton.
William Ellis.
Jon. Hays.
Luke Kay.
William Griffith.
Thomas Halsell.
Alexander Duvall.
William Brown.
Jnᵒ Hook.
Jno. Delashmut.
Elias Delashmut.
Robᵗ Owens.
Frail Pain.
Thomas Fee.
John Bailey.
Geo. Fee.
John Turner.
Nathaniel Tucker.
William Tucker.
Jno. Tucker.
Isaac Wells.
Edward Mobberly.
William Mobberly.
Clement Mobberly.
Geo. Williams.
Francis Halbert.
Andrew Cox.
Thomas Morris.
Giley Williams.
William Hunt.
Eleazer Hunt.
John Johnson.
Willᵐ Parry.
Charles Rosson.
Richard Ransom.
Robert Ewing.
Nathan Dawson.
John Powell.
Benj. Finiam.
John Valentine Presler.
John Hutson.
Thos. Johnston.

Paltis Foutch.
Jacob Foutch.
Jacob Matthews.
Jacob Hooff.
Geo. Gomph.
Jacob Stoner.
Chidⁿ Mathew.
Jos. Smith.
Peter Smith.
Francᵒ White.
Daniel France.
Abrahᵐ Miller.
Christⁿ Thomas.
Peter Hoofman.
Christian Citchadaner.
Joseph Broner.
Jno. Broner.
Jno. Teterlany.
Henry Knafe.
Jacob Knafe.
Leonard Baker.
Geo. Swinehart.
Vinberston Lion.
Jacob Fredrock.
Thos. Barnett.
Benj. Osborn.
Geo. Colton.
John Bell.
Jno. Fletcher.
Jno. Ward.
Thos. Compton.
Wᵐ Morris.
Samʳᶫ. Mackerly.
Samˡ Eads.
Isaac Hardee.
Jno. Mash.
Geo. Bare.
Thos. Prather.
Aaron Prather.
Wᵐ Swearingen.
Jos. Clapham.
Wᵐ Shepard.
Wᵐ Shepard, Jr.
Wᵐ Spirgen.
John Moore.
Wᵐ Moore.
Wᵐ Moore, Jr.
Geo. Moore.
Jno. Stull.
Henry Fricks.
Jno. Vandener.
Willᵐ Ward.
John Parsons.
Andrew Martin.
Geo. Ivill.
Jno. Cabis.
Wᵐ Black.
Hugh Rice.
Michael Jones.
Jno. Fowns.
Robert Howston.
Garratt Gobb.
Thos. Davis.
Saml. Davis.
James Faun.
Wᵐ Graham.

Wᵐ Healer.
Thos. Fletcher.
Garon Hambleton.
Wᵐ Pheby.
Thos. Wilkeson.
Jno. Fryer.
Rice Jenkins.
Charles Bussey.
Wᵐ Norris.

Samˡ Plummer.
Wᵐ Cook.
Stephen Hamton.
Jno. Wofford.
Jno. Watts.
Benjⁿ Warringanford.
John Smoot.
Thomas Beall, and other names not attainable."

Rev. Joseph Jennings became the first incumbent of the parish on the presentation of Governor Bladen, Nov. 23, 1742, and his successor, Rev. Samuel Hunter, was presented as incumbent to the parish by Governor Bladen, Dec. 11, 1746. In 1744 he had been appointed rector of Christ Church, Kent Island, and was transferred thence to Frederick.

In 1747 (Bacon, ch. 9) an act was passed

"empowering the Vestry men and church Wardens of All Saints' Parish in Prince George County, or of the county wherein the parish shall be, to purchase three separate acres of land in the said parish whereon to build a church and two chapels of Ease, and to empower the County Justices of Prince George County, or of the County wherein the parish shall be, to levy on the taxable inhabitants of the said parish the sum of three hundred pounds current money for the uses a' therein mentioned, namely, £200 for building the parish church at Frederick town, on Carroll creek, £50 towards building the chapel already begun between Monocacy and Seneca creek, and £50 towards erecting another chapel between Antietam and Conecocheague."

The chapel in the southern part of the parish, St. Peter's, was begun at this time, but the parish church and the other chapels were not. In 1753, Governor Sharpe informed Lord Baltimore that this parish would show 2215 taxables, whose thirty pence per poll would amount to £394.10 after deducting all charges, showing a population of 8860.

When Frederick County was created the parish ceased to belong to Prince George's County.

In 1750 an act was passed

"to enable the justices of Frederick County to levy a sum of money on the taxable inhabitants of All Saints' parish, in the said county, namely, £100 currency for finishing the Parish Church in Frederick town, and the minister of the said parish to perform divine service, etc., at the said parish church and at each of the two chapels of Ease belonging to the said parish on every third Sunday."

These chapels were many miles apart. The first church at Frederick was built on the old burial-ground, about a mile south of the present cemetery belonging to the church.

In the County Court records of December, 1749, there is an entry of the indenture of a boy to Rev. Samuel Hunter, second rector of All Saints'. There is also a record dated April, 1750, of his mark for cattle and hogs, and August 20th, of his purchase of a negro girl; and in 1752, of the sale of a town-lot

FREDERICK COUNTY.

of ground, No. 92, sixty feet by ninety-three. In the county records for 1754 there is an entry of his purchase of a negro man and of fifty acres of land; also of one hundred and fifty acres; and in 1755, of his buying a negro man and forty-three acres of land.

In a letter of Governor Sharpe's of June 4, 1759, he states that "some time ago" the parish of All Saints', Frederick, was vacated by the death of Mr. Hunter, that is, in 1758. He left no will, but the court record shows that his wife, Ann, became his administratrix, and credits herself with cash received from the vestry of All Saints' Parish. On the 11th of May, 1761, Mrs. Hunter was married to James Holmes.

Rev. Thomas Bacon was the third rector of All Saints'.[1]

After the death of Mr. Hunter the parishioners again addressed their petition to the Governor and Assembly to divide the parish, as follows:

"To his Excy Horatio Sharpe, Esq., Govr of Md., and the lower and upper houses of assembly of sd province now convened. The Petition of the Free-holders and Freemen of All Saints' Parish, in Frederick Co., humbly showeth:

"That whereas the aforesaid parish, from its vast extent and great numbers of people residing there, has rendered it impracticable for any one clergyman to discharge his function in such a manner as to improve and edify the people so fully and amply as christianity and the nature of the thing require, we are to inform your Excy and Honors that the 30 pence poll of the 1st parish amounts at present to near 80,000 lbs. of Tobo, and that this parish includes the whole county, except a small part between Seneca & Rock Creek, which being abstracted from the other, the parish remains then above 150 miles in length, besides its extent every way, as it is peopled at present. From this inconvenience the word of God and christian knowledge are much impeded and hindered. Numbers of the parishioners cannot go to church at all, and others who otherwise being well-wishers to the orthodox reformed religion of the church of England, have their children baptized by dissenting ministers, and others, again, join themselves in worship with other Sectaries as quakers.

"Your Petitioners therefore pray your Excellency and Honors to take our state and circumstances unto your most serious consideration, and grant that an Act may pass for dividing the said parish, which may be in force immediately after the death of the Rev. Saml Hunter, our present incumbent, that your petitioners may have the exercise of the word of God preached to us, and the sacrament duly administered to our edification and comfort. We pray for the dividing line to begin at the mouth of Monocacy, and to run up with the said creek till it intersects the Pennsylvania line. The lower part of which division will be a compact uniform parish, and would amount, by the number of taxables at present, to upwards of 27,000 lbs. Tobo, which we pray may be a distinct parish by another name, and your petitions, as in duty bound, will ever pray, etc.

"Alex. Pearre. Jno. Rawling.
Jona Wilson. Jno. Veatch.
Thos. Kirk. Chas. Brisorey.

[1] For a sketch of Rev. Thomas Bacon, see chapter on "Distinguished Men."

Wm Haies.
Joseph Harris.
Jas. Veatchguner.
Benj. Veatch.
Hendery Allison.
William Wilson.
Josias Beens.
Jno. Tannehill.
Thos. Hynton, Jr.
Vachel Henton.
Geo. Lynton, Jr.
Michael Dowden.
John Henton.
Stephen Hampton.
Thomas Henton, Sr.
Thomas Leaspear.
James Coffee.
Jacob Towsend, A.B.
Robt Constable.
Geo. Bussey.
George Norris.
John Jacobs.
Phillip Pindel.
William Saer.
Garah Davis.
Jonathan Workland.
Wadsworth Wilson.
Jeremiah Veatch.
Thos. Howard.
Thos. Appleton.
Alexr Magruder.
William Mackay.
James Beall.
Edward Nichols.
Gabriel Hughes.
Robt. Mitchell.
Ezekiel Goshen.
Charles Hayes.
Jeremiah Hayes.
James Veatch, Sr.
Daniel Veatch.
Ninman Veatch.
Jno. Morris.
Thomas Veatch.
John Johnson.
Barre Hoy.
Thos Johnson, Jr.
Thos. Stewart.
Hough Roby.
Edward Darnall.
Ephraim Davis.
Newton Chiswell.
John Harris.
Thos Birdwhistle.
Samuel Lenton.
Ninian Beall, Sr.
Thos. Walton.
Joseph Beall, of Ninian.
Nathl Beall.
Timothy Whitehead.
Lubaniah Wade.
Wm Bredghar.
Edwd Bussey.
Arthur Lee.
Gabriel Fitchgirl.
Jno. Veatch.

Richard Beall.
Edwd Wilson.
Edwd Jones.
Thos. Kirk, Jr.
Philip Coffee.
Jno. Armstrong.
Jno. Essex.
Jno. Malden, Jr.
Wm Nashon.
George Clark.
John Greenup.
Saml Casel.
Wm Beall.
Wonly Bean.
Philip Turner.
Nicholas Rhoades.
Samuel Plummer.
Edwd Wilson.
Jno. Plummer.
Gilbert Crum.
Barnet Cole.
Thomas Plummer.
George Hinkle.
Jeremiah Plummer.
John Allison.
Isaac Rew.
Abner Lewy.
Abraham Crum.
Gybert Crum.
Henry Field.
Zachariah Low.
Jas. Soper.
Nath. Wickham.
Daniel Kennedy.
Pool Wolf.
Joseph Justice.
George Truck.
Saml Read.
George Brown.
Richard Simpson.
Warfield Hall.
William Williams.
John Larmack.
Cornelius Crom.
Dennis Hensey.
Nicholas Traspah.
John Justice, Jr.
Wm McDonald.
Stephen Richard, Jr.
Andrew Young.
George Spangle.
Michael Null.
Thomas Laysdon.
Thos. Durbin.
John Durbin.
James Logue.
John Fowler.
Samuel Durbin.
Richard Willes.
William Durbin.
George Brown, Jr.
John Willes.
Daniel James.
Joseph Write.
George Becraft.
Amos Waite.

Jacob Nichols.
Edwd Beel.
Jas. McDonald.
John Justice, Sr.
Archibald Campbell.
George Hall.
Samuel Ellis.
Zachariah Ellis.
James Ellis.
Daniel Steward.
James Fuffe.
Thomas Ely.
John Allison, Jr.
Thomas Cour.
Matthew Hickman.
George Jewell.
Richard Meyrick.
John Talbot, Sr.
Griffith Meyrick.
John Walter.
Daniel Walter.
Willm Gabtford.
Joseph Locker.
Henry Hickman.
Davis Hickman.
Solomon Hickman.
Jno. Wilcoxon.
Isa Baker.
Jacob Baker.
John Fletchall.
Charles Nell.
Ezek^l Hickman.
Willm Layton.
William Hickman.
Stephen Hickman.
Isaac Eltinge.
Joshua Hickman, Jr.
James Gore.
James Remmer.
John Baxter.
Joseph Groves.
Charles Hopkins.
George Willison.
James M. Gore.
Checong Joyce.
James Riggs, Sen.
James Riggs, Jr.
Philip Byant.
James Buny.
Thos. Dawson.
Robt. Lamar.
Charles Coats.
Richard Taylor.
Silas Veatch.
W. Norris.
William Wheat, Jr.
Robt. Wilson.
William Summers.
Charles Watts.
John Lason.
Richard Kirby."

The same petition was afterwards presented with the amendment stating the whole amount of tobacco at 70,000 pounds, and the amount for the lower parish if divided at 34,000 pounds; also that the parish had now become vacant by the death of the Rev. Samuel Hunter. It was signed by

Edward Sprigg.
Jon^a. Wilson.
Joseph Beall.
Robt Lee.
Michael Dowden.
Richard Beall.
Newton Chiswell.
John Veatch.
Thomas Dawson.
Joseph Haness.
Samuel Ellis.
Charles Coats.
Ezekiel Goshen.
Zachariah Ellis.
Nathl Dowden.
Josiah Locker.
Charles Hoskins.
John Dowden.
Ephraim Davis.
Charles Hayes.
John Owen.
Joshua Hickman.
Wm Willson.
Josiah Willson.
James Ellis.
James Levington.
Jacob Duckett.
William Saer.
Silas Veatch.
Robt Willson.
Will Barker.
Thomas Conly.
James Gore.
William Osborn.
James Mannin.
Thomas Gore.
Robt. Masters.
Jeremiah Veatch.
James Veatch.
Daniel Veatch.
Isaac Baker.
William Coates.
Thomas Appleton.
John Wade.
George Wade.
Nathan Veatch.
Leonard Beall.
John Rawlins.
Thomas Howard.
Benjamin Veatch.
Solomon Stinson.
Thomas Burge.
Jared Stoaks.
George Hays.
Thomas Stoaks.
Jon. Markland.
Hugh Roby.
Clement Gore.
William Hays.
Jno. Norris.
George Howard.
Jacob Howard.
Nicholas Rhoades.
Edward Nichols.
Ninian Veatch.
George Jewell.
Rezin Howard.
Charles Adkins.
Charles Hays, Jr.
Alex^r Pearre.
Leon^a Wayman.
James Graham.
Wm Norris, Jr.
Robt Constable.

Governor Sharpe replied as follows:

"Being unwilling to give my assent to such an act before I could know whether it would be agreeable to his Lordship or not, I desired the gentlemen of the upper house to retain the petition on their hands. If his lordship approves thereof, they will prepare a bill and send it down at the next session."

On the 4th of May, 1760, the Governor in writing to Lord Baltimore said, "During the sessions I communicated to the gentlemen of the upper house your Lordship's pleasure relative to a division of All Saints' Parish, whereupon the Attorney-General prepared a bill for that purpose, which was sent to the lower house, but was there rejected because, as it was said, some of the Burgesses from Frederick County were of opinion that a division might be made more agreeable to the parishioners than proposed by the bill, and therefore nothing ought to be done therein till the parishioners could be consulted." The division line, it will be seen, as defined in the bill, was quite different from the one before asked for, the line proposed now running from the Potomac River to and with the ridge of the Catoctin Mountains until it intersected the temporary line, instead of the Monocacy River.

The act read as follows:

"An Act dividing All Saints' Parish, in Frederick County, and making a chapel of Ease a parish church.

"Whereas, the inhabitants of the upper part of All Saints' parish, in Frederick County, have by their petition to the present Genl Assembly represented that a very considerable part of the inhabitants of the said parish are by reason of the great extent thereof deprived of the benefit of public worship and hearing sermons & have therefore prayed that the s^d parish may be divided by a line drawn from the Potomac river to & with the ridge of the Catoctin Mountains until it intersects the temporary (Pennsylvania) line, and also that the Chapel of Ease now standing between Conecocheague and Antietam may be erected into a parish church.

"Be it therefore enacted, etc., that from and after the end of this present session of assembly, the aforesaid parish of All Saints' shall be and is hereby declared to be divided by a line as above described, and all West and North thereof is declared to be a separate parish by the name of All Souls' Parish, having all the benefits, privileges, powers, and authorities of any other parish, and the chapel spoken of be made the parish church."

As previously stated, the bill passed the Upper House, but failed in the Lower. It is not known at what date the presentation of Mr. Bacon was made, but it was somewhere near the end of 1758. He was placed in charge of the parish at first as curate, in accordance with a rule adopted by the Governor. In 1759, however, the parishioners petitioned for his induction, which would make him the permanent incumbent, and he was accordingly inducted.

In May, 1760, there occurred the great fire in Boston, by which two hundred and twenty families were rendered homeless. To send them aid Governor Sharpe issued an appeal to every congregation in the province. In response to this appeal the Rev. Mr. Bacon sent from the church and two chapels funds equal to ninety-five dollars; the Dunkard, sixteen dollars; the Presbyterian, in Frederick Town, twenty-four dollars; and the Lutherans, twelve dollars and fifty cents.

In 1761 a petition was sent to the General Assembly stating that the church in Frederick Town had been enlarged, but that the chapel below Monocacy was a crazy wooden building not worth repairing, and the chapel beyond the Antietam was decayed and not capable of holding one-third of the congregation and could not be enlarged, and asking a parish assessment of 120,000 pounds of tobacco to rebuild them; whether the petition was granted or not does not appear.

Three years before leaving Talbot County, Mr. Bacon had commenced his great work of compiling the laws of Maryland, showing what had been repealed and what were still in force. It was an undertaking of special value and importance to the clergy, for the church, as a legal establishment, was legislated for by the General Assembly, and without such a compilation no clergyman or vestryman could know when they were liable to incur the penalty of violated law or what their legal rights might be. From its commencement Mr. Bacon had given such time to it as he had been able, and we learn that on the 15th of February, 1762, he went to Annapolis in order to compare his manuscripts with the records. In 1765, after many difficulties and delays, Mr. Bacon brought out his compilation of the laws of Maryland. It is a folio volume of a thousand pages, and has ever since remained a standard authority. Its historical value is very great, since it is a voluminous record of the progress of Maryland from its earliest period for one hundred and thirty years.

Rev. George Goldie, curate of All Saints', was licensed by the Bishop of London for Virginia, Feb. 25, 1766, but appears to have come direct to Maryland. He became curate to Mr. Bacon, and was very popular with the congregation. Mr. Bacon left Talbot with his health much impaired, and the conclusion of his last public work did not find it improved. In July of 1767, Governor Sharpe speaks of him as advanced in years and declining in health. He lingered on, however, until the 24th of May, 1768, when he died in his seventieth year. He was buried in the old parish church at Frederick Town. At his death he left a widow and three daughters, who returned to Talbot County.

Three days after the death of Mr. Bacon (May 27th) the Rev. Bennett Allen[1] was appointed his successor. Mr. Allen's curates were Rev. Jeremiah Berry, Rev. Daniel McKennon, and Rev. Bartholomew Booth. Rev. Jeremiah Berry was a native of St. John's Parish, Prince George's County. After his ordination in England he was licensed by the Bishop of London, on Dec. 22, 1768, for Maryland. He did not arrive here until the spring of 1769, and soon after, it appears, became curate of All Saints', and officiated in the chapel below Monocacy, now St. Peter's Parish.

Mr. Berry was a Whig, and in 1777 took the oath of fidelity to the State of Maryland. He continued in his post till after the Revolution, and died, it is said, in 1783, leaving three sons,—Jeremiah, Nicholas, and William,—one of whom was the grandfather of Gen. Berry.

Rev. Daniel McKennon was from England, and was licensed by the Bishop of London, Dec. 22, 1768, the same day with Mr. Berry. On arriving in Maryland he became a curate to Mr. Allen, and was probably employed at Frederick Town, for, as stated in the *Maryland Gazette* of Jan. 23, 1771, Mr. Allen lived in the remote corner of the parish (that is, in Hagerstown), and did not appear to perform divine service in Frederick Town more than once or twice a year. Mr. McKennon remained as curate until January, 1774, when Governor Eden presented him to Westminster Parish, Anne Arundel County. During the Revolution he sailed for England, and was lost on his passage at sea, leaving his family in Maryland. There are now five of his descendants in the ministry of the church, among whom are the Rev. Dr. Walker, of South Carolina, and his brother, E. T. Walker, of Virginia.

The matter of the division of the parish came up again before the General Assembly in 1770, and an act was passed "to divide All Saints' Parish, in Frederick County, and to erect two new parishes by the names of Eden parish and Frederick parish." By the act nine commissioners were appointed to imme-

---

[1] For sketch of Bennett Allen, see chapter on "Distinguished Men."

diately divide the parish into three equal parts, respect being had to numbers, and to return a certificate of such division to be recorded in the County Court. The parish church was to be in one district, and each chapel of ease in another. Upon the removal of Rev. Bennett Allen, the incumbent, these three districts would become distinct parishes. The parish-church district was to retain the name of the old parish, the Monocacy district was to be called Eden Parish, and the Antietam district Frederick Parish. The freeholders of each parish were to meet at their respective churches on Easter Sunday after the said removal, to elect six vestrymen and two wardens. Hon. Robert Eden was at this time the Governor of the province, and the lower parish was named after him.

On the 4th and 15th of January, 1774, the vestry advertised in the *Maryland Gazette* that they intended petitioning the next General Assembly for an assessment to build a church where the old one then stood. In 1776 Frederick County was divided into three counties, and part of All Saints' Parish was thus thrown into Montgomery County and part into Washington County. By the constitution of 1776 the legal revenue of the clergy was made to cease on the 3d of November, though the church property in the parishes was reserved to the vestry. The clergy were thus left without any legal support.

According to the tenor of the act of 1770, when Mr. Allen vacated the parish, the lower and upper districts of this parish became respectively Eden Parish and Frederick Parish.

In 1777 the clergy were requested to take the prescribed oath of allegiance to the State of Maryland. This was done by Mr. Berry, and he continued to officiate in Eden Parish. There were now thirty-eight clergymen in the State, and all but nine or ten took the oath.

In 1779 the General Assembly passed the "Select Vestry Act," by which parishes were enabled to elect vestries, and when elected the parish property of whatever name was vested in them, and they were empowered to elect ministers and provide for their support. Rev. Francis Lauder removed to Frederick from Calvert. He was licensed by the Bishop of London for Maryland in 1771. On his arrival in the province he was placed in charge of Christ Church Parish, Calvert County, where he remained, with the exception of two years, until he removed to All Saints'. On the 22d of June, 1784, the first convention of the clergy and lay delegates of Maryland assembled at Annapolis, but it does not appear that Mr. Lauder was there. His ministry could not have been of long continuance, for the county records show that his will was made in 1785, and proved May 25th of that year. He was buried in the old churchyard. His will shows that he left a wife Mary, a son James, then in Georgia, and another son Francis, not yet twenty years old.

Rev. George Bower was rector of All Saints' in 1786, and also of Frederick Parish, Washington County. He appears to have resigned these parishes in 1788, and to have become the rector of Queen Caroline Parish, Anne Arundel County, now in Howard County. At the end of the year he returned to Antietam (Hagerstown), and henceforward resided there.

Although the lower part of All Saints' Parish had been made by an act of Assembly in 1770 a separate parish by the name of Eden Parish, and had ever after had its own minister, yet, whether from dislike to the name given it or for some other reason, the General Assembly in 1792 passed an act ignoring the former one, and providing for the division of All Saints' Parish in Montgomery and Frederick Counties, and erecting a parish out of the same by the name of St. Peter's Parish.

In 1793, Bishop Claggett made a visitation to All Saints' Parish, and on the 24th of March confirmed eleven persons. One of the names on the list of confirmations has affixed to it these words: "The first person I ever confirmed." This, therefore, was the first confirmation held by Bishop Claggett. It was also the first time the parish had ever been visited by a bishop.

In the report of Mr. Reed, the district visitor of this year (1798), he says, "In Frederick Town the church was in a serious state. There was no vestry in All Saints', and no information consequently could be had from that source."

St. Mark's, Zion, and St. John's Parishes.— Under the vestry act of 1798, and on the petition of a number of persons, the Diocesan Convention combined a part of All Saints' Parish with another charge, and gave to both the name of St. Mark's Parish.

Another report of Mr. Reed, the district visitor in 1800, says, "On Sunday, the 28th of May, I preached at Frederick Town to a small audience, mostly young men and boys. Religion is cold and dead. They have no vestry there, and I believe if it was not for our friend, Mr. Wm. Beall, the church would be extinct there. The house is in a most ruinous state, and destitute of common cleanliness. They have repaired the wall around the churchyard, and Mr. Bower preaches there every other Sunday."

Zion Parish was formed at the Diocesan Convention of May, 1804. A petition was presented from sundry persons residing in part of All Saints', Frederick, and St. Peter's, Montgomery County, desiring the convention to authorize them to constitute themselves a separate congregation, and it was resolved that the convention confirm the proceedings of the parish newly constituted by the above-mentioned petitioners, provided the vestries thereof obtain the approbation of the vestries of the parishes out of which it was formed.

We have seen that as early as 1770 the upper part of All Saints' Parish had been constituted a separate parish by the name of Frederick. In 1806, however, a petition was presented to the Diocesan Convention from sundry persons and inhabitants of this portion of All Saints' Parish, which lay in Washington County, praying to be allowed to constitute a separate cure by the name of St. John's Parish. The petition was granted, and the convention enacted that the whole of Washington County should constitute St. John's Parish, except that portion in said county which had been given to St. Mark's Parish.

The Rev. Mr. Bower, rector of All Saints' Parish, died in 1813. In a letter to the Rev. Dr. Kemp, dated Feb. 27, 1814, Hon. John Hanson Thomas thus speaks of the churches under his charge: "For several years before his (Mr. Bower's) death he officiated only in the church at this place and that on the Maryland tract, about twelve miles from hence. The old parish church is situated in a remote part of the town, very difficult of access in bad weather, and in a very uncomfortable state of decay. We have at considerable expense erected a new, commodious, handsome building in the centre of the town (about a mile distant from the old one), which is not yet finished. Several gentlemen have paid towards it $— each. About $4000 have been laid out, and our funds are exhausted, but we are devising means to raise the money, and nothing now is wanted to complete the church inside but the pews and pulpit."

On the 25th of October, 1814, J. S. Cook arrived at Frederick Town. He was a candidate for the ministry, but decided to open a school in Frederick. He asked to be appointed lay reader for All Saints', and his request was granted.

In 1815, Rev. Mr. McDowell, of New York, was elected rector, but declined.

Bishop Kemp warmly desired the election of the Rev. Joseph Jackson to the rectorship of All Saints', but the friends of the Rev. Thomas Howell were also urgent in pressing his name upon the congregation. Both parties, however, failed to accomplish their object, and the Rev. Frederick W. Hatch was elected rector. Mr. Hatch removed to Frederick from North Carolina, having been ordained a deacon by Bishop Clagget, in 1811.

In 1818, Mr. Hatch reported eighty-five communicants. In 1819 he removed to Virginia, but in 1830 became the rector of Washington Parish, District of Columbia. In 1834 and 1835 he was chaplain of the United States Senate. In 1836 he removed to the State of New York, and in 1858 went to reside with his son in California, and died there Jan. 14, 1860, upwards of seventy years of age.

Rev. John Johns became the rector of All Saints' in 1819. He was a native of Delaware, and a graduate of Princeton College, N. J. He was ordained deacon by Bishop White, May 6, 1819. In 1828 he resigned the parish, and became the rector of Christ Church, Baltimore, and subsequently was Bishop of Virginia.

Rev. John S. Stone became rector in 1828. He was a native of Connecticut; was ordained deacon Jan. 4, 1826. Rev. S. Douglass was elected to succeed Mr. Stone. He accepted the call, but soon resigned.

Rev. Thomas Jackson was chosen rector in May, 1830. He was a native of England. In 1835 he was stricken with paralysis, and died at Richmond, Va. Rev. Henry V. D. Johns, who succeeded him, was a native of Delaware, and a brother of Bishop Johns, of Virginia. He was a graduate of Princeton College, N. J., and of the General Theological Seminary. He was ordained deacon by Bishop White, July 28, 1826, and in 1833 became rector of All Saints'. In his report, rendered in 1834, he mentions that a parsonage had been finished, the church repaired and thoroughly furnished, a chapel built by J. Breen at Catoctin Furnace, and consecrated by Bishop Stone Oct. 25, 1833, and a missionary employed, who officiated not only at this chapel, but at Point of Rocks and at Brownsville, in Pleasant Valley. He died in 1836, aged fifty-nine, leaving a widow, three sons, and two daughters. He published eight or ten sermons and addresses and two small volumes of family prayers. Rev. Henry Keppler, a native of Maryland, was ordained deacon by Bishop Stone in 1837, and became rector of All Saints' in that year. He removed to Virginia in 1839. Rev. Upton Beall was chosen rector about the 1st of May, 1838. He was a native of Prince George's County, Md., and a graduate of the Virginia Theological Seminary. Rev. Joshua Peterkin became the rector of All Saints' in 1841. Mr. Peterkin was a native of Baltimore, and was ordained deacon by Bishop Moore in 1837, after having graduated at the Virginia Theological Seminary.

The Rev. Joshua Morsell became Mr. Peterkin's assistant November, 1842. Mr. Peterkin resigned in

1847, and his successor was the Rev. William W. Pendleton, a native of Virginia, and a graduate of the West Point Military Academy. He removed to Virginia in 1853, and during the civil war was an officer in the Confederate army, rising to the rank of brigadier-general.

Rev. Charles Seymour became rector of All Saints' Dec. 15, 1853. He was a graduate of the General Theological Seminary, and a native of New York. He was ordained deacon in 1844 by Bishop B. T. Onderdonk. His rectorship ceased July 1, 1862, and he was succeeded by Rev. Marmaduke M. Dillon, who entered on his charge Nov. 17, 1863, after a vacancy in the parish of more than eighteen months. Mr. Dillon was a native of England and had been an officer in the army. In 1866 he resigned, and went to the English colonial diocese of Nassau, West Indies.

The Rev. Osborne Ingle was chosen rector shortly before the convention of May 16, 1866. He is a native of Washington, D. C., a graduate of the Virginia Theological Seminary, and was ordained in 1863 by Bishop Johns, of Virginia. He removed to Baltimore in 1864, and became assistant minister at St. Paul's. In July of that year he was chosen rector of Memorial Protestant Episcopal Church, and from thence was called to Frederick. He is still the rector of All Saints' Parish. In 1871 he had for his assistant Rev. Joseph T. Colton. Following is the list of the rectors and assistant clergy of All Saints' since its formation:

From		To
Nov. 23, 1742	Joseph Jennings	1745
Dec. 11, 1745	Samuel Hunter	1758
1758	Thomas Bacon	1768
1767	George Goldie (curate)	1772
May 27, 1768	Bennett Allen	1770
1769	Daniel McKennon (curate)	1774
1769	Jeremiah Berry (curate)	1783
1782	Francis Louder	1785
1786	George Bower	1813
July 1, 1815	Frederick W. Hatch, D.D.	1820
1820	John Johns	1828
Dec. 25, 1828	John S. Stone, D.D.	1829
May, 1829	Thomas Jackson	1833
1833	Henry V. D. Johns, D.D.	1836
1837	Henry S. Keppler	1838
May, 1838	Upton Beall	1841
1841	Joshua Peterkin, D.D.	1847
1847	William W. Pendleton, D.D.	1853
Dec. 15, 1853	Charles Seymour	1862
Nov. 17, 1863	Marmaduke M. Dillon	1866
May, 1866	Osborne Ingle (present rector)	

Lay delegates to Diocesan Conventions, and number of communicants reported.

Year.	No. Communicants.	Year.	No. Communicants.
1811. T. Mason.		1821. John Graham	83
1812. J. H. Thomas.		1822. Richard Potts	83
1816. Charles Mann	72	1823. " "	92
1817. John Graham.		1824. " "	94
1818. Richard Potts	85	1825. John Graham	108
1819. " "		1826. W. B. Tyler	108
1820. " "	85	1827. ———	124
1828. Richard Potts	128	1851. Dr. R. Dorsey	152
1829. John Graham	107	1852. Ross Johnson	153
1830. Richard Potts	107	1853. W. B. Tyler	180
1831. T. W. Johnson	106	1854. Dr. W. B. Tyler	154
1832. W. J. Ross	120	1855. " "	138
1833. Richard Potts.		1856. ———	154
1834. ———	135	1857. W. J. Ross	163
1835. Richard Potts	136	1858. G. R. Dennis	163
1836. " "	136	1859. W. J. Ross	171
1837. R. H. Marshall	117	1860. C. E. Trail	194
1838. Richard Potts } T. W. Johnson }	108	1861. No convention.	
		1862. ———	178
1839. W. J. Ross	98	1863. ———	178
1840. Richard Potts	91	1864. R. H. Marshall	154
1841. W. J. Ross	98	1865. ———	165
1842. ———	128	1866. G. R. Dennis	176
1843. Dr. Johnson	146	1867. Dr. W. S. McPherson	179
1844. Dr. R. Dorsey	146		
1845. T. W. Johnson	152	1868. G. R. Dennis	163
1846. W. J. Ross	148	1869. G. W. Delaplane	177
1847. Lewis Medtart	150	1870. ———	217
1848. ———	145	1871. R. M. McGill	231
1849. ———	147	1872. G. R. Dennis	239
1850. Richard Potts	151	1873. " "	229

On the 22d of June, 1811, the vestry advertised for proposals to build a new church upon a neat, moderate plan, about 60 feet long and 40 feet wide, and on March 19, 1814, was advertised the lottery for finishing the new church, viz.:

5000 tickets at $3=$15,000, less twenty per cent.=$3000, the sum to be raised; Managers, Philip Thomas, John Graham, George Baer, John H. Thomas, Richard Potts, John Tyler, Thomas Shaw, William Ross, Benjamin Rutherford.

Oct. 13, 1819, a family vault in the graveyard was built. On the 10th of April, 1855, the corner-stone of the present elegant church was laid, the principal feature of the occasion being an able address by Rev. Dr. Johns. On Jan. 3, 1856, the church was opened for divine services, and the sum of twenty-three thousand dollars had been paid in for the cost of erection, and the other contributions towards the same object were one thousand and eighty-six dollars, as per report of 1856.

Evangelical Reformed Church.—This church was established by the German immigrants from the Palatinate, who settled on the present site of Frederick City prior to 1740. No records of the church, however, have been preserved earlier than 1747.

In May of that year, when Rev. Michael Schlatter visited Frederick, he found a German Reformed organization, which had existed for some considerable time without a pastor. He speaks of Frederick as a newly-laid-off town. He preached in "a new and yet unfinished church," and administered the holy communion to ninety-seven persons. This was already the second church, the first having already grown too small or gone to decay.

This second church was consecrated May 14, 1747, and stood at the lower end of what is now known as the old Reformed graveyard near Patrick Street.

From the baptismal record it is evident that this congregation had, if not a stated ministry, at least one occasional supply. The earliest baptismal record preserved is that of Elizabeth, daughter of Adam and Barbara Stull, born Feb. 6, 1747, from which time on the records of this famous church are reasonably full and complete.

John Thomas Schley was the first teacher of this congregation. He was born Aug. 31, 1712, at Mertzheim, in Germany, and married, in January, 1735, Margaret Wintz. She died in June, 1790, and Mr. Schley November 25th following. They lived in wedlock fifty-five years, had nine children, five of whom survived their parents. He was a lay reader in the church, and a man of good education and rare discernment, and for forty-five years was the mainstay of the church. From him descended the large and influential Schley families, so well and favorably known in the political, military, agricultural, and ecclesiastical history of Maryland. In the absence or sickness of the pastors Mr. Schley often officiated, and next to the pastor was the person of whom spiritual and temporal advice and support were sought.

Rev. Theodore Frankenfeld was pastor from 1753 to 1755. He arrived in Frederick May 4, 1753, and preached his introductory sermon on the first Sunday after his arrival. He continued his services to the close of 1755, about which time he died, and was buried in the old graveyard of the church. He was succeeded by Rev. John Conrad Steiner in 1756, who remained in charge a little less than three years. He reported one hundred and ninety-six communicants on Easter Sunday, 1759. Rev. Philip William Otterbein was the next pastor, and commenced his labors in 1760, and continued for about five years. During his pastorate, in 1761, Stephen Ramsberg and Jacob Shower purchased from Christian Lowndes in the name and for the use of the congregation, the lot on which the Evangelical Reformed Church buildings, including the present parsonage, now stand, and in the following year a stone parsonage was erected thereon. In 1764 the third house of worship was built, the original walls of which are still partially preserved in the church and chapel, in which stands the town-clock. The site for the church and graveyard was the gift of Daniel Dulany, and was deeded to Stephen Ramsberg, John Brunner, George Hoffman, and George Linginfelter, elders of the church, and to their successors forever upon the sole condition that it should not be applied to any other purpose than that for which it was given. The building committee of this church was composed of John Thomas Schley, Frederick Witman, Jacob Brunner, and Valentine Adams. Its dimensions were sixty feet long, forty-five wide, and eight high, with steeple sixty feet high. It was built of stone, the materials of which were hauled by the congregation to the spot where the building was erected. Its original cost was six hundred and eighty-four pounds currency. The materials of the old church were sold to John Thomas Schley for ten pounds.

Rev. Charles Lange became pastor in February, 1766, and continued for nearly two years. The next in the succession was Rev. Frederick L. Henop. His pastorate continued fourteen years, during the most trying period of American history. It was an age of heroes and heroines, whose unwritten history remains a precious legacy to their descendants. In 1770 the first organ was purchased for one hundred and ninety-three dollars and thirty-seven cents. In 1775, Jacob Bantz presented to the congregation the principal part of the present Reformed graveyard, lying west of Bantz, and between Second and Third Streets. In 1778 two bells were placed in the steeple, which were bought in London, England, with fixtures, for one hundred and thirty pounds English currency.

Rev. John Runkel succeeded Mr. Henop. He preached his introductory sermon Dec. 5, 1784. During his stay there was considerable dissension in the congregation, as is shown in the following advertisement, which appeared Jan. 2, 1794:

"Notice is hereby given by the vestery of the High Dutch Reformed Congregation in Frederick town; a rumour being spread that evil-minded persons intended to use violence on the property of said congregation. We, the said vestery, being regularly elected, installed and served as such a number of years; being, therefore, authorized and constrained by the deeds on said congregation's property, as likewise the long-established rules of said congregation adopted and underwritten. Being desirous to preserve, love and peace, exhort all who may have been led astray to consider, we dare not violate our trust, and are therefore under necessity to notify them that if violence is used we must seek protection under God by the laws of our country. John Brunner, of Henry, Joseph Doll, John Brunner, Jacob Rohr, Jacob Metzger, Henry Baer, Jacob Brunner."

In Bartgis' *Maryland Gazette* (in which the above appeared) we find the following under date of Jan. 9, 1794:

"Mr. Printer,—In your last paper I found (in the corner where you generally place the public notices and advertisements) a 'notice given by the Vestry of the high Dutch Ref. Congregation in Fredk Town, etc.,' a notice that must command the attention of the ignorant, and awe the timid into submission by conceiving that the vestry of the High Dutch Ref. Congregation must be something very great and powerful. Let the persons who form that vestry inquire whether the Presbyterians either of ancient or modern times have had or now can have a vestry, since they were always governed by elders and deacons. Then, Mr. Printer, it is to be wished that the spelling of the vestery may be contracted into vestry, and that period 'being desirous to preserve, love and peace, exhort all who have been led astray, etc.,' be better explained. Upon the whole, we expect to see a better harmony of words and sentences with a true explanation of 'to preserve, love and peace,' since it is unintelligible with a comma after 'preserve,' and uncertain whether 'love and peace' are verbs or substantives.

"The mention of 'evil-minded persons,' who are said 'to have an intention to use violence on the property of said congregation' imports that the said vestry suppose themselves and some of their adherents the High Dutch (I think they might have written German) Ref. Congregation, excluding the majority, who cannot swallow their bigotry, nor submit (especially in a free country) to the yoke of their spiritual tyranny. It is to be wished that their differences might be brought to an happy issue, or else that the laws of our country might finally settle them so that the public may hereafter not be imposed on by notices of that kind. And if, Mr. Printer, you intend to insert every 'rumour spread' we are able to furnish you with a great number of rumours, and by your favour to enlarge your *Gazette* from half a sheet to a whole one. I am, etc.,

"OBSERVATOR."

"The editor, mindful of his business, is pleased to inform *Observator* that in future he wishes him to address the *Vestry* or *Party* concerned; his *Press* is still open to any person or party, and by sending their pieces with the author's name, so that in future a proper account may be made, due attention will be paid. The *Gazette* will be enlarged in due time, and the editor does not doubt of the encouragement both of the *Observator and Vestry-men*."

What the specific cause of dissension was does not fully appear, but it seems to have been subsequently removed, as the congregation was not divided, but continued to flourish under the original organization. On Feb. 22, 1800, the church was used for the delivery of ex-Governor Thomas Johnson's funeral oration on George Washington.

In 1801, Mr. Runkel retired with the privilege of naming his own successor. He selected Rev. Daniel Wagner, who remained from October, 1802, until October, 1810. In 1807 the steeple was remodeled, and the wood-work and spire, which are still standing, were put up by Stephen Steiner as architect and contractor. The pulpit at first was on the west side and then on the south. The first stairs to the galleries were on the outside, the steeple standing outside of the edifice; but afterwards the wings were built up to the steeple, making the church square in shape. In the first church a door opened from the rear portion into the graveyard. About the time of this remodeling the original bells were superseded by two of a larger size cast in New Haven, Conn., but they proved inferior in tone to the old ones.

The next pastor was Rev. Jonathan Helfenstein, who continued from 1811 to 1828. In August, 1821, a catechising society was formed, which was the earliest type of a Sunday-school known in the congregation. In 1822 and '23 the church edifice was remodeled by Mr. Hart as architect, at a cost of two thousand five hundred dollars. The interior of the church was changed in appearance by transferring the pulpit from the west side to the south end of the church. In 1825 the English language was given prominence in the services by calling an assistant pastor, Rev. Samuel Helfenstein, Jr., who was to preach exclusively in English. The arrangement agreed upon was three English sermons to one in German. The assistant, however, remained only two or three years.

Rev. John H. Smaltz was pastor from July, 1829, to October, 1833. During his pastorate the German service was given up, and English alone was used at the Sunday services.

Rev. Charles Reighley was next in the succession from September, 1833, to near the close of 1835, and during this period restlessness and discontent prevailed.

Rev. Daniel Zacharias, D.D., who came next, preached his first sermon on the first Sunday in April, 1825, and continued pastor to the day of his death, March 31, 1873, an unbroken period of thirty-eight years. In 1836 the recesses were built to the side of the steeple and the stairways to the galleries were placed in them. A slate roof was also put on the edifice. In 1839 a back building was added to the parsonage. In 1840 the present organ, manufactured by Fith & Hall, of New York, was purchased by the "Ladies' Sewing Society" for twelve hundred dollars. In the same year also the Frederick congregation became a self-sustaining charge, and then the system of renting pews and sittings was first introduced. Dr. Zacharias now began to preach German occasionally, and gathered back the scattered German members. In 1843, Rev. Isaac Gerhart was called to Frederick as German pastor, and continued some six and a half years. The church was incorporated in 1848, in which year the congregation determined to erect a new church edifice upon the site of the lecture-room and sexton's house. In addition to this a lot thirty feet front by one hundred and forty feet deep was purchased from Mr. Eichelberger for fifteen hundred dollars. The corner-stone was laid June 12, 1848. Its architect was John Wall, of Baltimore. It was dedicated June 8, 1850, and cost in money twenty-four thousand dollars, though its real value cannot be estimated because of the amount of work done and materials furnished as contributions to the church. The building is on the style of the Erechtheium, and has two beautiful and well-proportioned towers in imitation of the Lantern of Demosthenes. In front is a handsome portico. The steps leading to this portico are from the immense granite-quarries of Woodstock, and were furnished by Messrs. Sumwalt & Green, of

Baltimore. The iron railing was supplied by Bechtol & Co., of New York. The basement is divided into a large lecture-room, a vestry-room, pastor's room, library for the Sunday-school, and apportionments for wood and coal. The main body of the building contains one hundred and eighteen pews arranged in three blocks, with aisles between. The side galleries are also supplied with pews, and are entered from the eastern and western towers. The organ-gallery (containing a handsome organ purchased at a cost of about four thousand dollars) is well arranged for the comfort of the choir, and is separated from the side galleries so as to prevent intrusion. The building committee was composed of Dr. Daniel Zacharias, John Kunkel, and Gideon Bantz. Charles Haller acted as master builder.

On the morning of the consecration the edifice was filled to overflowing. The dedication services were conducted by the pastor, Rev. Dr. Zacharias, and Rev. Alfred Nevin, of Chambersburg, preached from the text, "The glory of this last house shall be greater than of the former."

"The Orphans' Home Board" of the church was incorporated Jan. 13, 1873, and what was known as the Wilson property, adjoining the church on the west side, was bought for $5000, but never used for the purpose intended.

The present pastor is Rev. E. R. Eschbach, who commenced his labors June 14, 1874. On Oct. 11, 1874, the church erected a handsome monument to the memory of Dr. Daniel Zacharias on his grave in Mount Olivet Cemetery, at a cost of $1034.05. In October, 1876, the church edifice was refrescoed, repainted, and recarpeted, at a cost of $1828.43.

The old organ was also replaced by a new one manufactured by Messrs. Johnson & Son, of Westfield, Mass., costing $4000.

In 1880 the steeple of the old German church was repaired and painted, and in 1881 an elegant chapel was constructed for the Sunday-school and other purposes at a cost of twelve thousand dollars. This is built on the old German church-lot, and a portion of the walls of the old church thereon form a part of the new chapel, which is known as Trinity Chapel. Work was commenced May 11, 1881, and the corner-stone was laid with appropriate ceremonies on Saturday, July 9, 1881. The sermon was preached by Rev. Theodore Apple, D.D., of Lancaster, Pa. Rev. Dr. Eschbach, pastor of the church, followed with a full and explicit history of the church from 1845 to 1881. Rev. D. Diehl, Rev. Dr. Leech, Rev. Osborne Ingle, Rev. Mr. Hammond, Rev. C. W. Stinespring, and Rev. Mr. Cauliflower also assisted in the exercises.

At the conclusion of the services in the church the congregation repaired to the chapel, where services were conducted by Dr. Eschbach according to the rites of the church. The following articles were then placed in a tin box and deposited in the stone: history of the congregation, Bible, order of worship and hymn-book of the Reformed Church, Sunday-school hymn-book, constitution of the church, revised New Testament, copies of newspapers, etc.

Evangelical Lutheran Church.—The records of the church date back to Aug. 22, 1737, but German Lutherans had probably settled in this neighborhood some years earlier. The settlers brought their Bibles, catechisms, and hymn-books with them, and as soon as possible invited ministers of their faith to visit the settlement, in order that they might preach to them, baptize their children, and administer the sacrament. On the 31st of October, 1736, Rev. Gabriel Neasman, pastor of a Lutheran Church in Philadelphia, visited the little community. The congregation had already effected an organization, but no church record had been kept prior to this. A substantially-bound book was purchased, and entries of baptisms were commenced. The first baptism upon record is that of George Frederick Unsult, born Aug. 6, 1737, baptized on the 22d of the same month by Rev. Mr. Wolf. From 1748 to 1763 the record bears among others the names of Bechtel, Schley, Culler, Angelberger, and Metzger.

June 24, 1777, a constitution was adopted and signed by the church wardens—John George Lay, John Stirtzman, John Michael Roemer, George Michael Hoffman, Peter Apple, and Henry Six—and twenty-six communicants; total, thirty-four male members. The constitution provided that no person should preach in the church who could not furnish adequate credentials of ordination and ministerial character and standing. Prior to this date the congregation had erected a wooden church edifice on Church Street, on the eastern corner of the lot of ground deeded to the congregation by Daniel Dulany. From this time the congregation grew steadily. In 1757, Rev. Bernard Michael Houseal was pastor, and served the church for several years.

In 1753 the congregation began to make arrangements for a larger and more substantial stone edifice, which was soon afterwards commenced. The work, however, was arrested by the French and Indian war, and was not finished until 1762. The church was dedicated by Rev. John Christopher Hortwick on Trinity Sunday, 1762. In addition to the services of Rev. Messrs. Houseal and Hortwick, other clergymen furnished occasional preaching. April 28, 1771, Rev.

John Andrew Krug became pastor, and served the church for over twenty-five years. The congregation steadily advanced in numbers and prosperity. The Revolutionary war interrupted its growth for a time, as many of the men were enlisted in the army. Rev. Mr. Krug was born in Germany, March 19, 1732, a month later than George Washington, and was about thirty-nine years of age when he became pastor of this church. He died May 30, 1796, in the sixty-fifth year of his age.

Rev. Mr. Wildbahn became pastor Dec. 4, 1796, and continued in charge until June 4, 1798.

Dec. 1, 1799, Rev. Frederick Moeller became pastor. August, 1800, the church contracted with Stephen Steiner to erect a church steeple for the sum of seventeen hundred dollars. Rev. F. Moeller resigned the charge June, 1802. His successor was Rev. Frederick William Jazinsky, who was educated in the universities of Germany, and as a young man had served as an officer in the armies of Frederick the Great of Prussia.

July 17, 1808, Rev. David F. Schaeffer, a young man who had just completed his theological studies, became pastor. He was a person of remarkable social and ministerial qualities, and the congregation grew rapidly under his active ministry.

On Aug. 8, 1812, the corner-stone of a union church for the Lutheran and Reformed congregations was laid on land presented by Mr. Waltz, near the old meeting-house on Carroll's Manor. Rev. S. Helfenstein preached in German, and Rev. David F. Schaeffer in English.

A lottery for Emmanuel Evangelical Lutheran Church at Frederick was organized about this time. There were 2500 tickets @ $2.50 = $6250; discount of twenty-six per cent. = $1625 to be raised; managers, F. Heisely, Dr. Bogen, G. Creager, Jr., Wm. Michael, David Morkell, Peter Burkhart, John S. Miller, Charles Schell, H. Zicle, J. Medtart, J. Fesaler, F. Loehr, M. Kelb, J. Dill, and F. Mantz.

The services of the church had been conducted in the German language until the year 1810, when Mr. Schaeffer introduced occasional services in English. On the 18th of September, 1820, a Sunday-school was organized by Mr. Schaeffer. The young men and ladies of the church took an active part in this new enterprise. Among the most active were Cyrus Mantz, Philip Reich, George Engelbrecht, Jacob Engelbrecht, Edward Trail, Augustus Ebert, John Winter, Emanuel Greenwald, John H. Hoffman, Mary K. Baer, Lydia Ramsburg, Henrietta Emmett, and others.

In 1825 the church was enlarged by an addition of twenty-eight feet to the north end.

A number of young men from this church became students of theology and ministers of the gospel. Among them are the following: Rev. Dr. C. P. Krauth, the first president of Pennsylvania College, Rev. Messrs. Meyerheffer, D. J. Hauer, W. Jenkins, Daniel Jenkins, J. Winter, D. P. Rosenmiller, J. N. Hoffman, Benjamin Keeler, C. F. Schaeffer, John Kehler, Michael Wachter, Jacob Medtart, Francis J. Ruth, —— Roof, Emanuel Greenwald, W. H. Harrison, James Horkey, Sidney Horkey, J. J. Sumon, P. L. Harrison, J. F. Prolest, George Prolest, Thomas M. Kemp, Jeremiah Frazier, A. I. Weddel, John Gladhill, Jesse Winecoff, J. G. Martz, George A. Nixdorff, Cyrus Waters. The pastors of the church have been—

Bernhard Michael Houseal, 1757; John Christopher Hortwick, 1762; John Andrew Krug, April, 1771; Rev. —— Wildbahn, Dec. 4, 1796; Rev. F. Moeller, December, 1799; Rev. Frederick William Jazinsky, 1802; Rev. D. F. Schaeffer, July, 1808; Rev. Simeon W. Horkey, January, 1837; Rev. Dr. George Diehl, July, 1851.

The church buildings have been a wooden church erected in 1741–46, stone church 1754–60, enlarged 1825. The present large brick church, extreme length ninety-five feet, width seventy-five feet, with seating capacity for eleven hundred persons, is in the Norman Gothic style, with two steeples in front, each one hundred and fifty feet in height. The Sunday-school and lecture-room are in the rear of the church; the building is a two-story structure. The lower room is forty-two by seventy feet, and the upper story comprises a large infants' school-room, young men's prayer-meeting room, and the pastor's study.

The congregation owns two graveyard lots. The one on which the church stands extends one hundred and thirty feet from Church Street to Second. The other is on the eastern suburb of the town. The congregation owns also several hundred acres of mountain land in Allegany. The parsonage, a good brick building, is located near the church on Church Street. The present church edifice was erected in 1854 and 1855, the corner-stone having been laid on Saturday afternoon, Aug. 26, 1854. Its cost was twenty-five thousand dollars. The building committee were John Loats, L. Coppersmith, Michael Keefer, George Smith, and Jacob Morkell. Among the largest contributors were Henry Nixdorff, Joseph Routzahn, Lewis Coppersmith, John Loats, Lewis Birely, Jacob Morkell, Joshua Dill, Lewis Kemp, David J. Morkey, Nancy Motter, George S. Greashow, J. W. L. Corty, and John Morkell.

The present lecture and Sunday-school rooms were enlarged at a cost of four thousand dollars in 1855.

The church was renovated and improved in 1858 by excavating the cellar and adding a new furnace. The church was used as a hospital by the United States army in the winter of 1862 and 1863, and subsequently was refrescoed and renovated. In 1870 the exterior and interior were repainted and otherwise improved at a cost of two thousand five hundred dollars. In 1872 a new organ was purchased for two thousand six hundred dollars. In 1878 a new roof was put on and other improvements made, and in 1879 the church was refrescoed and new carpets were procured.

The congregation numbers five hundred and fifty members, of whom four hundred and fifty are communicants. The Sunday-school numbers over seven hundred pupils and ninety teachers and officers. The church also has a mission-school in the west end of the town, with seventy pupils, under the care of Messrs. Nixdorff and Shaffner, Mrs. Frazier, and Miss Keller. The large Sunday-school connected with the church is under the control of the pastor, Rev. George Diehl, D.D., who is *ex officio* president. W. M. Hardt is superintendent; J. M. Ebberts, secretary; Mrs. Bowie Doll, Mrs. Parson, Mrs. Corty, and Miss Mary K. Baer, managers; Messrs. Morkey and Storm, librarians. Among the teachers are Messrs. Levy Maught, John M. Ebbert, J. H. Bennett, David Young, Nat. Nagel, J. D. Hone, L. M. Engelbrecht, C. F. Kreh, C. B. Fox, H. A. Hahn, Lewis Keefer, T. Chilcoate, L. Duvall, J. N. Loy, J. B. Gorratt, D. Costeel, N. M. Nixdorff, H. Haller, George Zimmen, and Misses Rice, Hone, Engelbrecht, Fout, Davidson, Doll, Haller, Ebert, Street, Hardt, Nixdorff, Schroyer, Tabler, and Hahn.

The infant school, numbering over two hundred and thirty scholars, is under the control of Messrs. J. M. Hardt, George F. Miller, and John Fleming, and Misses Hone, Bennett, Haller, and Zacharias.

Among the families that are prominent and active members of the church may be mentioned the Engelbrechts, Hardts, Nixdorffs, Levys, Markeys, Bennetts, Sumons, Hallers, Titlows, Getzendanners, Smiths, Millers, Groshows, Reifsniders, Fraziers, Zimmermans, Schleichs, Whips, Groves, Paceleys, Trundles, Keefers, Eberts, Londerkins, De Granges, Rizers, Hiteshews, Otts, Duvalls, Corteys, Garratts, Parsons, Stiallmons, Foutses, Wisongs, Fesslers, Hahns, Krehs, Eislers, Railings, Lembrights, Moberlys, Grabenhorsts, Eichelbergers, Goffs, Renners, Chilcoates, Dolls, Simmonses, Chamberses, Routzahns, Kolles, Cullers, Busheys, Johnsons, Moores, Schaffners, Warners, Yingers, Boumgoodners, and Lochners. Among the prominent members recently lost by death are John Loats, John Reifsnider, J. M. Busley, John D. Getzendanner, Philip M. Engelbrecht, B. L. Storm; and by removals from the town, Dr. Bruce Thomas and Basil Delashmutt. The present officers are Rev. George Diehl, D.D., pastor and president of the church council; Thomas M. Haller, secretary; and L. M. Nixdorff, treasurer. The church council, in addition to the pastor, are George S. Groshaw, William S. Miller, L. M. Nixdorff, John T. Moore, David Derr, Col. H. Culler, W. Irvin Parson, J. P. Renner, George A. Schroeder. The organist of the church is Miss Lucille Reich. The choir is under the direction of William Schroeder and Miss Fannie B. Hone, assisted by Messrs. Elkins, Keeler, Stone, and Schroeder, and Misses Tabler, Moberly, Fessler, Kreh, James, and Bartgis.

Methodist Episcopal Church.—The first circuit formed, embracing the whole country west of Baltimore, was called Frederick. There is no evidence of Methodist services having been held in the town of Frederick before 1770, when it was visited by Robert Strawbridge and the Rev. John King. After that, however, it was regularly visited by the circuit preachers. A society was organized, among whom John Haggerty was the most active, and who subsequently became a distinguished preacher. While Methodism grew with the population in various parts of the circuit, the progress in Frederick was comparatively slow. For more than thirty years after its introduction there were only about thirty members. In 1792 the first church was built, of boards, on West Second Street, and afterwards a second one of brick was erected on the same lot, now or lately owned by the Methodist Protestant Church. In 1841 the third edifice was erected on East Church or Second Street, which in 1864 and 1865 gave way to the present elegant and commodious structure, adjoining which is a substantial and tasteful parsonage.

The pastors (as far as discoverable) have been:

1773, John King; 1774, Philip Gatch, William Duke; 1775, William Waters, Robert Strawbridge; 1776, Freeborn Garretson, Martin Rodda; 1777, Samuel Sprague, Caleb Peddicord; 1779, Richard Garretson, William Glendenning; 1780, Thomas Foster, William Waters; 1781, Charles Scott, Jonathan Forrest; 1782, Philip Cox, Michael Ellis; 1783, Ignatius Pigman, William Phœbus; 1784, John Magary, Isaac Smith; 1785, William Ringgold, Samuel Breeve; 1786, Michael Ellis, Joseph Cromwell; 1787, Jonathan Forrest, Benton Riggin; 1788, Eliphalet Reed, George Callahan; 1789, John Hill; 1790, Jonathan Forrest, John Simmons; 1791, Jonathan Forrest, Thomas Bell; 1792, Aquila Garretson, John Chalmers; 1793, Joshua Wells, Thomas Boyd; 1794, Martin Hill, Charles Burgoon.

Frederick Circuit was first formed by the second Methodist Conference held in America, which met at Philadelphia, May 25, 1774. Among the five preachers taken into full connection there was Philip Gatch, one of the earliest of native American preachers. He was born March 2, 1751, in the Twelfth District of Baltimore County, and was the son of George Gatch, who married a Miss Burgin, whose ancestors came from Burgundy and settled near Georgetown, Kent Co., not far from Sassafras River. Philip's grandfather, Godfrey Gatch, emigrated from Prussia in

1725. Rev. Philip Gatch preached in connection with William Duke, a young man, a few weeks on Frederick Circuit, then containing only a hundred and seventy-five members, and extending from Baltimore County to the western boundary of the province, and south to and including Georgetown, D. C. He was then sent to Kent County to take the place of Rev. Abraham Whitworth, expelled for bad conduct. In the latter part of the year 1774 he returned to Frederick, and continued until the close of Conference year. One Saturday evening, in going to his Sunday appointment, he had to pass by a tavern, when he was attacked by two ruffians and forced into the inn to drink liquor, but refused. The men falling into a quarrel between themselves, Mr. Gatch escaped and went on his way. In the following year he was sent to Kent Circuit, but Mr. Strawbridge, one of the two preachers on the Frederick Circuit that year, being under necessity of going to Baltimore, Mr. Gatch and he exchanged, and the former returned to Frederick for the third time. He suffered bitter persecution, but did not falter, and even ventured to preach at a place where a short time before two Baptist preachers had been taken from the stand and maltreated. At one of his appointments, between Bladensburg and Baltimore, he was seized by a mob and tarred and feathered, from which treatment his eyes never fully recovered. Such were some of the trials the faithful preachers of this church had then to undergo; but this last outrage excited public indignation to such an extent that nothing of a similar nature ever again occurred to the preachers of any denomination. Mr. Gatch in 1777 was stationed in Virginia, on Sussex Circuit, where he was inhumanly treated by two men, who nearly dislocated his shoulders. By these and the previous injuries received on the Frederick Circuit he was disabled from an active itinerancy, and was located by the Conference of 1778. On Jan. 14, 1778, he married Elizabeth, daughter of Thomas Smith, of Powhatan County, Va., to which State he removed in 1788, and continued to preach there locally. In 1797 he removed to Clermont County, Ohio, where he organized the first Methodist society or church in that county. In 1802 he was a member of the Constitutional Convention that formed the first constitution of Ohio, under which it was admitted into the Union in 1803. From 1803 to 1824 he was one of the associate judges of the Court of Common Pleas. He died Dec. 28, 1835. Such was the first regular preacher on the Frederick Circuit, a man whose Christian and private and public life was of so high an order that Judge John McLean, of the United States Supreme Court, wrote and published his life, under the title of "Memoirs of Rev. Philip Gatch."

In 1857 the Baltimore Conference was divided, and Frederick Station became one of the appointments of the East Baltimore Conference. The pastors since 1860 have been:

1860, McKendree Riley; 1861–62, B. F. Crever; 1863–64, Wilfred Downs; 1865, Dr. Hicks; 1866 and 1867, James Curns; 1868, Richard Hinkle.

In 1869 the Frederick Station was again incorporated into the old Baltimore Conference by the transfer of the Maryland appointments of the East Baltimore Conference. The ministers in charge of the station since then have been:

1869 and 1870, Richard Hinkle; 1871 to 1874, Job A. Price; 1874 to 1877, Alfred H. Ames, M.D.; 1877 to 1879, W. T. L. Welch; 1879 to 1882, S. V. Leech, D.D.

Statistics of 1881.—Probationers, 12; full members, 265; local preachers, 2; children, 10; deaths, 5; parsonages, 2; present indebtedness, $5180 (on church property); Sunday-school officers and teachers, 43; Sunday-school scholars, 257; collected for missions from church, $144.70; collected for missions from Sunday-school, $185.38; collected for ministerial support, $1770.

Presbyterian Church.—The Frederick Presbyterian Church has nearly reached its one hundredth year of existence, having been established in 1782. We have sought in vain for records concerning the first edifice in use by this congregation, the old building which stood within the graveyard at the end of West Fourth Street. It was a plain brick structure, with brick floor, high-backed pews and lofty pulpit, and tradition says that the bricks were brought from England. The people who gathered there to worship God from distant parts of the county were chiefly descendants of the Scotch-Irish settlers in the Cumberland Valley.

The minister who was instrumental in organizing the first congregation was the Rev. Stephen B. Balch, D.D., who was the pastor of the church at Georgetown, D. C., from 1780 to 1833. Mr. Balch came a distance of forty miles once or twice a month to minister to the congregation, and manifested the keenest interest in the progress and welfare of the church many years after, as is shown by a letter written to Henry McCleary in 1803. The names of many associated with this organization in its early history have been lost, but the following seem to have been prominent, viz.: the families of Bailly, Reynolds, Fleming, McCleary, Dean, White, Ritchie, Bryan, McPherson, Hoff, Neill, McLanahan, Buckey, Sanderson, McElfresh, Graham, Howard, Snyder, Thompson, Boyd, Robertson, Ross, and Mormon.

These names were associated with the organization as early as 1800.

The Rev. David Baird succeeded Dr. Balch. About this time the General Assembly of the church made a special effort to occupy fields that were promising in Western Maryland and the Valley of Virginia.

The Rev. Cunningham N. Sample, who was licensed to preach in April, 1793, was appointed April, 1795, by the General Assembly, and ordered to discharge his mission on the Western Shore of Maryland. Subsequently he was directed by the Presbytery to preach at Frederick and Pipe Creek.

The report by Mr. Sample of his work, presented April, 1795, met the approbation of the Presbytery; but we find that the Assembly of 1796 did not approve his course, because "he had not pursued the route pointed out to him." In 1799 a letter was received from Mr. Sample stating that he had retired from the ministry, and had engaged in a secular employment. During the ministry of Mr. Sample, Abraham Hoff, John Neill, Hugh Reynolds, and Henry McCleary were elected elders, and David Bryan deacon.

The next minister who served the church was the Rev. Samuel Knox, of the Presbytery of Belfast, Ireland. The earliest information concerning this pastor to which we have had access is found in the records of the Frederick Academy. In May, 1797, Mr. Knox was elected president of that institution. Whether he was called to this position after or before he was called to the church we are unable to state. In 1803, Mr. Knox retired from the church, and in the same year resigned his position in the academy. In 1804 the Presbytery of Baltimore, with which his church has always been connected, instructed its commissioners to the General Assembly to represent "the advantages which might probably result to the cause of religion from the appointment of a missionary to itinerate on the Western Shore and on the waters of the Potomac."

For a period of four or five years there was no regular pastor, and only occasional preaching.

In 1809 the Rev. Patrick Davidson, of the Presbytery of Carlisle, was called to the vacant pulpit. Mr. Davidson was a graduate of Dickinson College, was licensed by New Castle Presbytery in 1797, and served the churches of Fagg's Manor, Tom's Creek, and Pipe Creek prior to his removal to Frederick.

In August, 1809, Mr. Davidson was elected principal of Frederick Academy, and probably entered upon his work as pastor in Frederick in the year 1810. But it was not until 1815 that he was dismissed from the Presbytery of Carlisle and installed as pastor of the Frederick Church. In 1817 the congregation considered the question of the removal of the church to a more eligible place, and Dec. 20, 1819, a site for the new church was bought of Mrs. Susan Keller, and deeded to Henry McCleary, Joseph Fleming, John McPherson, John Ritchie, and John Reynolds, in trust for the church. The church edifice was not completed until 1825, and not dedicated until after 1827, probably during the ministry of the Rev. Mr. McCullough.

In 1830 the following persons were appointed elders, viz.: John Ritchie, John White, and Robert McCleary. Oct. 9, 1824, the pastoral relation was dissolved by the death of Mr. Davidson. From this time until September, 1830, the church was without a pastor, and the following ministers acted as supplies for brief periods, viz.: Rev. J. W. McCullough, Rev. Mr. Mines, Rev. Mr. McIntosh, and Rev. Mr. Galloway.

In September, 1830, Rev. I. G. Hamner, D.D., received a unanimous invitation to become pastor. Dr. Hamner was of Princeton Theological Seminary, and had for contemporaries in that institution such men as Albert Barnes, J. W. Alexander, David McKinney, Theodore D. Woolsey, Edward N. Kirk, and others well known throughout the country.

Dr. Hamner had been in Fayetteville, N. C., as pastor, and came to Frederick when this church was in a very depressed condition. Under Dr. Hamner's pastorate, however, it rapidly improved, and the children, who up to this time had received instruction in a Sunday-school conducted by Presbyterians and Episcopalians, were gathered into a school of their own. Of the fifty persons admitted to membership during his brief ministry, seven have acted as ruling elders in the church. Four members were ordained and installed as elders before Dr. Hamner resigned his position as pastor, viz.: J. E. Woodbridge and Chester Coleman, in December, 1831; David B. Devitt, in January, 1833; and James L. Davis, in June, 1833.

In June, 1833, Dr. Hamner resigned, to take charge of the Fifth Presbyterian Church, Baltimore. Having served that church for many years, he afterwards became pastor of churches in New Haven, Conn., and Newark, N. J.

From June, 1833, to November, 1834, the pulpit was supplied by Revs. T. P. C. Shellman and Joseph Smith. At the latter date Rev. Philo F. Phelps, a graduate of Princeton Theological Seminary, was called as pastor, and entered upon his duties as such in 1835.

In December, 1835, Lloyd Dorsey, M.D., and Samuel R. Hogg were ordained elders. On the 8th of October the following persons were elected trustees according to the provisions of the charter: John Bailey, L. P. W. Balch, and Thomas Gurley, for one year; Robert McCleary, Albert Ritchie, and Wm. R. Sanderson, for two years; Frederick A. Schley, J. P. Thompson, and Moses Worman, for three years.

Mr. Phelps' pastorate was brief, extending over about two years. From Frederick he went to Florida, and thence to Lansingburg, N. Y., where he died in 1841.

Mr. William Blood took charge of the church in 1837. He remained one year, but was not installed as pastor.

For some months after this the pulpit was supplied, by direction of Presbytery, by the following ministers from Baltimore: Rev. J. G. Hamner, D.D., Rev. J. C. Backus, D.D., Robert J. Breckenridge, D.D., and George W. Musgrove, D.D.

Rev. Joseph Smith was elected pastor July 24, 1838, and in August of the same year principal of the Frederick Academy. Dr. Smith was a graduate of Jefferson College, studied theology with Rev. Dr. Hill, of Winchester, Va., and spent one year at Princeton. He had for contemporaries in the Theological Seminary, Dr. Hodge, Dr. Wm. Nevin, Bishops Johns and McIlvaine, of the Episcopal Church, Dr. Schumacher, of the Lutheran Church, and others.

In June, 1843, the Rev. John Miller became pastor. He graduated from Princeton College in 1836, and from the Theological Seminary in 1839. On Jan. 2, 1844, a free day-school was started under the direction of Mr. Miller. It opened with nearly forty scholars, and soon increased to seventy. For its support and management the ladies of the church formed an organization by electing Mrs. Patrick Davidson president, Mrs. Samuel Tyler secretary, and Mrs. Edward Shriver treasurer. The following constituted the board of managers: Mrs. Reynolds, Mrs. John White, Mrs. Moses Worman, Mrs. McLanahan, Mrs. R. McCleary, Miss C. Reynolds, Miss M. Eichelberger, Miss Margaret Sanderson, Miss Emma Reigart, Mrs. Charles Shriver, Miss M. Davidson, Miss Eliza Montz, Miss E. Berger, Miss J. H. Williams, Mrs. Wilson, Mrs. Thompson, Mrs. M. Hood.

Nor was this the only school started by Mr. Miller. A letter received from Peter McMortin, now of Michigan, informs us that he started a classical school through the solicitation of Mr. Miller, that most of his patrons were connected with this church, and that Dr. Albert Ritchie was so much interested in this school that he vacated his office that it might be used for a school-room. In 1845 the congregation decided to build a parsonage, and Edward Shriver, Seth Nichols, and George J. Fisher were appointed a building committee.

The lot on which the parsonage is built was bought of Frederick H. Schley, and the house was built by the voluntary contributions of the members.

In 1847 the frame house now occupied by Mr. Renner was bought of Mrs. Sarah English. About the same time the church was repaired and the iron fence put up around it. In December, 1848, Mr. Miller resigned his charge, after having accomplished much that has proved of permanent benefit to the church. Mr. Miller's successor was the Rev. Joseph M. Atkinson, who was educated at Princeton College and Seminary. Mr. Atkinson had served the churches of Sheperdstown and Smithville, Va., and was installed pastor of this church July, 1849. In September, 1853, Jonathan Tyson and Charles M. Miller were ordained as elders. In December, 1855, Rev. Jacob Kerr received a call, but declined it. He was invited to act as supply, and acted in that capacity for one year. In October, 1857, Rev. J. B. Ross accepted a call to become pastor. In the following year the church was renovated and improved. The walls were frescoed, the front and the windows were remodeled, and a new furnace and chandelier were introduced at a cost of two thousand eight hundred and twenty dollars. Mr. Ross resigned his charge in October, 1862.

For one year and a half after the dissolution of the pastoral relation the church was without a pastor. During several months of this period the edifice was used by the government for hospital purposes. The number of sick and wounded after the battle of Antietam, which occurred Sept. 17, 1862, was so great that all the public buildings, the school-houses, and several of the churches were needed for their accommodation. After several months had passed the government restored the church to the trustees, but such was the excitement that the session did not begin to make arrangements to secure a pastor until January, 1864.

At that time they sent for Rev. Robert H. Williams, who had two churches in charge in Harford County. He accepted, and preached his first sermon as pastor on the first Sabbath of May. On the following evening he was installed as pastor by Rev. C. Dickson, D.D., G. P. Hays, D.D., and Rev. Griffith Owen.

Before a month of Mr. Williams' ministry had passed arrangements were made for the organization of a mission Sabbath-school. For a long time this school was under the superintendence of the pastor, and afterwards was in charge of Simon Parsons and

James Hogg. So successful was this school that another was soon opened, under the superintendence of Henry K. Cormack, on All Saints' Street. The temperance society, which was organized in 1866, was composed principally of the boys of the Sabbath-school, and became the nucleus of the Good Templars, and afterwards the Temple of Honor, the only temperance organization now in the city.

The Young Men's Christian Association of Frederick was reorganized in 1868, and from that time to this the young men of this church have been among its prominent and most useful members.

The Sewing Society was reorganized, and Miss Charlotte Baer acted for a long time as its prominent officer. The youngest association of the congregation is the Ladies' Missionary Society.

In May, 1867, William Dean was installed as elder, and in July, 1867, Adam Gault and A. Y. McCormick, M.D., were ordained as deacons.

In January, 1872, C. W. Ely and C. H. Hill were ordained elders, and George Dean and C. G. Meyers deacons. In January, 1876, G. F. S. Zimmerman and T. Lynn Davis were ordained elders. The trustees who served the church during Mr. Williams' ministry were the following, viz.: E. H. Rockwell, Grayson Eichelberger, Edward Shriver, James Hergeshiemer, Adam Gault, G. J. Doll, G. F. S. Zimmerman, David M. Kinney, M.D., Simon Parsons, Jacob Tyson, Henry Markey, Hiram Schisler, W. L. Morris, William Worman, Perry McCleary, Frederick Duvall, and Samuel H. Brown.

Mr. Williams retired in 1880, and in the spring of 1881, Rev. Irwin P. McCurdy was called. The elders for 1881 were Charles W. Ely, Charles H. Hill, George Zimmerman; Deacons, George W. Means and Charles G. Meyers.

The Baptist Church.—Following is a copy of the covenant of the first Baptist congregation in Frederick Town:

"The Covenant agreed upon, entered into, and signed by the Baptist Church of Jesus Christ at Frederick Town, State of Maryland, the 10th day of July, 1790. We, the subscribers, inhabitants of Frederick County in the State aforesaid being constituted into a church agreeable to the order of the Baptists some time about the first of July in the year of our Lord 1773, having been by misfortune deprived of our records, from the time of our constitution until now, do, for the glory of God, and our own peace and comfort, covenant and agree to and with each other, to maintain, stand by, and defend the following essential doctrines, and observe the rules of discipline hereunto annexed; that is to say in general we hereby declare our assent to all those doctrines contained in the Baptist Confession of Faith adopted by the Baptist Association at Philadelphia in the year 1742, and lately reprinted by their order; which we receive as comprehending the articles of our faith, believing it to be agreeable to the word of God; (at least in its essential parts) we recommend it to the perusal of one another, our families and friends. But in particular we profess to believe in the following very essential doctrines." (Here follows the articles of belief.)

Members' Names.

Thos. Beatty, deceased.
Wm. Gilmore, deceased April 25, 1806.
James Beatty, dismissed.
John Whiteneck, dism'd.
Elinor Gregg, dism'd.
Catharine Gilmore, dec'd.
Elizabeth Coleman, dismissed 1795.
Penelope Hill, dismissed 1798.
Richard Hopewell, dismissed 1806.
Ruth Gassaway, dism'd.
Abraham Wood, dismissed 1795.
Sarah Hyatt, deceased.
Wm. Simkins, dismissed.
Susannah Powell, dec'd.
Sarah Hedge, dismissed.
Rachel H. Bronson, dismissed 1806.
Edward Ward, dec'd.
Geo. McMins, dismissed.
Luke Barnerd, excommunicated Nov., 1799; restored June 11, 1803.
Rebecca Barnerd, excommunicated 1803.
Wm. Parkinson, dism'd 1806.
Elizabeth Harley, dism'd.
Hannah Albaugh, dec'd.
Marion Knight (wife of Moses), excom'd.
Negro, Ben Bronson, dismissed 1806.
Sarah Bond, excluded.
Negro, Charles Adams, dismissed 1806.
Negro, Sarah, dismissed.
Sarah Scott, excluded Dec. 26, 1825.
Wm. B. Martin, dism'd.
Mary Barton, dismissed.
John Bagant, dismissed.
Catharine Baygant, dismissed.
Wm. Gilmore, Jr., dism'd.
Joshua Johnson, excluded Dec. 26, 1828.
Sophia Duvall, dismissed 1805.
Isabella Low, excommunicated Dec. 26, 1828.
Conrad Keller, deceased.
Elizabeth Keller.
Lydia Braidy, dismissed 1805.
James Braidy, dismissed 1805.
Thomas Ritchie, rec'd by letter from New York, Sept. 21, 1827.
Catherine Estworthy, Nov. 5, 1827.
Patty Dean, Nov. 5, 1827.
Henry Randall (by letter), Nov. 5, 1827.
Isabella Randall, Nov. 5, 1827; deceased 1828.
Luke Forrest, rec'd from Ebenezer Church, Feb. 4, 1828.
Henry Lease.
Ann Bannister, received by baptism; dis. 1830.
Nancy Hill (colored).
Mary Davis.
Elder Wm. Parkinson, received by letter from First Baptist Church, New York, Oct. 31, 1840; dism'd July 7, 1841.
Mary Ward, deceased.
Ezekiel Beatty, deceased June 10, 1792.
Elijah Beatty, excommunicated July 23, 1796.
Sarah Gassaway, dec'd.
Ruth Bainbridge, dism'd 1794.
Abraham ——, deceased.
Math. Harley, deceased.
Keziah Davis, deceased.
Posthumous Claggett, dismissed.
Mary Claggett, dism'd.
Alexander Ogle, dism'd.
Mary Ogle, dism'd.
Milld^d Smith, excluded Dec. 26, 1818.
Negro, Sarah Hopewell, dismissed 1806.
Negro, Catherine Stuart, dismissed 1806.
Thos. Morgan, dismissed 1793.
Negro "John," deceased.
Thomas Hill, excom'd.
Sarah Maynard, deceased.
James Walling, dism'd.
Priscilla Tillard, deceased.
Fender Smith (black woman), excluded.
Maria Hyatt, deceased.
Sarah Tillard, deceased.
Isabella Paxton, deceased.
Polly West, dism'd 1805.
Geo. Sedwick, dismissed 1806.

Polly Ritchie, received by letter; dism'd by letter to New York; received 1833.
Jacob Lease, Jr.
Mary Geyer, received by letter; excluded Dec. 26, 1828.
John Welsh, rec'd by letter Oct. 5, 1811; dec'd.
Mary M. Holmes, excom'd Dec. 26, 1828.
Mary Ann English.
Joseph Trapnell, May 23, 1827; excommunicated July 25, 1829.
Harriett Trapnell, May 23, 1827.
Aaron Bannister, dism'd 1830.
John Bannister, Aug. 19, 1827.
Millie Grayson, by bapt'm.
Daniel Lease, received by baptism Dec. 26, 1828.
John Roderick, rec'd by baptism Dec. 26, 1828.
Richard English, received by baptism 1828.
Elizabeth Dean, received by baptism 1829.
Enos B. Reese.
Cassandra Wickham, received by letter from the Baptist Church at Salem, Dec. 21, 1831.

It appears that the old covenant and records up to 1790 had been taken away by John Beatty.

On the 10th of July, 1790, Wm. Gilmore was chosen deacon, and Thomas and James Beatty trustees. The latter were ordered to have the deed for the meeting-house lot made to them and their successors. Absalom Bainbridge was licensed to preach in the same year. April 21, 1791, Elijah Beatty was appointed clerk. Sept. 24, 1794, Alex. Ogle and Posthumous Claggett were chosen additional trustees. Jan. 21, 1797, full license was given Wm. Parkinson to preach; July 22, 1797, George Grice was elected deacon, *vice* Wm. Gilmore, resigned.

The records from 1790 to 1841 (the last found) do not give the names of the preachers, but are mostly taken up with additions to the church and dismissions and excommunications therefrom, with other routine church affairs.

As far as can be learned the early preachers were Absalom Bainbridge, 1790; Wm. Parkinson, 1796; Jeremiah Moore, 1805; —— Ledwicks, 1809; John Welch, 1811; Plummer Waters, Jr., 1818; Joseph H. Jones, 1836.

St. John's Catholic Church.—To write fully the history of St. John's Catholic Church and residence is to give the history of Catholicism in Frederick County. All the churches in the county have been more or less connected with St. John's. St. Joseph's, on the Manor, and the churches of Petersville, Liberty, and Middletown, are its offshoots. St. John's is also associated with the churches of Mount St. Mary's and Emmittsburg, as having had for a number of years the same pastor, the Rev. John Dubois, afterwards Bishop of New York. By the middle of the last century a number of Catholics had settled in the Monocacy Valley. They were principally of English origin, having come directly from England or from the lower counties of the State. Many of them were tenants on Carroll's Manor, on the Monocacy, and these formed the nucleus of St. Joseph's Parish, at present under the charge of the fathers of the Novitiate. A large portion of the English settlers belonged to the Established Church, but in this particular locality (the Manor) the Catholics were probably in the majority, as Mr. Carroll, no doubt, was anxious that his religion should get a foothold in Frederick Valley. That most of them were from the lower part of the State is shown by the fact that the names frequently occurring on the old baptismal and marriage records are those belonging to St. Mary's, Charles, Calvert, and Prince George's Counties. Other Catholics were drawn to Frederick County in order to escape the rigors of the penal laws, which were in full force in the rest of the province. In enumerating the Catholic population of Frederick one hundred years ago the German Catholics have also to be taken into the reckoning. These immigrants came from Germany and Pennsylvania about the middle of the last century. Some Hessians settled in Frederick Town at the end of the Revolutionary war, but of these very few were Catholics. There were also a few Irish Catholics scattered through the county.

John Cary, whose name is signed to a deed for a lot on which the original chapel was built, appears to have been an Irishman. The deed is in favor of Father George Hunter, and bears date Oct. 2, 1765. In the document it is stated that for and in consideration of the payment of five shillings, current money, the title is given to the lot above mentioned. This same lot had some years previously cost the seller forty or fifty times that amount. Mr. Cary was a merchant, as appears from the deed. The spiritual needs of this congregation were supplied as well as circumstances permitted by the fathers from St. Thomas' Mission, near Port Tobacco, then and for a long time after the residence of the superior of the Jesuits in Maryland. The fathers of this mission had stations, churches, or residences through Maryland, Virginia, Pennsylvania, and a part of New York. Most likely Frederick Valley was for some time attended directly from St. Thomas'. The father who was appointed for the work used, no doubt, to make long excursions, which would take in the Catholics of what is now the District of Columbia, of Montgomery and Frederick Counties, along the banks of the Potomac River. After the mission was begun at Conewago some German father would perhaps go to Frederick Town, a distance of forty miles, to administer the sacraments to the faithful of his nationality.

In the course of time the number of Catholics increased, especially in Frederick Town, and it became necessary to build a residence and chapel. This residence and chapel were accordingly erected in 1763 by Father John Williams, an English Jesuit. Very little is known about this father. He came to the mission of Maryland on June 9, 1758, in company with Fathers James Framback and James Pellentz, the founders of the congregation at Conewago. How long Father Williams remained at Frederick and who was his immediate successor is uncertain. He returned, most probably, to Europe, as his name is not mentioned among the nineteen ex-Jesuits in Maryland in 1774. There is reason to believe that Father George Hunter was the successor of Father Williams, from the fact that his name occurs in the deed already mentioned. It may be objected that Father Hunter was superior of the order in Maryland at the time, 1765, and that the deed was consequently made out in his name. This reasoning is not conclusive, for it is doubtful whether Father Hunter was superior in 1765. It is known that he was superior and vicar-general in 1794, but this was after his return to Maryland. Nor were deeds always made out in the name of the superior, as will be seen farther on. In Campbell's list of ex-Jesuits, alluded to before, Father James Frambach is set down as the pastor of Frederick Town in the year 1773. The mission intrusted to Father Framback was no easy one, as the whole of Western Maryland and the upper part of Virginia formed his parish, entailing upon him long and perilous expeditions to visit the Catholics scattered through this extensive territory. Sick calls over mountains and rivers for fifty and sixty miles must have been very trying for one who had already been on the laborious Maryland Mission nearly twenty years. He slept generally beside his horse, in order to be prepared for a sudden flight, and on one occasion, when on a visit to a Catholic family in Virginia, he barely escaped with his life by the fleetness of his horse in carrying him through the waters of the Potomac. He was fired upon by his pursuers before he reached the Maryland side of the river, but escaped unhurt. Father Framback was a German, and came to the mission in 1758. He died at St. Inigoes, Aug. 26, 1795, in the seventy-third year of his age.

Father James Walton succeeded Father Framback. This statement is made on the authority of a deed for a part of the Novitiate property, which was executed in 1779.

Father Walton was an Englishman, and came to Maryland in the year 1776, and died at St. Inigoes in 1803, aged sixty-five.

The first residence erected now forms part of the Novitiate. It was a two-story brick building, and included on the first floor three rooms and a passage, and had a front of about fifty-five feet. The second floor was used as a chapel, and has since been used as the library of the Tertian fathers, the chapel of the Blessed Virgin, and the fathers' recreation-room. Many years afterwards a basement was added to the building by the grading of the street. This was the work of Father McElroy. The small chapel of Father Williams was for nearly forty years the only place of worship for the Catholics of Frederick County. The fathers remained in Frederick Town after the suppression of the Jesuits, or at least went thither now and then. Father Walton, the last father of whom we have any record as having been there, died in 1803, but some time before his death the chapel was attended by the Rev. John Dubois. As the fathers of the old society were yearly growing fewer, and the number of Catholics was constantly becoming larger, many of the more distant churches were given up to secular priests. St. John's fell into good hands. The Rev. John Dubois is too conspicuous in the history of the church in the United States to need any notice here. He began to administer to the spiritual wants of St. John's congregation about 1792. He had also under his care the Catholics about Emmittsburg, and those of Montgomery County, Martinsburg, Western Maryland, and Virginia; and, in fact, was for a long time the only priest between Baltimore and St. Louis. "Some of his congregation," we are told, "came to Frederick to attend mass and receive the sacraments from distances of twenty, forty, and sixty miles; and when any of them were ill or dying the indefatigable pastor journeyed these distances on horseback, and sometimes on foot, to carry the consolations of religion to them. His missionary labors were extraordinary; he spared no pains, labor, or fatigue in the discharge of the sublime duties which heaven assigned him. After the exhausting fatigues of his ministry in town he scoured the country in quest of souls, entering into the minute details of instructing and catechising the children and servants, etc."

One of the first undertakings of the new pastor was to build a church in place of the small upper room in the residence. The work was begun in the year 1800. The people thought him mad, and even Mr. Taney, afterwards chief justice, who was a member of his congregation, said, "We all thought that the means could not be raised to pay for such a building; that the church would never be completed, and if completed, would never be filled with Catholics."

The church was a brick building, eighty-two feet in length and forty-five feet in breadth, and having been torn down in part in 1859 and rebuilt and transformed, has since been used by the Junior Fire Company as an infirmary. Much difficulty was met by Rev. Mr. Dubois in paying for the church. The usual means were resorted to, and in 1804 a lottery authorized by the State was resorted to, but with little success. The announcement was as follows:

"Lottery to complete Church of St. John's, Fred'k-Town, 4800 tickets @ $5 = $24,000, subject to deduction of 15 per cent. Managers, J. Dubois, Henry Darnall, Joseph Smith, Samuel Lilly, George Baer, jun., Peter Mantz, Roger B. Taney. Frederick, Febr'y 3, 1804. Tickets to be had of managers, or at the stores of Messrs. John McPherson, Francis Mantz, Jacob Steiner, Henry Koontz, Jr., John and Isaac Mantz, John Baily, George Baer, and William C. Hobbs."

The Rev. Mr. Dubois remained in Frederick until 1806, when he removed to Emmittsburg, and from this place most probably went to Frederick once or twice a month. Things continued in this state until Father Francis Malevie, of the Society of Jesus, took charge. This occurred in 1811. The church continued to grow, especially in the more distant stations, and it became necessary a few years later to build small churches in several parts of the county. The German element had become more numerous in Frederick, but the English and Irish names were still in the majority. During the years that had passed since the Revolution a great many slaves had been brought into the county, and as a number of them were Catholics, their instruction in religious duties entailed no trifling burden on the pastor. The church of St. John's was still unfinished, and was even unsafe. The interior was not plastered, and the roof had been so poorly made that it had begun to sink. Supports from within had become a matter of necessity, as the side walls, yielding to the weight, were pressed out. Father Malevie had the church plastered in 1812, and the roof was secured by means of wooden columns.

Father Malevie was born Dec. 1, 1770. His naturalization papers speak of him as a native of Russia, and a subject of the emperor of that country. In early life he entered the order of St. Francis of Assisi, but on account of the troubles in France at the end of the last century he was forced, on the dispersion of his order, to live in the world as a secular priest. In 1804, with the permission of the Holy See, he entered the society in Russia. While yet a novice he was sent to the United States, and was the first Jesuit who came from Russia to this country. Father Malevie was allowed to take his last vows on the 29th of June, 1815. On his return to Frederick he continued the work which he had been doing so well. The next undertaking worthy of note was the building of St. Joseph's Church on the Manor, about seven miles from Frederick. The work was finished in 1820. The lot of ground for the church and graveyard, with a portion of the funds, no doubt, for the building itself, was a gift to the father from Charles Carroll of Carrollton. There is not, perhaps, a piece of land in Frederick County that has for its size more conspicuous names connected with it than the St. Joseph's property. First, the gift already mentioned; then another was made by the Pattersons, another by the Harpers and McTavishes; and finally, in 1853, another by Mary Ann, Marchioness of Wellesley. The document by which the marchioness conveyed the property has an international character, as it had to pass through the office of the American consul in England, the Hon. Mr. Ingersoll. St. Joseph's congregation has always been under the charge of the Jesuit fathers, who have attended it from their residence in Frederick, or from the Novitiate.

In 1821, Mr. Coale, a prominent Catholic of Liberty, a town about twelve miles from Frederick, offered a lot of ground for a church. Father Malevie, with the approbation of the superiors, accepted it, and a building was begun. The work, however, went on very slowly, and was not completed until after his death. This church has, with the exception of two or three years, been always attended by the Jesuit fathers of Frederick. A few years ago the old building was torn down, and a new one was erected at a cost of fifteen thousand dollars. Gen. Coale, the son of the donor of the lot, bore all the expenses of the new church.

Father Malevie died Oct. 3, 1822.

Several gentlemen, among whom was Mr. Taney, addressed a letter to the father superior, asking him to retain Father McElroy. The request was granted, and thus was begun a career of usefulness which, if we consider the resources at hand, has scarcely been equaled in any city in the country. Father McElroy found the congregation small, the church sadly in need of repair, the residence old and weather-beaten, and after twenty-three years of arduous labor he left the congregation large and flourishing, whilst the old church had given way to one of the finest edifices in the State, and the old two-story residence had been greatly enlarged and was doing service as a Novitiate of the society. The new residence on Church Street, the buildings for St. John's Literary Institution, and the school and orphanage of the Sisters of Charity, gave proof also of the energy and skill of the pastor of St. John's. It is an easy matter to show financial tact in large cities with liberal congregations, but it was quite a task to build churches and schools in Frederick fifty years ago, as money was scarce, and the little to be had was to be used with consummate ability in order to accomplish anything at all commensurate with the necessities of the case. Towards the end of 1823 negotiations were begun with the superior of the Sisters of Charity for the establishment of a community in Frederick. The help the Sisters could render to the pastor for school purposes was much needed. Early in 1824 five Sisters arrived from Emmittsburg, and were domiciled in a wretched log cabin, built in the days of the Revolution, on what is now the convent property. This had but two rooms on the first floor and a miserable attic overhead. The school was opened, however, a notice having previously been inserted in the papers to this effect, viz.:

"St. John's Female Benevolent and Frederick Free School will be opened on the 3d of January, 1824. Reading, writing, and needle-work, etc., will be taught. All denominations admitted."

In 1825 it became necessary to build a larger establishment for the Sisters, to serve for a school and an orphan asylum. After strenuous labor the work was done and paid for, and provision was secured for the maintenance of the orphans. During this year (1825) Father McElroy had as his assistant Father P. W. Walsh, who was much needed, as the congregation in Frederick alone was enough for one priest. The help of another father became more imperative next year, when a church was built at Petersville. The land for this church was given by Mr. West, a Protestant gentleman. The fathers from Frederick still supply this congregation. A few years ago the old log building was enlarged. The colored people form the larger part of the congregation. Of late years a great deal has been done for the religious education of the colored children by the efforts of a young lady, who, though wealthy and admired by the world, has given herself entirely to this good work.

On Aug. 7, 1828, the corner-stone of St. John's Literary Institute was laid. In 1829 the classes were begun, and soon St. John's College became the rival of Georgetown, and remained so until 1853, when it received a check by the expulsion of a large number of students at one time.

St. John's has given many members to the society and to the legal and medical professions, including some of the most distinguished names in this city and State. The school is still in existence. A charter was obtained from the Legislature in 1829, together with an annual donation of three hundred dollars. This sum is still paid by the comptroller of the State. The pastor had done a great deal towards finishing and beautifying the old church in Frederick, but on account of the increase in the congregation it was thought advisable to extend the front of the church fifteen or twenty feet and erect galleries. This plan was proposed to the people in 1830, and all readily agreed to contribute to the work. Several builders were consulted about the contemplated addition, and were unanimous in expressing the opinion that it would be a waste of money, and advised rather the tearing down of the old church and the erection of a new one. The project was abandoned for some time for want of money. In 1832 the new plan was put before the congregation, and four thousand dollars were subscribed. To this amount was added a legacy of another thousand dollars. Very Rev. Father Peter Kenney, superior and visitor, was consulted, and after an interchange of opinions it was finally resolved, in January, 1833, that the work should be undertaken, and the site changed from that on which the old church stood to the lot on the opposite side of the street. Works on architecture were obtained from Georgetown, and with the aid of these Father McElroy and Mr. Tehan, a well-known builder of those days, fixed upon a plan for the new edifice. The form was to be that of a Latin cross, the nave to be one hundred and thirty-six feet in length and forty-nine in width, the transept ninety-four feet in length and forty-nine in width; length of nave to transept, sixty-three feet; height from floor to ceiling, forty feet. The society's church in Gardinier Street, Dublin, was used as a model for the ground-plan, though St. John's is considerably larger.

The corner-stone was laid in the northeast angle of the nave on St. Joseph's day, 1833. The work went on amid the greatest difficulties, but subscriptions, loans, legacies, and contributions from the employés of the Baltimore and Ohio Railroad and Chesapeake and Ohio Canal enabled the pastor to finish the building by 1837. Among the presents recorded for the altar were a dozen candlesticks and two crucifixes. These cost twelve hundred francs, and were sent by Very Rev. John Roothaur, general of the society.

On the 26th of April St. John's was consecrated with the usual impressive services of the Catholic Church. The steeple of St. John's was completed in 1854 by Father Burchard Villiger, and a few years ago the interior of the church was restored and beautified. During the erection of the church the Novitiate was transferred from White Marsh to the residence of the clergy in Frederick. The change was proposed almost jokingly by Father McElroy to Very Rev. Father Kenney in 1832. The latter received the suggestion in earnest, and determined to carry out the idea. He would have done so at the time but for his recall to Ireland. Very Rev. Father McSherry, the successor of Father Kenney, had the same views, and in 1833 a large addition was made to the residence. This addition consisted in placing another story on the old building, and the extension of the west end from what is now the rector's sitting-room to the passage leading to the refectory. The wing now used by the novices, together with the chapel, was added by Father Samuel Barber. The east extension, from the pastor's room to the alley, was made by the Very Rev. Father Brocord. The infirmary wing was added by Father Paresce in 1859. From time to time the establishment of the Sisters had been enlarged to meet the wants of the orphans and the school. A large addition was made about the year 1827, and this last effort of Father McElroy for the education of the young was attended with highly satisfactory results. The school building was burned down in 1845, but was soon replaced by another. In 1839 we find Father James Ryder acting as the assistant of Father McElroy in the church and in the school, where he was prefect and teacher of French and writing.

Father Thomas Lilly succeeded Father McElroy in September, 1845. The assistants were Fathers George Villiger, Stonestreet, Meredith, Jenkins, Finotti, and Bogue. During the three years that followed the church and college continued to flourish. Quite a number of colored adults were received into the church by Father Lilly.

In 1846 the Sisters of Charity withdrew, and were replaced by the Nuns of the Visitation from Georgetown. The convent of the Visitation is now among the finest establishments of education in the city. The school enjoys a fine reputation here and elsewhere. The Sisters also maintain an excellent free school.

In 1848, Father Charles H. Stonestreet became the successor of Father Lilly. The assistants at different times during the year were Fathers Bogue, Finotti, and Ciampi. During the presidency of Father Stonestreet the Very Rev. Francis Dzierozynski, who was looked upon by all as a saintly man, died at the residence. Father Dzierozynski was a native of Orsani, in Poland, and was born on the 3d of June, 1777.

Father Thomas Mullaly was appointed the successor of Father Stonestreet at the end of 1850. Under his administration it became necessary to expel so large a number of students from the college that it began to decline, and has since been used merely as a school for the city. The president of the college was also the pastor of the church. The pastors after Father Mullaly were Fathers Villiger, Samuel Barber, Hippolyte, De Neckere, Blenkinsop, and McAtee. The assistants during this period, from 1853 to 1860, were at different times, Fathers Bogue, Duddy, and Tuffer.

In 1860 the residence on Church Street was rented out, and the fathers and brothers connected with the church and college took up their abode in the Novitiate, where they have since remained. The pastors who followed Father Sourin, who had charge of the church from 1860 to 1870, were Fathers O'Kane, Smith, Jenkins, Ciampi, Fulmer, and lastly Father Stonestreet, who, after an absence of twenty-five years, returned to the church as its parish priest.

The outlying missions during all these years have not been neglected. New churches have been built and the old ones enlarged. Five years ago the present pastor of the missions concluded to build a small church in Middletown, seven miles from Frederick. Recently a small church was built near the town of Urbana. It is intended principally for the use of a colony of colored people who have settled in that community.

German Reformed Church.—Under the ministration of Rev. John H. Smaltz, pastor of the Evangelical Reformed Church from 1829 to 1833, services in the German language ceased, and were conducted in English. From that time the Germans professing the Reformed faith had no regular preaching until 1843, in which year Rev. Isaac Gerhart was settled as pastor, and continued for six years. In 1849, Rev. E. W. Meister became the pastor and remained until 1851. He was succeeded by Rev. Mr. Reineke, who continued until 1855. His successor was Rev. John Knelling, who preached about a year, and from that time to 1861 the congregation was without regular stated preaching. Rev. F. H. Schwart then was pastor until 1863, and was followed by Rev. G. W. Glessner, who remained until 1867. Rev. J. C. Hauser was the next pastor, from 1867 to 1872, when he was succeeded by Rev. Herman Billfeld, the present pastor in charge. From 1850 to April, 1881, services were conducted in the old Reformed church, and since then in Kemp Hall, corner of Market and Church Streets. This church belongs to the German Synod of the Reformed Church of the United States. It has a prosperous Sunday-school, under Jacob Nottnagel as superintendent. The church membership numbers eighty persons.

Methodist Protestant Church.—The Methodist Protestant Church in the United States was organized in the year 1829 in Baltimore.

Rev. Josiah Varden was a missionary of this church in Frederick City in 1859, in which year a society was organized there as the result of his labors. Nineteen members first constituted the Frederick Methodist Protestant Church, and the first regular pastor was Rev. Peter Lightfoot, who remained until 1860. His successor was Rev. Edward G. Drinkhouse, who continued two years, and was followed by Rev. David A. Sherman as pastor for the next two, and Rev. William S. Hammond for two more. Rev. J. K. Nichols was pastor for four years, succeeded by Rev. J. D. Wilson in 1870, who remained one year. The next was Rev. S. G. Valliant for one year, followed by Rev. C. H. Littleton until 1876, when Rev. W. W. White took charge. Mr. White was succeeded by C. O. Mervin, who remained about six months. There has been no pastor since 1878, when the church building on East Church Street, formerly the property of the Methodist Episcopal Church, was closed. In the spring of 1881 the church and parsonage were transferred by the four remaining trustees to the Conference Missionary Society. For four years preceding April, 1881, the parsonage was occupied by Rev. J. E. Maloy, who had a circuit in the country, but did not preach in this church, and since then by Rev. J. L. Mills, who has the circuit occupied by Mr. Maloy. When the church closed, in 1878, its membership was thirty, but the organization may now be said to have disbanded.

Trinity M. E. Church, South.—Until 1836 Frederick was in the circuit (except one or two years when found non-sustaining) embracing several appointments in the county. That year it was made a station by the Methodist Episcopal Church (South) Conference, and Rev. Samuel Bryson was appointed pastor. Under his ministry the work expanded, and the station has ever since been self-sustaining. At first the Methodist Episcopal Church (South) occupied the small brick church on West Church Street, now held by the Methodist Protestant congregation. The Trinity congregation now have a finer and more commodious building on East Church Street, built in 1865, under the pastorate of Rev. W. W. Hicks.

In 1860 the General Methodist Conference, at Buffalo, introduced into the discipline the new chapter on slavery. Its action was offensive to many members, who regarded it as an innovation upon Methodist usages. Some of these withdrew and united with other churches. The Baltimore Conference, which met in Staunton in 1861, by resolutions protested against the action of the General Conference, withdrew therefrom, and remained independent till 1866, when it formally united with the Methodist Episcopal Church, South, at Alexandria, Va. Those who withdrew from the Methodist Episcopal Church in Frederick City determined in 1865 (soon after the war) to form a society and join the Methodist Episcopal Church, South. The first services were held in the beginning by Rev. John Hall, of Baltimore Conference, in private houses, and afterwards in the large three-story house occupied by Messrs. Shilling & Young as a bakery, situated on East Patrick Street, near the corner of Carroll. Junior Hall was temporarily secured as a place of worship, and services were held whenever ministerial help could be obtained. Rev. George G. Smith, of Georgia, and Rev. John Poisal, of Baltimore Conference, and others aided in this way till Dec. 16, 1866, when a society was regularly organized by Rev. Samuel Register, D.D., presiding elder of Baltimore Conference, Methodist Episcopal Church, South. The following were the first fourteen and original members: William B. Shilling, Mary Shilling, Joseph Shawen, John R. Torreyson, James W. Pearre, S. Marion Pearre, John T. Sinn, Catharine C. Sinn, Robert H. Burton, Ann Burton, Jane Holland, William Eberts, Godfrey Koontz, and W. Nash Young. In order to have a permanent place of worship the hall belonging to and over the store of R. H. Macgill, corner of East Patrick and Market Streets, was leased. This place having been fitted up, was formally dedicated by Rev. S. S. Rozell, D.D., in January, 1867. The full cost of fitting up the hall was paid that day. Among the outside friends who helped in the work William Tregoe is mentioned as having painted the hall free, also R. Brown Henderson as having been active in securing a place of worship on former occasions. The first Quarterly Conference was held February 21, 1867, presided over by Rev. Eugene R. Smith, from Texas Conference, who had been appointed pastor of the work January 6th, and who was reappointed at the Annual Conference in March following. This year the congregation prospered greatly, and in March, 1868, sixty-six members were reported. The pastor for 1868 was Rev. Samuel Kepler. On Dec. 7, 1868, J. W. Pearre, Charles Howard, and Lloyd T. Macgill were chosen to select a site whereon to build a church. On Jan. 5, 1869, under an act of incorporation, Edward Howard, Edward Sinn, Godfrey Koontz, J. W. Pearre, D. G. Crise, Alexander A. D. Warfield, Thomas H. O'Neal, J. R. Torreyson, and W. B. Shilling were elected trustees. In 1869 the church had eighty members, and Rev. Samuel Kepler continued pastor. In 1870, Rev. Maybury G. Balthis was appointed pastor, but owing to ill health resigned, and was succeeded by Rev. J. C. Hummer, who supplied the charge until the Conference met. On Dec. 15, 1870, the trustees purchased of W. L. Duvall and wife a house and lot for eight hundred and thirty-seven dollars, and one adjoining from John A. Simmons for two thousand four hundred and thirty-seven dollars, situated on East Second Street, where the church now stands. Frederick Zumstein contracted to build the new church for eight thousand eight hundred and forty-five dollars according to the plans furnished free by John C. Harkness, an architect of Washington, D. C. The corner-stone was laid with Masonic ceremonies by Columbia Lodge, No. 58, A. F. and A. M., June 6, 1871, on which occasion Rev. William E. Munsey, D.D., of Baltimore, delivered the address in the German Reformed church, which had been tendered for the day. The new church was dedicated Sunday, Jan. 21, 1872. Rev. James A. Duncan, D.D., president of Randolph-Macon College, preached in the morning, and Rev. S. S. Rozell, D.D., of Washington City, in the afternoon, and Rev. Dr. Duncan again at night. In 1871 and 1872, Rev. J. C. Hummer was pastor, and in 1873, Rev. George T. Tyler, under whose ministrations thirty persons professed religion and thirty-five accessions to the church were made. Rev. George T. Tyler continued pastor in 1874, 1875, and in 1876. In 1877 the pastor was Rev. S. S. Rozell; 1878, J. Asbury Regester; 1879 and 1880, Rev. A. Ezra Brandenbaugh, and in 1881, Rev. H. P. Hamill.

Quin's African Methodist Episcopal Church. —This church was rebuilt in 1876, and is now a tasteful and commodious edifice.

Asbury Methodist Episcopal Church. —This church is on All Saints' Street. It was erected in 1818. An addition was made to it in 1850, and it was renovated in 1870. It stands well back in a large yard, part of which is used as a cemetery. Among the persons buried here we find Elizabeth, wife of Jonathan Murdock, born Aug. 1, 1796, died Aug. 3, 1878. Rev. Nicholas Smith, died Dec. 9, 1827, aged sixty-five years. Rev. Henry Cole, died Sept. 10, 1850, aged fifty-five, and Hannah, his wife, Feb. 23, 1871, aged seventy-eight. William Brown, born Sept. 29, 1800, died April 2, 1877. Rev. Solomon Snodden, born March 6, 1810, died February, 1852.

Cemeteries. —The cemeteries in and near Frederick City are those of the Lutheran Church, Mount Olivet, All Saints', the German Reformed Church, the Shriver Family Burying-Ground, and the Presbyterian and Catholic Cemeteries. Of these the principal one is Mount Olivet, and the oldest that of the Lutheran Church.

Lutheran Cemetery. —This cemetery lies in the rear of the Lutheran church, on Church Street, and is the oldest cemetery in Frederick. From its tombstones we gather the following:

Michael Reamer, born in 1715, died Nov. 25, 1800.
Christina Buckey, wife of Matthias Buckey, born July 18, 1752, died Nov. 10, 1808.
John Ebbert, born July 24, 1772, died April 1, 1851, and Rebecca, his wife, born July 21, 1776, died Oct. 30, 1822.
Jacob Fout, born Sept. 9, 1765, died March 21, 1807.
Baltzer Fout, born April 28, 1779, died March 24, 1830, and his wife Mary, born Sept. 24, 1787, died Nov. 25, 1821.
Adam Link, born 1721, died April 24, 1805.
Benj. Winter, Sr., born Dec. 10, 1761, died June 27, 1817.
"Frederick Birely, died 1806, aged 57 years.

"'Verses on tombstones are but idly spent,
The living character's the monument.'"

Hannah Zeiler, born April 3, 1779, died Aug. 27, 1797.
Anna Maria Zeiler, born March 13, 1745, died March 28, 1814.
Henry Zeiler, born Oct. 25, 1743, died Oct. 28, 1823.
Daniel Miller, son of John and Magdalen Miller, born Sept. 5, 1796, died April, 1803.
Sophia Kolb, wife of M. Kolb, born Sept. 15, 1772, died May 12, 1819.
Catharine, wife of John Kolb, died July 19, 1829, aged 65 years.
Catharine M. Kimball, born in Mayence, Germany, Sept. 10, 1745, died May 18, 1831.
Her daughter, Mrs. Anna Marie B. Morris, of Baltimore, died Dec. 2, 1834, aged 71.
Mary, wife of Francis Mantz, born June 3, 1754, died May 12, 1818.
Peter Myerheffer, born Jan. 12, 1758, died April 28, 1831.
John Adam Rees, born October, 1757, died Feb. 27, 1819.
John Lambert, born Nov. 28, 1764, died Oct. 10, 1810.
Anna Margaretha, wife of John L. Hoff, born June 18, 1726, died Oct. 6, 1811.
Mary M., wife of Conrad Doyle, died April 5, 1829, aged 75.
Conrad Englebrecht, died Feb. 2, 1819, aged 61.
Margaret Englebrecht, died Sept. 8, 1836, aged 76.
Samuel Miller, born March 26, 1726, died April 18, 1808.
Christiana Lowe, born Feb. 14, 1772, died April 8, 1829.
Adam Hart, born Dec. 12, 1767, died Jan. 24, 1804, and his wife Elizabeth, born Nov. 19, 1770, died May 24, 1835.
"In sure and certain hope of the resurrection of eternal life, sleepeth here William House, a native of Elsass (Alsace), in Germany. He emigrated to this town Anno Domini 1750. He departed this life on the 1st of March, A.D. 1822, aged 89 years 3 months and 3 days."
Sophia Dorothea Brimm, born Feb. 16, 1758, died Feb. 22, 1826.
William Markell, born Feb. 26, 1760, died May 4, 1816, and Mary, his wife, born May 8, 1760, died Sept. 23, 1832.
Conrad Markell, born 1721, died Sept. 3, 1782.
Susan Emmitt, born Nov. 19, 1764, died Nov. 15, 1787.
Jacob Shellman, born Feb. 6, 1757, died Nov. 29, 1840.
Henry Kehler, Sr., died July 14, 1851, aged 81, and his wife Mary M., died Nov. 2, 1841, aged 62.
Dorothea Koontz, born 1734, died March 4, 1798.
George Peltz, born Nov. 12, 1786, died Aug. 12, 1802.
Jacob Datiesman, born Dec. 17, 1781, died July 23, 1802.
Jacob Lowe, Sr., born Sept. 30, 1748, died Sept. 25, 1796.
Jacob Medtart, born May 14, 1752, died April 19, 1821, and his wife Mary Magdalena, died in 1802, aged 44.
Samuel Nixdorff, born in Bethlehem, Pa., April 18, 1745, died March 1, 1824.
David Preisch, born Oct. 9, 1764, died (not legible).
"In memory of John Adam Krug, born March 19, 1732, died

March 30, 1796, aged 64 years and 11 days. Pastor here for 25 years."

His wife, Henrietta Krug, born June 26, 1751, died March 26, 1822, and his son, Daniel Krug, born June 5, 1793, died July 2, 1859.

Susanna Barbara Huntschum, born April 6, 1728, died Jan. 3, 1774.

Susanna, wife of Michael Hauser, died April 18, 1826, aged 69.

Maria Barbara Derr, daughter of F. Riehl, born Nov. 3, 1772, died June 7, 1826.

All Saints' Cemetery.—Most of the bodies buried here have been removed to Mount Olivet Cemetery. We give nearly all yet remaining in this old graveyard:

Sarah Maulsby, wife of Dr. David I. Maulsby, born Feb. 24, 1807, died Jan. 2, 1880.

Alexander Truscott, died April 10, 1840, aged 53 years, and Kate, his wife, April 15, 1840, aged 55, both natives of England.

Elias Boteler, born Sept. 15, 1767, died Oct. 14, 1807, and Anna Maria Boteler, born July 5, 1806, died Oct. 15, 1807.

George Alcock, a native of Nottingham, England, died Dec. 15, 1852, aged 76 years.

Sarah McPike, died Jan. 28, 1784.

One stone headed by a Masonic badge has this inscription: "William Sanders, died October 18, 1827, aged 41 years." Arm Sherwood, died April 5, 1829, aged 42 years, natives of England.

Mark Bishop, born Sept. 30, 1786, died Oct. 16, 1836.

James Brice, died Aug. 14, 1834, aged 27.

Margaret Howard, died March 7, 1844, aged 65.

Margaret, wife of Col. James Johnson, died Sept. 5, 1813, aged 64 years.

The tombstone of Gen. Roger Nelson, who died June 6, 1815, aged 56 years, is nearly illegible, and covered partially by bushes and briers. It records his services in the Revolution, his participation in the battles in the Carolinas, and his presence at the surrender of Yorktown, and notes his services in Congress and on the bench, but its words are not clearly legible. Beside him lies the youngest son of Roger and Eliza Nelson, who died Jan. 27, 1823, aged 19 years.

Mount Olivet Cemetery.—This beautiful cemetery, lying just south of the city and abutting on Market Street, has an attractive situation, and is kept in excellent order. It was incorporated Oct. 4, 1852, with the following incorporators: Richard H. Marshall, Richard Potts, William J. Ross, W. B. Tyler, James Whitehill, Charles E. Trail, Andrew Boyd, John Sifford, John J. Boyd, John A. Steiner, George J. Fisher, Alfred J. Brengle, Grason Eichelberger, John Loats, Henry Lorentz, Lewis C. Coppersmith. Its first officers were William J. Ross, president, who continued as such up to May 2, 1876, when on account of impaired health he resigned. His successor was Valentine S. Bruner, who still holds that position. The secretary and treasurer, elected Dec. 2, 1852, was Lawrence J. Brengle, who held those offices until his death in 1874, when he was succeeded by the present incumbent, Thomas M. Markell. William S. Duvall has been its superintendent from its organization, and resides in the keeper's dwelling, at the main entrance to the cemetery. The directors for 1881 are V. S. Bruner, William J. Ross, Francis Markell, L. E. Hedges, Lewis M. Nixdorff, L. V. Scholl, Thomas E. Pope, A. H. Hunt, Jacob D. Haw. The interments up to May 7, 1881, were three thousand six hundred and eighty-seven, besides nearly four hundred soldiers of the opposing armies of the civil war of 1861-65. The Confederate dead are buried in the western portion of the grounds in a row, with neat tombstones, and number about three hundred and nine. The Federal dead are interred in the eastern part, and are of a smaller number, many having been removed by the general government to "Antietam Cemetery." Mount Olivet Cemetery was organized upon ten thousand dollars capital by a joint-stock company, but the capital was subsequently returned to the stockholders, and it is now operated and controlled by the lot-owners, each of whom has a vote and a voice in its management and in the election of officers. It was laid out by the well-known Baltimore surveyor, James Belden. It is subdivided into eighteen sections, marked on its plates by the letters of the alphabet, from A to R inclusive, and each of these sections is divided into lots, numbered consecutively from one up to five hundred or more, as the size of the division may warrant. Two graves are conspicuous in the cemetery, viz.: those of Francis Scott Key, author of the "Star Spangled Banner," and his wife. On Mr. Key's slab is the inscription,—

"Francis Scott Key,
Born Aug. 9th, 1780.
Died January 11th, 1843."

And on that of his wife,

"Mary Tayloe Key,
Born May 26, 1784. Died May 18, 1859."

In the rear are the graves of Francis Scott Key, Jr., who died April 4, 1866, and Simon Frazier Blunt, a son-in-law, deceased in 1854. Key's remains, with those of his wife, were removed from Greenmount Cemetery, Baltimore, after the war. It is a matter of some surprise that no monument has ever been erected over his remains.

German Reformed Church Cemeteries.—The site for this graveyard and the church was the gift of Daniel Dulany. On May 11, 1881, the day the excavations of this graveyard were begun for removing all the remaining tombstones in it, preparatory to the erection of a chapel, the inscriptions of the following stones were obtained:

"Magdalina Schmidt, born 1707. Departed 1754. Blessed are the dead who die in the Lord from henceforth, yea, saith the Spirit, that they may rest from their labors, and their works do follow them." The slab of Abraham Miller, with an angel and hour-glass beautifully carved at its head, says he was born Aug. 24, 1707, and departed Sept. 20, 1754, aged 47 years and 27 days. A well-preserved stone, with figures of two angels hovering over the tomb, with a scroll, shows that Jacob Steiner, born 1713, departed this life in 1748. Then follows the verse, "Blessed are the dead who die," etc., and at the bottom the words *memento mori*." Another tells that Valentine Schwartz, Jr., born 25 May, 1772, died 12 February, 1806; and another that Susannah Schwartz, consort of Valentine Schwartz, died March 19, 1827, aged 89 years and 10 months. This is thought to have been one of the last stones put up in this burying-ground. One of the old black-slate stones, remarkably well preserved, has the following: "In memory of Mary Baer, daughter of John Kimball. Departed this life March, 1768, aged 32." One "to the memory of George Baer, Senior, a native of Germany," was illegible as to farther words. One to the memory of Jacob, son of Jacob Mather and his wife Rachel, shows that he was born Nov. 19, 1776, and died March 21, 1778. Another, to Margaretha Schley, tells that she was born Nov. 9, 1779, died Aug. 10, 1780, daughter of John Jacob Schley and Anna Maria, his wife. This was made of sandstone, and had wreaths of flowers at its head. Another marks the grave of Anna Maria Bärin, born Aug. 25, 1780, died Aug. 18, 1781, daughter of Henry and Elizabeth Bärin. A little double stone records that Peter Dofler, born Oct. 15, 1771, died Oct. 14, 1772; and Anna Maria Dofler, born Oct. 22, 1769, died Oct. 12, 1772. One tells of Margaret Gibbs, wife of Jacob Faubel, who died Feb. 22, 1795, aged 29 years, 7 months, and 9 days. The following two are only partially legible, viz.: John Schwartz, son of Valentine Schwartz, born Nov. 26, 1760, and Johan Valentine Schwartz, born in Martzheim, Jan. 8, 1725.

There were other stones, whose inscriptions were so faded and worn out as to be utterly illegible. The above are all that could be obtained, and most of these were in the German language. A great many were sunk deep into the earth, and their inscriptions were defaced beyond recognition.

On the western side of the city, and not exceeding a quarter of a mile from its centre, is another graveyard of the German Reformed Church, in which the members of that denomination have been buried for a great many years. It is surrounded by a stone wall about six feet high, which incloses a little more than two acres, very nearly square, having a frontage of about three hundred feet on Bentz Street, and sloping westward to the depression through which runs Carroll Creek. It is in full view of the Catoctin Mountains. In the northeast corner there are two walled inclosures studded with evergreen trees of considerable size. There are two entrances, the northern and principal one being near West Third Street. From this a straight roadway runs to the western border of the grounds. Proceeding along this roadway to a point about half-way to the end of the road, and turning to the south, an inclosure is reached surrounded by an open-worked iron fence. Inside there are six mounds. The most prominent of the tombstones marks the resting-place of Harriet Youer, who died in 1874, aged 77 years. Next to this, on the south, is a low gray stone, on which is the insciption:

"Barbara Fritchie, died Decr. 18, 1862, aged 96 years." Another gray stone shows that John C. Fritchie, the husband of Barbara, died Nov. 10, 1849, aged 69 years. The other three occupants of the lot are Samuel Youer, born Dec. 3, 1776, and died July 31, 1819; Ann Maria, wife of Samuel Youer, born March 28, 1773 (date of death sunk below the surface of the earth); and Margaret Stover, died Nov. 23, 1857, aged 86 years.

Among others buried in this cemetery are the following:

Christiana Metzger, born in Lancaster County, Pa., July 14, 1766, and died Sept. 20, 1847, and her son, Jacob Metzger, born Jan. 1, 1789, who died Oct. 5, 1853.

Peter Bofler, born Aug. 15, 1731, died Oct. 31, 1803.

Henry Steiner, register of wills, died May 18, 1825, aged 49 years, 10 months, 25 days.

Richard Mills, born Aug. 4, 1760, died March 27, 1823.

Jacob Folger, born Oct. 17, 1786, died Nov. 30, 1818.

Henry Weinmiller, born Nov. 25, 1746, died Dec. 26, 1808.

Woodward Evitt, died Sept. 29, 1830, aged 71.

David Levy, died Dec. 16, 1806, aged 39.

Andrew Shriver, born Aug. 30, 1778, died Jan. 16, 1805.

Jacob Steiner, died Sept. 11, 1832, aged 70, and his wife, Margaret, died Dec. 8, 1834, aged 70.

Henry Koontz, died Nov. 29, 1831, aged 67, and his wife, Margaret, April 10, 1815, aged 50.

John Gephart, died Oct. 27, 1842, aged 82, and his wife, Elizabeth, April 3, 1818, aged 63.

Edward Salmon, born Aug. 19, 1747, died June 29, 1809.

Maria Phebe Sinn, died Nov. 18, 1811, aged 70.

Peter Hardt, died Jan. 6, 1821, aged 63.

Christian Steiner, born Jan. 14, 1797, died Feb. 25, 1862, and his wife, Rebecca, born April 20, 1802, died April 21, 1862.

John Bruner, born Jan. 14, 1745, died Feb. 25, 1819. Elizabeth, his daughter, and wife of Christian Scholl, born June 13, 1775, died March 20, 1821. Ann Mary, his daughter, and wife of Abraham Kemp, born Jan. 2, 1779, died July 21, 1855. Abraham Kemp, born Oct. 16, 1786, died May 26, 1868.

John Bruner, died Dec. 4, 1821, aged 47, and Catharine, his wife, April 17, 1863, aged 80.

Henry Thomas, born 1790, died Nov. 2, 1859.

David Schley, third son of John Schley, died Oct. 15, 1852, aged 55, and Anna Mary, his wife, Oct. 29, 1828, aged 24.

George Houck, died Oct. 22, 1867, aged 92, and his wife, Catharine, died July 4, 1838, aged 56.

Barbara Bruner, died Feb. 1, 1836, aged 84.

Nicholas Holtz, born June 10, 1762, died Aug. 3, 1849, and his wife, Susanna, May 22, 1840, aged 74.

Caspar Mantz, born April 8, 1718, died Feb. 28, 1791.

Francis Mantz, born Jan. 26, 1749, died May 22, 1823.

Caspar Mantz, born June 23, 1776, died Oct. 31, 1839.

George Baer, died April 3, 1834, aged 70, and his wife, Catherine, March 15, 1853, aged 85.

Daniel Hauser, died Aug. 18, 1832, aged 84.

At the head of a neat tablet is the figure of a man writing at his desk in his study, and below is this inscription:

"Erected by the members of the German Reformed Church of Frederick and vicinity in memory of the late Jonathan Helfentein, for 17 years their esteemed pastor. He departed this life September 23, 1829, aged 45 years."

Jacob Weist, Sr., born July 17, 1788, died July 5, 1847.

Mary Levy, wife of Jacob Levy, born Jan. 8, 1769, died April 7, 1798.

Jacob Bentz, born 1749, died Dec. 24, 1783, and his wife, Margaret, January, 1806.

George Trisler, died Sept. 9, 1845, aged 77.

Mary, wife of Michael Trisler, died April 5, 1828, aged 87.

Rosanna, wife of George Trisler, born Nov. 19, 1799, died Oct. 12, 1826.

Stephen Ramsburg, born Feb. 24, 1781, died Nov. 8, 1857.

John Ramsburg, died Jan. 29, 1807, aged 66, and his wife, Ann Mary, Jan. 14, 1825, aged 84.

Conrad Reitmyer, born in Reading, Berks Co., Pa., March 14, 1762, died July 22, 1842, and his wife, Susanna, born Dec. 18, 1758, died Nov. 8, 1830.

Jacob Hiteshew, born Feb. 14, 1760, died May 11, 1835.

Catherine, wife of Gideon Young, born July 19, 1780, died Sept. 8, 1863.

John Baer, of Henry, born Sept. 12, 1785, died Aug. 14, 1828.

Frederick Getz, born in Lancaster, Pa., March 13, 1781, died Sept. 13, 1824.

Elias Brunner, born Oct. 14, 1756, died June 28, 1826.

Andrew Zimmerman, born Sept. 24, 1754, died July 19, 1826.

The Shriver Family Burying-Ground.—David Shriver married Rebecca Ferree, daughter of Abraham Ferree, who in 1736 married a Miss Eltinge, from Esopus, N. Y., her parents being Low Dutch. This Abraham Ferree (or Ferrie) was the son of Philip Ferree, and grandson of Mary Ferree, whose maiden name was Mary Warrinbuer. The latter died in Conestoga township, Lancaster Co., Pa., in 1716. She had resided in Lindon, near the river Rhine, in France, but after her husband's death went to London with her children, and thence to America. The tombs in this graveyard are as follows:

Abraham Shriver, born in 1771, and died July 29, 1848. His wife, Ann Margaret, who died Dec. 26, 1840, aged 63. Dr. William Eltinge Shriver, their son, who died April 24, 1859, aged 40. Charles, their son, who died Feb. 17, 1849, aged 31. Abraham, infant son of above Charles and Ann Eliza Shriver, who died Jan. 24, 1839; Samuel S., another infant son, who died Aug. 11, 1841; Abraham, their third and infant son, who died Jan. 6, 1844; and Charles E., their last son, who fell in battle in the Confederate army, Aug. 23, 1863, in his 18th year. Elizabeth Lydia, wife of Edward Shriver, died Dec. 2, 1860, aged 52 years. Frederick Stoever and Philip Abraham, sons of Edward and Elizabeth Lydia Shriver, the former dying Oct. 19, 1845, aged 11 months, and the latter Dec. 7, 1838, aged 4 months. Mary, wife of Charles Wilson, and daughter of Abraham and Margaret Shriver, died Nov. 5, 1853, aged 43. Ann Margaret Campbell and her infant daughter, Maria, wife and daughter of Charles A. Campbell, and daughter and granddaughter of Abraham and Margaret Shriver. The mother died April 29, 1832, and the daughter 23d July following.

Martha Snowden, the faithful colored nurse of Edward and Elizabeth Shriver, died Nov. 25, 1855, aged 28.

The following also appears:

"Here lies interred the body of Abe Brighton, who died January 30, 1847, aged about 60 years, the early, continued, and much attached servant of the Shriver family."

Presbyterian Cemetery.—This old burying-ground, on West Fourth Street, was laid out nearly a century ago, but interments are rarely made in it now. Among those buried there are the following:

Rev. Patrick Davidson, born Oct. 9, 1775, died Oct. 9, 1824; Mary, his wife, who died Oct. 13, 1850, and Charlotte, his eldest daughter, who died Aug. 22, 1846, aged 46 years.

Catharine Boston, a native of Havant, Hampshire, England, died Aug. 15, 1833, aged 39.

Jonathan Webster Dusten, a native of New Hampshire, died April 15, 1820, aged 28.

Sarah Norton, born at Farmington, Conn., May 21, 1794, died Jan. 16, 1815.

Elizabeth, wife of Robert Elliott, LL.D. and A.M., principal of Frederick Academy, died May 15, 1821, aged 46.

Hugh Reynolds, died July 23, 1804, aged 52.

Col. John Ritchie, died Nov. 15, 1826, aged 69, and his wife, Ann, died Dec. 15, 1826, aged 57.

Henry McCleery, died Nov. 25, 1819, aged 70, and his wife, Martha, Dec. 12, 1813, aged 59.

Andrew McCleery, born Nov. 21, 1777, died July 9, 1853.

Thomas H. Howard, born Feb. 28, 1789, died Sept. 26, 1852.

Rev. Samuel Knox, died Aug. 31, 1832, aged 76, and his wife, Zeraiah, July 26, 1839, aged 56.

John Bayly, born Aug. 16, 1775, died April 14, 1844, and his wife, Elizabeth, born Nov. 3, 1781, died Dec. 31, 1845.

James Robertson, a native of Scotland, died April 23, 1823, aged 54.

Catholic Cemetery.—This burial-ground lies on East Fourth Street, and is beautifully situated. Among those buried there are

Col. James McSherry, author of the "History of Maryland," who was born July 29, 1819, and died July 13, 1869.

Outerbridge Horsey, who died June 7, 1842, aged 66 years, and his wife, Eliza D. Lee Horsey, who died July 5, 1862, aged 80.

Judge Madison Nelson, who died Jan. 1, 1870, aged 67.

Dr. Joseph A. Smith, born June 19, 1831, died Oct. 25, 1860.

Leonard Smith, born March 29, 1794, died July 2, 1849, and Eliza, his wife, born Dec. 19, 1795, died Nov. 26, 1875.

Barbara Wenz, born Aug. 5, 1809, died June 30, 1873.

Joseph H. Deck, died Aug. 12, 1863, aged 63.

Victoire Vicendiere, born Oct. 3, 1776, died Jan. 22, 1854.

Adelaide V. Lowe, died March 29, 1861, aged 72.

Michael Byrne, died March 28, 1859, aged 67, and Rebecca, his wife, Sept. 5, 1855, aged 56.

John Tehan, born Nov. 21, 1796, died Sept. 3, 1868.

Peter Hagen, died Feb. 6, 1850, aged 77, a native of Carlinborn, County Louth, Ireland, and his wife, Anna, born March 26, 1794, died July 5, 1847.

William Lee, born June 23, 1775, died July 8, 1845.

Priests and Students.

Father John McElroy, S.J., died Sept. 12, 1877, aged 96.

Father Josephus Duverney, S.J., born Dec. 30, 1806, died Nov. 14, 1878.

Joannes Walsh, S.J., died April 21, 1875, aged 22.

Father Jacobus Pinasco, S.J., died Oct. 22, 1873, aged 38.

Father Michael Tuffer, S.J., died Jan. 16, 1873, aged 76.

E. Patritius Forhan, S.J., born Feb. 28, 1819, died Nov. 15, 1869.

Georgius Howse, S.J., died March 20, 1865, aged 39.

Thomas H. Kane, S.J., born July 9, 1851, died Aug. 30, 1878.

Julianus Fairfax, born Dec. 14, 1841, died Jan. 23, 1875.

Novitiate Scholars.

Michael O. Walsh, S.J., died June 15, 1876, aged 20.

James F. Hallahan, S.J., died Feb. 16, 1876, aged 22.

Joannes Alfredus Gough, S.J., died Feb. 3, 1876, aged 20.

Aloysius Bennassai, S.J., born Sept. 4, 1858, died Oct. 26, 1879.

Jacobus Brophy, S.J., died June 12, 1865, aged 21.

Martinus J. O'Neil, S.J., died June 21, 1876, aged 20.

CHAPTER XXVII.

THE PRESS OF FREDERICK.

DURING the Revolution no papers were published in the counties outside of Baltimore and Annapolis. But after the Revolutionary struggle was over and independence was achieved the first newspaper was printed in Frederick.

The first press or printing-office brought to Frederick County was introduced by Matthias Bartgis, of Philadelphia, and opened by him in North Market Street, Frederick Town, Md., in 1779. Mr. Bartgis served his apprenticeship to the printing business with Bradford, in Philadelphia, the contemporary of Dr. Benjamin Franklin, and removed to Frederick with the good wishes of Bradford and Franklin, as offering a good field for a printing-office and the establishment of a newspaper.

With the approbation and encouragement of Governor Thomas Johnson, Governor Thomas Sim Lee, Gen. Roger Nelson, Abraham Faw, George Murdoch and others, the first newspaper ever published in Frederick County was by Matthias Bartgis, Jan. 4, 1786, issued from his office in North Market Street, entitled the *Maryland Chronicle, or Universal Advertiser*. It was issued every Wednesday, at the rate of sixpence per copy, or eleven shillings and three pence per annum. It had a circulation of about one hundred and fifty copies to commence with. At that period there was no regularly established post-office, and the papers were sent to subscribers outside of Frederick Town, Baltimore, Hagerstown, Winchester, etc., by private post.

The following is the heading, etc., of the third number issued:

(Vol. I.)   THE   (No. 3.)

MARYLAND CHRONICLE,
OR THE
UNIVERSAL ADVERTISER.

Qui nova desiderat, pervolvat viscera nostra: Affero delicias fortuitosque casus.

(Published every Wednesday.)
Wednesday, January 18, 1786.
Price six Pence.

Subscriptions for this paper are taken by Mr. Benjamin Musgrove, in Liberty Town; Mr. Nicholas Tschudy, in Baltimore; Mr. John Morris, in York Town; Mr. Wendel Keller, in Hanover Town; Mr. Patrick McSherry, in Little's Town; Mr. William Renner, in Tawney Town; Mr. Frederick Stemple, in Middle Town; Mr. Frederick Geyger, in Funk's Town; Mr. John Ragen, in Hager's Town; Mr. John Hoeflich, in New Castle; Mr. David Harvey, in Sharpsburg; Mr. Cornelius Wynkoop, in Shepherd's Town; Mr. David Lush, in Leesburg; Mr. Alexander Rodgers, in Martinsburg; Mr. Henry Baker, in Winchester; Mr. Solomon Jones, in Prince William County; Mr. Hugh McDowell, in Staunton, Virginia; and by the editor, Matthias Bartgis.

P.S.—I purpose, should sufficient encouragement offer, to establish a Post from this place to Winchester, to carry my English and German News-Papers to Funk's Town, Hager's Town, Sharpsburg, Shepherd's Town, Martinsburg, and Winchester.

The title of the paper was subsequently changed to the *Maryland Gazette, or Frederick County Advertiser*, in 1792.

The first number under this title was issued May 22d, and was a folded sheet the size of letter-paper. Its price was seven shillings and sixpence per annum.

In 1794 the name was changed to the *Federal Gazette*, and in 1801 to the *Republican Gazette*, and continued with this title until 1820, when Mr. Bartgis sold out his interest in the paper and retired.

Mr. Bartgis, during the time of his connection with a printing-office and newspaper in Frederick Town, published for a number of years the "Poor Robin Almanac," Lutheran hymn and prayer-books, a "History of the Revolution in Scriptural Style," and sundry other books and pamphlets. He also printed and published from 1803 to 1813 a paper called *The Hornet*, in English and German, with the motto,—

"To true Republicans I will sing,
But aristocrats shall feel my sting."

When he retired from business, Mr. Bartgis sold his interest in the paper to Robert Ritchie and John Macgill, by whom it was continued for several years. During his connection with the office, Mr. Bartgis had for a partner in 1811 his son, Matthias E. Bartgis, and William B. Burke in 1817.

Mr. Bartgis was not a brilliant writer, but was a good printer, and was conversant with the English, German, French, and Latin languages. He was a liberal-hearted man, and a little eccentric at times. He was extensively acquainted in Frederick County, but did not accumulate great wealth during his connection with the printing business. He died about the year 1825, at his residence near the old paper-mill, on the Tuscarora, owned by himself, and was buried about three miles northwest of Frederick, in the old Trout (now Cronise's) burying-ground.

Robert Ritchie and John Macgill took charge of the *Republican Gazette* after the retirement of Matthias Bartgis, and edited and published it for three or four years. In the year 1823 the firm of Ritchie & Macgill was dissolved. Robert Ritchie continued the *Republican Gazette* until his death.

Mr. Bartgis published in his paper the Constitution of the United States as adopted by the National Convention at Philadelphia, and Washington's first message to Congress. He personally knew Washington, Franklin, and Lafayette.

Rights of Man.—John Winter, who was a practical printer, schoolmaster, etc., published the *Rights of Man* in Frederick Town and County from 1790 to 1802. He also taught school in Bentztown, near the old market-house. He was a Washingtonian Federalist of the old school. He left Frederick Town for several years, but returned in August, 1806. He was very fond of attending barbecues on the banks of

Monocacy and Bush Creek on the Fourth of July. Mr. Winter was a native of one of the lower counties of Maryland, and was said to be a distant relative of Henry Winter Davis.

He had a son, also named John Winter, as eccentric as himself, who carried around the *Rights of Man* and delivered them to the subscribers of that paper. He generally went bareheaded and barefooted.

The Key.—In 1798, 1799, and 1800, Dr. John D. Cary, of Frederick Town, published a small paper in book form, entitled *The Key*, in compliment to Gen. John Ross Key,—a Key to unlock the secrets of men's hearts. His nephew, Hon. George Cary, emigrated from Frederick Town to Georgia, and was subsequently chosen a member of Congress from that State. Its first number was issued Jan. 13, 1798, and was printed at the office of the *Federal Gazette*, in Market Street.

Frederick Town Herald.—In 1802, John P. Thompson, a practical printer, from Carlisle, Pa., at the solicitation of the late Judge Richard Potts, Col. William Campbell, Dr. Philip Thomas, Col. John McPherson, George Baer, Dr. Francis Brown Sappington, and other leading Federalists, removed to Frederick and established the *Frederick Town Herald*. Its first number was issued June 23, 1802. He published it for a period of about thirty years, and sold the office to William Ogden Niles, of Baltimore, son of Hezekiah Niles, of *Niles' Weekly Register*. Mr. Niles edited and published the paper for four or five years, and then sold it to Ezekiel Hughes, son of Jeremiah Hughes, of Annapolis, Md. Mr. Niles was a good writer, and especially upon the subject of the tariff, American tonnage, navigation, and commerce was well posted. He left Frederick and removed to Washington City, when he changed his notions upon the subject of a tariff, became a sort of free-trader, and obtained a situation in the Treasury Department under Hon. Robert J. Walker, Secretary of the Treasury in the days of James K. Polk's administration. Mr. Niles, Peter G. Washington, and Robert H. Bogardus, of New York, aided Mr. Walker very much in framing the free-trade tariff of 1846, which passed Congress. He died in Washington City some years ago.

Ezekiel Hughes succeeded Mr. Niles in the publication and editorship of the *Herald*. He published it for a number of years, and took into partnership with him Mr. Levely. It was published for eight or ten years by Hughes & Levely, and afterwards by Thomas Turner. From Mr. Turner it passed into the hands of George D. Miller, a practical printer, a native of Queen Anne's County, on the Eastern Shore, and Col. Thomas Sappington, at one time a member of the House of Delegates, State senator, and register of wills of this county. These gentlemen printed and published it for several years, and then sold the office to Lewis F. Coppersmith, son-in-law of the late Isaac Baugher, and projector of the Coppersmith building, corner of Market and Church Streets. From Coppersmith it passed into the hands of George W. Beckenbaugh and Charles B. Woodward, then to Beckenbaugh and William L. W. Seabrook, etc., and afterwards into the hands of the late Capt. John W. Heard. But in 1860 and 1861 it advocated the secession movement, for which, in 1861, it was suppressed by a military order of the department commander, and the materials, fixtures, files, etc., sold, and purchased by Elihu H. Rockwell, of Frederick.

Col. Sappington, Mr. Miller, Mr. Coppersmith, and Capt. John W. Heard died some years ago. Mr. Hughes, Mr. Seabrook, and Mr. Beckenbaugh are still living,—Mr. Hughes, at Washington, D. C.; Mr. Beckenbaugh, at Fairview, Washington Co., Md.; and Mr. Seabrook, at Westminster, Carroll Co., Md.

Republican Advocate.—In 1803, John B. Colvin, at the request of Gen. Samuel Smith and Hon. William Pinkney, of Baltimore, and Thomas Hawkins and Samuel Duvall, of Frederick County, commenced the publication of a paper in Frederick Town and County called the *Republican Advocate*. It was continued until 1808–9. Mr. Colvin was a native of Albany, N. Y., and during the contest in 1800 between Adams and Jefferson for President published the *Daily Advertiser*, in Baltimore, in support of Jefferson. In 1807 he left Frederick Town and removed to Washington City, where he established and published *The Monitor, National Register*, and other papers. In 1824 he edited the *Washington City Gazette*, in support of William H. Crawford for the Presidency. He was a brilliant and forcible writer, and was the author of the letters signed "Numa," addressed to John Randolph of Roanoke. He compiled the "Magistrate's Guide" for the use of justices of the peace in Maryland. He was a great linguist, and employed for a number of years in the State Department, Washington City, under Adams and Monroe. He was the confidential friend of Jefferson, Madison, and Monroe during their administrations. In the years 1804, 1805, 1806, and 1807, when he resided in Frederick and published the *Republican Advocate*, the Federalists made no opposition to the Republican ticket, but in the next year, 1808, elected their ticket by four hundred majority to the Legislature.

Silas Engles, a practical printer, succeeded Mr. Colvin in the publication of the *Republican Advocate*. In 1811 the paper ceased to exist.

Independent American Volunteer.—In 1807 the *Independent American Volunteer* made its appearance in Frederick Town, edited and published by William B. Underwood. The *Volunteer* was continued for a year or two, then merged into the *Republican Advocate*, and in 1811 both papers were discontinued. Mr. Underwood then went from Frederick Town to Baltimore, where for a short period he published the *Minerva*, a literary and scientific paper. From Baltimore he went to Carlisle, Pa., where he commenced the publication of the *American Volunteer* as a Democratic paper, which is still in existence.

A German Paper.—March 14, 1810, a German Republican paper issued its first number, then suspended for two or three weeks to give the people time to subscribe, when it was to have been issued regularly.

The Genius of Liberty was published at Uniontown, in Frederick County, by Charles Sower in 1812. It was a paper devoted to the interests of the Federal party. It was published until 1815, when it took the name of the *Star of Federalism*, and the office was removed to Frederick Town. It was published in that place up to the year 1821, when Charles Sower died. In the faction fight between the two wings of the old Federal party in this county,—"Hansonites" and "Taneyites,"—Mr. Sower supported the "Hansonite" wing. He was a genial, clever gentleman and a good printer, and published several novels.

The Plain Dealer, by Charles T. Melsheimer, was published in Frederick Town from 1812 to 1815. It was an aggressive Federal paper, and was violently opposed to the war of 1812-14. The Hon. John Hanson Thomas and Hon. Alexander Contee Hanson contributed largely to its columns. The father of Mr. Melsheimer also published a German paper in Frederick Town.

The Westminster Chronicle, by —— ——, was published for a year or two at Westminster, then in Frederick County, in 1818.

Family Gazette.—In 1820 a small paper, called the *Family Gazette*, was published in Frederick by George Kolb and William Daugherty. It was chiefly devoted to religious affairs.

The Family Visitor, a literary paper, was published in Frederick Town by George F. Stayman. It was edited in good part by the Rev. Mr. Harkey.

The Examiner was started in May, 1813, and edited and published by Samuel Barnes from his office in Patrick Street, under the title of the *Political Examiner and Public Advertiser*. Mr. Barnes was born in Queen Anne's County, and served his time in the printing business in the office of the Baltimore *American*. In 1811, in connection with Baptiste Irvine, he edited and published the Baltimore *Daily Whig*. At the request and instance of Gen. Samuel Smith and Hon. William Pinkney, of Baltimore, and Gen. Joseph Swearingen, Gen. Thomas C. Worthington, Thomas Hawkins, Dr. Grafton Duvall, Joshua Cockey, and other leading Republicans of Frederick County, he removed to Frederick, and commenced the publication of the *Examiner*. He was nominated a candidate on the Republican ticket for the House of Delegates in 1819, but was defeated. In 1824, 1825, and 1826 he was elected to the House of Delegates from Frederick County. He was a candidate in 1827 on the Adams and Clay ticket, but was defeated. Mr. Barnes was a warm friend and admirer of Henry Clay. After he sold the office in 1832 to George E. Woodbridge, he removed to Baltimore, where he edited the *Daily Chronicle* and *Daily Clipper*, papers published in that city. He was a member of the Masonic fraternity, and one of the old defenders of Baltimore in 1812. Mr. Barnes, David Schley, Frederick A. Schley, and Charles H. Kiefer, who were at one time connected as editors and proprietors of this paper, are all dead. Neilson Poe, John H. Williams, Thomas Haller, David M. Smith, editors and former proprietors, are still living; as also Messrs. Harry C. Keefer and Charles E. Knauf, its present editors and publishers. *The Examiner* is a weekly paper. The whole number of issues up to June 15, 1881, is stated at 3975, which number divided by 52 would give 76 volumes and 23 numbers over. In the opposite corner the volume is stated to be the 77th, No. 24. So that in that long period the paper has never failed to make its weekly appearance, and it now presents a hale and vigorous countenance. It is the largest and most widely-circulated paper in Western Maryland, and its advertising and job-printing were never more lucrative than now. Its editors and proprietors are constantly making it more useful, interesting, and entertaining. In 1816 it supported James Monroe and Daniel D. Tompkins for President and Vice-President (Lawrence Brengle and John Buchanan were then elected for this district).

In 1820 it supported the re-election of the same candidates; in 1824 it advocated the election of Henry Clay and Nathan Sandford for the two highest positions of the government (Dr. William Zollickoffer, of Frederick, and William Gabby, of Washington County, being the electors of those districts); in

1828 it supported John Quincy Adams and Richard Rush. The county that year gave Adams about four hundred majority over Jackson. In 1832 it advocated the election of Henry Clay and John Sargeant, and in 1836 that of William Henry Harrison and Francis Granger; in 1840, Harrison and Tyler—"Tippecanoe and Tyler too"—were at its mast-head; in 1844, Clay and Frelinghuysen were its candidates; in 1848, Gen. Taylor and Millard Fillmore; in 1852, Gen. Scott and William A. Graham; in 1856, Millard Fillmore and Andrew Jackson Donelson; and in 1860, John Bell and Edward Everett. Then came the great Rebellion, in which it espoused the side of the Union, and rendered great services to the government by its manly and patriotic course. It supported in 1864, Abraham Lincoln and Andrew Johnson; in 1868, Gen. Grant and Schuyler Colfax; in 1872, Gen. Grant and Henry Wilson; in 1876, R. B. Hayes and William A. Wheeler; and in 1880, J. A. Garfield and Chester A. Arthur.

It is scarcely necessary to add that it is thoroughly Republican in its political tone. It has always been conservative but outspoken, and its honorable history is closely interwoven with that of the county, whose best interests it has so ably advocated in the three-quarters of a century of its existence.

While in Frederick, in 1828, Mr. Barnes published a campaign paper at *The Examiner* office called the *Anti-Jacksonian*, the leading writers for which were Dr. Henry Staley, William V. Morgan, and Dr. Grafton Duvall.

In 1833, Mr. Barnes sold out his office to George Woodbridge, of Connecticut, a gentleman who afterwards became a prominent preacher at Richmond, Va. Mr. Woodbridge edited the paper for a short time, and then sold out the establishment to Mr. Neilson Poe, now judge of the Orphans' Court in Baltimore, the son of Jacob Poe, and a native of Frederick County.

In 1838 or 1839, Mr. Poe, who studied law in the office of the late William Gwynn, of Baltimore, tired of the editorial profession, after gallantly supporting the Whig party and the election of William Cost Johnson to Congress, removed to Baltimore City and resumed the vocation of the law.

John H. Williams and William W. Markell succeeded Mr. Poe in the publication of *The Examiner*. Mr. Markell shortly afterwards withdrew from the paper on account of ill health. Mr. Markell died soon afterwards, and Mr. Williams continued the paper on his own account until 1849.

In 1849, David Schley and Thomas Haller succeeded Mr. Williams. In 1852, David Schley died, and Frederick Schley purchased his interest, and continued up to 1858, when Charles H. Keefer purchased an interest, and the firm of Schley, Haller & Co. then commenced.

In 1863, on account of ill health, Thomas Haller sold his interest in *The Examiner* office to Charles E. Knauff, and the firm then was Schley, Keefer & Co. In 1865, Frederick Schley retired from the paper, and David M. Smith purchased his interest, and the firm then was Keefer, Smith & Co., and continued so until Nov. 22, 1875, when Charles H. Keefer and Charles E. Knauff purchased his interest, and he retired. Charles H. Keefer was killed by a railroad accident June 12, 1877, and was succeeded by his talented brother, Harry C. Keefer.

During the years 1813 and 1814, in the months of August and September,—the war period,—the paper was published twice a week.

During the editorial career of Barnes, Woodbridge, Poe, Williams, David Schley, Frederick Schley, Charles H. Keefer, and others, as the advocate of the old Republican, Whig, American, and modern Republican parties, *The Examiner* has maintained a "bold front." It is now the oldest paper in the county, and has the most extensive patronage of any in the county.

The Republican Citizen.—The *Republican Citizen and State Advertiser* was commenced at Westminster in May, 1821, by George W. Sharp, who removed to Westminster from Marietta, Lancaster Co., Pa. After publishing the paper a short time in Westminster, Mr. Sharp removed the office to Frederick Town, Md. The paper while published there first supported Wm. H. Crawford for the Presidency as the "regular nominee" of the Republican party, but in 1828 and 1832 supported the claims of Gen. Andrew Jackson to the Presidency. Mr. Sharp continued to publish the paper until 1832, when he sold it to Dr. Samuel H. McKeeban, of Emmittsburg. This gentleman died in 1833, and the paper passed into the hands of Peter H. Brown, son of Matthew Brown, of Fleecy Dale, Frederick County. When Mr. Brown retired from the *Citizen* office the paper became the property of Messrs. Frederick Rigney and Wm. M. B. McLanahan.

From Rigney & McLanahan, about the year 1843, the *Citizen* passed into the hands of John W. Baughman, who continued to edit and publish it to the day of his death. For a short period J. Lawson Norris was connected with Mr. Baughman as associate editor. Upon the death of John W. Baughman, in 1872, the *Citizen* passed into the hands of his two sons, L. Victor and J. Wm. Baughman, under the firm of Baughman Brothers, by whom it is now edited and published.

During the Presidential campaigns the *Citizen* has uniformly supported the nominations regularly made according to the usages of the Democratic party,—Crawford, Jackson, Van Buren, Polk, Cass, Pierce, Buchanan, Breckenridge, McClellan, Seymour, Greeley, Tilden, and Hancock.

John W. Baughman was arrested by the Federal authorities in 1862, and incarcerated at the Old Capitol in Washington, and released on the day of the battle of Bull Run, through the intercession of his most intimate friends, Hon. Henry May and Robert J. Brent, of Baltimore City. In 1863 the *Citizen* was suspended from the United States mails for nine months, by order of Postmaster-General Montgomery Blair. In 1864, Mr. Baughman was arrested by Gen. Hunter, his paper suppressed, his property confiscated, and he sent beyond the Federal lines. A few days after, by order of Maj. John I. Yellott, provost-marshal of Frederick, Mrs. Baughman and her children were banished from home, and sent beyond the Federal lines, in Clark County, Va. The publication of this old-established journal was resumed in August, 1865, by John W. Baughman. For sixty years this paper has been the acknowledged organ of the Democratic party of the county, and in ability and in successful business management is not surpassed by any paper in Maryland. It is a four-page sheet of thirty-two columns, and makes a specialty of the latest and newsiest local events, while its reputation for well-written editorials gives it high rank among the journals of the State.

John W. Baughman was a native of "Merryland Tract" in Frederick County. At thirteen years of age he came to Frederick City. His father was a highly respectable farmer, his grandfather being captain of a vessel which brought many of the original settlers of Frederick County to this country. In early life young Baughman was thrown upon his own personal resources. He entered as a clerk the store of Francis Leuber, a merchant in Frederick, and a little later spent two years at St. John's Institution (now college), where he received all the academic education he ever obtained. He then returned to his commercial occupation, and was engaged for several years in Frederick and in Baltimore City. After reaching manhood he formed a partnership with a young merchant in Baltimore in the commission business, and by his untiring industry and strict integrity he succeeded in building up one of the largest trades in Baltimore. Though he did not acquire wealth, he won a reputation in Baltimore for honor, intelligence, and genial disposition which procured him troops of friends, who loved and honored him to the hour of his death, and who will long cherish his memory.

About 1841–42 he commenced (at the suggestion

JOHN W. BAUGHMAN.

of the friend of his boyhood, ex-Governor Lowe) the study of the law under Gen. James M. Coale. Two years later he was admitted to the bar, and formed a law partnership with Governor Lowe, which continued until he assumed the editorial duties of the *Republican Citizen* in 1845. Having married most happily in 1844 (Mary Jane, daughter of Baker Jamison, one of the most prominent and well-known citizens of the county, who was connected with oldest Catholic families of Maryland, and whose daughter was regarded as one of the most attractive women in this section of the State), and finding the practice of the legal profession by two young beginners hardly adequate to the support of a family, he was persuaded by his friends to purchase the *Citizen*. His public life as a journalist for twenty-five years is too well known to the people of Frederick, of the county, and of the State, to need further comment than that he was at all times "a fearless champion of popular rights, the brave defender of civil and religious liberty."

During the administration of Mr. Lowe as Governor of Maryland, John W. Baughman filled the office of inspector-general of flour at Baltimore, then the principle flour mart of the Union.

Under the administration of President Buchanan,

without solicitation, he was appointed appraiser-general of the port of Baltimore. He was averse to office-seeking and even to office-holding; in the two instances above mentioned his friends, knowing well his fitness and merits, fairly forced him to accept the places put at his disposal.

Mr. Baughman had always been a pronounced Democrat, and through his journal taken a leading part in the politics of the State.

During the civil war he passed through a stormy existence. After imprisonment in the Old Capitol, suppression of his paper from the mails, mobs at his office, insults to his wife and family, he was finally arrested, his property confiscated, and he banished beyond the Federal lines, his wife and four children (the eldest, Victor, being in the Southern army) sent to follow him a few days after. He was one of the boldest and most fearless writers in the State, and a true and ardent friend of the South. During his banishment he was placed in the Third Auditor's office in Richmond by his warm friend Gen. Breckenridge, then Secretary of War; his son William was with him, he being a member of the Richmond defenders. Mrs. Baughman, with her daughters, Mary Louisa, and Corinne, and her youngest son Charles H. S., spent their banishment with Col. Dearmont, a kind and well-known citizen of Clark County, Va. L. Victor, the eldest son, was a member of Capt. McAleer's company of the Maryland line, and remained with the infantry until the army crossed to the south bank of the James River. He participated in the battles of Malvern Hill and Gaines' Farm. He afterwards joined Company D, First Maryland Cavalry, under Capt. Welsh, and was with Early and Breckenridge in their raid through Maryland in 1864, as also the famous Chambersburg raid, and was captured at Moorfield, Va., and imprisoned in Camp Chase, Ohio, for nine months, being exchanged in March, 1865, just prior to the fall of Richmond. After the war Mr. J. W. Baughman and family returned to their home and friends, and he to his editorial duties. He was welcomed with open arms and glad hearts by the Democracy of Frederick County, who ever delighted to honor him. Only a few weeks before his death the party elected him as a delegate from his Congressional district to the National Democratic Convention in Baltimore (which convention nominated Greeley for the Presidency), but he was unable to attend, on account of an illness contracted in the South, from which he never recovered. He died July 31, 1872. His wife is still living in Frederick.

L. Victor Baughman, the eldest child, was colonel on the staff of Governors James Black Groome and John Lee Carroll, prominent in the politics of the State, and a delegate to the Cincinnati Convention which nominated Hancock in 1880. He was married on the 27th of September, 1881, to Helen M. Abell, fourth daughter of Hon. A. S. Abell, the veteran publisher and proprietor of the Baltimore *Sun*. J. William Baughman is also well known in his county and State, is still single, and was unanimously elected reading clerk of the House of Delegates of the State in 1882.

Charles H. Stonestreet Baughman married in 1872 the eldest daughter of Capt. J. W. Heard, and is associated with his brothers. The two daughters are single, and live with their mother.

Lutheran Evangelical Intelligencer.—In 1824, '25, and '26, George W. Sharp printed the *Lutheran Evangelical Intelligencer* at the *Citizen* office, a paper edited by Rev. David F. Schaeffer, LL.D., of Frederick.

The Reservoir and Public Reflector.—In 1824, John Magill commenced a paper called *The Reservoir and Public Reflector*, and advocated the introduction of a supply of fresh mountain water into Frederick Town. In other respects the *Reservoir* was a literary paper, but did not touch upon political matters.

Intellectual Regale and Evening Companion. —In 1824, '25, and '26 there was a small paper published in Frederick by the printer apprentices, called the *Intellectual Regale and Evening Companion*. It was devoted to fun and amusement. The publishers of the paper were George, Richard, Wm. Weber, Wm. Janvier, Samuel Davidson, B. S. Bulfinch, Thompson Bennett, and others.

Political Intelligencer and Public Advertiser.—In 1825, Charles Nagle commenced the publication of a paper called the *Political Intelligencer and Public Advertiser*. It had a brief existence. Henry Bickley, then a schoolmaster of Frederick, chiefly contributed to its columns.

The People, a Jacksonian campaign paper, was published in Frederick in 1828, the chief contributors to which were Hon. Francis Thomas, Hon. Madison Nelson, David Schley, and others.

The Regulator.—In 1831, Samuel Davidson, a practical printer, son of the Rev. Patrick Davidson, of Frederick, commenced the publication of a paper at Taneytown, in Frederick County, called *The Regulator*. He published the paper for several years and then sold the office to Col. John K. Longwell, who published it a short time and then changed the name to the *Carrolltonian*, and removed it to Westminster to advocate the division of Frederick County and formation of Carroll County. The paper is now called the *American Sentinel*, a Republican paper printed at Westminster. Mr. Davidson removed to the State of Ohio.

The Sentinel.—In 1833, James Maxwell, a printer, published a paper in Frederick Town entitled *The Sentinel*, devoted principally to the election of James Dixon, Esq., to Congress, and the defeat of Hon. Francis Thomas, but failed in the effort. The *Sentinel* did not last long.

Frederick Times.—In 1835, Col. James M. Shellman published a paper in Frederick Town called the *Frederick Times*. Edward A. Lynch, a well-known lawyer and Whig orator of the county, was connected with him for a short time as associate editor. Col. Shellman removed to Westminster.

Frederick Visitor.—The *Frederick Visitor* was published in Frederick by Thomas Haller in 1838. He also published a paper called the *Olive Branch* in 1843 in connection with Thomas C. Prince. It was edited by Revs. Daniel Zacharias, John L. Pettis, and Simon W. Harkey.

The Times and Democratic Advocate.—After Mr. Van Buren, in 1837, advocated the divorce of Bank and State, and the establishment of the Independent Treasury, the Conservative party in Congress, under the lead of William C. Rives, Nathaniel P. Tallmage, and others, commenced organizing throughout the country. In 1837 *The Times and Democratic Advocate* was commenced in Frederick by Barzelia Marriott, and published by him for several years. Christian Getzendanner succeeded him in the publication of this paper. It was regarded as a faction paper in the ranks of the Democratic party, and did not make much headway. Through the opposition of Hon. Francis Thomas and others, the paper soon ceased to exist.

Frederick News.—In 1845, Coombs & Wheeler published the *Frederick News* in Frederick. It was devoted to literary affairs and local topics, and claimed to be the cheapest paper published in the State: seventy-five cents per month.

Maryland Union.—The *Democratic Union* was established in Frederick City in 1853 by Col. William P. Maulsby, a member of the Frederick County bar, who continued to edit and publish it until August, 1855, when he disposed of the office to Dr. John W. Geyer, who changed its name to that of the *Maryland Union*. Dr. Geyer published the *Maryland Union* until June, 1857, when he sold the office to Gen. Bradley T. Johnson, Charles Cole, and Clarke Koontz. The health of Koontz failing he soon retired from the business, and died in less than a year after he started into it. His interest having been purchased by Mr. Cole, the paper was published and the business conducted by Johnson & Cole until shortly after the nominations of Stephen A. Douglas and John C. Breckenridge for President, when, as Johnson preferred Breckenridge, and Cole preferred Donglas, Johnson withdrew, and afterwards entered the service of the Southern Confederacy, where he soon rose to the rank of a brigadier-general. After the withdrawal of Johnson a young and promising lawyer, by the name of James T. Smith, associated for a short time with Mr. Cole in the publication of the *Maryland Union*. He was a man of high spirit and dauntless courage, and became first lieutenant of Capt. Faithful's company of the Union army in 1863, and was killed in the battle of Gettysburg on the 4th of July of the same year. Since then the *Maryland Union* has been under the exclusive management and control of Charles Cole. It is a Democratic Conservative newspaper, firm in its political convictions, and bold at all times in the expression of its sentiments, but never running to extremes. Hence, in 1860, it supported Douglas for President, and when the war between the North and the South broke out it espoused the cause of the Union and rendered effective service. It could not, however, indorse *all* that had been done by authority of the government during the war, and its criticisms having offended some of those in power who entertained different views, its editor and his family, together with about twenty-five other families of Frederick City, were arrested by order of Gen. Hunter, to be sent South across the lines three days thereafter, but President Lincoln disapproved the order, and it was finally revoked. No *Maryland Union* was issued for that week, and it was the only week in which that paper failed to make its appearance from June, 1857, to the present time.

Frederick Republican.—In 1867 a small advertising and news sheet called *The Advertiser*, published by Marcellus M. Shaffner, John W. Ebert, and David H. Moberly, made its appearance in Frederick. For six or eight months it was published daily,—being the first daily published in the city.

In 1868 it was purchased by Col. George W. Z. Black, who changed the name to the *Frederick Republican*, advocated negro suffrage, and made it an uncompromising Republican journal. It did not succeed very well. In 1871 it was discontinued, the office being sold to a printing establishment in Philadelphia. Col. Black was appointed postmaster of Frederick at the commencement of Grant's administration, held the position for several years, resigned, and went to Washington City.

Sunday Morning Visitor.—In 1870, John W. Ebert and Foster S. McBride started a printing-office in Frederick and published a paper called the *Sunday Morning Visitor*, devoted to temperance and Christianity. It was discontinued after a year or so.

Maryland Herald.—In 1870 the *Maryland Herald*, by Samuel L. Gouverneur, made its appearance from the office purchased from Ebert & McBride. It was started as an independent paper, "Independent in all things—Neutral in nothing." It warmly indorsed the Liberal Republican movement in 1872, and supported Horace Greeley for President. The paper did not survive long afterwards. Mr. Gouverneur, a grandson of President Monroe, now resides in Washington City.

The Frederick Times, a weekly paper, was commenced in Frederick and the first number issued on the 4th of January, 1876, by David M. Smith, previously connected for a few years with the *Examiner* office. Mr. Smith shortly afterwards sold out his interest in the office to the Frederick Publishing Company, John W. Kauffman, editor.

It is now published by Kauffman & Bouldin. Their daily paper, the only one in the county, and a sprightly, newsy, and enterprising sheet, is in its fourth volume.

The Moon.—This is a four-page weekly amateur journal, devoted to literature, poetry, local affairs, etc. Fifty cents per annum. It is in its second volume, and is published by P. & T. McCleery, No. 177 North Market Street.

Miscellaneous.—There were a number of ephemeral papers published in Frederick County, in old Federal and Republican times, merely as campaign papers for a month or two, and also in the election contests between Hon. Francis Thomas and his opponents. Notably, a so-called Democratic sheet published by Jacob Markell, John Sifford, Henry Boteler, and others, in support of Mr. Thomas as an Independent Democrat for Congress.

Several small sheets have been published for a short time by the young ladies of the Frederick Female Seminary, etc., and by other parties, as literary and juvenile productions.

The following persons are among the well-known and authenticated contributors to the Frederick County press, from the appearance of the first number of the *Maryland Chronicle, or Universal Advertiser*, Jan. 4, 1786, down to the present time:

Samuel Knox, D.D., S. Selby (2), Mountjoy Bayly, Thomas Johnson, Thomas Sim Lee, Legh Masters, Henry Ridgely Warfield, Richard Potts, George Trisler, Henry Williams, William Patterson, William Murdock Beall, Abraham Faw, Gen. Roger Nelson, Roger Brooke Taney, Benjamin Ogle, Lawrence Brengle, Dr. John Tyler, William T. T. Mason, John Hanson Thomas, Frederick A. Schley, Samuel Duvall, Dr. Grafton Duvall, Gen. T. C. Worthington, Henry Bickley, Richard Brooke, Dr. Henry Staley, Wm. V. Morgan, Matthew Brown, Thomas Hawkins, Dr. Lewis H. Steiner, Hon. John Ritchie, J. Mortimer Kilgour, Gen. James M. Coale, Dr. Wm. Zollickoffer, Abraham Shriver, Alexander C. Hanson, Thomas Hawkins, Hon. Madison Nelson, Hon. Francis Thomas, Hon. Enoch Louis Lowe, James Dixon, Wm. H. Hinks, L. P. W. Balch, Dr. Jacob Baer, Dr. John W. Geyer, Samuel Tyler, LL.D., Rev. D. F. Schaeffer, Wm. F. Lynch, U.S.N., Rev. Simeon W. Harkey, Rev. John McElroy, S.J., Rev. Daniel Zacharias, D.D., John H. McElfresh, Prof. H. Winchester, Abner Ritchie, Patrick O'Neill, Frederick Houck, Benjamin S. Rutherford, Wm. C. Hoffman, James McSherry, Edward B. Baltzell, Capt. H. Clay Naill, Charles Hammond, Milton G. Urner, Col. Charles E. Trail, Dr. Geo. Diehl, Rev. R. H. Williams, Prof. Nathaniel Vernon, Frederick Houck.

The following is a list of poets native of or connected with Frederick County:

David Steiner, George Trisler, John Winter, Dr. John D. Cary, Francis Scott Key, Edgar Allen Poe, Benjamin S. Bulfinch, William V. Morgan, Mrs. Emily N. Maulsby, Mrs. Nellie Eyster, Miss Inez Biser, Miss Tennie Wachter, Hon. George Cary, Prof. George H. Miles, Col. Charles E. Trail, Patrick O'Neill, Frederick Houck.

Notes on Frederick Printers and Members of the Press.—Overton Harne attained the greatest age of any printer connected with the press of Frederick County. He died in 1873, at the residence of his son, between Hagerstown and Williamsport, at the advanced age of ninety-seven. He served apprenticeship at the printing business with Matthias Bartgis, in Frederick Town, in the year 1797.

William Noland, who served his time with John B. Colvin at the printing business in Frederick Town *Republican Advocate* office, 1803-7, was one of the swiftest type-setters and most extensive tramp printers in the country. He was known all over the United States. Born near Noland's Ferry, Frederick Co. Died at Georgetown, D. C.

Matthew Brown, of Fleecy Dale, Frederick Co., was long connected with the press of Baltimore City and Frederick County. He wrote considerably, and devoted much of his time to agriculture and wool-growing.

John P. Thompson, the richest printer in Frederick County, was president of the Frederick County Bank, and worth about one hundred thousand dollars when he died.

John B. Colvin was considered the ablest editor, but poorest in a pecuniary point of view, ever connected with the press of Frederick County. He published the *Republican Advocate* in 1803-7. He died in Washington City in 1827.

John Porter died in Rockville, Montgomery Co., Md., where he published a paper and kept a hotel.

Wm. B. Burke published the *Maryland Journal* in Rockville in 1827. He warmly supported the re-election of John Quincy Adams in 1828. His paper was the organ of the party.

George Richard Weber, who served as apprentice with Ritchie & Magill in Frederick Town, published a paper called the *Illinois Register*, at Springfield, Sangamon Co., Ill., a paper still in existence. He was intimately acquainted with Abraham Lincoln. William Weber, his brother, who also served his time in the same office, published the *Hagerstown Mail*, was a member of the House of Delegates for Washington County, and published the *Alleganian*. He now lives in Cumberland.

John Rigdon, who served his time at the printing business with George W. Sharp, in Frederick, went West, and became a Methodist preacher, and succeeded very well.

George W. Sharp, editor of the *Citizen*, removed West to Delaware County, Ohio, started a woolen-factory in that place, was elected to the Ohio Legislature in 1842, and was made chairman of the Committee on Banks and Banking. He died in Ohio.

George F. Stayman, who served his time with Mr. Sharp, printed a Democratic paper in Delaware County, Ohio. He now resides in Piqua, Miami Co., Ohio.

William Ritchie, who edited and published the *Republican Gazette* in 1823–24, etc., was clerk of the tax commissioners of Frederick County for many years, brother-in-law of Ezra Mantz, and son of William Ritchie, formerly clerk of Frederick County Court.

Augustus H. Krauth, who served an apprenticeship in Frederick with John Magill at the *Reservoir* office, went to New York, and was at one time one of the proprietors of the *New York Sunday Mercury*. His brother, Frederick Krauth, published a paper in Alameda County, Cal.

Charles Nagle, editor of the *Political Intelligencer*, afterwards worked in the office of the *Vicksburg (Miss.) Sentinel*, in 1839 and 1840.

Mr. Janvier was from Princeton, N. J. He served his time in the *Frederick Town Herald* office. Mr. John P. Thompson was his uncle.

John T. Jackson, who was an apprentice with William Ogden Niles, in Baltimore, and worked with him in Frederick, in the *Herald* office, went to California in 1849, worked in the *Picayune* office in San Francisco in 1851, and at the time of the great fire, when the office was burnt up, went to the placer diggings, or gold-mines.

George D. Miller was born in Queen Anne's County, Md. He served with Capt. Matthews, editor of the *Kent Bugle*, in Chestertown, Kent Co., and worked in Philadelphia and New York as a journeyman printer. He was for several years connected with Col. John K. Longwell, of Westminster, in the publication of the *Carrolltonian* newspaper; and afterwards with Col. Thomas Sappington in the publication of the *Frederick Herald*.

Frederick Schley, who for a number of years was connected with *The Examiner* newspaper as chief editor, was a strong and vigorous writer. He died Jan. 24, 1875, and lies buried in Mount Olivet Cemetery. A beautiful monument of Italian marble has recently been placed over his grave.

Dr. John D. Cary, who published the *Key* in 1798–1800, was noted for many good qualities. Capt. Lewis Green and Capt. Henry Brish, who married two of his daughters, moved to Tiffin, Seneca Co., Ohio. Frederick Green, son of Capt. Lewis Green, and great-grandson of Jonas Green, of the *Maryland Gazette*, Annapolis, was elected to Congress from the Tiffin District, Ohio, some years ago. In 1846, or thereabouts, *The Cleveland Herald* published in its paper the contents (entire) of the *Maryland Gazette*, published at Annapolis in 1776.

Charles Hammond was a native of New Market District, Frederick Co., was a lawyer in Ohio, and at one time (during the war of 1812–14) published the *Ohio Federalist*, St. Clairsville, Belmont Co., Ohio, and afterwards the *Liberty Hall and Cincinnati Gazette*, published in Cincinnati, Ohio. Mr. Hammond was one of the ablest editors and lawyers in Ohio. He was a warm friend of Henry Clay. He was also a great friend of John Hanson Thomas, of Frederick Town.

Henry S. Geyer, son of John Geyer, saddler, of Frederick Town, nephew of Daniel Sheffey and Lawrence Brengle, first mayor of Frederick Town, wrote considerable for the Frederick Town papers. He studied law in Frederick, and had some knowledge of the printing business. He moved to Staunton, Augusta Co., Va.; from there to St. Louis, Mo., where he wrote considerable for the *Missouri Republican*, and in 1833 was one of the editors of the St. Louis *Times*. He was a member of the convention of Missouri which framed the first constitution of that State. In 1850 he was elected to the United States Senate from Missouri over the Hon. Thomas Hart Benton, defeating "Old Bullion," a senator of thirty years' standing, the first time he was defeated in Missouri for the United States senatorship. John Geyer, Daniel Sheffey, and Lawrence Brengle published a "Diary" of events in Frederick County from 1776 to 1795, after the manner of Jacob Engelbrecht. That

"Diary" was last seen in the possession of Jonas Geyer, a son of John Geyer, brother-in-law of Lawrence Brengle, and brother of Henry S. Geyer.

William M. B. McLanahan, at one time connected with the *Republican Citizen* office as editor and publisher, went West, and became acquainted with Col. Theodore O'Hara, editor of the Frankfort (Ky.) *Yeoman.* With Col. O'Hara, Crittenden, and others he joined the "Lopez Expedition" against the city of Havana, Cuba, in 1851. With Narcisso Lopez, the expedition was captured by the Spaniards, and Lopez, Crittenden, O'Hara, Victor Kerr, McLanahan were captured by the Spaniards, charged and convicted with being filibusters, and were "garroted."

Toler Wolfe, who worked for a considerable time as a journeyman printer in the *Herald and Citizen* office, and in Winchester, Va., and Washington, D. C., went to Cincinnati, Ohio, where he worked for a considerable time, and then emigrated to the Rocky Mountains and Oregon. He was a great friend of George Trisler.

Alexander Sterett, printer, was last heard of at Natchez, Miss., working on the *Mississippi Free-Trader*.

David F. Smith, a printer, keeps a variety store, the "Temple of Fancy," in Frederick City.

Silas Engles, printer and editor of the *Republican Advocate*, died in Frederick Town.

Robert Laird, for many years foreman of the *Frederick Town Herald* office, in the days of John P. Thompson, was a printer, and a member of the Presbyterian Church. When he left Frederick he went to Pittsburgh, Pa.

H. L. Brady, printer, formerly connected with the *Valley Register* office, Middletown, is now publishing and editing the *Morgan Mercury*, in Morgan County, W. Va.

Col. John K. Longwell, formerly connected with the Taneytown *Regulator* and *Carrolltonian* newspaper, is now president of one of the national banks of Westminster. He is also one of the directors in the Western Maryland Railroad.

Jerome Barney, son of A. Barney, formerly of this county, is now publishing a paper at San Rafael, Marin Co., Cal., *The San Rafael Herald*.

William B. Lynch, Esq., brother of Judge John A. Lynch, is publishing a Democratic paper in Leesburg, Loudon Co., Va.

George Martin, printer, who served his time with Charles Nagle in the office of the *Political Intelligencer and Public Advertiser*, Frederick Town, went West many years ago, and his whereabouts are unknown. He is a brother-in-law of J. Alfred Ritter.

John Robinson and Scott Kennedy Young are working in the Government printing-office at Washington City.

George Baltzell is a teacher in the public schools of the city of Frederick.

Judge Jona. D. English, printer, is a farmer in Creagerstown District.

Thomas O'Leary, printer, is working in the Government signal-office, Boston, Mass.

John S. Zittle is publishing the *Shepherdstown Register*, at Shepherdstown, Jefferson Co., W. Va.

Thomas Turner is publishing a Democratic paper at Upper Marlboro', Prince George's Co., called *The Prince Georgian*.

Col. James McSherry, who contributed to the *Olive Branch, Herald*, and other papers of this county, was, as we said, the author of the "History of Maryland," and of several other works of marked interest.

The Old and New Printers, Editors, and Publishers connected with the Press of Frederick County.—Mathias Bartgis, John Winter, Overton Harne, Mathias E. Bartgis, William B. Burke, Benj. Franklin Bartgis, John P. Thompson, Silas Engles, John B. Colvin, Wm. B. Underwood, John D. Carey, Charles Sower, Wm. Noland, Benj. S. Bullfinch, Robert Laird, Allen Prater Duvall, John Porter, Samuel Davidson, Robert Ritchie, John Magill, Wm. Y. Magill, Wm. Daugherty, Wm. Janvier, Samuel Barnes, George Woodbridge, Charles Nagle, George Martin, Thomas Haller, Thomas C. Prince, Neilson Poe, William Need, Thompson Bennett, Mathew Brown, George W. Sharp, George R. Weber, Wm. Weber, George Handley, Wm. V. Morgan, Dr. S. H. McKeehan, Peter H. Brown, Barzelai Marriott, Christopher Getzendanner, Jas. Maxwell, James Bartgis, John Bartgis, Mathias E. Bartgis, Jr., Thomas O'Leary, George Baltzell, James M. Shellman, Jonathan D. English, John Rigdon, Marcellus M. Shaffner, Frederick Rigney, David F. Smith, George Colegate, John K. Longwell, C. T. Melsheimer, George F. Stayman, Thomas Sappington, George D. Miller, Alexander Sterrett, Wm. Ogden Niles, John T. Jackson, Wm. M. B. McLanahan, Charles B. Woodward, Augustus H. Krauth, Jerome Barney, Frederick Krauth, Wm. B. Lynch, John Robinson, Geo. W. Beckenbaugh, Wm. L. W. Seabrook, Eugene Schley, Theo. N. Engelbrecht, Spencer C. Jones, John Fletchall, Joseph Walker, Wm. Coombs, Charles H. Long, Oscar Candler, Lewis Sinn, Geo. Carlton Rhoderick, H. L. Brady, Jacob T. C. Miller, J. S. L. Rodrick, Joshua Keefer, Joshua Ruth, David Schley, Frederick Schley, Alfred Schley, George Schley, John Schley, Ferdinand Albaugh, George U. Graff, Charles Cole, Charles Edwin Cole, Lamertine Cole, Wm. P. Maulsby, Josiah Harrison, Henry T. Mahler, John F. A. Fox, David L. Elkins, J. Edward Doll, Toler Wolfe, Frank P. Gephart, Albert Rhodes, George W. Ebberts, John W. Ebert, Harry C. Keefer, John K. Hanshaw, Miles Hard, John S. Zittle, Samuel Hard, Charles W. Tabler, Eugene L. Haller, James D. Murphy, Charles E. Haller, George W. Z. Black, Wm. W. Markell, David H. Moberly, William T. Cochran, Foster S. McBride, Charles E. Knauff, Charles H. Keefer, David M. Smith, Samuel L. Gouverneur, Isaiah Wolffersberger, John Levely, —— Wheeler, Scott Kennedy

Young, Alexander McLean, Michael Slayman, John H. Williams, John W. Baughman, L. Victor Baughman, J. Wm. Baughman, J. Lawson Norris, John W. Heard, Alexander P. Beatty, John W. Kauffman, Edward A. Lynch, Benjamin H. Scott, Hon. George Cary, Clarke Koontz, Rev. David F. Schaeffer, Rev. Simeon W. Harkey, W. W. Rhoderick, Charles Krumbaugh, Wm. Fauble, Wm. Montgomery, Wm. Chapple, Robert Schley, Charles E. Liggett, Thomas McLain, George Melambre, Dr. John W. Geyer, John H. Thomas, Bradley T. Johnson, Vincent Ryan, Christopher Myers, William Austin, Francis T. Strailman, John Kaufman, James Knocks, George Trisler, Charles E. Shearer, Thomas Turner, George Kolb, Lewis F. Coppersmith, Henry Bickley, Ezekiel Hughes, James T. Smith, Francis Campbell, Thomas Turner, James McSherry, Charles E. Simmons, Melvin E. Doll, Wm. F. T. Brenner.

CHAPTER XXVIII.

BANKS AND OTHER FINANCIAL INSTITUTIONS.

IN 1787, owing to the large amount of "Continental money" which had been issued during the Revolutionary war, and which had depreciated to such an extent that it became almost worthless, gold and silver became very scarce, in fact, almost disappeared from circulation. The House of Delegates of Maryland in order to relieve the stringency passed a bill for the emission of a large amount of paper money. It excited the community very much, as it was calculated to unsettle all the fixed values of land, houses, and stock, and other property in the State and county. The Senate rejected the bill as fraught with much mischief. At a meeting held at Frederick Town, which was largely attended, in February, 1787, the following action was taken:

"FREDERICK COUNTY, Feb. 14, 1787.

"At a respectable meeting of the inhabitants of Frederick County, held at Frederick-Town this day, at the request of their delegates, expressed by public advertisements; the abstract of the bill for an emission of paper money on loan, published by the House of Delegates with their address thereon; the message of the Senate accompanying the return of that bill, and their message of the twentieth of January being read, THOMAS SIM LEE, Esq., in the chair, and HENRY WILLIAMS, secretary, the following RESOLVES were entered into.

"This meeting having taken under consideration the abstract of the bill for an emission of paper money on loan, together with the address of the House of Delegates, are of opinion that an emission of paper money on the plan proposed would not be attended with any real advantage to the people of this country, or the community in general, but that it might ultimately plunge us into disgrace and ruin, by adding to the evils we already suffer.

"Therefore, Resolved, That it is the opinion of this meeting, that the Senate acted wisely in rejecting the bill in question, that the reasons assigned on the subject in their message to the House of Delegates clearly evince to us the propriety of their conduct, and proves that in their deliberation they possessed a firm regard for the welfare and happiness of the people at large, as well as for the dignity and honor of the State, which justly entitles them to the approbation and thanks of their constituents.

"*Resolved*, That this meeting highly approve of the conduct of three of the delegates of this county, in opposing the passage of the said bill, and that it is hereby recommended to the other delegate who voted in favor of it, to co-operate with them in the opposition should a similar bill be introduced at the next session.

"*Resolved*, That this meeting approve of the conduct of the Senate, in rejecting the bill for the relief of debtors; which we conceive would have had a direct tendency to destroy confidence between individuals, pervert the streams of justice, and give a fatal stab to our commercial interests.

"*Resolved*, That we also approve of the conduct of the Senate, in refusing the bill for suspending the law which justly secures permanent salaries to the chancellor and judges agreeably to the spirit of the constitution.

"*Resolved*, That it is the ardent desire of this meeting to see our excellent constitution preserved inviolate, it being happily calculated to diffuse the blessings of freedom and to secure equal rights—and therefore we are of opinion that every attempt made by either branch of the Legislature to infringe any constitutional privilege of the other ought to be discountenanced.

"*Resolved*, That it is the opinion and wish of this meeting that every reasonable exertion should be made by the Legislature at this critical period to succor and strengthen the Federal government of the United States, as well as the government of this State; that we will cheerfully render our assistance as far as our circumstances will admit, and that we have full confidence the necessary aids may be afforded without adopting oppressive measures, while the produce of our land sells for its real value in specie, provided the resources of the State are called forth and judiciously applied.

"*Resolved*, That this meeting will pay due obedience to the laws, and will endeavor to preserve good order in the community.

"*Resolved*, That this meeting will further make known our sentiments to our immediate representatives on the subjects proposed for our consideration by instructions.

"*Resolved*, That the chairman be requested to sign the proceedings of this meeting, and that they be published in the *Maryland Chronicle*, and *Baltimore Journal*.

"THOMAS S. LEE,
"*Chairman*.
"HENRY WILLIAMS, *Secretary*."

It will be seen from the foregoing that the business men of Frederick had thoroughly mastered the leading principles of a sound system of finance, and to the continuous application of similar rules and methods through a long series of years the community in large measure is indebted for its present prosperity. To the banks of Frederick, indeed, the city may be said to owe its existence, for had it not been for them Frederick would in all probability have been burned by the Confederate forces during the advance into Maryland in 1864. Concerning this event the late Jacob Engelbrecht, in his diary, says,—

"Our old city of Frederick was captured by the rebel forces under Gen. Jubal Early on Saturday, July 9, 1864. They first

EZRA HOUCK.

entered about six o'clock A.M. from the west. We had no army to protect us except two or three thousand, while the rebels had from ten to fifteen thousand men. Gen. Early levied a contribution on the city of two hundred thousand dollars, which I am told was paid on Saturday."

The money was obtained from the banks, and the corporation became responsible for its payment. Thus by their assistance was averted the threatened destruction of the city at the hands of the enemy. The amounts contributed by the several banks were in proportion to their capital stock. By act of Legislature in 1865 it was provided that one-half of the amount loaned should be reimbursed with interest. As they were all in a sound condition, the unexpected assessment in no way affected their solvency or credit. The banks of Frederick, indeed, are remarkable for the systematic and careful manner in which their affairs are managed.

Ezra Houck is remembered now and will be long remembered as a prominent figure in the list of Frederick City's eminent financiers. For forty-six years he was closely associated with the administration of the affairs of the Farmers' and Mechanics' National Bank, and for many years previous to his death he was a director in that institution, as well as its president from 1872 until he died in 1878. He was born in Frederick City, July 30, 1802. His father, George Houck, was born in Frederick County, Md., in 1775, and died in the county in 1867, aged ninety-two years. His grandfather came to Maryland from Germany during the latter half of the eighteenth century, and took a place among the pioneers of Frederick County. Ezra Houck's early school education was limited to a brief season at the Frederick Academy, and comprised in its benefits to him but little more than the rudimentary elements. While yet a school-boy he exchanged his school life for a life upon his father's farm, located a few miles from Frederick. There he spent a few subsequent years in rural pursuits, but at the age of twenty returned to the city and took service in the county clerk's office. In 1826 he married Catharine, daughter of Jacob Bentz, of Frederick County, and upon his marriage removed to his father's old farm, where until about 1832 he employed his time and energies in the cultivation of the soil. In the year named he determined to abandon farming, and accordingly removed to Frederick, where he entered the Farmers' and Mechanics' Bank as book-keeper, having meanwhile briefly occupied the bench as judge of the Orphans' Court. From the day he entered the bank until the day of his death he devoted himself closely and unceasingly to its affairs, to the exclusion of participation in any other business interests. He was for many years a director of the bank, vice-president for a few years previous to 1872, and in that year succeeded Dr. William Tyler as president of the institution. His administration was conspicuous for the display of a signal ability, and until his death, April 8, 1878, he was the bank's president. Business interests were to him such absorbing matters that he steadily declined to take a prominent part in the conduct of public concerns, albeit he was frequently chosen as alderman. He was, moreover, president of the Mutual Insurance Company, and of the Frederick and Woodsborough Turnpike Company. He was one of the founders of the Junior Fire Company, and for some years its president. He was during life a zealous member of the Reformed Church, and long one of its elders. In the erection of the present fine Reformed church edifice he acted as a vigorous member of the building committee.

In politics he was a stanch Democrat, and affiliated with the Democracy always. Mr. Houck's children numbered eleven, of whom nine are living, six daughters in Frederick City and three sons, Ezra, George, and James, upon their farms in Frederick County. Ezra lives upon the old homestead near Frederick City. Mr. Houck's home in the city was the stone mansion now the residence of his widow, with whom his marital companionship covered the extended space of fifty-one years. That mansion is reputed to be an hundred years or more old, and to have known as occupants but three families during all that time, although it has never been vacant.

Following are sketches of all the banks of Frederick, given in the order of their formation:

The Central National Bank was organized in 1808 as a branch of the Farmers' Bank of Maryland, whose principal office was located at Annapolis. The Frederick branch gradually became so prosperous that it determined to sever its connection with the Farmers' Bank, and accordingly it obtained a charter as the Central Bank, Jan. 2, 1854. It was organized as a national bank May 15, 1865. The officers are: President, Richard H. Marshall (for many years one of the judges of the Circuit Court); Cashier, Henry Williams; Directors, Richard H. Marshall, George M. Potts, Lewis M. Thomas, Wm. Downey, Wm. S. Meiller, Fairfax Schley, Chas. W. Ross, John A. Lynch, Wm. G. Baker, and Wm. J. Worman. The following are the predecessors of the above-mentioned presidents and cashiers: president from 1808 to 1831, John Tyler; to 1850, Wm. Ross; to 1858, Richard Potts; to 1859, Wm. B. Tyler; to 1878, R. Y. Stokes. Cashiers: from 1808 to 1830, Thos. Shaw;

to 1838, J. McPherson; to 1848, Cyrus Mantz; to 1861, Godfrey Mantz; to 1875, P. Storm; to 1878, P. M. Englebrecht. Mr. Wm. H. Miller is the teller, a genial and accommodating gentleman, as well as an energetic and reliable business man. The bank's New York correspondent is the Park National Bank. In the adjustment of the Confederate loan the bank lost $27,000. The building owned and occupied by the bank is of brick, and is strong and substantial in appearance. It is pleasantly and centrally located, and is a very valuable property. The bank has a capital stock paid in of $200,000, a surplus fund of $40,000, and $10,546.61 of undivided profits.

The Farmers' and Mechanics' National Bank was organized in 1817 as a branch of Westminster Bank, with the well-known Dr. Wm. Tyler as president, which position he retained for fifty-five years, until his death, April 26, 1872. The beneficial results of his management have been amply demonstrated by the unusual success which has attended the operations of the bank. In 1828 the institution received its charter as an independent concern, to be known as the Farmers' and Mechanics' Bank of Frederick County. Continuing the policy upon which it was first conducted, the institution developed steadily in the volume of business and in strength and stability. In July, 1865, under the national banking act, it became the Farmers' and Mechanics' National Bank. Upon the death of Dr. Tyler, Mr. Ezra Houck, who had been connected with the bank for forty years, accepted the presidency, and directed the affairs with ability until his death, April 8, 1878. His successor is Col. Chas. E. Trail, a highly-respected citizen of Frederick. The high business standing of the institution and the fact that it has not paid less than twelve per cent. dividends since 1862 provide a sufficient commentary upon Col. Trail's qualifications as a financial manager. Mr. Samuel Nixdorff has performed the duties of cashier with tact and discrimination since 1877. His predecessors have been Ezra Mantz, Wm. M. Beall, Thomas W. Morgan, Thomas M. Markell, and John Wm. Bierly. The directors are Col. Chas. E. Trail, George Markell, A. H. Hunt, V. S. Brunner, W. Winebrenner, C. Staley, Samuel H. Brown, Wm. F. Johnson, Hon. M. G. Urner, George S. Groshon, Joseph G. Miller, and Philip Reich. By the Confederate raid the bank lost $17,000. Its New York correspondent is the Park National Bank. The bank is centrally located, and is a very popular institution. It has a capital stock of $125,000 paid in, a surplus fund of $40,000, and undivided profits to the amount of $22,560.79.

Charles Edward Trail, president of the Farmers' and Mechanics' National Bank, has all his life been a resident of Frederick City, where he was born Jan. 28, 1826. His paternal ancestors emigrated to America from Scotland more than a century and a half ago, and, with his maternal ancestors (the Ramsburgs), were numbered among the earliest settlers and founders of Frederick County. Their descendants have contributed largely to the peopling of the Frederick and Middletown Valleys, and to-day are numerous among the representative people of that section of the county. Mr. Trail's father (Edward) was born in Montgomery County, Md., in 1798, and died in 1876, aged seventy-nine, leaving his widow, Lydia Christine (Ramsburg), to survive him. She was born in Frederick City in 1802, and is still a resident of her native place, hale and active, at the age of eighty.

In 1851, Mr. Trail married Ariana, youngest daughter of Col. John H. McElfresh and Theresa Mantz, whose ancestors, the Mantzes, coming from Germany, were prominent in Frederick County's early settlement. He received a classical education at Frederick College, and in 1847 entering upon the study of law with Joseph M. Palmer, was admitted to the bar in 1849. Ill health compelled him to abandon his law practice after three years of arduous labor, and in 1851 he sought the recreating influences of a European tour. Upon his return he devoted himself to the care of his large landed interests, which embraced the ownership of a half-dozen of the most fruitful farms in Frederick County. In 1860 he was chosen president of the Isabella Gas Company, and became eventually the sole owner of the property of that corporation. In 1863 he was elected a member of the House of Delegates, and in 1864 to the Senate, in which body he served until 1867. Although urged to stand for a senatorial renomination, he declined.

Desiring a reform in the municipal administration of his native city, Mr. Trail successfully originated, in 1870, a movement in which he bore a large share as president of the board of aldermen for three years. During this time the present fine city hall was erected, Mr. Trail being chairman of the building committee. As a member of the board of trustees of the State Deaf and Dumb Institute, he was mainly instrumental in the adoption of the fine design for that edifice, and as chairman of the building committee, performed his duties to the entire satisfaction of the board and the Legislature of Maryland. In 1870 he became actively interested in the construction of the Frederick and Pennsylvania Line Railroad, and after serving as director for several years, was in 1878 elected president of the road. That position he

still occupies. In 1876 he was called to be the president of the board of trustees of the Frederick Female Seminary, an institution under the supervision of the State. In 1878 he succeeded Ezra Houck as president of the Farmers' and Mechanics' National Bank, which under his prudent management enjoys a very high reputation, and is most successfully conducted.

In 1877 he was severely injured in a railroad collision, in which a number of persons were killed, but after several months' confinement entirely recovered.

Mr. Trail's inclinations have always been of a literary character, and in early manhood he was a frequent writer for the press and for the leading magazines of that day.

He built in 1855 a residence, then very far in advance of the prevailing architecture of Frederick, but the example he set bore bountiful results in its subsequent emulation by others and the present high standard of building improvements in the town. His children, three sons and four daughters, are all living. In religious faith he is an Episcopalian. Previous to the late civil war he was a stanch Whig, stood firmly for the Union during that struggle, and since then has sustained the principles of the Republican party. To the cares and ambitions of a busy life he has added the useful purposes of a public-spirited citizen, and enjoys the satisfaction of occupying a prominent place among the promoters of the public welfare.

The Frederick County National Bank is justly ranked among the most solid financial institutions of Frederick County. Organized in 1818 as a State bank, its early affairs were conducted with marked ability. Its presidents were John Graham, 1818; John P. Thompson, 1833; A. B. Hanson, 1850. Its cashiers were George Baer, 1818, who had previously represented his people in the United States Congress; Henry Doyle, 1833; William B. Tyler, 1842; L. J. Brengle, 1845; Henry Schley, 1845; John H. Williams, 1850. Under these several managements the bank was enabled to disburse large earnings as dividends to its stockholders. Its management at the present time consists of the following officers: President, John H. Williams, elected in 1867, having rendered valuable services as cashier for seventeen years previous; Cashier, Perry B. McCleery, who was appointed at the same time; Directors, Lewis Bruner, Z. T. Gittenger, G. B. Hammond, P. L. Pyler, Calvin Page, John T. Quynn, C. C. Smith, John H. Williams, and J. Alfred Ritter. This bank suffered a loss, with its contemporaries, from the invading Southern army to the extent of twenty thousand dollars. Its principal New York correspondent is the Importers' and Traders' National Bank. The building owned and occupied by the bank is attractive in appearance, and is well located on the principal street of the city. The interior appointments are exceptionally well arranged and substantial. Under its present management the bank is in a thoroughly healthy and prosperous condition.

It has a capital stock of $150,000 paid in, a surplus fund of $50,000, and undivided profits amounting to $9823.78.

The Frederick County Bank was entered on the last Saturday night in May, 1841, and robbed of nearly one hundred and eighty thousand dollars in specie, bonds, and notes. The specie taken was entirely in gold, and consisted of eagles, half-eagles, sovereigns, etc. Maryland six per cent. bonds, numbered from 1113 to 1118, inclusive, were also stolen, which, with the coupons attached, amounted to six thousand dollars. The rest of the plunder consisted of two certificates of six per cent. Maryland stock of three thousand dollars each, and two of four thousand dollars each, and eleven five per cent. sterling bonds of the State of Maryland, numbered from 865 to 875, inclusive, amounting to twelve thousand two hundred and twenty-two dollars. The notes of the bank taken were of the denominations of $5, $10, $20, $50, and $100. Some fifty thousand dollars in silver which was in the vault remained untouched. The institution for a few days ceased doing business, and a statement from its affairs was as soon as possible laid before the public. The capital was but one hundred and seventy-five thousand dollars, so that the robbers took more than the actual capital of the institution. A key was found in the creek, near the city mill, on Sunday morning following the robbery. A dark-lantern of rude construction was also discovered. The key was filed off and filled up until it was made to fit the lock of the exterior door of the bank quite as well as the key which belonged to it. The lamp did not appear to be the production of an experienced workman, and looked as if it had been in service before. Two men were seen taking a box to the corner of the bank, where they seated themselves on the box, for the purpose, it is supposed, of keeping watch while the robbers were progressing with the work. A spur with the straps broken was found in the vault.

The progress of the robbers was impeded by seven locks, some of them of the most complex construction. The street-door must have been entered before, and the men doubtless worked for some weeks in discovering the secret springs in the three locks of the vault, and in taking impressions for the purpose of making suitable keys. All the contents of the iron chest in the vault were taken without any discrimination, including some of the issues of the Frederick corporation, notes that were laid aside as unfit for use, being worn out, etc. Of the silver, none of which was in the chest, they took but ten dollars.

Mr. Doyle, the cashier, swore to a statement, made before Judge Shriver, of the manner in which he always kept the keys of the institution, etc., and testified that when he went into the bank on Monday morning he found nothing disarranged, and was not made sensible of the robbery until, during the course of the morning, he opened the iron chest in the inner vault and found the contents gone. An extra from the Frederick *Herald* office said, "We would advise the public not to sacrifice their notes, as they will doubtless be paid in full," and in another paragraph offers to take them in payment for accounts at that office.

Nearly the whole amount of which the bank was robbed was recovered through negotiation by letter between the attorney of the robbers at New York and the officers of the bank. This correspondence was commenced by the attorney, who made a proposition in behalf of his clients, to which the officers were disposed to accede if nothing better could be done. Accordingly, Dr. Tyler and Mr. Beall, directors of the bank, proceeded to New York during the week, and there concluded the negotiations with a compromise which, it is stated, left the rogues in possession of all the gold they carried off, some ten thousand dollars, and nine thousand dollars paid by the bank for the recovery of securities and notes amounting in value to upwards of one hundred and sixty thousand dollars. The particulars of the negotiation are given as follows:

"Some three or four weeks after the robbery the officers of the bank received a communication, postmarked Philadelphia, consisting of a sheet of letter-paper, on which were pasted printed letters, words, and phrases clipped from a newspaper, and so placed as to form intelligible sentences.

"At the head was an advertisement that had been published about five years previous, showing by what means the robbery of a jewelry-store had been compromised in New York. Beneath this was a communication, made up partly of words, but chiefly of letters, proposing negotiations for the return of the money and securities stolen, which, if the bank was disposed to enter into, it was to signify the same by an advertisement in the New York *Courier and Enquirer*. This proposition ended with the adage, 'Delays are dangerous.' On the margin the following laconic and significant hint was displayed, '☞ Wanted, $52,000!' Upon the receipt of this letter Officer Ridgely was sent for, and it was given into his possession by the officers of the bank. He took it to Philadelphia, and having consulted with High Constable Young, it was resolved to await another move. Soon after a publication appeared in the New York *Herald* reflecting on the officers of the bank, and a communication followed, postmarked Philadelphia, which referred to the article in the *Herald*, and suggested the means of showing to the world that the robbery was not committed by the officers of the bank. In order to prove that the real robber was the correspondent, this communication was accompanied by a correct sketch of the front-door key of the bank. This letter was also referred to the officers, Ridgely and Young, and the latter suggested the propriety of waiting a little longer before any action was taken, at the same time expressing the confident belief that the communication would speedily be followed by a letter from a lawyer. This opinion the officers delivered to the officers of the bank, with the request that if such a letter be received information should be given to them, and they would at once take measures that would insure the recovery of the money and the apprehension of the thieves. This the bank, it is stated, pledged itself to do.

"Nothing definite or satisfactory resulted until the 19th of June, when the following letter was received, postmarked New York City:

"'NEW YORK, June 16, 1841.

"'H. DOYLE, ESQ.:

"'*Dear Sir*,—My aid and assistance have been asked with reference to the loss of the Frederick County Bank on the 22d of May last. If you, or the president, or some person acting for the bank, could have a personal interview with me I have no doubt I could arrange matters in a satisfactory manner. It would afford me great pleasure to be the means of effecting a restitution of the heavy loss which the bank sustained on that occasion. Respectfully yours,

"'WILLIAM WILEY.'

"'P.S.—I can be seen personally or a letter may be addressed to me at 47 Howard Street.'

"Upon the receipt of the above the board of directors appointed Dr. William Bradley Tyler and William A. Beall, of Frederick, both stockholders in the bank, to proceed to New York, with a view of conferring with Mr. Wiley, and gave to these two gentlemen a power of attorney to receive the funds, and pay the reward according to the amount given, if they should prove successful. Dr. Tyler and Mr. Beall on the same day started for the city of New York, and arrived there on the ensuing night about eleven o'clock. Early on Monday morning Mr. Wiley was seen by the agents of the bank, who found him engaged in the duties of his office, which were those of an associate justice of one of the inferior courts of the city of New York. He was also a lawyer, practicing in the courts of that city. The agents were received by Mr. Wiley with the assurance that no difficulty should be thrown in the way of a speedy recovery of the plundered funds of the bank. Mr. Wiley requested the delay of a few days, as the individual professing to know something about the funds was absent at the South. Nothing was heard until Wednesday evening, when Wiley called on the agents, who agreed to pay eight per cent. for the restoration of the lost issues of the bank. Wiley went away, and in the morning notified the agents that he would accept their offer. It was still not in his power to say on what day they could come into possession, but pledged himself to deliver the notes and securities at the earliest possible moment. Nothing more was heard until Saturday morning, when Wiley called on Messrs. Tyler and Beall saying that he was prepared to deliver the property of the bank. Mr. Wiley then went to the New York Bank, and in the presence of Mr. Beall requested the cashier to go with them and assist in counting the money. He also procured the aid of Mr. Hearn, a respectable merchant in Broadway, as they passed along. The place of appointment was a front room in the hotel standing on the corner of Broadway and Howard Streets, where they all assembled, viz.: Dr. Tyler, Mr. Beall, Mr. Wiley, Mr. Seal (clerk to

Mr. Wiley's court), Mr. Halsey, cashier of the New York Bank, and Mr. Hearn, the Broadway merchant. Mr. Wiley then left the room for a few minutes, and returned with a leather valise, which was found to contain the recovered funds, all sealed up in a single package. The envelope was opened, and the money counted by the above-named gentlemen. This took place on Saturday morning. After the counting was finished the funds were delivered to Messrs. Tyler and Beall, who paid Mr. Wiley the percentage on the issues as agreed on, and by the evening cars they returned home with their lost treasure. The bank again commenced business. The robbers kept in their possession $10,049 in gold, $7052 in notes and bills, $2500 of canal scrip belonging to individuals, $1542 in Frederick County bank-notes, in all $21,143. In the transactions leading to the recovery of the money there was no promise of indemnity or impunity, no pledge to relax the efforts of justice, no intimations that exertions to apprehend the robbers and bring them to punishment would be in the slightest degree diminished, no permission to keep the funds not delivered, and, in a word, no compromise of any kind was made, nor was anything done or said by the agents of the bank that would not bear the test of public scrutiny. Wiley, the agent for the robbers, would give no information further than that the vaults were opened by false keys, and that six persons were concerned. The bank withdrew all former rewards, and offered a reward of five thousand dollars for the detection of the robbers and twenty per cent. for the recovery of the residue of the money, but it does not appear that anything was ever accomplished in that direction."

The Frederick Town Savings Institution was chartered March 7, 1828. Its name conveys very clearly the main object of its organization. That the design of its founders has been realized in a marked degree may be readily inferred from the very favorable report of 1881. It carries on a legitimate banking business in loans, discounts, deposits, collections, and exchange, and the ability of the management is shown in the fact that it annually pays from its earnings as dividends to its stockholders about eight per cent. Special deposits are received, on which three per cent. is allowed. The officers are: President, Lewis Markell; Secretary, George H. Wolfe; Directors, Lewis Markell, Dr. L. H. Steiner, Joseph Cronise, N. D. Haner, M. E. Doll, H. W. Bentz, George Metzger, George W. Miller, and Steiner Schley. From the organization up to the date of the present management the following have served as president and secretary, viz.: Presidents, Jacob Baer, 1828; Stewart Gaither, 1831; W. S. McPherson, 1831; William J. Ross, 1844. Secretaries, John McPherson, 1828; David Steiner, 1831; Daniel Hughes, 1832; George Engelbreght, 1833; Lewis Ramsburg, 1842; B. A. Cunningham, 1865; Lewis V. Scholl, 1875. Under their management the bank has always held a prominent place among monetary institutions, and its solvency and good standing has never been doubted. In July, 1858, this bank made a change in its method of transacting business. Interest was no longer allowed on larger deposits than five dollars. The receipt of weekly deposits was discontinued, but special deposits were received, to be withdrawn after a given notice from the bank. This institution was the largest loser of any in the city by the requisition of the Confederate troops in 1864, for in making a settlement with the corporation it was found that the bank was "out" forty-one thousand dollars. The Baltimore correspondence is mostly carried on with the National Mechanics' Bank. Mr. Markell, the president, is a wealthy and prominent citizen of Frederick, and possesses the confidence and respect of the entire community, while the secretary, Mr. Wolfe, who was formerly connected with the Union Bank in Baltimore, is a skillful financier. With a working capital of six hundred thousand dollars, and under the management and direction of such officers and managers, the signal success that has attended the career of the Frederick Town Savings Institution becomes readily accounted for, and a future of equal prosperity and usefulness would seem to be assured.

The Franklin Savings-Bank received its charter in 1856, and passed successfully through the great financial crisis of 1857. For eighteen years David Markell conducted the affairs of the bank as president, being succeeded by Andrew Boyd in 1874. Mr. Boyd served in this capacity for three years, and was succeeded by the present executive officer, A. D. O'Leary, who has had long expeience in monetary affairs. William H. Nicodemus, the efficient secretary, has held this position for five years. His predecessors have been Andrew Henderson, previous to 1874, and William M. Hardt for the next year. No interest is paid on transient deposits, but special deposits are received, on which three per cent. is allowed. Weekly deposits become stock in six months, and dividends are disbursed on these. The demand by Early, in 1864, cost the bank nineteen thousand dollars. The bank's working capital is $200,000. Its Baltimore correspondent is the Third National Bank. The directors are well-known and prominent citizens, as follows: John H. Keller, A. J. Wilcoxon, A. L. Eader, A. T. Rice, James Hergesheimer, Henry E. Hanshaw, G. W. B. Shreiner, Henry D. O'Leary.

The First National Bank was incorporated under the National Banking Act of 1865, with a capital stock of $100,000, and during its entire career has been rated among the best-managed monetary concerns in the country. So successful has it been that it has paid its stockholders a yearly dividend of twelve per cent., and has per its last report a surplus and profits of $30,629.28. The management has undergone comparatively few changes. Its first president,

Lawrence J. Brengle, filled that position until his death, in 1874. His successor, Thomas Gorsuch, the cashier during the first nine months of the bank's existence, was elected a representative to the General Assembly, and was for some time assessor of internal revenue, and for six years previous to 1879 was clerk of the Circuit Court. Mr. Gorsuch still holds the position of president. In the last campaign (fall of 1881) he was the Republican candidate for comptroller of Maryland, but was defeated by Thomas J. Keating. The cashier is Thomas Markell, one of Frederick's most active business men. Ira Tyler has held the position as teller since Jan. 1, 1867, to the entire satisfaction of all connected with the bank. William K. Zimmerman has been the discount clerk for ten years past. The board of directors is composed of Thomas Gorsuch, Charles B. S. Levy, Lycurgus E. Hedges, William H. Falconer, George Joseph Doll, Charles J. Lewis, Joseph Rousten, John L. Nicodemus, and George Houck. Its New York correspondent is the Park National, and its Baltimore correspondent the First National. The bank has a capital stock paid in of $100,000, a surplus fund of $20,000, and undivided profits amounting to $10,629.28.

Among those who are identified with private banking interests of Frederick City may be named Thomas Clagett, who was born in Clarksburg District, Montgomery Co., Md., April 21, 1813.

Ninian M., his father, was a native of Maryland, being born in 1768, in Prince George's County. He married, after removing to Montgomery County, Margaret Burgess, daughter of Edward Burgess, a captain of the Continental army. He died in 1841, at the residence of his son Thomas, aged seventy-three years. She died about 1844, aged about seventy-two years.

Thomas Clagett moved from Montgomery to Frederick County in 1839, in Urbana District, and came to Frederick City in 1866. His maternal grandfather, Edward Burgess, was one of the first judges of Montgomery County. Several of his ancestors were prominent officials in the early days of Western Maryland. The Clagett family is of English, and the Burgess of Scotch descent.

Thomas Clagett married, in 1837, Cynthia Norwood, daughter of Thomas Norwood, a native of Frederick County, Md., but of English descent. She was born April 25, 1815. Born of this union were the following children: Edward Thomas, Jan. 16, 1838, he went South during the civil war, and was never heard from; Sarah Ann, Sept. 30, 1839, married Henry O. Talbott, of Poolesville, and lives in Charlestown, Jefferson Co., W. Va.; Jane, born July 25, 1841, married Thomas N. Harwood, of Frederick County, and now living in Frederick City; Rebecca, born March 19, 1843, living at home with her parents; William Henry, Dec. 27, 1844, married to Jane Prater, of Greenville, Bond Co., Ill., where he now resides; Margaret B., born Sept. 26, 1846, married Charles T. Remsburg, a farmer of Middletown Valley, Frederick Co., Md., where she now resides; Louisa, born Oct. 6, 1848, married to S. Theodore Stauffer, of Walkersville, and died Feb. 18, 1870; Jesse, born May 15, 1851, married to Mary S. Price, daughter of Thomas W. Price, of Philadelphia, Pa., and resides in Baltimore; Mary, born Aug. 14, 1853, married to Dr. Edward Bowlus, of Middletown, now of Frederick; Samuel M., born Aug. 12, 1857, living with parents.

Mr. Clagett's boyhood, and in fact the greater portion of his life, was passed in agricultural pursuits, except from 1835 to 1838, when engaged in a mercantile business in Damascus, Montgomery Co. From 1838 until 1866 he was an extensive and successful grower of tobacco, being one of the largest shippers to market of "up-country tobacco" in the State during those years, and since 1866 he has been engaged as a banker and broker in Frederick City; never has been an office-seeker or office-holder.

Of Mr. Clagett's four sisters and one brother none are now living. Rebecca, Ann, and Jane married and moved to Ohio, where they died; Mary died young, about 1821, aged sixteen; John was born Nov. 28, 1815, and died about 1829.

The Mutual Insurance Company of Frederick County was incorporated by an act of the General Assembly passed at its December session, 1843, with the following incorporators, viz.: William J. Ross, Patrick Tormey, Lawrence J. Brengle, Lewis Medtart, Zachariah T. Windsor, Edward Trail, Hugh McAleer, William H. Albaugh, Calvin Page, Francis Leuber, Ezekiel Hughes, David Boyd, Joseph Deck, John Wilcoxon, William F. Johnson, John Ramsburg, Philip Hauptman, Robert Boner, George Hoskins, George Dertzabaugh, Baldwin Albaugh. Its object was to insure against loss or damage by fire their respective dwelling-houses, other buildings, merchandise, household furniture, and other property.

On May 7, 1844, the following directors were elected: Lawrence J. Brengle, president; Patrick Tormey, secretary and treasurer; and David Boyd, Lewis Medtart, Z. T. Windsor, William H. Albaugh, Calvin Page, Edward Trail, William J. Ross, Hugh McAleer, Francis Leuber, Ezekiel Hughes, directors. It has been in successful operation twenty-eight years,

RES. AND OFFICE OF THOMAS CLAGETT,
FREDERICK, MD.

and annually writes the insurance of a large part of the best property of the county.

Its directors for 1881 (elected in May) are George Markell, president and treasurer; Philip Reich, Calvin Page, George W. Delaplane, James McSherry (counsel), David Frazier (agent), Francis Markell, Charles E. Trail, Joseph Cronise, Joseph G. Miller, Thomas R. Jarboe, James Houck, directors. Its secretary, George W. Cramer, has held that position for the past twenty years.

The Improvement Land and Building Association was chartered May 15, 1868, with the following charter members: David C. Martin, David M. Smith, Milton G. Urner, Charles W. Miller. Its first officers were—

President, J. William Birely; Vice-President, David C. Winebrenner; Secretary, E. A. Gittinger; Treasurer, John T. Quynn; Directors, J. William Birely, Daniel Getzendanner, Jr., David C. Winebrenner, John C. Hardt, A. H. Aubert, John T. Quynn, George W. Cramer, E. A. Gittinger, Augustus L. Eager, Jacob Heintz, Ethan A. Cramer, David H. Kolb; Solicitor, Milton G. Urner.

The officers for 1881 are—

J. William Birely, president; D. C. Winebrenner, vice-president; Francis Markell, treasurer; George W. Cramer, secretary; Walter Saunders, agent; M. G. Urner, solicitor; Directors, J. William Birely, D. C. Winebrenner, John T. Quynn, Val. S. Brunner, P. B. Kunkel, Francis Markell, Lewis M. Nixdorff, John A. Lynch, John C. Hardt, A. H. Aubert, David H. Kolb, and G. W. Cramer.

The Mutual Aid Association elected the following officers in 1881:

Lloyd T. Macgill, president; Albert W. Burkhart, vice-president; Christian H. Eckstein, secretary; Thomas N. Harwood, treasurer; Dr. Thomas Turner, medical director; Charles T. Darner, Horatio Zittle, general agents; Examining Committee, Dr. Thomas Turner, Dr. Lloyd T. Macgill, Christian H. Eckstein; Board of Actuaries, A. W. Burkhart, Thomas Clagett, Joshua Ahalt, Horatio Zittle, Charles W. Miller; Directors, Dr. Lloyd T. Macgill, Albert W. Burkhart, C. H. Eckstein, Thomas Clagett, Charles W. Miller, Dr. Thomas Turner, Joshua Ahalt, Thomas N. Harwood, Horatio Zittle, Charles T. Darner.

CHAPTER XXIX.

SECRET ORDERS, BENEVOLENT SOCIETIES, ETC.

SCARCELY any other city in the country is better supplied than Frederick with organizations for the relief of distress, and for the mutual assistance, encouragement, and social enjoyment of their members. There are two Masonic lodges, one commandery of Knights Templar, a lodge of Knights of Pythias, a tribe of the Independent Order of Red Men, a lodge and encampment of Odd Fellows, a Catholic beneficial society, a Young Men's Christian Association, a lodge of Knights of Honor, a council of the United American Mechanics, a post of the Grand Army of the Republic, and several other deserving organizations.

Hiram Lodge, No. 28, A. F. and A. M., was the first Masonic lodge in Frederick County of which there is any authentic record. It was organized in February, 1799. Dr. John Fischer, of Frederick City, was the first Grand Inspector for Frederick County, and was a member of this lodge. He represented it in the Grand Lodge of 1808, the date of its last representation. The following citizens were members of Hiram Lodge: Henry Bair, Tobias Butler, George Baltzell, Nicholas Fridinger, John B. Faulkner, Joseph McCully, Henry Schell, Henry R. Warfield, Elias Boteler, James Huey, William Robinson, Jacob Stephens, Samuel Harris, Samuel Sharp, Richard L. Head, John L. Harding, E. H. Stone, Mountjoy B. Luckett, Henry Bantz, Richard Butler, Francis Clarke, John Gantt, James S. Hook, James Neale, Adam Schisler, Joab Waters, Henry Ebbert, George Lipper, Joseph Hays, John Gibbony, Moses Shaw, Thomas C. Worthington, Robert Erskine, Benjamin Stallings, Samuel Philpot, Roger Nelson, Jacob Bayer, Jr., Dr. John Fischer, Ambrose Goslin, John Hinkle, James Philips, John Tyler, Alexander Whitacre, John Houston, Samuel Woods, Morris Jones, Arthur Tanzey, Frederick C. Hap, John M. Beatty, George Graff, Alexander C. Harrison, William Thomas Morris.

The house in which Hiram Lodge met cannot now be ascertained. Of these members of the lodge some were quite prominent in Masonry and distinguished in the State. George Baltzell was the tax collector of Frederick County for a number of years, and secretary of his lodge. Henry R. Warfield was a prominent lawyer and member of the Frederick bar. He represented the district in the Congress of the United States. James Neale kept a tavern in 1801, where the Central Hotel is now kept. Roger Nelson was a captain in the Revolutionary war, and received eighteen wounds. He was also a member of Congress from this district, was judge of the Frederick County Court, and afterwards clerk of the same court. He was the Grand Junior Warden in 1799; Deputy Grand Master of the Grand Lodge from 1801 to 1805. Dr. John Tyler and Dr. John Fischer were prominent physicians. Henry Bayer, Henry Bantz, Arthur Tanzey, Thomas C. Worthington, John Houston, and Adam Schisler took an active part in organizing Columbia Lodge in 1815. Tobias Butler was at one time clerk of the County Court. Thomas C.

Worthington was a member of Congress from this district in the year 1824. Mountjoy B. Luckett was a prominent young physician, and died in New Orleans in 1809.

A lodge called Mark Lodge worked under a dispensation in 1817, but was not chartered.

Columbia Mark Lodge, No. 10, was chartered Jan. 11, 1820, and expired in January, 1824.

Columbia Lodge, No. 58, A. F. and A. M., was organized in 1815, on the petition of Joseph Swearingen, Jacob Bayer, Henry Bantz, Thomas C. Worthington, Adam Schisler, Matthew Murray, William Bantz, Adam Korn, and James F. Houston. The Grand Lodge of Maryland granted a charter bearing date Nov. 7, 1815, authorizing William Bantz, Adam Schisler, and Samuel Barnes to organize Columbia Lodge, No. 58, in Frederick Town. Under this warrant a number of Masonic brethren, on the 8th day of December, 1815, met at the house of James F. Houston in Frederick Town. There is some doubt as to the exact location of this house; one statement is that it is the house on the south side of East Patrick Street now occupied by Charles E. Worthington as a boarding-house, and by Messrs. Besant & Knott as a grocery-store. This house was built by Job Hant in 1811 or 1812. Another account is that it was the house on the southeast corner of Market and Second Streets, now occupied by the Farmers' and Mechanics' National Bank. The facts and statements gathered from the oldest inhabitants of Frederick seem to point to the bank property as the more probable location of the John Houston house. Arthur Tanzey acted as "W. M." *pro tem.*, Adam Schisler, S. W.; Samuel Barnes, J. W.; James F. Houston, Sec.; Joseph Swearingen, Treas.; Matthew Murray, S. D.; Thomas C. Worthington, J. D. The brethren present were William Bantz, John Houston, Adam Korn, John Houston, George Attie, Basil Murray. A lodge was then opened, and the following were installed as the first officers:

William Bantz, W. M.; Adam Schisler, S. W.; Samuel Barnes, J. W.; James T. Houston, Sec.; Joseph Swearingen, Treas.; Matthew Murray, S. D.; Thomas C. Worthington, J. D.

Jacob Bayer was appointed Tyler for the next meeting. The lodge then closed to meet again on Dec. 17, 1815, when the by-laws were adopted and the above officers elected. The lodge next met on St. John's day, Dec. 27, 1815, in a room in Henry Bantz's house. This house is still standing on the south side of Second Street, between Market and Public Streets, and is owned by Judge William P. Maulsby. The officers elected at the previous meeting were installed on this occasion.

About the 1st of May, 1819, the lodge moved to the house of Henry Baer. This is the house on the north side of East Patrick Street, in which the Fessler family now lives. It is an old frame house plastered on the outside, and was built by John Shellman near the middle of the last century.

On the 15th of March, 1821, the lodge moved to the house of Samuel Webster. This house is on the northeast corner of Patrick and Market Streets. The lodge was held over the store-room, then occupied by Samuel Webster as a boot and shoe store, but now occupied by D. S. S. Thomas as a drug-store.

Some time during the year 1823 the lodge moved to a building on the east side of Market Street between Third and Fourth Streets, then owned by a Mrs. Smith. It is the building now occupied by the Degrave Brothers as a tobacco-store, and is the next house south of David C. Winebrenner's dry-goods and grocery-stores. The lodge met here until it dissolved, in 1830.

On Dec. 29, 1824, Gen. Lafayette was received by his Masonic brethren in the house of Henry Bantz on Second Street, where this lodge had its second place of meeting. William Baer presented this lodge a Masonic apron, which now hangs over the chair of the Junior Warden. To this apron is attached a cord with these words:

"This apron belonged to William Baer, and was worn by Gen. Lafayette when introduced to Columbia Lodge of A. Y. Masons at Frederick City, Md., in December, 1824, William Baer acting Marshal and Master of Ceremonies. He was introduced by Wm. Baer to W. M. Dr. Jacob Baer."

The lodge received Gen. Lafayette, with his son, George W. Lafayette, and his private secretary, in the west room of Col. McPherson's lower floor or parlor. The house is now owned by the Hon. Richard Marshall.

During this period Masonry was in a languishing condition, so much so that the brethren of Columbia Lodge thought it advisable to cease their meetings, and on June 7, 1830, held their last communication under the charter of 1815.

Robert W. Middleton, the secretary at this last meeting, renounced Freemasonry, and on July 8, 1830, one month after the meeting, went to Gettysburg, the hot-bed of anti Masonry in Pennsylvania, and printed a newspaper called *The Anti-Masonic Star*.

There is no evidence of the existence of any Masonic lodge in this county from the year 1830 to 1843.

In 1842, a number of Masons met in the old school-house on the north side of Church Street, between Market and Public Streets, on the lot on which the new German Reformed church now stands, for the purpose of memorializing the Grand Lodge for a renewal of the charter of Columbia Lodge. The following signed the memorial, viz.: Thomas C. Worthington, A. B. Hanson, D. Rolls, Caspar Quynn, Adolphus Fearhake, David Boyd, John W. Dorsey, Thomas Carr, Thomas C. Brashears, Abdiel Unkefer, Thos. W. Morgan, John Kefauver, of G., A. Barney, Ezra Bantz, Lloyd Dorsey, Henry Baer, John H. Fout, Jacob Roat, Nicholas Turbutt, Wm. D. Jenks, G. M. Eichelberger, Geo. Salmon, N. H. Owings,—23.

All the memorialists are now dead except A. Fearhake and John H. Fout. Oct. 23, 1843, a number of Masons met in the old Methodist Episcopal church on the north side of West Church Street, near Bentz Street. This building has lately been modernized and greatly improved, and is at present used and owned by the Methodist Protestant Church. At this meeting Caspar Quynn acted as chairman, A. Barney secretary. Anthony Kimmell stated the object of the meeting was the resuscitation of Columbia Lodge, and to secure a permanent house for its use.

Oct. 26, 1843, the brethren met, Caspar Quynn in the chair, and A. Barney secretary, and adjourned to a room prepared for them in the house of George Koontz. This house is on the west side of Market Street, the second building south of Church Street. It is now occupied by Bernard Rosenour, and is used as a dwelling and shoe-store.

The present charter, bearing date Nov. 6, 1842, and empowering G. M. Eichelberger to act as W. M., David Boyd, S. W., Thomas C. Brashear as J. W., to open Columbia Lodge, No. 58, was produced and read. These officers were then installed by D. G. Master Kimmell, and the lodge opened in regular form.

G. M. Eichelberger, W. M.; David Boyd, S. W.; Thos. C. Brashear, J. W.; A. Barney, Sec. *pro tem.*; Caspar Quynn, S. D.; M. E. Bartgis, J. D.; Solomon Albaugh, Tyler.

The brethren present were A. Kimmell, A. Fearhake, Geo. Salmon, Geo. Zollinger, John Kefauver, Wm. D. Jenks, M. Bedtman, Rezin Stevens, John Sifford. A. Barney was chosen secretary and installed.

Dec. 18, 1843, the lodge met, and went into an election for officers to serve the next six months. Caspar Quynn was elected W. M., Thomas W. Morgan, S. W., and William D. Jenks, J. W. George Salmon was appointed S. D., and H. Fearhake, J. D.

Several of the meetings just mentioned were held in David Boyd's house on Market Street, on the south corner of Market Space. This building is now owned and occupied by A. C. McCardell. About this time the lodge moved to the hall which had been prepared for its use in the old Methodist Episcopal church on Church Street.

On July 6, 1857, the lodge rented a room in the McGill Building, on the southeast corner of Market and Patrick Streets, for five years, at seventy-five dollars per annum, for its use.

On June 19, 1865, the lodge held its first meeting in the hall in the old Episcopal church on Public Street.

Sept. 22, 1865. The lodge proceeded to the Methodist Episcopal church on East Church Street to lay the corner-stone of the new church, which was done with the usual Masonic ceremonies. D. G. Master John A. Lynch officiating.

May 31, 1871. The lodge assisted the Grand Lodge in laying the corner-stone of the "Deaf and Dumb Institute" in Frederick City. Grand Master John H. B. Latrobe officiating.

June 6, 1871. The lodge laid the corner-stone of "Trinity Chapel of the Methodist Episcopal Church, South." A. Fearhake, Jr., officiating.

Nov. 6, 1871. The lodge sent to the sufferers by the great fire in Chicago the sum of eight hundred and forty-six dollars, contributed by the members.

Anthony Kimmell was Grand Senior Warden of the Grand Lodge in 1832, '33, '34, '35; Deputy Grand Master in 1842, '43, '44, '57; Most Worshipful Grand Master, 1859. John A. Lynch was Deputy Grand Master in 1864. C. N. S. Levy is now Grand King of the Grand Chapter.

From June, 1815, to 1830, eight Ancient Masons united with the lodge, one hundred and twelve were made Masons, and sixteen rejected. From 1843 to 1880, sixty-five Ancient Masons joined the lodge; one hundred and ninety-eight were initiated, passed and raised.

Columbia Lodge has had thirty-three W. M., forty-five S. W., fifty-three J. W., and, from 1843 to 1880, eleven secretaries and fifteen treasurers. From 1843 to 1880 there have been four hundred and forty-six applications for membership and initiation; of this number, one hundred and forty-nine were rejected. From 1843 to 1863, one hundred and sixty-nine applications, thirteen rejected; 1860 to 1880, two hundred and seventy-seven applications, one hundred and thirty-six rejected. In 1865 there were twenty-six rejections.

Lynch Lodge, No. 163, A. F. and A. M.—June 5, 1873, Grand Master Latrobe granted a dispensation to Benjamin H. Schley, W. M., Steiner Schley, S. W., and Peter S. Bantz, J. W., to make Masons and form a new lodge. Nov. 18, 1873, the Grand Lodge issued a regular charter to Lynch Lodge, No. 163, named in honor of Judge John A. Lynch.

The first officers were:

W. M., Benjamin H. Schley; S. W., Steiner Schley; J. W., Philip Stern; Sec., Charles F. Kreh; Treas., Julius Neuwahl; S. D., Harry C. Keefer; J. D., George A. Abbott; Tyler, F. T. Rhodes.

At a special communication of this lodge, Past Deputy Grand Master John A. Lynch, under authority from Grand Master Latrobe, constituted the lodge and installed the aforesaid officers. It holds its meetings in the hall of Columbia Lodge, and numbers thirty active and zealous Masons.

The officers for 1881 are:

W. M., Isaac Lowenstein; S. W., Isaiah N. Loy; J. W., Jacob J. Sahm; Sec., George E. Myer; Treas., Julius Neuwahl.

Jacques de Molay Commandery, No. 4.—This commandery commenced under a dispensation dated Nov. 23, 1867. The officers in the dispensation were George A. Hanson, E. C.; Peter S. Bantz, Gen.; and J. Alfred Ritter, Capt.-Gen.

Sept. 18, 1868, the Grand Commandery granted a regular charter to Jacques de Molay Commandery, No. 4, and its first officers were the same as in the dispensation.

The officers for 1881 are:

E. C., John A. Lynch; Gen., Charles C. Smith; Capt.-Gen., M. E. Getzendanner; P., Adolphus Fearhake, Jr.; Sec., F. A. Markey; S. W., W. V. Albaugh; J. W., C. V. S. Levy; S. B., George W. Cramer; Std. B., C. F. A. Fox; W., William N. Young; Sent., F. F. Rhodes.

Enoch Royal Arch Chapter, No. 23.—Enoch Chapter, No. 10, was chartered Nov. 15, 1820, and was last represented in the Grand Chapter in 1827 by Daniel Kolb, Adolphus Fearhake, Sr., and Francis Thomas.

Enoch Chapter, No. 23, commenced under a dispensation dated in May, 1866. The officers named in the dispensation were George A. Hanson, High Priest, Allen G. Quynn, King, and William N. Young, Scribe. Nov. 13, 1866, the Grand Chapter granted it a regular charter, and the first officers under it were the same as in the dispensation.

The officers for 1881 are:

H. P., Philip Stern; K., William N. Young; S., W. V. Albaugh; R., F. A. Markey; Treas., H. Goldenberg; C. H., J. W. Griffin; P. S., A. Fearhake, Jr.; R. A. C., C. S. V. Levy; M. 3d V., I. Lowenstein; M. 2d V., C. C. Smith; M. 1st V., John A. Lynch.

Mountain City Lodge, No. 29, Knights of Pythias.—This lodge was instituted Feb. 12, 1869. The grand officers' names affixed to the charter are:

G. W. Stoddard, G. C.; E. R. Davis, V. G. C.; C. F. Abbott, V. G. P.; H. P. Barnes, G. B.; F. Turner, G. K. R. & S.; J. B. Hurst, G. G.; A. S. Walton, G. O. S.; John Muth, G. O. S. The charter members were L. Vanfosson, J. M. Ebberts, W. A. Simmons, G. N. Hauer, H. F. Steiner, E. A. Kramer, J. C. Hardt, J. W. Brubaker, J. A. Steiner, J. M. Miller, F. W. Slugh, T. M. Holbruner, H. M. Keefer.

Starwart Conclave, S. P. K., No. 3.—This conclave, formerly called Stoddard, was organized May 17, 1869. The grand officers who signed the charter were:

James Bond, G. C.; John J. Ward, G. Sec. The charter members were William A. Simmons, David M. Smith, James N. Walter, John Simmons, P. L. Hiteshew, C. W. Tabler.

Alpha Temple of Honor, No. 2.—Officers elected in May, 1881, for the ensuing term:

W. C. T., I. P. Suman; W. V. T., J. J. Bielfeld; W. R., G. W. Tyson; W. A. R., W. H. Keller; W. F. R., I. F. Steiner; W. Tr., A. R. Yeakle; W. U., W. V. Miller; W. D. U., B. E. Veitch; W. G., W. F. Kuhn; W. S., T. P. Rice; W. Chaplain, F. B. Sappington; W. R. H. S., Charles Patten, Jr.; W. L. H. S., J. S. Quinn; P. W. C. T., D. S. Rice.

Chippewa Tribe, No. 19, I. O. O. R.—On the twenty-sixth Sun of the Buck Moon, in Grand Sun 5610, the Grand Council of the Improved Order of Red Men of Maryland issued its dispensation to form Chippewa Tribe, No. 19, to the following pale-faces:

Samuel Snyder, J. W. Suman, John D. Zieler, L. M. Wolf, William T. Duvall, William H. Hiteshew, George R. Kephart, W. Moling, George W. Dertsbauch, O. Nurz, P. R. Shaffner, J. V. Hollebaugh, M. Albaugh, George Albaugh, Jacob Lillich.

The aforesaid dispensation was signed by

William H. Ford, G. S.; Thomas Sprigg, G. S. S.; William H. Cox, G. J. S.; John T. Alexander, G. P.; John L. Booker, G. C. of R.; B. W. Ferguson, G. K. of W.

Its first officers, elected on the Third Sun of the Flower Moon (May, 1850), were:

S., Samuel Snyder; S. S., Israel W. Suman; J. S., John D. Zeiler; C. of R., William H. Hiteshew; K. of W., Lewis W. Wolf; P., William T. Duvall.

In 1851, after one year's organization, it numbered thirty-one members. This order is a beneficial institution, and in Maryland, with its thirty-five tribes, expended in charities in 1880, $10,153.46. This tribe has a present membership of one hundred and eighty, and meets every Thursday evening at its commodious and elegant hall on Market Street. Its officers for semi-annual term ending June 30, 1881, were:

S., Frank T. Davis; S. S., George W. Vanfossen; J. S., Charles Smallwood; C. of R., John H. Bennett; K. of W.,

John C. Hart; Rep. to Great Council of Md., Edward A. Gittinger.

Its receipts for the year 1880 were $1407.47, of which there was paid out for relief of brothers, $606; of widows, $230; of orphans, $10; and for burying the dead, $45; total charities expended, $891.

In case of the sickness of a member, the tribe pays him three dollars a week.

It has a well-selected library of 1121 volumes.

Frederick Lodge, American Order United Workingmen, No. 14.—The officers of this lodge for the term ending December, 1881, are:

P. M. W., Isaac Lowenstein; M. W., W. Nash Young; Foreman, W. B. Starm; A. F., D. Lowenstein; Receiver, George E. Meyer; Financier, J. W. Griffin; Guard, I. Lowenstein; Recorder, D. M. Scholl; I. W., F. A. Markey; O. W., P. W. Shafer; Trustee, McClintock Young.

This lodge was instituted in May, 1880.

Mount Olive Encampment, No. 9, Independent Order Odd-Fellows.—This encampment was instituted May 21, 1846. Charter members, David Schley, Casper Mantz, Thomas A. Fleming, W. S. Brown, C. Sheppard, W. S. Davis.

Its charter was granted by the following grand officers: Past Grand Masters, J. Meares, Richard Marley, H. Mathoit, Levi Taylor, J. J. Johnson; G. Patriarch, John Hamilton; G. H. Priest, William Bayley; Senior Warden, J. G. Waters; Scribe, N. T. Dushane; Treasurer, A. E. Warner; Junior Warden, John J. Sharp; and Secretary, James Patterson. Its Chief Patriarchs have been:

1846, David Schley; 1847, Casper Mantz, Thomas A. Fleming; 1848, W. C. Smallwood, J. H. Jones; 1849, Samuel Tyler, G. Beckenbaugh; 1850, W. R. Marsh, W. S. Bantz; 1851, J. A. Ritter, C. Cole; 1852, J. A. Steiner, C. F. A. Fox; 1853, C. Fox, William Mahony; 1854, Jesse J. Hunt; 1855, Thomas Haller; 1856, George Hoskin; 1857, Frederick Keefer; 1858, William F. Johnson; 1859, John G. Sinn; 1860, John T. Sinn; 1861, Christopher Wahner; 1862, Thomas M. Holbruner; 1863, Frederick Sargess; 1864, G. W. Davis; 1865, Henry L. Zeigler; 1866, Philip M. Englebrecht; 1867, C. Wahner; 1868, W. H. Zeigler; 1869, D. C. Martin; 1870, G. A. Abbott; 1871, Job K. Sheppard; 1872, William A. Simmons; 1873, E. A. Gittinger; 1874, Philip Stern; 1875, C. B. Fox; 1876, Charles A. Bruner; 1877, Lewis Koester; 1878, A. J. Fromke; 1879, S. Kingsbaker; 1880, Peter Ross.

The officers for 1881 are:

C. P., Philip Stern; H. P., A. J. Fromke; S. W., F. S. Hopewood; J. W., J. J. Grahe; Scribe, William A. Simmons; Treas., E. A. Gittinger.

Membership, thirty-five. C. Sheppard was scribe for the first term in 1846, and was succeeded by Henry B. Fissler, who served until 1872, since which time William A. Simmons has been scribe.

Adam Lodge, No. 35, I. O. O. F.—Its dispensation was allowed May 15, 1841. Its charter was granted July 16, 1841, by Richard Marley, M. W. G. M.; Levi Taylor, R. W. D. G. M.; W. G. Cook, R. W. G. S.; J. J. Johnson, W. G. W; John Robinson, W. G. T.; and by Past Grand Masters James L. Ridgely, Aug. Mathiot, Robert Neilson, A. E. Warner, J. Maris, and Past Grand Secretary Thomas Wildey. The charter members were John Kefauver, of G., Caspar Quynn, George A. Cole, Anthony Kimmel, Charles Nixon, Ezra Bantz, William Slater.

The first officers were:

Casper Quynn, N. G.; William Slater, V. G.; John Kefauver, of G., Sec.; Ezra Bantz, Treas.

The Noble Grands have been:

1841, Caspar Quynn, William Slater; 1842, J. M. Harding, W. C. Martin, George Salmon, F. A. Rigney; 1843, Caspar Mantz, W. S. Brown, Charles J. Fox, David Schley; 1844, J. W. Reynolds, Godfrey Koontz, W. Geyer, A. K. Mantz; 1845, P. L. Storm, T. H. O'Neal, H. B. Fessler, Hamilton Stier; 1846, R. W. Philips, T. A. Fleming, John A. Steiner, P. Goodmanson; 1847, N. T. Haller, George McCahan; 1848, J. H. Jones, J. L. Norris; 1849, W. S. Bantz, J. C. O'Neal; 1850, J. C. O'Neal, George Hoskins; 1851, Charles Cole, J. H. Bangs; 1852, M. R. Marsh, T. F. Cockey; 1853, J. A. Ritter, A. H. Hunt; 1854, J. T. Moore, Z. J. Gittinger; 1855, W. H. Derr, Frederick Keefer; 1856, John Rhodes, John G. Sinn; 1857, J. M. Ebert, P. M. Englebrecht; 1858, William Mahony, W. F. Johnson; 1859, Gideon Bantz, P. B. McCleery; 1860-72, record-book mislaid; 1873, John H. Bruner, J. E. Rice; 1874, Philip Stern, D. M. Main; 1875, H. G. Sleeper, G. H. Zimmerman; 1876, Lewis Koester, C. A. Bruner; 1877, B. F. Phoebus, C. Edwin Cole; 1878, Solomon Kingsbaker, Julius Neuwahl; 1879, T. C. Lauderkin, C. F. Fleming; 1880, Walter Saunders, J. I. Duvall; 1881, T. H. Haller, Francis Brengle.

The secretaries have been:

1841, F. A. Rigney; 1842, T. H. O'Neal, A. K. Mantz, G. W. Sands; 1843, James Reynolds, M. R. Marsh, G. S. Groshon; 1844, H. B. Fessler, Casper Mantz; 1845-47, J. M. Ebert; 1847-55, J. D. Faubel; 1855, A. H. Hunt; 1856, P. M. Englebrecht; 1857-60, M. R. Marsh; 1860-73, record-book missing; 1873-78, W. G. Cole; 1878-82, W. H. Zeigler.

The officers for 1881 (2d term) are:

N. G., Francis Brengle; V. G., John H. Cutshaw; Sec., William H. Zeigler; Treas., Albert T. Rice.

St. John's Beneficial Association.—The idea of forming a beneficial or benevolent association connected with St. John's Church was first entertained in 1852, and on the 12th day of December of the same year such a society was formed. Each member is entitled to four dollars per week as benefits while sick, and on the death of a member the sum of fifty dollars is paid his widow or legal representatives to defray his funeral expenses. It has other special benevolent features, and for more than thirty years has been engaged in benevolent works. Its incorporators were Col. James McSherry, William M. Merrick, John A. Smith, William Walsh, Lewis Logue, Hugh L. McAleer, Charles Smith, and John Buckfelder, who obtained an act of incorporation July 6, 1854. Its officers have been:

1853.—Pres., James McSherry; Vice-Pres., James Kerrigan; Sec., W. R. Sappington; Treas., John A. Smith.
1854.—Pres., James McSherry; Vice-Pres., W. M. Merrick; Sec., A. W. Marriott; Treas., William Walsh.
1855-56.—Pres., James McSherry; Vice-Pres., Henry Pampel; Sec., L. M. Ryan; Treas., William Walsh.
1857-58.—Pres., James McSherry; Vice-Pres., H. A. Hazer; Sec., L. M. Ryan; Treas., William Walsh.
1859-66.—Pres., James McSherry; Vice-Pres., H. A. Hazer; Sec., F. A. Whaner; Treas., William Walsh.
1866.—Pres., James McSherry; Vice-Pres., James McSherry, Jr.; Sec., F. A. Whaner; Treas., William Walsh.
1867-70.—Pres., James McSherry, Jr.; Vice-Pres., Thomas Barry; Sec., F. A. Whaner; Treas., William Walsh.
1870-76.—Pres., James McSherry; Vice-Pres., Lewis Burke; Sec., F. A. Whaner; Treas., William Walsh.
1876-80.—Pres., James McSherry; Vice-Pres., Lewis Burck; Sec., Joseph F. Eisenhauer; Treas., William Walsh.
1880.—Pres., James McSherry; Vice-Pres., N. J. Wilson; Sec., J. F. Eisenhauer; Treas., William Walsh.
1881.—Pres., James McSherry; Vice-Pres., N. J. Wilson; Sec., J. F. Eisenhauer; Treas., William Walsh; Messenger, Charles E. Bruchey.

It has had but two presidents,—father and son,—Col. James McSherry and Capt. James McSherry, the latter since 1867. It holds a stated meeting every month, and an annual meeting on the second Sunday of January, when the yearly election of officers takes place by ballot.

Fredonia Council, No. 46, Order of United American Mechanics.—On Feb. 6, 1874, the State Council of the "O. U. A. M." issued a dispensation to establish Fredonia Council, No. 46, to the following charter members, viz.: M. C. Winchester, George R. Wisong, Frank P. Ingram, C. H. Eckstine, Charles Patten, John P. Renner, Edgar L. Miller, Charles E. Ingram, J. Edward Rice, Tobias Haller, E. S. Harding, C. T. Albaugh, N. S. Tyson, and Philip H. Nussbaum; signed and countersigned by John G. Mitchell, Councilor, and John W. Holden, Secretary.

Its first officers were:

Jun. Ex. Councilor, N. S. Tyson; C., John C. Motter; V. C., M. C. Winchester; Rec. Sec., J. Edward Rice; Fin. Sec., F. P. Ingram; Treas., Philip H. Nussbaum.

It has a membership of eighty-five, and meets every Friday evening in its hall in the Kemp Building, in the third story thereof. It pays four dollars per week benefits to sick members, and on the death of a member each member has to pay the family of the deceased one dollar. It has a library of three hundred and twenty-six volumes, purchased by penny assessments of a penny a week on each member. The officers for semi-annual term ending July 1, 1881, are:

Sen. Ex. Councilor, J. C. Motter; Jun. Ex. Councilor, Trago W. Lauderkin; C., Charles E. Kemp; V. C., Lewis Byer; Rec. Sec., C. H. Eckstein; Fin. Sec., John H. Bennett; Treas., Wm. C. Birely.

Reynolds Post, No. 2, Grand Army of the Republic, was organized at the close of the civil war. Its commander for 1881 is Gen. John A. Steiner, and the chairman of its executive committee is Col. C. W. F. Vernon, surveyor of the port of Baltimore. May 30th is the national Decoration Day of Union graves, and it was attended in 1881 with ceremonies and exercises surpassing in extent those of any previous year. In Frederick the graves of the dead were covered with flowers, and the entire ceremonies were conducted under the auspices of Reynolds Post. A poem appropriate to the occasion was read by Hon. William H. Hinks, and an oration was delivered by Rev. S. V. Leech, D.D. Sacred anthems were sung by the choir, under the direction of Lieut. Geo. E. Greenwood. The "old flag" was planted over Barbara Fritchie's grave, which was covered with flowers. Capt. Wm. Glessner was chairman of the committee on decoration of Mount Olivet, Gideon Staley of the committee on outside decorations, and Maj. O. A. Horner of the committee on flowers.

Confederate Monumental and Memorial Associations.—The first call for a meeting to organize a Ladies' Confederate Monumental Association was responded to by a number of ladies, and the following were the proceedings of the first meeting held:

Aug. 7, 1879, in response to a notice issued by Capt. Owings, president of the Confederate Memorial Association, the following ladies met at the residence of that gentleman for the purpose of organizing an association, having the object in view of creating a fund of money sufficient to enable them to erect a monument to the "unknown" deceased Confederate soldiers interred at Mount Olivet Cemetery: Mrs. B. F. Brown, Mrs. A. J. Delashmutt, Mrs. L. M. Nixdorff, Mrs. N. Owings, Mrs. W. N. Young, Mrs. E. L. Eader, and Misses Davidson and A. R. Fout. The meeting was organized and the following officers elected: President, Mrs. John H. Williams; First Vice-President, Mrs. B. F. Brown; Second Vice-President, Mrs. J. H. Gambrill; Secretary, Mrs. A. L. Eader; Treasurer, Mrs. Nicholas Owings. The meeting adjourned to meet Aug. 11, 1869, when there were present Mrs. John H. Williams, president; Mrs. J. H. Gambrill, second vice-president; Mrs. A. E. Eader, Secretary; and Mrs.

A. J. Delashmutt, Mrs. Frank Clingan, Mrs. Ellen Howard, Mrs. N. Owings, Mrs. W. Nash Young, Mrs. J. S. W. Jarboe, Mrs. Henry Williams, Miss A. R. Font, Miss Lucy Boteler, Miss Janie Williams, Miss Ella Shriver, Miss Davidson, Miss Emma Gittinger, Miss Cockey. On motion the organization was designated as the "Ladies' Confederate Monumental Association of Frederick County, Md."

Two ladies from each district in the county were appointed to act as vice-presidents. A committee was appointed to solicit subscriptions throughout the city, and at the same time it was decided to establish a dining pavilion at the Agricultural Fair Grounds during the fair, for the purpose of increasing the funds. The results of the collection and proceeds of dining parlor and Pen-Mar excursion amounted to $1429. The proceeds of the musical entertainment at City Hall, May 30, 1880, were applied to the renovation of the three hundred and nine Confederate graves, and paying for the foundation of a monument, etc., to the forty "unknown" Confederate dead. The "Confederate Memorial Association" co-operated with the ladies throughout.

The officers of the "Confederate Memorial Association" for 1881 are:

President, Nicholas Owings; Vice-President, L. Victor Baughman; Secretary, Wm. Nash Young; Managers, R. Brown Henderson, James McSherry, Frederick J. Nelson, G. F. Clingan, Wm. Nash Young, Peter Sahm, A. P. Works, F. C. Knott, Henry Williams, John W. Brosius, Charles Ritter, Nicholas Owings, A. L. Boteler, Wm. T. Besant, F. Marion Faubel.

On June 2, 1881, the monument was unveiled. Preparations had been made upon an extensive scale for the entertainment of guests, but as the day was rainy the programme was carried out under unfavorable conditions.

At 10.30 o'clock a special arrived from Baltimore, bearing large delegations from the Murray Confederate Association and the Society of the Army and Navy of the Confederate States in Maryland, under the command of Capt. McHenry Howard and Gen. Bradley T. Johnson, and led by Charle's Band. The Winchester Rifles, Linganore Guards, and other organizations came in on earlier trains. At 2.30 o'clock the ceremonies were opened.

The oration delivered by Hon. James A. Buchanan, of Baltimore, at the City Hall, was well received. The monument was unveiled at Mount Olivet Cemetery by Miss Owings, daughter of Capt. Owings; Miss Gambrill, daughter of James H. Gambrill; Miss Quynn, daughter of the late Allen Quynn; and Miss Clingan, daughter of G. F. Clingan.

The statue is of Carrara marble, and was made in Italy, the base being granite; height of monument fifteen feet from the ground, and cost fourteen hundred dollars, Mr. Batterson being the contractor. The inscriptions on the panels are as follows:

ON FIRST PANEL.

"Erected A.D. 1880, by the Ladies' Monumental Association of Frederick County, in honor of the soldiers of the Confederate army who fell in the battles of Antietam and Monocacy and elsewhere, and who are buried here."

RIGHT PANEL.

"Soldiers rest, thy warfare o'er,
Sleep the sleep that knows not breaking,
Dream of battle-fields no more,
Days of danger, nights of waking."

LEFT PANEL.

"To the unknown soldiers whose bodies here rest. We cannot inscribe their names upon tablets of stone, but we may hope to read them in a purer and an unchangeable record."

REAR PANEL.

"Their praises will be sung
In some yet unmoulded tongue,
Far on in summers that we shall not see."

Ladies' Relief Association.—During the war of 1861–65 the ladies of Frederick organized the "Ladies' Relief Association," with Mrs. Gideon Bantz as president, for lending aid to the medical officers of the Federal forces quartered near the city in their treatment of sick and disabled soldiers, by preparing such delicacies as are most relished by invalids. It originated in a call published in the *Examiner* of Aug. 21, 1861, and on October 21st fifty ladies met and organized. Seven committees were appointed, who had each the duty of securing the articles required for the sick on a specified day of the week. They visited the hospitals in the morning, and saw that the articles furnished were properly disposed of. After the battles of South Mountain and Antietam, in September, 1862, Gettysburg, in July, 1863, and Monocacy, in July, 1864, with thousands of wounded soldiers here and in the neighborhood, this association performed an immense labor, and its deeds of good were engraved on many a suffering heart.

Various other Societies.—Eastern Star Grange, No. 5, was organized several years ago, and its Master is George William Smith, and its Secretary, James A. Brown. "The Mechanical Library" and "Young Men's Christian Association," both instituted years ago, are in a flourishing condition. The Knights of Honor have a good lodge, No. 603.

Protestant Episcopal Orphan Asylum.—This elegant structure was erected in 1840, by the aid of fairs and the public donations for that purpose, the lot on which the building is located having been presented for this object by Mrs. Eleanor Potts. The building cost nearly five thousand dollars, and for a short period after its erection was occupied by the Chesapeake and Ohio Canal Company as their office. The office of this company was removed in 1840 from the city of Washington to Frederick, which from its central position was the most proper location. Great credit is due to the ladies of the Episcopal Church for the energy and patience displayed in the establishment of this institution, which for two decades has been doing a noble work.

CHAPTER XXX.

PROMINENT INSTITUTIONS AND EVENTS.

THE Barracks, for many years one of the features of Frederick, were built during the Revolutionary war, and in the midst of a fine, green lot, beautifully located on an eminence overlooking the whole of Monocacy, or Frederick Valley. The city is spread out below it, the spires of its numerous churches and its more lofty edifices meeting the eye on the one side, while the rich and luxuriant fields of one of the most productive valleys in the world may be seen on the other. The Barracks were used as a place of confinement for prisoners taken with Burgoyne at Saratoga, and next for the Hessians who were captured at Yorktown. Numerous huts were erected in addition to the Barracks, all of which were removed before 1840. The Barracks were next occupied by the French prisoners of "L'Insurgent," captured by the "Constellation" during the *quasi*-war with France. While the Hessians were there some of the more intelligent became enamored with the beauty and the advantages of the country, and made their escape, so that they were left behind when their fellow-prisoners were marched off, and from this stock descended a numerous and vigorous progeny.

The Barracks were long partly occupied by the State armorer, and the rooms rented out to tenants. On the Barracks Hill lay the old cannon, which had been famous among the boys from time immemorial. It was brought here to celebrate the peace of 1783, and was used in 1841 as the "Great Baby Waker" by Dertzabaugh, and for the celebration of the Fourth of July and other popular rejoicings. This piece of ordnance was among the first cannon cast in Maryland during the Revolutionary war, and was an eighteen-pounder. It was cast at Mount Ætna Furnace, six miles north of Hagerstown. From 1868 for three or four years the State Deaf and Dumb Asylum occupied the Barracks buildings, until their present institution was erected on the Barracks grounds.

From 1840 and for several years afterwards a portion of the Barracks (which belonged to the State) were used by special permission of the Legislature by Messrs. Jenks & Ramsburg as a cocoonery. They had a white mulberry orchard, consisting of ten acres, in an adjoining lot. The State granted them the use of the Barracks buildings to test the experiment of silk-culture, then creating so much discussion throughout the country. W. D. Jenks began operations and planted his trees in 1837. Feb. 28, 1840, the reels were put up. During the year sewing silk was made equal to that of foreign manufacture. After the flyer was in operation, gold-stripe vesting was manufactured in considerable quantities.

The Old Town-Clock.—In perusing the musty records of Frederick we find that the solemn tones of the town-clock first pealed forth in 1807. It was constructed by that faithful chronicler of local incidents in early days and "goodly artisan," Frederick Heisley. According to a contemporary description, it was "a noble piece of mechanism, and doth greatly excite the curiosity of our town-folk." What interesting scenes the old clock must have witnessed during the seventy-four long years of its existence! It is a seven-day time-piece, and has been wound up by John Fessler and his son nearly ever since its erection.

Washington and Lafayette in Frederick.—Gen. Washington first visited Frederick Town in April, 1755, as one of Gen. Braddock's aides, and again in 1791, when on his way from Mount Vernon to Philadelphia, at that time the seat of the national government. During his second visit he was formally received and entertained by the people of Frederick. On reaching the hill near the farm now owned by Henry Scholl he was met by a company of horsemen from Frederick, headed by Maj. Mountjoy Bayley, chief marshal, and comprising many of the most influential and respectable citizens of the county. The President was conducted up to Barracks Hill, through the town and up Market Street to Brother's tavern, and then to Rich Hill, the residence of Governor Thomas Johnson. There was a brilliant illumination in honor of the event. The following is the correspondence which passed between Gen. Washington and a committee of citizens of Frederick County. Referring to this correspondence, the *Rights of Man*, published in Frederick Town in 1791, said,—

"This illustrious character during his short stay in Frederick Town, in this State, was treated with marks of high respect and great affection by the respectable citizens of this flourishing town. Previous to his departure, which public business obliged him to hasten, the following address (drawn in great haste) was presented to him, to which he was pleased to return an answer exhibiting as usual fresh proofs of his greatness and goodness."

The correspondence is as follows:

"To the President of the United States:

"*Sir*,—The inhabitants of Frederick take the liberty of congratulating you upon your safe arrival at this place, and to assure you that it gives them sincere pleasure to have this opportunity of expressing that veneration and attachment which they have always felt, and still feel, for your person and character as a patriot, a statesman, a soldier, and a fellow-citizen. They have, sir, a lively sense of gratitude for that long series of services which you have so ably exhibited on the public stage."

In reply Washington said:

"Your ascription of my public services overrates their value; and it is justice to my fellow-citizens that I should assign the eminent advantages of our political condition to another cause, —to their valor, wisdom, and virtue. From the first they derive their freedom; the second has been proved by their independence in national prosperity; the last, I trust, will long protect their social rights and insure their individual happiness. That your participation of these advantages may realize your best wishes is my sincere prayer.

"George Washington.
"Messrs. Murdoch, Beall, Potts, Thomas, and McPherson."

After leaving Frederick Town, in July, 1791, on his way to Philadelphia, Gen. Washington passed through Woodsborough, Ladiesburg, and York Road Station to Middleburg and Taneytown, Hanover, etc. In passing through what is now known as Carroll County he remained part of the afternoon and overnight at "Terra Rubra," the hospitable mansion of Maj. John Ross Key, near Middleburg, where a large concourse of people had assembled to greet him. Many who had seen service with him in the days of '76, and who knew him personally, and admired his military and civil career, hastened to take him by the hand and bid him welcome. He was escorted from Frederick Town by ex-Governors Thomas Johnson and Thomas Sim Lee, Maj. Mountjoy Bayley, and others.

After breakfast on the morning after the night spent at Maj. Key's, ex-Governor Johnson announced that the general would say a few words to his friends before he left.

"My countrymen," said Washington, deeply affected, "I am about to leave your good land, your beautiful valleys, your refreshing streams, and the Blue Hills of Maryland, which stretch out before me. I cannot leave you, fellow-citizens, without thanking you again and again for your kind greeting; for the true and devoted friendship you have shown me. When in the darkest hours of the Revolution, of doubt and gloom, the succor and support I received from the people of Frederick County always cheered me. It always awoke a responsive echo in my breast. I feel the emotion of gratitude beating in my heart,— my heart is too full to say more. God bless you all."

Washington was a first-rate farmer and always took a lively interest in agricultural pursuits. At that time Frederick County (before it was divided) was the largest wheat-growing county in the United States, and its grain crop of 1791 was particularly fine. That and other facts which fell under his observation prompted Washington, in a letter written shortly after to Sir John Sinclair, of Great Britain, to state that "Frederick County was the Garden Spot of the United States."

A funeral tribute to Washington's memory was paid on the 22d of February, 1800, at Frederick, in conformity with the military orders received from Maj.-Gen. Charles Cotesworth Pinckney, of Charleston, S. C., addressed to Brig.-Gen. Mountjoy Bayley, of Frederick Town, commanding the Federal troops in Western Maryland. There was an immense attendance from all parts of the county and from distant points of Frederick.

Gen. John Eager Howard, of Baltimore, Charles Carroll of Carrollton, Col. William Washington, Maj. Paul Bentalou, and Sergt. Lawrence Everhart, were in the procession. Ex-Governor Thomas Sim Lee, Hon. Benjamin Ogle, Governor of Maryland, and Hon. George Baer, Jr., member of Congress, were seated with Thomas Johnson, orator of the day, in a carriage drawn by four white horses and draped in mourning.

The exercises began with the discharge of sixteen guns from the artillery, commanded by Capt. William Clements, and half-hour guns were fired until the procession moved. About eleven o'clock the line of procession was formed opposite Capt. Valentine Brother's, and moved in the following order:

An advance guard of four dragoons.
Capt. Nelson's cavalry, commanded by Cornet Daniel Hauer, Jr.
The General's horse dressed in black.
Federal Troops under the command of Capt. Val. Brother.
Federal officers.
Music.
Military officers in uniform.
Physicians.
Clergy.
The Bier and Pall-Bearers.
Sixteen young ladies in mourning representing the sixteen
States in grief.
Committee of Arrangements.
Masonic Brethren.
The Rev. Samuel Knox, principal of the academy, followed
by the other tutors, and upwards of one hundred
pupils in mourning.

The procession moved down Market Street to the Square, and then up Patrick Street. When arrived in front of the German Presbyterian church the whole halted and opened to the right and left. The bier was then conveyed into the cemetery and three volleys fired over it by Capt. Brother's command. In the church Thomas Johnson delivered an eloquent oration upon the life and services of his friend and associate General Washington.

In the summer of 1824, Lafayette, with his son, George Washington Lafayette, and Mr. Le Vasseur, his private secretary, sailed from Havre in the ship "Cadmus," Capt. Allyn, and arrived in the city of New York on the 15th of August of that year. His advent was the signal for universal rejoicing. Party spirit was hushed, patriotic ardor alone prevailed, and an era of good feeling pervaded the entire land.

Frederick County was one of the foremost communities to do him honor, and among the citizens who were particularly active in urging an appropriate reception were Messrs. William P. Farquhar, Samuel Barnes, editor of the Frederick *Examiner*, Joshua Cockey, Henry Kemp, Joseph M. Cromwell, John Lee, Henry Ridgely Warfield, Stephen Steiner, and John Kunkel. John Kunkel and his son Hon. Jacob M. Kunkel were in their day conspicuous men in the history of Western Maryland.

Hon. Jacob M. Kunkel was born in Frederick, July 24, 1822, and in that city died, April 7, 1870. His great-grandfather, John Kunkel, was a colonel in the army of Frederick the Great, and about 1732 emigrated to America. Soon afterwards he purchased of Richard and Thomas Penn, proprietors of the province, a tract of land in Lancaster County, Pa. The letters patent and the land itself are still in the possession of his descendants. He was an old man when the war of the Revolution opened, and although he himself could not go, he sent six of his seven sons to the Continental army. One of them fell at the battle of the Brandywine. Jacob, the fifth son, was a dragoon, and while upon detached service on the banks of the Delaware was with a companion suddenly surprised by a small command of British horse. The young dragoon, however, was equal to the emergency; shooting the commanding officer of the enemy dead on the spot, he leaped upon the latter's horse, and before the men could recover from their surprise was pushing on across the river, and so luckily escaped. In the holsters of his equine prize he found two silver-mounted pistols marked "J. P." One of the weapons is yet in the possession of the Kunkel family. The eldest son, William (grandfather of Hon. J. M. Kunkel), served at the defense of Fort Mifflin, on Mud Island.

Jacob M. Kunkel's father, John Kunkel, came to Frederick Town in 1809, and engaging first in business as a distiller, was later extensively engaged in tanning, which he followed until his death, July 13, 1861. It may suffice to show in what esteem he was held to say that he was known far and wide as "Honest John Kunkel." He was in the service a few months during 1812 as a light-horseman, and in 1820 was a member of the board of aldermen of Frederick. His wife was Elizabeth Baker, of Lancaster County, Pa., whose ancestors did valiant service in the Revolutionary struggle. One of her uncles was a colonel in the Federal army.

Jacob M. Kunkel's early education was obtained at St. John's Catholic Seminary. Ill health obliged him to desist from his studies, and in 1835, he journeyed to the West in company with Rev. Charles Reighly, a former pastor of the German Reformed Church of Frederick, and under his tuition pursued his education at Monroe, Mich., during the following two or three years. Upon his return to Frederick about 1838 he entered Frederick College, and completed his education at the University of Virginia, Charlottesville, where he graduated with high honors. He was a member of the Jefferson Literary Society of the university, and one of its officers.

In 1844 he entered upon the study of the law with Joseph M. Palmer, and in October, 1845, was admitted to the Frederick bar. Later he became a law partner of ex-Governor Francis Thomas, and for many years conducted a successful legal practice. Jan. 3, 1848, in Frederick, he married Anna Mary, eldest daughter of Dr. John H. McElfresh, of Frederick City, one of the wealthiest and most influential landholders of Frederick County.

In 1849, Jacob M. Kunkel was nominated by the Democratic party to the State Senate, having for his opponent the late Gideon Bantz, reputed at that time to be the most popular Whig in the county, and gaining the election, served during his four years' term with much distinction. In 1857 he was elected by the Democracy to the Thirty-fifth Congress, defeating Hon. H. W. Hoffman, the Know-Nothing candidate, who had himself in 1855 beaten Hon. W. T. Hamilton for Congress. In 1859, Messrs. Kunkel and Hoffman were again rival congressional candidates, and, as before, Hoffman was compelled to strike his colors to his old competitor. Mr. Kunkel participated in the exciting incidents of 1861, and true to the doctrine of States rights, vehemently opposed the theory of coercion and centralization. At the expiration of his congressional term, with the session of 1861, he found his health sorely impaired, and thenceforward held himself retired from active political life, albeit he continued zealously to advocate, by such means as lay in his power, the principles of Democracy and the

JACOB M. KUNKEL.

interests of his party's candidates. He was esteemed throughout the State as a conscientious politician of high integrity and patriotic purposes. In bearing he was the polished and scholarly gentleman, genial in his hospitality and warm and lasting in his friendships. The latter years of his life were mainly spent in literary and scientific pursuits, amid the treasures of a large and valuable private library. Until 1866 he was a partner with his brother, John B., at Catoctin Furnace, and found occupation for his leisure also in the management of his landed estates. He was a member of the Protestant Episcopal Church, and at one time a vestryman therein. As already recorded, he died April 7, 1870. His widow survived him a little more than eight years, dying Dec. 12, 1878. Of their three children, a son and daughter died in youth. The remaining son, John I. Kunkel, resides with his family in the old Kunkel mansion in Frederick.

When it became definitely settled that Lafayette would visit Frederick, triumphal arches were erected, and the town was handsomely decorated with flags, bunting, etc. A handsome pavilion was also erected at the corner of Market and West Church Streets, the interior being tastefully ornamented with crimson silk, banners, etc.

Messrs. George Baer, Dr. John Tyler, Col. John McPherson, Gen. Thomas Contee Worthington, John L. Harding, and James F. Houston were appointed a committee to visit Baltimore and see Gen. Lafayette in order to perfect the arrangements for his visit. The day was fixed, and everything made ready for the demonstration. On the 29th of December, 1824, Gen. Lafayette, accompanied by his suite and Col. John H. Barney, Capt. Dubois, Mr. Matelin, Hezekiah Niles, Gen. Shepherd C. Leakin, John S. Skinner, and others, arrived in a stage at the Monocacy bridge late in the evening, where a large crowd was gathered to greet him. By the time Lafayette and his escort reached the city Frederick was thronged with an immense concourse of people. All sections of the county and adjoining counties were represented, and many had come from Virginia, Pennsylvania, South Carolina, and other States.

On the following day a dinner was given Lafayette at Talbott's City Hotel, Col. John McPherson presiding. A grand ball concluded the festivities.

After the general had left the country and returned to France, John S. Skinner, of Baltimore, had a number of agricultural seeds, and a collection of fowls, live 'possums, partridges, 'coons, etc., forwarded to him by a ship laden with tokens of national esteem. Among others, Mr. Philip Reich, of Frederick, sent him four or five ears of corn of a fine variety. This was highly prized, as the general had heartily enjoyed some corn-bread which he had eaten at Talbott's hotel. The receipt of the corn was acknowledged in his own handwriting, as follows:

"LAGRANGE, May 29, 1827.

"I am to acknowledge your kind letter of November 18th, and the welcome receipt of several precious kinds of corn, which are just arrived in time to be seasonably planted. While I feel as a farmer the merit of this gift, I have a particular pleasure in this obligation to you, and beg you, my dear sir, to accept my best thanks, with the assurance of my most sincere and friendly regard.
"LAFAYETTE.
"PHILIP REICH, ESQ."

The original of this letter is now in the hands of the Engelbrecht family, of Frederick.

The general left Frederick on the last day of December, 1824, accompanied by the mayor and some members of the committee of arrangements. He arrived at Rockville the same evening, and reached Georgetown on the 1st of January, 1825, where he was met by his old friend, James Monroe, the President of the United States. In a letter from Lagrange to a lady of Frederick, he declared that his reception there, on account of the incidents connected with it, was the most agreeable to his feelings of any he had received while in this country.

Gen. Lafayette was a very prominent member of the Masonic fraternity, and the apron which he wore while here among his brethren was presented to him by the late William Baer, and is now in possession of Columbia Lodge, of Frederick.

Centennial Celebration at Frederick.—On the 28th of June, 1876, was celebrated the one hundredth anniversary of the adoption by the Maryland Convention at Frederick of the resolution instructing the Maryland delegates to Congress to vote for the resolution declaring the provinces free and independent States. The convention assembled at Frederick on the 21st of June, 1776, and took the first decided action on the part of the colony looking to an armed contest with Great Britain. In the early part of 1876 a notice was issued calling for a meeting of citizens to take steps to commemorate the centennial anniversary of the county. On February 22d a meeting was accordingly held at the court-house. Gen. John A. Steiner was made temporary chairman, and the following permanent organization effected: President, Hon. John Ritchie; Vice-Presidents, James H. Gambrill and Col. Wm. Richardson; Secretary, H. K. Carmack; Treasurer, Wm. H. Falconer. A resolution was adopted authorizing the appointment of a County Central Centennial Committee, and the following persons were selected:

Hon. Richard H. Marshall, Hon. John A. Lynch, Gen. James M. Coale, Gen. Edward Shriver, Wm. J. Ross, Hon. Lewis H. Steiner, Frederick J. Nelson, Col. Charles E. Trail, Col. George R. Dennis, Dr. Fairfax Schley, John H. Williams, Milton G. Urner, C. V. S. Levy, James McSherry, J. W. Pearre, Hon. Wm. H. Hinks, Rev. George Diehl, D.D., Rev. John McCaffrey, D.D., Rev. R. H. Williams, Rev. E. R. Eschbach, D.D., Rev. O. Ingle, Rev. A. H. Ames, Rev. Charles Stonestreet, Rev. George T. Tyler, Rev. S. Gobricher, Rev. C. H. Littleton, Rev. J. L. Grimm, George F. Webster, Wm. P. Maulsby, Jr., F. Brengle, Noah Bowlus, J. E. R. Wood, J. C. Motter, Charles Cole, C. H. Keefer, J. Wm. Baughman, J. W. Kauffman, Otis Tyler, John Loats, George M. Potts, Calvin Page, P. B. Kunkel, Gideon Bantz, McClintock Young, Jacob Byerly, Henry Pampel, Benjamin Stewart, Edward Koontz, Gabriel Beckley, Col. J. T. Sinn, H. F. Steiner, Thos. M. Wolfe, Peter Sahm, C. C. Smith, Mayor Moberly, ex-Mayor Ebert, A. O. Baugher, Prof. Hackleton, Philip Stern, S. Kingsbacker, H. T. Mahler, G. W. Tyson, W. L. Duvall, C. Lerch, John H. Lampe, Lewis Koester, John C. Hardt, A. J. Wilcoxon, A. J. Delashmutt, Thomas E. Pope, Lewis Bruner, Adolphus Fox, J. Fenton Thomas, John Eisenhauer, Wm. Simmons, M. N. Rohrback, Aug. L. Eader, Prof. J. Engelbrecht, Philip M. Engelbrecht, L. S. Clingan, Z. James Gittinger, J. Alfred Ritter, John H. Abbott, Charles Kreh, Charles W. Miller, Benjamin Blackston, Wm. P. Rice, Thomas W. Morgan, John Kunkel, Henry M. Nixdorff, Wm. Need, Thomas Gorsuch, Dr. Wm. T. Wootton, Wm. F. Johnson, George W. Smith, Col. John B. Thomas, Edward Eichelberger, Louis Schley, L. O. Delashmutt, William C. Johnson.

The district committees were:

Buckeystown, No. 1.—Capt. Chiswell, William G. Baker, Otho Keller, John Delashmutt, Dr. Henry K. Fulton.

Middletown, No. 3.—George C. Roderick, John W. White, Vincent Sanner, Asa Bowlus, Dr. Charles J. Baer.

Creagerstown, No. 4.—Joshua Biggs, John W. Shaw, John W. Staub, Charles Stevens, Jacob Miller.

Emmittsburg, No. 5.—James M. Dwenn, Samuel Motter, Maj. Horner, David Agnew, Isaac S. Annan.

Catoctin, No. 6.—John W. Hoover, James C. Clarke, Daniel W. Blickenstaff, Daniel Leatherman, Dr. Lamar.

Urbana, No. 7.—Hon. Samuel Hinks, Charles E. Worthington, C. K. Thomas, Thomas A. Smith, Baker Jamison.

Liberty, No. 8.—Henry Baker, J. S. L. Roderick, Peter Lugenbeel, G. Gaither, Harry Boyle.

New Market, No. 9.—Dr. J. Downey, Grafton B. Hammond, Melville P. Wood, Hamilton Stier, William W. Ogborn.

Hauver's, No. 10.—Harvey Buhrman, Lewis Crawford, Valentine Harbaugh, Peter Hauver, Jos. B. Brown.

Woodsboro', No. 11.—Jacob M. Newman, John Snyder, L. N. Phillips, J. Hull Bowers, William Carmack.

Petersville, No. 12.—Hon. Outerbridge Horsey, M. W. Fout, Job M. Miller, Charles F. Wenner, John Morrison.

Mount Pleasant, No. 13.—E. L. Cramer, Dr. Stone, Joseph Routzahn, James Riddlemoser, David M. Scholl.

Jefferson, No. 14.—L. Culler, Columbus Dade, Ezra M. Thomas, Robert Boteler, George T. Whip.

Mechanicstown, No. 15.—John Landers, Dr. W. White, George H. Johnson, Maj. Charles A. Damuth, Charles E. Cassell.

Jackson, No. 16.—Upton Buhrman, Joseph Brown, Daniel V. Harp, Dr. G. W. Boteler, Jonas Doub.

Johnsville, No. 17.—Lot Hartsock, Ephraim Stoner, Thomas Jones, Maurice L. Starr, A. Henry Norris.

Woodville, No. 18.—Evan Wilson, Frederick S. Clary, William R. Dorsey, Moses Doty, Dr. J. Bromwell.

On the 25th of March (1876), the two hundred and forty-second anniversary of the landing of the Maryland Pilgrims, the committee met, and determined to hold the celebration in Frederick on the 28th of June, the hundredth anniversary of the order of the Convention of Maryland to her delegates to the Provincial Congress to vote for the declaration severing the connection of this with the mother-country.

At a subsequent meeting of the central committee, sub-committees were appointed to solicit contributions to defray the expenses necessarily incident to a proper observance of the day, and a programme was adopted, Col. S. Carmack being appointed chief marshal, with Col. Wm. Richardson and Lewis S. Clingan as aides, and Gen. Edward Shriver officer of the day.

It is needless to say that the citizens responded liberally to the solicitation for material aid, as they were determined to make their celebration in every way worthy of the event commemorated, and their patriotic efforts were crowned with the most gratifying success.

At three o'clock on the morning of the 28th the bells rang forth a merry hallelujah chorus, the rich diapasons of St. John's Catholic, the several fire-bells, the St. John's Reformed, and the chiming *Swelt* tones of the Evangelical Lutheran forming a perfect harmony with the dignified and majestic sub-bass of the Episcopal and Evangelical Reformed. All the public buildings and many private residences wore an aspect of floral loveliness at an early hour. Conspicuous in variety and beauty of ornamentation were the City and Central Hotels, Dill House, and Novitiate, all being profuse in loyal insignia. At the Novitiate a large streamer bearing the inscription "Ad Te Omnes Gentes Venient" (To Thee all Nations Come) was suspended from a fourth story window to the opposite side of the street. St. John's College was also gayly dressed. At 8 A.M. the different fire companies, tradesmen, and various organizations assembled on North Market Street, the right resting on Sixth. About 9.30 A.M. the procession moved down Market Street in the following order:

Squad of Policemen.
Chief Marshal—Col. Samuel Carmack.
Aides—Col. William Richardson and Lewis S. Clingan.
Frederick Cornet Band.
Orators, Poet, Clergy.
Old Soldiers of 1812.
Judges of Circuit Court and County Officers.
Middletown Cornet Band.
Mayor, Aldermen, and Common Council.

CORNELIUS STALEY.

Independent Hose Company, No. 1
(having three engines drawn by horses, and two reels handsomely decorated with flowers, flags, etc., drawn by members of the company. An Indian chief in full costume, accompanied by a squaw, surmounted the first engine. On the second appeared a young lady representing the Goddess of Liberty; on the third four full-rigged sailor-boys. Eighty-six members of this company were in the line of march, each wearing a green badge).

Junior Fire Company.
(Engine drawn by four horses, and two hose-carriages, which had been recently painted, were all tastefully decorated. The engine was manned by four sons of America, dressed in Continental costume. Their uniform consisted of dark pantaloons, white shirts, straw hats, trimmed with pink ribbon, and red cuffs, inscribed "Junior." Thirty-seven little girls in white, in an open wagon, supplemented the display of the Junior Fire Company.)

Chippewa Tribe, No. 19, I. O. R. M.,
With war-clubs, tomahawks, bows and arrows, etc.
Delaware Tribe, No. 19, of Berlin, Md.
Frederick City Lodge, Knights of Pythias.
The Harrugari Order.
Woodsborough Band.
Fredonia Council, No. 46, O. U. A. M.,

followed by a large number of tastefully-decorated wagons, representing various trades and business interests of the city.

The programme of exercises at the Court-house Square was as follows:

Martial Music—"Hail Columbia."
Organization.
Prayer—By Rev. Dr. George Diehl.
Centennial Hymn.
Martial Music—"America."
President's Address—Hon. John Ritchie.
Hymn—"Our Country."
Martial Music—"Washington's March."
Reading of Declaration of Independence—By Dr. Lewis H. Steiner.
Hymn—"Star Spangled Banner."
Poem—By Col. Charles E. Trail.
Hymn—"My Country 'Tis of Thee."
Martial Music—"Yankee Doodle."
Address—By James McSherry.
Hymn—"Hail Columbia."
Martial Music—"Marseillaise."
Address—By Milton G. Urner.
Hymn—"Voices of Freedom."
Martial Music—"Our Flag is There."
Prayer—By Rev. R. H. Williams.
Hymn—"Before the Lord We Bow."
Doxology—"Praise God," etc.
Benediction—Rev. E. R. Eschbach.

Nearly every private residence in the city, as well as the stores and public buildings, were decorated with bunting, flowers, etc.

One of the interesting features of the day was the presence of a number of the veterans of the war of 1812, among whom were the following:

John Degrange and John Pampell, of Capt. Nicholas Turbott's company; Frederick Hawman, of Capt. George W. Grit's company; Reuben Grove, of Capt. John Brengle's company; Daniel Heffner, of Capt. Joseph's Wood's company; Jacob Aubert, of Capt. Jacob Getzendanner's company; George Marquert, of Capt. Davidson's company, D. C. Mr. Marquert is a native of Frederick Town, but was attached to Capt. Davidson's company of the District of Columbia. Capt. Davidson's infantry, Capt. Stull's rifles, and Capt. George Peter's artillery formed a brigade of the District of Columbia militia. Francis Scott Key, of Georgetown, and George Peabody were high privates in Capt. Stull's company. Mr. Marquert mustered with Key and Peabody, and cherished a friendly recollection for the great philanthropist and the author of the "Star Spangled Banner."

At night there was a handsome display of fireworks, followed by a brilliant centennial ball.

Cornelius Staley, one of the best-known of Frederick County's citizens, was born near Frederick City, Oct. 22, 1808, and traces his ancestry back through at least three generations of Frederick County citizens, his great-grandfather having come from Germany shortly after 1740. His grandfather, Jacob, was born about 1747, and his father, John, in 1777. Frederick County was likewise the birthplace of his maternal grandfather, whose daughter Margaret, born 1780, was the mother of the subject of this notice. Cornelius Staley was married Nov. 17, 1829, in Washington County, to Ruanna, daughter of Adam and Catharine Snively, of the county last named. Their living children are Mrs. Marietta C. Doub and Mrs. Antoinette F. Gambrill. Mr. Staley's life from birth has been passed almost exclusively upon the farm, and it is his boast that he has earned the right to be considered a true "son of the soil." His education was limited to the benefits derived from the common schools of the day, and as he was trained in the religious faith advocated by the United Brethren in Christ, so in that faith he has ever steadfastly continued. Political honors have never been to his liking, for in the humble and quiet pursuits of his business as an agriculturalist he has found the greater satisfaction of winning golden opinions as a citizen and neighbor. He was, however, persuaded in 1836 to accept from the Governor of Maryland an appointment for three years as justice of the peace. In 1841 he was chosen to the Legislature, and in 1843 a member of the board of county commissioners. Mr. Staley's military record includes a brief experience in 1844 as first lieutenant of the Ringgold Dragoons, a famous military organization of that day. For many years he has been a stanch supporter of and laborer for the best interests of the County Agricultural Society. He served as president of the society in 1859 and 1860, and is at present a member of the board of managers.

Water-Works.—At an election held March 28, 1825, at "Talbott's Hotel," for directors of the Frederick Water Company, the following were chosen for the ensuing year: John McPherson, John Kunkel, Gideon Bantz, Stephen Steiner, John L. Harding, Abraham Shriver, William Tyler, and Henry Koontz. On the 31st they examined the neighboring sources of water, and on April 18th opened the subscription-books for stock at the Branch Bank. John McPherson was elected president of the board, and Thomas Shriver, superintendent of the works.

The directors were as follows:

In 1826, John McPherson, Abraham Shriver, John Kunkel, Jacob Shriver, William C. Russell, Thomas W. Morgan, William Tyler, Henry Koontz; in 1827, John McPherson, Richard Potts, John Kunkel, Henry Koontz, Thomas Carlton, D. Schley, Rev. D. A. Schaeffer, William Tyler; in 1828, John McPherson, Richard Potts, David F. Schaeffer, William Tyler, William B. Tyler, Henry Koontz, John Kunkel, John Baltzell.

The last election for directors, as far as learned from the minutes of this company, was held March 23, 1838, when the following were chosen: Richard Potts, William Tyler, George Baltzell, Gideon Bantz, W. R. Sanderson, Frederick Nursz, John C. Fritchie, Lewis Medtart. The water was brought partly in wooden pipes from a spring two and a half miles northwest of the city to a reservoir one mile distant from the corporation, and thence supplied to the town. It was very inadequate to the public wants.

In 1839 the city took into consideration the question of building works, and an act of the Assembly of that year granted it the franchise for a lottery of $75,000, which it sold to parties in Baltimore for the benefit of its water-works fund. In 1844, by act of December of that year, the city borrowed $30,000 to aid in the construction of the works, and in October of 1845 made another loan of $8000 to complete them. These works cost about $90,000. From the receiver at the foot of the mountain to the works proper is a distance of two and a half miles, and from thence to the city about one mile.

The building of the water-works began Sept. 19, 1844, and were completed Nov. 22, 1845.

The principal engineer was F. Erdman; assistant engineer, Geo. Erdman; and superintendents, Winchester Clingan, Wm. Baltzell, and Samuel Carmack.

The following were the aldermen and councilmen under whose administration they were built:

Aldermen, Gideon Bantz, Ezra Houck, Peter S. Storm, Calvin Page, David J. Markey; Councilmen, Jacob Keller, Henry Boteler, Geo. Koontz, Wm. Kolb, Peter Goodmanson, Daniel Derr, Henry Young.

Gas-Works.—In October, 1849, Geo. R. Fischer prepared to furnish Frederick City with illuminating gas. A large number of hands were put to work in laying pipes on Patrick, Church, and Court Streets. The entire work was completed in a few weeks, and gas was used in the city before New Year's. This was the feeble beginning of the Isabella Gas Company, which during an existence thus far of thirty-three years has passed beyond the most sanguine expectations of its organizers, and proved untrue the evil predictions of those who first prophesied its failure. Hon. Charles E. Trail has been its president for many years. The Citizens' Gas Company was organized in October, 1878. Its officers have been from its organization as follows: President, G. J. Doll; Treasurer, C. V. S. Levy; Directors, F. P. Carlin, Calvin Page, C. V. S. Levy, G. J. Doll. Its works are on East Patrick Street.

Among those who have been identified with the material interests of Frederick, and who have aided by their capital and influence works of public improvement, is William Michael Feaga. He comes of Revolutionary stock, and boasts an ancestry in Frederick County extending back to 1783, when his grandfather, Philip Feaga, a German, located a farm near Frederick City. He was one of the Hessian allies in the British army during the Revolution, and in common with hundreds of his fellow-countrymen, resolved, upon the termination of the campaign, to make America his home. In 1788 he purchased the place now owned by Wm. M. Feaga, rebuilt the mill he found there, and resided upon the property until his death, which took place about 1827. His son George—born in May, 1786, and deceased in 1865—was father to the worthy gentleman whose name heads this article, and whose birth occurred on the old homestead June 4, 1820. Mr. Feaga's maternal grandfather was Jacob Trout, himself born in Frederick County, whither *his* father came from Germany and made his home in the then dense wilderness. Jacob Trout was a captain in the war of the Revolution, and as a further instance of how the Feaga blood flowed bright and quickly in the stormy days, it may be remarked that old Philip Feaga walked from Frederick to Baltimore, determined to enlist for the fight, but, unfortunately for his hopes, was rejected because of his extreme age. One of his sons (Frederick) fought in that war, while of Jacob Trout's sons John entered the war of 1812, and Jacob, Jr., the campaign against the Indians, in which he was doubtless killed, since he was not heard of afterward. William M. Feaga received his school education from the district pedagogue, and from his youth to the present day has milled and farmed upon the old homestead, save for a period of two years, 1866-67, when he filled the office of collector and treasurer of the county. The mill now carried on by him, it may be interesting to note, has been in possession of a Feaga ever since 1788. To the opening of the war of the Rebellion he was an unflinching Jackson Democrat. With the sounding of the war tocsin he cast his allegiance on the side of the Union,

WILLIAM MICHAEL FEAGA.

and when the war closed he gave his adherence to the Republican party. Trained in the Lutheran faith, he has steadily upheld it by his influence and countenance. In 1844 he married Susanna Maria, daughter of Frederick Ramsburg, a veteran of the war of 1812, and one of Frederick County's early settlers. By his marriage with Miss Ramsburg, Mr. Feaga had nine children, of whom six are living. The sons are Edmund Pendleton, Elmer Butler, and Josiah Ramsburg. After a union of thirty-three years, Mr. Feaga lost his wife, Dec. 20, 1877. Oct. 18, 1881, he married again, choosing for his second consort Miss Hester Ann Rogers Preston, daughter of Charles Preston. Her father was born near Frederick City in 1789, where *his* father, Francis (an Englishman), made a settlement many years before. Mrs. Feaga's maternal grandfather was Thomas Baldwin, a native of Annapolis, and a descendant of one of the earliest comers to the Eastern Shore of Maryland.

The Great Flood.—On July 24, 1848, occurred the most terrible flood ever experienced in Frederick City. Fortunately no lives were lost, but the damage to property amounted to nearly half a million dollars. The rain commenced falling on the night previous, and continued some time, soaking the ground to a considerable depth, but on the next morning (Friday) about eight o'clock it fell in torrents, and rained without intermission until after dinner, and in less than half an hour Market Street was covered with water, and by ten o'clock it was sweeping through the lower part of the city at a fearful rate, carrying off bridges, stables, tan-yards, outhouses, and even dwellings. The water in Carroll Creek rose so rapidly that the people in that section of the city did not have time to remove a thing from their houses, and the consequence was a great many lost everything they had. Among the heavy losers were John Loats and Gideon Bantz, the damage to their tan-yards being very great, as they both lost considerable quantities of leather and bark, independent of the injury done their buildings and machinery. Messrs. Hardt & Keefer lost a large amount of lumber. The residents in the vicinity of the creek suffered heavily. The house of Mr. Beckley was washed away as the last member of his family was leaving. The livery-stables, confectionery-shops, millinery-stores, and other places of business on South Market Street from the corner of Patrick to car corner suffered terribly, Hood & Crane losing a number of buggies, with many other valuable articles. On West Patrick Street the damage was equally as great. All the houses from George Smith's, on the other side of the Bentztown bridge, to Lewis H. Doll's tobacco-store were flooded, causing a great injury to furniture, carpeting, etc., and sweeping away the contents of gardens and fences, pavements, porches, and numerous back buildings. The corner of the house adjoining the creek on the south side of the street was carried away, and other buildings in the immediate vicinity were so much damaged that they had to be torn down and rebuilt. Ramsburg & Bro. were heavy sufferers. The water in their store ran over the counter and destroyed large quantities of groceries and other articles. The boot and shoe store of L. M. Nixdorff suffered considerably, as did all in that neighborhood. The beer establishment of John Lipps was so damaged as to necessitate rebuilding. Farther up the same side of the street the rush of the water was fearful, and on the opposite side it reached the second story of some houses, knocking topsy-turvy everything it came in contact with. In Brewers' Alley the destruction was very great. Mr. Peter Bear was a heavy loser. The bridge over the creek at this point was swept away, together with seven other bridges in different sections of the city, which cost over $20,000 to rebuild. Following the creek from Brewers' Alley down to Market Street, and thence to Carroll Street, nothing but ruin and destruction met the eye. The barrel-factory of G. Koontz, on Carroll Street, together with a lot of barrels and cooper stuff, was washed away, involving a heavy loss to the proprietor, and throwing many employés out of work. The house of Joseph Nelson was completely flooded, and it was only by the timely assistance rendered that his family were saved from drowning. That part of S. G. Groshon's warehouse adjoining the creek was swept off, also the back building of the house occupied by Mrs. Dayhoff. Many valuable horses were lost, among them two of Gideon Bantz', one of Mrs. Norris', one of Dr. Fairfax Schley's, one of Oliver Myers', one of Jacob Schmidt's, one of L. M. Hildebrand's, and one of Peter Bear's. It is impossible to give a list of all who suffered. F. Y. Rhodes and family, finding the water about to inundate their premises, started to find a place of safety, and had scarcely got across the bridge ere it fell into the sweeping current. His store was drenched from the floor to the ceiling, destroying the major part of his confectioneries, with other injuries to carpets, etc. Charles E. Myers, while attempting to rescue some horses in the stable of his brother across the creek, was obliged by the rising waters to seek refuge on the top of the stable, and was only relieved from his perilous position by a rope thrown to him. A. M. Baughman, employed at the foundry of McClintock Young, started home, wading in the water, but was caught up and carried down on driftwood to the stone bridge on the Baltimore pike, where the drift lodged. In this way he was enabled to escape. Mrs. Pampel, seeking to escape from her house on West Patrick Street, was barely rescued just as the advancing waters were about to carry her off. Mrs. Paris Corey, of West Patrick Street, came near being lost in escaping from the lower to the higher part of her house. The damage in Middletown Valley was immense, being over one hundred and fifty thousand dollars; also along the Linganore, where not a mill-dam was left. Capt. John Spargo, a merchant at New London, was accidentally drowned while attempting to save some property. For over a week following all railroad communication with Baltimore was cut off, and the mails were greatly impeded and delayed.

Notable Storms.—The first week of March, 1767, was remarkable for its heavy storms. On Monday evening, the 2d, it rained hard; on Tuesday, the 3d, there was another heavy rain and high, destructive wind; on the 4th, 5th, and 6th there was more rain and a severe wind from the northeast. By these heavy rains the rivers and streams were swollen so much above their usual height that many bridges, mills, and dams were swept away, and much other damage done. The tide rose at Annapolis to a very great height. On Saturday, the 7th, two persons attempting to ride across Patapsco Falls were drowned, and Joseph Goodman, a blacksmith, while fording a stream was also lost. In one part of the Potomac the river rose forty-five feet higher than it had been in the summer, and the Monocacy rose about fifteen feet. Many houses, cattle, horses, etc., were carried away and lost. In the sugar-lands the flood made prodigious havoc, about four hundred hogsheads of tobacco being destroyed. There was another flood on the 5th of October, 1786, the creek which runs through the town rising suddenly in the night, many persons not being apprised of the danger had their stock carried away by the current. Several persons whose dwellings bordered on the creek, and who were confined to their beds with sickness, came near perishing before assistance could be afforded them. People who had resided near the Monocacy for sixty years stated that the waters of that creek rose ten feet higher than was ever before known, and the inhabitants sustained considerable losses, as many dwelling-houses, grist-mills, and saw-mills were destroyed or carried off.

May 16, 1803, there was a tremendous hail-storm, accompanied with thunder and lightning. The weather during the previous six weeks had been unusually cold, and the fruits were destroyed by the frost. Some of the hail-stones measured three and a half inches in circumference.

June 26, 1826, there was a freshet in Carroll's Creek, and considerable damage was done to the gardens of Jacob Englebrecht, Mr. Retmyer, Joseph Talbott, and Dr. Duvall, with others. Along the Monocacy hay, wheat sheaves, rye, logs, fences, etc., were swept away.

April 20, 1828, another flood in Carroll's Creek.

May 26, 1828, another severe hail-storm, hail falling as large as pigeon-eggs.

Sept. 29, 1837, freshet in Carroll's Creek.

March 5, 1838, another flood in the creek; gardens overflowed, and many houses full of water.

Nov. 2, 1846, there was a flood in Carroll's Creek, the highest since 1821.

Oct. 7, 1847, there was another fearful freshet; bridges were swept away, gardens washed out, and buildings damaged.

Aug. 12, 1848, there was another great freshet in the creek.

Aug. 6, 1855, high water in the Monocacy within five feet of the tops of the abutments of the bridge.

Feb. 2, 1876.—The wind-storm which passed over the county and city of Frederick between two and six o'clock A.M., and which came directly from the west, was one of the most terrible and destructive ever experienced in that section of the country. For several hours it raged with unabated fury, and created the greatest consternation in almost every household. Quite a number of houses, stables, etc., in the city were unroofed and otherwise damaged, and the débris scattered in the streets and gardens. The steeple of the Episcopal church, one hundred and thirty-five feet high, was blown down, and in falling crushed a portion of the roof of the Central National Bank building, occupied by Col. G. R. Dennis, the president of the bank, and his family as a residence. Fortunately no one was injured. The damage to both buildings was between three thousand and four thousand dollars.

The State Deaf and Dumb Institution had a number of window-glasses broken and the roof slightly injured, and considerable damage was done to Montevue Hospital. In the country a great deal of loss was incurred. At Jefferson a church steeple was blown down, and at Mechanicstown the Lutheran church was completely unroofed. Numerous houses also were damaged at these and other towns, and a number of fine stables and barns in the country were partially demolished. Among the latter were those of Nelson B. Ramsburg, Rev. A. E. Wallis, and Thomas Anderson. The destruction of fencing, etc., was very great, and at various places the roads were blockaded by large trees which had been torn up by the roots.

Record of Events.—In July, 1757, Alexander McKeafy and Samuel Wilson were shot and killed near Frederick Town. This was probably during the Indian war. On the 22d of October, 1773, four convicts who had murdered their master, Archibald Moffmar, were executed at Frederick.

In December, 1798, Upton Bruce, a member of the House of Delegates from Frederick County, asked leave to bring in a bill entitled an "Act for the gradual abolition of slavery." There was some opposition developed, and Mr. Bruce withdrew his motion.

In November, 1763, about twenty Indians made an inroad into the "Great Cove" and killed Christopher Fiddler, Charles Stewart, and Thomas Enery, burning the house of William Nox, taking him and his family of eight persons prisoners, and murdering one of his children. They were pursued but escaped.

1819.—Methodist Episcopal Church camp-meeting began on Mr. John Devilbiss' farm, near Lewistown.

Oct. 4th.—Great Masonic procession.

1820.—German Reformed Synod met, in May.

The Catoctin Mountain, northwest of town, on fire, extending ten miles, and was extinguished by a heavy snow falling, April 2d.

August 27th.—Annual Methodist Episcopal Church camp-meeting in progress on land of John Devilbiss, near Lewistown.

November 18th.—Officers of First Frederick Dragoons elected, viz.: Captain, John McPherson, Jr.; First Lieutenant, John Rigney; Second Lieutenant, Thomas J. Graham; Cornet, George McLane.

Artillery: Captain, Lewis Green; First Lieutenant, John Buckey; Ensign, Matthias E. Bartgis.

First Frederick Guards: Captain, James F. Houston; First Lieutenant, Samuel Webster; Ensign, William Russell.

1821.—January 30th. Samuel Frey, the "converted Jew," preached in Reformed church.

March 21st.—The jury in the case of Abraham Shivers vs. *The Political Examiner*, for libel, returned a verdict of "not guilty."

July 2d.—Freshet carried off part of the stone bridge on Market Street, at Hallerstown, and was very high on Patrick Street as far as Reitmyer's on the turnpike.

July 23d.—The water in Carroll Creek was higher than it had been for thirty-three years, and William Perry lost two horses in the flood while attempting to cross the road between Ezra Dill's and William Springer's. The water in Market Street was as high as George Bentz', and in Patrick up to Jacob Scales'.

September 1st.—Two large Republican barbecues held, one on Maryland Tract, the other at Trout's place, four miles northwest.

September 3d.—Lutheran State Synod met in Frederick.

September 14th.—The first number of *Republican Citizen and State Advertiser* appeared.

September 18th.—A band of music was formed, composed of John Englebrecht, George Lowe, William Englebrecht, J. D. England, Ezra Doll, Adam Wolffe, Eli Moberly, Jacob Englebrecht, Charles Heckert.

September.—General prevalence of fever and ague.

September 24th.—Bell procured for court-house steeple.

1822.—January 1st. The "Mathenian Association" selected the following managers: Cyrus Mantz, George Englebrecht, William Jenkins, Jr., Edward Trail, Philip Reich.

February.—The attempted impeachment of Judge Abraham Shriver, of the Fifth Judicial District, by the Legislature resulted in his acquittal.

March 24th.—Doctor Horwitz was giving lessons in Hebrew.

May.—Capt. Thomas W. Morgan commanded the "Independent Blues."

August 3d.—"Harmonic Band" organized.

September 6th.—Camp-meeting began on land of John Larkin, seven miles from town.

December 17th.—The dwelling-house of Jacob Weinbrenner burned with all the contents, and family barely saved their lives.

1823.—January 20th. Col. Steiner circulated a petition to have a bridge built over the Potomac at Harper's Ferry.

April 25th.—Roger Brooke Taney had a public sale of his household goods, preparatory to his departing to Baltimore to locate.

May 31st.—William Patterson (negro) was publicly whipped at court-house for stealing from his master.

June 26th.—A fire in the house of B. S. Pigman, on Court Street, occupied by A. Bladen as dwelling, and by Francis Thomas and Benjamin Price as law offices.

July 4th.—General celebration, reading of Declaration of Independence by James M. Shellman, and an oration by Benjamin Price.

July 12th.—Lutheran Church purchased of Worthington Johnson twenty and three-quarter acres of land at the east end of Church Street for a graveyard, at five hundred dollars.

July 15th.—Col. A. Fenwick, Dr. William Howard, and William Price, canal commissioners, left Frederick for Poplar Springs to locate the canal. The cavalcade consisted of two wagons and sixty hands.

August 5th.—Mr. Jenkins and his horses were killed by lightning at Mr. Kephart's tavern during a hail-storm, in which hail fell larger than hen's eggs.

August 13th.—Meeting of canal delegates from different cities at court-house to organize for Ohio and Chesapeake Canal. The committee from Frederick were John Graham, John McPherson, Grafton Duvall, William Goldsborough, B. S. Pigman, William Tyler, and Singleton Duvall, who was secretary of the meeting.

September 4th.—Col. John McPherson purchased the mill of the late James Robertson, at the mouth of Linganore Creek, near Monocacy bridge, for thirty-five thousand five hundred dollars.

September 26th.—Political meeting addressed by W. P. Farquhar, Dr. Henry Baker, Benjamin Yingling, William Schley, and Frederick Darkis.

October 8th.—Market opened at Bentztown market-house.

December 15th.—Gen. Winfield Scott passed through Frederick.

1824.—January 7th. Great excitement about ghosts seen in the tavern-stand lately kept by Charles Humrichouse, but none of the spirits were caught.

May 1st.—Militia parade-officers: Captains, James S. Weaver, Jacob Houck, Samuel Houston, Samuel Webster, David Springle, Winchester Clingan, Philip Pypher; Lieutenants Thomas Dean, Henry Stowell, Daniel Kolb, George Lowe, Eli Moberly, Thomas Dean, Levi Davis; Ensigns, J. J. McCully Augustus F. Ebert, William Doherty.

May 25th.—Gen. Andrew Jackson, of Tennessee, passed through Frederick.

October 4th.—"Warren Greens," "Frederick Blues," artillery, and a troop of horse marched to Baltimore to welcome Lafayette.

December 7th.—An attempt made to rob the Winchester mail four miles from town.

December 29th.—Marquis de Lafayette arrived in Frederick at four P.M. He was received with as much pomp and parade as in any other city.

1825.—January 1st. At election of officers of "Mathenian Association," George Englebrecht was chosen president, J. N. Hoffman secretary, and John Cook treasurer.

April 9th.—In the Lutheran graveyard, at the east end of Church Street, recently laid off in lots twelve feet square and sold at twelve dollars a lot, was buried Miss Prudencia Ebert, daughter of John Ebert, the first interment in this burial-ground.

April 20th.—Corner-stone laid for the rebuilding and enlarging of Lutheran church.

May 27th.—William Peter Pauli appointed letter-carrier and penny post for Frederick Town and vicinity.

May 26th.—Cattle-show at Mrs. Cooekerley's tavern, Monocacy bridge, at which Geo. M. Conradt was awarded five dollars for best piece of carpeting, Geo. Wissinger two dollars for best linen, and John Hall two dollars for best piece of diaper.

June 13th.—The addition to Frederick at west end of Patrick Street was laid out by Col. Stephen Steiner and Stephen Ramsburg. It is now called "Battle Town," from a small encounter between Col. Steiner and Stephen Klein, the first resident of the addition. The people first called it "Stephensburg," from the three Stephens connected with it as aforesaid. After that it was called "Ratsville," from the great number of rats in its vicinity.

June 17th.—Anthony St. John Baker, British consul-general; Hon. Mr. De Malitz, Russian secretary of legation; and Mrs. Iturbide, ex-Empress of Mexico, passed through town.

July 4th.—Richard H. Marshall delivered the oration at the court-house. There was a barbecue at "Bentz' Pump."

August 15th.—Lewis Medtart appointed postmaster, *vice* Col. James Fisher Houston, resigned, and removed the office to his dwelling next the market-house.

August 24th.—Francis Scott Key delivered an address at the Reformed church.

November 18th.—The Duke of Saxe-Weimar was in Frederick; called on Rev. D. F. Schaeffer and John Schley; then went to Washington.

1826.—June 2d. All Saints' Church used its new organ for the first time, made by Wilfred Hall, of Philadelphia, for seven hundred dollars.

July 4th.—The day celebrated by addresses by L. P. W. Walsh and Rev. D. F. Schaeffer.

July 2d.—General meeting of sorrow in memory of Thomas Jefferson and John Adams, who died on July 4, 1826. Suspension of all business. Oration at Lutheran church by Dr. John Tyler. The citizens all wore crape on their left arms for thirty days. All the military companies and various orders and societies marched in the procession from the court-house to the church. All arrangements were made by a committee appointed at the "town-meeting" on the 16th, viz.: Geo. Baer, Col. John McPherson, Col. John Ritchie, Maj. John Graham, Maj. Peter Mantz, John Schley, William Ross, Grafton Duvall, John L. Harding, John Kunkel, Stephen Steiner, Geo. Baltzell, and Geo. W. Evitt.

September 17th.—Carter, a young Cherokee Indian (half-breed), addressed the Sunday-schools.

1727.—January 23d. "Orphan Society" organized; officers elected, President, Charles Cassini; Secretary, Aug. F. Ebert; Treasurer, John Englebrecht.

July 6th.—The oldest man in Frederick was Daniel Hauer, Sr., born in Lotheringen, Germany, Aug. 24, 1769. He came to America a passenger on the same ship with Baron DeKalb, and settled in Frederick in 1771.

October 25th.—"The Young Men's Bible Society of Frederick County" elected the following directors: from Lutheran Church, Geo. Englebrecht, A. F. Egbert, John Hanshaw, Jacob Englebrecht; from Episcopalian, Clottworthy Birnie, Jr., John A. Donne, Wm. J. Ross, Thos. Shriver; from German Reformed, Dr. Henry Staley, Lewis Ramsbaugh, Wm. Helfenstein, Seth Thomson; from Presbyterian, J. M. Shelman, Dr. Albert Ritchie, Robt. McLaird, J. G. McNeely; from Methodist, Godfrey Koontz, Geo. Koontz, Geo. Salmon, and Wm. Marvin.

1828.—April 19th. A black man of Dr. Tyler's, while digging clay in the doctor's brickyard, found a box of money, containing, as supposed, about two thousand dollars in specie.

July 4th.—James M. Cole delivered the oration. Baltimore and Ohio Railroad formally commenced at Baltimore by Charles Carroll of Carrollton, and at Washington the Ohio and Chesapeake Canal began by President J. Q. Adams.

December 5th.—Jonathan Edwards Woodbridge opened a school at Prospect Hill, one mile west of town, at Schnertzell's old building.

1829.—January. Balloon ascension.

February 8th.—Andrew Jackson, President-elect, arrived in Frederick *en route* to Washington, and stayed over-night at Talbott's tavern.

February 23d.—Municipal vote at election: for mayor, Thomas Carlton 324, Geo. Kolb 208; for aldermen, Geo. Schultz 233, Jacob Faubel 227, Geo. W. Evitt 223, Samuel Carmack 223, John Kunkel 206 (all five were elected), Henry Kemp 205, Frederick Stoner 204, Jacob Englebrecht 204, Andrew Hein 197, Geo. Hauer 144, Geo. Houck 130, David Boyd 116, John McDonald 104, Jacob Brunner 88, Peter Kephart 51, N. Turbutt 15.

March 16th.—Henry Clay arrived in Frederick, and on the 18th the Adams men gave him a dinner.

May 16th.—Jacob Rohr appointed postmaster by President Jackson, *vice* Lewis Medtart.

July 2d.—Very cold, and on June 29th light snow.

About 1829 an entire family named Newey, seven in number, residing on the South Mountain, Frederick County, near Smithsburg, was murdered by a man named Markley, who was tried before Chief Justice John Buchanan, and convicted and hung in Frederick County.

1830.—June 7th. Work on the branch of the railroad from Frederick to Frederick Junction began.

August 4th.—Methodist camp-meeting began on land of David Bowlus, near High Knob.

August 17th.—The troop of horse under Capt. W. S. McPherson called out to suppress a rebellion of laborers on the railroad. Capt. Carmack's company of infantry also went.

September 17th.—Laying of track on the railroad began near the depot.

October 31st.—United States General Synod of Lutheran Church met at Frederick.

John Nelson appointed in October special minister to Naples by President Jackson.

December 1st.—Baltimore and Ohio Railroad opened as far as Frederick.

December 3d.—Trains began running regularly to Baltimore.

1832.—February 27th. Municipal election: for mayor, Thos. Carlton 298, Lewis Medtart 236; for aldermen, Daniel Kolb 300, Gideon Bantz 292, Thos. W. Morgan 257, David Boyd 217, Abraham Kemp 200, Casper Quynn 176, Jacob Faubel 117, Geo. W. Ent 108, Samuel Carmack 106, Andrw Heim 93, Wm. Kolb,

Sr., 77, John Kunkel 70, George Shultz 69, William Fisher 62, Henry Nixdorff 59. John S. Miller, Frederick Goehler, Lewis Birely, N. Turbutt, John McDonald, John Fressler, and Philip Hauptman each had less than 59. The councilmen elected by wards were: 1st, George Wissinger; 2d, Wm. Small; 3d, Jacob Keller; 4th, Philip Rohr; 5th, Samuel B. Lewis; 6th, George B. Shope; 7th, William Ely.

April 18th.—Railroad from Monocacy Viaduct to Point of Rocks finished.

April 23d (Easter Monday).—The "Columbus" car went from Frederick to Point of Rocks, first trip, with fifty passengers.

May 21st.—The streets lighted for the first time with lamps, and Clement Hilton and John Haller appointed lighters.

June 23d.—Three military companies formed: "Everhart Grays," commanded by Capt. Samuel Carmack; "Independent Blues," by Capt. Wm. Small; and "Worthington Blues," by Morris J. Jones.

July 4th.—The day was one of humiliation and prayer, with services in the churches, on account of the cholera prevailing all over the land.

July 5th.—Jacob Hart purchased of the Levy Court the old almshouse in Bentztown for two thousand four hundred dollars.

August 5th.—Camp-meeting in progress near Lewistown, on Mr. Devilbiss' land.

October 17th.—Jacob Ijams killed on the railroad by being run over by the engine while asleep on the track near Crum's farm.

In September and October, 1832, the cholera prevailed to an alarming extent in Frederick City. There were sixty-two deaths recorded in fifty-two days, and there were probably others not recorded.

That dreadful scourge, scarlet fever, prevailed for over two months, and during the time of the cholera mostly. It proved as fatal to children as the cholera among the grown people. It subsided in the latter part of November, 1832.

December 4th.—Lawrence Noland run over by the cars, between Frederick and Point of Rocks, and instantly killed.

1833.—April 22d. The celebrated Indian chief Black Hawk, his two sons, the Prophet, and two warriors stayed at Frederick all night.

August 23d.—Eight hundred and sixty-seven houses in Frederick, a gain of two hundred and twenty since June 27, 1817.

November 13th.—Falling stars in greatest profusion.

1834.—April 4th. A negro preached in Lutheran church.

April 15th.—A woman preached in Methodist church.

April 17th.—Rev. John Newland Maffett preached.

May 13th.—A sailor painted Reformed church steeple, and on the top of steeple fired off a pistol and drank a health to the town. On May 25th lightning struck above the steeple, shattering the top.

September 12th.—Mr. Simpson ascended in a balloon from academy yard and went three-fourths of a mile.

September 20th.—Lutheran camp-meeting in Loudon County, Va., at which hundreds from Frederick attended.

November 4th.—Sale of the estate of the late John Brien at public vendue, viz.: Ritchie's farm south of town, 328 acres, to Wm. Lorman, $80.30 per acre; the mansion-house fronting the court-house to F. A. Schley, $7050; the four houses (or block), the corner to Dr. R. E. Dorsey, $2025, second to James Raymond, $1710, third to J. M. Cole, $1690, fourth to E. A. Lynch, $2390; lot in Second Street, next to Presbyterian church, to Mahlon Talbott, $1700; "Hermitage Farm," of 748 acres, to John Schley, $26,367; (Lilly's) triangular farm south of town, 35 acres, to E. B. McPherson, $2400; and the mountain land to Wm. Lorman at $6.60 per acre.

December 10th.—Dr. Lewis Weltzsheimer, an apothecary in 1800, died.

1836.—July 4th. Celebration: two companies, under Capts. Hoskins and Small, one from Baltimore, and one from Winchester, marched in the procession; oration by Wm. P. Mausby, and in the afternoon barbecue at Monocacy.

August 23d.—Mill Alley, or Bentz Street, paved with stones.

September 2d.—Hallerstown bridge built.

October 27th.—Railroad accident near Henry Doyle's plantation; ten persons injured, but none killed.

Gen. Santa Anna stopped at Roberts' tavern.

1837.—February 13th. Duel fought at Bladensburg between Wm. Cost Johnson and Wm. Schley,—the former wounded in the knee, and the latter receiving merely a flesh wound.

March 8th.—Ex-President Jackson passed through Frederick Town *en route* to Tennessee; was received by two companies of militia.

United Brethren's camp-meeting at Cornelius Staley's began.

September 30th.—Some forty Fox and Sac Indians, with Keokuk, Black Hawk, and other chiefs, passed through town to Washington.

October 24th.—President Van Buren at Roberts' tavern.

1838.—February 12th. Ball at Roberts' tavern; managers, Michael Byrnes, Ezra Bentz, George Hoskins, John Rigney, Alfred F. Brengle, Charles Shriver, Samuel Duer, Henry Houck, Joseph Stallings, Calvin Page, Dennis Ferry, Peter H. Brown, Charles Hammond, David C. Steiner, W. G. Cole, Ambrose Ingram, Christian Smith, of George, William Kolb.

1839.—January 1st. At the County Temperance Convention, Dr. Lloyd Dorsey was chosen president, and Dr. William M. Kemp secretary.

June 26th.—New bridge built over the creek in Brew House Alley.

August 26th.—"Junior" Fire Company got its new engine; it was tried, and threw water over the steeple of German Reformed church.

1841.—President elect, Gen. Harrison, arrived February 5th, and stayed all night at Dorsey's City Hotel. On a rostrum before the hotel he addressed a vast crowd, and caught the cold that caused his death April 4th following.

A military convention composed of delegates representing thirty-one uniform volunteer companies of Maryland was held in Frederick on the 20th of October, 1841. Maj.-Gen. George H. Steuart was president.

August 1st.—New Methodist Episcopal church corner-stone laid, with an address by Rev. John Rice.

1842.—May 2d. First public procession of Adams Lodge, No. 35, I. O. O. F.

1847.—June. First use of ether in Frederick by Dr. Samuel Tyler on a colored man.

May 25th.—The German Reformed Church celebrated its centennial anniversary, with an address by its pastor, Rev. Dr. Daniel Zacharias.

1848.—May 30th. Military Court of Enquiry into conduct of Maj.-Gen. Gideon J. Pillow, composed of Col. Nathan Towson, president, and Gen. Caleb Cushing and Col. William G. Belknap. There were present Gens. John A. Quitman, Winfield Scott, James Shields, D. E. Twiggs, Franklin Pierce, Col. W. S. Harney, and other distinguished officers.

1849.—April 23d. Jacob Faubel appointed postmaster, *vice* John Rigney, in office since Jan. 1, 1839.

1850.—Vote for mayor, February 25th: James Bartgis 367, John Bender 243, William Lowe 90, George Salmon 88.

June 24th.—Frederick Schley brought from China a Chinese boy, "Mock Alloo," to be educated, but he returned to Canton, China, March, 1852.

1851.—February 2d. Asbury African church consecrated.

April 20th.—The "Junior" Hall finished.

1853.—February 28th. Vote for mayor: James Bartgis 358, David J. Markey 194, John Bender 184, Jacob Hart 78.

April 11th.—John Jacob Smith appointed postmaster.

1854.—March 31st. Water at the artesian well in the mountain came out at the surface.

May 30th.—The first corpse buried in Mount Olivet Cemetery was that of Mrs. Ann Crawford.

September 29th. Basil E. Dorsey and F. M. Grunis purchased the City Hotel of N. B. Harding for twenty-one thousand dollars.

1855.—May 24th. Bethel church, colored, was commenced in East Third Street, William S. Bennett the builder.

1856.—February 25th. Vote for city officers: Mayor, Lewis Brunner 467, Ormond F. Butler 463; Aldermen, Ezra Houck 489, Henry Butler 483, George Smith 469, J. Alfred Ritter 469, William S. Bennett 463, Thomas H. O'Neil 460, D. H. Haller 458, James Whitehill 425.

May 18th.—Twelve cases of smallpox.

1859.—February 28th. Vote for mayor: William G. Cole 552, Henry Houck 518.

May 25th.—The old Catholic steeple built in 1805 taken down.

1860.—Frederick's population: white males, 2980; white females, 3337; free colored males, 558; free colored females, 696; colored slaves, both sexes, 443. Total, 8054.

Fires.—1763. Capt. Evan Sheby's house, together with his furniture and a large store of provisions, was burned accidentally early in December.

May 3, 1786.—Almshouse in Bentz Town burned.

June 26, 1797.—The right wing of the Barracks entirely destroyed.

May 31, 1801.—Stables of Capt. James Neall's tavern burned.

Feb. 1, 1825.—Log house of Joseph Payne, on Sixth Street, burned.

June 1, 1826.—Fire broke out in stable of Francis Kleimert, on Second Street, and consumed all his and Joshua Dill's property, Lewis Wetzheimer's house, kitchen, and stable, the late George Kessler's two houses, the dwelling occupied by Mrs. Reynolds, making altogether six dwellings, with other buildings attached. Mr. Dill lost six hundred dollars in currency, and Mr. Kleimert between three and four thousand dollars in specie.

June 5, 1826.—John Schindler's mill in Middletown burned.

July 30, 1829.—William Motter's barn, near Middletown, struck by lightning and burned, together with all his crop of grain, etc.

April 1, 1830.—Talbott's tavern (City Hotel) damaged by fire.

Nov. 23, 1836.—George Broadrup's paper-mill burned.

Feb. 28, 1838.—Moses Warman's large barn, one mile from town, burned.

Sept. 24, 1839.—Fire in factory of George M. Conradt, head of Patrick Street.

March 22, 1841.—Fire in stable back of lecture-room of Reformed church, and by severe work a conflagration prevented.

Jan. 25, 1853.—Fitzhugh & Snyder's iron-foundry burned; twenty hands thrown out of employment.

June 21, 1854.—John Bartholow's tannery burned.

Aug. 14, 1855.—Delaplane's mill, near Buckeystown, burned; rebuilt, and again burned for third time June 28, 1858, the first fire having been Aug. 7, 1824.

Dec. 7, 1857.—Michael Keefer's mill and distillery burned.

May 8, 1861.—Court-house burned.

Sept. 13, 1862.—The jail burned.

Barbara Freitchie.—Sept. 10, 1862, a portion of the Confederate army, under the command of Gen. Thomas J. ("Stonewall") Jackson, marched through some of the streets of Frederick on their way to the battle-field of Sharpsburg. An incident, real or assumed, of that march led to the poem of John G. Whittier, called "Barbara Freitchie," which, no matter what happens, will always be quoted in connection with Frederick City. This poem is as follows:

"Up from the meadows rich with corn,
   Clear in the cool September morn,

"The clustered spires of Frederick stand,
   Green-walled by the hills of Maryland.

"Round about them orchards sweep,
   Apple and peach-tree fruited deep,

"Fair as a garden of the Lord
   To the eyes of the famished rebel horde.

"On that pleasant morn of the early fall
   When Lee marched over the mountain wall,

"Over the mountains, winding down,
   Horse and foot, into Frederick-town,

"Forty flags with their silver bars,
   Forty flags with their silver stars,

"Flapped in the morning wind: the sun
   Of noon looked down, and saw not one.

"Up rose old Barbara Freitchie then,
   Bowed with her fourscore years and ten.

"Bravest of all in Frederick-town,
   She took up the flag the men hauled down.

"In her attic window the flag she set,
   To show that one heart was loyal yet.

"Up the street came the rebel tread,
   'Stonewall' Jackson riding ahead.

"Under his slouched hat, left and right
   He glanced: the old flag met his sight.

"'Halt!'—the dust-brown ranks stood fast;
   'Fire!'—out-blazed the rifle-blast.

"It shivered the window, pane and sash;
   It rent the banner with seam and gash.

"Quick, as it fell, from the broken staff
   Dame Barbara snatched the silken scarf;

"She leaned far out on the window-sill,
   And shook it forth with a royal will.

"'Shoot, if you must, this old gray head,
   But spare your country's flag,' she said.

"A shade of sadness, a blush of shame,
   Over the face of the leader came;

"The nobler nature within him stirred
 To life at that woman's deed and word:

"'Who touches a hair of yon gray head
 Dies like a dog! March on!' he said.

"All day long through Frederick Street
 Sounded the tread of marching feet;

"All day long that free flag tost
 Over the heads of the rebel host.

"Ever its torn folds rose and fell
 On the loyal winds that loved it well;

"And through the hill-gaps sunset light
 Shone over it with a warm good-night.

"Barbara Freitchie's work is o'er,
 And the rebel rides on his raids no more.

"Honor to her, and let a tear
 Fall, for her sake, on 'Stonewall's' bier.

"Over Barbara Freitchie's grave
 Flag of freedom and union wave;

"Peace and order and beauty draw
 Round thy symbol of light and law;

"And ever the stars above look down
 On thy stars below in Frederick-town." [1]

---

[1] Such poetry is not only above criticism, it is of no use to criticise it. Occasions equally with places are embalmed by it. As long as the name of Frederick City lasts the poem of Barbara Freitchie will be quoted in connection with it. This is immortality,—not of place, but of the poet's gift. It is part of the poet's power. He suffers, starves, is ignored, contemned, but something in his lines survives him, and that something, be it correct or incorrect, is too strong for criticism. Byron's satire on immortality, "die on the field of glory and have your name spelt wrong in the Gazette," exactly suits the sort of notoriety which Frederick City has earned by Mr. Whittier's poem of "Barbara Freitchie." We do not propose to quarrel with it. What sense would there be in doing that, any more than in quarreling with the flow of Niagara Falls or the contour of the Chesapeake Bay? But we do propose to set the facts right about "Barbara Freitchie," and we are sure that Mr. Whittier will thank us for so doing. His conscience is almost as strong as his poetic vigor, and he would rather not write poetry at all than take for his themes events not only improbable in themselves, but which, under the circumstances, had he known them, he would perceive could never have happened.

For example, had Mr. Whittier studied the history of the Antietam campaign closer he would have known that at the hour when Jackson marched through Frederick nobody was up, and Barbara Freitchie could not have seen whether her flag was flying or not. In the second place, at this time the rebel horde was not "famished."

In the third place, it is not only a great piece of nonsense, but very unjust, both to "Stonewall" Jackson and his men, to assume, as Mr. Whittier unconsciously seems to do, that Gen. Jackson was not sincerely, loyally, even fanatically, a believer in the righteousness of his cause. To suppose that a shade of sadness or a blush of shame could or would overcome his cheek or arrest his purposes at sight of the "old flag" is almost as ridiculous as to imagine that he would waste the powder and ball of a regiment or brigade in firing at it. "Stonewall" Jackson would certainly have done neither. He treasured his ammunition far too dearly, and if he thought about the subject at all, it was simply how he could save his cartridges for the foemen ravaging the valleys where he had spent his infancy.

In the fourth place, no such incident ever occurred. There was a flag, there was a Barbara Freitchie, and that is all there is of it. The proofs of this are ample and satisfactory. It would not be needful to adduce them but for the way in which the poem seems to indict the character of "Stonewall" Jackson and his men. We have nothing to say of their acts and the consequences flowing from them, but there are too many of those famous warriors still living in Western Maryland for their motives to be safely impugned. It is for their sake and in their behalf that we apply "the iconoclastic hand of fact" to Mr. Whittier's verses. Happily, the objects of those verses, equally with the author of them, will not suffer from any scrutiny. Thus much premised, let us arrange the contradictory circumstances confronting the Barbara Freitchie myth.

(1) As to the *time*. Unfortunately for Mr. Whittier, he indicates that in a very precise way. "Forty flags," he tells us, "flapped in the morning wind,"—at noon "not one." It was high noon, therefore, upon his hypothesis, when old Barbara Freitchie rose and hung out her flag. As a rule, persons of Mrs. Freitchie's age, as Mr. Whittier has forgotten, are the earliest risers. Still, she might have overslept herself upon this particular occasion, so momentous to the extremely loyal. If she had been awake, as it is presumable she was, at a peculiarly early hour of the dawn, say 5.15 A.M., she would have seen "Stonewall" Jackson "riding ahead" in front of "the rebel horde." That was the hour when it is alleged he passed by her house, and of that particular fact we have explicit evidence, presently to be produced. At 5.15 A.M. on Sept. 15, 1862, the "Hagerstown Almanac" tells us, the sun was about twenty-five minutes below the horizon, and consequently, unless the morning twilight was particularly clear and bright (which it seldom is, even on high ground, until at least a month later, and probably never is in the valley of the Monocacy), it would have been very hard to see a large flag, much less a little one, at that hour. That particular minute, however, was the one of "Stonewall" Jackson's passing. Proof: an autograph note of Jackson's, written impromptu nearest the point to which he came in passing through that neighborhood,—a note addressed to his friend Mrs. Ross, a daughter of Governor McDowell, of Virginia, which reads like a drum-head message, to wit:

"Regret not being permitted to see Dr. and Mrs. Ross, but could not expect to have that pleasure at so unseasonable an hour.
"T. J. JACKSON.
"SEPT. 10, 1862, 5¼ A.M."

This ought to satisfy all doubters.

But other proof is behind. Jackson and his command were by no means moving on the route Mr. Whittier gives them to

---

CHAPTER XXXI.

FREDERICK COUNTY DISTRICTS AND VILLAGES.

Their Settlement, Gradual Development, and Present Prosperity.

IN certain portions of England the subdivisions of a county or "shire" were called "hundreds," from the fact that they were supposed to contain one hundred families, one hundred freemen, or one hundred manors.

The term was adopted at an early date in this country, and is still in use in the State of Delaware. It was also used in Maryland in the early days of the province, but was superseded by the word "district." The following were the hundreds, or election districts, in Frederick County in 1798:

---

the battle-field of Antietam, "over the mountain wall," which does not exist. It was one of the famous general's inconceivable "flank" movements, the object being to invest and capture Harper's Ferry. Consequently we know that he was coming eastward, and that when he penned the note to Mrs. Ross, at her door, he was passing down Second Street, north of Patrick Street, his command having entered Frederick by way of Mill Alley from the north, reaching Patrick Street on the west side of Carroll Creek. It thus happens that there was a mill-stream, to say nothing of other incumbrances, between Gen. Jackson's line of march and Barbara Freitchie's residence, which was on Patrick Street east of the bridge. If Jackson's command did not pass the spot at all, if the hour when he went through Frederick was too early for even large objects to be distinguished, if Jackson was no such man at all as the story assumes, what becomes of the legend?

But there is more of it. Miss Esmeralda Boyle has set to work systematically to investigate the matter, as if it really were of some importance. She records the fact that she was a "rebel," and thought so much of Lee and his army that she got up in time to see them pass through. Lee's column, in her words, halted in front of her house, which was on West Patrick Street, "directly opposite Mrs. Freitchie's," long enough to permit Jackson's column to pass through. This took quite a time, and Miss Boyle says, "All the time that Gen. Lee stopped in front of Mrs. Freitchie's house I saw no flag waving. If there had been I certainly should have seen it; and as for Gen. Jackson, he did not pass over the bridge, but passed up another street."

Miss Boyle rather intimates that Mrs. Barbara Freitchie would have been the last person to do such a conspicuous act, and that she would have disclaimed the notoriety which Whittier has pinned upon her name. But upon this point it is best to give her own language, or rather that which she quotes, the words of Jacob Engelbrecht, once mayor of Frederick-town, and for thirty-six years opposite neighbor of Barbara Freitchie, and a strong Union man. She was always "a nice old lady," he says, "born in Lancaster, Pa., Dec. 3, 1766, and died in Frederick, Md., Dec. 18, 1862. She lost her husband in 1846, never had any children, and her neighbors seem never to have heard about the flag-raising, one way or another, until the publication of the poem. She was a 'Union woman,' and it is their impression that she did use a small flag some days after, when McClellan's army came through the town."

Mr. Englebrecht further says, "When Gen. Lee passed through our city with his army, I was very anxious to see all I could. I therefore posted myself at one of the up-stairs windows, where I had a full view of all that passed below in the street. When Gen. Lee got in front of Mrs. Freitchie's house, and also in front of mine, he and his whole army halted, and I afterwards ascertained (this, you know, was in West Patrick Street) that Gen. 'Stonewall' Jackson and his army had passed. All the time that Gen. Lee stopped in front of Mrs. Freitchie's house I saw no flag waving. If there had been I certainly would have seen it; and as for Gen. Jackson, he did not pass over the bridge, but passed up another street. . . . I was at the front window up-stairs nearly the whole time the invading troops were passing; hardly ate my meals, except when one corps had passed; there was a stoppage of sometimes an hour or two; moreover, I was anxious to know what length of time it would take them to pass."

Dr. Samuel Tyler (the biographer of Chief Justice Taney) says "Stonewall" Jackson never "passed Barbara Freitchie's house, but passed down Mill Alley from the north of Frederick, and entered Patrick Street on the west side of Carroll Creek, while Barbara Freitchie's house was out of his way from his encampment. He and his staff passed down Second Street, north of Patrick Street, and he dismounted from his horse and wrote on a card the note given above, and rode off to Mill Alley, and down it to Patrick Street." In regard to the flag which Mrs. Freitchie did wave when McClellan's army passed through the town he says,—

"While Gen. Reno, who was killed at South Mountain, was passing Barbara Freitchie's house with the United States troops, as I have heard, a little girl held at the window a small United States flag. Barbara Freitchie was at the window then, about ninety-six years old, and it is likely out of these facts the imaginative informant gave Whittier the ideas of the poem. All that relates to the Confederate general and his troops is pure fiction."

Maj. H. Kyd Douglas, now a leading member of the Hagerstown bar, and who was during the late war on Gen. "Stonewall" Jackson's staff, says,—

"Jackson's corps crossed the Potomac into Maryland Sept. 5, 1862, and on that day an admiring civilian of Western Maryland presented the general with a large gray horse. The next morning, when he tried to ride him, he became unmanageable, and in rearing fell backward upon the general, who was so severely hurt that it was some time before he sufficiently recovered to be moved. He was then placed in an ambulance, and turned his command over to Gen. D. H. Hill. Jackson stopped about three miles short of Frederick, and established his headquarters in Best's Grove, as also did Gens. Lee and Longstreet. He did not go into Frederick that day, and certainly was not ' riding ahead' of the 'rebel tread' which passed through Frederick to the other side. While encamped near Frederick he kept closely to his tent, seeing very few of the many citizens who called on him. On Sunday night he asked Majs. Douglas and Morrison of his staff to go to church with him, and was taken to town in an ambulance. There being no service in the Presbyterian church, he went to hear Dr. Zacharias at the Evangelical Reformed church, and, as usual, went to sleep. On the morning of the 10th Jackson's corps was put in motion, and the general went to Frederick in an ambulance, and then mounted his horse. While the army was passing through, he rode with Maj. Douglas to the house of Dr. Ross, the Presbyterian pastor, and left a note for him with a servant, with instructions to deliver when the doctor got up, but not to awake him for the purpose. This being done, he went directly, and by the shortest cut, to the Hagerstown pike, and put himself at the head of the column. Nothing like that which is related by Mr. Whittier ever occurred, and Gen. Jackson and Barbara Freitchie never saw each other."

There is nothing more to say in regard to this matter, we think, except to quote Mr. Whittier himself. In a card of his, published in the *Boston Advertiser*, he says that he has no wish to prolong a doubtful controversy. "It seems to be admitted by those who deny the main incident of the ballad that the venerable Union woman did not hesitate to make a way through the Confederate soldiers at her door, applying to them epithets more energetic than polite, and that she had a Union flag in her house. If she did not show it on that occasion, so much the worse for Frederick City." And so say we all.

No. 1.—Unity and Burnt House Woods.
" 2.—Israel Creek and Manor.
" 3.—Pipe Creek and Westminster.
" 4.—Sugar Loaf and Linganore.
" 5.—Lower Monocacy.
" 6.—Taneytown and Pipe Creek.
" 7.—Upper and Middle Monocacy.
" 8.—Kittoctin and Tom's Creek.
" 9.—Lower and Middle Kittoctin.

At first, and for thirty years, the "hundreds" were divisions simply for road supervisors, constables, tax collectors, etc., and the elections were not held in them, but at the "county-seat." They lasted four days. Afterwards the elections were held in the "hundreds," and on one day only. The election districts now are:

1, Buckeystown; 2, Frederick; 3, Middletown; 4, Creagerstown; 5, Emmittsburg; 6, Catoctin; 7, Urbana; 8, Liberty; 9, New Market; 10, Hauver's; 11, Woodsborough; 12, Petersville; 13, Mount Pleasant; 14, Jefferson; 15, Mechanicstown; 16, Jackson; 17, Johnsville; 18, Woodville; 19, Linganore; 20, Lewistown.

In order to avoid confusion we will take them in numerical order as above.

BUCKEYSTOWN DISTRICT, No. 1.

Buckeystown, or Election District No. 1, was originally bounded as follows: "Beginning at the mouth of Monocacy River; thence up Potomac River to the highest ridge of Catoctin Mountain; thence along the top of said mountain to the main road leading from Frederick Town to Newtown (Trap); thence with said road to the North Branch of Ballenger's Creek (above John Hoffman's mill); then down said creek to Monocacy River; then up said river to the main road crossing from Frederick Town to Georgetown and the city of Washington; then with said road to the line of division between Frederick and Montgomery Counties; then with said line to the mouth of the Monocacy, aforesaid." In 1848 its eastern limits were curtailed by the formation of Urbana District, No. 7, and it is at present bounded by the Monocacy River on the east, by the Potomac on the south, the Catoctin Mountain on the west, and Ballenger's Creek on the north. Jefferson District, No. 14, adjoins it on the west, Frederick District, No. 2, on the north, and Urbana District, No. 7, on the east. The district is situated in the southern part of the county. The first land taken up in the district was by the father of Charles Carroll of Carrollton, and was known as "Carroll's Manor," a name by which this part of the district is still distinguished. Carroll's Manor originally contained fifteen thousand acres, and embraced a wide area of extremely rich and fertile territory, extending from Catoctin Mountain and the Potomac River on the west and south to the high ground and Monocacy on the east. For many years the manor remained almost exclusively in the hands of descendants and collateral branches of the Carroll family, and as late as 1840 the greater portion of it was still owned by the Tuckers, Jacksons, Lees, the Marchioness of Wellesley, and Mrs. Harper. At that date Mrs. Harper's revenues from the rent of her portion of the estate amounted to eight thousand dollars a year. Some of the Carroll heirs still retain an interest in portions of the old manor. Among the earliest settlers were the Buckeys, from whom the district took its name, the Thomases, Lucketts, Delashmutts, Kemps, Harwoods, Dutrows, Johnsons, Michaels, Padgetts, Snouffers, Spechts, Trundles, Whites, Sinns, Besants, Stunkles, Duvalls, Delaplanes, and the Nicodemus family.

The Lucketts were of English extraction, and were prominent in the early history of the district. One of the family, Capt. Wm. Luckett, commanded a company of Frederick militia during the French and Indian war, and in 1758 was stationed at Fort Frederick, with his command, by order of Governor Sharpe. Levin Luckett, the only grandson of Capt. Wm. Luckett, married Miss Letitia Peyton, of Loudon County, Va., whither he subsequently removed. Some of the pioneer settlers were of English extraction, but at least half of them were Germans or of German descent.

Buckeystown Village. — Buckeystown Village, which owes its name to the first settlers on the site which it now occupies, is situated on the Baltimore and Ohio Railroad, about six miles from Frederick City, and is near the old United States road, over which Braddock marched to his famous defeat, and which was formerly the great thoroughfare between the North and the South.

The first actual settlers, George and Michael Buckey, were of German origin, and both took up lands in the neighborhood of the village in 1775. George Buckey owned the land which the village now occupies, and may be regarded as its founder. He built the first tannery in the district, which remained in his family until 1834, when it was sold to Daniel Baker. It is now owned by Daniel Baker & Sons, and consumes more than eight hundred tons of bark annually. Although it has been in operation for more than a hundred years, its ownership has been confined to the Buckey and Baker families. The three large limekilns of F. C. Thomas & Co., O. J. Keller, and M. J. Grove, are situated in the vicinity of the village, and give employment to seventy-five laborers. They ship large quantities of lime to Montgomery and Howard Counties.

The village contains two churches, one of the Methodist Protestant and the other of the Methodist Episcopal denomination. The former was dedicated Sept. 15, 1867, and cost five thousand dollars. Its pastors have been:

William S. Hammond, two years; J. K. Nicholls, three and a half years; J. L. Kilgore, six months; Jacob Wilson, one year; C. H. Littleton, four years; J. E. Maloy, four years; W. R. Mills, called in 1881.

Its Sunday-school superintendent is Judge A. W. Nicodemus.

The Methodist Episcopal church was completed and dedicated in 1839 by Bishop Beverly Waugh. It had been erected years before by Ignatius Davis, a zealous member of the denomination, but was not entirely finished until the above date. Before its dedication its pastors were:

John A. Gere, two years; Francis McNeill, one year; Robert Cadden, one year.

Since then it has been under the charge of the following pastors and assistants:

Pastors.—William Butler, two years; Jonathan Cleary, two years; Henry G. Dill, two years; Isaac Collins, two years; —— Holland, two years; John N. Henning, two years; John G. Brooke, two years; James Brads, two years; David Trout, one year; David Thomas, one year; John Anderson, William Taylor, J. M. Spangler, John P. Hall, George Stevenson, Charles F. Thomas, M. L. Smizer, A. R. Miller, J. W. Smith, W. H. Reed, D. G. Miller, G. W. Feelemyer, Reuben Kolb, D. M. Browning. *Assistants.*—Joseph Parker, two years; B. Doll, one year; L. M. Consor, one year; —— Brent, one year; John M. Jones, one year; —— Dulin, one year; John Boggs, one year; —— Fulton, one year; J. R. Dubrow, two years; G. W. Cooper, one year; Moncure D. Conway, one year; W. H. Waring, one year; L. M. Gardner, one year; Ellis T. Teal, one year; John Geyer, one year; J. W. Kelley, B. G. W. Reed, —— Essenberg, C. D. Smith.

In 1863 the circuit was divided, and it is now composed of Urbana, Ijamsville, Point of Rocks, Koontz Chapel, and Buckeystown.

Between the village and the Monocacy there is a rich deposit of marl, composed of lime and earthy substances.[1]

The physicians are Drs. B. Poole and H. J. Boone, and the merchants J. H. Delashmutt & Bro. and A. J. McKenna. No intoxicating liquors have been sold in the village for nearly forty years.

Adamstown is a thriving village on the Baltimore and Ohio Railroad, nine miles from Frederick, and sixty-four from Baltimore. It is situated on a portion of the fertile territory of the old Carroll Manor, and was named in honor of Adam Kohlenberg, who settled there in 1840. The first white settler was Daniel Rhodes, who laid out lots south of the railroad. Mr. Snouffer was the next settler, and he was followed by Mr. Oswell and Thomas Thomas.

The Sugar Loaf and Catoctin Mountains can be plainly seen from the village, and the Monocacy and Tuscarora Rivers flow in the vicinity. The Reform church, built in 1869, is the only place of worship; its pastors have been Revs. W. F. Colliflower, eight years; Simon S. Miller, eight; and N. H. Skiles (present incumbent), six. Its physicians are J. D. Thomas and W. H. Johnson. The latter is a grandson of Maj. Roger Johnson, of Revolutionary fame, and grand-nephew of Governor Thomas Johnson. The merchants are John P. Hess and Thomas Hayden.

Point of Rocks is at the southwestern boundary of the district, upon the Potomac River and the Chesapeake and Ohio Canal, and at the junction of the main stem and the Metropolitan Branch of the Baltimore and Ohio Railroad. The situation is one of romantic beauty, and the place is associated with some of the most memorable events of the late war. The village was formerly situated about a mile from its present location, on the Washington and Hagerstown roads, and was called "Trummelstown." It was partially destroyed by fire, but was recalled to life by the Baltimore and Ohio Railroad, removed to its present location, and rechristened Point of Rocks. It was laid out Aug. 23, 1835, by H. G. O'Neal for Charles Johnson. It contains three churches,—Catholic, Methodist Episcopal, and African Methodist Episcopal church,—two hotels,—the American and St. Charles,—and several stores and restaurants.

The Catholic church was erected in 1881, and is a neat and commodious structure, under the charge of Father De Wolf. The Methodist Episcopal church was built in 1865, and belongs to the Buckeystown and Urbana circuit. Its present pastor is Rev. D. M. Browning. The merchants are Thomas & Spalding and B. D. Chambers, and the physician, Dr. R. W. Trapnell. St. Paul's Protestant Episcopal church is situated about a mile from Point of Rocks, on the old Hagerstown road. St. Paul's Parish was created in 1844, with the following boundaries:

"Beginning at the Potomac River east of John Barnett's farm and running up with Poplar Branch until it intersects the public road leading from Hook's tobacco-house to Hawkins', now Grove's mill; then with said road until it intersects the road leading from the Point of Rocks to Jefferson; then across said road, between the lands of B. Moffit and N. Luckett, to the Ridge road on the top of the Catoctin Mountain, where it intersects the line of All Saints' Parish; then eastwardly along the said Ridge road to where it is crossed by Ballanger's Creek; thence

---

[1] Monocacy is an Indian name, signifying "right ear," in contradistinction to Linganore, the "left ear." It is usually a gentle and quiet stream, but in time of freshets rises suddenly, and to a great height.

DANIEL BAKER.

with said creek to its junction with the Monocacy River, and down therewith to its mouth; thence up the Potomac River to the place of the beginning."

Its ministers since 1841 have been:

1841, Rev. J. H. Morrison; 1842, Rev. Olcutt Bulkley; 1845, Rev. Richard H. Phillips; 1849, Rev. Asa Colton; 1856, Rev. Meyer Lewin; 1858, Rev. William A. Smallwood, D.D.; 1863, Rev. Joseph Trapnell, Jr.

Greenfield Mills is two and a half miles from Tuscarora Station, on the Metropolitan Branch of the Baltimore and Ohio Railroad, and four from Adamstown. The well-known Greenfield Mills are located here and operated by Roberts Brothers. James F. Beall is postmaster and merchant.

Licksville is one mile from Tuscarora Station on the Metropolitan Branch of the Baltimore and Ohio Railroad, and near the Potomac River and Chesapeake and Ohio Canal. J. C. Lamar is the postmaster and merchant, and S. H. Hempstone station agent.

Lime Kiln, a station of the Baltimore and Ohio Railroad, is four and a half miles from Frederick City, and sixty and one-quarter miles from Baltimore. It is the largest manufacturing and shipping point of lime in the county. In its vicinity are several of the finest dairies in the State. It contains but one store, the proprietors of which are M. J. Grove & Son.

Among the points of interest in the district is the family residence of Henry A. Johnson, which was built before the Revolutionary war. On his farm is the family burying-ground, which is the oldest in the district, and in which repose the remains of Thomas Johnson, uncle of Hon. Wm. Cost Johnson, John Johnson, and John Johnson, of John.

The public school-teachers of the district for the term ending April 15, 1881, were:

School No. 1, 52 pupils, Carrie V. Higgins; No. 2, 82 pupils, W. R. McDaniel, G. W. Blessing, assistant; No. 3, 30 pupils, H. R. Biser; No. 4, 32 pupils, W. T. Ennis; No. 5, 64 pupils, F. R. Neighbors; No. 6, 60 pupils, C. W. Wright; No. 7, 40 pupils, Katie E. Weeking; No. 1 (colored), 63 pupils, J. H. Robinson; No. 2, 45 pupils, Charles Lyles.

The magistrates are:

Ezra Michael, of Adamstown; Wm. P. Allmuth, of Licksville; Dr. J. Boone, of Buckeystown; Wm. F. Gatton, of Point of Rocks.

The constable is:

William H. Krantz.

The Tuscarora Creek Region.—A pleasant drive of about five miles in a northwesterly direction from Frederick City, through a rich and fertile country, and over a splendid turnpike road, places one in the "Tuscarora" region, whose principal stream yet bears the name of the once powerful but now extinct tribe of Indians who inhabited that section. From this stream, Tuscarora Creek, the city of Frederick receives its principal supply of water, which is conveyed through pipes to the receiving-house at the base of the Catoctin Mountains, and thence to the reservoir at Frederick. This improvement was completed in 1870. Here also during the latter half of the eighteenth century was established the first paper-manufactory in Maryland, and within a quarter of a mile distant, on the Tuscarora, were erected by Nicholas Zimmerman, George Burkhart, and George Boyer, respectively, three paper-mills, all once doing a brisk business in the manufacture of wrapping, printing, and writing-paper; bank-note paper also was made at them. The ruins of these mills are still to be seen. The region is abundantly supplied with numerous springs of excellent water. Here also are the celebrated "Yellow Springs," "Montonqua," or medicine-water, as it was called by the Indians. These waters were held in great esteem by the red man, and on account of their reputed virtues in healing the sick, inspiring their warriors with strength and courage, and endowing their hunters with luck for the chase, they were regarded as the fountain of the "Great Spirit."

It is said that previous to going to battle, or on the hunt, and upon various other occasions, the Indians resorted thither and practiced, in conjunction with a free use of the waters of the Montonqua, various charms and incantations to aid them in their enterprises. And here, tradition says, once a year during the "Flower's Moon" (May) the diseased Indians were brought for cure, and were subjected by the "medicine-men" of the tribe to a variety of ceremonies, such as bathing three times a day (sunrise, meridian, and sunset) in the waters of the Montonqua, drinking the blue oily substance floating on the surface, and having their bodies anointed with a deep orange-colored pigment made from its thick and slimy yellow deposits.

Here also is said to have been located a kind of general "headquarters" for the various tribes when great events were to be celebrated, a council of war held, or a treaty concluded. The Indians held sacred the ground near the "Fountain of the Great Spirit," and a treaty there ratified was regarded as doubly binding. An Indian village once occupied a site near by, and many relics of its rude inhabitants, such as stones for grinding meal, stone hatchets, arrows, etc., have been found. During the times of the first white settlers (the first half of the eighteenth century) and in later years the springs were a place of general resort for social gatherings from the region round about.

On holidays and various festive occasions persons came from many miles, and it is said to have been no uncommon thing to see gathered beneath the umbrageous foliage of the surrounding forest scores and even hundreds of the pioneers, together with no inconsiderable sprinkling of friendly red men, who frequently came to gaze in wonder and astonishment upon the advancing tide of civilization which was destined to so soon sweep them from their favorite hunting-grounds. Wrestling was a favorite sport, in which the savages also took part.

There are several other mineral waters near by, one of them being a sulphur spring of considerable virtue. Doubtless in course of time the vicinity will become a favorite summer resort, for the salubrity of the climate, the beautiful scenery, easy accessibility, and close proximity to our Eastern cities combine to make it a delightful spot for health and pleasure.

The Tuscarora region is also supposed to contain valuable mineral deposits, such as stove-coal, iron ore, copper, lead, graphite, and silver and gold, small quantities of each having been discovered at various times and by different persons within the last quarter of a century. Considerable efforts were made by the late William C. Hoffman and several other enterprising gentlemen to discover a workable vein of stove-coal, but as yet without any great success, the quantities found being too small to justify the expense of mining. A copper-mining company was formed some time since, but after sinking several shafts in the vicinity of "High Knob," on the Catoctin Mountain, it finally abandoned the effort. A similar failure attended the experiments of a company prospecting for gold in the vicinity of "White Rock."

In this connection the following tradition survives, viz.: "A Mr. Hedges, one of the first settlers of this region, was an excellent shot with the rifle and a great favorite with the Indians. While out with them on a hunting expedition on one occasion his supply of bullets became exhausted, and one of the Indians after a short absence returned with a 'chunk of lead,' apparently clipped from a rock, from which 'slugs' were made and the chase resumed." A number of searches have been made in recent years for the supposed "lead rock" in this vicinity, but as yet without success. Although some of the land in this region was taken up in the early part of the last century (as shown by some of the parchment "grants," sealed with the provincial seal of Maryland, and still extant in the hands of the descendants of these hardy pioneers), the tide of immigration did not set in very strongly until about the middle of the century.

On the crest of the "Catoctin Range" we find the "High Knob," a peak of fifteen hundred and thirty feet in altitude. This knob is an abrupt termination of one of the spurs of the mountain, and is distant about seven miles on the west from Frederick City. It commands a beautiful view of Harper's Ferry gap, and a large portion of both Frederick or Monocacy and Middletown or Catoctin Valleys, and during the late war was used by the Federal army as a signal-station. A few miles farther northward, on the eastern slope of the same range, is the "White Rock," a huge pile of granite, rising almost perpendicularly from a ledge of rocks on the mountain-side to more than twice the height of the tallest trees in the surrounding forest. The Indian name of this rock is Koomawauwa, or Thunder Stone, from a superstition prevalent among the red men that here the "Great Spirit" stands upon the rock and pounds the skies to produce thunder. The White Rock is a place of considerable local notoriety, and is a favorite spot for picnics, excursions, etc., from many miles around. From its summit the beholder is at one glance enabled to obtain a sublime view of the entire valley of the Monocacy. Towns, villages, forests, fields, roads, and bridges, the courses of the streams, etc., are plainly delineated, the landscape being dotted with bright-colored barns and pleasant farm-houses. The distant "Sugar Loaf" and the winding Potomac may also be seen, with the far-off mountains of Virginia on the south, the low blue hills of the Linganore on the east, and the region of Gettysburg, Round Top, and the dimly-outlined peaks of Pennsylvania on the north. In the rear towers silent the lofty range of old Catoctin.

On the summit of these rocks the declaration of peace with England after the war of 1812 was celebrated by the inhabitants of the neighboring country with martial music, speeches, and feasting throughout the day, and a grand "bon-fire" and "mountain illumination" which lasted through the entire night.

The spot, tradition says, was once the scene of a terrible tragedy. About a quarter of a century before the white settler had made his first entrance into this part of the country two young warriors became enamored with the daughter of their chieftain. A quarrel and deadly feud arose. The Indian maiden finally made a decisive choice and gave the coveted pledge of love's acceptance—the "keousa," a milk-white arrow decorated by her own deft hand with fanciful festoons of hair from her locks—to the favored swain. The rejected suitor determined to revenge his failure on his rival. He had not long to wait ere chance afforded him an opportunity to gratify his passion. The maiden and her lover, now betrothed, repaired, as was the custom of their tribe, to the rock to celebrate the nup-

"SPRING BANK,"
RESIDENCE OF GEORGE HOUCK,
FREDERICK DISTRICT, FREDERICK CO., MD.

tial rites and invoke the smiles of the "Great Spirit" on their union. The discarded suitor placed himself in ambush near by, and when the opportune moment arrived sprang upon them and hurled the maiden over the cliff. A desperate combat ensued between the two warriors, who struggled to the edge of the cliff and tumbled over. All three were killed.

Another tragedy occurred here during the latter half of the eighteenth century. On a beautiful summer morning a gay group of young men and maidens of the vicinity met at the "Yellow Springs" for a sort of picnic. After enjoying themselves for some time in dancing and other amusements, a trip to the White Rock, about two miles distant, was proposed and acceded to by a number of the party, who at once wended their way up the mountain. The rock was reached, and after spending some time there they started homeward. Before proceeding on their way one of the young ladies discovered that she had lost her handkerchief, which she supposed had been left on the rock. Her companion, a young man named Hedges, to whom she was betrothed, volunteered to go back, and the party waited by the wayside. A considerable time having elapsed without his return, several of the young men started back to see what detained him, and to their horror discovered his lifeless remains lying under a large rock which had rolled down on him, crushing him to death. It was supposed that he attempted to climb upon the rock by a nearer way than the usual ascent, and in some manner loosened the rock, which fell upon him and killed him. His companions having procured assistance removed the rock, gathered up his body in a sheet as best they could, and conveyed it to his home near the foot of the mountain. The young man was the descendant of one of the first settlers in this region. His body was buried in the old burying-ground of the Hedges family, near the Yellow Springs.

FREDERICK DISTRICT, No. 2.

Frederick, or District No. 2, originally had the following boundaries:

"Beginning at the mouth of Ballanger Creek; thence up Monocacy River to the mouth of Fishing Creek; then by a straight line to Stephen Stoner's saw-mill on said creek; thence up said creek to the Big Spring, the head-water thereof; thence by a west course to the highest ridge on the Catoctin Mountain; thence with the top of said mountain to the main road leading from Frederick to Jefferson; thence with said road to Ballanger's Creek, above John Hoffman's mill; thence down said creek to the beginning."

Among the earliest settlers were immigrants from Germany, among them John Thomas Schley, the Brunners, Shellmans, Kemps, Raymers, Groshes, Foutses, Houcks, Holtzs, Steiners, Reichs, Bentzs, Brengles, Mantzs, Conradts, Youngs, and Kolbs. Monocacy Manor was settled by persons from Southern Maryland, and it is more than probable that English immigrants and Maryland pioneers were established in this section some years before the Germans came. Frederick District, as it existed before the formation of Lewistown, was bounded by Creagerstown District on the north, Woodsborough, Mount Pleasant, and New Market on the east, Urbana and Buckeystown on the south, Jefferson, Middletown, Jackson, and Catoctin on the west. Lewistown District is north of it. It is divided from the districts on the west by the Catoctin Mountains, and from thence on the east by the Monocacy River. It is centrally located with reference to other portions of the county, and its soil is very productive and its scenery highly picturesque. The city of Frederick is situated in the southeastern portion, and there are the following villages in the district, viz.: Hamburg in the north, Shookstown and Fairview in the west, and Frederick Junction in the southeast. The country is thickly studded with farms, and is traversed by numerous roads.

George Houck's residence, near Harmony Grove, in Frederick District, is one of the finest and most costly in Frederick County. It is a red-brick structure of Romanesque architecture, set in the midst of expansive and well-kept grounds, and affording from its observatory a magnificent view of Frederick Valley, the Catoctin Range, Sugar-Loaf Mountain, and South Mountain. It is supposed that on a clear day the eye may reach from the elevation mentioned to a distance of at least forty miles up and down the valley. The house was erected in 1881, and contains all the modern improvements that judiciously-expended wealth could obtain or refined taste suggest. The work was all done by home mechanics, and was under Mr. Houck's personal supervision and direction. It has a front of forty-five feet, and a depth of forty-two feet six inches, with an attached building thirty-two feet deep. There are nineteen handsomely-finished and roomy apartments, each especially designed for comfort and convenience. There is a fine brick stable, forty-five by twenty, with ample room for four horses and four cows. This residence stands upon Mr. Houck's farm, which contains two hundred and six acres of cleared land, but forms no portion of the farm buildings. These, some distance beyond, include a substantial and handsome red-brick house and red-brick barn, with other surroundings in keeping with the high architectural standard sought to be observed. Mr. Houck's farm adjoins the farms of his brothers

Ezra and James, the three making an aggregate of seven hundred acres of some of the most valuable farming lands in Maryland.

In the western portion is High Knob, a spur of the Catoctin Mountain, fifteen hundred and thirty feet in height. Nearly all the local history of this district has already been given in the chapters of Frederick City.

The teachers for the term ending April 13, 1881, were:

District No. 1, 58 pupils, A. B. Holtz; No. 2, vacant; No. 3, 69 pupils, E. Oliver Belt; No. 4, 62 pupils, H. F. Leving; No. 5, 47 pupils, E. L. Molineaux; No. 6, 75 pupils, A. B. Forney; ——, 43 pupils, Annie Bartgis; No. 7, 45 pupils, D. R. Stauffer; No. 8, 22 pupils, Sue M. Garratt.

From Aug. 28 to Sept. 3, 1810, was held the first camp-meeting, at Francis Hoffman's farm, between Frederick and New Town ("Trap"), about seven miles from the former and two and a half from the latter.

Just outside of Frederick City, on the Jefferson road, is W. O. DeNegre's house, said to have been built of brick imported from England by one of the Dulanys, but not finished for occupancy until the beginning of the present century. On the Georgetown turnpike, about half a mile south of Frederick, at "Locust Level," is the beautiful residence of the late Jacob Lewis. He was born April 7, 1804, in Goshen township, Chester Co., Pa., but at the time of his death, Sept. 15, 1878, resided at Locust Level. His father was also named Jacob Lewis, and married Hannah Meredith. His grandfather was David Lewis, a relative of Dr. Benjamin Rush. His grandmother was Mary Cloyd. His paternal ancestors came from Wales, and those of his mother from England.

In 1838 he married Delia Smith, daughter of Elisha Sandford and Elizabeth (Burtsall) Smith. Their children are John S., who resides in Harrisonburg, Va.; Hannah More, now Mrs. G. W. M. Crook, lives in Baltimore; William Reese, died aged twenty in 1865; H. Thorpe, lives in Cumberland, Md.; Francis Irwin, lives in Frederick City, Md.; Mary Elizabeth, now Mrs. S. M. Hartsuch, lives in Washington, D. C.; Martha L., now Mrs. J. W. C. Sitz, lives in Baltimore; Sandford I., lives in Chicago, Ill.; Charles Lee, died in infancy. Delia Lewis, wife of Jacob Lewis, died Oct. 18, 1853.

On the 3d of April, 1862, Jacob Lewis married Elizabeth Winger, daughter of Joseph and Esther (Buckwall) Winger. Karl M. Winger, great-grandfather of Elizabeth Winger Lewis, came from the canton of Zurich, Switzerland, in 1736, and purchased lands of William Penn, one of which tracts is now owned by unbroken title by his descendants. Their children are Anetta Esther, Rush Ransom, Emogine E., Jacob, who died in infancy in 1868, Cloyd, and J. Winger and J. Latta, who died in infancy in 1874.

Jacob Lewis was educated in Chester County, Pa., and in Baltimore County, Md. He was a member of the Methodist Protestant Church, which he joined in 1826 in Baltimore County, and was one of its trustees. In Frederick County, however, he and his family attended the Protestant Episcopal Church. In politics he was a Democrat, and during the war was a Union man. He was a successful farmer, and is a large land-owner. Jacob Lewis was the youngest of three children. His father died while he was an infant; afterwards his mother married Benjamin Reese, whose ancestors were English Friends. He was an extensive miller, but failing in business the family removed to Baltimore County in 1814. Jacob did much towards supporting his mother, and was untiring in his efforts to purchase her a home, which he succeeded in doing. In 1831 he went to Genesee County, N. Y., where he was a successful farmer, and in a few years was able to buy a good farm. He bought and sold land with profit. After living there seventeen years he moved to Frederick, Md., and in the Urbana District bought several tracts of land, together over one thousand acres. After a residence there of seven years he sold the land for twenty thousand dollars, more than he paid for it. At the time of his death he was a large land-owner in Frederick County, and also owned a farm near Baltimore City. As a man of business he was energetic and successful. He was jovial and possessed much native wit. He was kind and generous to the poor, no one of whom ever appealed to him for aid unheeded. During the civil war voters were questioned as to whether they had aided the Southern troops in any way, if they had fed them, and when this interrogatory was put to Mr. Lewis he replied that he had. The judge said, "I presume you were compelled to?" "Oh, no!" was his reply, "I will feed a hungry man without any compulsion." At which there was an outburst of laughter, with the hearty response from the judge of election, "Come on and vote! Come on and vote!" In his family he was kind, sympathetic, and indulgent, a Christian in deeds more than in words. He died suddenly of heart-disease, on Sunday morning, Sept. 18, 1878.

In 1872, H. C. Brown removed from Clinton County, Pa., to Frederick County, Md., having purchased in the latter section the old Gen. Brengle

Jacob Lewis

"LOCUST LEVEL."
RESIDENCE OF THE LATE JACOB LEWIS, FREDERICK DISTRICT, FREDERICK CO., MD.

"BELLE-VUE."
RESIDENCE OF H.C. BROWN, FREDERICK DIST. FREDERICK CO. MD,

property, lying in the Frederick Valley, on the Monocacy, one and a half miles distant from Frederick City. The farm-house, a small brick structure, had been built by Gen. Brengle, and well-authenticated report made its age date from 1816. In 1878, Mr. Brown materially improved and enlarged it to its present proportions. It is now a two-story, roomy brick edifice, of attractive appearance, occupying a gentle elevation about three hundred yards removed from the public highway. The numerous and well-constructed farm-buildings include a barn, measuring seventy-five by fifty-six feet. It was built in 1879. Mr. Brown has in his farm two hundred and thirty acres, of which all are cleared and excellently well watered. Its close proximity to Frederick City makes it, of course, more than ordinarily valuable. The staple crop is wheat, of which from ninety to one hundred acres are sown each year. Mr. Brown is one of the model farmers of Frederick County, and is reckoned among the most successful. He was bred an agriculturist, and that he has shown what spirited energy and experienced judgment can do for a farmer, illustrates forcibly the value of keeping abreast of the times and employing the fruits of the advanced ideas of the age.

Montevue Hospital is situated in this district. The first almshouse was in Bentztown, and was built before 1770. It burned down May 3, 1786. The next one was built on West Patrick Street, Frederick Town, just opposite the market-house, and situated on the site of what is now J. H. Ramsburg's carriage-factory. On April 13, 1832, the inmates of the old almshouse in the city were removed to the new one, about two miles in the country, northwest of the city. This building was erected in 1830–31, by John Shipman (carpenter), who contracted to do the work for thirteen thousand dollars. Henry Steiner was appointed its overseer.

Montevue Hospital was built in 1870, at a cost of about one hundred and twenty-five thousand dollars. The following have been the superintendents since 1862:

1862–68, Lewis Yonson; 1868–70, George Hinkle; 1870–72, V. H. Freaner; 1872–76, George P. Ramsburg; 1876–80, C. F. Fleming; 1880, Henry Snider.

The number of inmates May 21, 1881, were:

	Males.	Females.	Total.
County inmates	77	59	136
Colored "	25	15	40
Transient "	4	1	5
Travelers	2	0	2

Among the handsome residences in this district is that of Col. C. K. Thomas. The fine brick mansion occupies a handsome elevation overlooking the Monocacy, about three and a half miles from Frederick City. The farm tract was in the possession of the Marshall family upwards of one hundred years ago, and in the patent is called "Araby," by which name it is still known. James Marshall (a Scotchman) built the house now occupied by Col. Thomas, and according to the best obtainable evidence must have erected it as early at least as 1780. Not only historic in respect to age, Col. Thomas' mansion is doubly historic as a landmark in the chain of stormy events that marked the progress of the civil war of 1861–65, for it was upon and about the farm that the battle of Monocacy was fought, July 9, 1864.

Col. Thomas (a native of Frederick County, and a merchant in Baltimore to 1860) removed from that city in the year named to "Araby," in search of a spot where the turmoils and distractions would not be felt. As it turned out he found considerable distraction at "Araby" after a while. The farm mansion was a position that both Federal and Confederate forces strove for. The Federals occupied it at the opening of the action, but were dislodged by the enemy after a severe cannonading. During the bombardment, which lasted from 9.30 A.M. to 3.30 P.M., the house was much battered. A portion of the wall of the dining-room (in which latter apartment the Union sharpshooters were posted) was beaten down, and in that room, as well as in the library and dining-room, are still visible great indentations made by shells and rifle-shots. The west side of the structure suffered the most damage, but altogether the injury was by no means as great as it was feared it would be. Eight shells penetrated the interior, and the marks they left, as well as the shells themselves, are preserved as eloquent relics of that eventful day. During the fight Col. Thomas' family, with the family of Mr. Gamble, occupied safe quarters in the cellar. After the Confederates abandoned the position, Gen. Grant and eight major-generals (including Hunter, Ricketts, Wright, Crook, and Sheridan) assembled in an upper room of the mansion over the library and held a council of war. Mrs. Thomas breakfasted with Gen. Grant the morning after that council, and remembers how Grant said to her the war would last at least a year longer, but not more. Events proved the correctness of his prophecy. The forces engaged at the battle of the Monocacy are reported to have aggregated twenty thousand, and the guns about forty. Something like seven hundred prisoners were taken, and five hundred men killed. About three hundred were buried upon Col. Thomas' place, and afterwards removed. Among those buried on the farm were

Gens. Lamar and Ferry and Lieut. Van Valkenburg. Previous to the battle of Gettysburg, Gen. Hancock halted his command at "Araby," *en route* to the battle-field, and made Col. Thomas' house his headquarters the better portion of three days.

MIDDLETOWN DISTRICT, No. 3.

Middletown, or Election District No. 3, was formerly considerably larger than at present, but its area has been lessened by the creation of other districts from its territory.

At present it is bounded on the east by the Catoctin Mountain, separating it from Frederick District, on the north by Jackson District, on the west by South Mountain, separating it from Washington County, and on the south by Peterville and Jefferson Districts.

The first settlers in the district were English, but they were quickly followed by Germans, who soon owned most of the lands, and formed more than three-fourths of the population down to the Revolution. The two earliest settlers were the Penbridge brothers, who in 1740 took up lands near the present residence of Joseph Hedges, on what was called "Turkey Range." Among the first pioneers were Jacob Flook, Conrad Young, Conrad Crone, the Shafers, Robert Johnson, Gen. Joseph Swearengin, Henry Kefauver, the Bowluses, Coblentzes, Routzahns, Collinses, Derrs, Wieres, Remsburgs, Keplers, Castles, Smeltzers, Ahalts, Larentzes, and Rudys.

Braddock marched with part of his army through Middletown District, and rested his troops on the Catoctin range at what has since been known as "Braddock's Spring." This district suffered greatly from the ravages of civil war, and the battle of South Mountain was fought within its limits. Many residences in the vicinity of the battle-ground were injured by the hot fire of shot and shell, among them that of Mrs. Col. Henry R. Smeltzer (the daughter of Sergt. Everhart, of Revolutionary fame), which was pierced by a cannon-ball. Lamb's Mountain is the highest peak of this range of the Blue Ridge, and is eighteen hundred feet in height.

Middletown takes its name from the fact that it is midway between Frederick and Boonsboro'. It is situated between the Catoctin and Blue Ridge Mountains, in the beautiful and fertile Middletown Valley, and is on the old national pike, eight miles west of Frederick City, and one mile from the Catoctin Creek. It was laid out just after the close of the Revolution by Margaret Crone, who owned the land on which the town now stands. The first settlers in the town were Jacob Lorentz and Frederick Stemple. Among other early settlers were Abraham Miller, who died in 1836, Mr. Litler, Michael Bickenbaugh, Valentine Bowlus, Daniel Rhodes, Michael Keller, Caspar and Adam Herring, Aaron Suman, and Jacob Alexander. The first blacksmith was Thomas Powell. The first physician was Dr. Lewis Creager, who was succeeded by Drs. Thomas Springer and Jacob Coblentz. The first teacher was Horatio O'Neal, and the second a Mr. Dorcas. The first tavern was kept by Jonathan Levy, on the site now occupied by the residence of Adam Smith. The earliest wagon-maker was Thomas Murray; cabinet-maker, Christian Sifford. The first tannery was owned by Michael Motter. The two oldest houses are those of Lloyd Hiett and Adam Herring. The first stone-mason was Jacob Kritzer. Frederick Stemple kept the first store, and Frederick Staley had a distillery four miles distant. Bowlus' mill and cotton-factory was near "Spoonsville."

Middletown and the district in which it is situated were largely represented in camp and field during the war of 1812. Among those who raised companies and participated in the battle of Bladensburg were Capts. Jacob Alexander, Thomas Murray, Daniel Shawen, and Daniel Marker. Abraham Miller, father of Daniel Miller, married, in 1792, Susan Creager, daughter of Capt. Daniel Creager, distinguished in the Revolution. Daniel Miller was born in Middletown in 1806, and married Catherine, daughter of Perry Herbert, a soldier in the war of 1812. He is the father of C. W. Miller, postmaster of Frederick.[1]

The battle of South Mountain was fought in plain view of Middletown. Gen. Rutherford B. Hayes, who was severely wounded in this engagement, was conveyed to the house of Jacob Rudy, a resident of Middletown, where he remained for several weeks.[2]

On the 4th of March, 1834, an act was passed by the General Assembly by which "the citizens of Middletown, Keller's addition to Middletown, Grove's addition to Middletown, and Wise's addition to Middletown, in Frederick County," were constituted a body corporate "by the name of the Burgess and

---

[1] The method of raising money by lottery for public enterprises was a favorite one in Middletown, as in other parts of the State, in former times. Thus, in February, 1803, a lottery was held to raise four hundred dollars to purchase a fire-engine. There were two thousand tickets at one dollar each, and sixteen hundred dollars were distributed in prizes. The managers were Frederick Stemple, Sr., Thomas Powell, Peter Suman, Henry Stemple, and Samuel Shoup.

[2] In February, 1851, a large meeting was held at Middletown in favor of forming a new county out of the southwestern part of Frederick and the southeastern part of Washington County, and committees were appointed to memorialize the Constitutional Convention on the subject, but after some agitation of the matter the effort was abandoned.

"ARABY."
RESIDENCE OF COL. C. K. THOMAS, URBANA DISTRICT, FREDERICK CO., MD.

Commissioners of Middletown." Since the incorporation the town officers have been:

1834, Burgess, Jacob Hoffman; Clerk, S. G. Harbaugh. 1836, Burgess, John Sifford; Clerk, Jacob Hoffman. 1838, Burgess, John Appleman; Clerk, James Williamson; Commissioners, Adam Keller, S. L. Geisinger, Peter Wise, Jacob Lorentz, J. H. Miller. 1840, Burgess, George Baer; Commissioners, James Cook, Van Swearingen, Michael Keller, Jacob Young, Joseph Wise. 1841, Burgess, J. T. C. Miller; Commissioners, Jacob Wise, D. Middlemoser, Thomas Nottingham, Jacob Young, Geo. Baer; Clerk, D. C. Herring. 1842, Burgess, Jacob Weaver; Commissioners, S. Trigg, M. Rhoderick, Henry Cochran, Peter Young, Joseph Powers; Clerk, Wm. Ervin. 1843, Burgess, J. T. C. Miller; Clerk, J. W. Walker. 1845, Burgess, J. G. Protzmen; Clerk, A. Keller; Constable, John Kisselring; Commissioners, S. L. Geisinger, W. T. Ervin, Peter G. Schlosser, P. H. Thomas. 1846, Burgess, P. G. Schlosser; Commissioners, J. T. C. Miller, James Stevens, Joshua Korrick, Jacob Kuhn. 1848, Burgess, Peter Young; Clerk, A. P. Ingram; Commissioners, D. H. Herring, Townsend Barber, L. H. Herring, James Stevens; 1850, Burgess, J. T. C. Miller; Commissioners, Lawson Alexander, J. Cullen, Henry Lighter, Wm. Zittle, S. L. Geisinger; Clerk, C. P. Young; Constable, Robert Thomas. 1851, Burgess, P. H. Thomas; Clerk, A. Keller; Commissioners, L. H. Herring, T. Barber, Christian Remsburg, J. Cullen, C. J. Baer. 1852, Burgess, P. H. Thomas; Commissioners, H. Herring, Alex. Weaver, P. G. Schlosser, G. Bowlus, Joseph Wise. 1853, Burgess, W. T. Ervin; Commissioners, L. H. Herring, S. L. Geisinger, C. J. Baer, H. Lighter, Wm. Kefauver. 1854, Burgess, W. T. Ervin; Commissioners, D. C. Herring, S. L. Geisinger, H. Lighter, Wm. Kefauver, C. J. Baer, P. Young. 1855, Burgess, W. T. Ervin; Commissioners, P. Young, Allen Sparrow, Joshua Crick, Jonathan Biser, P. G. Schlosser. 1856, Burgess, H. Boyer; Commissioners, G. W. Crouse, Samuel Toms, Joseph Wise, Joshua Carrick, Wm. Kefauver. 1857, Burgess, W. T. Ervin; Commissioners, Wm. Kefauver, Samuel Bowlus, P. G. Schlosser, Joseph Wise, C. Ramsburg. 1858, Burgess, Joshua Carrick; Commissioners, H. Lighter, Samuel Toms, C. J. Baer, Wm. Kefauver. 1859, Burgess, H. Boyer; Commissioners, Jonathan Biser, John Derr, Wm. Boteler, W. T. Ervin, Joseph Wise. 1860, Burgess, P. G. Schlosser; Commissioners, T. Barber, James Chamberlin, Jacob Cullen, L. Alexander, Wm. Kefauver. 1861, Burgess, P. G. Schlosser; Commissioners, L. Alexander, Joseph Wise, Alex. Weaver, John Derr, James Chamberlin. 1862, Burgess, Ezra Minnick; Commissioners, Jonathan Biser, Joseph Wise, David Coblentz, Jacob Rudy, John Derr. 1863, Burgess, W. T. Ervin; Commissioners, D. Coblentz, J. Biser, Allen Sparrow, John Derr, Joseph Wise. 1864, Burgess, W. T. Ervin; Commissioners, John Alexander, Alex. Weaver, Samuel Toms, J. M. Brandenburg, Wm. P. Winbigler. 1865, Burgess, John W. White; Commissioners, Jonathan Biser, L. H. Herring, E. Minnick, Adam Keller, Jacob Rudy. 1866, Burgess, Peter W. Shafer; Commissioners, John Linthicum, W. N. Wachter, Carlton Rudy, Geo. Kesselring, Andrew Boist. 1867, Burgess, P. W. Shafer; Commissioners, Adam Keller, Thos. H. Willard, J. D. Fink, J. E. Young, J. Toms. 1868, Burgess, W. W. Perry; Commissioners, J. H. T. Rudy, T. H. Willard, J. D. Fink, John Derr, Alex. Weaver. 1869, Burgess, Ezra Minnick; Commissioners, Asa Bowlus, Samuel Leaver, J. F. Chamberlin, C. W. Koogle, Arthur McQuade. 1870, Burgess, George Ingram; Commissioners, Wm. Cullen, Joel Brandenburg, J. E. Young, H. Kefauver, Jacob Rudy. 1871, Burgess, George Ingram; Commissioners, John Alexander, Joel Brandenburg, J. E. Young, H. Kefauver, John Cutler. 1872, Burgess, P. W. Shafer; Commissioners, C. E. Wise, J. E. Young, T. C. Rudy, C. A. Heagy, J. Alexander. 1873, Burgess, Geo. Ingram; Commissioners, C. A. Heagy, C. W. Koogle, J. E. Young, J. Alexander, G. V. Crouse. 1874, Burgess, Geo. Ingram; Commissioners, G. H. Kefauver, C. W. Koogle, John Alexander, Vincent Sanner, G. V. Crouse. 1875, Burgess, Allen Sparrow; Commissioners, G. H. Kefauver, C. E. Wise, Joseph Gaver, C. A. Heagy, C. W. Koogle. 1876, Burgess, Allen Sparrow; Commissioners, C. E. Wise, Samuel Leaver, Geo. Shearer, Arthur McQuade, P. W. Shafer. 1877, Burgess, Allen Sparrow; Commissioners, J. W. Damer, Joseph Gaver, John Tracy, Samuel Leaver, Henry Miller. 1878, Burgess, Allen Sparrow; Commissioners, C. A. Heagy, John Tracy, D. S. Kapler, J. W. Damer, John Derr. 1879, Burgess, C. A. Heagy; Commissioners, D. S. Kapler, G. W. Gaver, C. E. Wise, F. K. Stone, John Tracy. 1880, Burgess, Allen Sparrow; Commissioners, Samuel Leaver, S. S. Thompson, Ezra Derr, Charles Gaver, Charles Nienmyer. 1881, Burgess, H. S. Stephens; Commissioners, Samuel Leaver, D. S. Kapler, C. E. Wise, E. V. Boileau, G. W. Tracy; Clerk, S. N. Young.

Zion Lutheran Church.—The southern part of Middletown Valley was settled by persons from Prince George's County and Calvert, but a few German families occupied the lands around Middletown. These families belonged to the Lutheran and German Reformed denominations, and formed the nucleus of Zion congregation. Its first place of worship stood two miles west of the town, on the lands of Daniel Ahalt. There is still a graveyard partially inclosed about this primitive church, where lie many of the ancestors of those who worship in the present edifice. The first church was a joint one used by the Lutherans and German Reformers. It was a rude log structure, thirty by thirty feet, and was erected about 1755. It was taken down in 1790. It was used both for religious worship and as a parochial school. The fifty acres on which the church was built were either purchased of or given by Henry Kefauver. The land was deeded in trust to Jacob Flook for the German Reformed congregation, and to Conrad Young, father of Henry Young, for that of the Lutherans. But inasmuch as there was then no law in Maryland allowing churches to hold over two acres of real estate, forty-eight acres of it fell into the hands of James Shawn. He was sued for it, but gained the suit, and held it and sold it for eighty dollars per acre. The two congregations occupied the church some twenty years. Conrad Young served fifteen years as trustee, and lived to be ninety-seven years old and his wife ninety-three. About 1775 the German Reformed congregation left the church and built a log edifice in Middletown, near the site of its present church, and gave the privilege to the Lutherans to worship in it jointly with them. This second church was jointly occupied by the two congregations until it needed repairing. Then it was used as a school-house, and was afterwards sold. The German Reformers built a third church, a log structure, near the second one, and gave permission to the Lutherans to occupy it jointly with them, but the latter determined to erect a church of their own. After considerable discussion as to the site, the Lutherans built the fourth church, but first Lutheran church proper, in Middletown, on a lot presented by Conrad Crone.

It had a steeple, bell, and organ. The bell was purchased by Conrad Young from a man-of-war ship. It became broken, and a second one was bought by the young men of the congregation, which was presented in 1841 to the Jefferson Church. For the building of the church many farmers made contributions of wheat, which was made into flour and sold. The church was built during the pastorate of Rev. John Andreas Krug (about 1783), and was taken down during the ministry of Rev. Johann George Graeber, having stood about thirty-five years. The second Lutheran church proper, or fifth church from its organization, was built during Mr. Graeber's ministry. It had a steeple made at Shepherdstown, Va., which was hauled to Middletown by George and Michael Bowlus and Jacob Crone. It was a brick structure, and the wife of Rev. Mr. Graeber lies buried under it. This church cost over nine thousand dollars, and was built in part by lottery. It was repaired in Rev. Mr. Wachter's ministry, which extended from 1836 to 1843. The bells, purchased in Philadelphia during the pastorate of Rev. Mr. Schnee, weighed over eleven hundred pounds. The sacramental cup, lined with gold, was presented by Mrs. Hiestern as a memorial of her husband. This church was consecrated Sept. 24, 1815, and called Zion. The clergymen present, besides the pastor, were Rev. Mr. Kurtz, of Baltimore, and Rev. Dr. Schaeffer, of Frederick. Mr. Kurtz preached to a congregation of twelve hundred people. The first Lutheran preacher known to have been located in the valley was Rev. Nicodemus. The following have been the regular pastors of this church:

1. Rev. Frederick Gerresheim, who lived in Middletown. He arrived Dec. 16, 1779, and resigned in July, 1782. Previous to his ministry the congregation had had occasional supplies from various preachers, but only with long intervals between them.

2. Rev. John Andreas Krug arrived Sept. 18, 1782. He lived in Frederick, but served this congregation.

3. Rev. Jacob Goering, who lived at Hagerstown. He served one year, and was called to York, Pa. He was an eloquent and learned man and a distinguished Oriental scholar.

4. The name of the fourth pastor, who remained six months, is not given on the church records.

5. Rev. Dr. John George Schmucker, father of Prof. S. S. Schmucker, of Gettysburg College, and author of a work on Revelations.

6. Rev. Johann George Graeber arrived June 2, 1796, and resigned July 1, 1819. During his ministry the stone parsonage was built. His charge was composed of Middletown, Boonsboro', Ringer's Church, Jefferson, Loudon County, Va., near Lewistown, and Schaaf's school-house, between Jefferson and Burkittsville.

7. Rev. Johannes Kachler took charge July 1, 1819, and resigned Oct. 18, 1821.

8. Rev. Jacob Schnee arrived March 15, 1822, and departed April, 1827.

9. Rev. Abraham Reck arrived Aug. 15, 1827, and resigned April 3, 1836.

10. Rev. Michael Wachter, from June, 1836, to Sept. 19, 1843.

11. Rev. Charles A. Hay, from Jan. 11, 1844, to Nov. 3, 1844, when he was called to a professorship at Gettysburg, where he yet remains.

12. Rev. David F. Bittle, from May, 1845, to 1852. He was the founder and president of Roanoke College, Va., and largely identified with educational matters in Maryland and Virginia.

13. Rev. J. Rosenberg, from Dec. 11, 1852, to Sept. 27, 1853.

14. Rev. John McCron, D.D., from Nov. 27, 1853, to Aug. 1, 1855.

15. Rev. Philip Rizer, from October, 1855, to August, 1857.

16. Rev. C. M. Klink, from October, 1857, to June, 1861. During his ministry the present church edifice, seating fully fifteen hundred people, was erected at a cost of thirty thousand dollars. The corner-stone was laid in 1859. It is one of the largest, finest, and best-arranged churches in the country.

17. Rev. Lloyd Knight, from Dec. 29, 1861, to June 28, 1862.

18. Rev. William D. Strobel, D.D., from April 10, 1863, to June 15, 1867.

19. Rev. M. J. Alleman, from May 1, 1868, to April 3, 1869.

20. Rev. Daniel Steck, D.D., from Sept. 1, 1870, to March, 1875. He died in June, 1881.

21. Rev. Joseph Hawkins, from April 15, 1875, to April 16, 1876.

22. Rev. L. A. Mann, the present pastor, born in Loudon County, Va., graduated at Roanoke College, studied theology at Gettysburg, pastor eight years at Marion, Va., six at Burkittsville, and came to this church April 25, 1876.

In 1782 the church had 86 communicants, and in 1829, 155. During Rev. Mr. Bittle's pastorate the lecture-room and second parsonage was built, also the Mount Tabor church, in this district. During Mr. Mann's ministry a church has been erected at Harmony costing three thousand dollars, which was dedicated on Ascension Day, 1880. Mount Tabor and Harmony are only stations, both being parts of the Middletown congregation. Zion Sunday-school was organized Dec. 2, 1827. Its first superintendent was Rev. S. G. Harbaugh, a native of Middletown, and for many years State librarian of Ohio. The second was Daniel Remsburg, and the third and present one is Samuel Derr.

Evangelical Reformed Church.—The records of this church go back to 1755. An account of the first three churches occupied by the Reformed congregation has already been given in the preceding sketch of the Lutheran Church. The first teacher in the parochial school was Mr. Mintz, in 1755, and the first burying-ground was called "Gott's Acker." The present church was erected in 1818 and 1819. The corner-stone was laid July 2, 1818, the spire put up October 27th of the same year, and the building was consecrated June 27, 1819. It was built under the superintendence of Peter Coblentz, and during the pastorate of Rev. Jonathan W. Helfenstein. The following members of the Frederick Singing Society were present at its consecration and sang:

Margaret Bentz, Sophia Doll, Mary Rohr, Elizabeth Bentz, Charlotte Steiner, Ann Sophia Koontz, Margaret Fessler, Elizabeth L. Conradt, Christiana Conradt, Ann Louisa Hauser, Miriam Hart, Catherine Englebrecht, George Englebrecht, John G. Happner, Peter Doll, George Schultz, John Koontz, Jacob Cronise, David Schley, John Krauth, George M. Conradt, Jr., Jacob Englebrecht, T. F. Conradt, Dr. G. Weise, Jacob Smith, William Englebrecht.

The Sunday-School Union was organized at a meeting held Dec. 29, 1830, of which Peter Coblentz was chairman, and S. G. Harbaugh secretary. Its board of managers were:

First class, Benjamin Routzahn, Jacob Baer, W. H. Harbaugh; second class, H. G. O'Neal, Peter Coblentz, David Smith; third class, S. G. Harbaugh, Henry Fite, Jacob Meinel.

Each of the above took his turn and served a month in course. The present superintendent is Charles H. Coblentz. Until 1830 the ministers in charge were the Frederick pastors, who officiated in the following order:

1. Rev. John Conrad Steiner, from 1756 to 1759. He died in Philadelphia, July 1, 1762, aged fifty-five years.
2. Rev. William Otterbein, from 1760 to 1765.
3. Rev. Charles Lange, from 1760 to 1768. He administered the sacrament "across the First mountain," at a school-house, to Adam Ryell, Elias Williard, Franz Oster, George Cost, and others.
4. Rev. Frederick L. Henop, from 1769 to 1783.
5. John W. Runkel, from 1784 to April 1, 1802. Mr. Runkel officiated at Middletown Jan. 11, 1799, at the funeral of Melchior Gessier, aged one hundred and ten years.
6. Rev. Daniel Wagner, from 1802 to October, 1810.
7. Jonathan Helfenstein, from 1811 to 1828. In 1825 he introduced English into part of the services.

In 1830 this congregation became a separate charge and church by itself, and since then its pastors have been:

1. Rev. John C. Bucher, from Jan. 1, 1830, to 1842.
2. Rev. A. P. Freese, from Aug. 1, 1842, to 1845.
3. Rev. E. F. McCauley, from Oct. 11, 1845, to December, 1855.
4. Rev. G. W. Glessner, from Oct. 11, 1856, to 1861.
5. Rev. F. A. Rupley, from June 27, 1861, to 1876.
6. Rev. T. F. Hoffmeier, from 1876 to the present time.

Rev. Mr. Bucher in his ministry of twelve and a half years baptized seven hundred and forty-five persons, confirmed four hundred and eighty-four, buried two hundred and sixty, and married two hundred and one couples. The elders elected April 17, 1843, were Jacob Thomas, Peter White; deacons, Jacob Koogle, Jonathan Keller. In April, 1844, the elders elected were Peter Shafer; the deacons, Samuel Bowlus, Philip Coblentz, P. C. Wise.

Methodist Episcopal Church.—This church was organized about the beginning of the century. The first edifice was burned. The second one, a brick structure, was erected about 1830, and was occupied in conjunction with the United Brethren. In 1853 was begun the construction of the present edifice, a substantial and neat building. It was dedicated on the last Sunday in May, 1855. The clergymen present were Revs. John A. Collins, presiding elder of the Cumberland District, Littleton F. Morgan, and J. P. Cook, of Baltimore, and James Brads, of York, Pa. The dedicatory sermons were preached by Rev. Mr. Cook in the afternoon, and Rev. Mr. Morgan in the evening. The collections during the day reached two thousand four hundred dollars. The old church was transferred to the United Brethren. In 1829 Frederick Circuit embraced Middletown, and so continued until 1858, when Middletown and Jefferson were formed into a circuit, and in the same year Berlin, Knoxville, and Sandy Hook were attached. There were then one hundred and fifty-nine members. The pastors since 1858 have been:

1858, John Anderson; 1859, Revs. Meminger and Gray; 1860-61, A. A. Eskridge and Savage; 1862, L. D. Heron; 1863, Charles Kalfus and J. B. Van Meter; 1864, C. F. Thomas and C. D. Smith; 1865, H. C. Pardue, J. D. Moore; 1866, H. C. Pardue (a parsonage was built this year costing fifteen hundred dollars); 1867-69, A. M. Kester; 1870-72, S. M. Hartsock; 1873 to 1876, A. J. Bender; 1876 to 1879, W. G. Herbert; 1879-80, J. H. Marsh; 1881, John L. Walsh.

The circuit is now composed of Middletown, Jefferson, and Petersville. The superintendents of the Sunday-school are L. H. Herring and L. W. Wright.

United Brethren Church.—This congregation bought the old Methodist Episcopal church edifice in 1853, in which it had up to then a part interest, and which it had helped to build a quarter of a century previous. Its preacher is Rev. C. H. Mott.

The Catholic Church is a commodious edifice which was built several years ago, but has no resident pastor.

Rev. G. W. Jenkins is the pastor of the African Methodist Episcopal Church.

Cemeteries.—In the old Lutheran cemetery the tombstones show that

Thomas Castle, born Oct. 24, 1729, died Oct. 24, 1805; Adam Routzahn died May 5, 1827, aged 90 years, 7 months, and 20 days; Catharine Routzahn, born 1736, died June, 1831, and left 9 children, 63 grand and 150 great-grandchildren; John Philip Sheffer, born July 28, 1776, died Dec. 9, 1844; John Floyd, Sr., born 1766, died April, 1826.

In the new Lutheran graveyard the following are buried:

Christiana Weire, born 1765, died July 1, 1852; John Kepler, born January, 1773, died July 28, 1849, and his wife, Mary Magdalen, born Nov. 22, 1770, died June 28, 1840.

German Reformed cemetery:

Jacob Smith, born 1761, died Dec. 17, 1819; Jacob Crone, born 1759, died Sept. 23, 1834; Jacob Schedt, born June 28, 1724, died Aug. 22, 1794; Peter Coblentz, born Feb. 28, 1732, died June 9, 1808; John H. Oldfather, born near Lewisburg, Preble Co., O., and fell at South Mountain, Sept. 14, 1862. He was a member of Company I, Twelfth Ohio Regiment U.S.A.

In the Methodist Episcopal graveyard are:

Rev. Thomas Fulton, died Dec. 1, 1850, aged 36; John Bowlus, born May 22, 1773, died Feb. 9, 1850; Sarah, wife of Robert Pettingall, born Jan. 20, 1787, died March 31, 1850, and Robert Pettingall, born in the parish of Runnall, county of Norfolk, England, July 7, 1787, died Dec. 2, 1837; William Perry, born Nov. 17, 1787, died Aug. 31, 1836; Henry Young, born May 21, 1789, died Nov. 23, 1859, and his wife, Hannah, born Oct. 28, 1779, died July 27, 1862; George Routzahn, born July 6, 1774, died July 12, 1867.

In this burying-ground lie the remains of Sergt. Lawrence Everheart, whose career in the Revolutionary war has been narrated in a preceding chapter. Above his grave a monument has been erected by his relatives. It is of marble, and is about twelve feet high. On the front of the base is the inscription,—

"Lawrence Everheart, ordained a minister of the gospel of the M. E. Church by Bishop Asbury, A.D. 1808."

And on the right side of the base is the following:

"Sergeant Lawrence Everheart, born May 6, 1755, died Aug. 6, 1840, in his 86th year.

"A veteran of the Revolution, the rescuer of Washington at the battle of the Cowpens, he assisted at the most remarkable battles during the war, and in the battle of Brandywine, when Lafayette was wounded, he and Sergeant Wallace rescued him from his perilous situation, and carried him about two miles to the house of a friend. He served from the beginning to the close of the Revolution. He was generous and just in all the relations of life."

On the front of the shaft is carved a shield bearing the Stars and Stripes, and on the opposite side of the shaft is a cluster of roses. Beside him lies his wife, whose tombstone has this inscription:

"Mary Everheart, born Oct. 1755, died July 3, 1847. Our conversation is in Heaven, from whence also we look for the Savior."

About a mile from the cemetery, near Middletown, and on the pike to Frederick, lives the surviving child of Sergt. Lawrence Everheart by his wife Mary, viz., Mrs. Col. Henry R. Smeltzer, a venerable lady of eighty-two years.

Catoctin Lodge, No. 113, I. O. O. F.—This lodge was instituted May 8, 1868, by Grand Master John Q. A. Herring and Grand Secretary J. B. Escaville. The date of the charter is May 6, 1868. The charter members were Jacob Rudy, G. L. Routzahn, W. N. Wachter, Thomas H. Williard, Horatio Zittle, William H. Young. Its first officers were:

N. G., Jacob Rudy; V. G., G. L. Routzahn; Sec., W. N. Wachter; Treas., Thomas H. Williard; R. S. N. G., W. H. Young; L. S. N. G., John E. Crone; O. G., J. J. Williamson; I. G., C. E. Schildtknecht; R. S. S., A. C. Bregonier; L. S. S., David Groff; W., W. W. Perry; Con., H. Zittle; Chaplain, P. W. Shafer.

The first four initiations were Lloyd H. Herring, Rev. A. M. Kester, George Kesselring, Isaiah Toms. The following have been the Noble Grands:

1868, G. L. Routzahn; 1869, Horatio Zittle, W. N. Wachter, 1870, John E. Crone, W. H. Miller; 1871, Samuel Leaver, T. W. Koogle; 1872, C. H. Coblentz, John D. Miller; 1873, Thomas H. Willard, C. E. Wise; 1874, John F. Shafer, George C. Huffer; 1875, J. W. Long, P. W. Shafer; 1876, W. H. Norris, Dr. J. E. Beatty; 1877, John L. Sigler, J. D. Fink; 1878, George D. Castle, S. H. Pettingall; 1879, Cyrus T. Biser, D. L. Koogle; 1880, John H. Kepler, John C. Stone; 1881, G. M. Koogle, D. B. Routzahn.

The office of secretary was filled from 1868 to 1875 by P. W. Shafer, and since then it has been occupied by W. N. Wachter. The officers for the term ending December, 1881, are:

N. G., D. B. Routzahn; V. G., J. C. Keller; Sec., W. N. Wachter; Treas., T. W. Koogle; Marshal, J. D. Miller; Chaplain, Noah Routzahn; W., J. E. Crone; Con., G. W. Castle; R. S. N. G., J. D. Miller; L. S. N. G., Samuel Leaver; R. S. V. G., J. W. Long; L. S. V. G., D. L. Koogle; I. G., D. W. Lighter; O. G., C. E. Neinmyer; R. S. S., C. W. Koogle; L. S. S., S. P. Flair.

The number of members is 116, and the aggregate of accumulated funds is $1872.23.

The lodge meets every Saturday night. The district deputies are W. N. Wachter, Dr. J. E. Beatty, H. Zittle. It has a library of three hundred and sixty volumes.

Valley Encampment, No. 34, I. O. O. F.—This encampment was instituted Feb. 6, 1877, by William L. Schley, Grand Patriarch, and John M. Jones, Grand Scribe, assisted by Joseph Hoffstetter, G. J. W., and Charles H. Gatch, P. G. P. The charter members were W. N. Wachter, John H. Grove, W. T. Grove, R. S. Delaughter, John F. Shafer, G. C. Shafer, Dr. J. E. Beatty. Its officers have been:

1877, C. P., W. N. Wachter; H. P., John H. Grove; S. W., W. T. Grove; J. W., R. S. Delaughter; Scribe, J. F. Shafer; Treas., G. C. Shafer. 1878, C. P., John H. Grove; H. P., W. T. Grove; S. W., R. S. Delaughter; J. W., J. F. Shafer; Scribe, W. N. Wachter; Treas., G. C. Shafer. 1879, C. P., W. T. Grove; H. P., R. S. Delaughter; S. W., J. F. Shafer; J. W., G. C. Shafer; Scribe, W. N. Wachter; Treas., J. C. Stone. 1880, C. P., R. S. Delaughter; H. P.,

J. F. Shafer; S. W., G. C. Shafer; J. W., J. H. Kepler; Scribe, W. N. Wachter; Treas., J. C. Stone. 1881, C. P., J. F. Shafer; H. P., J. H. Kepler; S. W., J. L. Sigler; J. W., J. C. Stone; Scribe, W. N. Wachter; Treas., R. S. Delaughter.

The number of members is 13, and the encampment meets on the first and third Tuesdays of every month in I. O. O. F. Hall. W. N. Wachter is R. W. District Deputy Patriarch.

Middletown Lodge, No. 19, A. O. U. W.—This lodge was instituted Jan. 18, 1881, by Deputy Grand Master Isaac Lowenstein, assisted by P. M. W. J. W. Griffin and George E. Myers. Its charter members and officers are:

P. M. W., Rev. L. A. Mann; M. W., Dr. J. E. Beatty; G. F., John D. Main; O., George C. Roderick; Recorder, W. N. Wachter; Financier, A. C. Bregonier; Receiver, C. L. Gaver; Guide, H. E. Sparrow; I. W., Dr. E. M. Bowlus; O. W., T. C. Rudy.

The number of members is 13. The lodge meets on the first and third Friday evenings in every month at I. O. O. F. Hall.

Independent Order Good Templars.—This lodge was instituted in 1867, by Rev. Mr. Ackerman, of Hagerstown. The first Chief Templar was W. W. Cunningham; Vice Templar, Mrs. Rev. Pardoe. It maintained its organization some four years. Subsequently it was rechartered as "Good Samaritan Lodge, No. 15," by Rev. Mr. Poulson, of Baltimore, and remained in existence till about 1880.

The teachers in the district for the term ending April 15, 1881, were:

School No. 1, 46 pupils, Joseph Remsburg; No. 2, 49 pupils, T. F. Gaver; 33 pupils, Clara Pettingall, assistant; No. 3, 173 pupils, Thomas J. Lamar, S. N. Young (first assistant), J. W. Castle (second assistant); No. 4, 40 pupils, J. H. T. Rudy; No. 5, 60 pupils, David Ansherman; No. 6, 47 pupils, L. M. Kepler; No. 7, 34 pupils, L. W. McBride; No. 8, 44 pupils, C. L. Grove; No. 9, 27 pupils, C. T. Guyton; No. 10, 52 pupils, L. M. Warrenfeltz. No. 1 (colored), 24 pupils, Bettie Colson; No. 2 (colored), 31 pupils, J. R. Bruner.

The magistrate for the district is Ezra Minnick, and the constable is Samuel Leaver.

In 1839, Jacob T. C. Miller commenced at Middletown the publication of a paper called the *Catoctin Enterprise*. He published it for several years, and it then passed into the hands of H. L. Brady. It is now called the *Valley Register*, published by G. Carlton Rhoderick. It is decidedly Republican in its politics. It is a very good local paper, well conducted, and claims to have the largest circulation in Middletown Valley of any paper published in the county.

CREAGERSTOWN DISTRICT, No. 4.

Creagerstown, or Election District No. 4, originally had the following boundaries: "Beginning at the mouth of Fishing Creek; thence up Monocacy River to the main road, crossing said river at formerly Price's, but now Knoof's ford; thence with the main road until it intersects the main road from Creagerstown to Emmittsburg, near Benjamin Ogle's old place; then with a straight line down towards a warehouse near Owings' Creek, built by James Ogle, deceased; thence with said Owings' Creek to the south branch thereof; thence with it until it intersects the lines of No. 10; then with the lines of No. 10 until it shall intersect the former lines of No. 4, and then with them to the beginning." Originally, therefore, the district was bounded on the north by Mechanicstown and Emmittsburg Districts, on the east by Woodsborough, on the south by Frederick, and on the west by Catoctin. But subsequently Lewistown District was formed, in part out of its territory, and now bounds it on the south. Creagerstown District was settled about 1750 by the Creagers (then spelt Kriegers), Kolbs, Beattys, Hoffmans, Gusharns, Zimmermans, Lillys, Dohmers, Reids, Protsmans, Campbells, Millers, Shrupps, Wilhides, Maj. Head, Hammetts, Fundenbergs, Cullers, Bollers, Bickels, and others. A large majority of the earliest settlers were Germans, and many of them from Pennsylvania. John Creager owned the land where the village stands, and laid it off before the Revolution into lots for a town. Isaac Kolb, in 1775, built his house, where his son, Mathias Kolb, now resides. He died in 1829. The Beattys owned nearly all the land about town, and were very prominent in the settlement of the district. Among the best citizens of this section of the county is John Culler, who was born in Middletown Valley, Frederick Co., Md., Dec. 24, 1806. His father, John Culler, married Anna Mary Coblentz, both natives of the Middletown Valley. His father died at the age of seventy-two, and his mother at forty-six, and both are buried in the valley where they were born. The grandfather, Michael Culler, came from Pennsylvania, and married a Miss Smith. John Culler, the subject of this sketch, married Maria Smith, daughter of John Smith. She was born in May, 1810, and died Dec. 11, 1872. They were married March 7, 1833. Their children are Ann Maria, born Dec. 25, 1833, and died May 31, 1852; Charlotte Elizabeth, born March 10, 1835, married John William Long, and is the mother of seven children. They are farmers, and reside near Jefferson. His only son, John Harmon Culler, born April 7, 1837, is married and lives on the old homestead, a farm of two hundred and eighty-four acres, and has seven children. In religious connection John Culler is a Lutheran, and in politics has been a Whig, and afterwards an American, during the war a strong Union man, and is now a Republican.

JOHN CULLER.

While residing the greater part of his life in Maryland, he has traveled very extensively over the States of the Union. For thirty-eight years he pursued farming, and since 1846 has been engaged until 1881 in mercantile business. Having been successful in both he retired from business, May, 1881.

Creagerstown is situated at what was formerly the junction of the Baltimore and Pittsburgh road with the Washington and Buffalo road. It was a great stage point until the building of the Frederick and Emmittsburg Railroads, and in its palmy days supported four well-kept taverns. The first German Reformed church was built in 1791, and the present edifice in 1834. The Winebrennarian church was erected in 1866. Before the organization of the districts of Hauver's, Emmittsburg, Mechanicstown, Lewistown, Catoctin, and Woodsboro', all created out of its original territory, people had to go to Creagerstown from a distance of ten or fifteen miles to vote, and often at these large gatherings serious fights occurred. A very large tannery was in operation here between 1785 and 1810. Among the first settlers in the village were the Eckmans and Housemans. Three-quarters of a century ago a large brewery was operated where now is the property of Dr. Zimmerman. Michael Rimike, a wealthy old bachelor, was one of the large land-owners. John R. Curtis, up to 1854, was for long years a magistrate and one of the leading citizens of the district. The village was in olden times the great centre of militia musters, cornstalk trainings, wrestling matches, and fisticuff encounters. The stages that ran through the place were those of Thompson & Tate, of Gettysburg, Pa., Mealy & Sim, and Ulrich & Son. The physicians have been Drs. Johnson, James Liggett, in 1834; Watters, Hull, and William Zimmerman. Maj. Head, a Revolutionary soldier, died in 1834. Col. Cramer, an officer in the Revolution, lived between the village and Utica; Capt. Shryock served in the war of 1812. Samuel Grunis, of English descent, was an early pioneer of note. The village is pleasantly situated on the Emmittsburg road, twelve miles north of Frederick, one and a half from Monocacy River, and two from Loy's Station, on the Western Maryland Railroad. The merchants are J. L. Miller (postmaster) and William J. Cramer & Son. H. J. Krise keeps a good hotel. The magistrates of the district are H. J. Krise, Creagerstown; A. T. Norris, Rocky Ridge. In the old graveyard at the village are a few graves of old pioneers, of which we notice:

John Flowers, born June 24, 1731, died Jan. 5, 1805; Frederick Eichelberger, born 1763, died Aug. 7, 1838; Frederick W. Shriver, born Feb. 8, 1744, died Feb. 27, 1820; Charles Shrupp, died Oct. 15, 1822, aged 75 years, 9 months, and 20 days; Eva Catharina Beckinbaugh, born Sept. 3, 1780, died Dec. 6, 1854.

Col. Jacob Creager used to relate many incidents derived from his father of the conflicts of the Tories and Whigs in the days of the Revolution. All that section of country leading from Frederick to Catoctin Furnace and Harman's Gap and the Creagerstown District was studded with a thick belt of woods. But few roads were open, and persons had to be very cautious how they made their way through the tangled thickets. Robbers and Tory emissaries were known to invest many of these secret hiding-places, and the champions of the Whig cause were begirt with danger on every side. Col. Creager was authorized to watch the Tories, and succeeded at length in breaking up the gang who had for two years annoyed the patriots by their midnight warfare of pillage, and by carrying information to the enemy in distant States.

The teachers for the term ending April, 1881, were:

School No. 1, 57 pupils, Marian E. Eichelberger; No. 2, 47 pupils, J. H. Seabrook; No. 3, 52 pupils, John M. Parrell; No. 4, 31 pupils, James W. Robinson.

Rocky Ridge Village is at the junction of the Emmittsburg with the Western Maryland Railroad,

fifty-one miles from Baltimore, seven from Emmittsburg, and sixteen from Frederick. W. H. Albaugh is postmaster. The Lutheran and German Reformed Churches are respectively supplied by Revs. W. C. Wise and Henry Wissler, of Mechanicstown. The Baptists have a neat church and a good congregation. Among the oldest and most prominent settlers in this neighborhood, and in fact in Frederick County, are the Biggs family. Joshua Biggs, who has been so closely identified with the best interests of Western Maryland, was born Jan. 1, 1821, in what was then a part of Frederick County, on a farm within a few miles of his present residence, Rocky Ridge, on the Western Maryland Railroad, in Creagerstown District. His father, William Biggs, of Jacob, was born Sept. 24, 1793, on a farm on the east of the Monocacy, and now in Carroll County, about three miles from Rocky Ridge. His mother was Sarah Haines, born July 4, 1794, near what is now Lenwood Station, Western Maryland Railroad. His grandfather, Jacob Biggs, died many years ago; the grandfather of his mother was William Haines, a member of the Society of Friends. His ancestors on both sides emigrated to this country from England. His wife, Phebe S. Morrison, to whom he was married on the 11th of November, 1856, was of Scottish descent; her grandparents came to this country during the war of 1812; her maternal ancestors derive their origin from the Bruces of Scotland. Joshua Biggs was inspector of public schools of Frederick County from 1851 to 1865, and he has been a director of the Western Maryland Railroad since 1866. In early life he devoted several years to teaching and the study of medicine, but engaged in agricultural pursuits in 1856, and commenced operating a merchant mill, and gained reputation as a miller by the introduction of improved machinery and in the manufacture of high grade flour. In 1870, on the completion of the Western Maryland Railroad to Rocky Ridge, he built a residence and warehouse at that point, which is on his paternal estate and at the junction of the Emmittsburg Railroad, and is now engaged in superintending the business at that point, together with the merchant mill, and cultivating a large landed estate of five hundred acres surrounding his residence.

His children are William Haines, Robert Bruce, James Sheridan, and David Morrison. William H. is married, and in business at Rocky Ridge. Robert Bruce is a student of law at the University of Maryland, and the other children are with their parents.

His education was obtained in the schools of the county and at Gettysburg College. He is a member of the Reformed Church. He was before the late war a Whig; during the war he was a Union man, but differing from his political friends on questions of reconstruction of the Union, he became and continues a Democrat. He was elected to the House of Delegates from Frederick County by the Union party for the sessions of 1861 and 1862, and was re-elected and served in the session of 1864. He was elected to the Senate by the Democrats in 1867, and served in the sessions of 1868 and in 1870.

Owen's Creek Village is near Loy's Station, on the Western Maryland Railroad. The postmaster is C. W. Loy, dealer in agricultural implements. Drs. J. L. Miller and J. W. Devilbiss are the resident physicians. The industries are: G. W. Shaw, J. Martin, millers; John Campbell, D. S. Loy, M. D. Loy, blacksmiths; James Dorsey, A. Hines, Walter Carl, carpenters.

EMMITTSBURG DISTRICT, No. 5.

Emmittsburg, or Election District No. 5, has the following boundaries: "Beginning at that ford on Monocacy River formerly called Price's, but now Knoof's Ford; thence with the main road until it intersects the main road leading from Creagerstown to Emmittsburg, near Benjamin Ogle's old place; then by a division line drawn towards a wash-house on Owing's Creek, above the ford on said creek, formerly built by James Ogle, deceased; thence up said Owing's Creek to the south branch thereof; then up the said south branch to the lines of No. 10, and with the lines of No. 10 reversed to the Pennsylvania line; then with said line to Rock Creek; then with said creek to Monocacy River; then down said river to the beginning." Its boundaries, therefore, are Pennsylvania on the north, Carroll County on the east, Creagerstown and Mechanicstown Districts on the south, and Mechanicstown and Hauver's on the west. The district is situated in the northeastern portion of the county. The only town is that of Emmittsburg, besides which are the villages of Bridgeport and Motter's. The western section near Carrick's Knob is the most thickly settled portion of the county. Near by is Round Top, seventeen hundred feet high.

William Elder, a Catholic, who emigrated from St. Mary's County and was the first white man who settled in the district, gave the name of "St. Mary's Mount" to a portion of Carrick's Knob. He located himself at the foot of the Blue Ridge in 1734, then the abode of numerous Indians and the haunt of wild beasts. He called his place "Pleasant Level." Here he built a house, reserving one room for religious services, which he called a chapel. This room was equal in size to all the rest of his house. He was there joined by his family and a few friends from St. Mary's County. Mr. Elder was a devout Catholic, and his chapel was the home for all weary travelers and a delightful resort for all professing his faith. Hospitality was religiously practiced by this good family and their descendants. The little congregation was often visited by priests from St. Mary's, and later from Conewago and Frederick, and sometimes by Father Matthew Ryan, from Path Valley, Pa., until 1807, when St. Mary's church was built. The old mansion stood until about 1852.

Mr. Elder was born in Lancashire, England, in 1707, and emigrated to St. Mary's County not earlier than 1728, and not later than 1732. In 1739 death invaded the home of this pioneer, taking from him the mother of his five children. Her maiden name was Ann Wheeler, and she was married to Mr. Elder in England. She bore him four boys and one daughter. The first son, William, married a Miss Wickham. The second, Guy, was twice married, and by his second wife had thirteen children, viz., Joseph, Judith, James, Polly, Benjamin, Patsey, Ellen, Rebecca, Guy, Priscilla, Edward, Thomas, and George, of whom the first four went to Kentucky. Charles, third son of the emigrant, married Julia Ward, of Charles County. The fourth child, Mary, married Richard Lilly, of Virginia, and through her children the family became connected with that of the McSherrys of Virginia. The fifth child, Richard, married Phœbe Deloyvier.

In 1744, William Elder married Jacoba Clementina, daughter of Arnold Livers. This gentleman, an Englishman by birth, had been an active and noted partisan of James II. Upon the collapse of that monarch's cause he had been obliged to flee from his native land, and became the proprietor of a large estate in Maryland, called "Arnold's Delight," on Owing's Creek. It is said of Arnold Livers, in explanation of the singular name given by him to his daughter, that he had registered a vow that his first child, whether boy or girl, should be called James. The good priest to whom the child was presented for baptism found no difficulty in complying with the father's wishes, and so the babe was christened Jacoba Clementina. Livers in his flight from England carried this child with him. She bore to William Elder four sons and two daughters, named Elizabeth, Arnold, Thomas, Ignatius, Ann, and Aloysius. It was from the second named that the title for the farm upon which now stands the structure known as Mount St. Mary's College was derived. In the old Catholic cemetery, about half a mile below St. Mary's College and near the town of Emmittsburg, three stones mark the graves of William, Ann Wheeler, and Jacoba Clementina Elder. The inscriptions, which are still distinct, record their names and dates of births and deaths: William Elder, born in 1707, died April 22, 1775; Ann Wheeler Elder, born 1709, died Aug. 11, 1739; Jacoba Clementina Elder, born 1717, died Sept. 19, 1807. Thomas, the third child of William Elder by his second wife, was born Jan. 4, 1748, and married, in 1771, Elizabeth Spalding, a sister of Basil Spalding, of Charles County, and shortly after that event removed to and occupied a farm in Harbaugh's Valley, where he lived for twenty-eight years, and where his family of eleven children were born. The names of these in the order of their birth were:

1. Anne, or Nancy, born July 1, 1772, lived single, and died in 1844.

2. Basil Spalding, born Oct. 22, 1773, married Elizabeth Snowden, Nov. 18, 1801, and died in Baltimore, Oct. 13, 1869 (his wife having died Jan. 20, 1860).

3. Catharine, born March 7, 1776, was the second wife of Joseph Gardiner, of Nelson County, Ky. Three of her stepchildren became Sisters of Charity, of the Nazareth Community, and of these the late Mother Frances Gardiner was for many years superior of the sisterhood.

4. William Pius, born May 4, 1778, died in Baltimore, Aug. 22, 1799.

5. Clementina, born June 16, 1780, married Richard Clarke, and died Aug. 21, 1851.

6. Ignatius, born July 21, 1782, married Monica Greenwell.

7. Theresa, born March 1, 1785, died unmarried, Dec. 19, 1816.

8. Thomas Richard, born June 14, 1789, married Caroline Clements, and died July 11, 1835.

9. Christiana, born Oct. 30, 1791, married John B. Wright.

10. Mary Elizabeth, born May 15, 1794, married John Tarboe.

11. Maria M., born April 11, 1791, married John Howell.

To the second of the above—Basil Spalding Elder and his wife Elizabeth (Snowden)—were born thirteen children, of whom three died in infancy. Of the other ten, Eleanora became a Sister of Charity; another daughter, Mrs. Jenkins, died in Havana in 1846; another, Mrs. Baldwin, in Baltimore, in 1872. Of their male children seven survive,—Francis W., in Baltimore; Basil T., in St. Louis; James C., in Baton Rouge, La.; Joseph E., in Denver, Col.; Thomas S., in New Orleans; William Henry, Bishop of Cincinnati; and Charles D., in New Orleans.

It was in 1799 that Thomas Elder broke up his establishment in Harbaugh's Valley and removed to Kentucky, accompanied by all his children except Basil S., then engaged in business in Baltimore.

James Elder, the first Catholic of his name to emigrate to Kentucky, was born in this district in 1760, and was the son of Guy, and grandson of William Elder. He married Ann Richards, and immediately went to Kentucky, where he settled on Hardin's Creek. His brother William in a few months joined James in his Kentucky home. James Elder died Aug. 15, 1845, and Ann, his wife, Jan. 8, 1857. Ann Wheeler, the wife of William Elder the emigrant, died in her thirty-fourth year, of consumption, the hardships of her husband's pioneer life proving too much for her frail constitution. There being no undertakers, necessity compelled them to hollow out a chestnut-tree, and in this rude coffin the remains of this good woman were deposited.

After the Elders the first pioneers were Scotch-Irish, then Irish and German settlers began pouring in. Among the earliest settlers were the Emmitts, Shieldses, Williamses, Baughers (Isaac and Joseph, successful merchants), Grovers, Troxells, Hayses, Harrits, Weltys, Weavers, Danners, Agnews, Zimmermans, etc.

The Biggs and Troxell Families.—The first member of the Biggs family in Maryland came from England and settled in New Jersey. He afterwards removed to Frederick County, about 1750, and settled where Biggs' Ford on the Monocacy now is. After some time he sold his farm and settled on the Monocacy, between the mouths of Pipe Creek and Tom's Creek, where he bought fifteen hundred acres of land, extending from Pipe Creek to the mouth of Tom's Creek. He lived here with two of his sons, William and Benjamin Biggs. Benjamin sold his interest to his brother William and moved to Western Virginia, where he raised a large family. His eldest son, Benjamin, resided near West Liberty. He became a general, and with his brothers was engaged in the Indian wars. His brother, Zachariah Biggs, laid off Ohio into sections, and kept the land-office in Steubenville, Ohio. Frederick, the seventh son of William Biggs, and grandson of the emigrant, bought the farm called "Rich Revel," owned by William, on the Monocacy, opposite the mouth of Stony Branch, of Lieut. George Need, an officer in the Revolution in the company of Capt. Benjamin Ogle.

Frederick Biggs married Mary Wilson, daughter of Joseph Wilson, and died in 1840, aged seventy-one years and nine months. He was the father of the late William Biggs, the great-grandson of the emigrant.

Prior to the Revolutionary war Peter Troxell, Sr., bought of Indian Tom—from whom the well-known creek derived its name—the tract of land of which Richard Offut now owns part. Near this tract Mathias Martin, from Germantown, Pa., settled. Mr. Martin's farm in later years was owned by Peter Sebold. Mr. Martin married a daughter of Peter Troxell, and their daughter, Mary Magdalena, became the wife of Lewis Motter. John Troxell was the eldest son of Peter Troxell. To him is ascribed the building of Troxell's mills, which stand near the junction of Tom's Creek and Flat Run (now the property of Mr. Eisenhart), and which have a historic interest. Before and during the Revolutionary war political meetings were held in the mills. William Elder, the second son of the old pioneer, was a leading spirit at these gatherings. He was an orator by nature, and many a stirring appeal in behalf of the colonies was made by him. In 1779 we find William Elder captain in the Revolutionary army. Many of Mr. Troxell's descendants are now residing in Emmittsburg. He and his wife died there, and are buried in the graveyard attached to the Elias church. John Troxell died in 1836, in his eighty-third year.

Tom's Creek Presbyterian Church.—Some years before the founding of Emmittsburg, a thrifty colony of Scotch-Irish Presbyterians located themselves near Mason and Dixon's line, in what was then called York County, Pa., now Adams. These men were used to hardships, and were robust and healthy, and of industrious and economical habits. They soon crossed the border into Frederick County, and built a church on Tom's Creek Hundred, about a mile and a half from the then embryo town of Emmittsburg. These settlers were ardently attached to the doctrines of their forefathers, and it is a singular coincidence that the two creeds most bitterly opposed to each other in Scotland and Ireland, the Catholic and the Presbyterian, should have been planted side by side in the Emmittsburg District of Frederick County before they were established in any other portion of Western Maryland.

The minutes of the Presbytery of Donegal show that the Rev. Robert McCordie was appointed to supply at "Monokasy" on the second Sabbath of September, 1760. This is the first notice of preaching within the bounds of the congregation. There was also a congregation at Pipe Creek, and we find that the Presbytery being in session "at Mr. Duffield's meeting-house," in Carlisle, April 27, 1761, a "supplication" for supplies was presented from Tom's Creek. The response, if any, of the Presbytery is not recorded. On June 24th, Tom's Creek again asked for supplies. A similar request was at the same time presented from Pipe Creek. The Presbytery thereupon appointed Rev. John Beard to preach at Tom's Creek on the first Sabbath in October. The service held at Tom's Creek in accordance with this appointment, early in October, 1761, was most probably the first within the bounds of the congregation. In November, 1761, Rev. Robert McCordie was appointed to supply Tom's Creek once each in the months of December, February, and April; and at the spring meeting a further appointment was made for the month of May. In November, 1762, it was ordered that the Rev. Samuel Thompson supply Tom's Creek Church on the second Sabbath of that month, and that the Rev. Robert Smith supply Tom's Creek on the second Sabbath of April. Robert Smith was one of the pioneers of Presbyterianism in the southern part of Pennsylvania and the adjacent portions of Maryland. He came from Londonderry, Ireland, in 1730, and became the pastor of the churches of Pequea and Leacock, Pa. He also founded and maintained a classical school at Pequea, where his life was chiefly spent.

April 17, 1763, Tom's Creek and Pipe Creek asked leave to apply to the Presbytery of New Brunswick for a young man to supply them. The answer to this request is not recorded, but the Rev. Samuel Thompson was appointed to preach at Tom's Creek on the third Sabbath of June, and the Rev. Robert Smith on the first Sabbath of September.

This church was supplied during the next autumn and winter by William Edmiston and John Slemons, licentiates of the Presbytery of Philadelphia, and by the Rev. Robert Smith. For the summer of 1764, Mr. Slemons had three appointments at Pipe Creek and two at Tom's Creek. The Rev. Samuel Thompson also preached at the latter place in October. Messrs. Edmiston and Magaw subsequently renounced Presbyterianism and took orders in the Episcopal Church. The former became rector of St. Thomas', Frederick Co., Md., and the latter rector of St. Paul's, Philadelphia.

At a meeting of the Presbytery, Oct. 24, 1764, a controversy began respecting the boundary line between the two congregations of Tom's Creek and Pipe Creek. Each church charged the other with encroaching on its territorial limits. After hearing their mutual complaints the Presbytery advised the parties to maintain harmony, and appointed the Rev. Messrs. John Roan and Samuel Thompson, with Elders James Murphy and Samuel Eddy, a committee to meet at Tom's Creek on the second Wednesday of November to determine the bounds between said congregations. Accordingly a meeting was held, at which the following agreement was entered into:

"We, the subscribers, commissioners of Lower Marsh, Tom's Creek, and Piney Creek congregations, being met this 25 of April, 1765, in order to treat respecting the division lines between said congregations, have agreed that a line being drawn straight from Marsh Creek meeting-house to that of Tom's Creek, a line crossing that line at right angles at the end of four and a half miles from Marsh Creek meeting-house, and extended on the one side to Tom's Creek, and on the other till it intersect Piney Creek congregation, shall be the division line between said congregations; and that the division line between Marsh Creek congregation and that of Piney Creek shall be midways between the meeting-houses of said congregations. Witness our hands this day and year above written. *Et sic subscribitur.*

"JOHN ALEXANDER, WILLIAM COCHRAN,
"SAMUEL MCFARRAN, JOHN MCKINLEY,
"WILLIAM SHIELDS, JAMES MCGINLEY,
"ANDREW HART, WILLIAM PORTER."

During the next five years Tom's Creek and Piney Creek had occasional supplies, appointed chiefly at the stated meetings of the Presbytery in April and October. Andrew Bay, John Slemons, John Craighead, Hezekiah James Balch, Samuel Thompson, and Robert Cooper were among their preachers.

Hezekiah James Balch was born in Harford County, Md., in 1746. He graduated at Nassau Hall, 1766, and was licensed the following year by the Donegal Presbytery. After ordination by the same Presbytery, in 1769, he went on a mission to the South, and became a pastor of Rocky River and Poplar Tent Churches, in North Carolina. He was a member of the famous Mecklenburg Convention, held May 19, 1775, and was one of three Presbyterian ministers appointed to prepare resolutions for the action of the convention. The other two were Dr. Ephraim Brevard and William Kennon, and all three were graduates of Princeton. The "declaration" framed by this trio of Presbyterian ministers, and adopted by the patriotic citizens of Mecklenburg, contained in it the germ of the grander national act of July 4, 1776. Mr. Balch died in the summer of 1775. He was an elder brother of the Rev. Stephen Bloomer Balch, D.D., for many years pastor of "Georgetown on Potomac," and who preached at an early day in Frederick. The committee met at Tom's Creek on the fourth Tuesday in June, 1771, all the members being present except Mr. Craighead and Elder Dill. Mr. Cooper was chosen moderator, and Mr. Duffield clerk. The commissioners from Piney Creek were Patrick Watson, Abraham Heytor, Benjamin McKinley, James Galt, and James Hunter; from Tom's Creek, William Blair, William Shields, William Brown, and Samuel Emmit.

When the committee and parties came together there were two subjects of dispute to be considered. The first was that Piney Creek desired a separation from Tom's Creek and the settlement of a pastor of their own, whereas Tom's Creek favored the continuance of the previous union and the joint settlement of a pastor. After a patient and full hearing of the arguments on both sides, the committee decided this first question in favor of Piney Creek and dissolved the union.

The second subject of controversy was that of the boundary line between the two congregations. In April, 1765, this question was considered and apparently settled by agreement of the commissioners of the three congregations of Lower Marsh Creek, Tom's Creek, and Piney Creek, but a closer inspection of the terms of that agreement shows that the lines then determined were those between Marsh Creek and Piney Creek, and between Marsh Creek and Tom's Creek respectively, and not the line between Tom's Creek and Piney Creek, which the committee was now called to consider. The settlement of this long-continued dispute involved the question of priority of organization, it being conceded that the older congregation had the right to have its wishes respected as to the line of division. The committee decided that the claim of Tom's Creek to priority was valid, and hence gave judgment in favor of making the Monocacy the dividing line instead of Stony Ridge.

The first pastor of Tom's Creek was the Rev. Hezekiah Balch. The call was placed in his hands Aug. 15, 1775, and was accepted the next day. It was accompanied with subscriptions amounting to £112 9s. 6d., the congregation agreeing to pay a salary of £100. The installation services took place Oct. 16, 1775, and were conducted by the Rev. Amos Thompson and the Rev. John Slemons.

In April, 1778, the Rev. Mr. Balch, pastor of the Tom's Creek Church, assigned as a reason for absence from the previous meeting that he "was at camp."

After being released from his charge, Mr. Balch took a dismission to the Presbytery of Hanover, in Virginia. Rev. Hezekiah Balch, D.D., was born in Harford County, Md., in 1741. He entered the College of New Jersey in 1758, graduated there in 1762, and was licensed by the Presbytery of New Castle in 1768 or 1769. He labored for some time within the bounds of the Hanover Presbytery, and was ordained as an evangelist by that body March 8, 1770.

The pulpit again being vacant, the Presbytery appointed supplies for Tom's Creek for the next six months, and regularly thereafter while without a pastor.

In October, 1780, a paper signed by forty members of the Lower Marsh congregation was presented to the Presbytery, asking leave to unite with Tom's Creek in forming the same pastoral charge. Action upon this paper was deferred until the next April, when the proposed union was effected with the concurrence of Tom's Creek.

The following year, 1781, the congregation called the Rev. Matthew Woods to become its pastor. This call Mr. Woods declined, and accepted one from Hanover, Dauphin Co., Pa. The same congregation called on, April 8, 1783, Rev. John McKnight. It was accompanied with subscription papers amounting to £180; Marsh Creek agreeing to pay £85, and Tom's Creek £95, but each congregation claiming a discharge upon the payment of £75 per annum. Each congregation also promised a gratuity of fifty bushels of wheat upon Mr. McKnight's acceptance of the call. Overtures were at the same time made to Mr. McKnight from South Branch, Del., and Patterson Creek, Va., and from Bullskin and Coal Spring Churches, but after consideration he formally accepted the proposals of Lower Marsh Creek and Tom's Creek. His installation took place on the second Wednesday of November, 1783, at the Lower Marsh Creek Church, the Rev. James Martin and the Rev. John Block conducting the services. Mr. McKnight's labors continued nearly six years, and were eminently acceptable to the people of his charge. In 1789 he was called to be a colleague of the Rev. Dr. John Rodgers, pastor of the United Presbyterian Churches of New York City. The salary offered was £400.

The Presbytery met Sept. 8, 1789. Dr. Rodgers appeared as the commissioner of the congregations, and urged the Presbytery to put the call into Mr. McKnight's hands. The commissioners from Marsh Creek (James McYaughy, Benjamin Reed, and Reynolds Ramsey) and from Tom's Creek (William Shields, William Porter, and John Witherow) protested very earnestly against Mr. McKnight's removal.

After mature deliberation the Presbytery determined to place the call in his hands. He accepted it, and the pastoral relation was thereupon dissolved.

He was dismissed October 7th, and was installed December 2d over his new charge in New York. Dr. McKnight's pastorate in New York continued twenty years, at the end of which time he removed to a small farm which he had purchased for a residence in the neighborhood of Chambersburg, Pa. He continued to preach as a supply until 1822, but declined any regular settlement after leaving New York.

He was born near Carlisle, Pa., Oct. 1, 1754, graduated at Nassau Hall, under the presidency of Dr. Witherspoon, in 1773, and studied theology under the direction of the Rev. Dr. Robert Cooper. He was licensed and ordained by the Presbytery of Donegal, and labored in Virginia before his settlement in Lower Marsh and Tom's Creek congregations. The degree of Doctor of Divinity was conferred upon him by Yale College in 1791, and in 1795 he was moderator of the General Assembly. He became president of Dickinson College in 1815, but resigned the office after having held it for a little more than a year. Two of his sons entered the ministry. His death occurred Oct. 21, 1823, in the seventieth year of his age.

After a vacancy of two years, Lower Marsh Creek and Tom's Creek applied to the Presbytery for leave to prosecute a call for William Paxton, then a licentiate under the care of the Presbytery of New Castle. The request was granted, and the services of Mr. Paxton secured. He was taken under the care of the Presbytery of Carlisle, at Upper Marsh Creek, on the 7th of June, 1792, and was ordained and installed at Lower Marsh Creek on the 3d of October, 1792. Dr. Robert Davidson preached the ordination sermon, the Rev. James Long presided and gave a charge to the candidate. The services were held in a grove near the Marsh Creek church, where a temporary pulpit and seats were provided for the accommodation of an assembly exceeding the capacity of the house of worship.

Mr. Paxton ministered to the united congregations with great assiduity for four years, when Lower Marsh Creek became desirous of obtaining his undivided time and labors. Application was made Oct. 4, 1796, to have the connection with Tom's Creek dissolved, Marsh Creek alone offering to raise a support of one hundred and fifty pounds. Tom's Creek earnestly remonstrated against any disturbance of the existing relation. After a full and patient hearing of Mr. Paxton and of the commissioners on both sides, the Presbytery decided to grant the request of Marsh Creek. The pastoral relation with Tom's Creek was accordingly dissolved. Mr. Paxton was the son of a respectable farmer of Lancaster County, Pa. He was born April 1, 1760, and his early life was devoted to agricultural employments. He served in the Revolutionary war, and was in the battle of Trenton. He prosecuted his studies, literary and theological, at the Strasburg Academy, under the direction of Rev. Nathaniel W. Sample. His pastorate at Marsh Creek lasted forty-nine years. He was a man of decided ability, and a faithful preacher. The degree of Doctor of Divinity was conferred upon him by Dickinson College in 1826. His death occurred April 16, 1845. The Rev. William M. Paxton, D.D., pastor of the First Church of New York, is his grandson.

From 1796 to 1800 Tom's Creek was without a pastor. Among the supplies who preached during this period were Mr. Francis Herron, Mr. David McConaughy, and Mr. Matthew Brown. The two last named became respectively presidents of Washington and Jefferson Colleges in Western Pennsylvania. The next pastor of Tom's Creek was the Rev. Patrick Davidson, who was born in 1775. He graduated at Dickinson College, was introduced to the Presbytery of New Castle as a candidate by the Rev. Nathan Grier, Oct. 5, 1796, and was licensed by that body Oct. 5, 1797. He was ordained and installed pastor at Fagg's Manor, Pa., April 3, 1799. Owing to some "disagreeable circumstances rendering his situation uncomfortable" among that people the pastoral relation was dissolved, April 2, 1800. In the afternoon of the same day he obtained a dismission to the Presbytery of Carlisle, by which he was received Oct. 7, 1800, just two days before his acceptance of the call from Tom's Creek.

Mr. Davidson was elected principal of the Frederick Academy, Aug. 15, 1809. This position he accepted, and removed to Frederick in the autumn of that year, although the pastoral relation with the Tom's and Piney Creek Churches was not dissolved until Sept. 26, 1810. Out of this premature removal grew the complaint that he had left his congregations unsupplied during the winter of 1809–10. Mr. Davidson was dismissed to the Presbytery of Baltimore, Sept. 28, 1814, and remained in connection with that body until his death, which occurred Oct. 9, 1824. During his principalship of the Frederick Academy he supplied the Frederick Church, and preached occasionally at Pipe Creek and Creagerstown.

He accepted a call to Tom's Creek, Oct. 9, 1800, upon a salary of one hundred and fifty pounds. He was installed on the third Tuesday of the same month. The services were conducted by the Rev. John Slemons, who was appointed to preside; the Rev. William Paxton, who preached the sermon; and the Rev. David McConaughy, who gave the charge.

In October, 1801, the Piney Creek Church extended a call to Mr. Davidson, offering him £87 10s. for one-half his ministerial and pastoral services.

A commissioner informed the Presbytery that Tom's Creek had been consulted and had agreed that Mr. Davidson's services should be divided between the two congregations. The call was accordingly presented to Mr. Davidson, and upon his acceptance of it the arrangement was consummated.

Tom's Creek and Piney Creek were now, for the first time in a period of forty years, united under the same pastor. The union then established has been continued with entire harmony through successive pastorates for three-quarters of a century. Mr. Davidson's labors were continued in the two congregations until the autumn of 1809. The next pastor was the Rev. Robert Smith Grier. When Mr. Grier came into this region he was a licentiate of the Presbytery of New Castle. He appeared at Gettysburg, April 14, 1813, and obtained leave to labor in the bounds of the Presbytery of Carlisle. On April 12, 1814, he accepted calls to Tom's Creek and Piney Creek, each church promising him a salary of three hundred dollars.

In January, 1824, there were four ruling elders in the Tom's Creek Church, viz.: James Crocket, John Witherow, William Long, and William Bigham. In October of the same year John Stewart, Nathaniel Randolph, Joseph Kerr, and John Nichols were added to the Session, making eight in all. There were at this time one hundred and seven communicants. In 1839 the church edifice, which had stood one mile north of the village, was taken down and rebuilt in Emmittsburg, where the Tom's Creek Church has since worshiped.

The pastorate of Mr. Grier, though covering more than half a century, was a quiet, uneventful one. He lived during a large part of his ministry upon his farm, three miles north of Emmittsburg, and over the line separating Maryland and Pennsylvania. Conducting farming operations himself, he was in full sympathy with his parishioners, who were largely engaged in agricultural pursuits. At the close of the fiftieth year of his pastorate he preached a semi-centennial discourse, reviewing the history of his labors. On this occasion his brother, Rev. Dr. John C. Grier, and his two sons, Smith and Laverty, both of them Presbyterian ministers, were present and took part in the exercises.

Rev. Robert Smith Grier was the elder son of Rev. Nathan and Susannah (Smith) Grier. He was born at Brandywine Manor, Chester Co., Pa., May 11, 1790. His father was pastor of the Presbyterian Church at the Forks of the Brandywine. His preparative studies were pursued at the Brandywine Academy. He graduated at Dickinson College, Carlisle, September, 1809, and united with the church in 1810. He studied theology under his father's instruction, and was licensed by the Presbytery of New Castle in September, 1812. He was received under the care of the Presbytery of Carlisle, April 12, 1814, and the same day accepted calls to Tom's Creek and Piney Creek Churches. He was ordained Sept. 28, and installed Nov. 14, 1814. This was his only charge. Mr. Grier was buried in the Tom's Creek graveyard, which is one mile north of Emmittsburg. Mr. Grier was married three times. His first wife was Elizabeth Laverty, by whom he had two sons and three daughters, Susan, Mary, and Jane. Susan married Rev. John R. Marsden, an Episcopal minister. Mary is unmarried and a resident of Emmittsburg.

The other daughter is dead. Mrs. Grier died Sept. 25, 1830. Mr. Grier's second wife was Sarah Jane Annan, by whom he had one son and one daughter. The son died in early life. The daughter, Ann Margaret, became the wife of Maj. O. A. Horner, of Emmittsburg, and died Aug. 14, 1872.

His third wife was Mrs. Margaret Stewart, who still survives, and is an active and useful member of the Emmittsburg Church.

After the decease of Mr. Grier both churches were supplied for a few months by Rev. Daniel B. Jackson, then a licentiate, but now the pastor of Black River Falls Church, Wisconsin. Early in the summer of 1866 they were visited by the Rev. Isaac M. Patterson, pastor of the Annapolis Church, and a member of the Presbytery of Baltimore. This visit resulted in a call to the pastorate of both churches. Mr. Patterson commenced his labors early in August, and was installed at Piney Creek, November 13th, and on the next day at Emmittsburg. The Session of Tom's Creek consisted of the following elders: David Gamble, Nathaniel Grayson, John Witherow, William C. Landers, John J. Neeley, and Alexander L. Horner. Mr. Patterson's ministry lasted seven years, during which a parsonage property was bought and enlarged and improved at an outlay of four thousand six hundred and fifty dollars. Both houses of worship were remodeled and refurnished, involving a further expenditure of three thousand two hundred and fifty dollars. In April, 1867, the Session of Tom's Creek applied to the Presbytery for a change of ecclesiastical name. In response to this application the designation "Emmittsburg" was substituted for the well-known but less euphonious title of "Tom's Creek."

In the summer of 1873, Mr. Patterson resigned his pastoral charge, in order to accept a call to Milford, N. J., which is his present field of labor. The relations of the present pastor to the united churches of Emmittsburg, Piney Creek, and Taneytown were constituted in December, 1873, by a committee of the Presbytery of Baltimore.

Emmittsburg is situated in a beautiful section of Frederick County, on the east side of the Blue Ridge Mountains, one and a half miles from Mason and Dixon's line, and adjoining Adams County, Pennsylvania. The foundation of Emmittsburg dates back to 1786. It was then known by the name of Poplar Fields. The original population consisted of seven families, viz.: Richard Jennings, merchant; Adam Hoffman, hatter; John Rogers, tavern-keeper; Michael Smith, blacksmith; Frederick Baird, carpenter; James and Joseph Hughes, merchants and architects.

At that time the village consisted of only a few buildings, and was called "Silver Fancy." Subsequently William Shields built a house where Peter Hoke's store now stands, and this was the beginning of "Shields' addition." Capt. Jennings built the first house in the village. It was a one-story frame structure. The first brick house, adjoining the former, was also built by Capt. Jennings. This was taken down some years ago, and rebuilt by Isaac S. Annan & Co. In 1786, James and Joseph Hughes built the two houses on the northwest corner of the square at present occupied by their descendants. They also built houses on the lot now owned by George W. Rowe and John O'Donohue. They then built the Eagle Hotel (on the site now occupied by the Western Maryland), where many a weary traveler found rest. In after-years it was managed by Mrs. Margaret Agnew, who fell a victim to the cholera in 1853. James Hughes built the second brick house, on the northeast corner of the square, which, with many others, was burned in 1863, and rebuilt by Dr. Robert L. and J. C. Annan. This old mansion was the cradle of the Catholic Church in Emmittsburg, containing a room where the Catholic service was recited whenever practicable. It was visited at this period by Father Sufremont, of Conewago, and afterwards occasionally by Father Dubois, of Frederick. The third brick house was built by Frederick Baird, and is now the Presbyterian parsonage. Mr. Baird was a first-class mechanic, and his work in carving was of a superior character. The first tan-yard was built and owned by Christian Flamt, and sold by him in 1798 to Lewis Motter, of York County, Pa., father of the present owner. Mr. Motter came to Emmittsburg, Sept. 5, 1798. Here he raised a large family, and accumulated a considerable amount of property. He also filled many important positions of trust. John Ropley was at that time (in 1786) justice of the peace for three districts, Taneytown, Pipe Creek, and Emmittsburg. The first schoolmaster of the village was Thomas Cocklin. At the beginning of the century Martin Corcoran taught here, and there are some still living who are indebted to Miss Margaret Corcoran for their knowledge of "A, B, C's." Mr. Sanders was a subsequent teacher, and some of his descendants reside in the county. There is no one living who can recall the days spent under the guidance of a Cocklin or Mallady, and few indeed remember Master William Mullen and his mathematical academy on Church Street, or Isaac Burbank, whose daughter became the wife of the late distinguished Governor and senator of Indiana, Oliver P. Morton. But many can remember the amiable and gentlemanly Robert Crooks, also Oliver McClain and Mr. Walters. The town now has three schools, two public and one parochial. A large public school building has been erected lately at the West End. The colored school is taught in Lincoln Hall. St. Euphemia's Academy, conducted by the Sisters of Charity, has passed through its third year successfully, giving great encouragement to the devoted teachers, and a large and commodious building is about to be erected on St. Vincent's Avenue for this school. There are six flourishing Sunday-schools.

In the year 1786 the male inhabitants of the village and vicinity assembled at Hockinsmith's tavern, one and a half miles from town, now the home-place of David S. Gilliland, to deliberate concerning a change of name. Hon. John McGurgan being called to preside, proposed to change the name from "Poplar Fields" to "Emmittsburg" in honor of William Emmitt, one of the largest landholders in the district. All present threw up their hats, clapped their hands, and hurrahed for Emmittsburg. The company had quite a merry time, and having drunk the health of the newly-baptized town, returned home full of sanguine expectations as to the rapid growth of the infant settlement.

The name of the post-office was also changed from Poplar Fields to Emmittsburg. William Greenmeyer, who died in 1802, in the thirtieth year of his age, was the first postmaster. He was a son-in-law of John Troxell, who built the brick house adjoining the Eagle Hotel. This house was burned in 1863, rebuilt by Joshua Shorb, and is now owned by Isaac Hyder. The second postmaster was Patrick Reed, at the same time landlord of the Eagle Hotel. The third was a German by the name of Louff; the fourth, Joseph Hughes, Sr.; the fifth, Joachim Elder; the sixth, Dr. Augustus Taney; the seventh, Joachim Elder again, who was succeeded by Robert Crooks, James Knouff, Maj. O. A. Horner, and Samuel N. McMair.

In the year 1790 society in Emmittsburg was in a very crude state. Playing long bullets was the general exercise. The ladies excelled in spinning the cloth which served as garments for their families and servants. After the population increased, dancing-masters were introduced, and manners grew more refined, sociability became the order, and charity the ruling principle. On Saturday afternoons farmers came to town to transact their business, and after business devoted themselves to pleasure, visiting their friends, etc., and making it quite a holiday.

The Elias Church.—It is probable but by no means certain that the original building of Elias Church was erected in 1797. It was conjointly owned, and on alternate Sundays and other occasions used by the Evangelical Lutheran and the Reformed Church congregation.

The German Reformed and Lutheran Churches in this neighborhood were from the start, by reason of relationships existing among their members and the unity of language (both being German), so intimately associated that they held their church property in common, and in the main recognized but one form of government. Their first church was located on Tom's Creek, about two and a half miles from the town, where the Tom's Creek Methodist Episcopal church now stands.

The Elias church, which was built in 1797, enlarged in 1835, and remodeled in 1870, had at first a small spire, framed into the timbers of the roof, on the eastern gable. This was subsequently shattered by lightning, and the present steeple was built in 1814, Peter Troxell being the architect and George Smith doing the carpenter work. The principal portion of the funds were provided by a lottery. The charter and constitution of the organization was changed in 1850, when each congregation assumed its own government, the two still holding the buildings and grounds in common. The first Lutheran pastor was the Rev. Jonathan Ruthroff, who resided in Greencastle, Pa. The Rev. John G. Gropb succeeded him. He resided at Taneytown, where he died March 27, 1829, aged seventy, having been pastor for twenty-seven years. In 1826, Rev. John A. Hoffman became the associate of Rev. Gropb, and preached occasionally in the English language. On the resignation of Rev. Gropb in 1827 or 1828, Rev. Hoffman succeeded him. He resigned in 1833, and was succeeded by Rev. S. D. Finckle in 1834, who resigned in 1836, and was followed by Rev. Ezra Keller in 1837. Mr. Keller remained only one year, and was followed by Rev. Solomon Sentman, who continued from Jan. 7, 1841, to July 4, 1852. About this time the congregation was separated from the Taneytown charge, and was constituted the Emmittsburg charge, of which Rev. John Welfry became the first pastor. Mr. Welfry entered upon his duties Nov. 5, 1852, and resigned after serving two years. He was followed by Rev. George S. Collins as supply for six months from Nov. 6, 1854, when declining health necessitated the relinquishment of his charge.

Rev. Henry Bishop took charge Sept. 1, 1855, and served over seven years, resigning Dec. 8, 1862. He was followed April 1, 1863, by Rev. W. V. Gotwald, who continued until Feb. 2, 1866. Since then the Rev. E. S. Johnston has been pastor. During his ministration a parsonage has been purchased, and the general advancement of the charge has been greatly promoted.

Reformed Church.—The Reformed congregation, which occupied the Elias church conjointly with the Lutheran, had for their first pastor Rev. Valentine Nicodemus, who died at Taneytown at an advanced age about 1788. Rev. Lewis Heinch was the next. Rev. J. Ranhauser succeeded him, and was followed by Rev. Frederick Ranhauser, who preached his first sermon June 19, 1806, and resigned in 1816. The Rev. William Runkel commenced his ministry Nov. 3, 1816, and closed April 20, 1821. He died in the year 1832, aged eighty-four, and his remains repose in the Elias Church graveyard. Rev. David Bossler became pastor in 1821, and continued as such for a period of eleven years. Prior to this time the services were conducted almost exclusively in the German language. Rev. Elias Heiner began his ministry Oct. 20, 1833, and during his pastorate and since the English language has been used, with only occasional services in German. Dr. Heiner was for many years afterwards well known as pastor of the old Second Street Church in Baltimore City. Rev. Samuel R. Fisher next succeeded, and remained three years, closing his term Aug. 25, 1839. Dr. Fisher has long been known as the able and highly-efficient editor of the *Reformed Church Messenger*. Rev. A. P. Frazee followed Rev. Mr. Fisher, and remained from June 14, 1840, to July 24, 1842. Rev. William Philips was chosen pastor in 1842, and resigned in 1846. Rev. G. W. Aughinbaugh succeeded him in that year, and continued ten years. During his pastorate the town was visited by the cholera, and he evinced no small degree of courage and self-sacrifice in ministering to the suffering throughout the continuance of the epidemic. Dr. G. W. Aughinbaugh has been for several years past the president of Palatinate College in Pennsylvania. For several years following the church was without a regular pastor. During the year 1858, however, Rev. Elnathan E. Higbee officiated as supply. He has since become well known as a successful educator in classical and theological science, as a pulpit orator, and as president of Mercersburg College. Rev. Walter E. Krebs began his ministry Sept. 26, 1858, and remained four years. Rev. John M. Titzel entered upon his duties Nov. 16, 1862, and preached his farewell sermon on the third Sunday after the Epiphany, Jan. 26, 1873. On Easter-day of the same year Rev. A. R. Kremer was elected pastor, and was installed in his office on Whit-Monday, June 2d, following, and continued until 1881, when he was succeeded by Rev. William A. Ying, the present incumbent. In 1868 the Reformed congregation, having sold their interest in the Elias church to the Lutherans, began the erection of the building now known as the Church of the Incarnation, which was finished and dedicated July 31, 1869. On the 31st of March, 1873, the church spire was blown down during a violent wind storm, and preparations for rebuilding it commenced at once, and before many months had passed, the bell, which was uninjured by the fall, was again in place.

St. Joseph's Catholic Church.—Towards the close of the last century Rev. Matthew Ryan, passing through the village, on his way to Path Valley, suggested to Mr. Hughes the idea of building a church, and gave him ten dollars as the first subscription. Mr. Hughes went to work with a will, and in 1793 soon raised sufficient funds to commence the erection of the church. He was the architect and contractor, under the supervision of four trustees, viz.: Richard Jennings, Henry Arnold, Joseph and James Hughes. The two last gentlemen presented the lot upon which the church is built, including the cemetery where their bones now rest. Richard Jennings is also buried there. Father Frambach, from Frederick, and Father Sufremont, from Conewago, were the first priests who ministered to the wants of the people. They were also visited by Father Dubois. Father Dubois was succeeded by Father Matthew Ryan, a native of Kildare, Ireland, who was the first resident pastor of St. Joseph's Church. Father Ryan died on the 5th of January, 1817. Father Duhamel, who died in 1818, also administered to the congregation for some time. He was followed by Father Simon Gabriel Bruté, Rev. John F. Hickey, Father Thomas McCaffrey, and other zealous priests. In 1852 the church was taken in charge by the Lazarist Fathers, an order instituted by St. Vincent de Paul. In 1831, Father John Hickey enlarged the edifice, and in 1841, finding the congregation still increasing, determined to erect a larger structure. On the day that the old church was torn down Father Hickey was transferred to Baltimore, to the lasting regret of his flock. The labor of completing the new church devolved upon Rev. John McCaffrey, of Mount St. Mary's College, who entered upon it with zeal and energy. It was finished in 1842 (Mr. Tehan, of Frederick, architect), and dedicated on the feast of St. Michael of that year by Most Rev. Archbishop Eccleston, the sermon being preached by Rev. Father Ryder, of the Society of Jesus. A handsome steeple was erected in 1869, the design of which was furnished by the Rev. Father Burlando. The name of this church was St. Mary's until in 1808, Bishop Dubois having given that name to his mountain sanctuary, the church in town was placed under the patronage of St. Joseph. Ever since the foundation of St. Joseph's Church, excepting six months, the choir has been composed of the descendants of the original choir of 1793, a period of eighty-seven years.

On the 15th of January, 1851, the chapel was robbed of property valued at one thousand dollars, including a crucifix, golden chalices, etc.

Mount St. Mary's Catholic Church.—In 1807, James Hughes was appointed architect for Mount St. Mary's Church. To transport building materials over roads covered with brambles and whortleberry-bushes was a laborious undertaking, but the task was lightened by the cheering influence of Father Dubois. Some neighbors, not of the faith, gave their labor voluntarily; among these were John Rowe and Robert Fleming. The latter used to relate many amusing anecdotes of his friend Father Dubois.

The land was given by Joseph Elder, a grandson of the pioneer. In 1824, Father Dubois built a large seminary, which was unfortunately burned down. In the words of Dr. McCaffrey,—

"A noble edifice, the fruit of so many years' unparalleled exertions, was on the point of completion, and a hundred youthful students were ready to occupy it. The feast of Pentecost, on the 6th of June, 1824, came and passed away. The last rays of a bright sun, ere it set behind Mount St. Mary's Mount, had gilded the cross which rose from the cupola of this majestic structure. When the sun again appeared in the east it threw its cheerless beams on blackened walls and smouldering ruins. Startled by alarming cries at the dead of night from the tranquil slumbers which visit the good man at the close of a well-spent day, Mr. Dubois beheld at a glance the ruin of his hopes. His characteristic fortitude did not forsake him. Conquering the agonies of despair, he calmly gave directions or observed in silent grief the progress of destruction. Soon he pointed out some defects in the floor of the flaming edifice which he would remedy in the next; and this, too, though the snows of sixty winters had whitened his head, and he had gone beyond his present means in erecting the building which was destroyed. And again he realized his prediction. He had the public confidence and sympathy. God prospered all his labors, and a new college arose from the ashes of its predecessor."

Father Dubois not only finished it, although he remained only two years longer here, but he also presided over the erection of a still more spacious academy at St. Joseph's. Father Dubois was called away from his work in order to be consecrated Bishop of New York in 1826. He died in 1843. "All things whatsoever he did," says Father McCaffrey, "were fertilized by the dews of heaven, were watered from the fountains of divine grace, and prospered under the blessings of the most high God."

Mount St. Mary's College.—The appearance of this famous institution and its surroundings afford abundant evidence of the zealous efforts of the Fathers, who have labored unremittingly to make it a leading college of the church. From its lofty height Carrick's Knob looks down with majestic mien upon the extensive fertile plains outstretched below, and Tom's Creek winds its clear, silvery thread between its grassy banks. The Indian graves, the Grotto, the Devil's Den, and the Hermitage are the same as of yore, and the autumnal leaf on Mary's Mount displays all the gorgeous colors of autumn as when the early student first gazed upon the enchanting scene. But in place of the lowly log farm-house now stands an elegant mansion, bespeaking the comfort and competence of its inmates. Lime and deep plowing have made the soil generous in its yield. Orchards have grown up, and even vineyards are gladdening the heart of the thrifty cultivator. In 1808 the college opened in a small farm-house with seven scholars, gathered together by the Rev. John Dubois; now a cluster of spacious stone buildings form the material part of this famous college. Nearly two hundred students are annually trained within its walls, and thousands have gone forth from it in bygone years, and still bear an affectionate remembrance of their Alma Mater. It has sent forth, including the founder, thirteen bishops and archbishops, and more than one hundred and fifty priests.

On "Pleasant Level," near Hayfield, stands an old house, long used as a store, and now occupied by L. Dielman. This ancient building was converted by Father Dubois into a school, and was the beginning of the noted St. Mary's College. The school was removed a few years after to its present site by the advice of Bishop Dubourg. The present spacious and substantial buildings form a striking contrast with their humble beginning. The first students were John Lilly, of Conewago, James Clements, of Littlestown, Rev. John Hickey, of Frederick, and Dr. James A. Shorb. In 1809 the pupils at the Pennsylvania School, sixteen in number, were transferred to St. Mary's. In 1810, Father Dubois' pupils increased to forty, the next year to sixty, and in 1813 to eighty-five. Father Dubois' duties as a priest were partially relieved by the arrival and assistance of Mr. Duhamel, a French priest exiled to French Guiana, but who escaped and in 1809 came to St. Mary's.

In 1812, Rev. Simon Gabriel Bruté, a native of France, was stationed at St. Mary's as the spiritual director of the sisterhood of St. Joseph's, and filled the post of professor at St. Mary's College, which he held until 1815. He was the guiding spirit of the place. In recreation hours this indefatigable man laid out roads in the mountains with his own hands, even clearing off the stones. He also constructed the "Grotto" in a romantic part of the mountain above the college, where nature is seen in all her beauty. Huge rocks, overgrown with moss and projecting over a ravine, and crystal streams gurgling down the hillside in the midst of dense foliage and wild-flowers of various hues, combine to make a picture as lovely as it is unique. Father Bruté in 1815 was elected president of St. Mary's College of Baltimore, but resigned this position in 1818 to return to assist Father Dubois. Here he remained until consecrated Bishop of Vincennes, Ind., in 1834. He was born March 20, 1779, in the province of Little Brittany, France, and died June 28, 1839. The log houses of the school, increased to two rows, became too small, and new buildings were erected. As already stated these were destroyed June 6, 1824, by fire. In 1826, however, the new and larger building was completed, and Father Dubois opened the studies of the scholastic year within its walls. Father Dubois was succeeded as president by the Rev. Michael De Burgo Egan, who from his youth had been trained in the institution, over which he ruled with a spirit worthy of the teachings and example of his venerated master. Declining health, however, soon interrupted his labors. His successor was another pupil of Dubois and Bruté, the Rev. John B. Purcell, afterwards Archbishop of Cincinnati. In 1830, Dr. Purcell obtained the first charter for the college from the Maryland Legislature, making the institution a regular college; and in June, 1831, the first diplomas under the charter were given to the graduates. In 1832, Father Purcell was consecrated Bishop of Cincinnati. The college continued to progress under the direction of Rev. Francis B. Jamison and Rev. Thomas R. Butler until 1838, when Rev. John McCaffrey took the helm, to guide it to a still higher degree of prosperity than it had yet attained. In 1858 occurred the fiftieth anniversary of the college, and October 6th and 7th were days of jubilee and rejoicing by its assembled alumni from every part of the globe. Addresses were delivered by President McCaffrey and Hon. James McSherry, and poems were recited by George H. Miles and Rev. Charles C. Pise, D.D., the latter a Latin ode. President McCaffrey retired in 1871, and was succeeded by Rev. John McCloskey. The very Rev. Dr. John McCaffrey, for many years president of Mount St. Mary's College, died at two o'clock on the morning of Sept. 26, 1881, aged seventy-six years. Dr. McCaffrey was widely known throughout the United States from his long connection with Mount St. Mary's. He was born in Emmittsburg in 1805, and entered Mount St. Mary's College in 1821. After spending some years in the study of theology in the ecclesiastical seminary, he was ordained deacon in 1831. Through humility he remained in this order for seven years. He was advanced to the order of priesthood by Rt. Rev. Samuel Eccleston in 1838. The Archbishop of Baltimore was then a member of the college council, and nominated Dr. McCaffrey for the presidency of the college left vacant by the resignation of Rev. Thomas R. Butler. He assumed his place in the council and the presidency of the college March 19, 1838. This office he held continuously for over thirty years. In consequence of failing health he resigned in 1871. His first associates in the council were Rev. John Hickey, Rev. H. Xaupi, Rev. Philip Borgna, Rev. George Flaut, and the Rev. P. Corry. His brother, Rev. Thomas McCaffrey, was also associated with him till he died, Aug. 5, 1853. He taught theology in the seminary for several years while president, succeeding to the chair of theology previously held by Bishop Brute and Rev. Philip Borgna. In 1856 he began a new church on the college grounds, which financial embarrassment prevented him from completing. After his resignation of the presidency he continued to reside at the college, and occasionally, as his health would permit, taught his favorite classics. He left in MSS. some very valuable sermons, of which only three have been preserved in print. These are an oration on the landing of the pilgrims of Maryland, and funeral discourses relating to Bishops Dubois and Brute. His funeral took place at the college church on Thursday morning, Sept. 29, 1881. President McCloskey resigned in 1877, and Rev. John A. Watterson was elected president, and served until 1880, when he was made Bishop of Columbus, Ohio. Rev. John McCloskey then again resumed the presidency, but only for a few months, as death closed his labors on Christmas eve, 1880. His successor was Rev. Wm. Byrne, but in the spring of 1880 the institution became involved in serious financial difficulties, and was placed in the hands of Capt. James McSherry, as receiver. Father Byrne, however, still has charge of the educational administration. The college is situated at the base of the Blue Ridge Mountains, and is about a mile and a half from St. Joseph's, and nearly the same distance from the town. Its commencement exercises, held June 22 and 23, 1881, were unusually interesting, and were attended by large audiences, gathered from various portions of the country.

St. Joseph's College.—In 1809 the foundation of St. Joseph's institution of the Sisters of Charity and school for young ladies was begun by Mrs. Eliza Seton in a plain dwelling and with humble surroundings. Here Mother Seton and her band of devoted followers labored for years in their high and holy calling. Mrs. Seton died in 1821, in her forty-seventh year, regretted by all who had the happiness to know her. This incomparable woman was very beautiful, but cheerfully relinquished the world to devote herself to religious work. St. Joseph's to-day is undoubtedly one of the finest educational establishments in the United States. Its charter of incorporation was obtained in 1817 from the Maryland Legislature, through the influence of Robert Goodloe Harper. Among the many spots rendered interesting by legends of the past is a favorite resort in the grounds of this college, called the "Indian burying-ground." This spot, surrounded by forest-trees, has been converted by the Sisters of Charity into a lovely grotto, in which stands an image of the Virgin Mary.

This mother-house of the Sisters of Charity, like the acorn, has grown to a large tree, whose branches overshadow the most distant States of the Union, numbering one hundred and ten mission-houses. The Sisters also have charge of hospitals, orphanages, and schools. There are over eleven hundred members of the community belonging to St. Joseph's. It was in June, 1809, that Mother Seton removed a portion of her little community from Baltimore, and while the plain dwelling was being finished for them on their land in the valley they occupied the house in which Mr. Dubois had first resided, and which he vacated for the log college below it.

St. Joseph's now forms a magnificent cluster of buildings, located on a healthy, beautiful spot, and surrounded by lovely grounds. These, with its several hundred Sisters and nearly two hundred girls in the college, speak in no feeble voice of the beneficent results which may follow the self-sacrificing efforts of a single individual.

The commencement exercises of June 23, 1881, were the most successful in the long and eventful history of the institution.

The Methodist Episcopal Church.—In 1831 the Methodist church was erected, during the pastorate of Rev. Mr. Moreland, a native of Ireland, who settled at the base of the Blue Ridge Mountains, under the shadows of Carrick's Knob. Mr. Moreland was found dead in his gig one Sunday morning in August as he was on his way to officiate in the Methodist chapel on the banks of Tom's Creek. His remains were interred in the cemetery adjoining the new church in Emmittsburg, which he caused to be built. The first sermon delivered in this edifice was the funeral panegyric of Rev. Mr. Moreland. The present pastor is Rev. E. O. Eldridge.

Physicians.—The first physician in Emmittsburg was Dr. Reuch, who is buried in Tom's Creek graveyard. Dr. Brown settled on the banks of Tom's Creek some years before Dr. Reuch came to the village. Among those who became popular as medical practitioners was Robert I. Annan, who though not a pioneer was early on the ground. Dr. Annan was a pupil of the renowned Dr. Richard Rush, of Philadelphia, from whom he received his certificate of admission to the medical faculty on the 29th of April, 1789. He began the practice of his profession in Carroll's Lower Tract, where he was married, Nov. 29, 1790, to Mary Cochran (granddaughter of Wm. Cochran, who made the first purchase of that tract), and subsequently removed to Emmittsburg.

Dr. Annan's son, Dr. Andrew Annan, secured a practice almost equal to that of his father, and on retiring from professional life he transferred his business to his son, Robert L. There was also the "old doctor's" brother, Dr. Samuel Annan, distinguished as the founder of a medical school in Baltimore, and as a professor of medicine in Kentucky. The highly-esteemed and successful physician Dr. Jefferson Shields and Dr. Alexander Stewart, of Shippensburg, Pa. (Dr. Andrew Annan and Dr. Shields were partners for some time), also had a lucrative practice in this section. Dr. James W. Eichelberger, Sr., was also associated with Dr. Andrew Annan for a number of years. He has but recently retired, in a green old age, from the regular and active work of professional life, leaving as his successors his sons, Drs. Charles D. and James W. Eichelberger. Dr. William Patterson was early associated in the practice of his profession with the well-known Dr. James A. Shorb, who came here from Littlestown, Pa., and was one of the first students of Mount St. Mary's College. Dr. Patterson died on the 27th of May, 1876, at the age of seventy-four years and three days. Dr. Augustine Taney, whose father was an uncle of the late Chief Justice Taney, read medicine with old Dr. Swope, at Taneytown, and settled when a young man in Emmittsburg, where he became a highly-influential citizen. In the midst of his usefulness and prosperity he fell a victim to the cholera in 1853, at the age of fifty-six years. In addition to Dr. Shorb and Dr. Patterson, Dr. Wells, whose son and grandson are both physicians, Drs. Robert and Daniel Moore, Dr. John B. Brawner, Dr. Felix McNeal, Dr. John J. Grover, and Dr. Timothy Sweeney have been attending physicians at Mount St. Mary's and St. Joseph's at different times.

The present incumbent of this position, the well-known Dr. Brawner, is a lineal descendant of the first settlers of the neighborhood, the Elders and Livers. Dr. J. G. Troxell, though but recently settled here, has won the confidence and respect of a large circle, and resides between the college and Clairvaux, the summer resort.

Various Local Events.—Emmittsburg was incorporated by the General Assembly of Maryland, Jan. 13, 1825. Subsequently quite a number of amendments were added, and a revised, amended, and enlarged charter was passed March 10, 1854, which remains in force without any important change.

The town being so near the border suffered a great deal during the late war from the depredations of both armies, but was happily spared from being the scene of any conflicts.

On the night of June 16, 1863, however, a fire broke out in the livery-stables of Beam & Guthrie, which spread with terrible rapidity over a large portion of the village, and rendered many of its inhabitants homeless. It was not long, however, before new buildings arose from the ashes, and there are few vestiges of the conflagration now to be seen. The fire was discovered about eleven o'clock, in the loft of the stables, which were soon destroyed. The flames communicated to the dwellings of Mr. Adelsberger and Dr. Eichelberger, directly in front, and then laid waste the whole side of the street going east for about ten doors from the Square, when the houses directly opposite took fire and were also destroyed, the last one being the hotel of Mr. Wile, one of the largest in the State outside of the city of Baltimore. It was four stories high, and erected four years previous to its destruction. Messrs. D. and J. Adelsperger owned the first dwelling and store burned. They had built it but a few years before, and occupied it as a tin and house furnishing store. Dr. Eichelberger's, next door to them, was a large two-story brick building, directly on the corner of the Square and the road to Gettysburg. The next was the large dwelling on the opposite corner, occupied by Dr. Patterson, then the merchant tailor store of Patrick Kelly, together with his dwelling. The other houses destroyed were occupied by Messrs. Frank Magraw, James Hosplehorn, and Upton Koontz, Miss Zimmerman, Jacob Horner, Simon Mentzer, John Miller, James L. Wise, Mr. Winter, Mr. Morrison, Jesse Seabrooks, Jesse Nussear, Joshua Shorb (store-house and dwelling), and the City Hotel of D. Wile. The fire is supposed to have been the work of an incendiary. Most of the houses consumed were built of wood, and many of the occupants barely escaped with their lives, losing all their furniture and clothing. The burning of the City Hotel of Mr. Wile proved a great inconvenience at that particular time to the many visitors and friends of Mount St. Mary's College and St. Joseph's Academy, whose annual commencements took place the following week. There was one fire-engine in the place, which was worked and managed by the citizens when it was required, the water being supplied in buckets filled at the different wells and cisterns. Some years ago Block's old tavern, which stood at the head of Main Street, was torn down, and a new hotel, the Emmit House, was built in its place. A long, fine, wide street has been opened northward from this hotel, and has been built up mainly through the enterprise of Isaac Annan.

In October, 1838, a celebration was held in Emmittsburg by the Democratic Reformers in honor of the election of their Governor and majorities in both branches of the State Legislature. A dinner was given, at which John Jones presided and Dr. William Patterson acted as secretary. Among the guests was Hon. Francis Thomas. In the evening Mr. Thomas addressed the company, after which a procession was formed, under command of Maj. Harritt as marshal, and marched through the town.

The telegraph was introduced in 1866, and its wires have ever since been under the efficient management of the Misses Helman.

In 1875 a railroad connecting with the Western Maryland Road at Rocky Ridge was completed, but not until after the death of its first president, Joshua Motter. His successor was John A. Dwin, and in a few years, he having died, Rev. F. Goedry was elected, but his clerical duties preventing his giving the necessary time and labor to the road, he resigned, and the present incumbent, J. Taylor Motter, was chosen.

There are four large public halls,—Annan's on the Square, the band hall on Church Street, St. Vincent's, and Lincoln. The town has several stores, including one general merchandising establishment, two tin and stove-stores, three dry goods, three furniture establishments, three undertakers, three hotels, five shoe-shops, two tailors, one jewelry-store, two apothecaries, two confectioneries, three milliners, seven general stores, one gunsmith, two carriage-factories, two saddlery-shops, one clothing-store, one photograph-gallery, with many groceries, a marble and tan-yard, and several mechanical shops of varied industries.

The town is a favorite summer resort, owing to its healthfulness and the lovely scenery by which it is surrounded.

Filial Lodge, No. 62, A. F. and A. M., was located here. It was never represented in the Grand Lodge, and the record of its proceedings (if any ever existed) cannot be found.

Massasoit Tribe, No. 41, I. O. R. M., kindles the council fire every Saturday evening, 8th Run. Officers:

R. E. Hockensmith, P.; Daniel Gelwicks, Sach.; John G. Hess, Sen. S.; J. J. Mentzer, Jun. S.; John T. Gelwicks, C. of R.; Charles S. Zeck, K. of W.

Emerald Beneficial Association, Branch No. 1.—Monthly meetings, fourth Sunday in each month. Officers:

J. Thomas Bussey, Prest.; Thomas J. Henley, Vice-Prest.; Geo. F. Rider, Sec.; F. A. Adelsberger, Asst. Sec.; Dr. J. B. Brawner, Treas.

Junior Buiding Association.—The officers are:

Sec., J. Thomas Bussey; Directors, J. T. Hayes, Prest.; W. S. Guthrie, Vice-Prest.; John Witherow, W. H. Hoke, Daniel Lawrence, James A. Rowe, Charles J. Rowe, Joseph Waddles.

The town officers are:

Burgess, J. H. T. Webb; Commissioners, U. A. Lough, Charles S. Zeck, Daniel Sheets, James C. Annan, F. W. Lansinger, J. T. Long.

The first newspaper published in Emmittsburg was edited and printed by E. S. Riley, now of Annapolis, about 1841, and was called the *Emmitsburg Banner*. After publishing it for three months he sold out the paper and office to Troxell, Duphorne & McTale. In 1844, Mr. C. Grate published the *Emmitsburg Star*, a very interesting and useful sheet, which he continued several years. The *Mountain Echo*, a small paper, was published by young Lagarde in 1860 at Ingleside. The *Emmitsburg Chronicle* was established June 14, 1879, by Samuel Motter, a graduate of Princeton College, and is still edited and owned by him. It is an independent journal, fearless and outspoken, and one of the best local papers in Maryland. About 1845 a paper was started called the *Emmitsburg Gazette*. It took no active part in political affairs, but was chiefly devoted to local matters. It was published by Robert F. Crooks. It claimed that as Samuel Emmit spelled his name with only one "t," Emmitsburg should be spelled in the same way.

The teachers for the term ending April, 1881, were:

School No. 1, 45 pupils, C. N. Stern; No. 2, 55 pupils, J. F. Adelsberger; No. 3, 77 pupils, C. D. Hoover, Emma E. Motter, assistant; No. 4, 47 pupils, E. F. Smith; No. 5, 54 pupils, S. P. Ambrose; No. 6, 47 pupils, George Leyfold; No. 7, 58 pupils, W. C. Krise; No. 8, 42 pupils, F. C. Fox; No. 9, 20 pupils, Columbia Fraley; No. 10, 33 pupils, W. F. Miller. No. 1 (colored), 45 pupils, Cornelius Landers.

The justices of the peace are Michael C. Adelsberger, Henry Stokes, James Knouff, Eugene L. Rowe; Registrar, James A. Elder; Constable, Wm. H. Ashbaugh; School Trustees, Henry Stokes, E. R. Zimmerman, U. A. Lough.

Bridgeport is five miles from Emmittsburg, and near the Carroll County line. M. E. Correll is postmaster. Its industries are represented by Amos Bishop, Joseph Hobbs, John Long, George Ohler, carpenters; Sylvester Fink, Thomas Hawks, John Ohler, blacksmiths; William Gingell, William Starner, millers; Samuel Linaly, Benjamin Pool, merchants; Samuel Switzer, wool-manufacturer.

Motter's is on the Emmittsburg Railroad, and is three and a half miles from Rocky Ridge. Its location is pleasant, and the country about is fertile and productive. Among its business men are T. L. Naill, auctioneer and postmaster; J. T. Cretin, William Shriver, and Mrs. J. Walters, hotel-keepers; Lawrence Deilman, Naill & Fisher, merchants; W. H. Dorsey, Henry Lindsey, J. & W. Sheeley, masons; William Eisenhart, Henry Maxwell, millers; Dr. J. W. Hickey, dentist; Joshua Hobbs, David Wachter, Walters & Taylor, carpenters; R. S. Knode, harness-maker; Philip Stansberry, David Weaver, blacksmiths; Dr. James Troxell, physician; George W. Worthen, wheelwright; and James Worthen, plasterer.

CATOCTIN DISTRICT, No. 6.

By an act of General Assembly, passed Feb. 3, 1848, George Shutt, Jacob Young, of D., and Hiram H. Mullen were designated commissioners to lay out an election district out of those parts of Hauver's and Middletown contiguous to each other. On May 9, 1848, they laid out Catoctin, or Election District No. 6. Catoctin thus took the place of District No. 6 (Taneytown), which had been added to Carroll on the formation of that county.

From the boundaries established in 1848 it will be seen that Hauver's is on the north, Mechanicstown, Creagerstown, and Frederick on the east, Jackson on the south, and South Mountain on the west. The settlers were nearly all Germans, with some Swiss, who came into this district just prior to the French and Indian war. Among the first to settle were the Wolfs, Blessings, Hoovers, Groffs, Kuhns, Brandenburgs, Crouses, Myers, Stottlemyers, Leathermans, Buzzards, Markers, Harshmans, Shuffs, Hoffmans, Freys, and Reckers. They were a religious people, thrifty and hard-working, and soon opened up good farms and acquired comfortable homes. Many of the earliest settlers were Dunkers, or Tunkers, people of strong religious convictions and of a sturdy pioneer stock. This religious denomination arose in 1708 in the Palatinate, from eight persons who entered into a covenant with each other to meet regularly, to carefully and impartially examine the doctrines of the New Testament, and, by the help of God, to ascertain what are the obligations it imposes on professed followers. The result of these meetings was the formation of the society now generally known as the Dunkers. As stated in a preceding chapter, a settlement of the Dunkers was made in 1725 on the banks of the Cocalico Creek, in Lancaster Co., Pa., where the Reading road and Downingtown turnpike intersect it, in Ephrata township, and is well known by the name of "Kloster," or "Ephrata," or "Dunkertown," a nickname from the word Dunker, or Tunker, a corruption of Taeufer, Baptists. About twenty-five years after the settlement at Ephrata a number of the Tunker families removed to Frederick County and located in this district, among whom the Hoover family was most prominent.

The villages in this district are Wolfsville and Ellerton.

Wolfsville is six miles from Smithsburg, and near Catoctin Creek. It derives its name from the Wolf family, one of the earliest to settle in this neighborhood. On Feb. 6, 1851, a public meeting was held here to consider the propriety of forming a new county out of portions of Frederick and Washington Counties. The meeting was unanimously opposed to the new county project. Other districts falling within the range of the contemplated new county also held meetings and expressed themselves favorable to its formation, but the object was never accomplished.

South Mountain Lodge, I. O. O. F., No. 125, was instituted Oct. 28, 1873, of which H. S. Myers is secretary. John H. Mangans is postmaster at Wolfsville, and Dr. Lewis Lamar the resident physician. The merchants are Holter & Phleeger, J. W. Hoover, and F. Leatherman. The industries are D. Biser, N. Eccard, millers; G. H. Barkdall, John Myers, Lawson Kline, blacksmiths; A. W. Bartgis, J. G. Smith, shoemakers; J. A. Grove, carpenter; J. O. Hays, cooper; Mrs. E. Hoover, boarding-house; Scott T. Martin, huckster; Amanda S. Recher, Mrs. A. C. Stottlemyer, dressmakers; and J. N. Wolf, butcher. The churches are the Lutheran, German Reformed, Dunkerd, and United Brethren. Rev. Wm. R. Coursey, for many years in charge of the latter, died on July 1, 1881, in his seventy-eighth year, having preached in this neighborhood for over a third of a century.

Ellerton is near Catoctin Creek, and is nine miles from Smithsburg. The postmaster and merchant is Thomas F. Bittle; physician, Dr. L. Wachter. The industries are Josiah Harp, miller; Israel Delander, J. E. Palmer, undertakers; D. Wastler, Aaron Shipley, shoemakers; J. H. Moses, J. C. Palmer, Joseph Palmer, M. L. Weddle, James Weddle, carpenters; H. Poffenberger, Isaac Poffenberger, blacksmiths.

William Poole, one of the oldest citizens of the Valley, died on July 4, 1881, near this village, in his ninety-first year.

The teachers for the term ending April 15, 1881, were:

School No. 1, 52 pupils, John O. Hays; No. 2, 63 pupils, M. A. E. Biser; No. 3, 66 pupils, S. E. Grove, Hezekiah Harp, assistant; No. 4, 41 pupils, M. V. Easterday; No. 5, 25 pupils, C. L. Wachter; No. 6, 37 pupils, H. O. Ridmour; No. 7, 56 pupils, D. Gibbon; No. 8, 24 pupils, C. J. Stoleburger; No. 9, 46 pupils, W. E. Schildknecht.

URBANA DISTRICT, No. 7.

By an act of General Assembly, passed Feb. 28, 1848, John F. Simmons, James F. Johnson, and John H. Worthington were appointed commissioners to lay out an election district out of parts of Buckeystown (No. 1) and New Market (No. 9). On June 16, 1848, they established Urbana, or Election District No. 7, to fill the vacancy or number which Westminster once held before the creation of Carroll County, of which it formed a constituent part.

The district is in the southern portion of the county. Frederick and New Market Districts are on the north, New Market on the east, Montgomery County on the south, and Buckeystown on the west. The district was settled as early as 1730 by the Bealls, Murdochs, Cockeys, Worthingtons, Donalds, Duvalls, etc., who were followed by the Johnsons, McPhersons, Fearhakes, Rines, Brashears, Henrys, Moberlys, Simmonses, Dixons, and others. The first pioneers were of English origin, but afterwards many Germans came in.

Nathaniel Beall was among the first to locate, and married Ann Murdoch. Their son, Elisha Beall, was born in the district Jan. 4, 1745, and died Dec. 17, 1831. Elisha Beall's first wife was Susanna Murdoch, by whom he had no children. His second wife was Jane Perry, of Montgomery County, by whom he had eleven children, to wit:

1. Mary, born July 24, 1784.
2. Harriet, born April 27, 1786, died Aug. 14, 1834.
3. Eliza, born Aug. 15, 1787, died Nov. 28, 1850.
4. William Murdoch Beall, born March 16, 1789, died March, 1848; was sheriff of the county.
5. Perry Wilson, born July 20, 1799, died Sept. 8, 1821.
6. Cassandra, born March 22, 1792, died Oct. 9, 1839.
7. Jemima, born Sept. 20, 1793.
8. Rebecca, born Oct. 1, 1795, died 1871.
9. James Perry, born May 15, 1798, died 1802.
10. George Washington Beall, born April 15, 1801.
11. Jane Margaret, born July 6, 1804, died Sept. 25, 1821.

Jane Beall, mother of above children, died Sept. 11, 1819. Of the above, George W. Beall is the only survivor. He married Caroline Cockey, a daughter of William Cockey, by his wife, a Miss Graff, of Green Spring Valley, Baltimore Co. George W. Beall was born on the old Beall homestead, where William Johnson now resides.

The old stone mansion was built about 1810 by his father, Elisha Beall, and took the place of the old log house built by Nathaniel Beall before 1744. Geo. W. Beall's residence is a mile southwest of Ijamsville, and is on the survey called "Duvall's Forest."

Early Glass-Works.—In the *Maryland Journal* of May 22, 1789, appeared the following:

"THE AMERICAN GLASS MANUFACTORY AT NEW BREMEN.—The subscriber having completed his glass manufactory near Frederick Town, State of Maryland, on an extensive plan, is now able to furnish Glass, not only sufficient for the Consumption of this State, but also in great Part for the neighbouring States. He makes Window-Glass transparent and substantial, equal to the London Crown, an inferior Quality equal to the Bristol Crown; all kinds of Flint Glass, such as Decanters and Wine Glasses; Tumblers of all Sizes, and any other Sort of Table Glass. He also cuts Devices, Cyphers, Coats of Arms, or any other Fancy Figures on Glass, and in a short time hopes to be able to furnish Looking-Glasses of all Sizes. He takes this opportunity of returning his hearty and sincere Thanks to a patriotic Public for the Encouragement he has received in giving a Preference to the American Manufactured Glass, and hopes by due Attention to merit a Continuance of their favor.

"For the Convenience of Gentlemen who wish to purchase Glass either by the small or large Quantities, the Subscriber has provided a Warehouse in Frederick Town for the Reception and sale of his Glass, of which he has a large Quantity of all kinds on hand, and has appointed Mr. Abraham Faw his Agent for the Sale thereof, who will dispose of the same as low as possible, in payment of which he will receive Cash, good Bills on Phila. or Balto., or will Barter for assorted Merchandise, either in the Dry or Wet Good Line, or any Kind of Country Produce, and if required, will deliver Glass at any of the Sea-Port Towns in this or the neighbouring States; and any Orders for Glass received by Mr. Faw will be punctually attended to and speedily executed by the Public's obedient and humble servant,

"JOHN FREDERICK AMELUNG."

"NEW BREMEN, May 16, 1789.

"N.B.—The said Glass may also be had of Messrs. Thomas and Samuel Hollingsworth, Merchants, Balto."

These works were on Bennett's Creek, near "Park Mills."

Urbana Village.—Sixty years ago where this pleasant village stands (near the centre of the district) there were but two buildings, "Zion" Protestant Episcopal church, and the tavern kept by John Rine, which was on the lot now occupied by Thomas Dixon. John Rine was born Feb. 16, 1786, and married Mary Rine, a daughter of Casper Rine, a tenant on the Johnson farm. She was born Aug. 11, 1787. John and Mary Rine's daughter married William B. Dorsey, a son of Joshua Dorsey. The old Georgetown (D. C.) road passed through Urbana to Frederick. This village is three miles from Ijamsville and seven from Frederick. The merchants are Thomas A. Smith (postmaster) and J. J. Jamison & Sons; physician, Dr. E. E. Mullinix; millers, A. K. Simmons, Thomas Peters; saw-millers, G. Bussard, J. C. Keller.

The Methodist Episcopal Church was organized and built in 1833, and its erection was mainly due to the efforts of Mrs. Richard Thompson, formerly a Miss Gore, of Freedom, Howard Co. It is a part of the Buckeystown Circuit, and the present pastor is Rev. D. M. Browning.

The Catholic Church was originally an outlying mission of St. John's Church at Frederick, but subsequently the present elegant and commodious edifice was erected. The congregation is very large and constantly increasing, many of its members coming for ten miles around to attend services.

Zion Parish.—Zion Protestant Episcopal Parish was organized in 1802 out of All Saints' Parish. The first vestrymen were elected April 2, 1802, viz.: William Brashear, Elisha Beall, Thomas Sprigg, John Montgomery, Roger Johnson, John H. Simmons, Adam Kramer, and George Kesler. The limits of this parish were not definitely fixed until April 2, 1804, at which time the following were made to constitute its metes and bounds, viz.: " Beginning with the mouth of the Monocacy and running with the Frederick County line to the plantation of the late Wm. McCoy; from thence to Clarksburg; thence with the Georgetown road to Little Seneca; thence up Little Seneca to its source; thence to the head of the three runs; thence to the waters of the Linganore, and with the waters of said creek to the mouth; and from thence down the Monocacy to its mouth." The present stone structure was commenced in 1802, and when completed was consecrated by Bishop Claggett.

From 1832 to 1840 there was a parochial school. The rectors have been the following, viz.:

March 25, 1804.—John H. Reynolds; 1806, parish united with St. Peter's.

1810.— —— Chandler; parish united with St. Mark's.

1813.—William Gibson, resigned 1815; parish united with St. Peter's.

During the vacancy Charles Mann, a candidate for lay orders, acted as lay reader until 1817.

1818.—John Armstrong, resigned 1819; parish united with St. Peter's.

1819.—Wm. Armstrong, resigned 1820 to go to England; parish united with St. Peter's.

1820.—Spencer Wall, resigned 1821; parish united with St. Peter's.

1821.—Wm. Armstrong, until 1832; parish united with St. Peter's.

1832.—Mervin Allen, until 1833; parish united with St. Peter's. Mr. Allen's remains lay in the graveyard until 1880, when they were removed to Frederick, but the tombstone is still standing.

1833.— —— Bean; parish united with St. Peter's.

Feb. 7, 1836.—Jos. Trapnell, resigned 1844; parish united with St. Peter's.

March 22, 1844.—R. H. Phillips, resigned Feb. 8, 1847; parish united with St. Paul's.

Sept. 1, 1847.—Joshua Peterkin, resigned September, 1849; father of the bishop of West Virginia.

March, 1851.—Asa S. Colton, resigned 1852; parish united with St. Peter's.

September, 1854.—Wm. Armstrong, died April, 1857; buried in the graveyard.

October, 1857.—William Smallwood.

September, 1863.—W. F. M. Jacobs, resigned March 10, 1865.

Aug. 15, 1865.—Enoch Reed, resigned Sept. 2, 1866.

October, 1867.—James D. McCabe, resigned Aug. 16, 1873.

No date.—James Stephenson; parish united with New Market.

"Zion" Burying-Ground.—This cemetery adjoins the church. In a remote portion of the ground is the grave of a Confederate soldier, marked only with a slate stone now nearly hidden from view, on which is scratched, in a primitive manner,

"Lieut.-Col. Travener,
17th Va. Cavalry.
Died July 11, 1864."

This officer was mortally wounded at the battle of Monocacy. By his side lies his comrade in arms, a Maj. Smith, of the same regiment, who was shot in a skirmish at Urbana just after the battle of Monocacy, and who died a few days later. Over his grave a neat marble stone has been erected by his friends, bearing the inscription,—

"Frederick F. Smith.
Born at Ripley, Va.
Died July 12, 1864."

At another place is a tombstone inscribed to

"John Montgomery,
A soldier of ——
Born 1760. Died 1846,
Aged 85 yrs."

This stone is broken off at the word " of," but it is highly probable that Col. Montgomery participated in the Revolutionary war. His descendants are worthy and respected citizens of Urbana District.

Another inscription reads as follows:

"Sacred to the memory of
John Porter Blane
Born at Guiness near Ballynahinch
County Down, Ireland.
Died June 24, 1848, aged 42 yrs.
As teacher of Urbana Primary School
he was beloved by the children.
As a citizen he was devoted to the Institutions
of his adopted Country.
Reared to both the profession of law and
medicine with a mind of no ordinary cast
he commanded the admiration of his
friends and the respect of his enemies.
By one who knew him well this small
tribute is erected."

Another stone bears an inscription to

"Rev. Wm. Armstrong,
for 22 yrs rector of St. Matthews parish
Wheeling, W. Va., and 14 yrs. rector of
Zion parish. He died April 1, 1857, aged 69."

Quite alone in one corner of the churchyard is a tombstone with a ship graven on it and the following inscription:

"Sacred to the memory
of John S. Ordeman."

Mr. Ordeman is said to have been a brother of Capt. Herman D. Ordeman, of Frederick County, who commanded vessels.

Urbana Masonic Lodge.—Some time between the years 1790 and 1799 there was a Masonic lodge at "Fleecy Dale Factory," near the old "Glass-Works." The lodge meetings were held in a house kept by a Mr. Stanley as a tavern. This lodge is supposed to have been organized under the auspices of a John Frederick Amelung, an emigrant from the city of Bremen. Amelung came over to this country with two hundred German mechanics, as the agent of a company that commenced the manufacture of glass near Fleecy Dale. George Fearhake, the father of P. M. Adolphus Fearhake, Sr., was a member of this lodge, and came to this country in company with Mr. Amelung. A gentleman named Frew or Faw was the Master of the lodge. The records of this lodge cannot be found.

Iron Furnaces, Factories, etc.—In the southwestern part of the district, near the Monocacy, was the "Johnson Iron Furnace," built in 1774 by the four Johnson brothers,—Thomas, Baker, Roger, and James. This was in operation over a quarter of a century, and the remains of the establishment yet exist and show it to have been a very large furnace. On Bush Creek, in the northern part of the district, the Johnson brothers had a forge which was worked for many years. Extensive deposits of rich iron ore still exist in the district. During the Revolutionary era these furnaces were in active operation and proved of great benefit to the patriot cause, in behalf of which the Johnsons took a most active part in the field, in the cabinet, and in furnishing munitions of war for the Continental army.

Fountain Mills.—This place is situated near Bennett's Creek, two and a half miles from Monrovia. The large Price distillery is located here. The merchants are J. M. Davis (postmaster), Reuben Engle, and Samuel Hobbs. W. T. Turner and S. B. Davis run a flouring-mill, and Jonathan Jacobs has a carriage manufactory.

Park Mills.—This thriving point is on Bennett's Creek, three miles from Buckeystown, nine from Frederick, and sixty from Baltimore. A Methodist Episcopal Church, of Urbana Circuit, is located here. The merchants are Justus Martin (postmaster), S. H. Anderson, Brook Jamison, Moberly & Bro., Thomas Smith, and J. Sims. The other industries and professions are represented by Dr. E. E. Mullinix, physician; O. A. Millard, miller; Charles Dronenberg, D. M. Howard, John Moore, Horace Peters, blacksmiths.

Ijamsville.—This place was named after John Ijams, who owned the land on which the village was erected. It is on the Baltimore and Ohio Railroad, nine miles from Frederick. Most of the village is in New Market District, which is separated from that of Urbana by the railroad track. The mills, T. L. Crawford's store, and the blacksmith-shops of David Case and J. C. Dronenberg are in the Urbana part.

The Ijamsville Flour-Mills, located at Ijamsville, have been in existence for nearly a century under various proprietors. John Ijams was the original owner, and formerly conducted the business. The mill passed into the ownership and control of Mr. McComas in 1874, and was considerably enlarged and improved. It is now furnished with two sets of burrs. The power is supplied by Bush Creek, on the banks of which the mill is situated. Mr. McComas' son has lately been made a member of the firm. With a capacity of twenty-four barrels per day, the mill not only furnishes the local trade, but its brand is well known in the Baltimore market. The finest grades of choice family flour are made at these mills. The proprietor, Mr. McComas, is one of the most influential and enterprising men in the district and county.

The "Araby" Mills, at Frederick Junction, were founded in 1830 by Col. J. McPherson, who sold them to Jas. Gambrill in 1856. Mr. Gambrill is a characteristic American merchant, active, thorough, and full of energy and vim. A native of Howard County, Md., he removed to Frederick in 1849, and soon obtained a place in the front rank of its merchants and manufacturers. Immediately on coming into possession of the mills he added many improvements. The mills now consist of two buildings. The machinery is run by two overshot water-wheels, with a maximum of thirty horse-power each. Six or eight coopers are employed at the mills, whose capacity is about sixty barrels of flour per day.

In 1878, with characteristic energy, Mr. Gambrill enlarged his business by the purchase of the Frederick City Mill, thus increasing his production to forty-five thousand barrels per annum. The latter mill, with five run of burrs, is situated near the Baltimore and Ohio Railroad line. The power used is a sixty horse-power steam-engine, and the machinery is not excelled in the State. The mill produces the finest and best flour that can be made, having the advantage not only of improved machinery but of the grain of Frederick County, than which there is no better in the world. The special brands which are most popular are the "Best Araby" and the "Unsurpassed." The increase of business at the Frederick Mills has been from fifty to sixty per cent. Mr. Gambrill has as his assistants in the business his two sons, Messrs. Richard and C. P. Gambrill.

Araby, sometimes called Frederick Junction, is on the Baltimore and Ohio Railroad, three miles from Frederick. W. T. Mullinix is postmaster; F. B. Miller, assistant postmaster and dispatcher; W. T. Mullinix, railroad and express agent; Frank Mantz, train superintendent; John O'Brien, railroad foreman; Charles Reach, merchant; J. E. Devilbiss, cooper; Harry Hartman, blacksmith; W. H. Kemp, carpenter; J. H. Gambrill, Thos. Kenna, and C. Staley, millers.

The teachers for the year ending April 15, 1881, were:

School No. 1, 33 pupils, M. Virginia Ryan; No. 2, 52 pupils, J. W. Dixon; No. 3, 58 pupils, Georgia D. England; No. 4, 31 pupils, W. R. Winchell; No. 5, 30 pupils, Louisa Dutrow; No. 6, 26 pupils, J. V. Silance; No. 7, 40 pupils, J. H. Shipley. No. 1 (colored), 65 pupils, John H. Griffin; No. 2 (colored), 55 pupils, D. R. Hall.

The magistrates are Joseph Moberly, Francis Knott, and Isaac Davis.

The constables are Jacob Doneberg and —— Dixon.

In the southwestern portion of the district is the Sugar-Loaf Mountain, thirteen hundred feet in height. Bennett's Creek flows through the district from east to west, and the Monocacy River forms its western boundary. Bush Creek flows along the northern edge.

LIBERTY DISTRICT, No. 8.

Liberty, or District No. 8, originally had the following boundaries:

"Beginning at the fork of the Liberty and Annapolis road, and running down the old Annapolis road by Sheets' place and Hobbs' mill on the Linganore to a gate-post at the going into Dorsey's old quarter; thence east to the south branch of the Linganore; thence up said branch to Clary's mill; thence east to the Baltimore (now Carroll) County line; then with said line to the main branch of Sam's Creek; thence down it to Little Pipe Creek; thence down said creek to the mill formerly owned by Roop; thence with a straight line to Pine Tree, on the main road from Woodsborough to Liberty, and from said tree with a straight line to the beginning."

It is situated in the eastern portion of the county, and has Linganore District on the north and east, Woodville on the east, New Market on the south, and Mount Pleasant and Woodsborough on the west. Settlements were made in this district as early as 1732. "Gaither's Chance" of ten hundred and sixty-four acres was surveyed July 24, 1732, and "Hammond's Strife," of twelve hundred and thirty acres, Aug. 10, 1753. Among the earliest pioneers were the Howards, Dorseys, Upton Sheredine, Sollerses, John Wagner, the Hobbs, the Hammonds, Gaithers, John Young, Coales, Crabsters, Sweadners, Abram Jones, Clemsons, Thomas Warfield, Brashears, and Grafton Sheredine.

The Gaithers of Maryland came to America from Wales at a very early period. William Gaither, born Feb. 15, 1745, was an early settler in Montgomery County, and soon after that year purchased a tract of land in Frederick County called "Pleasant Fields," which is now the home and property of his grandson, Henry Chew Gaither. William Gaither married Elizabeth Davis, who was born Nov. 21, 1745. Mrs. Gaither resided before her marriage at "Greenwood," the family-seat of the Davises, and now the property of her grandson, Hon. A. Bowie Davis. After her marriage William Gaither removed to "Pleasant Fields," proposing to reside there permanently, but a short stay convinced him that he liked it less than he had expected, and accordingly he returned to Montgomery County, where he passed the remainder of his days, dying there May 1, 1804. His son, William, Jr., decided, on his father's return to Montgomery, to remain on the Frederick County farm, and continued to reside there. In the troubles growing out of the political agitation preceding the war of 1812, William Gaither, Jr., warmly espoused the cause of the anti-war party, and assisted Alexander Contee Hanson, Gen. Henry Lee, Gen. Lingan, and others in the defense of the *Federal Republican* office at Baltimore against the mob which afterwards broke into the Baltimore jail, killed Gen. Lingan, and maltreated Lee, Hanson, and others. On this occasion Mr. Gaither was seriously injured, and was left as being dead in the street. In order to satisfy himself that life was extinct, one of the rioters thrust a knife into his hand, and finding that he gave no sign of life abandoned him for some other victim. Mr. Gaither was finally rescued by friends, and after a tedious illness recovered. On becoming convalescent he returned to "Pleasant Fields," and spent the rest of his life there as a planter and farmer. He died suddenly on the 10th of April, 1834, and his widow died on the 29th of March, 1844. William Gaither, Jr., was one of eleven children,—seven daughters and four sons,—and was born Oct. 12, 1789. His wife (born April 22,

1796) was Margaret Ann, daughter of John Dorsey, whose ancestors were among the earliest settlers of that portion of Anne Arundel now known as Howard County. Their children were seven in number,—five sons and two daughters,—of whom one daughter and three sons are living. The latter are Henry C., John D., and George. Henry Chew Gaither, brother of William Gaither, Sr., was a colonel in the Revolutionary war, and was distinguished for his courage and patriotism. The small sum which he received in coin on account of his pay he had melted down and made into a large silver cup, on which was inscribed the history of its origin.

Henry C. Gaither, whose portrait accompanies this sketch, is the son of William Gaither, Jr., and the great-nephew of Col. Henry C. Gaither. He was born on the homestead Feb. 19, 1824, and was educated in part at the Brookville Academy, and completed his studies at the academy at Frederick. He then engaged in agricultural pursuits, in which he has continued ever since. Mr. Gaither has been eminently successful in his business, and in private life is one of the quietest, most unassuming, and kindliest of gentlemen. He is a man of great moral and social force, an intelligent observer of men and things, and a potent factor for good in his community. Mr. Gaither attached himself to the Methodist communion quite early in life, and about the beginning of the late civil war became a member of the Methodist Church South. He was a stanch Whig as long as the Whig party remained in existence, and when it became extinct transferred his allegiance to the Democracy, to whom he has ever since adhered. On the 18th of May, 1852, he married Juliet E., daughter of Ephraim H. Maynard, of Frederick County, a descendant of one of Maryland's oldest families. Juliet E. Maynard was born Aug. 28, 1830. Ephraim H. Maynard was born May 29, 1794, at the Maynard homestead, in the vicinity of "Pleasant Fields," where he lived and died. Mr. Gaither's mother, Juliet Higgins, born Oct. 3, 1803, was a daughter of Rev. James Lee Higgins, and her grandmother was Sophia Dorsey, afterwards Mrs. Sheredine. Her great-grandfather was Henry Maynard, who married Eleanor Howard.

Mr. and Mrs. Henry C. Gaither's children have been William Maynard Gaither, Juliet Elizabeth, now Mrs. Henry Norris, Margaret Anne Gaither, Richard Dorsey Gaither, lately deceased, Clara Gaither, Henry Chew Gaither, Jr., Thomas Hodgekiss Gaither, and Emma Maynard Gaither. Among Mr. Gaither's prized possessions is the silver goblet made of Revolutionary coin which Col. Henry C. Gaither left as an heirloom to the member of the family who should bear his name. One of Mr. Gaither's sons is also named Henry Chew, as stated above, and to him the goblet will be transmitted in accordance with Col. Gaither's wish.

Mr. Gaither's eldest brother, John D., was a member of the Maryland Constitutional Convention of 1851, being associated with the Hon. William Cost Johnson and ex-Governor Francis Thomas. The Gaither family is one of the most influential and refined in Western Maryland, and the old homestead, "Pleasant Fields," continues in the present, as in the past, to dispense a generous and charming hospitality. Mr. Gaither owns two fine farms, aggregating three hundred and fifty acres, and at one time was reckoned among the most extensive tobacco-growers of the county.

Liberty District at a very early period was strongly Federal in politics, and afterwards the Whigs had a preponderance of three to one of the votes. During the Revolutionary war, and for a long time afterwards, it was the largest slave-holding district of the county. On Dec. 18, 1760, "The Fountain Copper-Mines," the first discovered in Maryland, were successfully carried on.

The following notice appeared at the above date:

"Whereas Captain John Thompson and William Tipple each hold a part in the said mines in Frederick County, and as the same is now carried on by the said owners of the said mines, therefore, agreeable to articles, the said Thompson and Tipple are hereby requested to pay their arrears to our manager, Herman Husband, on the premises, without delay.

"By order of the Company.

"HERMAN HUSBAND."

On the 20th of November, 1765, a copartnership was entered into by Stephen Richards and John Stevenson, to raise copper ore from a tract of land of Stevenson's, called "Spring Garden," lying in Frederick County, under certain stipulations set forth in the agreement, to which Upton Sheredine and Christopher Carman were witnesses. James Smith was appointed manager, and having hired some hands, soon got to work, but with very little success until the year 1767, when some ore was shipped to London. On Aug. 17, 1779, an advertisement appeared in the newspapers stating that a plantation in Frederick County known as "Stevenson's Copper-Mine" was for rent, and that applications should be made at the "Deer Park" to John Stevenson. A vein of copper was discovered Nov. 4, 1837, on the lands of William C. Hobbs, between Liberty and New Market, which was worked by Isaac Tyson, Jr. In June, 1839, a rich and valuable copper-mine was opened on the land of Gen. James M. Coale.

HENRY C. GAITHER.

In 1864 the following prospectus of the "Liberty Copper-Mines" appeared:

"It is proposed to reopen the 'Liberty Copper-Mines,' situated in Frederick County, Maryland. These mines were formerly worked by Messrs. Evan T. Ellicott and the late Isaac Tyson, Jr. The smelting-furnace erected by these gentlemen on the premises is a sufficient assurance that the mines were of no ordinary richness in their yield of ore, yet the stagnation in all manufacturing enterprises at the time (1839), together with the low price of copper, then 17 cents (now 42 cents), the great difficulty and expense of transportation to a distant market, more than forty miles over country roads (now six miles to railroad), compelled them to abandon these works. The late Isaac Tyson, Jr., one of the most sagacious and successful mining men in this country, always regarded these mines as of great value. His executors have been induced to dispose of this property for the purpose of reopening and mining, on condition of their retaining a large interest in the same. The property of the company, independent of the $30,000 cash working capital, consists of about fifty acres of mineral land in fee, and the mineral right in fee to about five hundred acres adjoining, the engine-house, furnaces, the adit or funnel, more than half a mile in length, which drains the mines to the depth of sixty feet, and is said to have cost upwards of $40,000 to construct, together with thousands of dollars' worth of ores now on the surface, all go with the mines. The great peculiarity of this property consists of an immense and, from appearances, almost inexhaustible deposit of a black mineral earth, covering about thirteen acres, and containing more or less copper. But the shaft which is said to lead to the deposit of rich sulphurates, which, from testimony taken on the ground, is believed to exist at the depth of one hundred feet below the surface, will be at once reopened (samples of which, and also of the mineral earth, can be seen at the counting-room of the undersigned), and should it but half realize what tradition assigns to it, will place these mines among the most profitable in this country.

"GILDERSLEEVE & WHITRIDGE,
"No. 61 Second Street, Baltimore."

These mines, now called "The Maryland Copper-Mines," are in full operation, and are owned by Pope & Cole, of Baltimore. Capt. Samuel Hoskings is the superintendent. On them are large "Mill Concentrating Works." They lie two and a half miles from Liberty, the same distance from Johnsville, and three and a half from Woodsborough.

The old "Dollyhide Copper-Mills," just east of Liberty, have not been worked for many years, and the zinc-mines in the same neighborhood are not now in operation.

Among the most successful agriculturists of this beautiful country is Edward Hobbs, who was born at the "Downey" homestead, on property inherited by his mother, on July 4, 1838. The Downey homestead is in Liberty District, about a mile and a half northeast of New London, Frederick Co. The homestead of Edward Hobbs is called "Oakland," and his adjacent properties are "Spring Garden" and "Black Castle." His father, William Hobbs, was born Dec. 6, 1793, and died Sept. 15, 1871, at the residence of his daughter, Mrs. Laura Dorsey, near New Market. He was born at a homestead known as "White House," on Parr's Ridge, near Mount Airy. The mother of Edward Hobbs was Susan Dorsey, who was born at Drummine, a homestead near the village of New London, Nov. 26, 1804, and died in New Market, Sept. 10, 1861.

William Hobbs, Jr., father of Edward Hobbs, was a son of William Hobbs, Sr., who was a son of Samuel Hobbs, one of three brothers who settled near Mount Airy. William Hobbs, Sr., was the first coroner and school commissioner of Frederick County. He married twice,—by the first wife there was no issue; by the second wife, who was a daughter of the Hon. Basil Dorsey, then on the bench for Frederick County, he had six children, of whom William Hobbs, Jr., the father of Edward, was the youngest son. William Hobbs, Jr., was a gentleman of liberal education, and was not only conversant with the literature of the day, but was a ripe historical scholar. He commenced life in Baltimore as a dealer in tobacco, and was an intimate personal friend of Mr. Peabody and the Riggses. His health compelled him to return to the country, where he engaged in agriculture with very great success. He studiously avoided politics, although a man of pronounced principles.

Susan Hobbs, the mother of Edward Hobbs, was the daughter of Evan Dorsey and Susannah Lawrence. She was a lady of great refinement and culture. Added to her great sweetness of disposition, her constant charities made her greatly beloved.

Edward Hobbs, the subject of this sketch, was the fifth son of William Hobbs, Jr. At an early age he evinced a special fondness for agricultural pursuits. Having completed the ordinary course of mental training afforded by the system of primary schools, he completed a liberal course of studies at Calvert College. Upon his return from college he immediately entered upon an agricultural life. He had a natural fondness for the chase, an inherited trait of character, and for years he kept a fine pack of hounds. With this single divertisement he has permitted nothing to interfere with his agricultural pursuits. He is a man of restless and indomitable energy, of quick intelligence and observation, and stands to-day in the very front rank of agriculturists in this part of the State. He has always taken the liveliest interest in all schemes looking to the advancement of agriculture, and for years has been prominently connected with the Agricultural Society of Frederick County.

Though a very decided Democrat, he has had neither the leisure nor the inclination to engage in political life, his time being thoroughly occupied in looking after his handsome estate, and with such other considerations as might tend to advance the agricultural interests of the State. He is unmarried.

Liberty Town.—"Duke's Woods" was surveyed Aug. 29, 1739, and contained six hundred and thirty-three acres. On it Liberty Town was laid out by John Young, June 13, 1782. The plat consisted of two hundred and forty-six lots, each fifty by three hundred feet. All the lots between Nos. 47 and 69, inclusive, belonged to John Cochran, to whom Mr. Young had sold them as land before the town was laid out. Mr. Young sold these lots at eight dollars each, subject to a yearly ground-rent of one dollar, with the condition that each purchaser should build a house within two years or forfeit his lot. There are four principal streets,—Main and North, running east and west, and Walnut and Sycamore, north and south. John Young died without any family, and left all his estate by will to Richard Coale, who died in 1834. Of Richard Coale's three children, Richard, Dr. William, and Gen. James M. Coale, the latter only is living. He is an attorney-at-law, and is reputed to be the wealthiest man in the county. He has never married.

Elihu H. Rockwell was born in Middletown, Conn., July 15, 1790. In 1814 he came to Mount Pleasant, where on May 14th he began teaching school, in which he continued until November, 1820, when he removed to Liberty Town. He was sent to Frederick County by the father of Bishop Huntington. He taught at Liberty from November, 1820, to April, 1824, and was then for two years engaged in surveying. He then taught from April, 1826, to June, 1837, when he was appointed county surveyor. He removed to Frederick City in 1855, where he now resides in his ninety-second year, a hale and vigorous old man. He was married in July, 1837, to Mrs. Rachel Wiestling, widow of Rev. J. H. Wiestling.

Liberty District was in early days called, in common parlance, "Little Britain," a name given it in derision by the opponents of the Federalists, then largely in the majority. The three oldest persons living who were born in the town are Basil Sweadner, his brother, and Richard Galliver. One of the oldest houses is that of Basil Sweadner, built by Filley Markmam. The earliest store-keepers were Abram Crabster, Abram Jones, Thomas Sappington, Henry Stevenson, and David Foutz. Among the first tavern-keepers were John M. Daniel, Enoch Taylor, and John Prinkman. On May 15, 1807, John Ringland, formerly of Frederick, removed to Liberty and opened a tavern at the noted tavern-stand where Jacob Kiler lived. In 1819, Samuel Merritt kept the "Indian King" at the old stand previously occupied by William Myers. Of the earliest mechanics there are remembered Henry Sweadner, Mahlon Davis, and Mr. Bowhorn. Dr. Sappington practiced from 1775 to about 1815, and was succeeded by Dr. John Dorsey. Among the old-time preachers are Rev. Daniel Reese and Rev. Reynolds. The pioneer schoolmasters were Crosby, Joseph Penn, and Elihu H. Rockwell. In the year 1821 the Catholic church was erected, and Rev. Father Malevie, the priest at Frederick, was the first to hold services. The lot on which it was erected was presented by Richard Coale. A few years ago the old building was torn down and a new one built, at a cost of fifteen thousand dollars, by Gen. James M. Coale, who bore all the expense. "Lovers' Rock Graveyard," near the town, has a tradition that under the rock, long years ago, an old woman used to live, and on Horse-Head Rock, high in the air, is seen one of nature's most singular freaks, a perfect image of a horse set in the rock. "Fairview Cemetery" is one of the most tasteful and best-kept burying-grounds in the county. A Mr. Glissan gave the land for "Lovers' Rock Graveyard," and was buried in the solid rock, which was hollowed out for his tomb.

"Banner of Liberty."—In 1851, Alfred Schley, son of David Schley, started the *Banner of Liberty* at Liberty Town. He was not long connected with the establishment. It went into the hands of J. S. L. Roderick, by whom it is now conducted. The *Banner* is a newsy local paper, Republican in politics, and is conducted with marked skill and ability. It is in a flourishing condition. Mr. Roderick was postmaster from 1869 to 1880, when Edward Mitchell was appointed.

Another of the old families who emigrated to this district at an early period were the Clemsons. John Clemson, the present honorable representative of the family, was born July 17, 1826, upon the old Clemson estate, in Frederick County, known as "Ashmead," which Mr. Clemson still owns and occupies. His paternal grandfather, a veteran of the war of 1776, moved from Lancaster County, Pa., about 1775, to the present Clemson farm, and by various purchases speedily became possessed of one thousand acres in one tract. Upon that place he had his home ever after, dying at the age of ninety in 1846. His wife was a daughter of Mr. Haines, of Frederick County.

One of Mr. Clemson's nephews was Col. Clemson, of the war of 1812. Another nephew, Thomas Clemson, married one of John C. Calhoun's daughters, and was at one time *chargé d'affaires* at Belgium.

John Clemson had seven children, of whom John, Jr., was born on the homestead, Feb. 12, 1789. He

"CLEMMONT"
RESIDENCE OF JOHN CLEMSON JOHNSVILLE DIST., FREDERICK CO., MD

was a lifelong farmer, and died Jan. 10, 1860. He married Sophia, daughter of Thomas Price, of Baltimore County. She was born in Baltimore County, Dec. 5, 1798, and died April 13, 1872. Their children were two in number, of whom the only one

living is John Clemson, now residing on the Clemson farm. John Clemson, last named, attended school in Baltimore, later at Bristol College, Philadelphia, and subsequently at a private school near Baltimore, where he numbered among his classmates a boy who was afterwards well known as Hon. John Merriman. His educational term was completed at Mount St. Mary's College, near Emmittsburg, where he graduated in 1846. His inclination was for the legal profession, but yielding to his father's wishes, he determined to remain on the old farm, and thus pledged himself to the pursuits of agriculture for all time. May 15, 1855, he married, in Washington, D. C., Julia Louisa, daughter of Gen. Osborn Cross, of the United States army. Gen. Cross died in New York, July 15, 1876, and was buried from his daughter's home in Frederick County.

Military distinction marked the history of the Cross family and ancestry. Mrs. Clemson's uncle, Col. Truman Cross, is said to have been the first man killed in the Mexican war. Her brother, Edwin B. Cross, was a law student in New Haven when the war of 1861 opened, and enlisting at once in a Connecticut regiment, was complimented by the Governor of Connecticut with the present of full side-arm equipments, in recognition of the fact that he (Cross) was the only Southern man in the command. Mrs. Clemson's grandfather, Col. Bartholomew Von Schaumburg, came from England as one of the Hessian allies in the British army in 1776, but upon reaching America, and satisfying himself as to the merits of the conflict, went over to Washington's army, and was by Washington commissioned a lieutenant. He rose to be a colonel, and served with much gallantry through the campaign. Another of Mrs. Clemson's ancestors, Lieut. Joseph Cross, took part as an officer on board the frigate "Constitution" in the fight maintained by that vessel against the "Guerriere," and for his heroic services on that occasion was presented by the Legislature of Maryland with a sword, now in the possession of Miss Elizabeth Cross, of Baltimore.

In 1857, Mr. Clemson engaged in business in Alexandria as miller and distiller. He continued therein until the outbreak of hostilities in 1861 forced him to abandon his undertakings in that section and despoiled him of all his possessions there. In 1861 he returned to his farm in Frederick County, and since then has made it his home.

The old manor-house is a fine specimen of substantial stone architecture. Its walls are fully three feet in thickness, and although the structure is approaching its hundredth year, it seems, in its strength and solidity, likely to last another hundred years. Like the old-time mansion-houses, its apartments are roomy and sturdily embellished. A spirit of broad hospitality dwells within its ample recesses, and good cheer is mutely heralded in all its surroundings. Of Mr. Clemson's five children four are living. His political faith has always found him with the Democracy. Although trained in the Episcopal Church, he became a Catholic during his term at Mount St. Mary's College, and has thus since remained.

The school-teachers for the year ending April 15, 1881, were:

School No. 1, 127 pupils, G. M. Thomas, teacher; Ada Roederick, first assistant; S. Spurrier, second assistant; No. 2, 51 pupils, Mollie A. Biggs. No. 1 (colored), 53 pupils, J. A. Loud.

The fine brick school building at Liberty was erected in 1878, at a cost of some $5000.

The magistrates for the district are John E. Unkefever and Sidney Sappington.

Lafayette Lodge, No. 79, A. F. and A. M., was chartered in 1823, and was last represented in the Grand Lodge in May, 1831. Gen. Anthony Kimmel was at one time one of its active members.

Churches.—Before 1860, when Liberty Circuit was created, the Methodist Protestant Church was a part of the Pipe Creek Circuit.

Its pastors since 1860 have been:

1860, H. C. Cushing; 1862, J. T. Wall; 1864, D. A. Shermer; 1866, D. W. Bates; 1869, F. Swentzell; 1872, E. R. McGregor; 1874, J. Roberts; 1876, J. R. Nichols; 1877, J. K. Nichols; 1879, J. M. Brown.

Rev. William H. Koontz is pastor of the Methodist Episcopal Church.

"Dollyhide" Creek was named in honor of Miss Dolly Hide, daughter of an early settler named Hide, whose lands embraced two surveys,—"Hide and Seek" and "I Spy."

NEW MARKET DISTRICT, No. 9.

New Market, or Election District No. 9, has the following boundaries:

"Beginning at the fork on Monocacy where the main road crosses from Frederick to Georgetown; thence with the Monocacy to the mouth of Israel's Creek; then up said creek to the road leading from Frederick to Liberty; then with the said road to the old Annapolis road; then with the said road by Shields' place and Hobbs' mill, on Linganore, to a gate-post at the going into Dorsey's old quarter; thence east to the south branch of Linganore; thence up Linganore to Clarey's mill; thence east to the Baltimore County line; thence with said line to Parr's aforesaid main road, passing from Frederick Town to Georgetown; thence with said road to the beginning."

The district was taken from Liberty District. As now constituted it has Mount Pleasant and Liberty Districts on the north, Woodville on the east, Montgomery County and Urbana on the south and west, and Frederick and Mount Pleasant on the west. It is situated in the southeastern portion of the county. The Linganore Creek runs along the northern and the Monocacy along the western edge. The villages are New Market, Ijamsville, Bartonville, New London, and Kemptown.

Among the earliest settlers were the Dorseys, Hammonds, Plummers, Halls, Ballengers, Brashers, Howards, Shipleys, Owens, Maynards, Norrises, Johnsons, Griffiths, Poultneys, Jameses, Hobbses, Burketts (Burchards), Moberlys, and Hollands.

The Griffiths, who figure so prominently in the history of Western Maryland, were among the first settlers in the county. Lebbeus Griffith, Sr., who lives in this district, is the lineal descendant of the first settler. He has been a lifelong farmer of Frederick County and a widely-esteemed citizen. He was born in Montgomery County, Feb. 11, 1804. There also was his father, Howard Griffith, born in 1757, and there died Jan. 4, 1834. Lebbeus Griffith's grandfather was one of Montgomery County's pioneers. Howard Griffith was married in 1782 to Jemima, daughter of Mordecai Jacobs, of Prince George's County; she died Jan. 21, 1831. They had nine children. The only one living is Lebbeus Griffith, Sr., of Frederick County. He came to Frederick County in 1827, and married Mary Ellen, daughter of Philemon Griffith, a pioneer in Prince George's County, but then a dweller

on the place now owned by Lebbeus Griffith, Sr. On that farm Philemon Griffith died in 1839, aged eighty-two. By his marriage with Miss Griffith, Lebbeus Griffith had three children; two of them are living. June 30, 1835, Mr. Griffith's wife died. March 5, 1839, he married a second time, taking to wife Sarah Ann, daughter of Rev. John Wood, a native of Frederick County. By this second marriage there were six children; of them only one son and two daughters are living. The second Mrs. Griffith died Jan. 29, 1853; and Jan. 26, 1858, Mr. Griffith married his present wife, Ruth S., daughter of Seth W. Warfield, of Howard County, where he was born, as well as was his father before him. Eight children blessed the third union, and of the eight the living number five, three sons and two daughters. Mr. Griffith is therefore, as has been seen, the father of ten living children, of whom six reside in Frederick County. Three of Lebbeus Griffith's brothers, Mordecai, Howard, and Greenberry, fought on the Federal side in the campaign of 1812. His first wife's father, Philemon Griffith, was one of Washington's soldiers in the Revolution, and being taken prisoner by the British on Long Island was kept in confinement twelve months. Mr. Griffith has been a farmer from his youth up, and in the manifold cares consequent upon his arduous labors as a tiller of the soil has had but little inclination and less time to mingle in political strife or office-seeking, although he was for two years a valued and useful member of the board of county commissioners. In politics he has always been an unflinching Democrat. During the war he held himself aloof from advocacy of either side of the question, and in common with many others was compelled to endure much spoliation of property at the hands of Federals and Confederates alike. In religion he has always been a Baptist. For upwards of thirty years he has been an honored and prominent member of Fidelity Lodge, No. 154, I. O. O. F., of New Market.

The first tract of land patented in Liberty District was granted by Lord Baltimore in 1743 to John Dorsey, Jr., father of Basil and Samuel Dorsey. The first house built was erected for Basil Dorsey by a carpenter named McElfresh, and is still standing, having been remodeled, and is the residence of John T. Meredith. The descendants of many of the first settlers are yet remaining in the district, and several of them own the lands granted to their ancestors. Among the soldiers of the Revolution who achieved distinction were Col. Philemon H. Griffith, Greentree, Holland, and several of the Hammonds and Dorseys. In an old graveyard on the farm of Mr. Quynn lies Nathan T. Hammond, buried in 1754. The first mill for grinding flour was built by Anthony Poultney, and is on the site of the mill now owned by John D. Shearer, at Monrovia. Benjamin Johnson operated a glass manufactory on the property now owned by Messrs. Ramsbaugh, Detrick, & Sinn. The material for manufacturing the glass was procured on the land. The first tannery was that of a Mr. Garrison. Anthony Poultney conducted a button-factory, where were made metal and bone buttons. The first settlers lived in liberal style, many of them owning one and two hundred slaves, black and white. The district is separated from that of Mount Pleasant by Linganore Creek, named after an old Indian chief, the last of his tribe, who lived and died on its bank. The word Linganore means "left ear," and signifies the left ear of the Potomac, as the Monocacy does the "right ear." The other streams are Bush Creek and Ben's Branch. The New London flour-mill was built in 1804 by Evan Dorsey, and is on Ben's Branch. The Linganore mills were erected about the first of the century by a Scotchman named Robinson, who was afterwards killed by being thrown from his buggy. Delashmutt's mill, on Bush Creek, was built by a Mr. Reel. Upton Sheredine, the representative of this congressional district in Congress, married a daughter of Basil Dorsey, Sr., and died in 1800 without issue. He took a very active part in the war of the Revolution, and was buried near Liberty, on the farm of Luther Welch. John Dorsey, Jr., entered a tract of over six hundred acres of land, called "Dorsey's Search," and the Hammonds a large tract on what is called Long Branch. About 1780 there was an emigration to this district from Wrightsville, Pa., of the families of Davis, Wright, and others. During the "Whisky Insurrection" of 1794 the insurgents planted a "liberty pole" at Hagerstown, which was fearlessly cut down by a Revolutionary soldier, John Downey. Mr. Downey was going from his home, near Charlestown, Va., to a farm he owned in Franklin Co., Pa., and stopping at dinner in Hagerstown, observed the pole, and boldly, in the presence of those who had put it up, he cut it down, saying "he had fought through the war for independence, and now that it was secured he would not countenance any rebellion to the laws." He came out of the Revolution as a captain, having enlisted in his sixteenth year. He was one of the guard to escort to Frederick Town the Hessian prisoners captured by Washington at Trenton, N. J. His son William settled in New Market in 1814. The latter married a daughter of Basil Downey, and was the father of William Downey, the present large land-owner in the district. Before settling in New Market he had graduated at Princeton College, where he was a room and classmate of John J. Crittenden, and he subsequently read law with the distinguished Henry St. George Tucker, of Virginia. John James, prominent among the first settlers, entered large tracts of land on the head-waters of Ben's Branch and Linganore, and his granddaughter became the wife of the noted "Linganore Farmer," and one of Maryland's ablest men, Gen. Anthony Kimmel. In the war of 1812, Capt. Basil Dorsey commanded a company, with Benjamin Wright and a Mr. Hamilton as his lieutenants. About 1750 to 1770, William Hobbs was one of the leading men, and was popularly called "King Billy, king of the Convicts." He received this sobriquet from the fact of his constantly going to all the vessels arriving from the mother-country with transported convicts on board. These convicts were sold for a term of years, and Mr. Hobbs bought numbers of them, as also a number of "redemptioners." He thus secured his schoolmaster, shoemaker, blacksmith, tailor, fuller, wheelwright, carpenter, scrivener, etc. New Market continued up to the war of 1861–65 a very large slaveholding district, and next to Frederick has the largest population of any district in the county.

The last tract of land taken up and patented in the district was that of "Pleasant Valley," which was very heavily wooded. For this reason it was passed over by the pioneers, who sought land more easily cleared up. The first persons in the county to use lime for agricultural purposes were Basil Downey and Maj. S. P. James. In 1838 the real estate of Mrs. Cordelia H. Downey, consisting of two thousand three hundred and seventeen acres and twenty-four poles, was divided into six parts. These lands embraced parts or all of the surveys called "Peace and Plenty," "Resin Shipley's Discovery," Resurvey of "Darby's Delight," "Dorsey's Search," "Omission," "Good Meadow," "The Middle," "Well Timbered," "Outland," "Pleasant Valley," "Moab," "Hall's Choice," "Shingle Timber," "Hunting Lot" (granted to John Howard, of Gideon, Feb. 16, 1745), "Drummire" (granted to Basil Dorsey, Sr., May 18, 1798). "Darby's Delight" originally belonged to Joshua Waddington, of New York. Basil Dorsey, Sr., father of Cordelia H. Downey (formerly Dorsey), died in 1800. The dwelling—one and a half miles east of the town, in sight of the Baltimore and Frederick turnpike and the Baltimore and Ohio Railroad, and owned by the heirs of H. W. Dorsey Waters—was built on a very high hill by a Mr. McElfresh, the maternal ancestor of the Trails and Kunkels.

Nearly seventy-three years ago Eli Davis, now of this district, was born, in New Market District, Frederick Co., Nov. 5, 1809. His father, George Davis, was born in Lancaster County, Pa., Feb. 3, 1775, and removing while yet a young man to Montgomery County, Md., he engaged in mercantile business at Hyattstown, and from that place enlisted for the war of 1812. There he married Elizabeth, daughter of Eli Hyatt, and upon his marriage bought and made his home upon a farm in New Market District. He died May 10, 1850, upon the present Eli Davis' place. His widow died May 13, 1855. Of their twelve children eight are living,—four sons and four daughters. Eli Davis was the second son. His school education was gained in rural temples of learning. Aug. 18, 1831, he was married in Clarksburg, Montgomery Co., to Rachel, daughter of William Morsell, a member of the Society of Friends, and a native of Frederick County. Mr. Morsell was born on the present Eli Davis home farm April 13, 1778, and died there May 17, 1846. His father, William, came from Calvert County to Frederick County before the opening of the Revolution. Mr. Davis' marriage with Miss Morsell was a little romantic. The young pair conceived the notion that their marriage would be opposed by parental authority, and so they, deciding to brook no obstacle to their happiness, walked away to Clarksburg one fine morning and were wedded. As it happened they misjudged parental authority, and might have been married with numberless fatherly and motherly blessings had they but spoken out. The worthy old couple tell with much enjoyable zest the story of their elopement, and the trouble they might have saved themselves if they had been more trustful toward the old folks. Mrs. Davis was her father's only child, and upon his death inherited a considerable estate, which upon her marriage she deeded to her husband. He has added to the property, and ranks now among the large landholders of the county, his farming lands aggregating about eleven hundred acres. Mr. and Mrs. Davis have had eleven children,—nine sons and two daughters. Two of the sons and the two daughters are dead. Five of the living sons now occupy and work as many of their father's farms. Mr. Davis was bred a Baptist, but for many years has been a member of the Protestant Methodist Church. He has never taken part in public life, never served on a jury, and has ever given his closest attention to his agricultural duties. He has now, however, retired from active participation in the conduct of his farms, since he can count safely upon his sons' prudent care and management thereof. He was an old-line Whig. When the war came on he joined the Democracy, of whose principles he is a sterling advocate. During the war he occupied strictly neutral ground. Besides his farms he owns the Fountain mills property, earlier owned by William Morsell, in which he labored in his younger days.

Where the Monrovia mills are now located was once the seat of a woolen factory. George Burkett was a very early pioneer and very wealthy. He entered a great body of land, one survey of which was called "Peace and Plenty." When a member of the General Assembly at Annapolis, while at a party to which he had been invited, he was about to relate the fact of his having raised that year twenty-five hundred bushels of wheat, but having incidentally learned that Col. Lloyd, a member from the Eastern Shore, had produced *twenty-five thousand* bushels, he kept quiet, and did not tell of his prodigious feat. Rachel Plummer, who resides in the village, is a lineal descendant of Samuel Plummer, who took out his patent for land in this district from Thomas Bladen, Governor of the province, on June 17, 1743. Samuel Plummer died suddenly in Prince George's County, and was found by one of his slaves sitting under a tree dead. Soon after his widow and children removed

ELI DAVIS.

to Frederick County. His will, executed Jan. 13, 1754, devised his Frederick County lands as follows: to his eldest son, Thomas, "Hunting Lot," two hundred and twenty-six acres on Linganore; to his second son, Joseph, one hundred and eighty-seven acres on Bush Creek; to his third son, Samuel, "Food Plenty" and "Rocky Hill," of three hundred and eighteen acres, on Bush Creek; to his son Abraham, two hundred acres, part of "Hickory Plains," on Bush Creek; to his daughter Cassandra Ballinger, two hundred acres, of "Hickory Plains," on Bush Creek; to his daughter Sarah, one hundred and fifty-four acres, part of "Hickory Plains" and "Help;" to his son-in-law, Richard Holland, one hundred and ninety-eight acres, called "Rich Hill." Samuel Plummer had twelve children, and owned other lands in Frederick County besides the tracts above given. In 1747 the heirs of Samuel Plummer gave four acres to the Society of Friends (Quakers) for the erection of a meeting-house, which was immediately built of logs. The old log structure was taken down and replaced by the present edifice in 1852, on the same lot. It is situated near the railroad depot at Monrovia. The Plummers were Friends, and during the Revolutionary war suffered much from their adherence to their ancient principles. On one occasion the family was visited by British soldiers who took almost all the necessaries of life from them, but providentially for the family missed a roll of linsey just taken from the loom and placed behind the door. This the family soon converted into blankets, as the weather was very cold. Samuel Plummer was a large slave-holder, and his children retained their slaves until a rule was passed in their Society commanding all members to liberate them. The early proprietors were wealthy men who passed their time in fishing and hunting, as the streams abounded in trout and the forest in game.

John T. Williams, of this district, also ranks among the leading and most successful farmers of Frederick County. He was born in Urbana District, Dec. 23, 1825, where also his father, William A., was born in 1788, and died 1854. The ancestors of Mr. Williams came from England, and, as can be best ascertained, his grandfather, John Williams, was the pioneer of the name in Frederick County. Mr. Williams' maternal grandfather was James Hood, a native of what is now Howard County, as was his father before him. William A. Williams' wife (mother of John T. Williams) died in 1856, aged sixty-two. They had six children, and of them five are yet living. The book education acquired by John T. Williams was such as he obtained at the district school, and the practical training in life a useful and substantial experience upon his father's farm under his father's tuition. That his instruction yielded ample and profitable results his subsequent history and present station have abundantly testified. Oct. 27, 1853, he married Jane Elizabeth, daughter of Charles and Eleanor Hendry, of Frederick County. Mr. Hendry was a native of Virginia, where his ancestors were among the founders of the country. Mr. Hendry died in Frederick County in 1877. His widow is still living. Of Mr. Williams' six children, five survive—two sons and three daughters. Anthony K. (a son) occupies and manages one of his father's farms. The other children reside under the parental roof. Mr. Williams owns three farms and a mill property. Aside from a few years' experience as a silent partner in a mercantile house at Ijamsville, his attention has been exclusively devoted during life to his large agricultural interests. Those interests have fully occupied his time, and although county school commissioner in 1870–71, he has otherwise rigidly held himself aloof from participation in political or public life. Indeed, had he had even such inclination he esteemed his private business of too much value to neglect for other issues. In religious convictions he has always been a supporter of the Methodist Episcopal Church. Early in life he was a Whig. The war made him a Democrat. At the outbreak of hostilities he was a pronounced Union man, but circumstances forced him to espouse the Confederate cause, and, as a consequence, he was called upon to suffer the loss of much property.

New Market.—The following advertisement appeared in the Maryland newspapers of the spring of 1788:

"Laid out for a Town, to be called New Market, on Public road. Grading from Frederick Town to Baltimore about 9 miles from Frederick: Two principal streets in the Town are 66 ft., the other 50 ft. wide, three others 33 ft. wide. Lots are 66 ft. front, 165 feet back. There is reserved a lot of ground for a Market House and a church.

"The lots are to be sold by Nicholas Hall, living near Premises. Lots bounding on Main st. will be sold for £3 current money each. The lots back at Forty Shillings each; all subject to an annual ground rent of 5 shillings, to commence May 5, 1788."

It is supposed that this sale failed to be a success, as the town was really laid out June 1, 1793, by said Nicholas Hall, when the lots were leased for sixty-six and two-thirds cents each, with the privilege of buying the fee at any time. It has been asserted that William Plummer, in conjunction with said Hall, laid out the town in 1792, but the authority for this statement is not given. Rachel Plummer, the daughter of William, granddaughter of Thomas, and great-granddaughter of Samuel Plummer, the patentee and early settler, resides now in the house built by her father in 1790, before the town was laid out, it being then William Plummer's farm-house, and being in that part of the town known as "Plummer's part" of "New Market Plains." In 1880, Rachel Plummer sold the farm, which had never been out of the possession of the family, but reserved the dwelling and lot on which she lives.

The first house built in the village was put up by George Smith, a German, and was used for a tavern. It was located on the lot where Rev. Jesse Shreve now lives, and is still standing, and in good repair for a frame structure. Several of Smith's descendants still live in the district. William Downey's residence is on the site of the old button-factory, and that of Charles Roelky is where the old wrought-iron nail-factory stood. Dr. Belt Brashears was the first physician. In 1878 the Legislature incorporated the town by a special act.

The first five commissioners were elected in 1879, to wit: Isaac S. Russell, Dr. H. H. Hopkins, Dr. H. W. Dorsey, John T. P. Mount, Adam Boyer. In 1880 there were elected Francis Lickle (*vice* Boyer), Edward Houck (*vice* Dr. Hopkins, resigned), Thos. U. Lease (*vice* Mount, resigned), John T. Smith (*vice* Lickle, resigned). In 1881, F. Waltz was elected (*vice* Dr. H. W. Dorsey). The officers for 1881 are

John T. Smith (president), Thomas A. Lease (secretary), F. Waltz, Edward Houck, Isaac Russell (commissioners), and George Burgess (bailiff).

The physicians are Drs. H. W. Dorsey, Jesse W. Downey, E. W. Moberly, Isaac N. Wood, H. H. Hopkins. Postmistress, Mrs. P. O. H. Stier.

Churches.—The first Methodist Episcopal church, an old log structure, was erected about the last decade of the preceding century, and in 1821 gave way to the present commodious edifice. Revs. John Pitts and James L. Higgins were among the first preachers. The present pastor is Rev. W. A. Koontz, with Rev. J. C. Nicholson as assistant. The trustees are M. P. Trayer, John T. Lorne, John W. Rinehart, Joseph Molesworth, Thomas M. Walls, Thos. U. Lease, and James P. Molesworth. The superintendent of the Sunday-school is J. P. Molesworth.

The Methodist Episcopal Church South was organized in 1867. Its pastors have been:

1867, J. P. Hall; 1868, W. A. McDonald; 1870, J. T. Maxwell; 1871, A. Q. Flaherty; 1873, David Bush; 1876, W. R. Stringer; 1879, M. G. Balthis.

Grace Protestant Episcopal church was built in 1872. Its pastor is Rev. James Stevenson, S.T.D., who preached here before the building was erected.

The wardens are Dr. Harry W. Dorsey (senior) and Dr. J. W. Downey (junior). Vestrymen, Dr. H. W. Dorsey, William Downey, Dr. H. H. Hopkins, Dr. E. W. Moberly, Capt. J. W. Darsey, John D. Shearer, J. Johnson Downey, George Schell.

The Methodist Protestant Church was organized and its church edifice erected in 1831. Up to 1846 it formed a part of Pipe Creek Church Circuit. Its pastors have been:

1831, I. Ibbertson; 1832, I. Webster, C. W. Jacobs; 1833, W. Sexsmith; 1834, J. Warden, H. Doyle; 1835, H. Doyle, J. W. Everist, A. A. Lipscomb; 1836, J. S. Reese, W. J. Porter; 1838, E. Henkle; 1839, G. D. Hamilton; 1840, B. Appleby, G. D. Hamilton; 1841, J. S. Reese, J. T. Ward; 1842, J. R. Reese, J. Elderdice, P. L. Wilson; 1843, J. S. Reese, S. L. Rawleigh; 1844, W. Collier, J. L. McClean, J. D. Brooks; 1845, P. L. Wilson, J. K. Nichols; 1846, P. L. Wilson; 1847, H. P. Jordan; 1849, L. W. Bates, W. Reinecke; 1850, A. Baker; 1852, P. L. Wilson; 1854, A. Hammond (assistant); 1855, T. M. Wilson; 1856, C. Eversole (assistant); 1857, A. Baker (assistant); 1858, W. T. Wright, J. Clay (assistant); 1859, J. W. Charlton (assistant); 1860, A. D. Dick (assistant); 1861, J. K. Nichols, A. S. Eversole (assistant); 1862, D. Wilson, M. E. Hysore (assistant); 1863, J. D. Kinzer (assistant); 1864, S. T. Graham (assistant); 1865, J. Roberts, F. M. Hawkins (assistant); 1866, J. C. Stewart (assistant); 1867, J. E. Darby (assistant); 1868, R. S. Norris, G. D. Edmonson (assistant); 1869, H. C. Cushing, J. B. Butler (assistant); 1870, W. T. Dumm; 1872, S. F. Ferguson; 1873, G. F. Farring; 1874, C. T. Cochil; 1875, W. J. D. Lucas (assistant); 1876, T. A. King (assistant); 1877, S. J. Willey (assistant); 1878, J. Shreve, A. J. Walter (assistant); 1880, A. D. Murray (assistant); 1881, W. H. Stone (assistant).

This church is in a circuit of eight congregations, viz.: New Market, Mountain View, Mount Carmel, Kemptown (Providence), Central, Fairview, Pleasant Grove, and Montgomery County.

Total membership of circuit, 514; value of church property, $14,000.

The Asbury Methodist Episcopal church was built several years ago. Rev. Mr. Spredle is the pastor.

Masonic Lodges.—The first information we have of Masonry in this county comes from New Market, and dates back to a period antecedent to 1776. Since that time there have always been zealous Masons in this district. In the dwelling-house on the farm now owned by William Downey, near New Market, the first lodge of Freemasons in Western Maryland was held, prior to the American Revolution of 1776.

The meetings were held in a room up-stairs, which was painted blue, and the chart was painted on the chimney above the mantel-piece, with a frame of woodwork around it. Mr. Downey states that he has this from "reliable tradition," and that the chart was painted as described he has no doubt, as he heard it again and again from old inhabitants, who if now

living would be more than a hundred years old. The land on which the house stands was granted to a man named Turner, and was afterwards purchased by George Burchard (sometimes called Burkett). Subsequently it was purchased by Basil Dorsey, the grandfather of William Downey, and has been in his family for eighty or ninety years. Gen. Anthony Kimmel, in his lifetime, thought it was the first Masonic lodge in Western Maryland.

This house stands on a little tract anciently called "Turner's Forest," and said to have been the rendezvous of the Tories in the Revolutionary war. George Burchard subsequently purchased this tract, resurveyed it, and had it called "Peace and Plenty," the name it now retains.

William Downey, who is mentioned above, was born on the homestead farm which he now owns near the village of New Market in the Ninth Election District of Frederick County, on the 8th December, 1825. His father, William Downey, was born near Charlestown, W. Va., on the 18th of May, 1789, and his mother, Cordelia H. Dorsey, was born on the 19th day of February, 1798, on the old Dorsey homestead, near New Market. The paternal great-grandfather of William Downey was William Downey, of Scotch-Irish descent, who emigrated to this country and settled in Cumberland Valley, Pa. In religion he was a Presbyterian. John Downey, the grandfather, was born Aug. 20, 1753, and died 26th September, 1825. He enlisted in the army at the beginning of the Revolution, and served through the entire war, coming out with the rank of captain. He was detailed with his company to guard the Hessian prisoners taken at Trenton and sent to Frederick. He would never receive any pension for his services, considering that he fought for the liberty of his country, and that it would be a reproach to receive pay after the war was over. He was a man of great force of character. During the "Whisky Insurrection" the whisky boys planted a pole in Hagerstown. John Downey was passing through the town, and seeing the pole, he borrowed an axe, and, though threatened with death, he cut the pole down. He married Rubany Stocksdale, of Baltimore County.

There were three brothers by the name of Dorsey —Edward, John, and Thomas—who emigrated from England about 1670 or 1680 and settled in Anne Arundel County, Md., from whom are descended the Dorseys of Maryland and Kentucky.

John Dorsey, Jr., of Anne Arundel County, to whom was granted in 1741 a large tract of land then in Prince George's County, now in Frederick County, and known as "Dorsey's Search," was the maternal ancestor of William Downey. Among the children of John Dorsey, Jr., were Basil Dorsey, Samuel Dorsey, and John Dorsey. Basil married Miss Crochett, of Baltimore County, and left four sons and two daughters. His second son, Basil, the grandfather of William Downey, married a daughter of Nathan Harris, who was born in St. Mary's County, and was the son of Thomas Harris and Sarah Offutt. His wife was a Mrs. Dorsey, the widow of Capt. Philemon Dorsey; her maiden name was Lawrence, a descendant of Sir Thomas Lawrence, at one time secretary of the province of Maryland. By this marriage Basil Dorsey left one child, a daughter, Cordelia H., who married William Downey, the father of the subject of this sketch. Basil Dorsey, the great-grandfather of William Downey, was at one time a justice of the County Court of Frederick, and took a very prominent and decided part in favor of the colonies during their struggle for independence, and occupied many prominent positions in forwarding the cause of independence.

William Downey married, Feb. 11, 1847, Margaret Jane Wright, the daughter of Jesse Wright, of New Market. She was born Dec. 3, 1825. Her father's ancestors emigrated from the north of Ireland and settled in Pennsylvania, and founded Wrightsville, Pa. Her mother's ancestors were Germans, and settled at Frederick City. Her grandfather was Maj. Peter Mantz, of the Maryland Flying Camp of the Revolution, and he was for a number of years a judge of the Orphans' Court of Frederick County. Their children are Dr. Jesse W. Downey,[1] born March 24, 1848; Frank Downey, born April 15, 1859; Margaret Mantz Downey,[2] born Aug. 27, 1850; and Eliza Downey, born June 17, 1867.

William Downey, Sr., died in 1828, and William Downey, the subject of this sketch, then but three years old, resided with his mother. In 1839 he boarded with Nathan Nelson, and attended school at the Central School for one year. In 1840 he went to Dr. Francis Waters, D.D., who was the principal of Franklin Academy, in Baltimore County. Afterwards he went to the Light Street Academy, conducted by John Lug, and from thence to Dickinson College, Pennsylvania, thence to St. Mary's College, in Baltimore. He was clerk in the tobacco warehouse until 1845. In religion he is an Episcopalian, and in politics a Democrat. He has been a director of the Central National Bank of Frederick since 1861, and was a charter member of Philanthropic Lodge, A. F. and A. M., No. 168, and secretary since its organiza-

---

[1] Dr. J. W. Downey married a daughter of Maj. Denton Hammond, of New Market.

[2] Margaret Mantz Downey married Dr. Howard H. Hopkins, of Baltimore City.

tion. He took possession of his farm in 1845, and in four years brought the farm up to a high state of fertility by the use of lime burnt on the farm. In 1849 he removed to the village of New Market, and in 1851 engaged in merchandising, in which he continued until 1865, when, having purchased Monrovia Mills, he engaged for four years in milling, with decided success pecuniarily. Since 1869 he has been engaged in looking after his estate, which by repeated purchases has become very large, aggregating over twelve hundred acres. His mother divided her estate, which was some two thousand three hundred acres of land, among her children, the great bulk of which William Downey has purchased, and he is now of the sixth generation of his race that has owned it. It has now been in the family since Lord Baltimore granted it to his ancestors. William Downey has always been very diligent in business, and has always regarded real estate as the safest and most independent investment. In the midst of a busy life he has kept himself well read in general literature, and has always taken an active part in politics, but never would accept any office or nomination for an office.

Philanthropic Lodge, No. 50, was in operation at New Market to 1815. It was represented in the Grand Lodge in 1814 by Arthur Tanzey and J. H. Burgess. In 1817, Wm. Downey was W. M., Arthur Tanzey, S. W., and Ambrose Ingman, J. W., of this lodge. It was last represented in the Grand Lodge by Ambrose Ingman in 1820.

Philanthropic Lodge, No. 168, now working at New Market, is the successor to Philanthropic, No. 50, and took a new number only because a sufficient number of the old members could not be found to resuscitate the lodge under its original number. On Jan. 14, 1874, a dispensation was granted to William Downey, Geo. E. Talbott, Hamilton Steir, Thomas P. Mullinix, Dr. H. H. Hopkins, William R. Dorsey, Dr. Jesse W. Downey, Henry S. Lansdale, and D. W. Duvall to form a lodge at New Market. Dr. Jesse W. Downey was appointed W. M., Henry S. Lansdale, S. W., and William Downey, J. W. On the 12th of May, 1874, a regular charter was granted to Philanthropic Lodge, No. 168, and the same officers were retained as under the dispensation. The next Master elected was Dr. H. H. Hopkins, who has been successively followed by M. P. Wood, John D. Lickle, D. W. Duvall, and again by Dr. Jesse W. Downey. The officers for 1880 were:

Dr. Jesse W. Downey, W. M.; Charles McGill Luckett, S. W.; M. P. Wood, J. W.; William Downey, Sec.; John D. Shearer, Treas.; D. W. Duvall, S. D.; Frank Downey, J. D.; and John T. P. Mount, Tyler.

The officers for 1881, first term, were:

Dr. Thomas C. Worthington, W. M.; Charles McGill Luckett, S. W.; Frank Downey, J. W.; William Downey, Sec.; John D. Shearer, Treas.; Rev. Geo. D. Edmonson, S. D.; M. P. Wood, J. D.; and John T. P. Mount, Tyler.

The officers elected for term ending December, 1881, were:

W. M., M. P. Wood; S. W., Frank Downey; J. W., G. D. Edmonson; Sec., Wm. Downey; Treas., John D. Shearer; S. D., Dr. J. W. Downey; J. D., D. W. Duvall; Tyler, John T. P. Mount.

The lodge numbers 36 members. It meets on the first and second Wednesdays of each month.

Independent Order of Odd-Fellows.—Fidelity Lodge, No. 54, was instituted in 1847. Charter members, William P. Anderson, Hamilton Stier, Caleb Douty, Joseph Kemp, and Thomas Claggett. Its charter was signed by Grand Master John A. Thompson and Grand Secretary G. D. Tewksbury.

Its officers for term ending December, 1881, were:

N. G., Wm. H. Baker; V. G., N. M. Waters; Sec., James M. Rice; Treas., J. W. Downey, M.D.

Number of members, 57. It owns a fine hall valued at $2000, and has $600 surplus accumulated funds.

John E. McCahan, of this lodge, has been Grand Master of the State Grand Lodge.

Linganore Mill is the oldest in the county, having been in existence for over a century. There is no record of its earlier operations in existence. The present owner, C. C. Anders, received it as an inheritance from his father, who, in connection with Mr. Reifsnider, conducted it for some three years. Mr. Anders has had the mill since 1877. It is situated about three miles from Frederick, on the Monocacy Creek, and about half a mile from the National pike. It is five stories high, built of brick, and very substantial, having six runs of burrs, and three overshot-wheels twelve feet in diameter. The mill, which requires the attention of four millers, is run by water-power, and has a capacity of two hundred and forty barrels per day. In connection with the Linganore mill a farm of three hundred acres is cultivated, on which a portion of the grain used in the mill is grown. Only wheat is ground, and nothing but the best family brands is produced. Forty thousand barrels annually of fine flour are sent out from Linganore mill, and so wide-spread is its popularity that Mr. Anders finds a ready market for all he can produce in Frederick County and in Baltimore. The firm has an office and salesroom on Patrick Street, Frederick, where all orders are attended to. Linganore mill is an interesting local feature of Frederick County, as well as an important factor in its industrial prosperity.

The Monrovia Mills are situated upon the main stem of the Baltimore and Ohio Railroad, fifty miles from Baltimore, and while occupying a position unexcelled for the shipping of goods to any desired market, is no less accessible for the reception of the fine products of the agricultural region by which it is surrounded. The mill was originally built by Mr. Anthony Poultney, about a century ago, and afterwards rebuilt by D. Rinehart. Coming into Mr. Shearer's possession in 1869, it had the misfortune to be totally destroyed by fire in 1873. With the least possible delay it was rebuilt, and under the present management of Mr. Shearer it has enjoyed a steady and rapidly-growing business. The machinery, which is of the latest and best pattern, is operated by both steam and water-power, the former being obtained from a twenty-five horse-power engine, and the latter from Bush Creek, close to which the mill stands. There are two twelve-feet overshot-wheels and five runs of burrs, which give to the mill the capacity of one hundred barrels per day of twenty-four hours. The flour here produced is of a remarkably fine quality, and has a popularity which is not only local, but extends through this and the neighboring States to Rio Janeiro, Liverpool, and other points.

Monrovia is nine miles from Frederick. The station agent on the Baltimore and Ohio Railroad is W. W. Ogborn, and his assistant is J. W. Sullivan, who is postmaster. M. P. Wood is the merchant, and George D. Page the blacksmith. The celebrated lawyer, Charles Pitts, a grandson of Nicholas Hall, the original proprietor of New Market, was born here. On the old "Hall patent land" Anna W. Plummer still resides, the granddaughter of William Plummer, who was the grandson of Samuel Plummer, who in 1743 entered over two thousand acres of land at Monrovia and New Market.

Cromwell is three miles from Ijamsville, five from Frederick, and forty from Baltimore, and is pleasantly situated near Linganore Creek. It has one church, the Methodist Protestant, of which Rev. Jesse Shreeve is pastor. R. J. Starr is the postmaster and merchant; Eden Sheets and Jacob Brady, coopers; A. J. Carpenter and Zachariah Dailey, blacksmiths; Samuel Kolb, mason; and J. W. Duvall & Sons, wheelwrights.

Ijamsville is on the Baltimore and Ohio Railroad, fifty-two miles from Baltimore, and nine from Frederick. H. R. Lowderman is the merchant, station agent, and postmaster. The railroad divides the village, all south of the track being in Urbana District.

The Methodist Episcopal church was dedicated July 25, 1858, with appropriate ceremonies, and sermons by Revs. Thomas B. Sergeant and T. M. Reese. It is on the Urbana and Buckeystown Circuit. Its present pastor is Rev. D. M. Browning. The Sunday-school superintendent is J. T. McComas.

New London is four miles from Monrovia, and near Ben's Branch. It has two churches,—the Methodist Protestant, of which Rev. Jesse Shreeve is pastor, and the Methodist Episcopal, of which Rev. D. M. Browning is the preacher in charge. The merchants are Noah Barnes (postmaster), J. S. Maxwell, Mrs. R. Spargo, and Mrs. M. A. Webb.

Kemptown is situated near Bush Creek, four miles from Monrovia. It has one church,—Providence Methodist Protestant, of which Rev. Jesse Shreeve is pastor. The merchants are O. T. Fout and M. R. Lewis; postmaster, W. T. Lewis.

The teachers for the term ending April 15, 1881, were:

School No. 1, 64 pupils, Emma R. Garrott; No. 2, 51 pupils, J. B. Hyatt; No. 3, 59 pupils, C. M. Luckett; No. 4, 56 pupils, B. H. Riggs; No. 5, 34 pupils, G. D. Edmonston; No. 6, 73 pupils, J. T. Browning; No. 7, 25 pupils, Hannah Garrott; No. 8, 29 pupils, Ella S. Nelson. No. 1 (colored), 74 pupils, J. B. Washington; No. 2 (colored), 41 pupils, W. B. Johnson.

The magistrates are John T. Smith, Joel Hall, William Murphy; Constable, John Burgess.

HAUVER'S DISTRICT, No. 10.

Hauver's, or Election District No. 10, was laid out with the following boundaries, viz.:

"Beginning at the intersection of the State line dividing Washington and Frederick Counties; then with said line to the lines of District No. 5, at a stone on said line east of Jacob Trisler's; thence south fifteen degrees, west about four miles and a half, near Eyler's fields; thence south thirty-seven and a half degrees, west about two miles, near Smith's saw-mill; thence south twelve degrees, east about a quarter of a mile, to Smith's mill; thence south twenty-three degrees, west about two and a quarter miles, near Hauman's saw-mill; thence south thirty-one degrees, west about three and a half miles, near Buzzard's saw-mill; thence south forty-eight degrees, west about one mile; thence south twenty-seven degrees, west about one and a half miles; thence south about three-quarters of a mile to Ferran's swamp; thence south seventy degrees, west about two miles, to a black-walnut tree; thence north eighty-seven degrees, west about three and a quarter miles, to Mangins; thence north sixty-five degrees, west about three miles, to Black Rock, on the Washington County line; thence with the Washington County line to the beginning."

The district, therefore, is bounded on the north by Pennsylvania, on the east by Emmittsburg and Mechanicstown Districts, on the south by Catoctin, and on the west by Washington County. It is situated in the extreme northwestern portion of the county. The villages are Sabillasville and Foxville.

The first settlement in this district was made about the year 1758 or '59, by a Swiss colony in the southwest portion of Harbaugh's Valley, in the neighborhood of what is now called "Hauver's." It is a national instinct of the Swiss to love mountainous regions. Swiss soldiers, it is said, have died of homesickness for their Alps, and Swiss immigrants nearly always seek the more elevated lands. Hence the first Swiss pioneers in Frederick County passed by the fertile valleys and sought the lands on the sides of the Catoctin Mountains. The next settlers were the Harbaughs, in 1760 and '61. All this region was then a wilderness, for Frederick Town had only been laid out fifteen years before, and five years previous Chambersburg, Pa., was a small town on the outskirts of civilization. The whole country between Chambersburg and Frederick, including Conecocheague Valley, showed but here and there a small settlement. Rev. Michael Schlatter, who passed from Frederick to the above valley in 1748, speaks of all the region west of the South Mountain as presenting nothing but regions of grass, hazel-bushes, shrubbery, and crab-apple trees, and says the whole country was called "the barrens." Indians were still there, but friendly when they were not drunk. When George Harbaugh, the first settler, removed to the valley, which took its name from him, there was as yet no road in existence through it. The immigrants had to unload their effects and leave their wagons at the eastern end of the valley, where they made arrangements to convey their effects to the place of destination on sleds, and partly on pack-horses. The first of the noted family of Harbaugh to settle in America was Yost Harbaugh, a native of Switzerland. He arrived in 1736, and settled first in Maxatawny, a valley of Berks County, Pa., but about 1743 removed to the new settlement of Kreutz Creek, west of the Susquehanna. He died in April, 1762. He was twice married, and his children were as follows: By his first wife, George, Ludwig, Jacob, John, Henry, Yost; and by his second wife (named "Mary Liz" in his will), Leonard, Mary Elizabeth, Ann Margaret, and Ann Catherine. The emigrant, Yost Harbaugh, was a member of the German Reformed Church, and married his second wife in Pennsylvania in 1746. Of the above children, George Harbaugh was the first of the three brothers that removed to the valley. He was born in Switzerland in 1727, and came down from York County, Pa., to the valley in 1760 or '61, about the time of the establishment of "Mason and Dixon's line," which ended the disputes that so seriously interfered with the early settlers. He became a Moravian in his religious profession, which was perhaps occasioned from the comparative nearness of the Moravian settlement at Graceham. He came to his death by accidental drowning, somewhere in the head-waters of the Falls Creek, near the foot of what is called Mount Misery. His children were George, John, Anna Regina, Elizabeth, and a little daughter who, at the age of six years, was accidentally killed by the discharge of a gun. Of these children, George lived a while on the old homestead, and then removed to Bedford County, Pa. This George had a son, Jacob, a lame man, who kept tavern in Sabillasville; John lived at what is now Schultz's mill, and later went to Ohio; Anna Regina married a Mr. Eyler, resided in Eyler's Valley, and died in 1849, aged ninety-two years, and is buried at Graceham; Elizabeth married a Mr. Fetter, of Bethlehem, Pa. Ludwig, the second son of Yost Harbaugh, and the second Harbaugh to settle in the valley, was born in Switzerland in 1728. After his marriage he removed from York County, Pa., to near Weller's mill, just east of Mechanicstown. From thence he removed to Middletown Valley, where his first son, Christian, was born Jan. 14, 1753. Afterwards, about 1761, he removed to Harbaugh's Valley, and settled on the farm not far from and southwest of Sabillasville, formerly Zollinger's, but in 1856 owned by John Harbaugh, of Christian. Ludwig died Aug. 9, 1809, aged eighty-two years, and was buried in the graveyard on his own farm. His wife, Christiana, died Oct. 17, 1797, aged seventy years.

Their descendants were numerous. Of their children, Christian lived a short distance west of Sabillasville, and died March 23, 1836, aged eighty-three. He was buried at Graceham, and left one hundred and thirty children and grandchildren. He was a Moravian, as was his wife, a Miss Williard. Christian had ten children, Peter, Christian, John (a noted tanner), who lived on a farm south of Sabillasville owned by his grandfather Ludwig; Elias, Henry, who lived on the old homestead near Sabillasville; Alexander, Solomon, Elizabeth, Mary, Rebecca, Charlotte, who married a Mr. Willman and lived in Sabillasville, and Sabina. Ludwig's second son was Jacob Harbaugh, who lived on the top of the mountain northwest of Sabillasville. He was called "Mountain Jacob." His first wife was the widow of a Mr. Winters, her maiden name being Casebeer. She was married to Jacob Harbaugh. They both died in their ninety-second year, left no offspring, and are buried on their homestead. The third son, Henry, married on the Monocacy, and removed to near Lexington, Ky. The fourth son, Peter, was unmarried, and was accidentally drowned in a branch of the Monocacy. He was on the eve of being married, and on arriving at the creek on the way to the residence of his intended bride, he found it greatly swollen from the rain. He dismounted, and leaving his horse, attempted to cross in a small boat. The rolling current being too strong for him, carried him violently down the stream. He was found fourteen days afterwards in a drift of wood. The fifth child, Yost Harbaugh, lived in the valley (where Elias Harbaugh lately died). He belonged to the United Brethren, and died in 1837, aged sixty. His children were Thomas, William (who lived in the lower end of the valley), Daniel (who lived on the homestead on Friends' Creek), Elizabeth, Sarah, Sophia, and Margaret,—the three next to the last married respectively to Charles Smith, Henry Fitz, and John Nagel. Of Ludwig's other five children, John was gored to death by a bull when a boy, Elizabeth married a Mr. Rice, of Kentucky, and Margaret married Andrew Williard, south of Shutts' mills, where she died. They were both of the Moravian communion. The third son of the emigrant, Yost Harbaugh, and the third one to settle in the valley, was Jacob Harbaugh, born in Switzerland, Feb. 5, 1730. He was married, April, 1761, to Anna Margaretta Smith, daughter of George Smith. She was born April 3, 1740, and died March 18, 1803. Jacob moved to the valley in 1761, immediately after his marriage. He had bought land there previous to his removal. He settled on the farm on which he lived and died, towards the upper end of the valley, near where it opens out towards Frederick. It was subsequently occupied by his son Elias, and later, by his grandson Leonard. When Jacob purchased the land it was surrounded by a wilderness. There was but a small space cleared, on which stood a cabin, which had been erected by the previous occupants. There are two small graves in the orchard there, the children of the man who lived on it when Jacob bought the place. He bought the land of a Capt. Daniel Smith, who lived near the gap, towards the outlet of the valley, in the direction of Frederick. At this period the depredations of Indians were not infrequent. One of Capt. Smith's daughters was taken away by the Indians, and was so long absent that they could only recognize her on her return by a wart on the end of her tongue. After she had been recovered, she was of such a roving disposition that they could not keep her at home. She is buried at Litiz, in Lancaster County, Pa. On Dec. 22, 1764, Samuel Greybill deeded part of a tract of land called "Mount Olivet," containing three acres, to Jacob Harbaugh. This was an addition to his previous purchase. He paid five pounds for it, and it lay back of the graveyard. South of the house, in a meadow, Jacob planted an oak-tree in 1760, which stood until cut down in 1856 by the occupant of the place. At first all kinds of game and wild beasts were plentiful in the valley. The latter even ventured up to the houses in open day. In 1764, as Jacob Harbaugh's wife was engaged in taking bread from the bake-oven, she was suddenly surprised by the fierce attack of a wild-cat. A desperate contest ensued, but at length she came off victorious, causing the vicious animal to retreat. Jacob served some years as constable. On one occasion he was attacked by a band of men at "Money's tavern," which it seems was the place for holding magisterial courts, and one of them struck him in the eye with a stone, causing the loss of its sight. Jacob Harbaugh was a member of the Reformed German Church, and after it was organized worshiped at what is called "Apple's Church," instituted about 1790. His house was built about 1768, by his brother Leonard Harbaugh. His old clock (still standing in the room) was bought with Continental money, and the family Bible was printed in Nuremberg in 1770. He died April 28, 1818, and was buried by the side of his wife in the family graveyard back of the orchard on the homestead farm. Jacob Harbaugh's children were Anna Margaretta, born Jan. 27, 1762, married to Henry Snyder, near Chambersburg, Pa.; Jacob, born March 21, 1763, who lived in the lower end of the valley, and died Dec. 16, 1842, eighty years of age; John, born May 27, 1764, married Elizabeth Winters, and lived in the upper end of the valley; Susannah, born Nov. 6, 1765, and married Jacob Hoover, lived in the valley; Catherine, born March 6, 1767, and died in a good old age unmarried; Barbara, born March 12, 1768, and died Oct. 6, 1809; Julian, born June 21, 1769, and died Nov. 11, 1817; Anna Maria, born March 17, 1771, married John Shriver, near Lutersburg, and died March 3, 1873; Henry, born Aug. 22, 1772, and died Nov. 11, 1844; George Harbaugh, born March 17, 1774, and married Anna Snyder (near Boonsboro'), Jan. 2, 1801. He settled in Washington township, Franklin Co., Pa., near the Maryland line, on a tract of two hundred acres, being part of "The third Resurvey on Sarah's Delight" (eighteen hundred acres) granted by patent to Christopher Shockey by Frederick, Lord Proprietary of the province of Maryland, July 12, 1768. Two hundred acres of it were sold by Christopher to Valentine Shockey, and the latter, Feb. 13, 1787, sold it to Jacob Harbaugh, Sr., for £1000. The latter sold it to George Harbaugh, Sept. 1, 1804, for £1200. A small part of this two hundred acres extends across Mason and Dixon's line into Hauver's District. He built his house of stone in 1805.

George Harbaugh died Feb. 3, 1853. He had twelve children, of whom the tenth was Rev. Henry Harbaugh, D.D., born Oct. 25, 1817, and who was twice married, first to Louisa Goodrich, and after her death to Mary Louisa Linn. Yost, the eleventh child of Jacob Harbaugh, was born Jan. 21, 1776, and died Aug. 18, 1777. Yost, the twelfth child, was born March 17, 1778; married Elizabeth Maug, had seven children, lived at Fountain Dale Mill, and died April 28, 1817; the thirteenth child of Jacob, named Frederick, was born Nov. 1, 1779, and died in infancy; the fourteenth, Joseph, born Dec. 2, 1780, died in infancy; and the last and fifteenth was Elias, born Jan. 1, 1782. He was married Dec. 30, 1817, to Anna Catharine Pentzer. She was born Aug. 23, 1793, and died Feb. 15, 1849. Elias resided on his farm near Sabillasville, and died Aug. 4, 1854. He had nine children, all baptized and confirmed in the German Reformed Church. Yost, the sixth son of Yost Harbaugh, the emigrant, was born on Oct. 11, 1741, and served in Braddock's expedition, was at Bloody Run in the Indian wars, and a captain in the Revolution. Leonard, the first child of Yost Harbaugh, the emigrant, by his second wife, was born May 10, 1749. He removed to Baltimore in 1775, and in 1792 to Washington, D. C. He built the War and Treasury offices as they stood previous to their destruction by the British in 1814. He did part of the building of the President's house, and was many years engaged in large public enterprises, making the Potomac River navigable for long boats, etc. He died Sept. 22, 1822. Mary Elizabeth, the second child of Yost Harbaugh by his second wife, was born on Good Friday, 1753; married Godfrey Lenhart, and died Aug. 15, 1819. The third child, Anna Margaret, married a Mr. Bailey, and the fourth, Anna Catharine, a Mr. Brenisen.

The Hauvers, from whom this district took its name, were very early settlers, but came subsequently to the Harbaughs. They were of German origin, very numerous, and a thrifty people. Peter Hauver, a descendant of the old stock, has several times been in the Legislature as a member from this county. They are located in the southern and southeastern part of the district. In their neighborhood, at Hauver's (a straggling village), were formerly held the elections. At these violent troubles sometimes arose over candidates to be voted for, and for long years feuds existed between the mountaineers ("Swissers") and the inhabitants of the valley, in which many bloody encounters took place.

Peter Zollinger settled very early in this district, and was of Swiss birth, being one of the Palatinates who came by thousands after the French and Indian war. He owned the land on which Sabillasville was founded and which was then called Zollinger's Town. After his death the name was exchanged to Servillasville, in honor of his wife Servilla, a lady held in affectionate remembrance by the whole community, but in course of time the name became adulterated into "Sabillasville."

Valentine Shockey, son of Christopher Shockey, the patentee of eighteen hundred acres, a small part of which was in this county, and the balance in Pennsylvania, became a notorious counterfeiter. He flourished from about 1775 to 1804, when he was in the York County, Pa., jail, and there, while in prison, George Harbaugh purchased his farm. There is yet to be seen a cave near Mount Misery, east of the Great Falls, on Falls Creek, which is called Shockey's Cave, where he and his confederates made their money, and hid themselves in times when they were fearful of pursuit. This iniquitous business was carried on along these mountains during the whole of the last quarter of the eighteenth century. Shockey resided on the tract bought by George Harbaugh. His house stood between the present stone house and a barn. Once, when a posse were in hot pursuit of the counterfeiter, they came to his house in the evening, but he escaped to the mountain. They waited for some time, and then set fire to his house, with the hope that the sight of the flames would lure him from his hiding-place, and if he should come to the rescue, they might be able to capture him. The flames soon enveloped the building, and on the woods around and from the distant mountain shone the red glare of the burning house. From the side of the mountain Shockey looked down on the work of destruction, but he did not leave his retreat. Shockey was the leader of a terrible gang, whose exploits resounded from Baltimore to the Ohio River. About 1830, on Shockey's old farm, a zinc plate, the counterfeit type of a Continental note, was turned up by a harrow. The cave and the traditions concerning Shockey show him to have been a daring and desperate man, and the boldest of the counterfeiters who followed on the heels of the Revolution.

Sabillasville.—This pretty village is situated in the northern part of the district, and is on the Western Maryland Railroad. It lies about two miles from the Pennsylvania line, and nearly the same distance from the Washington County line. Dr. William F. Luckett, the resident physician, has been located here for ten years, and enjoys a large and lucrative practice. There are two churches,—German Reformed, Rev. H. Wissler, pastor; and United Brethren, Revs. J.

LYCURGUS PHILLIPS.

D. Freed and Wein, preachers in charge. R. S. Dupharne is the postmaster. A well-stocked store is kept by David and Lewis Crawford, and the village boasts of a good hotel, of which John Stern is the landlord. The village is beautifully located between two high mountains, and is in the midst of an orderly and intelligent community. The temperance local option law went into effect in this district in May, 1881.

From Mechanicstown the railroad grade ascends towards the Blue Ridge, and at every step of one's progress the scenery becomes grander and more picturesque. Above Mechanicstown, where the scaling of South Mountain begins, a high bridge is crossed, which affords a splendid view in every direction. At Sabillasville, by a piece of engineering skill in what is known as the "Horse-Shoe Curve," there is another magnificent view of the mountains and valley. The ascent gradually unfolds more and more of the panorama below, until passing "Blue Ridge Summit," fifteen hundred feet above tide-water, well known as a resort for excursionists, and near which are numerous hotels and springs, Waynesboro' Station is reached, where suddenly bursts on the view a scene of indescribable beauty,—the Cumberland Valley, a section of surpassing loveliness. Two miles distant is the famous "Crown Cliff," where the prospect is sublime. In the distance the hotel at Monterey Springs may be clearly distinguished, and smiling fields and dwellings and church-spires enliven the landscape, while the substantial Switzer barns add a characteristic feature to the picture for miles away. It was on this lofty summit that Mason and Dixon and their party, when running the line between the possessions of William Penn and Lord Baltimore, tarried a while to enjoy the chase in the midst of the magnificent scenery, then in all its primeval grandeur. Near by is "Hartman's Gap," through which Alan Cameron and the Tory refugees from Canada penetrated, under the guidance of the Indian chief "White Eyes," the ally of the British, in order to join the Hessians under Knyphausen and the British Tories under Gen. Gage and Lord Dunmore to destroy the town of Frederick. Sabillasville is on the old Gap road, the first one built over the mountains, and over which in olden times passed all the teams going from Catoctin Furnace to the Franklin County, Pa., forges and furnaces.

The teachers in the district for the term ending April, 1881, were:

School No. 1, 85 pupils, W. M. Martin, L. Eby assistant; No. 2, 50 pupils, J. M. Kiefer; No. 3, 35 pupils, E. M. G. Buhrman; No. 4, vacant; No. 5, 28 pupils, Theodore Smith.

Foxville is situated near the Washington County line, six miles from Smithsburg, six from Mechanicstown, and three from Smithfield, on the Western Maryland Railroad. It contains a Methodist Episcopal and a Lutheran church. Harvey Buhrman is postmaster. The merchants are H. T. Brown, Thomas C. Fox; physician, Dr. Harvey Buhrman; constable, H. Clay Hayes; shoemakers, Emanuel Prior, Elias Renner; blacksmith, Jacob Weller; carpenters, Henry Wolf, Upton Wolf.

WOODSBOROUGH DISTRICT, No. 11.

The boundaries of Woodsborough, or District No. 11, were established as follows: "Beginning at the forks of the Liberty and old Annapolis road, and running thence with a straight line to the pine-tree on the Woodsborough and Liberty road; thence with a straight line to the mill formerly owned by Roop on Little Pipe Creek; thence with said creek to the mouth thereof; then with the Monocacy to the mouth of Israel's Creek; thence with said creek to the road leading from Frederick to Liberty; thence with said road to the beginning." The district is in the northeastern portion of the county. On the north Double Pipe Creek separates it from Carroll County; on the east lie Johnsville and Liberty Districts; on the south Mount Pleasant; and on the west Frederick, Lewistown, and Creagerstown Districts, from which it is separated by the Monocacy River. The Frederick and Pennsylvania Line Railroad passes through the middle and northeastern portions. The villages are Woodsborough and Georgetown. The first settlers were the Woods, Cramers, Stouffers, Stimmels, Cronises, Shanks, Smiths, Dudderars, Fogles, Deleplanes, Locks, Albaughs, Krises, Millers, Phillips, and Winebrenners.

The paternal ancestor of Mr. Phillips, the first of the family in Maryland, came from England. John Phillips, grandfather to L. N. Phillips, was in the front rank of Frederick County pioneers. His son Noah, born in that portion of Montgomery County now embraced within the limits of Frederick County, moved in early life to the place now occupied by his son, Lycurgus N.

Noah Phillips married a daughter of John Campbell, of Frederick County. He died Feb. 8, 1863, aged eighty-five. His wife preceded him by nineteen years, dying April 9, 1844. But two of their children are living,—Lycurgus N., of Frederick County, and Mrs. Minerva Howard, of Baltimore.

Lycurgus N. Phillips was born March 28, 1822, upon the farm which is and always has been his home. His school-days covered a brief period under the instructions of the district pedagogue, and later a three years' term at Pennsylvania College. He was brought up to be a farmer, and has made farming a satisfactory and successful venture. Nov. 27, 1849, he married a daughter of Joseph Biggs, of Carroll County, of which his forefathers were dwellers for many years back. Of the thirteen children who have blessed the union of Mr. and Mrs. Phillips, eight are living,—five sons and three daughters,—and thus far they have remained steadily under the ancestral rooftree,—an unbroken family circle.

By religious faith Mr. Phillips is a Methodist. His first vote was cast for Henry Clay, and following the fortunes of the Whig party until the party became extinct, he joined the American, and ultimately the Republican party, to which he still adheres. He was chosen a Republican member of the first Legislature of Maryland after the war, and during his term of service acted with much zeal and marked ability as a member of four important committees. The evening of existence finds him philosophically in the enjoyment of the comforts that a life of labor and industrious energy has gained for him. As counsel and adviser his judgment is much deferred to, and as a citizen and neighbor he is held in high esteem.

Woodsborough District and town both take their name from Col. Joseph Wood. His father, Joseph Wood, the emigrant, was born in Gloucester, England, and on coming to America first settled in Cecil County, Md., on " Bohemia Manor." There he married his first wife, in January, 1734 or 1735, by whom he had five children :

1. Robert, born Aug. 12, 1736, and married Oct. 13, 1763, to Catharine, daughter of Nicholas Dorsey.
2. Sarah, born Jan. 10, 1739, married Nathaniel Wickham, and died July 11, 1777.
3. Joseph Wood (the colonel, from whom the name was given to district and town), born Sept. 17, 1743.
4. Mary, born Aug. 7, 1746, married Moses Hedges.
5. Catharine, born April 9, 1749.

Joseph Wood, the emigrant, married his second wife, Catharine Julien, Sept. 11, 1749, by whom he had six children :

1. Elizabeth, born Feb. 5, 1750, married Aug. 6, 1769, to Thomas Wilson.
2. Abraham, born Feb. 7, 1753.
3. John, born Nov. 29, 1754.
4. Rachel, born Feb. 5, 1757, married to Benjamin Barnhart.
5. Rebecca, born Sept. 12, 1759, and married to Thomas Reynolds.
6. Ruth, born Nov. 24, 1761.

Joseph Wood, the emigrant, removed from Cecil County to Hauver's District about 1755. He loaned the Continental Congress eight thousand dollars in silver to fight the war of independence. He was buried at Rocky Hill church, and his second wife (Catharine Julien) at a place one mile south of the town, on what is now the Miller property.

Col. Joseph Wood, the third child of the emigrant by his first wife, married, April 9, 1769, Ann, daughter of James Reed, by whom he had five children, viz. :

1. Mary, born June 25, 1772, and married to James Harlan.
2. Sarah, born June 21, 1774, married to Joshua, son of James and Elizabeth Harlan.
3. Elizabeth, born Feb. 10, 1777, died March 31, 1777.
4. Catharine, born March 2, 1778, and married to John Williams.
5. Joseph, the third of the name, born Jan. 9, 1781, and married to Nancy Grabill.

Robert, first child of Joseph Wood, the emigrant, had by his wife, Catherine Dorsey, the following children :

1. Sarah, born June 1, 1764.
2. Joseph, born May 19, 1765.
3. Nicholas, born May 13, 1766.
4. Martha, born Jan. 19, 1768.
5. Charles D., Sept. 29, 1769.
6. Amelia, born July 26, 1772.
7. Jesse, born Sept. 27, 1775.
8. Dennis, born Dec. 12, 1776.
9. Catherine, born Dec. 11, 1778.
10. Robert, born Dec. 15, 1781.

Joseph Wood, the third, had by his wife, Nancy Graybill, five children, viz. :

1. Charles, born Dec. 11, 1805, and married March, 1828, to Mary, daughter of John Saylor.
2. John, born August, 1809, married to Sophia Whenrich.
3. Joseph (fourth), born October, 1811, and married to Ruth Ann Houcke.
4. Sarah, married June 5, 1844, to Frederick Lock.
5. Moses.

Four Harlan brothers, Quakers, came from England to America, of whom one, not being satisfied, started home again, but instead went to Ireland, and was afterwards known as "Irish George." The other three located near Doe Run, in Chester County, Pa. Their names were William, James, and Caleb. One of them, James, married Elizabeth Webb, by whom he had the following children :

1. James, married to Mary Wood.
2. Steven, married to Catharine Wright.
3. Daniel, married to Mary Legget.
4. Mary, married to Mr. Woodward.
5. Elizabeth, married to Mr. Baldwin.
6. Joshua, married to Sarah Wood.

Joshua Harlan was born Aug. 17, 1763, and married Sarah Wood, January, 1792. He died Dec. 24, 1830, and she May 28, 1844. Their children were:

1. Nancy, born Oct. 5, 1792, died Jan. 22, 1859.
2. James Wood, born April 4, 1795, died April 7, 1861.
3. Joseph, born June 13, 1797.
4. Elizabeth, born Nov. 21, 1798.
5. Mary, born Nov. 21, 1803, died June, 1872.
6. Catharine, born Feb. 14, 1806.
7. Joshua George Washington and Thomas Jefferson (twins), born April 24, 1808.
8. John Madison, born Dec. 22, 1810, died Jan. 31, 1851.
9. Eliza Ellen, born Sept. 26, 1815, and married June 23, 1836, to Moses Anders, born Jan. 29, 1815, and son of Jacob Anders.

The children of Moses and Eliza E. Anders were:

1. John Marshall, born Jan. 16, 1838.
2. Francis M., born Sept. 5, 1840, died Dec. 27, 1845.
3. George W., born Oct. 30, 1842 (sergeant-major of Third Maryland Battalion in war of 1861-65).
4. Thomas J., born Nov. 23, 1844.
5. Charles, born Aug. 14, 1847.
6. Florence, born June 10, 1849, died Jan. 25, 1852.
7. Moses W., born May 12, 1851, died July 21, 1852.
8. Florence V., born May 20, 1854.
9. Aaron E., born July 10, 1857.
10. Moses H., born July 26, 1859, died Dec. 10, 1863.

John M., son of Moses Anders, married May, 1854, Margaret S., daughter of Paul Anders. Their children are John E., Moses S., Marshall E., Jessie L., Della C., and Gertrude M. Thomas J., fourth child of Moses Anders, married Susan E. Brumer, of Clark County, W. Va., Sept. 21, 1870, daughter of John and Emily Jane Brumer. Their children are John Caton, Stanley Matthews, Beulah M., and Roger K.

Prior to the Revolution of 1776, Col. Joseph Wood built what is known as the stone mills at Woodsborough, and erected a mansion of brick imported from England. This fine dwelling is still standing, and is occupied by David Albaugh. Another house of brick which Col. Wood erected is still standing, and is occupied by George M. Shaw. Col. Wood owned some fifteen hundred acres of land, a part of "Monocacy Manor," on a portion of which, near the northern boundary, the town was laid out.

Joseph Wood, the emigrant, had his fourteen hundred and fifty acres surveyed Jan. 10, 1748, and received his patent June 1, 1750.

Jacob Stimmel, born in Adams County, Pa., settled in the district about 1770, and his son, John B. Stimmel, now living, was born June 27, 1790. The latter is the father of ex-Constable Stimmel. John Winebrenner, a descendant of one of the first settlers, and founder of the religious sect known as Winebrennarians, was born in this district.

Woodsborough.—The first settlement or village was called "Woods Town," but the plat of Col. Wood, dated Feb. 7, 1786, laying out the town, designated it as "Woodsberry." Afterwards it was called "Woodsborough," and the word is generally spelled "Woodsboro'." It occupied some forty acres, and was laid off into eighty lots, each two hundred and forty-seven by sixty-six feet. The principal streets are Frederick, Second, and Third, thirty-three feet in width. There are two alleys sixteen and a half feet wide. Elizabeth is the central cross street between the two alleys. The town is most beautifully located in a bottom surrounded by hills, and is on the Frederick and Pennsylvania Railroad and Woodsborough turnpike, ten and a half miles from Frederick, and near Israel's Creek and Monocacy River. It lies in the midst of a fertile and salubrious country, diversified and undulating. The inhabitants point with affectionate pride to the old edifice which gave rest and refreshment to Gen. Washington when he encamped his foot-sore army on the adjacent hills, on their march to Philadelphia. The town was then on the great highway from the South, by way of Frederick, York, and Lancaster, to Philadelphia. The old house which served Washington for a headquarters was built of split logs, and filled in with mortar and stone. It became a tavern, and until 1855 bore the sign of Washington mounted on a charger with drawn sword in hand. It is yet standing, in good preservation, near the town, between the York and Creagerstown roads. Capt. G. W. Anders, a lineal descendant of Col. Wood, has in his possession the original plat of the town. Col. Wood died in the house where Mrs. Eliza Holbruner has lived for seventy years. The colonel at the beginning of the century built a Universalist church, which about twenty years ago was converted into a building for other purposes. The oldest living persons in the town born in its limits are Mrs. Catherine Hall (born Smith), Mrs. Eliza Holbruner (born Maxwell), and Mrs. Charlotte Donsife (born Shank), all three about seventy-five or seventy-six years of age.

Churches.—About a mile and three-quarters from Woodsborough, on the road to Johnsville, is Rocky Hill Lutheran and Reformed church. It was built in 1768, on a lot conveyed by Peter Baird, grandfather of Matthias Baird. It was an old-time two-story log structure, and fifty years after its erection was plastered and weather-boarded, and remains to this day in its primitive condition. Its pulpit, a square box four feet high, was put up in 1771. It is reached by a staircase. The galleries occupy three sides of the church. The whole building is in a good state of preservation, and bids fair to stand a century yet. It was built by the Lutherans, Reformers, and Presbyterians, but about 1800 the latter withdrew. Up to about 1830 the preaching was in the German language, and then for a number of years it alternated between German and English, and about 1840 began to be held exclusively in the latter tongue. Among its first pastors was Father Grubb, an early pioneer missionary preacher. From 1770 to 1815 the preachers were Rev. Grove, Rev. Wachter, and Rev. D. F. Schaeffer. Its present Sunday-school superintendent is Michael Fogle, and the assistant superintendent, Matthias Baird. Adjoining the church is the old burying-ground, which contains tombstones dating as far back as 1769. All the earlier inscriptions are in German.

Methodist services were held in the early part of the century at the old "Burnt Mills," and "at the house where Widow Gilbert lives." The first class-leader was George H. Hardman. The church was built in 1819, and J. A. Baker was the first superintendent of the Sunday-school after its organization, and so continued for many years. It belongs to the Liberty Circuit, West Baltimore District, of Baltimore Conference. Among the early preachers may be mentioned Revs. Nicholas Sneeden, Reynolds, John L. Given, Rowen, Larkins, George Hilt, Bard, Tabner Ball, Mercer, J. Cronin, James, Hanks, Philmyer, W. R. Mills, Gilmore, A. Riley. Since and including 1868 the pastors have been:

1868, Rev. Philmyer; 1869, Rev. Cullom; 1871, Rev. Charles Clever; 1873, Rev. William Buhrman; 1876, Rev. M. P. Cronin; 1879, Rev. W. H. Koontz.

The Lutheran Church was organized in 1838, under the auspices of Rev. Mr. Weiser, but services had been held for years previous by Rev. Dr. Harkey and others. Since and including 1857 its pastors have been:

1857, Rev. Beckley; 1863, Rev. S. W. Owen; 1871, Rev. B. F. Alleman; 1873, Rev. Michael Fair; 1875, Rev. A. R. Lentz; 1876, Rev. D. M. La Motte, who is the minister at present.

The Methodist Protestant Church was organized and built in 1832, and its present pastor is Rev. J. M. Brown.

The pastor of the Reformed Church is Rev. Mr. Hench, and his predecessor was Rev. Orange E. Lake.

The earlier physicians of the town were Drs. Baltzell, Henry Staley, Kuhn, Thomas Sinn, J. M. Geyer, H. L. Donsife. The present physicians are Drs. R. T. Hammond, W. H. Wagner, and H. K. Derr. Dr. Hammond has been in practice here forty years, and Dr. Wagner since 1853. The latter studied under Dr. Thomas Sinn at Liberty, and is a member of the Sydenham Society of London, England.

J. H. Baker has been postmaster since 1877. His predecessor for two years was Eugene Albaugh, before whom were Benjamin Smith, John Main, Jacob M. Wachter, George W. Shank, Benjamin Smith.

The school-teachers for the term ending April 15, 1881, were:

School No. 1, 33 pupils, Adam Roser; No. 2, 46 pupils, Minnie L. Seabrook; No. 3, 55 pupils, J. E. Dougherty; No. 4, 65 pupils, B. F. Hildebrand; No. 5, 117 pupils, M. J. Hendrickson, J. Callahan assistant; No. 6, 82 pupils, B. W. Stitely; No. 7, 42 pupils, Hattie A. Rinehart.

The magistrates are George W. Shank, J. H. Bowers, John A. Lock, Adam Birely.

New Midway is pleasantly situated on the Frederick and Pennsylvania Line Railroad. F. C. Renner is postmaster; Robert Barrick, constable; Jesse Bolder, builder; M. D. Butt, merchant; Charles Dougherty, blacksmith; E. Renner, wheelwright; Frank Strine, shoemaker; and F. C. Renner, fly-brush manufacturer.

Georgetown is located in the southwestern part of this district, and was named in honor of George Cramer. It is on the Frederick and Pennsylvania Railroad, but the station is called by the railroad Walkersville. All the territory of Georgetown proper, except four lots, is in Woodsborough district. F. B. Lewis keeps a store, and also deals in coal, lumber, etc., and is the station agent. This place is growing rapidly, and is one of the prettiest villages on the line of the railroad.

Monocacy Manor.—The General Assembly by various acts confiscated all the estates, real and personal, of parties attainted with treason during the Revolution. The lands thus confiscated were resurveyed and subdivided, and then sold by the State at public vendue. Among them was Monocacy Manor, in Frederick County, of 8983 acres, belonging to Daniel Dulany. This tract was confiscated by an act of November, 1780, and the sales thereof appropriated to the redemption of the certificates granted the soldiers of the "Maryland line." These certificates were received as specie in payment of the lands or lots thus purchased. The sale took place Oct. 10, 1781, and below is given the number of the lots, with acres in same, the tenant then in possession, and the names of purchasers.

Lots.	Acres.	Tenant.	To Whom Sold.	For in £.
1	54	Widow Shover	Gen. Williams	350
2	182	Wm. Smith	Col. P. Adams	1630
3	191	Geo. Devilbiss	John McHenry	1215
4	140	Geo. Devill, Jr.	Wm. Bailey	830
5	95	Peter Fisnot	"	510
6	113	Val. Mauk	"	560
7	28	Philip Weaver	"	190
8	140	Frederick Baker	Gen. Smallwood	1225
9	199	John Devilbiss	"	1560
10	165	Col. Wood	Col. Rawlings	1950
11	138	Widow Hedge	Col. J. Howard	1500
12	248	Jno. and Wm. Crum	Capt. Montgomery	2535
13	130	Peter Cramer	Col. J. Howard	760
14	41	Christian Barrick	Samuel Swearingen	403
15	130	Geo. Devilbiss	John Beall (for son)	1120

Lots.	Acres.	Tenant.	To Whom Sold.	For in £.
16	78	P. Wier	Wm. Whitcraft	760
17		Included.		
18	105	Wm. Smith	Capt. Jones	350
19 20	131	Jacob Keller	Capt. J. Lingen	450
21	114	Jacob Beaver	Joseph Dowson	800
22	85	James Hail	Col. J. Tootle	510
23	115	Michael Fireston	Dr. Pindell	750
24	153	Peter Hedge	Col. J. Howard	1200
25	150	Peter Barrick	Wm. Whitcraft	610
26	153	Jacob Barrick	Dr. Jenifer	540
27	103	John Barrick	Col. Ramsey	925
28	120	Chris. Barrick	Capt. Bruff	410
29	138	A. Adams	Col. Ramsey	1410
30	99	Michael Riddlemoser	Gen. Williams	325
31	88	Luke Barnard	"	750
32	125	John Manchey	"	1250
33	141	John Cooper	Maj. J. Gist	615
34	168	Daniel Buzzard	"	1015
35	209	J. and W. Cramer	Capt. Montgomery	1624
36	252	Robt. Fulton	Chas. Troxell	1835
37	128	Mrs. Springer	Col. J. Howard	830
38	11	Adam Snuke	Wm. Bailey	190
39	110	John Brown	Wm Bailey	705
40	126	Geo. Sexton	Capt. Baltzell	725
41	133	Geo. Rhodes	Capt. Trueman	780
42	95	Wm. Barrick	Capt. Williams	610
43	94	Han. Barrick	"	675
44	252	W. and H. Barrick	Gen. Williams	1100
45 46	117	A. Smith	Wm. Bailey	525
47	170	M. Shank	Capts. Williams and Brooke	1150
48	111	John Hoof	Col. Tootle	1030
49	128	Geo. Shank	Maj. Lynch	1205
50	7	Vacancy	Wm. Bailey	55
51	200	Geo. Earhart	Geo. Murdoch	2050
52	68	Col. J. Wood	Col. Wood	400
53 54	63	Col. J. Wood	Capt. Lynn	550
55 64	193	Chris. Hufford	Maj. Davidson	1300
56 57	198	Maj. Wood	Gen. Smallwood	1270
58	198	John Harlan	"	1265
59	157	John Renner	"	805
60 61 62	333	John Barrick and J. Wood	Wm. Whitcraft	3040
63	133	Thos. Brown	Col. P. Adams	750
64		Added.		
65	207	W. T. Hartzog	Maj. Davidson	735
66 67	261	Phil. Smith	Col. Woolford	1005
68	153	Peter Smith	James Smith	825
69	85	Peter Barrick	Gen. Williams	705
70	89	Vacancy	Col. Tootle	575
71	11	"	Jo. Dawson	603
72	25	"	Wm. Bailey	230
73	25	"	Col. Ramsey	195
74	17	"	"	110
75	48	"	Capt. J. Jones	375
76	10	"	Capt. Evans	90
77	32	Andrew Beamer	Col. Ramsey	410
78	24	Vacancy	Capt. Denny	115
79	28	W. Shover	Col. B. Mackall	315
80	70	Vacancy	Col. Ramsey	125
81	52	"	Capt. Evans	120
82	100	"	Col. Ramsey	105
83	42	"	Capt. J. Jones	120
84	47	Balsor Snider	Col. J. Wood	270
85	93	Col. Wood	Maj. Lynch	345

Total acres, 8983. Total of sale in money, £60,555.

A large number of lots in Frederick Town belonging to Daniel Dulany were also seized by the State and sold at the same time; also 300 acres called "Partnership," the property of John Buchanan.

PETERSVILLE DISTRICT, No. 12.

By an act of the General Assembly passed in December, 1829, Petersville, or Election District No. 12, was created by dividing Middletown (No. 3) into Nos. 3 and 12. The commissioners appointed in the said act to make this division were Patrick McGill, Col. J. Thomas, Benjamin West, George Bowlus, and George Willard. Its boundaries were established as follows:

"Beginning at a large stone planted on the dividing line between Washington and Frederick Counties, standing on the north side of the road leading from New Town (Trap) to Sharpsburg then leaving said dividing line, and running with that part of the south line of District No. 3 south seventy-two degrees east down the east side of said mountain, still continuing said course, passing by and leaving the dwellings and habitations designated in the following manner, viz.: Bechtell's, Michael Smith's, Samuel Gaver's, Henry Asherman's, and William House's dwellings on the north side of said line, and Goodman's, Jacob Smith's, Samuel Fink's, Edward Tritt's, Daniel Biser's, Eli James', John House's, and George Herring's on the south side of said line, still continuing said line until it strikes the Catoctin Creek to a large stone, now planted near the margin of said creek, and directly opposite a large poplar-tree, standing on the other side of said creek; then running down by and with the meanders of the said Catoctin Creek to the mouth thereof, at the Potomac River; then up said river till it intersects the Washington County line; thence with said line to the beginning."

This division was made March 22, 1831. Petersville District is situated in the extreme southwestern portion of the county. On the north lies Middletown District, and on the east Jefferson District, from which it is separated by the Catoctin Creek; on the south the Potomac River, along whose northern bank extends the Metropolitan Branch of the Baltimore and Ohio Railroad; and on the west the Blue Ridge, separating it from Washington County. It is abundantly watered by the Catoctin, the Potomac, and the Little Catoctin and their tributaries, and it forms the southwestern section of the smiling Middletown Valley. The villages are Petersville, situated near the centre, Burkittsville, Berlin, Knoxville, Weverton, and Broad Run. The earliest settlers in the district located themselves on the historic "Maryland Tract." They were either English immigrants or settlers from Maryland and Virginia, and were about equally divided into members of the Established Church of England and the Catholic Church. Among the first to settle were the Lees, Morrisons, Wests, Hilleary's, Claggetts, Cramptons, and Garretts, and afterwards the Deavers, Groves, Willards, Slifers, Botelers, Ahalts, Whipps, Shafers, and Alexanders. The dwelling-house of John Lee was built by the Rev. Mr. Booth, an Episcopal clergyman, for a seminary, and it happened to be so odd a structure that the people in the upper part of the valley suspected it to be a Tory rendezvous, and only through the efforts of Mr. Potts, of Frederick, were the hardy yeomanry restrained from tearing it down.

Petersville.—This place is two and a half miles from Knoxville, and twelve southwest of Frederick. It is situated in the centre of the Maryland Tract, between the South Mountain on the west and Catoctin on the east. The neighborhood has been for years a favorite summer resort. It has a refined and cultivated society, and was at one time the residence of Governor Lee, Hon. John Lee, and Governor Francis Thomas. The fine residence occupied by John Columbus O'Donnell possesses considerable historic interest, having been built in 1819 by Col. John Thomas, father of Governor "Frank" Thomas, and having remained in the possession for two generations of the widely-known and noted Thomas family. In 1861, Gen. Columbus O'Donnell, of Baltimore, purchased the property from Governor Thomas, and materially improved as well as embellished it. During the late civil war the house was occupied at various periods as the headquarters of Union generals, including Custer and Kilpatrick. It is situated on a commanding elevation close to the village of Petersville, and within a short distance of the battle-field of Antietam. From it may be had a fine view not only of Harper's Ferry Gap, but of a splendid expanse of mountain scenery. John Columbus O'Donnell, the present proprietor, has expended upon it the results of a generous taste and advanced ideas gained from extensive foreign travel.

The house, which now as heretofore is the abode of a generous and elegant hospitality, is situated in the midst of charming grounds, whose natural beauties have been greatly heightened by intelligent landscape gardening. The estate contains about three hundred acres, and is regarded as one of the most valuable in Frederick County.

William Gardner is the postmaster, and the resident physicians are Drs. John W. Hilleary and George W. West.

St. Mark's Parish.—This parish (Protestant Episcopal) is an offshoot from All Saints', at Frederick. Its creation has already been described in a preceding chapter. The rectors since and including 1800 have been:

1800-12, Rev. George Bower, also rector of All Saints'; 1814, Rev. John Chandler, also rector of St. Peter's; 1815-17, Rev. George Williams; 1819-21, Rev. William Westerman; 1822-28, Rev. John L. Bryan; 1829-31, Rev. Jared Rice; 1833-34, Rev. Mervin Allen; 1835-41, Rev. Richard H. Phillips; 1841, Rev. John Delaplane; 1842-44, Rev. Olcutt Bulkley; 1844-48, Rev. John Francis Hoff; 1848-52, Rev. Francis Marsh Baker; 1853-58, Rev. Alexander Magruder, Marbury; 1858-60, Rev. Robert Bean Sutton; 1860, Rev. Joseph Trapnell, Jr.

The Rev. Townsend Dade, of Eden, afterwards St. Peter's Parish, officiated on the Maryland Tract soon after the year 1783, and after him the rectors of that parish down to 1806.

For a sketch of Rev. John Chandler, see St. Peter's Parish. George Williams passed himself off as a clergyman, and was minister of this parish for nearly three years, but was discovered to be an impostor and compelled to leave. Rev. William Westerman was a native of the West Indies, and was ordained by Bishop White in 1818. He removed to Petersville in 1819. In 1821 he returned to the West Indies, and died there in 1859. Rev. John L. Bryan removed in 1822 from Virginia, of which he was a native. He was ordained deacon by Bishop Moore in 1818. In 1831 he removed to Ohio, and there died in 1866. Rev. Jared Rice was a native of Vermont, but ordained by Bishop Moore in 1828. He became rector of St. Mark's in 1829, and died in 1833, aged thirty-two years. He was a graduate of the Virginia Theological Seminary. No material for sketches of Rev. Mervin Allen and Rev. R. H. Phillips has been obtained. Rev. John Delaplane was a native of Pennsylvania, and a graduate of the Virginia Theological Seminary. He was ordained by Bishop Moore in 1834. He then became the minister of St. Thomas' Church, at Hancock, Washington Co. He was chosen rector of St. Mark's in 1841, and died that year, leaving a son and daughter. His wife subsequently married the Rev. J. Buck. Rev. Olcutt Bulkley, a native of Vermont, and graduate of the Virginia Theological Seminary, was ordained by Bishop Moore in 1837, and took charge of Christ Church Parish, Calvert County, Md. He removed to Petersville in 1840, and in 1842 and 1844 was rector of All Saints' Parish. He removed to Virginia, and disappeared from the clergy list in 1856.

Other Churches.—The Lutheran Church was erected in 1872. Its pastors have been Revs. L. A. Mann, 1872 to 1876; J. H. Turner, 1876 to 1880; and M. L. Beard, the present incumbent. The Methodist Episcopal congregation originally held its services in the school-house, but in 1859 purchased the public hall and converted it into a neat edifice. Its pastor is Rev. E. Smith. The Catholic Church has had a large membership from the first settlement of the district, when a congregation was formed. Its fine edifice has a commanding view of the country around. Rev. John Gaffney is the priest in charge.

Burkittsville.—This town is situated in the far-

MOUNT O'DONNELL.
RESIDENCE OF JNO. COLUMBUS O'DONNELL PETERSVILLE DIST. FREDERICK CO., MD.

famed Middletown Valley, at the foot of the Blue Ridge Mountains, two and a half miles from Claggett's, on the Baltimore and Ohio Railroad, and nine from Harper's Ferry. The climate is particularly beneficial to invalids, and the neighborhood is rapidly becoming a popular summer resort. It was first known as "Harley's Post-Office," but received its present name from Henry Burkitt, who owned the land on which the village was built. Mr. Harley kept the first store, some fifty years ago. The postmaster is Martin L. Hightman, and the physicians Drs. J. D. Garrott, Tilghman Biser, G. L. Staley, and T. E. Hardy.

The organization of the Lutheran congregation dates back to 1830. The edifice was erected in 1859, before which time the members worshiped with the Reformed congregation in the latter's building. It was first connected as a charge with Middletown, and later associated with Jefferson, but became a separate charge in 1857. Its pastors have been:

1857, Rev. G. A. Nixdorff; 1864, Rev. W. C. Wire; 1868, Rev. L. A. Mann; 1876, Rev. J. H. Turner; 1880, Rev. M. L. Heisler (supply); 1881, Rev. M. L. Beard.

The fine church edifice was built during the ministry of Rev. G. A. Nixdorff. Its Sunday-school superintendent is John Hightman.

The Reformed Church was established in 1829 by Rev. John C. Bucher, pastor of the Middletown Church. Its pastors have been Revs. G. L. Staley, Samuel Phillips, Moses Stewart (eleven years), H. I. Comfort (five years), and M. L. Shuford, since 1873. The pastor acts as the Sunday-school superintendent. The elders are Ezra Willard, Greenbury House, Henry H. Biser; the deacons, William Pearl, F. G. House, W. S. Flook. The congregation has a substantial parsonage. The cemetery, jointly held by the Reformed and Lutheran Churches, is now a public one for the use of all.

The Protestant Episcopal Church holds occasional religious services at Union Chapel, a commodious building, owned by Messrs. Wilcoxon & Levy, of Frederick. Rev. J. Trapnel, of St. Mark's Church, is the officiating minister.

The town has one of the most commodious public school-houses in the county, and its schools are not surpassed in efficiency by those of any place of its size in the State.

Burkittsville Female Seminary.—This institution, located at Burkittsville, was founded in 1866, by the Rev. W. C. Wire, A.M., a Lutheran clergyman, who continued to preside over the institution for some twelve years. The buildings, which were erected in 1866, consist of an elegant and substantial brick edifice seventy feet long and three stories high, with a wing thirty-six feet long, surmounted by a cupola which affords an extensive view of the surrounding country. The institution was formally opened on the 15th of October, 1866, and was incorporated by the General Assembly of Maryland in March, 1867. The number of pupils has steadily increased, and the sphere of its influence is annually widening. The course of study embraces all the branches essential to a practical and ornamental education. The collegiate course comprises three years, but pupils are advanced according to their progress, and not the time spent in the institution. The faculty consisted at first of Rev. W. C. Wire, A.M., principal; Mrs. M. J. Wire, vice-principal and superintendent; Miss M. H. Duphorne, mathematics, English branches, and botany; Miss M. A. Newlin, drawing and painting, and assistant in English; Miss M. A. Mackley, vocal and instrumental music. The annual sessions of the institution comprise ten months, commencing in September, and closing in June. Rev. J. H. Turner, D.D., succeeded Mr. Wire for two years, and Prof. M. L. Heisler is the present principal. He took charge of the institution in 1880.

Burkittsville Tannery.—Michael Weiner, a native of Bavaria, came to the United States in 1834, and having spent a few years as an employé at the Middletown tannery, purchased in 1846 the tannery at Burkittsville, belonging to E. H. Sleifer, who had bought it from the original proprietor, a Mr. Locker. Mr. Weiner has steadily maintained a reputation for the product of his works, which enables him to command for it the highest price in the market. Forty lay-away vats and five leaches enable the tannery to produce one thousand heavy hides per annum. Sole, harness, and upper leather and sheep and calf-skins of the best quality are made. Mr. Weiner has a good local trade, but finds his chief market in Baltimore. Since 1878 he has been assisted by his son, Henry M. Weiner, who has the personal management of the works.

Needwood Distillery.—Probably no whisky in the United States bears a better reputation than that produced at the Needwood distillery. It is noted everywhere for its purity and flavor, and commands a high price in the market. In 1850, Outerbridge Horsey, a native of Frederick County, began its manufacture, and from that time to this all his skill, knowledge, and energy and many costly experiments have been directed to the production of pure rye whisky. So closely has this policy been adhered to that the Needwood is said to be the only distillery in the United States which runs the entire year on one class of whisky. In 1862, when the hurricane of war swept over this beautiful section of the State, Mr. Horsey's business was destroyed, and much of his machinery carried off. When peace permitted a resumption of industries, Mr. Horsey set up new and improved machinery, erected a large brick warehouse with a capacity of three thousand barrels, and increased his facilities, after which he proceeded with the manufacture of his whisky. The Needwood Distillery is beautifully situated in the Blue Ridge Mountains, four miles from Knoxville, on the Baltimore and Ohio Railroad. The superintendent is James Dall. The market for Mr. Horsey's product comprises the trade of the entire country. The largest orders, however, come from New York, Boston, Chicago, Cincinnati, and the State of California. Nothing, it is said, gives such flavor and tone to whisky as age, aided by a sea voyage. For this reason Mr. Horsey never sends out raw or new whisky. Once made it is placed in the bonded warehouse, remaining in an even temperature, for months, often years, after which it is shipped to the seaboard, and thence around Cape Horn to the Pacific coast, where it remains for a year or two, after which it is brought back, rich in all the qualities that epicures require.

Ahalt's Distillery.—About the year 1848 the Hon. John Lee erected a flour-mill on the site of the above distillery, which is about four miles from Knoxville, the nearest railway station on the Baltimore and Ohio Railroad. This structure was afterwards remodeled into a saw-mill, and in 1879 again changed its form, and was made suitable to its present purpose by J. D. Ahalt. It is a well-known fact that the grain grown on the fertile plains of Frederick and Washington Counties is of a quality so fine that no matter what it is converted into it always produces the best of its kind. Recognizing this fact and comprehending its value, J. D. Ahalt started the above distillery for the manufacture of pure rye whisky. Mr. Ahalt will use none but the choicest selected rye, while his process is based upon the most improved methods, some of which are the results of costly scientific experiments made by himself. The whisky, after lying long enough to become mellow, will be shipped by sailing vessels to Rio Janeiro, receiving the benefit of a sea voyage to that point and return. The distillery is admirably located upon a lovely mountain slope, where clear spring-water is always obtainable.

Knoxville.—This town is on the Baltimore and Ohio Railroad, seventy miles from Baltimore and fifteen from Frederick. It is pleasantly situated on an easy slope, and is shielded from the winds by the surrounding hills. South Mountain is near, and on the Virginia side of the Potomac the mountains rise in picturesque grandeur. It has Methodist Episcopal, Lutheran, and Reformed Churches, supplied respectively by Revs. John W. Walsh, M. L. Beard, and M. L. Shuford. Robert Porter is postmaster, and Dr. John Reed physician. The merchants are J. M. Miller, W. T. Main, J. D. Main; shoemaker, S. W. Brooks; grain dealers, Darby & Rice; coal, I. N. Merchant; wheelwright, John Mitchell; blacksmiths, John W. Porter, G. E. Thomas; saddlery, Robert Porter; hotel, James Reely; butcher, Charles W. Schnetze.

Capt. H. T. Deaver, a native of Frederick County, and one of the best known of the residents of his section, lives on what is known as the old Richard Johnson place, one mile from the village of Knoxville. Richard Johnson (brother to Hon. William Cost Johnson) was a bachelor and a person of eccentric disposition. His farm contained two hundred acres, and was known as "Peri Land." Capt. Deaver bought the property of the Johnson estate in 1852, and in 1865 built the handsome, substantial, and roomy residence he now occupies. The two hundred acres originally in his purchase have been increased by him to five hundred. The house is a brick structure two and a half stories in height, and is situated on a picturesque elevation fully eight hundred feet above tide-water. The farm lies at the lower end of the Middletown Valley, and from its highest eminence, whereon the residence stands, may be seen portions of the States of Maryland, Virginia, and West Virginia, embraced in the counties of Loudon, Jefferson, Washington, Frederick, and Montgomery. Old Richard Johnson used to maintain, and stoutly, too, that he could see from his house seven counties and three States. In the distance may be seen Harper's Ferry Gap and the waters of the Potomac and the Shenandoah, while the towering elevations of Elk Ridge, Blue Ridge, and South Mountain rear their distant fronts within clear sight. Capt. Deaver has a handsomely-improved farm, and ranks among the most successful of agriculturists. Unusual care is taken of the grounds inclosing the mansion, and they form accordingly a feature of much importance in the general prospect.

St. John's Female Seminary, a select boarding-school for young ladies, located near Knoxville, is an offshoot of Mount Washington Female College, and was organized originally at Mount Washington, Baltimore Co., Md., in the spring of 1856. After being in successful operation from that date to the 19th of April, 1861, the school was disbanded by the force of

Residence of **Capt. H.T. Deaver** Petersville Dist., Frederick Co., MD.

"AUBURN."
RESIDENCE OF C. M. LEWIS, MOUNT PLEASANT DISTRICT, FREDERICK CO., MD.

circumstances arising out of the civil war. In 1864 the property known as "Tyrconnel," one of the most beautiful places in Frederick County, was secured for its use, and the school was reorganized in a new home. The buildings, however, were of limited capacity, affording accommodations for only a small number of pupils, but in 1874 a large additional building was erected for school purposes, making the school in every way more comfortable and efficient, and increasing its capacity to the number of thirty or more boarding scholars. The buildings are surrounded with extensive grounds artistically laid out and ornamented with flowers and trees in great variety. The school, which is not incorporated, was under the control of the Rev. George Lewis Staley, D.D., a clergyman of the German Reformed Church, until 1879. During the past two years it has not been in operation, but Professor Staley has used the buildings for a summer resort for boarders from the cities.

Berlin.—This village (Barry Post-Office) is on the Baltimore and Ohio Railroad, seventy-five miles from Baltimore, and fifteen from Frederick by county road. The town has great advantages for trade, and does a large business in grain, fertilizers, and coal. The merchant mills of Jordan, Wenner & Jordan are located here. There is a lodge of Knights of Pythias (Catoctin, No. 91), and one of Independent Order of Red Men (Delaware Tribe, 43). Rev. John Hall is pastor of the Methodist Episcopal Church, and William A. Barnard is postmaster. The merchants are Jordan, Wenner & Jordan, Boteler & Gross; builder, E. D. Barnard; blacksmith, W. A. Barnard; railroad and express agent, Lingan Boteler; butcher, Thos. Watt; shoemaker, Joseph Shilling; restaurant, T. B. Leopold.

Broad Run is pleasantly situated in the centre of the great Middletown Valley, seven miles from Knoxville, and is said to be surrounded by the richest land and most beautiful buildings in the county. John H. Grove is the merchant and postmaster; M. F. Fink and J. D. Whipp, millers; W. S. Keafauver, wagon-maker; Samuel Ahalt, G. W. Huffer, machinists; W. T. Grove, J. E. Flook, carpenters; J. C. and P. G. Cochran, blacksmiths.

The teachers of the district for the term ending April 15, 1881, were:

School No. 1, 36 pupils, Anna M. Werking; No. 2, 64 pupils, A. C. McBride, Fanny Hightman, assistant; No. 3, 41 pupils, John H. M. Claggett, C. S. Smith; No. 4, 34 pupils, M. E. Philpot; No. 5, 80 pupils, William Gittings, C. B. Carlisle, assistant; No. 6, 62 pupils, C. E. Miller, Alice M. Thomas; No. 7, 16 pupils, Ella V. Smith. No. 1 (colored), 43 pupils, Mary S. Jackson; No. 2 (colored), 34 pupils, Adelaide Dodson.

The magistrates are Israel Carnes, Burkittsville; James Meek, Petersville; Dr. John Reed, Knoxville.

S. L. Gouverneur, of this district, the grandson of ex-President James Monroe, and who had in his possession many of the important papers of that distinguished patriot and statesman, prepared for publication a work from the pen of Mr. Monroe addressed to his countrymen, and written after he had retired from public life.

MOUNT PLEASANT DISTRICT, No. 13.

By an act of the General Assembly passed April 19, 1852, Mount Pleasant, or Election District No. 13, was established out of parts of Liberty (8), New Market (9), and Woodsborough (11). The commissioners named in the act to lay it off were James S. Riddlemoser, George Murdoch, and John Myers. Its boundaries were made as follows: "Commencing at the mouth of the Linganore Creek; thence up said creek to the head of William Jones' mill-dam; thence with a straight line as near as may be to Jacob Harmiss' dwelling-house, on the road leading from Liberty Town to Brigg's ford on the Monocacy River; thence down said river to the place of beginning." The district is situated near the centre of the county, and is drained by Monocacy River and the Linganore and Israel Creeks. The villages are Mount Pleasant and Walkersville. On the north is Woodsborough District, on the east Liberty and New Market, on the south and west New Market and Frederick.

Among the families which settled in this district at an early period may be mentioned the Cramers, Stouffers, Routzahns, Diffindalls, Ramsburgs, Nicodemuses, Bealls, Derrs, Houcks, Koonses, Dorseys, Jacobs, and Shriners.

The residence of C. M. Lewis, about five miles distant from Frederick City, is a type of the substantial, hospitable, and comfortable old mansions with which the mind naturally associates the era of good cheer and genial warmth that characterized social life in the early days of Maryland history. It stands removed some distance from the highway, and is approached by a fine drive through a wooded avenue. There is about the old stone mansion an air that seems to bid the visitor a hearty welcome, and to bespeak, moreover, the comforting entertainment which abides within. The house was built in 1815 by Joshua Dorsey, whose daughter married Dr. Thomas Johnson about that time. In that house both Joshua Dorsey and Dr. Johnson died. The Dorseys and Johnsons were famous as royal entertainers, and at their fireside the leading families of that region frequently gathered and held at times high revel, while within the time-honored walls of the mansion many brilliant minds have discussed the topics of the time, and groups of merry-makers have enlivened its apartments. Mr. C. M. Lewis (by profession a master-machinist) purchased the property in 1875, and moved thither from Baltimore. There are one hundred and thirty-five acres of cleared and fruitful land, with most excellent improvements, attached to the premises. The farm itself lies in what is known as Glade Valley. Near by is an eminence much favored by sight-seers, from which one may obtain a delightful view of a broad stretch of picturesque landscape.

Mount Pleasant Village is on the Liberty road, six miles from Frederick, and three from Walkersville. It derives its name from its elevated site, from which not only Frederick City is seen, but also, on a clear day, the Potomac River, twenty-five miles distant. The Reformed Church was organized in 1869, and its edifice erected in 1870, under the auspices of Rev. A. R. Kremer. His successors as pastors were J. M. Souder, in 1875, and Rev. A. Shulenberger, the present incumbent, in 1876. Mr. Shulenberger also preaches at Rocky Hill and Union Chapel.

The merchants are C. A. Thomas (postmaster), J. T. Taylor, and James Riddlemoser. The physicians are Drs. D. E. Stone and J. H. Leib. The other industries are G. W. Buckey, tanner; John D. Damon, shoemaker; John Fitch, John Wagner, hucksters; D. S. Kemp, carpenter; A. Sheetenhelm, wheelwright; B. Stevens & Bro., blacksmiths; W. W. Wetker, cabinet-maker.

The Methodist Episcopal Church is attached to the Liberty Circuit.

Georgetown.—Four houses of this place are situated in Mount Pleasant District, one of which is that of Drs. William and Michael Zimmerman, another that of Rev. J. D. Freed. The United Brethren church was built in 1857, and its pastors have been:

1857, I. K. Statton, H. Tahelm; 1858, I. K. Statton, S. Evers; 1859, L. W. Matthews, W. Jackson; 1860, L. W. Matthews, T. F. Buschong; 1861, I. Baltzell, T. F. Buschong; 1862–64, W. T. Lower, J. W. Grimm; 1865, T. Stern, J. W. Grimm; 1866, T. Stern, J. D. Freed; 1867, J. Delphy, J. D. Freed; 1868, J. W. Kiracofe, J. W. Grimm; 1869, J. W. Kiracofe, J. E. Holt; 1870, J. K. Nelson, Rev. Zerman; 1871, J. K. Nelson, W. O. Smith; 1872–75, A. M. Evers; 1875–78, J. L. Grimm; 1878, Edras Ludwick, J. L. Grimm; 1879–81, William Beall; 1881, J. D. Freed.

Ceresville Flour-Mills.—The Ceresville mills and estate originally consisted of about six hundred acres of choice limestone land, situated about three and one-third miles northeast of Frederick, on the east bank of the Monocacy, where the waters of Israel Creek empty into the river. At the beginning of the present century the estate was owned by Gen. Williams, and between the years 1812 and 1816 he built the mansion-house in which Samuel Hoke, Jr., now resides, a saw-mill, and the present Ceresville flouring and grist-mills. The mill-house is built substantially of stone, 40 by 60 feet, and four stories high, with all the necessary machinery for manufacturing sixty barrels of flour per day, all of which is driven by the waters of Israel Creek by two overshot water-wheels sixteen feet high. The mansion-house was subsequently the home of Maj. Daniel Hughes, who distinguished himself in the Indian war in Florida, and of Charles Johnson, the father of Gen. Bradley T. Johnson.

The present proprietor of the mills is Edward A. Shriner, whose grandfather, Michael Shriner, resided on a farm near Unionville. Michael Shriner, whose ancestors came from Germany at a very early period, had three sons,—Cornelius, Basil, and Abram H.,—all of whom engaged in the milling business. Of these, Cornelius, the father of E. A. Shriner, leased the Ceresville mills in 1826, and purchased them in the following year. His first wife, who was the daughter of Christian Scholl, was married to him about this time. She died in 1838. His second wife, whom he married in 1841, was Mary P., daughter of George Barrick, who is still living. Of the first marriage, E. A. Shriner is the only child now living. Of the second marriage, two children,—Mary C. and G. W. B. Shriner—survive, the latter being engaged in the grocery business in Frederick. Cornelius Shriner was a farmer in early life, but afterwards became a miller, as stated. Before his death, which occurred on the 13th of September, 1854, he had amassed a large property, and was at the head of an extensive and flourishing business. In 1840, Cornelius Shriner bought a half-interest in the Linganore mills, and in 1844 purchased from Col. Edward Schley the Carroll Creek flouring-mills. In 1850 he purchased of Lewis V. Scholl the remaining interest in the Linganore mills and estate. Mr. Shriner resided for several years in Frederick City, and was a director in the Frederick County Bank for a number of years. For the greater portion of his life, however, he resided at the Ceresville mills, although his place of business was in Frederick. Mr. Shriner dealt largely in grain to supply the Linganore and Carroll Creek flouring-mills, and was among the largest manufacturers of flour in the State. He also dealt largely in grain and live-stock, which he shipped to Baltimore, where his son was associated with G. Sauerwein in the produce and commission house of G. Sauerwein & Co.

In 1854, while riding to church with his son George, Mr. Shriner was paralyzed and fell from his

E. A. Shriner

RESIDENCE AND MILL OF E. A. SHRINER,
MOUNT PLEASANT DISTRICT, FREDERICK CO., MD.

horse. He was taken home insensible, and after a brief illness died at the age of fifty-four years.

E. A. Shriner, eldest son of Cornelius Shriner, was born on the homestead at Ceresville, Jan. 24, 1830, and still resides there. Mr. Shriner received from his father a thorough training as a miller, and since his earliest youth has been engaged in that calling. In 1850 he was given an interest in the business, and in 1852 associated himself with G. Sauerwein in establishing in Baltimore the house of G. Sauerwein & Co., referred to above. In 1858 he was married to Margaret A., daughter of John Derr, of Frederick County, a descendant of the French Huguenots who fled to this country from the Palatinate early in the eighteenth century. Mr. Shriner succeeded to the ownership of the Ceresville mills upon the death of his father, and has continued to operate them ever since. Mr. Shriner's aspirations have never led him to seek political distinction, his business having always been the object of his assiduous care and interest, and he finds sufficient gratification in knowing that he has succeeded in largely developing and improving the extensive mill property which he has controlled and managed for nearly thirty years. Mr. Shriner has been identified with the Frederick and Liberty Turnpike Company for a number of years, and since 1869 has been the president of that corporation.

Mr. Shriner's residence and mill property are situated on the Liberty and Frederick turnpike, between three and four miles from Frederick. Originally they comprised a small stone house and a four-story stone mill. The latter succeeded a one-story brick mill that stood not far from the present mill on Israel's Creek, which dated its existence from about 1790. The stone mill was built in 1813. Cornelius Shriner improved and enlarged the residence by a brick addition. A number of other improvements have been made from time to time, and the mill at present is perfectly equipped and appointed in all respects. It is furnished with three burrs and one chopper, and manufactures flour by the latest patented process. It has a capacity for grinding fifty thousand bushels of wheat annually, and produces eight thousand barrels of flour every year, of which seven thousand are shipped to Eastern and other markets.

The neighborhood has been much improved by the construction of the Frederick and Woodsborough and the Liberty and Frederick Turnpike Road Companies, which centre at the Ceresville mills, and which were built at a cost of $50,000.

In the construction of these roads Mr. Shriner took an active interest, and served as director, and in the latter company as president. In the mean time the mills have been improved by the introduction of the latest machinery. The mill itself is as solid and substantial as the day it was built, and its long ownership in one family, who have given it their care and attention, has built up a reputation upon the merits of its products which is as solid as the mill itself. Situated in the heart of the "Garden of Maryland," where the cereals are the best, the products of the Ceresville mills have always been exceedingly popular.

Mr. Shriner has devoted all his time to the production of a perfectly pure article of flour, made only of the best wheat, and known in the Washington, D. C., and Baltimore markets as the "Ceresville, Bloomingdale, and E. A. Shriner brands of family flour."

Walkersville.—This village lies on the Woodsborough turnpike, adjoining Georgetown, and is six miles north of Frederick. It is one of the newest and at the same time one of the most attractive places in the county, and in the past three years over thirty substantial houses have been erected within its limits. It was named in honor of John Walker, who owned the land on which it was laid out. S. W. Stauffer is the postmaster, and Dr. J. D. Nicodemus the resident physician. J. Hanson Stauffer keeps a large drygoods store. Its beautiful location and proximity to the fine turnpike skirting it make it a favorite resort for drives and excursions from Frederick City.

The school-teachers of the district for the term ending April 15, 1881, were:

School No. 1, 30 pupils, Olivia E. Ever; No. 2, 46 pupils, Melissa J. Long; No. 3, 61 pupils, R. H. Harrover; No. 4, 35 pupils, George F. Thomas; No. 5, 59 pupils, R. T. Glisan; No. 6, 30 pupils, Bettie Roelke; No. 7, 86 pupils, C. Harry Anders, A. A. Wagner (assistant). No. 1 (colored), 44 pupils, Adelaide Chambers.

JEFFERSON DISTRICT, No. 14.

Jefferson, or District No. 14, was established by an act of the General Assembly passed in 1832, and was created out of Middletown (No. 3). The commissioners named in the act to make the division were Patrick McGill, Sr., Henry Culler, John Simmons, Jacob Thomas, of John, and Adam Lorentz. The district was laid out April 11, 1833, with the following boundaries: "Beginning at the Potomac River opposite the highest ridge on the Virginia shore; thence with said mountain bounding the western ridge, the highest part thereof, to a large forked sassafras-tree (marked) on the north side and very near the new public road leading from Jacob Feaster's mill, intersecting the turnpike road near Staub's dwelling-house, running from said tree north eighty-two degrees, west two miles and one-three-hundred-and-twentieth of a mile, intersecting the branch four perches north of the blacksmith-shop in Rockville; from thence with the meander of said stream until it intersects Catoctin Creek, where is now a marked large sycamore-tree and a stone planted on the north side of said branch opposite a ledge of rocks on the west side of Catoctin Creek; thence with the meanders of said Catoctin Creek until it intersects the Maryland and Virginia line, and with said line to the beginning."

By act of March 7, 1850, the dividing line between Frederick, Buckeystown, and Jefferson Districts was changed " to the eastern summit range of the Catoctin Mountains, crossing the Frederick and Harper's Ferry road at or near the sixth mile-post on said road from Frederick City." Jefferson District is in the southwestern section of the county; Middletown District skirts it on the north, Frederick and Buckeystown on the east, and Petersville and Middletown on the west. Its southern boundary is the Potomac River. The Catoctin Mountains extend through the eastern portion from north to south. The villages are Jefferson, Centreville, Lander Post-Office, and Catoctin Switch.

Among the earliest settlers were Capt. Marler, Stoneo Frazer, the Phillipses, Lamars, Thrashers, Simmonses, Delashmutts, Lakins, Cullers, Shawens, Easterdays, Castles, Ramsburgs, Shaeffers, Keafauvers, Motters, and Kesslers. The Johnson family did not settle in the district until about 1798. Thomas Johnson (2) was born Aug. 24, 1729, and died in Buckeystown District, Oct. 2, 1778. His wife was a Miss Thomas. Their children were John, Thomas, Richard, and William. The latter married in 1800 Catharine Cost, of Frederick. William Johnson was born about 1770, on his father's farm in Buckeystown District, but in 1798 removed to what is now Jefferson District, where he purchased four hundred acres of land, nearly all in woods, and was the first man to sow clover in the valley. William Johnson died in October, 1811, and left three sons,—Thomas, Richard, and William Cost Johnson. The latter became a prominent lawyer and politician. Col. Thomas Johnson is the only surviving son of the three sons of William Johnson. He was born on his farm, Feb. 15, 1801, was a colonel forty years in the militia, and served in 1861 in the Maryland Legislature as a member of the Lower House.

Jefferson.—In 1800 this town had only four dwellings, and was then known as the "Trap," and afterwards as "Newtown Trap." It was so called from the fact that it was a rough and dangerous settlement, in passing through which many a poor traveler was robbed and sometimes foully made way with. Hence it acquired a bad name in its early days.[1] It was incorporated by the Legislature of 1831–32, through the active efforts of William Cost Johnson, then one of the delegates of Frederick County. By general consent the naming of the new town was left to the oldest resident, Dr. Charles MacGill, who, notwithstanding the majority of the citizens desired to call it "Catoctin" (after the Indian tribe that once occupied the valley), named it after the illustrious Thomas Jefferson, of whom the doctor was a warm admirer. The town is an elevated, healthy point, twenty-six feet higher than Burkittsville, and one hundred and twenty-five above Harper's Ferry. In the beginning of the century and for years afterwards it was on the great thoroughfare from the North to the South, and the travel through it was immense. The first man to preach in Jefferson was a local preacher of the Methodist Episcopal Church named Martin, a brother of Luther Martin, Maryland's distinguished lawyer. Henry Culler was the first mayor of the town.

Churches.—The Lutheran church was built in 1841, and rebuilt in 1866, but previous to the first date preaching had been had for ten years, and at various times before. The pastors have been:

1831–34, Rev. A. Peck; 1834–35, Rev. J. Harpel; 1836–40, Rev. Wachter; 1841, Rev. Jesse Wincoff, Rev. C. C. Baughman; 1841–43, Rev. W. F. Eyster; 1845–53, Rev. D. J. Hauer; 1853–54, Rev. G. S. Collins; 1855–57, Rev. B. Appleby; 1857–58, Rev. E. Darsey; 1858–78, Rev. H. G. Bowers; 1878, May 1, Rev. W. H. Settlemyer, the present pastor. The Sunday-school superintendent is Dr. J. J. Culler. The elders are Daniel Culler, Basil Lewis, John W. Long; and the deacons, J. Henry Culler, William Shaff.

The Methodist Protestant church was built in 1843. Its present pastor is Rev. W. R. Mills, and its pastors previous to Rev. J. E. Maloy, Mr. Mills' predecessor, were those stationed at Frederick.

The Methodist Episcopal church was built in 1830, and for thirty years previous preaching was had at the old school-house or at dwelling-houses. Among the preachers before 1830 were Revs. Charles B. Young, James Reed, E. R. Veech, and J. R. Cadden, and since them Thomas McGee, William Butler, Joseph Parker, Aaron Clary, H. G. Dill, J. W. Langley, David Trout, L. M. Gardner, John Anderson, B. G. W. Reed. In 1858, Jefferson was united with Middletown Circuit.

The German Reformed Church was established in 1841. Aug. 16, 1841, Peter Hoffman and wife con-

---

[1] The commissioners by act of March 14, 1832, to blend Newtown Trap and New Freedom with the town of Jefferson were William Lynch, Levy Williss, and John W. Pratt.

veyed part of lot No. 43, eighty-two and a half by two hundred and seventeen and a half feet, to Sebastian Ramsburg, John Feaster, Sr., Henry Crum, John Stockman, Sr., Henry Stockman, Jacob Feaster, Jr., John Hemp, and John Stockman, of John, the consistory of the church then duly organized, as a site for a church, which was immediately erected. Rev. N. H. Skyles has been pastor since 1875, and his predecessor was Rev. S. S. Miller.

Rev. E. Jenkins is the pastor of the African Methodist Episcopal Church.

Post-office, Masonic Lodge, Etc.—C. E. Thomas has been postmaster since 1860, and before him three of his brothers, Emanuel, John, and Perry G., had held the office. This office has been most of the time in the Thomas family.

The great storm of Sept. 8, 1866, blew down the Methodist Protestant church, the Lutheran in part, as well as Dr. Crum's and Mrs. Anderson's houses in part. It was the most terrific wind-storm ever known in the valley.

St. Alban's Lodge, A. F. and A. M., No. 65, was located in New Town (now Jefferson), and was last represented in the Grand Lodge in November, 1820, by Samuel Cole (probably a proxy).

In the German Reformed cemetery, the oldest burying-ground, the following early settlers are buried, viz.: David Kemp, born Sept. 2, 1778, died Feb. 20, 1856, and Mary Kemp, his wife, born Dec. 20, 1782, died April 4, 1855; Thomas Lamar, born Dec. 19, 1777, and died Aug. 11, 1864.

Among other old families here interred are the Grosses, Barricks, Baers, Flooks, and Lakins.

The teachers of the district for the term ending April 15, 1881, were:

School No. 1, 16 pupils, Addie Currier; No. 2, 105 pupils, W. H. Meyers, Annie E. Sowers, assistant; No. 3, 40 pupils, C. W. Marriott. No. 1 (colored), 37 pupils, W. A. Thomas.

The physicians are Drs. G. W. Crum, J. H. Crum, J. J. Culler; merchants, S. M. Culler, S. E. Little, Isaac Walker; saw-mill, H. C. Biser; dentist, Dr. H. D. Mills; dealers in harness, saddles, etc., D. C. Shaff, A. D. Doty; miller, Basil Lewis; blacksmiths, R. F. Cochran, H. C. Wise, Peter Poole; tobacco and notions, W. V. Culler; undertakers, T. T. Thomas, J. G. Etchison & Son; tailor, C. E. Thomas; carpenters, F. S. Feaster, W. P. Stockman, F. Shaff.

MECHANICSTOWN DISTRICT, No. 15.

Mechanicstown, or Election District No. 15, was created by the act of May 27, 1852, out of parts of Creagerstown (4), Emmittsburg (5), and Hauver's (10). The commissioners designated in the act to lay it off were Frederick White, John Eyler, and Michael M. Ege. Its boundaries were made as follows: "Beginning at the summit of the Catoctin Mountain, near the furnace, and running thence to a point near the blacksmith-shop of Michael Zimmerman; thence from said shop along the public road to Thomas Metcalf's land; thence with a straight line to John R. Boller's house, including said house and the village of Graceham; thence along the public road leading from Mechanicstown to the Emmittsburg cross-road; thence along the Emmittsburg road to a point where the branch known as Beaver Dam crosses said road; thence in a straight line to a point north of John A. Martin's house; thence in a northern direction to William Boller's farm; thence with the Emmittsburg road, leading to Wolf's tavern, to the cross-road from Mechanicstown to Sabillasville; thence with a straight line to Harman's farm; thence with the south side of the road to the new-cut road near Gat's farm, and thence with a straight line to the place of beginning."

Mechanicstown District is situated in the northern part of the county, with Hauver's and Emmittsburg Districts on the north, Emmittsburg and Creagerstown on the east, Creagerstown on the south, and Catoctin and Hauver's on the west.

The early settlers were the Wellers, Creagers, Wilhides, Firors, and Rouzers, who came about 1750, with other pioneers. These were nearly all Germans. "Longatepaugh," a survey of two hundred and forty-nine acres, was patented to Lawrence Creager, July 17, 1779, and "Shoemaker's Knife," a tract of fifty-five acres, was granted July, 1746, to Philip Knavell. During the French and Indian war the early inhabitants of this region were on the extreme Western frontier, and suffered severely from the depredations of the savages.

The pleasant village of Mechanicstown is beautifully situated on the east of the pretty stream called Hunting Creek, which has its source in the Catoctin Mountain. It is fifty-two miles northwest from Baltimore, and about the same distance from Washington City, and sixteen north of Frederick. It lies at the base of the mountain. The first settlement dates back to 1751, when a few buildings were erected along the road leading from Hagerstown via "Harman's Gap" to Baltimore. Lots were then laid out by James and Lawrence Creager, who held nearly all the lands as far as the present village of Creagerstown.

The Weller family was the first that actually settled on the site of the present town. There were three Weller brothers, who came from Berks County, Pa., one of whom stopped here because of the very large and fine spring of water, now called the "Cold Spring."

The second settled in Virginia, and the third afterwards located in Kentucky. Jacob Weller settled on the site of Mechanicstown, and was a teamster in the Revolutionary war. The first hotel (now the "Gilbert House") was built in 1800, under the auspices of Jacob Weller, son of the first settler, and the first store was kept by Jacob Firor in 1806. At that period the present beautiful landscape was an almost uninterrupted forest, and game of various descriptions was so plentiful that it is said the good host, Mr. Weller, wishing to furnish his guests with a treat of squirrels, killed from one tree seventy-three of them.

At the beginning of the century the shrieks of the prowling wolf were heard at night, and the only response was the plaintive cry of the whip-poor-will.

In 1810 the first tan-yard was established by a Mr. Wampler. In 1811 the post-office was opened in a house built in 1805 by Mr. Ridenoure, and in 1842 was kept in the same log dwelling. In 1811 there was started by Jacob Weller an extensive edge-tool manufactory, the first one erected south of New York. It was built on Fishing Creek, and run by the above stream of water as a tilting-forge. Mr. Weller would start his "tilting-hammer" in the morning before daylight, and working on a cold piece of iron, would wake up the whole neighborhood with the fearful noise. He manufactured pump-augers, chisels, axes, etc. Many of his orders came from the Southern States and the West Indies. He made all of the mill-irons used at that day for miles around, and some of them can still be found with his name (Weller) branded on them. This factory continued until near 1850. In 1815 a large woolen manufactory was erected, and kept in successful operation for over forty years. In 1820 the celebrated Hunting Creek Tannery was built by Richard Jones, of Baltimore. It was of stone, two stories high, and the establishment comprised about two hundred vats constructed upon the patent reel principle, consumed annually over two thousand cords of bark, and required the labor of but fifteen men to manufacture twenty-five thousand sides of superior leather per annum. It was afterwards carried on by Capt. W. L. Jones, John Q. Hewlett, and others. There was another tannery in the town, beside two others contiguous, in all requiring five thousand cords of bark and a capital of one hundred and fifty thousand dollars. The first tannery is not now in operation. Samuel Stern had a tannery at the foot of the mountain, built about 1820.

The town derived its name from the fact that its population was composed principally of mechanics. The first lucifer-matches made in America were manufactured in this town. Their inventor and discoverer was Joseph Weller, who in 1825, at Frederick, purchased some matches of French importation. On his return home he started an investigation of the material, etc., and the result was his discovery of their ingredients and the manufacture of them immediately with the assistance of his brothers. They were twice burned out. The matches were peddled out through the country at twenty-five cents per package, and with the paper box of matches went a piece of sand-paper on which to ignite them. Many of the farmers drove away the peddlers with dogs, because they feared the burning of their houses and barns by this new invention. Great curiosity was excited as to the secret of their manufacture, but no one discovered it so as to compete with the Wellers. They were first made into blocks, subdivided at first by hand and later by machinery, and then dipped, one by one, into the brimstone mixture, etc., then left to dry, and the next day tied up in packages.

The town was incorporated in 1832, and the first burgess was Mr. Adlesperger. The records of the old incorporation are all lost. Mr. Park was burgess in 1842. In 1870 the Legislature passed an act repealing the first incorporation and creating a new one. The officers under the new charter have been as follows:

1870, Commissioners, G. W. Foreman, president; Leonard Picking, clerk; G. W. Stocksdale, John R. Rouzer, V. B. Osler, Frederick White. 1871, V. B. Osler, president; J. R. Rouzer, G. W. Foreman, G. W. Stocksdale, C. J. Creager, L. Picking, clerk; W. J. Black, assessor. 1872, L. Picking, president; William White, clerk; J. R. Rouzer, treasurer; G. J. Sigman, G. W. Foreman. 1873, V. B. Osler, president; Wm. White, clerk; J. R. Rouzer, treasurer; G. W. Foreman, G. J. Sigman. 1874, E. Little, president; E. L. Boblitz, clerk and treasurer; John Freeze, Alfred Troxell, Wm. Roy. 1875, D. S. Firor, president; G. W. Foreman, Joshua Stokes, Thomas Andrews, E. L. Boblitz, clerk and treasurer. 1876, J. H. Cover, president; E. L. Boblitz, clerk and treasurer; J. Cassell, V. B. Osler, G. W. Stocksdale, G. W. Foreman, assessor. 1877, V. B. Osler, president; A. Slick, D. C. Martin, J. N. Barton, vice G. W. Foreman, deceased; E. L. Boblitz, clerk and treasurer. 1878, A. Slick, president; E. M. Smith, W. A. Lynn, Wm. Lydie, A. Mitchell, clerk. 1879, A. Slick, president; W. C. Grimes, W. L. Armacost, Wm. Lydie, Wm. Six, S. H. Witherow, clerk. 1880, A. Slick, president; Wm. Six, Wm. Lydie, James Mackley, G. J. Sigman, E. L. Boblitz, clerk. 1881, J. H. Cover, president; A. Slick, P. N. Hammaker, G. W. Stocksdale, E. L. Boblitz, clerk; W. J. Black, assessor.

The assessment of 1880 shows the real estate to be valued at $165,493, upon which a tax of 15 cents on the $100 was levied.

In 1836 a disturbance took place between the citizens of Mechanicstown and the hands at Catoctin Iron Furnace. On Saturday, August 27th of that year, the furnace employés marched into Mechanicstown and commenced an attack on the citizens with bludgeons, stones, dirks, and other weapons. A bloody conflict ensued, which continued throughout the day. Finally the foe retreated, a number of them having been badly hurt.

There are five main roads leading to this village besides the great thoroughfare. A number of picturesque spots are to be seen in the vicinity, among them the falls of Hunting Creek, which rises in the Catoctin Mountain. On the same mountain a short distance from the falls is a rock resembling a chimney in shape and known as the Chimney Rock. It forms a fine observatory from which to view the lovely landscape outstretched below.

Catoctin Furnace is situated in the southern portion of the district, three miles from Mechanicstown. It was built in 1774 by the Johnson Brothers,—Thomas, Baker, Roger, and James,—upon a tract of seven thousand acres patented in 1770 to Leonard Calvert and Thomas Johnson. In 1793 the firm dissolved, and Thomas and Baker Johnson, two of the brothers, became the owners. In 1803, Baker Johnson bought out his brother, and leased the furnace to Benjamin Blackford and a Mr. Thornbury. Before the expiration of the lease Mr. Johnson died, and his executors sold the furnace to Willoughby and Thomas Mayberry in 1813. Willoughby Mayberry, however, soon became the sole owner. In 1820 it was purchased by John Brien, who vastly improved the property. Afterwards James Fitzhugh bought it, and then John B. Kunkel and brother, and for the past quarter of a century it has been worked by John B. Kunkel. He has recently built the third furnace, an anthracite one. The timber on these lands has been used in their third and fourth growth. The ore which is obtained is of the best quality of brown hematite. Abundant forests afford every facility for the making of charcoal. Fully three hundred wood-choppers and coal-makers and over a hundred miners are employed by the proprietor. The capacity of the furnace is twelve thousand tons of pig metal annually, which finds a ready market among the consumers for machinery, car-wheels, and for all foundry and rolling-mill purposes. Under the management of Col. Kunkel, the works are in the finest possible order, and the general system pursued is proved to be excellent by its very handsome and satisfactory results. Henry Hendricks, a colored man in Mechanicstown, has one of the old Catoctin stoves, made seventy years ago by Thornbury & Blackford. In 1801, Baker Johnson built near the furnace an elegant mansion, in which Dr. W. S. McPherson now resides.

John B. Kunkel, one of the foremost of iron manufacturers in Western Maryland, was born in Frederick City, Dec. 11, 1817, and in Frederick County has spent his life. His great-grandfather, William Kunkel, was a colonel in the Prussian army, and about 1732, emigrating to America, made his home in Lancaster County, Pa. Six of his seven sons served in the American army during the Revolution, and two lost their lives in the service, one at the battle of the Brandywine, and a second in a manner not positively ascertained, since his fate was never known. Of that son it is told that he was but eighteen years of age when he entered the service. He was a captive on board the Jersey prison-ship, and was so impressed with the terrible sufferings endured by the prisoners that upon his release and return home he vowed to his father that he would return to the army and fight until the last redcoat was driven from the country. From that hour he was never heard of.

The youngest son, William, grandfather to John B. Kunkel, lived and died upon the tract in Lancaster County originally located by Col. Kunkel.

William Kunkel the younger had three sons, of whom the eldest was John. In 1809 he moved to Frederick City, and engaged in business as a distiller. In 1828 he abandoned distilling and embarked his energies and capital in the manufacture of leather. His operations in that direction were of considerable importance, and employed not only a tannery owned by himself but other tanneries as well. He followed the trade of a tanner in Frederick until his death in that city in 1861, aged seventy-seven. His wife, a descendant of the Hoffmans of Lancaster County, Pa., died in Frederick in 1856. Her ancestors were active participants in the war of the Revolution. It is related of Jacob Hoffman, one of her uncles, that during the campaign he was frequently on the march barefooted, and that he wore twisted strands of hay in lieu of suspenders. John B. Kunkel was married in 1842 to a daughter of William Porter, of Philadelphia, once a member of the famous old-time firm of Bevan & Porter, shipping merchants. Mrs. Kunkel is a descendant of Governor John Redding, one of New Jersey's early Governors, and president of the Colonial Council in 1745. Governor Redding was a blood relative, through Lord Wilton, of Charles Stuart, of England.

The Catoctin Iron-Works, founded by the Johnsons about the Revolution, and now carried on and owned by John B. Kunkel, were purchased in 1858 by Mr. Kunkel's father, upon the dissolution of the firm of latest operators there, Fitzhugh & (J. M.)

Kunkel. The business was continued at Catoctin by Jacob M. and J. B. Kunkel until 1866, when Jacob M. retired. Since that time J. B. Kunkel has been the sole proprietor. The furnace has an annual capacity of ten thousand tons, and produces first-class forge and car-wheel metal. About eleven thousand acres of land are tributary to the works. Ore is obtained at a distance of about one mile and a half from the furnace, to which it is transported over a railway owned by Mr. Kunkel. The ores mined at these banks yield from thirty-eight to fifty per cent. in metallic iron. About one hundred men are regularly employed in the conduct of Mr. Kunkel's business. That business, as may be well understood, engages and has engaged his closest attention, and in its pursuit he has found neither time nor desire for the distractions of public life. He occupies a tastefully-appointed home at Catoctin, and there dispenses a genial hospitality. His living children number seven, of whom three sons are associated with him in the management of the works.

Catoctin (Protestant Episcopal) Church.—In 1855, Harriot Chapel was made an independent congregation. In 1855 it was enacted that the territory heretofore a portion of All Saints' Parish, Frederick County, and contained within the following metes and bounds, to wit: beginning for the same on the South Mountain, at the junction of the boundary line between the States of Maryland and Pennsylvania and the division line between Frederick and Washington Counties, in the State of Maryland, and running southwestwardly along the ridge of South Mountain to a point therein called Braddock's Gap; thence southeastwardly to Biggs' ford on Monocacy River; thence up said river to Devilbiss' ford; thence eastwardly along and with the county road (through and including the village of Walkerville) to Mount Pleasant, to the intersection of Tie's road with the main road from Frederick City to Liberty; thence still eastwardly with a straight line to a point where the division line between Frederick and Carroll Counties crosses the main road from Liberty to Freedom; thence northwardly with said last-mentioned line to the boundary line between the States aforesaid; and thence westwardly with the boundary line to the beginning, and to be named and known as the Catoctin Parish. The rectors have been:

1855, Rev. H. I. Windsor; 1854, Rev. J. A. Harrell; 1857, J. G. Jacocks; 1860, Rev. A. A. Curtis; 1861, Rev. —— Perryman; 1865, Rev. J. T. Chambers; 1868, Rev. R. C. Hall; 1870, Rev. Thomas Tongue; 1871, Rev. James B. Averett.

Rouzer's Tannery.—The father of Mr. Rouzer, the present proprietor of Rouzer's Tannery, was almost wholly without capital, and began with but few facilities and many obstacles to combat. Such, however, was his energy and tact that his business has enlarged and improved, until now the son of its founder owns and conducts one of the most important industries of Western Maryland. On the fine farm on which the tannery is located Mr. Rouzer was born and raised. The tannery has a capacity of five thousand to six thousand finished sides per annum. This tannery suffered the misfortune of being burnt down in November, 1853, but was promptly rebuilt the same year. The buildings now consist of the main house, two bark-sheds, two wagon-sheds, and a scale-house, all in good order. A switch belonging to the establishment runs to the Western Maryland Railroad, and affords ample facilities for shipping and receiving goods. Most of the hides tanned come from Texas, though some are received from South America, and the market being almost wholly in Baltimore, only a few are retailed within the county. The bark used comes from Fairfield and Cashtown, in Pennsylvania.

John Rouzer, one of the leading tanners of Western Maryland, was born Nov. 25, 1815, upon the property now occupied as his home, the fine residence he occupies having been built by his father in 1812. His father, Daniel, born in New Jersey in 1766, came to Maryland while a lad, and worked as an apprentice at the tanning business in Hagerstown and Frederick. At the age of twenty-seven—that is to say, in 1793—he made upon the present Rouzer place, near Mechanicstown, a start as a tanner on his own account. He was married twice. His first wife was Sophia, daughter of Peter Shover, one of Frederick County's early settlers. By that marriage there were ten children. The only one living is Henry Rouzer, of Mechanicstown, born in 1806. Sophia Rouzer died in 1810, and in 1814 Mr. Rouzer took a second helpmate in Julia, daughter of John Matthews, of Frederick County. She was born in 1779. Of the second marriage there were but three children,—John, born 1815; Eliza, born 1817; Sarah Ann, born 1819. John and Sarah Ann are still living. Daniel Rouzer was more or less actively engaged in tanning until his death, Aug. 18, 1850, aged eighty-four. His widow followed him four years later, Aug. 19, 1854. John Rouzer has passed his life upon the place where he was born. A brief season of schooling was followed by an early application to the trade pursued by his father, and he may be fairly said to have been bred a tanner. His yearning was for a thorough school education, but his father thought he could not spare his services from the business, and so in deference to paternal desire he denied himself the scholas-

tic training towards which his ambition inclined. For years he was his father's assistant, and ultimately becoming a partner, continued so until the father's death. Upon the settlement of the estate, Mr. Rouzer bought the tannery property, and since then has continued the business solely on his own account. In 1853 fire destroyed the tannery buildings, which were at once rebuilt upon a larger and much improved plan. About three thousand hides are tanned annually, the production being exclusively sole leather; and in their manufacture about nine hundred tons of bark are used. Mr. Rouzer married, in 1846, Phœbe T., daughter of John Landers, a comer to Frederick County in 1812. Mrs. Rouzer died six months after her marriage. After remaining a widower sixteen years, Mr. Rouzer married again, March 20, 1862, his second wife being Emma K., daughter of Nicholas Parrish, of Frederick County. Nicholas Parrish and his wife are still living in Mechanicstown. The children of the second marriage were nine, all sons; seven are living. Five are at school, and two (the youngest) at home. Mr. Rouzer was trained in the Lutheran faith, is now a zealous member of the church, and for many years has been an elder therein. Public life has never enticed him from the cares of a business to which he is wedded, and in which he finds a vast deal more of satisfaction than politics or office-holding could give. He did not take an active part in the civil war, but he was throughout a devoted Union man.

The Franklin Flour-Mills, located on the pike leading from Frederick, and fifteen miles from that city, is one of the most important and busy mills in the county. It was built by Jacob Firor in 1828, and in 1876 came into the possession of John Jones, a native of Frederick County. On assuming control of the mills he furnished them with improved machinery, which consists of two runs of wheat-burrs, operated by a fourteen-foot overshot water-wheel, eighteen-foot fall, with a capacity of fifty barrels per day of twenty-four hours. Owings' Creek, upon whose banks the mill is situated, supplies the power. The building is substantially built of brick, and is 40 by 50 feet, two and one-half stories high, and is in as good a condition as when built. Producing both patent and straight goods, Mr. Jones not only finds a brisk local market for them, but the "John Jones" brand is well known in the Baltimore and New York markets as a reliable and standard article.

Churches.—About 1765 the German Reformers and Lutherans united built a log church about a mile from Mechanicstown, which was called "Apple's Church." Its early records are lost. The first child baptized was Johann Adam, son of Jacob and Margaretta Momma, May 23, 1773. The next was Maria Barbara, daughter of Philip and Eva Catherina Ambros, July 23, 1773. The next was Anna Maria, daughter of Daniel Klingan and Anna Elizabeth Schmidt, Aug. 1, 1773, on which day Johann Heinrich, son of Johann Kupper Schmidt, was also baptized. On Dec. 15, 1793, eighteen members were added to the church. Among the first preachers were Revs. Rahawson and Bassler. Afterwards the ministers were Revs. Elias Heiner, S. R. Fisher, G. W. Aughimbaugh, and E. E. Higbee. In 1858 came Rev. H. I. Comfort, succeeded in 1867 by Rev. N. E. Gilds, who was followed in 1875 by Rev. Henry Wissler, the present pastor. For a long period Apple's Church and the church at Emmittsburg were a joint charge. Mr. Wissler has charge of five churches,— Trinity, and one at Creagerstown, Rocky Ridge, Sabillasville, and St. Jacob's, near Fountain Dale. In 1880 the Reformed congregation removed to the town, where its new edifice had been just completed. "Apple's Church" took its name from a family of Apples living in the neighborhood, who gave the land upon which to build the first meeting-house. This structure stood until about 1815, when the present one was built, which has several times since been repaired.

From 1765 to 1858 the Lutherans, in conjunction with the Reformers, worshiped at "Apple's Church." The names of the first preachers are not obtainable, but towards the last quarter of the past century Father Grubb was a regular preacher at this congregation. The present "Apple's Church" building was erected under his auspices about 1815, by funds largely subscribed by the Lutherans. He died over fifty years ago, having traveled extensively in preaching. He was also a doctor, and particularly noted in cases of fever and bilious colic. After him were Revs. Reuben Weiser, John J. Reifmensnyder, Wachter, George W. Anderson, and John Richards. A new church, the present structure, and the finest in the town, was dedicated in the spring of 1858, when the congregation left "Apple's Church." It was erected under the auspices of Rev. William Hunt. His successors have been Rev. S. Curtis, J. N. Unruh, Jacob Summers, and W. C. Wire, the latter the present pastor. This church has a membership of two hundred and fifteen. Up to about 1830 preaching was exclusively in the German language, and then for a few years it alternated between German and English, and finally was entirely of English. The first settlers of the district worshiped at "Apple's Church," and were mostly of German descent.

The Moravian church is a pretty frame structure,

and is supplied by Rev. E. W. Shields, of Graceham.

The United Brethren (Weller's) Church was organized in 1831, and on December 11th of that year the church edifice was consecrated. It was erected upon ground presented by Jacob Weller, who was born at Mechanicstown, Jan. 25, 1775, and died May 6, 1846. His first wife, Anna Margaret, was born Oct. 22, 1780, and his second, Mary Love, Sept. 8, 1795. Before the meeting-house was finished preaching was had in the old school-house. The first trustees were Jacob Weller, George Stokes, Henry Kemp, to whom, a few years later, were added Frederick Rider, Jacob Martin, and Reuben Osler. Its pastors have been Revs. Nelson, Glossbrenner, William Brown, Winebrenner, Isaac, George, and John Statton, W. T. Lower, Isaiah Baltzell, John Sand, William Knott, George Rymel, Bishop Markwood, Jacob Bastell, Gibbons, Matthews, McCabe, Darkies, J. D. Freed, Funk, Kneidick, William Evers, John W. Grimm (1861–65), C. I. B. Brane (1874–76), J. P. Funk (1876–77), J. D. Freed (1877–81), and Rev. Wein (1881), the present incumbent. This church is in a highly prosperous condition.

In 1859, on Whit-Monday, the beautiful Catholic church, situated on a commanding elevation near the railroad, was dedicated. The congregation is large, and the church flourishing. Its pastor up to 1880 was Rev. H. A. McMurdie, whose labors terminated that year by his decease.

The Methodist Episcopal Church organization was perfected in 1849, previous to which time services had been held in the school-house nearly opposite. The present edifice was erected in 1850, by Rev. B. C. Flowers, who, with Andrew Sefton and Tuisco Marlow, were three of the trustees. Its corner-stone was laid by Rev. S. S. Rozell, and the dedication sermon was preached by Rev. Henry Slicer.

In 1849 the presiding elder was Alfred Griffiths, and the preachers in charge Revs. John A. Henning and J. R. Debrow. In 1850 the pastors were Revs. George Brooke and J. R. Debrow, and in 1881, Rev. W. O. Eldridge, whose predecessor was H. P. West.

In 1861–62 a paper made its appearance in Mechanicstown called the *Family Visitor*, published by Isaiah Wolfersburger. It was tinctured with "secession" proclivities at the commencement of the civil war, and the paper was suppressed by the Union men of the town. The same gentleman afterwards published a Republican paper at Ellicott City, in Howard County, called the *American Progress*.

Societies.—In the summer of 1871, Grand Master Latrobe granted a dispensation to form a Masonic lodge at Mechanicstown. On Nov. 20, 1871, the Grand Lodge granted a charter to Acacia Lodge, No. 155. The officers in 1879 were:

W. M., D. C. Martin; S. W., Cost J. Carmack; J. W., John H. Rouzer: Sec., Van B. Osler; Treas., Geo. W. Stocksdale.

Good Samaritan Lodge, No. 46, I. O. O. F., was instituted at Emmittsburg, Oct. 23, 1845. Its charter members were George Zollinger, Peter Stein, John Burk, John B. Picking, and Lewis Colliflower. It was moved to Mechanicstown in 1849. The lodge hall was erected and completed Aug. 10, 1848. The building was occupied as a seminary, in which Rev. Sidney Harkey taught. The lodge rented the upper part until 1870, when by a special act of the Legislature it was empowered to purchase the building.

The first officers were:

N. G., J. G. Picking; V. G., J. Burke; Treas., Mr. Wilty; Sec., Joseph Abrams.

The officers for the term ending December, 1881, were:

N. G., Wm. Stix; V. G., Joshua Herring; Sec., John Landers; Treas., Van B. Osler.

Number of members, 70; accumulated funds, $250; and value of property, $2000.

Knights of Pythias Lodge, No. 67, was instituted June 2, 1871. Charter members, A. A. Moore, E. L. Suader, Dr. Wm. White, F. M. Uhler, Thomas Shaw, Emory Hubbard, S. R. Moore, M. A. Willard, J. Youson, J. H. Rouzer, Frederick White, J. W. Davidson, E. Baxter, J. L. King, J. S. Martin, Henry Willard, J. Eyler, J. W. Loy.

Its first officers were:

C. C., A. A. Moore; V.C., Dr. Wm. White; Prel., F. M. Uhler; M. A., J. H. Rouzer; K. R. S., E. L. Suader; M. F., S. A. Moore; M. Exch., J. W. Davidson; I. G., Thomas Shaw; O. G., M. A. Willard.

Officers for term ending June, 1881:

C. C., Wm. H. Stull; V. C., T. N. Eyler; Prel., E. M. Smith; M. A., G. W. Stimmel; K. R. S., C. Harman; M. F., John H. Rouzer; M. Exch., E. N. Cover; I. G., Wm. Miller; O. G., Horatio Fogle; P. C., Wm. H. Dammuth; Representative to Grand Lodge, John H. Rouzer.

The lodge meets in I. O. O. F. Hall every Friday evening. Number of members, 28; accumulated funds, $731.94.

Physicians.—The first resident physicians were Drs. Alexander Goldsborough and John Restler. The latter was a surgeon in Bonaparte's army, and after the battle of Waterloo came to America. Then followed Dr. E. Lincoln Brown. From 1845 to 1849, Drs. E. T. Curry and J. M. Geyer were in partnership. Dr. Joseph Biggs, who practiced here several years, removed in 1854. Dr. J. M. Geyer practiced from 1856 to 1861. Dr. George M. Zimmerman was here from 1862 to 1878, and Dr. Horatio N. Shultz from 1869 to 1874. Dr. M. E. Leatherman came in 1878. Dr. William White, who came in 1849, was born in Carroll County, and has been in continuous practice at Mechanicstown for thirty-two years.

Seminary.—The Mechanicstown Male and Female Seminary was established in 1874, under the care of the Middle Conference of the Lutheran Synod of Maryland. In the first year it had thirty-three students. Its principal for nearly all the time of its existence (over two years) was Rev. Victor Miller. The trustees were Dr. William White, president; John Rouzer, J. J. Henshaw, M.D., W. J. Black, George W. Stocksdale, Van B. Osler.

"Catoctin Clarion."—On the 4th of March, 1871, the *Catoctin Clarion*, published by William Need, made its appearance in Mechanicstown. It was a local paper, took but little part in politics, though the editor favored and voted for Horace Greeley for President in 1872. It was published for four years by the original proprietor, but on account of ill health he disposed of the office to Alexander P. Beatty.

Mr. Beatty bought the office July 23, 1875, and sold it Aug. 1, 1879, to E. L. Root and Charles E. Cassell, the latter being the editor. It is a sprightly sheet of neat appearance, and is conducted with ability. It is independent in sentiment.

Railroad, Express, Etc.—The Western Maryland Railroad was completed to this place in 1872, and the connection by rail of this hitherto inland town with the outside world gave a fresh impetus to the business of the town. Express connections were soon established and telegraph wires erected. From this time on the town, which in 1824 had but one store (kept by Charles Hoffman), grew very rapidly. Its fine scenery, delightful climate, and well-known salubrity make it an attractive summer resort, patronized by many from the cities. The site has been selected for the fine public-school building to be erected this year, and a new canning manufactory has been completed.

The teachers in the district for the term ending April 15, 1881, were:

School No. 1, 35 pupils, D. C. Weller; No. 2, 45 pupils, Mattie E. Youson; No. 3, 33 pupils, Jennie Selsam; No. 4, 46 pupils, John Landers; 64 pupils, E. L. Boblitz; 59 pupils, Frederick White; No. 5, 38 pupils, J. W. Davidson; No. 6, 40 pupils, J. W. Grinder; No. 7, 87 pupils, J. W. C. Zimmerman.

Justices of the Peace, Frederick White, Mechanicstown; Dr. W. S. McPherson, Catoctin; Calvin L. Firor, Greytown.

Graceham.—This ancient village is situated in the extreme eastern part of the district and near the Creagerstown boundary line. It is the seat of the first Moravian church in Maryland. The log dwelling for the first minister was completed in 1749, but preaching began in 1745, at the houses of the pioneers. On the 12th of September, 1768, twelve men felled and squared fifty-six logs for the first log church which was situated on Carroll's Manor. The day previous, Mr. Carroll, the proprietor of the Manor, through his agent, Joseph Johnson, gave a written instrument to Rev. R. Powell, granting ten acres of land on which to build this church, and also gave two pounds towards putting up the house. The house was raised October 11th and 12th. Mr. Powell moved into the house (which was a church and dwelling combined) on Dec. 1, 1768, and that day preached from this text, "He will betroth us unto Him forever." The building was not finished and consecrated until Oct. 16, 1773. Though preaching began in 1745, the first regular congregation was not formed until Oct. 6, 1758.

The Moravian ministers of this church have been as follows:

1745, Lórenz Tharntansen Nyberg, John H. Herzer; 1746, George Nieke; 1748, George Neiser; 1749, Swen Roseen; 1751, Mathaeus Renz; 1752, Richard Utley; 1755, Christian Richter; 1757, Valentine Haidt; 1758, —— Rundt; Oct. 6, 1758, Johann Michael Zahn (first regular pastor), died; 1762, Franz Böhler; 1764, Otto Krogstrup; 1767, Nicholaus H. Eberhard (died); 1778, R. Powell, —— Heffner; 1770, Richard Utley (died); 1771, Joseph Neiser; 1775, Johannes Schweishaupt; 1784, Daniel Sydrich (died); 1790, Gottlieb Senseman, Johann Friedrich Peter; 1791, Johann Martin Beck; 1796, Christian Friedrich Schaaf; 1798, Johann Friedrich Schlegel (died); 1805, Carl Gottlieb Blech; 1819, Johann Peter Kluge; 1827, Samuel Reineke; 1835, Samuel R. Huebner; 1839, Ambrose Randthaler; 1845, Edward Randthaler; 1849, Robert de Schweinitz, A. A. Reineke; 1854, Benjamin Ricksecker; 1859, Henry Bachman; 1861, Eugene P. Greider; 1867, Henry T. Bachman; 1870, Jesse Blickensderfer; 1873, L. P. Clewell; 1880, E. W. Shields.

We find the following first two baptisms on the church records (kept in German):

1. June 13, 1759, by Rev. John Michael Zahm, Ann Regina, daughter of George and Catharine Harbaugh. Witnesses, Regina Zahm, Casper Schmidt, Mr. Williar, Mr. Weller, Lorenz Krieger.

2. June 28, 1759, by same minister, Juliana, daughter of Casper and Christian Schmidt. Witnesses, Regina Zahm, Elizabeth Williar, Lorenz Krieger.

A few years later the following occur:

1. May 1, 1763, by Rev. Franz Böhler, Samuel, son of Robert and Sarah Toons (born March 29). Witnesses, Samuel Herr, Lorenz Krieger, Casper Schmidt, Catherina Böhler.

2. April 8, 1764, by Rev. John Daniel Sydrich, Mary Marga-

retha, daughter of George and Catherina Kast (born Sept. 29, 1763). Witnesses, Fanny Kast and Margaretha Sydrich.

3. Sept. 9, 1764, Joseph, son of Joseph and Mary Johnson (born July 2, 1764). Witnesses, Peter Stilley, Sarah Duckett, and Mary Sydrich.

4. April 5, 1767, by Rev. Joseph Powell, Martha, daughter of John and Ann Eson (born Feb. 15, 1767). Witnesses, Martha Powell, Mary Stilley, Joseph Johnson, and John Padgett.

The old log church gave way to the second building, which stood until 1822, on October 27th of which year the present church edifice was consecrated. It is a brick structure fifty by forty-two feet. The parsonage in front was erected of brick in 1798, and is the second one. In it and its predecessor were held the parochial schools of the church. The old graveyard is near by and is in a well-kept condition. The men are all buried on the right hand side (from the entrance) and the women on the left. Immediately in their rear are the children's graves, and still farther in the rear those of strangers or new members of the church. Up to a recent period the tombstones were all numbered.

The oldest one whose inscription is legible is No. 3, that of John Heinrich Krieger, born 17th May, 1749, died 25th May, 1764, aged fifteen years and eight days. No. 28 is that of Ludwig Protsman, born 1718, died 1778. No. 51 is that of Lorenz Krieger, born March 15, 1715, died Aug. 28, 1784. No. 395 is that of Philip William Boller, born March 6, 1766, died Dec. 9, 1848

There are three graves of three generations of the Siess family, father, son, and grandson, viz.: John George Siess, born March 23, 1754, in Heidelberg, Pa., died Oct. 14, 1823; his son, Godfrey Siess, born Feb. 9, 1765, in Heidelberg, Pa., died Aug. 4, 1841; his grandson, John Siess, born Oct. 26, 1794, died May 3, 1862. The latter was the father of the Rev. Dr. Siess, the eminent Lutheran divine and theological writer and author. The tombstone of Nicholaus Henry Eberhard, one of the pioneer Moravian ministers, shows the date of his birth to have been Jan. 2, 1723, and of his death April 8, 1770.

Graceham a century and a quarter ago was a noted religious seat, to which came hundreds of the pioneers for religious worship. At this time the men all carried rifles to defend themselves against the Indians or wild beasts.

Where O. L. Siess now lives, Godfrey Siess just after the Revolution had a snuff manufactory, the only one in the county outside of Frederick Town.

The Moravian buildings are on a rising ground at the eastern end of the village. To the right is seen a spring-house, where there are several never-failing springs of water. In the background appears a part of the mountain.

JACKSON DISTRICT, No. 16.

Jackson, or District No. 16, was laid off out of those parts of Catoctin (No. 6) and Middletown (No. 3) contiguous to each other by an act of the General Assembly passed May 25, 1852. The commissioners designated in the act to establish it were Capt. David Kailor, Daniel Main, and David Young, of D. Its boundaries were fixed as follows: "Beginning at the Frederick District line above George Blessing's, and running thence in a straight line as near as practicable to intersect the Catoctin Creek, where the road leading from Smithsburg to Frederick City crosses said creek, excluding the aforesaid George Blessing's dwelling; thence to the bridge lately built across the branch coming from Palmer's mill, on the road leading from the old Hagerstown road to Wolfville; thence to intersect the Washington County line above Jacob Renner, including said Renner; thence with said Washington County line until it intersects the turnpike leading from Frederick to Hagerstown; thence to Shoemaker's school-house; thence to Koogle's school-house; thence to intersect the road leading from Beallsville to Middletown at Kinney's mill; thence to intersect the Frederick District line above George W. Summers'; thence with the said Frederick District line to the point first mentioned above." Jackson District is situated in the western portion of the county, on the slope of South Mountain, and is south of Catoctin and north of Middletown Districts. On the east is Frederick District, and across the mountains on the west lies Washington County. The villages are Myersville, Jerusalem, and Beallsville. The first settlement was made before 1745, by the Flooks, Bowluses, Myers, Hoffmans, Buhrmans, Grossnickles, Remsburgs, Harmons, Smiths, Bisers, Toms, Koogles, Dutrows, Bussards, Delaughters, Derrs, Sumans, Gavers, Poffenbergers, etc. Nearly all these settlers were German immigrants, many of whom belonged to the German sectaries, including the Dunkers, the Mennonites, and others. There were also a number of Lutherans and German Calvinists. The immigrants were tenacious in the preservation of their language, religion, habits, and customs. They were also sturdy Republicans, and lived heartily upon their rich and carefully-cultivated lands. Their impress is still visible and their influence felt all over this district. The first man to preach the gospel in this district was Rev. Bernard Michael Houseal, the first Lutheran pastor at Frederick, or in the county. He crossed the Catoctin range on horseback as early as 1753, and preached the word of God to a few of the early settlers assembled in private dwellings of the pioneers.

Myersville.—This place is thirteen miles from Frederick and near Catoctin Creek. It took its name from the Myers family, one of the oldest in this section. Rev. C. H. Mott is pastor of the United

Brethren Church, and Rev. H. G. Bowers of the Lutheran. C. A. Buhrman is postmaster. The physician is Dr. L. M. Zimmerman, and the merchants Joseph Brown and Upton Buhrman. James W. Morgan is justice of the peace, George W. Main constable, and John Koogle surveyor. William Schildnecht has a tannery, A. R. Mowen a tin-shop, William Ludy a saw-mill, and B. F. Fout and Josiah Harp are the millers. Mrs. Caroline Biser keeps a boarding-house, and C. A. Buhrman a stationery-store. The village is filled with enterprising mechanics, and it is the chief seat of trade for a populous country for miles around.

When it was found that the Tories were gathering in large numbers at Castle's old building, near where Harmony Grove (Beallsville) is now located, in this district, the greatest consternation prevailed in Frederick Town. The bells were rung and the people convoked. A file of soldiers was immediately formed and dispatched to the hiding-place of the recusants. They were seized at once and brought to Frederick. A fair trial was instituted, and the Tories and spies underwent a searching examination. It was satisfactorily proven to the minds of the Committee of Safety that these men near Castle's were in communication with Knyphausen's men in the Jerseys and the Tories in Canada, that they gave information as to the situation of affairs in Frederick, and advised the British to seize upon the barracks, the magazine, and if necessary burn the town. Of the seven Tories tried three were hanged, and the Tory movement in the Middletown Valley was effectually suppressed.

The teachers in the district for the term ending April 15, 1881, were:

School No. 1, 38 pupils, C. H. Anversaght; No. 2, 50 pupils, C. C. Grossnickle; No. 3, 32 pupils, M. L. Rice; No. 4, 64 pupils, J. L. Lutz, H. E. Staley, assistant; No. 5, 81 pupils, D. U. Schildknecht, J. W. Wilson, assistant; No. 6, 41 pupils, T. L. Hauver; No. 7, 42 pupils, J. W. Gaver.

Harmony.—This pretty village is nine miles from Frederick, and is pleasantly situated in a healthy neighborhood, near Middle Creek. It contains a flourishing Dunker Church, one of the oldest in the county, and a Lutheran Church, the latter being part of the Middletown congregation. William B. Taylor is the postmaster, and with his son operates the woolen manufactory. The merchants are Joseph H. Bussard and George F. Williams. The other industries are E. Baker, Joseph Bebington, millwrights; Caton Blesson, M. Brandenburg, carpenters; G. Brady, G. W. Summers, millers; J. N. Brandenburg, blacksmith; J. E. Castle, George Harshman, shoemakers; D. Gladhill, wheelwright; George S. Harp, constable; P. R. Langdon, weaver; L. Rothanheafer, gunsmith; George Wachter, saddlery.

JOHNSVILLE DISTRICT, No. 17.

By an act of General Assembly of March 9, 1854, Johnsville, or Election District No. 17, was laid off and established out of parts of Liberty (No. 8) and Woodsborough (No. 11). It was laid out by Special Commissioners Nicholas Norris, Jacob Root, and Daniel S. Herring, as appointed in above act. Its boundaries were designated as follows: Commencing at or near the stone bridge across Pipe Creek near Diffendall's mill; thence by the most suitable line to the Hill school-house; thence to some point at or near the Copper-mine school-house; thence with the Copper-mine road to some point at or near Nicholas Norris' farm; from thence to Sam's Creek, the dividing line between Frederick and Carroll Counties; and thence with said dividing line to the place of beginning." The district, which is situated in the eastern portion of the county, is bounded by Carroll County on the north and east, Linganore District on the south, and Woodsborough District on the west. Among the early settlers were the Birely family, of German descent, numerous branches of which are found throughout the neighborhood and county. The Ilers were noted for their numbers and fine physical development. Peter Iler, who died in 1872, aged seventy years, left nine sons and twelve girls, all strong and hearty men and women. Of these sons not one weighed less than one hundred and eighty pounds. Mr. Iler never had a physician in his house for any of his twenty-one children. Among other pioneer families were the Fogles, Morts, Clemsons, Bastians, Stiteleys, Phillipses, Koonses, Shoemakers, Hammers, Snookses, Albaughs, McGuinises, Warners, Haughs, Carmacks, Johnsons, Norrises, Buckeys, Stoners, Bowmans, Foxes, Keefers, Martzes, Dutterds, Stulls, Renners, Crams, Flickingers, Bakers, and Grossnickles. The settlement in the district was first made about 1746.

Johnsville lies five miles from Union Bridge (Carroll Co.), and is pleasantly situated near Beaver Dam Creek. It took its name from the fact that when the village was first settled most of the Christian names of the first settlers were John. It has a large church of the Dunker congregation, a class of religionists very numerous in this district. Its physicians are Drs. Reuben Sidewell and his son, Frank H., and H. C. Devilbiss. The elder Dr. Sidewell was born in Chester County, Pa., and has had a large and lucrative practice here since 1846.

Western Maryland Lodge, I. O. O. F., was instituted in 1879, and has its hall over Dr. Sidewell's office. The merchants of the village are C. E. Saylor, Frank Smith, and J. Shrieve & Co. Over Mr. Saylor's large store is a fine town hall. In 1846, when the village was fairly established, there was but one mail a week. Now the village has two each day.

The Methodist Protestant Church was organized about 1840, and became a part of Pike Creek Circuit, which was created in 1829. We give a list of the pastors on the circuit from 1829 to 1881:

1829, D. E. Reese, Sr.; 1830, F. Stier, J. Hanson; 1831, I. Ibbertson; 1832, I. Webster, C. W. Jacobs; 1833, W. Sexsmith; 1834, J. Varden, H. Doyle; 1835, H. Doyle, J. W. Everist, A. A. Lipscomb; 1836, J. S. Reese, W. J. Porter; 1838, E. Henkle; 1839–40, G. D. Hamilton; 1840, B. Appleby; 1841, J. S. Reese, J. T. Ward; 1842, J. R. Reese, J. Elderdice, P. L. Wilson; 1843, J. S. Reese, S. L. Rawleigh; 1844, W. Collier, J. L. McLean, J. D. Brooks; 1845, P. L. Wilson, J. K. Nichols; 1847, J. Morgan, T. D. Valliant; 1848, W. Roby; 1849, D. E. Reese; 1850, T. L. McLean; 1851, H. P. Jordan, J. Roberts; 1852, H. J. Day; 1853, T. M. Wilson; 1854, J. A. McFadden; 1855, F. Schwentzell; 1856, N. S. Greenaway; 1857, J. T. Ward, J. T. Murray. In 1860 Liberty Circuit was created, consisting of Liberty, Johnsville, Woodsborough, and Walkersville. 1860, H. C. Cushing; 1862, J. T. Ward; 1864, D. A. Shermer; 1866, D. W. Bates; 1869, F. Swentzell; 1873, E. R. McGregor; 1874, J. Roberts; 1876, J. R. Nicholls; 1877, J. R. Nicholls; 1880, J. M. Brown.

Ladiesburg was so called because some sixty years ago its population comprised seven ladies and only one gentleman. The happy individual was Samuel Birely, who died in 1877, aged eighty-three years. The post-office was established in 1830.

It contains two dry-goods stores, one millinery-shop, one hay and straw-packing establishment, a shoe and blacksmith-shop, Adams Express office, and a water station on the Frederick Division of the Pennsylvania Railroad. It lies fourteen miles north of Frederick, within two miles of the Monocacy River, and near the Carroll County line. The surrounding country is agricultural in character. There are two churches, the Reformed and the Lutheran. The Winebrennarians have a congregation about a mile distant. A few Catholics are scattered throughout the neighborhood. The Dunkers, or German Baptists, are in large numbers a few miles south and east of the place. The location of the village is elevated and surrounded by hills, which are called the "Fox Mountains," or "Fox Hills." These hills are dotted with springs of the purest water, which seem to be inexhaustible. This portion of the county is believed to have been a favorite spot with the Indians. The descendants of persons who lived there a century ago speak of reminiscences related by their ancestors, in which reference was made to large numbers of Indian graves formerly seen on the surrounding hills. Arrow-heads of stone are common objects upon the surface of the ground. Along Big Pipe Creek, four miles distant, small elevations on the hillsides may still be seen which are supposed to be graves of the savages. Within three hundred yards of the village is an elevation on a level plain of about twenty acres, which is encircled by slight hills. It is about seven feet high, and ninety yards in diameter in the widest portion. The plain and surrounding hills resemble an immense amphitheatre. Near Claysville lava has been found in large quantities, which was evidently thrown out by a volcanic eruption many centuries ago.

On Nov. 16, 1826, John Evey had a saw-mill and marble quarry at Beaver Creek, then rented by Joseph Emmett, Jr. In June, 1777, Jacob Myers completed a wire-mill near Little Pipe Creek.

Dr. J. J. Leggett is the resident physician.

School-teachers in the district for term ending April 15, 1881:

School No. 1, 34 pupils, Luta O. Marks; No. 2, 84 pupils, D. E. Hammond, Jennie Booker (assistant); No. 3, 32 pupils, W. Emma Norris; No. 4, 22 pupils, N. M. Rice; No. 5, 28 pupils, Annie E. Kinzer; No. 6, 57 pupils, Martha J. Ecker; No. 7, 39 pupils, Alma O. Thomas.

WOODVILLE DISTRICT, No. 18.

Woodville, or Election District No. 18, was established according to an act of the Legislature adopted April 1, 1872, out of portions of New Market (No. 9) and Liberty (No. 8). Its boundaries were designated, to wit: " Commencing at the junction of the Buffalo road and Talbot's Branch; thence running with said branch to the crossing of the Unionville and Linganore public road; thence with said road to the old Annapolis road; thence with said Annapolis road to the intersection of the New Market road; thence with said road to Forest Grove school-house; thence with a straight line to the reservoir on the Baltimore and Ohio Railroad known as No. 13; thence to the tobacco-house on the Kemptown road formerly owned by Brook Buckstone; thence with the Kemptown road to Penn's shop on the Buffalo road; thence with the Buffalo road to the place of beginning." The territory comprising this district as it now stands was settled in part as early as 1740. It is situated in the southeast portion of the county, and is bounded by Carroll and Montgomery Counties and New Market and Liberty Districts. Among the first settlers may be mentioned the Clarys, Owens, Griffiths, Shipleys, Pooles, Vansants, Kimmels, and Lawrences. One of the first surveys was "Moab," granted to one of the Clarys about 1743. Judge Samuel Chase owned a large tract of land, on which he built a two-story log house to which he came during the summer. His place was called "Pleasant Hall." This house stood until a few years ago, and was where Richard Vansant now lives, west of Mount Airy. There are yet standing two rows of cherry-trees planted by Judge Chase, which are now very large.

Plane No. 4 is on the Baltimore and Ohio Railroad, forty-six miles from Baltimore, seventeen from Frederick, and near the source of Bush Creek. This is the last plane on the railroad from the east, and in the early days of the road the cars were pulled by horses to the summit and then "braked" down the grade. The railroad company has a large engine-house and two engines to help east-bound freight-trains over the planes, and have a coal-shute for coaling all engines on main stem First Division. The engine-house is two and a quarter miles east of this place. Two hundred tons of coal are daily loaded from the shutes into passing engines. B. G. Shipley is assistant superintendent of trains, and William R. Dorsey has charge of the coal-shute, which is worked with only six men. A. M. D. Mullinix is postmaster. P. G. M. Griffith keeps a general store, and Frank Bartholow operates a tannery.

Ridgeville is mostly in Carroll County, being divided from the Woodville District by the Buffalo road.

Woodville is three miles from Mount Airy, sixteen from Frederick, and thirty-three from Baltimore. F. S. Clary is merchant and postmaster; Dr. Richard S. Appington, physician; J. W. Condon, undertaker; J. Franklin, blacksmith; J. W. Harrison, J. H. Runkles, carpenters; E. Wilson, miller.

Linganore village is seven miles from Mount Airy. The postmaster is Thornton Poole, who married a daughter of the well-known Dr. Beall Owens, and who is the merchant of the place. Moses Douty and Samuel Reifsnyder are millers.

Sidney Grove Methodist Episcopal Church South, at Linganore, was organized in 1768. Its pastors have been:

1868, Rev. W. A. McDonald; 1870, J. T. Maxwell; 1871, A. Q. Flaherty; 1873, David Bush; 1876, W. R. Stringer; 1879, M. G. Balthis.

West Falls is three miles from Mount Airy, twenty from Frederick, and forty from Baltimore. The Methodist Episcopal Church belongs to the Unionville circuit. J. C. Douty is postmaster, and J. F. Hood assistant. The avocations embrace Dr. W. H. Gray, physician; J. F. Hood, merchant; J. A. Clary, miller; J. Rinehart, F. W. Gartrall, J. H. Devaull, carpenters; H. Demmitt, wheelwright; C. Bear, D. Bear, J. Butler, L. J. T. Dorsey, blacksmiths.

The teachers of the district for the term ending April 15, 1881, were:

School No. 1, 32 pupils, C. Eugenia Hanna; No. 2, 31 pupils, Martha E. Breneman; No. 3, 30 pupils, J. M. Hanna; 42 pupils, Sue M. Garrett; No. 4, 53 pupils, Bessie Mussetter. No. 1 (colored), 38 pupils, E. B. Oram.

Magistrates, Richard Vansant, Thornton Poole.

Parr's Springs.—At this noted resort the four counties of Frederick, Montgomery, Howard, and Carroll converge.

Mount Airy.—This place is in Carroll County, but is a large shipping station for Woodville District. The railroad grade from Plane No. 4 to this point is eighty-three feet to the mile.

LINGANORE DISTRICT, No. 19.

Linganore, or Election District No. 19, was laid out and established out of part of Liberty District (No. 8) by an act of General Assembly of March 29, 1878. Its boundaries were designated as follows: "Beginning at a white-oak tree at the intersection of the Copper-mine road with the Johnsville District line, running thence south to the spring-house of Henry Carter, thence with Spring Branch to New Liberty road, thence south to the bend in the public road west of the dwelling-house of William H. Baker, thence with said public road until it intersects the Woodville District line, thence with said line to the Carroll County line, thence with said Carroll County line until it intersects Johnsville District line, thence with said line to the place of beginning." This district was settled previous to 1752, and among the early families were those of Dudderars, Gaithers, Nails, Nicodemuses, Lugenbeels, Pearres, Ensors, Nussbaums, Devilbisses, Hammonds, Sappingtons, Bakers, Eckers. William Gaither came from Montgomery County and settled here at a very early period. His son William by his wife, a Mrs. Davis (née Howard), married a Miss Dorsey, and their son, John Gaither, is still living, one of the substantial men of the district.

Unionville.—This pretty village lies on the Liberty road, two miles east of Liberty and five from New Windsor, Carroll Co. The merchants are H. Lindsey and Norris & Urner. S. J. Norris is the postmaster. The physicians are Drs. G. R. Sappington and M. Whitehill. H. Brenneisen is the justice of the peace. The various industries are represented by P. Beach, J. C. Gilbert, shoemakers; Charles Brenneisen, painter; Brenneisen & Bro., photographers; J. E. Brenneisen, wagon-maker; B. Buckingham, J. Douty, blacksmiths; E. D. Danner, huckster; J. W. Enry, J. Whitehill, B. F. Nicodemus, millers; G. P. Gosnell, harness-maker; D. Hartsock, undertaker; J. A. Stitely, carpenter. The Methodist Episcopal Church is the largest and oldest in Unionville or vicinity, having been in existence for sixty years.

The Methodist Episcopal Church South, belonging to the Baltimore Annual Conference, was organized in 1868. The church edifice was dedicated in 1869, and is called "Pearre Chapel," after Rev. James Pearre, a wealthy and benevolent citizen, who built it at his own expense. Its pastors have been:

1868, W. A. McDonald; 1870, J. T. Maxwell; 1871, A. Q. Flaherty; 1873, David Bush; 1876, W. R. Stringer; 1879, M. G. Balthus. *Stewards.*—1870, J. R. Mills, D. W. Dudderar, H. C. Gaither; 1873, D. W. Dudderar, H. C. Gaither, C. B. Simpson, and present incumbents. C. B. Simpson was class-leader to 1875, and since then Rev. James Pearre.

This church is on a circuit composed of New Market, Sidney Grove, Denny's Post-office, Franklinville, and Unionville. This circuit has one parsonage and five church edifices, all built since 1868 and paid for. Circuit membership, 350.

May 15, 1868, a dispensation was granted to James D. McCabe, Edward D. Damer, John P. Naill, Wm. M. Naill, Lewis Kelly, David Nussbaum, David Glass, and John M. Glass to form a Masonic lodge. James D. McCabe was appointed W. M.; Edward D. Damer, S. W.; and John P. Naill, J. W. Nov. 16, 1868, the Grand Lodge issued a regular charter to Linganore Lodge, No. 137, at Unionville, retaining the same officers as under the dispensation. The officers for 1881 were:

W. M., Rufus W. Devilbiss; S. W., Peter Lugenbeel; J. W., George D. Norris; Sec., Daniel Hartsock; Treas., Peter Sluckbier.

Edward D. Damer, Past Master, was Worshipful Master for eleven years of this lodge.

Its membership is about 30.

David and Jonathan Lodge, No. 103, I. O. O. F., is one of the most flourishing in the county.

The school-teachers for the term ending April 15, 1881, were:

School No. 1, 54 pupils, Laura Garrott, E. Atkinson (assistant); No. 2, 67 pupils, H. L. Biell; No. 3, 30 pupils, Lillie Hill. *Colored schools.*—No. 2, 34 pupils, Fannie Sims; No. 3, 17 pupils, Louisa Locks.

Oak Orchard is five miles from New Windsor, Carroll Co. The ore-mines on the farm of Elijah C. Ensor have been reopened, and are superintended by John Smeltzer, of Wrightsville, Pa.

John T. Barnes is postmaster.

The industries are Noah I. Franklin, merchant; John E. Waltz, carriage-maker; John Summerville, undertaker; Jacob H. Naill, E. C. Ensor, millers; A. Alexander, blacksmith; M. L. Devilbiss, A. Miller, carpenters; W. H. Fisher, W. H. Garber, shoemakers; J. P. Naill, huckster.

David W. Naill, of this district, while a member of the State Senate, was the author of the inscription that the State put on the block it contributed to Washington's Monument, in Washington City, to wit: "Maryland,—the memorial of her regard for the Father of his Country, and of her cordial, habitual, and immovable attachment for the American Union." Mr. Naill's house, a stone structure, was built in 1771 by Solomon and Susan Miller, on a tract of land taken up in 1727 by James Carroll, and called "Park Hall." Mr. Naill was largely engaged in the milling business near Bethel church.

LEWISTOWN DISTRICT, No. 20.

By the act of April 5, 1878, of General Assembly, Lewistown, or Election District No. 20, was laid out and established out of portions of Frederick and Creagerstown Districts. Its designated boundaries are as follows: "Beginning at the southwest corner of Mechanicstown District line and running with said Election District line, bearing slightly northeast, to the crossing of the road leading from Eicholtz' mills to Lewistown, at a point near the dwelling-house of A. G. P. Wiles; thence in a southeasterly direction to the Woodsborough Election District line on the Monocacy River, touching the north corner of George L. Devilbiss' dwelling-house, and with the Woodsborough Election District line on a southerly course to Biggs' ford on the Monocacy River; thence bearing a northwesterly course to the north corner of Bethel Church; thence bearing still a northwesterly course to intersect the Catoctin Election District line at a point where the said line strikes the Hamburg road; and thence with Catoctin District line in a northerly direction to the place of beginning." It is bounded by Creagerstown on the north, Woodsborough on the east, Frederick on the south, and Catoctin on the west. This portion of the county was settled about 1745, and the early families were those of John Devilbiss, the Hills (soldiers in the Hessian regiments), Cronises, Schaeffers, Leathermans, Cramers, Ramsburgs, Poes, Wetzels, Eichelbergers, and Snooks. Simon Snook entered two large tracts of land on the Monocacy, and married Charlotte Keller. Their son Jacob, who died in 1811, was the father of the venerable Daniel Snook, now in his eighty-second year.

The Snooks' surveys were called "No help for my loss" and "Silver Mot."

In this district was the famous "Devilbiss Campmeeting Ground," near the foot of the mountain.

Once when Elder Gruber was holding there a big camp-meeting a mob of mountaineers came down and raised a disturbance by taking down the ropes of the tents and otherwise creating trouble. The Methodists, to avoid a repetition on the following day, tarred the ropes, by which means the offenders were recognized, as they got tar on their clothes in their second attempt to pull down the tents. The rioters then gathered together and marched around the grounds singing, "Old Daddy Gruber tarred the ropes, oh, glory Hallelujah," etc., and nearly broke up the meeting.

Lewistown.—Daniel Fundenberg laid out the village in 1815. The grist-mill now operated by John C. Derr was built about 1824 by John Brien, who subsequently sold it to Frederick A. Schley, who conveyed it to the present proprietor. Fishing Creek runs through the village, and on it is the woolen-factory of William B. Taylor & Son. It was built over fifty years ago by John Cronise, who in 1837 sold it with the land, nineteen and three-fourths acres, parts of surveys "Trifle" and "Ogle's Necessary Compact," to John W. Derr. While the latter owned it, and when operated by his tenant or lessee, Mr. Routzahn, it burned down. Mr. Derr rebuilt it, and afterwards sold the property to David Study, who later conveyed the same to Sarah A. Taylor, of whom the present proprietors purchased it in 1880. It manufactures carpets, coverlids, blankets, and woolen fabrics generally. The village is on the Emmittsburg road, ten miles from Frederick and five from Harmony Grove. It contains Lewistown Grange, No. 134, P. of H., of which George W. Miller is Master, and J. D. English, secretary. At an early date a distillery was located here and operated by a Mr. Eichelberger. O. T. Zimmerman has had a store here for twenty years, and the other merchant is A. N. Cramer, the postmaster, who came about three years ago. C. D. Keyser has a cabinet-shop, George H. Clem a hotel, and Dr. J. K. Waters is the physician.

The Methodist Protestant Church edifice was built in 1857, previous to which the congregation worshiped in a log house erected years ago, but now used by the Colored Methodist Episcopal Church for their services. The Methodist Protestant Church was organized in 1847 under the pastorate of Rev. P. L. Wilson, but previously Rev. Dr. John S. Reese had preached. The subsequent pastors were Revs. Mills, J. E. Maloy, Arnett, H. C. Littleton, D. Shirmer, Evans, Reese, and J. K. Nichols. Its Sunday-school superintendent is J. W. Clem. W. H. Todd has been trustee since its organization.

The Methodist Episcopal church, of which Rev. W. O. Eldridge is present pastor, was erected in 1833. It belongs to a circuit consisting of Emmittsburg, Mechanicstown, Maple Chapel, Tom's Creek, Middleburg, and Keys' School-house. Some of its pastors have been Revs. Isaac Collins, Holland, George Brooks, Joseph Prance, Joseph Cooper, Keith, D. Moore, W. H. Koontz, Heming, Maxwell, and West. It has a fine bell and organ. It is located near the village on a high hill, and commands one of the finest views in the county. The substantial brick school-house was built in 1868.

Utica.—This place is on the Emmittsburg and Frederick road, eight miles north of Frederick and three and a half from Walkersville, on the Frederick and Pennsylvania Line Railroad. The first settler near it was Valentine Bowersocks, who located in the neighborhood about 1770, and built the first house near the village. Jacob Cronise was the founder of the village, and erected the mill and stone mansion-house. The first store was kept by a Mr. Cole in 1830, and the present store is owned by A. M. Geesy. In 1830, William Todd, of Lancaster County, Pa., removed here and purchased the mill erected three years before. Mr. Todd built up the town, and his son, William H. Todd, now owns and operates the merchant-mill, which sends its flour to New York, Baltimore, and Philadelphia. St. Paul's Reformed and Lutheran church (jointly) was built in 1839. Its pastors are Revs. Shedrin A. Hedges (Lutheran) and Henck (Reformed). Mr. Hedges also preaches at Creagerstown and Bethel. O. T. Zimmerman is superintendent of the Reformed, and Andrew Walker of the Lutheran, Sunday-school. Revs. Summers and Unruh were former Lutheran pastors here. In olden times the Reformers, Dunkers, Lutherans, and Methodists used to worship in an old log church, to which was added, about 1800, a stone structure under the preaching of Rev. Nicholas Sneeden, a noted circuit-rider of frontier days. Dr. J. K. Waters is the only physician.

Augustus Clem started in 1876, at Utica, a small paper called the *Sunbeam*, which was published monthly with a limited circulation, but was afterwards merged into *The Visitor*. It is yet published, and is devoted to religious and literary matters.

Other Villages.—Hensonville is a village on the Emmittsburg road, five and a half miles from Frederick and two and a half from Harmony Grove. Its postmaster is W. H. Ramsburg. Its industries are H. A. Buckey, tanner; Gipson Dunlap, tailor; J. E. Palmer, wagon-maker; and William Frey and Daniel Sunday, lime-burners. By a special act of the Maryland Legislature liquors are prohibited from being sold within three miles of this village.

Harmony Grove, a pretty hamlet, is situated on the Frederick and Pennsylvania Line Railroad, two and a half miles from Frederick. It has a Methodist Protestant church and a public school. N. R. Plummer is postmaster, and keeps a grain-store, etc. J. C. Cronise, Thomas Miller, Abraham Trimmer, and W. J. Warman are millers; J. Metcalfe, millwright; and H. C. Grabenhorst, dairyman.

The school teachers of the district for the term ending April 15, 1881, were:

School No. 1, 115 pupils, J. P. Delander, Maggie Agnew, assistant; No. 2, 54 pupils, H. L. Gaver; No. 3, 58 pupils, L. H. Warrenfelts. No. 1 (colored), 33 pupils, Hiram Clapper.

Magistrates, Henry Eaton, Samuel Heffner.

In 1812, sub-committees from the different election districts met "in general committee" at the Washington Hotel, in Fredericktown, for the purpose of recommending four candidates for the General Assembly. Among the members we find the names of Ignatius Davis, Samuel M. Thomas, and John M. Cromwell from District No. 1; Col. Stephen Steiner, Henry Steiner, Otho Lawrence, and John Brengle from District No. 2; William Hillary, John S. Frazier, and Levin Hayes from District No. 3; James Johnson and Maj. William Head from District No. 4; Joseph Hewes, Dr. Robert L. Annan, and William Emmitt from District No. 5; John Ross Key and Joseph Taney from District No. 6; Gen. Robert Cummings, Col. Henry Barrick, Joshua Delaplaine, and Sebastian Graff from District No. 7; and Col. Philip McElfresh, Capt. Eli Brashear, Maj. Daniel James, and Basil Dorsey from District No. 9. Col. Philip McElfresh was appointed chairman, and Matthew Brown secretary, and it was unanimously decided to recommend Maj. John Graham, Ignatius Davis, Joshua Delaplaine, and Richard Potts to the voters of Frederick County. Political contests three-quarters of a century ago were not by any means free from the acerbities which so often disfigure the campaigns of our own day. In the memorable contest between George Baer and Gen. Samuel Ringgold, candidates for Congress in 1796, one of the most effective "points" made against the general was an alleged expression of his reflecting on the German element of the population. In those days "politics" was an expensive luxury—as it still continues to be—for any one who would spend his money. Of Gen. Ringgold, for instance, it is related that just before election he would ride all over the county in his carriage and four, and wherever he found a family in distress or a farm to be sold by the sheriff he would give the needed relief in hard cash, declaring, generally, that none of his constituents should suffer as long as he could prevent it.

MONTGOMERY COUNTY.

CHAPTER XXXII.

INTRODUCTORY.

The First Settlers—Indian Tribes—Erection of the County—Gen. Montgomery—The Character and Soil of the County—Geological Formations—The Rivers and Creeks—Original Land Grants—Social Progress—Crops and Population—Legislation.

THE territory now embraced by Montgomery County was originally a portion of Prince George's, but was segregated in 1748, when it became a portion of the new county of Frederick, created in that year, and comprising all the land lying west of a line drawn from the mouth of Rock Creek, through a portion of the District of Columbia, to the Patuxent River, an immense but comparatively unknown section of the State, which was destined eventually to be divided into six counties, and to comprise much of the most valuable territory in Maryland, and to contain a population which, for industry, enterprise, and all the elements which constitute the worth and importance of a community, is unsurpassed in America. That portion which now forms the county of Montgomery was partially settled very early in the history of the province of Maryland. The pioneers who came over in the "Ark" and the "Dove" and their immediate successors were an active, pushing race of people, who fully appreciated the gravity of the situation in which they had placed themselves. They knew their lives were to be toilsome and beset with many dangers and adversities, but the love of adventure which had brought them to the New World doubtless sustained their spirits under innumerable trials, and goaded their restless nature to fresh explorations. Many of them soon tired of the monotony of the peninsula, and in canoes and by bridle-paths over land worked their way to the interior of the country. The broad waters of the Potomac and Patuxent were invitingly open to them, and the sound as well as just and upright policy pursued towards the Indians by the early colonists reduced to a minimum the dangers from this source.

We have seen in the introductory to the history of Frederick County how Henry Fleet in 1625, nine years prior to the settlement of St. Mary's, ascended the Potomac to the head of navigation and was made captive by the Indians. In his journal he gives a very graphic description of the country, and those familiar with it will recognize in Tohoga the site of Georgetown, and in the place "where the river is not above twelve fathoms broad" the narrows immediately below the Little Falls and in the neighborhood of the bridge.

At the time of the first settlement of the province the Indians who inhabited the territory along the line of the Potomac, in the neighborhood of Rockville and the District of Columbia, belonged to the Piscataway confederacy, whose emperor was chief of all the tribes on the Potomac. Piscataway was originally the seat of this great chief and his tribe, and was situated on a creek of that name, about sixteen miles below Washington City. The Piscataway confederacy numbered at least six tribes, among which were the Pamunkies, Piscataways, and Anacostans. Deeds can be found recorded among the land records of Prince George's County, at Upper Marlboro, made by the emperor of the Piscataways to the purchasers of his land. The power of this great chief is shown in the fact that upon his arrival with his colonists in the Potomac in 1634, Governor Leonard Calvert found it necessary to leave his companions and go in person from St. Clement's Island to Piscataway to meet the emperor and treat with him about settling in his dominions. This Calvert did, previously to his landing at St. Mary's, and received from the great chief the celebrated answer, "I will neither bid you go nor stay." As we have shown in the history of Frederick County, the Jesuit priests of St. Mary's in 1643 sent Father White, one of their number, as a missionary to this tribe, and such was his success that among others he baptized the emperor and his family. He did not, however, remain long, as he, together with all the other priests, were driven out of the province during the ascendency and misrule of Ingle in 1645, under color of authority from the English Parliament.

But as early as when Father White was among the Piscataway tribes land had been taken up by some of the colonists on the creek below, where the town of Piscataway now stands. The first evidence we have of any great body of settlers in this neighborhood is to be found in the old vestry-book of Piscataway Parish, under date of Jan. 30, 1694, which is as follows: "By a sufficient and lawful authority the inhabitants of Piscataway parish, having met at the house of John Addison, Esq., in said parish, elected the said John Addison foreman, William Hatton, John Smith, William Hutchinson, William Tannehill, and John Swallwell to be vestrymen in said parish; and they ordered that the forty pounds per poll be paid to John Addison, Esq., and William Hutchinson, and that they do employ carpenters for building a church." The parish was created under the act of 1692, being one of the original thirty parishes into which the province of Maryland was then divided. The church was built at the head of Back Creek, which makes out from the Potomac River at what is now Fort Washington. The first rector was the Rev. George Tubman, and upon the creation of Prince George's County, in 1695, Piscataway Parish became its western half. In 1701, Mr. Tubman was succeeded by Rev. Robert Owen, and in 1710 he was followed by Rev. John Frazier, who married in the county, and afterwards purchased and settled on an estate called "Blue Plains," on the Maryland side of the Potomac, opposite Alexandria, Va.

The settlements in this neighborhood increased rapidly, and, as will be seen in the sketch of the Episcopal Church in this county, soon grew strong enough to erect a church building about where the town of Rockville now stands. At a very early period, perhaps about 1695, this immediate vicinity received a large accession to its population from the Scotch refugees, who, despairing of the fortunes of the House of Stuart, took refuge in large numbers in the province. From this colony, and those who followed them in 1715–17 and 1745, sprang many of the leading families of Montgomery and Prince George's Counties, their names attesting their strength. Such was their number and influence that about 1695 one of the county districts, or hundreds, as they were then called, was named "New Scotland."

In after-years the Six Nations, by the accession of the Tuscaroras, who inhabited the head-waters of the Potomac about Harper's Ferry, claimed title to a portion of the county, and no doubt gave names to the Senaca, Monocacy, and the Tuscarora streams, but had no permanent residence within the county borders. Besides deer, buffaloes, bears, and turkeys, this country also abounded in wolves, for as late as 1797 an act of Assembly was passed (for Montgomery County) offering a reward of thirty dollars for the head of every wolf over six months old, and four dollars for every one under that age. The first settlers speedily made clearings in the forest and reduced the land to cultivation, the remunerative prices obtained for tobacco (which could be nowhere else so successfully grown as in these lands) stimulating their enterprise. In fact, the growth of tobacco was pursued in Montgomery, as in other sections of the State, to such an extent that the lands were finally impoverished, and it was only by a radical change in the system of farming and in the character of the crops that Montgomery County has been raised to the standard of productiveness which it now maintains as one of the leading counties of Maryland. Many of the old houses, built of brick and stone, attest the possession of considerable wealth and great social refinement among the planters. The brick used in the construction of houses, churches, and public buildings generally were often brought from England as ballast by vessels returning after having taken out cargoes of tobacco from the "plantations." The farm-house of that day was generally a square substantial building with large halls and roomy, high-ceiled apartments, in which the planter dispensed a generous and often courtly hospitality. The table always contained an abundance of food, and the style of living was liberal, not to say prodigal. Farther up the county, in the section bordering on Frederick, many German immigrants from Pennsylvania settled, and these, together with the English and other colonists, were forced by their remoteness from navigable water to restrict themselves to timber for building purposes. In most cases these wooden buildings were large log cabins, chinked with clay or mortar, and having a chimney built on the outside, generally of stones or pieces of timber plastered with clay. These structures, though not inviting, were warm and dry in winter and cool in summer. All the barns and tobacco-houses were constructed on a similar plan. The log houses were seldom more than one story high, but they generally had large garret-rooms and a deep cellar.

In the unsettled districts the log cabin became what was known as a "half-faced camp," generally used by a hunter. This was a log cabin inclosed on three sides, the front being protected by a sort of veranda. The great advantage of these houses was their cheapness and the fact that they could be erected without the aid of a carpenter. As soon as the logs were collected and dressed the neighbors assembled, and the house was "raised" by their joint efforts. A jollification always ensued, much after the style of the apple-butter and quilting parties of New England, or the husking matches at the South. The furniture in these dwellings was, of course, of the simplest description, but in the houses of the planters farther south and east it was more costly, much of it being mahogany. Throughout Western Maryland the bed-room furniture consisted generally of painted bedsteads, with straw beds and feather beds for covering, and a chair or two. The housekeeping was always clean and neat, and the German housewife especially was noted for her skill in preparing butter and cheese, and for her industry and deftness in weaving and knitting. Apple and cherry orchards were to be found on nearly every farm, and the cellar was generally well stocked with excellent home-brewed beer and cider. Slave-labor was largely employed in Montgomery County, and colored labor continues to be generally used, although the farmers themselves and their families are almost invariably hard-working, thrifty, and energetic. In the old times the servants' "quarter" was not infrequently the largest building on the estate. Occasionally, however, it was a succession of cabins, each of which contained several families, though sometimes, as a special favor, one family was permitted to occupy a building alone. Vast tracts of land were tilled by single proprietors, but there was also a thrifty middle class, which had practically no existence as a farming community in the more southern counties, and to this class Montgomery owes in a great measure her present prosperity, although it is only just to add that many of her most industrious and successful farmers and business men are descendants of large planters of the last century. Montgomery, in fact, was particularly fortunate in the composition of her early population, which was a harmonious blending of the English colonists of wealth and influence and of those energetic German and Scotch-Irish settlers from the North who carved their fortunes with their hands. They multiplied and prospered, and nothing occurred to mar the harmony of their lives or disturb the even tenor of their way until the breaking out of the French war and the defeat of Braddock in 1755.

The invasion of the western frontier of the province by the French and the Indians from Fort Du Quesne created great excitement and anxiety while it lasted, but a force from the lower district of Frederick County (now Montgomery) under Col. Ridgely and Capt. Alexander Beall marched to the rescue and allayed the fears of the settlers. The rapid settlement of Frederick County and its unwieldy proportions soon suggested the propriety of a division to accommodate the necessities of the citizens, and on the 31st of August, 1776, Dr. Thomas Sprigg Wootton, a member of the State Convention, introduced a bill for the division of Frederick County into three distinct municipalities. The bill was read and ordered to lie on the table. It was called up and passed by a small majority, Sept. 6, 1776, and thus two new counties, Washington and Montgomery, were created. The language of the act relating to the latter is as follows:

"*Resolved*, That after the first day of October next such part of the said county of Frederick as is contained within the bounds and limits following, to wit: beginning at the east side of the mouth of Rock Creek, on the Potomac River, and running thence with the said river to the mouth of Monocacy, then with a straight line to Parr's Spring, from thence with the lines of the county to the beginning, shall be and is hereby erected into a new county called Montgomery County."

The county was formed at the outset of that fierce struggle which resulted in the independence of the colonies and the formation of a free government, and it was especially appropriate that it should take the name of one of the noblest heroes and patriots who fell during the contest. Richard Montgomery, from whom it was named, was born near Raphoe, Ireland, Dec. 2, 1736. He was commissioned as an officer of the British army when but eighteen years of age. He was at the siege of Louisburg in 1758, and acquitted himself with distinction in the expeditions against Martinique and Havana. In 1759 he shared in the glorious victory of Gen. Wolfe at Quebec, in which that brave soldier lost his life, and fought over the very spot probably where he was destined to lose his life in defense of the liberties of his country. In 1763 he revisited Europe, and in 1772 he emigrated to New York, where he married a daughter of Judge Robert R. Livingston and settled in Rhinebeck. He represented Dutchess County in 1775 in the Provincial Congress, and in the same year was commissioned brigadier-general. He was assigned to the expedition sent to Canada in the summer of 1775, and by reason of the illness of Gen. Schuyler assumed command. He captured Chambly, St. John's, and Montreal, and by the middle of November was in possession of the greater part of Canada. He formed a junction with Arnold's troops, December 4th, and laid siege to Quebec. Becoming convinced that it was impossible to conduct the siege to a successful issue with the small number of men at his command, he concluded to attempt the capture of the city by a *coup de main*, and at two o'clock on the morning of December 31st, Montgomery headed the attack on the town. He reached the first barrier, which was quickly carried, and pressed on the second, where he and his two aides fell dead from the discharge of the only cannon fired from this battery. Had he lived his daring attack would probably have been successful, but his death was the signal for a panic among the raw and undisciplined troops. Because of the estimation in which he was held by the enemy, some courtesies were extended to his remains, but the other officers were huddled into shallow graves with no coffins, and their remains were reinterred with the opening of spring to obviate the unpleasant odor which arose from them.

Ramsey, in his "History of the American Revolution," says,—

"Few men have ever fallen in battle so much regretted by both sides as Gen. Montgomery. His many amiable qualities had procured him an uncommon share of private affection, and his great abilities an equal proportion of public esteem. Being a sincere lover of liberty, he had engaged in the American cause from principle, and quitted the enjoyment of an easy fortune and the highest domestic felicity to take an active share in the fatigues and dangers of a war instituted for the defense of the community of which he was an adopted member. His well-known character was almost equally esteemed by the friends and foes of the side which he had espoused. In America he was celebrated as a martyr to the liberties of mankind; in Great Britain, as a misguided, good man, sacrificing what he supposed to be the rights of his country. His name was mentioned in Parliament with singular respect. Some of the most powerful speakers in that assembly displayed their eloquence in sounding his praise and lamenting his fate. Those in particular who had been his fellow-soldiers in the previous war expatiated on his many virtues. The minister himself acknowledged his worth, while he reprobated the cause for which he fell. He concluded an involuntary panegyric by saying, 'Curses on his virtues, they have undone his country!'

A monument of white marble was erected to his memory by order of Congress in front of St. Paul's church, New York. It bears this inscription:

"This Monument
Was erected by order of
Congress, 25th January, 1776,
To transmit to posterity
A grateful remembrance of the
Patriotism, conduct, enterprise, and
Perseverance
of Major-General
Richard Montgomery;
Who, after a series of success,
Amidst the most discouraging difficulties,
Fell in the attack
On Quebec,
31st of December, 1775,
Aged 38 years."

The remains of Gen. Montgomery, after remaining forty-two years in their original burying-place, were brought to the city of New York, July 8, 1818, and interred near the monument in St. Paul's church with great pomp and ceremony.

It may be naturally inferred that a people who would select such a name for their county would occupy no doubtful position in the contest then convulsing the colonies. Nowhere in the State was there exhibited more intense repugnance to the arbitrary measures of Great Britain or more ardent patriotism. The first public meeting in Frederick County was held at Hungerford's tavern (now Rockville, the county-seat of Montgomery), to take action in favor of American freedom and secure the repeal of the obnoxious laws. In the subsequent war Montgomery furnished a very large proportion of the troops which composed the Maryland line, and though many perished on the battle-fields of the Revolution, the following officers became members of The Society of the Cincinnati at the conclusion of the war: C. Ricketts, lieutenant; Lloyd Beall, captain; Samuel B. Beall, lieutenant; Henry Gaither, captain; Richard Anderson, captain; James McCubbin Lingan, captain; Richard Chiderson, captain; David Lynn, captain.

In addition to the members of that society there were Cols. Charles Greenbury Griffith and Richard Brooke; Capts. Edward Burgess and Robert Briscoe; Lieuts. Greenbury Gaither, John Gaither, Elisha Beall, Elisha Williams, John Lynn, and John Court Jones; Ensigns Thomas Edmondson, John Griffith, and William Lamar; and Quartermaster Richard Thompson.

Montgomery County is bounded on the north by Frederick and Howard Counties, on the east by the counties of Howard and Prince George's, on the south by District of Columbia and the Potomac River, and on the west by the Potomac River. The latter separates the county from the State of Virginia, and the Patuxent River forms the boundary line between Montgomery and Howard. The number of acres comprised within the present limits of the county is 242,356, of which about 175,000 acres are under cultivation, 60,000 are woodland, and the balance unimproved. The land is rolling in character, naturally fertile and productive, and very favorably situated for agricultural purposes. A network of fresh, limpid streams covers the surface of the county, affording ample power for milling purposes, as well as abundant water for farming and grazing. Aside from the Potomac and Patuxent Rivers, which bound the county respectively on the west and east, there are a large number of tributaries, among which are Rock Creek, Great, Little, and Dry Seneca, Little Monocacy, Muddy Branch, Broad Run, Bennett's and Crab's Creeks. The Washington Branch of the Baltimore and Ohio Railroad passes near the eastern boundary of the county, and the Metropolitan Branch of the same road runs almost directly through the centre from south to north. The Chesapeake and Ohio Canal, which follows the Potomac, runs along its southwest border, and it will thus be readily observed that Montgomery possesses unusual facilities for traffic with leading commercial centres.

Montgomery embraces an area of five hundred and eight square miles, which comprises all the varieties of soil formed from the disintegration of the volcanic rocks, such as red and white isinglass, hornblende, sometimes called rotten rock, mica slate, with the addition of a distinct variety known as the red lands, a valuable kind of soil, which results from the disintegration of red sandstone. Its soils have in them all of the elements of fertility, some in the largest proportions, and can be improved to a degree equal to the best Pennsylvania and New York lands. The progress made in the past two decades has shown this by noted examples of great improvement in apparently completely worn-out and impoverished soils. These with skill and care have become as productive as many of the best lands in the State, and at a cost less than is required to put in cultivation the wild lands of the West and Northwest, to which immigration, especially from foreign countries, has been directed. The soil varies greatly, the western or upper part of the county being a finely-cultivated and fertile region, while the more northern portion, although thickly settled, is a thinner and poorer soil. The eastern section, near to Howard and Prince George's Counties, is mostly a light sandy loam, with some clay lands, and exhibits, in its vast improvements about Sandy Spring, what may be accomplished by industrious, skillful tillage. These lands, which were formerly almost a wilderness, with only a nominal value, have become an excellent farming district. The part binding the District of Columbia, from its proximity to Washington, is being cultivated largely as market farms, to supply the great demands of the District population, and is the residence of many of the most wealthy and influential citizens of the national capital, who have sought the pure air of the country in preference to the marshes of the Potomac. The climate is temperate and favorable to general agriculture, and the winters are seldom too cold for out-door cattle-feeding. Oak in all its varieties, hickory, poplar, chestnut, pine, walnut, birch, maple, sycamore, and ash constitute the timber growths. Its chief products are wheat, corn, oats, and tobacco, large crops of the latter being raised in its western limits on the red lands. The splendid grass crops are favorable to the breeding of superior horses, cattle, sheep, and other live-stock, and from the herds in this county numerous specimens have been selected for exportation to other States. The best judges have pronounced it particularly valuable for wool-growing, and some of the Northern wool-growers are meditating its selection as a location for the pursuit of their calling. Gneiss, serpentine, red sandstone, intermixed with shale, limestone, trap, and quartz are the prevailing rock formations. Entering the county from the northwest, red sandstone makes its appearance, and is extensively quarried near the mouth of Seneca Creek; it is succeeded by argillites, and, within a short distance of Rockville, by the serpentine formation, containing beds of chromiferous iron. This is the centre of a group of primary rocks which occupies nearly the whole of the county, the rocks of this group being principally granitic,—gneiss, hornblende, micaceous and talcose slates of chromiferous iron, which are used for the production of pigments and dyes. Ores of manganese are found, and gold was discovered in 1848. Chrome ore is found and manufactured in the northern part. The

"SITKA FARM."
RESIDENCE OF H. M. HUTCHINSON, MONTGOMERY CO., MD.

Seneca sandstone is worked at the extensive quarries on the Chesapeake and Ohio Canal at the mouth of Seneca Creek. It was largely used in the construction of the canal, and also in the public buildings in Washington City, notably the Smithsonian Institute. It is easily quarried and dressed, being somewhat soft when first taken out. The county contains other fine building-stone, among which are excellent varieties of granite. Near Hyattstown, in the northwest, a quarry of roofing-slate has been opened. Copper ores have been discovered, and chrome ores occur at many points in a serpentine formation which stretches from near New Lisbon, in Carroll County, through Montgomery County, four miles west of Rockville, nearly to the Potomac River. The ore has been worked at several points, and is found to vary considerably in quality. From the extent of this formation, future explorations will no doubt develop these ores in the largest and richest quantities. Black oxide of manganese occurs one mile and a half west of Brookville, but the workings which were commenced were suspended.

The geographical situation of the county is excellent. Located midway between the level tide-water lands bordering on the Chesapeake and the mountainous country embraced within the shadows of the Blue Ridge and the Alleganies, it possesses the advantages of both. Without the miasma of the former, it has the sloping roads with easy grades and the healthy features of the latter without its hills and declivities.

Parr's Ridge enters Montgomery County at the northern corner, declining in elevation to the Potomac. At Damascus the elevation is seven hundred feet; at Clarkesburg, six hundred and fifty feet. The ridge at Barnesville is five hundred and fifty feet. It is drained on the northwest by Bennett's Creek into the Monocacy. Damascus is situated at the junction of Parr's Ridge and the Southeast Ridge, which forms the basin of Seneca Creek, the stream which draws or drains all its waters inside the county, and drains about one-third the whole area.

The Southeast Ridge to Laytonsville, where the elevation is six hundred and fifteen feet, divides the streams flowing into the Patuxent on the northeast from the streams forming the head-waters of Seneca on the southwest. From near Laytonsville the ridge divides, and one spur runs south to the Potomac. The ridge from Laytonsville to where the Metropolitan Branch road crosses it at an elevation of five hundred and fifteen feet divides the streams flowing into the Seneca on the northwest from the streams passing the head-waters of Rock Creek on the southeast.

At the Metropolitan Branch road the ridge divides and a spur runs west to Darnestown, where it has an elevation of four hundred and fifty feet. Thence the ridge runs southwest to the Potomac. This ridge divides the waters drained into the Seneca on the northwest side from the waters drained into Muddy Branch on the southeast side. The principal ridge (on the south side of the main road from the District of Columbia to Frederick City) again divides, and while the main ridge continues south of the Potomac, and from the southeast of the basin of Muddy Branch, it also forms the northwest side of the valley of Watts' Branch. The ridge from the junction or divide referred to runs southeast to the Potomac at Georgetown, and divides the waters flowing into Rock Creek on the northeast side. Rockville, the county-seat, is located on this ridge at an elevation of four hundred and fifty feet. At Rockville the ridge again divides, and the other side runs south to the Great Falls of the Potomac. This ridge forms the southeast side of the valley of Watts' Branch and the northwest side of the valley of Cabin John.

At the divide referred to at Laytonsville the ridge running south to Mechanicsville divides the waters of Hawling's River (a tributary of the Patuxent) on the northeast side from part of the head-waters on the southwest side that flow into the basin of Rock Creek. At Mechanicsville the ridge has an elevation of five hundred and forty feet. and again divides, one ridge running south, then turning to the southeast continues to the Potomac at Washington City, and forms the east and northeast side of the curve of the valley of Rock Creek, and the southwest side of the basin of the Northwest Branch.

The ridge running from Damascus through Laytonsville to Mechanicsville continues a southeast course through Sandy Spring to Spencerville, thence into the waters of Patuxent from the waters of the Northwest Branch.

The streams of the county, their fall and volume of water, next claim attention. As remarked above, Bennett's Creek derives its head-waters from the northwest side of Parr's Ridge. The main stream and tributaries have a water-power of about two hundred feet.[1] The Little Monocacy, also on the northwest

---

[1] The rivers of Maryland, with rare exceptions, took their names from the Indians who lived on their borders, and were generally given for some peculiarities which they possessed. Some of the streams which now course lazily through Montgomery, their beds filled up by the caving of the banks and the débris of innumerable forest-trees, were in the early days, before railroads and turnpikes were known, of paramount importance to those who tilled the soil in Montgomery and the neighboring counties. The Patuxent was navigable for con-

side of Parr's Ridge, has an available water-power of about one hundred feet. Southwest of the village of Poolesville (which has an elevation of about four hundred and fifty feet) Broad Run takes its rise, and has a water-power of fifty feet. The main stream of the Seneca has an available water-power of about two hundred and seventy-five feet; its tributary, Dry Seneca, and tributaries, about one hundred and fifty feet; Little Seneca has a fall of about one hundred and eighty feet; its tributary, Buck Lodge, about sixty feet; Ten-Mile Creek, about sixty feet,—making a total of three hundred feet. Long Draught has a water-power of about fifty feet; Gunners' Branch, about fifty feet; Wheatstone, over fifty feet; Cabin Branch, about fifty feet; Goshen Branch, about fifty feet; Wild Cat, fifty feet; Magruder's Branch, fifty feet; and Darby's Branch, fifty feet,—making a total for Seneca and tributaries of eleven hundred feet of available water-power. Seneca, at the junction with the Potomac, is one hundred and eighty feet above tide; below the mouth of Long Draught, two hundred and sixty-four feet; at the crossing of the Metropolitan Branch Road, two hundred and eighty feet; at Middlebrook, three hundred and eight feet; at the mouth of Goshen Branch, three hundred and forty-nine feet; at the mouth of Wild Cat, three hundred and seventy-five feet; at the mouth of Magruder's Branch, four hundred and thirty feet; and at Darby's Mill, about four hundred and fifty feet above tide.

The Patuxent, though larger than Seneca, derives a large portion of its head-waters from Howard County. The Cat-Tail Creek, its principal tributary, at its junction with the Patuxent, above Triadelphia, drains an area in Howard County of about eighteen thousand acres; while its principal, the Patuxent, above the junction drains an area in Howard and Montgomery Counties of about twenty-two thousand acres. Hawling's River, a tributary of the Patuxent, at the crossing of the Laytonsville and Unity road is about four hundred and fifty feet above tide; at A. B. Davis' mill, three hundred and seventy-five feet; at its junction with the Patuxent it is two hundred and ninety-four feet; its tributary, Ready Branch, has an available water-power of about fifty feet,—making a total for Hawling's River and tributaries of about two hundred feet. The Patuxent has a small available water-power near its source, five hundred and twenty-five feet above tide; near Triadelphia, three hundred and seventy-five feet; at its junction of Hawling's River, two hundred and ninety-four feet. The conjectural fall below the junction in the county is about seventy feet, making about three hundred feet of available water-power for the main stream, and a total for the Patuxent and tributaries of about five hundred feet.

The main stream of the Northwest Creek draws its head-waters from near Mechanicsville, and unites with the Potomac at Washington City, and has an approx-

---

siderable vessels as far up as Bladensburg. There is reason to believe that Henry Fleet, on his visit to this section, before the arrival of the colonists, pushed through the country as far as Little Monocacy, which was at that time a far more pretentious stream than is now the river into which it empties. It was capable of bearing on its bosom vessels of heavy burden, and was a powerful auxiliary to the farmer. Tradition says that the early settlers of Maryland and Virginia ascended this river as far as the falls at the old Hampton mill. The original Indian names were Menagassi, Menakessi, Monakessi, and Monockissey, which have been modernized into Monocacy. These words are derived from Maskane, strong and rapid; Mashanne, a rapid stream; and Okkehanne, a crooked or winding stream. Heckewelder, from these derivations, believes the meaning of Menagassi to be a rapid stream containing several great bends or windings.

Pa, or Paw, in the dialects of some of the tribes of the Five Nations, means small. Tuxet, or tuxent, conveys the idea of a place where something descends or falls, as a stream or river. Patuxent, therefore, means probably a stream or river small or narrow at the falls. The original name of the river Potomac was Pedhannock. *Ped* signifies waves or swells, frothing restlessly, as if driven by the winds, or forced along by a rapid current. *Cennhanne* means a stream flowing through pine-trees; *kithanne*, main or superior stream; *kithamme*, two streams flowing into one, as the North and South Branches of the Potomac, or the Potomac and Shenandoah. Both *hanne* and *hamme* have about the same meaning. *Pedhanne*, or *Pedhamme*, therefore, may signify a river or stream with high frothy waters or waves. Pedhammock, however, has been modernized into Potomac, and implies a stream issuing from a mountain. Webster defines the Potomac as "a place of the burning pine, resembling a council fire," and Heckewelder says the word Pedhammock, or Powtomok, signifies "they are coming by water." Between these two authorities there is a vast difference, and probably the best way to reconcile them is to combine their definitions, which would give as the meaning of the word "a river of high and frothy waves issuing from a mountain by the burning pine in two streams, which flow together and form the main stream of the country." *Kit*, in the language of the Delawares, signifies great; as kithamme, two great streams coming together, *hamme* being the plural of *hanne*, and the word may refer to the Shenandoah and Potomac coming together at Harper's Ferry. Three of the streams of the county have the name of Seneca, not presumably after the distinguished Roman philosopher of that name, as the Indians of that date never displayed any taste for or knowledge of the classics. The Indian word *shinnik* signifies story, and *banne* a river or stream. *Sinnike* is a derivation from the first name, and signifies the same. Both have been modernized into Senegar, and mean a story, creek, stream, or river, and the lapse of time has possibly caused the original name to be changed to Seneca. *Sinnipehella* includes the adjective, subject, predicate, and object, and signifies strong water rushing over rocks and stones. This is the original name of Seneca Falls, and gives color to the above inference, though the river might possibly have been named after the Seneca tribe of Indians, at one time so numerous and formidable in Western New York, as well as in Western Maryland.

imate fall in the county of two hundred feet. The Paint and Sligo have an approximate fall of two hundred feet in the county. Rock Creek is classed as next to the Patuxent and Seneca in fall and volume of water. The North Fork draws its head-waters from near Laytonsville, and to the junction with the East Fork, including its tributaries, Mill Branch has an available water-power of about fifty feet. The East Fork draws part of its head-waters from near Mechanicsville, thence to the junction with the North Fork near Rockville, and having an available water-power of one hundred feet. At the junction the elevation above tide-water is about two hundred and seventy-five feet; at Veirs' mill, two hundred and fifty; at the crossing of the Metropolitan Branch Railroad, two hundred and eleven feet; and thence to the Potomac, dividing Georgetown from Washington City. The total available water-power of Rock Creek is five hundred and twenty-five feet. Part of Rock Creek runs through the District of Columbia.

Fall Branch runs into the Potomac at the Little Falls, with about fifty feet of available water-power. Cabin John draws part of its head-waters from near Rockville, and runs south to the Potomac. The main stream and tributaries have an available water-power of two hundred and fifty feet. One of the longest and largest single arches in the world is thrown across this stream to convey water from the Great Falls on the Potomac to Washington. The crown of the arch is one hundred feet above the stream. Watts' Branch draws part of its head-waters from northwest of Rockville, and runs southwest to the Potomac. It has an available water-power of about two hundred feet.

Muddy Branch rises about the centre of the county, and runs southwest to the Potomac. It has an available water-power of about two hundred feet.

But, remarkable as the fall and volume of the streams in the county are, they are eclipsed by the astonishing available water-power of the Potomac. In extreme droughts hundreds of millions of gallons of water daily flow over the Great Falls; the average flow amounts to billions of gallons daily. At the mouth of Monocacy the elevation is two hundred feet above tide; at Seneca, one hundred and eighty feet; at the Great Falls, one hundred and fifty feet; and at this point the fall and volume of water is sufficient to drive every factory in New England.

Competent authority thinks that the Potomac has been from indefinite ages wearing away the right bank of the stream. Nearly all the meadows or lowlands are on the Maryland side, while the deep water and channel of the river are nearest to the Virginia side.

The Potomac is the southwestern boundary of Montgomery County for forty miles, and falls two hundred feet in that distance. The water to supply Washington City is drawn by an aqueduct from the Potomac above the Great Falls, at an elevation of one hundred and fifty feet, with a capacity to convey more than sixty-seven million gallons of water daily.

The strata of rocks and soil generally run from nearly northeast to southwest. The climate, like that of the State, may be called variable, as shown by the contrast between the intense and long-continued cold of the past winter and the mild winter that preceded it. The estimated annual average fall of rain is forty-one inches, but the late Benjamin Hallowell estimated it at forty-three inches. The extremes of rain-fall have varied from twenty-eight inches in 1822 to over sixty inches in subsequent years. The soil generally retains moisture to a far greater degree than limestone soils, and the deep clay loam is remarkable for producing a crop in the driest seasons. Five general or severe droughts have occurred during the present century, with an exact period of sixteen years intervening between each.

The general progress of settlement was to the north and westward. Among the first recorded patents is that of

Girls' Portion.—This was surveyed for Henry Darnell in 1688. It extends from Rock Creek eastward to O. H. P. Clark's farm, three and three-eighths miles. The Ashton and Sligo turnpike passes through the tract. The Silver Spring farm, the estate of the late F. P. Blair, and the residence of the Hon. Montgomery Blair, includes a portion of this tract; also the Silver Spring Station and Sligo. The Brookville and Washington turnpike crosses it.

Leeke Forest.—This additional tract of seven hundred and ten acres was surveyed for Col. Henry Dulany in 1688. It lies west of "Joseph's Park," on the west side of Rock Creek, and extends west one and seven-eighths miles. The Rockville and Georgetown turnpike passes through it. The farms of the late Samuel Perry and William Hudleston, on the old Georgetown road, and Bethesda church are included within its limits.

Hermitage.—Granted to William Joseph, May 2, 1689, for three thousand eight hundred and sixty acres. This grant lies on the east side of Rock Creek, and adjoins "Joseph's Park" on the north, extending from Viers' mill to the intersection of the Rockville and Washington turnpike with the Union Turnpike Company's road. The Brookville and Washington turnpike passes through it from the Watery Branch to one-fourth of a mile south of Mitchell's Cross-Roads. The city road from Rockville to Washington passes through it from Grove's farm to Aug. Burgdorf's farm, at the intersection of the Brookville and Washington turnpike. The Norwood turnpike traverses the tract from Kemp's store to Lyddane's farm, at its intersection with the Brookville and Washington turnpike. It embraces many fine farms and elegant residences. Lying to the east of "Hermitage" is

St. Winexburg, surveyed to John Woodcock, May 3, 1689, for five hundred acres, extending from the Northwest Branch at Kemp's mill westward one and one-half miles west of the Brookville and Washington turnpike. The road from Kemp's mill to Lyddane's farm and the Norwood turnpike passes through it. This grant includes the estate of the late William Pierce. Immediately north of "St. Winexburg" is located

Carroll's Forest, granted to Charles Carroll, May 3, 1689, consisting of five hundred acres. This tract was conveyed May 3, 1794, by Charles Carroll of Carrollton to John Connelly.

Joseph's Park was granted to William Joseph, May 20, 1689, containing four thousand two hundred and twenty acres. This tract lies on the east side of Rock Creek, and embraces Knowles' Station, Forest Glen Station, and Linden Station, including the farms of Alfred Ray, William A. Batchellor, and Carroll's, or St. John's Chapel. The Brookville and Washington turnpike passes through it from Augustus Burgdorf's farm nearly to Grace Church.

On the west side of Rock Creek, north of "Leeke Forest" and west of "Hermitage," is a tract called

Dan, granted to Thomas Brooke, Sept. 6, 1694, for three thousand six hundred and ninety-seven acres, extending from Rock Creek one and one-half miles west, and up the creek north two and seven-eighths of a mile. The Georgetown turnpike passes over it from Mr. Codwise's farm to that of the late Samuel Perry. The year following, attracted no doubt by the fertility of the bottom-lands lying on the banks of the Potomac, Richard Brightwell, with a more adventurous spirit than any of the previous settlers, and actuated by a noble impulse, ascended the Potomac River as far as the mouth, and above it, to the Great Seneca, and sought to establish a settlement far from his neighbors, where he and his friends could enjoy the pleasure and excitements of fishing and hunting. Here could be found in abundance buffaloes, bears, wolves, and deer, the Sugar-Loaf Mountain and the chain of hills that extend to the Monocacy River affording them ample shelter and protection from the skill and pursuit of the wily hunter. He located his grant between Edward's Ferry and the mouth of the Great Seneca, and named it

Brightwell's Hunting Quarter.—It was patented Aug. 29, 1695, and contained one thousand and eighty-six acres. It extended for about four miles along the Potomac River, and is now traversed through its whole length by the Chesapeake and Ohio Canal. The beginning of this tract was destroyed in the construction of the canal, but a suitable stone was planted in its stead at the bottom of the canal, which is known only to a few persons. For the next twenty-five years the course of settlements on Rock Creek continued west of the creek. West of "Joseph's Park" and south of "Leeke Forest" is situated

Clean Drinking, patented to John Coats, Oct. 1, 1699, for seven hundred acres. This tract extends down Rock Creek to Jones' Bridge. Walter C. Jones established a mill on this survey, and left his epitaph upon an old stone that still remains a monument of his folly. The inscription, though somewhat defaced by time, is still legible, and reads:

> "Here lies the body and bones
> Of old Walter C. Jones;
> By his not thinking
> He lost 'Clean Drinking,'
> And by his shallow pate
> He lost his vast estate."

Following the settlements on Rock Creek came those upon the Patuxent.

Bear Neck, granted to Benjamin Williams, March 26, 1700, for one hundred and fifty acres. Adjacent to this and lying to the south is

Maiden's Fancy, to Neal Clarke, surveyed Sept. 11, 1700, for five hundred and eighty acres. This tract is situated in the southeast corner of the county. Two miles above on the river is

Bear Bacon, surveyed for Mark Richardson, June 24, 1703, containing six hundred acres. The Ashton and Laurel road passes through this tract from the cemetery to Liberty Grove school-house. The next settlements were made in the southwestern part of the county, between Rock Creek and the Potomac River.

Friendship, patented to Thomas Addison and James Stoddart, Dec. 1, 1711, for three thousand one hundred and twenty-four acres. This land extends from near the Potomac and below Edmund Brooke's farm in a southeasterly and easterly direction across the Georgetown turnpike, north of Tennallytown, and up the pike northwesterly near to Bethesda Post-office, and contains many rich and valuable farms,—Allison Naipor's lands, and the farms of Richard Williams, Henry Loughborough, and others. The river road passes through from Rider's farm to near Tennallytown. Adjoining on the east lies

Charles and Thomas, surveyed for Charles Beale and Thomas Fletchall, April 8, 1715, containing four hundred and nineteen acres. The road from Tennallytown to Jones' Bridge runs through the land. On the north and west of Friendship lies another tract, called

Friendship, for Charles Beale and Thomas Fletchall, May 2, 1715, for one thousand three hundred and sixty-eight acres. This tract extends from the farms of L. A. Lodge in a northeast course as far as C. W. Lansdale's farm.

Clagett's Purchase, surveyed for Thomas Fletchall, April 10, 1715, contains seven hundred and seventy-two acres, and is situated west of "Clean Drinking" and south of "Leeke Forest." The Georgetown turnpike crosses the tract from the branch below Bethesda Church to nearly its intersection with the old Georgetown road. Immediately west of this is

Huntington, surveyed for Thomas Fletchall, Dec. 10, 1715, comprising three hundred and seven acres. It is divided by the old Georgetown road. West of "Leeke Forest" and west of "Huntington" comes

Contention, granted to William Fitz Redman, Feb. 15, 1715, containing six hundred and twenty acres, embracing the farms of Mr. Yeabower and others. North of "Hermitage" and east of Rock Creek is found

Bradford's Rest, granted to John Bradford, June 13, 1713, comprising two thousand six hundred and fifty-eight acres. Adjacent on the west lies the

Addition to Bradford's Rest, granted to Maj. John Bradford, Sept. 20, 1715, for five hundred and eighty four acres. And again the same lands resurveyed, with lands added, and called

Bradford's Rest, for Maj. John Bradford, June 10, 1718, containing four thousand eight hundred and ninety-two acres. This tract extends up Rock Creek north as far as William E. Muncuster's farm, and east as far as the late Roger Brooke's farm. The road from Rockville to Baltimore runs through the grant from William S. Brooke's farm to Granville Stabler's farm, three and one-half miles, and the Brookville and Washington turnpike runs through it from near Higgins' tavern nearly to Raines' store. The lands embrace many elegant farms, including those of Philip Riley, Charles Abert, the late Roger Brooke, A. R. Wadsworth, William S. Brooke, Hon. Allen Bowie Davis, A. H. Herr, and others.

The streams and water-courses seem to have attracted the attention of the early settlers, as is proved by the location of the grants. First comes Rock Creek, and then Northwest Branch, which was the next point selected by the emigrants, followed by the settlements along the Patuxent; after this came Watts' Branch and Hawling's River. The first settlement on Watts' Branch was

Dung Hill, surveyed for Walter Evans, Aug. 10, 1715, containing five hundred and thirty-six acres. It was situated on the Potomac, at the mouth of Watts' Branch. The Chesapeake and Ohio Canal runs through it, as does also the river road from near Watts' Branch to Cornell's farm. Immediately below this grant, lying along the Potomac, is

Thompson's Hop-yard, patented by John Thompson, Dec. 8, 1715, which embraced one hundred acres. This is but a short distance above the Great Falls.

Cool Spring Level was patented to Archibald Edmonston, April 28, 1717, containing five hundred and ninety-two acres. This tract is situated on the road from Offutt's Cross-Roads to the Great Falls. On the north of this road is

Allison's Park, surveyed for John Allison, June 10, 1715, embracing six hundred and twenty acres, and lying south of Watts' Branch. Adjacent to this is

Archibald's Lot, granted to James Moore, March 17, 1718. This tract lies on the road from Rockville to the Great Falls, and contains one hundred acres, and is embraced in the farm of Jacob Miller.

Younger Brother.—This tract lies west of

Watts' Branch, and was surveyed for William Offutt, Aug. 2, 1717, and contained six hundred acres, and comprises the farms of William Viers and Joseph T. Bailey. Following this is

Dispute, lying on the head-waters of Watts' Branch, surveyed for Charles and William Beall, Jan. 19, 1719, containing six hundred and seventy acres. An older tract lies to the east of this and is called the

Two Brothers, comprising twelve hundred acres, through which passes Watts' Branch and the road from Rockville to Darnestown. The next that claims attention on Watts' Branch is

The Exchange, for Arthur Nelson, granted March 10, 1718, for four hundred and eighteen acres, and again to the same person, Jan. 28, 1719,

The New Exchange, for one hundred and fifty acres. These two were resurveyed Dec. 20, 1721, and were called "Exchange and New Exchange Enlarged," for Arthur Nelson, and contained sixteen hundred and twenty acres. By this extension the tract extended down Watts' Branch a long distance, and embraced the site upon which Rockville was originally built. The road from Rockville to the Great Falls passed for more than two miles through the tract. The county poor-house farm, Judge Bouic's (O'Neal's), John E. Willson's, and other farms are included in the tract. North of "Dan," mentioned previously, is the

Addition to Dan, surveyed for Philip Lee, Dec. 10, 1717, containing five hundred and seventy-six acres, traversed by the Georgetown turnpike. Then came Joseph West and James Holmand, who joined in a copartnership and had a tract surveyed containing five hundred and thirty-five acres, and when they came to give it a name were troubled to select one that would give satisfaction to both partners,—each wanted his name selected for the tract, so as to appear on the records at Annapolis. Much was said on the subject by both parties. Finally a compromise was effected by mutual friends, who, taking their two Christian names, joined them with the copulative conjunction "and," which gave them

Joseph and James, and it was so patented, Oct. 15, 1718. It is situated on the road from Rockville to Gaithersburg, and embraces the farms of Samuel Clements and others.

In following the succession of settlements, it is necessary to return to the Northwest Branch, where Archibald Edmonston located

Easy Purchase, for which a patent was granted April 23, 1716, consisting of nine hundred acres, extending from the Northwest Branch to the West Point Branch. The Ashton and Sligo turnpike runs through the entire length of it, from John T. Baker's farm, below and near Colesville, to the late John Hopkins' farm, at the intersection of the Columbia road. Crossing to the east side of the Northwest Branch is located

Friendship Enlarged, for Alexander Beall, May 14, 1716, containing nine hundred and twenty acres, and extending from near the county line up to the north of Bond's mill, on the Ashton and Sligo turnpike. A short distance north of "Carroll's Forest," heretofore described, lies a tract called

Drumaldry, surveyed for James Beall, Sept. 16, 1715, for two hundred and twenty-five acres. It lies on the Northwest Branch, and embraces the farms of James Bonifant. On the Northwest Branch, and still north of this, James Beall was granted

Lay Hill, Aug. 17, 1716, containing one thousand two hundred and ninety-eight acres. The Northwest Branch runs through the tract, while the Norwood turnpike passes the entire length. The farms of Abraham Van Horn, A. J. Cashell, and others are situated on it. On the ridge dividing the headwaters of the Patuxent and Northwest Branch lies a tract embracing many farms, called

Snowden's Manor, surveyed for Richard Snowden, Dec. 10, 1715, containing one thousand acres. The Ashton and Sligo turnpike runs through the estate, also the road from Ashton to Laurel. The tract embraces the lands of William John Thomas, the farms of William Lee, Warwick Miller, Asa Stabler, and the farm and bone-mill of William Bond. A resurvey was made twenty-eight years after, and was called

Snowden's Manor Enlarged, for Richard Snowden, dated March 5, 1743, and embraced nine thousand two hundred and sixty-five acres. This manor contains some of the finest lands in the county. The Laurel road passes through it from Ashton, through Spencerville, to the cemetery near Liberty Grove church. The turnpike from Ashton to Winpenny's farm, near Colesville, runs upon it, while the Norwood turnpike passes through it from Joseph Moore's farm to Van Horn's farm. The Northwest Branch runs through the tract from near Ashton to Kemp's mill.

Charles and Benjamin, surveyed and granted to Charles Beall, July 2, 1718, containing two thousand two hundred and eighty acres. This tract extends from E. J. Hall's farm down the Brookville and Washington turnpike to Higgins' tavern, embracing the farms of B. D. Waters, Thomas Waters, Josiah W. Jones, Samuel Cashell, and others. The Episcopal church at Mechanicsville is located on this grant.

Beall's Manor, granted to Charles and William Beall, Feb. 14, 1720, embracing seventeen hundred and eighty-seven acres, situated on the head-waters of West Point Branch, beginning in Thomas Winpenny's yard, a mile north of Colesville, on the Ashton and Sligo turnpike. On it are located the farms of Thomas Winpenny, Mr. O'Hare, Lloyd Green, J. W. Bancroft, and others. Colesville stands on a tract adjacent to "Beall's Manor," surveyed about the same time, and called

Beall Christie, containing five hundred and six acres. Colesville is a thriving village of recent date.

Bear Garden Enlarged was surveyed for Archibald Edmonston, Nov. 10, 1716, containing twelve hundred and sixty-five acres. Adjoining this tract is

Deer Park, surveyed for Archibald Edmonston, Feb. 14, 1720, containing six hundred and eighty-two acres. This grant, including "Beall Christie," lies between the East Point and the West Point Branches, and embraces the farms of Julius Marlow and others. Adjacent to "Beall's Manor" is

Snowden Hill, granted to Richard Snowden in October, 1723, surveyed for five hundred and forty-six acres. The Columbia road passes by this tract, while it is well watered by the West Point Branch passing through it. Nancy Brown's farm and others are included, as also the road from John Leizar's to Nancy Brown's.

Charley Forest was granted to Maj. John Bradford, and contained one thousand two hundred and thirty acres, increased by

Addition to Charley Forest, surveyed for the same person, Sept. 16, 1720. These two united extend from Mechanicsville to within a short distance of where Snell's Bridge crosses the Patuxent River. The turnpike from Mechanicsville to Sandy Springs and Ashton passes over it, and from Ashton the road to Snell's Bridge and the road to Brighton traverses it.

On this tract is situated Sandy Springs and Ashton, including many valuable farms, viz.: Fair Hill Farm, at Mechanicsville, with the farms of William H. Farquhar, Alvin Gilpin, R. T. Bentley, and Edward Thomas. The tract is located on the dividing ridge that separates the head-waters of the Northwest Branch and Cabin Creek.

In following the order of dates in settlement Hawling's River is reached, when

Hygham is found granted to John Bradford, Feb. 23, 1720, surveyed for one hundred acres. Beginning from the same tree is

Gold's Branch, granted to Richard Snowden, July 30, 1722, for two hundred and fifty-seven acres. These two grants lie on Hawling's River, and constitute a portion of the farm of Allen Bowie Davis, his residence being located on the latter, through which the Westminster road passes, and also Gold Branch, a small tributary of Hawling's River.

Gittings' Ha! Ha! was surveyed for Thomas Spriggs and Richard Simmons, July 27, 1724, and contained five hundred and seventeen acres, lying on both sides of Hawling's River, embracing the farms of James T. Holland, Thomas John Holland, and William Brown. Adjoining this lies

Bordley's Choice, granted to Thomas Bordley, April 8, 1725, for one thousand acres. The Reedy Branch, an offshoot of Hawling's River, divides the tract and affords plenty of water to the farms of Thomas J. Holland, William Rigg, Thomas Rigg, and Brice Howard. The Brookville Academy is located on this survey. Adjoining this tract lies a grant originally

Brooke Grove, surveyed for James Brooke, Sept. 14, 1728, a resurvey of which was made for the same person Nov. 15, 1741, for three thousand one hundred and sixty-four acres. It was again resurveyed so as to include the adjacent vacancies, and named

Addition to Brooke Grove, and granted to James Brooke, Sept. 29, 1762. It contained seven thousand nine hundred and six acres. After this addition to his grove he had eleven thousand and sixty acres granted by patent and six thousand by purchase. This tract extends from Thomas J. Holland's farm some eight or nine miles in a northwesterly direction beyond the Big Seneca. The town of Brookville and Laytonsville are situated on it. The road from Brookville to Laytonsville passes through the tract, which embraces some of the finest farms in the county, including those of E. J. Hall, the late Dr. William B. Magruder, John Riggs, Charles Brooke, the late Walter Magruder, David L. Pugh, Thomas D. Gaither, and Samuel Riggs, of R. This was the largest tract of land owned by one person in the county, and gives an example of the wealth and influence enjoyed by these early princes of the manor. James Brooke was a descendant of Robert Brooke, who established a Protestant colony at Della Brooke, on the Patuxent, June 29, 1650, seventy-eight years prior to this date.

John and Sarah, surveyed for John Philburn, Dec. 21, 1724, and containing two hundred acres, includes the town of Unity.

Benjamin's Lot, surveyed for Benjamin Gaither, April 8, 1725, for five hundred and sixteen acres, is located on the Patuxent River. It embraces the town of Triadelphia, and includes the farms of Robert Brown and others. The Westminster road from Brookville passes through "Bordley's Choice," "Gold's Branch," "Addition to Brooke Grove," and "Benjamin's Lot" to the Patuxent bridge.

New Year's Gift was granted to Thomas Bordley, Oct. 11, 1726, for eleven hundred and forty-three acres, and is situated on the head-waters of Hawling's River. The road from Unity to Damascus runs through it, while it embraces the farms of the late Thomas Griffith, A. B. Worthington, Charles Hutton, and Richard H. Griffith.

With the granting of this tract there was a halt in the settlements along the Patuxent, Hawling's, and head-waters of the Big Seneca Rivers. But little activity was manifested until about 1741, when settlers poured in and the country rapidly filled up until 1775, when very little vacant land remained. Returning again to Rock Creek on the west side, and passing on down south of the road leading from Rockville to Baltimore,

Autra was surveyed for Caleb Litton, Jan. 18, 1720, containing four hundred and five acres, since which time Hon. Allen Bowie Davis has added a portion of this tract to his Rock Creek farm.

Easy Come By was surveyed for William Pottinger, and contained three hundred acres, granted to him Oct. 2, 1722. Adjacent to this is

Mill Land, surveyed for Edward Dawson, March 10, 1724, containing two hundred and fourteen acres, and is situated on the west of Rock Creek, and lies on the north side of the road from Rockville to Baltimore, and embraces the farm of the late Judge Richard J. Bowie and others. Three miles from Rockville, on the east of Rock Creek, and about one mile northeasterly from "Mill Land," lies

Boyd's Delay, surveyed Nov. 12, 1725, and granted to John Boyd, June 6, 1727. It contained two hundred and thirty-three acres, afterwards increased by the addition of several tracts, both by purchase and grant. Many of his descendants are in the county. His great-grandson, the late Rev. R. T. Boyd, an eminent divine, and one of the founders of the Methodist Protestant Church, was born on this estate in 1794. His widow is still living, and resides in Clarksburg. The lands embrace the farms of William E. Muncaster, Roger B. Farquhar, and James F. Barnsly.

Magruder's Hazard was surveyed for Samuel and John Magruder, Nov. 23, 1726. It contained one hundred acres.

Paradise was surveyed for Thomas Gittings, Sept. 17, 1728, for two hundred acres. These two tracts lie on the east side of Rock Creek. The road from Redland to Muncaster's mill passes through it.

Bernard's Desire was surveyed for Luke Bernard, Feb. 1, 1723, containing two hundred and thirty acres. The road from Rockville to Redland passes through this tract, as also through the farm of the late John Bean.

Wickham's and Pottinger's Discovery was surveyed for Nathan Wickham and Samuel Pottinger, Jan. 1, 1721, and contained one thousand acres. It is situated on Piney Branch, and embraces the farms of N. D. Offutt, Mary M. Dodd, Samuel Jones, and others.

Partnership was granted to Henry Massey and John Flint, April 4, 1722, and comprised two hundred acres, and adjoins "Dung Hill," heretofore mentioned. Watts' Branch runs through the land, which embraces at present the farm of Elbert Perry.

The Brothers' Industry was surveyed for James Wallace, April 16, 1722, for one thousand four hundred and twenty-nine acres, and includes the farms of Edwin Wallace, Solon Young, and others.

Deer Park was surveyed for Ralph Crabb, April 19, 1722, and contained four hundred and seventy acres. It lies on the ridge separating the head-waters of Muddy Branch from those of Whetstone Branch, and embraces a portion of Gaithersburg, a station on the Metropolitan Railroad, which since its incorporation as a city has rapidly improved.

Fellowship was surveyed for Nathan Wickham and Samuel Pottinger, March 10, 1723, and contained four hundred acres, and lies on the waters of Whetstone Branch, and embraces the farm of the late Charles Saffell, and the late Nathan Cook's home-farm.

Constant Friendship was granted to Joseph West and James Holmand in 1722. It lies near Rockville, and includes the lands of Levi Viers and others.

It will be seen that the first settlements, commencing in 1688, in this county were along the banks of Rock Creek, extending up both banks of the stream as far as Rockville. Thence they sought the Patuxent, and continued to spread along the banks of this fertile stream as far as Snell's Bridge. Then the country lying west of Rock Creek, towards the Potomac, and north and east of Rockville, seems to have attracted the attention of the settlers. Next came the flat red-lands along the Potomac, in the vicinity of Darnestown and Poolesville, which were surveyed and granted. Among the first was

Wickham's Good Will, surveyed for James Plummer in 1723, containing two hundred and seventy acres. This tract is situated on Muddy Branch, near where the road from Gaithersburg to Du Fief's farm crosses the stream, and embraces the farm of J. Hardesty.

The Joseph was granted to Joseph West, July 1, 1723, and contained three hundred acres, lying on Muddy Branch. The road from Rockville to Darnestown passes through the tract, which has its beginning at a stone at the northeast corner of the bridge over Muddy Branch.

Middle Plantation was surveyed for Daniel Dulany, May 30, 1724, and embraced seven hundred and twenty-two acres. This tract is situated at the mouth of Great Seneca, where the Chesapeake and Ohio Canal passes through it.

Magruder's and Beall's Honesty was granted to Daniel Magruder and Charles Beall, May 16, 1726, and contained one thousand seven hundred and twenty-six acres. It extends from "Leeke Forest" in a southwesterly direction to the Potomac River, and down the river to Edmond Brooke's farm, then returns with, or parallel with, "Friendship" and "Contention," before mentioned, and embraces the farm of William Reading. The Chesapeake and Ohio Canal passes through it.

Clever Wald Enlarged was surveyed for William Offutt, July 17, 1728. It contains two thousand acres, and embraces the farms of the late Philip Stone, George Bradley, Joshua W. Offutt, and others.

Goose Pond was surveyed for John Chittam, Nov. 4, 1726, for one hundred acres. It lies on the Potomac, a short distance above the Great Falls, and is traversed by the Chesapeake and Ohio Canal. Just below this, and immediately opposite the Great Falls, is

Bear Den, surveyed for William Offutt, April 4, 1729, and containing two hundred acres.

Prevention was granted Wm. Beall and others, July 4, 1727, for eleven hundred and eighty-two acres. Rock Creek runs through the tract. Viers' mill is located at the crossing of the Rockville and Washington road. It embraces the Rock Creek farm of Judge Bouic and others.

Saint Mary's was granted Caleb Litton, June 28, 1727, for sixty-seven acres. It lies south of Rockville, on the city road.

It has already been stated that the original Rockville stood on "Exchange and New Exchange Enlarged." The additions will now be given:

Valentine's Garden Enlarged was surveyed for Arthur Nelson, June 17, 1720, and contains nine hundred and fifty acres. The same was resurveyed, as follows:

Resurvey on Valentine's Garden Enlarged, for Henry Wright Crabb, April 10, 1753, for two thousand and eighty-five acres. On this tract stands the first addition to Rockville, and it lies mostly north and northwest of Rockville, and extends as far as the Washington Grove Camp-ground. Haymond's addition was surveyed for John Haymond, Nov. 10, 1743, and contained three hundred acres. On this tract lies the second addition to Rockville, embracing that portion of the town recently laid out in the vicinity of the Metropolitan Railroad depot and the Agricultural Fair Grounds.

About this time the tide of settlements commenced to extend up the Potomac, and a neighbor was found for Richard Brightwell, who located near Edward's Ferry in 1695. For twenty-six years he had braved the perils of his "Hunting Quarter," and during this time had seldom visited the lower settlements, being content with his dogs, pet bears, and deer for companions until "Concord" was granted to Daniel Dulany, April 26, 1721, for one thousand one hundred and six acres, which was located one mile above "Brightwell's Hunting Quarter," on the Potomac River, and one hundred yards above the mouth of Broad Run, where the line begins, and extends up the Potomac to some distance above White's Ferry, taking in most of the bottom-lands through which runs the Chesapeake and Ohio Canal.

Hanover was granted to Dr. Patrick Hepburn, March 16, 1722, for fifteen hundred acres, and situated on the head-waters of the Dry Seneca. It embraces the farms of Howard Griffith, Samuel Darby, the late Grafton Beall, and others.

Flint's Grove was surveyed for John Flint, July 4, 1722, and contained three hundred acres. It lies on Dry Seneca, and includes the farm of Thomas Fife.

Happy Choice was surveyed for William Black, May 20, 1724, for eleven hundred and eighty-six acres, and lies on the road from Barnesville to Rockville. William O. Sellman's farm and others are included in this tract.

Hopewell, granted to John Norress, Oct. 31, 1726, for three hundred acres, lies on the Little Monocacy, and is crossed by the road running from the mouth of Monocacy to Mount Ephraim, and is also joined by the farm of Wm. Price.

Jeremiah's Park, surveyed for Jeremiah Hays, Dec. 10, 1747, includes the site upon which Barnesville stands. Sellman's Station and Post-office, one mile from Barnesville, on the Metropolitan Railroad, also called Barnesville Station, are located on this tract.

Partnership, surveyed for Charles Diggs and John Bradford, April 16, 1728, for two thousand acres, lies on Dry Seneca, and embraces the farms of Thomas Darby, Robert H. C. Allnut, Samuel Dyson, F. S. Poole, John T. Fletchall, and others.

The Resurvey on Part of Forest, surveyed for Robert Peter, May 17, 1784, containing seventeen hundred and ninety-six and one-fourth acres, embraces the lands in and around Poolesville, the first house in which was built by John Poole in 1793.

Banks' Venture was surveyed for John Banks, Nov. 29, 1752, and contained one hundred acres, including the present site of Redland.

Abraham's Lot was granted to Cornelius Etting in 1732, on the Potomac River, near the mouth of Broad Run.

Killmain was granted to Daniel Carroll in 1735, and contains three thousand acres. It lies on the Conrad's Ferry road, and includes the lands of Ludowick Young's heirs and others.

John's Delight, granted and surveyed for John Harriss, June 14, 1755, embraces the lands in and adjacent to Martinsburg and Conrad's Ferry.

Conclusion, granted to Daniel Dulany in 1731, embraces the farms of Joseph Dawson, Frederick Dawson, Col. George W. Dawson, and others, all finely improved.

Turkey Thicket was granted to John Magruder, September, 1736, and embraces the farms of Zadok Magruder and others.

Benjamin's Square, granted to Benjamin Wallingford in 1743, includes the farms adjacent to Goshen.

Spring Garden, granted to Higison Belt in 1738, includes the farm of James Williams and the lands near Laytonsville.

Abel's Level, granted to Abel Brown in 1741, and Moore's Delight, granted to Benjamin Penn in 1748, lies on the headwaters of Great Seneca Creek, and embraces the farms of Col. Lyde Griffith and others.

Pork Plenty, if no Thieves, granted to Nathan Ward in 1753, lies on the Patuxent, and embraces the lands in and around Duvall's old mill.

Chestnut Ridge, granted to George Buchanan in 1732, embraced the lands in and adjacent to Germantown Station, on the Metropolitan Railroad.

Ralfo, granted to George Scott in 1740, includes a portion of Horace Waters' land and others.

Grandmother's Good Will, granted to John Crampton, lies on the Little Seneca, and adjoins the farm of George W. Israel, south of Clarksburg.

Cow-Pasture, surveyed for Henry Griffith, Feb. 10, 1761, for three thousand eight hundred and fifty-four and one-half acres, lies on both sides of Little Seneca Creek, near Clarksburg.

Peach-Tree Hill was granted to Richard Watts, Sept. 13, 1750, and contains seventy-five acres, and adjoins "Cow-Pasture." A resurvey was granted to include vacancies, and called

Errors Corrected, for Nicholas Ridgeley Warfield, May 23, 1792, and contains two hundred and twenty-eight and three-fourths acres. The Little Seneca Creek passes through the tract, as also the old Baltimore road from Barnesville to Neelsville. This is the home-farm and residence of Gassaway W. Linthicum, and is under fine cultivation.

Very Good, granted to John Dickinson in 1756, and **Bite the Biter,** granted to Samuel Saffell in 1756, are both near the village of Damascus.

Silent Valley, granted to Ellsworth Beane in 1756, lies east of Damascus.

Trouble Enough Indeed, granted to Thomas Whitten in 1766, contains two thousand four hundred and ninety-two acres. It lies between Clarksburg and Damascus, and embraces the lands near King's distillery.

By glancing at the map of the county, and selecting a point on the Patuxent east of Richard H. Griffith's residence as a starting-point, a line drawn to William Griffith's residence, on Hawling's River, thence to Brookville, thence to Redland, thence to Charles Saffell's residence, thence to F. A. Tschiffely's residence, thence to where the river crosses Watts' Branch, thence up the river road to the road from Poolesville to White's Ferry, thence west to the Potomac River, a tolerably well-defined boundary line of the settlements made before 1730 will be established, excepting a few settlements made on the head-waters of the Great Seneca and the Dry Seneca. Beyond this boundary line but very few settlements were made previous to 1741. Within these limits settlements progressed regularly as before, but after 1741 the settlements rapidly extended all over the county, so that by 1755 very little vacant land remained.

After this period only here and there a vacancy was discovered, and a resurvey on the adjoining tract would be made to include it.

From the earliest settlements to 1700 the grants were given as lying in Charles County; from 1700 to 1748, as lying in Prince George's; from 1748 to 1776, as lying in Frederick; and since 1776 all grants have been from Montgomery County. By a glance at the names of the first settlers it will be readily learned that Montgomery County was settled by a class of people far superior to the ordinary emigrant who reaches the shores of America in modern times and is shipped by contract to the West. In the majority of instances the settler was an educated gentleman with a cultured family, who had fled from the oppressions of wretched government and the persecutions of religious bigotry to secure freedom of thought and action in a virgin country where his precursors had established a secure asylum. He brought with him all his worldly goods, and he also contributed the refinements and æsthetic features of the social life he had abandoned. The Dulanys, Magruders, Bowies, Bouics, Viers, Clarks, Bealls, Bordleys, Gaithers, Brookes, Wallingfords, Wickhams, Browns, Wards, Darnells, Watkinses, Addisons, Stoddards, Evanses, Thompsons, Snowdens, Dawsons, Crabbs, Saffells, Wests, Diggs, Offutts, Bradfords, Carrolls, Buchanans, Scotts, Griffiths, Dickinsons, Beanes, Hayses, and Cramptons were the pioneers of Montgomery County, and the descendants of many of them are still among the most prominent and most respectable citizens of the county, thrifty, honest, intelligent, engaged in the same occupations as their sires, and frequently cultivating the same acres.

The material, social, and moral condition of Frederick County (embracing Montgomery, Allegany, and Garrett) about the period of the Revolution presents a vivid contrast to its present appearance and circumstances. Then it was the frontier county of the province, and its hardy sons were the pioneers of civilization. On its outskirts roamed the savage. Fort Cumberland was the rendezvous of the British and colonial army in 1755. Fort Necessity and the Great Meadows witnessed the conflict between the lilies of France and the lions of England. In 1758 Cherokees were slain on George's Creek and bounties paid for their scalps. Its centre was occupied by an industrious mechanical and agricultural people, comprised chiefly of Germans, while the lower district (now Montgomery) was settled and filled with an English people remarkable for the best traits that distinguished their mother-country. The first settlers and their descendants were hardy pioneers, familiar with the plow, the sickle, and the rifle. Their wives and daughters rode on pillons behind their husbands, fathers, and brothers to meeting, and a four-wheeled carriage was unknown in the limits of the county. Montgomery County has passed through three distinct phases of civilization since its settlement, or rather through two, and is now entered upon the third.

First were the old tobacco-planters, with their baronial estates and armies of slaves. They felled the native forests and planted the virgin soil in tobacco and Indian corn. This did very well so long as there was timber for the axe and new land for the hoe, and those old lords of manors were happy. They feasted and frolicked and fox-hunted, and made the most of life. These are what are known as "the good old times." But in less than a century after this system of denuding and exhaustion began there were no more forests to clear and no more new lands to till. Then succeeded the period of old fields and decaying worm-fences and mouldering homesteads. This saddest condition of the county had reached its climax about 1840, at which time the population reached its minimum. Then and before the lands bordering on the Rockville and Georgetown turnpike, the only paved road in the county, were, with the exception of Robert Dick's farm and one or two others, but a succession of uninclosed fields. During this period there was a constant stream of emigration from the county, some going to the cotton-fields of the South, but most to the fertile new lands of Kentucky and Missouri. Few enterprising young men settled on their fathers' farms, nor were they to blame, for the land would no longer yield its increase, and they had no means of renovating the soil. Montgomery land had become a synonym for poverty. This was not, however, universally true. The red-lands of Medley's, and those around Brookville and in the Friends' settlement at Sandy Spring, and on Hawling's River, with an occasional farm in other sections, had retained comparative fertility. That emigration, however, was not in vain. It added strength and intelligence to that movement which from the first settlement of the country has ever been in progress from the Atlantic to the Pacific, and furnished representative men to other States. The Lamars of the South, who have now (1881) a representative in the United States Senate, and the grandfather of Hon. Thomas H. Benton, of Missouri, were from this county.

The late Senators Edwards, of Illinois, and Garrett Davis, of Kentucky, and that brilliant commoner, Proctor Knott, besides a host of others who have filled distinguished positions at the bar, on the bench, and in every representative capacity throughout the Western States, were natives of this soil.

The Society of Friends in the neighborhood of Sandy Spring, who formed their settlement in the course of the decade preceding and following the middle of the eighteenth century, and who at every period of our history have done so much to promote the material development and intellectual advancement of our country, first abandoned the destructive system during the last quarter of the last century, probably induced thereto by the change then made in the character of their labor.

The same society, about 1845, or perhaps a few years earlier, introduced into this county the old Chinchi Island Peruvian guano. Its effect was magical. It had the properties of Aladdin's lamp.

No sooner were the people made aware that by application of this new fertilizer to their old worn-out lands they could be made to produce remunerative crops of cereals and grass, than they turned to their cultivation with the wonted energy of their race. This industry was greatly promoted by the Crimean war, which caused a material advancement in the prices of all kinds of farm products. From this epoch may be dated the cereal-growing period. New post-and-rail fences replaced the old zigzag affairs, old buildings were renovated and new ones erected, and the fields teemed with bountiful harvests. The decade from 1850 to 1860 was one of unrivaled prosperity to the people.

Then came the struggle between the sections, with all its blighting and devastating horrors. The young men again sought the tented field. The business of farming was in many localities suspended, fences were destroyed and farms laid waste by the marching and countermarching of armies and the general ravages of war. During this contest slavery was abolished, and at its close we entered upon the third era of our existence, the free labor period. The young men returned to their homes with muscles hardened and energies quickened by their martial experience. They accepted with cheerfulness the new order of things, and fully alive to the kindly properties of their native soil, and acquainted with the means of making it productive, went to work with a will, and already every vestige of that unfortunate struggle has been effaced, and now, with a larger population, the people are in a more advanced state of enlightenment and material prosperity than ever before. The buildings are better, the fences better, the churches better, handsomer, more numerous and more largely attended, the school-houses greatly multiplied and of superior construction, and the school system more thorough and efficient than any which preceded it.

Since the opening of the Metropolitan Branch of the Baltimore and Ohio Railroad half a million of dollars has been annually expended by the people in the purchase of lime, bone phosphates, and other fertilizers of a kindred character, resulting in a greatly-increased production of wheat and Indian corn. This gives employment to at least twenty-five mills, located on the various streams in the county, several of which are merchant-mills. Besides this, a large quantity of grain is annually exported in an unmanufactured state.

Market-gardening and fruit-growing, too, are becoming extensive industries here, and can nowhere else be more successfully prosecuted, the soil yielding abundantly and of the best quality all the vegetables and fruits common to a temperate climate. Wine production is also growing into quite a business, and cannot fail to prove successful, as this county is the home of many varieties of the wild grape and the native soil of the Catawba. These various industries must soon place the people in the very van of agricultural progress. There are purely local advantages, too, which will promote and accelerate the march of improvement. The Great Falls of the Potomac is the largest available water-power in the world, and its development and utilization for manufacturing purposes cannot fail to eventuate in the growth of a considerable town at that point.

The increase in population and commercial importance of Baltimore, connected as this county is with her by her great railway, must surely be felt here. But, above all, the overshadowing influence of the national capital must in time make this county all that its most ardent friends could desire. In 1850 the county contained 1051 farms, covering 162,815 acres improved and 111,122 acres unimproved lands, valued together at $3,084,361, and the value of farming implements and machinery was $134,179. The live-stock consisted of 4118 horses, 93 asses and mules, 4519 milch cows, 724 working oxen, 3523 other cattle, 9780 sheep, and 16,332 swine, valued in the aggregate at $394,678; and the amount of wool produced was $28,691, and of butter 245,927 pounds, and the value of animals slaughtered was $99,903. The crops of 1849–50 amounted to: wheat, 164,108 bushels; rye, 5157; Indian corn, 396,947; oats, 168,240; barley, 56; buckwheat, 6083; peas and beans, 589; Irish potatoes, 49,399; and sweet potatoes, 131 bushels; also hay, 8588 tons; clover-seed, 1036 bushels; and other grass-seed, 49 bushels; hops, 170 pounds; flax, 5510 pounds; and flaxseed, 701 bushels. The value of orchard products was $8513, and of market-garden products, $4470; wine, 75 gallons; silk-cocoons, 21 pounds; and beeswax and honey, 4334 pounds, are also found among the productions of the county. The value of home-made manufactures for the year was set down at $9802. There were at the date mentioned 80 industrial establishments in the county, with an aggregate invested capital of $137,810, consuming in the year raw material to the value of $219,372, employing on the average 179 males and 63 females, at an average monthly cost of $3870, and producing goods to the value of $331,167 in the year. Two-fifths of the capital was invested in milling operations, and one-fourth in the manufacture of cotton and wool. The following are the details of the principal occupations:

Business.	No.	Capital.	Hands.	Value of Products.
Agricultural implements	5	$1,350	10	$3,860
Blacksmiths	8	3,000	25	9,605
Cotton-factory	1	20,000	70	39,200
Woolen-factories	4	15,200	30	24,500
Mills, flour	6	25,050	13	124,945
" grist	25	43,300	25	72,722
" saw	15	12,050	15	15,852
Tanneries	3	3,900	9	9,668

And besides these there were in operation two boot and shoe factories, one cooperage, one engraving office, one bone-mill, two clover-mills, one paper-mill, one sumac-mill, one saddlery, one stone quarry, and one tin-shop. The gold-mine employed seven hands, and produced in the year $1596. The average wages to a farm-hand with board was eight dollars per month; to day labor seventy-five cents, or with board fifty cents; to a carpenter one dollar and twenty-five cents a day, and to a female domestic with board one dollar per week. The price of board for laboring men was one dollar and seventy-five cents a week. The value of real estate and personal property amounted to $4,523,800, and the taxes assessed thereon to $26,246; of which sum $13,128 was State tax, and $13,128 county tax. The number of paupers supported in the year ending June 1, 1850, was one hundred and eighteen, of which ninety-nine remained charged on the public at that date. Only one criminal was convicted during the year. The educational statistics of the county show that the number of primary and public schools was, on June 1, 1850, thirty-four, with the same number of teachers and seven hundred and fifty scholars; annual cost, $8006, of which $3007 was received from public funds and $4999 from other sources, and that the number of academies and other schools was six, with ten teachers and one hundred and sixty pupils; annual cost, $6530, of which $1060 was received from public funds and $5470 from other sources. The whole number of individuals that attended school in 1849–50 was 1264. One newspaper was published in the county, and there were eight libraries, containing 1657 volumes.

In striking contrast with the above are the statistics of the census for 1880 as far as they can be ascertained. The following is the population of the county by districts. Two districts have been created since the census was taken:

First Election District (Cracklin), 2419. Second Election District (Clarksburg), including the following places, 3652: Browningsville, village, 54; Clarksburg, village, 67; Damascus, village, 112; Gaithersburg, town, 43; Hyattstown, village, 48. Third Election District (Medley's), including the following villages, 4252: Edwards' Ferry, village, 36; Poolesville, village, 287. Fourth Election District (Rockville), including town of Rockville, 4203; Rockville, town, 688. Fifth Election District (Berry's), including the following villages, 3799: Colesville, village. 45; Spencerville, village, 84. Sixth Election District (Darnestown), including the village of Darnestown, 1658; Darnestown, village, 107. Seventh Election District (Bethesda), 1488. Eighth Election District (Mechanicsville), including the following villages, 3288: Ashton, village, 45; Brookville, village, 206; Cincinnati, village, 54; Sandy Spring, village, 50. Total population, 24,759.

The population of the county is given below for the successive decades from 1790 to 1880 inclusive. It will be observed that the career of Montgomery has not always been progressive. The impoverishment of the land from the excessive cultivation of tobacco retarded her growth at several periods, but since 1850 her prosperity has been continuous.

POPULATION.

	Total.	White.	Colored.
1790	18,003	11,679	6,324
1800	15,058	8,508	6,550
1810	17,980	9,731	8,249
1820	16,400	9,082	7,318
1830	19,816	12,103	7,713
1840	15,456	8,766	6,690
1850	15,860	9,435	6,425
1860	18,322	11,349	6,973
1870	20,563	13,128	7,434

1880.—Total, 24,759; males, 12,700; females, 12,059. Native, 24,390; foreign, 369; white, 15,608; colored, 9,151.

The following statistics of crops grown in Montgomery County during 1880 have been courteously furnished by the Census Bureau: buckwheat, acreage, 260; number of bushels, 3057; Indian corn, acreage, 35,287; number of bushels, 1,020,573; oats, acreage, 3126; number of bushels, 59,537; rye, acreage, 1785; number of bushels, 17,109; wheat, acreage, 35,673; number of bushels, 615,702; tobacco, acreage, 1053; number of pounds, 806,036.

The statistics of the census for 1880 show that Montgomery, with one exception, grows more wheat to the acre than any county in Maryland, the average yield being $17\frac{1}{2}$ bushels. Washington is the banner county in this regard, yielding $25\frac{3}{4}$ bushels per acre, while Frederick, which follows Montgomery in the order of production, gives an average of 17 bushels to the acre.

The following is the financial exhibit and levy for 1881.

The county commissioners met June 29, 1881, and signed the levy books. During the year the board held but thirty-two meetings, the number of meetings in past years having been between forty-five and forty-seven. The following shows the items of expense:

Pensions	$3,690.90
Insane paupers	3,078.38
Almshouse	4,070.45
Inquests	130.50
Pauper coffins	373.00
Circuit Court and jail	10,767.80
Orphans' Court	991.55
Registration	600.00
Election	317.00
Printing	1,610.00
Justice of the peace	319.74
Constables	786.42
Roads and bridges	13,896.87
Bounty bonds	1,207.25
Public schools	17,000.00
Discount	1,700.00
Sundries	1,932.05
Commissioners	1,331.00
Collectors	3,000.00
School-house at Gaithersburg	750.00
At Mannakee's	350.00
Total	$67,765.96

The collectors reported for the year $152,000 in new assessments, but the exemptions and withdrawals were so much as to leave only an increase of about $80,000. The taxable basis was $8,332,552.

The rate of State and county tax remained the same as in the preceding year, one dollar on the hundred.

Below is given in chronological order a list of the acts of the General Assembly of Maryland having reference to the interests of Montgomery County:

1787.—Georgetown incorporated.

1797 and 1800.—Acts to levy money for building a new jail.

1801.—To review the road from the mouth of Monocacy to Georgetown, through the lands of L. Luckett.

For laying out a road from J. Orme's to intersect the main road from William Darue's to Montgomery Court-house.

For removing prisoners to the new jail and selling the old.

1801 and 1802.—Creating the town of Rockville.

1803 and 1812.—Opening a road from Westminster through Montgomery County to Washington City.

1803.—For encouraging the killing of crows.

1804.—Laying out a road from Liberty Town, in Frederick County, to Hyattstown, and authorizing a lottery therefor.

For changing the road from Rockville to Potomac River.

1805.—Opening a road from Barnesville to Maccubbin's mill, to intersect the main road leading from Frederick Town to George Town, at or near Logtown.

For an addition to Rockville.

1806.—For a lottery to raise money to purchase a fire-engine and to purchase ground and build a school-house in Rockville.

1807.—For laying out a road from Richardson's mill to intersect the main road to Bladensburg.

A Board of Agriculture established.

1808.—For laying out a road from Crow's mill, on the Patuxent, by the Point Branch and the Northwest Branch, to intersect the line of the District of Columbia.

For laying out the town of Brookville.

Declaring to be a public road the road from Edwards' Ferry, on the Potomac, to the road through the Sugar Land Bottom from the mouth of Seneca to Conrad's Ferry.

1809.—For laying out a road from the lower end of William Darne's lane to intersect the road from J. Orme's plantation to the Montgomery court-house.

For creating the town of Hyattstown.

For making a turnpike from Ellicott's lower mills towards Georgetown.

For incorporating Rockville Academy.

For opening a road from the mouth of B. Gilpin's lane to intersect the old road to Montgomery court-house at or near A. Slater's.

1810.—For altering the road to Baltimore where it passes over the lands of P. B. Key.

For a lottery for opening and clearing the road from Westminster to Georgetown (through this county).

1811.—Creating the town of Barnesville.

Prescribing penalty on persons erecting booths or selling liquor within two miles of any Methodist camp or quarterly meeting.

1812.—For vacating the road from O. Trundle's, on Carroll's Manor, intersecting the public road at the mouth of the Monocacy.

1813.—Authorizing the Levy Court to appoint a constable for the town of Brookville.

1814.—For incorporating the trustees of Rockville Academy.

1815.—For laying out a road from a point on the road from Frederick Town to Noland's Ferry, to intersect the road from the mouth of Monocacy to Baltimore.

Incorporating a company to make a turnpike road from the mouth of Monocacy, through Montgomery County, to intersect the Baltimore and Frederick turnpike road at the Poplar Springs, in Anne Arundel County.

1816.—For alteration of the road from Georgetown to Rockville.

Levying money to complete the repairs on the jail.

For authorizing the proceedings of the Rockville Roman Catholic Church to be recorded and made valid.

For laying out a road from Unity to the establishment of Bentley & Co., called Triadelphia, and thence crossing the Patuxent into Anne Arundel County, to intersect the road from Roxbury to Elk Ridge Landing.

Appointing commissioners of the school fund.

1817.—For laying out a road from New Market, in Frederick County, to the District of Columbia line.

For conveying lands to the Society of Quakers for the establishment of a school.

For preventing geese and swine from going at large in Rockville, or within a quarter of a mile.

Incorporating companies to make certain turnpike roads through Montgomery and adjoining counties.

For laying out a road from New Market to intersect the Georgetown road near Griffith's lane, and thence to intersect the old Baltimore and Frederick road near H. Wayman's.

1818.—Repealing that part of an act of 1816 providing for the education of poor children in the county.

1833.—Authorizing George M. Chichester to keep a ferry from his lands in, over the Potomac River.

To open a road from Damascus to Rockville.

To open a road in Montgomery, Anne Arundel, and Baltimore Counties.

For restraining the sale of ardent spirits in Brookeville.

For opening a road from Greenfield, in Frederick County, to near Clarksburg.

1834.—Divisional line established between Frederick and Montgomery Counties.

Levy Court to appoint annually a bailiff in the village of Unity.

To keep in repair the Rockville and Washington turnpike road.

To provide for building a court-house.

1835.—Providing for the surrender of the road and bridges of Columbia Turnpike Company to Anne Arundel and Montgomery Counties.

1835 and 1837.—Providing for the instruction of youth in primary schools.

1836.—For opening road from the old Quaker road, near Henry Griffith's, to Lisbon, in Anne Arundel County.

1838.—Authorizing the erection of a bridge over the Patuxent River at Brown's Ford.

For establishing primary schools, in which one manager of said schools was to be appointed for each election district annually by county commissioners.

1841.—For building a bridge over the Patuxent River at Triadelphia factory.

To open a road from said bridge to intersect the road from Washington to Westminster.

1843.—Owners of lands through which Robinson's mill road passes to retain gates or erect others.

1839.—An act to promote the culture of the mulberry and the manufacture of silk in Montgomery County, and to incorporate a company by the name and style of the Montgomery Silk Company. Its capital stock not to be less than one thousand dollars nor more than fifty thousand dollars, divided into shares of twenty dollars each. The commissioners authorized to receive subscriptions were Thomas P. Stabler, Thomas McCormick, Lloyd Dorsey, Samuel Blunt, Greenbury Griffith, William T. Glaze, Thomas T. Wheeler, Thomas Poole, William Brewer, Adam Robb, Zachariah F. Johnson, William Tommilson, Francis Valdenar, Samuel D. Waters, and Thomas Gittings.

1825.—Ephraim Gaither, Richard H. Griffith, James Day, Baker Waters, William Brewer, Elisha W. Williams, Thomas P. Wilson, Otho Magruder, Roger Brooke, and Thomas Gettings appointed school commissioners to apply and distribute school fund for poor children.

1829.—An act appointing Zadoc Magruder, William McLannahan, and Thomas Gittings to inspect and purchase certificates of surveys, resurveys, plats, etc., essential to the land affairs of the county.

1836.—Thomas Gittings, W. O. Chappell, and William Chiswell to examine surveys, field-notes, etc., of Willy Janes, assistant surveyor of the county, and purchase such or all as may be of value to the county.

1868.—Incorporating Triadelphia Turnpike Company, also Savings Institution of Sandy Springs.

Appointing commissioners,—Francis Valdenar, of Montgomery, and William W. Hall, of Prince George,—to run, define, and mark the dividing lines between said counties.

1870.—Authorizing the repair of old jail or construction of new one.

Incorporating Washington, Colesville, and Ashton Turnpike Company.

1874.—Agricultural Society incorporated with following directors: Elisha J. Hall, Nathan S. White, Robert W. Carter, Edward W. Owen, George E. Brooke, Henry C. Hallowell, N. D. Offutt, Joseph P. Bailey, John T. De Sellum, William S. Brooke, and Thomas R. Suter.

1878.—Gaithersburg incorporated by act of April 5th.

1880.—Creating Districts Nos. 9 and 10, known as Gaithersburg and Great Falls Districts.

CHAPTER XXXIII.

COURTS AND COUNTY OFFICIALS.

Creation of the First Court—Erection of Court-House—First Court Proceedings—First Court Records—Early Marriages—Civil List—Elections.

IN the early part of 1777, Nathan Magruder, John Murdock, Henry Griffith, Thomas Cramphin, Jr., Zadoc Magruder, Allen Bowie, and John Wilson were appointed commissioners for Montgomery County to purchase a lot of land not exceeding four acres, at a place to be selected by a majority of the votes, for the purpose of building thereon a court-house and prison for the county. The place selected and long known as Montgomery Court-House was by act of 1801 designated Rockville. The town was then but a small hamlet, but is to-day a town of social and commercial importance. The old court-house was built shortly afterwards, and the first court held in 1779.

In 1798 an act was passed to divide the county into five election districts, and in 1799, Daniel Reintzell, Hezekiah Veitch, Thomas Fletchall, John Adamson, and Thomas Davis were appointed commissioners and made the division. The original districts were Berry, Cracklin, Rockville, Medley's, and Clarksburg, which remained the political divisions until 1878, when three new districts, Bethesda, Darnestown, and Mechanicsville, were formed, and in 1880 Gaithersburg and Great Falls Districts were laid out by an act of the General Assembly of Maryland.

The first County Court met at Leonard Davis', May 20, 1777, and was held by the following worshipful justices: Charles Jones, Elisha Williams, Richard Thompson, Edward Burgess, Samuel W. Magruder, William Deakins, James Offutt. Samuel Carnole was appointed court crier. A bond from Clement Beall, the new sheriff, signed by him, George Beall, Jr., and Hezekiah Magruder, was approved by the court. The second court was held May 29th, with same justices save Joseph Willson, in place of William Deakins. Brooke Beall, the clerk of the court, was ordered to take charge of the records and other papers belonging to his office until there was a sufficient public building provided for that purpose, or it was otherwise ordered by the Legislature. It was also ordered that the courts be held at the house of Leonard Davis until the erection of the court-house and prison, and that Davis find a sufficient house for the reception of prisoners by July 20th. The bond of Brook Beall as clerk, appointed by the first court, signed by him, Edward Burgess, and Samuel Wade Magruder, was approved.

The third court met August 12th, with the same justices on the bench as at first, save that Offutt was absent, but in his place were William Deakins, Thomas S. Wootton, and Phineas Campbell. The following grand jury, the first in the county, appeared and were sworn: Alexander Claggett (foreman), Henry Clarke, Herbert Wallace, James Stimpson, William Benson, Richard Hopkins, Benjamin Harris, Jr., Thomas McCubbin, Aaron Lanham, Daniel Henry, Basil Roberts, James Harbin, John Daley, Greenbury Gaither, Michael Litton, Benjamin Allison, James Higgins. The court bailiff was Benjamin Nicholls. Richard Potts and Baker Johnson were admitted to the bar as attorneys. On August 13th warrants were issued to Samuel Douglass as overseer of the "main road," in the room of Samuel Biggs.

The following bonds were given and licenses paid for tavern-keeping:

"State of Maryland
vs.
Lucy Oune, £40.
Saml. Turner, 40.
William Deakins, 40.

For Lucy Oune's keeping a sufficient house of entertainment, according to act of Assembly. Fine paid Sheriff & Clerk."

"Same
vs.
Nicholas Paul, £40.
John Watkins, 40.
Adam Burns, 40.

for N. Paul's keeping House of Entertainment. Fine paid Sheriff & Clerk."

Paul Hoy brought into court his servant Mary Riley, who had run away, and who was adjudged to serve her master two years after her present time of servitude had expired, also a further time of six months after the expiration of said two years, which six months was allowed her on payment of three pounds to her master as a fine for having base-born child. James Luter and Thomas Graves gave bonds for keeping taverns. The sureties of the former were Adam Burns and John Dowden; of latter, John Watkins and Adam Burns. On the oath of Ann Campbell, John Waters gave bond in twenty pounds, with John Randall as security, for his appearance at the next term. Leonard Richard brought into court his servant Ann Graham, to be adjudged for having a base-born child, and she was ordered to serve thirteen months in addition to her present servitude, and fined £3 7s. John Hewes was recognized to the next court in forty pounds, to be of good behavior towards Ninian Beall, with Benedict Woodward and Thomas Sparrow as sureties. John Jones, an orphan, aged three years, was bound unto William Nailor until his majority. Richard Downs, for running away from his master, Charles Murphy, was ordered to serve five months longer. Leonard Davis was licensed to keep tavern, with Charles Hungerford and Richard Crabb as sureties. Negro "Sampson," belonging to Thomas Lancaster Lansdale, and negro "Judea," of Jeremiah Oune, were set levy free. Brock Mockbie got a license to keep tavern, with Edward Burgess and Simon Nicholls as securities. Ann Giddings, for having a base-born child, was fined £1 10s. Philip Houser was appointed overseer of main roads, *vice* Ninian Beall (son of Ninian). "Dinah, a mulatto, aged three years," was sold to Simon Nicholls until her thirty-first year for twenty pounds; and "Dick Hodney," mulatto, aged one year, was sold to the same until his thirty-first year for ten pounds.

The justices of the court settled and adjusted the rates of liquors and other accommodations as follows:

	£	s.	d.
A hot diet for a gentleman, with a pint of beer or cider	0	3	0
Do. for a gentleman's servant, with do	0	2	6
A cold do. for a gent, with do	0	2	6
Do. for a gent's servant, with do	0	2	0
Lodging in a good bed, with clean sheets	0	0	9
Stablage with hay or fodder 24 hours for a horse	0	2	0
Pasturage 24 hours for a horse	0	0	9
Oats or corn per gall	0	1	0
West India Rum or Spirits per quart, sealed and made into Toddy, with loaf sugar	1	10	0
Do., or do. per gill	0	2	6
Peach Brandy per Quart	0	8	0
Apple & cherry do. per Quart	0	5	0
Whiskey per Quart	0	5	0
Madeira Wine per Quart	0	10	0
Claret per Quart	0	10	0
Red or white port or Lisbon per Quart	0	10	0
Teneriff per Quart	0	5	0
Good Lemmons apiece	0	0	6
Good Limes apiece	0	0	2
Good strong beer per Gallon	0	4	0
Good small do. per do	0	2	0
Good Cider per do	0	2	8

All liquors intermixed with Cherries not to exceed the above rates.

The following constables were appointed:

Upper part of Newfoundland Hundred		Aquila Duvall.
Lower part " "		John Holmes, Senr.
Upper part of Potomack "		William Davis.
Lower " " "		Bennett Woodward.
Seneca "		John Cook.
North West "		John Lee.
George Town "		Thomas Branham.
Rock Creek "		John Tannehill.
Sugar Land "		Thomas Dowden.
Sugar Loaf "		John Watts.
Linganore "		Hezekiah Griffith.

The following witnesses testified before the grand jury: Walter Smith Greenfield, Bennett Woodward, John Cook, Thomas Branham, John Watts, Hezekiah Griffith, William Davis, John Tannehill, Henry O'Neale, Ninian Beall (of Ninian), Mary Greenfield, Ann Giddings.

The court appointed George Beall, Jr., and Hezekiah Magruder "tobacco inspectors," who gave bonds with Zach. Magruder and Thomas Nicholls as sureties. (They were reappointed in 1778.)

The next County Court met Nov. 11, 1777. Present, Justices Charles Jones, Richard Thompson, James Offutt, Richard Beall, William Deakins. The following grand jury appeared: Elias Harding, Charles Murphy, John Flemming, Jr., John Thompson, Joshua Harbin, Thomas Veatch, Jonathan Tucker, William Parkin, George Offutt, Martin Fisher, William Willett, James Haislip, Zephaniah Offutt, Moses Oune, Edward Beall. The bailiff was Walter Magruder. Samuel Briggs was licensed to keep tavern upon payment of £3 15s., and gave bond, with Thomas Veatch and Wm. Blackmore as sureties. Josiah Russell and Samuel Irwin were admitted as attorneys. Ninian Beall was licensed to keep tavern, with John Suter and Samuel Biggs on his bond, also George Campbell, with Thomas Dowden and Samuel

Biggs as bondsmen. Henry Clark was appointed constable, *vice* John Lee, in Northwest Hundred. Daniel Henry was arrested for saying that he wished Hancock and Adams (John Hancock and Samuel Adams) were taken by the enemy, as they were the beginning of the war. On his examination by the court he was honorably discharged, the accusation being without the least foundation in fact.

Christian Bencers and Richard Callahan were recognized to the next term,—offenses not stated. The first criminal trial was that of James Vine for felony. He was found guilty, and sentenced to receive at the hands of the sheriff twenty lashes at the common whipping-post on his bare back, and be put five minutes in the pillory. Thomas Malone was bound over to the next court to keep the peace, especially towards Ninian Beall. Ann Willson was fined £1 for having a base-born child, Hugh Clifford £1 7s. for assault on Ninian Beall, and the latter £2 10s. 7d. for neglect of duty as overseer of the roads. In the case of Catherine McKay *vs.* Christopher Keyser, on her petition for freedom, she was declared free, her servitude having expired. Ann Woodward, for having a base-born child, was sold for seven years, and her child until it arrived at the age of thirty-one years, Archibald Allen being the purchaser for five pounds, and he released ten years of the child's servitude. George Mitchel was examined " for speaking inimical against the States," and in default of £2000 bail to appear at next court, was committed to the gaol. Benjamin Nicholls was ordered to take care of and provide for a negro man. In the case of George Gordon *vs.* Joseph Sim for his freedom, the latter was ordered to pay thirty shillings seven pence, the remaining part of Gordon's freedom dues. John Hutchinson was declared levy free. Hiram Kirk, an orphan, aged eleven, was bound unto Thomas Johns and Thomas Richardson until his majority, during which apprenticeship his masters were to learn him the cooper's trade, to read, write, and cipher as far as the rule of three, and when free, give him a set of cooper's tools and a decent suit of apparel. David Hurvey and Mary O'Neill were recognized to the next term of court.

The next court convened March 10, 1778, when the following grand jury were sworn: Ninian Beall Magruder, Van Swearingen, William Beall Magruder, William Clark, Anthony Wilcoxon, George Reed, James Slicer, John Belt, Samuel Beall Magruder, Edward Magruder, Nathan Holland, Thomas Sparrow, Thomas Lewis, George Beall, Benjamin Harris, James Duley. The court appointed Josiah Russell as prosecutor during its present sitting. Archibald Boyd was admitted as an attorney. The following persons appeared in court and took " the oath of fidelity and support to the State of Maryland:" William Holland, Nathan Thompson, John Litmor, Seth Gaither, Ananias Ogdon, Levi Hays.

At the August court, 1778, the justices sitting were Samuel Wade Magruder, Gerard Briscoe, Henry Gaither, Charles Jones, Walter Beall, Richard Thompson, Edward Burgess, Thomas Sprigg Wootton.

Christopher Buzby was convicted of felony by the following petit jury: John Wilcoxon, William O'Neale, Thomas Hays, Benoni Dawson, Basil Roberts, Henry Clark, Joseph Wheat, Sr., Nathaniel Crawford, Anthony Wilcoxon, Humphrey Godman, John Allison, Benjamin Harris, and was sentenced to receive on his bare back twenty lashes and stand ten minutes in the pillory. At the November court, 1778, Samuel Turner, Brooke Beall, and William Deakins, Jr., were appointed to view the road leading from Seneca into the new road from the mouth of Watts' Branch to Georgetown, for the purpose of building a bridge over said Watts' Branch. The court appointed Charles Jones and Walter Beall to agree with workmen to build a bridge over Rock Creek near Charles Jones'. Twenty pounds was levied to purchase a stone for the jail. The first petit jury which tried a criminal case was sworn in at the November court, 1777, to wit: James Perry, William Tannehill, Edward Wheeler, Charles Gassaway, Daniel Henry, Samuel Biggs, Thomas Tucker, John Wilcoxon, Philip Oune, Michael Litton, William Boyd, Anthony Wilcoxon, who convicted James Vine of felony. The first regular petit jurors summoned appeared at the August term, 1777, to wit: Samuel Turner, Thomas Nicholls, John Watkins, Charles Gassaway, Zachariah Offutt, Nathaniel Crawford, Charles Jones, Zachariah Thompson, John Hawkins, Walter Smith Greenfield, William Talbot, Joseph Magruder, Ninian Magruder, Stephen Kisor, Thomas Graves, Zephaniah Wallace, Jacob Upright, Richard Magruder, Joseph White, James Wallace, Joshua Harbin, John Ray, Samuel Brewer Magruder, Samuel Watson, Mark Elliott, and Michael Dowden, who for their two days' services received forty pounds of tobacco, the same as was allowed the grand jurors for that length of time.

At the March term, 1779, the justices sitting were Charles Jones, Phineas Campbell, Walter Beall, Henry Gaither, Joseph Wilson, George Cullom, S. W. Magruder. For indecent behavior to the court James Pelly was fined £5.

At the August term, 1779, the grand jury were Richard Wootton (foreman), Daniel Vears, Daniel Henry, William Howard, Samuel Watson, Elias Harding, Edward Wheeler, Wadsworth Willson,

Humphrey Godman, Hugh Riley, Henry Wilcoxon, William Fee, Van Swearingen, Mark Elliott, Nathan Linthicum, Alexander Catlett. The court crier appointed was John Ball. At the August term, 1780, Jonathan Nixon, Jr., was bailiff, and Luther Martin was admitted to practice as an attorney.

The first deed recorded was on July 3, 1777, from Benjamin Spyker, of George Town, to Andrew Reintzel, for lot No. 78 in George Town; consideration, £75. This indenture was acknowledged before Charles Jones and Richard Thompson, justices of the peace, who were witnesses to its execution.

On Aug. 9, 1777, a lease executed Sept. 7, 1776, between Thomas McCray (lessor) and Samuel Boone, whereby for five shillings was leased during the natural life of lessor 100 acres on Muddy Branch, adjoining lands of William Deakins, Edin Pancoast, and Alexander Campbell, was recorded. The third indenture was recorded August 12th, and dated July, 1777, from John Watson to John Reynell and Samuel Coats, conveying for £800 two tracts of land, the first on Sligo Branch, part of "Labyrinth," and containing 240 acres, and the second a tract patented by Lord Baltimore to John Watson, Aug. 2, 1766, called "Rockingham," and laid out for twelve acres. On the same day was recorded a deed from Ninian Beall to Alexander Catlett and his wife Susanna for 200 acres, called "Farewell," also for another tract of 179 acres. Also on same day was put to record a deed from Ninian Beall to Hardage Lane and his wife Rachel for 525 acres in one tract, 152½ acres called "Bachelor's Chance," and a third of 22½ acres of the resurvey on Rich Meadows. Also on same day was recorded a conveyance from Ninian Beall to Benjamin Edwards and his wife Margaret for 429 acres of resurvey on Gravelly Ridge and 271 acres of resurvey on Rich Meadows. The considerations in these three deeds were the grantees being the daughters and sons-in-law of the grantor. On same day was recorded the indenture of apprenticeship of Thomas Wall, son of Mary Wall, apprenticed to John McCormack for seven years to learn the art of a weaver. Said apprentice was to have two years' schooling, and at the expiration of his term of service have a new suit of wearing apparel agreeable to the customary wear of the country, and a new loom with the necessary utensils thereto belonging given him by his master, whom he had to serve with diligence and respect. On same day was recorded articles of agreement between William Collyar and Abraham Sansbury, whereby the latter sold to the former all his right of everything upon a plantation belonging to Jonathan Allison, or of which said Allison was overseer (only one bed and furniture, one servant-woman named Mary Ryan, a tea-kettle, the wool, and some leather), for £130. It was agreed, in case there was trouble in getting possession of the property or a lawsuit attending same, Sansbury should pay "the lawful boot" and not be entitled to the purchase-money.

The Levy Court in 1777 made an assessment for the building of a court-house and prison of 108,342 pounds of tobacco,—that is, 26 pounds upon each taxable,—the total taxables being 4167. The court ordered the sheriff to collect it, having decided that these sums of tobacco might in reason be paid and received.

Some insight into the early settlement of the county may be obtained from an examination of the wills recorded and the inventories of personal property and letters of administration and guardianship filed immediately after the establishment of the Orphans' Court. The first will admitted to probate in the new county was that of Edward Gaither, son of Benjamin, on June 11, 1777, before Samuel West, register of wills. It was dated March 26, 1777, and the four subscribing witnesses to its execution were John Ray, Jr., Benjamin Ray, John Suter, and Samuel Hardesty. The testator bequeathed to his son Benjamin one tract of land called "Gaither's Purchase," containing one hundred acres, also fifty-four acres of part of a tract called "What's Left." To his son Basil he bequeathed "Mitchell's Garden" of nineteen acres, one hundred and thirty acres of a tract called "Mitchell's Range," and two acres likewise in same "Range." To his son Eli the plantation on which the testator lived, of one hundred and ninety-eight and one-half acres, and to his sons Greenbury, Nicholas, Burgess, Jonsey, and Brice all the remaining part of "Mitchell's Range," all the first and second resurveys on "Mitchell's Range," the tract called "Gaither's Range," and the one named "Good Luck." The tract he was to have of Zachariah Linthicum to be equally divided among the last five sons. He left his copper still to his wife Elenor during her natural life, besides other properties. To his daughters Elenor Prather, Sarah Gaither, Casander Gaither, and Lyla Gaither he devised all his negroes, save the two to his wife during her life. The second will was recorded May 28, 1777, and was that of Samuel Saffell, dated Nov. 25, 1776. Its witnesses were Robert Dawe, Benjamin B. Kelly, and Griffith Davis. He gave to his children—Samuel, William, Ann, James, Joshua, Elizabeth, Charles, and Sarah—each a shilling, and to his wife Sarah, made the executrix, all his properties.

The following is a summary of the real and personal property, as returned by Assessor Enoch Green for taxation in 1793:

MONTGOMERY COUNTY.

	Georgetown, Lower Potomack, and Middle Potomack Hundreds, First District	Upper Potomack and Sugar-Land Hundreds, Second District	Sugar-Loaf and Linganore Hundreds, Third District	Lower Newfoundland, Rock Creek, and Northwest Hundreds, Fifth District	Upper Newfoundland and Seneca Hundreds, Fourth District	Total
Total Amount. (£ s. d.)	210,054 10 5	116,081 1 6	110,464 6 5	106,398 10 8	105,130 18 5	£648,129 7s. 6d.
Value of other Personal Property. (£ s. d.)	27,693 10 —	21,188 9 2	26,798 5 —	17,581 12 6	20,815 9 7	£114,077 6s. 3d.
Value. (£ s. d.)	1,180 16 8	133 10 10	103 15 —	284 7 6	270 10 5	£1,973 5s.
Silver Plate.	2834	320	249	682	649	4735
Value. (£)	3,330	2,663	1,896	2,358	2,408	£12,645 10s.
Male Slaves above 45 years, and Females above 36 years.	202	143	100	147	151	743
Value. (£)	2,521	2,845	1,812	1,822	1,666	£10,667 10s.
Male and Female Slaves under 8 years.	435	410	265	371	308	1789
Value. (£)	8,757	7,895	5,595	7,175	5,410	£34,832
Female Slaves from 14 to 36 years.	296	265	188	243	182	1174
Value. (£)	13,772	14,175	8,685	12,075	8,749	£57,456 10s.
Male Slaves from 14 to 45 years.	310	318	193	272	197	1290
Value. (£)	4,215	3,662	2,520	3,345	2,675	£16,417
Male and Female Slaves from 8 to 14 years.	282	245	168	223	179	1097
Value. (£ s. d.)	148,594 13 9	63,519 1 6	63,054 6 5	61,706 10 8	63,185 18 5	£400,060 10s. 10d.
Number of Acres.	48,268¾	60,359⅞	83,786⅞	67,721¼	65,986½	326,211⅝

The following wills were proven and recorded at the times mentioned,—all within the first three years after the creation of the county:

May 31, 1777, Ralph Hoult.
June 14, " John Fletchall.
July 25, " Ann Hoult.
June 17, " James Farrall.
Aug. 4, " Jasper Yost.
" 21, " William Willson.
May 22, " Nathan Offutt.
Feb. 19, 1778, Middle Smith.
" 2, " Henry Claggett.
" 4, " Richard Anderson.
March 4, " John Mullikin (painter).
" 21, " William Mullikin.
" 28, " Lodowick Davis.
April 14, " Thomas Claggett.
May 30, " Benjamin Prather.
" 2, " John Cook.
June 4, " Hugh Coupland.
Jan. 8, 1779, Eleven Hopkins.
Aug. 19, 1778, Richard Beall, of Samuel.
Oct. 5, " John Holmes.
May 12, " James Harbin.
Feb. 10, " Samuel West (register of wills).
Jan. 9, 1779, Archibald Edmondston.
" 27, 1778, John Fryer.
May 14, " James Sprigg.
March 21, " Thomas Prickett.
June 9, " James Gatton.
Feb. 9, 1779, Samuel Magruder, then of Prince George's County, where the will was dated Jan. 12, 1739.
Feb. 11, 1779, Thomas Cartwright.
July 4, " Robert Owen.
" 30, " William Shaw.
Aug. 4, " Benjamin Gatton.
" 30, " Catherine Ferguson.
Sept. 4, " Robert Constable.
Nov. 12, " William Davis, Sr.
Dec. 18, " Gabriel Baxter.
Feb. 8, 1780, Jane Maccollum.
March 11, " Robert Lashley.
" 15, " Henry Leeke.
" 15, " Nicholas Rhoades.
" 24, " George Beall.
" 29, " Elizabeth Butler.
May 22, " James Beall, son of Ninian.

The first inventory recorded is that of John Cook (an additional one), of ninety-five barrels of corn, valued at £38, Jan. 18, 1779. The next was of Joshua Hickman, amount £433. Then of Ambrose Cook, Jan. 8, 1779, of £1249 6s. 3¼d. Then of James Odel (appraised Aug. 12, 1763), of £348 16s. 10d. Of Jasper Yost, taken Aug. 27, 1777, for £216 10s. 4d. Robert Redmond's, March 10, 1778, of £66; John Fryer's, June 23, 1778, of £2 4s.; of Aaron Prather, March 7, 1777, of £328 2s. 2¼d.; of Edward Gaither, Feb. 6, 1778, of £484 9s.; and of William Willson, Aug. 28, 1777, of £459 4s. 9d.

At the June term, 1779, Charlotte Perry chose John Williams as her guardian, and Joseph West chose William O'Neale,—first two guardians appointed. This was the first Orphans' Court held, as the County Court had for previous two years transacted all probate business. At August term, Edward McDaniel, aged eight, was bound to Sarah Mitchell, and John Cannida to William Tracey. The first letters of administration were taken out at December term by Mary Hickman and Neal McGinnis on Arthur Hickman's estate. At the February term, 1780, the first citation was issued, and was for Jacob Reintzel to appear at the next term. At the same term an attachment for Samuel Hobbs and wife was issued. The business of the court in the first three years was small, but at the close of the Revolutionary war began to increase, when the sittings of the justices became longer and the minute-books full of the dull routine of court work.

The following is a list of marriage licenses for the first two years of which there is any record given. Prior to 1798 no records of marriages were made, or, if they were, they have been lost:

1798.
Feb. 10. Francis Piles and Ann Poole.
" 10. Richard Hudson and Nancy Wellen.
" 15. William Magruder and Lucy Williams.
" 16. Benjamin Davis and Elizabeth Thresher.
" 17. Michael Whealan and Elizabeth Nicholson.
" 19. John Peter and Eleanor Orme.
" 21. Thomas Hickman and Margaret Sowonor.
" 21. Alexander Offut and Anne Lowe.
" 26. John Gartsell and Lucretia Beall.
March 8. Peter Hawkins and Elender Williams.
" 9. William Worthington and Ruth Perry.
" 10. Christopher Sipe and Elizabeth Iglehart.
" 10. John Boyd and Mary Parmen.
" 14. William Darnes and Betsey Gahaive.
" 16. William Thomas and Peggy Fletcher.
" 21. Arnold Warfield and Margaret Browning.
" 24. William H. Gittings and Jane Murry.
" 28. Basil Macmewe and Sarah Walker.
" 31. Christopher A. Coall and Sarah Claton.
April 11. Brian Flaherty and Bridget Flaherty.
" 12. Thomas Crowley and Judy Conner.
" 14. John Miller and Eleanor Barnett.
" 20. Barton Enniss and Margaret Smith.
" 24. Thomas Watkins and Catherine Magruetry.
" 30. Thomas H. Willcoquen and Sarah Prather.
May 17. Walter Duvall and Sarah Duvall.
" 19. Charles Stewart and Chloe Ann Norton.
" 22. John B. James and Ruth Crawford.
" 22. William Stewart and Helen Beall.
" 22. Ignatius Davis and Margaret Wootton.
June 1. Zachariah Duley and Ann Lazenby.
" 2. William Prather and Elizabeth Adamson.
" 4. Collin Williamson and Mary Tatbo.
" 6. Henry O'Riley and Elizabeth Sewal.
" 21. James Long and Margaret Sanford.
" 25. Patrick Carroll and Ann Tarrell.
July 12. John All and Comfort Young.
" 20. Nathan Walker and Ann Beck.

Aug. 7. Justice Ridgway and Anne Artist.
" 22. Charles Riggs and Sarah Ervin.
" 23. Allin Macentosh and Eleaner Robey.
Sept. 11. Amos Scott and Anne West.
" 12. Benjamin Cross and Margaret Walker.
" 19. Henry Robert Whittaker and Mary Edwards.
" 24. Thomas Willson and Nancy Rankins.
Oct. 2. John Pringle and Elizabeth Hendley.
" 3. Dawson Cash and Jemimah Beene.
" 8. Basil Ferguson and Elizabeth Brashear.
" 8. Thomas Wheeler and Ruth Jackson.
" 11. Benjamin Summers and Virlinda Beckwith.
" 15. David O'Neale and Rebecca Lane.
" 17. James Baggerly and Elizabeth Smith.
" 18. Walter Hellen and Nancy Johnson.
" 23. Thomas Kennedy and Rosamond H. Thomas.
" 26. Stephen Penne and Elender Scrivnor.
" 26. Thomas Arnold and Mary Frazer.
" 29. Robert Wilson and Elender Shekells.
Nov. 1. Charles Sheats and Hannah Hobbs.
" 5. Thomas Buress and Linny Butt.
" 6. John Jones and Sarah Stewart.
" 7. Alexander Jones and Mary Waner.
" 19. John Thomas and Nancy Berry.
" 20. Israel Houser and Terry Hobbs.
" 23. Becra Ashton and Rachel Perry.
" 26. Joseph Crown and Mary Slater.
" 28. Jacob Cross and Dehilah Cross.
" 30. Benjamin Sharp and Henrietta Harriss.
Dec. 3. Thomas Dick and Margaret Peter.
" 4. Samuel Cicel and Sarah Belt.
" 8. Harrison Cleveland and Sarah Richard.
" 8. Benjamin Cracroft and Nelly Prather.
" 11. Charles Harvey and Rebecca King.
" 11. Aaron Poole and Hessa Browning.
" 12. Nathan Holland, Jr., and Martha Beall.
" 12. Joseph Astlen and Rachel Chiswell.
" 14. John Jackson and Easter Ellis.
" 17. Joseph Gue and Mary Hey.
" 17. John M. Cox and Eleanor Gray.
" 17. Basil Cohoo and Nancy Phillips.
" 18. Levi Lewis and Rebecca Winn.
" 18. Bennett Biven and Sarah Dougherty.
" 18. Roby Penn and Lucrecia Howes.
" 18. William Slater and Sarah Leatch.
" 20. George Ward and Ann Redman.
" 22. Edward Brashears and Ann Dyoon.
" 22. William Case and Eliza Kelly.
" 24. Conrad Heater and Barbara Gotert.
" 24. John Powell and Eleanor Steel.
" 24. John Campbell and Priscilla Oden.
" 26. Erazmus Hogdon and Jane Douglass.
" 26. Norris Read and Elizabeth Holland.
" 26. John Orme and Elizabeth Guines.
" 26. John Troop and Rebecca Moreley.
" 27. Joseph Brooke and Letitia Boone.
" 31. Charles Davis and Lawrady House.
1799.
Jan. 1. Alexander Campbell and Chloe Ann Boswell.
" 2. Benjamin Sedgwick and Susannah Nicholson.
" 5. John Bowman and Mary Hittle.
" 10. Richard Turner and Elizabeth Beall.
" 10. Daniel Carroll and Ann McCubbin.
" 12. James Hoben and Susannah Sewell.
" 12. James Collins and Nancy Whetzel.
" 13. Walter Jones and Elizabeth Harwood.

Jan. 15. Henry C. Wyvall and Ruth Duvall.
" 15. Jonas Austin and Ann Hoggins.
" 17. James Wilson Perry and Margaret Jones.
" 17. James Johnson and Ann Riney.
" 18. Jacob Snomley and Ellender Fluks.
" 19. Thomas Whalin and Ellender Carey.
" 21. John Adams, Jr., and Eleanor Colyer.
" 22. Charles Offutt Jones and Rebecca Offutt.
" 22. Thomas Gatton and Ruth Ray.
" 25. Benjamin Thompson and Elizabeth Hany.
" 28. Brice Lowry and Sarah Appleby.
" 28. Samuel Hedges and Eleanor McCoy.
" 29. John Trundle and Elizabeth Wells.
" 30. William Heath and Vorlinder Boswell.
" 30. William T. Beall and Eleanor Beall.
" 31. Rezin Shaw and Anna Crim.
Feb. 1. Richard Lewis and Elizabeth Beall.
" 4. James Groomes and Sarah Hing.
" 5. Daniel Ball and Elizabeth Carroll.
" 5. David Anderson and Margaret Thompson.
" 6. Richard Cissell and Charlotte Cissell.
" 6. William West and Nancy Offutt.
" 8. Walter Jenkins and Ruth Selby.
" 9. Abner Cloud and Susannah Smallwood.
" 13. Thomas Garrett and Elizabeth Fee.
" 13. John Austin and Casandria Odle.
" 18. John Arvin and Elizabeth Duvall.
" 19. Joshua Spurrier and Harriet Baker.
" 20. Thomas Sedgwick and Ann Atcherson.
" 23. Hezekiah Dison and Lucy Perry.
" 25. Carlton Belt, Jr., and Elizabeth Jones.
" 25. John Trundle and Mary Neatch.
" 25. Barroch Offutt and Nirlinda Offutt.
March 7. Brooks Edmonston and Deborah Orme.
" 14. James B. Crawford and Ann Allison.
" 18. Basil Waters and Ann P. Magruder.
" 20. Daniel Duty and Elizabeth Jinkins.
" 21. John George Baker and Amelia Jackson.
" 23. Levi Tucker and Susannah Collins.
" 28. Ignatius Jones and Viney Jones.
" 30. Stephen Bickett and Catharine Cliver.
April 2. Giles Easton and Elizabeth Nolen.
" 10. Thomas Hill and Eleanor Wheeler.
" 11. John Doran and Elizabeth Grantt.
" 11. John Nicholson and Tabitha Oden.
" 13. Charles Beatty and Vorlinder Offutt.
" 15. Tench Ringgold and Mary C. Lee.
" 18. Jessoll Leatch and Mary Litton.
" 22. Joseph Cope and Elizabeth Hennis.
" 25. James Davis and Anny Cisell.
May 10. Jonathon Gloyd and Hetty Limebarry.
" 20. Basil Trundle and Easter Hughs.
" 21. Edmund Riggs and Jane Willson.
" 26. Charles Griffith and Elizabeth Green.
" 29. Samuel Gatton and Mary Jarboe.
June 6. Samuel G. Jones and Mary Few.
" 12. George Warren and Sarah Ticker.
July 6. William Olliver and Rebecca Wilburn.
" 11. John Hymes and Virlinder Swain.
Aug. 5. Lenoard Piles Ozbun and Sarah Thresher.
" 7. Solomon Pelly and Massy Holland.
" 10. Nicholas Beckwith and Mary Butt.
" 28. Jacob Hoikman and Susannah Hall.
" 28. Jonathan Fry and Amelia Flatford.
Sept. 4. John Barney and Milly Brassford.
" 10. Richard Wells and Anne Belt.

Sept. 16. Washington Bowie and Ann Crabb Chue.
" 16. David Peter and Sarah Johns.
Oct. 8. Jacob Howard and Rachel Prather.
" 10. Laurence Lyddan and Mary Whealan.
" 14. Benjamin Dillaha and Rachel Slater.
" 24. George McCormick and Maria Bell.
" 25. William Wheeler and Ann Hill.
" 25. Thomas Warbough and Permelia Simpson.
Nov. 4. John Magruder and Mary Linthicum.
" 7. Joseph Fermelion and Sarah Hays.
" 13. John Hinchen and Margaret Brown.
" 13. Joseph Compton and Monarchy Tunnely.
" 17. William Levering and Susanna White.
" 20. Jesse Merchant and Elizabeth Dunn.
" 20. John Lyons and Sarah Welch.
" 23. James Bolton and Lucy Shaw.
" 25. Barton Harris and Elizabeth Casey.
" 26. Hardage Lane and Mary Greenfield.
" 27. John Wright and Elizabeth Downey.
" 30. Jonas Parsley and Eleanor Clayton.
Dec. 3. Rezin Darbey and Mary Waifield.
" 4. Ignatius Drury and Harriet Riding.
" 4. Nicholas Gray and Mary Hean.
" 5. Edward Douglass and Eleanor Maglue.
" 6. Henry Hewel and Rebecca Seaders.
" 9. James Magruder and Elizabeth Linthicum.
" 11. Barroch Prather and Casandra Swearingen.
" 12. Alexander Beall and Criscilla Harvey.
" 14. Azel Waters and Ercilla Holland.
" 14. Basil Moore and Anna Reindertz.
" 17. Jonathon Sparrow and Elizabeth Free.
" 17. Edward Godman and Sarah Douglass.
Dec. 18. Joseph Brown and Nancy Windsor.
" 18. John Perry and Jane Alnutt.
" 18. Thomas Stonestreet and Polly Nichols.
" 19. John Morris and Anne Green.
" 20. Charles Bevin and Sophia Moore.
" 21. Michael McElvane and Amelia Holland.
" 21. Hezekiah Vermilion and Elizabeth Gloyd.
" 21. Jonah Chamberlain and Susan Collins.
" 23. Richard Stewart and Elizabeth Remineton.
" 26. John Williams and Sarah Stone.
" 27. George H. Gloud and Elizabeth Boyd.
" 27. Samuel Gue and Rachel Mobly.
1800.
Jan. 1. William Ramsey and Margaret Herren.
" 2. Thomas Cook and Sally Maria Traverse.
" 4. Alexander Callico and Mary Sedgewick.
" 4. John Seaton and Ann Wise.
" 4. Giles Hill and Ann Newton.
" 9. Basil Poole and Ruthy King.
" 13. Edward Porter and Mary Heater.
" 14. John Laulam and Lucy Ray.
" 16. John Atcherson and Sylvia Perkins.
" 16. Camden Riley and Anne Ray.
" 17. Frederick Gaither and Jane Gaitrell.
" 18. Nathan James and Anne Buyton.
" 21. Nathan Orme and Polly Beall.
" 21. Ephraim Murphy and Mary Lewis.
" 21. Philip Cissell and Rachel Lizure.
" 21. Joseph Shelion and Julia Hill.
" 23. Solomon Holland and Margaret Gatton.
" 25. John Redman and Harriet Ward.
" 28. Benedict Beckwith and Elizabeth White.
" 29. Thomas James and Lydia Fowler.
Feb. 2. Benjamin Fowler and Judith Scott.

Feb. 5. William Brewer and Mary R. Chiswell.
" 5. Charles Mocklefresh and Elizabeth T. Chiswell.
" 10. Michael Harper and Rebecca Wheat.
" 22. Charles Williams and Elizabeth Shaw.
" 22. Philip Tosell and Mary Whealan.
" 22. Thomas Prather and Jenny Beall.
" 24. George Hoskins and Mary Read.

On June 2, 1812, Henry Harding was married at Rockville to Catharine Ann Robb by Father Plunkett.

On June 23, 1818, in Washington City, Judge Charles J. Kilgour, of Rockville, was married to Miss Louisa McIlhany, of Virginia.

On Feb. 22, 1844, in Barnesville, by Rev. M. Jones, the Rev. James C. Henning, of Methodist Episcopal Church, to Miss Alice Ann, youngest daughter of the late John Webster Wilson, of Baltimore.

A list of the officers of the county is given from the earliest period of which there is any record:

JUDGES OF THE CIRCUIT COURT.

Chief Judges.

1791, Richard Potts.
1793, William Craik.
1797, Richard Potts.
1801, William Craik.
1802, William Claggett.
1806, Jeremiah Townly Chase.
1826, Thomas Beall Dorsey.
1851, Nicholas Brewer (circuit judge).
1865, Samuel H. Berry (circuit judge).
1867, Madison Nelson (died Jan. 1, 1870).
1870, William P. Maulsby.
1870, Richard J. Bowie (died March, 1881).
1881, John Ritchie.

William P. Maulsby was appointed to serve until following election, as was also John Ritchie.

Associate Judges.

1791, Jeremiah Crabb.
1793, Benjamin Edwards.
1795, Thomas Plater.
1795, Richard Anderson.
1797, Charles C. Beatty.
1802, Patrick Magruder.
1803, William Holmes.
1803, Richard Turner.
1805, Richard Wootton.
1806, Richard Ridgely.
1806, Richard H. Harwood.
1818, Charles J. Kilgour.
1825, Thomas H. Wilkinson.
1838, Nicholas Brewer.
1867, William Veirs Bowie.
1867, John A. Lynch.

CLERKS OF CIRCUIT COURT.

1777, Brooke Beall.
1795, Upton Beall.
1827, Brice Selby.
1845, Samuel T. Stonestreet.
1851, James G. Herring.
1863, E. B. Prettyman.

SHERIFFS.

1777, Clement Beall.
1780, Simon Nicholls.
1783, John H. Nicholls.
1786, William Robertson.
1789, Benjamin W. Jones.
1792, Solomon Holland.
1795, Benjamin Ray, Jr.
1798, Benjamin W. Jones.
1801, Solomon Holland.
1804, Benjamin Ray, Jr.
1807, John Fleming.
1810, William Candler.
1813, Robert W. Fleming.
1816, Arnold T. Windsor.
1819, Brice Selby.
1822, William Clements.
1825, Henry Harding.
1828, Thomas F. W. Vinson.
1831, William O'Neall.
1834, Richard K. Waters.
1837, William O. Chappell.
1840, Henry Lilly.
1842, Thomas F. W. Vinson.
1843, D. H. Candler.
1846, William O. Chappell.
1849, William Thompson.
1851, Philip J. Connell.
1853, Matthew Fields.
1855, Silas Browning.
1857, John T. Benson.
1859, Samuel Gloyd.
1861, John T. Baker.
1862, Perrie Leizear.
1865, Zephaniah N. Jones.
1867, James H. Claggett.
1869, John T. Benson.
1871, Thomas Waters, of S.
1873, Edward H. Waters.
1875, Hilleary O. Higgins.
1877, Ambrose Clements.
1879, John H. Kelchner.

REGISTERS OF WILLS.

1777, Samuel West.
1778, Richard Wootton.
1779, Samuel Turner.
1808, Solomon Holland.
1839, James W. Anderson.
1847, Henry Harding.
1851, William Thompson, of R.
1857, Walter Adamson.
1858, John W. Spates.
1863, Robert W. Carter.

STATE'S ATTORNEYS.

1845, Richard J. Bowie.
1849, William Viers Bowie.
1867, George Peter.
1871, Spencer C. Jones.
1879, J. B. Henderson.

LEVY COURTS AND COUNTY COMMISSIONERS.

1799–1800.—Thomas Davis, Allen Bowie, John L. Summers, John Clarke, John B. Magruder, Charles Wayman, James Lockland.

1801.—Thomas Davis, John L. Summers, John Clarke, James Lockland, Thomas B. Beall, Adam King, Thomas Davis.

1802.—Thomas Davis, Allen Bowie, John L. Summers, John C. Clark, Henry Brooke, Æneas Campbell.

1803.—Henry Brooke, Edward Burgess, Richard West, Thomas B. Evans, Ozias Offutt, Henry Dorsey, Thomas Linsted.

1804.—Henry Brooke, Edward Burgess, Richard West, Thos. B. Evans, Ozias Offutt, Thos. Linsted, George Riley.

1805.—Henry Brooke, Edward Burgess, Ozias Offutt, Richard West, George Riley, Warren Magruder, Norman West.

1806.—Henry Brooke, Norman West, Richard West, Edward Burgess, George Riley, Warren Magruder, Robert Wright.

1807.—Henry Brooke, Edward Burgess, Norman West, Richard West, Warren Magruder, Henry Jones, Samuel Lane.

1808–12.—Norman West, Richard West, Edward Burgess, Warren Magruder, Henry Jones, Samuel Lane, James B. Brooke.

1813.—Henry C. Gaither, Richard Beall, William Darne, Thomas Gitting, Richard West, Thomas Fletchall, Lyde Griffith.

1814.—Jesse Wilcoxon, Richard Beall, William Darne, Thomas Gitting, Richard West, Thomas Fletchall, Lyde Griffith.

1815.—Eli Dorsey, Jesse Wilcoxon, William Darne, Thomas Gitting, Richard West, Thomas Fletchall, Lyde Griffith.

1816.—Thomas Gitting, Richard West, Lyde Griffith, Jesse Wilcoxon, Eli Dorsey, Benjamin Hussy, Alex. Warfield.

1817.—Thos. T. Wheeler, Thomas Gitting, Richard West, Lyde Griffith, Jesse Wilcoxon, Eli Dorsey, Alex. Warfield.

1818–19.—Thomas Gitting, Richard West, Lyde Griffith, Jesse Wilcoxon, Eli Dorsey, Thos. T. Wheeler, Alex. Warfield.

1820.—Richard West, Henry W. Dorsey, James Fletchall, John Busey, Thomas Anderson, Daniel Trundle.

1821.—Elijah Viers, Richard West, James Fletchall, John Busey, Thomas Anderson, Daniel Trundle.

1822.—Samuel Griffiths, Daniel Trundle, John Busey, James Fletchall, Richard West, Elijah Viers.

1823.—Richard Gitting, James Fletchall, Daniel Trundle, Samuel Griffith, Warren Magruder, Richard West.

1824–27.—Richard West, Richard Gitting, James Fletchall, Daniel Trundle, Samuel Griffith, Lloyd Magruder, Joshua Dorsey.

1827.—Richard West, James Fletchall, Daniel Trundle, Samuel Griffith, Lloyd Magruder, Joshua Dorsey, Roger Brooke.

1828.—Richard West, James Fletchall, Daniel Trundle, Roger Brooke, Horace Wilson, Henry Griffith.

1829.—Benjamin White, Richard West, James Fletchall, Daniel Trundle, Roger Brooke, Horace Wilson.

1830.—Joshua Dorsey, Greenbury Griffith, William C. Pearce, Burgess Willett, Wm. D. Poole.
1831-32.—Roger Brooke, Lloyd Magruder, Horace Wilson, Henry Griffith, Benj. White.
1833.—Lloyd Magruder, Horace Wilson, Henry Griffith, John L. Trundle, Edward Dawes.
1834.—Baker Waters, Lloyd Magruder, Henry Griffith, J. L. Trundle, Edward Dawes.
1835.—Thos. J. Perry, Edward Dawes, Henry Griffith, Baker Waters, John L. Trundle.
1836.—F. C. Clopper, Baker Waters, Edward Dawes, Baker Waters, J. L. Trundle.
1837-38.—Edward Dawes, Henry Griffith, Baker Waters, F. C. Clopper, Benj. White.
1839-41.—William Sellman, Henry Griffith, John T. Viers, Henry H. Young, Wm. C. Pearce.
1842.—E. W. Owen, C. H. Murphy, J. T. Viers, H. H. Young, Francis Valdenar.
1843-44.—Wm. Thompson, of R., C. H. Murphy, James Offutt, Elias Spalding, Francis Valdenar.
1845.—Francis Valdenar, Charles H. Murphy, Elias Spalding, William Thompson, of R., James Offutt.
1846-47.—C. H. Murphy, Henry H. Young, William Brown, Hazel B. Cashel, Benoni Dawson.
1848-49.—Zachariah Waters, Nathan C. Dickerson, Stephen M. Lyddane, Martin L. Gittings, John C. Gott.
1850-51.—John C. Gott, Benjamin E. Hughes, Nathan C. Dickerson, S. M. Lyddane, M. L. Gittings.
1852-53.—C. H. Murphy, S. M. Lyddane, John C. Gott, William Brown, Joshua C. Gilpin.
1854-55.—Julius West, Howard Griffith, C. H. Murphy, Nathan S. White, William Brown, of J.
1856-57.—Howard Griffith, William Brown, Samuel Riggs, of R., William H. Offutt, Thomas English.
1858-61.—Samuel Riggs, of R., John W. Shaw, William Chiswell, W. H. Offutt, William H. Spencer.
1861.—John T. Benson, W. A. Chiswell, William Groomes, John H. Gassaway, N. C. Dickerson.
1863.—Walter M. Talbot, Wm. W. Blunt, J. H. Gassaway, John L. Du Fief, Thomas Rawlings.
1865.—Thomas J. Holland, William Reid, Benjamin C. Gott, Joseph T. Bailey, Thomas Rawlings.
1867.—John L. Du Fief, Thomas J. Holland, Thomas Rawlings, William Reid, Benjamin C. Gott.
1869.—Thomas J. Holland, Solomon Dowden, E. G. Duley, Stephen M. Lyddane, Oliver H. P. Clark.
1871.—Samuel J. Cashell, Samuel Dowden, John H. Dade, Stephen M. Lyddane, Remus G. Dorsey.
1873.—Remus G. Dorsey, Horace Waters, J. H. Dade, S. M. Lyddane, Samuel S. Cashell.
1875.—David Griffith, Joseph Henderson, Richard G. White, John Saunders, Richard Cissell.
1877.—David Griffith, Joseph Henderson, Richard G. White, John Saunders, Thomas G. Hardesty. Jan. 3, 1879, Mr. White died, and William W. Poole was appointed by Governor Carroll to fill the vacancy.
1879.—George T. Waters, Solomon Dowden, William W. Poole, Joseph T. Bailey, Thomas G. Hardesty.

Joseph A. Taney, the efficient clerk to the board of county commissioners, has held that place for eighteen years.

Justices and Judges of the Orphans' Court.

1777-79.—Charles Jones, Thomas Sprigg Wootton, David Lynn, Edward Burgess, James Campbell.
1779-80.—Edward Burgess, Æneas Campbell, Joseph Willson, Charles Jones, William Deakins.
1780-83.—Charles Jones, Æneas Campbell, Richard Wootton, Joseph Willson, Edward Burgess.
1783-88.—Æneas Campbell, Richard Wootton, Joseph Willson, Edward Burgess.
1788-90.—Edward Burgess, Æneas Campbell, Joseph Willson, John Holmes, Richard Wootton.
1790-92.—Edward Burgess, Joseph Willson, John Holmes, Æneas Campbell, Lawrence O'Neale.
1792-94.—Thomas Cramphin, Thomas Johns, John Holmes.
1794-97.—John Holmes, Richard Wootton, Thomas Cramphin.
1797-98.—Thomas Cramphin, Richard Wootton, Benjamin Edwards.
1798-1800.—Thomas Cramphin, Richard Wootton, Daniel Reintzel.
1800-2.—Thomas Cramphin, Richard Wootton.
1802-3.—Richard Wootton, William Holmes.
1803-4.—Richard Wootton, Honore Martin, Samuel Griffith.
1804-10.—Honore Martin, Thomas Linsted, Robert Smith.
1810-12.—Honore Martin, Thomas Linsted, Walter B. Beall.
1812-13.—Thomas Davis, Richard Anderson, Brice Selby.
1813-14.—Thomas Davis, Henry Harding, Brice Selby.
1814-15.—Brice Selby, Henry Harding, Thomas J. Claggett.
1815-16.—Thomas Davis, Henry Harding, Thomas J. Claggett, Richard K. Watts.
1816-17.—William Darne, Henry Harding, Thomas J. Claggett.
1817-19.—Brice Selby, Henry Harding, William Darne.
1819-20.—Henry Harding, Thomas Lingan, William Darne.
1820-23.—Honore Martin, Richard K. Watts, Sr., George Magruder.
1823-28.—Honore Martin, Robert Wallace, Richard K. Watts, Sr.
1828-30.—Henry Harding, Willy James, Jesse Leach.
1830-31.—Robert Wallace, Samuel C. Veirs, John Adamson, Jr.
1831-34.—Henry Harding, Willy James, Jesse Leach.
1834-38.—Henry Harding, Jesse Leach, Thomas F. W. Vinson.
1838-39.—Henry Harding, Thomas F. W. Vinson, Philip G. Biays.
1839-42.—William O'Neale, Jr., Thomas F. W. Vinson, John Jones, of N.
1842-45.—Samuel C. Veirs, William O'Neale, Jr., John Jones, of N.
1845-47.—Henry Harding, Nathan Holland, Otho Magruder.
1847-48.—George W. Dawson, Otho Magruder, Allen B. Davis, Nathan Holland (*vice* Davis, resigned).
1848-51.—James W. Anderson, John Jones, of N., John T. Veirs.
1851-56.—Samuel C. Veirs, Otho Magruder, John Jones, of N.
1855-61.—Otho Magruder, John W. Anderson, Robert P. Dunlap, Hazel B. Cashell (*vice* Magruder in 1856).
1861-63.—Elijah Thompson, John W. Anderson, H. B. Cashell.
1863-67.—Samuel C. Veirs, John W. Anderson, William Thompson, of R.
1867-72.—William Thompson, of R., H. B. Cashell, A. H. Sommers.
1872-75.—Hazel B. Cashell, Edward W. Owen, A. H. Sommers.
1875-79.—E. W. Owen, A. H. Sommers, Samuel Darley.
1879-83.—Edward W. Owen, A. H. Sommers, R. G. Dorsey.

Officers in 1777.

Surveyor, William Bayley, Jr.; Coroners, Walter Beall, Simon Nicholls, Archibald Allein, Henry Gaither; Examiner-General, Francis Deakins; was appointed Feb. 16, 1782, examiner-general of the vacant soldiers' land, etc.

MEMBERS OF STATE CONSTITUTIONAL CONVENTIONS.

1776: First State Convention.—Thomas Sprigg Wootton, Jonathan Wilson, William Bayley, Jr., Elisha Williams.

1788: To ratify Federal Constitution.—Benjamin Edwards, Richard Thomas, Thomas Cramphin, William Deakins, Jr.

1851.—J. M. Kilgour, Allen Bowie Davis, Washington Waters, John Brewer, James W. Anderson.

1864.—Edmund P. Duvall, Thomas Lansdale, George Peter.

1867.—Greenbury M. Watkins, Nicholas Brewer, Samuel Riggs, of R., Washington Duvall.

MEMBERS OF CONGRESS.

1789-91, Jeremiah Crabb, Patrick Magruder, Thomas Plater; 1807-14, Philip Barton Key, Alexander Contee Hanson; 1816-20, George Peter, George C. Washington; 1849-53, Richard J. Bowie.

JUSTICES OF THE COUNTY COURT.

1777, Charles Jones, Thomas Sprigg Wootton, David Lynn, Edward Burgess, William Deakins, Henry Griffith, Elisha Williams, Joseph Williams, Æneas Campbell, Samuel Wade Magruder, Robert Owing, Francis Deakins, James Offutt, Thomas Cramphin, Richard Beall, Gerrard Briscoe, Allen Bowie, Charles Greenbury Griffith, Elias Harding, Richard Thompson.

STATE SENATORS FROM MONTGOMERY COUNTY.

1786, Benjamin C. Stoddert (elected, but did not accept); 1791, Benjamin C. Stoddert (he resigned, and Thomas Sim Lee elected Nov. 21, 1794); 1796, Uriah Forrest; 1821-24, Dr. John Wootton; 1831-34, Benjamin S. Forrest; 1836, Richard J. Bowie; 1838, Horace Willson; 1842-60, William L. Gaither; 1860-65, Washington Duvall; 1865, Thomas B. Lansdale; 1867, Isaac Young; 1868, Nicholas Brewer; 1870, W. O. Sellman; 1874, Nicholas Brewer; 1878, George Peter; 1882, Joseph T. Moore.

MEMBERS OF THE HOUSE OF DELEGATES FROM MONTGOMERY COUNTY.

1777.—Edward Burgess, Elisha Williams, William Bayly, Jr., Richard Crabb.

1779.—Edward Burgess, Thomas Cramphin, William Bayly, Thomas Sprigg Wootton.

1780.—Thomas Cramphin, William Bayly, Lawrence O'Neale, Charles Hungerford.

1781.—Edward Burgess, Charles Greenbury Griffith, William Bayly, Lawrence O'Neale.

1782.—Edward Burgess, Charles G. Griffith, Lawrence O'Neale, Benjamin Edwards.

1783.—Lawrence O'Neale, Benjamin Edwards, Edward Burgess, Thomas S. Wootton.

1784.—Thomas Cramphin, Lawrence O'Neale, Benjamin Edwards, Thomas Sprigg Wootton.

1785.—Lawrence O'Neale, Thomas S. Wootton, Thomas Beall, of George, Thomas Cramphin.

1786.—Edward Burgess, Lawrence O'Neale, William Holmes, John Hayman Nicholls.

1787.—Edward Burgess, Lawrence O'Neale, William Holmes, Charles G. Griffith.

1788.—Jeremiah Crabb, Thomas Cramphin, Jr., Lawrence O'Neale, William Dorsey.

1789-90, Edward Burgess, Jeremiah Crabb, Lawrence O'Neale, Uriah Forrest.

1791.—Lawrence O'Neale, Jeremiah Crabb, Francis Deakins, Thomas Turner.

1792-93.—Jeremiah Crabb, Lawrence O'Neale, John Threlkeld, Richard Wootton.

1794.—Lawrence O'Neale, Thomas Davis, David Luckett, Walter Brooke.

1795.—Thomas Davis, Edward Burgess, Lawrence O'Neale, Daniel Rentzel.

1796.—Daniel Rentzel, Elemeleck Swearingen, Lawrence O'Neale, David Luckett.

1797.—George Riley, Robert Swailes, Patrick Magruder, Robert P. Magruder.

1798.—John L. Summers, Robert P. Magruder, Elemeleck Swearingen, George Riley.

1799.—Robert P. Magruder, George Riley, Thomas Turner, Elemeleck Swearingen.

1800.—Robert P. Magruder, Thomas Davis, Hezekiah Veatch, Thomas Beall, of George.

1801.—Robert P. Magruder, Thomas Davis, Elemeleck Swearingen, Hezekiah Veatch.

1802.—Elemeleck Swearingen, Thomas Davis, Brice Selby, Hezekiah Veatch.

1803.—Elemeleck Swearingen, Thomas Davis, Hezekiah Veatch, John Linthicum.

1804.—Elemeleck Swearingen, John Linthicum, Brice Selby, Wm. Darne.

1805.—Wm. Carroll, Brice Selby, Richard Key Watts, John Linthicum.

1806.—Wm. Carroll, Richard Key Watts, Brice Selby, Wm. Darne.

1807.—Wm. Carroll, Wm. Darne, Benjamin Ray, Jr., John Linthicum.

1808.—Wm. Carroll, Henry Chew Gaither, Samuel Thomas, Jr., Hezekiah Veatch.

1809.—Henry C. Gaither, Samuel Thomas, Charles H. W. Wharton, Hezekiah Veatch.

1810.—Edward Owen, Henry C. Gaither, Abraham Jones, C. H. W. Wharton.

1811.—Abraham Jones, John H. Riggs, Edward Owen, Charles Evans.

1812-15.—Abraham Jones, Charles J. Kilgour, Richard J. Crabb, John H. Riggs.

1816.—Leonard Watkins, Zadock Lanahan, Richard K. Watts, George C. Washington.

1817-18.—Ephraim Gaither, George C. Washington, Benjamin S. Forrest, Ezekiah Linthicum.

1819.—George Peter, Ephraim Gaither, George C. Washington, Benjamin S. Forrest.

1820.—Ephraim Gaither, Henry Harding, Wm. Darne, Benjamin S. Forrest.

1821.—Benjamin S. Forrest, William Darne, John H. Riggs, Benjamin Duvall.

1822.—Archibald Lee, John A. T. Kilgour, Washington Duvall, Elisha Williams.

1823.—George Peter, Washington Duvall, John A. T. Kilgour, Elisha Williams.

1824.—Otho Wilson, J. H. Beall, Archibald Lee, J. W. Lansdale.

1825.—John W. Lansdale, Archibald Lee, Edward Hughes, Otho Willson.

1826.—Edward Hughes, Willey Janes, John P. C. Peter, John W. Lansdale.

1827-28.—Archibald Lee, John P. C. Peter, Edward Hughes, John W. Lansdale.

1829.—Thomas Gittings, Ephraim Gaither, Edward Hughes, Archibald Lee.

1830.—Henry Harding, Thomas Gittings, Horace Willson, Archibald Lee.

1831-32.—Henry Harding, Horace Willson, Thomas Gittings, Stephen N. C. White.

1833.—Otho Willson, John A. Carter, Stephen N. C. White, Henry C. Gaither.
1834.—Henry C. Gaither, Henry Harding, Thomas Gittings, David Trundle.
1835.—Robert M. Beam, Thomas Gittings, John W. Darby, David Trundle.
1836.—Henry Harding, John W. Darby, Samuel D. Waters, George W. Dawson.
1837.—Robert M. Beam, S. N. C. White, Henry Griffith, of L., L. A. Dawson.
1838.—Richard R. Waters, Robert T. Dade, Wm. M. Stewart, Wm. C. Wilson.
1839.—Wm. Lingan Gaither, Richard R. Waters. Robert T. Dade, John G. England.
1840.—John G. England, Thomas Gittings, Wm. L. Gaither, John C. Ott.
1841.—John W. Darby, John Braddock, Jr., John C. Gott, Thomas Gittings.
1842.—Lyde Griffith, Robert T. Dade, Alexander Kilgour, L. H. Worthington.
1843.—David Trundle, Alexander Kilgour, Lyde Griffith, Samuel D. Waters.
1844.—Wm. B. Howard, Samuel D. Waters, George C. Patterson, Alexander Kilgour.
1845.—Nathan Holland, James N. Allnut, George C. Patterson, Lloyd Dorsey.
1846.—Lyde Griffith, Nathan Holland, Washington Bonifant, James N. Allnut.
1847.—Thomas Neel, Alexander Kilgour, Washington Bonifant, James N. Allnut.
1849.—Washington Bonifant, Wm. T. Glaze, Stephen N. C. White, Alexander Kilgour.
1852-53.—Robert T. Dade, Alexander Kilgour.
1854.—Washington Bonifant, Washington Waters.
1856.—Charles A. Harding, Howard Duvall.
1858.—Washington Duvall, Nicholas Worthington.
1860.—Howard Griffith, Charles A. Harding.
1861.—(December session) Robert P. Dunlap, Allen B. Davis, (April session) Howard Griffith.
1862.—Allen Bowie Davis, Robert P. Dunlap.
1864.—Isaac Young, Benjamin F. Fawcett.
1865.—Benjamin F. Fawcett, Greenbury M. Watkins.
1867.—Enoch B. Hutton, Raymond W. Burche.
1868.—Samuel Riggs, of R., Nicholas D. Offutt, Thomas T. Conley.
1870.—George W. Hilton, John W. Veitch, Greenbury M. Watkins.
1872.—Samuel Riggs, of R., George W. Hilton, Oliver H. P. Clark.
1874.—O. H. P. Clark, Greenbury M. Watkins, John T. Fletchall.
1876.—Somerset O. Jones, William M. Canby, Howard Griffith.
1878.—William H. Canby, Howard Griffith, Montgomery Blair.
1880.—William Grady, Thomas J. Owens, George C. Patterson.
1882.—Thomas Waters, Joseph Dyson, John M. McDonald.

REGISTERS OF VOTERS, 1881.

First District, Albert G. Merriwether; Second, John H. Gibson; Third, William T. Jones; Fourth, Reynolds S. Patterson; Fifth, Samuel J. Hopkins; Sixth, Samuel W. Boswell; Seventh, Clayton Williams; Eighth, Robert M. Mackall; Ninth, James H. Claggett; Tenth, Oliver S. Maus.

DEPUTY SHERIFFS.

Samuel H. Jones, William B. Miller, John R. Miller, William O. Kingsbury, John Selby, J. M. Miles.

DEPUTY CLERKS OF COURT.

George R. Braddock, R. S. Patterson, A. D. Green.

JAILER.

W. O. Kingsbury.

SURVEYOR.

Charles F. Townsend.

CORONERS.

Edward W. Horner, M. J. Higgins.

OVERSEER AT ALMSHOUSE.

John P. Connell.

TRUSTEES OF THE POOR.

Gustavus Jones, J. A. Gloyd, Henry Pumphrey, H. Trail, Columbus Joy; Clerk, R. S. Patterson.

TAX COLLECTORS.

First District, John Allnutt; Second, J. L. Dowden; Third, Nathan D. Poole; Fourth, Joseph H. Bailey; Fifth, James L. Dorsey.

OFFICIALS IN 1860, NOT ELSEWHERE GIVEN.

Clerk to Commissioners, Uriah Forrest; Surveyor, James Anderson; Justices of the Peace: First District, Henry N. Harris, F. T. Browne, Benjamin R. Fish; Second, Joshua Purdam, P. M. Smith, James A. Crandle; Third, Samuel Darby, Samuel S. Hays, C. N. Mosburgh; Fourth, H. W. Viers, M. F. Harris, C. W. Lansdale; Fifth, Thomas Fawcett, Richard Cissel, James H. Brooke; Constables: First District, Richard Lowe, R. T. Mannake; Second, C. G. Waters, James Winroad; Third, Alex. E. Soper, James F. Poole; Fourth, John R. Miller, John Johnson; Fifth, H. O. Higgins, Jos. Hopkins; Road Supervisors: First District, William Thompson, of R.; Second, Obed Hurley; Third, Richard P. Spates; Fourth, William S. Wilson; Fifth, Nathan Shaw; Militia: Colonel, Lloyd Dorsey; Lieutenant-Colonel, J. W. Anderson; Coroner, Mortimer Moulden.

The Bar.—The following attorneys have been admitted to the Montgomery County bar, as shown by the "list-books" of the clerk's office:

1777.—Richard Potts, Baker Johnson.
1780.—Thomas Wilson Ridgeley, Jr., Luther Martin, Robert Smith, Davis Ross, William H. Dorsey, Edward Nicholls, John M. Gantt, John T. Mason.
1795.—James Johnson.
1797.—Henry Ridgely Warfield, William Claggett, Roger Perry, William Goldsborough.
1798.—Allen B. Duckett, Archibald Van Horn.
1799.—John Cottman.
1801.—Roger Brooke Taney, Francis Scott Key.
1803.—Philip Barton Key, B. S. Pigman, Richard K. Watts.
1805.—W. L. Brent, W. Chapman, Thos. Buchanan, Richard Ridgely.
1809.—Charles J. Kilgour, L. P. W. Balch.
1810.—Frederick A. Schley.
1816.—Henry Ashton, Mr. Boyle, W. M. Worthington, Zadok Magruder.
1821.—Charles L. W. Dorsey.
1828.—Lawrence A. Dawson, John J. Campbell, Richard J. Bowie, John Brewer, Samuel W. Beall.
1829.—B. S. Lear, John G. England (oldest member of the bar).
1830.—W. M. Stuart.
1831.—Richard S. Coxe.
1832.—Z. Collins Lee, Wm. H. Thompson, Joseph Braddock, Washington C. Calvert, Samuel W. Dorsey.

1834.—John H. McLefresh, P. Worthington, Edward Hammond, Robert W. Carter.
1835.—Reverdy Johnson.
1836.—James Brewer.
1837.—Joshua Morsell, Lewis B. Wootton, Somerrith Pinkney.
1838.—George C. Patterson.
1839.—John S. Tyson, E. A. Lynch, W. R. Harding, Wm. C. Gott.
1840.—William Viers Bouic.
1842.—M. H. Myerly, W. H. Dorsey.
1843.—W. P. Braddock, Robert Ould, Franklin Miner.
1844.—Hugh Carpenter, Jr., George A. Pearre, W. P. Preston.
1845.—John E. Addis, W. C. Brent.
1846.—M. G. Palmer, John T. Vinson, L. C. Valdeman.
1847.—B. T. B. Worthington, A. C. Campbell.
1849.—J. H. G. McCutchen, W. B. Chichester.
1850.—E. G. Day, W. T. Ewan, Edward Ewan, D. Ratcliffe, C. H. Petts, George Peter, Flavel S. Wootton, N. Brewer, Jr.
1852.—M. Thompson.
1855.—W. M. Merrick, J. E. Young.
1856.—J. W. Bittinger, Thomas Anderson.
1858.—J. F. Strother, John Pendleton, John L. Hays, E. C. Carrington.
1864.—Robert G. Thrift, D. E. H. Emary.
1865.—Edward Higgins, Thos. H. England, G. Fred. Mattox, Henry E. Wootton, Fred. J. Nelson, G. W. D. Anderson.
1866.—A. J. Smith, William P. Maulsby, Hattersley W. Talbott, John Bell Adams, Samuel A. Perry, John C. Parker.
1867.—J. Selby Clark.
1868.—Thomas Wilson, R. S. Davis, J. B. Henderson, Spencer C. Jones, A. H. Loughborough, Vestal Willowby, R. M. Williams, Fendal Marburg, Joseph H. Bradley, Grayson Eichelberger, Woodbury Wheeler, J. Randolph Quinn.
1869.—C. V. S. Levy, W. A. Gordon, Jr., Francis Miller, Thomas Donaldson, F. P. D. Sands, A. W. Wilson.
1870.—R. W. Abert, P. M. Moriarty, A. H. Hobbs, W. Veirs Bouic, Jr., Wm. Brewer, F. Schmidt, John M. Colby.
1872.—J. E. R. Wood.
1873.—John B. Brewer.
1874.—Charles Abert, Noah Bowlus, C. W. Beach, James W. Anderson, T. F. Miller, Charles Danforth, Edwin Linthicum, John C. Motter, J. V. L. Findlay, James McSherry, W. P. Maulsby, Jr., Milton G. Urner, John Ritchie, H. T. Taggart, J. F. Peter, R. Hawkins, G. Nelson.
1875.—G. T. Porter, J. H. Gordon, A. H. Blackiston, William Walsh, S. A. Coxe, Archibald Stirling, Jr., R. T. Semmes, William Price.
1876.—C. H. Stanbril, Montgomery Blair, James Doffly, J. P. Jordan, A. B. McKaig, Henry W. Hoffman, J. A. Cahill, R. H. Lerdon, Frank Almoney, J. W. Warren, C. H. Lawrence, Thos. J. McKaig, W. M. McKaig.
1877.—Washington Catlett, H. Hutton, H. P. Heath, William Bruce.
1879.—Sturges Davis, Fillmore Beall, Philip D. Laird, George R. Gott, G. E. Hamilton, Charles W. Prettyman, George E. Humes.
1880.—Richard R. Beall, J. F. Riley, Thos. G. Hayes, Lewis C. Smith, Thos. W. Brundige, Richard White, W. H. Manning, George W. Card.
1881.—John E. Smith, W. A. Hammond, W. W. Anderson.

The following records of important elections which have taken place in the county will be of interest to the reader:

Votes for Delegates to the State Convention of 1788 to adopt or reject the Federal Constitution.—Federal Ticket— Thomas Cramphin, 896; William Deakins, Jr., 894; Richard Thomas, 895; Benjamin Edwards, 891.

Anti-Federal Ticket—Edward Burgess, 313; Lawrence O'Neall, 312; William Holmes, 312; Henry Griffiths, 311. Total vote, 1209. Federal majority, 583.

Presidential and Congressional Election in 1789.—The first constitutional election for representatives to Congress and electors for President and Vice-President took place in January, 1789. The vote in Montgomery County was for eight Presidential electors—Chancellor John Rogers,[1] 320; Col. George Plater,[1] 322; Col. William Tilghman,[1] 321; William Richardson,[1] 314; Alexander C. Hanson,[1] 319; Robert Smith (attorney), 308; Dr. Philip Thomas,[1] 317; Dr. William Matthews,[1] 310; Jeremiah T. Chase, 5; Charles Ridgely, of William, 41; John Seney, 44; James Shaw, 38; William Paca, 40; Moses Rawlings, 6.

For Six Congressmen—Joshua Seney,[1] 353; Daniel Carroll,[1] 362; Benjamin Contee,[1] 318; George Gale,[1] 316; William Smith,[1] 310; Michael Jenifer Stone,[1] 278; George Dent, 84; Samuel Sterett, 37; John F. Mercer, 42; Abraham Faw, 2; William F. Murray, 42; Nathaniel Ramsey, 6.

Vote for President in 1856.

	Buchanan.	Fillmore.
Cracklin	161	220
Clarkesburg	159	304
Medley's	199	221
Rockville	359	256
Berry's	248	207
	1126	1208

Vote for President in 1860.

	Bell.	Breckenridge.	Douglas.	Lincoln.
Cracklin	205	130	44	3
Clarkesburg	313	163	17	
Medley's	210	187	23	
Rockville	260	384	9	
Berry's	167	261	6	47
	1155	1125	99	50

Majority for Bell, 30.

April 6, 1864, on the vote for calling a State Constitutional Convention, Montgomery County voted aye, 516; nay, 746.

October 12th, on the question of adopting the new constitution, the county voted aye, 422; nay, 1367.

November 8th of the same year, at the Presidential election, the county gave 496 votes for Abraham Lincoln, and 1542 for George B. McClellan.

Vote of the County for Governor in 1867.—Oden Bowie (Democrat), 1675; H. Lenox Bond (Republican), 320.

Vote of the County for President in 1868.—Horatio Seymour, 1745; U. S. Grant, 399.

Vote for President in 1872.

	Greeley.	Grant.
First District	310	391
Second District	281	314
Third District	456	384
Fourth District	637	408
Fifth District	437	452
	2121	1949

---

[1] Federalists.

Vote for Congressmen in 1874.

	Walsh.	Lowndes.
Cracklin	323	345
Clarkesburg	328	291
Medley's	504	345
Rockville	689	363
Berry's	399	388
	2253	1732

Majority for Walsh, 521.

Vote for Congressmen in 1876.

	Walsh.	McComas.
First District	392	394
Second District	379	323
Third District	598	365
Fourth District	898	465
Fifth District	586	551
Total	2853	2098

Vote for Congressmen in 1878.

	Peter.	Urner.	Resley.
Cracklin	214	246	6
Clarkesburg	330	367	2
Medley's	489	346	3
Rockville	526	315	5
Berry's	375	295	12
Darnestown	223	141	2
Bethesda	215	104	4
Mechanicsville	156	441	16
Total	2528	2255	50

Vote for Governor in 1871.

	Whyte (D).	Tome (R).
Cracklin	355	366
Clarkesburg	351	279
Medley's	484	346
Rockville	615	380
Berry's	452	462
Total	2257	1840

Vote for Governor in 1879.

	W. T. Hamilton.	J. A. Gary.
First District	276	233
Second District	367	311
Third District	455	345
Fourth District	511	316
Fifth District	374	305
Sixth District	213	150
Seventh District	184	103
Eighth District	212	417
Total	2592	2180

For Delegates.—William Grady, 2507; Thomas J. Owens, 2483; George C. Patterson, 2486; Joseph T. Moore, 2258; Upton Darby, 2327. Three elected.

For State Attorney.—James B. Henderson, 2551; James Dawson, 2197.

For Judges of Orphans' Court.—Remus G. Dorsey, 2553; Edward W. Owen, 2646; Abraham H. Sommers, 2534; William Brown, of James, 2266. Three elected.

For Clerk.—Elisha B. Prettyman, 2531; Philimon M. Smith, 2124.

For Register of Wills.—Robert W. Carter, 2635.

For County Commissioners.—Joseph T. Bailey, 2617; Solomon Dowden, 2579; Thomas G. Hardesty, 2535; William W. Poole, 2617; George T. Waters, 2623; Charles G. Porter, 2267. Five elected.

For Surveyor.—Charles F. Townsend, 2642.

Vote in 1880.

	President.		Congress.	
	Hancock.	Garfield.	Schley.	Urner.
First District	304	245	306	245
Second District	438	372	412	398
Third District	547	372	552	369
Fourth District	625	358	618	362
Fifth District	525	396	508	415
Sixth District	244	150	239	155
Seventh District	220	148	219	149
Eighth District	223	456	212	471
Total	3126	2497	3066	2564

Vote for and against Liquor License.

	For.	Against.
First District	255	267
Second District	279	463
Third District	344	512
Fourth District	404	544
Fifth District	282	608
Sixth District	103	275
Seventh District	120	234
Eighth District	114	534
Total	1901	3431

CHAPTER XXXIV.

EDUCATIONAL AND MISCELLANEOUS MATTERS.

The First Schools—Educational Statistics—Tobacco—Meteoric Shower—Patriotism of the People—Business Notes—Inns and Taverns—Centennial Celebration—Representative Men.

NOT much attention was given to popular education, or, more properly speaking, public-school education, in the early history of Maryland. The ancestors of the present generation were busily engaged in settling a new country. They made their money by toilsome methods, after having encountered great hazards and hardships. They were peculiarly self-dependent, and could not be taught the advantages to be derived by the community from the expenditure of their hard-earned substance for the education of those who were bound to them by no tie, and who had not aided in making it. King William's School was established at Annapolis in 1696 for instruction in Latin, Greek, and writing, and the trustees were styled the "Rectors and Visitors of the Free Schools of Maryland;" but their duties, aside from the management of the school in Annapolis, were probably not laborious. The masters of King William's School were required to teach as many poor children as the visitors should determine, but Annapolis, at that time one of the most important towns in the province, probably furnished as many scholars as this institution, with its limited resources, could instruct. An act of 1723 ordered the erection of public schoolhouses in all the counties, and there were schools established at several of the more populous and prominent points in the State; but it is easy to conjecture how impotent they were as auxiliaries to general education at a time when traveling was done on horseback and many of the most flourishing settlements were in the heart of the back country. The Assembly of 1763 declared that it was reasonable that education should be extended equally to the several parts of the province, and that there should be a public school erected in Frederick County, as well as in other counties. In order to build a house and other conveniences for a country school, it was enacted that there should be one acre purchased in Frederick Town, in Frederick County, and that Col. Thomas Cresap, Mr. Thos. Beatty, Mr. Nathan Magruder, Capt. Joseph Chapline, Mr. John Darnall, Col. Samuel Beall, and the Rev. Mr. Thos. Bacon be the visitors of the school, and are authorized to purchase the lot.

It was further enacted "that an equal dividend of the duties, taxes, etc., collected for the use of the county schools shall be paid to said visitors and applied to the purchase of said lots and buildings."

The school system, under the control of the Church of England, although tainted with the intolerance of the period, displays a commendable solicitude for the cultivation of the minds and morals of the youth of the colony. In the absence of collegiate institutions, private schools, conducted by learned men, ecclesiastical and lay, of all creeds, laid the foundation of scholastic knowledge. The more affluent youth were educated abroad, but the log school-house and the winter fireside developed the seeds of science in many minds, and produced a race of men possessed of extraordinary mental endowments and capacity for public affairs.

There was no literature in those days. But the public archives, the proceedings, courts, resolutions, and letters of public men embodied in the journals of the Convention, the legislation of the State immediately succeeding its organization as an independent sovereign power, the judicial opinions and the brilliant career of members of the bar educated before and after Martin, Pinkney, Wirt, Taney, Johnson, and men of that stamp attest that the fountains from which they drank were both pure and invigorating.

The first school of any reputation in Montgomery County was a seminary for young men in the Wallace or Magruder neighborhood, established towards the close of the Revolutionary war by James Hunt, a Presbyterian clergyman from Philadelphia, on his farm, called "Tusculum," now memorable as the Alma Mater of William Wirt. It was there that he was prepared, as far as scholastic training could prepare him, for that brilliant career which made his name one of the most illustrious in American annals.

Many of the families of that generation were educated there, and traditions and legends connected with them still cluster around the spot.

The next classical institution established in this county was the Rockville Academy, chartered in 1809, and the next the Brookville Academy, chartered in 1814. Both of these institutions are handsomely endowed by the State, and have been in successful operation ever since their foundation, and the refining and elevating influence they have exerted upon the youth of the county can scarcely be appreciated.

Many private institutions of learning of efficiency and reputation have since been established at Rockville, Brookville, Sandy Springs, Darnestown, and Poolesville, and the public-school system is the very best that could be devised. Involuntary ignorance is no longer possible, and ignorance of every kind is being rapidly eradicated.

Between 1830 and 1840 a general interest was awakened in regard to the education of the masses, and the germ of the present school system was very generally established in the counties of the State. In 1864 a cumbrous system of education was introduced, but its workings soon made it apparent that it was not fitted for the sections of Maryland embraced by it, and it was superseded or modified in most of the counties by the present method.

The following managers of the primary schools of Montgomery County met at the court-house June 19, 1839. Thomas Griffith, Benoni Dawson, and John A. Carter, the latter being made chairman. Uriah Forrest was appointed clerk to the board. The Legislature, at its session of 1838 and 1839, had passed an act establishing primary schools in the county, and had authorized the creation of this board to supervise the same. On July 8, 1839, the board divided the Third Election District into eight school districts, and adopted the division of the Fifth Election District into school districts as made by the commissioners in 1827. On Aug. 19, 1839, the board divided Rockville District, No. 4, into six school districts, and Medley's, No. 3, was slightly changed in its districts. The First and Second Districts, Cracklin and Clarkesburg, do not seem from the records to have come under this law, or had been divided into school districts by previous enactments.

The present free school system went into operation in this county in 1866, when the following board of school commissioners were selected: W. H. Farquhar, J. T. Dessellum, F. A. Dawson, J. N. Soper, Charles Abert. The secretary and treasurer was R. M. Williams. On April 29, 1868, the following

MONTGOMERY COUNTY.

board was appointed by the county commissioners: William Musser, B. B. Crawford, William T. Jones, Samuel Jones, R. W. Branch, with James Anderson as secretary, treasurer, and examiner. On Jan. 4, 1870, the following board was elected by the people: Samuel Jones, S. W. Davis, Edward Lewis, Isaac Young, Thomas Waters of S., who chose James Anderson as secretary, treasurer, and examiner. In January, 1872, the Circuit Court appointed the following board: Samuel Jones, W. T. Jones, and W. M. Talbot, who continued Mr. Anderson as examiner, secretary, and treasurer. In January, 1880, the court appointed the following board: Allen Bowie Davis, R. T. White, and Henry Renshaw, who appointed S. R. White as secretary, treasurer, and examiner.

The first law relative to free, or rather public, schools relative to this county was passed in 1827, but it proving seriously defective, gave way to the act of 1838 and 1839. This act provided for three managers, who had general supervision of all the public schools then existing or to be thereafter created. Some of the districts created under it were loth to accept the new system, and it never went into general or full operation.

The Teachers' Association of Montgomery County was permanently established on Sept. 8, 1881, at a meeting of teachers of which R. J. Green was secretary *pro tem*. The constitution and by-laws reported by the committee, William Grady, were adopted. These provide for holding four meetings of the association annually, on the first Friday after each regular meeting of the board of county school commissioners. Its officers consist of a president, vice-president, secretary, treasurer, and an executive committee of three. The first regular election of officers will be held on the first regular meeting of the school year, until when Messrs. Armstrong, Prettyman, and Venable were appointed to serve as the executive committee. Any white teacher teaching school in the county can become a member by signing the constitution and by-laws and paying an initiation fee of twenty-five cents, and agreeing to pay at each regular meeting a quarterly due of ten cents. The association is formed for interchange of views on teaching, improvements in school matters and discipline, lectures, discussions, and the general advancement of the teacher's profession.

The following is a summary of school statistics for the year ending Sept. 30, 1880:

Number of school-houses, frame	70
" " brick	1
" " log	11
" " stone	1
" fenced lots	7
Number of schools having outbuildings	76
" " " sufficient blackboards	78
" " " good furniture	78
" pupils for the year	4717

Receipts.

State school tax	$10,263.36
" free-school fund	2,672.26
" county school tax	9,349.44
Sales of books	422.08
State appropriation to colored schools	3,132.72
" " " "	1,044.24
Balance on hand Sept. 30, 1879	21.80
From collections on cash and orders	6,821.25
Balance to S. R. White, as per check	9.58
From various sources	354.00
	$33,291.41

Disbursements.

Teachers' salaries	$24,486.75
Fuel	467.82
Incidental expenses of school	254.86
Rent	60.00
Books and stationery	1,463.01
Interest	105.51
Salary of secretary, treasurer, and examiner in part for three years	2,748.44
Per diem of school commissioners in part for two years	364.40
Office-rent, furniture, seal, and fuel	47.22
Printing and advertising	71.25
Paid to colored schools	3,219.74
Attorneys' fees at Annapolis	25.00
Postage and stationery	26.89
Expense on bank deposits	6.47
Insurance on school-books and office	13.30
Expenses of school commissioners to Baltimore, 1879	48.00
Building, repairs, and furniture	170.38
Balance, cash on hand	5.97
	$33,291.41

COLORED SCHOOLS.

(Included in above, but here given separate.)

Receipts.

From State	$4,176.96

Which was disbursed for teachers' salaries, books, and other expenses.

Tobacco.—Tobacco was for many years the principal medium of exchange in the province and State of Maryland. Money was scarce in those early days, and the rate of exchange probably varied with the arrival of every ship. It was therefore necessary to settle upon some commodity which had an absolute intrinsic value on both sides of the ocean. Thus it happened that the salaries of officials, pastors, and teachers were always rated as so many pounds of tobacco, as were also the wages of mechanics and laborers. This was probably regarded as fortunate at that time, but no greater evil could have befallen the province. It gave an unhealthy stimulus to the cultivation of the tobacco crop to the exclusion of more necessary produce, and the very best lands in the State were rapidly exhausted by this veritable vampire and the injudicious tillage of the planters, the latter being unable to understand that land, like everything else, could be overworked. No county in the State suffered more than Montgomery from this cause.

In 1732 tobacco was made a legal tender at one

penny per pound, and one of the early acts prescribed a penalty of five hundred pounds of tobacco for a certain offense, and another a forfeit of two hundred pounds for Sabbath-breaking, another a fine of two thousand pounds for selling strong liquor on Sunday, except in cases of absolute necessity. There was a time when the cases of absolute necessity, as exhibited by the absolute prostration of the subjects thereof, were many, but these are now few in number, and the law for its rigid enforcement awaited the slow growth of public opinion up to the point which demanded and secured compliance with the requirements of the statute. A law, to be wise and efficient, need not necessarily be a reflection of public opinion,—it is often a teacher, an evangelist, to show the people their real need and duty. Another law imposed a fine of six hundred pounds of tobacco upon county clerks who should neglect their duty, and another regulated the rate in shillings and pence per one hundred pounds of tobacco, at which "fees and allowances, fines, forfeitures, and penalties given or made in tobacco should be computed;" that was twelve shillings sixpence. On a basis of dollars and cents, seven shillings and a sixpence, or sixty pounds of tobacco, were equal to one dollar. Students of advanced theories of modern as well as ancient finance will at once perceive the serious difficulties in the way of transacting business when the standard of value, the medium of exchange, was itself a commodity necessarily irregular, fluctuating, and unreliable, likely to be abundant at one time with a corresponding expansion in values, and scarce at another with corresponding shrinkage in other articles measured by it, with the usual embarrassment and distress. Another difficulty soon became apparent in the agricultural processes of the early fathers; the evils attendant invariably upon a system almost exclusively agricultural and the concentration of the productive energies of the people upon one article of produce came upon them. With few or no local manufacturing industries of any extent, and imperfect means of transportation over the "rolling roads" and bridle-paths of primitive times, it can readily be perceived that the early planters possessed few luxuries. The uncertain income from this one article of export and the fluctuation of the tobacco trade was one of the reasons assigned for the slow growth of the population of the province of Maryland under the royal government (after 1689, William and Mary of England). But after the first third of the eighteenth century people began to turn their attention to wheat-raising, and a mill for the manufacture of wheat-flour was built by James Brooke about 1737, near the junction of Hawling's River and the Patuxent. The ship-biscuit made at Brooke's bakery were consigned to agents at Bladensburg, Elkridge Landing, and Joppa, to supply vessels on their return voyage. An impetus was thus given to wheat-raising, and by 1774 the planters, instead of cultivating tobacco exclusively and awaiting the slow returns of European agents, raised wheat and corn for the market at hand, and as a contrast to the former meagre supplies and privations, there were brought into the stores of the large towns mathematical instruments, hardware, groceries, liquors, wines, glassware, fine and coarse linens, mirrors, India china dinner and tea sets, silk, satin, and brocade. Forty pounds of tobacco per head was at one time the tithe or tax levied for the support of the established church, and thirty pounds at another. In 1696, Mr. Gaddes arrived in the province, being sent out by his lordship the Bishop of London, and the Assembly appointed him to read prayers in some vacant parish, and made provision for his maintenance of ten thousand pounds of tobacco. In the same year the House concluded to build a church in Annapolis, and passed an act imposing a tax of "three pence per hundred on tobacco, to continue and be in force until the 12th day of May, which shall be in the year of our Lord God 1698, and to be applied to the building of ye church at Annapolis." As the population increased the revenue from the tax of forty pounds of tobacco became immense, and the tax was subsequently by law reduced to thirty pounds per head. After this law had expired an attempt to collect the old tithe of forty pounds was made, and strong opposition to its collection ensued. It was in regard to this matter that Charles Carroll and Daniel Dulany carried on their famous and sharp contests under the respective signatures of "First Citizen" and "Antilon;" the opinions of the former were supported by the people in the election which ensued, and their thanks were presented to him at public meetings held in Baltimore, Frederick, and Annapolis. All the court officers and other public officials were paid their salaries and fees in tobacco, and all taxes levied in this weed. Tobacco warehouses were established in various parts of the province and tobacco inspectors appointed,—all under the control of the Assembly.

As has been already said, the lands of Montgomery County yielded gradually to the strain of successive crops of tobacco, until at length it was discovered that the county, instead of making headway, was actually retrograding. This alarmed the property-holders. The culture of tobacco was in a great measure abandoned. Proper manures were utilized for strengthening the soil, careful tillage became the rule, and to-day there is no more prosperous county in the State.

Montgomery County Agricultural Society.—A meeting of the citizens of the county was held in Rockville, March 4, 1846. Otho Magruder was made president, Samuel Viers vice-president, and W. Viers Bouic secretary. The resolutions offered by Richard J. Bowie were adopted, viz.:

1st. That the interest of our county will be greatly promoted by the founding of an agricultural society for the whole county.

2d. That a committee of twenty-five persons from different parts of the county be selected by the chair to prepare the draft of a constitution for such an association, based on practical results, and to recommend such other steps as may in their judgment advance the objects of this meeting.

The committee appointed were, First District, Allen B. Davis, Roger Brooke, Sr., Dr. W. B. Magruder, Thomas Griffith, Ulysses Griffith; Second District, William Sellman, Dr. W. Waters, Lyde Griffith, Z. Waters, Samuel Blum; Third District, H. W. Talbott, William Chiswell, J. P. C. Peter, John Gott, John C. White; Fourth District, Nathan Loughborough, R. J. Bowie, J. T. Bayley, F. C. Clopper, G. M. Watkins; Fifth District, F. Valderman, Thomas Getting, Thomas Wilson, Edward Stabler, W. F. Stabler.

On June 1, 1846, the first officers were chosen: President, John P. C. Peter; Vice-Presidents, R. P. Dunlap, A. B. Davis, G. W. Dawson, F. Valderman, Dr. H. W. Wilson; Corresponding Secretary, J. Wanderson; Recording Secretary, W. Viers Bouic; Treasurer, Robert W. Cardiz; Executive Committee, W. H. Farquhar, S. C. Viers, Joseph T. Bayley, F. C. Clopper, Otho Magruder.

Since then the following have been successively chosen presidents: Allen Bowie Davis, Robert P. Dunlap, John L. Duflief, Richard J. Bowie, Joseph H. Bradley (who held the society together during the war and reorganized it at the close), Elisha J. Hall, John H. Gassaway, and Wm. S. Brooke.

The officers for 1881 were:

President, Wm. S. Brooke; Vice-Presidents, James C. Holland, James A. Boyd, Benjamin C. Goth, Dr. E. E. Stonestreet, John Bready, Wm. C. Hazel; Secretary, Charles W. Prettyman; Wm. Veirs Bouic, Jr.; Executive Committee, Joseph T. Bailey, Dr. F. Thomas, John E. Wilson, John H. Gassaway, George R. Rice; Commmittee of Reception, Wm. S. Brooke (president), W. W. Corcoran, Francis Valdenar, Charles Abert, Hon. W. V. Bouic, R. W. Carter, Geo. E. Brooke, O. H. P. Clark, Dr. William A. Waters, Asa M. Stabler, W. W. Blunt, N. D. Offutt, Ed. P. Thomas, George Peter, Hon. Montgomery Blair, H. C. Hallowell, U. S. White, Dr. Washington Waters, Capt. E. W. Owen, Thomas J. S. Perry, S. T. Stonestreet, John A. Baker, E. B. Prettyman, J. C. Holland, Americus Dawson, Hon. Elisha J. Hall (ex-president), Hon. A. B. Davis (ex-president), Hon. Joseph H. Bradley (ex-president), Hon. John H. Gassaway (ex-president); Chief Marshal, John A. Carter; Aides, Wm. R. Pumphrey, R. J. Lea; Assistants, N. D. Offutt, Jr., J. C. Bentley, Wm. Gilpin, H. H. Miller, Thomas Bailey, C. G. Wilson, Charles Veirs, Gustavus Jones, Jr., Frank Hallowell, J. L. Dowden, Ed. C. Peter, Granville Stabler.

Its twenty-eighth annual exhibition was held Sept. 7, 8, and 9, 1881, and was a creditable illustration of the progress made by the people of the county in everything relating to agriculture.

The grounds of the society are among the most commodious and beautiful in the State. They are located near the town of Rockville, and occupy some twenty acres.

No county in the State has given more careful and intelligent study to the development of the science of agriculture. The people of Montgomery are among the most cultured in Maryland, and for many years have seen and profited by the advantages of co-operation and interchange of views upon their paramount industry, the cultivation of the soil. At an early date farmers' clubs were organized in the districts and neighborhoods, and when the Grange movement was inaugurated the farmers of Montgomery enthusiastically welcomed its advent and enrolled themselves as members of the order.

In addition to their clubs and granges, a Farmers' Convention, embracing representatives of all the societies, and invited guests from abroad, is held annually, at which carefully-prepared papers are read upon the best methods of increasing the yield of crops or the proper management of stock; in short, upon all subjects having the remotest bearing upon the science in which they exhibit such pardonable pride.

The latest Farmers' Convention was held at the Lyceum, Sandy Spring, Jan. 18, 1881. The clubs and granges were fully represented, and there were a number of prominent visitors from Howard, Prince George's, and Washington Counties, and the State of Virginia. The officers were Henry C. Hallowell, president; Charles Aberts, Joseph T. Moore, John E. Wilson, Benjamin D. Palmer, Richard Waters, and W. B. Chichester, vice-presidents; Allen Farquhar, Charles F. Kirk, secretaries.

Maryland has generally been the pioneer in legislation looking to the moral health of her people. It is questionable whether self-interest or pure philanthropy has exercised a greater influence in the treatment of matters of this character; perhaps both have been controlling elements in securing legislation. Freedom of conscience caused an outpouring of emigrants of the better class from the mother-country.

Kind treatment of the Indians established confidence between the races, and enabled the whites to enjoy unmolested the possessions they acquired in the new province, and the punishment of drunkenness as a crime wrought a revolution in some localities which was highly beneficial to the material interests of the province. Tobacco was the staple, and in exchange for this commodity rum was introduced. Maryland tobacco became popular both in Old and New England. Old England sent brick for houses, clothing to wear, and implements to work with in exchange for it, and New England sent rum, molasses, codfish, and wooden ware. The Society of Friends were the first to see the evil of traffic in New England rum, and in 1688, as they could not reach those who manufactured the article, they advised their members not to trade for it nor to sell it to Indians. The bottle and Bible they said was an incongruous mixture. The Church of England soon followed in their footsteps, and drunkenness was declared by law to be a crime and punished as such. For non-enforcement of the law the magistrate was subject to a triple fine, and it was further enacted that any person who should revile the justice in the performance of his duty should forfeit five pounds, or be imprisoned one month without bail. The effect of this restraint was soon visible. Along with other operating causes it contracted the crop of tobacco, and led planters to the cultivation of cereals and the encouragement of domestic manufactures. In 1833, nearly two hundred years after the landing of the pilgrims in St. Mary's, the trustees of the Brookville Academy, an institution founded by the joint efforts of the Friends and the descendants of members of the Church of England, secured the passage of a law prohibiting the sale of intoxicating liquors in the town of Brookville or its vicinity, and their action has been sustained with singular unanimity by public opinion. The great shower of shooting-stars took place during this year, and great excitement was created in this portion of Maryland, many believing for a brief space that the end of the world was at hand, but it is nowhere recorded that this exercised any influence in hastening the passage of the bill.[1]

The citizens of Montgomery County responded with alacrity to the call of the country in 1812. The county furnished more than its quota of troops,

---

[1] The following account of a visit to an old Revolutionary hero, by Hon. Allen Bowie Davis, of Montgomery, and his graphic description of the meteoric shower which took place that night, Nov. 12, 1833, cannot fail to interest the reader:

"Five miles beyond Clopper's mill, on the Great Seneca, at early candle-light, I reined up at the farm of Charles Saffell, an old soldier, then eighty-four years of age, who had been a musician in the Revolutionary army. The old gentleman had a drum, fife, and fiddle, an old English musket, which he captured at the battle of Brandywine, and many other relics from the 'days that tried men's souls.' He was spending the calm evening of his long life in singing our long catalogue of heroes, yet unsung, and from his sweet flute, fife, and violin I ardently drank in the inspiring melodies of the Revolution. At the hour of ten o'clock I took the candle and a *row* of paper matches, about the length and appearance of a row of pins, and retired to a bed in an upper room. The matches were made by cutting out a piece of paper about three inches long and one wide, and making a dozen clips with a pair of scissors into one of the lower edges of the paper, so prepared as to extend about three-quarters of the distance across its width. This clipped edge was dipped into the combustible mixture, and when dry, all that was necessary to produce a flame was to tear off one of these clippings and draw its clipped ends gently along between the tip of the forefinger and the wall of your room, or over the surface of any rough substance. I struck the match, the first kind known in trade, and with a cheerful and glad heart lit the candle. I was soon under the cover, and yielded to 'tired nature's sweet restorer, but encountered a very singular and inexplicable experience, which I will mention, for I am writing facts, of which I ought not to be ashamed. The air being keen and frosty, three counterpanes were on the bed, and I slid under them, and made a survey of the surroundings in the dark room before trying my hand at sleep. On entering the room I discovered a wooden bolt on the door, and made it fast against intrusion; saw several chairs, other articles of furniture, and two windows only, over which curtains were hanging, one of them being at the back of the bed, within reach of the occupant. Trying my hand at sleep, I met with half success; but just at this stage of the proceeding, imagine my surprise when, by some unseen force, the three counterpanes were drawn violently from the bed to the floor. After recovering from my astonishment, I visited the ruins on the floor, recaptured the counterpanes, and coveted sleep once more. After a time I fell into a troubled doze, and down went the counterpanes again, with greater violence than at first. I sprang down after them, found the matches, lit the candle, and searched for the intruder, but no such party could be found, neither in nor under the bed, nor elsewhere in the room. I made up the bed again, got in, tried to sleep. After a long trial—I know not how long—I fell into a troubled slumber, but was suddenly roused by a terrific stream of unearthly light flashing through the window, curtain and all, and blazing over the room from floor to ceiling. Drawing the curtain aside, I beheld a great ball of fire, as large as the sun or moon, rushing from the direction of the zenith, and describing a circular or parabolic curve towards the far distant southwestern horizon. Hearing at the same time a great uproar among the servants down in the yard, I sprang from the bed to the next window, and looked out upon the great meteoric shower of Nov. 12 and 13, 1833. Rushing down into the yard, I saw a squad of frightened servants, so terrified, indeed, that they knew nothing save that the world was coming to an end. The old soldier appeared at the door, asked me to come into his room, and said it was nothing,—he had seen the like before. The shower continued until overpowered by daylight, the stars rushing down through space like snow-flakes, yet vastly more luminous. Fearful balls of fire shot madly towards the earth, like the pyrotechnic rocket shoots upward, consuming their substance in flight, or losing it by friction against the walls of air. Most of the meteors were as large and brilliant as the stars themselves, and it required no vivid imagination to suppose that these celestial bodies were then rushing to earth; for the which were under the command of Maj. George Peter, a brilliant officer and accomplished gentleman. At the battle of Bladensburg, in 1814, that most disastrous fiasco of modern times, the troops of Montgomery and Prince George's, under the command of Commodore Barney, aided by a body of seamen and marines, maintained their ground until they were overpowered by numbers and the commodore badly wounded and taken prisoner. The British proceeded to Washington, and burned the Capitol, the President's house, and many other buildings. President Madison was compelled to take flight, and sought safety in Brookville, Montgomery Co., whence he issued his dispatches. Among the interesting incidents connected with the British attack on Washington was the removal of the public archives to Montgomery County. Some panic-stricken citizens with half a dozen carts were moving out of the devoted city as the British fleet sailed up the Potomac. As they passed the War Office they were halted by a sentinel and the public records packed in the carts. The latter were driven rapidly to the old Rock Creek church under a guard of soldiers, and for several weeks, until all danger had vanished, the precious documents were faithfully guarded in that sacred edifice amid the tangled thickets and dense woods of the county, the citizens meanwhile providing the soldiers with the necessaries of life.

The feeling of uneasiness which prevailed prior to the breaking out of the great civil war in 1861 was keenly felt in Montgomery County. The citizens of this portion of Maryland were mainly descended from those who settled the wilderness in the seventeenth century, a hardy, determined, and educated people, likely to entertain strong convictions upon all matters of public interest, and to be willing and anxious to defend them when called in question. Their associations and sympathies were for the most part with the South, and, like the inhabitants of many of the older counties of Maryland, they had inherited from their ancestors strong States-rights principles. They did not, however, act with precipitation. Meetings were held and resolutions passed calling upon the patriots of both sections to use their influence for conciliation. When all hopes of a peaceful issue to the contest had fled, the young and adventurous flocked in numbers to Virginia and connected themselves with some of the many organizations then under arms to repel invasion. Among the large number who distinguished themselves on many bloody fields during the war it seems almost invidious to particularize, and yet a history of Montgomery County at this period would be incomplete without some mention of such men as Cols. Ridgely Brown, Elijah Veirs White, Benjamin S. White, and Gus Dorsey; Capts. Thomas Griffith, Festus Griffith, George W. Chiswell, and James Anderson; Lieut. Edward Chiswell, and Surg. Edward Wootton. Col. Brown crossed the Potomac at the

---

heavens blazed with an incessant discharge of fiery globes, that burst in countless numbers from the cloudless sky. Leaving the old soldier's house, I hurried on to Rockville, through Gaithersburg, looking all along the road for traces of the great phenomenon, some natural record or engraving of its occurrence, but could discover none, save in the eternal flint of words and memory. All whom I talked with on the way took a religious view of the case, none venturing an astronomical or meteorological solution of the great problem so suddenly sprung upon them. It was therefore generally believed that the time had come when 'the stars of heaven shall fall,' and when 'the powers of the heaven shall be shaken,' for the confusion was so great that not one could call to mind the fact that the great Egyptian, Grecian, Roman, and Jewish stars of empire and powers of heaven, referred to by the Great Teacher and Prophet, had fallen along the Mediterranean shores, to make way for other great stars of empire, climbing the canopy of nations, and holding their way westward.

"At Gaithersburg, and on the road from that village to Rockville, I met great numbers of people hurrying to and fro, that their knowledge might be increased. The theory that all the stars *were down*, and that not a luminary would blaze and twinkle in the heavens during the coming night, was generally supported by those who took a Biblical view of the matter on their 'own hook,' but such as had the least claim to common sense knew better, and sought an explanation somewhere outside of the lids of the Bible.

"About nine o'clock on the morning of the 13th I reined up before the old hotel in Rockville, and soon entered the bar-room, but I shall break down in the attempt to describe appearances in that room,—in front of the door, on the porch, in the street, and wagon-yard,—not that I did not see and remember well enough to do so, but that description was so beggared that no pen was, nor is, adequate to the task. I saw lawyers, physicians, ministers, farmers, wagoners, sportsmen in the chase and at the card-table, all repenting of their sins, confessing to one another, taking and denying positions, and covering up tracks. Certain of them confessed that when they first saw the raging meteoric shower cast its globes of fire to the ground, and against the outside walls and the windows of their room, they rushed from the card-table, cast their pack into the fire, and kneeled in prayer before a long-neglected throne of mercy. They prayed ardently, it is said, until the shower was overpowered by daylight; and, just as I entered the bar-room, I saw some of the accused coming down-stairs with elongated faces unwashed, uncombed hair, unbrushed clothing, unblacked boots, and caved-in beavers! One excited orator stood forth in the bar-room, and declared that every man who believed the big stars had fallen was a fool, for he had watched them during the whole time of the shower, and not one of them had forsaken its post in the heavens. 'When night comes,' said he, 'you may miss some of the little stars, but, my word for it, the big ones will be there.'

"Countrymen on their way to market declared that they saw great stars fall, explode, and bury their fragments in the earth. I soon left for Georgetown to gain experience there; and here, in conclusion, I remark, that persons grown up since the year 1833 can never obtain an adequate idea of the great meteoric shower, for it must be seen to be properly realized."

beginning of the war with twenty-three men and joined a Virginia regiment of cavalry under Col., afterwards Brig.-Gen., Thomas T. Mumford. He fought gallantly under this distinguished officer until the First Maryland Battalion of Cavalry was formed. He joined this regiment and was elected captain of a company, from which position he was promoted and made major, and upon the retirement of Cols. Smith and Howard, because of disabling wounds, took command of the battalion. He was killed in 1864.

Col. Brown has had few superiors in any age or country. He combined with exalted courage a rare degree of intelligence and a purity and gentleness of nature which would have been creditable to a Bayard. He was the idol of his men, and was the recipient of marked commendations from all the general officers under whom he served.

Montgomery County did not escape the vexations incident to the march of hostile armies. Both sides at times used her soil as a base of operations, and the farmers of that section on more than one occasion had cause to rue the day which had brought war with its train of horrors upon a peaceful and prosperous country. On the 21st of October, 1861, the ill-fated expedition which crossed the Potomac at Ball's Bluff was hurled back in disorder to the Montgomery side, and during that night the remnants were rescued from their perilous position in the centre of the Potomac by the First Maryland Regiment, under Col., afterwards Gen., John R. Kenly. In the latter part of June, 1863, the advanced guard of Lee's army, under Gen. Stuart, passed through the county, and the farmers were very generally stripped of their horses. In July, 1864, the forces under Gen. Early and Gen. Bradley T. Johnson marched to attack Washington, and the streets of Rockville were the scene of a spirited cavalry fight for several hours, which resulted in the Confederate troops holding the town. Several months after the foregoing, Capt. Walter Bowie, son of Col. W. W. W. Bowie, formerly of Prince George's County, an officer of Mosby's battalion, was killed in an ambuscade in Montgomery County upon his return from a raid in Southern Maryland. He was a gallant and dashing soldier.

Tavern-keepers Licensed in 1780.—Brock Mackbee, Elizabeth Riley, James Suter, Robert Owen, John Dowden, Ludwick Yost, John Beall, Jacob Reintzell.

Tavern-keepers in 1800.—Frederick Scholl, Henry Lansdale, Charles Rogers, William Dagrue, William Ogle, Theophilus Robey, Benjamin Gittings, John B. Medley, Christopher Coole, Adam Robb, Lewis Duvall, John Dells, Thomas Maccubbin, John Thomas, George Gloyd, John Thomas.

Storekeepers in 1800.—Honore Martin, Robert Smith, John Clarke, John H. Griffith, Joseph D. West, John Edwards, John Poole, Jr., Thomas Linsted & Co., Joseph Browning, Lemuel Shaw, John L. Summers, William Needham, Henry Gaither & Co., Peter Bouic, Charles C. Jones, Henry B. Harrell, Solomon Veirs, Edward Berry, Stephen Shaw, Richard James, William Willson & Co., Thomas Watkins, James Barnes, Lewis Browning & Co., John Getty, Edward House, Jeremiah Fowler, Thomas & Willson, Robert Wallace, John Penn, Henry Poole, Jesse Phillips, Charles Decanidre, John Henderson, Francis Ober, Levi Pigman, Robert Smith, Joshua Dorsey. The licenses of the tavern-keepers were six pounds per annum, and of the store-keepers three pounds.

Tavern-keepers in 1820.—Mary White, Andrew Graff, Joseph Neale, Osborn T. Willson, Elijah Martin, Mountjoy Scholl, Richard Butt, John McDonald, Benjamin Dritehett, John I. Bugh, Iver Campbell, William Spanow, Richard Ratliffe, Richard I. Bugh, John Minemiller, Mary Sands, Rodolph Magennis, Richard Spates, John Barnes, John Lansdale, James Syddane, Janaro S. Faire, Lewis Tabler, James E. Jones, John R. Griffith, Edward Clarke, Jane Gloyd, Richard Barnes, Nathan Trail, of William, Jacob Hoyle, William C. Veirs, John Lodge, John Adams, John Buxton, of Thomas, Levy Phillips, Joseph A. Murphy, Thomas C. Nicholls, Jasper Peddicord, Thomas Watkins, Samuel Hilton, Robert Crawford, Walter Stuart, Hezekiah Thompson, Hilleary Beall, Thaddeus White, Benjamin Perry, William Huddleston, Deborah Wallace.

Store-keepers in 1820.—Benjamin Burdett, Nancy Griffith, William Tucker, John Grantt, William T. Hempstone & Co., Thomas Anderson, William G. Penn, Evan Thompson, George Gassaway, Leonard Hays, Sr., John Braddock, Walter Stuart, Frederick and Richard Bowman, Mordecai Purdum, John Adamson, Jr., Camden R. Nicholls, Samuel C. Veirs, Richard Poole, Patrick Syddane, Benjamin Curran, William H. Hempstone, John Poole, Sr., Philemon Plummer, Overton Williams, Fielder Darnell, Leonard Green, Dennis Lachland, Basil Macgill, Benjamin Perry, John Candler, Henry Griffith, Samuel P. Richardson, Daniel Duvall, George W. Riggs.

The tavern rates in 1820, as established by the County Court, were as follows:

Breakfast for a Gentleman	$0.37½
" " Servant	25
Hot dinner for a Gentleman	50
Cold " " "	37½
Hot " " Servant	33⅓
Cold " " "	25
Madeira Wine per quart	1.25
Sherry " "	1.25
Port " "	1.00
Claret " "	1.00
All low wines "	75
Porter "	25
Country Porter "	25
" Strong beer "	12½
Small beer "	6¼
Cyder "	10
Spirit per gill	10
Rum "	10
French brandy per gill	12½
Whisky "	6¼
Oats or corn per gallon	12½
Stablage and hay 24 hours	37½
Lodging with clean sheets	25
Toddy made of spirit per quart	12½
Punch per quart	37½
Supper for a gentleman	50
" " Servant	25

Gold-Mines.—As far back as 1827, Prof. Ducatelle, a mineralogist of great note, declared that the region near the Great Falls, in Montgomery County, gave strong indications of the presence of gold. A few years afterwards, when Mrs. Trollope was writing out her notes upon American manners, while on a visit at the residence of Miss Stone, a German consul, Mr. Hitz, found traces of gold. About 1865 a gold-hunter from the Pacific slope found samples of free gold, and soon after a company purchased a tract of land, secured numerous samples, and commenced operations, but the quartz contained no gold. Another company sunk several shafts on the Forrest property, but failed to find gold in paying quantities. A company from Washington and Baltimore sunk a shaft one hundred feet deep on the canal. In October, 1869, a nugget of alluvial gold worth by estimation one hundred and seventy-five dollars was discovered on the farm of Robert Davidson, and was sent to the General Land Office for examination. It weighed nine and four-tenths ounces, eight pennyweights, and eleven grains. It was three and three-eighths inches in length, two and six-eighths in width, and averaged about one-half of an inch in thickness. The matrix was hard granite quartz, which was browned by the decomposition of iron pyrites.

In general aspect the quartz resembled that which was found and excavated from the ledge worked for some time by a company in the vicinity of the Great Falls, and corresponded in every respect with samples of gold-bearing quartz from the county previously deposited in the cabinet of the Land Office. The nugget was hardly covered with earth, in a loose, gravelly loam, resting on auriferous pieces of quartz.

The character of the rocks of this county is well exhibited by the section of them made by the Baltimore and Ohio Railroad. Beginning near Ellicott Mills, on the Patapsco River, in a perfect nest of granite traps and hornblende rocks, it is but a short space before an interruption of serpentine rocks is arrived at, which formation in another part of the State yields valuable deposits of chrome ore. Then more hornblende rocks, steatite, zalc slate, and granite, in which connection it is supposed the gold deposits exist. Where the rocks in their southwestern course cross at the Great Falls, it has been a periodical occurrence to find gold quartz, and the late Prof. Hitchcock, of Williams College, Massachusetts, after a visit to that remarkable place, said that the rocks are identical with the most celebrated auriferous deposits of other countries. Besides the geological features above referred to, this county has other claims to consideration from capitalists in the deposits of magnesian mineral for making epsom salts and calcined magnesia; in its beds of porcelain clay, or kaolin, for making queensware crockery; in its limestone and soapstone quarries, the latter giving employment to large works in Baltimore in preparing it for hearths, tables, shelves, linings for grates, bath-tubs, etc.; rich deposits of copper, magnetic oxide of iron, plumbago; and at Seneca Creek, the famous freestone quarries which in this part of the country supply the same material for buildings which in the East is derived from the Connecticut Valley. In 1870, ex-Governor McClurg, a member of Congress from Missouri, caught the gold fever, but after much prospecting gave up the effort. So it may be safely said that within the short period of five years over one hundred thousand dollars were spent in the county in searches for gold, all of which turned out to be a permanent and worthless investment. In 1871 a lad (the son of Robert G. Davidson), while herding some cattle on his father's farm, picked up a stone four or five inches long which contained free gold, and sold for one hundred and sixty-five dollars and forty-five cents. This led to further examination, and a rock of twelve to fourteen inches was discovered containing seven hundred dollars in gold. Mr. Davidson pursued his mining until 1876, when work was stopped, the results being unsatisfactory.

Three or four years ago, Mr. Davidson sold sixty-five acres to Bartlett, Merritt, Jones & Co., for seven thousand dollars. These gentlemen, after working a while, sold to a party in Baltimore, who formed a company known as the "Montgomery Mining Company," and William H. Brown, an extensive druggist in Baltimore, was elected president, under whose management the work was pushed vigorously. They had some thirty hands at work, sunk five shafts, varying from twenty to eighty feet in depth, from which thousands of tons of ore were taken. Two steam-engines of fourteen horse-power were kept constantly going. Various outbuildings, boarding-houses, superintendent's house, and stables were erected. A large stamp-mill, "Knowl's patent," was in full operation, and from this mill the gold bars were taken to the government mint for refining and stamping. H. C. Harrison, a miner of many years experience in Nevada, had entire superintendence and management of the works.

In May, 1879, Mr. Ellicott contracted to sell his farm to a gold company in New York for thirty-five thousand dollars, he investing one-fifth of the same in the company's stock, and arrangements were being matured for working the mine. The company failed to comply with the agreement, although their time was extended to June 9th. A large load of the ore was taken from this farm and sent to Philadelphia for examination, the company not being satisfied with the partial one made by Prof. Emmons, of Albany, N. Y. In the spring of 1880 a wealthy citizen of Pittsburgh paid a visit to the gold-mines, and, in company with another Pittsburgh capitalist, purchased a large interest in the company, and secured the adjoining farm of two hundred and four acres on the north. A mill with ten stamps was erected, and steam took the place of hand in bringing up the product of the mine. He at once commenced active operations. H. C. Harrison, an experienced miner from the West, was engaged as superintendent, and a force of men put to work deepening the shaft, which had already been sunk a short distance. Houses were built, and all the appliances of a gold-mine put to work within a few miles of the nation's capital. For some time the farmers did not object to a stranger prospecting for gold, but subsequently this was changed, and every farm was for sale and intruders kept off. The prices were not so exorbitant as one would expect from the promising development made in the vicinity. The Acker estate was sold to a Pittsburgh gentleman. The vein, according to the testimony of experts, ran a little east of north, diagonally across this estate, and thence into a farm of two hundred acres owned by Mr. Fawcett, who sold it to five men, three of whom were interested in the Montgomery mine, for sixteen thousand dollars.

The citizens of Montgomery County, in response to the resolutions adopted at a previous public meeting, assembled on the fair-grounds at Rockville, Sept. 6, 1876, to celebrate the centennial anniversary of the organization of the county. The following is a list of the committee in charge of the celebration:

A. B. Davis, chairman; W. W. Blunt, Dr. Nicholas Brewer, H. C. Hallowell, E. B. Prettyman, H. W. Talbott, J. T. Moore, I. Young, M. Wilson, Washington Bowie, Mrs. C. J. Maddox, Miss Rebecca D. Davis, Mrs. Dr. W. A. Waters, Miss Susan Dawson, Mrs. Mary B. Thomas, Misses Nannie Wootton, Ella Bowie, Mary Bowie, Jennie Hodges, Sallie Peter, E. Darne, Laura Muncaster, Grace Green, I. Anderson, Bookie Russell, Cora Stover, M. Dawson, Della Mans, Mollie Dice, Agnes Bailey, Blanch Braddock, Maggie Fields, Sidonia Pumphrey, Lillie Campbell, Mary Higgins, Nannie McCormack, Belle Almoney, T. Benning, Sallie Benning, Ida Adamson, Emma Kleindienst, Nannie Williams, and Estelle Bouie, William Brewer, Hon. W. Veirs Bouie, Sr., George Peter, Charles Albert, James B. Henderson, and Spencer C. Jones. The following gentlemen composed the executive committee: A. B. Davis, Esq., chairman; William Blunt, E. B. Prettyman, secretary; W. Viers Bouie, treasurer.

In addition to the speaking and festivities, it was determined to collect as many " centennial relics" as could be found and place them on exhibition.

The spacious building where were deposited in glass cases the various and antique curiosities which had been brought out for exhibition was crowded to its utmost capacity. Among the articles exhibited were several relics of Gen. Washington, the authenticity of which were unquestionable, among them a lock of his hair, a piece of wood from one of his coffins, autograph letters, also old chinaware, some pieces of which were rendered very interesting by the spicy inscriptions, which showed the bitter hostility of the makers to the famous Stamp Act.

Among the prominent citizens of the county present were Montgomery Blair, William Brewer, E. J. Hall, Caleb Stabler, Rev. Mr. Averitt, V. S. White, Sr., William Brown, R. R. Waters, S. T. Stonestreet, Hon. George A. Pearre, of Allegany County, John S. Miller, Francis Valdeman, Robert Peter, W. H. Talbott, Rev. J. F. Macken, John H. Clagett, Jr., Dr. Turner Wootten, Edward Higgins, Edward W. Owen, Dr. Wash. Waters, Col. J. W. Anderson, Elbert Perry, Hon. Joseph H. Bradley, Nathan Clagget, Capt. Thomas Griffith, George E. Brooke, Col. John H. Dade, Gustavus Jones, Samuel Riggs, of R., Samuel Higgins, Henry Renshaw, J. F. D. Magruder, Rev. D. Mason, Rev. R. T. Brown, Rev. John C. Dice, Nicholas Dawson, Dr. Cephas F. Willett, Pennel Palmer, Francis Miller, J. A. Taney, J. Purdum, and Mr. Tchaffaly.

At 11.45 A.M. Mr. Davis called the assembly to order, when a quintette of males sang "O Lord we are Thy people." The Rev. B. Barry, eighty-six years of age, the oldest minister of the Baltimore Conference, offered a touching prayer, concluding with the "Lord's Prayer," which was recited in concert by the people. Hon. A. B. Davis next delivered an address, and was followed by T. Anderson, who read an able, concise, and very interesting historical sketch of the county, to which the author of this volume is indebted for much valuable information. Henry C. Hallowell recited a beautiful poem prepared by himself for the occasion. The next thing in order was dinner, which was a most enjoyable feast, after which Judge Richard J. Bowie delivered an interesting address. Brief addresses were also made by Judge Pearre, Judge Jones, and Rev. Mr. Averitt. During the day Charles Abert read a number of letters received from well-known gentlemen, natives of Montgomery, giving reasons for inability to be present at the first centennial of the county. Nearly all the writers took occasion to express their warm love for the county. Among the clergymen present were Rev. Father Macken, of the Catholic Church, Rev. Mr. Brown, of the Episcopal Church, Rev. Mr. Averitt, and also the Rev. Mr. Brown, of the Methodist Church. At the close Dr. Wilson Magruder, leader of the choir, sang the doxology, and all joined in. Rev. Mr. Barry concluded the exercises by pronouncing the benediction.

Representative Men.—As has been already hinted in these pages, Montgomery County was favored with a superior class of settlers, the characteristics of some of whom will doubtless interest the reader.

Benjamin Stoddert, an eminent patriot, was born in Maryland in 1751, and died at Bladensburg, Dec. 17, 1813. He was a captain at the battle of Brandywine, and afterwards major in the Revolutionary war. He was the first Secretary of the United States Navy. For many years he was extensively engaged in mercantile pursuits in Georgetown, D. C. He continued Secretary of the Navy until Jan. 26, 1802. His father, Capt. Stoddert, was an old Indian fighter in Western Maryland, and gave his name to Fort Stoddert, in the West, before the Revolution.

Daniel Carroll, cousin of Charles Carroll of Carrollton, was born in Maryland, and died at Washington, D. C., in 1849, at a great age. He was a delegate to Congress from 1780 to 1784, and was a delegate from Maryland to the convention which framed the Constitution of the United States. He was a member of Congress in 1789–91, and was, in the latter year, appointed one of the commissioners for laying out the District of Columbia. His farm formed the site of the present city of Washington. His father, Daniel Carroll, died at Upper Marlboro', Feb. 27, 1751. In November, 1770, Charles Carroll, barrister, conveyed by deed of trust to H. Rozier, Notley Young, and Daniel Carroll one hundred and sixty acres of land, lying near the Eastern Branch of the Potomac River, for the purpose of laying out a town to be called Carrollsburg, now a part of Washington City. It was divided into two hundred and sixty-seven lots, with streets, lanes, alleys, and a public square of four acres for the use of the town. The terms of the sale were that each subscriber was to pay to the trustees six pounds sterling in bills of exchange or cash, for which he was to receive a ticket signed and numbered by them, which was to indicate the lot the holder was entitled to. Upon the receipt of this the holders of the tickets were to receive a deed in fee-simple from the trustees for the lot so drawn. Mr. Carroll reserved for himself six lots. The following notice appears in the *Maryland Journal* of Dec. 15, 1789:

"Mr. Daniel Carroll, Jun., of Montgomery County, being in a very infirm state of health, has thought proper to convey, in Trust, to the Subscribers his Estate, real and personal. His Creditors are requested to make known to the Trustees their several demands against the said Daniel Carroll, Jun.

"NOTLEY YOUNG,

"GEORGE DIGGES, *Trustees*."

Henry Gaither, a gallant soldier, was born in Montgomery County in 1757, and died at Georgetown, D. C., June 22, 1811. He was a captain in the Revolutionary army, and engaged in nearly every important battle of the war. He was appointed major of the "Levies of 1791," and served under Gen. Arthur St. Clair in his unfortunate expedition against the Miami Indians, which terminated in "St. Clair's Defeat," in November, 1791, in the Northwest Territory (Ohio). He was lieutenant-colonel of the third sub-legion from October, 1793, to June 1, 1802. He was a good soldier and an excellent disciplinarian. Gen. William Lingan Gaither, a prominent politician of Maryland, frequently a member of the Legislature, and president of the State Senate, was his son. He died in Montgomery County, Aug. 2, 1858.

Ninian Edwards was born in Montgomery County, Md., March, 1775, and was graduated at Dickinson College, Pennsylvania. He studied both medicine and law, and devoted himself to the practice of the latter. He removed to Kentucky, and was twice elected to the Legislature. He was appointed a circuit clerk, and afterwards judge of the General Court of Kentucky, of the Circuit Court, and of the Court of Appeals, and finally chief justice of the State, all of which appointments he received before he was thirty-two years of age. President Madison in 1809 appointed him governor of the Territory of Illinois, to which office he was three times reappointed. Before Congress adopted any measures of defense, Governor Edwards organized companies, supplied them with arms, built stockade forts, and established a line of posts from the mouth of the Missouri to the Wabash River. His Territory was thus prepared for defense. In 1816 he was appointed a commissioner to treat with the Indian tribes. When Illinois was admitted into the Union, he was elected a senator in Congress, serving from 1818 to 1824, when he was appointed minister to Mexico, but declined. In 1826 he was elected governor of the State of Illinois, which office he filled until 1831. He died of cholera, July 20, 1833.

Jared Williams was born in Montgomery County, Md., March 4, 1766, and died in Frederick County, Va., Jan. 2, 1831. He was elected to the Virginia House of Delegates in 1811, and served several terms. He was a representative in Congress from Virginia from 1819 to 1825; Presidential elector in 1829, and voted for Gen. Jackson, and was appointed by the Electoral College to transmit the vote to Washington.

John W. Jones was born at Rock Creek, Montgomery Co., Md., April 14, 1806. He was carried by his father to Kentucky, and educated at Carlisle Seminary. He attended the lectures at the Pennsylvania Academy, and received the degree of Doctor of Medicine from Jefferson College. In 1840 he was elected to the Georgia Legislature, and was a representative in Congress from 1847 to 1849. He was also a medical professor in the Atlantic Medical College. He enjoys the reputation of having done much for the cause of education in the States of Georgia and Alabama, of the latter of which he was at one time a citizen.

Patrick Magruder was born in Montgomery County, Md., in 1768, and was educated at Princeton College. He was a representative in Congress from Maryland from 1805 to 1807, and was clerk of the United States House of Representatives from 1807 to 1815, performing at the same time the duties of librarian. He died in Petersburg, Va., in 1819 or 1820.

James Dunlap was born in Georgetown, D. C., March 28, 1793, graduated at Princeton in 1811, and studied law with Francis S. Key, with whom he was afterwards associated in the practice, and acted as district attorney in 1833. He was recorder of Georgetown in 1838, appointed judge of the United States Circuit Court in 1845, and chief justice in 1856, and until 1863, when the court was abolished. His opinion in the admiralty case of the "Tropic Wind" attracted very great attention in the profession at home and abroad, and was complimented by Lord John Russell. He died near Georgetown, May 6, 1872.

Philip E. Thomas has been already noticed as the founder, and for many years as president, of the Baltimore and Ohio Railroad.

Mrs. Ann Poultney, relict of the late Charles Poultney, and sister of Philip E. Thomas, was remarkable for her culture, piety, and refinement. She was a prominent member and speaker of the Society of Friends.

Col. John Berry participated in the defense of Fort McHenry, Baltimore, when bombarded by the British in 1814, and whose well-directed guns caused the British to weigh anchor and drop down the river out of the reach of the artillery of the fort. For his gallantry on this occasion he attracted the attention of Maj.-Gen. Winfield Scott, and was offered promotion and a transfer to another important military post. He preferred, after successfully defending his adopted city, to return to private life, and devoted himself to the development of the patent fire-brick with his brother, Thomas L. Berry, which proved eminently successful and profitable. He accumulated a large fortune, leaving as his representatives Gen. John Sommerfield Berry and John Hurst, the successful dry-goods merchant, and president of the National Exchange Bank.

Elisha Riggs was for many years the head of the well known firm of Riggs, Peabody & Co., on Baltimore Street, near Hanover, afterwards Peabody, Riggs & Co., on German Street, in Baltimore, the elder partner moving to New York after aiding and establishing the well-known firm of Corcoran & Riggs, of Washington. He died leaving a fortune of a million and a half of dollars. George Peabody, at one time his clerk, afterwards his partner, had in the mean time removed to London, where in his successful efforts to maintain and uphold the credit and integrity of Maryland he laid the foundations of his own colossal fortune.

Samuel Riggs was the junior member of the same firm. He died in early life, leaving a fortune of three hundred thousand dollars.

John C. Clark, a native of this county, was a well-known merchant and banker in Baltimore. He left a large fortune of four hundred thousand dollars to St. John's Independent Church, on Liberty Street, which was removed to a magnificent site and a new church built on Madison Avenue, near the park.

George R. Gaither, of Baltimore, was also a native of this county. His large and handsome stores and warehouses on Baltimore, Hanover, German, Howard, Charles Streets, and elegant dwelling-houses on Cathedral Street, entitle him to be numbered among Baltimore's most opulent and substantial citizens. He left a very large fortune.

Israel H. B. A. and R. R. Griffith, from the same neighborhood, for many years flourished as successful merchants of Baltimore. Upon the death of the first named, investments in stocks and bonds to the amount of $445,000, it is said, were found in a trunk under his bed.

Rev. Thomas McCormick carried butter to market in the first refrigerator ever made, of which Thomas Moore, a member of the Society of Friends, then living in the neighborhood of Brookville, was the inventor, and for which he took out a patent about 1803. The first model was of small size, made for the purpose of carrying butter to market on horseback, as most of the marketing was done in that way in those days. The refrigerator consisted of a cedar tub of oval form, and about eighteen or twenty inches deep; in this was placed a tin box with the corners square, which would contain twenty-two prints of butter of one pound each, leaving space on each side between the tin and the wood for ice in small lumps. The outside of the wooden box was covered with rabbit-skin with the fur on, and over that was a covering of coarse woolen cloth. In this first refrigerator the butter was carried on horseback to the market at

Georgetown, D. C., a distance of twenty miles, in warm weather, hard and firm, and with ice enough left to give each purchaser a small lump. This butter, of course, commanded a higher price than any other. After this Mr. Moore made them of larger dimensions, and in a different manner, for family and dairy purposes. They were composed of two cedar square boxes, one of smaller size, and the space between them filled with pulverized charcoal well packed in; a tin box fastened to the inner side of the lid contained the ice, and the whole was covered with coarse woolen cloth. Thomas Jefferson, then President of the United States, some of the heads of departments, and other citizens of the District of Columbia, who had ice-houses, used Thomas Moore's patent refrigerators. In fourteen years his patent expired, when he gave the public the benefit of the same by not renewing it. This refrigerator was, however, of but little practical benefit to farmers generally, as not one in a hundred had such a useless appendage to his farm as an ice-house, so they went out of use for a number of years. Thomas Moore was a remarkable man. His father, Thomas Moore, came to this country early in the last century, first settled in Pennsylvania, where he married, and afterwards removed to Loudon County, Va., where he built a residence and called the place Waterford, after his native home. Here the son Thomas carried on for a time the business of a cabinet-maker, which he had learned. He then engaged in milling and merchandising in connection with his brother-in-law, James McCormick. About 1794 he removed to Maryland, having married Mary, daughter of Roger Brooke, of Brooke Grove, Montgomery Co. Here he commenced farming on the estate of his wife, and soon distinguished himself as a practical farmer. The State of Maryland is greatly indebted to him for many improvements in agriculture. Although the land was poor when he took possession of it, he soon had the model farm of the county and State. This farm is now owned by E. J. Hall, Esq., late president of the County Agricultural Society, who married a niece of Mary Moore. Persons came from long distances to see his farm and to witness the deep plowing with the mammoth plow of his own invention, his fine stock of cattle in fields of red clover, his meadows of timothy, fine fields of corn, the ground yellow with pumpkins, and the large pen of small-bone hogs fattened on pumpkins, corn, and slop boiled in a box. Charles Carroll, son of Charles Carroll of Carrollton, came on purpose to see the farm and its improvements. The proprietor being absent on the occasion, it devolved upon his twelve-year-old nephew to show the visitor around, which service was rewarded by the first silver dollar the farmer boy ever called his own. Thomas Moore, about this time, wrote a treatise on agriculture, and another on ice-houses and refrigerators, which proved of signal benefit to the State of his adoption. In 1805 he was employed by the corporation of Georgetown to construct the causeway from Mason's Island to the Virginia shore, for which he received $24,000, and completed the work in less than a year. After this he was employed by the United States government to lay out the great National road to the West. During the war with Great Britain, from 1812 to 1816, he took charge of the Union Manufacturing Works near Ellicott's Mills, as chief manager. About this time he, in connection with his two brothers in-law, Caleb Bentley and Isaac Biggs, purchased the site and erected the cotton-mills known as Triadelphia, in Montgomery County. This was not a profitable investment, the war closing soon after the factory went into operation. He was next called upon by the Board of Public Works of the State of Virginia to accept the position of chief engineer of the James River Canal. He also served in the same capacity in the Chesapeake and Ohio Canal, when, after making considerable progress, he contracted a fever so fatal to many on the Potomac, and came home to end his life with his family. From 1818 until his death, with much honor to himself and with great benefit to the public, and with the entire approbation of those to whom he was responsible, he occupied the office of principal chief engineer of Virginia. On the 3d of October, after a sickness of twelve days, he died, aged sixty-three years.

Thomas L. Reese, the father and grandfather of the well-known grocery firm now doing business in Baltimore, was for a number of years a highly-esteemed citizen of this county. In early life he was a clerk with the celebrated Johns Hopkins in the counting-room of their uncle, Gerard T. Hopkins, and often heard the great capitalist say when he came to Baltimore he had but five dollars in the world, but he had resolved to become a rich man. When about twenty-five years old he married Mary, daughter of Thomas Moore (above mentioned), and lived for six or eight years in Brookville engaged in mercantile life, filling several offices of honor and trust, and everywhere esteemed as a conscientious and upright man.

JOHNS HOPKINS.

From thence he returned to Baltimore, and became a partner in the wholesale grocery firm of Gerard T. Hopkins & Co. In 1833 he opened a retail store on Pratt Street, desiring to educate his sons in all the details of business, where he remained until 1844, when he retired from active life; but still by his daily counsel and advice aided his sons who succeeded him in building up the large business they are now doing. In early life he was often heard to say that he never desired to become a rich man, and although actively engaged for more than thirty years in mercantile life, during which he reared and educated a large family, he died in moderate circumstances, but leaving to posterity a legacy more valuable than any amount of earthly riches,—a good name.

Thomas J. S. Perry, the senior member of the dry-goods firm of Perry & Co., of Washington City, died Sept. 5, 1880. He was born in 1825 in Montgomery County, and went to Washington when a young man, and finished his education in the old Rittenhouse Academy. He shortly after entered into business as a member of the dry-goods firm of Perry & Ashby. Augustus E. Perry dying in 1876, he succeeded as the senior member of the firm of Perry & Brother, Mr. Ashby having withdrawn. Sept. 1, 1881, Seaton Perry, his nephew, withdrew, and the firm was changed to Perry & Co. Perry & Brother formed their partnership in 1840. Thomas was the last of five brothers.

Gen. Uriah Forrest, a distinguished Revolutionary officer, was born in St. Mary's County in 1756, but early in life removed to Montgomery, where he took an active interest in the affairs of the county. He attained the rank of lieutenant-colonel in the Maryland line, and received a wound at the battle of Germantown, from the effects of which he never recovered. He was appointed auditor of Maryland, member of the Continental Congress in 1786-87, and upon the adoption of the Federal Constitution came within one vote of defeating Charles Carroll of Carrollton for the United States Senate. He was a member of the Maryland House of Delegates in 1789 and 1790 from Montgomery County, a major-general of militia, a member of Congress in 1793-95, and at his death, near Georgetown, D. C., in July, 1805, was clerk of the Circuit Court for the District of Columbia.

Roger Brooke, an immediate descendant of one of the first settlers of the colony of Maryland, was noted for wit and humor, and though a Quaker he had, like Washington, a great fondness for his hounds and the fox-chase, and was one of the most successful farmers in the county. Mr. F. P. Blair, in an agricultural address, characterized him as a second Franklin.

Robert Pottinger and Dr. William B. Magruder, father of the late most excellent and valuable citizen and physician, Dr. William B. Magruder, of Brookville, were leading and prominent citizens of the county.

The two Drs. Duvall, father and son, were prominent and active in their profession, and as politicians and representatives of the county in the State Legislature.

The different State inspectors of tobacco appointed from Montgomery County were Richard H. Griffith, Philemon Griffith, John W. Darby, Francis Valdemar, Perry Etchinson, Greenberry S. Etchinson, and Robert S. Hilton.

Robert Sellman, of this county, was, before the repeal of the law, appointed State flour inspector. He so actively and faithfully discharged the duties of the office that, after the repeal of the law, he was and still is continued as private inspector at the request of the merchants of Baltimore.

Thomas F. W. Vinson, well and favorably known to the citizens of this county, was a fine specimen of the gentleman of the olden times. His pleasing manners at once put his friends as well as strangers at their ease in his presence. He was for many years sheriff of the county and one of the judges of the Orphans' Court.

Mr. James Holland, grandfather of the present Thomas J. Holland and Clagett Holland, was said strongly to resemble Gen. Washington in his personal appearance. As an auctioneer he was extensively known. The following names of citizens and families of the county are worthy of record and of being handed down to posterity and honorable recollection: William Darne, Dr. S. N. C. White, William Pool, A. S. Hayes, William Bennett, Brook Jones, Joseph I. Johnson, Nathan Hempston, Jacob Nicholls, Horatio Trundle, Hezekiah Trundle, Richard Harding, William Trail, T. C. Lannan, Rev. Thomas W. Green, Dr. Horatio Willson, Rev. Basil Barry, Allen Bowie Davis, the Fletchers, Dawsons, Griffiths, Platers, Whites, Waters, Darbys, Gittings, Gotts, Peters, Gues, Pooles, Huttons, Riggs, Owens, and Gorvilles.

Revolutionary Pensioners.—Capt. Gleeson, whose residence was a log cabin near Barnesville, was severely wounded in the right knee in a battle between the "Black Snake" and "Little Turtle," yet he scorned to receive the small rate of pension offered him by the government for his meritorious services, and he died in his log cabin, well convinced that republics are ungrateful.

James Carrant was the first Revolutionary soldier pensioned in Montgomery County. He was placed on the roll in compliance with the general invalid pension law approved June 7, 1785, and died Sept. 4, 1822.

MONTGOMERY COUNTY.   683

Francis Hutchinson was also a pensioner, but not Revolutionary. He belonged to the regular army of the United States. Samuel Harris was pensioned as a matross of the Revolutionary artillery, and died on the 19th of September, 1826. William A. Needham was also a Revolutionary pensioner, placed on the roll in 1808. William O'Neal was a private in the Maryland militia at some period not known, and placed on the pension-roll per act April 30, 1816, at the rate of forty-eight dollars per annum. Samuel B. White was a private in the Revolutionary army, pensioned per act June 7, 1785, and died Jan. 16, 1832. James White was also a pensioner per act June 7, 1785. He belonged to the Revolutionary army. All the soldiers named above were invalid pensioners, pensioned on account of wounds and disability received in the service of the United States in the line of their duty, and they honorably appear on Montgomery's roll of honor as good men tried and true.

The following Revolutionary soldiers residing in Montgomery County were pensioned by act of Congress approved the 18th of March, 1818. In order to obtain the benefit of this act they were required to prove nine months' service in the Continental army, and exhibit under oath a schedule showing that their property was worth no more than five hundred dollars. Another act was passed on the 1st of May, 1820, requiring the exhibition of another schedule, and if in the mean time their property had increased so as to exceed five hundred dollars in value they were dropped from the pension-roll. These acts of Congress were very distasteful to the old soldiers, for they looked upon them as offering a reward to soldiers for keeping themselves in poverty.

The first name in the county placed upon the pension-roll, in compliance with the act of 1818, was John Robbins, on the 6th of April, 1818, aged seventy-two years, at the rate of ninety-six dollars per annum. He belonged to the "Old Maryland Line," so distinguished in all the battles in which it took part. All the pensioners under this act, if privates, received ninety-six dollars per annum; if commissioned officers, they were allowed two hundred and forty dollars per annum. The second name placed on the roll was that of Joseph Roy, aged sixty-five years, also of the Maryland Continental Line. Then followed the names of Thomas Penfield, aged seventy-two years, who died Dec. 15, 1832; James Ervin, aged sixty-seven, who died June 28, 1827; George Field, aged eighty, time of death unknown; Robert Hurdle, aged seventy-five, time of death unknown; John Jordan, aged seventy-seven, time of death unknown; Henry Leeke, age not given, dropped from the roll per act May 1, 1820, time of death unknown. These were privates of the Maryland Line. James Campbell, of Virginia Line, aged seventy-one years, private, died Sept. 14, 1827; Beltz, or Lohr, Pennsylvania Line, aged seventy-six, private, died Feb. 27, 1827; Thomas Lingan, lieutenant, Maryland Line, aged sixty-seven, died May 28, 1825; William Layman, ensign, Maryland Line, aged eighty-one, dropped from the roll per act May 1, 1820, restored March 22, 1826, time of death unknown. The two officers last named were pensioned at the rate of two hundred and forty dollars per annum.

The following-named soldiers of the Revolutionary war, residing in Montgomery County, were pensioned per act of Congress approved June 7, 1832. The minimum rate of pension allowed a private under this act was twenty dollars per annum for six months' service in any department of the Revolutionary army, and increased *pro rata* according to the time of service, so as not to exceed the rate of eighty dollars per annum, the maximum, for two years service. No grade of officer was allowed more than six hundred dollars per annum for two years' service. Periods of service for less than two years were rated according to rank and time of service. Every soldier was entitled to a pension under this act without regard to the value of his property, and many who lost their pensions on the passage of the act of May 1, 1820, were restored by the act of 1832. All pensions under this act were made to commence on the 4th of March, 1831. Those pensioned were as follows:

Geo. Beckwith, sergeant, $32.50 per annum; Maryland Line; aged 74.

Rich. Barret, sergeant, $36.15 per annum; Maryland Line; aged 79.

Giles Easton, private, $30 per annum; Maryland Line; aged 73.

Gab. Galworth, private, $80 per annum; Maryland Line; aged 77.

Chas. Morris, corporal, $79.63 per annum; New York Line.

Chas. Saffell, musician, $88 per annum; Maryland Line; aged 84.

Joseph Warfield, lieutenant, $85.97 per annum; Maryland Line; aged 76.

Samuel Griffith, captain, $414 per annum; Maryland Line.

James Fling, private, $80 per annum; Virginia Line; aged 73.

Charles Saffell, the oldest man on the list, died in 1837.

All the pensioners named above belonged to the Revolutionary army under Washington, except one or two on the list of invalids, who acquired the right to pension for services in the Indian wars which soon followed the Revolution.

Shadrach Nugent, a famous colored man, was born near Rockville in 1761. His father was brought to this country from Guinea, and was called Bob,—"Mr. Crampton's Bob." His mother was an Irishwoman named Mary Nugent, who had been brought to America as a convict at the expense of a man with whom she served for seven years to pay the expense of her transportation. Besides Shadrach there were three other children by this marriage,—Eli, Millie, and Nellie,—all of whom were of much brighter complexion than Shadrach. When quite small Shadrach was bound out by his mother to George Graff, and when the Revolutionary war began he went as a body-servant with Mr. Graff, who was a lieutenant in an independent artillery company, of which the second lieutenant was McPherson, and captain, Steiner, both of Frederick. The company entered the field in full uniform, and the entire outfit, cannon included, was bought by members of the organization. When the government ordered a draft the company entered the service as regulars, and were ordered to Baltimore, whither Shadrach went with his master. Gen. Smith was in command at Baltimore, and old Shad said the town was in confusion because the rumor went that the "Britishers war gwine to burn us up." One day Lieut. Graff sent for Shadrach to come down to the marquee. "He tole me," says Shad, "if dem English come, to fill my canteen with water and his'n wid whisky, and hang bofe around my shoulders. When dey got a fightin' wid dem Britishers, he wanted me to stand right squar behind him and hand him whiskey to drink, and he said if I didn't do dat, as how he'd haul out his pistol and shoot me dead. Well, you just believe me, honey, I was scared, was I, and I had made up my mind if dem Britishers had come to jump down a gully, canteen and all, and git, kase I warn't gwine to be killed by the Britishers nor Massa George neider, and he would have killed me suah. Dem Dutch allus keeps dere word." When the war was closed Shadrach's master, who had married a Miss Mary Carlton, bought a farm three miles from Rockville, and afterwards gave Shadrach his free papers, and told him that he was twenty-one years of age. In the same year he went to seek his mother, and found her with his oldest sister, Millie, who was married to a farmer named Dick Robinson. Near Brookville a company had established what was called the Triadelphia Factory, and in a quarry near by they were breaking stone to build houses for the use of the establishment. In this quarry Shadrach worked for quite a while, and subsequently on different farms. When the war of 1812 broke out, and during its duration, he stayed with his sister at Brookville, and saw the light when the British burned Washington. His brother Eli, who was living with a Mr. Dodge in Georgetown, came to Brookville with his family, because "ebberbody in Washington was scared." Shadrach came to Washington in the year Madison was elected President. He says "it warn't much of a place den, honey; all de place whar I lives now was a swamp, and houses on Pennsylvania Avenue was mighty scarce." There he first worked at Lyon's mill, and subsequently for Joel Brown, a hatter, in Georgetown. He next drove a cart for George Brown, who was employed under Street Commissioner Corcoran, father of W. W. Corcoran. He got married in the year Jackson took his seat in the White House. Of his two children living the youngest is thirty-seven years old. He remembers all the Presidents who have been elected since he went to Washington, and often saw Jefferson Davis in the latter's house in G Street. He is in pretty good health, walks without a cane, can read the Bible, has good teeth, thin, white hair, and talks with considerable animation. One of his sons died while enlisted as a soldier in the war of the Rebellion, and another one, now living, is employed at the Ebbitt House. George M. Graff, the present owner of the farm on which Shadrach worked before 1776, and his brother are grandnephews of Lieut. Graff, Shadrach's master. The Graff place is on the Frederick road, three miles from Rockville. Shadrach remembers that when a little lad he occasionally went to Clarksburg, and that Capt. Buxton, who bought his mother, lived upon that road, where Mr. Buxton now resides, near Middlebrook. Until three years ago, for a score of years he was a daily occupant of some prominent corner on some chief thoroughfare in Washington, standing erect, selling his "History of the Moons," with a card on his breast inscribed as follows:

"Shadrach Nugent was encamped on Federal Hill, Baltimore, Md., with Lieutenant George Graff, of the Artillery, as his body servant, 102 years ago this July, 1879, when General Lafayette reinforced General Washington at Yorktown, Va. I was 16 years old then, and am 118 years old now."

Being for long years too aged to labor, he lived by the sale of his observations and predictions concerning the moon, from whence his title, proudly boasted of by him, "The Moon Man," is derived. His compilation of changes is said to be in most instances surprisingly accurate, and is as follows:

"A HISTORY OF THE MOONS.

"The three first moons in every new year's almanac is the three first spring moons; the two first spring moons always fulls cold, and they are the last cold fulls.

"And the three next will be the summer moons for a hundred years.

"And the three next will be the three fall moons for a hundred years.

"And the next three will be the three winter moons for a hundred years to come.

"And there is only twelve fulls of the moon in every year's almanac for a hundred years.

"And it don't make any difference what months the spring moons change in, the weather will be half spring and half winter.

"And when the moon changes with her points down, the change is stormy.

"And when she changes with her points up, she changes calmer.

"And every almanac has a date, and when the date is later, the moon changes with her points up, laying on her back.

"And when the almanac's date is earlier, the moon changes with her points down; stormy.

"The first moon in every new year's almanac is March's moon, and the second moon is April's, the third moon is May's, and the fourth moon is June's,—the first summer moon which fills for summer.

"In every year you get an almanac; the almanacs tell about the weather, and I tell about the moon.

"I have been going by the moons for more than a hundred years, and have made it a special study.

"And I am one hundred and nineteen years old in this year of 1880.

"SHADRACH NUGENT,
"*The Moon Man.*"

Necrology—The following record of deaths in the county, compiled from very early dates, will be interesting:

Died in 1790, Mrs. Martha Beatty, consort of Col. Charles Beatty, aged 54 years.

November, 1790.—John Claggett, Esq., aged 83.

October, 1797.—Roger Nelson, captain of the Republican Volunteer troop of Light Dragoons of Frederick, belonging to Gen. Bayley's brigade.

Aug. 10, 1804.—Mrs. Elizabeth Browning, near Clarkesburg, in her 73d year.

Sept. 6, 1804.—Jonathan Browning, husband of the above E. Browning, aged 79.

Jan. 25, 1827.—At his residence at Rockville, Col. Upton Beall, aged 58. He was for more than thirty years county clerk.

Aug. 22, 1837.—Judge Kilgour, an upright judge and estimable citizen. "He was on his return home to Rockville from one of his farms near Leesburg, Va., riding in a barouche or carriage, when it is supposed his horse took fright and ran off, and he was thrown out, and his skull fractured and otherwise injured, so that he died an hour afterwards."

April 3, 1834.—At Hyattstown, Hon. George Baer, for many years president of the Frederick County Bank, and formerly a member of the United States Congress.

Nov. 6, 1841.—At Georgetown, D. C., Clara, formerly a servant of Thomas Edmonston, Sr., deceased.

March 26, 1855.—William Carroll. In 1812 he was almost unanimously elected to the Legislature. Daniel Carroll, his grandfather, was one of the framers of the Constitution, although he was not in Congress when the Declaration of Independence was signed. He was a brother of the late Archbishop of Baltimore, the first bishop in the United States. Mr. Wm. Carroll's great-grandfather was a brother of Charles Carroll of Carrollton. Mr. Carroll during the close of his life was employed for some time in the Department of State at Washington, and afterwards served with credit as a magistrate in Baltimore.

April 11, 1856.—Hon. Otho Magruder, in his 63d year. He was at the time of his death one of the judges of the Orphans' Court. He also attended the late meeting of the District Presbytery in Alexandria, and was elected alternate commissioner to the General Assembly.

Aug. 2, 1858.—Hon. William Lingan Gaither, at Berkeley Springs. Senator Gaither had been long in public life, and was well known throughout the State as a gentleman of fine talents, a high sense of honor, and sterling integrity. He had frequently represented Montgomery County in both branches of the State Legislature, and at the time of his death was a member of the Senate, of which body for many years he was the presiding officer. He was also until recently a State director in the Baltimore and Ohio Railroad Company. He was stricken down by a violent attack of typhoid fever while discharging his duties in the city of Baltimore.

May 6, 1863.—John Spater, register of wills.

Aug. 12, 1871.—Matthew Fields, Esq., aged 56. He was the editor of the Rockville *Sentinel*, which paper had been under his management and edited by him for twenty years. He was esteemed both as a journalist and in private life. During the war his paper was twice suppressed, and Mr. Fields for a time confined in the old Capitol prison. In recognition of the estimation in which he was held, business in the town was suspended on the day of his funeral.

March, 1876.—Hon. Greenbury M. Watkins, at his home in Boscage, aged 69. Mr. Watkins was a member of the House of Delegates of Maryland in 1874. He had been for many years prominently connected with works of public improvement in the State, and was well known in the District of Columbia. In the Legislature of 1874 he was chairman of the Committee of Ways and Means. In early life he was connected with the construction of the Chesapeake and Ohio Canal, and was a director therein from 1872 until his death. He was one of the largest real estate owners in the county, and was elected to the Legislature in 1864. In the Constitutional Convention of 1867 he was on the Judiciary Committee. He was re-elected to the Legislature in 1870 and in 1874. He was actively engaged in the construction of the Western Maryland Railroad between Hagerstown and Williamsport.

Sept. 2, 1877.—Rev. Basil Barry, of the Baltimore Conference of the Methodist Episcopal Church, aged 88 years, at the residence of his son-in-law, Dr. E. C. Stonestreet. Mr. Barry had been a resident of Rockville for the past forty years, and was held in high esteem by all classes of citizens. He was the eldest but one of the members of the Baltimore Annual Conference. He entered the ministry in 1815, serving on the following circuits and appointments: Mahoning, Great Falls, Staunton, New River, Allegany, Auckwille, Severn, Calvert, Prince George's, and Harford. In 1825–26 he was in New York; 1827, Baltimore Circuit; 1828, Staunton; 1829–30, Montgomery; 1831, Chambersburg; 1832–33, Clear Spring, Pa.; 1834, Cumberland; 1835–36, Allegany; 1837–38, Rock Creek; 1839–40, Liberty; 1841–42, Great Falls; and 1843, on Montgomery. In 1844 he took a supernumerary relation, in which he continued until 1861, when he took a superannuated relation. Mr. Barry, notwithstanding his extreme old age, was always a regular attendant at the Conference of the church, and frequently preached from the pulpit when occasion required. His last public ministration was at the Washington Grove camp-meeting, near Gaithersburg.

CHAPTER XXXV.

THE DISTRICT OF COLUMBIA.

Georgetown—Its First Officers—Incorporated—Business Notes—The District of Columbia—Laying off Washington City—The Public Buildings.

GEORGETOWN, originally included within the limits of Frederick, and afterwards in Montgomery, was laid out in response to a petition of the people of Frederick County to the General Assembly, setting forth that there was a convenient site for a town at the mouth of Rock Creek, on "Patowmack" River, adjacent to the Inspection House, called George Gordon's Rolling House. In accordance with their desire the Legislature, by act of May 15, 1751, authorized Henry Wright Crabb, John Needham, John Claggett, James Perry, and David Lynn, commissioners, to lay out and erect a town on the Potomac River above the mouth of Rock Creek, in Frederick County, and empowered them to purchase sixty acres, "part of the tracts of land belonging to George Gordon and George Beall, at the place aforesaid, where it shall appear to them to be most convenient, and to survey the same into eighty lots, to be erected into a town, and to be called George Town."

For the advantage of the town and for the encouragement of the *back inhabitants*, the commissioners were authorized to hold two fairs annually for three successive days, during which every one attending the same should be free from arrest, except for felony or breach of the peace.

The first meeting of the commissioners was held on the 18th of September, 1751, when they appointed Alexander Beall clerk and surveyor, and Josiah Beall coroner.

The owners of the site of the projected town, however, declined to sell, and they were accordingly compelled to summon a jury and condemn the property for the public uses for which it was intended. The jury, which consisted of William Pritchett, Ninian Magruder, Nicholas Baker, James Beall, Nathaniel Magruder, Charles Clagett, Thomas Clagett, James Holman, Charles Jones, Zachariah Magruder, James Wallace, Basil Beall, William Williams, Alexander Magruder, William Wallace, and John Magruder, son of Alexander, appraised the land, awarding two hundred and eighty pounds currency to the owners, and the survey and plat were completed on the 27th of February, 1752, when the commissioners numbered the lots and named the streets and lanes. Messrs. Gordon and Beall were allowed the first choice in the selection of lots in the new town, and Mr. Gordon chose lots 48 and 52. Mr. Beall at first refused to recognize the authority of the commissioners, and finally selected lots Nos. 72 and 79 under protest.[1]

The land upon which Georgetown is situated was first patented by the proprietary of Maryland to Ninian Beall on Nov. 18, 1703. The original tract contained seven hundred and ninety-five acres, and was named the "Rock of Dunbarton." The patent recites that it was made in consideration of there being due to Beall five hundred acres under a warrant of the 19th of May, 1702. The land is described as lying in Prince George's County,

"beginning at the southeast corner tree of a tract of land taken for Robert Mason, standing by Potomac River side, at the mouth of Rock Creek, on a point running thence with said land N. N. West six hundred and forty perches, then east three hundred and twenty perches, thence south 6½° easterly four hundred and eighteen perches, then west twenty perches, then S. S. West one hundred and seventy-five perches, thence with a straight line by the creek and river to the first bound containing, and there laid out for seven hundred and ninety-five acres."

The town grew rapidly, and its port at one time was a formidable rival to Baltimore. Its exports from Oct. 1, 1789, to July 1, 1790, amounted to $260,962. The first addition to the town was Beall's sixty-one acres, made in 1783, followed in 1784 by twenty-four acres from Peter Beatty, Threlkeld, and Deakin.

Georgetown was not named after Gen. Washington, as is generally supposed, as the town was laid out while Washington was still a young man and before he had become famous. It is more likely it took its name from George II., King of Great Britain, towards whom all the provinces at this time were extremely loyal. In 1789 the town was incorporated, with Robert Peter, mayor, John Mackall Gantt, recorder, and Brooke Beall, Bernard O'Neal, Thomas Beall, of George, James McCubbin Lingan, John Threlkeld, and John Peter, aldermen, "so long as they shall behave themselves therein." Robert Peter died Nov. 15, 1860, at Georgetown, aged eighty-one years. He was succeeded as mayor by G. Lloyd Beall in 1798, who served to 1803. The first recorder, John Mackall Gantt, served from 1789 to 1809, when he was succeeded by James S. Morsell from 1809 to 1813. He was followed by Francis Scott Key from 1813 to

---

[1] The following notice appears in the *Maryland Gazette* of Feb. 27, 1752:

"M. G., Feb. 27, 1752.—Notice is hereby given that the land appointed by act of Assembly to be laid out into a town by the name of Georgetown, adjacent to the warehouse at the mouth of Rock Creek, in Frederick County, is accordingly laid out, and the lots will be sold on March 23d next, at the house of Joseph Belt, living in said town, at ten A.M.

"Per order of the Commissioners.

"ALEX. BEALL, *Clerk*."

1816. In 1790 there were only seventy-five post-offices in the United States, and Georgetown was one of them, but it has been ascertained that the office was in operation on the 5th of January, 1776. William B. Magruder was appointed postmaster at Georgetown, Feb. 16, 1790; Richard Forrest, April 1, 1797; Joseph Carlton, Feb. 1, 1799; Tristram Dalton, Jan. 1, 1803. James McCubbin Lingan was appointed collector of customs Oct. 1, 1790, and John Oakley, Oct. 1, 1801.

The first newspapers published in Georgetown were the *Weekly Ledger* in 1790; *Sentinel of Liberty*, by Green, English & Co., in 1796; and the *Federal Republican* in 1812.

In November, 1796, William B. Magruder had "a large assortment of fall goods from London and Liverpool" for sale at his store in Georgetown on "the Baltimore terms." In September of the same year Tench Ringgold was in the commission business at the same place. In February, 1791, Andrew Ellicott, attended by Benjamin Banniker, the colored astronomer and surveyor, arrived in the town to lay off the District of Columbia for the capital. Maj. Longeout, a French gentleman, who was employed by the President as an assistant, also arrived in Georgetown in March for the same purpose. On Aug. 18, 1796, Washington passed through Georgetown on his way to Philadelphia, but remained in Washington City all night. Died in Georgetown, Oct. 10, 1799, Mrs. Elizabeth Thomas, aged one hundred and seven years; also, on the 21st of January, 1805, Mrs. Mary Lee, wife of Thomas Sim Lee, the second Governor of Maryland, and daughter of Ignatius Diggs. The corner-stone of the western abutment of the Federal bridge at Georgetown (being the second corner-stone) over Rock Creek was laid on Aug. 4, 1792, by Uriah Forrest, mayor of Georgetown.

Georgetown is a suburb of Washington, and is situated on the Potomac, being divided from the capital by Rock Creek. It is beautifully located on a range of hills rising above the former river, and stretches in undulating beauty along its borders.

The Heights of Georgetown are lofty eminences overlooking the city from the north and west. Along these are many splendid villas, the residences of gentlemen of wealth and distinction, and extensive gardens in the highest state of cultivation. Nothing can surpass the splendor of the panorama here presented. Below reposes the city, to the north the metropolis, and as far as the eye can reach the silvery Potomac courses through the most beautiful scenery. The city presents many objects of attraction. Its ancient college, a Catholic institution, its nunnery, its various literary institutions, its splendid aqueduct, and other noted edifices are worthy of attention.

Georgetown College, D. C.—The site now occupied by Georgetown College was selected for the purpose a few years after the American Revolution of 1776 by Rev. John Carroll, then a missionary priest of the vicinity, and afterwards the first Bishop and Archbishop of Baltimore, the primatial See of the United States. Georgetown was then within the limits of Montgomery County, wherein still resided many of the former members of the Society of Jesus, who served the ancient missions of Maryland and Pennsylvania. Of these missioners Rev. Mr. Carroll was one. After the suppression of the society in 1773, the ex-Jesuits of Maryland had continued to hold the former estates of the society, and it was from the resources furnished by these estates that they now proposed to erect this first Catholic institution of learning in the United States. It was expected that the Catholic laity would assist the enterprise, but it does not appear that any important help, or, indeed, any help at all, was received from this source. The first building, which is still standing, was begun in 1788, the few acres of ground surrounding it which had been secured were paid for in 1789, and the structure was ready for occupancy in 1791. In that year the first president, Rev. Robert Plunkett, an English ex-Jesuit, was appointed and the first student entered, William Gaston, afterwards a distinguished jurist and legislator in North Carolina. Meanwhile, in 1790, the State of Maryland ceded to the Federal government the territory now known as the District of Columbia, including Georgetown. Thus the site selected by Congress for the capital of the United States was identical, or nearly so, with that previously selected by the proto-Catholic bishop for his college, or "academy," as he originally proposed it should be. Georgetown, which had been a town of some importance for many years before the District was created, is now only a suburb of the city of Washington, which has grown to be a city of one hundred and forty thousand inhabitants. A very few years after the opening of the college the accession of students from various parts rendered further accommodations necessary, and in 1797 a spacious building north of the former one was completed for the use of the boarders. It continues to be used for the same purpose.

Under the presidents succeeding Rev. Mr. Plunkett—Rev. Robert Molyneux, 1793-96, a native of England and a member of the former society; Rev. William L. Dubourg, 1796-99, one of the Sulpician refugees from France, afterwards Bishop of New Orleans, and finally Archbishop of Besançon, in France; and Rev. Leonard Neale, 1799–1806, formerly of the society and in after-years coadjutor and then successor to Archbishop Carroll in the See of Baltimore—the "academy" grew into a regularly organized college, with a liberal course of studies and a competent faculty of instruction. In 1806 the Society of Jesus was restored in Maryland, the college was transferred to its care, and became the mother-house of the society in the United States. Rev. Robert Molyneux, the first Jesuit superior, became at the same time president of the college, and died in office in 1808. He was succeeded as superior by Rev. Charles Neale, S.J., brother of Leonard, and as president by Rev. William Matthews, a secular priest, the first regularly settled Catholic pastor of Washington. He died in that city in 1854 at a very advanced age, greatly revered by both Protestants and Catholics. While a teacher in the college, in 1797–98, he had welcomed to the institution Gen. Washington, who called to return a visit paid him by members of the faculty of the time. Among these was an enthusiastic admirer of Washington's, the Abbé Flaget, afterwards the first Bishop of Bardstown and Louisville. Since the days of the first President of the United States, all, or nearly all, his successors in office have visited the college, and in many cases presided at its annual commencements. During Rev. Mr. Matthews' administration, 1808–12, a corps of instructors from Georgetown opened a classical school in the city of New York, which had great success during the few years it was in operation, but was given up in 1813, chiefly from the difficulty of procuring a succession of Jesuit teachers.

In 1812, Rev. John Grassi, S.J., a native of Italy, became superior of the mission and president of the college. Under the administration of this learned and distinguished man the college obtained from the Congress of the United States in 1815 its charter as a university. Its first graduates received their diplomas in 1817, from which period the annual commencements date. Shortly after an institution was opened in Washington by fathers from the college as an ecclesiastical seminary, but the enterprise not proving financially practicable, the building was used as a day-school, under the patronage of Rev. William Matthews, whose church (St. Patrick's) it adjoined. The school earned a high reputation, and was frequented by sons of the most distinguished men in Washington of that day. With varying fortunes, but with a career generally successful, it has subsisted to this time, but is now conducted on the grounds attached to St. Aloysius' Church, and is known as Gonzaga College. In 1817, Rev. Anthony Kohlmann, S.J., a native of Germany and an eminent theologian and controversialist, became superior of the mission, while the presidency of the college devolved for a year upon the Rev. Benedict J. Fenwick, S.J., a former student of the college, and then upon Father Kohlmann for two years, 1818–20, while the latter was still superior, 1817–21. This is the last instance in which the two offices were united. Rev. Enoch Fenwick, S.J., brother of Benedict, and like him educated at Georgetown, was president from 1820 to 1822, when he was succeeded by his brother.

The latter continued in office until his appointment in 1825 to the bishopric of Boston, in place of the venerated Cheverus. The presidents next succeeding, up to 1837, were Rev. Stephen L. Dubuisson, S.J., a native of France; Rev. William Feiner, S.J., a native of Germany, who died after a few months; Rev. John Beschter, also a native of Germany; and Thomas F. Mulledy, S.J., a former student of the college. The latter, in 1832, erected a large addition to the original college building, containing a refectory and chapel for the students, each occupying an entire floor, and a study-hall of the same dimensions above. Down to and including 1878 the annual commencements have been held in this hall. During Rev. Mr. Mulledy's incumbency the missions of Maryland were regularly erected into a province, and Rev. William McSherry, S.J., a former student of the college, was made the first provincial, 1833. On March 30th of the same year His Holiness Gregory XVI. empowered the faculty of the college to confer degrees in philosophy and theology, a privilege which no other American institution enjoyed until a very recent date. On the expiration of Rev. Father McSherry's term of office, in 1837, he succeeded Rev. Mr. Mulledy as president of the college, and died in office in 1839.

The succeeding presidents, up to 1848, were Rev. Joseph A. Lopez, S.J., a Spaniard, who died in office after a few months; Rev. James Ryder, S.J., a former student of the college, the founder, in 1830, while a professor in the college, of the Philodemic Society, and the most celebrated pulpit orator of his day; Rev. Samuel F. Mulledy, S.J., a former student of the college, brother of Thomas; and finally Rev. Thomas Mulledy himself, president for a second time, 1845–48. About the time of his accession, Bishop Benedict J. Fenwick established at Worcester, in his diocese, the College of the Holy Cross, and a colony from Georgetown, bearing with them a handsome donation of books from the old college to the new, constituted a portion of its first faculty. This college, although admitting only Catholic students, has been eminently successful, and has, besides, given from among its alumni a large number of priests to the dioceses of New England and to the society, only a minority of its graduates choosing secular professions. Although it is now in high favor with the authorities of Massachusetts, it was many years before its charter could be obtained, and in the mean time the diplomas granted to its graduates were conferred by Georgetown College. Father Mulledy added to the attractions of the college a villa, three miles distant, which continued for many years, or until 1871, to be the resort on holidays of students and teachers, and during the summer vacations the home of the scholastics from Georgetown and other colleges of the province. The property is still owned by the college, but is now leased to private parties.

Rev. James Ryder again became president in 1848, and held office until 1851. During his administration the medical department of the university was organized in Washington, and opened for students in May, 1851. He also built Trinity church, the large and handsome church of the parish, substituting it for the ancient structure which had been attended by fathers from the college since 1795. Subsequent pastors of the church have converted the latter into a parochial school-house. The astronomical observatory, on an eminence near the college and within its grounds, which had been begun under Father Ryder's former administration, was now completed, and was being ably served by Fathers de Vico, Secchi, and Sistini, refugees from the political agitations of 1848 in Italy, and has since been in charge of Rev. James Curley, S.J., under whom the eminent Secchi made his first astronomical observations at Georgetown. Besides these more important works, many local improvements both in the buildings and grounds were made by Father Ryder, and the area of the grounds was extended, so that they now embrace over one hundred and fifty-four acres, much of which is woodland, while the arable portions furnish supplies to the college. Ten acres of park adjoining the college continue to furnish a delightful resort for the students during hours of recreation.

In August, 1851, Rev. Charles H. Stonestreet, S.J., succeeded Father Ryder in the presidency. Father Stonestreet was a graduate of 1833. Being made provincial of Maryland a year after entering the presidency, he resigned that position to Rev. Bernard A. Maguire, S.J. The latter built in 1854 a structure nearly corresponding in dimensions with the one erected by Father Mulledy in 1832, and intended chiefly to accommodate the younger students, who were thenceforth separated from the older ones, with their study-rooms, dormitories, and class accommodations in the new buildings, and their play-ground adjoining. In 1853, during Father Maguire's administration, Loyola College, in Baltimore, was opened and supplied with professors from Georgetown and elsewhere. That college became in 1858 the residence of the provincials, and Georgetown ceased to be headquarters, although the schools of philosophy and theology for the scholastics of the province continued to be held here until 1869, with the exception of three years after 1860, when they were conducted at the newly-opened college in Boston, since devoted exclusively to secular teaching under fathers of the society.

The first president of Loyola College, Rev. John Early, S.J., succeeded Father Maguire as president of Georgetown in 1858, and held office during all the trying period of the civil war, 1861–65. Notwithstanding the departure of numerous students, chiefly those from the South, at the outbreak of the war, the occupation of the grounds by Federal soldiers for some weeks in 1861, and the conversion of many of the buildings into a military hospital during 1862–63, the exercises of the college were never intermitted; besides, in that period of excited feeling and divided preferences only extraordinary prudence on the part of the head of the college could have averted imminent dangers, Georgetown being on the border-line between the then contending parties.

In 1866, Father Maguire became president for a second time. He organized the law department of the university, which opened its classes in Washington in October, 1870. In the previous year, Woodstock College, in Baltimore County, Md., was opened as a general scholasticate for the United States, and thither the scholastics who had been pursuing their studies of theology or philosophy in Georgetown repaired, their professors accompanying them and forming the bulk of the new faculty.

Father Early returned as president in 1870, and in the following year assigned to the college students in philosophy the rooms vacated by those who had removed to Woodstock. These rooms have since been occupied in a similar manner by the successive members, year after year, of the same class. It is now proposed to extend this privilege to the members of other classes, and rooms are being prepared for the purpose in the new and as yet (May, 1880) unoccupied building. Father Early died suddenly, but not unprepared, in May, 1873, himself and his predecessor having between them governed the college for twenty-one years.

He was succeeded by the Rev. P. F. Healy, S.J.,

a graduate of Holy Cross College in 1850, who is (June, 1881) still in office. Under his administration important changes and improvements have been made in the studies of the college course, especially in science and in the advanced studies in English branches. Georgetown is now probably the only college in the United States, with the exception of the professedly scientific schools, where a course of two years in chemistry is insisted on before the student can gain his diploma. The courses in the medical and law schools of the university have also been extended and improved. In 1877 the foundations of an extensive stone structure, uniting the former college buildings, and with a frontage to the east of over three hundred feet, were laid. The building was completed in a little less than two years. It is being interiorly prepared for occupancy at the opening of the scholastic year, 1880–81, at least as to the class-rooms, eight in number and very spacious, and the private rooms for students, over sixty in number. The other apartments in the building, which is universally pronounced the finest college structure in the United States, will be a hall for commencements,—where that of 1879 was held,—capable of accommodating eighteen hundred persons; a library with a capacity for one hundred thousand volumes; a lecture-hall for physics capable of seating three hundred; a chemical laboratory, with ample annexes for class purposes; a museum; offices for the president and treasurer; a range of parlors, etc. The whole building will be heated by hot water. The central tower, two hundred and six feet in height, will serve as a ventilating shaft for the entire structure, and a tower at the southern extremity of the building, one hundred and forty-two feet in height, affords a magnificent view over the cities of Georgetown and Washington and the course of the Potomac River for many miles.

The former students of Georgetown College are residents of all parts of the United States, and even of foreign countries. They embrace men in every calling, not a few of whom are eminent, either socially or politically.

The Nunnery or Convent of the Visitation is situated on the heights contiguous to the eastern margin of the Potomac, and commands a view of that magnificent river and—at a distance—of the city of Washington. The building appropriated for the ladies' academy is of brick, between two hundred and three hundred feet in length by forty feet in breadth. It is a handsome structure, and in the interior a combination of elegance and neatness. These buildings occupy part of the side of an oblong square which contains an area of four or five acres, a portion of which is laid out as a botanic garden. There are other edifices of great extent on the same square, comprising the archbishop's residence, an elegant church, the convent and charity schools. The whole is under the direction of the Sisters of Visitation, and the course of instruction is one embracing all the accomplishments of the age.

Among other institutions of learning, the most distinguished were Mr. Abbott's English and Classical Academy and Miss English's Female Seminary, both in their several spheres schools of the highest order.

The aqueduct which conveys the Chesapeake and Ohio Canal over the Potomac is a stupendous work, and an attraction to all men of science. It was constructed under the superintendence of Maj. Turnbull, of the United States Topographical Engineers, and cost nearly two million dollars. The piers, nine in number, and thirty-six feet above high-water mark, are built of granite, and imbedded seventeen feet in the bottom of the river, with a foundation upon solid rock, so as to withstand the shock of the spring ice, which rushes furiously from the falls and narrows above, crushing with tremendous force against the bridge and sweeping everything movable before it. These piers, built in the most masterly manner, will bear up against any force that may be propelled against them. This aqueduct connects the great canal with the city of Alexandria, Va. Its length is fourteen hundred and forty-six feet.

The cemetery on the heights is also a great ornament to the city. It was laid out in 1849, at the expense and under the direction of W. W. Corcoran, the eminent banker, and a native of the District. It is known as Oak Hill Cemetery. A capacious mausoleum or public vault is situated in a central position, the front of which is of dressed granite in the Henry VIII. style of Gothic. The donor of the land also added to the cemetery a massive front iron railing, a gate-keeper's lodge in the Norman style, and an elegant Gothic chapel, adorned with beautiful stained glass.

Georgetown was formerly a port of some note, and had considerable trade, and is now quite a thriving business place. It is connected by canal or railroad with all parts of the Union.[1]

Most of the territory composing the District of Columbia, including the city of Georgetown and the

---

[1] The following appeared in the *Maryland Journal* of Feb. 26, 1783:

"NOTICE.

"The inhabitants of Montgomery County intend petitioning next General Assembly of Maryland for the removal of the court-house from the place where it then met to George Town."

site of the capital of the nation, was originally a portion of Montgomery County. Before all the States had ratified the Constitution it became a matter of serious deliberation in Congress where the permanent capital should be located. Maryland and Virginia were from the first eager claimants for the honor, and though the cession of the territory would entail a serious temporary loss on Montgomery County, the prospective advantages to be derived from the proximity of the national capital far outweighed any considerations of this character, and no opposition to the scheme was at any time developed.

Congress had hitherto held its sessions, according to the exigencies of the war, at Philadelphia, Baltimore, Lancaster, York, Princeton, Annapolis, Trenton, and New York, but it was now determined to fix its permanent seat, and settle the violent sectional discussions which continually arose upon the subject between the Northern and the Southern States. The necessity of selecting a residence in which the government might exercise sufficient authority to protect itself from abuse, insult, and violence had been generally admitted since June, 1783, when Congress was driven from Philadelphia by a mutiny of a part of the Pennsylvania line, for the purpose of compelling Congress to grant their arrears of pay. In this emergency a committee was appointed, with Alexander Hamilton at its head, to ask the executive of Pennsylvania for assistance, and they reported that the Philadelphia militia could not be depended on for protection, and that Congress was at the mercy of the mutineers. When this report was made, Messrs. Ward, Mercer, and others, " being much displeased, signified if the city would not support Congress it was high time to remove to some other place." After discussing the situation with Gen. St. Clair, Congress, on the next day, adjourned to Princeton. This adjournment made the establishment of a Federal capital a necessity, and it continued to be made the subject of discussion down to its final adoption, in 1790. On Oct. 7, 1783, Mr. Gerry introduced a resolution that the buildings for the use of Congress be erected on or near the banks of the Delaware or the Potomac, provided that a suitable place could be obtained for a Federal town, and that the right of soil and exclusive jurisdiction be vested in the United States. This statute was repealed on the 24th of April, 1784, and on the 30th of October following, while Congress was sitting at Trenton, they appointed three commissioners to lay out a district on either bank of the Delaware, " not more than eight miles above or below the falls." They were authorized to purchase soil, erect and complete in an " elegant manner" a Federal house, President's house, houses for the secretaries of foreign affairs, war, marine, and treasury, but owing to the resistance of Southern members no appropriation to carry out the provisions of the act was made, and the law was never carried into execution.

On the 13th of January, 1785, an effort was made to substitute the Potomac, which failed. On the 10th of May, 1787, Mr. Lee, of Virginia, offered a resolution " for erecting the necessary public buildings for the accommodation of Congress at Georgetown, on the Potomac River," which was lost. The new constitution of 1787 declared that Congress shall have power to exercise exclusive legislation over such a district, not exceeding ten miles square, as may, by the cession of States, become the seat of government.

No action was had under this provision of the Constitution until Dec. 23, 1788, when the General Assembly of Maryland passed " an act to cede to Congress a district of ten miles square in this State for the seat of government of the United States." By this act it was enacted " by the General Assembly of Maryland that the representatives of this State in the House of Representatives of the Congress of the United States, appointed to assemble at New York on the first Wednesday of March next, be and they are hereby authorized and required, on behalf of this State, to cede to the Congress of the United States any district in this State, not exceeding ten miles square, which the Congress may fix upon and accept for the seat of government of the United States."

On the 27th of December Virginia passed a similar resolution, but no action was taken by Congress upon the measure until the 5th of September, 1789, when a resolution passed the House of Representatives " that the permanent seat of government of the United States ought to be at some convenient place on the banks of the Susquehanna, in the State of Pennsylvania." In the debates to carry this resolution into effect much feeling was displayed by the Southern members, and particularly by those from Virginia. They earnestly contended that the bank of the Potomac was the most suitable location. Mr. Madison, in the course of the debate, went so far as to declare that if the proceedings of that day had been foreseen by Virginia that State might not have become a party to the Constitution. As it was a matter of great importance, Mr. Scott declared that " the future tranquillity and well-being of the United States depended as much on this as on any question that had or could come before the Congress," and Mr. Fisher Ames remarked that " every principle of pride and honor, and even of patriotism, was engaged."

"I confess," said Mr. Vinning, "to the House and to the world that, viewing this subject in all its circumstances, I am in favor of the Potomac. I wish the seat of government to be fixed there because I think the interests, the honor, and the greatness of the country require it. I look upon it as the centre from which those streams are to flow that are to animate and invigorate the body politic. From thence it appears to me that the rays of government will naturally divulge to the extremities of the Union. I declare that I look upon the Western territory in an awful and striking point of view. To that region the unpolished sons of earth are pouring from all quarters,—men to whom the protection of the law and the controlling form of government are equally necessary. From this consideration I conclude that the bank of the Potomac is the proper situation."

The bill passed the House by thirty-one ayes to nineteen nays, with an amendment striking out the word Susquehanna, and inserting a clause that the permanent seat of government should be established at Germantown, Pa., whenever that State or its citizens should agree to pay one hundred thousand dollars for the erection of public buildings. The bill went back to the Senate for the consideration of the amendment, and before the Senate could act upon it Congress adjourned.

The fact that the North had the preponderance of votes in Congress now aroused Maryland and Virginia, who determined to evoke the power of money. On the 3d of December, 1789, the Legislature of Virginia passed an act ceding to Congress a district for the location of the seat of government in that State, and on the 10th transmitted the same to the Assembly of Maryland. At the November session of 1790 the Legislature of Maryland passed the following resolution:

"*Whereas*, By a resolution of the General Assembly of Virginia, passed on the 10th day of December, 1789, it was proposed to the General Assembly of Maryland that the Assembly of Virginia will pass an act for advancing a sum of money not less than one hundred and twenty thousand dollars to the use of the general government, and to be applied in such manner as Congress shall direct towards erecting public buildings, the Assembly of Maryland, on their part, advancing a sum not less than three-fifths of the sum advanced by the said State of Virginia, which resolution came so late to the last General Assembly of Maryland that it could not be acted upon, and was therefore referred to this present session; and, whereas, this General Assembly doth highly approve of the object of the said resolution, and is desirous of doing everything required, on the part of Maryland, for carrying the same into effect, on a second reading of the said resolution,

"*Resolved*, That this House doth accede to the proposition contained in the said resolution of the Assembly of Virginia, and will advance to the President of the United States, for the purpose mentioned in the said resolution, the sum of seventy-two thousand dollars, payable to his order in three equal yearly payments."

At the same time, to secure the prompt payment of the sum advanced, the treasurer of the Western Shore was authorized to sell the "reserved lands westward of Fort Cumberland," and also the lands lying in Dorchester County, and now in the possession of the tribe of Choptank Indians, and "to sell and convey the right of this State to one hundred acres of land at Fort Frederick, in Washington County." New York and Philadelphia at the same time offered to continue their "elegant and convenient accommodations." New Jersey offered several suitable buildings at Trenton. Baltimore subscribed in fourteen days £20,000, which was subsequently increased to £40,000, towards the erection of all government edifices if the capital should be located in that city.

On the 31st of May, 1790, a bill was introduced into the Senate to determine "the permanent seat of Congress and the government of the United States."

Baltimore and Georgetown again pressed their claims, but the motion was finally carried that a site "on the river Potomac, at some place between the mouths of the Eastern Branch and the Conecocheague, be and the same is hereby accepted for the permanent seat of the government of the United States." Mr. Varnum says,—

"The debates on the several resolutions and bills elicited much warmth of feeling and sectional jealousy. Almost all were agreed that New York was not a suitable place, as not being sufficiently central.

"There was much division of sentiment as to the relative advantages of Philadelphia and Germantown, in Pennsylvania; Havre de Grace and a place called Wright's Ferry, on the Susquehanna; Baltimore, on the Patapsco; and Conecocheague, on the Potomac. The last two were about equally balanced for some time in the number of supporters. It was remarked by one of the members of Maryland that the people of the State were in the situation of Tantalus, uncertain which to prefer, the Susquehanna or the Potomac. Mr. J. Smith set forth the advantages of Baltimore, and the fact that its citizens had subscribed forty thousand dollars for public buildings. The South Carolinians offered an apparently whimsical objection to Philadelphia, to wit: the number of Quakers, who, they said, were eternally dogging the Southern members with their schemes of emancipation. Others ridiculed the idea of building palaces in the woods. Mr. Gerry, of Massachusetts, thought it highly unreasonable to fix the government seat in such a position as to have nine States out of thirteen to the northward of the place, and adverted to the sacrifices the Northern States were ready to make in being willing to go so far south as Baltimore. Mr. Page said New York was superior to any place he knew for the orderly and decent behavior of its inhabitants. The motion to insert Baltimore instead of the Potomac was negatived by a vote of thirty-seven to twenty-three."

The act "establishing the temporary and permanent seat of government of the United States" was finally passed on the 16th of July, 1790, by a vote of thirty-two to twenty-nine. The first section of this act provides

"that a district of territory not exceeding ten miles square, to be located as hereafter directed, on the river Potomac, at some place between the mouth of the Eastern Branch and Conecocheague, be and the same is hereby accepted for the permanent seat of government of the United States."

Thus it was that this "sugar-plum" was given to the South for their adoption of the "Assumption Bill," which Mr. Jefferson says was "a bitter pill" to the Southern States, and it was necessary that "some concomitant measure should be adopted to sweeten it a little to them."

In compliance with the act of Congress, President Washington, in 1790, visited Williamsport, Washington Co., but not liking the situation, he finally selected the present site as the future capital of the country. As the act passed by Congress required the district to be located above the mouth of the Eastern Branch, he procured on the 3d of March, 1791, the passage of an amendatory act, by which he was authorized to make

"any part of the territory below the said limit, and above the mouth of Hunting Creek, a part of said district, so as to include a convenient part of the Eastern Branch, and of the lands lying on the lower side thereof, and also the town of Alexandria, provided that no public buildings be erected otherwise than on the Maryland side of the Potomac."

On the 24th of January, 1791, President Washington, in compliance with the act of Congress, appointed Hon. Thomas Johnson and Hon. Daniel Carroll, of Maryland, and Dr. David Stewart, of Alexandria, Va., commissioners, and directed them to lay off "the Territory of Columbia." Having completed their task of selecting the site, the President, on the 30th of March following, located the district for the permanent seat of the government, and in a letter to Thomas Jefferson, Secretary of State, dated March 31, 1791, he gives the following result of his efforts:

"The terms entered into by me, on the part of the United States, with the landholders of Georgetown and Carrollsburg are that all the land from Rock Creek along the river to the Eastern Branch, and so upwards to or above the ferry, including a breadth of about a mile and a half, the whole containing from three to five thousand acres, is ceded to the public, on condition that when the whole shall be surveyed and laid off as a city (which Maj. L'Enfant is now directed to do) the present proprietors shall retain every other lot; and as for such part of land as may be taken for public use, for squares, walks, etc., they shall be allowed at the rate of twenty-five pounds per acre ($66.67), the public having the right to preserve such parts of the wood on the land as may be thought necessary to be preserved for ornament, the landholders to have the use and profits of all the grounds until the city is laid off into lots and sale is made of those lots, which by this agreement become public property. Nothing is to be allowed for the ground which may be occupied as streets or alleys."

Under the date of April 10th, Mr. Jefferson replied, rejoicing in the economy of the bargain:

"The acquisition of ground at Georgetown is really noble, considering that only £25 an acre is to be paid for any grounds taken for the public, and the streets not to be counted, which will in fact reduce it to about £19 an acre. I think very liberal reserves should be made for the public."

The territory thus selected by Washington was mainly owned by four planters,—Daniel Carroll, David Burns, Samuel Davidson, and Notley Young,—who conveyed their property on the 19th of June, 1791, to Thomas Beall, of George, and John M. Gantt, in trust to be laid out for a Federal city; and the said Thomas Beall, of George, and John M. Gantt were to convey to the commissioners, for the use of the United States forever, all the streets and such of the said squares, parcels, and lots as the President should deem proper for the use of the United States forever.

In carrying out the objects of the act of Congress, the commissioners on the 15th of April superintended the fixing of the first corner-stone of the District of Columbia at Jones' Point, near Alexandria, where it was laid with all the Masonic ceremonies usual at the time. And on the 29th of June following, agreeable to appointment, the President and the three commissioners, with a large number of gentlemen, met in "the Federal Town" to select the situations for the public buildings. "Jenkins' Hill, on the east side of Goose Creek, the property of Daniel Carroll, Jr.," was chosen as the site for the Capitol, and that part of the district called Hamburgh, near Burn's gate, was selected for the President's house.

The name which Washington City and the District of Columbia now bears was adopted by the first commissioners, for in a letter to Maj. L'Enfant, dated Georgetown, Sept. 9, 1791, they inform the engineer that they have agreed that the Federal district shall be called "the Territory of Columbia," and the Federal city "the City of Washington," and directs him to entitle his map accordingly.

On the 19th of December, 1791, the General Assembly of Maryland passed an act ceding to the United States for the permanent seat of government that portion of territory which lies in the State of Maryland, which together with that ceded by Virginia made a tract of ten miles square, bounded as follows:

"Beginning at Jones' Point, being the upper part of Hunting Creek, in Virginia, and at an angle, at the outset, of forty-five degrees west of the north, and running a direct line ten miles, for the first line; then beginning again at the same Jones' Point and running another direct line at a right angle with the first across the Potomac, ten miles, for the second line; then from the termination of the first and second lines, running two other direct lines, ten miles each, the one crossing the Eastern Branch and the other the Potomac, and meeting each other in a point, which has since been called the Territory of Columbia."

This act, although it ceded a portion of the territory of the State, did not rest the rights of its citizens on the provisions of the Constitution alone, but by the following clause it will be seen that the Legislature expressly reserves them in the articles of cession, and denies the power of Congress to interfere with the right of property. The act of cession declares—

"That all that part of the said Territory called Columbia which lies within the limits of this State shall be and the same is hereby acknowledged to be forever ceded and relinquished to the Congress of the United States, in full and absolute right and exclusive jurisdiction, as well of soil as of persons residing or to reside thereon, pursuant to the tenor and effect of the eighth section of the first article of the constitution of government of the United States; provided that nothing herein contained shall be so construed to vest in the United States any right of property in the soil as to affect the rights of individuals thereon, otherwise than the same shall or may be transferred by such individuals to the United States; and provided also that the jurisdiction of the laws of this State over the persons and property of individuals residing within the limits of the cessation aforesaid shall not cease or determine until Congress shall, by law, provide for the government thereof under their jurisdiction, in manner provided by the Article of the Constitution before recited."

As slavery was a species of property, and existed in the District of Columbia before this act of cession, it was regarded as included in the compact between the three sovereign powers,—sovereign and independent within their respective spheres, and qualified and competent to enter into a compact, and therefore not to be annulled without the consent of all the parties. Slavery existed in the District of Columbia before the Constitution and the laws to which it gave origin were framed, and the obligations which it was intended to enforce were recognized and declared to be in force before the government was established there. Maryland, Virginia, and the general government recognized this principle by various acts of legislation up to the time of its abolishment, and the Senate of Maryland reiterated this document as late as the year 1837, when they resolved, on Mr. Joseph S. Cottman's resolution,—

"That Congress does *not* possess the power to abolish slavery in the District of Columbia, and in the opinion of this Legislature the abolition of slavery in said District by Congress would be a violation of the terms and conditions upon which the cession of the District of Columbia was made to the Federal government; and in the event of such violation the territory included in said district ought, and of right will, revert respectively to the States of Virginia and Maryland."

On the 29th of September, 1792, President Washington authorized the commissioners to dispose of any lot or lots in the city of Washington at private sale, for such price and on such terms as they should think proper. No sales, however, took place of any consequence until the 23d of December, 1793, when a contract was made with Robert Morris, of Philadelphia, and James Greenleaf, of New York, for the sale of six thousand lots, averaging five thousand two hundred and sixty-five square feet each, and situated northeast and southwest of Massachusetts Avenue, for the sum of eighty dollars per lot, payable in seven equal annual installments, without interest, commencing on the 1st of May, 1794, and with a condition of building twenty brick houses annually, two stories high, and covering twelve hundred square feet each. This contract was afterwards modified by an agreement dated April 24, 1794, by which the payment of eighty thousand dollars and erecting the houses should rest on the joint bond of Morris, Greenleaf, and John Nicholson, and that one thousand lots should be conveyed to the said Morris and Greenleaf.

On the 18th of September, 1793, the southeast corner-stone of the north wing of the Capitol was laid with Masonic orders; George Washington, Worshipful Master of Lodge No. 22, Virginia, directing, assisted by the Grand Lodge of Maryland and several lodges under its direction. A volunteer company of artillery from Alexandria, with mayor and other corporate officers of Washington, Georgetown, and Alexandria, and a numerous body of citizens also participated in the ceremonies. The orator of the day was Joseph Claude, of Annapolis. The *Maryland Gazette* of September 26th informs us that at the conclusion of the ceremonies "the whole company retired to an extensive booth, where an ox of five hundred pounds' weight was barbecued, of which the company generally partook, with every abundance of other recreation."

We have already stated that as an inducement for the selection of this site Virginia advanced one hundred and twenty thousand dollars for the construction of the public buildings, and Maryland seventy-two thousand dollars. This sum was soon exhausted, and, moreover, Robert Morris and James Greenleaf, who had purchased large tracts of land, not only failed to pay the first installment, which fell due in May, 1795, but early in that year discontinued the buildings which they had commenced under their contract. The President, finding that the work on the public buildings must stop for the lack of funds, and that it would not be prudent to offer for sale so large a portion of the public property as would be necessary to raise the sums requisite to complete them, sent a message to Congress in 1796, in which he urged the propriety of authorizing the loan, secured by the city property, and if that should prove deficient, then Congress was to guarantee it. Congress approved of the measure, and authorized a loan under their guarantee to the amount of three hundred thousand dollars. But so low was the credit of the young capital, and so uncertain her further existence, that it was impossible to obtain the smallest loan. After various unsuccessful attempts to borrow money at home and abroad, Washington determined to make a personal application to the State of Maryland for a loan. In a letter to Governor John Hoskins Stone, dated Philadelphia, Dec. 7, 1796, he says,—

"Sir,—The attempts lately made by the commissioners of Washington City to borrow money in Europe for the purpose of carrying on the public buildings having failed, or been retarded, they have been authorized by me to apply to your State for a loan of $150,000, upon terms which they will communicate. Such is the present condition of foreign nations with respect to money that, according to the best information, there is no reasonable hope of obtaining a loan in any of them immediately, and application can now only be made in the United States upon this subject with any prospect of success, and perhaps nowhere with greater propriety than to the Legislature of Maryland, where, it must be presumed, the most anxious solicitude is felt for the growth and prosperity of that city which is intended for the permanent seat of government of America.

"If the State has in its power to lend the money which is solicited, I persuade myself it will be done, and the more especially at this time when a loan is so indispensable, that without it not only very great and many impediments must be induced in the prosecution of the work now in hand, but inevitable loss must be sustained by the funds of the city in consequence of premature sales of public property.

"I have thought I ought not to omit to state, for the information of the General Assembly, as well the difficulty of obtaining money on loan as the present necessity for it, which I must request the favor of you most respectfully to communicate."

Such was the influence of his name that Maryland, on the 4th of December, 1796, lent one hundred thousand dollars, to be used for the erection of the Capitol buildings; but so low was the credit of the general government that, as an additional guarantee of the repayment of the loan, the State required Gustavus Scott, William Thornton, and Alexander White, the three commissioners, in their individual capacity, to give bond of two hundred thousand dollars. On the 22d of December, 1797, the State lent them an additional sum of one hundred thousand dollars upon similar terms, and on the 23d of December, 1799, fifty thousand dollars more. As security for the latter sum, Gustavus Scott and William Thornton gave their individual bond, together with Uriah Forrest and James Maccubbin Lingan. On the third Monday of November, 1800, Congress opened its first session in the city of Washington.

Washington, the national metropolis of the United States, is beautifully and conveniently situated on a gentle undulating surface on the north bank of the Potomac, between Rock Creek and the Anacostia, or Eastern Branch. The city extends northwest and southeast for about four and a half miles, and from the east to the south for about two and a half miles.

The public buildings occupy the most elevated and convenient situations. The streets run north and south, east and west, crossing each other at right angles, with the exception of fifteen avenues, which are named after the States. The Capitol commands the streets called Maryland, Delaware, and Pennsylvania Avenues; the President's house those of Pennsylvania, Vermont, New York, and Connecticut, and all these different intersections eleven hundred and seventy squares. Pennsylvania Avenue, which stretches in a direct line from Georgetown to the Eastern Branch, passing the President's house to the Capitol, is four miles in length and one hundred and sixty feet in width between these edifices, and one hundred and thirty feet east of the Capitol and west of the President's house. The streets, which are from seventy to one hundred feet wide, give a fine appearance to the city. The whole area of the city is about three thousand and sixteen acres, and its circumference about fourteen miles.

The longitude of the capital was determined in 1821, by calculations made by William Lambert from observations conducted by William Elliot, under the authority of Congress, to be seventy-seven degrees one minute and forty-eight seconds (77° 1' 48") west from the observatory of Greenwich, and the latitude thirty-eight degrees fifty-five minutes and forty-eight seconds (38° 55' 48") north.

Washington is nearly surrounded by a fine amphitheatre of hills of moderate elevation, covered with trees and shrubbery, and commanding from many points picturesque scenery and extensive views of the Potomac, or "River of Swans," which, descending from the Allegany Mountains, and winding its way for nearly four hundred miles through a fertile and most attactive country, empties into the Chesapeake Bay, and finally through its ample waters mingles itself with the ocean. The environs of the city abound in the most eligible sites for villas and country-seats, and such will doubtless be multiplied as the advantages of the metropolis become more extensively known.

The public buildings of Washington are the Capitol, the Executive Mansion, the State offices, Treasury buildings, War offices, Navy offices, offices of the Secretary of the Interior, Post-office, office of the Attorney-General, National Observatory, the Arsenal, navy-yard, Smithsonian Institute, National Medical College, Columbian College, Coast Survey office, City Hall, National Institute, numerous churches, the hotels, and many others devoted to a variety of useful, literary, and benevolent purposes.

The Capitol is situated on an area of thirty acres, inclosed by an iron railing. The building stands on the western portion of this plot, and is so elevated as to command a view of the entire city, including Georgetown Heights, the windings of the Potomac, and the city of Alexandria. It was commenced in 1793, with Mr. Hallet as architect, who was succeeded in that capacity by Mr. Hadfield, Mr. Hoban, and Mr. Latrobe. During the embargo the works were suspended, and as the British subsequently demolished much of what had been accomplished by the above gentlemen, the government in 1815 found it necessary to reconstruct the whole edifice. It was finished as it now stands under the superintendence of C. Bullfinch. The exterior exhibits a rusticated basement of the height of the first story; the other two stories are comprised in a Corinthian elevation of pilasters and columns; these columns, which are thirty feet in height, form an advancing portico on the east, one hundred and sixty feet in extent, the centre of which is crowned with a pediment of eighty feet span, while a receding loggia one hundred feet in extent distinguishes the centre of the west front.

The building is surrounded by a balustrade of stone, and covered with a lofty dome in the centre and a flat dome on each wing. The dimensions of the buildings are, length of front three hundred and fifty-two feet four inches, depth of wings one hundred and twenty-one feet six inches, and the height to the top of the dome one hundred and forty-five feet. The cost up to 1828, when it may be said to have been completed, was nearly one million eight hundred thousand dollars. During the session of Congress, 1850-51, appropriations were made for the further enlargement of the Capitol by the addition of two new wings of two hundred and thirty-eight by one hundred and forty feet each wing, and the whole Capitol, including the space between the wings and the main building, covers an area of four and one-third acres. The corner-stone of the extension was laid by President Fillmore on the 4th of July, 1851, with Masonic ceremonies, on which occasion the Hon. Daniel Webster delivered a brilliant oration.

CHAPTER XXXVI.

INTERNAL IMPROVEMENTS IN MONTGOMERY COUNTY.

Public Roads and Bridges—Stage-Coaches—Railroads—Chesapeake and Ohio Canal.

FAR more attention appears to have been given by the people of Montgomery in early times to the improvement of the public roads than is frequently bestowed on them at the present time by the inhabitants of some of the counties. In 1777 the roads were laid out and the following persons appointed overseers, and it was not unusual for the overseers to be fined for neglect of duty, as has already been observed by the records of the court:

1. From the top of Strong Hill, above Henry Threlkeld's, to Thomas Graves'.—James Toppin.
2. From Thomas Graves' to Captain John Run, below James Offutt's mill.—Thomas Duley.
3. From the fork of the road above the plantation on the main road, belonging to George Reed, to Rock Creek bridge, by Charles Jones', and from said bridge to Aaron Lanham's and Charles Jones' gate, and from Thomas Graves' to Rock Creek ford, from thence to the county line which leads to the church.—Thomas Graves.
4. From Captain John Run, including the bridge crossway near Ninian Riley's, to the house *keeped* by Leonard Davis.—James Moore.
5. From Leonard Davis' to Rock Creek bridge, near James Smith's former plantation, and from Leonard Davis' to a bridge on Rock Creek near William Beckwith's, and from Rock Creek *Chappell* until it intersects the George Town road.—Ninian Riley.
6. From Thomas Graves' to Captain John Run, by James Moore's, and from Thomas Richardson's and Thomas Johns' mill to the main road that leads by the said James Moore's.—Joseph Gill.
7. From Captain John Meeting-house to the plantation of Zachariah McCubbin.—William Wallace, Sr.
8. From Leonard Davis' to Henry Claggett's, and from Leonard Davis' to the Muddy Branch, and from said Davis' to Joseph Wilson's quarter, and up to Luke Bernard's road.—Peter Brown.
9. From Seneca to the mill branch, and with the said road to the end.
10. From Sligo to Mrs. Carroll's plantation, to the county line on the church road, and out of that road to Sligo, to Walter Beall's mill, and out of the first road to Rock Creek bridge, near Mr. Charles Jones'.—Dent Summers.
11. From John Lee's, on Sligo, on the road to Bladensburg, to the county line, and from said Lee's to the cross-roads below Thomas Cramphin's, and from the Northwest, by Walter Beall's mill, on the direct road to church, to Sligo Branch.—John Watson.
12. From Muddy Branch to Seneca bridge, by Henry Cramphin's plantation, and from the fork of the road over the bridge to Graff's mill.—Ninian Beall, Philip Houser.
13. From John Fletchall's to John Willcoxon's road.—Benjamin Gatten.
14. From the eastermost side of the branch, where the bridge is, near Charles Hays', to Seneca, and from Charles Hays' bridge to Willcoxon's old road.—Benjamin Summers.
15. From Monocacy to the east side of the bridge near Charles Hays'.—Jeremiah Jacobs.
16. From Seneca bridge, near Lodwick Yoast's, to the county line above Little Bennett's Creek, and to the ford on Seneca above Richard Watts'.—John Fryer.
17. From Joseph Willson's quarter to the bridge on Seneca near Lodwick Yoast's.—James Raet.
18. From the bridge on Rock Creek to the cross-roads that leads by Mrs. Carroll's, and from Thomas Williams' mill to the Watery Branch, near where Thomas Roley liveth.—Thomas Nicholls, son of Thomas.

19. From Rock Creek bridge, going to the Chappell, until it intersects the road going to Swenford's bridge downwards, and down said road until it falls into the main road at Henry Wilson's.—Henry Davidson.

20. From James Brooke's to Bucey's road, and to Charles Williams' lower part of the road, from Brooke's to Williams'.

21. From the bridge near George Snell's to the fork of the road below Samuel Richardson's late dwelling plantation, and from there to cross Hawling's River, to intersect the road near Green's bridge.—George Darby.

22. From Green's bridge to the fork of the road commonly called Bucey's road, near Joshua Dorsey's quarter.—John Prather.

23. From the county line near Jonathan Nixson's to Walter Beall's mill, and from the said mill to Jeremiah Ducker's shop, from the said place across the Northwest Branch to the fork of the road near Richard Thomas' quarter.—Samuel Thomas, Jr.

24. From the northwest side of Captain John bridge to the centre of Watts' Branch bridge, from Mrs. Offut's plantation to the meeting-house on Captain John, from the said meeting-house to the road by Henry Claggett's to Leonard Davis' tavern.—Henry Claggett.

25. From Bennett's Creek to the new road that goes by Richardson's quarter to Halling's River.

26. From Jones' saw-mil to Graff's mill.—Adin Pancoast.

27. From Graff's mill to the centre of the crossway near Walter's, in the sugar lands.—William Evans.

28. From the centre of the crossway in the sugar lands, near Walter's, to John Fletchall's upper gate.—Gabriel Baxter.

29. All the streets and alleys in George Town to the top of the stony hill above Henry Threlkeld's, and from the end of the main street to the bridge over the mouth of Rock Creek.—Benjamin Notley Pierce.

30. From the Mill Branch to George Robinson's bridge, and the road that leads from William Beckwith's mill to Dent's mill.—Aaron Prather.

31. From the Bladensburg road near John Trundel's to the George Town road near John Claggett's, and from the Bladensburg road where the same turns off to George Town, below Allen Bowie's, to Sligo bridge near Mrs. Carroll's, and from Richardson's mill to the main road that leads by Andrew Heughs'.—Aaron Lanham.

32. From the road that leads from Graff's mill till it intersects the road from Little Monocacy by Henry Allison's.—Samuel Biggs, Samuel Douglass.

33. From the county line near Thomas Richardson's tavern to Snowden's Manor, from Snowden's Manor to the fork of the road near Jeremiah Ducker's shop, and from Snowden's Manor to the fork of the road above Richard Thomas' quarter.—John Thomas.

34. From the fork of the road below Seneca to the fork of the road above Richard Thomas' quarter.—Higginson Belt, Sr.

35. From the county line above Henry Ridgely's quarter down to the fork of the road commonly called Bucey's road.—William Owen.

36. From the eastermost side of Jacob's bridge until it intersects the Sugar Land road running from Graff's mill.—Benjamin McKoll.

Nothing more clearly attests the energy and enterprise of a community than the attention bestowed upon the roads and bridges, the highways of communication between different portions of the neighborhood and the outside world. It is one of the distinguishing features of general enlightenment.

In 1778 the Levy Court, at the November term, appropriated £100 for the erection of a bridge over Seneca Creek near Ludwick Yost's tavern, the same amount for the building of a bridge over Rock Creek near the Chapel, and a similar sum for a bridge over the same creek near the plantation of Charles Jones. It must not be imagined, however, that the fine system of roads which now makes traveling a pleasure rather than a burden in this portion of Maryland was immediately established.

The first roads of which there is any record were: The old Indian road from Washington to Frederick crossed Seneca ("Sinicar") Creek a few yards above the present county road crossing, and a road from Sandy Spring, a settlement commenced by James Brooke in 1726, which entered the highway from Frederick to Baltimore at Porter's tavern, a distance of eighteen miles. The first public roads mentioned in the county are the roads from Frederick to Georgetown, that from Georgetown to the mouth of the Monocacy, and the road from the mouth of Monocacy to Montgomery Court-house, in the act of Assembly of 1790 to straighten and amend the public roads in the several counties; and the road from the mouth of Watts' Branch to the same place, provided for in the loan granted to the several counties for road purposes by the act of Assembly of 1784.

The planters at that early period did not use wheeled vehicles, but attached a sapling to each end of a tobacco hogshead, and thus formed a pair of shafts, by which they hauled the hogshead for shipment to Europe, to Bladensburg, Georgetown, Elk Ridge, Sandy Springs, and Baltimore, and brought back their supplies of groceries and other necessaries on the backs of horses. Public highways were unknown. "Rolling roads," made by tobacco hogsheads which were rolled to the inspection warehouses, and bridle-paths, used by pack-horses, were the chief means of communication.

They even brought their annual supply of herring and shad in this manner. Their clothing and bed-linen were chiefly woven from home-grown flax and wool. Their personal travel was done exclusively on horseback.

The turnpike from Rockville to Georgetown, the first paved road in the county, was originally chartered in 1806, but was actually constructed under an amendatory act, containing the chief provisions of its present charter, passed 1817. The Union turnpike, leading from Washington to Brookville, was chartered in 1849. It has recently built several branch roads. The Washington, Colesville and Ashton turnpike road was chartered in 1870. The Conduit road, from

Georgetown to the Great Falls of the Potomac, has just been completed. It follows the line of the Washington Aqueduct, and crosses Cabin John Branch on a bridge of a single arch of the longest span in the world. This aqueduct is also a Montgomery work, having its source and almost its entire line within the limits of the county, and its permissive right from the State of Maryland.

The Columbia road runs from Washington to Westminster through Brookville. The old Baltimore road runs through the county, commencing on the Monocacy near its mouth. The river road runs along the Potomac from Georgetown to White's Ferry. The old Annapolis road runs from the Brookville turnpike near Mitchell's Cross-roads to Annapolis.

In 1791 the grand jurors at the November court were

Jesse Wharton, Samuel Hardesty, Samuel Williams, Joseph N. Chiswell, Lawrence O. Holt, Edward Crow, Alexander Whittaker, Burch Chesire, Zachariah Linthicum, Nicholas Payne, Benjamin Ricketts, Ninian Willett, Edward Hardinge, Zachariah Austin, John Ray, Jacob Williams, Edward Willett, Richard Conner.

In 1800, at November court, the grand jurors were

John Linthicum, Ignatius Waters, Frederick Linthicum, George Riley, John Wallace, John Dunlap, Robert Peter, Jr., Stephen Adams, Frederick Gaither, Isaac L. Lansdale, John H. Riggs, Daniel Beall, Basil Darby, William Willson, John B. Magruder, James O. Bowman, William Garrett, Henry Warring, Howard Griffith, Lawrence O. Holt, Thomas Riggs, of Samuel, Samuel Willson, Burgess Culver.

Western Mail-Stage.—In 1819 the Frederick Town mail-stage started from Mr. John Davis', Washington City, on Sundays, Tuesdays, and Thursdays, at two o'clock in the morning, calling at Mr. Tennison's (the Washington Hotel), at Mr. Oneite's (the Franklin House, in Washington City), at the stage-office (at the Union Tavern) in Georgetown, and breakfasted at Mr. Campbell's, at Rockville, and thence to Frederick Town, in time for the Western mail-stage. Returning, it left Mrs. Kimball's (the old stand), Frederick, on Mondays, Wednesdays, and Fridays, at 9 A.M., and arrived in Washington at an early hour those evenings. The fare through was four dollars. The passengers going by the above line were entitled to a preference for seats in the mail-stage from Frederick to Hagerstown, Pittsburgh, or Wheeling.

The first railroad in operation in Maryland it is said was built in Montgomery County. The rails were laid and a line of road four or five miles in length constructed to facilitate the transportation of stone from the great "White Quarry," at the foot of the Sugar-Loaf, for the building of an aqueduct by the Chesapeake and Ohio Canal Company over the river Monocacy at its junction with the Potomac. Excavations for the Baltimore and Ohio Railroad may have commenced before excavations for this little mountain road, but it is quite certain that here the first rails were laid, and here the first railroad in Maryland, and perhaps the first in the United States, was put in full operation. Iron rails were not used, but wooden, or "string-pieces," as they were called, consisting of nothing more than trunks of trees, generally oak, cut from twelve to sixteen feet long, so as to allow the diameter at the smaller end to be not less than eight or ten inches. Along the whole length of these string-pieces a groove or triangular trough was cut with an adze from the circumference to the centre, taking out a fourth part of the wood, which left two flat surfaces, forming a right angle at the heart or centre of the log. The trackway was graded, and the log or string-piece put down with one of its flat surfaces parallel with the surface of the ground, and the other perpendicular to it. The perimeter of the car-wheel ran on the flat surface of the groove or trough, and the outside or outward edge of the perimeter moved along the perpendicular surfaces of the string-piece on each side of the track, preventing it from running off. The track was firmly ballasted on the inner and outer side with blast-rock. A smooth path was made between the string-pieces to accommodate two horses abreast. No cross-ties were used, the weight of the string-pieces and stone ballast was sufficient to bind the track together. When one flat surface of the rail or string-piece was worn and split by the pressure of the wheel, the other was substituted by turning the rails "end for end," or from "side to side" of the track, and thus the road was repaired, until it became necessary to put in new string-pieces. The road was built up-hill and down, through a rough and mountainous country for the greater part of the way, very little grading being done. The cars consisted of plain wooden platforms only, supported by iron wheels and axles. One wheel or more on each car had cogs on the inside of the perimeter, into which an iron lever could play, so as to lock a wheel or two in going down-hill. The lever was held in the hands of the driver of the horses, and when the wheel or wheels were locked, the car, with its great load of hewn rock, would, to the relief of the horses, slide down the hill like a locked wagon on an earthen road. Snow was removed from the track by laborers with shovels. A car containing tools and provisions, with "gigger" cups and big jugs, was dispatched from each terminus of the road to clear off the snow, and when the two parties met on the road, double giggers were dealt out by the "grog boss," and great hilarity presently followed, unless the laborers happened to be hostile, and then an attempt might be made to repeat the battle of the Boyne.

The road was kept in active operation until the

aqueduct was finished, and then abandoned to decay. Most of the string-pieces, however, were soon seized by the mountaineers for firewood, and the ballast hauled off to build and repair stone fences.

The Baltimore and Ohio Railroad, the pioneer of all the great railroad systems of the world, is not strictly a Montgomery work, and its main stem nowhere touches the territory, but it skirts the entire eastern and northern frontier, and approaches nearly to the western confines, and is of vital importance to a large portion of the inhabitants of the county.

The Metropolitan Branch of the Baltimore and Ohio Railroad was chartered in 1865, and completed and operated in July, 1873. This road runs diagonally through the county from its northwest corner to the southeastern extremity, and is available for nearly every section. When its Hanover Switch Branch is constructed there will be no neighborhood in the county which is not within easy reach of either a railroad or a canal.

The Metropolitan Railroad Company was organized in 1853, to build a railroad from Georgetown, D. C., *via* Frederick to Hagerstown. The first meeting of the directors was held July 30, 1853, for the election of president, and at a subsequent meeting on August 11th the chief engineer was elected, who at once selected a corps of assistants and commenced the preliminary surveys. Another party was formed in November. The former was engaged on the lower division of the work, and the latter between Frederick and Hagerstown. From the rough nature of the country through which the road was required to be built, very careful examinations were found necessary, with a view of finding the most eligible and central route through Montgomery County, and at the same time to make selection of a line for location which would give general satisfaction to the several interests involved in the work. A very large amount of duty was satisfactorily performed by the engineer department. Five hundred and forty miles were carefully surveyed and estimated, while the whole distance from Georgetown to Hagerstown was but a little over seventy-five miles.

Besides the several routes surveyed, many reconnoissances were made, and crest-levels taken on Parr's Ridge, in Montgomery County, in all of which very favorable passes were found, and the line adopted for location proved to correspond almost with the exact terms of the charter. The amount of subscription on which this road was organized was five hundred thousand dollars, on which up to July, 1854, the payments to the commissioners amounted to fifty thousand nine hundred dollars.

The officers of the company for 1854 were:

President, Francis Dodge; Directors, John W. Maury, W. W. Corcoran, Joseph Bryan, George Parker, Washington City; Daniel Weisel, Hagerstown, Md.; M. Davis, Frederick County, Md.; F. C. Clopper, Montgomery County, Md.; A. H. Dodge, A. H. Pickrell, W. M. Boyce, David English, H. C. Matthews, Georgetown, D. C.; J. W. Deeble, secretary and treasurer; E. French, chief engineer; W. H. Grant, acting chief engineer.

The charter called for its location "from Georgetown by the most eligible and central route through Montgomery County, crossing the Baltimore and Ohio Railroad at a point not exceeding five miles from the Monocacy Viaduct, by the line of said railroad to Frederick City, in Frederick County, thence by the most convenient and practical route through Frederick and Washington Counties to Hagerstown."

Preliminary surveys were made of four lines, as follows, to the Baltimore and Ohio Railroad and city of Frederick:

Line No. 1.—The first line examined started from "Cox's Corner," in Georgetown, leaving the city on the west, crossing the head-waters of the small tributaries of the Potomac, and passing about three-quarters of a mile west of the village of Rockville; thence, taking a general course ranging a little to the west of the city of Frederick, it passed on the east side of the Sugar Loaf Mountain, descending Bennett's Creek, crossing the ridge between Bennett's Creek and the Monocacy River, and from the Monocacy River to the Baltimore and Ohio Railroad near Buckeystown Station. From thence the line took a direct course to the western part of the city of Frederick.

Line No. 2 was surveyed by the party returning from Frederick to Georgetown, and commenced at the Baltimore and Ohio Railroad at the point of crossing by the first line, and diverging westwardly from the first line, crossed the Monocacy River at a point about a mile north of the county line between Frederick and Montgomery Counties and west of the Sugar Loaf Mountain; thence to a point on the stream known as the "Long Draught," about six miles northwest of Rockville, where it crossed the first line (No. 1) and kept to the east until it reunited with it about one mile west of Rockville.

Line No. 3 was surveyed from Georgetown to Frederick, commencing at a higher elevation in Georgetown, above "Cox's Corner," near the northwestern limits of the city, and taking a more easterly direction from the starting-point than No. 1, ascending the ridge dividing the tributaries of the Potomac from those of Rock Creek, passing on the east side of the village of Rockville to the head-waters of the tributaries of Seneca Creek, and keeping for a greater part of the distance on Rock Creek or the eastern slope of the ridge; curving to the east of the general course in passing the tributaries last mentioned, the line crosses the Seneca, and passes to the east of Clarksburg, Hyattstown, and Urbanna, and strikes the Baltimore and Ohio Railroad on Bush Creek, about two miles southeast of the Monocacy Viaduct. Following mainly parallel with the Baltimore and Ohio Railroad to the Monocacy Station, it there crosses the main track of that road, and keeping on the west of the Frederick Branch, passes through the southern part of the city of Frederick to a point in common with the line first surveyed to that place.

Line No. 4 diverges to the west of No. 3 near Rockville, and passing about one-half mile east of Gaithersburg, crossing the

Georgetown and Frederick turnpike and Seneca Creek near Middlebrook, and striking No. 1 on the Seneca Ridge, between Seneca Creek and Little Seneca; thence in common with No. 1 to Ten-Mile Creek, where it diverges westwardly, taking a route across Parr's Ridge at a low pass about a mile east of Barnesville, and uniting with line No. 2 on the ridge between the Monocacy River and Little Monocacy.

In addition to these lines numerous subordinate lines have been run at various points between Georgetown and the Baltimore and Ohio Railroad, which are mainly as follows:

An improvement of No. 1, commencing at a lower elevation in Georgetown near Prospect Street, keeping more westwardly along the Potomac slope of the ridge, and uniting with No. 1 about five miles out of Georgetown.

An oblique cross line connecting No. 1 and No. 3 on the ridge between Georgetown and Rockville; it diverges eastwardly from the former at a point about seven and a half miles from Georgetown, and connects with the latter about three and a half miles south of Rockville.

A line diverging westwardly from No. 4 about a mile east of Gaithersburg, crossing the Georgetown and Frederick turnpike near Gaithersburg, and crossing the Seneca Creek about three-quarters of a mile above Clopper's mill, falls into line No. 4, on the Seneca Ridge.

A line diverging from line No. 4 on a spur of Parr's Ridge, between Ten-Mile Creek and Buck Lodge, and crossing Parr's Ridge by a considerable sweep to the east, descends along the head-waters of Little Monocacy in a westwardly direction, then turns northwardly and crosses the spurs of the Sugar Loaf near its western base, thence crossing Bennett's Creek and the Monocacy River connects with line No. 1, about half a mile west of the latter stream.

A line commencing on the Rockville Ridge for the purpose of shortening the most eastwardly line (No. 3) where it passes around the head-waters of the tributaries of Seneca Creek, and reuniting with that line on the Seneca Ridge, about one and one-fourth miles southeastwardly from Nealsville.

A line was also traced in the immediate valley of Rock Creek, commencing at the "Paper-mill bridge," and extending up the creek about three miles.

During the progress of the foregoing examinations a crest-line was run on Parr's Ridge, commencing near Clarksburg and terminating on the eastern bank of the Potomac River. Line No. 3, the middle line, was recommended as the most eligible route by the engineers, and the total expense of completing the road from Georgetown to Hagerstown was estimated at $3,465,000. The road was not built by this company owing to unforeseen difficulties, among which were the financial depression of 1857, and the civil war which ensued four years later. But by 1873 the Baltimore and Ohio Railroad had built and completed a branch from Washington to its main road at Washington Junction (Point of Rocks).

Richard Randolph located, as assistant engineer, the whole road, and was then transferred to the Virginia Valley Railroad. James A. Boyd had the first contract, which was for Section 11, Parr's Ridge, which is here two hundred and fifty feet lower than the Parr's Ridge on the main line; this was a deep cut three-fourths of a mile long, running from grade to thirty feet cut in one-fourth; then thirty feet for one-fourth of a mile; then running out in the next fourth of a mile. About the time this section was finished several of the next heaviest were put under contract. James A. Boyd took Sections 10, 12, 13, 14, 15, and 16. Henry Gantz, 17, 18, 19, and 20. E. D. Smith, Section 7, including the masonry of the bridge over Monocacy; the grade is ninety feet above low water over this stream, and there is a very heavy embankment on the west side. The greatest height is seventy feet, with a long rock cut on the east side, twenty to thirty feet deep for more than three-fourths of a mile. The iron superstructure for this Monocacy bridge was built by the company at their Mount Clare shops. It has three spans of two hundred feet each, and one of one hundred. This one-mile section cost, including graduations, masonry, and bridge superstructure, three hundred thousand dollars. Sections 1, 2, 3, 4, including the Calico Rocks, were built by the company's forces. Sections 5 and 6 by Bernard Riley, 8 and 33 by Peter McNamara, 9 by White and McArdle, 21 by Timothy Flaherty, 22 and 23 by B. R. Codwise, 24, 25, and 26 by Michael Buoy, 27 and 30 by Dennis Murphy, 28 and 29 by Timothy Cavan, 31, 32, and 33 by G. M. Watkins, 34 and 37 by Patrick McCabe, 35 by Alfred Ray, 36 and 39 by James Farward, 40 by Thomas A. Waters, and 41 and 42 by the company's force.

Not finding materials for bridges at the crossing of the Little Monocacy, Little and Big Seneca, these streams were crossed on trestles, constructed by the company's force. Little Monocacy and Big Seneca trestles are seventy feet high and Little Seneca one hundred and six. The intention is to replace these trestles, as they wear out, with permanent structures of stone and iron.

The maximum grade is fifty feet per mile, the minimum radius of curvature one thousand feet, and the elevation at Gaithersburg five hundred and sixteen feet above tide. The distance from Point of Rocks to Baltimore by the old line is sixty-nine miles, and from Point of Rocks to Baltimore *via* Washington, eighty miles.

All important passenger trains of the Baltimore and Ohio Company, including local and fast freight, pass over the Metropolitan Branch, affording unprecedented facilities to the people for personal travel and transportation of productions and supplies. There are twenty-eight stations on the road from Washington to Point of Rocks, or the Washington Junction, the intersection with the main stem, a distance of forty-two and a half miles, viz.:

METROPOLITAN BRANCH.

Stations.	Miles.	Stations.	Miles.
Washington	0	Rockville	16¼
Metropolitan Junction	1	Derwood	19
Queenstown	3¼	Washington Grove	20¾
Terra Cotta	4	Gaithersburg	21½
Stott's	4¼	Clopper's	24½
Brightwood	6¼	Germantown	26½
Silver Springs	7	Little Seneca	28½
Linden	9	Boyd's	29½
Forest Glen	9½	Barnsville	33¼
Ray's Quarry	9¾	Dickerson	35¾
Knowles'	11	Tuscarora	39
Windham's	13½	Sugar Loaf	41¾
Halpin	15½	Washington Junction	42¾

The Baltimore, Cincinnati and Western Maryland Railroad was chartered several years ago by the States of Ohio, West Virginia, Virginia, and Maryland, and, if built, will pass diagonally through the county from near Brighton, *via* Brookville, Gaithersburg, Darnestown, and Dawsonville to the Potomac at Edwards' Ferry, or mouth of Goose Creek, over a distance of thirty miles.

The Chesapeake and Ohio Canal.—When the war of the Revolution had ended, and the people began to think how best they could perpetuate the independence which had been gained after a seven years' arduous struggle, there were none who felt the task before them more difficult than the men of Maryland. In this emergency, George Washington, who, patriotic to his country in war, had shown himself equally so to his native State in peace, and even during the perils and dangers of military life had become impressed with the importance of opening a route to the West, turned, after retiring to private life, with fresh enthusiasm to his cherished scheme of making the Potomac navigable from Fort Cumberland to the Great Falls at Georgetown. In 1774 he had procured the passage of a law from the Virginia Legislature empowering the opening of the Potomac so as to make it navigable from tide-water to Wells' Creek, and, although the Legislature of Maryland objected to a concurrence in the law, the project seemed to favor success, when the battle of Lexington turned the attention of the colonists elsewhere, and the call of Gen. Washington to the field caused a temporary suspension of the movement. But as soon as the need for his military services had ended, he entered into an extensive correspondence with prominent gentlemen in Maryland, in order to try and secure their co-operation. On the 29th of March, 1784, he wrote to Mr. Jefferson, stating that ten years before he had been struck with the importance of the subject, and added, "My opinion coincides perfectly with yours regarding the practicability of an easy and short communication between the waters of the Ohio and Potomac,—of the advantages of that communication, the preference it has over all others, and of the policy there would be in the State of Maryland to adopt and render it facile." His ideas, as frequently expressed, were that unless artificial communications were formed to draw the future trade of the vast region beyond the Alleganies to Atlantic ports, either Spain, which held the mouth of the Mississippi, or England, which possessed the St. Lawrence, would secure it; that these communications must be made through Maryland, Virginia, New York, or Pennsylvania, and that if the two former did nothing, the latter would step in and win the prize. In the fall of 1784 he made a journey West on horseback, traveling in all six hundred and eighty miles, crossing the mountains by Braddock's road through Allegany County, Md., and returning through the valleys of the Cheat and Shenandoah Rivers. Soon after his return, in October of the same year, he sent a letter to the Governor of Virginia, in which he dwelt fully on the practicability of the scheme which he had previously suggested, and, in fact, it may be said, sketched, with a bold and free hand, the original outline of nearly all the internal improvements which have since been adopted by these sister States. His object was to link together these distant States by the strong bonds of a common interest, and to this task he addressed himself, addressing a letter to a member of Congress of similar import to that sent to the Governor of Virginia, and taking not only a commercial, but a national and political view of the subject.

The communication to the Governor of Virginia was submitted by him to the next Legislature of that State, and while it was being discussed by the members, Gen. Washington and the Marquis de Lafayette paid a visit to Richmond. Washington succeeded in the promise of the Legislature's support for the measure, and as the concurrence of Maryland was necessary, the Potomac being within her limits, he went to Annapolis, still with Lafayette, and laid his views before the Legislature there. A few days afterwards he wrote to Joseph Jones and James Madison, of the Virginia Legislature, recommending the appointment of deputies by the Legislatures of the two States to meet and agree upon a bill. The Virginia Legislature at once appointed Gen. Washington, Gen. Gates, and Col. Blackburn to go to Annapolis and confer with a similar committee from the Maryland Legislature, while the Maryland Legislature as soon as it went into session had the subject before it, and on Dec. 22, 1784, requested the Senate to appoint some of its members to join the gentlemen nominated by this House to meet and confer with the commissioners appointed by the State of Virginia. The Senate agreed to this, and appointed Thomas Stone, Samuel Hughes, and Charles Carroll of Carrollton to join John Cadwalader, Samuel Chase, John De Butts, George Digges, Philip Key, Gustavus Scott, and Joseph Dashiell, appointed by the House to meet and confer with the Virginia commissioners.

Gen. Washington and Gen. Gates went to Annapolis (Col. Blackburn being prevented by indisposition), and on Dec. 22, 1784, a conference was held, with Gen. Washington, chairman, and R. B. Latimer, clerk. Provisions looking to the establishment of the Potomac Company were unanimously agreed to, and bills in conformity with them afterwards drawn up, adopted, and passed by the Legislatures of the two States, each State at the same time authorizing a subscription for fifty shares of the capital stock, which both of them subsequently increased.

Messrs. Cadwalader, Chase, De Butts, Digges, Key, Scott, and Joseph Dashiell of the commissioners brought in the bill in accordance with the report of the convention, and Mr. Cadwalader delivered the bill to the speaker on the same day. By concurrent action of the two States the Potomac Company was then formed. The charter provided that the capital stock should consist of five hundred shares of one hundred pounds each, with power of enlargement if found necessary; that the navigation should be improved from tide-water to the highest practicable point on the North Branch or to Fort Cumberland, so as to permit the passage of boats drawing twelve inches of water; that the company should be authorized "to construct canals and erect such locks and perform such other work as they may judge necessary" for the purpose; that the work should be commenced in one year, and the improvements be completed from the Great Falls to Fort Cumberland in three years, and from the Great Falls to tide-water in two years, under the penalty of a forfeiture of charter.

Such was the public affection for Gen. Washington that within a few months nearly all of the capital stock was subscribed for. The company went into operation on May 17, 1785, Gen. Washington being its first president, and holding that position until he was called to the Presidency of the United States. Thomas Johnson and Thomas Sim Lee, the two first Governors of Maryland, were associated with him after the Declaration of Independence in the board of directors, and James Rumsey, who claimed to be the first discoverer of the practical application of steam to purposes of navigation, was general superintendent of the work. In the ensuing August operations were commenced, and no doubt those who prepared and helped to pass the acts of incorporation thought that three years and fifty thousand pounds sterling would be sufficient to complete the work on the proposed plan and within the specified limits. But when the three years had expired the work was only slightly advanced, and on application of the company acts were passed by the Legislatures of Maryland and Virginia in 1786 amending the charter and granting a further term of three years. In 1790 the term was again extended for three years, and so on from time to time until the year 1820, when the public became satisfied that the bed of the Potomac River could not by any expenditure at command be so improved as to answer the purposes intended.

When this decision had been arrived at the Board of Public Works of Virginia, in pursuance of a resolution of the General Assembly of Jan. 8, 1820, appointed Thomas Moore principal engineer, "to examine the waters of the Potomac above the upper line of the District of Columbia, and to explore the country between the Potomac and Ohio on the one side, and the Potomac and Rappahannock on the other, with a view to ascertain and report upon the practicability of effecting a communication by canal between the three rivers." Early in 1821 the States of Maryland and Virginia appointed a joint commission, consisting of Moses T. Hunter, William T. T. Mason, William Naylor, Athanasius Fenwick, and Elie Williams, "to examine the affairs of the Potomac Company, the state of navigation of the river Potomac, its susceptibility of improvement, and to make report whether the said company had complied with its charter granted by the two States, and its ability to comply within a reasonable time, and whether any, or what aid should be given to the company, and what would be the best means of effecting an improvement in the navigation of the said river." In July, 1822, assisted by Thomas Moore, civil engineer, of Virginia, they began their work, and in December following transmitted a report to the Governor of each of the States, by whom it was communicated to their respective Legislatures in January, 1823. The substance of it was that the Potomac Company had failed to comply with their charter; that they could not possibly effect the objects of their incorporation; that they had not only expended their capital and the tolls received, with the exception of a small dividend declared in 1822, but had incurred a heavy debt, which they could never discharge; that it would be imprudent and inexpedient to give them any further aid, and that the only alternative was to divest them of their charter and adopt some more effectual mode of improving the navigation of the river.

After reviewing the different kinds of improved inland navigation, the commissioners declared their preference for an independent canal, or still-water navigation, the cost of which from Little Falls to Fort Cumberland, a distance of one hundred and eighty-two miles, was estimated to be $1,578,954. Thomas Moore, civil engineer, of Virginia, having died before the survey was completed, Isaac Briggs, of Maryland, was appointed to fill his place. The commissioners recommended that Maryland and Virginia should each furnish one-half of the required sum, viz., $789,477, and proposed that the money, in the first instance, should be raised by the two States by loan for sixteen or twenty years. They expressed the opinion that the proposed canal, if constructed, would make Cumberland the entrepôt of the commerce of the West, and that nothing would be wanting to insure to the citizens of Baltimore the largest share of the advantages to accrue from it except a connection with that city by a lateral canal from the head of the Eastern Branch of the Potomac, or Bladensburg, to the Patapsco at Elkridge, supposed, by the required route, to be about twenty-five miles; or if it should accord more with the wishes and interest of the Baltimoreans to connect with the canal at a higher point of the Potomac, they suggested that a survey be made to test the practicability of a branch from the foot of the Catoctin Mountain, or any point below it, to Baltimore. What had been mere speculation in regard to the settlement and growth of the West in 1784 was in 1822 a substantial fact, and the importance of a convenient channel for trade and intercommunication had become obvious to all, and out of this general sentiment sprang the idea of the Chesapeake and Ohio Canal.

The advocates of this means of communication between the tide-waters of the Potomac and the Ohio River entered into the enterprise early in 1823 with great zeal and energy, and in accordance with the feeling which had been started in favor of the new project, the Potomac Company, on the 3d of February of the same year, adopted a resolution signifying their willingness to surrender their charter to a new company, and, during the same winter, acts were passed by the Legislatures of Maryland and Virginia to incorporate a joint-stock association, entitled "The Potomac Canal Company." These acts, however, proved abortive, because they did not provide for the necessary co-operation of the United States, as sovereign of the District of Columbia, and also because of disagreement in some of their provisions. The people of Baltimore, especially, objected to the Potomac Canal, because, under the bill in question, it was to terminate, as at present, in Georgetown, and the privilege was virtually denied them of tapping it so as to connect it with a canal to Baltimore if they so desired, and besides, the State was asked to cede to the company all its right to the waters of the river, thus virtually preventing the future connection of the canal with the city of Baltimore.

In order to bring about united action in the next session of the Legislatures of the two States, meetings were held in various parts of the country, the first being at Leesburg, Loudon Co., Va., on Aug. 25, 1823. It was followed by others both in Maryland and Virginia, and on Tuesday, Nov. 6, 1823, a convention was held at Washington City, with delegates from Maryland, Virginia, Pennsylvania, and the District of Columbia. Dr. Joseph Kent, of Prince George's County, a member of Congress, was chairman. The convention determined on the formation of a joint-stock company, with power to cut a canal from the tide-water of the Potomac, by way of Cumberland, to the mouth of Savage River, and ultimately to the navigable waters of the Monongahela or Ohio Rivers, also giving authority to the States of Maryland, Virginia, and Pennsylvania to make connections with it by lateral canals. Committees were also appointed to petition the Legislatures of these States and Congress for a concurrent act of incorporation and for assistance in constructing the works, the committee from Maryland consisting of Grafton Duvall, George Mason, of Charles, C. Thomas Kennedy, J. C. Herbert, and James Forrest. The name fixed upon was "The Chesapeake and Ohio Canal Company," and a resolution was also passed looking to the ultimate extension of the works to Lake Erie. A central committee, consisting of Charles Fenton Mercer, John Mason, Walter Jones, Thomas Swann, John McLean, Wm. H. Fitzhugh, H. L. Opie, Alfred H. Powell, P. C. Pendleton, A. Fenwick, John Lee, Frisby Tilghman, and Robert W. Bowie, was appointed to take charge of the whole subject and obtain the consent of the Potomac Company to the measure.

Memorials were accordingly sent to Congress and to the Legislatures of Maryland, Virginia, and Pennsylvania for an act of incorporation. In the mean time, however, a meeting was held in Baltimore on the 20th of December, 1823, to take into consideration "the expediency of promoting a connection between the Ohio and the Chesapeake at Baltimore by a canal through the District of Columbia," and also as to whether the citizens of Baltimore "preferred a canal to be made first to the Susquehanna River or to the Ohio." Gen. Robert Goodloe Harper made an exhaustive speech explaining his views "on the expediency of promoting a connection between the Ohio at

Pittsburgh and the waters of the Chesapeake at Baltimore, by a canal through the District of Columbia."

The reason for this difference in opinion and sentiment on the part of Baltimore is obvious. Georgetown, Alexandria, and Washington feared the advantages which Baltimore would have through improved communication with the West. Baltimore at that time enjoyed all the trade of Pennsylvania between the Susquehanna and the mountains, as well as the whole downward trade of that river, and that of Frederick and Washington Counties in Maryland, thus enabling her to leave Georgetown and Alexandria far behind. These advantages, however, she feared would be overcome by the small towns on the Potomac, and therefore the majority of citizens at the meeting referred to preferred a canal to the Susquehanna to one from Cumberland to Georgetown. On account of this strong opposition, and because the act submitted did not provide sufficiently for the connection of the Chesapeake and Ohio Canal with the city of Baltimore, the Maryland Assembly adjourned without passing the measure. On the 27th of January, 1824, the Virginia Legislature passed it, with amendments to remove the objections of Baltimore, and on Jan. 31, 1825, the Maryland Legislature confirmed it. On March 3, 1825, it was ratified by Congress, and on Feb. 9, 1826, by Pennsylvania.

On May 16, 1825, the Potomac Company surrendered their charter to the Chesapeake and Ohio Canal Company. By the amended charter the new company was authorized to construct a navigable canal of not less than forty feet at the surface, twenty-eight feet at the bottom, and not less than four feet deep from the tide-water of the Potomac in the District of Columbia to Cumberland, or the mouth of Savage Creek, and thence across the Allegany Mountains to some convenient point of navigation on the waters of the Ohio or its tributary streams. The company was also empowered to connect the canal by a branch improvement from the town of Cumberland to the Savage River, with a view to the development of the coal-fields at that point. Two years was allowed from the organization of the company for the commencement of the work, and twelve years from the date of its commencement for the completion of the section from tide-water to Cumberland. The capital stock was to be six million dollars, in sixty thousand shares of one hundred dollars each, with power of future enlargement. At the November session of Congress in 1823, the subject was laid before it by President Monroe, and that body, on April 3, 1824, appropriated thirty thousand dollars for necessary surveys, plans, and estimates. In May following the President appointed Brig.-Gen. Simon Bernard and Lieut.-Col. Totten, officers of the United States army, and John L. Sullivan, civil engineer, of Massachusetts, a board of internal improvements to designate the most suitable route for the canal. On Oct. 23, 1826, Gen. Bernard made a report, which was communicated by the President to Congress on December 7th following. It showed minutely the route of the canal from tide-water to the Ohio, with detailed estimate of its cost, as follows:

Sections.	Distances.		Ascent, Descent.	Number Locks.	Amount of Est.
	Miles.	Yards.	Feet.		
Eastern........			578	74	$8,177,081.05
Middle..........	70	1010	1961	246	10,028,122.86
Western........	85	440	619	78	4,170,223.78

The board divided the line into three sections,—eastern, middle, and western. The first began at Georgetown, running thence on the northern or Maryland side of the Potomac to Cumberland. The middle began at Cumberland and ended at the mouth of Castleman's River on the Youghiogheny. The western extended from thence to Pittsburgh.

Gen. Bernard estimated that in the first six years after the opening of the canal the advantages to be derived from it by augmentations in the value of lands, revenue from customs, etc., would amount to $81,625,585. The estimated cost of the several sections took the public mind, however, by surprise, and the commissioners who had been appointed to open books for subscription to the capital stock felt it prudent to defer the matter. The central committee again summoned the Canal Convention which met on Dec. 5, 1826, in Washington City, and adopted a resolution that a committee be appointed to submit an estimate of the cost of the canal, founded upon the report of the United States Board of Internal Improvement of Oct. 23, 1826, to the War Department. The following were appointed as the committee: A. Stewart, C. F. Mercer, J. B. Alexander, Chauncey Forward, Josiah Malin, John McHenry, James Adams, John Hoye, J. Mason, O. H. Williams, B. S. Pigman, John McPherson, and John McLean. Three days afterwards they reported that the United States engineers had been betrayed into great errors in their estimates, and that the work could be constructed for about one-half the amount of the estimate. The convention ordered that the report be printed, but it was viewed with distrust by the great mass of the community, and on March 3, 1827, a memorial signed by thirty-two members of Congress was presented to John Quincy Adams, President of the United States, requesting that the estimates both of the United States Board of Internal Improvement and of the Canal Convention Committee be submitted to practical civil engineers to reconcile their apparent disagreement and verify their accuracy. The President accordingly appointed James Geddes and Nathan S. Roberts, and their report of the cost of a canal from the upper boundary of Georgetown to Cumberland was transmitted to Congress on March 10, 1828. They made the distance one hundred and eighty-six and three-fourths miles, and presented estimates of a canal of three different dimensions, passing over nearly the same ground indicated by the United States engineers. The general estimates were as follows: for a canal forty feet in width at the surface and four feet deep, $4,008,005.28; for one forty-eight feet surface and five feet deep,—the dimensions upon which Gen. Bernard's estimate was based,—$4,330,991.68; and for a canal enlarged where practicable to sixty feet, with a proportional breadth at bottom and five feet deep, $4,479,346.93. This report was generally received as correct, and as its results had in the mean time been sufficiently known to justify such a proceeding, the commissioners on Oct. 1, 1827, opened books for subscription to the capital stock, and on that and the following day a considerable amount was subscribed.

At December session, 1825, the State of Maryland had passed a law authorizing a subscription to the capital stock to the whole amount of stock owned by the State in the Potomac Company, and of the debts due the State from the company, and also of $500,000 payable in current money, on condition, as regarded the money subscription, that Congress should subscribe one million dollars to the capital stock of the eastern section and secure a connection with the city of Baltimore. The condition requiring the United States subscription to the "capital stock of the eastern section" was repealed by the Legislature in March, 1827. In March, 1828, the same body passed a supplement, authorizing the treasurer to make the subscription payable in five per cent. State certificates whenever the commissioners on the part of the State should certify that the sum of $2,500,000 had been subscribed to the capital stock. By act of May 24, 1828, Congress authorized a subscription of one million dollars, and on the same day authorized the cities of Washington, Georgetown, and Alexandria to subscribe and pay for shares of stock in the company. The commissioners then called a general meeting of the stockholders in the city of Washington for the 20th of June, 1828. They reported at the meeting that there had been subscribed, payable in current money, the sum of $3,090,100, besides subscriptions to the amount of $190,149.77 in the stock of the Potomac Company. On the same day the Chesapeake and Ohio Canal Company was formally organized by the election of the following board: President, Hon. Charles Fenton Mercer, then a member of Congress from Virginia; Directors, Joseph Kent, Phineas Janney, Walter Smith, Peter Lenox, Andrew Stewart, and Frederick May. The western terminus of the canal was to be at Pittsburgh. On the 23d of June the board entered on their duties, and on the 25th of the same month appointed Benjamin Wright chief engineer, adopting the route which had been surveyed by the United States engineers and by Geddes and Roberts as the line of the canal between Georgetown and Cumberland. The 4th of July, 1828, was fixed upon for the celebration of the commencement of the work, and on that day John Quincy Adams, President of the United States, dug the first spadeful of earth from the site marked out for the channel of the canal.

On Aug. 15, 1828, the Potomac Company surrendered its charter and property to the Chesapeake and Ohio Canal Company, and on Sept. 1, 1828, work on the canal was commenced, the capital subscribed at that time being $3,609,400. In September, 1828, the canal was ordered to be extended to the mouth of Rock Creek, in Georgetown, and thence to the mouth of the Tiber, in Washington City.

An important item in the history of the canal may now be mentioned, namely, the controversy between the company and the Baltimore and Ohio Railroad Company. In June, 1827, the railroad company surveyed a route for their road from Baltimore to Point of Rocks, and thence up the Potomac Valley, over the same ground which had been surveyed with a view to the location of the canal. The canal company accordingly united with the Potomac Company, which had not then formally surrendered its charter, and on June 10, 1828, prayed an injunction against the railroad company, which was granted. On the 23d of the same month the railroad company obtained an injunction against the Chesapeake and Ohio and Potomac Companies. The controversy continued until 1832, when the Court of Appeals of Maryland decided the question in favor of the canal company. In May, 1833, an arrangement was effected between the companies, the chief feature of which was that the canal company would so locate the canal at different points below Harper's Ferry as to afford a passage for the railroad. The railroad company agreed to pay to the canal company two hundred and sixty-six thousand dollars, and not continue their road farther than Harper's Ferry until the canal should be, by 1840, extended to Cumberland. The friends of both works now began to co-operate together in favor of the prosecution of the canal. In February, 1833, the State of Virginia authorized a subscription to the capital stock of the canal company of two hundred and fifty thousand dollars, and on March 14, 1834, the State of Maryland authorized an additional subscription of one hundred and twenty-five thousand dollars, payable in five per cent. bonds of the State, and also a further subscription to the same amount in case Congress should subscribe one million dollars.

On Oct. 18, 1834, the citizens of Allegany County, Md., met in the court-house, Cumberland, to take steps leading to the further prosecution of the work. Wm. McMahon presided, with David Shriver and William Ridgely vice-presidents, and Thomas J. McKaig and James Smith secretaries. Resolutions were passed to hold a convention in the city of Baltimore on Dec. 8, 1834, to be composed of three or more delegates from Maryland, District of Columbia, and the several States taking an interest in the completion of the canal. The convention accordingly met, with George C. Washington, of Maryland, president; Elisha Whittlesey, of Ohio, Elisha Boyd, of Virginia, William A. Bradley, District of Columbia, and William Robinson, Jr., of Pennsylvania, vice-presidents; and John P. Kennedy and Joseph Shriver, of Maryland, secretaries. Among the delegates present were the following: Allegany County, David Shriver, John Hoge, M. C. Sprigg, S. P. Smith, M. N. Falls, Thomas J. McKaig, Joseph Shriver, James Smith, Thomas Perry, William Matthews, Robert Swan, Andrew Bruce, Alpheus Beall, John J. Hoffman, Richard Beall, R. C. Hollyday; Washington County, Joseph Galby, Frisby Tilghman, O. H. Williams, Robert Wason, John Blackford, Joseph I. Merrick, William Price, Daniel Weisel, Joseph C. Hays, John Welty, Charles A. Warfield, Andrew Kershner, John R. Dale, Michael A. Finley, Joseph Weast, Abraham Barnes, Isaac Nesbit, John O. Wharton, Joseph Hollman, Samuel M. Hitt, N. B. Robinson, Thomas Buchanan, Jr., Charles Wilson, William Holliday; Frederick County, Outerbridge Horsey, John Thomas, Richard Johnson, of William, John Cost, James Simmons, S. R. Waters, Roderick Dorsey, Plummer Ijams, Anthony Kimmell, John Kinser, Isaac Shriver, Washington Van Bibber, John McKalab, W. B. Gwynn, Isaac Baugher, John Stewart, Martin Eichelberger, William Todd, Jacob Poe, Brooke Baker, William Tyler, J. H. McElfresh, Thomas Carlton, George Bowlus, John Sifford. The principal acts of the convention consisted in the appointment of a committee to report on the "probable revenue of the canal," and a committee to report "an estimate of the probable cost, and the time required for its completion;" also, committees to memorialize Congress, the States of Maryland, Virginia, and Pennsylvania, and the authorities and citizens of Baltimore, for the necessary means to finish the canal to Cumberland. The committee on cost reported that the completion of the works is expected to carry the total cost of the eastern section of the canal to the amount of very near $6,500,000, and on this "estimate" was predicated the Maryland loan of December session, 1834. In regard to the time required for the construction of the works to Cumberland, the committee felt assured that if the line of seventy-eight miles below Cumberland were placed under contract, eighteen months, or two years at most, would suffice.

On the 7th of March, 1835, the Maryland House of Delegates, by a vote of 44 to 30, passed a bill providing for $2,000,000, the amount represented as necessary to complete the canal to Cumberland. The citizens of Baltimore assembled in town-meeting on the 10th of the same month, and adopted resolutions expressive of the hope that the Legislature would approve and pass the bill. On March 18th it was taken up in the Senate, and passed by a vote of two to one, thus becoming a law. The sum of $2,000,000 was granted in the form of a loan to the company, the State reserving the power to convert it into capital stock, at any future period, if deemed expedient. To secure payment of the principal and interest a mortgage was required to be given to the State on the lands, water-rights, etc., and this mortgage was executed on April 23, 1835. This loan caused an exultation among the friends of the canal corresponding with the importance that was attached to it, and in the spring of 1835 the engineers were directed to locate and make an estimate of the unfinished line to Cumberland, and on Jan. 6, 1836, C. B. Fisk and Messrs. Cruger and Purcel, who had been detailed for the purpose, reported that the aggregate cost would amount to $3,560,619.

On Jan. 30, 1836, a memorial was presented by the president and directors of the canal to the Maryland House of Delegates soliciting additional aid, showing that the deficiency of means to complete the canal amounted to $2,961,402. The memorial was referred to the Committee on Internal Improvements. On March 8th the chairman of the Committee of Ways and Means made a report, in which the completion of the canal to Cumberland was strongly recommended, and also offered a bill to carry his views into effect. It was taken up on the 29th of the month, and referred to the next General Assembly by a vote of 35 to 34, or, in other words, rejected. Two days afterwards a communication was presented by citizens of Baltimore, inclosing resolutions which had been passed at a mass-meeting that the prosperity of Baltimore and the advancement of the State depended mainly on the success of the measure. A select committee of five members, to whom the resolutions were referred, reported a bill similar to that which had been rejected, but before finally acting on the measure the Legislature adjourned, after appointing a joint committee of five, with instructions to investigate the subject and report by bill or otherwise after the recess.

On Monday, May 2d, an internal improvement convention was held in Baltimore, at which delegates were reported from Baltimore City and County, and from Frederick, Washington, Allegany, Anne Arundel, Montgomery, Prince George's, Charles, St. Mary's, Harford, Queen Anne's, Kent, and Worcester Counties. Resolutions were passed declaring that it was the duty of the State to supply the means for the speedy completion of the canal to Cumberland, and a committee was appointed to present them to the Legislature.

On May 20th the General Assembly of Maryland reassembled, and on May 25th the majority of the joint committee of both houses, to whom the subject of internal improvement had been committed, reported, urging the propriety of making no further appropriation to the canal company until the practicability of an eligible connection, by canal, with Baltimore, so as to give the Chesapeake and Ohio Canal an eastern terminus within the State of Maryland, had been ascertained. At this period the company had received but one-half of the $2,000,000 loan, only $121,000 of which had been disbursed for the construction of work done subsequent to the date of the act under which the loan was made, two-thirds of the residue having been applied to the payment of debts of the company, and to repairing the finished portion of the canal. The minority of the joint committee offered as a substitute for the majority report a bill embodying the views of the convention of May 2d, which was passed by the House on June 3d by a vote of 48 to 29, and on the following day was assented to by the Senate by a vote of 11 to 2. This was the law known as the $8,000,000, and it authorized subscriptions to the capital stock of the canal company to the amount of $3,000,000.

By the acceptance of the act the company was required to release the Baltimore and Ohio Railroad Company from the restriction which arrested it at Harper's Ferry, and allow the railroad to be constructed *pari passu* with, but without preceding, the canal along the valley of the Potomac. By the act $500,000 were subscribed to the Maryland Canal Company, but the subscription to the Chesapeake and Ohio Canal Company was not to be made until the Maryland Canal Company had certified that a sufficient amount had been subscribed to their stock to justify the commencement of the construction of their canal and to insure its completion by the most northern practicable route.

The citizens of Baltimore exhibited unusual manifestations of gratification at the success of the measure, but the act was not welcomed with the same satisfaction by the Chesapeake and Ohio Canal Company. The chief objections rested on the provision which required the Maryland Canal Company to construct their canal by the most northern practicable route, and exception was also taken to the clauses relating to the future construction of the Chesapeake and Ohio Canal and the Baltimore and Ohio Railroad. The subject was referred by the stockholders to a committee, who, on July 28, 1836, reported that it would be premature in the company to accept the act until the Maryland Canal Company had determined upon their route and an understanding had been effected with the Baltimore and Ohio Railroad Company.

The commissioners appointed to carry into effect the charter of the Maryland Company met in Baltimore, April 5, 1836, and adopted, for their canal, the route surveyed by Dr. Howard. By the 12th of May they had received subscriptions for 16,105 shares of $100 each, more than half the amount considered necessary for the construction of the work, and on May 18th the company duly organized by the election of a president and directors. George W. Hughes and Charles B. Fisk, engineers, who had been appointed to conduct a survey, made a joint report on July 26th, in which they came to the conclusion that the most northern practicable route from the Chesapeake and Ohio Canal to Baltimore was on or near the location traced by Dr. Howard in 1827, through the District of Columbia. The Maryland Canal Company adopted the route, and soon afterwards it was reported that 33,000 shares, amounting to $3,000,000, the full amount required, had been subscribed.

The stockholders of the Chesapeake and Ohio Canal Company met again on July 28th, and received the assent of the Baltimore and Ohio Railroad to certain propositions which had been made to them by the canal company in regard to an explanation or modification of the provisions of compromise. They also gave their consent to the several provisions of the Maryland act of December, 1835, declaring, however, that their acceptance of the act should not be final, until the Maryland Canal Company had entered into an agreement to connect their canal with the Chesapeake and Ohio Canal at a suitable point in Georgetown, and within three months give the required certificate in reference to the means for the commencement and completion of their work. These stipulations were at once satisfactorily arranged, and on August 1st the Chesapeake and Ohio Canal Company formally communicated their acceptance of the act to the Governor of the State, the Baltimore and Ohio Railroad Company having done so on July 26th. On September 9th the Maryland Canal Company certified that a sufficient amount of capital stock had been subscribed to justify the commencement of the construction of their work, and on September 21st the Chesapeake and Ohio Canal Company executed an instrument guaranteeing to the State, after the expiration of three years, a dividend of six per cent. per annum, payable semi-annually out of the net profits of the canal and works, on the amount authorized to be subscribed to its capital stock, and the treasurer of the State accordingly made the subscription of $3,000,000 to the capital stock of the company.

The act of 1835 authorized the city of Baltimore to subscribe to the capital stock of both the Maryland Canal Company and the Baltimore and Ohio Railroad Company. In regard to the first company the power was not availed of, but on Sept. 27, 1836, the city subscribed $3,000,000 to the capital stock of the railroad, with a proviso that the whole sum should be applied exclusively to the prosecution of the work from Harper's Ferry westward. The railroad recommenced operations, and adopting a route through Virginia, gave a wide berth to the canal and pushed forward their road to Cumberland, which they reached in November, 1842.

It may be of interest here to give a short summary of the movements which now took place in regard to the contemplated work of the Maryland Canal. After July, 1836, Messrs. Fisk and Hughes made a more minute survey, and on March 3, 1837, submitted a final report declaring the Westminster, Linganore, and Seneca routes impracticable, and declaring the most northern practicable route for an extension of the Chesapeake and Ohio Canal to Baltimore to be from Georgetown.

In September, 1836, Isaac Trimble was appointed by the city of Baltimore to examine localities and determine upon the practicability of a cross-cut canal within this State. In March, 1837, he made a report, in which he expressed the opinion that the Seneca route was practicable, the cost being estimated at $6,324,300. At the session of the Legislature in December, 1837, memorials were presented praying that the Maryland Canal Company be required to construct their works by way of Seneca and Patuxent Rivers, and the Committee on Internal Improvements were directed to inquire into the surveys that had been made. Messrs. Fisk, Hughes, and Trimble appeared before the committee and gave testimony. On the 8th of March, 1838, the Legislature by joint resolutions declared that the Maryland Canal Company were entitled to no subscriptions on the part of the State unless they would agree to locate their canal by the most northern practicable route of the routes by the valleys of the Monocacy and Patapsco, or by a route diverging from the Chesapeake and Ohio Canal, at the mouth of Seneca River, and authorized the Governor to direct a further survey of these routes to be made. In April following the Secretary of War granted the services of Col. J. J. Abert to make the necessary examinations. The conclusions of his report were that the Westminster, Linganore, and Seneca routes were each impracticable, but that there was a route, which he called the "Brookville route," connecting, on the one side, with the Seneca, at the mouth of Whetstone Branch, and on the other with the Patuxent, at the mouth of Hawlings' River, which was "practicable with due supply of water." He next proceeded to make an estimate of cost, and in February, 1839, reported that the length of the route was seventy miles, but that the estimate had only been made for twenty-one and three-fourths miles, this portion being computed to cost in round numbers $11,670,000, or more than five hundred thousand dollars per mile. He was then informed that it was unnecessary to proceed any further.

The subsequent proceedings which took place in carrying into effect the provisions of the act of 1835, ch. 395, may now be taken up. On the acceptance of the act by the canal and railroad companies the Governor and Council were authorized to appoint three commissioners to go to Europe and dispose of the stock of the State, out of the proceeds of which the subscriptions to the capital stock of the companies were to be paid. Six months after the passage of the act the commissioners were appointed, and in the spring of 1837 they departed on their mission. Owing, however, to the financial crisis, which was then somewhat advanced, it was found impracticable for them to dispose of the stock at the premium required by the act. The subject was brought before the Legislature in December, 1837, and that body passed resolutions to the effect, as regarded the Chesapeake and Ohio Canal Company, that the company should receive certificates of stock to the amount of $2,500,000, at the par value thereof, upon giving to the State treasurer a receipt in full payment of the $3,000,000 subscribed to the capital stock of the company under the act of 1835, and that the residue of the certificates, five hundred thousand dollars, should be retained by the treasurer as security for payment of the premium. These resolutions were acted upon, and the certificates issued to the company in April, 1838. The payment was not, however, made in current money, but in State securities, and the company transmitted $1,500,000 to its London agent with authority to sell, or failing in this to negotiate a loan. Another portion of the stock was advertised for sale in this country. But the precious metals had become scarce, and as the price of stocks necessarily fell, no offers were made here. In London, the objection to the securities was the form in which they were issued and the rate of interest that they bore, and the agent then advised a change of the six per cent. certificates into five per cent. sterling coupon bonds. The company, however, thought that public opinion would not sanction them in selling at a price far below that which they had contracted to pay the State, and so they determined to borrow money upon a hypothecation of the certificates of stock, and apply to the next Legislature for authority to change the form of the securities into an equivalent amount of five per cent. sterling bonds. The agent in London obtained large loans upon a hypothecation of the stock, in most instances at $87.50 on the $100. The contractors on the work, which was being pressed forward, were sustained by money borrowed from banks and the scrip or promissory notes of the company. The money received from the loans in England and the United States was applied to redemption of scrip, payment of arrears to contractors, regular estimates for work on the canal, and interest on the $2,000,000 loan from the State. Before the close of the year 1838 about four-fifths of the whole amount of certificates of stock delivered to the company by the State had been hypothecated.

At the December session, 1838, both the canal and railroad companies made application to the Legislature for authority to change the six per cent. certificates into five per cent. sterling bonds. The Chesapeake and Ohio Canal Company also asked further aid from the State, and submitted a "revised estimate" of the work yet required to be executed to finish the canal to Cumberland. The amount remaining to be done on Jan. 1, 1839, was, in round numbers, $3,450,000. In April, 1839, the 27½ miles between dam No. 5 and dam No. 6, at the Great Cacapon, were completed and navigation opened to the latter point, which continued to be the western terminus of the canal until its final completion to Cumberland in 1850. After the presentation of the memorials a committee was appointed to investigate the affairs of the company. They recommended that a proposition be made to Congress either for the general government to aid the company, or transfer to this State the interest of the United States in its capital stock, on condition that Maryland would provide the necessary means to finish the canal to Cumberland.

On April 5, 1839, an act was passed releasing the company from the twenty per cent. premium stipulated to be paid by it, and authorizing the commissioner of loans to issue to the company five per cent. sterling bonds to the amount of $3,200,000, as an equivalent for and in lieu of the $3,000,000 of six per cents. The company was required to redeem the six per cents. by a substitution of five per cents. where the former had been hypothecated, and return the whole amount to the State to be canceled. It was also required to pay the interest on the bonds for three years and execute a mortgage to the State to secure payment. Another act authorized an additional subscription to the capital stock of the company of $1,375,000, payable in five per cent. sterling bonds. These acts were promptly accepted by the company and their provisions complied with. On June 1, 1839, the means of the company, over and above its liabilities, were $2,087,139.94, and the cost of the work remaining to be done at that date was $2,935,103. On Nov. 9, 1839, the president of the company notified the Governor of Maryland that the board could not command the means to pay the interest on the bonds and at the same time comply with its other indispensable engagements. The company made a formal application to the next Legislature, which commenced in December, 1839, for further aid from the State, showing that the amount necessary to complete the fifty miles between dam No. 6 and Cumberland was $2,410,222. Two modes of relief were discussed by the Legislature,—one of them that the State bonds to be issued should be disposed of at par for money and the proceeds paid over to the company, the other that the bonds should be delivered to the company to be sold by them at par for money, or exchanged at their normal value for the evidences of debt of the company. Each, however, had its advocates, and between the two contending parties the whole measure fell to the ground, and the Legislature adjourned without making any appropriations.

The chief engineer represented to the company at this juncture that the losses likely to result from a total suspension of the works would amount to $1,000,000.

Contractors and merchants residing contiguous to the canal solicited a continuation of the works and an issue of scrip of the company. The company concluded to let the works proceed, and during the year 1840, and from January to April, 1841, issued scrip amounting to $555,400, without any pledge to sustain it.

At the session of the Legislature, December, 1840, another appropriation for aid was again asked for by the company. The sum of money still required to finish the canal to Cumberland was $1,825,892, and in addition it was said that, estimating the State bonds unsold at eighty per cent., the company would need $700,000, exclusive of the interest to the State, to redeem the scrip and pay arrears to contractors. The Legislature again adjourned without adopting any measure of relief.

The company now began to contract its operations on the canal and pay off the old loans by a sale of the five per cent. sterling bonds. The company transmitted a large number of these bonds to their London agent for sale, and bills of exchange were drawn upon him. The agent made considerable sales at a large discount, but failing to dispose of bonds sufficient to meet the drafts as they fell due, he pledged them at reduced rates. The company again began a hypothecation of the bonds in this country, and soon came a series of forced sales, exhaustion of appropriations, public complaints, private reproaches, and, finally, absolute discredit.

In March, 1841, an application was again made to the Legislature for further assistance, and an act was passed for an additional loan of $2,000,000, payable in the six per cent. stock or bonds of the State. The act, however, required the several companies of Allegany County to construct a railroad from the mines to the canal, and complete the same simultaneously with its completion to Cumberland, and also to guarantee payment to the company of at least $200,000 per annum for the transportation of their own coal on the canal. The securities offered by the coal and iron companies were, however, not deemed sufficient by the State treasurer, and the act proved abortive, and was subsequently repealed by the Legislature. At December session, 1841, another application for relief was made to the Legislature, but without success, and immediately after the adjournment of that body the contractors stopped work, and the prosecution of the work was not again resumed until after the passage of the act of March 10, 1845.

At the December session, 1842, the General Assembly of Maryland passed a law authorizing the State treasurer to sell its interests in the various companies which the State had sustained by its aid. He was authorized to sell the whole interest of the State in the canal, at that time amounting to $8,000,000, for $5,000,000, payable in State bonds bearing five per cent. interest, the company to secure to its creditors payment of their claims within twenty years from the date of transfer, with annual interest at six per cent. Advertisements of the sale were published in the leading cities of this country and Europe, but no bids were received, and the act became a dead letter.

In August, 1843, the company had reached its lowest point of depression. In addition to its liabilities to the State, its debts and obligations due to individuals amounted to $1,174,566.31, and some of its creditors had been reduced from affluence to absolute poverty. Eighteen and three-tenths miles of work had to be done to complete the canal to Cumberland, the cost of which was estimated at $1,545,000. In consequence of heavy breaches in the canal, produced by the great freshets of April and September, 1843, the deficit at the close of that year was unusually large. The whole revenues of the year amounted only to $47,635.51, and the current expenses to $83,792.80, showing an excess of expenses over income of $36,157.29.

In January, 1844, the company succeeded in rescuing from assumed forfeiture £15,500 of the sterling bonds which had been hypothecated in England in 1839, and a small amount of coupons overdue, which enabled it to discharge to a considerable extent debts for current expenses and put the canal in better order. An arrangement was also concluded with the Baltimore and Ohio Railroad Company, by which that company agreed to fix the charge for the transportation of coal at two cents per ton per mile from Cumberland to dam No. 6, there to be transferred to the canal. By this arrangement the tolls of the company for the year 1844 exceeded $50,000; but the agreement was, however, abandoned by the railway company in May, 1845.

A memorial was presented to the State Legislature at the December session, 1843, suggesting the waiver by that body of the State liens on the revenues of the canal, so as to empower the company to issue its bonds, with preferred liens on its revenues, to an amount not exceeding $2,000,000. The Legislature was, however, not prepared to adopt the measure, but at the December session, 1844, the application was renewed. Although the opposition to it was influential, there were members in the House of Delegates who fully appreciated the deep importance of the completion of the canal, and after a long and arduous struggle the act waiving the liens of the State was passed. It authorized the president and board of directors to borrow, or raise on the bonds of the company, secured by a pledge of revenues and tolls hereafter to accrue, such sums of money as would be required to pay for the completion of the canal to Cumberland, and also to pay the interest on the bonds issued under the act in aid of the net revenues until they became sufficient for the purpose, with a proviso that the whole amount of bonds issued should not exceed $1,700,000. The interest on the bonds, at the rate of six per cent. per annum, was to be made payable semi-annually, and the principal in not less than thirty-five years. So soon as the revenues should be more than sufficient to pay the interest on the bonds and on the certificates of debt issued to the creditors of the Potomac Company, which was not to exceed five thousand dollars per year, the company was to pay to the State treasurer out of the surplus net revenues such sum, not exceeding an average of twenty-five thousand dollars a year, dating from the 1st of January next after the completion of the canal to Cumberland, as might be necessary to constitute an adequate sinking fund, the treasurer to invest and accumulate the same until a sufficient amount should be obtained to pay the principal of the bonds that might be issued, which he was directed to pay at maturity. The act was, however, not to take effect until one or more of the companies of Allegany County should guarantee to the canal company an aggregate transportation on the entire length of the canal of not less than an average of one hundred and ninety-five thousand tons of tonnage per year for five years, dating from the end of six months after the canal had been completed to Cumberland.

In the charter of the canal company, prior to 1844, there was no express power given to it to borrow money for the construction or completion of the canal. Besides this, the time limited by the charter for its completion to Cumberland had expired in 1840, and no steps had been taken to procure amendments on these points. The president and board of directors, therefore, believing that the measure suggested by the company for the completion of the work would, sooner or later, prevail, memorialized the Legislature of Virginia at the session of 1843 for the passage of an act providing for the amendments indicated, and also enlarging the powers of the company in regard to extending the canal by a slack-water improvement to the mouth of Savage River. The Legislature of Virginia passed the bill on Jan. 20, 1844, providing for an extension of the time for completing the canal to Cumberland to Jan. 1, 1855, and conferring authority on the president and directors of the company to borrow money, issue bonds, and pledge the property and revenues of the company for payment of the same, with a proviso waiving the prior rights and liens of the State of Maryland under the mortgages which had been executed to it by the company. The assent of the Maryland Legislature was given to this act on Feb. 8, 1844, and it was confirmed by Congress, and approved by the President of the United States on Feb. 7, 1845.

At a general meeting of the stockholders of the company, held at Frederick on April 29, 1845, the act of the General Assembly of Maryland was accepted, and a mortgage executed to the State bearing date Jan. 8, 1846. The amendments to the charter, which have been described, were finally ratified by Congress, about one month before the passage of the act waiving the liens for the completion of the canal. On the 1st of December, 1842, the chief engineer estimated the amount required to complete the canal to Cumberland at $1,545,000, and another estimate in August, 1845, placing the amount at $1,404,471. By persevering exertions the full amount of guarantee required by the act was obtained from the incorporated companies of Allegany County, and the instruments of guarantee received the approval of the Governor and the Maryland State agents on July 29, 1845.

The act of 1844 did not place any money at the disposal of the company, but merely authorized the president and directors to issue the company's bonds, upon a pledge of its disencumbered revenues, to an amount not exceeding $1,700,000. Owing to the general depreciation of American securities, a sale of the bonds at par was unattainable, and resort was had to a contract payable in the bonds. On Sept. 25, 1845, the president and board of directors concluded an agreement in which, for the consideration of $1,625,000 of the bonds to be issued under the act of 1844, the contractors bound themselves within two years to finish the canal to Cumberland, to pay to a trustee, for the use of the company, in twenty-one monthly installments, one hundred thousand dollars in money, to enable the board to liquidate land claims and incidental expenses, and to pay the interest on the bonds to be issued until the work had been finished. Soon after the date of the contract the contractors began work between dam No. 6 and Cumberland, and prosecuted it until June, 1846, when, their private means being exhausted, and the Legislature having adjourned without passing an act to restore the credit of the State, they suspended operations.

One of the contractors now went to England and succeeded in arranging for a negotiation there, predicated upon the resumption of payment by Maryland. On March 8, 1847, the Legislature of Maryland passed a law for funding the arrears and paying the interest accruing on the State debt after October 1, 1847. The Legislature of Virginia passed an act on March 8, 1847, authorizing a guarantee of the bonds to the amount of three hundred thousand dollars, and the District cities and certain citizens of Alexandria subscribed on similar terms for one hundred thousand dollars of the bonds at their par value. The London parties, however, withdrew from their negotiations, on the ground that a change had taken place in the money market, and the prospects of the company were at this period discouraging. During the years 1846 and 1847 considerable damage was done to the canal by a series of freshets, particularly on the lower division, and the increased expense of mending the breaches thereby occasioned was exceedingly embarrassing.

On Oct. 13, 1847, the contractors, through the medium of three distinguished gentlemen of the North, succeeded in concluding a negotiation, by which, assuming that $600,000 of the bonds had been disposed of at par, they agreed to sell to certain parties in Boston, New York, and Washington City, at the rate of sixty cents on the dollar, $833,333 of the bonds they were to receive from the company at par, leaving still a margin of $191,667 of the bonds as a reserve fund. The Maryland State agents and the president and board of directors accordingly consented to issue and pay out the bonds as the work proceeded. Two of the original contractors withdrew from the copartnership after the execution of the contract for the completion of the canal, and Thomas G. Harris, of Washington County, Md., became associated with the remaining two, who were James Hunter, of Virginia, and William B. Thompson, of the District of Columbia, the three forming a firm under the name of Hunter, Harris & Co. In 1847 operations were resumed, and prosecuted under their management until March 11, 1850, when they were suspended in consequence of the pecuniary difficulties of the contractors. The suspension, however, only lasted a few days, the firm making an assignment of their interest in the contract for the benefit of their creditors. The work was again started, and continued until the middle of July, 1850, when the assignees abandoned it from inability to complete the canal with the remaining means that were applicable to the purpose.

On July 18th of the same year the president and board of directors entered into a new contract with Michael Byrne, of Frederick County, for the final completion of the canal. Mr. Byrne commenced the work promptly, and on Oct. 10, 1850, the canal was opened for the purpose of navigation throughout the entire line to Cumberland, and the through trade then commenced. He, however, still continued to press forward the work, which was then of an external character, and on Feb. 17, 1851, the final payment was made to him under his contract. From that period may be dated the completion of the Chesapeake and Ohio Canal to Cumberland.

The Chesapeake and Ohio Canal, between Georgetown and Cumberland, lies on the north or Maryland side of the river, and follows the valley of the Potomac throughout its entire length, except at Paw-Paw Bend, twenty-seven miles below Cumberland, where it passes through the mountain by a tunnel 3118 feet in length. From the Rock Creek basin in Georgetown to the basin at Cumberland is $184\frac{4}{10}$ miles, and the total rise from the level of mid-tide at Georgetown to the Cumberland basin is $609\frac{4}{10}$ feet. This ascent is overcome by 74 lift-locks and a tide-lock that connects Rock Creek basin with the Potomac. At the mouth of the Tiber, in Washington City, is another tide-lock which connects it with the Potomac River. The canal is constructed for a depth of six feet throughout. From Georgetown to Harper's Ferry it is sixty feet wide at the surface and forty-two feet at the bottom. From Harper's Ferry to dam No. 5, forty-seven miles, the width at the surface is fifty feet, and at the bottom thirty-two feet; and from dam No. 5 to Cumberland, seventy-seven and a half miles, the surface width is fifty-four feet, and the bottom thirty feet. The average lift of the locks is a little over eight feet. The locks are one hundred feet long and fifteen feet wide in the clear, and are capable of passing boats carrying one hundred and twenty tons (two thousand two hundred and forty pounds). The cost of the canal from the mouth of the Tiber, in Washington City, to the city of Cumberland, a distance of $185\frac{4}{10}$ miles, for construction, engineer expenses, lands, and other contingencies, amounted in the aggregate to the sum of $11,071,176.21, or $59,618.61 per mile.

On Thursday, Oct. 10, 1850, the opening of the canal for continuous navigation from Alexandria to Cumberland was commemorated at the latter place with imposing ceremonies. Among those who arrived in Cumberland to take part in the celebration were Gen. James M. Coale, president, and Messrs. John Pickall, William C. Johnson, William A. Bradley, George Schley, S. P. Smith, directors of the canal company; ex-Governor Sprigg, Gen. Tench Tilghman, and J. Van Lear, State agents; Hon. William D. Merrick, formerly United States senator from

Maryland; John L. Skinner, editor of *The Plow, the Loom, and the Anvil;* Henry Addison, mayor of Georgetown, and a number of gentlemen from various parts of Maryland and Virginia. On the morning of the celebration a procession was formed which marched through the streets to the canal-locks, and when everything had been arranged five canal-boats, laden with the product of the mines of Allegany County and destined for Eastern markets, passed through the locks. Mr. William Price then delivered an address, to which Gen. James M. Coale, president of the canal company, made a reply. The company then embarked on the canal-packet " Jenny Lind" and the canal-boat " C. B. Fisk," and proceeded down the canal, followed by the Eckhart Light Artillery, the coal-boats "Southampton," " Elizabeth," " Ohio," and " Delaware," belonging to the Merchants' Line of Messrs. McKaig & Agnew, and the " Freeman Rawdon," belonging to the Cumberland Line of Mr. Ward, bringing up the rear. The company disembarked at a large spring ten miles east of Cumberland, and then returned on board and partook of a collation prepared by a committee of the canal company,—Messrs. S. P. Smith, W. A. Bradley, and John Pickall. On their return to Cumberland they were entertained by the citizens at Barnum's Hotel, J. A. Hefelfinger, proprietor, and after the cloth had been removed, Hon. William Cost Johnson, the tried friend of the canal, and who, as chairman of the Committee of Internal Improvement of the House of Delegates, at December session, 1844, reported the act under which it was completed, rose and offered the following toast : " The Chesapeake and Ohio Canal and the Baltimore and Ohio Railroad: the former has happily reached its ebony harvest amid the coal-fields of the Alleganies ; may the latter journey vigorously on, westward, until it rejoices amid the golden plains of the far Californias."

A List of the Presidents, Directors, and Chief Officers of the Chesapeake and Ohio Canal Company from its organization in June, 1828, to its completion on Feb. 27, 1851.

Presidents.	Period of Service.	
	From	To
Charles Fenton Mercer	June 21, 1828	June 6, 1833
John H. Eaton	" 6, 1833	" 27, 1834
George C. Washington	" 27, 1834	" 3, 1839
Francis Thomas	" 3, 1839	April 2, 1841
Michael C. Sprigg	April 2, 1841	Dec. 3, 1842
Wm. Gibbs McNeill	Dec. 3, 1842	Aug. 17, 1843
James M. Coale	Aug. 17, 1843	Feb. 27, 1851
Directors.		
Joseph Kent	June 21, 1828	June 11, 1831
Phineas Janney	" "	" 2, 1840
Walter Smith	" "	" 3, 1839
Peter Lenox	" "	" 6, 1833

Presidents.	Period of Service.	
	From	To
Andrew Stewart	June 21, 1828	June 6, 1833
Frederick May	" "	" 11, 1831
William Price	June 11, 1831	" 27, 1834
John J. Albert	" "	Dec. 21, 1839
William Gunton	June 6, 1833	June 3, 1839
Richard H. Henderson	" "	" "
George Bender	June 27, 1834	April 29, 1835
M. St. Clair Clarke	" 15, 1835	June 22, 1836
Thomas Carbery	" 22, 1836	July 16, 1838
John Hoye	July 16, 1838	June 3, 1839
Thomas Perry	June 3, 1839	Dec. 21, 1839
James Carroll	" "	" "
Jacob G. Davies	" "	June 2, 1840
Joseph White	" "	" "
Robert P. Dunlop	Dec. 21, 1839	April 2, 1841
Washington Duvall	" "	June 2, 1840
John W. Maury	" "	" "
Frederick A. Schley	June 2, 1840	Declined.
James Swan	" "	April 2, 1841
John McPherson	" "	" "
William Lucas	" "	" "
William Tyler	" "	" "
Jacob Markell	July 22, 1840	" "
Frisby Tilghman	April 2, 1841	June 7, 1847
John R. Dall	" "	Aug. 5, 1842
John O. Wharton	" "	June 24, 1847
Daniel Burkhart	" "	" "
James M. Coale	" "	Aug. 17, 1843
John P. Ingle	" "	June 24, 1847
William Price	Aug. 5, 1842	
William Darne	June 4, 1844	July 23, 1845
Robert W. Bowie	July 23, 1845	June 7, 1847
William A. Bradley	June 24, 1847	
Henry Daingerfield	" "	
Wm. Cost Johnson	" "	
John Pickell	" "	
George Schley	" "	
Samuel P. Smith	" "	
Chief Engineers.		
Benjamin Wright	June 23, 1828	Nov. 13, 1830
Charles B. Fisk	April 12, 1837	Sept. 26, 1840
Ellwood Morris	Sept. 26, 1840	April 13, 1841
Charles B. Fisk	April 13, 1841	
Clerks.		
Asa Rogers	June 28, 1828	Declined.
John P. Ingle	July 5, 1828	July 9, 1840
Thomas Turner	" 9, 1840	Dec. 20, 1846
Walter S. Ringgold	Dec. 20, 1846	
Treasurers.		
Clement Smith	July 5, 1828	July 7, 1834
Robert Barnard	" 18, 1834	Nov. 14, 1840
Samuel Tyler	Nov. 14, 1840	April 13, 1841
Robert Barnard	April 14, 1841	June 4, 1841
M. C. Cramer	June 4, 1841	Aug. 6, 1841
Ezra Houck	Aug. 6, 1841	Sept. 15, 1841
Joseph Schell	Sept. 16, 1841	Dec. 22, 1841
Robert Barnard	Dec. 22, 1841	Feb. 13, 1846
Philemon Chew	Feb. 13, 1846	April 14, 1846
Lawrence J. Brengle	April 15, 1846	

The present president of the canal is Hon. Arthur Pue Gorman, one of the most distinguished of the living public men of Maryland, whose rare ability has placed him in the United States senate at the early age of forty-one. Mr. Gorman's rapid advancement has been the result of conspicuous talents, calm judgment, and keen appreciation of the opportunities of life. He was born in Woodstock, Howard Co., Md., on the 11th of March, 1839. His ancestors were descended from Presbyterian stock of the North of Ireland. John Gorman, his grandfather, came to the United States in 1784, and settled in Harrisburg, Pa. For a number of years he was engaged in cattle-trading between Harrisburg and Baltimore, and was attracted by the thriving prospects of the latter city, to which he finally removed and settled in "Old Town." Here was born Peter Gorman, the father of the senator, a sturdy, self-reliant, clear-headed man, with all the vigorous characteristics of that old Irish Presbyterian stock which furnished so much to the cause of liberty in this country during and after the war of the Revolution. Peter Gorman became one of the pioneers in the construction of that great enterprise, the Baltimore and Ohio Railroad, and was one of the early contractors who built the first section of the road.

It was while engaged in this undertaking that he found it necessary, in order to facilitate his work, to remove to Woodstock. Here he married Elizabeth A. Brown, daughter of John R. Brown, whose family had settled in the county when it was a part of Anne Arundel, in colonial days. Members of the Brown family had served with distinction in the Revolution and in the war of 1812, and its descendants were people of consequence in the county. One of the fruits of this marriage was Arthur P. Gorman, whose continued success in life has attracted general attention. Besides him, there were two sons and two daughters. Young Gorman was but six years of age when his father removed from Woodstock to the present homestead and residence of the senator, near Laurel. His father was at this time active and prominent in political affairs, was a great organizer, and exerted a very large influence. He was frequently sent as a delegate to the State conventions of his party, and represented the State in several national conventions, although he would never become a candidate for office. At an early day he identified himself with the Douglas Democracy, and became one of its recognized leaders in Maryland.

When young Gorman was thirteen years old his father, through his influence at Washington, aided by Gen. Hammond, the congressman from his district, and Governor W. T. Hamilton, who was also at that time a member of Congress, succeeded in having him appointed page in the House of Representatives, where he attracted the attention and won the friendship of Stephen A. Douglas, who had him transferred to the Senate. Senator Douglas at once became his patron and friend, and the young page, who was himself at a much later day to become a member of the Senate, learned his first lessons in the great problem of politics at the feet of this distinguished statesman. The observant and reflecting mind of the young page quickly caught and utilized the instructive wisdom evolved from the great discussions going on about him. No period in the history of the Senate could have better afforded him the opportunity for obtaining a clear insight into the theory of our government, its splendid possibilities and its great dangers, than that of the five years immediately preceding the war, and the career of Senator Gorman since has shown how well his mind imbibed the knowledge which was so liberally poured out to him, and how greatly the evolution of some of the greatest problems of our Constitution impressed his youthful but sturdy character.

Under the tutorship of Mr. Douglass young Gorman's mind and character expanded, and under the patronage of the same friend his fortunes were rapidly advanced. He was received as a member of the Illinois senator's family and became his private secretary. So well also did he commend himself to the favorable notice of the other senators that he was successively advanced to the positions of messenger, assistant doorkeeper, assistant postmaster, and finally postmaster. In the mean time he maintained his confidential relations with Senator Douglas, who could not fail to appreciate the extraordinary activity and good judgment of his young friend, whose ability as an organizer began to be conspicuous and command attention. When, therefore, Mr. Douglas was about to undertake that famous campaign in Illinois in which he was to meet Abraham Lincoln in a contest which attracted the breathless attention of the whole country, Mr. Gorman was asked to accompany him. From this undertaking he returned to Washington with a strong hold upon the confidence and esteem of the Douglas wing of the Democratic party, with which by this time he had become completely identified. In the ensuing session of Congress the great fight over the Kansas-Nebraska bill occurred, and the tact, calm judgment, activity, and physical powers of Mr. Gorman were relied upon by the Douglas Democrats to manage the voting strength of the friends of the bill, and to defeat, by keeping their organization in vigorous action, the filibustering efforts of its opponents.

His activity in this contest naturally aroused the hostility of the opponents of the measure, and strong efforts were at once made to have him removed from the postmastership of the Senate. These efforts were, however, of no avail. The charges which were preferred, after being submitted to Vice-President Breckenridge, were dismissed as not sustained, and it was decided that no cause for removal existed. At this time Peter Gorman was still closely connected with the Douglas Democrats in Maryland, and viewed with great satisfaction the considerable part which his son was taking in the interest of that party. The elder Gorman, although not a member of the Charleston Convention of 1860, was the recognized leader of the Douglas party at the convention, and it was his management which succeeded in nominating Mr. Douglas for the Presidency. The result is too well known to be more than referred to here. After the Breckenridge bolt, which divided the Democratic party and resulted in the election of Abraham Lincoln and civil war, the Gormans, father and son, adhered to the Union cause.

Peter Gorman died in 1862, shortly after his release from Libby Prison, Richmond, where he was confined by order of Governor Letcher. He had been sent by the government at Washington to Richmond for the purpose of preventing by his influence the passage of the ordinance of secession by the Virginia Legislature. Immediately upon his arrival, however, he was placed under arrest and sent to Libby Prison, from which he was not released until the State had seceded. His prison-life and the excitement of the scenes in which he was engaged affected his health and caused his death.

In the mean time his son had been retained in his position as postmaster of the Senate, although by the withdrawal of the Southern members the political complexion of that body had undergone a radical change and it was controlled by the Republican senators. He held his place throughout the war, and was engaged during that time in special work which required great tact and wise management.

The Committee on the Conduct of the War found his services especially valuable, and he was constantly being dispatched to important points for information to be used in the committee's investigation. Upon one occasion he found himself at Gen. Grant's headquarters, near Petersburg, Va., and witnessed the great mine explosion which occurred before that city. During all this time Mr. Gorman had been naturally drifting into the Conservative party, and after the close of the war he became one of the organizers of the Conservative party in Maryland. He took a very active part in the contest between the radical Republicans in the Senate and President Johnson, and successful efforts were made to remove him from his office, although they were nearly defeated by the strenuous efforts of Senator Wade, of Ohio, then President of the Senate. He was at once appointed collector of internal revenue in the Fifth Federal Collection District of Maryland, the appointment being obtained by Reverdy Johnson, Thomas A. Hendricks, Montgomery Blair, and several conservative Republican senators.

He assumed charge in September, 1866. It was one of the most extensive in the department, and was in arrears to the amount of one hundred and fifty thousand dollars. When he resigned the office this had been made up, all his accounts adjusted, and a settlement made in a very few weeks,—a record which was not surpassed by that of any other officer in the service. During his residence in his district he had taken great interest in local politics, and the internal knowledge that he had obtained of the conduct of public affairs in his long service at Washington gave him a decided advantage, which he well understood how to use. His first State office was a directorship in the Chesapeake and Ohio Canal, to which he was appointed in 1869, and at once took a very prominent part in the direction of the conduct of canal affairs. His administrative qualities were instantly recognized, and his influence in the board of directors became very great.

In the mean time he was elected a member of the House of Delegates from Howard County, Judge William M. Merrick being his colleague, and represented the county in the Legislature of 1870-72. He was re-elected to the next Legislature, and was chosen at the first session Speaker of the House. Almost immediately after the adjournment of the Legislature, Mr. Gorman's services to the canal, as one of its most astute and far-seeing directors, were recognized by his appointment to the presidency. The influence of the new president's administrative ability was at once manifest. He entered upon the discharge of his duties with the same zeal and sagacity which had characterized his life as an officer of the United States Senate, and which had so greatly advanced his fortunes. Under his management the affairs of the canal were placed in excellent condition.

In 1875 he was a candidate for the State senatorship, and was elected to succeed the Hon. John Lee Carroll, who was elected Governor of the State. By this time his talents as an organizer had been recognized by his party in the State, and in 1877 he was unanimously chosen chairman of the Democratic State Central Committee, a position which he has ever since held. In 1877 he was re-elected to the State Senate from Howard County, where his popularity had become unbounded. In the Senate he at once became the recognized leader of his party, and until his elevation to the United States Senate his influence at Annapolis was unbounded. He was always eager to advance the material interests of the State and the best interests of his people, and was most actively engaged in settling the difficulties which had for a long time existed between the State and the railroad corporations within its limits.

In 1880, when the Legislature met, it was a foregone conclusion that he was to succeed Hon. William Pinkney Whyte as United States senator in Congress, and he was elected to that high office by a unanimous vote, having received in the caucus nearly two-thirds of the Democratic voters present, constituting a very large majority of the Democratic members of the Legislature, and he took his place in the Senate on the 4th of March, 1881, being the youngest member of that body. His political course since his election to the Senate has been dignified and eminently creditable. He has held himself aloof from the contests of factions, and has maintained a most exemplary position of independence and conciliation.

It may be said of his management of the affairs of the canal, of which he is still president, that during the two first years of his administration it has yielded a net income of one hundred thousand dollars a year, which is more than double the amount yielded in any of the twenty years previous.

Mr. Gorman has been since his election to the Senate recognized by that body as a member worthy of the most exalted confidence, and he has been placed upon the most important committees.

Senator Gorman's private life has been uneventful. He is a man of strong domestic nature, in all the busy whirlpool of politics finding the chiefest pleasures of life in the bosom of his interesting family. His country residence at Laurel has for years been his retreat in which he sought rest and relief from the annoyances and fatigues of his public career. Since his election to the United States Senate he has taken possession of the house on Fifteenth Street so long occupied by ex-Governor Swann, and adjoining the somewhat famous residence of the late Fernando Wood, of New York. Here the senator disburses a generous hospitality to his personal and political friends.

The true manliness of Senator Gorman's character has never been fully appreciated, except by those who are fortunate enough to possess his intimate personal acquaintance. His views are broad and his judgment calm and serene. He seldom makes a false step, and never a foolish one. He possesses qualities of the highest grade of statesmanship, although circumstances have made him appear to be a politician.

His talents are not of the brilliant and showy character which attract the admiration of the multitudes, but are of that quiet, strong, and unostentatious nature which command the respect of men of high character and transcendent ability, among whom he is acknowledged to be a man of extraordinary judgment and force. His nature is generous and warm-hearted, but he is undemonstrative in his friendship, and although easy of approach is difficult of intimate acquaintance. His friends love him, and every one who is thrown within the circle of his influence is insensibly won by a persuasive power more easily felt than understood. He is a strong though not a brilliant writer and speaker, his force in debate being at times so tremendous as to wake the unwilling admiration of his opponents.

Those who imagine that Senator Gorman's ability as a politician is the strongest part of his character make a mistake, and in the great future which is before him he will display those other and higher qualities which have long commanded for him the unqualified admiration of those who know him best and are best qualified to pass judgment.

The following statement shows the amounts paid upon the subscriptions to the capital stock of the Chesapeake and Ohio Canal Company, and the balances that were due on the same to the 1st of November, 1850:

	Amount Subscribed.	Amount Paid.	Balances.
Subscriptions were made by the United States........................	$1,000,000	$999,990.00	$10.00
State of Maryland..................	5,000,000	5,000,000.00	
State of Virginia.....................	250,000	250,000.00	
Corporation of Washington......	1,000,000	1,000,000.00	
" Georgetown........	250,000	250,000.00	
" Alexandria.........	250,000	250,000.00	
" Shepherdstown...	2,000	2,000.00	
Individuals:			
Washington.................$233,600		185,586.80	48,013.20
Georgetown................... 229,700		196,532.63	33,167.37
Alexandria................... 47,300		34,938.00	12,362.00
Maryland...................... 40,700		25,951.71	14,748.29
Virginia 37,400		30,394.25	7,005.75
Pennsylvania 18,700	607,400	797.00	17,903.00
	$8,359,400	$8,226,190.39	$133,209.61

From the above statement it will be seen that the State of Maryland is the holder of five million dollars of the $8,226,593 composing the capital of the canal, holding fifty thousand shares of the stock, equal to about five-eighths of the whole capital stock.

On the 31st of December, 1866, the total cost of the canal had been $27,000,000. The State of Maryland held a first lien on the corpus of the canal, and a second lien on its tolls and revenues for $5,968,586.94, and besides that was entitled to preferred stock and guaranteed dividends for $10,806,250. The total indebtedness of the canal company to the State at the present time is about $22,000,000.

MONTGOMERY COUNTY DISTRICTS.

CHAPTER XXXVII.

CRACKLIN DISTRICT, No. 1.

Although Montgomery County was created in 1776, it was not divided into election districts until 1798, when an act of Assembly was passed for this purpose, which was confirmed in the following year. The returns of the commissioners appointed to lay off the districts under these acts is not of record, so that it is now impossible to indicate with certainty their original boundaries. In 1821, however, they were directed to be laid off anew, and under this division Cracklin District, No. 1, was assigned the following metes and bounds:

"Beginning at Mershberger's old mill on Patuxent, and running down Patuxent to the mouth of Hawling's River; then running up said river to the mouth of Reed's Branch, from thence to the head of the late Gerard Brooke's spring; thence to the pole bridge near where Cyrus, a black man, formerly kept a blacksmith-shop; then with a small road, leaving the house formerly owned by Surrett Dickerson on the right, until it intersects the road passing in front of Mrs. Magruder's house at the corner of her fence; thence with said road, leaving the house where the late Capt. Benjamin Ricketts did live on the right, until it intersects the Bladensburg road at the lower end of said Ricketts' plantation; then with the road through the place where Zadok Ricketts once lived to the head-waters of Muddy Branch; then down said branch to the Georgetown road; then with said road to Middlebrook Mills on Seneca; then up Seneca to the head thereof; then with a straight line by Darnall's spring to the main road; then with said road until it intersects a road leading by Benjamin Benton's; thence with said road to the beginning."

These boundaries continued unchanged until 1878, when a portion of the district was taken to form Mechanicsville, and in 1880 it was still further reduced by the creation of Gaithersburg District, No. 9.

Cracklin is bounded on the north by Clarksburg District, on the east by Howard County, on the south by Mechanicsville District, and on the northwest by Gaithersburg District. The Patuxent River divides it from Howard County, and Great Seneca Creek forms a part of its northern boundary line, separating it for a portion of the distance from Clarksburg District, No. 2. The land is well watered by Whetstone and Cabin Branches in the west, by Goshen Branch in the centre, Scott's Branch in the east, by Rock Creek in the southwest, and by Hawling's River, which rises in the district and flows southeast through Mechanicsville into the Patuxent.

Among the earliest settlers in the district were John Banks, Benjamin Wallingford, Benjamin Penn, and Higson Belt, who were followed by the Griffiths, the Darbys, Mackalls, Gaithers, Neels, Allnutts, Bells, Plummers, Popes, Riggs, Warfields, Bowmans, Stewarts, Crawfords, and the Waters'.

The first representative of the last-named family in Montgomery was Dr. Richard Waters, who was born about 1760 in Prince George's County. He served as a surgeon in the Revolutionary war, and was distinguished both as a surgeon and physician. At the close of the war he purchased a large estate, called "Spring Garden," in Montgomery County, on the road leading from Goshen to Gaithersburg. He married Miss Margaret Smith, of Prince George's, by whom he had several children, among whom were Somerset, a commission merchant of Baltimore, and for many years State tobacco inspector, and Hon. Richard Waters, who was born at the old homestead on the 19th of December, 1794. The latter became prominent in politics at an early age, and held many positions of trust and honor, filling the important office of sheriff with fidelity and efficiency, and representing his county in the State Legislature. In his canvass for the General Assembly he discovered that the State appropriation for the education of poor children was often misapplied by the trustees, and making this the great issue in his campaign, he was elected by an overwhelming majority. He at once directed his energies to the removal of the evil, and succeeded in securing the passage of a bill providing a general system of public education. This was the initial movement in the important work of establishing the present public-school system of the State, and Mr. Waters' services were so much appreciated by his constituents that on the expiration of his first term he was again chosen to represent them in the General Assembly. Mr. Waters left several children, some of whom are still living. His son Samuel is an eminent divine in the Missouri Conference of the Methodist Episcopal Church South, another, William, is the agent of the Adams Express Company in Cincinnati, a third, Somerset, is a leading physician in Carroll County, and has served several terms in the General Assembly, and a fourth, George, resides near the old homestead. His only daughter, Rebecca, married Jesse T. Higgins, formerly of Poolesville, and now a merchant of Baltimore.

Unity.—The village of Unity is situated near the southeastern boundary of the district, on a part of a tract of two hundred acres surveyed for John Philburn on the 21st of December, 1724, and called, after the curious fashion of that day, "John and Sarah," probably in honor of the first master and mistress of the estate. Unity was created by act of Assembly prior to 1806, but the first house, which is now occupied by Rezin Duvall, was not built until 1811.

In 1827 the village comprised six dwellings. William Price resided in the house now occupied by John G. Kinsey; Elisha R. Gaither lived in the house now the residence of Rezin Duvall; Philemon Plummer in that of Charles F. Townsend; Philemon Griffith in that of Mr. Nimrod Davis; Francis Simpson in the house now occupied by Francis Groomes, and Erasmus Daly in that of James E. Harvey. Garret Gaither, the first merchant known in this place, commenced business there as early as the year 1813. His place of business was situated between the residence of Mr. Nimrod Davis and the store of Colliflower & Harvey. The pioneer blacksmith of this vicinity was a man by the name of Smith. Hugh Anderson kept the first hotel in the place, occupying what is now the residence of Mr. Davis for that purpose. After a few years he was succeeded by Mr. Levi Chambers, who about the year 1818 sold out to Mr. Graff, by whom it was conducted until about 1860. Dr. Anderson settled here about 1831, and was the first resident physician of the town. Edward Bell, who was the pioneer teacher, and renowned as "a learned man" in those days, was succeeded in his duties by William Musgrove, who for many years was the schoolmaster of the neighborhood. Daniel Grant, the first shoemaker in the neighborhood, worked at his trade in the house now owned by Judson Balswaer. Unity boasted for many years the third oldest post-office in the county, but it was finally discontinued, and the mails are now received at Sunshine Post-office.

Bartholomew Protestant Episcopal Church is located about one mile from the village, on the road leading from Laytonsville to Unity. The congregation belonged originally to Prince George's Parish, and was organized in 1821. Among the founders and original members were Thomas Griffith, Henry Griffith, Henry C. Gaither, Thomas Davis, Nathaniel Clagett, and Jesse Wilcoxen. The church was erected about the time of the formation of the congregation, but was remodeled and otherwise improved in 1871. Among its pastors have been Rev. Mr. Allen, Rev. Levin Gills, who was its rector for many years, Rev. Chandler Hutton, Rev. Mr. Duncan, Rev. Dr. Mason, and Rev. Mr. Lorne. The vestrymen are Elisha Griffith, Col. Edward Owen, Richard Lansdale, Charles Higgins, John F. D. Magruder, F. Griffith.

The Presbyterian Church was erected in 1874, and is situated in the village of Unity. The congregation was organized the same year, prior to the building of the church, under the charge of Rev. Thomas Duncan. The erection of the church was chiefly due to Dr. James H. Maynard and Nimrod Davis, the former of whom solicited the greater part of the funds necessary for its construction, the latter giving the lot upon which the building stands. The original trustees were Elisha Griffith, Col. Edward Owen, Thomas Lansdale, Charles Higgins, John F. D. Magruder, Richard Lansdale, and F. Griffith. Rev. Mr. Duncan was succeeded as the pastor by the Rev. Dr. Mason, and he by Rev. Mr. Lorne. The congregation now numbers thirty-five members, and the officers are as follows: Treasurer, Richard Lansdale; Secretary, Charles Higgins. The vestry are the same as at its organization, with the exception of one deceased.

The Methodist Protestant Church (Mount Carmel) is located between Unity and Triadelphia.

Sunshine.—This is the post-office for the village of Unity, and is situated about ten miles from Gaithersburg and one mile from Unity.

Laytonsville.—This village is part of an addition to "Brooke Grove," surveyed for James Brooke, Sept. 4, 1728. The locality was originally settled by the Layton family among others, and to John L. Layton it is indebted for its name. It is situated seven miles from Gaithersburg, on the road leading from Goshen to Unity. F. L. Beall is the postmaster, and Dr. B. B. Crawford, born in Howard County, has been its physician for thirty years. The Methodist Episcopal Church was erected in 1867; the present pastor is Rev. J. Thomas Cross. Attached to the church is a cemetery, in which among others are the graves of Rev. Henry Walker, born Feb. 22, 1809, died March 16, 1877; Lizzie C., wife of George W. Mobley, born Sept. 24, 1843, died Dec. 5, 1875, aged thirty-two years, two months; Mollie F., wife of George W. Mobley, born Nov. 27, 1853, died Sept. 7, 1880. Brooke Chapel, near the village, was built in 1871, and rebuilt in 1879.

Goshen is situated five miles northeast of Gaithersburg, on Goshen Branch. The Goshen mills, which are located at this point, are under the care of J. S. Davis and J. W. Lewis. A. R. Martin is the postmaster.

The Methodist Episcopal Church South was erected in 1869–70, and was dedicated to divine worship Sunday, May 21, 1870, the dedication services being conducted by Rev. Dr. Munsey, of Baltimore City, assisted by other eminent clergymen. The burying-ground in the rear of the church contains among others the graves of

Rev. James Layne, born in Sussex County, Del., died March 1, 1840; joined the church of which he was a minister in 1792.

Joshua W. Dorsey, died June 6, 1875.

Mrs. M. A. E. Dorsey, born Aug. 14, 1814; died Sept. 5, 1817.

Wm. Thompson, born Feb. 14, 1812; died June 23, 1872.

Analine, wife of John M. Stewart, and daughter of Samuel and Nathaniel Pope, died Jan. 10, 1878.

Jerusha Waters, died May 2, 1879, aged 80.

Reuben Davis, died Oct. 13, 1877, aged 85.

Redland.—This point is two miles from Derwood Station on the Metropolitan Branch of the Baltimore and Ohio Railroad. H. S. Thompson and H. B. Penn are merchants,—the latter postmaster. The physicians are Drs. J. W. and J. Magruder. One mile north is situated Emory Grove Methodist Episcopal Church. Redland is on "Banks' Venture," surveyed for John Banks, Nov. 29, 1752.

Hazel B. Cashell, whose post-office is Redland, is one of the most prominent of Montgomery County's farmers and one of its largest landholders. He was born Nov. 5, 1808, in Montgomery County, about five miles from his present home. His father (George) emigrated to America from Ireland, and settled upon a farm in Montgomery County. He married Elizabeth, daughter of Hazel Butt, a native of Montgomery County. Their children numbered nine, of whom the living are Hazel B., Hamilton, Samuel, Jackson, Thomas, Mrs. Elizabeth Groomes, and Mrs. Emily Miller. George Cashell died in 1858, aged eighty-four. His widow died in 1860, aged seventy-two. Hazel B. Cashell resided with his father until he reached his twentieth year, when he leased of Samuel White a farm known as "Charles and Benjamin," and then began his first active experience as a farmer on his own account. Later he leased a farm of Roger Brooke, and in 1848, purchasing a farm of five hundred and thirty acres (his present home), he took up his residence thereon in 1849, and has there resided ever since. In 1847 he was elected county commissioner on the Democratic ticket, and served as such until 1851. In 1854 he was chosen judge of the Orphans' Court to fill the unexpired term of Judge Magruder, and thereafter Judge Cashell was chosen to the office for four successive terms of four years each. During the war of 1861–65, and while upon the bench, he was arrested by the Federal authorities upon a charge of treason to the government. He was tried by a military court and acquitted, but the Secretary of War disapproved the finding and remanded the case to the civil courts. The trial was therefore renewed before the United States Court sitting in Baltimore, Judge Cashell being in the interim allowed his liberty upon parole. The case was ended by an abandonment thereof by the government. Mr. Cashell has long ranked as a representative farmer, and beginning, as has been said, the pursuit of husbandry as a tenant, he is to-day the owner of fourteen hundred acres of valuable farming lands.

He has been twice married. His first wife was Caroline, daughter of James Groomes, of Montgomery County, to whom he was united in 1832. She bore him five children, of whom the survivors are four. James, Thomas, and Lycurgus, the living sons, are well-known Montgomery County farmers. In 1859, Mrs. Cashell died, and after a lapse of eleven years Mr. Cashell married for his second wife, in 1870, Harriet, daughter of Thomas and Mary Jones, of Caroline County, Va. The Joneses were among the early settlers in the Old Dominion, and bore a name that in that region has had an honorable place in history. By the second marriage there have been two children, both sons. Since 1866 Mr. Cashell has been president of the Rockville and Washington Turnpike Company.

Claysville.—This place is situated midway between Mount Zion and Laytonsville, and contains a store and several shops.

The school trustees and teachers for 1881 and 1882 are as follows:

Trustees.—No. 1, Franklin Groomes, J. F. D. Magruder, Dr. Maynard; No. 2, John W. Wallick, Alexander C. Jackson, Elisha Riggs, of S.; No. 3, John T. Warfield, J. Fenton Snoffer, William Magruder; No. 4, Justian Magruder, W. O. Householder, Charles Bready; No. 5, F. L. Bell, Charles H. Griffith, B. B. Crawford.

Teachers.—No. 1, S. W. Davis, Unity P. O.; No. 2, J. M. Woodfield, Damascus P. O.; No. 3, A. R. Martin, Goshen P. O.; No. 4, E. M. Hollend, Redland P. O.; No. 5, E. M. Beach, Laytonsville P. O.

There are two colored schools in the district. The magistrates are Samuel Biggs, of G., J. T. Warfield, J. W. Wallick.

CLARKESBURG DISTRICT, No. 2,

is bounded on the north by Frederick County, east by Howard County, south by Cracklin District, southwest by Gaithersburg District, and west by Darnestown and Medley Districts.

Into Great Seneca Creek, in its southwest, empty Magruder's and Wild-Cat Branches, while the Patuxent River separates it from Howard County. In its southwestern section flow Ten-Mile Creek, Cabin Branch, and Little Seneca Creek. In the north, Bennett's Creek flows into Frederick County, as does Little Bennett's Creek, and into the latter empty Wild-Cat and Soper's Branches.

As originally laid out it was bounded as follows:

Beginning near Benjamin Gaither's blacksmith-shop, and running with the road leading to Clopper's mill, the late Samuel Simmons', and the late Richard Hoggins', to the road leading from the mouth of Monocacy to Green's bridge on the east side of Joshua Perry's plantation, there with the road by John Willson's to the mouth of his lane, then with a north line to the line of Frederick County, then with said line to Parr's spring, then down Patuxent to Mershberger's old mill, then down Seneca to the beginning near Benjamin Gaither's blacksmith-shop.

In the formation of Gaithersburg District, in 1880, a small part of the territory of Clarkesburg was taken, thus reducing the above limits slightly.

The first settlers in the district were Ellsworth Beane, Samuel Saffell, Thomas Whitten, John Crampton, and Henry Griffith, who were soon followed by the Howards, Laytons, Neels, Claggetts, Warrings, Hyatts, Prices, Warfields, Tablers, Watkinses, Purdums, Windsors, Wateres, Kemps, Bealls, Darbys, Kings, Linthicums, Williamses, Lewises, and others.[1]

Greenbury Willson, on Aug. 1, 1811, had a mill in operation on the farm of Edward Magruder, on Wild-Cat Creek.

Clarkesburg, after which the district was called, is beautifully located on the Washington and Frederick road, thirty miles from Washington, fifteen from Frederick, and four and a half from Boyd's Station. The town occupies a portion of a tract of three hundred and eighty-five acres, surveyed on the 10th of February, 1761, for Henry Griffith, lying on both sides of Little Seneca Creek, and known originally as the "Cow-Pasture" survey. The first house was erected in 1780 by John Clark, whose daughter married William Wilson, the father of Leonidas Wilson, the present owner, who for a long time was a successful merchant of the place. It is now occupied by Lewis & Williams. Mr. Clark kept the first store. The first dwelling-house was that now occupied by Leonard Dent Shaw, in the upper part of the town, and was built in 1777. In the garden of Mr. Scholl, at the east end of the town, the celebrated Catawba grape, which has since gained such a world-wide reputation, was probably first cultivated in America. The property is now owned by Hon. George W. Hilton, and is annually visited by numbers of pomologists and curiosity-seekers. Dr. Horace Wilson was among the earliest physicians.

Before the era of railroads the town was on the direct road from the West to the national capital, and the stage-lines and many private conveyances on their way to and from those points passed through the place. At one time it contained three taverns,—one kept by Mrs. Schell, where L. D. Shaw lives, one by Mr. Pritchard (now the Thompson House), and the third by Mr. Griffith, where Hon. G. W. Hilton now resides.

Among the first blacksmiths was Benjamin Browning. John G. Clark, the founder of the town, came from the North. The oldest native inhabitant of the place is Leonidas Wilson, who was born in 1812. He is the son of William, grandson of John, and great-grandson of Jonathan Wilson, who came up from Prince George's County before or during the French and Indian war.

William H. Buxton is postmaster, and Drs. T. K. Galloway, R. H. Thompson, and William A. Waters physicians.

Methodist Episcopal Church.—The present neat brick edifice was built in 1853, and is on or near the site of the old log structure it succeeded. The first rude church building was erected between 1782 and 1784, and in it Bishop Asbury several times preached. Rev. Randolph R. Murphy, a native of Clarkesburg, is the present pastor, and is a son of one of the old pillars of the church.

In the cemetery adjoining the church are the following interments:

Charles H. Murphy, died Aug. 14, 1879, aged 82; and his wife, Julia, April 23, 1853, aged 49.

Maria Louise, wife of Obed Hurley, died April 16, 1861, aged 42; and Jane, wife of same, died Nov. 5, 1853, aged 59.

Freeborn G. Miles, born April 1, 1812, died Jan. 31, 1845.

Nancy W. Thompson, born Nov. 20, 1794, died May 20, 1866.

Synthia R. Thompson, died Feb. 20, 1870, aged 64.

Ann Elizabeth, wife of Philemon M. Smith, and daughter of Dr. Horace Wilson, died Jan. 29, 1875, aged 52.

Leah, wife of Dr. Horace Wilson, died June 22, 1842, aged 50.

Maria, wife of Rev. James G. Henning, born April 25, 1813, died Dec. 23, 1842.

John W. Beall, died Sept. 5, 1866, aged 63.

Howard Young, died Oct. 3, 1877, aged 66.

Nancy A., wife of Hezekiah Barber, died April 23, 1873, aged 68.

Martha Judy, died April 12, 1867, aged 75.

William Levi Hurley, died July 10, 1874, aged 76.

Prof. J. Mortimer Hurley, died April 8, 1879, aged 50.

"The Clark Private Burying-Ground" contains the remains of

John Clark, born August, 1752, died February, 1805; and Ann, his wife, died March 27, 1810, aged 61.

Gustavus Wilson, born Feb. 11, 1811, died 1812.

John Clark Wilson, born Aug. 25, 1802, died Dec. 6, 1803.

William Harris, nephew and adopted son of Rev. Buckley Carl, pastor of Presbyterian Church in Rahway, N. J., died May 5, 1817, aged 24.

---

[1] In the *Maryland Gazette* of 1754 appeared the following notice:

"Five Pounds Reward. Ran away, Sept. 12th, from the copper-works near Seneca Creek, in Frederick County, Maryland, a convict servantman, John Raner.

"JAS. PERRY, JOHN BOND.

"N.B.—Whoever takes up said servant, and brings him to Jas. Perry, near said works, at Rock Creek, in Frederick County, or to John Bond in Balto. Co., shall have £5 reward."

Clarkesburg Lodge, No. 100, I. O. O. F., was instituted Aug. 28, 1858, the charter being issued on that date to Rufus K. Waters, William P. Winsor, Dr. R. Thompson, C. R. Murphy, A. M. Layton. The lodge received three members into the fellowship at their first meeting, making a total of eight members. The first election of officers resulted in the choice of Dr. R. T. Thompson as Noble Grand, A. M. Layton as Secretary, Rufus K. Waters as Vice-Grand, and C. R. Murphy as Treasurer. Their hall was purchased in 1871 from C. R. Murphy. The lodge only numbers six members at present, though at one time the membership reached one hundred.

The present officers are G. W. Darby, Noble Grand; Nathan H. Darby, Vice-Grand; John H. Gibson, Treasurer; C. R. Murphy, Secretary; John Lemon, O. G.; William R. Winsor, P. G.

Methodist Episcopal Church South.—This congregation was formed in 1865 under the direction of Rev. J. P. Hall, who was its first pastor, and numbered about twenty-five members at the time of its organization.

Robert Smith followed Rev. Mr. Hall as pastor, and was assisted by Rufus Willson. In 1870, Rev. Benjamin F. Ball succeeded to the charge, and it was during his pastorate that the present church edifice was erected. The church was dedicated in 1871, Mr. Ball preaching the dedicatory sermon. In 1872, Rev. Mr. Tebbs became the pastor, and was succeeded in 1874 by William McDonald, who was assisted by Mr. A. C. McNair. In 1876, Rev. William Wade assumed charge of the church, and was followed by Rev. Mr. Gover and Rev. Mr. Watts, the present incumbent. The steward is C. R. Murphy, and the trustees are C. R. Murphy, John A. Lewis, Edward Lewis, W. W. Welch.

Clarkesburg Literary Association was established in 1879. President, C. R. Murphy; Vice-President, William R. Windsor; Treasurer, John S. Belt; Corresponding Secretary, Col. T. H. S. Boyd; Recording Secretary, Thomas A. Burdette.

Among the former prominent representatives of the Methodist Protestant Church in Clarkesburg was the Rev. Reuben T. Boyd. Mr. Boyd was born July 3, 1794, on the old estate of the Boyds, known as "Boyd's Delay," on Rock Creek, three miles east of Rockville. He studied for the ministry, and was authorized to preach the gospel in the Baltimore District of the Methodist Episcopal Church, Nov. 26, 1825. His certificate was signed by Rev. Joseph Frye, president, James R. Williams, secretary, and was renewed Dec. 30, 1826. For several years preceding and during this time a great reform was being agitated in the Methodist Episcopal Church, the object of which was a change in the form of government so as to admit of lay representation in the councils of the church.

Mr. Boyd took an active and zealous stand in behalf of the projected reform, and was a constant contributor to the columns of a paper published by William Stockton, father of the late Rev. Thos. Stockton, one of the most eminent pulpit orators of his day, and chaplain of the United States House of Representatives. This paper was published in the interest of the reformers, and soon brought down on them the censure of the bishop and elders of the church. The agitation finally resulted in the expulsion of eleven ministers for advocating the rights of the laity, Mr. Boyd being the youngest of the eleven. But the reformers were not to be crushed, and soon gathered around them a strong following. They assumed the name of the Associated Methodist Churches, and at the Maryland Annual Conference of Ordained Ministers and Lay Delegates, held in Baltimore, April 5, 1829, Mr. Boyd was ordained to the office of deacon, and authorized by the Conference to administer the ordinance of baptism, to assist the elder in the administration of the Lord's Supper, to celebrate marriage, and to preach and expound the Holy Scriptures. His certificate was signed by Rev. Nicholas Snethen, president, and Luther J. Cox, secretary.

At the Maryland Annual Conference of Ministers and Delegates, held in the city of Georgetown, D. C., April 8, 1832, Mr. Boyd was ordained to the office of elder in the new organization, which had changed its name to the Methodist Protestant Church, and authorized by the Conference to administer the ordinance of baptism, to assist the elder in the administration of the Lord's Supper, to celebrate marriage, and to preach and expound the Holy Scriptures.

His certificate on this occasion was signed by Rev. Eli Henkle, president, James Hanson, secretary. Mr. Henkle was the father of ex-Congressman Henkle, from the Fifth Maryland District. Their church membership increased rapidly, and new Conferences were formed, especially in the South and West. Feeling that his sphere of usefulness would be enlarged by removing to the West, Mr. Boyd was transferred to the Illinois Conference in 1838, and from there to the Ohio Conference in 1840, where he remained nine years. On Nov. 28, 1840, a license was issued by W. H. Harrison, then clerk of the court of Hamilton County, Ohio, and afterwards President of the United States, authorizing Mr. Boyd, as a regular ordained minister of the Methodist Protestant Church, to solemnize marriages throughout the State of Ohio.

He returned to the Maryland Conference in 1849, where he continued an active and efficient minister until 1859, when health failing him, he was placed on the superannuated roll of the Conference. After an active and continuous life of thirty-four years in the ministry he was compelled to seek rest. He bought property in Clarkesburg, and removed there with his family in 1859, spending the remaining days of his life in the happy enjoyment of a consciousness of a bright future beyond the grave. He died seated in his easy-chair, surrounded by his books and papers, on the 15th of February, 1865, in his seventy-third year. At peace with God and mankind, honored and respected by all, he left behind a record worthy of example. During his life he was a constant and voluminous writer, and his publications in the *Methodist Protestant and Western Recorder* attracted universal attention.

George W. Hilton, one of the most influential citizens of Clarkesburg, was born in Laytonsville, Oct. 2, 1823, and was educated in Georgetown, D. C. He taught school in the old mountain school-house in the Third District (Medley's), and subsequently in Clarkesburg and Cracklin Districts. In 1847 he was appointed deputy sheriff and collector, and held these positions until 1852, when he became a merchant in Damascus, where he prosecuted his business successfully for seven years. In 1859 he purchased property in Clarkesburg, and transferring his business to that place, continued it successfully until 1872, when he turned his attention to agricultural pursuits. He was elected to the Legislature in 1869, and was re-elected in 1871, serving on the committees on Corporations and Printing In 1877 he was appointed by Governor John Lee Carroll a member of the board of control and review for the revision of tax assessments, and performed the duties of the position with intelligence and efficiency. Mr. Hilton is a gentleman of large experience, fine judgment, and ability, and has won deserved popularity by the integrity of his private life, and the conscientious and upright manner in which he has discharged the public trusts committed to his hands.

Catawba Grape.—It has been claimed that this celebrated grape was originally discovered by the late Darius Claggett, of Washington City, D. C., in the mountains of Virginia, and that cuttings were brought by him to Georgetown, where he planted them in his garden. This claim, however, cannot be sustained, as it is susceptible of proof that Maj. Adlum was making wine of this grape in 1824, three years before Mr. Claggett first got his cuttings from Virginia. This will appear by reference to Maj. Adlum's book on native grapes and vines published in 1824, to be found in the Congressional Library, as well as from the last edition, published in 1827. W. Viers Bouic, in a letter published in *The Advocate*, says "he knew Mr. Claggett well, and never heard him claim to be the discoverer of the Catawba grape." He also knew Maj. Adlum, and heard him tell Jeremiah Orme, a native of Montgomery County, at that time an extensive grocer in Georgetown, D. C., that the Catawba wine which he offered to sell him was made from grapes from vines which were grown from cuttings obtained from the garden of Mr. Scholl, of Clarkesburg.

In the "American Encyclopedia," vol. iv. p. 555, it is claimed that the Catawba grape was first discovered in a wild state about the year 1801, near Ashville, Buncombe Co., N. C., near the head-waters of the Catawba River, and that about a quarter of a century later that grape was found by Maj. Adlum in a garden of a German near Washington, and that Gen. Day, of Rocky Mount, on the Catawba River, was the original transmitter of a few plants to Washington City, while a United States senator, some time previous to 1816.

The same work shows that through Maj. Adlum this grape found its way to Cincinnati, and thence was disseminated through the West and Southwest with great rapidity. In 1829 or 1830 the late Zakok Magruder, then a distinguished lawyer of Rockville, procured a number of plants from Maj. Adlum. All the vines in the old gardens of Rockville were obtained from Mr. Magruder, except those in the garden at Rose Hill farm, now owned by Miss Henrietta Dunlap. Those were procured by Mrs. Beall, who then owned the farm, from her brother, Singleton Wootton, late of New Market, Frederick Co., Md. Mr. Wootton got them from the original vine in the garden of Jacob Scholl at Clarkesburg. Jacob Scholl was the grandfather of John E. Willson. He was of German descent, but was born in Frederick County, Md., and kept a large hotel at Clarkesburg. He is the person alluded to in the "Encyclopedia" as the German from whose garden Maj. Adlum got his cuttings of this celebrated grape. Mountjoy Scholl, the only surviving child of Jacob Scholl, wrote to Mr. Bouic from Clarkville, Pike Co., Mo., under date of July 17, 1878, stating that he was born in 1792, at Clarkesburg, where his father then and long after resided. He cannot state the exact time, but when he was a small boy, a traveler who stopped all night at his father's hotel gave his father two grape-cuttings, which were planted in the garden, and from the vines thus raised Maj. Adlum obtained his cuttings. Maj.

Adlum told his father that he had been all over Europe hunting for this grape without success. He said it came from the Toke Mountains in Germany. Mr. Scholl says his father always called it Toke or Tokay. He never saw the word spelled, and is not certain that he has spelled it correctly, but he is positive it was never called Catawba. The first time he knew it to be called Catawba was in a newspaper article published in St. Louis after the grape had reached there from Cincinnati.

Hyattstown is situated on the old Frederick and Washington road, sixteen miles from Rockville, and seven miles from Monrovia. The first house erected in the town was that now occupied by H. Dutteral, which was built about the year 1800, and was then the residence of F. Poole. In 1811 the village comprised twelve houses. Among the families then residing there were those of Jesse Hyatt, H. Poole, Thomas Foster, George Cover, Levi Philips, Daniel Collins, and George Davis. Thomas Foster was the blacksmith, and his shop stood on the present site of Tabler's restaurant. Jacob Smith was the first carpenter of the place; Henry Poole the first storekeeper. Mr. Philips was the proprietor of the first hotel, and employed for the purpose the house now occupied by O. W. Dutteral. Mr. Hyatt succeeded Mr. Philips, but removed the hotel to the house now used as a store, etc., by Mr. Welsh. Mr. Collins was the first tailor in the village; he lived in a house that was situated upon what is now known as the Christian Church property. Samuel Soper was the pioneer school-teacher, and taught his few scholars in the old Methodist church. Warner Welsh was the principal merchant until 1856. The town was founded by and named in honor of Jesse Hyatt, who was born Dec. 14, 1763, and died Jan. 12, 1813. Since 1856 Hyattstown has improved rapidly, and now comprises several fine stores, etc. It was created by an act of Legislature in the year 1809.

Methodist Episcopal Church.—This old congregation was first organized in 1804. A lot was purchased from Eli Hyatt and wife, and a church was erected under the management of Samuel Hobbs, Basil Soper, Charles McElfresh, John Smith, and Joseph Benton. The building was a log structure, and stood upon the site of the present edifice. The congregation at its formation numbered about eighteen members. Of those who connected themselves with the church prior to 1819, Perry Browning is the only survivor. In 1852 the church was destroyed by fire, and in June, 1856, under the care of Rev. Charles Reed, the corner-stone of the present edifice was laid. The dedication took place in 1857, Rev. Benjamin F. Brown, the presiding elder, preaching the dedicatory sermon. The builder of the church was John Gardner, and the building committee consisted of William Browning, William McLain, and Jacob R. Smelser. The church is of brick, and two stories in height. The congregation was divided in 1865, but now numbers about fifty members. The steward is J. Nelson Soper; Trustees, Perry Browning, J. N. Soper, Zachariah Harris, Charles T. Browning, and James Corlett. Among the pastors of the church have been Revs. Francis Asbury, Enoch George, Beverly Waugh, Alfred Griffith, Frederick Stier, Hamilton Jefferson, Jesse Lee, Christopher Fry, James Paintey, Tobias Riley, Thomas Larkin, Job Gees, Caleb Reynolds, Basil Barny, Andrew Hemphill.

Among the graves in the burial-ground of the church are the following:

Philemon Smith, Sr., born Feb. 2, 1794, died March 14, 1879; Elizabeth, his wife, born Feb. 17, 1794, died March 16, 1824; Ava, second wife, born Jan. 29, 1802, died June 9, 1838.

John Gardner, died Nov. 11, 1879, aged 76; Eli, his wife, born Sept. 9, 1807, died Jan. 25, 1870.

Martha A., wife of Uriah M. Layton, and daughter of John and Elizabeth Gardner, born Oct. 29, 1834, died Oct. 11, 1864.

Warner Welsh, born June 24, 1818, died Aug. 11, 1875; Mary Ann, his wife, died Feb. 11, 1857, aged 32.

Mary A., wife of Asa Hyatt, died April 2, 1859, aged 62.

Asa Hyatt, born Dec. 11, 1787, died Aug. 20, 1848.

Wetson Lee Philips, died September, 1846, aged 45.

George Rhodes, born May 25, 1783, died Aug. 11, 1847; Ann Maria, his wife, born Dec. 1, 1789, died Aug. 5, 1849.

Martha J., wife of A. J. Tabler, and daughter of Joshua and Catherine Norwood, born May 1, 1829, died Jan. 21, 1868.

Harriet, wife of William Tabler, and daughter of John and Charlotte Smith, born May 9, 1817, died May 13, 1861.

Lewis Tabler, born June 28, 1781, died Aug. 4, 1847: Mary, his wife, and daughter of Gesard Christina Lee, born March 9, 1789, died Sept. 6, 1867.

Samuel S. Benton, born July 19, 1812, died April 11, 1865.

William Browning, died April 1, 1869, aged 72; Mary Browning died Aug. 3, 1879, aged 72.

Levino Hobbs, born Sept. 17, 1789, died Dec. 21, 1862.

John R. Lewis died March 25, 1879, aged 62.

Elizabeth A., wife of G. A. Darby, died Sept. 8, 1873, aged 38.

B. F., son of J. R. and A. E. Smeltzer, born Jan. 18, 1851, died March 2, 1873.

William McLain, born Oct. 27, 1803, died Dec. 12, 1872.

Harriet McLain, died Jan. 30, 1855, aged 44.

Evan T. Anderson, born Nov. 7, 1817, died June 7, 1863.

Adam Hagen, born May 22, 1853, aged 64.

Mary A., wife of John D. Krantz, born May 21, 1823, died Feb. 14, 1847.

Mary, wife of Barrock Hall, born June 8, 1761, died Dec. 22, 1854.

Margaret Nichols, wife of Camden R. Nichols, born June 22, 1803, died June 28, 1856.

Martha Garratt, born March 20, 1783, died Oct. 21, 1850.

Margaret P., wife of B. P. Philips, died March 30, 1864, aged 46.

Mahalia A. R. Orme, daughter of Mahalia and Middleton Kinney, died Sept. 4, 1862, aged 36.

Christian Church.—This church was established in 1840, the congregation worshiping in the houses of the different members until the erection of their church in 1845. Among the founders of the church were Eli Wolfe, William Richards, Charlotte Richards, Lavina Wolf, Sarah Hyatt, and Sarah A. Price. The first elders of the church were Eli Wolfe and William Richards. The church edifice, which was erected in 1845, stood upon the cemetery lot. In 1871, under the auspices of Rev. Alfred N. Gilbert, of Baltimore, they built a new two-story frame church, at a cost of three thousand dollars. The lot was donated by Jacob B. Thomas and wife, of Baltimore. On Aug. 20, 1871, the church was dedicated, and a reorganization effected with the following officers: Elder, Levi C. Ziegler; Deacons, Thomas Price, P. C. Dutrow, C. Harrison, Lutheran Norwood. The pastors of the church have been Neal McCollum, John P. Mitchell, and William H. Shell. At its reorganization the congregation numbered about forty members, and at present numbers thirty. The present officers are B. F. Hawkins, Thomas Price, Seymour Poole.

The cemetery of the Christian Church is situated in the outskirts of the town, on the old Frederick road, and contains the graves of

Jesse Hyatt, born Dec. 4, 1763, died Jan. 12, 1813.
Mary E., wife of E. G. Harris, born Aug. 29, 1846, died Sept. 8, 1876.
Eleanor Ann, wife of David A. Zeigler, born April 15, 1815, died Aug. 25, 1874.
Eli Wolfe, died June, 1871, aged 70.
Caroline Wolfe, died April, 1862, aged 60.
George Wolfe, born Aug. 20, 1806, died Oct. 27, 1868.
Charlotte Richards, born March 29, 1796, died Aug. 22, 1868.
Susan Fowler, died March 26, 1836, aged 18.

The Methodist Episcopal Church South was established in 1865, by Rev. John P. Hall. It began with twenty members, and now numbers sixteen. The first steward of the church was William B. Lewis, and the present steward is W. W. Welsh, who is also Sunday-school superintendent. The building is a frame structure, and was erected in 1876–77, at a cost of twelve hundred dollars. The pastors in charge have been Rev. J. P. Hall, Robert Smith, Benjamin F. Ball, Rev. Mr. Tebbs, Mr. McDonald, Wm. Wade, and Rev. Mr. Gover. Rev. Mr. Watts is the present pastor, and has been assisted by J. G. Greishen and John Miller.

Boyd's Station is on the Metropolitan Branch of the Baltimore and Ohio Railroad, seventy miles from Baltimore and thirty from Washington, D. C. As late as 1869 the site of the present flourishing town was still an unreclaimed waste. The former owner of the property on which the town is situated was Camden R. Nichols. The station takes its name from Capt. James A. Boyd, who, with James E. Williams and Mr. Lewis, have rapidly built up the place. The first house was built by James E. Williams. Capt. Boyd has expended over a hundred thousand dollars in improvements in the past few years. The location is very healthy, being over five hundred feet above the level of the sea. James E. Williams is postmaster, merchant, railroad and express agent, and F. P. Meigs, pomologist. Boyd Presbyterian church is a pretty frame structure, erected in 1876, of which Rev. James Henderson is pastor.

In the cemetery adjoining are only two tombstones:

William M. Williams, died Nov. 6, 1879, aged 34 years; and his wife, Florence M., died Sept. 20, 1879, aged 20 years.

Apiculture, Peach-Culture.—The keeping and propagation of bees in the county is assuming considerable importance. It requires but small capital and a very limited amount of labor, while attended with little or no risk. Bee-keeping has become a science, and those who patiently learn its ways have no fear of being stung. Neither are whole swarms of these industrious little creatures destroyed in order to secure their treasures of sweetness. On the contrary, they have really become pets of those who take a loving care of them. To such perfection has the art of raising honey been brought that not a bee is sacrificed in taking away the honey, while the comb is even saved. By a new and ingenious method, with a little machine, the fresh combs when taken from the hives are deftly unsealed and the honey extracted from the comb by the principle of suction, and the comb, perfectly uninjured, is returned to the hive to be filled again in a few days by the same bees. This honey is the purest known in the market, and is put up in sealed glasses. The feeding and keeping of bees is very easily learned, and is said by those employed in it to be a most delightful business. Two hundred and fifty dollars will stock a yard of bees that will with proper care annually yield one thousand dollars. Mahlon T. Lewis, of Clarkesburg, and Capt. F. P. Meigs, of Boyd's Station, are extensively engaged in the business.

Owing to the destruction of peach-trees by insects on the Peninsula, the peach, like the tobacco-plant, must continually seek new land, since soil that has been planted in peach-trees cannot be successfully replanted until it has been allowed a rest of many years. This is eventuating in the transfer from the Eastern Shore of the peach-culture to the uplands of Montgomery and adjoining counties.

Damascus.—This village is seven miles from

Mount Airy. In 1810 it contained three houses, one of which was occupied by Stephen Anderson, and another by James Whiffen, who kept a store at the place. Thomas Foster was the first blacksmith, and Evan Thompson the first school-teacher. The only physician living in Damascus is Dr. B. F. Lansdale, and the merchants are J. H. Claggett, Marcellus Etchinson, Luther N. King, and P. M. Smith, who is also postmaster. Damascus Grange, No. 80, is located here, of which Joseph M. Burdett is Master, and C. W. Browning, Secretary.

Methodist Episcopal Church.—The church edifice, a frame structure, was built in 1869. Rev. Randolph R. Murphy is pastor. In its cemetery are buried

George W. Gue, born March 4, 1815, died Feb. 26, 1879; and Sarah E., his wife, born April 3, 1819, died Jan. 27, 1875.

Aden H. B. Gue, died July 13, 1876, aged 31; and Ella, his wife, Sept. 5, 1877, aged 24.

Nathan B. Warthen, born Jan. 29, 1826, died Jan. 14, 1879; and Emma A., his wife, born July 3, 1846, died Feb. 19, 1872.

Rhoda Ann Warthen, born July 9, 1829, died Nov. 6, 1869.

Charlotte, wife of Thomas Young, born Sept. 28, 1808, died March 21, 1877.

Montgomery Lodge, No. 88, I. O. O. F.—This lodge was instituted Jan. 20, 1854, and held its first meeting in a room over P. M. Smith's store, Feb. 8, 1854. The charter was granted to Joseph Kemp, Green S. Etchinson, William Barnes, James S. Kemp, and Jeremiah T. Browning. At the first meeting the lodge comprised only the five charter members, who received and initiated two persons,— Grafton Watkins and Francis M. Waters. The following officers served the first year: N. G., Green S. Etchinson; V. G., James S. Kemp; Sec., J. Thomas Browning; Treas., William Barnes. At the meeting March 6th in the same year, F. M. Waters was chosen as R. S. N. G., and James Etchinson L. S.; Rufus Darby R. S. V. G., and Rufus Waters L. S. The successive officers have been as follows:

N. G.'s, G. S. Etchinson, Jos. S. Kemp, G. Watkins, G. W. Hilton, P. M. Smith, Jos. T. Johnson, L. Etchinson, L. M. Watkins, J. M. Etchinson, Rufus Darby, William Williams, C. F. Purdham, H. G. Warfield, N. B. Wartham, R. E. Burdock; V. G.'s, Jos. A. Kemp, Nicholas Darby, G. W. Hilton, J. Purdham, H. G. Warfield, L. Etchinson, L. M. Watkins, J. M. Etchinson, Rufus Darby, William Williams, C. F. Purdham, H. S. Dell, N. B. Walton, R. E. Burdock, J. W. Mites; Sec.'s, J. T. Browning, Grafton Watkins, Joseph Kemp, Eli M. Watkins, Joseph Kemp, P. M. Smith, James Smith, G. Watkins.

For the term beginning in January and ending in June, 1864, the following-named gentlemen served as officers:

N. G., G. S. Etchinson; V. G., Wm. Barnes; Sec., C. F. Purdam. From June, 1864, to January, 1865, N. G., Wm. Barnes; V. G., P. M. Smith; Sec., C. F. Purdam. From January to July, 1865, N. G., P. M. Smith; V. G., R. S. Hilton; Sec., C. F. Purdam. From July, 1865, to January, 1866, N. G., R. S. Hilton; V. G., C. F. Purdam; Sec., Joseph Kemp. From January to July, 1866, N. G., C. F. Purdam; V. G., J. W. Kemp; Sec., Joseph Kemp. From July, 1866, to January, 1867, N. G., J. C. W. Kemp; V. G., A. Baker; Sec., G. Watkins. From January to July, 1867, N. G., A. Baker; V. G., J. W. Watkins; Sec., G. Watkins. From July, 1867, to January, 1868, N. G., J. W. Watkins; V. G., H. B. Darby; Sec., L. M. Watkins. From January to July, 1868, N. G., H. B. Darby; V. G., Wm. Boyer; Sec., L. M. Watkins. From January to July, 1869, N. G., C. A. Pope; V. G., R. Burns; Sec., C. A. Purdam. From July, 1869, to January, 1870, N. G., R. Burns; V. G., J. W. Hover; Sec., J. W. Watkins. From January to July, 1870, N. G., R. E. Price; V. G., M. R. Lewis; Sec., J. C. W. Kemp. From July, 1870, to January, 1871, N. G., Joshua Purdam; V. G., J. C. W. Kemp; Sec., L. M. Watkins. From January to July, 1871, N. G., J. C. W. Kemp; V. G., J. W., Watkins; Sec., L. M. Watkins. From July, 1871, to January, 1872, N. G., J. W. Watkins; V. G., N. R. Darby; Sec., G. W. Watkins. From January to July, 1872, N. G., J. S. Kemp; V. G., L. M. Watkins; Sec., J. C. W. Kemp. From July, 1872, to January, 1873, N. G., H. G. Warfield; V. G., H. B. Willson; Sec., J. C. W. Kemp. From January to July, 1873, N. G., J. S. Kemp; V. G., L. M. Watkins; Sec., J. C. W. Kemp. From July, 1873, to January, 1874, N. G., L. M. Watkins; V. G., R. Burns; Sec., J. C. W. Kemp. From January to July, 1874, N. G., R. Burns; V. G., P. M. Smith; Sec., J. C. W. Kemp. From July, 1874, to January, 1875, N. G., P. M. Smith; V. G., Joseph A. Gue; Sec., J. C. W. Kemp. From January to July, 1875, N. G., Joseph A. Gue; V. G., N. R. Darby; Sec., C. F. Purdam. From July, 1875, to January, 1876, N. G., N. R. Darby; V. G., R. A. Hurley; Sec., J. C. W. Kemp. From January to July, 1876, N. G., R. A. Hurley; V. G., C. F. Purdam; Sec., J. C. W. Kemp. From July, 1876, to January, 1877, N. G., J. Hagar; V. G., R. A. Hurley; Sec., J. C. W. Kemp. From January to July, 1877, N. G., C. F. Purdam; V. G., R. A. Hurley; Sec., G. Watkins. From July, 1877, to January, 1878, N. G., R. A. Hurley; V. G., Joseph H. Lewis; Sec., J. C. W. Kemp. From January to July, 1878, N. G., P. M. Smith; V. G., William Williams; Sec., G. Watkins. From July, 1878, to January, 1879, N. G., William Williams; V. G., C. F. Purdam; Sec., R. A. Hurley. From January to July, 1879, N. G., R. A. Hurley; V. G., C. Watkins; Sec., J. C. W. Kemp. From July, 1879, to January, 1880, N. G., C. Watkins; V. G., H. B. Wilson; Sec., J. C. W. Kemp. From January to July, 1880, N. G., H. B. Wilson; V. G., William Williams; Sec., J. C. W. Kemp. From July, 1880, to January, 1881, N. G., R. A. Hurley; V. G., William Williams; Sec., J. C. W. Kemp. From January to July, 1881, N. G., C. Watkins; V. G., H. C. Edwards; Sec., J. C. W. Kemp. And the present officers are: N. G., J. Hagar; V. G., H. C. Edwards; Sec., J. C. W. Kemp; Treas., G. Watkins.

In 1869 the hall was erected at a cost of twelve hundred dollars; it was dedicated on July 20, 1876, the address being delivered by Dr. David A. Wilson, Grand Chaplain of the I. O. O. F., Grand Lodge of Maryland. The lodge is in a very flourishing condition, and numbers about twenty-six members in good standing. They have given several very successful and creditable celebrations and public installations.

Neelsville.—This place is situated on the Frederick and Washington road, between Gaithersburg and Clarkesburg. It takes its name from the Neel family, one of the oldest in this section.

Presbyterian Church.—This edifice, built in 1877, is a frame structure and of Swiss architecture. In its rear is the old frame church built about 1830. Rev. James Henderson is the pastor.

In the church graveyard are buried:

Johanna Fredericka, wife of Jacob F. Snyder, born Aug. 22, 1834, died Aug. 27, 1851.

Emma V., daughter of Wm. H. and Jane Benson, born May 9, 1856, died Jan. 11, 1881.

Savilla, wife of R. H. Bennett, born Oct. 25, 1827, died March 19, 1877.

Mary E., wife of G. F. Linthicum, died June 4, 1878, aged 28; and Ellinora G., wife of same, died March 2, 1880, aged 34.

Joshua Dorsey, born Jan. 20, 1825, died Feb. 8, 1877.

Middlebrook is on the Frederick road, near Big Seneca, eight miles from Rockville. George H. Clements is merchant and postmaster.

Cedar Grove is five miles northeast of Germantown. O. T. Watkins is merchant and postmaster. Salem Methodist Episcopal church is located here. White Oak chapel is on the road from Damascus to Goshen, and Cedar Grove Methodist Episcopal church on the road from Hyattstown to Damascus.

Browningsville.—This place is in the northern part of the district, five miles from Monrovia, eighteen from Rockville, thirty-seven from Baltimore, and near Bennett's Creek. It derives its name from the Browning family, who were among the earliest settlers in this vicinity. Near the village are the Bethesda Methodist Episcopal and Mountain View Methodist Protestant churches. The merchants are S. M. Benton & Brother, Reuben Engle, and Samuel Hobbs, the latter being also postmaster. Browning & Jacobs have a carriage-making establishment.

Claggettsville, so named from the Claggetts, who settled near it before 1750, is southeast of Browningsville. Montgomery chapel is located here, and here reside Capt. W. C. and John H. Claggett.

At Kingsville, in King's Valley, is King's distillery and saw-mill, operated by L. G. King.

The school trustees and teachers for 1881 and 1882 for this district are as follows:

Trustees.—No. 1, J. L. Duvall, John R. Mount, John I. Mullinix; No. 2, W. C. Claggett, Jackson Day, John Warfield; No. 3, Samuel Hobbs, Caleb Burdett, W. T. Browning; No. 4, A. G. Warfield, L. C. Zeigler, John N. Soper; No. 5, George W. Hilton, G. H. Gibson, J. S. Leamon; No. 6, James E. Williams, R. S. Umstead, Aloysius Reed; No. 7, Charles T. Purdam, Wm. E. Riggs, L. D. Watkins; No. 8, J. L. Duvall, James J. Bowman, J. G. Duvall; No. 9, Wm. T. Browning, C. F. Purdam, J. D. King.

Teachers.—No. 1, L. C. Hammond, Damascus P. O.; No. 2, —— Kemp, Damascus P. O.; No. 3, T. G. Day, Browningsville; No. 4, F. Prettyman, Hyattstown; No. 5, A. Ishemus, Gaithersburg; No. 6, W. H. Pace, Boyd's; No. 7, L. M. Watkins, Cedar Grove; No. 8, J. C. W. Kemp, Damascus; No. 9, J. T. Bryer, Browningsville.

There are four colored schools.

The magistrates are J. C. W. Kemp, John S. Belt, George W. Darby, J. D. Gardner.

The Claggetts were of English descent, and settled in Prince George's and other lower counties about 1665. Ninian M. Claggett, son of John Claggett, of Prince George's, married a daughter of Edward Burgess and settled in this district. He died in 1840, aged seventy-three years. His father-in-law, Edward Burgess, resided also in this district, and was a captain in the Revolution and one of the first justices of the County Court. Thomas Claggett, son of Ninian M. Claggett, was born in this district, and is a wealthy private banker in Frederick City.

MEDLEY DISTRICT, No. 3.

is bounded on the north by Frederick County and Virginia, east by Clarkesburg District, south by Darnestown District, and southwest and west by Virginia. From the State of Virginia it is separated on the west, southwest, and northwest by the Potomac River. Little and Big Seneca Creeks divide it from Darnestown District. Broad Run, Horse-pen Branch, Beaver Dam Branch, and Great Seneca Creek all empty into the Potomac. On the east Little Monocacy flows north and empties into the Potomac just below the point where the Monocacy joins the Potomac. Dry Seneca Creek, Russell's Branch, and Bucklodge Branch are in the south and southwest. The Chesapeake and Ohio Canal skirts its northern and western border.

Its boundaries, as defined by the survey of 1821, are as follows: Beginning at the mouth of Monocacy and running down the Potomac, including the islands, to the mouth of Seneca, then up Seneca to Clopper's mill, then with the line of the Second District to Frederick County line, then with said line to the beginning. This was one of the original five districts created by acts of 1798 and 1799, and its boundaries, as established by act of 1821, were not altered until 1878, when a portion of its southern territory was taken to help form Darnestown District, No. 6.

The first settlers in the district were John Haines, Cornelius Etting, Dr. Patrick Hepburn, John Norriss, Richard Brightwell, Robert Peter, Jeremiah Hays, the Dawsons, Brewers, Pooles, Spateses, Whites, Sellmans, Harrises, Remsburgs, Rawlingses, Dysons, Allnutts, Youngs, Joneses, Chiswells, Hempstones, Metzgers, Fishers, and others.

Isaac Young was born at Kilmaine, Medley Dis-

trict, Montgomery Co., Jan. 25, 1828, and now resides on a part of the same farm, called "Woodbine," near Poolesville Post-office. His father, David Young, son of Ludwick Young, was born on the homestead, near Hagerstown, Washington Co., Sept. 27, 1796. Ludwick Young and his wife, Catherine Shafer, disposed of their land in 1812, and purchased in Montgomery County, of Richard Hale, whither they moved in the same year, accompanied by their children,—six sons and two daughters,—John, Mary, Henry, David, Samuel, Amos, George, and Elizabeth. Ludwick Young was a very intelligent and successful farmer, and introduced improved agriculture with deep plowing and subsoiling, which attracted many persons to see the sod upturned by four horses in the plow. At his death, Sept. 24, 1820, his real estate was divided into six farms, and to each son was bequeathed a farm, the widow remaining with David at the homestead. She survived her husband until Oct. 25, 1825. David continued to occupy the homestead until his death, Aug. 21, 1879, and his widow, Phebe R., still resides there, in her eighty-fourth year. David Young first married, April, 1827, Matilda Chilton, born in 1800, a daughter of Joshua and Nancy Chilton, by whom he had three children, Isaac, William N., and Verlinda Catharine. They were early left without a mother, and in March, 1836, David Young married Phebe R. Donohoe, who still lives.

Isaac Young, the subject of this memoir, remained at home and received such training as is afforded on a well-regulated farm, and with the opportunity of attending the district school for six months in the year, from his twelfth to his eighteenth year. In 1846 he went to the Genesee Wesleyan Seminary, at Lima, Livingston Co., N. Y., where he prosecuted his studies with diligence until June, 1848, when he returned home, and for six years alternated between teaching, clerking, and farming, in the District of Columbia, in Danville, Ky., and in Illinois.

In 1854 he returned to Maryland, and on May 15, 1856, was married to Margaret Young, his cousin, at her father's residence, near Poolesville. His wife was the daughter of Joseph N. Chiswell, and was born Aug. 18, 1829. The young couple removed immediately after marriage to their present residence, and where eighteen months before there were only woods and marshes; by application and perseverance they built and improved their present mansion, and surrounded it with cultivated fields. Their children are Ella Lee, born March, 1863, who died on August 5th in the same year; Merlinda C., born June 7, 1864; Irene, born Jan. 11, 1870, died July 25th in the same year; and Lucretia, born June 20, 1871.

In the fall of 1863, Isaac Young was elected to represent his county in the House of Delegates of Maryland, and re-elected in 1866 to the Senate; in 1869 he was again renominated, but declined, in consequence of ill health in his family. He was appointed by Governor Bowie a director in the Chesapeake and Ohio Canal, and served during that executive term. He has always been most active in the cause of education, and his exertions in that behalf while in the Legislature were so appreciated and approved that he was placed upon the board of school commissioners by the suffrage of his fellow-citizens, as well as by appointment by the Legislature, and for several years has been a trustee of the Poolesville Academy. He has always been an active and charter member of the Order of Patrons of Husbandry of Poolesville, of which he was Worthy Master, and was made Lecturer of the grange at Barnesville; he was elected Worthy Master of the County Grange in 1879, and re-elected in 1880. He gave to the order the benefit of his time, talents, and experience, frequently addressing meetings and assemblies in his own county and in Frederick. As a farmer, he delighted in good cultivation, the rearing of fine stock, always procuring, as far as his means would permit, the best, and he was ever ready to give all in his power to promote the general welfare of his fellow-citizens, and he enjoys the confidence and esteem of all who know him.

Mr. Young is a conscientious and zealous member of the Presbyterian Church. This has been manifested since his connection with it, as he has been an elder in the church since 1856, and superintendent of the Sunday-school.

In politics he is a Democrat; strictly adhering to the principles of his party, he always voted the "ticket." He was a member of the State Convention when Tilden was nominated, and of the Congressional Convention in 1879. He has been a strong advocate of local option, making many speeches in 1880 in advocacy of that measure.

Among those connected with the early history of the district was William Darne, of "Mountain View," who removed from his home at the foot of Sugar-Loaf Mountain to Darnestown, to which he gave his name.[1]

Mr. Darne several times represented the county in the Legislature, and was a director in the Chesapeake and Ohio Canal. His farm contained about one hundred and fifty acres, watered by the Little Monocacy on the northeast, and bounded on the south and west

---

[1] One of Mr. Darne's daughters married Capt. Smoot, of the navy; another, Capt. Lacy, of the army; and another, Dr. Bell, of Montgomery.

by the county road, leading from Barnesville to Major Hempston's old brick mill. The lands of the Gotts and Plummers lay adjacent on the south, those of Abraham S. Hayes and Z. G. Harris on the east and southeast, and those of Colmore Offutt and Hanson Hayes on the north. Patrick McDade's old mill was located on Little Monocacy, about half a mile north of "Mountain View." McDade died about 1836.

On the old John Jay farm, over a mile from the mill, in an upper room of the two-story family dwelling, Thomas Veith taught school. He was a well-educated old gentleman, small in stature, of sharp visage, and dark, piercing eyes. He wore the old bell-crown hat and the long, drab surtout coat, without which the old gentlemen of the day could not pass in fashionable society, or think themselves fortified against the cold blasts blowing from the tall peak of Sugar-Loaf. From this old farm and school, in a direction bearing a degree or two west of north, about two miles distant, is "Braddock's Pass," through which the British general marched to the fort at the old furnace, where he crossed the Monocacy. From this pass along and up a deep ravine towards the old "Johnson House," built in the days of Governor Eden, not far from the furnace and ford, which are in Frederick County, the rails of the first railroad in Maryland were laid by the Chesapeake and Ohio Canal Company to transport stone from the quarry, at the foot of Sugar-Loaf, for the purpose of building an aqueduct over the Monocacy at its junction with the Potomac. On the road to Barnesville, at Hempstone's brick mill, was a small stone house, 12 by 16 feet, kept by the jolly Richard Venable Morton. Near the brick mill, on the north side of Little Monocacy, stood "Old Bethlehem" meeting-house. Here Revs. Basil Harry and Thomas W. Green were old-time preachers, and Daniel Price, Thomas Mulligan, and Z. G. Harris class-leaders. This old log structure fell into ruins in 1836.

Newport.—John Garrett laid out a town which he called Newport, on the west side of the mouth of the Seneca, in 1787, just above the Seneca Falls on the Potomac River, twenty-two miles above Georgetown. He disposed of the lots by lottery on Oct. 15, 1787, at five pounds per ticket. The town did not realize the hopes of its founder, and the place is now known as Seneca.

Barnesville is seventy-three miles from Baltimore, seventeen from Rockville, and one from the Metropolitan Branch Railroad, and is situated in the midst of a rich tobacco-growing region.

The site of this town, as well as Sellman's Station and Post-office (called also Barnesville Station), one mile from Barnesville, on the Metropolitan Railroad, is a part of a tract of land surveyed for Jeremiah Hays, Dec. 10, 1747. Barnesville was created by the General Assembly in 1811, and called in honor of William Barnes, who owned land here, and who subsequently removed to Ohio and laid out the town of Barnesville, in Belmont County in that State. Mr. Barnes built the first house on the lot upon which the residence of William Hilton now stands. The second house erected was that now occupied by Mrs. Sarah Claggett, and is a weather-boarded log building. The first store was kept by Leonard Hays, and the second by John Plummer. Among the first tavern-keepers were Benjamin Tucker and William Trail. Jacob Stiers kept the first blacksmith-shop in a house now owned by Solomon Plummer, and on the lot occupied by Zachariah Lloyd. About the earliest physician was Dr. Lisle. The oldest people now living in the town are the brothers Solomon and Leonard Plummer, aged respectively eighty-one and eighty-three years. They were born in the country, a few miles from Barnesville, and were the sons of John Plummer. Solomon Plummer married a Miss Knott, daughter of one of the first settlers, and when he first remembered the place, in 1805, it had but five or six houses. John Poole had a tannery establishment where William Sellman lives about 1810, and was succeeded in the same business by Ira Elder. John Plummer settled near the site of Barnesville in 1792, and Zachariah Knott and William Barnes before that time.[1]

One of the early inhabitants of Barnesville was Capt. James Gleeson. He served with distinction in the Revolutionary war, and was the hero of a hundred Indian battles, winning laurels under Gen. Wayne and under St. Clair in the disastrous campaign of 1792. He lived in the last house in the town on the right of the road leading northward towards the Sugar-Loaf Mountain. South of the "Old Captain" lived Silas Ward, who in 1828 was at the height of his fame. He lost his life by falling accidentally over the aqueduct at the mouth of the Monocacy. Next to his house was that of Frederick Nuse, who started at the "foot of Barnesville" as a dealer in furniture, but in fifteen years removed to Keokuk, Iowa, where he became the founder and builder of that city, and in the lumber business amassed a large fortune, still carried on by his son, George Ross Nuse. Two lots farther south lived Abraham S. Hays, a gentleman of the old school and magistrate for many years. He

---

[1] The two oldest residents of the town are Mrs. Mary J. Hawkins (daughter of William Trail), born there in 1823, and John W. Brown, who settled there in 1829.

held his courts generally in his parlor, and so quiet and orderly were the sessions that his family were never disturbed by boisterous litigants nor the pleadings of the learned counsel. No one witness was allowed to hear the testimony of another. In a northern and eastern direction from Squire Hays' residence was his farm of two hundred and fifty acres. Opposite his town dwelling was his blacksmith-shop, in which his slave "Old Ned" was the smith. On his farm, about a furlong to the eastward of the village, stood "Hays' School-house," subsequently called Barnesville Academy. It consisted of one room only, sixty feet long by thirty feet wide, built to accommodate about one hundred scholars. Old-style desks carefully made with drawers to keep the books in safe condition were ranged around the walls. Two tin-plate stoves, made for burning wood, half the cord-stick in length, warmed the hall; shelves extended all around the upper part of the walls near the ceiling for the storage of lunch-baskets, and nails were driven in the walls close under these shelves for the hanging up of cloaks, hats, bonnets, and shawls. The principal's desk was placed at the south end of the hall. From 1830 to 1836, the halcyon days of the academy, Thomas Carr Lannan, a graduate of Belfast College, Ireland, was the principal, and for a time Mr. Rogers and Mr. McGary, two young candidates for holy orders in the Catholic Church, his assistants.

Among the young ladies who graduated high in Mr. Lannan's classes were Miss Henrietta Harwood, whose home was near the mouth of the Monocacy, Miss Mary Plummer, Miss Caroline Murphy, Miss Martha Hayes, Miss Mary Nicholls, Misses Frances and Jane Trail, Sarah Ellen Hayes, Ellen Jones, Mary Pearre, Catharine Pearre, and Henrietta Wilcoxen. Among the young gentlemen who attended the academy at this period were Edward Hayes, Mortimor Trail, Oscar Trail, Thomas Nichols, Richard Belt, Thomas Harwood, John Sellman, Gassaway Grimes, Howard Sellman, Thomas Johnson, James Pearre, Thomas Austin, Stephen Jay, Pickering White, George Pearre, David Hershey, John Hershey, Lemuel Beall, Avery Bell, William Sellman, Robert Saffell, Hamilton Anderson, King Jay, Reuben Carley, Philemon Plummer. Gassaway Grimes, Richard Thompson, and John Reid belonged to the higher Latin and Greek classes. They entered upon the study of medicine, graduated, and attained high rank in the profession. Dr. Thompson now lives in Clarkesburg, and Dr. Reed in Washington County, Md. Dr. Grimes died in early life; not long after he commenced to practice, Oscar Trail, Edward Hays, Richard Belt, Thomas Johnson stood foremost in academical studies. Mr. Trail commenced the mercantile business in Baltimore, where he became a highly respected and successful merchant. Messrs. Hays, Belt, and Johnson embraced learned professions. George Pearre studied law in Frederick, and is now Judge Pearre, of Allegany County. John, William, and Robert Sellman were respectable and earnest scholars, and made successful business men. John removed to Baltimore, and has been a member of the City Council; Robert holds the position of inspector of flour in the same city; William, who still lives in Montgomery, has represented it in the Maryland Senate. John Hershey won all the Latin and Greek prizes, and became an eloquent divine. Another pupil was Hon. Allen Bowie Davis, who before eighteen years of age was the teacher at Murphy's and Komemburg's school-houses, not far from each other, on the northeastern slope of Sugar-Loaf Mountain, where he succeeded Thomas Ponder and Elisha M. Swift. About 1836, Mr. Lannan, the principal of Barnesville Academy, relinquished the school and removed to Missouri, where he remained a number of years. Not realizing his anticipations in the then far West, he returned to Montgomery, and died a few years since at Poolesville.

Among those whose names appear in the early history of the district is that of Jonathan Willson.

The "Willson family" came originally from Prince George's County, and either before or shortly after their arrival in Montgomery became the owners of a tract of land (about nine hundred and fifty acres) near what is now the division line between Montgomery and Frederick Counties. The tract still bears the name then given to it, "Willson's Inheritance," and its beginning, a large flat stone full four feet high, forms a conspicuous object on the left of the present road from Hyattstown to Barnesville. The tract is now owned by the Hershey family, John Sellman, and perhaps others. Here lived one hundred years ago Jonathan Willson, whose name appears as a member of the State Legislature when the county of Montgomery was formed. He almost accomplished a centennial in his own person, having lived to the age of ninety-eight years and a few months, the immediate cause of his death even then being the result of an accident. The family tradition is that he was a man of much intelligence, energy of character, and influence. His only son, John, who inherited the estate, lived in the house now occupied by C. R. Hershey. He also lived to the advanced age of ninety-three.

John had four sons and a daughter, who married a Dr. Magruder and became the mother of the late Dr. William B. Magruder, near Brookville, and of other children, ten in all, whose descendants are numerous and widely scattered. Of the sons, the eldest, John, lived and died on the paternal acres, a quiet, highly-esteemed "gentleman of the olden times" and a bachelor. He died in 1849, aged eighty-nine. The second son, Thomas P., settled in Rockville, was for many years a prominent merchant there, and died at that place about the year 1832. His descendants are now living in Frederick City and County. The fourth son, Charles, lived for many years in Medley District, first as a merchant at Poolesville, then on a farm which he purchased not far from the mouth of the Monocacy, which is now owned by the White family, and finally moved to the southern part of Kentucky, where he died. His descendants are to be found in Tennessee, Virginia, and Baltimore County, in this State. The third, William, very early in life engaged in merchandising in Clarkesburg, and continued the business uninterruptedly at the same stand for about forty-five years, dying in 1859, at the age of eighty-three. He married the eldest daughter of John Clark, one of the oldest residents of the village (which was named after him), and to his business upon his death William Willson succeeded. Leonidas Willson, his son, resides in Clarkesburg.

This Mr. Clark was the father of two sons, John and Nelson, who very early in life—John not yet being of adult age—removed from their native village to Baltimore, and immediately went into business on their own account, were each more than ordinarily successful, and died in the possession of considerable property, the fruit of energy, skill, and enterprise. Nelson, the younger of the two, died about twenty-four years since, in the prime of life, married, but without children. John died in 1867, at the age of seventy-four. He was singularly unfortunate in the death of his children. Of a family of nine, all of whom with one exception attained adult age, and several married, he had buried all several years before his death. After providing well for his grandchildren, all of whom are now living in Baltimore or its vicinity, and making other bequests, he left property to the value of half a million of dollars to a beneficiary society which at his instance had been incorporated in connection with St. John's Church of Baltimore. The family name became extinct with him, only female branches surviving.

Another prominent family in this district is that of the Gotts.

Benjamin Collinson Gott resides upon the farm where he was born, May 28, 1814. His father, Richard, was born March 25, 1776, in Anne Arundel County, from which locality he came with his father, Richard, to the present Gott farm, in Montgomery County, in 1792, since which time the property has been in possession of a Gott. Richard Gott the younger was a lieutenant in the war of 1812. He married Sarah Collinson, of Anne Arundel County, and became the father of thirteen children, of whom eleven grew to maturity. The living are Benjamin C., Thomas N., Mary C. White, and Elizabeth Ann Gott. Losing his wife by death, Richard Gott married for his second consort Miss Mackenzie, whose father was an officer in the United States navy. She died before her husband, whose death occurred in 1859, after he had passed his eighty-third birthday. By the second marriage there were no children. Benjamin C. Gott was bred a farmer, and a farmer has continued to be all his days. The tract of seven hundred acres left by his father he has increased to eight hundred and fifty. The stone house his father built in 1812, Benjamin Gott improved and enlarged and still occupies.

Mr. Gott has been married twice. His first wife was Susan E., daughter of George Darby, of Montgomery County. The two surviving of the three children of that marriage are George R. Gott, an attorney-at-law in Baltimore, and the wife of Dr. Stephen Beard, of Prince George's County. Mrs. Gott died May 28, 1855, and May 18, 1858, Mr. Gott married Mary R., daughter of William Cissel, of Montgomery County, where she was born, May 17, 1837. William Cissel lives near Poolesville.

Eight of the ten children born of the second marriage survive, seven of the eight being sons. Benjamin Gott has long enjoyed the distinction of being one of Montgomery County's representative farmers, and in matters appertaining to the field of advanced and profitable agriculture is a practical exponent and recognized authority. In his own quiet way, he makes his influence and example felt in the community to much better purpose perhaps than if he chose to seek a similar effect through the method of public life, for be it understood that his tastes run not in the last-named direction. Early a Whig and now a Democrat, he has always believed in a watchful interest in the government of affairs, local and national, but he is no lover of office. The only office he ever held was that of county commissioner, to which he was chosen, against his will, in 1864.

St. Mary's Catholic Church.—This church was organized and the edifice built in 1808, under the supervision of Father Plunkett, who then had charge of the mission, embracing the whole county. The present church building is the original structure with additions made at various times. This church was

under the charge of the priests resident at Rockville until 1869, when the present pastor, Rev. J. S. Birch, took charge of it. He also has St. Rose's Church under his care, and is the first resident priest and pastor of both. Father Birch, since his residence here, has completed the church edifice and parsonage, and shortly after his arrival had St. Mary's Hall built, which is used as a parochial school. The church is a solid and elegant oak building.

The ground on which the church property stands was a donation from Zachariah Knott, an early settler in the district. The membership of the church from its organization in 1808 has been almost entirely English.

Among the interments in the church cemetery are

James Moore, born June 6, 1789, died Aug. 18, 1870.
Columbus F. Wallace, died Feb. 7, 1862, aged 25.
Abigail Higgins, born in Cloyne, County Cork, Ireland, died Oct. 22, 1833, aged 25.
Zachariah Knott, died Nov. 23, 1820, aged 79.
William Edelin, died May 8, 1841, aged 56.
Henry Jones, born March 20, 1778, died Dec. 3, 1830; and his wife, Eleanor, born Aug. 3, 1778, died April 23, 1844.
John Beall, of L., born Dec. 23, 1781, died Aug. 26, 1831; and Charlotte, his wife, born Feb. 18, 1787, died Jan. 23, 1867; and their son, John R. Beall, born Sept. 8, 1823, and died Sept. 19, 1845.
Peter McGee, born in County Down, Ireland, died July 25, 1855, aged 55.
Lloyd S. Jones, born Aug. 4, 1807, died Feb. 9, 1863.
Sallie E., wife of Geo. H. Clements, died July 14, 1871, aged 32.
Maria, wife of John Carlin, born Sept. 5, 1808, died Jan. 5, 1879.
Adie E., wife of John T. Carlin, born Aug. 2, 1848, died Sept. 17, 1870.
Mary E., wife of Thomas Trundle, born Feb. 21, 1830, died May 9, 1862.
Hezekiah W. Trundle, born March 20, 1810, died April 20, 1863; and his wife, Emily A., born Dec. 21, 1814, died Nov. 7, 1878.
Ella, wife of James O. Trundle, born Dec. 22, 1839, died Oct. 20, 1860.
Otto T. Austin, born April 15, 1833, died Feb. 6, 1860.
Mary E., wife of Thomas Ward, died May 5, 1878, aged 55.
Robert T. Power, native of County Duncaven, town of Waterford, Ireland, died May 29, 1851, aged 58.
Rebecca, wife of George Redmond, and daughter of William Murphy, died Sept. 26, 1829, aged 20.
Anna Murphy, died May 29, 1852, aged 70.
Joanna V., wife of Stephen R. Austin, died July 13, 1875, aged 20.
Sophia C., wife of John L. T. Jones, died July 10, 1849, aged 22.
Teresa, wife of Brook Jones, born 1785, died July 20, 1876; and her husband, died July 19, 1850, aged 73.
Mary A. Jones, born April 19, 1814, died April 19, 1864.
Mary R., wife of James B. Reid, died Jan. 28, 1852, aged 68.
Emeline B., wife of Richard H. Jones, born ―― 25, 1812, and died Jan. 11, 1873.

Methodist Episcopal Church.—This two-story frame edifice was built in 1843. Its present pastor is Rev. Randolph R. Murphy. In the burying-ground in the rear are interred

Leonard Hays, born July 30, 1793, died April 24, 1864; and Eliza Hays, born June 28, 1807, died July 21, 1874.
Elisha Howard, died April 27, 1874, aged 84; and his wife, Eleanor, born July 12, 1791, died Feb. 8, 1873.
Laura V., wife of Richard T. Pyles, born Nov. 6, 1842, died Sept. 17, 1865.
Elizabeth M. Hawkins, died June 10, 1867, aged 22.
Jacob Nichols, born Oct. 2, 1788, died Nov. 25, 1857; and his wife, Sarah, born Feb. 19, 1798, died April 27, 1867.
Sarah Ellen, wife of Benjamin S. White, and daughter of Jacob and Sarah Nichols, died May 15, 1856, aged 26.
Hatton Browne, born Jan. 28, 1801, died Dec. 28, 1871; and his wife, Deborah, died Feb. 16, 1866, aged 73.
Abigail, wife of William Trail, born June 5, 1789, died May 10, 1857.
"Sacred to the memory of William Alexander, of Philadelphia, Corporal Co. H, 6th U. S. Cavalry. Killed Sept. 10, 1862. Erected by Union friends of Georgetown, D. C."
John H. T. Hays, born Oct. 8, 1813, died June 23, 1857.
Thomas L. Hays, born Nov. 20, 1816, died Oct. 4, 1873.
Sarah A. Plummer, born Sept. 20, 1820, died Feb. 26, 1873.
Mary Plummer, born May 4, 1817, died June 18, 1874.
Isaac Bell, of N. Y., died Aug. 17, 1844, aged 35; of English descent, and his mother's maiden name was Poole.
John Smith, born Dec. 18, 1801, died July 19, 1872.
Hester Ellen, wife of John T. McAbee, died Jan. 17, 1848, aged 18.
Elizabeth, wife of Jacob Feaster, died July 30, 1858, aged 70.
Philemon N. Plummer, born Dec. 16, 1815, died Oct. 26, 1861.
Syrah A. Plummer, died July 19, 1866, aged 35.
Mary Anne, wife of Colmore Offutt, born Feb. 6, 1788, died Sept. 2, 1845; and her husband, died Feb. 7, 1855, aged 67.
Williminer Harris, died Jan. 22, 1848, aged 54.
James P. Wade, born Aug. 7, 1825, died April 15, 1858.
James Edelin, born March 27, 1777, died March 21, 1852; and his wife, Eleanor, born Nov. 18, 1780, died Sept. 28, 1852.

Baptist Church.—Its edifice, a two-story frame building, was erected about 1869. Its pastor is Rev. D. E. Hatcher.

Protestant Episcopal Church.—This church building, a frame structure, was erected a few years ago, and is situated near the town on the road from Sellman's Station. Its pastor is Rev. H. Thomas, of Poolesville.

The Hayes Family Burying-Ground.—This graveyard is on land now owned by John W. Brown.

Leonard Hayes, died Sept. 14, 1822, aged 63; and his wife, Eleanor, Oct. 25, 1833, aged 73.
Elizabeth, wife of John A. Trundle, and daughter of Leonard and Eleanor Hayes, born Feb. 22, 1818, died Jan. 30, 1855.
Samuel S. Hayes, born April 2, 1787, died Sept. 5, 1857; and his wife, Anna, born Sept. 7, 1796, died March 8, 1855; Sarah, their daughter, born Dec. 28, 1823, died Jan. 17, 1847.
Martha M. Nichols, daughter of S. S. Hayes, and granddaughter of Leonard Hays, died Sept. 1, 1840, aged 17.

Barnesville Grange, No. 87.—This grange of Patrons of Husbandry was very early instituted. Its Master is E. J. Chiswell, and Secretary Otho Hayes.

R. T. Pyles is postmaster at Barnesville; the physicians are Drs. G. W. Bowlen and R. Vinton Wood.

Prominent at an early day among the residents of Barnesville and its vicinity was the Saffell family. W. T. R. Saffell, the author and historian, was born Sept. 18, 1818, about two miles south of Barnesville, on a farm called "Knott's Place," where his father, Lameck Saffell, resided at the time. Among the venerable residents in the vicinity at that period were William Darne, Dr. S. N. C. White, William Poole, Abraham S. Hayes, William Bennett, Brook Jones, Francis C. Clopper, Joseph I. Johnson, Nathan Hempstone, Jacob Nicholls, Horatio Trundle, Hezekiah Trundle, Richard Harding, William Trail, Thos. C. Lannan, the esteemed schoolmaster, Rev. Thos. Green, Dr. Horatio Willson, William Willson, and Rev. Basil Barry.

Charles Saffell, a Revolutionary soldier and pensioner, lived on a farm five miles north of Rockville, near Gaithersburg. He died there in 1837, at the age of ninety years. At the beginning of the Revolution he lived with his father, a French musician, in Prince George's County. From that county he marched to Annapolis and joined the regiment of the Maryland Flying Camp under command of Gen. Rezin Beall, and sailing to the Head of Elk, he marched northward in the company commanded by John Hawkins Lowe. Charles was a drummer, fifer, and bugler at the battles of Long Island, Fort Washington, Brandywine, Germantown, and Monmouth. He was an auctioneer, and in later days visited all parts of the country in that capacity. As a violinist, also, he amused himself in his feeble old age, and often reproduced the melodies of the Revolution.

Poolesville is situated on a portion of a survey made to Robert Peter, May 17, 1784, containing one thousand seven hundred and ninety-six acres, and known as "The Resurvey on part of Forest."

The Peter family originally came from Scotland, where they possessed considerable landed estates. Robert Peter, who emigrated to this country some time during the last century, was born in 1726, at Crossbasket Castle, Lanarkshire, Scotland, and died at his residence in Georgetown in 1806. Mr. Peter settled at Georgetown and was its first mayor, serving as such from 1789 to 1798. He was one of the younger sons of Thomas Peter, of Crossbasket, by Jane Dunlop, daughter of James Dunlop, of Garnkirke. James Dunlop's wife was Lilias Campbell, of Blytheswood, in Lanarkshire. Thomas Peter, father of Robert, was a younger son of Walter Peter, of Chapel Hall, in Mearnshire, in the northeast of Scotland, whose ancestors owned the estate from the Norman conquest. Robert Peter's wife, Elizabeth Scott, whom he married Dec. 27, 1767, was the daughter of Thomas Scott, of Malenie, Midlothianshire, who was the heir male of Buccleugh by his wife Isabel, daughter of Lord Fountainhall. George Scott was born at Malenie in 1700, and came to Maryland in 1730. In 1758 he was appointed for life sheriff for the counties of Charles, Prince George's, and Frederick, and farmer of Lord Baltimore's quit-rents and deputy commissary-general. He died in 1771. Robert Peter, like most of the tobacco merchants of Bladensburg and Georgetown, on the Potomac, was a Tory. At one time he was in danger of confiscation, but succeeded in retaining his estates. His nephew, Thomas Peter, was a captain in the British army, and was present at the siege of Yorktown. After the surrender he visited his uncle at Georgetown, and afterwards returned to Scotland and succeeded his father as the "laird" of Crossbasket. He maintained his connection with the British service, and died a general in the English army in 1830. His daughter, an only child, married Gen. Dirom, of Mount Annan, in Dumfriesshire.

George Peter, son of Robert Peter, and cousin of Gen. Thomas Peter, was born at Georgetown, Montgomery Co., now the District of Columbia, on the 28th of September, 1779. When only fifteen years of age he joined the Maryland troops in the campaign of 1794 against the Whisky Insurrectionists, but his parents sent a messenger to camp, and Gen. Washington hearing of the matter ordered him to be sent home. His youthful ardor, however, was gratified four years later, July, 1799, by his appointment as second lieutenant of the Ninth Infantry, U.S.A., by President Adams, and he enjoyed the distinction of receiving his commission from the hands of Gen. Washington at Mount Vernon. In February, 1801, he was promoted to a lieutenancy of artillery and engineers, and in November, 1807, to a captaincy of artillery. In May, 1808, he was transferred to the light artillery, and on the 11th of June, 1809, he resigned his commission.

In *Niles' Register* of May 15, 1847, an interesting description is given of the corps of Light or "Flying" Artillery organized by Capt. George Peter while in command at Fort McHenry, Baltimore, during the administration of President Jefferson. In July, 1808, the company was ordered to Washington and reviewed on the 4th of July. This was the first light-horse battery formed in the Federal service, and Maj. Peter always referred with special pride and gratification to the fact that he was specially selected by President Jefferson for that purpose. At the beginning of the war of 1812 President Madison tendered him a brig-

MAJ. GEORGE PETER.

adier-generalship, which the condition of his private affairs compelled him to decline; but in 1813 he volunteered his services and commanded a battalion of flying artillery. Among the privates in this battalion were George Peabody and Francis Scott Key, besides several others who afterwards became distinguished citizens. In writing of this battalion, W. W. Corcoran, the eminent banker, says the list of its members represented the wealth, worth, and talent of the town at that time. Previous to the war of 1812, Maj. Peter accompanied Gen. Wilkinson in the organization of the Territorial government of Missouri, leaving Washington April 1, 1805, and arriving at St. Louis on the 4th of July following. Maj. (then Lieut.) Peter established the first cantonment on the banks of the Missouri, at Bellefontaine, and fired the first salute on the return of Lewis and Clarke from their expedition to the Pacific. He also served under Gen. Wilkinson at New Orleans during Gov. Claiborne's administration, before Louisiana was admitted into the Union. His army life at St. Louis and New Orleans, and also at Niagara and Fort Columbus, N. Y., was the theme of many interesting and vivid reminiscences. Maj. Peter was also present as a witness at the trial of Aaron Burr.

In 1815 he was elected to Congress from the Sixth District of Maryland, but his seat was contested on the ground that he was not a resident of the congressional district. At that time he was a resident of Georgetown and a member of the Town Council, but had large farms in Maryland. The House of Representatives, however, decided in his favor, and admitted him to his seat. He was the first Democrat ever elected to Congress from the Sixth District of Maryland, and was re-elected in 1817, and again in 1828. He served several terms in the State Legislature, and in 1855 was elected by the Democratic party a Commissioner of Public Works for the State of Maryland. He was a man six feet in height, straight as an arrow, and of splendid physique. The portrait accompanying this sketch is copied from an original by St. Memin, and was taken when he was about twenty-five years of age. He always kept open house, his manner was always polite, dignified, and courteous, and his hospitable home was scarcely ever without company. He was married three times. His first wife was Ann Plater, of Maryland; his second, Agnes Freeland; and his third, Sarah Worfleet Freeland, of Petersburg, Va. Maj. Peter was one of the largest land-owners and farmers in Montgomery County, and carried on these farms up to the date of his death, which occurred at Montanverd near Darnestown, June 22, 1861. When he died, Maj. Peter was nearly eighty-two. Dr. Armistead Peter, a distinguished physician at Georgetown, D. C., and Hon. George Peter, of Montgomery County, are his sons.

In 1804 Poolesville comprised only three or four houses, occupied by the families of John Poole, Melton, and Campbell. The first house was erected in 1793 by John Poole, from whom the town received its name. He was the first merchant in the vicinity, and kept his store in his dwelling-house. The Melton family occupied the house now used by Wm. Poole. Campbell, who was a cabinet-maker, lived on the road near the millinery-shop of Mrs. Rice; the house is not in existence, having been destroyed some years ago.

The house which is now occupied by Mr. Cator was then used as a tavern and kept by a Mr. Riney, who was succeeded in the management by Mr. Fowler, who was followed by Mr. Taylor. Mr. Powell was the shoemaker, and Melton the tailor. Dr. Lyles was the first physician, and resided a short distance from the village. A Mr. Herbert was the pioneer schoolmaster, and taught in the old log school-house which stood upon the farm now owned by Dr. Gotts. Mr. Jarbel was his successor; they were both residents of the town. The Benson family, quite prominent in the early history of the district, resided upon the farm which is now occupied by Mr. Steiffer.

A town hall and public-school building was erected a few years prior to the late civil war, but was destroyed by fire. The first postmaster of the town was Dennis Locklin, who was succeeded by Philip Reed, Wm. Metzgar, and Samuel Cator, who has served in that capacity for twelve years.

Among the educational institutions of Poolesville is the Briarley Hall Boarding and Day School for young ladies. It was established in 1873, and is situated about three-fourths of a mile from the town. The principals are Mrs. M. E. and Miss W. E. Porter.

Presbyterian Church.—The Presbyterian Church of Poolesville was organized April 16, 1847. It consisted at first of only two members, Robert J. Graff and Mrs. Luyles, but others rapidly united with it. Rev. C. H. Nourse was instrumental in effecting the organization of the church, and continued in charge of it ten years. It was then served for several years by Rev. H. R. Smith, of Leesburg. During the war the regular services were much interrupted. For a time Rev. D. Motzer, of Darnestown, preached in the church. In the spring of 1868, Rev. C. N. Campbell, of Charlestown, W. Va., was invited to the church, and after preaching about one year was regularly installed pastor, and still continues in charge of the congregation. The fine church edifice was erected in 1848. The church now numbers thirty-four members. Robert J. Graff was the first elder. The elders at the present time are Isaac Young and Thomas Milford, and the deacons William Shafer and Eugene Hughes.

Baptist Church.—On Nov. 5, 1860, the following persons, who had been members of the Rockville Baptist Church, withdrew and formed a congregation in Poolesville: M. F. Williams, Emma Higgins, M. J. Hoskinson, M. J. Trundle, Wm. F. Jones, Greenbury Griffith, P. L. Trundle, R. P. Spates, and J. P. Bowie. W. T. Jones was chosen deacon, and J. P. Bowie, clerk. The church was incorporated Feb. 13, 1864, with the following gentlemen as incorporators: Wm. F. Jones, George D. Powell, John W. Booth, Jamer H. Money, James N. Miles. The congregation worshiped in the Presbyterian church until 1864, when a brick edifice, twenty-five by forty feet, was erected, which was dedicated on May 28, 1865, Mr. G. N. Samson, of Columbian College, delivering the dedicatory sermon, assisted by Elders White and G. F. Adams. The cost of this neat structure was about twelve hundred dollars. In September, 1865, Elder White, after having served the church as its minister since its organization, resigned. He had been untiring in his efforts to promote the interests of his charge, and his departure was greatly regretted. H. J. Chandler, of Norfolk, Va., was his successor, and occupied the pulpit until 1869. Mr. Davis followed him, but only remained a short time. The church was without a pastor for some time, but the vacancy was finally filled by Rev. Mr. Woodson, who was followed by Mr. Kearns. In 1876, C. L. Amy began his pastorate, which terminated by the succession of Mr. Hatcher, Nov. 1, 1880. The congregation now numbers about fifteen members. The deacon is Wm. T. Odds, and the clerk J. M. Meyers.

Methodist Episcopal Church.—This congregation, which is the pioneer church of all the denominations in this vicinity, was formed about 1816. Their church was erected in 1826, and is still standing, although it has several times been remodeled and repaired. The congregation was very prosperous and in an extremely flourishing condition until its division in 1866. Among the pastors of the church have been Rev. Mr. Hempfield, Rev. John A. Collins, Rev. Horace Holland, Rev. John W. Stout, Rev. Mr. Brown, Rev. Mr. Shipley, and Revs. William Hank, Robert Bean, John Lanhan, Gilbert, Phelps, Browning, Balaska, and Morgan. The steward of the church at present is Wm. Cissell; the trustees are Wm. Cissell, Samuel C. Cator, Richard Ashland. The congregation numbers about twelve. Rev. Mr. Murphy is the pastor.

The graveyard surrounding the church contains the remains of

A. P. Eversole, born April 27, 1836, died Aug. 13, 1864.
Mary E. Hyatt, died March 27, 1854, aged 25 years.
George F. Hughes, died Jan. 3, 1862.
John W. Hughes, died July 12, 1855, aged 66.
Ann West, wife of James W. Reed, died July 5, 1862, aged 32.
R. P. Spates, born Dec. 25, 1792, died March 5, 1863; Amelia, his wife, born 1795, died July 19, 1855.
Ellen Hiser, born in Shepherdstown, Sept. 4, 1808, died June 10, 1850.
Daniel Heffner, born 1782, died June 29, 1861.
Jane Hughes, died Aug. 7, 1857, aged 57.
Ruth Eagle, born 1817, died 1839.
Mary E. Gooley, born 1825, died 1845.
Elizabeth R. Leipley, born July 17, 1827, died Sept. 20, 1847.
Margaret A. D., wife of George N. Leapley, died Jan. 26, 1859, aged 31.

Methodist Episcopal Church South.—This congregation was formed on the division of the Methodist Episcopal Church in 1866. Prominent among the principal promoters of this church at that time were Ludwick Young, George Hughes, William Hughes, and John O. Merchant. The congregation at its first establishment numbered about twenty-four members, and was under the charge of Rev. John P. Hall. George Donohue and B. F. Reed were the stewards. They worshiped in the Baptist church until the erection of their own church in 1867. This church was dedicated in May, 1868, under the auspices of Samuel Register, the presiding elder of Baltimore. It is a neat frame structure, situated in the southwest part of the town, and cost about $1500. Previous to the erection of the church the congregation had increased to between twenty-five and thirty members, and after its completion and on the succession of Rev. Robert Smith to the pulpit increased to fifty members. Mr. Smith, who delivered his first sermon in 1868, was assisted during his two years of service by Rufus Willson, a young minister. In 1870, Benjamin F. Ball was appointed to this charge, and in 1872 was followed by Rev. Mr. Tebbs, who in turn was succeeded by Mr. McDonald in 1874. Rev. William Wade was the next pastor, and Rev. Mr. Lloyd assisted him in his duties. Rev. Mr. Gover, assisted by Mr. Willson, occupied the pulpit until the present minister, Rev. Mr. Watts, began his pastorate in 1880. The church numbers sixty members, and under its supervision is a large Sunday-school superintended by Mr. Devilbiss. The stewards of the church are Thomas Hoskinson and Etna Mouldin. The church belongs to the Montgomery Circuit.

St. Peter's Parish.—The congregation of St. Peter's was organized before or during the Revolutionary war, and prayers for peace were offered in the

Wm A Schaffer

church during that memorable period. In May, 1799, the following gentlemen were chosen vestrymen: John Poole, Jr., George B. Hayes, John White, Alexander Whitaker, Maj. John Harwood, Charles Crabb, Thomas Brown, and Col. David Luckett. Hugh Smith Dunn and Thomas Veatch, Jr., wardens; William Dunn, register. At their meeting May 13, 1799, a request was sent to Right Rev. T. J. Clagett to recommend a minister to the parish. John Poole was appointed to officiate as reader until the appointment of a minister.

On the 18th of August, 1799, Rev. Thomas Scott accepted a call and preached his first sermon to the congregation. He was employed at a salary of eighty-five pounds for one year from that date. He resigned in 1802, and the charge remained vacant until April 2, 1804, when the vestry made a contract with Rev. John Fowler Reynolds "to pay him for performing divine service, at the expiration of one year, the sum of two hundred and thirty dollars." During the vacancy the church was repaired and remodeled. Rev. Thomas Reed was the next pastor. In 1810, Rev. John Chandler was engaged, his term expiring in 1812, when, on July 26, 1819, Rev. William Armstrong began his pastorate. Rev. Spencer Wall preached here in 1821. In 1822 the congregation gave its support to the establishment of a theological seminary, a question which was then deeply agitating the Episcopal Church. During Mr. Armstrong's pastorate in 1823 a vestry-room was added to the church. Rev. Allen Mervin was the pastor in 1833, Rev. Mr. Bean in 1834, Rev. Joseph Tropnell in 1836, Rev. A. S. Colton in 1849, Rev. William Tropnell in 1860, followed by Rev. D. D. McCabe, Rev. John Towles, and the present pastor, Rev. Henry Thomas, who began his duties in 1878. The congregation numbers about fifty members. The wardens are Wallace Poole and N. Talbott; Vestrymen, F. S. Poole, John Jones, Dr. Thomas Schaeffer, L. I. Hays, Dr. Hellen, R. T. Pyles, Thomas Fryeffe, Thomas Story; Register, Dr. B. W. Walling. The original church edifice stood on what is now called Monocacy Cemetery.[1]

Poolesville Lodge, No. 115, I. O. O. F.—This lodge of I. O. O. F. was instituted on Thursday, July 8, 1869. The instituting ceremonies were conducted by Joseph B. Escaville, Grand Secretary of the Grand Lodge of Maryland. Its first officers were: N. G., Joseph W. Miles; V. G., R. T. Hillard; Sec., Dr. R. T. Gott; Treas., John R. Grimes. It has now surrendered its charter.

Among the prominent citizens residing in the neighborhood of Poolesville is William Augustus Schaeffer, of "Pleasant Grove." Mr. Schaeffer was born Jan. 31, 1831, near Boonsborough, Washington Co., of which county his father, Leonard Schaeffer, was likewise a native, the birth of the latter occurring Dec. 23, 1778. Leonard Schaeffer married (1806) Mary, daughter of Frederick Schroder, one of the earliest settlers in Funkstown. Leonard Schaeffer was for a number of years a successful merchant, and later in life was a farmer and miller. He died April 5, 1832; his widow, Sept. 20, 1853. They had fourteen children. The living are Gustavus, in Frederick County; Thomas and William A., of Montgomery County; Mrs. Ann Dorsey, of Baltimore; and Mrs. Caroline Hoffman, of Oregon.

William A. Schaeffer was but one year old when his father died, and to his mother's careful and excellent training he was indebted for the sterling principles that supported his struggling footsteps in early life and set him at last upon a sure foundation, from which he evolved the structure of a useful and profitable after-life. He was bred to farming pursuits, and obtained but a brief school experience. At the age of sixteen he chose to begin the task of supporting himself, and obtaining employment as clerk in a store in Frederick, where he remained four years. At the age of twenty he embarked in mercantile trade on his own account, at Utica Mills, Frederick Co., and successfully held his way as a merchant until 1857. In that year he disposed of his store business and bought a small unimproved farm near Utica Mills. That property he labored upon with industrious determination to increase its value, and succeeded so well that at the end of twelve years he sold it for just double the money it had cost him. He thereupon purchased the fine farm tract known as Pleasant Grove (near Poolesville), containing about three hundred and ten acres, and thereon has since had his home. To the improvement of his estate Mr. Schaeffer has given his close attention, and in the pursuit of his business cares has found neither time nor desire to seek public distinction by way of political strife or clamor for office. Sept. 13, 1853, he was married, by Rev. Jesse Shreve, to Emily Ann, daughter of John P. Gallion, a native of Harford County, Md., where

---

[1] On Oct. 20, 1794, Walter White conveyed by deed to St. Peter's Parish five-eighths of an acre of land, part of a tract called "Chappel Forest," adjoining an acre formerly conveyed to the trustees of the congregation of "Monocacy Chappel." The consideration stipulated in the indenture was three pounds ten shillings current money. The witnesses were Æneas Campbell and Lawrence O'Neale.

On June 5, 1830, John Adlam conveyed to the vestry of said parish ten and three-fourths acres, part of "Chappel Forest," for the sum of two hundred dollars. This indenture was witnessed by Daniel Duvall and Daniel J. Krommer.

he was born Jan. 17, 1800. His father and mother were natives of England. His wife was Elizabeth, daughter of Joshua Brown, of German descent. John P. Gallion died in Frederick County in 1876, sixteen years after the death of his wife. Their living sons and daughters are Mrs. W. A. Schaeffer, Mrs. Mary Cramer, Albert W. Gallion, and George F. Gallion. Of Mr. and Mrs. Schaeffer's children, those surviving are William L., Frank G., Elizabeth A., Mary N., and Thomas W.

Monocacy Cemetery and Beallsville.—Monocacy Cemetery was laid out upon the site of "Old St. Peter's Church," or, as it was frequently called, "Old Monocacy Chapel," an ante-Revolutionary relic and time-honored place of public worship, which must have been one of the first ever built in the State, as stones erected to the memory of the dead in the churchyard date back as far as 1735. Old St. Peter's church was built about the year 1737, was torn down and rebuilt on the same spot, and at the breaking out of the late civil war, in a very fair state of preservation, was used and occupied for religious purposes.

During the war the Federal cavalry frequently stabled their horses in it, burnt up the seats and weather-boarding, and otherwise damaged the building so as to render it unfit for service. Under these circumstances the vestry transferred their grounds to several public-spirited gentlemen to be used in common with other land adjacent purchased by them as a public cemetery, comprising about nine acres of land. In January, 1872, the association was chartered as "The Monocacy Cemetery Society of Montgomery County," with F. S. Poole, Dr. N. Brewer, W. W. Poole, Howard Griffith, N. W. Allnutt, John A. Jones, and Isaac Young as incorporators. At a subsequent election of the lot-holders a board of managers were elected, with Dr. N. Brewer as president and Isaac Young secretary and treasurer, which positions they still hold, with the same gentlemen above named as managers. This cemetery is located at Beallsville, a thriving village about two and a half miles from Barnesville Station on the Metropolitan Branch of the Baltimore and Ohio Railroad, some distance from Poolesville and the mouth of Monocacy River.

Among the graves in the cemetery are the following:

John Cross, died Sept. 13, 1838, aged 25 years, 7 months, and 23 days.

Hannah Lawrence, born Dec. 25, 1784, died Feb. 25, 1865.

Francis Bouslin, died July 4, 1829, aged 18.

Mary White, consort of Capt. James White, of Montgomery County.

William T. Johnson, born Feb. 17, 1818, died July 18, 1861; Sarah Ann, his wife, died Aug. 3, 1856, aged 62.

Sarah A., wife of Robert Sellman, born May 31, 1823, died Sept. 20, 1852.

Alonzo Sellman, born Sept. 17, 1844, died Oct. 27, 1878.

Wallace Sellman, born Nov. 12, 1842, died May 22, 1863.

Mary, consort of Capt. Clement T. Hilleary, died June 20, 1816, aged 32.

James S. Pleasants, died Oct. 6, 1863, aged 46.

Elisha Williams, died at Longwood, Sept. 1, 1854, aged 76.

Warren King, born Jan. 31, 1794, died June 12, 1871.

John D. Poole, born Sept. 4, 1828, died June 6, 1876.

John Scrimager, died November, 1830, aged 23.

Margaret A., wife of H. J. Norris, died July 9, 1881, aged 38.

Mrs. Harriet E. Vinson, died Sept. 10, 1850, aged 38.

Mary A. Benson, born Feb. 23, 1833, died June 1, 1872.

Mrs. Ann Vinson, died May 4, 1862, aged 73.

Mrs. Mary Vinson, died Nov. 11, 1861, aged 75.

Sarah Ann Gumaer, died Oct. 14, 1842, aged 25.

Rev. T. Dade, died Feb. 6, 1822, aged 80.

John Douglass, of Castlestewart, Wigtonshire, Scotland, died Nov. 21, 1832, aged 36.

Mary Cross, born Jan. 22, 1815; died Aug. 8, 1855.

John Cross, born Aug. 25, 1782, died Oct. 4, 1854.

Mrs. Mary Cross, died Feb. 6, 1845, aged 52.

Joseph Thomas Cross, died Aug. 4, 1842, aged 25 years, 4 months.

William Aprilton Cady, died April, 1861, aged 42.

John S. Mouly, died March 8, 1847, aged 48.

Benjamin Poole, died Dec. 6, 1843, aged 71; Ann W., his wife, died Oct. 4, 1852, aged 58.

Dorcas Hammontree, died Feb. 21, 1836, aged 37.

John Manly, died Nov. 25, 1816, aged 64; Mary, his wife, died June 18, 1823, aged 52.

Henry W. Talbott, born Nov. 12, 1789, died Feb. 7, 1859.

Charles A. H. Bowles, born Aug. 11, 1844, died Aug. 10, 1863.

Solomon Davis, died July 10, 1822, aged 48.

Robert Willson, born Sept. 13, 1762, died March 4, 1835; Eleanor, his wife, born July 21, 1773, died August, 1851.

Fannie E. Poole, born March 31, 1840, died March 11, 1860.

Colonel Robert T. Dade, born Oct. 4, 1786, died Feb. 17, 1873; Ruth, his wife, died March 11, 1864, aged 74.

Henrietta Dawson, died March 31, 1855, aged 76.

Henrietta Dayne, born March 24, 1818, died March 17, 1837.

Elizabeth Allnutt, died Aug. 6, 1872, aged 84 years, 9 days.

John R. Hall, born March 29, 1832, died June 9, 1880.

William R. Vinson, born Nov. 10, 1846, died June 15, 1880.

Gerhard Metzgar, born March 2, 1810, died Sept. 5, 1844.

Ann R., wife of B. T. Norris, born Sept. 20, 1801, died Feb. 19, 1860.

Amy Robertson, died March 9, 1865, aged 70.

Louisa M., wife of William B. Vinson, born July 23, 1819, died Sept. 3, 1880.

William D. Poole, born Aug. 8, 1808, died April 3, 1869; Rebecca, his wife, born Dec. 29, 1820, aged 71 years, 8 months.

James N. Allnutt, died June 1, 1854, aged 63; B. A., his wife, died Feb. 27, 1876, aged 64.

Thomas F. Chiswell, born Sept. 10, 1810, died May 7, 1851.

Mary E. Chiswell, born March 31, 1810, died Jan. 27, 1873.

Sarah A., wife of T. H. Poole, born Jan. 31, 1819, died Jan. 19, 1875.

William Poole, died June 29, 1878, aged 91.

Dr. Thomas Poole, died March 17, 1870, aged 66; Sarah A. E. Willson, his wife, born April 15, 1808, died June 21, 1844; Reginald, their son, died April 11, 1861, aged 28 years, 1 month, 7 days.

Martin Fisher, died Feb. 18, 1832, aged 37; Priscilla, his wife, died Feb. 3, 1880, aged 81 years, 9 months.

Joseph R. Fisher, died April 17, 1862, aged 43 years, 2 months, 24 days.

Wm. Metzgar, born Oct. 17, 1805, died Aug. 19, 1874.

Philip Metzgar, born Jan. 8, 1846, died March 29, 1862.

Nathan T. Metzgar, born June 11, 1842, died Oct. 23, 1875.

Catharine Hughes, died Nov. 15, 1874, aged 75.

Daniel T. Heffner, died Jan. 29, 1875, aged 60.

George N. Leapley, died Dec. 15, 1876, aged 65.

Susanna Mulligan, born Sept. 24, 1780, died May 23, 1873.

Geo. F. Metzgar, died March 5, 1872.

Alice Kraft, died April 27, 1872, aged 28.

Joseph N. Dawson, born Feb. 20, 1796, died July 10, 1869.

Elizabeth Dawson, born July 22, 1794, died Feb. 4, 1852.

Geo. W. Dawson, born Nov. 28, 1799, died Dec. 26, 1874.

Robert Doyne Dawson, born July 10, 1758, died Aug. 13, 1824.

Jos. H. Dawson, died March 20, 1857, aged 21 years, 11 months, 20 days.

Robert T. Dawson, died Sept. 11, 1874, aged 30 years, 2 months, 14 days.

Benoni Dawson, died Jan. 11, 1857, aged 53 years, 2 months, 19 days. Sarah, his wife, died April 17, 1879.

Jesse Vears, died March 19, 1871, aged 77.

Sophia Vears, died Dec. 23, 1875, aged 64.

Motley Vears, died Jan. 25, 1877, aged 28.

Benjamin F. Reed, died Aug. 20, 1874, aged 39 years, 11 months.

Warner Bollinger, born April 10, 1814, died Nov. 15, 1877; Mary, his wife, died Oct. 28, 1879, aged 66.

Samuel Young, died Oct. 18, 1877, aged 69.

Henrietta, wife of Peter Stang, born Dec. 9, 1853, died Sept. 13, 1877.

R. G. White, died Jan. 3, 1879, aged 52 years, 2 months, 17 days.

H. Henderson White, died July 1, 1862, aged 31 years, 8 months, 13 days.

Sarah White Richey, died Jan. 19, 1880.

Mrs. Martha Plater, wife of Dr. Nicholas Brevier, and daughter of E. W. Williams, Esq., died March 2, 1854, aged 23 years, 11 months.

Virgil M. Hickerson, died March 24, 1880, aged 23.

William Jones, born Jan. 31, 1800, died June 5, 1876.

Morgan Jones, born May 12, 1802, died September, 1876.

Dorcas A. Hoskinson, died Oct. 20, 1875, aged 49 years, 8 months, 27 days.

Beallsville.—This village is eighteen miles from Rockville, seventy from Baltimore, and three and a half from Sellman's Station. The place was first called Beall's Cross-roads. In 1872, John A. Belt opened a store here, and in 1878 was succeeded by Chiswell & Davis. The physicians are Drs. B. W. Walling, John W. Ayler, and R. T. Gott, and the postmaster, F. M. Griffith.

Among the best-known citizens in this neighborhood is Hon. Howard Griffith. Mr. Griffith is a gentleman of high character, of much practical ability, and of considerable experience in public affairs. A farmer by occupation, and taking great interest in the advancement of agricultural prosperity, he has been called on to serve in several public capacities. He was born March 20, 1821, near Goshen, Montgomery Co., Md., and resides near Beallsville, Montgomery Co., Md. He is the son of the late Maj. Greenbury Griffith, who commanded the Alexandria Artillery in the war of 1812, and was born near Goshen, May 20, 1787. His mother's maiden name was Prudence Jones, born Nov. 5, 1796, in Washington City, and now living, in her eighty-sixth year. His paternal grandfather was the late Howard Griffith, and his great-grandfather was the late Greenbury Griffith. His maternal grandfather was Charles Jones, of Ireland, who, espousing the cause of American independence, raised an Irish brigade, and fought gallantly in the American cause. Jan. 12, 1847, he married Sarah Newton Chiswell, a daughter of Capt. Wm. Chiswell, for many years county surveyor of Montgomery County. Her mother was Sarah, the daughter of Col. George W. F. Fletchall, of Montgomery County. There were four children by this marriage,—Charles G. and Julia, each married, and Georgiana and William, unmarried. On the 24th December, 1878, he married Angelica, the daughter of the late John Young, near Poolesville, in Montgomery County. He was educated at Goshen Seminary, under Prof. Wm. Musser. His family, on both sides of his ancestors, has been always connected with the Baptist Church. His maternal great-grandfather came from England to Providence Plantation with Roger Williams. He has represented his county in the Legislature in the sessions of 1860, and the extra session of 1861, and in 1876 and 1878. His politics have always been those of a Democrat, and so were those of his parents. By occupation he is a farmer and cattle broker, and he has met with very fair success in his business.

Dawsonville.—This place, named after the Dawson family, one of the oldest and most wealthy in the district, is four and a half miles from Boyd's Station. Pleasant Hill Lodge, No. 97, I. O. O. F., has just been removed here from Darnestown. Of Bethel and Seneca Baptist Churches, situated in the vicinity, Revs. Charles Yates, E. B. Wynn, Sr., and M. Urner are pastors. Dr. N. S. White is the physician; A. Williams, merchant; and H. C. Allnutt, postmaster.

The Allnutts are the largest landed proprietors in the district. Since the year 1750 the name has been identified with the history of what is now known as Montgomery County, and since that time too the land upon which the first of the name settled in the county has been in possession of his descendants. The progenitor of the family in Montgomery was James Allnutt, who came hither from Prince George's as early as, if not before, 1750, and made his home in the wilderness near the present site of Dawsonville. For his first wife he married Miss Lawrence, and for his second Miss Coberth. There were three sons by both marriages,—Lawrence, who married Eleanor Dawson; James, who married Belinda Dawson; and Jesse, who took Eleanor Chiswell to wife. The three brothers lived to be very old. James and Lawrence spent their lives near their native place. Jesse moved to Virginia, where he died at the age of eighty-seven. Lawrence (one of the three sons named) was grandfather to Benoni Allnutt, of Montgomery County, whose father (likewise named Lawrence) died in 1858. The surviving sons of Lawrence last mentioned are Nathan, Benjamin, and Benoni. Benoni Allnutt was born Jan. 2, 1835, about half a mile from his present home, upon a farm tract now owned by James N. and Benjamin W. Allnutt. Benoni resided at home until his father's death in 1858, and under the will received a farm, which now forms a portion of his present place. He took possession at once, and bestirred himself zealously to make his mark as a successful farmer. Nov. 20, 1860, he married Emily, daughter of Benoni Dawson, of Montgomery County. The Dawsons were known to Prince George's County before 1750, and in Montgomery County have been residents since about that time, for they came to this part from Prince George's about the time the Allnutts did. Thomas Dawson, great-grandfather to Mrs. Benoni Allnutt, was the first of the name to come hither. He located on property now owned and occupied by Americus Dawson, near Dawsonville, and owned by a Dawson since Thomas cleared it, about one hundred and thirty years ago. Thomas Dawson had two sons, Robert and Nicholas. The former volunteered, while yet a youth, as a soldier for the Revolutionary war. He was sorely wounded in action, but lived through the campaign and many years thereafter. The sword and scabbard worn by him during his service are still owned by his descendants. He had seven sons, of whom one was Dr. Benoni Dawson, a physician of high repute and father of Mrs. Benoni Allnutt. He married Sarah, daughter of Joseph W. Jones, who served through the Seminole war. He died in 1850, and his widow in 1878. Seven of their eleven children are living. The Jones' ancestry goes back to early times in Prince George's County, to which section Edward and Richard Jones emigrated from Wales early in America's history. It is worthy also of remark that Mrs. Benoni Allnutt boasts descent from Sir Isaac Newton; the first Newtons who came to Maryland being known to have been two children who were stolen by gypsies and carried from England to America.

Benoni Allnutt has devoted himself faithfully and to some purpose to the business of his life—farming. His possessions embrace one thousand valuable acres, lying within a model and handsomely improved farm. The success that has attended his efforts has come simply as the result of untiring industry and wisely, directed exertions. As a citizen, his influence is felt for good, and as a sterling member of the great army of useful workers, his example is acknowledged to be worthy of imitation. Mr. Allnutt's home is one of the finest in the county. His residence, built in 1871, was constructed of native stone, and is not only a handsome architectural specimen, but embodies all the comforts and conveniences that improved skill and refined taste could suggest.

Martinsburg.—This village is situated on "John's Delight," which was surveyed and granted to John Harriss, June 14, 1755. The merchants are Phillips Brothers and Reed & Offutt. James W. Reed is postmaster.

Dickerson.—This station is on the Metropolitan Branch Railroad, seventy-six miles from Baltimore and twenty from Rockville. Dr. W. D. Hellen is the physician, and W. H. Dickerson (after whom the place was named) is merchant and postmaster.

Monocacy.—This place is on the Monocacy River, near the crossing of the Metropolitan Railroad. Frederick Sellman is postmaster and merchant.

White's Ferry.—This ferry is on the Potomac River and Chesapeake and Ohio Canal. It is seven miles from Dickerson, fifteen from Rockville, and seventy from Baltimore. It takes its name from the old and well-known White family. L. C. White is postmaster, William Rollinson, ferryman, E. W. Mercer, merchant, and White & Wootton, grain dealers.

Edwards' Ferry.—This ferry is on the Potomac River, between Sycamore Landing and Ball's Bluffs. George W. Spates is postmaster.

Sellman's Station.—This station is on the Metropolitan Railroad, four miles west of Boyd's, nine east of the Point of Rocks, and one from Barnesville, for which it is the railway station. Samuel Darby is railroad and express agent.

School-Meetings.—In School District No. 2, on July 22, 1839, at a school-meeting held under the superintendence of manager Dr. Benoni Dawson, John Cross was elected president, and Elisha M. Swift clerk. The following trustees were then chosen: Colmore Williams, John Cross, and Jesse Viers. The meeting voted for an assessment on the district of eight hundred dollars, and that the new school-house be erected on the site of the previous one.

In District No. 6, on July 23d, at its meeting, Thomas G. Reid was elected president, and John A. Chiswell clerk. The trustees selected were Thomas Hall, Elias Spalding, John A. Chiswell.

In District No. 5, on July 15th, John Gott, Sr., presided at the meeting, and Nathan S. White was clerk. The trustees chosen were Joseph C. White, George Hoyle, and Nathan S. White.

On July 30th, in the Third District, Joseph J. W. Jones was president of the meeting, and Henry W. Talbott secretary. The trustees chosen were Joseph J. W. Jones, H. W. Talbott, and Richard A. Harding. The site selected for the school was on the land of Benjamin White, near a spring in the woods, and five hundred dollars for its construction was levied.

August 3d, in District No. 3, Abraham Hays was chosen president of the meeting, and John C. Gott clerk. The trustees elected were Thomas W. Hyde, William Baine, and John Gott. The former school-house near Barnesville was selected and ordered to be rented. Six hundred and fifty dollars was levied on the taxable property of the district.

In District No. 4, at the meeting of August 11th, James M. Dawson, Sr, was president, and J. M. Dawson, Jr., clerk. It adjourned without action to Aug. 9, 1840.

At a special meeting of District No. 8, on August 19th, its previous levy of six hundred and fifty dollars was reduced to three hundred and twenty-five dollars.

In District No. 1, at the meeting of August 20th, John P. C. Peter was president, and Thomas B. Dawson clerk. The trustees elected were John Dawson, William Dyson, and Lawrence Allnutt.

At a special meeting of District No. 2, on September 21st, the levy of previous meeting of eight hundred dollars was reduced to six hundred dollars, and at another meeting on October 2d, the old site for the school-house was selected by a vote of 18 to 2.

The school trustees and teachers for 1881 and 1882 are as follows:

Trustees.—No. 1, L. A. Darby, B. F. Dyson, J. H. Dawson; No. 2, Thomas T. Darby, Benoni Allnutt, Upton Darby; No. 3, R. W. Williams, D. J. Williard, W. T. Aud; No. 4, D. T. Ramsburg, Carson Hyatt, P. H. Kissburg; No. 5, W. T. Jones of I., Richard Stallings, W. A. Schaffer; No. 6, Leonidas Jones, Dr. Shreeve, B. F. White; No. 7, W. O. Sellman, S. S. Ways, Dr. V. Wood; No. 8, W. H. Cecil, John Phillmon, James Pearre; No. 9, J. C. White, John H. Lynch, W. W. White; No. 10, J. T. Norris, F. R. Hall, G. I. Ishemend; No. 11, Dr. W. D. Heten, Henry Sahall, P. H. Clements; No. 12, F. M. Griffith, A. Hempston, J. F. Waesche.

Teachers.—No. 1, T. W. Welsh, Dawsonville P. O.; No. 2, E. H. Darby, Darnestown P. O.; No. 3, Sallie Elgin, Poolesville P. O.; No. 4, J. E. Philips, Martinsburg P. O.; No. 5, J. P. Birnie, Martinsburg P. O.; No. 6, L. R. Gost, Dickerson P. O.; No. 7, Thomas Story, Barnesville P. O.; No. 8, J. H. Davis; No. 9, vacant; No. 10, C. R. Biggerly, Poolesville P. O.; No. 11, C. Pyles, Barnesville P. O.; No. 12, G. W. Feddall, Beallsville P. O.

There are four colored schools.

The magistrates are S. S. Hays, G. W. Chiswell, N. T. Talbott, S. George Donohoe.

ROCKVILLE DISTRICT, No. 4,

is bounded on the north by Darnestown District, northeast by Gaithersburg District, southeast by Cracklin District, east by Mechanicsville District, south by Berry and Bethesda Districts, and west by Great Falls District. Rock Creek flows through the southeast part of the district, and separates it from Mechanicsville and Berry Districts. Cabin John Creek, having its source near Rockville town, flows southwest into the Potomac. Watts' Branch, also having its head near Rockville, flows northwest into the Potomac. Crabb's and Mill Branches in the east empty into Rock Creek.

Under the act of 1821 the district was assigned the following metes and bounds:

Beginning at the mouth of Seneca, and running down Potomac, including the islands to the line of the territory of Columbia; then with said line to Rock Creek; then up said creek to Robertson's mill; then up the Bladensburg road until it intersects the line of the Second District at the lower end of the late Benjamin Ricketts' plantation; then with the line of the said Second District to Clopper's mill; then down Seneca to the beginning.

In 1878 part of the above territory on the north was taken to form Darnestown District, No. 6, and part on the south to form Bethesda. In 1880 a small part on the northeast was taken for the formation of Gaithersburg, and all its western limits taken to make Great Falls, No. 10. Thus from its original area one whole district has been created, and parts of three others.

Among the earliest settlers in the district were James Moore, Thomas and William Beall, Arthur Nelson, Edward Dawson, Joseph West, James Halmard, Caleb Litton, the Magruders, Viers, Graffs, and Watkinses.

Rockville, the county-seat, is situated in the eastern part of the district, on the Metropolitan Branch of the Baltimore and Ohio Railroad. It occupies a portion of a tract originally known as "Survey Exchange and New Exchange Enlarged," which was surveyed Dec. 20, 1721, for Arthur Nelson, and contained sixteen hundred and twenty acres.

When Montgomery County was created, Sept.

6, 1776, the town was a little hamlet, consisting of Charles Hungerford's tavern (kept subsequently by Leonard Davis), which is still standing, and occupied by Mrs. Susan Russell, whose grandfather, Joseph Wilson, built and owned it; the Anderson house, in which Miss Julia Anderson lives, and one or two others. The hamlet had no name until the erection of the county, when it was designated as Montgomery Court-House.

The first court was held at the house of Leonard Davis, the famous old Hungerford tavern, on the 20th of May, 1777.[1]

The old court-house was built shortly afterwards, and the first court held in it in 1779.

On Aug. 3, 1784, William Prather Williams purchased the land around the court-house, and immediately thereafter caused it to be laid off into streets and town-lots by Col. Archibald Orme, and called it Williamsburg. At the November session, 1801, of the Legislature an act was passed, which, after reciting that the titles to these lots were uncertain, because there was no record of the survey thereof made by Col. Orme, erected the place into a town called Rockville, and appointed commissioners to resurvey it. At the November session, 1802, there was a supplemental act passed, and in 1803 the commissioners caused the resurvey and a plan of the town to be made by William Smith, county surveyor. It was first meditated to call the town Wattsville, but Watts' Branch being regarded as too insignificant a stream, it was finally concluded to name it after its more pretentious neighbor, Rock Creek. The old Hungerford or Russell house is not only the oldest building in the place, but also from its associations the object of greatest interest to the antiquary. Mrs. Richard Wootton, a sister-in-law of Thomas Sprigg Wootton, who moved the erection of the county, danced in it at a ball given more than one hundred and ten years ago.[2]

The first addition to Rockville lies principally to the north and northward of the town, and is part of "Resurvey on Valentine's Garden Enlarged," which was surveyed April 10, 1753, for Henry Wright Crabb for two thousand and eighty-five acres. On March 4, 1873, the second addition was made to the town, and embraces that part recently laid out in the vicinity of the railroad depot and fair grounds. This new section is on "Hammond's Addition," which was surveyed for John Hammond, Nov. 10, 1743, and contained three hundred acres. The present court-house was erected about 1840. The first jail stood where Mrs. Almoney resides, nearly opposite the court-house, and the second on the present site of Rabbit's livery-stable.

The nearest mill was on Watts' Creek, and was owned by Mr. Perry, afterwards by Strove & Perry, then by Mr. Braddock, and was on the property now owned by Mr. Stonestreet. The oldest native inhabitant is George R. Braddock, deputy clerk of the court, who was born in 1818, in the house now occupied by Agnes Noland. The earliest merchant remembered was a Mr. Milsted, who was followed by John Braddock, who kept a store where Mrs. Bowie's boarding-school now stands. Subsequent storekeepers were Mr. Higgins and Mr. Adamson. John Lodge kept a tavern near the property now occupied by Fields & Rabbit, and was succeeded by William Sands. Dr. James Anderson was one of the earliest physicians. Benjamin S. Forrest was probably the oldest resident attorney. The first blacksmith's shop was that of William Braddock, who also kept a store where Dawson's store now stands. One of the earliest carpenters was Francis Kidwell, who lived on the site of the Montgomery Hotel, and built the court-house.[3]

The following list of lot-owners in Rockville (then called Williamsburg) in 1793 is taken from the assessment books:

Allen Bowie, 1 House and lott.
Enoch Beeson, 1 House and lott.
John Sutton Crawford, 2 unimproved lotts; 1 House and lott.
Walter Clagett, 1 unimproved lott.
Bryan Dayley, 1 House and lott.
Hezekiah Ford, 1 House and lott.
Dr. Joseph Hall, 1 House and lott.
Edward Harding, 1 House and lott.
Philip Jenkins, 2 Houses and lotts; 2 unimproved lotts.
John Lyons, 1 unimproved lott.

---

[1] Present, the worshipful Charles Jones, Samuel W. Magruder, Elisha Williams, William Deakins, Richard Thompson, James Offutt, and Edward Burgess; Brook Beall, clerk, and Clement Beall, sheriff.

[2] Address of T. Anderson, Esq., at Montgomery County Centennial Celebration.

[3] The glorious event of peace and independence was celebrated at the court-house, April 13, 1783, by eighty ladies and gentlemen, who participated in an elegant dinner. The "Hessian Band" from Frederick Town was in attendance. The following toasts were drank: 1. The United States in Congress; 2. Gen. Washington and the Northern Army; 3. Gen. Greene and the intrepid officers and soldiers of the Southern Army; 4. His Most Christian Majesty and the Queen and Royal Family of France; 5. Perpetual alliance and mutual good offices between France and America; 6. The Count De Rochambeau; 7. Marquis De Lafayette; 8. Chevalier De la Luzerne; 9. The Ministers of France and America at Paris; 10. Governor Paca and the State of Maryland; 11. The shades of those gallant heroes who nobly fell in defense of American liberty; 12. May literature, philosophy, and all the sciences meet with every encouragement from the Legislature of Maryland; 13. The truly virtuous and patriotic ladies of America, who rejected luxuries, and even the conveniences of life, for the salvation of their country.

Wm. Magrath, 1 House and lott.
Honore Martin, 2 Houses and lotts; 4 improved lotts.
Richard Morgan, 1 House and lott.
Nicholas Mudd, 2 unimproved lotts.
Francis Magruder, 1 unimproved lott.
Wm. Oneale, Sr., 5 unimproved lotts.
Caleb Summers, 1 House and lott; ½ lott improved.
John L. Summers, 2 one-half lotts and Houses; 1 improved lott; 2 unimproved.
Joseph Wilson, of J., 1 House and lott.
Joseph Willson (heirs), 1 House and lott; 2 unimproved lotts.
Wm. P. Williams, 13 unimproved lotts.
Thos. O. Williams, 11 unimproved lotts.
Elisha O. Williams, 11 unimproved lotts.
Edward O. Williams, 11 unimproved lotts.

The building of the Baltimore and Ohio Railroad gave a new impetus to the business prosperity and progress at Rockville, and in 1860 it was incorporated by the General Assembly and raised to the dignity of a city. As the records of the corporation prior to 1864 have been destroyed, it is therefore impossible to give the officers during that period.

The principal officers of Rockville from 1864 to 1881 have been as follows:

1864.—W. Viers Bouic, president, John H. Higgins, and M. Green; M. Morgan, clerk; and John B. Miller, bailiff.
1865.—William Viers Bouic, president; James W. Campbell, George Peter, commissioners; M. Morgan, clerk; and Melchisideck Green, chief bailiff.
1866.—Melchisideck Green, president; David H. Bouic, John H. Higgins, commissioners; M. Morgan, clerk; and Henry Lyday, chief bailiff.
1867.—William V. Bouic, president; George Peter, Richard M. Williams, commissioners; James F. Braddock, chief bailiff; and M. Morgan, clerk. Upon the resignation of Mr. Peter, O. Z. Muncaster was elected to the board.
1868.—John R. Miller, John H. Higgins, R. M. Williams, commissioners; Thomas G. Peddecord, chief bailiff; J. Davis, Jr., clerk.
1869.—M. Field, president; E. B. Prettyman, M. Green, commissioners; S. T. Mullican, chief bailiff; and R. S. Patterson, clerk.
1870.—M. Field, president; E. B. Prettyman, M. Green, commissioners; G. W. Dore, chief bailiff; and R. S. Patterson, clerk.
1871.—Same re-elected.
1872.—W. Viers Bouic, president; E. B. Prettyman, M. Green, commissioners; William Connell, chief bailiff; and R. S. Patterson, clerk.
1873.—W. Viers Bouic, president; Reuben A. Bagley, M. Green, commissioners; R. S. Patterson, clerk. James Bixton was elected chief bailiff, but declined, and William Connell was appointed to fill the place.
1874.—W. Viers Bouic, president; Reuben A. Bagley, M. Green, commissioners; R. S. Patterson, clerk; and William O. Kingsbury, chief bailiff.
1875.—Same re-elected.
1876.—W. Viers Bouic, president; M. Green, S. C. Jones, commissioners; H. W. Talbott, clerk; and James T. West, chief bailiff.
1877.—W. Viers Bouic, president; M. Green, S. C. Jones, commissioners; Henry Viete, chief bailiff; H. W. Talbott, clerk.
1878.—W. Viers Bouic, president; M. Green, J. P. Biggs, commissioners; H. W. Talbott, clerk; and Thomas F. Monday, chief bailiff.
1879.—Same re-elected.
1880.—W. Viers Bouic, who resigned, and was succeeded by N. D. Offutt, president; M. Green, Charles E. Sommers, commissioners; H. W. Talbott, clerk; and William O. Kingsbury, chief bailiff.
1881.—The present officers, Charles Sommers, N. D. Offutt, president, M. Green, commissioners; Mr. Kingsbury and Mr. Talbott, clerk and bailiff respectively.

Rockville boasts no less than three excellent local journals,—the Montgomery *Advocate*, the *Independent Montgomerian*, and the Montgomery County *Sentinel*.

The Advocate was established in November, 1872, by William B. Green, who published it until 1875, when he sold the paper and office to William Brewer. In 1879, Albert J. Almoney became associated with Mr. Brewer in its publication as editor and publisher. The *Advocate* is a neat four-page paper of thirty-two columns, edited with unusual ability. Special prominence is given to local news, in the collection of which it employs an able corps of correspondents in all sections of the county. It is a stanch supporter of the Democratic party.

The Independent Montgomerian was established by William B. and Walter O. Green in September, 1880, and on Saturday, Sept. 10, 1881, it entered on its second volume. It is a four-page sheet of thirty-six columns, and its motto, "Partiality to none, justice to all," indicates the broad principles upon which it is conducted. It is ably edited, and its columns are devoted largely to local news from every part of the county. W. B. Green was formerly of the Montgomery *Advocate*.

The Montgomery County Sentinel was established Aug. 11, 1855, by Matthew Fields, sheriff of the county. In the spring of 1864, Mr. Fields was arrested by the United States military authorities, and released in June following. During the three months of his arrest and imprisonment the paper was not published. George R. Braddock for a short time was its editor. Mr. Fields died in August, 1871. The paper is still owned by his widow, and is ably conducted by her son, William Fields. It is an excellent local journal, and a firm advocate of Democratic principles.

Rockville Journal and Maryland Journal.—The Rockville *Journal* was in January, 1836, edited by M. Stewart, who subsequently changed its name to the *Maryland Journal*. In 1855 the *Journal* was edited by Mr. Parker, and later managed and controlled by Kilgour, Wood & Co., and subsequently, by Angel & Gibbs. It suspended just before the late civil war. It was a Whig, and afterwards an American paper.

Mizpah Lodge, No. 144, A. F. and A. M.—This lodge was instituted in February, 1869. Its Worshipful Masters have been in the following order: Thomas J. Peddicord, Hattersly W. Talbott, Spencer C. Jones, E. Barrett Prettyman, William Brewer, Hattersly W. Talbott. The following were the charter members, and the lodges to which they originally belonged:

Thomas J. Peddicord, Patmos, No. 70, Md.; Hattersly W. Talbott, Patmos, No. 70, Md.; Spencer C. Jones, Rockingham Union, No. 27, Va.; Thomas N. Conrad, Patmos, No. 189, Va.; E. Barrett Prettyman, Olney, No. 141, Md.; Rev. Samuel R. White, Dawson, No. 16, D. C.; William Brewer, Olney, No. 141, Md.; James Anderson, Rockingham Union, No. 27, Va.

At the first meeting of the lodge for work, on Feb. 23, 1869, the following persons were initiated: Cooke D. Luckett, Reuben A. Bogley, Edward E. Stonestreet, M.D., and Thomas Anderson, all of whom in the following March were raised to the degree of a Master Mason. Spencer C. Jones was lodge secretary from its organization until July, 1881, when D. F. Owens was elected. The officers for the quarter beginning July 1, 1881, were:

W. M., Hattersly W. Talbott; S. W., William B. Green; J. W., Isaac R. Maus; Sec., Daniel F. Owens; Treas., Edward E. Stonestreet.

The lodge has a membership of forty-three, and meets every other Tuesday evening at its hall in the public-school building.
Richard G. White, who received the Master's degree March 19, 1872, died Jan. 3, 1879, and Charles M. Keys, who was admitted by demit from New Jerusalem Lodge, No. 9, D. C. In the winter of 1881 the lodge was entered by burglars, who stole the lodge jewels, made of silver, and valued at one hundred and fifty dollars.

Prince George P. E. Parish.—On the 12th of April, 1712, it was ordered by the vestry of St. John's Parish that the Rev. J. Frazer preach in the East Branch Hundred once a month on Sunday. This was the hundred west of the Eastern Branch of the Potomac, and extended to the Paint Branch. This appears to have been the beginning of what was afterwards known as Rock Creek Church. Mr. Frazer's monthly services continued until 1719, when steps were taken towards building a chapel of ease. At the request of the inhabitants of Eastern Branch and Rock Creek Hundreds, Mr. Frazer appointed Sept. 8, 1719, for them to meet and make choice of a site and contribute towards the erection of a chapel. Accordingly, twenty-seven persons assembled, and unanimously selected a place " near James Keas', on John Cash's or Capt. Beall's land." The subscriptions were: in tobacco, John Bradford, 1000 pounds; William Smith, 400; George Bussy, 300; Thomas Stump, 250; L. Morgan, 250; William Harbine, 250; James Hook, 200; Richard Hooker, 200; John Henerick, 100; Walter Evans, 300; Matthew Markland, 200; and John Reed, 100,—making 3550 pounds. In money, " W. F." subscribed £3; Thomas Lucas, £2; William Blatterly, £1 10s.; Henry Thickpenny, £15; William Thompson, Isaac Harden, Leonard Howell, Groves Tomlin, John Harden, John Chilton, James Moor, Thomas Wilson, each £1; William Williams, Philip Evans, and Benjamin Thrasher, 10s. each,—in all, £17 5s. Subsequently 800 pounds of tobacco were subscribed, and £27 15s., and John Bradford gave 100 acres of land, on which the chapel was erected. On the 10th of February, 1724, the vestry ordered 1000 pounds of tobacco for the repair of the church. This proves that a chapel had been built, and so long before that it needed repairing. In 1726 St. John's Parish was divided: Piscataway and New Scotland Hundreds, containing 791 taxables, yielding 31,640 pounds of tobacco, were constituted St. John's Parish, and the Eastern Branch, Rock Creek, and Potomac Hundreds, having 791 taxables, yielding 21,800 pounds of tobacco, were constituted a new parish, named Prince George Parish, and the chapel at Rock Creek was made the parish church for the new parish. The act creating the new parish was passed by the General Assembly in July, 1726, and it was provided that the division should go into effect from and after " the fourth Tuesday of November next following." The parish embraced all the country northwest of a line " beginning with the mouth of the Eastern Branch of the Potomac, and running up therewith to the fork thereof, and thence continuing the course of the East Branch to its head, and by a straight line until it strikes the Patuxent River."

It therefore comprised all the territory now embraced in Montgomery, Frederick, and Washington Counties, part of Carroll County, and part of the District of Columbia. It was, however, a frontier parish, and had not more than two thousand four hundred inhabitants. On the 3d of December, 1826, the freeholders of the parish came together at the parish church at Rock Creek, afterwards known as St. Paul's, and chose a vestry, as follows: Nathaniel Wickham, John Flint, John Powell, Joseph Chew, James Holmes, and John Pritchard. Caleb Lutton and William Harbin were elected church-wardens, and William Jackson, register. Mr. Frazer, whose efforts had done so much towards building up the church, and who seems to have been an industrious, conscientious man, terminated his connection with the Rock Creek Church in 1726, and restricted himself to St.

John's Parish. On the 29th of December, 1726, the Rev. George Murdoch, a native of Prince George's County, received his appointment as rector of Prince George Parish. On Sunday, January 8th following, he held his first service. On the next Tuesday the vestry met and received his letters of induction from Governor Charles Calvert.

Mr. Murdoch was ordained deacon at St. Paul's Cathedral, London, Feb. 20, 1724, by Dr. Gibson, then Bishop of London, and priest by the same bishop, February 29th of the same year, in the royal chapel of St. James'. At the time of his ordination he was a married man, and had a family. After returning to this country he went to Virginia and had a parish there, probably St. James', Northam, Goochland Co. On the same day on which he was received as rector the vestry of Rock Creek Church engaged Mr. George Beall to build a "vestry house," sixteen feet by twelve, having eight feet pitch, for two thousand five hundred pounds of tobacco, and to put a plank floor in the church, which before had been without one. On the 3d of April the vestry consented that Mr. Murdoch should preach every third Sunday in some convenient place to the upper inhabitants of the parish. This was probably not far from the present town of Rockville, and the building is said to have stood on the present site of the graveyard, near the former residence of the late Judge R. J. Bowie.

On the 28th of May the vestry sent for a large folio Bible and a Book of Common Prayer. On the 1st of August they procured a record book for registering their proceedings, and ordered a well to be dug and fourteen pews to be put up. In February, 1728, certain residents of the upper portion of the parish petitioned the Governor and Council for permission to fix the site of the proposed new church, alleging that they had not been properly treated by the vestry with regard to the matter. The petition was granted and a meeting of the freeholders was held, and it was decided that the chapel at Rock Creek was to be the parish church. The subscribers for building the proposed chapel in the upper part of the parish were Joseph West, Thos. Sheppard, John West, John Rogers, William Smith, Ignatius Perrot, Benjamin Thrasher, Nathaniel Wickham, Sr., Luke Barnard, John Nelson, Jeremiah Plomer, Bryan Kelly, Samuel Pottinger, James Edmondson, Nathaniel Wickham, Jr., Stephen Hampton, Caleb Lytton, Joseph Gold, Arthur Nelson, Robert Pottinger, Wm. West, Thomas Thompson, William Sheppard, Jeremiah Dickinson, Samuel Richards, Charles Perry. On the 7th of November, 1738, Thomas Williams offered two acres of land upon which to build a chapel of ease, and it was accepted. The land was situated one mile east of Rockville. A chapel was evidently erected upon it some time prior to November, 1743, for under that date we find that the vestry agreed to petition the court for an assignment of twelve pence per poll towards building a new church and defraying parish charges. In the following year an act was passed by the General Assembly constituting the chapel a chapel of ease and the former church the parish church. The church near Rockville was uniformly termed Rock Creek Chapel, and the parish church was denominated Rock Creek Church, both being near Rock Creek, though twelve miles apart.

At a meeting of the vestry on the 11th of April, 1748, it was determined that Rock Creek chapel was to have divine service every other Sunday, and that the services at Paint chapel should be discontinued.

Paint chapel stood on the boundary line which now divides Montgomery from Prince George's County and not far from the Patuxent. Hence it was often called "Paint Chapel on the Patuxent." It was erected, not by the public funds, but by private contributions, and there is no record as to when it was built. Up to 1748 occasional services were held there, but, as we have seen, they were discontinued in favor of Rock Creek chapel. In 1748 Frederick County was created, and the parish of Prince George embraced the whole of the new county and a portion of Prince George's County. In 1749 Rev. Richard Hartwell assisted Mr. Murdoch as curate. In 1750, for the accommodation of the increasing congregation at the Rock Creek chapel, a gallery was built. Early in 1751 mention is made of the Rev. Moses Tabbs, curate. In the following year Mr. Tabbs became the rector of William and Mary Parish, St. Mary's County. There is also a record in 1751 of the death of Mr. Alexander Magruder, a prominent vestryman. Several improvements were made at the chapel in the same year, such as an addition to the pulpit, the removal of the desk, etc. In 1756 the vestry had imposed on them the duty of returning to the Governor a list of the bachelors in the parish. A law had been passed by the General Assembly taxing all bachelors; the tax being designed to assist in raising money for the French and Indian war. Those bachelors worth three hundred pounds and over were taxed twenty shillings, and those worth over one hundred pounds and under three hundred pounds, five shillings. This tax was continued for six consecutive years.

The following is a list of the bachelors returned by the vestry, with their residences as far as known, valuation of property, and the years in which they were taxed:

Hugh Riley, Rock Creek, £300; 1756.
William Wallis, Jr., £200; 1756, 1757.
William Offutt (3), Falls of Potomac, £350; 1756.
Nathaniel Magruder, Inspector, Rock Creek, £350; 1756, 1757.
Robert Peters, Georgetown, £300; 1756, 1757, 1758, 1759, 1760, 1761, 1762.
Anthony Holmead, north of Rock Creek, £1000; 1756, 1757, 1758, 1759, 1760, 1761.
Walter Evans, Eastern Branch Ferry, £300; 1756, 1757, 1758, 1759, 1760, 1761, 1762.
Barton Lucas, Eastern Branch Ferry, £150; 1756 (300), 1757, 1762.
James Colmore, Paint Branch, £500; 1756, 1757, 1758, 1759, 1760, 1761, 1762.
William Needham, £700; 1756, 1757, 1758, 1759.
Ludwick Davis, head of Seneca, £300; 1756, 1758, 1759, 1760.
Robert Beall, of James, North West Branch, £140; 1756, 1757, 1758, 1759, 1760, 1761, 1762.
Alexander Beall, of James, North West Branch, £150; 1756, 1757, 1758, 1759, 1760 (200), 1761, 1762.
James Brooke, Jr., B's mile, £300; 1756, 1757, 1759 (500).
Joseph Perry, North West Branch, £200; 1756.
John Riggs, Hallery River, £100; 1756, 1757, 1758, 1759, 1760 (300).
Zach. Offutt, Great Falls, £100; 1756, 1757, 1758, 1759, 1760, 1761, 1762.
Robert Mundell, Georgetown, £300; 1756, 1757.
Arch^d Orme, Rock Creek, £300; 1756, 1757, 1758, 1759, 1760, 1761, 1762.
Thomas Offutt, Great Falls, £300; 1757, 1758, 1759, 1761.
Dawson Cash, East Branch, £100; 1757, 1758, 1759.
Roger Brooke, Hallery River, £100; 1757.
Jno. Murdock, Lower Falls, £1000; 1757, 1758, 1759, 1760.
Thomas Davis, on Seneca, £100; 1757.
Sam Perry, of Ignatius, £100; 1757, 1758.
Thomas Riggs, Hallery River, £100; 1758, 1759 (200), 1760, 1761, 1762.
Benj. Adams, £100; 1758.
Wm. Queen, £100; 1758, 1759.
Charles Carroll, £2000; 1758.
Stephen Garbo, R. Creek, £100; 1758.
Alexander Hall, £100; 1758, 1759, 1760, 1761, 1762.
Nathl Pigman, £100; 1758.
John Flint, Goose Creek, £100; 1759, 1760, 1761.
Thomas Lansdale, £300; 1759, 1760, 1761, 1762.
Dr. Comshot, £100; 1759.
S. W. A. G. Cornish, £100; 1760, 1761, 1762.
Aaron Lanham, Paint Creek, £100; 1760, 1761, 1762.
Wm. Murphy, Great Falls, £300; 1760.
Jas. Wallace, £100; 1761.
Thos. Conn, £500; 1761, 1762.
Marsen Duvall, Rock Creek, £500; 1761.
Clement Beall, £300; 1761, 1762.
John Wilcox, on Rock Creek, £100; 1761.
Thomas Johns, £1000; 1761, 1762.
John Watson, Georgetown, £300; 1761, 1762.
Richard Brooke, Hallery River, £500; 1761, 1762.
Richard Cheney, £300; 1761, 1762.
Rev. A. Williamson, £300; 1762.
Ephraim Davis, £300; 1762.
Wm. Lynn, £100; 1762.
E. Jenkins, £100; 1762.
Alexander Cash, £100; 1762.
Thomas Windham, £100; 1762.

In 1757 the following petition from King George and Prince George Parishes was presented to the Governor, praying the erection of a new parish:

"*To his Excellency Horatio Sharpe, Esq., Governor and Commander-in-chief on and over the Province of Maryland, and to the Honorable the upper and lower houses of Assembly.*

"The humble petition of Sundry of the Freeholders of King George's and Prince George's parishes most humbly shewith that they live at so great a distance from the said parish churches that they nor their families cannot go to hear divine service, and that the per pole of the two parishes is sufficient to maintain three ministers; therefore your humble petitioners pray that your honors will take it into your pius consideration and create a parish out of the two above mentioned, according to the bounds specified below, after the death of either of the present incumbents, the Tobacco arising in that part of the parish may be applied towards the building of a church in the parish erected, and your humble petitioners as in duty bound will ever pray, &c.

"The bounds of   parish to include the north part of King George's parish and the south part of Prince George's parish, bounded with the north side of the Eastern Branch from the north thereof unto the ferry thereon, and with the road that leads from thence to the westernmost bounds of Queen Anne's parish, with the bounds thereof northward unto Patuxent river, and with the said river westward unto a bridge thereon near Peter Murphy's; then with a straight line to northeast main fork of the Fall's branch, and with the said branch into Potomack river, and with the said river to the north of the Eastern branch. We also pray that the place for the churchstand may be [determined] by the freeholders of the said parish, and as may be appointed for that purpose, and at the dwelling-house of Mr. William Selby's, being near the centre of the parish.

"Edward E. Brownen, Jr., Chrst. C. Hyatt, Leonard Wayman, Sr., Leonard Wayman, Jr., Richard Lansdale, James Crow, James Wallace, William Wallace, William Hall, Saml Prather, Richard Isaac, Henry Culver, Richard Welsh, Johnson T. Turner, Weaver B. Barnes, Benoni Fowler, Jonah Elson, Lewis Duvall, Shadrach Turner, Thomas Welsh, Jas. Walker, Wm. Wilson Selby, Philip Yocker, Seth Hyatt, Thomas Mobley, Thomas Jack, Hez^k Magruder, Joseph Jones, Charles Jones, John Tyson, John Cuthwright, John Caster, John Ray, Jr., Wm. Foam, Jr., Thos. Hoskinson, F. . . . , Jas. Ramsey, Peregrine May, . . . Wm. Brown, John Flint, Daniel Lewis, Hugh Thomas, Francis Edwards, John Smith Prather, Thomas Catterall, Jas. O. M   , Jeremiah Prather, Ar. . . . , William Beall, John . . . Trundle, . . . Bunnet, . . . Thomas Lucas, Jr., John Ray, Thos. Nichols, Jr., Simon Nichols, Geo. Beall, Jr."

The petition was not granted.

A similar petition was presented in 1758, but the Governor did not lay it before the General Assembly. This petition was as follows:

"*To His Excellency Hon^o Sharpe, Esq., Governor and Commander in chief on and over the Province of Maryland, and the Honble the Upper and Lower Houses of Assembly:*

"The petition of the vestrymen, church wardens, and freeholders of Prince George Parish, in Frederick County, sheweth—

"That the parish is so extensive, which makes it so inconvenient, that the chief or greatest part of the inhabitants thereof can but very seldom repair to public worship to the great discouragement of religion and virtue, and we therefore take leave, as the said parish is now very sufficient to support two ministers, to pray your honors will make an act to divide the said parish by a line drawn from the lower falls of Potomack to William Richardson's bridge that crosses Patuxent River by said Richardson's dwelling plantation, or at any other place your honors or your greater wisdom may think more convenient, and your petitioners in duty bound will pray.

"Nathan Magruder, Robert Owen, James White, Samuel Magruder, Jr., Sam. Owen, Hezekiah Magruder, William Fee, Edward Gaither, Zadock Magruder, James Beall, S.N., Samuel White, Jr., William Spiers, Sr., Edward Owen, Sr., Richard Gattrall, Francis Gattrall, John Holmes, Richard Thrads, Daniel Williams, Edward Lowry, Nathan Holland, William Holland, Edward Owen, Jr., Basil Adams, Samuel West, Willi Dent, John Banks, Benj. Holland, Wm. Rickette, James Perry, Nathaniel Offutt, Philip Casey, James Casey, Ralph Holt, Henry Burgess, Thomas Davis, Robert Beall, S.N., Joseph West, Sr., Benj. Kelley, John Jones, John West, Benj. West, William Williams, Sr., William Davis, Sr., George Rea, Wm. Brown, John Hopkins, James Hopkins, Richard Hopkins, Wm. Pritchett, John Pritchett, Michael Carter, Kensey Gittings, William Offutt (3), Thos. Offutt, Simon Nicholls, Benj. Perrey, Edward Doring, Thom. Nicholls, Sr., Joshua Busey, James Burnes, Tho. Harris, Wm. Hall, John Maddox, Alex. Jackson, Robt. Buchan, Wm. Peerce, Arch^d Orme, Chas. Jones, Numan Tannehill, Hugh Tomlinson, Thos. Dowden, Edw. V. Harven, Jere. M. Macknear, Wm. Young, Geo. Beall, Geo. Beall, Jr., Nathaniel Magruder, R^d Thompson, Joseph Belt, Josi Beall, Jno. Gibson, Robert Peter, John Crossthwaite, John Kindrick, John Baptist Lovelis, Edm. Riggs, Henry Claggett, James Roberts, Wm. Boyd, Thomas Cleland, Elisha Williams, William Davis, John Cook, Josiah Jones, Wm. Jones, Joseph Glaze, John Swann, Richard Anderson, Jas. T. Turbley, Nichs. Baker, Clementius Baker, John Cheshire, Burtch Cheshire, Richard Allison, Peregrine Mackness, Jr., James Ray, Frances Wodard, Hugh Wilson, Thomas Trunal, James Tomlinson, James Evens, Reynolds Allen, Zach. White, Dawsen Cash, John Cash, John Wight, Henry Duly, John Ray, Sr., Clement Beale, John Brown, Thomas Cramphin, John Beale, Thomas Pearce, John Clagett, Walter S. Greenfield, John Briscoe, Thomas Thomas, John Sniffords, Walter Evans, Jeremiah Riley, Eliphas Riley, David Burns, John Maclean, Norman Riley, John Ray, Jr., John Hearbin, John Ferguson, Vachel Medcalfe, Osburn Talburt, Jr., James Wallace, Jr., Richard Bowes, Thomas Allison, Benj. Allison, Leonard Johnson, Ezl. O'Neall, James Mack, Anthony Holmead, Samuel Duvall."

In May, 1761, a petition was presented to the Governor and Assembly for a levy on the taxables of the parish for a new chapel on the branch of the Patuxent known as Hawling's River. This would seem to indicate that there was a chapel already there. Thus, therefore, there were four Episcopal Churches within the limits of the present county of Montgomery prior to 1761. The petition is as follows:

"*To His Excellency Hon^o Sharpe, Esq., Governor and Commander in chief in and over the province of Maryland, and To the Hon^l the Upper and lower Houses of Assembly at this time convened:*

"The petition of the vestry and inhabitants of Prince George parish, in Frederick and Prince George County, humbly shewith, that the parishoners residing in and upon the neighborhood of a Branch of the Patuxent, commonly called Hawlings river, are in the greatest want of a chapel of Ease.

"This petition, therefore, most humbly prayeth that his Excl^n and the Hon^l the Upper and Lower Houses of Assembly would be graciously pleased to pass an act to empower Frederick and Prince George Counties to levy upon the taxable inhabitants of Prince George parish such sum of money as to their Honors it may appear sufficient for erecting a new chapel, to be located upon or near the branch of the Patuxent commonly called Hawlings river, and his Excl^o and their Honors petitioners as in duty bound shall ever pray.

"Signed by Order of the Vestry . . . May . . . 1761, pr.

"SIMON NICHOLS, *Regr.*

"Robert Lemar, William Waters, William Lucas, Thomas Riggs, Peter Pierce, Elisha Riggs, Richard Fitzgerald, Robert Owen, John Musgrove, Ru Thranh, David Lynn, David Carlisle, Jr., Aquila Standford, Charles Case, Michael Ashfordouden, William Holland, Arnold Holland, Ephraim Davis, John Riggs, Samuel Brown, John Acred, Richard Macklepsh, Abel Acred, Chas. Calihorn, Edward Gaither, Christopher Hyat, John Prather, Zach^a Spiers, Henry Gaither, Jr., Nathaniel Ward, Lewis Duvall, Sr., John Pierce Duvall, Aquila Duvall, Edward Crow, Samuel Farmer, John Owen, Robert Daw, James Sargent, Snowden Sargent, Mathew Pigman, Daniel Williams, Calder Hayman, Thomas Davis, Lodowick Davis, John Forrest Davis, William Phillips, Charles Penn, Edward Penn, Benjamin Gaither, Henry Lecke, Stephen Gatherill, John Holland, Henry Lecke, Jr., Joseph Lecke, George Gue, Thomas Gartherill, Josias Holland, Frances Gartherill, Aaron Gartherill, Benjamin Darby, George Darby, Thomas Johnson, William Johnson, Edward Chambey, William Richardson, William Mace, Richard Clarke, George Bowman, Uriah Virgen, John Lanham, Valentine Felton, John Barns, Jacob Barns, Nathan Holland, Samuel White, Joseph Richardson, Robert Kendall, James Kendall, Gerd^d Briscoe, Sam. Richardson, Hugh Thomas, Richard Berry, Henry Gaither, Sr., Frederick Bowman, Darby Murphy."

In 1758, Rev. Thomas Johnson was Mr. Murdoch's curate, probably succeeding Mr. Tabbs. Mr. Johnson left in 1759, and was succeeded by the Rev. Clement Brooke. Mr. Murdoch died in February, 1761, after a ministry of thirty years. Some of his descendants still reside in Montgomery County, and one of them married the Hon. Richard Potts, of Frederick. He is said to have reached the age of nearly ninety years. Rev. Alexander Williamson was temporarily appointed curate in his stead. Mr. Williamson was the son of the Rev. James Williamson, of All Saints' Parish, Frederick County. At the end of a year he was inducted as rector of the parish. In the preceding year Edward Owen, William Dent, William Williams, and H. W. Crabb built a gallery in the new part of Rock Creek chapel, which was confirmed to their use and as their property.

In 1764 it was agreed that a vestry-house should be built at Rock Creek Chapel. About 1767 the Rev. Joseph Thiekeld came to the parish from Virginia and lived at Rock Creek, but it does not appear that he was employed in any clerical capacity. On the 24th of March, 1767, it was agreed to erect a third addition to Rock Creek chapel. This was a structure twenty feet square to be added in front. A petition was also presented to the General Assembly for permission to build a brick church. In 1769 this petition was repeated, and in the following year twenty-six pews were ordered to be built in Rock Creek chapel. Thus far, however, they were unable to procure the consent of the State government to the erection of the proposed brick church. On the 10th of October, 1771, Daniel, of St. Thomas Jenifer, delivered a petition from the Upper to the Lower House, praying that the rector, vestry, and freeholders of Prince George Parish be empowered to levy ninety-six thousand pounds of tobacco for building a new church at the place where the old church then stood. A bill was prepared and passed both houses granting the subject matter of the petition, but the vestry did not immediately proceed to put it into execution. A bill subsequently passed the Assembly for the division of Prince George's County, but it does not appear to have been carried into effect.

Rev. John Bowie, a native of Maryland, having received orders, was licensed by the Bishop of London on the 28th of July, 1771, and on his return to this country became curate for Mr. Williamson. In 1772, Mr. Williamson's health failed, and he was forced to sail for Barbadoes. Mr. Bowie left the parish soon after, and in 1773 was appointed to a parish in Worcester County. Having signified his loyalty to the Crown, though afterwards an earnest sympathizer with the cause of his fellow-citizens, he was subjected to much harsh treatment at the hands of the revolutionists, but was finally permitted to reside in Montgomery County with his brother, Allen Bowie, ancestor of Hon. A. Bowie Davis, and afterwards officiated as rector in Worcester, Dorchester, and Talbot Counties. In 1774 the vestry advertised for contractors to erect a new church in place of the old one. The edifice was to be fifty feet square, with a pitch of twenty-four feet. The walls were to be twenty-two inches thick in the first story and eighteen in the second. The foundation was to be of stone, three feet thick, and the roof to be of cypress shingles. The next curate was the Rev. Thomas Read, a native of Matthews County, Va. Mr. Read was ordained and licensed by the Bishop of London, and soon after his return to America became the assistant of Mr. Williamson. He remained in this capacity until 1776, when the church livings were abolished by the provisional government of the Revolution. One year later he became the rector of St. Ann's, Annapolis.

Mr. Williamson, rector of Prince George Parish, retired about the same time to his estate, about five miles above Georgetown, where, being a man of wealth, he built a handsome residence, which afterwards fell into the possession of Judge Dunlop, who lived there for a number of years. About 1777, Mr. Read left Annapolis and returned to Prince George Parish. On the 14th of October, 1779, he married Sarah Magruder, of Montgomery County, daughter of Samuel Wade and Lucy Magruder. The walls of the church at Rock Creek were completed and the roof finished prior to 1775, but the Revolution coming on work was suspended, and the building remained in an uncompleted state for a number of years.

In the *Maryland Journal* of June 27, 1780, the following notice appeared:

"The subscribers, appointed by the contributors for the purpose of employing a clergyman of the Protestant Church to officiate at Rock Creek Church, in Montgomery County, give notice that a very genteel salary will be given to any gentleman of that profession by application to Jos. Wilson, Elias Harding, Thomas Johns, Thomas Cramphin, Jr., Richard Wootton, James Perry, Elijah O. Williams, *Trustees*."

In the Diocesan Convention of 1789 the parish was represented by the rector, Mr. Read, and by Mr. Deakins as lay delegate. In the following year Mr. Read was made a member of the standing committee of the diocese. In 1790, Mr. Read's parish had a population of fifteen thousand and four places of public worship. In August, 1790, the vestry proposed building a chapel where the old Rock Creek chapel stood.

In 1794 Prince George Parish was divided, and all the territory lying within the boundaries of the District of Columbia was constituted a separate parish called Washington Parish. Rock Creek, or St. Paul's Church, thus fell into the District of Columbia, together with all the territory lying between the northern boundary of Washington City and the northern boundary of the District of Columbia. About 1795, Rev. Joseph Jackson, a native of the North of England, became the assistant for Mr. Read. Mr. Jackson had previously been teacher of a school at Barnaby Manor, the residence of the Rev. Henry Addison, during which time he also acted as lay reader at Hawling's River and Paint Chapels, Montgomery County. Mr. Jackson remained as curate for Mr. Read about a year. In 1797 the Rev. William Swann became the assistant in Prince George Parish, and officiated at Hawling's Run and Paint Chapels. Mr. Swann remained about a year, but for three years officiated partially at Hawling's Run and Paint Chapels, combining these charges with St. Peter's and Zion, in

Frederick. Subsequently he removed to Westminster Parish, where he conducted a school. In 1798, Mr. Read began to preach at Seneca Chapel, at Middlebrook, north of Rockville, on the Frederick road. The land had been presented by a Mr. Benson, and on it a frame building had been erected. In 1801 the vestry decided to build the proposed new church, to replace the old Rock Creek chapel, and in 1802 contracted with William Orr for the work. The structure was to be of brick, and was to cost £825. Subsequently the vestry agreed to give Mr. Orr the material in the old structure in addition to the money subscribed. On the 1st of August, 1803, the vestry examined the work of the new chapel, and determined to endeavor to raise a subscription for the repair of the Rock Creek church. On the records the death is noted of Mr. Allen Bowie, long an active and influential member of the vestry. The chapel was not finished for some time afterwards. In 1806 Rock Church complained to Bishop Claggett that Mr. Read had told them that he should henceforth restrict his ministrations to Rock Creek Chapel, and had advised them to employ another minister, but that afterwards he had informed them that he did not intend to relinquish the glebe lands which belonged to Rock Creek Church. Bishop Claggett replied that it was not legally competent for Mr. Read to relinquish the glebe, as he was merely a tenant at will. Subsequently Mr. Read officiated alternately at Rock Creek Church and Rock Creek Chapel. On the 11th of September, 1808, the new chapel was so far advanced that it was consecrated by Bishop Claggett with the name of Christ Church. In his journal the bishop states that the new chapel was situated near the site of the old one. After the consecration he confirmed twenty-nine persons, and a sermon was preached by the Rev. Dr. Contee, rector of William and Mary Parish, Charles County.

The deed of consecration states that the ancient wooden fabric had been found a few years ago so much decayed as to be unfit for use, but that "several benefactors had contributed to the erecting and completely finishing a new, spacious, and elegant two-story brick fabric," and that the vestry had, by their solemn act and deed, given and returned back to God "all their right, title, claim, and interest in and to the said building," and that therefore the bishop had consecrated it to the service of God.

About 1809 Rock Creek Church appears to have been without a regular pastor, as we find that Franklin Anderson, a law student in the office of Francis Scott Key, afterwards the author of the "Star-Spangled Banner," in Washington, acted as lay reader there, and that Mr. Key also served in the same capacity until 1820. In 1811 Paint Chapel was established as a separate congregation, and was authorized by the convention to take the name of Zion Church. In the same year a petition was presented to the Diocesan Convention from Rock Creek Church, asking to be constituted a separate parish, but the convention refused, on the ground that, in granting the petition, it might be considered as having transferred the Prince George Parish glebe to the new parish.

One year later a petition was presented to the Diocesan Convention asking for the erection of a new parish from the Hawling's River congregation. Leave was granted to form themselves into a separate congregation under the general incorporation act. The new parish was named St. Bartholomew's. Its boundaries, however, were not finally established until 1839.

In October, 1812, the vestry of Prince George addressed a note to Francis C. Clopper, complaining that he had converted Seneca chapel into a stable and carriage-house. It seems that Mr. Clopper had appropriated the chapel and land to his own use, although both had been given to the parish by William Benson. This would seem to indicate that the chapel had not been used for some time. The difficulty appears to have arisen from the fact that Mr. Benson died intestate, without having given a deed for the land. Possibly the confusion and trouble arose from the difficulties preceding the resignation of Mr. Read, which was handed to the vestry in April, 1814. Mr. Read resigned because "the parishioners would not be governed according to the discipline of the Protestant Episcopal Church," and because there seemed "no probability of my (his) being any longer profitable to them." Mr. Read did not cease his ministerial labors, however, but became the rector of St. Bartholomew's, or Hawling's River Parish. He continued as pastor for two years and then resigned, after which he resided on his farm, three miles north of Rockville, on the Frederick road, until his death, which occurred on the 5th of January, 1838, in the ninetieth year of his age.

Mr. Read was succeeded by the Rev. Alfred Henry Dashiell, who preached every other Sunday at Rock Creek chapel. In the following year (1815) it was agreed to raise a subscription of two thousand dollars for building a new church at Rockville. In 1817, Mr. Dashiell resigned the pastorate and removed to Virginia. The parish was vacant for some time, and during the interval the Rev. Mr. Addison officiated at intervals at Rock Creek church. No vestry having been elected on Easter Monday, the parishioners, in

November, 1818, after due notice, met at Rock Creek church and elected a vestry. A few days after, the new vestry held a meeting and determined to repair Rock Creek chapel. Subsequently, however, it was decided to be inexpedient to attempt the repair of the chapel, and that it was "wholly unsafe to perform divine worship in it." It was added, that besides "the bad arrangement and plan of the building, it seems now in a state of ruin." The vestry therefore decided to recommend the erection of a new edifice, and addressed the bishop of the diocese, requesting him to authorize the sale of the glebe lands and to select a minister for the church at Rockville. The bishop consented to the sale of the glebe, and a committee was appointed to settle any dispute that might arise in connection with the proposed transaction.

On the 1st of March, 1821, Solomon Holland conveyed to Prince George Parish vestry a deed in fee-simple for the lot on which the present church stands. It contained five thousand six hundred and seventy square feet of land, and was conveyed solely for the erection of the church, and not to be used as a burial-place. This tract was a part of lots numbered six and seven on the plat of Rockville. This deed was witnessed by Jesse Leach and Richard T. O. Waters, and recorded April 24, 1821, and the consideration was five dollars.

In the same year the Rev. Thomas G. Allen was chosen rector. Mr. Allen was a native of New York, but had studied for the ministry under the Rev. Dr. Wilmer, of Alexandria, and had been ordained by Bishop Moore, of Virginia. He settled in Virginia and married there, and removed thence to Prince George Parish. On the 20th of February, 1821, a contract was entered into for the erection of a new church at Rockville, to cost one thousand nine hundred and ninety-five dollars, exclusive of plastering and painting inside. On the 22d of September, 1822, the church, which had been completed, was consecrated and named Christ Church. In 1827 the trouble with Francis C. Clopper concerning Seneca chapel was adjusted by an arrangement that Clopper should furnish the timber and scantling for a new frame church in place of the structure which he had transferred into a stable and carriage-house, and that the church should be at once rebuilt.

On the 29th of January, 1828, John Taylor and his wife, Anne, conveyed to the parish through its rector and vestrymen, Charles J. Kilgour, George C. Washington, Benjamin S. Forest, James Anderson, Jr., Arnold J. Windsor, John Cook, Richard Butt, and John Adamson, one acre and fifty-two perches, part of a tract called "Middlebrook." The consideration was five dollars, and the deed was witnessed by James Ord and R. S. Briscoe. Later in the same year Mr. Allen resigned. After a vacancy of five months the Rev. Henry C. Knight was called to the parish, and accepted the charge. He was then only a deacon, but on the 20th of December, 1828, he was ordained priest by Bishop Henry M. Onderdonk, of Pennsylvania. Mr. Knight had charge of Bartholomew's, in connection with Prince George Parish. At the end of a year he removed to Massachusetts, and was succeeded by the Rev. Levin J. Gilliss, who officiated both at Rockville and at St. Bartholomew's, Hawling's River. Mr. Gilliss was a native of Somerset County, and had been ordained deacon by Bishop Kemp on the 24th of May, 1818. He had previously been rector of Queen Anne's, and afterwards of St. Paul's Parish, in Prince George's County. During all these years nothing had been done with the glebe lands of the parish, and no mention is made on the records of Rock Creek Church.

From this it is evident that the three last rectors of the parish did not officiate there. It was, however, still the parish church of Prince George Parish. From other sources it is learned that from 1817 the Rev. Mr. Addison, the Rev. C. C. Addison, and the Rev. Mr. McCormick officiated there. At the suggestion of the Rev. Dr. Ethan Allen, in the spring of 1828, a vestry was elected for Rock Creek Church, who sent a delegate to the Diocesan Convention, who was admitted to a seat. Dr. Allen, who was the rector of the church at Rockville, also officiated there at irregular intervals. In 1829 another delegate was sent to the convention, but his seat was contested on the ground that it was merely a chapel and had no regular minister. Dr. Allen, however, demonstrated to the convention that Rock Creek church was not a chapel, but the parish church itself. The delegate was allowed to retain his seat, but the right of representation was not accorded to the church. In 1830, Rock Creek Church presented itself again to the convention with a rector, the Rev. Mr. Ash, and a lay delegate, and after considerable discussion it was constituted a separate church and granted the right of representation. In 1833, Mr. Gilliss, rector of Prince George and St. Bartholomew's, reported to the convention that considerable repairs had been made to the churches in both his parishes, and that a neat and comfortable parsonage had been built at Rockville.

Mr. Gilliss continued rector for fourteen years. His ministry was one of quiet progress and great usefulness. In 1844 he removed to Washington

City, where he assisted in organizing and establishing the Church of the Ascension. He was succeeded by the Rev. Edward Wayler, a native of England, ordained by Bishop Griswold in 1837, who came to the parish from Pennsylvania. Mr. Wayler did not officiate at St. Bartholomew's, which was henceforth disassociated from the church at Rockville. In his report in 1845 he stated that the interior of the church had been renovated, a more convenient vestry-room made, and a new fence put around the yard. He only remained one year, and was succeeded by the Rev. George F. Worthington, a native of Anne Arundel County. Mr. Worthington was ordained by Bishop Doane, of New Jersey, Aug. 24, 1840, and was for some years in charge of St. John's in the Valley and Sherwood Chapel, Baltimore County, and afterwards was located at Catonsville, where he organized St. Timothy's Church. Mr. Worthington occasionally officiated at Seneca chapel, Middlebrook, in addition to performing his regular parish duties. In May, 1847, a bell was purchased for the church at Rockville, and in 1849 the parsonage was repaired and funds were procured for the purchase of an organ. In the spring of that year he was succeeded by the Rev. David Kerr, a native of Talbot County. Mr. Kerr was a graduate of the General Theological Seminary, and was ordained deacon by Bishop Stone, afterwards priest. He officiated in various churches until 1849, when he was called to the rectorship of the Rockville Church. In 1852 he resigned, and subsequently withdrew from the ministry. He died about 1877. Mr. Kerr was succeeded by the Rev. Lorenzo S. Russell, a native of Massachusetts, who reported in 1854 that the chancel had been enlarged and new altar-desks and furniture provided. Mr. Russell was ordained by Bishop Whittingham on the 24th of February, 1850, and took charge of St. Philip's Church, Laurel, whence he removed to the Rockville Parish. The present rector is the Rev. Benjamin F. Brown. In addition to the parish church at Rockville and the old church, St. Paul's, Rock Creek, there have been created from time to time St. Bartholomew's, or Hawling's River Church, St. Mark's, or Paint Chapel, St. John's, Mechanicsville, St. Peter's, St. Alban's, and Seneca Chapel. The history of St. Bartholomew's has already been given in connection with that of Rock Creek Church. St. Peter's, or Zion Parish, was originally known as Eden Parish, and before its creation as a parish was the Monocacy District of All Saints'. It embraced portions of what are now Frederick and Montgomery Counties, lying between the Monocacy and Seneca Creeks. Subsequently the parish was divided into two parishes,— St. Peter's, in Montgomery, and Zion, in Frederick. The two, however, appear to have formed one charge. The present church at Rockville is still known as Christ Church, the parish church of Prince George Parish.

Interments in Protestant Episcopal Church (now Rockville) Cemetery:

Edward Stonestreet, born May 1, 1855, died June 20, 1876.
Rev. Basil Barry, died Sept. 2, 1877, aged 88.
Martha W., his wife, died Feb. 2, 1860, aged 59.
Mary L. Offutt, wife Nicholas D. Offutt, and daughter of Dr. John Ward M. Anderson, died Dec. 25, 1876, aged 37 years, 1 month, 16 days.
Lucinda, wife of James R. Benson, died Dec. 23, 1879, aged 59 years, 11 months.
Catharine Beatty, died Sept. 15, 1861, aged 23.
William R. Saye, died Feb. 1, 1864, aged 43.
Edwin B. Miller, died Nov. 18, 1880, aged 21.
William Braddock, died Sept. 11, 1830, aged 41 years, 19 days.
Eliza, his wife, died March 29, 1878, aged 82 years, 1 month, 16 days.
Henry H. Young, born Sept. 17, 1776, died March 9, 1854.
Rebecca M. Young, died in 1822, aged 45.
Elizabeth Young, died 1842, aged 31.
Upton Beall, died Jan. 25, 1827, aged 57.
Jane Neale, his wife, died Aug. 2, 1849, aged 56.
Matilda B. Lee, their first daughter, died Feb. 6, 1870, aged 58.
Jane Elizabeth, their second daughter, died Nov. 3, 1863, aged 48.
Ursula Willcoxen, born March 2, 1800, died Sept. 13, 1876.
Robert Connell, died Aug. 10, 1868, aged 74.
Henry Hilleary, died July 19, 1792, aged 54.
Sarah, wife Thomas Johns, died July 2, 1782, aged 32.
Richard and Henry Bowle, March 27 and December, 1800, aged 18 and 26.
Cassaway Perry, born July 24, 1787, died July 26, 1837.
John Harding, born March 23, 1683, died Jan. 2, 1752.
John H. Higgins, born April, 1815, died June 17, 1870.
Elizabeth K. Kilgour, died April 21, 1860, aged 73.
Maria A. Beatty, born Oct. 29, 1811, died June 14, 1874.
Edward Beatty, died March 24, 1864, aged 23 years, 6 months.
Laura W. Holland, born Sept. 18, 1814, died March 25, 1861.
Zachariah Holland, born Oct. 26, 1806, died July 20, 1867.

Rockville Presbyterian Church.—Its pastors have been:

1761–93, Rev. James Hunt; 1793–1800, Rev. Adam Freeman; 1800–5, Rev. Conrad Spence, D.D.; 1805–14, Rev. Samuel Martin, D.D.; 1814–20, Rev. Joshua T. Russell; 1822–52, Rev. Dr. Mines, with Rev. Randolph A. Smith as co-pastor from 1846; 1852–59, Rev. William T. Smith; 1859–75, Rev. Edward H. Cumpston; 1875 to present time, Rev. Parke P. Flournoy.

Among the families connected with this church have been the Magruders, Gattons, Brewers, Ann Searle, Joneses, Hollands, Belts, Graffs, De Sellums, Ormes, Rickettses, Talbotts, Treadwells, Martins, Spateses, Hughes, Dunlaps, Mineses, Bealls, Johnsons, Russells, Muncasters, Almoneys, etc. This and the Bethesda Church are offshoots of "Cabin John Church," established in 1723 by Rev. John Orme, V.D.M. For a full history in detail of the Rockville, Bethesda, and Cabin John Churches, see Bethesda District, where, under the head of "Bethesda Presbyterian Church," a very elaborate account is given, covering a period of one hundred and twenty years, with references to the earliest Presbyterian families.

St. Mary's Catholic Church.—Up to the year 1866, when the learned Dr. Chappelle was assisted by the zealous Father Sullivan, Montgomery County was but a single parish, under the control of one priest.

The Catholics of Montgomery have always been fortunate in the appointment of their ministers, from the venerated Father Redmond, under whose auspices was laid the corner-stone of St. Mary's church, down to the present dignified and respected incumbent, Father Cunningham. The exact date of the erection of St. Mary's is not known, but the cornerstone was laid by Bishop Whitfield, assisted by the pastor, Father Redmond, in the latter part of 1817. Before the completion of the building, however, Father Redmond was called to another field of labor. Father Carroll succeeded him, and under his administration the church was rapidly completed. From this time to the present there has been little of historical importance in connection with the church.

Among the pastors of the church have been the venerable Father Piot, now a very old man, residing at St. Charles' College, Howard County, Md.; Father Thos. Foley, afterwards Bishop of Chicago, now deceased; Father McManus, now pastor of St. John's Church, Baltimore; Father Dougherty, now stationed at Ellicott City; Father Didier, now pastor of St. Vincent's Church, one of the most flourishing in Baltimore; Father Chappelle, since honored with the title of Doctor of Divinity, and now pastor of St. Joseph's Church, Baltimore; Father Sullivan, lately appointed pastor of St. Peter's Church, Washington, D. C.; Father Boyle, the eloquent pastor of St. Matthew's, Washington, D. C.; Father Starr, chancellor of the diocese, Cathedral, Baltimore; Father Mackin, assistant pastor St. Martin's Church, Baltimore; Father Casper Schmidt, stationed at Elk Ridge, Md.

But little change has been made in the original church edifice. Father Mackin built a room to the west of the sanctuary the size of the sacristy on the east, which is used for a Sunday-school. Just west of the church is the graveyard, which is susceptible of much improvement at a small cost. The congregation of St. Mary's numbers about eight hundred members.

Among the graves in the cemetery are those of the following persons:

J. Clayton Bael, born Sept. 21, 1854, died March 15, 1881.
William H. Bohrer, died Oct. 2, 1874, aged 22.
Amelia J. G., wife of Robert Clester, died April 4, 1878, aged 26.
Richard Bean, died Nov. 17, 1879, aged 45 years, 2 months.
John Bean, born March 25, 1798, died aged 73 years, 9 months, 1 day; Mary, his wife, born Aug. 7, 1797, died May 2, 1866.
Mary J., wife of M. Morgan, born Nov. 18, 1835, died Feb. 9, 1874.
Nicholas Brooke, died Nov. 5, 1852, aged 46; Mary Ann, his wife, died Jan. 15, 1870, aged 58.
Mrs. Eleanor Brooke, died Oct. 11, 1842, aged 74.
Horatio James, died May 15, 1870, aged 68.
Wm. G. Robertson, born March 17, 1819, died June 26, 1861.
Michael Fitzgerald, died Dec. 7, 1855.
Rebecca, wife of Charles S. Hunter, died Dec. 19, 1856.
Maria Dugan, died Aug. 21, 1857, aged 73.
Charles Beckwith, died May 7, 1856, aged 67.
Joseph Gingal, born June 7, 1810.
Wm. J. Flock, born Aug. 5, 1849, died Jan. 2, 1872.
Samuel Gloyd, Sr., born Oct. 24, 1800, died July 3, 1875.
Ellen J. Viers, died Dec. 4, 1867, aged 39.
J. Davis, Sr., died Sept. 19, 1870, aged 68.
Frances Flock, died Sept. 4, 1863, aged 56.
John Ph. Flock, born March 8, 1836, died Oct. 31, 1871.
Anthony Kleindienst, died June 17, 1863, aged 33; Mary C., his wife, born Nov. 24, 1834, died Aug. 7, 1877.
James L. Grier, born July 2, 1834, died Jan. 24, 1857.
Elizabeth, wife of Wm. Gamble, died Sept. 1, 1871, aged 63 years, 5 months.
Martha, wife of L. W. Finch, died Aug. 15, 1870, aged 32.
Margaret, wife of Thos. Lyddane, born Feb. 19, 1824, died March 1, 1880.
James E. Lyddane, born Nov. 16, 1815, died Nov. 29, 1863.
James N. Lyddane, born Sept. 21, 1838, died Aug. 14, 1875.
M. S. Macdonald, died Jan. 5, 1874, aged 84.
Hy. Clements, died April 5, 1855; Jane Clements, died Oct. 16, 1848; Teresa J. Clements, died Sept. 6, 1844; Elizabeth Clements, died Sept. 19, 1844; Mary Clements, died Sept. 20, 1844.
Elizabeth A., wife of Bennett Abel, of St. Mary's County, Md., died July 11, 1860, aged 71.
Lemuel Clements, born Oct. 16, 1794, died Nov. 1, 1880.
John Scott, born at Chestertown, Md., March 26, 1789, died in the county, Aug. 19, 1843.
Mary E. Boswell, born May 1, 1823, died Dec. 15, 1855.
Catherine E. Lowe, born May 1, 1833, died Dec. 3, 1879.
Martha Gaither, born Dec. 3, 1802, died Feb. 27, 1876.

Before the erection of St. Mary's, Father Plunkett, in 1804, celebrated service at the residence of Mr. Digges, near Bladensburg, visited Carroll's chapel, now St. John's church, and held services at the residence of Harry Bevans. He remained in charge of the mission in this county for about ten years. His successor was Father Redmond, S.J., in 1814, who in 1817 built St. Mary's church. He visited Barnesville, St. John's, and Mr. Gardiner's, at Hawling's River (now St. Peter's); also Richard Bowie's, two miles east of Rockville, and remained four years. His successor, Rev. Francis Xavier Carroll, who resided at Rockville, had charge of all the missions of the county, and remained two years. Rev. John De Vas came in 1820. For fifteen years he had charge of all the missions, but his health failing he then attended St. Rose's congregation only, living with a family named Peddicora, where he said mass every Sunday. He left in 1844, and became a professor in Georgetown College. Father B. S. Piot then had charge for three years, and was succeeded by Father Gallagher, who built St. Rose's church and remained until 1846. Rev. Thomas Foley was pastor from 1846 to 1847; Father McManus, 1847 to 1849; Father King, in 1849, who died the same year; Father McGuire, 1849 to 1851; Rev. F. X. Boyle, 1851 to 1854; Rev. J. J. Dougherty, who built St. Peter's church, 1854 to 1861; Rev. E. Didier, 1863 to 1866; Rev. P. L. Chappelle, 1866 to 1871. Then the mission of Montgomery County was divided. The succeeding pastors were Revs. Mackin, Casper Schmidt, J. A. Cunningham, and Father Gallen, present incumbent.

Baptist Church.—The church edifice was erected in 1823, and rebuilt in 1861.

On the 19th of August, 1821, the following persons withdrew from the old Seneca Baptist Church, which was under the pastoral care of Elder Plummer Waters, assigning, among other reasons, their dissent from the views of the pastor on the subject of *missions*: William Clingan, Jesse Leach, Willie James, William Brewer, William Chiswell, Mary R. Braddock, Mary R. Brewer, Sarah Chiswell; and these, with Joseph H. Jones, William Sedgwick, Martha Jones, Prudence Jones, Sarah Leach, Abraham Stallings, Sarah Stallings, were constituted a regular Baptist Church, Oct. 20, 1821, by Rev. John Healy, pastor of the Second Baptist Church, Baltimore; Rev. Obediah B. Brown, pastor of the First Baptist Church, Washington, D. C.; and Rev. Thomas Barton, pastor of the Second Baptist Church, Washington, D. C. Elder J. H. Jones was elected pastor of the new congregation, and William Sedwick assistant. The latter was afterwards regularly ordained by request of the church, and Jesse Leach and William Chiswell were elected deacons, and Willie James clerk.

By a formal resolution a branch of this church was established near Dr. William Brewer's, to be called Upper Bethel. The name under which the church was organized in Rockville was "Bethel Baptist Church." The first addition after the organization was Edward Anderson.

The church joined the Baltimore Association, and reported in their first letter a membership of eighteen. Miss Margaret Pierce, who is still living, was received and baptized Oct. 20, 1822.

Dec. 30, 1831, by a resolution, the church resolved that the upper branch be called "Bethel," and the lower, "Rockville" Baptist Church. The last record by the clerk (Willie James) was May 4, 1837.

Prior to 1851, Elder Jones resigned, having served as pastor for about twenty-four years, during which time the church reached a membership of sixty-nine, by letter and baptism, as shown by the records.

For some years the church was without a regular pastor, receiving the ministrations of such as were invited to visit them, among whom were Dr. Samson, Dr. Cole, Dr. Adams, Rev. C. Meadows, and others. The membership was reduced to nine. In May, 1851, Rev. F. L. Kregel was called to the pastorate, and ordained by Revs. J. M. W. Williams, G. F. Adams, and J. H. Philips, and Charles Spates was elected deacon. An evangelist, Rev. N. B. Collins, held a series of meetings, which revived the interest and doubled the membership, and it became a member of the Maryland Union Baptist Association. Mr. Kregel resigning after a period of about three years, Elder Thomas Jones was chosen pastor in February, 1855, and continued his labors until his health compelled him to leave, in the fall of 1858. In May of this year, Edward M. Viers was elected deacon, and still serves.

During the pastorate of Rev. Thomas Jones the church regained considerable strength. During his stay of nearly four years the membership increased from eighteen to seventy-three.

In January, 1859, a committee was appointed to purchase a lot and collect funds to erect a house at what is now called Mount Zion, where in 1860 a neat house, thirty by forty feet, was erected and dedicated free of debt. In January, 1859, Elder S. R. White, then a student of Columbian College, was invited as a supply. In June following he was called to the care of the church, and September 10th following entered upon his duties as pastor. During his pastorate the church has licensed three of her members to preach, all of whom were ordained, and one of whom, Rev. J. L. Lodge, D.D., of Newark, N. J., is still in the pastorate. Three houses of worship have been erected,—one at Poolesville, one at Georgetown, and one at Mount Zion, the two former becoming separate organizations. The Baptist Church in Georgetown, D. C., was also the result of efforts by the pastor of this church and two of its members. The house of worship in Rockville has been rebuilt and enlarged at a cost of three thousand five hundred dollars, and has now a neat and commodious audience-room, with baptistery, organ, tower, and bell.

During his pastorate of nearly twenty-one years Mr. White baptized two hundred and eighty-seven persons, preached one hundred and thirty-nine funeral sermons, married one hundred and thirty-four couples. The present membership is one hundred and seventy-seven. The officers are E. M. Viers and R. A. Bagley, deacons; D. H. Bouic, clerk and treasurer. Rev. D. E. Hatcher, present pastor, was called in 1879.

The burying-ground is on the right of the church, and among those buried there are

Col. Thomas F. W. Vinson, died Sept. 8, 1843, aged 58.
Brice Selby, died April 15, 1844, aged 70.
Charles Spates, died Oct. 15, 1873, aged 83. His tombstone was erected by the Baptist Church, of which he was a deacon thirty years; and his wife, Ruth, born June 17, 1788, and died Oct. 13, 1866.
Samuel Clark Viers, died Nov. 8, 1872, aged 75; and his wife, Julianna, born May 24, 1794, died Nov. 27, 1878.
William Braddock, died Oct. 31, 1850, aged 47.
Virginia Sophia Sommers, died May 17, 1872, aged 44.
Peter A. Bouic, died Jan. 10, 1859, aged 57.
William Nelson Austin, died Sept. 23, 1864, aged 72.
Charles Smith, died Aug. 13, 1845, aged 28.
John, second son of William and Mary R. Brewer, born Sept. 14, 1804, died July 10, 1866.
Ellen Brewer, wife of Spencer C. Jones, and daughter of John and Elizabeth S. Brewer, born July 22, 1845, died July 21, 1876.
Isaac Riley, died July 5, 1850, aged 76.
B. F. Riley, born Dec. 24, 1845, died Aug. 21, 1872.
William R. Hance, died April 2, 1878, aged 60.
Wallace A. Bohrer, died February, 1864, aged 17.
Cornelia L. Bohrer, died Sept. 10, 1874, aged 49.

Rockville Christian Church.—This church had its origin about the year 1820, mainly through the efforts of Elder William McClenahan, who at that time stood at the head of the English department of the Rockville Academy, which position he filled most acceptably for many years. He was an able teacher and zealous expounder of the word of God. His wife (Elizabeth) and his sisters (Mary and Sarah) and his mother were all co-workers in establishing the church in Rockville. About the year 1835, Elder McClenahan immersed a number of persons, who were received into church fellowship, among whom were his daughters (Elizabeth Ann and Mary Jane), Miss Elizabeth Braddock (afterwards married to John R. Miller), Mrs. Mary Granger, Mrs. Sarah Jacobs, William Braddock, Benjamin Daily and his wife and son, since deceased, Robert Carroll and wife, and John Kelly and wife. From the year 1835 to 1858 the congregation held their meetings part of the time at the Rockville Academy, but most of the time at the private residences of some of its members.

During this period the church has experienced many vicissitudes of religious fortune, losing many members by death, removal, and other causes, whose places have been filled by gradual accessions of new converts.

On the 10th day of July, 1858, the trustees of the Rockville Presbyterian Church sold and conveyed to William Braddock their house of worship, located on the northwest corner of Jefferson and Adams Streets, and in August of the same year William Braddock agreed, for a valuable consideration, to convey the same to "The Rockville Christian Church."

On the 15th day of August, 1866, articles of incorporation were duly executed and recorded in the clerk's office of the Circuit Court for Montgomery County, and on the 26th day of September following Mrs. Roberta V. Braddock, administratrix of William Braddock, in pursuance of the agreement entered into by her late husband, executed to the trustees a deed for the aforenamed property, which the congregation has since used and still use as a place of public worship. The house has been from time to time repaired and improved, externally and internally; recently a baptistery has been added thereto, and arrangements are now nearly effected for more improvements of the interior.

The congregation has had the ministerial services of many visiting brethren from different parts of the country, in addition to those regularly employed, the latter serving in the following order: Joseph Braddock, at the time of his death and for several years previous, principal of the Rockville Academy; Elder John L. T. Holland, of Virginia; Elder Alexander Anderson, of Scotland; Elder J. W. Kemp, of Ohio; Elder D. Sommer, of Maryland; Elder William H. Schell, present pastor.

At a regular meeting of the church, held in pursuance of the articles of incorporation, on the 9th day of July, 1878, the following officers were elected, who still hold their places:

Pastor, Elder William H. Schell; Elders, John R. Miller and John W. Horner; Deacons, George R. Braddock, Edward Horner, E. Gilmore Duley, and Hezekiah Trail; Trustees, John R. Miller, Hezekiah Trail, George R. Braddock, Edward Horner, and E. Gilmore Duley; Clerk, George R. Braddock; Treasurer, Hezekiah Trail.

Elder Schell has been the regular pastor for three years. A flourishing Sunday-school is connected with the church. The congregation at present numbers sixty-eight members.

Methodist Episcopal Church South.—The brick church, built many years ago, after the division of the church in 1844 fell into the possession of the Methodist Episcopal Church, and is now occupied by the colored congregation. In 1867 and 1868, under the pastorate of Rev. James E. Armstrong, the present frame edifice was built. Since the organization of the church in 1865 it has had the following pastors:

1866, John A. Gilbert, L. C. Miller; 1867, James E. Armstrong, H. H. Kennedy; 1868–69, James E. Armstrong, Asbury R. Martin; 1870, Dabney Ball, D.D., John A. Curren; 1871–75, P. H. Whisner, B. W. Bond; 1875–78, John C. Dice, C. W. Brown; 1878, John C. Dice, L. R. Green; 1879, G. T. Tyler, L. R. Green; 1880–81, G. T. Tyler, F. M. Strother.

This church forms a circuit with seven other churches,—Emory, Goshen, Brookville, Gaithersburg, Darnestown, Potomac Chapel, and Harris' School-house.

Rockville Lyceum.—Officers for 1881:

President, J. W. Warren; Vice-President, W. V. Bouic, Jr.; Secretary, A. M. Fletcher; Treasurer, E. C. Peter; General Committee, D. Laird, Rev. S. R. White, E. C. Peter, Mrs. A. Wood, and Miss Agnes Matlack.

Rockville Academy.—The second classical institution established in Montgomery County was the Rockville Academy. The first school of any reputation in the county was a seminary for young men in the Wallace or Magruder neighborhood, established near the close of the Revolutionary war by Rev. James Hunt, a Presbyterian clergyman, on his farm, called "Tusculum," now memorable as the Alma Mater of William Wirt. It was there that he was prepared, as far as scholastic training could prepare him, for that brilliant career which has made his name one of the most illustrious in American annals.[1] After Mr. Hunt's death in 1793 there was in the county no school in which any instruction beyond the rudiments of English education was pretended to be taught. The rising generation, whose parents were able to incur the expense, were sent to Frederick, Bladensburg, or Georgetown for education. In a few families tutors were employed, who gave instruction in the higher branches. Sparse as the schools were then, the earliest records of the county show that a class of men then existed who were most accomplished clerks. Penmanship was brought to great perfection; manuscripts were executed with the regularity, beauty, and precision of type; language was used with accuracy, conciseness, and perspicuity,—in fine, learning, although not generally disseminated as now, had its disciples, who were familiar with "the well of English undefiled." The germ of the Rockville Academy was first developed in an act of the General Assembly passed in 1805, and re-enacted in 1806. Upton Beall, Honore Martin, Lewis Beall, Thomas Linsted, Thomas P. Willson, Richard Anderson, and Solomon Holland were appointed commissioners to raise the sum of two thousand five hundred dollars by lottery for the purpose of purchasing a lot to erect a school-house and buy a fire-engine. The sum to be raised, though comparatively small, considered in relation to the then population and property of the county, was equivalent to five times its present value. The scheme authorized by the Legislature was successfully executed. A beautiful lot was purchased, on which a substantial brick building was erected, which remains a plain but permanent monument with which the names of its projectors should ever be associated in grateful remembrance. To give stability to the institution and enlarge its usefulness, its founders and patrons obtained in 1809 a charter incorporating Richard Anderson, Solomon Holland, Lewis Beall, Jesse Leach, James Anderson, John Wootton, Joseph Elgar, and Honore Martin as "trustees of the Rockville Academy, in Montgomery County." The trustees were empowered to hold real and personal estate to an amount not exceeding five thousand dollars in annual value; to appoint professors, teachers, and assistants for instructing students and scholars "in the vernacular and learned languages, and such sciences and branches of education as they shall think proper." The Assembly in 1811 appropriated the sum of eight hundred dollars, to be paid annually to the trustees on condition that they should educate eight indigent pupils free of charge. The first principal was Rev. John Breckenridge, of Pennsylvania, a minister of the Presbyterian Church, and during his administration the academy acquired considerable reputation. Pupils were attracted from remote points, while its influence enlarged as its patronage increased. Rev. John Mines, D.D., whose personal character and attainments were calculated to impress his pupils with high regard and profound respect, was principal twenty-five years. After he declined a re-election, for ten years, and until about 1857, the time of his death, he exercised a general oversight over the institution. Rev. William McClenahan, head of the English department and colaborer of Dr. Mines, was afterwards president of Princeton College. The records of the academy having been lost during the civil war, a full list of the principals and assistants cannot be given. For seventy-two years, without any material intermission, the academy has instructed from thirty to sixty students annually. Through the filial affection and generosity

---
[1] T. Anderson's Centennial Oration.

of one of its sons, the late Julius West, a beautiful and valuable farm near Rockville was, about 1868, devised to the academy in perpetual trust for educational purposes. In 1869 the academy was under the control of Rev. Thomas N. Conrad. His successor, the present principal, is Prof. Cooke D. Luckett, a graduate of the University of Virginia. Its board of trustees are Col. James W. Anderson, president; Hon. George Peter, secretary; Robert W. Carter, Esq., treasurer; Maj. J. G. England, Hon. W. Viers Bouic, E. B. Prettyman, N. D. Offutt, H. W. Talbott. The institution is divided into junior, intermediate, senior, and classical departments. The sessions are of ten months' duration, at the close of which gold medals are given for the highest standing in each department. Students are prepared for college, university, or active business pursuits of life.

Mutual Building Association of Montgomery County.—This association was incorporated April 22, 1879, with the following gentlemen as incorporators: Spencer C. Jones, John J. Higgins, Hezekiah Trail, William H. Rabbitt, D. F. Owens, R. A. Bagley, J. B. Edmonston. The stock of the association is limited to six hundred shares, of the par value of one hundred dollars per share, of which no member is allowed to hold more than twenty unredeemed shares. Two hundred and thirty-one of the shares are held by the members.

The total receipts for the first year were $3015; for the second year, $3325.30.

The following officers have served the association:

1879.—President, Spencer C. Jones; Vice-President, John J. Higgins; Secretary and Treasurer, Hattersly W. Talbott; Solicitor, James Dawson; Board of Directors, Spencer C. Jones, John J. Higgins, Hezekiah Trail, Reuben A. Bagley, John B. Edmondson, Dr. D. F. Owens, and William H. Rabbitt.

1880.—President, D. F. Owens; Vice-President, John J. Higgins; Secretary and Treasurer, H. W. Talbott; Solicitor, C. W. Prettyman; Directors, Dr. D. F. Owens, J. J. Higgins, Hezekiah Trail, John B. Edmondson, William H. Rabbitt, Dr. E. E. Stonestreet, S. B. Haney.

The present officers are: President, E. E. Stonestreet; Vice-President, J. J. Higgins; Secretary and Treasurer, H. W. Talbott; Solicitor, C. W. Prettyman; Directors, B. F. Owens, J. J. Higgins, Hezekiah Trail, W. H. Carr, W. R. Pumphrey, W. H. Rabbitt, S. B. Haney.

Rockville Library Association.—This association was organized in 1871, with the following officers: President, Richard J. Bowie; Secretary, Spencer C. Jones; Treasurer, William Viers Bouic. Its library and rooms were in the rear of the law-office of Anderson & Bouic.

Rockville Division, No. 49, S. of T.—This division existed for many years, and its officers in 1873 were:

W. P., R. A. Sheckel; W. A., H. C. England; R. S., J. F. Peter; A. R. S., W. W. Russell; F. S., A. T. Davis; Chaplain, Rev. S. R. White; Treas., R. A. Bouic; C., C. W. Prettyman; A. C., W. R. Pumphrey; I. S., Charles Abert; O. S., J. F. Braddock; P. W. P., M. Morgan.

Prominent among the citizens of Rockville for many years was Samuel C. Viers, who was born near Dawsonville, August, 1798. When young he removed to Baltimore, where he engaged in the mercantile business with Charles Diffenderfer, whose youngest sister he married in 1819. He remained in business in Baltimore until 1833, when he removed to a farm purchased by him on Rock Creek. In early life he served many years as magistrate, and was postmaster of Rockville under Van Buren's administration, from 1837 to 1841. He was appointed chief judge of the Orphans' Court by Governor Grason. In 1851 he was elected by the people judge of this court, and re-elected in 1853. He enlarged the town by the erection of a large number of dwelling-houses, and to his enterprise Rockville owes much of its present prosperity. He joined the Baptist Church in 1824, under Elder J. H. Jones, and died Nov. 8, 1872, in the seventy-fourth year of his age.

Another distinguished citizen of Rockville was the late Hon. Richard Johns Bowie. Judge Bowie was born in Georgetown, D. C., June 23, 1807, and was the son of Washington and Margaret Bowie. His father was a leading importing merchant of that town, where his childhood was spent. A pupil of Dr. Carnahan, who afterwards became president of Princeton College, he acquired an education, and commenced the study of law in his native town, in the office of Clement Cox, and was admitted to the bar at the youthful age of nineteen. He chose Montgomery County as his field of legal labor, and the following year removed to Rockville. His ability found almost instant recognition in the quick flow towards him of a lucrative practice, and in a little while he was admitted to the bar of the United States Supreme Court. The Whig doctrine found in him an earnest advocate, and Henry Clay a warm admirer.

On the 19th of November, 1836, the college of senatorial electors assembled at Annapolis, as provided by the constitution of the State, and Richard J. Bowie was elected a member of the Senate of Maryland. This was his first entrance into public life. Though then quite a young man (under thirty years of age), he was thought by the college of electors worthy to be ranked by the side of such associates as

John V. L. McMahon, William Price, Richard Thomas, William Schley, James B. Ricaud, and the other distinguished men whose name and fame are identified with the Legislature of Maryland. The Senate of 1836, it is high honor to say of it, was unsurpassed for talents by any which ever assembled in Maryland. In that body Mr. Bowie held a prominent position, a conclusive evidence of his ability and worth, and took a leading part in many of the important measures agitated at the session of 1836 and 1837.

When the celebrated Bemis case occurred, and the demand for the surrender of Bemis' associates made by the Executive of Pennsylvania had been communicated by the Governor of Maryland to the General Assembly, with a view to obtain its advice upon the delicate and momentous question at issue, Mr. Bowie was one of the committee of conference between the two houses to whom the subject was referred; and it was he who drew up the resolutions which were subsequently adopted by both branches of the Legislature. Those resolutions asserted on behalf of the South the very rights afterwards conceded by the enactment of the Fugitive Slave Law; and the principles thus set forth by the youthful senator of Maryland were afterwards sanctioned to their fullest extent by the Supreme Court of the United States, in its decision of the case of Prigg and the Commonwealth of Pennsylvania. The length of these resolutions precludes their insertion here, but they may easily be referred to in the volume of the laws of December session, 1837. They were offered by Mr. Bowie, in a spirit of compromise, at a time when more violent measures had been suggested for the action of our Legislature, and when it required the exercise of the utmost prudence to preserve the friendly relations between the two States, and at the same time secure the rights of the citizens of our own. It will be remembered that the amended constitution of Maryland was adopted by the Legislature at the sessions of 1836, 1837. The amendments then enacted were considered satisfactory to the most ultra reformers of that day. They provided for the election of a Governor and senators by the people; the abolishment of the life tenure of clerks and registers, and their appointment for a term of seven years; an increase of representation to Baltimore and the larger counties. This was the reform demanded at that day, and it received the cordial support of Mr. Bowie.

By the operation of this amended constitution Mr. Bowie's term of service in the State Senate was reduced from five years to two. He retired from the Legislature with the session ending in the spring of 1838, and was never afterwards a member of either branch of that body.

In 1839, Mr. Bowie was selected by the Whigs of the district, composed of Frederick and Montgomery Counties, as their representative to the National Convention at Harrisburg. He went there the zealous supporter of the nomination of Henry Clay. The mode adopted by convention in making the nomination was to vote by States, the majority giving the whole vote of a State. Mr. Bowie had proposed, and advocated with much zeal, the plan of voting per capita,—that is, for each individual member of the convention to be entitled to cast his own vote.

Had this motion prevailed it is generally understood that Henry Clay would have obtained the nomination, and his friends afterwards deeply regretted that they had not sustained Mr. Bowie's motion. A nomination of Henry Clay at that election would have certainly made him President of the United States. After the nomination of Gen. Harrison, Mr. Bowie was placed on the electoral ticket, and with his colleagues from Maryland had the honor of voting for the hero of Tippecanoe.

From the time of his retirement from the State Senate in 1838 to the election of 1849, Mr. Bowie continued to devote himself to his profession, in which he attained a very high position, being not only the leading member of the bar of his own county, but also a frequent and distinguished practitioner before the Court of Appeals. In 1844 he was chosen prosecuting attorney for Montgomery County, and remained in that office until he was sent to Congress. In 1849 he was nominated by the Whig Convention of the district composed of St. Mary's, Prince George's, Charles, Calvert, Anne Arundel, and Montgomery Counties as a candidate for the House of Representatives, and elected in October of that year. While in Congress Mr. Bowie was emphatically a working man. He also frequently participated in the debates, and many of his printed speeches would do credit to any one of the ablest statesmen of the country.

To Mr. Bowie belongs the honor of having been the first member of the House of Representatives who took ground in favor of Mr. Clay's compromise bill. He made a beautiful and thrilling speech in its favor, which was highly complimented at the time.

Another speech delivered by him during his term was one (made Feb. 14, 1851) on the "River and Harbor bill," in which he strongly advocated the true national and Maryland side of the question.

In the fall of 1851, Mr. Bowie was re-elected to Congress. Though his opponent was an able and popular member of his own party, Mr. Bowie received the unprecedented majority of 774, and in his own election district all but 14 votes of some 300 polled.

Among the speeches delivered by him during his second term was one on the Homestead bill, made April 26, 1852, and one on the foreign policy of the government, made Feb. 25, 1853. As a member of the Committee on Claims, Mr. Bowie prepared several important reports. One of these, accompanied by a bill, failed of success from the delays of a Congress too much interested in the question of President-making to devote much of its time to the immediate interests of the general public constituency.

At the nominating convention of his congressional district, held in 1853, he declined to accept a third nomination, which there was every reason to think would have been cheerfully tendered him.

Upon the expiration of his second congressional term he was put in nomination as the Whig candidate for the governorship of Maryland against T. Watkins Ligon, the Democratic nominee, and suffered defeat. The power and influence of the Whig party was now on the decline, and Judge Bowie, in common with many others, retired from active participation in politics. The outbreak of the civil war awoke him, however, to the influence of the old active spirit, and as a devoted Union man he caused his voice and counsel to be heard and felt. In 1863 he was elevated to the bench as a member of the Court of Appeals, and as one of that body displayed such eminent judicial learning that Governor Bradford appointed him chief judge of the court. That high place he retained until the adoption of the new State constitution of 1867. In that year he was the Republican candidate for chief judge of the Sixth District against Madison Nelson, but at that election no Republican candidate was successful. Upon Judge Nelson's death, Judge Bowie was elected, in November, 1871, to be chief judge of the Circuit Court, and again became a member of the Court of Appeals.

During the tenth year of his service he was stricken with a fatal illness, and died at his home in Montgomery County, March 12, 1881. Up to within a year of his death he was remarkably active, and attended with regularity the sessions of the court. An obituary published at the time of his death recited that "few men in this State have more justly and in a greater degree enjoyed the honor and esteem of their fellow-citizens without distinction of party than Judge Bowie in his long public career. He was everywhere, and by all with whom he came in contact, recognized as a man of unblemished integrity, a nice sense of honor, never seeking political office, but belonging to that class of men, of whom few are now to be met with, who believed in the principle that the office should seek the man, and it frequently sought *him*. The trust reposed in him by his fellow-citizens was never betrayed. Though a consistent Whig, and afterwards an ardent Republican, he could always command votes from the opposition whenever a candidate for any office, and as a member of the Legislature, member of Congress, and as judge he discharged the duties of each position in a manner reflecting credit upon himself as well as upon his State." His widow (daughter of Gen. Otho H. Williams, of Hagerstown, one of the most distinguished citizens of Western Maryland) survives him, and resides at "Glen View," the home farm, near Rockville.

St. Mary's Institute.—This young ladies' boarding-school in 1869 was under the charge of Misses Dugan and Walley. It is now conducted by Mrs. Bowie and Miss Gardener.

Rockville Cemetery Association.—Its officers for 1881 were:

Hon. R. J. Bowie, president; Wm. V. Bowie, Jr., secretary and treasurer; W. R. Pumphrey, superintendent; Wm. V. Bowie, Jr., James B. Henderson, Hezekiah Trail, N. D. Offutt, E. B. Prettyman, Dr. E. E. Stonestreet, directors.

The school trustees and teachers for 1881 and 1882 are as follows:

Trustees.—No. 1, I. G. England, Jr., D. H. Bouic, E. O. Edmonston; No. 2, J. T. Bayley, T. W. Stonestreet, J. R. Benson; No. 3, S. C. Veirs, James Gingles, Sylvester James; No. 4, Wm. Atwood, —— Wagner, W. H. Magruder; No. 5, W. R. Gaither, Henry Ansley, R. Watkins.

Teachers.—No. 1, J. L. Armstrong, Rockville P. O.; No. 2, C. B. Clements, Rockville P. O.; No. 3, C. G. Petty, Mount Rose P. O.; No. 4, B. E. Braddock, Mount Rose P. O.; No. 5, Milford Offutt, Rockville P. O.

There are two colored schools.

The magistrates are Chandler Keys, J. W. M. Kiger, M. Morgan, S. W. Magruder.[1]

Montrose.—This point is near Randolph Station, on the Metropolitan Branch of the Baltimore and Ohio Railroad. Charles A. Lochte, John Magruder, and Mrs. M. Heley, merchants. The latter is postmistress.

---

[1] The Mounted Rifle Company organized at Rockville elected, Dec. 17, 1859, the following officers: Captain, R. J. Bowie; First Lieutenant, W. Viers Bouic; Second Lieutenant, J. L. Dufief; Third Lieutenant, George Peter, Jr.; Ensign, Charles M. Price; First Sergeant, Henry Hurley; Second Sergeant, John T. Kilgour; Third Sergeant, M. Green; Fourth Sergeant, J. T. Bayley; First Corporal, Cornelius Bean; Second Corporal, William J. Ricketts; Third Corporal, William Atwood; Surgeon, Dr. A. H. Sommers; Secretary, S. A. Matlack; Treasurer, J. W. Spates.

BERRY DISTRICT, No. 5.

This district is bounded on the north by Mechanicsville District, on the east by the Patuxent River, dividing it from Prince George's County, on the south by the District of Columbia, and on the west by Bethesda and Rockville Districts. On the northwest Rock Creek divides it from Rockville District. Paint Branch, Sligo Branch, and Northwest Branch of the Potomac flow southeast into Prince George's County. The boundaries of the district until 1878 were as follows: Beginning at the mouth of Hawling's River and running down Patuxent to Prince George's County line, then with said line to the Territory of Columbia, then with said Territory to Rock Creek, then up Rock Creek to Robertson's mill, then up the Bladensburg road until it intersects the line of the First District at the lower end of Benjamin Ricketts' plantation, then with the line of the Second District reversed to the beginning.

The limits of the district were reduced in 1878 by the erection of Mechanicsville, which was formed in that year from portions of Berry and Cracklin Districts.

Among the earliest settlers in the district were William Joseph, Alexander Beall, Richard Snowden, Neal Clark, the Duvalls, Dorseys, Cashells, Rileys, Kemps, Van Horns, Bonifants, Stablers, Hardings, Shaws, and Fawcetts.

School-Meetings.—At a school-meeting of School District No. 2, held Sept. 5, 1839, Thomas Fawcett was president, and John McCutchen, clerk. Washington Duvall, John McCutchen, George D. Spencer, Thomas and William Valdenar were appointed a committee to ascertain the number of white children between the ages of six and sixteen years and select a site for a school, and report at the next meeting. At an adjourned meeting on the 13th the committee reported eighty-two children, and recommended for the school-house site the one near a spring situated east of the road leading from Colesville to the Burnt Mills, west of the Paint Branch, north of John Selby's residence, and south of the house then occupied by John Mullican, known as Patrick Arme's old place. The trustees selected were Thomas Fawcett, George B. Scaggs, George D. Spencer. Three hundred dollars were levied.

The First School District held its meeting on September 14th, at the house of David Parker, at Leesboro', of which Robert Y. Brent was president, and Charles Bunting, clerk. Adjourned until March 3, 1840.

The meeting of the Second District was held September 12th, of which John Cook was president, and John Brewer, clerk. Adjourned to June, 1840, without any further action.

District No. 4, on September 4th, held its meeting, of which Eden Beall was president, and Richard S. Anderson, clerk. The trustees elected were Richard S. Anderson, Eden Beall, and John Rabbitt. A committee was appointed to ascertain the legal number of school youths and look out a site for a new school-house, and report at the January meeting following. Four hundred dollars was levied.

Drumeldra.—On July 18, 1831, Abraham Brooke, Elizabeth Lukens, and Hannah Lukens opened a boarding-school for girls at this point, near Colesville. Being but fourteen miles from Washington City, and having an able corps of teachers, it was for many years one of the best institutions in the State.

Spencerville is seven miles from Laurel, twelve from Rockville, twenty-five from Baltimore, and near the Patuxent River. The town derives its name from Wm. A. Spencer, who founded it in 1850. The first store of general merchandise was established and conducted by John Gainer. He was succeeded by Joseph Mabbitt about 1860, and the store is now owned by Andrew McCoy. In 1869, Mr. Chaney founded the business that is now so successfully carried on by Messrs. Chaney & Fair. Austin Black was the pioneer blacksmith of the vicinity. The post-office was established about 1860 by William Spencer. Wm. H. Phair is the present postmaster, having been appointed in February, 1881. Liberty Grove Grange, No. 50, P. of H., is located in the place, of which John E. Phair is the Master, and Wm. Rich, secretary. Dr. Charles H. Waters is the physician. The land in the vicinity of this village produces from fifteen to thirty-five bushels of wheat, and eight to twelve barrels of corn, and two tons of hay to the acre.

Union Cemetery Association.—This association was formed about 1862. The present officers are: President, C. W. Rich, and Secretary, W. H. Phair. The cemetery is situated about two miles west of Spencerville, on the road leading to Burtonsville. Among the graves inclosed within its limits are those of

Mary Louisa, wife of Griffith M. Smith, died May 2, 1862, aged 36 years, 2 days.
Joseph Green, born Sept. 5, 1855, died Aug. 27, 1880.
Hiram Spencer, died April 23, 1870, aged 32.
Charles Dickinson, died Jan. 5, 1858, aged 31.
Amelia, his wife, died April 8, 1861, aged 31.
Sarah T., wife of William H. Spencer, died Sept. 12, 1865, aged 66.
Mary A., wife of Charles S. Burns, born Jan. 9, 1849, died Nov. 23, 1876.

George Reigle, Sr., died July 2, 1861, aged 73 years, 2 months, 26 days.

Eve, his wife, died June 4, 1863, aged 74 years, 9 months, 8 days.

J. M. Reigle, died Sept. 8, 1860, aged 25.

John D. Rich, died May 8, 1859, aged 60.

John Alex. Bennett, died May 21, 1860, aged 25.

Belinda, wife of Asher D. Bennett, died Oct. 15, 1861, aged 56.

Joseph Soper, born Feb. 6, 1817, died Feb. 16, 1878.

Lawrence Reigle, died March 6, 1865, aged 54 years, 4 months, 6 days.

Wm. H. Reigle, died Dec. 8, 1870, aged 21 years, 21 days.

H. Clay Pierce, died May 29, 1871, aged 35 years.

Spencerville Circuit of the Methodist Episcopal Church is composed of portions of circuits, and was first called Sandy Spring Circuit, in 1865, the Rev. John W. Cornelius being then in charge of it.

The circuit extends from the parsonage to Liberty Grove, one and a half miles; from Liberty Grove to Mount Pisgah, six miles; from the parsonage to Zion, four miles; from Zion to Oakwood, five miles; from Oakwood to Ashton, three miles.

Liberty Grove appointment for many years belonged to the circuit below, including Laurel (Prince George's Co.), Lavady, Elk Ridge. The circuit was called Laurel-Patuxent. Oakwood belonged to Rockville Circuit for years. Mount Pisgah belonged to the same circuit with which Liberty Grove was connected.

There was a circuit, which existed a short time, made up of Friendship, Federal's, Zion, Oakwood, and Sharp Street (colored). The Conference, in 1865, gave the circuit its present form, and appointed Rev. John W. Cornelius to the charge. The succeeding appointment was Rev. E. B. Richardson, who did much in the way of building up the circuit. He paid a heavy debt on Oakwood church, and built the Zion church, or rather completed it, as it was only a frame structure. He built Mount Pisgah, and he built Ashton after organizing the society. The class-leaders of the churches at present are: Liberty Grove, Wm. H. Phair; Oakwood, Joseph H. Ziegler; Ashton, Rev. James M. Haslup; Mount Pisgah, James I. Turner.

The ministers from 1870 of the circuit have been:

1870–73, Joseph A. McCauley, presiding elder; J. P. Wilson, pastor in charge; 1873–76, William F. Speake, presiding elder; Charles O. Cook, pastor in charge; 1876–78, B. P. Brown, presiding elder; J. W. Smith, pastor in charge; 1878 (and present), B. P. Brown, presiding elder; J. S. M. Haslup, pastor in charge.

We give a sketch of its congregations:

Old Federal Church is in the bounds of and belongs to the Spencerville Circuit, and is a half-mile south of Colesville. It is said by many persons to be the oldest Methodist Episcopal church now standing in Maryland, and that the Annual Conference met within its walls. From its pulpit the word of life has been dispensed by some of the mighty men of the Methodist Episcopal Church. Here Bishop Asbury preached Christ and the resurrection within its walls to the many who came to hear, and here the eloquent McKendrie pointed men to Christ and bade them look and live. Sneathing Shin, Roberts Emory, George Sewell, J. A. Collens, and many other distinguished divines have also officiated here. The old church is no longer used for public worship.

Mount Pisgah.—This is the next oldest congregation on the circuit. It is regarded as the best church on the circuit, and is considered by many the best country church in the county. This is the third church built here in a short space of time, the two former having been destroyed by fire. In the vicinity of these are some attractive country-seats owned by persons living in Washington City, who attend service at the church. Among the former members were ex-Secretary of United States Treasury, McCullough and family.

Oakwood.—For a number of years the ministers preached in a small school-house. The Rev. Wm. P. Magruder, M.D., who was for a considerable period a member of the Baltimore Conference, and who on account of ill health was obliged to stop preaching, located near this appointment and joined this class, and about 1867 or 1868 commenced a protracted meeting, which resulted successfully. After this the desire of the people was *a new church*. The enterprise was undertaken by the Rev. J. W. Cornelius, and in a short time a church was erected, and dedicated by Rev. Dr. Littleton Morgard and Rev. A. Manship, of Philadelphia. The congregation is renowned for its liberality.

Liberty Grove.—This in a number of particulars is the best appointment on the circuit. They have a neat church, with a Sunday-school room below. The congregation is very large, and numbers two classes. The people are very liberal and kind-hearted.

Ashton.—In 1868 there was no appointment here, but in the following year Rev. E. Richardson commenced preaching in a small church belonging to the African Methodist Episcopal Church. When the winter came on a protracted meeting was held, which resulted in the conversion of many persons and the erection of a church edifice. A short time before the Conference of 1869, Bishop Ames preached in the church, and collected money to complete it.

Zion is situated in the county of Prince George's, and was connected with this circuit at its formation.

Colesville.—This village, named in honor of the Cole family, who very early settled in the neighborhood, is six miles from Silver Spring Station on the Metropolitan Branch of the Baltimore and Ohio Railroad, thirteen from Rockville, thirty from Baltimore, and near Paint Branch. It is located on "Beall Christie," granted to Charles and William Beall in 1720, and consisting of five hundred and six acres. The merchants are Mrs. A. Graff and John L. Bradford,—the latter postmaster. "Federal Methodist Episcopal church," already mentioned, a half-mile south of the village, was built just at the close of the Revolution, but is not now used for worship, having been supplanted by the Andrews Methodist Episcopal church, erected in 1868 and 1869. This is a one-story frame structure, at the western end of the village. Its pastors have been Revs. Messrs. Armstrong, McDonald, Hatteway, Smith, Jones, Porterfield, Haslip, and Wolf. The superintendent of the Sunday-school is Benjamin Fawcett, assisted by James Ziegler. The trustees are William Shaw, Francis Lazenby, and Benjamin Fawcett. In its cemetery are buried Thomas Fawcett, born March 8, 1794, died Jan. 18, 1871, and his wife, Lydia, born June 28, 1800, died Feb. 14, 1874; Joseph Fawcett, born Aug. 15, 1836, died Feb. 20, 1874; Eliza Fawcett, born June 26, 1835, died Jan. 6, 1871; Ann F. Kidwell, born Nov. 10, 1841, died Jan. 2, 1880. Charles Cunningham was the first blacksmith in Colesville, and was succeeded by Allen Reed in 1868.

Burtonsville.—This place is five and a half miles from Laurel, and was named in honor of Isaac Burton, who owned most of the land surrounding the hamlet. The post-office was established some twelve years ago. The store was started in 1868 by Alexander Sims, who was succeeded by Burton & Carr, they by Mr. Chaney, and he by Bruce Small. Isaac Burton is postmaster, and Dr. Charles Waters, physician. Liberty Grove M. E. Church, which is situated in the vicinity, is described under "Spencerville Circuit."

St. Mark's P. E. Church, or chapel, belongs to Silver Spring Parish, and was erected in 1876. It is situated near Fairland Post-office, at the intersection of the Annapolis and Columbia roads.

Four Corners is a village two miles from Silver Spring Station on the Metropolitan Branch of the Baltimore and Ohio Railroad. It contains a Methodist Episcopal Church South, built about 1871, of which Rev. Mr. Wolf is pastor. The merchants are George H. Jarboe and William E. Manakee. Lewis Miller is postmaster.

Knowels' is on the Metropolitan Branch of the Baltimore and Ohio Railroad, five miles from Rockville and fifty-one from Baltimore. The postmaster is Joshua Carrick.

Wheaton is near Forest Glen Station on the Metropolitan Branch of the Baltimore and Ohio Railroad. The merchants are D. C. Anderson, Thomas Bean, Charles Davis, Samuel Jones, Richard Mitchell, Alfred Ray, and George Plyer,—the latter postmaster. Dr. Charles Osman is the physician.

Burnt Mills.—This hamlet is situated on the Colesville turnpike, and contains several shops.

Mitchell's Cross-roads is on the Brookville turnpike, and contains a post-office, store, and several shops.

St. John's Catholic Church (Carroll's Chapel).—The church edifice is a neat brick structure, situated at Forest Glen Station on the Metropolitan Branch of the Baltimore and Ohio Railroad. The church was organized prior to 1790 by Bishop Carroll, and around it cluster many interesting memories of that pious and distinguished prelate. Here came from Virginia and Maryland many of the oldest and best families to worship. Among the dead interred in its ancient burial-ground are the following:

John Rabbitt, born Feb. 22, 1779, died March 29, 1863.
Rebecca Rabbitt, born Aug. 10, 1785, died March 5, 1876.
Martha E. Barnes, wife of John T. Barnes, died Sept. 6, 1865, aged 32.
Mary E., consort of Joseph L. Carroll, and daughter of James W. Fling, died Jan. 11, 1863, aged 38.
Susan A., wife of George Kemp, died Dec. 17, 1874, aged 46 years, 10 months, and 27 days.
Lucinda Burrows, died Sept. 29, 1873, aged 66.
Lloyd A. Burroughs, died Nov. 7, 1833, aged 30.
Ann Leydone, consort of Patrick Leydone, died Jan. 26, 1843, aged 25.
Julia Ann Donaugho, born in the County Galway, Ireland, died June 2, 1846, aged 76.
John Donougho, born in the County Galway, Ireland, died Sept. 15, 1852, aged 83.
Patrick Donougho, died 1812, aged 18.
Timothy Donougho, born April 25, 1800, died July 22, 1829.
Bridget Donougho, born March 4, 1804, died June 4, 1854.
Margaret Donougho, born July 24, 1807, died June 27, 1874.
Julia, wife of Josiah Bell, and daughter of J. and P. Ingram, died at Washington, D. C., March 21, 1874, aged 40.
Annie McDonald, died Feb. 21, 1858, aged 23.
Lewis Ratcliff, died Aug. 8, 1849, aged 44 years, 9 months, and 7 days.
Charles Bunting, born July 1, 1785, died Sept. 18, 1833.
Susan M. Bunting, born Feb. 21, 1801, died May 25, 1874.
Lucretia, wife of J. N. Norton, born Sept. 28, 1829, died July 12, 1876.
William B. Mickum, died Nov. 25, 1866, aged 38.
Charles E. Brent, born at Washington, D. C., 1827, died Dec. 6, 1867.
Anna M., relict of Robert Leroy Livingstone, of New York, died Feb. 27, 1865, at New York City, aged 73.
Eleanor Carroll, wife of Daniel Carroll, died Feb. 3, 1796, aged 92.
Ann Brent, relict of Robert Brent, Esq., and daughter of Daniel Carroll, born July 13, 1733, died November, 1804.

William Brent, born at Aquia, Stafford Co., Va., died in Washington, D. C., Dec. 15, 1848, aged 73.

Elizabeth Brent, his wife, born in Charles Co., Md., died in Washington, D. C., March 29, 1863, aged 63.

"Edward and Priscilla Neal."

Catharine Digges, relict of George Digges, born in Stafford Co., Va.

John White, died Jan. 1, 1855, aged 59.
Sarah J. White, born March 4, 1799, died Sept. 7, 1856.
James M. White, died June 19, 1853, aged 30.
Charles V. Coopard, born July 14, 1777, died Nov. 13, 1861.
Mary E. Coopard, born Sept. 2, 1802, died May 9, 1864.
Michael Connolly, died March, 1854, aged 78.
Sarah Lyons, died Nov. 2, 1800, aged 29.
"Mark Whelan," son of Nick Whelan.
Margaret Fahy, died Aug. 22, 1800.
Mary Whalen, died Dec. 27, 1830, aged 60.
Elizabeth Barnes, died July 7, 1861, aged 76.
Julian Whelan, died June 25, 1832, aged 35.
Sarah Sweney, died Jan. 6, 1831, aged 80.
Bridget Connelly, died Dec. 4, 1829, aged 52.
John O. Conner, died 1832, aged 33.
Martin Conner, born 1750, died 1829; Sarah, his wife, born 1745, died 1814.
Matilda Haverson, died July 21, 1859, aged 60.
Phil. Fenwick, born Dec. 12, 1789, died Oct. 21, 1863; and wife, Mary Ann, born March 18, 1799, died Sept. 21, 1848.
Catharine, daughter of Pat. and Nora Welsh, died June, ——, aged 15.
William D. Barrett, died July 18, 1829, aged 30.
Notley Moreland, died Aug. 27, 1863, aged 60.
Notley Moreland, Jr., died Nov. 5, 1857, aged 20.
George R. Carroll, died Aug. 7, 1858, aged 45.
William Carroll, born June 12, 1782, died Feb. 21, 1855.
George A. Carroll, M.D., died July 18, 1844, aged 56.
Ann Carroll, born April 17, 1777, died July 29, 1862.
Elizabeth Digges Carroll, born Aug. 4, 1753, died Jan. 27, 1843.
Daniel Carroll, died on June 19, 1790.
William Dudley Diggs, born 1790, died Jan. 17, 1830, aged 59.
Norah, his wife, born 1791, died July 17, 1864.
Theo. Mosher, born Dec. 4, 1824, died July 26, 1878.
Sarah Hayes Brent, daughter of Robert Y. and Harriet Brent, died April 28, 1862.
William Cottringer Brent, died Sept. 13, 1860, aged 56.
Harriet, wife of Robert Y. Brent, died Oct. 10, 1865, aged 64.
Robert Young Brent, died Dec. 7, 1855, aged 67.

The corner-stone of the church was laid Aug. 9, 1849, by Archbishop Eccleston, when Rev. John P. Donelan preached the sermon.

Silver Spring Parish and Grace Protestant Episcopal Church.—In 1858, Silver Spring Parish was formed out of Rock Creek Parish. Its rectors since 1862, when the elegant frame edifice was erected, have been as follows: 1862-65, Rev. McEnheimer; 1865-70, Rev. John Wiley; 1870 to present time, Rev. James B. Averitt. This church has three chapels, —St. Mark's, on Columbia road, built in 1876; St. John's, at Bethesda, erected in 1876; and St. Mary's, on the Brookville road, built in 1881. The principal persons instrumental in the formation of this parish in 1858 were Montgomery Blair, Josiah Harding, O. H. P. Clark, Hopkins Anderson, Mrs. Admiral S. P. Leland, William H. Batchelor. The venerable journalist, Francis P. Blair, Sr., was baptized and received into this church, in his residence at Silver Spring, in an upper chamber, where hung Sully's picture of his revered mother. The vestrymen of the church are Montgomery Blair, Joseph H. Bradley, Dr. James H. Davidson, Spencer Watkins, Horatio Carroll, William Riley, Jr., Julius Marlow, Franklin Pilling; and the wardens are Richard T. Ray and John Davidson. Its rector, Rev. James B. Averitt, was born in 1835 in North Carolina, and graduated at the university of that State, and also in the law school under Chief Justice R. M. Pearson. He served four years in the Confederate army, and was several years principal of the Winchester, Va., Seminary for Young Ladies. When he took the pastorate the church had forty-one, and now has two hundred and twenty communicants. The three chapels already mentioned have been built during his rectorship. Previous to his removal to this parish he had charge for several months of the Catoctin Mission of Frederick County. In the cemetery attached to the church are the remains of

W. P. Jackson, died Sept. 17, 1873, aged 23.
Deborah W. Ganby, born Dec. 5, 1802, died Dec. 6, 1864.
Eleanor Winthem, aged 36.
Elizabeth Winthem, aged 81.
Anna Winthem, aged 77.
Charlotte G. Cousins, born April 11, 1793, in London, England, died Feb. 18, 1874.
Adolph M. Wilhelm Bergfield, born July 10, 1828, died Jan. 30, 1874.
Mary, wife of Charles B. Graves, born Oct. 10, 1855, died June 23, 1880.
John G. Fiddler, born April 23, 1823, died March 4, 1874.
Nancy Jones, died Feb. 20, 1873, aged 55.
George J. Schmidt, born Sept. 7, 1827, died June 27, 1877.

Sligo —This place is on the Brookville turnpike, near Silver Spring Station on the Metropolitan Branch of the Baltimore and Ohio Railroad, and is six miles from Washington. James L. Dorsey is postmaster, and Drs. Josiah Harding and C. G. Stone, physicians. The merchants are J. L. Dorsey, Samuel Jackson, and A. L. Graves. The Methodist Episcopal and Methodist Protestant congregations have each a neat frame church edifice. Sligo and Silver Spring Station are both on the survey of "Girl's Portion," which was surveyed for Col. Henry Dulany in 1688. It extended from Rock Creek eastward to O. H. P. Clark's farm, three and three-eighths miles. The Ashton and Sligo turnpike passes through this tract, and the Brookville and Washington turnpike crosses it. The

Blair estate, "Silver Spring," is included in this survey.

St. Joseph's Park lies on the east side of Rock Creek, and embraces Knowles' Station, Forest Glen Station, and Linden Station, including the beautiful farms of Alfred Ray, William A. Batchelor, and Carroll's or St. John's chapel. The Brookville and Washington turnpike passes through it, from Augustus Burgdorf's farm nearly to Grace Protestant Episcopal church.

St. Joseph's Park comprises a tract of land granted May 20, 1689, to William Joseph, containing four thousand two hundred and twenty acres.

The school trustees and teachers for 1881 and 1882 are as follows:

Trustees.—No. 1, Aquila Windham, Cephas Hurley, Maurice Weller; No. 2, J. C. Willson, J. B. Childs, Thos. Cissel; No. 3, Wm. E. Shaw, Joseph Hopkins, John M. Clark; No. 4, James Bonifant, W. F. Lagenby, Perry Luthwan; No. 5, Richard Waters, L. H. Duvall, W. H. Spencer; No. 6, W. P. Miller, Dr. Thomas, Wm. T. Bond; No. 7, Frank Mulhem, J. G. Cashell, Jackson Cashell; No. 8, O. P. H. Clark, Thos. Hardesty, Columbus Joy; No. 9, Benj. Fawcett, —— Keiler, J. Marlow; No. 10, H. Linkins, W. B. Weller, Edward Rabbitt; No. 11, W. H. Manneke, P. P. Flournoy, R. H. Perry.

Teachers.—No. 1, Mary D. Hardy, Wheaton P. O.; No. 2, E. S. C. Weaver, Sligo P. O.; No. 3, Cyrus Grady, Burnt Mills P. O.; No. 4, C. N. Warfield, Colesville P. O.; No. 5, Frank Miller, Spencerville P. O.; No. 6, A. T. Porter, Sandy Spring P. O.; No. 7, Wm. Grady, Sandy Spring P. O.; No. 8, F. P. Clark, Silver Spring P. O.; No. 9, H. S. Rennolds, Fairland P. O.; No. 10, Mercy A. Griffin, Norbeck P. O.; No. 11, A. R. Wingate, Bethesda P. O.

There are three colored schools.

The magistrates are John T. Baker, Causin Condict, James C. Haviland, Samuel R. Carr.

DARNESTOWN DISTRICT, No. 6.

This district was created Feb. 14, 1878, and was formed from portions of Medley and Rockville Districts. Its metes and bounds are as follows:

"Beginning at the crossing of Little Seneca Creek by the county road leading from Gaithersburg to Barnesville, and running down and with said Little Seneca Creek until it empties into Great Seneca Creek; thence down and with said Great Seneca Creek until it empties into the Potomac River; thence down and with said Potomac River to the mouth of Watts' Branch; thence up and with said Watts' Branch to the mouth of Piney Branch; thence up and with said Piney Branch until the same is crossed by the public road near the residence of Mrs. Upton West; thence down and with said public road in the direction of Darnestown, until the same intersects the road known as the Du Tirf mill road; then with and up said road, as it is described in the plat recorded in Liber J. G. H., number seven, folio six hundred and three, of the land records of said Montgomery County, until the same intersects the Gaithersburg and Barnesville road, near Gaithersburg; then with said Gaithersburg and Barnesville road in the direction of Barnesville to the place of beginning, to include Harris and Watkins Islands in the Potomac River."

This district is bounded on the north and northwest by Medley District, west by the Potomac River and Virginia, south by Great Falls and Rockville Districts, and east by Clarkesburg and Gaithersburg Districts. Little and Great Seneca Creeks separate it from Medley District, and Piney Branch from Great Falls District. The other streams are Muddy Branch, flowing west into the Potomac, and Long Draught, northwest into Great Seneca Creek.

The earliest settlers were Walter Evans, James Plummer, John Chitten, William Offutt, the Dawsons, Pumphreys, Joneses, Wests, Du Fiefs, Purdums, Crosses, Vincents, Rices, Higginses, and Bentons.

Darnestown.—This town lies five miles from Germantown, and was named in honor of William Darne. The oldest house belongs to the heirs of William Darne, and is occupied by Edward Green. The first store was kept by John Candler, and the first tavern by Andrew Barneycloe. Dr. Edwards was the first resident physician. John Doud was the first blacksmith, and the first wheelwright-shop was carried on by Samuel Leeke, with whom Richard Hopple, his successor, and the present wheelwright, learned his trade. John Candler was the first postmaster, and J. S. Windsor is the present. Dr. Thomas Williams is the resident physician, and Dr. R. B. Beall, dentist. James S. Windsor and James F. Poole are the merchants. Darnestown Grange, No. 33, is located here, of which L. A. Darby is Master, and E. L. Tschiffely, secretary. Pleasant Hill Lodge, No. 97, I. O. O. F., was instituted at Pleasant Hill, where its meetings were held until after the war, when it was removed to this town. In September, 1881,—no meetings having been held here for several months,—the lodge was removed to Dawsonville.

The Presbyterian church, a frame structure, was built in 1855. The successful establishment of this church was chiefly the result of the faithful labors of its first and efficient pastor, Rev. Metzger. After his death Rev. James Henderson became pastor, who was succeeded by Rev. Charles Beach, and he by Rev. Henry Brown, the present incumbent.

In the rear of the church is a graveyard, in which are interred

Mary E. Warfield, born Sept. 18, 1820, died Dec. 27, 1880.
Wm. W. Warfield, born Sept. 17, 1858, died Nov. 8, 1874.
Mary A., wife of James Offutt, born Nov. 3, 1819, died April 6, 1879.
Elizabeth R., wife of Elbert Perry, born Dec. 3, 1820, died Feb. 18, 1880.
Bessie L., daughter of C. H. and Celia E. Vincent, died Oct. 6, 1880, aged 7 years.
Elizabeth Claggett, died Dec. 7, 1872, aged 79.
Susan E. Claggett, died Feb. 5, 1872, aged 58.
Fannie E. Hays, died June 1, 1863.

Rose R. Offutt, died March 28, 1870, aged 19.

George H. Peter, born July 7, 1809, died May 23, 1880.

Ann, wife of M. F. Harris, born Dec. 30, 1810, died July 30, 1878.

John Israel, only son of J. P. and M. C. Philips, died Feb. 19, 1862, aged 15.

An elegant monument and stone bears this inscription:

"Sacred to the memory of Andrew Small, born Aug. 28, 1794, in Lochee, Parish of Liff, Scotland, died in Washington City, D. C., April 6, 1847. In the year 1829, Mr. Small emigrated to America, and by industry and economy accumulated considerable wealth. Firmness of purpose, strictness of integrity, and sincerity were the leading traits of his character. Having purchased an estate in this county, he became much interested in the religious and educational interests of the Darnestown Presbyterian Church and community, and during his life made a liberal donation for the support of the gospel in this place. By his will he left to the trustees of the church means for the endowment of the Andrew Small Academy, and very liberally provided for the support of the Sunday-school and the widows and orphans of the church and community. He died a peaceful death. His last words were to the effect that he relied alone on the blood of Christ for salvation."

Andrew Small Male and Female Academy.—This institution is near the Presbyterian church. It grew out of a parochial school established and maintained for some years by the church. Mr. Andrew Small, a native of Scotland, but then residing in Georgetown, D. C., becoming acquainted with the neighborhood while filling a contract for making that part of the Chesapeake and Ohio Canal which passes near by, and admiring the commendable efforts of the people to improve their educational facilities, was induced to leave to the Presbyterian Church the large bequest of forty thousand dollars. The larger part of this munificent sum was directed to be devoted to the erection of a suitable building for a school and the partial endowment of an institution which would bring the advantages of a liberal education within the reach of the whole community. The academy building—the largest school building in the county, and built of brick—was finished and first occupied in 1869, two years after Mr. Small's death. The institution was named after its liberal founder. The first principal was Prof. M. L. Venable, of Southern Virginia. He continued in charge four years, and was succeeded by the present incumbent, Rev. C. N. Campbell, who has had the advantage of a thorough collegiate training, having graduated with distinction at Princeton College. He is a Presbyterian clergyman. The institution is a boarding-school for both boys and girls, and numbers some sixty pupils, about one-third of whom are boarders. It is managed by a self-perpetuating board of trustees, duly incorporated, of whom F. A. Tschiffely is president, and G. R. Rice, secretary. The funds are, however, controlled by the trustees of the church, who are elected annually. The generous design of its establishment was to furnish to the people of Darnestown and the surrounding region a Christian school of high grade at moderate rates. Through Mr. Small's donation this effort has been accomplished. The course of instruction is full and thorough, preparing boys for college or for business, and affording to young ladies the means of a liberal education. Prof. Campbell is assisted by an able corps of teachers, and at the end of the scholastic year a public examination of a week is held in all the studies of the year. An annual public exhibition closes the school year, when certificates of proper deportment and of scholarship are given to those who deserve them. Prizes for the best compositions in the several classes are also awarded, and such other honors as are deemed proper.

Baptist Church.—This log edifice was built over a half-century ago by the Methodists, but for several years has been used by the Baptist congregation. Near it are the graves of the following persons:

Elizabeth Truman and her infant baby, wife and child of Josiah Truman, who died April 25, 1852, aged 22 years.

Elizabeth, wife of Samuel T. Magruder, died July 5, 1881, aged 65.

Mrs. Sarah Dorsey, born Feb. 9, 1800, died Dec. 20, 1879.

Worthington, only son of S. T. and Elizabeth Magruder, born July 30, 1848, died Sept. 29, 1854.

James Hawkins, Jr., died Dec. 29, 1855, aged 58.

Ara, wife of James Hawkins, died May 2, 1848, aged 57.

Ellen Maria, wife of Nathaniel Claggett, died Oct. 10, 1848, aged 23; and Ann Elizabeth, wife of same, died Dec. 29, 1857, aged 27.

Joseph C. Hawkins, died May 3, 1849, aged 28.

Daues Norris, born May 28, 1786, died Jan. 18, 1867.

Elizabeth Padgett, died April 1, 1879, aged 60.

John H. Lewis, born Oct. 4, 1787, died Aug. 1, 1872; and his wife Lucinda, born Nov. 23, 1793, died Dec. 7, 1873; and their daughter, Catherine Cadwell, born Dec. 1, 1824, died May 24, 1846.

Susan Stewart, died June 30, 1853, aged 75.

Seneca Baptist church is at the mouth of Great Seneca Creek, and is a neat stone structure. Its pastor is Rev. Mr. Hatchey, of Virginia, who also preaches at the Baptist church between Darnestown and Germantown,—a new frame edifice.

The school trustees and teachers for 1881 and 1882 are as follows:

Trustees.—No. 1, M. B. Montgomery, Geo. R. Rice, Winfield Magruder; No. 2, J. F. Poole, Wm. H. Rice, Wm. H. Vincent; No. 3, H. A. Pumphrey, R. H. Bennett, Jacob Snider.

Teachers.—No. 1, J. F. Burn, Rockville P. O.; No. 2, Dr. T. E. Williams, Darnestown P. O.; No. 3, H. C. Hickerson, Germantown P. O.

There are two colored schools. The magistrates are Edward L. Hays, Samuel Higgins.

ALFRED RAY.

Hunting Hill.—This post-office is forty miles from Baltimore, sixteen from Georgetown, D. C., and four from Rockville. J. B. Ward is merchant and postmaster; E. Holland, teacher; a cooper, blacksmith, and T. H. Herrington, carpenter.

BETHESDA DISTRICT, No. 7.

This district was created by an act March 20, 1878, and was formed from portions of Rockville, the Fourth, and Berry, the Fifth, Districts. Its metes and bounds are as follows:

"Beginning on the Potomac River at the point where the dividing line between Montgomery County and the District of Columbia crosses the same; then running with said dividing line in a northeasterly direction until the same crosses near the residence of Hon. Montgomery Blair; then with the said dividing line in a southeasterly direction until the same is crossed by the turnpike leading from Brookville to Washington City; then with said turnpike in a northerly direction until the same is crossed by the Metropolitan Branch of the Baltimore and Ohio Railroad; then with said railroad in a westerly direction until the same crosses the county road east of Rock Creek and near Newport Mills; then with said county road until it intersects the turnpike leading from Rockville to Georgetown; then with a straight line to the intersection of the Orendorff mill road with the old Georgetown road, near the residence of Isaac O. Rabbitt; then with said Orendorff mill road until the same is crossed by Thomas' Run; then down and with said Thomas' Run until the same empties into Cabin John Creek; then down and with said Cabin John Creek until the same empties into the Potomac River; then down and with the Potomac River to the place of beginning."

This district is bounded on the north and northwest by Great Falls District, north by Rockville District, east by Berry District, south by the District of Columbia, and west by the Potomac River and Virginia. Cabin John Creek and Thomas' Run separate it on the north from Great Falls and Rockville Districts. Rock Creek flows southerly in the east into the District of Columbia, while flowing westwardly are Bowie's Run into Cabin John Creek, Naylor's Branch into the Potomac, and Falls Branch into Receiving Reservoir.

The first settlers were Thomas Fletchall, Thomas Addison, James Stoddart, the Wilsons, Youngs, Austins, Councilmans, Loughboroughs, Beans, Renshaws, Pyles, Gingells, Andersons, Williamses, Huddlestons, Lawrences, and Rays.

Alfred Ray, prominent in Montgomery as a farmer and stock-raiser, comes of one of the oldest of Maryland's families, following, indeed, his ancestry upon either side back to the time of Lord Baltimore's possession of the province. The Rays were of the first Protestant settlement made in what is now Anne Arundel County, and were active and zealous members of the Church of England.

Enos Ray, who was born in Anne Arundel County, moved to the District of Columbia about 1830. He had rendered excellent service as a soldier of the war of 1812, and in recognition of that service received from the government two sections of land. His wife was Sarah, daughter of Anthony L. Moreland, of Anne Arundel County, whose progenitors are supposed to have located in Anne Arundel County about the time Lord Baltimore came over. The Morelands afterwards became prominent landholders in Montgomery County. Enos Ray's wife died in 1826. He married for his second wife, Elizabeth, daughter of Archibald Osborn, of the District of Columbia.

Of the children by the first marriage the only one living is William Ray, of Montgomery County. Of the ten children by the second marriage, seven survive. Enos Ray died in April, 1881, aged eighty-nine. Longevity was in his ancestors a common thing. His grandmother Ray lived to be one hundred and four. Mr. Ray's wife died in April, 1880, aged eighty-four.

William Ray above named was born in the District of Columbia, Jan. 16, 1824. He attended school at Columbian College, his preceptor being the well-known Dr. Samson. William Ray's father was a very successful farmer, and owned so much land that he was enabled to give each of his children a farm. Thus, William, at the age of twenty-eight, received a farm located in the District, and entered at once upon active experience as a practical farmer. He lived upon the District farm until 1863, when he purchased the Montgomery County farm-tract known as "Highland," situated about nine miles distant from Washington. "Highland" was for years owned by the Brent estate, and from 1816 to the date of Mr. Ray's purchase was held by the Federal government, from the Congress of which, indeed, Mr. Ray obtained his title. To the six hundred and forty acres originally included in "Highland" Mr. Ray has added one hundred acres, and much enhanced the value of the property by material and valuable improvements. He gives especial attention to the growth of grass and dairying, but carries on likewise general farming upon a liberal scale. About one hundred head of stock are regularly maintained upon the place. From 1852 to 1863 Mr. Ray filled the important office of tax collector of the District of Columbia, and in the years 1862 and 1863 was United States revenue assessor for the District. The holding of public office, however, has never been to his taste. He has fulfilled important tasks as a railway contractor, and among other undertakings built the bridges on the Baltimore and

Ohio Railroad between Washington and Point of Rocks, graded the road-bed between Forest Glen and Washington, and extended most of the arches on the Baltimore and Ohio Railroad between Baltimore and Washington.

He has been twice married. His first wife was Lydia A., daughter of Capt. James White, of the District of Columbia. His second marriage was with Miss Ella M., daughter of Nicholas Gatch (died 1878) and Ann Merryman (died 1881), of Baltimore County. For five generations the Gatch family has been represented in Baltimore County. An old document, still in the possession of the descendants, testifies that Dec. 26, 1727, Godfrey Gatch (who came from Prussia to Maryland) and Maria, his wife, were authorized by Governor Leonard Calvert to pass unmolested and uninterrupted through the province, conditioned upon their "behaving themselves according to law." The land then owned by Godfrey Gatch in Baltimore County is now owned in part by Mrs. William Ray. Mr. and Mrs. Ray have nine children living.

Silver Spring—The Blair Family.—Hon. Francis Preston Blair, the veteran journalist and editor of the *Globe* during Jackson's administration, was attracted to Silver Spring under singular circumstances. He had purchased a very fine saddle-horse, Selim, of Gen. William Lingan Gaither, another of Montgomery's representative men, who had repeatedly served his native county with credit and ability in both branches of the State Legislature. In taking a ride with his daughter beyond the limits of the District of Columbia and in the lower part of Montgomery County, Selim became frightened, threw his rider, and ran down among the thick growth of pines in the valley to the west of the road. Mr. Blair followed, and found the horse fast to a bush, which had caught the dangling reins of the bridle. Near the spot he spied a bold fountain bubbling up, the beautiful white sand sparkling in the water like specks of silver. Mr. Blair became so charmed with the spot and the spring that he resolved at once, if possible, to possess it. He sought its owner, and soon a bargain was made at what was then considered a good price by the seller, but in the eyes of Mr. Blair as very cheap. These are the circumstances which led to the proprietorship of the far-famed and classic seat of Silver Spring, where its owner, venerable and distinguished, spent in easy retirement the last twenty-five years of his long and eventful life, and died peacefully, full of years and honors, at the advanced age of eighty-seven, Oct. 18, 1876.[1]

---

[1] "Centennial Celebration of Montgomery County."

Mr. Blair was born in 1789 in Abingdon, Va., and early in life settled in Kentucky, where he married Eliza Violetta Howard Gist, the fourth daughter of Col. Nathaniel Gist, who was a colonel in the Virginia line during the Revolutionary war, and died early in the present century at an old age. Col. Gist left two sons, Henry Carey and Thomas Cecil Gist; and his eldest daughter, Sarah Howard, married Hon. Jesse Bledsoe, a United States Senator from Kentucky, and a distinguished jurist, whose grandson, B. Gratz Brown, was the Democratic candidate for Vice-President in 1872; his second daughter, Anne (Nancy) Gist, married Col. Nathaniel Hart, a sister of Mrs. Henry Clay; his third daughter married Dr. Boswell, of Lexington, Ky.; and his fifth daughter married Benjamin Gratz, of the same place. Mrs. Blair's father, Col. Nathaniel Gist, was the third child of Christopher Gist, who married Sarah Howard, the second daughter of Joshua and Joanna O'Carroll, by whom he had four children: Nancy, who died unmarried, and Thomas, Nathaniel, and Richard. Christopher, with his sons Nathaniel and Richard, was with Braddock on the fatal field of Monongahela, and for his services received a grant of twelve thousand acres of land from the King of Great Britain.

It is said that the third brother, Thomas, was taken prisoner at Braddock's defeat, and lived fifteen or sixteen years with the Indians in Canada. Richard settled in South Carolina, where he married, and was killed at the battle of South Mountain. Thomas Gist after his release from captivity lived with his father on the grant in Kentucky, and became a man of note, presiding in the courts till his death, about 1786. Col. Nathaniel Gist, father of Mrs. Blair, married Judith Carey Bell, of Buckingham County, Va. Christopher Gist, the father of Nathaniel, because of his knowledge of the country on the Ohio and his skill in dealing with the Indians was chosen to accompany Washington on his mission in 1753, and it was from his journal that all subsequent historians derive their account of that expedition. Christopher was the son of Richard Gist, who in 1705 married Zipporah Murray, and who became surveyor of the Western Shore, and was one of the commissioners in 1729 for laying off Baltimore Town, and was presiding magistrate in 1736. This Richard was the only child of Christopher Gist, who died in Baltimore County in 1691, and whose wife, Edith (Cromwell), died in 1694.

The Gists were early emigrants to Maryland, and took an active part in the affairs of the province. Francis P. Blair took an active interest in the politics of the country up to the year of his death. In 1860 he was one of the Republican delegates from Maryland to the Chicago Convention that nominated President Lincoln. His son, Gen. Francis P. Blair, Jr., many years represented St. Louis in the National House of Representatives, and was a major-general in the Union army, in which, in the civil war, he served with distinction. He was the Democratic candidate for Vice-President in 1868. Hon. Montgomery Blair, son of Francis P. Blair, Sr., resides at Silver Spring, at the old Blair seat. He is one of the most distinguished lawyers in the country. He was a strong Union man, and supported President Andrew Johnson in the great fight made by the Republican party to impeach him. Since then he has been identified with the Democratic party, of which to-day the country has no abler adherent.

He was born in Franklin County, Ky., on May 10, 1813, and graduated at West Point in 1835. Entering the Second Artillery, he served in the Florida war, but resigned on May 20, 1836. He studied law, and began practice in St. Louis in 1837. He was United States District Attorney for Missouri in 1839–43, and was judge of the Court of Common Pleas, 1843–49. In 1842 he was also mayor of St. Louis. In 1852 he removed to Maryland, and was a delegate from the then Sixth Congressional District to the Chicago Convention in 1860 that nominated Abraham Lincoln. From March, 1861, to Sept. 23, 1864, he was United States Postmaster-General. He was the only member of Mr. Lincoln's cabinet who opposed the surrender of Fort Sumter in 1861. He opposed strenuously the arrest of private citizens during the war and the reconstruction measures, including the Wade-Davis bill. In 1863, in a speech at Rockville, Montgomery Co., he publicly denounced the principles of those measures. This speech, which was widely published, gave great offense to the Republicans, and was approved by the Democrats. There was a strong Republican pressure to force his withdrawal from the cabinet, but he had the fullest confidence of Mr. Lincoln to the last. In October, 1864, the resignation of Mr. Blair, which had been tendered long before, was accepted. In 1865, Mr. Blair organized the movement that restored self-government to the people of Maryland. In 1877 he was elected to the House of Delegates, and took the lead in all important measures affecting the best interests of his State and county. His most notable efforts were to secure a protest against, or an investigation of, the title of Mr. Hayes to the Presidency, and to economize by reducing expenses in our State affairs. In the Legislature Mr. Blair was one of the ablest and hard-working members. To his personal influence was due the passage of the resolutions by both branches of the Legislature directing the attorney-general of the State to take legal steps looking to the adjudication by the Supreme Court of the right of Mr. Hayes to the Presidency. Before the repeal of the Missouri Compromise he had been a Democrat, but afterwards attached himself to the Republican party, and was removed by President Buchanan from the office of solicitor of the Court of Claims, to which he had been appointed by President Pierce. Mr. Blair participated in the argument before the Supreme Court of all the great constitutional questions since 1853, such as the test oath law, the enforcement act, etc. In the famous Dred Scott case he was counsel for the plaintiff. Mr. Blair is now one of the ablest statesmen in the country, of tall and commanding figure, of pleasing manners, great intelligence, and public spirit.

Cabin John.—This town is on the Chesapeake and Ohio Canal, nine miles from Rockville, forty-eight from Baltimore, and derives its name from Cabin John Creek,—originally Captain John,—which here enters the Potomac River. This creek is crossed by a stone-arch bridge, of a single arch, the longest span in the world. It was built by the government to carry water from the Great Falls of the Potomac to Washington. This magnificent structure crosses the creek at a height of one hundred and one feet. It is erected of immense blocks of granite, with Seneca parapets and coping, and leaps the ravine in a single arch of two hundred and twenty feet, with fifty-seven and a half feet rise from the springing line. It is twenty feet wide, and its extreme length four hundred and twenty feet. It cost two hundred and thirty-seven thousand dollars. It is the largest stone-arch bridge in the world, the second being part of the Grosvenor bridge, with a span of two hundred feet, which crosses the river Dee. It was constructed by Gen. M. C. Meigs, during the administration of Jefferson Davis as Secretary of War under President Pierce. For a long time the name of Mr. Davis was among those inscribed on a stone tablet which marks the bridge, but by the official order of Secretary Simon Cameron it was erased at the beginning of the late war, and is now truly conspicuous by its absence.

Bethesda Presbyterian Church.—The Presbyterian congregations of Rockville and Bethesda form one church, organically and historically. They have one bench of elders and one communion roll, though they are distinct congregations, worshiping in different churches. The name of the church was originally Captain John, latterly called Cabin John. Of the early history of the church very little can be gathered, as one or two of the first volumes of the records have been lost. The date of the organization of the church is unknown, but there is reason to believe that the church existed prior to the Revolutionary war. The father of one of the elders (Mr. De Sellum) was baptized by the Rev. James Hunt, pastor of Captain John Church. He was born in 1773. Mr. Hunt's name occurs for the first time in the records of the Presbyterian Church in 1761. Whether at that time he was pastor of Cabin John on the one hand, or whether the church existed before he became minister, we are unable to decide. The impression is that he was the first minister, and that the church had its origin about 1761. The first pastor, Rev. James Hunt, was born in Hanover County, Va., where his father, about 1740, was one of four seceders from the established church who formed a Presbyterian Society, whose first pastor was Rev. Samuel Daviss. Mr. Hunt, in 1783, had lived for a considerable time at his residence, some three miles west of Bethesda church, on his farm, which was called by the classic name Tusculum.

At this date his school was one of high standing, and doubtless widely known in the State. It seems he sustained his family partly by the revenue from this school while nursing the infant church, which was probably unable to give him an adequate support. Among his pupils was William Wirt. We have the following concerning Wirt's early days from "Kennedy's Life of Wirt." In 1783 (says he) "I was removed from the grammar school of Mr. Dent, in Charles County, to that of the Rev. Mr. Hunt, in Montgomery County." The author continues: "Wirt remained at Mr. Hunt's school in Montgomery County until it was broken up in 1787. During the last two years of this period he was an inmate of Mr. Hunt's family."

Mr. Hunt seems to have exercised a happy influence over the character of his pupils. He was a man of cultivated mind, liberal education, and philosophical temper. He possessed a pretty good library, a thing uncommon in those days. He had, besides, a pair of globes and philosophical apparatus. He was communicative, and quick to appreciate the taste of his scholars, and from all accounts kindly and indulgent in his intercourse with them. Young Wirt found much in this association to advance him on his way. He acquired some insight into astronomy, some taste for physics, some relish for classical study, but, above all, some sharpness of appetite for the amusement afforded by "the run of the library." He studied law with William P. Hunt, son of Rev. James Hunt, at Montgomery County Court-house.

On the stone which marks Mr. Hunt's grave at the site of old Cabin John church are engraved the words:

"In memory of the Rev. James Hunt, who departed this life the 2d of June, 1793, aged 62 years.

"He was set apart to the work of the ministry early in life, in which he continued till death, laboring for the good of souls and the glory of his Heavenly Master.

"'Be ye followers of me as I was of Christ Jesus. By grace ye are saved.'"

The successor of Mr. Hunt occupied his place a comparatively short time, dying in the year 1800. His name was Adam Freeman. He was succeeded by one of the most remarkable men the Presbyterian Church has ever produced in this country,—Dr. Conrad Speece. His connection with the church was a short one, and ended in 1805. Dr. Speece spent the greater part of his ministerial life in Virginia, where he is still remembered by many of the elder people as a preacher of great power. He was a man of originality and genius. Of the fourth pastor, Dr. Samuel Martin, no particulars can be learned, except that his connection with the Presbytery of Baltimore, and doubtless with this church, ceased in 1814.

He was succeeded by the Rev. Joshua T. Russell. Some of the oldest members of the church still remember him as a man of unusual oratorical powers. During his ministry occurs the following entry in the record book, dated Dec. 14, 1818:

"*Whereas*, The Session are fully persuaded of the importance of family worship, and of the duty of each member of the church to maintain such worship, as prescribed in the Directory, chap. xv. 3, 4; *and whereas*, They have reason to fear that this duty is too much neglected by the members of this church; therefore,

"*Resolved*, That two members of the Session be appointed as a committee to inquire of all male members of this church who are heads of families whether this duty is regularly attended to in their families, and that they report to Session the result of their inquiries at their next meeting."

Under date of Jan. 2, 1819, is recorded the report of the committee, which was to the effect that they had found only one member who entirely neglected family worship, and another who had occasionally neglected it. "The Session," says the record, "conversed with the latter, and received encouragement that he would in future be constant in the discharge of this duty. A committee was also appointed to converse with the neglector and endeavor to persuade him to maintain family prayer in the future."

The day following, Jan. 3, 1819, there was a very solemn communion, in which eight persons were admitted to the Lord's table. Rev. Elias Harrison preached the sermon to a very large congregation. In one of his letters he states that he often preached to more than one thousand persons at Cabin John church.

In 1820 a committee was appointed by the Session to consult with gentlemen in the neighborhood now occupied by Bethesda congregation as to the propriety of erecting a meeting-house in the vicinity of Mr. McCubbin's, and to propose the organization of a congregation there as a branch of Cabin John Church.

After 1820 there seems to have been no pastor for two years, and it was perhaps in this interim that the Rev. John Breckenridge preached to the congregation in the Bethesda neighborhood. During the time of his supplying this church the first Bethesda church was built.

Dr. Carnahan, afterwards president of Princeton College, also ministered to the church at this time, though never its pastor.

In 1822, Dr. Mines, whose memory is fragrant among the members at this day, began a pastorate of thirty-five years. His name is inscribed on the tablet which is a prominent object in the Rockville church. Dr. Mines performed the double duty of pastor and teacher. He was for a long time principal of Rockville Academy, and in this position was as efficient as in his work in the church. Says a late contributor to the Montgomery *Sentinel*, "In the academy he had a continuous re-election for twenty-five years, and had to decline by reason of age and infirmity (he being about forty years of age when he took charge), but he had a general oversight until the day of his death."

Under his principalship the academy prospered, and took high rank in general education and the preparatory collegiate course. His pupils are now among the most worthy citizens, filling the posts of the farmer, mechanic, lawyer, judge, preacher, and physician. Two of his sons and five pupils were brought into the church and entered the ministry.

During the summer vacation of the academy he generally held a protracted meeting, sometimes in the woods, where churches were not convenient, and with good result. In social life he was a pattern worthy of imitation, hospitable, cheerful, bright, and happy. During the latter years of his ministry Dr. Mines was assisted by Rev. Randolph A. Smith, who became co-pastor in 1846. During his co-pastorate the church at Bethesda was consumed by fire. It was built of unhewn stone, and stood within what is now the cemetery.

Through the indefatigable efforts of Mr. Smith the adjoining parcel of land on the south, consisting of about thirty acres, was purchased, and the present commodious church edifice built on a much more eligible site than that occupied by the first building. Mr. Smith also accomplished the building of a comfortable mansion about four hundred yards south of the church.

In the year 1852 the Rev. William T. Eva became pastor of the church. He is described by those who knew him as a hard student, an excellent preacher, and a most faithful pastor in every respect. The church prospered greatly under his ministration. In one year about forty persons were added to the congregation. He is now pastor of a very large church in Philadelphia. He resigned the charge of the Bethesda and Rockville Church in 1857.

In 1859 the Rev. Edward H. Cumpston became pastor. During his pastorate, in 1864, the membership of the church was larger than ever before, numbering one hundred and eighty-six, according to the statistical report. He resigned the charge in 1874, and is now pastor of the Presbyterian Church at Hancock, Md.

The present pastor, Rev. Parke P. Flournoy, entered upon his work, April 1, 1875. The elders in office in 1818, the date of the earliest sessional records, were Thomas Scott, William Scott, Osgood Offutt, and Richard Gatton. Nicholas Clopper was ordained 3d January, 1819; Otho Magruder and Zachariah Gatton, Oct. 1, 1820; William Talbott, 1845; Richard Cromwell, 1846; O. W. Treadwill and William Gibbs, 1856; Isaac Hawn, March 1, 1857; Greenbury Watkins, March 1, 1857; C. W. Lansdale, in 1857; John Breiver and W. M. Talbott, May 12, 1861; Frederick L. Moore and Julian Magruder, in 1866. Most of these are deceased. The elders of the church now living are C. W. Lansdale, J. Lewis Bohrer, and Henry Renshaw, who attend Bethesda Church, and John T. De Seelum, W. M. Talbott, and Julian Magruder, who attend Rockville Church. Mr. Moore removed to Georgetown some years ago. The deacons are George Huddleston and Clayton Williams, at Bethesda, and George M. Graffat, Rockville.

For many years Cabin John church was the only one within convenient distance of a large population. Among the families connected with the church at Cabin John as members, attendants, or supporters in the past and present are the Gattons, Claggetts, Spateses, Magruders, Offutts, Scotts, Cloppers, Fishers, Perrys, Bradleys, Muncasters, Youngs, Ormes, Douglasses, Willits, Lodges, Peterses, Bealls, Councilmans, Douds, Washingtons (George C.), Watkinses, and Searles; among the names connected with the Bethesda branch are the Dunlops, Bradleys, Belts, McCubbinses, Lairds, Huddlesons, Magruders, Youngs, Wilsons, Lodgeses, Tomlinsons, Bohrers, Williamses,

Hugheses, Holmeses, Syleses, Tomlinsons, Wallaces, Renshaws, Watkinses, Spateses, Joneses, Burnetts, Shoemakers, Laffboroughs; while the Rockville Church reckons on its lists such names as those of the Magruders, Gattons, Brewers, Anne Searle, Jones, Hallards, Belts, Groffs, De Seelums, Ormes, Rickettses, Talbotts, Treadwells, Martins, Spateses, Hughes, Dunlaps, Mineses, Bealls, Johnsons, Russells, Muncasters, Almoneys, etc. In addition to these offshoots of Cabin John Church, Neilsville, Darnestown, Poolsville, and Hermon Churches may be counted as its branches, as Cabin John Church was the first Presbyterian Church in the county.

The ancestors of the congregations now comprising these churches worshiped at Cabin John Church, and it is believed that Rev. John Orme, V.D.M., as early as 1723, established the Cabin John Mission, when Montgomery was part of Prince George's County, he being in charge of the Upper Marlborough Presbyterian Church at that date, and known to be a frequent visitor in the vicinity of Rockville, where he married, and where many of his descendants are still living.

The Bethesda church is on the Rockville turnpike, two miles northwest of Bethesda Post-office, and is the old survey of "Leeke Forest," surveyed for Col. Henry Dulany in 1688. This tract lies west of " St. Joseph's Park," on the west side of Rock Creek, and extends west one and seven-eighths miles. The farms of the late Samuel Perry and William Huddleston, on the old Georgetown road, are also in this survey.

Bethesda Post-office.—This place is on the Rockville and Georgetown road, five and a half miles from Georgetown, and three and a half from Knowles'. The merchants are C. B. Peirce and R. C. Lester,—the latter postmaster. Hon. Joseph H. Bradley, the distinguished lawyer of Washington City, has an elegant seat near here, and among the prominent farmers of this region are Spencer Watkins, H. G. and James Carroll, William Councilman, George and William Huddleston, the Renshaw Brothers, the Wilsons and Gingells.

Mount Zion Baptist Church is near Magruder's school-house, and was dedicated Sept. 8, 1861, Rev. Dr. Samson, of Washington, D. C., preaching the sermon. It belongs to the Rockville Circuit, and its pastors have been Revs. S. R. White and D. H. Hatchey.

Concord Methodist Episcopal Church is situated near Cabin John, and on the road leading to Offutt's Cross-roads.

St. John's Chapel is near Bethesda Post-office, and was erected in 1876. It belongs to the Silver Spring Parish, and is a mission of the Grace P. E. Church. Its pastor is Rev. James B. Averitt.

The school trustees and teachers for 1881 and 1882 are as follows:

Trustees.—No. 1, J. H. Davidson, G. H. Dodge, O. Sommers; No. 2, M. H. Austin, W. H. Pyles, Erasmus Perry; No. 3, John Botner, William Councilman, M. Wilson; No. 4, J. D. W. Moore, Robert Davidson, W. T. Lynch.

Teachers.—No. 1, Thomas L. Venable, Bethesda P. O.; No. 2, R. V. Griffith, Bethesda P.O.; No. 3, M. L. Venable, Bethesda P. O.; No. 4, E. C. Hobbs, Cabin John P. O.

The magistrates are C. W. Lansdale and J. H. Dodge.

Bethesda Church Cemetery contains the remains of Rebecca Perry, the wife of Elbert Perry, died March 17, 1856, aged 68 years; Wesley L. Magruder, died May 20, 1877, aged 63 years; Mary Ann Levis, born Dec. 8, 1808, died March 30, 1875.

MECHANICSVILLE DISTRICT, No. 8.

This district was created by an act of the General Assembly of 1878, and was formed from portions of the Cracklin District, No. 1, and Berry, No. 5. Its metes and bounds are as follows:

"Beginning at Brown's bridge, on the Patuxent River, and following the county road known as the Limekiln road to its crossing of Ashton and Coalesville turnpike; then with the continuation of said Limekiln road to Holland's Corner; then with the Norwood branch of the Union turnpike to the crossing at Holland's branch; then continuing with said Limekiln road to the Brookville and Washington turnpike; thence with the said pike to the Baltimore and Rockville road; then with said Baltimore and Rockville road to the bridge crossing Rock Creek; then following up and with the eastern branch of Rock Creek to the bridge crossing said creek at William E. Muncaster's mill; then with the county road leading to the village of Redland, to where the said road crosses the western branch of Rock Creek, at what was formerly known as Ricketts' ford; then following up and with said western branch of Rock Creek to where it crosses the road leading from Rockville to Unity, near the farm of Walter M. Talbot; then following said road to its intersection with the road leading from Mechanicsville to Laytonsville, near the residence of Fletcher R. Veatch; then following the road leading from Laytonsville to Brookville to the crossing of a public road near the Catholic church and the village of Mount Zion; then with said public road to Hawling's River, near the residence of Thomas D. Gaither; then down and with Hawling's River to the Westminster road, near Allen Bowie Davis' mill; then with the said Westminster road to the intersection of the road leading to Triadelphia, north of the store of Frederick O. Gaither; thence with the said road to the bridge across the Patuxent River at the village of Triadelphia; then down and with said Patuxent River to Brown's bridge, the place of beginning."

The district is bounded on the north by Cracklin District, west by Rockville District, south by Berry District, and east by the Patuxent River, separating it from Howard and Prince George's Counties. In the north Gold and Ready Branches flow into Hawling's River, which flows southeast into the Patuxent. Rock Creek in the northwest separates it from Cracklin District, and in the southwest the North Branch of Rock Creek divides it from Rockville District.

First Settlers.—The earliest settlement in this district was made by Robert Brooke, who established a Protestant colony, June 29, 1650, of forty persons, including his wife and ten children, on the Patuxent River. Among the subsequent settlers were James Brooke, a descendant of the above, John Bradford, Benjamin Gaither, Thomas Sprigg, Richard Simmons, John Boyd, Thomas Gittings, Thomas Davis, the Stablers, Waterses, Barnesleys, Magruders, and Farquhars.

The Quakers, or Friends, found in Maryland province a refuge and home from their persecutors. In Massachusetts laws had been passed that prescribed them as a "cursed sect." They were there imprisoned without bail, and sentenced to banishment upon pain of death. They were to be maimed, whipped, and "men or women to have their tongues bored through with a red-hot iron." These persecutions led George Fox, a zealous leader of the sect, to come to Maryland; being delighted with the country, and learning that the laws and liberal policy of the province placed no restrictions on religious liberty, he remained in the colony, and preached the doctrines of his sect both to the settlers and the Indians. The members of the General Assembly and the Council, men of distinction, justices of the peace, and even the heir of the proprietary himself, came to listen to him preach. The Friends established settlements or meetings through Prince George's and Montgomery Counties, and accomplished a great deal towards promoting the material development and intellectual advancement of the region. The first house built by the Friends in Montgomery County was by James Brooke, on "Brooke Grove," surveyed for him Sept. 4, 1728, and resurveyed Nov. 15, 1741. It contained three thousand one hundred and fifty-four acres, and was again resurveyed, Sept. 29, 1762, for Mr. Brooke, so as to include adjacent property, which resurvey contained seven thousand nine hundred and six acres. After this addition to his Grove he had eleven thousand and sixty acres granted by patent, and six thousand by purchase, and owned at the time of his death nearly twenty thousand acres. This tract extends from Thomas J. Holland's farm some eight or nine miles in a northwesterly direction, beyond the Big Seneca. The town of Brookville, named after the Brookes, which was founded in 1780, and Laytonsville are situated in it.

The road from Brookville to Laytonsville passes through this tract, which embraces some of the finest farms in the county, including those of E. J. Hall, the late Dr. William B. Magruder, John Riggs, Charles Brooke, the late Walter Magruder, David L. Pugh, Thomas D. Gaither, and Samuel Riggs, of R. This was the largest tract of land owned by one person in the county, and gives an example of the wealth and influence enjoyed by the early leaders of the Friends' Society. On and near "Brooke Grove" the Friends gathered in sufficient numbers to establish a flourishing "meeting," and more than a century ago they took a step that distinguished them from surrounding communities by the emancipation of their slaves. The house is occupied at present by William J. Schofield. By their patient industry and perseverance, combined with their intellectual culture, social intercourse, agricultural knowledge, their fidelity to the principles of moral truth and human advancement, the Quakers, or Friends, have left an impress upon the character of the whole people of the county, a stimulus to their aims and energies.

The Lloyds, the Thomases, the Snowdens, the Richardsons, the Shipleys, and many other families came, it is supposed, from the Principality. The Severn and the Wye (in Talbot County), upon which the Hon. Edward Lloyd resided, were no doubt named after the rivers of Wales, in honor of his native country. The Thomases, it is said, first lived on Kent Island, but according to the earliest recorded information we have been able to obtain, they resided in Anne Arundel, near Thomas' Point, about 1655. Philip, the emigrant, was a privy councilor, and many of his descendants held high public positions, including Philip Evan Thomas, the projector and first president of the Baltimore and Ohio Railroad. The Snowdens arrived about 1660. They were the ancestors of the large family living in Prince George's and this county. The Richardsons resided many generations upon West River. They came probably about 1655. The Shipleys, a family of planters in Anne Arundel, and subsequently in Montgomery and Carroll Counties, arrived at a period but little later; and two of the largest families of Maryland, the Magruders and Beales, undoubtedly came from Scotland. So also did the Bowies, the Edmonstons, and other families. The Magruders arrived about 1655. One of their earliest seats was upon the western branch of the Patuxent. Alexander, the emigrant, died about 1680, leaving six children,—Alexander, Nathaniel, James, John, Samuel, and Elizabeth. The Beales came some time after the Magruders. Col. Hinton Beale was the earliest. One of the oldest residents in the county is Edward Stabler, born in 1795. He has been postmaster at Sandy Spring for fifty years, and is probably the oldest postmaster in the United States. He was the originator and founder of the Mutual Fire Insurance Company of Montgomery County, organized in 1848. About 1841, Caleb Stabler purchased four hundred acres at two dollars and five cents per acre. This land was without house or fencing, but he built a comfortable two-story log house, and called his place "Drayton." This place, under his skillful culture, became a garden-spot, and was subsequently divided by its venerable owner into six parts, and each of his sons and sons-in-law built and settled on his portion, the old people retaining the homestead. This family reclaimed an almost barren waste and converted it into one of the most fertile and beautiful farms in the county.

Among the tracts of land surveyed early in the eighteenth century was "Benjamin's Lot," granted to Benjamin Gaither in 1725, part of which is now the famous Triadelphia mill property, which was founded in 1809 by three brothers-in-law, Isaac Briggs, Thomas Moore, and Caleb Bentley, and is now the residence of Hon. Thomas Lansdale. This gentleman was born in Berry District in 1808; moved to Ohio early in life, and returned to Savage Factory, in Anne Arundel, now Howard, County, and was extensively engaged there in mechanical operations for a number of years. He was one of the inventors and builders of the first wood-planing machines. He also invented the metallic yoke for swing-bells. He came to Triadelphia in 1842, remained five years, and went to Ellicott's Mills, on the Patapsco River, in Baltimore County, to build, superintend, and operate the granite factory. He was the first manager who introduced steam into a factory for heating purposes, which he did about the year 1852, exciting the surprise and admiration of the visitors from different parts of the country interested in such matters. This factory was burned down twice, rebuilt, and finally swept away by the destructive flood of 1868, which left hardly a vestige behind to mark the site of its repeated calamities. Being unsuccessful in his efforts to gain control of the granite works by purchase, he returned to Triadelphia about the year 1856. From that time until war, fire, and flood had made many changes in that, as in other localities simultaneously visited, Triadelphia was a busy, thriving, and attractive village of three hundred or four hundred inhabitants and about thirty dwellings, besides the large three-story stone cotton-factory, saw, plaster, bone, and grist-mills, store, and mechanical shops. Mr. Lansdale was a member of the State Constitutional Convention of 1864, and was elected to the Senate of Maryland in 1865. He was active in lending his aid to various public works for the material advancement of the State and county, and liberal in fostering local institutions designed to promote the welfare of the people. He died in 1878.

Prominent among the noble band whose deeds have added lustre to the name and fame of the Friends' Society of Sandy Springs and of Montgomery County, stands the commanding figure of Benjamin Hallowell, philosopher, philanthropist, orator, farmer, and teacher; gifted with an extraordinary variety of knowledge, prominent in the many fields of investigation in which he exerted his powerful energies, and prosecuting his researches with one ultimate end, the happiness of his fellow-creatures. He was born in Montgomery County, Pa., in 1799; came to Montgomery County, Md., in 1819, as a teacher of the Friends' school at Frederick Hill; in 1824 he established a school at Alexandria, and received among his pupils many who have since attained position and honor. In the summer of 1842, Mr. Hallowell came to live upon his farm, "Rockland," near Sandy Springs, upon a tract of poor land, which by judicious draining, fertilizing, and grass-seeding he completely reclaimed. In 1859 he was unanimously elected first president of the Maryland State Agricultural Society College without his knowledge or consent. Shortly afterwards he took up his residence in the county. He was prominent in organizing the Farmers' Club of Sandy Springs, the first meeting of which was held at the residence of Richard T. Bentley. In 1846 he delivered an address at the first regular meeting of the Agricultural Society of Montgomery County, and was a frequent lecturer before various associations on scientific and agricultural subjects. He was Professor of Chemistry in the Medical Department of Columbian College, Washington, a member of the American Philosophical Society of Philadelphia, and one of the foremost in the Baltimore Yearly Meeting to adopt plans for the improvement of the condition of the Indians on our Western borders. He died in 1877, in the seventy-eighth year of his age, regretted and beloved by all who knew him, and leaving behind him a name which will be perpetually fragrant with the aroma of a long life of labor for others and good will towards men.

Caleb Bentley was another of the early residents of the district. He was born in 1762 in Chester County, Pa., and kept the first store in Brookville and Sandy Springs. He died in 1852. He belonged to the Society of Friends.

Another of the early inhabitants, Rev. Thomas McCormick, was born in Loudon County, Va., in

"GREENWOOD"
RESIDENCE OF ALLEN BOWIE DAVIS EIGHTH DIST. MONTGOMERY CO. MD.

1792, and when six years old was taken by his uncle, Thomas Moore, with whom he remained until his fourteenth year. He was then taken by his father to Baltimore, where he learned the trade of a carpenter. In 1817 he built the fine mansion of E. J. Hall, and was subsequently engaged in the mercantile business until 1829, when he purchased a farm, "Longwood," near Brookville, where he spent fifteen years. He carried butter to market in the first refrigerator ever made,—the patent of Thomas Moore, who died in 1823.

John Thomas, who sixty years ago lived about six miles from Triadelphia, near Green's bridge over the Patuxent, established an interesting industry for the collection of pine sap from the pine-trees in the adjacent forests. This was done by removing a small chip from the foot of the tree, near the root; the opening thus made would receive the falling sap, which was gathered in the morning, taken to Mr. Thomas, who paid ten cents an ounce for it. The revenue derived from this source was, however, not sufficient to meet the expectations of the projector, and it was abandoned.

Ephraim Davis settled and built in 1755 in Mechanicsville District, on what is now the "Greenwood" estate. During President Washington's administration his son, Thomas Davis, who was born Dec. 10, 1769, raised a company and marched to Pennsylvania in 1794 to help suppress the "Whisky Insurrection." While thus engaged he was elected to the Legislature, and frequently thereafter filled the same position. He was also elector of the Senate under the old constitution, and a member of the Governor's Council. He served as a justice of the peace, a member of the board of tax commissioners, judge of the Levy and Orphans' Court, and also as one of the associate judges of the County Court before the change requiring all three of the judges to be taken from the legal profession. He was likewise a noted conveyancer and surveyor. He was one of the founders and trustees of the Brookville Academy and of St. Bartholomew's Protestant Episcopal Church, in whose vestry and communion he died in 1833, aged sixty-five years. His son, Allen Bowie Davis, was born Feb. 16, 1809, and resides on the old homestead, "Greenwood," which has been in the family since 1755. He succeeded his father in the board of trustees of Brookville Academy. In 1840 he was elected a member of the State Board of Public Works, in which he exercised his influence in favor of the representation of the minority and the abolition of political agencies in the management of public trusts. In 1850 he was elected to the State Constitutional Convention, and was made one of the first trustees of the State Agricultural Society, and subsequently president of the board. About the same time he was elected president of the Montgomery Manufacturing Company of Triadelphia, with encouraging financial results in his administration. As president of the County Agricultural Society he introduced reforms and changes which were instrumental in laying the foundation for its growth and prosperity. In 1849 he obtained the charter of the Brookville and Washington Turnpike Company, and served sixteen years as its president. In 1863 he was elected to the Legislature, and made chairman of the Committees on Roads and Agriculture. During his term of office he extended the prohibitory liquor law over an area greater than that embraced in its early provisions, with a corresponding improvement in the health, morals, and prosperity of the people. About 1869 he was elected president of the State Agricultural Society, and presided at the first meeting for its organization. In January, 1880, he was appointed by the court one of the public school commissioners, and is now the president of the board. Mr. Davis has been twice married. His first wife, Rebecca Comfort, was the eldest daughter of Chief Justice Thomas Beale Dorsey, of Elk Ridge. She died in 1836, and in 1839 Mr. Davis married his present wife, Hester Ann Wilkens, the daughter of William Wilkens, formerly an eminent dry-goods merchant of Baltimore City. Mr. Davis is a model farmer, and his beautiful estate, "Greenwood," is one of the garden spots of Montgomery County.

St. Bartholomew's Protestant Episcopal Parish.—It is strange that none of the four parishes within the county possesses even a record of its metes and bounds. Formerly the whole county was comprised by Prince George Parish, the parish church, called Rock Creek church, standing where the cemetery now is, near the residence of the late Judge Bowie. In 1758 a petition, numerously signed by the Browns, Gartrells, Griffiths, Riggses, Davises, and others, was presented to Governor Sharpe and his Council for permission to lay off a parish and erect a "chapel of ease" on a branch of the Patuxent, called Hawling's River, the petitioners stating that they were too remote from the parish church at Rock Creek, and were able to erect a church and support a minister if their petition was granted. Consent was given, and a chapel erected very near the site of the present St. Luke's church, Crowtown. All traces of the building are gone, and with the exception of Mr. William Brown, who was baptized in the church, there is probably no one in the neighborhood who remembers the edifice.

St. Bartholomew's Parish was carved out of Prince

George's in 1821 by the Diocesan Convention of that year. Its bounds were as follows: "Beginning at a bridge near Harry W. Dorsey's, on Seneca River, running with the road by John Belt's to Snell's bridge, on the Patuxent, including the upper part of Montgomery County, lying between the Seneca and Patuxent Rivers." The next year, 1822, the convention extended the boundaries "to include the farm of Jonathan Duly, lying on the road from John Belt's to Snell's bridge." The boundaries of the parish have since been changed, but its present extent cannot be definitely ascertained. But though the parish was not formally erected until 1821, the churchmen of this section seem to have acted as if the parish had legal existence, for on Easter Monday, 1813, a meeting of the parishioners was held at Bowman's store for the election of vestrymen, and the following persons were chosen: Thomas Davis, Ephraim Gaither, James Whiffing, Edward Burgess, John H. Riggs, Rezin Darby, H. C. Gaither, and Anthony Ricketts.

At a special meeting held June 7th, of the same year, Thomas Davis was chosen the first lay delegate to attend the "convention to be held in Baltimore on Whit-Sunday."

May 2, 1814, the vestry resolved that "on the fourth Monday of that month the vestry shall meet at Bowman's store, to select a site for the church." A list of adjourned meetings fills up the time (from which it appears the lack of quorums is not a modern evil) till Aug. 13, 1814, when a committee, consisting of H. C. Gaither and Henry Griffith, was appointed to contract for building a church "according to the determined plan." The next year (Aug. 7, 1815) Frederick Bowman was added to the building committee, a fact showing that the church was then still incomplete. Indeed, from the fact that the first order for the payment of "any bills that may be presented" is dated as late as Nov. 6, 1815, it is probable that the building was not begun till the summer of that year. But by Easter Monday, 1816, such progress had been made that the parishioners could meet at the church for the election of vestrymen, yet it stood unfinished several years, for as late as March 13, 1819, Frederick Gaither, Jesse Wilcoxon, and H. C. Gaither were directed to contract for "plastering and for any carpenter's work necessary in connection therewith." This work was pushed with dispatch, for on May 9, 1819, application was made to Bishop Kemp to consecrate the church, and the ceremony was performed the same day. As the application was made on the very day of the consecration, the bishop must have come on a "visitation," the pre-notification of which to the vestry was the occasion of stirring them up to complete the house according to the order of March 13th. If the present rule, that a church cannot be consecrated till it is out of debt, was then in force, this church must have been fully paid for at the time of the bishop's visit. Previously, however, there had been some difficulty in collecting some of the subscriptions, for on Nov. 8, 1817, the vestry directed legal proceedings to be taken against all delinquents who should not pay the amount promised by them by December 11th, and the order was directed to be "set up in all convenient places." However, with all its delays and struggles, the church was at last completed, and still stands on Hawling's River, about two miles east of Laytonsville. From its beginning to 1843 this church was associated with the one at Rock Creek, subsequently at Rockville, in the employment of a minister.

The first minister was a Mr. Wheaton, from Dec. 13, 1818, to December, 1819. Aug. 7, 1820, the vestry elected Rev. Thomas G. Allen "*for one year.*"

It appears from the vestry-book that Mr. Allen visited the parish without a formal invitation, bringing a "certificate of standing" from Bishop Kemp. (Perhaps the bishop had been applied to to recommend some one.) Mr. Allen preached his trial sermon August 6th, and was called to the charge of the church the next day. He continued until 1828, being re-elected from year to year. Rev. H. C. Knight was elected in his place. It is not said whether he accepted. If so, he remained but a year, for Sept. 20, 1829, the Rev. Levin J. Gillis was chosen. He continued till 1843. Mr. Gillis seems to have caused the severance of this church from the one at Rockville in 1844. April 4, 1844, the Rev. O. Hutton, D.D., was called. He took charge June 1st, and continued therein until 1861, when he resigned. Yet there is another minute, accepting the doctor's resignation, dated July 19, 1866. We suppose that, owing to the war or for other reasons, the first resignation was withdrawn, though there is no record of the fact. But parish records are proverbially fragmentary. When the doctor assumed the rectorship St. John's Church, Mechanicsville, was associated with St. Bartholomew's. The exact date of the building of St. John's cannot be ascertained, but in the resolution of association, at the time of calling Dr. Hutton, it is spoken of as "the chapel recently erected near Mechanicsville." After Dr. Hutton's resignation St. John's was for a short time connected with the Rockville Church, but soon returned to its former association, which still continues. Revs. Tinsley and Poindexter held short rectorships, and were followed by Rev. Thomas Duncan in 1868 to 1874 or

'75. By his energy and devotion St. Luke's, at Crowtown, and the chapel at Unity were built, supplying pressing needs to those communities. Mr. Duncan was succeeded by Dr. Mason in 1875, but ill health compelled him to resign in a little more than one year. On Easter Sunday, 1877, the Rev. Mr. Laird entered upon the charge, and continues to hold it. He is very energetic in his labors, and has met with deserved success.

On Feb. 19, 1825, Margaret Brooke conveyed by deed to the vestry of St. Bartholomew's Parish one acre of land, being a part of a tract called "The Addition to Brooke Grove," bounded northerly by a tract called "Tusculum," and southerly by the public road, and including the church of said parish and the burying-ground and yard to the church attached. The consideration of the indenture was twenty-five dollars, and it was witnessed by Richard Butt and Benjamin Higgins.

Sandy Spring.—The village of Sandy Spring is eight miles east of Rockville and eleven from Laurel, and is situated in the midst of a settlement of Friends. The village derives its name from a spring half a mile south of it, the waters of which were formerly considered especially adapted for washing and scouring purposes.

The name of the village and neighborhood has caused among strangers a double deception. On first hearing it they conceive it to be a regular watering-place, and the agricultural traveler expects to find it a light, sandy soil, the very opposite of which is soon made apparent to his conception by the condition of the winter roads. It appears from the earliest land warrants laid in this section that the first settlements were commenced just after the beginning of the last century. The tract of land called "Snowden Manor," that now forms the resting-place of all the families in the eastern and southeastern part of this section, was surveyed for Richard Snowden, Dec. 10, 1715, and contained one thousand acres. The Ashton and Sligo turnpike runs through the estate, and the road from Ashton to Laurel. The tract embraces the lands of William John Thomas, the farms of William Lee, Warwick Miller, Asa Stabler, and the farm and bone-mill of William Bond. "Beall's Manor," adjoining it on the south, was granted Feb. 14, 1720, to Charles and William Beall, and contained seventeen hundred and eighty-seven acres. It is situated on the head-waters of West Point Branch, beginning in Thomas Winpenny's house-yard, a mile north of Colesville, on the Ashton and Sligo turnpike. On it are located the farms of Thomas Winpenny, Mr. O'Hare, Lloyd Green, J. W. Barcroft and others.

The "Charles and Benjamin" tract, beginning at a point not far from Hawling's River, and extending nearly through the heart of the neighborhood, beyond its southeastern border, was surveyed and granted to Charles Beall, July 2, 1718, and comprised two thousand two hundred and eighty acres. This tract extends from Hon. E. J. Hall's farm down the Brookville and Washington turnpike to Higgin's tavern, embracing the farms of Z. D. Waters, Thomas Waters, Josiah W. Jones, Samuel Cashell, and others. "Charley Forest," of twelve hundred and thirty acres, was granted to Maj. John Bradford. The "Addition to Charley Forest" was surveyed to Maj. Bradford, Sept. 16, 1720. These two surveys united extend from Mechanicsville to within a short distance of Snell's bridge. The turnpike from Mechanicsville to Sandy Spring and Ashton, and the road to Snell's bridge, as also that to Brighton, passes through it.

On this tract are situated Sandy Spring and Ashton, including the valuable farms of "Fair Hill," and those of William H. Farquhar, Albin Gilpin, R. T. Bentley, Edward Thomas, and many others. The tract is located on the dividing ridge that separates the head-waters of the Northwest Branch and Cabin Creek. When the first settlements were made an unbroken forest covered the whole region, except in a few spots where the wigwams of the natives showed a little patch of corn or tobacco. The forest then was not like that of the present day, filled with the undergrowth that mars its beauty. As an illustration of this, it is related that on one occasion a horse escaped from one of the settlers on the place next above the present residence of Thomas P. Stabler, and came down towards the spring through the woods. Its owner was able to follow the animal the whole distance by the tracks left in the clear soil of the forest, where *only* large trees grew. No Indian burial-places or Indian remains have ever been discovered in the vicinity, but arrow-heads and a few rude culinary utensils have been turned up in the fields from time to time. Evidences of the existence of various wild denizens of the woods are still present in the names given to many of the first tracts of land taken up in the county. "Bear Den," "Deer Park," "Wolf Den," and designations similar to these are quite numerous, while "Bear Bacon," a very ancient tract lying on the Laurel road, directly east of "Snowden Manor," serves as a significant indication of the uses to which these wild beasts were put before the introduction of domestic animals. In the minutes of the ancient "Monthly Meeting," held at "The Cliffs," on Herring Creek, is contained the first mention of a meeting of Friends at Sandy Spring, which probably occurred in the Seventh month and 27th day of 1753. The first members composing this meeting appear to have belonged to the Brooke and Thomas families. It was in 1742 that Richard Snowden, proprietor of "Snowden Manor," conveyed five hundred acres of its northwestern part to Philip Thomas.

Roger Brooke was born at Brooke Grove, in Montgomery (then Frederick) County, on the 24th of November, 1774. His ancestor was Robert Brooke, who emigrated from England in 1650. Robert Brooke was born in London on the 3d of June, 1602, and his wife, Mary Baker, was a native of Battel, in Sussex. They were married on the 25th of February, 1627. Their children were Baker, Mary, Thomas, and Barbara. Robert Brooke's second wife was Mary, second daughter of Roger Mainwaring, Dean of Worcester. Their children were Charles, Roger, Robert, John, Mary, William, Ann, and Francis. On the 29th of June, 1650, Robert Brooke arrived in Maryland with his wife and ten children. Besides these were the following servants: men-servants, Mark King, Mark Lovely, William Bradney, Philip Harwood, Richard Robinson, Anthony Kitchen, William Jones, John Clifford, James Leigh, Benjamin Hammond, Robert Sheale, Thomas Joyce, Henry Peere, Thomas Elstone, Edward Cooke, Ambrose Briggs, Robert Hooper, William Hinson, John Bocock, David Brown, Henry Robinson; maid-servants, Anne Marshall, Katherine Fisher, Elizabeth Williamson, Margaret Watts, Abigail Montague, Eleanor Williams, and Agnes Neale. Robert Brooke was then forty-eight years of age. He was the first settler on the Patuxent, and located himself about twenty miles up the river, at a place which was afterwards known as Delabrook, and in 1652 removed to an adjoining estate, which he named Brooke Place. After his arrival in Maryland three children were born,—Basil, who died on the day of his birth, and Eliza and Henry, twins. Robert Brooke died on the 20th of July, 1656, and his widow died on the 29th of November, 1663. Soon after reaching Maryland, Robert Brooke was appointed commander of Charles County, and was chosen by Cromwell's commissioners Governor of Maryland. Early in the next century, James Brooke, a descendant of Robert Brooke, born at Battel Creek, Feb. 21, 1705, removed to the locality known as Sandy Spring neighborhood, in what is now Montgomery County. His father was Roger Brooke, Jr., son of Roger Brooke, who was the son of Robert Brooke. James Brooke patented large tracts of land, over twenty thousand acres in all, on which his children settled. Roger Brooke, the subject of this sketch, was his grandson, and occupied the house built by his father, who bore the same name, within a mile of the original mansion of James Brooke, the first permanent settler in that part of Maryland.

At the age of sixteen his father's death left him with many cares and responsibilities, his mother and five sisters being still at home, each with considerable landed estates, requiring much attention, from the fact that they had all been worked down by the culture of tobacco. In 1804, Roger Brooke was married to Mary Pleasants Younghusband, who was born March 10, 1770, near Richmond, Va. She was the daughter of Isaac Younghusband, a native of England, who had been the captain of a merchant vessel trading between Liverpool and Richmond. At the latter place the captain became acquainted with and married Mary Pleasants, whose ancestors removed from England to Virginia in 1668. She was the daughter of Thomas Pleasants and Mary Jordan. After the death of his first wife in 1838, Roger Brooke married, in 1840, Sarah T. Gilpin, a daughter of Bernard Gilpin. His education was only such as the common schools afforded, but he had been trained with the utmost care by his intelligent and pious mother, Mary Matthews, who, born near Monocacy, Md., was married to Roger Brooke's father in 1758, and survived him eighteen years. Five children were born to Roger Brooke, of whom four outlived him. The elder, a daughter, was married to Dr. Charles Farquhar; the second, also a daughter, to Elisha John Hall, who, like his brothers-in-law, Roger and George E. Brooke, has been widely known as an active and successful farmer. In this respect the children followed the occupation of their father, whose life was devoted to the pursuits of agriculture.

A somewhat notable fact in this connection is that all the descendants of Roger Brooke have remained in the same locality, and all the male members of the family have devoted themselves exclusively to farming, and have succeeded remarkably in improving their lands and increasing their productive capacity. The children of Roger Brooke were Sarah B., who married Dr. Charles Farquhar; Mary B., who married Elisha John Hall; Roger, who died some years ago; and George E. Of Mrs. Farquhar's children there are now living Anna F., wife of Charles H. Brooke, her second cousin; Roger B., Mary Edith, Charles, Granville, and Eliza Elgar Farquhar. Of Mrs. Hall's children there are now living Mary Kate, wife of Samuel A. Janney, and Louisa P., wife of George F. Nesbitt. Roger Brooke married Sara Pleasants, of Virginia, and their surviving children are William L., Martha R., wife of Frederick Stabler;

Roger Brooke

Mary P., Walter, Roger, Deborah, and Albin. George E. Brooke married Eliza Jordan, and their children now living are Alice, wife of James P. Stabler; Charles, and Annie.

Roger Brooke may be regarded as a pioneer in adopting the improved system of farming in Maryland. He devoted much of his time and attention to planting orchards, draining low grounds, ridding the fields of the stones with which they were heavily encumbered, and procuring improved stock. His industry and his progressive policy first showed the possibility of redeeming the poverty-stricken lands of this region of Maryland. The convincing evidence of his method of farming was that it proved remunerative. The profits of one farm enabled him gradually to purchase several additional estates, it being his conviction through life that the safest investment for money was in land. He was a prominent member and promoter of the agricultural societies, both county and State, and in the infancy of the latter he exerted himself with vigor and effect in its behalf. Although preferring always the quiet and independence of home-life, his interests were not confined to that narrow space, but extended to national questions, both of a political and economic character. For more than fifty years he was a subscriber to the *National Intelligencer* of Washington, and frequently wrote short articles for that paper, which the editors gladly received. He never failed to cast his vote on the day of election, encouraging the young men always to do likewise. His connection with politics extended thus far, but no farther. He would not accept any office except that of member of "the Levy Court," as the board of county commissioners was then called.

Roger Brooke was one of those men gifted by nature with a mind that assures its own education. This was exhibited to a remarkable degree in the knowledge which he acquired of nature and nature's productions, from the feathered songster to the tiniest flower of the forest. Although he was entirely unacquainted with the literature of botany, there seemed to be not a single plant to be found in field or woods that he could not name, and with whose qualities, especially its medical properties, he was unacquainted. It was no doubt owing to his love of nature and outdoor life, added to his fondness for sport, inherited from a long line of British ancestry, that he became noted for a lively interest in fox-hunting, which continued nearly to the close of his life. This interest, however, never seemed to interfere with his religious duties, to which he was steadily devoted in youth, manhood, and old age. From his birth he was attached to the Society of Friends, and fully indorsed their doctrines and principles. To his influence, and that of his associates, may be attributed the order and sobriety which have thus far characterized the neighborhood where he resided. He was, however, remarkably social in his nature, offering to friends and strangers of all sects and conditions a hospitality seldom surpassed. Being gifted with a rich humor, and possessing a fund of anecdotes laid up in an unequaled memory, his society was sought and enjoyed by a great variety of persons, from the patriot and statesman down to the humblest neighbor on the adjoining lands. In his latter days he often remarked that few people had realized more enjoyment than he, and in his old age it was his great pleasure, seated with a friend beneath the sturdy old sycamore which so aptly illustrated the rugged strength of his character, to relate the varied experiences of his long and eventful life, or to discourse of those topics with which experience and a careful study of men and things had made him so conversant. In connection with this sycamore, it is related that, returning home from mill on one occasion, while still a lad, he got into an altercation with a boy, and having wrested from his antagonist a small sycamore shoot or sapling, bore it home in triumph, and planted it before the door of his father's dwelling. Before his death the sapling had grown to be a large and vigorous tree, beneath whose shade he whiled away many a pleasant hour. On the 31st of December, 1860, he died, calmly and peacefully, having attained the age of eighty-six years, and his remains were laid with those of his forefathers. In accordance with his oft-reiterated wish, the spot remains unmarked by any stone or monument.

The Brookes continue as in the past to be one of the most influential families in Western Maryland. The late Chief Justice Taney's mother was the daughter of Roger Brooke, one of the descendants of Robert Brooke, the emigrant, and the family connection is very extensive.

The Brooke family, like the Calverts, were Catholic, and the first to change his faith to Protestantism was James Brooke, who on June 5, 1725, married Deborah, eldest daughter of Richard and Elizabeth Snowden, of the Society of Friends. As elsewhere stated, James Brooke, in 1728, settled in this neighborhood, leaving his relatives behind in the lower counties. Roger Brooke, Sr., son of James Brooke, married Mary Elgar. It is said that when James Brooke built his house, in 1728–29 (still standing, and owned by William J. Schofield), it was the only frame house between this point and Canada. When James Brooke was hunting, in 1756, with six dogs, they came upon a very large panther. The ferocious beast attacked the dogs and laid them sprawling on every side of him. At this juncture, it is said, the old man came up, and fired ineffectually on the enraged animal, which now turned upon him. He endeavored to reload, but found he had shot away his last bullet, it being during the French and Indian war, when there was a scarcity of ammunition. But the men of those days were trained for all such emergencies. Cutting off one of the metal buttons of his coat, he dropped it down the capacious mouth of his old musket and blazed away at the panther, striking him right between the eyes, and killing the beast at once. Tobacco was the principal agricultural staple, but an act of the Assembly required every planter to put out annually two acres of corn, in order to avert any famine. Richard Snowden at one time had twenty-four tobacco-houses on one tract of land. For a number of years there was only one pair of boots in the settlement, such was the simplicity of manners and of living. This rare article was in the possession of the head of the Thomas family, and was loaned out in the spirit of brotherly kindness to such of the neighbors as were about to undertake the serious enterprise of a journey to Annapolis. It is also known that a single great-coat served the purposes of the whole community for similar important occasions.

The Friends' meeting-house had no fire for years, and when it was first proposed to have a stove in it a vehement opposition arose as a piece of hurtful indulgence. At length the advocates of the innovation prevailed. It happened that on the first meeting-day after the stove was put up no fire was kindled in it, and one of the elders who had opposed most strongly the introduction of the stove coming along, spread his hands wide over it, and feeling no heat, exclaimed, "Oh, the dumb idol!" and at the same time taking off his great-coat, laid it across the stove and took his seat. The next "meeting-day" being a cold one, a fire was made in the stove, and the same Friend coming in, ignorant of the change, pulled off his great-coat at the door, setting an example to the effeminate ones, and stalking up the aisle, again threw his coat across the stove, and took his place in the gallery. A slight commotion ensued among the younger members, and impressed at so extraordinary a manifestation he lifted his eyes, and saw his outer garment enveloped in smoke. The idol was no longer dumb.

The Friends in general took no active part in the Revolution, but were rather suspected of leaning to the cause of the mother-country. Not so, however, was it with the people here. The Brookes in particular—a race of large, stalwart men, trained up in the love of independence—went in heart and hand for the patriot cause. One of the sons of the old patriarch, James Brooke, became a colonel in the Continental army, and was of course dismissed from the meeting for this breach of faith. Evan Thomas, born in 1738, then resided in the old brick house near Colesville, and attended regularly the Sandy Springs meeting, of which he was a solid and faithful minister. At the beginning of the Revolution he entered the exciting political arena, and was elected a member of the first convention that met at Annapolis. Being re-elected, the conviction was soon forced upon his mind that the convention's resolves meant war, and he retired from the path into which events were leading him and came back to the tenets of his faith. But a thorny road it proved to him for years. For preaching without secular authority he was forcibly dragged from the gallery where he stood, fined and imprisoned; but the next meeting-day after his release he was again at his post. One of his sons was Hon. Philip Evan Thomas, the projector of the Baltimore and Ohio Railroad, and to the erection of the Friends' meeting-house in 1817 he contributed five hundred dollars.

A year or two afterwards came the establishment of the Fair Hill Boarding-School. Contemporaneous with the introduction of fertilizers a "Farmers' Club" was established, about 1845, and these combined agencies have resulted in a wonderful improvement of the soil in this neighborhood, and in the agricultural methods of the surrounding farmers. The famous "Lyceum" did much to stimulate investigation, and no location in Maryland can boast better-tilled farms, more elegant improvements, or people of broader and more liberal culture than Sandy Spring and the adjacent region.

Friends' Meeting-house.—The first edifice was a frame structure, built about 1742, and which, with some additions and repairs, remained standing until 1817, when the present substantial brick edifice was built. In the graveyard attached are interred the remains of

Mahlin Kirk, died 4th mo. 13, 1860, aged 76.
Albert G. Palmer, born Aug. 23, 1829, died March 6, 1860.
Joseph Gilpin, born May 7, 1780, died March 29, 1858.
H. Russell Stabler, born 8th mo. 4, 1853, died 2d mo. 15, 1857.
Martha A. Stone, died 12th mo. 21, 1855.
Jacob Weller, born Jan. 3, 1806, died Sept. 13, 1876.
Roger Brooke, born 10th mo. 5, 1810, died 3d mo. 15, 1868.
Catherine Chandlee, died 2d mo. 10, 1872, aged 78.
Wilson Scott, died 6th mo. 4, 1872, aged 54.
Mary Pleasants, born 1st mo. 13, 1825, died 9th mo. 8, 1869.
Elizabeth T. Kirk, born 6th mo. 1, 1825, died 10th mo. 4, 1869.

Rebecca N. Palmer, born Aug. 2, 1804, died Aug. 6, 1867.

William P. Palmer, M.D., born Nov. 19, 1792, died Dec. 27, 1869.

Archibald D. Moore, born 2d mo. 8, 1841, died 5th mo. 27, 1864.

Mary H. Brooke, died June 29, 1864, aged 25 years.

Wm. Thomas, born 8th mo. 20, 1848, died 1874.

Sarah M. Sullivan, born October, 1839, died Sept. 23, 1875.

John J. Osburn, born Oct. 30, 1841, died Feb. 4, 1880.

Sas. H. Stone, born 24th of 6th mo., 1813, died 8th of 12th mo., 1880.

Hannah C. Pierce, born 3d mo. 29, 1789.

Joshua Pierce, born 16th of 3d mo., 1781, died 1863.

Hannah G. Birdsall, born 20th of 5th mo., 1803, died 22d of 3d mo., 1877.

Mortimer Osburn, born March 30, 1810, died April 8, 1875.

Virginia F. Moore, born 20th of 3d mo., 1841, died 10th of 3d mo., 1873.

Benjamin J. Hallowell, died 7th of 9th mo., 1877, aged 78 years, 21 days.

Margaret E. Hallowell, died 1st of 5th mo., 1873, aged 76 years, 8 months, 13 days.

Jacob W. Ziegler, died Sept. 16, 1805.

George Brooke, born 5th of 8th mo., 1846, died 1st of 1st mo., 1876.

Edward S. Hallowell, died 18th of 3d mo., 1866, aged 18.

Timothy Kirk, died 15th of 10th mo., 1865, aged 87.

Anna H. Moore, died 22d of 8th mo., 1863.

J. Edgar Hallowell, died June 12, 1863, aged 27.

W. T. Parnsley, died Aug. 11, 1863, aged 22.

Warwick Guion Miller, died 1860, aged 28.

The first store in Sandy Spring was kept by Caleb Bentley. The Orthodox meeting-house was erected in 1880. The Sandy Spring Lyceum occupies a neat building near the Friends' meeting-house. The other organizations here are the Montgomery County Branch of the Prisoners' Aid Society, the Enterprise Farmers' Club, the Montgomery Farmers' Club, the Sandy Spring Horticultural Society, the Sandy Spring Home Interest Society, and the Sandy Spring Young Folks' Sociable.

On June 10, 1734, a tract of land called "Rockland," of one hundred and seventy-four acres, was granted Allen Farquhar, which now embraces part of Union Bridge, a thriving town of Carroll County. In 1735, Allen Farquhar sold this land to his son, William Farquhar, who became one of the leading business men in what is now Carroll, then a part of Frederick County. From him descended Amos, father of William H. Farquhar. The latter married Margaret, daughter of Isaac and Hannah (Brooke) Briggs. The Farquhar family has been in this country for nearly two centuries, and have always been zealous members of the Society of Friends. William H. Farquhar, the leading representative of the family in the county, is one of the best farmers in Montgomery.

The Mutual Fire Insurance Company of Montgomery County, one of the largest mutual fire insurance companies in Maryland, is located at Sandy Spring. It was incorporated by the General Assembly at its December session of 1847. The incorporators and first directors were Edward Stabler, Dr. William P. Palmer, George E. Brooke, Robert R. Moore, William H. Farquhar, Joseph Gilpin, Richard T. Bentley, Joshua Peirce, Edward Lee, Samuel Ellicott, Henry Stabler, Francis P. Blair, Sr., and Caleb Stabler. From its organization its president has been Edward Stabler, and its secretary and treasurer Robert R. Moore, now assisted by Thomas L. Moore. In 1876 the directors were:

Edward Stabler, William H. Farquhar, B. Rush Roberts, Henry C. Hallowell, Joseph T. Moore, Sandy Spring; Nathan S. White, Dawsonville; Isaac Hartshorne, Brighton; Charles Abert, Norbeck; James B. Matthews, Matthews' Store, Howard County; Thomas F. Shepherd, Uniontown, Carroll County; Robert B. Dixon, Easton, Talbot County; William J. Albert, Catonsville, Baltimore County; William Downey, New Market, Frederick County.

The directors of the company in 1881 were:

Edward Stabler, president; Wm. Hy. Farquhar, Sandy Spring, Montgomery County; James B. Matthews, Glenwood, Howard County; Thomas F. Shepherd, Uniontown, Carroll County; Isaac Hartshorne, Brighton, Montgomery County; Henry C. Hallowell, Sandy Spring, Montgomery County; Robert B. Dixon, Easton, Talbot County; Joseph T. Moore, Sandy Spring, Montgomery County; Charles Abert, Norbeck, Montgomery County; Asa M. Stabler, Spencerville, Montgomery County; Richard T. Bentley, Sandy Spring, Montgomery County; W. B. Chichester, Olney, Montgomery County; Charles G. Porter, Sandy Spring, Montgomery County.

A General Statement of the Operations of The Mutual Fire Insurance Company of Montgomery County, Md., from June 1, 1848, to May 1, 1876.

COUNTIES.	Amount Insured.	Amount of Premium Notes.	Losses by Fire.	Rate per cent. of Loss on Premium Notes.
Montgomery	$3,893,305	$270,331	$81,430	30 7/10
Howard	2,779,101	192,793	40,919	21 2/10
Frederick	2,246,459	146,062	47,431	32 5/10
Baltimore	2,211,885	154,774	17,309	11 1/10
Talbot	2,119,390	147,280	39,783	
Carroll	1,908,295	128,307	16,260	27
Prince George's	1,694,244	114,274	36,859	12 7/10
Anne Arundel	1,157,178	74,385	43,200	32 5/10
Queen Anne	638,170	44,050	19,238	58
District of Columbia	531,409	34,144	5,869	43 7/10
Caroline	255,340	20,179	2,300	17 1/10
St. Mary's	116,380	7,984	None.	11 7/10
Allegany	98,940	7,991	2,202	
Washington	94,573	5,552	3,215	27 5/10
Charles	69,408	4,252	2,861	58
Calvert	47,571	2,632	2,035	
Harford	20,650	1,632	None.	
Garrett	14,275	1,462	19	
Cecil	11,260	896	55	
Dorchester	6,800	459	None.	
Kent	1,546	80	1,250	
Somerset	825	49	None.	
	$19,917,004	$1,359,568	$362,235	

Report showing the Condition of the Mutual Fire Insurance Company of Montgomery County, Md., to Jan. 1, 1881.

Amount insured Jan. 1, 1880	$13,434,891.83	
Increase of risks during the year	280,837.00	
		$13,715,728.83
Amount of premium notes Jan. 1, 1880	$913,770.65	
Increase of premium notes during the year	23,052.56	
		$936,823.21

Estimated Assets.

City of Baltimore stock 1890 at par	$20,000.00	
United States 4 per cent. consols	26,000.00	
Northern Central Railroad bonds (gold interest)	6,000.00	
Northern Central Railroad bonds (currency interest)	2,000.00	
		$54,000.00
Interest on premium notes now due and payable on or before thirty days from the first Monday in January, at 4 per cent.	$37,472.92	
Interest on investment 1881	2,720.00	
Interest on investment now due	740.00	
Office and lot at Sandy Spring	1,557.86	
Rents	50.00	
Cash in the National Park Bank drawing interest	16,544.88	
Cash on hand and due by agents	2,586.72	
		61,672.38
		$115,672.38

Liabilities.

Claims for losses by fire, adjusted and unadjusted	$4,250.00	
Directors and Executive Committee attending meetings and mileage, 1880	469.40	
		4,719.40
		$110,952.98

William Pennill Palmer, one of the first incorporators of the Mutual Fire Insurance Company of Montgomery County, and one of its best citizens, was descended from John Palmer and Mary Southey, who came from England to Pennsylvania about 1680. Their son, John Palmer, married Martha Yeardy, and Moses Palmer, the son of John and Martha, married Abigail Sharpless, whose son, Moses Palmer, born in Concord, April 12, 1757, and died Aug. 29, 1840, married Hannah Pennill, born Dec. 17, 1770, and died Aug. 3, 1801, the daughter of John Pennill and Sarah Meredith. William Pennill Palmer, the son of this last marriage, was born in Concord, Chester Co. (now Delaware Co.), Pa., Nov. 19, 1792, and was educated at the Friends' School at Westtown. He made several voyages to England and one to China, as captain's clerk. He studied medicine under Drs. Chapman and Rush, and was graduated from the University of Pennsylvania in 1815, in which year he settled in Brookville, Montgomery Co., Md., where he practiced his profession in conjunction with Dr. Henry Howard until the spring of 1822. He purchased that year "Woodlawn," near Sandy Spring Post-office, to which he removed, and there continued to reside till his death, Dec. 27, 1869. He married, Sept. 26, 1822, Martha Gray, daughter of William Gray and Rachel Hill, of Gray's Ferry, Pa., who died in 1825, leaving two sons,—William Gray Palmer, now practicing medicine in Washington, D. C., and Moses Gray Palmer, attorney-at-law, St. Louis, Mo. May 17, 1831, he married Cleora Duvall, daughter of Dr. Benjamin Duvall (of Montgomery County, who was born April 13, 1768, and died Feb. 19, 1857), and Deborah Mordent Jackson (a descendant of one of the Mordents, Earls of Warwick), born Feb. 13, 1768, and died Dec. 16, 1851. Cleora, now in her seventy-seventh year, lives at "Woodlawn," having around her three children, survivors of nine, and a fair allotment of grandchildren.

Dr. Palmer was a member of the Society of Orthodox Friends till his second marriage, when he was "read out of meeting" for marrying a non-member. He was a lifelong Democrat, but never held nor aspired to any political office. He was from 1844 to his death one of the directors of the Mutual Fire Insurance Company of Montgomery County. While eminently successful in his general practice,—covering a period of fifty-two years,—he was held in especial esteem as a surgeon and obstetrician. He was peculiarly fitted for a country pioneer physician, with a sound mind in a sound body, a quick and vigorous intellect, an iron constitution, with energy and willpower. He always made his visits on horseback, and never knew any distinction between those who paid and those he called "God Almighty's patients." Of Dr. Benjamin Duvall the following obituary notice recalls the virtues of an early physician and prominent citizen of Western Maryland:

"With feelings of more than ordinary grief we record the death of Dr. Benjamin Duvall, in the ninetieth year of his age, which transpired at his late residence in this county on the 19th of February last (1857). His life was one of long usefulness, and by his death our county has been deprived of the services of a skillful and attentive physician. Dr. Duvall commenced the practice of medicine in 1788, and was very successful in his profession, accumulating a large property, which he well husbanded and improved. He voted at every Presidential election since the adoption of the Federal Constitution, not excepting the last, when he was brought in his carriage and voted for Mr. Buchanan. He was a Federalist till 1824, at which time he voted for Gen. Jackson, and from that time to his death was a true Democrat. He represented the county in the Legislature in 1821, with Forrest, Darne, and Riggs. The deceased was all his life of active constitution physically and mentally, and at the time of his death was fully possessed of his mental faculties. He has left behind him numerous descendants and a large circle of friends."

Savings Institution of Sandy Spring.—This institution was incorporated by an act of Assembly approved by the Governor March 28, 1868. The incorporators were Caleb Stabler, R. T. Bentley, Joseph T. Moore, Albar Gilpin, Robert R. Moore, H. C. Hallowell, William H. Farquhar, B. Rush Roberts, P. T. Stabler, Francis Miller, William John Thomas, Samuel Ellicott, Warwick P. Miller, Isaac Hartshorne, Warwick M. Stabler, Henry Stabler, William W. Moore, Charles Stabler, Charles G. Por-

ter, Robert M. Stabler, Edward Lee, Samuel P. Thomas, James S. Hallowell, Asa M. Stabler, Charles H. Brooke, and B. H. Miller.

The officers in 1881 were:

President, Caleb Stabler; Vice-President, Wm. John Thomas; Secretary, Allen Farquhar; Treasurer, Joseph T. Moore; Directors, W. W. Owen, Roger B. Farquhar, Caleb Stabler, Joseph T. Moore, Alban Gilpin, William H. Farquhar, Isaac Hartshorne, William John Thomas, Charles Stabler, Benjamin H. Miller, Asa M. Stabler, Charles F. Kirk, Richard T. Bentley, Robert R. Moore, H. C. Hallowell, William W. Moore, Philip T. Stabler, Warwick M. Stabler, Charles G. Porter, Charles H. Brooke, A. G. Thomas, Albert Chandlee, Benjamin D. Palmer, John H. Strain, Bernard McCrossen. The first vice-president was Joseph T. Moore; first treasurer, R. T. Bentley; and first secretary, Robert R. Moore.

Report of the Savings Institution of Sandy Spring, Montgomery County, for the year ending March 1, 1881.

Balance as shown by the Twelfth Annual Report, March 1, 1880.. $103,088.14

Receipts for the Past Year.

Cash received from depositors............................	$46,051.97
" " " interest on investments.......	6,851.44
" " " committee on Marietta and Cincinnati R. R. bonds............................	3.36
Amount found over in cash of our late treasurer.	1.40
Total receipts for the year........................	$52,908.17

Payments for the Past Year.

Cash paid depositors........................	$14,677.24
Amount of interest paid depositors for the year ending March 1, 1880........	4,048.05

Expenses for the Year.

Rent of boxes in Safe Deposit Company.............................	$15.00
Rent of banking-house...........	25.00
Taxes, State and county, $108.98; books, printing, and expressage, $32.15.......	141.13
Postage, $6.50; desk for secretary, $7.00; janitor, $1.35; sundries, $1.90................	16.75

Salaries.

President...................	$100.00	
Vice-President.............	25.00	
Treasurer...................	125.00	
Secretary...................	125.00 $375.00	$572.88

Total payments for the year..........	$19,298.17	$19,298.17
Gain for the year........................	$33,610.00	33,610.00
Showing amount on hand March 1, 1881............		$136,698.14

Held and Invested as follows:

Par.		Cost.
$23,000	Missouri State stocks..........................	$23,243.75
10,000	Northern Central R. R. gold bonds......	10,150.36
9,000	Pittsburgh & Connellsville R. R. 7 per cent. bonds................................	9,148.75
6,000	U. S. 4 per cent. consols, 1907...............	5,976.25
5,000	Virginia State consols.....................	3,556.25
3,000	Baltimore & Ohio R. R. bonds, 1885......	3,017.50
2,000	Loan on Hudson River R. R. bonds.......	2,000.00
5,000	New Jersey Central R. R. 1st consol bonds............................	5,080.50
1,500	Equitable Trust Company 7 per cent. bonds............................	1,530.00
1,000	Central Ohio R. R. bonds.....................	1,015 00
1,000	Northern Central R. R. currency bonds	850.00
400	Third National Bank stock of Baltimore	431.50
$66,900	stocks and bonds. Costing	$65,999.86
	Deeds of trust and mortgages on real estate......	57,525.00
	Cash in the National Park Bank of New York City, drawing interest.................	11,015.06
	Cash in the Farmers' and Planters' Bank of Baltimore........................	1,019.57
	Cash in the treasurer's hands............................	1,138.65
		$136,698.14

This Amount is Due by the Institution, as follows:

To the credit of depositors on March 1, 1881......	128,098.99	
To the credit of interest account after deducting last year's expenses, from which interest to depositors will be declared for year ending March 1, 1881..	6,278.56	
Profit and loss, or surplus owned by the institution...	2,320.59	$136,698.14

Olney.—This pretty town, often called Mechanicsville, is eight miles from Rockville, on the Brookville and Washington turnpike. The first house built in the neighborhood was "Fair Hill," which also was formerly the name of the town. The first settlers were Whitson Canby and William Kelley. The latter came about 1800 from Newtown, Bucks Co., Pa., and carried on a blacksmith and wheelwright-shop. From the same place shortly afterwards came Moses Barnsley. The latter was father of James F. Barnsley, born here in 1816, and who has been the toll-gate keeper since 1861. Benedict H. Daley kept the first store. Enoch Bell was the first blacksmith. William Starkey kept tavern in 1830. Liquor was always sold in the store until 1837, when J. D. Barnsley became the proprietor and refused to sell liquors, since which time none has been retailed in the place.

William B. Barnsley devoted his life to hard work as a mechanic in the village of Mechanicsville, and not only achieved an enviable record as the author of his own fortunes, but amassed in his business a handsome competence. He was born Dec. 19, 1814, in Mechanicsville, Montgomery Co., whither his father, Moses (born Feb. 22, 1789), moved from Bucks County, Pa., in 1806, when he was but seventeen years of age, for the purpose of taking service with his brother-in-law, William Kelly, a wheelwright in Mechanicsville. Moses followed the business of blacksmithing and wheelwrighting in Mechanicsville from 1806 to 1840. Then he retired to his farm, and there died, Dec. 22, 1844. John, father to Moses Barnsley, came from England to America upon a promise from his uncle (living in Bucks County) that he (the latter) would adopt John as his son and heir if he would come over and live with him. John grew to be one of the wealthy farmers of Bucks County, and was an ardent patriot during the Revolution, and gave largely of his wealth to assist the cause of his adopted country. Moses Barnsley married Elizabeth, daughter of Jonathan Dooley, of Montgomery County, Pa., where Mr. Dooley's ancestors, the De Lacourts (French Huguenots), were among the earliest settlers. The first of the name (De Lacourt) in Montgomery County lived within twelve miles of Triadelphia, and bequeathed a farm to each of his ten children. Moses Barnsley's living children are James F., John J., Margaret A. R., and Elizabeth C. William B. died July 13, 1878. He was bred to the business of wheelwrighting and blacksmithing, just as was his father before him, and for thirty years he followed it assiduously.

Mr. Barnsley never married. He resided with his

William B Barnsley

sister Margaret, to whom he left the bulk of his possessions. His life was uneventful, but, better, it was useful. He found his satisfaction in pursuing in a successful way the duties concerned with the progress of his business, and in doing well whatever he set his hand to do. He was a valued member of the community in which he lived, a counselor whose wise and experienced judgment was often sought, and a spirited advocate of the theory of public progress.

William McPherson was the first school-teacher, and was succeeded by Amos Farquhar, Phineas Paxton, Richard and Mary Kirk. The town is built on a small tract of forty-seven acres, granted to Richard Brooke, July 28, 1763, and called after George III.

St. John's Protestant Episcopal Church.—This church was erected prior to 1844, and was built during the rectorship of Rev. Levin J. Gillis, of St. Bartholomew's Parish. He was succeeded by Rev. O. Hutton, D.D., in 1844, who was succeeded by Revs. Tinsley and Poindexter, and they by Rev. Thomas Duncan, in 1868, who remained till Easter Sunday in 1877, when the present incumbent, Rev. Dr. Laird, was called. In the cemetery are the graves of

George Hinkey, born Dec. 20, 1826, died March 4, 1866.
Nathan Childs, born Nov. 17, 1799, died June 16, 1871.
Elizabeth A. Hutton, born June 5, 1815, died Jan. 29, 1874.
Emily Umstead, born May 1, 1819, died May 1, 1876.
William B. Barnsley, born Dec. 19, 1814, died July 13, 1878.
Alfred B. Griffith, died July 8, 1862, aged 41 years.
Jeffrey P. T. Magruder, died July 14, 1880, aged 40 years.
Elizabeth Singleton Griffith, born April 28, 1838, died April 10, 1876.
Dr. J. Wilson Magruder, died July 14, 1880, aged 40 years.
Harriet Griffith, born May 17, 1800, died Aug. 12, 1874.
William J. Neel, born July 25, 1844, died Jan. 19, 1873.
Dr. William B. Magruder, born Nov. 2, 1802, died Jan. 21, 1873.
Mary A. Magruder, died Dec. 23, 1852, aged 46 years, 26 days.
Grafton Holland, born April 16, 1800, died March 24, 1855.
Ellen, his wife, born Dec. 24, 1808, died March 3, 1877.
Matthew Hannah, died Dec. 12, 1857, aged 97.
Elizabeth Hannah, died April 19, 1857, aged 94.

The church is on the survey of Charles and Benjamin, granted to Charles Beall July 2, 1718, which contained two thousand two hundred and eighty acres.

Olney Lodge of Ancient Free and Accepted Masons, No. 141, was instituted several years ago, and it and Mizpah, No. 144, are the only two Masonic lodges in the county.

Olney Grange, No. 7, of Patrons of Husbandry, of which Joseph T. Moore is Master, and Mrs. C. H. Farquhar, Secretary, is one of the oldest in the county. The store is kept by Williams & Boyer, and R. S. Kirk is postmaster. Dr. William E. Magruder is the physician, and Dr. F. H. Manakee, dentist.

Dr. William B. Magruder, who resided in Mechanicsville District, Montgomery County, for a number of years, was one of the most active and influential citizens of that section of the State. He was born Nov. 2, 1802, and died on the 21st of January, 1873, aged about seventy years. Dr. Magruder was one of the best-known men in the county, and enjoyed the confidence and respect of the entire community. He was a member of the famous Magruder family of Southern Maryland, which emigrated to this country nearly two hundred years ago. Near Washington City was a settlement known as "New Scotland," from the fact that it was settled largely by emigrants from Scotland. It afterwards became a hundred of Prince George's County. Of the Scotch families which located themselves in this vicinity, the Magruders and the Beales were among the most conspicuous. The Magruders settled on the Patuxent, and their descendants are now scattered over various portions of Maryland and Virginia. Among the prominent members of the family have been Judge Alexander Contee Hanson Magruder, Gen. J. B. Magruder, the distinguished Confederate officer, and Judge Daniel

R. Magruder; Dr. William B. Magruder's son, Dr. William E. Magruder, who resides near Olney, or Mechanicsville, and who enjoys a large and lucrative practice. Another son, Bowie Magruder, is a successful farmer. Besides Dr. William E. Magruder, there are two other physicians named Magruder who have lived in Montgomery County,—Dr. Wilson Magruder, who resides at "Redlands," and Dr. Julian Magruder, who formerly lived near Rockville, but who recently removed to Ohio. Both these gentlemen are distant relatives of Dr. William E. and Bowie Magruder.

Mount Zion is in the northwestern part of the district, on the Cracklin District line. It contains a small frame Catholic church, and Mount Zion Methodist Episcopal church, colored. Near the latter is buried Rev. L. D. Snowden, of the Methodist Episcopal Church, who died Dec. 5, 1875, aged forty-nine years.

Triadelphia.—This place is ten miles from Hood's Mills, fourteen from Rockville, twenty-five from Baltimore, and near the Patuxent River. A. H. Brown is the merchant, and Thomas F. Lansdale, postmaster. The town was laid out on "Benjamin's Lot," surveyed for Benjamin Gaither, April 8, 1725, and containing five hundred and sixteen acres. It is located on the Patuxent River, and includes the farms of Robert Brown and others. The Triadelphia Cotton-mill was established in 1809 by three brothers-in-law, Isaac Briggs, Caleb Bentley, and Thomas Moore, but ceased operations after the war of 1812.

Brighton is fifteen miles from Laurel, fourteen from Rockville, and twenty-six from Baltimore. Of Brighton Grange, No. 60, Isaac Hartshorne is Master, and Ella M. Lansdale, Secretary. The merchants are Edward Peirce & Co., the senior member of the firm being the postmaster. Dr. Jeremiah Nichols is the physician.

For an account of St. Luke's Protestant Episcopal Church, see St. Bartholomew's Parish, under this district.

Brookville.—This town is ten miles from Rockville, and was created by an act of the Legislature in 1808. The land on which it is situated was the property of Richard Thomas, Thomas Moore, and Henry Howard. It took its name from the Brooke family, who settled in the neighborhood in 1728. Richard Thomas built the mill in 1794, and in 1801 erected his house, the first in the town, and which is now the rectory of the Protestant Episcopal church. Caleb Bentley kept the first store. Dr. Henry Howard was the first physician. Mr. Murphy was the first blacksmith, and John McCauley the second. A Dr. Lukens practiced there before Dr. Howard, but did not reside in the place. Richard Thomas, the first settler and founder of the town, married Deborah Brooke. Among other early settlers were Brice and George Gassaway, the latter of whom kept store. The first teacher was Robert Stuart. The oldest native of the place is Roger Thomas, born in 1803. The present physicians are Drs. J. S. Martin and Artemus Riggs. In the beginning of the century, David Newlin had a grist, saw, clover-seed, and flaxseed-mill, and before that had a fulling-mill on the Hawling's River. Thomas Moore, at whose instance the town was created by the Assembly in 1808, married Mary Brooke, and built the house now occupied by Hon. E. J. Hall.

Methodist Episcopal Church.—This edifice was built about 1838. Among its pastors have been Revs. Richard Browne, Paynter, and Harris.

Methodist Protestant Church.—This congregation was formed under the care of Rev. Thomas McCormick, one of the seceding ministers from the old Methodist Episcopal Church. About 1830 he, with his family, removed to this place, and in 1833 the church edifice was erected, it being the first church built in the town. Hanson and Henry Brown were the contractors and builders. Among the very few members of the congregation at its organization were Wm. and Henry Brown, Mrs. McCormick, and Hannah McCormick. The church edifice was remodeled in 1871. The present pastor is J. W. Matthews, assisted by Rev. G. F. Berring.

Salem Methodist Protestant Church Cemetery contains the remains of

Margaret Parsley, born March 22, 1782, died Feb. 26, 1879.
Agnes Connell, born November, 1790, died September, 1870.
Nelson Sullivan, born Feb. 19, 1812, died Nov. 13, 1874.
John Wesley Baker, died June 2, 1872, aged 72.
Emily Neuden, born Dec. 29, 1813, died Dec. 13, 1873.
David Newlin, born Jan. 7, 1769, died July 3, 1852.
William S. Newlin, born April 24, 1836, died Feb. 12, 1855.
John Whiteside, Jr., born in County Down, Ireland, died in Brookville, March 14, 1863, aged 28.
Artemus Neuden, born Nov. 28, 1802, died May 15, 1852.
Mary, his wife, born Jan. 15, 1803, died Dec. 21, 1854.
Christina Ludwigham, died Nov. 28, 1861, aged 53.
James L. Whiteside, born in County Down, Ireland, June 15, 1795, died May 17, 1859.
Mary A., wife of John Hill, born Sept. 21, 1784, died April 1, 1868.

Methodist Episcopal Church South.—This congregation was formed in 1865, and worships in the Methodist Episcopal church. There is a colored congregation of the Protestant Episcopal Church in the town under the charge of Rev. Dr. Laird.

Brookville Circulating Library Association

was instituted at a meeting held Feb. 17, 1849, at which Rev. Orlando Hutton was chairman, and J. O. Williamson, secretary. The first permanent officers of the association were A. Bowie Davis, president; E. J. Hall, treasurer; J. C. Williamson, secretary; and Dr. William B. Magruder, F. Gartrell, R. Riggs, Samuel Ellicott, directors. The stock was taken up by private subscription, each stockholder becoming a member and entitled to his share of the property of the association. Elisha Riggs, of New York City, generously purchased a very large amount of the stock and presented it to his relatives in the county. John A. Riggs is the president, John W. Whiteside the secretary and treasurer, and Rev. Orlando Hutton, B. W. Howard, E. W. Owen, and R. W. Gartrell the directors.

Brookville Academy.—This institution was chartered by the Legislature in 1815, by act of January 2d of that year. The first trustees were Thane Davis, John H. Riggs, Caleb Bentley, William H. Dorsey, Ignatius Waters, Thomas Riggs, and David Newline. The first principal was Robert Stuart, succeeded, in 1822, by Samuel O. Bumstead; in 1827, by Moses Woodward; in 1828, by Thomas Haggerty; in 1829, by George T. Bigelow; and in 1831, by William Hill.

Since then the principals have been: 1834, N. C. Brooks; 1836–51, Elisha J. Hall; 1851, D. L. House; 1851–63, E. B. Prettyman; 1863–65, Professor Burns; 1865–69, J. Duncan Parkinson, J. Llewellyn Massey; 1869–79, Samuel H. Coleman; 1879–80, Edwin M. Magruder; 1880–81, William H. Thomas; 1881, present incumbent, Rev. C. K. Nelson, D.D., for many years a learned professor of St. John's College, Annapolis. The officers and trustees for 1881 were: President, E. J. Hall; Treasurer, Z. D. Waters; Secretaries, Dr. James S. Martin, Thomas J. Holland, John A. Riggs, Capt. J. Strain, Rev. Orlando Hutton, D.D. Hon. Allen Bowie Davis was twenty-six years president of the board. The first academy building, a brick structure and now occupied by the I. O. O. F. lodge, was relinquished in 1869 for the new and large edifice near the town, on the road to Unity. The academy is situated one-half mile north of Brookville. Its location is a remarkable healthy and beautiful region, seven hundred feet above tide-water.

In 1833 the trustees, at the suggestion of Professor Henry Howard, petitioned the Legislature to prohibit the sale of intoxicating liquors in the vicinity of the academy, and the request was granted, but coupled with the condition that the continuance of the prohibition should depend upon the wishes of the people in the immediate neighborhood. The condition was cheerfully accepted by the board, and from that time to the present no one has ever asked for the repeal of the law. Allen Bowie Davis, who was a member of the board of trustees of the academy, says, "The signing of that petition was among the first public acts of my life, and I now proudly look back on it as the best." For a long time this law stood solitary and alone in its glory. It was the first permanent and continuous law of its kind in Maryland, and probably in the United States. Its benefit to the academy and surrounding neighborhood was so marked and advantageous that other schools and neighborhoods in many sections of the State have followed the example of Brookville and obtained similar laws. Thus quietly but surely has the work progressed, until now some six or eight entire counties have adopted the same principle. In 1862 the prohibitory laws were extended to Cracklin District, Emory Chapel, and Sandy Spring, nearly one-fifth of the county.

Brookville Lodge, No. 50, I. O. O. F.—"Triadelphia Lodge," No. 50, I. O. O. F., was chartered by the Right Worshipful Lodge of Maryland, Oct. 22, 1846, with the following charter members: John L. Heckrote, William Lee, B. Burton, Owen Dorsey, Thomas Lucy, and George Kinsey. In accordance with a deputation of the R. W. Grand Master of Maryland, Archer Ropes, Past Grand John Wollen of Patuxent Lodge, No. 45, opened in Triadelphia the Grand Lodge of Maryland by proclamation, assisted by Past Grand J. A. McNew and others, on Dec. 25, 1846. At this meeting the above charter members deposited their cards, and Triadelphia Lodge was regularly instituted. The first officers were: N. G., John S. Heckrote; V. G., Owen Dorsey; Secretary, Thomas Lucy; and Treasurer, John Cook. The lodge then elected Hiram Warrell, Rufus H. Speake, Thomas C. Miller, and Elisha Riggs to take the degrees, of whom Miller, Riggs, and Warrell were initiated at that meeting. The first trustees were Elisha Riggs, Hiram Warrell, and B. Burton. The hall occupied by the lodge was the property of the Montgomery Manufacturing Company, and was used for the meetings until Jan. 23, 1864, when the lodge was removed to Brookville, four miles from Triadelphia. Here the lodge held its first meeting, Jan. 30, 1864, with the following officers: N. G., Z. Waters; V. G., John Whiteside; Secretary, John C. Colliflower; Treasurer, E. J. Hill. On March 26th, J. W. Whiteside was elected secretary, vice Colliflower, resigned, and has held that position, with brief intermissions, ever since. The hall now occupied by

Phil Chase Riley

the lodge was purchased Nov. 6, 1869, of the trustees of the academy. The number of members initiated by Triadelphia Lodge up to the time of its removal to Brookville was one hundred and forty. The name of Triadelphia Lodge was changed to that of Brookville, May 7, 1864. The number of members initiated since the removal to Brookville has been eighty-six, and the present membership is fifty. The officers for second term of 1881 were: N. G., Andrew Shafer; V. G., Thos. Lishear; Sec., J. W. Whiteside; Treas., E. A. Parsley; D. D. Grand Master, Z. D. Waters.

The oldest member is John Whiteside, who has belonged to the order thirty-five years; the next oldest, R. W. Gartrell; the third, James Townsend; the fourth, H. N. Harris; and the fifth, J. C. Colliflower. From this lodge sprang Rainbow, No. 16, of Lisbon, Howard Co.; Clarkesburg, No. 88; Montgomery, No. 100; and Concord (now defunct), located in Rockville. This lodge was the first instituted in the county. During the existence of Triadelphia Lodge it had several large and pleasant celebrations, which were participated in by its sister lodges; but the most important and largest was held by Brookville Lodge, Aug. 29, 1866, the year after the close of the war, in which the Grand Lodge took part, as well as all the subordinate and sister lodges of this and adjoining counties. The speakers were Josiah L. Baucher, G. M.; Henry T. Garey, P. G. M.; and Joseph B. Escaville, Grand Secretary of Maryland; and Grand Representative Havener J. Sweet, of Washington. Six hundred Odd-Fellows marched in the procession. This was the last public appearance of Grand Master Baucher, whose death occurred shortly afterwards.

Ashton.—This village lies one mile southeast of Sandy Spring, and is located on the historical survey of "Addition to Charley Forest," surveyed for Maj. John Bradford, Sept. 16, 1720. The first store was kept by Porter & Stable, and is now conducted by R. C. Thomas. Bernard Gilpin, father of Joshua C. Gilpin, owned part of the land on which the village stands. He settled here in 1790. William Thomas owned most of the other land in the vicinity. He was the son of Richard Thomas, Jr., born in this county, but whose father, Richard Thomas, Sr., removed from St. Mary's County. For an account of the Ashton Methodist Episcopal Church, see Spencerville Circuit, under Berry District.

Norbeck.—This place is five miles from Rockville. James Rannie is the merchant; John A. Bennett, postmaster and store-keeper; C. P. Cashell, carriage-maker; Charles W. Nicholls and W. Burris, carpenters; and James G. Gill, blacksmith.

Philander Chase Riley, residing upon a fine farm near Norbeck, is a native of the city of Washington, where he was born Feb. 26, 1832. His ancestry in America is allied to the history of Accomac County, Va., where his grandfather, John, was born, and where also his father, Thomas Robinson Riley, had his birth,—1785. The latter removed from Accomac County to Washington about 1825. His wife was Elizabeth Cropper, daughter of John Blackstone and Elizabeth Wise, of Accomac County. Seven of their ten children are living. Thomas Robinson Riley, like his father before him, was a landed proprietor in Virginia. When he made Washington his home he became identified with the business of steamboating,—an interest that was in those days one of considerable importance and value as a busy industry. After a career of active usefulness he died in Washington in 1846. At the age of seventeen Philander C. Riley (having been educated at Rittenhouse Academy, Washington) embarked in business in Washington with his brother Thomas, and as a business partner was concerned with him and his brother William from 1850 to 1870. In the last-named year he determined to retire from trade, for he had grown weary of it, and desiring, moreover, to spend the residue of his days as a landholder and agriculturist in perpetuation and recognition of the examples of his ancestors, he purchased the farm property he now owns and at once made it his home. The place contains about six hundred acres, and when he bought it was but little more than a barren common. Lending himself with earnest will to the task of embellishing and improving his estate, he created the present highly-cultivated and finely-improved farm, than which few are to be found of more pronounced excellence or more finished appointment. Mr. Riley's ambition has been and is to foster with all his capacity the best interests of agriculture, and to make his farm a model. To that end he has given himself most diligently to the task, and enjoys the present satisfaction of knowing that his efforts have been neither misdirected nor unrewarded. A lifelong Democrat, he has ever kept a place among progressive citizens in observing with solicitude and watchful interest the progress of political history, while he has at no time been wanting in the emphatic expression of his political faith, but beyond that and into the field of political honors his desires have never led him, nor indeed would the allegiance he owes to his private affairs permit him that indulgence. Nov. 10, 1868, Mr. Riley married Virginia Covington, daughter of Benjamin Frank Smith and Matilda Rebecca Price, of the District of Columbia. The Smiths were early settlers in Maryland,—Dr. Joseph Sim Smith (Mrs. Riley's grandfather) being of the widely-known physicians of his day. Capt. Benjamin Price (Mrs. Riley's maternal grandfather) fought with much gallantry on the Federal side during the war for American independence, and in recognition of his meritorious services received a sword that is now in the possession of Dr. Christopher Johnson, of Baltimore.

Rockland Seminary.—In 1858 the Alexandria Boarding-School of the learned Benjamin Hallowell closed, and in the same year Francis Miller, one of the principals of the Alexandria school, and a son-in-law of its head, opened a boarding-school for boys at "Stanmore." In the same year Henry C. Hallowell removed to the Hallowell estate, "Rockland." In 1867, Mrs. Caroline H. Miller opened a girls' school at Stanmore, while her husband was studying and practicing law, the boys' school having been discontinued. In 1878, the school at Stanmore having closed, Henry C. Hallowell opened a boarding-school for young ladies at Rockland. Mr. Hallowell graduated at Yale College in 1852, with Francis Miller, whose sister Sarah he married, and who married his sister, Caroline H. Hallowell. Mr. Miller is of the noted Washington City law firm of Riddle, Miller & Padgett.

The institution is designed to be a select school, in which girls can obtain a thorough education under judicious and careful superintendence. The principal, as stated, is a graduate of Yale College, and was associated with his brother, Benjamin Hallowell, in the Alexandria Boarding-School. The buildings are well arranged for a boarding-school, and for the comfort and health of the scholars. They are situated in Sandy Spring neighborhood, about eighteen miles northwest of Washington City, and twenty-eight miles from Baltimore.

The district school trustees and teachers for 1881 and 1882 are as follows:

Trustees.—No. 1, R. T. Bentley, Z. J. Davis, J. T. Moore; No. 2, W. W. Owen, J. D. Berry, C. T. Bunnby; No. 3, J. C. Holland, Gus. Jones, G. W. Dorsey; No. 4, B. W. Howard, W. B. Miller, William Mobly; No. 5, J. W. Jones, R. W. Young, Granville Farquhar; No. 6, William Brown, of J., W. C. Gartril, J. F. Holland.

Teachers.—No. 1, F. P. Davis, Sandy Spring P. O.; No. 2, G. A. Umstead, Olney P. O.; No. 3, F. W. Ball, Brookville P. O.; No. 4, B. L. Coan, Brookville P. O.; No. 5, Adele Bamly, Olney P. O.; No. 6, W. W. Waters.

There are four colored schools.

The magistrates are Alfred F. Fairall, Henry N. Harris.

GAITHERSBURG DISTRICT, No. 9.

This district was erected April 10, 1880, and was formed from portions of the First, or Cracklin, Second, or Clarksburg, Fourth, or Rockville, and Sixth, or Darnestown, Districts. Its metes and bounds are as follows:

"Beginning for the same at the cross-roads in the village of Germantown, and running thence with the Neelsville road to the Georgetown and Frederick road; thence across said Georgetown and Frederick road to the road leading from the Neelsville Presbyterian church to the old Baltimore road; thence with the said road to its intersection with the old Baltimore road; thence with the said old Baltimore road to Seneca bridge; thence with the road leading from said Seneca bridge to Rockville via the village of Redland to where the said road is crossed by Mill Branch, near the farm of William O. Householder; thence with a straight line to the intersection of the Georgetown and Frederick road with what is known as the Gaither road, between the residences of George M. Graff and Lemuel Clements; thence with said Gaither road to its intersection with the Rockville and Darnestown, near the residence of Thomas W. Stonestreet; thence with said Rockville and Darnestown road, in the direction of Darnestown, to its intersection with what is known as the Quince Orchard road, near the Quince Orchard Schoolhouse; thence with the said Quince Orchard road to its intersection with the Gaithersburg and Barnesville road, near the St. Rose's Catholic church; thence with the said Gaithersburg and Barnesville road, in the direction of Barnesville, to the place of beginning."

The district is bounded on the north by Clarksburg and Darnestown Districts, east by Clarksburg and Cracklin Districts, south by Cracklin and Rockville Districts, and west by Rockville and Darnestown Districts. Flowing westward through it are Great Seneca Creek and Gunner's Run and Long Draught Creek, the two latter emptying into the former.

The first two settlers in the district were Ralph Crabb and George Buchanan, who were soon followed by the Gaithers, Claggetts, Selbys, Suters, Walkers, Thompsons, Reeds, Bensons, Gassaways, Gloyds, Waters, Williams, Bennetts, Briggs, Cooks, Smalls, Days, Codwises, Mills, and Cloppers.

Francis Cassatt Clopper, a prominent representative of the last-named family, was born in Baltimore on the 26th of July, 1786. His early life was passed in York, Pa., but while yet a boy he went to Philadelphia to begin his business career. When only eighteen he was sent by his employers to New Orleans to collect moneys due them there and at intermediate points. The trip was made on horseback, through a wild frontier country, alone, or with such chance companions as he might meet upon the road, but his mission was successful, and he brought back the money quilted in his vest. This was but the first of many like it. On July 8, 1811, he was married to Ann Jane Byrne, of Philadelphia, and in the following year he purchased the farm in Montgomery County upon which he resided until his death, the family having moved there in the same year, making a continuous residence of fifty-seven years.

NATHAN COOKE.

The original grants of the tracts of land comprised in the purchase date back to 1748, and formed part of their manor of Conecocheague, or, as one of them has it, of "Calverton." The lands are described as lying upon "Sinicar" Creek, near the ford known as the "Indian Ford," and it is said that the old Indian road from Washington to Frederick crossed Seneca a few yards above the present county road crossing.

The land at one time belonged to the Benson family, but about 1804 was sold to Zachariah McCubbin, from whom Mr. Clopper purchased it. Other tracts were bought from parties at a later date. The original foundation of the mill is not known. One was standing in 1812 upon the site of the present saw-mill. His public spirit was a prominent feature of Mr. Clopper's character, as he was always interested in some project for the advancement of the county. The last twenty years of his life were expended almost entirely in efforts to procure the construction of a railroad through the county. He was connected with the organization of the original Metropolitan Railroad Company, and when that failed in the business depression of 1857, he called the attention of the president of the Baltimore and Ohio Railroad to the advantages of the route to his company, and procured a reconnoissance to be made and a report, which later were followed up by the construction of the road. He died in 1868, after a married life of fifty-seven years.[1]

The Cook family is also among the oldest in this district. Nathan Cook, Sr., was born in Montgomery County, near Gaithersburg, June 21, 1803, and died Sept. 18, 1869, after a life of usefulness in a sphere wherein he found much honor and respect. His father died while Nathan was but a lad, and his mother (Rachel, daughter of Col. Magruder) married for her second husband Henry Dorsey. By the first marriage there were four children, and by the second six. Young Nathan was trained in book-learning by Rev. Mr. Reed, an Englishman of considerable capacity as a tutor, and thereafter studied at Rockville, but the spirit of industrious ambition was too strong within him to lend his attention long to the school-desk, and so at an early age he set himself earnestly to the business of farming, to which he had determined to devote his life.

It was well that he did so, for at the age of twenty-one he found himself, by inheritance, the possessor of a farm known as "Gray Rock," near Gaithersburg, where he continued thereafter to reside until his death. Thanks to his rugged experience he was well fitted to assume his new responsibilities, and easily managed his property, so that it improved in value and yielded him a handsome revenue. Nov. 17, 1825, he married Elizabeth, daughter of Dr. Zadock Magruder, of Montgomery County, of which he was a native, and in which he was for many years a leading physician. Mrs. Cook survives her husband, and still resides at "Gray Rock." Of their four children two are living, Nathan P. and Rachel D. Nathan Cook, Sr., never sought public distinction, and ever studiously avoided participation in political strife or race for office, although more than once besought to stand as a candidate. His interests were turned to pleasanter and quieter paths. His philanthropy and his large-hearted sympathy for the poor were known and reverenced far and near, and to the practical illustration of those virtues he gave himself with conspicuous devotion. His ear was always attuned to listen to the distressed, his energies quick to find the abode of deserving poverty, and his hand ever ready to succor the needy. Not only did he exert himself privately as the dispenser of aid and comfort to suffering humanity, but for twenty years he was one of the alms-house trustees, the president of the board at the time of his death, and steadily an earnest laborer on behalf of the beneficent purposes embodied in the institution. In his death the poor lost indeed a watchful friend. He stood high in the confidence of his neighbors, and was frequently called upon to settle estates, in the performance of which duty he gained much approval for his wise judgment and careful management.

Germantown is eleven miles from Rockville, sixty-seven from Baltimore, and one from Germantown Station, on the Metropolitan Branch of the Baltimore and Ohio Railroad. The post-office is at the station, of which Thomas N. Henderson is postmaster, and John H. Gassaway is railroad and express agent. Germantown takes its name from the fact of its first settlement having been made by German families, notably by Frederick Snyder, Frederick Richter, and Peter Hogan. H. D. Waters is the village merchant. The Methodist Episcopal church is a commodious two-story frame structure. In the burial-ground at its side are interred Mary E. Metz, born Sept. 16, 1814, died July 20, 1879; Martha J., daughter of G. T. and M. W. Leaman, died July 17, 1876, aged three years and nine months. The place was formerly in Clarkesburg and Darnestown Districts. Joseph A. Taney, for the past eighteen years clerk to the county commissioners, resides on the Rockville road near the village. Germantown Station is part of survey Chestnut Ridge, granted to George Buchanan in 1732.

Gaithersburg.—This town lies partly in the survey

---

[1] "Centennial Celebration of Montgomery County."

of "Deer Park," surveyed for Ralph Crabb, April 19, 1722, which contained four hundred and twenty acres. It takes its name (as does also the district) from Benjamin Gaither, who built the first house in its limits in 1802. This house stood on the site of the residence of Mrs. Rebecca Ann Gloyd, and on the lot is a large oak-tree over two centuries old. Mr. Gaither was born near Anity in 1764, was magistrate for a long term of years, and died in 1838, aged seventy-four years. He had six children, of whom one is Col. James B. Gaither, for a long time one of the best-known magistrates of the country. In 1826 there were only three or four houses in the town. Robert Crawford kept the first hotel, and the first three storekeepers were, respectively, Benjamin Thompson, John Lowe, and Samuel Gloyd. The village was called Gaithersburg up to 1850, when its name was changed to Forest Oak, by which it was known until the completion of the Metropolitan Branch Railroad, in 1873, when the old name was restored. A new public school building, a fine frame structure, has just been completed, which is two stories high, and forty by twenty-four feet.

The Methodist Episcopal church, a two-story frame edifice, was built in 1846 and '47. Its pastor is Rev. Mr. Cross. The Methodist Episcopal Church South was erected in 1867, and is called "Forest Chapel." It is a beautiful frame structure. In its rear is "Forest Oak Cemetery," established in 1879, in which are the following interments:

Mary, wife of J. N. Benton, born June 28, 1840, died March 25, 1869.
Anthony Ricketts, born Nov. 10, 1823, died May 6, 1877.
Walter Montgomery, son of William E. and Sarah A. Selby, born July 13, 1875, died March 28, 1879.
Margaret A., daughter of David and Margaret Carlisle, died July 31, 1880, aged 4 years and 4 months.

This church belongs to the Rockville Circuit, and its pastors for 1881 were Revs. G. T. Tyler and F. M. Strother.

The Protestant Episcopal church, a handsome Gothic structure, was completed in 1881, and is supplied by the rector of the Rockville church, Rev. Mr. Brown. The town contains an excellent hotel, a large frame building, erected in 1881 by Juan Boyle, its proprietor. It is three stories high, near the Protestant Episcopal church, and in a beautiful grove. It has already become a popular resort for summer boarders. Over a thousand tons of fertilizers are sold and delivered in Gaithersburg annually to the neighboring farmers. J. Sprigg Pool has a large grain warehouse, and his shipments of wheat have reached a hundred thousand bushels annually. The well-known Darby mill is only a mile distant. C. F. Hogan has lately erected an extensive building, in which he carries on carriage-making, and employs some dozen hands. John Nicholls has a large harness, saddle, and trunk-making establishment in the lower story of "Diamond Hall," a large hall owned by John A. Diamond, the upper story of which is used for public meetings and entertainments.

Gaithersburg Grange is a flourishing lodge, of which John T. De Sellum is secretary. Henry Ward is postmaster, Dr. E. C. Etchison, physician, and J. Sprigg Poole, railroad and express agent. The merchants are John A. Belt, T. J. Owen, Ward & Fulks, and Gloyd & Amiss.

Gaithersburg is increasing in trade and population faster than any other place in the county, and is attracting many business men from other parts.

St. Rose Catholic Church is situated on the Rockville road, midway between Gaithersburg and Germantown, and is attended by a large congregation. It is an outgrowth of the Rockville Mission.

Gaithersburg is situated about midway between the Point of Rocks and Washington City. Six public roads converged at this point, of which one is the Great Western road, from the District of Columbia to Frederick City. Near the town will be the junction of the projected cross railroad to Baltimore City. A large number of new buildings have lately been erected, and building lots are in active demand.

Among the former well-known residents in the vicinity of Gaithersburg was Dr. Thomas Patterson. He was born in Franklin County, Pa., and married Jane Clarke, sister of the late Matthew St. Clair Clarke, clerk of the National House of Representatives three terms. Dr. Patterson practiced medicine a short time in Martinsburg, Va., and then removed to Washington, D. C., where he became librarian of the Congressional Library. He remained there in this position twenty-seven years, residing part of the time in Hagerstown, Md. In 1831 he removed to this county, near Gaithersburg, where he died in 1847, at an advanced age. He left a large family, some of whom are still residents of the State.

Corporation and Officers.—The town was incorporated by an act of the General Assembly passed April 5, 1878, with the following metes and bounds: Beginning at a stone planted on the west side of the Goshen road, a little east of Diamond Hall, and run thence with said road to the southern limits of the Metropolitan Branch Railroad; thence with said railroad, on the south side thereof, to a lot of land belonging to the late Charles Saffell; thence across said lot and the Georgetown and Frederick road to a stone on Remus G. Dorsey's land; thence with the outlines of said Dorsey's land to the new cut road, known as the Fitzgerald road; thence to a stone on Chestnut Street; thence by a straight line to a stone on the dividing line between Wade and Lanahan; thence with said line to the Frederick and Georgetown road; thence across said road to a stone on a line between the lands of Giles Eastern and Ignatius Thomas Fulks; thence with said line to a stone; thence with a straight line to the beginning. The first election after the act of incorporation was held on the first Monday in May, 1878, and resulted in the selection of the following officers:

Commissioners, Henry Ward (president), James B. Gaither, William Gloyd, Reuben Burriss; Bailiff, John Burriss.

The corporation officers since that period have been:

1879.—Commissioners, Dr. E. C. Etchison (president), Henry Ward, Reuben Burriss, S. S. Gloyd, James B. Gaither; Bailiff, John Burriss.
1880.—Commissioners, H. C. Ward (president), M. M. Benton, James B. Gaither, Reuben Burriss, Dr. E. C. Etchison; Bailiff, Leonard Buxton.
1881.—Commissioners, S. S. Gloyd (president), Giles Eastern, C. H. Duvall, Ignatius T. Fulks, Remus G. Dorsey; Bailiff, William E. English.
E. L. Amiss has been the corporation clerk since 1878.

The school trustees and teachers of Gaithersburg District for 1881 and 1882 are as follows:

Trustees.—No. 1, Samuel Gloyd, R. B. Briggs, N. J. Walker; No. 2, G. H. Henden, Z. Dowden, W. H. Benson; No. 3, Samuel Higgins, E. L. T. Saffield, J. H. Garrett.

Teachers.—No. 1, E. S. Amiss, Gaithersburg P. O.; No. 2, R. J. Green, Germantown P. O.; No. 3, Dorsey Peter, Darnestown P. O.

There are two colored schools in the district. J. B. Gaither is the magistrate.

The Washington Grove Camp-Meeting Association of the District of Columbia and Maryland was chartered March 30, 1874, with the following incorporators:

F. Howard, William R. Woodward, J. T. Mitchell, B. H. Steinmetz, Thomas Somerville, J. W. Wade, M. G. Emery, Alexander Ashley, R. H. Willett, W. M. Talbot, J. G. Warfield, E. F. Simpson, J. A. Ruff, Thomas H. Langley, W. R. Hunt, Thomas P. Morgan, Henry T. Whalen, G. Thomas Woodward, J. R. Riggles, W. H. Griffith, John Lanahan, G. G. Baker, B. Peyton Brown, T. H. Davis, and J. Henry Wilson.

It is a stock association, with the capital stock fixed at twenty thousand dollars, divided into one thousand shares at twenty dollars a share. One share entitles the owner to the privilege of a tent-site, and five shares to a cottage site.

The tract consists of two hundred and sixty-eight acres, and is located on what is known as Parr's Ridge, on the line of the Metropolitan Railroad, twenty and one-half miles from Washington. The first camp was held Aug. 13, 1873. Among the first officers were

Dr. Flodoardo Howard, president; W. R. Woodward, vice-president; E. F. Simpson, secretary; J. A. Ruff, treasurer. The present officers are Thomas P. Morgan, president; W. R. Woodward; E. F. Simpson; B. H. Steinmetz, treasurer.

The organization is under the control of the Methodist Episcopal Church, but persons of all denominations unite with them, and are heartily welcomed.

GREAT FALLS DISTRICT, No. 10.

This district was created by act of April 10, 1880, and was formed out of a portion of Rockville, or Fourth District. Its metes and bounds are as follows:

"Beginning at the mouth of Cabin John Creek; thence up and with said Cabin John Creek to the mouth of Thomas' Run; thence up and with said Thomas' Run until the same is crossed by the Orendorff mill road; thence with a straight line to where Piney Branch is crossed by the public road near the residence of Mrs. Upton West; thence down and with said Piney Branch until it empties into Watts' Branch; thence down and with said Watts' Branch until it empties into the Potomac River; thence down and with said Potomac River to the place of beginning."

This district is bounded on the north by Darnestown District, northwest, west, and southwest by the Potomac River, dividing it from Virginia, south by Bethesda District, and east by Rockville District. Rock Run flows southwest into the Potomac, as does also Cabin John Creek, which divides it from Bethesda on the southwest; Thomas' Run, separating it from Bethesda District on the south, flows west into Cabin John Creek; Watts' Branch, flowing northwest, empties into the Potomac, and into Watts' Branch empties Piney Branch, which, on the north, divides the district from Darnestown District.

The first settlers were John Thompson, the Moores, Claggetts, Perrys, Offutts, Trundles, McCormicks, Padgetts, Pearces, Stones, Woodbridges, Hintons, Hardestys, Harrisons, Connells, some of whom settled prior to the year 1700.

Offutt's Cross-roads.—This place is six miles from Rockville, and two and a half from Great Falls. It derives its name from the Offutt family, one of the first to settle in the district. The physicians are Drs. B. Offutt and C. F. Willett; the postmistress is Phœbe E. Welsh. Near the village is Potomac chapel (Methodist Episcopal Church), of which G. T. Tyler and F. M. Strother are the pastors. Near this church are the graves of Rev. James Hunt and his wife. Their tombstones bear the following inscriptions:

"In memory of Rev. James Hunt, who departed this life the 2d of June, 1793, aged sixty-two years. He was set apart to the work of the ministry early in life. He continued till death laboring for the good of souls and for the glory of his heavenly Master.

> Be ye followers of me,
> As I was of Christ Jesus.
> By grace are ye saved,
> But strive to enter in at the straight gate."

Mr. Hunt was preceptor of "Tusculum Academy," the first institution of learning in the county, and one of his pupils was William Wirt.

"In memory of Mrs. Ruth Hunt, who departed this life the 17th of May, 1793, aged 67 years. Devoted herself to the service of religion, and continued through a long life a bright example of Christian piety. She was a woman of sorrows and acquainted with grief, being the greater part of her days the subject of affliction, which refined her as fire for dwelling in the mansion of the Holy and Blessed.

> I've tryed the strength of death at last,
> And here I lie under a cloud;
> But I shall rise above the skies
> When the last trump shall sound."

Near the grave of Mr. and Mrs. Hunt are those of

Edith W., daughter of J. W. and Alberta A. Claggett, born Sept. 29, 1869, died Dec. 16, 1878.

William Alexander, died July 14, 1876, aged 39.

Between Rock Run and Cabin John Creek, and near Seven Locks on the Potomac River, is Herman Presbyterian church, a neat frame edifice with a tall steeple.

Great Falls is on the Chesapeake and Ohio Canal and Potomac River. It is nine miles from Rockville, forty-nine from Baltimore, and derives its name from the falls of the Potomac River at this place. It is a part of "Bear Den," surveyed for Wm. Offutt, April 4, 1729. Dr. J. W. Carahe is the resident physician, J. W. Carroll, the hotel-keeper, and Howard A. Garrett, merchant.

Cromelin Lodge, No. 89, Knights of Pythias, was instituted June 13, 1874, and its charter granted Jan. 28, 1875. The charter members and first officers were O. S. Maus, P. C.; H. A. Garrett, P. C.; E. E. Fisher, V. C.; J. W. Carroll, Prelate; Wm. G. Connell, M. of E.; Everett Ellis, M. of F.; John Minnis, M. at A.; John Collins, I. G.; Daniel Harvell, O. G.; O. S. Maus, K. R. S.

The officers for 1881 are:

C. C., R. Minniss; V. C., R. G. Connell; Prelate, John Collins; M. of E., George Cummings; M. of F., Samuel Mansfield; K. of R. and S., H. A. Garrett; P. C., J. W. Carroll; M. at A., O. S. Maus; I. G., A. F. Soper; O. G., J. T. Pennyfiel; Janitor, Levi Hill; Trustees, Wm. G. Connell, J. Minnis, O. S. Maus; Relief Committee, R. Minniss, R. G. Connell, J. Collins, William Priestly, M. W. Downs, T. F. Monday, E. E. Fisher.

The lodge has $713.42 of accumulated funds, and meets on Saturday evening from October to April, and the remainder of the year on Thursday evenings.

The school trustees and teachers for 1881 and 1882 are as follows:

Trustees.—No. 1, A. C. Fawcett, W. G. Connell, T. W. Shogen; No. 2, R. G. Connell, J. W. Carroll, Wm. Bull; No. 3, J. H. Claggett, D. W. Cramer, Henry Claggett.

Teachers.—No. 1, E. C. Crockett, Potomac P. O.; No. 2, C. E. Higgins, Potomac P. O.; No. 3, S. E. Kilgour.

The magistrate is R. G. Davidson.

Great Falls Division, No. 50, Sons of Temperance, was chartered April 5, 1873, and continued in active operation some four years.

Its charter members were John W. Carroll, John Collins, Robert McNair, John Minnis, Thomas Hill, George W. Cummings, Everitt Ellis, John Kelly, James W. Evely, Edward E. Fisher, Basil T. Henly, Thomas Sullivan, Francis Fisher, Frank Soper.

The gold-mines of Montgomery County, of which a full account is given elsewhere, are in the vicinity of Great Falls.

END OF VOLUME I.

www.ingramcontent.com/pod-product-compliance
Lightning Source LLC
Chambersburg PA
CBHW080526300426
44111CB00017B/2626